书名题签：韩启德

中華科學技術大詞典

— 医学卷 —

全国科学技术名词审定委员会　编

名誉总主编　路甬祥
总　主　编　白春礼

2019年·北京

图书在版编目(CIP)数据

中华科学技术大词典.医学卷/全国科学技术名词审定委员会编.—北京:商务印书馆,2019
ISBN 978-7-100-17571-5

Ⅰ.①中… Ⅱ.①全… Ⅲ.①科学名词—名词术语—中国—词典②医学—科学名词—名词术语—中国—词典 Ⅳ.①H03②R-61

中国版本图书馆CIP数据核字(2019)第115584号

权利保留,侵权必究。

中华科学技术大词典
医学卷
全国科学技术名词审定委员会 编

商 务 印 书 馆 出 版
(北京王府井大街36号 邮政编码100710)
商 务 印 书 馆 发 行
北京中科印刷有限公司印刷
ISBN 978-7-100-17571-5

2019年6月第1版　　开本 787×1092　1/16
2019年6月北京第1次印刷　印张 71½
定价:215.00元

《中华科学技术大词典》

编辑委员会

名誉总主编：路甬祥

总 主 编：白春礼

副 总 主 编（以姓氏笔画为序）：

　　孙寿山　李济生　张礼和　张伯礼　张焕乔　陆汝钤

　　陈运泰　武　寅

常务副总主编：刘　青

编辑委员会委员（以姓氏笔画为序）：

丁一汇	于殿利	才　磊	王　杰	王　璞	王存忠
王英杰	仇伟立	叶大年	代晓明	白春礼	冯　军
曲爱国	朱　星	朱建平	乔格侠	任图生	邬　江
刘　青	刘功臣	刘志荣	刘连安	刘虎威	孙寿山
严加安	严海军	李宇明	李胜利	李济生	余桂林
辛德培	汪朝光	宋　彤	张　晖	张玉森	张礼和
张先恩	张伯礼	张柏春	张晓林	张焕乔	陆汝钤
陈　竺	陈运泰	陈超志	武　寅	周明鑑	周洪波
饶克勤	娄　宇	洪定一	顾红雅	奚大华	高素婷
唐绪军	陶文沂	黄　行	黄群慧	韩布新	程　晓
储成才	温昌斌	谢地坤	路甬祥	裴亚军	潘书祥

《中华科学技术大词典·医学卷》

编辑委员会

主　编：陈　竺

副主编：饶克勤　朱建平　张玉森

编辑委员会委员（以姓氏笔画为序）：

于　欣　王　奎　王　琦　王方正　王永炎　区永欣
牛远杰　田嘉禾　匡仁安　朱　蕾　朱明炜　朱建平
华桂茹　刘又宁　许润三　那彦群　孙殿军　苏　旭
李迎新　李国平　李经纬　励建安　张玉森　陆德铭
陈　杰　陈　竺　陈　实　侯春林　饶克勤　敖英芳
徐　浩　徐建光　高学敏　黄龙祥　黄跃升　崔丽英
蒋朱明　傅　瑜　谢　鸣

《中华科学技术大词典》项目部

主　任：张　晖

副主任：代晓明

成　员：吴　顿　白　杨　王　海

路甬祥序

全国科学技术名词审定委员会(以下简称"全国科技名词委")在其成立30多年来工作的基础上,对科学技术名词审定工作和海峡两岸科技名词对照工作的成果进行系统梳理,编纂出版《中华科学技术大词典》,有利于发挥其规范科学技术名词和加强海峡两岸各领域交流的重要作用。同时,也是全国科技名词委工作成果的重要展示。

科学技术名词作为科学技术概念的语言表达,产生于科技领域,应用于社会各个方面,是科技和经济社会融合发展的结晶。通过科学技术名词的规范表述,促进科技理论、知识和思想的传播交流,这是科学技术名词工作的根本宗旨。科学技术名词也是中华文化宝库的重要组成部分,它凝结着人类智慧和中华民族的创造,映射出科学技术和人类文明进步的轨迹。做好科学技术名词审定、公布、推广等各方面工作,有利于传承弘扬中华优秀科学文化,提高全民族科学文化素养,促进社会文明和谐发展,促进国际经济政治、科技文化的交流与合作。依托全国科技名词委30多年来的工作成果,在会聚数千位科技专家和学术精英的智慧结晶、融合现代科学和中华文化的新理念之基础上,编纂出版《中华科学技术大词典》,必将在普及现代科学技术和传承中华优秀文化中发挥积极作用,也具有宝贵的历史价值。

编纂一部集科技名词规范成果之大成的大型工具书,是当前科技名词规范化工作发展的需要。我国科技名词审定工作从全国科技名词委成立伊始,已经在基础科学、工程技术、农业、医学、人文社会科学等领域审定公布了130多种、40多万条的学科规范名词,出版了近30个学科的海峡两岸科技名词对照本,为我国科技发展和两岸科教文化交流发挥了重要的基础性作用。但是,以往的公布和出版工作都是分学科进行的,其优势是有利于开展审定工作,方便单个学科或行业领域的使用,而不足之处在于次序分散,不利于跨学科,以及综合性、交叉性学科领域的使用,也不利于科技名词的系统认知和社会普及。将这些名词系统分类和编纂集成,有利于学科向综合性、交叉性、系统性方向发展和创新。因而,编纂一部综合性的科学技术名词工具书,既是审定公布工作的深化与延伸,也是响应社会各界规范使用科技名词的基本诉求,必将在促进科技文化交流和实现协同创新方面发挥十分重要的作用。

科学技术名词也是海峡两岸科教文化交流的重要载体。由于历史的原因,海峡两岸分隔近70年,其间正是现代科技大发展时期,新名词术语层出不穷,两岸专家分别定名,形成大量名词术语之间的差异。台湾大学一位气象学教授曾举例说,两岸用同一种语言,但对于同样的气象探测设备,大陆称"无线电探空气球",台湾称"雷保";对于同样的云层气象条件,台湾称"逸入",大陆称"夹卷",造成学术交流的障碍。凡此种种概念相同而称谓不同的情况,约占科技名词术语三分之一以上,严重影响到两岸科技、文化、教育、经贸等各领域的交流和发展。海峡两岸各界对名词术语差异所造成的语言障碍都普遍有相似的经历和深刻的认识。1993年4月,两岸第一次"汪辜会谈"顺乎民意,把探讨"海峡两岸科技名词统一"列入了共同协议之中。随之全国科技名词委制定了《关于开展海峡两岸科学技术名词统一工作的意见》,决定加强与台湾地区学者和有关机构的交流合作,促进两岸科技名词的交流对照与统一工作。此后20多年来,两岸科技名词工作成绩斐然,已先后出版了近30种分学科的"海峡两岸名词对照本"。本次编纂出版《中华科学技术大词典》,广泛收集审选了各学科名词,成为囊括近百个学科、约50万条科技名词的综合性大词典。它的问世,将面向海峡两岸民众,释疑解惑,互动交流,协同科学认知,增进文化认同,为两岸科学文化等各领域的交流合作架起桥梁。它是促进科技创新发展,促进中华文化传承,促进两岸交流与祖国统一的科学文化工程,也是两岸专家学者的共同愿望,意义重大、影响深远。

《中华科学技术大词典》的出版,是两岸专家相互配合、共同努力的结果。双方专家也在这次合作中加深了相互了解,取得了广泛共识。大词典的问世是两岸学术界和专家合作的成果,是海峡所不能阻断的科教文化交流的缩影。我相信在两岸专家共同努力下,两岸科教文化的交流会呈现更加良好的局面。

《中华科学技术大词典》的出版,是我国科学技术名词规范化事业不断发展的重要见证,也是两岸科技文化交流中具有重要意义的盛事。故为序,以示衷心祝贺!

路甬祥

2018年8月28日

白春礼序

历经两岸专家学者多年来的共同努力,《中华科学技术大词典》即将问世了,这是两岸科技名词交流对照工作的一件盛事,也是两岸科教文化、经济社会等各个领域交流合作的一项基础工作,我感到由衷的欣慰。

中华文字是历史渊源的载体、民族精神的血脉,是人类文化的瑰丽成果。它不同于西方拼音文字,构成了中国人独有的思维方式和文化传统,使海峡两岸及中华文化圈内所有人民引为自豪。

科学技术名词是中华文化的重要组成部分,许多科学技术名词的定名都折射出中华文化艰辛的发展历程。特别是近代以来,中华民族历经苦难,举步维艰,大批先辈科学家肩负着沉重的历史责任,化解万难,在引进消化西方先进科技概念的基础上,结合中国的文化传统,创制了一大批具有中华文化品位和特点的名词术语,为我国近代科技跟上世界科技的发展创造了条件。

尽管经过了近70年的两岸分隔,但共同的历史传统和语言文化,无时无刻不在提醒着人们,海峡两岸同根同源、同文同宗,都是中华文明的继承者、弘扬者。但是,由于两岸社会长期处于相互隔绝的状态,其间正是全球科学技术飞速发展的历史时期,对于人类社会在相互学习、共同发展中产生的科学技术概念,两岸使用同样的文字却分别定名,其表达科学技术概念的词素词义,悄然发生了不同的演变,给两岸人民带来了交流的障碍,影响了两岸科教文化、经济贸易、人文社会等领域的交流合作。早在30年前恢复交流后不久,就有大陆学者关注到两岸科技名词的不同发展路径,意识到两岸科技名词的差异是造成两岸认知差距的原因之一,因而呼吁从促进计算机信息处理的角度出发,积极研究并推进海峡两岸科技名词的统一,消除语言障碍。

科技名词交流是海峡两岸专家学者的共同呼声。1993年首轮"汪辜会谈"达成的协议中就有探讨两岸科技名词统一的内容。全国科学技术名词审定委员会始终积极、稳妥地推动此项工作,这一举措也逐步得到两岸科技界的广泛认同。多年来两岸合作增加,交往频繁,文化上水乳交融,大陆和台湾地区科技名词交流互鉴,不少过去为一方独有的名词术语,已经逐步从分歧趋于一致。在此形势下,两岸合作编纂一部涵盖科学与技术各领域名词术语的科学技术大词典正逢其时。

2010年7月,两岸科学技术领域专家学者议定,在前期合作的基础上,合编《中华科学技术大词典》等辞书;同时双方协商决定利用信息技术,采用云计算平台开展数据库建设。在两岸专家学者多轮协商并形成共识的基础上,大词典编纂工作得以全面展开。

《中华科学技术大词典》的编纂突出了基础性、通用性、实用性,以广泛收录全球通用的现代科技概念为主,适当收录一些双方各自特有的名词术语,反映两岸科学技术名词差异,以方便两岸科技交流和一般民众使用,并为学习汉语的外国人提供帮助。同时为便于两岸读者使用,对于两岸不同的通用字形采取了分别呈现的形式。这种安排不仅便于双方大众阅读,同时也有助于双方逐步了解对方用字用词的现实情况,以达到化异为同的目的。几年来两岸专家学者实事求是、相互尊重、学风严谨、科学务实,奉献了各自的学识和心智,在两岸文化交流合作中又迈出坚实的一步。我们这次编纂出版《中华科学技术大词典》,既是过去两岸科技名词工作的延续,也为今后在更大的领域开展两岸学术交往,为科技文化、经济社会的进一步交流合作创造了基础条件。多年来的两岸科技名词交流实践充分说明,罔顾历史,无论是对传统文化的否定与切割,还是出于政治私利操控的"去中国化",都经不住历史长河的冲刷,终将因得不到公众的支持而烟消云散。维护两岸和平发展是两岸同胞的民意主流,本次编纂工作一直得到台湾方面有关机构和广大专家学者的协助与支持,编纂成果也将为两岸各界共享,成为促进两岸关系和平发展的一件鲜活的、生动的实例。

《中华科学技术大词典》集科学与技术领域名词术语之大成,汇聚了两岸无数专家学者的智慧,必将发挥传承与弘扬中华文化的历史和现实作用。经过两岸专家学者的不懈努力,《中华科学技术大词典》即将出版,借此机会,我谨向30多年来支持和参与科技名词工作的两岸专家学者致以诚挚的敬意!向参与此次词典编纂工作的所有专家学者,向全国科学技术名词审定委员会事务中心和词典项目部的同仁们,向支持本词典出版的国家出版基金规划管理办公室和投入精干队伍保障出版质量的商务印书馆,表示由衷的感谢!

白春礼

2019年夏

前　言

2009年7月,以"推进和深化两岸文化教育交流合作"为主题的第五届两岸经贸文化论坛在长沙举行,倡议两岸民间合作编纂中华语文工具书。2010年7月,两岸合编中华语文工具书第二轮会谈决定,两岸合编的工具书由语言文字领域拓展到科学技术领域,以全国科学技术名词审定委员会(以下简称"全国科技名词委")和台湾教育研究院为实施者,组织两岸专家合作编纂《中华科学技术大词典》。2011年3月,两岸专家共同提出编纂出版《中华科学技术大词典》的总体方案。2013年12月,《中华科学技术大词典》正式纳入《2013—2025年国家辞书编纂出版规划》,2016年6月《中华科学技术大词典》获得国家出版基金项目支持。

《中华科学技术大词典》成立编辑委员会,由白春礼院士担任总主编,路甬祥院士为名誉总主编。同时设立词典项目部,负责编纂的日常组织工作。各领域先后共有500多位专家学者参加了本词典的编纂和审定。

《中华科学技术大词典》在全国科技名词委审定公布的130多种学科名词和已出版的近30种海峡两岸科技名词对照本的基础上,参考台湾方面公布的名词数据库资料编纂而成。全书共收录96个学科,约50万条科技名词;并实现大陆名与台湾名,中文名和英文名的对照功能。全书按照学科领域和学科特点,共分为10卷,即数理化卷、地学卷、生物学卷、工程技术卷(上、中、下)、农业卷、医学卷、社会科学卷、人文科学卷。

本词典收录的各学科名词具有以下特点:一是在全国科技名词委公布名词的基础上,参照台湾方面的收词范围扩展而来,基本上反映出海峡两岸科学技术发展现状;二是体现了规范性,充分利用科技名词规范化工作的成果;三是注重科学文化的传承,既收录了当代科学技术领域的科技名词,也适当收录了反映中国近代以来科学和文化发展脉络的科技名词。本词典是两岸专家学者对多年来科技名词领域交流、对照和统一工作成果的一次大规模整理和总结,是两岸合作编写工具书的最新成果,是两岸专家学者的智慧结晶,是两岸共同弘扬中华文化的一次重要实践。

本词典作为两岸专家共同参与编纂的工具书,契合了两岸科学技术发展的现实需求,为两岸在科技、教育、文化、经贸等方面的交流合作提供了必不可少的对照性词汇,可成为两岸各领域交流的参考和依据。同时,可用作全球华语地区科技界人士的参考读物。

本词典编纂期间,编审专家以严肃的科学态度,认真工作,持之以恒,默默奉献。台湾教育研究院及台湾各学科的部分专家学者参与了词目编选,特别是对台湾名、英文名等进行了仔细审读。在此,我们向他们表示衷心的感谢。

《中华科学技术大词典》涉及学科广泛,尤其是进行如此大规模的两岸科技名词梳理、遴选、编纂及全面对照,没有先例,难度巨大,编纂中难免会有疏漏错误之处,欢迎广大专家学者和读者批评指正。

《中华科学技术大词典》编辑委员会

2019年3月1日

《中华科学技术大词典·医学卷》编纂说明

《中华科学技术大词典·医学卷》(以下简称《医学卷》)是《中华科学技术大词典》的第8卷。《医学卷》的收词,以全国科学技术名词审定委员会审定的各专业医学名词为基础,按国家学科分类标准,增补了基础医学、预防医学、临床医学、军事医学、人体解剖学、药学、中医药学的相关名词。同时参照医学主题词表、国际疾病分类、医学百科全书等权威医学著作,添加、调整了相关名词。全书收词80000余条,结构系统、完整。全部词条按照大陆名音序排序,以便查检。

根据《中华科学技术大词典》编委会的总体安排,于2016年7月至2018年10月,分别按照工作程序,经过四轮审稿和三次编校:一是对存在的格式、书写、拼写、翻译不准确等问题进行校正;二是对两岸名词概念不对应以及不适合作为科技名词的词汇,进行了必要的调整、替代和删除;三是对特别基础、重要、常用的词进行了增收,分卷编辑据此加以校核,形成初审稿。之后由《中华科学技术大词典》项目部进行数据处理,重点进行各学科词条合库、查重和筛选,形成二审稿。针对二审稿,第二次组织专家深入细致地审查,解决初审遗留问题,检查处理编辑加工过程中的疏漏,形成三审稿,并由分卷主编第三次组织专家审校。为保证书稿质量,再次请《中华医学杂志》(英文版)编辑进行审查,并由项目部进行三校;台湾地区用词送台湾专家进行了审查,体现了两岸专家密切合作的精神风范。在此基础上形成了终审稿,由分卷主编和副主编再次把关,报送《中华科学技术大词典》编辑委员会审查批准,交由商务印书馆出版。

《中华科学技术大词典》项目部和全国科学技术名词审定委员会事务中心各审定室的同志们对词典的编纂出版给予了大力的支持。从组建分卷编辑委员会开始,他们就积极参与,协助联系专家,承担了提供稿件资料、协助组织召开编委会、开展专项检查、誊录与复核编校意见等多项繁杂工作。

参加医学名词审定的专家数以千计,因篇幅的原因,编辑委员会主要由主持各专业学科名词审定的主任委员组成。在此,我们向所有为词典编纂、出版工作做出贡献的专家、学者和同人们表示衷心的感谢。

由于时间仓促,编者水平有限,难免有各种不足和差错,诚望读者批评指正。

《中华科学技术大词典·医学卷》编辑委员会

2019年5月16日

目　　录

凡例 ··· 2

词目首字音序索引 ·· 4

词目首字笔画索引 ·· 12

词典正文 ·· 1—1105

附录 ·· 1107

　　国际单位制 ·· 1109

　　希腊字母表 ·· 1112

　　地质年代表 ·· 1113

　　元素周期表 ·· 1114

词目英文索引

（二维码）

凡 例

1. 词条收录

1.1 本词典所收词条涵盖基础科学、工程技术、农业科学、医学、社会科学、人文及其他领域共计96个学科,例如数学、物理学、化学、天文学、地质学、测绘学、动物学、植物学、航天科学技术、建筑学、机械工程、电子学、材料科学技术、资源科学技术、农学、土壤学、医学、中医药学、经济学、法学、语言学、教育学等。

1.2 本词典收录的词条包括海峡两岸通用的,以及海峡两岸有差异的科学技术名词共约50万条。

1.3 本词典收录的词条按照科学技术相关学科领域归类,共分为10卷。依次为数理化卷、地学卷、生物学卷、工程技术卷(上、中、下)、农业卷、医学卷、社会科学卷、人文科学卷。

2. 词条构成

2.1 本词典所收词条由词目(中文)及其对应的英文构成。

2.2 词目采用两岸名称对照的形式,大陆名列前,台湾名列后,中间以"/"分隔。例如:

电灼式印刷机/放電式列印機

拉克斯-密格拉蒙定理/拉克斯-米爾格雷定理

2.3 词目的字形,分别采用两岸各自通用的字形。例如:

自然循环/自然循環

作业控制中心/作業控制中心

2.4 词目中的大陆名有两条(或以上)同义词时,分别以两条(或以上)词目列出。例如:

背景/背景

本底/背景

2.5 词目中的大陆名对应两条(或以上)台湾同义词时,台湾名在词目中并行排列,中间以逗号隔开。例如:

出口融资/出口融資,籌集出口資金

横节理/横節理,交錯劈理,Q節理

2.6 词目中的大陆名对应两个(或两个以上)台湾名概念时,对应的台湾名分别以①②……列出。例如:

质量/ ①質量,②品質

槽轮/ ①間歇工作輪,星形輪,日內瓦輪,②有槽帶輪

2.7 词目中大陆名和台湾名中"[ ]"内的字为可省略部分。例如:

等离[子]体动力学/電漿動力學

2.8 词目中大陆名和台湾名中"( )"内的汉字、西文字母、阿拉伯数字、罗马数字为该词的特殊标注(如天体名的备注、化合物结构标示、数学概念的符号标识等)。例如:

虹神星(小行星7号)/虹神星(7號小行星)

聚(β-氨基丙酸)/聚(β-胺基丙酸)

广义(g,k)特征标/廣義(g,k)特徵[標]

2.9 本词典收录的词条不单独标出所属学科。

3. 词目排序

3.1 词目按大陆名的首字汉语拼音字母次序排列，首字同音的按笔画排列，笔画少的在前，多的在后；笔画相同的按起笔笔形（横、竖、撇、点、折）的次序排列，起笔笔形相同的按第二起笔笔形的次序排列，以此类推。首字相同的按第二字的汉语拼音字母次序排列，以此类推。

3.2 词目中含有西文字母或阿拉伯数字、罗马数字时，按词目中的汉字汉语拼音排序；词首或词中的西文字母或阿拉伯数字、罗马数字一律不参加排序。

4. 词目对应的英文（或其他外文）

4.1 词目对应的外文主要为英文，也有极少量的其他文种词语或字母。例如拉丁文、法文、德文及希腊字母等。遇有其他外文时，遵从其特殊形式。

4.2 词目对应的英文，在词目之后列出。例如：

计算机辅助设计/電腦輔助設計 computer-aided design

4.3 词义相同的英文并行排列，中间以逗号隔开。例如：

粗钢/粗鋼 crude steel, raw steel

4.4 英文名词一般采用单数形式，必须或习惯采用复数形式的英文名词除外。

4.5 以人名、地名等命名的专有名词，其对应的英文，首字母为大写。

4.6 英文如有英美拼法差异时，一般采用美式拼法。

4.7 英文中出现拉丁文词时，一般遵从各学科领域的格式惯例。例如：

肠产毒性大肠杆菌/腸產毒性大腸桿菌 enterotoxigcnic *Escherichia coli*（生物学卷）

南方古猿/南[方古]猿 *Australopithecus*（地学卷）

奥斯特线虫属/牛胃絲蟲屬 *Ostertagia*（农业卷）

尺头/尺頭 caput ulnare（拉）（医学卷）

4.8 英文中出现汉语拼音转写词语时，一般遵从汉语拼音分词习惯。例如：

芎菊上清丸 xiongju shangqing pills

4.9 中医穴位名，根据国家标准 GB/T 12346-2006《腧穴名称与定位》和 GB/T 13734-2008《耳穴名称与定位》确定，并与国际标准一致。例如：

昆仑/昆侖 kunlun, BL60

枕/枕 zhen, AT3, occiput

5. 附录

本词典后附有国际单位制、希腊字母表、地质年代表、元素周期表。

6. 索引

6.1 本词典列有词目首字音序索引和词目首字笔画索引。

6.2 本词典附有词目英文索引（扫描二维码查取）。

词目首字音序索引

(字右边的号码指词典正文的页码)

A		bai		被	29	别	47	C		插	66	衬	76	触	89
		白	12			ben		bin		茶	67	cheng		chuan	
		百	16	奔	29	宾	48			查	67	撑	76	川	90
a		柏	17	贲	29	濒	48	ca		搽	67	成	77	氚	90
吖	1	摆	17	本	30	殡	48	擦	63	察	67	承	79	穿	90
阿	1	败	17	苯	30	髌	48			侘	67	城	79	传	91
锕	3	拜	17	beng		鬓	48	cai		chai		乘	79	船	92
ai		ban		崩	32	bing		猜	63	拆	67	程	79	喘	92
哀	3	扳	17	绷	32	冰	48	才	63	柴	67	澄	79	串	92
埃	3	班	17	泵	32	槟	49	材	63	chan		橙	79	chuang	
癌	4	斑	18	bi		丙	49	财	63	掺	67	chi		创	92
矮	4	瘢	18	逼	32	秉	50	裁	63	缠	67	痴	80	疮	93
艾	4	坂	18	鼻	32	柄	50	采	63	蝉	67	池	80	窗	93
爱	5	板	18	比	37	屏	50	彩	63	蟾	67	弛	80	床	93
嗳	5	半	19	吡	38	禀	50	踩	63	镜	67	迟	80	chui	
an		伴	21	笔	38	并	50	菜	63	产	67	持	80	吹	93
安	5	瓣	21	必	38	病	51	蔡	63	铲	70	匙	81	垂	93
桉	6			毕	38	bo		can		颤	70	尺	81	捶	95
氨	6	bang		闭	39	拨	53	参	63	chang		齿	82	槌	95
鞍	8	邦	22	庇	39	波	53	餐	63	菖	70	耻	83	锤	95
铵	8	棒	22	荜	40	玻	54	残	63	猖	70	赤	84	chun	
按	8			铋	40	剥	54	蚕	64	长	70	炽	84	春	95
胺	9	bao		秘	40	菠	55	惨	64	肠	71	瘦	84	椿	96
暗	9	包	22	草	40	播	55			尝	74	瘾	84	纯	96
		孢	23	莼	40	伯	55	cang		常	74			唇	96
ang		胞	23	痹	40	泊	55	仓	64	偿	74	chong		醇	97
昂	9	薄	24	蔽	40	柏	56	苍	64	场	74	冲	84		
盎	9	饱	24	壁	40	勃	56	藏	64	怅	74	充	85	chuo	
		保	25	避	40	铂	56					茺	85	戳	97
ao		抱	25	臂	40	博	56	cao		chao		虫	85		
凹	9	豹	25			搏	56	操	64	超	74	重	85	ci	
鳌	9	鲍	25	bian		薄	56	糙	64	巢	76			词	97
奥	9	暴	25	边	41	跛	56	嘈	64	朝	76	chou		瓷	97
澳	10	爆	26	砭	42			槽	64	潮	76	抽	86	慈	97
懊	10			萹	42	bu		草	64	炒	76	稠	86	磁	97
		bei		编	42							臭	86	雌	98
B		杯	26	蝙	42	卜	56	ce		che				次	98
		卑	26	鞭	42	补	56	侧	65	车	76	chu		刺	99
		悲	26	扁	43	捕	58	测	66	扯	76	出	87		
ba		北	26	苄	43	哺	58	策	66	撤	76	初	88	cong	
八	11	贝	26	变	44	不	58					除	88	葱	99
巴	11	备	27	便	45	布	60	cen		chen		锄	89	从	99
拔	12	背	27	辨	45	步	62	参	66	臣	76	雏	89	丛	99
菝	12	钡	28	标	45	部	62	岑	66	尘	76	处	89		
钯	12	倍	28	表	46					辰	76	杵	89	cou	
靶	12	悖	29	鳖	47			ceng		沉	76	楮	89	腠	100
										层	66	陈	76	储	89	cu	
				biao				cha		晨	76	怵	89	粗	100
								叉	66					卒	100
								差	66						

词目首字音序索引 5

促	100	dang		雕	138	dui		乏	177	feng		蛤	243
猝	101	当	122	吊	138	队	151	伐	178	丰	204	G		隔	243
醋	101	党	123	调	139	对	151	法	178	风	204			膈	243
簇	102	dao		die		兑	153	发	178	枫	206	ga		镉	244
		刀	123	跌	139	dun		fan		封	206	伽	224	葛	244
cuan		氘	123	迭	139	蹲	153	帆	178	砜	207	钆	224	个	245
攒	102	导	123	叠	139	炖	153	番	178	峰	207	gai		各	245
窜	102	岛	123	碟	139	钝	153	翻	179	锋	207	垓	224	铬	245
cui		捣	123	蝶	139	盾	153	凡	179	蜂	207	改	224	gei	
催	102	到	123	ding		顿	153	钒	179	冯	207	钙	224	给	245
脆	103	倒	123	丁	140	duo		烦	179	缝	207	盖	225	gen	
淬	103	盗	123	钉	141	多	153	樊	179	fo		概	225	根	245
翠	103	稻	124	疔	141	夺	159	繁	179	佛	207	gan		跟	246
cun		de		耵	141	堕	159	反	179	fou		干	225	geng	
存	103	得	124	酊	141	惰	159	返	179	否	207	甘	226	更	247
寸	103	锝	124	顶	141			犯	181	fu		肝	227	庚	247
cuo		德	124	定	142	E		饭	181	夫	207	坩	232	耿	247
搓	103	deng		锭	143			泛	181	呋	207	苷	232	梗	247
撮	103	灯	124	dong		e		范	182	肤	208	柑	232	gong	
痤	103	登	124	东	143	阿	160			麸	208	酐	232	工	247
挫	103	等	124	冬	143	俄	160	fang		跗	208	疳	232	弓	248
锉	103	邓	125	氡	143	莪	160	方	182	孵	208	杆	232	公	248
错	103	镫	125	动	143	哦	160	芳	183	敷	208	感	233	功	249
				冻	146	鹅	160	防	183	弗	208	橄	234	攻	249
D		di		胨	147	蛾	160	房	184	伏	209	干	234	供	249
		低	125	洞	147	额	160	仿	184	扶	209	绀	235	肱	249
da		滴	127	dou		恶	161	纺	184	服	209	gang		宫	251
哒	104	狄	127	兜	147	厄	161	放	185	佛	209	冈	235	巩	251
搭	104	迪	127	斗	147	扼	161	fei		茯	209	刚	235	汞	252
达	104	敌	128	抖	147	苊	161	飞	187	氟	209	肛	235	共	252
打	104	涤	128	豆	147	呃	161	非	187	浮	210	纲	237	贡	253
大	104	笛	128	痘	147	恶	162	菲	190	匐	210	钢	237	gou	
dai		抵	128	窦	147	鄂	163	鲱	190	辐	210	岗	237	佝	253
呆	109	底	128	du		遏	163	肥	190	福	211	杠	237	沟	253
代	109	骶	128	督	148	噁	163	腓	191	蝠	211	gao		钩	253
带	110	地	130	毒	148	腭	163	榧	192	府	211	高	237	狗	253
待	111	递	131	独	149	噩	164	肺	192	俯	211	睾	240	枸	253
袋	111	第	131	读	149	鳄	164	狒	199	辅	211	膏	242	构	253
戴	111	蒂	133	渎	149	en		废	199	腑	212	糕	242	gu	
黛	111	缔	133	犊	149	恩	165	沸	199	腐	212	藁	242	孤	253
dan		碲	133	堵	149	蒽	165	费	199	父	212	告	242	姑	254
丹	111	dian		杜	149	er		痱	199	负	212	锆	242	菇	254
担	111	颠	133	妒	150	儿	165	fen		妇	212	ge		箍	254
单	111	癫	133	度	150	耳	166	分	199	附	213	戈	242	古	254
耽	116	典	134	镀	150	二	170	芬	203	复	214	疙	242	谷	254
胆	116	点	134	duan				吩	203	副	216	咯	242	股	255
但	120	碘	134	端	150	F		酚	203	赋	218	哥	242	骨	257
淡	120	电	135	短	150			坟	203	傅	218	鸽	242	钴	263
弹	120	垫	138	段	151	fa		焚	203	富	218	割	242	蛊	263
蛋	121	淀	138	断	151	发	176	粉	203	腹	218	革	242	鼓	263
氮	122	靛	138	煅	151			奋	203	鳆	223	格	242	鸪	264
膻	122			锻	151			粪	203	覆	223			臌	264
		diao													
		凋	138												

固	265	蛤	278	猴	296	hui		棘	338	碱	366	捷	386	鸠	412
雇	266			骺	296	灰	316	集	339	见	367	睫	386	九	412
	gua		hai	后	297	挥	316	蒺	339	间	367	截	387	久	412
瓜	266	海	278	厚	299	恢	316	嵴	339	建	368	姐	387	灸	412
刮	266	酰	280	候	300	回	316	嫉	339	剑	368	解	387	韭	412
胍	266	氦	280	鲎	300	茴	318	几	339	健	368	介	388	酒	412
寡	266	害	280		hu	蛔	318	己	340	渐	368	戒	388	旧	414
挂	266		han	呼	300	毁	318	挤	340	践	368	芥	388	枢	414
	guai	鼾	280	忽	301	汇	318	脊	340	腱	368	界	388	救	414
乖	266	含	280	狐	301	会	318	麂	344	溅	369	疥	388	厩	414
拐	266	寒	281	弧	301	绘	319	计	344	鉴	369		jin		ju
怪	266	汉	281	胡	301	彗	319	记	345	键	369	斤	388	居	414
	guan	汗	282	壶	302	秽	319	技	345	箭	369	今	388	疽	414
关	266	颔	282	葫	302	惠	319	季	345		jiang	金	388	鞠	414
观	269		hang	槲	302	喙	319	剂	345	江	370	津	390	局	414
官	269	杭	282	蝴	302		hun	济	345	将	370	筋	390	桔	415
冠	269	航	282	糊	302	昏	319	继	345	姜	370	紧	390	菊	415
管	270	颃	282	虎	302	婚	319	寄	346	豇	370	堇	391	橘	416
贯	270		hao	琥	302	浑	319	绩	347	浆	370	锦	391	咀	416
惯	270	蒿	282	互	302	魂	319		jia	僵	371	进	391	沮	416
灌	270	毫	282	户	302	混	319	加	347	缰	371	近	392	枸	416
	guang	豪	283	护	302		huo	夹	348	桨	371	浸	393	矩	416
光	271	壕	283		hua	豁	320	痂	348	降	371	禁	393	举	416
胱	273	号	283	花	303	活	321	家	348	绛	371	噤	393	巨	416
广	273	耗	283	划	304	火	322	嘉	350	酱	371		jing	拒	418
	gui		he	华	304	获	322	荚	350		jiao	茎	393	具	418
归	273	诃	283	滑	304	霍	323	颊	350	交	371	京	393	剧	418
圭	273	呵	283	化	305	藿	323	甲	351	郊	373	经	393	距	418
龟	273	禾	283	划	307			岬	356	胶	373	荆	398	惧	418
规	274	合	283	华	307	══ J ══		贾	356	椒	374	惊	398	锯	419
硅	274	何	283	桦	307			钾	356	焦	374	晶	398	聚	419
鲑	274	和	283		huai		ji	假	357	嚼	375	睛	399		juan
诡	274	河	284	怀	307	击	324	驾	361	角	375	精	399	蠲	420
鬼	274	核	284	槐	307	饥	324	架	361	绞	377	鲸	404	卷	420
癸	274	颌	284	踝	307	机	324	嫁	361	铰	377	井	404	狷	420
贵	274	貉	286	坏	308	肌	324		jian	矫	377	肼	404	绢	420
桂	274	领	286		huan	鸡	329	尖	361	脚	378	颈	404		jue
桧	275	赫	287	还	308	奇	329	坚	361	搅	378	径	408	决	420
	gun	褐	287	环	309	积	329	间	361	校	378	净	408	觉	420
辊	275	鹤	287	寰	312	姬	330	肩	362	较	378	胫	408	绝	420
滚	275		hei	缓	312	基	330	艰	364	教	378	痉	409	掘	421
	guo	黑	287	幻	312	畸	332	监	364	酵	378	竞	410	厥	421
郭	275		heng	换	313	箕	332	兼	364		jie	敬	410	蕨	421
锅	275	亨	289	唤	313	稽	332	缄	364	阶	378	静	410		jun
瘑	275	恒	289	患	313	激	332	煎	364	疖	378	境	412	军	421
国	275	横	289		huang	吉	333	睑	364	接	378	镜	412	均	421
腘	275		hong	肓	313	级	333	检	364	节	379		jiong	君	422
果	275	轰	290	慌	313	极	333	减	364	杰	380	炯	412	菌	422
过	276	烘	290	黄	313	即	334	剪	365	拮	380			皲	422
		红	290	煌	315	急	334	睑	365	洁	380		jiu	峻	422
══ H ══		虹	293	磺	315	疾	338	简	366	结	380	旧	412		
		洪	294		hou					桔	386	纠	412		
	ha		hou	喉	294										
哈	278														

词目首字音序索引

K

ka
咖 423
卡 423
咔 424
咯 424

kai
开 424
揩 425
凯 425
铠 425

kan
龛 425
堪 425
坎 425
砍 425
莰 425

kang
康 425
糠 426
亢 426
抗 426

kao
考 432
烤 432
靠 432

ke
苛 432
柯 432
科 432
颏 433
颗 433
髁 434
壳 434
咳 434
可 434
渴 435
克 435
刻 436
客 436
氪 437

ken
肯 437

keng
坑 437

kong
空 437
孔 438
恐 438

空 438
控 438

kou
芤 438
口 438
叩 443
扣 443

ku
枯 443
哭 443
苦 443
库 443

kua
夸 444
胯 444
跨 444

kuai
块 444
快 444

kuan
宽 444
髋 444
款 445

kuang
狂 445
矿 445
框 446
眶 446

kui
盔 447
窥 447
奎 447
葵 447
喹 447
蝰 447
溃 447

kun
昆 448
醌 448

kuo
扩 448
括 448
阔 448
廓 448

L

la
拉 449
腊 449

蜡 449
辣 449

lai
来 449
莱 450
赖 450

lan
兰 450
阑 450
蓝 451
篮 451
榄 451
烂 451
滥 451

lang
郎 451
狼 451
朗 452

lao
劳 452
牢 452
痨 452
老 452
铑 453
烙 453
落 453
酪 453

le
乐 453
勒 453

lei
雷 454
镭 454
累 454
蕾 454
肋 454
泪 456
类 457

leng
棱 459
冷 459

li
厘 460
离 460
梨 461
犁 461
罹 461
藜 461
黧 461
李 461
里 461
理 462

锂 462
鲤 462
鳢 462
力 462
历 462
厉 462
立 462
丽 463
利 463
沥 464
疠 464
荔 464
栗 464
蛎 464
粒 464
痢 464
羚 464

lian
连 464
帘 465
莲 465
联 465
廉 466
鲥 466
镰 466
敛 467
脸 467
练 467
炼 467
恋 467
链 467

liang
良 468
莨 468
凉 469
梁 469
量 469
两 469
亮 470
量 470

liao
疗 470
撩 470
燎 470
钉 470
鸼 470
鹩 470
列 470
劣 470
烈 470
猎 470
裂 470

lin
邻 471
林 471
临 471
淋 472
磷 475
鳞 477

lin
淋 477
膦 477

ling
灵 477
苓 478
铃 478
凌 478
菱 478
羚 478
零 478
岭 478
另 478
领 478

liu
刘 478
留 478
流 478
琉 480
硫 480
瘤 482
柳 482
六 482

long
龙 482
聋 483
笼 483
隆 483
癃 483

lou
蒌 483
蝼 483
瘘 483
漏 483

lu
卢 484
芦 484
炉 484
鸬 484
颅 484
鲈 487
卤 487
鲁 487
陆 487
鹿 487
路 487

辘 487
露 487

lü
驴 487
吕 487
铝 487
律 487
虑 487
绿 487
葎 488
氯 488
滤 490

luan
卵 490
孪 490
卵 490
乱 493

lun
伦 493
轮 493
论 493

luo
罗 494
萝 494
啰 494
逻 494
螺 494
裸 495
瘰 495
洛 495
骆 495
络 495
落 495

M

ma
麻 496
马 497
吗 499
蚂 499

mai
埋 499
迈 499
麦 499
脉 500
唛 501

man
满 501
螨 501

曼 501
蔓 502
漫 502
慢 502

mang
芒 505
盲 505
莽 506

mao
猫 506
毛 506
矛 509
锚 509
冒 509
帽 509
瞀 509

mei
玫 509
眉 509
梅 510
湄 511
媒 511
煤 511
酶 511
霉 512
每 512
美 512
镁 513
袂 513

men
门 513
闷 514

meng
虻 514
萌 514
蒙 514
朦 514
礞 514
蒙 514
猛 514
锰 514
蠓 514
孟 514
梦 514

mi
咪 514
弥 514
迷 515
猕 516
醚 516
糜 516

米 517
脒 517
觅 517
泌 517
秘 518
密 518
嘧 518
蜜 518

mian
绵 518
棉 519
免 519
勉 521
娩 521
面 521

miao
描 523
眇 523
缪 523

mie
灭 524

min
民 524
敏 524

ming
名 524
明 524
鸣 524
命 524

mo
模 524
膜 525
摩 526
磨 526
蘑 526
末 526
没 526
莫 526
墨 527
默 527
磨 527
貘 527

mu
模 527
母 527
牡 528
拇 528
姆 528
踇 528
木 528
目 529
沐 530
苜 530

词目首字音序索引

牧	530	鲇	549	鸥	568	碰	578	蒲	594	qiang		驱	627	任	644
钼	530	黏	549	呕	568		pi	浦	594	羌	613	屈	627	韧	644
募	530	捻	552	偶	568	批	578	普	594	枪	613	祛	627	妊	644
幕	530	碾	552	藕	568	披	578	谱	594	腔	613	躯	628		ri
慕	530	念	552			砒	578	蹼	595	蜣	613	趋	628	日	647
暮	530		niang		P	劈	578	瀑	595	强	613	曲	628		rong
穆	530	酿	552			皮	578	曝	595	蔷	614	瞿	629	茸	648
			niao		pa	枇	584			羟	614	蠼	629	荣	648
	N	鸟	552	爬	569	铍	584		Q	强	615	取	629	绒	648
		尿	553	帕	569	疲	584				qiao	龋	629	容	648
	na	脲	558		pai	啤	584		qi	乔	616	去	629	溶	648
拿	531	溺	558	拍	569	脾	585	七	596	荞	616		quan	熔	650
那	531		nie	排	569	蜱	587	期	596	桥	616	圈	630	蝾	650
纳	531	捏	558	哌	570	匹	587	漆	596	巧	616	全	630	融	650
钠	531	啮	558	派	570	痞	587	齐	596	翘	616	泉	633		rou
	nai	镊	558		pan	屁	587	奇	596	鞘	616	拳	633	柔	650
奶	531	镍	558	潘	570		pian	歧	596		qie	蜷	633	揉	650
奈	531	颞	558	攀	570	偏	587	祈	596	切	616	醛	633	鞣	650
耐	532		ning	盘	570	胼	588	脐	596	茄	617	颧	633	肉	650
萘	532	宁	560	蹒	570	片	589	骑	598	切	617	犬	634		ru
	nan	柠	560	蟠	571		piao	棋	598	怯	617	劝	634	如	652
男	532	凝	560	判	571	漂	589	旗	598		qin		que	铷	652
南	533	拧	562	泮	571	瓢	589	蕲	598	侵	617	炔	634	濡	652
难	533		niu	襻	571	漂	589	鳍	598	亲	617	缺	634	蠕	652
喃	533	牛	562		pang	嘌	589	企	598	芹	618	雀	635	乳	652
赧	533	扭	563	彷	571	漂	589	杞	598	芩	618	确	635	入	658
	nang	纽	563	庞	571		pin	启	598	秦	618		qun	褥	658
囊	533	钮	563	旁	571	拼	589	起	598	禽	618	群	635		ruan
	nao		nong	膀	571	贫	589	气	598	噙	618			软	658
蛲	534	农	563	螃	574	频	589	汽	603		qing		R	阮	660
脑	534	浓	563	胖	574	品	589	契	603	青	618				rui
瑙	540	脓	563		pao		ping	器	603	轻	620		ran	蕤	661
臑	540	弄	565	抛	574	乒	589	憩	603	氢	620	然	636	锐	661
	nei		nu	炮	574	平	589		qia	倾	621	燃	636	瑞	661
内	540	努	565	跑	574	评	591	掐	603	清	621	染	636		run
	nen	胬	565	泡	574	苹	591	恰	603	鲭	622		rang	闰	661
嫩	548	怒	565	疱	574	屏	591	髂	603	情	622	让	637	润	661
	neng		nü		pei	瓶	591		qian	氰	623		rao		ruo
能	548	女	565	胚	575		po	千	605	庆	623	饶	637	若	661
	ni	衄	566	培	576	泼	591	迁	605		qiong	桡	637	弱	661
尼	548		nuan	佩	576	珀	591	牵	605	穷	623	绕	638		
呢	548	暖	566	配	576	破	591	铅	605	穹	623		re		S
泥	548		nüe		pen	魄	591	荨	605	琼	623	惹	638		
鲵	548	疟	566	喷	577		pou	前	605		qiu	热	638		sa
拟	548	虐	567	盆	577	剖	591	钱	611	丘	624		ren	撒	662
逆	548		nuo		peng		pu	钳	611	秋	625	人	641	臊	662
匿	549	挪	567	烹	578	扑	592	潜	612	蚯	625	壬	644	萨	662
腻	549	诺	567	彭	578	铺	592	浅	612	球	625	仁	644		sai
溺	549			蓬	578	仆	592	芡	612	巯	626	忍	644	腮	662
	nian		O	硼	578	脯	592	茜	613	鼽	626	刃	644	塞	662
年	549	欧	568	膨	578	葡	592	嵌	613		qu	认	644	噻	663

鳃	663	少	682	始	723	shuai		髓	759	tao	
赛	663	绍	683	士	723	衰	744	岁	760	逃	774
san		哨	684	世	723	率	744	碎	760	桃	774
三	663	she		示	723	shuan		隧	760	陶	774
伞	668	舌	684	势	723	闩	744	sun		淘	774
散	668	蛇	687	试	723	栓	744	孙	760	套	774
sang		舍	687	视	723	shuang		损	760	te	
桑	668	设	687	拭	728	双	744	suo		特	774
嗓	669	社	687	柿	728	霜	748	娑	761	teng	
sao		舍	688	是	728	爽	748	梭	761	疼	776
扫	669	射	688	适	728	shui		羧	761	滕	776
瘙	669	摄	688	室	729	水	748	缩	761	藤	776
臊	669	麝	688	铈	729	睡	751	所	762	ti	
se		shen		舐	729	shun		索	762	剔	776
色	669	申	688	释	729	吮	751	锁	762	梯	776
涩	671	伸	688	嗜	729	顺	751			锑	776
啬	671	身	689	噬	732	瞬	752	—T—		踢	776
铯	671	参	689	螫	733	shuo				提	776
塞	671	砷	689	shou		说	752	ta		啼	776
sen		深	689	收	733	朔	752	他	764	蹄	776
森	671	神	690	手	734	硕	752	铊	764	体	777
seng		审	697	守	736	si		塌	764	剃	778
僧	671	肾	697	首	736	司	752	濌	764	替	779
sha		胂	706	寿	736	丝	752	塔	764	嚏	779
杀	671	渗	706	受	736	私	753	踏	764	tian	
沙	671	葚	706	授	737	思	753	tai		天	779
纱	672	sheng		售	737	斯	753	胎	764	添	780
砂	672	升	706	兽	737	锶	754	台	767	田	780
痧	672	生	706	瘦	737	撕	754	苔	767	恬	780
鲨	672	声	711	shu		嘶	754	太	768	甜	780
shai		圣	711	书	737	死	754	肽	768	填	780
筛	672	剩	712	枢	737	四	754	钛	768	tiao	
晒	673	shi		叔	737	似	756	泰	769	挑	781
shan		尸	712	梳	737	饲	756	酞	769	条	781
山	673	失	712	舒	738	song		tan		调	781
珊	673	虱	713	疏	738	松	756	贪	769	跳	782
栅	674	狮	713	输	741	崧	757	瘫	769	tie	
闪	674	施	713	蔬	741	su		弹	769	贴	782
疝	674	湿	713	熟	741	苏	757	痰	769	萜	782
扇	674	蓍	715	暑	742	诉	757	檀	770	铁	782
善	674	十	715	蜀	742	素	757	坦	770	咕	782
膳	674	石	717	鼠	743	速	757	毯	770	ting	
鳝	674	时	718	薯	743	宿	757	叹	770	听	782
shang		识	718	曙	743	粟	758	炭	770	烃	783
伤	674	实	718	术	743	塑	758	碳	771	廷	783
商	675	拾	720	束	743	suan		探	771	停	783
上	676	食	720	树	743	酸	758	tang		葶	784
尚	681	蚀	722	竖	743	蒜	759	汤	772	挺	784
shao		莳	723	腧	743	算	759	羰	772	艇	784
烧	682	史	723	数	743	sui		唐	772	tong	
苕	682	矢	723	漱	744	随	759	糖	772	通	784
杓	682	使	723	shua		岁		烫	774	同	784
				刷	744					桐	787
										铜	787
										童	787
										酮	787
										瞳	787
										统	788
										桶	788
										筒	788
										痛	788
										tou	
										偷	789
										头	789
										投	791
										骰	792
										透	792
										tu	
										凸	793
										秃	793
										突	793
										图	794
										徒	794
										涂	794
										屠	794
										土	794
										吐	795
										钍	795
										兔	795
										菟	795
										tuan	
										团	795
										tui	
										推	795
										癫	795
										腿	795
										退	796
										蜕	796
										褪	796
										tun	
										吞	796
										豚	796
										臀	796
										tuo	
										托	797
										拖	798
										脱	798
										驼	800
										妥	800
										椭	800
										拓	800
										唾	800

—W—

wa
挖 802
蛙 802
娃 802
瓦 802
袜 802

wai
歪 802
外 802

wan
弯 808
蜿 809
豌 809
丸 809
完 809
顽 809
烷 809
挽 810
晚 810
脘 810
万 810
腕 810

wang
尪 811
亡 811
王 811
网 811
往 812
妄 812
忘 812
望 812

wei
危 813
威 813
微 813
煨 815
韦 815
违 816
围 816
维 816
伪 817
苇 817
尾 817
纬 818
委 818
萎 818
猥 819
痿 819

鲔	819			苋	866	新	897	眩	917	厌	955	移	973	荧	1001
卫	819	— X —		现	866	囟	900		xue	咽	955	遗	974	萤	1001
未	820			限	866	信	900	削	917	验	955	疑	976	营	1001
位	821		xi	陷	866		xing	靴	917	焰	955	乙	976	蝇	1002
味	821	西	839	腺	867	兴	900	学	917	燕	955	已	979	影	1002
畏	821	吸	840		xiang	星	900	雪	917		yang	以	979	瘿	1002
胃	821	希	841	乡	869	猩	901	鳕	917	羊	955	钇	980	应	1003
喂	826	昔	841	相	869	行	901	血	917	阳	956	蚁	980	硬	1003
蔚	826	析	841	香	869	形	901		xun	杨	958	倚	980		yong
魏	826	息	841	箱	870	型	902	熏	930	佯	958	酏	980	拥	1005
	wen	硒	842	镶	870	醒	902	寻	930	疡	958	义	980	痈	1005
温	826	悉	842	响	870	杏	902	巡	931	洋	958	艺	980	庸	1005
瘟	828	烯	842	向	870	幸	902	荨	931	烊	958	异	980	永	1005
文	828	稀	842	项	870	性	902	循	931	仰	958	抑	984	涌	1005
纹	828	犀	842	相	871		xiong	鲟	931	养	958	呓	985	蛹	1005
闻	828	锡	842	象	871	凶	904	训	931	氧	958	易	985	用	1005
蚊	828	溪	842	像	871	兄	904	驯	931	痒	960	疫	985		you
吻	828	豨	842	橡	871	芎	904	蕈	931	样	960	益	985	优	1005
稳	828	蜥	842		xiao	汹	904			恙	960	逸	986	忧	1006
问	829	膝	842	肖	871	胸	904	— Y —			yao	意	986	幽	1006
	weng	习	843	逍	871	雄	910			夭	960	溢	986	尤	1006
翁	829	席	843	消	871	熊	910		ya	腰	960	薏	986	由	1006
鎓	829	洗	843	硝	873		xiu	丫	932	摇	962	翳	986	邮	1006
	wo	徙	844	小	873	休	910	压	932	遥	962	翼	986	油	1006
涡	829	喜	844	哮	884	修	910	押	933	咬	962	癔	987	疣	1007
窝	829	戏	844	笑	884	羞	911	鸦	933	药	962		yin	铀	1007
蜗	829	系	844	效	884	袖	911	鸭	933	要	965	因	988	蚰	1007
肟	830	细	844		xie	嗅	911	牙	933	钥	965	阴	988	游	1007
沃	830	郄	849	楔	884	溴	911	芽	940		ye	茵	995	有	1008
卧	830	隙	849	歇	884		xu	蚜	941	耶	965	音	995	右	1010
握	830		xia	蝎	884	须	912	哑	941	椰	965	殷	996	幼	1012
	wu	虾	849	协	885	虚	912	雅	941	噎	965	铟	996	诱	1012
乌	830	侠	849	邪	885	需	913	亚	941	野	965	银	996	釉	1013
污	830	峡	850	胁	885	徐	914	氩	943	叶	965	淫	996		yu
巫	831	狭	850	偕	885	许	914	夜	966	龈	996	淤	1013
钨	831	下	850	斜	885	醑	914		yan	射	966	引	996	瘀	1013
屋	831	夏	856	谐	886	旭	914	咽	943	液	966	吲	997	于	1014
无	831		xian	携	886	叙	914	胭	945	腋	967	饮	997	余	1014
吴	835	仙	856	鞋	886	续	914	烟	945		yi	蚓	997	盂	1014
蜈	835	先	856	缬	886	絮	914	阉	946	一	968	隐	998	鱼	1014
五	835	纤	861	泄	886	蓄	914	淹	946	伊	968	瘾	999	渔	1015
午	836	氙	864	泻	886		xuan	延	946	衣	968	茚	999	逾	1015
伍	836	掀	864	谢	886	宣	914	严	947	医	969	印	999	榆	1015
武	836	酰	864	薤	886	喧	914	言	947	依	969		ying	与	1015
舞	836	鲜	864	蟹	886	玄	914	岩	947	咿	970	英	999	宇	1015
戊	837	弦	864		xin	悬	915	炎	948	铱	970	婴	999	羽	1015
芴	837	涎	864	心	887	漩	916	沿	948	噫	970	罂	1000	雨	1015
物	837	衔	865	芯	897	璇	916	研	948	懿	970	樱	1000	禹	1015
误	838	痫	865	辛	897	选	916	盐	949	仪	970	鹦	1000	语	1015
恶	838	嫌	865	欣	897	癣	916	颜	950	怡	970	膺	1000	玉	1015
雾	838	显	865	锌	897	癫	917	衍	950	怡	970	鹰	1000	芋	1015
寤	838							眼	950	胰	970	迎	1001	郁	1015
												荥	1001	育	1016

彧	1016	熨	1026	贬	1032	蛰	1035	栀	1047	钟	1069	柱	1079	姊	1089
浴	1016			乍	1032	赭	1035	脂	1047	肿	1069	祝	1079	籽	1089
预	1016	— Z —		诈	1032	褶	1036	蜘	1049	种	1070	疰	1079	紫	1089
欲	1016			栅	1032	浙	1036	执	1049	中	1070	蛀	1079	自	1090
阈	1016			炸	1032	蔗	1036	直	1050	仲	1071	铸	1079	字	1095
喻	1016	za		痄	1032	zhen		值	1052	众	1071	筑	1079	眦	1095
御	1016	杂	1027	榨	1032	贞	1036	职	1052	种	1071	zhua		zong	
愈	1017	zai		zhai		珍	1036	植	1053	重	1072	抓	1079	宗	1095
鹬	1017	灾	1027	摘	1032	真	1036	跖	1054	zhou		爪	1079	综	1095
yuan		甾	1027	窄	1032	砧	1038	止	1055	舟	1073	zhuan		棕	1095
鸢	1017	栽	1027	zhan		诊	1038	纸	1055	周	1073	专	1080	腙	1095
渊	1017	再	1027	粘	1032	枕	1039	指	1055	粥	1074	转	1080	鬃	1095
元	1017	在	1028	詹	1033	疹	1040	趾	1057	轴	1074	zhuang		总	1095
芫	1017	载	1028	谵	1033	阵	1040	枳	1058	肘	1074	桩	1081	纵	1096
园	1017	zan		展	1033	鸩	1040	酯	1058	帚	1075	装	1081	zou	
员	1017	暂	1028	战	1033	振	1040	至	1058	咒	1075	壮	1081	走	1096
原	1017	赞	1028	站	1033	震	1041	志	1058	绉	1075	状	1081	奏	1097
圆	1021	zang		zhang		镇	1041	制	1059	昼	1075	撞	1081	zu	
缘	1021	脏	1028	张	1033	zheng		质	1059	皱	1075	zhui		足	1097
猿	1021	藏	1029	章	1033	争	1041	炙	1059	骤	1075	椎	1081	阻	1098
远	1021	zao		樟	1033	征	1041	治	1059	zhu		锥	1083	组	1099
院	1023	凿	1029	长	1033	怔	1041	栉	1060	朱	1075	坠	1083	祖	1101
yue		早	1029	掌	1033	蒸	1041	桎	1060	侏	1075	缀	1083	zuan	
约	1023	枣	1030	帐	1035	整	1041	致	1060	珠	1075	赘	1083	钻	1101
月	1023	蚤	1030	胀	1035	正	1042	秩	1061	诸	1075	zhun		zui	
乐	1024	藻	1030	障	1035	证	1044	掷	1061	猪	1075	准	1083	嘴	1101
阅	1024	皂	1030	瘴	1035	郑	1044	痔	1061	蛛	1076	zhuo		最	1101
越	1024	造	1030	zhao		政	1044	窒	1061	潴	1076	灼	1084	罪	1102
yun		噪	1030	招	1035	症	1044	蛭	1061	竹	1076	浊	1084	醉	1102
晕	1024	燥	1030	朝	1035	zhi		智	1061	逐	1076	啄	1084	zuo	
云	1024	躁	1031	沼	1035	支	1044	痣	1061	主	1076	着	1084	左	1102
匀	1024	ze		照	1035	汁	1046	滞	1062	煮	1078	zi		佐	1104
芸	1024	泽	1031	罩	1035	芝	1046	置	1062	助	1078	咨	1084	作	1104
允	1024	zeng		zhe		枝	1046	稚	1062	住	1078	姿	1084	坐	1105
孕	1024	曾	1031	遮	1035	知	1046	zhong		贮	1079	资	1084	唑	1105
运	1025	增	1031	折	1035	肢	1046	中	1062	注	1079	滋	1084	做	1105
晕	1026	zha		辄	1035	织	1047	终	1069	驻	1079	子	1085		
		扎	1032												

词目首字音序索引 **11**

词目首字笔画索引

(字右边的号码指词典正文的页码)

一画		尸	712		617	亢	426	右	1010		1024	**六画**			307
一	968	己	340	方	802	布	182		60	犯	181	邦	22	迈	499
乙	976	已	979	瓦	1055	闩	744	戊	837	外	802	动	143	毕	39
二画		弓	248	止	682	火	322	龙	482	处	89	圭	273	至	1058
二	170	子	1085	少	647	斗	147	平	589	冬	143	吉	333	贞	1036
十	715	卫	819	日	1062	计	344	灭	524	鸟	552	扣	443	尘	76
丁	140	女	565	中	1070	户	302	东	143	包	22	考	432	尖	361
七	596	刃	644	贝	27	认	644	卡	423	饥	324	托	797	劣	470
八	11	飞	187	冈	235	心	887	北	26	主	1076	老	452	光	271
人	641	习	843	内	540	尺	81	凸	793	立	462	巩	251	当	122
入	658	叉	66	水	748	引	996	卢	484	冯	207	执	1049	早	1029
儿	165	马	497	见	367	巴	11	旧	414	玄	914	扩	448	吐	794
几	339	乡	869	午	836	孔	438	归	273	闪	674	扫	669	虫	85
九	412	**四画**		牛	562	队	151	目	529	兰	450	地	130	曲	628
刀	123	丰	204	手	734	以	979	叶	965	半	19	场	74	团	795
力	462	王	811	气	598	允	1024	甲	351	汁	1046	耳	166	吕	487
三画		开	424	毛	506	邓	125	申	688	汇	318	芋	1015	同	784
三	663	井	404	壬	644	劝	634	电	135	头	789	共	252	吊	138
干	225	天	779	升	706	双	744	号	283	汉	281	芍	682	因	988
	234	夫	207	夭	960	书	737	田	780	宁	560	芒	505	吸	840
于	1014	元	1017	长	70	幻	312	由	1006	让	637	亚	941	吁	1
工	247	无	831		1033	**五画**		卟	56	训	931	芝	1046	吗	499
土	794	韦	815	仁	644	玉	1015	史	723	必	38	芎	904	岁	760
士	723	云	1024	片	589	未	820	兄	904	记	345	机	324	帆	178
才	63	专	1080	仆	592	末	526	叩	443	永	1005	过	276	回	316
下	850	扎	1032	化	305	示	723	另	478	司	752	臣	76	刚	235
寸	103	艺	980	斤	388	击	324	叹	770	尼	548	再	1027	网	811
大	104	木	528	爪	1079	打	104	凹	9	民	524	协	885	肉	650
与	1015	五	835	反	179	巧	616	四	754	弗	208	西	839	钆	224
万	810	支	1044	介	388	正	1042	矢	706	出	87	压	932	钇	980
上	676	不	58	父	212	扑	592	失	712	奶	531	厌	955	年	549
小	873	犬	634	从	99	功	248	乍	1032	加	347	在	1028	朱	1075
口	438	太	768	今	388	去	629	禾	283	皮	578	百	16	氘	123
山	673	区	626	凶	904	甘	226	丘	624	边	41	有	1008	先	856
千	605	历	462	分	199	世	723	代	109	孕	1024	存	103	廷	783
川	90	尤	1006	乏	177	艾	4	仙	856	发	176	夸	444	舌	684
个	245	厄	161	公	248	古	254	仪	970	圣	711	夺	159	竹	1076
久	412	匹	587	仓	64	节	379	白	12	对	151	灰	316	迁	605
凡	179	车	76	月	1023	本	30	他	764	台	767	达	104	乔	616
丸	809	巨	416	风	204	术	743	瓜	266	矛	509	列	470	传	91
广	273	牙	933	丹	111	可	434	丛	99	纠	412	死	754	乒	589
亡	811	戈	242	匀	1024	丙	49	用	1005	母	527	成	77	休	910
门	513	比	37	乌	830	左	1102	印	1005	幼	1012	夹	348	伍	836
丫	932	互	302	六	482	厉	462	乐	453	丝	752	邪	885	伏	209
义	980	切	616	文	828	石	717					划	304	优	1005

伐	178	闭	39	吞	796	苄	43	员	1017	肛	235	忧	1006	纸	1055
延	946	问	829	远	1021	芳	183	听	782	肘	1074	怅	74	纹	828
仲	1071	羊	955	违	816	严	947	吩	203	肠	71	松	756	纺	184
任	644	并	50	韧	644	芦	484	吻	828	龟	273	快	444	纽	563
伤	674	关	266	运	1025	芯	897	吹	93	免	519	完	809	八画	
伦	493	米	517	扶	209	劳	452	呗	997	狂	445	牢	452	环	309
华	304	灯	124	技	345	克	435	别	47	狄	127	穷	623	武	836
	307	汗	282	坏	308	苊	438	吮	751	角	375	灾	1027	青	618
仰	958	污	830	扼	161	苏	757	岗	237	鸠	412	良	468	现	866
仿	184	江	370	拒	418	杆	232	帐	1035	条	781	证	1044	玫	509
伪	817	池	80	批	578	杠	237	岑	66	卵	490	诃	283	表	46
自	1090	汤	772	扯	76	杜	149	财	63	灸	412	启	598	盂	1014
伊	968	兴	900	走	1096	材	63	针	1036	岛	123	评	591	规	274
血	917	宇	1015	贡	253	杏	902	钉	141	迎	1001	补	56	柑	232
向	870	守	736	汞	252	巫	831	钊	470	饭	181	初	88	拓	800
囟	900	字	1095	攻	249	杓	682	氙	864	饮	997	社	687	拔	12
似	756	安	5	赤	84	极	333	氚	90	系	844	识	718	坦	770
后	297	军	421	折	1035	杞	598	牡	528	言	947	诈	1032	担	111
行	901	许	914	抓	1079	李	461	告	242	冻	146	诉	757	押	933
舟	1073	论	493	坂	18	杨	958	乱	493	状	1081	诊	1038	抽	86
全	630	农	563	扳	17	更	247	利	463	亨	289	词	97	拐	266
会	318	设	687	坎	425	束	743	秃	793	床	93	君	422	拖	798
杀	671	寻	930	均	421	豆	147	私	753	库	443	灵	477	拍	569
合	283	那	531	抑	984	两	469	每	512	庇	40	即	334	顶	141
企	598	导	123	抛	574	丽	463	体	777	疗	141	层	66	拆	67
众	1071	异	980	投	791	医	969	何	283	疗	470	屁	587	拥	1005
伞	668	弛	80	坟	203	辰	76	佐	1104	疠	378	尿	553	抵	128
创	92	孙	760	坑	437	否	207	但	120	应	1003	尾	817	势	723
肌	324	阵	1040	抗	426	还	308	伸	688	冷	459	迟	80	抱	25
肋	454	阳	956	抖	147	岜	811	作	1104	序	914	局	414	拉	449
杂	1027	收	733	护	302	来	449	伯	55	辛	897	改	224	幸	902
危	813	阶	378	壳	434	连	464	低	125	肓	313	张	1033	拧	562
旭	914	阴	988	志	1058	步	62	佝	253	忘	812	陆	487	招	1035
负	212	防	183	块	444	卤	487	住	1078	闰	661	阿	1	披	578
名	524	如	652	扭	563	坚	361	位	821	间	361		160	拨	53
各	245	妇	212	声	711	肖	871	伴	21		367	陈	76	拇	528
多	153	戏	844	拟	548	时	718	身	689	闷	514	阻	1098	盯	141
争	1041	羽	1015	芫	1017	吴	835	皂	1030	羌	613	附	213	耶	965
色	669	观	269	苇	817	呋	207	佛	207	判	571	坠	1083	取	629
壮	1081	红	290	芸	1024	助	1078	伽	224	兑	153	妊	644	苷	232
冲	84	纤	861	苊	161	里	461	近	392	灼	1084	姊	1089	苦	443
冰	48	驯	931	芽	940	吱	985	彷	571	沐	530	妒	150	苯	30
庆	623	约	1023	芘	38	呆	109	返	181	沥	464	努	565	昔	841
刘	478	级	333	苋	866	呕	568	余	1014	沙	671	忍	644	苛	432
齐	596	巡	931	花	303	园	1017	希	841	汽	603	鸡	329	若	661
交	371			芹	618	呃	161	坐	1105	沃	830	纬	818	苹	591
衣	968	七画		芥	388	围	816	谷	254	汹	904	驱	627	苜	530
次	98	寿	736	芩	618	吡	38	妥	800	泛	182	纯	96	英	999
产	67	麦	499	芬	203	足	1097	含	280	没	526	纱	672	苓	478
决	420	形	901	苍	64	邮	1006	邻	471	沟	253	纲	237	茚	999
充	85	进	391	苋	837	男	532	肝	227	沉	76	纳	531	范	182
妄	812	戒	388	芡	612	串	92	肟	830	怀	307	纵	1096	直	1050

词目首字笔画索引

茄	617	昂	9	舍	687	庚	247	实	718	珀	591	标	45	竖	743
茎	393	昃	412		688	废	199	试	723	珍	1036	柑	232	削	917
苔	767	咔	424	金	388	净	408	郎	451	珊	673	枯	443	尝	74
林	471	呫	782	命	524	盲	505	肩	362	玻	54	栉	1060	是	728
枝	1046	迪	127	郐	849	放	185	房	184	毒	148	柯	432	眇	523
杯	26	典	134	采	63	刻	436	衬	76	型	902	柄	50	眨	1032
枢	737	固	265	觅	517	育	1016	视	723	拭	728	枢	414	哑	941
枇	584	咀	416	受	736	郑	1044	祈	596	挂	266	相	869	显	865
杵	89	咒	1075	乳	652	卷	420	诡	274	封	206		871	冒	509
析	841	呼	300	贪	769	单	111	建	368	持	80	查	67	星	900
板	18	鸣	524	念	552	炖	153	寻	1075	拮	380	枳	1058	哒	104
松	756	呢	548	贫	589	炒	76	居	414	项	870	柏	17	畏	821
枪	613	咖	423	肼	404	炎	948	刷	744	城	79		56	胃	821
枫	206	岩	947	肤	208	炉	484	屈	627	政	1044	栀	1047	贵	274
构	253	罗	494	朊	660	炔	634	弧	301	贲	29	枸	253	界	388
杭	282	岬	356	肺	192	浅	612	弥	514	挺	784		416	虹	293
杰	380	帕	569	肢	1046	法	178	弦	864	括	448	栅	674	虾	849
枕	1039	岭	478	肽	768	泄	886	承	79	拾	720		1032	虮	514
卧	830	凯	425	肱	249	河	284	孟	514	挑	781	柳	482	蚁	980
刺	99	败	17	肿	1069	泪	456	孤	253	指	1055	柱	1079	思	753
枣	1030	贮	1079	胀	1035	沮	416	孢	23	垫	138	柿	728	蚂	499
雨	1015	图	794	股	255	油	1006	降	371	挤	340	柠	560	品	589
郁	1015	钍	795	肥	190	泊	55	限	866	垓	224	树	743	咽	943
矿	445	钒	179	服	209	沿	948	姑	254	拼	589	勃	56		955
奈	531	制	1059	胁	885	泡	574	姐	387	挖	802	要	965	咻	970
奔	29	知	1046	周	1073	注	1079	始	723	按	8	酊	141	响	870
奇	329	迭	139	昏	319	泮	571	姆	528	挥	316	威	813	哌	570
	596	垂	93	鱼	1014	泻	886	虮	713	挪	567	歪	802	哈	278
奋	203	牧	530	兔	795	泌	517	驾	361	荆	398	研	948	咯	242
欧	568	物	837	狐	301	泥	548	参	63	茸	648	厘	460		424
轰	290	乖	266	忽	301	沸	199		66	革	242	厚	299	咬	962
转	1080	刮	266	狗	253	沼	1035		689	茜	613	砒	578	咳	434
轮	493	和	283	狒	199	波	53	艰	364	荚	350	砂	672	咪	514
软	658	季	345	备	27	泼	591	线	866	荜	40	泵	32	炭	770
到	123	委	818	炙	1059	泽	1031	绀	235	带	110	砭	42	峡	850
鸢	1017	秉	50	饱	24	治	1059	练	467	草	64	砍	425	贴	782
非	187	供	249	饲	756	怔	1041	组	1099	茧	364	砜	207	骨	257
叔	737	使	723	饴	970	怯	617	细	844	茵	995	面	521	幽	1006
歧	596	侠	849	变	43	怵	89	织	1047	茴	318	耐	532	钙	224
肯	437	侧	65	京	393	性	902	终	1069	荞	616	奎	447	钛	768
齿	82	侏	1075	庞	571	佛	209	绐	1075	茯	209	牵	605	钝	153
虎	302	佩	576	夜	966	怪	266	驻	1079	茶	67	鸥	568	钟	1069
肾	697	依	969	府	211	怡	970	绊	21	荛	85	残	63	钡	28
尚	681	伴	958	底	128	学	917	驼	800	荣	648	轴	1074	钢	237
具	418	侘	67	疟	566	宗	1095	绍	683	荧	1001	轻	620	钠	531
味	821	卑	26	疠	464	定	142	经	393	荥	1001	鸦	933	钥	965
果	275	质	1059	疝	674	审	697	贯	270	荨	605	韭	412	钨	831
昆	448	欣	897	疙		官	269	绐	1027		931	背	27	钩	253
国	275	往	812	疡	958	空	437	九画		胡	301	战	1033	钮	563
呵	283	爬	569	剂	345		438	契	603	荔	464	点	134	钯	12
明	524	径	408	卒	100	帘	465	奏	1097	南	533	虐	567	拜	17
易	985	所	762	郊	373	穹	623	春	95	药	962	临	471	矩	416

词目首字笔画索引

氡	143	蚀	722	恢	316	泰	769	栓	744	哨	684	蚶	566	疲	584
氟	209	弯	808	恍	316	秦	618	桧	275	哭	443	徒	794	痊	409
氢	620	孪	490	恬	780	珠	1075	桃	774	恩	165	徐	914	脊	340
选	916	将	370	恰	603	班	17	格	242	蚤	9	殷	996	效	884
适	728	哀	3	举	416	素	757	桩	1081	唑	1105	航	282	离	460
香	869	亮	470	觉	420	匿	549	校	378	唤	313	拿	531	唐	772
种	1070	度	150	宣	914	蚕	64	核	284	峰	207	耸	757	凋	138
	1071	疣	1007	室	729	顽	809	样	960	圆	1021	爱	5	颁	282
秋	625	疥	388	宫	251	栽	1027	桉	6	峻	422	豹	25	瓷	97
科	432	疮	93	突	793	捕	58	根	245	钱	611	翁	829	资	1084
重	85	疫	985	穿	90	振	1040	索	762	钳	611	脐	444	凉	469
	1072	咨	1084	客	436	载	1028	或	1016	钴	263	胰	970	站	1033
复	214	姿	1084	冠	269	起	598	哥	242	钻	1101	胱	273	剖	591
段	151	亲	617	语	1015	盐	949	速	757	钼	530	脑	945	竞	410
便	44	音	995	扁	42	捏	558	豇	370	钾	356	胼	662	部	62
顺	751	施	713	袂	513	埋	499	栗	464	铀	1007	脆	103	旁	571
修	910	闻	828	祛	627	损	760	贾	356	铁	782	脂	1047	旅	487
保	25	差	66	祖	1101	挫	103	酎	232	铂	56	胸	904	阅	1024
促	100	养	958	神	690	捋	487	配	576	铃	478	脏	1028	羞	911
俄	160	美	512	祝	1079	换	313	酏	980	铅	605	脐	596	恙	960
信	900	姜	370	误	838	挽	810	唇	96	铈	729	胶	373	瓶	591
泉	633	类	457	诱	1012	热	638	夏	856	铊	764	脑	534	拳	633
鬼	274	迷	515	鸩	1040	恐	438	砹	1038	铋	40	胼	588	粉	203
侵	617	籽	1089	说	752	捣	123	砷	689	铍	584	脒	517	益	985
禹	1015	前	605	退	795	壶	302	破	591	缺	634	胺	9	兼	364
盾	153	首	736	屋	831	埃	3	原	1017	氩	943	脓	563	朔	752
待	111	逆	548	昼	1075	耻	83	套	774	氦	280	狷	420	烤	432
衍	950	总	1095	屏	50	耿	247	逐	1076	氧	958	狼	451	烘	290
律	487	炼	467			591	耽	116	烈	470	氨	6	留	478	烦	179
须	912	炽	84	费	199	荻	425	较	378	特	774	皱	1075	烧	682
叙	914	炸	1032	眉	509	莽	506	鸱	286	造	1030	凌	478	烟	945
剑	368	炮	574	除	88	莱	450	顿	153	乘	79	挛	490	烙	453
逃	774	烂	451	院	1023	莲	465	致	1060	敌	128	恋	467	烊	958
食	720	烃	783	娃	802	莳	723	柴	67	舐	729	桨	371	递	131
盆	577	剃	778	怒	565	莫	526	鸬	484	积	329	浆	370	浙	1036
胚	575	洁	380	架	361	载	160	虑	487	秩	1061	衰	744	浦	594
胨	147	洪	294	癸	274	荷	284	监	364	秘	40	高	237	酒	412
胆	116	浊	1084	蚕	1030	获	322	紧	390		518	郭	275	娑	761
胂	706	洞	147	柔	650	恶	161	逍	871	透	792	席	843	消	871
胍	266	测	66	绒	648		162	党	123	笔	38	准	1083	涡	829
胞	23	洗	843	结	380		838	唛	501	笑	884	症	1044	海	278
胖	574	活	321	绕	638	莨	468	晒	673	值	1052	痄	232	涂	794
脉	500	涎	864	绘	319	真	1036	眩	917	倾	621	病	51	浴	1016
胫	408	派	570	给	245	框	446	哮	884	倒	123	疸	414	浮	210
胎	764	染	636	绛	371	桂	274	鸭	933	候	300	疾	338	涤	128
匍	592	洛	495	骆	495	桔	386	哺	58	俯	211	痄	1032	流	478
勉	521	济	345	络	495		415	剔	776	倍	28	疹	1040	润	661
狭	850	洋	958	绝	420	桡	637	晕	1024	健	368	痈	1005	浸	393
狮	713	浑	319	绞	377	桎	1060		1026	臭	86	疼	776	烫	774
独	149	浓	563	统	788	桐	787	蚜	941	射	688	疱	574	涩	671
急	334	津	390		十画	桥	616	蚊	828		966	疰	1079	涌	1005
饶	637	恒	289	耗	283	桦	307	蚓	997	息	841	痂	348	悖	29

害	280	接	378	辄	1035	犁	461	烹	578	寄	346	揉	650	翘	616
宽	444	掷	1061	辅	211	秽	319	麻	496	宿	757	斯	753	悲	26
家	348	控	438	颅	484	移	973	痔	1061	窒	1061	期	596	紫	1089
宾	48	掀	470	虚	912	笼	483	痒	960	密	518	联	465	凿	1029
窄	1032	探	771	雀	635	笛	128	康	425	鞍	422	甚	706	掌	1033
容	648	掘	421	常	74	第	131	庸	1005	谐	886	葫	302	暑	741
朗	452	掺	67	眶	446	敏	524	鹿	487	屠	794	散	668	最	1101
诸	1075	职	1052	眦	1095	做	1105	盗	123	弹	120	惹	638	量	469
诺	567	基	330	匙	81	偕	885	章	1033			募	530		470
读	149	菝	12	晨	76	袋	111	商	675	堕	159	葛	244	脸	365
扇	674	菱	478	眼	950	偿	74	旋	915	随	759	萆	488	喷	577
袜	802	董	391	悬	914	偶	568	望	812	蛋	121	葡	592	喃	533
袖	911	勒	453	野	965	偷	789	率	744	隆	483	敬	410	晶	398
被	29	黄	313	曼	501	售	737	馘	1016	隐	998	葱	99	喹	447
调	139	萘	532	晚	810	停	783	阉	946	婚	319	葶	784	遏	163
	781	菲	190	啄	1084	偏	587	着	1084	婿	565	蒂	133	践	368
剥	54	菖	70	距	418	躯	628	羚	478	颈	404	萎	483	跖	1054
展	1033	萌	514	趾	1057	兜	147	羟	614	绩	347	落	453	跌	139
剧	418	萜	782	啮	558	假	357	盖	225	续	914		495	跗	208
弱	661	萝	494	蛎	464	徙	844	粘	1032	骑	598	蒿	42	跑	574
陶	774	菌	422	蚰	1007	得	124	粗	100	维	816	朝	76	跛	56
陷	867	萎	818	盅	263	衔	865	粒	464	绵	518		1035	蹄	528
姬	330	革	40	蚯	625	盘	570	断	151	绷	32	葵	447	遗	974
娩	521	菜	63	蛀	1079	船	92	剪	365	综	1095	棒	22	蛙	802
通	784	菟	795	蛇	687	斜	885	兽	737	绿	487	楮	89	蛴	534
能	548	菊	415	累	454	龛	425	烯	842	缀	1083	棱	459	蛭	1061
难	533	菠	55	鄂	163	鸽	242	烷	809	巢	76	棋	598	蛔	318
预	1016	萤	1001	患	313	敛	467	清	621	**十二画**		椰	965	蛛	1076
桑	668	营	1001	啰	494	悉	842	添	780	琥	302	植	1053	蛞	448
绢	420	萨	662	唾	800	欲	1016	淋	472	琼	623	森	671	蛤	243
验	955	菇	254	啤	584	彩	63		477	斑	17	焚	203		278
绦	774	梦	514	逻	494	领	478	湨	149	替	779	椅	980	喂	826
继	345	梗	247	崩	32	脚	378	淹	946	款	445	椒	374	喘	92
十一画		梅	510	婴	999	脯	592	渐	368	堪	425	椎	1081	喉	294
彗	319	检	364	圈	630	豚	796	混	319	搽	67	棉	519	喻	1016
球	625	梳	737	铑	453	脸	467	渊	1017	塔	764	棕	1095	啼	776
理	462	梯	776	铝	487	脱	798	淫	996	搭	104	椭	800	喧	914
麸	208	桶	788	铜	787	脘	810	渔	1015	揞	425	惠	319	喙	319
琉	480	梭	761	铟	996	脉	558	淘	774	越	1024	逼	32	嵌	613
堵	149	救	414	铠	425	匐	210	液	966	趋	628	粟	758	帽	509
描	523	啬	671	铬	245	象	871	淬	103	超	74	棘	338	赋	218
捷	386	副	216	铯	671	逸	986	淤	1013	提	776	硬	1003	黑	287
排	569	酞	769	铰	377	猜	63	淡	120	博	56	硝	873	铸	1079
捶	95	酚	203	铱	970	猪	1075	淀	138	喜	844	确	635	铺	592
掇	533	硅	274	铲	70	猎	470	深	689	彭	578	硫	480	链	467
推	795	硒	842	铵	8	猫	506	梁	469	插	66	厥	421	锁	762
掀	864	硕	752	银	996	猖	70	渗	706	煮	1078	裂	470	锄	89
授	737	盔	447	铷	652	猝	101	情	622	蛩	1035	雄	910	锂	462
捻	552	爽	748	矫	377	猕	516	惧	419	裁	63	颊	350	锅	275
教	378	厩	414	氪	437	猛	514	惊	398	搓	103	辊	275	铑	242
掊	603	聋	483	甜	780	减	364	惨	64	搅	378	暂	1028	铖	160
培	576	雪	917	梨	461	毫	282	惯	270	握	830	雅	941	锉	103

锋	207	然	636	登	124	雾	838	鼠	742	溪	842	磁	97	瘘	483
锌	897	装	1081	缄	364	辐	210	催	102	滚	275	稀	842	瘟	669
锐	661	痣	1061	缓	312	输	738	像	871	溢	986	殡	48	辣	449
锑	776	痨	452	缔	133	督	148	微	813	溶	648	需	913	端	150
锎	3	痘	147	编	42	频	589	愈	1017	溺	549	雌	98	旗	598
短	150	痞	587	缘	1021	鉴	369	遥	962		558	龈	996	精	399
智	1061	痢	464	**十三画**		睛	399	领	282	鲨	300	颗	433	熔	650
氰	623	痤	103	瑞	661	睫	386	腻	549	塞	662	嘈	64	漆	596
氮	122	痛	865	瑙	540	睡	751	膝	100		671	嘌	589	漱	744
毯	770	痧	672	魂	319	嗜	729	腰	960	窥	447	蜡	449	漂	589
氯	488	痛	788	摄	688	嗯	163	腮	662	窦	147	蜥	842	漫	502
犊	149	童	787	填	780	暖	566	腭	163	裸	495	蝇	1002	潇	1076
鹅	160	颏	433	搏	56	歇	884	腹	218	福	211	蜘	1049	滴	127
剩	712	阑	450	鼓	263	暗	9	腺	867	群	635	蜱	587	漩	916
程	79	阔	448	摆	17	照	1035	腧	743	障	1035	蜷	633	漏	483
稀	842	善	674	携	886	畸	332	腿	795	嫉	339	蝉	67	慢	502
等	124	普	594	摇	962	跨	444	詹	1033	嫌	865	蜿	809	赛	663
筑	1079	粪	203	蒜	759	跳	782	鲇	549	嫁	361	嘧	518	寨	266
策	66	道	124	薯	715	路	487	鲈	487	叠	139	罂	1000	察	67
筛	672	曾	1031	靴	917	跟	246	鲍	25	缝	207	瓴	128	蜜	518
筒	788	焰	955	靶	12	蜈	835	猿	1021	缠	67	鹋	264	瘠	838
筋	390	滞	1062	蓝	451	蜗	829	触	89	**十四画**		锶	754	褐	287
傅	218	湿	713	幕	530	蛾	160	解	387	静	410	锻	151	褪	796
集	339	温	826	蔼	165	蜂	207	雒	89	赘	1083	镀	150	谱	594
焦	374	渴	435	莨	40	蜢	613	酱	371	嘉	350	镁	513	隧	760
储	89	溃	447	蓬	578	蜕	796	禀	50	赫	287	舞	836	嫩	548
奥	9	溅	369	蒿	282	蛹	1005	痱	199	截	387	稳	828	翠	103
御	1016	滑	304	蒺	339	嗅	911	痹	40	境	412	熏	930	熊	910
循	931	游	1007	蓄	914	嗳	5	廓	448	摘	1032	箍	254	瞀	509
艇	784	滋	1084	蒲	594	嗓	669	瘠	275	聚	419	箕	332	缩	761
舒	737	湄	511	蒙	514	置	1062	痴	80	酱	614	算	759	缪	523
逾	1015	慌	313	蒸	1041	罪	1102	痿	819	慕	530	管	270	**十五画**	
领	286	惰	159	楔	884	罩	1035	瘀	1013	暮	530	僧	671	璇	916
釉	1013	割	242	椿	96	蜀	742	痰	769	蔓	502	鼻	32	撕	754
番	178	寒	281	禁	393	嵴	339	廉	466	蔡	63	魄	591	撒	662
释	729	富	218	槭	451	骰	792	麂	344	蔗	1036	睾	240	撩	470
禽	618	窜	102	槐	307	错	103	新	897	蔽	40	膜	525	撑	76
腈	399	窝	829	槌	95	锚	509	意	986	蔚	826	膈	243	撮	103
腊	449	窗	93	榆	1015	锝	124	羧	761	榷	192	膀	571	赭	1035
腓	191	窘	412	概	225	锡	842	数	743	模	524	鲑	274	播	55
腘	275	雇	266	赖	450	锤	95	煎	364		527	鲔	819	撞	1081
脾	585	谢	886	酮	787	锥	1083	塑	758	槟	49	鲜	864	撤	76
腋	967	犀	842	酰	864	锦	391	慈	97	榨	1032	鲟	931	增	1031
腑	212	强	613	酯	1058	锭	143	煤	511	酵	378	疑	976	鞋	886
腙	1095		615	酪	453	键	369	煨	815	酶	511	孵	208	鞍	8
腔	613	粥	1074	感	233	锯	419	煅	151	酰	280	豪	283	蕨	421
腕	810	疏	738	碘	134	锰	514	煌	315	酿	552	膏	242	蕤	661
腱	368	隔	243	硼	578	矮	4	满	501	酸	758	遮	1035	蕲	598
鲁	487	隙	849	碎	760	稚	1062	滤	490	碟	139	腐	212	蔬	741
猩	901	媒	511	碰	578	稠	86	滥	451	碱	366	瘦	84	横	289
狼	819	絮	914	雷	454	筒	366	溻	764	碳	771	瘟	828	槽	64
猴	296	赦	626	零	478	毁	318	溴	911	碲	133	瘦	737	樱	1000

词目首字笔画索引

樊	179	墨	527	澄	79	磺	315	瘿	1002	瞳	787	鹞	1017	蟾	67
橡	871	骷	296	懊	10	霍	323	瘴	1035	嚏	779	骤	1075	髋	444
槲	302	镍	558	额	160	餐	63	癃	483	曙	743	十八画		髌	48
樟	1033	镇	1041	褥	658	噤	393	瘾	999	蹒	570	鬓	1095	鳕	917
橄	234	镉	244	鹤	287	嘴	1101	凝	560	螺	494	藕	568	蟹	886
敷	208	镍	558	谵	1033	蹄	776	辨	45	髁	434	鞭	42	颤	70
豌	809	镒	829	熨	1026	螨	501	糙	64	髀	40	鞣	650	癣	917
醋	101	镓	350	劈	578	螃	574	糖	772	镫	125	藜	461	瓣	21
醌	448	靠	432	缬	886	器	603	糕	242	黏	549	藤	776	鳖	47
醇	97	稽	332	十六画		噪	1030	燎	470	魏	826	覆	223	爆	26
醉	1102	稻	124	靛	138	噬	732	燃	636	簇	102	礞	514	二十画及以上	
碾	552	箱	870	鳌	9	噎	970	濒	48	繁	179	瞿	629	鬟	48
震	1041	箭	369	操	64	噻	663	激	332	黛	111	蟠	571	躁	1031
霉	512	僵	371	颞	558	罹	461	寰	312	舝	280	髂	603	蠕	652
辘	487	德	124	鞘	616	鹦	1000	褶	1036	貘	527	镭	454	嚼	375
暴	25	膝	842	燕	955	默	527	壁	40	膦	264	镰	466	鳘	461
噎	965	滕	776	薤	886	镜	412	避	40	朦	514	翻	179	鳝	674
嘶	754	鲤	462	蕾	454	赞	1028	缰	371	臊	669	臑	540	鳞	477
影	1002	熟	741	薯	743	憨	603	十七画		膻	122	鳍	598	谵	970
踝	307	摩	526	薏	986	穆	530	戴	111	臁	466	鹰	1000	癫	795
踢	776	瘛	84	薄	24	篮	451	螯	733	鳃	663	癔	987	灌	270
踏	764	瘪	18		56	魁	626	壕	283	鳄	164	瀑	595	露	487
踩	63	瘤	482	颠	133	膨	578	擦	63	糜	516	戳	97	髓	759
蝶	139	瘫	769	噩	164	膳	674	鞠	414	膺	1000	十九画		癞	133
蝶	650	瘸	466	橙	79	臌	477	藏	64	癌	18	攒	102	麝	688
蝴	302	颜	950	橘	416	雕	138		1029	癌	4	藿	323	蠹	462
蝠	211	羰	772	整	1041	鲭	622	藁	242	糠	426	蘑	526	囊	533
蛙	447	糊	302	融	650	鲱	190	檀	770	燥	1030	藻	1030	镜	67
蝎	884	潜	612	瓢	589	鲵	548	臀	986	濡	652	攀	570	镶	870
蝮	223	潮	76	醛	633	鲸	404	磷	475	豁	320	曝	595	颧	633
蟆	483	鲨	672	醒	902	磨	526	霜	748	臀	796	蹼	595	躅	420
蝙	42	澳	10	醚	516			螭	629	臂	40	蹲	153	欅	571
噙	618	潘	570	醌	914	瘵	495	瞬	752	翼	986	蠓	514	蠼	629

A

吖丁啶类/吖丁啶類　azetidines
吖啶/吖啶　acridine
吖啶橙/吖啶橙　acridine orange
吖啶黄/吖啶黄　acridine yellow
吖啶类/吖啶類　acridines
吖啶生物碱/吖啶生物鹼　acridine alkaloid
吖啶琐辛/吖啶瑣辛　akrinol
吖庚因类/吖庚因類　azepines
吖辛因类/吖辛因類　azocines
阿巴前列素/阿巴前列素　arbaprostil
阿贝折射计/阿貝折射計　Abbe refractometer
阿苯达唑/阿苯達唑　albendazole
阿伯克龙比综合征/艾伯克症候群，澱粉樣變性　Abercrombie syndrome
阿布德尔哈尔顿透析/Abderhalden 氏透析　Abderhalden dialysis
阿布拉米病/Abrami 氏病　Abrami disease
阿-蔡计数池/亞貝·蔡司計數池　Abbe-Zeiss counting cell
阿达帕林/阿達帕林，類維生素 A 酸　adapalene
阿德诺西林/阿德諾西林　amdinocillin
阿狄森瘢痕瘤/Addison 氏瘢瘤　Addison keloid
阿狄森色素沉着过度/Addison 氏色素沈著過度　Addisonian hyperpigmentation
阿狄森综合征/愛迪生氏症候群　Addisonian syndrome
阿迪综合征/Adie 氏症候群　Adie syndrome
阿蒂斯反应/阿圖斯氏反應　Arthus reaction
阿蒂斯现象/阿圖斯氏現象　Arthus phenomenon
阿-蒂综合征/Achard-Thiers 二氏症候群　Achard-Thiers syndrome
阿-杜病/Aran-Duchenne 二氏病　Aran-Duchenne disease
阿-杜肌萎缩/Aran-Duchenne 二氏肌萎縮　Aran-Duchenne muscular atrophy
阿多尼丁/福壽草苷，福壽草素　adonidin
阿多甾醇/阿多甾醇　adosterol
阿恩特-舒尔茨定律/安-舒二氏定律　Arndt-Schulz law
阿尔比纳斯肌/Albinus 氏肌　Albinus muscle
阿尔茨海默病/阿茲海默症　Alzheimer disease
阿尔茨海默染剂/阿茲海默氏染劑　Alzheimer stain
阿尔茨海默细胞/阿茲海默氏細胞　Alzheimer cell
阿尔茨海默疫苗/阿茲海默疫苗　Alzheimer vaccine
阿尔盖·罗伯逊瞳孔[征]/Argyll Robertson 氏瞳孔　Argyll Robertson pupil
阿尔曼尼-埃布斯泰因细胞/阿-埃二氏細胞　Armanni-Ebstein cell
阿尔梅达病/Almeida 氏病　Almeida disease
阿尔珀斯病/阿爾珀斯病　Alpers disease
阿尔塞弗溶液/Alsever 氏溶液　Alsever solution
阿尔陶森试验/艾瑟森氏試驗　Althausen test
阿尔特曼-格什法/歐特門遜氏法　Altmann-Gersh method
阿尔新蓝/阿辛藍　Alcian blue
阿尔新蓝染色/阿辛藍染色　Alcian blue stain
阿尔孕酮/阿爾孕酮　algestone
阿法罗定/阿法羅定　alphaprodine
阿菲波菌属/軍院菌屬　*Afipia*
阿芬太尼/阿芬太尼　alfentanil
阿佛丁麻醉/阿佛丁麻醉　Avertin anesthesia
阿弗他口炎/鵝口瘡口炎　stomatitis aphthosa
阿弗他溃疡/口瘡潰瘍　aphthous ulcer
阿弗他腺周炎/口周圍腺炎　periadenitis aphthae
阿格纽夹板/Agnew 氏夾板　Agnew splint
阿根廷出血热/阿根廷出血熱　Argentinian haemorrhagic fever
阿洪病/暗洪病，自發性斷趾病　Ainhum
阿-基畸形/Arnold-Chiari 氏變形　Arnold-Chiari malformation
阿-基脑畸形/小腦扁桃體下疝畸形　Arnold-Chiari malformation
阿卡波糖/阿卡波糖　acarbose
阿科斯塔病/高山症　Acosta disease
阿-克病/Apert-Crouzon 氏病　Apert-Crouzon disease
阿克尔隆德变形/亞克倫氏變形　Akerlund deformity
阿克罗宁/阿克羅寧　acronine
阿拉伯吡喃糖/阿拉伯膠糖，樹膠醛醣　arabopyranose
阿拉伯茶叶碱/阿拉伯茶葉鹼　katine
阿拉伯胶浆/阿拉伯樹膠漿　acacia mucilage

阿拉伯胶素/阿拉伯膠素　arabin
阿拉伯胶糖浆/阿拉伯膠糖漿　acacia syrup
阿拉伯树胶/阿拉伯樹膠　acacia
阿拉伯酸盐/阿拉伯膠鹽酸　arabate
阿拉伯糖/阿拉伯膠糖　arabinose
阿拉伯糖醇/阿拉伯糖醇　arabite
阿拉伯糖苷/阿糖胞苷　arabinoside
阿拉伯糖尿/阿拉伯膠糖尿　arabinosuria
阿拉伯糖酸/阿拉伯糖酸,樹膠糖酸　arabonic acid
阿拉伯糖中毒/阿拉伯膠糖過多症　arabinosis
阿拉伯酮糖/阿拉伯酮醣　arabinulose
阿拉伯象皮病/阿拉伯象皮病　true elephantiasis
阿拉伯医学/阿拉伯醫學　Arabic medicine
阿拉日耶综合征/Alagille 症候群　Alagille syndrome
阿拉霉素/阿拉黴素　alamethicin
阿兰岛病/阿蘭德島病　Aland island disease
阿兰绿色癌/Aran 氏綠色癌　Aran green cancer
阿利贝尔瘢痕瘤/假瘢瘤　Alibert keloid
阿利马嗪/阿利馬嗪　trimeprazine
阿林厄姆溃疡/Allingham 氏潰瘍　Allingham ulcer
阿留申水貂病/阿留申水貂病　Aleutian Mink disease
阿留申水貂病病毒/阿留申水貂病病毒　Aleutian Mink disease virus
阿路德林/異丙烷腺上腎素　aludrine
阿洛糖/阿洛糖　allose
阿洛西林/阿洛西林　azlocillin
阿义马林/阿馬林　ajmaline
阿马托/銨甲苯　amatol
阿米巴/阿米巴　ameba
阿米巴病/阿米巴病,變形蟲病　amebiasis
阿米巴的/阿米巴的　amoebic
阿米巴淀粉酶/阿米巴澱粉酵素　amebadiastase
阿米巴肺脓肿/阿米巴肺膿腫　Amebic abscess of lung
阿米巴痢疾/阿米巴痢疾,變形蟲痢疾　Amebic dysentery
阿米巴瘤/阿米巴腫　ameboma
阿米巴[性]包囊/阿米巴囊腫　amebic cyst
阿米巴[性]肺炎/阿米巴性肺炎　amebic pneumonia
阿米巴[性]肝脓肿/阿米巴性肝膿腫　amebic liver abscess
阿米巴[性]肝炎/阿米巴性肝炎　amebic hepatitis
阿米巴[性]结肠炎/阿米巴性結腸炎　amebic colitis
阿米巴[性]阑尾炎/阿米巴性闌尾炎　amebic appendicitis
阿米巴样/阿米巴樣　ameboid
阿米巴样[神经]胶质/阿米巴狀膠質　ameboid glia
阿米巴样[神经]胶质瘤/阿米巴樣神經膠質瘤　ameboid glioma
阿米巴样运动/阿米巴樣運動　ameboidism
阿米根/胺精　amigen
阿米雷司/阿米雷司　aminorex
阿米洛利/阿米洛利　amiloride
阿米芹属/阿米芹屬　Ammi
阿米三嗪/阿米三嗪　almitrine
阿米替林/阿米替林　amitriptyline
阿米妥/安密妥　amytal
阿明/乙基磷酸對硝基苯乙酯　armin
阿莫地喹/阿莫待喹,卡莫喹　amodiaquine
阿莫沙平/阿莫沙平　amoxapine
阿莫西林/羥氨苄青黴素　amoxicillin
阿姆斯勒方格表/阿姆斯勒方格表　Amsler grid
阿姆斯特丹型侏儒/阿姆斯特丹型侏儒　Amsterdam type dwarfism
阿那佐林钠/測血容量指示劑　anazolene sodium
阿尼普酶/阿尼普酶　anistreplase
阿尼齐科夫细胞/Anitschkow 氏細胞　Anitschkow cell
阿诺病/Hanot 氏病　Hanot disease
阿诺德韧带/Arnold 氏韌帶　Arnold ligament
阿诺德神经/Arnold 氏神經　Arnold nerve
阿诺尔德-基亚里畸形/阿諾德-希阿里畸形　Arnold-Chiari malformation
阿诺特水褥/Arnott 氏墊　Arnott bed
阿诺-肖法尔综合征/阿-肖二氏症候群　Hanot-Chauffard syndrome
阿诺综合征/Hanot 氏症候群　Hanot syndrome
阿片/鴉片　opium
阿片酊/鴉片酊,鴉片酊劑　opium tincture
阿片类镇痛药/阿片類鎮痛藥　opioid analgesics
阿片相关性障碍/阿片相關性障礙　opioid-related disorder
阿片样受体/阿片樣受體　opioid receptor
阿片样肽类/阿片樣肽類　opioid peptides
阿朴阿托品/阿朴阿托品,衍阿托品　apoatropine
阿朴啡类/阿朴啡類　aporphines
阿朴啡类生物碱/阿朴啡類生物鹼　aporphine alkaloid
阿朴吗啡/阿朴嗎啡,衍嗎啡　apomorphine
阿朴乌头碱/阿朴烏頭素,衍烏頭素　apaconitine
阿普加评分/阿帕嘉氏新生兒評分　Apgar score
阿普林定/阿普林定　aprindine
阿普洛尔/阿普洛爾　alprenolol
阿普唑仑/阿普唑侖　alprazolam
阿奇红霉素/疊氮紅黴素　azithromycin

阿屈膦酸盐/阿屈膦酸鹽　alendronate
阿曲库铵/阿曲庫銨　atracurium
阿柔比星/阿柔比星　aclarubicin
阿瑟综合征/Aase 氏症候群　Aase syndrome
阿什曼现象/阿什曼現象　Ashman phenomenon
阿施夹/Asch 氏夾板　Asch splint
阿是穴/阿是穴　ashi point
阿司咪唑/阿司咪唑　astemizole
阿司帕坦/阿司帕坦　aspartame
阿司匹林/阿斯匹靈,乙醯水楊酸　aspirin
阿斯科利疗法/亞克利氏療法　Ascoli treatment
阿斯曼病灶/阿斯曼病灶　Assmann foci
阿斯佩格综合征/阿斯佩格症候群　Asperger syndrome
阿-斯综合征/亞-斯二氏症候群　Adams-Stokes syndrome
阿苏埃罗疗法/亞斯羅氏療法　asuerotherapy
阿糖胞苷/阿糖胞苷　ara-C
阿糖呋喃胞苷三磷酸/阿糖呋喃胞苷三磷酸　arabinofuranosylcytosine triphosphate
阿糖核苷类/阿糖核苷類　arabinonucleosides
阿糖腺苷/阿糖腺苷　vidarabine
阿糖腺苷磷酸盐/阿糖腺苷磷酸鹽　vidarabine phosphate
阿特拉嗪/阿特拉嗪　atrazine
阿替洛尔/阿替洛爾　atenolol
阿托品/阿托品　atropine
阿托品性结膜炎/阿托品性結膜炎　atropine conjunctivitis
阿托品衍生物/阿托品衍生物　atropine derivative
阿瓦德微管型膜式氧合器/阿瓦德微管型膜式氧合器　Awad tubular membrane oxygenator
阿韦利斯综合征/阿韋利斯症候群　Avellis syndrome
阿维 A/阿維 A　acitretin
阿维 A 酯/阿維 A 酯　etretinate
阿魏/阿魏　asafetida, Chinese asafetida
阿魏化痞膏/阿魏化痞膏　awei huapi plaster
阿希赫斯特夹板/Ashhurst 氏夾板　Ashhurst splint
阿昔洛韦/阿昔洛章　aciclovir
阿孝夫细胞/Aschoff 氏細胞　Aschoff cell
阿孝夫小体/阿紹夫小體　Aschoff body
阿歇尔综合征/Ascher 氏症候群　Ascher syndrome
阿扬溶液/Hayem 氏溶液　Hayem solution
阿耶罗菌属/阿耶羅菌屬　Ajellomyces
阿耶萨综合征/Ayerza 氏症候群　Ayerza syndrome
阿扎胞苷/阿扎胞苷　azacitidine
阿扎丙宗/阿扎丙宗　apazone

阿扎胆醇/阿扎膽醇　azacosterol
阿扎呱隆/阿扎呱隆　azaperone
阿扎立平/阿扎立平　azaribine
阿扎尿苷/阿扎尿苷　azauridine
阿扎培汀/氮佩汀　azapetine
阿扎他定马来酸盐/阿剳他定馬來酸鹽　Azatadine maleate
阿卓糖/右羥己糖　altrose
阿卓糖酸/羥己糖酸　altronic acid
阿祖林/可哥鹼　azurin
阿佐霉素/含氮黴素　azotomycin
锕射气/錒射氣　actinium emanation
哀苦/哀苦　sorrow feeling
埃/埃　angström
埃宾豪斯试验/埃賓豪斯氏試驗　Ebbinghaus test
埃波拉病毒/Ebola 病毒　Ebola virus
埃伯纳液/Ebner 氏液　Ebner liquid
埃博拉出血热/伊波拉出血熱,伊波拉病毒病　Ebola hemorrhagic fever
埃博拉疫苗/埃博拉疫苗　Ebola vaccine
埃布斯泰因肥胖病饮食[疗法]/Ebstein 氏飲食　Ebstein diet
埃布斯坦综合征/埃布斯坦症候群　Ebstein syndrome
埃-当二氏病/Ehlers-Danlos 二氏病　Ehlers-Danlos disease
埃德尔曼细胞/Edelmann 氏細胞　Edelmann cell
埃-德肌营养不良/Emery-Dreifuss 二氏肌肉失養症　Emery-Dreifuss muscular dystrophy
埃迪瞳孔/埃迪瞳孔　Adie pupil
埃窦斯综合征/Eddowes 氏症候群　Eddowes syndrome
埃尔布点/Erb 氏點　Erb point
埃尔布-杜兴麻痹/埃-杜二氏麻痺　Erb-Duchenne paralysis
埃尔布痉挛性截瘫/Erb 氏痙攣性截癱　Erb spastic paraplegia
埃尔布麻痹/Erb 氏麻痺,臂神經叢麻痺　Erb palsy
埃尔布-夏科病/埃-夏二氏病,痙攣性失調症　Erb-Charcot disease
埃尔利希反应/Ehrlich 氏反應　Ehrlich reaction
埃尔斯纳哮喘/Elsner 氏氣喘　Elsner asthma
埃及牛乳糖/牛乳糖　tewfikose
埃及血吸虫/埃及血吸蟲　Schistosoma haematobium
埃及血吸虫病/埃及血吸蟲病　Schistosomiasis haematobia
埃及伊蚊/埃及蚊,黃熱蚊　Aedes aegypti
埃可病毒/埃可病毒　Echovirus

埃可病毒感染/埃可病毒感染　Echovirus infection
埃可病毒疹/埃可病毒疹　Echovirus eruption
埃克瘘/Eck氏瘘管　Eck fistula
埃克斯纳丛/Exner氏丛　Exner plexus
埃里希体病/埃里希體病　Ehrlichiosis
埃利斯韧带/Ellis氏韌帶　Ellis ligament
埃利希侧链学说/埃利希側鏈學說　Ehrlich side chain theory
埃利希-海因茨粒/埃利希氏顆粒,埃-海二氏顆粒　Ehrlich-Heinz granule
埃伦美厄烧瓶/歐倫麥氏燒瓶,錐形瓶　Erlenmeyer flask
埃梅特[弯]针/Emmet氏針　Emmet needle
埃默特-盖尔霍恩子宫托/空杆子宫托　Emmert-Gellhorn pessary
埃内贝尔征/安娜贝兒徵　Hennebert sign
埃瑟移植物/埃瑟氏移植物　Esser graft
埃[舍利]希杆菌属/Escherich氏菌屬,大腸桿菌屬　Escherichia
埃[舍利]希杆菌族/埃歇利氏菌族　Escherichieae
埃氏放线菌/eriksonii氏放線菌　Actinomyces eriksonii
埃斯马赫止血带/Esmarch氏止血帶　Esmarch tourniquet
埃托啡/羥戊甲嗎啡　etorphine
埃文斯综合征/埃文斯症候群　Evans syndrome
癌/癌　carcinomata
癌变/癌變　carcinomatous change
癌的/癌的　carcinomatous
癌基因/致癌基因,腫瘤形成基因　oncogene
癌基因蛋白质类/癌基因蛋白質類　oncogene proteins
癌胚抗原/癌胚抗原　carcino-embryonic antigen
癌前病变/癌前期病灶　precancerous lesion
癌前黏膜白斑病/癌前期白斑角化症　precancerous leukokeratosis
癌前[期]的/癌前的　precancerous
癌前[期]非痣样黑色素细胞瘤/癌前期非痣樣黑色素細胞瘤　precancerous non-naevoid melanocytoma
癌前[期]黑变病/癌前期黑變症　precancerous melanosis
癌前状态/癌前狀態,癌前況況　premalignant condition, precancerous condition
癌切除术/癌切除術　carcinectomy
癌肉瘤/癌肉瘤　carcinosarcoma
癌栓/癌栓　cancer plug
癌细胞/癌細胞　cancer cell

癌细胞溶解/癌溶解,癌崩解　carcinolysis
癌细胞栓子/癌片栓子　cancer embolus
癌相关性水疱/癌相關性水皰　cancer-related bullae
癌性脊髓病/癌性脊髓病　carcinomatous myelopathy
癌性甲状腺肿/癌性甲狀腺腫　carcinomatous goiter
癌性角化病/癌性角化症　cancer keratosis
癌性溃疡/癌性潰瘍　carcinomatous ulcer
癌性心包炎/癌性心包炎　carcinomatous pericarditis
癌血[症]/癌血症　canceremia
癌症/癌症　cancer
癌症医护设施/癌症醫護設施　cancer care facility
癌症疫苗/癌症疫苗　cancer vaccine
癌转移/癌轉移　cancerometastasis
癌状的/癌狀的　carcinomatoid
矮糠/羅勒　basil
矮胖体型/矮胖體型,肥短體型　pyknic type
矮树痒/矮樹癢　scrub itch
矮小病/矮小病　runt disease
矮小幻觉/顯小性幻覺　lilliputian hallucination
矮小[身材]/矮小畸形,侏儒　microsomatia
矮妖精貌综合征/矮妖精貌症候群,多諾霍氏症候群　leprechaunism
矮壮素/矮壯素　chlormequat
艾比肌/降下唇肌　Aeby muscle
艾波特-罗森管/亞-羅二氏管　Abbott-Rawson tube
艾波特-米勒管/亞-米二氏管　Abbott-Miller tube
艾伯特病/Albert氏病　Albert disease
艾迪生病/艾迪生病　Addison disease
艾迪生病危象/艾迪生氏病危象,腎上腺危象　Addisonian crisis
艾迪综合征/艾迪氏症候群　Adie syndrome
艾杜糖/艾杜糖　idose
艾杜糖醛酸/艾杜糖醛酸　iduronic acid
艾杜糖醛酸硫酸酯酶/艾杜糖醛酸硫酸酯酶　iduronate sulfatase
艾杜糖醛酸酶/艾杜糖醛酸酶　iduronidase
艾附暖宫丸/艾附暖宫丸　aifu nuangong pills
艾灸/艾灸　moxa-wool moxibustion
艾科植物/艾科植物　mugwort
艾伦-多伊西试验/艾-道二氏試驗　Allen-Doisy test
艾美球虫属/艾美耳球蟲　*Eimeria*
艾绒/艾絨　moxa wool
艾萨克综合征/以撒克候群　Isaac syndrome
艾森门格尔病/艾森門格病　Eisenmenger disease
艾森门格尔综合征/艾森門格症候群　Eisenmenger syndrome
艾氏剂/愛德林　aldrin
艾属/艾屬　*Artemisia*

艾司唑仑/艾司唑侖　estazolam
艾斯库累普/艾司古拉庇護師　aesculapius
艾条/艾條　moxa stick
艾条灸/艾條灸　moxa stick moxibustion
艾叶/艾葉　argy wormwood leaf
艾炷/艾炷　moxa cone
艾炷灸/艾炷灸　moxa-cone moxibustion
艾滋病/愛滋病,後天性免疫不全症候群　acquired immuno deficiency syndrome, AIDS
艾滋病痴呆复合征/愛滋病癡呆複合徵　AIDS dementia complex
艾滋病·肺肾阴虚证/愛滋病·肺腎陰虛證　AIDS with lung-kidney yin deficiency pattern
艾滋病·肺卫受邪证/愛滋病·肺衛受邪證　AIDS with pattern of lung-defense phase affected by pathogen
艾滋病·脾肾两虚证/愛滋病·脾腎兩虛證　AIDS with spleen-kidney deficiency pattern
艾滋病·脾胃虚弱证/愛滋病·脾胃虛弱證　AIDS with spleen-stomach weakness pattern
艾滋病·气虚血瘀证/愛滋病·氣虛血瘀證　AIDS with pattern of qi deficiency and blood stasis
艾滋病·痰蒙心窍证/愛滋病·痰蒙心竅證　AIDS with pattern of phlegm clouding heart orifice
艾滋病相关复合征/愛滋病相關疾病　AIDS-related complex
艾滋病相关机会致病菌感染/愛滋病相關機會致病菌感染　AIDS-related opportunistic infection
艾滋病相关淋巴瘤/愛滋病相關淋巴瘤　AIDS-related lymphoma
艾滋病相关肾病/愛滋病相關腎病　AIDS-related nephropathy
艾滋病血清诊断/愛滋病血清學診斷　AIDS serodiagnosis
艾滋病疫苗/愛滋病疫苗　AIDS vaccine
爱德华菌属/Edwards 氏菌屬　Edwardsiella
爱德生试验/愛德生試驗　Adson test
爱迪生病/愛迪生氏病　Addison disease
爱泼斯坦-巴尔病毒/Epstein-Barr 二氏病毒　Epstein-Barr virus
爱泼斯坦-巴尔病毒感染/Epstein-Barr 病毒感染　Epstein-Barr Virus infection
爱泼斯坦-巴尔病毒核抗原/Epstein-Barr 病毒核抗原　Epstein-Barr Virus nuclear antigen
爱泼斯坦肾变病/Epstein 氏腎病　Epstein nephrosis
爱泼斯坦小节/Epstein 氏珍珠　Epstein pearl
爱泼斯坦异常/Epstein 氏異常　Ebstein anomaly
爱泼斯坦综合征/Epstein 氏症候群　Epstein syndrome
爱斯基摩皮炎/北極洋皮炎　kallak
嗳气/噯氣,打嗝　belch, belching
嗳气·肝胃不和证/噯氣·肝胃不和證　belching with pattern of disharmony between liver and stomach
嗳气·脾胃虚寒证/噯氣·脾胃虛寒證　belching with pattern of deficiency-cold of spleen and stomach
嗳气·食积证/噯氣·食積證　belching with food retention pattern
嗳气·胃阴虚证/噯氣·胃陰虛證　belching with pattern of stomach yin deficiency
嗳气·胃中痰火证/噯氣·胃中痰火證　belching with pattern of phlegm-fire in stomach
安吖啶/安吖啶　amsacrine
安贝氯铵/安貝氯銨　ambenonium chloride
安瓿/安瓿　ampule
安瓿封口/安瓿熔封　ampule sealing
安瓿灌封机/安瓿充填機　ampule filling and sealing machine
安瓿灌注/安瓿充填　ampule filling
安波霉素/二黴素　ambomycin
安德烈森溃疡病饮食/Andresen 氏潰瘍病飲食　Andresen diet
安德鲁病/Andrews 氏病　Andrews disease
安德鲁斯试验/安德魯氏試驗　Andrewes test
安德森夹/安德森氏夾板　Anderson splint
安德施神经/Andersch 氏神經　Andersch nerve
安第斯山地病/南美洲安第斯山地病　Andes disease
安定/鎮靜　tranquilize
安定麻醉[法]/安定麻醉法　neuroleptanesthesia
安定麻醉剂/安定麻醉劑　neuroleptanesthetic
安定药/安定藥,鎮靜劑,安神藥　tranquilizer, tranquilizing agent
安定镇痛[法]/安定止痛法　neuroleptanalgesia
安东尼 A 及 B 型/安東尼 A 及 B 型　Antoni types A and B
安东综合征/安東症候群　Anton syndrome
安-法病/Anderson-Fabry 氏病　Anderson-Fabry disease
安非拉酮/安非拉酮　diethylpropion
安非他酮/安非他酮　bupropion
安福消肿膏/消炎糊劑　antiphlogistine
安抚胶体浴/安撫膠體浴　soothing colloid bath
安格尔错𬌗分类/安格爾錯𬌗分類　Angle classification of malocclusion
安格尔夹/Angle 氏夾板　Angle splint
安[格尔]氏带环/Angle 氏環　Angle band
安宫牛黄丸/安宮牛黃丸　angong niuhuang pill,

Peaceful Palace Bovine Bezoar Pill
安魂定魄/安魂定魄 calming the mind
安静的/静的,宁静 quiet
安静状态/静止狀態 resting state
安克洛酶/安克洛酶 ancrod
安坤赞育丸/安坤贊育丸 ankun zanyu pills
安乐死/安樂死 euthanasia
安南溃疡/Annam 氏潰瘍 Annam ulcer
安尼奥廷/動情素 Amniotin
安匹林/安匹林 empirin
安普莱茨技术/Amplatz 氏技術 Amplatz technique
安普罗铵/安普羅銨 amprolium
安曲霉素/安麴黴素 anthramycin
安全措施/安全措施 security measure
安全带伤/安全帶傷 seat belt injury
安全范围/安全範圍 safety range
安全界限/安全界限 margin of safety
安全开颅圆锯/可避免損傷腦組織的圓鋸,可避免損
  傷腦組織的環鑽鋸 abaptiston
安全面切盘/安全面切盤 safe sided disc
安全评价/安全評估 safety evaluation
安全期/安全期 safe period
安全期计划生育法/安全期計劃生育法 natural
  family planning method
安全气囊皮炎/安全氣囊皮膚炎 airbag dermatitis
安全套/保險套 condom
安全性/安全性 safety
安全性行为/安全性行爲 safe sex
安全因素/安全因素 safety factor
安全用药/安全用藥 safe medication
安沙霉素类/安沙黴素類 ansamycins
安神补心丸/安神補心丸 anshen buxin pills
安神法/安神法 tranquil lization method
安神剂/安神劑 sedative, tranquillizing formula
安神止痛[法]/醒覺除痛法 ataralgesia
安氏I类错𬌗/安氏I類錯𬌗 Angle class I
  malocclusion
安氏II类错𬌗/安氏II類錯𬌗 Angle class II
  malocclusion
安氏III类错𬌗/安氏III類錯𬌗 Angle class III
  malocclusion
安斯巴彻尔单位/安巴赫氏單位 Ansbacher unit
安他唑啉/安他唑啉 antazoline
安胎/安胎 tranquilizing fetus to prevent miscarriage
安特罗弗尔/安特羅弗爾 antrophore
安慰性的/安撫的 soothing
安慰药/安慰劑 placebo
安慰治疗效应/安慰劑效應 placebo effect

安西他滨/安西他濱 ancitabine
安息香/安息香 benzoin
安息香试验/安息香試驗 benzoin test
安息香树胶/樹膠安息香 gum benzoin
桉胶/紅樹膠 eucalyptus gum
桉树胶/基諾 kino
桉树属/桉樹屬 *Eucalyptus*
桉烷倍半萜类/桉烷倍半萜類 eudesmane
  sesquiterpenes
桉油/桉[葉]油 eucalyptus oil
氨/胺 ammonia
氨吖啶/胺基吖啶 aminoacridine
氨苯蝶啶/三胺苯蝶啶 triamterene
氨苯砜/胺苯碸 dapsone, diaminodiphenylsulfone
氨苯磺胺类/胺苯磺胺類 sulfanilamides
氨苯胂酸/胺基苯胂酸 arsanilic acid
氨苯酞胺/胺苯酯胺 amphotalide
氨苯唑/胺苯唑 amiphenazole
氨苄西林/安比西林,胺苄青黴素 ampicillin
氨苄西林抗药性/胺苄西林抗藥性 ampicillin
  resistance
氨茶碱/胺基非林,乙烯二胺茶葉素 aminophylline
氨氮/胺氮 ammonia nitrogen
氨丁三醇/緩血酸胺,三羥甲基氮甲烷
  tromethamine
氨发酵/胺發酵 ammoniacal fermentation
氨苷菌素/胺基殺菌素 aminosidine
氨合物/胺合物 ammoniate
氨化硝酸银/胺化硝酸銀 ammoniated silver nitrate
氨环己西林/環青黴素 cyclacillin
氨基/胺基 amino
氨基吖啶类/胺基吖啶類 aminoacridines
氨基苯磺酸锌/胺苯磺酸鋅 zinc sulfanilate
氨基苯甲酸/胺基安息香酸 aminobenzoic acid
氨基苯甲酸丁酯/胺基安息香酸丁酯 butyl
  aminobenzoate
氨基比林/胺基吡啉 amidopyrine
氨基比林试验/胺基吡啉試驗 aminopyrine test
氨基比林N-脱甲酶/胺基吡啉N-脱甲酶
  aminopyrine N-demethylase
氨基吡啶类/胺基吡啶類 aminopyridines
氨基丙腈/胺基丙腈 aminopropionitrile
氨基醇/胺基醇 alkamine
氨基氮/胺基氮 amino nitrogen
氨基蝶呤/胺基喋呤 aminopterin
氨基丁酸/胺基丁酸 aminobutyric acid
氨基多肽酶/胺基多肽酶 aminopolypeptidase
氨基蒽醌类染料/胺基蒽醌類染料

aminoanthraquinone dye
氨基酚类/胺基酚類　aminophenols
氨基甘氨酸尿/胺基甘胺酸尿　aminoglycinuria
氨基甘露糖/胺基甘露糖　epichitosamine
氨基苷/胺基苷類,胺基配糖　aminoglycoside
氨基硅烷键合硅胶/胺基烷矽鍵結矽膠　amino chemically bonded silica
氨基合成酶/胺基合成酶　amido-ligase
氨基核苷嘌呤霉素/胺基核苷嘌呤黴素　puromycin aminonucleoside
氨基磺酸/胺基苯磺酸　sulfamic acid
氨基磺酸铵/胺基磺酸銨　ammonium sulfamate
氨基己酸/胺基己酸　aminocaproic acid
氨基己糖/胺基己糖　amidohexose
氨基己糖多糖/糖胺聚糖　glycosaminoglycan
氨基己糖苷酯酶/胺基己糖苷酯酶　hexosaminidase
氨基甲酸/胺基甲酸,胺基碳酸　carbamic acid
氨基甲酸羟苯丁酯/胺基甲酸羥苯丁酯　hydroxyphenamate
氨基甲酸血红蛋白/胺基碳酸血紅素　hemoglobin carbamate
氨基甲酰反应/碳醯胺基酸　carbamino reaction
氨[基]甲酰血红蛋白/碳醯胺基血紅素　carbaminohemoglobin
氨基喹/胺基喹　aminoquin
氨基喹啉类/胺基喹啉類　aminoquinolines
氨基联苯化合物/胺基聯苯化合物　aminobiphenyl compound
氨基磷酸酶/磷酸胺酶　phosphaminase
氨基硫脲比色法/胺基硫脲比色法　thiosemicarbazide colorimetry
氨基马尿酸类/胺基馬尿酸類　aminohippuric acids
氨基咪唑甲酰胺/胺基咪唑醯胺　aminoimidazole carboxamide
氨基[末]端[的]/胺基末端的　aminoterminal
氨基萘磺酸/萘胺磺酸　naphthionic acid
氨基脲类/胺基脲類　semicarbazides
氨基偶氮甲苯/胺基偶氮甲苯　aminoazotoluene
氨基嘌呤/胺基嘌呤　aminopurine
6-氨基青霉烷酸/6-胺基青黴[烷]酸　6-amino-penicillanic acid, 6-APA
氨基噻唑/胺基噻唑　aminothiazole
氨[基]三唑/胺唑　amitrole
氨基水解酶类/胺基水解酶類　aminohydrolases
氨基水杨酸/胺基水楊酸　aminosalicylic acid
氨基水杨酸钙/胺基水楊酸鈣　calcium aminosalicylate
氨基酸/胺基酸　amino acid

氨基酸重复序列/胺基酸重複序列　amino acid repetitive sequence
氨基酸代谢病/胺基酸缺陷病　aminoacidopathy
氨基酸过多[症]/胺基酸病理性過多症　aminosis
氨基酸活化酶/胺基酸活化酶　amino acid-activating enzyme
氨基酸类/胺基酸類　amino acids
氨基酸类药物/胺基酸類藥物　amino acids drug
氨基酸氯甲基酮类/胺基酸氯甲基酮類　amino acid chloromethyl ketones
氨基酸萘基酰胺酶类/胺基酸萘基醯胺酶類　amino acid naphthylamidases
氨基酸尿[症]/胺基酸尿　aminoaciduria
氨基酸谱/胺基圖表　aminogram
氨基酸取代/胺基酸取代　amino acid substitution
氨基酸[使用]频率/胺基酸頻率　amino acid frequency
氨基酸受体/胺基酸受體　amino acid receptor
氨基酸特征结构/胺基酸特徵結構　amino acid motif
氨基酸序列/胺基酸序列　amino acid sequence
氨基酸序列同源性/胺基酸序列同源性　amino acid sequence homology
氨基酸血/胺基酸血症　aminoacidemia
氨基酸氧化还原酶类/胺基酸氧化還原酶類　amino acid oxidoreductases
氨基酸异构酶类/胺基酸異構酶類　amino acid isomerases
氨基酸酯混合物/胺基酸酯混合物　amino acid ester mixture
氨基酸转运系统/胺基酸轉運系統　amino acid transport system
氨基酸组成/胺基酸組成　amino acid composition
氨基酸组成分析仪/胺基酸組成分析儀　amino acid composition analyzer
氨[基]肽酶/胺基勝肽酵素　aminopeptidase
氨基糖/胺[基]糖　amino sugar
氨基糖苷类/胺基糖苷類　aminoglycosides
氨基糖苷类抗生素/胺基糖苷類抗生素　aminoglycoside antibiotics
氨基糖苷肾病/胺基糖苷腎病　aminoglycoside nephropathy
氨基糖类/胺基糖類　amino sugars
氨基乙酰丙酸/胺基乙醯丙酸　aminolevulinic acid
7-氨基头孢烷酸/7-胺基頭孢烯酸　7-amino cephalosporanic acid
7-氨基脱乙酰氧头孢烷酸/7-胺基脫乙醯氧頭孢烷酸　7-amino-deacetoxycephalosporanic acid, 7-ADCA

氨基酰化/胺基醯化 aminoacylation
氨基酰化酶/胺基醯化酶 aminoacylase
氨基氧乙酸/胺基氧醋酸 aminooxyacetic acid
氨基乙醇类/胺醇 amino alcohols
氨基乙磺酸缺乏/胺基乙磺酸缺乏 taurine deficiency
氨基乙腈/胺基乙腈 aminoacetonitrile
氨基乙酸二羟化铝/二羥胺基醋酸鋁 dihydroxyaluminum aminoacetate
5-氨基乙酰丙酸/5-胺基乙醯丙酸 5-aminolevulinic acid
氨基异丁酸类/胺基異丁酸類 aminoisobutyric acids
氨己烯酸/胺己烯酸 vigabatrin
1-氨-4-甲氨蒽醌/1-胺-4-甲胺蒽醌 1-amino-4-methylaminoanthraquinone
氨甲苯酸/胺甲苯酸 aminomethylbenzoic acid
2-氨-2-甲-1-丙醇处理虫胶液/2-胺-2-甲-1-丙醇處理蟲膠液 2-amino-2-methyl-1-propanol treated shellac solution
氨甲蝶呤/胺甲喋呤 amethopterin
氨甲环酸/胺甲環酸 tranexamic acid
氨甲酸羟苯乙酯/胺甲酸羥苯乙酯 styramate
氨甲酸叔己酯/甲基戊醇碳醯胺 emylcamate
氨甲酸酯类/胺甲酸酯類 carbamates
氨甲酰胆碱/胺甲醯膽鹼,卡巴可林 carbocholine
氨甲酰甲胆碱/氯貝膽鹼 bethanechol
氨甲酰甲胆碱化合物/胺甲醯甲膽鹼化合物 bethanechol compound
氨甲酰磷酸合酶/胺甲醯磷酸合成酶 carbamoyl-phosphate synthase
氨甲酰磷酸合酶Ⅰ缺乏病/胺甲醯磷酸合酶Ⅰ缺乏病 carbamoyl-phosphate synthaseⅠdeficiency disease
氨甲酰磷酸盐/胺甲醯磷酸鹽 carbamyl phosphate
氨解[作用]/胺解 aminolysis
氨磷汀/胺磷汀 amifostine
氨硫脲/胺硫尿素,結核安,縮胺硫脲類 thioacetazone, thiosemicarbazone
氨鲁米特/胺麩精 aminoglutethimide
氨氯地平/胺氯地平 amlodipine
氨尿/胺尿症 ammoniuria
氨尿嘧啶/胺嘧啶 aminometradine
氨排泄/胺漏 ammonirrhea
氨皮炎/胺皮膚炎 ammonia dermatitis
氨曲南/胺曲南 aztreonam
氨水烧伤/胺水燒傷 aqueous ammonia burn
氨水杨酸/胺水楊酸 mesalamine
氨肽酶类/胺肽酶類 aminopeptidases
氨肟/胺腭 amidoxime

氨酰胆碱/胺醯膽鹼 imbretil
氨酰基脯氨酸二肽酶缺乏[症]/脯胺酸肽酶缺乏 prolidase deficiency
氨酰基转移核糖核酸合成酶类/胺醯基 tRNA 合成酶類 amino acyl-tRNA synthetases
氨酰转移酶类/胺醯轉移酶類 aminoacyl transferases
2-氨-4-硝苯酚/2-胺-4-硝苯酚 2-amino-4-nitrophenol
2-氨-5-硝苯酚/2-胺-5-硝苯酚 2-amino-5-nitrophenol
氨硝酸银溶液/含胺硝酸銀溶液 ammoniacal silver nitrate solution
氨性尿/胺性尿 ammoniacal urine
氨溴索/胺溴索 ambroxol
氨血[症]/胺血症 ammonemia
氨乙吡唑/胺乙吡唑 ametazole
氨乙基/胺乙基 aminoethyl
氨乙基膦酸/胺乙基磷酸 aminoethylphosphonic acid
鞍背/鞍背 dorsum sella
鞍背点/鞍背點 klition
鞍膈/鞍膈,蝶鞍橫膈 diaphragma sellae, diaphragm of sella turcica
鞍基/鞍,部分假牙之斷面或一部分 saddle
鞍结节/鞍結節 tuberculum sellae
鞍结节脑膜瘤/鞍結節腦膜瘤 tuberculum sellae meningioma
鞍栓/馬鞍狀栓塞 saddle embolism
鞍形头/鞍狀頭,斜[頂]頭 clinocephalism
鞍中突/中床狀突 middle clinoid process
鞍[状]鼻/鞍狀鼻,凹陷鼻 saddle nose
鞍状峰/鞍狀峰 saddle back
鞍状关节/鞍狀關節 sellar joint, saddle joint, saddle articulation
鞍状阻滞麻醉/鞍狀隔斷麻醉法 saddle block anesthesia
铵/銨 ammonium
按抚法/按撫法 stroking
按摩/按摩,推拿 massage
按摩膏/按摩膏 massage cream
按摩浴缸/按摩浴缸 jacuzzi
按钮/按鈕 button
按蚊属/瘧蚊 Anopheles
按蚊族/瘧蚊亞科,阿諾斐雷蚊亞科 Anophelini
按需型起搏器/按需型起搏器 demand pacemaker
按压法/按壓法 pressure manipulation
按诊/按診 body palpation
按诊疗收费计划/按診療收費計劃 fee-for-service

plan
胺/胺　amine
胺碘酮/胺碘酮　amiodarone
胺化作用/胺化作用　amination
胺甲萘/萘基甲基胺基甲酸酯　carbaryl
胺能神经元/胺能神經元　aminergic neuron
胺尿[症]/胺尿症　aminuria
暗产色菌/暗產色菌株　scotochromogen
暗带/牙釉質之橫斷層　diazone
暗点/[眼前]暗點,盲點　scotoma
暗点测定[法]/暗點測量法　scotometry
暗点发生/暗點化　scotomization
暗点计/暗點計　scotometer
暗点描记器/暗點描記器　scotomagraph
暗点性眩晕/暗點性眩暈　scotodinia
暗光盲/暗光盲　twilight blindness
暗光眼球震颤/眼球之暗光震顫　darkness tremor
暗盒/片匣　cassette
暗褐菌素/視網膜棕質,視褐素　fuscin
暗间隙/暗間隙　dark space
暗霉素/尼拉黴素　nebramycin
暗色孢科/暗色孢科　Dematiaceae
暗色丝孢霉病/暗褐色絲菌病　phaeohyphomycosis
暗示/暗示　suggestion
暗示解惑疗法/暗示解惑療法　suggestion and puzzel removing therapy
暗示疗法/暗示療法　suggestion therapy, suggestive medicine
暗视觉/暗[光]視力,夜間視覺　scotopic vision, noctovision
暗视视网膜电图/暗視視網膜電圖　scotopic electroretinogram
暗视野聚光器/暗視野聚光器　darkfield condenser
暗视野显微镜/暗視野顯微鏡　darkfield microscope, dark field microscope
暗视野[显微]镜检术/暗視野顯微鏡檢查　darkfield microscopy
暗[视]野照明/暗視野照明,黑地照明法　darkfield illumination
暗视阈值反应/暗視閾值反應　scotopic threshold response
暗适应/暗光適應　dark adaptation
暗适应计/暗適應計　dark adaptometer
暗室俯卧试验/暗室俯臥試驗　darkroom prone test
暗室试验/暗室試驗　darkroom test
暗影试验/影子試驗　shadow test
昂丹司琼/昂丹司瓊　ondansetron
盎格尔西假腿/安格斯氏假腿　Anglesey leg

凹痕/凹陷,壓陷　pitting
凹间韧带/凹間韌帶,小窝間韌帶　interfoveolar ligament
凹入/壓痕,鋸齒狀缺痕　indentation
凹透镜/凹透鏡　minus lens
凹凸透镜/凹凸透鏡　concavoconvex lens
凹陷瘢痕/凹陷瘢痕　depressed scar
凹陷骨折/凹陷骨折　depressed fracture
凹陷甲/指甲點狀凹陷,趾甲點狀凹陷　nail pitting
凹陷性疤痕/凹陷性疤痕　pitted scar
凹陷性病变/凹陷性病變　excavated lesion
凹陷性骨折/凹陷性骨折　depressed fracture
凹柱镜片/凹柱鏡片　concave cylindrical lens
凹状甲/凹狀甲　coilonychia
螯合剂/螯合劑　chelating agent
螯合疗法/螯合療法　chelation therapy
螯合酶/螯合酶　chelatase
螯合物/螯合物　chelate
螯合[作用]/螯合[作用]　chelation
奥本海姆征/奥本海姆徵　Oppenheim sign
奥伯试验/奥伯試驗　Ober test
奥布赖恩肉芽肿/O'Brien氏肉芽腫　O'Brien granuloma
奥布赖恩运动不能/O'Brien氏暫時肌麻痺　O'Brien akinesia
奥迪肌/Oddi氏肌　Oddi muscle
奥迪括约肌/奥迪括約肌　sphincter of Oddi
奥迪括约肌成形术/奥迪括約肌成形術　plastic repair of Oddi sphincter
奥迪括约肌功能障碍/奥迪括約肌功能障礙　sphincter of Oddi dysfunction
奥迪括约肌切开术/奥迪括約肌切開術　sphincterotomy of Oddi
奥迪括约肌狭窄/奥迪括約肌狹窄　stenosis of Oddi sphincter
奥尔巴赫神经丛/Auerbach氏叢　Auerbach plexus
奥尔波特综合征/Alport症候群　Alport syndrome
奥尔布赖特病/Albright病　Albright disease
奥尔布赖特遗传性骨营养不良/Albright氏遺傳性骨發育不良　Albright hereditary osteodystrophy
奥尔布赖特综合征/Albright氏症候群　Albright syndrome
奥尔德里奇/歐德里奇　Aldrich
奥尔德里奇合剂/歐德里奇合劑　Aldrich mixture
奥尔德里奇综合征/歐德里奇症候群　Aldrich syndrome
奥尔菲拉解剖学博物馆/奥菲拉氏解剖學博物館　Orfila museum

奥尔马赫固定液/Ohlmacher 氏固定液　Ohlmacher fixing fluid
奥尔梅病/Olmer 氏病　Olmer disease
奥尔舍夫斯基管/歐塞基氏管　Olshevsky tube
奥尔特加细胞/Hortega 氏細胞，小神經膠質細胞　Hortega cell
奥尔特溶液/Orth 氏溶液　Orth solution
奥尔西-格罗科法/奥-格二氏法　Orsi-Grocco method
奥芬铵/奥芬銨　oxyphenonium
奥芬那君/鄰甲基苯海拉明　orphenadrine
奥夫雷希特病/Aufrecht 氏病　Aufrecht disease
奥夫伦病/Owren 氏病　Owren disease
奥古蛋白/奥古蛋白　orgotein
奥克巴胺/奥克巴胺　octopamine
奥克斯纳环/Ochsner 氏環　Ochsner ring
奥克斯纳肌/Ochsner 氏肌　Ochsner muscle
奥克斯纳疗法/Ochsner 氏療法　Ochsner treatment
奥勒通/奥勒通，丙酸睾酮油劑　oreton
奥利耶-蒂尔施移植物/歐-泰二氏移植物　Ollier-Thiersch graft
奥利耶病/Ollier 氏病　Ollier disease
奥罗泼希病毒/Oropouche 病毒　Oropouche virus
奥罗亚热/奥洛耶熱　Oroya fever
奥美拉唑/奥美拉唑　omeprazole
奥尼翁尼翁病毒/歐尼安尼安氏病毒　O'nyong-nyong virus
奥尼亚型单纯性大疱性表皮松解症/歐格納型單純性大皰性表皮鬆解症　Ogna variant of epidermolysis bullosa simplex
奥皮奇异现象/奥比氏奇異現象　Opie paradox
奥匹呱醇/奥匹呱醇　opipramol
奥曲肽/奥曲肽　octreotide
奥赛动物/奥賽氏動物　Houssay animal
奥赛现象/奥賽氏現象　Houssay phenomenon
奥沙那胺/環氧乙基己醯胺　oxanamide
奥沙尼喹/奥沙尼喹　oxamniquine
奥沙西泮/奥沙西泮　oxazepam
奥斯古德-施拉特病/奥-史二氏病　Osgood-Schlatter disease
奥斯勒病/Osler 氏病　Osler disease
奥斯皮茨征/Auspitz 氏徵象　Auspitz sign
奥斯汀・弗林特杂音/奥斯汀・弗林特氏雜音　Austin Flint murmur
奥索利酸/奥索利酸　Oxolinic acid
奥特纳综合征/Ortner 氏症候群　Ortner syndrome
奥托骨盆/鄂圖骨盆　Otto pelvis
奥西那林/奥西那林　orciprenaline
奥昔麻黄碱/奥昔麻黃鹼　oxyfedrine
奥昔嘌醇/奥昔嘌醇　oxypurinol
奥硝唑/奥硝唑　ornidazole
奥[扎尔德]曼森线虫/曼森線蟲屬　*Mansonella ozzardi*
澳大利亚抗原/澳大利亞抗原　Australian antigen
澳大利亚 X 脑炎/澳洲 X 腦炎　Australian X encephalitis
澳洲钩端螺旋体病/澳洲鉤端螺旋體病　Pomona fever
澳洲胶/澳洲膠　Australian gum
澳洲 X 脑炎病毒/澳洲 X 病病毒　Australian X disease virus
懊恼/懊憹　heat sensation in the chest and restlessness

B

八倍体/八倍體　octoploid
八段锦/八段錦　eight-sectioned exercise
八法/八法　eight methods
八风/八風　bafeng, EX-LE10
八纲/八綱　eight principles
八纲辨证/八綱辨證　pattern identification of eight principles
八会穴/八會穴　eight influential point
八角枫碱/安钠巴鬆,新煙鹼　anabasine
八角茴香/八角茴香　Chinese star anise
八廓/八廓　eight regions
八脉交会穴/八脈交會穴　eight confluence point
八邪/八邪　baxie, EX-UE9
八旬老人/八旬老人　octogenarian
八珍汤/八珍湯　bazhen decoction
八珍益母丸/八珍益母丸　bazhen yimu pills
八阵/八陣　eight tactical arrays
八正合剂/八正合劑　bazheng mixture
八正散/八正散　bazheng powder
八字脚/八字腳　splay foot
八字形缝合/八字形縫合　figure eight suture
八字形结/八字形結　figure-eight tie
巴巴可鱼毒草/巴巴可魚毒植物　barbasco
巴贝虫病/巴貝蟲病　babesiasis
巴比妥/巴比妥　barbital
巴比妥类静脉麻醉药/巴比妥類静脈麻醉藥　barbiturate intravenous anesthetic
巴比妥酸/巴比妥酸　barbituric acid
巴比妥酸盐/巴比妥鹽　barbiturate
巴宾斯基反射/巴賓斯基反射　Babinski reflex
巴宾斯基-纳若特综合征/Babinski-Nageotte 二氏症候群　Babinski-Nageotte syndrome
巴宾斯基征/巴賓斯徵　Babinski sign
巴宾斯基综合征/Babinski 氏症候群　Babinski syndrome
巴波霉素类/班貝黴素類　bambermycins
巴伯斯指间毛窦/理髮師指尖毛竇　barber interdigital hair sinus
巴布科针/Babcock 針　Babcock needle
巴德病/布德氏病,Budd 氏病　Budd disease, Budd cirrhosis
巴德肝硬变/布德氏病,Budd 氏病　Budd disease, Budd cirrhosis
巴德黄疸/布德氏黄疸,Budd 氏黄疸　Budd jaundice
巴德特-别德尔综合征/巴-比二氏症候群,勞比二氏症候群　Bardet-Biedl syndrome
巴迪内韧带/Bardinet 氏韌帶　Bardinet ligament
巴蒂斯塔缩容心脏成形术/巴蒂斯塔縮容心臟成形術　Batista volume reducing cardioplasty
巴豆/巴豆　croton fruit
巴豆毒蛋白/巴豆毒質　crotin
巴豆酸/巴豆酸　crotonic acid
巴豆酸盐类/巴豆酸鹽類　crotonates
巴豆中毒/巴豆中毒　crotonism
巴多林管口/Bartholin 氏前口　Bartholin anus
巴多林孔/Bartholin 氏孔　Bartholin foramen
巴多林腺/Bartholin 氏腺　Bartholin gland
巴多林腺囊肿/Bartholin 氏腺囊腫　Bartholin cyst
巴尔干流感/巴爾干半島病,巴爾干流行性感冒　Balkan grippe
巴尔干肾病/巴爾干腎病　Balkan nephropathy
巴尔干式夹板/巴爾干夾　Balkan splint
巴尔干式架/巴爾干支架　Balkan frame
巴尔科夫韧带/Barkow 氏韌帶　Barkow ligament
巴洛病/Barlow 氏病　Barlow disease
巴尔姆咳/Balme 氏欬嗽　Balme cough
巴特疝/Barth 氏疝氣　Barth hernia
巴尔通绷带/Barton 繃帶　Barton bandage
巴尔通体病/巴爾通體病　bartonelliasis
巴尔通体感染/巴爾通體感染　Bartonella infection
巴尔通体属/巴爾通體屬　*Bartonella*
巴伐利亚夹/Bavarian 夾板　Bavarian splint
巴甫洛夫小胃/巴甫洛夫囊　Pavlov pouch
巴戟天/巴戟天　morinda root
巴津病/Bazin 氏病　Bazin disease
巴柯碱/巴柯鹼　paucine
巴克动脉瘤/Park 氏動脈瘤　Park aneurysm
巴克莱-希尔-奎伊综合征/巴克莱-希爾-奎伊症候群　Buckley-Hill-Quie syndrome
巴拉圭茶碱/巴拉圭茶素　yerbine
巴拉尼试验/巴拉尼試驗　Barany test
巴莱病/Ballet 氏病　Ballet disease

巴兰斯征/巴蘭斯徵　Ballance sign
巴雷特食管/巴雷特食管　Barrett esophagus
巴林顿核/巴林頓核　Barrington nucleus
巴林格尔病/Ballingall 氏病　Ballingall disease
巴林特综合征/巴林特症候群　Balint syndrome
巴龙霉素/巴龍黴素　Paromomycin
巴洛病/巴羅病　Balo disease
巴氯芬/巴氯芬　Baclofen
巴拿马热/巴拿馬熱　Panama fever
巴-帕综合征/Bartholin-Patau 氏症候群　Bartholin-Patau syndrome
巴-皮综合征/Bard-Pic 二氏症候群　Bard-Pic syndrome
巴曲酶/巴曲酶　Batroxobin
巴萨万特垫/巴薩威特墊　cushion of passavant
巴塞尔解剖学名词/巴賽爾解剖學名詞　Basle nomina anatomica
巴氏合金/Babbitt 氏金屬　Babbitt metal
巴斯德菌病/巴斯德桿菌病　pasteurellosis
巴斯德菌感染/巴斯德菌感染　Pasteurella infection
巴斯德菌属/巴斯德拉菌屬　*Pasteurella*
巴斯德菌族/巴斯德桿菌目　Pasteurelleae
巴斯德培养液/Pasteur 氏液　Pasteur fluid
巴斯德溶液/Pasteur 氏溶液　Pasteur solution
巴斯刷牙法/巴斯刷牙法　Bass method of tooth brushing
巴特癌/Butter 氏癌　Butter cancer
巴特综合征/巴特症候群　Bartter syndrome
巴腾病/Batten 氏病　Batten disease
巴托林管/Bartholin 氏管　duct of Bartholin
巴西副球孢子菌/巴西副球孢子菌　Paracoccidioides brasiliensis
巴西副球孢子菌素/巴西副球孢子菌素　paracoccidioidin
巴西果蛋白/巴西果蛋白　excelsin
巴西鸡吸虫/雞吸蟲　Typhlocoelum cucumerinum
巴西利什曼原虫/巴西利什曼體　Leishmania brasiliensis
巴西尼疝修补术/巴西尼疝修補術　Bassini herniorrhaphy
巴西疟原虫/猿瘧蟲　Plasmodium brasilianum
巴西试验/巴西試驗　brazilian test
巴西天疱疮/巴西天皰瘡　Brazilian pemphigus
巴西芽生菌/巴西芽生菌　Blastomyces brasiliensis
巴西芽生菌病/巴西芽生黴菌病　blastomycosis brasiliensis
巴西锥体虫病/巴西錐蟲病　Brazilian trypanosomiasis

巴西棕榈蜡/巴西棕櫚蠟　carnauba wax
巴亚尔热线/放線間纖維叢　Baillarger line
巴泽多病/Basedow 氏病,凸眼性甲狀腺腫　Basedow disease
巴泽多病者/巴塞杜氏病患者　basedowian
拔毒生肌散/拔毒生肌散　badu shengji powder
拔管法/拔喉管法　extubation
拔罐疗法/拔罐療法　cupping therapy
拔毛镊/拔毛鑷,拔毛鉗　epilating forceps
拔毛癖/拔毛癖,拔鬚髮狂　trichotillomania
拔伸牵引/拔伸牽引　traction by pulling and extension
拔髓针/鉤狀抽髓針　barbed broach
拔牙[法]/拔牙[法]　tooth extraction
拔牙钳/拔牙鉗,齒鉗　dental forceps
拔牙学/拔牙學　exodontics
拔牙学家/拔牙專家　exodontist
菝葜配质/菝葜配糖基,菝葜配糖苷　smilagenin
菝葜皂苷/洋菝葜素　smilacin
钯/鈀　palladium
钯离子比色法/鈀離子比色法　palladium ion colorimetry
靶/靶　target
靶酶模型/靶酶模式　target enzyme model
靶器官/靶器官　target organ
靶细胞/靶細胞,目標細胞　target cell
靶向制剂/靶向製劑　targeting preparation
靶心率/靶心率　target heart rate
靶行为/標的行爲　target behavior
靶组织/標的組織　target tissue
靶组织反应/靶組織反應　target response
白斑病/白斑病　leucoderma
白斑症/白斑症　leucopathy
白疕/白疕,牛皮癬　psoriasis, white crust
白疕·血热内蕴证/白疕·血熱內蘊證　white crust with pattern of internal amassment of blood heat
白疕·血虚风燥证/白疕·血虛風燥證　white crust with pattern of wind-dryness due to blood deficiency
白疕·瘀滞肌肤证/白疕·瘀滯肌膚證　white crust with pattern of stasis stagnating in skin
白扁豆/白扁豆　hyacinth bean
白驳风/白駁風,白斑病　vitiligo
白驳风·肝气郁结证/白駁風·肝氣鬱結證　vitiligo with liver qi stagnation pattern
白驳风·气血两虚证/白駁風·氣血兩虛證　vitiligo with qi-blood deficiency pattern
白驳风·气滞血瘀证/白駁風·氣滯血瘀證　vitiligo with pattern of qi stagnation and blood stasis

白布绷带/白洋布繃帶　calico bandage
白痴/白癡　idiocy
白带[病]/白帶[病]　leucorrhea disease, white vaginal discharge
白带过多/白帶漏　leukorrhagia
白带·寒湿凝滞证/白帶·寒濕凝滯證　leucorrhea disease with pattern of stagnation and congelation of cold-damp
白带·脾气虚证/白帶·脾氣虛證　leucorrhea disease with pattern of spleen qi deficiency
白带·肾阳虚证/白帶·腎陽虛證　leucorrhea disease with pattern of kidney yang deficiency
白带·湿热下注证/白帶·濕熱下注證　leucorrhea disease with pattern of downward diffusion of damp-heat
白带·痰湿内盛证/白帶·痰濕內盛證　leucorrhea disease with pattern of internal exuberance of phlegm-damp
白带丸/白帶丸　baidai pills
白蛋白/白蛋白　albumin
白蛋白 A/白蛋白 A　albumin A
白蛋白 X/白蛋白 X　albumin X
白蛋白铋/蛋白[化]铋　bismuth albuminate
白蛋白的/蛋白素的　albuminous
白蛋白定量法/蛋白定量法　albuminimetry
白蛋白定量器/蛋白定量計　albumimeter
白蛋白反应/白蛋白反應　albuminoreaction
白蛋白分解/蛋白質分解　albuminolysis
白蛋白过多/白蛋白過多症　hyperalbuminosis
白蛋白过少/白蛋白過少症　hypoalbuminosis
白蛋白类/白蛋白類　albumins
白蛋白尿/蛋白[素]尿　albuminuria
白蛋白凝集素/白蛋白凝集素　albumin agglutinin
白蛋白球蛋白比率/白蛋白球蛋白比率　A-G ratio
白蛋白受体/白蛋白受體　albumin receptor
白蛋白痰/痰内含蛋白　albuminoptysis
白蛋白细胞/白蛋白細胞　albuminous cell
白蛋白性肿胀/白蛋白性腫脹　albuminius swelling
白蛋白血症/白蛋白素血症　albuminemia
白蛋白衍生物/白蛋白衍生物　derived albumin
白蛋白溢/蛋白漏　albuminorrhea
白点病/白點病　white-spot disease
白点状慢性结膜炎/草原性結膜炎　prairie conjunctivitis
白点状视网膜变性/白點狀視網膜變性　albescent punctate degeneration of retina
白癜风/白癜風,白斑[病]　vitiligo
白顶囊肿/白顶囊腫　white-domed cyst

白豆蔻/白豆蔻　cardamon fruit
白垩/白堊,天然堊　chalk
白垩的/白堊的　chalky
白垩合剂/白堊合劑　chalk mixture
白垩性痛风/白堊性痛風　chalky gout
白恶露/白惡露　white lochia
白发/白髮　canities
白发症/白毛症　poliosis
白凡士林/白凡士林　albolene
白矾/白礬　alum
白放线菌素/白色放射線菌素　actinomycetin
白肺/白色肺炎　white lung
白痱/白痱,白粟疹,晶狀粟疹　miliaria alba
白[蜂]蜡/白蠟　bleached beeswax
白附子/白附子　giant typhonium rhizome
白鲑精蛋白/白魚精蛋白　coregonin
白果/白果　ginkgo seed
白果中毒/白果中毒　ginkgo seed poisoning
白喉/白喉　diphtheriae
白喉棒状杆菌/白喉桿菌　corynebacterium diphtheriae
白喉毒素/白喉毒素　diphtheria toxin
白喉后的/白喉後的　postdiphtheritic
白喉后狭窄/白喉後狹窄　postdiphtheritic stenosis
白喉·火毒炽盛证/白喉·火毒熾盛證　diphtheria with blazing fire-toxin pattern
白喉禁忌/白喉禁忌　contraindications of diphtheria
白喉抗毒素/白喉抗毒素　diphtheria antitoxin
白喉溃疡/白喉性潰瘍　diphtheritic ulcer
白喉类毒素/白喉類毒素　diphtheria toxoid
白喉-破伤风-百日咳菌苗/白喉-破傷風-百日欬菌苗　diphtheria-tetanus-pertussis vaccine
白喉-破伤风菌苗/白喉-破傷風菌苗　diphtheria-tetanus vaccine
白喉-破伤风-脱细胞百日咳菌苗/白喉-破傷風-脫細胞百日欬菌苗　diphtheria-tetanus-acellular pertussis vaccine
白喉三不可/白喉三不可　three inhibitions of diphtheria
白喉性多神经病/白喉性多發性神經病變　diphtheritic polyneuropathy
白喉性耳炎/白喉性耳炎　otitis diphtheritica
白喉性喉炎/白喉性喉炎　diphtheritic laryngitis
白喉性坏死/白喉性壞死　diphtheritic necrosis
白喉性结膜炎/白喉性結膜炎　diphtheritic conjunctivitis
白喉性膀胱炎/白喉桿菌性膀胱炎　croupous cystitis
白喉性咽峡炎/白喉性咽炎　angina diphtheritica

白喉性阴道炎/白喉性陰道炎　diphtheritic vaginitis
白喉·疫毒犯表证/白喉·疫毒犯表證　diphtheria with pattern of epidemic toxin assailing exterior
白喉·疫毒凌心证/白喉·疫毒凌心證　diphtheria with pattern of epidemic toxin attacking heart
白喉·疫毒伤阴证/白喉·疫毒傷陰證　diphtheria with pattern of epidemic toxin injuring yin
白槲鞣酸/槲皮鞣酸　quercitannic acid
白虎汤/白虎湯　baihu decoction
白花蛇舌草/白花蛇舌草　oldenlandia
白化病/白化病,白化症,白公病　albinism
白化病患者/白化病患　albino
白化病眼底/白眼底　albinotic fundus
白桦/白樺　birch
白桦焦油/樺焦油　birch tar
白桦油/白樺油　betula oil
白环俞/白環俞　baihuanshu, BL30
白肌/白肌　white muscle
白肌病/白肌病　white muscle disease
白肌纤维/白肌纖維　white muscle fiber
白及/白及　common bletilla rubber
白甲/白甲病　leukonychia
白坚木碱/白堅木鹼　aspidospermine
白坚木属/白堅木屬　Aspidosperma
白交通支/白交通支　white communicating branches
白芥/白芥　white mustard
白芥子酸/芥子酸　sinapinic acid
白金/白金　platinum
白睛/白睛　white of the eye, bulbar conjunctiva and sclera, white eye
白睛病/白睛病　disease in white of the eye, disease of bulbar conjunctiva, disease of white eye
白睛混赤/白睛混赤　bulbar conjunctival and ciliary hyperemia, turbid reddening of white of the eye
白睛青蓝/白睛青藍　blueish white of the eye, blue sclera, late-stage scleritis
白睛溢血/白睛溢血　hemorrhagic white eye, subconjunctival ecchymosis, subconjunctival hemorrhage
白睛溢血·热客肺经证/白睛溢血·熱客肺經證　hemorrhagic white of the eye with pattern of heat lodging in lung channel
白睛溢血·阴虚火旺证/白睛溢血·陰虛火旺證　hemorrhagic white of the eye with pattern of yin deficiency and fire effulgence
白蜡树苷/白蠟樹苷　fraxin
白乐君/巴留特林　paludrine
白藜芦/白藜蘆　white hellebore

白蔹/白蘞　Japanese ampelopsis root
白蛉/白蛉　sandfly
白蛉病毒属/白蛉病毒　Phlebovirus
白蛉叮伤/白蛉叮傷　sandfly bite
白蛉皮炎/白蛉皮膚炎　harara
白蛉热/白蛉熱,沙蚊屬　phlebotomus fever
白蛉热病毒/白蛉熱病毒　phlebotomus fever virus
白蛉热那不勒斯病毒/白蛉熱那不勒斯病毒　sandfly fever Naples virus
白蛉属/白蛉屬　Phlebotomus
白毛舌/白毛舌　white hairy tongue
白茅根/白茅根　cogon grass rhizome
白茅属/白茅　Imperata
白霉/白黴　white mold
白膜/白膜　tunica albuginea
白膜侵睛/白膜侵睛　white membrane invading black of the eye, phlyctenular keratoconjunctivitis, white membrane invading eye
白膜炎/白膜炎　albuginitis
白内障/白内障　cataracta
白内障瓣状摘出术/白内障瓣狀摘出術　flap extraction of cataract
白内障硅胶摘出术/白内障矽膠摘出術　silicoextraction of cataract
白内障后无晶状体/白内障後無晶狀體　postcataract aphakia
白内障截囊术/白内障挑開術　discission of cataract
白内障镜片/白内障透鏡　cataract lens
白内障冷冻摘出术/白内障冷凍摘出術　cryoextraction of cataract
白内障囊内摘出术/白内障囊内摘出術　intracapsular extraction of cataract
白内障囊外摘出术/白内障囊外摘出術　extracapsular extraction of cataract
白内障线状摘出术/白内障線狀摘出術　linear extraction of cataract
白内障性抑郁症/白内障性抑鬱症　couching for cataract
白内障压下术/白内障壓下術　depression of cataract depression
白内障摘出术/白内障摘出術　extraction of cataract
白念珠菌/白念珠菌　Candida albicans
白千层/白千層　cajeput
白前/白前　willowleaf rhizome
白曲霉/白麴黴菌　Aspergillus candidus
白三烯拮抗剂/白三烯拮抗劑　leukotriene antagonist
白三烯类/白三烯類　leukotrienes
白三烯受体/白三烯受體　leukotriene receptor

白[色]/白色　white
白色表浅性甲癣/白色表淺性甲癬　white superficial onychomycosis
白色痤疮/白色痤瘡　acne alba
白色的/白色的　albicans
白色海绵状斑痣/白色海綿狀斑痣　white sponge naevus
白色花斑癣/白色變色糠疹　pityriasis versicolor alba
白色划痕现象/白色劃紋現象　white dermographism
白色坏疽/白色壞疽　leukonecrosis
白色角化病/白色角化病　leukokeratosis
白色糠疹/白糠疹　pityriasis alba
白色毛结节菌病/毛乾白節病　white piedra
白色尿胆素/白色尿膽質　leukourobilin
白色皮肤划痕现象/異位性皮膚炎皮紋　white dermatographia
白色皮片/蒼白色移植片,無血管移植片　white graft
白色皮片排斥/白色皮片排斥　white graft rejection
白色皮片缺血/白色皮片缺血　white graft ischemia
白色丘疹型大疱性表皮松解症/白色丘疹型水皰性表皮鬆解症　albopapular form of epidermolysis bullosa
白色丘疹样/白色丘疹樣　albopapuloid
白色水肿/白斑水腫　leukoedema
白色萎缩/白色萎縮　white atrophy
白色萎缩症/白色萎縮症　atrophie blanche
白色血栓/白色血栓　white thrombus
白色衍生物/白色衍生物　leukoderivative
白色叶状斑/白楊葉斑　ash-leaf macule
白色月经/白色月經　white menstruation
白色肿/關節白腫　white swelling
白色足分支菌病/白色足菌病　white mycetoma
白涩症/白澀症　dry eye, dry astringent eye, xerosis conjunctivitis
白涩症・肺阴虚证/白澀症・肺陰虛證　dry eye with lung yin deficiency pattern
白涩症・肝肾阴虚证/白澀症・肝腎陰虛證　dry eye with liver-kidney yin deficiency pattern
白涩症・脾胃湿热证/白澀症・脾胃濕熱證　dry eye with pattern of dampness-heat in spleen and stomach
白涩症・邪热留恋证/白澀症・邪熱留戀證　dry eye with lingering pathogenic heat pattern
白芍/白芍　debark peony root
白髓/白髓　white pulp
白苔/白苔　white fur
白檀油醇/白檀油醇　amyrol

白体/白體　corpus albicans
白头翁/白頭翁　Chinese pulsatilla root
白头翁脑/白頭翁腦　anemonol
白头翁素/白頭翁素　anemonin
白头翁汤/白頭翁湯　baitouweng decoction
白头翁中毒/白頭翁中毒　anemonism
白秃疮/白禿瘡,白癬　tinea blanca
白秃疮・风盛血燥证/白禿瘡・風盛血燥證　tinea blanca with pattern of wind excessiveness and blood dryness
白豚鼠/白化豚鼠　albino guinea pig
白网状质/白網狀質　white reticular formation
白薇/白薇　blackend swallowwort root
白细胞/白血球　leukocyte, white blood cell
白细胞层/白血球集合層　leukocytic cream
白细胞动力学/白血球動力學　leukokinetics
白细胞毒素/白血球毒素　leukocytotoxin
白细胞毒性/毒害白血球性　leukotoxicity
白细胞毒血清/毒白血球性血清　leukotoxic serum
白细胞分核计数/白血球分核計數,有絲無絲白血球計數法　filament-nonfilament count
白细胞分离术/白細胞分離術　leukocyte reduction procedure
白细胞隔离/白細胞隔離　leukocyte sequestration
白细胞共同抗原/白細胞共同抗原　leukocyte common antigen
白细胞管型/白細胞管型　white cell cast
白细胞滚动/白細胞滾動　leukocyte rolling
白细胞过多/白血球極度過多症　hyperleukocytosis
白细胞计数/白血球計數　leukocyte count
白细胞计数器/白血球計數器　leukocytometer
白细胞减少/白細胞減少　leucocytopenia
白细胞减少的/白血球減少的　hypoleukocytic
白细胞减少性白血病/白血球減少性白血病　leukopenic leukemia
白细胞减少性咽峡炎/低白血球性咽峽炎　hypoleukocytic angina
白细胞减少指数/白血球減少指數　leukopenic index
白细胞介素/白細胞介素,間白素　interleukin
白细胞介素-2/白細胞介素-2　interleukin-2
白细胞介素-6/白細胞介素-6　interleukin-6
白细胞介素受体/白細胞介素受體　interleukin receptors
白细胞聚集体/白細胞聚集體　leukocyte aggregate
白细胞L1抗原复合物/白細胞L1抗原複合物　leukocyte L1 antigen complex
白细胞颗粒/白血球小粒　plasmasome
白细胞疗法/白血球療法　leukocytotherapy

白细胞瘤/白血球瘤　leukocytoma
白细胞黏附缺陷综合征/白細胞黏附缺陷症候群　leukocyte-adhesion deficiency syndrome
白细胞黏附受体/白細胞黏附受體　leukocyte-adhesion receptor
白细胞黏着反应/白細胞黏著反應　leukocyte adherence reaction
白细胞尿/白血球尿　leukocyturia
白细胞凝集素/白血球凝集素　leukoagglutinin
白细胞趋向性/白血球趨向性　leukocytotaxis
白细胞去除术/白血球透析術　leukapheresis
白细胞缺乏的/白血球低於正常的　aleukemic
白细胞缺乏性白血病/白血球缺乏性白血病　aleukemic leukemia
白细胞溶解/白血球崩解　leukocytolysis
白细胞溶素/溶白血球素　leukocytolysin
白细胞三烯/白細胞三烯　leukotriene
白细胞渗出学说/柯恩漢氏學說　emigration theory
白细胞生成/白血球生成　leukopoiesis
白细胞输注/白細胞輸注　leukocyte transfusion
白细胞弹性蛋白酶/白細胞彈性蛋白酶　leukocyte elastase
白细胞调节素/白細胞調節素　leukoregulin
白细胞停滞/白細胞停滞　leukostasis
白细胞系/白血球系　leucon
白细胞像/白血球像　leukogram
白细胞学/白血球學　leukocytology
白细胞血小板减少/白血球血小板减少　leukothrombopenia
白细胞移动/白血球運動　leukokinesis
白细胞移动抑制因子/白細胞移動抑制因子　leukocyte migration inhibitory factor
白细胞异常色素减退综合征/白細胞異常色素減退症候群　Chediak-Higashi syndrome
白细胞抑制因子/白血球抑制因子　leukocyte inhibitory factor
白细胞游出/白血球移出　leukocytoplania
白细胞游走抑制因子/白細胞遊走抑制因子　leukocyte migration-inhibitory factor
白细胞郁滞/白血球鬱滯　cytostasis
白细胞增多/白血球增多症　leukocytosis
白细胞粘连抑制试验/白細胞粘連抑制試驗　leukocyte adherence inhibition test
白细胞障碍/白細胞障礙　leukocyte disorder
白细胞组织增生/白血球增生病　leukoblastosis
白鲜皮/白鮮皮　cortex dictam
白线/白線　white line
白线疝/白線疝　hernia of white line

白线支座/白線支座　adminiculum lineae albae
白屑风/白屑風　white-scaled wind
白屑风·风热血燥证/白屑風·風熱血燥證　white-scaled wind with pattern of wind-heat and blood dryness
白屑风·脾胃湿热证/白屑風·脾胃濕熱證　white-scaled wind with pattern of dampness-heat in stomach and spleen
白癣/白癬　tinea alba
白血病/白血病　leukemia
白血病病毒/白血病病毒　leukovirus
白血病基因表达调控/白血病基因表達調控　leukemic gene expression regulation
白血病浸润/白血病浸潤　leukemic infiltration
白血病前期/白血病前期　preleukemia
白血病生成/白血病生成　leukemogenesis
白血病性裂隙/白血病性血像間斷　hiatus leukemicus
白血病性肉瘤病/白色肉瘤症　leukosarcomatosis
白血病性视网膜炎/白血病性視網膜炎　leukemic retinitis
白血病样反应/白血病[樣]反應　leukemoid reaction
白血病疹/白血病疹　leukemid
白翳黄心内障/白翳黄心内障　silver cataract with yellowish center
白英/白英　climbing nightshade
白脂肪组织/白脂肪組織　white adipose tissue
白芷/白芷　dahurian angelica root
白质/白質　white matter
白质后连合/白質後連合　posterior white commissure
白质脑炎/腦白質炎　leukoencephalitis
白质前连合/白質前連合　anterior white commissure
白昼残留印象/白晝殘留像　day residue
白昼失声/白晝失音　nyctophonia
白术/白朮　largehead atractylodes rhizome
白浊/白濁，淋病　gonorrhea, white turbidity
百白咳毒素/百白欬毒素　pertussis toxin
百病始生/百病始生　treatise on origin of diseases
百部/百部　stemona root
百草枯/百草枯　paraquat
百分饱和度/百分飽和度　percent saturation
百骸/骨　bones
百合/百合　lily bulb
百合病/百合病　baihe disease, disease of all vessels, lily disease
百合固金汤/百合固金湯　baihe gujin decoction
百会/百會　baihui, DU20

百里酚肽/麝香草酚酞　thymolphthalein
百里香/百里香　thyme
百里香属植物/百里香屬植物　*Thymus* plant
百慕大群岛耐火海绵皮炎/百慕達群島耐火海綿皮膚炎　Bermuda fire sponge dermatitis
百日咳/百日欬　chin cough
百日咳菌苗/百日欬疫苗　pertussis vaccine
百日咳样咳嗽/百日欬樣的，類百日欬　pertussoid
百岁老人/百歲老人　centenarian
柏油样粪/柏油狀糞　tarry stool
柏油样囊肿/柏油狀囊腫　tarry cyst
柏子仁/柏子仁　Chinese arborvitae kernel
柏子养心丸/柏子養心丸　baizi yangxin pills
摆动的/振动的　pendular
摆动反应/擺動反應　hunting reaction
摆动负重相/擺動負重相　swing phase
摆动假说/不穩定假說　wobble hypothesis
摆动性眼球震颤/擺動狀眼球震顫　pendular nystagmus
摆[摇运]动/擺動，運動　pendular movement
败毒散/敗毒散　baidu powder
败毒梭菌/敗血梭狀芽孢桿菌　Clostridium septicum
败酱草/敗醬草　atrina glass
败血病性脑膜炎/敗血病性腦膜炎　septicemic meningitis
败血症/敗血病　septicemia
拜沃特综合征/Bywater 氏症候群　Bywater syndrome
扳法/扳法　pulling manipulation
扳机效能/引發活動　triggered activity
扳机指/扳機指，彈機指　trigger finger
扳颈手法/扳頸手法　neck-pulling manipulation
班伯格液/Bamberger 氏液　Bamberger fluid
班布里奇反射/班布里氏反射　Bainbridge reflex
班德夹板/Bond 氏夾板　Bond splint
班德劳气褥/Bandeloux 氏墊　Bandeloux bed
班蒂综合征/脾性貧血　Banti syndrome
班氏试验/斑格氏試驗　Bang test
班氏吴策线虫/人血絲蟲，班克洛氏絲蟲　Wuchereria bancrofti
班廷减肥膳食/Banting 氏食療　Banting diet
斑/斑點　macula, blotch
斑驳病/白斑病，斑狀皮膚　piebald skin
斑[点]的/斑的　macular
斑点杂交/斑點雜交　dot blot hybridization
斑点再浓集/斑點再濃集　spot reconcentration
斑点状钙化软骨发育不良/斑點狀鈣化軟骨發育不良　chondrodysplasia calcificans punctata

斑点状骨病/斑點狀骨　spotted bone
斑点状角膜营养不良/角膜退化并有灰點沈積　macular corneal dystrophy
斑点状痛/皮斑樣疼痛　spot pain
斑点状疹/斑疹　macular eruption
斑痕/斑痕　stigma
斑痕形成/斑痕形成　stigmatization
斑块/斑[塊]　plaque
斑块状副银屑病/斑塊狀副銀屑病　parapsoriasis en plaque
斑块状水疱鳞屑性湿疹/斑塊狀水皰鱗屑性濕疹　patchy vesiculosquamous eczema
斑马鱼蛋白质类/斑馬魚蛋白質類　zebrafish proteins
斑马状色素沉着/斑馬狀色素沈著　zebra-like hyperpigmentation
斑蝥/斑蝥　cantharides
斑蝥虫病/甲蟲[寄生]病　canthariasis
斑蝥皮炎/斑蝥皮炎　blister beetle dermatitis
斑蝥属/斑蝥屬　*Cantharis*
斑蝥素/斑蝥素　cantharidin
斑蝥酸/斑蝥酸　cantharidic acid
斑蝥酸盐/斑蝥酸鹽　cantharidate
斑蝥中毒/斑蝥中毒　cantharidism
斑虻属/斑虻屬　*Chrysops*
斑片/斑[片]　patch
斑片的/片狀的　patchy
斑片试验/斑片試驗　patch test
斑丘疹/斑丘疹　maculopapule, maculopapular eruption
斑色的/斑色的　versicolor
斑色胎儿/斑色胎，先天性魚鱗癬胎兒　harlequin fetus
斑氏环路/斑氏環路　Bain circuit
斑氏丝虫病/斑氏絲蟲病　filariasis bancrofti
斑似的/斑點的　blotchy
斑蝥/斑蝥　blister beetle
斑蝥酊/斑蝥酊　cantharides tincture
斑贴试验/貼膚試驗　patch test
斑贴试验试剂盒/貼膚試驗組　patch testing kit
斑秃/簇圓禿　alopecia areata
斑纹/條痕　stripe
斑纹毛/斑紋毛　brindled hair
斑纹心/斑貓狀心，斑色心　tabby cat heart
斑纹性麻风/斑紋性麻風　macular leprosy
斑形秃发/斑形禿髮　alopecia Celsi
斑性梅毒疹/斑性梅毒疹　syphilid maculosa
斑性荨麻疹/斑狀蕁麻疹　urticaria maculosa

斑岩脾/紫質狀脾　porphyry spleen
斑釉[症]/釉質雜色病，釉質斑駁病　poikilodentosis, mottled enamel
斑疹/斑疹　macula
斑疹狼疮/斑疹狼瘡　lupus maculosus
斑疹热/斑疹熱　spotted fever
斑疹伤寒/斑疹傷寒　typhus
斑疹伤寒立克次体/斑疹傷寒立克次氏體　Rickettsia typhi
斑疹伤寒小结/斑疹傷寒小結　typhus nodule
斑疹伤寒性口溃疡/口型[斑疹]傷寒　stomatotyphus
斑疹伤寒疫苗/斑疹傷寒疫苗，流行性傷寒立克次體死菌疫苗　typhus vaccine
斑脂翳/斑脂翳　adherent leucoma, fat patch nebula
斑痣/斑痣　spilus
斑痣性错构瘤病/母斑症　phacomatosis
斑状/斑狀　maculosa
斑状白色萎缩症/斑塊狀白色萎縮症　atrophie blanche en plaque
斑状淀粉样变性/斑狀澱粉樣變性症　macular amyloidosis
斑状结核瘤/斑狀結核瘤　tuberculoma en plaque
斑状梅毒疹/斑狀梅毒疹　macular syphilide
斑状皮肤松弛症/斑狀皮膚鬆弛症　anetoderma maculosa
斑状皮肤萎缩/斑狀皮萎病　atrophoderma maculatum
斑状特发性皮肤萎缩/斑狀特發性皮膚萎縮　atrophia cutis idiopathica maculosa
斑状萎缩/斑狀萎縮　macular atrophy
斑状阴茎黑变症/斑狀陰莖黑變症　macular penile melanosis
斑[状阴]影/斑駁　mottling
斑状硬斑病/斑狀硬斑病　morphea en plaque
斑状紫癜/斑狀紫癜病　purpura maculosa
瘢痕/瘢痕　scar, cicatrices
瘢痕癌/瘢痕癌　carcinoma of scar
瘢痕的/瘢痕的　cicatricial
瘢痕疙瘩/瘢痕疙瘩，蟹足腫　cheloid
瘢痕疙瘩性痤疮/瘢痕疙瘩性痤瘡　acne keloidalis
瘢痕疙瘩性毛囊炎/蟹足腫性毛囊炎　folliculitis keloidalis
瘢痕疙瘩性芽生菌病/瘢疤芽生黴菌病　keloidal blastomycosis
瘢痕灸/瘢痕灸　scarring moxibustion
瘢痕瘘/瘢痕瘻管　cicatricial fistula
瘢痕挛缩/瘢痕攣縮　cicatricial contracture

瘢痕切除术/瘢痕切除術　cicatrectomy
瘢痕切开术/瘢痕切開術　cicatricotomy
瘢痕去除[术]/疤痕去除　scar removal
瘢痕上皮/瘢痕上皮　cicatricial epithelium
瘢痕松解植皮术/瘢痕鬆解植皮術　lysis of cicatricial contracture and skin grafting
瘢痕体质/瘢痕體質　scar diathesis
瘢痕形成/結疤　scarring
瘢痕性肥大/瘢痕性肥大　cicatricial hypertrophy
瘢痕性红斑/成瘢性紅斑，紅瘢病　ulerythema
瘢痕性红斑性皮肤萎缩/疤痕性紅斑性皮萎病　atrophoderma ulerythematosa
瘢痕性基底细胞上皮瘤/瘢痕性基底細胞上皮瘤　cicatricial basal cell epithelioma
瘢痕性脊柱侧凸/瘢痕性脊柱側彎　cicatricial scoliosis
瘢痕性睑内翻/瘢痕性瞼內翻　cicatricial entropion
瘢痕性睑外翻/瘢痕性瞼外翻　cicatricial ectropion
瘢痕性交界型大疱性表皮松解症/疤痕性交界性水疱性表皮鬆解症　cicatricial junctional epidermolysis bullosa
瘢痕性角化症/疤痕性角化症　cicatrix keratoses
瘢痕性脑回/腦迴瘢痕，瘢痕狀腦迴　ulegyria
瘢痕性秃发/疤痕性禿髮　scarring alopecia
瘢痕性脱发/瘢痕性禿髮　alopecia cicatrisata
瘢痕性狭窄/瘢痕性狹窄　cicatricial stenosis
瘢痕性纤维瘤病/疤痕性纖維瘤病　cicatricial fibromatosis
瘢痕组织/瘢痕組織　scar tissue
瘢痕组织填充法/瘢痕組織填充法　scar tissue buttressing method
瘢瘤性毛囊炎/瘢瘤性毛囊炎　keloidalis
癍/斑　macula
阪口试验/阪口試驗　Sakaguchi test
板/板　plate
板层巩膜缩短术/板層鞏膜縮短術　lamellar scleral resection
板层骨/板層骨，片層骨，層性骨　lamellar bone
板层角膜移植片/板層角膜移植片　lamellar corneal graft
板层角膜移植术/層狀角膜成形術　lamellar keratoplasty
板层状/層的　lamellar
板层状鳞癣/層狀魚鱗癬　lamellar ichthyosis
板齿/板齒　incisor teeth
板电泳/平板電泳　plate electrophoresis
板股后韧带/板股後韌帶　posterior meniscofemoral ligament

板股前韧带／板股前韌帶 anterior meniscofemoral ligament
板后部／板後部 postlaminar part
板口线虫病／板口線蟲病，美洲鉤蟲病 necatoriasis
板叩诊［法］／叩診板用法 pleximetry
板块样真皮纤维瘤／板塊樣真皮纖維瘤 plaque form dermal fibroma
板框式压滤器／板框式壓濾器 plate and frame filter press
板蓝根／板藍根 isatis root
板蓝根颗粒／板藍根顆粒 banlangen granules
板内部／板內部 intralaminar part
板内核群／板內核群 intralaminar nuclear group of thalamus
板前部／板前部 prelaminar part
板前支／板前支 prelaminar branch
板球股／板球股病 cricket thigh
板上丛／板上叢 plexus epilamellaris
板纹蜡／片形蠟 carding wax
板炎／板炎，馬蹄葉炎 laminitis
板样背／板樣背 flat back
板样腹／木腹 wooden belly
板样甲状腺炎／木樣甲狀腺炎 woody thyroiditis
板障／板障 diploe
板障管／板障管 diploic canal
板障静脉／板障靜脈 diploic vein
板障支／板障支 diploic branch
板状强直／板狀強直 boardlike rigidity
半孢子／半孢子，半芽孢 hemispore
半薄切片／半薄切片 semithin section
半保留复制／半保留複製 semiconservative replication
半暴露疗法／半暴露療法 semiexposure method
半鼻再造术／半鼻再造術 hemirhinoplasty
半闭式装置／半閉式裝置 semiclosed system
半边莲／半邊蓮 Chinese lobelia herb
半表半里／半表半裡 half-exterior and half-interior
半侧痉挛／半身痙攣 hemispasm
半侧弱视／半側弱視 hemiamblyopia
半侧舌头萎缩／半側舌頭萎縮 hemilingual atrophy
半侧舌炎／半側舌炎,偏側舌炎 hemiglossitis
半侧味觉丧失／偏側味覺缺失 hemiageusia
半成品／半成品 intermediate product
半成形便／半成形便 semiformed stool
半翅目／半翅蟲類 Hemiptera
半蛋白胨／半蛋白腖 hemipeptone
半导体／半導體 semiconductor
半导体激光疗法／半導體雷射療法 semi-conductor laser therapy
半毒素／半毒素 hemitoxin
半纺锤丝／半梭狀纖維,半梭形纖維 half-spindle fiber
半分生孢子／半分生孢子 deuteroconidium
半俯卧位／半伏臥位 semiprone position
半复粒淀粉／半複粒澱粉 half compound starch granule
半复消色差物镜／半複消色差物鏡 semiapochromat
半肝切除术／半側肝切除術 hemihepatectomy
半钩甲／半鉤甲 hemionychogryphosis
半固定桥／半固定橋 semi-fixed bridge
半固定桥连接体／半固定橋連接體 semi-fixed connector
半关节成形术／半關節成形術 hemiarthroplasty
半管／半管 semicanal
半胱氨酸／半胱胺酸,硫胱胺酸 cysteine
半胱氨酸蛋白酶抑制剂／半胱胺酸蛋白酶抑制劑 cysteine proteinase inhibitor
半胱氨酸合酶／半胱胺酸合酶 cysteine synthase
半胱氨酸内肽酶类／半胱胺酸內肽酶類 cysteine endopeptidases
半胱氨酸天冬氨酸蛋白酶／半胱天冬酶 caspases
半胱氨酰多巴／半胱胺醯多巴 cysteinyldopa
半胱胺／半胱胺 cysteamine
半规管／半規管 semicircular duct
半规管单脚／半規管單腳 crus membranaceus simplex ductus semicircularis
半规管固有膜／半規管固有膜 proper membrane of semicircular duct
半规管壶腹／半規管的壺腹 ampulla of semicircular canal
半规管基底膜／半規管基底膜 basal membrane of semicircular duct
半规管开窗术／半規管開窗術 fenestration of semicircular canal
半规管轻瘫／半規管輕癱 canal paresis
半合成青霉素类／半合成青黴素類 semi-synthetic penicillins
半合成头孢菌素类／半合成頭孢菌素類 semi-synthetic cephalosporins
半合子／半接合子 hemizygote
半合子状态／半接合子狀態 hemizygosity
半殆／半咬合 half occlusion
半喉切除术／半喉切除術 hemilaryngectomy
半环扁尾蛇毒素类／半環扁尾蛇毒素類 erabutoxins
半昏迷／半昏迷 semicoma
半奇静脉／半奇靜脈 hemiazygos vein

半畸形/部分畸形　demimonstrosity
半棘肌/半棘肌　semispinalis, musculus semispinalis
半脊椎/半脊椎　hemivertebra
半寄生物/半寄生物　semiparasite
半间日疟/半間日瘧　semitertian malaria
半腱肌/半腱肌　semitendinosus
半解剖式牙/半解剖式牙　semianatomic tooth
半精密支托/半精密支托　semiprecision rest
半开放麻醉法/半開放麻醉法　semiopen anesthesia
半开放装置/半開放裝置　semiopen system
半抗原/半抗原,不完全抗原　hapten
半抗原抑制试验/半抗原抑制試驗　hapten inhibition test
半窥镜/半窺鏡　semispeculum
半醌/半醌　semiquinone
半流质饮食/半流質飲食　semiliquid diet
半硫丸/半硫丸　banliu pills
半卵圆中心/半卵中心　semioval center
半麻醉/半麻醉,矇睡　seminarcosis
半埋入横褥式缝合/半埋入橫褥式縫合　half buried horizontal mattress suture
半脉症/半脈症　hemisphygmia
半梦游症/半夢行　hemisomnambulism
半密闭麻醉法/半密閉麻醉法　semi-closed anesthesia
半面[关节]/半[個關節]面　demifacet
半面痉挛/半面痙攣　hemi-facial spasm
半明胶蛋白/半明膠蛋白　semiglutin
半膜肌/半膜肌　semimembranosus, musculus semimembranosus
半膜肌囊/半膜肌囊　bursa of semimembranosus
半脾移植/半脾移植　hemisplenic transplantation
半片阅读镜/半片閱讀鏡　pulpit spectacle
半桥粒/半橋粒　hemidesmosome
半切牙术/半切牙術　tooth hemisection
半球间裂隙/半球間裂隙　fissura interhemispherica
半球形乳房/半球形乳房　hemispherical breast
半球形视野计/半球形視野計　hemispherical perimeter
半球形状的/半球形的　hemispherical
半染色体/半染色體　hemichromosome
半乳多糖/半乳糖原　galactogen
半乳聚糖/半乳糖複合物,複半乳糖　galactan
半乳糖/半乳糖　galactose
半乳糖胺/乳胺糖　galactosamine
半乳糖醇/半乳糖醇,衛矛醇,甜醇　galactitol
半乳糖苷/半乳糖苷,半乳糖配糖體　galactoside
半乳糖苷酶/半乳糖苷酶　galactosidase

半乳糖固定/半乳糖固定作用　galactopexy
半乳糖激酶/半乳糖激酶　galactokinase
半乳糖磷酸类/半乳糖磷酸類　galactosephosphates
半乳糖氯醛/半乳糖氯醛　galactochloral
半乳糖耐量/半乳糖耐量　galactose tolerance
半乳糖脑苷脂/半乳糖腦苷,半乳糖腦苷脂類　galactocerebroside
半乳糖尿/半乳糖尿　galactosuria
半乳糖凝集素类/半乳糖凝集素類　galectins
半乳糖醛酸/半乳糖醛酸　galacturonic acid
半乳糖脎/半乳糖脎　galactosazone
半乳糖神经酰胺类/半乳糖神經醯胺類　galactosylceramides
半乳糖神经酰胺酶/半乳糖神經醯胺酶　galactosylceramidase
半乳糖酸/半乳糖酸　galactonic acid
半乳糖脱氢酶类/半乳糖脫氫酶類　galactose dehydrogenases
半乳糖性白内障/半乳糖性白內障　galactose cataract
半乳糖血症/半乳糖血症　galactosemia
半乳糖氧化酶/半乳糖氧化酶　galactose oxidase
半乳糖脂类/半乳糖脂類　galactolipids
半乳糖转移酶/半乳糖基轉移酶　galactosyltransferase
半舌切除术/偏側舌切除術　hemiglossectomy
半身不遂/半身不遂,偏癱　hemiplegia
半身裹法/半身裹法　half pack
半身汗出/半身汗出　hemihidrosis
半身无汗/半身無汗　hemianhidrosis
半身照射/半身照射　hemibody irradiation
半食/半食　half diet
半手套状绷带/半手套狀繃帶　demigauntlet bandage
半数抑制浓度/半數抑制濃度　inhibitory concentration 50
半数有效量/半數有效劑量　50% effective dose, ED 50
半数致死量/半數致死[劑]量　median lethal dose, lethal dose 50, LD 50
半数致死浓度/半數致死濃度　median lethal concentration, LC 50
半数致死时间/半數致死時間　median lethal time, LT 50
半数中毒量/半數中毒[劑]量　median toxic dose, TD 50
半衰期/半衰期　half life
半缩醛/半縮醛　hemiacetal
半胎盘/半胎盤　semiplacenta

半弹性硬蛋白/半彈力蛋白　hemielastin
半体内试验/擬體內試驗　ex vivo test
半调整性殆架/半調整性咬合器　semiadjustable articulator
半萜/半萜　hemiterpene
半同胞/半同胞　halfsib
半脱位/半脫[位],不全脫位　semiluxatio, subluxation
半微量天平/半微量天平　semi-micro balance
半无脑/半頭畸形　hemicephalia
半无脑畸胎/半頭畸胎　hemicephalus
半无心畸胎/半心畸胎　hemiacardius
半下颌畸形/半下頜畸形　hemignathia
半下颌骨切除术/單側下頜骨切除術　hemimandibulectomy
半夏/半夏　pinellia tuber
半夏白术天麻汤/半夏白尤天麻湯　banxia baizhu tianma decoction
半夏厚朴汤/半夏厚朴湯　banxia houpu decoction, pinellia and magnolia bark decoction
半夏曲/半夏麴　fermented pinellia
半夏秫米汤/半夏秫米湯　pinellia and sorghum decoction
半夏泻心汤/半夏瀉心湯　banxia xiexin decoction
半夏中毒/半夏中毒　pinellia tuber poisoning
半纤维素/半纖維素　hemicellulose
半心畸形/半心畸形　hemicardia
半醒幻觉/半醒的幻覺　hypnopompic hallucination
半醒状态/半醒狀態　hypnopompic state
半醒状态的/半醒狀態的　postdormital
半羽肌/半羽肌　unipennate muscle
半圆形的/半圓形的　semicircular
半圆应力/半圓應力　semicircular stress
半月板回旋挤压试验/半月板迴旋擠壓試驗　McMurray's test
半月板切除术/關節半月板切除術　meniscectomy
半月板炎/關節半月板炎　meniscitis
半月板研磨试验/半月板研磨試驗　meniscus trituration test
半月板重力试验/半月板重力試驗　meniscus gravity test
半月板周部/副半月板　parameniscus
半月板周炎/副半月板炎　parameniscitis
半月瓣弧缘/半月瓣弧影　lunulae of semilunar valves
半月瓣小结/半月瓣小結　nodules of semilunar valves
半月骨/半月骨　semilunar bone

半月裂孔/半月裂孔　semilunar hiatus
半月平面/半月平面　planum semilunatum
半月神经节切除术/半月神經節切除術　gasserectomy
半月体/半月體,玻璃體　glass body
半月纤维软骨/半月狀纖維軟骨　semilunar fibrocartilage
半月线/半月線　linea semilunaris
半月线疝/史格爾氏疝　spigelian hernia
半月形处女膜/月狀形處女膜　lunar hymen
半月征/彎月徵象　meniscus sign
半月皱襞/半月皺襞　plica semilunaris
半月状束/半月狀束　semilunar tract
半枝莲/半枝蓮　barbated skullcup herb
半知菌类/不完全菌綱　fungi imperfecti
半肢/半肢[畸形]　hemimelia
半肢畸胎/半肢畸胎　hemimelus
半肢畸形/半肢骨骺發育異常畸形　hemimelia
半椎体/半脊椎畸形　hemivertebra
半自由寄生物/半自由寄生物　cenosite
伴刀豆球蛋白A/伴刀豆球蛋白A　concanavalin A
伴发的/伴發的　concomitant
伴发性阑尾炎/伴發性闌尾炎　concomitant appendicitis
伴发症状/伴發症狀　concomitant symptom
伴侣蛋白类/監控蛋白類　chaperonins
伴清蛋白/附蛋白素　conalbumin
伴X染色体的/X性聯的　X-linked
伴X[染色体]基因/X染色體基因　X-linked gene
伴随/伴隨　accompany
伴随负电位/伴隨負電位　contingent negative variation
伴随免疫/伴隨免疫性　concomitant immunity
伴同肺炎[发生]的/并肺炎發生的　synpneumonic
伴行静脉/并行靜脈　accompanying vein
伴性的/性聯的　sex-linked
伴性性状/性聯特性　sex-linked character
伴性遗传/性聯遺傳　sex-linked inheritance
伴肿瘤性皮肤病/伴腫瘤性皮膚病　paraneoplastic dermatosis
伴肿瘤性肢端角化病/伴腫瘤性肢端角化症　acrokeratosis paraneoplastica
绊创膏/粘連的硬膏劑　adhesive plaster
绊舌/絆舌　ankyloglossia
瓣闭锁不全/瓣閉鎖不全　valvular incompetence
瓣口反流面积/瓣口反流面積　regurgitant valve orifice area
瓣[膜]/瓣[膜]　flap, valve

瓣膜变形/瓣膜變形　valvular deformity
瓣膜成形术/瓣膜成形術　valvoplasty
瓣膜刀/瓣膜刀　valvotome
瓣膜的/瓣膜的,瓣的　valvular
瓣膜反流/瓣口反流　valvular regurgitation
瓣膜关闭不全/瓣閉鎖不全　valvular incompetence
瓣膜口狭窄/瓣狹窄　valvular stenosis
瓣膜隆起/瓣膜隆起　valve swelling
瓣膜切开术/瓣切開術,瓣膜切斷術　valvotomy
瓣膜上的/瓣膜上的　supravalvular
瓣膜上主动脉狭窄/瓣上主動脈狹窄　supravalvular aortic stenosis
瓣膜下主动脉狭窄/瓣下主動脈狹窄　subvalvular aortic stenosis
瓣膜血栓/瓣狀血栓　valvular thrombus
瓣膜杂音/瓣膜雜音　valvular murmur
瓣膜整形术/瓣膜整形術　valvuloplasty
瓣膜阻塞/瓣膜阻塞　valvular obstruction
瓣性心内膜炎/瓣性心內膜炎　valvular endocarditis
瓣中瓣人工瓣植入术/瓣中瓣人工瓣植入術　valve in valve prosthetic valve implantation
瓣周漏/瓣周漏　perivalvular leakage
瓣状内障摘出术/瓣狀摘出術　flap extraction
瓣状切断术/瓣狀截斷術　flap amputation
邦尼埃综合征/Bonnier 症候群　Bonnier syndrome
邦威尔三角/鮑威爾氏三角　Bonwill triangle
棒杆菌感染/棒桿菌感染　corynebacterium infection
棒杆菌属/棒狀桿菌屬　Corynebacterium
棒节/棒節　club
棒球/棒球　baseball
棒球肩/棒球肩病　baseball shoulder
棒曲霉/棒狀麴菌　Aspergillus clavatus
棒曲霉素/棒麴黴素,開放青黴素　patulin
棒酸/棒酸　clavulanic acid
棒状杆菌感染/棒狀桿菌感染　corynebacterium infection
棒状物/桿　shaft
包被性瘤/隱囊性瘤　encysted tumor
包被性脂肪坏死/包被性脂肪壞死　encapsulated fat necrosis
包藏性髓石/包藏性髓石　embedded denticle
包虫囊叩响/包蟲囊叩響　hydatid resonance
包虫囊疹/包蟲囊疹　hydatid rash
包虫囊震颤/包蟲囊震顫　hydatid thrill
包虫囊肿/包蟲囊　hydatid cyst
包虫囊状的/包蟲囊狀的　hydatidiform
包虫皮内试验/包蟲皮內試驗　Casoni test
包裹/被膜形成,包以被膜　encapsulation

包裹的/以被膜包覆的,包膜的　encapsulated
包裹性脓胸/包被性蓄膿　encapsulated empyema
包裹性胸膜炎/包裹性胸膜炎,被囊胸膜炎,包繞性胸膜炎　encysted pleurisy
包涵/包涵　inclusion
包涵囊肿/包涵囊腫　inclusion cyst
包涵体/包涵體　inclusion body
包涵体病毒/包涵體病毒　inclusion virus
包涵体肌炎/包涵體肌炎　inclusion body myositis
包涵体结膜炎病毒/包涵體結膜炎病毒　inclusion conjunctivitis virus
包涵体性结膜炎/包涵體結膜炎　inclusion conjunctivitis
包涵性皮样囊肿/包涵性皮樣囊腫　inclusion dermoid
包合物/包合物　clathrate
包煎/包煎　wrap-boiling
包茎/包莖　phimosis
包埋/包埋　embedding
包埋材模型/包被管型,圍模　investment cast
包膜/被膜　peplos
包膜病毒/包膜病毒,套膜病毒　envelope virus
包膜下肾切除术/包膜下腎切除術　subcapsular nephrectomy
包囊/包囊　encapsulation
包囊孢子/孢子囊孢子　sporangiospore
包囊虫病/包蟲病　hydatid disease
包囊形成/隱囊狀態,被囊現象　encystment
包囊性脓肿/被囊性膿腫　encysted abscess
包皮/包皮　foreskin
包皮背侧切开术/包皮背側切開術　dorsal slit of prepuce
包皮变应性水肿/包皮變應性水腫　allergic edema of prepuce
包皮成形术/包皮成形術,包皮造形術　posthioplasty
包皮垢结石/包皮石,包皮凝塊　preputial concretion
包皮垢石/包皮垢石　postholith
包皮过长/包皮過長　redundant prepuce
包皮环切[术]/包皮環割術,環割術,環狀切除術　circumcision
包皮环切术者/環切術專家　peritomist
包皮结石/包皮結石　calculus of prepuce
包皮切开术/包皮切開術　preputiotomy
包皮系带/包皮繫帶　frenulum of prepuce
包皮腺/包皮腺　preputial gland, odoriferous crypts of prepuce
包皮腺炎/泰森氏腺炎,陰莖頭腺炎　tysonitis
包皮炎/包皮炎　posthitis

包鞘囊肿/包鞘囊腫 thecal cyst
包绕的/隱囊的,皮囊的 encysted
包绕性腹股沟疝/被囊性腹股溝疝 encysted hernia
包绕性水囊肿/被囊性水囊 encysted hydrocele
包胎盘/包胎盤 placenta capsularis
包蜕膜/包蜕膜,翻蜕膜 decidua capsularis
包蜕膜性前置胎盘/包蜕膜性前置胎盤 placenta capsular praevia
包围性腹膜炎/被囊性腹膜炎 encysted peritonitis
包衣锅/錠衣鍋 coating pan
包衣片剂/錠衣著[劑] coated tablet
包扎/包扎,包敷 dressing
包扎固定疗法/包扎固定療法 bandage-fixing therapy
包扎疗法/包扎療法,封閉敷料 occlusive dressing
包装缺陷突变体/包装缺陷突變體 package defective mutant
包装细胞/包被細胞 incasing cell
包装细胞株/包裝細胞株 packaging cell line
包装信号/包裝信號 packaging signal
孢囊柄/孢子囊梗 sporangiophore
孢子/孢子 spores
孢子残渣/孢子殘渣 sporal residuum
孢子虫/孢子蟲,芽孢蟲 sporozoon
孢子虫病/孢子蟲病 sporozoosis
孢子管/孢子管 sporoduct
孢子浆/孢子漿 spore plasma
孢子卵囊/孢子卵囊 oocysts
孢子囊/孢子囊 sporangium
孢子凝集反应/孢子凝集作用 sporoagglutination
孢子生殖周期/孢子生殖週期 sporogenic cycle
孢子丝菌病/孢子絲菌病 sporotrichosis
孢子丝菌病样分枝杆菌病/孢子絲菌樣分枝桿菌病 sporotrichoid mycobacteriosis
孢子丝菌病样结节/孢子絲菌病樣結節 sporotrichoid nodule
孢子丝菌病样莱什曼病/孢子絲菌病樣萊什曼病 sporotrichoid leishmaniasis
孢子丝菌病样诺卡菌病/孢子絲菌病樣諾卡菌病 sporotrichoid nocardiosis
孢子丝菌属/胞子絲菌屬 *Sporothrix*
孢子丝菌性下疳/孢子絲菌下疳 sporotrichotic chancre
孢子体/孢子體 sporozoite
孢子形成/孢子形成 sporulation
孢子悬浮液/孢子懸液 spore suspension
胞壁酸类/胞壁酸類 muramic acids
胞壁酰二肽/胞壁醯二肽 muramyldipeptide

胞壁酰五肽羧肽酶/胞壁醯五肽羧肽酶 muramoylpentapeptide carboxypeptidase
胞壁质酶/溶菌酶 muramidase
胞苷/胞核戊苷,胞嘧啶核苷 cytidine
胞苷二磷酸/胞苷二磷酸 cytidine diphosphate
胞苷二磷酸胆碱/胞苷二磷酸膽鹼 cytidine diphosphate choline
胞苷二磷酸二甘油酯类/胞苷二磷酸二甘油酯類 cytidine diphosphate diglycerides
胞苷-磷酸/胞苷-磷酸 cytidine monophosphate
胞苷-磷酸 N-乙酰神经氨酸/胞苷-磷酸 N-乙醯神經胺酸 cytidine monophosphate N-acetylneuraminic acid
胞苷三磷酸/三磷酸胞核嘧啶核苷 cytidine triphosphate
胞苷酸类/胞苷酸類 cytosine nucleotides
胞苷脱氨酶/胞核戊苷脱胺基酵素 cytidine deaminase
胞宫/胞宫,子宫 uterus, womb
胞宫湿热证/胞宫濕熱證 pattern of dampness-heat in uterus, pattern of dampness-heat in womb
胞宫虚寒证/胞宫虚寒證 pattern of deficiency-cold in uterus, pattern of deficiency-cold in womb
胞管肾纲感染/胞管腎亞綱感染 secernentea infection
胞肓/胞肓 baohuang, BL53
胞间连丝/胞間連絲 plasmodesmata
胞间黏附分子/胞間黏附分子 intercellular adhesion molecule
胞间桥/细胞間橋 cell bridge
胞间腺毛/胞間腺毛 interspace glandular hair
胞间液/組織液 tissue fluid
胞睑病/胞瞼病 eyelid disease
胞睑外翻/胞瞼外翻 ectropion
胞浆蛋白/原形質蛋白質 plasmosin
胞浆内的/细胞漿内的 intracytoplasmic
胞浆溶解作用/细胞質溶解 endolysis
胞浆素酸/胞漿素酸 plasminic acid
胞浆素原活化体/血漿蛋白原活化因數 plasminogen activator
胞块/塊 mass
胞磷胆碱/胞磷膽鹼 citicoline
胞轮振跳/胞輪振跳 twitching eyelid, blepharospasm, twitching of eyelid
胞轮振跳·心脾两虚证/胞輪振跳·心脾兩虛證 twitching eyelid with heart-spleen deficiency pattern
胞轮振跳·血虚生风证/胞輪振跳·血虛生風證 twitching eyelid with pattern of blood deficiency

generating wind
胞脉/胞脈　uterine vessels
胞门/胞門　uterine ostium
胞嘧啶/胞嘧啶　cytosine
胞[嘧啶核]苷酸/胞[嘧啶]核苷酸　cytidylic acid
胞嘧啶脱氨酶/胞嘧啶脫胺酶　cytosine deaminase
胞膜先破/胞膜先破　premature rupture of amnion
胞内分枝杆菌/細胞内分枝桿菌　Mycobacterium intracellulare
胞内分枝杆菌肺病/胞内分枝桿菌肺病　pulmonary disease due to Mycobacterium intracellularis
[胞]内酶/[胞]内酶　endoenzyme
胞器/胞器　organelle
胞腔/胞腔　cell lumen
胞肉粘轮/胞肉粘輪　sticking of cornea and eyelid
胞生痰核/胞生痰核　phlegm nodule in eyelid, chalazion, phlegmatic nodule in eyelid
胞生痰核·痰热蕴结证/胞生痰核·痰熱蘊結證　phlegm nodule in eyelid with phlegm-heat amassment pattern
胞胎/胞胎　fetus with placenta and umbilical cord
胞体/胞體，細胞體　cell body
胞体分裂/胞體分裂　cytodieresis
胞体树突/胞體樹狀突　cytodendrite
胞铁[色]素/胞鐵色素　cytosiderin
胞吐作用/胞吐作用　exocytosis
胞吞作用/胞吞作用　endocytosis
[胞]外酶/[胞]外酶　ectoenzyme, lyoenzyme
胞虚如球/胞虛如球　ball-like edema of eyelid, puffiness of eyelid
胞咽/胞咽　cytopharynx
胞衣/胞衣　afterbirth
胞衣不下/胞衣不下　retention of placenta
胞衣不下·寒凝证/胞衣不下·寒凝證　retention of placenta with cold congelation pattern
胞衣不下·气虚证/胞衣不下·氣虛證　retention of placenta with qi deficiency pattern
胞衣不下·血瘀证/胞衣不下·血瘀證　retention of placenta with blood stasis pattern
胞饮/胞飲　pinocytosis
胞饮的/胞飲的　pinocytotic
胞饮泡/胞飲泡　pinocytotic vesicle
胞饮小泡/胞飲小泡　pinocytic vesicle
胞饮作用/胞飲作用　pinocytosis
胞质/胞質　periplasm
胞质蛋白质类/胞質蛋白質類　periplasmic proteins
胞质分裂/胞質分裂　cytokinesis
胞质结构/胞質結構　cytoplasmic structure

胞质结合蛋白质类/胞質結合蛋白質類　periplasmic binding proteins
胞质内精子注射/精子細胞漿内的注射　intracytoplasmic sperm injection
胞质[内生活]环/細胞漿内循環　cytoplasmic cycle
胞质溶解/胞質破裂　plasmarrhexis
胞质融合/胞漿接合,胞質接合　plasmatogamy
胞质网/胞體質網,胞體質絲　cytoreticulum
胞质网丝/細胞漿絲質,細胞漿網質　cytomitome
胞质小泡/胞質小泡　cytoplasmic vesicle
胞质小体/分離體　aposome
胞质液化/胞質液化　plasmatosis
胞质逸出/胞漿綻裂,胞漿迸出　plasmoptysis
胞质运动/胞質循流　cytoplasmic streaming
胞质皱缩性/胞漿分離性　plasmolyzability
胞肿如桃/胞腫如桃　peach-like swelling of eyelid, severe inflammatory edema of eyelid
胞肿如桃·风热袭表证/胞腫如桃·風熱襲表證　peach-like swelling of eyelid with pattern of wind-heat assaulting exterior
胞肿如桃·热毒炽盛证/胞腫如桃·熱毒熾盛證　peach-like swelling of eyelid with blazing heat-toxin pattern
薄板/片狀　sheet
薄壁组织/薄壁組織　parenchyma
薄层板贮箱/薄層板貯箱　plate storage rack
薄层电泳法/薄層電泳法　thin-layer electrophoresis
薄层色谱法/薄層層析法　thin-layer chromatography, thin layer chromatography
薄层移植物/層狀移植物　lamellar graft
薄唇/薄唇　thin lip
薄中厚皮片/薄[的]中厚皮片　thin intermediate thickness free skin graft
薄红细胞/薄紅血球,扁紅血球　leptocyte
薄红细胞血症/扁紅血球症　leptocytosis
薄厥/薄厥　sudden syncope, syncope due to rage
薄皮/薄皮　thin skin
薄皮瓣移植术/薄皮瓣移植術　transplantation of thin skin flap
薄束/薄束　fasciculus gracilis
薄束核/薄束核　gracile nucleus
薄束结节/薄束結節　gracile tubercle
薄苔/薄苔　thin fur
薄血管翳/薄血管翳　thin pannus
薄釉质/薄釉質　dwarfed enamel
薄纸样胎/紙樣胎兒,壓扁胎兒　paper-doll fetus
饱和/飽和　saturation
饱和的/飽和的　saturated

饱和甘汞电极/飽和甘汞電極 saturated calomel electrode
饱和染液/飽和染液 saturated staining solution
饱和溶液/飽和溶液 saturated solution
饱和脂肪酸/飽和脂肪酸 saturated fatty acid
饱和脂酸甘油化物/飽和脂酸甘油化物 saturated fatty acid glyceride
保持器/保持器 apparatus retention
保存的/保存的 preservative
保存液/保存液 preservation solution
保肝药/保肝藥 hepatoprotective
保和丸/保和丸 baohe pills
保护绷带/保護繃帶 protective bandage
保护床/保護床 protection bed
保护蛋白/保護蛋白質 protective protein
保护的/保護的 protective
保护敷料/保護性敷料 protective dressing
保护膏/保護膏 protective paste
保护基/保護基 protective group
保护胶体/保護膠質 protective colloid
保护疗法/庇護療法 protective therapy
保护酶/防衛酵素 protective ferment
保护性胶体学说/保護性膠體學說 theory of protective colloid
保护性抗体/保護性抗體 protective antibody
保护性抗原/保護性抗原 protective antigen
保护性免疫/保護性免疫 protective immunity
保护性膳食/防衛性飲食 protective diet
保护性阻滞/保護性阻滯 protective block
保健操/保健操 conditioning exercise
保健工作者/健康照顧工作者 health-care worker
保健灸/保健灸 health preserving moxibustion, keeping fit moxibustion
保健药品/保健用品 health care medicine
保健原理/保健原理，衛生原理 hygiogenesis
保留隙口/滯留間隔 retention gap
保留灌肠/保留灌腸 retention enema
保罗-米克斯特管/保-米二氏管 Paul-Mixter tube
保密性/隱密性 confidentiality
保守疗法/保守療法,姑息療法 conservative treatment
保守序列/保守序列 conserved sequence
保塔罗管/Botallo 氏管 duct of Botallo
保卫细胞/保衛細胞 guard cell
保温/保温 incubation
保温箱/保温箱 incubators
保险/保險 insurance
保险范围/保險範圍 insurance coverage

保险机构/保險機構 insurance carriers
保险赔偿费/保險賠償費 insurance benefits
保险索赔审核/保險索賠審核 insurance claim review
保险套下疳/保險套下疳 condom chancre
保险统计分析/保險統計分析 actuarial analysis
保险选择偏倚/保險選擇偏倚 insurance selection bias
保心药/保心藥 cardioprotectant
保幼激素类/保幼激素類 juvenile hormones
保育院校/保育院校 nursery school
抱轮红赤/抱輪紅赤 ciliary hyperemia, reddening surrounding the black of the eye
抱头火丹/抱頭火丹 head erysipelas
抱头火丹·毒邪内攻证/抱頭火丹·毒邪內攻證 head erysipelas with pattern of toxin attacking inward
抱头火丹·风热化火证/抱頭火丹·風熱化火證 head erysipelas with pattern of wind-heat transforming into fire
抱膝/抱膝 knee-cap fixing ring
豹斑[皮]综合征/Leopard 症候群 Leopard syndrome
豹纹状眼底/豹紋狀眼底 leopard fundus
鲍比夹板/Bowlby 氏夾板 Bowlby splint
鲍恩病/鮑恩病 Bowen disease
鲍恩样光线性角化病/波文樣日光性角化症 Bowenoid actinic keratosis
鲍恩样丘疹病/鮑恩樣丘疹病 bowenoid papulosis
鲍鲁溃疡/包魯潰瘍 Bauru ulcer
鲍曼肌/Bowman 肌 Bowman muscle
鲍曼膜/Bowman 氏膜 Bowman membrane
鲍曼饮食/Bauman 氏飲食 Bauman diet
鲍文病样/類 Bowen 氏病的 Bowenoid
暴喘/暴喘 sudden dyspnea
暴发的/暴發的 eruptive
暴发型/暴發型 fulminant type
暴发型肝炎/暴發性肝炎 fulminant hepatitis
暴发型痢疾/暴發性痢疾 fulminant dysentery
暴发型脑膜炎球菌败血症/暴發型腦膜炎球菌敗血症 fulminating meningococcemia
暴发型脑膜炎球菌脑膜脑炎/暴發型腦膜炎球菌腦膜腦炎 fulminating meningococcal meningoencephalitis
暴发性/暴發性,猛暴性 fulminating
暴发性痤疮/暴發性痤瘡 acne fulminans
暴发性的/暴發性的 fulminant
暴发性红斑痤疮/暴發性酒渣 rosacea fulminans
暴发性脊髓炎/爆發性脊髓炎 foudroyant myelitis

暴发性阑尾炎/暴發性闌尾炎　fulminating appendicitis
暴发性缺氧/暴發性缺氧症　fulminating anoxia
暴发性紫癜/暴發性紫癜病　purpura fulminans
暴发子痫/暴發子癇　fulminant eclampsia
暴风客热/暴風客熱　fulminant wind-heat invasion, acute catarrhal and allergic conjunctivitis, sudden wind and invading fever
暴风客热·风热并重证/暴風客熱·風熱并重證　fulminant wind-heat invasion with pattern of equal predomination of wind and heat
暴风客热·风重于热证/暴風客熱·風重於熱證　fulminant wind-heat invasion with pattern of wind predominating over heat
暴风客热·热重于风证/暴風客熱·熱重於風證　fulminant wind-heat invasion with pattern of heat predominating over wind
暴咳/暴欬,暴嗽　sudden cough
暴力/暴力　violence
暴力牵引/暴力牽引　violent traction
暴痢/暴痢　fulminant dysentery
暴聋/暴聾,突發性耳聾,突發性聽覺喪失　sudden deafness, sudden hearing loss
暴露/曝露　exposure
暴露赤眼生翳/曝露赤眼生翳　exposure keratitis, nebula due to exposed cornea
暴露赤眼生翳·肝经风热证/曝露赤眼生翳·肝經風熱證　nebula due to exposed cornea with pattern of wind-heat in liver channel
暴露赤眼生翳·肝肾阴虚证/曝露赤眼生翳·肝腎陰虛證　nebula due to exposed cornea with liver-kidney yin deficiency pattern
暴露疗法/曝露療法　exposure method
暴露性角膜炎/曝露性角膜炎,兔眼性角膜炎　exposure keratitis
暴盲/暴盲　sudden blindness, sudden visual loss
暴盲·肝经实热证/暴盲·肝經實熱證　sudden blindness with pattern of excessive heat in liver channel
暴盲·肝气郁结证/暴盲·肝氣鬱結證　sudden blindness with liver qi stagnation pattern
暴盲·肝肾阴虚证/暴盲·肝腎陰虛證　sudden blindness with liver-kidney yin deficiency pattern
暴盲·肝阳上亢证/暴盲·肝陽上亢證　sudden blindness with liver yang hyperactivity pattern
暴盲·脾肾阳虚证/暴盲·脾腎陽虛證　sudden blindness with spleen-kidney yang deficiency pattern
暴盲·气血瘀阻证/暴盲·氣血瘀阻證　sudden blindness with pattern of qi-blood stasis and obstruction
暴盲·痰瘀互结证/暴盲·痰瘀互結證　sudden blindness with pattern of intermingled phlegm and stasis
暴怒伤阴/暴怒傷陰　violent rage damaging yin
暴吐/暴吐　fulminant vomiting
暴喜伤心/暴喜傷心　overwhelming joy impairing heart
暴喜伤阳/暴喜傷陽　overjoy damaging yang
暴泻/暴瀉　fulminant diarrhea
暴喑/暴喑　sudden loss of voice
爆发性减压/爆炸式減壓　explosive decompression
爆发抑制/爆發抑制　burst suppression
爆裂骨折/爆裂骨折　bursting fracture
爆裂声/爆聲,小的尖銳聲　crackle
爆裂性骨折/爆裂性骨折　blow-out fracture
爆炸气浪/爆炸氣浪　blast
爆炸伤/爆炸傷　explosive injury
爆炸性肺震荡/胸爆炸傷　blast chest
爆震伤/爆震傷　blast injury
爆震性聋/爆震性聾　explosive deafness
杯芳烃/杯芳烴　calixarene
杯冠化合物/杯冠化合物　crown compound
杯盘比/杯盤比　cup disc ratio
杯伞菌素/杯傘菌素　clitocybine
杯状耳/杯狀耳　cup ear
杯状细胞/杯狀細胞　beaker cell
杯状子宫托/杯狀子宮托　cup pessary
卑怯/卑怯　guilt complex due to heart blood insufficiency, timidity
卑格米侏儒症/卑格米侏儒症　Pygmy dwarfism
悲/悲[慟]　grief
悲哀疗法/悲哀療法　sorrow therapy
悲胜法/悲勝法　sorrow therapy to overcome anger
悲胜怒/悲勝怒　sorrowing to overcome anger
悲忧伤肺/悲憂傷肺　melancholy impairing lung
悲郁/悲鬱　stagnation caused by grief
悲则气消/悲則氣消　excessive sorrow leading to qi consumption, grief causing qi consumption
悲中/悲中　stroke due to grief
北豆根/北豆根　asiatic moonseed rhizome
北非洲回归热螺旋体/北非洲回歸熱螺旋體　Borrelia berbera
[北美]金缕梅粉/[北美]金縷梅粉　witch hazel powder
[北美]金缕梅精/[北美]金縷梅精　witch hazel distillate

北美鲜黄莲/北美鮮黃蓮　Jeffersonia diphylla
北美芽生菌病/北美芽生菌病　north American blastomycosis
北美洲回归热螺旋体/北美洲回歸熱螺旋體,諾維氏螺旋體　Borrelia novyi
北沙参/北沙参　coastal glehnia root
北亚蜱传斑疹伤寒/北亞蜱傳斑疹傷寒　North Asian tick borne typhus
贝-伯-肖三氏病/Besnier-Boeck-Schaumann 三氏病　Besnier-Boeck-Schaumann disease
贝-达脱位/Bell-Dally 二氏脱位　Bell-Dally dislocation
贝德纳尔瘤/Bednar 氏瘤　Bednar tumor
贝迪克综合征/Benedict 氏症候群　syndrome of Benedict
贝恩顿绷带/Baynton 氏繃帶　Baynton bandage
贝尔肌/Bell 氏肌　Bell muscle
贝尔痉挛/Bell 氏抽搐,面肌抽搐　Bell spasm
贝尔疗法/貝爾療法　Bell treatment
贝尔麻痹/Bell 氏麻痺　Bell palsy
贝尔-马让迪定律/貝-馬二氏準則,貝爾氏準則　Bell-Magendie law
贝尔纳管/Bernard 氏管　Bernard duct
贝尔纳综合征/Bernard 氏症候群　Bernard syndrome
贝尔神经/Bell 氏神經　Bell nerve
贝尔坦韧带/Bertin 氏韌帶　Bertin ligament
贝尔托洛蒂综合征/Bertolotti 氏症候群　Bertolotti syndrome
贝尔脱位/Bell 氏脱位　Bell dislocation
贝尔西食管裂孔疝修补术/貝爾西食管裂孔疝修補術　Belsey hiatal hernia repair
贝尔现象/貝爾現象　Bell phenomenon
贝格尔感觉异常/Berger 氏感覺異常　Berger paresthesia
贝格尔细胞/卵巢門細胞　Berger cell
贝格矫治器/貝格矯治器　Begg appliance
贝格曼[胶质]细胞/伯格曼[膠質]細胞　Bergmann cell
贝赫切特综合征/Behcet 氏症候群　Behcet syndrome
贝卡里法/培卡里法　Beccari process
贝壳甲综合征/貝殼甲症候群　shell nail syndrome
贝壳杉烷二萜类/貝殼杉烷二萜類　kaurane diterpenes
贝壳硬蛋白/甲殼素　conchiolin
贝壳状耳/貝殼狀耳　shell ear
贝可皮质醇/貝可皮質醇　beclomethasone
贝克尔黑变病/Becker 氏黑變症　Becker melanosis
贝克尔色素性毛痣/Becker 氏色素性有毛母斑　Becker pigmented hairy nevus
贝克尔痣/Becker 氏母斑　Becker nevus
贝克尔综合征/Becker 氏症候群　Becker syndrome
贝克费尔德滤菌器/貝克斐特濾器,伯克飛特氏濾器　Berkefeld filter
贝克肌营养不良/貝克肌營養不良　Becker muscular dystrophy
贝克猫肺炎病毒/Baker 氏貓肺炎病毒　Baker feline pneumonitis virus
贝克囊肿/Baker 氏囊腫　Baker cyst
贝克三体征/贝克三體徵　Beck triad
贝克痣/貝克痣　Becker nevus
贝拉尔韧带/Bérard 氏韌帶　Berard ligament
贝勒病/Byler 氏病　Byler disease
贝类/貝　shellfish
贝利尼导管/Bellini 氏管　duct of Bellini
贝利尼韧带/Bellini 氏韌帶　Bellini ligament
贝利斯效应/Bayliss 效應　Bayliss effect
贝娄病/貝婁病　baleri
贝罗凯体/維洛凱氏體　Verocay body
贝美格/貝美格　bemegride
贝母/貝母　fritillaria bulb
贝母瓜蒌散/貝母瓜蔞散　beimu gualou powder
贝母碱/貝母鹼　verticine
贝那替秦/貝那替秦　benactyzine
贝内迪克特综合征/貝内迪克特症候群　Benedikt syndrome
贝内特骨折/班奈特骨折　Bennett fracture
贝内特角/班奈特氏角　Bennett angle
贝内特运动/班奈特氏運動　Bennett movement
贝内特脱位/Bennett 氏脱位　Bennett dislocation
贝-塞综合征/Bernard-Sergent 二氏症候群　Bernard-Sergent syndrome
贝特朗试剂/矽鎢酸試劑　Bertrand reagent
贝特曼紫癜/Bateman 氏紫癜　Bateman purpura
贝托莱液/Berthollet 氏液　Berthollet fluid
贝叶斯定理/貝葉斯定理　Bayes theorem
贝佐尔德脓肿/貝佐爾德膿腫　Bezold abscess
备急千金要方/備急千金要方　Important Prescriptions Worth a Thousand Gold for Emergency, Essential Recipes for Emergent Use Worth a Thousand Gold
备解素/備解素,終補體活素　properdin
备填洞/已修形窩洞　prepared cavity
备用医院/備用醫院　packaged hospital
背[部]/背[部]　back
背部痤疮/背部痤瘡　acne dorsalis
背部过激综合征/背部過激症候群　angry back

syndrome
背部损伤/背部損傷　back injury
背部弹力蛋白纤维瘤/背部彈力纖維瘤
　　elastofibroma dorsi
背侧被盖核/背側被蓋核　dorsal tegmental nucleus
背侧肠系膜/背側腸繫膜　dorsal mesentery
背侧的/背側的　dorsalis
背侧跗骨间韧带/背側跗骨間韌帶　dorsal intertarsal
　　ligament
背侧副橄榄核/背側副橄欖核　dorsal accessory
　　olivary nucleus
背侧横掌间韧带/背側橫掌間韌帶　dorsal transverse
　　intermetacarpal ligament
背侧横跖间韧带/背側橫蹠間韌帶　dorsal transverse
　　intermetatarsal ligament
背侧结节/背側結節　dorsal tubercle
背侧近侧跖间韧带/背側近端蹠間韌帶　dorsal
　　proximal intermetatarsal ligament
背侧面/背側面　dorsal surface
背侧丘脑/背側丘腦　dorsal thalamus
背[侧]屈/向背彎曲,背曲　dorsiflexion
背侧腕间韧带/背側腕間韌帶　dorsal intercarpal
　　ligament
背侧掌间韧带/背側掌間韌帶　dorsal
　　intermetacarpal ligament
背侧支/背側支　dorsal branch
[背侧支]内侧皮支/[背側支]内側皮支　medial
　　cutaneous branch
背侧总肠系膜/背總腸繫膜　dorsal common
　　mesentery
背侧总环状韧带/背側總環狀韌帶　dorsal common
　　annular ligament
背侧纵束/背側縱束　dorsal longitudinal fasciculus
背[侧]纵柱/背[側]縱柱　dorsal longitudinal column
背唇/背唇　dorsal lip
背法/背法　back-packing manipulation
背沟/背溝　dorsal groove
背肌/背部諸肌　muscle of back
背夹/背夾板　back splint
背景活动/背景活動　background activity
背景荧光/背景螢光　background fluorescence
背疽/背疽　carbuncle of back
背阔肌/背闊肌,闊背肌　latissimus dorsi
背阔肌肌皮瓣/背闊肌肌皮瓣　latissimus dorsi
　　myocutaneous flap
背阔肌腱下囊/背闊肌腱下囊　subtendinous bursa of
　　latissimus dorsi
背冷/背冷　coldness in back

背裂/背裂　dorsal fissure
背面/背面　facies dorsalis
背内侧核/背内側核　dorsomedial nucleus
背区/背區　back region
背热/背熱　hotness in back
背神经/背神經　dorsal nerve
背损伤/背損傷　back injury
背痛/背痛　backache
背驮式肝移植/背馱式肝移植　piggyback liver
　　transplantation
背外侧被盖区/背外側被蓋區　laterodorsal
　　tegmental area
背外侧的/背外側的　dorsolateral
背外侧束/背外側徑　dorsolateral fasciculus,
　　dorsolateral tract
背系膜/背腸繫膜,背臟繫膜　dorsal mesentery
背向后的/背向後的　dorsoposterior
背向前的/背向前的　dorsoanterior
背心系膜/背側心繫膜　dorsal mesocardium
背心型体积描记器/背心型體積描記器　jerkin
　　plethysmography
背胰/背胰　dorsal pancreas
背胰管/後胰腺管　dorsal pancreatic duct
背胰芽/背胰芽　dorsal pancreatic bud
背俞穴/背俞穴　back-shu point
背肢畸胎/背肢畸胎,背部寄生肢　notomelus
背中线的/背中線的　dorsomedian
背主动脉/背主動脈　dorsal aorta
钡/鋇　barium
钡餐/鋇餐　barium meal
钡放射性同位素/鋇放射性同位素　barium
　　radioisotope
钡化合物/鋇化合物　barium compound
钡剂休克/鋇劑休克　barium shock
钡石灰/鋇石灰　baralyme
钡盐/鋇鹽　barium salt
倍半硫化物/半硫化物,三硫化物　sesquisulfide
倍半萜/倍半萜　sesquiterpene
倍半萜类/倍半萜類　sesquiterpenes
倍量[剂]型/倍量[劑]型　double strength
倍硫磷/倍硫磷　fenthion
倍氯米松/倍氯米松　beclomethasone
倍频吸收带/多頻吸收帶　multiple frequency
　　absorption band
倍数/倍數　multiple
倍数核/倍數核　amphikaryon
倍他洛尔/倍他洛爾　betaxolol
倍他米松/貝皮質醇　betamethasone

倍他米松17-戊酸酯/倍他米松17-戊酸酯 betamethasone 17-valerate
倍他司汀/倍他司汀 betahistine
倍他唑/倍他唑 betazole
悖德痴愚者/精神错乱,性道德缺失 moral imbecile
悖德精神病/悖德精神病,悖德狂 moral insanity
被动安乐死/被動安樂死 passive euthanasia
被动病例发现/被動病例發現 passive case finding
被动错觉/受動性錯覺 passive illusion
被动的/被動的 passive
被动攻击型人格障碍/被動攻擊型人格障礙 passive-aggressive personality disorder
被动过敏反应/被動過敏反應 passive anaphylaxis
被动免疫/被動免疫性 passive immunity
被动免疫法/被動免疫[法] passive immunization
被动凝集[反应]/被動凝集[反應] passive agglutination
被动皮肤过敏反应/被動皮膚過敏反應 passive cutaneous anaphylaxis
被动溶血/被動溶血 passive hemolysis
被动睡眠/被動睡眠 passive sleep
被动体验/被動體驗 passive experience
被动萎缩/被動萎縮 passive atrophy
被动性白细胞增多/被動性白血球增多 passive leukocytosis
被动性失禁/被動性失禁 passive incontinence
被动性水肿/被動性水腫,瘀血性水腫 passive edema
被动性违拗/被動拒絕症,被動違拗症 passive negativism
被动性血块/被動性血塊 passive clot
被动性运动/被動運動 passive motion
被动血凝反应/被動性血球凝集作用 passive hemagglutination
被动运动/被動練習 passive exercise
被动致敏/被動敏感化,被動性起敏作用 passive sensitization
被动转移/被動轉移 passive transfer
被动转移试验/被動轉移試驗 passive transfer test
被动转运/被動轉運 passive transport
被动状态/被動狀態 passive state
被覆黏膜/被覆黏膜 lining mucosa
被覆上皮/被覆皮膜 covering epithelium
被盖/蓋 tegmentum
被盖背侧交叉/背側被蓋交叉 dorsal tegmental decussation
被盖的/被蓋的 tegmental
被盖辐射/被蓋輻射 tegmental radiation
被盖腹侧交叉/腹側被蓋交叉 ventral tegmental decussation
被盖脊髓束/被蓋脊髓徑 tegmentospinal tract
被盖区/被蓋部 tegmental region
被盖束/被蓋徑 tegmental tract
被盖细胞/被蓋細胞 tegmental cell
被盖中部/被蓋中部 midtegmentum
被盖中央束/被蓋中央徑 central tegmental tract
被害妄想/被害感,被迫妄想,迫害妄想 delusion of persecution
被截肢者/被截肢者 amputee
被控制感/被控制感 feeling of being controlled
被窥视恐怖/被視恐懼症 scopophobia
被膜/[被]膜 tunica
被膜剥除术/被膜剝脫術 decapsulation
被膜下淋巴窦/被膜下淋巴竇 subcapsular sinus
被囊动物/被囊類動物 tunicate
被囊细胞/被膜細胞 amphicyte cell
被殴打妇女/被毆打婦女 battered women
被窃妄想/被竊妄想 delusion of being stolen
被褥支架/被褥支架 bed arch
被[受]污染的/汙染的 contaminated
被吸附物/被吸附物 adsorbate
被遗弃儿童/被遺棄兒童 abandoned child
被影响体验/被影響體驗 experience of being influenced
被子植物/被子植物 angiosperm
被子植物素/被子植物素 angiospermin
奔马痨/奔馬癆 galloping consumption
奔马律/奔馬律 gallop
奔豚/奔豚 kidney amassment, running piglet
奔豚·肝气犯肺证/奔豚·肝氣犯肺證 kidney amassment with pattern of liver qi invading lung
奔豚·肝气犯脾证/奔豚·肝氣犯脾證 kidney amassment with pattern of liver qi invading spleen
奔豚气/奔豚氣 running piglet
奔走步态/變速步伐 metadromic progression
贲门/賁門 ①cardia, cardiac orifice ②benmen, CO3
贲门部/賁門部 cardiac part
贲门成形术/賁門成形術 cardioplasty
贲门窦/賁門竇 cardiac antrum
贲门肌切开术/賁門肌切開術 cardiomyotomy
贲门痉挛/賁門痙攣 cardiospasm
贲门扩张器/賁門擴張器 cardiodilator
贲门扩张术/賁門擴張術 cardiodiosis
贲门括约肌/賁門括約肌 cardiac sphincter
贲门淋巴环/賁門淋巴環 lymphatic ring of cardia,

cardiac lymph ring
贲门上部/賁門上部　epicardia
贲门松弛/賁門鬆弛　cardiochalasia
贲门狭窄/賁門狹窄　preventricular stenosis
贲门腺/[胃]賁門腺　cardiac gland
本草/本草　①herbal medicine, Bencao ②medicinal works
本草备要/本草備要　Bencao Beiyao
本草从新/本草從新　Bencao Congxin
本草待诏/本草待詔　Consultant for medical affairs
本草纲目/本草綱目　Compendium of Materia Medica
本草纲目拾遗/本草綱目拾遺　Supplement to Compendium of Materia Medica
本草经集注/本草經集注　Bencaojing Jizhu
本草经疏/本草經疏　Bencaojing Shu
本草考证/本草考證　Herbal Textual
本草品汇精要/本草品滙精要　Collected Essentials of Species of Materia Medica
本草拾遗/本草拾遺　A Supplement to Materia Medica
本草图经/本草圖經　Bencao Tujing
本草衍义/本草衍義　Augmented Materia Medica
本达固定液/Benda氏固定液　Benda fluid
本胆烷醇酮/本膽烷醇酮　Etiocholanolone
本底辐射/背景放射,背景輻射　background radiation
本地疟/本地瘧　autochthonous malaria
本地性感染/本地性感染　autochthonous infection
本经配穴法/本經配穴法　association of affected channel, association of affected meridian, combination of affected channel, combination of affected meridian
本经取穴/本經取穴　point selection along affected channel, point selection along affected meridian
本内迪克特试剂/本内迪克特試劑　Benedict reagent
本神/本神　benshen, GB13
本生阀/本生閥　Bunsen valve
本生吸收系数/本生氏吸收係數,布森氏係數　Bunsen coefficient
本斯·琼斯[白蛋白]尿/Bence Jones氏尿　Bence Jones urine
本特利调温氧合器/本特利調溫氧合器　Bentley temptrol oxygenator
本体感觉/本體感覺　proprioceptive sense, proprioception
本体感神经肌肉易化法/自受性神經肌肉促進作用　proprioceptive neuromuscular facilitation

本体感受器/本體刺激受器,自受器　proprioceptor
本托尔手术/本托爾手術　Bentall operation
本质的/本質的　essential
本周蛋白/本瓊氏蛋白質　Bence Jones protein
本周蛋白尿/本瓊氏蛋白尿　Bence Jones proteinuria
苯氨基甲酸酯类/苯胺基甲酸酯類　phenylcarbamates
苯胺/苯胺　amino benzene, aniline
苯胺癌/苯胺癌　aniline carcinoma
苯胺氮芥/苯胺氮芥　aniline mustard
苯胺黑/苯胺黑　benzalin
苯胺化合物/苯胺化合物　aniline compound
苯胺基萘磺酸类/苯胺基萘磺酸類　anilino naphthalenesulfonates
苯胺瘤/苯胺瘤　aniline tumor
苯胺羟化酶/苯胺羥化酶　aniline hydroxylase
苯胺水溶液/苯胺水溶液　aniline-water solution
苯胺油/苯胺油　aniline oil
苯胺中毒/苯胺中毒　anilinism
苯胺紫/苯胺紫,錦葵紫　mauvein
苯巴比妥/苯基巴比妥酸　phenobarbital
苯吡喃类/苯吡喃類　benzopyrans
苯丙氨酸/苯丙胺酸　phenylalanine
苯丙氨酸氨裂解酶/苯丙胺酸胺裂解酶　phenylalanine ammonia-lyase
苯丙氨酸加单氧酶/苯丙胺酸單一氧化酶　phenylalanine monooxygenase
苯丙氨酸tRNA连接酶/苯丙胺酸tRNA連接酶　phenylalanine-tRNA ligase
苯丙氨酸羟化酶/苯丙胺酸羥化酶　phenylalanine hydroxylase
苯丙氨酸羟化酶缺乏/苯丙胺酸羥化酶缺乏　phenylalanine hydroxylase deficiency
苯丙胺/安非他命　amphetamine
苯丙胺相关性障碍/苯丙胺相關性障礙　amphetamine-related disorders
苯丙醇胺/苯丙醇胺　phenylpropanolamine
苯丙氮䓬类/苯丙氮䓬類　benzodiazepines
苯丙砜/苯丙碸　solasulfone
苯丙酮类/苯丙酮類　propiophenones
苯丙酮尿/苯丙酮尿症　phenylpyruvicaciduria
苯丙酮尿症/苯酮酸尿症　phenylketonuria
苯丙酮酸/苯丙酮酸　phenylpyruvic acid
苯丙酮酸性白痴/苯丙酮酸性智力缺陷　phenylpyruvic amentia
苯丙酮酸性精神幼稚症/苯基丙酮酸性癡愚,苯丙酮酸性精神發育不全　phenylpyruvic imbecility
3-苯丙烯醛/3-苯丙烯醛　cinnamaldehyde

苯丙香豆素/苯丙香豆素　phenprocoumon
苯并芘/苯并芘　benzoapyrene
苯并芘类/苯并芘類　benzopyrenes
苯并芘羟化酶/苯并芘羥化酶　benzopyrene hydroxylase
苯并噁嗪类/苯并噁嗪類　benzoxazines
苯并噁唑/苯并噁唑　benzoxazoles
苯并蒽/苯并蒽　benzanthracene
苯并二氮䓬受体拮抗药/苯二氮七環衍生物受體拮抗藥　benzodiazepine receptor antagonist
苯并呋喃类/苯呋喃類　benzofurans
苯并红紫/苯紅紫　benzopurpurine
苯并环庚烯类/苯并環庚烯類　benzocycloheptenes
苯并咪唑类/苯咪唑類　benzimidazoles
苯雌酚/苯雌酚　benzestrol
苯丁酸氮芥/苯丁酸氮芥　chlorambucil
苯丁酮类/苯丁酮類　butyrophenones
苯噁洛芬/苯噁洛芬　benoxaprofen
苯二胺/苯二胺　phenylenediamine
苯二胺类/苯二胺類　phenylenediamines
苯二氮䓬类/苯二氮䓬類　benzodiazepines
苯二氮䓬酮类/苯二氮䓬酮類　benzodiazepinones
苯二甲酸类/苯二甲酸類　phthalic acids
苯福林/脱羟肾上腺素　phenylephrine
苯汞化合物/苯汞化合物　phenylmercury compounds
苯汞基/苯汞基,苯汞化合物　phenylmercuric
苯呱利定/苯呱利定　phenoperidine
苯呱利多/苯呱利多　benperidol
苯海拉明/苯海拉明　benadryl
苯海索/苯海索　benzhexol
苯琥胺/苯琥胺　phensuximide
苯环利定/苯環利定　Phencyclidine
苯环利定滥用/苯環利定濫用　phencyclidine abuse
苯环利定受体/苯環利定受體　phencyclidine receptor
苯黄酮类/苯黄酮類　benzoflavones
苯磺酸盐类/苯磺酸鹽類　benzenesulfonates
苯基/苯基　phenyl
苯［基］丙氨酸氮芥/苯丙胺酸氮芥　phenylalanine mustard
苯基硼酸/苯基硼酸　phenyloboric acid
苯基水杨酸/苯水楊酸　phenylsalicylic acid
苯基乙醇胺 N-甲基转移酶/苯基乙醇胺 N-甲基轉移酶　phenylethanolamine N-methyltransferase
苯甲二氮䓬健忘症/二氮平健忘症　diazepam amnesia
苯甲磺酰基氟化物/苯甲磺醯基氟化物　phenylmethylsulfonyl fluoride
苯甲吗啉酮/苯甲嗎啉酮　fenmetramide
苯甲醛/苯甲醛　benzaldehyde
苯甲醛醑/苯甲醛醑　benzaldehyde spirit
苯甲酸/苯甲酸,安息香酸　benzoic acid
苯甲酸铵/安息香酸銨　ammonium benzoate
苯甲酸苄酯/苯甲酸苯甲酯,安息香酸甲苯　benzyl benzoate
苯甲酸苄酯洗液/苯甲酸苯脂洗劑　benzyl benzoate lotion
苯甲酸雌二醇/安息香酸雌二醇　estradiol benzoate
苯甲酸类/苯甲酸類　benzoic acids
苯甲酸铝/苯甲酸鋁　aluminium benzoate
苯甲酸钠/安息香酸鈉　sodium benzoate
苯甲酸 β-萘酯/安息香酸萘酚　betanaphthyl benzoate
苯甲酸盐/苯甲酸鹽　benzoate
苯甲烃铵化合物/苯扎胺化合物　benzalkonium compound
苯甲酰胺类/苯甲醯胺類　benzamides
苯甲酰胺酶/苯甲醯胺酶　benzamidase
苯甲酰胆碱/苯甲醯膽鹼　benzoylcholine
苯甲酰磺胺/苯甲醯磺胺　sulfabenzamide
苯甲酰［基］/苯甲醯基,安息香醯基　benzoyl
苯甲酰甲醛/苯甲醯甲醛　phenylglyoxal
苯甲酰精氨酸-2-萘酰胺/苯甲醯精胺酸-2-萘醯胺　benzoylarginine-2-naphthylamide
苯甲酰精氨酸硝基苯胺/苯甲醯精胺酸硝基苯胺　benzoylarginine nitroaniline
苯甲酰喹/苯甲酸喹寧醇　benzoxiquine
苯甲酰葡萄糖醛酸/苯醯醛醣酸　benzoyl glucuronic acid
苯甲异噁唑青霉素/苯甲異噁唑青黴素　oxacillin
苯肼/苯肼　phenylhydrazine
苯肼中毒性贫血/苯肼中毒性貧血　phenylhydrazine anemia
苯醌/苯醌　quinone
苯醌类/苯醌類　benzoquinones
苯赖加压素/苯賴加壓素,苯丙胺酸賴胺酸加壓素　felypressin
苯疗法/安息香酸劑療法　benzotherapy
苯邻二甲酰亚胺类/苯鄰二甲醯亞胺類　phthalimides
苯硫脲/苯硫尿素　phenylthiourea
苯六羧酸/苯六甲酸　mellitic acid
苯基吗啡类/苯嗎吩烷類　benzomorphans
苯脲化合物/苯脲化合物　phenylurea compound
苯葡萄糖醛苷酸/葡萄醛酸酚酯　phenylglycuronic acid

苯醛/苯甲醛　benzoic aldehyde
苯醛绿/苯醛綠　benzaldehyde green
苯乳酸/苯乳酸　phenyllactic acid
苯噻啶/苯噻啶　pizotyline
苯噻二嗪类/苯噻二嗪類　benzothiadiazines
苯噻唑基硫脲/苯噻唑基硫脲　phenylthiazolylthiourea
苯妥英/雙苯丙脲　phenytoin
苯妥英钠/二苯乙内醯尿素鈉　phenytoin sodium
苯妥英龈增生/達蘭丁牙齒增生　dilantin gingival hyperplasia
苯烷胺生物碱/苯烷胺生物鹼　phenylalkylamine alkaloid
苯溴马隆/苯溴馬隆　benzbromarone
苯亚甲基/苯亞甲基　benzylidene
苯衍生物/苯衍生物　benzene derivative
苯氧乙基青霉素/苯氧乙烷基青黴素　phenethicillin
苯氧乙酸盐类/苯氧乙酸鹽類　phenoxyacetates
苯乙胺类/苯乙胺類　phenethylamines
苯乙呱啶酮/苯乙呱啶酮　glutethimide
苯乙基丙二酰胺/苯乙基丙二醯胺　phenylethylmalonamide
苯乙基醇/苯乙醇　phenylethyl alcohol
苯乙肼/苯乙肼　phenelzine
苯乙醚类/苯乙醚類　phenyl ethers
苯乙双胍/苯乙雙胍　phenformin
苯乙酸/苯醋酸　phenylacetic acid
苯乙酸乙酯/苯乙酸乙酯　ethyl phenylacetate
苯乙酸酯类/苯乙酸酯類　phenylacetates
苯乙酮/苯乙酮　acetophenone
苯乙酮类/苯乙酮類　acetophenones
苯乙烯/苯乙烯　styrene
苯乙烯共聚物/苯乙烯共聚物　styrene copolymer
苯乙酰胺/苯乙醯胺　phenylacetamide
苯乙酰脲/醋醯尿素苯　phenacemide
苯异丙基腺苷/苯異丙基腺苷　phenylisopropyladenosine
苯茚胺/苯茚胺　phenindamine
苯茚二酮/苯茚二酮　phenindione
苯扎贝特/苯扎貝特　bezafibrate
苯扎托品/苯扎托品　benztropine
苯中毒/苯中毒,石油精中毒　benzolism
苯佐卡因/胺基苯甲酸乙酯　benzocaine
苯唑拉胺/苯唑拉胺　benzolamide
崩解/分解,分裂　disintegration
崩解剂/崩散劑　disintegrating agent
崩解[作用]/崩散[作用]　disintegration
崩漏/崩漏　metrorrhagia and metrostaxis, metrorrhagia, metrostaxis
崩漏•脾虚证/崩漏•脾虛證　metrorrhagia and metrostaxis with spleen deficiency pattern
崩漏•肾阳虚证/崩漏•腎陽虛證　metrorrhagia and metrostaxis with pattern of kidney yang deficiency
崩漏•肾阴虚证/崩漏•腎陰虛證　metrorrhagia and metrostaxis with pattern of kidney yin deficiency
崩漏•血热证/崩漏•血熱證　metrorrhagia and metrostaxis with blood heat pattern
崩漏•血瘀证/崩漏•血瘀證　metrorrhagia and metrostaxis with blood stasis pattern
崩蚀性溃疡/崩蝕性潰瘍　phagedenic ulcer
崩蚀性溃疡的/蝕瘡狀的　phagedenic
崩蚀性脓皮症/崩蝕性膿皮症　phagedenic pyoderma
崩蚀性软下疳/崩蝕性軟下疳,蝕瘡性軟下苷　phagedenic chancroid
崩中/崩中　metrorrhagia
绷带/繃帶　bandage
绷带法/繃帶法　bandaging
绷带固定/繃帶固定　bandage fixation
绷带卷/卷繃帶　roller bandage
泵式充氧器/合氧器唧筒　pump-oxygenator
泵衰竭/泵衰竭　pump failure
逼尿肌反射亢进/壓迫肌性反射過強　detrusor hyperreflexia
逼尿肌无反射/逼尿肌無反射　detrusor areflexia
鼻/鼻　nose
鼻按摩法/鼻按摩法　nasal massage
鼻孢子虫属/鼻芽孢菌屬　*Rhinosporidium*
鼻孢子菌病/鼻孢子菌病　rhinosporidiosis
鼻背/鼻背,鼻梁　back of nose, nasal dorsum
鼻背点/鼻背點　sellion
鼻背动脉/鼻背動脈　dorsal nasal artery, dorsal artery of nose
鼻绷带/鼻繃帶　nasal bandage
鼻变态反应/鼻變態反應　nasal allergy
鼻病/鼻病　nasal disease, nose disease
鼻部/鼻部　nasal part
鼻部切诊/鼻部切診　palpation of nose
鼻部闻诊/鼻部聞診　auscultation and olfaction of nose
鼻部纤维性丘疹/鼻部纖維性丘疹　fibrous papule of nose
鼻侧裂/鼻側裂　lateral cleft nose
鼻侧偏盲/鼻側偏盲　nasal hemianopsia
鼻侧软骨/鼻側軟骨　nasal lateral cartilage
鼻侧视网膜/視網膜鼻部　nasal retina
鼻侧突/鼻外突　lateral nasal process

鼻测量计/量鼻儀　nasograph
鼻插管法/鼻插管法　nasal intubation
鼻长/鼻長　nasal length
鼻成形术/鼻成形術　rhinoplasty
鼻冲洗/鼻沖洗　nasal irrigation
鼻充血减轻剂/鼻充血減輕劑　nasal decongestants
鼻出血/鼻出血　epistaxia
鼻吹药法/鼻吹藥法　method of nasal insufflation
鼻唇成形术/鼻唇成形術　nasolabioplasty
鼻唇的/鼻與唇的　nasolabial
鼻唇沟/鼻唇溝　nasolabial sulcus, nasolabial groove
鼻唇角/鼻唇角　nasal labial angle
鼻唇淋巴结/鼻唇淋巴結　nasolabial lymph node
鼻唇囊肿/鼻唇囊腫　nasolabial cyst
鼻胆管引流[术]/鼻膽管引流[術]　nasobiliary drainage
鼻导管给氧/鼻導管給氧　nasal catheter oxygen inhalation
鼻道/鼻道　nasal cavity
鼻道狭窄/鼻道狹窄　rhinostenosis
鼻的/鼻的　nasal
鼻堤/鼻丘　agger nasi, nasoturbinal concha
鼻疔/鼻疔　nasal ding, nasal furunculosis
鼻动脉/鼻動脈　nasal artery
鼻窦/鼻竇　paranasal sinuses
鼻窦疾病/鼻竇疾病　paranasal sinus disease
鼻窦痰包/鼻竇痰包　phlegmatic mass in nasal sinus
鼻窦炎/鼻竇炎　sinusitis
鼻窦炎口服液/鼻竇炎口服液　bidouyan koufuye, bidouyan mixture
鼻窦支气管炎/鼻副竇支氣管炎　sinobronchitis
鼻窦支气管综合征/鼻竇支氣管症候群　sinobronchial syndrome
鼻窦肿瘤/鼻竇腫瘤　paranasal sinus neoplasms
鼻额部脑迷离瘤/鼻額部腦迷離瘤　encephalochoristoma naso-frontalis
鼻额角/鼻額角　nasal frontal angle
鼻额静脉/鼻額靜脈　nasofrontal vein
鼻腭长神经/鼻腭長神經　long nasopalatine nerve
鼻腭的/鼻與腭的　nasopalatine
鼻腭短神经/鼻腭短神經　short nasopalatine nerves
鼻腭沟/鼻腭溝　nasopalatine groove
鼻腭管/鼻腭管　nasopalatine canal, nasopalatine duct
鼻腭管囊肿/鼻腭管囊腫, 正中前上腭囊腫　nasopalatine duct cyst
鼻腭神经/鼻腭神經, Cotunnius 氏神經　nasopalatine nerve, nerve of Cotunnius
鼻耳窘迫综合征/鼻耳窘迫症候群　nose-ear distress syndrome
鼻肥大/鼻肥大　hypertrophic nose
鼻副软骨/鼻副軟骨　accessory nasal cartilages
鼻疳/鼻疳　nasal gan disease, nasal malnutrition, nasal vestibulitis and eczema
鼻疳·肺经蕴热证/鼻疳·肺經蘊熱證　nasal gan disease with pattern of heat amassment in lung channel
鼻疳·湿热上蒸证/鼻疳·濕熱上蒸證　nasal gan disease with pattern of dampness-heat steaming upward
鼻疳·阴虚血燥证/鼻疳·陰虛血燥證　nasal gan disease with pattern of yin deficiency and blood dryness
鼻干/鼻乾　dry nose
鼻高/鼻高　nasal height
鼻槁/鼻槁, 萎縮性鼻炎　atrophic rhinitis, withered nose
鼻槁·肺肾阴虚证/鼻槁·肺腎陰虛證　withered nose with lung-kidney yin deficiency pattern
鼻槁·脾气虚证/鼻槁·脾氣虛證　withered nose with spleen qi deficiency pattern
鼻槁·燥邪犯肺证/鼻槁·燥邪犯肺證　withered nose with pattern of dryness assailing lung
鼻隔/鼻隔　nasal septum
鼻根/鼻根　root of nose, nasal root
鼻根部脑膨出/鼻根部腦膨出　nasofrontal encephalocele
鼻根点/鼻根點　nasion
鼻根点陷凹/鼻根點陷凹　nasion excavation
鼻骨/鼻骨　nasal bone
鼻骨骨折复位钳/鼻骨骨折復位鉗　nasal bone fracture reduction forcep
鼻骨间缝/鼻骨間縫　internasal suture
鼻骨孔/鼻孔　nasal foramina
鼻骨筛骨沟/鼻骨篩骨溝, 鼻神經溝　nasal groove
鼻灌洗液/鼻灌洗液　nasal lavage fluid
鼻鼾/鼻鼾　snore, snoring
鼻颌沟/鼻頜溝　nasomaxillary groove
鼻横沟/鼻橫溝　transverse nasal groove
鼻横线/鼻橫紋　striae nasi transversa
鼻红粒病/鼻紅粒病　granulosis rubra nasi
鼻喉科学/鼻喉科學　laryngorhinology
鼻后滴注/鼻後滴液法　postnasal drip
鼻后棘/鼻後棘　posterior nasal spine
鼻后镜检查[法]/鼻後孔檢視法　posterior rhinoscopy

鼻后孔/鼻後孔　posterior nare, choana
鼻后孔闭锁/鼻後孔閉鎖　atresia of choana
鼻后孔填塞术/鼻後孔填塞術　postnasal packing
鼻后孔息肉/鼻後孔息肉　choanal polyp
鼻后上内侧支/鼻後上内側支　medial posterior superior nasal branches
鼻后上外侧支/鼻後上外側支　lateral posterior superior nasal branch
鼻后外侧动脉/鼻後外側動脈　posterior lateral nasal artery
鼻后外侧及中隔动脉/鼻後外側及中隔動脈　lateral and septal posterior nasal artery
鼻后下支/鼻後下支　posterior inferior nasal branch
鼻呼吸/鼻[式]呼吸　nasal respiration
鼻呼吸困难/鼻呼吸困難　nasal dyspnea
鼻坏疽/壞疽性鼻炎,走馬鼻疳　cancrum nasi
鼻坏死/鼻壞死　rhinonecrosis
鼻肌/鼻肌　nasalis, musculus nasalis
鼻肌横部/鼻肌橫部　transverse part of nasalis
鼻肌翼部/鼻肌翼部　alar part of nasalis
鼻[基]板/鼻[基]板　nasal placode
鼻激发试验/鼻激發試驗　nasal provocation test
鼻疾病/鼻疾病　nose disease
鼻棘/鼻棘　nasal spine
鼻棘点/鼻棘點　nasospinale
鼻嵴/鼻嵴　nasal crest
鼻夹/鼻夾　nasal splint
鼻颊裂/鼻頰裂　nasobuccal cleft
鼻甲/[鼻]甲　turbinate
鼻甲刀/鼻甲刀　conchotome
鼻甲骨/鼻甲骨　scroll bone
鼻甲海绵丛/鼻甲海綿叢　cavernous plexus of conchae
鼻甲嵴/鼻甲嵴　conchal crest
鼻甲切除术/鼻甲切除術　turbinectomy
鼻甲切开术/鼻甲切斷術　turbinotomy
鼻甲炎/鼻甲炎　conchitis
鼻尖/鼻尖　apex of nose, nasal tip
鼻尖点/鼻尖點　rhinion
鼻尖蝶形切口/鼻尖蝶形切口　nasal tip butterfly incision
鼻尖肥大/鼻尖肥大　nasorostral hypertrophy
鼻尖下垂鼻/鼻尖下垂鼻　drooping nose
鼻尖形态/鼻尖形態　contour of nasal tip
鼻疖/鼻癤　nasal furuncle
鼻疖·火毒内陷证/鼻癤·火毒内陷證　nasal furuncle with pattern of fire-toxin sinking inward
鼻疖·邪毒外袭证/鼻癤·邪毒外襲證　nasal furuncle with pattern of external assault by pathogenic toxin
鼻结核/鼻結核　tuberculosis of nose
鼻睫根/鼻睫根　nasociliary root
鼻睫神经/鼻睫神經　nasociliary nerve
鼻睫神经痛/鼻睫神經痛　nasociliary neuralgia
鼻睫[状]的/鼻睫的　nasociliary
鼻睫状神经/鼻睫狀神經　nasociliary nerve, nerve nasociliaris
鼻镜/鼻鏡　rhinoscope
鼻镜检查/鼻鏡檢查,鼻窺器檢查　rhinoscopy
鼻疽杆菌/鼻疽桿菌　corynebacterium mallei
鼻菌/鼻菌　nose cancer
鼻菌·火毒蕴结证/鼻菌·火毒蘊結證　nose cancer with fire-toxin amassment pattern
鼻菌·痰瘀互结证/鼻菌·痰瘀互結證　nose cancer with pattern of intermingled phlegm and stasis
鼻科学/鼻科學　rhinology
鼻孔/鼻[前]孔　nare, nostril
鼻孔闭锁/鼻孔閉鎖　atretorrhinia
鼻孔底/鼻孔底　nasal floor
鼻孔开大肌/鼻孔擴張肌　dilator muscle of nose
鼻孔扩张器/鼻孔擴張器　rhineurynter
鼻孔美容术/鼻孔美容術　narial cosmesis
鼻孔外翻/鼻孔外翻　ectropion of nostril
鼻孔狭窄/鼻孔狹窄　stricture of nostril
鼻孔症状/鼻孔症狀　nostril symptom
鼻宽/鼻寬　nasal breadth
鼻泪沟/鼻淚溝　nasolacrimal groove
鼻泪管/鼻淚管　nasolacrimal canal, nasolacrimal duct, ductus nasolacrimalis
鼻泪管襞/淚皺襞　lacrimal fold
鼻泪管插管术/鼻淚管插管術　nasolacrimal duct intubation
鼻泪管口/鼻淚管口　orifice of nasolacrimal duct
鼻泪管狭窄/鼻淚管狹窄　stenosis of nasolacrimal duct
鼻泪管阻塞/鼻淚管阻塞　obstruction of nasolacrimal duct
鼻梁/鼻梁　bridge of the nose
鼻梁形态/鼻梁形態　contour of nasal bridge
鼻裂/鼻裂　bifid nose
鼻隆凸/鼻隆凸　nasal eminence
鼻瘘/鼻瘻　nasal fistula
鼻漏/鼻漏　rhinorrhea
鼻毛/鼻毛　hair of vestibule of nose
鼻美容术/鼻美容術　aesthetic rhinoplasty
鼻面/鼻面　nasal surface
鼻面角/鼻面角　nasal facial angle

鼻囊/鼻囊　nasal capsule
鼻囊软骨/鼻囊軟骨　nasal capsule cartilage
鼻脑脊液瘘/顱竇瘘　craniosinus fistula
鼻脑膜脑膨出/鼻腦膜腦膨出　nasal meningoencephalocele
鼻内侧支/鼻内側支　medial nasal branch
鼻内的/鼻内的　intranasal
鼻内麻醉/鼻内麻醉　intranasal anesthesia
鼻内投药/鼻内投藥　intranasal administration
鼻内支/鼻内支　internal nasal branch
鼻内注射/鼻内注射　nasal injection
鼻黏膜/鼻黏膜　mucous membrane of nose, nasal mucosa
鼻[黏膜]干燥/鼻乾燥　xeromycteria
鼻黏膜嗅区/鼻黏膜嗅部　olfactory region of nasal mucous membrane
鼻黏膜炎/鼻黏膜炎　endorhinitis
鼻衄[病]/鼻衄[病],鼻出血,流鼻血　epistaxis, nose bleeding disease
鼻衄·肺经风热证/鼻衄·肺經風熱證　nose bleeding with pattern of wind-heat in lung channel
鼻衄·肝火上炎证/鼻衄·肝火上炎證　epistaxis with pattern of flaring up liver fire, nose bleeding with pattern of liver fire flaring upward
鼻衄·肝肾阴虚证/鼻衄·肝腎陰虛證　nose bleeding with liver-kidney yin deficiency pattern
鼻衄·脾不统血证/鼻衄·脾不統血證　nose bleeding with pattern of spleen failing to control blood
鼻衄·气血两虚证/鼻衄·氣血兩虛證　epistaxis with pattern of deficiency of both qi and blood
鼻衄·热邪犯肺证/鼻衄·熱邪犯肺證　epistaxis with pattern of heat pathogen invading lung
鼻衄·胃火炽盛证/鼻衄·胃火熾盛證　epistaxis with pattern of blazing stomach fire, nose bleeding with stomach fire blazing pattern
鼻衄·心火炽盛证/鼻衄·心火熾盛證　nose bleeding with blazing heart fire pattern
鼻衄·阴虚火旺证/鼻衄·陰虛火旺證　epistaxis with pattern of exuberant fire due to yin deficiency
鼻旁的/鼻旁的　paranasal
鼻旁窦/鼻旁竇　paranasal sinus
鼻偏斜/鼻偏斜　nasal deviation
鼻前棘/前鼻棘　anterior nasal spine
鼻前棘点/鼻前穴　acanthion
鼻前孔/鼻前孔　anterior nares
鼻前孔闭锁/鼻前孔閉鎖　atresia of anterior naris
鼻前孔狭窄/鼻前孔狭窄　stricture of anterior naris
鼻前庭/鼻前庭　nasal vestibule

鼻前庭囊肿/鼻前庭囊腫　nasal vestibular cyst
鼻前外侧支/鼻前外側支　lateral anterior nasal branch
鼻前囟弓/鼻前囟弧　nasobregmatic arc
鼻腔/鼻腔　nasal cavity
鼻腔闭锁/鼻腔閉鎖　atresia nasi
鼻腔测压/鼻腔測壓　rhinomanometry
鼻腔干燥/鼻腔乾燥病　mycteroxerosis
鼻[腔]镜/鼻[腔]鏡　conchoscope
鼻腔黏膜给药/鼻腔黏膜給藥　nasal administration
鼻腔筛漏斗/鼻腔篩漏斗　ethmoidal infundibulum of cavity of nose
鼻腔填塞疗法/鼻腔填塞療法　therapy of plugging into nasal cavity
鼻切迹/鼻切跡　nasal notch
鼻切开术/鼻切開術　rhinotomy
鼻丘细胞/鼻丘細胞　agger nasi cell
鼻鼽/鼻鼽,過敏性鼻炎　allergic rhinitis
鼻鼽·肺经伏热证/鼻鼽·肺經伏熱證　allergic rhinitis with pattern of latent heat in lung channel
鼻鼽·肺气虚寒证/鼻鼽·肺氣虛寒證　allergic rhinitis with lung qi deficiency-cold pattern
鼻鼽·脾气虚证/鼻鼽·脾氣虛證　allergic rhinitis with spleen qi deficiency pattern
鼻鼽·肾阳虚证/鼻鼽·腎陽虛證　allergic rhinitis with kidney yang deficiency pattern
鼻区/鼻部　nasal region
鼻软骨/鼻軟骨　nasal cartilages
鼻塞/鼻塞　nasal obstruction, stuffy nose
鼻[塞测]压计/鼻塞測壓計,鼻腔壓力測量儀　rhinomanometer
鼻塞语音/鼻塞語音　stomatolalia
鼻塞支气管音/鼻吸氣性支氣管聲　sniffling bronchophony
鼻塞[子]/鼻塞　rhinobyon
鼻煽/鼻煽　flapping of nasal wings
鼻[伤风]病毒/鼻傷風病毒　coryza virus
鼻上颌窦痛/鼻上頜竇痛　rhinantralgia
鼻上颌窦炎/鼻上頜竇炎　nasoantritis
鼻上颌缝/鼻頜縫　nasomaxillary suture
鼻深/鼻深　nasal depth
鼻神经/鼻神經　nasal nerve
鼻神经功能病/鼻神經官能症　rhinoneurosis
鼻神经沟/鼻神經溝　groove for nasal nerve
鼻神经胶质瘤/鼻神經膠質瘤　nasal glioma
鼻神经节/鼻神經節　nasal ganglion
鼻石/鼻石　rhinolith
鼻石病/鼻石症　rhinolithiasis

鼻水肿/鼻水腫　rhinedema
鼻饲[法]/經鼻哺養法　nasal feeding
鼻酸/鼻酸　irritating sensation in nose
鼻损伤/鼻損傷　injury of nose, nasal trauma
鼻缩小成形术/鼻縮小成形術　reductive rhinoplasty
鼻涕/鼻涕　snivel
鼻填塞术/鼻填塞術　nasal tamponade
鼻通气管/鼻通氣管　rhinophore
鼻通气检验镜/鼻通氣檢驗鏡　nasographic mirror
鼻痛/鼻痛　rhinalgia
鼻涂敷法/鼻塗敷法　coating method for nose
鼻外侧支/鼻內侧支　lateral nasal branch
鼻外静脉/鼻外靜脈　external nasal vein
鼻外支/鼻外支　external nasal branch
鼻窝/鼻窝,嗅窝　nasal pit
鼻雾化吸入法/鼻霧化吸入法　method of nasal spray inhalation
鼻吸试验/嗅聞試驗　sniff test
鼻息肉/鼻息肉　nasal polyp
鼻息肉病/鼻息肉病　nasal polyposis
鼻息肉·寒湿凝聚证/鼻息肉·寒濕凝聚證　nasal polyp with pattern of cold-dampness congelation and aggregation
鼻息肉·湿热蕴结证/鼻息肉·濕熱蘊結證　nasal polyp with dampness-heat amassment pattern
鼻下点/鼻下點　subnasale
鼻腺/鼻腺　nasal gland
鼻小柱/鼻小柱　nasal columella
鼻[小]柱正中切口/鼻[小]柱正中切口　nasal midcolumella incision
鼻性哮喘/鼻性氣喘　nasal asthma
鼻嗅疗法/鼻嗅療法　smelling therapy
鼻血管收缩药/鼻血管收縮藥　nasal vasoconstrictor
鼻血瘤/鼻血瘤　hematoma of nose
鼻血瘤·肝郁化火证/鼻血瘤·肝鬱化火證　hematoma of nose with pattern of liver depression transforming into fire
鼻压计/鼻壓力計　nasomanometer
鼻牙槽囊肿/鼻與齒槽囊腫　nasoalveolar cyst
鼻咽/鼻咽,咽之鼻部　nasal part of pharynx, nasopharynx
鼻咽癌/鼻咽癌　nasopharyngeal carcinoma, NPC
鼻咽癌·火毒蕴结证/鼻咽癌·火毒蘊結證　nasopharyngeal carcinoma with fire-toxin amassment pattern
鼻咽癌·气血凝结证/鼻咽癌·氣血凝結證　nasopharyngeal carcinoma with pattern of qi-blood coagulating and intermingling

鼻咽癌·痰浊凝聚证/鼻咽癌·痰濁凝聚證　nasopharyngeal carcinoma with pattern of phlegm-turbidity coagulation and aggregation
鼻咽癌·正虚毒滞证/鼻咽癌·正虛毒滯證　nasopharyngeal carcinoma with pattern of healthy qi deficiency and toxin stagnation
鼻咽道/鼻咽道　nasopharyngeal meatus
鼻咽的/鼻咽的　nasopharyngeal
鼻咽电极/鼻咽電極　nasopharyngeal electrode
鼻咽沟/鼻咽溝　nasopharyngeal groove
鼻咽管/鼻咽管　meatus nasopharyngeus
鼻咽疾病/鼻咽疾病　nasopharyngeal disease
鼻咽镜/鼻咽鏡　nasopharyngoscope
鼻咽镜检查[法]/咽鼻部檢查法　pharyngorhinoscopy
鼻咽黏膜利什曼病/黏膜萊什曼病　espundia
鼻咽清毒颗粒/鼻咽清毒顆粒　biyan qingdu granules
鼻咽通气管/鼻咽通氣管　nasopharyngeal airway
鼻咽血管纤维瘤/鼻咽血管纖維瘤　nasopharyngeal angiofibroma
鼻咽炎/鼻咽炎　rhinopharyngitis
鼻咽肿瘤/鼻咽腫瘤　nasopharyngeal neoplasm
鼻炎/鼻炎　coryza
鼻炎片/鼻炎片　biyan tablets
鼻眼裂/鼻眼裂　naso-ocular facial cleft
鼻痒/鼻癢　rhinocnesmus, nose itching
鼻异物/鼻異物　foreign body entering nose
鼻翼/鼻翼　wing of nose, alae nasi
鼻翼大软骨/鼻翼大軟骨　major alar cartilage of nose
鼻翼耳屏线/鼻翼耳屏線　ala-tragus line
鼻翼沟/鼻翼溝　paranasal ala sulcus
鼻翼切开术/鼻翼切開術　alatomy
鼻翼缺损/鼻翼缺損　defect of nasal ala
鼻翼软骨/鼻翼軟骨　nasal alar cartilage
鼻翼扇动/鼻翼扇動　flaring of alae nasi
鼻翼小软骨/鼻翼小軟骨　minor alar cartilage of nose
鼻音/鼻音　nasal voice
鼻银沉着病/鼻銀沈著病　argyria nasalis
鼻蝇蛆病/鼻蛆病,蛆性鼻炎　peenash
鼻硬结病/鼻硬結病　rhinoscleroma
鼻用吸入器/鼻用吸入器　nasal inhaler
鼻阈/鼻閾　nasal limen
鼻渊/鼻淵　acute and chronic sinusitis, sinusitis
鼻渊·胆腑郁热证/鼻淵·膽腑鬱熱證　sinusitis with pattern of heat stagnation in gallbladder-fu
鼻渊·肺经风热证/鼻淵·肺經風熱證　sinusitis with

鼻渊·肺气虚寒证/鼻淵·肺氣虛寒證　sinusitis with lung qi deficiency-cold pattern, pattern of wind-heat in lung channel

鼻渊·肺气虚寒证/鼻淵·肺氣虛寒證　sinusitis with lung qi deficiency-cold pattern

鼻渊·脾气虚证/鼻淵·脾氣虛證　sinusitis with spleen qi deficiency pattern

鼻渊·脾胃湿热证/鼻淵·脾胃濕熱證　sinusitis with pattern of dampness-heat in spleen and stomach

鼻缘/鼻緣　nasal margin

鼻粘连/鼻粘連　nasal synechia

鼻真菌病/鼻真菌病　rhinomycosis

鼻蒸气吸入法/鼻蒸氣吸入法　method of nasal vapor inhalation

鼻正中裂/鼻正中裂　median cleft nose

鼻指数/鼻指數　nasal index

鼻窒/鼻窒　nasal obstruction disease, chronic rhinitis, nasal blockade

鼻窒·肺经蕴热证/鼻窒·肺經蘊熱證　nasal obstruction disease with pattern of heat amassment in lung channel

鼻窒·肺脾气虚证/鼻窒·肺脾氣虛證　nasal obstruction disease with spleen-lung qi deficiency pattern

鼻窒·气滞血瘀证/鼻窒·氣滯血瘀證　nasal obstruction disease with pattern of qi stagnation and blood stasis

鼻中隔/鼻中隔　nasal septum

鼻中隔鼻成形术/鼻中隔鼻成形術　septorhinoplasty

鼻中隔成形术/鼻中隔成形術　septoplasty

鼻中隔穿孔/鼻中隔穿孔　perforation of nasal septum

鼻中隔刀/鼻中隔刀　septatome

鼻中隔骨部/鼻中隔骨部，骨性鼻中隔　bony part of nasal septum, bony septum of nose

鼻中隔骨棘/鼻中隔骨棘　spur of nasal septum

鼻中隔骨脊/鼻中隔骨脊　ridge of nasal septum

鼻中隔后支/鼻中隔後支　posterior septal branch

鼻中隔厚度计/鼻中隔厚度計　septometer

鼻中隔降肌/鼻中隔降肌　depressor muscle of septum of nose

鼻中隔膜部/鼻中隔膜部　membranous part of nasal septum

鼻中隔黏膜下切除术/鼻中隔黏膜下切除術　submucous resection of nasal septum

鼻中隔脓肿/鼻中隔膿腫　nasal septal abscess

鼻中隔偏曲/鼻中隔彎曲　deflection of nasal septum

鼻中隔前支/鼻中隔前支　anterior septal branch

鼻中隔切除术/鼻中隔切除術　septectomy

鼻中隔切开术/鼻中隔切開術　septotomy

鼻中隔软骨/鼻中隔軟骨　septal cartilage of nose, nasal septal cartilage

鼻中隔软骨部/鼻中隔軟骨部　cartilaginous part of nasal septum

鼻中隔血肿/鼻中隔血腫　hematoma of nasal septum

鼻中隔炎/鼻中隔炎　nasoseptitis

鼻中隔支/鼻中隔支　nasal septal branch

鼻中突/鼻內突　median nasal process

鼻肿瘤/鼻腫瘤　nose neoplasm

鼻周期/鼻週期　nasal cycle

鼻注入/鼻注入　nasal injection

鼻准/鼻準，鼻尖　nasal apex

比昂基综合征/Bianchi 氏症候群　Bianchi syndrome

比奥呼吸/比奧呼吸　Biot respiration

比表面积/比表面積　specific surface area

比布龙解蛇毒药/Bibron 氏解毒藥　Bibron antidote

比尔斑/Bier 氏點　Bier spot

比尔罗特肥大/Billroth 氏肥大　Billroth hypertrophy

比尔罗特吻合[术]/比爾羅特吻合[術]　Billroth anastomosis

比尔默贫血/Biermer 氏貧血　Biermer anemia

比尔绍夫斯基征/比爾紹夫斯基徵　Bielschowsky sign

比尔神经节细胞/Beale 氏神經節細胞　Beale ganglion cell

比尔阻断术/Bier 氏阻斷術　Bier block

比弗征/比弗徵　Beevor sign

比呱立登/比呱立登　Biperiden

比混浊法/濁度試驗法　turbidity method

比活/比活性　specific activity

比积/比容　specific volume

比基尼综合征/Picchini 氏症候群　Picchini syndrome

比吉洛韧带/Bigelow 氏韌帶　Bigelow ligament

比较病理学/比較病理學　comparative pathology

比较解剖学/比較解剖學　comparative anatomy

比较免疫学/比較免疫學　comparative immunology

比较胚胎学/比較胚胎學　comparative embryology

比较生理学/比較生理學　comparative physiology

比较心理学/比較心理學　comparative psychology

比较组织学/比較組織學　comparative histology

比里骨/Pirie 氏骨，距舟骨　Pirie bone

比例危险度模型/比例危險度模型　proportional hazards model

比率/比率，比例　ratio

比目鱼肌/比目魚肌　soleus, musculus soleus

比目鱼肌腱弓/比目魚肌腱弓　tendinous arch of soleus

比目鱼肌线/比目魚肌線　soleal line
比内-西蒙测验/比-西測驗　Binet-Simon test
比尼霉素/二硝黴素　biniramycin
比气道传导率/比氣道傳導率　specific airway conductance
比热/比熱　specific heat
比萨液/Piazza 氏液　Piazza fluid
比色测定/比色測定　colorimetric determination
比色单/比色單　shade prescription
比色滴定法/比色滴定法，測色滴定法　colorimetric titration
比色法/比色法　colorimetric method, colorimetry
比色计/比色計　chromometer
比色溶液/比色溶液　colorimetric solution
比色座/比較器　comparator block
比沙可啶/比沙可啶　bisacodyl
比沙孔/Bichat 氏孔　Bichat foramen
比顺应性/比順應性　specific compliance
比斯综合征/Pins 氏症候群　Pins syndrome
比索洛尔/比索洛爾　bisoprolol
比特性黏度/比固有黏度　specific intrinsic viscosity
比托斑/比托斑　Bitot spot
比吸收/特殊吸收　specific absorption
比旋光度/比旋[光度]　specific optical rotation
比耶鲁姆暗点/比耶魯姆暗點　Bjerrum scotoma
比重/比重　specific gravity
比重测定法/比重瓶測量法　pyknometry
比重秤/比重天平　specific gravity balance
比重瓶法/比重瓶法　pycnometric method
比佐泽罗红细胞/Bizzozero 氏紅血球　Bizzozero red cell
芘类/芘類　pyrenes
吡贝地尔/吡貝地爾　piribedil
吡啶/吡啶　pyridine
3,4-吡啶二[羧]酸/吡啶二元酸　cinchomeronic acid
吡啶类/吡啶類　pyridines
吡啶硫胺/吡塞胺　pyrithiamine
吡啶生物碱/吡啶生物鹼　pyridine alkaloid
吡啶羧酸类/吡啶羧酸類　picolinic acids
吡啶酮类/吡啶酮類　pyridones
吡多辛/吡哆醇，抗皮炎素，維生素 B6　pyridoxine
吡哆胺/吡哆胺　pyridoxamine
吡哆胺磷酸氧化酶/吡哆胺磷酸氧化酶　pyridoxamine phosphate oxidase
吡哆醛/吡哆醛　pyridoxal
吡哆醛激酶/吡哆醛激酶　pyridoxal kinase
吡哆酸/吡哆酸　pyridoxic acid
吡咯/吡咯[圜]　pyrrole
吡咯布他明/吡咯布他明　pyrrobutamine
吡咯汗疱疹/吡咯汗皰疹　pyrrolopompholyx
吡咯类/吡咯類　pyrroles
吡咯啉羧酸还原酶类/吡咯啉羧酸還原酶類　pyrroline carboxylate reductases
吡咯米酸/吡咯米酸　piromidic acid
吡咯尼群/吡咯尼林　pyrrolnitrin
吡咯齐定生物碱类/吡咯齊定生物鹼類　pyrrolizidine alkaloids
吡咯烷类/吡咯烷類　pyrrolidines
吡咯烷生物碱/吡咯生物鹼　pyrrolidine alkaloid
吡咯烷酮/吡咯烷酮　pyrrolidone
吡咯烷酮类/吡咯烷酮類　pyrrolidinones
吡咯烷酮羧酸/吡咯烷酮羧酸　pyrrolidone carboxylic acid
吡咯细胞/吡咯細胞　pyrrol cell
吡呱酸/吡呱酸　pipemidic acid
吡卡酯/吡啶醇氨甲酸酯　Pyridinolcarbamate
吡喹酮/吡喹酮　praziquantel
吡拉明/吡拉明　pyrilamine
吡拉西坦/吡拉西坦　piracetam
吡拉辛/吡拉辛　pyracin
吡硫醇/吡硫醇　pyrithioxine
吡硫锌/匹塞翁鋅　zinc pyrithione
吡罗昔康/吡羅昔康　piroxicam
吡那地尔/吡那地爾　pinacidil
吡喃/吡喃[圜]　pyran
吡喃共聚物/吡喃共聚物　pyran copolymer
吡喃类/吡喃類　pyrans
吡喃葡[萄]糖/吡喃葡[萄]糖，吡喃糖　glucopyranose
吡喃糖/吡喃糖　pyranose
吡喃酮/吡喃酮，二氧化烯陸圜　pyrone
吡喃香豆素类/吡喃香豆素類　pyranocoumarins
吡喃[型]半乳糖/吡喃糖型半乳糖　galactopyranose
吡嗪/吡嗪　pyrazine
吡嗪酰胺/吡嗪醯胺　pyrazinamide
吡维铵化合物/吡維銨化合物　pyrvinium compound
吡唑类/吡唑類　pyrazoles
吡唑啉酮类/吡唑啉酮類　pyrazolones
笔毛动脉/筆毛動脈　penicillar artery
必备药物/必備藥物　essential drug
必需氨基酸/必需胺基酸　essential amino acid
必需氨基酸类/必需胺基酸類　essential amino acids
必需氨基酸疗法/必需胺基酸療法　essential aminoacid therapy
必需微量元素/必需微量元素　essential trace element

必需脂肪酸/必需脂肪酸　essential fatty acid
必需脂肪酸类/必需脂肪酸類　essential fatty acids
必要基因/必要基因　essential genes
毕赤酵母/畢赤酵母　pichia
毕业护士/受訓護理人員　trained nurse
闭合/閉合　closure
闭合复位术/閉合復位術，不切開回復術　closed reduction
闭合皮瓣/閉合皮瓣　closed skin flap
闭合容积/閉合容積　closing volume
闭合容量/閉合容量　closing capacity
闭合伤/閉合傷　closed injury
闭合性骨折/封閉性骨折　closed fracture
闭合性颅骨骨折/閉合性顱骨骨折　closed fracture of skull
闭合性颅脑[损伤]综合征/閉合性顱腦損傷症候群　closed head syndrome
闭合性气胸/閉合氣胸　closed pneumothorax
闭合性头部损伤/閉合性頭部損傷　closed head injury
闭合循环麻醉/閉合循環麻醉　closed-circuit anesthesia
闭角型青光眼/閉角型青光眼　angle-closure glaucoma
闭经/閉經，停經，月經異常停止　amenorrhea
闭经·肝肾两虚证/閉經·肝腎兩虛證　amenorrhea with pattern of deficiency of both liver and kidney
闭经·寒凝血瘀证/閉經·寒凝血瘀證　amenorrhea with pattern of cold congelation and blood stasis
闭经·气血两虚证/閉經·氣血兩虛證　amenorrhea with pattern of deficiency of both qi and blood
闭经·气滞血瘀证/閉經·氣滯血瘀證　amenorrhea with pattern of qi stagnation and blood stasis
闭经·痰湿阻滞证/閉經·痰濕阻滯證　amenorrhea with pattern of stagnation and blockade of phlegm-damp
闭经·阴虚血燥证/閉經·陰虛血燥證　amenorrhea with pattern of yin deficiency and blood dryness
闭孔/閉孔　obturator foramen
闭孔动脉/閉孔動脈　obturator artery
闭孔动脉耻骨支/閉孔動脈恥骨支　pubic branch of obturator artery
闭孔动脉后支/閉孔動脈後支　posterior branch of obturator artery
闭孔动脉前支/閉孔動脈前支　anterior branch of obturator artery
闭孔沟/閉孔溝　obturator groove
闭孔后结节/閉孔後結節　inferior obturator tubercle, posterior obturator tubercle
闭孔肌试验/閉孔肌試驗　obturator test
闭孔嵴/閉孔嵴　obturator crest
闭孔筋膜/閉孔筋膜　obturator fascia
闭孔静脉/閉孔靜脈　obturator vein
闭孔淋巴结/閉孔淋巴結　obturator lymph node
闭孔膜/閉[孔]膜　obturator membrane
闭孔内肌/閉孔內肌　obturator internus, internal obturator muscle
闭孔内肌腱下囊/閉孔內肌腱下囊　subtendinous bursa of obturator internus
闭孔内肌神经/閉孔內肌神經　nerve to internal obturator
闭孔内肌坐骨囊/閉孔內肌坐骨囊　sciatic bursa of obturator internus
闭孔前结节/閉孔前結節　anterior obturator tubercle
闭孔疝/閉孔疝　obturator hernia
闭孔神经/閉孔神經　obturator nerve
[闭孔神经]后支/[閉孔神經]後支　posterior branch of obturator nerve
闭孔神经前支/閉孔神經前支　anterior branch of obturator nerve
闭孔外肌/閉孔外肌　obturator externus, external obturator muscle
闭孔支/閉孔支　obturator branch
闭口印模/閉口印模　close-mouth impression
闭膜管/閉膜管　obturator canal
闭囊壳/閉囊殼　cleistothecium
闭襻性肠梗阻/閉襻性腸梗阻　closed loop intestinal obstruction
闭塞/閉塞，咬合，堵塞　obliteration, occlusion
闭塞部/閉塞部　occlusive part
闭塞性鼻音/閉塞性鼻音　closed rhinolalia
闭塞性动脉内膜炎/閉塞性動脈內膜炎　endarteritis obliterans
闭塞性动脉硬化/閉塞性動脈硬化　arteriosclerosis obliterans
闭塞性干燥性龟头炎/乾性閉塞性陰莖頭炎　balanitis xerotica obliterans
闭塞性肝静脉内膜炎/閉塞性肝靜脈內膜炎　endophlebitis hepatica obliterans
闭塞性静脉炎/閉塞性靜脈炎　obliterating phlebitis
闭塞性细支气管炎/阻塞性細支氣管炎　bronchiolitis obliterans
闭塞性细支气管炎机化性肺炎/阻塞性細支氣管炎機化性肺炎　bronchiolitis obliterans organizing pneumonia
闭塞性心包炎/閉塞性心包炎　obliteration

pericarditis
闭塞性心肌病/閉塞性心肌病 obliterative cardiomyopathy
闭塞性血栓/閉塞性血栓 occluding thrombus
闭塞性血栓性脉管炎/血栓塞性血管炎 thromboangiitis obliterans
闭塞性扎法/阻塞性結扎 occluding ligature
闭式二尖瓣交界分离术/閉式二尖瓣交界分離術 closed mitral commissurotomy
闭式二尖瓣交界扩张器/閉式二尖瓣交界擴張器 dilator for closed mitral commissurotomy
闭式循环装置/閉式循環裝置 closed circuit system
闭式引流灌洗/閉式引流灌洗 closed suction-irrigation
闭式引流[术]/密閉式引流 closed drainage
闭锁的/閉鎖的,無孔的 imperforate
闭锁堤/閉鎖堤 terminal bar
闭锁殆/咬合過深,閉式咬合 closed bite
闭锁黄体/閉鎖黄體 atretic corpus luteum
闭锁[畸形]/閉鎖 atresia
闭锁卵泡/閉鎖卵泡 atresic follicle, atretic follicle
闭锁综合征/閉鎖症候群 locked-in syndrome
闭胸心脏按压/閉胸心臟按壓 close chest cardiac massage
闭眼垂直写字试验/閉眼垂直寫字試驗 blind-folded vertical writing test
庇护/庇護 shelter
荜茇/蓽茇 long pepper
荜澄茄/畢澄茄 cubeb
荜澄茄素/畢澄茄素 cubebin
荜澄茄酸/畢澄茄酸 cubebic acid
荜澄茄中毒/畢澄茄中毒 cubebism
铋/鉍 bismuth
铋餐/鉍餐 bismuth meal
铋沉着症/鉍沈著症 bismuthia
铋毒性龈炎/鉍性齦炎 bismuth gingivitis
铋色素沉着/鉍色素沈著 bismuth-induced pigmentation
铋酸/鉍酸 bismuthic acid
秘鲁香胶/秘魯香膏 balsam of Peru
秘鲁疣/秘魯疣 verruca peruviana
萆薢/萆薢 poison yam
萆薢分清饮/萆薢分清飲 bixie fenqing drink
蓖麻蛋白/蓖麻毒蛋白,蓖麻毒[素] ricin
蓖麻油/蓖麻油 castor oil
蓖麻油酸鲸蜡酯/蓖麻油酸鯨蠟酯 cetyl ricinoleate
蓖麻油酸类/蓖麻油酸類 ricinoleic acids
蓖麻油酸双酚A型环氧树脂酯/蓖麻油酸雙酚A型環氧樹脂酯 bisphenol A type epoxy resin ricinoleate
蓖麻油酸盐/蓖麻油酸鹽 ricinoleate
蓖麻中毒/蓖麻中毒 ricinism
蓖麻子/蓖麻子 castor bean, castor seed
痹病/痺病,關節痛 arthralgia, bi disease
蔽光疗法/遮光療法 scototherapy
壁/壁 wall
壁层/壁層 parietal layer
壁腹膜/腹膜壁層 parietal peritoneum
壁龛/龕 niche
壁内的/壁内的 intramural
壁内动脉瘤/壁内動脈瘤 intramural aneurysm
壁内神经丛/壁内神經叢 intramural plexus
壁内神经节/壁内神經節 intramural ganglion
壁旁神经节/壁旁神經節 paramural ganglion
壁虱/壁蝨 tick
壁虱属/壁蝨屬 Ixodes
壁蜕膜/壁蛻膜,真蛻膜 decidua parietalis
壁外性压迫/壁外性壓迫 extrinsic compression of wall
壁细胞/壁細胞 parietal cell
壁细胞迷走神经切断术/壁細胞迷走神經切斷術 parietal cell vagotomy
壁胸膜/壁層胸膜 parietal pleura
避孕/避孕[法] contraception
避孕剂/避孕劑 contraceptive
避孕器械/避孕器械 contraceptive device
避孕套/避孕套 condoms
避孕行为/避孕行爲 contraception behavior
避孕药/避孕藥 contraceptive, contraceptive agent
避孕药后闭经/避孕藥後閉經 postpill amenorrhea
避孕疫苗/避孕疫苗 contraceptive vaccine
髀关/髀關 biguan, ST31
臂/臂 arm
臂不全畸胎/臂不全畸胎 perobrachius
臂丛/臂[神經]叢 brachial plexus
臂丛干/臂叢幹 trunk of brachial plexus
臂丛根/臂叢根 roots of brachial plexus
臂丛股/臂叢股 divisions of brachial plexus
臂丛后束/臂叢後束 posterior cord of brachial plexus
臂丛麻痹下丛型/Klumpke氏麻痺 Klumpke paralysis
臂丛内侧束/臂叢内側束 medial cord of brachial plexus
臂丛上干/臂叢上幹 superior trunk of brachial plexus

臂丛神经病/臂叢神經病　brachial plexus neuropathies
臂丛[神经]麻痹/臂麻痹　brachial plexus paralysis
臂丛神经牵拉试验/臂叢神經牽拉試驗　Eaten's test
臂丛神经损伤/臂神經叢損傷　brachial plexus injury
臂丛神经炎/臂叢神經炎　brachial plexus neuritis
臂丛束/臂叢束　cords of brachial plexus
臂丛锁骨上部/臂叢鎖骨上部　supraclavicular part of brachial plexus
臂丛锁骨下部/臂叢鎖骨下部　infraclavicular part of brachial plexus
臂丛外侧束/臂叢外側束　lateral cord of brachial plexus
臂丛下干/臂叢下幹　inferior trunk of brachial plexus
臂丛中干/臂叢中幹　middle trunk of brachial plexus
臂丛综合征/臂症候群　brachial syndrome
臂丛阻滞麻醉/Kulenkampff 氏麻醉　Kulenkampff anesthesia
臂的/肱的　brachial
臂过小者/臂小畸形者　microbrachius
臂后骨筋膜鞘/臂後骨筋膜鞘　posterior osseofascial compartment of arm
臂后皮神经/臂後皮神經　posterior brachial cutaneous nerve
臂后区/臂後部　posterior brachial region
臂间倒位/臂間倒位　pericentric inversion
臂筋膜/臂筋膜,肱筋膜　brachial fascia
臂力摆荡/臂運動　brachiation
臂淋巴腺/臂腺　brachial gland
臂麻痹/臂麻痹　brachial palsy
臂臑/臂臑　binao, LI14
臂内侧肌间隔/臂内側肌間隔　medial brachial intermuscular septum
臂内侧肌间韧带/臂内側肌間韌帶　medial intermuscular ligament of arm
臂内侧皮神经/臂内側皮神經　medial brachial cutaneous nerve, medial cutaneous nerve of arm
臂内倒位/臂内倒位　paracentric inversion
臂旁核/臂旁核　parabrachial nucleus
臂旁内侧核/臂旁内側核　medial parabrachial nucleus
臂旁外侧核/臂旁外側核　lateral parabrachial nucleus
臂前骨筋膜鞘/臂前骨筋膜鞘　anterior osseofascial compartment of arm
臂前区/臂前部　anterior brachial region
臂上静脉/臂上靜脈　superior gluteal vein
臂上神经/臂上神經　superior gluteal nerve
臂神经丛/臂神經叢　plexus brachialis
臂神经丛阻滞/臂叢阻滞　brachial plexus block
臂神经痛/臂神經痛　brachial neuralgia
臂损伤/臂損傷　arm injury
臂痛/臂痛　brachialgia, arm pain
臂外侧肌间隔/臂外側肌間隔　lateral brachial intermuscular septum
臂外侧肌间韧带/臂外側肌間韌帶　lateral intermuscular ligament of arm
臂外侧上皮神经/臂外側上皮神經　superior lateral brachial cutaneous nerve
臂外侧下皮神经/臂外側下皮神經　inferior lateral brachial cutaneous nerve
臂弯曲/臂彎曲　brachiocyllosis
臂痈/臂癰　arm abscess
臂痈·火毒炽盛证/臂癰·火毒熾盛證　arm abscess with blazing fire-toxin pattern
臂痈·气血两虚证/臂癰·氣血兩虛證　arm abscess with qi-blood deficiency pattern
臂指数/臂指數　arm index
边缘/邊緣　edge
边缘变性/邊緣變性　rim degeneration
边缘病病毒/邊緣病病毒　border disease virus
边缘层/邊緣層　marginal layer
边缘的/[邊]緣的　marginal
边缘窦/邊緣竇　marginal sinus
边缘封闭区/邊緣封閉區　border seal area
边缘肝素化/邊緣肝素化　marginal heparinization
边缘脊/緣脊　marginal ridge
边缘溃疡/邊緣性潰瘍　marginal ulcer
边缘前置胎盘/邊緣前置胎盤　placenta praevia marginalis
边缘区/[邊]緣帶　marginal zone
边缘韧力/邊緣強度　edge-strength
边缘适应/邊緣適應　marginal adaptation
边缘胎盘/邊前置胎盤　marginal placenta
边缘系/邊緣系統　limbic system
边缘细胞/邊緣細胞　border cell
边缘小体/緣小體　marginal corpuscle
边缘性环形角膜溃疡/邊緣性環形角膜潰瘍　marginal ring ulcer of cornea
边缘性前置胎盘/邊緣性前置胎盤　marginal placenta praevia
边缘性人格障碍/邊緣性人格障礙　borderline personality disorder
边缘性龈炎/齦緣炎　marginal gingivitis
边缘性营养不良/邊緣性營養不足　marginal

dystrophy
边缘修整印模/邊緣塑形　border molding
边缘叶/邊緣葉　limbic lobe
边缘叶脑炎/邊緣葉腦炎　limbic encephalitis
边缘龈/邊緣齦,游離齦　marginal gingiva
边缘运动/邊緣運動　border movement
边缘支/邊緣支　marginal ramus
边缘状态/邊緣狀態　borderline state
砭镰法/砭鐮法　stone-needling method
砭石/砭石　stone needle
萹蓄/萹蓄　common knotgrass herb
编码/編碼　code for, encode
编码区/編碼區　coding region
编织骨/編織骨,網狀骨　woven bone
编织疗法/編織療法　weaving therapy
蝙蝠咬狂犬病/副狂犬病,亞瘋犬病　paralyssa
鞭虫病/鞭蟲病　trichuriasis
鞭击法/拍打療法　fustigation
鞭毛/鞭毛　flagella, flagellum
鞭毛虫/鞭毛蟲　flagellate
鞭毛虫病/鞭毛蟲病　flagellate disease
鞭毛虫类/鞭毛蟲類　flagellata
鞭毛虫[性]痢疾/鞭毛蟲痢疾　flagellate dysentery
鞭毛蛋白/鞭毛蛋白　flagellin
鞭毛凝集素/鞭毛凝素　flagellar agglutinin
鞭毛体/鞭毛體　flagellated body
鞭毛细胞/鞭毛細胞　flagellate cell
鞭毛形成/鞭毛形成　enflagellation
鞭毛亚门感染/鞭毛亞門感染　Mastigophora infection
鞭毛轴丝/鞭毛軸絲　axoneme
扁长头/扁長頭　platystencephalism
扁耳/扁平耳　flat ear
扁股骨/扁股　platymeria
扁瘊/扁瘊,扁平疣　verruca plana
扁瘊·风热毒蕴证/扁瘊·風熱毒蘊證　verruca plana with pattern of wind-heat toxin amassment
扁瘊·气滞血瘀证/扁瘊·氣滯血瘀證　verruca plana with pattern of qi stagnation and blood stasis
扁肌/扁肌　flat muscle
扁胫骨/扁脛骨　platycnemia
扁卷螺/扁卷螺類　planorbid
扁颅/頭顱壓扁法　platycrania
扁颅底/扁後腦,腦後壓扁　platybasia
扁平的/扁平的　planus
扁平骨/扁骨　flat bone
扁平骨盆/扁骨盆　flat pelvis
扁平黄[色]瘤/扁平黄色瘤　xanthoma planum, plane xanthoma
扁平角膜/扁平角膜　flat cornea
扁平髋/扁平髋　coxa plana
扁平狼疮/扁平狼瘡　lupus planus
扁平卵圆管/扁平卵圓管　flat-oval tube
扁平丘疹/扁平丘疹　planus papule
扁平蠕虫感染/扁平蠕蟲感染　flat worm infection
扁平上皮网状细胞/扁平上皮網狀細胞　flattened epithelial reticular cell
扁平湿疣/扁平濕疣　condyloma
扁平手/扁平手　flat hand
扁平双极细胞/扁平雙極細胞　flat bipolar cell
扁平苔藓/扁平苔蘚　lichen planus
扁平微笑曲线/扁平微笑曲線　flat smile curve
扁平细胞/扁平細胞　flat cell
扁平型/扁平型　platypelloid type
扁平眼压计/壓平眼壓計　applanation tonometer
扁平蝇/扁平蠅　flat fly
扁平疣/扁平疣　flat wart
扁平指甲/扁平指甲　platonychia
扁平趾甲/扁平趾甲　platonychia
扁平足/扁平足　pes planus, flat foot
扁平足者/扁平腳者,平蹠腳者　sarapus
扁鹊/扁鵲　Bianque
扁蠕虫/扁蠕蟲　Platyhelminth
扁桃/扁桃　almond
扁桃[仁]油/杏油　almond oil
扁桃酸类/扁桃酸類　mandelic acids
扁桃酸盐/杏仁酸鹽　mandelate
扁桃体/扁桃體,扁桃腺　tonsil
扁桃体白喉/白喉扁桃腺炎　diphtherial tonsillitis
扁桃体半孢子菌病/扁桃腺半芽孢菌病　tonsillohemisporosis
扁桃体病/扁桃腺病　amygdalopathy
扁桃体穿刺/扁桃腺穿刺　tonsil puncture
扁桃体刀/扁桃腺手術刀　amygdalotome
扁桃体的/扁桃體的,扁桃腺的　amygdaline, tonsillar
扁桃体镜检查/扁桃腺檢視法　tonsilloscopy
扁桃体囊/扁桃體囊　tonsillar capsule
扁桃体念珠菌病/扁桃腺串珠菌病　tonsillomoniliasis
扁桃体切除器/扁桃腺切除器　tonsillectome
扁桃体切除术/扁桃腺切除術　tonsillectomy
扁桃体上窝/扁桃體上窝,扁桃腺上窩　supratonsillar fossa
扁桃体神经/扁桃腺神經　tonsillar nerve
扁桃体石/扁桃腺石　amygdalolith
扁桃体窝/扁桃體窝　tonsillar fossa, tonsillar pit

扁桃体腺样增殖体切除术/扁桃腺及腺體切除術 tonsilloadenoidectomy
扁桃体小窝/扁桃體小窩 tonsillar fossula
扁桃体性白血病/扁桃體性白血病 amygdaline leukemia
扁桃体性哮喘/扁桃腺性氣喘 amygdaline asthma
扁桃体压碎术/扁桃腺壓碎術 amygdalothrypsis
扁桃体炎/扁桃腺炎 tonsillitis
扁桃体隐窝/扁桃體隱窩 tonsillar crypt, tonsil crypt
扁桃体隐窝电烙术/扁桃體隱窩電烙法 electrocryptectomy
扁桃体真菌病/扁桃腺黴菌病 tonsillomycosis
扁桃体支/扁桃體支 tonsillar branch
扁桃体肿瘤/扁桃體腫瘤 tonsillar neoplasms
扁桃体周脓肿/扁桃腺周膿腫 peritonsillar abscess
扁桃体周炎/扁桃腺周圍炎 peritonsillitis
扁头/扁頭,矮頭 chemocephalia
扁纤毛虫属/扁纖毛蟲屬 Opalina
苄胺类/苄胺類 benzylamines
苄胺氧化酶/苄胺氧化酶 benzylamine oxidase
苄醇/苯甲醇 benzyl alcohol
苄达明/苄達明 benzydamine
苄二甲胍/苄二甲胍 bethanidine
苄非他明/苄非他明 benzphetamine
苄酚宁化合物/苄酚寧化合物 bephenium compounds
苄氟噻嗪/苯氟噻嗪 bendroflumethiazide
苄环烷/苄環烷 bencyclane
苄基化合物/苄基化合物 benzyl compound
苄基异喹啉类/苄異喹啉類 benzylisoquinolines
苄基异喹啉生物碱/苄基異喹啉生物鹼 benzylisoquinoline alkaloid
苄基紫精/苄基紫精 benzyl viologen
苄氯乙胺/二苯氯乙胺 dibenzylchlorethamine
苄脒类/苄脒類 benzamidines
苄普地尔/苄普地爾 bepridil
苄丝肼/苄絲肼 benserazide
苄索氯铵/苄索氯銨 benzethonium chlorid
苄烯化合物/苄烯化合物 benzylidene compound
苄星青霉素 G/苄星青黴素 G,比西林 Benzathine Penicillin G
变白/變白 blanch
变动性呼吸/變動性呼吸 metamorphosing respiration
变化性/變異性 variability
变力状态/變力狀態 inotropic state
变量/變數 variable

变量校正/變數校正 variate calibration
变色/變色 discoloration
变色性皮癣/色癬菌病 chromophytosis
变色牙/變色牙 discolored tooth
变时现象/變時現象,變速性 chronotropism
变兽妄想/變狼妄想 lycanthropy
变数串联重复/變數串聯重複 variable number of tandem repeat
变态/變態 metamorphosis
变态的/變態的 metamorphic
变态反应/變態反應,過敏反應 allergy
变[态反]应病/過敏性病 allergosis
变[态反]应性的/過敏性 allergic
变[态反]应性脉管炎/過敏性脈管炎 allergic angiitis
变[态反]应性血管炎/過敏性血管炎 allergic vasculitis
变态反应学/過敏病學 allergology
变态反应学家/過敏病學家 allergologist
变态心理学/變態心理學 abnormal psychology
变位酶/變酵素,催化酵素 mutase
变温动物/變溫動物 heterotherm
变形/變形,變態,歪扭 deformations, metamorphosis, distortion
变形阿米巴/變形阿米巴,變形變形蟲 amoeba proteus
变形变[态反]应性/變型變應性 metallergy
变形虫样运动/變形蟲樣運動 ameboid motion
变形杆菌感染/變形桿菌感染 proteus infection
变形杆菌群/變形桿菌群 proteus group
变形杆菌属/變形桿菌屬 Proteus
变形菌族/變形菌族 Proteeae
变形细胞/變形細胞 ameboid cell
变形性骨炎/變形性骨炎 osteitis deformans
变形性骨炎样的/Paget 氏病樣的 pagetoid
变形性骨炎样网状细胞增多症/Woringer-Kolopp 氏病 Woringer-Kolopp disease
变形性关节炎/變形性關節炎 arthritis deformans
变形性肌张力障碍/變形性肌緊張不足 dystonia musculorum deformans
变形性脊柱炎/畸形性脊椎炎 poker back
变形序列征/變形序列徵 deformation sequence
变形再生/重組性再生 morphallactic regeneration
变形综合征/Proteus 症候群 Proteus syndrome
变性/變性,變質 denaturation, degeneration
变性醇/變性醇,變性酒精 denatured alcohol
变性蛋白/變性蛋白質 denatured protein
变性[蛋白]胨/變性蛋白腖 metapeptone

变性反应/變性反應　reaction of degeneration
变性高铁血红蛋白/變性高鐵血紅素　cathemoglobin
变性剂/變性劑　denaturant
变性胶原性斑块/變性膠原性板塊　degenerative collagenous plaque
变性结核菌素/改良型結核菌素　tuberculinose
变性明胶/變性明膠　metagelatin
变性囊肿/變性囊腫　degeneration cyst
变性弹力蛋白/變性彈力蛋白,變性彈性組織　elacin
变性型涎腺肿大[症]/變性型涎腺腫大[症]　degenerative sialosis
变性血管翳/變性血管翳　degenerative pannus
变性[作用]/變質,變性　denaturation
变旋[现象]/變旋　mutarotation
变压呼吸器/變壓呼吸器,壓力呼吸器　barospirator
变移上皮/變移上皮　transitional epithelium
变异/變異　variation
变异减速/變異減速　variable deceleration
变异菌株/細菌之變異型　dissociant
变异体/變異體,變種　variant
变异型心绞痛/變異型心絞痛　variant angina pectoris
变异性红斑角化病/變異性紅斑角皮症　erythrokeratoderma variabilis
变异性图案状红斑角皮症/變異性圖案狀紅斑角皮症　erythrokeratodermia figurata variabilis
变应性白细胞破碎性血管炎/過敏性白血球破碎性血管炎　allergic leukocytoclastic vasculitis
变应性鼻窦炎/過敏性鼻竇炎　allergic sinusitis
变应性鼻炎/過敏性鼻炎　allergic rhinitis
变应性反应/過敏性反應,變應性反應　allergic reaction
变应性间质性肾炎/過敏性間質性腎炎　allergic interstitial nephritis
变应性睑缘炎/過敏性瞼緣炎　allergic blepharitis
变应性接触性唇炎/過敏性接觸性唇炎　allergic contact cheilitis
变应性接触性皮炎/過敏性接觸性皮炎　allergic contact dermatitis
变应性接触性荨麻疹/過敏性接觸性蕁麻疹　allergic contact urticaria
变应性结膜炎/過敏性結膜炎　allergic conjunctivitis
变应性口腔溃疡/過敏性口潰瘡　allergic canker sore
变应性脑炎/過敏性腦炎　allergic encephalitis
变应性膀胱炎/過敏性膀胱炎　allergic cystitis
变应性皮肤血管炎/過敏性皮膚血管炎　allergic cutaneous vasculitis
变应性前列腺病/過敏性前列腺病　allergic prostatosis
变应性肉芽肿病/過敏性肉芽腫病　allergic granulomatosis
变应性肉芽肿性血管炎/過敏性肉芽腫性血管炎　Churg-Strauss syndrome
变应性湿疹/過敏性濕疹　allergic eczema
变应性湿疹性接触性皮炎/過敏性濕疹性接觸性皮膚炎　allergic eczematous contact dermatitis
变应性系统性血管炎/過敏性系統性血管炎　allergic systemic vasculitis
变应性小动脉炎/過敏性小動脈炎　arteriolitis allergica
变应性哮喘/過敏性氣喘　allergic asthma
变应性血管炎/過敏性血管炎　hypersensitivity angiitis
变应性药疹/過敏性藥疹　allergic drug eruption
变应性支气管肺曲霉菌病/過敏性支氣管肺麴黴菌病　allergic bronchopulmonary aspergillosis
变应性直肠炎/過敏性直腸炎　allergic proctitis
变应性紫癜/變應性紫癜病,過敏性紫癜病　allergic purpura
变应原/變應原,過敏原　allergen
变应原浸出物/過敏反應原浸出物　allergenic extract
变应原性/變應原性,過敏原性　allergenicity
变应原性接触性唇炎/過敏原性接觸性唇炎　allergenic contact cheilitis
变应原性物质/致敏性物質　allergenic substance
变应疹/變應疹　allergid
变蒸/變蒸　steaming changes in infant, changing steaming in infant, growing fever and perspiration
变证/變證　deteriorated case
变质疗法/變質療法　allassotherapy
变质特征/變質特徵　stigma of degeneracy
便秘/便秘　constipation
便秘[病]/便秘[病]　constipation
便秘绞痛/積糞絞痛　stercoral colic
便秘恐怖/恐糞積症　coprostasophobia
便秘·气虚证/便秘·氣虛證　constipation with qi deficiency pattern
便秘·血虚证/便秘·血虛證　constipation with blood deficiency pattern
便秘·阳虚证/便秘·陽虛證　constipation with yang deficiency pattern
便秘药/便秘藥　emplastic
便秘·阴虚证/便秘·陰虛證　constipation with yin deficiency pattern
便脓血/便膿血　passing stool with pus and blood

便士重量/便士重量 pennyweight
便溏/稀糞 loose stool
便携式电话/可攜式電話 cellular phone
便携式监测/可攜式監測 ambulatory monitoring
便携式心电描记术/可攜式心電描記術 ambulatory electrocardiography
便携式血压监测/可攜式血壓監測 ambulatory blood pressure monitoring
便血/便血 hematochezia, hemafecia
便血·肠风伤络证/便血·腸風傷絡證 hematochezia with pattern of intestinal wind injuring collaterals
便血·脾胃虚寒证/便血·脾胃虛寒證 hematochezia with pattern of deficiency-cold of spleen and stomach
便血·气不摄血证/便血·氣不攝血證 hematochezia with pattern of failure of qi to keep blood
便血·胃肠积热证/便血·胃腸積熱證 hematochezia with pattern of accumulated heat in stomach and intestine
便血·胃肠湿热证/便血·胃腸濕熱證 hematochezia with pattern of damp-heat in stomach and intestine
辨别学习/辨別學習 discrimination learning
辨别阈/辨別閾 differential threshold
辨别阈差试验/辨別閾差試驗 difference limen difference test
辨别阈试验/辨別閾試驗 difference limen test
辨病论治/辨病論治 treatment based on disease differentiation
辨出血/辨出血 differentiating bleeding
辨带色/辨帶色 distinguishing color of vaginal discharge
辨结节/辨結節 differentiating nodule
辨经质/辨經質 observing menstrual property
辨距障碍/辨距不良 dysmetria
辨溃疡/辨潰瘍 differentiating ulcer
辨麻木/辨麻木 differentiating numbness
辨梦/辨夢 dream interpretation
辨脓/辨膿 differentiating pus
辨痛/辨痛 differentiating pain
辨血量/辨血量 observing menstrual volume
辨血色/辨血色 observing menstrual color
辨痒/辨癢 differentiating itching
辨语聋/聽語聾,精神[性]聾 word deafness
辨证/辨證 pattern identification, syndrome differentiation
辨证论治/辨證論治 treatment based on pattern identification
辨证取穴/辨證取穴 point selection based on pattern identification
辨肿块/辨腫塊 differentiating lump
辨肿块大小/辨腫塊大小 differentiating size of lump
辨肿块活动度/辨腫塊活動度 differentiating movablity of lump
辨肿块界限/辨腫塊界限 differentiating sideline of lump
辨肿块内容物/辨腫塊內容物 differentiating content of lump
辨肿块疼痛/辨腫塊疼痛 differentiating pain of lump
辨肿块位置/辨腫塊位置 differentiating location of lump
辨肿块形态/辨腫塊形態 differentiating shape of lump
辨肿块质地/辨腫塊質地 differentiating texture of lump
标本/標本 specimen, manifestation and root cause
标本兼治/標本兼治 treating both manifestation and root cause of disease
标本制备/標本製備 specimen handling
标本中气/標本中氣 manifestation, root cause and medial qi
标称质量/標稱質量 nominal mass
标记/標記 marker
标记化合物/標記化合物 labeled compound
标记基因/標記基因,標識基因 marker gene
标记抗生物素蛋白-生物素法/標記抗生物素蛋白-生物素法 labeled avidin-biotin method, LAB method
标记染色体/標記染色體 marker chromosome
标记疫苗/標記疫苗 marker vaccine
标准比色液/標準比色液 standard color solution
标准操作规程/標準作業程序 standard operating procedure, SOP
标准对数视力表/標準對數視力表 standard logarithmic visual acuity chart
标准化/標準化 standardization
标准化疗方案/標準化療方案 standard chemotherapy regimen
标准还原溶液/標準還原溶液 normal reducing solution
标准碱过剩/標準鹼過剩 standard base excess
标准近视力表/標準近視力表 standard near vision chart
标准抗毒素/標準抗毒素 normal antitoxin
标准[离]差/標準差 standard deviation
标准培养[物]/標準培養[物] type culture

标准品/標準物質　standard substance
标准曲线/標準曲線　standard curve
标准容积/標準容積　standard volume
标准溶液/標準溶液　standard solution
标准膳食/標準飲食　standard diet
标准视力表/標準視力表　standard visual acuity chart
标准碳酸氢盐/標準重碳酸鹽　standard bicarbonate
标准误[差]/標準誤[差]　standard error
标准氧化溶液/標準氧化溶液　normal oxidizing solution
表玻璃/表[面]玻璃　watch glass
表层坏死/表層性壞死　superficial necrosis
表次黄嘌呤/表次黄嘌呤　episarkin
表达/表現　expression
表达载体/表現[型]載體　expression vector
表睾酮/表睾酮　epitestosterone
表观分布容积/擬似分布體積　apparent volume of distribution
表观黏度/表觀黏度　apparent viscosity
表观盐皮质激素过多综合征/表觀鹽皮質激素過多症候群　apparent mineralocorticoid excess syndrome
表寒/表寒　exterior cold
表寒里热/表寒裡熱　exterior cold with interior heat
表寒里热证/表寒裡熱證　pattern of exterior cold and interior heat
表里辨证/表裡辨證　pattern differentiation of exterior and interior
表里分消/表裡分消　eliminating pathogens by diaphoresis and purgation respectively
表里俱寒证/表裡俱寒證　pattern of cold in both exterior and interior
表里俱热证/表裡俱熱證　pattern of heat in both exterior and interior
表里配穴法/表裡配穴法　exterior-interior points association, exterior-interior points combination
表里双解/表裡雙解　expelling pathogens from both interior and exterior
表里双解剂/表裡雙解劑　formula for relieving both exterior and interior disorders
表里同病/表裡同病　simultaneous exterior and interior patterns
表氯醇/表氯醇　epichlorohydrin
表美雌醇/表美雌醇　epimestrol
表面/表面　surface
表面标记/表面標記　markings surface
表面等离子体共振/表面等離子體共振　surface plasmon resonance
表面辐照/表面照射　surface irradiation
表面活性/表面活性　surface activity
表面活性剂/表面活性劑　surfactant, surface-active agent
表面解剖学/表面解剖學　surface anatomy
表面抗原/表面抗原　surface antigen
表[面卵]裂/表面分裂　superficial cleavage
表面麻醉/表面麻醉　superficial anesthesia
表面免疫球蛋白/表面免疫球蛋白　surface immunoglobulin
表面能/表面能　surface energy
表面上皮/表面上皮　superficial epithelium
表面特性/表面特性　surface property
表面特征/表面特徵　surface character
表面吞噬作用/表面吞噬作用　surface phagocytosis
表面无痛法/表面止痛法，滲透止痛法　permeation analgesia
表面癣菌属/表皮癬菌屬　*Epidermophyton*
表面移植物/表面移植物　surface graft
表面张力/表面張力　surface tension, tension surface
表皮/表皮，外皮　epidermis, cuticle
表皮包涵囊肿/表皮包涵囊腫　epidermal inclusion cyst
表皮剥脱/表皮剥脱　excoriation
表皮层/外皮層　cuticular layer
表皮成形术/表皮成形術，補皮術　epidermatoplasty
表皮的/表皮的　epidermal
表皮多囊病/表皮多囊病　epidermal polycystic disease
表皮发育不良/表皮發育障礙　epidermodysplasia
表皮分离层/表皮之分離層　stratum disjunction
表皮附件/表皮附屬器　epidermal appendage
表皮更新时间/表皮更新時間　epidermal turnover time
表皮黑[色]素单位/表皮黑[色]素單位　epidermal melanin unit
表皮化/表皮化　epidermidalization
表皮坏死溶解/表皮壞死鬆解　epidermal necrolysis
表皮嵴/表皮嵴　epidermal ridge
表皮角质层/表皮角質層　horny layer of epidermis
表皮瘤/表皮瘤　epidermoid tumor
表皮霉菌病/表皮黴菌病　epidermomycosis
表皮囊肿/表皮囊腫　epidermal cyst
表皮内的/表皮內的　intraepidermal
表皮内上皮瘤/表皮內上皮瘤　intra-epidermal epithelioma
表皮内嗜中性 IgA 皮肤病/表皮内嗜中性球甲型球

蛋白皮膚病　intraepidermal neutrophilic IgA dermatosis
表皮葡萄球菌/表皮葡萄球菌　staphylococcus epidermidis
表皮生成/表皮生成　epidermopoiesis
表皮生长因子/表皮成長因子　epidermal growth factor
表皮生长因子受体/表皮生長因子受體　epidermal growth factor receptor
表皮松解的/表皮鬆解的　epidermolytic
表皮松解毒素/表皮鬆解毒素　epidermolytic toxins
表皮松解角化过度症/脱皮性角化過度　epidermolytic hyperkeratosis
表皮松解性棘皮瘤/表皮鬆解性棘皮瘤　epidermolytic acanthoma
表皮松解性角化过度型鱼鳞病/表皮鬆解性角化過度型魚鱗病　epidermolytic hyperkeratotic ichthyosis
表皮松解[症]/表皮鬆解　epidermolysis
表皮脱落的/表皮剥傷的　excoriated
表皮脱落性的/剝落的　exfoliative
表皮萎缩/表皮萎縮　epidermal atrophy
表皮细胞更新速率/表皮細胞更新速率　epidermal cell turnover rate
表皮细胞坏死/表皮細胞壞死　epidermal cell necrosis
表皮再植/表皮再植　reepithelialization
表皮下的/表皮下的　subepidermal
表皮下基底带/表皮下基底帶　subepidermal basement zone
表皮下结节性纤维化/表皮下結節性纖維化　subdermal nodular fibrosis
表皮癣[菌病]/皮癣　epidermophytosis
表皮癣菌素/表皮癣菌素　epidermophytin
表皮癣菌疹/表皮癣菌疹　epidermophytid
表皮芽/表皮芽　epidermal bud
表皮炎/表皮炎　epidermitis
表皮样癌/表皮樣癌　epidermoid cancer, epidermoid carcinoma
表皮样的/表皮樣的　epidermoid
表皮样囊肿/表皮樣囊腫　epidermoid cyst
表皮样组织细胞瘤/表皮樣組織細胞瘤　epithelioid histiocytoma
表皮移植片/表皮移植物　epidermic graft
表皮真皮[交]界/表皮真皮交界　epidermal-dermal junction
表皮痣/表皮痣　epidermal nevus
表皮痣综合征/表皮母斑症候群　epidermal nevus syndrome
表浅的/淺[層]的　superficial
表浅狼疮/表淺狼瘡　lupus superficialis
表浅性扁桃体炎/扁桃腺淺層炎　superficial tonsillitis
表浅性毛囊炎/表淺性毛囊炎　superficial folliculitis
表浅脂肪瘤样痣/表淺性脂肪瘤母斑　nevus lipomatous superficialis
表情倒错/表情錯亂,擬態不倫　paramimia
表情肌/表情肌　mimetic muscle
表情肌痉挛/演戲狀痙攣　histrionic spasm
表情线/表情線　expression lines
表情性麻痹/表情肌麻痺　histrionic paralysis
表情样痉挛/表情肌痙攣　mimic spasm
表情障碍/表情障礙,擬態不能　dysmimia
表热/表熱　exterior heat
表热里寒/表熱裡寒　exterior heat with interior cold
表热里寒证/表熱裡寒證　pattern of exterior heat and interior cold
表柔比星/表柔比星　epirubicin
表实/表實　exterior excess
表实证/表實證　exterior excess pattern
表位/表位　epitope
表位作图/表位作圖　epitope mapping
表现变异性/表現變異性　variable expressivity
表现度/表現度　expressivity
表现焦虑量表/表現焦慮量表　manifest anxiety scale
表小皮/薄表皮　epidermicula
表邪入里/表邪入裡　exterior pathogens involving interior
表型/表型　phenotype
表型定位[法]/表型定位[法]　phenotype mapping
表型模拟/表型模擬者,模擬特性　phenocopy
表型组/表型群　phenome
表虚/表虚　exterior deficiency
表虚证/表虚證　exterior deficiency pattern
表演状抽搐/作態狀抽搐　gesticulatory tic
表异孕烷醇酮/孕尿男性素　epiallopregnanolone
表证/表證　exterior pattern
鳖甲/鱉甲　turtle carapace
鳖甲煎丸/鱉甲煎丸　biejiajian pills
别构部位/異型位點　allosteric site
别构调节/別構調節　allosteric regulation
别构效应/異構效應　allosteric effect
别赫捷列夫征/別赫捷列夫徵　Bechterew sign
别络/別絡　connecting collaterals
别嘌呤醇/別嘌呤醇　allopurinol

别孕二醇/異黃體脂醇　allopregnandiol
别孕烯醇酮/異妊娠烯醇酮　allopregnenolone
别孕[甾]烷/異妊娠素　allopregnane
宾氏试验/賓氏試驗　Bing test
宾斯旺格病/賓斯旺格病　Binswanger disease
濒死/瀕死　articulo mortis
濒死肠套叠/死後套叠　postmortem intussusception
濒死的/瀕死的　agonal
濒死期白细胞增多/瀕死期白血球增多, 終期白血球增多　agonal leukocytosis, terminal leukocytosis
濒死期感染/瀕死期感染　agonal infection
濒死期血栓/瀕死期血栓　agony thrombus
濒死期血栓形成/瀕死栓塞　agonal thrombosis
濒死前的/瀕死前的　preagonal
濒死心律/瀕死心律　agony rhythm
濒死性腹水/瀕死性腹水　preagonal ascites
殡仪业者/殯殮業者, 收殮業者　mortician
殡葬事宜/殯葬事宜　mortuary practice
殡葬仪式/殯葬儀式　funeral rite
髌底/髕底　base of patella
髌反射计/膝蓋反射計　patellometer
髌股疼痛综合征/髕股疼痛症候群　patellofemoral pain syndrome
髌骨/髕骨, 膝蓋骨　patella
髌[骨]的/髕骨的, 膝蓋骨的　patellar
髌骨骨折/髕骨[骨]折　patellar fracture
髌[骨]固定术/髕骨固定術　patellapexy
髌骨关节面/髕骨關節面　articular surface of patella
髌骨摩擦试验/髕骨摩擦試驗　patellar rubbing test
髌骨前面/髕骨前面　anterior surface of patella
髌骨切除术/髕骨切除術　patellectomy
髌骨软骨软化症/髕骨軟骨軟化症　chondromalacia patellae
髌骨软骨软化症・风寒湿阻证/髕骨軟骨軟化症・風寒濕阻證　chondromalacia patella with wind-cold-dampness obstruction pattern
髌骨软骨软化症・肝肾亏虚证/髕骨軟骨軟化症・肝腎虧虛證　chondromalacia patella with liver-kidney deficiency pattern
髌骨软化症/髕骨軟化症　patellar chondromalacia
髌骨脱位/髕骨脫位　patellar dislocation
髌骨下脂肪垫/髕骨下脂肪墊　infrapatellar fat pad
髌骨中点/髕骨中點　patella center
髌滑膜襞/髕滑膜襞　patellar synovial fold
髌尖/髕尖　apex of patella
髌腱断裂/髕腱斷裂　rupture of patellar tendon
髌面/髕面　patellar surface
髌内侧滑膜襞/髕內側滑膜襞　medial patellar synovial fold
髌内侧支持带/髕內側支持帶　medial patellar retinaculum
髌前滑膜炎/髕前黏液囊炎　prepatellar bursitis
髌前滑囊/髕骨前囊　prepatellar bursa
髌前滑囊炎/髕前滑囊炎　prepatellar bursitis
髌前腱下囊/髕前腱下囊　subtendinous prepatellar bursa
髌前筋膜下囊/髕前筋膜下囊　subfascial prepatellar bursa
髌前囊炎/髕前水瘤　hygroma prepatellare
髌前皮下囊/髕前皮下囊　subcutaneous prepatellar bursa
髌韧带/髕韌帶　patellar ligament
髌上滑膜襞/髕上滑膜襞　suprapatellar synovial fold
髌上囊/髕[骨]上囊　suprapatellar bursa
髌外侧支持带/髕外側支持帶　lateral patellar retinaculum
髌网/髕網　patellar rete
髌下滑膜襞/髕下滑膜襞　infrapatellar synovial fold
髌下囊/髕下囊　infrapatellar bursa
髌下皮下囊/髕下皮下囊　subcutaneous infrapatellar bursa
髌下深囊/髕下深囊　deep infrapatellar bursa
髌下支/髕下支　infrapatellar branch
髌下脂肪垫损伤/髕下脂肪墊損傷　infrapatellar fat-pad injury, injury of infrapatellar fat pad
髌下脂体/髕下脂體　infrapatellar fat pad
髌阵挛/膝陣攣　patellar clonus
鬓疽/鬢疽　carbuncle of temple
冰床罩/冰支架　ice cradle
冰岛格陵兰地方性热病/冰島及丹麥之地方性熱病　Kriim fever
冰点测定器/測冰點器　cryoscope
冰点降低/凝固點降低　freezing point depression
冰冻的/冰凍的　frozen
冰冻麻醉/冰凍麻醉　ice anesthesia
冰冻盆腔/冰凍樣骨盆　frozen pelvis
冰冻切片/冰凍切片　frozen section
冰冻蚀刻/冷凍蝕刻　freeze-etching
冰晶石/冰晶石　cryolite
冰内生物/冰內生物　pagon
冰硼散/冰硼散　bingpeng powder
冰片/冰片, 樟腦醇　borneol, camphyl alcohol
冰片烷类/冰片烷類　bornanes
冰水疗法/冰水療法　ice water treatment
冰瑕翳/冰瑕翳　ice nebula
冰[样]的/冰狀的　glacial

槟榔/檳榔　areca seed
槟榔癌/檳榔癌　betel cancer
槟榔碱/檳榔素　arecoline
丙氨酸/丙胺酸　alanine
丙氨酸氨基转移酶/丙胺酸轉胺酶　alanine aminotransferase, alanine transaminase
丙氨酸 tRNA 连接酶/丙胺酸 tRNA 連接酶　alanine-tRNA ligase
丙氨酸外消旋酶/丙胺酸外消旋酶　alanine racemase
丙氨酸转氨酶/丙胺酸轉胺酶　alanine aminotransferase, alanine transaminase
丙氨酰亮氨酸/丙胺醯亮胺酸　alanyl-leucine
丙胺卡因/丙胺卡因　prilocaine
丙胺类/丙胺類　propylamines
丙胺太林/丙胺太林　propantheline
丙吡胺/丙吡胺　disopyramide
丙醇胺类/丙醇胺類　propanol amines
丙醇类/丙醇類　propanols
丙碘酮/丙碘酮　propyliodone
丙二醇/丙二醇　propylene glycol
丙二醇脱水酶/丙二醇脫水酶　propanediol dehydratase
丙二硫化硫胺素/丙二硫化硫胺素　thiamin propyldisulfide
丙二醛/丙二醛　malondialdehyde
丙二酸/丙二酸　malonic acid
丙二酸盐类/丙二酸鹽類　malonates
丙二酰辅酶 A/丙二醯輔酶 A　malonyl coenzyme A
丙二酰[基]/丙二醯基　malonyl
丙谷胺/丙穀胺　proglumide
丙环啶/丙環啶　procyclidine
丙磺舒/丙磺舒　probenecid
丙基/丙[烷]基　propyl
丙卡巴肼/丙卡巴肼　procarbazine
丙卡特罗/丙卡特羅　procaterol
丙硫氧嘧啶/丙烷基硫尿嘧啶　propylthiouracil
丙硫异烟胺/丙硫異煙胺　prothionamide
丙氯拉嗪/丙氯拉嗪　prochlorperazine
丙米嗪/托法尼, 鹽酸丙咪嗪, 伊米帕明　tofranil, imipramine
丙内酯/乙丙酸內酯　propiolactone
丙泮尼地/丙泮尼地　propanidid
丙泊酚/異丙酚　propofol
丙嗪/丙嗪　promazine
丙炔酸/丙炔酸, 炔丙酸　propiolic acid
丙酸/丙酸　propionic acid
丙酸苯酯类/丙酸苯酯類　phenyl propionates
丙酸放线菌/丙酸放線菌　Actinomyces propionicus
丙酸杆菌属/丙酸桿菌　*Propionibacterium*
丙酸睾酮/初油酸睾脂酮, 丙酸睾丸脂酮　testosterone propionate
丙酸类/丙酸類　propionic acids
丙酸氯倍他索/丙酸倍氯鬆　clobetasol propionate
丙酸血/丙酸血　propionicacidemia
丙酸盐类/丙酸鹽類　propionates
丙酸酯/丙酸酯　propionate
丙酸蛛网菌/丙酸蛛菌　Arachnia propionica
丙糖/丙糖, 三碳糖　triose
丙糖磷酸异构酶/丙糖磷酸異構酶　triose-phosphate isomerase
丙酮/丙酮　acetone
丙酮不溶性抗原/不溶於丙酮的抗原　acetone-insoluble antigen
丙酮二酸/二羥基丙二酸　mesoxalic acid
丙酮化合物/丙酮化合物　acetonide
丙酮化合[作用]/丙酮化　acetonation
丙酮尿/丙酮尿　acetonuria
丙酮醛/丙酮醛　pyruvaldehyde
丙酮酸/丙酮酸　pyruvic acid
丙酮酸激酶/丙酮酸激酶　pyruvate kinase
丙酮酸激酶缺乏症/丙酮酸激酶缺乏　pyruvate kinase deficiency
丙酮酸羧化酶/丙酮酸鹽羧基酶　pyruvate carboxylase
丙酮酸羧化酶缺乏症/丙酮酸羧化酶缺乏症　pyruvate carboxylase deficiency disease
丙酮酸脱氢酶/丙酮酸脫氫酶　pyruvic dehydrogenase
丙酮酸脱氢酶复合物/丙酮酸脫氫酶複合物　pyruvate dehydrogenase complex
丙酮酸脱氢酶复合物缺乏症/丙酮酸脫氫酶複合物缺乏症　pyruvate dehydrogenase complex deficiency disease
丙酮酸脱羧酶/丙酮酸鹽脫羧基酶　pyruvate decarboxylase
丙酮酸血[症]/丙酮酸血症　pyruvemia
丙酮酸盐/丙酮酸鹽　pyruvate
丙酮酸氧化酶/丙酮酸氧化酶　pyruvate oxidase
丙酮糖尿/丙酮醣尿症　acetonglycosuria
丙酮血[症]/丙酮血症　acetonemia
丙烷/丙烷　propane
丙戊酸/丙戊酸　valproic acid
丙戊酸钠/丙戊酸鈉　sodium valproate
丙烯/丙烯　propene
丙烯除虫菊酯/愛利斯林　allethrin
丙烯基/丙烯基　propenyl

丙烯晶状体/丙烯透鏡　acrylic lens
丙烯腈/丙烯腈　acrylonitrile
丙烯腈共聚物/丙烯腈共聚物　acrylonitrile copolymer
丙烯吗啡/阿羅啡　allorphine
丙烯醛/丙烯醛　acrolein
丙烯酸/丙烯酸　acrylic acid
丙烯酸单体/丙烯酸的單體　acrylic monomer
丙烯酸单体引发皮炎/丙烯酸的單體應的皮膚炎　acrylic monomer-induced dermatitis
丙烯酸的/丙烯酸的　acrylic
丙烯酸丁酯/丙烯酸丁酯　butyl acrylate
丙烯酸聚合物/丙烯酸鹽聚合物　acrylate polymer
丙烯酸树脂类/丙烯酸樹脂類　acrylic resins
丙烯酸树脂铝粉/丙烯酸樹脂鋁粉　acrylic resin coated aluminium powder
丙烯酸树脂盘/丙烯酸樹脂盤　acrylic resin tray
丙烯酸树脂贴面/丙烯酸樹脂貼面　acrylic resin veneer
丙烯酸塑料/丙烯酸塑膠　acrylic plastics
丙烯酸烷酯/丙烯酸烷酯　alkyl acrylate
丙烯酸烷酯共聚物/丙烯酸烷酯共聚物　alkyl acrylate copolymer
丙烯酸盐/丙烯酸鹽　acrylate
丙烯酸盐类/丙烯酸鹽類　acrylates
丙烯酸酯基托/丙烯酸樹脂鹽基質　acrylic resin base
丙烯酸酯夹板/丙烯酸脂夾　acrylic splint
丙烯酸酯甲冠/丙烯酸酯甲冠　acrylic jacket crown
丙烯酸[酯]类聚合物/丙烯酸聚合物　acrylic polymer
丙烯酸酯磨钻/丙烯酸酯磨鑽　plastic bur
丙烯酸酯填塞/丙烯酸酯填塞　acrylic resin packing
丙烯酸酯牙/丙烯酸酯牙　acrylic tooth
丙烯酰胺/丙烯醯胺　acrylamide
丙型病毒性肝炎/丙型病毒性肝炎　viral hepatitis type C
丙型肝炎/丙型肝炎　hepatitis C
丙型肝炎抗体/丙型肝炎抗體　hepatitis C antibody
丙型肝炎抗原/丙型肝炎抗原　hepatitis C antigen
丙亚胺/丙亞胺　razoxane
丙氧芬/右丙氧芬　propoxyphene
丙氧卡因/丙氧卡因　propoxycaine
丙种/丙型,伽馬　gamma
丙种球蛋白/丙種球蛋白,丙型球蛋白　gamma globulin
丙种球蛋白缺乏血症/血γ球蛋白缺乏　agammaglobulinemia

秉风/秉風　bingfeng, SI12
柄曲菌素/柄麴菌素　sterigmatocystin
柄胸结合/柄胸結合　manubriosternal synchondrosis
柄胸联合/柄胸聯合　manubriosternal symphysis
屏气发作/屏氣發作　breath holding spell
屏气试验/屏氣試驗　breath holding test
禀赋/稟賦　natural endowment
禀赋不足/稟賦不足　insufficiency of natural endowment
禀赋异常/稟賦異常　abnormal natural endowment
并病/并病　disease of one channel involving another channel
并唇[畸形]/并唇畸形　synchilia
并[存]意识/副意識,附意識　coconsciousness
并耳[畸形]/并耳畸形　synotia
并发病/并發性病　complicating disease
并发的/并發的　complicated
并发疟/混合瘧　hybrid malaria
并发脱位/并發脫位,合并脫位　complicated dislocation
并发先兆子痫/并發先兆子癇　superimposed preeclampsia
并发性白内障/并發性白内障　complicated cataract
并发症/并發症　complication
并发子痫/并發子癇　superimposed eclampsia
并甲/并甲　synonychia
并列心脏移植/并列心臟移植　parallelled cardiac transplantation
并列性抑制/共濟壓制,協調抑制　coordinate repression
并四苯类/并四苯類　naphthacenes
并头联胎畸形/并頭連胎畸形　synencephaly
并腿畸胎/并腿畸胎　sympus
并腿[畸形]/并肢畸形　symmelia
并行收缩/異常心臟收縮　parasystole
并行线面测量器/平行儀　parallelometer
并月/并月　bimonthly menstruation
并肢/并肢　synpodia
并殖吸虫病/并殖吸蟲病　paragonimiasis
并指分离术/指蹼分離術　dactylolysis
并指[畸形]/并指[畸形]　zygodactyly, syndactyly
并指畸形伴外胚层发育不良/并指畸形伴外胚層發育不良　syndactyly with ectodermal dysplasia
并指缺指畸形/不全并指畸形　ectrosyndactyly
并指者/并指畸形者　syndactylus
并趾[畸形]/并趾[畸形]　zygodactyly, syndactyly
并趾畸形伴外胚层发育不良/并趾畸形伴外胚層發育不良　syndactyly with ectodermal dysplasia

并趾缺趾畸形/不全并趾畸形　ectrosyndactyly
并趾者/并趾畸形者　syndactylus
病/病　ill
Rust 病/Rust 氏病　Rust disease
病案/病歷記錄　medical record
病案簿/病歷本　casebook
病案附注/病案附注　medical commentary
病案管理员/病案管理員　medical record administrator
病案教学制/個案教學制,病案制　case system
病案连锁/病案連鎖　medical record linkage
病案讨论/病案討論　casuistics
病程/病程　disease process
病程记录/病程記錄　progress note
病床/病床　bed
病床利用率/病床利用率　bed occupancy
病床调整/病床調整　bed conversion
病的/病的　sick
病窦综合征/病竇症候群　sick sinus syndrome
病毒/病毒　virus
B 病毒/B 病毒　B virus
病毒包涵体/病毒包涵體　viral inclusion body
病毒包膜蛋白质类/病毒包膜蛋白質類　viral envelope proteins
病毒包膜突起/病毒被膜粒　peplomer
病毒变异/病毒變異　virus variation
X 病毒病/X 病毒病　virus-X disease
病毒出血热/病毒出血性發熱　virus hemorrhagic fever
病毒蛋白质类/病毒蛋白質類　viral proteins
病毒的/病毒的　viral
病毒非结构蛋白质类/病毒非結構蛋白質類　viral nonstructural proteins
病毒复制/病毒複製　virus replication
病毒干扰/病毒干擾　viral interference
病毒感染后肾炎/病毒感染後腎炎　postviral infectious nephritis
病毒固定[作用]/病毒固定法　viropexis
病毒核心蛋白质类/病毒核心蛋白質類　viral core proteins
病毒基因/病毒基因　viral gene
病毒基因表达调控/病毒基因表達調控　viral gene expression regulation
病毒基因组/病毒基因組　virus genome
病毒基质蛋白质类/病毒基質蛋白質類　viral matrix proteins
病毒激活/病毒啟動　virus activation
病毒结构蛋白质类/病毒結構蛋白質類　viral structural proteins
病毒抗体/病毒抗體　viral antibody
病毒抗药性/病毒抗藥性　viral drug resistance
病毒抗原/病毒抗原　virus antigen
病毒颗粒/病毒脂蛋白體　virosome
病毒粒质/病毒粒質　viroplasm
病毒粒子/病毒粒子　virion
病毒灭活/病毒滅活　virus inactivation
病毒尿/病毒尿　viruria
病毒培养/病毒培養　virus cultivation
病毒潜伏期/病毒潛伏期　virus latency
病毒融合蛋白质类/病毒融合蛋白質類　viral fusion proteins
病毒生理学/病毒生理學　viral physiology
病毒受体/病毒受體　virus receptor
病毒体疫苗/病毒體疫苗　virosome vaccine
病毒调控蛋白质类/病毒調控蛋白質類　viral regulatory proteins
病毒脱落/病毒脱落　virus shedding
病毒尾蛋白质类/病毒尾蛋白質類　viral tail proteins
病毒细胞转化/病毒細胞轉化　viral cell transformation
病毒相关性血细胞吞噬综合征/病毒性血球吞噬症候群　virus-associated-hemophagocytic syndrome
病毒性癌基因蛋白质类/病毒性癌基因蛋白質類　viral oncogene proteins
病毒性出血热/病毒性出血熱　viral hemorrhagic fever
病毒性出血性败血症/病毒性出血性敗血症　viral hemorrhagic septicemia
病毒性肺炎/病毒性肺炎　viral pneumonia
病毒性腹泻/病毒性腹瀉　viral diarrhea
病毒性肝炎/病毒性肝炎　viral hepatitis
病毒性肝炎疫苗/病毒性肝炎疫苗　viral hepatitis vaccine
病毒性横痃/病毒性横痃　virus bubo
病毒性呼吸道感染/病毒性呼吸道感染　viral respiratory infection
病毒性疾病/病毒性疾病　virus disease
病毒性脊髓炎/病毒性脊髓炎　viral myelitis
病毒性角膜炎/病毒性角膜炎　viral keratitis
病毒性结膜炎/病毒性結膜炎　viral conjunctivitis
病毒性脑膜炎/病毒性腦膜炎　viral meningitis
病毒性脑炎/病毒性腦炎　viral encephalitis
病毒性皮肤疾病/病毒性皮膚疾病　viral skin disease
病毒性葡萄膜炎/病毒性葡萄膜炎　viral uveitis
病毒性胃肠炎/病毒性胃腸炎　viral gastroenteritis

病毒性细支气管炎/病毒性細支氣管炎　viral bronchiolitis
病毒性心包炎/病毒性心包炎　viral pericarditis
病毒性心肌炎/病毒性心肌炎　viral myocarditis
病毒性性传播疾病/病毒性性傳播疾病　viral sexually transmitted disease
病毒性血凝集/病毒性血球凝集作用　viral hemagglutination
病毒性眼感染/病毒性眼感染　viral eye infection
病毒学/病毒學　virology
病毒学家/病毒學家　virologist
病毒血凝素类/病毒血凝素類　viral hemagglutinins
病毒血症/病毒血症　viremia
病毒抑制药/病毒抑制藥　virostatic
病毒疫苗/病毒疫苗　viral vaccine
病毒诱导/病毒誘導　virus induction
病毒再活化/病毒再活化　virus reactivation
病毒载量/病毒載量　viral load
病毒载体/病毒載體　viral vector
病毒整合/病毒整合　virus integration
病毒致细胞病变/病毒致細胞病變　viral cytopathogenic effect
病毒装配/病毒裝配　virus assembly
病发于阳/病發於陽　disease arising from yang
病发于阴/病發於陰　disease arising from yin
病感失认[症]/病感失憶症　anosognosia
病害性鞣质/病理性鞣酸　pathologic tannin
病患行为/生病行爲　illness behavior
病机/發病機制　pathogenesis
病机学说/病機學説　theory of pathogenesis
病菌/病菌　germ
病菌学说/病菌説　germ theory
病理变态反应/病理性過敏　pathologic allergy
病理带/病理帶　pathological band
病理反应性/病態反應化　pathergy
病理过程/病理過程　pathologic processes
病理解部学/病理解剖學　morbid anatomy
病理生理学/病理生理學　pathophysiology
病理生物学/病理生物學　pathobiology
病理形态学/病理形態學　pathomorphology
病理性白细胞增多/病理性白血球增多　pathologic leukocytosis
病理性代谢/病之新陳代謝　pathometabolism
病理性肥大/病理性肥大　pathological hypertrophy
病理性骨脱矿质/病理性骨脱礦質　pathologic bone demineralization
病理性骨折/病理性骨折　pathological fracture
病理性𬌗/病理性𬌗　pathologic occlusion
病理性激情/病理性激情　pathological affect
病理性扩张/病理性擴張　pathologic dilatation
病理性强直/病理性強硬　pathologic rigidity
病理性肾结核/病理性腎結核　pathological renal tuberculosis
病理性缩窄/病理性縮窄　pathologic constriction
病理性脱钙作用/病理性脱鈣作用　pathologic decalcification
病理性脱位/病理性脱位　pathological dislocation
病理性吸收/病理性吸收　pathological absorption
病理性心境恶劣/病理性心境惡劣　dysphoria
病理性新生血管化/病理性新生血管化　pathologic neovascularization
病理性眼球震颤/病理性眼球震顫　pathological nystagmus
病理性眼震/病理性眼震　pathologic nystagmus
病理性有丝分裂/病理性有絲分裂　pathologic mitosis
病理性赘述/病理性贅述　circumstantiality
病理性醉酒/病理性醉酒　pathological drunkenness
病理学/病理學　pathology
病理[学]的/病理的　pathological
病理学各论/病理學各論，病理分論　special pathology
病理学家/病理學家　pathologist
病理学总论/病理學總論，病理通論　general pathology
病理移位/病理移位　pathological migration
病理状态/病理狀態　pathological state
病历室/病案室　record room
病例/病例　case
病例报告/病案報告　case report
病例对照研究/病例對照研究　case control study
病例发现/病例發現　case-finding
病例发现延误/病例發現延誤　delay in case finding
病例管理/病例管理　case management
病脉/病脈　abnormal pulse
病媒接种诊断法/宿主接種診斷法，異體診斷法　xenodiagnosis
病情记录/病情論，疾病論　pathography
病情学/病情學　nosography
病情学家/病情學家　nosographer
病人/病人　patient
病人辩护/病人辯護　patient advocacy
病人参与/病人參與　patient participation
病人出院/病人出院　patient discharge
病人扶持器/病人昇降器　hoist bed
病人隔离/病人隔離　patient isolation

病人隔离装置/病人隔離裝置　patient isolator
病人管理/病人管理　case management
病人管理率/病人管理率　case management rate
病人护送服务/病人護送服務　patient escort service
病人护养法/病人營養法，護病法，病人護理法　nosotrophy
病人教育/病人教育　patient education
病人角色/病人角色　sick role
病人控制镇痛/病人控制鎮痛　patient-controlled analgesia
病人遴选/病人遴選　patient selection
病人满意度/病人滿意度　patient satisfaction
病人模拟/病人模擬　patient simulation
病人权利/病人權利　patient right
病人入院/病人入院　patient admission
病人识别系统/病人識別系統　patient identification system
病人选择自由条例/病人選擇自由條例　patient freedom of choice law
病人延误/病人延誤　patient's delay
病人医护管理/病人醫護管理　patient care management
病人医护连续性/病人醫護連續性　continuity of patient care
病人医疗护理/病人醫療護理　patient care
病人医疗护理计划/病人醫療護理計劃　patient care planning
病人医疗小组/病人醫療小組　patient care team
病人依从/病人依從　patient compliance
病人再入院/病人再入院　patient readmission
病人中心医护/病人中心醫護　patient-centered care
病人转送/病人轉送　transportation of patient
病人转诊/病人轉診　patient transfer
病人自己决定条例/病人自己決定條例　patient self-determination act
病色/病色　sick complexion
病色相克/病色相克　mutual restriction between disease and complexion
病史记录/病史記錄　medical history taking
病室护士/病房護理人員　hospital nurse
病损/病損　impairment
病态/病態　pathosis
病态肥胖症/病性肥胖　morbid obesity
病细胞综合征/病細胞症候群　sick cell syndrome
病因/病因　cause of disease
病因辨证/病因辨證　pattern identification of etiology
病因疗法/原因療法　causal treatment
病因学说/病因學說　etiology

病因预防/原因預防法　causal prophylaxis
病原/病原　pathogen
病原的/致病的　pathogenic
病原体/主使因數，主因　causative agent
病灶/病灶　lesion
病灶感染/病灶傳染，局部性感染　focal infection
病灶内切除[术]/病灶內切除[術]　intralesional excision
病灶内输注/病灶內輸注　intralesional infusion
病灶内治疗/病灶內治療　intralesional therapy
病灶内注射/病灶內注射　intralesional injection
病灶性病/局部病灶　focal disease
病灶性黏蛋白病/局部黏液素病　focal mucinosis
病灶硬化性骨髓炎/局部硬化性骨髓炎　focal sclerosing osteomyelitis
病征/徵象　sign
病症/病症　disorder
拨开/用針挑開　tease
拨络法/撥絡法　plucking tendon manipulation
拨云退翳丸/撥雲退翳丸　boyun tuiyi pills
波茨-史密斯-吉布森手术/波-史-吉三氏手術　Potts-Smith-Gibson operation
波动面/波動面　cove plane
波动说/波浪學說　undulatory theory
波尔定碱/波耳多鹼　boldine
波尔顿点/伯爾頓氏點　Bolton point
波尔多因/波耳多苷　boldoin
波尔泽特夹/Porzett 氏夾板　Porzett splint
波格斯-萨洛蒙试验/波-薩二氏試驗　Porges-Salomon test
波济综合征/Pozzi 氏症候群　Pozzi syndrome
波浪状呼吸/波浪性呼吸音　wavy respiration
波利策法/波利策法　Politzer method
波伦序列征/波倫序列徵　Poland sequence
波伦综合征/波倫症候群　Poland syndrome
QRS-波群/QRS 複合波　QRS complex
波士顿皮疹/波士頓皮疹　Boston exanthem
波氏小脓肿/Pautrier 氏微小膿瘍　Pautrier microabscess
波数/波數　wave number
波数计/高頻電流之振動率描記器　ondometer
波斯溃疡/Persian 潰瘍　Persian ulcer
波斯湾综合征/波斯灣症候群　Persian Gulf syndrome
波坦综合征/Potain 氏症候群　Potain syndrome
波特倒转术/派特爾氏轉向術　Potter version
波特动脉瘤/Pott 氏動脈瘤　Pott aneurysm
波特骨折/Pott 氏骨折，腓骨下端骨折　Pott fracture

波特疗法/派特氏療法　Potter treatment
波替疝/Petit氏疝　Petit hernia
波瓦散病毒/波瓦森病毒　Powassan virus
波瓦生脑炎/波瓦生腦炎　Powassan encephalitis
波希鼠李苷/普希鼠李苷,歐鼠李苷　purshianin
波希鼠李皮/美鼠李皮　Cascara
波形蛋白/波形蛋白　vimentin
波状脉/波狀脈　undulating pulse
波状热/波型熱　melitensis
波状热[性]皮炎/Brucellum氏桿菌性紅斑　erythema brucellum
波状外形的/起伏狀的　contoured
玻璃/玻璃　glass
玻璃罐/玻璃罐　glass cup
玻璃化/玻璃化作用　vitrification
玻璃离聚物黏固剂/玻璃離聚物黏固劑　glass ionomer cement
玻璃离子黏固剂/玻璃離子黏固劑　glass ionomer cement
玻璃膜/玻璃膜　glassy membrane
玻璃丝发/玻璃絲髮　spun glass hair
玻璃碳/玻璃碳　vitreous carbon
玻璃碳种植体/玻璃碳種植體　vitreous carbon implant
玻璃糖质/玻璃糖質　hyaloidin
玻璃体/玻璃體　vitreous body
玻璃体变性/玻璃體變性　vitreous degeneration
玻璃体出血/玻璃體出血　vitreous hemorrhage
玻璃体穿刺术/玻璃體穿刺法　hyalonyxis
玻璃体动脉/玻璃體動脈　hyaloid artery
玻璃体房/玻璃體房　vitreous chamber
玻璃体管/玻璃體管　hyaloid canal, vitreous canal
玻璃体后脱离/玻璃體後脫離　posterior detachment of vitreous
玻璃体混浊/玻璃體混濁　vitreous opacity
玻璃体基质/玻璃體基質　vitreous stroma
玻璃体剪/玻璃體剪　vitreous scissor
玻璃体膜/玻璃體膜　hyaloid membrane
玻璃体囊/玻璃體囊　vitreous capsule
玻璃体内注射/玻璃體內注射　intravitreal injection
玻璃体黏液质/玻璃體黏質　hyalomucoid
玻璃体镊/玻璃體鑷　vitreous forcep
玻璃体浓缩/玻璃體濃縮　vitreous condensation
玻璃体脓肿/玻璃體膿腫　vitreous abscess
玻璃体牵引/玻璃體牽引　vitreous retraction
玻璃体腔/玻璃[狀]體房,玻璃狀體腔　vitreous chamber
玻璃体切除器/玻璃體切除器　vitreous cutter

玻璃体切除术/玻璃體切除術　vitrectomy
玻璃体切开术/玻璃體切開術　vitreotomy
玻璃体缺损/玻璃體殘缺　coloboma of vitreous
玻璃体疝/玻璃體疝　vitreous hernia
玻璃体脱出/玻璃體脫出　prolapse of vitreous
玻璃体脱离/玻璃體脫離　detachment of vitreous
玻璃体窝/玻璃體窩　hyaloid fossa
玻璃体细胞/玻璃體細胞,透明細胞　hyalocyte
玻璃体液/玻璃體液,透明液　vitreous humor
玻璃体液化/玻璃體液化　liquefaction of vitreous
玻璃体移植术/玻璃體移植術　vitreous transplantation
玻璃体置换术/玻璃體置換術　vitreous replacement
玻璃调合板/玻璃調合板　glass slab
玻璃纤维皮炎/玻璃纖維皮炎　glass fiber dermatitis
玻璃纤维织物/玻璃纖維織物　glass fiber cloth
玻璃样变性/玻璃樣變性　glassy degeneration
玻璃样动脉/類玻璃體動脈　hyaloid artery
玻璃样液/玻璃狀液　vitreous humor
玻璃状体基质/玻璃體基質　vitreous stroma
玻利维亚出血热/玻利維亞出血熱　Bolivian hemorrhagic fever
玻连蛋白/玻連蛋白　vitronectin
玻连蛋白受体/玻連蛋白受體　vitronectin receptor
玻片/玻片　slide
玻片培养/玻片培養　slide cultivation
玻片试验/玻片試驗　slide test
玻片压诊法/壓視法　diascopy
玻瓶培养/瓶内培養　flask culture
玻状的/玻璃狀的　glassy
剥痂术/剝痂術　denudation of eschar
剥离/剝離,剝落　stripping
剥离性动脉瘤/剝離性動脈瘤　dissecting aneurysm
剥落/剝落　abruptio
剥落性发疹性扁平苔藓/剝落性發疹性扁平苔蘚　exfoliative and exanthematous lichen planus
剥毛工哮喘/棉纖維吸入性氣喘　stripper asthma
剥膜术/剝膜術　stripping of membrane
剥苔/剝苔　eroded fur
剥脱活检/剝脫活檢　strip biopsy
剥脱性唇炎/脫皮性唇炎　exfoliative cheilitis
剥脱性骨软骨炎/分割性骨軟骨炎　osteochondritis dissecans
剥脱性角质松解症/剝脫性角質鬆解症　exfoliative keratolysis
剥脱性狼疮/剝脫性狼瘡　lupus exfoliativus
剥脱性皮炎/剝落性皮膚炎　dermatitis exfoliativa
剥脱性舌痛/剝落性舌痛,慢性舌乳頭炎

glossodynia exfoliativa
剥脱性湿疹/剥脱性濕疹　eczema exfoliativum
剥脱性食管炎/剥脱性食管炎　exfoliative esophagitis
剥脱性胃炎/剥脱性胃炎　exfoliative gastritis
剥脱性银屑病/剥落性乾癬　exfoliative psoriasis
剥脱性龈炎/脱屑性齦炎　desquamative gingivitis
剥脱性子宫内膜炎/脱落性子宫内膜炎　exfoliative endometritis
剥脱综合征/剥脱症候群　exfoliation syndrome
菠菜绿粪/菠菜狀糞　spinach stool
菠萝/鳳梨　pineapple
菠萝蛋白酶/鳳梨酵素　bromelain
菠萝试验/鳳梨試驗　pineapple test
播散/散播　dissemination
播散性痤疮/散播性痤瘡　acne disseminata
播散性带状疱疹/散布性帶狀疱疹　disseminated herpes zoster
播散性单纯疱疹/散布性單純疱疹　disseminated herpes simplex
播散性的/散布性，彌漫性，播散的　disseminated
播散性豆状皮肤纤维瘤病/散播性豆狀皮膚纖維瘤 dermatofibrosis lenticularis disseminata
播散性骨硬化病/播散性骨硬化病　osteosclerosis disseminata
播散性汗孔角化病/播散性汗孔角化病　disseminated porokeratosis
播散性坏死/播散性壞死　diaspironecrosis
播散性黄色瘤/播散性黄色瘤　xanthoma disseminatum
播散性脊髓炎/播散性脊髓炎　disseminated myelitis
播散性渐进性[细胞]坏死/散布性壞死　diaspironecrobiosis
播散性结核/擴散性結核，急性粟粒結核　disseminated tuberculosis
播散性狼疮/散布性狼瘡　lupus disseminatus
播散性年幼型颌骨纤维发育不良/散布型幼年型颌骨纖維化發育不全　disseminated juvenile fibrous dysplasia of the jaws
播散性盘状红斑狼疮/播散性盤狀紅斑狼瘡　disseminated discoid lupus erythematosus
播散性皮肤纤维瘤/散布性皮膚纖維瘤　disseminated dermatofibroma
播散性浅表光线性汗孔角化病/播散性淺表光線性汗孔角化病　disseminated superficial actinic porokeratosis
播散性神经性皮炎/播散性神經皮膚炎　disseminated neurodermatitis
播散性嗜酸[细胞]性胶原病/播散性嗜酸[细胞]性膠原病　disseminated eosinophilic collagen disease
播散性粟粒性皮肤结核/播散性粟粒性皮膚結核　tuberculosis cutis miliaris disseminata
播散性脱发/散布性禿髮　alopecia disseminata
播散性无变应性皮肤利什曼病/播散性無反應性皮膚萊什曼病　disseminated anergic cutaneous leishmaniasis
播散性纤维性骨炎/播散性纖維性骨炎　osteitis fibrosa disseminata
播散性炎/散布性炎症　disseminated inflammation
播散性真菌感染/播散性真菌感染　disseminated fungal infection
伯氨喹/原奎寧　Primaquine
伯贝克颗粒/伯貝克顆粒　Birbeck granule
伯醇/一級醇　primary alcohol
伯恩伯格弓/伯恩格氏弓　Birnberg bow
伯恩哈特感觉异常/Bernhardt氏感覺異常　Bernhardt paresthesia
伯恩海姆综合征/Bernheim氏症候群　Bernheim syndrome
伯格病/Buerger氏病　Buerger disease
伯基特淋巴瘤/Burkitt氏淋巴瘤　Burkitt lymphoma
伯基特疝/Birkett氏疝　Birkett hernia
伯克霍尔德菌感染/伯霍爾德桿菌感染　Burkholderia infections
伯克疗法/伯爾克氏療法　burquism
伯克肉样瘤/Boeck氏類肉瘤　Boeck sarcoid
伯鲁里溃疡/Buruli氏潰瘍　Buruli ulcer
伯纳-霍纳综合征/伯-霍二氏症候群　Bernard-Horner syndrome
伯纳特溶液/Burnett氏溶液　Burnett solution
伯纳特消毒液/Burnett氏消毒液　Burnett disinfecting fluid
伯努利方程/Bernoulli公式　Bernoulli equation
伯沙奋特杆/Passavant氏隆起　Passavant bar
伯氏疏螺旋体/伯氏疏螺旋體　Borrelia burgdorferi
伯氏疏螺旋体感染/伯氏疏螺旋體感染　Borrelia Burgdorferi infection
伯氏疏螺旋体组/伯氏疏螺旋體組　Borrelia burgdorferi group
伯特绦虫病/伯特條蟲病　bertielliasis
伯特歇尔细胞/伯特歇爾細胞　Boettcher cell
伯廷骨/Bertin氏骨　Bertin bone
泊非霉素/泊非黴素　porfiromycin
泊利噻嗪/多噻嗪　polythiazide
泊洛沙姆/泊洛沙姆　poloxamer
泊洛扎林/泊洛扎林　poloxalene
泊松分布/普森分布　Poisson distribution

柏格节律/Berger 氏節律　Berger rhythm
柏林水肿/Berlin 氏水腫　Berlin edema
柏林综合征/Berlin 氏症候群　Berlin syndrome
勃起/勃起　erection
勃起不能/勃起不能　astyphia
勃起的/勃起的　erectile
勃起组织/勃起組織　erectile tissue
勃起组织癌/勃起組織癌　erectile carcinoma
勃起组织瘤/勃起組織瘤　erectile tumor
铂化合物/鉑化合物　platinum compound
铂极/鉑極　platinode
铂铱针/鉑銥針　platinum-iridium needle
博代杆菌百日咳/博德氏桿菌百日欬　Bordetella pertussis
博代杆菌感染/博德氏桿菌感染　Bordetella infection
博代杆菌属毒力因子/博德氏桿菌屬毒力因數　*Bordetella* virulence factor
博丹斯基单位/波丹斯基氏單位　Bodansky unit
博恩霍尔姆病/布恩霍姆氏病,流行性肋膜痛　Bornholm disease
博尔德穆尔食管吻合术/博爾德莫爾食管吻合術　Beordmore anastomosis of esophagus
博尔纳病/Borna 病　Borna disease
博尔施双眼绷带/Borsch 繃帶　Borsch bandage
博赫达勒克[裂]孔/Bochdalek 氏孔　foramen of Bochdalek
博克哈特脓疱病/Bockhart 氏膿痂疹　Bockhart impetigo
博克神经/Bock 氏神經　Bock nerve
博来霉素/博來黴素　Bleomycin
博士/博士　doctor
博氏线/博氏線　Beau line
博氏综合征/Beau 氏症候群　Beau syndrome
博塔洛孔/Botallo 氏孔　Botallo foramen
博塔洛韧带/Botallo 韌帶　Botallo ligament
博特金病/Botkin 病　Botkin disease
博弈论/博弈論　game theory
搏动/搏動　pulsation
搏动的/搏動的　pulsating
搏动灌注/搏動灌注　pulsatile perfusion
搏动式人工呼吸器/搏動式人工呼吸器　pulsator
搏动性脓胸/搏動性膿胸,搏動性蓄膿　pulsating empyema
搏动[性疼]痛/搏動痛　throbbing pain
搏动性血肿/搏動性血腫　pulsatile hematoma
搏动性眼球突出/跳動性凸眼　pulsating exophthalmos
搏动血流/搏動血流　pulsatile flow
搏动血流泵/搏動血流泵　pulsatile flow pump
薄膜/薄膜　film
薄膜分散法/薄膜分散法　film dispersion method
薄膜舌/薄膜舌　filmy tongue
薄膜衣/膜衣　film coat
薄膜衣片剂/膜衣錠[劑]　film coated tablet
薄膜蒸发器/薄膜蒸發器　membrane evaporator
跛行/跛行　limp, claudication
薄荷/薄荷　peppermint
薄荷脑/薄荷腦　menthol
薄荷脑樟脑/樟薄荷腦　mentholated camphor
卟吩/卟吩　porphin
卟吩胆色素/卟吩膽色素　porphobilin
卟啉/卟啉,吡咯紫質,胞體紫質　porphyrin
卟啉病/卟啉病,吡咯紫質沈著病,卟啉代謝病　porphyria, porphyrinopathy
卟啉尿/卟啉尿症,吡咯紫質尿症　porphyrinuria
卟啉血/卟啉血症,吡咯紫質血症　porphyrinemia
卟啉原/吡咯紫質原　porphyrinogen
卟啉原类/卟啉原類　porphyrinogens
卟啉症/紫質症　porphyria
补偿感应/補償性誘導　complementary induction
补偿曲线/補償性彎　compensating curve
补偿曲线曲度/補償曲線曲度　prominence of compensating curve
补偿性肥大/補充性肥大　complementary hypertrophy
补偿循环/補償循環　compensatory circulation
补充的/補充的　complementary
补充及替代医疗/輔助及另類醫療　complementary and alternative medicine
补充矿质/補充礦質　remineralization
补充疗法/補充療法　complementary therapy
补充细胞/補充細胞,儲備細胞　complementary cell, reserve cell
补充运动区/補充運動區　supplimentary motor area
补法/補法　tonifying method
补肺阿胶汤/補肺阿膠湯　bufei ejiao decoction
补复性骨炎/補復性骨炎　restitutive osteitis
补骨脂/補骨脂　malaytea scurfpea fruit
补骨脂素/補骨脂素　psoralen
补呼气量/補呼氣量　expiratory reserve volume
补剂/補劑　tonifying formula
补空性肥大/補空性肥大　hypertrophy ex vacuo
补料/補料　feeding
补料速率/補料速率　feed rate
补脾/補脾　invigorating the spleen
补脾益肺/補脾益肺　invigorating spleen for

benefiting lung
补脾益气/補脾益氣 invigorating spleen and replenishing qi
补片移植物/補釘移植物 patch graft
补气/補氣，尾吹氣 invigorating vital energy, make up gas
补气固脱/補氣固脱 invigorating qi for relieving desertion
补气剂/補氣劑 qi-supplementing formula
补气明目/補氣明目 benefiting qi for improving eyesight
补气升提/補氣昇提 invigorating qi for ascending
补气养血/補氣養血 benefiting qi and nourishing blood
补肾/補腎 invigorating the kidney
补肾安胎/補腎安胎 tonifying kidney for preventing miscarriage
补肾固齿/補腎固齒 tonifying kidney to strengthen tooth
补肾固齿丸/補腎固齒丸 bushen guchi pills
补肾明目/補腎明目 tonifying kidney for improving eyesight
补肾纳气/補腎納氣 improving inspiration by invigorating the kidney
补肾摄精/補腎攝精 invigorating kidney for consolidating semen
补肾调经/補腎調經 invigorating kidney for regulating menstruation
补授法/補授法 complementary feeding
补体/補體 complement
补体单位/補體單位 complement unit
补体固定现象/補體固定現象 fixation phenomenon
补体活化酶类/補體活化酶類 complement activating enzymes
补体激活/補體活化 complement activation
补体结合/補體結合，補體固定 complement fixation, alexin fixation
补体结合反应/補體固定反應 complement fixation reaction
补体结合试验/補體結合試驗 complement fixation test
补体灭活/補體的滅能作用 inactivation of complement
补体膜攻击复合物/補體膜攻擊複合物 complement membrane attack complex
补体偏离/補體轉向 complement deviation
补体溶血活性测定/補體溶血活性測定 complement hemolytic activity assay

补体 3b 受体/補體 3b 受體 complement 3b receptor
补体 3d 受体/補體 3d 受體 complement 3d receptor
补体受体/補體受體 complement receptor
补体系统/補體系統 complement system
补体抑制因子/補體抑制因子 complement inhibitor
补体因子 B/補體因數 B complement factor B
补吸气量/補吸氣量 inspiratory reserve volume
补习教学/補習教學 remedial teaching
补血/補血 replenishing blood
补血固脱/補血固脱 replenishing blood for relieving depletion
补血剂/補血劑 blood-supplementing formula
补血润燥/補血潤燥 nourishing blood for moistening dryness
补血养肝/補血養肝 replenishing blood and nourishing liver
补血养心/補血養心 replenishing blood for nourishing heart, tonifying blood and nourishing the heart
补血药/補血藥 hematonic
补阳/補陽 tonifying yang
补阳还五汤/補陽還五湯 buyang huanwu decoction
补阳剂/補陽劑 yang-supplementing formula
补养药疗法/姑息給藥法，保守給藥法 conservative medication
补液/補液 fluid replacement
补液量计算公式/補液量計算公式 fluid replacement formula
补液疗法/補液療法 fluid replacement therapy
补[益]法/補[益]法 invigoration method
补益肺气/補益肺氣 replenishing and restoring lung qi
补益肝脾/補益肝脾 invigorating liver and spleen
补益肝气/補益肝氣 benefiting liver qi
补益肝肾法/補益肝腎法 tonifying and replenishing liver and kidney
补益剂/補益劑 supplementing and boosting formula
补益精髓/補益精髓 strengthening and nourishing marrow and essence
补益脾肾/補益脾腎 invigorating spleen and kidney
补益肾气/補益腎氣 invigorating kidney qi
补益心肺/補益心肺 invigorating heart and lung
补益心肝/補益心肝 invigorating heart and liver, tonifying the heart and liver
补益心脾/補益心脾 invigorating heart and spleen, tonifying the heart and spleen
补益心气/補益心氣 benefiting heart qi, tonifying heart qi

补益心肾/補益心腎　invigorating heart and kidney, supplementing heart and kidney
补阴/補陰　invigorating yin
补阴剂/補陰劑　yin-supplementing formula
补阵/補陣　supplementing array
补中益气/補中益氣　invigorating spleen-stomach and replenishing qi
补中益气汤/補中益氣湯　buzhong yiqi decoction
捕虫草酶/捕蟲植物酵素　azerin
捕获/捕捉　capture
哺乳动物/哺乳動物　mammal
哺乳动物染色体/哺乳動物染色體　mammalian chromosome
哺乳动物学/哺乳動物學　mammalogy
哺乳动物正呼肠孤病毒/哺乳動物正呼腸孤病毒　mammalian orthoreovirus
哺乳困难/哺乳困難　dystithia
哺乳期/哺乳期　lactation
哺乳期[乳腺]脓肿/哺乳期乳房膿腫　milk abscess
哺乳性盲/哺乳性盲　lactation blindness
哺乳性视神经炎/哺乳性視神經炎　lactation optic neuritis
哺乳性子宫萎缩/哺乳性子宮萎縮　lactation atrophy
哺育细胞/哺育細胞　nurse cell
不安静的/不安靜的,不寧的　restless
不饱和溶液/不飽和溶液　unsaturated solution
不饱和膳食脂肪类/不飽和膳食脂肪類　unsaturated dietary fats
不饱和脂肪类/不飽和脂肪類　unsaturated fats
不饱和脂肪酸/不飽和脂肪酸　unsaturated fatty acid
不饱和脂肪酸类/不飽和脂肪酸類　unsaturated fatty acids
不变态类/不變形態類　ametabolon
不成熟的/不成熟的　immature
不成熟儿/未成熟嬰兒　immature infant
不当牙科治疗/不當牙科治療　faulty dental
不得眠/不得眠　inability to sleep
不等互换/不等互換　unequal crossing over
不等联体双胎/不等聯體雙胎　unequal conjoined twins
不等面关节/不等面關節　incongruent articulation
不等渗溶液/不等滲溶液　anisotonic solution
不等隐斜/不等隱斜　anisophoria
不等折光性/不等折光性　anisotropic property
不等支原体/殊異支原體　mycoplasma dispar
不典型[的]/非典型的　atypical
不典型性/不典型,異型　atypism
不典型增生/不典型增生　atypical hyperplasia

不定性骨囊肿/不定性骨囊腫　indefinite bone cyst
不动的/不動的　nonmotile
不动杆菌/不動桿菌　Acinetobacter
不动杆菌感染/不動桿菌感染　Acinetobacter infection
不动关节/不動關節　coarticulation
不动情期/不動情期　anestrus
不动性白细胞增多/不動性白血球增多　nonmotile leukocytosis
不断的/不斷的　constant
不对称/不對稱　asymmetry
不对称的/不對稱的　asymmetric
不对称的对称/不對稱的對稱　asymmetric symmetry
不对称合成/不對稱合成　asymmetric synthesis
不对称联体儿/不對稱聯體兒　asymmetric conjoined twins
不对称乳房/不對稱乳房　asymmetrical breast
不对称散光/不對稱散光　asymmetrical astigmatism
不对称伸缩振动/不對稱伸縮振動　asymmetrical stretching vibration
不对称萎缩/不對稱萎縮　atrophy asymmetric
不对称吸收/不對稱吸收　asymmetric resorption
不发育/不發育　aplasia
不分层皮质/不分層皮質　unlaminated cortex
不分裂细胞/不分裂細胞　non-diving cell
不规则的/不規則的　atactic
不规则骨/不規則骨,異形骨　irregular bone
不规则疟/不規則瘧　malaria irregularis
不规则散光/不規則散光　irregular astigmatism
不规则牙本质/不規則牙本質,次生牙本質　irregular dentin
不规则眼球震颤/不規則眼球震顫　irregular nystagmus
不规则致密结缔组织/不規則致密結締組織　dense irregular connective tissue
不含黑色素的/無黑色素的　amelanotic
不含蔗糖的/不含蔗糖的　sucrose-free
不合理用药/不合理用藥　non-rational use of drug
不和谐/不一致　dissonance
不挥发物/不揮發物　non-volatile matter
不活动基因/靜止基因　silent gene
不活动状态/不活動狀態　inactive state
不加热血清反应素试验/不加熱血清反應素試驗　unheated serum reagin test
不间断护理/持續性照護　continuing care
不减数分裂/未減數分裂　ameiosis
不健康的/不健康的　unhealthy

不均等卵裂/不等裂　unequal cleavage
不均分配补偿/不均分配補償　disproportionate share reimbursement
不均匀放射/不均匀輻射　heterogeneous radiation
不开放医院/不開放醫院　closed hospital
不可重配/不可重配　non rep
不可复性关节盘前移/不可復性關節盤前移　anterior meniscus displacement without reduction
不可复性关节盘移位/不可復性關節盤移位　disc displacement without reduction
不可逆胶体/不可逆膠體　irreversible colloid
不可逆凝胶/不可逆性凝膠　irreversible gel
不可逆效应/不可逆效應　irreversible effect
不可逆性/不可逆性　irreversibility
不可逆性竞争性拮抗/不可逆性競爭性拮抗　irreversible competitive antagonism
不可逆性水胶体/不可逆性水膠體　irreversible hydrocolloid
不可逆指示剂/不可逆指示劑　irreversible indicator
不可渗透的/不透水的　impervious
不可调节式𬌗架/不可調型咬合器　non-adjustable articulator
不[可]通透的/無法穿透的　impermeable
不可吸收性物质/不可吸收性物質　nonresorbable material
不连接的/未接合的　unconnected
不连接性骨折/不連接性骨折　disunited fracture
不连胸骨的/不連胸骨的　asternal
不连续沉淀/不連續之沈澱　discontinuous precipitation
不连续毛细血管/不連續毛細管　discontinuous capillary
不联会/接合不能,聯會不能　asynapsis
不良/不良　dys
不良刺激/劣性刺激　pessimal stimulation
不良的/不良的　adverse
不良反应/不良反應　untoward reaction, adverse reaction
不良反应阈/不良反應閾限　threshold of adverse effect
不良冠/不良牙冠　faulty crown
不良建筑物综合征/不良建築物症候群　sick building syndrome
不良接触/不良接觸　faulty contact
不良填补性牙龈炎/不良填補性牙齦炎　faulty fillings in gingivitis
不良性溃疡/不良性潰瘍　unhealthy ulcer
不良修复/不良修復　faulty restoration

不灵敏核极化转移增益法/不靈敏核的極化轉移增益法　insensitive nucleus enhancement by polarization transfer, INEPT
不寐[病]/不寐　insomnia
不寐·肝火扰心证/不寐·肝火擾心證　insomnia with pattern of liver-fire disturbing heart
不寐·肝郁血虚证/不寐·肝鬱血虛證　insomnia with pattern of liver depression and blood deficiency
不寐·痰热内扰证/不寐·痰熱內擾證　insomnia with pattern of internal disturbance of phlegm-heat
不寐·胃气不和证/不寐·胃氣不和證　insomnia with pattern of stomach qi disharmony
不寐·心火炽盛证/不寐·心火熾盛證　insomnia with pattern of blazing heart-fire
不寐·心脾两虚证/不寐·心脾兩虛證　insomnia with pattern of heart-spleen deficiency
不寐·心肾不交证/不寐·心腎不交證　insomnia with pattern of incoordination between heart and kidney
不寐·心虚胆怯证/不寐·心虛膽怯證　insomnia with pattern of heart deficiency and timidity
不灭性/不滅性,不可毀滅的　indestructibility
不明热/不明熱　pyrexia of unknown origin
不耐酒/不耐酒,無耐酒力　alcoholic intolerance
不耐热抗体/不耐熱抗體　heat labile antibody
不耐性反应/不耐性反應　intolerance reaction
不内外因/不内外因　neither internal nor external cause, non-endo-non-exogenous cause
不能复苏的/不能復甦的　irresuscitable
不能手术的/不能手術的　inoperable
不宁腿综合征/不寧腿症候群　restless legs syndrome
不凝性/不凝,不能凝固　incoagulability
不排卵/無排卵,無卵性行經　anovulation
不排卵的/不排卵的　anovular
不平衡/不平衡　imbalance
不平衡易位/不平衡易位　unbalanced translocation
不全并指/不全并指　incomplete syndactyly
不全病毒颗粒/病毒微粒　viromicrosome
不全的/不完全的　incomplete
不全骨折/不全骨折　infraction
不全流产/不全流產　incomplete abortion
不全麻痹性眼球震颤/眼肌輕度麻痺性眼球震颤　paretic nystagmus
不全盲/不全盲　incomplete blindness
不全偏盲/不完全偏盲　incomplete hemianopia
不全食物/不適當飲食　faulty diet
不全脱位/不完全脱位,部分脱位　incomplete dislocation, partial dislocation

不燃物/不燃物　incombustible
不燃性/不燃燒性,不能燃燒性,防火性　incombustibility
不染色的/拒染的,忌染的　achromatophil
不染色性/拒染性,忌染性　achromatophilia
不容/不容　burong, ST19
不溶[解]的/不溶的　insoluble
不溶性/不溶性　insolubility
不溶性微粒/微粒物質　particulate matter
不伤害/不傷害　non-maleficence
不射精/不射精　failure of ejaculation
不识人/不識人　coma
不舒服/不適　malaise
不随意的/不隨意的　involuntary
不随意肌/不隨意肌　involuntary muscle
不通气引流法/不通氣引流法　air-tight drainage
不同时的/不同步的　asynchronous
不透光性/不透光性　optical opacity
不透明/混濁　opacity
不外显/不外顯　nonpenetrance
不完全白化病/類白化病　albinoidism
不完全唇裂/不完全唇裂　clefts incomplete lip
不[完]全蛋白质/不完全蛋白質　incomplete protein
不完全骨折/不完全骨折　incomplete fracture
不完全抗体/不完全抗體　incomplete antibody
不完全瘘/不全瘘,單口瘘　incomplete fistula
不完全卵裂/不完全卵裂,不全裂　incomplete cleavage, meroblastic cleavage
不完全色盲/不完全色盲,部分色盲　partial color blindness
不完全疝/不完全疝　incomplete hernia
不[完]全外显/不[完]全外顯　incomplete penetrance
不完全显性/不完全顯性　incomplete dominance
不完全型/不完全型　incomplete form
不完全性心脏传导阻滞/不完全心傳導阻滯　incomplete heart block
不妄作劳/不妄作勞　avoiding overstrain
不卫生的/不衛生的　insanitary
不闻香臭/不聞香臭　loss of smell
不稳的/不穩定　unstable
不稳定的/不穩定的,易變的　labile
不稳定骨折/不穩定骨折　unstable fracture
不稳定酸/不穩定酸　labile acid
不稳定型心绞痛/不穩定型心絞痛　unstable angina
不稳定性/不穩定性,不安定　instability
不稳定性高血压/底線性高血壓　labile hypertension
不稳定性萎缩瘢痕/不穩定性萎縮瘢痕　unstable atrophic scar
不吸收缝线/不吸收性縫線　nonabsorbable suture
不显汗/不自覺性出汗,隱汗　insensible perspiration
不显形的/隱形的　adelomorphous
不显性感染/無症狀性感染　silent infection
不相容性/不相容性　incompatibility
不消化粪/不消化性糞　lienteric stool
不锈钢根管治疗器械/不銹鋼根管治療器械　stainless steel endodontic instrument
不锈钢牙套/不銹鋼牙套　crown steel
不需氧脱氢酶/厭氧脱氫酵素　anaerobic dehydrogenase
不许可的/不被允許的　inadmissible
不易移位性骨折/不易移位性骨折　fracture favorable
不应期/不應期　refractory stage
不应性/不應性　refractoriness
不应状态/不應狀態　refractory state
不育/不[生]育　infertility
不育大孢子菌病/不育大孢子菌病,單芽孢囊菌病　adiaspiromycosis
不育细胞/無生殖能力細胞　sterile cell
不育性孢虫囊/不育性包蟲囊　sterile cyst
不育症/不孕症　sterility disease
不愈合骨折/不愈合骨折　ununited fracture
不孕症/不孕症　infertility
不孕症·肝气郁结证/不孕症·肝氣鬱結證　infertility with pattern of liver qi depression
不孕症·肝肾阴虚证/不孕症·肝腎陰虛證　infertility with pattern of liver-kidney yin deficiency
不孕症·脾肾阳虚证/不孕症·脾腎陽虛證　infertility with pattern of yang deficiency of spleen and kidney
不孕症·肾气虚证/不孕症·腎氣虛證　infertility with pattern of kidney qi deficiency
不孕症·痰湿阻滞证/不孕症·痰濕阻滯證　infertility with pattern of stagnation and blockade of phlegm-damp
不孕症·瘀血内阻证/不孕症·瘀血内阻證　infertility with pattern of internal blockade of static blood
不皂化物/不皂化物　non-saponifiable matter
不整齐扑动/不規則性心房撲動　impure flutter
不正常红细胞增多症/不正常紅血球增多症　inappropriate polycythemia
不转位/非旋轉,未[能]旋轉　nonrotation
不足/不足,短缺　deficit
布安[固定]溶液/Bouin 氏溶液　Bouin solution
布安[固定]液/Bouin 液　Bouin fluid
布巴病/蒲巴病,皮膚黏膜利什曼病　buba

布比卡因/布比卡因　Bupivacaine
布-布二氏移植物/Blair-Brown 二氏移植物　Blair-Brown graft
布袋丸/布袋丸　budai pill
布地奈德/布地奈德　Budesonide
布恩斯韧带/Burn 韌帶　Burn ligament
布尔病/Buhl 氏病　Buhl disease
布尔达赫径/Burdach 氏徑　Burdach tract
布尔纳维病/Bourneville 氏病　Bourneville disease
布尔内维尔-普林格病/Bourneville-Pringle 氏病　Bourneville-Pringle disease
布尔热里韧带/Bourgery 韌帶　Bourgery ligament
布酚宁/布酚寧　nylidrin
布佛雷溃疡/Bouveret 潰瘍　Bouveret ulcer
布佛雷综合征/Bouveret 症候群　Bouveret syndrome
布赫瓦尔德萎缩/Buchwald 氏萎縮　Buchwald atrophy
布巾/布巾　napkin
布-津病/Brill-Zinsser 氏病　Brill-Zinsser disease
布凯活动滤线器/布基氏遮光闌,布-波二氏光板　Bucky diaphragm
布克利嗪/安其敏　buclizine
布枯/布枯葉　buchu
布拉地新/布拉地新　bucladesine
布拉克斯顿·希克斯征/布拉克斯頓·布雷希氏徵象　Braxton Hicks sign
布拉洛尔/布拉洛爾　bupranolol
布拉什菲尔德斑/Brushfield 氏斑　Brushfield spot
布喇格反射/Bragg 氏反射　Bragg reflection
布莱德福架/布萊福德氏架　Bradford frame
布莱克窝洞分类/布萊克窩洞分類　Black classification of cavity
布莱洛克-陶西格手术/布-陶二氏手術　Blalock-Taussig operation
布赖斯-蒂切卵/布-提二氏卵　Bryce-Teacher ovum
布赖特盲/Bright 氏盲　Bright blindness
布赖特杂音/Bright 氏雜音　Bright murmur
布兰汉姆心动过缓/Branham 氏心搏徐緩　Branham bradycardia
布兰汉姆征/Branham 氏徵象　Branham sign
布兰维尔耳/Blainville 氏耳　Blainville ear
布朗架/布朗架　Brown frame
布朗三角图形法/布朗三角圖形法　Brown triangle method
布朗氏移植片/Braun 移植物　Braun graft
布朗运动/布朗運動　Brownian movement
布劳吻合[术]/布勞吻合[術]　Braun anastomosis
布-勒肿瘤/Buschke-Lowenstein 氏腫瘤　Buschke-Lowenstein tumor
布雷菲德菌素 A/布雷菲德菌素 A　Brefeldin A
布雷谢骨/Breschet 骨　Breschet bone
布里索病/Brissaud 氏病　Brissaud disease
布里索脊柱侧凸/Brissaud 氏脊柱側彎　Brissaud scoliosis
布里索-马里综合征/Brissaud-Marie 二氏症候群　Brissaud-Marie syndrome
布立马胺/布立馬胺　burimamide
布利索-西卡综合征/布-賽二氏症候群　Brissaud-Sicard syndrome
布林顿病/Brinton 病　Brinton disease
布卢姆综合征/布盧姆症候群,Bloom 症候群　Bloom syndrome, Blum syndrome
布鲁顿丙种球蛋白缺乏血症/Bruton 氏無伽馬球蛋白血症　Bruton agammaglobulinemia
布鲁格施综合征/Brugsch 氏症候群　Brugsch syndrome
布鲁赫膜/Bruch 氏膜　Bruch membrane
布鲁津斯基征/布魯津斯基徵　Brudzinski sign
布鲁克病/Brooke 氏病　Brooke disease
布鲁克公式/布魯克公式　Brooke formula
布鲁克瘤/Brooke 氏腫瘤　Brooke tumor
布鲁曼病/Blumenthal 氏病　Blumenthal disease
布鲁霉素/布魯黴素　bluensomycin
布伦纳手术/布雷納氏手術　Brenner operation
布伦尼曼综合征/Brenneman 氏症候群　Brenneman syndrome
布伦斯病/Bruns 氏病　Bruns disease
布伦斯综合征/Bruns 氏症候群　Bruns syndrome
布伦希尔得病毒/布倫希爾病毒　Brunhilde virus
布罗德曼皮质区/布羅德曼皮質區　cortical areas of Brodmann
布罗迪脓肿/Brodie 氏膿瘍　Brodie abscess
布罗迪-特伦德伦堡试验/Brodie-Trendelenburg 氏試驗　Brodie-Trendelenburg test
布罗静脉/Burow 氏靜脈　Burow vein
布罗卡共济失调/布洛卡運動失調　Broca ataxia
布罗卡回/布洛卡迴　Broca gyrus
布罗卡失语/布洛卡氏失語症　Broca aphasia
布罗卡语言区/布洛卡語言區　speech area of Broca
布罗姆修复术/布羅姆修復術　Brom repair
布罗溶液/Burow 氏溶液　Burow solution
布洛芬/布洛芬　ibuprofen
布洛克综合征/Brock 氏症候群　Brock syndrome
布美他尼/布美他尼　Bumetanide
布尼亚病毒科感染/布尼亞病毒科感染　Bunyaviridae infection

布尼亚维拉病毒/布尼安維拉病毒　Bunyamwera virus
布萨卡结节/布薩卡結節　Busacca nodules
布舍瑞林/布舍瑞林　Buserelin
布施克硬肿病/布施克硬腫病　scleredema of Buschke
布氏姜片虫/伯斯基氏薑片蟲　Fasciolopsis buski
布氏菌变应原/布氏桿菌素　Brucellergen
布氏菌病/布氏桿菌病，布鲁士桿菌病　Brucellosis
布氏菌菌苗/布氏桿菌菌苗　Brucella vaccine
布他拉莫/布他拉莫　butaclamol
布他哌嗪/布他呱嗪　butaperazine
布替罗星硫酸盐/硫酸丁醯苷菌素　Butirosin sulfate
布托啡诺/布托啡諾　butorphanol
布托沙明/布托沙明　butoxamine
布汪巴热/Bwamba 熱　Bwamba fever
布汪巴热病毒/Bwamba 熱病毒　Bwamba fever virus
布-魏病/Brushfield-Wyatt 二氏病　Brushfield-Wyatt disease
布-旺移植片/Braun-Wangensteen 二氏移植片　Braun-Wangensteen graft
布夏尔结节/布夏爾結節　Bouchard node
布歇病/Bouchet 病　Bouchet disease
布质磨片/布板,布盤　cloth disk
步幅/步幅　pace
步廊/步廊　bulang, KI22
步数计/計步器　pedometer
步态/步態,步式　gait
步态电图/步態電圖　electrobasogram
步态电图描记器/步態記錄器　electrobasograph
步态分析/步態分析　gait analysis
步态共济失调/步態共濟失調　gait ataxia
步态描记器/異態步式記錄器　basograph
步态失调/步態失調　gait apraxia
步态训练/步態訓練　gait training
步行/步行　walking
步行不能/步行不能　abasia
步行辅助器/步行輔助器　walker
步行训练/步行訓練　ambulation training
步骤/步驟　procedure
部分/部分　fraction
部分变性反应/部分變性反應　reaction of partial degeneration
部分不应状态/部分不應狀態　partial refractory state

部分肠梗阻/部分腸梗阻　partial intestinal obstruction
部分促凝血酶原时间/部分促凝血酶原時間　partial thromboplastin time
部分单侧性雀斑样痣/局部單側性色素小斑症　partial unilateral lentiginosis
部分蛋白/部分蛋白質　partial protein
部分的/部分的　partial
部分发育缓慢/部分發育遲鈍　bradyauxesis
部分发作/部分發作　partial seizure
部分房室传导阻滞/部分房室傳導阻斷　partial atrioventricular block
部分分裂卵原肠胚/偏裂原腸胚　merogastrula
部分感觉缺失/部分感覺缺失　partial anesthesia
部分梗阻/部分阻塞　partial obstruction
部分骨折/部分骨折　partial fracture
部分冠/部分冠　partial crown
部分激动药/部分激動藥　partial agonist
部分拮抗药/部分拮抗藥　partial antagonist
部分颈部清扫术/部分頸部廓清術　partial neck dissection
部分抗原/部分抗原　partial antigen
部分盲/部分性盲,部分視覺　meropia
部分脾移植/部分脾移植　partial splenic transplantation
部分前置胎盘/部分前置胎盤　incomplete placenta previa
部分缺失/部分缺失　excalation
部分缺肢畸形/部分下肢缺損　meromelia
部分三体/部分三套體　partial trisomy
部分失神经支配/部分失神經支配　partial denervation
部分听骨链[重建]赝复物/部分聽骨鏈[重建]贗複物　partial ossicular replacement prosthesis
部分无颅[畸形]/部分無顱畸形　meroacrania
部分性癫痫/部分性癲癇　partial epilepsy
部分性房室通道/部分性房室通道　partial atrioventricular canal
部分性前置胎盘/部分性前置胎盤　partial placenta praevia
部分阻滞/部分阻滯　partial block
部门间关系/部門間關係　interdepartmental relation
部[位]/部,區　region

C

擦除的/擦落的　abrasive
擦除术/磨擦　attrition
擦法/擦法　scrubbing manipulation
擦烂/擦爛,擦疹　intertrigo
擦烂[性]湿疹/擦爛性濕疹,對磨性濕疹　eczema intertrigo, eczema intertriginosum
擦皮器/擦皮器　dermabrader
擦破/擦破　abrasion
擦伤/擦傷　brush burn
擦伤性水疱/摩擦性水皰　friction blister
擦拭法细胞学检查[术]/擦拭法細胞學檢查[術]　abrasive cytologic examination
擦拭清洁剂/磨磋性清潔劑　abrasive cleanser
擦浴/擦浴　ablution
猜疑性精神病/懷疑性精神病　doubting insanity
才能试验/才能試驗　aptitude test
材料/材料　materials
材料试验/材料試驗　materials testing
财务管理/財務管理　finance management
裁缝踝/裁縫師踝　tailors ankle
采采蝇病/採採蠅病,非洲錐蟲病　tsetse-fly disease
采海绵潜水夫病/採海綿潛水伕病　sponge-fisher disease
采蘑菇者肺/採蘑菇者肺　mushroom-picker lung
采收/採收,採集　collection
采收期/採收期　collection period
采蕈者病/採蕈者病　mushroom worker disease
采制/採製　collection and preparation
彩斑状的/雜色的,斑駁的　variegated
彩线试验/絨線試驗　worsted test
踩法/踩法　treading manipulation
菜花样乳头状瘤/菜花樣乳頭狀瘤病　florid papillomatosis
菜花状耳/花椰菜樣耳　cauliflower ear
菜末蜡/馬來蟲　Malay bug
菜农皮炎/菜農皮膚炎　vegetable-farmer dermatitis
菜乌紫病/菜烏紫病　pickles cyanosis
菜油甾醇/葉子脂醇　campesterol
蔡斯腺/Zeis氏腺體　gland of Zeis
参比标准/參考標準　reference standard
参比电极/參考電極　reference electrode

餐叉样畸形/餐叉樣畸形　fork-form deformity
餐后的/餐後的,進食後的　postprandial
残存/殘存　survival
残端妊娠/殘餘妊娠　stump pregnancy
残根/殘根　residual root
残毁尸体色情[狂]/虐屍淫狂,虐屍色情　necrosadism
残毁性关节炎/殘毀性關節炎　arthritis mutilans
残毁性狼疮/殘毀性狼瘡　lupus mutilans
残毁性麻风/癩性麻瘋,毀形性麻瘋　lepra mutilans
残基/殘基　residue
残疾/無能力,能力喪失　disability
残疾保险/殘疾保險　disability insurance
残疾儿童/殘疾兒童　disabled children
残疾鉴定/殘疾鑒定　disability evaluation
残疾人/殘疾人　disabled person
残疾人牙科医疗/殘疾人牙科醫療　dental care for disabled
残疾人语言交往辅助器/殘疾人語言交往輔助器　communication aids for disabled
残角子宫/殘角子宮　rudimentary horn of uterus
残留的/殘餘的,剩餘的　residual
残留结石/殘留結石　residual stone
残留溶剂/殘留溶媒　residual solvent
残留听力/殘留聽力　residual hearing
残留微粒性疾病/殘留微粒性疾病　remnant particle disease
残留型精神分裂症/殘留型精神分裂症　residual schizophrenia
残留性中耳炎/殘留性中耳炎　residual otitis media
残留谵妄/殘留譫妄　residual delirium
残气量/餘氣量　residual volume
残缺/殘缺　mutilation
残缺性畸形/殘缺性畸形　malformation by defect
残髓/殘髓　residual pulp
残髓炎/殘髓炎　residual pulpitis
残胃/殘胃　gastric remnant
残遗骨/殘遺骨　rudimentary bone
残遗晶状体/殘遺晶狀體　rudiment lens
残遗器官/殘遺器官,殘器　vestigial organ
残余感染/殘餘感染　residual infection

残余囊肿/殘餘囊腫　residual cyst
残余脓肿/殘餘膿腫　residual abscess
残余体/殘餘體　residual body
残余牙槽嵴/殘餘牙槽脊　residual alveolar ridge
残余肿瘤/殘餘腫瘤　residual neoplasm
残障/殘障　handicap
残肢/殘肢　meromelia, stump
残肢幻觉/殘肢幻覺　phantom limb hallucination
残肢神经痛/殘肢神經痛　stump neuralgia
蚕肠线/蠶腸線　silkworm gut
蚕豆病/蠶豆病　favism
蚕豆嘧啶葡糖苷/大巢豆素　vicine
蚕蛾醇/蠶醇　bombykol
蚕沙/蠶沙　silk-worm droppings
蚕食性角膜溃疡/蠶食性角膜潰瘍　rodent corneal ulcer
蚕甾醇/蠶蛹固醇　bombicesterol
惨戚/慘戚　feeling miserable
仓德克-阿希海姆试验/宋-阿二氏驗孕試驗　Zondek-Aschheim test
仓廪之本/倉廩之本　root of granary, spleen and stomach
苍白/蒼白　pallor
苍白的/蒼白的　pale
苍白密螺旋体/梅毒螺旋體　treponema pallidum
苍白球/蒼白球　globus pallidus
苍白球变性/蒼白球變性　pallidal degeneration
苍白球的/蒼白球的　pallidal
苍白球化学破坏术/蒼白球化學切除術　chemopallidectomy
苍白球切除术/淡蒼球切除術,淡蒼球化學摘除術　pallidectomy
苍白球切开术/淡蒼球切開術　pallidotomy
苍白球丘脑化学破坏术/蒼白球與丘腦化學切除術　chemopallidothalamectomy
苍白球支/蒼白球支　branches of globus pallidus
苍白球中脑综合征/蒼白球中腦症候群　pallidomesencephalic syndrome
苍白球综合征/蒼白球症候群　pallidal syndrome
苍白色高血压/蒼白色高血壓　pale hypertension
苍白[色]窒息/蒼白窒息　asphyxia pallida
苍白细胞棘皮瘤/蒼白細胞棘皮瘤　pale cell acanthoma
苍白血栓/蒼白血栓　pale thrombus
苍白移植物反应/蒼白移植物反應　white graft reaction
苍耳散/蒼耳散　cang'er powder
苍耳子/蒼耳子　Siberian cocklebur fruit

苍术/蒼朮　atractylodes rhizome
苍术苷/蒼朮苷　atractyloside
藏精气而不泻/藏精氣而不瀉　storing essence without leaking
藏毛病/藏毛病　pilonidal disease
藏毛的/藏毛的,潛毛的　pilonidal
藏毛窦/藏毛竇　pilonidal sinus
藏毛瘘管/藏毛瘻管　pilonidal fistula
藏毛脓肿/藏毛膿腫　pilonidal abscess
操练椅/運動治療椅　plint
操纵基因/操縱基因　operator gene
操纵基因区/操縱基因區　operator region
操纵子/操縱子　operon
操作式条件反射/操作式條件反射　operant conditioning
糙面内质网/糙面內質網　rough endoplasmic reticulum
糙皮病/癩皮病,玉蜀黍病　pellagra
糙皮病的/糙皮病的　pellagrous
糙皮病患者/癩皮病患者　pellagrin
糙皮病舌炎/糙皮病舌炎　glossitis pellagra
糙皮病学/癩皮病學　pellagrology
糙苔/糙苔　rough fur
嘈杂/嘈雜　gastric upset
嘈杂[病]/嘈雜[病],胃脘嘈雜　gastric discomfort, stomach upset
嘈杂·胃气虚证/嘈雜·胃氣虛證　stomach upset with qi deficiency pattern
嘈杂·胃热证/嘈雜·胃熱證　stomach upset with stomach heat pattern
嘈杂·胃阴虚证/嘈雜·胃陰虛證　stomach upset with yin deficiency pattern
嘈杂·血虚证/嘈雜·血虛證　stomach upset with blood deficiency pattern
槽式导管/槽式導管　railway catheter
槽式缘/槽式緣　chamfer margin
槽牙/槽牙　bicuspid teeth
草/草　grass
草氨酸/草胺酸　oxamic acid
草醋酸盐类/草醋酸鹽類　oxaloacetates
草地皮炎/草地皮膚炎　meadow dermatitis
草豆蔻/草豆蔻　katsumada galangal seed
草果/草果　fruit of caoguo
草履虫属/草履蟲屬　*Paramecium*
草履虫素/草履蟲素　paramecin
草绿色链球菌/草綠色鏈球菌　Streptococcus viridans
草绿色链球菌感染/草綠色鏈球菌感染　viridans

streptococcal infection
草莓/草莓　strawberry
草莓舌/莓狀舌　strawberry tongue
草莓汁/草莓汁液　strawberry juice
草莓状血管瘤/草莓狀血管瘤　strawberry hemangioma
草莓状痣/草莓狀痣　strawberry nevus
草秣室装填夫肺/草秣室裝填夫肺　silo-filler lung
草酸/草酸,乙二酸　oxalic acid
草酸铵/草酸銨　ammonium oxalate
草酸钙/草酸鈣　calcium oxalate
草酸钙结石/草酸鈣結石　calcium oxalate stone
草酸类/草酸類　oxalic acids
草酸尿/草酸[鹽]尿　oxaluria
草酸铈/草酸鈰　cerium oxalate
草酸性痛风/草酸性痛風　oxalic gout
草酸盐/草酸鹽　oxalate
草酸盐沉积病/草酸鹽沈積症　oxalosis
草酸盐处理/草酸鹽處置法　oxalation
草酸盐血/草酸鹽血　oxalated blood
草酸盐血浆/草酸鹽血漿　oxalate plasma
草酸中毒/草酸[鹽]中毒　oxalism
草乌/草烏　kusnezoff monkshood root
草席病/草席病　straw mattress disease
草酰胺/乙二醯胺　oxamide
草酰乙酸类/草醯乙酸類　oxaloacetic acids
草酰乙酸盐/草醯乙酸鹽　oxaloacetate
草药/草藥　herb
草药-药物相互作用/草藥-藥物相互作用　herb-drug interaction
草药医派/本草醫派,自然醫學派　physiomedicalism
草药医学/草藥醫學　herbal medicine
草原病/草原病　veldt sickness
侧柏酮/側柏酮　thujone
侧柏叶/側柏葉　Chinese arborvitae twig and leaf
侧板/側板　lateral disc
侧板中胚层/側板中胚層,側面板狀中胚層　lateral plate mesoderm
侧半规管/側半規管　ductus semicircularis lateralis
侧[壁]动脉瘤/管側動脈瘤　lateral aneurysm
侧侧吻合[术]/側側吻合[術]　side-to-side anastomosis
侧唇/側唇　lateral lip
侧窦血栓形成/側竇血栓形成　lateral sinus thrombosis
侧窦血栓性静脉炎/側竇血栓性靜脈炎　lateral sinus thrombophlebitis
侧窦乙状部沟/側竇乙狀部溝　lateral groove for sigmoidal part of lateral sinus
侧耳/側耳　pleurotus
侧[方]暗间隙/側[方]暗間隙　lateral dark space
侧方关系/側方關係　lateral relation
侧方𬌗/側方𬌗　lateral occlusion
侧方平衡/側方平衡　lateral equilibration
侧方平衡𬌗/側方平衡𬌗　lateral balanced occlusion
侧[方]脱位/側脱位　lateral dislocation
侧方压缩/側方壓縮　lateral condensation
侧方运动/側運動　lateral movement
侧副沟/側副溝　collateral sulcus
侧副管/側副管　collateral vessel
侧副隆起/側副隆凸　collateral eminence
侧副韧带/側副韌帶　collateral ligaments
侧副三角/側副三角　collateral trigone
侧副支/側副支　collateral branch
侧弓反张/側弓反張　pleurothotonos
侧角/側角　lateral horn
侧块/側塊　lateral mass
侧链/側鏈　side chain, lateral chain
侧链学说/側鏈[學]說　side-chain theory
侧裂隙/側裂隙　fissura collateralis
侧貌分析/側貌分析　profile analysis
侧貌描记器/側貌描記器　silhouetter
侧面的/外側的　lateral
侧脑沟/側腦溝　lateral cerebral sulcus
侧脑室/側腦室　lateral ventricle
侧脑室后角/側腦室後角　posterior horn of lateral ventricle
侧脑室脉络丛/側腦室脈絡叢　choroid plexus of lateral ventricle
侧脑室脉络丛支/側腦室脈絡叢支　choroidal branches of lateral ventricle
侧脑室内侧静脉/側腦室內側靜脈　medial vein of lateral ventricle
侧脑室前角/側腦室前角　anterior horn of lateral ventricle
侧脑室乳突分流/側腦室乳突分流　ventriculomastoid shunt
侧脑室外侧静脉/側腦室外側靜脈　lateral vein of lateral ventricle
侧脑室下角/側腦室下角　inferior horn of lateral ventricle
侧脑室下静脉/側腦室下靜脈　inferior ventricular vein
侧脑室造瘘术/側腦室造瘺術　lateral ventriculostomy
侧脑室中央部/側腦室中央部　central part of lateral

ventricle
侧内皮垫/側内皮墊　lateral endothelial cushion
侧平衡/側平衡　lateral balance
侧韧带/側韌帶　collateral ligament
侧视内镜/側視内鏡　sideviewing endoscope
侧位肾盂造影术/側臥腎盂攝影術　lateral pyelography
侧卧位/側臥位　lateral decubitus, lateral position
侧下丘脑区/側下丘腦區　lateral hypothalamic area
侧向滑动瓣/側向滑動瓣　lateral sliding flap
侧向髁导斜度/側向髁導斜度　inclination of lateral condylar guidance
侧向髁道斜度/側向髁道斜度　lateral condyle path inclination
侧延龋/側向齲蝕　lateral caries
侧移动/側向移動　lateral excursion
侧翼序列/側翼序列　flanking sequence
侧影显露/側影顯露　profile emergence
侧扎法/側面結扎　lateral ligature
侧褶/側褶　lateral fold
侧支/側支　collateral branch
侧支呼吸/側支呼吸　collateral respiration
侧支性充血/側支性充血　collateral hyperemia
侧支循环/側支循環　collateral circulation
侧支循环动脉/側支循環動脈　collateral artery
侧柱/側柱　lateral column
测定/測定,鑑定,分析　assay
测谎/測謊　lie detection
测角计/測角計　goniometer
测力法/測力法　ergometry
测力图/肌力描記波,肌功波　ergogram
测量模型/測量模型　measurement model
测量器/測量器,調查員　surveyor
测颅法/測顱術　cephalometry
测膜镜/測薄膜鏡　leptoscope
测热辐射器/熱射線計　pyroscope
测算疗法/測算療法,計數療法　metrotherapy
测痛计/測痛計　dolorimeter
测微法/測微法,量微法　micrometry
测微辐计/測微輻射計,輻射微量計　radiomicrometer
测微计/測微計,量微器　micrometer
测压法/測壓法　manometry
测压性传导阻滞/測壓性傳導阻滯　manometric block
测验/試驗,檢查　test
策动心理学/策動心理學　hormic psychology
策尔韦格综合征/Zellweger 氏症候群　Zellweger syndrome
参差表面描绘术/參差表面描繪術　fractography
岑克尔变性/岑克爾氏變性　zenkerism
岑克尔溶液/Zenker 氏溶液　Zenker solution
层/層　lamina, stratum, layer
层板状的/分層的　laminated
层叠状血栓/層疊狀血栓　stratified thrombus
层级/層級,分層　hierarchy
层流洁净工作台/層流清淨檯　laminar flow clean bench
层流洁净室/層流清淨室　laminar flow clean room
层片硬结/薄層性硬結　laminate induration
层析/層析法　chromatography
层粘连蛋白/層粘連蛋白　laminin
层粘连蛋白受体/層粘連蛋白受體　laminin receptor
叉/叉　fork
叉状的/叉狀的　furcal
叉状神经/叉狀神經　furcal nerve
差别的/差別的　differential
差别基因表达/差別基因表達　differential gene expression
差别基因决定/差別基因決定　differential gene determination
差别生长/差別性生長　differential growth
差动力/差動力　differential force
差热分析/差熱分析　differential thermal analysis
差示温度计/差示溫度計　differential thermometer
差式扫描量热法/差式掃描量熱法　differential scanning calorimetry
差向异构化/差向異構化　epimerization
差向异构体/差向異構體　epimer
差异感觉/異感性,不等感性　heteresthesia
插钉术/釘固術　nailing
插管法/插管法,喉管插入法　intubation
插管前准备/插管前準備　preintubation preparation
插管钳/插管鉗　intubating forcep
插管术/插管術　encheiresis
插管术者/施插管者　intubationist
插管芯/插管芯　intubating stylet
插入/插入　insertion
插入导管/插入導管　catheterize
插入的/插入的　intercalated
插入物/插入物　insert
插入细胞/插入細胞　peg cell
插入[性]期外收缩/插入性期外收縮　interpolated extrasystole
插入序列/插入序列　introns
插入诱变/插入誘變　insertional mutagenesis

插烯物/插烯物　vinylog
插语症/插語症　embolalia
茶/茶　tea
茶苯海明/茶苯海明　dimenhydrinate
茶积/茶積　abdominal mass due to tea addiction
茶剂/茶劑　medicinal tea
茶碱/茶鹼　theophylline
茶癖病/茶癖病　teataster disease
茶树油/茶樹油　tea tree oil
查多克征/查多克徵　Chaddock sign
查尔林综合征/Charlin氏症候群　Charlin syndrome
查尔酮/查爾酮　chalcone
查加斯病/Chagas氏病　Chagas disease
查科三联征/查科三聯徵　Charcot triad
查帕病/卻巴病　chappa
搽剂/搽劑,擦劑　liniment
察目验伤法/察目驗傷法　method by inspecting eyes to examine an injury
佗傺/佗傺　absent-mindedness
拆分/分割,解析　resolution
拆分剂/分割劑　resolving agent
柴葛解肌汤/柴葛解肌湯　chaige jieji decoction
柴胡/柴胡　Chinese thorowax root
柴胡口服液/柴胡口服液　chaihu oral liquid
柴胡疏肝散/柴胡疏肝散　bupleurum powder for relieving liver qi, chaihu shugan powder
掺药/摻藥　dusting powder medicine
掺药法/摻藥法　dusting powder drug method
掺杂物/摻雜［物］　adulterant
缠缚疗法/纏縛療法　binding therapy
缠喉风/纏喉風　tangling throat wind
缠丝痧/纏絲痧　winding filament sha disease
蝉蜕/蟬蛻　cicada slough
蟾蜍疗法/蟾酥毒素療法　bufotherapy
蟾蜍甾/蟾蜍類固醇　bufanolide
蟾蜍中毒/蟾蜍中毒　phrynin poisoning
蟾毒素/蟾［酥］毒素　bufotoxin
蟾毒色胺/蟾酥皮腺素　bufotenin
蟾皮病/蟾皮病　phrynoderma
蟾腮腺素/蟾酥腮腺素　bufin
蟾酥/蟾酥　toad venom
蟾酥甾类/蟾酥甾類　bufanolides
镵针/鑱針　shear needle
产补体白细胞/產補體白血球　alexocyte
产程/產程　labor
产程图/產程圖　partogram
产出性的/產生性的　productive
产次/產次　parity

产道/產道　birth canal
产道裂伤/產道裂傷　laceration of birth canal
产地加工/產地加工　processing in production place
产毒性/產毒性　toxigenicity
产毒性腹泻/產毒性腹瀉　toxigenic diarrhea
产房/產房　delivery room
产妇/產婦　parturient
产妇死亡率/產婦死亡率,母死亡率　maternal mortality
产妇卫生保健服务/產婦衛生保健服務　maternal health services
产后/分娩後的　postpartum
产后保健/產後保健　postnatal care
产后病/產後病　puerperal disease
产后病脉/產後病脈　morbid postpartum pulse
产后病诊法/產後病診法　diagnostics for postpartum disease
产后常脉/產後常脈　regular postpartum pulse
产后出血/產後出血　postpartum hemorrhage
产后垂体功能不全综合征/Sheehan氏症候群　Sheehan syndrome
产后大便难/產後大便難　puerperal constipation
产后大便难·脾肺气虚证/產後大便難·脾肺氣虛證　postpartum constipation with pattern of qi deficiency of spleen and lung
产后大便难·血虚津亏证/產後大便難·血虛津虧證　postpartum constipation with pattern of blood deficiency and fluid depletion
产后发狂/產後發狂　postnatal mania
产后发热/產後發熱　puerperal fever
产后发热·感染邪毒证/產後發熱·感染邪毒證　postpartum fever with pattern of pathogenic toxin
产后发热·气虚证/產後發熱·氣虛證　postpartum fever with qi deficiency pattern
产后发热·外感证/產後發熱·外感證　postpartum fever with exogenous infection pattern
产后发热·血虚证/產後發熱·血虛證　postpartum fever with blood deficiency pattern
产后发热·血瘀证/產後發熱·血瘀證　postpartum fever with blood stasis pattern
产后发育/出生後發育　postnatal development
产后忿/產後忿　postnatal emotional stress
产后腹痛/產後腹痛　postpartum abdominal pain
产后腹痛·寒凝血瘀证/產後腹痛·寒凝血瘀證　postpartum abdominal pain with pattern of cold congelation and blood stasis
产后腹痛·气血两虚证/產後腹痛·氣血兩虛證　postpartum abdominal pain with pattern of

deficiency of both qi and blood
产后宫缩痛/產後宮縮痛　after-pains
产后恍惚/產後恍惚　postnatal absent-minded
产后惊悸/產後驚悸　postnatal palpitation
产后精神病/產後精神病　postpartum psychosis
产后痉/產後痙　postpartum convulsion, postpartum tetanus
产后痉病/產後痙病　postpartum convulsion disease
产后痉病•感染邪毒证/產後痙病•感染邪毒證　postpartum convulsion disease with pattern of pathogenic toxin
产后痉病•阴血不足证/產後痙病•陰血不足證　postpartum convulsion disease with pattern of yin blood insufficiency
产后狂越/產後狂越　postnatal mania
产后麻瞀/產後麻瞀　postnatal numbness of the body
产后目病/產後目病　postpartum eye disease
产后目病•肝气郁结证/產後目病•肝氣鬱結證　postpartum eye disease with liver qi stagnation pattern
产后目病•气血两虚证/產後目病•氣血兩虛證　postpartum eye disease with qi-blood deficiency pattern
产后目病•瘀血凝滞证/產後目病•瘀血凝滯證　postpartum eye disease with pattern of static blood coagulation and stagnation
产后尿毒症/產後尿毒症　puerperal uremia
产后尿血/產後尿血　postpartum hematuria
产后脓毒病/產後敗血病　puerperal sepsis
产后破伤风/產後破傷風　puerperal tetanus
产后期/產後期　postpartum period
产后乳腺炎/產後乳腺炎　postpartum mastitis
产后三禁/產後三禁　three contraindications for postpartum treatment
产后三审/產後三審　observing three postpartum items
产后伤暑/產後傷暑　postpartum summerheat affection
产后身痛/產後身痛　postpartum body pain, postpartum pain of body
产后身痛•风寒证/產後身痛•風寒證　postpartum body pain with wind-cold pattern
产后身痛•肾虚证/產後身痛•腎虛證　postpartum body pain with kidney deficiency pattern
产后身痛•血虚证/產後身痛•血虛證　postpartum body pain with blood deficiency pattern
产后身痛•血瘀证/產後身痛•血瘀證　postpartum body pain with blood stasis pattern
产后室/分娩恢复室　postdelivery room
产后输卵管闭塞/產後輸卵管閉塞　puerperal tubal occlusion
产后脱发/產後禿髮　postpartum alopecia
产后小便不通/產後小便不通　postpartum retention of urine
产后小便不通•气虚证/產後小便不通•氣虛證　postpartum retention of urine with qi deficiency pattern
产后小便不通•气滞证/產後小便不通•氣滯證　postpartum retention of urine with qi stagnation pattern
产后小便不通•肾虚证/產後小便不通•腎虛證　postpartum retention of urine with kidney deficiency pattern
产后小便不通•血瘀证/產後小便不通•血瘀證　postpartum retention of urine with blood stasis pattern
产后小便淋痛/產後小便淋痛　postpartum stranguria, postpartum strangury
产后小便淋痛•肝经郁热证/產後小便淋痛•肝經鬱熱證　postpartum strangury with pattern of heat stagnating in Liver Channel
产后小便淋痛•肾阴虚证/產後小便淋痛•腎陰虛證　postpartum strangury with pattern of kidney yin deficiency
产后小便淋痛•湿热[蕴结]证/產後小便淋痛•濕熱[蘊結]證　postpartum strangury with pattern of accumulation and binding of damp-heat
产后小便频数/產後小便頻數　postpartum frequent urination, postpartum frequent urine
产后小便频数•气虚证/產後小便頻數•氣虛證　postpartum frequent urination with qi deficiency pattern
产后小便频数•肾虚证/產後小便頻數•腎虛證　postpartum frequent urination with kidney deficiency pattern
产后小便失禁/產後小便失禁　postpartum enuresis
产后小便失禁•产伤证/產後小便失禁•產傷證　postpartum enuresis with pattern of birth injury
产后小便失禁•气虚证/產後小便失禁•氣虛證　postpartum enuresis with qi deficiency pattern
产后小便失禁•肾虚证/產後小便失禁•腎虛證　postpartum enuresis with kidney deficiency pattern
产后心烦/產後心煩　postnatal vexation
产后休止期脱发/產後休止期落髮　postpartum telogen effluvium

产后虚羸/產後虛羸　postpartum debility
产后虚羸·肺肾阴虚证/產後虛羸·肺腎陰虛證　postpartum debility with pattern of yin deficiency of lung and kidney
产后虚羸·脾肾阳虚证/產後虛羸·脾腎陽虛證　postpartum debility with pattern of yang deficiency of spleen and kidney
产后虚羸·气虚证/產後虛羸·氣虛證　postpartum debility with qi deficiency pattern
产后虚羸·血虚证/產後虛羸·血虛證　postpartum debility with blood deficiency pattern
产后血崩/產後血崩　massive postpartum hemorrhage, postpartum haemorrhage
产后血崩·产伤证/產後血崩·產傷證　massive postpartum hemorrhage with pattern of birth injury
产后血崩·气不摄血证/產後血崩·氣不攝血證　massive postpartum hemorrhage with pattern of failure of qi to keep blood
产后血崩·血热内扰证/產後血崩·血熱內擾證　massive postpartum hemorrhage with pattern of internal disturbance of blood heat
产后血崩·瘀血内阻证/產後血崩·瘀血內阻證　massive postpartum hemorrhage with pattern of internal blockade of static blood
产后血栓形成/產後血栓形成　puerperal thrombosis
产后血晕/產後血暈　postpartum anemic fainting, postpartum hemorrhagic syncope
产后血晕·血虚气脱证/產後血暈·血虛氣脫證　postpartum hemorrhagic syncope with pattern of qi collapse due to blood deficiency
产后血晕·血瘀气逆证/產後血暈·血瘀氣逆證　postpartum hemorrhagic syncope with pattern of qi counter-flowing and blood stasis
产后遗粪/產後遺糞　puerperal incontinence of feces
产后抑郁·肝气郁结证/產後抑鬱·肝氣鬱結證　postpartum depression with pattern of liver qi depression
产后抑郁·心脾两虚证/產後抑鬱·心脾兩虛證　postpartum depression with pattern of heart-spleen deficiency
产后抑郁·瘀血内阻证/產後抑鬱·瘀血內阻證　postpartum depression with pattern of internal blockade of static blood
产后抑郁[症]/產後抑鬱[症]　postnatal depression, postpartum depression
产后喑/產後喑　postpartum dysphonia
产后痈/產後癰　postpartum abscess
产后郁冒/產後鬱冒　postnatal depression and vertigo
产后躁狂/產後躁狂　puerperal mania
产后阵痛/產後痛　dolores postpartum
产后子宫内膜炎/產後子宮內膜炎　puerperal endometritis
产后子宫炎/子宮病,產褥性子宮炎　metria
产后子痫/產後子癇　eclampsia postpartum
产后自汗盗汗/產後自汗盜汗　postpartum spontaneous and night sweating, spontaneous sweating and night sweating after childbirth
产后自汗盗汗·气虚证/產後自汗盜汗·氣虛證　postpartum spontaneous and night sweating with qi deficiency pattern
产后自汗盗汗·阴虚证/產後自汗盜汗·陰虛證　postpartum spontaneous and night sweating with yin deficiency pattern
产黄青霉/產黃青黴菌　Penicillium chrysogenum
产碱杆菌属/產鹼桿菌屬　*Alkaligenes*
产科/產科　department of obstetrics
产科出血/產科出血　obstetric hemorrhage
产科的/產科的　obstetrical
产科护理/產科護理　obstetrical nursing
产科接生/產科接生　obstetric delivery
产科结合径/產科直徑,真直徑　obstetric conjugate
产科麻醉/產科麻醉　obstetrical anesthesia
产科取胎术/產科取胎術　obstetrical extraction
产科听诊/產科聽診法　obstetric auscultation
产科外科手术/產科外科手術　obstetric surgical procedures
产科学/產科學　obstetrics
产科医师/產科醫師　obstetrician
产科医院/產科醫院　maternity hospital
产科真空吸胎术/產科真空吸胎術　obstetrical vacuum extraction
产科镇痛/產科鎮痛　obstetrical analgesia
产力异常/產力異常　abnormal uterine action
产量/產量　output
产酶棒状杆菌/酵素棒狀桿菌　corynebacterium enzymicum
产气/[组织或器官内]產氣　aerosis
产气的/氣性的　aerogenic
产气夹膜杆菌/產氣夾膜桿菌　perfringens
产气夹膜梭菌/產氣夾膜梭狀芽孢桿菌　Clostridium perfringens
产气菌/產氣菌　aerogen
产前/產前　antepartum
产前保健/產前保健,產前護理　antenatal care
产前暴露迟发效应/產前暴露遲發效應　prenatal

exposure delayed effect
产前超声检查/產前超聲檢查 prenatal ultrasonography
产前出血/產前出血 antepartum hemorrhage
产前发育/出生前發育 prenatal development
产前诊断/產前診斷 prenatal diagnosis
产前子痫/產前子癇 eclampsia antepartum
产钳/產[科]鉗 obstetrical forcep
产钳术/產鉗術 obstetric forcep delivery
产青霉素酶淋病性奈瑟氏菌/產生青黴素酶的淋病雙球菌 penicillinase producing Neisseria gonorrhoeae
产热/熱之產生,產熱作用 thermogenesis
产褥病/產褥病,產後病 puerperalism
产褥护士/產褥護士,產婦護理人員,產後護士 monthly nurse
产褥期/產褥期,產後期 puerperal state
产褥期的/產後的,產褥的 puerperal
产褥期感染/產後感染 puerperal infection
产褥期疾病/產褥期疾病 puerperal disorder
产褥期精神病/產褥精神病,產後精神病 puerperal psychosis
产褥期乳腺炎/產後乳腺炎 puerperal mastitis
产褥期子宫炎/產褥性子宮炎 puerperal metritis
产褥期子痫/產後子癇 puerperal eclampsia
产褥热/產褥熱 childbed fever
产褥性滑膜炎/產褥性滑膜炎 puerperal synovitis
产褥性失语/產褥性失語 puerperal aphasia
产褥性猩红热/產褥猩紅熱 puerperal scarlatina
产伤/產傷 birth injury
产伤麻痹/分娩癱瘓 birth palsy
产伤性麻痹/產科麻痺 obstetric paralysis
产生变应性化合物/產生過敏的化合物 allergy-producing compound
产生胶原的/產生膠原的 collagenous
产生焦痂的/產生焦痂的 escharotic
产生菌/生產菌 producing strain
产生色素的/產生色素的 pigment-producing
产生色素细胞/產生色素的細胞 pigment-producing cell
产时子痫/產時子癇 eclampsia intrapartum
产式/產式 labor presentation
产物/產物 product
产幼虫/產幼蟲 larviposition
产院/產院 birthing center
铲形手/鏟形手 spade hand
颤搐/牽搐,抽筋 twitch
颤动线/振動線 vibrating line

颤抖/顫抖 jitter
颤音/震顫性發音困難 tromophonia
颤振·肝风内动证/顫振·肝風內動證 tremor disease with pattern of internal stirring of liver wind
颤振·气血两虚证/顫振·氣血兩虛證 tremor disease with pattern of deficiency of both qi and blood
颤振·髓海不足证/顫振·髓海不足證 tremor disease with pattern of marrow sea insufficiency
颤振·痰热动风证/顫振·痰熱動風證 tremor disease with pattern of wind stirring due to phlegm-heat
颤振·血瘀风动证/顫振·血瘀風動證 tremor disease with pattern of moving wind due to blood stasis
颤振·阳气虚衰证/顫振·陽氣虛衰證 tremor disease with pattern of yang qi exhaustion
菖蒲苦苷/白菖[蒲]素 acorin
猖獗龋/猖獗齲 rampant caries
长臂/長臂 long-arm
长臂猿白血病病毒/長臂猿白血病病毒 gibbon ape leukemia virus
长波紫外线/長波紫外線 long-wave ultraviolet
长春胺/長春胺 vincamine
长春地辛/長春地辛 vindesine
长春花生物碱类/長春花生物鹼類 vinca alkaloids
长春碱/長春鹼 vinblastine
长春新碱/長春新鹼 vincristine
长唇子宫颈/獏嘴狀子宮頸 tapiroid cervix
长顶盖/長頂蓋 long coping
长[度]/長度 length
长放线状的/長放射狀的 longiradiate
长骨干的/長骨幹的 diaphyseal
长冠牙/牛牙症 taurodontism
长[管]骨/長骨 long bone
长光程吸收池/長光程貯液槽池 long path cell
长核苷酸组件/長核苷酸元件 long interspersed nucleotide element
长肌/長肌 long muscle
长 Q-T 间期综合征/長 Q-T 間期症候群 long Q-T syndrome
长脚/長腳 long crus
长结肠/長結腸[畸形] dolichocolon
长结合上皮/長結合上皮 long junctional epithelium
长颈者/長頸[畸形] dolichoderus
长链酰基 CoA 脱氢酶/長鏈醯基 CoA 脫氫酶 long-chain acyl-CoA dehydrogenase
长脉/長脈 long pulse
长膜壳绦虫/縮小包膜蟲,縮小條蟲 Hymenolepis diminuta
长膜壳绦虫病/長膜殼條蟲病 hymenolepiasis

diminuta
长期毒性／長期毒性 long-term toxicity
长期糖尿病综合征／長期糖尿病症候群 long-term diabetic syndrome
长期医疗／長期醫療 long-term care
长期医疗保险／長期醫療保險 long-term care insurance
长期抑制／長期抑制 long-term depression
长期照料／長期照料 long-term care
长潜伏期肝炎／長潛伏期肝炎 long-incubation hepatitis
长强／長強 changqiang, DU1
长时程增强／長時程增強 long-term potentiation
长收肌／内收長肌 adductor longus
长寿／長壽 longevity
长寿膳食／含穀類飲食 macrobiotic diet
长寿商／長壽商 longevity quotient
长寿水平／長壽水準 longevity level
长[统]袜／長襪 stocking
长头／長頭 long head
长头的／長頭的 dolichocephalic
长突[神经胶质]细胞／長放射形細胞 longiradiate cell
长尾单鞭滴虫／長尾單鞭蟲 Cercomonas longicauda
长尾精子／長尾精子,長絲精子 nematospermia
长吸呼吸／長吸式呼吸 apneusis
长效甲状腺刺激物／長效甲狀腺刺激物 long-acting thyroid stimulator
长效胰岛素／長效型胰島素鋅懸液,胰島素晶懸液,緩慢胰島素 lente insulin, ultralente insulin
长叶薄荷酮／胡薄荷酮 pulegone
长针／長針 long needle
长正中／長正中 long centric
长中央动脉／長中央動脈 long central artery
长轴观／長軸觀 long-axis view
肠／腸 bowel
肠癌／腸癌 intestinal cancer
肠闭锁／腸閉鎖 intestinal atresia
肠痹／腸痹 intestinal painful impediment
肠壁囊样积气症／腸壁囊樣積氣症 pneumatosis cystoides intestinalis
肠壁黏膜[层]突出／腸壁黏膜突出,黏膜疝 mucosal hernia
肠壁疝／腸壁疝,李希特氏疝 parietal hernia
肠病／腸病 enteropathy
肠病毒感染／腸病毒感染 enteroviral infection
肠病发生机理／腸病之發生 enteropathogenesis
肠病性／腸病性 enteropathica

肠病性关节炎／腸病性關節炎 enteropathic arthritis
肠病性肢端皮炎／胃腸性肢皮炎 acrodermatitis enteropathica
肠病学／腸學 enterology
肠道病原体／腸病原 enteropathogen
肠侧侧吻合[术]／腸側側吻合[術] side-to-side intestinal anastomosis
肠肠吻合术／腸與腸造口吻合術 enteroenterostomy
肠肠系膜闭塞／腸與腸繫膜阻塞 enteromesenteric occlusion
肠肠系膜的／腸與腸繫膜的 enteromesenteric
肠成形术／腸造形術 enteroplasty
肠虫性阑尾炎／腸蟲性闌尾炎,寄生蟲性闌尾炎 helminthic appendicitis
肠重复畸形／腸重複畸形 duplication of intestine
肠穿刺术／腸穿刺術 enterocentesis
肠穿孔／腸穿孔 intestinal perforation
肠丛／腸叢 enteric plexus
肠促胰酶素／胰外分泌激素 pancreozymin
肠促胰液素／小腸胰泌素 secretin
肠袋虫属／纖毛蟲屬 *Balantidium*
肠胆囊切开术／腸膽囊切開術 enterocholecystotomy
肠刀／腸刀 enterotome
肠道／腸道 intestinal tract
肠道病毒／腸病毒 enteric virus
肠道病毒感染／腸道病毒感染 enterovirus infection
肠道出血／腸出血 intestinal hemorrhage
肠道孤儿病毒／腸性孤獨型病毒 enteric orphan virus
肠道清洗／洗腸 intestinal lavage
肠道透析／腸道透析 intestinal dialysis
肠道细菌内毒素移位／腸道細菌內毒素移位 endotoxin translocation from intestine
肠道细菌移位／腸道細菌移位 bacterial translocation from intestine
肠道营养／腸道營養 enteral nutrition
肠的／腸的 enteric, intestinal
肠动静脉畸形／腸動靜脈畸形 arteriovenous malformation of bowel
肠动描记法／腸運動記錄 enterography
肠动描记器／腸運動記錄器 enterograph
肠动[描记]图／腸動描記圖 enterogram
肠毒素／腸毒素,腸細胞毒 enterotoxin
肠毒血症／腸毒血症 enterotoxemia
肠端侧吻合[术]／腸端側吻合[術] end-to-side intestinal anastomosis
肠端端吻合[术]／腸端端吻合[術] end-to-end intestinal anastomosis

肠段移植物/腸段移植物　intestinal segment graft
肠放射性损伤/腸放射性損傷　radiation injury of intestine
肠分泌物/腸分泌物　intestinal secretion
肠缝术/腸縫合術　enterorrhaphy
肠缝线/腸縫線　catgut suture
肠肝固定术/腸肝固定術　enterohepatopexy
肠肝循环/肝腸循環　hepato-enteric circulation, enterohepatic circulation
肠肝炎/腸肝炎　enterohepatitis
肠杆菌科/腸細菌科　Enterobacteriaceae
肠杆菌科感染/腸桿菌科感染　Enterobacteriaceae infection
肠杆菌属/腸桿菌屬　*Enterobacter*
肠杆菌素/腸菌素　enterobactin
肠干/腸幹　intestinal trunk
肠梗塞/腸梗塞　intestinal infarction
肠梗阻/腸阻塞　intestinal obstruction
肠沟/腸溝　intestinal groove
肠垢/腸垢　putrid stool
肠管旁淋巴结/腸管旁淋巴結　juxtaintestinal lymph node
肠肌层/腸肌層　myenteron
肠肌层的/腸肌層的　myenteric
肠肌丛/腸肌叢　myenteric plexus, plexus myentericus
肠肌神经丛/腸肌神經叢　myenteric nervous plexus
肠激肽/腸激肽　enterokinin
肠疾病/腸疾病　intestinal disease
肠假性梗阻/腸假性梗阻　intestinal pseudo-obstruction
肠浆膜炎/腸漿膜炎　seroenteritis
肠绞痛/腸絞痛　intestinal colic
肠节/腸胚節　enteromere
肠结核/腸結核　tuberculosis of intestine
肠痉挛/腸痙攣　intestinal spasm
肠[窥]镜/腸内視鏡，檢腸鏡　enteroscope
肠扩张/腸擴張，腸膨脹　enterectasis
肠兰[伯]氏鞭毛虫/腸蘭伯氏鞭毛蟲，蘭伯氏賈第蟲　Lamblia intestinalis
肠淋巴管扩张/腸淋巴管擴張　intestinal lymphangiectasia
肠瘘/腸瘻　intestinal fistula
肠鳗状虫/腸鰻狀蟲　Anguillula intestinalis
肠面/腸面　intestinal surface
肠鸣/腸鳴　borborygmus
肠囊瘤/腸囊瘤　enterocystoma
肠囊肿/腸囊腫　enteric cyst

肠内分泌细胞/腸内分泌細胞　enteroendocrine cell
肠内菌丛/腸内菌叢，腸内微生物　intestinal flora
肠内空虚/無糞便[形成]　acoprosis
肠内泌素/腸内泌素　duodenal autacoid
肠内吸收/腸内吸收　enteral absorption
肠内引流式胰腺移植/腸内引流式胰腺移植　enteric drainage pancreas transplantation
肠黏膜/腸黏膜　intestinal mucosa
肠黏膜炎/腸黏膜炎　endoenteritis
肠扭转/腸扭轉　intestinal volvulus
肠旁路术/腸旁路術　intestinal bypass
肠旁路综合征/腸分流症候群　bowel bypass syndrome
肠膀胱的/腸與膀胱的　enterovesical
肠膀胱瘘/腸膀胱瘻管　enterovesical fistula
肠膀胱疝/腸膀胱疝氣，腸膀胱赫尼亞　enterocystocele
肠胚外翻畸形/腸胚外翻畸形，原腸胚外翻　extrogastrulation
肠皮肤的/腸及皮膚的　enterocutaneous
肠蜣螂病/腸甲蟲病　scarabiasis
肠切除术/腸切除術　intestinal resection
肠切开术/腸切開術　enterotomy
肠球菌/腸球菌　enterococci
肠球菌感染/腸球菌感染　enterococcal infection
肠球菌血症/腸球菌血症　enterococcemia
肠蛆病/腸蛆病　enteromyiasis
肠缺血/腸缺血　ischemia of intestine
肠缺血综合征/腸缺血症候群　intestinal ischemic syndrome
肠绕道综合征/腸繞道症候群　bowel bypass syndrome
肠热病/腸熱病　enteroidea
肠热症/腸熱病　enteric fever
肠绒毛/腸絨毛　intestinal villus
肠绒毛促动素/腸絨毛激素　villikinin
肠溶片剂/腸衣錠[劑]　enteric coated tablet
肠溶丸剂/腸用丸劑，避胃丸劑　enteric pill
肠溶衣/腸衣　enteric coat
肠沙/腸沙，腸砂　intestinal sand
肠疝切开术/腸疝切開術　hernioenterotomy
肠神经系统/腸神經系統　enteric nervous system
肠神经炎/腸神經炎　enteroneuritis
肠渗血/腸滲血　enterostaxis
肠生的/腸原的　enterogenous
肠石/腸石　enterolith
肠石病/腸石病　enterolithiasis
肠嗜铬细胞/腸嗜鉻細胞，腸親鉻細胞

enterochromaffin cell
肠嗜铬样细胞/腸嗜鉻樣細胞 enterochromaffin-like cell
肠肽酶/腸肽酶 enteropeptidase
肠罩/腸罩 female abdominal mass
肠炭疽/腸炭疽 intestinal anthrax
肠套叠/腸套疊 intussusception
肠体腔/腸體腔 enterocoele
肠痛/腸痛 enteralgia
肠外瘘/腸皮瘘 enterocutaneous fistula
肠外置术/腸外置術 intestinal exteriorization
肠胃外吸收/非肠胃道吸收 parenteral absorption
肠胃型流行性感冒/腸胃型流行性感冒 gastrointerstinal influenza
肠胃炎/腸胃炎,胃腸炎 enterogastritis
肠胃胀气/胃腸氣積 flatulence
肠吻合[术]/腸吻合術,腸接合術 intestinal anastomosis
肠紊乱/腸紊亂 bowel disturbance
肠吸附/腸蓄積 enterosorption
肠吸收/腸吸收 intestinal absorption
肠息肉/腸息肉 intestinal polyp
肠息肉病/腸息肉病 intestinal polyposis
肠系膜/腸繫膜 mesentery, mesenterium
肠系膜穿透疝/腸繫膜穿透疝 transmesenteric hernia
肠系膜的/腸繫膜的 mesenteric
肠系膜动脉/腸繫膜動脈 mesenteric artery
肠系膜动脉闭塞/腸繫膜動脈閉塞 mesenteric arterial occlusion
肠系膜动脉栓塞术/腸繫膜動脈栓塞術 mesenteric artery embolization
肠系膜动脉性肠阻塞/腸繫膜血管性腸阻塞 arteriomesenteric ileus
肠系膜动脉血栓形成/腸繫膜動脈血栓形成 mesenteric artery thrombosis
肠系膜缝术/腸繫膜縫合術 mesenteriorrhaphy
肠系膜根/腸繫膜根 radix of mesentery
肠系膜梗塞/腸繫膜梗塞 mesenteric infarction
肠系膜固定术/腸繫膜固定術 mesenteriopexy
肠系膜间丛/腸繫膜間叢 intermesenteric plexus
肠系膜间的/腸繫膜間的 intermesenteric
肠系膜绞痛/腸繫膜絞痛 mesenteric angina
肠系膜静脉/腸繫膜靜脈 mesenteric vein
肠系膜静脉血栓形成/腸繫膜靜脈血栓形成 mesenteric venous thrombosis
肠系膜裂孔疝/腸繫膜裂孔疝 mesenteric hiatal hernia
肠系膜淋巴结/腸繫膜淋巴結 mesenteric lymph node, mesenteric glands
肠系膜淋巴腺炎/腸繫膜淋巴腺炎 mesenteric lymphadenitis
肠系膜囊肿/腸繫膜囊腫 mesenteric cyst
肠系膜切除术/腸繫膜切除術 mesenterectomy
肠系膜疝/腸繫膜疝 mesenteric hernia
肠系膜上丛/腸繫膜上叢 superior mesenteric plexus
肠系膜上动脉/腸繫膜上動脈 superior mesenteric artery
肠系膜上动脉压迫综合征/腸繫膜上動脈壓迫症候群 superior mesenteric artery compression syndrome
肠系膜上静脉/腸繫膜上靜脈 superior mesenteric vein
肠系膜上淋巴结/腸繫膜上淋巴結 superior mesenteric lymph node
肠系膜上神经节/腸繫膜上神經節 superior mesenteric ganglion
肠系膜下丛/腸繫膜下叢 inferior mesenteric plexus, plexus mesentericus inferior
肠系膜下动脉/腸繫膜下動脈 inferior mesenteric artery
肠系膜下静脉/腸繫膜下靜脈 inferior mesenteric vein
肠系膜下淋巴结/腸繫膜下淋巴結 inferior mesenteric lymph node
肠系膜下神经节/腸繫膜下神經節 inferior mesenteric ganglion
肠系膜血管闭塞/腸繫膜血管閉塞 mesenteric vascular occlusion
肠系膜血管性肠梗阻/腸繫膜血管性腸阻塞 angiomesenteric ileus
肠系膜血管血栓形成/腸繫膜血栓形成 mesenteric thrombosis
肠系膜炎/腸繫膜炎 mesenteritis
肠系膜折叠术/腸繫膜折疊術 mesenteriplication
肠系膜中央淋巴结/腸繫膜中央淋巴結 central mesenteric lymph node
肠细胞/腸細胞 enterocyte
肠狭窄/腸狹窄 intestinal stenosis
肠下垂/腸下垂 enteroptosis
肠下垂体型/腸下垂體型 habitus enteroptoticus
肠腺/腸腺,腸濾泡 intestinal follicle, intestinal gland
肠腺炎/腸腺炎 enteradenitis
肠消化不良/腸消化不良 intestinal indigestion
肠型流感/腸型流行性感冒 intestinal influenza

肠性白血病/腸性白血病　intestinal leukemia
肠性毒血症/糞中毒,糞血症　scatemia
肠性脓毒症/腸性敗血症　sepsis intestinalis
肠性消化不良/腸性消化不良　intestinal dyspepsia
肠性眩晕/腸性眩暈　intestinal vertigo
肠性幼稚型/腸性幼稚型　intestinal infantilism
肠旋转不良/腸旋轉不良　malrotation of intestine
肠血管病/腸血管病　vascular disease of bowel
肠血管发育异常/腸血管發育異常　angiodysplasia of bowel
肠血管异常/腸血管異常　vascular abnormality of intestine
肠炎/腸炎　enteritis
[肠]炎性腹泻/炎性腹瀉　inflammatory diarrhea
肠液/腸液　intestinal juice
肠衣片剂/腸衣片劑　enteric-coated tablet
肠抑胃素/腸抑胃素　enterogastrone
肠抑胃肽/腸抑胃肽　gastric inhibitory polypeptide
肠易激综合征/腸易激症候群　irritable bowel syndrome
肠阴道的/腸與陰道的　enterovaginal
肠阴道瘘/腸陰道瘻管　enterovaginal fistula
肠痈/腸癰　acute appendicitis, intestinal abscess
肠痈·气滞血瘀证/腸癰·氣滯血瘀證　intestinal abscess with pattern of qi stagnation and blood stasis
肠痈·热毒炽盛证/腸癰·熱毒熾盛證　intestinal abscess with blazing heat-toxin pattern
肠痈·瘀滞化热证/腸癰·瘀滯化熱證　intestinal abscess with pattern of static blood and stagnated qi transforming into heat
肠郁滞/腸停滯　enterostasis
肠源性发绀/腸原性發紺病　enterogenous cyanosis
肠源性感染/腸原性感染　enterogenic infection
肠源性囊肿/腸原性囊腫　enterogenous cyst
肠源性脂肪代谢障碍/腸管脂肪營養異常,腸性脂質失養症　intestinal lipodystrophy
肠源性自体中毒/腸原中毒　enterotoxication
肠运动描记器/腸蠕動描繪器　ecterograph
肠造口术/腸造口術,腸造瘻術　enterostomy
肠粘连切开术/腸粘連切開術　synechtenterotomy
肠粘连松解术/腸粘連分離術　enterolysis
肠胀气/腸氣鼓,鼓肠　intestinal tympanites
肠[真]菌病/腸黴菌病　enteromycosis
肠中毒/腸性中毒　intestinal intoxication
肠周腔/腸周腔,原腸腔　perienteron
肠子宫肛门/腸道子宮肛門　entero-uterine anus
肠子宫内膜异位/腸子宮內膜異位　endometriosis in bowel

尝味[者]基因/嘗味基因　taster gene
常规变异型免疫缺陷/尋常變異性免疫缺乏　common variable immunodeficiency
常规尿分析/常規尿分析　routine urinalysis
常规医学/常規醫學　conventional medicine
常规遮盖法/常規遮蓋法　conventional occlusion
常规诊断试验/常規診斷試驗　routine diagnostic test
常年性鼻炎/常年性鼻炎　perennial rhinitis
常年性变应性鼻炎/常年性變應性鼻炎　perennial allergic rhinitis
常染色体/體染色體　autosome
常染色体的/體染色體的　autosomal
常染色体显性多囊肾/體染色體顯性多囊腎　autosomal dominant polycystic kidney
常染色体显性皮肤疾病/體染色體顯性皮膚疾病　autosomal dominant skin disorder
常染色体显性视神经萎缩/體染色體顯性視神經萎縮　autosomal dominant optic atrophy
常染色体显性遗传/體染色體顯性遺傳　autosomal dominant inheritance
常染色体性遗传/體染色體性遺傳　autosomal heredity
常染色体隐性/體染色體隱性　autosomal recessive
常染色体隐性多囊肾/體染色體隱性多囊腎　autosomal recessive polycystic kidney
常染色体隐性皮肤疾病/體染色體隱性皮膚疾病　autosomal recessive skin disorder
常染色体隐性遗传/體染色體隱性遺傳　autosomal recessive inheritance
常染色质/常染色質,真染色質　euchromatin
常色/常色　normal complexion
常山/常山　antifeverile dichroa root
常思狂走/常思狂走　manic running
常温心脏手术/常溫心臟手術　normothermic heart surgery
常现棘唇[线]虫/常現棘唇絲蟲　Dipetalonema perstans
偿还途径/償還途徑　reimbursement mechanism
场发射/場發射　field emission
场流分馏法/場流分餾法　field flow fractionation
场透镜/向場透鏡　field lens
怅然/悵然　deep sadness
超薄切片/超薄切片　ultrathin section
超薄切片机/超薄切片機　ultramicrotome
超闭合[牙]/超閉合[牙]　overclosure
超变区/超變區　hypervariable region

超常传导/超常傳導　supernormal conduction
超常激动/超常激動　supernormal excitation
超常增生/過度增生　hyperplasia
超重振/超重振　over recruitment
超雌/過雌性　superfemale
超短波疗法/超短波療法　ultrashort wave therapy
超短波透热[疗]法/超短波透熱[療]法　ultrashort wave diathermy
超二倍体/超二倍體　hyperdiploid
超反应性/反應過強的　hyperergia
超感知觉/感覺外認識,感覺外反應　extrasensory perception
超高压电子显微镜/超高壓電子顯微鏡　ultrahigh voltage electron microscope
超关节夹板固定/超關節夾板固定　splint fixation over joint
超广谱/超廣譜　superspectrum
超[过]滤[作用]/超過濾　ultrafiltration
超耗氧/額外氧,超額氧　excess oxygen
超基因/超基因　super gene
超极化/超極化,高極化作用　hyperpolarization
超极化阻滞/超極化阻滯　hyperpolarization block
超急性排斥反应/超急性排斥反應　hyperacute rejection
超减力毒素/超低毒素　ultratoxon
超接种/超接種　hypervaccination
超抗原/超強抗原,上層抗原　superantigen
超临界液相色谱法/超臨界液相色譜法　supercritical fluid chromatography
超螺旋/超螺旋　superhelix, supercoil
超滤/超濾　ultrafiltration
超滤膜/超過[濾]膜　ultrafiltration membrane
超滤器/超濾器　ultrafilter
超滤液/超濾液　ultrafiltrate
超媒体/超媒體　hypermedia
超免疫性/高度免疫性,免疫性過度　hyperimmunity
超免疫状态/超免疫狀態　hyperimmune state
超免疫[作用]/高度免疫法,超免疫法　hyperimmunization
超敏感性细胞/超敏感性細胞　supersensitized cell
超排卵/排卵過多　superovulation
超平面/超平面　hyperplane
超气态/超氣態　ultragaseous state
超热力学/超熱力學　extrathermodynamics
超射线透射性/放射性透穿力　hyperlucency
超声波离子导入机/超音波離子導入機　ultrasonic ion transport machine
超声波图/超音波圖　ultrasonogram

超声波性白内障/超音波性白內障　ultrasonic cataract
超声电子计算机切面显像[术]/超音電子電腦切面顯像[術]　ultrasonic computer tomography
超声腹腔镜/超音腹腔鏡　ultrasonic laparoscope
超声混合器/超音波混合器　ultrasonic mixer
超声间动电疗法/超音間動電療法　ultrasound-diadynamic electrotherapy
超声监测/超音監測　ultrasonic monitoring
超声检查/超音波檢查法　ultrasonography
超声洁治器/超音波刮牙器　ultrasonic scaler
超声洁治术/超音波牙結石刮除術　ultrasonic scaling
超声疗法/超音療法　ultrasonic therapy
超声美容术/超音美容術　ultrasonic cosmesis
超声内镜/超音內鏡　ultrasonic endoscope
超声内镜检查/腔内超音檢查　endosonography
超声频率/超音波頻率　supersonic frequency
超声全息/超音全息　ultrasonic holography
超声乳化白内障吸除术/晶狀體乳化法　phacoemulsification
超声扫描术/超音波掃描術　sonography
超声束/超音束　ultrasonic beam
超声碎石术/超音碎石術　ultrasonic lithotripsy
超声损伤/超音損傷　ultrasound injury
超声调制中频电疗法/超音調製中頻電療法　ultrasound-modulated medium frequency electrotherapy
超声透入疗法/超音透入療法　phonophoresis
超声雾化吸入法/超音霧化吸入法　ultrasonic atomizing inhalation
超声吸脂[术]/超音吸脂[術]　ultrasonic liposuction
超声心动描记术/超音波心臟動態診斷[法]　echocardiography
超声诊断/超音診斷　ultrasonic diagnosis
超声振荡器/超音波振盪器　ultrasonator
超视病毒/超視病毒　invisible virus
超视域幻视/超視域幻視　extravisual hallucination
超[数]排卵/超級排卵,超量排卵,排卵過旺　superovulation
超数染色体/超數染色體　supernumerary chromosome
超速离心/超速離心　ultracentrifugation
超速离心法/超速離心法　ultracentrifugation
超速抑制/超速抑制　overdrive suppression
超吞噬的/超吞噬的　hyperphagocytic
超吞噬细胞/超吞噬細胞　hyperphagocytic cell
超吞噬作用/超吞噬現象　ultraphagocytosis

超微量化学/超微量化學　ultramicrochemistry
超微病毒/濾過[性]病毒　ultramicroscopic virus
超微结构/超微結構,微細構造,超微組織　ultrastructure
超微结构病理学/超微結構病理學　ultrastructural pathology
超微粒/超微膠粒　ultramicron
超微粒灰黄霉素/超微粒灰黃黴素　ultramicrosize griseofulvin
超我/超我　superego
超显微镜/超顯微鏡　ultramicroscope
超氧化物类/超氧化物類　superoxides
超氧化物歧化酶/超氧化物歧化酶　superoxide dismutase
超氧阴离子/過氧化物陰離子　superoxide anion
超铀元素/超鈾元素　transuranium
超预防/超預防法　ultraprophylaxis
超重力/超重力　hypergravity
超最适度/超最適度,最適度以上　supraoptimum
巢/巢　nest
朝鲜蓟/朝鮮薊　artichoke
潮波/潮波　tidal wave
潮的/潮的　tidal
潮红/潮紅　flush
潮[流]气/潮流氣　tidal air
潮霉素 B/潮黴素 B　hygromycin B
潮气量/潮氣容量　tidal volume
潮热/潮熱　tidal fever
潮式呼吸/陳-施二氏呼吸　Cheyne-Stokes respiration
潮式引流法/膀胱潮式引流　tidal drainage
炒炭/炒炭　carbonizing by stir-frying
炒[制]/炒　stir-frying
车轮型/車輪型　cart-wheel pattern
车前草/車前草　plantain herb
车前子/車前子　plantago seed, plantain seed
车轴关节/車軸關節　pivot joint, trochoid joint, trochoidal articulation
扯裂[术]/撕開法,扯裂法　divulsion
撤退出血/撤退出血　withdrawal bleeding
臣使之官/臣使之官　pericardium as the minister organ
臣药/臣藥　minister drug
尘埃病/塵病　dust disease
尘埃计算器/大氣塵埃計[算器]　coniometer
尘埃性哮喘/塵埃性氣喘　dust asthma
尘埃学/塵埃學　coniology
尘肺/肺塵埃沈著病,塵肺症　pneumoconiosis
尘肺病/塵肺症　coal-miners disease
尘螨属抗原/塵蟎屬抗原　*Dermatophagoides* antigen
尘细胞/塵埃細胞　dust cell
辰砂/朱砂　cinnabar
沉淀/沈澱　precipitation
沉淀法/沈澱法　precipitation method
沉淀剂/沈澱劑　precipitant
沉淀类毒素/沈降類毒素　precipitated toxoid
沉淀素/沈澱素　precipitin
沉淀素反应/沈澱素反應　precipitin reaction
沉淀素试验/沈澱[素]試驗　precipitin test
沉淀碳酸钙/沈澱碳酸鈣　precipitated calcium carbonate
沉淀物/沈澱物　precipitated
沉淀性抗体/沈澱性抗體　precipitating antibody
沉积/沈積　deposition, deposit
沉积物/沈積物　accretion
沉积症/蓄積病　accumulation disease
沉积[作用]/沈著,沈積　deposition
沉降/沈降　sedimentation
沉降平衡/沈降平衡　sedimentation equilibrium
沉降谱/離心沈降型　sedimentation pattern
沉降时间/沈降時間　sedimentation time
沉降试验/沈降試驗　sedimentation test
沉降速度/沈降速度　sedimentation velocity
沉降系数/沈降係數　sedimentation coefficient
沉脉/沈脈　deep pulse
沉默的/静的　silent
沉香/沈香　Chinese eaglewood
沉渣/沈渣　sediment
陈化/陳化　aging
陈旧[性]骨折/陳舊[性]骨折　old fracture
陈旧性会阴裂伤修补术/陳舊性會陰裂傷修補術　repair of old perineal laceration
陈旧性神经鞘瘤/古老神經鞘瘤　ancient schwannoma
陈旧[性]脱位/陳舊性脱位　old dislocation
陈旧性心肌梗死/陳舊性心肌梗死　old myocardial infarction
陈皮/陳皮　dried tangerine peel
陈-施[托克斯]精神病/契-史二氏精神病　Cheyne-Stokes psychosis
晨僵/晨僵　morning stiffness
衬垫夹板/襯墊夾板　padded splint
衬里皮瓣/襯裡皮瓣　lining skin flap
衬细胞/沿竇細胞　littoral cell
撑开牵引[术]/撐開牽引[術]　distraction

撑口器/撑口器　mouth prop
撑起夹/撑起夾　cock-up splint
成白细胞/母白血球　leukoblast
成斑[点]/成斑,斑點狀態　maculation
成孢子细胞/成孢子細胞,芽孢細胞　sporoblast
成本效益分析/成本效益分析　cost-benefit analysis
成层胶/成層膠　spacer gel
成初乳小体/初乳小體,初乳母細胞　galactoblast
成串期前收缩/成串期前收縮　salvo premature beat
成单核细胞/單核母細胞　monoblast
成单核细胞瘤/單核母細胞瘤　monoblastoma
成对刺激/成對刺激　couple stimulation
成对孔/接合孔　conjugate foramen
成对联想学习/成對聯想學習　paired-associate learning
成对期前收缩/成對期前收縮　couplets premature beat
成骨不全/成骨不全,骨發生不全　osteogenesis imperfecta
成骨层/骨原層　osteogenic layer
成骨骼的/骨骼生成的　skeletogenous
成骨骨肉瘤/骨母細胞骨肉瘤　osteoblastic osteosarcoma
成骨区/成骨區　zone of ossification
成骨细胞/成骨細胞　osteogenic cell, osteoblast
成骨细胞的/骨母細胞的　osteoblastic
成骨细胞瘤/成骨細胞瘤,骨母細胞瘤　osteoblastoma
成骨细胞肉瘤/成骨細胞肉瘤　osteoblastic sarcoma
成骨性癌/成骨性癌　osteoblastic cancer
成骨的/骨性的,骨原的　osteogenic
成骨质/成骨質,造骨質　osteogen
成骨组织/成骨組織　osteogenic tissue
成黑[色]素细胞/成黑素細胞　melanoblast
成黑素细胞病/黑母細胞症　melanoblastosis
成红细胞/紅血球母細胞　erythroblast
成红细胞减少症/紅血球母細胞缺乏症　erythroblastopenia
成红细胞瘤/母紅血球瘤　erythroblastoma
成红细胞瘤病/母紅血球瘤病　erythroblastomatosis
成活/成活　take
成肌细胞/成肌細胞　myoblasts
成肌细胞的/肌母細胞的　myoblastic
成肌细胞瘤/肌胚細胞[性肌]瘤　myoblastic myoma
成肌纤维细胞瘤/肌纖維母細胞瘤　myofibroblastoma
成脊索细胞瘤/脊索胚癌,脊索胚瘤　chordoblastoma
成绩不良/成績不良　underachievement

成键[分子]轨道/鍵結軌域　bonding molecular orbital
成浆细胞/成漿細胞,漿母細胞　plasmablast
成交感神经细胞/交感神經母細胞　sympathetoblast
成交感神经细胞瘤/交感神經母細胞瘤　sympathicoblastoma
成交感细胞/成形交感細胞　sympathetic formative cell
成胶原细胞/膠原母細胞　collagenoblast
成角/角度形成　angulation
成角折顶/成角折頂　angulation and bending manipulation
成巨核细胞/巨核胚細胞　megakaryoblast
成淋巴细胞的/淋巴胚細胞的　lymphoblastic
成淋巴细胞淋巴瘤/淋巴母細胞淋巴瘤　lymphoblast lymphoma
成淋巴细胞瘤/淋巴胚細胞瘤　lymphoblastoma
成淋巴细胞瘤病/淋巴胚細胞瘤病　lymphoblastomatosis
成淋巴细胞瘤疹/淋巴胚細胞瘤疹　lymphoblastomid
成淋巴细胞性白血病/淋巴母細胞性白血病　lymphoblastic leukemia
成淋巴细胞增多[症]/淋巴胚細胞過多病,母淋巴球過多病　lymphoblastosis
成卵黄细胞/卵黄母細胞　lecithoblast
成卵细胞/卵芽細胞　ooblast
成免疫细胞/免疫母細胞　immunoblast
成免疫细胞淋巴结病/免疫母細胞淋巴結病　immunoblastic lymphadenopathy
成膜体/成膜體　phragmoplast
成脑[脊]膜细胞瘤/腦膜胚細胞瘤　meningoblastoma
成内皮细胞瘤/内皮胚瘤,内皮母細胞瘤　endothelioblastoma
成年人/成年人　adult
成年型/成年型　adult-onset
成年型糖尿病/成年型糖尿病　maturity-onset diabetes
成黏液细胞/成黏液素細胞,黏液素母細胞,肥胖細胞　mucinoblast
成黏液细胞瘤/黏液胚細胞瘤　myxoblastoma
成胚卵黄/成形卵黄,構胎卵黄,構造卵黄　formative yolk
成胚细胞/胚細胞　embryoblast
成皮细胞/皮胚　dermoblast
成脾细胞/成脾細胞,脾母細胞　splenoblast
成品/最終產品　finished product

成品控制/最終產品管制　finished product control
成品托盘/成品托盤　ready-made tray
成平滑肌瘤/母平滑肌瘤　leiomyoblastoma
成群的/簇集的　agminate
成人呼吸窘迫症/成人呼吸窘迫　adult respiratory distress
成人呼吸窘迫综合征/成人呼吸窘迫症候群　adult respiratory distress syndrome
成人畸胎瘤/成人畸胎瘤　adult teratoma
成人口腔正畸学/成人口腔正畸學　adult orthodontics
成人尿布/成人尿布　adult diaper
成人期/成人期　adulthood
成人丘疹性肢端皮炎/成人丘疹性肢端皮膚炎　adult papular acrodermatitis
成人 T 细胞淋巴瘤/成人 T 細胞淋巴瘤　adult T-cell lymphoma
成人 T 细胞性白血病/成年 T 細胞白血病　adult T-cell leukemia
成人型幽门肥大/成人型幽門肥大　adult hypertrophy of the pylorus
成人型早老症/成人早衰老　adult progeria
成人硬化病/布希克氏成人硬化病　scleredema adultorum
成人硬皮病/成人硬皮病　scleroderma adultorum
成人原发结核感染/成人原發結核感染　adult primary tuberculous infection
成软骨细胞/成軟骨細胞,軟骨母細胞　chondroblast
成软骨细胞瘤/軟骨母細胞瘤　chondroblastoma
成色素细胞/成色素細胞,色素母細胞　chromatoblast
成少突胶质细胞/成少突膠質細胞　oligodendroblast
成少突神经胶质细胞/寡樹突膠質母細胞,間膠質母細胞　oligoblast
成神经管细胞/成神經管細胞　medulloblast
成[神经]胶质细胞/成[神經]膠質細胞,神經膠母細胞　glioblast
成神经节细胞/神經結胚細胞　esthesioblast
成神经膜细胞/神經膜胚細胞　lemmoblast
成神经细胞/神經原細胞,神經母細胞　neuroblast
成肾组织/腎元組織　nephrogenic tissue
成视细胞/視母細胞　optoblast
成室管膜细胞/室管膜胚細胞,室管膜成膠質細胞　ependymoblast
成嗜铬细胞/嗜鉻母細胞　pheochromoblast
成嗜铬细胞瘤/成嗜鉻細胞瘤　pheochromoblastoma
成熟促进因子/成熟促進因子　maturation-promoting factor

成熟儿/成熟嬰兒　mature infant
成熟儿童/成熟兒童　adult children
成熟分裂/成熟分裂,減數分裂　maturation division
成熟卵/成熟卵　ovium
成熟卵核/成熟卵核　deuthyalosome
成熟卵泡/成熟卵泡,赫拉夫卵泡　mature follicle
成熟免疫/成年期免疫性　maturation immunity
成熟期/成熟期　maturation phase
成熟期卵核/成熟期卵核　metanucleus
成熟受阻/成熟受阻,細胞成熟停止　anacmesis
成熟细胞/成熟細胞　mature cell
成熟型畸胎瘤/成熟畸胎瘤　mature teratoma
成熟障碍/成熟障礙　dysmaturity
成松果体细胞瘤/松果腺胚瘤　pinealoblastoma
成髓细胞/骨髓母細胞　myeloblast
成髓细胞白血病/骨髓母細胞性白血病　myeloblastic leukemia
成髓细胞瘤/骨髓母細胞瘤　myeloblastoma
成髓细胞瘤病/骨髓母細胞瘤病　myeloblastomatosis
成髓细胞血症/骨髓母細胞血症　myeloblastemia
成髓细胞组织增生/成髓細胞組織增生病,骨髓母細胞組織增生病　myeloblastic leukosis
成团反应/凝聚反應　conglobation reaction
成[吞]噬细胞/吞噬母細胞　phagocytoblast
[成]外胚层裂球/外胚層分裂球　ectomere
成纤维细胞/成纖維細胞,纖維母細胞　fibroblast
成纤维细胞的/纖維母細胞的　fibroblastic
成纤维细胞瘤/纖維母細胞瘤　fibroblastoma
成纤维细胞生长因子/纖維母細胞成長因子　fibroblast growth factor
成纤维细胞生长因子受体/纖維母細胞生長因子受體　fibroblast growth factor receptor
成纤维细胞性风湿病/纖維母細胞性風濕病　fibroblastic rheumatism
成腺细胞/腺胚細胞,腺母細胞　adenoblast
成星形胶质细胞/成星形膠質細胞,星形膠質母細胞　astrocytoblast
成星形细胞/星[形]母細胞　astroblast
成形便/成形糞　formed stool
成形带环/已成型環帶　contoured band
成形的/成形的　formative
成形发育/器官成形,器官之形態發育　morphophyly
成形剂/成形劑　plasticizers
成形器/成形器　former
成形钳/成形鉗　contouring pliers
成形手术/成形手術,造形手術　plastic operation
成形性虹膜炎/成形性虹膜炎　plastic iritis
成形性心内膜炎/成形性心内膜炎　plastic

endocarditis
成形性胸膜炎/成形性胸膜炎　plastic pleurisy
成形性血块/成形性血塊　plastic clot
成形质/原漿綢質　morphoplasm
成型板/印模板　die plate
成型片/成型片　matrix band
成型片夹/成型片夾　matrix holder
成血管层/成血管層　angioderm
成血管囊/血管囊腫　angiocyst
成血管内皮细胞瘤/血管内皮母細胞瘤　hemangioendothelioblastoma
成血管细胞/血管母細胞,血管胚細胞　angioblast
成血管细胞瘤/血管母細胞瘤　hemangioblastoma
成血管细胞瘤病/血管母細胞瘤病　hemangioblastomatosis
成血管组织/成血管組織　angioblastic tissue
成血细胞/血球原細胞,血球母細胞　hemocytoblast
成血细胞性白血病/血母細胞性白血病　hemocytoblastic leukemia
成血小板物质/血小板素　thrombon
成牙[本]质细胞/牙質母細胞　odontoblast cell, odontoblast
成牙本质细胞层空泡性变/牙質母細胞層空泡性變　vacuolar degeneration of odonto-blastic layer
成牙本质细胞突/牙質母細胞突,成齒質細胞突　odontoblastic process, odontoblast process
成牙骨质细胞/牙骨質母細胞　cementoblast
成牙质细胞瘤/牙質母細胞瘤　dentinoblastoma
成羊膜细胞/羊膜母細胞　amnioblast, amniogenic cell
成胰岛细胞/胰島母細胞,胰島胚細胞　nesidioblast
成胰岛细胞瘤/胰島母細胞瘤　nesidioblastoma
成瘾/上瘾　addiction
成瘾的/上瘾的　addictive
成瘾行为/成瘾行爲　addictive behavior
成瘾性/成癮性　addiction
[成釉器]中间层/中間層　stratum intermedium
成釉细胞癌/釉質母細胞癌　ameloblastic carcinoma
成釉细胞瘤/釉質母細胞瘤　ameloblastoma
成釉细胞肉瘤/釉質母細胞肉瘤　ameloblastic sarcoma
成釉细胞纤维瘤/釉質母細胞纖維瘤　ameloblastic fibroma
成釉细胞纤维肉瘤/釉質母細胞纖維肉瘤　ameloblastic fibrosarcoma
成釉细胞纤维牙瘤/釉質母細胞纖維牙瘤　ameloblastic fibro-odontoma
成釉细胞牙瘤/釉質母細胞性牙瘤　ameloblastic odontoma
成釉细胞牙肉瘤/釉質母細胞牙肉瘤　ameloblastic odontosarcoma
成釉[质]细胞/釉質母細胞　ameloblast
成釉质细胞突/釉質母細胞突　ameloblast process
成员/會員　member
成脂[肪]细胞/脂母細胞,脂胚細胞　lipoblast
成脂细胞瘤/脂胚細胞瘤　lipoblastoma
成组织细胞/組織胚細胞　histioblast
承扶/承扶　chengfu, BL36
承光/承光　chengguang, BL6
承浆/承漿　chengjiang, RN24
承浆疔/承漿疔　chengjiang ding, furuncle on chengjiang point
承筋/承筋　chengjin, BL56
承灵/承靈　chengling, GB18
承满/承滿　chengman, ST20
承泣/承泣　chengqi, ST1
承山/承山　chengshan, BL57
城市斑疹伤寒/城市斑疹傷寒　shop typhus
乘车者眩晕/乘車性眩暈　riders vertigo
程控刺激/程序控制刺激　programmed electrical stimulation
程控额外刺激/程序控制額外刺激　programmed extrastimulation
程控扫描/程序控制掃描　programmed scanning
程序波长检测器/可程控波長檢測器　programmable wavelength detector
程序设计语言/程序設計語言　programming languages
程序性衰老/程序性衰老　programmed aging
程序性细胞死亡/程序性細胞死亡　programmed cell death
澄清度/澄明度　clarity
澄清剂/澄清劑　clarificant
澄心静默/澄心静默　meditation
澄心静默疗法/澄心静默療法　meditation
澄源/澄源　treating root cause for arresting uterine hemorrhage
橙花醇/橙花醇　nerol
橙花油/橙花油　neroli oil
橙皮苷/橙皮苷　hesperidin
橙皮苷结晶/橙皮苷結晶　hesperidin crystal
橙皮糖浆/橙皮糖漿　orange syrup
橙皮油/柑皮油,甜橙皮油　orange oil
橙[色]/橙　orange
橙色血质/血棕晶質,血棱晶膽色素質　hematoidin
橙酮/橙酮　aurone

痴呆/癡呆,失智　dementia
痴呆・禀赋不足证/癡呆・禀賦不足證　dementia with pattern of defects in natural endowment
痴呆・脾肾气虚证/癡呆・脾腎氣虛證　dementia with pattern of qi deficiency of spleen and kidney
痴呆・脾虚湿困证/癡呆・脾虛濕困證　dementia with pattern of damp retention due to spleen deficiency
痴呆・气血两虚证/癡呆・氣血兩虛證　dementia with pattern of deficiency of both qi and blood
痴呆・髓海不足证/癡呆・髓海不足證　dementia with pattern of marrow sea insufficiency
痴呆・痰浊上扰证/癡呆・痰濁上擾證　dementia with pattern of upward disturbance of phlegm-turbidity
痴呆・心肝火旺证/癡呆・心肝火旺證　dementia with pattern of exuberant fire of heart and liver
痴呆・血瘀气滞证/癡呆・血瘀氣滯證　dementia with pattern of blood stasis and qi stagnation
痴呆者/癡呆者　dement
痴愚/癡愚,愚鈍　imbecility
痴愚者/中癡者　imbecile
池/池　cistern, pool
弛缓性截瘫/弛緩性截癱　flaccid paraplegia
弛缓性膀胱/失張膀胱　atonic bladder
弛缓药/弛緩藥　relaxant
弛张疟/弛張瘧　malaria remittens
迟钝精子/遲鈍精子　muzzled sperm
迟钝性白痴/遲鈍性白癡　torpid idiot
迟钝性抑郁症/遲滯性抑鬱　retarded depression
迟发反应/遲發反應　late response
迟发佝偻病/遲發性佝僂病　late rickets
迟发型变态反应/遲發性過敏　delayed allergy
迟发型超敏反应/延遲性過敏性,遲發性過敏性　delayed hypersensitivity
迟发型反应/延遲反應　delayed reaction
迟发型皮肤反应/遲發型皮膚反應　delayed cutaneous reaction
迟发型转白反应/延遲褪色反應　delayed-blanch reaction
迟发性超敏反应/遲發性高敏感反應　delayed hypersensitivity reaction
迟发性发绀/遲發性發紺　delayed cyanosis
迟发性淋巴水肿/晚發性淋巴水腫　lymphedema tarda
迟发性皮肤卟啉病/遲發性皮膚卟啉症　porphyria cutanea tarda
迟发性压力性荨麻疹/遲發性壓力性蕁麻疹　delayed pressure urticaria
迟发性运动障碍/遲發性運動障礙　tardive dyskinesia
迟发性转白现象/遲發性轉白現象　delayed blanch phenomenon
迟发幼稚型/晚發幼稚型,退化性幼稚型　tardy infantilism
迟发症状/遲發症狀　delayed symptom
迟缓/遲緩　retardation
迟缓充盈/遲緩充盈　delayed filling
迟缓受精/遲緩受精　delayed fertilization
迟缓真杆菌/遲緩真桿菌　Eubacterium lentum
迟脉/遲脈　slow pulse
迟萌/遲萌　delayed eruption of tooth
迟效制剂/遲效製劑　delayed-action preparation
迟牙/遲齒　wisdom tooth
迟延的/遲延的　tardive
迟延胚胎植入/遲延胚胎植入　delayed embryo implantation
迟延性发绀/遲延性發紺　tardive cyanosis
迟延性休克/遲發性休克　deferred shock
迟延移植片/延期移植物　delayed graft
持箔器/持箔器　foil carrier
持久斑疹性毛细血管扩张/持久發疹性斑狀毛細血管擴張　telangiectasia macularis eruptiva perstans
持久性的/持久的　persistent
持久性豆状角化过度病/持久性豆狀角化過度病　hyperkeratosis lenticularis perstans
持久性光反应/持久性光反應　persistent light reaction
持久性红斑/持久性紅斑　erythema perstans
持久性棘层松解性皮病/持久性棘層鬆解皮膚病　persistent acantholytic dermatosis
持久性痉挛/固定性痙攣　fixed spasm
持久性蒙古斑/持久性蒙古斑　persistent Mongolian spot
持久性浅表皮炎/持久性表淺皮膚炎　persistent superficial dermatitis
持久性全身性淋巴腺病/全身持久性淋巴腺病　persistent generalized lymphadenopathy
持久性色素异常性红斑/持久性變色紅斑　erythema dyschromicum perstans
持久性手足脓疱病/持久性手足膿皰症　persistent pustulosis of hands and feet
持久性图状红斑/持久性圖狀紅斑　erythema figuratum perstans
持久性掌跖脓疱病/持久性掌蹠膿皰症　persistent palmoplantar pustulosis
持石器/持石器　litholabe
持续被动性运动疗法/持續被動性運動療法

continuous passive motion therapy
持续不卧床腹膜透析/連續性非臥床腹膜透析 continuous ambulatory peritoneal dialysis
持续低流量给氧/持續低流量給氧 continuous administration of low flow oxygen
持续低温灌注/持續低温灌注 continuous hypothermical perfusion
持续骶管麻醉/持續性脊尾麻醉法 continuous caudal anesthesia
持续释放制剂/持效性釋出製劑 extended release preparation
持续痛/持續痛 persistent pain
持续无排卵/持續無排卵 chronic anovulation
持续吸引引流/持續吸引引流 continuous suction drainage
持续型间日疟/持續型間日瘧 biduotertian
持续性脊髓麻醉/持續性脊髓麻醉 continuous spinal anesthesia
持续性皮炎/持續性皮膚炎 dermatitis perstans
持续性胎儿循环/持續性胎兒循環 persistent fetal circulation
持续性胎儿循环综合征/持續性胎兒循環症候群 persistent fetal circulation syndrome
持续性心动过速/恆久性心搏過速 constant tachycardia
持续性心律失常/連續性心律不整 continuous arrhythmia
持续性枕横位/持續性枕橫位 persistent occipitotransverse position
持续性枕后位/持續性枕後位 persistent occipitoposterior position
持续性肢端皮炎/持續性肢端皮膚炎 acrodermatitis perstans
持续言语/持續言語,語句反復症 perseveration
持续正压呼吸/連續正壓呼吸 continuous positive pressure breathing
持续正压通气/持續正壓通氣 continuous positive pressure ventilation
持续植物人状态/持續植物人狀態 persistent vegetative state
匙/匙 spoon
匙突/匙突 cochleariform process
匙形挖器/匙狀挖出器 excavator spoon
匙针/匙針 spoon needle
匙针疗法/匙針療法 spoon needle therapy
匙状甲/匙狀甲 spoon nails
尺背指神经/尺背指神經 ulnar dorsal digital nerve
尺侧/尺側 ulnar

尺侧半肢畸形/尺側半肢畸形 ulnar hemimelia
尺侧返动脉/尺返動脈 ulnar recurrent artery
尺侧返动脉后支/尺側返動脈後支 posterior branch of ulnar recurrent artery
尺侧返动脉前支/尺側返動脈前支 anterior branch of ulnar recurrent artery
尺侧副韧带/尺側副韌帶,肘肘韧带 ulnar collateral ligament, ligamentum collaterale ulnare, brachiocubital ligament
尺侧屈腕肌/尺側屈腕肌 flexor carpi ulnaris
尺侧上副动脉/尺側上副動脈 superior ulnar collateral artery
尺侧腕骨/尺側腕骨 ulnar carpal bone
尺侧腕屈肌/尺側腕屈肌 flexor carpi ulnaris
尺侧腕屈肌尺骨头/[尺側腕屈肌]尺骨頭 ulnar head of flexor carpi ulnaris
尺侧腕屈肌肱骨头/[尺側腕屈肌]肱骨頭 humeral head of flexor carpi ulnaris
尺侧腕韧带/尺側腕韌帶 ulnar carpal ligament
尺侧腕伸肌/尺側伸腕肌 extensor carpi ulnaris
尺侧腕伸肌尺骨头/[尺側腕伸肌]尺骨頭 ulnar head of extensor carpi ulnaris
尺侧腕伸肌肱骨头/[尺側腕伸肌]肱骨頭 humeral head of extensor carpi ulnaris
尺侧腕伸肌腱鞘/尺側伸腕肌腱鞘 tendinous sheath of extensor carpi ulnaris
尺侧下副动脉/尺側下副動脈 inferior ulnar collateral artery
尺侧掌骨点/尺側掌骨點 metacarpale ulnare
尺动脉/尺動脈 ulnar artery
[尺动脉]腕掌支/[尺動脈]腕掌支 palmar carpal branch
尺骨/尺骨 ulnar bone
尺骨粗隆/尺骨粗隆 ulnar tuberosity, tubercle of ulna
尺骨的/尺骨的 ulnar
尺骨干骨折/尺骨幹骨折 fracture of shaft of ulna, ulna shaft fracture
尺骨骨间缘/尺骨骨間緣 interosseous border of ulna
尺骨骨折/尺骨骨折 ulnar fracture
尺骨关节盘/尺骨關節盤 articular disc of ulna
尺骨冠突/尺骨冠突 coronoid process of ulna
尺骨后面/尺骨後面 posterior surface of ulna
尺骨后缘/尺骨後緣 posterior border of ulna
尺骨茎突/尺骨莖突 styloid process of ulna
尺骨内侧面/尺骨內側面 medial surface of ulna
尺骨前面/尺骨前面 anterior surface of ulna

尺骨前缘/尺骨前緣　anterior border of ulna
尺骨上1/3骨折合并桡骨头脱位/尺骨上1/3骨折合并橈骨頭脫位　fracture of upper 1/3 of ulna combined with dislocation of head of radius
尺骨体/尺骨體　shaft of ulna
尺骨头/尺骨頭　head of ulna, ulnar head
尺骨鹰嘴骨折/尺骨鷹嘴骨折　olecranal fracture
尺骨鹰嘴滑囊炎/尺骨鷹嘴滑囊炎　bursitis of olecranon, synovitis of olecranon
尺箕/尺箕　ulnar loop
尺静脉/尺靜脈　ulnar vein
尺偏手/尺偏手　ulnar clubhand
尺切迹/尺骨切跡　ulnar notch
尺桡骨干双骨折/尺橈骨幹雙骨折　double fracture of shafts of ulna and radius, ulnoradial shaft fractures
尺神经/尺神經　ulnar nerve
尺神经病/尺神經病　ulnar neuropathies
尺神经沟/尺神經溝　sulcus for ulnar nerve, groove of ulnar nerve
尺神经肌支/尺神經肌支　muscular branch of ulnar nerve
尺神经交通支/尺神經交通支　communicating branch with ulnar nerve
尺神经浅支/尺神經淺支　superficial branch of ulnar nerve
[尺神经]深支/深[神經]支　deep branch
尺神经压迫综合征/尺神經壓迫症候群　ulnar nerve compression syndrome
尺神经掌支/[尺神經]掌支　palmar branch of ulnar nerve
尺神经指背神经/尺指背神經　dorsal digital nerve of ulnar nerve
尺神经指掌侧固有神经/尺指神經掌側固有神經　proper palmar digital nerves of ulnar nerve
尺神经指掌侧总神经/尺指神經掌側總神經　common palmar digital nerves of ulnar nerve
尺头/尺頭　caput ulnare(拉)
尺腕侧副韧带/尺腕側副韌帶　ulnar collateral ligament of carpus
尺腕掌侧韧带/尺腕掌側韌帶　palmar ulnocarpal ligament, flexor retinaculum
尺泽/尺澤　chize, LU5
尺指神经掌侧副神经/尺神經掌側指副神經[支]　collateral palmar digital nerve of ulnar nerve
齿/[牙]齒　dens, tooth
齿槽/齒槽　alveolus of teeth
齿槽风/齒槽風　jaw wind, maxillary osteo-myelitis

齿槽风·气血两虚证/齒槽風·氣血兩虛證　jaw wind with qi-blood deficiency pattern
齿槽风·邪热炽盛证/齒槽風·邪熱熾盛證　jaw wind with blazing pathogenic heat pattern
齿槽骨炎/齒槽骨炎　dentoalveolar osteitis
齿槽管/齒槽管　alveolar channel
齿槽内囊肿/齒槽內側囊腫　medial alveolar cyst
齿迟/齒遲　retardation in tooth eruption
齿齼/齒齼　dentin hypersensitiveness
齿错位/齒錯位　transposition of teeth
齿的/齒的　dental
齿窦/齒竇　dental sinus
齿垩质/齒堊質　bony substance of tooth
齿发育不良/齒化生異常　dental dysplasia
齿槁/齒槁　withering teeth
齿根/齒根　tooth root
齿更/齒更　dental transition
齿垢密螺旋体/齒垢密螺旋體　Treponema denticola
齿2/3 殆/齒2/3 咬合　two third occlusion
齿痕舌/齒痕舌　teeth-printed tongue
齿坏死/齒壞死　dental necrosis
齿豁/齒豁　gomphiasis, loose tooth
齿坚/齒堅　firm tooth
齿间夹/齒間夾板　interdental splint
齿间细胞/齒間細胞　interdental cell
齿颈/齒頸　dental neck
齿科内分泌学/齒科內分泌學　endocrinodontia
[齿科用]抽髓针/根管針,抽髓針　nerve broach
齿列增生/齒列增生　denture hyperplasia
齿裂/齒裂　fissured tooth
齿轮泵/齒輪泵　gear pump
齿轮现象/齒輪現象　cogwheel phenomenon
齿轮样强直/齒輪狀強硬　cogwheel rigidity
齿轮征/齒輪徵象　cogwheel sign
齿轮状呼吸音/齒輪狀呼吸音　cogwheel respiration
齿螺旋体/齒螺旋體　Treponema dentium
齿内在耗损/內生性齒吸收　internal resorption of teeth
齿衄/齒衄　gum bleeding
齿衄[病]/齒衄[病]　gum bleeding, gum bleeding disease
齿衄·脾不统血证/齒衄·脾不統血證　gum bleeding with pattern of spleen failing to control blood
齿衄·胃火炽盛证/齒衄·胃火熾盛證　gum bleeding with blazing stomach fire pattern, gum bleeding with pattern of blazing stomach fire
齿衄·阴虚火旺证/齒衄·陰虛火旺證　gum bleeding with pattern of exuberant fire due to yin deficiency,

gum bleeding with pattern of yin deficiency and fire effulgence
齿乳突/齒乳突　dental papillae
齿痛/齒痛　dentalgia, toothache
齿突凹/齒凹　dental fovea of atlas
齿突后关节面/齒突後關節面　posterior articular facet of dens
齿突尖/齒突尖　apex of dens, odontoid process
齿突尖韧带/齒突尖韌帶　apical ligament of dens, apical odontoid ligament
齿突前关节面/齒突前關節面　anterior articular facet of dens
齿突韧带/牙樣骨韌帶　odontoid ligament
齿突韧带联合/橫韌帶與齒突的　syndesmo-odontoid
齿线/齒線　dentate line
齿龄/齒齡　bruxism, teeth grinding
齿龄·气血两虚证/齒齡·氣血兩虛證　teeth grinding with qi-blood deficiency pattern
齿龄·胃腑积热证/齒齡·胃腑積熱證　teeth grinding with pattern of stomach-fu heat accumulation
齿龄·小儿疳积证/齒齡·小兒疳積證　teeth grinding with pattern of infantile malnutrition and food stagnation
齿龄·心火炽盛证/齒齡·心火熾盛證　teeth grinding with blazing heart fire pattern
齿-眼-皮肤综合征/齒-眼-皮膚症候群　dento-oculocutaneous syndrome
齿样骨/牙樣骨　odontoid bone
齿龈增生/齒齦增生　gum hypertrophy
齿釉沟/齒釉溝　enamel groove
齿釉质形成不全/牙釉質發育不良　enamel dysplasia
齿质瘤/齒質瘤　dentinoid tumor
齿质细胞/齒質細胞　dentinal cell
齿质原纤维/牙本質原纖維　dentinogenic fiber
齿中央咬合/齒中央咬合　central occlusion
齿周韧带/齒周韌帶　periodontal ligament
齿状的/齒狀的　dentate
齿状骨折/齒狀骨折　dentate fracture
齿状核/齒狀核　dentate nucleus
齿状核门/齒狀核門　hilum of dentate nucleus
齿状红核束/齒狀紅核束　dentatorubral tract
齿状回/齒狀迴　dentate gyrus
齿状丘脑束/齒狀丘腦束　dentatothalamic tract
齿状韧带/齒狀韌帶　denticulate ligament, denticulate dentate ligament
齿状线/齒狀線　dentate line
耻股韧带/恥股韌帶　pubofemoral ligament
耻骨/恥骨　pubis
耻骨成形术/恥骨造形術　pubioplasty
耻骨的/恥骨的　pectineal, pubic
耻骨腹膜肌/恥骨腹膜肌　pubicoperitoneal muscle
耻骨弓/恥骨弓　pubic arch
耻骨弓角度/恥骨弓角度　angle of subpubic arch
耻骨[弓]下的/恥骨下的　subpubic
耻骨弓状韧带/恥骨弓狀韌帶　arcuate pubic ligament
耻骨骨炎/恥骨骨炎　osteitis pubis
耻骨关节/恥骨關節　articulation of pubis
耻骨后间隙/恥骨後間隙　retropubic space
耻骨后前列腺切除术/恥骨後前列腺切除術　retropubic prostatectomy
耻骨后疝/恥骨後疝　hernia retropubica
耻骨肌/恥骨肌　musculus pectineus
耻骨肌疝/恥骨肌疝　pectineal crural hernia
耻骨肌线/恥骨線　pectineal line
耻骨嵴/恥骨嵴　pubic crest
耻骨间盘/恥骨間盤　interpubic disc
耻骨结节/恥骨結節　pubic tubercle
耻骨筋膜/恥骨筋膜　fascia pectinea
耻骨静脉/恥骨靜脈　pubic vein
耻骨联合/恥骨聯合　pubic symphysis
耻骨联合点/恥骨聯合點　symphysion
耻骨联合分离/恥骨聯合分離　pubic symphysis diastasis, separation of the pubic symphysis
耻骨联合缝术/恥骨連合縫合法　symphyseorrhaphy
耻骨联合面/恥骨聯合面　symphysial surface of pubis
耻骨联合腔/恥骨聯合腔　pubic symphysis cavum
耻骨联合切除术/恥骨連合切除術　symphysiectomy
耻骨联合切开刀/恥骨連合刀　symphysiotome
耻骨联合切开术/恥骨連合切開術　symphysiotomy
耻骨联合软骨/盆軟骨　pelvisternum
耻骨联合松解术/恥骨聯合鬆解術　symphysiolysis
耻骨膀胱肌/恥骨膀胱肌　pubovesical muscle, musculus pubovesicalis
耻骨膀胱韧带/恥骨膀胱韌帶　pubovesical ligament
耻骨前列腺肌/恥骨前列腺肌　puboprostatic muscle, musculus puboprostaticus
耻骨前列腺韧带/恥骨前列腺韌帶,恥骨攝護腺韌帶　puboprostatic ligament
耻骨前韧带/恥骨前韌帶　anterior pubic ligament
耻骨韧带/恥骨韌帶　pubofemoral ligament
耻骨疝/恥骨下股疝　pectineal hernia
耻骨上经膀胱前列腺切除术/恥骨上及經由膀胱之前列腺切除術　suprapubic transvesical prostatectomy

耻骨上膀胱切开取石术/恥骨上膀胱切開取石術 suprapubic cystolithotomy
耻骨上膀胱造口术/恥骨上膀胱造口術 suprapubic cystostomy
耻骨上膀胱针刺吸引术/恥骨上膀胱針刺吸引術 suprapubic needle aspiration of bladder
耻骨上前列腺切除术/恥骨上前列腺切除術 suprapubic prostatectomy
耻骨上韧带/恥骨上韌帶 superior pubic ligament
耻骨上支/恥骨上支 superior ramus of pubis
耻骨梳/恥骨梳 pecten pubis
耻骨梳韧带/恥骨梳韌帶 pectineal ligament
耻骨体/恥骨體 body of pubis
耻骨尾骨肌/恥骨尾骨肌 musculus pubococcygeus
耻骨下角/恥骨下角 subpubic angle
耻骨下疝/恥骨下疝 subpubic hernia
耻骨下脱位/恥骨下脱位 subpubic dislocation
耻骨下支/恥骨下支 inferior ramus of pubis
耻骨阴道肌/恥骨陰道肌 pubovaginalis, musculus pubovaginalis
耻骨支/恥骨支 pubic branch
耻骨直肠肌/恥骨直腸肌 musculus puborectalis
耻区/恥部 pubic region
耻尾肌/恥尾肌 pubococcygeus
耻坐骨/恥坐骨 pubo-ischiadic bone
赤白带/赤白帶 red and white vaginal discharge
赤带[病]/赤帶[病] red vaginal discharge
赤带·肾阴虚证/赤帶·腎陰虛證 red vaginal discharge with pattern of kidney yin deficiency
赤带·湿热下注证/赤帶·濕熱下注證 red vaginal discharge with pattern of downward diffusion of damp-heat
赤带·心肝火旺证/赤帶·心肝火旺證 red vaginal discharge with pattern of exuberant fire of heart and liver
赤带·血虚证/赤帶·血虛證 red vaginal discharge with blood deficiency pattern
赤道/赤道 equator
赤道板/中緯板 equatorial plate
赤地衣素/地衣紅質 erythrin
赤根驱虫草素/赤根草素 spigeline
赤脉传睛/赤脈傳睛 ciliary hyperemia, red vessel spreading to black of the eye
赤霉素/赤黴素 gibberellin
赤膜/赤膜 red membrane
赤膜下垂/赤膜下垂 drooping pannus, prolapse of red membrane, trachomatous pannus
赤曲菌/赤麴黴菌 Aspergillus ruber

赤芍/赤芍 peony root
赤石脂/赤石脂 halloysite
赤水玄珠/赤水玄珠 Black Pearl from Red River
赤丝虬脉/赤絲虯脈 red tangled vessel
赤藓醇/赤蘚醇 erythritol
赤藓醇基/紅蘚醇根 erythrityl
赤藓醇四硝酸酯/赤蘚醇四硝酸酯 erythrityl tetranitrate
赤藓红/赤藻紅,紅螢素 erythrosin
赤藓糖/赤蘚糖 erythrose
赤藓酮糖/赤蘚酮醣 erythrulose
赤小豆/赤小豆 rice bean
赤游丹/赤游丹 red wandering erysipelas, wandering erysipelas
赤游丹·毒传心肝证/赤游丹·毒傳心肝證 wandering erysipelas with pattern of toxin invading heart and liver
赤游丹·毒在肌肤证/赤游丹·毒在肌膚證 wandering erysipelas with pattern of toxin invading muscle and skin
炽灼残渣/熾灼殘渣 residue on ignition
瘈脉/瘈脈 chimai, SJ18
瘈疭/瘈[疭] clonic convulsion, tugging and slackening
冲动/衝動,壓出 impulse
冲动发放/衝動發放狀態 incitogram
冲动控制障碍/衝動控制障礙 impulse control disorder
冲动行为/衝動行爲 impulsive behavior
冲动型人格障碍/衝動型人格障礙 impulsive personality disorder
冲动性[行为]障碍/衝動異常 impulse disorder
冲服/沖服 administered after dissolved
冲击波伤/衝擊波損傷 blast injury
冲浪者结节/衝浪者結節 surfer nodule
冲力比/衝力比 punch force ratio
冲脉/衝脈 thoroughfare channel, thoroughfare vessel, Chong Vessel, Chong Channel
冲门/衝門 chongmen, SP12
冲任不固/衝任不固 insecurity of thoroughfare and conception channels, unconsolidation of Chong and Conception Channels
冲任不固证/衝任不固證 pattern of unconsolidation of Chong and Conception Channels
冲任不调/衝任不調 disharmony of Chong and Conception Channels, disharmony of thoroughfare and conception channels
冲任不调证/衝任不調證 pattern of disharmony of

Chong and Conception Channels
冲任虚寒/沖任虛寒　deficiency-cold of thoroughfare and conception channels
冲任虚损/沖任虛損　debility of thoroughfare and conception channels
冲突/衝突　conflict
冲洗/沖洗，灌洗　douche, rinsing
冲洗法/沖洗法　irrigation therapy
冲洗法细胞学检查[术]/沖洗法細胞學檢查[術]　lavage cytologic examination
冲洗疗法/沖洗療法　douche therapy
冲洗器/注洗器　irrigator
冲阳/沖陽　chongyang, ST42
冲浴/淋水療法　affusion
充气过度/膨脹過度　hyperinflation
充气夹板/充氣夾板　inflatable splint
充气抗休克服/氣囊式抗休克大衣　pneumatic antishock garment
充气尿道镜检查/充氣尿道鏡檢術　aerourethroscopy
充气膀胱镜/膀胱充氣鏡檢器　aerocystoscope
充气膀胱镜检查/膀胱充氣鏡檢法　aerocystoscopy
充气 X 射线体层照相术/肺部 X 光攝影法　pneumotomography
充气胃镜检查/胃充氣內鏡檢查　pneumogastroscopy
充气造影术/充氣 X 光攝影法　pneumoradiography
充气造影照片/充氣 X 光照片　pneumoroentgenogram
充气止血带/氣性壓血帶　pneumatic tourniquet
充实换气法/充滿換氣法　plenum ventilation
充填剂/充填劑　plug
充填器/充填器　plugger
充填移植物/充填移植物　filler graft
充血/充血　hyperemia
充血的/充血的　congestive
充血试验/充血試驗　hyperemia test
充血性痤疮/充血性痤瘡　congestive acne
充血性寒战/充血性寒顫　congestive chill
充血性溃疡/充血性潰瘍　congestive ulcer
充血性皮脂漏/充血性皮脂漏　seborrhea congestiva
充血性痛经/充血性痛經　plethoric dysmenorrhea
充血性头痛/充血性頭痛　congestive headache
充血性心力衰竭/充血性心衰竭　congestive heart failure
充溢性失禁/充溢性失禁　overflow incontinence
充盈缺损/充盈缺損　filling defect
充盈性膀胱测压/充盈性膀胱測壓　filling cystometry
充注型乳房植入体/充注型乳房植入體　inflatable breast prosthetic implant
充注型阴道模具/充注型陰道模具　inflatable vaginal stent
茺蔚子/茺蔚子　motherwort fruit
虫/蟲　bug
虫白蜡/蟲白蠟　Chinese wax
虫积/蟲積　parasitic amassment
虫积小肠证/蟲積小腸證　pattern of ascariasis of small intestine
虫瘕/蟲瘕　parasitic abdominal mass
虫胶/蟲膠　shellac
虫胶板/蟲蠟基牙托　shellac base
虫媒病毒/蟲媒病毒　arbovirus
虫媒病毒病/蟲媒病毒病　arbovirus disease
虫媒病毒感染/蟲媒病毒感染　arbovirus infection
虫媒病毒脑炎/蟲媒病毒腦炎　arbovirus encephalitis
虫媒传染病/蟲媒傳染病　arthropodborne infectious disease
虫霉病/蟲黴菌病　entomophthoromycosis
虫蚀样边缘/蟲蝕樣邊緣　eroded edge
虫兽伤/蟲獸傷　bitten by animal and insect, injury by animal and insect
虫痒/蟲癢　worm itching
虫蚀/蟲蛀　rotten due to insect bites
重瓣胃/重瓣胃　omasum
重瓣胃炎/重瓣胃炎　omasitis
重搏切迹/主動脈凹痕　aortic notch
重叠/重疊　overlap
重叠峰/重疊峰　fused peaks, overlapped peaks
重叠缝合/重疊縫　overlapping suture
重叠感染/重疊感染　superinfection
重叠构像/重疊構象　eclipsed conformation
重叠结缔组织病/重疊性結締組織疾病　overlapped connective tissue disease
重叠杂音/重複雜音　reduplication murmur
重叠植皮术/重疊植皮術　overlapping skin grafting
重叠综合征/重疊症候群　overlap syndrome
重腭/重腭　swollen upper palate
重方/重方　compound recipe
重复 DNA/重複 DNA　repetitive DNA
重复包扎/重複包扎　tie-over dressing
重复肠梗阻/重複腸阻塞　ileus duplex
重复基因/重複基因　duplicate gene
重复毛/多生毛　pili multigemini
重复尿道/重複尿道　duplication of urethra
重复膀胱/重複膀胱　duplication of bladder
重复 X 射线[照]片/重複 X 射線片　diplogram
重[复]肾/重[複]腎，複腎[畸形]　double kidney

重复肾盂/重複腎盂 duplication of pelvis
重复输精管/重複輸精管 duplication of vas deferens
重复输尿管/重複輸尿管 duplication of ureter
重复性/重複性,再现性 repeatability
重复性开放式涂抹试验/重複性開放式敷用試驗 repeat open application test
重复序列/重複序列 repetitive sequence
[重]复足/[重]複足 duplication of foot
重寄生[现象]/重寄生現象 hyperparasitism
重寄生物/附寄生物,再寄生物 hyperparasite
重睑/重瞼 double eyelid
重睑成形术/重瞼成形術 construction of double eyelid
重建/重建 reconstruction
重建性直肠结肠切除术/重建性直腸結腸切除術 restorative proctocolectomy
重建总离子流/重建總離子流 reconstruction total ion current, reconstruction TIC
重结晶/再结晶 recrystallization
重颏/雙頦 double chin
重楼玉钥/重樓玉鑰 Jade Key to the Secluded Chamber
重舌/重舌 double tongue, sublingual swollen tongue
重舌·胎毒内蕴证/重舌·胎毒内蘊證 double tongue disease with pattern of internal amassment of fetal toxin
重舌·心脾积热证/重舌·心脾積熱證 double tongue disease with pattern of heart-spleen heat accumulation
重肾双输尿管/重腎雙輸尿管 duplication of kidney and ureter
重调/重調 readjustment
重瞳/重瞳,雙瞳畸形 dicoria, double pupil
重吸收作用/重吸收[作用] reabsorption
重新试验反应/重新試驗反應 retest reaction
重演律/重演律,重演说 recapitulation law
重演学说/重演說 recapitulation theory
重折光质/重折光質 anisotropic substance
重组/重組 recombination
重组 DNA/重組 DNA recombinant DNA
重组病毒/重組病毒 reassortant virus
重组蛋白质类/重組蛋白質類 recombinant proteins
重组干扰素 γ/重組干擾素 γ recombinant interferon-gamma
重组红细胞生成素/重組紅細胞生成素 recombinant erythropoietin
重组集落刺激因子/重組集落刺激因子 recombinant colony-stimulating factor
重组粒细胞集落刺激因子/重組粒細胞集落刺激因子 recombinant granulocyte colony stimulating factor
重组粒细胞巨噬细胞集落刺激因子/重組粒細胞巨噬細胞集落刺激因子 recombinant granulocyte macrophage colony-stimulating factor
重组率/重組率 recombination fraction
重组酶类/重組酶類 recombinases
重组频率/重組頻率 recombination frequency
重组染色体/重組染色體 recombinant chromosome
重组融合蛋白质类/重組融合蛋白質類 recombinant fusion proteins
重组体/重組體 recombinant
重组异倍性/重組異倍性 recombination aneuploidy
重组质粒/重組質粒 recombinant plasmid
重组子/重組子 recon
重组组织型纤溶酶原激活剂/重組體組織漿胞素原活化劑 recombinant tissue type plasminogen activator
抽掣痛/抽掣痛 dragging pain
抽搐/抽搐 tic, convulsion
抽搐性运动障碍/抽搐性運動障礙 tic disorder
抽动秽语综合征/抽動穢語症候群 Gilles de la Tourette syndrome
抽空换气法/抽空換氣法 vacuum ventilation
抽空进样/抽空進樣 vacuum injection
抽气罐/吸盤 suction cup
抽气通风/抽空換氣法 exhausting ventilation
抽屉试验/抽屜試驗 drawer test
抽吸/吸引,吸入 suction
抽吸活组织检查/針吸式活組織檢驗 aspiration biopsy
抽吸器/抽吸器,吸引器 aspirator
抽血注射预防[反应]法/體外血液去敏感法 exohemophylaxis
抽样研究/抽樣研究 sampling study
稠度试验/稠度試驗,堅實度試驗 consistence test
稠度计/稠度計 consistometer
臭鼻菌苗/臭鼻疫苗 ozaena vaccine
臭鼻症/臭鼻症 ozena
臭虫/臭蟲 bedbug
臭虫叮咬/臭蟲叮咬 bedbug bite
臭虫属/臭蟲屬 Cimex
臭虫痒症/臭蟲癢 cimicosis
臭汗/臭汗 fetid sweat
臭汗症/臭汗症 osmidrosis
臭味/臭味 foetor

臭腺/臭腺,氣味腺　scent gland, odoriferous gland
臭[性月]经/臭性月經　bromomenorrhea
臭氧/臭氧　ozone
臭氧发生器/臭氧發生器　ozonator
臭氧分解/臭氧分解　ozonolysis
臭氧化物/臭氧化物　ozonide
臭氧计/臭氧計　ozonometer
臭氧检验器/臭氧檢查器　ozonoscope
臭氧探测仪/臭氧探測儀　ozonesonde
臭氧乙醚/臭氧乙醚　ozone-ether
出定/出定　exiting the Ding
出汗/發汗　diaphoresis
出汗不良型类天疱疮/異汗樣類天皰瘡　dyshidrosiform pemphigoid
出汗期/出汗期　sweating stage
出汗性血管瘤/出汗性血管瘤　sudoriparous angioma
出口/出口　outlet
出口横径/出口橫徑　transverse outlet
出口后矢状径/出口後矢狀徑　posterior sagittal diameter of outlet
出口平面/出口平面　pelvic outlet plane
出口综合征/出口症候群　outlet syndrome
出球小动脉/出球小動脈　efferent glomerular arteriole
出射点/出射點,眼點　eyepoint
出生后的/出生後的　postnatal
出生后发育/生後發育,産後發育　postnatal development
出生后免疫/出生後免疫　postnatal immunity
出生率/出生率,生產率　birth rate
出生率降低/降低出生率　denatality
出生前发育/產前發育　prenatal development
出生前生活/子宮内生活　intrauterine life
出生缺陷/先天[性]缺陷　birth defect
出生时低体重婴儿/出生時低體重嬰兒　low birth weight infant
出生顺序/出生順序　birth order
出生体重/出生體重　birth weight
出生证/出生證　birth certificate
出血/出血　bleeding
出血大疱性咽峡炎/出血水皰性咽峡炎　angina bullosa haemorrhagica
出血的/出血的　hemorrhagenic, hemorrhagic
出血点/出血點　hemorrhagic spot
出血遏制/出血遏制　arrest of hemorrhage
出血囊肿/出血囊腫　hemorrhagic cyst
出血时间/出血時間　bleeding time
出血素/出血素,溶内皮素　hemorrhagin

出血素质/出血素質　hemorrhagic diathesis
出血性/出血性的　haemorrhagic
出血性败血症/出血性敗血病　hemorrhagic septicemia
出血性胆囊炎/出血性膽囊炎　hemocholecystitis
出血性耳炎/出血性耳炎　otitis haemorrhagica
出血性腹膜炎/出血性腹膜炎　hemorrhagic peritonitis
出血性肝炎/出血性肝炎　hemorrhagic hepatitis
出血性梗死/出血性梗塞,紅色梗塞　hemorrhagic infarct
出血性梗死形成/出血性梗塞形成　hemorrhagic infarction
出血性骨髓炎/出血性骨髓炎　hemorrhagic osteomyelitis
出血性疾病/出血性疾病　hemorrhagic disease
出血性脊髓病/出血性脊髓病　hemorrhagic myelopathy
出血性脊髓空洞症/出血性脊髓空洞病　hematomyelopore
出血性脊髓炎/出血性脊髓炎　hemorrhagic myelitis
出血性溃疡/出血性潰瘍　hemorrhagic ulcer
出血性脑上部灰质炎/出血性腦上部灰質炎　polioencephalitis haemorrhagica superior
出血性脑炎/出血性腦炎　hemorrhagic encephalitis
出血性疟/出血性瘧　hemorrhagic malaria
出血性贫血/出血性貧血　hemorrhagic anemia
出血性青光眼/出血性青光眼　apoplectic glaucoma
出血性肾炎/出血性腎炎　hemorrhagic nephritis
出血性肾盂肾炎/出血性腎盂腎炎　hemorrhagic pyelonephritis
出血性输卵管炎/出血性輸卵管炎　hemorrhagic salpingitis
出血性天花/出血性痘　variola haemorrhagica
出血性天疱疮/出血性天皰瘡　pemphigus haemorrhagica
出血性胃肠炎/出血性胃腸炎　gastroenteritis hemorrhagica
出血性胃炎/出血性胃炎　hemorrhagic gastritis
出血性心包炎/出血性心包炎　hemorrhagic pericarditis
出血性休克/出血性休克　hemorrhagic shock
出血性血小板增多/出血性血小板增多症　hemorrhagic thrombocythemia
出血性荨麻疹/出血性蕁麻疹　urticaria haemorrhagica
出血性胰腺炎/出血性胰腺炎　hemorrhagic pancreatitis

出血性阴茎异常勃起/出血性勃起　stymatosis
出血性障碍/出血性障礙　hemorrhagic disorder
出血性紫癜/出血性紫癜病　purpura haemorrhagica
出血指数/出血指數　bleeding index
出牙/出齒　eruption
出牙迟延/生牙延緩　delayed dentition
出牙过早/出牙過早　precocious dentition
出牙期痉挛/出牙期痙攣　tooth spasm
出芽/芽生的　budding
出院规划/出院準備服務　discharge planning
出针/出針　needle withdrawal
出疹/發疹　eruption
初卟啉/初卟啉　etioporphyrins
初产/初產　primiparity
初产妇/初產婦　primipara
初潮/初潮　menarche
初次感染/初次感染　primary infection
初次免疫应答/首次免疫反應　primary immune response
初发的/初發的,始基的　primordial
初[发]腭/初腭,原腭　primary palate
初发性妄想/初發性妄想　primordial delirium
初发雅司疹/初發雅司疹　mamanpian
初骨/初骨,原骨　primitive bone
初级代谢产物/初級代謝產物　primary metabolite
初级辐射/初級輻射線　primary radiation
初级骨单位/初級骨單位　primary osteon
初级骨化中心/初級骨化中心　primary ossification center
初级骨髓/初級骨髓　primary bone marrow
初级骨髓腔/初級骨髓腔　primary marrow cavity
初级骨小梁/初級骨小梁　primary bone trabecula
初级护理保健/初級護理保健　primary nursing care
初级集合管/初級集合管　primary collecting duct
初级记忆/初級記憶　primary memory
初级精母细胞/初級精母細胞　primary spermatocyte
初级淋巴小结/初級淋巴小結　primary lymphoid nodule
初级卵黄囊/初級卵黃囊　primary yolk sac
初级卵黄细胞/初級卵黃細胞　primary yolk cell
初级卵母细胞/初級卵母細胞　primary oocyte
初级卵泡/初級卵泡,原卵泡　primary follicle
初级绒毛干/初級絨毛幹　primary stem villus
初级溶酶体/初級溶體　primary lysosome
初级卫生保健/初級衛生保健　primary health care
初级性索/原始生殖索　primary sex cord
初级眼保健/初級眼保健　primary eye care
初级支气管/初級支氣管　primary bronchus
初经迟延/月經遲來　delayed menstruation
初经过早/早來月經　precocious menstruation
初经前期/初經前期　premenarche
初磷脂/初磷脂　protagon
初模型/初模型　preliminary cast
初期疮/初期瘡　primary sore
初期的/原發的　primary
初期脊椎前移/脊椎滑脫症前驅症　prespondylolisthesis
初期结核病/潛伏結核　pretuberculosis
初期麻醉/初期麻醉　primary anesthesia
初期外科处理/初期外科處理　primary surgical care
初热/起始熱　initial heat
初乳/初乳　colostrum, colostric fluid
初乳小体/初乳小體　colostrum corpuscle
初乳溢/初乳漏,初乳溢流　colostrorrhea
初筛/預篩　prescreening
初生不乳/初生不乳　unable to suck in newborn
初生不啼/初生不啼　newborn asphyxia
初生大便不通/初生大便不通　lack of neonatal meconium
初生肛门内合/初生肛門內合　neonatal anal blockade
初生口噤/初生口噤　neonatal lockjaw
初生木质部/初生木質部　primary xylem
初生目闭/初生目閉　closed eyes in newborn
初生女婴阴道出血/初生女嬰陰道出血　neonatal vaginal bleeding
初生皮层/初生皮層　primary cortex
初生乳核/初生乳核　neonatal mammary nodule
初生肾缩/初生腎縮　retraction of testes in newborn
初生态/初生態,新生態　nascent state
初生无皮/初生無皮　skin erosion in newborn
初生小便不通/初生小便不通　neonatal anuria
初始淋巴管/初始淋巴管　initial lymphatic vessel
初始强化治疗阶段/初始強化治療階段　initial intensive phase of treatment
初始循环/原始循環　primitive circulation
初纤维/原絲,原細纖維　protofibril
初印模/初模　preliminary impression
初原肠胚/原囊胚,初囊胚　archigastrula
初原纤维/原原纖維,基原纖維　protofibril
初孕妇/初孕婦　primigravida
初治/初治　initial treatment
初治方案/初治方案　initial treatment regimen
初种/初種　primary vaccination
除颤器/除顫器　defibrillator
除虫菊属/除蟲菊屬　*Pyrethrum*

除虫菊酮/除蟲菊酮　pyrethron
除虫菊酯类/除蟲菊酯類　pyrethrins
除臭剂/除臭劑　deodorant
除臭鸦片/除臭鴉片　deodorized opium
除臭液/除臭液　deodorant solution
除臭作用/除臭作用　deodorization
除胆固醇[作用]/除膽脂醇法　decholesterinization
除氮/脱氮　denitrogenation
除管/拔管　extubate
除管法/除管法　detubation
除极/去極化作用,去偏極　depolarization
除极期/去極化期　depolarization phase
除甲状腺功能/除去甲狀腺功能　dethyroidize
除蜡法/除蠟法　deceration
除[皮肤]色素剂/皮膚色素消褪藥　hypopigmenter
除去器/除去器,消除器　remover
除湿通络/除濕通絡　eliminating dampness and dredging channels
除湿止带/除濕止帶　eliminating dampness and arresting leucorrhea
除套管术/拔除插管法,套管移除去　decannulation
除外诊断/除外診斷法,刪除診斷法　diagnosis by exclusion
除胰腺/除胰,切除胰臟　depancreatize
除莠剂/除莠劑　herbicide
除脏术/內臟剜除術,剜臟術　evisceration
除中/除中　pseudo good appetite
除皱术/除皺術　rhytidectomy
锄形洁治器/鋤刮器　hoe scaler
雏埃及小体/雛埃及小體　Aegyptianella pullorum
雏囊/雛囊　brood capsule
处方/處方　formula, prescription
处方法/處方法　prescribing method
处方费/處方費　prescription fee
处方集/處方集　formulary
处方设计前工作/處方設計前工作　preformulation
处方药/處方藥　prescription drug
处女/處女　virgin
处女恐怖/少女不明事理之恐懼　parthenophobia
处女膜/處女膜　hymen
处女膜闭锁/處女膜閉鎖　atresia hymenalis
处女膜缝术/處女膜縫合術　hymenorrhaphy
处女膜痕/處女膜痕　hymenal carunculae
处女膜口/處女膜口　hymenal orifice
处女膜破裂/處女膜破裂　defloration
处女膜破裂性肾盂炎/破貞性腎盂炎　defloration pyelitis
处女膜切除术/[處女]膜切除術　hymenectomy
处女膜切开术/處女膜切開術　hymenotomy
处女膜修复[术]/處女膜修復[術]　hymen repair
处女膜炎/處女膜炎　hymenitis
处女型B细胞/處女型B細胞　virgin B cell
处女型T细胞/處女型T細胞　virgin T cell
杵臼关节/杵臼關節,球窝關節　spheroidal joint, enarthrosis
杵臼关节炎/杵臼關節炎,球窝關節炎　enarthritis
杵状变/杵狀膨大　clubbing
杵状甲/杵狀甲　club nail
杵状毛/杵狀毛　club hair
杵状指/杵狀指　clubbing of digit, clubbed finger
杵状指甲/杵狀指甲　nail clubbing
杵状趾/杵狀趾　clubbing of digit, clubbed toe
杵状趾甲/杵狀趾甲　nail clubbing
楮实子/楮實子　papermulberry fruit
储备/儲備,儲量　reserve
储[备溶]液/儲備原液　stock solution
储备性受体/儲備性受體　spare receptor
储藏细胞/儲藏細胞　storage cell
储存反应/貯積反應　depot reaction
储存佐剂/儲存佐劑　depot forming adjuvant
储花粉室/花粉[儲藏]室　pollenarium
储能生长/生長,長育　bioplasia
怵惕/怵惕　fearful and alert
触/觸　touch
触发型起搏/觸發型起搏　triggered pacing
触幻觉/觸幻覺　haptic hallucination
触角沟/觸角溝　antennal groove
触角征象/觸角徵象　antenna sign
触觉/觸覺　tactile sense
触觉半月板/觸覺半月板　meniscus tactus
触觉测量法/觸覺測定法　esthesiometry
触觉测量器/觸覺計　esthesiometer
触觉迟钝/觸覺遲鈍,鈍觸　amblyaphia
触觉的/觸覺的　haptic, tactile
触觉感受器/接觸受器　contact receptor
触觉过敏/觸覺過敏,觸覺增強　hyperpselaphesia
触觉减退/觸覺減退,觸覺遲鈍　hypopselaphesia
触觉缺失/觸覺缺失　tactile anesthesia
触觉失认[症]/觸摸感失認症　tactile agnosia
触觉细胞/觸細胞　tactile cell
触觉小体/觸覺小體　tactile corpuscle
触觉小珠/觸覺小球　tactile elevation
触觉性失语/觸覺性失語症　tactile aphasia
触觉学/觸覺論　haptics
触觉震颤/觸覺震顫　tactile fremitus
触觉助听器/觸振交談器　teletactor

触叩诊/觸叩診　palpatopercussion
触酶试验/觸酶試驗　catalase test
触器/觸[覺]器　tactor
触染性痘疮/觸染性痘瘡　contagious ecthyma
触染性毛囊角化病/接觸傳染性毛囊角化病
　keratosis follicularis contagiosa
触染性脓疮/接觸傳染性臁瘡　ecthyma contagiosum
触染性脓疱病/傳染性膿皰病　impetigo contagiosa
触染性软疣/觸染性軟疣　molluscum contagiosum
触染性炭疽/觸染性炭疽　contagious anthrax
触痛/觸痛　haphalgesia
触物感痛症/觸物灼熱感　asphalgesia
触细胞/觸小體　touch cell
触小板/觸小板　tactile disc
触须/貓犬鬚　vibrissae
触诊/觸診[法]　palpation
触珠蛋白/血紅素結合素　haptoglobin
触珠蛋白类/觸珠蛋白類　haptoglobins
川贝母/川貝母　tendrilleaf fritillary bulb
川贝枇杷糖浆/川貝枇杷糖漿　chuanbei pipa syrup
川楝子/川楝子　szechwan chinaberry fruit
川木通/川木通　armand clematis stem
川牛膝/川牛膝　medicinal cyathula root
川崎病/川崎氏疾病　Kawasaki disease
川乌/川烏　common monkshood mother root
川芎/川芎　Sichuan lovage rhizome
川芎茶调散/川芎茶調散　chuanxiong chatiao
　powder
氚/氚　tritium
穿刺/穿刺,刺傷　puncture
穿刺法/穿刺法　puncture method
穿刺骨折/穿刺骨折　punctured fracture
穿刺培养/針刺培養　needle culture
穿刺术/穿刺術　paracentesis
穿刺性糖尿病/穿刺型糖尿病,第四腦室穿刺性糖尿
　病　puncture diabetes
穿刺针/穿刺針　puncture needle
穿动脉/穿動脈　perforating artery
穿腭类/穿腭類　hyperotreti
穿耳洞后/穿耳洞後　following ear piercing
穿骨切断术/斷骨截斷術　diaclastic amputation
穿拐痨/穿拐痨　tuberculous arthritis of the ankle
　joint
穿静脉/穿[透]靜脈　perforating vein
穿孔/穿孔　perforation
穿孔的/穿刺的　punctured
穿孔卡片系统/穿孔卡片系統　punched-card system
穿孔器/穿孔器　perforator
穿孔性的/穿孔的,穿通的　perforating
穿孔性腹膜炎/穿孔性腹膜炎　perforative peritonitis
穿孔性巩膜软化/穿孔性鞏膜軟化　scleromalacia
　perforans
穿孔性骨折/穿孔性骨折　perforating fracture
穿孔性阑尾炎/穿孔性蘭尾炎　perforative
　appendicitis
穿孔性皮肤病/穿孔性皮膚病　perforating
　dermatosis
穿颅器/穿顱器　transforator
穿颅术/穿顱法　transforation
穿黏膜种植体/穿黏膜種植體　transmucosal implant
穿皮神经/穿皮神經　perforating cutaneous nerve
穿山甲/穿山甲　pangolin scales
穿梭载体/穿梭載體　shuttle vector
穿通的/穿通的　perforans
穿通管/穿通管,福爾克曼管　perforating canal
穿通通路/穿通通路　perforant pathway
穿通纤维/穿通纖維　perforating fiber
穿通性癌/面皮癌　boring cancer
穿通性腓动脉/腓骨穿通動脈　perforating peroneal
　artery
穿通性钙化性弹力纤维病/穿孔性鈣化彈性纖維病
　perforating calcific elastosis
穿通性环状肉芽肿/穿孔性環狀肉芽腫　perforating
　granuloma annulare
穿通性溃疡/穿孔性潰瘍　perforating ulcer
穿通性类风湿结节/穿孔性類風濕結節　perforating
　rheumatoid nodule
穿通性毛囊炎/穿孔性毛囊炎　perforating folliculitis
穿通性龋/穿孔性齲　penetrating caries
穿通性弹力纤维瘤/穿孔性彈性纖維瘤　perforating
　elastoma
穿通性弹性假黄瘤/穿孔性彈性纖維假黃瘤
　perforating pseudoxanthoma elasticum
穿透[的]/穿透的　penetrate, penetrating
穿透伤/穿透傷　perforating wound
穿透式电子显微镜/穿透式電子顯微鏡
　transmission electron microscope
穿透性角膜移植术/穿入性角膜成形術　penetrating
　keratoplasty
穿透性溃疡/穿透性潰瘍　penetrating ulcer
穿透性胎盘/侵蝕粘連胎盤　placenta percreta
穿透性头部损伤/穿透性頭部損傷　penetrating head
　injury
穿透性眼损伤/穿透性眼損傷　penetrating eye injury
穿透支原体/穿透支原體　mycoplasma penetrans
穿下颌种植体/穿下頜種植體　tansmandibular

implant
穿心莲/穿心蓮 common andrographis herb
穿心莲片/穿心蓮片 chuanxinlian tablets
穿支/穿支 perforating branch
传病媒介/病媒,載體 vector
传播/傳[播] transmission
传播性搏动/傳播性搏動 transmitted pulsation
传播性胃肠炎/可傳染性胃腸炎 transmissible gastroenteritis
传播性胃肠炎病毒/傳播性胃腸炎病毒 transmissible gastroenteritis virus
传播性血栓/傳布性血栓 propagated thrombus
传出的/輸出的 efferent
传出神经/離中神經 centrifugal nerve, efferent nerve
传出神经纤维/傳出神經纖維 efferent nerve fiber
传出神经元/傳出神經元 efferent neuron
传出束/輸出徑 efferent tract
传出通路/傳出通路 efferent pathway
传出阻滞/釋出性阻滯 exit block
传导/傳導 conduction
传导比例/傳導比例 conduction ratio
传导不可逆性/傳導不可逆性 irreversibility of conduction
传导动脉/傳導動脈,大動脈幹 conducting artery
传导放电/傳導放電 conductive discharge
传导骨/傳導骨 conduction bone
传导麻醉/傳導麻醉法 conduction anesthesia
传导热/傳導熱 conductive heat
传导热疗法/傳導熱療法 conductive heat therapy
传导系统/傳導系統 conduction system
传导性/傳導性,傳導力 conductibility
传导性聋/傳導性聾 conductive deafness
传导性失语/傳導性失語症 conduction aphasia
传导性听觉丧失/傳導性聽覺喪失 conductive hearing loss
传导之官/傳導之官 official of transportation
传化物而不藏/傳化物而不藏 digesting and transporting food and drink without storing essence
传能线密度/傳能線密度 linear energy transfer
传染/傳染 infection
传染病/傳染病 communicable disease
传染病控制/傳染病控制 communicable disease control
传染病学/傳染病學 lemology
传染的/有傳染性的 communicable
传染途径/傳染途徑 routes of infection
传染性痤疮/傳染性痤瘡 contagious acne

传染性单核[白]细胞增多[症]病毒/傳染性單核白血球增多症病毒 infectious mononucleosis virus
传染性单核细胞增多症/傳染性單核細胞增多症 infectious mononucleosis
传染性肝炎病毒/傳染性肝炎病毒 infectious hepatitis virus
传染性核酸/傳染性核酸 infectious nucleic acid
传染性红斑/傳染性紅斑 erythema infectiosum
传染性黄疸/傳染性黃疸,感染性黃疸 icterus infectious
传染性角结膜炎/傳染性角結膜炎 infectious keratoconjunctivitis
传染性口角炎/傳染性口角炎 perleche
传染性淋巴细胞增多症/傳染性淋巴細胞增多症 infectious lymphocytosis
传染性黏液瘤病/感染性黏液瘤病 infectious myxomatosis
传染性皮肤疾病/傳染性皮膚疾病 infectious skin disease
传染性腔上囊病病毒/傳染性腔上囊病病毒 infectious bursal disease virus
传染性软疣病毒/接觸傳染性軟疣病毒 molluscum contagiosum virus
传染性湿疹样皮炎/傳染性濕疹樣皮炎 infectious eczematoid dermatitis
传染性胸膜肺炎/傳染性胸膜肺炎 contagious pleuropneumonia
传染性血栓形成/感染性血栓形成 infective thrombosis
传染性胰腺坏死病毒/傳染性胰腺壞死病毒 infectious pancreatic necrosis virus
传染性支气管炎病毒/傳染性支氣管炎病毒 infectious bronchitis virus
传染源/傳染源 sources of infection
传入单位/傳入的單位 afferent unit
传入的/傳入的 afferent
传入神经/傳入神經,向心神經 afferent nerve, centripetal nerve
传入神经纤维/傳入神經纖維 afferent nerve fiber
传入神经元/傳入神經元 afferent neuron
传入神经阻滞/去傳入神經法 deafferentation
传入束/傳入束 afferent tract
传入通路/傳入通路 afferent pathway
传入支阻断/傳入支阻斷 afferent block
传入阻滞/進入性阻滯 entrance block
传送带接口/傳送帶界面 moving belt interface
传统药/傳統藥 traditional drug
传统医学/傳統醫學 traditional medicine

船员踝肿/船员踝部浮肿症　deck ankles
喘/呼吸困难　dyspnea
喘鸣/喘鳴,嘯聲　stridor
喘鸣的/喘鳴的　stridulous
喘胀/喘脹　dyspnea and distension
串联重复序列/串聯重複序列　tandem repeat sequences
串联游离皮瓣/串聯游離皮瓣　free skin flap in series
串扰/串擾　crosstalk
串线伤/同側穿孔創傷　seton wound
串线针/串線針　seton needle
串雅内编/串雅内編　Internal Therapies of Folk Medicine
串雅外编/串雅外編　External Therapies of Folk Medicine
串珠肋/串珠肋　rachitic rosary
串珠蛇舌状虫/串珠蛇洞頭蟲　Armillifer moniliformis
串珠状/連珠狀　beaded
串珠状痤疮/串珠狀痤瘡　varicose acne
串珠状的/串珠狀的　moniliform
创口缝术/創傷縫合術　traumatonesis
创面/創面　wound surface
创面活组织检查术/傷口活組織檢查法　wound biopsy
创面菌群/創面菌群　wound flora
创伤/創傷　trauma
创伤病理学/創傷病理學　pathology of trauma
创伤弹道学/創傷彈道學　wound ballistics
创伤的/創傷的,外傷的　traumatic
创伤感染/創傷感染　traumatic infection
创伤后代谢反应/創傷後代謝反應　posttraumatic metabolic response
创伤后的/創傷後的,外傷後的　posttraumatic
创伤后癫痫/創傷後癲癇　posttraumatic epilepsy
创伤后骨萎缩/創傷後骨萎縮　Sudeck atrophy
创伤后脊柱后凸/創傷後脊柱後凸　posttraumatic kyphosis
创伤后脑综合征/創傷後腦症候群　posttraumatic brain syndrome
创伤后气管狭窄/創傷後氣管狹窄　posttraumatic tracheal stenosis
创伤后人格障碍/創傷後人格障礙　posttraumatic personality disorder
创伤后头痛/創傷後頭痛　posttraumatic headache
创伤后营养不良/創傷後營養不良　wound dystrophy
创伤后应激障碍/創傷後應激障礙　posttraumatic stress disorder
创伤后肿瘤/創傷後腫瘤　posttraumatic neoplasms
创伤后综合征/創傷後症候群　posttraumatic syndrome
创伤免疫学/創傷免疫學　immunology of trauma
创伤评分/創傷評分　trauma score
创伤外科学/創傷外科學　traumatic surgery
创伤细菌学/創傷細菌學　bacteriology of trauma
创伤性出血/創傷性出血　traumatic hemorrhage
创伤性大脑出血/創傷性大脑出血　traumatic cerebral hemorrhage
创伤性动脉瘤/創傷性動脈瘤　traumatic aneurysm
创伤性窦道/創傷性瘻　traumatic sinus
创伤性发热/創傷性發熱　traumatic fever
创伤性睾丸炎/創傷性睾丸炎　traumatic orchitis
创伤性膈疝/創傷性膈疝　traumatic diaphragmatic hernia
创伤性骨囊肿/創傷性骨囊腫　traumatic bone cyst
创伤性骨折/創傷性骨折　traumatic fracture
创伤性关节炎/創傷性關節炎　traumatic arthritis
创伤[性]殆/創傷殆,創傷性咬合　traumatic occlusion
创伤性滑膜炎/創傷性滑膜炎　traumatic synovitis
创伤性滑膜炎·风寒侵袭证/創傷性滑膜炎·風寒侵襲證　traumatic synovitis with wind-cold invasion pattern
创伤性滑膜炎·痰湿阻络证/創傷性滑膜炎·痰濕阻絡證　traumatic synovitis with pattern of phlegm-dampness obstructing collateral
创伤性滑膜炎·血瘀气滞证/創傷性滑膜炎·血瘀氣滯證　traumatic synovitis with pattern of blood stasis and qi stagnation
创伤性疾病/創傷病　traumatic disease
创伤性截肢/創傷性截斷　traumatic amputation
创伤性精神病/創傷性精神病　traumatic psychosis
创伤性口炎/創傷性口炎　traumatic stomatitis
创伤性颅内出血/創傷性顱内出血　traumatic intracranial hemorrhage
创伤性脑病/創傷性腦病變　traumatic encephalopathy
创伤性脑出血/創傷性脑出血　traumatic brain hemorrhage
创伤性脑干出血/創傷性脑幹出血　traumatic brain stem hemorrhage
创伤性气急/創傷性氣促,創傷性窒息　traumatopnea
创伤性气胸/創傷性氣胸　traumatic pneumothorax

创伤性神经病/創傷性神經病變　traumatic neuropathy
创伤性神经衰弱/創傷性神經衰弱　traumasthenia
创伤性水肿/創傷性水腫　traumatic edema
创伤性脱发/創傷性禿髮　traumatic alopecia
创伤性文身/創傷性文身　traumatic tattoo
创伤性心包压塞/創傷性心包壓塞　traumatic pericardial tamponade
创伤性休克/創傷性休克　traumatic shock
创伤性牙殆/創傷性牙殆　traumatic dental occlusion
创伤性蝇蛆病/創傷性蠅蛆病　traumatic myiasis
创伤性应激障碍/創傷性應激障礙　traumatic stress disorder
创伤性谵妄/創傷性譫妄　traumatic delirium
创伤性窒息/創傷性窒息　traumatic asphyxia
创伤性蛛网膜下腔出血/創傷性蛛網膜下腔出血　traumatic subarachnoid hemorrhage
创伤性子宫粘连/創傷性子宮粘連　traumatic uterine adhesion
创伤修复/創傷修復　repair in trauma
创伤学/創傷學科　traumatology
创伤严重度指数/創傷嚴重度指數　trauma severity indice
创伤药/創傷藥,治創藥　vulnerary
创伤愈合/創傷愈合　healing of wound
创伤[原]性的/造成創傷的,致創傷的　traumatogenic
创伤诊治中心/創傷診治中心　trauma center
创伤指数/創傷指數　trauma index
创伤治疗/創傷治療　trauma care
创伤治疗法/創傷治療法　traumatotherapy
创伤治疗学/創傷治療學,外傷治療法　traumatherapy
疮/瘡　sore
疮痂/瘡痂　scab
疮痨性溃疡/瘡癆性潰瘍　tuberculous ulcer
疮疡/瘡瘍　sore and ulcer
疮疡补法/瘡瘍補法　benefiting method for healing of sore and ulcer, sore-ulcer-tonifying therapy
疮疡补托法/瘡瘍補托法　promoting method with tonification
疮疡透托法/瘡瘍透托法　direct promoting method
疮疡托法/瘡瘍托法　promoting pustulation of sore and ulcer by strengthening vital qi, sore-ulcer-promoting therapy
疮疡消法/瘡瘍消法　resolving method for sore and ulcer, sore-ulcer-resolving therapy
窗/窗　window
窗孔式叶状骨内植入体导缘/刃形骨內植體之窗式導緣　fenestrated leading edge of blade endosseous implant
窗口图解技术/窗口圖解技術　window diagram technique
床/床　bed
床边试验/床邊試驗　bedside test
床边视野计/臥床視野計　bed perimeter
床旁诊断化验信息系统/床旁診斷化驗資訊系統　point-of-care systems
床上运动/床上運動　bed exercise
床外因素/床外因素　extra-bed factor
床形的/床狀的　clinoid
吹鼻疗法/吹鼻療法　nose-insufflating therapy
吹玻璃工人病/吹玻璃工人病　glass-blower disease
吹玻璃工人肺气肿/吹玻璃工人肺氣腫　glass-blower emphysema
吹耳疗法/吹耳療法　ear-insufflating therapy
吹风冷却/吹風冷卻　windchill
吹风[气]样杂音/吹氣狀雜音　blowing murmur
吹管/吹管　pipe
吹号者疣/吹號者疣　trumpeter wart
吹喉疗法/吹喉療法　larynx-blowing therapy
吹口哨状唇畸形/吹口哨狀唇畸形　whistling lip deformity
吹气性杂音/吹氣性雜音　whiffing murmur
吹气样呼吸音/吹氣樣呼吸音　blowing respiration
吹入麻醉/灌氣麻醉法　insufflation anesthesia
吹入器/吹入器,吹藥器　insufflator
吹药法/吹藥法　blowing drug method
垂腭/垂腭,懸雍垂延長　falling palate
垂耳/垂耳　lop ear
垂腹/垂腹　venter propendens
垂肩畸形/垂肩畸形　dropped shoulder abnormality
垂盆草/垂盆草　stringy stonecrop herb
垂屏式氧合器/垂屏式氧合器　screen oxygenator
垂前/垂前　chuiqian, anterior ear lobe, LO4
垂熔玻璃滤器/垂熔玻璃濾器　sintered glass filter
垂体/[腦下]垂體　pituitary
垂体胺/垂體胺　hypophamine
垂体柄/[腦下]垂體莖　hypophyseal stalk
垂体卒中/[腦下]垂體中風　pituitary apoplexy
垂体促性腺素类/[腦下]垂體促性腺素類　pituitary gonadotropins
垂体的/[腦下]垂體的　hypophyseal, hypophysial
垂体 ACTH 分泌过多/[腦下]垂體 ACTH 分泌過多　pituitary ACTH hypersecretion
垂体功能不全性肥胖症/[腦下]垂體機能不全性肥

胖症　pituitary adiposity
垂体功能减退/[脑下]垂體機能不足　hypohypophysism
垂体功能亢进/[脑下]垂體機能亢進　hyperhypophysism, hyperpituitarism
垂体功能缺失/[脑下]垂體缺失，腦下垂體缺失病　apituitarism
垂体功能试验/垂體功能試驗　pituitary function test
垂体功能障碍/[脑下]垂體功能障礙　pituitarism
垂体管/[脑下]垂體管　hypophyseal duct
垂体后叶激素类/[脑下]垂體後葉激素類　hypophysis posterior lobe hormones, posterior pituitary hormones
垂体[后叶]液/[脑下]垂體後葉溶液　posterior pituitary solution
垂体激素类/[脑下]垂體激素類　hypophysis hormones, pituitary hormones
垂体激素释放激素类/[脑下]垂體激素釋放激素類　pituitary hormone-releasing hormones
垂体激素释放兴奋药/[脑下]垂體激素釋放興奮藥　hypophysis hormone release stimulant
垂体激素释放抑制激素类/[脑下]垂體激素釋放抑制激素類　pituitary hormone release inhibiting hormones
垂体激素受体/[脑下]垂體激素受體　pituitary hormone receptor
垂体激素调节激素受体/[脑下]垂體激素調節激素受體　pituitary hormone-regulating hormone receptor
垂体疾病/[脑下]垂體疾病　pituitary disease
垂体冷凝破坏法/[脑下]垂體冷凝破壞法　cryohypophysectomy
垂体瘤/[脑下]垂體瘤　pituitary tumor
[垂体]滤泡细胞/濾泡細胞　follicular cell
垂体门静脉/[脑下]垂體門靜脈　hypophyseoportal vein
垂体门静脉系统/[脑下]垂體門靜脈系統　portal vein of hypophysis
垂体门脉的/[脑下]垂體門脈的　hypophyseoportal
垂体门脉循环/[脑下]垂體門脈循環　hypophyseoportal circulation
垂体囊肿/[脑下]垂體囊腫　hypophyseal cyst
垂体前叶/[脑下]垂體前葉　anterior pituitary
垂体前叶激素类/腦下垂體前葉激素類，前葉垂體激素　anterior pituitary hormones, hypophysis anterior lobe hormones
垂体前叶样激素/[脑下]垂前葉樣激素　anterior pituitary like substance

垂体切除术/[脑下]垂體切除術　hypophysectomy
垂体软骨/[脑下]垂腺軟骨　hypophyseal cartilage
垂体上动脉/[脑下]垂體上動脈　superior hypophysial artery
垂体神经部/[脑下]垂體神經部　pars nervosa
垂体肾上腺功能试验/[脑下]垂體腎上腺功能試驗　pituitary-adrenal function test
垂体肾上腺系统/[脑下]垂體腎上腺系統　pituitary-adrenal system
垂体-肾上腺轴/[脑下]垂體腎上腺軸　pituitary-adrenal axis
[垂体]嗜碱性细胞/嗜鹼性細胞　basophilic cell
垂体嗜酸细胞/[脑下]垂體嗜酸性細胞　oxyphilic cell of hypophysis
[垂体]嗜酸性细胞/嗜酸性細胞　acidophilic cell
垂体窝/[脑下]垂體凹　hypophysial fossa
垂体细胞/[脑下]垂體細胞　pituicyte
垂体下动脉/[脑下]垂體下動脈　inferior hypophysial artery
垂体腺癌/[脑下]垂體腺癌　pituitary carcinoma
垂体腺瘤/[脑下]垂體腺瘤　pituitary adenoma
垂体协作激素/[脑下]垂體協助素　pituitary synergist
垂体性闭经/[脑下]垂體性停經　pituitary amenorrhea
垂体性恶病质/[脑下]垂體性惡病質　hypophysial cachexia
垂体性高血压/[脑下]垂體性高血壓　pituitary hypertension
垂体性黏液水肿/[脑下]垂腺性黏液水腫　pituitary myxedema
垂体性尿崩症/[脑下]垂體性尿崩症　pituitary diabetes insipidus
垂体性无睾症/[脑下]垂體性無睾現象　pituitary eunuchism
垂体性眼病/[脑下]垂體性眼病　pituitarigenic oculopathy
垂体性侏儒/[脑下]垂體性侏儒　hypophysial dwarf
垂体性侏儒症/[脑下]垂體性侏儒症　pituitary dwarfism
垂体炎/[脑下]垂體炎　hypophysitis
垂体照射/[脑下]垂體照射　pituitary irradiation
垂体肿瘤/[脑下]垂體腫瘤　pituitary neoplasms
垂体综合征/[脑下]垂體症候群　pituitary syndrome
垂腕畸形/垂腕畸形　wristdrop deformity
垂直板/垂直板　perpendicular plate
垂直参考线/垂直輔助線　vertical reference line
垂直层流洁净室/垂直式層流潔淨室　vertical

laminar flow clean room
垂直传递/遺傳之垂直傳遞　vertical transmission
垂直的/垂直的　vertical
垂直疾病传播/垂直疾病傳播　vertical disease transmission
垂直截骨术/垂直截骨術　vertical osteotomy
垂直距离/垂直距離,垂直尺度　vertical dimension
垂直性眼球震颤/垂直性眼球震顫　vertical nystagmus
垂直性隐斜/垂直性隱斜　vertical phoria
垂直眩晕/垂直眩暈　vertical vertigo
垂直轴/垂直軸　vertical axis
垂直阻生/垂直阻生　vertical impaction
垂足畸形/垂足畸形　equinus foot
捶胸整脉术/捶胸整脈術　thump version
槌状指/槌狀指　mallet finger
槌状指畸形/槌狀指畸形　mallet finger deformity
槌状趾畸形/槌狀趾畸形　mallet toe deformity
锤/錘　hammer
锤骨/錘骨　malleus
锤骨柄/錘骨柄　manubrium of malleus
锤骨后襞/錘骨後皺襞　posterior malleolar fold
锤骨颈/錘骨頸　neck of malleus
锤骨前襞/錘骨前皺襞　anterior malleolar fold
锤骨前韧带/錘骨前韌帶　anterior ligament of malleus
锤骨前突/錘骨前突　anterior process
锤骨切除术/錘骨切除術　sphyrectomy
锤骨上韧带/錘骨上韌帶　superior ligament of malleus
锤骨头/錘骨頭　head of malleus
锤骨外侧韧带/錘骨外側韌帶　lateral ligament of malleus, axis ligament of malleus
锤骨外侧突/斜側突　lateral process of malleus
锤击样颤搐/錘擊狀痙攣　malleation
锤前韧带/錘前韌帶　ligamentum mallei anterius
锤手麻痹/錘手麻痺　hammer palsy
锤凸/錘凸　malleolar prominence
锤纹/錘紋　malleolar stria
锤型/錘型　plectron
锤造冠/錘造冠　swaged crown
锤造金属全冠/錘造金屬全冠　swaged metal full crown
锤状趾/錘狀趾　hammer toe
锤状趾综合征/錘狀趾症候群　hammer toe syndrome
春/春　spring
春黄菊属/洋甘菊屬　Anthemis
春季肺水肿/春季肺水腫　vernal edema of lung
春季结膜炎/春季結膜炎　vernal conjunctivitis
春季卡他性眼炎/春季眼炎　spring ophthalmia
春季脑炎/春季腦炎　vernal encephalitis
春季疹/春季疹　spring eruption
春霉素 B/春黴素 B　vernamycin B
春温/春溫　spring warm disorder, spring warmth
春温夹滞/春溫夾滯　spring warmth complicated with food stagnation
春温•内闭外脱证/春溫•內閉外脫證　spring warmth with pattern of internal blockade and external collapse
春温•气营两燔证/春溫•氣營兩燔證　spring warmth with pattern of blazing heat in both qi and nutrient phases
春温•热结气虚证/春溫•熱結氣虛證　spring warmth with pattern of heat binding and qi deficiency
春温•热结阴亏证/春溫•熱結陰虧證　spring warmth with pattern of heat binding and yin insufficiency
春温•热扰胸膈证/春溫•熱擾胸膈證　spring warmth with pattern of heat stagnation in chest and diaphragm
春温•热盛动风证/春溫•熱盛動風證　spring warmth with pattern of wind stirring by exuberant heat
春温•热盛动血证/春溫•熱盛動血證　spring warmth with pattern of bleeding caused by blazing heat
春温•热陷心包证/春溫•熱陷心包證　spring warmth disease with pattern of heat invading pericardium
春温•热与血结证/春溫•熱與血結證　spring warmth with pattern of binding of heat and blood
春温•热郁胆腑证/春溫•熱鬱膽腑證　spring warmth with pattern of heat stagnation in gallbladder
春温•热灼胸膈证/春溫•熱灼胸膈證　spring warmth with pattern of heat burning in chest and diaphragm
春温•热灼营血证/春溫•熱灼營血證　spring warmth with pattern of toxin entering nutrient and blood phases
春温•肾阴虚证/春溫•腎陰虛證　spring warmth with pattern of kidney yin deficiency
春温•邪留阴分证/春溫•邪留陰分證　spring warmth with pattern of pathogen retained in yin

phase
春温·虚风内动证/春溫·虛風內動證　spring warmth with pattern of internal stirring of deficient wind
春温·阳明腑实证/春溫·陽明腑實證　spring warmth with pattern of excess of Yangming fu-viscera
春温·阳明热盛证/春溫·陽明熱盛證　spring warmth with pattern of exuberant heat in Yangming
春温·阴虚火旺证/春溫·陰虛火旺證　spring warmth with pattern of exuberant fire due to yin deficiency
椿皮/椿皮　cortex ailanthi, tree-of-heaven bark
纯的/純的　pure
纯度/純度　purity
纯多糖/全糖類　holosaccharide
纯合体交配/同品種異系交配　incross
纯合性/純合性, 同型接合性　homozygosity
纯合子/純合子, 同種胚子, 同質接合子　homozygote
纯红细胞再生障碍/純紅細胞再生障礙　pure red cell aplasia
纯化/純化　purification
纯培养/純培養　pure culture
纯阳之体/純陽之體　infantile body of pure yang
纯阴结/純陰結　pure yin binding
纯音测听法/純音測聽法　pure-tone audiometry
纯音筛选测听[法]/純音篩選測聽[法]　pure-tone screening audiometry
纯音听阈均值/純音聽閾均值　pure-tone average
唇/唇　lip
唇癌/唇癌　cheilocarcinoma
唇板/唇板　labial lamina
唇瓣/唇瓣　lip flap
唇鞭毛虫病/唇鞭蟲病　chilomastigiasis
唇不全裂/唇不全裂　incomplete cleft lip
唇部/唇部　labial part
唇侧倾斜/唇側傾斜　labioclination
唇侧翼缘/唇側凸緣　labial flange
唇侧龈/唇面齦　labial gingiva
唇侧折牙/唇側折牙　labial fracture
唇成形术/唇造形術, 補唇術　cheiloplasty
唇挡/唇擋　lip bumper
唇的/唇的　labial
唇低线/唇低線　lip low line
唇疔/唇疔　ding of lip, lip furuncle
唇动描记器/唇動描記器　labiograph
唇读/唇讀　lip reading

唇萼薄荷/胡薄荷　pennyroyal
唇反/唇反　cheilectropion
唇风/唇風　lip wind, chronic cheilitis, labial wind
唇风·脾虚血燥证/唇風·脾虛血燥證　lip wind with pattern of spleen deficiency and blood dryness
唇风·胃经风热证/唇風·胃經風熱證　lip wind with pattern of wind-heat in stomach channel
唇干裂/唇乾裂　cheilosis
唇干燥/唇乾燥　xerocheilia
唇杆/唇側槓　labial bar
唇高线/唇高線　lip high line
唇弓/唇弓　labial arch
唇弓脊/唇弓脊　ridge of labial arch
唇沟/唇溝　labial groove
唇沟板/唇[齒]溝　lip furrow band
唇颌腭裂[畸形]/裂唇頜腭畸形, 狼咽　cheilognathopalatoschisis
唇颌裂[畸形]/裂唇頜畸形, 兔唇　cheilognathoschisis
唇颌面裂[畸形]/裂唇頜面畸形　cheilognathoprosoposchisis
唇红/唇紅　vermillion of the lip
唇红缘/唇紅緣　vermilion border
唇后联合/唇後連合　posterior labial commissure
唇厚度/唇厚度　lip thickness
唇及舌头不自主运动障碍/嘴唇及舌頭不自主運動障礙　buccal lingual masticatory dyskinesia
唇疾病/唇疾病　lip diseases
唇间擦烂/唇擦爛　intertrigo labialis
唇角化病/嘴唇角化病　keratosis labialis
唇颈脊/唇頸脊　labiocervical ridge
唇癌/唇癌　lip cancer
唇口成形术/唇口造形術, 唇口修補術　cheilostomatoplasty
唇联合/唇連合　commissura labiorum
唇裂/唇裂, 裂唇　cleft lip, chapped lip
唇裂[畸形]/裂唇畸形, 兔唇　cheiloschisis
唇裂矩形[唇]瓣修复术/唇裂矩形[唇]瓣修復術　cleft lip repair by quadrilateral lip flap technique
唇裂三角[唇]瓣修复术/唇裂三角[唇]瓣修復術　cleft lip repair by triangular lip flap technique
唇裂手术减张弓/羅格氏弓　Logan bow
唇裂术后继发畸形/唇裂術後繼發畸形　postoperative secondary deformity of cleft lip
唇裂修复术/唇縫合術　cheilorrhaphy
唇裂序列征/唇裂序列徵　cleft lip sequence
唇裂针/唇裂針　harelip needle
唇瘘/唇瘻　labial fistula

唇面/唇面 labial surface
唇面[龋]洞/唇面龋齿腔洞 labial cavity
唇黏膜/唇黏膜 labial mucosa
唇[皮缘]中点/唇[皮缘]中點 labrale
唇牵开器/唇牽開器 lip retractor
唇前联合/唇前連合 anterior labial commissure
唇舌弓矫治器/唇舌弓矯治器 labiolingual appliance
唇湿/唇濕 cheilitis
唇四白/唇四白 perilabial zone
唇外翻/唇外翻 eclabium
唇完全裂/唇完全裂 complete cleft lip
唇系带/唇繫帶 labial frenum
唇线/唇線 lip line
唇腺/唇腺 labial gland
唇[向]𬌗/齿唇侧咬合 labial occlusion
唇向移位/唇向移位 labioplacement
唇血管镜/唇血管鏡 angiocheiloscope
唇炎/唇炎 cheilitis
唇音滥用/唇音濫用,不當使用唇音 labialism
唇龈板/唇齦板 labiogingival lamina
唇龈的/唇齦的 labiogingival
唇龈沟/唇齦溝 labiogingival groove
唇龈切口/唇齦切口 labiogingival incision
唇语/唇語 lip language
唇缘/唇緣 labial margin
唇运动学/唇運動學 labiology
唇粘连/唇粘連 ankylocheilia
唇真菌病/唇黴菌病 labiomycosis
唇支/唇支 labial branch
唇肿/唇腫 swollen lip
唇肿·风寒外袭证/唇腫·風寒外襲證 swollen lip with pattern of external assault by wind-cold
唇肿·风热袭表证/唇腫·風熱襲表證 swollen lip with pattern of wind-heat assaulting exterior
唇肿瘤/唇腫瘤 lip neoplasms
唇珠/唇珠 vermilion tubercle
唇足虫目/唇足蟲目 Chilopoda
醇的/酒精的 alcoholic
醇苷/醇苷 alcoholic glycoside
醇基/醇基 alcohol group
醇解/醇解 alcoholysis
醇类/醇類 alcohols
醇酶/釀醇酵素,酒精酶 alcoholase
醇醚氯仿混合液麻醉/醇醚氯仿混合液麻醉 alcohol-chloroform-ether mixture anesthesia
醇尿/醇尿,酒精尿 alcoholuria
醇溶蛋白/酒精可溶[性]蛋白質 alcohol-soluble protein
醇溶谷蛋白/禾穀蛋白類 prolamin
醇溶性浸出物/乙醇抽提物 ethanol-soluble extractive
醇溶液/醇溶液 alcoholic solution
醇酸树脂/醇酸樹脂 alkyl resin
醇脱氢酶/乙醇脱氫酶,乙醇脱氫酵素 alcohol dehydrogenase
醇血症/醇血症 alcoholemia
醇氧化还原酶类/醇氧化還原酶類 alcohol oxidoreductases
醇诱发的/誘發的酒精反應 alcohol-induced
醇中毒/醇中毒 ethanolism
戳法/戳法,踩法 stamping manipulation
戳伤/戳傷,刺傷 stab wound
词汇性失语/言语的失語症 verbal aphasia
词联想测验/詞聯想測驗 word association test
词义性痴呆/失義性癡呆 semantic dementia
词组重复症/語句重複症 choreophrasia
瓷边缘/瓷邊緣 porcelain margin
瓷高嵌体/瓷高嵌體 ceramic onlay
瓷甲冠/瓷甲冠 porcelain jacket crown
瓷嵌体/瓷嵌體 ceramic inlay
瓷贴面/瓷貼面 porcelain veneer
瓷牙/瓷牙 porcelain tooth
慈善/行善 beneficence
慈善医院/慈善醫院 voluntary hospital
磁带录音录像/磁帶錄音錄影 tape recording
磁共振波谱学/磁共振波譜學 magnetic resonance spectroscopy
磁共振成像/磁共振成像 magnetic resonance imaging
磁共振血管造影术/磁共振血管造影術 magnetic resonance angiography
磁共振胰胆管造影术/磁共振胰膽管造影術 magnetic resonance cholangiopancreatography
磁控[电子]管/磁電管 magnetron
磁疗法/磁力療法 magnetotherapy
磁频率/磁頻率 magnet rate
磁倾针/磁傾針 dipping needle
磁石/磁石 magnetite
磁体种植体/磁體種植體 magnetic implant
磁铁吸出[法]/磁鐵吸出[法] magnet extraction
磁性的/磁的 magnetic
磁性固位/磁性固位 magnetic retention
磁性伸缩/磁伸縮 magnetoconstriction
磁性衔铁/磁性銜鐵 armature keeper
磁性眼内异物/磁性眼内異物 intraocular magnetic foreign body

磁朱丸/磁朱丸　cizhu pills
磁阻/磁阻　reluctance
雌氮芥/雌氮芥　estramustine
雌二醇/雌二醇,二羟雌性素　estradiol
雌二醇拮抗剂/雌二醇拮抗劑　estradiol antagonist
雌二醇受体/雌二醇受體　estradiol receptor
雌二醇同源物/雌二醇同源物　estradiol congener
雌二醇脱氢酶类/雌二醇脱氫酶類　estradiol dehydrogenases
雌激素/雌性素　estrin
雌激素高脂血症/雌激素高脂血症　estrogenic hyperlipidemia
雌激素过多/動情素過多症,血內動情素過多　hyperestrinism
雌激素拮抗剂/雌激素拮抗劑　estrogen antagonist
雌激素类/雌激素類　estrogens
雌激素试验/雌激素試驗　estrogen test
雌激素受体/雌激素受體　estrogen receptor
雌激素受体调节剂/雌激素受體調節劑　estrogen receptor modulator
雌激素替代疗法/雌激素替代療法　estrogen replacement therapy
雌激素与肌酐比值/雌激素與肌酐比值　estrogen/creatinine ratio
雌蕊/雌蕊　pistil
雌三醇/雌三醇　estriol
雌四醇/雌四醇　estetrol
雌酮/雌酮　estrone
雌烷类/雌烷類　estranes
雌烯类/雌烯類　estrens
雌烯三醇/雌烯三醇　estrenol
雌性不育/雌性不育　female infertility
雌性激素/雌性激素,雌性賀爾蒙　female sex hormone
雌[性]配子/雌配子　female gamete
雌[性]原核/雌性原核　female pronucleus
雌雄间体/中間性　sex intergrade
雌雄异体的/雌雄異體　diecious
雌[甾]激素/雌激素　estrogen
次胞质体/次胞質體　deuterosome
次苯基/伸苯基　phenylene
次卟啉/次卟啉　deuteroporphyrin
次的/次的　the second
次腭/續腭　secondary palate
次甘氨酸/次甘氨酸　hypoglycin
次高铁血红素/次高鐵血紅素　kopratin
次黄嘌呤/次黄嘌呤　hypoxanthine
次黄嘌呤磷酸核糖转移酶/次黄嘌呤磷酸核糖轉移酶　hypoxanthine phosphoribosyltransferase
次磺酸类/次磺酸類　sulfenic acids
次级/次級的,續發的,次發的　secondary
次级代谢产物/次級代謝產物　secondary metabolite
次级放射/次級放射　secondary radiation
次级苷/次級苷　secondary glycoside
次级骨单位/次級骨單位　secondary osteon
次级骨化中心/次級骨化中心　epiphyseal ossification center, secondary ossification center
次级骨髓/次級骨髓　secondary bone marrow
次级骨髓腔/次級骨髓腔　secondary marrow cavity
次级骨小梁/次級骨小梁　secondary bone trabecula
次级集合管/次級集合管　secondary collecting duct
次级记忆/次級記憶　secondary memory
次级[间质]细胞/次級[間質]細胞　secondary interstitial cell
次级精母细胞/次級精母細胞　secondary spermatocyte
次级淋巴小结/次級淋巴小結　secondary lymphoid nodule
次级卵黄囊/二級卵黄囊　secondary yolk sac
次级卵母细胞/次級卵母細胞　secondary oocyte
次级卵泡/次級卵泡　secondary follicle
次级绒毛干/次級絨毛幹　secondary stem villus
次级溶酶体/次級溶體　secondary lysosome
次级乳糖酶缺乏/次級乳糖酶缺乏　secondary lactase deficiency
次级性索/次級性索　secondary sex cord
次级营养素/間接營養物　secondary nutrient
次[级]支气管/次支氣管　secondary bronchus
次级致癌物/次級致癌物　secondary carcinogens
次尖/上腭白齒之上次尖　hypocone
次髎/次髎　ciliao, BL32
次裂/次裂[隙]　secondary fissure, fissura secunda
次磷酸/次亞磷酸,低亞磷酸　hypophosphorous acid
次磷酸类/次磷酸類　phosphinic acids
次磷酸锰/次磷酸亞錳　manganese hypophosphite
次磷酸盐/低亞磷酸鹽,次亞磷酸鹽　hypophosphite
次硫酸盐/次硫酸鹽,亞硫酸鹽　hyposulfite
次氯酸/次氯酸　hypochlorous acid
次氯酸钠/次氯酸鈉　sodium hypochlorite
次氯酸钠烧伤/次氯酸鈉燒傷　sodium hypochlorite burn
次氯酸盐/次氯酸鹽,低氯酸鹽　hypochlorite
次氯血红素/亞血晶素　deuterohemin
次桥基/次橋基　secondary abutment
次全鼻再造术/次全鼻再造術　subtotal nose reconstruction

次胂酸/次胂酸　arsinic acid
次生木质部/次生木質部　secondary xylem
次生皮质/次生皮質　secondary cortex
次声频率/音波下頻率　infrasonic frequency
次水杨酸盐/次水楊酸鹽　subsalicylate
次碳酸铋/次碳酸鉍　bismuth subcarbonate
次硝酸铋/次硝酸鉍　bismuth subnitrate
次小尖/上腭白齒之上末尖　hypoconule
次溴酸/次溴酸　hypobromous acid
次要淋巴细胞刺激基因座/次要淋巴細胞刺激基因座　minor lymphocyte stimulatory loci
次要组织相容性基因座/次要組織相容性基因座　minor histocompatibility loci
次要组织相容性抗原/次要組織相容性抗原　minor histocompatibility antigen
次要组织相容性系统/次要組織相容性系統　minor histocompatibility system
次最适度/次適度　suboptimum
刺/刺　stab
刺胞动物/刺胞動物　cnidaria
刺檗碱/刺檗鹼　oxycanthine
刺创引流/戳穿引流　stab wound drain
刺戳创伤/刺戳創傷　stab wound
刺法/刺法　acupuncture technique
刺法灸法学/刺法灸法學　subject of acupuncture and moxibustion technique
刺槐毒蛋白/刺槐毒素　robin
刺激/刺激[作用]　stimulation, stimulus
刺激参数/刺激參數　stimulation parameter
刺激泛化/刺激泛化　stimulus generalization
刺激过敏/興奮過度,刺激感受性過強　hyperirritability
刺激剂/刺激劑　irritant
刺激加速性神经/刺激加速性神經　excito-acceleratory nerve
刺激麻醉性毒/刺激兼麻醉性毒物　acronarcotic poison
刺激模式/刺激範型　stimulus pattern
刺激强度/刺激強度　stimulation intensity
刺激神经/刺激神經　excitor nerve
刺激试验/刺激試驗　irritant test
刺激[性]的/刺激物,刺激的　irritant
刺激性放射[疗法]/刺激性輻射療法　irritative radiation
刺激性接触性皮炎/刺激性接觸性皮炎　irritant contact dermatitis
刺激性皮炎/刺激性皮炎　irritant dermatitis
刺激性泻药/刺激性瀉藥　irritant laxative
刺激抑制性神经/刺激抑制性神經　excito-inhibitory nerve
刺金合欢胶/刺金合歡膠　cape gum
刺禁/刺禁　contraindication of needling
刺灸法/刺灸法　techniques of acupuncture and moxibustion
刺李/刺梅　Prunus spinosa
刺络拔罐/刺絡拔罐　pricking and cupping
刺入冷冻法/刺入冷凍法　penetration freezing
刺手/刺手　needle-holding hand
刺鼠螨/刺鼠蟎　spiny rat mite
刺痛/刺痛　stabbing pain
刺痛反应/刺痛反應　smarting reaction
刺梧桐树胶/梧桐膠　Karaya gum
刺五加/刺五加　root and vine of manyprickle acanthopanax
刺五加片/刺五加片　ciwujia tablets
刺细胞/刺絲母細胞　cnidoblast
刺痒的/發癢的　urticant
刺状红细胞增多/棘細胞症,棘紅血球增多症　acanthocytosis
葱豉汤/蔥豉湯　congchi decoction
葱恙虫/蔥恙蟲　onion mite
从化/從化　transformation in accord with constitution
从命自动症/從命自動症　command automatism
从性基因/從性基因　sex-conditioned gene
从性性状/從性性狀　sexinfluenced trait
从阳化热/從陽化熱　heat transformed from yang
从阴化寒/從陰化寒　cold transformed from yin
从欲/從欲　desire satisfaction, self indulgence
从欲疗法/從欲療法　desire satisfaction
从欲顺意疗法/從欲順意療法　desire and wish satisfaction
从治/從治　paradoxical treatment
丛/叢　plexus
丛集性头痛/偏頭神經痛　cluster headache
丛林斑疹伤寒/叢林型斑疹傷寒,日本恙蟲病　scrub typhus
丛林热/叢林熱　jungle fever
丛林型斑疹伤寒/叢林斑疹傷寒,島嶼病,恙蟲病　island disease
丛密绒毛膜/葉狀絨毛膜　chorion frondosum
丛状的/叢狀的　plexiform
丛状神经瘤/叢狀神經瘤　plexiform neuroma
丛状神经纤维瘤/叢狀神經纖維瘤　plexiform neurofibroma
丛状梭形细胞痣/叢狀梭狀細胞痣　plexiform

spindle cell nevus
丛状纤维组织细胞瘤/叢狀纖維組織細胞瘤　plexiform fibrohistiocytic tumor
丛状型成釉细胞瘤/叢狀型成釉細胞瘤　plexiform ameloblastoma
丛状血管病/簇集性血管瘤　tufted angioma
腠理/腠理　striae and interstitial space
粗糙疙瘩皮肤病/團塊皮膚病　lumpy skin disease
粗糙呼吸音/粗糙呼吸音　harsh respiration
粗糙链孢霉/粗糙鏈孢黴　Neurospora crassa
粗糙皮肤病病毒/粗糙皮膚病病毒　lumpy skin disease virus
粗糙食物/粗糙食物　roughage
粗糙心包/毛狀心包　shaggy pericardium
粗糙型菌落/粗糙型菌落　rough colony
粗糙杂音/粗糙雜音　rough murmur
粗大震颤/粗大震顫　coarse tremor
粗干啰音震颤/粗乾啰音震顫，支氣管性震顫　rhonchal fremitus
粗肌丝/粗肌絲　thick myofilament
粗隆/粗隆　tuberosity
粗面内质网/粗糙内質網　rough endoplasmic reticulum
粗球孢子菌/粗球孢子菌　Coccidioides immitis
粗涩杂音/摩鉎狀雜音　rasping murmur
粗湿啰音/粗濕啰音　coarse rale
粗丝切断钳/粗絲切斷鉗　heavy gauge side cutter
粗提物/粗抽提物　crude extract
粗腿病/粗腿病　thick leg disease
粗线/粗線　linea aspera
粗线期/粗線期　pachytene stage
粗杂呼吸音/粗糙呼吸音　rude respiration
卒发/驟起　sudden onset
卒腹痛/卒腹痛　sudden abdominal pain
卒聋/卒聾　sudden deafness
卒痛/卒痛　sudden pain
卒心痛/卒心痛　sudden precordial pain
卒中/猝發，中風　stroke
卒中发作/中風發作　apoplectic stroke
卒中型炭疽/中風狀炭疽　apoplectic anthrax
卒中性眩晕/中風性眩暈　apoplectic vertigo
促鼻液剂/引嚏藥，引涕藥　errhine
促病毒[繁殖]素/促病毒素　stimulon
促肠液激素/小腸分泌素　enterocrinin
促大肠杆菌素因子/促大腸桿菌素因子　colicinogen
促胆酸盐生成的/促膽質生成的，生成膽酸的　cholanopoietic
促蛋白合成类固醇/促合成代謝性類固醇　anabolic steroid
促蛋白尿的/引起蛋白尿的　albuminuretic
促淀粉酶/促澱粉酵素　auxoamylase
促分泌剂/催泌藥　succagogue
促分泌素/促泌素　secretagogue
促黑[色]素激素细胞/促黑激素細胞　melanotroph
促黑素细胞激素/促黑色素細胞激素　melanocyte-stimulating hormone
促黄体激素/黄體[成長]激素　luteinizing hormone
促黄体素释放素/促黄體素釋放素　luteinizing hormone-releasing hormone
促黄体素释放素试验/促黄體素釋放素試驗　luteinizing hormone-releasing hormone test
促甲状腺激素细胞/促甲狀腺激素細胞　thyrotroph, TSH cell
促甲状腺素/促甲狀腺素　thyrotropin
促甲状腺素瘤/促甲狀腺素瘤　thyrotropinoma
促甲状腺素释放激素/促甲狀腺素釋放激素　thyrotropin-releasing hormone
促甲状腺素释放激素受体/促甲狀腺素釋放激素受體　thyrotropin-releasing hormone receptor
促甲状腺素释放素试验/促甲狀腺素釋放素試驗　thyrotropin releasing hormone test
促甲状腺素释放兴奋试验/促甲狀腺素釋放興奮試驗　thyrotropin releasing hormone stimulation test
促甲状腺素受体/促甲狀腺素受體　thyrotropin receptor
促甲状腺素兴奋试验/促甲狀腺素興奮試驗　thyrotropin stimulation test
促结缔组织生成的/促進結締組織增生的　desmoplastic
促进剂/促進劑　accelerant
促进阶段/促進階段　promoting stage
促流泪素/促流淚素　lacrimalin
促瘤生长[现象]/促瘤生長[現象]　tumor enhancement
促卵泡成熟激素/促卵泡成熟激素　follicle-stimulating hormone
促[卵]受精膜生成素/促卵受精素　oocytin
促脉/促脈　abrupt pulse, irregular-rapid pulse
促尿氯排泄药/利氯尿劑　chloruretic
促尿钠排泄肽类/促尿鈉排洩肽類　natriuretic peptides
促尿钠排泄药/促尿鈉排洩藥　natriuretic
促尿锶排泄/尿排鍶作用　strontiuresis
促尿酸尿药/促尿酸尿藥　uricosuric agent
促凝血酶/凝血激酶　thrombokinase
促凝药/促凝藥　coagulants

促皮质素/促皮質素,促肾上腺皮质素剂 corticotropin
促乳激素细胞/激乳腺素細胞 mammotroph, prolactin cell
促肾上腺皮质的/促腎上腺皮質的 adrenocorticotropic
促肾上腺皮质激素类药/促腎上腺皮質激素類藥 corticotropins
促肾上腺皮质激素凝胶/促腎上腺皮質激素凝膠 corticotropin gel
促肾上腺皮质激素受体/促腎上腺皮質激素受體 corticotropin receptor
促肾上腺皮质激素细胞/促腎上腺皮質激素細胞 ACTH cell, corticotroph
促肾上腺皮质激素腺瘤/促腎上腺皮質激素腺瘤 adrenocorticotropic hormone adenoma
促肾上腺皮质激素兴奋试验/促腎上腺皮質激素興奮試驗 adrenocorticotropin stimulation test
促肾上腺皮质素/促腎上腺皮質素 adrenocorticotropic hormone
促肾上腺皮质素瘤/促腎上腺皮質素瘤 corticotropinoma
促肾上腺皮质素释放激素/促腎上腺皮質釋放激素 corticotropin-releasing hormone
促肾上腺皮质素释放激素受体/促腎上腺皮質素釋放激素受體 corticotropin-releasing hormone receptor
促肾上腺皮质素释放素试验/促腎上腺皮質素釋放素試驗 corticotropin releasing hormone test
促[肾上腺]小球激素/促小球激素,促腎上腺腎絲球激素 glomerulotropin
促肾上腺性/促腎上腺 suprarenotropism
促生育素类/促生育素類 menotropins
促生长素受体/促生長素受體 somatotropin receptor
促衰变因子/衰退加速因子 decay-accelerating factor
促同化神经/合成代謝神經,同化神經 anabolic nerve
促吞噬肽/促吞噬肽 tuftsin
促胃动素/促胃動素 motilin
促胃液素/胃激素,胃分泌活素 gastric secretin
促效药/促效劑 agonist
促性腺激素类/促性腺激素類 gonadotrophins
促性腺激素释放激素/促性腺激素釋放激素 gonadotropin-releasing hormone
促性腺激素受体/促性腺激素受體 gonadotropin receptor
促性腺激素细胞/促性腺激素細胞 gonadotroph
促性腺激素兴奋药/促性腺激素興奮藥 gonadotrophin stimulant
促性腺激素增强因子/促性腺激素增強因子 synprolan
促性腺素/促性腺素 gonadotropin
促性腺素类/促性腺素類 gonadotropins
促性腺素瘤/促性腺素瘤 gonadotropinoma
促孕激素/助孕素 gestagen
促组织血流增多剂/循環促進劑 hyperkinemic
猝出血性视网膜炎/猝出血性視網膜炎 apoplectic retinitis
猝倒样状态/猝倒樣狀態 cataleptoid state
猝倒症/猝倒症 cataplexy
猝发性气体放电/猝發性氣體放電 sudden gaseous discharge
猝发疹/猝發疹,玫瑰疹 exanthema subitum
猝灭荧光测定法/淬熄螢光光度測定法 quenching fluorometry
猝死/猝死 sudden death
醋氨苯砜/醋胺苯碸 acedapsone
醋氨酚/對位乙醯胺基酚 acetaminophen
醋苯阿尔孕酮/醋苯阿爾孕酮 algestone acetophenide
醋的/醋的 acetic
醋地高辛/乙醯地高辛 acetyldigoxin
醋碘苯酸/醋碘苯酸 acetrizoic acid
醋丁洛尔/醋丁洛爾 acebutolol
醋磺己脲/乙醯苯磺醯環己尿素 acetohexamide
醋甲胆碱化合物/醋甲膽鹼化合物 methacholine compound
醋甲唑胺/甲醋唑胺 methazolamide
醋霉菌/醋黴菌 acetic fungus
醋美沙朵/醋美沙朵 methadyl acetate
醋溶性白蛋白/醋溶性白蛋白 acetosoluble albumin
醋酸/醋酸 acetic acid
醋酸铵/醋酸銨 ammonium acetate
醋酸铵溶液/醋酸銨溶液 ammonium acetate solution
醋酸苯汞/醋酸苯汞 phenylmercuric acetate
醋酸[比重]计/醋酸定量器 acetimeter
醋酸地衣红/醋酸地衣紅 aceto-orcein
醋酸丁酯/醋酸丁酯 butyl acetate
醋酸发酵/醋發酵 acetic fermentation
醋酸反应/醋酸反應 acetic acid reaction
醋酸氟轻松/氟新諾龍[丙酮醋酸]酯 fluocinonide
醋酸氟孕酮/醋酸氟孕酮 flurogestone acetate
醋酸钙/醋酸鈣 calcium acetate
醋酸酐/醋酸酐,無水醋酸 acetic anhydride
醋酸间甲酚酯/醋酸間位甲酚 metacresol acetate

醋酸可的松/醋酸可的松　cortisone acetate
醋酸铝/醋酸鋁　aluminum acetate
醋酸铝溶液/醋酸鋁溶液　aluminum acetate solution
醋酸氯地孕酮/醋酸氯地孕酮　chlormadinone acetate
醋酸美仑孕酮/美侖孕酮乙酸鹽　melengestrol acetate
醋酸钠溶液/醋酸鈉溶液　sodium acetate solution
醋酸氢化可的松/醋酸氫化可的松，乙酸氫皮質酮　hydrocortisone acetate
醋酸氢化可的松软膏/乙酸氫化可的松軟膏　hydrocortisone acetate ointment
醋酸醛/醋酸醛　acetic aldehyde
醋酸[生成]酶/醋酸酶　acetolase
醋酸铊/醋酸鉈　thallium acetate
醋酸铁/醋酸鐵　iron acetate
醋酸铁铵溶液/鐵和醋酸銨溶液　iron and ammonium acetate solution
醋酸戊酯/醋酸戊酯　amyl acetate
醋酸纤维素电泳/醋酸纖維素電泳　cellulose acetate electrophoresis
醋酸纤维素膜/乙醯纖維素膜　acetyl cellulose membrane
醋酸纤维素膜电泳/醋酸纖維薄膜電泳　cellulose acetate membrane electrophoresis
醋酸盐/醋酸鹽　acetate
醋酸盐激酶/醋酸鹽激酶　acetate kinase
醋酸酯/醋酸酯　acetic ester
醋酰胺/醋醯胺　acetic acid amide
醋硝香豆素/醋硝香豆素　acenocoumarol
醋蒸/醋蒸　steaming with vinegar
醋制/醋制　processing with vinegar
醋炙/醋炙　stir-frying with vinegar
醋竹桃霉素/三乙醯夾竹桃黴素　troleandomycin
醋煮/醋煮　boiling with vinegar
簇虫后胞/簇蟲後胞　deutomerite
簇虫前胞/簇蟲前胞　primite
簇集性毛囊炎/簇集性毛囊炎　agminate folliculitis
簇晶/簇晶　cluster crystal
簇状痤疮/簇集性痤瘡　acne agminata
簇状秃发/圓形禿髮　pelade
攒竹/攢竹　cuanzhu, BL2
窜痛/竄痛　scurrying pain
催产剂/催產藥　parturifacient
催产素/催產素　oxytocin
催产素激惹试验/催產素激惹試驗　oxytocin challenge test
催产素受体/催產素受體　oxytocin receptor
催产素注射剂/催產素注射劑　oxytocin injection
催产药/催產藥　ecbolic, oxytocic
催化部位/催化部位　catalytic site
催化的/催化的　catalytic
催化剂/催化劑　accelerator
催化抗体/催化抗體　catalytic antibody
催化热滴定/催化熱滴定　catalytic thermometric titration
催化域/催化域　catalytic domain
催化作用/催化[作用]，接觸作用　catalysis
催激素药/催激素劑　hormonagogue
催泪弹烧伤/催淚彈燒傷　tear gas burn
催泪剂/催淚劑　lacrimator
催泪瓦斯/催淚瓦斯　tear gas
催眠/催眠　hypnogenesis, hypnosis
催眠暗示/催眠性暗示　hypnotic suggestion
催眠的/催睡的　hypnagogic
催眠毒素/催眠毒素　hypnotoxin
催眠后暗示/催眠後暗示　posthypnotic suggestion
催眠[精神]分析/催眠分析術　hypnoanalysis
催眠疗法/催眠療法　hypnotherapy
催眠麻醉法/催眠麻醉法　hypnosis anesthesia
催眠麻醉[精神]分析/催眠麻醉分析　hypnonarcoanalysis
催眠术/催眠　hypnosis
催眠术士/催眠術士，催眠師　hypnotist
催眠性昏睡/催眠性昏睡　trance coma
催眠性迷睡/催眠性迷睡　hypnotic trance
催眠性迷睡者/催眠夢遊者　somnipathist
催眠性睡眠/催眠性睡眠　hypnotic sleep
催眠学/催眠學，睡眠學　hypnology
催眠样状态/催眠樣狀態　hypnoidal state
催眠药/催眠藥　hypnotic, soporific
催眠状态/催眠狀態　hypnotic state
催脓剂/催膿劑　suppurantia
催脓药/釀膿藥　maturant
催气/催氣　promoting arrival of qi
催乳[激]素/催乳[激]素，泌乳素　galactin
催乳剂/催乳劑　galactopoietic
催乳素瘤/催乳激素細胞腺瘤　prolactinoma
催乳素受体/催乳素受體　prolactin receptor
催乳药/催乳藥，催乳劑　galactopoietic
催生/催生　expediting child delivery
催嚏剂/催嚏藥　sternutatory
催吐剂/催吐劑　vomitive
催吐药/催吐藥　emetic
催涎/催涎　ptyalize
催涎药/催涎藥　ptyalagogue

催欲药/催欲藥　aphrodisiacs
脆的/易碎的　brittle
脆发[症]/脆髮症　brittle hair, trichorrhexis
脆骨/骨脆弱　brittle bone
脆甲/脆甲　brittle nail
脆甲症/爪甲脆折　onychorrhexis
脆弱类杆菌/脆弱類桿菌　bacteroides fragilis
脆双核阿米巴/脆二核阿米巴　dientamoeba fragilis
脆碎度/脆度　friability
脆性骨综合征/脆性骨症候群　brittle bone syndrome
脆性红细胞/脆弱紅血球,易碎紅血球　fragilocyte
脆性红细胞增多/脆弱紅血球形成　fragilocytosis
脆性角膜综合征/脆性角膜症候群　brittle cornea syndrome
脆[性]X染色体/脆[性]X染色體　fragile X chromosome
脆性位点/脆性位點　fragile site
脆性X综合征/脆性X症候群　fragile X syndrome
淬/淬　quenching, tempering
淬火/淬煉　quenching
翠雀次碱/飛燕草素　delphinoidine
存储/備藏,貯積　storage
存活率/存活率　survival rate
存活率分析/存活率分析　survival rate analysis
寸/寸　cun
寸关尺/寸關尺　cun-guan-chi, bar and cubit, inch
寸口/寸口　cunkou, site for taking wrist pulse
搓法/搓法　kneading manipulation, twisting manipulation
撮空/撮空　groping in the air
撮口/撮口　locked jaw
痤疮/痤瘡,粉刺　acne
痤疮棒杆菌/痤瘡棒狀桿菌　Corynebacterium acne
痤疮丙酸杆菌/痤瘡丙酸桿菌　Propionibacterium acne
痤疮炎/痤瘡炎　acnitis
痤疮样瘢痕性红斑/痤瘡樣疤痕性紅斑　ulerythema acneiforme
痤疮样的/痤瘡樣　acneiform
痤疮样梅毒疹/痤瘡樣梅毒疹　syphilid acneformis
痤疮样脓疱/痤瘡樣膿皰　acneiform pustule
痤疮样疹/痤瘡樣疹　acneiform eruption
痤疮样疹诱发因子/痤瘡樣疹誘發因子　acneiform-inducing agent
痤疮样痣/痤瘡樣痣　nevus acneformis
挫伤/挫傷　contusion
挫伤性白内障/挫傷性內障　contusion cataract
挫伤性肺炎/挫傷性肺炎　contusion pneumonia
挫折/挫敗,阻撓　frustration
锉/銼修　filing
锉锯状喘鸣/鋸木狀嘯鳴　stridor serraticus
错读[症]/錯讀症,讀書障礙　paralexia
错构瘤/錯構瘤　hamartoma
错构胚细胞瘤/缺陷胚瘤　hamartoblastoma
错𬌗/錯咬　false occlusion
错𬌗模拟矫治𬌗架/錯𬌗模擬矯治𬌗架　typodont
错觉/錯覺　illusion
错配/錯配　mismatching, mispairing
错听/錯聽　otosis
错位/錯位,異位　malposition
错位长出/錯位長出　maleruption
错误/錯誤　error
错误投射/投影錯誤　erroneous projection
错语/錯語,中樞性失語症　paraphasia
错语性失语症/錯語性失語症　paraphemia
错语[症]/言語錯亂,亂語症　paraphasia

D

哒嗪类/噠嗪類　pyridazines
搭肩试验/搭肩試驗　Dugas sign
达顿病/Dutton 氏病，錐蟲病　Dutton disease
达尔林普尔病/Dalrymple 氏病　Dalrymple disease
达尔文耳/Darwin 氏耳　Darwin ear
达尔文结节/達爾文結節　Darwinian point
达-格病/Duchenne-Griesinger 二氏病　Duchenne-Griesinger disease
达金-卡莱尔法/達-卡二氏法　Dakin-Carrel method
达金溶液/Dakin 氏液　Dakin fluid
达卡巴嗪/達卡巴嗪　Dacarbazine
达里埃病/Darier 氏病　Darier disease
达林病/Darling 氏病　Darling disease
达玛烷/達瑪烷　dammarane
达玛脂/丹馬樹脂　Dammar resin
达那唑/達那唑　danazol
达内什病毒/Danysz 氏病毒　Danysz virus
达氏螺旋体/Duttoni 氏螺旋體　Treponema duttoni
达托霉素/達托黴素　daptomycin
达维多夫氏细胞/Davidoff 氏細胞　Davidoff cell
达佐霉素/重氮黴素　duazomycin
打谷者肺/農夫肺　thresher lung
打鼾/打鼾　snoring
打呵欠/呵欠　hiation
大斑块副银屑病/大斑塊副銀屑病　large plaque parapsoriasis
大包/大包　dabao, SP21
大孢子/大型孢子，巨芽胞　macrospore
大便滑脱/大便滑脫　incontinence of feces
大便艰难/大便艱難　difficulty in defecation
大便秘结/大便秘結　constipation
大便失禁/大便失禁　fecal incontinence
大补阴丸/大補陰丸　dabuyin pill
大柴胡汤/大柴胡湯　dachaihu decoction
大肠/大腸　large intestine
大肠癌/大腸癌　large intestine cancer
大肠癌·肝肾阴虚证/大腸癌·肝腎陰虛證　large intestine cancer with pattern of liver-kidney yin deficiency
大肠癌·脾肾气虚证/大腸癌·脾腎氣虛證　large intestine cancer with pattern of qi deficiency of spleen and kidney
大肠癌·湿热蕴毒证/大腸癌·濕熱蘊毒證　large intestine cancer with pattern of damp-heat and amassing poison
大肠癌·瘀毒内结证/大腸癌·瘀毒內結證　large intestine cancer with pattern of internal binding of static blood and poison
大肠杆菌/大腸桿菌　Escherichia coli
大肠杆菌病/大腸菌病　colibacillosis
大肠杆菌蛋白质类/大腸桿菌蛋白質類　Escherichia coli proteins
大肠杆菌毒素/大腸桿菌毒素　colitoxin
大肠杆菌毒素中毒/大腸桿菌毒素中毒　colitoxicosis
大肠杆菌毒血症/大腸桿菌毒血症　colitoxemia
大肠杆菌感染/大腸桿菌感染　coli infection
大肠杆菌菌苗/大腸桿菌菌苗　Escherichia coli vaccine
大肠杆菌菌血症/大腸菌血症　colibacillemia
大肠杆菌黏着素/大腸桿菌黏著素　Escherichia coli adhesin
大肠杆菌尿/大腸菌尿［症］　colibacilluria
大肠杆菌群/大腸桿菌群　coliform bacteria
大肠杆菌噬菌体/大腸桿菌噬菌體　Coliphage
大肠杆菌素/大腸桿菌素　colicin
大肠杆菌素产生/產生大腸桿菌素　colicinogeny
大肠杆菌性脑膜炎/大腸桿菌性腦膜炎　Escherichia coli meningitis
大肠杆菌性脓毒病/大腸桿菌性敗血病　colisepsis
大肠杆菌性膀胱肾盂炎/大腸菌性膀胱腎盂炎　colicystopyelitis
大肠杆菌性膀胱炎/大腸菌性膀胱炎　colicystitis
大肠杆菌性肾炎/大腸桿菌性腎炎　colinephritis
大肠梗阻/大腸梗阻　large bowel obstruction
大肠寒结/大腸寒結　cold accumulation of large intestine
大肠惊/大腸驚　convulsion due to large intestine disorders
大肠热结/大腸熱結　heat accumulation of large intestine
大肠热结证/大腸熱結證　pattern of heat accumulated in large intestine

大肠伤寒痢疾菌群/大腸傷寒痢疾菌類　colon-typhoid-dysentery group
大肠湿热/大腸濕熱　dampness-heat of large intestine
大肠湿热证/大腸濕熱證　pattern of dampness-heat in large intestine
大肠虚寒/大腸虛寒　deficiency-cold of large intestine
大肠液亏/大腸液虧　fluid insufficiency of large intestine
大肠俞/大腸俞　dachangshu, BL25
大承气汤/大承氣湯　dachengqi decoction
大出血/大出血,血漏　hemorrhoea, massive hemorrhage
大定风珠/大定風珠　dadingfengzhu pill
大动脉/大動脈　large artery
大动脉错位/大動脈錯位　malposition of great artery
大动脉炎/大動脈炎　Takayasu arteritis
大豆蛋白质类/大豆蛋白質類　soybean proteins
大豆磷脂/大豆磷脂　soybean phospholipid
大豆食品/大豆食品　soy food
大都/大都　dadu, SP2
大敦/大敦　dadun, LR1
大多核白细胞/巨嗜中性白血球,巨多核白血球　giant neutrophil
大多角骨/大多角骨　trapezium bone, greater multangular
大多角骨结节/大多角骨結節　tubercle of trapezium bone
大多孔室脂质体/大多孔室脂質體　macrovesicle liposome
大腭孔/大腭孔　foramen greater palatine
大发作/大發作　grand mal
大方/大方　major prescriptions
大方脉/大方脈　medical department for adult
大肺性气肿/大肺性氣腫　large-lunged emphysema
大[分]裂球/大分裂球,大型分裂細胞　macromere
大分子物质/大分子物質　macromolecular substance
大分子中性氨基酸转运子/大分子中性胺基酸轉運子　large neutral amino acid-transporter
大风子油酸/大風子[油]酸　chaulmoogric acid
大风子油酸乙酯/大風子酸乙酯　antileprol
大腹皮/大腹皮　areca peel
大根香叶烷倍半萜类/大根香葉烷倍半萜類　germacrane sesquiterpenes
大宫之人/大宫之人　atypical earth-phase person, more gentle
大骨节病/大骨節病,卡-貝二氏病,地方性變形性骨關節病　Kaschin-Beck disease, osteoarthrosis deformaris endemica
大骨空/大骨空　dagukong, EX-UE5
大骨盆/大骨盆　greater pelvis
大观本草/大觀本草　Daguan Bencao
大汗/大汗　profuse sweating
大汗腺/頂漿腺　apocrine gland
大汗腺癌/頂漿腺癌　apocrine carcinoma
大汗腺单位/頂漿腺單位　apocrine sweat unit
大汗腺囊瘤/頂漿囊瘤　apocrine hydrocystoma
大汗腺囊腺瘤/頂漿腺囊腺瘤　apocrine cystadenoma
大汗腺囊肿/頂漿腺囊腫　apocrine cyst
大汗腺痣/頂漿腺母斑　apocrine nevus
大汗腺潴留性囊肿/頂漿腺滯留性囊腫　apocrine retention cyst
大核/大核,滋養核　macronucleus
大颌病/巨頜病　lumpy jaw
大颌弓间距/大頜間距　large interarch distance
大赫/大赫　dahe, KI12
大横/大橫　daheng, SP15
大花寄生草汁/大花寄生草汁　hypocist
大环化合物/大環化合物　macrocyclic compound
大环内酰胺类/大環內醯胺類　macrocyclic lactams
大环内酯类/大環內酯　macrolide
大环内酯类抗生素/巨環內酯類抗生素　macrolide antibiotic
大环生物碱/巨環生物鹼　macrocyclic alkaloid
大黄/大黄　rhubarb root and rhizome
大黄蜂/大黄蜂　hornet
大黄附子汤/大黄附子湯　dahuang fuzi decoction
大黄牡丹汤/大黄牡丹湯　dahuang mudan decoction
大黄素/大黄素,大黄苷　emodin
大黄䗪虫丸/大黄䗪蟲丸　dahuang zhechong pills
大茴香子/茴香實　aniseed
大活络丹/大活絡丹　dahuoluo pills
大集合物/大集合物　macroaggregate
大戟科/大戟科　Euphorbiaceae
大戟中毒/大戟中毒　euphorbia poisoning
大蓟/大薊　Japanese thistle herb, Japanese thistle root
大建中汤/大建中湯　dajianzhong decoction
大胶质/大神經膠質　macroglia
大角/大角　greater cornu, greater horn
大角咽部/大角咽部　ceratopharyngeal part
大角咽肌/大角咽肌　ceratopharyngeal muscle
大脚风/大腳風　elephantiasis of leg
大结节/大結節　greater tubercle
大结节嵴/大結節嵴　crest of greater tubercle

大结胸证/大結胸證　chest binding pattern with heat and fluid, major chest binding pattern
大静脉/大靜脈　large vein
大巨/大巨　daju, ST27
大角之人/大角之人　atypical wood-phase person, more amiable and modest
大颗粒淋巴细胞/大顆粒淋巴細胞,大粒性淋巴球　large granular lymphocyte
大孔树脂/巨孔樹脂　macroporous resin
大口/大口　large mouth
大口疮性溃疡/大口瘡性潰瘍　aphthous ulcer major
大块的/大塊的　massive
大块肝坏死/大塊肝壞死　massive hepatic necrosis
大块骨质溶解/大量骨質溶解　massive osteolysis
大块解剖/大塊解剖　block dissection
大块切骨术/大塊截骨術　block osteotomy
大块萎缩/大塊萎縮　massive collapse
大块性坏死/大塊壞死　massive necrosis
大理石/大理石　marble
大理石骨/大理石狀骨　marble bone
大理石骨病/大理石狀骨病　marble bone disease
大理石状态/大理石狀態　marble state
大理石状纹理/大理石狀紋理　marbleization
大连接体/主要接合部　major connector
大蠊属/大蠊屬　*periplaneta*
大量灭菌疗法/大量滅菌療法　massive sterilizing therapeutics
大量培养/大量培養　mass culture
大淋巴细胞/大淋巴細胞,巨淋巴球　large lymphocyte
大淋巴细胞增多/巨淋巴球增多,巨淋巴球生成　macrolymphocytosis
大陵/大陵　daling, PC7
大菱形肌/大菱形肌　rhomboideus major, greater rhomboid muscle
大流行病/大流行病　pandemic disease
大流行动物病/動物病大流行　panepizootic
大流行情况/大流行狀態　pandemicity
大流行性流感/大流行性流感冒　pandemic influenza
大麻/大麻　cannabis
大麻二酚/大麻二酚　cannabidiol
大麻酚/大麻油醇　cannabinol
大麻酚类/大麻酚類　cannabinoids
大麻酚受体/大麻酚受體　cannabinoid receptor
大麻滥用/大麻濫用　marijuana abuse
大麻树脂/大麻樹脂　charas
大麻中毒/大麻中毒,大麻成癮　cannabism

大麻子样结石/大麻子狀結石　hemp seed calculus
大麦醇溶蛋白/大麥蛋白　hordein
大满月/大滿月　one hundred days after delivery
大面积刺激/大面積刺激　areal stimulation
大脑/大腦　cerebrum
大脑半球/大腦半球　cerebral hemisphere
大脑半球皮质切除术/大腦半球皮質切除術　cerebral hemicorticectomy
大脑半球切除术/大腦半球切除術　cerebral hemispherectomy
大脑半球神经胶质增生/大腦半球神經膠質增殖病　hemispheric gliosis
大脑半球优势/大腦優勢　cerebral dominance
大脑部/大腦部　cerebral part
大脑刺激/大腦刺激　cerebral irritation
大脑大静脉/大腦大靜脈　great cerebral vein
大脑大静脉池/大腦大靜脈池　cistern of great cerebral vein
大脑大静脉动脉瘤样畸形/大腦大靜脈動脈瘤樣畸形　aneurysmal malformation of vein of Galen
大脑导水管/大腦導水管　cerebral aqueduct
大脑的/大腦的　cerebral
大脑动脉/大腦動脈　arteriae cerebri
大脑动脉丛/大腦動脈叢　plexus arteriae cerebri
大脑动脉淀粉样变性病/大腦動脈澱粉樣變性症　cerebral arterial amyloidosis
大脑动脉环/大腦動脈環　cerebral arterial circle
大脑额叶/大腦額葉　frontal lobe of cerebrum
大脑轭/大腦隆凸　cerebral juga
大脑分水界性梗塞/大腦分水界性梗塞　watershed infarction
大脑弓状纤维/大腦弓狀纖維　cerebral arcuate fiber
大脑沟/大腦溝　cerebral sulci
大脑横裂/大腦橫裂　cerebral transverse fissure
大脑横裂隙/大腦橫裂隙　fissura transversa cerebralis
大脑后动脉/大腦後動脈　posterior cerebral artery
大脑后动脉梗塞/大腦後動脈梗塞　posterior cerebral artery infarction
大脑后动脉交通后部/大腦後動脈交通後部　postcommunicating part of posterior cerebral artery
大脑后动脉交通前部/大腦後動脈交通前部　precommunicating part of posterior cerebral artery
大脑后动脉终部/大腦後動脈終部　terminal part of posterior cerebral artery
大脑回/大腦回　cerebral gyri, convolution of cerebrum
大脑脊髓外侧径/大腦脊髓外側徑　lateral

cerebrospinal tract
大脑脚/大腦腳 cerebral peduncle
大脑脚底/大腦腳底 crus cerebri
大脑脚横静脉/大腦腳橫靜脈 transverse peduncular vein
大脑脚静脉/大腦腳靜脈 peduncular vein
大脑脚内侧静脉/大腦腳內側靜脈 medial peduncular vein
大脑脚切断术/大腦腳切開術 pedunculotomy
大脑脚外侧静脉/大腦腳外側靜脈 lateral peduncular vein
大脑脚支/大腦腳支 peduncular branch
大脑脚综合征/大腦腳症候群 syndrome of cerebral peduncle
大脑脚纵静脉/大腦腳縱靜脈 longitudinal peduncular vein
大脑静脉/大腦靜脈 cerebral vein
大脑局部缺血/大腦局部缺血 cerebral ischemia
[大脑]联合中枢/聯合中樞 association center
大脑镰/大腦鐮 cerebral falx
大脑镰脑膜瘤/大腦鐮腦膜瘤 cerebral falx meningioma
大脑镰皱褶/大腦鐮皺摺 fold falx cerebri
大脑面/大腦面 cerebral surface
大脑内的/大腦內的 intracerebral
大脑内静脉/大腦內靜脈 internal cerebral vein
大脑内培养/大腦內培養 intracerebral culture
大脑内视大径/大腦內視大徑 intracerebral optic tract
[大脑皮层]联合区/聯合區 association area
大脑[皮层]性共济失调/大腦性行動失調症 cerebral ataxia
大脑皮质/大腦皮質 cerebral cortex
大脑皮质功能区/大腦皮質功能區 functional area of cortex
大脑皮质坏死/腦皮質性壞死 cerebrocortical necrosis
大脑皮质性脑炎/腦皮質炎 cortical encephalitis
大脑前动脉/大腦前動脈 anterior cerebral artery
大脑前动脉丛/大腦前動脈叢 plexus arteriae cerebri anterioris
大脑前动脉梗塞/大腦前動脈梗塞 anterior cerebral artery infarction
大脑前动脉交通后部/大腦前動脈交通後部 postcommunicating part of anterior cerebral artery
大脑前动脉交通前部/大腦前動脈交通前部 precommunicating part of anterior cerebral artery
大脑前交通动脉/大腦前交通動脈 anterior communicating artery of cerebrum
大脑前静脉/大腦前靜脈 anterior cerebral vein
大脑前联合/大腦前連合 anterior commissure of cerebrum
大脑浅静脉/大腦淺靜脈 superficial cerebral vein
大脑上的/大腦上的 epicerebral
大脑上静脉/大腦上靜脈 superior cerebral vein
大脑上淋巴道/大腦上淋巴道 epicerebral lymph tract
大脑深静脉/大腦深靜脈 deep cerebral vein
大脑生理学/腦生理學 cerebrophysiology
大脑髓质/大腦髓質 cerebral medullary substance
大脑炭疽/大腦炭疽 cerebral anthrax
大脑凸面脑膜瘤/大腦凸面腦膜瘤 cerebral convexity meningioma
大脑外侧沟/大腦外側溝 lateral sulcus of cerebrum
大脑外侧裂/大腦外側裂隙 fissura cerebri lateralis
大脑外侧窝/大腦外側窩 lateral cerebral fossa
大脑外侧窝池/大腦外側窩池 cistern of lateral cerebral fossa, cistern of lateral fossa of cerebrum
大脑窝/大腦窩 cerebral fossa
大脑下静脉/大腦下靜脈 inferior cerebral vein
大脑小脑裂/大腦小腦間裂隙 fissura cerebrocerebellaris
大脑性跛/大腦性跛 cerebral claudication
大脑性感觉过敏/大腦性感覺過敏 cerebral hyperesthesia
大脑性感觉缺失/大腦性感覺缺失 cerebral anesthesia
大脑性呼吸/大腦式呼吸 cerebral respiration
大脑性痉挛/大腦性痙攣 cerebral spasm
大脑[性]盲/大腦性盲 cerebral blindness
大脑性偏身麻木/大腦性單側麻木 cerebral hemianesthesia
大脑性书写不能/大腦性書寫不能 cerebral agraphia
大脑性瘫痪/大腦性麻痺 cerebral palsy, cerebral paralysis
大脑叶/大腦葉 cerebral lobes
[大脑]右半球/右半球 right hemisphere
大脑中动脉/大腦中動脈 middle cerebral artery
大脑中动脉丛/大腦中動脈叢 plexus arteriae cerebri mediae
大脑中动脉梗塞/大腦中動脈梗塞 middle cerebral artery infarction
大脑中动脉瘤/大腦中動脈瘤 middle cerebral artery aneurysm
大脑中静脉/大腦中靜脈 middle cerebral vein

大脑中浅静脉/大腦中淺静脉 superficial middle cerebral vein
大脑中深静脉/大腦中深静脉 deep middle cerebral vein
大脑[中枢]定位/大腦區域定位法 cerebral localization
大脑中央灰质/大腦中央灰質 gray substance of central cerebrum
大脑纵隔/大腦縱隔 mediastinum cerebri
大脑纵裂/大腦縱裂 fissura longitudinalis cerebri
大[内]收肌孔/大内收肌孔,腱裂孔 opening in adductor magnus muscle
大疱/大皰 bulla
大疱触染性脓疱病/大皰性傳染性膿皰病 impetigo contagiosa bullosa
大疱的/大皰的 bullosa
大疱生成/大皰症 bullosis
大疱形成/大皰形成 bullae formation
大疱性扁平苔藓/大皰性扁平苔蘚 bullous lichen planus
大疱性表皮松解/大皰性表皮鬆懈 epidermolysis bullosa
大疱性淀粉样变性病/水皰性澱粉樣變性症 bullous amyloidosis
大疱性冻疮/大皰型凍瘡 pernio bullous
大疱性多形[性]红斑/水皰性多形性紅斑 erythema multiforme bullosum
大疱性肺气肿/皰性氣腫 bullous emphysema
大疱性鼓膜炎/大皰性鼓膜炎 bullous myringitis
大疱性鼓膜炎·风热外袭证/大皰性鼓膜炎·風熱外襲證 bullousmyringitis with pattern of external assault by wind-heat
大疱性鼓膜炎·肝火上扰证/大皰性鼓膜炎·肝火上擾證 bullous myringitis with pattern of liver fire disturbing upward
大疱性红斑狼疮/水皰性紅斑狼瘡 bullous lupus erythematosus
大疱性角膜病变/大皰性角膜病變 bullous keratopathy
大疱性接触性皮炎/水皰性接觸性皮膚炎 bullous contact dermatitis
大疱性类天疱疮/大皰性類天皰瘡 bullous pemphigoid
大疱性脓疱病/大皰性膿瘡病 bullous impetigo, impetigo bullosa
大疱性荨麻疹/大皰性蕁麻疹 bullous urticaria, urticaria bullosa
大疱性鱼鳞病样红皮病/水皰性魚鱗癬樣紅皮病 bullous ichthyosiform erythrodermia
大疱性鱼鳞病样角化过度/水皰性魚鱗癬樣過度角化症 bullous ichthyosiform hyperkeratosis
大疱性紫癜/大皰性紫癜病 purpura bullosa
大疱疹/大皰疹 bullous eruption
大片吸虫/巨瓜仁蟲 fasciola gigantica
大奇论篇/大奇論篇 Discussion on Magics
大气暴露室/大氣暴露室 atmosphere exposure chamber
大气爆发性损伤/大氣衝擊波損傷 atmospheric blast injury
大气的/大氣的 atmospheric
大气压/大氣壓力,氣壓 atmospheric pressure
大气压离子化/大氣壓離子化 atmospheric pressure ionization
大切片刀/大切片刀 macrotome
大秦艽汤/大秦艽湯 daqinjiao decoction
大青叶/大青葉 dyers woad leaf
大山楂丸/大山楂丸 dashanzha bolus
大商之人/大商之人 atypical metal-phase person, more sharp-eyed
大舌下腺管/大舌下腺管 major sublingual duct
大嗜酸粒细胞瘤/大嗜酸粒細胞瘤 oncocytoma
大收肌/内收大肌 adductor magnus
大手术/大手術 major surgery
大鼠冠状病毒/大鼠冠狀病毒 rat coronavirus
大蒜/[大]蒜 garlic
大蒜瓣/蒜莖型 garlic clove
大蒜素/大蒜素 allicin
大提琴阴囊/大提琴陰囊 cello scrotum
大体的/大體的 gross
大体观/肉眼外型 gross appearance
大体解剖学/大體解剖學 gross anatomy
大头[畸形]/大頭[畸形] macrocephaly
大头瘟/大頭瘟 fever with swollen head, swollen-head epidemic
大头瘟·毒盛肺胃证/大頭瘟·毒盛肺胃證 swollen-head epidemic with pattern of toxin exuberant in lung and stomach
大头瘟·胃阴虚证/大頭瘟·胃陰虛證 swollen-head epidemic with pattern of stomach yin deficiency
大头瘟·邪犯肺卫证/大頭瘟·邪犯肺衛證 swollen-head epidemic with pattern of pathogen invading lung-defense phase
大腿长/大腿長 thigh length
大腿滚动试验/大腿滾動試驗 thigh rolling test
大腿美容术/大腿美容術 aesthetic thigh surgery
大唾液腺/大唾液腺 major salivary gland

大腕骨/大腕骨　great carpal bone
大网络树脂/巨網路樹脂　macroreticular resin
大网膜/大網膜　greater omentum
大网膜瓣/大網膜瓣　omentum flap
大网膜及肠系膜囊肿/大網膜及腸繫膜囊腫
　　omental cyst and mesenteric cyst
大网膜输尿管成形术/大網膜輸尿管成形術
　　omentoureteroplasty
大网膜移植术/大網膜移植術　omentum grafting
大网膜移植物/大網膜移植物　omentum graft
大细胞癌/大細胞癌　large cell carcinoma
大细胞部/大細胞部　magnocellular part
大细胞淋巴瘤/大細胞淋巴瘤　large-cell lymphoma
大细胞性贫血/大紅血球性貧血　macrocytic anemia
大小便失禁/大小便失禁,糞尿失禁　gatism
大小迥异联胎畸胎/大小迥異連胎畸形　heteralius
大小[双]头畸胎/大小頭連胎　heterocephalus
大小体联胎畸胎/不全寄生胎,大小體連胎
　　heteradelphus
大小知觉/大小知覺　size perception
大笑/笑　laughter
大笑不能[症]/哄笑不能　aphonogelia
大笑疗法/大笑療法　laughter therapy
大[型]动物区系/大型動物　macrofauna
大型分生孢子/大型頂端芽孢　macroconidium
大[型]植物区系/大[型]植物區系　macroflora
大学医院/大學醫院　university hospital
大血管错位/大血管錯位　transposition of great
　　vessel
大血藤/大血藤　sargentgloryvine stem
大叶性肺炎/大葉性肺炎　lobar pneumonia
大翼/大翼　greater wing
大阴唇/大陰唇　greater lip of pudendum
大隐静脉/大隱靜脈　great saphenous vein
大隐静脉瓣功能试验/大隱靜脈瓣功能試驗
　　Brodie-Trendelenburg test
大迎/大迎　daying, ST5
大于胎龄儿/大於胎齡兒　large for gestational age
　　infant
大羽之人/大羽之人　atypical water-phase person,
　　more contented
大圆肌/大圓肌　musculus teres major
大圆肌腱下囊/大圓肌腱下囊　subtendinous bursa of
　　teres major
大约/大約　circa
大枣/大棗　Chinese date
大张皮移植术/大張皮移植術　large sheet skin
　　grafting
大折返/大折返　macroreentry
大针/大針　big needle
大枕孔/大枕孔　foramen occipitale magnum
大智妄想/大智妄想,智慧狂　sophomania
大钟/大鐘　dazhong, KI4
大杼/大杼　dazhu, BL11
大转子/大轉子　greater trochanter
大转子点/大轉子點　trochanterion
大椎/大椎　dazhui, DU14
大锥蝽/大錐蝽　Panstrongylus megistus
大眦漏/大眥漏　internal canthus leaking eye
呆手/呆手,死狀手　dead hand
呆小病/呆小症,矮呆病　cretinism
呆小病样的/呆小症樣的　cretinoid
呆小病样发育异常/呆小病樣發育異常,呆小病性發
　　育障礙　cretinoid dysplasia
呆小病样水肿/呆小病狀水腫　cretinoid edema
代偿失调/代償機能衰敗　decompensation
代偿性出血/代替性出血　vicarious hemorrhage
代偿[性]的/代償的　compensatory
代偿性多汗症/代償性多汗症　compensatory
　　hyperhidrosis
代偿性肥大/代償性肥大　compensatory hypertrophy
代偿性咯血/替代性欬血　vicarious hemoptysis
代偿性红细胞增多/代償性紅血球增多症
　　compensatory polycythemia
代偿性呼吸/替代性呼吸　vicarious respiration
代偿性呼吸音/小兒樣呼吸　supplementary
　　respiration
代偿性脊柱侧弯/代償性脊柱側彎　compensatory
　　scoliosis
代偿性间歇/代償性間歇　compensatory pause
代偿性碱中毒/代償性鹼毒症　compensated alkalosis
代偿性气肿/代償性氣腫　complementary
　　emphysema
代偿性酸中毒/代償性酸中毒　compensated acidosis
代偿性萎缩/代償性萎縮　compensatory atrophy
代偿性心脏肥大/代償性心臟肥大　compensatory
　　hypertrophy of the heart
代偿性月经/代償性月經,替代性行經,倒經
　　vicarious menstruation
代际关系/代際關係　intergenerational relation
代脉/代脈　regularly intermittent pulse
代森锌/乙硫鋅　zineb
代授法/代授法　feeding with substitute
代替物/取代物　substitute
代替[药]疗法/替代性藥療法　substitutive
　　medication

代谢/代謝　metabolism
代谢测定床/代謝測定床　metabolic bed
代谢产物/代謝產物　metabolite
代谢当量/代謝當量　metabolic equivalent
代谢的/代謝的　metabolic
代谢反应/代謝反應　metabolic response
代谢疾病/代謝疾病　metabolic disease
代谢减退/代謝減退,新陳代謝不足,代謝活力減少　hypometabolism
代谢亢进/新陳代謝過盛　hypermetabolism
代谢清除率/代謝清除率　metabolic clearance rate
代谢调节/代謝調節　metabolic regulation
代谢途径/代謝途徑　metabolic pathway
代谢性白内障/代謝性白內障　metabolic cataract
代谢性骨疾病/代謝性骨疾病　metabolic bone disease
代谢性肌病/代謝性肌病　metabolic myopathy
代谢性碱中毒/代謝性鹼毒症　metabolic alkalosis
代谢性降解/代謝性降解　metabolic degradation
代谢性颅病/代謝性顱病　metabolic craniopathy
代谢性脑疾病/代謝性腦疾病　metabolic brain disease
代谢性皮肤疾病/代謝性皮膚疾病　metabolic skin disease
代谢性酸中毒/代謝性酸毒症　metabolic acidosis
代谢中间产物/代謝中間產物　metabolic intermediate
代谢终产物/代謝終產物　metabolic end product
代谢综合征/代謝症候群　metabolic syndrome
代用品/代用品　substitute
带/條帶,繫帶　strap
带病原状态/帶菌狀態　carrier state
带刺毛虫皮炎/帶刺毛蟲皮炎　stinging caterpillar dermatitis
带蒂黑色素瘤/有莖的黑色素瘤　pedunculated melanoma
带蒂毛囊错构瘤/有莖的毛囊錯構瘤　pedunculated follicular hamartoma
带蒂皮瓣/帶蒂皮瓣　pedicle skin flap
带蒂皮瓣转移阴道形成术/帶蒂皮瓣轉移陰道形成術　construction of vagina by pedicled skin grafting
带蒂组织移植术/帶蒂組織移植術　pedicled tissue grafting
带蒂组织移植物/帶蒂組織移植物　pedicled tissue graft
带发皮片/帶髮皮片　hair-bearing free skin graft
带发皮片簇植术/帶髮皮片簇植術　punched hair-bearing free skin grafting
带发皮片移植术/帶髮皮片移植術　hair-bearing free skin grafting
带缝线针/帶縫線針　swedged needle
带感觉神经皮瓣/帶感覺神經皮瓣　neuro-sensory skin flap
带环就位器/帶環就位器　band seater
带环去除钳/帶環去除鉗　band removing plier
带菌学/菌媒學　phorology
带孔牙/帶孔牙　diatoric tooth
带脉/帶脈　daimai, belt channel, belt vessel, GB26
带脉失约/帶脈失約　belt channel dysfunction
带旁核/帶旁核　paratenial nucleus
带配子体者/瘧蟲帶菌者　gametocyte carrier
带石针/帶石針　mounted stone
带条叩诊/狹條式叩法　strip percussion
带下/帶下　leukorrhea, morbid vaginal discharge
带下病/帶下病　leukorrheal diseases, morbid vaginal discharge
带下病诊法/帶下病診法　diagnostics for woman's disease
带下过多/帶下過多　profuse vaginal discharge
带下过少/帶下過少　oligo-vaginal discharge
带下过少・肝肾两虚证/帶下過少・肝腎兩虛證　oligo-vaginal discharge with pattern of deficiency of both liver and kidney
带下过少・血枯瘀阻证/帶下過少・血枯瘀阻證　oligo-vaginal discharge with pattern of blood depletion and blockade of static blood
带下史/帶下史　history of vaginal discharge
带血管蒂甲状旁腺移植/帶血管蒂的甲狀旁腺移植　vascularized parathyroid transplantation
带血管蒂肾上腺移植/帶血管蒂的腎上腺移植　vascularized adrenal transplantation
带氧酶/帶氧酵素　oxyphorase
带状/帶狀　band form
带状层/帶狀層　stratum zonale
带状粪/帶狀糞　ribbon stool
带状弓/帶狀弓　ribbon arch
带状光检影镜/帶狀光檢影鏡　streak retinoscope
带状肌/帶狀肌　ribbon muscle
带状角膜病/帶狀角膜病　band keratopathy
带状角膜炎/帶狀角膜炎　band keratitis
带状静脉形成不良/帶狀靜脈形成不良　venous malformations zosteriform
带状溃疡/帶狀潰瘍　girdle ulcer
带状疱疹/帶狀皰疹　shingles
带状疱疹病毒/帶狀皰疹病毒　herpes zoster virus
带状疱疹后的/皰疹後的　postherpetic

[带状]疱疹后神经痛/[帶狀]皰疹後神經痛 post-herpetic neuralgia
带状疱疹样的/帶狀的,帶疹狀的 zosteriform
带状疱疹样雀斑样痣/帶狀小痣樣痣 zosteriform lentiginous nevus
带状色谱/帶狀層析法 strip chromatography
带状视网膜检影法/帶狀光檢影[法] streak retinoscopy
带状胎盘/帶狀胎盤 zonary placenta
带状痛/帶狀痛 girdle pain
带状网状色素过度沉着/帶狀網狀色素過度沈著 zosteriform reticulate hyperpigmentation
带状银屑病/帶狀銀屑病 psoriasis zosteriformis
待产室/候產室 labor room
待验/待驗 guarantine
袋形缝术/袋形縫術 marsupialization
袋状皮瓣/袋狀皮瓣 marsupial skin flap
戴奥辛/戴奥辛 dioxin
戴特斯细胞/戴特斯氏細胞 Deiters cell
戴维森分流术/大衛森分流術 Davidson shunt
戴维斯移植皮片/大衛斯氏移植片 Davis graft
戴元礼/戴元禮 Dai Yuanli
黛蛤散/黛蛤散 daige powder
丹-伯病/Danielssen-Boeck 二氏疾病 Danielssen-Boeck disease
丹达特咬合器/丹達特咬合器 Dentatus articulator
丹迪-沃克综合征/丹迪-沃克症候群 Dandy-Walker syndrome
丹迪综合征/丹迪症候群 Dandy syndrome
丹毒/丹毒 erysipelas
丹毒的/丹毒的 erysipelatous
丹毒毒素/丹毒毒素 erysipelas toxin
丹毒·风热毒蕴证/丹毒·風熱毒蘊證 erysipelas with pattern of wind-heat toxin amassment
丹毒·肝脾湿火证/丹毒·肝脾濕火證 erysipelas with pattern of dampness-fire in spleen and liver
丹毒·湿热毒蕴证/丹毒·濕熱毒蘊證 erysipelas with pattern of dampness-heat toxin amassment
丹毒丝菌感染/丹毒絲菌感染 Erysipelothrix infections
丹毒·胎火蕴毒证/丹毒·胎火蘊毒證 erysipelas with pattern of fetal fire amassing toxin
丹毒性咽峡炎/丹毒性咽峽炎 angina erysipelatosa
丹毒样癌/類丹毒癌瘤 carcinoma erysipeloides
丹佛体制/丹佛體制 Denver system
丹磺酰化合物/丹磺醯化合物 dansyl compound
丹吉尔病/塔吉爾氏病 Tangier disease
丹木斯/丹木斯 diamox
丹尼尔/丹尼耳 daniell
丹尼尔电池/Daniell 氏電池 Daniell cell
丹尼特饮食/Dennett 氏飲食 Dennett diet
丹尼斯·布朗夹/Denis Browne 氏夾板 Denis Browne splint
丹尼斯法/德尼斯氏法 Denis method
丹曲林/丹曲林 dantrolene
丹参/丹参 Salvia miltiorrhiza, danshen root
丹参注射液/丹参注射液 danshen injection
丹氏浓缩器/丹氏濃縮器 Danish concentrator
丹溪心法/丹溪心法 Danxi's Mastery of Medicine
丹酰氯/二甲胺基萘磺醯氯 dansyl chloride, DANS-Cl
丹栀逍遥散/丹栀逍遥散 danzhi xiaoyao san
丹栀逍遥丸/丹栀逍遥丸 danzhi xiaoyao pills
担架/擔架 stretcher
担轮幼虫/擔輪幼蟲 trochophore
担子/擔子,孢子囊 basidium
担子孢子/擔子芽孢,擔孢子 basidiospore
担子菌纲/擔子菌綱 Basidiomycetes
单氨基单羧酸类氨基酸尿症/單胺基單羧酸類胺基酸尿症 monoamine mono-carboxylic group aminoaciduria
单胺氧化酶/單胺氧化酶 monoamine oxidase
单胺氧化酶抑制剂/單胺氧化酶抑制劑 monoamine oxidase inhibitor
单孢子囊菌素/單芽孢囊菌素 haplosporangin
单倍二倍性/單倍二倍性 haplodiploidy
单倍核/單倍核 hemikaryon
单倍期/單倍期,單數相 haplophase
单倍体/單倍體 haploid
单倍体数/單倍體數 haploid number
单倍体相同的供者/單倍體相同的供者 haploidentical donor
单倍体组/單倍體組 haploid set
单倍性/單倍體性,單套染色體性 haploidy
单倍真菌病/單芽孢囊菌病 haplomycosis
单鼻孔/單鼻孔 single nostril
单臂畸胎/單臂畸胎 monobrachius
单臂畸形/單臂畸胎 monobrachia
单臂卡环/單臂卡環 one-arm clasp
单鞭滴虫/單鞭蟲 cercomonad
单波脉/單波脈 monocrotic pulse
单波脉[现象]/單搏現象 monocrotism
单不饱和脂肪酸类/單不飽和脂肪酸類 monounsaturated fatty acids
单侧唇裂/單側唇裂,單側裂唇 unilateral cleft lip
单侧的/單側的 unilateral

单侧多发性囊肿/單側多發性囊腫　unilateral multicystic disease
单侧腭裂/單側腭裂　unilateral cleft palate
单侧发育不良/單側發育不良　hemidysplasia
单侧肥大/單側肥大　unilateral hypertrophy
单侧肺不发生/單側肺不發生　unilateral pulmonary agenesis
单侧膈肌麻痹/單側膈肌麻痺　unilateral paralysis of diaphragm
单侧膈膨升/單側膈膨昇　hemidiaphragmatic eventration
单侧两性畸形/單側半陰陽　unilateral hermaphroditism
单侧聋/單側聾　hemianacusia
单侧平衡/單側平衡　unilateral equilibration
单侧气胸/單側氣胸　unilateral pneumothorax
单侧擒拿法/單側擒拿法　unilateral grasping massage for throat disease
单侧透明肺综合征/單側透明肺症候群　unilateral hyperlucent lung syndrome
单侧舞蹈病/單側舞蹈病,半身舞蹈病　hemilateral chorea
单侧性脊髓损伤/單側性脊髓損傷　spinal unilateral injury
单侧性听觉丧失/單側性聽覺喪失　unilateral hearing loss
单侧性优势/一侧优势　lateral dominance
单侧性痣/單側性痣　nevus unius lateris
单侧痣/單側痣　nevus unius lateralis
单侧痣样毛细血管扩张/單側痣狀毛細管擴張　unilateral nevoid telangiectasia
单侧痣样毛细血管扩张综合征/單側痣樣毛細血管擴張症候群　unilateral nevoid telangiectasia syndrome
单层扁平上皮/單層扁平上皮　simple squamous epithelium
单层布裹法/單層布裹法　one sheet pack
单[层]分子膜/單膜片　monofilm
单层立方上皮/單層立方上皮　simple cuboidal epithelium
单层鳞状上皮/鋪磚狀上皮　tessellated epithelium
单层培养/單層培養　monolayer culture
单层上皮/單層上皮　simple epithelium
单层纤毛柱状上皮/單層纖毛柱狀上皮　simple ciliated columnar epithelium
单层脂质体/單層微脂粒　unilamelar liposome
单层柱状上皮/單層柱狀上皮　simple columnar epithelium

单冲压片机/單銃壓錠機　single punch tablet machine
单纯癌/單純性癌　carcinoma simplex
单纯病/單純病　haplopathy
单纯超滤/單純超濾　isolated ultrafiltration
单纯痤疮/單純痤瘡　acne simplex
单纯蛋白质/單純蛋白質　simple protein
单纯感染/單純感染　simple infection
单纯梗死/缓和性梗塞　bland infarct
单纯黄疸/單純黃疸　icterus simplex
单纯结节性肥胖病/單純結節性肥胖病　adiposis tuberosa simplex
单纯近视散光/單純近視性散光　simple myopic astigmatism
单纯糠疹/單純糠疹,白糠疹　pityriasis simplex
单纯恐怖症/單純恐怖症　simple phobia
单纯滤泡囊肿/單純濾泡囊腫　simple follicular cyst
单纯脓疱病/單純膿疱病　impetigo simplex
单纯疱疹/單純疱疹　herpes simplex
单纯疱疹病毒/單純疱疹病毒　herpes simplex virus
单纯疱疹病毒感染/單純疱疹病毒感染　herpes simplex
单纯疱疹病毒疫苗/單純疱疹病毒疫苗　herpes simplex virus vaccine
单纯疱疹脑炎/單純疱疹腦炎　herpes simplex encephalitis
单纯皮肤组织细胞增生病/單純皮膚組織細胞增生症　pure cutaneous histiocytosis
单纯扑动/规则性心房震颤,纯心房撲動　pure flutter
单纯溶液/單純溶液　simple solution
单纯乳房切除术/單純乳房切除術　simple mastectomy
单纯乳突切开术/單純乳突切開術　simple mastoidotomy
单纯塞尔托利细胞综合征/生殖細胞發育不全症候群,單純 Sertoli 氏細胞症候群　Sertoli-cell-only syndrome
单纯散光/單純散光　simple astigmatism
单纯外源性胃炎/單純外源性胃炎　simple exogenous gastritis
单纯萎缩/單純萎縮　simple atrophy
单纯腺瘤/單純腺瘤　adenoma simplex
单纯型大疱性表皮松解[症]/單純型大疱性表皮鬆解[症]　epidermolysis bullosa simplex
单纯型精神分裂症/單純型精神分裂症　simple schizophrenia
单纯性/單純性　simplex

单纯性白细胞增多/單純[性]白血球增多 pure leukocytosis
单纯性鼻炎/單純性鼻炎 simple rhinitis
单纯性唇炎/單純性唇炎 cheilitis simplex
单纯性大疱性表皮松解症/單純性水皰性表皮鬆解症 epidermolysis bullosa simplex superficialis
单纯性肥大/單純性肥大 simple hypertrophy
单纯性肺嗜酸细胞浸润症/單純性肺嗜酸細胞浸潤症 simple pulmonary eosinophilia
单纯性骨折/單純[性]骨折 simple fracture
单纯性汗腺棘皮瘤/單純[性]汗腺棘皮瘤 hidroacanthoma simplex
单纯性滑膜炎/單純[性]滑膜炎 simple synovitis
单纯性回状红斑/單純性迴狀紅斑 erythema simplex gyratum
单纯性集群性憩室病/單純性集群性憩室病 simple massed diverticulosis
单纯性甲状腺肿/單純性甲狀腺腫 simple goiter
单纯性睑炎/單純性瞼炎 blepharitis simplex
单纯性腱鞘囊肿/單純[性]腱鞘囊腫 simple ganglion
单纯性近视/單純性近視 simple myopia
单纯性溃疡/單純[性]潰瘍 simple ulcer
单纯性淋巴管瘤/單純[性]淋巴管瘤 lymphangioma simplex
单纯性毛细管瘤/單純性微血管瘤 simple capillary hemangioma
单纯性脑膜炎/單純[性]腦膜炎 simple meningitis
单纯性尿道炎/單純性尿道炎 simple urethritis
单纯性气胸/單純性氣胸 pneumothorax simplex
单纯性雀斑痣/單純性雀斑痣 lentigo simplex
单纯性肾囊肿/單純性腎囊腫 simple cyst of kidney
单纯性脱位/單純[性]脱位 simple dislocation
单纯性腺性唇炎/單純性腺性唇炎 cheilitis glandularis simplex
单纯性小痣/單純性小痣 simple lentigines
单纯性心动过速/單純性心搏快速 simple tachycardia
单纯性心内膜炎/單純性心内膜炎 simple endocarditis
单纯性性腺发育障碍症/單純性性腺發育障礙症 pure gonadal dysgenesis
单纯性血管瘤/單純性血管瘤 hemangioma simplex
单纯性哑/非聾性啞 audimutism
单纯性咽峡炎/單純性咽峽炎 angina simplex
单纯性阅读障碍/單純性閱讀障礙 pure alexia
单纯性紫癜/單純[性]紫癜病 purpura simplex
单纯疣/單純疣 verruca simplex
单纯远视散光/單純遠視性散光 simple hyperopic astigmatism
单唇裂/單裂唇 single harelip
单点刺激/單點穿刺性刺激 punctual stimulation
单碘酪氨酸/單碘酪胺基酸 monoiodotyrosine
单独的/單獨的,孤立的 solitary
单端孢霉烯类/單端孢黴烯類 trichothecenes
单端固定桥/單端固定桥 cantilever fixed bridge
单耳听觉/單耳聽覺 monaural hearing
单耳听力不全/單耳聽覺不全 otohemineurasthenia
单耳响度平衡试验/單耳響度平衡試驗 monaural loudness balance test
单发性皮脂腺囊瘤/單純性皮脂腺囊瘤 steatocystoma simplex
单方/單方 simple recipe
单房棘球蚴病/單房性包蟲囊病 unilocular hydatid disease
单房性的/單房的 unilocular
单房性囊肿/單房囊腫 unilocular cyst
单肺移植/單肺移植 single lung transplantation
单分散气雾形成接口/單分散氣霧形成界面 monodisperse aerosol generation interface, MAGIC
单分支管状腺/單分支管狀腺 simple branched tubular gland
单分支泡状腺/單分支泡狀腺 simple branched acinar gland
单付费者系统/單付費者系統 single-payer system
单股反链病毒目感染/單負病毒目感染 mononegavirales infection
单腹胀大/氣脹,鼓脹 tympanites
单睾丸者/單睾者 monorchid
单睾吸虫病/單睾吸蟲病 haplorchiasis
单睾症/單睾丸症 monorchidism
单个/單一 single
单个型/單個型 single pattern
单骨脚/單骨脚 simple bony crus
单骨纤维发育不良/單一骨骼纖維化發育不全 monostotic fibrous dysplasia
单骨性/單骨性的 monostotic
单关节/單關節 simple joint, simple articulation
单关节炎/單關節炎 mono-articular arthritis
单管泡状腺/單管泡狀腺 simple tubuloacinar gland
单管状腺/單管狀腺 simple tubular gland
单光子发射电子计算机体层扫描/單光子激發斷層掃描 single-photon emission computed tomography
单行排列细胞模型/單行排列細胞的範型 Indian-file cell pattern

单核白细胞/單核白細胞　mononuclear leukocyte
单核的/單核的　mononuclear
单核苷酸/單核苷酸　mononucleotide
单核苷酸多态性/單核苷酸多態性　single nucleotide polymorphism
单核母细胞白血病/單核母細胞性白血病　monoblastic leukemia
单核吞噬细胞系统/單核吞噬細胞系統　mononuclear phagocyte system, MPS
单核细胞/單核細胞　mononuclear cell, monocyte
单核细胞的/單核球的　monocytic
单核细胞发生/單核細胞生成　monocytopoiesis
单核细胞化学吸引蛋白质类/單核細胞化學吸引蛋白質類　monocyte chemoattractant proteins
单核细胞减少[症]/單核血球減少症　monocytopenia
单核细胞-巨噬细胞集落生成单位/單核細胞-巨噬細胞集落形成單位　colony-forming unit-monocyte-macrophage
单核细胞生成/單核血球製成　monocytopoiesis
单核细胞性白血病/Naegeli氏白血病,單核血球白血病　Naegeli leukemia
单核细胞性类白血病反应/單核細胞性白血病樣反應　monocytic leukemoid reaction
单核细胞增多/單核白血球增多　mononuclear leukocytosis
单核细胞增多症/單核白血球增多症　mononucleosis
单核因子/單核因子　monokine
单颌全口义齿/單頜全口義齒　single complete denture
单环β-内酰胺类/單環β-内醯胺類　monobactams
单簧管或竖笛吹奏者唇炎/吹木簫者唇炎　clarinettist cheilitis
单肌炎/單肌炎　monomyositis
单基因病/單基因病　monogenic disease
单极成神经细胞/單極神經母細胞　unipolar neuroblast
单极导联/單極導程　unipolar lead
单极的/單極的　unipolar
单极电凝[术]/單極電凝[術]　monopolar coagulation
单极电灼术/單極電灼術　monopolar electric cautery
单极神经细胞/單極神經細胞　unipolar nerve cell
单极神经元/單極神經原　unipolar neuron
单极细胞/單極細胞　unipolar cell
单剂量包装/藥品單一劑量包裝　unit dose package
单甲基肼/單甲基肼　monomethylhydrazine
单价抗体/單價抗體　univalent antibody

单价体/一價的,單價的　univalent
单价血清/單價血清　monovalent serum
单价疫苗/單價菌苗　univalent vaccine
单尖牙/單尖齒　unicuspid
单键/單鍵　single bond
单角的/單角的,僅一角的　monangle
单角子宫/單角子宮[畸形]　unicornuate uterus
单晶体/單晶體　solitary crystal
单精入卵/孤精入卵,單精受精　monospermy
单菌性感染/單種感染　monoinfection
单克隆抗体/單株抗體　monoclonal antibody
单克隆抗体类/單株抗體類　monoclonal antibodies
单克隆学说/單一細胞衍生的學說　monoclonal hypothesis
单孔/單孔　single foramen
单孔目动物/單孔動物　monotreme
单口瘘/單口瘻,盲瘻　blind fistula
单蜡膏/單蠟劑　simple cerate
单链构型多态性/單鏈構型多態性　single strand conformation polymorphism
单磷酸/單磷酸鹽　monophosphate
单卵孪生/單卵孿生　monozygotic twins, monozygotic twinning
单卵双生/單卵雙生　monozygotic twins
单卵双胎儿/單卵雙胎兒　monovular twins
单卵种/單卵種　monovulatory species
单盲法/單盲法　single-blind method
单面洞/單面齲齒腔洞　simple cavity
单面双头畸胎/單面雙頭畸形　miopus
单膜脚/單膜腳　simple membranous crus
单能辐射/單一能量輻射線　monoenergetic radiation
单能性/偏能的　unipotency
单宁类/單寧類　tannins
单宁酸铋/鞣酸鉍　bismuth tannate
单泡脂肪细胞/單泡脂肪細胞　unilocular adipose cell
单泡状腺/單泡狀腺　simple acinar gland
单胚叶瘤/單胚層瘤　monodermoma
单脐动脉脐带/單臍動脈臍帶　single umbilical artery of cord
单[潜]能细胞/單潛能細胞　unipotent cell
单腔支气管导管/單腔支氣管導管　single lumen endobronchial tube
单亲/單親　single parent
单亲二体性/單親二體性　uniparental disomy
单亲家庭/單親家庭　single-parent family
单曲管状腺/單曲管狀腺　simple coiled tubular gland
单躯联胎/軀體連胎,單軀畸胎　somatodidymus

单绒毛膜双胎/單絨毛膜雙胎　monochorionic twin pregnancy
单乳头肾/單乳頭腎　unipapillary kidney
单乳胸/單乳腺胸　amazon thorax
单色辐射/單色輻射　monochromatic radiation
单色觉眼/單色眼,單色視覺　monochromatic eye
单色盲分光镜/分光檢色器　spectrocolorimeter
单神经病/單神經病　mononeuropathy
单神经炎/單神經炎　mononeuritis
单声带炎/單聲帶炎　monocorditis
单式显微镜/單顯微鏡　simple microscope
单视/單視　haplopia
单手进针法/單手進針法　needle-inserting with single hand
单酸甘油脂/單酸甘油脂　monoglyceride
单胎妊娠/單胎妊娠　singleton pregnancy
单态的/單形性的　monomorphic
单态氧/單態氧　singlet oxygen
单瘫/單癱,單麻痺　monoplegia
单糖/單糖　monosaccharide
单糖浆/單糖漿,白糖漿　simple syrup
单糖类/單糖類　monosaccharides
单糖转运蛋白质类/單糖轉運蛋白質類　monosaccharide transport proteins
单体/單體　monomer
单体畸胎/單畸胎　single monster
单体GTP结合蛋白质类/單體GTP結合蛋白質類　monomeric GTP-binding proteins
单体联胎/單體連胎　monosomian
单体网格蛋白装配蛋白质类/單體網格蛋白裝配蛋白質類　monomeric clathrin assembly proteins
单体型/單型　haplotype
单体性/單數染色體　monosomy
单体诱发的/單體誘發的　monomer-induced
单萜/單萜　monoterpene
单萜类/單萜類　monoterpenes
单头的/單頭的,一頭的　uniceps
单头联胎/單頭連胎　monocephalus
单突触反射/單突觸反射　monosynaptic reflex
单腿半蹲试验/單腿半蹲試驗　single leg semisquatting test
单腿独立试验/單腿獨立試驗　single leg standing test
单腿跳跃试验/單腿跳躍試驗　single leg skipping test
单维生素缺乏病/單種維生素缺乏病　monavitaminosis
单位/單位　unit
单位格子/單位格子　unit cell
单位量/單位制　unitage
单位膜/單位膜　unit membrane
单细胞腺/單細胞腺　unicellular gland
单纤维肌电图学/單纖維肌電圖學　single fiber electromyography
单酰基甘油酯脂酶类/單醯基甘油酯脂酶類　monoacylglycerol lipases
单腺/單[細胞]腺　simple gland
单向阀/單向閥　check valve
单向交叉抗药性/單向交叉抗藥性　monodirectional cross resistance
单向扩散试验/單向擴散試驗　single diffusion test
单向型口咽通气管/單向型口咽通氣管　one way oropharyngeal airway
单向性心传导阻滞/單向性心傳導阻滯　unidirectional heart block
单向阻滞/單向性傳導阻滯　unidirectional block
单相反应/單相反應　uniphasic reaction
单相抑郁[症]/單相抑鬱　unipolar depression
单硝酸硫胺素/單硝酸硫胺素　thiamin mononitrate
单小叶/單小葉　simple lobule
单小叶性肝硬变/單小葉性肝硬變　unilobular cirrhosis
单心房/單心房　single atrium
单心室/單一心室　single ventricle
单心室性房室连接/單心室性房室連接　univentricular atrioventricular connections
单星体/單星[體]　monaster
单形性腺瘤/單形性腺瘤　monomorphic adenoma
单形牙/單形牙,單純齒冠　haplodont
单性生殖/無精生殖　parthenogenesis
单牙牙种植体/單牙牙種植體　single-tooth dental implant
单眼复视/單眼[性]複視　monocular diplopia
单眼视觉/單眼視覺,單眼視力　monocular vision
单眼视野/單眼視野　monocular visual field
单眼注视/單眼注視　monocular fixation
单眼紫癜/單眼紫癜　purpura cyclops
单羊膜囊双胎/單羊膜囊雙胎　monoamnionic twin pregnancy
单液电池/單液電池　one-fluid cell
单一骨折/單一骨折　single fracture
单一性垂体前叶功能不全/單一性垂體前葉功能不全　isolated deficiency of anterior pituitary hormone
单一性促黄体素缺乏症/單一性促黃體素缺乏症　isolated luteinizing hormone deficiency
单一性促甲状腺素缺乏症/單一性促甲狀腺素缺乏

症　isolated thyrotropin deficiency
单一性促卵泡素缺乏症/單一性促卵泡素缺乏症　isolated follicular stimulating hormone deficiency
单一性促肾上腺皮质素缺乏症/單一性促腎上腺皮質素缺乏症　isolated corticotropin deficiency
单一性促性腺素缺乏症/單一性促性腺素缺乏症　isolated gonadotropin deficiency
单一性骨囊肿/單一性骨囊腫　solitary bone cyst
单一性生长素缺乏症/單一性生長素缺乏症　isolated growth hormone deficiency
单一症状性癔病/單症狀性癔病　monosymptomatic hysteria
单乙醇胺/單乙醇胺　monoethanolamine
单音[测听]弦/單弦琴,單弦音響測定器　monochord
单音调言语/單音調言語　plateau speech
单硬脂酸乙二醇酯/單硬脂酸乙二醇酯　ethyleneglycol monostearate
单油酸山梨醇多乙烯/單油酸山梨醇多乙烯　polyoethylene sorbitol mono-oleate
单羽肌/單羽肌　unipennate muscle
单语症/單語症　monophasia
单元型/單元型　haplotype
单原子分子/單原子性分子　monatomic molecule
单折射板/單折射板　isotropous disc
单针透析/單針透析　single-needle dialysis
单症状/單一症狀　monosymptom
单症状的/單症狀的　monosymptomatic
单肢感觉异常/單肢感覺倒錯　monoparesthesia
单肢轻瘫/單肢輕病,局部輕麻痹　monoparesis
单肢[手足]徐动症/單[側]肢瘈病　monathetosis
单肢投掷症/單肢投擲症　monoballismus
单直管状腺/單直管狀腺　simple straighted tubular gland
单轴畸胎/單軸性畸胎　monoaxial monster
单轴神经元/單軸神經元　monaxon
单足畸胎/單足畸胎　monopus
单足[畸形]/單足畸形　monopodia
耽误/耽誤　delay
胆/膽　gallbladder
胆癌/膽癌　gallbladder cancer
胆茶碱/茶鹼膽鹼　oxtriphylline
胆翠质/膽綠質　choleprasin
胆道/膽道　biliary tract
胆道闭锁/膽道閉鎖　biliary atresia
胆道测压[术]/膽道測壓[術]　manometry of biliary tract
胆道出血/膽道出血　hemobilia

胆道感染/膽道感染　infection of biliary tract
胆道梗阻/膽道梗阻　obstruction of biliary tract
胆道蛔虫病/膽道蛔蟲病　biliary ascariasis
胆道疾病/膽道疾病　biliary tract disease
胆道贾第虫病/膽道賈第蟲病　giardiasis of biliary tract
胆道减压术/膽道減壓術　decompression of biliary tract
胆道口括约肌炎/奥迪氏括約肌炎　odditis
胆道黏液腺/膽道黏液腺　hepatic gland
胆道脓肿/膽道膿瘍　biliary abscess
胆道闪烁显像[术]/膽管閃爍攝影法　cholescintigraphy
胆道外科手术/膽道外科手術　biliary tract surgical procedure
胆道肿瘤/膽道腫瘤　biliary tract neoplasm
胆蒽/膽蒽　cholanthrene
胆矾/膽礬,硫酸銅　blue stone
胆骨化醇/膽利鈣醇,維生素 D3　cholecalciferol
胆固醇/膽固醇,膽脂醇　cholesterol
胆固醇病/膽脂醇病　cholesterin disease
胆固醇侧链断裂酶/膽固醇側鏈斷裂酶　cholesterol side-chain cleavage enzyme
胆固醇产生/膽脂醇產生　cholesterogenesis
胆固醇沉积症/膽脂醇代謝病　cholesterol lipoidosis
胆固醇沉着病/膽固醇沈著病　cholesterolosis
胆固醇沉着性变性/膽硬脂性變性,膽硬脂蓄積過多　cholesteatosis
胆固醇基/膽硬脂基　cholesteryl
胆固醇结晶栓塞/膽固醇晶體栓塞　cholesterol crystal embolization
胆固醇结石/膽固醇結石　cholesterol stone
胆固醇逆向转运/反向膽固醇運輸　reverse cholesterol transport
胆固醇尿/膽固醇尿症　cholesterinuria
胆固醇 7-α-羟化酶/膽固醇 7-α-羥化酶　cholesterol 7-alpha-hydroxylase
胆固醇生成/膽固醇合成　cholesterolopoiesis
胆固醇栓塞/膽固醇栓塞　cholesterol embolism
胆固醇性水胸/膽固醇性水胸　cholesterohydrothorax
胆固醇性胸腔积液/膽固醇性胸腔積液　cholesterol pleural effusion
胆固醇血[症]/膽固醇血症　cholesteremia
胆固醇抑制剂/膽固醇抑制劑　cholesterol inhibitor
胆固醇酯类/膽固醇酯類　cholesterol esters
胆固醇酯酶/膽固醇酯酶　cholesterol esterase
胆固醇酯贮积病/膽固醇酯貯積病　cholesterol ester

storage disease
胆固醇粥样动脉硬化/膽固醇粥樣動脈硬化　cholesterol atherosclerosis
胆管/膽管，膽道　bile duct
胆管癌/膽管癌　carcinoma of bile duct
胆管病/膽管病　cholepathia
胆管测压造影[术]/膽管測壓造影[術]　manometric cholangiography
胆管丛/膽道叢　biliary plexus
胆管的/膽道的　biliary
胆管肝细胞瘤/膽管肝[細胞]瘤　cholangiohepatoma
胆管疾病/膽管疾病　bile duct disease
胆管空肠吻合术/膽管空腸造口吻合術　cholangiojejunostomy
胆管扩张/膽管擴張　cholangiectasis
胆管瘤/膽管瘤　cholangioma
胆管内置管扩张[术]/膽管内置管擴張[術]　biliary stent dilatation
胆管脓肿/膽管膿腫　bile duct abscess
胆管切开术/膽管切開術　cholangiotomy
胆管胃吻合术/膽管胃造口吻合術　cholangiogastrostomy
胆管腺瘤/膽管腺瘤　bile duct adenoma
胆管小肠吻合术/膽管小腸造口吻合術　cholangioenterostomy
胆管性肝炎/膽管肝炎　cholangiohepatitis
胆管炎/膽管炎，膽道炎　cholangitis
胆管炎性脓肿/膽管炎性膿腫　cholangitic abscess
胆管造口术/膽管造口術，膽管造瘻術　cholangiostomy
胆管造内口术/膽管造内口術　internal hepatocholangiostomy
胆管造外口术/膽管造外口術　external hepatocholangiostomy
胆管造影片/膽囊及膽管X光像　cholangiogram
胆管造影术/膽管X光攝影法　cholangiography
胆管肿瘤/膽管腫瘤　bile duct neoplasm
胆管周围炎/膽管周圍炎　pericholangitis
胆褐素/膽棕質　bilifuscin
胆红素/膽紅素，膽紅質　bilirubin
胆红素脑病/膽紅素腦病　bilirubin encephalopathy
胆红素尿/膽紅素尿症　bilirubinuria
胆红素性梗死/膽紅素性梗塞　bilirubin infarction
胆红素血[症]/膽紅素血症　bilirubinemia
胆红素盐/膽紅素鹽　bilirubinate
胆黄褐素/膽黃褐質，膽茶色質，不純膽紅素　bilifulvin
胆黄素/膽黃質　biliflavin
胆火不得卧/膽火不得臥　insomnia due to gallbladder fire
胆碱/膽鹼，膽汁素　choline
胆碱激酶/膽鹼激酶　choline kinase
胆碱疗法/膽素療法　choline treatment
胆碱磷酸胞苷酰转移酶/膽鹼磷酸胞苷醯轉移酶　choline-phosphate cytidylyltransferase
胆碱磷酸化酶/膽鹼磷酸化酶　choline phosphorylase
胆碱磷酸酶/膽磷酸鹽酵素　choleophosphatase
胆碱能的/膽鹼能的，膽鹼激素性的　cholinergic
胆碱能激动剂/膽鹼能激動劑　cholinergic agonist
胆碱能拮抗剂/膽鹼能拮抗劑　cholinergic antagonist
胆碱能神经元/膽鹼能神經元　cholinergic neuron
胆碱能受体/膽鹼能受體　cholinergic receptor
胆碱能纤维/膽鹼能纖維　cholinergic fiber
胆碱能性荨麻疹/膽鹼能蕁麻疹　cholinergic urticaria
胆碱能药/膽鹼能藥　cholinergic
胆碱缺乏症/膽鹼缺乏症　choline deficiency
胆碱受体阻滞药/膽鹼受體阻滯藥　cholinoreceptor blocker
胆碱脱氢酶/膽鹼脱氫酶　choline dehydrogenase
胆碱O-乙酰转移酶/膽鹼O-乙醯轉移酶　choline O-acetyltransferase
胆碱酯酶/膽鹼酯酶　cholinesterase
胆碱酯酶活化药/膽鹼酯酶活化藥，膽鹼酯酶再啟動劑　cholinesterase reactivator
胆碱酯酶抑制药/膽鹼酯酶抑制劑　cholinesterase inhibitor
胆碱酯酶痣/膽鹼酯酶痣　cholinesterase nevus
胆绞痛/膽絞痛　biliary colic
胆[结]石/膽石　gallstone
胆经郁热/膽經鬱熱　heat stagnated in the gallbladder meridian, stagnated heat of gallbladder channel
胆经郁热证/膽經鬱熱證　pattern of heat stagnation in the gallbladder meridian, pattern of stagnated heat of gallbladder channel
胆惊/膽驚　convulsion due to gallbladder disorder
胆瘘/膽瘻　biliary fistula
胆绿素/膽綠素　biliverdine
胆绿素盐/膽綠素鹽　biliverdinate
胆南星/膽南星　bile arisaema
胆囊/膽囊　gallbladder
胆囊癌/膽囊癌　carcinoma of gallbladder
胆囊病/膽囊病　cholecystopathy
胆囊肠瘘/膽囊腸瘻　cholecystoenteric fistula
胆囊超声显像[术]/膽囊超聲顯像[術]

cholecystosonography
胆囊弛缓/膽囊弛緩,膽囊無張力　cholecystatony
胆囊穿孔/膽囊穿孔　perforation of gallbladder
胆囊胆管造影照片/膽囊與膽管 X 光像
　　cholecystocholangiogram
胆囊底/膽囊底　fundus of gallbladder
胆囊电烙/膽囊電烙術　electrocholecystocausis
胆囊动脉/膽囊動脈　cystic artery
胆囊缝合术/膽囊縫合術　cholecystorrhaphy
胆囊钙化/膽囊鈣化　calcification of gallbladder
胆囊固定术/膽囊固定術　cholecystopexy
胆囊管/膽囊管　cystic duct, cystic gall duct
胆囊管缝合术/膽囊管縫合術　cysticorrhaphy
胆囊管切开术/膽囊管切開術　cysticotomy
胆囊管石切除术/膽囊管石切除術
　　cysticolithectomy
胆囊回肠吻合术/膽囊迴腸造口吻合術
　　cholecystoileostomy
胆囊积脓/膽囊積膿　empyema of gall-bladder
胆囊积气/膽囊積氣　pneumogallbladder
胆囊积水/膽囊積水　hydrops of gallbladder
胆囊积血/血性膽囊　hemocholecyst
胆囊疾病/膽囊疾病　gallbladder disease
胆囊结肠瘘/膽囊結腸瘻管　cholecystocolonic fistula
胆囊结肠切开术/膽囊結腸切開術
　　cholecystocolotomy
胆囊结肠吻合术/膽囊結腸造口吻合術
　　cholecystocolostomy
胆囊结肠造口吻合术/膽囊結腸吻合術
　　cystocolostomy
胆囊结石病/膽囊結石病　cholecystolithiasis
胆囊颈/膽囊頸　neck of gallbladder
胆囊静脉/膽囊靜脈　cystic vein
胆囊镜检查[术]/膽囊鏡檢查[術]　cholecystoscopy
胆囊局限性腺肌瘤样增生/膽囊局限性腺肌增生
　　focal adenomyomatous hyperplasia of the
　　gallbladder
胆囊空肠吻合术/膽囊空腸造口吻合術
　　cholecystojejunostomy
胆囊扩张/膽囊擴張　cholecystectasia
胆囊淋巴结/膽囊淋巴結　cystic lymph node
胆囊囊肿/膽囊囊腫　gall cyst
胆囊扭转/膽囊扭轉　torsion of gallbladder
胆囊排空/膽囊排空　gallbladder emptying
胆囊切除术/膽囊切除術　cholecystectomy
胆囊切除术后综合征/膽囊切除術後症候群
　　postcholecystectomy syndrome
胆囊切开术/膽囊切開術　cholecystotomy

胆囊神经丛/膽囊神經叢　cystic plexus
胆囊肾盂吻合术/膽囊腎盂造口吻合術
　　cholecystnephrostomy
胆囊十二指肠结肠襞/膽囊十二指腸結腸皺襞
　　cholecystoduodenocolic fold
胆囊十二指肠韧带/膽囊十二指腸韌帶
　　cysticoduodenal ligament
胆囊十二指肠吻合术/膽囊十二指腸造口吻合術
　　cholecystoduodenostomy
胆囊收缩素/膽囊收縮素,激膽囊素　cholecystokinin
胆囊收缩素受体/膽囊收縮素受體　cholecystokinin
　　receptor
胆囊碎石术/膽囊石搗碎術　cholecystolithotripsy
胆囊体/膽囊體　body of gallbladder
胆囊胃吻合术/膽囊胃造口吻合術
　　cholecystgastrostomy
胆囊窝/膽囊窩　fossa for gallbladder
胆囊下垂/膽囊下垂　cholecystoptosis
胆囊腺管/Luschka 氏管　Luschka duct
胆囊小肠缝合术/膽囊小腸縫合術
　　cholecystenterorrhaphy
胆囊小肠吻合术/膽囊小腸造口吻合術
　　cholecystenteroanastomosis
胆囊型伤寒/膽囊型傷寒　cholecystotyphoid
胆囊[穴]/膽囊[穴]　dannang, EX-LE6
胆囊炎/膽囊炎　cholecystitis
胆囊淤积/膽囊淤積　gallbladder stasis
胆囊运动障碍/膽囊收縮障礙　biliary dyskinesia
胆囊造口术/膽囊造口術,膽囊造瘻術
　　cholecystostomy
胆囊造影术/膽囊 X 光攝影法　cholecystography
胆囊造影照片/膽囊 X 光像　cholecystogram
胆囊肿瘤/膽囊腫瘤　gallbladder neoplasm
胆囊周围脓肿/膽囊周圍膿腫　pericholecystic
　　abscess
胆囊周炎/膽囊周圍炎　pericholecystitis
胆囊自切除/自體膽囊切除術　autocholecystectomy
胆气/膽氣　gallbladder qi
胆气不足/膽氣不足　insufficiency of gallbladder qi
胆气不足证/膽氣不足證　pattern of gallbladder qi
　　insufficiency
胆器[官]/膽泌器　biliary apparatus
胆怯/膽怯　timidity
胆青素/膽藍質　cholecyanin
胆色素/膽色素,膽色質　bile pigment
胆色素生成/膽色素生成　cholechromopoiesis
胆色素原/膽色素原　porphobilinogen
胆色素原合酶/膽色素原合酶　porphobilinogen

synthase
胆色素原尿/膽色素原尿　porphobilinogenuria
胆石/膽[道結]石　gallstones
胆石病/膽石病　cholelithiasis
胆石切除术/膽石取出術　cholelithotomy
胆石通胶囊/膽石通膠囊　danshitong capsule
胆石性肠梗阻/膽石性腸梗阻　gallstone ileus
胆石性绞痛/膽石絞痛　gallstone colic
胆石性消化不良/膽石性消化不良　cholelithic dyspepsia
胆俞/膽俞　danshu, BL19
胆酸/膽酸　cholic acid
胆酸螯合剂/膽酸螯合劑　bile acid sequestrant
胆酸类物质排出增多/利膽物質分泌作用　cholaneresis
胆酸钠/膽酸鈉　sodium cholate
胆酸盐生成/膽酸鹽生成　cholanopoiesis
胆土素/膽土質　bilihumin
胆烷类/膽烷類　cholanes
胆烯类/膽烯類　cholenes
胆系协同失调/膽道共濟失調　biliary dyssynergia
胆小管/膽小管　bile canaliculus
胆小管炎/細膽管炎　cholangiolitis
胆虚/膽虛　insufficiency of gallbladder qi
胆虚气怯/膽虛氣怯　insufficiency of gallbladder qi, insufficiency of gallbladder qi causing timidity
胆血胸/膽血胸　cholohemothorax
胆血症/膽血症　cholemia
胆胰分泌转流术/膽胰分泌轉流術　biliopancreatic diversion
胆胰管汇合异常/膽胰管匯合異常　choledochopancreatic junction anomaly
胆影葡胺/膽影葡胺　biligrafin
胆郁/膽鬱　stagnation pattern of gallbladder qi
胆郁痰扰/膽鬱痰擾　gallbladder qi stagnation and phlegm disturbance, stagnated gallbladder qi with disturbing phlegm
胆郁痰扰证/膽鬱痰擾證　pattern of gallbladder qi stagnation with phlegm disturbance, pattern of stagnated gallbladder qi with disturbing phlegm
胆甾醇性心包炎/膽固醇性心包炎　cholesterol pericarditis
胆甾二烯醇类/膽甾二烯醇類　cholestadienols
胆甾二烯类/膽甾二烯類　cholestadienes
胆甾烷/膽甾烷　cholestane
胆甾烷醇/膽甾烷醇　cholestanol
胆甾烷类/膽甾烷類　cholestanes
胆甾烷酸/膽烷酸,去羥基膽酸　cholanic acid
胆甾烷酮类/膽甾烷酮類　cholestanones
胆甾烯/膽烯　cholestene
胆甾烯酮 5α 还原酶/膽甾烯酮 5α 還原酶　cholestenone 5 alpha-reductase
胆甾烯酮类/膽甾烯酮類　cholestenones
胆胀/膽脹　gallbladder distention
胆胀·胆腑郁热证/膽脹·膽腑鬱熱證　gallbladder distention with pattern of heat stagnation in gallbladder
胆胀·肝胆气郁证/膽脹·肝膽氣鬱證　gallbladder distention with pattern of qi stagnation of liver and gallbladder
胆胀·肝胆湿热证/膽脹·肝膽濕熱證　gallbladder distention with pattern of damp-heat in liver and gallbladder
胆胀·气滞血瘀证/膽脹·氣滯血瘀證　gallbladder distention with pattern of qi stagnation and blood stasis
胆胀·阳虚郁滞证/膽脹·陽虛鬱滯證　gallbladder distention with pattern of yang deficiency and qi depression
胆胀·阴虚郁滞证/膽脹·陰虛鬱滯證　gallbladder distention with pattern of yin deficiency and qi stagnation
胆汁/膽汁　bile
胆汁的/膽汁的　bilious
胆汁反流/膽汁返流　bile reflux
胆汁反流性胃炎/膽汁反流性胃炎　bile reflux gastritis
胆汁分泌/膽汁之分泌　biliation
胆汁[分泌]过多/膽汁過多,膽分泌過旺　hypercholia
胆汁粪/膽性糞　bilious stool
胆汁疗法/膽汁療法　choletherapy
胆汁内胆固醇增多/膽硬脂排洩量增多　cholesteroleresis
胆汁内异质分泌/膽汁內異質分泌　syncholia
胆汁黏稠综合征/膽汁黏稠症候群　biliary hyperviscosity syndrome
胆汁尿/膽尿症　choleuria
胆汁浓缩综合征/濃縮膽汁症候群　inspissated bile syndrome
胆汁溶解度试验/膽汁可溶性試驗　bile solubility test
胆汁生成/膽汁生成,膽汁形成　biligenesis
胆汁栓塞/膽汁栓塞　bile thrombus
胆汁素质/膽病體質　bilious diathesis
胆汁酸/膽汁酸　bile acid

胆汁[酸]盐/膽[酸]鹽　bile salt
胆汁性腹膜炎/膽汁性腹膜炎　bile peritonitis
胆汁性肝硬化/膽汁性肝硬變　biliary cirrhosis
胆汁性绞痛/膽汁性絞痛　bilious colic
胆汁性呕吐/吐膽症,膽汁嘔吐　bilious vomiting, cholemesis
胆汁性呕吐物/膽性吐物,膽色嘔吐物　bilious vomit
胆汁性瘙痒[症]/膽汁性搔癢[症]　biliary pruritus
胆汁性消化不良/膽汁性消化不良　bilious dyspepsia
胆汁胸/膽[汁]胸　cholothorax
胆汁循环/膽汁循環　bile circulation
胆汁盐/膽汁鹽　bile salt
胆汁移行倒错/膽汁排洩障礙[性黃疸]　parapedesis
胆汁溢流/膽汁溢流　overflow of gall
胆汁引流/膽汁引流　biliary drainage
胆汁淤积/膽汁淤積　cholestasis
胆汁障碍/膽汁障礙　dyscholia
胆汁正常/膽汁正常　eucholia
胆汁质/黃膽質　bilious temperament
胆脂瘤/膽硬脂瘤　cholesteatoma
胆主决断/膽主決斷　gallbladder governing decision
胆紫素/膽紫質　bilipurpurin
胆总管/膽總管　common bile duct, ductus choledochus
胆总管部分切除术/總膽管切除術　choledochectomy
胆总管成形术/總膽管造形術　choledochoplasty
胆总管端端吻合术/總膽管兩部分吻合術　choledochocholedochostomy
胆总管缝合术/總膽管縫合術　choledochorrhaphy
胆总管肝管吻合术/總膽管肝管造口吻合術　choledochohepatostomy
胆总管梗阻/總膽管梗阻　obstruction of common bile duct
胆总管回肠吻合术/總膽管迴腸造口吻合術　choledochoileostomy
胆总管疾病/總膽管疾病　common bile duct disease
胆总管结石/總膽管結石　calculus of common bile duct, choledocholith
胆总管结石病/總膽管結石病　choledocholithiasis
胆总管空肠吻合术/總膽管空腸造口吻合術　choledochojejunostomy
胆总管[窥]镜/總膽管鏡　choledochoscope
胆总管扩张/總膽管擴張　choledochectasia
胆总管括约肌/總膽管括約肌　sphincter of common bile duct
胆总管囊肿/總膽管囊腫　choledochal cyst
胆总管囊肿切除术/總膽管囊腫切除術　choledochocystectomy
胆总管切开术/總膽管切開術　choledochotomy
胆总管十二指肠吻合术/總膽管十二指腸造口吻合術　choledochoduodenostomy
胆总管石切除术/總膽管結石取出術　choledocholithotomy
胆总管碎石术/總膽管石摧碎術　choledocholithotripsy
胆总管探查[术]/總膽管探查[術]　exploration of common bile duct
胆总管胃吻合术/總膽管胃造口吻合術　choledochogastrostomy
胆总管狭窄/總膽管狹窄　stenosis of common bile duct
胆总管小肠吻合术/總膽管小腸造口吻合術　choledochoenterostomy
胆总管炎/總膽管炎　choledochitis
胆总管异常扩张/總膽管擴大　megacholedochus
胆总管造口术/總膽管造口術,膽總管造瘻術　choledochostomy
胆总管造影照片/總膽管X光照片　choledochogram
胆总管肿瘤/總膽管腫瘤　common bile duct neoplasms
但寒不热/但寒不熱　chill without fever
但热不寒/但熱不寒　fever without chill
但欲寐/但欲寐　analeptic, somnolence
淡/淡　tasteless
淡白舌/淡白舌　pale tongue
淡豆豉/淡豆豉　fermented soybean
淡红舌/淡紅舌　pink tongue
淡红猪圆线虫/淡紅豬圓蟲　Hyostrongylus rubidus
淡黄青霉多糖/淡黃青黴多醣　luteose
淡漠/淡漠　indifference
淡漠的/淡漠的,冷淡的,漠然的　apathic
淡漠型甲[状腺功能]亢[进]/無表情的甲狀腺高能症　apathetic hyperthyroidism
淡漠性痴呆/木訥性癡呆　apathetic dementia
淡漠性抑郁/淡漠性抑鬱,淡漠性憂鬱　apathic depression
淡渗利湿/淡滲利濕　promoting diuresis with drugs of tasteless flavor
淡水/淡水　fresh water
淡竹叶/淡竹葉　lophatherum herb
淡紫色发绀/向日散狀發紺　heliotrope cyanosis
弹道系数/彈道係數　ballistic coefficient
弹片伤/炮彈傷　shell wound
弹式测热计/彈筒式量熱器,卡計彈　bomb calorimeter
弹丸状乳腺/彈丸狀胸　shotty breast

弹状病毒/彈狀病毒　rhabdovirus
弹状病毒科感染/彈狀病毒科感染　Rhabdoviridae infection
蛋氨酸吸收障碍综合征/甲硫胺酸吸收障礙症候群　methionine malabsorption syndrome
蛋白/卵白　egg white
蛋白 C/蛋白質 C　protein C
C 蛋白/C 蛋白　C protein
N 蛋白/N 蛋白　N protein
蛋白沉积[症]/蛋白質蓄積,蛋白質沈著　proteinosis
蛋白促生长肽/助生長質　streptogenin
蛋白代谢/蛋白質新陳代謝　proteometabolism
蛋白胆汁症/蛋白膽汁症　albuminocholia
蛋白蛋白/卵蛋白素　egg albumin
蛋白丢失性肠病/蛋白丟失性腸病　protein-losing enteropathy
蛋白胨/蛋白腖　peptone
蛋白胨溶液/蛋白腖溶液　peptone solution
蛋白胨性荨麻疹/蛋白腖性蕁麻疹　peptone urticaria
蛋白反应热/蛋白熱　protein fever
蛋白分选信号/蛋白分選信號　protein sorting signal
蛋白激酶 C/蛋白[質]激酶 C　protein kinase C
蛋白激酶类/蛋白[質]激酶類　protein kinases
蛋白激酶抑制剂/蛋白[質]激酶抑制劑　protein kinase inhibitor
蛋白激素/蛋白質性激素　proteohormone
蛋白甲基转移酶类/蛋白甲基轉移酶類　protein methyltransferases
蛋白碱/蛋白贋鹼類　leukomaine
蛋白碱血/蛋白贋鹼血症　leukomainemia
蛋白结合/蛋白結合　protein binding
蛋白结合碘/蛋白結合碘　protein-bound iodine
蛋白精氨酸 N-甲基转移酶/蛋白精胺酸 N-甲基轉移酶　protein-arginine N-methyltransferase
蛋白聚糖类/蛋白聚糖類　proteoglycans
蛋白抗原/蛋白質抗原　proteantigen
蛋白赖氨酸 6-氧化酶/蛋白賴胺酸 6-氧化酶　protein-lysine 6-oxidase
蛋白酪氨酸激酶/蛋白酪胺酸激酶　protein tyrosine kinase
蛋白酪氨酸试验/蛋白酪胺基酸試驗　protein tyrosin test
蛋白硫酸软骨素类/蛋白硫酸軟骨素類　proteochondroitin sulfates
蛋白酶/蛋白酶　protease
蛋白酶激活受体/蛋白酶啟動受體　proteinase-activated receptor
蛋白酶解/蛋白酶解　proteolysis

蛋白酶体内肽酶复合物/蛋白酶體內肽酶複合物　proteasome endopeptidase complex
蛋白酶抑制药/蛋白酶抑制藥　protease inhibitor
蛋白尿/蛋白尿　proteinuria
蛋白尿恐怖/蛋白尿恐懼症　albuminurophobia
蛋白尿性多尿症/蛋白尿多尿症　diabetes albuminurinicus
蛋白尿性黑矇/蛋白尿性黑矇　albuminuric amaurosis
蛋白溶菌素/蛋白溶菌素　proteinidin
蛋白色素/蛋白色素,蛋白色質　proteinochrome
蛋白商/蛋白係數　protein quotient
蛋白水解[产]物/蛋白[質]水解產物　protein hydrolysate
蛋白水解酶/蛋白質分解酵素,分解蛋白酵素　proteolytic enzyme
蛋白水解药/蛋白水解藥　proteolytic
蛋白同化甾类/促脂肪合成類固醇　anabolic steroids
蛋白消化/蛋白質消化　proteopepsis
蛋白性骨炎/蛋白性骨炎　osteitis albuminosa
蛋白性肾炎/蛋白性腎炎　albuminous nephritis
蛋白血[症]/蛋白血症　proteinemia
蛋白样变性/蛋白樣變質　albuminoid degeneration
蛋白样痰/蛋白樣痰　sputum albuminoid
蛋白异常血症/蛋白異常血症　dysproteinemia
蛋白银/銀蛋白　argentoproteinum
蛋白原/蛋白母質,蛋白質原　proteinogen
蛋白脂质/蛋白脂質　proteolipid
蛋白脂质类/蛋白脂質類　proteolipids
蛋白[质]/蛋白質,蛋白類,蛋白體　protein
蛋白质变性/蛋白質變性　protein denaturation
蛋白质沉降分析/蛋白質沈降分析　sedimentation analysis of protein
蛋白质代谢/蛋白質代謝　protein metabolism
蛋白质二硫化物还原酶/蛋白質二硫化物還原酶　protein disulfide reductase
蛋白质二硫化物异构酶/蛋白質二硫化物異構酶　protein disulfide isomerase
蛋白[质]分泌细胞/蛋白分泌細胞　protein-secretory cell
蛋白质复性/蛋白質複性　protein renaturation
蛋白质工程/蛋白質工程　protein engineering
蛋白质构象/蛋白質構象　protein conformation
蛋白质[过敏]病/異種蛋白病　protein sickness
蛋白质合成抑制药/蛋白質合成抑制藥　protein synthesis inhibitor
蛋白质激酶/蛋白質激酶　protein kinase
蛋白质剪接/蛋白質剪接　protein splicing

蛋白质结构同源性/蛋白質結構同源性　protein structural homology
蛋白质结合/蛋白質結合　protein binding
蛋白质酪氨酸磷酸酶/蛋白質酪胺酸磷酸酶　protein-tyrosine-phosphatase
蛋白质类/蛋白質類　proteins
蛋白质类药物/蛋白質類藥物　protein drug
蛋白[质]疗法/蛋白質療法　proteotherapy
蛋白质能量缺乏症/蛋白質能量缺乏症　protein-energy deficiency
蛋白质能量营养不良/蛋白質能量營養不良　protein-energy malnutrition
蛋白质皮肤炎/蛋白質皮膚炎　protein dermatitis
蛋白质前体/蛋白質前體　protein precursor
蛋白质缺乏/蛋白質缺乏　protein deficiency
蛋白[质]缺乏症/蛋白過少,蛋白缺乏症　hypoproteinosis
蛋白质生物合成/蛋白質生物合成　protein biosynthesis
蛋白质数据库/蛋白質資料庫　protein database
蛋白质丝氨酸苏氨酸激酶/蛋白質絲胺酸蘇胺酸激酶　protein-serine-threonine kinase
蛋白质相互作用图/蛋白質相互作用圖　protein interaction mapping
蛋白质序列分析/蛋白質序列分析　protein sequence analysis
蛋白[质]学/蛋白質學　proteinology
蛋白质亚单位/蛋白質亞單位　protein subunit
蛋白质亚型/蛋白質亞型　protein isoform
蛋白质异戊二烯化/蛋白質異戊二烯化　protein isoprenylation
蛋白质印迹法/蛋白質印跡法　western blotting
蛋白质杂交/蛋白質雜交　protein hybridization
蛋白质折叠/蛋白質折疊　protein folding
蛋白质阵列分析/蛋白質陣列分析　protein array analysis
蛋白质致敏[作用]/蛋白質起敏作用　protein sensitization
蛋白质转运/蛋白質轉運　protein transport
蛋白质足迹法/蛋白質足跡法　protein footprinting
蛋白质组/蛋白質組　proteome
蛋白质组学/蛋白質組學　proteomics
蛋黄/蛋黃　egg yolk
蛋黄反应/卵黃反應　egg yellow reaction
蛋壳状甲/卵殼狀甲　eggshell nail
蛋类/蛋類　eggs
蛋类过敏/蛋類過敏　egg hypersensitivity
氮/氮　nitrogen
氮丙啶类/氮丙啶類　aziridines
氮迟滞/氮遲滯　nitrogen lag
氮川三醋酸/氮川三醋酸　nitrilotriacetic acid
氮代谢/氮代謝　nitrogenous metabolism
氮放射性同位素/氮放射性同位素　nitrogen radioisotope
氮分配试验/氮分配試驗　nitrogen partition test
氮分子激光疗法/氮分子雷射療法　nitrogen molecular laser therapy
氮化合物/氮化合物　nitrogen compound
氮化物/氮化物　nitride
氮化[作用]/氮化作用,氮化物生成　nitridation
氮芥化合物/氮芥化合物　nitrogen mustard compound
氮蓝四唑/四唑氮藍　nitroblue tetrazolium
氮啉类/氮啉類　azirines
氮霉素/氮黴素　azomycin
氮鸟嘌呤/氮雜鳥嘌呤　azaguanine
氮尿/氮尿症　azoturia
氮平衡/氮平衡　nitrogen equilibrium, nitrogen balance
氮同位素/氮同位素　nitrogen isotope
氮酮/氮酮　azone
氮血热/氮血熱　azothermia
氮血[症]的/高氮血症的　azotemic
氮循环/氮循環　nitrogen cycle
氮氧甲基/氮氧甲基　uret
氮溢/氮漏　azotorrhea
氮杂化合物/氮雜化合物　aza compound
氮杂茂类/氮雜茂類　azoles
氮杂烃铵/氮雜烴銨　azamethonium
氮质过多症/氮質過多病　azotenesis
氮质血症/高氮血症　azotemia
氮族转移酶类/氮族轉移酶類　nitrogenous group transferases
膻中/膻中　danzhong, RN17
膻中疽/膻中疽　carbuncle of chest center, danzhong carbuncle
当归/當歸　Angelica sinensis, Chinese angelica
当归补血汤/當歸補血湯　danggui buxue decoction
当归流浸膏/當歸流浸膏　danggui extract
当归六黄汤/當歸六黃湯　danggui liuhuang decoction
当归龙荟丸/當歸龍薈丸　danggui longhui pills
当归属/當歸屬　*Angelica*
当归四逆汤/當歸四逆湯　danggui sini decoction
当量溶液/當量溶液,定規液　normal solution
当量盐溶液/當量鹽溶液,定規鹽溶液　normal

saline solution
当洛斯病/Danlos 氏病　Danlos disease
当洛斯综合征/Danlos 症候群　Danlos syndrome
当阳/當陽　dangyang, EX-HN2
党参/黨參　tangshen
刀刺般的/撕裂性的　lancinating
刀刺样痛/刀刺狀痛,撕裂性痛　lancinating pain
刀豆/刀豆　jack bean
刀豆氨酸/刀豆胺基酸　canavanine
刀豆氨酸酶/刀豆胺基酸酶　canavanase
刀缘完成/刀緣完成　knife-edge finish
刀针/刀針　knife needle
氘/氘　deuterium
氘核/氘核　diplon
氘化/氘化　deuterate
氘[化]脂/含氘脂肪　deuterofat
氘交换测定/氘交換測定　deuterium exchange measurement
导赤散/導赤散　daochi powder
导电性/導電性　electric conductivity
导钉牵伸术/加釘牽伸法　nail extension
导管/導管　vessel, ductus, duct
导管癌/管癌　ductal carcinoma
导管保持器/導管保持器,导管架　catheterostat
导管插入术/導管插入術　catheterization
导管的/管狀的　ductal
导管后型主动脉缩窄/導管後型主動脈縮窄　coarctation of aorta
导管乳头状瘤/導管乳頭狀瘤　duct papilloma
导管消融术/導管消融術　catheter ablation
导管引流/導管引流　canula drainage
导静脉/導靜脈　emissary vein
导尿管插入术/導尿管插入術　urinary catheterization
导尿术/導尿法　urethral catheterization
导平面/導平面　guiding plane
导热析气计/熱傳導性測量儀　catharometer
导热性/導熱性　thermal conductivity
导数分光光度法/導數分光光度法　derivative spectrophotometry
导水管/導水管　aqueduct
导水管扩张术/導水管擴張術　dilatation of aqueduct
导水管狭窄/導水管狹窄　aqueduct stenosis
导水管周围灰质/導水管周圍灰質　periaqueductal gray matter
导向系统/導向系統　guidance system
导药法/導藥法　guiding medicinal method
导液法/導液法,穿刺引流法　hydrocenosis

导引套针/導引套針　piloting trocar
导欲/導欲　desire satisfaction, encouraging desires
导之以其所便/導之以其所便　enlightening and consoling
岛部/島部　insular part
岛长回/島長迴　long gyrus of insula
岛动脉/島動脈　insular artery
岛短回/島短迴　short gyri of insula
岛盖部/蓋部　frontal operculum, opercular part
岛盖顶部/額頂蓋　frontoparietal operculum
岛盖额部/額蓋　frontal operculum
岛环状沟/島環狀溝　circular sulcus of insula
岛回/島迴　insular gyri
岛静脉/島靜脈　insular vein
岛叶/島葉　insular lobe
岛阈/島閾　limen insulae, limen of insula
岛中央沟/島中央溝　sulcus centralis insulae
岛状筋膜瓣/島狀筋膜瓣　island fascial flap
岛状皮瓣/島狀皮瓣　island skin flap
岛状物/島狀物　island
岛状移植物/島狀移植物　island graft
捣碎的/搗碎的　comminuted
捣碎器/攪碎器,混合器　blender
到处求医/到處求醫　doctor shopping
到处求医癖/Munchausen 氏症候群　Munchausen syndrome
到院死亡/到院死亡　dead on arrival
倒凹区/倒凹區　undercut area
倒错/倒錯,失常　perversion
倒翻转移/倒翻轉移　tumbling transfer
倒钩卡环/倒鉤卡環　reverse hook clasp
倒钩形切口/倒鉤形切口　reverse hook incision
倒睫/倒睫　trichiasis
倒睫拔除[法]/亂睫矯正法　illaqueation
倒睫性眼睑炎/棘樣眼瞼炎　echinophthalmia
倒捻子/都念子,山竹　mangosteen
倒捻子素/都念子素,山竹素　mangostin
倒位环/倒位環　inversion loop
倒圆锥形帽/倒圓錐形帽　phrygian cap
倒置位/倒置位　prone jackknife position
倒置显微镜/倒置式顯微鏡　inverted microscope
倒置阻生/倒置阻生　inverted impaction
倒锥钻/倒錐鑽　inverted cone bur
盗汗/盜汗　night sweat, night sweating
盗汗·气阴两虚证/盜汗·氣陰兩虛證　night sweating with pattern of deficiency of both qi and yin
盗汗·心血虚证/盜汗·心血虛證　night sweating with pattern of heart blood deficiency

盗汗·阴虚火旺证/盜汗·陰虛火旺證　night sweating with pattern of exuberant fire due to yin deficiency
盗血现象/盜血現象　steal phenomenon
道/道　meatus
道德/道德　morals
道德困境/倫理困境　ethical dilemma
道地药材/道地藥材　genuine regional drug
道尔顿/道爾頓　dalton
道尔顿-亨利定律/道-亨二氏定律　Dalton-Henry law
道格拉斯韧带/Douglas 氏韌帶　Douglas ligament
道格拉斯移植物/Douglas 氏移植物　Douglas graft
道路交通事故/道路交通事故　road traffic accident
道上棘/道上棘　suprameatal spine
道上三角/道上三角　suprameatal triangle
道上小凹/道上小凹　suprameatal foveola
道氏综合征/Down 氏症　Down syndrome
道义职责/道義職責　moral obligation
稻[白]米病/白米病　rice disease
稻农皮炎/稻農皮炎　rice farmer dermatitis
稻芽/稻芽　germinated rice-grain
得气/得氣　arrival of qi, reaching or feeling the qi
得神/得神　fullness of vitality, presence of vitality
锝化合物/錒化合物　technetium compounds
德-杜麻醉/Drain-Dumenil 二氏吸入麻醉　Drain-Dumenil anesthesia
德尔菲技术/德爾菲技術　Delphi technique
德戈棘皮瘤/Degos 氏棘皮瘤　Degos acanthoma
德戈斯病/Degos 氏病　Degos disease
德国麻疹/德國麻疹　German measles
德卡姆病/Dercum 氏病　Dercum disease
德-克麻痹/德-克二氏麻痺　Dejerine-Klumpke paralysis
德拉菲尔德[固定]液/Delafield 氏液　Delafield fluid
德拉根多夫试剂/德拉根多夫試劑,碘化鉍鉀試劑　Dragendorff reagent
德莱-布里翁系统/德莱-布里翁系統　Delay-Brion system
德朗热综合征/de Lange 氏症候群　de Lange syndrome
德雷斯巴赫综合征/Dresbach 氏症候群　Dresbach syndrome
德-李现象/德-李二氏現象　Dejerine-Lichtheim phenomenon
德里疖/德里癤　Delhi boil
德里辛/德里辛　dericin
德林克人工呼吸器/德林克氏呼吸機　Drinker respirator
德-鲁综合征/Déjerine-Roussy 二氏症候群　syndrome of Déjerine-Roussy
德·谬塞征/de Musset 氏徵象　de Musset sign
德普伊夹/Depuy 氏夾板　Depuy splint
德乔治序列征/德喬治序列徵　DiGeorge sequence
德斯诺斯病/Desnos 氏病　Desnos disease
德索绷带/Desault 氏繃帶　Desault bandage
德瓦尔鼓泡式氧合器/德瓦爾鼓泡式氧合器　De Wall bubble oxygenator
灯火灸/燈火灸　burning rush moxibustion, rush-fire cauterization
灯笼病/燈籠病　lantern disease
灯刷形染色体/燈刷狀染色體　lampbrush chromosome
灯丝/燈絲　filament
灯心草/燈心草　common rush
登豆疮/登豆瘡,疱疹樣膿皰病　impetigo herpetiformis
登豆疮·气阴两虚证/登豆瘡·氣陰兩虛證　impetigo herpetiformis with qi-yin deficiency pattern
登豆疮·热入营血证/登豆瘡·熱入營血證　impetigo herpetiformis with pattern of heat entering nutrient-blood
登弗姆林营养指标/登弗林度標　Dunfermline scale
登革出血热/出血性登革熱　dengue hemorrhagic fever
登革热/登革熱　dengue fever
登革热病毒/登革熱病毒　dengue fever virus
登革热休克综合征/登革熱休克症候群　dengue fever shock syndrome
登记/登記,註冊　register
登克尔手术/登克爾手術　Denker operation
等孢子球虫病/等孢子球蟲病　isosporiasis
等比例白细胞减少/等比白血球減少　isohypocytosis
等比例白细胞增多/等比白血球增多　isohypercytosis
等比例白细胞正常/等比例白血球正常　dinormocytosis
等臂染色体/同染色體　isochromosome
等长收缩/等長收縮　isometric contraction
等长舒张/等長弛緩　isometric relaxation
等长运动/等長運動　isometric exercise
等电沉淀/等電沈澱　isoelectric precipitation
等电点/等電點　isoelectric point
等电聚焦/等電聚焦　isoelectric focusing
等幅中频电疗法/等幅中頻電療法　undamped medium frequency electrotherapy
等高线色谱图/等高層析圖　contour chromatogram

等离点/等離點 isoionic point
等离子体刀/等離子體刀 plasma scalpel
等离子体解吸质谱法/等離子體脫附質譜法 plasma desorption mass spectrometry, PDMS
等流量容积/等流量容積 volume of isoflow
等密度离心法/等密度離心法 isopycnic centrifugation
等面关节/等面關節 congruent articulation
等氢离子溶液/等氫離子溶液 isohydric solution
等热量食物/等熱[量]食物 isodynamic food
等容舒张/等容弛緩 isovolumetric relaxation
等容舒张期/等容舒張期 isovolumic relaxation phase
等渗溶液/等滲溶液 isotonic solution
等渗调节/等滲調節 isoosmotic adjustment
等渗性/等透,等渗透壓 isosmoticity
等时节律/同步節律 isochronal rhythm
等式/等式 equation
等视力线/等視力線 isopter
等视线/等視線 visual isopter
等速肌力测定/等速肌力測定 isokinetic muscle strength test
等速运动/等速運動 isokinetic exercise
等位基因/等位基因 allele
等位基因的/等位基因的 allelic
等位基因失衡/等位基因失衡 allelic imbalance
等位性/對偶性 allelism
等温法/等溫法 isothermal method
等温感觉/等溫覺 isothermognosis
等吸光点法/等吸光點法 isosbestic point method
等像透镜/等影像透鏡 iseikonic lens
等效径/等效徑 equivalent diameter
等效[应]/等效應 isoeffect
等压点/等壓點 equal pressure point
等张溶液/等張溶液 isotonic solution
等张收缩/等張收縮 isotonic contraction
等张性[肌纤维]长度增加/肌肉過長 mecystasis
邓纳姆溶液/Dunham氏溶液 Dunham solution
镫骨/鐙骨 stapes, stirrup bone
镫骨襞/鐙骨襞 stapedial fold
镫骨成形术/鐙骨整形術 stapedioplasty
镫骨底/鐙骨底 base of stapes
镫骨底固定肌/鐙骨底固定肌 fixator muscle of base of stapes
镫骨底环带/鐙骨基底環狀韌帶 annular ligament of base of stapes
镫骨后脚/鐙骨後腳 posterior crus of stapes
镫骨环状韧带/鐙骨環狀韌帶 annular ligament of stapes, annular ligament of digits of stapes
镫骨肌/鐙骨肌 stapedius
镫骨肌腱切断术/鐙骨肌腱切斷術 stapediotenotomy
镫骨肌神经/鐙骨神經 stapedial nerve
镫骨肌支/鐙骨肌支 stapedial branch
镫骨膜/鐙骨膜 membrane of stapes
镫骨前脚/鐙骨前腳 anterior crus of stapes
镫骨切除术/鐙骨切除術 stapedectomy
镫骨神经/鐙骨神經 stapedial nerve
镫骨松动术/鐙骨鬆動術 stapediolysis
镫骨头/鐙骨頭 head of stapes
镫骨外科手术/鐙骨外科手術 stapes surgery
镫骨造孔术/鐙骨切斷術 stapedotomy
镫骨足板部分切除术/鐙骨足板部分切除術 partial stapedecotomy
镫形吻合/鐙連接 stirrup anastomosis
低白蛋白血症/低白蛋白血症,血白蛋白過少 hypoalbuminemia
低倍镜/低倍鏡 low power lens
低比重溶液/低比重溶液 hypobaric solution
低丙球蛋白血症/血丙型球蛋白過少 hypogammaglobulinemia
低补体血性肾小球肾炎/低補體血性腎小球腎炎 hypocomplementemic glomerulonephritis
低草酸盐饮食/低草酸鹽飲食 low-oxalate diet
低常温度/低常溫度 subnormal temperature
低常状态/低常狀態 subnormality
低出生率/低出生率 oligonatality
低促性腺素性闭经/低促性腺素性閉經 hypogonadotropic amenorrhea
低促性腺素性功能减退症/促性腺激素分泌不足,性腺機能不足 hypogonadotropic hypogonadism
低蛋白血症/低蛋白血症 hypoproteinemia
低蛋白饮食/低蛋白[質]飲食 low-protein diet
低氮尿性肾病/低氮尿性腎病 hypazoturic nephropathy
低碘化物/低碘化物,次碘化物 subiodide
低电解质血/血電解質過少 hypoelectrolytemia
低电压[X射线]摄影术/定位攝影術 senography
低度/低度的,輕度的 low-grade
低度近视/低度近視 low myopia
低度淋巴瘤/低度淋巴瘤 low-grade lymphoma
低度远视/低度遠視 low hypermetropia
低分化成肌纤维细胞肉瘤/低度分化之肌纖維母細胞肉瘤 low-grade myofibroblastic sarcoma
低分子量肝素/低分子量肝素 low-molecular-weight heparin

低分子量激肽原/低分子量激肽原　low-molecular-weight kininogen
低钙击面征/低鈣擊面徵　chvostek sign
低钙束臂征/低鈣束臂徵　trousseau sign
低钙血症/低鈣血症,血鈣過少　hypocalcemia
低共熔点/低共熔點　eutectic point
低共熔混合物/低共熔混合物　eutectic mixture
低级物/低級物　lower member
低剂量耐受[性]/低劑量耐受[性]　lowdose tolerance
低甲状腺素血症/低甲狀腺素血症　hypothyroxinemia
低钾性周期性麻痹/低鉀性週期性麻痺　hypokalemic periodic paralysis
低钾[血]性碱中毒/低血鉀性鹼毒症　hypokalemic alkalosis
低钾血症/低鉀血症,血鉀過少　hypokalemia
低钾血症肾病/血鉀過少性腎病　hypokalemic nephrosis
低碱溶液/低鹼溶液　hypobasic solution
低磷试验/低磷試驗　phosphorus deprivation test
低磷酸/次磷酸　hypophosphoric acid
低磷酸血症骨病/低磷酸血症骨病　hypophosphatemic bone disease
低磷[酸盐]血性骨软化症/低磷[酸鹽]血性骨軟化症　hypophosphatemic osteomalacia
低磷酸酯酶症/磷酸酶過少　hypophosphatasia
低磷血症/血磷酸鹽過少,低磷酸鹽血症　hypophosphatemia
低流量血液透析/低流量血液透析　low flow hemodialysis
低硫酸盐/最低硫酸鹽,亞硫酸鹽　protosulfate
低氯性氮血症/低氯性氮血症　hypochloropenic azotemia
低氯血症/低氯血症　hypochloraemia
低镁血症/低鎂血症,血鎂過少　hypomagnesemia
低免疫性/低免疫性,免疫性降低　hypoimmunity
低敏感性/敏感減輕　hyposensitivity
低钠血症/低鈉血症,血鈉過少　hyponatremia
低钠饮食/低鈉飲食　low-sodium diet
低钠综合征/低鈉症候群　low sodium syndrome
低能/低能　feeblemindedness
低凝血酶血[症]/低凝血酶血症　hypothrombinemia
低凝血酶原血症/低凝血酶原血症　hypoprothrombinemias
低嘌呤饮食/低嘌呤飲食　low purine diet
低频电疗法/低頻電療法　low frequency electrotherapy
低频电疗美容术/低頻電療美容術　low frequency electrotherapy cosmesis
低频[率]/低頻率　low frequency
低频脉冲电疗法/低頻脈衝電療法　low frequency impulse current therapy
低气压病/低氣壓病　hypobarism
低强度激光/低強度雷射　low level laser
低热量饮食/低熱量飲食　low calorie diet
低熔[金属]铸型/合金假齒熔製法　cheoplasty
低熔铸牙/低熔鑄齒　cheoplastic teeth
低乳糖乳/糖尿病人飲用乳　diabetic milk
低色素性贫血/低色性貧血　hypochromic anemia
低色小红细胞性贫血/小紅血球低色性貧血,低色性小球性貧血　hypochromic microcytic anemia
低肾素型高血压/低腎素型高血壓　low renin hypertension
低肾素症/低腎素症　hyporeninism
低渗溶液/低張溶液　hypotonic solution
低生育力/低生育力　subfertility
低视力/低視力　low vision
低输出量心衰竭/低輸出量心衰竭　low-output heart failure
低输出综合征/低心輸出量症候群　low-output syndrome
低碳酸血症/血碳酸過少　hypocapnia
低体温的/低溫的　hypothermic
低铁血色素/低鐵血色素　ferrohemochrome
低酮血症/低酮血症　hypoketonemia
低位产钳术/低位產鉗產　low forcep delivery
低位钳/低位鉗　low forcep
低位微笑/低位微笑　low smile
低温/低温　hypothermia
低温电子显微镜检查/低温電子顯微鏡檢查　cryoelectron microscopy
低温防护剂/低温防護劑　cryoprotective agent
低温冷藏组织贮存/低温冷藏組織貯存　tissue storage by refrigeration
低温麻醉/低温性麻醉法　hypothermic anesthesia
低温生物学/低温生物學　cryobiology
低温下溶血性抗体疾病/低温下溶血性抗體疾病　cold hemolytic antibody disease
低温下氧耗定律/低温下氧耗定律　Van't Hoff law
低温心搏停止[法]/低温心搏停止　cryocardioplegia
低温心脏停搏液/低温心臟停搏液　cryocardioplegic solution
低温阻滞/冷卻阻斷　cryogenic block
低硝酸盐/最低硝酸鹽,亞硝酸鹽　protonitrate
低效能利尿药/低效能利尿劑　low ceiling diuretic

低心排血量/低心排血量　low cardiac output
低心排血量综合征/低心排血量症候群　low cardiac output syndrome
低血钙性白内障/低血鈣性白內障　hypocalcemic cataract
低血容量性休克/血容積過少性休克　hypovolemic shock
低血容量症/循環血量減少　hypovolaemia
低血糖病/血糖過少病　hypoglycemosis
低血糖昏迷/低血糖昏迷　hypoglycemic coma
低血糖性白内障/低血糖性白內障　hypoglycemic cataract
低血糖性休克/低血糖休克　hypoglycemic shock
低血糖症/低血糖症,血糖過少,血糖減少　hypoglycemia
低血糖[症]的/低血糖的　hypoglycemic
低血压/低血壓　hypotension
低血压的/低血壓的　hypotensive
低血压性麻醉/低血壓性麻醉法　hypotensive anesthesia
低血氧性缺氧/低血氧性缺氧　hypoxic hypoxemia
低压电损伤/低壓電損傷　low voltage electrical injury
低压梯度泵/低壓梯度泵　low pressure gradient pump
低亚硫酸/低亞硫酸　hydrosulfurous acid
低盐饮食/低鹽飲食　low-salt diet
低盐综合征/低鹽症候群　low-salt syndrome
低眼压/低眼壓　ocular hypotension
低氧/低氧,缺氧　hypoxia
低氧化物/低氧化物,次氧化物　suboxide
低氧性酸中毒/低氧性酸中毒　hypoxic acidosis
低氧血/低氧血　hypoxemia
低氧血症/血氧缺乏　anoxemia
低氧症/低氧症　hypoxidosis
低音聋/低音聾　bass deafness
低音胸语音/失音性胸語音　aphonic pectoriloquy
低应答个体/低應答個體　low responder
低张力性子宫功能不良/低張性子宮收縮異常　hypotonic uterine dysfunction
低β脂蛋白血症/血β-脂蛋白過少,低β-脂蛋白血症　hypobetalipoproteinemia
低脂[肪]膳食/低脂飲食　low fat diet
低脂血症/低脂血症　hypolipidemia
低置胎盘/低置胎盤　low-lying placenta
低重/低重　hypogravity
滴/滴　drop
滴鼻法/滴鼻法　method of nosedrop
滴鼻剂/滴鼻劑　nasal drop
滴鼻疗法/滴鼻療法　nose-dripping therapy
滴虫病/滴蟲病,梨形蟲病　trichomoniasis
滴虫感染/滴蟲感染　trichomonas infection
滴虫性包皮阴茎炎/滴蟲性包皮陰莖頭炎　trichomonal balanoposthitis
滴虫性尿道膀胱炎/滴蟲性尿道膀胱炎　trichomonal urethrocystitis
滴虫性前列腺炎/滴蟲性前列腺炎　trichomonal prostatitis
滴虫[性]阴道炎/滴蟲[性]陰道炎　trichomonas vaginitis
滴定法/滴定法　titration
滴定分析法/滴定分析法　titrimetry
滴定剂/滴定劑　titrant
滴定液/滴定液　volumetric solution, VS
滴耳法/滴耳法　method of eardrop
滴耳剂/滴耳劑,耳滴劑,耳藥水　ear drop
滴耳疗法/滴耳療法　ear-dripping therapy
滴管/滴器　dropper
滴酒法/滴酒法　alcohol fire cupping, alcohol fire method
滴落征象/滴落徵象　drip sign
滴滤池/濾濾器　percolating filter
滴丸剂/滴丸劑　dripping pill
滴眼剂/滴眼劑　eye drop
滴眼药水法/滴眼藥水法　application of eyedrop
滴药法/滴藥法　dripping method
滴注/滴注　drip
滴注法/滴入,滴灌,滴注　instillation
滴注记录单/滴注記錄單　drip sheet
滴注器/滴注器　instillator
滴状扁平苔藓/滴狀扁平苔癬　lichen planus guttata
滴状病灶/滴狀病灶　guttate lesion
滴状副银屑病/滴狀副銀屑病　guttate parapsoriasis
滴状银屑病/滴狀牛皮癬　psoriasis guttata
滴状硬斑病/滴狀硬斑病　guttate morphea
滴嘴状细胞/承霤口狀細胞　gargoyle cell
狄克试验/狄克氏試驗　Dick test
狄克血清/狄克氏血清　Dick serum
狄氏剂/地特靈　dieldrin
迪博斯克比色计/杜博克氏比色計　Duboscq colorimeter
迪厄拉富瓦病/Dieulafoy氏病　Dieulafoy disease
迪-厄综合征/Duchenne-Erb二氏症候群　Duchenne-Erb syndrome
迪格奥尔格综合征/DiGeorge症候群　DiGeorge syndrome

迪皮特朗骨折/Dupuytren 氏骨折　Dupuytren fracture
迪皮特朗夹/Dupuytren 氏夾板　Dupuytren splint
迪皮特朗挛缩/Dupuytren 氏攣縮　Dupuytren contracture
迪皮特朗阴囊水肿/Dupuytren 氏陰囊水腫　Dupuytren hydrocele
迪皮特朗足病/Dupuytren 氏足病　Dupuytren disease of the foot
迪普莱综合征/Duplay 氏症候群　Duplay syndrome
迪特尔危象/迪特爾危象　Dietl crisis
迪特里希狭窄/Dittrich 氏狹窄　Dittrich stenosis
迪瓦恩结肠造口术/迪瓦恩結腸造口術　Devine colostomy
迪韦尔内骨折/Duverney 氏骨折　Duverney fracture
迪歇恩综合征/Duchenne 氏症候群　Duchenne syndrome
迪-约综合征/Dubin-Johnson 二氏症候群　Dubin-Johnson syndrome
敌敌畏/二氯福　dichlorvos
涤纶/達克龍　dacron
涤纶编织人造血管/達克龍編織人造血管　dacron woven graft
涤纶缝线/達克龍縫線　dacron suture
涤纶毛滤器/達克龍毛濾器　dacron wool filter
涤痰汤/滌痰湯　phlegm cleansing decoction
涤痰息风/滌痰息風　clearing phlegm for calming endogenous wind, eliminating phlegm and checking wind
笛音/笛音　syrigmophonia
抵抗感觉/抵抗感覺　sense of resistance
抵抗[力]/抵抗　resistance
抵抗运动/自動對抗阻力之運動　active resistive exercise
抵抗株/耐藥菌株　resistant strain
底凹/牙冠之底凹　basilar pit
底板/底板　floor plate
底部/底部　basal part
底部切除术/底部切除術　fundectomy
底段上静脉/底段上靜脈　superior basal vein
底段下静脉/底段下靜脈　inferior basal vein
底段总静脉/底段總靜脈　common basal vein
底前蝶骨/底前蝶骨　basipresphenoid bone
底丘脑/丘腦底部　subthalamus
底丘脑核/底丘腦核　subthalamic nucleus
底丘脑束/底丘腦束　subthalamic fasciculus
底突/底突　basilar process
底蜕膜/底蜕膜　decidua basalis

底蜕膜性前置胎盘/底蜕膜性前置胎盤　placenta basal praevia
底物/受質　substrate
底物特异性/受質特異性　substrate specificity
底物循环/受質循環　substrate cycling
底细胞/底部細胞　floor cell
骶[部]痛/薦痛　sacrodynia
骶部弯曲/骶部彎曲,薦部彎曲　sacral curve
骶丛/薦叢　sacral plexus
骶粗隆/薦骨粗隆　sacral tuberosity
骶段/[骨盆之]薦段　sacral segment
骶副交感核/薦副交感核　sacral parasympathetic nucleus
骶沟/薦溝　sacral groove
骶骨/骶骨,薦骨　sacrum, sacral bone
骶骨背面/薦骨背面　posterior surface of sacral bone
骶骨底/骶骨底,薦骨底　base of sacrum
骶骨耳状面/薦骨耳狀面　auricular surface of sacrum
骶骨骨折/薦骨骨折,薦椎骨折　sacral fracture, sacrum fracture
骶骨岬/薦骨岬　promontory of sacrum
骶骨尖/薦尖,骶尖　apex of sacrum
骶骨角/薦角　sacral horn
骶骨旁的/薦骨旁的　parasacral
骶骨前移/薦骨前移　sacrolisthesis
骶骨切除术/薦骨切除術　sacrectomy
骶骨上关节突/薦骨上關節突　superior articular process of sacrum
骶骨痛/薦骨痛　hieralgia
骶骨脱位/薦骨脫位,薦異位　hierolisthesis
骶骨[下部]切开术/薦骨切開術　sacrotomy
骶管/薦管,骶管　sacral canal
骶管裂孔/骶管裂孔,薦管裂孔　sacral hiatus
骶[管]麻醉/薦管麻醉法　sacral anesthesia
骶管阻滞/薦管阻滯　caudal block
骶管阻滞麻醉/薦椎阻斷麻醉法　sacral block
骶横位/薦橫位　sacrotransverse
骶后孔/骶後孔,薦後孔　posterior sacral foramen
骶后位/薦後位　sacroposterior
骶后纵切肛门成形术/薦後縱切肛門成形術　posterior sacral sagittal anoplasty
骶会阴肛门成形术/薦會陰肛門成形術　sacroperineal anoplasty
骶棘肌/薦棘肌　sacrospinous muscle
骶棘韧带/薦棘韌帶　sacrospinous ligament
骶脊髓/薦脊髓　sacral spinal cord
骶岬淋巴结/薦岬淋巴結　lymph node of

promontory
骶尖/薦骨尖,骶骨尖　tip of sacral bone
骶角/骶角,薦角　sacral horn
骶结节韧带/薦結節韌帶　sacrotuberous ligament
骶结节韧带镰突/骶結節韌帶鐮狀突　ligamentous falx
骶静脉丛/薦靜脈叢　sacral venous plexus
骶髋关节炎/薦尾關節炎　sacrocoxitis
骶联体/薦聯體　sacropagus
骶淋巴结/薦淋巴結　sacral lymph node
骶瘘/薦椎瘻　sacral fistula
骶内脏神经/內臟薦神經　sacral splanchnic nerve
骶旁麻醉/薦旁麻醉　parasacral anesthesia
骶旁阻滞/薦旁阻斷麻醉　parasacral block
骶盆面/薦盆面　sacropelvic surface
骶髂骨间韧带/薦髂骨間韌帶　interosseous sacroiliac ligament
骶髂关节/薦髂關節　sacroiliac joint, iliosacral articulation, sacroiliac articulation
骶髂关节错缝/薦髂關節脫位　dislocation of sacroiliac joint
骶髂关节分离试验/薦髂關節分離試驗　Patrick test
骶髂关节损伤/薦髂關節損傷　sacroiliac joint injury
骶髂后长韧带/薦髂後長韌帶　long posterior sacroiliac ligament
骶髂后短韧带/薦髂後短韌帶　short posterior sacroiliac ligament
骶髂后韧带/薦髂後韌帶　posterior sacroiliac ligament
骶髂前韧带/薦髂前韌帶　anterior sacroiliac ligament
骶前孔/薦前孔　anterior sacral foramen
骶前麻醉/薦前麻醉　presacral anesthesia
骶前神经/薦前神經　presacral nerve
骶前神经切除术/薦前神經切除術　presacral neurectomy
骶前神经切断术/薦前神經切斷術　presacral neurotomy
骶前位/薦前位　sacroanterior
骶区/薦部　sacral region
骶曲/薦曲　sacral curvature, sacral flexure
骶神经/薦神經　sacral nerve
骶神经丛/薦神經叢,薦靜脈叢　plexus sacralis
骶神经后支/薦神經後支　posterior branch of sacral nerve
骶神经节/薦神經節　sacral ganglion
骶神经前支/薦神經前支　anterior branch of sacral nerve
骶外侧动脉/薦外側動脈　lateral sacral artery

骶外侧动脉脊支/薦外側動脈脊支　spinal branch of lateral sacral artery
骶外侧嵴/薦外側嵴　lateral sacral crest
骶外侧静脉/薦外側靜脈　lateral sacral vein
骶外侧支/薦外側支　lateral sacral branch
骶尾背侧肌/薦尾背側肌　dorsal sacrococcygeal muscle
骶尾部/薦尾部　sacrococcygeal region
骶尾部畸胎瘤/薦尾部畸胎瘤,骶骨與髂骨畸胎瘤,薦椎尾骨畸胎瘤　sacrococcygeal teratoma
骶尾部畸胎瘤·肾气虚证/薦尾部畸胎瘤·腎氣虛證　sacrococcygeal teratoma with kidney qi deficiency pattern
骶尾部畸胎瘤·湿热下注证/薦尾部畸胎瘤·濕熱下注證　sacrococcygeal teratoma with pattern of dampness-heat diffusing downward
骶尾部囊肿窦/薦尾部囊腫竇　cystic sinus of sacrococcygeal region
骶尾的/薦椎與尾骨的　sacrococcygeal
骶尾窦/尾骨竇　coccygeal sinus
骶尾腹侧肌/薦尾腹側肌　musculus sacrococcygeus ventralis
骶尾骨/薦尾骨　sacrococcyx
骶尾骨间关节盘/薦椎尾骨間關節盤　sacrococcygeal disc
骶尾骨痛/薦尾骨痛　sacrocoxalgia
骶尾关节/薦尾關節　sacrococcygeal joint, sacrococcygeal articulation
骶尾后肌/薦尾後肌　posterior sacrococcygeal muscle
骶尾后浅韧带/薦尾後淺韌帶　superficial posterior sacrococcygeal ligament
骶尾后深韧带/薦尾後深韌帶　deep posterior sacrococcygeal ligament
[骶尾]角间韧带/[薦尾]角間韌帶　intercornual ligament
骶尾联合/薦尾聯合　sacrococcygeal joint
骶尾瘘/薦椎尾骨瘻　sacrococcygeal fistula
骶尾囊肿/薦尾囊腫　sacrococcygeal cyst
骶尾前肌/薦尾前肌　anterior sacrococcygeal muscle
骶尾前韧带/薦尾前韌帶　anterior sacrococcygeal ligament
骶尾区/薦尾區　sacro-coccyx region
骶尾外侧韧带/薦尾外側韌帶　lateral sacrococcygeal ligament
骶翼/骶翼,薦翼　ala of sacrum
骶正中动脉/薦正中動脈　median sacral artery
骶正中嵴/骶正中嵴,薦正中嵴　median sacral crest
骶正中静脉/薦正中靜脈　median sacral vein

骶中动脉/薦中動脈　coccygeal artery
骶中间嵴/骶中間嵴,薦中間嵴　intermediate sacral crest
骶中静脉/骶中静脈,薦中静脈　middle sacral vein
骶椎/骶椎,薦椎　sacral vertebra
骶椎的/薦椎的　sacral
骶椎结节韧带/薦椎結節韌帶　sacrotuberous ligament
骶椎裂/薦椎裂　bifid sacrum
骶椎尾骨韧带/薦椎尾骨韌帶　sacrococcygeal ligament
骶椎坐骨韧带/薦椎坐骨韌帶　sacrosciatic ligament
地阿诺/丹醇　deanol
地奥司明/布枯葉素　diosmin
地奥心血康胶囊/地奥心血康膠囊　di'ao xinxuekang capsules
地百合属/地百合屬　*Helonias*
地板/地板　floor
地板层/地板層　floor layer
地贝卡星/地貝卡星　dibekacin
地仓/地倉　dicang, ST4
地产药材/地産藥材　native drug
地蒽酚/地蒽酚　anthralin
地尔硫䓬/地爾硫䓬　diltiazem
地伐西匹/地伐西匹　devazepide
地方病/地方病　endemic disease
地方病学/地方病學,風土病學　endemiology
地方的/地方性的,流行的　endemic
地方兽疫性肝炎/地方性動物肝炎　enzootic hepatitis
地方性斑疹伤寒/地方性斑疹傷寒,鼠性斑疹寒熱　endemic typhus
地方性斑疹伤寒热/地方性斑疹傷寒熱　endemic typhus fever
地方性呆小病/地域性呆小症　endemic cretinism
地方性动物病/地方性動物病　enzootic disease
地方性多形性荨麻疹/多形性地方性荨麻疹　urticaria multiformis endemica
地方性跟骨肥大/地方性跟骨肥大　endemic hypertrophy
地方性甲状腺肿/地方性甲狀腺腫　endemic goiter
地方性绞痛/地方性絞痛　endemic colic
地方性精索炎/地方性精索炎　endemic funiculitis
地方性溃疡/地方性潰瘍　endemic ulcer
地方性流行性感冒/地方性流行性感冒　influenza nostras
地方性麻痹性眩晕/局部麻痺性眩晕　endemic paralytic vertigo

地方性梅毒/地方性梅毒　endemic syphilis
地方性牛血尿/地方性牛血尿　enzootic bovine hematuria
地方性牛造白细胞组织增生/地方性牛造白細胞組織增生　enzootic bovine leukosis
地方性兽病/動物地方病　enzootic
地方性血尿/地方性血尿　endemic hematuria
地方性荨麻疹/地方性蕁麻疹　urticaria endemica, endemic urticaria
地方性蚤传斑疹伤寒/地方性蚤傳斑疹傷寒　endemic flea-borne typhus
地方性猪脑脊髓炎/地方性豬腦脊髓炎　enzootic porcine encephalomyelitis
地芬尼多/地芬尼多　difenidol
地芬尼泰/地芬尼泰　diamfenetide
地芬诺酯/地芬諾酯　diphenoxylate
地肤子/地膚子　belvedere fruit
地氟醚/地氟醚　desflurane
地高辛/毛地黃素　digoxin
地高辛配基/長葉毛地黃配質　digoxigenin
地骨皮/地骨皮　cortex lycii radicis, Chinese wolfberry root-bark
地黄饮子/地黃飲子　dihuang drink
地机/地機　diji, SP8
地锦草/地錦草　creeping euphorbia
地考喹酯/地考喹酯　decoquinate
地喹氯铵/地喹氯銨　dequalinium
地拉韦定/地拉韋定　delavirdine
地拉草/地拉草　dilazep
地蜡/地蠟精　ceresin
地理病理学/地理病理學　geographic pathology
地理医学/地理醫學　geographic medicine
地龙/地龍　earthworm
地美环素/地美環素　demeclocycline
地美炔酮/地美炔酮　dimethisterone
地美硝唑/二甲硝唑　dimetridazole
地面/地面　ground
地奈德/地奈德　desonide
地诺前列素/地諾前列素　dinoprost
地诺前列酮/地諾前列酮　dinoprostone
地气/地氣　earth qi
地区卫生计划/地區衛生計劃　regional health planning
地区卫生教育中心/地區衛生教育中心　area health education center
地区医疗规划/地區醫療規劃　regional medical program
地屈孕酮/地屈孕酮　dydrogesterone

地塞米松/地塞米松　dexamethasone
地塞米松抑制试验/地塞米松抑制試驗　dexamethasone suppression test
地上植物组成部分/地上植物組成部分　aerial plant component
地舍平/地舍平　deserpidine
地鼠涎腺炎病毒/地鼠涎腺炎病毒　hamster salivary-gland disease virus
地丝菌病/地絲菌病,土毛菌病　geotrichosis
地丝菌属/土毛菌屬　Geotrichum
地图舌/地圖舌　graphic tongue
地图样舌/地圖狀舌　geographic tongue
地图状头颅/地圖狀頭顱　maplike skull
地五会/地五會　diwuhui, GB42
地西泮/苯甲二氮䓬　diazepam
地昔帕明/去鬱敏,脱甲丙咪嗪　desipramine
地衣/地衣　lichens
地衣红/地衣紅　orcein
地衣酸/地衣酸,松蘿素　usnein
地衣形菌素/地衣形菌素　licheniformin
地衣紫/地衣紅質　cudbear
地榆/地榆　garden burnet root
地榆抽提液/地榆抽提液　burnet extract
地榆槐角丸/地榆槐角丸　diyu huaijiao pills
地中海病/地中海病,庫利氏貧血　mediterranean disease
地中海贫血/地中海貧血　thalassemia
地中海热/地中海熱　mediterranean fever
地中海膳食/地中海膳食　mediterranean diet
地中海[性]贫血/地中海型貧血　mediterranean anemia
地中海疹热/地中海疹熱　mediterranean exanthematous fever
地佐环平马来酸盐/地卓西平馬來酸鹽　dizocilpine maleate
递减传导/遞減傳導　decremental conduction
递减反应/遞減反應　decrement response
递减型杂音/漸弱雜音　decrescendo murmur
递增起搏/遞增起搏　incremental pacing
第八脑神经/第八腦神經　the eighth cranial nerve
第八凝血因子/第八凝血因子　blood coagulation factor Ⅷ
第二产程/第二產程　the second labor stage
第二穿动脉/第二穿動脈　the second perforating artery
第二次孕妇/二[次]孕婦　secundigravida
第二代抗抑郁药/第二代抗抑鬱藥　the second generation antidepressive agents
第二房间隔/第二[房間]隔　septum secundum
第二房间孔/第二[房間]孔　foramen secundum
第二鼓膜/第二鼓膜　secondary tympanic membrane
第二级重寄生物/第二級再寄生物　the second degree hyperparasite
第二级死骨/第二度死骨　secondary sequestrum
第二极体/第二極體　the second polar body
第二肋/第二肋　the second rib
第二肋间后动脉/第二肋間後動脈　the second posterior intercostal artery
第二螺旋板/次螺旋板　secondary spiral lamina
第二磨牙/第二臼齒　the second molar
第二躯体感觉区/第二軀體感覺區　secondary somatosensory area
第二躯体运动区/第二軀體運動區　secondary somatomotor area
第二视区/第二視區　the second visual area
第二心音/第二心音　the second sound
第二心音固定分裂/第二心音固定分裂　fixed splitting of the second heart sound
第二心音逆分裂/第二心音逆分裂　paradoxical splitting of the second heart sound
第二信使系统/第二信使系統　the second messenger system
第二跖骨/第二蹠骨　the second metatarsal bone
第二趾/第二趾　the second digit of foot
第二趾背内侧神经/第二趾背內側神經　dorsal medial nerve of the second toe
第九次孕妇/九[次]孕婦　nonigravida
第六病/第六病　the sixth disease
第六次孕妇/六[次]孕婦　sextigravida
第六感/第六覺　the sixth sense
第六性病/第六性病　the sixth venereal disease
第七次孕妇/七[次]孕婦　septigravida
第七感/第七覺　the seventh sense
第七颈神经根综合征/第七頸神經根症候群　middle radicular syndrome
第三产程/第三產程　the third labor stage
第三穿动脉/第三穿動脈　the third perforating artery
第三次孕妇/第三胎孕婦　tertigravida
第三的/第三的　ternary
第三腓骨肌/第三腓骨肌　peroneus tertius, the third peroneal muscle
第三跗骨/第三跗骨　the third tarsal bone
第三级死骨/第三度死骨　tertiary sequestrum
第三磨牙/第三磨牙　the third molar
第三脑室/第三腦室　the third ventricle

第三脑室脉络丛/第三腦室脈絡叢　choroid plexus of the third ventricle, plexus choroideus ventriculi tertii
第三脑室脉络丛支/第三腦室脈絡叢支　choroidal branch of the third ventricle
第三脑室脉络组织/第三腦室脈絡組織　tela choroidea of the third ventricle
第三脑室前部造瘘术/第三腦室前部造瘺術　anterior the third ventriculostomy
第三视区/第三視區　the third visual area
第三腕骨/第三腕骨　the third carpal bone
第三楔状骨/第三楔骨　the third cuneiform bone
第三心音/第三心音　the third sound
第三性腺/第三性腺　the third gonad
第三循环系统/第三循環　the third circulation
第三腰椎横突综合征/第三腰椎橫突症候群　the third lumbar transverse process syndrome, transverse process pattern of the third lumbar vertebra
第三腰椎横突综合征·风寒湿阻证/第三腰椎橫突症候群·風寒濕阻證　the third lumbar transverse process syndrome with wind-cold-dampness obstruction pattern
第三腰椎横突综合征·肝肾亏虚证/第三腰椎橫突症候群·肝腎虧虛證　the third lumbar transverse process syndrome with liver-kidney deficiency pattern
第三腰椎横突综合征·血瘀气滞证/第三腰椎橫突症候群·血瘀氣滯證　the third lumbar transverse process syndrome with pattern of blood stasis and qi stagnation
第三掌骨茎突/第三掌骨莖突　styloid process of the third metacarpal bone
第三者满意/第三者滿意　the third-party consent
第三枕神经/第三枕神經　the third occipital nerve
第三跖骨/第三蹠骨　the third metatarsal bone
第三趾/第三趾　the third digit of foot
第三转子/第三粗隆,第三轉節　the third trochanter
第十二脑神经/第十二腦神經,舌下神經　the twelfth cranial nerve
第十脑神经/第十顱神經,迷走神經　the tenth cranial nerve
第十三凝血因子a/第十三凝血因子a　blood coagulation factor XIII a
第四/第四　the fourth
第四穿动脉/第四穿動脈　the fourth perforating artery
第四的/第四的　quaternary
第四脑神经/第四顱神經,滑车神經　the fourth cranial nerve
第四脑室/第四腦室　the fourth ventricle
第四脑室带/第四腦室帶　tenia of the fourth ventricle
第四脑室带静脉/第四腦室帶靜脈　vein lining the the fourth ventricle
第四脑室盖/第四腦室蓋　tegmen of the fourth ventricle
第四脑室脉络丛/第四腦室脈絡叢　choroid plexus of the fourth ventricle
第四脑室脉络丛支/第四腦室脈絡叢支　choroidal branch of the fourth ventricle
第四脑室脉络组织/第四腦室脈絡組織　tela choroidea of the fourth ventricle
第四脑室髓纹/第四腦室髓紋　striae medullares of the fourth ventricle
第四脑室外侧孔/第四腦室外側孔,基-雷二氏孔　lateral aperture of the fourth ventricle, Key-Retzius foramen
第四脑室外侧隐窝静脉/第四腦室外側隱窩靜脈　vein of the lateral recess of the the fourth ventricle
第四脑室正中沟/第四腦室正中溝　median sulcus of the fourth ventricle
第四脑室正中孔/第四腦室正中孔　median aperture of the fourth ventricle
第四期梅毒/第四期梅毒　quaternary syphillis
第四视区/第四視區　the fourth visual area
第四腕骨/第四腕骨　the fourth carpal bone
第四心音/第四心音　the fourth sound
第四跖骨/第四蹠骨　the fourth metatarsal bone
第四趾/第四趾　the fourth digit of foot
第五病/第五疾病　the fifth disease
第五性病/第五性病　the fifth venereal disease
第五腰椎动脉/最下腰動脈　the fifth lumbar artery
第五跖骨/第五蹠骨　the fifth metatarsal bone
第五跖骨粗隆/第五蹠骨粗隆　tuberosity of the fifth metatarsal bone
第五跖骨基底部骨折/第五蹠骨基底部骨折　Jones fracture
第一产程/第一產程　the first labor stage
第一穿动脉/第一穿動脈　the first perforating artery
第一代杂种病/第一代雜種病　F1 disease
第一房间隔/第一[房間]隔　septum primum
第一房间孔/第一[房間]孔　foramen primum
第一级房室传导阻滞/第一級房室傳導阻滯　the first-degree atrioventricular block
第一级死骨/第一度死骨　primary sequestrum

第一极体/第一極體　the first polar body
第一急救者/第一急救者　the first responder
第一肋/第一肋　the first rib
第一肋间后动脉/第一肋間後動脈　the first posterior intercostal artery
第一肋胸肋结合/第一肋胸肋結合　sternocostal synchondrosis of the first rib
第一目/第一目　the first order
第一期愈合/第一期愈合　healing by the first intention
第一躯体感觉区/第一軀體感覺區　primary somatosensory area
第一躯体运动区/第一軀體運動區　primary somatomotor area
第一鳃弓复杂性缺损/第一鰓弓複雜性缺損　the first branchial arch complex defect
第一鳃弓综合征/第一鰓弓症候群　the first arch syndrome
第一神经元/第一神經單位,原始神經單位　protoneuron
第一视区/第一視區　primary visual area
第一听区/第一聽區　primary auditory area
第一楔骨/第一楔骨　the first cuneiform bone
第一心音/第一心音　the first sound
第一掌骨拇指化术/第一掌骨拇指化術　pollicization of the first metacarpal bone
第一跖背动脉/第一蹠背動脈　the first dorsal metatarsal artery
第一跖骨/第一蹠骨　the first metatarsal bone
第一跖骨粗隆/第一蹠骨粗隆　tuberosity of the first metatarsal bone
第一跖足底总动脉/第一蹠足底總動脈　the first common plantar metatarsal artery
第一至第五掌骨/第一至第五掌骨　metacarpal bones Ⅰ-Ⅴ
蒂/蒂　pedicle
蒂巴因/蒂巴因　thebaine
蒂比耶日-魏森巴赫综合征/Thibierge-Weissenbach 二氏症候群　Thibierge-Weissenbach syndrome
蒂策综合征/Tietze 氏症候群　Tietze syndrome
蒂德曼神经/Tiedemann 氏神經　Tiedemann nerve
蒂的/蒂的　peduncular
蒂尔施移植物/Thiersch 氏移植物　Thiersch graft
蒂菲耶试验/塔斐爾氏試驗　Tuffier test
蒂夹/蒂夾　pedicle clamp
蒂勒综合征/Thiele 氏症候群　Thiele syndrome
蒂默综合征/Timme 氏症候群　Timme syndrome
蒂内尔征/蒂內爾徵　Tinel sign
蒂生成/莖之發生,生蒂　pedicellation
蒂状瓣/蒂狀瓣　pedicle flap
蒂状移植物/蒂狀移植物　double-end graft
缔合/結合反應　association reaction
缔合胶体/結合膠體　association colloid
碲化汞-碲化镉复合半导体检测器/硫化汞-碲化鎘複合[物]半導體檢測器　mercury cadmium telluride detector, MCT detector
碲酸/碲酸　telluric acid
碲酸盐/碲酸鹽　tellurate
颠倒性畸形/顛倒性畸形　malformation by perversion
颠茄/顛茄　belladonna
颠茄酊/顛茄酊　belladonna tincture
颠茄生物碱类/顛茄生物鹼類　belladonna alkaloids
颠茄叶/顛茄葉　banewort
颠茄硬膏/顛茄硬膏　belladonna plaster
癫病/癲病,抑鬱性精神病　depressive psychosis, schizophrenia
癫病·肝气郁结证/癲病·肝氣鬱結證　depressive psychosis with pattern of liver qi depression
癫病·气虚痰结证/癲病·氣虛痰結證　depressive psychosis with pattern of qi deficiency and phlegm binding
癫病·气阴两虚证/癲病·氣陰兩虛證　depressive psychosis with pattern of deficiency of both qi and yin
癫病·痰气郁结证/癲病·痰氣鬱結證　depressive psychosis with pattern of phlegm-qi stagnation and binding
癫病·心脾两虚证/癲病·心脾兩虛證　depressive psychosis with pattern of heart-spleen deficiency
癫病·阴虚火旺证/癲病·陰虛火旺證　depressive psychosis with pattern of exuberant fire due to yin deficiency
癫狂/癲狂　insanity, on mania
癫狂病/癲狂病,瘋狂病,躁鬱症精神病　crazy disease, manic-depressive psychosis
癫痫/癲癇　epilepsy
癫痫持续状态/癲癇持續狀態　epileptic state
癫痫大发作/癲癇大發作　major epilepsy
癫痫发作/癲癇發作　attack of epilepsy
癫痫发作后的/癲癇後的　postepileptic
癫痫后谵妄/癲癇後譫妄　delirium postepilepticum
癫痫患者/患癲癇者　epileptic
癫痫替代症状/癲癇替代症候　epileptic equivalent
癫痫先兆/癲癇先兆　epileptic aura
癫痫小发作/癲癇小發作　petit mal epilepsy

癫痫[小发作]性失神/癲癇小發作失神　absentia epileptica
癫痫性痴呆/癲癇性癡呆　epileptic dementia
癫痫性痤疮/癲癇性痤瘡　epileptic acne
癫痫性喊叫/癲癇喊叫　epileptic cry
癫痫性幻觉/癲癇性幻覺　epileptic hallucination
癫痫性肌阵挛/癲癇性肌陣攣病　myoclonia epileptica
癫痫性精神病/癲癇性精神病　epileptic psychosis
癫痫性狂暴/癲癇性狂暴　furor epilepticus
癫痫性神游/癲癇性神遊　epileptic fugue
癫痫性眩晕/癲癇性眩暈　epileptic vertigo
癫痫性谵妄/癲癇性譫妄　delirium epilepticum
癫痫学/癲癇學　epileptology
癫痫样波型/癲癇樣波型　epileptiform pattern
癫痫样的/癲癇狀的　epileptiform
癫痫样人格障碍/癲癇型人格障礙　epileptoid personality disorder
癫痫样震颤/癲癇狀震顫　epileptoid tremor
典型痛风/尋常痛風　regular gout
点/點　dot, point
点凹甲/點凹甲　pitted nail
点彩/彩斑　stippling
点彩舌/點彩舌　dotted tongue
点刺法/點刺法　swift pricking blood therapy
点滴覆膜孢酵母/點滴覆膜孢酵母　Saccharomycopsis guttulatus
点滴灌肠法/點滴灌腸法　proctoclysis
点滴酵母/戈氏酵母菌　Saccharomyces guttulatus
点滴静脉输液法/點滴静脈注射法　drip phleboclysis
点裂隙龋洞/小凹裂溝窩洞　pit and fissure cavity
点磨法/點磨法　spot grinding
点头/點頭　nutation
点头痉挛/點頭痙攣　eclampsia nutans
点突变/點突變　point mutation
点隙/凹痕,痘凹,凹陷　pit
点穴法/點穴法　finger pointing manipulation
点压法/點壓法　point pressing method
点眼疗法/點眼療法　eye dripping therapy
点眼药法/點眼藥法　topical eye medication
点眼药粉法/點眼藥粉法　application of eye powder
点样器/點樣器　sample applicator
点指数/點指數　vertex degree
点状凹陷甲/點狀凹陷甲　stippled nail
点状白内障/點狀内障　punctate cataract
点状玻璃体炎/點狀玻璃體炎　punctate hyalitis
点状出血/點狀出血　punctate hemorrhage
点状痤疮/點狀痤瘡　acne punctata
点状的/點狀的,斑點的　punctate
点状骨骺发育不良/點狀骨骺發育異常　dysplasia epiphysialis punctata
点状角化病/點狀角化病　punctate keratosis
点状角膜炎/點狀角膜炎　punctate keratitis
点状角皮症/點狀角皮症　punctate keratoderma
点状皮片/點狀皮片　pinch free skin graft
点状[皮下]出血/點狀皮下出血,瘀斑性出血　petechial hemorrhage
点状软骨发育异常/點狀軟骨發育異常　chondrodysplasia punctata
点状视网膜炎/點狀視網膜炎　punctate retinitis
点状外渗/點狀外滲　punctiform extravasation
点状物质/點狀質　dotted substance
点状先天性软骨营养不良/點狀先天性軟骨失養　chondrodystrophia congenita punctata
点状小痣/點狀小痣　speckled and lentiginous nevus
点状银屑病/點孔狀乾癬　psoriasis punctata
点状硬皮病/點狀硬皮病　guttate scleroderma
点状掌跖角化病/點狀掌蹠角化病　keratosis punctata palmoplantaris
碘奥酮/碘奥酮　iodopyracet
碘[苯]酚/碘酚[合劑]　iodophenol
碘苯类/碘苯類　iodobenzenes
碘苯酸盐类/碘苯酸鹽類　iodobenzoates
碘吡啶酮类/碘吡啶酮類　iodopyridones
碘泊酸盐/碘泊酸鹽　ipodate
碘醋酸盐类/碘醋酸鹽類　iodoacetates
碘痤疮/碘痤瘡　iodine acne
碘达胺/碘達胺　iodamide
碘胆固醇/碘膽脂醇　iodocholesterol
碘蛋白类/碘蛋白類　iodoproteins
碘酊/碘酊　tincture of iodine
碘定量法/碘定量法　iodimetry
碘仿/碘仿　iodoform
碘仿反应/碘仿反應　iodoform reaction
碘仿中毒/碘仿中毒　iodoformism
碘放射性同位素/碘放射性同位素　iodine radioisotope
碘附/碘附　iodophor
碘甘卡酸/碘甘卡酸　ioglycamic acid
碘苷/碘苷　idoxuridine
碘海醇/碘海醇　iohexol
碘化铋奎宁/碘化鉍奎寧　quinine bismuth iodide
碘化铋吐根碱/碘化鉍吐根素　emetine bismuth iodide
碘化淀粉/含碘澱粉,碘制澱粉　amylum iodatum
碘化汞砷溶液/碘化汞砷溶液　arsenic and mercuric

iodide solution
碘化合物/碘化合物　iodine compound
碘化钾/碘化鉀　potassium iodide
碘化钾碘溶液/碘化鉀碘溶液　IKI solution
碘化钾汞/碘化鉀汞　potassiomercuric iodide
碘化钾溶液/碘化鉀溶液　potassium iodide solution
碘化硫/碘化硫　sulfur iodide
碘化钠/碘化鈉　sodium iodide
碘化麝香草脑/碘化麝香草腦　thymol iodide
碘化十烃季铵/碘化十烴季銨　decamethonium iodide
碘化烃类/碘化烴類　iodinated hydrocarbons
碘化物/碘化物　iodide
碘化物过氧化物酶/碘化物過氧化物酶　iodide peroxidase
碘化亚铜/碘化亞銅　cuprous iodide
碘化乙酰/碘化乙醯基　acetyl iodide
碘化油/碘化油　iodized oil
碘化作用/碘化作用　iodination
碘甲磺酸钠/碘甲磺酸鈉　methiodal sodium
碘甲烷/碘化甲烷　methyl iodide
碘甲状腺功能减退症/碘甲狀腺功能減退症　iodine hypothyroidism
碘甲状腺功能亢进症/碘原性甲狀腺機能亢進　iodine-induced hyperthyroidism
碘甲状腺球蛋白/碘甲狀腺球蛋白　iodothyroglobulin
碘克沙酸/碘克沙酸　ioxaglic acid
碘拉葡胺/碘拉葡胺　iothalamate meglumine
碘疗法/碘療法　iodotherapy
碘硫尿嘧啶/碘硫尿嘧啶　iothiouracil
碘硫酸盐/碘硫酸鹽　iodosulfate
碘绿/碘綠質　iodine green
碘马尿酸/碘馬尿酸　iodohippuric acid
碘马尿酸钠/碘馬尿酸鈉,希普蘭　hippuran
碘尿/碘尿　ioduria
碘帕醇/碘帕醇　iopamidol
碘羟喹啉磺酸/碘羥喹啉磺酸,羅雷丁　iodoxyquinoline sulfonic acid
碘氰吲哚洛尔/碘氰吲哚洛爾　iodocyanopindolol
碘球蛋白/碘球蛋白　iodoglobulin
碘溶液/碘溶液　iodine solution
碘酸/碘酸　iodic acid
碘酸钠/碘酸鈉　sodium iodate
碘酸盐/碘酸鹽　iodates
碘他拉酸/碘拉酸　iothalamic acid
碘同位素/碘同位素　iodine isotope
碘性甲状腺功能亢进/碘性巴塞多氏病　jodbasedow

碘血/碘血症　iodemia
碘乙酸/碘乙酸　iodoacetic acid
碘乙烷/碘化乙烷　hydriodic ether
碘乙酰胺/碘乙醯胺　iodoacetamide
碘油造影术/碘油檢影術　iodolography
碘源/碘源　propiodal
碘疹/碘皮病　iododerma
碘值/碘價　iodine number
碘中毒/碘中毒　iodism
碘中毒性腮腺炎/碘性腮腺炎　iodine mumps
碘紫癜/碘紫癜　purpura iodica
电按摩法/電按摩法　electromassage
电按摩器/電按摩器　electromassor
电病理学/電病理學　electropathology
电测压计/電測壓計　electromanometer
电沉积/電沈著法,電鍍法　electrodeposition
电池/電池　battery cell
电除毛法/電除毛法　electro-epilation
电触诊[法]/電觸診法　galvanopalpation
电穿刺术/電穿刺術　electroparacentesis
电穿孔/電穿孔　electroporation
电穿孔[作用]/電致孔[作用]　electroporation
电磁波/電磁波　electromagnetic wave
电磁波谱/電磁波光譜　electromagnetic spectrum
电磁辐射/電磁輻射　electromagnetic radiation
电磁疗法/電磁療法　electromagnetotherapy
电磁流量计/電磁流量計　electromagnetic flowmeter
电磁频率/電磁頻率　electromagnetic frequency
电磁天平/電磁天平　electromagnetic balance
电刺激/電刺激　electric stimulation
电刺激疗法/電刺激療法　electric stimulation therapy
电[刺激]收缩性/肌肉之受電收縮性　electrocontractility
电刺激术/電刺激術　electrostimulation
电催化[作用]/電催化作用　electrocatalysis
电刀/電刀　electrotome
电刀胆囊切除术/膽囊電切除術　electrocholecystectomy
电导测定法/傳導測量術　conductometry
电的/電的　electric
电动取皮机/電動取皮機　electric dermatome
电动剃须刀/電動刮鬍刀　electric razor
电镀工业/電鍍工業　electroplating industry
电反应测听[法]/電反應測聽[法]　electric response audiometry
电反应降低/電激無反應狀態　parelectronomy
电放射测量计/電放射計　electroradiometer

电复律/心电复律　electroversion
电干燥法/電乾燥法　electrodesiccation
电光膀胱镜/電膀胱鏡　electrocystoscope
电光谱描记术/電光譜圖測定　electrospectrography
电光谱图/電光譜圖　electrospectrogram
电光性盲/電光盲　electric-light blindness
电光性眼炎/電光性眼炎　electric ophthalmia
电光治疗/電光療法　electric light treatment
电合成[法]/電合成法　electrosynthesis
电荷/電荷　electric charge
电荷密度/電荷密度　charge density
电荷转移/電荷轉移　charge transfer
电荷转移光谱/電荷轉移光譜　charge-transfer spectrum
电弧/電弧　electric arc
电弧烧伤/電弧燒傷　electric arc burn
电化学疗法/電化學療法　electrochemotherapy
电击/電擊　stroke lightning
电击伤/電擊傷　electric injury
电击性白内障/電傷性白內障　electric cataract
电击性内障/閃電性內障　lightning cataract
电击样痛/閃電狀痛　fulgurant pain
电击样舞蹈病/電擊性舞蹈病,電擊狀舞蹈病　electric chorea
电机械分离/電機械分離　electrical mechanical dissociation
电极/電極　electrode
电记波摄影术/電心動記錄法　electrokymography
电记波照相器/電心動記錄器　electrokymograph
电鉴定生死法/生死電驗法,電流辨生死法　electrobioscopy
电接触烧伤/電接觸燒傷　electric contact burn
电解池/電解池　electrolytic cell
电解代谢/電解物代謝　electrolyte metabolism
电解分析/電分析　electroanalysis
电解渗入法/電解滲入法　dielectrolysis
电解脱毛/電解脫毛　electrolytic depilation
电解针/電解針　electrolysis needle
电解质类/電解質　electrolytes
电解质平衡液/電解質平衡液　balanced electrolyte solution
电解质缺乏综合征/電解質缺乏症候群　electrolyte deficiency syndrome
电解质紊乱/電解質紊亂　electrolyte disturbance
电解质转移/電解質轉移　electrolyte shift
电解[作用]/電氣解析　electrolysis
电解[作用]的/電解的　electrolytic
电紧张/電緊張　electrotonus
电紧张性电流/緊張電流　electrotonic current
电紧张性收缩/電張性攣縮　galvanotonic contraction
电惊厥疗法/電痙療法　electroconvulsive therapy
电抗休克/電抗休克　electric countershock
电缆式神经移植术/電纜式神經移植術　cable nerve grafting
电缆式神经移植物/索狀神經移植物　cable graft
电烙器/電烙器　electric cautery
电烙切断术/電烙截斷術　galvanocaustic amputation
电离/電離　ionization
电离常数/離子常數　ionization constant
电离辐射/電離輻射　ionizing radiation
电离性白内障/電離性白內障　ionizing cataract
电量/電量　electric quantity
电疗法/電療[法]　electrotherapy
电疗式睡眠/電療式睡眠　electrotherapeutic sleep
电疗学家/電療學家　electrotherapeutist
电流的/電流的　galvanic, voltaic
电流收缩性/電流收縮性　galvanocontractility
电[流]睡眠/電流性睡眠　electric sleep
电流性眩晕/電流性眩暈　voltaic vertigo
电麻醉/電流性知覺缺失　electric anesthesia
电脉冲刺激[法]/電脈衝刺激[法]　electric pulse stimulation
电免疫扩散/電免疫擴散法　electroimmunodiffusion
电描记术/電子攝影　electrography
电描记图/電描記圖　electrogram
电凝法/電凝法　electrocoagulation
电凝术/電擊凝固　electric coagulation
电喷雾接口/電噴霧接口　electrospray interface
电起搏法/以節律器刺激心跳動　electroaugmentation
电气流/電氣流　electric souffle
电迁移进样/電遷移進樣　electromigration injection
电切除术/電切除法　electroresection
电切割/電切割法　electrosection
电切术/電切除　electrocision
电热喉镜/電熱喉鏡　thermolaryngoscope
电热疗法/電熱療法　electrothermotherapy
电热偶温度计/電熱偶溫度計　electric couple thermometer
电热器/電熱機　electrotherm
电热梳性秃发/電熱梳性禿髮　hot-comb alopecia
电热温度计/電溫度計　thermelometer
电热针/電熱針　moxibustion with electric warming needles
电融合/電融合　electrofusion
电烧伤/電燒傷　electric burn

电渗/電滲　electroosmosis
电渗析/電透析　electrodialysis
电渗[现象]/用電透入法,藥物電透法,電滲透　electroendosmosis
电生理学/電生理學　electrophysiology
电生理学的/電生理學的　electrophysiologic
电生理研究/電生理研究　electrophysiological study
电声门描记[法]/電聲門描記[法]　electroglottography
电声探子/電探針　electric probe
电声[异物]定位器/電聲異物定位器　electroacoustic locator
电视辅助外科手术/電視輔助外科手術　video-assisted surgery
电视辅助胸外科手术/電視輔助胸外科手術　video-assisted thoracic surgery
电视显微镜检查/電視顯微鏡檢查　video microscopy
电视胸腔镜手术/電視胸腔鏡手術　video assisted thoracic operation
电水浴疗法/電水浴療法　hydroelectric bath therapy
电睡眠疗法/電睡眠療法　electrosleep therapy
电碎石术/電波碎石術　electrolithotrity
电损伤/電損傷　electric injury
电体操疗法/電體操療法　electro gymnastic therapy
电透药法/電透藥法　electro medication
电透照检查/電光透照檢查法　electrodiaphany
电突触/電突觸　electrical synapse
电外科学/電外科學　electrosurgery
电位测定法/電位測定法　potentiometry
电位滴定法/電位滴定法　potentiometric titration
电位过低/電位過低　hypopotentia
电味觉测定[法]/電味覺測定[法]　electrogustometry
电味觉测定仪/電味覺測定儀　electrogustometer
电兴奋疗法/電興奮療法　electroexcitation therapy
电休克/電擊,電氣休克,電震法　electric shock
电休克治疗/電氣休克療法,電震療法　electric shock therapy
电压/電壓　electric tension
电压门控钾通道/電壓門控鉀通道　voltage-gated potassium channel
电压调控性通道/電壓調控性通道　voltage operated channel
电鳐/電鰩　torpedo
电影磁共振成像/電影磁共振成像　cine magnetic resonance imaging
电影X射线摄影术/活動X光像攝影術,X光活動攝影術　cineradiography
电影[性]眼/電影性眼　klieg eye
电应激性/電應激性,應電性　electric irritability
电泳/電泳　electrophoresis
电泳疗法/電泳療法　electrophoresis
电泳迁移位移试验/電泳遷移位移試驗　electrophoretic mobility shift assay
电泳图/電泳圖　electrophoretogram
电泳图型/電泳圖型　electrophoretic pattern
电圆锯/電[環]鋸　electrotrephine
电针刺/電針灸,以電流行針　electro-acupuncture
电针刀/電割針　acusector
电针疗法/電針療法　electro-acupuncture therapy
电针麻醉/電針麻醉　electro-acupuncture anesthesia
电针切开术/電針割治法　acusection
电针仪/電針儀　electro-acupuncture therapeutic apparatus
电诊断法/電診[斷]法　electrodiagnosis
电诊断学/電診學　electrodiagnostics
电诊断医学/電診斷醫學　electrodiagnostic medicine
电震颤按摩/電振按摩法　electrovibratory massage
电[植]皮刀/電皮刀　electrodermatome
电助听训练器/人工電喉　electrophonoide
电灼疗法/電閃擊法　electrofulguration
电灼术/電灼術　electrocautery
电子传递复合物Ⅰ/電子傳遞複合物Ⅰ　electron transport complex Ⅰ
电子传递链/電子傳遞鏈　electron transport chain
电子传递链复合蛋白质类/電子傳遞鏈複合蛋白質類　electron transport chain complex proteins
电子电位计/電子電位計　electronic potentiometer
电子构型/電子構型　electronic configuration
电子喉/電子喉　electronic larynx
电子减肥仪/電子減肥儀　electron slimming machine
电子磨砂机/電子磨砂機　electron abrasing machine
电子内镜检查[术]/電子內鏡檢查[術]　electronic endoscopy
电子能损谱学/電子能損譜學　electron energy-loss spectroscopy
电子染色/電子染色　electron staining
电子束疗法/電子束療法　electron beam therapy
电子探针微区分析/電子探針微區分析　electron probe microanalysis
电子探针显微分析仪/電子探針微分析器　electron probe microanalyzer
电子透明/電子透明　electron-lucent
电子透明带/電子透明帶　electron-lucent zone
电子显微镜/電子顯微鏡　electron microscope
电子显微镜检查/電子顯微鏡檢查,電子顯微術

电子显微镜术/電子顯微術,電子顯微鏡檢查 electron microscopy
电子显微照片/電子顯微攝影 electron micrograph
π电子效应/π電子效應 π electron effect
电子业/電子工業 electronics industry
电子跃迁/電子躍遷 electron transition
电子脂肪分解[术]/電子脂肪分解[術] electrolipolysis
电子致密/電子致密 electron-dense
电子致密带/電子致密帶 electron-dense zone
电子致密小体/電子致密小體 electron-dense body
电子转移黄素蛋白质类/電子轉移黃素蛋白質類 electron-transferring flavoproteins
电子自旋共振/電子自旋共振 electron spin resonance
电子自旋共振谱学/電子自旋共振譜學 electron spin resonance spectroscopy
电阻温度计/電阻溫度計 resistance thermometer
垫/墊 pad
垫层/襯墊組織 cushion
垫料/墊料 padding
垫棉法/墊棉法 cotton pad drainage
垫上运动/墊上運動 mat exercise
垫枕法/墊枕法 pillow-support treatment
垫枕练功法/墊枕練功法 functional exercise of spinal extensor in supine position
淀粉/澱粉 starch, amylum
淀粉半纤维素/澱粉半纖維質 amylohemicellulose
淀粉绷带/澱粉繃帶 starch bandage
淀粉当量/澱粉當量 starch equivalent
淀粉分解/澱粉分解 amylolysis
淀粉分解的/分解澱粉的 amylolytic
淀粉分解酶/澱粉分解酵素 amylolytic enzyme
淀粉甘油/澱粉甘油 glycerin of starch
淀粉合成作用/澱粉合成作用 amylosynthesis
淀粉合酶/澱粉合酶 starch synthase
淀粉糊精/澱粉糊精,紅糊精 amylodextrin
淀粉粒/澱粉粒 starch granule
淀粉磷酸化酶/澱粉磷酸分解酶 amylophosphorylase
淀粉酶/澱粉酶 diastase
淀粉酶测定法/澱粉酵素測定法 diastasimetry
淀粉酶解/澱粉水解 amylorrhexis
淀粉酶尿/澱粉酶尿 amylasuria
淀粉酶清除率/澱粉酶清除率 clearance of amylase
淀粉酶试验/澱粉酶試驗 amylase test
淀粉尿/多糖尿 amylosuria

淀粉凝固酶/澱粉凝結酵素,澱粉凝結酶 amylocoagulase
淀粉凝胶电泳/澱粉凝膠電泳 starch gel electrophoresis
淀粉葡萄糖苷酶缺乏/澱粉葡萄糖苷酶缺乏 amylo glucosidase deficiency
淀粉溶质/澱粉溶質 amylogen
淀粉生成/澱粉合成 amylogenesis
淀粉水解物/糖分解物 glucidtemns
淀粉[糖化]酶/澱粉分解酵素 diastatic ferment
淀粉消化不良/澱粉消化不良 amylodyspepsia
淀粉血症/澱粉血症 amylemia
淀粉样变性/澱粉樣變性,蠟樣變性 amyloidosis, amyloid degeneration
淀粉样病/澱粉樣病 amyloid disease
淀粉样蛋白/澱粉樣蛋白 amyloid
淀粉样β蛋白/澱粉樣β蛋白 amyloid beta-protein
淀粉样蛋白环/澱粉樣蛋白環 amyloid ring
淀粉样β蛋白前体/澱粉樣β蛋白前體 amyloid beta-protein precursor
淀粉样蛋白血[症]/澱粉樣蛋白血症 amyloidemia
淀粉样肝/澱粉樣肝 albuminoid liver
淀粉样瘤/澱粉樣瘤 amyloid tumor
淀粉样神经病[变]/澱粉樣神經病[變] amyloid neuropathy
淀粉样肾/澱粉樣腎 amyloid kidney
淀粉样肾变病/類澱粉腎病 amyloid nephrosis
淀粉样体/澱粉樣小體 corpora amylacea
淀粉溢/澱粉瀉 amylorrhea
淀粉转葡糖苷酶缺乏/澱粉轉葡萄糖苷酶缺乏 amylo-transglucosidase deficiency
淀粉阻滞剂/澱粉阻滯劑 starch blocker
靛/靛青 indigo
靛酚反应/靛基酚反應 indophenol reaction
靛酚酶/靛基酚酵素 indophenolase
靛酚试验/靛基酚試驗 indophenol test
靛苷/靛苷 indican
靛红/靛紅 isatin
靛红尿/靛紅尿 indirubinuria
靛卡红试验/靛洋紅試驗 indigo carmine test
靛蓝二磺酸钠/靛藍二磺酸鈉 indigotindisulfonate sodium
靛蓝二磺酸盐/二磺酸靛藍 indigotindisulfonate
靛糖/靛苷質 indiglucin
凋落的/脱落的,蜕的 deciduous
雕刻[蜡]块/雕刻塊 carving block
雕刻疗法/雕刻療法 carving therapy
吊床式绷带/吊床繃帶 hammock bandage

吊床样/吊床樣　hammock form
吊韧带/吊韌帶　hammock ligament
调查/調查，测量　survey
跌打损伤/跌打損傷　wound
跌打丸/跌打丸　dieda pills
跌打万花油/跌打萬花油　dieda wanhua oil
跌倒/跌倒　falling
跌倒发作/跌倒發作　drop attack
跌伤/跌傷　falling injury
迭代目标转换因子分析法/替代目標轉換因子分析法　iterative target transform factor analysis method
叠氮化钠/疊氮化鈉　sodium azide
叠氮化氢/偶氮亞胺化物，三氮化氫　azoimide
叠氮化物/疊氮化物　azide
叠氮酸/疊氮酸　hydrazoic acid
叠缝带环/疊縫帶環　lap band
叠盖/瓦狀重疊　imbrication
叠盖线/疊蓋線　imbrication line
叠加分辨率图示法/疊加解析圖示法　overlapping resolution map
叠片磁铁/疊片磁鐵　laminated magnet
叠瓦癣/馬拉巴癬　Malabar itch
叠瓦状的/疊瓦狀的　imbricated
叠瓦状细胞/複疊細胞　imbricated cell
叠趾畸形/疊趾畸形　overlapping toe deformity
碟状脸/碟狀面容　dish face
蝶鞍/蝶鞍　sella turcica
蝶鞍扩大/蝶鞍擴大　enlarged sella
蝶鞍上/蝶鞍上的　suprasellar
蝶鞍上囊肿/蝶鞍上囊腫　suprasellar cyst
蝶鞍上脑膜瘤/鞍上腦膜瘤　suprasellar meningioma
蝶导静脉孔/蝶導静脈孔，蝶導血管孔　emissary foramen
蝶底骨/底蝶骨　basisphenoid bone
蝶点/蝶點　sphenion
蝶顶窦/蝶頂竇　sphenoparietal sinus
蝶顶缝/蝶頂縫　sphenoparietal suture
蝶啶/蝶翅色質　pteridine
蝶窦/蝶竇　sphenoidal sinus, sphenoid cell
蝶窦口/蝶竇口　aperture of sphenoidal sinus
蝶窦切除术/蝶竇切除術　sphenoidectomy
蝶窦切开术/蝶竇切開術　sphenoidotomy
蝶窦炎/蝶竇炎　sphenoid sinusitis
蝶窦中隔/蝶竇中隔　septum of sphenoidal sinus
蝶额缝/蝶額縫　sphenofrontal suture
蝶轭/蝶軛　jugum sphenoidale
蝶腭长神经/蝶腭長神經　long sphenopalatine nerve

蝶腭动脉/蝶腭動脈　sphenopalatine artery, nasopalatine artery
蝶腭[骨]的/蝶骨與腭的　sphenopalatine
蝶腭孔/蝶腭孔　sphenopalatine foramen
蝶腭切迹/蝶腭切跡　sphenopalatine notch
蝶腭神经节切除术/[蝶腭]神經節切除術　meckelectomy
蝶腭神经节阻断/蝶腭神經節阻斷　sphenopalatine ganglion block
蝶腭神经痛/蝶腭神經痛，斯路德氏神經痛　sphenopalatine neuralgia
蝶腭综合征/蝶腭症候群　sphenopalatine syndrome
蝶耳骨化中心/蝶耳骨化中心　sphenotic center
蝶骨/蝶骨　sphenoid bone, alar bone
蝶骨部/蝶骨部　sphenoid part
蝶骨大脑面/蝶骨大腦面　cerebral surface of sphenoid bone
蝶骨大翼/蝶骨大翼　greater wing of sphenoid bone
蝶骨电极/蝶骨電極　sphenoidal electrode
蝶骨顶缘/蝶骨頂緣　parietal margin of sphenoid bone
蝶骨骨髓炎/蝶骨髓炎　esosphenoiditis
蝶骨海绵窦沟/蝶骨海綿竇溝　cavernous groove of sphenoid bone
蝶骨互连双胎[畸形]/蝶骨連胎　sphenopagus
蝶骨基底沟/蝶骨基底溝　basilar groove of sphenoid bone
蝶骨脊脑膜瘤/蝶骨脊腦膜瘤　sphenoid ridge meningioma
蝶骨甲/蝶骨甲　concha sphenoidalis
蝶骨颈动脉沟/蝶骨頸動脈溝　carotid groove of sphenoid bone
蝶骨眶面/蝶骨眶面　orbital surface of sphenoid bone
蝶骨鳞缘/蝶骨鱗緣　squamosal margin of sphenoid bone
蝶骨颞面/蝶骨顳面　temporal surface of sphenoid bone
蝶骨颞下嵴/蝶骨顳下嵴　infratemporal crest of sphenoid bone
蝶骨颞下面/蝶骨顳下面　infratemporal of sphenoid bone surface
蝶骨前部/蝶骨前部，前蝶骨　presphenoid
蝶骨鞘突/蝶骨鞘突　vaginal process of sphenoid bone
蝶骨颧缘/蝶骨顴緣　zygomatic margin of sphenoid bone
蝶骨上颌面/蝶骨上頜面　maxillary surface of

sphenoid bone
蝶骨体/蝶骨體　body of sphenoid bone
蝶骨小翼/蝶骨小翼　lesser wing of sphenoid bone
蝶骨翼切迹/蝶骨翼切跡　pterygoid fissure, pterygoid notch
蝶骨翼突/蝶骨翼突　pterygoid process of sphenoid bone
蝶骨翼窝/蝶骨翼窩　pterygoid fossa of sphenoid bone
[蝶骨]翼状突/翼狀突　pterygoid process
蝶骨舟状窝/蝶骨舟狀窩　scaphoid fossa of sphenoid bone
蝶颌窝综合征/蝶頜窩症候群　sphenomaxillary fossa syndrome
蝶后骨/蝶後骨　postsphenoid bone
蝶棘/蝶骨棘　spine of sphenoid bone
蝶嵴/蝶嵴　sphenoidal crest
蝶甲/蝶甲　sphenoidal concha
蝶甲骨/蝶甲骨　sphenoturbinal bone
蝶角/蝶角　sphenoidal angle
蝶犁缝/蝶犁縫　sphenovomerine suture
蝶鳞缝/蝶鱗縫　sphenosquamosal suture
蝶呤/喋呤　pterin
蝶[呤]氨苯甲酰二谷氨酸/蝶醯二麩胺酸　pteroyldiglutamic acid
蝶[呤]氨苯甲酰三谷氨酸/蝶醯三麩胺酸　pteroyltriglutamic acid
蝶颧缝/蝶顴縫　sphenozygomatic suture
蝶筛缝/蝶篩縫　sphenoethmoidal suture
蝶筛结合/蝶篩結合　sphenoethmoidal synchondrosis
蝶筛隐窝/蝶篩隱窩　sphenoethmoidal recess
蝶上颌缝/蝶頜縫　sphenomaxillary suture
蝶突/蝶突　sphenoidal process
蝶下颌韧带/蝶下頜韌帶　sphenomandibular ligament
蝶酰二谷氨酸/狄奥普特靈,蝶醯二榖胺酸　diopterin
蝶酰三谷氨酸/喋呤氨苯甲醯三榖胺酸　teropterin
蝶小舌/蝶骨小舌　lingula of sphenoid, sphenoidal lingula
蝶囟/蝶囟　sphenoid fontanelle
蝶形槽浴/蝶形槽浴　butterfly shaped tank bath
蝶形骨折/蝶形骨折　butterfly fracture
蝶形皮疹/蝶形疹　butterfly rash
蝶岩间裂隙/蝶岩間裂隙　fissura sphenopetrosa
蝶岩结合/蝶岩軟骨結合　sphenopetrosal synchondrosis
蝶岩裂/蝶岩裂　sphenopetrosal fissure
蝶翼骨/蝶翼骨,蝶内大翼的　alisphenoid
蝶蛹/蛹　chrysalis
蝶缘/蝶緣　sphenoidal margin
蝶枕沟/蝶枕底溝　sphenobasilar groove
蝶枕结合/蝶枕軟骨結合　sphenooccipital synchondrosis
蝶枕裂隙/蝶枕間裂隙　fissura spheno-occipitalis
蝶状狼疮/蝴蝶狀狼瘡　butterfly lupus
蝶嘴/蝶嘴　sphenoidal rostrum
丁胺卡那霉素/丁胺卡那黴素　amikacin
丁胺类/丁胺類　butylamines
丁苯那嗪/丁苯那嗪　tetrabenazine
丁苯羟酸/丁苯羥酸　bufexamac
丁丙诺啡/丁丙諾啡　buprenorphine
丁醇/丁醇　butanol
丁醇类/丁醇類　butanols
丁二胍/丁雙胍　buformin
丁二烯/丁二烯　butadiene
丁公藤/丁公藤　obtuseleaf erycibe stem
丁基/丁基　butyl
丁基氯醛/丁氯醛　butyl chloral
丁卡因/四卡因　tetracaine
丁硫氨酸/丁硫胺酸　buthionine
丁硫醇/丁硫醇　butylmercaptan
丁螺环酮/丁螺環酮　buspirone
丁萘夫汀/丁萘夫汀　bunaftine
丁羟茴香醚/丁羥茴香醚　butylated hydroxyanisole
丁羟甲苯/丁羥甲苯　butylated hydroxytoluene
丁氰酯/丁氰酯　bucrylate
丁醛糖/丁醛醣　aldotetrose
丁酸/丁酸,酪酸　butanoic acid
丁酸倍氯松/丁酸倍氯鬆　clobetasol butyrate
丁酸苯酯类/丁酸苯酯類　phenylbutyrates
丁酸类/丁酸類　butyric acids
丁酸锰/丁酸錳　manganese butyrate
丁酸生成发酵/丁酸發酵　butyric fermentation
丁酸盐/丁酸鹽,酪酸鹽　butyrate
丁酸乙酯试验/丁酸乙酯試驗　ethyl butyrate test
丁糖/丁糖,四碳糖　tetrose
丁酮类/丁酮類　butanones
丁烷/丁烷　butane
丁烷类/丁烷類　butanes
丁烯/丁烯　butylene
丁烯二醇类/丁烯二醇類　butylene glycols
丁酰胆碱酯酶/丁醯膽鹼酯酶　butyrylcholinesterase
丁酰 CoA 脱氢酶/丁醯 CoA 脱氫酶　butyryl-CoA dehydrogenase
丁香/丁香　clove

丁香酚/丁香油酚　eugenol
丁香柿蒂汤/丁香柿蒂湯　dingxiang shidi decoction
丁香油/丁香油　oil of clove
丁香油酚敷料/丁香油酚敷料　eugenol dressing
丁香油印模材/丁香油印模材　eugenol impression material
丁型[病毒性]肝炎/丁型[病毒性]肝炎　viral hepatitis type D, delta agent hepatits
丁溴巴比妥/丁溴丙烯巴比妥酸　butallylonal
丁溴东莨菪碱/丁溴東莨菪鹼　hyoscine butylbromide
丁字带/丁字帶　T-shaped bandage
钉/釘　peg
钉板型种植体/釘板型種植體　staple implant
钉合吻合/釘合吻合　stapled anastomosis
钉嵌体/釘嵌體　pinlay
钉突样改变/釘突樣改變　spikes projecting
钉形固位/釘形固位　pin retention
钉形固位体/暗釘固位體，針形固位體　pinledge retainer
钉翳/釘翳　anterior synechia leukoma, nail nebula
钉状牙/釘狀牙　peg tooth
疔疮/疔瘡　ding, deep-rooted sore, hard furuncle
疔疮·火毒炽盛证/疔瘡·火毒熾盛證　ding with blazing fire-toxin pattern
疔疮·火毒蕴结证/疔瘡·火毒蘊結證　ding with fire-toxin amassment pattern
耵耳/耵耳，中耳炎　impacted cerumen, ceruminal ear, otitis media
耵聍/耳垢　cerumen
耵聍分泌过多/耳垢過多　ceruminosis
耵聍溶解/耳垢溶解　ceruminolysis
耵聍栓塞/耳垢阻塞外耳道　ceruminal impaction
耵聍腺/耳垢腺　ceruminous gland
耵聍腺瘤/耳垢腺瘤　ceruminoma
耵聍性聋/耳垢性聾症　ceruminous deafness
酊[剂]/酊[劑]　tincture
酊剂制备/酊劑製配　tincturation
顶/頂，蓋　roof
顶板/頂板　roof plate
顶部/頂部　cupular part
顶部的/頂部的　apical
顶部入路/頂部入路　parietal approach
顶部胸廓成形术/頂部胸廓成形術　apical thoracoplasty
顶导静脉/頂導靜脈　parietal emissary vein
顶端测压型心导管/頂端測壓型心導管　manometer-tipped cardiac catheter

顶封/頂封　tip-seal
顶盖脊髓的/四叠体脊髓的　tectospinal
顶盖脊髓束/頂蓋脊髓束　tectospinal tract, tractus tectospinalis
顶盖前区/頂蓋前區，中腦頂蓋　pretectal area
顶盖细胞/頂蓋細胞　roof cell
顶盖小脑束/四叠體小腦徑　tectocerebellar tract
顶盖延髓束/頂蓋延髓束　tectobulbar tract
顶骨/頂骨　parietal bone
顶骨侧窦沟/頂骨側竇溝　lateral groove for lateral sinus of parietal bone
顶骨导静脉/頂骨導靜脈　parietal emissary vein
顶骨的/頂骨的　parietal
顶骨蝶角/頂骨蝶角　sphenoidal angle of parietal bone
顶骨额角/頂骨額角　frontal angle of parietal bone
顶骨额缘/頂骨額緣　frontal border of parietal bone
顶骨鳞缘/頂骨鱗緣　squamosal border of parietal bone
顶骨上矢状窦沟/頂骨上矢狀竇溝　sulcus sagittalis ossis parietalis
顶骨矢状缘/頂骨矢狀緣　sagittal border of parietal bone
顶骨外面/頂骨外面　external surface of parietal bone
顶骨乙状窦沟/頂骨乙狀竇溝　sulcus sinus sigmoidei ossis parietalis
顶骨枕角/頂骨枕角　occipital angle of parietal bone
顶骨枕缘/頂骨枕緣　occipital border of parietal bone
顶核/頂核　fastigial nucleus
顶核桥延束/頂核橋延束　fastigiobulbar tract
顶后静脉/頂後靜脈　posterior parietal vein
顶后内侧静脉/頂後內側靜脈　posteromedial parietal vein
顶回/頂迴　parietal gyrus
顶间沟/頂間裂隙，頂骨間溝，頂葉間裂　interparietal fissure
顶间骨/頂間骨　interparietal bone, os interparietale
顶浆分泌物/頂漿腺分泌物　apocrine secretion
顶浆分泌细胞/頂漿細胞　apocrine cell
顶浆分泌腺炎/頂漿分泌腺炎　apocrinitis
顶浆分泌性痤疮/頂漿腺痤瘡　apocrine acne
顶浆腺色汗症/頂漿腺色汗症　apocrine chromhidrosis
顶浆腺纤维瘤/頂漿腺纖維瘤　apocrine fibroadenoma
顶浆腺腋臭汗症/頂漿腺腋臭汗症　apocrine bromhidrosis

顶浆样汗腺/頂漿樣汗腺　apocrine sweat gland
顶角/頂角　parietal angle
顶结节/頂結節　parietal tuber
顶空浓缩进样器/頂空濃縮進樣器　head-space concentrating injector
顶孔/頂骨孔　parietal foramen
顶孔间点/頂穴,頂囟　obelion
顶裂/頂裂　capping
顶盲端/頂盲端　cupular cecum
顶泌汗腺/頂泌汗腺　apocrine sweat gland
顶泌腺/頂泌腺　apocrine gland
顶内沟/頂内溝　intraparietal sulcus
顶颞后斜线/頂顳後斜線　dingnie houxiexian, MS7, posterior oblique line of vertex-temporal
顶颞前斜线/頂顳前斜線　dingnie qianxiexian, MS6, anterior oblique line of vertex-temporal
顶旁1线/頂旁1線　dingpangxian Ⅰ, MS8, lateral line 1 of vertex
顶旁2线/頂旁2線　dingpangxian Ⅱ, MS9, lateral line 2 of vertex
顶前静脉/頂前静脈　anterior parietal vein
顶前内侧静脉/頂前内側静脈　anteromedial parietal vein
顶切迹/頂切跡　parietal incisure, parietal notch
顶区/頂骨部　parietal region
顶乳突缝/頂乳突縫　parietomastoid suture
顶上区/頂上區　superior parietal area
顶上小叶/頂上葉　superior parietal lobule
顶体/頂體,頭巾　acrosome
顶体蛋白/頂體蛋白　acrosin
顶体反应/頂體反應　acrosome reaction
顶体后环/頂體後環　postacrosomal ring
顶体后致密板/頂體後致密板　postacrosomal dense lamina
顶体粒/頂體顆粒　acrosomal granule
顶体酶/頂體酶　acrosomal enzyme
顶体内膜/頂體内膜　inner acrosomal membrane
顶体泡/頂體泡　acrosomal vacuole, acrosomal vesicle
顶体期/頂體期　acrosomal phase
顶体素/頂體素　acrosin
顶体外膜/頂體外膜　outer acrosomal membrane
顶体下间隙/頂體下間隙　subacrosomal space
顶臀长/頂臀長度　crown-rump length
顶下沟/頂下溝　subparietal sulcus
顶下区/頂下區　inferior parietal area
顶下小叶/頂下葉　inferior parietal lobule
顶先露/頂骨產式　parietal presentation
顶叶/頂葉　parietal lobe
顶叶后动脉/頂後動脈　posterior parietal artery
顶叶静脉/頂静脈　parietal vein
顶叶前动脉/頂前動脈　anterior parietal artery
顶叶与枕叶的/頂葉與枕葉的　parietooccipital
顶叶与枕叶性失语症/頂枕葉失語症　parietooccipital aphasia
顶叶支/頂支　parietal branch
顶缘/頂緣　parietal margin
顶枕的/頂枕的,頂葉與枕葉的　parietooccipital
顶枕动脉/頂枕動脈　parietooccipital artery
顶枕沟/頂枕溝　parietooccipital sulcus
顶枕间裂隙/頂枕間裂隙　fissura parietooccipitalis
顶枕入路/頂枕入路　parietooccipital approach
顶枕支/頂枕支　parietooccipital branch
顶质分泌/頂端分泌的　apocrine
顶中线/頂中線　dingzhongxian, MS5, middle line of vertex
顶踵长/頂踵長度　crown-heel length
定标器/定標器　scaling block
定长状态/肌纖維長度固定之狀態　metrostasis
定喘/定喘　dingchuan, EX-B1
定喘汤/定喘湯　dingchuan decoction
定点诱变/定點誘變　site-directed mutagenesis
定魂魄/定魂魄　calming the mind
定界叩诊/定界叩診　definitive percussion
定惊悸/定驚悸　relieving palpitations
定居寄生物/[固]定寄生物　ecoparasite
定居巨噬细胞/定居巨噬細胞　resident macrophage
定菌[作用]/定菌作用　bacteriopexia
定量沉淀试验/定量沈澱試驗　quantitative precipitation test
定量的/定量的　quantitative
定量构效关系/定量構效關係　quantitative structure activity relationship, QSAR
定量冠状动脉摄影术/定量冠狀動脈攝影術　quantitative coronary arteriography
定量雾化吸入器/定量霧化吸入器　metered dose inhaler
定量吸入气雾剂/定量吸入氣化噴霧劑　metered dose inhalation aerosol
定量吸入器/定量吸入器　metered-dose inhaler
定量药理学/定量藥理學　quantitative pharmacology
定魄/定魄　calming the mind
定期的/定期的,週期的　periodic
定群调查/定群調查　cohort study
定时不能/對時間之感覺失常　chronotaraxis
定时扩散[脊髓麻醉]术/定時擴散術　time diffusion

technique
定时障碍/時間辨別障礙　dyschronism
定位缝合/定位縫合　key approximation suture
定位觉缺失/定位覺缺失　topoanesthesia
定位平面/定位平面　plane of orientation
定位平面斜度/定位平面斜度　inclination of plane of orientation
定痫丸/定癇丸　epilepsy relieving pill
定向分子进化/定向分子進化　directed molecular evolution
定向力/定向力, 辨向力　orientation
定向筛选/定向篩選　directed screening
定向听诊器/複式聽診器　symballophone
定向细胞/定向細胞　committed cell
定向诱变/定向誘變　site directed mutagenesis
定向[造血]干细胞/定型[造血]幹細胞　committed hemopoietic stem cell
定向障碍/定向力缺失, 定向力障礙　disorientation
定向组织捐赠/定向組織捐贈　directed tissue donation
定性的/定性的　qualitative
定性叩诊/定性叩診　qualitative percussion
定性研究/定性研究　qualitative research
定义/定義　definition
定影法/定影法　shadowing
定植/移生　colonization
定植感染/移生感染　colonization infection
定志丸/定志丸　dingzhi pill, mind stabilizing pill
定着细胞/定著細胞　fixed cell
锭剂/錠劑　morsulus, lozenge
东部马脑脊髓炎病毒/東部馬腦脊髓炎病毒　eastern equine encephalomyelitis virus
东方传统医学/東方傳統醫學　oriental traditional medicine
东方的/東方的　oriental
东方疖/巴格達瘤　Bagdad boil
东方马脑脊髓炎/東方馬腦脊髓炎　eastern equine encephalomyelitis
东方马脑炎/東部馬腦炎　eastern equine encephalitis
东方毛圆线虫/東方毛狀圓蟲　Trichostrongylus orientalis
东非昏睡病/東非睡眠病　East African sleeping sickness
东莨菪碱/東莨菪素, 歐莨菪素　scopolamine
东莨菪碱衍生物/東莨菪鹼衍生物　scopolamine derivative
东莨菪亭/東莨菪副素　scopoletin
东医宝鉴/東醫寶鑒　Treasured Mirror of Oriental Medicine
L-冬氨酸/L-天冬胺酸　L-aspartic acid
冬虫夏草/冬蟲夏草　Cordyceps sinensis, Chinese caterpillar fungus
冬瓜串/冬瓜串　upper arm abscess
冬瓜皮/冬瓜皮　Chinese waxgourd peel
冬瓜子/冬瓜子　waxgourd seed
冬季的/冬季的　hiemal
冬季咳/冬季欬嗽　winter cough
冬季瘙痒[症]/冬令搔癢　pruritus hiemalis
冬季性关节炎/冬令關節炎　arthritis hiemalis
冬季痒疹/冬季癢疹　prurigo hiemalis
冬葵子/冬葵子　Fructus Malvae（拉）
冬令的/冬令的　hiemalis
冬令红斑角质松解/冬季紅斑角質解離症　erythrokeratolysis hiemalis
冬令脓疱性肢皮炎/冬季膿皰性肢端皮膚炎　acrodermatitis pustulosa hiemalis
冬令皮炎/冬季皮膚炎　dermatitis hiemalis
冬令瘙痒/冬令搔癢症, 凍癢症　frost-itch
冬眠/冬眠　hibernation
冬眠合剂/鎮定混合劑　lytic cocktail
冬青素/冬青素　ilicin
冬温/冬温　warm disease in winter, winter warmth
氡[射]线照片/居里圖　curiegram
氡子体/氡子體　radon daughter
动触反应/動觸反應　pulsations and sensations reaction
动磁场疗法/動磁場療法　dynamic magnetic field therapy
动关节/動關節, 黏液腔關節　abarthrosis
动合子/卵動子, 授胎蟲, 孕蟲　ookinete
动幻觉/運動性幻覺　kinesthetic hallucination
动机/動機　motivation
动静结合/動靜結合　combination of motion and quiescence
动静脉的/動靜脈的　arteriovenous
动静脉分流/動靜脈分流　arteriovenous shunt
动静脉分流术/動靜脈分流術　arteriovenous shunt operation
动静脉畸形/動靜脈畸形　arteriovenous malformation
动静脉交叉现象/動靜脈交叉現象　arteriovenous crossing phenomenon
动静脉扩张/動靜脈擴張　phlebarteriectasia
动静脉连续性杂音/動靜脈連續性雜音　arteriovenous continous murmur
动静脉瘤/動靜脈瘤　arteriovenous aneurysm

动静脉瘘/動靜脈瘻　arteriovenous fistula
动静脉内瘘/動靜脈內瘻　internal arteriovenous fistula
动静脉外瘘/動靜脈外瘻　external arteriovenous fistula
动静脉吻合/動靜脈吻合　arteriovenous anastomoses, arteriovenous anastomosis
动静脉血管瘤/動靜脈性血管瘤　arteriovenous hemangioma
动静脉血体外膜式氧合/動靜脈血體外膜式氧合　arteriovenous extracorporeal membrane oxygenation
动静脉血氧差/動靜脈血氧差　arteriovenous oxygen difference
动静脉血氧合/動靜脈血氧合　arteriovenous oxygenation
动觉/動覺,运动感觉　kinesthesis
动觉的/運動覺的　kinesthetic
动觉记忆/動覺記憶　kinesthetic memory
动力蛋白 ATP 酶/動力蛋白 ATP 酶　dynein ATPase
动力蛋白质类/動力蛋白質類　dynamins
动力的/動力的,動力學的　dynamic
动力精神病学/動力精神病學　dynamic psychiatry
动力式夹板/動力式夾板,活動性夾板　dynamic splint
动力性肠梗阻/肌力過強性腸阻塞,動力性腸梗塞　dynamic ileus, hyperdynamic ileus
动力性黄疸/動力性黃疸　dynamic jaundice
动力性尿路梗阻/動力性尿路梗阻　dynamic obstruction of urinary tract
动力性心肌成形术/動力性心肌成形術　dynamic cardiomyoplasty
动力性运动/動力性運動　dynamic exercise
动力性杂音/動力性雜音　dynamic murmur
动力悬吊/動力懸吊　dynamic suspension
动力障碍/動力障礙　dyskinesis
动粒/著絲點　kinetochore
动脉/動脈　①artery, arteria ②tremulous pulse
动脉泵/動脈泵　arterial pump
动脉闭塞性疾病/動脈閉塞性疾病　arterial occlusive disease
动脉病/動脈病　arteriopathy
动脉病毒感染/動脈病毒感染　arterivirus infection
动脉插管[术]/動脈插管[術]　arterial cannulation
动脉成形术/動脈成形術,動脈造形術　arterioplasty
动脉出血/動脈出血　arterial hemorrhage
动脉胆道瘘/動脈膽道瘻　arteriobiliary fistula
动脉导管/動脈導管　ductus arteriosus, arterial duct
动脉导管三角/動脈導管三角　ductus arteriosus triangle
动脉导管未闭/動脈導管未閉　patent ductus arteriosus
动脉的/動脈的　arterial
动脉动脉瘘/動脈動脈瘻　arterio-arterial fistula
动脉分支灌注/動脈分支灌流　arterial limb perfusion
动脉缝合术/動脈縫合術　arteriorrhaphy
动脉钙化/動脈鈣化　arteriosteogenesis
动脉干/動脈幹　truncus arteriosus
动脉干分隔不均/動脈幹分隔不均,動脈幹不等分裂　unequal division of truncus arteriosus
动脉干永存/動脈幹永存　persistent truncus arteriosus
动脉沟/動脈溝　arterial groove
动脉骨化/動脈骨化　arteriostosis
动脉冠/動脈冠　vasocorona
动脉管路/動脈管路　arterial line
动脉管路滤器/動脈管路濾器　arterial line filter
动脉管路气泡捕集器/動脈管路氣泡捕集器　arterial bubble trap
动脉灌注管路/動脈灌注管路　arterial perfusion line
动脉坏死/動脈壞死　arterionecrosis
动脉环/動脈環　arterial circle
动脉肌瘤病/動脈肌瘤病　arteriomyomatosis
动脉夹层/動脈剥離　arterial dissection
动脉痉挛/動脈痙攣　arteriospasm
动脉瘤/動脈瘤　aneurism
动脉瘤成形术/動脈瘤成形術　aneurysmoplasty
动脉瘤缝闭术/動脈瘤縫合術　aneurysmorrhaphy
动脉瘤结扎术/動脈瘤結扎術　aneurysmodesis
动脉瘤切除术/動脈瘤切除術　aneurysmectomy
动脉瘤切开术/動脈瘤切開術　aneurysmotomy
动脉瘤素质/動脈瘤體質　aneurysmal diathesis
动脉瘤性骨囊肿/動脈瘤狀骨囊腫　aneurysmal bone cyst
动脉瘤性静脉曲张/動脈瘤性靜脈曲張　aneurysmal varix
动脉瘤性咳/動脈瘤性欬嗽　aneurysmal cough
动脉瘤性纤维性组织细胞瘤/動脈瘤性纖維性組織細胞瘤　aneurysmal fibrous histiocytoma
动脉瘤样骨囊肿/動脈瘤樣骨囊腫　aneurysmal bone cysts
动脉瘤杂音/動脈瘤雜音　aneurysmal murmur
动脉瘤造影[术]/動脈瘤造影[術]　aneurysmography
动脉瘤针/動脈瘤針　aneurysm needle

动脉瘤震颤/動脈瘤震顫 aneurysmal thrill
动脉毛细血管/動脈微血管 arterial capillary
动脉毛细[血]管纤维变性/動脈微血管纖維變性 arteriocapillary fibrosis
动脉囊/主動脈囊 aortic sac
动脉内化疗/動脈内化療 intraarterial chemotherapy
动脉内膜/動脈内膜 endarterium
动脉内膜病/動脈内膜病變 endarteropathy
动脉内膜切除术/動脈内膜切除術 endarterectomy
动脉内膜炎/動脈内膜炎 endarteritis
动脉内膜硬化/内膜炎性動脈硬化 intimal arteriosclerosis
动脉内输注/動脈内輸注 intra-arterial infusion
动脉内注射/動脈内注射 intra-arterial injection
动脉扭转术/動脈扭轉止血法 arteriostrepsis
动脉旁路术/動脈旁路術 arterial bypass
动脉喷血描记法/動脈噴血描記法,血液衝動描記法 hemautography
动脉喷血描记图/動脈噴血描記圖 hemautograph
动脉钳/動脈鉗 artery forcep
动脉切除术/動脈切除術 arterectomy
动脉切开术/動脈切開術 arteriotomy
动脉球/動脈球 bulbus arteriosus
动脉热交换器/動脈熱交換器 arterial heat exchanger
动脉韧带/動脈韌帶 arterial ligament
动脉韧带淋巴结/動脈韌帶淋巴結 lymph node of arterial ligament
动脉[散射]痛/動脈痛 arteralgia
动脉上的/動脈上的 eparterial
动脉上支气管/動脈上支氣管 ramus bronchialis eparterialis
动脉生成/動脈生成 arteriogenesis
动脉石/動脈石 arteriolith
动脉输血/動脈輸血法 arterial transfusion
动脉输液/動脈輸液 arterial infusion
动脉束/動脈束 arterial tract
动脉树/動脈樹 arterial tree
动脉外膜/動脈外膜 adventitia
动脉外膜的/動脈外膜的 adventitial
动脉外膜真皮/動脈外膜的真皮 adventitial dermis
动脉网/動脈網 arterial rete
动脉狭窄/動脈狭窄 narrowing of artery
动脉下的/動脈下的 hyparterial
动脉下支气管/動脈下支氣管 hyparterial bronchus
动脉心瘤/動脈心瘤 arterio-cardiac aneurysm
动脉性/動脈性 arteriosity
动脉性溃疡/動脈性潰瘍 arterial ulcer
动脉性心系膜/動脈性心繫膜 arterial mesocardium
动脉学/動脈學 arteriology
动脉血/動脈血 arterial blood
动脉血二氧化碳分压/動脈血二氧化碳分壓 arterial partial pressure of carbon dioxide
动脉血返回/動脈血返回 arterial blood reentry
动脉血气分析/動脈血氣分析 arterial blood gas analysis
动脉[血]压/動脈血壓 arterial pressure
动脉血氧饱和度/動脈血氧飽和度 arterial oxygen saturation
动脉血氧分压/動脈血氧分壓 arterial partial pressure of oxygen
动脉压/動脈内張力,動脈壓力,動脈血壓 arterial tension
动脉压监测/動脈壓監測 arterial blood pressure monitoring
动脉炎/動脈炎 arteritis
动脉移植/動脈移植 artery transplantation
动脉移植物/動脈移植物 arterial graft
动脉异位/動脈異位,動脈變位 arteriectopia
动脉音描记法/動脈音響描記法 phonarteriography
动脉音图/動脈音響圖 phonarteriogram
动脉硬化/動脈硬化 arteriosclerosis
动脉硬化的/動脈硬化的 arteriosclerotic
动脉硬化性精神病/動脈硬化性精神病 arteriosclerotic psychosis
动脉硬化性脑疾患/動脈硬化性腦障礙 arteriosclerotic brain disorder
动脉硬化性肾/動脈硬化腎 arteriosclerotic kidney
动脉硬化性肾炎/動脈硬化性腎炎 arteriosclerotic nephritis
动脉硬化性眩晕/動脈硬化性眩暈 arteriosclerotic vertigo
动脉圆锥/動脈圓錐 conus arteriosus, arterial cone
动脉圆锥切除术/動脈圓錐切除術 infundibulectomy
动脉圆锥支/動脈圓錐支 branch of arterial conus
动脉杂音/動脈雜音 arterial murmur
动脉造影术/動脈X光攝影法 arteriography
动脉造影照片/動脈[X光]像 arteriogram
动脉针/動脈針 artery needle
动脉中层炎/動脈中層炎,動脈中膜炎 mesarteritis
动脉中层硬化/動脈中層硬化 medial arteriosclerosis
动脉周围丛/動脈周圍叢 periarterial plexuses
动脉周围交感神经切除术/動脈周圍交感神經切除術 periarterial sympathectomy

动脉周围淋巴鞘/動脈周圍淋巴鞘,圍動脈淋巴鞘 periarterial lymphatic sheath
动脉周[围]炎/動脈周圍炎 periarteritis
动脉粥样变性/動脈粥樣變性,粥瘤狀變性 atheromasia, atheromatous degeneration
动脉粥样化的/動脈粥樣化的,粥瘤的 atheromatous
动脉粥样硬化/動脈粥瘤硬化,粥腫狀硬化 atherosclerosis
动脉粥样硬化的/動脈粥樣硬化的 atherosclerotic
动脉粥样硬化栓塞/動脈粥瘤性栓塞 atheroembolism
动脉贮血室/動脈貯血室 arterial reservoir
动脉贮血室截流活瓣/動脈貯血室截流活瓣 arterial reservoir check valve
动脉注射/動脈注射 intra-arterial injection
动脉转位术/動脈轉位術 arterial switch procedure
动情后期/動情後期 metestrus
动情间期/動情間期 diestrus
动情期/動情期 estrus
动情期[变]化/動情激素化 estrinization
动情期测定/動情期測定 estrus detection
动情期同步化/動情期同步化 estrus synchronization
动情前期/動情前期,求偶前期 proestrus
动时痛/動時酸痛 oxycinesia
动丝测微计/絲測微計 filar micrometer
动速测量器/速度計,記速器 tachymeter
动态暗间隙/動態暗間隙 dynamic dark space
动态肺顺应性/動態肺順應性 dynamic lung compliance
动态干扰电疗法/動態干擾電療法 dynamic interferential electrotherapy
动态检影[法]/動態檢影[法] dynamic retinoscopy
动态镜/動態鏡 zoescope
动态镜检查/動態鏡檢查 stroboscopy
动态镜盘/動態鏡盤 stroboscopic disk
动态平衡/動態平衡 dynamic balance
动态屈光/動態折射 dynamic refraction
动态人口学/動態人口統計學 dynamic demography
动态心电图/動態心電圖 ambulatory electrocardiogram
动物病毒/動物病毒 animals virus
动物毒素/動物毒素 zootoxin
动物极/動物極 animal pole
动物解剖学家/動物解剖學家,動物解剖者 zootomist
动物流行病/動物流行病 epizootic disease
动物性的/動物性的 zoogenous
动物[性]移植物/動物移植物 zooplastic graft
动物组织成术/動物組織移植術 zooplasty
动纤毛/動纖毛 kinocilium
动形怡神/動形怡神 body exercise to have a cheerful mood
动形悦情法/動形悅情法 body exercise to achieve cheerful mood
动眼肌/動眼肌 oculomotor muscle
动眼痉挛/動眼痙攣 oculogyral spasm
动眼神经/動眼神經 oculomotor nerve
动眼神经副核/[副交感]動眼神經副核 accessory nucleus of oculomotor nerve
动眼神经根/動眼神經根 oculomotor root
动眼神经沟/動眼神經溝 sulcus of oculomotor nerve
动眼神经核/動眼神經核 nucleus of oculomotor nerve
动眼神经疾病/動眼神經疾病 oculomotor nerve disease
动眼神经交叉性偏瘫/動眼神經交叉性偏癱 hemiplegia oculomotoria alternans
动眼神经上支/[動眼神經]上支 superior branch of oculomotor nerve
动眼神经下支/[動眼神經]下支 inferior branch of oculomotor nerve
动眼神经支/動眼神經支 branch of oculomotor nerve
动作电位/動作電位 action potential
动作过慢/動作徐緩 bradypragia
动作过速/動作快速,動作急促 tachypragia
动作失调/共濟官能喪失,共濟不能 incoordination
动作性震颤/動作性震顫 action tremor
冻疮/凍瘡 pernio, chilblain
冻疮·寒凝化热证/凍瘡·寒凝化熱證 chilblain with pattern of cold congelation transforming into heat
冻疮·寒凝血瘀证/凍瘡·寒凝血瘀證 chilblain with pattern of cold congelation and blood stasis
冻疮·寒盛阳衰证/凍瘡·寒盛陽衰證 chilblain with pattern of yang declining due to cold excessiveness
冻疮·气虚血瘀证/凍瘡·氣虛血瘀證 chilblain with pattern of qi deficiency and blood stasis
冻疮样红斑狼疮/凍瘡樣紅斑狼瘡 chilblain lupus erythematosus
冻疮样狼疮/凍瘡狀狼瘡 chilblain lupus
冻疮综合征/凍瘡症候群 perniotic syndrome
冻干法/凍乾法 freeze-drying
冻干卡介苗/凍乾卡介苗 Bacillus Calmette-Guérin

vaccine, freeze-dried BCG vaccine
冻干器/凍乾器　lyophilizer
冻僵/凍僵　frozen stiff
冻[结]伤/凍[結]傷　congelation
冻结显示/凍結顯示　freeze-frame
冻伤/凍瘡　frostbite
冻伤性红斑/凍瘡性紅斑　erythema pernio
冻伤性荨麻疹/凍傷性蕁麻疹　urticaria congelation
冻蚀法/凍蝕法　freeze-etching
胨毒素/腖毒素　peptotoxin
胨分解/腖分解　peptolysis
胨化/腖化作用　peptonization
胨抗凝血素/腖酵素　peptozym
胨类/腖類　peptones
胨尿/腖尿症　peptonuria
胨休克/[蛋白]腖休克　peptone shock
胨血浆/[蛋白]腖血漿　peptone plasma
洞壁/洞壁　cavity wall
洞衬剂/洞襯裏　cavity lining
洞穿缺损/洞穿缺損　through and through defect
洞面/腔洞表面　cavosurface
洞面角/洞面角　cavosurface angle
洞斜面/傾斜邊, 斜角　bevel
洞穴病/礦穴病　cave sickness
兜腮痈/兜腮癰　preauricular and parotid abscess
斗形纹/渦, 環生體　whorl
抖法/抖法, 顛法　shaking manipulation
豆氨酸/豆胺酸　conavanine
豆钩韧带/豆鉤韌帶　pisohamate ligament
豆核襻/豆狀襻　lenticular ansa
豆核束/豆核束　lenticular fasciculus
豆蔻/豆蔻　cardamom
豆球蛋白/豆球蛋白　legumin
豆乳/豆乳　soy milk
豆薯苷/豆薯苷　pachyrhizid
豆血红蛋白/豆血紅蛋白　leghemoglobin
豆油/大豆油　soybean oil
[豆]芫菁属/豆芫青屬　Epicauta
豆甾醇/豆甾醇　Stigmasterol
豆掌韧带/豆掌韌帶　pisometacarpal ligament
豆状/豆狀　lenticulare
豆状癌/扁豆狀癌　lenticular carcinoma
豆状骨/豆狀骨　lenticular bone of hand
豆状核/豆狀核　lentiform nucleus
豆状核变性/豆狀核變性　lenticular degeneration
豆状核病/Wilson 氏病　Wilson disease
豆状核后部/豆狀核後部　retrolentiform part
[豆状核]壳/殼　putamen

豆状核内髓板/[豆狀核]內髓板　medial medullary lamina of lentiform nucleus
豆状核外髓板/[豆狀核]外髓板　lateral medullary lamina of lentiform nucleus
豆状核纹状体动脉/豆狀核紋狀體動脈　lenticulostriate artery
豆状核下部/豆狀核下部　sublentiform part
豆状核性失语症/豆狀核性失語症　lenticular aphasia
豆状皮肤纤维瘤/豆狀皮膚纖維瘤　dermatofibroma lenticulare
豆状乳头/豆狀乳頭　lentiform papillae
豆状绦虫/豌豆狀條蟲　Taenia pisiformis
豆状突/豆狀突　lentiform nodule
痘/痘, 膿皰　pox
痘病毒/痘病毒　poxvirus
痘病毒科感染/痘病毒科感染　Poxviridae infection
痘疮样坏死性痤疮/痘瘡樣壞死性痤瘡　acne necrotica varioliformis
痘疮样胃炎/痘瘡樣胃炎　gastritis varioliformis
痘痕/痘痕　pockmark
痘苗病毒/牛痘苗, 牛痘毒　vaccinia virus
痘样痤疮/痘瘡狀痤瘡　acne varioliformis
痘疹入眼/痘疹入眼　smallpox involving eye
痘疹样类牛皮癣/萎縮性類牛皮癬, 痘狀類牛皮癬　parapsoriasis atrophicans
窦/竇　antrum
窦刀/竇切開刀　antrotome
窦道/竇道　sinus tract, deep blind fistula
窦道·气血两虚证/竇道·氣血兩虛證　sinus tract with qi-blood deficiency pattern
窦道·余毒未清证/竇道·餘毒未清證　sinus tract with uncleared remnant toxin pattern
窦的/竇的　sinusal
窦房瓣/竇房瓣　sinoatrial valve
窦房传出阻断/竇房傳出阻斷　sinoatrial exit block
窦房传导时间/竇房傳導時間　sinoatrial conduction time
窦房传导阻滞/竇房性傳導阻滯　sinoatrial heart block
窦房的/竇房的　sinoatrial
窦房节律/竇房節律　sinoatrial rhythm
窦房结/竇房結　sinuatrial node, sinoatrial node
窦房结传导阻滞/竇房結傳導阻斷　sinoatrial block
窦房结动脉/竇房結動脈　sinoatrial node artery
窦房结功能衰竭/竇房結功能衰竭　sinus node failure
窦房结功能障碍/竇房結功能障礙　sinus node

dysfunction
窦房结恢复时间/竇房結恢復時間　sinus node recovery time
窦房结细胞/竇房結細胞　sinus nodal cell
窦房结折返性心动过速/竇房結折返性心動過速　sinoatrial nodal reentry tachycardia
窦房结支/竇房結支　branch of sinuatrial node
窦房孔/竇房孔　sinoatrial orifice
窦房折返性心动过速/竇房折返性心動過速　sinoatrial reentry tachycardia
窦隔/竇隔　sinus septum
窦汇/竇匯　confluence of sinus
窦结节/竇結節　sinus tubercle
窦结折返/竇房結性回路　sinus nodal reentry
窦腔 X 射线照相术/竇腔 X 射線照相術　sinography
窦切除术/竇切除術　antrectomy
窦切开术/竇切開術　sinusotomy
窦神经/竇神經　sinus nerve
窦室传导/竇室傳導　sinoventricular conduction
窦性传导阻滞/竇性傳導阻滯　sinus block
窦性间歇/竇性停止　sinus pause
窦性静止/竇性靜止　sinus standstill
窦性停搏/[房]竇停止　sinus arrest
窦性心动过缓/竇性心搏徐緩　sinoatrial bradycardia, sinus bradycardia
窦性心动过速/竇性心搏快速,單純性心搏快速　sinus tachycardia
窦性心律/竇性節律　sinus rhythm
窦性心律失常/竇性節律不齊　sinus arrhythmia
窦炎/竇炎　sinuitis
窦样管/竇樣管　sinusoid vessel
窦阴道球/竇陰道球　sinovaginal bulb
窦周间隙/竇周間隙,迪塞間隙　perisinusoidal space
窦状毛细管/竇狀微血管　sinusoidal capillary
窦状隙/竇狀的　sinusoid
窦组织细胞增多症/淋巴結組織細胞增多　sinus histiocytosis
督脉/督脈　governor channel, governor vessel
督脉虚损/督脈虛損　governor channel insufficiency
督俞/督俞　dushu, BL16
毒/毒　toxin
毒扁豆碱/毒扁豆鹼,毒扁豆素　physostigmine
毒扁豆碱中毒/毒扁豆素中毒　physostigminism
毒翅虫属/隱翅蟲屬　Paederus
毒虫螫伤/毒蟲螫傷　insect bite
毒簇/毒簇,帶毒體　toxophore
毒[蛋白]胨/毒[蛋白]腖　toxopeptone
毒蛋白[质]/毒蛋白質　toxoprotein
毒胡萝卜内酯/毒胡蘿蔔内酯　thapsigargin
毒火犯耳证/毒火犯耳證　pattern of toxic fire invading ear
毒菌溶血苷/條蕈素,白蕈毒　phallin
毒空木毒/毒空木毒　toot poison
毒理病理学/毒物病理學　toxicological pathology
毒理学/毒理學　toxicology
毒理学家/毒理學家　toxicologist
毒理遗传学/毒理遺傳學　toxicogenetics
毒力/毒力　virulence
毒力因子类/毒力因子類　virulence factor
毒马钱碱/南美箭毒樹鹼　toxiferine
毒毛花苷 G/烏本箭毒苷,毒毛旋花苷　ouabain
毒毛旋花苷/毒毛旋花子配糖體　strophanthin
毒毛旋花子/毒毛旋花子,毒毛旋花屬,羊角拗屬　Strophanthus
毒毛旋花子苷元/毒毛旋花苷　strophanthidin
毒漆树/毒性鹽膚木　poison sumac
毒芹[毒]素/野芹毒質　cicutoxin
毒球蛋白/毒球蛋白　toxoglobulin
毒入营血证/毒入營血證　pattern of toxin entering the nutrient and blood aspects, pattern of yingfen and xuefen invaded by toxin
毒蛇类/毒蛇類　venenosa
毒蛇咬伤/毒蛇咬傷　venomous snake bite
毒蛇咬伤·风毒证/毒蛇咬傷·風毒證　venomous snake bite with wind-toxin pattern
毒蛇咬伤·风火毒证/毒蛇咬傷·風火毒證　venomous snake bite with pattern of wind-fire toxin
毒蛇咬伤·火毒证/毒蛇咬傷·火毒證　venomous snake bite with fire-toxin pattern
毒树脂/毒樹脂　toxiresin
毒素/毒素　toxin
毒素防御素/菌毒防禦素　toxophylaxin
毒素拮抗蛋白/毒素拮抗蛋白,菌毒防禦素　toxicosozin
毒素-抗毒素/毒素抗毒素合劑　toxin-antitoxin
毒素抗毒素合剂/毒素抗毒素混合物　toxin-antitoxin mixture
毒素谱/毒素譜　toxin spectrum
毒素溶液/毒素溶液　toxin solution
毒素受体/毒素受體　toxoreceptor
毒素[性]病/毒素[性]病　toxinosis
毒[素]原/毒素原　toxogen
毒素治疗/毒素治療　toxitherapy
毒素中和试验/毒素中和試驗　toxin neutralization test
毒莴苣浓汁/臭萬苣膏,野萬苣膏　lettuce opium

毒物/毒物　poison, toxicant
毒物代谢/毒物代謝　toxicant metabolism
毒物动力学/毒物動態學,毒動學　toxicokinetics
毒物的/毒物的,有毒的　toxic
毒物分布/毒物分布　distribution of toxicant
毒物监测/毒物監測　monitoring of poison
毒物恐怖/毒物恐懼症,中毒恐懼症　toxicophobia
毒物中和/定毒力,中和毒素力　toxicopexis
毒效应/中毒效應　toxic effect
毒性/毒性　toxicity
毒性当量/毒物當量　toxic equivalent
毒性反应/毒性反應　toxic reaction
毒性甲状腺腺瘤/毒性甲狀腺腺瘤　toxic thyroid adenoma
毒性甲状腺肿/毒性甲狀腺腫　toxic goiter
毒性结节性甲状腺肿/毒性結節性甲狀腺腫　toxic nodular goiter
毒性口炎/毒性口炎　stomatitis venenata
毒[性]酶/毒酵素　toxenzyme
毒性试验/毒性試驗　toxicity test
毒性试验指导原则/毒性試驗基準　guideline for toxicity study
毒性药品/毒性物質　poisonous substance
毒性症状/毒性症狀　sign of toxicity
毒性作用/毒性作用　toxic action
毒血症/毒血症　toxemia
毒血症的/毒血症的　toxemic
毒血症性黄疸/毒血症性黄疸　toxemic jaundice
毒蕈碱/毒蕈素　muscarine
毒蕈碱激动剂/毒蕈鹼激動劑　muscarinic agonist
毒蕈碱拮抗剂/毒蕈鹼拮抗劑　muscarinic antagonist
毒蕈碱受体/毒蕈鹼受體　muscarinic receptor
毒蕈中毒/毒蕈中毒　mushroom poisoning, poisonous mushroom poisoning
毒[药]片剂/毒藥錠劑　toxitabellae
毒液/蟲毒　venom
毒油综合征/毒性油症候群　toxic oil syndrome
毒莠定/毒莠定　picloram
毒鱼刺伤/毒魚刺傷　venomous fishes sting
毒鱼豆素/捕魚樹葉　piscidin
毒原/毒原　toxogen
毒甾醇/毒甾醇　toxisterol
毒蜘蛛舞蹈病/塔蘭登毒蛛病,跳舞病　tarantism
毒蛛中毒/毒蛛中毒　latrodectism
毒作用/毒作用　toxic action
独活/獨活　Heracleum
独活寄生汤/獨活寄生湯　duhuo jisheng decoction
独立带/獨立帶　free band
独立守神/獨立守神　mental auto-adjustment
独立行医协会/獨立行醫協會　independent practice associations
独立缘/獨立緣　free border
独生子女/獨生子女　only child
独特位/特發位　idiotope
独特型/獨特型　idiotype
独眼畸胎/獨眼　cyclops
独眼[畸形]/獨眼畸形　cyclopia
独阴/獨陰　duyin, EX-LE11
独有决定簇/獨有決定簇　private determinant
独有特异性/獨有特異性　private specificity
独语/獨語　soliloquy
读唇/唇讀法　lip-reading
读框/讀框　reading frame
读心症/讀心症　mindreading
读音分节/讀音分節　syllabize
读乐谱不能/讀樂譜不能,音樂性失讀症　musical alexia
渎职/瀆職　malfeasance
犊鼻/犢鼻　dubi, ST35
犊肉样疹/犢肉樣疹　veal skin
堵鼻鼓气法/Valsalva 氏操作　Valsalva maneuver
堵耳试验/堵耳試驗　Sullivan occlusion test
杜贝尔溶液/Dobell 氏溶液,複方硼酸鈉溶液　Dobell solution
杜布瓦饮食/DuBois 氏飲食　DuBois diet
杜-雷定律/杜-雷二氏定律　DuBois-Reymond law
杜鹃花毒素/杜鵑花毒素　androdedotoxin
杜兰德病/Durand 氏病　Durand disease
杜朗特病/Durante 氏病,骨脆弱　Durante disease
杜罗济埃杂音/Duroziez 氏雜音　Duroziez murmur
杜罗济埃征/Duroziez 氏徵象　Duroziez sign
杜诺凡氏溶液/Donovan 氏溶液　Donovan solution
杜诺凡小体/Donovan 氏體　Donovan body
杜-尚综合征/Dubreuil-Chambardel 二氏症候群　Dubreuil-Chambardel syndrome
杜氏肌营养不良/杜氏肌營養不良　Duchenne muscular dystrophy
杜氏利什曼原虫/黑熱病原蟲　Leishmania donovani
杜松焦油/杜松焦油　cade oil
杜松[实]/杜松[實]　juniper berry
杜松苔/杜松苔屬　haircap
杜松油/杜松油　juniper oil
杜瓦瓶/迪華瓶　Dewar flask
杜兴-埃尔布麻痹/埃-杜二氏麻痺,杜-歐二氏麻痺　Duchenne-Erb paralysis
杜仲/杜仲　eucommia bark, cortex eucommiae

杜仲胶/杜仲膠　Gutta-Percha
妒忌/妒忌　jealousy
度量/度量　measure
度硫平/度硫平　dothiepin
镀/鍍　plating
镀银染色法/鍍銀染色法　silver staining method
端侧吻合[术]/端側吻合[術]　end-to-side anastomosis
端端吻合[术]/端端吻合[術]　end-to-end anastomosis
端黄卵/端黄卵　anisolecithal ovum, telolecithal egg
端基异构体/端基差向異構體　anomer
端极染色法/偏極染法　polar staining
端静脉/終端静脈　terminal vein
端粒/染色體終端　telomere
端粒结合蛋白质类/端粒結合蛋白質類　telomere-binding proteins
端脑/端腦,終腦　telencephalon
端脑分化/端腦化　telencephalization
端脑曲/端腦曲　telencephalic flexure
端盘吸虫/端盤吸蟲　amphistome
端式结肠造口术/端式結腸造口術　terminal colostomy
端坐呼吸/端坐呼吸,直體呼吸　orthopnea
短臂/短臂　short arm
短柄产钳/短柄産鉗　leniceps
短波/短波　short wave
短波疗法/短波療法　short wave therapy
短波透热法/短波透熱法　radiathermy
短波紫外线/短波紫外線　short-wave ultraviolet
短肠/短腸　short gut
短肠综合征/短腸症候群　short bowel syndrome
短程化学疗法/短程化學療法　shortcourse chemotherapy
短床连续展开/短床連續展開　short-bed continuous development
短杆菌酪肽/短桿菌酪肽　tyrocidine
短杆菌属/短桿菌屬　Brevibacterium
短杆菌素/短杆菌素,酪毛黴素　tyrothricin
短杆菌肽/短桿菌肽　gramicidin
短骨/短骨　short bone
短颌/短頜畸形　brachygnathia
短肌/短肌　short muscle
短脚/短腳　short crus
短颈/短頸　brevicollis
短颈性营养不良/短頸營養不良　dystrophia brevicollis
短肋/短肋骨　short rib

短肋多指畸形综合征/短肋多指畸形症候群　short rib-polydactyly syndrome
短肋多趾畸形综合征/短肋多趾畸形症候群　short rib-polydactyly syndrome
短脉/短脈　short pulse
短膜虫属/短膜蟲屬　Crithidia
短膜壳绦虫病/短膜殼蟲病　hymenolepiasis nana
短纽/短紐　vinculum breve
短期毒性/短期毒性　short-term toxicity
短期培养/短期培養　short-term culture
短期心理疗法/短期心理療法　brief psychotherapy
短气/短氣,氣急,呼吸短促　shortness of breath
短屈肌/短屈肌　breviflexor
短散在核苷酸元件/短分散核苷酸元件　short interspersed nucleotide element
短时记忆/短時記憶　short-term memory
短时性肿胀/短時性腫脹　fugitive swelling
短食管/短食管　short esophagus
短收肌/内收短肌　adductor brevis
短头/短頭　short head
短头的/短頭的　brachycephalic
短头[畸形]/短頭畸形　brachycephalism
短突的/短突的　breviradiate
短突细胞/短突細胞　breviradiate cell
短袜/短襪　socks
短尾派/短尾派　brachyura
短暂表达/短暫表達　transient expression
短暂的/短暫的,不穩定的　evanescent, transient
短暂热/一日熱,短暫性熱　ephemeral fever
短暂热病毒/短暫熱病毒　ephemeral fever virus
短暂完全性遗忘/短暫完全性遺忘　transient global amnesia
短暂性脑缺血发作/短暫性腦缺血發作　transient ischemic attack
短增量敏感指数/短增量敏感指數　short increment sensitivity index
短阵快速脉冲刺激/短陣快速脈衝刺激　burst stimulation
短阵快速起搏/心跳過速整律　burst pacing
短肢/短肢[畸形]　phocomelia
短指[畸形]/短指[畸形]　brachydactylia, brachydactyly
短趾[畸形]/短趾[畸形]　brachydactylia, brachydactyly
短中央动脉/短中央動脈　short central artery
短中指畸形/短中指畸形　brachymesophalangy
短中趾畸形/短中趾畸形　brachymesophalangy
短轴索/短神經單位　short neuron

短肘后肌/短肘後肌 short anconeus muscle
短 P-R 综合征/短 P-R 症候群 short P-R syndrome
段间部/段間部,節間部 intersegmental part
段内部/段内部 intrasegmental part
断层解剖学/斷層解剖學 sectional anatomy
断层摄影的/斷層攝影的 tomographic
断耳疮/斷耳瘡 severing auricle sore, pyogenic auricular perichondritis, sore severing auricle
断耳疮·热毒腐耳证/斷耳瘡·熱毒腐耳證 severing auricle sore with pattern of heat-toxin eroding ear
断耳疮·邪毒外袭证/斷耳瘡·邪毒外襲證 severing auricle sore with pattern of external assault by pathogenic toxin
断离性肾盂输尿管成形术/斷離性腎盂輸尿管成形術 dismembered ureteropelvioplasty
断裂/斷裂,碎裂 fragmentation
断裂反应/斷裂反應 cleavage reaction
断裂热点/斷裂熱點 breakage hot spot
断裂性心肌炎/斷裂性心肌炎 fragmentation myocarditis
断[毛]发癣菌/斷髮毛癬菌 Trichophyton tonsurans
断面特征/斷面特徵 cut surface character
断奶/斷奶 weaning
断乳腹泻/斷奶性腹瀉 diarrhea ablactatorum
断片定位[法]/斷片定位[法] fragmentation mapping
断脐术/臍帶切開術 omphalotomy
断乳/斷乳,斷奶 ablactation
断[胎]头器/[胎兒]斷頭器 decapitator
断头术/[胎兒]斷頭術 decapitation
断续刺激/斷續刺激 interrupted stimulation
断续排尿/尿液淋瀝 urinary stuttering
断续性多次排粪/零碎性排便 fragmentary defecation
断续性呼吸音/斷續性呼吸音 cogwheel breathing sound
断续言语/斷繞言語 scanning speech
断音言语/斷音言語 staccato speech
断肢存在幻觉/自我軀體存在感 autosomatognosis
断肢性掌跖角皮症/斷肢性掌蹠角皮症 mutilating palmoplantar keratoderma
断肢再植/斷肢再植 replantation of amputated limb
断指再植/斷指再植 replantation of amputated finger
断趾再植/斷趾再植 replantation of amputated toe
煅/煅 calcining
煅淬/煅淬 calcining and quenching
煅炭/煅炭 carbonizing by calcining
煅[制]/煅燒 calcining
锻炼/鍛煉 exercise
队列研究/隊列研究 cohort study
对氨苯酚/對胺苯酚 p-aminophenol
对氨苯乙酮/對胺苯乙酮 para-midoacetophenone
对氨基苯磺酸/對胺基苯磺酸,磺胺酸 sulfanilic acid
对氨基苯磺酸类/對胺基苯磺酸類 sulfanilic acid
对氨基苯磺酰胺/對胺苯磺醯胺 sulfanilamide
对氨基苯[甲]酸/對胺安息香酸 para-aminobenzoic acid
对氨基苯甲酸盐/對胺安息香酸鹽 para-aminobenzoate
对氨基苯甲酸乙酯/對胺基苯甲酸乙酯 ethyl-p-aminobenzoate
对氨基马尿酸盐/對胺馬尿酸鹽 para-aminohippurate
对氨基水杨酸/對胺水楊酸 para-aminosalicylic acid
对氨基水杨酸钠/對胺基水楊酸鈉 sodium para-aminosalicylate
对氨邻甲苯酚/對胺鄰甲苯酚 p-amino-o-cresol
对半甲/對半甲 half and half nail
对半卡环/對半卡環 half and half clasp
对苯二胺皮炎/對苯二胺皮炎 para-phenylene diamine dermatitis
对比敏感度/對比敏感度 contrast sensitivity
对比敏感度函数/對比敏感度函數 contrast sensitivity function
对比染色/對比[法],復染[法] counterstaining
对比支气管肺活量测定法/對比支氣管肺量測定法 differential bronchospirometry
对边𬌗/對緣咬合 edge-to-edge occlusion
对苄氯酚/對苄氯酚 benoquin
对苄氧酚/莫諾苯宗 monobenzone
对丙烯基苯酚/對[羥基]丙烯酚 anol
对侧偏瘫/對側偏癱 contralateral hemiplegia
对侧性水肿/對側水腫 collateral edema
对称/對稱 symmetry
对称部/對稱部 antimere
对称的/對稱的 symmetrical
对称联体儿/對稱聯體兒 symmetric conjoined twins
对称散光/對稱散光 symmetrical astigmatism
对称伸缩振动/對稱伸縮振動 symmetrical stretching vibration
对称突触/對稱突觸 symmetrical synapse
对称性进行性白斑病/對稱性進行性白斑症 symmetrical progressive leucopathy
对称性进行性红斑角化病/對稱性進行性紅斑角化病 symmetrical progressive erythrokeratoderma

对称性联胎/雙連對稱畸胎　diplopagus
对称性突触/對稱性突觸　symmetrical synapse
对称因素/對稱因素　symmetry factor
对称肢体大小不等/左右肢不等　anisomelia
对冲骨折/對沖骨折,對側傷骨折　fracture by contrecoup
对冲性损伤/對沖性損傷　contrecoup injury
对端并生/對端并生　telobiosis
对耳轮/對耳輪,迎輪　antihelix
对耳轮横沟/對耳輪橫溝　transverse groove of antihelix
对耳轮脚/對耳輪腳　crura of antihelix
对耳轮上脚/對耳輪上腳　superior crura of antihelix
对耳轮弹力纤维性结节/對耳輪彈力纖維變性結節　elastotic nodule of antihelix
对耳轮弹性组织结节/對耳輪彈性組織結節　elastotic nodule of antihelix
对耳轮窝/對耳輪窩　fossa of antihelix
对耳轮下脚/對耳輪下腳　inferior crura of antihelix
对耳屏/對耳屏　antitragus
对耳屏耳轮裂/對耳屏耳輪裂　antitragohelicina fissure
对耳屏肌/對耳屏肌　antitragicus, muscle of antitragus
对耳屏及耳轮间裂/對耳屏及耳輪間裂　fissura antitragohelicina
对二甲氨苯甲酸戊酯/對二甲胺苯甲酸戊酯　amyl p-dimethylamino benzoate
对二甲氨苯甲酸 2-辛酯/對二甲胺苯甲酸 2-辛酯　2-ethylhexyl p-dimethylamino benzoate
对二甲氨基苯甲醛/對二甲胺苯甲醛　paradimethylaminobenzaldehyde
对光敏感的/對光敏感的　photosensitive
对极染色法/兩極染法　bipolar staining
对甲酚/對位甲酚　paracresol
对甲基水杨酸/對木餾油酸,羥基甲苯酸　para-cresotic acid
对角径/[骨盆]對角徑　diagonal conjugate
对角应力/對角應力　diagonal stress
对抗疗法/對抗[治]療法　allopathy
对抗牵伸术/對抗牽伸術　contraextension
对抗牵引/對抗牽引　countertraction
对抗[性]的/拮抗的　antagonistic
对抗药/對抗藥,拮抗劑　antagonistic drug
对口穿刺术/對側穿側　counterpuncture
对口切开/對側切開　contraincision
对流/對流　convection
对流放电/對流放電　convective discharge

对流免疫电泳/對流免疫電泳　counter immunoelectrophoresis
对流热/對流熱　convective heat
对硫磷/對硫磷　parathion
对氯苯氨基丙酸/對氯苯胺基丙酸　para-chlorophenylalanine
对氯苯丁胺/對氯苯丁胺　chlorphentermine
对氯酚/對氯酚　parachlorophenol
对萘酚苯甲醇/對萘酚苯甲醇　p-naphtholbenzein
对内反应作用/內應性　interofection
对偶皮瓣/對偶皮瓣　double transposition skin flap
对胚极/對胚極　abembryonic pole
对屏尖/對屏尖　apex of antitragus
对脐发疽/對臍發疽　contra-umbilicus carbuncle
对羟苯甲酸类/對羥苯甲酸類　parabens
对羟苯羟乙酸/羥基杏仁酸　parahydroxymandelic acid
对羟苯乙酸/對羥基苯乙酸　p-oxyphenylacetic acid
对羟基苯甲酸丙酯/對羥基苯甲酸丙酯　propylparaben
对羟基苯甲酸丁酯/對羥基苯甲酸丁酯　butyl parahydroxybenzoate
对羟基苯甲酸甲酯/[對]羥基苯甲酸甲酯　methylparaben
对羟基苯甲酸乙酯/對羥基苯甲酸乙酯　ethyl parahydroxybenzoate
对切殆/對切殆　end-to-end occlusion
对数期/對數[增殖]期　logarithmic phase
对位缝合/接合缝法　apposition suture
对位交叉构象/對位交叉構象　staggered conformation
对向肌/對向肌,對抗肌　opponens
对斜面夹板/雙斜面夾　double inclined plane splint
对氧磷/對氧磷　paraoxon
对乙酰氨基酚/對乙醯胺基酚　paracetamol
对乙酰氨基水杨酸盐/對乙醯胺基水楊酸鹽　acetyl salicylic acid
对应因子分析/對應因數分析　correspondence factor analysis
对应指长短不均/手指不等長　anisodactyly
对应趾长短不均/脚趾不等長　anisodactyly
对映体过量/對映體過量　enantiomeric excess, EE
对映现象/對映現象　enantiotropy
对映性变化/對映體變化　enantiotropic change
对映选择性/對映選擇性　enantioselectivity
对映[异构]体/對映[異構]體　enantiomer
对掌成形术/對掌成形術　opponensplasty
对照动物/對照動物　control animal

对照品/對照物質 reference substance
对照生药/對照生藥 authentic crude drug
对照实验/對照實驗 control experiment
对照液/校核液 control solution
对症取穴/對症取穴 symptomatic point selection
对跖的/對蹠的 antipodal
兑端/兌端 duiduan, DU27
兑入/兌入 mix
蹲踞姿势/蹲踞姿勢 squatting posture
蹲位/蹲位,屈膝蹲踞姿勢 kneeling-squatting position
炖[制]/燉 stewing
钝剥离/鈍器組織分離 blunt dissection
钝钩/鈍鉤 blunthook
钝锯齿状/鈍鋸齒狀 crenation
钝锯齿状红细胞/皺縮紅血球 burr cell
钝伤/鈍傷 blunt trauma
钝痛/鈍痛 dull pain
钝头扁平苔藓/鈍頭扁平苔藓 lichen planus obtusus
钝缘支动脉/鈍緣支動脈 obtuse marginal artery
盾甲状疝/盾甲狀疝 thyroidal hernia
盾式分布/盾狀[之陰毛]分布 escutcheon
盾状毛/盾狀毛 peltate hair
盾状胸/盾狀胸 shield-like chest
顿挫痘疮/頓挫痘瘡 variola abortiva
顿挫型/頓挫型 abortive form
顿挫型带状疱疹/頓挫型帶狀皰疹 abortive zoster
顿挫性脊髓痨/頓挫性脊髓癆 abortive tabes
顿挫性收缩/頓挫收縮 aborted systole
顿服/頓服 draught, administered at draught
顿咳/頓欬 whooping cough
顿咳·肺脾气虚证/頓欬·肺脾氣虛證 whooping cough with pattern of qi deficiency of lung and spleen
顿咳·肺阴虚证/頓欬·肺陰虛證 whooping cough with pattern of lung yin deficiency
顿咳·痰火阻肺证/頓欬·痰火阻肺證 whooping cough with pattern of phlegm-fire blocking lung
顿咳·邪犯肺卫证/頓欬·邪犯肺衛證 whooping cough with pattern of pathogen invading lung-defense phase
多巴胺/多巴胺 dopamine
多巴胺激动剂/多巴胺激動劑 dopamine agonist
多巴胺拮抗剂/多巴胺拮抗劑 dopamine antagonist
多巴胺能神经元/多巴胺能神經元 dopaminergic neuron
多巴胺β羟化酶/多巴胺β羥化酶 dopamine beta-hydroxylase

多巴胺摄取抑制剂/多巴胺攝取抑制劑 dopamine uptake inhibitor
多巴胺受体/多巴胺受體 dopamine receptor
多巴胺药/多巴胺藥 dopamine agent
多巴胺乙型羟化酶缺乏/多巴胺乙型羥化酶缺乏 dopamine beta-hydroxylase deficiency
多巴酚丁胺/多巴酚丁胺 dobutamine
多巴脱羧酶/多巴色素去羧基酶 dopa decarboxylase
多倍体/多倍體 polyploid
多倍体细胞/多倍體細胞 polyploid cell
多倍性/多倍性 polyploidy
多鼻窦切除术/多鼻旁竇切除術 polysinusectomy
多鼻窦炎/多鼻竇炎 polysinusitis
多边形的/多角的 polygonal
多变量校正/多變量校正 multivariate calibration
多病同发/多發病 polypathia
多波长直线回归法/多波長線性回歸法 multi-wavelength linear regression method
多波脉/多脈搏 polycrotic pulse
多不饱和脂肪酸/多不飽和脂肪酸 polyunsaturated fatty acid
多层片剂/多層錠劑 multilayer tablet
多层脂质体/多層微脂粒 multilamelar liposome
多产妇/多產婦 grand multipara
多重人格/多重人格 multiple personality
多重人格障碍/多重人格障礙 multiple personality disorder
多处创伤/多處創傷 multiple trauma
多处切断术/多處截斷術 multiple amputation
多处痛觉/複痛覺 polyalgesia
多次[曝光]X射线照相术/複式X光照相術 polisography
多次内反射/多次内反射 multiple internal reflection, MIR
多次肾移植/多次腎移植 multiple renal transplantation
多次行经/多次行經,月經次數增多 plurimenorrhea
多簇受体/多簇受體 pluriceptor
多蛋白复合物/多蛋白複合物 multiprotein complexes
多氮化合物/多氮化合物 polyazin
多导电极/多導電極 multilead electrode
多道睡眠描记术/多種睡眠描記法 polysomnography
多底物类似物/多酶受質類似物 multisubstrate analog
多动秽语综合征/多動穢語症候群 tourette syndrome

多动脉炎/多發性動脈炎　polyarteritis
多动脉炎肾病/多動脈炎腎病　polyarteritic nephropathy
多窦炎/多竇炎　polysinuitis
多度悬胶[体]/多種懸液，複懸液　polysuspensoid
多恩-休格曼试验/道蘇氏試驗　Dorn-Sugarman test
多尔心室成形术/多爾心室成形術　Dor remodeling ventriculoplasty
多耳[畸形]/多耳畸形　pleonotia
多发对称性脂肪瘤病/多發對稱性脂肪瘤病　multiple symmetric lipomatosis
多发伤/多發傷　multiple injury
多发神经炎性精神病/多種神經炎性精神病　polyneuritic psychosis
多发性/多發性　multiplex
多发性斑状色素沉着症/多發性斑狀色素沈著症　pigmentation macularis multiplex
多发性病变/多發性病變　multiple lesions
多发性错构瘤综合征/多發性錯構瘤症候群，多發性缺陷瘤症候群　multiple hamartoma syndrome, cowden syndrome
多发性对称性脂肪瘤样病/多發性對稱性脂肪瘤樣病　multiple symmetrical lipomatosis
多发性梗塞性痴呆/多發性腦梗塞癡呆　multi-infarct dementia
多发性骨髓瘤/多發性骨髓瘤　multiple myeloma
多发性关节炎/多發性關節炎　multiple arthritis
多发性汗腺脓肿/多發性汗腺膿腫　multiple sweat gland abscess
多发性肌炎/多肌炎　polymyositis
多发性畸形/多發性畸形　multiple abnormalities
多发性静脉扩张/多發性靜脈擴張　multiple phlebectasia
多发性卡普西出血性血管瘤/Kaposi 氏多發性出血性血管瘤　multiple hemorrhagic hemangioma of Kaposi
多发性口面糜烂性外胚层病/多腔性糜爛性外胚層病　ectodermosis erosiva pluriorificialis
多发性毛囊周围性纤维瘤/多發性毛囊周圍性纖維瘤　multiple perifollicular fibroma
多发性毛盘状瘤/多發性毛盤狀瘤　multiple trichodiscoma
多发性囊状结核性骨炎/多發性囊狀結核性骨炎　osteitis tuberculosa multiplex cystica
多发性脑梗死性痴呆/多發性腦梗死性癡呆　multiinfarct dementia
多发性内分泌瘤病/多發性內分泌瘤病　multiple endocrine neoplasia
多发性内分泌肿瘤/多發性內分泌腫瘤　multiple endocrine neoplasis
多发性内分泌肿瘤综合征/多發性內分泌腫瘤症候群　multiple endocrine neoplasia syndrome
多发性黏液瘤病/多發性黏液瘤　myxomatosis
多发性[皮下]小脂瘤/多數小脂瘤病　polymicrolipomatosis
多发性皮脂囊肿/多發性皮脂囊腫　steatocystoma multiplex
多发性丘疹状毛发上皮瘤/多發性丘疹狀毛髮上皮瘤　trichoepithelioma papulosum multiplex
多发性色素斑综合征/多發性色素斑症候群　multiple lentigines syndrome
多发性上皮瘤/多發性上皮瘤　multiple epithelioma
多发性神经病/多發性神經病　polyneuropathy
多发性神经根病/多發性神經根病　polyradiculopathy
多发性神经根神经病/多神經根神經病　polyradiculoneuropathy
多发性特发性出血性肉瘤/多發性特發性出血肉瘤　multiple idiopathic hemorrhagic sarcoma
多发性外生骨疣/多發外生骨疣　multiple exostosis
多发性网状青斑/多發性網狀青斑　asphyxia reticularis multiplex
多发性纤维毛囊瘤/多發性纖維毛囊瘤　multiple fibrofolliculomas
多发性纤维上皮增生/多發性纖維上皮增生　multiple fibroepithelial hyperplasia
多发性遗传性外生骨疣/多發性遺傳性外生骨疣　multiple hereditary exostose
多发性硬化/多發性硬化　multiple sclerosis
多发性脂肪瘤/多發性脂肪瘤　multiple lipoma
多房棘球绦虫/多房性孢囊蟲　echinococcus multilocularis
多房棘球蚴病/多房棘球蚴病　echinococcosis multilocularis
多房水疱/複合水泡，複室性水泡　compound vesicle
多房性/多房的　multilocular
多房性囊性肾瘤/多房性囊性腎瘤　multilocular cystic nephroma
多房性囊肿/複合囊腫，多房囊腫　compound cyst
多房性膀胱/多房性膀胱　multilocular bladder
多分散胶体/多分散膠體，複分散質　polydispersoid
多酚/多酚　polyphenol
多睾者/多睾者　polyorchis
多睾[畸形]/多睾[畸形]　polyorchidism
多根的/多根的　multirooted
多功能程控/多功能程式控制　multiprogrammability

多功能美容机/多功能美容機　multifunctional cosmetic instrument
多股丝/多股絲　multistrand wire
多骨的/多骨的　polyostotic
多骨膜炎/多骨膜炎　polyperiostitis
多骨纤维发育不良/多骨纖維發育不良　polyostotic fibrous dysplasia
多关节的/多數關節的　polyarthric
多关节痛/多發性關節痛　polyarthralgia
多关节痛风/多數關節痛風　polyarticular gout
多关节炎/多關節炎　polyarthritis
多管听诊器/多管聽診器　stethopolyscope
多汗[症]/多汗[症]　hyperhidrosis
多核白细胞/多核白血球　polycyte
多核苷酸/多核苷酸　polynucleotide
多核苷酸酶/多核苷酸酶　polynucleotidase
多核苷酸腺苷酰转移酶/多核苷酸腺苷醯轉移酶　polynucleotide adenylyltransferase
多核糖核苷酸类/多核糖核苷酸類　polyribonucleotides
多核糖体/多核糖體　polyribosome
多核细胞/多核細胞　polykaryocyte
多花水仙碱/多花水仙鹼　tazettine
多滑膜炎/多滑膜炎　polysynovitis
多化学品过敏/多化學品過敏　multiple chemical sensitivity
多环芳香族烃/多環芳香族烴　polycystic aromatic hydrocarbons
多环化合物/多環化合物　polycyclic compound
多黄卵/多黃卵　megalecithal ovum
多肌病/多肌病變　polymyopathy
多肌麻痹/多肌麻痺　polyplegia
多肌痛/多肌痛　polymyalgia
多肌阵挛病/多肌陣攣病　polyclonia
多基因/多基因　polygene
多基因病/多基因病　polygenic disease
多基因的/多基因的　polygenic
多基因高胆固醇血症/多基因性高膽固醇血症　polygenic hypercholesterolemia
多基因遗传/多基因遺傳　polygenic inheritance
多基因族/多基因族　multigene family
多极成神经细胞/多極神經母細胞　multipolar neuroblast
多极电凝[术]/多極電凝[術]　multipolar electrocoagulation
多极神经元/多極神經元　multipolar neuron
多极有丝分裂/多心性核分裂　multicentric mitosis
多棘慢复合波/多棘慢複合波　multiple spike and slow wave complex
多脊髓畸形症/多脊椎畸形　polydysspondylism
多甲[畸形]/多爪甲畸形,多甲症　polyonychia
多价变态反应/多價性過敏　polyvalent allergy
多价抗血清/多價抗血清　polyvalent antiserum
多价血清/多價血清　multipartial serum
多价疫苗/多價疫苗　polyvalent vaccine
多腱滑囊炎/多肌腱滑囊炎　polytendinobursitis
多腱炎/多腱炎　polytendinitis
多浆膜炎/多發性漿膜炎　multiple serositis
多焦点镜片/多焦點鏡片　multifocal lens
多角形细胞/多角細胞　polygonal cell
多节指/多節指　hyperphalangia
多节趾/多節趾　hyperphalangia
多经取穴/多經取穴　point selection form multiple channels, point selection form multiple meridians
多精入卵/多精入卵　polyspermy
多聚蛋白质类/多聚蛋白質類　polyproteins
多聚谷氨酸/聚穀氨酸　polyglutamic acid
多聚甲醛/三聚甲醛　paraformaldehyde
多聚甲醛干髓剂/多聚甲醛乾髓劑　paraformaldehyde pulp mummifying agent
多聚酶/聚合酶　polymerase
多聚嘧啶区结合蛋白质/多聚嘧啶區結合蛋白質　polypyrimidine tract-binding protein
多聚体/聚合物體　polymer
多菌传染/多種感染,多菌性感染　multi-infection
多克隆活化因子/多克隆活化因子　polyclonal activator
多克隆抗淋巴细胞血清/多克隆抗淋巴細胞血清　polyclonal antilymphocyte serum
多克隆抗体/多克隆抗體　polyclonal antibody
多孔可塑性夹/多孔可塑性夾　poroplastic splint
多孔菌素/多孔蕈素,松蕈素　polyporin
多孔细胞/有孔細胞　porous cell
多孔性/多孔性　porosity
多块状物的/多處小瘤的　lumpy
多勒病/Dohle氏病　Dohle disease
多肋切断膈切开术/多肋式膈切開術　polypleurodiaphragmotomy
多类寄生虫感染/多種寄生蟲病　polyparasitism
多列睫/多列睫,多行睫　polystichia
多裂肌/多裂肌　multifidi, musculi multifidi
多磷酸盐类/多磷酸鹽類　polyphosphates
多瘤/多瘤　polyoma
多瘤病毒/多瘤病毒　polyomavirus
多瘤病毒感染/多瘤病毒感染　polyomavirus infection

多瘤病毒转化抗原/多瘤病毒轉化抗原 polyomavirus transforming antigen
多卵种/多卵種 polyovulatory species
多氯联苯化合物/多氯聯苯化合物 polychlorinated biphenyls
多毛/多毛症,毛髮過多 hypertrichosis
多毛的/多毛的,被毛的 hairy, pilous
多毛耳/多毛耳 hairy ear
多毛畸胎/多毛畸胎 hair monster
多毛细胞白血病/髮狀細胞白血病 hairy cell leukemia
多毛真菌酸/多毛真菌酸 hirsutic acid
多毛症/多毛症 hypertrichosis, hirsutism
多毛肘/多毛之手肘 hairy elbow
多梅毒疹/多梅毒疹 polysyphilide
多媒体/多媒體 multimedia
多酶复合物/多酶複合物 multienzyme complex
多寐[病]/多寐[病] somnolence
多寐·脾气虚证/多寐·脾氣虛證 somnolence with pattern of spleen qi deficiency
多寐·湿困脾胃证/多寐·濕困脾胃證 somnolence with pattern of dampness retaining in spleen and stomach
多寐·痰浊闭阻证/多寐·痰濁閉阻證 somnolence with pattern of blockade of phlegm-turbidity
多寐·阳气虚衰证/多寐·陽氣虛衰證 somnolence with pattern of yang qi exhaustion
多寐·瘀血闭阻证/多寐·瘀血閉阻證 somnolence with pattern of blockade of static blood
多梦/多夢 dreamfulness, dreaminess
多面体的/多面狀的 polyhedral
多面形细胞/多面形細胞 polyhedral cell
多敏感性/多種敏感性 multisensitivity
多拇[指]畸形/多拇[指]畸形 multipollicalism
多纳特-兰兹泰纳试验/道-蘭二氏試驗 Donath-Landsteiner test
多囊胞性卵巢综合征/多囊胞性卵巢症候群 polycystic ovary syndrome
多囊的/多囊的 polycystic
多囊肝/多囊肝 polycystic liver
多囊瘤/多囊瘤 polycystoma
多囊卵巢病/多囊胞性卵巢疾患 polycystic ovary disease
多囊卵巢综合征/多囊[胞性]卵巢症候群 polycystic ovarian syndrome
多囊卵巢综合征·肝经湿热证/多囊卵巢症候群·肝經濕熱證 polycystic ovary syndrome with damp-heat in liver channel
多囊卵巢综合征·气滞血瘀证/多囊卵巢症候群·氣滯血瘀證 polycystic ovary syndrome with qi stagnation and blood stasis
多囊卵巢综合征·肾虚证/多囊卵巢症候群·腎虛證 polycystic ovary syndrome with kidney deficiency
多囊卵巢综合征·痰湿阻滞证/多囊卵巢症候群·痰濕阻滯證 polycystic ovary syndrome with stagnation and blockade of phlegm-damp
多囊肾/多囊腎 polycystic kidney, multilocular cyst of kidney
多囊肾疾病/多囊腎疾病 polycystic kidney disease
多囊性肾发育不良/多囊性腎發育不良 multicystic dysplastic kidney
多囊性纤维性发育不良/多囊性纖維性結構不全 polycystic fibrous dysplasia
多囊状膀胱/多囊狀膀胱 sacculated bladder
多瑙河地区流行性肾病/多瑙河地區流行性腎病 Danubian epidemic nephropathy
多内分泌腺瘤病/多内分泌腺瘤病 multiple endocrine adenomatosis
多能病毒/多能病毒 pluripotent virus
多能的/多能的,有多種作用的 pluripotent
多能血清/多作用抗毒血清 polyerg
多能造血干细胞/多潛能造血幹細胞 pluripotential hematopoietic stem cell, pluripotential hemopoietic stem cell
多能状态/多能狀態 pluripotent state
多年生的/常年的 perennial
多黏菌素/多黏桿菌素 polymyxin
多尿[期]/多尿[症] polyuria, diuresis stage
多尿型肾[功能]衰竭/多尿型腎[功能]衰竭 polyuric renal failure
多尿症/多尿症 hyperuresis
多诺霍综合征/Donohue氏症候群 Donohue syndrome
多潘立酮/多潘立酮 Domperidone
多泡体/多泡體 multivesicular body
多泡脂肪细胞/多泡脂肪細胞 multilocular adipose cell
多胚/多胚,多胎 polyembryony
多片切片机/多片切片機 polymicrotome
多普勒超声/杜卜勒超音波 Doppler ultrasound
多普勒超声检查/杜卜勒超聲檢查 Doppler ultrasonography
多普勒超声心动描记术/杜卜勒超聲心動描記術 Doppler echocardiography
多普勒超声血流探测仪/杜卜勒超聲血流探測儀 Doppler ultrasonic blood stream detector

多普勒激光血流探测仪/杜卜勒雷射血流探測儀 Doppler laser blood stream detector
多普勒效应/杜卜勒效應 Doppler effect
多器官功能衰竭/多器官功能衰竭 multiple organ failure
多器官功能障碍综合征/多器官功能障礙症候群 multiple organ dysfunction syndrome
多器官联合移植/多器官聯合移植 combined multiple organ transplantation
多[潜]能干细胞/多[潛]能幹細胞 multipotent stem cell, pluripotent stem cell
多[潜]能细胞/多潛能細胞 pluripotent cell
多羟环己烷/多羥環己烷 cyclotol
多X染色体综合征/多X染色體症候群 poly X syndrome
多染[色]性变性/多染細胞變性 polychromatophilic degeneration
多染色质状态/體細胞多倍性 polysomaty
多染细胞/多染細胞,多色細胞 polychromatophil cell
多染性/多染性 polychromatophilia
多染性成红细胞/嗜多色素性母紅血球 polychromatophilic erythroblast
多染[性]的/多染的,嗜多種色素的 polychromatophilic
多染性红细胞/[嗜]多色性紅血球 polychromatic erythrocyte
多染[性]细胞/多染細胞 polychromatophil
多染[性]细胞增多/多染細胞增多 polychromatosis
多染[性]细胞增多症/多染細胞增多症 polychromatocytosis
多人指导心理疗法/多人指導心理療法 multiple psychotherapy
多柔比星/多柔比星 doxorubicin
多乳房/多乳房 multimammas
多乳房病/多乳房病,多乳頭病 supernumerary breast
多乳头/多乳頭 supernumerary nipple
多软骨病/多軟骨病 polychondropathia
多软骨炎/多軟骨炎 polychondritis
多塞平/多塞平 doxepin
多色的/多色的 polychromatic, polychromic
多色素性黄疸/多色性黃疸 pleochromic jaundice
多色细胞/多色細胞 polychromatic cell
多色[现象]/雜染性 pantochromism
多色性角化不全/多樣性角化不全 parakeratosis variegata
多杀巴斯德菌/敗血性巴斯德拉菌 Pasteurella multocida
多沙普仑/多沙普侖 doxapram
多沙唑嗪/多沙唑嗪 doxazosin
多神经病/多[發性]神經病 polyneuropathy
多神经根神经炎/多神經根神經炎 polyradiculoneuritis
多神经根炎/多神經根炎 polyradiculitis
多神经肌炎/多神經肌炎 polyneuromyositis
多神经痛/多神經痛 polyneuralgia
多神经炎/多發性神經炎 multiple neuritis
多神经炎的/多神經炎的 polyneuritic
多神经炎型遗传性运动失调/多發性神經炎型動作失調性遺傳病 heredopathia atactica polyneuritiformis
多食/貪食 polyphagia
多室模型/多室模型 multi-compartment model
多手[畸形]/多手畸形 polycheiria
多受体/多受體 polyceptor
多塑性的/多塑性的 polyplastic
多塑性细胞/多塑性細胞 polyplastic cell
多胎/多胎,一胎多子 multiplets, multifetation
多胎产/多胎生產 multiple birth
多胎产后代/多胎產後代 multiple birth offspring
多胎儿/多胎兒 multiple fetuses
多胎妊娠/多胎妊娠 multiple pregnancy
多胎妊娠减少/多胎妊娠減少 multifetal pregnancy reduction
多态性/多態性 polymorphism
多态性信息含量/多態性資訊含量 polymorphism information content
多肽/多肽 polypeptide
多肽毒综合征/多肽毒症候群 polypeptidotoxique syndrome
多肽类药物/多肽類藥物 polypeptide drug
多肽酶/多肽酶 polypeptidase
多肽脑脊液症/脊液含多肽症 polypeptidorrhachia
多肽血[症]/多肽血症 polypeptidemia
多糖/多醣 polysaccharide
多糖包被/多醣包被 glycocalyx
多糖类/多醣類 polysaccharides
多糖裂合酶类/多醣裂合酶類 polysaccharidelyases
多体的/多體的 polysomic
多体畸胎/多體畸胎 polysomatous monster
多体[畸形]/多體畸形 polysomia
多体性/多體性 polysomy
多萜/多萜 polyterpene
多萜醇/多萜醇 dolichol
多萜醇-磷酸甘露糖/多萜醇-磷酸甘露糖 dolichol

monophosphate mannose
多萜醇磷酸酯类/多萜醇磷酸酯類 dolichol phosphates
多瞳/多瞳病 polycoria
多头绷带/多頭繃帶,多尾帶 many-tailed bandage, scultetus bandage
多头绷带法/多頭繃帶法 multitailed bandaging
多头肌/多頭肌 multicipital muscle
多头绦虫属/多頭條蟲 Multiceps
多头蚴病/共尾條蟲病 coenurosis
多腿畸胎/多腿畸胎 polyscelus
多唾/多唾 profuse spittle
多维检测/多維檢測 multidimensional detection
多西环素/去氧羥四環素 doxycycline
多西拉敏/多西拉敏 doxylamine
多希肢端色素沉着/Dohi 氏肢端色素沈著症 acropigmentation of Dohi
多烯类抗生素/多烯類抗生素 polyene antibiotic
多烯色素/多烯色素 polyene pigment
多系统萎缩/多系統萎縮 multiple system atrophy
多细胞层/多細胞層 cell rich zone
多细胞动物病/多細胞動物病 metazoal disease
多细胞动物的/多細胞動物的 metazoal
多细胞动物感染/多細胞動物感染 metazoal infestation
多细胞体/细胞簇 multicell
多细胞腺/多[細]胞腺 multicellular gland
多涎/多涎 sialism
多线染色体/多軸絲束染色體 polytene chromosome
多腺病/多腺病 polyadenopathy
多腺苷二磷酸核糖聚合酶类/聚 ADP 核糖聚合酶類 poly(ADP-ribose) polymerases
多腺苷酸化/多腺苷酸化 polyadenylation
多腺瘤/多腺瘤 polyadenoma
多腺瘤病/多腺瘤病 polyadenomatosis
多腺体自身免疫综合征/多腺體性自體免疫症候群 polyglandular autoimmune syndrome
多腺性的/多腺的 pluriglandular
多腺性综合征/多腺性症候群 pluriglandular syndrome
多腺炎/多腺炎 polyadenitis
多相反应/多相反應 heterogeneous reaction
多相筛查/多相普檢 multiphasic screening
多小脑回/小腦迴過多 polymicrogyria
多效蒸馏水器/多效蒸餾水器 multiple-effect still
多形的/多形的,複式的 polymorphous
多形核白细胞/多形核白血球 polymorphonuclear leukocyte
多形核的/多形核的 polymorphonuclear
多形核细胞/多形核細胞 polymorphonuclear cell
多形红斑/多形紅斑 erythema multiforme
多形淋巴瘤/多形性淋巴瘤 pleomorphic lymphoma
多形态的/多形態的 polymorphic
多形退行发育/多相退行發育 polyphasic anaplasia
多形细胞/多形細胞 polymorphous cell
多形[细胞]层/多形[細胞]層 polymorphic layer
多形性/多形性 pleomorphic, pleomorphous
多形性成胶质细胞病/多形性神經膠質母細胞瘤 glioblastoma multiforme
多形性低度恶性腺癌/多形性低度惡性腺癌 polymorphous low-grade adenocarcinoma
多形性红斑/多形性紅斑 erythema multiforme
多形性类天疱疮/多形性類天皰瘡 pleomorphous pemphigoid
多形性日光疹/多形性日光疹 polymorphic sun light eruption
多形性肉芽肿/多形性肉芽腫 granuloma multiforme
多形性网状内皮细胞增生症/多形性網狀內皮細胞增生症 polymorphic reticuloendotheliosis
多形性网状细胞增生病/多形網狀細胞增生症 polymorphic reticulosis
多形性纤维瘤/多形性纖維瘤 pleomorphic fibroma
多形性腺瘤/多形腺瘤 pleomorphic adenoma
多形性疹/多形性疹 polymorphous eruption
多型的/多型的 multipartial
多性杂种/複性雜種,多對基因雜種 polyhybrid
多溴联苯类/多溴聯苯類 polybrominated biphenyls
多血管炎/多血管炎 polyangiitis
多血[症]/多血病 polyemia
多言癖/多言癖 lalorrhea
多言[症]/多言症 polyphrasia
多阳之人/多陽之人 person with predominant yang
多样性类银屑病/多樣性類乾癬 parapsoriasis variegata
多药抗药性/多種抗藥性 multiple drug resistance
多药耐药相关蛋白质类/多藥耐藥相關蛋白質類 multidrug resistance-associated proteins
多叶胎盘/多葉胎盤 placenta multipartita
多因素病/多因素障礙 multifactorial disorder
多因素决定/多因素決定 overdetermination
多因子病/多因子病 multifactorial disease
多因子遗传/多因子遺傳 multifactorial inheritance
多阴之人/多陰之人 person with predominant yin
多用夹板/多用夾板 multifunctional splint
多余骨/多餘骨 supernumerary bone

多羽肌/多羽肌,複羽狀肌　multipennate muscle
多语症/多語症　talking sickness
多元分析/多元分析　multivariate analysis
多元论者/多元論者　polyphyletist
多元酸/多價酸　polyacid
多原发性肿瘤/多原發性腫瘤　multiple primary neoplasms
多源性羧化酶缺乏/多源性羧化酶缺乏　multiple carboxylase deficiency
多源性心律/多源性心律　multifocal rhythm
多掌骨[畸形]/多掌骨　polymetacarpia
多枝的/分枝状的　ramous
多肢畸胎/多肢畸胎　polymelus
多肢[畸形]/多肢[畸形]　polymelia
多脂树脂/多脂樹脂　polyester resin
多脂皂/多脂肥皂　superfatted soap
多脂猪病/油豬病　greasy pig disease
多跖骨[畸形]/多蹠骨　polymetatarsia
多指/多指　polydactyly
多指并指[畸形]/多指并指畸形　polysyndactyly
多指畸形/多指畸形　hyperdactyly
多趾/多趾　polydactyly
多趾并趾[畸形]/多趾并趾畸形　polysyndactyly
多趾畸形/多趾畸形　hyperdactyly
多酯类/多酯類　polyesters
多中心网状[内皮系统]组织细胞瘤病/内皮系统多中心性網狀組織細胞瘤病　multicentric reticulohistiocytosis
多中心性/多中心性　multicentricity
多中心研究/多中心研究　multicenter study
多种波动描记器/多種描記器　polygraph
多种波动[描记]图/多種描記圖　polygram
多种发育障碍/多種發育障礙　polydysplasia
多种分泌障碍/多種內分泌障礙　pluridyscrinia

多种菌感染/多種菌感染　polyinfection
多[种可]凝集性/多凝集性　polyagglutinability
多种耐药结核/多種耐藥結核　multidrug-resistant tuberculosis
多[种]内分泌腺腺瘤病/多種內分泌腺腺瘤病　polyendocrinoma
多种能力/多種能力,多種作用　pluripotentiality
多种维生素缺乏病/多種維生素缺乏病　polyavitaminosis
多种血细胞减少/多種血球減少,成形不全性貧血　pluricytopenia
多种药物疗法/雜湊給藥,合并給藥　polypharmacy
多种语言能力/多種語言能力　multilingualism
多种增生不良型大疱性表皮松解症/多種發育異常性水皰性表皮鬆解症　epidermolysis bullosa polydysplastica
多轴突[神经]细胞/多軸突細胞　polyaxon
多轴诊断系统/多軸診斷系統　multiaxial system
多足虫/多足蟲　myriapod
多足[畸形]/多足[畸形]　polypodia
多组分光谱分析/多組分光譜分析法　multicomponent spectrophotometry
夺获心搏/擄獲搏動　capture beat
夺气/奪氣　faint low voice
堕胎/堕胎　induced abortion
堕胎的/堕胎的　abortive
堕胎·胎堕不全证/堕胎·胎堕不全證　early abortion with incomplete abortion pattern
堕胎·胎殒难留证/堕胎·胎殞難留證　early abortion with dead fetus pattern
堕胎药/堕胎藥　abortifacient, abortifacient agents
堕胎者/堕胎者　abortionist
惰性气体/惰性氣體　inert gas
惰性气体麻醉/惰性氣體麻醉　inert gas narcosis

E

阿胶/阿膠　ass hide glue
阿胶黄连汤/阿膠黃連湯　ass hide glue and coptis decoction, ejiao huanglian decoction
俄国春夏脑炎病毒/俄國春夏腦炎病毒　Russian spring-summer encephalitis virus
莪术/莪朮　zedoary rhizome
锇处理/加锇酸作用　osmification
锇化合物/錒化合物　osmium compound
锇酸/錒酸　osmic acid
锇酸盐/錒酸鹽　osmate
鹅不食草/鵝不食草　small centipeda herb
鹅膏菌素类/鵝膏蕈類　amanitins
鹅膏蕈氨酸/鵝膏蕈胺酸　ibotenic acid
鹅肌肽/鵝肌肽　anserine
鹅颈畸形/鵝頸畸形　swan neck deformity
鹅口疮/鵝口瘡　oral thrush, white mouth, thrush
鹅口疮·热毒攻喉证/鵝口瘡·熱毒攻喉證　thrush with pattern of heat-toxin attacking throat
鹅口疮·心脾积热证/鵝口瘡·心脾積熱證　thrush with pattern of accumulated heat in heart and spleen
鹅口疮·虚火上浮证/鵝口瘡·虛火上浮證　thrush with upward floating of deficient fire
鹅口疮状心白斑/鵝口瘡狀心白斑　thrush breast
鹅卵石状苔藓/鵝卵石狀苔蘚　pebbly lichenification
鹅牛磺胆酸/鵝牛磺膽酸　chenotaurocholic acid
鹅皮样变/鵝皮斑　cutis anserina
鹅脱氧胆酸/鵝去氧膽酸　chenodeoxycholic acid
鹅掌风/鵝掌風　goose-web wind, tinea manuum
鹅掌风·风湿蕴肤证/鵝掌風·風濕蘊膚證　goose-web wind with pattern of wind-dampness amassing in skin
鹅掌风·血虚风燥证/鵝掌風·血虛風燥證　goose-web wind with pattern of wind-dryness due to blood deficiency
鹅掌样病/鵝掌狀手病　anserine disease
鹅脂/鵝脂　adeps anserinus
鹅足丛/鵝足叢　anserine plexus
鹅足囊/鵝足囊　anserine bursa
蛾皮炎/蛾皮炎　moth dermatitis
额板障静脉/額板障靜脈　frontal diploic vein, vena diploica frontalis
额鼻缝/額鼻縫　frontonasal suture
额鼻管/額鼻管　frontonasal duct
额鼻突/額鼻突　frontonasal prominence, nasofrontal process
额部痤疮/額部痤瘡　acne frontalis
额部发缘脱发/額部髮緣禿髮　alopecia liminaris frontalis
额部联胎/額部連胎　metopagus
额部入路/額部入路　frontal approach
额的/額的　frontal
额顶岛盖/額頂[島]蓋　Operculum frontoparietale（拉）
额顶入路/額頂入路　frontoparietal approach
额顶叶岛盖/額頂葉島蓋　frontoparietal operculum
额豆[状]核性失语/額豆狀核失語症　frontolenticular aphasia
额窦/額竇　frontal sinus
额窦口/額竇口　aperture of frontal sinus
额窦切开术/額竇切開術　frontal sinusotomy
额窦痛/額竇痛　metopantralgia
额窦炎/額竇炎　sinusitis frontalis
额窦中隔/額竇中隔　septum of frontal sinus
额发/額髮　forelock
额缝/額縫　frontal suture, metopic suture
额缝点/額縫點　metopion
额腹/額腹　frontal belly
额沟/額溝　frontal groove
额骨/額骨　frontal bone
额骨盲孔/額骨盲孔　foramen caecum ossis frontalis
额骨内板增生病/額骨內肥厚　hyperostosis frontalis interna
额骨内面/額骨內面　internal surface of frontal bone
额横皱纹/額橫皺紋　transverse frown line
额后静脉/額後靜脈　posterior frontal vein
额后内侧静脉/額後內側靜脈　posteromedial frontal vein
额肌/額肌　frontal muscle
额肌瓣悬吊术/額肌瓣懸吊術　frontalis muscle flap suspension operation
额极/額極　frontal pole

额嵴/額嵴 frontal crest
额角/額角 frontal angle
额结节/額結節 frontal tuber, frontal eminence
额静脉/額靜脈 frontal vein
额孔/額孔 frontal foramen
额泪缝/額淚縫 frontolacrimal suture
额鳞/額鱗 frontal squama
额梅毒疹/梅毒冠,额部梅毒疹 corona veneris
额面/額[平]面 frontal plane
额内侧回/額內側迴 medial frontal gyrus
额颞点/額顳點 frontotemporale
额颞入路/額顳入路 frontotemporal approach
额旁1线/額旁1線 epangxian I, MS2, lateral line 1 of forehead
额旁2线/額旁2線 epangxian II, MS3, lateral line 2 of forehead
额旁3线/額旁3線 epangxian III, MS4, lateral line 3 of forehead
额皮脂溢疹/脂漏冠 corona seborrhoeica
额皮质性失语/額皮質性失語 frontocortical aphasia
额前骨/額前骨 prefrontal bone
额前静脉/額前靜脈 anterior frontal vein
额前内侧静脉/額前內側靜脈 anteromedial frontal vein
额钳/額鉗 frontal forcep
额桥束/額葉橋腦束 frontopontine tract
额切迹/額切跡 frontal notch
额切面/額切面 frontal section
额区/額部 frontal region
额颧缝/額顴縫 frontozygomatic suture
额筛缝/額篩縫 frontoethmoidal suture
额上沟/額上溝 superior frontal sulcus
额上颌缝/額頜縫 frontomaxillary suture
额上回/額上迴 superior frontal gyrus
额神经/額神經 frontal nerve
额痛/額痛 metopodynia
额突/額突 frontal process
额外刺激/額外刺激 extrastimulation
额外甲状旁腺/額外[副]甲狀腺 supernumerary parathyroid gland
额外肾/額外腎,多腎 supernumerary kidney
额外心音/額外心音 extra heart sound
额外牙/額外牙,額外齒 supernumerary tooth
额外肢畸胎/額外肢連胎 melodidymus
额下沟/額下溝 inferior frontal sulcus
额下回/額下迴 inferior frontal gyrus
额下回岛盖部/額下迴島蓋部 opercular part of inferior frontal gyrus
额下回眶部/額下迴眶部 orbital part of inferior frontal gyrus
额下回三角部/額下迴三角部 triangular part of inferior frontal gyrus
额下入路/額下入路 subfrontal approach
额先露/額產式 brow presentation
额眼区/額眼區 eye motor area of frontal lobe
额叶/額葉 frontal lobe
额叶底内侧动脉/額底內側動脈 basomedial frontal artery
额叶底外侧动脉/額底外側動脈 basolateral frontal artery
额叶癫痫/額葉癲癇 frontal lobe epilepsy
额叶后内侧支/額後內側支 posteromedial frontal branch
额叶脓肿/額葉膿腫 frontal abscess
额叶前内侧支/額前內側支 anteromedial frontal branch
额叶前皮质/額葉前皮質 prefrontal cortex
额叶切除术/額葉切除術 frontal lobectomy
额叶性共济失调/額葉性失調 frontal ataxia
额叶中内侧支/額中內側支 mediomedial frontal branch
额缘/額緣 frontal margin
额枕束/額枕束 frontooccipital fasciculus
额支/額支 frontal branch
额指数/額指數 frontal index
额中部的/額中部的 mediofrontal
额中点/額中點 metopion
额中回/額中迴 middle frontal gyrus
额中静脉/額中靜脈 middle frontal vein
额中线/額中線 ezhongxian, MS1, middle line of forehead
额中央内侧静脉/額中央內側靜脈 centromedial frontal vein
额纵皱纹/額縱皺紋 vertical frown line
恶心/噁心 nausea
恶心感觉缺失/噁心感覺缺失 nausea anesthesia
恶心性祛痰药/噁心性祛痰藥 nauseous expectorant
厄尔布麻痹/厄爾布麻痺 Erb paralysis
扼颈性麻醉/扼頸性麻醉 Japanese anesthesia
苊类/苊類 acenaphthenes
呃逆[病]/呃逆[病] hiccup, hiccough
呃逆·脾肾阳虚证/呃逆·脾腎陽虛證 hiccough with pattern of yang deficiency of spleen and kidney
呃逆·脾胃阳虚证/呃逆·脾胃陽虛證 hiccough with pattern of yang deficiency of spleen and stomach
呃逆·气滞痰阻证/呃逆·氣滯痰阻證 hiccough with

呃逆·气滞证/呃逆·氣滯證 hiccough with qi stagnation pattern — pattern of qi stagnation and phlegm blockade
呃逆·气滞证/呃逆·氣滯證 hiccough with qi stagnation pattern
呃逆·实证/呃逆·實證 excessive hiccough
呃逆·胃寒证/呃逆·胃寒證 hiccough with stomach cold pattern
呃逆·胃火证/呃逆·胃火證 hiccough with stomach fire pattern
呃逆·胃阴虚证/呃逆·胃陰虛證 hiccough with pattern of stomach yin deficiency
呃逆·虚证/呃逆·虛證 deficient hiccough
恶变前纤维上皮瘤/癌前期纖維上皮瘤 premalignant fibroepithelioma
恶病质/惡病質,惡液質 cachexia
恶病质的/惡病質的 cachectic
恶病质反应/惡病質反應 cachexia reaction
恶病质腹泻/惡病質性腹瀉 cachectic diarrhea
恶病质[性]痤疮/惡病質性痤瘡 acne cachecticorum
恶病质性坏疽性臁疮/惡病質性壞疽性臁瘡 ecthyma gangrenosum cachecticorum
恶病质性水肿/惡病質性水腫 cachectic edema
恶病质性脱发/惡病質性禿髮 alopecia cachectica
恶病质性幼稚型/惡病質性幼稚型 cachectic infantilism
恶病质性紫癜病/病質性紫癜病 cachectic purpura
恶露/惡露,產後排出物 lochia
恶露不净/惡露不淨 prolonged lochiorrhea
恶露不净·气虚证/惡露不淨·氣虛證 prolonged lochiorrhea with qi deficiency pattern
恶露不净·血热证/惡露不淨·血熱證 prolonged lochiorrhea with blood heat pattern
恶露不净·血瘀证/惡露不淨·血瘀證 prolonged lochiorrhea with blood stasis pattern
恶露不下/惡露不下 lochioschesis
恶露不下·寒凝血瘀证/惡露不下·寒凝血瘀證 lochioschesis with pattern of cold congelation and blood stasis
恶露不下·气血两虚证/惡露不下·氣血兩虛證 lochioschesis with pattern of deficiency of both qi and blood
恶露不下·气滞血瘀证/惡露不下·氣滯血瘀證 lochioschesis with pattern of qi stagnation and blood stasis
恶露过多/惡露過多 lochiorrhagia
恶露细胞/惡露細胞 lochiocyte
恶露障碍/不良惡露 dyslochia
恶露潴留/惡露停滯,惡露不下 lochioschesis
恶脉/惡脈 superficial phlebitis, varicose vein
恶色/惡色 malignant complexion
恶丝虫病/惡絲蟲病 dirofilariasis
恶丝虫属/血直絲蟲屬 Dirofilaria
恶性/惡性 malignancy
恶性白喉/惡性白喉,劇重白喉 diphtheria gravis
恶性变/惡性變 malignant change
恶性成釉细胞瘤/惡性成釉細胞瘤 malignant ameloblastoma
恶性单型性组织细胞瘤/惡性單型性組織細胞瘤 malignant monomorphic histiocytoma
恶性的/惡性的 pernicious
恶性痘疮/惡性痘瘡 variola maligna
恶性多形性腺瘤/惡性多形性腺瘤 malignant pleomorphic adenoma
恶性高热/惡性高溫 malignant hyperthermia
恶性高血压/惡性高血壓 malignant hypertension
恶性黑棘皮病/惡性黑棘皮病 malignant acanthosis nigricans
恶性黑[色]素瘤/惡性黑[色]素瘤 malignant melanoma
恶性黄疸/惡性黃疸,重症黃疸 malignant jaundice
恶性混合瘤/惡性混合瘤 malignant mixed tumor
恶性畸胎瘤/惡性畸胎瘤 malignant teratoma
恶性甲状腺肿/惡性甲狀腺腫 malignant goiter
恶性间日疟/惡性間日瘧 malignant tertian malaria
恶性间质性黑色素瘤/惡性間質性黑色素瘤 malignant mesenchymal melanoma
恶性卡他/惡性卡他 malignant catarrh
恶性卡他热病毒/惡性卡他熱病毒 malignant catarrhal fever virus
恶性溃疡/惡性潰瘍 malignant ulcer
恶性蓝痣/惡性藍痣 malignant blue nevus
恶性类癌综合征/惡性類癌症候群 malignant carcinoid syndrome
恶性淋巴管内皮瘤/惡性淋巴管內皮瘤 malignant lymphangioendothelioma
恶性淋巴瘤/惡性淋巴瘤 malignant lymphoma
恶性淋巴肉芽肿/惡性淋巴肉芽腫 lymphogranuloma malignum
恶性瘤/惡性瘤,癌 malignant tumor
恶性梅毒/惡性梅毒 lues maligna
恶性脓疱/惡性膿皰 malignant pustule
恶性脓皮病/惡性膿皮病 malignant pyoderma
恶性疟[疾]/惡性瘧 pernicious malaria
恶性疟原虫/鐮狀瘧蟲 Plasmodium falciparum
恶性疟原虫感染/惡性瘧原蟲感染 falciparum infection
恶性呕吐/惡性嘔吐 pernicious vomiting

恶性贫血/惡性貧血　pernicious anemia
恶性葡萄胎/侵犯性葡萄胎　chorioadenoma destruens
恶性前的/惡性前的　premalignant
恶性雀斑样痣/惡性小痣　lentigo maligna
恶性雀斑样痣黑[色]素瘤/惡性雀斑樣痣黑[色]素瘤　lentigo maligna melanoma
恶性肉芽瘤杆菌/惡性肉芽瘤桿菌　corynebacterium granulomatis maligni
恶性色素细胞瘤/惡性色素細胞瘤　malignant chromatophoroma
恶性肾小球肾炎/惡性腎絲球腎炎　malignant glomerulonephritis
恶性肾硬化/惡性腎硬化　malignant nephrosclerosis
恶性嗜中性白细胞减少病/惡性嗜中性白血球減少病　malignant neutropenia
恶性水疱/惡性水皰　malignant vesicle
恶性水肿/惡性水腫　malignant edema
恶性胎块/惡性胎塊　mole-malignant
恶性炭疽/惡性炭疽　malignant anthrax
恶性天花/惡性天花　malignant smallpox
恶性透明细胞汗腺腺瘤/惡性明亮細胞汗腺瘤　malignant clear cell hidradenoma
恶性秃发/惡性禿髮　malignant alopecia
恶性突眼/惡性眼球凸出　malignant exophthalmos
恶性外耳道炎/惡性外耳道炎　malignant external otitis
恶性网状内皮细胞增生/惡性網狀內皮細胞增生病　malignant reticulo-endotheliosis
恶性萎缩性丘疹病/惡性萎縮性丘疹　malignant atrophic papulosis
恶性纤维组织细胞瘤/惡性纖維組織細胞瘤　malignant fibrohistiocytoma
恶性腺瘤/惡性腺瘤　malignant adenoma
恶性心内膜炎/惡性心內膜炎　malignant endocarditis
恶性型/惡性型　malignant form
恶性胸腔积液/惡性胸腔積液　malignant pleural effusion
恶性血管内皮[细胞]瘤/惡性血管內皮瘤　malignant hemangioendothelioma
恶性血小板减少症/惡性血小板減少症　malignant thrombocytopenia
恶性循环/惡性循環　vicious circle
恶性咽峡炎/惡性咽峽炎,壞疽性咽峽炎,惡性鎖咽　malignant angina, cynanche maligna
恶性营养不良症/紅孩病　kwashiorkor
恶性紫癜/惡性紫癜病　malignant purpura
恶性组织细胞病/惡性組織細胞病　malignant histiocytic disorder
恶性组织细胞增多症/惡性組織細胞增多　malignant histiocytosis
恶液质/惡液質,體液不調　dyscrasia
恶液质的/惡液質的,體液不調的　dyscrasic
恶液质性骨折/惡液質骨折　dyscrasic fracture
恶中/惡中　noxious parapoplexy
鄂木斯克出血热/鄂木斯克出血熱　Omsk hemorrhagic fever
鄂木斯克出血热病毒/Omsk出血熱病毒　Omsk hemorrhagic fever virus
遏抑物/抑制因子　suppressor
噁二唑类/噁二唑類　oxadiazoles
噁嗪类/噁嗪類　oxazines
噁唑类/噁唑類　oxazoles
噁唑酮/噁唑酮,氧氮雜戊酮　oxazolone
噁唑烷酮类/噁唑烷酮類　oxazolidinones
腭/腭,口蓋　palate
腭凹/腭凹　fovea palatinae
腭扁桃体/腭扁桃體　palatine tonsil
腭扁桃体原基/腭扁桃腺原基　primordium of palatine tonsil
腭不全裂/腭不全裂　incomplete cleft palate
腭侧根/上臼齒之腭側根　palatine root
腭成形术/腭造形術,腭修補術,補腭術　palatoplasty
腭垂/腭垂　uvula
腭垂肌/腭垂肌,懸雍垂肌　musculus uvulae
腭大动脉/腭大動脈　greater palatine artery, major palatine artery
腭大沟/腭大溝　greater palatine sulcus
腭大管/腭大管　greater palatine canal
腭大孔/腭大孔　greater palatine foramen
腭大孔注射法/腭大孔注射法　greater palatine foramen injection
腭大神经/大腭神經　greater palatine nerve
腭的/腭的　palatal
腭动描记器/腭動描記器　palategraph
腭动描记术/腭動描記法　palatography
腭发生/腭發生　palatogenesis
腭帆/腭帆　velum palatinum, palatine velum
腭帆提肌/提腭帆肌　levator veli palatini
腭帆张肌/張腭帆肌　tensor veli palatini
腭帆张肌囊/腭帆張肌囊　bursa of tensor veli palatini
腭帆张肌神经/腭帆張肌神經　nerve to tensor veli palatine, nerve of tensor veli palatini
腭反射/腭反射　palatal reflex

腭缝/腭縫　palatine raphe
腭杆/腭桿　palatal bar
腭沟/腭溝　palatine sulcus, palatine groove
腭骨/腭骨　palatine bone
腭骨垂直板/腭骨垂直板　perpendicular plate of palatine bone
腭骨蝶突/腭骨蝶突　sphenoidal process of palatine bone
腭骨腭沟/腭骨腭溝　palatine groove of palatine bone
腭骨眶突/腭骨眶突　orbital process of palatine bone
腭骨筛嵴/腭骨篩嵴　ethmoidal crest of palatine bone
腭骨水平板/腭骨水平板　horizontal plate of palatine bone
腭骨锥突/腭骨錐突　pyramidal tuberosity of palatine bone
腭横襞/腭橫襞　transverse palatine fold
腭横缝/腭橫縫　transverse palatine suture
腭后点/腭後點　staphylion
腭后神经/腭後神經　posterior palatine nerve
腭肌/腭肌　muscle of palate
腭棘/腭棘　palatine spine
腭嵴/腭嵴　palatine crest
腭腱膜/腭腱膜　palatine aponeurosis
腭降动脉/腭降動脈　descending palatine artery
腭降动脉咽支/腭降動脈咽支　pharyngeal branch of descending palatine artery
腭角/腭角　palatal anguli
腭口属/腭口屬　*Cheiracanthus*
腭口线虫病/腭口線蟲病　gnathostomiasis
腭扩张术/腭擴張術　palatal expansion technique
腭裂/腭裂　cleft palate
腭裂后推修复术/腭裂後推修復術　closure of cleft palate by Dorrance push back operation
腭裂减张切口修复术/腭裂減張切口修復術　closure of cleft palate by von Langenbeck operation
腭裂四瓣修复术/腭裂四瓣修復術　closure of cleft palate by Wardill four-flap operation
腭裂系列治疗/腭裂系列治療　cleft palate team approach
腭裂修复术/腭縫合術　palatorrhaphy
腭裂语音/腭裂語音　cleft palate speech
腭隆凸/腭隆凸　palatine tori
腭麻痹/腭麻痺　palatoplegia
腭面/腭面　palatal surface, palatine surface
腭黏膜下裂/腭黏膜下裂　submucosal cleft palate
腭脓肿/腭膿腫　palatal abscess
腭前孔注射法/腭前孔注射法　anterior palatine foramen injecion
腭前神经/腭前神經　anterior palatine nerve
腭鞘沟/腭鞘溝　palatovaginal sulcus
腭鞘管/腭鞘管　palatovaginal canal
腭切迹/腭切跡　palatine incisure
腭乳头囊肿/腭乳頭囊腫　cyst of palatine papilla
腭筛缝/腭篩縫　palatoethmoidal suture
腭上颌缝/腭頜縫　palatomaxillary suture
腭舌弓/腭舌弓　palatoglossal arch
腭舌肌/腭舌肌　palatoglossus
腭升动脉/腭昇動脈　ascending palatine artery
腭十字点/腭十字穴　staurion
腭突/腭突　palatine process
腭外静脉/腭外静脈　external palatine vein
腭完全裂/腭完全裂　complete cleft palate
腭腺/腭腺　palatine gland
腭小动脉/腭小動脈　lesser palatine artery
腭小房/腭小房　palatine cell
腭小管/腭小管　lesser palatine canal
腭小孔/腭小孔　lesser palatine foramina
腭小神经/小腭神經　lesser palatine nerve
腭悬雍垂肌/腭懸雍垂肌　palatostaphylinus
腭咽闭合/腭咽閉合　velopharyngeal closure
腭咽闭合不全/腭咽閉合不全　velopharyngeal incompetence
腭咽的/咽腭帆　velopharyngeal
腭咽缝术/腭咽縫合術　staphylopharyngorrhaphy
腭咽弓/腭咽弓　palatopharyngeal arch
腭咽肌/腭咽肌　palatopharyngeus
腭咽门诸肌/腭咽門諸肌　muscle of palate and fauces
腭炎/腭炎　palatitis
腭圆枕/腭隆凸　palatine torus
腭正中缝/腭正中縫, 中腭縫　median palatine suture
腭正中囊肿/腭中囊腫　median palatal cyst
腭中部的/中腭部的　mediopalatine
腭中神经/中腭神經　middle palatine nerve
腭肿瘤/腭腫瘤　palatal neoplasm
腭皱/腭皺　palatal rugae
腭阻塞器/腭阻塞器　palatal obturator
噩梦/噩夢　horrible dream, nightmare
鳄泪综合征/鱷淚症候群　crocodile tear syndrome
鳄梨抽提液/鱷梨抽提液　avocado extract
鳄梨油/鱷梨油　avocado oil
鳄梨油脂酸乙酯/鱷梨油脂酸乙酯　avocado fatty acid ethyl ester
鳄皮状鳞癣/鱷皮病, 鱷皮狀魚鱗癬　alligator skin, crocodile skin, ichthyosis sauroderma

鳄鱼泪/鱷淚 crocodile tear
鳄鱼泪综合征/假哭性症候群，鱷魚淚症候群 crocodile tear syndrome
鳄嘴钳/鱷魚鉗 alligator forcep
恩贝酸/恩貝酸 embelin
恩布酯/恩布酯 enbucrilate
恩氟烷/安氟醚 enflurane
恩格尔曼夹/Engelmann 氏夾板 Engelmann splint
恩卡尼/恩卡尼 encainide
恩前列素/恩前列素 enprostil
恩维霉素/恩維黴素 enviomycin
蒽/蒽環 anthracene
蒽酚/蒽酚 anthranol
蒽环类/蒽環類 anthracyclines
蒽环类抗生素/蒽環類抗生素 anthracycline antibiotic
蒽醌/蒽醌 anthraquinone
蒽醌苷/蒽醌苷 anthraquinone glycoside
蒽类/蒽類 anthracenes
蒽酮/蒽酮 anthrone
儿茶/兒茶 catechu, black catechu, cutch
儿茶酚/兒茶酚 catechol
儿茶酚胺/兒茶酚胺，鄰苯酚胺 catecholamine
儿茶酚胺能神经元/兒茶酚胺能神經元 catecholaminergic neuron
儿茶酚胺受体/兒茶酚胺受體 catecholamine receptor
儿茶酚雌激素类/兒茶酚雌激素類 catechol estrogens
儿茶酚 O-甲基转移酶/兒茶酚 O-甲基轉移酶 catechol O-methyltransferase
儿茶酚类/兒茶酚類 catechols
儿茶酚氧化酶/兒茶酚氧化酶 catechol oxidase
儿茶鞣酸/兒茶鞣酸 catechutannic acid
儿茶素/兒茶素，兒茶酸 catechin
儿科护理学/兒科護理學 pediatric nursing
儿科学/兒科學 pediatrics
儿科医师助理/兒科醫師助理 pediatric assistant
儿科医院/兒科醫院 pediatric hospital
儿科重症监护[治疗]病房/兒科重症監護[治療]病房 pediatric intensive care unit
儿童/兒童 child
儿童保健/兒童健康照護 child health care
儿童保健服务/兒童保健服務 child health service
儿童辩护/兒童辯護 child advocacy
儿童大疱性皮肤病/兒童水皰性皮膚炎 bullous dermatosis of child
儿童多动综合征/兒童多動症候群 child hyperkinesis syndrome
儿童多动综合征·肝肾阴虚证/兒童多動症候群·肝腎陰虛證 child hyperkinesis syndrome with liver-kidney yin deficiency
儿童多动综合征·脾虚肝旺证/兒童多動症候群·脾虛肝旺證 child hyperkinesis syndrome with spleen deficiency and liver hyperactivity
儿童多动综合征·痰火扰神证/兒童多動症候群·痰火擾神證 child hyperkinesis syndrome with phlegm-fire disturbing spirit
儿童多动综合征·心脾两虚证/兒童多動症候群·心脾兩虛證 child hyperkinesis syndrome with heart-spleen deficiency
儿童多动综合征·心肾不足证/兒童多動症候群·心腎不足證 child hyperkinesis syndrome with insufficiency of heart and kidney
儿童发育/兒童發育 child development
儿童发育学/兒童學 pedology
儿童发育学家/兒童專家 pedologist
儿童反应性障碍/兒童反應性障礙 child reactive disorder
儿童福利/兒童福利 child welfare
儿童抚养/兒童撫養 child rearing
儿童抚育/兒童撫育 child care
儿童关节疡/兒童關節瘍 pedarthrocace
儿童行为/兒童行為 child behavior
儿童行为障碍/兒童行為障礙 child behavior disorder
儿童脊髓性肌萎缩/兒童脊髓性肌萎縮 spinal muscular atrophies of child
儿童监护/兒童監護 child custody
儿童精神病学/兒童精神病學 child psychiatry
儿童精神分裂症/兒童型精神分裂症 child schizophrenia
儿童口腔保健/兒童口腔保健 dental care for children
儿童口腔医学/兒童牙科 pediatric dentistry
儿童口腔正畸学/兒童口腔正畸學 pediatric orthodontics
儿童慢性大疱性皮肤病/小兒慢性皰性皮疹 chronic bullous dermatosis of child
儿童期精神病/幼年精神病，青年精神病 neophrenia
儿童丘疹性肢端皮炎/兒童丘疹性肢端皮炎 papular acrodermatitis of child
儿童湿疹/兒童濕疹 child eczema
儿童死亡率/兒童死亡率 child mortality
儿童心理学/兒童心理學 child psychology
儿童牙科学/兒童牙科學 pediadontia

儿童营养障碍/兒童營養障礙 child nutrition disorders
儿童硬皮肌炎/兒童硬皮肌炎 child sclerodermatomyositis
儿童语言/兒童語言 child language
儿童指导/兒童指導 child guidance
儿童指导诊所/兒童指導診所 child guidance clinics
耳/耳 ear, auris
耳背肺/耳背肺 erbeifei, P2, lung of posterior surface
耳背肝/耳背肝 erbeigan, P4, liver of posterior surface
耳背沟/耳背溝 erbeigou, PS, groove of posterior surface
耳背脾/耳背脾 erbeipi, P3, spleen of posterior surface
耳背肾/耳背腎 erbeishen, P5, kidney of posterior surface
耳背心/耳背心 erbeixin, P1, heart of posterior surface
耳被囊/胚胎聽囊 auditory capsule
耳鼻喉科学/耳鼻喉科學 otorhinolaryngology
耳鼻喉科学家/耳鼻喉科學家 otolaryngologist
耳鼻喉外科手术/耳鼻喉外科手術 otorhinolaryngologic surgical procedures
耳鼻科学/耳鼻科學 otorhinology
耳鼻咽喉疾病/耳鼻咽喉疾病 otorhinolaryngologic disease
耳鼻咽喉科学/耳喉科學 otolaryngology
耳鼻咽喉肿瘤/耳鼻咽喉腫瘤 otorhinolaryngologic neoplasm
耳闭/耳閉 blocked ear, ear block
耳闭·脾虚湿困证/耳閉·脾虛濕困證 ear block with pattern of spleen deficiency and dampness retention
耳闭·气滞血瘀证/耳閉·氣滯血瘀證 ear block with pattern of qi stagnation and blood stasis
耳病/耳病 otopathy, ear disease
耳病性神经衰弱/耳病性神經衰弱 otoneurasthenia
耳病性眩晕/耳性眩暈 ab aure laeso vertigo
耳部吹药法/耳部吹藥法 method of ear insufflation
耳部带状疱疹/耳部帶狀皰疹 herpes zoster oticus
耳部切诊/耳部切診 palpation of ear
耳部清洁法/耳部清潔法 method of ear cleaning
耳部弹力组织性结节/耳彈力纖維變性結節 elastotic nodule of the ear
耳部疼痛性结节/耳部疼痛性結節 painful nodule of the ear
耳部涂敷法/耳部塗敷法 coating method for ear
耳部闻诊/耳部聞診 auscultation and olfaction of ear
耳超荷试验/耳超荷試驗 aural overload test
耳成形术/耳造形術 otoplasty
耳齿发育不良/耳齒發育不良 otodental dysplasia
耳虫/耳蟲 ear wig
耳出血/耳出血,耳溢血 otorrhagia
耳疮/耳瘡 ear sore, diffusion of otitis externa, sore of external auditory meatus
耳疮·风热夹湿证/耳瘡·風熱夾濕證 ear sore with pattern of wind-heat complicated by dampness
耳疮·肝胆湿热证/耳瘡·肝膽濕熱證 ear sore with pattern of dampness-heat in liver and gallbladder
耳疮·血虚风燥证/耳瘡·血虛風燥證 ear sore with pattern of wind-dryness due to blood deficiency
耳垂/耳垂 auricular lobule, auricle lobule, earlobe
耳垂缺损/耳垂缺損 defect of earlobe
耳垂皱褶/耳垂皺褶 earlobe crease
耳大神经/耳大神經 great auricular nerve
耳大神经后支/耳大神經後支 posterior branch of great auricular nerve
耳大神经前支/耳大神經前支 anterior branch of great auricular nerve
耳带疮/耳帶瘡 zoster oticus
耳带疮·肝胆湿热证/耳帶瘡·肝膽濕熱證 zoster oticus with pattern of dampness-heat in liver and gallbladder
耳带疮·邪毒外袭证/耳帶瘡·邪毒外襲證 zoster oticus with pattern of external assault by pathogenic toxin
耳带状疱疹/耳帶狀皰疹 zoster oticus
耳道/耳道 auditory meatus
耳道闭合/耳道閉合 otocleisis
耳道成形术/耳道成形術 meatoplasty
耳道点/耳道點,耳穴 auriculare
耳道内助听器/耳道內助聽器 in-the-canal hearing aid
耳的/耳的 aural
耳底/耳底 bottom of external acoustic meatus, ear bottom
耳底骨/耳底骨 basiotic bone
耳点/耳點 auriculare
耳疔/耳疔 ding of external auditory meatus, furuncle of external auditory meatus
耳窦/耳竇 auricular sinus
耳毒理学/耳毒理學 ototoxicology
耳毒性/耳毒性 ototoxicity
耳毒性聋/耳毒性聾 ototoxic deafness

耳朵假囊肿/耳朵假囊腫　pseudocyst of the ear
耳-腭-指/耳-腭-指　oto-palato-digital
耳防护器/耳防護器　ear protective device
耳幅指数/耳幅指數　auricular index
耳杆剂/耳桿劑　aurinarium
耳根/耳根　ear root
耳根毒/耳根毒　acute retroauricular lymphadenitis
耳根上点/耳根上點　otobasion superius
耳根下点/耳根下點　otobasion inferius
耳垢/耳垢　ear wax
耳垢的/耳垢的　ceruminous
耳骨泡/骨性泡　bulla ossea
耳郭冻疮/耳郭凍瘡　ear frostbite
耳郭枯槁/耳郭枯槁　withered auricle
耳郭痰包/耳郭痰包　phlegmatic nodule of auricle, pseudocyst of auricle
耳郭痰包·痰浊凝聚证/耳郭痰包·痰濁凝聚證　phlegmatic nodule of auricle with pattern of phlegm-turbidity coagulation and aggregation
耳和髎/耳和髎　erheliao, SJ22
耳后动脉/耳後動脈　posterior auricular artery
耳后附骨痈/耳後附骨癰　postauricular subperiosteal abscess
耳后附骨痈·热毒壅盛证/耳後附骨癰·熱毒壅盛證　postauricular subperiosteal abscess with pattern of heat-toxin congestion and excessiveness
耳后附骨痈·正虚毒滞证/耳後附骨癰·正虛毒滯證　postauricular subperiosteal abscess with pattern of healthy qi deficiency and toxin stagnation
耳后肌/耳後肌　auricularis posterior
耳后静脉/耳後靜脈　posterior auricular vein
耳后神经/耳後神經　posterior auricular nerve
耳后瘀血斑/耳後瘀血斑　Battle sign
耳后助听器/耳後助聽器　behind-the-ear hearing aid
耳弧/耳弧　auricular arc
耳化脓/耳化膿　otopyosis
耳级助听器/耳級助聽器　ear level hearing aid
耳疾病/耳疾病　ear disease
耳甲/耳甲　auricular concha
耳甲成形术/耳甲成形術　conchiplasty
耳甲隆起/耳甲[殼]隆起　eminence of auricular concha
耳甲腔/耳甲腔　cavity of auricular concha
耳甲艇/耳甲艇　cymba of auricular concha
耳尖/耳尖　ear apex, erjian, EX-HN6
耳间衰减/耳間衰減　interaural attenuation
耳检验/耳檢驗　auricular docimasia
耳胶原性丘疹/耳膠原性丘疹　collagenous papule of the ear
耳疖/耳癤　ear furuncle, furuncle of ear
耳疖·风热邪毒证/耳癤·風熱邪毒證　ear furuncle with wind-heat pathogenic toxin pattern
耳疖·肝胆湿热证/耳癤·肝膽濕熱證　ear furuncle with pattern of dampness-heat in liver and gallbladder
耳结核/耳結核　tuberculosis of ear
耳结节点/耳結節點　tuberculare
耳界切迹/耳界切跡　terminal notch of ear
耳镜/耳鏡　otoscope
耳镜检查/耳鏡檢法　otoscopy
耳菌/耳菌　ear cancer
耳菌·气滞血瘀证/耳菌·氣滯血瘀證　ear cancer with pattern of qi stagnation and blood stasis
耳菌·湿毒蕴结证/耳菌·濕毒蘊結證　ear cancer with dampness-toxin amassment pattern
耳科学/耳科學　otology
耳科诊断技术/耳科診斷技術　otological diagnostic technique
耳壳痰包/耳殼痰包　phlegmatic nodule of auricle, phlegm cover auricle
耳孔/耳孔　ear hole, external acoustic meatus
耳廓/耳廓　pinna of ear
耳廓成形术/耳廓成形術　pinnaplasty
耳廓的/耳廓的　auricular
耳廓附件/耳廓附件,副耳　auricular appendage
耳廓复合组织游离移植术/耳廓複合組織游離移植術　auricular compound tissue free grafting
耳廓横肌/耳廓橫肌　transversus auricularis, musculus transversus auriculae
耳廓后点/耳廓後點　postaurale
耳廓后沟/耳廓後溝,後耳環溝　posterior sulcus of auricle
耳廓后韧带/耳廓後韌帶　posterior auricular ligament
耳廓肌/耳廓肌　muscles of auricle
耳廓假囊肿/耳廓假囊腫　pseudocyst of the auricle
耳廓尖/耳廓尖,達爾文氏尖　apex of auricle, tip of ear, Darwinian apex
耳廓结节/耳廓結節,達爾文結節　auricular tubercle
耳廓前点/耳廓前點　preaurale
耳廓前韧带/耳廓前韌帶,前耳廓韌帶　anterior auricular ligament
耳廓缺损/耳廓缺損　defect of auricle
耳廓韧带/耳廓韌帶　auricular ligament
耳廓软骨/耳廓軟骨　conchal cartilage
耳廓三角/耳廓三角　auricular triangle

耳廓上韧带/耳廓上靭帶,上耳廓韧带 superior auricular ligament
耳廓缩小成形术/耳廓縮小成形術 reductive otoplasty
耳廓斜肌/耳廓斜肌 obliquus auricularis, musculus obliquus auriculae
耳廓再造术/耳廓再造術 reconstruction of auricle
耳廓锥[状]肌/耳廓錐[狀]肌 musculus pyramidalis auriculae
耳螨病/耳恙蟲病 otoacariasis
耳螨属/耳恙蟲屬 Otodectes
耳裂/耳裂 split ear
耳流脓/耳流膿 purulent ear discharge
耳聋/[耳]聾 deafness
耳聋[病]/耳聾[病] deafness disease
耳聋·风邪外袭证/耳聾·風邪外襲證 deafness with pattern of external assault by wind
耳聋·肝火上扰证/耳聾·肝火上擾證 deafness with pattern of liver fire disturbing upward
耳聋-蓝巩膜-骨脆综合征/Dighton-Adair 二氏症候群 Dighton-Adair syndrome
耳聋·气血两虚证/耳聾·氣血兩虛證 deafness with qi-blood deficiency pattern
耳聋·气滞血瘀证/耳聾·氣滯血瘀證 deafness with pattern of qi stagnation and blood stasis
耳聋·肾精亏虚证/耳聾·腎精虧虛證 deafness with kidney essence deficiency pattern
耳聋·痰火郁结证/耳聾·痰火鬱結證 deafness with phlegm-fire stagnation pattern
耳聋治肺/耳聾治肺 healing deafness by treating lung
耳聋左慈丸/耳聾左慈丸 erlong zuoci pills
耳瘘/耳瘻 auricular fistulae, ear fistula
耳瘘管/耳瘻管 aural fistula
耳瘘·气虚邪恋证/耳瘻·氣虛邪戀證 ear fistula with pattern of qi deficiency and lingering pathogen
耳瘘·邪毒外袭证/耳瘻·邪毒外襲證 ear fistula with pattern of external assault by pathogenic toxin
耳漏/耳漏 otorrhea
耳颅/耳顱 otocranium
耳轮/耳輪 helix
耳轮大肌/耳輪大肌 helicis major
耳轮棘/耳輪棘 spine of helix
耳轮脚/耳輪腳 crus of helix
耳轮脚沟/耳輪腳溝 sulcus of crus of helix
耳轮结节/耳輪結節 helix tubercle
耳轮切迹肌/耳輪切跡肌 muscle of helicine notch
耳轮尾/耳輪尾 tail of helix

耳轮小凹/耳凹 ear pit
耳轮小肌/耳輪小肌 helicis minor
耳轮小结软骨皮炎/耳輪結節性軟骨皮膚炎 chondrodermatitis nodularis helicis
耳毛/耳毛 hair of external acoustic meatus
耳毛霉菌病/耳白黴菌病 otomucormycosis
耳霉菌病/耳黴病 Hong Kong ear
耳门/耳門 ①tragus ②ermen, SJ21
耳迷根/耳迷根 ermigen, root of ear vagus, R2
耳迷路炎/耳迷路炎 otitis labyrinthica
耳面瘫[病]/耳面癱[病] otogenic facial paralysis disease
耳面瘫·风中经络证/耳面癱·風中經絡證 otogenicfacial paralysis with pattern of wind striking channel and collateral
耳面瘫·气虚血瘀证/耳面癱·氣虛血瘀證 otogenic facial paralysis with pattern of qi deficiency and blood stasis
耳鸣/耳鳴 tinnitus
耳鸣[病]/耳鳴[病] tinnitus disease
耳鸣·风邪外袭证/耳鳴·風邪外襲證 tinnitus with pattern of external assault by wind
耳鸣·肝火上扰证/耳鳴·肝火上擾證 tinnitus with pattern of liver fire disturbing upward
耳鸣·脾胃气虚证/耳鳴·脾胃氣虛證 tinnitus with spleen-stomach qi deficiency pattern
耳鸣·肾精亏虚证/耳鳴·腎精虧虛證 tinnitus with kidney essence deficiency pattern
耳鸣·痰火郁结证/耳鳴·痰火鬱結證 tinnitus with phlegm-fire stagnation pattern
耳鸣图/耳鳴圖 tinnitogram
耳鸣掩蔽器/耳鳴掩蔽器 tinnitus masker
耳模/耳模 ear mold
耳膜/耳膜 tympanic membrane
耳囊/耳軟骨囊 otic capsule
耳囊软骨/耳囊軟骨 otic capsule cartilage
耳内肌/耳内肌 intra auricular muscle
耳[内]积水/耳積水 hydrodis
耳[内]镜/耳内鏡 otoscope
耳内流脓/耳内流膿 purulent discharge in ear
耳内助听器/耳内助聽器 in-the-ear hearing aid
耳黏液溢/耳黏液漏 otoblennorrhea
耳钳/耳鉗 aural forcep
耳颞[部]的/耳與顳的 auriculotemporal
耳颞神经/耳顳神經 auriculotemporal nerve
耳颞神经交通支/耳顳神經交通支 communicating branch with auriculotemporal nerve
耳颞综合征/耳顳症候群 auriculotemporal

syndrome
耳脓溢/耳膿漏 otopyorrhea
耳衄/耳衄 ear bleeding
耳蜱病/耳壁蝨屬 otiobiosis
耳屏/耳屏,耳珠 tragus
耳屏板/耳屏板 tragal lamina
耳屏点/耳屏點 tragion
耳屏肌/耳屏肌,耳珠肌 tragicus, muscle of tragus
耳屏间切迹/耳屏間切跡 intertragic notch
耳屏上结节/耳屏上結節 supratragic tubercle
耳前的/耳前的 preauricular
耳前动脉/耳前動脈 anterior auricular artery
耳前窦道/耳前竇道 preauricular sinus
耳前肌/耳前肌 auricularis anterior, anterior auricular muscle
耳前肌节/耳前肌節 preotic myotome
耳前静脉/耳前靜脈 anterior auricular vein
耳前淋巴结/耳前淋巴結 preauricular lymph node
耳前切迹/耳前切跡 anterior notch of ear
耳前神经/耳前神經 anterior auricular nerve
耳前庭/耳前庭 vestibule of ear
耳前支/耳前支 anterior auricular branch
耳切开术/耳解剖術 ototomy
耳丘/耳丘,耳結節 auricular hillock
耳区/耳郭部 auricular region
耳蛆病/耳蛆病 otomyiasis
耳曲霉/耳麴菌 Aspergillus auricularis
耳乳突炎/耳乳突炎 otomastoiditis
耳软骨/耳軟骨 ear cartilage
耳软骨膜炎/耳軟骨膜炎 auricular perichondritis
耳软骨峡/耳軟骨峽 cartilaginous isthmus of ear
耳软骨性丘疹/耳軟骨性丘疹 cartilaginous papule of the ear
耳软骨炎/耳軟骨炎 auricular chondritis
耳塞/耳塞 ear plug
耳三角窝隆起/耳三角窩隆凸 triangular eminence
耳上点/耳上點 superaurale
耳上肌/耳上肌 auricularis superior, musculus auricularis superior
耳深动脉/耳深動脈 deep auricular artery
耳神经节/耳神經節 otic ganglion
耳神经节副交感根/耳神經節副交感根 parasympathetic root of otic ganglion
耳神经节感觉根/耳神經節感覺根 sensory root of otic ganglion
耳神经节交感根/耳神經節交感根 sympathetic root of otic ganglion
耳神经节运动根/耳神經節運動根 motor root of otic ganglion
耳神经科学/耳神經病學 otoneurology
耳神经痛/耳神經痛 otoneuralgia
耳神经外科/耳神經外科 otoneurosurgery
耳石/耳石 otolith
耳石病/[内]耳石病 otolithiasis
耳石膜/耳石膜 otolithic membrane
耳石诱发电位/耳石誘發電位 otolithic evoked potential
耳损伤/耳損傷 ear trauma
耳筒/耳筒,助聽筒 ear trumpet
耳痛/耳痛 earache, ear pain
耳痛风石/耳痛風石 auricular tophus
耳外骨/耳外骨 petromastoid
耳外科手术/耳外科手術 otologic surgical procedure
耳妄闻/耳妄闻 acoasm, auditory hallucination
耳窝/聽凹 auditory pit
耳窝螺旋韧带/耳蝸螺旋韌帶 spiral ligament of cochlea
耳蜗/[耳]蝸 cochlea
耳蜗的/耳蝸的 cochlear
耳蜗电图/耳蝸電圖 electrocochleogram
耳蜗动脉丝球/耳蝸動脈絲球 arterial glomeruli of cochlea
耳蜗毒性/耳蝸毒性 cochleotoxicity
耳蜗管/耳蝸管 periotic duct, cochlear duct
[耳蜗管]弓状部/[耳蝸管]弓狀部 pars arcuata
[耳蜗管]梳状部/[耳蝸管]梳狀部 pars pectinata
耳蜗后疾病/耳蝸後疾病 retrocochlear disease
耳蜗疾病/耳蝸疾病 cochlear disease
耳蜗神经核/耳蝸神經核 cochlear nucleus
耳蜗水管/耳蝸水管 cochlear aqueduct
耳蜗外植入术/耳蝸外植入術 extracochlear implantation
耳蜗微音电位/耳蝸微音電位 cochlear microphonic potential
耳蜗细胞/耳蝸細胞 cochlear cell
耳蜗性聋/耳蝸性耳聾 cochlear deafness
耳蜗炎/耳蝸炎 cochleitis
耳蜗植入术/耳蝸植入術 cochlear implantation
耳蜗植入物/耳蝸植入物 cochlear implant
耳息肉/耳息肉 otopolypus
耳下点/耳下點 subaurale
耳下淋巴结/耳下淋巴結 infraauricular lymph node
耳显微外科/耳顯微外科 otomicrosurgery
耳性咳/耳性欬嗽 ear cough
耳性青光眼/耳性青光眼 auricular glaucoma
耳性眩晕/耳性眩暈,聽覺性暈眩 auditory vertigo

耳性眼球震颤/耳性眼球震顫　aural nystagmus
耳眩晕[病]/耳眩暈[病]　otogenic vertigo disease
耳眩晕·风邪外袭证/耳眩暈·風邪外襲證　otogenic vertigo with pattern of external assault by wind
耳眩晕·肝阳上亢证/耳眩暈·肝陽上亢證　otogenic vertigo with liver yang hyperactivity pattern
耳眩晕·寒水上泛证/耳眩暈·寒水上泛證　otogenic vertigo with pattern of cold-water flooding upward
耳眩晕·上气不足证/耳眩暈·上氣不足證　otogenic vertigo with pattern of upper-qi insufficiency
耳眩晕·髓海不足证/耳眩暈·髓海不足證　otogenic vertigo with marrow sea insufficiency pattern
耳眩晕·痰浊中阻证/耳眩暈·痰濁中阻證　otogenic vertigo with pattern of phlegm-turbidity obstructing middle-jiao
耳穴/耳穴　auricular point
耳血管炎/耳血管炎　angiotitis
耳血肿/耳血腫　boxer ear
耳压疗法/耳壓療法　ear-pressure therapy
耳咽管/耳咽管　tuba auditiva
耳咽管沟/耳咽管溝　sulcus tubae auditivae
耳咽管含气小房/耳咽管含氣小房　cellulae pneumaticae tubae auditivae
耳咽管咽肌/耳咽管咽肌　musculus salpingopharyngeus
耳炎/耳炎　otitis
耳炎的/耳炎的　otitic
耳炎性脑膜炎/耳炎性腦膜炎　otitic meningitis
耳痒/耳癢　ear itching, itching in ear
耳隐窝病/耳隱窩病　attic disease
耳硬化病/耳硬化　otosclerosis
耳用制剂/耳製劑　aural preparation
耳语测听[法]/耳語測聽[法]　whispered sound audiometry
耳语声/耳語聲　whispered voice
耳语响/唯語響,低語響　whispering resonance
耳语音/胸耳語音　whispered pectoriloquy
耳语支气管音/支氣管耳語聲,低微支氣管聲　whispered bronchophony
耳胀/耳脹　ear distention
耳胀·风邪外袭证/耳脹·風邪外襲證　ear distention with pattern of external assault by wind
耳胀·肝胆湿热证/耳脹·肝膽濕熱證　ear distention with pattern of dampness-heat in liver and gallbladder
耳针刺/耳針刺　ear acupuncture
耳针疗法/耳針療法　ear-acupuncture therapy
耳针麻醉/耳針麻醉　ear-acupuncture anesthesia

耳真菌病/耳黴菌病　otomycosis
耳支/耳支　auricular branch
耳支交通支/耳支交通支　communicating branch with auricular branch
耳-指甲-腓骨综合征/耳-指甲-腓骨症候群　oto-onycho-peroneal syndome
耳中/耳中　erzhong, ear center, HX1
耳肿瘤/耳腫瘤　ear neoplasm
耳舟/耳舟　scapha
耳舟隆起/耳舟隆起　eminence of scapha
耳周的/[内]耳周圍的　periotic
耳周囊/耳組織周圍囊　periotic capsule
耳周围骨/耳周圍骨　periotic bone
耳状附件/耳狀附件　auricular appendix
耳状面/耳狀面　auricular surface
耳坠/耳墜　ear lobule
耳卒聋/耳卒聾　sudden deafness
耳组织切除术/耳組織切除術　otectomy
二氨基氨基酸类/二胺基胺基酸類　diamino amino acids
二氨基二磷脂/二胺二磷脂　diaminodiphosphatide
二氨基庚二酸/二胺基庚二酸　diaminopimelic acid
二氨基磷脂/二胺單磷脂　diaminomonophosphatide
二氨基酸/二胺基酸　diamino acid
二氨基乙酸/二胺基醋酸　diaminoacetic acid
二胺类/二胺類　diamines
二胺尿/二胺尿　diaminuria
二白/二白　erbai, EX-UE2
二杯试验/二杯試驗　two-glass test
二倍核/二倍數核　diploid nucleus
二倍卵片发育/倍數無卵核發育　diploid merogony
二倍期/二倍數期,雙染色體核期　diplophase
二倍体/二倍體　diploid
二倍体细胞/二倍體細胞　diploid cell
二倍稀释/二倍稀釋　doubling dilution
二倍性/具兩套同系染色體　diploidy
二倍性生物/具雙倍數染色體者　diplont
二苯胺/二苯胺　diphenylamine
二苯胺[基]偶氮苯/二苯胺偶氮苯　diphenylamino-azo-benzene
二苯氮䓬类/二苯氮䓬類　dibenzazepines
二苯二丁对蒽二酚/二苯二丁對蒽二酚　dibenz-dibutyl anthraquinol
二苯哌啶丁醇/二苯哌啶丁醇　diphenidol
二苯环庚烯类/二苯環庚烯類　dibenzocycloheptenes
二苯基硫脲/二苯硫脲　diphenylthiourea
二苯己三烯/二苯己三烯　diphenylhexatriene
二苯甲基化合物/二苯甲基化合物　benzhydryl

compound
二苯甲酮/二苯甲酮 benzophenone
二苯甲酮类/二苯甲酮類 benzophenones
二苯卡巴肼/二苯卡巴肼 diphenylcarbazide
二苯硫氮䓬类/二苯硫氮䓬類 dibenzothiazepines
二苯硫䓬类/二苯硫䓬類 dibenzothiepins
二苯氯[化]胂/二苯氯次砷 diphenylchlorarsine
二苯脲/二苯脲 carbanilide
二苯氰[化]胂/二苯氰化砷 diphenylcyanarsine
二苯氧氮䓬类/二苯氧氮䓬類 dibenzoxazepines
二苯氧䓬类/二苯氧䓬類 dibenzoxepins
二苯乙酸类/二苯乙酸類 diphenyl acetic acids
二苯茚酮/二苯乙醯茚滿二酮 diphenadione
二- dl -吡咯烷酮甲酸铝/二- dl -吡咯啶酮甲酸鋁 aluminium di-dl-pyrrolidone carboxylate
二臂联胎/二臂畸形連胎 dibrachius
二便不通/二便不通 anuria and constipation
二便失调/二便失調 abnormal urination and defecation
二丙诺啡/二丙諾啡 diprenorphine
二丙酸雌二醇/二丙酸雌二醇 estradiol dipropionate
二丙烯巴比土酸/二丙烯基巴比妥酸 diallylbarbituric acid
二波长分光光度法/二波長分光光度法 dual wavelength spectrophotometry
二波脉/雙重搏動的脈搏,重搏脈 dicrotic pulse
二波[脉]的/雙重搏動的 dicrotic
二层胚盘/二層性胚盤 bilaminar blastoderm
二产/第二次生產 secundiparity
二产妇/二[次]產婦 secundipara
二陈汤/二陳湯 erchen decoction
二重感染/重複感染,雙重感染 superinfection
二醇/二元醇 diol
二醇类/二醇類 glycols
二次化学平衡/二次化學平衡 the second chemical equilibrium
二次混合印模/二次混合印模 double mix impression
二次离子质谱法/二次離子質譜法 secondary ion mass spectrometry, SIMS
二次探查手术/二次探查手術 the second-look surgery
二次突变假说/二次突變假說 Knudson hypothesis
二次印模/二次印模 double impression
二氮/二氮 dinitrogen
二氮嗪/二氮嗪 diazoxide
二碘仿/二聚碘仿 diiodoform
二碘化物/二碘化物 diiodide

二碘咔唑/二碘咔唑 diiodocarbazol
二碘羟基喹啉/雙碘羥基喹啉 diiodohydroxyquin
二碘水杨酸/二碘水楊酸 diiodosalicylic acid
二碘顺芜酸乙酯/碘化芥子酸乙菌 iodobrassid
二碘荧光素/雙碘螢光素 diiodofluorescein
二叠体旁核/二疊體旁核 parabigeminal nucleus
二丁基/二丁基 dibutyl
二度房室传导阻滞/第二級房室傳導阻滯 second-degree atrioventricular block
二度烧伤/二度燒傷 the second degree burn
二噁茂类/二噁茂類 dioxoles
二噁茂烷类/二噁茂烷類 dioxolanes
二噁烷类/二噁烷類 dioxanes
二噁辛类/二噁辛類 dioxins
二蒽酮/二蒽酮 dianthrone
二芳基庚烷类/二芳基庚烷類 diarylheptanoids
二分裂/二分裂,各半分裂 binary fission
二分神经细胞/二分神經細胞 binary nerve cell
二分体/二分體 dyad
二氟苯隆/二氟苯隆 diflubenzuron
二氟可龙/二氟可龍 diflucortolone
二氟尼柳/二氟尼柳 diflunisal
二腹的/二腹的 digastric
二腹肌/二腹肌 digastric, biventer muscle
二腹肌沟/二腹肌溝 digastric groove
二腹肌后腹/二腹肌後腹 posterior belly of digastric
[二腹肌]前腹/[二腹肌]前腹 anterior belly of digastric
二腹肌三角/二腹肌三角 digastric triangle
二腹肌神经/二腹肌神經 digastric nerve
二腹肌窝/二腹肌窝 digastric fossa
二腹肌支/二腹肌支 digastric branch
二腹小叶/二腹小葉 biventral lobule
二高辛可宁/二高辛可寧 dihomocinchonine
二根叉受累/二根叉侵犯 bifurcation involvement
二根分叉部/二分叉 bifurcation
二核苷磷酸类/二核苷磷酸類 dinucleoside phosphates
二核苷酸/二核苷酸 dinucleotide
二环化合物/二環化合物 bicyclo compound
二环己基碳二亚胺/二環己基碳二亞胺 dicyclohexylcarbodiimide
二环乙烷基碳化二亚胺/二環乙烷基碳化二亞胺 dicyclohexyl carbodiimide
二级蛋白质结构/二級蛋白質結構 secondary protein structure
二级结构/二級結構,次生構造 secondary structure
二级弹线牵引/二級彈線牽引 class II elastic

二级弯折/二級彎折　the second order bend
二级异常殆/二級異常咬合　class Ⅱ malocclusion
二级异常殆第一分类与第二分类/二級異常咬合第一分類與第二分類　division 1 and 2 class Ⅱ malocclusion
二极管/二極管　diode
二甲胺/二甲胺　dimethylamine
二甲胺四环素色素沉着/米諾四環素色素沈著　minocycline pigmentation
二甲苯/二甲基苯　dimethylbenzene
二甲苯胺/二甲苯胺　xylidine
二甲苯二胺/二甲苯二胺　xylylenediamine
二甲苯酚/二甲[基]酚　xylenol
二甲苯基/二甲苯基　xylyl
二甲苯类/二甲苯類　xylenes
二甲苯茚满胺/二甲苯茚滿胺　dimefadane
二甲基乙酰胺/二甲基醯胺　dimethyl acetamide
二甲菲/二甲菲　dimethylphenanthrene
二甲胍/二甲基胍　dimethylguanidine
二甲磺酸丁酯/二甲磺酸丁酯　busulfan
二甲基/二甲基　dimethyl
二甲基苯基呱嗪碘化物/二甲基苯基呱嗪碘化物　dimethylphenylpiperazinium iodide
二甲基苯甲酸/二甲基苯甲酸　mesitylenic acid
二甲基苯甲酰甘氨酸/二甲基苯甲醯甘胺酸　mesityluric acid
二甲基丙基反转移酶/二甲基丙基反轉移酶　dimethylallyltransferase
二甲基二硫代氨基甲酸酯/二甲基二硫代胺基甲酸酯　dimethyldithiocarbamate
二甲基甲酰胺/二甲基甲醯胺　dimethylformamide
二甲基肼类/二甲基肼類　dimethylhydrazines
二甲基聚硅氧烷类/二甲基聚矽氧烷類　dimethylpolysiloxanes
二甲基亚硝胺/二甲基亞硝胺　dimethylnitrosamine
二甲聚硅氧烷/二甲聚矽氧烷　simethicone
二甲磷/二甲基磷　dimethyl phosphine
二甲秋水仙酸/二甲基秋水仙酸　dimethylcolchicinic acid
二甲胂腈/氰化二甲次砷　cacodyl cyanide
二甲胂酸/臭砒酸,二甲次砷酸　cacodylic acid
二甲胂酸盐/臭砒酸鹽,二甲砷酸鹽　cacodylate
二甲双胍/二甲雙胍　metformin
二甲双酮/二甲噁唑烷二酮　dimethadione
二甲缩醛/二甲縮醛　dimethylacetal
二甲酮/二甲酮　dimethyl ketone
二甲亚砜/二甲基亞砜　dimethyl sulfoxide
二甲氧基苯乙胺/二甲氧基苯乙胺　dimethoxyphenylethylamine
二甲茚定/二甲茚定　dimethindene
二价体/二價體　bivalent
二价阳离子/二價陽離子　divalent cation
二尖瓣/二尖瓣,僧帽瓣　bicuspid valve
二尖瓣瓣环/二尖瓣瓣環　mitral annulus
二尖瓣瓣膜切开术/二尖瓣切開術,僧帽瓣切開術　mitral valvotomy
二尖瓣闭锁/二尖瓣閉鎖,僧帽瓣閉鎖　mitral atresia
二尖瓣病素质/二尖瓣病質,僧帽瓣病質　mitralism
二尖瓣的/二尖瓣的,僧帽狀的,僧帽瓣的　mitral
二尖瓣反流/二尖瓣反流,僧帽瓣[口]反流　mitral regurgitation
二尖瓣梗阻/二尖瓣梗阻,僧帽瓣梗阻　mitral obstruction
二尖瓣关闭不全/二尖瓣閉鎖不全,僧帽瓣閉鎖不全　mitral incompetence
二尖瓣口面积/二尖瓣口面積,僧帽瓣面積　mitral valve orifice area
二尖瓣口钮孔状/二尖瓣鈕孔,僧帽瓣鈕孔　mitral buttonhole
二尖瓣上环/二尖瓣上環,僧帽瓣上環　supramitral ring
二尖瓣脱垂/二尖瓣瓣膜脫落,僧帽瓣瓣膜脫落　mitral valve prolapse
二尖瓣狭窄/二尖瓣狹窄,僧帽瓣狹窄　mitral stenosis
二尖瓣狭窄阴影/二尖瓣病象,僧帽瓣病象　mitralization
二尖瓣压力梯度/二尖瓣梯度,僧帽瓣梯度　mitral gradient
二尖瓣杂音/二尖瓣雜音,僧帽瓣雜音　mitral murmur
二尖瓣置换术/二尖瓣置換術,僧帽瓣置換術　mitral valve replacement
二间/二間　erjian, LI2
二阶/二階　the second order
二进制/二進位　binary system
二精入卵/雙精卵,雙受精　dispermy
二聚水/二聚水　dihydrol
二聚体/二聚體　dimer
二聚作用/二聚作用　dimerization
二联搏动/二聯搏動　coupled beat
二联孢子球虫/二聯孢子蟲　isospora bigemina
二联律/二聯律　bigeminy
二联脉/二聯脈　pulsus bigeminus
二联体/二聯體　diad
二联性精神病/二聯性精神病　folie a deux

二裂鼻/雙鼻[畸形],雙分鼻　bifid nose
二裂舌/雙分舌,分歧舌,裂舌　bifid tongue
二裂输尿管/二裂輸尿管　bifid ureter
二裂阴茎/二裂陰莖,分叉陰莖　bifid penis
二磷酸甘油酸类/二磷酸甘油酸類
　　diphosphoglyceric acids
二磷酸核糖腺苷抗体试验/二磷酸核糖腺苷抗體試驗　ADP-ribose antibody test
二磷酸盐类/二磷酸鹽類　diphosphates
二磷酸转移酶类/二磷酸轉移酶類
　　diphosphotransferases
二膦酸盐类/二膦酸鹽類　diphosphonates
二硫赤藓糖醇/二硫丁四醇　dithioerythritol
二硫代氨基甲酸酯/二硫代胺基甲酸酯
　　dithiocarbamate
二硫化二氢/二硫化氫　hydrogen disulfide
二硫化碳/二硫化碳　carbon disulfide
二硫化物/二硫化物　disulfide
二硫苏糖醇/二硫蘇糖醇　dithiothreitol
二硫酸盐/二硫酸鹽　dithionite
二硫硝基苯甲酸/二硫硝基苯甲酸
　　dithionitrobenzoic acid
二氯丙醇/二氯丙醇　dichlorhydrin
二氯醋酸/二氯醋酸　dichloroacetic acid
2,6-二氯靛酚滴定法/2,6-二氯靛酚滴定法　2,6-dichlorindophenol titration
二氯二苯二氯乙烷/二氯二苯二氯乙烷
　　dichlorodiphenyl dichloroethane
二氯二苯二氯乙烯/二氯二苯二氯乙烯
　　dichlorodiphenyl dichloroethylene
二氯二氟甲烷/二氯二氟甲烷,氟氯烷
　　dichlorodifluoromethane
二氯酚酸/二氯酚酸　diclofenac
二氯化物/二氯化物　dichloride
二氯甲醛肟/二氯甲肟　dichloroformoxime
二氯甲烷/二氯代甲烷　methylene chloride
二氯四氟乙烷/二氯四氟乙烷
　　dichlorotetrafluoroethane
二氯乙腈/二氯乙腈　dick
二氯乙酸盐/二氯乙酸鹽　dichloroacetate
二氯乙烷类/二氯乙烷類　dichloroethanes
二氯乙烯类/二氯乙烯類　dichloroethylenes
二氯异丙去甲肾上腺素/二氯異丙腎上腺素
　　dichloroisoproterenol
二卵双生/二卵雙生　dizygotic twins
二脒那秦/二脒那秦　diminazene
二妙散/二妙散　ermiao powder
二钠/二鈉　disodium

二钠酞酚酞/二鈉酞酚酞　sodophthalyl
二萘嵌苯/二萘嵌苯　perylene
二胚层胚盘/二胚層胚盤　bilaminar germ disc
二期缝合/次期縫合,第二期縫合　secondary suture
二期梅毒/[第]二期梅毒　secondary syphilis
二期切断术/第二期截斷術　secondary amputation
二期小肠移植/二期小腸移植　two-stage intestine transplantation
二期愈合/二期愈合　secondary healing
二期愈合前庭成形术/二期愈合前庭成形術
　　secondary epithelization vestibuloplasty
二腔观/二腔觀　two-chamber view
二羟苯丙氨酸/二羥苯基丙胺酸
　　dihydroxyphenylalanine
二羟苯基异丙氨基乙醇/二羥苯基異丙胺基乙醇
　　metaproterenol
二羟丙酮/二羥丙酮　dihydroxyacetone
二羟丙酮磷酸/磷酸二氫丙酮　dihydroxyacetone phosphate
二羟胆钙化醇类/二羥膽鈣化醇類
　　dihydroxycholecalciferols
二羟二氢苯并芘类/二羥二氫苯并芘類
　　dihydroxydihydrobenzopyrenes
二羟[基]/二羥基　dihydroxy
二羟基蒽酚/二羥基蒽酚　dioxyanthranol
二羟尿囊素铝/二羥尿囊素鋁　aluminium dihydroxy allantoinate
二羟色胺类/二羥色胺類　dihydroxytryptamines
二羟硬脂酸/二羥硬脂酸　dihydroxystearic acid
二氢吡啶类/二氫吡啶類　dihydropyridines
二氢卟啉/二氫卟啉　dihydroporphyrin
二氢β刺桐定碱/二氫β刺桐定鹼　dihydro-beta-erythroidine
二氢蝶啶还原酶/二氫蝶啶還原酶　dihydropteridine reductase
二氢蝶酸合酶/二氫蝶酸合酶　dihydropteroate synthase
二氢可待因酮/二氫可待因　dihydrocodeinone
二氢硫辛酰胺脱氢酶/二氫硫脂醯胺脫氫酶
　　dihydrolipoamide dehydrogenase
二氢路提丁/二氫路提丁　dihydrolutidine
二氢麦角碱/二氫麥角鹼　dihydroergotoxine
二氢麦角碱甲磺酸盐类/二氫麥角獨鹼甲磺酸鹽類
　　ergoloid mesylates
二氢尿嘧啶脱氢酶/二氫尿嘧啶脫氫酶
　　dihydrouracil dehydrogenase
二氢乳清酸酶/二氫乳清酸酶　dihydroorotase
二氢乳清酸氧化酶/二氫乳清酸氧化酶

dihydroorotate oxidase
二氢石蒜碱/二氫石蒜鹼 sekisanine
二巯丙醇/二巰丙醇 dimercaprol
二巯丙磺钠/二巰丙磺鈉 unithiol
二巯琥珀酸/二巰琥珀酸 succimer
二巯基化物/雙硫氫基 dithiol
二人用内镜/兩人用内診鏡 observerscope
二肉豆蔻磷脂酰胆碱/二肉豆蔻磷脂醯膽鹼 dimyristoylphosphatidylcholine
二肉豆蔻酸铝/二肉豆蔻酸鋁 aluminium dimyristate
二蕊紫苏属/二蕊紫蘇屬 *Collinsonia*
二噻扎宁/二噻寧 dithiazanine
二色视者/兩[原]色視者 dichromat
二-α-生育酚亚油酸/二-α-生育酚亞油酸 di-α-tocopheryl linoleate
二十二醇/二十二醇 behenyl alcohol
二十二碳六烯酸类/二十二碳六烯酸類 docosahexaenoic acids
二十六烷/二十六烷 hexacosane
二十四[烷]酸/二十四烷酸 lignoceric acid
二十碳五烯酸/二十碳五烯酸 eicosapentaenoic acid
二十碳-9-烯酸/鳕油酸,廿碳稀酸 gadoleic acid
二室模型/二室模型 two-compartment model
二室性水囊/二室性水囊 bilocular hydrocele
二酸/二酸 diacid
二羧基氨基酸尿/二羧基胺基酸尿 dicarboxylic aminoaciduria
二羧酸氨基酸类/二羧酸胺基酸類 dicarboxylic amino acids
二羧酸类/二羧酸類 dicarboxylic acids
二羧酸转运子/二羧酸轉運子 dicarboxylic acid transporter
二肽/二肽 dipeptide
二肽基肽酶类/二肽基肽酶類 dipeptidyl peptidases
二肽类/二肽類 dipeptides
二肽酶/二肽酵素 dipeptidase
二糖/二糖 disaccharide
二糖类/二糖類 disaccharides
二糖酶类/二糖酶類 disaccharidases
二糖尿/雙糖尿 disacchariduria
二体/二體[染色體] disome
二萜/二萜 diterpene
二萜类/二萜類 diterpenes
二酮/複酮,雙酮 diketone
二头的/兩頭的 bicipital
二头肌/二頭肌 bicipital muscle
二头肌沟/二頭肌溝 bicipital groove
二头肋/二頭肋 bicipital rib
二维定量构效关系/二維定量構效關係 two-dimensional quantitative structure activity relationship, 2D-QSAR
二戊烯/二戊烯 diamylene
二烯丙巴比妥/阿洛巴比妥 allobarbital
二烯烃类/二烯烴類 alkadienes
二酰胺/二醯胺 diamide
二酰甘油胆碱磷酸转移酶/二醯甘油膽鹼磷酸轉移酶 diacylglycerol cholinephosphotransferase
二酰甘油激酶/二醯甘油激酶 diacylglycerol kinase
二酰脲/雙醯脲 diureide
二相反应/複相反應 biphasic reaction
二相气雾剂/二相氣噴霧劑 two-phase aerosol
二项分布/二項分布 binomial distribution
二硝基氨基酚/二硝基胺基酚,胺基二硝基酚 dinitroaminophenol
二硝基苯/二硝基苯 dinitrobenzene
二硝基苯类/二硝基苯類 dinitrobenzenes
二硝基酚/二硝基酚 dinitrophenol
二硝基酚类/二硝基酚類 dinitrophenols
二硝基氟苯/二硝基氟苯 dinitrofluorobenzene
二硝基甲酚/二硝基甲酚 dinitrocresol
二硝基氯苯/二硝基氯苯 dinitrochlorobenzene
二硝基水杨酸试剂/二硝基水楊酸試劑,桑納氏試劑 dinitrosalicylic acid reagent
二硝酸盐/二硝酸鹽 dinitrate
二硝托胺/二硝托胺 dinitolmide
二小叶的/兩小葉的 bilobular
二性霉素/二性黴素 amphotericin
二溴丁酮/二溴丁酮 dibromoketone
二溴甘露醇/二溴甘露醇 mitobronitol
二溴化物/二溴化物 dibromide
二溴磷/二溴磷 naled
二溴三氯甲烷/二溴三氯甲烷 bromotrichloromethane
二溴卫矛醇/二溴衛矛醇 mitolactol
二溴乙烯/二溴乙烯 ethylene dibromide
二盐基性的/二鹽基性的 dibasic
二盐酸奎宁/二鹽酸奎寧 quinine dihydrochloride
二盐酸组胺/二鹽酸組織胺 histamine dihydrochloride
二氧化氮/二氧化氮 nitrogen dioxide
二氧化硅/二氧化矽 silicon dioxide
二氧化硫/二氧化硫 sulfur dioxide
二氧化酶/二氧化酶 dioxygenase
二氧化钛/二氧化鈦 titanium dioxide
二氧化碳/二氧化碳 carbon dioxide

二氧化碳半融雪/二氧化碳雪水　carbon dioxide slush
二氧化碳分压/二氧化碳分壓　partial pressure of carbon dioxide
二氧化碳激光疗法/二氧化碳雷射療法　carbon dioxide laser therapy
二氧化碳激光器/二氧化碳雷射器　carbon dioxide laser
二氧化碳监测仪/二氧化碳分壓測量計　capnometer
二氧化碳结合力/二氧化碳結合力　carbon dioxide-combining power
二氧化碳疗法/二氧化碳治療　carbonic therapy
二氧化碳麻醉/二氧化碳麻醉　carbon dioxide narcosis
二氧化碳描记术/二氧化碳濃度偵測法　capnography
二氧化碳描记图/二氧化碳濃度描記波　capnogram
二氧化碳培养/二氧化碳培養　carbon dioxide incubation
二氧化碳吸附剂/二氧化碳吸收劑　carbon dioxide absorber
二氧化碳性酸中毒/二氧化碳性酸中毒　carbon dioxide acidosis
二氧化碳雪/二氧化碳雪　carbon dioxide snow
二氧化碳浴/二氧化碳浴　carbon dioxide bath
二氧化碳总含量/二氧化碳總含量　total carbon dioxide content
二氧化钍/二氧化釷　thorium dioxide
二氧化物/二氧化物　dioxide
二氧化硒/二氧化硒　selenium dioxide
二氧化乙酰基/二氧化乙醯基　acetyl dioxide
二叶胎盘/二葉胎盤　duplex placenta
二叶窝/二葉窩　bilobed pit
二叶性囊胚/雙囊胚　diblastula
二叶主动脉瓣/二葉主動脈瓣　bicuspid aortic valve
二液界面/二液界面　dineric interface
二乙胺/二乙胺　diethylamine
二乙丙苯嗪/二乙基胺丙酚噻　ethopropazine
二乙基苯二甲酸酯/鄰苯二甲酸二乙酯　diethyl phthalate
二乙基亚硝胺/二乙基亞硝胺　diethylnitrosamine
二乙嗪/雙乙嗪　diethazine
二乙醛/乙二醛　biformyl
二乙色胺/二乙色胺　diethyltryptamine
二乙烯/雙乙烯基，聯乙烯基　divinyl
二乙烯醚/二乙烯醚　divinyl ether
二乙酰/二乙醯基　diacetyl
二硬脂酸乙二醇酯/二硬脂酸乙二醇酯　ethyleneglycol distearate
二元汞合金/二元素汞合金　binary amalgam
二元论者/二元論者　dualist
二元素合金/二元素合金　binary alloy
二元素合金系统/二元素合金系統　binary alloy system
二元素酸/二元[素]酸　binary acid
二至丸/二至丸　erzhi pills
二轴突[神经]细胞/二軸突細胞　diaxon
二棕榈酸抗坏血酯/二棕櫚酸抗壞血酯　ascorbyl dipalmitate
二足联胎/兩足連胎　dipus

F

发病机制/病之發生,發病原理,疾病發生論 pathogenesis
发病率/發病率 incidence
发病率计算法/罹病率計演算法 nosometry
发病率记录器/發病率記錄器 pathometer
发病年龄/發病年齡 age of onset
发赤药/發赤藥 rubefacient
发否黏液丸虫/費弗氏黏液丸蟲 Myxobolus pfeifferi
发绀/發紺,青紫 cyanosis
发绀的/發紺的 cyanotic
发绀型心绞痛/發紺性心絞痛 hypercyanotic angina
发光/發光 luminescence
发光测定法/發光測定法 luminescent measurement
发光蛋白质类/發光蛋白質類 luminescent proteins
发光尿/光尿症,尿發光 photuria
发光强度/發光強度 luminous intensity
发光物质/發光物質 luminescent agent
发汗药/發汗藥 sudorific, hidrotic
发汗浴/[催]汗浴 sweat bath
发红/發紅 redness
发酵/發酵 fermentation
发酵参数/發酵參數 fermentation parameter
发酵的/發酵的 zymotic
发酵动力学/發酵動力學 fermentation kinetics
发酵工程/發酵工程 fermentation engineering
发酵工艺/發酵技術 fermentation technology
发酵罐/發酵罐 fermentor
发酵花生饼/發酵花生餅 ontjom
发酵阶段/發酵階段 fermentation stage
发酵酶蛋白/發酵素 apozymase
发酵培养基/發酵培養基 fermentation medium
发酵试验/發酵試驗 fermentation test
发酵糖定量器/發酵糖量度器 saccharascope
发酵糖量计/發酵測糖器 fermentation saccharimeter
发酵性消化不良/發酵性消化不良 fermentative dyspepsia
发酵性血栓/發酵性血栓 ferment thrombus
发酵液/發酵液 fermentation broth
发酵支原体/發酵黴漿菌 Mycoplasma fermentans
发酵周期/發酵周期 fermentation period
发酵[作用]/發酵[作用],釀化 fermentation
发狂/發狂 mania
发冷期/寒冷期 cold stage
发明妄想/發明妄想 delusion of invention
发怒/發怒 anger
发暖剂/發暖藥 calefacient
发泡液/發泡液 blistering liquid
发疱疗法/發泡療法 vesiculation therapy
发情周期/動情週期,求偶週期 estrous cycle
发热/發熱,發燒,體溫上昇 pyrexia, fever
发热穿刺/發熱穿刺 heat puncture
发热疗法/發熱療法 fever therapy
发热期/發熱期 hot stage
发热性黄疸/發熱性黃疸 febrile jaundice
发热性惊厥/發熱性驚厥 febrile seizure
发热性精神病/熱病性精神病 febrile psychosis
发散透镜/發散透鏡 diverging lens
发射型计算机体层摄影术/發射型電腦體層攝影術 emission-computed tomography
发生器/發生器 generator
发声/發音 phonation
发声过强/發聲過強 supraenergetic phonation
发声过弱/發音過弱 subenergetic phonation
发声痉挛/發音痙攣 phonic spasm
发声困难/發音困難,發音障礙 dysphonia
发声器官/發聲器 vocal apparatus
发声无力/發音無力 phonasthenia
发声正常/發音正常 orthophony
发现/發現,所見 finding
发香质/产气味物質 odorivector
发泄/[精神]發洩 catharsis
发芽阶段/發芽階段 germination stage
发炎后色素过度沉着症/發炎後色素過度沈著症 postinflammatory hyperpigmentation
发颐/發頤 acute suppurative parotitis, suppurative parotitis
发颐·热毒内陷证/發頤·熱毒內陷證 suppurative parotitis with pattern of heat-toxin sinking inward
发颐·热盛酿脓证/發頤·熱盛釀膿證 suppurative parotitis with pattern of suppuration due to heat

exuberance
发颐·湿热蕴结证/發頤·濕熱蘊結證 suppurative parotitis with dampness-heat amassment pattern
发颐·正虚毒恋证/發頤·正虛毒戀證 suppurative parotitis with pattern of healthy qi deficiency and lingering toxin
发音分节的/發音[分節]的 syntactic
发音障碍/發音障礙,構音不全 articulation disorder, pararthria
发育/發育,長成 development
发育不良性表皮角化病/發育異常性表皮角化症 dysplastic epidermal keratosis
发育不良性巨输尿管/發育不良性巨輸尿管 dysplastic megaloureter
发育不良性皮肤骨瘤病/發育異常性皮膚骨瘤病 dysplastic cutaneous osteomatosis
发育不良性痣/發育異常性母斑 dysplastic nevus
发育不全/發育不全 agenesis
发育不全的/發育不全的 aplastic
发育不全心/發育不全心 hypoplastic heart
发育不全性侏儒/發育不全性侏儒 ateliotic dwarf
发育毒理学/發育毒理學 developmental toxicology
发育儿科学/發育兒科學 developmental pediatrics
发育沟/發育溝 developmental groove
发育过度/發育過度 hyperevolutism
发育过度性畸形/發育過度性畸形 malformation by excess
发育过慢/發育徐緩 bradygenesis
发育基因/發育基因 developmental gene
发育激素/發育激素 auximone
发育剂/發育劑 auxetic
发育力/發育力,生長力 plastodynamia
发育能力/胚胎預期發育力 prospective potency
发育期基因表达调控/發育期基因表達調控 developmental gene expression regulation
发育[潜能]梯度/發育[潛能]梯度 developmental potential gradient
发育生物学/發育生物學 developmental biology
发育停顿/發育停止 arrest of development
发育线/發育線 developmental line
发育型/發育型 developmental pattern
发育性白痴/發育期白癡 developmental idiocy
发育性白内障/發育性白內障 developmental cataract
发育性骨疾病/發育性骨疾病 developmental bone disease
发育性青光眼/發育性青光眼 developmental glaucoma
发育性痛/發育性痛 growing pain
发育遗传学/發育遺傳學 developmental genetics
发育异常/發育障礙,發育不全 dysplasia, heteroplasia
发育异常性黑色素细胞痣/發育異常性黑色素細胞痣 dysplastic melanocytic nevus
发育异常痣综合征/發育異常痣症候群 dysplastic nevus syndrome
发育障碍/發育障礙 developmental disability
发育障碍病/身體發育異常 dysgenopathy
发育障碍的/矮小的 stunted
发育中心/發育中心 developmental center
发缘点/發緣點 trichion
发胀/脹滿感 fullness
发疹病病毒/發疹病病毒 exanthematous disease virus
发疹型药疹/發疹性藥疹 exanthematous drug eruption
发疹性毳毛囊肿/發疹性毳毛囊腫 eruptive vellus hair cyst
发疹性汗管瘤/發疹性汗管瘤 eruptive syringoma
发疹性汗腺腺瘤/發疹性汗腺腺瘤 hidradenoma eruptiva
发疹性滑膜炎/發疹性滑膜炎 exanthematous synovitis
发疹性黄[色]瘤/發疹性黄色瘤 eruptive xanthoma
发疹性棘皮瘤/發疹性棘皮瘤 eruptive acanthoma
发疹性家族性舌乳突炎/發疹性家族性舌乳突炎 eruptive familial lingual papillitis
发疹性毛细血管瘤/發疹性微血管瘤 eruptive capillary hemangioma
发疹性细胞痣/發疹性痣細胞母斑 eruptive cellular nevi
发疹性脂溢性角化症/發疹性脂漏性角化症 eruptive seborrheic keratose
发疹性组织细胞瘤/發疹性組織細胞瘤 eruptive histiocytoma
发作/發作 attack, insult
发作性红斑/發作性紅斑 episodic erythema
发作性淋巴细胞减少症伴淋巴细胞毒性抗体/發作性淋巴球減少症伴淋巴細胞毒性抗體 episodic lymphopenia with lymphocytotoxic antibody
发作性睡眠/發作性睡病,麻醉樣昏睡 paroxysmal sleep
发作性睡[眠]病/發作性睡病,催眠樣昏睡 sleep paroxysmal, hypnolepsy
发作性睡眠状态/發作性睡眠狀態 hypnoleptic state
乏-帕小体/Vater-pacini 氏小體 Vater-pacini

corpuscle
乏气[压]层/乏氣壓層　aeropause
乏氧呼吸/缺氧性呼吸　anaerobic respiration
伐木工皮炎/伐木者皮膚炎　friente
法半夏/法半夏　processed pinellia tuber
法伯尔综合征/Faber 氏症候群　Faber syndrome
法伯病/Farber 氏病　Farber disease
法布里病/法布里病　Fabry disease
法布里综合征/Fabry 氏症候群　Fabry syndrome
法定传染病/法定傳染病　notifiable disease
法定监护人/法定監護人　legal guardian
法定盲/法定盲　legal blindness
法定名称/法定名稱　official name
法耳卡德纳/法耳卡德納　falcadina
法倔唑/法倔唑　fadrozole
法拉第电流/法拉第電流　Faradaic current
法-拉综合征/Favre-Racouchot 氏症候群　Favre-Racouchot syndrome
法兰克福平面/法蘭克福平面　Frankfurt plane
法兰绒绷带/法蘭絨繃帶　flannel bandage
法兰特溶液/Farrant 氏溶液　Farrant solution
法兰西标度/法式度標　French scale
法洛病/Fallot 氏病　Fallot disease
法洛三联症/法洛氏三聯症　trilogy of Fallot
法洛四联症/法洛氏四聯症候群,四聯畸形　tetralogy of Fallot
法洛五联症/法洛氏五聯症　pentalogy of Fallot
法洛综合征/Fallot 氏症候群　Fallot syndrome
法律实施/法律實施　law enforcement
法律责任/法律責任　legal obligation, legal liability
法莫替丁/法莫替丁　famotidine
法尼醇/法尼醇,麝子油醇　farnesol
法齐奥-隆德病/Fazio-Londe 二氏病　Fazio-Londe disease
法齐奥-隆德萎缩/Fazio-Londe 二氏萎縮　Fazio-Londe atrophy
法氏囊/法伯利氏囊　bursa of fabricius
法特管/Vater 氏管　duct of Vater
法医病理学/法醫病理學　forensic pathology
法医弹道学/法醫彈道學　forensic ballistics
法医毒理学/法醫毒理學　forensic toxicology
法医科学/法醫科學　forensic science
法医人类学/法醫人類學　forensic anthropology
法医学/法醫學　legal medicine
法医遗传学/法醫遺傳學　medicolegal genetics
法札溴铵/法劑溴銨　fazadinium
发/髮　capillus
发部乳突状皮炎/髮區乳突狀皮膚炎　dermatitis papillaris capillitii
发迟/髮遲　retardation in hair growth
发-齿综合征/髮-齒症候群　trichodental syndrome
发根黑点病/髮根黑點病　thysanotrix
发际疮/髮際瘡　hairline sore, hairline boils, multiple folliculitis of nape
发际[线]/髮際[線]　hairline
发结节病/結節性脆髮病　trichonodosis
发内癣菌/毛内癣菌　endothrix
发纽结病/纏髮疾病　kinky hair disease
发外孢子/毛外孢子　ectothrix spore
发外的/毛外的　ectothrix
发外感染/毛外感染　ectothrix infection
发癣菌病的/髮癣菌的　trichophytic
发癣菌素/髮癣菌素　trichophytin
发癣菌疹/髮癣疹　trichophytid
发癣霉/毛癣菌　trichophyton
发蛀脱发/髮蛀脫髮　androgenetic alopecia, insect bitten alopecia
发蛀脱发•肝肾两虚证/髮蛀脫髮•肝腎兩虛證　insect bitten alopecia with liver-kidney deficiency pattern
发蛀脱发•湿热上蒸证/髮蛀脫髮•濕熱上蒸證　insect bitten alopecia with pattern of dampness-heat steaming upward
发蛀脱发•血热风燥证/髮蛀脫髮•血熱風燥證　insect bittenalopecia with pattern of blood heat and wind-dryness
发蛀脱发•血虚风燥证/髮蛀脫髮•血虛風燥證　insect bitten alopecia with pattern of wind-dryness due to blood deficiency
帆状附着/帆狀附著,膜狀附著　velamentous insertion
帆状胎盘/帆狀胎盤　velamentous placenta
番红花/番紅花　crocus
番荔枝/蕃荔枝　sirikaya
番茉莉/番茉莉　manaca
番木瓜/番瓜樹,木瓜　papaw
番木瓜消化酶/木瓜酵素　papoid
番茄/番茄　tomato
番茄红素/番茄紅素,番茄紅質　lycopene
番茄红素血症/番茄紅素血　lycopenemia
番茄瘤/蕃茄狀瘤　tomato tumor
番茄素/番茄素　tomatin
番痧/番痧　filthy sha disease
番泻属植物/番瀉屬植物　Senna plant
番泻叶/番瀉葉　senna, senna leaf
番泻叶苷/番瀉葉苷　sennoside

番泻叶素/番瀉葉素　sennatin
番泻叶糖剂/番瀉藥糖劑　electuary of senna
番泻叶提取物/番瀉葉提取物　senna extract
翻出型肛门外吻合巨结肠根治术/翻出型肛門外吻合巨結腸根治術　swenson procedure
翻花疮/翻花瘡　cauliflower-like sore, squamous cell carcinoma
翻身床/翻身床　stryker frame
翻译后蛋白质加工/轉譯後蛋白質加工　post-translational protein processing
翻译肽链起始/翻譯肽鏈起始　translational peptide chain initiation
翻译肽链延伸/翻譯肽鏈延伸　translational peptide chain elongation
翻译肽链终止/翻譯肽鏈終止　translational peptide chain termination
翻转/翻轉,逆轉　reversal
翻转法内镜检查[术]/翻轉法内鏡檢查[術]　reverse method of endoscopy
凡士林皮炎/凡士林皮膚炎　petrolatum dermatitis
凡士林纱布/凡士林紗布,軟石蠟紗布　petrolatum gauze
钒化合物/釩化合物　vanadium compound
钒酸/釩酸　metavanadic acid
钒酸铵-浓硫酸试液/釩酸銨-濃硫酸溶液　mandelin test solution
钒酸盐/釩酸鹽　vanadate
钒中毒/釩中毒　vanadiumism
烦渴/劇渴　polydipsia
烦乱/煩亂　feeling terribly upset
烦满/煩滿　vexation and chest fullness
烦悗/煩悗　oppressed feeling
烦热/煩熱　vexing fever
烦惋/煩惋　oppressed feeling
烦心/煩心　vexation
烦冤/煩冤　feeling upset
烦躁/煩躁　dysphoria, restlessness
樊尚感染/Vincent氏感染　Vincent infection
樊尚氏疏螺旋体/包柔疏螺旋體　Borrelia vincentii
樊尚微生物/Vincent氏微生物　Vincent organism
樊尚牙周咽峡炎/Vincent氏牙周咽峽炎　Vincent periodontal angina
樊尚咽峡炎/Vincent氏咽峽炎,戰壕咽病　Vincent angina
繁睾吸虫病/繁睾吸蟲病　achillurabainiasis
繁殖/繁殖　breeding
繁殖的/繁殖的　proligerous
繁殖囊肿/繁殖囊腫　proligerous cyst

繁殖期/繁殖期　idiophase
反暗示/反暗示,對抗暗示　countersuggestion
反苯环丙铵/反苯環丙銨　tranylcypromine
反搏动术/對抗搏動法　counterpulsation
反常刺激/反常刺激　paradoxical stimulation
反常呼吸/反常呼吸　paradoxical respiration
反常偏侧/反常偏側　paradoxical lateralization
反常收缩/逆理收縮　paradoxical contraction
反常栓塞/逆理栓塞　paradoxical embolism
反常睡眠/非常規睡眠　paradoxical sleep
反衬色/對照色　contrast color
反重振/反重振　decruitment
反唇疗/反唇疗　ding inside lip
反磁性屏蔽/反磁性遮罩　diamagnetic shielding
反错构象/反錯構象　anticlinal conformation
反代型/相反鑄型　counterdie
反盗血现象/反盗血現象　reverse steal phenomenon
反叠构象/反叠構象　antiperiplanar conformation
反复生殖/重生,再生　iteroparity
反复性心动过速/交互性心搏快速　reciprocating tachycardia
反复性血尿/再發性血尿　recurrent hematuria
反杠杆原理/反槓桿原理　inverse lever rule
反关脉/反關脈　ectopic radial pulse
反光试验/反光試驗　catoptric test
反规性散光/反常散光,背例散光　astigmatism against the rule
反𬌗/反咬合　cross bite
反𬌗曲线/反咬合曲線　reverse curve
反𬌗弹力圈/反咬合彈力圈　crossbite elastics
反回力卡环/反回力卡環　reverse back-action clasp
反急跳/反急跳　counter-jerk
反甲/反甲,凹甲,匙狀甲　koilonychia
反键[分子]轨道/反鍵[分子]軌域　antibonding molecular orbital
反角/反角　contra-angle
反节律/逆節律　reversed rhythm
反恐怖症/對抗恐懼症　counterphobia
反馈调节/迴饋調節　feedback regulation
反馈抑制/迴饋抑制　feedback inhibition
反馈阻遏/迴饋壓抑　feedback repression
反粒子/反粒子　antiparticle
反流的/反流的,回流的　regurgitant
反流分布法/反流分布法　countercurrent distribution
反流分数/反流分數　regurgitant fraction
反流提取倾析机/反流提取傾析機　countercurrent extraction decanter
反流性黄疸/反流性黃疸　regurgitating jaundice,

regurgitation jaundice
反流性巨输尿管/反流性巨輸尿管　reflux megaloureter
反流性肾病/反流性腎病　reflux nephropathy
反流性食管炎/反流性食管炎　reflux esophagitis
反流性杂音/回流性雜音　regurgitation murmur
反流血流量/反流血流量　regurgitant blood flow
反论/自相矛盾之論　paradox
反论的/反論的　paradoxical
反模板/反模板　antitemplate
反门控去偶/反門控去偶　inverted gated decoupling
反蒙森曲线/反蒙森曲線　anti-Monson curve
反密码子/反密碼子　anticodon
反扭转/負扭轉　negative torsion
反求遗传学/逆遺傳學　reverse genetics
反社会性人格障碍/反社會性人格障礙　antisocial personality disorder
反射/反射　reflex, jerking
反射光/反射光　reflected light
反射光学/反射光學,光線反射論　catoptrics
反射弧/反射弧　reflex arc
反射计/反射計,反射檢查器　anacamptometer, reflexometer
反射减弱/反射減弱,反射過弱　hyporeflexia
反射亢进/反射過強,反射增強　hyperreflexia
反射疗法/反射療法　reflexotherapy
反射描记器/反射描記器　reflexograph
反射式检影镜/反射式檢影鏡　reflecting retinoscope
反射紊乱/不正常反射　parareflexia
反射显微镜/反射顯微鏡　reflecting microscope
反射消失/反射消失　areflexia
反射性癫痫/反射性癲癇　reflex epilepsy
反射性骨萎缩/反射性骨萎縮　reflex bone atrophy
反射性幻想/反射性幻覺　reflex hallucination
反射性回路/反射性回路　reflected reentry
反射性交感神经营养障碍/反射性交感神經營養障礙　reflex sympathetic dystrophy
反射性交感营养不良/反射交感性失養症　reflex sympathetic dystrophy
反射性咳/反射性欬嗽　reflex cough
反射性排卵/反射性排卵　reflex ovulation
反射性膀胱/反射性膀胱　reflex bladder
反射性气喘/反射性氣喘　reflex asthma
反射性神经痛/反射性神經痛　reflex neuralgia
反射性脱发/反射性禿髮　reflex alopecia
反射性无尿/反射性無尿　reflex anuria
反射性消化不良/反射性消化不良　reflex dyspepsia
反射性心动过速/反射性心搏快速　reflex tachycardia
反射性心绞痛/反射性心絞痛　reflex angina
反射性抑制/反射性抑制　reflex inhibition
反射学/反射學　reflexology
反射阈计/反射閾計　liminometer
反射运动/反射運動　reflex motion
反射增进频率/反射增進頻率　recruitment frequency
反射作用/反射作用　reflex action, reflection
反渗透/逆滲透　reverse osmosis
反式/反式　trans
反式构象/反式構象　transoid conformation
反式激活/反式啟動　trans-activation
反式激活因子类/反式啟動因子類　trans-activators
反式剪接/反式剪接　trans-splicing
反式脂肪酸/反式脂肪酸　trans fatty acid
反式作用因子/反式作用因子　transacting factor
反酸/胃酸逆流　acid regurgitation
反跳/反跳　rebound
反跳痛/反跳痛,反彈痛　rebound tenderness, rebounding pain
反胃[病]/反胃[病]　regurgitation, stomach reflux
反胃·脾胃虚寒证/反胃·脾胃虛寒證　stomach reflux with pattern of deficiency-cold of spleen and stomach
反胃·痰浊阻滞证/反胃·痰濁阻滯證　stomach reflux with pattern of blockade of phlegm-turbidity
反胃·胃热证/反胃·胃熱證　stomach reflux with stomach heat pattern
反胃性呕吐/反胃性嘔吐　regurgitant vomiting
反胃·血瘀积结证/反胃·血瘀積結證　stomach reflux with pattern of accumulation and binding of static blood
反响过强/反響過強,共鳴過強　hyperresonance
反响减弱/反響減弱　decreased resonance
反响增强/反響增強　increased resonance
反向插入/反向插入　inverted insertion
反向重复[序列]/反向重複[序列]　inverted repeat
反向传播/反向傳播　back propagation
反向的/反向的　inversa
反向分流/反轉性分流　reversed shunt
反向隔离/反向隔離　reverse isolation
反向过敏[反应]/反向過敏[反應]　reversed anaphylaxis
反向回力牙钩/反向迴力牙鉤　reverse back action clasp
反向偏斜/歪斜偏向,眼球之歪斜　skew deviation
反向蚀斑试验/反向蝕斑試驗　reverse plaque assay
反向斜面/反向斜面　contra bevel

反向主动脉缩窄/反向主動脈縮窄 reversed coarctation
反向转位/反向轉位 reversed rotation
反向转运物/反向轉運物 antiporter
反相/逆相 reversed phase
反相色谱法/逆相層析法 reverse-phase chromatography
反笑线/反笑線 reverse smile line
反效等位基因/反作用對偶基因 antimorph
反效应/逆作用,反功效 contrary effect
反义寡核苷酸/反義寡核苷酸 antisense oligonucleotide
反义寡核糖核苷酸类/反義寡核糖核苷酸類 antisense oligoribonucleotides
反义寡脱氧核糖核苷酸类/反義寡去氧核糖核苷酸類 antisense oligodeoxyribonucleotides
反义链/反義鏈 antisense strand
反抑细胞/反抑細胞 veto cell
反抑制/反抑制 retroinhibition
反应/反應 reaction, response
C-反应蛋白质/C反應蛋白 C-reactive protein
反应泛化/反應泛化 response generalization
反应分裂/分裂動力論 schizokinesis
反应过度/過度反應 overresponse
反应时间/反應時間 reaction time
反应素/反應素 reagin
反应特性改变/反應性異常 allobiosis
反应物/反應物 reactant
反应行为/反應行爲 respondent behavior
反应性/反應性 reactivity
反应性出血/反應性出血 reactionary hemorrhage
反应性穿通性胶原病/反應性穿通性膠原病 reactive perforating collagenosis
反应[性]的/反應的 reactive
反应性低血糖/反應性低血糖 reactional hypoglycemia
反应性附着障碍/反應性附著障礙 reactive attachment disorder
反应性关节炎/反應性關節炎 reactive arthritis
反应性坏死毒性脑膜炎/反應性壞死毒性腦膜炎 meningitis necrotoxica reactiva
反应性浆细胞增多/反應性漿細胞增多 reactive plasmacytosis
反应性结节性增生症/反應性結節性增生 reactive nodular hyperplasia
反应性精神障碍/反應性精神障礙 reactive disorder
反应性木僵/反應性木僵 reactive stupor
反应性偏执状态/反應性偏執狀態 reactive paranoid state
反应性乳突状增生/反應性乳突狀增生 reactive papillary hyperplasia
反应性血管内皮瘤病/反應性血管内皮細胞瘤病 reactive angioendotheliomatosis
反应性血糖过低/反應性血糖過低 reactive hypoglycemia
反应性抑郁[症]/反應性抑鬱 situational depression
反应性意识错乱/反應性意識錯亂 reactive confusion
反应性组织细胞增多/反應性組織細胞增多 reactive histocytosis
反应抑制/反應抑制 reactive inhibition
反应状态/反應狀態 reactive state
反折胎盘/厚緣胎盤 placenta reflexa
反折头/反折頭 reflected head
反证/反證 disprove
反治/反治 paradoxical treatment
反治法/反治法 retrograde treatment
反中微子/反中微子 antineutrino
反中子/反中子 antineutron
反转绷带/反轉繃帶 reversed bandage
反转点/反轉點 reversal point
反转过敏反应/反常過敏性,逆轉過敏性 inverse anaphylaxis
反转录/反轉錄 reverse transcription
反转录病毒/反[轉]錄病毒 retrovirus
反转录酶/反轉錄酶,逆轉錄酶 reverse transcriptase
反转录因子/反轉錄因子 retroelement
反转录转座子/反轉錄轉座子 retrotransposon
反转韧带/反轉韌帶 reflected ligament
反转型网状肢端色素沉着症/反轉型網狀肢端色素沈著症 acropigmentation reticularis inversa
反转型银屑病/反轉型乾癬 psoriasis inversa
反足细胞/對蹠細胞 antipodal cell
反佐药/反佐藥 contrary drug
返神经/返神經 recurrent nerve
返祖现象/返祖性,隔代遺傳 atavism
犯罪恐怖/犯罪恐懼症 peccatiphobia
犯罪受害者/犯罪受害者 crime victim
犯罪心理学/犯罪心理學 criminal psychology
饭匙倩/飯匙倩 habu
饭店/飯店 restaurant
饭后服/飯後服 administered after meal, post cibum, p.c.
饭后期间/飯後期間 postprandial period
饭前/飯前 ante cibum
饭前服/飯前服 administered before meal, ante

cibum, a.c.
饭醉[病]/飯醉[病]　post-meal somnolence
泛醇/泛醯醇　panthenol
泛发性白糠疹/廣泛性白色糠疹　extensive pityriasis alba
泛发性扁平黄瘤/全身性扁平黄瘤　generalized plane xanthoma
泛发性发疹性组织细胞瘤/全身性發疹性組織細胞瘤　generalized eruptive histiocytoma
泛发性肥大细胞增多症/全身性肥大細胞增多症　generalized mastocytosis
泛发性淋巴细胞[与]组织细胞性浸润/廣泛性淋巴組織細胞浸潤症　generalized lymphohistiocytic infiltration
泛发性特发性毛细血管扩张/全身特發性毛細血管擴張　generalized essential telangiectasia
泛发性硬斑病/全身性硬斑病　generalized morphea
泛红如妆/泛紅如妝　flush face
泛化/泛化　generalization
泛磺酸/泛磺酸　thiopanic acid
泛恐怖症/普遍性恐怖，普遍恐懼症　panophobia
泛醌/泛醌　ubiquinone
泛生论/泛生説　pangenesis
泛嗜性病毒/親全身性病毒　pantropic virus
泛素/泛素　ubiquitin
泛素蛋白连接酶复合物/泛素蛋白連接酶複合物　ubiquitin-protein ligase complex
泛素蛋白连接酶类/泛素蛋白連接酶類　ubiquitin-protein ligases
泛素激活酶类/泛素啟動酶類　ubiquitin-activating enzymes
泛素结合酶类/泛素綴合酶類　ubiquitin-conjugating enzymes
泛素硫酯酶/泛素硫酯酶　ubiquitin thioesterase
泛酸钙/泛酸鈣　calcium pantothenate
泛酸盐/泛酸鹽　pantothenate
泛昔洛韦/抗濾兒　famciclovir
泛酰巯基乙胺/泛醯巰基乙胺　pantetheine
泛影钠/泛影鈉,二乙醯胺基三碘苯甲酸鈉　hypaque sodium
泛影葡胺/泛影葡胺　diatrizoate meglumine
泛影酸盐/泛影酸鹽,二乙醯胺基三碘苯甲酸鹽　diatrizoate
泛油/泛油　extensive diffusion of oil
范布肯姆综合征/van Buchem 氏症候群　van Buchem syndrome
范布伦病/van Buren 氏病　van Buren disease
范德格拉夫器/范德葛氏器　van de Graaff machine

范德赫夫综合征/van der Hoeve 氏症候群　van der Hoeve syndrome
范德瓦尔斯半径/范德瓦半徑　van der Waals radius
范吉柯顿氏法/范格胡頓氏法　van Gehuchten method
范科尼贫血/范科尼貧血　Fanconi anemia
范科尼综合征/Fanconi 氏症候群　Fanconi syndrome
范氏氨基氮测定法/范氏胺基氮測定法　van Slyke method
范斯莱克试验/范斯萊氏試驗　van Slyke test
范特斯解毒剂/Fantus 氏解毒藥　Fantus antidote
范围/範圍,視野　field
范型/範型　pattern
范型脱发/範型脱髮　patterned baldness
方部/方部　quadrate part
方波气流型态/方波氣流型態　square wave flow pattern
方差/方差　variance
方差分析/方差分析　analysis of variance
方寸匕/方寸匕　tool for weighing medicine in ancient China
方肌/方肌　musculus quadratus
方剂/方劑,處方　prescription
方剂学/方劑學　prescriptions of Chinese materia medica
方肩/方肩　square shoulder
方晶/方晶　solitary crystal
方颅/方顱　enlarged square skull
方论/方論　discourse on prescription
方盛衰论篇/方盛衰論篇　Treatise on Qi Deficiency of Zang-fu Organs
方丝弓矫治器/方絲弓矯治器　edgewise appliance
方丝弓锁槽式带环/邊緣鎖槽式帶環　edgewise bracket band
方形管/方形管　rectangular tube
方形肌/方形肌　quadrate muscle
方形矫正弓线/方形矯正弓線　edgewise archwire
方形接合/方形接合　butt
方形结节/方形結節　quadrate tubercle
方形膜/方形膜　quadrangular membrane
方形韧带/方形韌帶　quadrate ligament, ligamentum quadratum
方形丝/方形絲　edgewise wire
方形小叶后部/方形小葉後部　posterior quadrangular lobule
方形小叶前部/方形小葉前部　anterior quadrangular lobule
方形牙弓/方形牙弓　square dental arch

方叶/方葉 quadrate lobe
芳基胺/芳基胺 arylamine
芳基胺 N-乙酰转移酶/芳基胺 N-乙醯轉移酶 arylamine N-acetyltransferase
芳基二烷基磷酸酶/芳基二烷基磷酸酶 aryldialkylphosphatase
芳基磺基转移酶/芳基磺基轉移酶 arylsulfotransferase
芳基磺酸类/芳基磺酸類 arylsulfonic acids
芳基磺酸盐类/芳基磺酸鹽類 arylsulfonates
芳基甲酰胺酶/芳基甲醯胺酶 arylformamidase
芳基硫酸酯酶类/芳基硫酸酯酶類 arylsulfatases
芳基烃羟化酶类/芳基烴羥化酶類 aryl hydrocarbon hydroxylases
芳基烃受体/芳基烴受體 aryl hydrocarbon receptor
芳基烷基胺 N-乙酰转移酶/芳基烷基胺 N-乙醯轉移酶 arylalkylamine N-acetyltransferase
芳烷基/芳烷基 aralkyl
芳香氨基酸类/芳香胺基酸類 aromatic amino acids
芳香-L-氨基酸脱羧酶类/芳香-L-胺基酸脱羧酶類 aromatic-L-amino-acid decarboxylases
芳香化湿/芳香化濕 resolving dampness with aromatics
芳香化浊/芳香化濁 eliminating turbid pathogen with aromatics
芳香混合物/芳香混合物 fragrance mix
芳香基硫酸酯酶/芳香基硫酸酯酶 arylsulphatase
芳香剂/芳香劑 flavoring agent, aromatic
芳香开窍/芳香開竅 inducing resuscitation with fragrant materials, resuscitation with aromatics
芳香苦味药/芳香苦味劑 aromatic bitters
芳香疗法/芳香療法 aromatherapy
芳香酶/芳香酶 aromatase
芳香酶抑制剂/芳香酶抑制劑 aromatase inhibitor
芳香酶抑制药/芳香酶抑制藥 aromatase inhibitor
芳香水剂/芳香水劑 aromatic water
芳香烃类/芳香烴類 aromatic hydrocarbons
芳香烃羟化酶/芳香烴羥化酶 aryl hydrocarbon-hydroxylase
芳香系/芳香族 aromatic series
芳香性氨基酸/芳香族胺基酸 aromatic amino acid
芳香族多环碳氢化合物/芳香族多環碳氫化合物 aromatic polycyclic hydrocarbons
芳[香族]基胂酸/芳香基胂酸 arylarsonic acid
芳香族硫酸/芳香族硫酸 elixir of vitriol
芳香族溶液/芳香族溶液 aromatic solution
芳香族酸/芳香酸 aromatic acid
芳香族烃/芳香烴 aromatic hydrocarbon

防氨面罩/防氨面具 kupramite
防病/疾病預防 disease prevention
防风/防風 divaricate saposhnikovia root
防风草/防風草 parsnips
防风通圣散/防風通聖散 fangfeng tongsheng powder
防风通圣丸/防風通聖丸 fangfeng tongsheng pills
防辐射药/防輻射藥 radioprotector
防腐法/防腐[法] antisepsis
防腐敷料/防腐敷料 antiseptic dressing
防腐剂/防腐劑 preservative
防腐溶液/防腐溶液 antiseptic solution
防腐无菌法/李斯特氏法則 listerism
防腐性注射液/[屍體之]防腐注射法 preservative injection
防护服/防護衣 protective clothing
防护手套/防護手套 protective gloves
防护牙托/口護套 mouth guard
防护眼镜/[防]護眼鏡 protective spectacle
防护装置/防護裝置 protective device
防护作用/防衛作用 peltation
防己/防己 Stephania tetrandra
防己黄芪汤/防己黄芪湯 fangji huangqi decoction
防结石的/阻止結石的,防治結石病的 antilithic
防空壕足/避難足 shelter foot
防盲/防盲 prevention of blindness
防龋[齿]药/防齲[齒]藥 anticariogenic
防晒剂/防曬劑 sunscreen agent, sunscreen
防晒乳液/防曬乳液,防曬黑劑 suntan lotion
防晒系数/防曬係數 sun protection factor
防声器/避噪音器 antiphone
防衰剂/治萎縮藥 anatrophic
防痛步态/止痛性步態 antalgic gait
防痛反应/避痛反應 antalgic reaction
防萎缩性肾切开取石术/防萎縮性腎切開取石術 anatrophic nephrolithotomy
防卫/防衛 defense
防卫细胞/防衛細胞 protective cell
防异毒素/防異毒素 allotoxin
防御反应/防衛反應 defense reaction
防御环/防禦圈 defensive circle
防御机制/防禦機制 defense mechanism
防御[力]崩溃/防衛力崩潰 defense rupture
防御力减退/防衛力減退 apophylaxis
防御力减退期/防禦力減退期 apophylactic phase
防御素/防禦素 phylaxin
防御素类/防禦素類 defensins
防御[素]学/防禦[素]學 phylaxiology

防御细胞/防禦細胞　defense cell
防御性精神病/防禦性精神病　defensive psychosis
防御性精神神经病/防禦性精神神經病　defensive psychoneurosis
防御医学/防禦醫學　defensive medicine
防皱带/除皺帶　antiwrinkle band
防撞装置/防撞装置　anti-bumping device
防紫外线剂/防紫外線藥　ultraviolet screening agent
房的/房的　atrial
房间隔/心房間隔,心耳間隔　interatrial septum
房间隔切除术/心房間隔切除術　atrial septectomy
房间隔缺损/房間隔缺損　atrial septal defect, atrial heart septal defect
房间隔缺损合并二尖瓣裂/房間隔缺損合并二尖瓣裂　atrial septal defect with cleft mitral valve
房劳/房勞　excessive sexual intercourse
房劳尿血/房勞尿血　hematuria due to sexual intemperance
房事淡漠/房事淡漠,無性戀　asexuality, low sexual desire
房室瓣/房室瓣　atrioventricular valve, AVV
房室传导/房室傳導　atrioventricular conduction
房室传导阻滞/房室傳導阻滯　atrioventricular block
房室的/房室的　auriculoventricular
房室垫/房室墊　atrioventricular cushion
房室分离/心房心室電傳導獨立　atrioventricular dissociation
房室隔/房室隔　atrioventricular septum
房室沟/房室溝　atrioventricular groove, AVG
房室管/房室管　atrioventricular canal, AVC
房室管永存/房室管永存,永久性房室管　persistent atrioventricular canal
房室肌束/Kent氏束　Kent bundle
房室交互心动快速/房室迴旋性心搏快速　atrioventricular reciprocating tachycardia
房室交界区/房室交界處,房室結合　atrioventricular junction
房室交界区心动过速/房室交界心搏過速,房室結合心搏過速　atrioventricular junctional tachycardia
房室交界区心律/房室交界心律,房室結合心律　atrioventricular junctional rhythm
房室交界区逸搏节律/房室結合逸脱節律　atrioventricular junctional escape rhythm
房室结/房室結　atrioventricular node
房室结动脉/房室結動脈　atrioventricular node artery
房室结合节律/房室結合節律　atrioventricular junctional rhythm
房室结合早期收缩/房室結合早期收縮　premature atrioventricular junctional complex
房室结律/房室結節律　atrioventricular nodal rhythm
房室结内折返性心动过速/房室結内折返性心動過速　atrioventricular nodal reentry tachycardia
房室结双径路/房室結雙徑路　dual atrioventricular nodal pathway
房室[结性]节律/房室節律　atrioventricular rhythm
房室结性心动过速/房室心搏過速　atrioventricular tachycardia
房室结支/房室結支　branch of atrioventricular node
房室径/房室徑　atrioventricular pathway
房室静脉/房室靜脈　atrioventricular vein
房室孔/房室孔,房室口　atrioventricular orifice, auriculoventricular orifice
房室口/房室口,房室孔　atrioventricular orifice, auriculoventricular orifice
房室[收缩]间期/心房室間期　auriculoventricular interval
房室束/房室束　atrioventricular bundle, atrioventricular band
房室顺序型起搏/房室順序型起搏　atrioventricular sequential pacing
房室同步/房室同步　atrioventricular synchrony
房室折返性心动过速/房室折返性心動過速　atrioventricular reentry tachycardia
房室支/房室支　Rami atrioventriculares(拉)
房束旁道/房束旁道　atriofascicular tract
房水/水狀液　aqueous humor
房水静脉/液樣靜脈　aqueous vein
房水流畅系数/房水流暢係數　coefficient of outflow facility
房水闪光/房水閃光　aqueous flare
房水生成速度/房水生成速度　rate of flow
房性心动过速/前房心搏快速　atrial tachycardia
房性逸搏性心律/前房性逸脱節律　atrial escape rhythm
仿生材料/仿生材料　biomimetic materials
仿生学/生物機械學　bionics
仿细胞内液型液/仿細胞内液型液　intracellulartype solution
仿细胞外液型液/仿細胞外液型液　extracellulartype solution
纺锤菌素/紡錘菌素　netropsin
纺锤剩体/紡錘剩體　mitosome
纺锤丝/梭狀纖維　spindle fiber
纺锤体/紡錘體　spindle

纺锤恙虫/紡錘恙蟲　spinning mite
纺锤状白内障/紡錘狀白內障　spindle cataract
纺织工咳/紡織工欬　weaver cough
纺织品皮炎/紡織品皮膚炎　textile dermatitis
放冲复合伤/放冲複合傷　radiation blast combined injury
放出/放出　emit
放大腹腔镜检查[术]/放大腹腔鏡檢查[術]　magnifying laparoscopy
放大镜/放大鏡　magnifying lens
放大内镜检查[术]/放大内鏡檢查[術]　magnifying endoscopy
放大试验/[规模]放大　scale-up
放电/放電　electric discharge
放弃[治疗]/中止治療　abandonment
放射变应原吸附/放射性過敏性吸附　radioallergosorbent
放射测量术/放射性測量　radiometry
放射碘化血清白蛋白/放射碘化血清白蛋白　radioiodinated serumalbumin
放射毒理学/放射毒理學　radiotoxicology
放射对比介质/放射性顯影劑　radiocontrast media
放射对称/放射對稱　radiation symmetry
放射冠/放射冠,輻射冠　corona radiata
放射核素心血管显像/放射核種心臟血管照相術　radionuclide angiocardiography
放射后纤维化/放射性纖維化　radiation fibrosis
放射化学/放射化學　radiochemistry
放射剂量分次/放射劑量分次　dose fractionation
放射科医师/放射科醫生　radiologist
放射量测定仪/輻射計　radiometer
放射量计/X射線之用量表,劑量計　dosage meter
放射疗法/放射療法　radiotherapy
放射免疫测定[法]/放射免疫測定法,放射免疫分析法　radioimmunoassay
放射免疫沉淀测定/放射免疫沈澱測定　radioimmunoprecipitation assay
放射免疫沉淀[法]/放射免疫沈澱[法]　radioimmunoprecipitation
放射免疫电泳[法]/放射免疫電泳[法]　radioimmunoelectrophoresis
放射免疫疗法/放射免疫療法　radioimmunotherapy
放射免疫吸附试验/放射免疫吸附試驗　radioimmunosorbent test
放射免疫显像/放射免疫顯像　radioimmunodetection
放射脑电描记法/放射腦電圖描記法　radioencephalography
放射配体测定/放射配體測定　radioligand assay

放射平衡/放射平衡　radioactive equilibrium
放射烧伤/放射燒傷　radiation burn
放射摄影术/X射線照像術　radiography
放射生态学/放射生態學　radioecology
放射生物学/放射生物學　radiobiology
放射衰变/放射性衰變　radioactive decay
放射外科手术/放射外科學,鐳外科學　radiosurgery
放射物[质]/放射物質　radiogen
放射线工作者癌/放射線工作者癌　roentgenologist cancer
放射线核素肾图/放射線核素腎圖　radionuclide renogram
放射线菌疾病/放射線菌疾病　ray-fungus disease
放射线疗法/放射線療法,光療法　actinotherapy
放射心电描记法/放射心電圖描記法　radioelectrocardiography
放射性/放射性　radioactivity
放射性沉降物/放射性沈降物　radioactive fallout
放射[性]的/放射性的　radioactive
放射性碘/放射性碘　radioactive iodine
放射性碘标记血清白蛋白/放射性碘標記血清白蛋白　radio-iodinated serum albumin
放射性碘化钠溶液/放射性碘化鈉溶液　sodium radio-iodide solution
放射性毒血症/放射線中毒症　actinotoxemia
放射性肺炎/放射性肺炎　radiation pneumonia
放射性废弃物/放射性廢物　radioactive waste
放射性骨坏死/放射性骨壞死　osteoradionecrosis
放射性过敏原吸附试验/放射性過敏原吸附試驗　RAST
放射性核纯度/放射性核純度　radionuclide purity
放射性核素/放射性核素　radionuclide
放射性核素发生器/放射性核素發生器　radionuclide generator
放射性核素膀胱输尿管反流试验/放射性核素膀胱輸尿管反流試驗　radionuclide vesicoureteral reflux test
放射性核素肾图/放射性核素腎圖　radionuclide renogram
放射性核素显像/放射性核素造影術　radionuclide imaging
放射性核素心室显像术/放射性核素心室顯像術　radionuclide ventriculography
放射性核素血管显像术/放射性核素血管顯像術　radionuclide angiography
放射性坏死/放射性壞死　radiation necrosis
放射性脊髓病/放射性脊髓病　radiation myelopathy
放射性脊髓炎/放射性脊髓炎　radiation myelitis

放射性胶体金/放射性膠體金　radioactive gold colloid
放射性结肠炎/放射性結腸炎　radiation colitis
放射性金溶液/放射性金溶液　radiogold solution
放射性空气污染/放射性空氣汙染　radioactive air pollution
放射性空气污染物/放射性空氣汙染物　radioactive air pollutant
放射性溃疡/放射性潰瘍　radiation ulcer
放射性磷酸钠溶液/放射性磷酸鈉溶液　sodium radio-phosphate solution
放射性浓度/放射性濃度　radioactive concentration
放射性皮炎/放射性皮膚炎　radiation dermatitis
放射性氰钴胺溶液/放射性氰酸鈷胺明溶液　radiocyanocobalamin solution
放射性神经炎/放射線神經炎　actinoneuritis
放射性肾炎/放射性腎炎　radiation nephritis
放射性食品污染/放射性食品汙染　radioactive food contamination
放射性示踪剂/放射性示蹤劑,放射性示蹤物　radioactive tracer
放射性水污染/放射性水汙染　radioactive water pollution
放射性水污染物/放射性水汙染物　radioactive water pollutant
放射[性损]伤/輻射損傷　radiation injury
放射性同位素/放射性同位素　radioisotope, radioactive isotope
放射性同位素扫描/放射性同位素掃描　radioisotope scanning
放射性同位素肾图术/放射性同位素腎圖檢查　radioisotope renography
放射性同位素稀释技术/放射性同位素稀釋技術　radioisotope dilution technique
放射性同位素远距离疗法/放射性同位素遠距離療法　radioisotope teletherapy
放射性同位素诊断技术/放射性同位素診斷技術　radioisotope diagnostic technique
放射性痛/放射性痛　irradiation of pain, radiating pain
放射性土壤污染物/放射性土壤汙染物　radioactive soil pollutant
放射性脱发/放射線性禿髮　radiation alopecia
放射性污染物/放射性汙染物　radioactive pollutant
放射性小肠炎/放射性小腸炎　radiation enteritis
放射性心包炎/放射性心包炎　radiation pericarditis
放射性修复/放射性修復　radiorepair
放射性药物/放射性藥物　radiopharmaceuticals
放射性元素/放射性元素　radioactive elements
放射性元素蜕变/放射性元素蛻變,放射性衰變　radioactive disintegration
放射性造影剂/放射性造影劑　radiocontrast medium
放射性指示剂/放射指示劑　radioactive indicator
放射性治愈性/放射性治療力　radiocurability
放射学/放射學　radiology
放射学工艺学/放射學工藝學　radiologic technology
放射学信息系统/放射學資訊系統　radiology information system
放射药剂学/放射藥劑學　radiopharmaceutics
放射照相的/放射線攝影的　radiographic
放射治疗剂量/放射治療劑量　radiotherapy dosage
放射肿瘤学/癌症放射療學　radiation oncology
放射状[的]/放射狀　radial
放射状角膜切开术/放射狀角膜切開術　radial keratotomy
放射状韧带/放射狀韌帶　radiate ligament
放射状牙质/皺齒質　plicadentin
放射自显影[术]/放射自顯影[法]　autoradiography
放射自显影照片/放射性同位素示蹤圖　radioautogram
放松的/放鬆的,鬆弛的　relaxed
放松运动/放鬆運動　relaxation exercise
放线杆菌病/放線桿菌病　actinobacillosis
放线杆菌属感染/放線桿菌感染　*Actinobacillus* infection
放线菌/放線菌　actinomycete, ray fungus
放线菌病/放線菌病　actinomycosis
放线菌病的/放線菌病的　actinomycotic
放线菌病性阑尾炎/放線菌性闌尾炎　actinomycotic appendicitis
放线菌病性足菌肿/放線菌性足菌腫　actinomycotic mycetoma
放线菌的/放線菌的　actinomycetic
放线菌科/放線菌科　Actinomycetaceae
放线菌目/放線菌目　Actinomycetales
放线菌目感染/放線菌目感染　Actinomycetales infection
放线菌噬菌体/放線菌噬菌體　actinophage
放线菌属/放線菌屬　*Actinomyces*
放线菌素/放線菌素　actinomycin
放线菌素 C/放線菌素 C　actinomycin C
放线菌素 D/放線菌素 D　actinomycin D
放线菌体素/放線菌體素　actinomycotin
放线菌酮/放射菌酮　actidione
放线菌性前列腺炎/放線菌性前列腺炎　actinomycotic prostatitis

放线菌肿/放線菌瘤 actinomycoma
放线菌足菌肿/放線菌足菌腫 actinomycetic mycetoma
放线状肋胸韧带/放線狀肋胸韌帶 radiate costosternal ligament
放血/放血 bloodletting
放血疗法/放血療法 blood letting therapy
飞法/飛法 needle-handle twisting
飞机式夹板/飛機式夾板 airplane splint
飞盲症/飛盲症 flight blindness
飞沫传染/飛沫傳染 droplet infection
飞腾八法/飛騰八法 method of eight flight
飞行病/高空神經官能病 flying sickness
飞行器/飛機 aircraft
飞行时差反应综合征/時差症候群 jet lag syndrome
飞燕草子/飛燕草子 larkspur
飞扬/飛揚 feiyang, BL58
飞扬喉/飛揚喉 hematoma of upper palate, hematoma of uvula
飞蝇幻视/飛蠅幻視 muscae volitantes
非凹陷性水肿/非壓陷性水腫 non-pitting edema
非巴比妥类静脉麻醉药/非巴比妥類靜脈麻醉藥 non-barbiturate intravenous anesthetic
非瘢痕灸/無瘢痕灸 non-scarring moxibustion
非板[状]骨/非板狀骨,網狀骨 nonlamellated bone
非闭塞性肠梗死/非閉塞性腸梗死 non-occlusive intestinal infarction
非搏动灌注/非搏動灌注 non-pulsatile perfusion
非哺乳动物胚胎/非哺乳動物胚胎 non-mammalian embryo
非程序DNA合成/非程序DNA合成 unscheduled DNA synthesis
非处方药/非處方藥 nonprescription drug, over the counter drug, OTC drug
非穿透伤/非穿透傷 non-perforating wound
非磁性眼内异物/非磁性眼內異物 intraocular nonmagnetic foreign body
非代偿性碱中毒/非補償性鹼中毒 uncompensated alkalosis
非代偿性酸中毒/非補償性酸中毒 uncompensated acidosis
非蛋白氮/非蛋白氮 non-protein nitrogen
非倒凹区/非倒凹區 non-undercut area
非等温法/非等溫法 non-isothermal method
非典型暴发性紫癜/非典型猛爆性紫癜症 atypical purpura fulminans
非典型分枝杆菌病/非典型分枝桿菌病 atypical mycobacteriosis
非典型化脓性肉芽肿/非典型化膿性肉芽腫 atypical pyogenic granuloma
非典型假胆碱酯酶/非典型假膽鹼酯酶 atypical pseudocholinesterase
非典型假肉瘤性皮肤组织细胞瘤/非典型假肉瘤性皮膚組織細胞瘤 atypical pseudosarcomatous cutaneous histiocytoma
非典型褥疮性纤维增生症/非典型褥瘡性纖維增生症 atypical decubital fibroplasia
非典型色素性紫癜/非典型色素性紫癜 atypical pigmented purpura
非典型失神发作/非典型失神發作 atypical absence seizure
非典型湿疣/非典型濕疣 atypical condylomata
非典型髓质瘤/非典型髓質瘤 atypical hyloma
非典型痛风/非典型痛風 atypical gout
非典型纤维黄[色]瘤/非典型纖維黃[色]瘤 atypical fibroxanthoma
非典型性分枝杆菌感染/非典型性分枝桿菌感染 atypical mycobacterium infection
非典型性结核病/非典型結核病 atypical tuberculosis
非典型性纤维组织细胞瘤/非典型纖維組織細胞瘤 atypical fibrohistiocytoma
非典型疣状心内膜炎/非典型性贅疣狀心內膜炎 atypical verrucous endocarditis
非典型鱼鳞癣样红皮症/非典型魚鱗癬樣紅皮症 atypical ichthyosiform erythroderma
非电离辐射/非電離輻射 nonionizing radiation
非定形的/無定形的 amorphous
非动性白细胞/非活動性白血球 nonmotile leukocyte
非毒性结节性甲状腺肿/非毒性結節性甲狀腺腫 nontoxic nodular goiter
非对称/非對稱 dissymmetry
非对称突触/非對稱突觸,格雷I型突觸 asymmetrical synapse
非对称性同侧偏盲/非對稱性偏盲 incongruous hemianopia
非对称性突触/非對稱性突觸 asymmetrical synapse
非对映[立体]异构物/雙星同質異構物 diastereoisomer
非对映[立体]异构[现象]/雙星同質異構物作用 diastereoisomerism
非对映体过量/非對映體過量 diastereomeric excess, DE
非对映[异构]体/非對映異構體 diastereomer
非翻译区/非翻譯區 untranslated region

非肝性的/非肝性的 anhepatic
非肝性黄疸/非肝性黄疸 anhepatic jaundice
非肝原的/非肝原的 anhepatogenous
非肝原性黄疸/非肝原性黄疸 anhepatogenous jaundice
非格司亭/非格司亭 filgrastim
非梗阻性肥厚型心肌病/非梗阻性肥厚型心肌病 non-obstructive hypertrophic cardiomyopathy
非工作侧/非工作侧 non-working side
非佝偻病性弓形腿/非佝僂病性弓形腿 non-rachitic bowleg
非骨化性纤维瘤/非骨化性纖維瘤 non-ossifying fibroma
非骨连接性斜颈畸形/非骨連線性斜頸畸形 non-synostotic plagiocephaly
非贯通伤/非穿通創傷 non-penetrating wound
非过敏性/非過敏性 non-allergic
非过敏性制剂/非過敏性製劑 non-allergic agent
非核酸依赖肽生物合成/非核酸依賴肽生物合成 nucleic acid-independent peptide biosynthesis
非黑瘤皮肤癌/非黑色瘤的皮膚癌 non-melanoma skin cancer
非呼吸性酸中毒/非呼吸性酸中毒症 non-respiratory acidosis
非活体移植/非活體移植 non-viable transplantation
非霍奇金淋巴瘤/非霍奇金淋巴瘤 non-hodgkin lymphoma
非机械性眼外伤/非機械性眼外傷 non-mechanical ocular injury
非肌肌球蛋白ⅡA型/非肌肌球蛋白ⅡA型 non-muscle myosin type ⅡA
非激活状态/非啟動狀態 unactivated state
非季节性变应性鼻炎/非季節性過敏性鼻炎 non-seasonal allergic rhinitis
非家族性网状内皮肉芽肿综合征/網狀内皮系腫瘤症候群 Abt-Letterer-Siwe syndrome
非甲型肝炎/非甲型肝炎 non-A hepatitis
非键[分子]轨道/非鍵[分子]軌域 nonbonding molecular orbital
非交通性脑积水/非交通性腦積水,阻塞性水腦 non-communicating hydrocephalus
非胶质尘肺症/非膠質塵肺症 non-collagenous pneumoconiosis
非角化复层扁平上皮/非角化複層扁平上皮 nonkeratinized stratified squamous epithelium
非接触式眼压计/非接觸式眼壓計 non-contact tonometer
非结核性分枝杆菌病/非結核性分枝桿菌病 non-tuberculous mycobacteriosis
非姐妹染色单体/非姐妹染色單體 non-sister chromatid
非解剖式牙/非解剖式牙 non-anatomic tooth
非精原细胞瘤/非精原細胞瘤 non-seminoma
非竞争性抑制/非競爭性抑制 non-competitive inhibition
非均相反应/非均相反應 inhomogeneous reaction
非均相液体药剂/非均相液體製劑 nonhomogeneous liquid preparation
非颗粒型内质网/無顆粒性内質網 agranular endoplasmic reticulum
非快速眼球转动睡眠/非快速眼球轉動睡眠 non-rapid eye movement sleep
非溃疡性睑炎/非潰瘍性眼瞼炎 non-ulcerative blepharitis
非郎格尔汉斯细胞组织细胞增多症/非郎格爾漢斯細胞組織細胞增多症 non-Langerhans-cell histiocytosis
非类固醇消炎药/非類固醇消炎藥 non-steroidal antiinflammatory drug
非粒性白细胞/非粒性白血球 non-granulocyte
非淋[球]菌性尿道炎/非淋[球]菌性尿道炎 non-gonococcal urethritis
非洛地平/非洛地平 felodipine
非麻醉镇痛药/非麻醉鎮痛藥 non-narcotic analgesics
非那吡啶/非那吡啶 phenazopyridine
非那二醇/氯苯甲基丁烷二醇 phenaglycodol
非那特利/非那特利 finasteride
非那西丁/非那西汀 phenacetin
非那西托林/非那西托林 phenacetolin
非那佐辛/非那佐辛 phenazocine
非钠依赖有机阴离子转运子/非鈉依賴有機陰離子轉運子 sodium-independent organic anion transporter
非尼拉敏/非尼拉敏 pheniramine
非牛顿流体/非牛頓流體 non-Newtonian fluid
非脓毒性栓塞/非膿毒性栓塞 bland embolism
非诺多泮/非諾多泮 fenoldopam
非诺洛芬/苯氧基氢化阿托酸 fenoprofen
非诺特罗/非諾特羅 fenoterol
非平面摇摆振动/非平面摇擺振動 wagging vibration
非前列腺肥大性前列腺病态/虛性前列腺阻礙 prostatisme sans prostate
非去极化/非去極化 non-depolarization
非染色质/非染色質,细胞核的非染質 achromatin

非染[色]质溶解/非染質崩解　achromatolysis
非热带性口炎性腹泻/非熱帶性口炎性腹瀉　non-tropical sprue
非人性化行为/人性喪失，無人性　dehumanization
非妊娠期绒毛膜癌/非妊娠期絨毛膜癌　non-gestational choriocarcinoma
非色素上皮/非色素上皮　nonpigmented epithelium
非肾上腺性女性假两性畸形/非腎上腺性女性假兩性畸形　non-adrenal female pseudohermaphroditism
非嗜铬性副神经节/非嗜鉻性副神經節　non-chromaffin paraganglia
非手性分子/非手性分子　achiral molecule
非水疱性脓痂疹/非水皰性膿痂疹　non-bullous impetigo
非水溶剂/非水溶劑　nonaqueous solvent
非丝连多形核白细胞/無連絲多形核白血球　nonfilament polymorphonuclear
非梭状芽孢杆菌的/非梭狀芽孢桿菌的　non-clostridial
非梭状芽孢杆菌气性坏疽/非梭狀芽孢桿菌氣性壞疽　non-clostridial gas gangrene
非羧基酸类/非羧基酸類　non-carboxylic acids
非特异疗法/非特異療法　phlogotherapy
非特异性刺激/非特異性刺激　nonspecific stimulation
非特异性蛋白质/非特異性蛋白質　nonspecific protein
非特异性的/非特異性的　nonspecific
非特异性睾丸炎/非特異性睾丸炎　nonspecific orchitis
非特异性疗法/非特異性療法　nonspecific therapy
非特异性免疫/非特異性免疫性　nonspecific immunity
非特异性尿道炎/非特異性尿道炎　nonspecific urethritis
非特异性膀胱炎/非特異性膀胱炎　nonspecific cystitis
非特异性输血/非特異性輸血　nonspecific blood transfusion
非特异性心包炎/非特異性心包炎　nonspecific pericarditis
非体外循环冠状动脉旁路移植术/非體外循環冠狀動脈旁路移植術　off-pump coronary artery bypass
非酮性高甘氨酸血症/非酮性高甘胺酸血症　non-ketotic hyperglycinemia
非酮症高渗高糖性昏迷/非酮症高滲高糖性昏迷　non-ketogenic hyperosmolar hyperglycemic coma

非透壁性心肌梗死/非透壁性心肌梗死　non-transmural myocardial infarction
非透析治疗/非透析治療　non-dialytic treatment
非吸烟烟草/非吸煙煙草　smokeless tobacco
非细菌性的/非細菌性的　abacterial
非细菌性膀胱炎/非細菌性膀胱炎　nonbacterial cystitis
非细菌性栓塞性心内膜炎/非細菌性栓塞性心内膜炎　abacterial thrombotic endocarditis
非细菌性心内膜炎/非細菌性心内膜炎　nonbacterial endocarditis
非细菌性血栓性心内膜炎/非細菌性血栓型心内膜炎　nonbacterial thrombotic endocarditis
非细菌性赘疣状心内膜炎/非細菌性贅疣狀心内膜炎　nonbacterial verrucous endocarditis
非纤维状胶原/非纖維狀膠原　non-fibrillar collagen
非线性映射/非線性映射　nonlinear mapping
非腺毛/非腺毛　nonglandular hair
非消化道给药/注射給藥　parenteral administration
非小细胞肺癌/非小細胞肺癌　non-small-cell lung carcinoma
非协调的异种移植/非協調的異種移植　discordant xenotransplantation
非心因性的/非心因性的　non-cardiogenic
非心源性肺水肿/非心源性肺水腫　non cardiogenic pulmonary edema
非性病梅毒/非性病梅毒　non-venereal syphilis
非性病硬化性淋巴管炎/非性病硬化性淋巴管炎　non-venereal sclerosing lymphangitis
非胸腺依赖区/非胸腺依賴區　thymus independent area, thymus independent region
非胸腺依赖性免疫不全/非胸腺依賴性免疫不全　thymus independent deficiency
非选择性蛋白尿/非選擇性蛋白尿　non-selective proteinuria
非血红素铁蛋白质类/非血紅素鐵蛋白質類　non-heme iron proteins
非血小板减少性紫癜/非血小板減少性紫癜病　non-thrombocytopenic purpura
非牙源性囊肿/非牙源性囊腫　non-odontogenic cyst
非炎性水肿/非炎性水腫　non-inflammatory edema
非药物处方/非藥物處方　non-drug prescription
非医疗美容/非醫療美容　non-medical cosmetics
非医学专业实习人员职务/非醫學專業實習人員職務　non-medical internship
非依赖性分化/自主分化，獨立分化　independent differentiation
非胰岛素依赖型糖尿病/非胰岛素依賴型糖尿病

non-insulin-dependent diabetes mellitus
非乙型肝炎/非乙型肝炎　non-B hepatitis
非抑制性胰岛素样活性/非抑制性胰島素樣活性　non-suppressible insulin-like activity
非语言交流/非語言交流　non-verbal communication
非预期药物不良反应/非預期不良反應　nonpredictable adverse drug reaction
非甾类雌激素类/非甾類雌激素類　non-steroidal estrogens
非甾类堕胎药/非甾類墮胎藥　non-steroidal abortifacient agent
非甾体消炎药/非類固醇消炎藥　non-steroid anti-inflammatory drug
非阵发性心动过速/非陣發性心動過速　non-paroxysmal tachycardia
非镇静组胺H1拮抗剂/非鎮靜組胺H1拮抗劑　non-sedating histamine H1 antagonists
非整倍配合/非整倍配合　aneugamy
非整倍体/非整倍體　aneuploid
非整倍体细胞/非整倍體細胞　aneuploid cell
非整倍性/非整倍性　aneuploidy
非正式社会控制/非正式社會控制　informal social control
非正中𬌗/咬合不正　acentric occlusion
非正中𬌗间记录/非正中𬌗間記錄　eccentric interocclusal record
非正中颌骨关系/偏位性頜關係　eccentric jaw relation
非指导性治疗/非指導性治療　non-directive therapy
非酯化脂肪酸类/非酯化脂肪酸類　non-esterified fatty acids
非治疗性人类实验/非治療性人類實驗　nontherapeutic human experimentation
非治疗性塑身术/非治療性塑身術　nontherapeutic body modification
非痣样良性黑色素上皮瘤/非痣樣良性黑色素上皮瘤,非母斑樣良性黑色素上皮瘤　non-naevoid benign melanoepithelioma
非洲出血热/非洲出血熱　African hemorrhagic fever
非洲传统医学/非洲傳統醫學　African traditional medicine
非洲防己酸/非洲防己酸,古倫朴酸　calumbic acid
非洲昏睡病/非洲昏睡病　lethargus
非洲马瘟/非洲馬瘟　African horse-sickness
非洲脑膜炎/非洲腦膜炎　African meningitis
非洲睡眠病/非洲睡眠病　African sleeping sickness
非洲锥虫病/非洲錐蟲病　African trypanosomiasis
非洲组织胞浆菌病/非洲組織漿菌病　African histoplasmosis
非专利药/學名藥,俗名藥　generic drug
非自身/非[抗原]自質　not-self
非自愿绝育/非自願絕育　involuntary sterilization
非阻塞性肠系膜缺血/非閉合性腸繫膜缺血　non-occlusive mesenteric ischemia
非阻塞性黄疸/非阻塞性黄疸　non-obstructive jaundice
非组蛋白染色体蛋白质类/非組蛋白染色體蛋白質類　non-histone chromosomal proteins
菲/菲　phenanthrene
菲茨综合征/Fitz氏症候群　Fitz syndrome
菲德勒心肌炎/Fiedler氏心肌炎　Fiedler myocarditis
菲啶类/菲啶類　phenanthridines
菲啶生物碱/菲啶生物鹼　phenanthridine alkaloid
菲尔绍淋巴结/菲爾紹淋巴結　Virchow lymph node
菲尔绍细胞/Virchow氏細胞,麻風細胞　Virchow cell
菲-勒综合征/Fiessinger-Leroy氏症候群　Fiessinger-Leroy syndrome
菲利普斯肌/Phillips氏肌　Phillips muscle
菲绕啉类/菲繞啉類　phenanthrolines
菲什伯格浓缩试验/費希伯氏濃縮試驗　Fishberg concentration test
鲱精蛋白/鯡精蛋白　clupeine
肥疮/肥瘡,黃癬　favus
肥疮·湿热毒蕴证/肥瘡·濕熱毒蘊證　favus with pattern of dampness-heat toxin amassment
肥达反应/肥達反應　Widal reaction
肥达试验/肥達試驗　Widal test
肥达综合征/Widal氏症候群　Widal syndrome
肥大/肥大,肥厚　hypertrophy
肥大的/肥大的　hypertrophic
肥大软骨细胞/肥大軟骨細胞　hypertrophic chondrocyte
肥大细胞/肥大細胞,肥胖細胞　mast cell
肥大细胞白血病/肥大細胞白血病　mast-cell leukemia
肥大细胞病/肥胖細胞病　mast-cell disease
肥大细胞瘤/肥胖細胞瘤　mastocytoma
肥大细胞肉瘤/肥大細胞肉瘤　mast-cell sarcoma
肥大细胞增多/肥大細胞增多,著色性蕁麻疹　mastocytosis
肥大性肺性骨关节病/班-馬二氏病,肺性肥大性骨關節病　Bamberger-Marie disease
肥大性脊椎炎/肥厚性脊椎炎　hypertrophic spondylitis
肥大性狼疮/肥厚性狼瘡　lupus hypertrophicus

肥大性气肿/肥大性氣腫　hypertrophic emphysema
肥大性血管瘤/肥大性血管瘤　hypertrophic angioma
肥大性牙髓炎/肥大性牙髓炎　hypertrophic pulpitis
肥大性硬化/阿諾氏肝硬變，肥大性[肝]硬變　hypertrophic cirrhosis
肥儿丸/肥兒丸　fei'er pills
肥厚性瘢痕/肥厚性瘢痕，肥大性瘢痕　hypertrophic cicatrix, hypertrophic scar
肥厚性鼻炎/肥厚性鼻炎　hypertrophic rhinitis
肥厚性扁平苔藓/肥厚性扁平苔蘚　hypertrophic lichen planus
肥厚性痤疮/肥厚性痤瘡　acne hypertrophica
肥厚性单一神经病变/肥厚性單一神經病變　hypertrophic mononeuropathy
肥厚性腹膜炎/肥厚性腹膜炎　pachyperitonitis
肥厚性[睾丸]鞘膜炎/肥厚性睾丸鞘膜炎　plastic vaginalitis
肥厚性骨膜炎/肥厚性骨膜炎　pachyperiostitis
肥厚性关节炎/肥厚性關節炎　hypertrophic arthritis
肥厚性腱鞘炎/肥厚性腱鞘炎　tenosynovitis hypertrophica
肥厚性盆腔腹膜炎/肥厚性骨盆腹膜炎　pachypelviperitonitis
肥厚性鞘膜炎/肥厚性鞘膜炎　pachyvaginalitis
肥厚性湿疹/肥厚性濕疹　eczema hypertrophicum
肥厚性输卵管卵巢炎/肥厚性輸卵管卵巢炎　pachysalpingo-ovaritis
肥厚性胃炎/肥厚性胃炎　hypertrophic gastritis
肥厚性心肌病/肥厚性心肌病　hypertrophic cardiomyopathy
肥厚性阴道炎/肥厚性陰道炎　pachyvaginitis
肥厚性幽门狭窄/肥厚性幽門狹窄　hypertrophic pyloric stenosis
肥厚阻塞型心肌病心肌切除术/肥厚阻塞型心肌病心肌切除術　myectomy in hypertrophic obstructive cardiomyopathy
肥料棒状杆菌/肥料棒狀桿菌　corynebacterium fimi
肥胖/肥胖　corpulence, obesity
肥胖病/肥胖病　adiposis, obesity
肥胖病膳食/肥胖病飲食　obesity diet
肥胖病学/超體重學　bariatrics
肥胖·脾肾阳虚证/肥胖·脾腎陽虛證　obesity with pattern of yang deficiency of spleen and kidney
肥胖·脾胃郁热证/肥胖·脾胃鬱熱證　obesity with pattern of stagnated heat in spleen and stomach
肥胖·脾虚不运证/肥胖·脾虛不運證　obesity with pattern of impaired transportation due to spleen deficiency
肥胖·气滞血瘀证/肥胖·氣滯血瘀證　obesity with pattern of qi stagnation and blood stasis
肥胖·生殖无能性营养不良/肥胖·生殖無能性營養不良　dystrophia adiposogenitalis
肥胖·生殖性萎缩/肥胖·生殖性萎縮　adiposogenital dystrophy
肥胖·痰湿内盛证/肥胖·痰濕內盛證　obesity with pattern of internal exuberance of phlegm-damp
肥胖·通气低下综合征/肥胖·通氣低下症候群　obesity-hypoventilation syndrome
肥胖性端坐呼吸/肥胖性直體呼吸　pimelorthopnea
肥胖性佝偻病/肥胖性佝僂病　fat rickets
肥胖性呼吸困难/肥胖性呼吸困難　liparodyspnea
肥胖性生殖器退化/肥胖生殖性變性，肥胖生殖性營養不良　adiposogenital degeneration, adiposogenital dystrophy
肥胖性生殖器退化综合征/肥胖性生殖無能症候群　adiposogenital syndrome
肥胖性震颤/肥胖性震顫　fat thrill
肥胖[症]/肥胖症　adiposity
肥气/肥氣　liver amassment
肥皂/肥皂　soap
肥皂水灌肠/肥皂水灌腸劑　soapsuds enema
肥皂性结肠炎/肥皂性結腸炎　soap colitis
肥皂样囊肿/肥皂樣囊腫　soap cyst
肥皂樟脑搽剂/肥皂樟腦擦劑　opodeldoc
腓侧/腓側　fibular
腓侧副韧带/腓側副韌帶　fibular collateral ligament
腓侧跖骨点/腓側蹠骨點　metatarsale fibulare
腓肠/腓腸　calf
腓肠部萎缩/無腿畸形，小腿萎縮　acnemia
腓肠动脉/腓腸肌動脈　sural artery
腓肠肌/腓腸肌　gastrocnemius
腓肠肌内侧头/腓腸肌內側頭　medial head of gastrocnemius, caput mediale musculi gastrocnemii
腓肠肌内侧头腱下囊/腓腸肌內側頭腱下囊　subtendinous bursa of medial head of gastrocnemius
腓肠肌外侧囊/腓腸肌外側囊　lateral brusa of gastrocnemius muscle
腓肠肌外侧头/腓腸肌外側頭　lateral head of gastrocnemius
腓肠肌外侧头腱下囊/腓腸肌外側頭腱下囊　subtendinous bursa of lateral head of gastrocnemius
腓肠静脉/腓腸肌靜脈　sural vein
腓肠内侧肌/腓腸內側肌　medial gastrocnemius muscle
腓肠内侧皮神经/腓腸內側皮神經　medial sural cutaneous nerve, medial cutaneous nerve of calf

腓肠神经/腓腸神經　sural nerve
[腓肠神经]跟外侧支/[腓腸神經]跟外側支　lateral calcanean branch
腓肠外侧皮神经/腓腸外側皮神經　lateral sural cutaneous nerve, lateral cutaneous nerve of calf
腓动脉/腓動脈　fibular artery, peroneal artery
[腓动脉]跟外侧支/[腓動脈]跟外側支　lateral calcaneal branch
腓骨/腓骨　fibula, calf bone
腓骨的/腓骨的　peroneal
腓骨第三肌/腓骨第三肌　musculus peroneus tertius
腓骨短肌/腓骨短肌　peroneus brevis, musculus peroneus brevis
腓骨干骨折/腓骨幹骨折　fibula shaft fracture, fracture of fibular shaft
腓骨骨间缘/腓骨骨間緣　interosseous border of fibula
腓骨骨折/腓骨骨折　fibular fracture
腓骨后面/腓骨後面　posterior surface of fibula
腓骨后缘/腓骨後緣　posterior border of fibula
腓骨肌滑车/腓骨肌滑車　peroneal trochlea
腓骨肌间韧带/腓骨肌間韌帶　fibular intermuscular ligament
腓骨肌上支持带/腓骨肌上支持帶　superior peroneal retinaculum
腓骨肌下支持带/腓骨肌下支持帶　inferior peroneal retinaculum
腓骨肌总腱鞘/腓骨肌總腱鞘　common sheath of peronei
腓骨颈/腓骨頸　neck of fibula
腓骨内侧嵴/腓骨内側嵴　medial crest of fibula
腓骨内侧面/腓骨内側面　medial surface of fibula
腓骨前缘/腓骨前緣　anterior border of fibula
腓骨切迹/腓骨切跡　fibular notch
腓骨神经损害/腓骨神經病灶　peroneal nerve lesion
腓骨体/腓骨體　shaft of fibula
腓骨头/腓骨頭　fibular head, head of fibula
腓骨头点/腓骨頭點　caput fibula point
腓骨头关节面/腓骨頭關節面　articular surface of fibular head
腓骨头后韧带/腓骨頭後韌帶　posterior ligament of fibular head
腓骨头尖/腓骨頭尖　apex of fibular head
腓骨头前韧带/腓骨頭前韌帶　anterior ligament of fibular head, anterior ligament of head of fibula
腓骨外侧面/腓骨外側面　lateral surface of fibula
腓骨长短肌腱滑脱/腓骨長短肌腱滑脱　sliding of long and short muscle tendon of fibula
腓骨长肌/腓骨長肌　peroneus longus, long fibular muscle
腓骨长肌腱沟/腓骨長肌腱溝　sulcus for tendon of peroneus longus
腓骨长肌足底腱鞘/腓骨長肌蹠側腱鞘　plantar tendinous sheath of peroneus longus
腓骨滋养动脉/腓骨滋養動脈　fibubar nutrient artery, nutrient artery of the fibula
腓关节面/腓關節面　fibular articular facet
腓肌萎缩/腓肌萎縮　peroneal atrophy
腓静脉/腓静脈　fibular vein, peroneal vein
腓淋巴结/腓淋巴結　fibular lymph node
腓浅神经/腓淺神經　superficial peroneal nerve, superficial fibular nerve
腓浅神经病/腓淺神經病　peroneal neuropathies
腓浅神经肌支/腓淺神經肌支　muscular branch of superficial peroneal nerve
腓浅神经趾背神经/腓淺神經趾背神經　dorsal digital nerve of foot of superficial peroneal nerve
腓深神经/腓深神經　deep peroneal nerve, deep fibular nerve
腓深神经背外侧神经/腓深神經背外側神經　dorsal lateral nerve of deep peroneal nerve
腓深神经第二趾背内侧神经/腓深神經第二趾背內側神經　dorsal medial nerve of the second toe of deep peroneal nerve
腓深神经肌支/腓深神經肌支　muscular branch of deep peroneal nerve
腓深神经趾背神经/腓深神經趾背神經　dorsal digital nerve of foot of deep peroneal nerve
腓神经/腓神經　peroneal nerve
[腓神经]跟内侧支/[腓神經]跟內側支　medial calcanean branch
腓神经交通支/腓神經交通支　communicating branch of peroneal nerve
腓腨发/腓腨發　calf cellulitis, pyogenic carbuncle of calf
腓总神经/腓總神經　common peroneal nerve, common fibular nerve
榧子/榧子　grand torreya seed
肺/肺　lung
肺癌/肺癌　lung cancer
肺癌·气阴两虚证/肺癌·氣陰兩虛證　lung cancer with pattern of deficiency of both qi and yin
肺癌·痰湿蕴肺证/肺癌·痰濕蘊肺證　lung cancer with pattern of phlegm-damp amassing in lung
肺癌·阴虚热毒证/肺癌·陰虛熱毒證　lung cancer with pattern of yin deficiency and heat-poison

肺癌•瘀阻肺络证/肺癌•瘀阻肺絡證　lung cancer with pattern of static blood blocking lung collateral
肺巴斯德菌病/肺巴斯德菌病　pneumonic pasteurellosis
肺包虫囊肿/肺包蟲囊腫　hydatid cyst of lung
肺孢子虫病/肺孢子蟲病　pneumocystis carinii pneumonia
肺痹/肺痹　lung bi
肺表面活性剂/肺表面活性劑　pulmonary surfactant
肺表面活性物质相关蛋白质类/肺表面活性物質相關蛋白質類　pulmonary surfactant-associated proteins
肺病/肺病　pneumonopathy
肺病疗法/肺病療法　pneumonotherapy
肺病学/肺臟學　pulmonology
肺不张/肺膨脹不全　atelectasis
肺藏魄/肺藏魄　lung storing corporeal soul, lung storing inferior spirit
肺肠炎/肺炎兼腸炎　pneumoenteritis
肺肠炎病毒/肺腸炎病毒　pneumoenteritis virus
肺朝百脉/肺朝百脈　lung connecting all vessel
肺尘埃沉着性结核病/炭末沈著性肺結核　anthracotic tuberculosis
肺尘中毒症/塵埃中毒病　coniotoxicosis
肺充气机/肺灌氣機　lungmotor
肺充血/肺充血　pulmonary congestion
肺出血/肺出血　pneumorrhagia
肺出血-肾炎综合征/古巴士德氏症候群　Goodpasture syndrome
肺穿刺术/肺穿刺術　pneumocentesis
肺吹气法/肺吹氣法　insufflation of lung
肺丛/肺叢　pulmonary plexus, pulmonalis
肺错构瘤/肺錯構瘤　pulmonary hamartoma
肺大疱/肺大皰　bullae
肺单位/肺單位　lung unit
肺的/肺的　pneumonic
肺底/肺底　base of lung
肺底后侧段支气管/肺底後小葉支氣管　bronchus segmentalis basalis posterior
[肺底]心段支气管/心葉支氣管　cardiac bronchus
肺底内侧小叶支气管/肺底內側小葉支氣管　bronchus segmentalis basalis medialis
肺底前小叶支气管/肺底前小葉支氣管　bronchus segmentalis basalis anterior
肺底外侧小叶支气管/肺底外側小葉支氣管　bronchus segmentalis basalis lateralis
肺动静脉瘘/肺動脈與靜脈瘻　pulmonary arteriovenous fistula

肺动脉/肺動脈　pulmonary artery
[肺动脉]半月瓣弧缘/[肺動脈]半月瓣弧緣　lunula of semilunar valve
[肺动脉]半月瓣小结/[肺動脈]半月瓣小結　nodule of semilunar valve
肺动脉瓣/肺動脈瓣　valve of pulmonary trunk, pulmonary valve
肺动脉瓣闭锁不全/肺動脈瓣閉鎖不全　pulmonary valve insufficiency
肺动脉瓣二叶瓣/肺動脈瓣二葉瓣　bicuspid pulmonary valve
肺动脉瓣发育不全/肺動脈瓣發育不全　agenesis of pulmonary valve
肺动脉瓣反流/肺動脈瓣反流　pulmonary regurgitation, pulmonic regurgitation
肺动脉瓣关闭不全/肺動脈閉鎖不全　pulmonary incompetence
肺动脉瓣前半月瓣/肺動脈瓣前半月瓣　anterior semilunar valve of pulmonary trunk
肺动脉瓣切开术/肺動脈瓣切開術　pulmonary valvotomy
肺动脉瓣上狭窄/肺動脈瓣上狹窄　supravalvular pulmonary stenosis
肺动脉瓣狭窄/肺動脈瓣狹窄　pulmonary valve stenosis
肺动脉瓣下狭窄/肺動脈瓣下狹窄　subvalvular pulmonary stenosis
肺动脉瓣性心内膜炎/肺動脈瓣性心內膜炎　pulmonic endocarditis
肺动脉瓣右半月瓣/肺動脈瓣右半月瓣　right semilunar valve of valve of pulmonary trunk
肺动脉瓣杂音/肺動脈瓣雜音　pulmonic murmur
肺动脉瓣左半月瓣/肺動脈瓣左半月瓣　left semilunar valve of valve of pulmonary trunk
肺动脉闭锁/肺動脈閉鎖　pulmonary artery atresia, pulmonary atresia
肺动脉不发育/肺動脈不發育　agenesis of pulmonary artery
肺动脉杈/肺動脈杈　bifurcation of pulmonary trunk
肺动脉窦/肺動脈竇　sinus of pulmonary trunk
肺动脉干/肺動脈幹　pulmonary trunk
肺动脉高[血]压/肺循環血壓過高　pulmonary hypertension
肺动脉高压危象/肺動脈高壓危象　pulmonary hypertensive crisis
肺动脉环束术/肺動脈環束術　pulmonary artery banding
肺动脉口/肺動脈口　orifice of pulmonary trunk,

pulmonary orifice
肺动脉漏斗状狭窄/肺動脈漏斗狀狹窄　infundibular pulmonary stenosis
肺动脉狭窄/肺動脈狹窄　pulmonary artery stenosis, stenosis of pulmonary artery
肺动脉楔压/肺動脈楔壓　pulmonary artery wedge pressure
肺动脉血流[量]/肺動脈血流　pulmonary blood flow
肺动脉压/肺動脈壓　pulmonary artery pressure
肺动脉杂音/肺動脈雜音　pulmonary murmur
肺动脉指数/肺動脈指數　pulmonary artery index
肺段切除术/肺段切除術　segmental resection of lung
肺段支气管/肺段支氣管　segmental bronchi
肺段支气管支/肺段支氣管支　segmental bronchial branch
肺恶/肺惡　critical condition of lung
肺恶寒/肺惡寒　lung being averse to cold
肺风粉刺/肺風粉刺　lung-wind acne
肺风粉刺・肺经风热证/肺風粉刺・肺經風熱證　lung-wind acne with pattern of wind-heat in lung channel
肺风粉刺・肝经郁热证/肺風粉刺・肝經鬱熱證　lung-wind acne with pattern of heat stagnation in liver channel
肺风粉刺・热毒夹瘀证/肺風粉刺・熱毒夾瘀證　lung-wind acne with pattern of heat-toxin complicated by stasis
肺风粉刺・湿热蕴结证/肺風粉刺・濕熱蘊結證　lung-wind acne with dampness-heat amassment pattern
肺风粉刺・痰瘀互结证/肺風粉刺・痰瘀互結證　lung-wind acne with pattern of intermingled phlegm and stasis
肺缝术/肺縫合術　pneumonorrhaphy
肺[浮沉]检验/肺浮沈檢驗　pulmonary docimasia
肺疳/肺疳　lung gan disease
肺隔离症/肺隔離　pulmonary sequestration
肺膈面/肺膈面　diaphragmatic surface of lung
肺根/肺根　radix of lung, root of lung
肺梗死/肺梗塞形成　pulmonary infarction
肺功能测试/肺功能測試　pulmonary function testing
肺功能检查/肺功能檢查　pulmonary function test
肺沟/肺溝　sulcus pulmonalis
肺固定术/肺胞腔壁固定手術　pneumonopexy
肺过敏性脉管炎/肺過敏性脈管炎　pulmonary hypersensitivity vasculitis

肺合大肠/肺合大腸　lung being connected with large intestine
肺黑变病/肺黑變病　pneumomelanosis
肺呼吸/肺呼吸　pulmonary respiration
肺坏疽/肺壞疽　necropneumonia
肺换气/肺換氣　pulmonary gas exchange
肺活检/肺活檢　lung biopsy
肺活量/肺活量　vital capacity
肺及大肠辨证/肺及大腸辨證　pattern identification of lung and large intestine
肺疾病/肺疾病　lung disease
肺棘球蚴病/肺棘球蚴病　pulmonary echinococcosis
肺尖/肺尖　apex of lung
肺尖后段支气管/肺尖後小葉支氣管　bronchus segmentalis apicoposterior
肺尖上段支气管/肺尖上小葉支氣管　bronchus segmentalis apicalis superior
肺尖萎陷术/肺尖萎陷術　apicolysis
肺尖下段支气管/肺尖下小葉支氣管　bronchus segmentalis subapicalis
肺尖支气管/肺尖支氣管　apical bronchus
肺间质纤维化/肺間質纖維化　pulmonary interstitial fibrosis
肺结核/肺結核　pulmonary tuberculosis
肺结核[X射线]条痕/肺結核條痕　tramitis
肺结节病/肺結節病　pulmonary sarcoidosis
肺解剖分流量/肺解剖分流量　anatomical pulmonary shunt
肺惊/肺驚　convulsion due to lung disorder
肺静脉/肺靜脈　pulmonary vein
肺静脉闭塞性疾病/肺靜脈閉塞性疾病　pulmonary veno-occlusive disease
肺静脉畸形引流/先天異常肺靜脈回流　anomalous pulmonary venous drainage
肺静脉口/肺靜脈口　orifices of pulmonary vein
肺厥/肺厥　lung syncope
肺开窍于鼻/肺開竅於鼻　lung opening at nose
肺空洞镜/肺空洞鏡　cavernoscope
肺空洞镜检查/肺空洞鏡檢法　cavernoscopy
肺叩响/肺叩響　pulmonary resonance
肺阔韧带/肺闊韌帶　broad ligament of lung
肺痨/肺癆　lung consumption, pulmonary tuberculosis
肺痨・肺阴虚证/肺癆・肺陰虛證　lung consumption with pattern of lung yin deficiency
肺痨・气阴两虚证/肺癆・氣陰兩虛證　lung consumption with pattern of deficiency of both qi and yin

肺痨·阴虚火旺证/肺癆·陰虛火旺證 lung consumption with pattern of exuberant fire due to yin deficiency

肺痨·阴阳两虚证/肺癆·陰陽兩虛證 lung consumption with pattern of deficiency of both yin and yang

肺肋面/肺肋面 costal surface of lung

肺量测定法/肺量測定法 spirometry

肺淋巴结/肺淋巴結 pulmonary lymph node

肺瘘/肺瘻 pulmonary fistula

肺络损伤/肺絡損傷 damage of collaterals in lung

肺毛滴虫/肺滴蟲 Trichomonas pulmonalis

肺毛细血管/肺微血管 pulmonary capillary

肺毛细血管楔[嵌入]压/肺微血管楔壓 pulmonary capillary wedge pressure

肺毛细血管血氧分压/肺微血管血氧分壓 pulmonary capillary partial pressure of oxygen

肺门/肺門 hilum of lung

肺门结核/肺門結核 hilum tuberculosis

肺门淋巴结结核/肺門淋巴結結核 hilar lymphonode tuberculosis

肺门腺体肿大/肺門腺體腫大 hilar gland enlargement

肺门血管搏动过度/肺門血管搏動過度 hilar dance

肺门血管结扎/肺門血管結紮 ligation of hilar vessel

肺门炎/肺門炎 hilitis

肺弥散/肺彌散 diffusion of lung

肺弥散能力/肺彌散能力 pulmonary diffusing capacity

肺面/肺面 pulmonary surface

肺囊虫/肺囊蟲 pneumocystis

肺囊虫感染/肺囊蟲感染 pneumocystis infection

肺囊虫属/肺囊蟲屬 *Pneumocystis*

肺囊虫性肺炎/肺囊蟲性肺炎 pneumocystis pneumonia

肺内侧面/肺内側面 medial surface of lung

肺内侧小叶支气管/肺内側小葉支氣管 bronchus segmentalis medialis

肺内麻醉/肺内麻醉 pulmonary anesthesia

肺念珠菌病/肺念珠菌症 pneumonomoniliasis

肺脓肿/肺膿腫 lung abscess

肺泡/肺泡 pulmonary alveoli, pulmonary alveolus

肺泡壁/肺泡壁 alveolar wall

肺泡蛋白沉积症/肺泡蛋白質沈著 pulmonary alveolar proteinosis

肺泡的/肺泡的 alveolar

肺泡隔/肺泡隔 alveolar septum

肺泡鼓响/肺泡鼓響 vesiculotympanic resonance

肺泡呼吸音/肺泡呼吸音 vesicular respiration

肺泡间孔/肺泡[間]孔 pulmonic alveolar vent

肺泡巨噬细胞/肺泡巨噬細胞 alveolar macrophage, pulmonary alveolar macrophage

肺泡空洞性呼吸音/肺泡空洞呼吸音 vesiculocavernous respiration

肺泡孔/肺泡孔 alveolar pore

肺泡毛细血管膜/肺泡微血管膜 alveolar-capillary membrane

肺泡毛细血管阻断/肺泡微血管阻斷 alveolar capillary block

肺泡囊/肺泡囊 alveolar sac

肺泡期/肺泡期 alveolar period

肺泡气/肺泡氣 alveolar gas

肺泡上皮/肺泡上皮 alveolar epithelium

肺泡X射线照相术/肺泡X光攝影法 pneumoalveolography

肺泡通气不足/肺泡通氣不足 alveolar hypoventilation

肺泡通气过度/肺泡通氣過度 alveolar hyperventilation

肺泡通气量/肺泡換氣 alveolar ventilation

肺泡微结石症/肺泡微結石症 pulmonary alveolar microlithiasis

肺泡无效腔/肺泡無效腔 alveolar dead space

肺泡细胞/肺泡細胞 alveolar cell

肺泡细胞癌/肺泡細胞癌 alveolar cell cancer

肺泡细胞瘤/肺泡細胞瘤 alveolar cell tumor

肺泡[小]管/肺泡管 alveolar duct

肺泡性肺不张/肺泡性肺不張 alveolar atelectasis

肺泡性叩响/肺泡叩響 vesicular resonance

肺泡[性]气肿/肺[泡]氣腫 alveolar emphysema

肺泡性哮喘/肺泡性氣喘 alveolar asthma

肺泡性支气管炎/肺泡性支氣管炎 vesicular bronchitis

肺泡炎/肺泡炎 alveolitis

肺泡样软组织瘤/肺泡樣軟組織瘤 alveolar soft part tumor

肺泡音/肺泡音 vesicular murmur

肺泡支气管呼吸音/肺泡支氣管呼吸音 vesiculobronchial respiration

肺泡中心细胞/肺泡中心細胞 centroalveolar cell

肺胚细胞瘤/肺胚細胞瘤 pulmonary blastoma

肺膨出/肺質膨出,肺赫尼亞 pneumatocele

肺膨胀不全/膨脹不全,肺不張 atelectasis

肺脾两虚/肺脾兩虛 deficiency of both lung and spleen

肺气/肺氣　lung qi
肺气不宣/肺氣不宣　failure of lung qi in dispersion
肺气虚/肺氣虛　deficiency of lung qi
肺气虚证/肺氣虛證　pattern of deficiency of lung qi
肺气压伤/肺氣壓傷　pulmonary barotrauma
肺气阴两虚证/肺氣陰兩虛證　pattern of deficiency of both qi and yin of lung
肺气肿/肺氣腫　pulmonary emphysema
肺气肿性哮喘/氣腫性氣喘　emphysematous asthma
肺牵张感受器/肺牽張感受器　pulmonary stretch receptor
肺前丛/前肺神經叢　anterior pulmonary plexus
肺前小叶支气管/肺前小葉支氣管　bronchus segmentalis anterior
肺切除术/肺切除術　pneumonectomy
肺切开术/肺切開術　pneumonotomy
肺热病/肺熱病　lung heat disease
肺热病·肺胃热盛证/肺熱病·肺胃熱盛證　lung heat disease with pattern of exuberant heat in lung and stomach
肺热病·风热犯肺证/肺熱病·風熱犯肺證　lung heat disease with pattern of wind-heat invading lung
肺热病·气阴两虚证/肺熱病·氣陰兩虛證　lung heat disease with pattern of deficiency of both qi and yin
肺热病·热陷心包证/肺熱病·熱陷心包證　lung heat disease with pattern of heat invading pericardium
肺热病·痰热壅肺证/肺熱病·痰熱壅肺證　lung heat disease with pattern of phlegm-heat congesting lung
肺热病·邪陷正脱证/肺熱病·邪陷正脱證　lung heat disease with pattern of interior invasion of pathogen and vital qi collapse
肺热肠燥证/肺熱腸燥證　pattern of lung heat and intestine-dryness
肺热炽盛证/肺熱熾盛證　pattern of exuberance of lung heat
肺热血瘀证/肺熱血瘀證　pattern of blood stasis due to lung heat
肺热阴虚证/肺熱陰虛證　pattern of yin deficiency due to lung heat
肺韧带/肺韌帶　pulmonary ligament
肺韧带淋巴结/肺韌帶淋巴結　lymph node of pulmonary ligament
肺容量测定/肺容量測定　lung volume measurement
肺[容]量计/測肺容量器　pulmometer
肺蠕虫/肺蟲　lung worm
肺软化/肺軟化　pneumomalacia
肺善/肺善　favorable condition of lung
肺上沟瘤/肺溝瘤　pulmonary sulcus tumor

肺上沟综合征/肺上溝症候群　superior pulmonary sulcus syndrome
肺上小叶支气管/肺上小葉支氣管　bronchus segmentalis superior
肺X射线[照]片/肺X光照片　pneumonograph
肺X射线照相术/肺X光攝影法　pneumonography
肺肾气虚/肺腎氣虛　qi deficiency of lung and kidney
肺肾气虚证/肺腎氣虛證　pattern of qi deficiency of lung and kidney
肺肾相生/肺腎相生　mutually promotion of lung and kidney
肺肾阴虚/肺腎陰虛　yin deficiency of lung and kidney
肺肾阴虚证/肺腎陰虛證　pattern of yin deficiency of lung and kidney
肺肾综合征/Goodpasture氏症候群　Goodpasture syndrome
肺生理分流量/肺生理分流量　physiological pulmonary shunt
肺失清肃/肺失清肅　impaired depurative descending of lung qi
肺石/肺結石　lung stone
肺石板屑沉着病/石板屑沈著病　schistosis
肺石病/肺石症　pneumolithiasis
肺石墨沉着病/肺石墨沈著病　graphite pneumoconiosis
肺食管旁淋巴结/肺食管旁淋巴結　pulmonary juxta-esophageal lymph node
肺嗜酸粒细胞增多/肺嗜酸粒細胞增多　pulmonary eosinophilia
肺鼠疫/肺鼠疫　pneumonic plague
肺俞/肺俞　feishu, BL13
肺衰/肺衰　lung failure
肺栓塞/肺栓塞　pulmonary embolism
肺水/肺水　lung edema
肺水·肺气虚寒证/肺水·肺氣虛寒證　lung edema with pattern of deficiency-cold of lung qi
肺水·风邪遏肺证/肺水·風邪遏肺證　lung edema with pattern of wind pathogen inhibiting lung
肺水·痰热壅肺证/肺水·痰熱壅肺證　lung edema with pattern of phlegm-heat congesting lung
肺水肿/肺水腫　edema of lung
肺顺应性/肺順應性　lung compliance
肺司呼吸/肺司呼吸　lung controlling breathing
肺松解术/肺鬆解術　pneumonolysis
肺弹性/肺彈性　elastance of lung
肺弹性回缩压/肺彈性回縮壓　lung elastic recoil pressure

肺通气/肺通氣　pulmonary ventilation
肺通气灌流比率/換氣灌注比率　ventilation-perfusion ratio
肺外侧小叶支气管/肺外側小葉支氣管　bronchus segmentalis lateralis
肺外的/肺外的　extrapulmonary
肺外科手术/肺外科手術　pulmonary surgical procedure
肺外性咳/肺外欬嗽　extrapulmonary cough
肺外氧合/肺外氧合　extrapulmonary oxygenation
肺外支气管/肺外支氣管　extrapulmonary bronchus
肺为贮痰之器/肺爲貯痰之器　lung being reservoir of phlegm
肺萎陷/肺陷落　collapse of the lung
肺痿/肺痿　lung wilt disease, atrophic lung disease, lung flaccidity
肺痿·虚寒证/肺痿·虛寒證　lung wilt disease with deficiency-cold pattern
肺痿·虚热证/肺痿·虛熱證　lung wilt disease with deficiency-heat pattern
肺吸虫/肺吸蟲　lung fluke
肺吸虫病/肺吸蟲病　paragonimiasis
肺吸收/肺吸收　pulmonary absorption
肺系膜/肺繫膜　mesopulmonum
肺细胞/肺細胞　pneumonocyte
肺下的/肺下的　subpulmonic
肺下缘/肺下緣　inferior border of lung
肺纤维化/肺纖維化　pulmonary fibrosis
肺腺瘤/肺腺瘤　pulmonary adenoma
肺腺瘤病/肺腺瘤病　pulmonary adenomatosis
肺小舌/肺葉小舌　lingula of lung
肺小叶/肺小葉　pulmonary lobule
肺小叶周围炎/肺小葉周圍炎　perilobulitis
肺楔形切除术/肺楔形切除術　wedge resection of lung
肺楔血管摄影术/肺楔血管攝影術　pulmonary wedge angiography
肺楔压/肺楔壓　pulmonary wedge pressure
肺斜裂[隙]/肺斜裂[隙]　oblique fissure of lung
肺心病/肺心症　pulmonary heart disease
肺心病综合征/肺性心病症候群　cor pulmonale syndrome
肺心痛/肺心痛　true heart pain with cold limbs caused by lung disease
肺型疟疾/肺型瘧疾　pneumopaludism
肺性P波/肺性P波　P pulmonale
肺性发绀/肺發紺　pulmonary cyanosis
肺性发声/發音困難　pneumophonia
肺性骨关节病/肺性骨關節病　pulmonary osteoarthropathy
肺胸膜/肺胸膜　pulmonary pleura
肺胸膜壁层固定术/肺胸膜壁層固定術　pneumopleuroparietopexy
肺胸膜炎/肺胸膜炎　pneumonopleuritis
肺血管疾病/肺血管疾病　pulmonary vascular disease
肺血管造影术/肺血管X光線攝影法　pneumoangiography
肺血管[造影]照片/肺血管攝影照片　pneumoangiogram
肺血管阻力/肺血管阻力　pulmonary vascular resistance
肺血管阻塞/肺血管阻塞　pulmonary vascular obstruction
肺血栓栓塞症/肺血栓栓塞症　pulmonary thromboembolism
肺血栓形成/肺血栓形成, 肺栓塞　pulmonary thrombosis
肺循环/肺循環, 小循環　pulmonary circulation
肺芽/肺芽　lung bud
肺炎/肺炎　pneumonitis
肺炎败血病/肺炎敗血病　pneumosepticemia
肺炎并发脓胸/肺炎并發膿胸　synpneumonic empyema
肺炎病毒感染/肺炎病毒感染　pneumovirus infection
肺炎喘嗽/肺炎喘嗽　pneumonia with dyspneic cough
肺炎喘嗽·变证/肺炎喘嗽·變證　deteriorated case of pneumonia with dyspneic cough
肺炎喘嗽·常证/肺炎喘嗽·常證　regular case of pneumonia with dyspneic cough
肺炎喘嗽·肺脾气虚证/肺炎喘嗽·肺脾氣虛證　pneumonia with dyspneic cough with pattern of qi deficiency of lung and spleen
肺炎喘嗽·风寒袭肺证/肺炎喘嗽·風寒襲肺證　pneumonia with dyspneic cough with pattern of wind-cold invading lung
肺炎喘嗽·风热犯肺证/肺炎喘嗽·風熱犯肺證　pneumonia with dyspneic cough with pattern of wind-heat invading lung
肺炎喘嗽·痰热壅肺证/肺炎喘嗽·痰熱壅肺證　pneumonia with dyspneic cough with pattern of phlegm-heat congesting lung
肺炎喘嗽·邪陷厥阴证/肺炎喘嗽·邪陷厥陰證　pneumonia with dyspneic cough with pattern of pathogen invading Jueyin
肺炎喘嗽·心阳虚衰证/肺炎喘嗽·心陽虛衰證

pneumonia with dyspneic cough with pattern of heart yang exhaustion
肺炎喘嗽•阴虚肺热证/肺炎喘嗽•陰虛肺熱證 pneumonia with dyspneic cough with pattern of yin deficiency and lung heat
肺炎后的/肺炎後的 metapneumonic
肺炎后脓胸/肺炎後膿胸 metapneumonic empyema
肺炎脑炎/肺炎兼腦炎 pneumoencephalitis
肺炎球菌病/肺炎雙球菌病 pneumococcosis
肺炎球菌的/肺炎球菌的 pneumococcal
肺炎球菌多糖/肺炎球菌多醣體 pneumococcus polysaccharide
肺炎球菌感染/肺炎球菌感染 pneumococcal infection
肺炎球菌菌苗/肺炎球菌菌苗 pneumococcal vaccine
肺炎球菌尿/肺炎雙球菌尿症 pneumococcosuria
肺炎球菌溶解/肺炎雙球菌溶解 pneumococcolysis
肺炎球菌属/肺炎雙球菌 *Pneumococcus*
肺炎球菌性肺炎/肺炎雙球菌性肺炎,大葉肺炎 pneumococcal pneumonia
肺炎球菌性溃疡/肺炎球菌性潰瘍 pneumococcal ulcer
肺炎球菌性脑膜炎/肺炎球菌性腦膜炎 pneumococcic meningitis
肺炎球菌性脓胸/肺炎球菌性蓄膿 pneumococcal empyema
肺炎球菌血症/肺炎雙球菌血症 pneumococcemia
肺炎性假瘤/肺炎性假瘤 pulmonary inflammatory pseudotumor
肺炎衣原体/肺炎衣原體 Chlamydophila pneumoniae
肺炎支原体/肺炎黴漿菌 Mycoplasma pneumoniae
肺阳/肺陽 lung yang
肺氧弥散量/肺氧彌散量 diffusion capacity for oxygen of lung
[肺]叶间积脓/葉間蓄膿 interlobar empyema
肺叶切除术/肺葉切除術 pulmonary lobectomy
肺叶支气管/肺葉支氣管 lobar bronchi
肺一氧化碳弥散量/肺一氧化碳彌散量 diffusion capacity for carbon monoxide of lung
肺移植/肺移植 lung transplantation
肺阴/肺陰 lung yin
肺阴虚/肺陰虛 deficiency of lung yin
肺阴虚证/肺陰虛證 pattern of deficiency of lung yin
肺硬币病变/肺硬幣病變 pulmonary coin lesion
肺硬变/肺硬變 pneumonocirrhosis
肺硬化性血管瘤/肺硬化性血管瘤 pulmonary sclerosing hemangioma
肺痈/肺癰,肺膿瘍 abscess of lung, lung abscess
肺痈•成痈期/肺癰•成癰期 abscess formation stage of lung abscess
肺痈•初期/肺癰•初期 initial stage of lung abscess
肺痈•恢复期/肺癰•恢復期 recovery stage of lung abscess
肺痈•溃脓期/肺癰•潰膿期 rupture stage of lung abscess
肺郁/肺鬱 stagnancy pattern of lung qi
肺源性脑病/肺原性腦病 pulmonary encephalopathy
肺源性心脏病/肺源性心臟病 cor pulmonale
肺胀/肺脹 lung distention
肺胀•肺肾气虚证/肺脹•肺腎氣虛證 lung distention with pattern of qi deficiency of lung and kidney
肺胀•寒痰阻肺证/肺脹•寒痰阻肺證 lung distention with pattern of internal blockade by cold-phlegm
肺胀•寒饮射肺证/肺脹•寒飲射肺證 lung distention with pattern of cold fluid hitting lung
肺胀•脾肾阳虚证/肺脹•脾腎陽虛證 lung distention with pattern of yang deficiency of spleen and kidney
肺胀•热痰内闭证/肺脹•熱痰內閉證 lung distention with pattern of internal blockade by heat-phlegm
肺胀•痰热壅肺证/肺脹•痰熱壅肺證 lung distention with pattern of phlegm-heat congesting lung
肺胀•脱证/肺脹•脫證 lung distention with collapse pattern
肺真菌病/肺黴菌病 pulmonary mycosis
肺震伤/肺震傷,肺震蕩 pulmonary concussion
肺蒸散/肺蒸散 pulmonary transpiration
肺支原体/肺支原體 mycoplasma pulmonis
肺志忧/肺志憂 lung being associated with worry
肺终芽/肺終末球 pneumonere
肺肿瘤/肺腫瘤 lung neoplasm
肺中毒性呼吸/肺中毒性呼吸 pneumotoxic respiration
肺主皮毛/肺主皮毛 lung governing skin and hair
肺主气/肺主氣 lung governing qi
肺主肃降/肺主肅降 lung governing purification and descending
肺主通调水道/肺主通調水道 lung governing regulation of water passages
肺主宣发/肺主宣發 lung governing diffusion

肺主治节/肺主治節　lung governing management and regulation
肺紫癜/肺紫癜病　lung purpura
肺总量/肺總量，總肺量　total lung capacity
肺阻力/肺阻力　lung resistance
肺组织胞浆菌病/肺組織胞漿菌病　pulmonary histoplasmosis
狒狒/狒狒　baboon
狒狒属/狒狒屬　*Papio*
狒狒综合征/狒狒症候群，對稱性過敏性接觸皮膚炎　baboon syndrome
废弃物处理/廢棄物處理　waste management
废物排除/廢物排除　metasyncrisis
废用胎盘/廢離胎盤　placenta obsoleta
废质性脾炎/廢質性脾炎　spodogenous splenitis
沸程/沸程　boiling range
沸点检醇器/沸點檢醇器　zeoscope
沸泡音/氣泡音　bubbling rale
沸石/沸石　zeolite
费城染色体/費城染色體　Philadelphia chromosome
费尔蒂综合征/費爾蒂症候群　Felty syndrome
费拉格复苏术/Flagg 氏復甦術　Flagg resuscitation
费拉塔细胞/Ferrata 氏細胞　Ferrata cell
费莱格尔病/Flegel 氏病，持久性豆狀過度角化　Flegel disease
费兰韧带/Ferrein 氏韌帶　Ferrein ligament
费里-波特定律/費-波二氏定律　Ferry-Porter law
费林反应/菲林反應　Fehling reaction
费林试验/菲林試驗　Fehling test
费林液/菲林溶液　Fehling solution
费米共振/費米共振　Fermi resonance
费希尔悬吊床/Fisher 氏床　Fisher bed
痱子/痱子，粟[粒]疹　sudamen, miliaria
痱子粉/痱子粉　prickly heat powder
痱子·热毒证/痱子·熱毒證　miliaria with heat-toxin pattern
痱子·暑湿证/痱子·暑濕證　miliaria with summerheat-dampness pattern
分贝/分貝　decibel
分辨力/分辨力，分辨本領　resolving power
分布/分布　distribution
分布广的/廣播的，蔓延的　widespread
分布速率常数/分布速率常數　distribution rate constant
分布性白细胞增多/分布性白血球增多　distribution leukocytosis
分步沉淀/分段沈澱　fractional precipitation
分侧肾功能试验/分側腎功能試驗　split-renal function test
分层/分層　demixing
分层分组/分層分組　hierarchic classification
分层[模型]解剖学/分層模型解剖學　clastic anatomy
分层皮瓣/分層皮瓣　split thickness flap
分层皮肤移植片/分層皮膚移植片　split thickness skin graft
分层皮移植片/分層皮膚移植物　split-skin graft
分层皮质/分層皮質　laminated cortex
分层血栓/分層血栓　laminated thrombus
分层移植物/分層移植物　split-thickness graft
分叉拇指/分叉狀拇指　bifid thumb
分叉韧带/分歧韌帶　bifurcated ligament
分叉型肾盂/分叉型腎盂　bifid pelvis
分叉型输尿管/分叉型輸尿管　bifid ureter
分次照射/分量照射法　fractionated irradiation
分段包埋/分段包埋　sectional investment
分段充填法/分段充填法　segmented condensation method
分段刮宫术/分段刮宮術　fractional curettage of uterus
分段夹/分段夾板　sectional splint
分段截骨术/分段截骨術　segmental osteotomy
分段性阻断/分段性阻斷　segmental block
分段印模/分段分壓模　sectional impression
分房[性]脓胸/分房性蓄膿　loculated empyema
分服/分服　taken separately
分割的/分割的　dissecting
分割呼吸/分離性呼吸管　divided respiration
分割性子宫炎/分割性子宮炎　dissecting metritis
分隔局限性阑尾炎/跳島性闌尾炎　skip appendicitis
分隔术/分隔術　septation operation
分光光度法/分光光度測定法　spectrophotometry
分光光度计/分光光度計　spectrophotometer
分光光度荧光计/螢光分光光度計　spectrophotofluorometer
分光镜/分光鏡　spectroscope
分化/分化　differentiation
分化抗原/分化抗原　differentiation antigen
分化群抗原/分化群抗原　cluster of differentiation antigen
分化细胞/高級細胞　noble cell
分级沉淀/分級沈澱　fractional precipitation
分级[分离]/分級[分離]　fractionation
分级培养法/分種培養，分開培養　fractional culture
分级运动试验/分級運動試驗　graded exercise test
分峙/分峙　crista dividens

分剂辐射/分劑輻射 fractionation radiation
分间隔离法/小室法 cubicle method
分节孢子/分節芽胞 arthrospore
分节导管/分節導管 vertebrated catheter
分节管/分節管 segmental duct
分节核细胞/分葉核細胞 segmented cell
分节器/分節器 segmental organ
分节性感觉缺失/分段性感覺缺失 segmental anesthesia
分解/分解 disintegrate, decomposition
分解代谢/分解代謝 catabolism
分解代谢产物/分解代謝產物 catastate
分解代谢的/分解代謝的,異化的 catabolic
分解代谢过度/分解代謝過度,異化過度 hypercatabolism
分解代谢阻遏/分解代謝壓抑 catabolic repression
分解点/分解點 decomposition point
分解性代谢/分解性代謝 catabolism metabolism, destructive metabolism
分界/分介 demarcation
分界面/分介面 interface
分筋/分筋 adhesion separation manipulation
分开性脱位/分開性脱位 divergent dislocation
分类[法]/分類 classification
分类进食/分類進食 dissociated diet
分离/分離 separation, disjunction, isolation
分离层/分離層 stratum disjunctum
分离灌注/分離灌注 isolation perfusion
分离剂/分離介質 separating medium
分离胶/分離凝膠 separation gel
分离焦虑/分離焦慮 separation anxiety
分离麻醉/分離麻醉,分離性感覺缺失 dissociation anesthesia
分离模具/分離模具 die
分离盘/分離盤 lightening disk
分离培养基/分離培養基 isolation medium
分离式腭带/分離式腭帶 split palatal strap
分离式腭杠/分離式腭槓 split palatal bar
分离式义齿/分離式義齒 disjunct denture
分离丝/分離絲 separating wire
分离细胞/隔離細胞 isolated cell
分离型精神障碍/分離型精神障礙 dissociative disorder
分离型癔症/分離性癔病 dissociative hysteria
分离性干扰/分離性干擾 dissociation interference
分离性感觉缺失/分離性感覺缺失 dissociated anesthesia
分离性黄疸/分離性黄疸 dissociated jaundice

分离性天花/稀疏痘 discrete smallpox
分离性吸收/分離性吸收 disjunctive absorption
分离性障碍/多種人格障礙 dissociative disorder
分离液/分離介質,分離劑 separating medium
分离运动/分離運動 isolated movement
分离指/分離指 separated finger
分离趾/分離趾 separated toe
分立二发射极/分立二發射極 discrete dynode
分量系数/分量係數 coefficient of partage
分裂/分裂 fission, splitting
分裂产物/分裂產物 fission product
[分裂]后期/[分裂]後期 anaphase
[分裂]间期/間期 interphase
[分裂]末期/[細胞分裂]末期 telophase
分裂耐受[性]/分裂耐受[性] split tolerance
[分裂]前期/前期 prophase
分裂潜能/潛在的分裂 division potential
分裂情感性精神病/感情分裂性精神病 schizoaffective psychosis
分裂球/分裂球 blastomere
分裂球变扁/分裂球變扁 cytarme
分裂式扩大树脂板/分裂式擴大樹脂板 split expansion plate
分裂手/裂手[畸形] cleft hand
分裂细胞/分裂細胞 segmentation cell
分裂象/分裂象 mitotic figure
分裂型人格障碍/分裂型人格障礙 schizoid personality disorder
分裂性人格者/類精神分裂的,輕微型精神分裂症 schizoid
[分裂]中期/[細胞分裂]中期 metaphase
分流/分流 split, shunt
分流分数/分流分數 shunt fraction
分流性发绀/分流性發紺 shunt cyanosis
分流性肾炎/分流性腎炎 shunt nephritis
分馏/分餾 fractional distillation
分馏法/化學分離法 fractionation
分米波疗法/分米波療法 decimeter wave therapy
分泌部/分泌部 secretory portion
分泌成分/分泌物組成部分 secretory component
分泌导管/分泌管 secretory duct
分泌的/分泌的 secretory
分泌过多/分泌過多 hypersecretion
分泌过少/分泌過少,分泌減少 hyposecretion
分泌功能异常/内分泌官能異常 pathocrinia
分泌颗粒/分泌粒 secretory granule
分泌率/分泌率 secretory rate
分泌毛细管/分泌毛細管 secretory capillary

分泌免疫球蛋白 A/分泌免疫球蛋白 A　secretory immunoglobulin A
分泌囊肿/分泌囊腫　secretory cyst
分泌黏液的/分泌黏液的　muciparous
分泌片/分泌片　secretory piece
分泌期/分泌期　secretory phase
分泌神经/分泌神經　secretory nerve
分泌神经元/分泌神經元　secretory neuron
分泌停止/分泌受抑,機能停止　apolepsis
分泌物/分泌物　discharge
分泌物潴留/分泌物瀦留　ischesis
分泌细胞/分泌細胞　secretory cell
分泌小泡/分泌小泡　secretory vesicle
分泌型 IgA/分泌型 IgA　secretory IgA
分泌型蛋白尿/分泌型蛋白尿　secretory proteinuria
分泌性中耳炎/分泌性中耳炎　secretory otitis media
分泌学/分泌學　crinology
分泌障碍/分泌障礙　dyscrinism
分泌组织/分泌組織　secretory tissue
分娩/分娩　childbirth, delivery
分娩发动/分娩發動　labor onset
分娩过程/分娩過程　obstetric labor
分娩机制/分娩機制　mechanism of labor
分娩急速/急速分娩　oxytocia
分娩恐怖/生育恐懼症　tocophobia
分娩力计/分娩力計　parturiometer
分娩力描记法/陣痛描記法　tocography
分娩力[描记]图/产力描記器　tocodynagraph
分娩日期规律/預產期規則　delivery date rule
分娩时/分娩時,分娩中　intrapartum
分娩时出血/分娩時出血　intrapartum hemorrhage
分娩疼痛/陣痛　labor pain
pH 分配假说/pH 分配假說　pH-partition hypothesis
分配色谱法/分配層析法,分配色層分析法　partition chromatography
分配误差/分配誤差　error of allocation
分配系数/分配係數　partition coefficient
分批补料发酵/分批補料發酵　fed-batch fermentation
分批发酵/分批發酵　batch fermentation
分期切除[术]/分期切除[術]　excision in stage
分期修复/分期修復　staged repair
分歧髁头/分歧髁頭　bifid condyle
分歧锥/分叉部錐體　bifurcation cone
分清泌浊/分清泌濁　separating clear and excreting turbid
分区医疗/分區醫療　district medical care
分散/分散　dispersion
分散的/分散的　disperse
分散胶体/散膠體　dispersion colloid
分散圈/分散環　circle of dispersion
分散式合金/分散式合金　dispersion alloy
分散胎盘/彌漫性胎盤　diffuse placenta
分散透镜/分散透鏡　dispersing lens
分散系[统]/分散系[統]　disperse system
分散细胞/分散細胞　dispersed cell
分散相/分散相　dispersed phase
分散相合金/分散相合金　dispersed alloy
分散性主动脉瓣下狭窄/分散性主動脈瓣下狹窄　discrete subaortic stenosis
分散质/分散質　dispersate
分升/十分之一公升,公合　deciliter
分生孢子/分生孢子　conidiospore
分生孢子器/分生孢子器　pycnidium
分生组织/分生組織　meristem
分生组织瘤/分生組織瘤　meristoma
分数[剂]量/分量劑量　fractionation dose
分碎术/切碎法,分碎法　morcellation
分体生殖/體細胞生殖　somatic reproduction
分析/分析　analysis
分析杆/分析桿　analyzing rod
分析化学/分析化學　analytical chemistry
分析天平/分析天平　analytical balance
分析障碍/分析障礙　disturbance of analysis
分析质量控制/分析品管　analytical quality control
分消走泄/分消走洩　elimination of pathogens through purgation and diuresis
分牙器/分牙器　tooth separator
分牙术/分牙術　bicuspidization
分叶的/分葉的　segmented
分叶肝/分葉肝　hepar lobatum
分叶核白细胞/多形核白血球　lobocyte
分叶皮瓣/分葉皮瓣　lobulated skin flap
分叶肾/分葉腎　lobulated kidney
分叶胎盘/分葉胎盤　furcate placenta
分[音]节不能/不能分節,不分節狀態　amerism
分支/分支　branch
分支孢子菌病/分支芽孢菌病　cladosporiosis
分支[传导]阻滞/細分支傳導阻斷　divisional block
分支代谢途径/分支代謝途徑　branched metabolic pathway
分支的/分支的　branched, ramose
分支杆菌糖脂/分支桿菌糖脂　mycoside
分支聚体/分支聚體　branched polymer
分支菌脂酸/分支菌脂酸　nastinic acid
分支酸/分支酸　chorismic acid

分支酸盐变位酶/分支酸鹽變位元酶 chorismate mutase
分支同质聚体/分支同質聚體 branched homopolymer
分支 DNA 信号扩增试验/分支 DNA 信號擴增試驗 branched DNA signal amplification assay
分支性传导阻滞/心室内傳導衝動阻斷 arborization block
分支状癌/分支狀癌 ramose cancer
分支阻滞/分支阻滯 fascicular block
分枝杆菌病/分枝桿菌病 mycobacterial disease, mycobacteriosis
分枝杆菌感染/分枝桿菌感染 mycobacterium infection
分枝杆菌科/分枝桿菌科 Mycobacteriaceae
分枝杆菌噬菌体/分枝桿菌噬菌體 Mycobacteriophage
分枝杆菌属/分枝桿菌屬 *Mycobacterium*
分枝杆菌素/分枝桿菌素 Mycobacillin
分枝杆菌性溃疡/分枝桿菌性潰瘍 mycobacterial ulcer
分枝杆菌佐剂/分枝桿菌輔劑,弗羅恩特氏完全輔劑 mycobacterial adjuvant
分枝菌酸/分枝菌酸 mycolic acid
分枝犁头霉/分枝犁頭黴 *Absidia ramosa*
分枝丝菌病/分枝絲菌病 cladothricosis
分植体/分植體 interplant
分钟间隔连续静脉肾盂造影[术]/分鐘間隔連續静脈腎盂造影[術] minute sequence intravenous pyelography
分钟间隔连续尿路造影[术]/分鐘間隔連續尿路造影[術] minute sequence urography
分钟量/一分鐘容量 minute volume
分桩冠/分柱冠 split-dowel crown
分子/分子 molecule
分子病/分子病 molecular disease
分子病理学/分子病理學 molecular pathology
分子层/分子層 molecular layer
分子层纹/分子層紋 stria of molecular layer
分子创伤学/分子創傷學 molecular traumatology
分子簇/分子簇 molecular group
分子大小/分子大小 molecular size
分子的/分子的 molecular
分子动力学/分子動力學 molecular dynamics
分子分散溶液/分子分散溶液 molecular disperse solution
分子轨道/分子軌域 molecular orbital
分子疾病/分子疾病 molecule disease
分子几何[结构]/分子幾何[結構] molecular geometry
分子间[的]/分子間的 intermolecular
分子间力/分子間力 intermolecular force
分子间力反应能/分子間力反應能 intermolecular force interaction energy
分子监控蛋白类/分子監控蛋白類 molecular chaperones
分子结构/分子結構 molecular structure
分子进化/分子進化 molecular evolution
分子静电势/分子静電勢 molecular electrostatic potential
分子克隆/分子克隆 molecular cloning
分子力/分子力 molecular force
分子力学/分子力學 molecular mechanics
分子连接性/分子連接性 molecular connectivity
分子连接性指数/分子連接性指標數 molecular connectivity index
分子量/分子量 molecular weight, relative molecular mass
分子量排除极限/分子量排除極限 molecular weight exclusion limit
分子流行病学/分子流行病學 molecular epidemiology
分子免疫学/分子免疫學 molecular immunology
分子模拟/分子模擬 molecular mimicry
分子模型/分子模型 molecular model
分子内[的]/分子内[的] intramolecular
分子内裂合酶类/分子内裂合酶類 intramolecular lyases
分子内氧化还原酶类/分子内氧化還原酶類 intramolecular oxidoreductases
分子内转移酶类/分子内轉移酶類 intramolecular transferases
分子胚胎学/分子胚胎學 molecular embryology
分子热/分子熱 molecular heat
分子容积/分子容 molecular volume
分子筛/分子篩 molecular sieve
分子生物学/分子生物學 molecular biology
分子式/分子式 molecular formula, formula molecular
分子死亡/分子死 molecular death
分子探针/分子探針 molecular probe
分子探针技术/分子探針技術 molecular probe technique
分子拓扑/分子拓撲學 molecular topology
分子细胞遗传学/分子細胞遺傳學 molecular cytogenetics

分子序列数据/分子序列資料　molecular sequence data
分子药理学/分子藥理學　molecular pharmacology
分子遗传学/分子遺傳學　molecular genetics
分子引力/分子[間]吸引力　molecular attraction
分子育种/分子育種　molecular breeding
分子运动/分子運動　molecular motion
分子杂交/分子雜交　molecular hybridization
分子折射度/分子折射度　molecular refraction
分子诊断技术/分子診斷技術　molecular diagnostic technique
分子蒸馏/分子蒸餾　molecular distillation
分子脂肪/分子性脂肪　molecular fat
分组/分組　grouping
分组心理疗法/分組心理療法　group psychotherapy
芬苯达唑/芬苯達唑　fenbendazole
芬地林/芬地林　fendiline
芬氟拉明/芬氟拉明　fenfluramine
芬-洪溃疡/Fenwick-Hunner 氏潰瘍　Fenwick-Hunner ulcer
芬克洛宁/苯氯寧　fenclonine
芬美曲秦/芬美曲秦　phenmetrazine
芬森浴/紫外光浴,芬森氏浴　Finsen bath
芬太尼/芬太尼　fentanyl
芬特明/芬特明　phentermine
芬替克洛/硫雙氯酚　fenticlor
芬维 A 铵/芬維 A 銨　fenretinide
芬香圣草糖浆/芳香北美聖草糖漿　aromatic Yerba santa syrup
吩嗪类/吩嗪類　phenazines
吩噻嗪/吩噻嗪　dibenzothiazine
酚/酚　phenol
酚苄明/酚苄明　phenoxybenzamine
酚的/酚的　phenolic
酚苷/酚苷　phenolic glycoside
酚红排泄倒置/酚紅排洩倒置　inversion of phenolsulfonphthalein excretion
酚磺酸钠/酚磺酸鈉　sodium phenolsulfonate
酚磺酸铜/酚磺酸銅　copper phenolsulfonate
酚磺酸锌/酚磺酸鋅　zinc phenolsulfonate
酚磺酞/酚磺酞,酚紅　phenolsulfonphthalein
酚磺乙胺/酚磺乙胺　ethamsylate
酚类/酚類　phenols
酚酶/酚酶,酚酵素　phenolase
酚噻嗪类/酚噻嗪類　phenothiazines
酚噻嗪诱发运动困难/酚噻嗪引起運動困難　phenothiazine induced dyskinesia
酚酞/酚酞　phenolphthalein

酚酞试验/酚酞試驗　phenolphthalein test
酚妥拉明/酚妥拉明　phentolamine
酚妥拉明试验/酚妥拉明試驗　phentolamine test
酚盐/酚化物　phenolate
酚樟脑/樟腦酚　phenol camphor
酚酯类/酚酯類　phenol esters
坟墓/墳墓　grave
焚化/焚燒法　incineration
粉饼/粉餅　compact powder
粉尘/粉末　dust
粉刺/粉刺,痤瘡　acne, comedone
粉刺癌/粉刺癌　comedo carcinoma
粉刺性痤疮/粉刺性痤瘡　acne comedo
粉刺性乳痈/粉刺性乳癰　comedomastitis, plasma cell mastitis
粉刺性乳痈·热毒蕴结证/粉刺性乳癰·熱毒蘊結證　plasma cell mastitis with heat-toxin amassment pattern
粉刺性乳痈·余毒未清证/粉刺性乳癰·餘毒未清證　plasma cell mastitis with uncleared remnant toxin pattern
粉刺样痣/粉刺痣　comedo nevus
粉刺状乳腺炎/粉刺性乳腺炎　comedomastitis
粉红病/慢性汞中毒　pink disease
粉红单端孢/粉紅單端孢黴菌　Trichothecium roseum
粉红头孢霉/粉紅頭孢黴　Cephalosporium roseum
粉花疮/粉花瘡　cosmetic dermatitis
粉化/粉化　efflorescence
粉黄色斑/角膜之鮭色斑,赭斑　salmon patch
粉剂/粉劑　powder
粉瘤囊肿/粉瘤性囊腫　atheromatous cyst
粉螨/家羔蟲　food mite
粉螨属/粉螨　Acarus
粉末吸入剂/粉末型吸入劑　powder inhalation
粉末衍射/粉末衍射　powder diffraction
粉碎/粉碎　comminution, pulverization
粉碎机/粉碎機　pulverizer, grinder
粉碎染色体/粉碎染色體　pulverized chromosome
粉碎性骨折/粉碎性骨折　comminuted fracture
粉体[工]学/粉體[工]學　powder technology
粉羔虫/粉羔蟲　meal mite
粉衣层/底衣層　sub-coat
粉针剂/注射用無菌粉末　sterile powder for injection
粉状孢子/粉狀孢子　aleuriospore
奋力综合征/勞力症候群　effort syndrome
粪便/糞[便]　feces
粪便检验法/糞便檢視法　scatoscopy

粪便嵌顿/糞塊嵌塞　fecal impaction
粪便学/糞學　coprology
粪卟啉/糞紫質　stercoporphyrin
粪卟啉类/糞紫質類　coproporphyrins
粪卟啉尿/糞紫質尿　coproporphyrinuria
粪卟啉原/糞紫質原　coproporphyrinogen
粪卟啉原氧化酶/糞紫質原氧化酶　coproporphyrinogen oxidase
粪卟啉症/糞紫質症　coproporphyria
粪产碱杆菌/鹼性糞便菌　Alcaligenes faecalis
粪臭素/糞臭質,甲基吲哚　Skatole
粪的/糞的　fecal
粪肥/糞肥　manure
粪积性消化不良/糞積性消化不良　feculent dyspepsia
粪抗体/糞抗體　coproantibody
粪类圆线虫/腸擬圓蟲,糞擬圓蟲　Strongyloides stercoralis
粪瘤/糞瘤　fecal tumor
粪瘘/糞瘻　stercoral fistula, fecal fistula
粪石/糞石　fecalith
粪石性阑尾炎/糞性闌尾炎　stercoral appendicitis
粪性溃疡/糞壓性潰瘍　stercoraceous ulcer
粪性脓肿/糞性膿腫　fecal abscess
粪圆[线虫]属/類圓蟲屬　*Strongyloides*
粪[甾]醇/糞脂醇　coprostanol
丰加霉素/豐加黴素　toyocamycin
丰隆/豐隆　fenglong, ST40
丰唐手术/豐唐手術　Fontan operation
风/風　wind
风池/風池　fengchi, GB20
风赤疮痍/風赤瘡痍　vesiculated dermatitis of eyelid, wind-red sore
风赤疮痍・风火上攻证/風赤瘡痍・風火上攻證　wind-red sore with pattern of wind-fire attacking upward
风赤疮痍・气阴两虚证/風赤瘡痍・氣陰兩虛證　wind-red sore with qi-yin deficiency pattern
风赤疮痍・湿热壅盛证/風赤瘡痍・濕熱壅盛證　wind-red sore with pattern of dampness-heat congestion and excessiveness
风赤疮痍・血虚风燥证/風赤瘡痍・血虛風燥證　wind-red sore with pattern of wind-dryness due to blood deficiency
风搐/風搐　wind tetany
风毒入络证/風毒入絡證　pattern of wind-toxicity invading collaterals
风毒证/風毒證　wind-toxicity pattern

风痱/風痱　apoplectic aphasia
风府/風府　fengfu, DU16
风关/風關　wind pass
风寒犯头证/風寒犯頭證　pattern of wind-cold invading head
风寒化热证/風寒化熱證　pattern of heat transformed from wind-cold
风寒湿痹/風寒濕痹　arthralgia caused by wind-cold-damp pathogens, wind-cold-damp bi, wind-cold-dampness arthralgia
风寒束表证/風寒束表證　pattern of exterior tightened by wind-cold
风寒袭鼻证/風寒襲鼻證　pattern of wind-cold invading nose
风寒袭肺/風寒襲肺　wind-cold attacking lung
风寒袭肺证/風寒襲肺證　pattern of wind-cold attacking lung
风火犯齿证/風火犯齒證　pattern of wind-fire invading teeth
风火热毒证/風火熱毒證　pattern of wind-fire and heat-toxicity
风火眼/風火眼　wind fire eye
风惊悸/風驚悸　convulsion due to wind
风惊恐/風驚恐　fright due to wind
风厥/風厥　wind syncope
风科/風科　department of wind
风轮/風輪　wind wheel
风轮赤豆/風輪赤豆　wind-wheel red bean, fascicular keratitis, red wind wheel
风轮赤豆・肝经实热证/風輪赤豆・肝經實熱證　wind-wheel red bean with pattern of excessive heat in liver channel
风轮赤豆・脾虚肝旺证/風輪赤豆・脾虛肝旺證　wind-wheel red bean with pattern of spleen deficiency and liver hyperactivity
风轮赤豆・阴虚火旺证/風輪赤豆・陰虛火旺證　wind-wheel red bean with pattern of yin deficiency and fire effulgence
风门/風門　fengmen, BL12
风秘/風秘　wind constipation
风牵偏视/風牽偏視　paralytic strabismus, wind-induced squint
风牵偏视・风痰阻络证/風牽偏視・風痰阻絡證　wind-induced squint with pattern of wind-phlegm obstructing collateral
风牵偏视・风邪中络证/風牽偏視・風邪中絡證　wind-induced squint with pattern of wind striking collateral

风牵偏视·肝阳化风证/風牽偏視·肝陽化風證　wind-induced squint with pattern of liver yang transforming into wind
风牵偏视·脉络瘀阻证/風牽偏視·脈絡瘀阻證　wind-induced squint with pattern of stasis and obstruction of vessel and collateral
风热疮/風熱瘡,玫瑰糠疹　pityriasis rosea, wind-heat sore
风热疮·风热蕴肤证/風熱瘡·風熱蘊膚證　wind-heat sore with pattern of wind-heat amassing in skin
风热疮·血热风盛证/風熱瘡·血熱風盛證　wind-heat sore with pattern of blood heat and wind excessiveness
风热犯鼻证/風熱犯鼻證　pattern of wind-heat invading nose
风热犯耳证/風熱犯耳證　pattern of wind-heat invading ear
风热犯肺/風熱犯肺　wind-heat invading lung
风热犯肺证/風熱犯肺證　pattern of wind-heat invading lung
风热犯目证/風熱犯目證　pattern of wind-heat invading eye
风热犯头证/風熱犯頭證　pattern of wind-heat invading head
风热侵[咽]喉证/風熱侵[咽]喉證　pattern of wind-heat invading throat
风热袭表证/風熱襲表證　pattern of exterior attacked by wind-heat
风热牙疳/風熱牙疳　wind-heat gum gan disease, wind-heat ulcerative gingivitis
风热阻络证/風熱阻絡證　pattern of wind-heat blocking collaterals
风瘙痒/風搔癢　wind itching, pruritus cutanea, pruritus due to wind pathogen
风瘙痒·湿热蕴结证/風搔癢·濕熱蘊結證　wind itching with dampness-heat amassment pattern
风瘙痒·血热风盛证/風搔癢·血熱風盛證　wind itching with pattern of blood heat and wind excessiveness
风瘙痒·血虚风燥证/風搔癢·血虛風燥證　wind itching with pattern of wind-dryness due to blood deficiency
风瘙痒·瘀血阻滞证/風搔癢·瘀血阻滯證　wind itching with pattern of static blood obstruction and stagnation
风善行数变/風善行數變　wind being mobile and changeable
风胜则动/風勝則動　predominate wind causing motion
风湿病/風濕病　rheumatism
风湿病膳食/致風濕飲食　rheumatic diet
风湿病学/風濕病學　rheumatology
风湿病样的/類風濕的　rheumatoid
风湿犯头证/風濕犯頭證　pattern of wind-dampness invading head
风湿化热证/風濕化熱證　pattern of heat transformed from wind-dampness
风湿挟毒证/風濕挾毒證　pattern of wind-dampness with toxicity
风湿凌目证/風濕凌目證　pattern of wind-dampness invading eye
风湿热/風濕熱　rheumatic fever
风湿热痹/風濕熱痹　arthralgia caused by wind-damp-heat pathogens, wind-damp-heat bi
风湿素质/含風濕潛質的　rheumatic diathesis
风湿痛/風濕痛　rheumatic pain
风湿型伤寒/關節型傷寒　arthrotyphoid
风湿性边缘性红斑/風濕性邊緣性紅斑　erythema marginatum rheumaticum
风湿性的/風濕的　rheumatic
风湿性多肌痛/風濕病性多肌痛　polymyalgia rheumatica
风湿性关节炎/風濕性關節炎　rheumatic arthritis
风湿性滑膜炎/風濕性滑膜炎　synovitis rheumatica
风湿性环状红斑/風濕性環狀紅斑　erythema annulare rheumaticum
风湿性肌萎缩/風濕性萎縮　rheumatic atrophy
风湿性疾病/風濕性疾病　rheumatic disease
风湿性脊柱侧凸/風濕性脊柱側彎　rheumatic scoliosis
风湿性[全]心炎/風濕性[全]心炎　rheumatic carditis
风湿性水肿/風濕性水腫　oedema rheumaticum
风湿性痛风/風濕性痛風　rheumatic gout
风湿性小结/風濕性小結　rheumatic nodule
风湿性心包炎/風濕性心包炎　rheumatic pericarditis
风湿性心内膜炎/風濕性心內膜炎　rheumatic endocarditis
风湿性心脏病/風濕性心臟病　rheumatic heart disease
风湿性咽峡炎/風濕性咽峽炎　angina rheumatica
风湿性紫癜/風濕病性紫瘢病　rheumatica purpura
风市/風市　fengshi, GB31
风水/風水　wind edema
风水相搏证/風水相搏證　pattern of fighting of wind

with water
风痰入络证/風痰入絡證　pattern of wind-phlegm invading collaterals
风痰上扰证/風痰上擾證　pattern of wind-phlegm invading upward
风痰哮/風痰哮　wind-phlegm wheezing
风痰证/風痰證　wind-phlegm pattern
风痛/風痛　wind pain
风团/風團，風疹塊,蕁麻疹團　wind patches
风为百病之长/風爲百病之長　wind being primary pathogen
风温/風溫　wind-warm disorder
风温[病]/風溫病　wind-warm disease
风温•肺热病/風溫•肺熱病　wind-warm disease with lung heat
风温•肺热发疹证/風溫•肺熱發疹證　wind-warm disease with pattern of eruption due to lung heat
风温•寒包火证/風溫•寒包火證　wind-warm disease with pattern of cold enveloping fire
风温•内闭外脱证/風溫•內閉外脫證　wind-warm disease with pattern of internal blockade and external collapse
风温•热炽阳明证/風溫•熱熾陽明證　wind-warm disease with pattern of blazing heat in Yangming Channel
风温•热结肠腑证/風溫•熱結腸腑證　wind-warm disease with pattern of heat binding in intestine
风温•热陷心包证/風溫•熱陷心包證　wind-warm disease with pattern of heat invading pericardium
风温•神闭腑实证/風溫•神閉腑實證　wind-warm disease with pattern of spirit blockade and fu-viscera excess
风温•痰热结胸证/風溫•痰熱結胸證　wind-warm disease with pattern of chest-binding by phlegm-heat
风温•胃热伤阴证/風溫•胃熱傷陰證　wind-warm disease with pattern of stomach heat injuring yin
风温•邪犯肺卫证/風溫•邪犯肺衛證　wind-warm disease with pattern of pathogen invading lung-defense phase
风温•邪热壅肺证/風溫•邪熱壅肺證　wind-warm disease with pattern of pathogenic heat congesting lung
风温•余邪伤阴证/風溫•餘邪傷陰證　wind-warm disease with pattern of yin injury by lingering pathogen
风溪/風溪　fengxi, wind stream
风险/危險　risk

风险胎儿/風險胎兒　fetus at risk
风险调节/風險調節　risk adjustment
风箱声/風箱音　bellows sound
风箱[状杂]音/風箱雜音,風箱聲　bellows murmur
风哮/風哮　wind wheezing
风邪/風邪　wind pathogen
风泻/風瀉　wind diarrhea
风心痛/風心痛　wind heart pain
风信子/風信子　hyacinth
风性开泄/風性開洩　wind pathogen being characterized by opening-dispersing
风性主动/風性主動　characteristic of wind being mobile
风选/風選　selection in wind
风眩/風眩　wind vertigo
风痒/風癢　wind itching
风易伤阳位/風易傷陽位　wind being apt to attack yang portion of body
风懿/風懿　wind stroke
风油精/風油精　wind medicated oil
风燥/風燥　wind dryness
风疹/風疹,德國麻疹　rubella
风疹病毒/風疹病毒　rubella virus
风疹病毒感染/風疹病毒感染　rubivirus infection
风疹[后]综合征/風疹後症候群　postrubella syndrome
风疹•气营两燔证/風疹•氣營兩燔證　rubella with pattern of blazing heat in both qi and nutrient phases
风疹•邪毒内盛证/風疹•邪毒內盛證　rubella with pattern of internal exuberance of pathogenic toxin
风疹•邪犯肺卫证/風疹•邪犯肺衛證　rubella with pattern of pathogen invading lung-defense phase
风疹性白内障/風疹性白內障　rubellar cataract
风疹性视网膜炎/風疹性視網膜炎　rubella retinitis
风疹疫苗/風疹疫苗　rubella vaccine
风证/風證　wind pattern
风中经络证/風中經絡證　pattern of wind invading channel
风肿/風腫　wind swelling
枫糖尿病/楓糖漿尿病　maple syrup urine disease
枫香脂/楓香脂　beautiful sweetgum resin
封闭敷料/封閉敷料　occlusive dressing
封闭抗体/封閉抗體　blocking antibody
封闭疗法/封閉療法　block therapy
封闭生态系统/封閉生態系統　closed ecological system
封闭试验/封閉試驗　blocking test

封闭循环学说/封閉循環學說　closed circulation theory
封闭因子/封閉因子　blocking factor
封固/封固　mounting
封固剂/封固劑　mountant
封口/熔封　sealing
封口机/熔封機　sealing machine
封髓丹/封髓丹　feng sui micropills
封锁线/隔斷線　cordon
砜类/碸類　sulfones
砜综合征/碸症候群　sulphone syndrome
峰不对称度/峰不對稱度　peak asymmetry
峰重叠/峰重疊　peak overlapping
峰谷/峰谷　peak valley
峰浓度/峰濃度　peak concentration
峰时间/峰時間　peak time
峰值呼气流速/最高呼氣流速　peak expiratory flow rate
锋电位/鋒電位　spike potential
锋针/鋒針　lance needle
蜂毒疗法/蜂毒療法　apiotherapy, bee-toxin therapy
蜂毒明肽/蜂毒明肽　apamin
蜂毒素/蜂螫毒素　apitoxin
蜂毒肽/蜂毒肽　melitten
蜂毒液类/蜂毒液類　bee venoms
蜂房/蜂房　honeycomb
蜂房状癌/蜂房狀癌　carcinoma alveolar
蜂胶/蜂巢臘膠　propolis
蜂蜡/蜂蠟　beeswax
蜂蜜/蜂蜜　honey
蜂王浆/蜂王漿　royal jelly
蜂窝/蜂窩　honeycomb
蜂窝肺/蜂巢狀肺　honeycomb lung
蜂窝[组]织炎的/蜂窩組織炎的　phlegmonous
蜂窝[组]织炎性喉炎/蜂窩組織炎性喉炎　phlegmonous laryngitis
蜂窝[组]织炎性睑缘炎/蜂窩組織炎性瞼炎　blepharitis phlegmonosa
蜂窝[组]织炎性溃疡/蜂窩組織炎性潰瘍　phlegmonous ulcer
蜂窝[组]织炎性阑尾炎/蜂窩組織炎性闌尾炎　phlegmonous appendicitis
蜂窝[组]织炎性脓肿/蜂窩組織炎性膿瘍　phlegmonous abscess
蜂窝[组]织炎性胃炎/蜂窩組織炎性胃炎　phlegmonous gastritis
蜂窝[组]织炎性腺炎/蜂窩組織淋巴腺炎　adenophlegmon

蜂窝状癌/蜂窩狀癌　areolar cancer
蜂窝[组]织炎/蜂窩組織炎　phlegmon
蜂音器疗法/蜂音器療法　kinesiphony
蜂蜇伤/蜂蜇傷　bee sting
蜂蜇[伤中]毒/蜂中毒　apisination
冯·埃布纳线/馮·埃布納線　von Ebner line
冯·埃布纳腺/馮·埃布納腺　von Ebner gland
冯·贝曼疝/von Bergmann 氏疝　von Bergmann hernia
冯·库普弗尔细胞/von Kupffer 氏細胞　von Kupffer cell
冯·雷克林豪森病/von Recklinghausen 氏病　von Recklinghausen disease
缝[合]/縫[合]　suture
缝合技术/縫合技術　suture technique
缝合韧带/縫韌帶　sutural ligament
缝合吻合/縫合吻合　sutured anastomosis
缝[合]针/縫針　suture needle
缝[间]骨/縫[間]骨　sutural bone
缝匠肌/縫匠肌　sartorius, musculus sartorius
缝匠肌腱下囊/縫匠肌腱下囊　subtendinous bursa of sartorius
缝皮钉/縫皮釘　skin staple
缝纫痉挛/縫紉痙攣　sewing spasm
缝线/縫線　suture
缝线包压法/縫線包壓法　bolus tie-over dressing
缝线肉芽肿/縫線肉芽腫　suture granuloma
缝线珠镊/縫合壓子　shot compressor
缝扎/縫扎　transfixion
缝扎法重睑成形术/縫扎法重瞼成形術　doubling eyelid operation by suture and ligation method
缝[际]/縫際　raphe
缝隙/裂隙　slit
缝隙出血/縫隙出血　slit hemorrhage
缝隙连接/間隙連接　gap junction
缝性白内障/縫內障　sutural cataract
佛波醇类/佛波醇類　phorbols
佛波醇酯类/佛波醇酯類　phorbol esters
佛罗里达马水蛭/佛羅里達馬水蛭　Florida horse leech
佛手/佛手　finger citron
否定性/否定性　negativity
夫妇的/夫婦的　conjugal
夫精人工授精/夫精人工授精　artificial insemination by husband, AIH
夫西地酸钠/褐黴酸鈉鹽,梭鏈孢酸鈉　sodium fusidate, fusidate sodium
呋喃/呋喃　furfuran

呋喃果糖/果呋糖　fructofuranose
呋喃基糖酰胺/呋喃基糖醯胺　furylfuramide
呋喃类/呋喃類　furans
呋喃硫胺/呋喃硫胺　fursutiamine
呋喃糖/呋喃糖　furanose
呋喃妥因/硝基呋喃妥因　nitrofurantoin
呋喃西林/呋喃西林　nitrofurazone
呋喃[型]葡萄糖/呋喃[型]葡萄糖,呋喃糖　glucofuranose
呋喃唑酮/呋喃唑酮　furazolidone
肤色/膚色　skin color
肤蝇[类]/膚蠅[類],牛蠅　botfly
肤蝇[类]幼虫/膚蠅幼蟲　bot
麸炒/麩炒　stir-frying with bran
跗/跗　tarsus
跗骨/跗骨　tarsal bone, tarsus
跗骨背侧韧带/跗骨背側韌帶　dorsal ligament of tarsus, dorsal ligament of tarsus
跗骨的/跗骨的,瞼板的　tarsal
跗骨窦/跗骨竇　tarsal sinus, tarsal canal
跗骨骨间韧带/跗骨骨間韌帶　interosseous ligament of tarsus
跗骨骨折/跗骨骨折　tarsal fracture
跗骨间关节/跗骨間關節　tarsotarsal joint
跗骨深韧带/跗骨深韌帶　deep ligaments of tarsus
跗骨痛/跗痛,足痛　tarsalgia
跗骨脱位/跗骨脱位　tarsectopia
跗骨折骨术/跗骨折斷術　tarsoclasis
跗骨足底韧带/跗骨蹠側韌帶,足骨間韌帶　plantar ligament of tarsus
跗关节/跗關節　tarsal joint
跗管综合征/跗管症候群　tarsal tunnel syndrome
跗横关节/跗橫關節　transverse tarsal joint
跗内侧动脉/跗內側動脈　medial tarsal artery
跗内侧韧带/跗內側韌帶　medial tarsal ligament
跗旁组织/跗旁組織　paratarsium
跗三角骨/跗三角骨　triangular bone of tarsus
跗外侧动脉/跗外側動脈　lateral tarsal artery
跗阳/跗陽　fuyang, BL59 point
跗跖背侧韧带/跗蹠背側韌帶　dorsal tarsometatarsal ligaments
跗跖关节/跗蹠關節　tarsometatarsal joint, tarsometatarsal articulations
跗跖关节扭伤/跗蹠關節扭傷　sprain of tarsometatarsal joint
跗跖关节脱位/跗蹠關節脱位　dislocation of tarsometatarsal joint
跗跖足底韧带/跗蹠蹠側韌帶　plantar tarsometatarsal ligament
跗中央骨/踝中央骨　ankle central bone
孵育/孵育　incubation
敷擦法/擦敷法,擦藥　entripsis
敷金属[法]/敷金屬法　metallization
敷料车/敷料車　dressing cart
敷料引流管/包敷管　dressed tube
敷脐疗法/敷臍療法　umbilical compress therapy
敷贴/敷貼　application
敷贴疗法/敷貼療法　application therapy, plastering therapy
敷贴型裂头蚴病/敷貼性裂頭蚴病　application sparganosis
敷贴[用]/敷貼[用]　application
敷眼疗法/敷眼療法　eye compress therapy
敷药法/敷藥法　application method
弗尔顿夹板/Fulton 氏夾板　Fulton splint
弗格森切口/弗格森切口　Fergusson incision
弗格森疝修补术/弗格森疝修補術　Fergusson herniorrhaphy
弗吉尔神经痛/Fothergill 氏神經痛　Fothergill neuralgia
弗-克运动失调/Fergusson-Critchley 二氏運動失調　Fergusson and Critchley ataxia
弗-库细胞/Foa-Kurloff 二氏細胞　Foa-Kurloff cell
弗拉克体力测验/弗萊克氏試驗　Flack test
弗莱彻主义/弗賴爾飲食主義　Fletcherism
弗莱克西希束/Flechsig 氏徑　Flechsig tract
弗莱舍环/弗萊舍環　Fleischer ring
弗莱试验/弗雷氏試驗　Frei test
弗莱综合征/Frey 氏症候群　Frey syndrome
弗兰克尔矫治器/弗蘭克爾矯治器　Frankel appliance
弗兰克尔试验/弗蘭克爾試驗　Frankel test
弗勒德韧带/Flood 氏韌帶　Flood ligament
弗勒明[组织固定]液/Flemming 氏固定液　Flemming fixing fluid
弗-拉手术/弗-拉二氏手術　Fredet-Ramstedt operation
弗雷利克液/Fralick 氏液　Fralick fluid
弗雷泽-斯皮勒手术/弗-史二氏手術　Frazier-Spiller operation
弗里德赖希共济失调/弗里德賴希共濟失調　Friedreich ataxia
弗里德赖希足/Friedreich 氏足　Friedreich foot
弗里德里希森-沃特豪斯综合征/弗-華二氏症候群　Friderichsen-Waterhouse syndrome
弗里德曼病/Friedmann 氏病　Friedmann disease

弗里克绷带/Fricke 氏繃帶　Fricke bandage
弗里斯贝格韧带/Wrisberg 氏韌帶　Wrisberg ligament
弗里斯贝格神经/Wrisberg 氏神經　Wrisberg nerve
弗里-威尔逊法/弗里-威爾遜法　Free-Wilson method
弗林德鼠白血病病毒/弗林德鼠白血病病毒　Friend murine leukemia virus
弗林特杂音/Flint 氏雜音　Flint murmur
弗鲁安综合征/Froin 氏症候群　Froin syndrome
弗罗利希综合征/弗勒赫利希症候群　Frohlich syndrome
弗罗梅尔病/Frommel 氏病　Frommel disease
弗洛朗斯结晶/弗羅倫氏晶　Florence crystal
弗洛伊德学派的/佛洛德氏學說的, 佛洛德[派學者]的　Freudian
弗洛伊德学说/佛洛德學說　Freudian theory
弗氏佐剂/弗洛德氏佐劑　Freund adjuvant
伏打电堆/伏特電堆　voltaic pile
伏尔托利尼病/Voltolini 氏病　Voltolini disease
伏格特综合征/Vogt 氏症候群　Vogt syndrome
伏隔核/伏隔核　nucleus accumbens septi
伏梁/伏梁　heart amassment
伏脉/伏脈　deep-sited pulse
伏气春温/伏氣春温　spring warmth caused by latent pathogenic qi
伏气春温兼新感证/伏氣春温兼新感證　spring warmth caused by latent qi triggered by newly contracted cold pathogen
伏暑/伏暑　latent summerheat
伏暑·热陷心包证/伏暑·熱陷心包證　latent summerheat with pattern of heat invading pericardium
伏暑伤寒/伏暑傷寒　latent summerheat disease with cold damage
伏暑·卫气同病证/伏暑·衞氣同病證　latent summerheat with pattern of involving both defense and qi phases
伏暑·卫营同病证/伏暑·衞營同病證　latent summerheat with pattern of involving both defense and nutrient phases
伏暑·邪结肠腑证/伏暑·邪結腸腑證　latent summerheat with pattern of pathogen bound in intestine
伏暑·邪在少阳证/伏暑·邪在少陽證　latent summerheat with pattern of pathogen involving Shaoyang Channel
伏暑·心热下移小肠证/伏暑·心熱下移小腸證　latent summerheat with pattern of heart heat descending into small intestine
伏天灸/伏天灸　moxibustion in dog days
伏兔/伏兔　futu, ST32
伏兔疽/伏兔疽　Futu abscess
伏邪/伏邪　hidden pathogen
伏邪温病/伏邪温病　warm disease caused by incubating pathogens
伏饮/伏飲　latent fluid retention
伏蝇属/玻璃蠅屬　Phormia
扶突/扶突　futu, LI18
扶正固本/扶正固本　supporting the healthy energy, strengthening and consolidating body resistance
扶正解表/扶正解表　strengthening body resistance for relieving exterior pattern
扶正解表剂/扶正解表劑　formula for strengthening body resistance for relieving exterior
扶正祛邪/扶正祛邪　strengthening vital qi to eliminate pathogenic factor
扶助/援助　aid
扶助脉动/扶助脈動　dependent beat
服从预先规定/服從預先規定　advance directive adherence
服药过量/過[度劑]量　overdose
服药食忌/服藥食忌　food taboo in drug application
怫忾/怫憤　qi stagnancy
怫郁/怫鬱　oppressive feeling
茯苓/茯苓　Indian bread
茯苓丸/茯苓丸　fuling pills
氟胞嘧啶/氟胞嘧啶　flucytosine
氟苯类/氟苯類　fluorobenzenes
氟比洛芬/氟比洛芬　flurbiprofen
氟醋酸盐/氟醋酸鹽　fluoroacetate
氟放射性同位素/氟放射性同位素　fluorine radioisotope
氟芬那酸/氟滅酸　flufenamic acid
氟奋乃静/氟奮乃靜　fluphenazine
氟伏沙明/氟伏沙明　fluvoxamine
氟骨病/氟骨症　fluorosis of bone
氟硅酸/[氫]氟矽酸　fluosilic acid
氟桂利嗪/氟桂利嗪　flunarizine
氟化反应/氟化作用　fluoridation
氟化钙/氟化鈣　calcium fluoride
氟化合物/氟化合物　fluorine compound
氟化钠/氟化鈉　sodium fluoride
氟化烃类/氟化烴類　fluorinated hydrocarbons
氟化物/氟化物　fluoride
氟化物中毒/氟中毒　fluoride poisoning

氟化亚锡/二價錫氟化物　stannous fluoride
氟化甾类/氟化甾類　fluorinated steroids
氟甲睾酮/氟羥甲基睾丸素　fluoxymesterone
氟甲噻嗪/氰甲基磺胺苯駢噻嗪啶　flumethiazide
氟卡尼/氟卡尼　flecainide
氟康唑/氟康唑　fluconazole
氟可龙/氟可龍　fluocortolone
氟磷酸/磷酸氟　fluorophosphate
氟罗沙星/氟羅沙星　fleroxacin
氟氯西林/氟氯西林　floxacillin
氟马西尼/氟馬西尼　flumazenil
氟米龙/去氧氟化甲基去二氫可體酮　fluorometholone
氟米松/氟甲松,二氟甲基潑尼松龍　flumethasone
氟尿苷/氟尿苷　floxuridine
氟尿嘧啶/氟尿嘧啶,氟二氧嘧啶　fluorouracil
氟哌啶醇/氟呱啶醇　haloperidol
氟哌利多/氟呱利多　droperidol
氟泼尼龙/氟化去二氧可體酮　fluprednisolone
氟氢可的松/氟化羥基可的松　fludrocortisone
氟氢缩松/氟化羥基氫化可體酮　flurandrenolone
氟司必林/氟司必林　fluspirilene
氟他胺/氟他胺　flutamide
氟碳化合物/氟碳化合物　fluorocarbon
氟碳聚合物/氟碳聚合物　fluorocarbon polymer
氟替尔/六氟二乙酯　flurothyl
氟脱氧尿苷酸/氟去氧尿苷酸　fluorodeoxyuridylate
氟脱氧葡萄糖/氟去氧葡萄糖　fluorodeoxyglucose
氟烷/氟烷　halothane
氟西奈德/二氟羥去二氫可體酮丙醯　fluocinolone acetonide
氟西泮/氟西泮　flurazepam
氟西汀/氟西汀　fluoxetine
氟硝西泮/氟硝西泮　flunitrazepam
氟性皮疹/氟皮病　fluoroderma
浮白/浮白　fubai, GB10
浮髌试验/浮髕試驗　floating patella test
浮动肋骨/浮動肋骨　floating rib
浮动拇指/浮動拇指　floating thumb
浮肋/浮[動弓]肋,椎肋　floating rib
浮络/浮絡　superficial collaterals
浮脉/浮脈　floating pulse
浮萍/浮萍　common ducksmeat herb
浮球感/浮動診法,浮球感診胎法　ballottement
浮石/浮石　pumice stone
浮郄/浮郄　fuxi, BL38
浮小麦/浮小麥　immature wheat

浮游髌/浮動髕　floating patella
浮游动物/浮游動物　zooplankton
浮游生物/浮游生物,游動生物　plankton
浮游植物/浮游植物　phytoplankton
匐行恶丝虫/匐行惡絲蟲　Dirofilaria repens
匐行的/匐行的,爬行的　serpiginous
匐行性动脉瘤/蜿蜒動脈瘤　serpentine aneurysm
匐行性回状红斑/匐行性迴[紋]狀紅斑　erythema gyratum repens
匐行性角膜溃疡/匐行性角膜潰瘍　serpent ulcer of cornea
匐行性溃疡/爬行性潰瘍,潛蝕性潰瘍　creeping ulcer
匐行性狼疮/匐行性狼瘡　lupus serpiginosus
匐行性皮炎/匐形性皮膚炎　dermatitis repens
匐行性软下疳/匐行性軟下疳　serpiginous chancroid
匐行性秃发/匐行性禿髮　ophiasis
匐行性血管瘤/匐行性血管瘤　angioma serpiginosum
匐行性血栓形成/匐行性血栓形成　creeping thrombosis
匐行疹/匐行疹　creeping eruption
匐行置换/匐行置換　creeping substitution
匐支青霉菌素/匐支青黴菌素　statolon
辐辏痉挛/輻輳痙攣　convergence spasm
辐射/輻射,放射　radiation
辐射病/輻射線病　radiation sickness
辐射对称/輻射對稱　radial symmetry
辐射防护/輻射防護　radiation protection
辐射防护剂/輻射防護劑　radiation-protective agent
辐射感应性/輻射感應性　photechy
辐射冠/放線冠　corona radiata
辐射剂量/輻射劑量　radiation dosage
辐射剂量效应关系/輻射劑量效應關係　radiation dose-response relationship
辐射监测/輻射監測　radiation monitoring
辐射链/輻射鏈　radial link
辐射灵敏度/放射線敏感度　radiosensitivity
辐射灭菌/輻射滅菌　radiation sterilization
辐射耐受性/輻射耐受性　radiation tolerance
辐射能/輻射能　radiant energy
辐射嵌合体/輻射嵌合體　radiation chimera
辐射热疗法/輻射熱療法　radiant heat therapy
辐射热内障/熱光內障　heat-ray cataract
辐射散射/輻射散射　radiation scattering
辐射事故/輻射事故　radiation accident
辐射损伤/放射線損傷　radiation damage

辐射损失/輻射損失　radiation loss
辐射卫生/輻射衛生　radiologic health
辐射物[质]/輻射物　radiant
辐射线/輻射線　radiatio
辐射效应/輻射效應　radiation effect
辐射性白内障/輻射性白内障　radiational cataract
辐射性白血病/輻射性白血病　radiation-induced leukemia
辐射性白血病病毒/輻射性白血病病毒　radiation leukemia virus
辐射性肺炎/輻射性肺炎　radiation pneumonitis
辐射性畸形/輻射性畸形　radiation-induced abnormality
辐射性肿瘤/輻射性腫瘤　radiation-induced neoplasm
辐射遗传学/輻射遺傳學　radiation genetics
辐射杂交图谱/輻射雜交圖譜　radiation hybrid mapping
辐射增敏药/輻射增敏藥　radiation-sensitizing agent
辐照后角化症/輻照後角化症　postirradiation keratosis
辐状纤维/輻狀纖維　radiate fiber
福贝斯病/Forbes 氏病　Forbes disease
福代斯斑/福代斯斑點　Fordyce spot
福代斯病/Fordyce 氏症　Fordyce disease
福尔根反应/富爾根反應　Feulgen reaction
福尔克曼管/Volkmann 氏管　Volkmann canal
福尔克曼夹/Volkmann 氏夾板　Volkmann splint
福尔克曼手挛缩/Volkmann 氏攣縮　Volkmann contracture
福尔马林/福馬林　formalin
福尔马林-岑克尔溶液/Zenker 氏甲醛溶液　formol-Zenker solution
福尔马林-米勒液/Müller 氏甲醛液　formol-Müller fluid
福格蒂取栓导管/福格蒂取栓導管　Fogarty embolectomy catheter
福格特线/佛依特線　Voigt line
福格特综合征/福格特症候群　Voigt syndrome
福克斯夹/Fox 氏夾板　Fox splint
福勒-墨菲疗法/弗-默二氏療法　Fowler-Murphy treatment
福雷尔被盖区/福雷爾被蓋區　tegmental region of Forel
福利车间/福利車間　sheltered workshops
福尼奥溶液/Fonio 氏溶液　Fonio solution
福瑟吉尔手术/弗沙吉氏手術　Fothergill operation
福氏纳格里阿米巴原虫/福氏耐格里原蟲　Naegleria fowleri
福斯曼抗体/弗斯門氏抗體　Forssman antibody
福维尔综合征/福維爾症候群　Foville syndrome
福辛普利/福辛普利　fosinopril
福修斯晶状体环/瓦斯爾氏晶狀體環　Vossius lenticular ring
蝠臭虫/蝠臭蟲　Cimex pipistrella
府舍/府舍　fushe, SP13
俯卧试验/俯臥試驗　prone test
俯卧位/俯臥位　prone position
辅骨/髆　condyle, fibula and radius
辅肌动蛋白/輔肌動蛋白　actinin
α-辅肌动蛋白/α-輔肌動蛋白原　alpha actinin
辅基/輔基　prosthetic group
辅料/輔料　adjuvant material
辅酶/輔酶,輔酵素　coenzyme
辅酶 A/輔酶 A　coenzyme A
辅酶测定器/輔酶測定器　coenzymometer
辅酶类/輔酶類　coenzymes
辅酶 A 连接酶类/輔酶 A 連接酶類　coenzyme A ligases
辅酶 A 转移酶类/輔酶 A 轉移酶類　coenzyme A-transferases
辅羧酶/輔羧酶　cocarboxylase
辅线/輔線　accessory line
辅药/輔藥　excipient
辅因子/輔因子　cofactor
辅音不清/子音不清　smudging
辅致癌作用/助癌生成　cocarcinogenesis
辅助病毒/輔助病毒　helper virus
辅助蛋白质/輔助蛋白質　auxiliary protein
辅助放射疗法/輔助放射療法　adjuvant radiotherapy
辅助化学疗法/輔助化學療法　adjuvant chemotherapy
辅助疗法/輔助療法　adjuvant therapy
辅助色板/輔助色板　accessory shade guide
辅助生活设施/輔助生活設施　assisted living facility
辅助生殖技术/輔助生殖技術　assisted reproductive technique
辅助通气/輔助通氣　assisted ventilation
辅助细胞/輔助細胞　accessory cell
辅助[性]肝移植/輔助[性]肝移植　auxiliary liver transplantation
辅助性 T[淋巴]细胞/輔助[型]T 細胞, T 型輔助細胞　helper T cell, Th cell
辅助[性]心脏移植/輔助[性]心臟移植　auxiliary cardiac transplantation
辅助循环/輔助循環　assisted circulation

辅阻遏物/辅抑制剂,辅抑制物　corepressor
辅佐性/輔佐性　adjuvanticity
腑病及脏/腑病及臟　fu-viscera disease involving zang-viscera
腐胺/腐肉鹼,腐物毒　putrescine
腐败变性/腐敗變性　putrid degeneration
腐败的/腐敗的　putrefactive
腐败毒/腐敗毒　putromaine
腐败脓毒病/腐化性敗血病　putrefactive sepsis
腐败小鳗线虫/腐敗性鰻狀蟲　Anguillulina putrefaciens
腐败性腹泻/腐敗性腹瀉　putrefactive diarrhea
腐败性污水/腐敗性糞汗　septic sewage
腐草霉素类/腐草黴素類　phleomycins
腐臭性溃疡/腐臭性潰瘍　putrid ulcer
腐烂性口炎/腐爛性口炎　putrid sore mouth
腐皮遮睛/腐皮遮睛　rotten membrane covering eye
腐肉/腐肉　sphacelus
腐[肉分]离/腐離　slough
腐生菌/腐物寄生菌　saprophyte
腐生葡萄球菌/腐生葡萄球菌　S. saprophyticus
腐生真菌/腐物寄生性真菌　saprophytic fungi
腐尸碱/腐屍鹼　saprin
腐蚀/腐蝕　corrosion
腐蚀标本/腐蝕標本　corrosion preparation
腐蚀的/腐蝕的　corrosive
腐蚀剂/腐蝕劑　caustic
腐蚀箭/腐蝕箭　caustic arrow
腐蚀解剖/腐蝕解剖學　corrosion anatomy
腐蚀疗法/腐蝕療法　eroding therapy
腐蚀性动脉瘤/腐蝕性動脈瘤　erosive aneurysm
腐蚀性溃疡/壞疽性口炎　corrosive ulcer
腐蚀性食管狭窄/腐蝕性食管狹窄　caustic stricture of esophagus
腐蚀性探条/腐蝕性探條　caustic bougie
腐蚀性胃炎/腐蝕性胃炎　corrosive gastritis
腐蚀药/腐蝕藥,糜爛藥　erosive medicine
腐蚀药把持器/腐蝕性藥把持器　portcaustic
腐蚀铸型/腐蝕鑄型　corrosion casting
腐蚀作用/腐蝕作用　caustic effect
腐苔/腐苔　curdy fur
腐蹄病/牛羊之腐腳病,腳壞死病　foot rot
腐[物寄]生的/腐生的　saprophytic
腐鱼尸碱/腐魚煙鹼　septicine
腐脏毒胺/腐肉毒素　mydatoxine
腐脏尸胺/腐臟毒　mydaleine
腐殖酸/腐土酸,腐黑酸　humic acid
腐殖质类/腐植質類　humic substances

腐组织毒/腐毒　zymoid
父代母育综合征/产翁現象　couvade syndrome
父母的/父母親的　parental
父母授权/父母授權　in potentate parentis
父亲/父親　father
父亲暴露/父親暴露　paternal exposure
父亲的/父親的　paternal
父亲年龄/父親年齡　paternal age
父亲年龄效应/父親年齡效應　paternal age effect
父亲行为/父親行爲　paternal behavior
父系遗传/父系遺傳　paternal inheritance
父性表型/父性表型　patromorph
父子关系/父子關係　father-child relation
负变株/負突變株　negative mutant
负氮平衡/負氮平衡　negative nitrogen balance
负的/負的　negative
负反馈/負反饋　negative feedback
负荷剂量/速效劑量　loading dose
负荷[试验]/負荷試驗　loading
负荷运动/負荷運動　load exercise
负离子/陰離子　negative ion
负链/負鏈　minus strand
负平衡/負性平衡　negative balance
负染色/負染色[法]　negative staining
负调节/負性調節　negative accommodation
负调节基因/負調節基因　negative regulator gene
负透镜/負透鏡　negative lens
负向流性/負向流性　negative rheotaxis
负性心动图/負心動波　negative cardiogram
负压通气机/負壓通氣機　negative-pressure ventilator
负压引流法/負壓引流法　negative pressure drainage
负优生学/負優生學　negative eugenics
负责任/負責性　accountability
负重运动/負重運動　weight loading exercise
妇产科学/婦產科學　obstetrics and gynecology
妇产科诊断技术/婦產科診斷技術　obstetrical and gynecological diagnostic technique
妇科外科手术/婦科外科手術　gynecologic surgical procedure
妇科学/婦科學　gynecology
妇乐颗粒/婦樂顆粒　fule granule
妇女/婦女　women
妇女卫生/婦女衛生　women's health
妇女卫生保健服务/婦女衛生保健服務　women's health service
妇人大全良方/婦人大全良方　Complete Effective Prescriptions for Women's Diseases, Furen Daquan

Liang Fang
妇人脏躁/婦人臟躁　hysteria
妇人症瘕/婦人症瘕　pelvic mass in woman
妇人症瘕·毒热证/婦人症瘕·毒熱證　pelvic mass in woman with poison-heat pattern
妇人症瘕·气滞证/婦人症瘕·氣滯證　pelvic mass in woman with qi stagnation pattern
妇人症瘕·肾虚血瘀证/婦人症瘕·腎虛血瘀證　pelvic mass in woman with pattern of kidney deficiency and blood stasis
妇人症瘕·湿热瘀阻证/婦人症瘕·濕熱瘀阻證　pelvic mass in woman with pattern of blockade of damp-heat and static blood
妇人症瘕·痰湿瘀结证/婦人症瘕·痰濕瘀結證　pelvic mass in woman with pattern of binding of phlegm-damp and static blood
妇人症瘕·血瘀证/婦人症瘕·血瘀證　pelvic mass in woman with blood stasis pattern
妇外科/婦科手術　gynecological surgery
妇炎平胶囊/婦炎平膠囊　fuyanping capsule
妇幼保健中心/婦幼保健中心　maternal-child health center
附壁性血栓/附壁性血栓　parietal thrombus
附壁血栓/壁血栓　mural thrombus
附分/附分　fufen, BL41
附睾/附睾　epididymis, epididymidis
附睾窦/附睾竇　sinus of epididymis
附睾分泌蛋白质类/附睾分泌蛋白質類　epididymal secretory proteins
附睾附件/附睾附件　appendix of epididymis
附睾睾丸炎/附睾睾丸炎　epididymoorchitis
附睾管/附睾管　duct of epididymis, epididymal duct
附睾结核/附睾結核　tuberculosis of epididymis
附睾类腺瘤/附睾類腺瘤　adenomatoid tumor of epididymis
附睾梅毒/附睾梅毒　syphilis of epididymis
附睾迷管/Haller 氏迷管　Haller aberrant duct
附睾囊腺瘤/附睾囊腺瘤　cystadenoma of epididymis
附睾切除术/附睾切除術　epididymectomy
附睾切开术/附睾切開術　epididymotomy
附睾肉瘤/附睾肉瘤　sarcoma of epididymis
附睾上韧带/附睾上韌帶　superior ligament of epididymis
附睾输精管切除术/附睾輸精管切除術　epididymodeferentectomy
附睾体/附睾體　body of epididymis
附睾头/附睾頭　head of epididymis
附睾尾/附睾尾　tail of epididymis

附睾系膜/附睾繫膜　mesoepididymis
附睾下韧带/附睾下韌帶　inferior ligament of epididymis
附睾腺瘤/附睾腺瘤　adenoma of epididymis
附睾小叶/副睾小葉　lobules of epididymis
附睾炎/附睾炎　epididymitis
附睾造影[术]/附睾造影[術]　epididymography
附睾支/附睾支　epididymal branch
附睾肿瘤/附睾腫瘤　tumor of epididymis
附骨/附屬骨　accessory bone
附骨疽/附骨疽　bone-attaching abscess, suppurative osteomyelitis
附骨疽·脓毒蚀骨证/附骨疽·膿毒蝕骨證　bone-attaching abscess with pattern of purulent toxin eroding bone
附骨疽·热毒炽盛证/附骨疽·熱毒熾盛證　bone-attaching abscess with blazing heat-toxin pattern
附骨疽·湿热阻滞证/附骨疽·濕熱阻滯證　bone-attaching abscess with pattern of dampness-heat obstruction and stagnation
附骨疽·正虚毒滞证/附骨疽·正虛毒滯證　bone-attaching abscess with pattern of healthy qi deficiency and toxin stagnation
附骨痰/附骨痰　bone-attaching phlegm, phlegmatic osteomyelitis, tuberculosis of hip joint
附红细胞体病/紅血球附體病　eperythrozoonosis
附加的/添加的　additional
附加关节/附加關節　supplementary articulation
附加径路/附加徑路　accessory pathway
附加囊/附加囊　adventitious cyst
附加体/附加體　episome
附加性月经/附加性行經　supplementary menstruation
附加音/附加音　adventitious sound
附加饮食/增添食物　addition diet
附加作用/附加作用　adjection
附件/附件,附屬器　adnexa, appendage
附件癌/附屬器癌　adnexal carcinoma
附件的/附件的,附屬器的　adnexal
附件发生/附屬器發生　adnexogenesis
附件腺癌/附屬器腺癌　adnexal adenocarcinoma
附件炎/附屬器炎　appendagitis
附件痣/附屬器痣　adnexal nevus
附件周围的/附屬器周圍的　periadnexal
附脐静脉/附臍靜脈　paraumbilical veins
附舌骨囊肿/附舌骨囊腫　adhyoid cyst
附属骨骼/附屬骨骼　appendicular skeleton
附属肌/附屬肌　appendicular muscle

附属屈肌/附屬屈肌　accessory flexor muscle
附属生殖管道/附屬生殖管道　accessory reproductive duct
附属生殖腺/附屬生殖腺　accessory reproductive gland
附属腺/副腺　accessory gland
附体/附體　possession
附头联胎/附頭連胎　heterodidymus
附于舌骨的/附於舌骨的　adhyoid
附肢骨骼/附肢骨骼　appendicular skeleton
附着/附著　attachment
附着斑/附著斑　attachment plaque
附着板/附著板　lamina affixa, attachment plate
附着核糖体/附著核糖體　attached ribosome, bound ribosome
附着髓石/附著髓石　adherent denticle
附着胎盘/附著胎盤　placenta apposita
附着龈/附著齦　attached gingiva
附着增加/附著增加　attachment gain
附子/附子　prepared common monkshood branched root
附子理中丸/附子理中丸　fuzi lizhong pills
复臂[畸形]/複臂畸形　dibrachia
复层扁平上皮/複層扁平上皮　stratified squamous epithelium
复层立方上皮/複層立方上皮　stratified cuboidal epithelium
复层上皮/複層上皮　laminated epithelium, stratified epithelium
复层纤毛柱状上皮/複層纖毛柱狀上皮　stratified ciliated columnar epithelium
复层柱状上皮/複層柱狀上皮　stratified columnar epithelium
复唇[畸形]/複唇畸形　dicheilia
复等位基因/複等位基因　multiple allele
复发/復發,再發　relapse
复发的/再發的　recurring
复发缓解性多发性硬化/復發緩解性多發性硬化　relapsing-remitting multiple sclerosis
复发率/復發率　relapse rate
复发性阿弗他口炎/復發性阿弗他口炎　recurrent aphthous stomatitis
复发性阿弗他溃疡/復發性阿弗他潰瘍　recurrent aphthous ulcer
复发性斑疹伤寒/復發性斑疹傷寒　Brill-Zinsser disease
复发性出血/復發性出血,再發性出血　recurrent hemorrhage, recurring hemorrhage
复发性单纯疱疹/復發性單純皰疹　recurrent herpes simplex
复发性胆总管结石病/復發性膽總管結石病　recurrent choledocholithiasis
复发性的/復發的　recurrent
复发性多软骨炎/復發性多軟骨炎　relapsing polychondritis
复发性二期梅毒/二期復發梅毒　relapsing secondary syphilis
复发性风湿病/再發性風濕病　palindromic rheumatism
复发性坏死性黏膜腺周炎/復發壞死性黏膜腺周炎　periadenitis mucosa necrotica recurren
复发性急性发炎发作/復發性急性發炎發作　recurrent acute inflammatory episode
复发性假下疳/再發性假下疳　pseudochancre redux
复发性结节性非化脓性脂膜炎/韋-克二氏病,再發性發熱結節性非化膿脂層炎　Weber-Christian disease
复发性局灶性手掌脱皮/復發性局部手掌脱屑　recurrent focal palmar peeling
复发性口疮溃疡/復發性口瘡潰瘍　recurrent aphthous ulcer
复发性溃疡/復發性潰瘍　recurrent ulcer
复发性溃疡性喉炎/復發性潰瘍性喉炎　relapsing ulcerative laryngitis
复发性阑尾炎/復發性闌尾炎　relapsing appendicitis
复发性肉芽肿性皮炎伴嗜酸细胞增多/嗜伊紅球增生性復發性肉芽腫性皮膚炎　recurrent granulomatous dermatitis with eosinophilia
复发性肾盂肾炎/復發性腎盂腎炎　recurrent pyelonephritis
复发性嗜酸粒细胞增多性肌周炎/復發性嗜伊紅球增生性肌周圍炎　relapsing eosinophilic perimyositis
复发性手脚掌汗腺炎/復發性手腳掌汗腺炎　recurrent palmoplantar hidradenitis
复发性脱位/再發性脱位　recurrent dislocation
复发性下疳/復發性下疳　chancre redux
复发性线状棘层松解性皮病/復發性線狀棘皮層鬆懈皮膚病　relapsing linear acantholytic dermatosis
复发性翼状胬肉/復發性翼狀胬肉　recurrent pterygium
复发性婴儿指纤维瘤/復發性嬰兒指纖維瘤　recurrent infantile digital fibroma
复发性婴儿趾纤维瘤/復發性嬰兒趾纖維瘤　recurrent infantile digital fibroma
复发性肿瘤/再發性瘤　recurrent tumor

复方/複方　compound recipe, compound prescription
复方安息香酊/複方安息香酊　compound benzoin tincture
复方氨基酸/複方胺基酸　compound amino acid
复方白垩散/複方白堊散劑　compound chalk powder
复方白松可待因糖浆/複方可待因白松糖漿　compound white pine syrup with codeine
复方白松糖浆/複方白松糖漿　compound white pine syrup
复方草珊瑚含片/複方草珊瑚含片　compound caoshanhu tablets
复方橙皮酊/複方橙皮酊　compound orange spirit
复方丹参滴丸/複方丹參滴丸　compound danshen dripping pills
复方丹参片/複方丹參片　compound danshen tablets
复方丹参注射液/複方丹參注射液　compound danshen injection
复方胆通片/複方膽通片　compound dantong tablets
复方碘[溶]液/複方碘溶液　compound iodine solution
复方番泻叶浸剂/黑飲劑　black draft
复方甘草/複方甘草　compound liquorice
复方甘草散/複方甘草散　compound licorice powder
复方合剂/複方合劑　drug combination
复方磺胺甲噁唑/複方磺胺甲噁唑　compound sulfamethoxazole
复方甲酚溶液/複方甲酚溶液　compound cresol solution
复方浸膏/複合浸膏　compound extract
复方氯化钠/複方氯化鈉　compound sodium chloride
复方硼酸钠/複方硼酸鈉　compound sodium borate solution
复方氢氧化铝/複方氫氧化鋁　compound aluminium hydroxide
复方泻丸/複方瀉丸　compound cathartic pill
复方药物/複合劑　compound medicine
复关节/複關節　compound joint, compound articulation
复管泡状腺/複管泡狀腺　compound tubuloacinar gland
复管状腺/複管狀腺　compound tubular gland
复合半抗原/複合半抗原　complex hapten
复合蛋白[质]/複合蛋白質　compound protein
复合的/複合的　compound
复合动脉瘤/複合動脈瘤　compound aneurysm
复合固定桥/複合固定橋　compound fixed bridge
复合混合物/複合混合物　complex mixtures
复合结核菌组/複合結核菌組　mycobacterium tuberculosis complex
复合抗原/複合抗原　complex antigen
复合颗粒细胞/複合顆粒細胞　compound granule cell
复合毛囊/複合毛囊　compound follicle
复合皮瓣/複合皮瓣　compound skin flap
复合伤/複合傷　combined injury
复合树脂/複合樹脂　composite resin
复合糖/糖軛合物　glycoconjugate
复合体/複合體　complex
复合填料/複合填料　composite filling
复合透镜/複透鏡　compound lens
复合脱位/複合脫位　compound dislocation
复合维生素 B/複合維生素 B, 維生素 B 複體　vitamin B complex
复合先露/複合式産式　compound presentation
复合苋紫溶液/複方莧紫素溶液　compound amaranth solution
复合型乳剂/複合型乳劑　multiple emulsion
复合性单纯骨折/複合性單純骨折　complex simple fracture
复合性动脉瘤/複合性動脈瘤　mixed aneurysm
复合性腱鞘囊肿/複合性腱鞘囊腫　compound ganglion
复合性局部疼痛综合征/複合性局部疼痛症候群　complex regional pain syndrome
复合性口疮病/口瘡綜合徵　complex aphthosis
复合性胃和十二指肠溃疡/複合性胃和十二指腸潰瘍　combined gastric and duodenal ulcer
复合牙色/複合牙色　composite tooth color
复合眼镜/複合眼鏡　compound spectacles
复合杂合子/複合雜合體　compound heterozygote
复合脂蛋白型高脂血症/複合脂蛋白型高脂血症　multiple lipoprotein-type hyperlipidemia
复合组织移植[术]/複合組織移植[術]　composite tissue transplantation
复极/再極　repolarization
复极化相/再極化時期　repolarization phase
复旧/復舊　recovery method for arresting uterine hemorrhage
复孔绦虫病/犬兩殖器條蟲病　dipylidiasis
复粒淀粉/複粒澱粉　compound starch granule
复溜/複溜　fuliu, KI7
复拇畸形/複拇畸形　thumb duplication
复拇指/複拇指　duplication of the thumb
复能/使再活動　reactivate
复泡状腺/複泡狀腺　compound acinar gland
复强反应/複強反應　booster reaction

复曲面透镜/托力克鏡　toric lens
复染剂/複染劑　counter stain
复染色法/複染法，對比染法　double staining
复式显微镜/複式顯微鏡　compound microscope
复视/複視　diplopia
复视计/複視計　diplopiometer
复视试验/複視試驗　diplopia test
复手[畸形]/單臂複手畸形　dicheiria
复手[畸形]者/單臂複手畸形者　dicheirus
复苏后综合征/復甦後症候群　postresuscitation syndrome
复苏器/復甦器　resuscitator
复苏术/復甦　resuscitation
复苏学/復甦學　reanimatology
复苏医嘱/復甦醫囑　resuscitation order
复体畸胎/複體畸胎，連胎　compound monster
复听/復聽　diplacusia
复头卷带/複頭卷帶　double handed roller bandage
复位/復位，放回　reposition
复位器/復位器　repositor
复位手法/復位手法　reduction manipulation
复位术/復位　reduction
复温/復溫　rewarming
复腺/複腺　compound gland
复消色差透镜/復消[色]差透鏡　apochromatic lens
复型膜技术/複型膜技術　replica techniques
复性/复性　renaturation
复性近视散光/近視性複性散光　compound myopic astigmatism
复性散光/複性散光　compound astigmatism
复性远视散光/複性遠視散光　compound hyperopic astigmatism
复眼/複眼　compound eye
复元活血汤/復元活血湯　fuyuan huoxue decoction
复原性男子女乳症/復原性男子女乳症　rehabilitation gynecomastia
复杂并指/并發性并指畸形　complicated syndactyly
复杂并趾/并發性并趾畸形　complicated syndactyly
复杂部分发作/複雜部分發作　complex partial seizure
复杂部分性癫痫/複雜部分性癫痫　complex partial epilepsy
复杂充填/複雜充填　complex filling
复杂骨折/複雜骨折　complicated fracture
复杂易位/複雜易位　complex translocation
复肢畸胎/複肢畸形怪胎　dimelus
复肢[畸形]/複肢畸形　dimelia
复制/複製　replication
复制叉/複製叉　replicating fork
复制技术/複製技術　copying processe
复制起点/複製起點　replication origin
复制体/複製體　replisome
复制脱氧核糖核酸/去氧核糖核酸複製　copy DNA
复制型/複製型　replicating form
复制子/複製子　replicon
复制综合征/複製症候群　duplication syndrome
复治方案/複治方案　retreatment regimen
复足[畸形]/複足畸形　dipodia
副阿拉伯胶素/副阿拉伯膠素　pararabin
副半奇静脉/副半奇靜脈　accessory hemiazygos vein
副闭孔动脉/副閉孔動脈　accessory obturator artery
副闭孔神经/副閉孔神經　accessory obturator nerve
副变应原/副過敏原　parallergin
副[病]因/副病因，助發病因　synaetion
副产物/副產物　by-product
副垂体/副腦下垂體　parahypophysis
副丛/副叢　accessory plexus
副大风子酸盐/大風子油酸鹽　hydnocarpate
副胆管/副膽管　accessory bile duct
副蛋白/副蛋白　paraprotein
副蛋白类/副蛋白類　paraproteins
副蛋白血症/副蛋白血症　paraproteinemia
副的/副的　accessory
副淀粉/副澱粉　paramylum
副痘疹病毒/副痘疹病毒　parapoxviruse
副多角骨/副多角骨　accessory multangular bone
副耳/副耳　accessory ear
副耳郭/副耳郭　accessory auricle
副耳珠/副耳珠　accessory tragus
副肝管/副肝管　accessory hepatic duct
副感觉/副感覺　concomitant sense
副膈神经/副膈神經　accessory phrenic nerve
副沟/副溝　supplemental groove
副核/副核　accessory nucleus
副核仁/副核仁　paranucleolus
副黄体素/副黄體素　paralutein
副黄体素细胞/副黄體素細胞　paralutein cell
副肌/副肌　supernumerary muscle
副肌强直/副肌強直　paramyotonia
副肌球蛋白/副肌漿球蛋白，副肌凝蛋白　paramyosin
副肌球蛋白原/副肌凝蛋白原　paramyosinogen
副基底/旁基底　parabasal
副基底层/旁基底層　parabasal layer
副激素/副激素　parahormone
副甲状腺/副甲狀腺　accessory thyroid gland

副甲状腺组织/副甲狀腺組織　accessory thyroid tissue
副交感部/副交感部　parasympathetic part
副交感根/副交感根　parasympathetic root
副交感神经/副交感神經　parasympathetic nerve
副交感[神经]的/副交感神經的　parasympathetic
副交感神经功能/副交感神經功能　parasympathetic function
副交感神经节/副交感神經節　parasympathetic ganglion, parasympathetic ganglia
副交感神经素/副交感素　parasympathin
副交感神经系统/副交感神經系統　parasympathetic nervous system
副交感神经阻断术/副交感神經阻斷術　parasympathectomy
副交感神经阻滞药/副交感神經阻斷藥　parasympatholytic
副交感支/副交感支　parasympathetic branch
副角蛋白/副油粒蛋白　pareleidin
副结核/類結核病　paratuberculosis
副结核[杆]菌素/副結核菌素,副結核菌苗　johnin
副精囊/副精囊　accessory seminal vesicle
副孔/副孔　accessory foramen
副肋/副肋　accessory rib
副泪腺/副淚腺　accessory lacrimal gland
副裂/附屬分裂　accessory cleavage
副流感病毒/副流行性感冒病毒　parainfluenza virus
副流感2型病毒/副流行性感冒第二型病毒　parainfluenza 2 virus
副流感疫苗/副流感疫苗　parainfluenza vaccine
副流行性感冒/副流行性感冒　parainfluenza
副脑膜炎球菌/副腦膜炎球菌　parameningococcus
副脑膜炎球菌性脑膜炎/副腦膜炎球菌性腦膜炎　parameningococcus meningitis
副黏病毒科感染/副黏病毒科感染　paramyxoviridae infection
副黏蛋白/副黏蛋白　paramucin
副黏液病毒/副黏液病毒　paramyxovirus
副黏液病毒病/副黏液病毒病　paramyxovirus disease
副黏液瘤样小体/副黏液瘤樣小體　paramyxoma-like body
副尿道/副尿道　paraurethra
副尿道管/副尿道管　paraurethral duct
副凝集素/副凝集素　para-agglutinin
副牛痘病毒/副牛痘病毒　paravaccinia virus
副牛痘[疹]/副牛痘,亞牛痘疹　paravaccinia
副胚层/副胚葉　parablast

副皮质区/副皮質區　paracortical area
副脾/副脾　accessory spleen
副脐静脉/副臍靜脈　paraumbilical vein
副球孢子菌/副球孢子菌屬　Paracoccidioides
副球孢子菌性/副球孢子菌性　paracoccidioidal
副球孢子菌性肉芽肿/巴西副球黴菌性肉芽腫　paracoccidioidal granuloma
副球蛋白/副球蛋白　fibroplastin
副球蛋白尿/副球蛋白尿　paraglobulinuria
副屈肌/副屈肌　accessiflexor
副染色质/核成形質,副核染質　karyoplastin
副韧带/副韌帶　accessory ligament
副乳房/副乳房　accessory breast
副软骨瘤/副軟骨瘤　parachondroma
副腮腺/副腮腺　accessory parotid gland
副伤寒/副傷寒　paratyphoid
副伤寒丙/副傷寒丙　paratyphoid C
副伤寒甲/副傷寒甲　paratyphoid A
副伤寒乙/副傷寒乙　paratyphoid B
副神经/副神經　accessory nerve
副神经干/副神經幹　trunk of accessory nerve
副神经核/副神經核　accessory nucleus
副神经疾病/副神經疾病　accessory nerve disease
副神经脊髓根/副神經脊髓根　spinal root of accessory nerve
副神经节瘤/副神經節瘤　paraganglioma
副神经淋巴结/副神經淋巴結　accessory nerve lymph node
副神经颅根/副神經顱根　cranial root of accessory nerve
副神经性[痉挛性]斜颈/副神經痙攣　accessory cramp
副神经元/副神經元,旁神經元　paraneuron
副肾上腺/副腎上腺　accessory suprarenal gland
副生小指/後小指　postminimus
副生小趾/後小趾　postminimus
副生殖管/副生殖管　paragenital duct
副生殖器/副生殖器　paragenitalis
副生殖器的/副生殖器的　paragenital
副胎盘/副胎盤　accessory placenta
副头静脉/副頭靜脈　accessory cephalic vein
副骰骨/副骰骨　accessory cuboid bone
副突/[脊椎骨]副突　anapophysis
副突变/副突變　paramutation
副卫细胞/副衛細胞　subsidiary cell
副[下]橄榄核/副[下]橄欖核　accessory olivary nucleus
副纤维/副纖維　accessory fiber

副纤维素/副木纖維質 paracellulose
副现象/副現象 epiphenomenon
副猩红热/副猩紅熱 parascarlatina
副胸腺/副胸腺 accessory thymus
副胸腺组织/副胸腺組織 accessory thymic tissue
副血清反应/副血清反應 paraserum reaction
副血友病/亞血友病 parahemophilia
副胰管/副胰管，胰副管 accessory pancreatic duct
副胰[腺]/副胰[腺] accessory pancreas
副胰组织/副胰組織 accessory pancreatic tissue
副缢痕/副縊痕 secondary constriction
副隐静脉/副隱靜脈 accessory saphenous vein
副征/副徵象 accessory sign
副中肾管/副中腎管 paramesonephric duct
副中肾管存留综合征/副中腎管存留症候群 persistent Müllerian duct syndrome
副中肾管综合征/副中腎管症候群 Müllerian duct syndrome
副中肾管组织退化因子/副中腎管組織退化因子 Müllerian regression factor
副肿瘤内分泌综合征/副腫瘤內分泌症候群 paraneoplastic endocrine syndrome
副肿瘤性/伴腫瘤性 paraneoplastic
副肿瘤性多发性神经病/腫瘤旁多發性神經病 paraneoplastic polyneuropathy
副肿瘤性小脑变性/副腫瘤性小腦變性 paraneoplastic cerebellar degeneration
副肿瘤综合征/伴腫瘤症候群 paraneoplastic syndrome
副椎静脉/副椎靜脈 accessory vertebral vein
副作用/副作用 side effect
赋权/賦權 empowerment
赋形剂/賦形劑 excipient, vehicle
傅里叶变换红外谱学/傅立葉變換紅外譜學 Fourier transform infrared spectroscopy
傅里叶分析/傅立葉分析 Fourier analysis
傅青主女科/傅青主女科 Fu Qingzhu's Obstetrics and Gynecology
富贵病/富貴病 royal malady
富集/富集 enrichment
富集培养基/增菌培養基 enrichment medium
富克斯斑/富克斯斑 Fuchs spot
富勒烯/富勒烯 fullerene
富尼埃坏疽/弗爾尼壞疽 Fournier gangrene
富尼埃试验/弗爾尼試驗 Fournier test
富血小板血浆/富血小板血漿 platelet rich plasma, PRP
富营养化/優養化 eutrophication

腹/腹[部] abdomen, belly
腹哀/腹哀 fuai, SP16
腹壁/腹壁 abdominal wall
腹壁部分切除术/腹壁部分切除術 laparectomy
腹壁成形术/腹壁成形術 abdominoplasty
腹壁动脉/腹壁動脈 epigastric artery
腹壁多脂症/腹壁多脂症 abdominal adiposity
腹壁缝合术/腹壁縫合術 celiorrhaphy
腹壁感染/腹壁感染 infection of abdominal wall
腹壁坏死性筋膜炎/腹壁壞死性筋膜炎 necrotizing fascitis of abdominal wall
腹壁间层疝/腹壁間疝 interparietal hernia
腹壁裂[畸形]/腹裂 abdominal fissure
腹[壁]瘘/腹[壁]瘺 abdominal fistula
腹壁脓肿/腹壁膿腫 mural abscess
腹壁膀胱陷凹/腹壁膀胱陷凹 abdominovesical pouch
腹壁皮肤松垂/腹壁皮膚鬆垂 abdominal chalastodermia
腹壁皮肤脂肪切除术/腹壁皮膚脂肪切除術 abdominal dermolipectomy
腹壁浅动脉/腹壁淺動脈 superficial epigastric artery
腹壁浅静脉/腹壁淺靜脈 superficial epigastric vein
腹壁切开/剖腹術切開法 celiotomy incision
腹壁全裂/完全腹裂 hologastroschisis
腹[壁]疝/腹疝 laparocele
腹壁上动脉/腹壁上動脈 superior epigastric artery
腹壁上静脉/腹壁上靜脈 superior epigastric vein
腹壁深动脉/腹壁深動脈 deep epigastric artery
腹壁深静脉/腹壁深靜脈 deep epigastric vein
腹壁外动脉/腹壁外動脈，旋髂深動脈 external epigastric artery
腹壁围裙状松垂[畸形]/腹壁圍裙狀鬆垂[畸形] abdominal apron deformity
腹壁下动脉/腹壁下動脈 inferior epigastric artery
腹壁下动脉耻骨支/腹壁下動脈恥骨支 pubic branch of inferior epigastric artery
腹壁下静脉/腹壁下靜脈 inferior epigastric vein
腹壁下淋巴结/腹壁下淋巴結 inferior epigastric lymph node
腹壁硬纤维瘤/腹壁硬纖維瘤 desmoid of abdominal wall
腹壁肿瘤/腹壁腫瘤 abdominal wall tumor
腹壁子宫固定术/子宮腹壁固定術 ventrohysteropexy
腹病/腹腔病 celiopathy
腹病性腮腺炎/腹病性腮腺炎 celiac parotitis

腹部/腹部　abdominal part, abdoment
腹部触诊/腹部觸診　abdominal touch
腹部多脏器移植/腹部多臟器移植　abdominal multivisceral transplantation
腹部放射摄影术/腹部放射攝影術　abdominal radiography
腹部寄生胎/腹部寄生胎　epigastric parasitus
腹部寄生肢畸胎/腹部寄生肢,腹肢畸胎　gastromelus
腹部绞痛/腹部絞痛　spasm of abdomen
腹部结核/腹部結核　abdominal tuberculosis
腹部联胎/腹部連胎　gastrodidymus
腹部内伤/腹部內傷　internal injury of abdomen
腹部脓肿/腹部膿腫　abdominal abscess
腹部皮下静脉/腹部皮下靜脈　subcutaneous vein of abdomen
腹[部]球[状]感/腹球感　globus abdominalis
腹部损伤/腹部損傷　abdominal injury
腹部外科/腹部外科　abdominal surgery
腹部外硬纤维瘤/腹部外硬纖維瘤　extra-abdominal desmoid
腹部纤维瘤病/腹部纖維瘤病　abdominal fibromatosis
腹部硬满/腹部硬滿　hard and full in abdomen
腹部肿瘤/腹部腫瘤　abdominal neoplasm
腹部[主动脉]脉搏/腹部脈搏,腹部搏動　abdominal pulse
腹部综合征/腹部症候群　abdominal syndrome
腹侧/腹側　ventro
腹侧被盖区/腹側被蓋區　ventral tegmental area
腹侧[的]/腹側的　ventral
腹侧核/腹側核　ventral nucleus
腹侧核群/腹側核群　ventral nuclear group
腹侧面/腹側面　ventral surface
腹侧牵引/向腹側引動　ventriduction
腹侧网状核/腹側網狀核　ventral reticular nucleus
腹侧主动脉/腹側主動脈　ventral aorta
腹[侧]纵柱/腹[側]縱柱　ventral longitudinal column
腹肠系膜/腹側腸繫膜　ventral mesentery
腹唇/腹唇　ventral lip
腹卒中/腹部性中風　abdominal apoplexy
腹带/腹帶　belly band
腹的/腹腔的　celiac
腹蒂/腹蒂　abdominal stalk
腹垫/腹墊　abdominal pad
腹动脉/腹腔動脈　coeliac artery
腹反射/腹反射　abdominal reflex

腹干/腹腔幹　coeliac trunk
腹髂动脉阻塞病/腹髂動脈阻塞病　aortoiliac occlusive disease
腹股沟/腹股溝　groin
腹股沟不全疝/腹股溝不完全疝　incomplete inguinal hernia
腹股沟部瘢痕挛缩/腹股溝部瘢痕攣縮　scar contracture of inguinal region
腹股沟翻转韧带/翻轉腹股溝韌帶　reflex inguinal ligament
腹股沟反转韧带/Colles 氏韌帶　Colles ligament
腹股沟腹膜前疝/腹股溝腹膜前疝　preperitoneal inguinal hernia
腹股沟股疝/Holthouse 氏疝　Holthouse hernia
腹股沟管/腹股溝管　inguinal canal
腹股沟管环/腹股溝環　annulus abdominalis
腹股沟管括约肌/腹股溝括約肌　inguinal sphincter
腹股沟管浅环/腹股溝管淺環　superficial inguinal ring
腹股沟管深环/腹股溝管深環　deep inguinal ring
腹股沟后韧带/腹股溝後韌帶　posterior inguinal ligament
腹股沟棘皮瘤/腹股溝棘皮瘤　acanthoma inguinale
腹股沟脊/腹股溝脊　inguinal crest
腹股沟溃疡/鼠蹊潰瘍　groin ulcer
腹股沟镰/腹股溝鐮　inguinal falx, falx inguinalis
腹股沟淋巴丛/腹股溝淋巴叢　plexus inguinalis
腹股沟淋巴结/腹股溝淋巴結　inguinal lymph node
腹股沟淋巴结炎/淋巴腺紅腫　bubo
腹股沟淋巴结炎的/淋巴腺紅腫的　bubonic
腹股沟淋巴肉芽肿/腹股溝淋巴肉芽腫　lymphogranuloma inguinale
腹股沟淋巴肉芽肿病毒/腹股溝淋巴肉芽腫病毒　virus of lymphogranuloma inguinale
腹股沟内侧窝/腹股溝內側窩　medial inguinal fossa
腹股沟前韧带/腹股溝前韌帶　anterior inguinal ligament
腹股沟浅淋巴结/腹股溝淺淋巴結　superficial inguinal lymph node
腹股沟区/腹股溝區,腹股溝部　inguinal region
腹股沟全疝/腹股溝全疝　complete inguinal hernia
腹股沟韧带/腹股溝韌帶,鼠蹊韌帶　inguinal ligament
腹股沟肉芽肿/腹股溝肉芽腫　granuloma inguinale
腹股沟三角/腹股溝三角　inguinal triangle
腹股沟疝/腹股溝疝　inguinal hernia
腹股沟上内侧浅淋巴结/腹股溝上內側淺淋巴結　superomedial superficial inguinal lymph node

腹股沟上外侧浅淋巴结/腹股溝上外側淺淋巴結 superolateral superficial inguinal lymph node
腹股沟深淋巴结/腹股溝深淋巴結,腘深淋巴結 deep inguinal lymph node
腹股沟生殖韧带/生殖腹股溝韌帶 genitoinguinal ligament
腹股沟水囊/腹股溝水囊 inguinal hydrocele
腹股沟痛/腹股溝痛 bubonalgia
腹股沟突出/腹股溝疝氣,腹股溝腫大 bubonocele
腹股沟外侧窝/腹股溝外側窩 lateral inguinal fossa
腹股沟下浅淋巴结/腹股溝下淺淋巴結 inferior superficial inguinal lymph node
腹股沟斜疝/間接腹股溝疝 indirect inguinal hernia
腹股沟支/腹股溝支 inguinal branches
腹股沟直疝/直接腹股溝疝 direct inguinal hernia
腹股沟子宫疝/腹股溝子宮膨出 hysterobubonocele
腹冠状的/腹冠狀的 abdominal coronary
腹横肌/腹橫肌 transversus abdominis, musculus transversus abdominis
腹横筋膜/腹橫筋膜 transverse fascia
腹后核/腹後核 ventral posterior nucleus
腹后内侧核/腹後内側核 ventral posteromedial nucleus
腹后外侧核/腹後外側核 ventral posterolateral nucleus
腹厚/腹厚 abdominal thickness
腹会阴拖出肛门成形术/腹會陰拖出肛門成形術 abdominoperineal pull through anoplasty
腹肌/腹[部諸]肌 muscle of abdomen, abdominal muscle
腹肌发育缺陷综合征/腹肌發育缺陷症候群 abdominal musculature deficiency syndrome
腹肌沟区/腹肌溝區,腹股溝區 inguinal region
腹肌腱膜/腹腱膜 abdominal aponeurosis
腹肌痛/腹肌痛 myalgia abdominis
腹肌炎/腹肌炎 celiomyositis
腹结/腹結 fujie, SP14
腹筋怒张/腹筋怒張 abdominal varicosis
腹颈反流/腹頸反流 abdominojugular reflux
腹菌类/腹菌 gasteromycetes
腹痨/腹癆 abdominal phthisis
腹肋/腹肋 abdominal rib
腹裂/裂腹[畸形] gastroschisis
腹瘤/腹部腫瘍,腹部瘤 celioma
腹露青筋/腹露青筋 venous engorgement on abdomen
腹面/腹面,腹側景 ventral aspect
腹鸣/腹鳴 borborygmus

腹膜/腹膜 peritoneum
腹膜壁层/腹膜壁層 parietal peritoneum
腹膜襞/腹膜皺襞 peritoneal folds
腹膜病/腹膜病 peritoneopathy
腹膜成形术/腹膜造形術,腹膜修補術 peritoneoplasty
腹膜刺激征/腹膜刺激徵 peritoneal irritation sign
腹膜的/腹膜的 peritoneal
腹膜腹肌间积水/腹膜腹肌間積水 hydrepigastrium
腹膜固定术/腹膜固定術 peritoneopexy
腹膜后的/腹膜後的 retroperitoneal
腹膜后间隙/腹膜後間隙 retroperitoneal space
腹膜后腔炎/腹膜後間隙炎 retroperitonitis
腹膜后淋巴结切除术/腹膜後淋巴結切除術 retroperitoneal lymphadenectomy
腹膜后淋巴囊/腹膜後淋巴囊 retroperitoneal lymph sac
腹膜后淋巴囊肿/腹膜後淋巴囊腫 retroperitoneal lymphocele
腹膜后脓肿/腹膜後膿腫 retroperitoneal abscess
腹膜后腔/腹膜後腔 retroperitoneum
腹膜后腔积气/腹膜後腔積氣 pneumoretroperitoneum
腹膜后疝/腹膜後疝 retroperitoneal hernia
腹膜后纤维化/腹膜後纖維化 retroperitoneal fibrosis
腹膜后肿瘤/腹膜後腫瘤 retroperitoneal neoplasm
腹膜后注气造影[术]/腹膜後充氣造影術 retroperitoneal pneumography
腹膜会阴筋膜/腹膜會陰筋膜 peritoneoperineal fascia
腹膜疾病/腹膜疾病 peritoneal disease
腹膜假黏液瘤/腹腔假黏液瘤 pseudomyxoma peritonei
腹膜巨噬细胞/腹膜巨噬細胞 peritoneal macrophage
腹膜内的/腹膜内的 intraperitoneal
腹膜内膀胱破裂/腹膜内膀胱破裂 intraperitoneal rupture of bladder
腹膜内注射/腹膜内注射 peritoneal injection
腹膜钮/腹膜鈕 peritoneal button
腹膜旁的/腹膜旁的 paraperitoneal
腹膜旁疝/腹膜旁疝 paraperitoneal hernia
腹膜旁肾切除术/腹膜旁式腎切除術 paraperitoneal nephrectomy
腹膜前的/腹膜前的 preperitoneal
腹膜前疝/腹膜前疝 preperitoneal hernia
腹膜腔/腹膜腔 peritoneal cavity

腹[膜]腔积脓/腹腔積膿,膿腹　pyoperitoneum
腹膜腔内输法/腹膜轉輸法　peritoneal transfusion
腹[膜]腔输液术/腹膜輸液法　peritoneoclysis
腹膜腔游动体/腹膜腔滑動體,腹膜腔鼠　peritoneal mouse
腹膜腔注射/腹膜腔注射　peritoneal injection
腹膜鞘突/腹膜鞘管　sheathing canal
腹膜切开术/腹膜切開術　peritoneotomy
腹膜渗出/腹膜滲液　peritoneal effusion
腹膜痛/腹膜痛　peritonealgia
腹膜透析/腹膜透析　peritoneal dialysis
腹膜透析液/腹膜透析液　peritoneal dialysis solution
腹膜外层炎/腹膜外層炎　ectoperitonitis
腹膜外间隙/腹膜外間隙　extraperitoneal space
腹膜外筋膜/腹膜外筋膜　extraperitoneal fascia
腹膜外膀胱破裂/腹膜外膀胱破裂　extraperitoneal rupture of bladder
腹膜外剖宫产术/腹膜外剖腹産術　extraperitoneal cesarean section
腹膜外器官/腹膜外器官　extraperitoneal organ
腹膜下阑尾炎/腹膜下闌尾炎　subperitoneal appendicitis
腹膜炎/腹膜炎　peritonitis
腹膜液/腹膜液　peritoneal fluid
腹膜隐窝/腹膜隱窩　peritoneal recess
腹膜脏层/腹膜臟層　intestinal peritoneum
腹膜造影术/腹膜X線照像術　peritoneography
腹膜粘连/腹膜粘連　peritoneal adhesion
腹膜脂膜炎/腹膜脂膜炎　peritoneal panniculitis
腹膜肿瘤/腹膜腫瘤　peritoneal neoplasm
腹膜自体成形术/腹膜被覆術　peritoneal autoplasty
腹内侧核/腹内側核　ventromedial nucleus
腹内附胎/腹内[寄生]胎　engastrius
腹内寄生畸胎/腹内無形畸胎　gastroamorphus
腹内器官炎/腹部臟器炎　celitis
腹内疝/腹内疝　internal abdominal hernia
腹内斜肌/腹内斜肌　obliquus internus abdominis, external oblique muscle of abdomen
腹皮下静脉/腹皮下静脈　abdominal subcutaneous vein
腹皮痈/腹皮癰　belly abscess
腹前壁腹膜/腹前壁腹膜　peritoneum of anterior abdominal wall
腹前壁综合征/前腹壁症候群　anterior abdominal wall syndrome
腹前核/腹前核　ventral anterior nucleus
腹前皮神经/腹皮前神經　anterior cutaneous nerve of abdomen
腹腔/腹腔　abdominal cavity
腹腔穿刺术/腹部穿刺術　abdominocentesis
腹腔丛/腹腔叢　celiac plexus
腹腔动脉压迫综合征/腹腔動脈壓迫症候群　celiac artery compression syndrome
腹腔灌洗/腹腔灌洗　peritoneal lavage
腹腔积气/腹腔積氣　gas inflation of abdomen
腹腔积血/腹腔積血　hemoperitoneum
腹腔静脉分流术/腹膜静脈分流　peritoneovenous shunt
腹腔镜/腹腔鏡　laparoscope
腹腔镜胆囊切除术/腹腔鏡膽囊切除術　laparoscopic cholecystectomy
腹腔镜检查/腹腔鏡術　laparoscopy
腹腔镜治疗[术]/腹腔鏡治療[術]　therapeutic laparoscopy
腹腔淋巴结/腹腔淋巴結　celiac lymph node, celiac gland
腹腔内出血/腹腔内出血　intraperitoneal hemorrhage
腹腔内妊娠/腹腔内妊娠　abdominal gestation
腹腔内疝/腹膜内疝　intra-abdominal hernia
腹腔内引流式胰腺移植/腹腔内引流式胰腺移植　free drainage intraperitoneal pancreas transplantation
腹腔内注射/腹腔内注射　intraperitoneal injection
腹腔脓肿/腹膜腔膿腫　peritoneal abscess
腹腔切开术/腹腔切開術　incision of abdomen
腹腔妊娠/腹腔妊娠　abdominal pregnancy
腹腔神经节/腹腔神經節　celiac ganglion
腹腔心异位/腹腔心異位　ectopia cordis abdominalis
腹腔支/腹腔支　celiac branch
腹疝/腹壁疝　ventral hernia
腹上部的/上腹部的　epigastric
腹上区/腹上部　epigastric region
腹上窝/腹上窩　epigastric fossa
腹神经/腹腔神經　celiac nerve
腹神经丛/腹腔神經叢　plexus celiacus
腹式呼吸/腹式呼吸　abdominal respiration
腹式呼吸运动/腹式呼吸運動　abdominal breathing exercise
腹水/腹水,水腹　ascites
腹水液/腹水液,水腹液　ascitic fluid
腹通谷/腹通谷　futonggu, KI20
腹痛[病]/腹痛[病]　abdominal pain
腹痛·肝气郁结证/腹痛·肝氣鬱結證　abdominal pain with pattern of liver qi depression
腹痛·寒实证/腹痛·寒實證　abdominal pain with cold excess pattern

腹痛·酒积证/腹痛·酒積證　abdominal pain with alcoholism pattern
腹痛拒按/腹痛拒按　abdominal pain refusing to pressure
腹痛·气虚证/腹痛·氣虛證　abdominal pain with qi deficiency pattern
腹痛·热积证/腹痛·熱積證　abdominal pain with heat accumulation pattern
腹痛·湿热[蕴结]证/腹痛·濕熱[蘊結]證　abdominal pain with pattern of accumulation and binding of damp-heat
腹痛·实热证/腹痛·實熱證　abdominal pain with excessive heat pattern
腹痛·食积证/腹痛·食積證　abdominal pain with food retention pattern
腹痛·痰积证/腹痛·痰積證　abdominal pain with pattern of phlegm accumulation
腹痛·瘀血证/腹痛·瘀血證　abdominal pain with static blood pattern
腹痛·中脏虚寒证/腹痛·中臟虛寒證　abdominal pain with pattern of deficiency-cold in spleen and stomach
腹外侧核/腹外側核　ventral lateral nucleus
腹外侧肌/腹外側肌　ventrolateral muscle
腹外侧区/腹外側部　lateral region of abdomen
腹外疝/腹外疝　external abdominal hernia
腹外斜肌/腹外斜肌　obliquus externus abdominis, musculus obliquus externus abdominis
腹外斜肌反射/腹外斜肌反射　obliquus reflex
腹围/腹圍　abdomen circumference
腹位心/腹位心　abdominal heart
腹系膜/腹腸繫膜, 腹臟繫膜　ventral mesentery
腹下部的/腹下的　hypogastric
腹下丛/腹下叢　hypogastric plexus
腹下动脉/腹下動脈　hypogastric artery
腹下神经/腹下神經　hypogastric nerve
腹线/腹線　abdominal line
腹泻/腹瀉, 洩瀉　diarrhea
腹泻性消化不良/洩瀉性消化不良　lienteric dyspepsia
腹心系膜/腹側心繫膜　ventral mesocardium
腹型流感/腸胃型流行性感冒　abdominal influenza
腹型偏头痛/腹性偏頭痛　abdominal migraine
腹型紫癜/腹部紫癜病　purpura abdominalis
腹性癫痫/腹性癲癇　abdominal epilepsy
腹性气喘/腹性氣喘　abdominal asthma
腹胸联胎/腹胸連胎　gastrothoracopagus
腹胰/腹胰　ventral pancreas

腹胰管/腹胰管　ventral pancreatic duct
腹胰芽/腹胰芽　ventral pancreatic bud
腹与会阴的/腹與會陰的　abdominoperineal
腹胀[病]/腹脹[病]　abdominal distension
腹胀·肺热证/腹脹·肺熱證　abdominal distension with lung heat pattern
腹胀·肺虚证/腹脹·肺虛證　abdominal distension with lung deficiency pattern
腹胀·肝火证/腹脹·肝火證　abdominal distension with liver fire pattern
腹胀·肝肾两虚证/腹脹·肝腎兩虛證　abdominal distension with pattern of deficiency of both liver and kidney
腹胀·脾实证/腹脹·脾實證　abdominal distension with excessive spleen pattern
腹胀·脾虚证/腹脹·脾虛證　abdominal distension with spleen deficiency pattern
腹胀·肾虚证/腹脹·腎虛證　abdominal distension with kidney deficiency pattern
腹胀·湿热[蕴结]证/腹脹·濕熱[蘊結]證　abdominal distension with pattern of accumulation and binding of damp-heat
腹胀·食积证/腹脹·食積證　abdominal distension with food retention pattern
腹胀·痰饮证/腹脹·痰飲證　abdominal distension with phlegm-fluid retention pattern
腹胀·脏寒证/腹脹·臟寒證　abdominal distension with cold zang-viscera pattern
腹诊/腹診　abdominal examination
腹诊推拿/腹診推拿　massage for abdominal diagnosis
腹直肌/腹直肌　rectus abdominis
腹直肌分离/腹直肌分離　diastasis recti abdominis
腹直肌旁切口/外腹直肌切開　lateral rectus incision
腹直肌鞘/腹直肌鞘　sheath of rectus abdominis
腹直肌鞘弓状线/道格拉斯氏線　Douglas line
腹直肌鞘后层/腹直肌鞘後層　posterior layer of sheath of rectus abdominis
腹直肌鞘前层/腹直肌鞘前層　anterior layer of sheath of rectus abdominis
腹直肌鞘血肿/腹直肌鞘血腫　rectus sheath hematoma
腹中间核/腹中間核　ventral intermediate nucleus
腹中痞块/腹中痞塊　mass in abdomen
腹主动脉/腹主動脈, 腹大動脈　abdominal aorta, ventral aorta, abdominal aortic
腹主动脉丛/腹主動脈叢　abdominal aortic plexus

腹主动脉瘤/腹主動脈瘤　abdominal aortic aneurysm
腹足类动物/腹足動物　gastropod
蝮蛇/蝮蛇　viper
蝮蛇毒溶血卵磷脂/卵磷脂眼鏡蛇毒溶血素　cobra lecithid
覆盖试验/屏障試驗　screen test
覆盖物/覆蓋物　mantle
覆盖义齿/覆蓋式假牙　overlay denture
覆㿽/齒疊咬　overlapping occlusion
覆膜/覆膜　tectorial membrane
覆盆子/覆盆子　palmleaf raspberry fruit
覆以皮壳的/覆以皮殼的　encrusted

G

伽伐尼电流/賈法尼的電流　Galvanic current
伽马/伽馬,丙型　gamma
伽马射线/伽馬射線　gamma ray
钆-二乙撑三胺五乙酸/钆-DTPA　gadolinium-diethylene triamine pentaacetic acid, gadolinium-DTPA
垓居里/垓居里　teracurie
改良根治性乳房切除术/改良根治性乳房切除術　modified radical mastectomy
改良黑勒贲门肌切开术/改良的黑勒賁門肌切開術　modified Heller operation
改良井出氏试验/改良之檢查梅毒試驗　Bio Lab test
改良菱形皮瓣/改良菱形皮瓣　modified rhomboid skin flap
改良乳突根治术/改良乳突根治術　modified radical mastoidectomy
改良式箭头卡环/改良式箭頭卡環　modified arrow head clasp
改良威德曼翻瓣术/改良威德曼翻瓣術　modified Widman flap surgery
钙/鈣　calcium
钙沉积过多/鈣固定過度　hypercalcipexy
钙沉积过少/鈣固定不足　hypocalcipexy
钙代谢/鈣代謝　calcium metabolism
钙代谢障碍/鈣代謝障礙　calcium metabolism disorder
钙胆汁/含鈣膽汁　calcibilia
钙蛋白酶/卡配因　calpain
钙动用/激鈣作用　calciokinesis
钙放射性同位素/鈣放射性同位素　anxiety disorder
钙负荷试验/鈣負荷試驗　calcium infusion test
钙-钙调蛋白依赖性蛋白激酶/鈣-調鈣蛋白依賴性蛋白激酶　calcium-calmodulin dependent protein kinase
钙硅沉着病/鈣矽沈著症　calcicosilicosis
钙化/鈣化　calcification
钙化不全/鈣化不全　hypocalcification
钙化醇/鈣化醇,骨化醇,維生素 D2　ergocalciferol, calciferol
钙化的/鈣化的　calcific, calcified

钙化防御/鈣過敏　calciphylaxis
钙化合物/鈣化合物　calcium compound
钙化软骨/鈣化軟骨　calcified cartilage
钙化纤维性假瘤/鈣化纖維性假瘤　calcifying fibrous pseudotumor
钙化性滑囊炎/鈣化性黏液囊炎　calcific bursitis
钙化性腱膜纤维瘤/鈣化腱膜纖維瘤　calcifying aponeurotic fibroma
钙化性结节/鈣化性結節　calcified nodule
钙化性尿道炎/石化性尿道炎　urethritis petrificans
钙化性软骨营养不良/鈣化性軟骨失養　chondrodystrophia calcificans
钙化性心包炎/鈣化性心包炎　pericarditis calculosa
钙化血栓/鈣化的血栓　calcified thrombus
钙化牙源性囊肿/鈣化牙源性囊腫　calcifying odontogenic cyst
钙化脂肪瘤/石化性脂瘤　lipoma petrificans
钙激动钾通道/鈣啟動鉀通道　calcium-activated potassium channel
钙拮抗药/鈣拮抗藥　calcium antagonist
钙结合蛋白质类/鈣結合蛋白質類　calcium-binding proteins
钙结合微丝蛋白/鈣結合微絲蛋白　gelsolin
钙粒蛋白A/鈣粒蛋白A　calgranulin A
钙粒蛋白B/鈣粒蛋白B　calgranulin B
钙联结蛋白/鈣聯蛋白　calnexin
钙敏感受体/鈣敏感受體　calcium-sensing receptor
钙黏着蛋白/鈣黏蛋白　cadherin
钙黏着蛋白类/鈣黏蛋白類　cadherins
钙尿/鈣尿　calciuria
钙平衡/鈣平衡　calcium balance
钙球/鈣球　calcospherite
钙球蛋白/鈣球蛋白　calcoglobulin
钙缺失/鈣缺失　calciprivia
钙乳胆汁/石灰膽液　milk of calcium bile
钙调蛋白/調鈣蛋白,鈣調素　calmodulin
钙调蛋白结合蛋白质类/調鈣蛋白結合蛋白質類　calmodulin-binding proteins
钙调节激素类/鈣調節激素類　calcium regulating hormones
钙调磷酸酶/鈣神經素　calcineurin

钙通道/鈣通道 calcium channel
钙通道激动药/鈣通道激動藥 calcium channel agonist
钙通道拮抗剂/鈣通道拮抗劑 calcium channel antagonist
钙通道阻滞剂/鈣離子通道阻斷劑 calcium channel blocker
钙同位素/鈣同位素 calcium isotope
钙网蛋白/鈣網蛋白 calreticulin
钙小球/鈣小球 calcoglobule
钙信号/鈣信號 calcium signaling
钙血症/鈣血症,血鈣過高 calcemia
钙盐/鈣鹽 calcium salt
钙质沉着症/石灰沈著病,鈣質沈著 calcinosis
钙质的/鈣質的 calcigerous
钙质减少/體內鈣減少,鈣不足 calcipenia
钙质浸润/鈣質浸潤 calcium infiltration
钙质性痛风/鈣化痛風 calcium gout
钙质转移/石灰性轉移 calcareous metastasis
盖壁/蓋壁 tegmental wall
盖[玻]片/蓋片,覆蓋玻片 coverglass
盖革[离子]计数器/加格氏離子計數器 Geiger counter
盖脊式桥体/蓋脊式橋體 ridge-lap pontic
盖拉德-阿尔特缝术/蓋-亞二氏縫合手術 Gaillard-Arlt suture
盖伦绷带/Galen 氏繃帶 Galen bandage
盖伦学说/蓋倫學說 Galenism
盖伦派医学/Galen 派醫學 Galenic medicine
盖膜/蓋膜 tectorial membrane
盖髓/齒髓護蓋 pulp capping
盖罩麻醉法/蓋罩麻醉法 closed method anesthesia
概念形成/概念形成 concept formation
概然寿命/可能壽命 probable life
干板 X 射线摄影术/乾板放射線照相術 xeroradiography
干冰/乾冰,二氧化碳雪 dry ice
干槽症/拔齒後之乾性齒槽 dry socket
干垂体粉/乾垂體粉 desiccated pituitary substance
干垂体后叶/腦垂體後葉 hypophysis sicca
干耵聍/乾厚耳垢 inspissated cerumen
干法制粒/乾法造粒 dry granulation
干敷料/乾敷料 dry dressing
干疳/乾疳 chronic infantile malnutrition, severe gan disease
干裹法/乾布裹法 dry pack
干烘舌/烘乾舌,乾燥舌 baked tongue
干姜/乾薑 dried ginger, zingiber

干脚气/乾腳氣 dry beriberi, weak foot due to dryness
干酵母/乾酵母 dried yeast
干菌量/乾菌重 dry cell weight
干咳/乾欬 dry cough
干酪/乳酪 cheese
干酪变性/乾酪變性 tyrosis
干酪性/乾酪化 caseation
干酪性鼻窦炎/乾酪性鼻竇炎 caseous sinusitis
干酪性鼻炎/乾酪性鼻炎 caseous rhinitis
干酪性肾炎/乾酪性腎炎 nephritis caseous
干酪样鼻炎/乾酪狀鼻炎 rhinitis caseosa
干酪样的/乾酪樣的 caseous
干酪样肺炎/乾酪樣肺炎,乾酪狀肺炎 caseous pneumonia
干酪样骨炎/乾酪樣骨炎 caseous osteitis
干酪样坏死/乾酪樣壞死 caseation necrosis
干酪样肾炎/乾酪樣腎炎 caseous nephritis
干酪中毒/乾酪中毒 tyrotoxism
干卵巢粉/乾卵巢粉 desiccated ovary substance
干麦芽浸膏/乾燥麥芽浸膏 candol
干凝胶/乾膠體 xerogel
干呕/乾嘔 retching
干皮病/乾皮病,皮膚乾燥症 xeroderma
干皮样病/乾皮樣病 xerodermoid
干漆/乾漆 dried lacquer
干丘疹/乾丘疹 dry papule
干扰/干擾 interference
干扰电疗法/干擾電療法 interferential electrotherapy
干扰量度法/干涉度量法 interferometry
干扰肾排泄/干擾腎排洩 interference with renal excretion
干扰素/干擾素 interferon
干扰素类/干擾素類 interferons
干扰素受体/干擾素受體 interferon receptor
干扰素诱导剂/干擾素誘導劑 interferon inducer
干扰现象/干涉現象 interference phenomenon
干扰性分离/干擾性分離 dissociation by interference
干扰性殆接触/中斷性咬合接觸 interceptive occlusal contact
干热灭菌/乾熱滅菌 dry heat sterilization
干涉显微镜/干涉顯微鏡 interference microscope
干涉显微镜检查/干涉顯微鏡檢查 interference microscopy
干涉仪/干涉儀,干涉計 interferometer
干尸化/乾屍化 mummification

干尸化坏死/乾屍化壞死　mummification necrosis
干尸化牙髓/牙髓乾酪化　mummified pulp
干湿球湿度计/空氣濕度計,冷卻式氣濕計　psychrometer
干湿球温度计/乾濕球溫度計　catathermometer
干髓术/乾髓術　mummification of pulp
干胃粉/乾胃粉　ventriculin
干物镜/乾接物鏡　dry objective
干陷/乾陷　dryness inward collapse
干性骨疽/乾性骨疽　dry caries
干性关节炎/乾性關節炎　arthritis sicca
干性滑膜炎/乾性滑膜炎　dry synovitis
干性坏疽/乾性壞疽　dry gangrene
干性坏死/乾性壞死　dry necrosis
干性截断术/乾性截斷術,無血截斷術　dry amputation
干性糠疹/乾糠疹　pityriasis sicca
干性啰音/乾水泡音　dry rale
干性皮肤/乾性皮膚　dry skin
干性湿疹/乾性濕疹　dry eczema
干性心包炎/乾性心包炎　dry pericarditis
干性胸膜炎/乾性肋膜炎　dry pleurisy
干性血管翳/乾性血管翳　dry pannus
干性油/快乾油　drying oil
干性综合征/乾燥症候群　sicca syndrome
干眼病/乾眼病　xerophthalmia
干眼膏/乾燥眼藥,眼用油膏　xerocollyrium
干眼综合征/乾眼症候群　dry eye syndrome
干羊膜/羊膜成形質　amnioplastin
干预/干預,介入　intervention
干预性研究/干預性研究　intervention study
干燥/乾燥　drying
干燥棒状杆菌/乾燥棒狀桿菌　Corynebacterium xerosis
干燥[病]/乾燥[病]　xerosis
干燥[病]的/乾燥的　xerotic
干燥法/乾燥法,除濕法　desiccation
干燥剂/乾燥劑,除潮劑　desiccant
干燥明矾/乾燥明礬　exsiccated alum
干燥器/乾燥器,除濕器,收濕器　desiccator
干燥失重/乾燥減重　loss on drying
干燥速率/乾燥速率　dry rate
干燥性鼻炎/乾燥性鼻炎　rhinitis sicca
干燥性喉炎/乾性喉炎,慢性喉炎　laryngitis sicca
干燥性角结膜炎/乾性角膜結膜炎　keratoconjunctivitis sicca
干燥性角膜炎/乾性角膜炎　keratitis sicca
干燥性湿疹/乾性濕疹　xerotic eczema

干燥性咽炎/乾性咽炎　pharyngitis sicca
干燥窑病/乾燥窯病　oast house disease
干支/干支　heavenly stems and earthly branches
干皱/乾皺,乾枯　kraurosis
干装柱法/管柱乾裝法　dry packing method
甘/甘　sweet
甘氨茶碱钠/甘膠鈉茶鹼製劑　theoglycinate
甘氨胆酸/甘膽酸　glycocholic acid
甘氨酸/甘胺酸　glycine
甘氨酸类药/甘胺酸類藥　glycine agent
甘氨酸tRNA连接酶/甘胺酸tRNA連接酶　glycine-tRNA ligase
甘氨酸羟甲基转移酶/甘胺酸羥甲基轉移酶　glycine hydroxymethyltransferase
甘氨酸受体/甘胺酸受體　glycine receptor
甘氨脱氧胆酸/甘胺去氧膽酸　glycodesoxycholic acid
甘氨酰色氨酸试验/諾-費二氏試驗　Neubauer-Fischer test
甘丙肽受体/甘丙肽受體　galanin receptor
甘丙肽样肽/甘丙肽樣肽　galanin-like peptide
甘草/甘草　glycyrrhiza uralensis, liquorice root
甘草次酸/甘草次酸　glycyrrhetinic acid
甘草酸/甘草酸　glycyrrhizic acid
甘草糖浆/甘草糖漿　licorice syrup
甘草味胶/甘草味膠　sarcocol
甘汞/甘汞　calomel
甘菊/甘菊　chamomile
甘菊环烃/甘菊藍　azulene
甘蓝/甘藍　cabbage
甘蓝性甲状腺肿/甘藍性甲狀腺腫　cabbage goiter
甘磷酸胆碱/甘磷酸膽鹼　glycerylphosphorylcholine
甘露醇/甘露醇　mannitol
甘露醇氮芥/甘露醇氮芥　mannomustine
甘露醇磷酸盐类/甘露醇磷酸鹽類　mannitol phosphates
甘露醇脱氢酶/甘露醇脱氫酶　mannitol dehydrogenase
甘露多糖/聚甘露糖　mannocarolose
甘露庚酮糖/甘露庚酮醣　mannoheptulose
甘露聚糖/甘露蜜　mannan
甘露酸/甘露蜜醇酸　mannitic acid
甘露糖/甘露糖　mannose
甘露糖二酸/甘露蜜糖二酸　mannosaccharic acid
甘露糖苷/甘露糖苷　mannoside
甘露糖苷过多症/甘露糖苷貯積症　mannosidosis
甘露糖苷酶/甘露糖苷酶　mannosidase
甘露糖苷酶缺乏病/甘露糖苷酶缺乏病

mannosidase deficiency disease
甘露糖基糖蛋白内切 β-N-乙酰氨基葡糖苷酶/甘露糖基糖蛋白内切 β-N-乙醯胺基葡糖苷酶 mannosyl-glycoprotein endo-beta-N-acetylglucosaminidase
甘露糖基转移酶类/甘露糖基轉移酶類 mannosyltransferases
甘露糖结合外源凝集素/甘露糖結合外源凝集素 mannose-binding lectin
甘露糖磷酸盐类/甘露糖磷酸鹽類 mannosephosphates
甘露糖-6-磷酸异构酶/甘露糖-6-磷酸異構酶 mannose-6-phosphate isomerase
甘露糖醛酸/甘露糖醛酸 mannuronic acid
甘露糖酸/甘露蜜糖酸 mannonic acid
甘露糖腙/甘露糖腙 mannohydrazone
甘露消毒丹/甘露消毒丹 ganlu xiaodu micropills
甘麦大枣汤/甘麥大棗湯 ganmai dazao decoction, wheat and jujube decoction, liquorice
甘珀酸/甘珀酸 carbenoxolone
甘薯/甘薯 batatas
甘松/甘松 nardostachys root
甘松香/甘松香 spikenard
甘素/甘味精 dulcin
甘遂/甘遂 gansui root
甘温除热/甘溫除熱 relieving fever with sweet and warm-natured drugs
甘硝石精/甘硝石精 sweet solution of niter solution
甘[乙]醇酸/甘醇酸 glycolic acid
甘油/甘油 glycerin
甘油苯醚/甘油苯醚 autodyne
甘油二酯类/甘油二酯類 diglycerides
甘油[基]/甘油基 glyceryl
甘油基醚类/甘油基醚類 glyceryl ethers
甘油激酶/甘油激酶 glycerol kinase
甘油磷酸铁/甘油磷酸鐵 iron glycerophosphate
甘油磷酸脱氢酶/甘油磷酸脫氫酶 glycerolphosphate dehydrogenase
甘油-3-磷酸 O-酰基转移酶/甘油-3-磷酸 O-醯基轉移酶 glycerol-3-phosphate O-acyltransferase
甘油磷酸盐脱氢酶/甘油磷酸鹽脫氫酶 glycerolphosphate dehydrogenase
甘油磷酸脂类/甘油磷酸脂類 glycerophospholipids
甘油磷酯类/甘油磷酯類 glycerophosphates
甘油醛/甘油醛 glyceraldehyde
甘油醛-3-磷酸脱氢酶类/甘油醛-3-磷酸脫氫酶類 glyceraldehyde-3-phosphate dehydrogenases
甘油醛-3-磷酸酯/甘油醛-3-磷酸酯 glyceraldehyde-3-phosphate

甘油三酯/三酸甘油酯 triglyceride
甘油三酯类/三酸甘油酯類 triglycerides
甘油试验/甘油試驗 glycerol test
甘油-水洗剂/甘油-水洗劑 glycerol-water lotion
甘油酸类/甘油酸類 glyceric acids
甘油酯/甘油酯 glyceride
甘油酯类/甘油酯類 glycerides
肝/肝[臟] liver
肝癌/肝癌 liver cancer
肝癌发生/肝癌形成 hepatocarcinogenesis
肝癌·肝气郁结证/肝癌·肝氣鬱結證 liver cancer with pattern of liver qi depression
肝癌·肝肾阴虚证/肝癌·肝腎陰虛證 liver cancer with pattern of liver-kidney yin deficiency
肝癌·肝阴虚证/肝癌·肝陰虛證 liver cancer with pattern of liver yin deficiency
肝癌·脾虚湿困证/肝癌·脾虛濕困證 liver cancer with pattern of damp retention due to spleen deficiency
肝癌·气滞血瘀证/肝癌·氣滯血瘀證 liver cancer with pattern of qi stagnation and blood stasis
肝癌·湿热蕴毒证/肝癌·濕熱蘊毒證 liver cancer with pattern of damp-heat and amassing poison
肝板/肝板 hepatic plate, liver plate
肝被膜/肝被膜 Glisson capsule
肝被膜下出血/肝被膜下出血 subcapsular hemorrhage of liver
肝痹/肝痹 liver bi
肝 DNA 病毒科感染/嗜肝 DNA 病毒科感染 hepadnaviridae infection
肝病患者/肝病者 hepatopath
肝病口臭/肝病口臭 liver breath
肝病前期水肿/肝病前期水腫 prehepatic edema
肝病性佝偻病/肝病性佝僂病 hepatic rickets
肝病性肾病/肝病性腎病 hepatic nephropathy
肝病性眩晕/肝病性眩暈 villous vertigo
肝卟啉病/肝卟啉病,肝性紫質病 hepatic porphyria
肝藏魂/肝藏魂 liver storing soul
肝藏血/肝藏血 liver storing blood
肝测量法/肝臟測量法 hepatometry
肝肠联合移植/肝腸聯合移植 combined liver and intestine transplantation
肝肠吻合术/肝腸吻合術 hepatoenterostomy
肝肠循环/肝腸循環 hepato-enteric circulation
肝出血/肝出血 hepatorrhagia
肝丛/肝叢 hepatic plexus
肝胆辨证/肝膽辨證 pattern identification of liver

and gallbladder
肝[胆]管/肝管　hepatic duct
肝胆管肠吻合术/肝膽管腸吻合術　hepatic portoenterostomy
肝胆管炎/肝膽管炎　hepatocholangeitis
肝胆囊结肠韧带/肝膽囊韌帶　hepatocystocolic ligament
肝胆湿热/肝膽濕熱　dampness-heat of liver and gallbladder
肝胆湿热证/肝膽濕熱證　pattern of dampness-heat of liver and gallbladder
肝胆实热/肝膽實熱　excessive heat of liver and gallbladder
肝胆水疱脓疱性发疹/肝膽水皰膿皰性發疹　hepatobiliary vesiculopustular eruption
肝胆汁/丙種膽液　C bile
肝的/肝的　hepatic
肝蒂/肝蒂　hepatic pedicle
肝淀粉样变性/肝澱粉樣變性　amyloidosis of liver
肝动脉/肝動脈　hepatic artery
肝动脉造影[术]/肝動脈造影[術]　hepatic arteriography
肝豆状核变性/肝[臟]豆狀核變性　hepatolenticular degeneration
肝豆状核的/肝豆狀核的　hepatolenticular
肝窦状隙/肝竇狀隙　hepatic sinusoid, liver sinusoid
肝短静脉/肝短靜脈　short hepatic vein
肝段/肝段　segment of liver
肝恶/肝恶　critical condition of liver
肝恶风/肝惡風　liver being averse to wind
肝二氧化碳充气照相术/静脈注射二氧化碳後偵測肝內二氧化碳濃度法　capnohepatography
肝肺综合征/肝肺症候群　hepatopulmonary syndrome
肝粉/肝粉　hepar siccatum
肝风内动证/肝風內動證　pattern of liver wind stirring up internally
肝缝术/肝縫合術　hepatorrhaphy
肝腹膜炎/肝腹膜炎　hepatoperitonitis
肝疳/肝疳　liver gan disease
肝膈面/肝膈面　diaphragmatic surface of liver
肝梗死/肝梗死　infarction of liver
肝功能不全/肝機能不全　hepatic insufficiency
肝功能亢进/肝機能亢進　hyperhepatia
肝功能试验/肝機能試驗　liver function test
肝功能衰竭/肝功能衰竭　liver failure
肝功能障碍/肝機能障礙　dyshepatia
肝固定术/肝固定術　hepatopexy
肝固有动脉/肝固有動脈　proper hepatic artery
肝固有动脉右支/肝固有動脈右支　right branch of proper hepatic artery
肝固有动脉中间支/肝固有動脈中間支　intermediate branch of proper hepatic artery
肝固有动脉左支/肝固有動脈左支　left branch of proper hepatic artery
肝固有淋巴结/肝固有淋巴結　proper hepatic lymph node
肝冠状韧带/肝冠狀韌帶　coronary ligament of liver
肝管胆管空肠吻合术/肝管膽管空腸吻合術　hepaticocholangiojejunostomy
肝管胆总管和胆囊切除术/肝管總管及膽囊切除術　cholangiocholecystocholedochectomy
肝管胆总管吻合术/肝管膽囊吻合術　hepaticocholedochostomy
肝管空肠吻合术/肝管空腸吻合術　hepaticojejunostomy
肝管[切开]取石术/肝管切開取石術　hepaticolithotomy
肝管切开术/肝管切開術　hepaticodochotomy
肝管十二指肠吻合术/肝管十二指腸吻合術　hepaticoduodenostomy
肝管碎石术/肝管碎石術　hepaticolithotripsy
肝管胃吻合术/肝管胃吻合術　hepaticogastrostomy
肝管[小]肠吻合术/肝管腸吻合術　hepaticoenterostomy
肝合胆/肝合膽　liver being connected with gallbladder
肝黑变病/肝黑病變　hepatomelanosis
肝红细胞生成性卟啉病/肝造紅血球性吡咯紫質沈著病　hepatoerythropoietic porphyria
肝后部/肝後部　posterior part of liver
肝火不得卧/肝火不得臥　insomnia due to liver fire
肝火炽盛证/肝火熾盛證　pattern of exuberance of liver fire
肝火燔耳证/肝火燔耳證　pattern of liver fire invading ear
肝火犯肺/肝火犯肺　liver fire invading lung
肝火犯肺证/肝火犯肺證　pattern of liver fire invading lung
肝火上炎/肝火上炎　liver fire flaring up
肝火上炎证/肝火上炎證　pattern of liver fire flaring up
肝积水/肝臟積水，水肝　hydrohepatosis
肝疾病/肝疾病　liver disease
肝棘球蚴病/肝棘球蚴病　hepatic echinococcosis
肝检查/檢肝法　hepatoscopy

肝绞痛/肝絞痛　hepatic colic
肝结肠韧带/肝結腸韌帶　hepatocolic ligament
肝结核/肝結核　hepatic tuberculosis
肝经风热/肝經風熱　wind-heat of liver channel
肝经湿热/肝經濕熱　dampness-heat of liver channel
肝经湿热证/肝經濕熱證　pattern of dampness-heat of liver channel
肝经郁热/肝經鬱熱　stagnated heat of liver channel
肝惊/肝驚　convulsion due to liver disorders
肝颈静脉的/肝頸靜脈的　hepatojugular
肝颈静脉反流[征]/肝頸回流　hepatojugular reflux
肝静脉/肝靜脈　hepatic vein
肝静脉闭塞性疾病/肝靜脈閉塞性疾病，肝臟靜脈阻塞病　hepatic veno-occlusive disease, veno-occlusive disease of the liver
肝静脉窦/肝靜脈竇　hepatic venous sinus
肝静脉梗阻/肝靜脈梗阻　hepatic venous obstruction
肝静脉括约肌/肝靜脈括約肌　hepatic sphincter
肝静脉血栓形成/肝靜脈血栓形成　hepatic vein thrombosis
肝静脉炎/肝靜脈炎　hepatophlebitis
肝静脉造影术/肝靜脈顯影術　hepatophlebography
肝局限性结节性增生/肝局限性結節狀增生　focal nodular hyperplasia of the liver
肝巨噬细胞/肝的吞噬細胞，柯弗氏細胞　Kupffer cell
肝厥/肝厥　liver syncope
肝开窍于目/肝開竅於目　liver opening at eye, liver opening into eye
肝阔韧带/肝闊韌帶　broad hepatic ligament
肝痨/肝癆　liver consumption
肝镰状韧带/肝鐮狀韌帶　falciform ligament of liver
肝裂/肝裂　hepatic fissure
肝淋巴结/肝淋巴結　hepatic lymph node
肝磷酸化酶激酶缺乏/肝臟磷酸酶激酶缺乏　hepatic phosphorylase kinase deficiency
肝磷酸化酶缺陷/肝臟磷酸酶缺乏　hepatic phosphorylase deficiency
肝瘘/肝瘻　hepatic fistula
肝慢性阻性充血/肝慢性阻性充血　chronic passive congestion of liver
肝盲管/胎兒肝盲管　hepatic cecum
肝毛细线虫病/肝毛細線蟲病　capillariasis hepatica
肝梅毒/肝梅毒　lues hepatis
肝门/肝門　porta hepatis
肝门静脉/肝門靜脈　hepatic portal vein
肝门静脉右支/肝門靜脈右支　right branch of hepatic portal vein
[肝门静脉右支]尾状叶支/[肝門靜脈右支]尾狀葉支　caudate branch
肝门静脉左支/肝門靜脈左支　left branch of hepatic portal vein
肝内胆管/肝內膽管　intrahepatic bile ducts
肝内胆管结石/肝內膽管結石　calculus of intrahepatic duct
肝内胆管结石病/肝石病　hepatolithiasis
肝内胆管扩张症/Caroli氏病　Caroli disease
肝内胆汁淤积/肝內膽汁淤積　intrahepatic cholestasis
肝脓肿/肝膿腫　liver abscess
肝胚细胞瘤/肝母細胞瘤　hepatoblastoma
肝膨出/肝膨出　hepatocele
肝脾病/肝脾病　hepatosplenopathy
肝脾测量法/肝脾測量法　hepatosplenometry
肝脾纤维化/肝脾纖維化　hepato-lienal fibrosis
肝脾炎/肝脾炎　hepatosplenitis
肝脾[肿]大/肝脾腫大，巨肝脾　hepatolienomegaly
肝片吸虫病/肝片吸蟲病　fascioliasis hepatica
肝片形吸虫/肝片形吸蟲　fasciola hepatica
肝破裂/肝破裂　hepatorrhexis
肝脐韧带/肝臍韌帶　hepatoumbilical ligament
肝气/肝氣　liver qi
肝气不舒/肝氣不舒　impeded flow of liver qi
肝气不舒证/肝氣不舒證　pattern of impeded flow of liver qi
肝气不足/肝氣不足　liver qi insufficiency
肝气犯脾/肝氣犯脾　liver qi invading spleen
肝气犯胃/肝氣犯胃　liver qi invading stomach
肝气横逆/肝氣橫逆　counterflow and transverse attack of liver qi
肝气逆/肝氣逆　counterflow of liver qi
肝气盛/肝氣盛　excessive liver qi
肝气实/肝氣實　excessive liver qi
肝气虚/肝氣虛　liver qi deficiency
肝气虚证/肝氣虛證　pattern of liver qi deficiency
肝气郁/肝氣鬱　liver qi depression
肝气郁结/肝氣鬱結　liver qi stagnation
肝气郁结证/肝氣鬱結證　pattern of liver qi stagnation
肝憩室/肝憩室　hepatic diverticulum
肝前部/肝前部　anterior part of liver
肝前性血蛋白过少/肝前性血蛋白過少　prehepatic hypoproteinemia
肝切除/切除肝　hepatectomize
肝切除术/肝切除術　hepatectomy
肝切开术/肝切開術　hepatotomy

肝热病/肝熱病　liver heat disease
肝韧带/肝韌帶　ligament of liver, hepatic ligament
肝溶液/肝溶液　liver solution
肝软化/肝軟化　hepatomalacia
肝闰管/肝閏管　hering duct
肝三角韧带/肝三角韌帶　triangular ligament of liver
肝色素沉着/色素肝　pigmented liver
肝闪烁扫描图/肝掃描圖　hepatoscan
肝善/肝善　favorable condition of liver
肝上部/肝上部　superior part of liver
肝神经节/肝神經節　hepatic ganglion
肝肾的/肝與腎的　hepatorenal
肝肾联合移植/肝腎聯合移植　combined liver and kidney transplantation
肝肾韧带/肝腎韌帶　hepatorenal ligament
肝肾同源/肝腎同源　homogeny of liver and kidney
肝肾型糖原贮积病/肝腎型糖原貯積病　hepatorenal glycogen storage disease
肝肾炎/肝腎炎　hepatonephritis
肝肾阴虚/肝腎陰虛　liver-kidney yin deficiency
肝肾阴虚证/肝腎陰虛證　pattern of liver-kidney yin deficiency
肝肾隐窝/肝腎隱窩　hepatorenal recess
肝肾[肿]大/肝腎腫大, 巨肝腎　hepatonephromegaly
肝肾综合征/肝腎症候群　liver-kidney syndrome
肝盛/肝盛　excessive liver qi
肝十二指肠韧带/肝十二指腸韌帶　hepatoduodenal ligament, angiomesenteric band
肝十二指肠吻合术/肝十二指腸吻合術　hepatoduodenostomy
肝石/肝石　hepatolith
肝石切除术/肝石切除術　hepatolithectomy
[肝]实质性黄疸/實質性黃疸　parenchymatous jaundice
肝俞/肝俞　ganshu, BL18
肝素/肝素　heparin
肝素测定系统/肝素測定系統　heparin assay system
肝素辅助因子/肝素輔助因子　heparin cofactor
肝素化/肝素化　heparinization
肝素化逆转/肝素化逆轉　heparinization reversal
肝素拮抗药/肝素拮抗藥　heparin antagonist
肝素裂合酶/肝素溶解酶　heparin lyase
肝素涂覆管道/肝素塗覆管道　heparin coated tubing
肝素血/肝素血症　heparinemia
肝素盐/肝素鹽　heparinate
肝索/肝索　hepatic cord
肝糖原/肝糖原　liver glycogen

肝糖原贮积病/糖原質病　glycogen disease
肝提取物/肝提取物　liver extract
肝体阴用阳/肝體陰用陽　liver being substantial yin and functional yang
肝铁质沉着/肝鐵質沈著　hepatic siderosis
肝痛/肝痛　hepatalgia
肝外胆管/肝外膽管　extrahepatic bile duct
肝外胆管闭锁/肝外膽管閉鎖　extrahepatic biliary atresia
肝外胆汁淤积/肝外膽汁淤積　extrahepatic cholestasis
肝外血管床阻塞/肝外血管床阻斷　extrahepatic-bed block
肝微粒体/肝微粒體　liver microsome
肝为刚脏/肝爲剛臟　liver being bold and firm viscera
肝尾状突/肝尾狀結節, 肝尾狀凸　caudal tubercle of liver
肝痿/肝痿　liver flaccidity
肝胃不和证/肝胃不和證　pattern of incoordination between liver and stomach
肝胃韧带/肝胃韌帶　hepatogastric ligament
肝胃十二指肠韧带/肝胃十二指腸韌帶　hepatogastroduodenal ligament
肝温/肝溫　liver warm disease
肝吸虫病/肝瓜仁蟲病, 肝蛭病　hepatic distomiasis
肝细胞/肝細胞　hepatic cell, hepatocyte, liver cell
肝细胞癌/肝細胞癌　hepatocellular carcinoma
肝细胞的/肝細胞的　hepatocellular
肝[细胞]毒素/肝細胞毒素　hepatotoxin
肝细胞瘤/肝細胞瘤　hepatoma
肝细胞溶解/肝細胞溶解　hepatolysis
肝细胞生长因子/肝細胞生長因子　hepatocyte growth factor
肝细胞腺瘤/肝細胞腺瘤　hepatocellular adenoma
肝细胞型/肝細胞型　hepatocellular type
肝细胞性黄疸/肝細胞性黃疸　hepatocellular jaundice
肝细胞移植/肝細胞移植　hepatocyte transplantation
肝下垂/肝下垂　hepatic ptosis
肝下阑尾/肝下闌尾　subhepatic appendix
肝下盲肠/肝下盲腸　subhepatic cecum
肝下隐窝/肝下隱窩　subhepatic recess
肝下缘/肝下緣　inferior border of liver
肝纤维附件/肝纖維附件　fibrous appendix of liver
肝纤维化/肝纖維化　hepatic fibrosis
肝纤维膜/肝纖維膜　fibrous membrane of liver
肝纤维囊/肝纖維囊　hepatobiliary capsule

肝线粒体/肝線粒體　liver mitochondria
肝腺泡/肝腺泡　liver acinus
肝小叶/肝小葉　lobule of liver, hepatic lobule
肝小叶间动脉/肝小葉間動脈　interlobular artery of liver
肝小叶间静脉/肝小葉間静脈　interlobular vein of liver
[肝]小叶内性黄疸/肝小葉内性黄疸　intralobular jaundice
肝小叶中央静脉/肝小葉中央静脈　central vein of hepatic lobule
肝心联合移植/肝心聯合移植　combined liver and heart transplantation
肝心痛/肝心痛　true heart pain with cold limbs caused by liver disease
肝星状细胞/肝星狀細胞　stellate cell of liver
肝型糖原磷酸化酶/肝型糖原磷酸化酶　liver form glycogen phosphorylase
肝性毒血症/肝性毒血症　hepatotoxemia
肝[性]昏迷/肝[性]昏迷　hepatic coma
肝[性]昏迷前期/肝[性]昏迷前期　hepatic precoma
肝性脑病/肝性腦病　hepatic encephalopathy
肝性神经病变/肝性神經病變　hepatic neuropathy
肝性肾小管性酸中毒/肝性腎小管性酸中毒　hepatic renal tubular acidosis
肝性肾小球硬化/肝性腎小球硬化　hepatic glomerulosclerosis
肝性水肿/肝性水腫　hepatic dropsy
肝性死亡/肝性死亡　liver death
肝胸膜的/肝與胸膜的　hepatopleural
肝胸膜瘘/肝肋膜瘻　hepatopleural fistula
肝休克/肝休克　liver shock
肝虚/肝虚　liver deficiency
肝虚雀目/肝虚雀目　liver-deficiency sparrow eye
肝虚雀目·肝血虚证/肝虚雀目·肝血虚證　liver-deficiency sparrow eye with liver blood deficiency pattern
肝虚雀目·脾失健运证/肝虚雀目·脾失健運證　liver-deficiency sparrow eye with pattern of spleen failing to transport
肝虚证/肝虚證　liver deficiency pattern
肝血/肝血　liver blood
肝血不足/肝血不足　insufficiency of liver blood
肝血吸出术/肝血吸取法　hepatophlebotomy
肝血虚/肝血虚　liver blood deficiency
肝血虚证/肝血虚證　pattern of liver blood deficiency
肝循环/肝循環　liver circulation
肝炎/肝炎　hepatitis

肝炎病毒/肝炎病毒　hepatitis virus
肝炎后肝硬化/肝炎後肝硬化　posthepatitic cirrhosis
肝炎抗体/肝炎抗體　hepatitis antibody
肝炎抗原/肝炎抗原　hepatitis antigen
肝阳/肝陽　liver yang
肝阳化风/肝陽化風　hyperactive liver yang causing wind
肝阳化风证/肝陽化風證　pattern of hyperactive liver yang causing wind
肝阳偏旺/肝陽偏旺　hyperactivity of liver yang
肝阳上亢/肝陽上亢　liver yang hyperactivity
肝阳上亢证/肝陽上亢證　pattern of liver yang hyperactivity
肝阳虚/肝陽虚　liver yang deficiency
肝阳虚证/肝陽虚證　pattern of liver yang deficiency
肝样变/肝樣變　hepatization
肝叶/肝葉　lobes of liver
肝胰襞/肝胰皺襞　hepatopancreatic fold
肝胰管/肝胰管　hepaticopancreatic duct
肝胰壶腹/肝胰管壺腹,法透氏壺腹　hepatopancreatic ampulla, ampulla of Vater
肝胰壶腹括约肌/肝胰管壺腹括約肌　musculus sphincter ampullae hepatopancreaticae
肝胰联合移植/肝胰聯合移植　combined liver and pancreas transplantation
肝胰腺/肝胰腺　hepatopancreas
肝移植/肝移植　liver transplantation
肝阴/肝陰　liver yin
肝阴虚/肝陰虚　liver yin deficiency
肝阴虚阳亢证/肝陰虚陽亢證　pattern of liver yin deficiency and liver yang hyperactivity
肝阴虚证/肝陰虚證　pattern of liver yin deficiency
肝硬化/肝硬化　hepatic cirrhosis, liver cirrhosis
肝硬化性幼稚型/肝硬化性幼稚型　hepatic infantilism
肝痈/肝癰,肝膿腫　liver abscess
肝右部/肝右部　right part of liver
肝右管/肝右管,右肝管　right hepatic duct
[肝右管]前支/[肝右管]前支　anterior branch
肝右静脉/肝右静脈　right hepatic vein
肝右叶/肝右葉　right lobe of liver
肝郁/肝鬱　liver depression
肝郁火旺/肝鬱火旺　liver qi stagnation and blazing fire
肝郁火旺证/肝鬱火旺證　pattern of liver qi stagnation and blazing fire
肝郁脾虚/肝鬱脾虚　liver qi stagnation and spleen deficiency

肝郁脾虚证/肝鬱脾虛證　pattern of liver qi stagnation and spleen deficiency
肝郁气滞聚证/肝鬱氣滯聚證　accumulation disease with pattern of liver depression and qi stagnation
肝郁失音/肝鬱失音　dysphonia due to liver depression
肝郁血虚证/肝鬱血虛證　pattern of liver qi stagnation and blood deficiency
肝郁血瘀证/肝鬱血瘀證　pattern of liver qi stagnation and blood stasis
肝原的/肝原的　hepatogenic
肝原性黄疸/肝原性黃疸　hepatogenic jaundice
肝圆韧带/肝圓韌帶　ligamentum teres hepatis
肝圆韧带裂/肝圓韌帶裂　fissure for ligamentum teres hepatis
肝圆韧带切迹/肝圓韌帶壓跡　notch for ligamentum teres hepatis
肝再生/肝再生　liver regeneration
肝[脏]病/肝病　hepatopathy
肝[脏]病[状态]/肝病體質　hepatism
肝脏毒理学/肝臟毒理學　hepatotoxicology
肝脏毒物/肝毒物　hepatotoxicant
肝脏检查/肝臟檢驗　hepatic docimasia
肝[脏]浆膜炎/漿液性肝炎　serohepatitis
肝脏面/肝臟面　visceral surface of liver
肝造口术/肝造口術,肝造瘻術　hepatostomy
肝支/肝支　hepatic branch
肝志怒/肝志怒　liver being associated with anger
肝质疗法/肝[劑]療法　hepatotherapy
肝中间静脉/肝中間靜脈　intermediate hepatic vein
肝中央静脉/肝中央靜脈　central vein of liver
肝[肿]大/肝腫大,巨肝　hepatomegalia, hepatomegaly
肝肿瘤/肝腫瘤　liver neoplasm
肝周炎/肝周圍炎　perihepatitis
肝主筋/肝主筋　liver dominating tendon, liver governing tendons
肝主谋虑/肝主謀慮　liver governing design of strategy
肝主升发/肝主昇發　liver governing ascending and dredging
肝主疏泄/肝主疏洩　liver controlling conveyance and dispersion, liver governing free flow of qi
肝著/肝著,肝鬱血瘀證　liver fixity, liver-qi stagnation and blood stasis
肝总动脉/肝總動脈　common hepatic artery
肝总管/肝總管,總肝管　common hepatic duct
肝总淋巴结/肝總淋巴結　common hepatic lymph node
肝左管/肝左管,左肝管　left hepatic duct
[肝左管]内侧支/[肝左管]內側支　medial branch
肝左静脉/肝左靜脈　left hepatic vein
肝左叶/肝左葉　left lobe of liver
坩埚/坩堝　crucible
坩埚形成座/坩堝形成座　crucible former
苷/苷,配糖體　glycoside
苷树脂/苷樹脂　glycosidal resin
苷元/苷元　aglycone
柑橘属/柑橘屬　Citrus
柑皮症/胡蘿蔔素沈著病　aurantiasis
酐类/酐類　anhydrides
疳病/疳病　infantile malnutrition
疳积/疳積　gan disease with food stagnation, infantile malnutrition
疳积上目/疳積上目　infantile malnutrition involving eye
疳积上目·脾肾阳虚证/疳積上目·脾腎陽虛證　infantile malnutrition involving eye with spleen-kidney yang deficiency pattern
疳积上目·脾虚虫积证/疳積上目·脾虛蟲積證　infantile malnutrition involving eye with pattern of spleen deficiency and worm stagnation
疳积上目·脾虚肝热证/疳積上目·脾虛肝熱證　infantile malnutrition involving eye with pattern of spleen deficiency and liver heat
疳积上目·湿热犯目证/疳積上目·濕熱犯目證　infantile malnutrition involving eye with pattern of dampness-heat assailing eye
疳气/疳氣　gan qi, mild gan disease, mild infantile malnutrition
疳证/疳證　gan disease, infantile chronic malnutrition
疳肿胀/疳腫脹　gan disease with edema and abdominal distention
杆单元/桿單元　bar unit
杆关节/桿關節　bar joint
杆菌/桿菌　bacilli
杆菌病/桿菌病　bacillary disease
杆菌的/桿菌的　bacillary
杆菌尿/桿菌尿,細菌尿　bacilluria
杆菌培养/桿菌培養　bacilliculture
杆菌溶素/桿菌溶素　bacilysin
杆菌属/桿菌屬　Bacillus
杆菌素/桿菌素　bacillin
杆菌肽/枯草桿菌素　Bacitracin
杆菌性坏死/桿菌性壞死　bacillary necrosis

杆菌性痢疾/桿菌痢疾　bacillary dysentery
杆菌性血管瘤病/桿菌性血管瘤病　bacillary angiomatosis
杆菌血症/桿菌血症　bacillemia
杆菌样巴尔通体/桿菌樣巴爾通體　Bartonella bacilliformis
杆线虫目感染/杆線蟲目感染　Rhabditida infection
杆形卡环/閂狀扣　bar clasp
杆状病毒/桿狀病毒　baculovirus
杆状核细胞/桿狀核細胞　stab cell
杆状瘤/桿狀瘤　rhabdoid tumor
杆状双极细胞/桿狀雙極細胞　rod bipolar cell
感官性眩晕/感官性眩暈　special sense vertigo
感官艺术疗法/感官藝術療法　sensory art therapy
感官知觉/感官知覺　perception sense
感光计/感光計　sensitometer
感光喷嚏/光照性噴嚏　photoptarmosis
感光细胞/感光細胞　photoreceptor cell
感光性卤化物/感光性鹵化物　photohalide
感光[作用]/感光作用, 受光作用　photoreception
感胶离子[顺]序/易溶離子順序　lyotropic series
感觉/[感]覺　sense, sensation
感觉迟钝/感覺遲鈍　dysesthesia
感觉错乱/感覺異常　paresthesia
感觉点环/感覺環　sensory circle
感觉分离/末梢感覺變異　peripheral dissociation
感觉感受器/感覺感受器　sensory receptor
感觉根/感覺根　sensory root
感觉过敏/感覺過敏　hyperesthesia
感觉过敏的/感覺過敏的　hyperesthetic
感觉级/感覺級　sensation level
感觉计/感覺計　sensimeter
感觉减退/感覺減退, 感覺遲鈍　hypesthesia
感觉径/感覺徑　sensory tract
感觉麻痹性膀胱/感覺麻痺性膀胱　sensory paralytic bladder
感觉皮层/感覺皮質　sensory cortex
感觉器[官]/感覺器[官]　sensory organ
感觉缺失/感覺刺激剥奪　sensory deprivation
感觉缺陷性白痴/感官缺陷性白癡　sensorial idiocy
感觉上皮/感覺上皮　sensory epithelium
感觉神经/感覺神經　sensory nerve
感觉神经病/感覺神經病變　sensory neuropathy
感觉神经传导速度/感覺神經傳導速度　sensory nerve conduction velocity
感觉神经的/感覺神經的　neurosensory, sensorineural
感觉神经节/感覺神經節　sensory ganglia
感觉神经末梢/感覺神經末梢　sensory nerve ending
感觉神经细胞/感覺神經細胞　neurosensory cell
感觉神经元/感覺神經元　sensory neuron
感觉视紫质/感覺視紫質　sensory rhodopsin
感觉系统药/感覺系統藥　sensory system agent
感觉细胞/感覺細胞　sense cell
感觉性代谢/感覺性新陳代謝作用　sensorimetabolism
感觉性共济失调/感覺性失調症　sensory ataxia
感觉性神经病/感覺性官能症　esthesioneurosis
感觉性失用症/感覺性失用症　sensory apraxia
感觉性失语[症]/感覺性失語症, 記言不能　sensory aphasia
感觉性谵妄/感覺性譫妄　sensory delirium
感觉移动性/感覺運動性　sensomobility
感觉异常/感覺異常, 感覺顛倒　paraesthesia
感觉异常的/感覺異常的　paresthetic
感觉异常性股痛/感覺異常性股痛　meralgia paresthetica
感觉异常性股痛综合征/Roth 氏症候群　Roth syndrome
感觉异常性幻肢/異感幻肢　pseudomelia paraesthetica
感觉与运动能力缺失/感覺與運動能力缺失　anesthecinesia
感觉阈/感覺閾　sensory threshold
感觉障碍/感覺障礙　sensation disorder
感觉正常/感覺正常, 知覺正常　euesthesia
感觉中枢/感覺中樞　center sense
感冒/感冒　common cold
感冒·表寒里热证/感冒·表寒裡熱證　common cold with pattern of exterior cold and interior heat
感冒病毒/傷風病毒　common cold virus
感冒·风寒证/感冒·風寒證　common cold with wind-cold pattern
感冒·风热证/感冒·風熱證　common cold with wind-heat pattern
感冒·气虚证/感冒·氣虛證, 氣虛感冒　common cold with qi deficiency pattern
感冒·暑湿证/感冒·暑濕證, 暑濕[内蘊]證　common cold with summerheat-damp pattern
感冒·血虚证/感冒·血虛證　common cold with blood deficiency pattern
感冒·阳虚证/感冒·陽虛證　common cold with yang deficiency pattern
感冒·阴虚证/感冒·陰虛證　common cold with yin deficiency pattern
感染/感染　infection

感染方式/感染方式　mode of infection
感染后脑脊髓炎/感染後腦脊髓炎　postinfectious encephalomyelitis
感染后脑炎/感染後腦炎　postinfectious encephalitis
感染控制/感染控制　infection control
感染控制人员/感染控制人員　infection control practitioner
感染伤口/感染性創傷,染毒創傷　infected wound
感染衰竭性精神病/感染衰竭性精神病　infection exhaustion psychosis
感染性动脉瘤/感染性動脈瘤　infectious aneurysm
感染性肺动脉瘤/感染性肺動脈瘤　infectious pulmonary aneurysm
感染性腹泻/感染性腹瀉　infectious diarrhea
感染性骨疾病/感染性骨疾病　infectious bone disease
感染性关节炎/傳染性關節炎　infectious arthritis
感染性黄疸/感染性黃疸　infectious jaundice
感染性疾病/感染性疾病　infectious disease
感染性间质性肾炎/感染性間質性腎炎　septic interstitial nephritis
感染性腱鞘炎/感染性腱鞘炎　infectious tenosynovitis
感染性溃疡/感染性潰瘍　infectious ulcer
感染性流产/敗血症性流產　septic abortion
感染性黏液瘤/感染性黏液瘤　infectious myxoma
感染性葡萄膜炎/感染性葡萄膜炎　infectious uveitis
感染性缺肢畸形/傳染性肢不全症　infectious ectromelia
感染性妊娠并发症/感染性妊娠并發症　infectious pregnancy complication
感染性栓塞动脉瘤/細菌栓塞性動脈瘤　embolomycotic aneurysm
感染性栓子的/感染性栓子的　embolomycotic
感染性水肿/感染性水腫　infectious edema
感染性胃肠炎/感染性胃腸炎　gastroenteritis infectiosa
感染性胃炎/感染性胃炎　infectious gastritis
感染性哮喘/感染性氣喘　infectious asthma
感染性心肌炎/感染性心肌炎　infectious myocarditis
感染性心内膜炎/感染性心内膜炎　infectious endocarditis
感染性血栓/感染性血栓　infectious thrombus
感染性造血坏死病毒/感染性造血壞死病毒　infectious hematopoietic necrosis virus
感受器/神經受體　nerve receptor
感受型失语症/接受性失語症　receptive aphasia
感叹号状[毛]发/驚嘆號狀毛　exclamatory pointed hair
感音神经敏度级/感音神經敏度級　sensorineural acuity level
感音神经性聋/感覺神經性聾　sensorineural deafness
感音神经性听觉丧失/感音神經性聽覺喪失　sensorineural hearing loss
感应电触诊法/感應電觸診法　faradopalpation
感应电疗法/感應電療法　faradization
感应电热疗法/感應電熱療法　inductothermy
感应电热器/感應電熱器　inductotherm
感应电收缩性/感應電流收縮性　faradocontractility
感应电休克/感應電休克　induction shock
感应电应激性/感應電應激性　faradic irritability
感应力/感應力　radiesthesia
感应器/感應器,感應機　inductorium
感应性精神病/感應性精神病　induced psychosis
感应性精神障碍/感應性精神障礙　shared paranoid disorder
感知幻觉/認知幻覺　hallucination of perception
感知觉训练/感知覺訓練　sensory and perceptual training
感知性防御/感知性防禦　perceptual defense
感知障碍性精神病/異感性精神病　allopsychosis
橄榄/橄欖　olive
橄榄耳蜗束/橄欖耳蝸束　olivocochlear tract
橄榄核套/橄欖核套　amiculum of olive
橄榄红核小脑性萎缩/橄欖紅核小腦性萎縮　olivorubrocerebellar atrophy
橄榄后沟/橄欖後溝　retroolivary sulcus
橄榄后静脉/橄欖後靜脈　retroolivary vein
橄榄后区/橄欖後區　retroolivary area
橄榄脊[髓]束/橄欖脊[髓]徑　olivospinal tract
橄榄霉素类/橄欖黴素類　olivomycins
橄榄球员/橄欖球員　rugby player
橄榄体脑桥小脑变性/橄欖體橋腦及小腦變性　olivopontocerebellar degeneration
橄榄体脑桥小脑的/橄欖體橋腦小腦的　olivopontocerebellar
橄榄体脑桥小脑萎缩/橄欖體橋腦小腦萎縮　olivopontocerebellar atrophy
橄榄体小脑束/橄欖小腦徑　olivocerebellar tract
橄榄小脑纤维/橄欖小腦纖維　olivocerebellar fiber
橄榄状的/橄欖狀的　olivary
干骺端/幹骺端　metaphysis
干骺端的/幹骺端的　metaphyseal
干骺端炎/幹骺端炎　metaphysitis
干骺续连症/幹骺續連症　metaphyseal aclasia

干细胞/幹細胞　stem cell
干细胞性白血病/幹細胞性白血病,胚細胞性白血病　embryonal leukemia, stem cell leukemia
干细胞移植/幹細胞移植　stem cell transplantation
干细胞因子/幹細胞因子　stem cell factor
绀红皮病/紅藍腫,紅紺腫　erythrocyanosis
绀色脾/紺色脾　cyanotic spleen
冈比亚马锥虫病/岡比亞馬錐蟲病　Gambian horse sickness
冈恩综合征/Gunn 氏症候群　Gunn syndrome
冈宁夹/Gunning 氏夾板　Gunning splint
冈上肌/岡上肌　supraspinatus, musculus supraspinatus
冈上肌肌腱炎/岡上肌肌腱炎　tendinitis of supraspinatus muscle
冈上肌腱炎/岡上肌腱炎　tendonitis of supraspinatus muscle
冈上肌综合征/岡上肌症候群　supraspinatus syndrome
冈上窝/岡上窩　supraspinous fossa
冈下肌/岡下肌　infraspinatus
冈下肌腱下囊/岡下肌腱下囊　subtendinous bursa of infraspinatus muscle
冈下窝/岡下窩　infraspinous fossa
刚果地板蛆/剛果地板蛆　Congo floor maggot
刚果红/剛果紅　Congo red
刚果红试验/剛果紅試驗　Congo red test
刚果锥虫/剛果錐蟲　Trypanosoma congolense
刚痉/剛痙　anhidrotic convulsion
刚柔/剛柔　toughness and gentleness
刚柔有辨/剛柔有辨　differentiation of masculinity and mansuetude
肛凹/肛室,原始肛　proctodeum
肛瓣/肛瓣　anal valve
肛表/直腸溫度計　rectal thermometer
肛部痛/肛痛,直腸痛　proctalgia
肛道/肛道,原肛　anal pit
肛道窝/原肛窩　proctodeal pit
肛动脉/肛動脈　anal artery
肛窦/肛竇　anal sinus
肛沟/肛溝　anal groove
肛管/肛管　anal canal
肛管癌/肛管癌　cancer of anal canal
肛管狭窄/肛管狹窄　anal stenosis
肛管直肠环/肛管直腸環　anorectal ring
肛后肠/肛後腸　postanal gut
肛静脉/肛門靜脈　anal vein
肛[恋]期/肛門期　anal stage
肛裂/肛裂　anal fissure
肛裂·气滞血瘀证/肛裂·氣滯血瘀證　anal fissure with pattern of qi stagnation and blood stasis
肛裂·血热肠燥证/肛裂·血熱腸燥證　anal fissure with pattern of blood heat and intestine dryness
肛裂·阴虚津亏证/肛裂·陰虛津虧證　anal fissure with pattern of yin deficiency and fluid insufficiency
肛瘘/肛瘻　anal fistula
肛瘘·湿热下注证/肛瘻·濕熱下注證　anal fistula with pattern of dampness-heat diffusing downward
肛瘘·阴虚火旺证/肛瘻·陰虛火旺證　anal fistula with pattern of yin deficiency and fire effulgence
肛瘘·正虚邪恋证/肛瘻·正虛邪戀證　anal fistula with pattern of healthy qi deficiency and lingering pathogen
肛[门]/肛門　anus
肛门闭锁/肛門閉鎖[畸形],鎖肛　imperforate anus, atresia ani
肛门闭锁会阴瘘/肛門閉鎖會陰瘻　anal atresia with perineal fistula
肛门闭锁尿道瘘/肛門閉鎖尿道瘻　anal atresia with urethral fistula
肛门闭锁前庭瘘/肛門閉鎖前庭瘻　anal atresia with vestibular fistula
肛门闭锁阴道瘘/肛門閉鎖陰道瘻　anal atresia with vaginal fistula
肛门不发生/肛門不發生,肛門發育不全　anal agenesis
肛门成形术/肛門成形術,肛門造形術　anoplasty
肛门的/肛門的　anal
肛门环箍术/肛門環箍術　anal wiring
肛门会阴的/肛門與會陰的　anoperineal
肛门会阴瘘/肛門會陰瘻　anoperineal fistula
肛门疾病/肛門疾病　anus disease
肛门镜/肛門鏡　anoscope
肛门镜检查[术]/肛門鏡檢法　anoscopy
肛门溃疡/肛門潰瘍　anal ulcer
肛门扩张器/肛門擴張器　anal dilator
肛门括约肌成形术/肛門括約肌成形術　anal sphincteroplasty
肛门裂/肛門裂傷　anal fissure
肛门挛急/肛門攣急　contracture of anus
肛门内括约肌/肛門內括約肌　sphincter ani internus, internal sphincter muscle of anus, internal anal sphincter
肛门排尿/肛尿症,肛門洩尿　urochezia
肛门膀胱瘘/肛門膀胱瘻　archocystosyrinx
肛门前移/肛門前移　anteceding anus

肛门瘙痒症/肛門搔癢　pruritus ani
肛门臊瘊/肛門臊瘊　condyloma of anus
肛门生殖器带/肛門生殖器帶　anogenital band
肛门生殖器区/肛門生殖器區　anogenital region
肛门生殖器疣/肛門生殖器疣　anogenital wart
肛门失禁/肛門失禁,大便失禁　anal incontinence, incontinence of feces
肛门失禁•脾虚不固证/肛門失禁•脾虛不固證　anal incontinence with pattern of unconsolidation due to spleen deficiency
肛门失禁•肾虚不固证/肛門失禁•腎虛不固證　anal incontinence with pattern of unconsolidation due to kidney qi deficiency
肛门湿疮/肛門濕瘡　anal eczema
肛门湿疮•脾虚湿困证/肛門濕瘡•脾虛濕困證　anal eczema with pattern of spleen deficiency and dampness retention
肛门湿疮•热毒壅盛证/肛門濕瘡•熱毒壅盛證　anal eczema with pattern of heat-toxin congestion and excessiveness
肛门湿疮•湿热下注证/肛門濕瘡•濕熱下注證　anal eczema with pattern of dampness-heat diffusing downward
肛门湿疮•血虚风燥证/肛門濕瘡•血虛風燥證　anal eczema with pattern of wind-dryness due to blood deficiency
肛门湿疡/肛門濕瘍　eczema of anus
肛门湿疹/肛濕疹　eczema ani
肛门梳带/肛門梳帶　pecten band
肛门梳切开术/肛門硬結切開術　pectenotomy
肛门梳[纤维]硬结/肛梳硬結　pectenosis
肛门梳炎/肛門梳炎　pectenitis
肛门脱垂/肛門脫垂　prolapse of anus
肛门外括约肌/肛門外括約肌　external anal sphincter, external sphincter muscle of anus
肛门尾骨的/肛門與尾骨的　anococcygeal
肛门狭窄/肛門狹窄　anal stenosis, stricture of anus
肛门狭窄•大肠湿热证/肛門狹窄•大腸濕熱證　anal stenosis with pattern of dampness-heat in large intestine
肛门狭窄•气滞血瘀证/肛門狹窄•氣滯血瘀證　anal stenosis with pattern of qi stagnation and blood stasis
肛门狭窄•热结肠燥证/肛門狹窄•熱結腸燥證　anal stenosis with pattern of intestine dryness due to heat accumulation
肛门血管扩张/肛門血管擴張　hemangiectasis of anus

肛门炎/肛門炎　anusitis
肛门阴道闭锁/肛門陰道閉鎖　atresia ani vaginalis
肛门直肠/肛門直腸部　anorectum
肛门直肠不发生/肛門直腸不發生,肛門直腸發育不全　anorectal agenesis
肛门直肠的/肛門與直腸　anorectal
肛门直肠瘘/肛門直腸瘻　anorectal fistula
肛门直肠脓肿/肛門直腸膿腫　anorectal abscess
肛门直肠炎/肛門直腸炎　anorectitis
肛门直肠综合征/肛門直腸症候群　anorectal syndrome
肛门肿瘤/肛門腫瘤　anus neoplasm
肛门周围/肛門周圍　perianal area
肛膜/肛膜　anal membrane
肛囊/肛囊　anal sacs
肛区/肛門部　anal region
肛乳头/肛乳頭　anal papilla
肛乳头炎/肛乳頭炎　anal papillitis
肛神经/肛神經　anal nerve
肛梳/肛梳　anal pecten
肛掏粪/肛掏糞　back-raking
肛提肌/肛舉肌,提肛門肌　levator ani muscle
肛提肌腱弓/肛提肌腱弓　tendinous arch of levator ani
肛尾丛/肛尾叢　anococcygeal plexus
肛尾缝/肛尾縫　anococcygeal raphe
肛尾韧带/肛尾韌帶　anococcygeal ligament
肛尾神经/肛尾神經　anococcygeal nerve
肛腺肿瘤/肛腺腫瘤　anal gland neoplasm
肛液溢/肛[液]漏　proctorrhea
肛异位/肛異位　ectopia ani
肛隐窝/肛隱窩　anal crypt
肛痈/肛癰　anorectal abscess, perianal or perirectal abscess
肛痈•火毒炽盛证/肛癰•火毒熾盛證　anorectal abscess with blazing fire-toxin pattern
肛痈•热毒蕴结证/肛癰•熱毒蘊結證　anorectal abscess with heat-toxin amassment pattern
肛痈•阴虚毒恋证/肛癰•陰虛毒戀證　anorectal abscess with pattern of yin deficiency and lingering toxin
肛[欲]期施虐欲/肛式施虐淫　anal sadism
肛直肠线/肛直腸線　anorectal line
肛直角/肛直角　anorectal angle
肛周鲍温病/肛門周圍的 Bowen 氏症　perianal Bowen disease
肛周大汗腺腺瘤/肛門周圍的大汗腺腺瘤　perianal apocrine gland adenoma

肛周的/肛門周圍的 perianal
肛周念珠菌病/肛門周念珠菌病 perianal candidiasis
肛周脓肿/肛門周膿腫 perianal abscess
肛周佩吉特病/肛門周圍的Paget氏病 perianal Paget disease
肛周皮炎/肛門周圍的皮膚炎 perianal dermatitis
肛周腺/肛周腺 perianal gland
肛周疣/肛門周圍的疣 perianal wart
肛柱/肛柱 anal column
纲/綱 class
钢/鋼 steel
钢水烧伤/鋼水燒傷 burn by molten steel
钢丝发病/鋼絲髮病 steely hair disease
钢丝夹板/鋼絲夾板 wire splint
钢丝探子/鋼絲探針 wire probe
钢铁般的/鋼鐵般 steely
岗哨细胞/哨細胞 sentinel cell
杠杆子宫托/挺狀子宮托 lever pessary
杠杆作用力/槓桿作用力 leverage
高安动脉炎/Takayasu氏動脈炎 Takayasu arteritis
高氨血症/高胺血症 hyperammonemia
高半胱氨酸/類胱胺酸, 高半胱胺酸 homocysteine
高倍镜/高倍鏡 high power lens
高苯丙氨酸血症/血苯丙胺酸過多, 高苯丙胺酸血症 hyperphenylalaninemia
高比重尿/尿比重增加, 重尿症 baruria
高比重溶液/高比重溶液 hyperbaric solution
高丙种球蛋白血症/血內丙型球蛋白過多 hypergammaglobulinemia
高草酸尿症/高草酸尿症 hyperoxaluria
高产率/高產率, 多產率 plurinatality
高成本工艺学/高成本工藝學 high-cost technology
高处眩晕/懸崖眩暈 height vertigo
高雌激素血[症]/高雌激素血症, 高血雌激素症 hyperestrogenemia
高促性腺素性闭经/高促性腺素性閉經 hypergonadotropic amenorrhea
高促性腺素性功能减退症/高促性腺素性功能減退症 hypergonadotropic hypogonadism
高催乳素血症/高催乳激素血症 hyperprolactinemia
高胆固醇血症/高膽固醇血症 hypercholesterolemia
高胆红素血症/高膽色素血症 hyperbilirubinemia
高蛋白饮食/高蛋白飲食 high-protein diet
高地疗法/高地療法, 高空療法 hypsotherapy
高碘酸/高碘酸, 過碘酸 periodic acid
高碘酸裂解/高碘酸裂解 periodate cleavage
高碘酸-希夫染剂/過碘酸Schiff氏染色 periodic acid-Schiff stain
高碘酸-希夫染色反应/高碘酸-雪夫染色反應 periodic acid-Schiff reaction
高淀粉酶血症/血澱粉酶過多 hyperamylasemia
高动力的/高動力的 hyperdynamic
高动力循环状态/高動力循環狀態 hyperkinetic circulatory state
高动脉压/高動脈壓 arterial hypertension
高度/高度 altitude, height
高度等张性/肌之等張性過度, 高等張性 hyperisotonia
高度发绀的/高度發紺的 hypercyanotic
高度近视/高度近視 high myopia
高度淋巴瘤/高度淋巴瘤 high-grade lymphoma
高度远视/高度遠視 high hypermetropia
高度阻滞/高度阻滯 advanced block
高腭穹/高腭穹 high arched palate
高尔夫球员足/高爾夫球員足 golfer foot
高尔基复合体/高爾基複合體 Golgi complex
高尔基-马佐尼小体/高爾基-馬佐尼小體 Golgi-Mazzoni corpuscle
高尔基期/高爾基期 Golgi phase
高尔基体/高爾基體 Golgi apparatus
高尔基体外侧网络/高爾基體外側網路 trans-Golgi network
高尔基细胞/高爾基細胞 Golgi cell
高尔基Ⅰ型神经元/高爾基Ⅰ型神經元 Golgi type Ⅰ neuron
高尔基Ⅱ型神经元/高爾基Ⅱ型神經元 Golgi type Ⅱ neuron
高尔斯病/Gowers氏病 Gowers disease
高尔斯溶液/Gowers氏溶液 Gowers solution
高尔斯束/Gowers氏徑 Gowers tract
高尔斯综合征/Gowers氏症候群 Gowers syndrome
高分辨气相色谱法/高解析氣相色譜法, 高解析氣相層析法 high resolution gas chromatography, HRGC
高分辨显带/高分辨顯帶 high resolution banding
高分化细胞/高分化細胞 noble cell
高分子多孔小球/聚合物多孔小珠 porous polymer bead
高分子量激肽原/高分子量激肽原 high-molecular-weight kininogen
高分子溶液/高分子溶液 macromolecular solution
高分子药物/聚合物藥物 polymer drug
高风雀目/高風雀目 high-wind sparrow eye, primary pigmentary degeneration of retina, sparrow eye
高风雀目·肝肾阴虚证/高風雀目·肝腎陰虛證

high-wind sparrow eye with liver-kidney yin deficiency pattern
高风雀目·脾气虚证/高風雀目·脾氣虛證 high-wind sparrow eye with spleen qi deficiency pattern
高风雀目·脾肾阳虚证/高風雀目·脾腎陽虛證 high-wind sparrow eye with spleen-kidney yang deficiency pattern
高风雀目·气滞血瘀证/高風雀目·氣滯血瘀證 high-wind sparrow eye with pattern of qi stagnation and blood stasis
高峰淀粉酶/高峰氏澱粉酶 Taka-diastase
高峰时间/峰距時間 apex time
高峰酸排出量/高峰酸排出量 peak acid output
高钙尿症/高鈣尿症,尿鈣過多 hypercalciuria
高钙血性尿毒症/高鈣血性尿毒症 hypercalcemic uremia
高钙血症/高鈣血症,血鈣過多 hypercalcemia
高钙血症肾病/高鈣血症腎病 hypercalcemic nephropathy
高甘油三酯血症/高三酸甘油酯血症,血三酸甘油酯過多 hypertriglyceridemia
高弓足/空凹足 pes cavus
高骨/高骨 protruding bones
高胱氨酸/高胱胺酸 homocystine
高胱氨酸尿/高胱胺酸尿 homocystinuria
高胱氨酸血/高胱胺酸血症 homocystinemia
高肌肽/高肌肽 homocarnosine
高级神经活动/高級神經活性 higher nervous activity
高级糖基化终产物/高級糖基化終産物 advanced glycosylation end product
高剂量耐受[性]/高劑量耐受[性] high dose tolerance
高加索人[的]/高加索人 Caucasian
高甲状腺素血症/血甲狀腺素過多,高甲狀腺素血 hyperthyroxinemia
高钾血性周期性麻痹/高鉀血性週期性麻痺 hyperkalemic periodic paralysis
高钾血症/高鉀血症,血鉀過多 hyperkalemia
高降钙素血症/高降鈣素血症 hypercalcitoninemia
高精氨酸/高精胺酸 homoarginine
高精氨酸血症/血高精胺酸症 hyperargininemia
高静脉压/高靜脈壓 venous hypertension
高空碱中毒/高山鹼毒症 altitude alkalosis
高空近视/高空近視 higt altitude myopia
高空缺氧/高空缺氧症 altitude anoxia
高空牙痛/高空牙痛 aero-odontalgia
高赖氨酸血症/高賴胺酸血症 hyperlysinemia

高酪氨酸血症/高酪胺酸血症,血酪胺酸過多 hypertyrosinemia
高乐斯征/Gowers氏徵象 Gowers sign
高良姜/高良薑 lesser galangal rhizome
高磷[酸盐]血症/血磷酸鹽過多,高磷酸鹽血 hyperphosphatemia
高磷[酸盐]血症肾病/高磷[酸鹽]血症腎病 hyperphosphatemic nephropathy
高龄初产妇/高齡初産婦 elderly primipara
高氯化物/過氯化物 perchloride
高氯酸/過氯酸 perchloric acid
高氯酸盐/過氯酸鹽 perchlorate
高氯血症/高氯血症 hyperchloremia
高氯血症酸中毒/血氯過多性酸毒症 hyperchloremic acidosis
高镁血症/高鎂血症,血鎂過多 hypermagnesemia
高锰酸钾/過錳酸鉀 potassium permanganate
高锰酸盐/過錳酸鹽 permanganate
高密度脂蛋白缺乏/高密度脂蛋白缺乏 high density lipoprotein deficiency
高免疫球蛋白E综合征/高免疫球蛋白E症候群 hyperimmunoglobulin E syndrome
高钠血症/血鈉過多 hypernatremia
高钠饮食/高鈉飲食 high sodium diet
高能放射疗法/高能放射療法 high-energy radiotherapy
高能量冲击波/高能量衝擊波 high-energy shock wave
高能磷酸化合物/高能磷酸化合物 high-energy phosphate compound
高黏滞综合征/高黏滯症候群 hyperviscosity syndrome
高尿酸血症/高尿酸血症,血尿酸過多 hyperuricemia
高尿酸血[症]的/高尿酸血症的 hyperuricemic
高尿酸血症肾病/高尿酸血症腎病 hyperuricemic nephropathy
高凝性/高凝固性 hypercoagulability
高凝状态/高凝固狀態 hypercoagulable state
高频/高頻率 high frequency
高频电疗法/高頻電療法 high frequency electrotherapy
高频电疗美容术/高頻電療美容術 high frequency electrotherapy cosmesis
高频电美容仪/高頻電美容儀 high frequency cosmetic instrument
高频率血型/高頻率血型 high frequency blood group

高频喷射通气/高頻噴射通氣　high frequency jet ventilation
高频听觉丧失/高頻聽覺喪失　high-frequency hearing loss
高频通气/高頻通氣　high frequency ventilation
高频胸壁压迫/高頻胸壁壓迫　high frequency chest wall compression
高频震荡/高頻震蕩　high frequency oscillation
高频正压通气/高頻正壓通氣　high frequency positive pressure ventilation
高普兰综合征/Gopalan 氏症候群　Gopalan syndrome
高起鳞癣/豪豬狀魚鱗癬　ichthyosis hystrix
高气压病/高壓症　hyperbarism
高迁移率族蛋白质类/高遷移率族蛋白質類　high mobility group proteins
高嵌体/高嵌體　onlay
高球蛋白血[症]/高血球蛋白症　hyperglobulinemia
高球蛋白血症[性]紫癜/高球蛋白血症[性]紫瘢症　hyperglobulinemic purpura
高热/高熱　hyperpyrexia
高热量饮食/高熱量飲食　high calorie diet
高热性气促/熱喘氣　thermopolypnea
高热性日射病/過高熱性日射病　hyperpyrexial insolation
高溶血性黄疸/溶血過多性黃疸　hyperhemolytic jaundice
高山病/高山病　mountain disease
高山肺水肿/高山性肺水腫　high altitude pulmonary edema
高山腹泻/高山腹瀉　hill diarrhea
高山疗法/高山療法，山地療法　orinotherapy
高山溶液/Takayama 氏溶液　Takayama solution
高肾素型高血压/高腎素型高血壓　high renin hypertension
高渗葡萄糖溶液/高滲葡萄糖溶液　hypertonic glucose solution
高渗溶液/高滲溶液　hypertonic solution
高渗盐水/高滲鹽水　hypertonic saline solution
高渗盐水试验/高滲鹽水試驗　hypertonic saline test
高渗盐水注射/高張鹽水注射　hypertonic saline injection
高生物素/高生物素　homobiotin
高输出量心衰竭/高輸出量心衰竭　high-output heart failure
高丝氨酸/高絲胺酸，類絲胺酸　homoserine
高丝氨酸脱氢酶/高絲胺酸脱氫酶　homoserine dehydrogenase
高速离心/高速離心　high speed centrifugation
高速子弹伤/高速子彈傷　high speed bullet wound
高弹性/彈性過高　hyperelastica
高碳酸血/血碳酸過多　hypercapnia
高糖皮肤病/皮膚糖尿病　skin diabetes
高糖膳食/碳水化物豐富飲食　high-carbohydrate diet
高田-荒试验/高田-荒二氏試驗　Takata-Ara test
高铁红细胞/含鐵[紅]血球　siderocyte
高铁环六肽/鐵絡環肽　ferrichrome
高铁血红蛋白/變性紅血球素，變性血紅素　methemoglobin
高铁血红蛋白血症/變性血紅素血症　methemoglobinemia
高铁血红素白蛋白/血黑質白蛋白，血質蛋白　hematin albumin
高铁血色原/高鐵血色素　ferrihemochrome
高铜汞合金/高銅汞合金　high copper amalgam
高危/高危險　high risk
高危儿/高危兒　high risk infant
高危人群/高危人群　high risk group
高危妊娠/高危妊娠　high risk pregnancy
高位髌骨/高位髕骨　patella alta
高位产钳术/高位産鉗産　high forcep delivery
高位肩胛/高位肩胛　high scapula
高位盲肠/高位盲腸　high cecum
高位钳/高位鉗　high forcep
高位微笑/高位微笑　high smile
高位牙/齒之上挺　supraversion
高温计/高溫計　pyrometer
高温浴/過熱浴　hyperthermal bath
高狭腭/高狹腭　hypsistaphylia
高香草酸/高香草酸，類梵尼酸　homovanillic acid
高效薄层色谱法/高效薄層層析法　high performance thin-layer chromatography, HPTLC
高效抗逆转录病毒治疗/高效抗逆轉録病毒治療　highly active antiretroviral therapy
高效空气过滤器/高效空氣過濾器　high efficiency particle air filter
高效能利尿药/高效能利尿藥　high ceiling diuretic
高效液相色谱法/高效液相層析法　high performance liquid chromatography, HPLC
高歇病/Gaucher 氏病，家族性脾性貧血　Gaucher disease
高歇细胞/Gaucher 氏細胞　Gaucher cell
高心排血量/高心排血量　high cardiac output
高血胆固醇症/高血膽固醇症　hypercholesterolaemia
高血糖高渗性非酮性昏迷/高血糖高滲性非酮性昏

迷　hyperglycemic hyperosmolar non-ketotic coma
高血糖性糖元分解因子/高血糖分解糖原質因子　hyperglycemic-glycogenolytic factor
高血糖症/高血糖症,血糖過高　hyperglycemia
高血压/高血壓,血壓過高　hypertension
高血压患者/高血壓者　hypertensive
高血压-间脑综合征/高血壓-間腦症候群　hypertensive-diencephalic syndrome
高血压脑病/高血壓性腦病　hypertensive encephalopathy
高血压脑出血/高血壓腦出血　hypertensive cerebral hemorrhage
高血压缺血性溃疡/高血壓缺血性潰瘍　hypertensive ischemic ulcer
高血压危象/高血壓危象　hypertensive crisis
高血压心脏病/高血壓性心臟病　hypertensive heart disease
高血压性红细胞增多症/高血壓性紅血球增多症　polycythemia hypretonica
高血压性颅内出血/高血壓性顱内出血　hypertensive intracranial hemorrhage
高压舱/高壓艙　hyperbaric cabin
高压电损伤/高壓電損傷　high voltage electrical injury
高压灭菌器/高壓蒸氣滅菌器　autoclave
高压性神经综合征/高壓性神經症候群　high pressure neurological syndrome
高压氧/高壓氧　high pressure oxygen
高压氧疗/高壓氧療　hyperbaric oxygen therapy
高压液相色谱法/高壓液相色譜法　high pressure liquid chromatography
高眼压/眼壓過高　ocular hypertension
高胰岛素血[症]/高胰島素血症;高血胰島素症　hyperinsulinemia, hyperinsulinism
高音听诊器/選音聽診器　phonoselectoscope
高应答个体/高應答個體　high responder
高原/高原　plateau
高原病/高空病,高山症　altitude sickness
高原性低血压/高原性低血壓　high altitude hypotension
高原性心脏病/高原性心臟病　high altitude heart disease
高甾类/高甾類　homosteroid
高张的/高張的,高滲透壓的　hypertonic
高张力/高張力　high tension
高张溶液/高張溶液　hypertonic solution, hyperosmotic solution
高张性膀胱/高張性膀胱　hypertonic bladder

高张性子宫功能障碍/子宫收縮異常　hypertonic uterine dysfunction
高褶虹膜型青光眼/高褶虹膜型青光眼　plateau iris glaucoma
高褶型虹膜/高褶型虹膜　plateau iris
高震按摩机/高震按摩機　high amplitude massor
高脂蛋白血症/高脂蛋白血症　hyperlipoproteinaemia
高脂蛋白血症Ⅰ型/高脂蛋白血症Ⅰ型　hyperlipoproteinemia type Ⅰ
高脂蛋白血症Ⅱ型/高脂蛋白血症Ⅱ型　hyperlipoproteinemia type Ⅱ
高脂[肪]饮食/高脂肪飲食　high fat diet
高脂质血[症]/血内脂質過多　hyperlipidemia
高直位/高直位　sincipital presentation
高阻抗管道/高阻抗管道　high impedance tube
睾/睾[丸]　testicle
睾内酯/睾内酯　testolactone
睾提肌/提睾肌　cremaster, cremaster muscle, cremasteric coat of testis
睾提肌动脉/提睾動脈　cremasteric artery
睾提肌筋膜/提睾筋膜　cremasteric fascia
睾酮/睾固酮,睾丸硬脂酮　testosterone
睾酮5-α-还原酶/睾固酮5-α-還原酶　testosterone 5-alpha-reductase
睾酮同源物/睾固酮同源物　testosterone congener
睾丸/睾丸　testicle, testis
睾丸癌/睾丸癌　carcinoma of testis
睾丸白膜/睾丸白膜　tunica albuginea testis
睾丸白膜层疝/睾丸白膜層疝　hernia of the tunica albuginea
睾丸表皮样囊肿/睾丸表皮樣囊腫　epidermoid cyst of testis
睾丸病/睾丸病　orchidopathy
睾丸颤搐/睾丸跳動　orchichorea
睾丸成形术/睾丸造形術　orchidoplasty
睾丸丛/睾丸叢　testicular plexus
睾丸挫伤/睾丸挫傷　contusion of testis
睾丸的/睾丸的　testicular
睾丸动脉/睾丸動脈　testicular artery
睾丸动脉输尿管支/睾丸動脈輸尿管支　ureteric branch of testicular artery
睾丸发育不全/睾丸發育不全　testicular dysgenesis, testicular hypoplasia, hypoplasia of testis
睾丸反向/反向睾丸　inverted testis
睾丸非生殖细胞瘤/睾丸非生殖細胞瘤　non-germinal cell tumor of testis
睾丸附睾切除术/睾丸副睾[丸]切除術　orchidoepididymectomy

睾丸附件/睾丸附件 appendix of testis, testicular adnexa
睾丸附件扭转/睾丸附件扭轉 torsion of testicular appendage
睾丸功能减退/睾丸機能不足 hypo-orchidism
睾丸功能开始/男性性功能建立,男性性功能開始 leydigarche
睾丸功能亢进/睾丸機能過狂 hyperorchidism
睾丸固定术/睾丸固定術 orchidopexy
睾丸核酸/睾丸核酸 testicular nucleic acid
睾丸积液肉样肿/睾丸積水肉腫 hydrosarcocele
睾丸畸胎癌/睾丸畸胎癌 teratocarcinoma of testis
睾丸畸胎瘤/睾丸畸胎瘤 teratoma of testis
睾丸畸形/睾丸畸形 deformity of testis
睾丸激素/睾丸激素 testoid
睾丸激素类/睾丸激素類 testicular hormones
睾丸疾病/睾丸疾病 testicular disease
睾丸计/睾丸测量器 orchidometer
[睾丸]间质/[睾丸]間質 interstitial tissue of testis
睾丸间质细胞/睾丸間質細胞 interstitial cell of leydig
睾丸间质细胞发育不全/睾丸間質細胞發育不全 leydig cell aplasia
睾丸间质细胞机能减退/睾丸間質細胞機能不足,雄性素分泌不足 hypoleydigism
睾丸间质细胞机能缺失/莱迪格氏症 aleydigism
睾丸交叉异位/睾丸交叉異位 crossed testicular ectopia
睾丸结核/睾丸結核 tuberculosis of testis
睾丸精母细胞瘤/睾丸精母細胞瘤 spermatocytic seminoma of testis
睾丸精原细胞瘤/睾丸精原細胞瘤 seminoma of testis
睾丸决定基因/睾丸決定基因 testicular determining gene
睾丸瘤/睾丸瘤 testicular tumor, testiculoma
睾丸梅毒/睾丸梅毒 syphilis of testis
睾丸母细胞瘤/睾丸母細胞瘤 orchioblastoma
睾丸囊状附件/睾丸囊狀附件 vesicular appendix of testis
睾丸内分泌功能减退/睾丸低能 hypo-orchidia
睾丸女性化/睾丸女性化 testicular feminization
睾丸女性化综合征/睾丸女性化症候群 testicular feminization syndrome
睾丸旁横纹肌肉瘤/睾丸旁橫紋肌肉瘤 paratesticular rhabdomyosarcoma
睾丸胚胎癌/睾丸胚胎癌 embryonal carcinoma of testis
睾丸鞘膜/睾丸鞘膜 tunica vaginalis of testis
[睾丸]鞘膜壁层/總鞘膜 parietal layer of tunica vaginalis
睾丸鞘膜低位穿刺术/陰囊下部穿刺術 hyposcheotomy
睾丸鞘膜积液/睾丸鞘膜積液,睾丸鞘膜積水 hydrocele of testis, hydrocele of tunica vaginalis
睾丸鞘膜纤维瘤/睾丸鞘膜纖維瘤 fibroma of testicular tunica
睾丸鞘膜炎/睾丸鞘膜炎 perididymitis
[睾丸]鞘膜脏层/本鞘膜 visceral layer of tunica vaginalis
睾丸切除术/睾丸切除術,摘睾術 orchiectomy
睾丸切开术/睾丸切開術 orchidotomy
睾丸缺如综合征/睾丸缺如症候群 absent testis syndrome
睾丸绒毛膜癌/睾丸絨毛膜癌 choriocarcinoma of testis
睾丸融合/睾丸融合[症] synorchidism
睾丸肉样肿/睾丸肉腫 sarcocele
睾丸疝/睾丸疝 hernia testis
睾丸[神经]痛/睾丸[神經]痛 orchioneuralgia
睾丸生殖细胞瘤/睾丸生殖細胞瘤 germinal cell tumor of testis
睾丸实质/睾丸實質 parenchyma of testis
睾丸输出小管/睾丸輸出小管 efferent ductules of testis
睾丸损伤/睾丸損傷 injury of testis
睾丸痛/睾丸痛 orchialgia
睾丸脱位/睾丸脱位 dislocation of testis
睾丸外膜/睾丸外膜 epiorchium
睾丸网/睾丸網 rete testis
睾丸网乳头状腺癌/睾丸網乳頭狀腺癌 papillary adenocarcinoma of rete testis
睾丸萎缩/睾丸萎縮 atrophy of testis
睾丸系膜/睾丸繫膜 mesorchium
睾丸下垂/睾丸下垂 orchidoptosis
睾丸下降/睾丸降下 orchiocatabasis
睾丸下降不全/睾丸下降不全 incomplete orchiocatabasis
睾丸腺癌/睾丸腺癌 adenocarcinoma of testis
睾丸小隔/睾丸小隔 septulum testis
睾丸小叶/睾丸小葉 lobule of testis, testicular lobule
睾丸性休克/睾丸休克 testicular shock
睾丸血管膜/睾丸血管膜 tunica vasculosa testis
睾丸炎/睾丸炎 orchitis, testitis
睾丸移植/睾丸移植 testis transplantation

睾丸移植物/睾丸移植物　testis graft
睾丸异位/睾丸異位　ectopia of testis
睾丸引带/睾丸引帶　gubernacular cord, gubernaculum testis, chorda gubernaculum
睾丸硬变/睾丸硬瘤　orchioscirrhus
睾丸右静脉/睾丸右靜脈　right testicular vein
睾丸真菌病/睾丸真菌病　mycosis of testis
睾丸制剂疗法/睾丸製劑療法　orchidotherapy, testicular therapy
睾丸中毒症/睾丸中毒　testitoxicosis
睾丸肿瘤/睾丸腫瘤　testicular neoplasm
睾丸纵隔/睾丸縱隔　mediastinum testis
膏肓/膏肓　gaohuang, inter cardiodia-phragmatic part, B43, BL43
膏粱厚味/膏粱厚味　greasy and surfeit flavor
膏淋/膏淋　stranguria due to chyluria, unctuous strangury
膏淋·脾虚气陷证/膏淋·脾虛氣陷證　unctuous strangury with pattern of spleen deficiency and qi collapse
膏淋·肾阳虚证/膏淋·腎陽虛證　unctuous strangury with pattern of kidney yang deficiency
膏淋·肾阴虚证/膏淋·腎陰虛證　unctuous strangury with pattern of kidney yin deficiency
膏淋·湿热下注证/膏淋·濕熱下注證　unctuous strangury with pattern of downward diffusion of damp-heat
膏摩/膏摩　ointment rubbing
膏伤珠陷/膏傷珠陷　sinking of eyeball
膏药/膏藥　medicinal paste, plaster
膏药疗法/膏藥療法　plaster therapy
膏滋/膏滋　oral thick paste
糕剂/餅狀物　cake
藁本/槁本　Chinese lovage
告之以其败/告之以其敗　informing patient of the severity of disease
锆肉芽肿/錯肉芽腫　zirconium granuloma
戈布莱细胞/杯狀細胞　goblet cell
戈德布拉特高血压/Goldblatt 氏高血壓　Goldblatt hypertension
戈登夹板/Gordon 氏夾板　Gordon splint
戈登征/戈登徵　Gordon sign
戈尔茨综合征/Goltz 氏症候群　Goltz syndrome
戈尔德贝格饮食/Goldberger 氏飲食　Goldberger diet
戈尔林综合征/Gorlin 症候群　Gorlin syndrome
戈拉碘胺/戈拉碘銨　Gallamine Triethiodide
戈勒姆病/戈勒姆病　Gorham disease

戈莱检测器/戈雷檢測器　Golay detector
戈莱柱/戈雷柱　Golay column
戈洛帕米/戈洛帕米　Gallopamil
戈瑟兰骨折/Gosselin 氏骨折　Gosselin fracture
戈舍瑞林/戈舍瑞林　Goserelin
戈谢病/戈謝病　Gaucher disease
疙瘩瘟/疙瘩瘟　nodular pestilence
咯利普兰/咯利普蘭　rolipram
咯嗪/咯嗪　alloxazine
哥伦比亚 SK 病毒/哥倫比亞 SK 病毒　Columbia SK virus
哥伦比亚蜱传斑疹热/哥倫比亞壁蝨熱　Colombia tick fever
哥特式弓描记器/哥特式弓描記器　Gothic arch tracer
鸽痘病毒/鴿痘病毒　pigeon pox virus
割处再生/切面再生　epimorphosis
割裂基因/割裂基因　split gene
割治法/割治法　cutting method
革兰染色/革蘭氏染色法　Gram stain
革兰溶液/革蘭氏溶液　Gram solution
革兰[氏]阳性[的]/革蘭氏陽性的　Gram-positive
革兰[氏]阳性菌感染/革蘭氏陽性菌感染　Gram-positive Bacterial infection
革兰[氏]阴性[的]/革蘭氏陰性的　Gram-negative
革兰[氏]阴性菌感染/革蘭氏陰性菌感染　Gram-negative Bacterial infection
革兰[氏]阴性菌毛囊炎/革蘭氏陰性菌毛囊炎　Gram negative folliculitis
革脉/革脈　tympanic pulse
革螨皮炎/革蟎皮炎　gamasid dermatitis
革蜱属/刺皮壁蝨屬　*Dermacentor*
革制夹/革製夾板　leather splint
格斗者疱疹/格鬥者皰疹　herpes gladiatorum
格尔森食物/Gerson 氏飲食　Gerson diet
格哈特综合征/Gerhardt 氏症候群　Gerhardt syndrome
格-赫饮食/Gerson-Herrmannsdorfer 二氏飲食　Gerson-Herrmannsdorfer diet
格拉代尼戈综合征/Gradenigo 氏症候群　Gradenigo syndrome
格拉非宁/格拉非寧　Glafenine
格拉司琼/格蘭塞隆　granisetron
格拉斯哥昏迷量表/格拉斯哥昏迷量表　Glasgow coma scale
格拉斯哥昏迷评分/格拉斯哥昏迷評分　Glasgow coma score
格拉斯哥预后评分/格拉斯哥預後評分　Glasgow

outcome scale
格莱细胞/Gley 氏細胞　Gley cell
格劳卡苷/格勞卡苷　glaucarubin
格勒试验/蓋萊試驗　Gelle test
格雷厄姆·斯蒂尔杂音/格雷厄姆·斯蒂爾雜音　Graham Steell murmur
格雷夫斯病/Graves 氏病　Graves disease
格雷夫突眼病/Graves 氏突眼病　ophthalmic Graves disease
格雷·特纳征/格雷·特納徵　Grey Turner sign
格雷西刮治器/格雷西刮治器　Gracey curette
格里豪病/Greenhow 氏病　Greenhow disease
格列本脲/格列本脲　glibenclamide
格列吡嗪/格列吡嗪　glipizide
格列齐特/格列齊特　gliclazide
格林-巴利综合征/格-巴二氏症候群　Guillain-Barre syndrome
格林登病/Grindon 氏病　Grindon disease
格林费尔特疝/Grynfelt 氏疝　Grynfelt hernia
格隆溴铵/格隆溴銨　Glycopyrrolate
格鲁伯疝/Gruber 氏疝　Gruber hernia
格鲁布性鼻炎/浮膜性鼻炎　croupous rhinitis
格鲁布性的/浮膜的, 哮吼性的　croupous
格鲁布性肺炎/格鲁布性肺炎　croupous pneumonia
格鲁布性喉炎/哮吼性喉炎　croupous laryngitis
格鲁布性结肠炎/浮膜性結腸炎　croupous colitis
格鲁布性胃炎/浮膜性胃炎　croupous gastritis
格伦手术/Glenn 氏手術　Glenn operation
格罗斯病/Gross 氏病, 直肠成囊病　Gross disease
格罗斯试验/Gross 氏試驗　Gross test
格式塔疗法/格式塔療法　gestalt therapy
格式塔学说/格式塔學説　gestalt theory
格思里肌/Guthrie 氏肌　Guthrie muscle
格思里试验/格思里試驗　Guthrie test
格斯特曼综合征/Gerstmann 氏症候群　Gerstmann syndrome
格瓦思米油醚[直肠]麻醉/Gwathmey 氏油醚麻醉法　Gwathmey oil-ether anesthesia
格致余论/格致餘論　Supplementary Treatise on Knowledge and Practice, Further Discourses on the Properties of Things
格子细胞/格子細胞　gitter cell
格子形切口/格子形切口　gridiron incision
蛤蚌毒素/蛤蚌毒素　saxitoxin
蛤贝充血毒[素]/蜊毒[素]　mytilocongestin
蛤贝毒/蛤毒　clam poison
蛤蚧/蛤蚧　tokay gecko
蛤蚧定喘丸/蛤蚧定喘丸　gejie dingchuan pills
蛤壳/蛤殼　clam shell
蛤仔毒素/貝毒素　venerupin
隔侧尖/隔側尖　septal cusp
隔侧乳头肌/隔側乳頭肌　septal papillary muscle
隔代遗传/隔代遺傳　skipped generation
隔核/隔核　septal nucleus
隔离/隔離　sequestration, isolation
隔离病室/隔離病室, 隔離病房　isolation ward
隔离层/隔離層　sealing coat
隔离的/隔離的　isolated
隔离灌注/隔離灌注　isolated organ perfusion
隔离抗原/隔離抗原　sequestered antigen
隔离群/隔離　isolate
隔离霜/隔離霜　barrier cream
隔离性囊肿/隔離性囊腫　sequestration cyst
隔离引流/腹部防炎引流　quarantine drain
隔膜的/中隔的　septal
隔区/隔區　septal area
隔室/隔室　compartment
隔室传真装置/投影機　scialyscope
隔室化/胞内之隔室化　compartmentalization
隔室模型/隔室模型　compartment model
隔束/隔束　septal band
隔体记忆/隔體記憶　telemnemonike
隔物灸/隔物灸　sandwiched moxibustion
隔缘的/中隔缘的　septomarginal
隔缘肉柱/隔緣肉柱　septomarginal trabecula
隔缘束/隔緣束　septomarginal fasciculus
膈/膈, 橫膈膜　diaphragm
膈丛/膈叢　phrenic plexus, diaphragmatic plexus
膈大动脉/膈大動脈　great phrenic artery
膈的/膈膜的　diaphragmatic
膈动描记器/膈動描記器　phrenograph
膈恶性肿瘤/膈惡性腫瘤　malignant tumor of diaphragm
膈腹神经/膈腹神經　phrenicoabdominal nerve
膈腹支/膈腹支　phrenicoabdominal branch
膈弓状韧带/膈弓狀韌帶　arcuate diaphragmatic ligament
膈关/膈關　geguan, BL46
膈呼吸/膈呼吸　diaphragmatic respiration
膈肌/膈肌　diaphragmatic muscle
膈肌肋部/膈肌肋部　costal part of diaphragm
膈肌内侧弓状韧带/膈肌内側弓狀韌帶　medial arcuate ligament of diaphragm
膈肌腔静脉孔/膈肌腔靜脈孔　vena caval foramen of diaphragm
膈肌食管裂孔/膈肌食管裂孔　esophageal hiatus of

diaphragm
膈肌外侧弓状韧带/横膈膜外側弓狀韌帶 lateral arcuate ligament of diaphragm
膈肌胸骨部/膈肌胸骨部 sternal part of diaphragm
膈肌腰部/膈肌腰部 lumbar part of diaphragm
膈肌右脚/膈肌右腳 right crus of diaphragm
膈肌正中弓状韧带/膈肌正中弓狀韌帶 median arcuate ligament of diaphragm
膈肌中心腱/膈肌中心腱 central tendon of diaphragm
膈肌主动脉裂孔/膈肌主動脈裂孔 aortic hiatus of diaphragm
膈肌左脚/膈肌左腳 left crus of diaphragm
膈脚/膈腳,膈柱 pillar of diaphragm
膈结肠固定术/膈式結腸固定術 phrenocolopexy
膈结肠韧带/膈結腸韌帶 phrenicocolic ligament
膈良性肿瘤/膈良性腫瘤 benign tumor of diaphragm
膈裂孔疝/裂孔疝 hiatus hernia
膈面/膈面 diaphragmatic surface, facies diaphragmatica
膈膜/[横]膈膜 diaphragma
膈膜韧带/膈膜韌帶 diaphragmatic ligament
膈膜心形韧带/膈膜心形韌帶 cordiform ligament of diaphragm
膈膨出/横膈突出 diaphragmatic eventration
膈膨升/膈膨昇 eventration of diaphragm
膈膨升折叠术/膈膨昇折疊術 plication of eventration of diaphragm
膈破裂/膈破裂 rupture of diaphragm
膈扑动/膈撲動 diaphragmatic flutter
膈疝/膈疝氣,膈赫尼亞,膈突逸 diaphragmatic hernia, diaphragmatocele
膈疝修补/膈疝修補 repair of diaphragmatic hernia
膈上动脉/膈上動脈 superior phrenic artery
膈上静脉/膈上靜脈 superior phrenic vein
膈上淋巴结/膈上淋巴結 superior phrenic lymph node
膈上淋巴结后群/膈上淋巴結後群 posterior group of superior phrenic lymph node
膈上淋巴结前群/膈上淋巴結前群 anterior group of superior phrenic lymph node
膈上淋巴结外侧群/膈上淋巴結外側群 lateral group of superior phrenic lymph node
膈上憩室/横膈上憩室 epiphrenic diverticulum
膈神经/膈神經 phrenic nerve, diaphragmatic nerve
膈神经抽出术/[膈]神經撕除法 phrenic avulsion
膈神经丛/膈神經叢 plexus phrenicus
膈神经电刺激呼吸/電膈神經式呼吸 electrophrenic respiration
膈神经核/膈神經核 phrenic nucleus
膈神经节/膈神經節 phrenic ganglia
膈神经麻痹/膈神經麻痺 diaphragmatic paralysis
膈神经切除术/膈神經切除術 phrenicectomy
膈神经切断术/膈神經切斷術 phrenicotomy
膈神经心包支/膈神經心包支 pericardiac branch of phrenic nerve
膈神经压轧术/膈神經壓軋術 phrenemphraxis
膈式呼吸运动/膈式呼吸運動 diaphragmatic breathing exercise
膈俞/膈俞 geshu, BL17
膈痛/膈痛 diaphragmalgia, diaphragmatic pain
膈胃的/膈與胃的 phrenogastric
膈胃综合征/膈胃症候群 phrenogastric syndrome
膈下垂/膈下垂 phrenoptosis
膈下动脉/膈下動脈 inferior phrenic artery, diaphragmatic artery
膈下静脉/膈下靜脈 inferior phrenic vein
膈下淋巴结/膈下淋巴結 inferior phrenic lymph nodes
膈下脓肿/横膈下膿腫 subphrenic abscess
膈下腔/膈下腔 hypophrenium
膈下异常肺静脉连接/膈下異常肺靜脈連接 infradiaphragmatic anomalous pulmonary venous connection
膈下隐窝/膈下隱窩 subphrenic recesses
膈心包炎/膈心包炎 phrenopericarditis
膈性腹膜炎/膈腹膜炎 diaphragmatic peritonitis
膈胸膜/膈胸膜 diaphragmatic pleura, diaphragmatic part
膈胸膜筋膜/膈胸膜筋膜 phrenicopleural fascia
膈运动波/膈波 phrenic wave
膈折叠术/膈折疊術 diaphragmatic plication
膈中心腱/膈中心腱 cordiform tendon of diaphragm
膈周炎/横膈周圍炎 periphrenitis
膈周[组织]炎/膈[旁]炎 paraphrenitis
膈状子宫托/膈狀子宮托 diaphragm pessary
膈纵隔隐窝/膈縱隔隱窩 phrenicomediastinal recess
镉/鎘 cadmium
镉尘肺/鎘塵肺 cadmiosis
镉放射性同位素/鎘放射性同位素 cadmium radioisotope
镉化合物/鎘化合物 cadmium compound
镉中毒/鎘中毒 cadmium poisoning
葛根/葛根 kudzuvine root
葛根芩连汤/葛根芩連湯 gegen qinlian decoction

葛根汤/葛根湯　gegen decoction
葛洪/葛洪　Ge Hong
个别托盘/個別托盤　individual tray
个别正常殆/個別正常咬合　individual normal occlusion
个人保健服务/個人保健服務　personal health service
个人的/個人的　personal
个人监护/人員監測　personnel monitoring
个人满足/個人滿足　personal satisfaction
个体发生/個體發生　ontogenesis, ontogeny
个体发育免疫学/個體發育免疫學　ontogenyimmunology
个体基因型变异/個體基因型變異　idiotypic variation
个体形成区/個體形成區　individuation field
个性/個性　individuality
个性定向力障碍/個性定向力障礙　autopsychical disorientation
个性发展/個性的發生　individuation
个性量表/個性量表　personality inventory
个性排牙法/個性排牙法　personalized alignment
个性牙排列/個性牙排列　personalized tooth alignment
各部配列式/各部配列式　memberment
各部位肿瘤/各部位腫瘤　neoplasm by site
各部血压不等/各部血壓不等　anisopiesis
各代增长指数/世代指數　generation index
各类血细胞增多/全部血球增多症　pancytosis
各向异性/各異方性　anisotropy
各向异性带/各向異性層　anisotropic band
各向异性屏蔽/非均質屏蔽　anisotropic shielding
铬/鉻　chrome
铬肠线/鉻製腸線　chromic catgut
铬毒性溃疡/鉻毒性潰瘍　chrome sore
铬放射性同位素/鉻放射性同位素　chromium radioisotope
铬合金/鉻合金　chromium alloy
铬化合物/鉻化合物　chromium compound
铬溃疡/鉻潰瘍　tanner ulcer
铬皮炎/鉻皮炎　chromium dermatitis
铬酸/鉻酸　chromic acid
铬酸钾/鉻酸鉀　potassium chromate
铬酸烧伤/鉻酸燒傷　chromic acid burn
铬酸盐/鉻酸鹽　chromate
铬酸盐类/鉻酸鹽類　chromates
铬同位素/鉻同位素　chromium isotope
给药/給［藥］　administer

给药错误/給藥錯誤　medication error
给药方案/給藥方案　dosage regimen
给药途径/給藥途徑　route of administration
给药系统/給藥系統　medication system
根/根　①root ②root of pulse
根癌土壤杆菌/根癌土壤桿菌　Agrobacterium tumefacien
根岸脑炎/根岸腦炎　Negishi encephalitis
根被/根被　velamen
根本的/根本的　radical
根侧牙周囊肿/根側牙周囊腫　lateral periodontal cyst
根的/根的　radicular
根度病/大鼻病　goundou
根分叉部缺损/根分叉部缺損　furcation defect
根固位体/根固位體　radicular retainer
根管闭塞/根管閉塞　obturation of root canal
根管长度测量仪/根管長度測量儀　root canal length meter
根管冲洗剂/根管沖洗劑　root canal irrigant
根管充填/根管充填　root canal obturation
根管充填材料/根管充填材料　root canal filling materials
根管充填银尖/根管充填銀尖　root canal silver point
根管锉/根管銼　root canal file
根管封闭/根管封閉　root canal sealing
根管口/根管口　root canal orifice
根管疗法/根管療法　root canal therapy
根管内封药/根管內封藥　intracanal medicament
根管内预备/根管內預備　intracanal preparation
根管内种植体/根管植入物　endodontic implant
根管针/根管針　root canal broach
根管制备/根管製備　root canal preparation
根管钻/根管鑽　root canal reamer
根迹维管束/根跡維管束　root trace bundle
根尖断裂/根尖折　apex fracture
根尖刮除术/牙尖刮除術　apical curettage
根尖片/根尖照片　periapical film
根尖切除术/根尖切除術　apicoectomy
根尖隙/根尖隙　apical space
根尖下的/根尖下的　subapical
根尖下截骨术/根尖下截骨術　subapical osteotomy
根尖纤维/尖端纖維　apical fiber
根尖牙周炎/根尖周膜炎　apical periodontitis
根尖炎/根尖炎　apicitis
根尖诱导形成术/根尖誘導形成術　apexification
根尖周疾病/根尖周疾病　periapical disease
根尖周囊肿/根尖周囊腫　periapical cyst

根尖周脓肿/牙根周膿腫　periapical abscess
根尖周肉芽肿/根尖周肉芽腫　periapical granuloma
根尖周吸收/牙根尖吸收　periapical resorption
根尖周牙骨质异常增生/根尖周牙骨質異常增生　periapical cemental dysplasia
根尖周炎/根尖牙周炎　periapical periodontitis
根尖周组织/根尖周組織　periapical tissue
根间截骨术/根間截骨術　interradicular osteotomy
根间纤维/根間纖維　interradicular fiber
根脚/根腳　root of swollen sore
根结/根結　root and knot
根茎/根[莖]　rhizome
根螨属/根菌屬　Rhizoglyphus
根霉菌属/酒麴菌屬　Rhizopus
根内固位体/根内固位體　intra-radicular retainer
根盘/根盤　hard base of swollen sore
根皮苷/根皮苷　phlorhizin
根皮苷处理/受根皮苷影響　phlorhizinize
根皮苷试验/根皮苷試驗　phlorizin test
根皮素/根皮素　phloretin
根鞘/根鞘　root sheath
根芹菜/根芹菜　Apium graveolens
根丝体/根絲體　rhizoplast
根向复位瓣术/根向復位瓣術　apically repositioned flap surgery
根治性颈清扫术/根治性頸清掃術　radical neck dissection
根治性淋巴结清扫术/根治性淋巴結清掃術　radical lymphatic node dissection
根治性膀胱切除术/根治性膀胱切除術　radical cystectomy
根治性前列腺切除术/根治性前列腺切除術　radical prostatectomy
根治性全肺切除术/根治性全肺切除術　radical pneumonectomy
根治性乳房切除术/根治性乳房切除術　radical mastectomy
根治性肾切除术/根治性腎切除術　radical nephrectomy
根状假足/根足　rhizopodium
跟/跟　heel
跟[部]痛/跟痛　calcaneodynia
跟反射/叩跟反射　heel-tap reflex
跟腓韧带/跟腓韌帶　calcaneofibular ligament
跟骨/跟骨　calcaneus, heel bone
跟骨的/跟骨的　calcaneal
跟骨沟/跟骨溝　calcaneal sulcus, interosseous groove of calcaneus
跟骨骨刺/跟骨骨刺　heel spur
跟骨骨突炎/跟骨凸炎　calcaneoapophysitis
跟骨骨折/跟骨骨折　calcaneal fracture, calcaneous fracture, fracture of calcaneus
跟骨结节/跟結節　calcaneal tuberosity, calcaneal tubercle
跟骨结节内侧突/跟結節内側突　medial process of calcaneal tuberosity
跟骨结节外侧突/跟結節外側突　lateral process of calcaneal tuberosity
跟骨前结节/跟骨前結節　anterior tubercle of calcaneus
跟骨体/跟骨體　calcaneal body
跟骨炎/跟骨炎　calcaneitis
跟骨瘀点/跟骨部瘀點　calcaneal petechiae
跟后黏液囊炎/跟後黏液囊炎　retrocalcaneal bursitis
跟腱/跟腱　tendo calcaneus
跟腱断裂/跟腱斷裂　rupture achilles tendon, rupture of achilles tendon
跟腱反射松弛时间测定/跟腱反射鬆弛時間測定　achilles reflex time
跟腱缝术/跟腱縫合術　achillorrhaphy
跟腱挛缩/跟腱攣縮　contracture of achilles tendon
跟腱囊/跟腱囊　bursa of tendo calcaneus, achilles bursa
跟腱[黏液]囊炎/跟腱囊炎　achillobursitis
跟腱痛/跟腱痛　achillodynia
跟腱炎/跟腱炎　achilles tendinitis, calcaneal tendonitis
跟腱张力试验/跟腱張力試驗　achilles tendon tension test
跟胫韧带/跟脛韌帶　calcaneotibial ligament
跟距骨桥/跟距骨橋　talocalcaneal bridge
跟内侧支/跟内側支　medial calcanean branch
跟皮下囊/跟皮下囊　subcutaneous calcaneal bursa
跟区/跟部　calcaneal region
跟随试验/跟隨試驗　pursuit test
跟痛症/跟痛症,足跟痛　heel pain
跟痛症·风寒湿阻证/跟痛症·風寒濕阻證　heel pain with wind-cold-dampness obstruction pattern
跟痛症·肝肾亏虚证/跟痛症·肝腎虧虛證　heel pain with liver-kidney deficiency pattern
跟痛症·血瘀气滞证/跟痛症·血瘀氣滯證　heel pain with pattern of blood stasis and qi stagnation
跟骰背侧韧带/跟骰背側韌帶　dorsal calcaneocuboid ligament
跟骰关节/跟骰關節　calcaneocuboid joint, calcaneocuboid articulation

跟骰内侧韧带/跟骰内側韌帶	medial calcaneocuboid ligament
跟骰韧带/跟骰韌帶	calcaneocuboid ligament
跟骰足底韧带/跟骰蹠側韌帶	plantar calcaneocuboid ligament
跟突/跟突	calcaneal process
跟外侧支/跟外側支	lateral calcanean branch
跟网/跟網	calcaneal rete
跟膝试验/跟膝試驗	heel-knee test
跟支/跟支	calcaneal branch
跟舟背侧韧带/背側跟舟韌帶	dorsal calcaneonavicular ligament
跟舟韧带/跟舟韌帶	calcaneonavicular ligament
跟舟外侧韧带/跟舟外側韌帶	lateral calcaneonavicular ligament
跟舟下韧带/跟舟下韌帶	ligamentum calcaneonavicular plantare
跟舟跖侧韧带/彈性韌帶,跟舟下韌帶	spring ligament
跟舟足底韧带/跟舟蹠側韌帶	plantar calcaneonavicular ligament
更代细胞/更代細胞	substituting cell
更迭的/交互的	alternating
更年安片/更年安片	gengnian'an pills
更年期/更年期	climacter
更年期精神病/衰敗期精神病	involutional psychosis
更年期性交困难/更年期性交困難	climacteric dyspareunia
更年期抑郁症/更年期抑鬱症	major depressive disorder
更年期忧郁[症]/退化性抑鬱	involutional depression
更年期月经/更年期的月經	climacteric menstruation
更年期综合征/更年期症候群	climacteric syndrome
更生霉素/更生黴素	dactinomycin
更昔洛韦/更昔洛韋	ganciclovir
庚巴比妥/庚基巴比妥	heptabarbital
庚醇/庚醇	heptanol
庚二酸/庚二酸	pimelic acid
庚醛/庚醛	heptanal
庚酸/庚酸	enanthylic acid
庚酸睾酮/庚酸睾酮,長效睾丸脂酮	testosterone enanthate
庚酸类/庚酸類	heptanoic acids
庚酸盐/庚酸鹽	heptylate
庚糖/庚糖	heptose
庚糖尿/庚糖尿	heptosuria
庚酮糖/酮庚糖	ketoheptose
庚烷/庚烷	theolin
庚烷类/庚烷類	heptanes
庚珠蛋白/庚球蛋白	heptoglobin
庚珠蛋白血/庚球蛋白血症	heptoglobinemia
耿氏交叉征/耿氏交叉徵	Gunn crossing sign
梗塞后/梗塞後	postinfarction
梗塞后心脏破裂/梗塞後心臟破裂	postinfarction heart rupture
梗塞周围传导阻滞/梗塞周圍傳導阻滯	periinfarction block
梗阻/阻塞,梗塞	obstruction
梗阻的/阻塞的,梗塞的	obstructive
梗阻性肥厚型心肌病/阻塞性肥厚型心肌病	obstructive hypertrophic cardiomyopathy
梗阻性呼吸困难/阻塞性呼吸困難	obstructive dyspnea
梗阻性阑尾炎/阻塞性闌尾炎	obstructive appendicitis
梗阻性脑积水/阻塞性水腦	obstructive hydrocephalus
梗阻性尿路病/阻塞性尿路病	obstructive uropathy
梗阻性膀胱/阻塞性膀胱	stammering bladder
梗阻性肾病/阻塞性腎病	obstructive nephropathy
梗阻性痛经/阻塞性痛經	obstructive dysmenorrhea
工厂事故/工業意外	industrial accident
工程/工程	engineering
工业安全/工業安全	industrial safety
工业毒理学/工業毒理學	industrial toxicology
工业废弃物/工業廢棄物	industrial waste
工业杀真菌剂/工業殺真菌劑	industrial fungicide
工业损伤/工業損傷	industrial injury
工业卫生/工業衛生學	industrial hygiene
工业性皮炎/工業性皮膚炎	industrial dermatitis
工业药学/工業藥學	industrial pharmacy
工业医学/工業醫學	industrial medicine
工业中毒/工業中毒	industrial poisoning
工艺疗法/工藝療法	art and craft therapy
工余保健服务/工餘保健服務	after-hours care
工娱疗法/工娛療法	occupation recreational therapy
工作安排忍受/工作安排忍受	work schedule tolerance
工作侧/工作側	working side
工作侧接触/工作側接觸	working contact
工作侧髁/工作側髁	working condyle
工作侧咬合/工作側咬合	working bite
工作负荷量/工作負荷量	workload
工作狂/工作癖患者	ergomaniac
工作疗法/工作療法	work therapy

工作模型/工作模型　working cast
弓长/牙弓長度　arch length
弓动脉/主動脈弧,主動脈弓　aortic arch
弓杆/牙弓槓,齒列槓　arch bar
弓蛔虫病/毒蛔蟲病　toxocariasis
弓收缩/弓收縮　arch construction
弓丝/弓線　arch wire
弓丝成型器/成弓器　arch former
弓体/弓體　bow
弓下陷足/下陷足　sag foot
弓形/弓形　arch form
弓形虫病/毒漿體原蟲病,弓蟲病　toxoplasmosis
弓形虫染色试验/弓形蟲染色試驗　Sabin-Feldman dye test
弓形虫素皮内试验/弓形蟲素皮內試驗　toxoplasmin test
弓形的/弓形的　arcuate
弓形动脉/弓形動脈　arcuate artery
弓形集合小管/弓形集合[小]管　arched collecting tubule
弓形静脉/弓狀靜脈　arcuate vein
弓形切口/弓形切口　crossbow incision
弓形体素/弓蟲素,毒胞漿液　toxoplasmin
弓形腿支具/弓形腿支具　bow leg brace
弓形纹/弓形紋　arch
弓形原虫脑脊髓炎/弓形原蟲腦脊髓炎　toxoplasmic encephalomyelitis
弓形肢体/弓形肢體　bowed limb
弓形子宫/弓形子宮[畸形]　uterus arcuatus
弓形足/弓形足　hollow foot
弓样病灶/弓樣病灶　arciform lesion
弓状的/弓樣的　arciform
弓状动脉/弓狀動脈,弓形動脈　arcuate artery
弓状核/弓狀核　arcuate nucleus
弓状嵴/弓形嵴　arcuate crest
弓状静脉/弓狀靜脈,弓形靜脈　arcuate vein
弓状扩张性紫癜/弓狀擴張性紫癜　purpura telangiectasia arciformis
弓状隆起/弧狀隆凸　arcuate eminence
弓状皮肤红斑/弓形真皮性紅斑　arcuate dermal erythema
弓状韧带/弓狀韌帶　arcuate ligament
弓状下窝/弧形下凹　subarcuate fossa
弓状纤维/弧纖維　arcuate fiber
弓状线/弓狀線　arcuate line
公费牙科医疗/公費牙科醫療　state dentistry
公费医疗/公醫制度　state medicine
公共机构伦理学/公共機構倫理學　institutional ethics
公共卫生/公共衛生,公眾衛生　public health
公共卫生部/公共衛生部　ministry of public health
公共卫生工作/公共衛生實施,公共衛生實踐　public health practice
公共卫生管理/公共衛生管理　public health administration
公共卫生护理学/公共衛生護理學　public health nursing
公共卫生信息学/公共衛生資訊學　public health informatics
公共卫生学生/公共衛生學生　public health student
公共卫生牙科学/公共衛生牙科學　public health dentistry
公共卫生牙医/公共衛生牙醫師　public health dentist
公共卫生院校/公共衛生院校　public health school
公共卫生专业教育/公共衛生專業教育　public health professional education
公开的/公開的　overt
公立医院/公立醫院　government hospital
公式/公式　formula
公孙/公孫　gongsun, SP4
公务的/公務的　official
功劳木/功勞木　Chinese mahonia stem
功劳叶/功勞葉　mahonia leaf
功率/功率　power
功能/功能　function
功能残气量/功能殘氣量　functional residual capacity
功能错乱/官能異常,功能異常　parafunction
功能的/功能的　functional
功能锻炼/功能鍛煉　functional exercise
功能分化/機能分化　functional differentiation
功能𬌗/齒工作咬合　working occlusion
功能恢复/功能恢復　functional rehabilitation
功能极性/動極性　dynamic polarity
功能夹板/功能性夾板　functional splint
功能减弱/官能減弱,運用力減少　miopragia
功能减退/機能減退,機能不足　hypofunction
功能亢进/機能亢進　hyperfunctioning
功能缺失/機能缺失　afunction
功能缺失的/機能缺失的　afunctional
功能失调性下丘脑性闭经/功能失調性下丘腦性閉經　functional hypothalamic amenorrhea
功能位/功能位　functional position
功能性刺激/官能性刺激　functional irritation
功能性出血/功能性出血　functional bleeding

功能性磁共振成像术/功能磁共振造影　functional magnetic resonance imaging, FMRI
功能性蛋白尿/功能性蛋白尿　functional proteinuria
功能性电刺激/功能性電刺激　functional electric stimulation
功能性反流/官能性反流　functional regurgitation
功能性肥大/功能性肥大　functional hypertrophy
功能性干扰/機能性干擾　functional interference
功能性𬌗/齒功能正常性咬合　functional occlusion
功能性𬌗平面/功能性𬌗平面　functional occlusal plane
功能性幻觉/功能性幻覺　functional hallucination
功能性黄疸/功能性黃疸　functional jaundice
功能性活动矫正器/功能性活動矯正器　activator appliance
功能性活化剂/機能性活化質　functional activator
功能性疾病/機能性病　dynamic disease
功能性脊柱侧凸/功能性脊柱側彎　functional scoliosis
功能性矫治器/功能性矯治器　functional appliance
功能性结肠疾病/功能性結腸疾病　functional colonic disease
功能性精神病/官能性精神病　functional psychosis
功能性颈清扫术/功能性頸廓清術　functional neck dissection
功能性痉挛/官能性痙攣　functional spasm
功能性盲/功能性盲　functional blindness
功能性神经外科[学]/功能性神經外科[學]　functional neurosurgery
功能性失语/功能性失語症　functional aphasia
功能性听觉丧失/功能性聽覺喪失　functional hearing loss
功能性痛经/機能性痛經　functional dysmenorrhea
功能性萎缩/功能性萎縮　functional atrophy
功能性消化不良/功能性消化不良　functional dyspepsia
功能性心血管病/功能性心血管疾病　functional cardiovascular disease
功能性阳痿/功能性陽痿　functional impotence
功能性异染色质/偶發性異染色質　facultative heterochromatin
功能性应力/機能性應力　functional stress
功能性杂音/官能性雜音　functional murmur
功能[性]障碍/功能性障礙　functional disturbance
功能性正畸矫正器/功能性正畸矯正器　functional orthodontic appliance
功能性肿瘤/功能性腫瘤　functional tumor
功能训练/功能訓練　functional training

功能异常/機能異常　parasthenia
功能印模/功能印模　functional impression
功能障碍/機能障礙,官能不良　dysfunction
功能[障碍]性子宫出血/功能不良性子宮出血　dysfunctional uterine bleeding
功能正常/運用正常,官能正常　orthergasia
功能正常甲状腺病综合征/甲狀腺官能病症候群　euthyroid sick syndrome
功能状态/功能狀態　functional status
攻补兼施/攻補兼施　reinforcement and elimination in combination
攻击性的/攻擊性的　aggressive
攻击性行为障碍/攻擊性行爲障礙　aggressive behavior disorder
[攻]下法/[攻]下法　purgation method
攻下冷积/攻下冷積　treating coagulated cold by purgation
攻下逐瘀/攻下逐瘀　eliminating blood stasis by catharsis
攻阵/攻陣　offensive array
供卵/供卵　donor egg
供能[食]物/可當能源的食物或其他物質　dynamophore
供体/供體　donor
供体角膜/供體角膜　donor's cornea
供血动脉夹闭术/供血動脈夾閉術　clipping of feeding artery
供血皮瓣/供血皮瓣　permanent blood carrying skin flap
供血者/供血者　blood donor
供盐过多/供鹽過多　hyperchloridation
供应者-倡导者组织/供應者-宣導者組織　provider-sponsored organization
供者特异性输血/供者特異性輸血　donor specific blood transfusion
供者选择/供者選擇　donor selection
供者预处理/供者預處理　donor pretreatment
肱尺关节/肱尺關節　humeroulnar joint
肱尺头/肱尺頭　humeroulnar head
肱动脉/肱動脈　brachial artery
肱动脉搏动/肱動脈搏動　brachial dance
肱动脉脉搏/肱動脈脈搏　brachial artery pulse
肱动脉脉搏图/肱脈圖　brachiogram
肱动脉听诊器/肱動脈聽診器　brachial stethoscope
肱二头肌/肱二頭肌　biceps brachii
肱二头肌长头/肱二頭肌長頭　long head of biceps brachii
肱二头肌长头肌腱滑脱/肱二頭肌長頭肌腱滑脱

dislocation of long head tendon of brachial biceps

肱二头肌长头肌腱炎/肱二頭肌長頭肌腱炎 myotenositis of long head of biceps brachii, tenovaginitis of long head of biceps brachii

肱二头肌长头腱断裂/肱二頭肌長頭腱斷裂 rupture of long head of brachial biceps

肱二头肌短头/肱二頭肌短頭 short head of biceps brachii

[肱]二头肌反射/[肱]二頭肌反射 biceps reflex

肱二头肌滑液鞘/肱二頭肌滑液鞘 synovial sheath of biceps brachii

肱二头肌腱断裂/肱二頭肌腱斷裂 rupture of tendon of biceps brachii

肱二头肌腱沟/肱二頭肌溝 bicipital groove of humerus

肱二头肌腱膜/肱二頭肌腱膜 bicipital aponeurosis

肱二头肌抗阻力试验/肱二頭肌抗阻力試驗 Yergason test

肱二头肌内侧沟/肱二頭肌內側溝 medial bicipital sulcus

肱二头肌桡骨囊/肱二頭肌橈骨囊 bicipitoradial bursa

肱二头肌外侧沟/肱二頭肌外側溝 lateral bicipital sulcus

肱骨/肱骨 humerus, humeral bone

肱骨大结节骨折/肱骨大結節骨折 fracture of greater tuberosity of humerus

肱骨的/肱骨的 humeral

肱骨副韧带/肱骨副韌帶 accessory ligament of humerus

肱骨干骨折/肱骨幹骨折 fracture of shaft of humerus, humeral shaft fracture

肱骨骨折/肱骨骨折 humeral fracture

肱骨关节盂韧带/肱骨關節盂韌帶 glenoid ligament of humerus

肱骨后面/肱骨後面 posterior surface of humerus

肱骨滑车/肱骨滑車 trochlea of humerus

肱骨肌管/肱骨肌管 humeromuscular tunnel

肱骨假颈/肱骨假頸 false neck of humerus

[肱骨]结节间沟/肱骨結節間溝 intertubercular groove of humerus

肱骨解剖颈/肱骨解剖頸 anatomical neck of humerus

肱骨髁/肱骨髁 condyle of humerus

肱骨髁间骨折/肱骨髁間骨折 humeral intercondylar fracture, intercondylar fracture of humerus

肱骨髁上骨折/[肱骨]髁上骨折 humeral supracondylar fracture, supracondylar fracture of humerus

肱骨髁上突/肱骨髁上突 supracondylar process of humerus

肱骨内侧髁上嵴/肱骨內側髁上嵴 medial supracondylar ridge of humerus

肱骨内侧缘/肱骨內側緣 medial border of humerus

肱骨内髁/肱骨內髁 funny bone

肱骨内上髁/肱骨內上髁 medial epicondyle of humerus

肱骨内上髁骨折/肱骨內上髁骨折 fracture of medial epicondyle of humerus, humeral internal epicondyle fracture

肱骨内上髁炎/肱骨內上髁炎 humeral internal epicondylitis, internal humeral epicondylitis

肱骨体/肱骨體 shaft of humerus

肱骨体前内侧面/肱骨體前內側面 anteromedial surface of shaft of humerus

肱骨体前外侧面/肱骨體前外側面 anterolateral surface of shaft of humerus

肱骨头/肱骨頭 head of humerus

肱骨外侧缘/肱骨外側緣 lateral border of humerus

肱骨外科颈骨折/肱骨外科頸骨折 fracture of surgical neck of humerus, humeral surgical neck fracture

肱骨外髁骨折/肱骨外髁骨折 humeral external condyle fracture

肱骨外上髁/肱骨外上髁 lateral epicondyle of humerus

肱骨外上髁骨折/肱骨外上髁骨折 fracture of lateral epicondyle of humerus

肱骨外上髁炎/肱骨外上髁炎 external humeral epicondylitis, humeral external epicondylitis

肱骨外上髁炎·风寒阻络证/肱骨外上髁炎·風寒阻絡證 humeral external epicondylitis with pattern of wind-cold obstructing collateral

肱骨外上髁炎·气血两虚证/肱骨外上髁炎·氣血兩虛證 humeral external epicondylitis with qi-blood deficiency pattern

肱骨外上髁炎·湿热蕴结证/肱骨外上髁炎·濕熱蘊結證 humeral external epicondylitis with dampness-heat amassment pattern

肱骨小结节/肱骨小結節,肱骨内结节 internal tubercle of humerus

肱骨小头/肱骨小頭 capitulum of humerus, capitate eminence

肱骨小头骨折/肱骨小頭骨折 capitellum fracture

肱骨滋养动脉/肱骨滋養動脈 humeral nutrient artery, nutrient artery of the humerus

肱关节/肱關節　articulation of humerus
肱横韧带/肱骨橫韌帶　transverse humeral ligament
肱肌/肱肌　brachialis, brachial muscle
肱静脉/肱静脈　brachial vein
肱淋巴结/肱淋巴結　brachial lymph node
肱桡关节/肱橈關節　humeroradial joint, humeroradial articulation
肱桡肌/肱橈肌　brachioradialis, brachioradial muscle
肱桡韧带/肱橈韌帶　brachioradial ligament
肱三头肌/肱三頭肌　triceps brachii, musculus triceps brachii
肱三头肌长头/肱三頭肌長頭　long head of triceps brachii
肱三头肌腱下囊/肱三頭肌腱下囊　subtendinous bursa of triceps brachii
肱三头肌内侧头/肱三頭肌內側頭　medial head of triceps brachii
肱三头肌外侧头/肱三頭肌外側頭　lateral head of triceps brachii
肱深动脉/肱深動脈　deep brachial artery
肱头/肱頭　humeral head
宫角妊娠/子宮角妊娠　cornual pregnancy
宫颈残端切除术/宮頸殘端切除術　excision of cervical stump
宫颈成熟/宮頸成熟　cervical ripening
宫颈成形术/子宮頸造形術　tracheloplasty
宫颈刮片/宮頸刮片　cervical scraping smear
宫颈管刮片/宮頸管刮片　endocervical scraping smear
宫颈环扎术/宮頸環扎術　cervical cerclage
宫颈活检/宮頸活檢　cervical biopsy
宫颈扩张术/宮頸擴張術　dilatation of the cervix
宫颈黏膜碘试验/宮頸黏膜碘試驗　Schiller test
宫颈黏液/宮頸黏液　cervix mucus
宫颈黏液检查/宮頸黏液檢查　cervical mucus examination
宫颈黏液精液相合试验/米-庫二氏試驗　Miller-Kurzrok test
宫颈旁阻滞术/子宮頸旁阻斷麻醉　paracervical block
宫颈切除术/宮頸切除術　amputation of cervix
宫颈切开/子宮頸分裂術　discission of cervix uteri
宫颈妊娠/子宮頸[管]妊娠　cervical pregnancy
宫颈上皮内瘤样病变/宮頸上皮內瘤樣病變　cervical intraepithelial neoplasia
宫颈息肉/宮頸息肉　cervical polyp
宫颈腺/子宮頸腺　cervical glands
宫颈腺囊肿/Naboth氏囊腫,子宮頸腺囊腫　Naboth cyst
宫颈修补术/子宮頸縫合術　trachelorrhaphy
宫颈炎/子宮頸炎　cervicitis
宫颈锥切术/宮頸錐切術　conization of cervix
宫口扩张/宮口擴張　dilatation of cervix
宫内避孕器/宮內避孕器　intrauterine device
宫内避孕器排出/宮內避孕器排出　intrauterine device expulsion
宫内发育迟缓/宮內發育遲緩　intrauterine growth retardation
宫内感染/宮內感染　intrauterine infection
宫内感染结核病/宮內感染結核病　intrauterine infective tuberculosis
宫内人工授精/宮內人工授精　intrauterine insemination, IUI
宫腔镜/子宮鏡　hysteroscope
宫腔镜检查/子宮鏡檢查　hysteroscopy
宫腔吸片/宮腔吸片　hystero cavity aspirating smear
宫缩乏力/子宮無力　uterine inertia
宫缩应激试验/宮縮應激試驗　contraction stress test
宫外孕/宮外孕　eccyesis pregnancy
巩膜/鞏膜　sclera, sclerae
巩膜层间充填/鞏膜層間充填　scleral interlaminar implant
巩膜层间切除术/鞏膜層間切除術　interlamellar scleral resection
巩膜成形术/鞏膜造形術　scleroplasty
巩膜穿刺术/鞏膜穿刺術　sclerocentesis
巩膜刀/鞏膜刀　sclerotome
巩膜沟/鞏膜溝　scleral sulcus, scleral furrow
巩膜固有质/鞏膜固有質　proper substance of sclera
巩膜黑变病/鞏膜黑變病　scleral melanosis
巩膜虹膜切除术/鞏膜虹膜切除術　sclerectoiridectomy
巩膜虹膜切开术/鞏膜虹膜切開術　scleriritomy
巩膜虹膜炎/鞏膜虹膜炎　scleroiritis
巩膜坏死/鞏膜壞死　scleral necrosis
巩膜环扎术/鞏膜環扎術　scleral encircling operation
巩膜环钻/鞏膜環鑽　scleral trephine
巩膜环钻术/鞏膜環鑽術　scleral trephining
巩膜黄染/黃疸的鞏膜　icteric sclera
巩膜疾病/鞏膜疾病　scleral disease
巩膜构架组织/鞏膜構架組織　scleral framework
巩[膜]角膜/鞏角膜　sclerocornea
巩膜角膜部/鞏膜角膜部　corneoscleral part
巩膜角膜虹膜炎/鞏膜角膜虹膜炎　sclerokeratoiritis
巩膜接触镜/鞏膜接觸鏡　scleral contact lens
巩膜结膜炎/鞏膜結膜炎　scleroconjunctivitis

巩膜静脉/鞏膜静脈 scleral vein
巩膜静脉窦/鞏膜静脈竇 scleral venous sinus
巩膜距/鞏膜距 scleral spur
巩膜扣带术/鞏膜扣帶術 scleral buckling
巩膜脉络膜炎/鞏膜脈絡膜炎 sclerochoroiditis
巩膜膨隆/鞏膜膨隆 scleral ectasia
巩膜破裂/鞏膜破裂 scleral rupture
巩膜葡萄肿/鞏膜葡萄腫 scleral staphyloma
巩膜切除虹膜分离术/鞏膜切除虹膜分離術 sclerectoiridodialysis
巩膜切除术/鞏膜切除術,硬部切除术 sclerectomy
巩膜切开术/鞏膜切開術 sclerotomy
巩膜软化/鞏膜軟化 scleromalacia
巩膜筛板/鞏膜篩板 cribriform plate of sclera
巩膜缩短术/鞏膜縮短術 scleral shortening
巩膜透热法/鞏膜透熱法 scleral diathermy
巩膜外层/鞏膜上層 episcleral layer
巩膜外层炎/上鞏膜炎,外鞏膜炎 episcleritis
巩膜外动脉/鞏膜外動脈 episcleral artery
巩膜外静脉/鞏膜外静脈 episcleral vein
巩膜外隙/鞏膜外隙 episcleral space
巩膜炎/鞏膜炎 scleritis
巩膜咬切器/鞏膜咬切器 scleral punch
巩膜造口术/鞏膜造口術 sclerostomy
巩膜棕黑层/鞏膜棕黑層 lamina fusca sclerae
汞/汞 mercury
汞苯甲酸酯类/汞苯甲酸酯類 mercuribenzoates
汞毒性口炎/汞性口角炎 mercurial stomatitis
汞毒性溃疡/汞毒性潰瘍 mercurial ulcer
汞毒性龈炎/汞毒性齦炎 mercurial ulitis
汞放射性同位素/汞放射性同位素 mercury radioisotope
汞非林/汞非林 mercurophylline
汞合金/汞合金 amalgam
汞合金匙/汞合金匙 amalgam spoon
汞合金充填器/汞合金充填器 amalgam plugger
汞合金代型/汞合金鑄模 amalgam die
汞合金搅拌机/汞合金研製器 amalgamator
汞合金输送器/汞合金輸送器 amalgam carrier
汞合金纹身/汞齊紋身 amalgam tattoo
汞弧/汞弧 mercury arc
汞化合物/汞化合物 mercury compound
汞利尿药/汞利尿藥 mercurial diuretic
汞皮炎/汞皮炎 mercury dermatitis
汞撒利/墨沙利爾 mersalyl
汞色素沉着/汞色素沈著 mercury pigmentation
汞同位素/汞同位素 mercury isotope
汞溴红/紅溴汞 merbromin

汞制剂/汞劑 mercurial
汞中毒/汞中毒 mercury poisoning
汞中毒性坏死/汞中毒壞死 mercurial necrosis
汞中毒性精神病/汞毒性精神病 hydrargyromania
共病现象/共病現象 comorbidity
共沉淀素/共同沈澱素 coprecipitin
共扼雌激素类/共扼雌激素類 conjugated estrogens
共轭/共軛,接合[作用] conjugation
共轭肌/協合肌 yoked muscle
共轭焦点/共軛焦點 conjugate focus
共轭梯度法/共軛梯度法 conjugate gradient method
共轭亚油酸类/共軛亞油酸類 conjugated linoleic acids
共沸点/共沸點 azeotropic point
共沸法/共沸法 azeotropic method
共沸[混合]物/共沸[混合]物 azeotrope
共沸蒸馏/共沸蒸餾 azeotropic distillation
共合成/共合成 co-synthesis
共济失调/共濟不能 ataxia
共济失调步态/共濟不能性步態,失調性步態 ataxic gait
共济失调的/運動失調的 ataxic
共济失调计/共濟失調計 ataxiameter
共济失调毛细血管扩张症/運動失調微血管擴張症 ataxic telangiectasia
共济失调型失语症/共濟不能性失語症 ataxic aphasia
共济失调性毛细血管扩张/毛細血管擴張性失調 ataxia telangiectasia
共价键/共價鍵 covalent bond
共焦显微镜检查/共焦顯微鏡檢查 confocal microscopy
共聚体/共聚物 copolymer
共鸣的/共鳴的 consonant
共鸣电火花疗法/共鳴電火花療法 resonant electric spark therapy
共溶剂/共溶劑 cosolvent
共生/共生 symbiosis
共同沉淀/共沈澱 coprecipitate
共同房室瓣/共同房室瓣 common atrioventricular valve
共同房室通道/共同房室通道 common atrioventricular canal
共同径路/共同徑路 common pathway
共同抗原/共同抗原 common antigen
共同培养技术/共同培養技術 coculture technique
共同性内斜/共同性内斜 concomitant esotropia
共同性外斜/共同性外斜 concomitant exotropia

共同性斜视/共同斜視　concomitant strabismus
共同依赖性/共同依賴性　codependency
共同阵挛性痉挛/共同陣攣性痙攣　synclonic spasm
共显性/等顯性　codominance
共有决定簇/共有決定簇　public determinant
共有特异性/共有特異性　public specificity
共有序列/共有序列　consensus sequence
共振吸收/共振吸收　resonance absorption
共振[现象]/共響　resonance
共振效应/共振效應　resonance effect
共脂肪酶类/共脂肪酶類　colipases
共转染/共同感染　cotransfection
贡博-菲利普三角/Gombault-Philippe 二氏三角　Gombault-Philippe triangle
佝偻病/佝僂病　rickets, rachitis
佝偻病的/佝僂病的　rachitic
佝偻病·肺脾气虚证/佝僂病·肺脾氣虛證　rickets with pattern of qi deficiency of lung and spleen
佝偻病·肝肾阴虚证/佝僂病·肝腎陰虛證　rickets with pattern of liver-kidney yin deficiency
佝偻病·脾肾气虚证/佝僂病·脾腎氣虛證　rickets with pattern of qi deficiency of spleen and kidney
佝偻病·脾虚肝旺证/佝僂病·脾虛肝旺證　rickets with pattern of spleen deficiency and liver hyperactivity
佝偻病性骨疏松/佝僂病性骨疏鬆　rachitic osteoporosis
佝偻病性脊柱侧凸/佝僂病性脊柱側彎　rachitic scoliosis
沟/溝　vallecula
沟凹封闭剂/坑縫封閉物　pit and fissure sealant
沟后部/溝後部　postsulcal part
沟裂龈瘤/溝裂齦瘤　epulis fissuratum
沟前部/溝前部　presulcal part
沟通的/溝通的　communicating
沟通技能/溝通技巧　communication skill
沟形夹/溝狀夾板　gutter splint
沟缘束/溝緣束　sulcomarginal fasciculus
沟状骨折/溝狀骨折　gutter fracture
沟状伤/溝狀傷　gutter wound
沟状中线甲营养不良/溝樣中線甲失養症　dystrophia unguis mediana canaliformis
钩/鈎　uncus
钩虫/鈎蟲　hookworm
钩虫病/鈎蟲病　AAA disease, ancylostomiasis
钩虫感染/鈎蟲感染　hookworm infection
钩虫皮病/鈎蟲癬病　coolie itch
钩虫皮炎/鈎蟲皮炎　ancylostomatic dermatitis
钩虫痒病/土癬　ground itch
钩端螺旋体病/細螺旋體病　leptospirosis
钩端螺旋体尿/[鈎端]螺旋體尿　leptospiruria
钩端螺旋体肾病/鈎端螺旋體腎病　leptospiral nephropathy
钩端螺旋体属/鈎端螺旋體屬　*Leptospira*
钩端螺旋体[性]黄疸/膽性[類]傷寒　bilious typhoid
钩割法/鈎割法　hook-cutting therapy
钩骨/鈎骨　hamate bone
钩骨钩/鈎骨鈎　hamulus of hamate bone, hook of hamate bone
钩[骨]掌[骨]韧带/鈎掌韌帶　hamatometacarpal ligament
钩回静脉/鈎回靜脈　vein of uncus
钩束/鈎束　uncinate fasciculus
钩藤/鈎藤　gambir plant nod
钩突/鈎突　uncinate process
钩吻碱甲/鈎吻鹼,黃素馨素　gelsemine
钩吻中毒/鈎吻中毒　gelsemism, gelsemium poisoning
钩形切口/鈎形切口　hook incision
钩压法[止血]/鈎壓止血法　uncipressure
钩针/鈎針　hooked needle
钩针手/執鈎針手　main en crochet
钩状骨/鈎狀骨　hooked bone
狗传染性肝炎/狗傳染性肝炎　hepatits contagiosa canis
狗脊/狗脊　cibot rhizome
狗皮膏/狗皮膏　goupi plaster
枸杞子/枸杞子　barbary wolfberry fruit
构巢曲霉菌/小巢狀麴菌　Aspergillus nidulans
构成式/構造式　constitutional formula
构成细胞/構成細胞　formative cell
构词性失写症/構詞性失寫症　verbal agraphia
构架/架構　framework
构思障碍/構思障礙　dyssymbolia
构象分析/構象分析　conformational analysis
构象效应/構象效應　conformational effect
构象异构/構象異構　conformational isomerism
构象异构体/構象異構體　conformer
构效关系/構效關係　structure-activity relationship
构型/構型　configuration
构音不全/構音不能,構音障礙　anarthria
构音困难/構音困難,發音不良　dysarthria
构音困难手笨拙综合征/構音困難手笨拙症候群　dysarthria clumsy hand syndrome
孤雌卵块发育/孤雌無卵核發育　parthenogenetic merogony

孤雌生殖/孤雌生殖　parthenogenesis
孤独/孤獨　loneliness
孤独性障碍/孤獨性障礙　autistic disorder
孤儿病毒/孤病毒　orphan virus
孤儿院/孤兒院　orphanages
孤束核脊髓束/孤立脊徑　solitariospinal tract
孤立淋巴滤泡/孤立淋巴濾泡　solitary lymphatic follicle
孤立淋巴小结/孤立淋巴小結　solitary lymphoid nodule
孤立肾/單腎　solitary kidney
孤立性暴发性[精神]障碍/孤僻,暴躁障礙　isolated explosive disorder
孤立性非特异性溃疡/孤立性非特異性潰瘍　isolated nonspecific ulcer
孤立性肥大细胞增多症/孤立性肥大細胞增多症　solitary mastocytosis
孤立性和播散性表皮松解性棘皮瘤/孤立性和散播性表皮鬆解性棘皮瘤　solitary and disseminated epidermolytic acanthoma
孤立性淋巴细胞瘤/孤立性淋巴細胞瘤　solitary lymphocytoma
孤立性毛发上皮瘤/孤立性毛髮上皮瘤　solitary trichoepithelioma
孤立性毛囊角化症/單一毛囊角化症　isolated dyskeratosis follicularis
孤立性肾囊肿/孤立性腎囊腫　solitary renal cyst
孤立性血管角质瘤/孤立性血管角化瘤　solitary angiokeratoma
孤束/孤束　solitary tract
孤束核/孤束核　nucleus of solitary tract, solitary nucleus
姑息的/姑息的,舒緩的　palliative
姑息疗法/姑息療法　palliative care
菇/菇,蕈　mushroom
箍围疗法/箍圍療法　therapy of encircling lesion with drugs
箍围药/箍圍藥　encircling paste
古柏线虫/庫柏絲蟲屬之寄生蟲　cooperid
古典式电诊断法/古典式電診斷法　classical electrodiagnosis
古典式剖宫产术/古典式剖宮產術　classical cesarean section
古今医案按/古今醫案按　Comments on Ancient and Modern Case Records
古今医统大全/古今醫統大全　Medical Complete Book: Ancient and Modern
古柯/古柯　coca

古柯鞣酸/古柯鞣酸　cocatannic acid
古柯叶/古柯葉　spadic
古老血肿/古老血腫　ancient hematoma
古老痣/古老痣　ancient nevus
古龙水/古龍水　cologne
古马夫蒂夫细胞/鄰腎小球細胞　Goormaghtigh cell
古奇夹板/Gooch 氏夾板　Gooch splint
古热罗综合征/Gougerot 氏症候群　Gougerot syndrome
古特拉斯病/Guiteras 氏病　Guiteras disease
古铜色的/青銅色的　bronzed
古细菌病毒/古細菌病毒　archaeal viruse
古细菌蛋白质类/古細菌蛋白質類　archaeal proteins
古细菌基因/古細菌基因　archaeal gene
古细菌基因表达调控/古細菌基因表達調控　archaeal gene expression regulation
古细菌基因组/古細菌基因組　archaeal genome
古细菌抗体/古細菌抗體　archaeal antibody
古细菌抗原/古細菌抗原　archaeal antigen
古细菌染色体/古細菌染色體　archaeal chromosome
谷氨基酸脱氢酶/麩胺基酸脱氫酶　glutamic dehydrogenase
谷氨酸/麩胺酸　glutamic acid
谷氨酸-半胱氨酸连接酶/麩胺酸-半胱胺酸連接酶　glutamate-cysteine ligase
谷氨酸草酰乙酸转氨酶/麩醯胺酸草醯乙酸轉胺酶　glutamic oxaloacetic transaminase
谷氨酸合酶/麩胺酸合酶　glutamate synthase
谷氨酸 tRNA 连接酶/麩胺酸 tRNA 連接酶　glutamate-tRNA ligase
谷氨酸钠/麩胺酸鈉　sodium glutamate
谷氨酸受体/麩胺酸受體　glutamate receptor
谷氨酸羧肽酶Ⅱ/麩胺酸羧肽酶Ⅱ　glutamate carboxypeptidase Ⅱ
谷氨酸脱氢酶/麩胺酸去氫酶　glutamate dehydrogenase
谷氨酸脱羧酶/麩胺酸去羧酶　glutamate decarboxylase
谷氨酸盐/麩胺酸鹽　glutamate
谷氨酸盐类/麩胺酸鹽類　glutamates
谷氨酰氨肽酶/麩胺醯胺肽酶　glutamyl aminopeptidase
谷氨酰胺/麩胺醯胺　glutamine
谷氨酰胺-果糖-6-磷酸转氨酶/麩胺醯胺-果糖-6-磷酸轉胺酶　glutamine-fructose-6-phosphate transaminase
谷氨酰胺连接酶/麩胺醯胺連接酶　glutamate-ammonia ligase

谷氨酰胺酶/麩胺醯胺酶 glutaminase
谷疸/穀疸 dietary jaundice
谷蛋白/麩蛋白 gluten
谷蛋白敏感性肠病/麩膠敏感性腸病 gluten-sensitive enteropathy
谷的/谷的,溝的 vallecular
谷淀粉酶/穀澱粉酶,禾穀酵素 cerealin
谷固醇血症/穀固醇血症 sitosterolemia
谷胱甘肽/麩胺基硫 glutathione
谷胱甘肽二硫化物/麩胺基硫二硫化物 glutathione disulfide
谷胱甘肽过氧化酶/麩胺基硫過氧化酶 glutathione peroxidase
谷胱甘肽合酶/麩胺基硫合酶 glutathione synthase
谷胱甘肽还原酶/麩胺基硫還原酶 glutathione reductase
谷胱甘肽转移酶/麩胺基硫轉移酶 glutathione transferase
谷精草/穀精草 pipewort flower
谷粒支原体/穀粒黴漿菌 mycoplasma granularum
谷硫磷/穀硫磷 azinphosmethyl
谷芽/穀芽 millet sprout
谷痒病/穀癢病,草席病 straw itch
谷痒症/穀癢症 grain itch
谷甾醇/穀甾醇 sitosterol
股/股,大腿 thigh
股白肿/股白腫 phlegmasia alba dolens
股薄肌/股薄肌 gracilis muscle
股薄肌移植术/股薄肌移植術 gracilis transplantation
股薄肌转移肛门括约肌成形术/股薄肌轉移肛門括約肌成形術 gracilis muscle transfer and anal sphincteroplasty
股丛/股叢 femoral plexus
股的/股的 femoral
股动脉/股動脉 femoral artery
股动脉腘动脉分流术/股動脉膕動脉分流 femoropopliteal bypass
股动脉脉搏/股動脉脈搏 femoral artery pulse
股二头肌/股二頭肌 biceps femoris, biceps muscle of thigh
股二头肌长头/股二頭肌長頭 long head of biceps femoris
股二头肌短头/股二頭肌短頭 short head of biceps femoris
股二头肌囊/股二頭肌囊 bursa of biceps femoris
股二头肌上囊/股二頭肌上囊 superior bursa of biceps femoris
股二头肌下腱下囊/股二頭肌下腱下囊 inferior subtendinous bursa of biceps femoris
股方肌/股方肌 quadratus femoris, musculus quadratus femoris
股方肌神经/股方肌神經 nerve to quadratus femoris
股骨/股骨 femur, thigh bone
股骨凹/股骨窩 femoral fossa
股骨粗隆间骨折/股骨轉子間骨折 intertrochanteric fracture of femur
股骨粗线/股骨粗線 linea aspera of femur
股骨干骨折/股骨幹骨折 femoral shaft fracture, fracture of shaft of femur
股骨骨折/股骨折 femoral fracture
股骨环状韧带/股骨環狀韌帶 annular ligament of femur
股骨会阴部脱位/髖關節之會陰脫骭 luxatio perinealis
股骨解剖颈/股骨解剖頸 anatomical neck of femur
股骨颈/股骨頸 neck of femur, femur neck
[股骨颈]干角/[股骨頸]幹角 collodiaphyseal angle, neck-shaft angle of femur
股骨颈骨折/股骨頸骨折 femoral neck fracture, fracture of neck of femur
股骨颈缺血性坏死/股骨頸缺血性壞死 femoral neck avascular necrosis
股骨距/股骨距 femoral calcar
股骨髁骨折/股骨髁骨折 fracture of femoral condyle
股骨髁间骨折/股骨髁間骨折 intercondylar fracture of femur
股骨髁上骨折/股骨髁上骨折 femoral supracondylar fracture, supracondylar fracture of femur
股骨卵圆窝/股卵圓孔 fossa ovalis femoris
股骨内踝骨折/Stieda氏骨折 Stieda fracture
股骨内髁/股骨內髁 interal articular femoral condyle
股骨内上髁/股骨內上髁 medial epicondyle of femur
股骨前倾角/股骨前傾角 anteversion angle of femur
股骨体/股骨體 shaft of femur
股骨头/股骨頭 femoral head, femur head
股骨头凹/股骨頭凹 fovea of femoral head
股骨头骨骺骨软骨病/股骨頭骨骺骨軟骨病 legg-calve-perthes disease
股骨头坏死/股骨頭壞死 femur head necrosis
股骨头坏死·风寒湿阻证/股骨頭壞死·風寒濕阻證 femoralhead necrosis with wind-cold-dampness

obstruction pattern
股骨头坏死·肝肾亏虚证/股骨頭壞死·肝腎虧虛證 femoralhead necrosis with liver-kidney deficiency pattern
股骨头坏死·气血两虚证/股骨頭壞死·氣血兩虛證 femoralhead necrosis with qi-blood deficiency pattern
股骨头坏死·痰湿阻络证/股骨頭壞死·痰濕阻絡證 femoralhead necrosis with pattern of phlegm-dampness obstructing collateral
股骨头坏死·血瘀气滞证/股骨頭壞死·血瘀氣滯證 femoralhead necrosis with pattern of blood stasis and qi stagnation
股骨头缺血性坏死/股骨頭缺血性壞死 ischemic necrosis of head of femur
股骨头韧带/股骨頭韌帶 ligament of head of femur
股骨外髁/股骨外髁 external articular femoral condyle
股骨外上髁/股骨外上髁 lateral epicondyle of femur
股骨下滋养动脉/股骨下滋養動脈 inferior nutrient artery of femur
股骨肿瘤/股骨腫瘤 femoral neoplasm
股骨滋养动脉/股骨滋養動脈 femoral nutrient artery, nutrient artery of the femur
股管/股管 femoral canal, crural canal
股腘静脉/股膕靜脈 femoropopliteal vein
股后皮神经/股後皮神經 posterior femoral cutaneous nerve
股后区/股後部 posterior region of thigh
股环/股環 femoral ring
股环隔/股環隔 femoral septum
股肌/股肌 femoral muscle
股静脉/股靜脈 femoral vein
股静脉内侧回旋支/股靜脈內側迴旋支 medial circumflex femoral vein
股静脉血栓形成/股靜脈血栓形成 femoral thrombosis
股疽/股疽 thigh abscess
股蓝肿/股藍腫 phlegmasia cerulea dolens
股内侧肌/股內側肌 vastus medialis
股内侧肌间隔/股內側肌間隔 medial femoral intermuscular septum
股内侧肌间韧带/股內側肌間韌帶 medial intermuscular ligament of thigh
股内侧肌支/股內側肌支 medial femoral muscle branch
股内侧静脉/股內側靜脈 medial femoral vein
股内侧区/股內側部 medial region of thigh
股内收肌群损伤/股內收肌群損傷 injury of adductor of femur
股前皮静脉/股前皮靜脈 anterior femoral cutaneous vein
股前区/股前部 anterior region of thigh
股鞘/股鞘 femoral sheath
股三角/股三角 femoral triangle
股疝/股疝 crural hernia
股深动脉/股深動脈 deep femoral artery
股深静脉/股深靜脈 deep femoral vein
股神经/股神經 femoral nerve
股神经病/股骨神經病變 femoral neuropathy
股神经肌支/股神經肌支 muscular branch of femoral nerve
股神经牵拉试验/股神經牽拉試驗 femoral nerve stretching test
股神经前皮支/股神經前皮支 anterior cutaneous branch of femoral nerve
股四头肌/股四頭肌 quadriceps femoris
股四头肌成形术/股四頭肌成形術 quadricepsplasty
股四头肌肌腱/股四頭肌肌腱 tendon of quadriceps muscle of thigh
股痛/股痛 meralgia
股外侧肌/股外側肌 vastus lateralis
股外侧肌间隔/股外側肌間隔 lateral femoral intermuscular septum
股外侧肌间韧带/大腿外側肌間韌帶 external intermuscular ligament of thigh
股外侧静脉/股外側靜脈 lateral femoral vein
股外侧皮神经/股外側皮神經 lateral femoral cutaneous nerve, lateral cutaneous nerve of thigh
股癣/股癬 tinea cruris
股阴痛/股陰痛 thigh pain
股支/股支 femoral branch
股直肌/股直肌 rectus femoris
股直肌反折头/股直肌反折頭 reflected head of rectus femoris
股直肌直头/股直肌直頭 straight head of rectus femoris
股中间肌/股中間肌 vastus intermedius
股肿/股腫 deep vein thrombosis, thigh swelling
股肿·气虚湿阻证/股腫·氣虛濕阻證 thigh swelling with pattern of qi deficiency and dampness obstruction
股肿·气虚血瘀证/股腫·氣虛血瘀證 thigh swelling with pattern of qi deficiency and blood stasis
股肿·气滞血瘀证/股腫·氣滯血瘀證 thigh swelling with pattern of qi stagnation and blood stasis

股肿·湿热下注证/股腫·濕熱下注證　thigh swelling with pattern of dampness-heat diffusing downward
骨/骨　bone
骨板/骨板　bone lamella
骨半规管/骨半規管　bony semicircular canal
骨痹/骨痹　bone bi, bone bi-disease
骨痹·风寒湿阻证/骨痹·風寒濕阻證　bone bi with pattern of blockade of wind-cold-dampness
骨痹·风湿热郁证/骨痹·風濕熱鬱證　bone bi with pattern of wind-damp-heat stagnation
骨痹·肝肾阴虚证/骨痹·肝腎陰虛證　bone bi with pattern of liver-kidney yin deficiency
骨痹·气血两虚证/骨痹·氣血兩虛證　bone bi with pattern of deficiency of both qi and blood
骨痹·肾虚髓亏证/骨痹·腎虛髓虧證　bone bi with pattern of marrow insufficiency and kidney deficiency
骨痹·痰瘀互结证/骨痹·痰瘀互結證　bone bi with pattern of intermingling of phlegm and static blood
骨痹·阳虚寒凝证/骨痹·陽虛寒凝證　bone bi with pattern of yang deficiency and cold congelation
骨痹·瘀血闭阻证/骨痹·瘀血閉阻證　bone bi with pattern of blockade of static blood
骨瘭疽/骨瘭疽　bone felon
骨病/骨病　osteonosus, bone disease, osteopathy
骨病理学/骨病理學　osteopathology
骨病性脊柱侧凸/骨病性脊柱側彎　osteopathic scoliosis
骨病医学/骨病醫學　osteopathic medicine
骨部/骨部　bony part
骨擦感/骨擦感　bone friction feeling
骨擦音/骨擦音　bony crepitus
骨测量法/骨測量法，测骨法　osteometry
骨层/骨層　osteoplaque
骨成形瓣/骨成形瓣　osteoplastic flap
骨成形不全/骨形成不全，骨發育不全　anosteoplasia
骨成形的/骨成形的　osteoplastic
骨成形术/骨造形術，骨修補術　osteoplasty
骨成形性囊状纤维性骨炎/骨成形性囊狀纖維性骨炎　osteitis fibrosa osteoplastica
骨成形性死骨切除/骨造形死骨剔出術　osteoplastic necrotomy
骨齿发育不良/骨齒發育不全　skeletodental dysplasia
骨重建/骨重建　bone remodeling
骨出血/骨出血　osteorrhagia
骨穿刺术/骨穿刺術　osteostixis
骨传导音/骨傳導音　bone conduction sound
骨刺/骨刺　bony spur
骨刺丸/骨刺丸　guci pills
骨脆症/成骨不全症　osteopsathyrosis
骨错缝/骨錯縫　dislocation of bone, mild malposition of bone and joint
骨代用品/骨代用品　bone substitute
骨单位/骨單位　osteon
骨单位骨板/骨單位骨板　osteon lamella
骨导/骨傳導　bone conduction
骨导听力计/骨傳音計　osseosonometer
骨导听力检查/骨傳導檢法　osseosonometry
骨导助听器/骨導助聽器　ossiphone
骨的/骨的　osseous
骨钉/骨釘　bone nail
骨动脉瘤/骨動脈瘤　bone aneurysm
骨度/骨度　bone-length measurement
骨度折量定位法/骨度折量定位法　proportional bone measurement
骨端/肢，端　extremity
骨恶性纤维组织细胞瘤/骨惡性纖維組織細胞瘤　malignant fibrous histiocytoma of bone
骨腭/骨腭　bony palate
骨发育/骨發育　bone development
骨发育不良/骨質發育不良　osseous dysplasia
骨发育不全/骨發育不全，成骨不全　dysostosis
骨发育不全性骨折/發育性不全骨折　agenetic fracture
骨发育异常/骨發育異常　osteodysplasty
骨发育障碍矮小症/致密骨發育不全　pyknodysostosis
骨肥大症/骨肥大症　osteohypertrophy
骨肥厚/骨肥厚　hyperostosis
骨分离/骨分離　osteodiastasis
骨缝术/骨縫合術　osteorrhaphy
骨复折术/骨折分離手術　anarrhexis
骨钙素/骨鈣蛋白質　osteocalcin
骨钙质缺乏/骨[内鈣]質耗損　osteohalisteresis
骨感觉/骨覺　simesthesia
骨干/骨幹　diaphysis
骨干[部分]切除术/骨幹切除術　diaphysectomy
骨干发育不良/骨幹發育異常　diaphyseal dysplasia
骨干骺融合/骨幹骺湊合手術　diaphyseal-epiphyselfusion
骨干炎/骨幹炎　diaphysitis
骨骼/骨骼　ossature
骨骼肌/骨骼肌　skeletal muscle, somatic muscle
骨骼肌成肌细胞/骨骼肌成肌細胞　skeletal myoblast

骨骼肌肌球蛋白/骨骼肌肌球蛋白　skeletal muscle myosin
骨骼肌松弛药/骨骼肌鬆弛藥　skeletal muscle relaxant
骨骼肌卫星细胞/骨骼肌衛星細胞　skeletal muscle satellite cell
骨骼肌纤维/骨骼肌纖維　skeletal muscle fiber
骨骼肌心室/骨骼肌心室　skeletal muscle ventricle
骨骼论/骨骼論　skeletography
骨骼系统/骨骼系統　skeletal system
骨骼学家/骨骼學家　osteologist
骨骼折损/骨骼折損　bone fracture and injury
骨鲠/骨鯁　bone sticking
骨骨膜的/骨與骨膜的　osteoperiosteal
骨骨膜炎/骨質骨膜炎　osteoperiostitis
骨骨膜移植物/骨與骨膜移植物　osteoperiosteal graft
骨鼓传导/骨鼓傳導　osteotympanic conduction
骨固定钢丝/骨固定鋼絲　bone wire
骨关节病/骨關節病　osteoarthropathy
骨关节端切除术/骨關節切開術　ostearthrotomy
骨关节结核/骨關節結核　osteoarticular tuberculosis, tuberculosis of bone and joint, tuberculous osteoarthropathy
骨关节结核·气血两虚证/骨關節結核·氣血兩虛證　osteoarticular tuberculosis with qi-blood deficiency pattern
骨关节结核·阳虚痰凝证/骨關節結核·陽虛痰凝證　osteoarticular tuberculosis with pattern of yang deficiency and phlegm coagulation
骨关节结核·阴虚内热证/骨關節結核·陰虛內熱證　osteoarticular tuberculosis with pattern of yin deficiency and internal heat
骨关节炎/骨關節炎　osteoarthritis
骨管性面神经炎/輸卵管神經炎　fallopian neuritis
[骨]骺/骨骺　epiphysis
骨骺板/骨骺板　epiphyseal plate
骨骺点状发育不良/康拉迪病　Conradi disease
骨骺发育不良/骨骺發育異常　epiphyseal dysplasia
骨骺分离/骨骺分離　epiphyseal separation
骨骺损伤/骨骺損傷　epiphyseal injury
骨骺脱离/骨骺脫離　slipped epiphyse
骨骺线/骨骺線　epiphyseal line
骨骺增生/骨骺增生　epiphyseal hyperplasia
骨壶腹/骨壺腹　bony ampullae
骨滑膜炎/骨滑膜炎　osteosynovitis
骨化/骨化　ossification
骨化醇类/骨化醇類　ergocalciferols
骨化的/骨化，成骨　ossific
骨化二醇/骨化二醇　calcifediol
骨化过度/骨化過度　pleonosteosis
骨化内障/骨性内障　bony cataract
骨化脓/骨化膿　ostempyesis
骨化软骨膜/骨化軟骨膜　perisclerium
骨化三醇/鈣三醇　calcitriol
骨化三醇受体/骨化三醇受體　calcitriol receptor
骨化性骨炎/骨化性骨炎　osteitis ossificans
骨化性肌炎/骨化性肌炎　myositis ossificans, ossificans myositis, ossifying myositis
骨化性脑膜炎/骨化性腦膜炎　meningitis ossificans
骨化性纤维瘤/骨化性纖維瘤　ossifying fibroma
骨化性脂肪瘤/骨化性脂瘤　lipoma ossificans
骨化中心/骨化中心　ossification center
骨坏死/骨壞死　osteonecrosis
骨灰/骨灰　bone ash
骨基质/骨基質　bone matrix
骨基质明胶/骨基質明膠　bone matrix gelatin
骨疾病/骨疾病　bone disease
骨棘球蚴病/骨孢蟲[囊]病　osteohydatidosis
骨痂/骨痂　bony callus
骨痂形成不全/骨痂形成不全　hypoporosis
骨痂形成性软化/骨痂形成性軟化病　porotic malacia
骨架/骨架　skeleton
骨间/骨間的　interosseous
骨间背侧肌/骨間背側肌　dorsal interossei
骨间背侧腱膜/骨間背側腱膜　dorsal interosseous aponeurosis
骨间背侧神经/骨間後神經　posterior interosseous nerve
骨间返动脉/骨間返動脈　recurrent interosseous artery
骨间后动脉/骨間後動脈　posterior interosseous artery
骨间后静脉/骨間後靜脈　posterior interosseous vein
骨间肌征/骨間肌徵象　interossei sign
骨间前动脉/骨間前動脈　anterior interosseous artery
骨间前静脉/骨間前靜脈　anterior interosseous vein
骨间前神经/骨間前神經　anterior interosseous nerve
骨间韧带/骨間韌帶　interosseous ligament
骨间纤维软骨/結合性纖維軟骨，海綿狀纖維軟骨　connecting fibrocartilage
骨间缘/骨間緣　interosseous border
骨间掌侧肌/骨間掌側肌　palmar interossei, palmar interosseous muscle

骨间掌侧筋膜/骨間掌側筋膜　palmar interosseous fascia
骨间总动脉/骨間總動脈　common interosseous artery
骨间足底肌/骨間蹠側肌　plantar interossei
骨胶/骨膠　bone gelatin
骨胶原/骨膠原　ossein
骨胶[原]纤维/骨膠[原]纖維　bone collagen fiber
骨脚/骨腳　bony crura
骨节/骨節,生骨板　scleromere
骨结合/骨性連合,骨性接合　synostosis
骨静脉炎/骨静脈炎　osteophlebitis
骨巨细胞瘤/骨巨細胞瘤　giant cell tumor of bone
骨剧痛/劇性骨痛　osteocope
骨科/骨外科　department of orthopedics
骨科手法/骨科手法　orthopedic manipulation
骨科学/骨科學　osteology
骨科医院/骨科醫院　osteopathic hospital
骨库/骨庫　bone bank
骨蜡/骨蠟　bone wax
骨龄/骨骼成熟年齡　bone age
骨领/骨領　bone collar
骨瘤/骨瘤　bone tumor, osteoma, stony tumor sticking to bone
骨瘤病/骨瘤病　osteomatosis
骨瘤·脾肾两虚证/骨瘤·脾腎兩虛證　bone tumor with spleen kidney deficiency pattern
骨瘤·气血瘀阻证/骨瘤·氣血瘀阻證　bone tumor with pattern of qi-blood stasis and obstruction
骨瘤·热毒壅滞证/骨瘤·熱毒壅滯證　bone tumor with pattern of heat-toxin congestion and stagnation
骨瘤·肾虚痰凝证/骨瘤·腎虛痰凝證　bone tumor with pattern of kidney deficiency and phlegm coagulation
骨瘤·阴毒壅滞证/骨瘤·陰毒壅滯證　bone tumor with pattern of yin toxin congestion and stagnation
骨瘘/骨瘻　bone fistula
骨颅/骨[性頭]顱　osteocranium
骨论/骨論　osteography
骨螺丝/骨螺絲　bone screw
骨螺旋板/骨螺旋板　osseous spiral lamina
骨螺紫/紫螺酸銨,紫脲酸銨　murexide
骨梅毒/骨梅毒　osseous syphilis
骨迷路/骨質迷路,迷路骨性囊　bony labyrinth
骨密度/骨密度　bone density
骨密质/骨密質,密質骨　compact bone, cortical bone, dense bone
骨膜/骨膜　periosteum

骨膜板/骨膜板　periosteal lamella
骨膜刀/骨膜刀　periosteotome
骨膜的/骨膜的　periosteal
骨膜缝术/骨膜縫合術　periosteorrhaphy
骨膜骨/骨膜性骨　periosteal bone
骨膜骨炎/骨膜骨炎　periostosteitis
骨膜骨赘/骨膜骨贅　periosteophyte
骨膜骨赘形成/骨膜骨贅形成　periostosis
骨膜瘤/骨膜瘤　periosteoma
骨膜瘤形成/骨膜瘤形成　periosteosis
骨膜内骨折/骨膜內骨折　intraperiosteal fracture
骨膜切开术/骨膜切開術　periosteotomy
骨膜上浸润麻醉/骨膜上浸潤麻醉　supraperiosteal infiltration anesthesia
骨膜外面的/骨旁的,骨膜外的　parosteal
骨膜下的/骨膜下的　subperiosteal
骨膜下骨/骨膜下骨　subperiosteal bone
骨膜下骨折/骨膜下骨折　subperiosteal fracture
骨膜下横骨折/骨膜下橫骨折　fracture en rave
骨膜下浸润麻醉/骨膜下浸潤麻醉　subperiosteal infiltration anesthesia
骨膜下麻醉/骨膜下麻醉　subperiosteal anesthesia
骨膜下牙种植/骨膜下牙種植　subperiosteal dental implantation
骨膜下植入桥基/骨膜下植入橋基　subperiosteal implant abutment
骨膜下种植体/骨膜下種植體　subperiosteal implant
骨膜芽/骨膜芽　periosteal bud
骨膜炎/骨膜炎　cortical osteitis
骨膜移植物/骨膜移植物　periosteal graft
骨囊肿/骨囊腫　bone cyst
骨内板/骨内板　endosteal lamella
骨内袋/骨内袋　intrabony pocket
骨内的/骨内的　intraosseous
骨内动脉瘤/骨内動脈瘤　osteoaneurysm
骨内固定器种植体/骨内固定器種植體　endosseous stabilizer implant
骨内[静脉]血栓形成/骨内血栓形成　osteothrombosis
骨内麻醉/骨内麻醉法　intraosseous anesthesia
骨内膜/骨内膜,骨内衣,骨髓膜　endosteum
骨内膜炎/骨内膜炎　endosteitis
骨内输注/骨内輸注　intraosseous infusion
骨内牙种植/骨内牙種植　endosseous dental implantation
骨内叶状闭口种植体/骨内葉狀閉口種植體　endosteal blade-close implant
骨内叶状开口种植体/骨内葉狀開口種植體　endosteal blade-vent implant

骨内种植术/骨内種植術　endosseous implantation
骨内种植体/骨内種植體　endosteal implant
骨黏合剂/骨黏合劑　bone cement
骨黏合线/骨黏合線　bone cement line
骨黏素/骨黏液素　osseomucin
骨排列不齐/骨排列不齊　bone malalignment
骨旁骨肉瘤/骨膜外骨肉瘤　parosteal osteosarcoma
骨佩吉特病/柏哲德變形性骨炎　Paget disease of bone
骨盆/骨盆　pelvis
骨盆部脊椎炎/骨盆脊柱炎　pelvospondylitis
骨盆测量/骨盆測法,骨盆量法　pelvimetry
骨盆测量器/骨盆計　pelvimeter
骨盆出口/骨盆出口,骨盆下口　exitus pelvis, inferior pelvic strait
骨盆出口狭窄/骨盆出口狭窄　contracted pelvic outlet
骨盆丛/骨盆叢　pelvic plexus
骨盆底/骨盆底　pelvic floor
骨盆点/骨盆點　pelvic spot
骨盆骨/骨盆骨　pelvic bone
骨盆骨折/骨盆骨折　pelvic fracture
骨盆横径/骨盆橫徑　transverse diameter of pelvis
骨盆回旋试验/骨盆迴旋試驗　pelvic rotation test
骨盆挤压分离试验/骨盆擠壓分離試驗　pelvic compression and separation test
骨盆结核/骨盆結核　tuberculosis of pelvis
骨盆静脉曲张/骨盆靜脈腫　pelvic varicocele
骨盆镜/骨盆內視鏡　pelviscope
骨盆毛细血管/骨盆的微血管　pelvic capillary
骨盆面/骨盆面　pelvic surface
骨盆内测量/骨盆內測法　internal pelvimetry
骨盆内的/骨盆內的　intrapelvic
骨盆[内外径]合并测量法/骨盆聯合測法　combined pelvimetry
骨盆内移截骨术/骨盆內移截骨術　Chiari procedure
骨盆内脏神经/骨盆內臟神經　pelvic splanchnic nerve
骨盆平面/骨盆平面　pelvic plane
骨盆器官热疗器/骨盆器官加溫器　pelvitherm
骨盆器械测量法/骨盆器測法　instrumental pelvimetry
骨盆前列腺囊韧带/骨盆前列腺囊韌帶　pelviprostatic capsular ligament
骨盆腔/骨盆腔　pelvic cavity
骨盆切开术/骨盆切開術,盆骨切開術　pelvisection
骨盆倾斜度/骨盆傾度,骨盆傾角　inclination of pelvis

骨盆入口/骨盆入口,骨盆上口　superior pelvic strait
骨盆入口狭窄/骨盆入口狭窄　contracted pelvic inlet
骨盆上口/骨盆上口　pelvic inlet, superior pelvic aperture
骨盆肾/骨盆肾,腰肾　pelvic kidney
骨盆胎头测量法/骨盆内胎頭測演算法　pelvicephalometry
骨盆胎头X射线测量术/骨盆内胎頭X光測演算法　pelvicephalography
骨盆痛/骨盆痛　pelvic pain
骨盆外测量/骨盆外測法　external pelvimetry
骨盆下口/骨盆下口　inferior pelvic aperture, pelvic outlet
骨盆斜度计/骨盆傾角計　cliseometer
骨盆斜径/骨盆斜徑　oblique diameter of pelvis
骨盆型/骨盆型　pelvic type
骨盆粘连/骨盆内粘連　pelvic adhesion
骨盆直肠的/骨盆直腸的　pelvirectal
骨盆直肠窝脓肿/骨盆直腸膿腫　pelvirectal abscess
骨盆直径/骨盆直徑　anteroposterior diameter of pelvis, true conjugate diameter of pelvis
骨盆指量法/骨盆指測法　digital pelvimetry
骨盆轴/骨盆軸　pelvic axis
骨盆纵裂/骨盆縱裂　diastematopyelia
骨膨胀症/骨膨脹　osteoectasia
骨皮质/骨皮質　cortical bone
骨破坏/骨破壞　osteoclasia
骨牵引/骨[骼]牵引　skeletal traction
骨钳/骨鉗　bone forceps
骨嵌入移植术/骨嵌入移植術　inlay bone grafting
骨切除术/骨切除術　osteoectomy
骨肉瘤/骨肉瘤　osteosarcoma
骨软骨病/骨發育不良病　osteochondrosis
骨软骨发育不良/骨軟骨發育不良　osteochondrodysplasia
骨软骨骨折/骨軟骨骨折　osteochondral fracture
骨软骨瘤/骨軟骨瘤　osteochondroma
骨软骨瘤病/骨軟骨瘤病　osteochondromatosis
骨软骨肉瘤/骨軟骨肉瘤　osteochondrosarcoma
骨软骨纤维瘤/骨軟骨纖維瘤　osteochondrofibroma
骨软骨炎/骨軟骨炎　osteochondritis
骨软骨营养不良/骨軟骨營養不良　chondroosteodystrophy
骨软骨原细胞/骨軟骨原細胞　osteochondrogenic cell
骨软化性萎缩/骨軟化性萎縮　halisteretic atrophy
骨软化[症]/骨[質]軟化症,軟骨病　malacosteon
骨扫描/骨掃描　bone scan

骨闪烁测量/骨閃爍測量　bone scintimetry
骨伤病机/骨傷病機　pathogenesis of orthopedics and traumatology
骨烧伤/骨燒傷　burn of bone
骨神经痛/骨神經痛　osteoneuralgia
骨生成/骨生成　osteogenesis
骨生长因子/骨生長因子　skeletal growth factor
骨嗜酸细胞肉芽肿/骨嗜酸細胞肉芽腫　mignon eosinophilic granuloma
骨松质/骨鬆質,鬆質骨　cancellous bone, spongy bone
骨髓/骨髓　medulla ossium
骨髓白细胞/骨髓[系]白血球　myeloplast
骨髓病的/脊髓病的　myelopathic
骨髓病性贫血/骨髓原性貧血　myelopathic anemia
骨髓匙/骨髓匙　marrow spoon
骨髓的/骨髓[樣]的　myeloid
骨髓多核巨细胞/骨髓多核巨細胞　myeloplaque
骨髓发育不良/骨髓發育不良　osteomyelodysplasia
骨髓疾病/骨髓疾病　bone marrow disease
骨髓检查/骨髓檢查　bone marrow examination
骨髓净化/骨髓淨化　bone marrow purging
骨髓痨性护胸甲状麻木/骨髓癆性護胸甲狀麻木　tabetic cuirass
骨髓疗法/髓質療法　myelotherapy
骨髓瘤/骨髓瘤　myeloma
骨髓瘤蛋白/骨髓瘤性蛋白質　myeloma protein
骨髓瘤蛋白质类/骨髓瘤蛋白質類　myeloma proteins
骨髓瘤球蛋白/骨髓瘤球蛋白　myeloma globulin
骨髓瘤细胞/骨髓瘤細胞　myeloma cell
骨髓腔骨化/髓腔硬化　centro-osteosclerosis
骨髓腔积血/骨髓腔出血　hematosteon
骨髓腔内插钉术/骨髓内釘固定　intramedullary nailing
骨髓肉瘤病/骨髓肉瘤病　myelosarcomatosis
骨髓 X 射线照相术/骨髓 X 光攝影術　osteomyelography
骨髓外浆细胞瘤/髓外漿細胞瘤　extramedullary plasmacytoma
骨髓外造血/骨髓外造血　extramedullary hemopoiesis
[骨]髓细胞/骨髓細胞　marrow cell
骨髓细胞毒素/骨髓細胞毒素,溶髓細胞毒素　myelotoxin
骨髓细胞组织增生/骨髓細胞組織增生病　myelocytic leukosis
骨髓纤维化/骨髓纖維變性　myelofibrosis

骨髓性白血病/骨髓性白血病　myelogenous leukemia
骨髓性骨病/骨髓性骨病　myelogenic osteopathy
骨髓性红细胞过多症/骨髓性紅血球過多症　myelopathic polycythemia
骨髓性假白血病/骨髓性假白血病　myelogenous pseudoleukemia
骨髓炎/骨髓炎　carious osteitis, osteomyelitis
骨髓衍生细胞/骨髓衍生細胞　bone marrow derived cell
骨髓依赖淋巴细胞/骨髓依存性淋巴球　bone marrow-dependent lymphocyte
骨髓移植/骨髓移植　bone marrow transplantation
骨髓硬化/骨髓硬化　myelosclerosis
骨髓增生的/骨髓增生的　myeloproliferative
骨髓增生性疾病/骨髓增生性疾病　myeloproliferative disease
骨髓增生性综合征/骨髓增生性症候群　myeloproliferative syndrome
骨髓增生异常综合征/骨髓增生異常症候群　myelodysplastic syndrome
骨髓增殖性疾病/骨髓增殖性疾病　myeloproliferative disorder
骨髓中毒性/毒害骨髓性　myelotoxicity
骨髓肿瘤/骨髓腫瘤　bone marrow neoplasm
骨髓组织/骨髓組織　myeloid tissue
骨髓组织增生/骨髓組織增殖　myeloidosis
骨髓祖代细胞/骨髓祖代細胞　myeloid progenitor cell
骨碎补/骨碎補　fortune's drynaria rhizome
骨碎裂/骨碎裂　osteomiosis
骨贴附移植术/骨貼附移植術　onlay bone grafting
骨痛/骨痛　ostalgia, osteodynia
骨突病/骨凸病　apophyseopathy
骨突的/骨凸的　apophyseal
骨突炎/骨凸炎　apophysitis
骨突折断/骨凸折斷　apophyseal fracture
骨脱矿质技术/骨脱礦質技術　bone demineralization technique
骨外成釉细胞瘤/骨外成釉細胞瘤　extraosseous ameloblastoma
骨外的/骨外的　extraosseous
骨外骨肉瘤/骨外骨肉瘤　extraosseous osteosarcoma
骨萎缩/骨萎縮　bone atrophy
骨细胞/骨細胞　bone cell, osteocyte
骨下袋/骨下袋　infrabony pocket
骨下袋植骨术/骨下袋植骨術　bone grafting for infrabony pocket

骨纤维发育不良/纖維性骨結構不全　fibrous dysplasia of bone
骨纤维瘤病/骨纖維瘤病　osteofibromatosis
骨纤维软骨肉瘤/骨纖維軟骨肉瘤　osteofibrochondrosarcoma
骨陷窝/骨陷窩,骨腔隙　bone lacuna
骨小管/骨小管　canaliculi of bone, bone canaliculus
骨小梁/骨小梁　bone trabecula
骨形态生成蛋白/骨成形性蛋白質　bone morphogenetic protein
骨性半规管/骨性半規管　osseous semicircular canals
骨性鼻后孔/骨性鼻後孔　bony posterior nasal aperture
骨性鼻腔/骨性鼻腔　bony nasal cavity
骨性[鼻]中隔/骨性鼻中隔　osteoseptum
骨性分类/骨性分類　osseous classification
骨性关节炎/骨性關節炎　osteoarthritis
骨性关节炎·风寒湿阻证/骨性關節炎·風寒濕阻證　osteoarthritis with wind-cold-dampness obstruction pattern
骨性关节炎·肝肾亏虚证/骨性關節炎·肝腎虧虛證　osteoarthritis with liver-kidney deficiency pattern
骨性关节炎·瘀血阻络证/骨性關節炎·瘀血阻絡證　osteoarthritis with pattern of static blood obstructing collateral
骨性叩响/骨叩響　osteal resonance
骨性颞下颌关节强直/骨性顳下頜關節強直　bony ankylosis of TMJ
骨性牙质/骨[狀]齒質　osteodentin
骨学/骨學　osteology
骨血管发育不良/骨血管發育不全　osteovascular dysplasia
骨血色素沉着/骨血色病　osteohemachromatosis
骨血栓静脉炎/骨血栓性靜脈炎　osteothrombophlebitis
骨牙粘连/粘連牙　ankylosed tooth
骨牙质瘤/骨齒質瘤　osteodentinoma
骨延长术/骨延長術　bone lengthening
骨炎/骨炎　ostitis
骨盐/骨礦質　bone mineral, bone salt
骨样癌/骨樣癌　carcinoma osteoid ossificans
骨样动脉瘤/骨樣動脈瘤　osteoid aneurysm
骨样骨瘤/骨樣骨瘤　osteoid osteoma
骨样心/骨樣心　bony heart
骨样牙本质/骨樣牙本質　osteoid dentin
骨样牙骨质/骨性齒質　osteocementum
骨样组织/骨樣組織　osteoid tissue

骨移植/骨移植　bone transplantation
骨移植术/骨移植法　bone grafting
骨移植物/骨移植物　osseous graft
骨隐窝/骨隱窩　bone crypt
骨营养/骨營養　osteotrophy
骨营养不良/骨營養不良　osteodystrophia
骨营养不良性关节病/骨營養不良性關節病　osteodystrophic arthropathy
骨硬蛋白/骨擬蛋白素　osseoalbumoid
骨硬化/骨質石化　osteosclerosis
骨硬化病/骨質石化病　osteopetrosis
骨原细胞/骨原細胞　osteoprogenitor cell
骨圆凿/骨圓鑿　bone gouge
骨再生/骨再生　bone regeneration
骨再折/再骨折　refracture
骨凿/骨鑿　osteotome
骨粘连蛋白/骨結合素　osteonectin
骨折/骨折,斷折　fracture
骨折板/骨折板　fracture board
骨折不连接/骨折未愈合　ununited fracture
[骨折]不愈合/骨不愈合　nonunion
骨折床/骨折床　fracture bed
骨折钉/骨折釘　fracture nail
骨折·肝肾亏虚证/骨折·肝腎虧虛證　fracture with liver-kidney deficiency pattern
骨折固定术/骨折固定術　fracture fixation
骨折后发热/骨折熱　fracture fever
骨折后期疗法/骨折後期療法　fracture treatment in later stage
[骨折]畸形愈合/骨連接不正,骨折畸形愈合　malunion, malunion of fracture
骨折夹板/骨折夾板　fracture splint
骨折连接/骨折之連接　union of fracture
骨折·气血两虚证/骨折·氣血兩虛證　fracture with qi-blood deficiency pattern
骨折三期论治法/骨折三期論治法　treatment method of fracture in three stages
骨折脱位/骨折脫位　fracture dislocation
骨折箱/骨折箱　fracture box
骨折性水疱/骨折性水皰　fracture bulla
骨折学/骨折學,骨折論　agmatology
骨折·血瘀气滞证/骨折·血瘀氣滯證　fracture with pattern of blood stasis and qi stagnation
[骨折]延迟愈合/連接遲緩,骨折遲緩愈合　delayed union
骨折愈合/骨折愈合　fracture healing, union of fracture
骨折早期疗法/骨折早期療法　fracture treatment in

early stage
骨折中期疗法/骨折中期療法　fracture treatment in middle stage
骨针/骨針　bone spicule
骨蒸/骨蒸　bone steaming, hectic fever
骨整合/骨結閤　osseointegration
骨脂瘤/骨脂瘤　osteolipoma
骨脂软骨瘤/骨脂軟骨瘤　osteolipochondroma
骨质减少/骨質稀少　osteopenia
骨质迷离瘤/骨質迷離瘤　osseous choristoma
骨质溶解/骨質溶解,骨組織崩解　osteolysis
骨质溶解的/骨質溶解的,蝕骨的　ossifluent
骨质疏松/骨稀鬆病,骨疏鬆病　osteoporosis
骨质疏松伴结缔组织痣/骨質疏鬆伴結締組織痣　osteoporosis associated connective tissue naevus
骨质疏松症·脾气虚证/骨質疏鬆症·脾氣虛證　osteoporosis with spleen qi deficiency pattern
骨质疏松症·肾阳虚证/骨質疏鬆症·腎陽虛證　osteoporosis with kidney yang deficiency pattern
骨质疏松症·肾阴虚证/骨質疏鬆症·腎陰虛證　osteoporosis with kidney yin deficiency pattern
骨质疏松症·血瘀气滞证/骨質疏鬆症·血瘀氣滯證　osteoporosis with pattern of blood stasis and qi stagnation
骨质吸收/骨吸收　bone resorption
骨质稀疏性骨炎/骨質稀疏性骨炎　diffuse-rarefying osteitis
骨质象牙化/象牙質變性　eburnation
骨质形成/骨質形成　ostosis
骨[质]营养不良/骨發育不全　osteodystrophy
骨质再生/纖維質骨化　inostosis
骨质增生性骨炎/骨質增生性骨炎　formative osteitis
骨肿瘤/骨[腫]瘤　bone neoplasms, osseous tumor, tumour of bone
骨周炎/骨旁組織炎　parosteitis
骨赘/骨贅　osteophyma
骨赘病/骨贅形成　osteophytosis
骨组织/骨組織　bone tissue, osseous tissue
骨组织肿瘤/骨組織腫瘤　bone tissue neoplasm
钴/鈷　cobalt
钴胺酰胺类/鈷胺醯胺類　cobamides
钴尘肺/鈷塵肺　cobaltosis
钴放射性同位素/鈷放射性同位素　cobalt radioisotope
钴铬钼合金/鈷鉻鉬合金　vitallium
钴黄/鈷黃　aureolin
钴炮/鈷放射球　cobalt bomb

钴皮炎/鈷皮炎　cobalt dermatitis
钴同位素/鈷同位素　cobalt isotope
蛊/蠱　parasitic tympanites
蛊毒/蠱毒　toxin produced by poisonous parasites
蛊毒病/蠱毒病　parasite poison disease
蛊吐血/蠱吐血　hematemesis caused by poisonous parasites
鼓部/鼓部　tympanic part, pars tympanica
鼓槌体/鼓槌體　drumstick
鼓大棘/鼓大棘　greater tympanic spine
鼓镫连结/鼓鐙連接　tympanostapedial syndesmosis
鼓窦/鼓竇　tympanic sinus
鼓窦鼓室炎/鼓室竇炎　antrotympanitis
鼓窦炎/耳竇炎　otoantritis
鼓沟/鼓溝　tympanic sulcus
鼓环/鼓環　tympanic anulus, tympanic ring
鼓环点/鼓環點　tympanion
鼓环桥/鼓環橋　annulus bridge
鼓鳞裂/鼓鱗裂　tympanosquamous fissure
鼓膜/鼓膜　tympanic membrane
鼓膜按摩/鼓膜按摩　drum massage, tympanic membrane massage
鼓膜成形术/鼓膜成形術　myringoplasty
鼓膜穿刺术/鼓膜穿刺　tympanocentesis
鼓膜穿孔/鼓膜穿孔　tympanic membrane perforation
鼓膜刀/鼓膜刀　myringotome
鼓膜固定术/鼓膜固定術　myringostapediopexy
鼓膜后隐窝/鼓膜後隱窩　posterior recess of tympanic membrane
鼓膜紧张部/鼓膜緊張部　tense part of tympanic membrane
鼓膜霉菌病/鼓膜黴菌病　myringomycosis
鼓膜破裂/鼓膜破裂　myringorupture
鼓膜脐/鼓膜臍　umbo of tympanic membrane
鼓膜前隐窝/鼓膜前隱窩　anterior recess of tympanic membrane
鼓膜切除术/鼓膜切除術　myringectomy
鼓膜切开术/鼓膜切開術　myringotomy
鼓膜上隐窝/鼓膜上隱窩　superior recess of tympanic membrane
鼓膜松弛部/鼓膜鬆弛部　flaccid part of tympanic membrane
鼓膜外层炎/鼓膜外層炎　myringodermatitis
鼓膜纤维软骨环/鼓膜纖維軟骨環　fibrocartilaginous ring of tympanic membrane
鼓膜炎/鼓膜炎　myringitis
鼓膜造孔术/鼓膜造孔術　tympanostomy

鼓膜张肌/鼓膜張肌　tensor tympani
鼓膜张肌半管/鼓膜張肌半管　semicanal for tensor tympani, cochleariform fossa
鼓膜张肌神经/鼓膜張肌神經　nerve to tensor tympani, nerve of tensor tympani
鼓膜振动器/振動治聾器　vibrophone
鼓膜支/鼓膜支　branch of tympanic membrane
鼓膜锥隆起/鼓錐隆凸　pyramid of tympanum
鼓泡氧合柱/鼓泡氧合柱　bubble oxygenating column
鼓切迹/鼓切跡　tympanic notch
鼓乳裂/鼓乳突裂　tympanomastoid fissure
鼓舌骨/鼓舌骨　tympanohyal
鼓式取皮机/鼓式切皮器　drum dermatome
鼓室/鼓室　tympanic cavity, tympanum
鼓室丙烯酸酯成形术/鼓室丙烯成形術　tympanoacryloplasty
鼓室成形术/鼓室成形術　tympanoplasty
鼓室唇/鼓室唇　tympanic lip
鼓室丛/鼓室叢　plexus tympanicus
鼓室丛切除术/鼓室交感神經叢切除術　tympanosympathectomy
鼓室导抗图/鼓室壓圖　tympanogram
鼓室的/鼓室的　tympanic
鼓室盾板/鼓室盾板　tympanic scute
鼓室盖/鼓蓋　tegmen tympani
鼓室后动脉/鼓後動脈　posterior tympanic artery
鼓室积气/鼓室積氣　pneumotympanum
鼓室积水/鼓室積水　hydrotympanum
鼓室积血/鼓室積血　hemotympanum
鼓[室]阶/鼓階　scala tympani
鼓室静脉/鼓室靜脈　tympanic vein
鼓室隆起/鼓室隆起　tympanic swelling
鼓室脉络球/鼓室脈絡球　glomus tympanicum
鼓室迷路固定术/鼓室迷路固定術　tympanolabyrinthopexy
鼓室黏膜/鼓室黏膜　mucosa of tympanic cavity
鼓室前动脉/鼓前動脈　anterior tympanic artery
鼓室球瘤/鼓室球瘤　glomus tympanicum tumor
鼓室乳突炎/鼓室乳突炎　tympanomastoiditis
鼓室上动脉/鼓上動脈　superior tympanic artery
鼓室上隐窝/鼓上隱窩　epitympanum
鼓室神经/鼓室神經　tympanic nerve, nervus tympanicus
鼓室神经节/鼓室神經節　tympanic ganglion
鼓室神经痛/鼓室神經痛　tympanic neuralgia
鼓室切开术/鼓室探查術　tympanotomy
鼓室通气管/鼓室通氣管　grommet
鼓室下动脉/鼓下動脈　inferior tympanic artery
鼓室小房/鼓室小房　tympanic cells, cellulae tympanicae
鼓室小管/鼓小管　tympanic canaliculus
鼓室硬化/鼓膜硬化症　tympanosclerosis
鼓手麻痹/鼓手麻痺　drummer palsy
鼓索/鼓索[神經]　chorda tympani
鼓索襞/鼓索襞　fold of chorda tympani
鼓索交通支/鼓索交通支　communicating branch with chorda tympani
鼓索神经/鼓索神經　chorda tympani nerve
鼓索小管/鼓索小管　canaliculus for chorda tympani
鼓索小管鼓室口/鼓索小管鼓室口　tympanic aperture of canaliculus for chorda tympani
鼓索性涎/鼓室[性]涎　chorda saliva
鼓响/鼓響　tympanic resonance
鼓小房/鼓小房　tympanic cell
鼓小棘/鼓小棘　lesser tympanic spine
鼓型过滤机/鼓型過濾機　drum filter
鼓性叩响/鼓性叩響　tympanitic percussion resonance
鼓音/鼓音　tympany
鹘眼凝睛/鶻眼凝睛　staring falcon eye, exophthalmos, falcon fixed eye
鹘眼凝睛·气郁化火证/鶻眼凝睛·氣鬱化火證　staring falcon eye with pattern of stagnated qi transforming into fire
鹘眼凝睛·气滞痰凝证/鶻眼凝睛·氣滯痰凝證　staring falcon eye with pattern of qi stagnation and phlegm coagulation
鹘眼凝睛·阴虚血瘀证/鶻眼凝睛·陰虛血瘀證　staring falcon eye with pattern of yin deficiency and blood stasis
臌胀[病]/[腹部]鼓脹　tympanites
臌胀·肝脾血瘀证/臌脹·肝脾血瘀證　tympanites with pattern of blood stasis of liver and spleen
臌胀·肝肾阴虚证/臌脹·肝腎陰虛證　tympanites with pattern of liver-kidney yin deficiency
臌胀·寒湿凝滞证/臌脹·寒濕凝滯證　tympanites with pattern of stagnation and congelation of cold-damp
臌胀·脾肾阳虚证/臌脹·脾腎陽虛證　tympanites with pattern of yang deficiency of spleen and kidney
臌胀·脾虚湿困证/臌脹·脾虛濕困證　tympanites with pattern of damp retention due to spleen deficiency
臌胀·气滞湿阻证/臌脹·氣滯濕阻證　tympanites with pattern of qi stagnation and dampness

retention
臌胀·水热蕴结证/臌脹·水熱蘊結證 tympanites with pattern of accumulation and binding of water-heat
臌胀·阴虚水停证/臌脹·陰虛水停證 tympanites with pattern of water retention due to yin deficiency
臌胀·瘀结水留证/臌脹·瘀結水留證 tympanites with pattern of blood stasis binding and water retention
臌胀·正虚邪恋证/臌脹·正虛邪戀證 tympanites with pattern of lingering pathogen due to vital qi deficiency
固崩止带剂/固崩止帶劑 formula for arresting leucorrhea and metrorrhagia
固表止汗/固表止汗 consolidating exterior for arresting sweating
固表止汗剂/固表止汗劑 formula for consolidating exterior for arresting sweating
固齿/固齒 strengthening teeth
固冲汤/固沖湯 guchong decoction
固冲止带/固沖止帶 consolidating Chong Vessel for stopping leukorrhagia
固唇器/固唇器 labiotenaculum
固醇/固醇 sterol
固氮酶/氮催化酶 nitrogenase
固氮酶还原酶/雙氮酶還原酶 dinitrogenase reductase
固氮铁钼蛋白/固氮鐵鉬蛋白 molybdoferredoxin
固氮作用/氮固定 nitrogen fixation
固定/固定 fixation
固定半径/定半徑 radius fixus
固定绷带/固定繃帶 immovable bandage
固定[病位]性癔病/固定性癔病 fixation hysteria
固定带/固定環 anchor band
固定垫/固定墊 pressure pad
固定毒株/固定病毒 fixed virus
固定方法/固定方法 fixation method
固定敷裹/固定敷料 fixed dressing
固定化酶/固化酶 immobilized enzyme
固定化细胞/固定化細胞 immobilized cells
固定肌/固定肌 fixation muscle
固定剂/固定劑 fixative
固定矫治器/固定矯治器 fixed appliance
固定痉挛/固定痙攣 lock spasm
固定巨噬细胞/固定巨噬細胞,固著型巨噬細胞 fixed macrophage
固定开睑器/固定開瞼器 stop speculum
固定连接体/固定連接體 rigid connector

固定黏膜/固定黏膜 immobile type mucosa
固定频率起搏器/固定頻率起搏器 fixed rate pacemaker
固定桥/弓形牙橋 fixed bridge
固定绒毛/固定絨毛,固著絨毛 anchoring villus
固定溶液/固定溶液 fixing solution
固定式眼架/固定檢眼鏡 phoroscope
固定视野/固定視野 field of fixation
固定[术]/固定[法],固定手術 fixation
固定吞噬细胞/固著性吞噬細胞 sessile phagocyte
固定细胞/固定細胞 fixed cell
固定相涂布/固定相塗布 stationary phase coating
固定性药疹/固定藥疹 fixed drug eruption
固定修复术/固定修復術 fixed prothesis
固定血膜/固定性血液塗片 fixed blood film
固定液/固定液 fixation fluid
固定义齿修复学/固定義齒修復學 fixed prosthodontics
固定疹/固定疹 fixed eruption
固化剂/固化劑 curing agent
固结/固結 consolidation
固经丸/固經丸 gujing pills
固经止血/固經止血 consolidating channel for hemostasis
固涩法/固澀法 astringing method
固涩剂/固澀劑 astringent formula
固涩敛乳/固澀斂乳 astringing for arresting lactation
固摄止血/固攝止血 astringing for hemostasis
固缩红细胞/固縮紅血球 pyknocyte
固缩后的/[紅血球]皺縮後的 postpycnotic
固体/固體 solid
固体病理学/固體病理學 solidistic pathology
固体分散物/固態分散劑 solid dispersion
固体绿/固體綠,孔雀綠 solid green
固体囊状汗腺腺瘤/固體囊狀汗腺腺瘤 solid cystic hydradenoma
固体溶液/固態溶液,固態溶劑,固溶體 solid solution
固体食物/固體食物 solid diet
固位/固定 immobilization
固位带环/固位帶環 attachment band
固位器/固位器 retaining device
固位体/保留器,保持器 retainer
固位形/固位形 retention form
固位指/固位指 retention finger
固相反应/固態反應 solid state reaction
固相酶/固相酶 insoluble enzyme

固相酶类/固相酶類　immobilized enzymes
固有层/固有層　lamina propria
固有肠系膜/固有腸繫膜　proper mesentery
固有缝间骨/固有縫間骨　proper epactal bone
固有结缔组织/固有結締組織　connective tissue proper
固有口腔/固有口腔　oral cavity proper
固有滤过作用/固有過濾　built-in filtration
固有酶/固有酵素　constitutive enzyme
[固有]食管腺/[固有]食管腺　esophageal gland proper
固有束/基束　basis bundle
固有小指伸肌/固有伸小指肌　proper extensor muscle of the fifth digit
固有心率/固有心率　inherent heart rate
固有牙槽骨/固有牙槽骨　proper alveolar bone
固阵/固陣　securing array
固着绒毛/固定絨毛　anchoring villus
雇员保健福利计划/雇員保健福利計劃　employee health benefit plan
雇主承担保健费用/雇主承擔保健費用　employer health cost
瓜氨酸/瓜胺酸　citrulline
瓜氨酸尿/西瓜胺基酸尿　citrullinuria
瓜氨酸血症/西瓜胺基酸血症　citrullinemia
瓜蒂散/瓜蒂散　guadi powder
瓜尔涅里包涵体/瓜爾涅里包涵體　Guarnieri inclusion body
瓜瓠瘟/瓜瓠瘟　gourd-like pestilence
瓜蒌/瓜蔞　snakegourd fruit
瓜蒌皮/瓜蔞皮　snakegourd peel
瓜蒌子/瓜蔞子　snakegourd seed
瓜鲁病毒/Guaroa 病毒　Guaroa virus
瓜纳瑞托病毒/瓜納瑞託病毒　Guanarito virus
瓜藤缠/瓜藤纏　erythema nodosum, vine tangling
瓜藤缠·寒湿瘀滞证/瓜藤纏·寒濕瘀滯證　vine tangling with pattern of cold-dampness stasis and stagnation
瓜藤缠·气滞血瘀证/瓜藤纏·氣滯血瘀證　vine tangling with pattern of qi stagnation and blood stasis
瓜藤缠·湿热下注证/瓜藤纏·濕熱下注證　vine tangling with pattern of dampness-heat diffusing downward
刮/刮　scrape
刮匙/刮匙　curette
刮除术/刮除術　curettement
刮法/刮法　needle-handle scraping
刮宫术/子宫内膜刮除術　dilatation and curettage
刮痧疗法/刮痧療法　scrapping therapy
刮痧损伤/刮沙損傷　coin-rubbing injury
刮治/刮治　scaling
胍/胍　guanidine
胍丁胺/精胺　agmatine
胍法辛/胍法辛　guanfacine
胍类/胍類　guanidines
胍那苄/胍那苄　guanabenz
胍乙啶/胍乙啶　guanethidine
胍唑/胍那唑　guanazole
寡核苷酸类/寡核苷酸類　oligonucleotides
寡核苷酸探针/寡聚核苷酸探針　oligonucleotide probe
寡核苷酸序列分析/寡核苷酸序列分析　oligonucleotide array sequence analysis
寡核糖核苷酸类/寡核糖核苷酸類　oligoribonucleotides
寡聚体/寡聚體　oligomer
寡克隆区带/寡克隆區帶　oligoclonal bands
寡霉素类/寡黴素類　oligomycins
寡肽/寡肽　oligopeptide
寡肽类/寡肽類　oligopeptides
寡糖/寡糖　oligosaccharide
寡糖类/寡糖類　oligosaccharides
寡脱氧核糖核苷酸类/寡去氧核糖核苷酸類　oligodeoxyribonucleotides
寡欲/寡欲　having few worldly desire
挂号/掛號　registration
挂号处/報到處　registration office
挂线法/掛線法　seton cutting method
挂线疗法/掛線療法　therapy of cutting with thread ligation
乖戾精神病/乖僻精神病　parergastic
拐杖/拐杖　crutch
拐杖瘫痪/拐杖癱瘓　crutch palsy
怪脉/怪脈　paradox pulse
怪僻的/怪癖的　eccentric
关冲/關沖　guanchong, SJ1
关格/關格　anuria and vomiting, dysuria and frequent vomiting
关格·脾肾气虚湿热内蕴证/關格·脾腎氣虛濕熱內蘊證　dysuria and frequent vomiting with pattern of qi deficiency of spleen and kidney and internal retention of damp-heat
关格·肾衰邪陷证/關格·腎衰邪陷證　dysuria and frequent vomiting with pattern of pathogen invasion due to kidney failure

关格·虚风内动证/關格·虛風內動證 dysuria and frequent vomiting with pattern of internal stirring of deficient wind
关格·阳虚寒湿内蕴证/關格·陽虛寒濕內蘊證 dysuria and frequent vomiting with pattern of internal retention of cold-damp due to yang deficiency
关格·阳虚湿浊内蕴证/關格·陽虛濕濁內蘊證 dysuria and frequent vomiting with pattern of internal retention of damp-turbidity due to yang deficiency
关格·浊邪侵犯上焦证/關格·濁邪侵犯上焦證 dysuria and frequent vomiting with pattern of turbid pathogen invading upper jiao
关格·浊邪侵犯下焦证/關格·濁邪侵犯下焦證 dysuria and frequent vomiting with pattern of turbid pathogen invading lower jiao
关格·浊邪侵犯中焦证/關格·濁邪侵犯中焦證 dysuria and frequent vomiting with pattern of turbid pathogen invading middle jiao
关键点/關鍵點 key point
关键工艺/關鍵制程 critical process
关键期/關鍵期 critical period
关节/關節 arthrosis, articulartion, joint
关节凹/關節凹 articular fovea
关节板滑脱/關節板滑脱 slip meniscus
关节半月板/關節半月板 articular meniscus
关节变形/關節變形 deformed joint
关节病/關節病 arthrosis
关节病变/關節病變 arthropathy
关节病理学/關節病理學 arthropathology
关节病素质/關節病質 arthritism
关节病型/關節病型 arthropathica
关节病型银屑病/關節病型乾癬 arthropathic psoriasis
关节病性银屑病/關節病性銀屑病 psoriasis arthropathica
关节病性指弯曲/關節病性指彎曲 arthropathy-camptodactyly
关节病性指弯曲综合征/關節病性指彎曲症候群 arthropathy-camptodactyly syndrome
关节病性趾弯曲/關節病性趾彎曲 arthropathy-camptodactyly
关节病性趾弯曲综合征/關節病性趾彎曲症候群 arthropathy-camptodactyly syndrome
关节不稳定性/關節不穩定性 joint instability
关节成形术/關節成形術,關節造形術 arthroplasty
关节充气造影术/關節充氣攝影術 arthropneumography
关节充气[造影]照片/充氣關節X光線照片 pneumarthrogram
关节穿刺术/關節穿刺術 arthrocentesis
关节唇/關節唇 articular labrum
关节丛/關節叢 plexus articularis
关节刀/關節刀 arthrotome
关节的/關節的 articular
关节点/關節點 articulare
关节动度测量法/關節運動測定法 arthrometry
关节动度计/關節測定器 arthrometer
关节发育不良/關節發育障礙 arthrodysplasia
关节分离/關節分離 dislocation of articular process
关节风湿病/關節風濕病 arthrorheumatism
关节钙化/關節鈣化 articular calcification
关节感觉/關節感覺 joint sense
关节骨偏斜/關節錯列 clinarthrosis
关节骨炎/關節骨炎 arthrosteitis
关节骨折/關節骨折 joint fracture
关节刮术/關節刮術 erasion of a joint
关节红肿/關節紅腫 redness and swelling of joint
关节滑膜炎/關節滑膜炎 arthrosynovitis
关节化脓/關節化膿 arthroempyesis
关节活动度/關節活動度 range of motion
关节活动度测量/關節活動度測量 measurement of range of motion
关节活动范围/關節活動範圍 articular range of motion
关节肌/關節肌 articular muscle
关节积脓/關節積膿 empyema articuli
关节积水/關節積水 hydrarthrosis
关节积血/關節積血 hemarthrosis
关节积脂血病/脂血關節症 lipohemarthrosis
关节疾病/關節疾病 joint disease
关节间纤维软骨/關節間纖維軟骨 fibroplate
关节僵硬/關節僵硬,關節硬化 arthrosclerosis, joint stiffness
关节结节/關節結節 articular tubercle
关节镜/關節鏡 arthroscope
关节镜检查/關節鏡檢查 arthroscopy
关节离断术/關節截斷術 disarticulation
关节挛缩/關節彎曲,關節強硬 arthrogryposis
关节螺旋体病/關節螺旋體病 spirochetosis arthritica
关节面/關節面 articular surface
关节面骨折/關節面骨折 articular surface fracture
关节[面]刮[除]术/關節刮除術 arthroxesis
关节囊/關節囊 articular capsule

关节囊成形术/關節囊造形術　capsuloplasty
[关节]囊缝合术/[關節]囊縫術　capsulorrhaphy
关节囊内骨折/關節囊内骨折　intracapsular fracture
关节囊内强直/囊内性關節粘連　intracapsular ankylosis
关节囊切除术/關節囊切除術　articular capsulectomy
关节囊切开术/關節囊切開術　articular capsulotomy
[关节]囊外的/關節囊外的　extracapsular
关节囊外骨折/關節囊外骨折　extracapsular fracture
关节囊外强硬/囊外性關節粘連　extracapsular ankylosis
关节囊纤维膜/關節囊纖維膜　fibrous membrane of articular capsule
关节内[触觉]小体/關節小體　articular corpuscle
关节内的/關節内的　intra-articular
关节内骨折/關節内骨折　intra-articular fracture
关节[内窥]镜/關節内視鏡　arthroscope
关节内陷/關節内陷　arthrokatadysis
关节内注射/關節内注射　intra-articular injection
关节盘/關節盤　articular disc
关节盘炎/關節間盤炎　discitis
关节腔/關節腔　articular cavity
关节腔充气[透视]法/關節腔充氣法　pneumoserosa
关节强硬恐怖/關節粘連恐懼症　ankylophobia
关节强直/關節强直,關節粘連　ankylosis
关节切除术/關節切除術,關節截除術　arthrectomy
关节切开术/關節切開術　arthrotomy
关节屈度计/關節屈度計　fleximeter
关节韧带/關節韌帶　articular ligament
关节融合/關節融合　fusion of joint
关节融合术/關節融合術　arthrodesis
关节软骨/關節軟骨　articular cartilage
关节软骨板/關節軟骨板　articular lamella
关节软骨钙沉着病/關節軟骨鈣沈著症　chondrocalcinosis articularis
关节软骨炎/關節軟骨炎　arthrochondritis
关节烧伤/關節燒傷　burn of joint
关节X射线照片/關節X光照片　arthrogram
关节神经/關節神經　articular nerve
关节神经痛/關節神經痛　articular neuralgia
关节石/關節結石　arthrolith
关节松弛/關節鬆弛　arthrochalasis
关节松解术/關節鬆解術　arthrolysis
关节痛/關節痛　arthralgia
关节痛风/關節痛風　articular gout
关节头/關節頭　articular head
关节突关节/關節突[間]關節　zygapophysial joint
关节脱位/關節脱位　dislocation of joint
关节外的/關節外的　abarticular
关节外痛风/非關節性痛風　abarticular gout
关节窝/關節窝　articular fossa, glenoid fossa
关节性胼胝/關節胼胝　articular callosity
关节学/關節學　arthrology
关节血管环/關節血管環　articular vascular circle
关节血管网/關節血管網　articular vascular rete
关节炎/關節炎　arthritis
关节炎患者/關節炎患者　arthritic
关节炎性痤疮/關節炎性痤瘡　arthritic acne
关节炎性红斑/關節炎性紅斑　erythema arthriticum
关节炎[性皮]疹/關節炎疹　arthritide
关节炎性银屑病/關節炎性乾癬　arthritic psoriasis
关节炎支原体/關節炎支原體　mycoplasma arthritidis
关节疡/關節疽　arthrocace
关节音图/關節移動之音像圖　acoustigram
关节硬化/關節硬化,關節僵硬　arthrosclerosis, joint stiffness
关节游离体/關節游離體　joint loose body
关节盂/關節盂　glenoid cavity
关节盂面/關節盂面　glenoid surface
关节盂韧带/關節盂韌帶　glenoid ligament
关节盂下脱臼/關節盂下脱位　subglenoid dislocation
关节盂缘/[關節]臼緣　ambo
关节[与]甲发育不良/關節及指(趾)甲發育不良　arthro-onychodysplasia
关节[与]眼病/關節與眼病　arthro-ophthalmopathy
关节造口术/關節造口術,關節造瘻術　arthrostomy
关节造影术/關節X光攝影術　arthrography
关节粘连/關節粘連　synarthrophysis
关节支/關節支　articular branch
关节脂肪组织炎/關節脂肪組織炎　lipoarthritis
关节制动术/關節制動手術　arthroereisis
关节肿大/關節腫大　arthrocele
关节周肌萎缩/關節萎縮　arthritic atrophy
关节周围的/關節周圍的　periarticular
关节周围骨折/關節周圍骨折　periarticular fracture
关节周围囊肿/關節周圍囊腫　periarticular cyst
关节周围炎/關節周圍炎　periarthritis
关节注气检查法/關節注氣檢查法　hydropneumogony
关节赘疣/關節贅疣,關節小體,關節鼠　arthrophyte
关节阻断/關節阻斷　articular block
关连性萎缩/關聯性萎縮　correlated atrophy
关门/關門　guanmen, ST22
关木通/關木通　Manchurian dutchmanspipe stem

关系妄想/關係妄想 delusion of reference
关元/關元 guanyuan, RN4
关元俞/關元俞 guanyuanshu, BL26
观测线/觀測線 survey line
观法/觀法 guan cultivation or reflection method
观念倒错/觀念倒錯 ideophrenia
观念的/觀念力的,聯想力的 ideational
观念性失用[症]/聯想障礙性失用症 ideational apraxia
观神色/觀神色 inspection of vitality and complexion
观想/觀想 immersive thinking
观隐/觀隱 observing interior
官方医学代表团/官方醫學代表團 official medical mission
官能团/官能基 functional group
官能团保留指数/官能團滯留指數 functional retention index
冠/冠 crown
冠额指数/頂額指數 coronofrontal index
冠缝点/冠縫點 coronale
冠醚类/冠醚類 crown ethers
冠内固位/冠内固位 intracoronal retention
冠内固位体/冠内固位體 intracoronal retainer
冠内空隙/冠内空隙 intracoronal space
冠颞点/冠顳點 stephanion
冠桥学/冠橋學 crown and bridge prosthetics
冠丝虫病/冠絲蟲病,蠕蟲皮膚病 stephanofilariasis
冠套连接杆/中位構造連接桿 mesostructure conjunction bar
冠突/冠狀突 coronoid process
冠突窝/喙狀窩 coronoid fossa
冠外固位/冠外固位 extracoronal retention
冠向复位瓣/冠向復位瓣 coronally repositioned flap
冠心病监护治疗病房/冠心病監護治療病房 coronary care unit
冠心病重症监护病房/冠心病重症監護病房 coronary care unit
冠心苏合丸/冠心蘇合丸 guanxin suhe pills
冠形锯/冠狀鋸,環鋸 crown saw
冠周炎/齒冠周圍齦炎 pericoronitis
冠状/冠[狀] corona
冠状病毒感染/冠狀病毒感染 coronavirus infection
冠状病毒科感染/冠狀病毒科感染 Coronaviridae infection
冠[状]的/冠狀的 coronary
冠状垫/冠狀墊 coronary cushion
冠状动静脉瘘/冠狀動靜脈瘻 coronary arteriovenous fistula

冠状动脉/冠狀動脈 coronary artery
冠状动脉斑块切除术/冠狀動脈斑塊切除術 coronary atherectomy
冠状动脉闭塞/冠狀動脈閉塞 coronary occlusion
冠状动脉侧支血流/冠狀動脈側支血流 coronary collateral flow
冠状动脉侧支循环/冠狀動脈側支循環 collateral coronary circulation
冠状动脉导管/冠狀動脈導管 coronary catheter
冠状动脉盗血综合征/冠狀動脈盜血症候群 coronary steal syndrome
冠状动脉分流术/冠狀動脈分流術 coronary artery bypass
冠状动脉功能不全/冠狀動脈功能不全 coronary insufficiency
冠状动脉灌注/冠狀動脈灌注 coronary perfusion
冠状动脉后降支/後降冠狀動脈 posterior descending coronary artery
冠状动脉疾病/冠狀動脈疾病 coronary arterial disease
冠状动脉流入血流/冠狀動脈流入血流 coronary arterial inflow
冠状动脉瘤/冠狀動脈瘤 coronary aneurysm
冠状动脉瘘/冠狀動脈瘻 coronary artery fistula
冠状动脉内血栓溶解/冠狀動脈內血栓溶解 intracoronary thrombolysis
冠状动脉旁路移植术/冠狀動脈旁路移植術 coronary artery bypass grafting
冠状动脉栓塞/冠狀動脈栓塞 coronary embolism
冠状动脉完全性动脉化旁路移植术/冠狀動脈完全性動脈化旁路移植術 coronary total arterialized bypass grafting
冠状动脉无再灌注现象/冠狀動脈無再灌注現象 coronary no reperfusion phenomenon
冠状动脉狭窄/冠狀動脈狹窄 coronary stenosis
冠状动脉性传导阻滞/冠狀動脈性傳導阻滯 coronary block
冠状动脉血流/冠狀動脈血流 coronary blood flow
冠状动脉血栓形成/冠狀動脈血栓 coronary thrombosis
冠状动脉血吸引装置/冠狀動脈血吸引裝置 coronary suction device
冠状动脉循环/冠狀[動脈]循環 coronary circulation
冠状动脉炎/冠狀動脈炎 coronaritis
冠状动脉异常起源/冠狀動脈異常起源 anomalous origin of coronary artery
冠状动脉硬化/冠狀動脈硬化 coronary

arteriosclerosis
冠状动脉再狭窄/冠狀動脈再狹窄　coronary restenosis
冠状动脉粥样硬化性心脏病/冠狀動脈粥樣硬化性心臟病　coronary atherosclerotic heart disease
冠状动脉综合征/冠狀動脈症候群　coronary syndrome
冠状窦/冠狀竇　coronary sinus
冠状窦瓣/冠狀竇瓣　valve of coronary sinus
冠状窦口/冠狀竇口　orifice of coronary sinus
冠状窦逆行灌注/冠狀竇逆行灌注　coronary sinus retrograde perfusion
冠状缝/冠狀縫　coronal suture, arcuate suture
冠状沟/冠狀溝　coronary sulcus
冠状骨/冠狀骨　coronary bone
冠状静脉/冠狀靜脈　coronary vein
冠状静脉窦型房间隔缺损/冠狀靜脈竇型房間隔缺損　coronary sinus atrial septal defect
冠状面/冠狀面　coronal plane
冠状切口/冠狀切口　coronal incision
冠状韧带/冠狀韌帶　coronary ligament
冠状血管/冠狀血管　coronary vessel
冠状血管畸形/冠狀血管畸形　coronary vessel anomaly
冠状血管痉挛/冠狀血管痙攣　coronary vasospasm
冠状血管扩张药/冠狀血管擴張藥　coronary vasodilator
冠状血管造影术/冠狀血管造影術　coronary angiography
冠状血管阻力/冠狀血管阻力　coronary vascular resistance
冠状轴/冠狀軸　frontal axis
管/管　canal, duct
管胞/管胞　tracheid
管道工痒症/鉛管工人發癢症　plumber itch
管的/管的　tubal
管碟法/圓筒平碟法　cup-plate method
管间的/管間的　intertubular
管口外科医师/孔口專家　orificialist
管理服务组织/管理服務組織　management service organization
管理医疗规划/管理醫療規劃　managed care program
管囊肿/管囊腫　tubulocyst
管内部/管內部　intracanalicular part
管内的/管內的　intraductal
管扭转/管扭轉　tubotorsion
管泡状腺/管泡狀腺　tubuloacinar gland

管球反馈系统/管球回饋系統　tubuloglomerular feedback system
管球失衡/管球失衡　glomerulotubular imbalance
管腺泡癌/管腺泡癌　ducto-acinar carcinoma
管形石膏/管形石膏　plaster cast
管形牙/管形牙　tube tooth
管型/管型　cast
管型尿/管型尿　cylindruria
管性呼吸音/管性呼吸音　tubular breathing sound
管牙[毒蛇]类/管牙類　solenoglypha
管样的/管樣的　syringoid
管状/管[狀]的　tubular
管状鼻/管狀鼻　proboscis-like nose
管状肠重复畸形/管狀腸重複畸形　tubular intestinal duplication
管状大汗腺腺瘤/管狀頂漿腺腺瘤　tubular apocrine adenoma
管状动脉瘤/管狀動脈瘤,圓柱樣動脈瘤　tubular aneurysm
管状囊肿/管狀囊腫　tubular cyst
管状视野/管狀視野　tubular visual field
管状腺/管狀腺　tubular gland
管状腺瘤/管狀腺瘤　canalicular adenoma
管状移植物/管狀移植物　rope graft
管状中柱/管狀中柱　siphonostele
贯穿缝合/貫穿縫法　through and through suture
贯穿褥式缝合/貫穿褥式縫合　transfixing mattress suture
贯穿引流法/貫通引流　through drainage
贯声门癌/貫聲門癌　transglottic carcinoma
贯通伤/穿入性創傷,穿通創傷　penetrating wound
贯通性创伤/貫通性創傷　penetrating wound
惯性背卧位/背臥無力姿　dorsal inertia position
灌肠剂/灌腸劑　enema
灌肠疗法/灌腸療法　enema therapy
灌肠器/灌腸器　enemator
灌流/灌流　perfusion
灌流套管/灌流套管　perfusion cannula
灌木病/灌木病　bush disease
灌木皮炎/灌木皮膚炎　bush dermatitis
灌水膀胱镜检查/灌水膀胱鏡檢查　water cystoscopy
灌洗/灌洗　lavage, irrigation
灌洗液/灌洗液　irrigating solution
灌注/灌注　perfusion
灌注不足/灌流過緩　hypoperfusion
灌注充分/灌注充分　adequacy of perfusion
灌注肺/灌注肺　perfusion lung
灌注后综合征/灌注後症候群　postperfusion

syndrome
灌注机/灌注機　perfusion unit
灌注损伤/灌注損傷　perfusion injury
灌注压/灌流壓力　perfusion pressure
灌注液/灌流液　perfusate
灌装机/充填裝機　filling machine
光/光　light
光斑贴试验/光斑貼試驗　photo-patch test
光变态反应皮炎/光變態反應皮炎　photoallergic dermatitis
光变性血红蛋白/光變性血紅素　photomethemoglobin
光变应性/光過敏性　photoallergy
光变应性的/對光過敏的　photoallergic
光变应性接触性皮炎/光過敏性接觸性皮膚炎　photoallergic contact dermatitis
光变应性药疹/光過敏性藥疹　photoallergic drug eruption
光变应原/光過敏原　photoallergen
光波听诊器/光波聽診器　photostethoscope
光传导作用/光傳導作用　phototransduction
光磁性/光磁　photomagnetism
光刺激/光刺激　photic stimulation
光催化[作用]/光催化[作用]　photocatalysis
光存储设备/光存放裝置　optical storage device
光导纤维透照器/光導纖維透照器　fiberoptic transilluminator
光电比色计/光電比色計　electrophotometer
光电比浊计/光電比濁計　photoelectric nephelometer
光电二极管阵列检测器/光電二極管陣列檢測器　photodiode array detector, DAD
光电反射计/光電反射計　photronreflectometer
光电管/光電池　photoelement
光电振动/光電震蕩　photoelectric vibration
光电子/光電子　photoelectron
光定位/光定位　light projection
光动力的/光動力的　photodynamic
光动力反应/光動力反應　photodynamic reaction
光动力灭活法/光動力去活性法　photodynamic inactivation
光动力学/光動力學　photodynamics
光动力学疗法/光動力學療法　photodynamic therapy
光动现象/趨光性，向光性　photodromy
光毒反应/光毒反應　phototoxic reaction
光毒性/光毒性　phototoxicity
光毒性的/光毒性的　phototoxic
光毒性反应/光毒性反應　phototoxic reaction

光毒性焦油皮炎/光毒性焦油皮炎　phototoxic tar dermatitis
光毒性接触性皮炎/光毒性接觸性皮膚炎　phototoxic contact dermatitis
光毒性皮炎/光毒性皮炎　phototoxic dermatitis
光毒性药[物]疹/光毒性藥[物]疹　phototoxic drug eruption
光度滴定法/光度滴定法　photometric titration
光度计/光度計　light meter
光反应/光[力]反應　photoreaction
光反应现象/光反應現象　photoreaction phenomenon
光分离置换法/光分離置換法　photopheresis
光复活[作用]/光再活化[作用]　photoreactivation
光感/光感　light perception
光感受器/光感受器　photoreceptor
光固化复合树脂/光固化複合樹脂　light-cured composite
光固化树脂/光固化樹脂　light-cured resin
光固化装置/光固化裝置　light curring unit
光管/光管　light pipe
光过敏/感光性，光敏感性　photosensitivity
光过敏反应/光過敏反應　photo sensitive reaction
光过敏疾患/光過敏疾患　photosensitivity disorder
光过敏性反应/光過敏性反應　photoallergic reaction
光汗症/光汗症　phosphoridrosis
光合磷酸化/光致磷酸化作用　photophosphorylation
光合物/光[力]產物　photoproduct
光合作用/光合作用　photosynthesis
光合作用中心复合蛋白质类/光合作用中心複合蛋白質類　photosynthetic reaction center complex proteins
光滑的/光滑的　glossy
光滑髓针/平滑抽髓針　smooth broach
光滑型菌落/平滑菌落,S 菌落　S colony
光化的/光化的　actinic
光化辐射/光化學性輻射線　photochemical radiation
光化力/光化力　actinicity
光化射线/光化射線　actinic ray
光化线透性/光化線傳導性　diactinism
光化性癌/光化性癌　actinic carcinoma
光化性光/光化性光　actinic light
光化性眼炎/光化性眼炎　actinic ray ophthalmia
光化学的/光化學的　photochemical
光化学疗法/光化學療法　photochemotherapy
光化学氧化剂/光化學氧化劑　photochemical oxidants
光幻视/光幻視　phosphene
光回溯反应/光回溯反應　photorecall reaction

光活化作用/光活化作用　photo-activation
光活性的/光敏感的　photoactive
光获取蛋白复合物/光獲取蛋白複合物　light-harvesting protein complex
光肌阵挛反应/光肌陣攣反應　photo myoclonic response
光加强作用/光加強作用　photoaugmentation
光甲剥离/光甲剥離　photo-onycholysis
光接触性/光接觸性　photocontact
光接触性皮炎/光接觸性皮膚炎　photocontact dermatitis
光解/光解　photolysis
光解物/光解物　photolyte
光紧张/光性緊張　phototonus
光紧张的/光緊張的　phototonic
光紧张性/光緊張性　phototonicity
光惊厥反应/光驚厥反應　photo convulsive response
光觉/光覺　light sense
光觉测定[法]/光覺檢法,光視檢查　photoptometry
光觉计/光覺計　photoptometer
光觉检查[法]/光覺檢查[法]　examination of light sense
光老化/光老化　photo-aging
光量子/光量子　quantum of light
光量子血液疗法/光量子血液療法　photo-quantum blood therapy
光疗法/光線療法　phototherapy
光疗小室/光療小室　phototherapy cabinet
光密度测定法/密度描記法　densitometry
光免疫学/光免疫學　photoimmunology
光面内质网/光面内質網　smooth endoplasmic reticulum
光敏/光敏,對光敏感　photosensitize
光敏反应/光敏感性反應　photosensitivity reaction
光敏感性皮肤病/光敏感性皮膚病　photosensitive dermatosis
光敏[感]性皮炎/光敏[感]性皮膚炎,光敏性皮炎　photosensitivity dermatitis
光敏感性疹/光敏感性皮疹　photosensitive eruption
光敏感药/光敏感藥　photosensitizing agent
光敏疗法/光敏療法　photosensitization therapy
光敏色素/[植物]光敏素　phytochrome
光敏湿疹/光敏感性濕疹　photosensitive eczema
光敏药物/光敏感藥物　photosensitive drug
光敏作用/光致敏作用　photosensitization
光明/光明　guangming, GB37
光凝固[术]/光凝固[術],光凝固[作用]　photocoagulation, light coagulation

光漂白作用/光漂白作用　photobleaching
光谱/光譜　spectrum
光谱差减法/光譜差減法　spectral subtraction method
光谱分析/光譜分析　spectrum analysis
光谱核型分析/光譜核型分析　spectral karyotyping
光谱检索/[光]譜檢索　spectral search
光谱鉴定法/光譜鑒別法　spectrographical identification
光谱学/光譜學　spectroscopy
光热分解/光熱解　photothermolysis
光散射/光散射　light scattering
光扫描图/光掃描　photoscan
光扫描仪/光掃描器　photoscanner
光生物学/光生物學　photobiology
光声机/聽音辨光器　optophone
光试验/光試驗　phototesting
光视蛋白/光視蛋白　photopsin
光视紫[红]质/光視紫質　lumirhodopsin
光适应/明光適應,明視力　photopia
光适应眼/光適應眼　light-adapted eye
光束聚焦装置/光束聚焦裝置　beam condenser
光束疗法/光線療法,射線療法　beam therapy
光体积描记术/光體積描記術　photoplethysmography
光通量/發光量　luminous flux
光痛/光[灼]痛　photalgia
光秃的/光秃的　bald
光稳定性/光安定性　light stability
光吸收杂质/吸光雜質　light-absorbing impurity
光纤喉镜/光纖喉鏡　fiberoptic laryngoscope
光线疗法/光療法　lucotherapy
光线调准/光線調準　collimation
光线性扁平苔藓/光線性扁平苔癬　lichen planus actinicus
光线性唇炎/日光唇炎　actinic cheilitis
光线性类网状细胞增多症/光化類網狀細胞增多症　actinic reticuloid
光线性肉芽肿/光線性肉芽腫　actinic granuloma
光线性弹性组织变性/光線性彈性組織變性　actinic elastosis
光性荨麻疹/光性蕁麻疹　urticaria photogenica
光学纯度/光學純度　optical purity
光学的/光學的　optical
光学活性/光學活性　optical activity
光学镜片/光學玻璃　optical glass
光学体层摄影术/光學體層攝影術　optical tomography

光学显微镜/光學顯微鏡　light microscope
光学显微镜术/光學顯微鏡方法　light microscopy, LM
光学相干体层摄影术/光學相干體層攝影術　optical coherence tomography
光学中心/光學中心　optical center
光药理学/光藥[理]學　photopharmacology
光药物/光藥物　photodrug
光药物反应/光藥物反應　photodrug reaction
光药物皮炎/光藥物皮膚炎　photodrug dermatitis
光泳现象/光子電泳法　photophoresis
光诱发的疾病/光引起的疾病　photo-induced disorder
光原性癫痫发作/光引起性發作　photogenic seizure
光泽苔藓/光澤苔蘚　lichen nitidus
光泽性角化不全/光澤性角化不全　parakeratosis brillante
光增敏剂/光增敏劑　photosensitizing agent
光照保护法/光照保護法　photoprotection
光照变色性/照光變色性　photochromy
光照产色性/光生色性　photochromogenicity
光照期/光週期　photoperiod
光照射/光滲　irradiation of light
光照射损伤/光照射損傷　light injury
光照性红斑/光照性紅斑,曝光紅斑　photoerythema
光照性皮肤病/光照性皮膚病　photodermatosis
光照性皮炎/光照性皮膚炎　photodermatitis
光照性视网膜炎/光照性視網膜炎　photoretinitis
光阵发反应/光陣發反應　photo paroxysm response
光致癌/光致癌作用　photocarcinogenesis
光致发光/光照發光　photoluminescence
光[致]复活[作用]/光照復能作用　photoreactivation
光致敏剂/光敏感劑　photosensitizer
光周期与青春期/光週期與青春期　photoperiod and puberty
光锥/光線錐體　pyramid of light
光子/光子　photon
光子吸收测定法/光子吸收測定法　photon absorptiometry
胱氨酸/胱胺酸　cystine
胱氨酸病/胱胺酸病　cystinosis
胱氨酸结模体/胱胺酸結構基元　cystine knot motif
胱氨酸结石/胱胺酸結石　cystine stone
胱氨酸尿/胱胺酸尿症　cystinuria
胱氨酸血/胱胺酸血症　cystinemia
胱胺/胱胺　cystamine
胱硫醚/胱硫醚　cystathionine
胱硫醚合成酶/胱硫醚合成酶　cystathionine synthetase
胱硫醚β合成酶缺乏/胱硫醚β合成酶缺乏　cystathionine β-synthase deficiency
胱硫醚β合成酶/胱硫醚β合成酶　cystathionine β-synthase
胱硫醚γ裂合酶/胱硫醚γ裂合酶　cystathionine γ-lyase
胱硫醚尿/胱硫醚尿,半胱胺甲硫胺酸尿症　cystathioninuria
广场恐怖症/廣場恐懼症,空室恐懼症　agoraphobia
广泛性儿童发育障碍/廣泛性兒童發育障礙　pervasive child development disorder
广泛性获得性黑变病/廣泛性獲得性黑變病　universal acquired melanosis
广泛性焦虑症/廣泛性焦慮症　generalized anxiety
广泛性蓝斑样色素沉着/廣泛性藍斑樣色素沈著　extensive blue patch-like pigmentation
广泛性毛囊错构瘤/廣泛性毛囊錯構瘤　generalized follicular hamartoma
广防己/廣防己　Radix Aristolochiae Fangchi(拉)
广藿香/廣藿香　cablin patchouli herb
广基型/廣泛連著的　sessile
广金钱草/廣金錢草　snowbell-leaf tickclover herb
广谱/廣譜　broad spectrum
广谱抗生素/廣譜抗生素　broad spectrum antibiotic
广食性寄生物/廣養性寄生物　eurytrophic parasite
广视野膀胱镜/廣視野內視鏡　panendoscope
广视野膀胱镜检查法/廣視野膀胱鏡檢查法　panendoscopy
广州管圆线虫病/廣州管圓線蟲病　angiostrongyliasis cantonensis
归挤法/歸擠法　total pressing manipulation
归经/歸經　channel entry, channel tropism
归来/歸來　guilai, ST29
归脾汤/歸脾湯　guipi decoction, returning to spleen decoction
圭尔帕饮食/Guelpa氏飲食　Guelpa diet
圭亚那利什曼原虫/圭亞那利什曼原蟲　Leishmania guyanensis
龟背/龜背　hunchback
龟背痰/龜背痰　tortoise-back phlegm, chronic vertebral suppurative abscess, thoracic spine tuberculosis
龟甲/龜甲　tortoise carapace and plastron
龟龄集/龜齡集　guilingji capsules
龟鹿二仙胶/龜鹿二仙膠　guilu erxian glue
龟头/龜頭　glans
龟头包皮炎/陰莖頭包皮炎　balanoposthitis

龟头成形术/陰莖頭造形術,陰莖頭成形術　balanoplasty
龟头后天性静脉扩张/龜頭後天性靜脈擴張　acquired phlebectasia of the glans penis
龟头脓溢/陰莖頭膿漏　balanorrhagia
龟头膨出/陰莖頭膨出　balanocele
龟头下裂/龜頭下裂　glandular hypospadia
龟头炎/龜頭炎　balanitis
规避性抑郁病/規避性憂鬱症　aversion depression
规定酒精/標準酒精　proof spirit
规定日剂量/規定之日劑量　defined daily dose
规定饮食/規定飲食　regimen diet
规格/規格　specification
规律的/規則的　regular
规律用药率/規律用藥率　regularity rate of treatment
规则散光/規則散光　regular astigmatism
规则致密结缔组织/規則致密結締組織　dense regular connective tissue
硅尘肺/磚石匠肺病　mason lung
硅沉着病/矽土沈著病,矽肺病　silicosis
硅沉着性假结核瘤/矽沈著性假結核瘤　pseudotuberculoma silicoticum
硅肺/肺石末沈著病　pneumosilicosis
硅肺结核/石末沈著性結核病　silicotuberculosis
硅氟化物/矽氟化物　silicofluoride
硅化合物/矽化合物　silicon compound
硅剂/矽療劑　silicea
硅胶/矽膠　silica gel
硅胶 G/矽膠 G　silica gel G
硅胶 H/矽膠 H　silica gel H
硅胶柱色谱法/矽膠柱層析法　silica gel column chromatography
硅结节/矽結節　siliconic nodule
硅凝胶/矽凝膠　silicone gel
硅凝胶肉芽肿/矽凝膠肉芽腫　silicone gel granuloma
硅凝胶乳房植入术/矽凝膠乳房植入術　silicone gel filled breast prosthetic implantation
硅肉芽肿/矽肉芽腫　silica granuloma
硅酸/矽酸　silicic acid
硅酸钙/矽酸鈣　calcium silicate
硅酸铝/矽酸鋁　aluminium silicate
硅酸铝类/矽酸鋁類　aluminum silicates
硅酸镁类/矽酸鎂類　magnesium silicates
硅酸盐/矽酸鹽　silicate
硅酸盐黏固剂/矽酸填充劑　silicate cement
硅碳棒/矽碳棒　globars
硅铁[合金]/矽鐵　ferrosilicon
硅酮/矽酮　silicone
硅酮树脂/矽酯樹脂　silicone resin
硅土绷带/矽土繃帶　silica bandage
硅烷类/矽烷類　silanes
硅钨酸/矽鎢酸　silicotungstic acid
硅橡胶/矽化物橡膠　silicone rubber
硅橡胶印模材料/矽橡膠印模材料　silicone rubber impression material
硅氧烷类/矽氧烷類　siloxanes
硅油/矽化物油　silicone oil
硅藻土/矽藻土　diatomite
硅藻土尘肺症/矽藻土塵肺症　diatomite disease
硅藻土纤维变性/矽藻土纖維變性　diatomite fibrosis
鲑精蛋白/鮭精蛋白　salmine
鲑隐孔吸虫/住鮭小吸蟲　Nanophyetus salmincola
诡辩性思维/詭辯性思維　sophistic thinking
鬼笔环肽/鬼筆環肽　phalloidine
鬼臼毒素/普達非倫毒質　podophyllotoxin
鬼臼[根]/足葉草根　mandrake root
鬼臼树脂/普達非倫脂　podophyllin
鬼臼树脂复合涂料/普達非倫複合塗料　podophyllin compound paint
癸二酸/癸二酸　sebacic acid
癸酸/癸酸　capric acid
癸酸二乙醇酰胺/癸酸二乙醇醯胺　capric acid diethanolamide
癸酸甘油三酯/三癸酸甘油酯　capric acid triglyceride
癸酸类/癸酸類　decanoic acids
癸酸盐/癸酸鹽　caprate
癸酸盐类/癸酸鹽類　decanoates
癸烷/癸烷,十碳烷　decane
贵要静脉/貴要靜脈　basilic vein, ulnar cutaneous vein
贵要正中静脉/貴要正中靜脈,正中貴要靜脈　median basilic vein
桂附地黄丸/桂附地黃丸　guifu dihuang pills
桂附理中丸/桂附理中丸　guifu lizhong pills
桂利嗪/桂利嗪　cinnarizine
桂皮/桂皮　cortex cinnamomi
桂皮酸盐/肉桂酸鹽　cinnamate
桂皮酸乙酯/桂皮酸乙酯　ethyl cinnamate
桂皮酰/桂醯基　cinnamyl
桂皮油/桂皮油,肉桂油　cassia oil
桂油香水/桂油香水　bay rum
桂枝/桂枝　cassia twig

桂枝茯苓丸/桂枝茯苓丸　guizhi fuling pills
桂枝甘草龙骨牡蛎汤/桂枝甘草龍骨牡蠣湯　guizhi gancao longgu muli decoction, decoction of cinnamon twig with liquorice, dragon's bone and oyster shell
桂枝汤/桂枝湯　guizhi decoction
桧萜醇/薩界檜醇　sabinol
辊轴刀/皮膚移植調整厚度用刀　Humby knife
滚法/滾法　rolling manipulation
滚法推拿/滾法推拿　rolling massage
滚筒泵/滾筒幫浦　roller pump
滚丸/滾丸動作　pill-rolling
滚子泵/滾子泵　roller pump
郭[霍]氏疟原虫/猩猩瘧蟲　Plasmodium kochi
锅包衣/鍋包衣　pan coating
瘑疮/瘑瘡　palmoplantar pustulosis
国公酒/國公酒　guogong wine
国际癌症研究署/國際癌症研究署　International Agency for Research in Cancer
国际标准品/國際標準品　international standard substance
国际残损、残疾和健康分类/國際身心障礙分類系統　ICIDH
国际单位/國際單位　international unit, IU
国际单位制/國際單位制　international system of units
国际护士理事会/國際護士理事會　international council of nurse
国际疾病分类法/國際疾病分類法　international classification of disease
国际教育交流/國際教育交流　international educational exchange
国际药学联合会/國際藥學聯合會　International Pharmaceutical Federation, FIP
国际烛光/國際燭光　international candle
国家卫生组织/國家衛生組織　National Institutes of Health
国家中医药管理局/國家中醫藥管理局　State Administration of Traditional Chinese Medicine
腘的/膕的　popliteal
腘动脉/膕動脈　popliteal artery
腘动脉瘤/膕動脈瘤　popliteal aneurysm
腘弓状韧带/膕弓狀韌帶　arcuate popliteal ligament
腘肌/膕肌　popliteus, musculus popliteus
腘肌沟/膕肌溝　groove for popliteus, popliteal groove
腘肌囊/膕肌囊　popliteal bursa
腘肌下隐窝/膕肌下隱窩　subpopliteal recess

腘筋膜/膕筋膜　popliteal fascia
腘静脉/膕靜脈　popliteal vein, vena poplitea
腘淋巴结/膕淋巴結　popliteal lymph node
腘面/膕面　popliteal surface
腘囊肿/膕囊腫　popliteal cyst
腘蹼综合征/膕蹼症候群　popliteal web syndrome
腘浅淋巴结/膕淺淋巴結　superficial popliteal lymph node
腘深淋巴结/膕深淋巴結　deep popliteal lymph node
腘神经/膕神經　popliteal nerve
腘绳肌腱/膕旁腱，腿後腱　hamstring
腘外侧神经/膕外神經　external popliteal nerve
腘窝/膕窩　popliteal fossa, popliteal cavity
腘窝囊肿/膕窩囊腫　popliteal cyst
腘斜韧带/膕斜韌帶　oblique popliteal ligament
腘翼状赘蹼赘肉/膕窩翼狀贅肉症候群　popliteal pterygium syndrome
果孢子/果孢子　carpospore
果酱色脓/果醬色膿　anchovy sauce pus
果酱状血块/果漿血凝塊　currant jelly clot
果酱状血栓/果漿狀血栓　currant jelly thrombus
果胶/果膠　pectin
果胶[甲]酯酶/果膠酯酶　pectinesterase
果胶类/果膠類　pectins
果胶酶/果膠酵素，植物膠酵素，溶果膠酶　pectase
果胶酸/果膠酸，植物膠酸　pectic acid
果胶糖/果膠糖，植物膠糖　pectose
果胶胰岛素/果膠胰島素　pectin insulin
果聚糖/聚左旋糖　levulosan
果聚糖类/果聚糖類　fructans
果螨属/果蟎屬　Carpoglyphus
果皮/果皮　pericarp
果肉/果肉　pulp
果实/果實　fruit
果食者/果食[主義]者　fruitarian
果食主义/果食主義　fruitarianism
果酸/果酸　fruit acid
果糖/果糖　fructose
果糖胺/果糖胺，果胺糖　fructosamine
果糖不耐受/果糖不耐受　fructose intolerance
果糖-二磷酸酶/果糖-二磷酸酶　fructose-bisphosphatase
果糖-二磷酸醛缩酶/果糖-二磷酸醛縮酶　fructose-bisphosphate aldolase
果糖二磷酸盐类/果糖二磷酸鹽類　fructosediphosphates
果糖分解/果糖分解　fructolysis
果糖基/果糖基　fructosyl

果糖激酶/果糖致活酵素　fructokinase
果糖激酶类/果糖激酶類　fructokinases
果糖激酶缺乏/果糖激酶缺乏　fructokinase deficiency
果糖甲苯脎/甲苯左旋糖脎　methylphenyl levulosazone
果糖-6-磷酸/果糖-6-磷酸酯　fructose-6-phosphate
果糖磷酸类/果糖磷酸類　fructose phosphates
果糖耐量试验/左旋糖耐量試驗　levulose tolerance test
果糖尿/果糖尿　fructosuria
果糖脎/果糖脎　fructosazone
果糖酮酸/果糖酮酸　fructuronic acid
果糖血[症]/果糖血症　fructosemia
果蝇蛋白质类/果蠅蛋白質類　drosophila proteins
果蝇胶蛋白质类/果蠅膠蛋白質類　drosophila glue proteins
果中毒/果中毒　fruit poisoning
过饱和/過飽和,使過度飽和　supersaturate
过饱和结晶学说/過飽和結晶學説　theory of supersaturation and nucleation
过饱和溶液/過飽和溶液　supersaturated solution
过饱和[现象]/過度飽和,飽和過度　supersaturation
过饱性绞痛/過飽性絞痛　crapulent colic
过长𬌗/齒過長咬合　supra occlusion
过程分析/過程分析　process analysis
过程评价/過程評價　process assessment
过程质量控制/製程管制　in-process control
过迟长出/過遲長出　retarded eruption
过醋酸盐/過醋酸鹽　peracetate
过碘酸希夫反应/希夫氏過碘酸反應　periodic acid-Schiff reaction, PAS reaction
过碘酸-希夫染色阳性的/過碘酸 Schiff 氏染色陽性的　periodic acid-Schiff-positive
过碘酸-希夫染色阳性的沉淀物/過碘酸 Schiff 氏染色陽性的沈澱物　periodic acid-Schiff-positive deposits
过度/過度　excess, hyper
过度不全角化/過度不完全角化　hyperparakeratosis
过度成熟/過[度成]熟　postmaturity
过度成熟的/過度成熟的　postmature
过度灌注综合征/過度灌注症候群　luxury perfusion syndrome
过度呼吸性手足搐搦/換氣過度性肢搦病　hyperventilation tetany
过度角化[症]/過度角化　hyperkeratosis
过度可动综合征/過度可動症候群　hypermobility syndrome
过度溶血的/過度溶血的　hyperhemolytic
过度生长/過度生長　overgrowth
过度嗜睡性障碍/過度嗜睡性障礙　disorders of excessive somnolence
过度外展综合征/外展過度症候群　hyperabduction syndrome
过度作用/作用過度　over-effect
过渡呼吸音/轉移性呼吸音　transitional respiration
过渡监护治疗病房/過渡監護治療病房　intermediate care unit
过渡态/過渡態　transition state
过渡态类似物/過渡態類似物　transition state analog
过渡型/過渡型　transitional type
过分冲动障碍/過分衝動障礙　hyperkinetic impulse disorder
过剂量/超過劑量規定　overdosage
过继免疫/過繼[性]免疫　adoptive immunity
过继免疫疗法/過繼免疫療法　adoptive immunotherapy
过继耐受[性]/過繼耐受[性]　adoptive tolerance
过继转移/過繼轉移　adoptive transfer
过经/過經　disease transmitting from one channel to another
过客病毒/過客病毒　passenger virus
过量/過量　overdose, luxus
过量代谢/過量代謝　excess metabolism
过量消耗/過量消耗　luxus consumption
过量胰岛素/過量胰島素　luxus insulin
过磷酸盐/重磷酸鹽　superphosphate
过硫化物/過硫化物　persulfide
过硫酸/過氧單硫酸　peroxymonosulfuric acid
过硫酸铵/過硫酸銨　ammonium persulfate
过硫酸盐/過硫酸鹽　persulfate
过路白细胞/過路白細胞　passenger leukocyte
过氯酸盐释放试验/過氯酸鹽釋放試驗　perchlorate discharge test
过滤/過濾　filtration
过滤灭菌/過濾滅菌　filtration sterilization
过滤作用/濾過法　filtration
过敏毒素/過敏毒素　anaphylotoxin
过敏毒素反应/過敏毒素反應　anaphylatoxis
过敏毒素中毒/過敏毒素中毒,過敏性中毒　anaphylatoxism
过敏反应/過敏反應　anaphylactic response, anaphylaxis
过[敏反]应的/過敏反應的　pathergic, anaphylactic

过[敏反]应化/過敏反應化　pathergization
过敏抗体/過敏性抗體　anaphylactic antibody
过敏素/過敏素　sensibilisin
过敏素原/過敏素原　taraxigen
过敏性鼻炎/過敏性鼻炎　anaphylactic rhinitis
过敏性反应/過敏性反應　anaphylactic reaction
过敏性坏疽/過敏性壞疽　anaphylactic gangrene
过敏性溃疡/過敏性潰瘍　erethistic ulcer
过敏性慢反应物质/過敏性慢反應物質　slow reacting substance of anaphylaxis
过敏性皮炎/過敏性皮膚炎　allergic dermatitis
过敏性肉芽肿性反应/過敏性肉芽腫性反應　allergic granulomatous reaction
过敏性体质/過敏性體質　allergic predisposition
过敏性心肌炎/過敏性心肌炎　hypersensitivity myocarditis
过敏性休克/過敏性休克　anaphylactic shock
过敏性血管炎/過敏性血管炎　hypersensitivity vasculitis
过敏性亚脓毒病/過敏性亞膿病毒　subsepsis allergica
过敏性[样]的/類似過敏性的　anaphylactoid
过敏性诊断法/過敏性診斷法　anaphylodiagnosis
过敏性中毒/過敏性中毒　anaphylactic intoxication
过敏性紫癜/過敏性紫癜病　anaphylactoid purpura
过敏性紫癜肾炎/過敏性紫癜腎炎　Henoch-Schönlein purpura nephritis
过敏样反应/假過敏性反應,類過敏反應　anaphylactoid reaction
过敏原/過敏原　sensitizin
过硼酸/過硼酸　perboric acid
过硼酸钠/過硼酸鈉　peroxydol
过硼酸盐/過硼酸鹽　perborate
过期产/過期產,逾期產　post-term birth
过期产儿/過期產兒　post-term infant
过期妊娠/過期妊娠　post-term pregnancy, prolonged pregnancy
过剩信息学说/過剩資訊學說　redundant information theory
过熟儿/過熟兒　postmature infant
过熟卵泡/過熟卵泡　postmature follicle
过熟内障/過熟內障　hypermature cataract
过熟婴儿/過熟嬰兒　postmature infant
过酸盐/過酸鹽　persalt
过压薄层色谱法/過壓薄層層析法　overpressure thin-layer chromatography
过氧苯甲酰/過氧化苯甲醯　benzoyl peroxide
过氧化酶体激增剂/過氧化酶體激增劑　peroxisome proliferator
过氧化镁/過氧化鎂　magnesium peroxide
过氧化氢/過氧化氫　hydrogen peroxide
过氧化氢酶/觸酶　catalase
过氧化氢酶缺乏症/缺觸酶症　acatalasia
过氧化氢溶液/過氧化氫溶液　hydrogen peroxide solution
过氧化氢试验/過氧化氫試驗　hydrogen peroxide test
过氧化物/過氧化物　peroxide
过氧化物酶/過氧化酶　peroxidase
过氧化物酶-抗过氧化物酶复合物法/過氧化酶-抗過氧化酶複合物法　peroxidase antiperoxidase complex method, PAP method
过氧化物酶体/過氧化物酶體　peroxisome
过氧化物酶体病/過氧化物酶體病　peroxisomal disease
过氧化物酶体类/過氧化物酶體類　peroxisomes
过氧化物酶体失调/過氧化物酶體失調　peroxisomal disorder
过氧化物酶体增殖物启动受体/過氧化物酶體增殖物啟動受體　peroxisome proliferator-activated receptor
过氧化乙酰/過氧化乙醯　acetyl peroxide
过氧化脂质类/過氧化脂質類　lipid peroxides
过氧化值/過氧化價　peroxide value
过乙酸/過乙酸　peracetic acid
过用/過用　overuse
过用殆/齒官能過旺性咬合　hyperfunctional occlusion
过载/過負荷　overload
过早绝经/過早絕經　premature menopause
过早衰老/過早衰老　premature aging

H

哈伯德浴池/哈巴德氏池　Hubbard tank
哈迪-温伯格平衡/遺傳平衡　Hardy-Weinberg equilibrium
哈尔明碱/駱駝蓬鹼　harmine
哈尔瓦克斯效应/霍爾瓦克效應　Hallwachs effect
哈尔宗病/哈爾宗病　halzoun
哈佛管/哈佛氏管　haversian canal
哈夫病/哈夫病,海灣病　Haff disease
哈弗里尔热/哈佛希熱　Haverhill fever
哈弗系统/哈佛氏系統　Haversian System
哈格多恩扁头针/Hagedorn 氏針　Hagedorn needle
哈金斯试验/哈金斯氏試驗　Huggins test
哈-克综合征/Hadfield-Clarke 二氏症候群　Hadfield-Clarke syndrome
哈勒沃登-施帕茨综合征/Hallervorden-Spatz 二氏症候群　Hallervorden-Spatz syndrome
哈里森沟/Harrison 氏溝　Harrison groove
哈里森抗麻醉品法案/哈里森氏反麻醉品法案　Harrison Antinarcotic Act
哈里斯带[膜]/Harris 氏韌帶　Harris band
哈里斯综合征/Harris 氏症候群　Harris syndrome
哈林顿溶液/Harrington 氏溶液　Harrington solution
哈罗普饮食/Harrop 氏飲食　Harrop diet
哈马灵/野芸香副鹼,二氫駱駝蓬鹼　harmaline
哈霉素/哈黴素　hamycin
哈蒙德病/Hammond 氏病　Hammond disease
哈蒙德夹/Hammond 氏夾板　Hammond splint
哈米特方程/哈米特方程式　Hammett equation
哈姆迪溶液/Hamdi 氏溶液　Hamdi solution
哈瑙咬合关系组合图/哈瑙咬合關係組合圖　Hanau articulation quint
哈奇森夏令痒疹/哈奇森夏令癢疹　summer prurigo of Hutchinson
哈钦森齿/Hutchinson 氏齒　Hutchinson teeth
哈钦森黑色素雀斑/哈欽森黑色素雀斑　Hutchinson's melanotic freckle
哈钦森瞳孔/哈欽森瞳孔　Hutchinson pupil
哈钦森牙/哈欽森牙　Hutchinson teeth
哈钦森征/哈欽森徵象　Hutchinson sign
哈氏棒手术/哈氏棒手術　Harrington rod operation
哈特尔[疗]法/哈特爾氏療法　Hartel treatment
哈特曼溶液/Hartman 氏溶液　Hartman solution
哈特纳普病/哈特納普病　Hartnup disease
哈西奈德/哈辛諾耐　halcinonide
蛤蟆瘟/蛤蟆瘟　toad-like pestilence
蛤蟆油/蛤蟆油　rana oviduct
海岸丹毒/海岸丹毒　coastal erysipelas
海豹瘟热病毒/海豹瘟熱病毒　phocine distemper virus
海豹肢畸形/海豹肢畸形　phocomelia
海豹[状]指/海豹指　seal finger
海贝皮炎/海貝皮炎　marine shell dermatitis
海贝咬伤/海貝咬傷　marine shells bite
海草皮炎/海草皮膚炎　dermatitis caused by seaweed
海蟾蜍毒素/海蛤蟆毒　marinobufagin
海葱次苷/海葱次甙　proscillaridin
海葱苷/海葱素　scillaren
海葱糖苷/海葱糖苷　scilliroside
海葱甾/海葱類固醇　scillanolide
海葱中毒/海葱中毒　scillism
海胆刺伤/海膽刺傷　sea urchin sting
海胆肉芽肿/海膽肉芽腫　sea urchin granuloma
海胆色素/海膽色素　echinochrome
海岛锡生藤碱/海島錫生藤鹼　insularine
海登海因细胞/Heidenhain 氏細胞　Heidenhain cell
海蝶刺伤/海蝶刺傷　sea butterflies sting
海丁格尔视刷/海丁格内視刷　Haidinger brush
海恩茨体/海恩茨體　heinz body
海风藤/海風藤　kadsura pepper stem
海弗利克极限/海弗克極限　Hayflick limit
海-海病/Hailey-Hailey 氏病　Hailey-Hailey disease
海金沙/海金沙　Japanese climbing fern spore
海克替啶/海克替啶　hexetidine
海-克征/海-克二氏徵象　Heim-Kreysig sign
海葵触须毒[素]/海葵毒素　actinotoxin
海葵刺伤/海葵刺傷　sea anemone sting
海葵毒[素]/海葵毒[素]　congestin
海葵素/海葵素　thalassin
海葵形溃疡/海葵潰瘍　sea anemone ulcer
海葵正铁血红素/海葵血紅素　actinohematin
海拉细胞/HeLa 氏細胞　HeLa cell

海蓝色组织细胞/海藍色組織細胞 sea-blue histiocyte
海狸香/海狸香 castoreum
海利奥辛/海利奧辛 heliosin
海硫因类/海硫因類 thiohydantoins
海龙/海龍 pipefish
海仑[青霉菌]素/海侖青黴菌素 helenine
海论/海論 Treatise on Audio-visual Abnormality
海洛因/海洛因,二乙醛嗎啡 heroin
海洛因依赖/海洛因依賴 heroin dependence
海洛因瘾/海洛因癮 heroinism
海马/海馬 hippocampus, sea horse
海马槽/海馬槽 alveus of hippocampus
海马多林/血基質素 hematolin
海马沟/海馬溝 hippocampal sulcus
海马回/海馬[旁]迴 hippocampal gyrus
海马回沟切开术/海馬迴溝切除術 uncotomy
海马回疣/海馬迴疣 verruca gyri hippocampi
海马结构/海馬結構 hippocampal formation
海马旁回/海馬旁迴 parahippocampal gyrus
海马旁回钩/海馬旁迴鈎 uncus of parahippocampal gyrus
海马伞/海馬傘 fimbria of hippocampus
海马始基/海馬始基 hippocampal rudiment
海马苔藓纤维/海馬苔蘚纖維 hippocampal mossy fiber
海马体裂隙/海馬體裂隙 fissura hippocampi
海马足/海馬趾 Pes hippocampi(拉)
海曼肾炎/海曼腎炎 Heymann nephritis
海绵/海綿 sponge
海绵采集者皮炎/海綿採集者皮炎 sponge fishers dermatitis
海绵层水肿/海綿狀水腫 spongiosis
海绵除鲠器/海綿捕鯁器 sponge probang
海绵刺伤/海綿刺傷 sponge sting
海绵丛/海綿叢 carvernous plexus
海绵窦/海綿竇 cavernous sinus
海绵窦沟/海綿竇溝 cavernous groove
海绵窦孔/海綿竇孔 cavernous foramen
海绵窦脑膜瘤/海綿竇腦膜瘤 meningioma of cavernous sinus
海绵窦血栓形成/海綿竇栓塞 cavernous sinus thrombosis
海绵窦支/海綿竇支 branch of cavernous sinus
海绵窦综合征/海綿體靜脈竇症候群 cavernous sinus syndrome
海绵骨小梁/海綿骨小梁 trabecula of spongy bone
海绵间窦/海綿體間竇 intercavernous sinuses

海绵皮层/海綿皮層 spongy cortex
海绵塞条/海綿塞條,海綿塞子 sponge tent
海绵肾/髓質海綿腎 medullary sponge kidney
海绵体/海綿體 corpus cavernosum
海绵体部/海綿體部 cavernous part, spongy part
海绵体静脉/海綿體靜脈 cavernous vein
海绵体膜/海綿體膜 spongy membrane
海绵体中隔/海綿體中隔 septum of cavernous body
海绵样动脉瘤/海綿樣動脈瘤 spongy aneurysm
海绵移植物/海綿移植物 sponge graft
海绵硬蛋白/海綿蛋白 spongin
海绵渔夫病/海綿漁夫病 sponge fisherman disease
海绵质/海綿質 spongioplasm
海绵质增生/海綿質增生 hyperspongiosis
海绵状/海綿狀 spongiform
海绵状癌/海綿狀癌 cavernous cancer
海绵状的/海綿狀的 spongy
海绵状虹膜炎/海綿質狀虹膜炎 spongy iritis
海绵状淋巴管瘤/海綿狀淋巴管瘤 cavernous lymphangioma
海绵状瘤/海綿狀瘤 cavernous tumor
海绵状脑/海綿狀腦 status spongiosus
海绵状脑白质营养不良/海綿狀腦白質營養不良症,卡納萬氏病 spongiform leukodystrophy
海绵状脓疱/海綿狀膿皰 spongiform pustule
海绵状水疱/海綿狀水皰 spongiform vesicle
海绵状微脓疡/海綿狀微膿瘍 spongiform microabscesse
海绵状血管淋巴管瘤/海綿狀血管淋巴管瘤 cavernous hemolymphangioma
海绵状血管瘤/海綿狀血管瘤 angioma cavernosum
海绵状脂肪瘤/海綿狀脂肪瘤 cavernosum lipoma
海绵状痣/海綿狀痣 nevus cavernosus
海绵组织/海綿組織 spongy tissue
海姆利希手法/海立克氏技巧 Heimlich maneuver
海鸥鸣样杂音/海鷗鳴樣雜音 seagull murmur
海螵蛸/海螵蛸 cuttlebone
海螵蛸棒摩擦法/海螵蛸棒摩擦法 method of rubbing with cuttlebone
海泉/海泉 haiquan, EX-HN11
海参毒素/海參素 holothurin
海生毒素类/海生毒素類 marine toxins
海虱/海蝨 sea lice
海石蕊紫/苔色素 archil
海水皮炎/海洋皮層炎 marine dermatitis
海水浴/海水浴 seawater bath
海水浴耳病/海濱耳炎 beach ear
海水浴疗法/海洋療法 thalassotherapy

海水浴[皮]疹/海水浴疹　sea bather eruption
海水浴荨麻疹/海水性蕁麻疹　urticaria maritima
海松酸/海松脂酸　pimaric acid
海索苯定/海索苯定　hexobendine
海索比妥/環己烯巴比妥　hexobarbital
海索那林/海索那林　hexoprenaline
海桐皮/海桐皮　cortex erythrinae
海湾病/海灣病　bay sickness
海星/海星　starfish
海熊类/海熊類　fur seals
海洋生药学/海洋生藥學　marine pharmacognosy
海洋微生物/海洋微生物　marine microorganism
海洋药物/海洋藥物　marine drug
海药本草/海藥本草　Oversea Materia Medica
海伊韧带/Hey 氏韌帶　Hey ligament
海伊疝/Hey 氏疝　Hey hernia
海因-梅丁病/海-梅二氏病　Heine-Medin disease
海因斯-布朗试验/海-布二氏試驗　Hines-Brown test
海鱼分枝杆菌/海洋分枝桿菌　mycobacterium marinum
海藻/海藻　seaweed
海藻萃取液/海藻萃取液　seaweed extract
海藻粉/海藻粉　seaweed powder
海藻皮炎/海藻皮炎　seaweed dermatitis
海藻糖/海藻糖　trehalose
海藻糖酶/海藻糖酶　trehalase
海蜇/海蜇　jellyfish
海蜇皮炎/海蜇皮炎　jellyfish dermatitis
酰基辅酶/酰基輔酶　acyl coenzyme
氦镉激光疗法/氦鎘雷射療法　helium-cadmium laser therapy
氦氖激光疗法/氦氖雷射療法　helium-neon laser therapy
氦氖激光器/氦氖雷射器　helium-neon laser
害虫诱惑剂/害蟲誘惑劑　metarchon
鼾病/鼾病　snoring disease
鼾声呼吸/鼾聲呼吸　stertorous respiration
鼾音/鼾音　rhonchus
鼾音的/鼾音的　rhonchial
含氨银液/含氨銀液　ammoniacal silver solution
含氮的/偶氮　azo
含碘蛋白质/含碘蛋白質　iodized protein
含服/含服　buccal
含氟磨光糊剂/含氟磨光糊劑　fluoride-containing polishing paste
含钙脊液/脊髓液內含鈣　calciorrhachia
含钙细胞/含鈣細胞　calcigerous cell

含胶体的/含膠體的　rhagiocrine
含胶体细胞/含膠體細胞　rhagiocrine cell
含空泡的/含空泡的　physaliferous
含孔的/含孔的,有孔的　foraminated
含量测定/含量測定　assay
含量均匀度/劑量單位含量均一度　uniformity of dosage units
含硫石灰溶液/硫化石灰溶液,硫酸石灰溶液　sulfurated lime solution
含硫酸类/含硫酸類　sulfur acids
含氯的/含氯的　chlorinated
含氯苏打/含氯蘇打,氯制蘇打　chlorinated soda
含氯苏打溶液/含氯蘇打溶液　chlorinated soda solution
含毛囊肿/含毛囊腫　pilocystic cyst
含尿脓肿/含尿膿腫,尿液性膿腫　urapostema
含硼砂的/含硼砂的　borated
含气窦/骨內之氣竇　air sinus
含气骨/含氣骨　pneumatic bone
含气囊肿/含氣囊腫　air cyst
含气[X 射线]管/氣體 X 射線管　gas tube
含气小房/咽鼓管氣房　tubal air cell
含石棉物质/含石綿物質　asbestos-containing material
含嗜碱性点彩红细胞/嗜鹼紅血球　basoerythrocyte
含漱法/含漱法　method of rinsing mouth
含水的/含水的　hydrous
含水煅石膏/水化石膏　hydrocal
含水酒精/水與酒精的　hydroalcoholic
含水无晶形成氧化硅/含水無晶形成氧化矽　amorphous silicon oxide hydrate
含水羊毛脂/含水羊毛脂　adeps lanae hydrosus
含水油膏/含水油膏　hydrous ointment
含锑药剂/含銻藥劑　antimonial
含铁小结/鐵沈著性小結　siderotic nodule
含铁血黄素/血[黃]鐵質　hemosiderin
含铁血黄素沉着症/血鐵質沈積症　hemosiderosis
含铁血黄素巨噬细胞/含鐵細胞　siderophore
含铁血黄素尿症/血鐵質尿　hemosiderinuria
含羞草氨酸/含羞草胺酸　mimosine
含血褐质的/血褐質的　hemapheic
含牙的/含齒的　dentigerous
含牙囊肿/含齒囊腫　dentigerous cyst
含氧量低的/含氧量低的,缺氧的　hypoxic
含氧酸/含氧酸　oxygen acid
含氧酸盐/含氧酸鹽,氧基酸鹽　oxysalt
含药宫内避孕器/含藥宮內避孕器　medicated intrauterine device

含药糖浆/加藥糖漿　medicated syrup
含樟脑的/含樟腦的　camphorated
寒/寒　cold
寒包热哮/寒包熱哮　heat wheezing enveloped by cold
寒带气候/寒冷氣候　cold climate
寒厥/寒厥,冷厥　cold type of cold limbs, cold syncope, syncope due to excessive cold
寒冷变态反应/寒冷性過敏　cold allergy
寒冷病/寒冷病　cryopathy
寒冷感/惡寒　creeping chill
寒冷型恶性疟/寒冷型惡性瘧　algid pernicious fever
寒冷性荨麻疹/寒冷性蕁麻疹　cold urticaria
寒冷性脂膜炎/寒冷性脂膜炎　cold panniculitis
寒凝胞宫证/寒凝胞宮證　pattern of coagulated cold in uterus, pattern of coagulated cold in womb
寒凝冲任/寒凝沖任　cold congealing in thoroughfare and conception channels
寒凝证/寒凝證　coagulated cold pattern
寒疟/寒冷瘧　cold malaria
寒热错杂/寒熱錯雜　intermingled cold and heat
寒热错杂证/寒熱錯雜證　pattern of intermingled heat and cold
寒热起伏/寒熱起伏　alternative chill and fever
寒热如疟/寒熱如瘧　chill and fever similar to malaria
寒热往来/寒熱往來　alternate attacks of chill and fever
寒热真假/寒熱真假　true-false of cold and heat
寒疝/寒疝　cold colic in abdomen and vulva
寒湿困脾/寒濕困脾　cold-dampness disturbing spleen
寒湿困脾证/寒濕困脾證　pattern of cold-dampness disturbing spleen
寒湿痢/寒濕痢　cold-damp dysentery
寒湿证/寒濕證　cold-dampness pattern
寒湿阻络证/寒濕阻絡證　pattern of cold-dampness blocking collaterals
寒实结胸证/寒實結胸證　chest binding pattern with cold fluid
寒食散/寒食散　powder taken cold
寒痰证/寒痰證　cold-phlegm pattern
寒痰阻肺证/寒痰阻肺證　pattern of cold-phlegm obstructing lung
寒痛/寒痛　cold pain
寒下剂/寒下劑　cold cathartic formula
寒邪/寒邪,寒淫,陰寒　cold pathogen
寒邪犯胃证/寒邪犯胃證　pattern of cold pathogen attacking stomach
寒性坏疽/冷凍壞疽　cold gangrene
寒性溃疡/冷性潰瘍　cold ulcer
寒性凝滞/寒性凝滯　cold having property of coagulation and stagnation
寒性脓肿/寒性膿腫　cold abscess
寒性收引/寒性收引　cold having property of contraction
寒性哮喘/寒性哮喘　cold asthma
寒易伤阳/寒易傷陽　cold pathogen being apt to attack yang
寒疫/寒疫　cold pestilence
寒因寒用/寒因寒用　treating false-cold pattern with cold methods
寒饮停肺证/寒飲停肺證　pattern of cold fluid retained in lung
寒战/寒顫　shivering
寒战疟/寒顫瘧　shaking ague
寒者热之/寒者熱之　treating cold pattern with heat methods
寒阵/寒陣　cold array
寒证/寒證　cold pattern
寒滞肝脉证/寒滯肝脈證　pattern of cold accumulated in liver channel
寒滞经脉证/寒滯經脈證　pattern of cold accumulated in channel
寒中/寒中　cold parapoplexy
寒肿/寒腫　cold swelling
汉城病毒/漢城病毒　Seoul virus
汉德病/Hand 氏病　Hand disease
汉德-许勒尔-克里斯琴病/Hand-Schüller-Christian 三氏病　Hand-Schüller-Christian disease
汉德-许勒尔-克里斯琴综合征/Hand-Schüller-Christian 三氏症候群　Hand-Schüller-Christian syndrome
汉德综合征/Hand 氏症候群　Hand syndrome
汉科克生物心脏瓣膜/漢科克生物心臟瓣膜　Hancock heart valve bioprosthesis
汉勒带/Henle 氏帶　Henle band
汉勒襻/Henle 氏環　Henle loop
汉勒韧带/Henle 氏韌帶　Henle ligament
汉勒细胞/Henle 氏細胞　Henle cell
汉密尔顿绷带/Hamilton 氏繃帶　Hamilton bandage
汉密尔顿焦虑量表/漢密爾頓焦慮量表　Hamilton anxiety scale
汉密尔顿抑郁量表/漢密爾頓抑鬱量表　Hamilton depressive scale
汉普顿驼峰/Hampton 氏隆起　Hampton hump

汉森病/Hansen 氏病　Hansen disease
汉森单位/漢森氏單位　Hanson unit
汉施方程/漢施方程式　Hansch equation
汉坦病毒/漢坦病毒　hantavirus
汉坦病毒肺综合征/漢坦病毒肺症候群　hantavirus pulmonary syndrome
汉坦病毒感染/漢坦病毒感染　hantavirus infection
汗/汗　sudor
汗闭/汗閉止,止汗　ischidrosis
汗闭性外胚层发育不良/無汗外胚層發育不全　anhidrotic ectodermal dysplasia
汗臭/汗臭　bromhidrosis
汗的/汗的　sudoral
汗多亡阳证/汗多亡陽證　yang depletion pattern due to profuse sweating
汗多胃燥证/汗多胃燥證　stomach dryness pattern due to profuse sweating
汗法/[大量]發汗,出汗　diaphoresis
汗管囊瘤/汗管囊瘤　syringocystoma
汗管囊腺瘤/汗管囊腺瘤　syringocystadenoma
汗管纤维腺瘤/汗管纖維腺瘤　syringofibroadenoma
汗孔/汗孔　sweat pore, sweat foramen
汗孔癌/汗孔癌　porocarcinoma
汗孔汗腺腺瘤/汗孔汗管瘤　porosyringoma
汗孔角化病/汗管角化,線狀汗孔角化症　porokeratosis
汗孔扩大/汗孔擴大　pore dilation
汗孔瘤/汗孔瘤　poroma
汗孔样汗腺瘤/汗孔樣汗腺瘤　poroid hidradenoma
汗毛/汗毛　fine hair
汗疱疹/汗皰　pompholyx
汗疱状湿疹/汗皰濕疹　dyshidrotic eczema
汗热病/汗熱病,流行性粟粒疹熱　English sweating sickness
汗酸/汗酸　hidrotic acid
汗脱/汗脱　sweating collapse
汗浙疮/汗浙瘡　erythema intertrigo
汗腺/汗腺　sweat gland, eccrine gland
汗腺癌/汗腺癌　carcinoma of sweat gland
[汗腺]暗细胞/暗細胞　dark cell
汗腺臭汗症/汗腺臭汗症　eccrine bromhidrosis
汗腺管/汗管　ductus sudoriferus
汗腺管周炎/汗腺周圍炎　perisyringitis
汗腺疾病/汗腺疾病　sweat gland disease
汗腺淋巴腺瘤/汗腺淋巴腺瘤　adenolymphoma of the sweat gland
汗腺鳞状汗管变形症/汗腺鱗狀汗管變形症　eccrine squamous syringometaplasia
汗腺螺旋腺癌/汗腺螺旋腺癌　spirocarcinoma
汗腺螺旋腺上皮瘤/汗腺螺旋腺上皮瘤　spiroepithelioma
汗腺毛发血管瘤痣/汗腺毛髮血管瘤痣　eccrine-pilar angiomatous nevus
[汗腺]明细胞/亮细胞,透明细胞　clear cell
汗腺囊瘤/汗腺囊瘤　hydrocystoma
汗腺囊瘤病/汗腺囊瘤病　hidrocystomatosis
汗腺色汗症/汗腺色汗症　eccrine chromhidrosis
汗腺先天性血管瘤/汗腺先天性血管瘤　congenital hemangioma of eccrine sweat gland
汗腺腺瘤/汗腺瘤　hidradenoma
汗腺炎/汗腺炎　hydradenitis
汗腺真皮管腺瘤/汗腺真皮管腺瘤　eccrine dermal duct adenoma
汗腺肿瘤/汗腺腫瘤　sweat gland neoplasm
汗疹性湿疹/多汗濕疹　eczema sudamen
汗证/汗證　sweating disease
汗中枢/汗中樞　sweat center
颔厌/頷厭　hanyan, GB4
杭纳溃疡/Hunner 氏潰瘍　Hunner ulcer
杭廷顿病/杭廷頓病　Huntington disease
航海坏血病/海上壞血病,海員壞血病　sea scurvy
航空病/航空病　air sickness
航空性肺气肿/航空性肺氣腫　aeroemphysema
航空性中耳炎/高空中耳炎　otitic barotrauma
航空牙科学/高空牙科學　aerodontia
航空医学/航空醫學　air medicine
航空中耳炎/飛行員中耳炎,航空性中耳炎　aero-otitis media
航天医学/宇宙醫學　aerospace medicine
航线/航線　airline
颃颡/頏顙　nasopharynx
颃颡岩/鼻咽癌　carcinoma of nasopharynx
蒿芩清胆汤/蒿芩清膽湯　haoqin qingdan decoction
毫安[培]计/毫安培計　milammeter
毫单位/毫單位　milliunit
毫伏[特]/毫伏特　millivolt
毫居里小时/毫居里小時　millicurie-hour
毫拉德/毫雷得　millirad
毫朗伯/毫朗伯　millilambert
毫伦琴/毫侖琴　milliroentgen
毫毛/毫毛,柔毛　vellus hair
毫米波疗法/毫米波療法　millimeter wave therapy
毫渗量/毫滲量　milliosmolarity
毫升/毫升　mil, milliliter
毫针/毫針　filiform needle
毫针刺法/毫針刺法　technique of filiform needle

acupuncture
豪厄尔-若利小体/豪-賈二氏小體　Howell-Jolly bodies
豪氏钳/豪氏鉗　How pliers
豪斯顿肌/Houston氏肌　Houston muscle
壕沟足/戰壕足病　trench foot
13［号染色体］三体综合征/三染色體13症，唇裂-眼畸形症候群　trisomy 13 syndrome
耗碘量/耗碘量　iodine consumption
耗竭性萎缩/衰竭性萎縮　exhaustion atrophy
耗水量/耗水量　water consumption
耗血/耗血　hematozemia
耗氧热量计/測氧熱量計　oxycalorimeter
耗脂［性］肉芽肿/噬脂細胞肉芽腫　lipophagic granuloma
诃子/訶子　medicine terminalia fruit
呵欠/呵欠　yawning
禾木胶/禾木膠　acaroid gum
合/合　he
合胞体的/融合細胞的　syncytial
合胞体瘤/融合細胞瘤　syncytioma
合［胞］体细胞/融合體細胞　syncytial cell
合胞体滋养层/葉外層　plasmoditrophoblast
合并的/合并的　combined
合并附属器肿瘤/合并附屬器瘤　combined adnexal tumor
合并感染/并行感染　concurrent infection
合并麻醉/合并麻醉　combined anesthesia
合并伤/合併傷　associated injury
合并性失语/混合性失語症　combined aphasia
合并性硬化/脊髓後索與側索之合并性硬化　combined sclerosis
合并痣/合并痣　combined nevus
合病/合病　disease involving two or more channels
合成/合成　synthetic
合成代谢/合成代謝，構成性代謝　anabolic metabolism, constructive metabolism
合成蛋白质/合成蛋白質　synthetic protein
合成观测计/液體接合檢查鏡　synthescope
合成后期/合成後期　post-synthetic phase
合成基因/合成基因　synthetic gene
合成抗菌药/合成抗菌藥　synthetic antibacterial drug
合成抗原/合成抗原　synthetic antigen
合成酶/合成酶　synthetase
合成期/合成期　synthetic phase
合成前列腺素类/合成前列腺素類　synthetic prostaglandins
合成前列腺素内过氧化物/合成前列腺素內過氧化物　synthetic prostaglandin endoperoxide
合成前期/合成前期　presynthetic phase
合成染色体/合成染色體　artificial chromosome
合成树脂/合成樹脂　synthetic resin
合成树脂皮炎/合成樹脂皮炎　synthetic resin dermatitis
合成纤维/合成纖維　synthetic fiber
合成橡胶印模材料/合成橡膠印模材料　elastomeric impression material
合成疫苗/合成疫苗　synthetic vaccine
合法流产/合法流産　legal abortion
合格牛乳/驗訖乳，檢定乳　certified milk
合谷/合谷　hegu, LI4
合谷疗/合谷疗　Hegu ding
合骨/内髁　medial malleolus
合骨法/合骨法　bone-rejoining manipulation
合欢花/合歡花　albizia flower
合欢皮/合歡皮　silktree albizia bark
合剂/合劑，混合物　mixture
合金/合金　alloy
合理医学/理性醫學　rational medicine
合理用药/合理用藥　rational use of drug
合霉素/合黴素　syntomycin
合体细胞/融合細胞　syncytium
合体滋养/融合細胞滋養層，合胞體滋養層　syncytiotrophoblast
合［穴］/合穴　he-sea point
合阳/合陽　heyang, BL55
合页皮瓣/合頁皮瓣　hinge skin flap
合脂酶/合脂酵素　lipese
合子/［接］合子　zygote
合子输卵管内移植/受精卵輸卵管植入　zygote intra-fallopian transfer, ZIFT
合作行为/合作行爲　cooperative behavior
何杰金氏棒状杆菌/Hodgkinii氏棒狀桿菌　corynebacterium Hodgkinii
何首乌/何首烏　fleeceflower root
和/和　demulcent therapy
和法/和法　harmonizing method
和合率/一致率　concordance rate
和剂局/和劑局　Bureau for Compounding
和剂局方/和濟局方　Heji Ju Fang
和解/和解　reconciliation
和解表里/和解表裡　reconciling exterior and interior
和［解］法/和［解］法　reconciliation method
和解少阳剂/和解少陽劑　reconciling shaoyang formula

和胃降逆/和胃降逆　harmonizing stomach for descending adverse qi
和胃燥湿剂/和胃燥濕劑　formula for harmonizing stomach and drying dampness
和阵/和陣　harmonizing array
和中/和中　regulating the middle warmer
河车大造丸/河車大造丸　heche dazao pills
河盲/河盲症　river blindness
河豚毒素/河豚毒素　tetrodotoxin
河豚毒酸/河豚毒酸　tetrodonic acid
河豚中毒/河豚中毒　fugu poisoning, balloon fish poisoning
荷包缝合/荷包縫合　purse string suture
荷包牡丹碱/比苦苦靈鹼　bicuculline
荷荷芭油/荷荷芭油　jojoba oil
荷叶/荷葉　lotus leaf
核/核　nucleus
核板/核板　nuclear disc
核被膜/核被膜,核套膜　nuclear envelope
核不均-核糖核蛋白类/核不均-核糖核蛋白類　heterogeneous-nuclear ribonucleoproteins
核磁共振/核磁共振　nuclear magnetic resonance
[核]磁共振成像/核磁共振影像　nuclear magnetic resonance imaging
核[大小]不均/細胞核大小不均　anisokaryosis
核袋[肌]纤维/核袋[肌]纖維　nuclear bag fiber
核蛋白类/核蛋白類　nucleoproteins
核蛋白体/核蛋白體,核糖體　ribosome
核蛋白质/核蛋白質　nucleoprotein
核蛋白质类/核蛋白質類　nuclear proteins
核毒素/核酸毒素　nucleotoxin
核断裂/核崩解　karyoclasis
核反应堆/核反應爐　nuclear reactor
核纺锤体/核紡錘體,核梭　nuclear spindle
核分裂抑制剂/核分裂抑制劑　mitotic inhibitor
核辐射检查法/核輻射檢查法　curioscopy
核苷/核苷　nucleoside
核苷 Q/核苷 Q　nucleoside Q
核苷二磷酸还原酶/核苷二磷酸還原酶　ribonucleoside diphosphate reductase
核苷二磷酸激酶/核苷二磷酸激酶　nucleoside-diphosphate kinase
核苷二磷酸糖类/核苷二磷酸糖類　nucleoside-diphosphate sugars
核苷类/核苷類　nucleosides
核苷类抗生素/核苷類抗生素　nucleoside antibiotic
核苷磷酸化酶/核苷磷酸化酶　nucleoside-phosphorylase

核苷磷酸激酶/核苷磷酸激酶　nucleoside-phosphate kinase
核苷酶/核苷酵素　nucleosidase
核苷三磷酸酶/核苷三磷酸酶　nucleoside-triphosphatase
核苷酸/核苷酸　nucleotide
核苷酸还原酶类/核苷酸還原酶類　ribonucleotide reductases
核苷酸基/核苷酸基　nucleotidyl
核苷酸基转移酶类/核苷酸基轉移酶類　nucleotidyltransferases
核苷酸类/核苷酸類　nucleotides
核苷酸类药物/核苷酸藥物　nucleotide drug
核苷酸酶/核苷酸酵素　nucleotidase
核苷酸图谱/核苷酸圖譜　nucleotide mapping
核苷酸脱氨酶类/核苷酸脱胺酶類　nucleotide deaminases
核苷酸转运蛋白质类/核苷酸轉運蛋白質類　nucleotide transport proteins
核苷脱氨酶类/核苷脱胺酶類　nucleoside deaminases
核苷转运蛋白质类/核苷轉運蛋白質類　nucleoside transport proteins
核固缩/核濃縮,[核]凝縮　karyopyknosis
核[过]大/核過大　karyomegaly
核后环/核後環　postnuclear ring
核黄疸/核質性黃疸,色素腦病變　kernicterus, nuclear jaundice
核黄素/核黄素　riboflavine
核黄素合酶/核黄素合酶　riboflavin synthase
核黄素缺乏/核黄素缺乏　riboflavin deficiency
核黄素缺乏病/乳黄素缺乏病,核酸糖黄素缺乏病　ariboflavinosis
核黄素血症/核黄素血症　ariboflavinaemia
核基质/核基質　nuclear matrix
核基质附着区结合蛋白质类/核基質附著區結合蛋白質類　matrix attachment region binding proteins
核基质结合区/核基質結合區　matrix attachment region
核基质相关蛋白质类/核基質相關蛋白質類　nuclear matrix-associated proteins
核间束/核間徑　internuncial tract
核间性眼肌瘫痪/内眼肌麻痺　internuclear ophthalmoplegia
核碱基转运蛋白质类/核鹼基轉運蛋白質類　nucleobase transport proteins
核角蛋白/核角素　nucleokeratin
核接合/核結合　karyapsis

核聚变/核聚變 nuclear fusion
核抗原/核抗原 nuclear antigen
核壳蛋白质类/核殼蛋白質類 nucleocapsid proteins
核壳[体]/核殼 nucleocapsid
核孔/核孔 nuclear pore
核孔复合蛋白质类/核孔複合蛋白質類 nuclear pore complex proteins
核孔复合体/核孔複合體 nuclear pore complex
核链[肌]纤维/核鏈[肌]纖維 nuclear chain fiber
核裂变/[原子]核裂變 nuclear fission
核裂产物/核裂產物,分裂產物 fission product
核帽结合蛋白质复合物/核帽結合蛋白質複合物 nuclear cap-binding protein complex
核酶/核酶 ribozyme
核膜/核膜 karyotheca, nuclear membrane
核内包涵体/核内包涵體 intranuclear inclusion body
核内复制/核内複製 endoreduplication
核内间隙/核内間隙 intranuclear space
核内体/核内體 endosome
核内有丝分裂/核内有絲分裂 endomitosis
核破裂/核破裂,核崩解 karyorrhexis
核染色细胞/核染色細胞 karyochrome cell
核染质/核染質 mitoplasm
核染质溢出/核染質溢出 chromidiosis
核仁/核仁 nucleole, nucleolus
核仁管系统/核仁管系統 nucleolar channel system
核仁内小体/内核仁 endonucleolus
核仁旁染色质/核仁附著染色質 nuclcolus associated chromatin
核仁溶解/核之溶解 pyrenolysis
核仁素/核仁素 nucleolin
核仁随体/附核仁 nucleolar satellite
核仁小斑/核仁小斑 nucleololus
核仁小体/核仁小體 entosthoblast
核仁组成区/核仁組成區 nucleolus organizer region
核仁组成中心/核仁組織導體 nucleolar organizer
核仁组织区/核仁組織區 nucleolar organizing region
核溶解/核溶解 nuclear solution
核上性眼肌瘫痪/核上性眼肌癱瘓 supranuclear ophthalmoplegia
核[深]染色细胞/核色細胞 karyochrome
核生成/核生成 karyogenesis
核嗜色性/核嗜色性 caryochrome
核素疗法/核素療法 nucleotherapy
核素[注射]动物/核素動物 nuclein animal
核酸/核酸 nucleic acid
核酸变性作用/核酸變性作用 nucleic acid denaturation
核酸重复序列/核酸重復序列 nucleic acid repetitive sequence
核酸复性/核酸複性 nucleic acid renaturation
核酸构象/核酸構象 nucleic acid conformation
核酸合成抑制剂/核酸合成抑制劑 nucleic acid synthesis inhibitor
核酸金属化物/核酸金屬化物 nucleide
核酸扩增技术/核酸擴增技術 nucleic acid amplification technique
核酸类/核酸類 nucleic acids
核酸类药物/核酸類藥物 nucleic acid drug
核酸磷酸酶/核酸磷酸酶,核苷酸酵素 nucleophosphatase
核酸酶/核酸酵素 nuclease
核酸酶保护测定/核酸酶保護測定 nuclease protection assay
核酸内切酶/核酸内切酶 endonuclease
核酸前体/核酸前體 nucleic acid precursor
核酸数据库/核酸資料庫 nucleic acid database
核酸探针/核酸探針 nucleic acid probe
核酸调控序列/核酸調控序列 nucleic acid regulatory sequence
核酸序列同源性/核酸序列同源性 nucleic acid sequence homology
核酸异源双链分子/核酸異源雙鏈分子 nucleic acid heteroduplexe
核酸杂交/核酸雜交 nucleic acid hybridization
核酸组蛋白/核組織蛋白 nucleohistone
核糖/核糖 ribose
核糖醇/阿束醇 ribitol
核糖蛋白/核糖蛋白 nucleoglucoprotein
核糖核蛋白/核糖核[酸]蛋白 ribonucleoprotein
核糖核苷/核糖核苷 ribonucleoside
核糖核苷酸/核糖核苷酸 ribonucleotide
核糖核酸/核糖核酸 ribonucleic acid, RNA
核糖核酸病毒/核糖核酸病毒 ribonucleic acid virus
核糖核酸酶/核糖核酸酶 ribonuclease
核糖核酸调控序列/核糖核酸調控序列 ribonucleic acid regulatory sequence
核糖基/核糖基 ribosyl
核糖基化/核糖基化 ribosylation
核糖霉素/核糖黴素 ribostamycin
核糖体/核糖體 ribosome
核糖体蛋白质 S6/核糖體蛋白質 S6 ribosomal protein S6
核糖体蛋白质 S6 激酶类/核糖體蛋白質 S6 激酶類 ribosomal protein S6 kinases
核糖体蛋白质类/核糖體蛋白質類 ribosomal

proteins
核糖体基因型/核糖體基因型　ribotyping
核糖体移码/核糖體移碼　ribosomal frameshifting
核桃仁/核桃仁　English walnut seed
核铁质/核鐵質　karyogen
核酮糖/核酮醣　ribulose
核酮糖二磷酸羧化酶/核酮醣二磷酸羧化酶　ribulose-bisphosphate carboxylase
核酮糖磷酸类/核酮醣磷酸類　ribulose-phosphates
核吞噬作用/[細胞]核吞噬作用　phagokaryosis
核外染色粒/核外染色粒　chromidium
核外染色质/核外染色質　chromidial substance
核外染色质网/核外染質網　chromidial net
核网/核網[質]　karyoreticulum
核网期/核網期　dictyotene stage
核网丝/核網絲,核染质　karyomitome
核微粒体/核微粒　karyomicrosome
核物理学/核子物理學　nuclear physics
核吸收/核吸收　nuclear absorption
核系/原核　karyonide
核纤层/核纖層　nuclear lamina
核纤层蛋白 A 型/核纖層蛋白 A 型　lamin type A
核纤层蛋白 B 型/核纖層蛋白 B 型　lamin type B
核纤层蛋白质类/核纖層蛋白質類　lamins
核小体/核小體　nucleosome
核心家庭/核心家庭　nuclear family
核心运动概念/核心運動概念　leading circle concept
核心脏病学/核子心臟學　nuclear cardiology
核形/核形,核式　Karyomorphism
核型/核型　karyotype
核型原子/核原子　nuclear atom
核性白内障/核性内障　nuclear cataract
核性别/性核　nuclear sex
核性眼肌瘫痪/神經核性眼肌麻痺　nuclear ophthalmoplegia
核液/核液,核漿　karyenchyma
核[液]泡/核[液]泡　nuclear vacuole
核医学/核醫學　nuclear medicine
核异常/核變異　dyskaryosis
核右移/血球成熟系列向右轉移　shift to the right
核增生/核增生　nucleosis
核质/核質　karyoplasm, nucleoplasm
核质比率/核原漿比值　karyoplasmic ratio
核周体/核周體　perikaryon
核桩冠/核樁冠　post crown with core
核左移/血球成熟系列向左移轉　shift to the left
𬌗叉/咬合叉　bite fork
𬌗的/咬合的　occlusive

𬌗干扰/咬合干擾　occlusal interference
𬌗夹板/咬合夾板　occlusal splint
𬌗面/𬌗面,咬合面　occlusal surface, masticatory surface
𬌗[面]的/閉塞的,咬合的　occlusal
𬌗面间的/咬合面間的　interocclusal
𬌗平衡/咬合平衡　occlusal balance
𬌗球形/閉合之球面形　spherical form of occlusion
𬌗下面/次咬合面　subocclusal surface
𬌗线/咬合線　occlusion line
𬌗型/咬合型　occlusal pattern
𬌗应力/咬合應力　occlusal stress
颌/頜　jaw
颌部寄生胎/頜部寄生胎　polygnathus
颌成形术/下頜造形術　genyplasty
颌导板/頜導板　gnatho-guide plate
颌动瞬目综合征/頜動瞬目症候群　jaw winking syndrome
颌骨/頜骨　jaw bone
颌骨骨折/頜骨折　jaw fracture
颌骨固定技术/頜骨固定技術　jaw fixation technique
颌骨间关系/頜骨間關係　jaws relation
颌骨正中关系/中央性頜關係　centric jaw relation
颌骨中枢癌/頜骨中樞癌　central carcinoma of jaw
颌关系记录/頜骨關係記錄　jaw relation record
颌后缩/頜後縮　retrognathia
颌畸形/頜畸形　jaw abnormality
颌疾病/頜疾病　jaw disease
颌间瘢痕挛缩/頜間瘢痕攣縮　intermaxillary cicatricial contracture
颌间垂直关系/頜間垂直關係　vertical relation of jaws
颌间固定/頜間固定　intermaxillary fixation
颌间间隙/頜間隙　intermaxillary space
颌间距离/上下頜弓間距　interarch distance
颌间挛缩/頜間攣縮　intermaxillary contracture
颌间牵引/頜間牽引　intermaxillary traction
颌间水平关系/頜間水平關係　horizontal relation of jaw
颌间支抗/頜間支抗　intermaxillary anchorage
颌髁/頜髁　condyle of jaw
颌裂/頜裂　cleft jaw
颌面侧位投照术/頜面側位投照術　lateral position roentgenography of maxillo-facial region
颌面发育不全/頜面發育不全　mandibulofacial dysplasia
颌面畸形/頜面畸形　maxillofacial abnormalities
颌面假体/頜面補缺術　maxillofacial prosthesis

颌面假体植入/頜面假體植入　maxillofacial prosthesis implantation
颌面美容外科学/頜面美容外科學　maxillofacial cosmetic surgery
颌面修复学/面部補缺學　maxillofacial prosthetics
颌囊肿/頜囊腫　jaw cyst
颌内动脉/內上腭動脈　internal maxillary artery
颌内支抗/頜內支抗　intermaxillary anchorage
颌旁寄生胎/頜旁寄生胎　paragnathus
颌舌骨脊/頜舌骨脊　mylohyoid ridge
颌[跳]反射/頜[跳]反射　jaw-jerk reflex
颌外支抗/頜外支抗　extramaxillary anchorage
颌下/頜下　submaxillary
颌下蜂窝[组]织炎/頜下蜂窩組織炎　submaxillary phlegmon
颌下腺/頜下腺　submandibular gland
颌下腺疾病/頜下腺疾病　submandibular gland disease
颌下腺涎/頜下腺涎　submaxillary saliva
颌下腺炎/頜下腺炎　submaxillaritis
颌下腺造影侧位投影术/頜下腺造影側位投影術　lateral position of submandibular gland sialography
颌下腺肿瘤/頜下腺腫瘤　submandibular gland neoplasm
颌下痈/頜下癰，頜下膿腫　submandibular abscess
颌学/頜學　gnathology
颌运动/頜運動　jaw movement
颌肿瘤/頜腫瘤　jaw neoplasm
赫伯登结节/赫伯登結節　Heberden node
赫伯登哮喘/Heberden 氏氣喘　Heberden asthma
赫蒂希-罗克受精卵/赫-洛二氏卵　Hertig-Rock ova
赫尔维韧带/Helvetius 氏韌帶　ligament of Helvetius
赫尔辛基宣言/赫爾辛基宣言　Helsinki declaration
赫尔辛斯基紫外线照射/Huldshinsky 氏放射療法　Huldshinsky radiation
赫-霍病/赫-霍二氏病，赫特氏病　Herter-Heubner disease
赫克斯海默反应/Herxheimer 氏反應　Herxheimer reaction
赫克斯海默热/Herxheimer 熱病　Herxheimer fever
赫克通现象/海克頓氏現象　Hekteon phenomenon
赫勒丛/Heller 氏叢　Heller plexus
赫利奥多罗斯绷带/Heliodorus 氏繃帶　Heliodorus bandage
赫利茨病/Herlitz 症　Herlitz disease
赫利固定液/Helly 氏[固定]液　Helly fluid
赫林试验/赫寧氏試驗　Hering test
赫林体/赫林氏體　Herring body

赫鲁比前置镜/赫魯比前置鏡　Hruby preset lens
赫曲霉毒素类/赫麴黴毒素類　ochratoxins
赫特维希上皮根鞘/赫德威氏上皮牙根鞘　Hertwig epithelial root sheath
赫胥黎层/赫胥黎氏層　Huxley layer
褐肺病/褐肺　brown lung
褐黄病/褐黃病　ochronosis
褐黄病性关节炎/褐黃病性關節炎　ochronotic arthritis
褐色萎缩/褐色萎縮，棕色萎縮　brown atrophy
褐色硬变/褐色硬結，棕色硬結　brown induration
褐铁矿/褐鐵礦　limonite
褐尾蠹/褐尾蠹　brown-tail moth
褐尾蠹皮炎/因蛾毛刺激而生的皮膚炎　brown-tail moth dermatitis
褐藻类/褐藻類　brown algae
褐脂/褐脂　brown fat
鹤顶/鶴頂　heding, EX-LE2
鹤节/鶴節　crane's joint
鹤虱/鶴蝨　common carpesium fruit
鹤膝风/鶴膝風　arthrosis like crane knee
鹤膝痰/鶴膝痰　crane's knee phlegm, tuberculosis of knee joint
黑暗产色性/黑暗產色性　scotochromogenicity
黑暗癖/黑暗癖　scotophilia
黑暗性眼球震颤/黑暗性眼球震顫　darkness nystagmus
黑白混血儿/黑白混血兒　mulatto
黑斑病/黑變病，黑皮病　melasma
黑变病/黑變病，黑色素沈著症　melanosis
黑变病的/黑變病的　melanotic
黑变性瘭疽/黑變性瘭疽　melanotic whitlow
黑布拉病/Hebra 氏病　Hebra disease
黑布拉红糠疹/Hebra 氏紅色糠疹　pityriasis rubra of Hebra
黑长尾猴/黑長尾猴　Cercopithecus aethiops
黑刺肉芽肿/黑刺肉芽腫　blackthorn granuloma
黑[点]癣/黑[點]癬　black dot ringworm
黑尔姆霍尔茨韧带/Helmholtz 氏韌帶　Helmholtz ligament
黑尔姆霍尔茨学说/哈姆赫茲氏學說　Helmholtz theory
黑尔综合征/Hare 氏症候群　Hare syndrome
黑粪症/黑糞症　melena
黑风内障/黑風內障　black wind glaucoma
黑寡妇蜘蛛/黑寡婦蜘蛛　black widow spider
黑光/黑光　black light
黑胡椒/黑胡椒　black pepper

黑棘皮病/黑色棘皮病　acanthosis nigricans
黑棘皮瘤/黑色素棘皮瘤　melanoacanthoma
黑加尔征/黑加爾徵　Hegar sign
黑甲/黑甲　melanonychia
黑角蝇属/住血蟲　Haematobia
黑芥/黑芥　black mustard
黑芥子硫苷酸/黑芥酸　myronic acid
黑芥子硫苷酸钾/黑芥酸鉀　potassium myronate
黑芥子硫苷酸盐/黑芥酸鹽　myronate
黑芥子酶细胞/芥子酶細胞　myrosin cell
黑睛/黑睛,黑仁,黑眼　black eye, cornea and iris
黑睛病/黑睛病　cornea disease, disease of black of eye
黑糠疹/黑色糠疹　pityriasis nigra
黑勒贲门肌切开术/黑勒賁門肌切開術　Heller operation
黑绿头苍蝇/黑綠頭蒼蠅　black blowfly
黑麻疹/黑麻疹　rubeola nigra
黑麦/黑麥,裸麥　rye
黑麦碱/黑麥鹼　secalin
黑麦糖/麥角糖　secalose
黑麦哮喘/裸麥氣喘　rye asthma
黑毛舌/黑舌[病]　black hairy tongue
黑矇/黑矇　amaurosis
黑矇的/黑矇的　amaurotic
黑内尔症状/海納氏症狀　Haenel symptom
黑尿/黑尿[症]　black urine
黑尿热/黑尿熱　blackwater fever
黑皮病/黑皮病　sowda
黑皮性图案状慢性红斑/黑皮性圖案狀慢性紅斑　erythema chronicum figuratum melanodermicum
黑皮炎/黑皮炎　melanodermatitis
黑皮质素受体/黑皮質素受體　melanocortin receptor
黑曲菌/黑麴菌　Aspergillus nigra
黑热病/黑熱病　black sickness, dumdum fever
黑人男性丘疹性疹/黑人男性之丘疹性皮疹　papular eruption in black male
黑软海绵素A/黑軟海綿素A　okadaic acid
黑塞尔巴赫韧带/Hesselbach氏韌帶　Hesselbach ligament
黑塞尔巴赫疝/Hesselbach氏疝　Hesselbach hernia
黑色的/黑色的　nigricans
黑色干性坏死/炭疽性壞死　anthraconecrosis
黑色过度角化症/黑色過度角化症　hyperkeratosis nigricans
黑色黄疸/黑黃疸　black jaundice
黑色角化病/黑色角化病　keratosis nigricans
黑色毛结节菌病/毛幹黑節病　black piedra
黑色内障/黑色內障　black cataract
黑色泥状粪/汙泥狀糞　caddy stool
黑色呕吐/黑吐[症]　melanemesis
黑色呕吐物/黑色[嘔]吐物　black vomit
黑色丘疹性皮肤病/黑色丘疹性皮膚病　dermatosis papulosa nigra
黑[色]松脂/黑瀝青　naval pitch
黑色素/黑[色]素　melanin
黑色素癌/黑色素癌　carcinoma nigrum
黑色素过度沉着/黑色素過度沈著　hypermelanosis
黑色素过少/皮膚色素減少症　hypomelanism
黑色素过少症/組織黑色素減少病,白斑病　hypomelanosis
黑[色]素颗粒/黑色素顆粒　melanin granule
黑色素瘤/黑[色]瘤　melanoma
黑色素色素沉着过度/黑色素的色素沈著過度　melanotic hyperpigmentation
黑色素神经外胚瘤/黑色素沈著性神經外胚層瘤　melanotic neuroectodermal tumor
黑[色]素体/黑素體　melanosome
黑[色]素细胞/黑[色素]細胞　melanocyte
黑[色]素小体/黑素體,黑素粒　melanosome
黑[色]素絮状反应/黑素凝絮反應　melanoflocculation
黑色萎缩/黑色萎縮　black atrophy
黑色萎缩症/黑色萎縮症　atrophie noire
黑色氧化铁[剂]/黑鐵氧化物,黑色氧化鐵　black oxide of iron, black iron oxide
黑色硬结/黑色硬結　black induration
黑砂糖/黑砂糖　black sugar
黑舌病/黑舌病　black-tongue disease
黑死病/黑死病　black death
黑[素]癌/黑[色素]癌　melanocarcinoma
黑[素]沉淀反应/黑素沈澱反應　melanoprecipitation
黑素成釉细胞瘤/黑釉質母細胞瘤　melanoameloblastoma
黑素类/黑素類　melanins
黑[素]瘤病/黑瘤病　melanomatosis
黑素尿/黑尿症　melanuria
黑素缺失症/無黑色素症　amelanosis
黑[素]肉瘤/黑肉瘤　melanosarcoma
黑素上皮癌/黑上皮瘤　melanoepithelioma
黑素生成/黑素生成　melanogenesis
黑素细胞/黑素細胞載色體　melanophore
黑素细胞刺激激素/黑素細胞刺激激素　melanocyte-stimulating hormone
黑素细胞刺激素/激黑細胞素　melanophorin
黑素细胞的/黑色素細胞的　melanocytic

黑素细胞瘤/黑素細胞瘤　melanocytoma
黑素细胞增多症/黑色素細胞增生症　melanocytosis
黑素细胞痣/黑色素細胞母斑,黑色素細胞痣　melanocytic nevus
黑素纤维瘤/黑色素纖維瘤　melanofibroma
黑素原/黑素原　melanogen
黑酸尿的/黑尿病的　alkaptonuric
黑酸尿症/黑酸尿症　alkaptonuria
黑髓/黑骨髓　black marrow
黑苔/黑苔　black fur
黑嚏根草/黑藜蘆　black hellebore
黑头粉刺/黑頭粉刺　blackhead
黑希特现象/赫希特氏現象　Hecht phenomenon
黑血[症]/黑色素血症　melanemia
黑氧化钛/黑氧化鈦　titanium oxide black
黑夜睛明/黑夜睛明　day blindness
黑夜恐怖/黑夜恐懼症　noctiphobia
黑夜锥虫/夜行錐蟲　Trypanosoma noctuae
黑翳如珠/黑翳如珠　descemetocele
黑蝇/黑蠅　blackfly
黑掌/黑掌　black palm
黑芝麻/黑芝麻　black sesame
黑质/黑質　substantia nigra, black substance
黑质网状部/黑質網狀部　reticular part of substantia nigra
黑质支/黑質支　branch of substantia nigra
黑质致密部/黑質致密部　compact part of substantia nigra
黑踵病/足跟瘀斑　black heel
亨德拉病毒/亨德拉病毒　Hendra virus
亨德森-哈塞尔巴赫方程式/漢-哈二氏方程式　Henderson-Hasselbalch equation
亨德森-琼斯病/漢-瓊二氏病　Henderson-Jones disease
亨勒层/亨勒層　Henle layer
亨勒多角骨/Henle 氏多角骨　trapezoid bone of Henle
亨勒内侧副韧带/Henle 氏内側副韌帶　medial accessory ligament of Henle
亨勒襻/亨勒襻　loop of Henle
亨尼波病毒/亨尼波病毒　Henipavirus
亨尼波病毒感染/亨尼波病毒感染　Henipavirus infection
亨诺赫-舍恩莱因紫癜/亨-史二氏紫瘢病　Henoch-Schonlein purpura
亨诺克/Henoch 氏　Henoch
亨森细胞/亨森氏細胞　Hensen cell
亨特病/亨特病　Hunt disease
亨特[肌]萎缩/Hunt 氏萎縮　Hunt atrophy
亨特韧带/Hunter 氏韌帶　Hunter ligament
亨特舌炎/Hunter 氏舌炎　Hunter glossitis
亨特神经痛/Hunt 氏神經痛　Hunt neuralgia
亨特纹状体综合征/Hunt 氏症候群　Hunt striatal syndrome
亨廷顿舞蹈症/亨廷頓舞蹈症　Huntington chorea
亨辛韧带/Hensing 氏韌帶　Hensing ligament
恒定区/恆定區　constant region
恒基托/恆基托　permanent base-plate
恒久型/恆久型　permanent form
恒冷箱切片/恆冷箱切片　cryostat section
恒冷箱切片机/恆冷箱切片機　cryostat microtome
恒磨牙/附加齒　accessional teeth
恒乳双生牙/二生齒列　diphyodontic gemination
恒压电池/恆久電池　constant cell
恒压软组织扩张术/恆壓軟組織擴張術　constant pressure soft tissue expansion
恒牙/恆齒,永久齒　permanent teeth
恒牙槽/恆牙齒槽　permanent alveolus
恒牙列/恆牙　permanent dentition
横部/橫部　transverse part
横产/橫産　cross birth
横产式/橫産式　transverse lie
横川后殖吸虫/橫川後殖吸蟲　Metagonimus ovatus
横川后殖吸虫病/橫川後殖吸蟲病　metagonimiasis yokogawai
横的/橫的　transverse
横笛吹奏者颌/橫笛吹奏者下巴　flautist chin
横动脉/橫動脈　transverse artery
横窦/橫竇　transverse sinus
横窦沟/橫竇溝　sulcus for transverse sinus
横窦脑膜瘤/橫竇腦膜瘤　transverse sinus meningioma
横断面解剖学/橫斷面解剖學　cross-sectional anatomy
横断面研究/橫斷面研究　cross-sectional study
横断性脊髓病/橫貫性脊髓病　transverse myelopathy
横断性视神经炎/橫斷性視神經炎　transverse optic neuritis
横跗关节/橫跗關節　transverse tarsal articulation
横膈疝/膈疝　diaphragmatic hernia
横膈上食管扩张术/橫膈上食道擴張術　supradiaphragmatic esophageal dilatation
横骨/橫骨　hyoid bone, henggu, KI11
横贯性脊髓炎/橫貫性脊髓炎　transverse myelitis
横肌/橫肌　transversalis

横嵴/橫嵴 transverse crest
横脊/橫脊 transverse ridge
横结肠/橫結腸 transverse colon
横结肠系膜/橫結腸繫膜 mesentery of transverse part of colon
横结肠造口术/橫結腸造口術 transverse colostomy
横径/橫徑 transverse diameter
横裂/橫裂 transverse fissure
横面骨折/橫面骨折 transverse facial fracture
横桥/[肌]橫橋 cross bridge
横切片/橫切片 transverse section
横韧带/橫韌帶 transverse ligament
横褥式缝合/橫褥式縫合 transverse mattress suture
横束/橫束 transverse fasciculi
横头/橫頭 transverse head
横突/橫突 transverse process
横突后结节/橫突後結節 posterior tubercle of transverse
横突棘肌/橫突棘肌 transversospinale
横突间肌/橫突間肌 intertransversarii, intertransverse muscle
横突间前肌/橫突間前肌 musculi intertransversarii anteriores
横突间韧带/橫突間韌帶 intertransverse ligament
横突孔/橫突孔 transverse foramen
横突肋凹/橫突肋凹 transverse costal fovea
横突前结节/橫突前結節 anterior tubercle of transverse process
横纹肌/橫紋肌 striped muscle, striated muscle
横纹肌错构瘤/橫紋肌錯構瘤 striated muscle hamartoma
横纹肌瘤/橫紋肌瘤 myoma striocellulare
横纹肌盘/橫紋肌盤 striated muscle disc
横纹肌溶解/橫紋肌溶解 rhabdomyolysis
横纹肌肉瘤/橫紋肌肉瘤 rhabdosarcoma
横纹肌细胞的/橫紋肌纖維細胞的 striocellular
横纹肌样肾母细胞瘤/橫紋肌樣腎母細胞瘤 rhabdomyoid Wilms tumor
横纹掌跖角皮症/橫紋蹠掌角皮症 striated palmoplantar keratoderma
横狭点/狹穴 stenion
横纤维/橫行纖維 horizontal fiber
横线/橫線 transverse line
横小管/橫小管 transverse tubule
横[形]骨折/橫[形]骨折 transverse fracture
横掌股间韧带/橫掌間韌帶 transverse metacarpal interosseous ligament
横针牙/橫針齒 cross-pin teeth

横支/橫支 transverse branch
横指同身寸/橫指同身寸 4-finger-breadth measurement
横置带环/橫置帶環 translocating band
横阻/橫阻 transverse arrest
横坐标/橫坐標 abscissa
轰炸休克/炸彈休克 bomb shock
烘焙/烘焙 bake, cure
烘干/烘乾 drying by baking
烘烙[疗]法/烙熱法 chauffage
红白血病/紅白血病 erythroleukemia
红斑/紅斑 erythema
红斑痤疮/紅斑性痤瘡 rosacea
红斑的/紅斑的 erythematous
红斑角皮病/紅斑角皮症 erythrokeratodermia
红斑狼疮/紅斑[性]狼瘡 lupus erythematosus
红斑狼疮试验/紅斑狼瘡試驗 lupus erythematosus test
红斑狼疮性脂膜炎/紅斑狼瘡性脂膜炎 lupus erythematosus panniculitis
红斑量/紅斑量 erythema dose
红斑软烂性口炎/紅斑軟爛性口炎 erythematopultaceous stomatitis
红斑水肿性反应/紅斑[性]水腫反應, 弗榭氏反應 E-E reaction
红斑型天疱疮/紅斑性天皰瘡 pemphigus erythematosus
红斑性弓形环状肉芽肿/紅斑性弓形環狀肉芽腫 erythematous arcuate granuloma annulare
红斑性酒渣鼻/紅斑性酒渣鼻 erythematous rosacea
红斑性湿疹/紅斑性濕疹 eczema erythematosum
红斑性天疱疮/紅斑性天皰瘡, 塞-阿二氏症候群 Senear-Usher syndrome
红斑性头痛/頭部紅痛病 erythromelalgia of head
红斑性肢痛病/紅斑性肢痛病 red neuralgia
红斑疹/紅斑疹 erythematous eruption
红斑[疹]毒素/玫紅毒素 erythrogenic toxin
红宝石刀/紅寶石刀 ruby knife
红宝石激光疗法/紅寶石雷射療法 ruby laser therapy
红宝石激光器/紅寶石雷射器 ruby laser
红背蜘蛛/紅背蜘蛛 red-back spider
红玻璃试验/紅玻璃試驗 red glass test
红唇/紅唇 vermilion
红唇皮肤交界处/紅唇皮膚交界處 vermilion-cutaneous junction
红唇切除术/唇紅緣切除術 vermilionectomy
红大戟/紅大戟 knoxia root

红带毒蛛/中亞毒蛛　kara-kurt
红豆蔻/紅豆蔻　galanga galangal fruit
红恶露/紅惡露,血性惡露　lochia cruenta
红发/紅髮　rutilism
红凡士林油/紅色凡士林　red petrolatum
红骨髓/紅骨髓　red bone marrow, red marrow
红光疗法/紅光療法　red light therapy
红汗/紅汗　hematohidrosis
红核/紅核　red nucleus, rubrum
红核橄榄束/紅核橄欖束　rubroolivary tract
红核脊髓的/紅核與脊髓的　rubrospinal
红核脊髓束/紅核脊髓徑　rubrospinal tract
红核网状束/紅核網徑　fasciculi rubroreticulares
红核支/紅核支　branch of red nucleus
红蝴蝶疮/紅蝴蝶瘡,紅斑性狼瘡　lupus erythematosus, red butterfly sore
红蝴蝶疮·脾肾阳虚证/紅蝴蝶瘡·脾腎陽虛證　lupus erythematosus with spleen-kidney yang deficiency pattern
红蝴蝶疮·脾虚肝旺证/紅蝴蝶瘡·脾虛肝旺證　lupus erythematosus with pattern of spleen deficiency and liver hyperactivity
红蝴蝶疮·气滞血瘀证/紅蝴蝶瘡·氣滯血瘀證　lupus erythematosus with pattern of qi stagnation and blood stasis
红蝴蝶疮·热毒炽盛证/紅蝴蝶瘡·熱毒熾盛證　lupus erythematosus with blazing heat-toxin pattern
红蝴蝶疮·阴虚内热证/紅蝴蝶瘡·陰虛內熱證　lupus erythematosus with pattern of yin deficiency and internal heat
红花/紅花　carthamus tinctorius, safflower
红花素/紅花酸　carthamic acid
红花油/紅花子油　Safflower Oil
红肌/紅肌　red muscle
红肌纤维/紅肌纖維　red muscle fiber
红酵母/[黏]紅酵母　Rhodotorula glutinis
红酵母病/紅酵母病　rhodotorulosis
红景天/紅景天　rose-boot
红糠疹/紅色糠疹　pityriasis rubra
红绿色盲/紅綠色盲,道爾頓氏症　red-green blindness, daltonism
红绿色弱/紅綠色弱　dyserythrochloropsia
红毛角化病/紅毛角化病　keratosis pilaris rubra
红霉素/紅黴素　erythromycin
红霉素乳糖酸盐/乳糖酸紅黴素　erythromycin lactobionate
红木色潮红/紅木色潮紅　mahogany flush
红尿症/紅尿症　erythruria
红皮病/紅皮病　erythroderma
红皮病性肥大细胞增多症/紅皮病性肥大細胞增多症　erythrodermic mastocytosis
红皮病性银屑病/牛皮癬紅皮病　erythroderma psoriaticum
红皮型银屑病/紅皮型乾癬　psoriasis erythroderma
红皮症/紅皮症　erythrodermia
红芪/紅芪　manyinflorescenced sweetvetch root
红球菌属/紅球菌　Rhodococcus
红人[颈]综合征/紅人[頸]症候群　red man neck syndrome
红色的/淡紅色的　erythroid
红色恶露/紅色惡露　red lochia
红色海绵/紅色海綿　red sponge
红色幻视/紅色幻視,紅光幻視　erythrophose
红色角质松解症/紅斑角質解離症　erythrokeratolysis
红色觉变常/紅色覺變常,紅色弱　protanomalopia
红色恐怖/懼紅症　erythrophobia
红色滤光片疗法/紅色濾光片療法　red filter treatment
红色盲/第一原色色盲,紅色色盲　protanopsia, red blindness
红色盲者/紅色盲者　protanope
红色毛癣菌/紅色毛癬菌　trichophyton rubrum
红色弱/紅色弱　protanomalia
红色素细胞/紅色素細胞,紅色顆粒細胞　allophore
红色素细胞反应/紅色素細胞反應　erythrophore reaction
红色脱屑性疾病/紅色脫屑性疾病　erythematous desquamating disorder
红色萎缩/紅色萎縮　red atrophy
红色血栓/紅色血栓　red thrombus
红色原圆线虫/紅色原圓線蟲　Protostrongylus rufescens
红痧/紅痧　sha disease with red eruption
红舌/紅舌　red tongue
红参/紅參　red ginseng
红湿疹/紅濕疹　eczema rubrum
红十字会/紅十字會　red cross
红视症/紅視[症]　erythropsia
红丝赤缕/紅絲赤縷　red threads
红丝疔/紅絲疔　acute lymphangitis, red filament
红丝疔·火毒入络证/紅絲疔·火毒入絡證　red filament with pattern of fire-toxin entering collateral
红丝疔·火毒入营证/紅絲疔·火毒入營證　red filament with pattern of fire-toxin entering nutrient phase

[红]粟疹/紅色粟粒疹　miliaria rubra
红髓/紅髓　red pulp
红痛/紅痛症　erythralgia
红外光吸收参比图谱/紅外光吸收對照光譜　infrared reference spectra
红外线/紅外線　infrared ray
红外线分光光度法/紅外線分光光度法　infrared spectrophotometry
红外[线]辐射/紅外[線]輻射　infrared radiation
红外线疗法/紅外線療法　infrared therapy
红外线热像仪/紅外線熱像儀　infrared thermograph
红外线性白内障/紅外線性白內障　infrared cataract
红系细胞/類紅血球　erythroid cell
红系祖细胞/紅系祖細胞　erythroid progenitor cell
红细胞/紅血球　red blood cell, erythrocyte
红细胞包涵体/紅血球包涵體　erythrocyte inclusion
红细胞爆裂型集落生成单位/紅血球爆裂集落形成單位　erythrocytic burst-forming unit, BFU-E
红细胞变形性/紅血球變形性　erythrocyte deformability
红细胞病/紅血球病　erythropathy
红细胞不均/紅血球大小不一　anisocytosis
红细胞成髓细胞血症/母紅血球骨髓血球增多症　erythromyeloblastosis
红细胞沉降/紅血球沈降　erythrosedimentation
红细胞沉降反应/紅血球沈降反應　erythrocyte sedimentation reaction
红细胞沉降率/紅血球沈降率　erythrocyte sedimentation rate
红细胞除去法/紅血球除去法　erythropheresis
红细胞叠积/紅血球疊積　erythrocyte aggregation, erythrocyte rouleaux
红细胞动力学/紅血球動力學　erythrokinetics
红细胞毒素/紅血球毒素　erythrotoxin
红细胞发生/紅血球產生,紅血球發生,紅血球生成　erythrogenesis, erythropoiesis
红细胞发生不能/紅血球成形不能　anerythroplasia
红细胞分解/紅血球分解　diastasemia
红细胞分裂/紅血球分裂　erythrocytoschisis
红细胞杆状小体/紅血球桿狀小體　erythroconte
红细胞管型/紅血球管型　red cell cast
红细胞基质/紅血球基質　discostroma
红细胞集结/紅血球凝結　sympexis
红细胞集落生成单位/紅血球[族]群形成單位　erythrocytic colony forming unit, CFU-E
红细胞计数/紅血球計數　erythrocyte count
红细胞计数器/紅血球計數器,紅血球測量計　erythrocytometer
红细胞寄生物/紅血球寄生物　erythroparasite
红细胞减少/紅血球過少症　erythrocytopenia
红细胞浆质/紅血球漿質　endosoma
红细胞聚集/紅血球聚集　erythrocyte aggregation
红细胞膜/紅血球膜　erythrocyte membrane
红细胞内期/紅血球期　erythrocytic phase
红细胞黏附试验/紅血球黏附試驗　red cell adhesion test
红细胞平均容量/紅血球平均容量　mean corpuscular volume
红细胞平均血红蛋白量/平均血球血紅素量　mean corpuscular hemoglobin
红细胞破坏/紅血球破壞　hemocatheresis
红细胞破坏反应/血球崩解反應　hemoclastic reaction
红细胞破坏性休克/血液崩解休克　hemoclastic shock
红细胞破碎/紅血球破碎　erythroclasis
红细胞钱串形成/紅血球之緡錢狀排列　impilation
红细胞容量/紅血球容量　erythrocyte volume
红细胞溶解/紅血球毀滅,紅血球被噬　erythrocatalysis
红细胞溶解的/紅血球崩解的　hemoclastic
红细胞生成/紅血球生成　erythropoiesis
红细胞生成不全/紅血球生成不全　erythrogenesis imperfecta
红细胞生成不足/紅血球製造缺乏,紅血球產生及發育不能　anerythropoiesis
红细胞生成的/製造紅血球的　erythropoietic
红细胞生成素/紅血球生成素　erythropoietin
红细胞生成素受体/紅血球生成素受體　erythropoietin receptor
红细胞生成素原/紅血球生成素原　erythropoietinogen
红细胞生成性卟啉病/造紅血球性吡咯紫質沈著病　porphyria erythropoietica
红细胞生成性粪卟啉症/紅血球生成性糞紫質病　erythropoietic coproporphyria
红细胞生成性尿卟啉[过多]症/紅血球生成性尿紫質病　erythropoietic uroporphyria
红细胞生成性原卟啉病/紅血球生成性原卟啉病　erythropoietic protoporphyria
红细胞失色症/紅血球失色病　lymphoplasmia
红细胞输注/紅血球輸注　erythrocyte transfusion
红细胞衰老/紅血球衰老　erythrocyte aging
红细胞糖苷脂/紅血球糖苷脂　globoside
红细胞调理素/紅血球調理素　erythrocyto-opsonin
红细胞同种抗体/紅血球同種抗體,血同種抗體

hemisoantibody
红细胞铜蛋白/紅血球銅蛋白　erythrocuprein
红细胞外型疟原虫/紅血球外原形體　exoerythrocytic plasmodium
红细胞系/紅血球系　erythron
红细胞镶嵌性/紅血球鑲工態　erythrocyte mosaicism
红细胞性肝性原紫质病/紅血球性肝性原紫質病　erythro-hepatic protoporphyria
红细胞性微血管/紅血球性微血管　erythrocytic capillary
红细胞阴离子交换蛋白/紅血球陰離子交換蛋白　erythrocyte anion exchange protein
红细胞影/紅血球[血]影　blood ghost, erythrocyte umbra
红细胞郁积/紅血球停滯　erythrostasis
红细胞增多[症]/紅血球增多[症], 紅血球過多症　erythrocythemia, erythrocytosis
红细胞脂蛋白/紅血球脂蛋白　elinin
红细胞指数/紅血球指數　erythrocyte indice
红细胞皱缩/紅血球皺縮　echinosis
红苋/紅莧　amaranth dye
红溴汞溶液/紅溴汞溶液　merbromin solution
红须发/紅色過度, 紅髮特徵　erythrism
红癣/紅癬　erythrasma
红牙/紅牙　erythrodontia
红氧还蛋白类/紅色還原蛋白類　rubredoxins
红移/紅移　red shift
红晕/紅暈　aula
红藻氨酸/海人酸, 紅藻胺酸　kainic acid
红藻氨酸受体/紅藻胺酸受體　kainic acid receptor
红藻类/紅藻　red algae
红疹毒素/狄克氏毒[素]　Dick toxin
红肢病/紅肢症　erythromelia
红紫酸/尿紫酸　purpuric acid
红紫酸盐/紫酸鹽　purpurate
虹彩/虹彩, 虹膜　iris
虹[彩]视/虹暈幻視　halo vision
虹彩状红斑/虹膜狀紅斑　erythema iris
虹膜/虹膜　iris
虹膜闭锁/虹膜閉鎖　atresia iridis
虹膜襞/虹膜襞　fold of iris
虹膜病/虹膜病　iridopathy
虹膜部分切除术/虹膜[部分]切除術　iritoectomy
虹膜成形术/虹膜成形術　iridoplasty
虹膜出血/虹膜出血　iridemia
虹膜大环/虹膜大環　greater ring of iris
虹膜刀/虹膜刀　iridotome

虹膜动脉大环/虹膜動脈大環　greater arterial circle of iris
虹膜动脉小环/虹膜動脈小環　lesser arterial circle of iris
虹膜肥厚/虹膜肥厚　iridauxesis
虹膜分离/虹膜分離　detached iris
虹膜分离切除术/虹膜切除内緣分離術　iridectomesodialysis
虹膜复位器/虹膜復位器　iris repositor
虹膜根部断离/虹膜鬆解術　iridodialysis
虹膜根部分离术/虹膜根部分離術　coredialysis
虹膜[根部]脱离/虹膜解離　iridodiastasis
虹膜巩膜切开术/虹膜鞏膜切開術　iridosclerotomy
虹膜钩/虹膜鉤　iris hook
虹膜固定术/虹膜鎖縛術　iridesis
虹膜贯穿术/虹膜貫穿術　transfixion of iris
虹膜红变/虹膜紅變　rubeosis of iris
虹膜后面/虹膜後面　posterior surface of iris
虹膜后黏着分开术/瞳孔鬆解術, 虹膜粘連鬆解術　corelysis
虹膜后色素层/虹膜後色素層　entiris
虹膜后粘连/虹膜後粘連　posterior synechia
虹膜环形粘连/虹膜環狀粘連　circular synechia
虹膜基质/虹膜基質　iris stroma
虹膜疾病/虹膜疾病　iris disease
虹膜剪/虹膜剪　iris scissor
虹[膜]角膜分离术/虹[膜]角膜分離術　sphincterolysis
虹膜角膜巩膜切除术/虹膜角膜鞏膜切除術　iridocorneosclerectomy
虹膜角膜角/虹膜角膜角　iridocorneal angle
虹膜角膜角隙/虹膜角膜角隙　spaces of iridocorneal angle
虹膜角膜炎/虹膜角膜炎　iridokeratitis
虹膜结核/虹膜結核　tuberculosis of irides
虹膜睫状体脉络膜炎/虹膜睫狀體脈絡膜炎　iridocyclochoroiditis
虹膜睫状体切除术/虹膜睫狀體切除術　iridocyclectomy
虹膜睫状体炎/虹膜睫狀體炎　iridocyclitis
虹膜晶状体囊炎/虹膜晶狀體囊炎　iridocapsulitis
虹膜裂/虹膜缺損　coloboma of iris
虹膜麻痹/虹膜麻痺　iridoparalysis
虹膜脉络膜炎/虹膜脈絡膜炎　iridochoroiditis
虹膜囊切除术/虹膜囊切除術　iridocystectomy
虹膜囊肿/虹膜囊腫　iris cyst
虹膜内翻/虹膜内翻　iridentropium
虹膜内缘黏着部分离/虹膜内緣分離術

iridomesodialysis
虹膜镊/虹膜鉗　iris forcep
虹膜疱疹/虹膜皰疹　herpes iris
虹膜膨隆/虹膜膨隆　iris bombe
虹膜膨胀/虹膜膨脹　iris bombe
虹膜劈裂症/虹膜劈裂症　iridoschisis
虹膜前面/虹膜前面　anterior surface of iris
[虹膜]前缘层/[虹膜]前緣層　anterior border layer
虹膜前粘连/虹膜前粘連　anterior synechia
虹膜嵌顿术/虹膜嵌頓術　iridencleisis
虹膜切除/虹膜切除　iridectomize
虹膜切除术/虹膜切除術　iridectomy
虹膜切开术/虹膜切開術　iridotomy
虹膜全粘连/虹膜全部粘連　total synechia
虹膜软化/虹膜軟化　iridomalacia
虹膜色/虹膜色　eye color
虹膜色素剥脱综合征/虹膜色素剥脱症候群　exfoliation syndrome
虹膜色素痣/虹膜色素痣　pigmented nevus of iris
虹膜疝/虹膜疝　hernia of the iris
虹膜式光阑/虹膜式光圈　diaphragm iris
虹膜收缩肌/虹膜縮肌　iridoconstrictor
虹膜梳状韧带/虹膜梳狀韌帶　pectinate ligament of iris
虹膜撕脱/虹膜撕除術　iridoavulsion
虹膜松解术/虹膜鬆解　iridolysis
虹膜瞳孔膜/虹膜瞳孔膜　iridopupillary membrane
虹膜瞳孔膜存留/虹膜瞳孔膜存留　persistent iridopupillary membrane
虹膜痛/虹膜痛　iridalgia
虹膜投影/虹膜投影　iris shadow
虹膜突出/虹膜突出　iridocele
虹膜退色/虹膜白斑病,虹膜脱色病　vitiligo iridis
虹膜脱出/虹膜脱出　prolapse of iris
虹膜脱垂/虹膜脱垂　iridoptosis
虹膜外翻/虹膜外翻　iridectropium
虹膜小环/虹膜小環　lesser ring of iris, lesser circle of iris
虹膜学/虹膜學　iridology
虹膜炎/虹膜炎　iritis
虹膜异色症/虹膜異色症　heterochromia iridium
虹膜异位/虹膜異位　iridectopia
虹膜粘连分离术/虹膜粘連分離術　synechiolysis
虹膜粘连[切开]刀/虹膜粘連刀　synechotome
虹膜展开术/虹膜牽張術　iridotasis
虹膜诊断法/檢視虹膜診病法　iridiagnosis
虹膜震颤/虹膜震顫　tremulous iris
虹膜中层/虹膜中層　mesiris

虹膜肿/虹膜腫大　iridoncus
虹膜肿瘤/虹膜腫瘤　iris neoplasm
虹膜周边粘连/虹膜周邊粘連　peripheral synechia
虹[色]细胞/虹色細胞　iridocyte
虹视/虹色幻视,虹晕　iridization
虹吸[管]/虹吸[管]　syphon
洪脉/洪脈　full pulse, surging pulse
喉/喉　larynx, throat
喉癌/喉癌　cancer of larynx
喉白斑病/喉白斑病　leukoplakia of larynx
喉瘢痕性狭窄/喉瘢痕性狹窄　cicatricial stricture of larynx
喉痹/喉痺　pharyngitis, throat obstruction
喉痹·肺肾阴虚证/喉痺·肺腎陰虛證　throat obstruction with lung-kidney yin deficiency pattern
喉痹·肺胃热盛证/喉痺·肺胃熱盛證　throat obstruction with pattern of heat exuberance in lung and stomach
喉痹·风邪外袭证/喉痺·風邪外襲證　throat obstruction with pattern of external assault by wind
喉痹·脾肾阳虚证/喉痺·脾腎陽虛證　throat obstruction with spleen-kidney yang deficiency pattern
喉痹·脾胃气虚证/喉痺·脾胃氣虛證　throat obstruction with spleen-stomach qi deficiency pattern
喉痹·痰瘀互结证/喉痺·痰瘀互結證　throat obstruction with pattern of intermingled phlegm and stasis
喉病/喉病　laryngopathy
喉部分切除术/喉部分切除術　partial laryngectomy
喉测量法/喉測量法　laryngometry
喉插管术/喉導管插入法,喉插管法　laryngeal catheterization
喉成形术/喉造形術　laryngoplasty
喉出血/喉出血　laryngorrhagia
喉喘鸣/喉管嘯鳴　laryngeal stridor
喉次全切除术/喉次全切除術　subtotal laryngectomy
喉刀/喉刀　laryngotome
喉底/喉底　bottom of throat, posterior pharyngeal wall
喉电描记[法]/喉電描記[法]　electrolaryngography
喉动描记器/喉動描記器　laryngograph
喉动态镜/喉動態鏡,聲帶振動鏡　laryngostroboscope
喉动态镜检查[法]/喉動態鏡檢查[法]　laryngostroboscopy

喉返回支/喉頭返回支　recurrent layngeal branch
喉返神经/喉返神經,迴喉神經　recurrent laryngeal nerve
喉返神经气管支/喉返神經氣管支　tracheal branch of recurrent laryngeal nerve
喉返神经损伤/喉返神經損傷　recurrent nerve injury
喉返神经咽支/喉返神經咽支　pharyngeal branch of recurrent laryngeal nerve
喉风/喉風　throat wind
喉缝术/喉縫合術　laryngorrhaphy
喉干燥[症]/喉乾燥　laryngoxerosis
喉感应电疗法/喉感應電療法,電胸療法　electropneumatotherapy
喉关/喉關　throat pass, fauce, throat bar
喉关节/喉關節　laryngeal joint
喉关痈/喉關癰,扁桃體周膿腫　abscess of throat pass, peritonsillar abscess
喉核/喉核,扁桃腺　node of throat, palatine tonsil, tonsil
喉厚皮病/聲帶肥厚　pachydermia laryngis
喉呼吸/喉呼吸　laryngeal respiration
喉肌/喉肌　muscle of larynx, laryngeal muscle
喉[肌]痉挛/喉痙攣,聲門痙攣　laryngospasm
喉肌无力/喉肌無力　myasthenia laryngis
喉疾病/喉疾病　laryngeal disease
喉角化病/喉角化病　laryngeal keratosis
喉结/喉結　laryngeal prominence, laryngeal protubcrance
喉结核/喉結核　tuberculosis of larynx
喉结节点/喉結節點　larynx point
喉结皮下囊/喉結皮下囊　subcutaneous bursa of laryngeal prominence, hyoid bursa
喉痉挛性咽峡炎/喉痙攣性咽峡炎　thymic angina
喉镜/喉鏡　laryngoscope
喉镜检查/喉鏡檢查　laryngoscopy
喉镜检查专家/喉鏡檢查專家　laryngoscopist
喉菌/喉菌　carcinoma of larynx
喉科擒拿疗法/喉科擒拿療法　holding massage in laryngological department
喉科十六绝症/喉科十六絕症　sixteen fatal symptoms in pharyngolaryngology
喉科学/喉科學　laryngology
喉科学家/喉科專家　laryngologist
喉科指掌/喉科指掌　Guide Book for Laryngology
喉咳/喉欬　throat cough
喉口/喉口　aperture of larynx
喉扩张器/喉頭擴張器　laryngeal dilator
喉裂/喉裂　cleft larynx

喉裂开术/喉中部切開術　laryngofissure
喉瘤/喉瘤　tumor of throat
喉啰音/喉水泡音　laryngeal rale
喉麻痹/喉麻痺　laryngoparalysis
喉面罩/喉面罩　laryngeal masks
喉描记[法]/喉照相術　laryngography
喉鸣/喉鳴　laryngeal stridor
喉模型/喉模型　laryngophantom
喉囊肿/喉囊腫　laryngeal cyst
喉黏膜/喉黏膜　laryngeal mucosa
喉黏液溢/喉黏液溢　laryngorrhea
喉脓囊肿/喉膿囊腫　laryngopyocele
喉蹼/喉部網狀組織　laryngeal web
喉气管沟/喉氣管溝　laryngotracheal groove
喉气管憩室/喉氣管憩室　laryngotracheal diverticulum
喉气管切除术/喉氣管切除術　laryngotracheal resection
喉气管切开术/喉氣管切開術　laryngotracheotomy
喉气管炎/喉氣管炎　laryngotracheitis
喉气管支气管镜检查/喉氣管支氣管鏡檢查　laryngotracheobronchoscopy
喉气管支气管炎/喉氣管支氣管炎　laryngotracheobronchitis
喉前淋巴结/喉前淋巴結　prelaryngeal lymph node
喉前庭/喉前庭　vestibule of larynx
喉前庭炎/喉前庭炎　laryngovestibulitis
喉腔/喉腔　laryngeal cavity
喉切除患者/喉切除患者　laryngect
喉切除术/喉切除術　laryngectomy
喉切开术/喉切開術　laryngotomy
喉全切除术/喉全切除術　total laryngectomy
喉肉芽肿/喉肉芽腫　laryngeal granuloma
喉乳头状瘤病/喉乳頭狀瘤病　laryngeal papillomatosis
喉软骨/喉軟骨　laryngeal cartilage
喉软骨膜炎/喉軟骨膜炎　perichondritis of larynx
喉[软骨]软化/喉軟化　laryngomalacia
喉上动脉/喉上動脈,上喉動脈　superior laryngeal artery
喉上静脉/喉上靜脈　superior laryngeal vein
喉上神经/喉上神經,上喉頭神經　superior laryngeal nerve
喉上神经内支交通支/喉上神經内支交通支　communicating branch with internal branch of superior laryngeal nerve
喉上神经痛/喉上神經痛　superior laryngeal neuralgia

喉 X 射线[照]片／喉 X 光片　laryngogram
喉神经／喉神經　laryngeal nerve
喉神经襞／喉神經皺襞　fold of laryngeal nerve
喉神经丛／喉神經叢　laryngeal plexus
喉声振动检查器／喉音振動測驗器　opeidoscope
喉室／喉室　ventricle of larynx, laryngeal sinus
喉室声带切除术／喉室皺裂軟骨切除術　ventriculocordectomy
喉室脱垂／喉室脫垂　prolapse of laryngeal ventricle
喉水肿／喉水腫　laryngeal edema
喉弹性圆锥切开术／喉彈力圓錐切開術　coniotomy
喉听诊音／喉聽診音　laryngophony
喉痛／喉痛　laryngalgia
喉危象／喉危象　laryngeal crisis
喉窝／喉窩　tonsillar fossa
喉息肉／喉息肉　laryngeal polypus, vocal cord polyp
喉狭窄／喉狹窄　laryngostenosis
喉下垂／喉下垂　laryngoptosis
喉下动脉／喉下動脈　inferior laryngeal artery
喉下静脉／喉下靜脈　inferior laryngeal vein
喉下神经／下喉神經　inferior laryngeal nerve
喉下神经交通支／喉下神經交通支　communicating branch with inferior laryngeal nerve
喉[下]咽部／喉咽下部　laryngohypopharynx
喉纤维弹性膜／喉纖維彈性膜　laryngeal fibroelastic membrane
喉腺／喉腺　laryngeal gland
喉小囊／喉小囊　laryngeal saccule
喉小窝／喉小窩　alveolus laryngeus
喉性眩晕／喉病性眩暈　laryngeal vertigo
喉性眩晕综合征／喉性眩暈症候群　laryngeal vertigo syndrome
喉癣／喉癬　lichenoid erosion of throat, throat tuberculosis, membranous pharyngitis
喉癣·肺肾阴虚证／喉癬·肺腎陰虛證　lichenoid erosion of throat with lung-kidney yin deficiency pattern
喉癣·气阴两虚证／喉癬·氣陰兩虛證　lichenoid erosion of throat with qi-yin deficiency pattern
喉咽／喉咽部　laryngeal part of pharynx, laryngopharynx
喉咽腔／咽喉腔　pharyngolaryngeal cavity
喉咽切除术／咽喉切除術　laryngopharyngectomy
喉咽支／喉咽支　rami laryngopharyngeales
喉炎／喉炎　angina laryngea
喉痒／喉癢　throat itching
喉异感症／喉異感症　paresthesia laryngis
喉暗／嘶啞　hoarseness

喉瘖／喉瘖　hoarseness disease
喉瘖·肺脾气虚证／喉瘖·肺脾氣虛證　hoarseness disease with spleen-lung qi deficiency pattern
喉瘖·肺肾阴虚证／喉瘖·肺腎陰虛證　hoarseness disease with lung-kidney yin deficiency pattern
喉瘖·风寒袭肺证／喉瘖·風寒襲肺證　hoarseness disease with pattern of wind-cold assaulting lung
喉瘖·风热犯肺证／喉瘖·風熱犯肺證　hoarseness disease with pattern of wind-heat assailing lung
喉瘖·痰热壅肺证／喉瘖·痰熱壅肺證　hoarseness disease with pattern of phlegm-heat congesting lung
喉瘖·血瘀痰凝证／喉瘖·血瘀痰凝證　hoarseness disease with pattern of blood stasis and phlegm coagulation
喉硬结病／喉硬结　laryngoscleroma
喉痈／喉癰　throat abscess
喉痈·气阴耗损证／喉癰·氣陰耗損證　throat abscess with qi-yin consumption pattern
喉痈·热毒搏结证／喉癰·熱毒搏結證　throat abscess with heat-toxin intermingling pattern
喉痈·热腐成脓证／喉癰·熱腐成膿證　throat abscess with pattern of suppuration due to heat exuberance
喉晕厥／喉性暈厥　laryngeal syncope
喉造口瘘／喉造口瘻　laryngostomic fistula
喉罩／喉罩　laryngeal mask
喉中间腔／喉中間腔　intermedial cavity of larynx
喉中痰鸣／喉中痰鳴　wheezing due to retention of phlegm in throat
喉肿瘤／喉腫瘤　laryngeal neoplasm
喉周炎／喉周圍炎　perilaryngitis
喉阻塞／喉阻塞　laryngeal obstruction
猴病毒／猴病毒　simian virus
猴肠道孤病毒／猴腸道孤病毒　enteric cytopathogenic monkey orphan virus
猴痘／猴痘　monkey pox
猴痘病毒／猴痘病毒　monkeypox virus
猴空泡病毒／猴空泡病毒　simian vacuolating virus
猴类免疫缺陷病毒／猴類免疫缺陷病毒　simian immunodeficiency virus
猴疟疾／猴瘧　monkey malaria
骺／骺　epiphysis
骺板／骺板　epiphyseal plate
骺的／骺的　epiphyseal
骺骨干固定术／骺固定術　epiphysiodesis
骺骨折／骺折　epiphyseal fracture
骺软骨／骺軟骨　epiphyseal cartilage
骺[软骨]板／骺[軟骨]板　epiphyseal cartilage plate
骺软骨结合／骺軟骨結合　epiphyseal synchondrosis

骺脱离/骺脫離　epiphysiolysis
骺线/骺線,骨端線　epiphyseal line
骺炎/骺炎　epiphysitis
后/後　posterior
后半规管/後半規管　ductus semicircularis posterior, posterior semicircular duct
后半月板股骨韧带/後半月板股骨韌帶　ligamentum meniscofemorale posterius
后半月瓣/後半月瓣　posterior semilunar valve
后备方案/後備方案　reserved regimen
后壁/後壁　posterior wall
后部/後部　posterior part
后部反光照明法/後部反光照明法　retroillumination
后侧皮神经/後側皮神經　posterior cutaneous nerve
后侧阴道痉挛/後陰道痙攣　posterior vaginismus
后侧中沟/後副正中溝　posterior paramedian groove
后层/後層　posterior layer
后肠/後腸　hindgut
后肠管/後腸管　metagaster
后肠激素/後腸激素　proctodone
后成论/後成論,漸成論　postformation theory
后出胎头产钳术/後出胎頭產鉗術　forceps delivery of aftercoming head
后除极/後去極化　afterdepolarization
后穿质/後穿質　posterior perforated substance
后床突/後床突　posterior clinoid process
后唇/後唇　posterior lip
后错𬌗/後縮咬合　retrusive occlusion
后代病毒/後代病毒　progeny virus
后的/後的　posterior
后底段/後底段　posterior basal segment
后底段支气管/後底段支氣管　posterior basal segmental bronchus
后底支/後底支　posterior basal branch
后电流/後電流　aftercurrent
后电位/後遺電位　afterpotential
后蝶骨/後蝶骨　postsphenoid
后顶/後頂　houding, DU19
后窦/後竇　posterior sinus
后端/後端　posterior extremity
后端子代/後子體　opisthe
后段/後段　posterior segment
后段动脉/後段動脈　posterior segmental artery
后段支气管/後段支氣管　posterior segmental bronchus, bronchus segmentalis posterior
后发性白内障/繼發性內障　after cataract
后方医院/後方醫院,基地醫院　base hospital
后房/後房　posterior chamber
后负荷/後負荷　afterload
后腹/後腹　posterior belly
后概率/後概率　posterior probability
后感觉/後遺感覺　afterimpression
后睾吸虫病/後睾吸蟲病　opisthorchiasis
后根/後根　posterior root
后根动脉/後根動脈　posterior radicular artery
后根静脉/後根靜脈　posterior root vein
后跟关节面/跟骨後關節面　posterior calcanean articular surface
后弓/後弓　posterior arch
后巩膜葡萄肿/後鞏膜葡萄腫　posterior scleral staphyloma
后巩膜炎/後鞏膜炎　posterior scleritis
后股/後股　posterior divisions
后骨壶腹/後骨壺腹　posterior bony ampulla
后骨性半规管/後骨性半規管　posterior osseous semicircular canal
后固定缝线术/後固定縫線術　posterior fixation suture
后固有束/後固有束　posterior fasciculus proprius
后关节面/後關節面　posterior articular facet
后𬌗/齒後位咬合　posterior occlusion
后壶腹神经/後壺腹神經　posterior ampullary nerve
后壶腹神经切除术/後壺腹神經切除術　posterior ampullary neurectomy
后踝/後踝關節　hough
后基底[脑膜炎]性凝视/後基底[腦膜炎]性凝視　postbasic stare
后极/後極　posterior pole
后极白内障/後極性內障　posterior polar cataract
后脊髓小脑后束/後脊髓小腦徑　tractus spinocerebellaris posterior
后继性运动/後繼性運動　aftermovement
后尖/後尖　posterior cusp
后降支/後降支　posterior descending branch
后交叉韧带/後交叉韌帶　posterior cruciate ligament
后交通动脉/後交通動脈　posterior communicating artery
后交通静脉/後交通靜脈　posterior communicating vein
后角/後角　occipital horn, posterior horn
后角底/後角底　base of posterior horn
后角固有核/後角固有核　nucleus proprius of posterior horn
后角尖/後角尖　apex of posterior horn
后角颈/後角頸　neck of posterior horn
后角球/後角球　bulb of posterior horn

后角头/後角頭 head of posterior horn
后角细胞/後角細胞 posterior horn cell
后角缘层/後角緣層 marginal layer of posterior horn
后脚/後腳 posterior crus
后结节/後結節 posterior tubercle
后结膜动脉/後結膜動脈 posterior conjunctival artery
后颈的/後頸的 nuchal
后距关节面/距骨後關節面 posterior talar articular surface
后连合/[大脑]後連合 posterior commissure
后淋/久淋,老白濁 gleet
后[颅凹]脑膜炎/小腦區腦膜炎,後腦膜炎 posterior meningitis
后颅窝/後顱窩 posterior cranial fossa
后路刺囊术/囊後切開術 posterior discission
后马托品/後馬托品 homatropine
后面/後面 posterior surface, facies posterior
后膜壶腹/後膜壺腹 posterior membranous ampulla
后莫辛可宁/後馬辛可尼 homocinchonine
后囊白内障/後囊白内障 posterior capsular cataract
后脑/後腦 metencephalon
后脑突出/腦後膨出 notencephalocele
后脑突出畸胎/腦後膨出畸胎 notencephalus
后内侧核/後内側核 posteromedial nucleus
后内侧中央动脉/後内側中央動脈 posteromedial central artery
后尿道瓣膜/後尿道瓣 posterior urethral valve
后尿道淋病/後尿道淋病 posterior urethral gonorrhea
后尿道炎/後尿道炎 posterior urethritis
后旁正中核/後旁正中核 posterior paramedian nucleus
后葡萄膜炎/後葡萄膜炎 posterior uveitis
后期迟延/後期遲延 anaphase lag
后期反应/後期反應 late phase reaction
后期染色体/後期染色體 metachromosome
后期修复/後期修復 late repair
后穹窿穿刺术/後穹窿穿刺 culdocentesis
后丘脑/丘腦後部 metathalamus
后屈/後屈 postexion
后乳头肌/後乳頭肌 posterior papillary muscle
后鳃体/後鰓體 ultimobranchial body
后筛窦/後篩竇 posterior ethmoidal sinus
后上牙槽动脉/後上齒槽動脈 posterior superior alveolar artery
后神经孔/後神經孔 posterior neuropore
后肾/後腎 definite kidney
后肾管/後腎管 metanephric duct
后肾帽/後腎帽 metanephric cap
后肾组织帽/後腎組織帽 metanephric tissue cap
后升支/後昇支 posterior ascending branch
后生动物/複細胞動物 metazoon
后生皮层/後生皮層 metaderm
后十二指肠/後十二指腸 metaduodenum
后视觉/視覺遺留,後遺視覺,遺視 aftervision
后室间沟/後室間溝 posterior interventricular groove
后室间静脉/後室間靜脈 posterior interventricular vein
后室间支/後室間支 posterior interventricular branch
后释放/後放 afterdischarge
后束/後束 posterior cord
后送分类/後送分類 transportation triage
后随链/後隨鏈 lagging strand
后索/後索 posterior funiculus
后弹力层膨出/角膜後彈力層膨出 descemetocele
后体腔/後胚腔 metacoeloma
后天的/後天的 acquired
后天[获得]性疾病/後天性疾病 acquired disease
后天畸形/後天畸形 acquired deformity
后天近视/後天近視 acquired myopia
后天淋巴水肿/後天性淋巴水腫 acquired lymphedema
后天免疫性/後天免疫性 acquire immunity
后天缺损/獲得性缺陷,後天性缺陷 acquired defect
后天散光/後天散光 acquired astigmatism
后天性并指/後天性并指 acquired syndactyly
后天性并趾/後天性并趾 acquired syndactyly
后天性卟啉病/後天性吡咯紫質沈著病 acquired porphyria
后天性癫痫/後天性癲癇,獲得性癲癇 acquired epilepsy
后天性盲/後天性盲 acquired blindness
后天性梅毒/後天性梅毒 acquired syphilis
后天性皮肤松垂症/後天性皮膚鬆垂症 acquired cutis laxa
后天性憩室/後天性憩室 acquired diverticulum
后天性溶血性黄疸/後天性溶血性黄疸 acquired hemolytic icterus disease
后天性色素细胞痣/後天性色素細胞性母斑 acquired nevomelanocytic nevus
后天性疝/後天疝 acquired hernia
后天性水疱性表皮松解症/後天性水皰性表皮鬆解

症　acquired epidermolysis
后天性线状真皮黑色素细胞增生症/後天性線狀真皮黑色素細胞增生症　acquired linear dermal melanocytosis
后天之精/後天之精　acquired essence
后突/後突　posterior process
后推术/後推術　push-back operation
后退的/後移的　retrocedent
后退接触位/後退接觸位　retruded contact position
后脱位/[向]後脱位　backward dislocation, posterior dislocation
后外侧的/後外側的　posterolateral
后外侧沟/後外側溝　posterolateral sulcus, posterolateral groove
后外侧核/後外側核　posterolateral nucleus
后外侧后核/後外側後核　retroposterolateral nucleus
后外侧开胸术/後外側開胸術　posterolateral thoracotomy
后外侧裂/後外側裂　posterolateral fissure
后外侧囟/後外側囟　posterolateral fontanelle
后外侧中央动脉/後外側中央動脈　posterolateral central artery
后外弓状纤维/後外弓狀纖維　posterior external arcuate fiber
后溪/後溪　houxi, SI3
后下/後下　decocted later
后下丘脑/後下丘腦　posterior hypothalamus
后陷凹镜/後陷凹鏡　culdoscope
后陷凹镜检查/凹陷鏡檢法　culdoscopy
后腺支/後腺支　posterior glandular branch
后向性心力衰竭/倒行性心衰竭　backward heart failure
后像/後像　afterimage
后小尖/後小尖，上臼齒外中尖　metaconule
后效抑制/後效抑制　residual inhibition
后效应/後遺效應　after effect
后斜角肌/後斜角肌　scalenus posterior, musculus scalenus posterior
后囟/後囟　posterior fontanelle, posterior fontanel
后牙/後齒　posterior teeth
后牙言语空隙/後牙言語空隙　posterior teeth speech space
后叶/後葉　posterior lobe
后叶垂体/後葉垂體　posterior pituitary gland
后叶垂体激素类/後葉垂體激素類　posterior pituitary hormones
后叶激素运载蛋白类/後葉激素運載蛋白類　neurophysins

[后叶]加压素类/血管昇壓素類　vasopressins
后移/後移　retroposition
后遗畸形/後遺畸形　sequel deformity
后遗色[觉]/後遺色　incidental color
后遗眼球震颤/後遺眼球震顫　after nystagmus
后遗征/後遺徵象　commemorative sign
后阴/後陰，肛門　anus
后原肠胚/後原腸胚　metagastrula
后缘/後緣　posterior border
后褶柱/後皺襞　posterior column of ruga
后[枕]囟/後[枕]囟　posterior occipital fontanelle
后正中隔/後正中隔　posterior median septum
后正中沟/後正中溝　posterior median sulcus
后正中静脉/後正中靜脈　posteromedian vein
后正中线/後正中線　posterior median line
后支/後支　posterior branch
后知觉/後遺知覺　afterperception
后殖吸虫病/偏殖器吸蟲病　metagonimiasis
后中间沟/後中間溝　posterior intermediate sulcus
后终静脉/後終靜脈　posterior terminal vein
后主静脉/後主靜脈　posterior cardinal vein
后柱/後柱　posterior column
后纵隔/後縱隔　posterior mediastinum, mediastinum posterius
后纵韧带/後縱韌帶　posterior longitudinal ligament
后纵韧带骨化/後縱韌帶骨化　ossification of posterior longitudinal ligament
厚壁分生孢子/厚壁分生孢子　chlamydoconidia
厚壁组织/厚壁組織，厚膜組織　sclerenchyma
厚层皮移植物/厚層皮移植物　thick-split graft
厚唇/厚唇　thick lip
厚[的]中厚皮片/厚[的]中厚皮片　thick intermediate thickness free skin graft
厚[度]/厚度　thickness
厚甲/厚甲　pachyonychia
厚角组织/厚角組織　collenchyma
厚膜孢子/厚膜孢子　chlamydospore
厚皮/厚皮　thick skin
厚皮性骨膜病/厚性骨膜病　pachydermoperiostosis
厚皮症/厚皮症　pachydermia
厚朴/厚朴　cortex magnoliae officinalis, official magnolia bark
厚朴花/厚朴花　official magnolia flower
厚朴温中汤/厚朴温中湯　houpu wenzhong decoction
厚苔/厚苔　thick fur
厚苔舌/厚苔舌　encrusted tongue
厚涂片法/厚塗片法　method of thick smear
厚血管翳/厚血管翳　thick pannus

厚硬性阴囊疝/厚硬性陰囊赫尼亞　porocele
候气/候氣　waiting for qi arrival
鲎试验/鱟試驗　limulus test
呼肠病毒/呼腸病毒　reovirus
呼肠病毒科感染/呼腸病毒科感染　Reoviridae infection
呼出气/呼出氣　expired gas
呼气/呼氣　exhalation
呼[气]的/呼氣的　expiratory
呼气活瓣/呼氣活瓣　expiratory valve
呼[气]肌/呼氣肌　expiratory muscle
呼气困难/呼氣困難　expiratory dyspnea
呼气流量峰值/呼氣流量峰值　peak expiratory flow
呼气末正压/吐氣末正壓　positive end-expiratory pressure
呼气末正压通气/呼氣末正壓通氣　positive end expiratory pressure
呼气试验/呼氣試驗　breath test
呼气推迟/呼氣延緩　expiratory flow retard
呼气性杂音/呼氣性雜音　expiratory murmur
呼吸/呼吸　breathing
呼吸爆发/呼吸爆發　respiratory burst
呼吸病毒感染/呼吸病毒感染　respirovirus infection
呼吸补泻/呼吸補瀉　reinforcing-reducing method by respiration
呼吸不足/呼吸不足,呼吸淺慢　hypopnea
呼吸超敏反应/呼吸超敏反應　respiratory hypersensitivity
呼吸代谢/呼吸代謝　respiratory metabolism
呼吸道/呼吸道　respiratory tract
呼吸道出血/呼吸道出血　hemorrhage from respiratory tract
呼吸道感染/呼吸道感染　respiratory tract infection
呼吸道合胞病毒/呼吸道合胞病毒　respiratory syncytial virus
呼吸道合胞病毒疫苗/呼吸道合胞病毒疫苗　respiratory syncytial virus vaccine
呼吸道合胞体/呼吸道融合細胞　respiratory syncytial
呼吸道合胞体病毒/呼吸道融合細胞病毒　respiratory syncytial virus
呼吸道合胞体病毒感染/呼吸道合胞體病毒感染　respiratory syncytial virus infection
呼吸道疾病/呼吸道疾病　respiratory tract disease
呼吸道瘘/呼吸道瘺　respiratory tract fistula
呼吸道黏膜/呼吸道黏膜　respiratory mucosa
呼吸道肉芽肿/呼吸道肉芽腫　respiratory tract granuloma
呼吸道烧伤/呼吸道燒傷　respiratory tract burn
呼吸道通气术/呼吸道切開術　aeroporotomy
呼吸道肿瘤/呼吸道腫瘤　respiratory tract neoplasm
呼吸动力学/呼吸動力學　pneumodynamics
呼吸锻炼/呼吸鍛煉　breathing exercise
呼吸防护装置/呼吸防護裝置　respiratory protective device
呼吸功/呼吸功　work of breathing
呼吸功能不全/呼吸功能不全　respiratory insufficiency
呼吸功能试验/呼吸功能試驗　respiratory function test
呼吸过大/呼吸過大　exaggerated respiration
呼吸过度/呼吸過度　hyperpnea
呼吸过慢/呼吸徐緩　bradypnea
呼吸缓慢/緩慢呼吸　slow respiration
呼吸机/呼吸器　respirator
呼吸肌/呼吸肌　respiratory muscle
呼吸急促/呼吸急促　tachypnea
呼吸加速/呼吸加速　accelerated respiration
呼吸加速中枢/呼吸加速中樞　panting center
呼吸间断/呼吸間斷　anaerosis
呼吸监护病房/呼吸監護病房　respiratory care units
呼吸减少/呼吸減少　spanopnea
呼吸觉/呼吸覺　respiratory sense
呼吸痉挛/呼吸痙攣　respiratory spasm
呼吸窘迫/呼吸窘迫　respiratory distress
呼吸窘迫综合征/呼吸窘迫症候群　respiratory distress syndrome
呼吸叩诊/呼吸式叩法　respiratory percussion
呼吸困难/呼吸困難　dyspneic respiration
呼吸困难的/呼吸困難的　dyspneic
呼吸力学/呼吸力學　mechanics of breathing
呼吸链/呼吸鏈　respiratory chain
呼吸量检视法/呼吸量檢視法　spiroscopy
呼吸量检视器/呼吸量檢視器　spiroscope
呼吸疗法/呼吸療法　respiratory therapy
呼吸率/呼吸率　rate of respiration
呼吸麻痹/呼吸麻痺　respiratory paralysis
呼吸酶/呼吸酶　respiratory enzyme
呼吸描记法/呼吸運動描記法　spirography
呼吸[描记]图/呼吸運動圖　spirogram
呼吸频率/呼吸頻率　ventilatory frequency
呼吸气量描记器/呼吸容積描記器　aeroplethysmograph
呼吸区/呼吸部　respiratory region
呼吸热量计/呼吸熱量計　respiration calorimeter
呼吸容量/换气量　respiratory capacity

呼吸商/呼吸商　respiratory quotient, RQ
呼吸深度/呼吸深度　depth of respiration
呼吸生理过程/呼吸生理過程　respiratory physiologic process
呼吸生理现象/呼吸生理現象　respiratory physiologic phenomena
呼吸生理学/呼吸生理學　respiratory physiology
呼吸声门/呼吸聲門　respiratory glottis
呼吸试验/呼吸試驗　breath test
呼吸树/呼吸樹　respiratory tree
呼吸衰竭/呼吸衰竭　failure of respiration
呼吸速度测定器/呼吸氣流測量器　pneumotachometer
呼吸停止/呼吸停止　respiratory arrest
呼吸无效腔/呼吸無效腔　respiratory dead space
呼吸系病毒/呼吸系病毒　respirovirus
呼吸系数/呼吸係數　respiratory coefficient
呼吸系统/呼吸系統　respiratory apparatus, respiratory system
呼吸系统毒理学/呼吸系統毒理學　respiratory toxicology
呼吸系统畸形/呼吸系統畸形　respiratory system abnormality
呼吸系统疾病/呼吸系統疾病　respiratory system disorder
呼吸系统结核病/呼吸系統結核病　tuberculosis of respiratory system
呼吸系统药/呼吸系統藥　respiratory system agent
呼吸系统诊断技术/呼吸系統診斷技術　respiratory system diagnostic techniques
呼吸细支气管/呼吸細支氣管　alveolar bronchiole
呼吸心动描记法/呼吸心動描記　pneumocardiography
呼吸兴奋药/呼吸興奮藥　respiration stimulant
呼吸性/呼吸的　respiratory
呼吸性碱中毒/呼吸性鹼中毒　respiratory alkalosis
呼吸性酸中毒/呼吸性酸中毒　respiratory acidosis
呼吸性细支气管/呼吸性細支氣管　respiratory bronchiole
呼吸性心律不齐/呼吸性心律不整　respiratory arrhythmia
呼吸性杂音/呼吸性雜音　respiratory murmur
呼吸音/呼吸音　respiratory sound
呼吸音减弱/呼吸音減弱　diminished respiration
呼吸音消失/呼吸音消失　absent respiration
呼吸运动/呼吸練習　breathing exercise
呼吸[运动]计/呼吸計　respirometer
呼吸[运动]描记器/呼吸運動描記器　pneoscope

呼吸增强/呼吸增強　augmented respiration
呼吸障碍/呼吸障礙　respiration disorder
呼吸指数/呼吸指數　spiro-index
呼吸中枢/呼吸中樞　respiratory center
呼吸转运/呼吸轉運　respiratory transport
呼吸阻力/呼吸阻力　respiratory resistance
忽略性肩先露/忽略性肩先露　neglected shoulder presentation
狐惑[病]/狐惑[病],贝切特[氏]症候群,Behcet氏症候群　Behcet's syndrome, huhuo disease
狐惑·肝脾湿热证/狐惑·肝脾濕熱證　Behcet's syndrome with pattern of dampness-heat in liver and spleen
狐惑·肝肾阴虚证/狐惑·肝腎陰虛證　Behcet's syndrome with liver-kidney yin deficiency pattern
狐惑·脾肾阳虚证/狐惑·脾腎陽虛證　Behcet's syndrome with spleen-kidney yang deficiency pattern
狐脑炎病毒/狐腦炎病毒　fox encephalitis virus
狐疝/狐疝　indirect hernia
弧/弧　arc
弧度/弧度　radian
弧菌病/弧菌病　vibriosis
弧菌感染/弧菌感染　vibrio infection
弧菌属/弧菌屬　*Vibrio*
弧菌性败血病/弧菌性敗血症　vibrio septicemia
弧形暗点/弧形暗點　arcuate scotoma
弧形斑/弧形斑　conus
弧形切口/弧形切口　curved incision
弧形视野计/弧形視野計　arc perimeter
弧影/孤影,小月斑,月窪　lunule
弧状菌/支架真菌　bracket fungus
胡瓜油/胡瓜油　cucumber oil
胡黄连/胡黃連　figwortflower picrorhiza rhizome
胡椒/胡椒　piper nigrum, pepper fruit
胡椒基丁醚/胡椒基丁醚　piperonyl butoxide
胡椒碱/胡椒鹼　piperine
胡椒酸/胡椒酸　piperic acid
胡椒中毒/胡椒中毒　piperism
胡狼类/胡狼類　jackals
胡芦巴/胡蘆巴　fenugreek, fenugreek seed
胡萝卜/胡蘿蔔　carota
胡萝卜属/胡蘿蔔屬　*Daucus*
胡萝卜素/胡蘿蔔素　carotin, carrotene
胡萝卜素黄皮病/胡蘿蔔素黃皮症　carotenoderma
胡萝卜素酶/胡蘿蔔素酵素　carotenase
胡萝卜素性黄皮病/胡蘿蔔素沈著,橘色皮　carotinosis, carotenemia

胡萝卜烷/胡蘿蔔烷　dancane
胡萝卜油/胡蘿蔔油　carrot oil
胡米胺/胡米胺　ethidium
胡宁病毒/胡寧病毒　junin virus
胡施克韧带/Huschke 氏韌帶　Huschke ligament
胡施克胃胰韧带/胡施克胃胰韌帶　gastropancreatic ligament of Huschke
胡说综合征/胡說症候群　nonsense syndrome
胡桃壳粉/胡桃殼粉　walnut shell power
胡桃皮酸/胡桃酸　juglandic acid
壶腹/壺腹　ampulla
壶腹顶/壺腹頂　ampullar cupula
壶腹沟/壺腹溝　ampullar groove
壶腹骨脚/壺腹骨腳　ampullar bony crura
壶腹后神经/壺腹後神經　posterior ampullar nerve
壶腹嵴/壺腹嵴　ampullary crest, crista ampullaris
壶腹嵴顶/壺腹嵴頂　cupula of ampullary crest
壶腹膜脚/壺腹膜腳　ampullar membranous crura
壶腹憩室/壺腹膨部　diverticula ampullae
壶腹前神经/壺腹前神經　anterior ampullar nerve
壶腹上神经/壺腹上神經　superior ampullar nerve
壶腹炎/壺腹炎　ampullitis
壶腹[状]的/壺腹狀的　ampullary
壶腹状动脉瘤/壺腹狀動脈瘤　ampullary aneurysm
葫芦状瘤/葫蘆狀瘤　hourglass tumor
槲寄生素/槲寄生黏質　viscin
槲皮素/槲皮素　quercetin
槲叶毒葛/毒槲　poison oak
蝴蝶状肺/蝶狀肺　butterfly lung
糊粉粒/糊粉粒　aleurone grain
糊剂/糊劑　paste
糊剂绷带/糊劑繃帶　paste bandage
糊精/糊精　dextrin
糊精类/糊精類　dextrins
糊精酶/糊精酵素　dextrinase
糊精尿/糊精尿　dextrinuria
糊精铁/糊精鐵　dextriferron
糊丸/糊丸　flour and water paste pill
糊状便/糊狀便　mushy stool
虎斑溶解/虎斑小體溶解　tigrolysis
虎斑状视网膜/虎斑狀視網膜　tigroid retina
虎口三关/虎口三關　three passes at the first web space, three passes at tiger-mouth
虎须疗/虎鬚疔　ding beside philtrum
虎牙/虎牙　canine teeth
虎杖/虎杖　polygonum cuspidatum, giant knotweed rhizome
琥珀色/琥珀色　amber

琥珀酸/琥珀酸　succinic acid
琥珀酸酐类/琥珀酸酐類　succinic anhydrides
琥珀酸 CoA 连接酶类/琥珀酸 CoA 連接酶類　succinate-CoA ligases
琥珀酸脱氢素/琥珀酸脫氫素　succinic dehydrogenase
琥珀酸脱氢酶/琥珀酸脫氫酶　succinate dehydrogenase
琥珀酸盐/琥珀酸鹽　succinates
琥珀酰亚胺类/琥珀醯亞胺類　succinimides
琥珀型突变/琥珀型突變　amber mutation
琥乙红霉素/琥乙紅黴素　erythromycin ethylsuccinate
互变[现象]/互變現象　interconversion
互变异构/互變異構　tautomerism
互变异构酶/互變異構酶　tautomerase
互变异构体/互變異構體,互變異構物　tautomer
互补 DNA/互補 DNA　complementary DNA
互补碱基/互補鹼基　complementary base
互补决定区/互補決定區　complementarity determining region
互补链/互補鏈　complementary strand
互补 DNA 探针/互補 DNA 探針　complementary DNA probe
互补位/互補位　paratope
互补 DNA 文库/互補 DNA 文庫　complementary DNA library
互补性/互補性　complementarity
互补作用/互補作用　complementation
互斥相/互斥相　repulsion phase
互换不能/互換不能　failure reciprocity
互生/相依生活,互賴生活,共生　mutualism
互生生物/相依生活者,共生生物　mutualist
互引相/互引相　coupling phase
户籍簿/戶籍簿　domiciliary register
户口普查/戶口普查　general household survey
户外生活/戶外生活　open air life
护场/護場　protecting field
护耳器/護耳器　ear protector
护肤/護膚　skincare
护理/護理　nursing care
护理方法学研究/護理方法學研究　nursing methodology research
护理工作/護理工作　nursing service
护理工作保险/護理工作保險　nursing service insurance
护理估计/護理估計　nursing assessment
护理管理人员/護理管理人員　nurse administrator

护理管理研究/護理管理研究　nursing administration research
护理过程/護理過程　nursing process
护理记录/護理記錄　nursing record
护理教育/護理教育　nursing education
护理教育研究/護理教育研究　nursing education research
护理理论/護理理論　nursing theory
护理伦理学/護理倫理學　nursing ethics
护理美学/護理美學　nursing aesthetics
护理评价研究/護理評價研究　nursing evaluation research
护理人员/護理人員　nursing staff
护理信息学/護理資訊學　nursing informatics
护理学经济学/護理學經濟學　nursing economics
护理学立法/護理學立法　nursing legislation
护理学模型/護理學模型　nursing model
护理学生/護理學生　nursing student
护理学史/護理學史　history of nursing
护理学图书馆/護理學圖書館　nursing library
护理学许可证/護理學許可證　nursing licensure
护理学学会/護理學學會　nursing society
护理学院教师实习/護理學院教師實習　nursing faculty practice
护理学哲学/護理學哲學　nursing philosophy
护理研究/護理研究　nursing research
护理院校/護理院校　nursing school
护理院校全体教工/護理院校全體教工　nursing faculty
护理诊断/護理診斷　nursing diagnosis
护理质量审核/護理品質審核　nursing audit
护理专业/護理專業　nursing specialty
护生/護生,見習護理人員　probationer nurse
护士/護士　nurse
护士病人关系/護士病人關係　nurse-patient relation
护士长/負責護理人員　charge nurse
护士作用/護士作用　nurses' role
护胸甲/胸甲,護心甲　cuirass
护指/護指　guard finger
花/花　flower
花斑/花斑　piebaldism
花斑曲霉菌/雜色麴菌　Aspergillus versicolor
花斑胎/花斑胎　harlequin fetus
花斑癣/花斑癬,變色糠疹　tinea versicolor
花斑眼镜蛇/花斑眼鏡蛇　harlequin
花斑眼镜蛇状颜色变化/花斑眼鏡蛇狀顏色變化　harlequin color change
花斑[状]的/白化症的　piebald
花苞/花苞　flower bulbs
花痴/花癡　anthomaniac
花癫/花癲　anthomaniac, sexual psychosis
花顶部/花頂部　flowering top
花朵形梅毒疹/花朵狀梅毒疹　corymbose syphilid
花粉/花粉　pollen
花粉变应原/花粉過敏原　pollen allergen
花粉病/花粉病　pollinosis
花粉超敏反应/花粉超敏反應　pollen hypersensitivity
花粉管/花粉管　pollen tube
花粉抗毒素/花粉[抗毒]素　pollantin
花粉抗原/花粉抗原　pollen antigen
花粉皮炎/花粉皮炎　dermatitis due to pollen
花粉性气喘/花粉性氣喘　pollen asthma
花冠点状白内障/花冠點狀白內障　coronary punctate cataract
花冠状白内障/冠狀內障　coronary cataract
花匠/花匠　florists
花椒/花椒　pricklyash peel
花结/花結　cockade
花结形的/花結形的　cocardiform
花结状反应/結核菌素皮內試驗反應,羅梅爾氏試驗　cockade reaction
花柳病/性病　venereal disease
花柳毒淋/花柳毒淋,淋病　gonorrhea
花柳毒淋・膀胱湿热证/花柳毒淋・膀胱濕熱證　gonorrhea with pattern of dampness-heat in bladder
花柳毒淋・肾气不固证/花柳毒淋・腎氣不固證　gonorrhea with pattern of unconsolidated kidney qi
花柳毒淋・湿热毒蕴证/花柳毒淋・濕熱毒蘊證　gonorrhea with pattern of dampness-heat toxin amassment
花柳毒淋・正虚毒恋证/花柳毒淋・正虚毒戀證　gonorrhea with pattern of healthy qi deficiency and lingering toxin
花青苷类/花青苷類　anthocyanins
花蕊石/花蕊石　ophicalcite
花色苷/花色苷　anthocyanin
花色素/花色素　anthocyanidin
花色素苷/花藍苷,花青質　anthocyanin
花色素苷尿/花青素尿　anthocyaninuria
花色素苷血症/花藍苷血　anthocyaninemia
花生过敏/花生過敏　peanut hypersensitivity
花生凝集素/花生凝集素　peanut agglutinin
花生仁吸入性支气管炎/花生支氣管炎　arachidic bronchitis
花生四烯酸/花生四烯酸　arachidonic acid

花生四烯酸盐/花生四烯酸鹽　arachidonate
花生四烯酸盐5-脂氧合酶/花生四烯酸鹽5-脂氧合酶　arachidonate 5-lipoxygenase
花生四烯酸盐脂氧合酶类/花生四烯酸鹽脂氧合酶類　arachidonate lipoxygenases
花生酸/花生酸　eicosanoic acid
花生酸类/花生酸類　eicosanoic acids
花生油/花生油　arachis oil
花纹状白斑病/範型白皮症　patterned leukoderma
花纹状红斑/圖案狀紅斑　figurate erythema
花心风/花心風　anthomaniac
花形细胞/花形細胞　flower cell
花椰菜/花椰菜　cauliflower
花叶病/斑駁病　mosaic disease
花叶[病]病毒/花葉病病毒　mosaic virus
花翳白陷/花翳白陷　keratohelcosis, petal nebula, petaloid nebula with a sunken center
花翳白陷·肺肝风热证/花翳白陷·肺肝風熱證　petaloid nebula with a sunken center with pattern of wind-heat in lung and liver channel
花翳白陷·肝胆湿热证/花翳白陷·肝膽濕熱證　petaloid nebula with a sunken center with pattern of dampness-heat in liver and gallbladder
花翳白陷·阳虚寒凝证/花翳白陷·陽虛寒凝證　petaloid nebula with a sunken center with pattern of yang deficiency and cold congelation
花翳白陷·阴虚火旺证/花翳白陷·陰虛火旺證　petaloid nebula with a sunken center with pattern of yin deficiency and fire effulgence
花状内障/花狀内障　floriform cataract
划船手/劃船手　pulling-boat hand
划痕/劃痕　scratch
划痕试验/刮劃試驗　scratch test
划痕性荨麻疹/劃紋性蕁麻疹　urticaria graphica
华顿管/Wharton氏管　Wharton duct
华尔敦颌下腺管/Wharton氏頜下腺管　submaxillary ducts of Wharton
华法林/殺鼠靈　Warfarin
华盖/華蓋　huagai, RN20
华氏温标/華氏溫標　Fahrenheit thermometric scale
华氏温度计/華氏溫度計　Fahrenheit thermometer
华支睾吸虫/中華肝吸蟲　Clonorchis sinensis
华支睾吸虫病/華支睾吸蟲病　clonorchiasis
滑车/滑車　trochlea
滑车凹/滑車小凹　trochlear fovea
滑车棘/滑車棘　trochlear spine, trochlear hamulus
滑车切迹/滑車切跡　trochlear notch
滑车上凹/滑車上凹　supratrochlear depression
滑车上的/滑車上的　supratrochlear
滑车上动脉/滑車上動脈　supratrochlear artery
滑车上静脉/滑車上靜脈　supratrochlear vein
滑车上淋巴结/滑車上淋巴結　supratrochlear lymph node
滑车上神经/滑車上神經　supratrochlear nerve
滑车上肘肌/滑車上肘肌　epitrochleoanconeus muscle
滑车神经/滑車神經　trochlear nerve
滑车神经核/滑車神經核　nucleus of trochlear nerve
滑车神经疾病/滑車神經疾病　trochlear nerve disease
滑车神经交叉/滑車神經交叉　decussation of trochlear nerve
滑车神经支/滑車神經支　trochlear branch
滑车下神经/滑車下神經　infratrochlear nerve
滑动/滑動　glide, gliding movement
滑动关节/滑動關節　gliding articulation
滑动肌丝学说/滑動纖維理論　sliding filament theory
滑动腱/脱腱病，溜腱病　slipped tendon
滑动肋/滑動肋　slipping rib
滑动切片机/滑動式切片機　sliding microtome
滑动性疝/滑動性疝　parasaccular hernia
滑动性食管裂孔疝/滑動性食管裂孔疝　sliding hiatal hernia
滑管/滑管　sliding tube
滑剂/滑劑　lubricating formula
滑肩症/滑落肩　slipped shoulder
滑精[病]/滑精，遺精　spermatorrhea, night emission
滑脉/滑脈　slippery pulse
滑面内质网/平滑内質網　smooth endoplasmic reticulum
滑膜/滑[液]膜　synovial membrane
滑膜襞/滑膜皺襞　synovial fold
滑膜层/滑膜層　synovial layer
[滑膜]成纤维细胞样细胞/滑膜成纖維細胞樣細胞　synovial membrane fibroblast-like cell
滑膜关节/滑膜關節　synovial joint
滑膜活检/滑膜活檢　synovial biopsy
[滑膜]巨噬细胞样细胞/滑膜巨噬細胞樣細胞　synovial membrane macrophage-like cell
滑膜瘤/滑膜瘤　synovioma
滑膜囊/滑液囊，黏液囊　synovial bursa
滑膜囊肿/滑液囊腫　synovial cyst
滑膜鞘/滑膜鞘　synovial sheath
滑膜切除术/滑膜切除術　synovectomy

滑膜韧带/滑膜韌帶　synovial ligament
滑膜绒毛/滑膜絨毛　villi synoviales
滑膜[绒毛]切除术/滑膜絨毛切除術　villusectomy
滑膜肉瘤/滑液性肉瘤　synovial sarcoma
滑膜软骨瘤病/滑液膜軟骨瘤病　synovial chondromatosis
滑膜突出/滑膜突出　synovial hernia
滑膜细胞/滑膜細胞　synovial cell
滑膜下的/滑膜下的　subsynovial
滑膜下囊肿/滑膜下囊腫　subsynovial cyst
滑膜炎/滑膜炎　synovitis
滑膜[皱]襞/分泌黏液突，黏液脊　synovial process
滑囊炎/滑囊炎　bursal synovitis
滑肉门/滑肉門　huaroumen, ST24
滑入/滑入　slide in
滑润剂/潤滑藥　lubricant
滑疝/滑動性疝　sliding hernia
滑石/滑石　talc
滑石[尘]肺/肺滑石沈著病　talc pneumoconiosis
滑石沉着病/滑石病　talcosis
滑石粉肉芽肿/滑石粉肉芽腫　talc granuloma
滑胎/滑胎　habitual abortion
滑胎・脾肾气虚证/滑胎・脾腎氣虛證　habitual abortion with pattern of qi deficiency of spleen and kidney
滑胎・气血两虚证/滑胎・氣血兩虛證　habitual abortion with pattern of deficiency of both qi and blood
滑胎・血瘀证/滑胎・血瘀證　habitual abortion with blood stasis pattern
滑苔/滑苔　slippery fur
滑脱/滑脱　olisthe
滑泄/滑洩　lingering diarrhea
滑行截骨术/滑行截骨術　sliding osteotomy
滑液/滑液　synovial fluid, synovia
滑液蛋白/滑液蛋白　synovin
滑液的/滑液的　synovial
滑液囊/滑囊，黏液囊　synovial bursa
滑液囊周炎/滑膜囊旁組織炎　parasynovitis
滑液支原体/滑液支原體　mycoplasma synoviae
滑泽皮/光滑皮　leiodermia
化虫丸/化蟲丸　huachong pill
化橘红/化橘紅　pummelo peel
化脓/化膿　pyesis
化脓的/化膿的　suppurative
化脓痛/化膿痛　suppuration pain
化脓性白肿/化膿性白腫　tumor albus pyogene
化脓性鼻窦炎/化膿性鼻竇炎　purulent sinusitis
化脓性鼻炎/化膿性鼻炎　purulent rhinitis
化脓性玻璃体炎/化膿性玻璃體炎　hyalitis suppurativa
化脓性顶浆腺炎/化膿性頂漿腺炎　apocrinitis suppurativa
化脓性肺炎/化膿性肺炎　suppurative pneumonia
化脓性腹膜炎/化膿性腹膜炎　purulent peritonitis
化脓性肝脓肿/化膿性肝膿腫　pyogenic liver abscess
化脓性肝炎/化膿性肝炎　purulent hepatitis
化脓性骨炎/化膿性骨炎　suppurative osteitis
化脓性关节炎/化膿性關節炎　suppurative arthritis, pyogenic arthritis
化脓性汗腺炎/化膿性汗腺炎　suppurative hidradenitis
化脓性滑膜炎/化膿性滑膜炎　purulent synovitis, suppurative synovitis
化脓性甲沟炎/化膿性甲溝炎　pyogenic paronychia
化脓性甲状腺炎/化膿性甲狀腺炎　suppurative thyroiditis
化脓性溃疡/化膿性潰瘍　suppurative ulcer
化脓性阑尾炎/化膿性闌尾炎　purulent appendicitis
化脓性门静脉炎/門靜脈膿血症　portal pyemia
化脓性脑膜炎/化膿性腦膜炎　purulent meningitis
化脓性黏液囊肿/化膿性黏液囊腫　suppurating mucocele
化脓性葡萄膜炎/化膿性葡萄膜炎　suppurative uveitis
化脓性肉芽肿/化膿性肉芽腫　granuloma pyogenicum
化脓性乳腺炎/化膿性乳腺炎　suppurative mastitis
化脓性腮腺炎/化膿性腮腺炎　pyogenic parotitis
化脓性舌扁桃体炎/化膿性舌扁桃腺炎　lingual quinsy
化脓性肾炎/化膿性腎炎　suppurative nephritis
化脓性肾盂肾炎/化膿性腎盂腎炎　suppurative pyelonephritis
化脓性肾盂炎/化膿性腎盂炎　suppurative pyelitis
化脓性胃炎/化膿性胃炎　purulent gastritis
化脓性膝关节炎/化膿性膝關節炎　septic knee
化脓性心包炎/化膿性心包炎　suppurative pericarditis
化脓性血栓性静脉炎/化膿性血栓性靜脈炎　suppurative thrombophlebitis
化脓性炎/化膿性炎症　purulent inflammation
化脓性眼内炎/化膿性眼內炎　suppurative endophthalmitis
化脓性胰腺炎/化膿性胰腺炎　purulent pancreatitis
化脓性指头炎/指端化膿　whitlow

化脓性趾头炎/趾端化膿 whitlow
化脓性中耳炎/化膿性中耳炎 suppurative otitis media
化生/化生 metaplasia
化生的/組織變形 metaplastic
化生性骨化/增生性骨化 metaplastic ossification
化生性息肉/化生性息肉 metaplastic polyp
化湿和中/化濕和中 removing dampness for regulating stomach
化痰开窍/化痰開竅 dissipating phlegm for resuscitation, waking up patient from unconsciouness by resolving phlegm
化痰散结/化痰散結 dissipating phlegm and resolving masses
化痰消瘿/化痰消瘿 dissipating phlegm for eliminating goiter
化痰消瘀/化痰消瘀 dissipating phlegm and eliminating blood stasis
化学/化學 chemistry
化学癌形成/化學性癌生成 chemical carcinogenesis
化学病理学/化學病理學 chemical pathology
化学剥脱除皱术/化學剝脫除皺術 chemical exfoliative rhytidectomy
化学剥脱术/化學換膚 chemical peeling
化学不育剂/化學滅生劑 chemosterilants
化学成分/化學成分 chemical constituent
化学成分确定的培养基/化學性界定培養基 chemically defined medium
化学刺激/化學刺激 chemical irritation
化学刺激物/化學性刺激物 chemical irritant
化学的/化學的 chemical
化学发光/化學發光 chemiluminescence
化学发光测定法/化學發光測定法 chemiluminescent measurement
化学发光免疫分析法/化學發光免疫分析法 chemiluminescence immunoassay, CLIA
化学发光自显影/化學發光自顯影 chemiluminescent autography
化学番木瓜[蛋白]酶/化學番木瓜[蛋白]酶 chemopapain
化学反应动力学/化學反應動力學 chemical kinetics
化学反应方程式/化學方程式 chemical equation
化学防爆药/化學防爆藥 chemical riot control agent
化学分化/化學分化 chemo-differentiation
化学感觉/化學感覺 chemical sense
化学感受体/化學性接受體 chemoceptor
化学感受体瘤/化學受體瘤 chemodectoma
化学感受[作用]/化學感受力 chemoreception

化学睾丸切除[术]/化學睾丸切除[術] chemical castration
化学合成/化學合成 chemosynthesis
化学机械性操作/化學機械性操作 chemomechanical preparation
化学鉴别/化學鑒別 chemical identification
化学键/化學鍵 chemical bond
化学键合相/化學鍵合相 chemically bonded phase
化学交感神经切除术/交感神經化學破壞術 chemical sympathectomy
化学结构式/化學公式 chemical formula
化学紧张/化學性緊張 chemical tonus
化学进化/化學進化 chemical evolution
化学抗生素/化學抗生素劑 chemobiotic
化学烙术/化學烙術 chemical cautery
化学疗法/化學療法 chemotherapeutics
化学落叶剂/化學落葉劑 chemical defoliants
化学免疫学/化學免疫學 chemoimmunology
化学免疫抑制/化學免疫抑制 chemical immunosuppression
化学凝固[法]/化學凝固法 chemocoagulation
化学胚胎学/化學胚胎學 chemical embryology
化学配伍禁忌/化學配伍禁忌,化學性不相容 chemical incompatibility
化学平衡/化學平衡 chemical equilibrium
化学趋向素/趨化性 chemotaxins
化学溶液/化學溶液 chemical solution
化学烧伤/化學品灼傷 chemical burn
化学烧伤全身中毒/化學燒傷全身中毒 intoxication after chemical burn
化学神经解剖学/化學神經解剖學 chemical neuroanatomy
化学渗透[作用]/滲透膜化學作用,滲透化學現象 chemosmosis
化学特异性/化學專一性 chemical specificity
化学突触/化學突觸 chemical synapse
化学脱色/化學脱色 chemical depigmentation
化学外科/化學外科 chemosurgery
化学吸引/化學吸引力 chemical attraction
化学-细菌致龋理论/化學與細菌致齲說 chemico-parasitic theory of dental caries
化学性白皮症/化學性白皮症 chemical leukoderma
化学性胞质流动/化學性胞質流動 chemodynesis
化学性垂体切除术/化學性垂體切除術 chemical hypophysectomy
化学性刺激/化學性刺激 chemical stimulation
化学性肺炎/化學性肺炎 chemical pneumonitis
化学性蜂窝组织炎/化學性蜂窩組織炎 chemical

化学性腹膜炎/化學性腹膜炎　chemical peritonitis
化学性角化症/化學性角化症　chemical keratose
化学性拮抗/化學性拮抗　chemical antagonism
化学[性]解毒剂/化學解毒劑　chemical antidote
化学性菌斑控制/化學性菌斑控制　chemical plaque control
化学性黏着/化學性黏著　chemical adhesion
化学性膀胱炎/化學性膀胱炎　chemical cystitis
化学性水污染/化學性水汙染　chemical water pollution
化学性水污染物/化學性水汙染物　chemical water pollutant
化学[性损]伤/化學性傷害　chemical injury
化学[性]雾/化學性霧影　chemical fog
化学性吸入损伤/化學性吸入損傷　chemical inhalation injury
化学性眼外伤/化學性眼外傷　chemical ophthalmic injury
化学性眼外伤·热邪侵目证/化學性眼外傷·熱邪侵目證　chemical ophthalmic injury with pattern of heat invading eye
化学性抑制/化學性抑制　chemical depression
化学性子宫内膜破坏法/化學性子宫内膜破壞術　chemical hysterectomy
化学修饰/化學修飾　chemical modification
化学血清疗法/血清化學療法　chemoserotherapy
化学药品/化學藥品　chemical drug
化学[药物]预防/化學預防法　chemoprophylaxis
化学医学[派]/經典派化學醫學法,古代化學療法　chemiatry
化学应激性/化學應激性,應藥性　chemical irritability
化学诱变剂/化學突變劑,化學突變原　chemical mutagen
化学预防/化學預防　chemoprevention
化学元素/化學元素　ultimate principle
化学约束/化學約束　chemical restraint
化学战/化學戰　chemical warfare
化学战药物/化學戰藥物　chemical warfare agent
化学脂膜炎/化學脂層炎　chemical panniculitis
化学止血剂/化學止血劑　chemical styptic
化学制剂/化學性製劑　chemical preparation
化[学治]疗/化學治療　chemotherapy
化[学治]疗的/化學療法的　chemotherapeutic
化[学治]疗后/化學治療後　post chemotherapy
化[学治]疗剂/化學治療劑　chemotherapeutic agent
化[学治]疗药/化學療法藥物　chemotherapeutic drug
化学致癌剂/化學致癌物　chemical carcinogens
化瘀明目/化瘀明目　expelling blood stasis for improving eyesight
化瘀明目法/化瘀明目法　resolving stasis to brighten eye
化妆品/化妆品　cosmetic
化妆品痤疮/化妆品痤瘡　cosmetic acne
化妆品皮肤病/化妆品皮膚病　cosmetic dermatosis
化妆品皮肤损害/化妆品皮膚損害　cosmetic skin damage
化妆品性痤疮/化妆品性痤瘡　acne cosmetica
化装癣/偽裝癬　tinea incognito
划界叩诊板/劃記叩診板　plessigraph
划线培养/劃線培養　streak cultivation
划线培养平皿/劃線培養平碟　streak plate
华佗/華佗　Hua Tuo
华佗再造丸/華佗再造丸　huatuo zaizao pills
桦蕈/樺蕈　bakkola
怀布尔-帕拉德体/懷布爾-帕拉德體　Weibel-Palade body
怀俄明/懷俄明　Wyoming
怀尔德饮食/Wilder氏飲食　Wilder diet
怀特黑德手术/懷特黑德手術　Whitehead operation
怀孕/受孕　conception
槐苷/芸香素　sophorin
槐花/槐花　pagodatree flower
槐花散/槐花散　huaihua powder
槐碱/刺槐素　sophorine
槐角/槐角　Japanese pagodatree pod
槐角丸/槐角丸　huaijiao pills
踝/踝　①ankle ②huai, AH3
踝部骨折/踝骨折　fracture of malleolus
踝反射/踝反射　ankle jerk
踝沟/踝溝　lateral malleolar sulcus
踝骨/踝骨　ankle bone
踝骨下关节/踝骨下關節　subtalar articulation
踝关节/踝關節　talocrural articulation
踝关节内外侧副韧带损伤/踝關節内外側副韌帶損傷　sprain of medial and lateral ligaments of ankle joint
踝关节扭伤/踝關節扭傷　sprain ankle joint, sprain of ankle joint
踝管综合征/踝管綜合徵　tarsal tunnel pattern
踝后区/踝後區　back part of ankle
踝扭伤/踝扭傷　ankle sprain
踝前内侧动脉/踝内前動脈　medial anterior malleolar artery

踝前区/踝前區　front part of ankle
踝上的/髁上的　supracondylar
踝损伤/踝損傷　ankle injury
踝外侧环状韧带/踝外側環狀韌帶　external annular ligament of ankle
踝外侧韧带/踝外側韌帶　ankle lateral ligament
踝阵挛/踝陣攣，踝痙攣　ankle clonus
坏病/壞病　mistreated disease
坏疽/壞疽　gangrene
坏疽螺旋体/壞疽螺旋體　Treponema gangrenosum
坏疽热棒状杆菌/壞疽熱棒狀桿菌　Corynebacterium necrophorum
坏疽性/壞疽的　gangrenous
坏疽性鼻炎/壞疽性鼻炎　rhinitis gangrenosa
坏疽性胆囊炎/壞疽性膽囊炎　gangrenous cholecystitis
坏疽性龟头炎/壞疽性龜頭炎　balanitis gangrenosa
坏疽性坏死/壞疽性壞死　gangrenous necrosis
坏疽性睑炎/壞疽性瞼炎　blepharitis gangrenosa
坏疽性疖/壞疽性癤　furunculus gangraenescens
坏疽性口炎/壞疽性口角炎　gangrenous stomatitis
坏疽性溃疡/壞疽性炎　cancrum, sloughing ulcer
坏疽性阑尾炎/壞疽性闌尾炎　gangrenous appendicitis
坏疽性牛痘/壞疽性牛痘　vaccinia gangrenosa
坏疽性脓疮/壞疽性臁瘡　ecthyma gangrenosum
坏疽性脓皮病/壞疽性膿皮病　gangrenous pyoderma
坏疽性膀胱炎/壞疽性膀胱炎　gangrenous cystitis
坏疽性皮炎/壞疽性皮炎　dermatitis gangrenosa
坏疽性气肿/壞疽性氣腫　gangrenous emphysema
坏疽性水痘/壞疽性水痘　varicella gangrenosa
坏疽性咽炎/潰瘍性咽炎　ulcerated sore throat
坏疽性直肠结肠炎/直腸結腸壞疽　chiufa
坏疽性紫癜/壞疽性紫瘢症　purpura gangrenosa
坏死/壞死　necrosis, necrotize
坏死斑/壞死斑　ecthyma gangrenosa
坏死的/壞死的　necrotic
坏死毒素/壞死毒素　necrotoxin
坏死后肝硬化/壞死性肝硬變　postnecrotic cirrhosis
坏死溃疡性牙龈炎/壞死性潰瘍性齦炎　necrotizing ulcerative gingivitis
坏死溃疡性龈口炎/壞死性潰瘍齦口炎　necrotizing ulcerative gingivostomatitis
坏死松解/壞死溶解　necrolysis
坏死松解性游走性红斑/壞死鬆解性遊走性紅斑　necrolytic migratory erythema
坏死素/壞死素　necrosin
坏死[物质]囊肿/壞死囊腫　necrotic cyst

坏死性/壞死性　necrotica
坏死性痤疮/壞死性痤瘡　acne necrotica
坏死性的/壞死[性]的　necrotizing
坏死性动脉炎/壞死性動脈炎　necrotizing arteritis
坏死性冻疮/壞死性凍瘡　necrotized chilblain
坏死性蜂窝[组]织炎/壞死性蜂窩性組織炎　necrotizing cellulitis
坏死性骨炎/壞死性骨炎　necrotic osteitis
坏死性红斑/壞死性紅斑　necrotic erythema
坏死性喉炎/壞死性喉炎　necrotic laryngitis
坏死性脊髓炎/壞死性脊髓炎　necrotic myelitis
坏死性筋膜炎/壞死性筋膜炎　necrotizing fasciitis
坏死性溃疡/壞死性潰瘍　necrotic ulcer
坏死性前巩膜炎/壞死性前鞏膜炎　necrotizing anterior scleritis
坏死性丘疹样结核疹/壞死性丘疹樣結核疹　papulonecrotic tuberculide
坏死性肉芽肿/壞死性肉芽腫　necrotizing granulomas
坏死性肾乳头炎/壞死性腎乳頭炎　necrotic renal papillitis
坏死性涎腺化生/壞死性涎腺化生　necrotizing sialometaplasia
坏死性小肠结肠炎/壞死性腸炎，假膜性腸炎　necrotizing enterocolitis
坏死性血管炎/壞死性血管炎　necrotizing vasculitis
坏死性咽峡炎/壞死性咽峽炎　angina gangraenosa
坏死性胰腺炎/壞死性胰腺炎　necrotizing pancreatitis
坏死性脂膜炎/壞死性脂層炎　necrotizing panniculitis
坏死性紫癜/壞死性紫瘢症　purpura necrotica
坏死原的/發自腐質的　necrogenic
坏死组织激素/壞死組織內泌素　necrohormone
坏死[组织]切除术/壞死物切除術　necrectomy
坏血病/壞血病　scorbutus
坏血病的/壞血病的　scorbutic
坏血病贫血/壞血病性貧血　scorbutic anemia
坏血病性痤疮/壞血病性痤瘡　acne scorbutica, lichen lividus
坏血病性溃疡/壞血病性潰瘍　scorbutic ulcer
坏血病龈炎/壞血病齦炎　scorbutic gingivitis
还原/還原　reducing
还原剂/還原劑　reducing agent
还原酶/還原酶　reducing enzyme
5-α还原酶/5-α還原酶　5α-reductase
α还原酶/α還原酶　α-reductase
还原铁/還原鐵　reduced iron

环/環　cycle
P-环/P環　P loop
QRS环/QRS環　QRS loop
T环/T環　T loop
环巴比妥/環巴比妥　phanodorn
环板/環板　basic lamella
环孢霉素/環孢靈　cyclosporin
环孢霉素A肾病/環孢黴素A腎病　cyclosporine A nephropathy
环孢子虫/環孢子蟲　cyclospora
环扁桃酯/環扁桃酯　cyclandelate
环丙沙星/環丙沙星　ciprofloxacin
环丙烷/環丙烷　cyclopropane
环丙孕酮/環丙孕酮　cyproterone
环菠萝烷/環木波羅烷　cycloartane
环层/環層　circular layer
环层小体/[帕氏]環層小體　pacinian corpuscle
环氮氧化物/環氮氧化物　cyclic N-oxides
环蝶呤/環蝶翅色質　cyclopterin
环丁烷类/環丁烷類　cyclobutanes
环芬尼/環芬尼　cyclofenil
环庚烷类/環庚烷類　cycloheptanes
环癸烷类/環癸烷類　cyclodecanes
环行运动/環形運動,旋轉運動　circus movement
环形纤维/環狀纖維　circular fiber
环核苷酸类/環核苷酸類　cyclic nucleotides
环核苷酸调节蛋白激酶类/環核苷酸調節蛋白激酶類　cyclic nucleotide-regulated protein kinases
环痕孢子/環痕孢子　annellospore
环糊精包合物/環糊精包合物　cyclodextrin inclusion compound
环糊精类/環糊精類　cyclodextrins
环化/環化　cyclization
环化酶/環化酶　cyclase
环肌/環肌　circular muscle
环己氨磺酸类/環己胺磺酸類　cyclamates
环己氨基磺酸钙/環乙烷胺基磺酸鈣　calcium cyclamate
环己胺类/環己胺類　cyclohexylamines
环己醇类/環己醇類　cyclohexanols
环己酮类/環己酮類　cyclohexanones
环己烷/環己烷　cyclohexane
环己[烷]氨[基]磺酸盐/環己烷胺基磺酸鹽　cyclamate
环己烷类/環己烷類　cyclohexanes
环己烷烃基树脂/環己烷烯基樹脂　cyclohexane alkyl resin
环己烯巴比妥/安速眠　enhexymal
环己烯巴比妥钠/環己烯巴比妥鈉　sodium hexobarbital
环己烯亚胺/克菌丹　captan
环加氧酶抑制药/環加氧酶抑制藥　cyclooxygenase inhibitor
环甲关节/環甲關節　cricothyroid joint
环甲关节囊/環甲關節囊　capsule of cricothyroid joint
环甲肌/環甲肌　cricothyroid, cricothyroid muscle
环甲肌斜部/環甲肌斜部　oblique part of cricothyroid
环甲肌支/環甲肌支　cricothyroid branch
环甲肌直部/環甲肌直部　straight part of cricothyroid
环甲卡因/環甲卡因　cyclomethycaine
环甲膜穿刺/環甲膜穿刺　thyrocricoid puncture
环甲膜切开气管插管/環甲膜切開氣管插管　cricothyrotomy endotracheal intubation
环甲膜切开术/環甲狀膜切開術　cricothyroid laryngotomy
环甲韧带/環甲韌帶　cricothyroid ligament
环甲软骨切开术/環甲軟骨切開術,甲狀軟骨切開術　cricothyroidotomy
环甲杓韧带/環甲杓韌帶　cricothyroarytenoid ligament
环甲正中韧带/環甲正中韌帶　median cricothyroid ligament
环节动物/環節動物　annulata
环节动物纲/環節動物網　Annelida
环境/環境　environment
环境暴露/環境暴露　environmental exposure
环境病/環境病　environmental illness
环境病理学/環境病理學,風土病理學　environmental pathology, geopathology
环境毒理学/環境毒理學　environmental toxicology
环境[对细胞]影响记录法/環境對細胞之影響記錄法　hylergography
环境监测/環境監測　environmental monitoring
环境控制装置/環境控制裝置　environment control unit
环境疗法/環境潛化療法　milieu therapy
环境设计/環境設計　environment design
环境危害/環境危害　environment hazard
环境微生物学/環境微生物學　environmental microbiology
环境卫生/環境衛生　environmental health
环境污染/環境汙染　environmental pollution
环境污染物/環境汙染物　environmental pollutant

环境养生/環境養生　choice and creation of healthy environment
环境药理学/環境藥理學　environmental pharmacology
环境医学/環境醫學　environmental medicine
环境因素诱发疾病/環境因素誘發疾病　disorder of environmental origin
环境致癌物/環境致癌物　environmental carcinogen
环境致畸因子/環境致畸因子　environmental teratogen
环孔板/環孔板　annulate lamella
环孔片层/環形片層　annulate lamella
环亮氨酸/環白胺酸　cycloleucine
环裂亚目/環列亞目　Cyclorrhapha
环磷酸腺苷/環腺苷酸單磷酸　cyclic adenosine monophosphate
环磷酰胺/環磷醯胺　endoxan
环磷氧化物/環磷氧化物　cyclic P-oxide
环硫氧化物/環硫氧化物　cyclic S-oxide
环卵沉淀试验/環卵沈澱試驗　circum-oval precipitating test
环醚类/環醚類　cyclic ethers
环鸟苷单磷酸/環鳥苷單磷酸　cyclic guanosine mono phosphate
环喷托酯/環噴托酯　cyclopentolate
环染细胞/環染細胞　gyrochrome
环绕结扎术/末梢栓結術　circumferential wiring
环绕颧骨结扎术/環繞顴骨結扎術　circumzygomatic wiring
环绕颧骨悬吊上颌术/環繞顴骨懸吊上頜術　circumzygomatic wire suspension of maxilla
环绕下颌结扎术/環繞下頜結扎術　circummandibular wiring
环噻嗪/環噻嗪　cyclothiazide
环杓侧肌/環杓外側肌　lateral cricoarytenoid muscle
环杓关节/環杓關節　cricoarytenoid joint, cricoarytenoid articulation
环杓关节囊/環杓關節囊　capsule of cricoarytenoid joint
环杓关节炎/環杓關節炎　cricoarytenoid arthritis
环杓后肌/環杓後肌　posterior cricoarytenoid muscle
环杓后韧带/環杓後韌帶　posterior cricoarytenoid ligament
环蛇毒素类/環蛇毒素類　bungarotoxins
环AMP受体蛋白质/環AMP受體蛋白質　cyclic AMP receptor protein
环枢[关节]半脱位/環樞[關節]半脱位　subluxation of atlantoaxial joint
环水杨酰苯胺/環水楊醯苯胺　cyclic salicylanilide
环丝氨酸/環絲胺酸　cycloserine
环缩耳/環縮耳　constricted ear
环肽类/環肽類　cyclic peptides
环糖/環糖　cyclose
环套息肉切除术/環套息肉切除術　snaring polypectomy
环跳/環跳　huantiao, GB30
环跳疽/環跳疽　Huantiao abscess, suppurative coxitis
环跳疽·气虚血瘀证/環跳疽·氣虛血瘀證　Huantiao abscess with pattern of qi deficiency and blood stasis
环跳疽·热毒炽盛证/環跳疽·熱毒熾盛證　Huantiao abscess with blazing heat-toxin pattern
环跳疽·湿热蕴结证/環跳疽·濕熱蘊結證　Huantiao abscess with dampness-heat amassment pattern
环跳疽·阴寒凝滞证/環跳疽·陰寒凝滯證　Huantiao abscess with pattern of yin cold congelation and stagnation
环烃类/環烴類　cyclic hydrocarbons
环烷类/環烷類　cycloparaffins
环戊噻嗪/環戊噻嗪　cyclopenthiazide
环戊烷/環戊烷　cyclopentane
环戊烯壬酸/環戊烯壬酸　alepric acid
环烯醚萜/環烯醚萜　iridoid
环烯醚萜苷/環烯醚萜苷　iridoid glycoside
环烯醚萜类/環烯醚萜類　iridoids
环纤维/環纖維　circular fiber
环香豆素/環香豆素　coumarin
环项发/環項髮　cervicle cellulitis
环辛烷类/環辛烷類　cyclooctanes
环形暗点/環形暗點　ring scotoma
环形绷带/環狀繃帶　circular bandage
环形的/環狀的　circinate
环形发/環狀毛　circle hair
环形红斑/環狀紅斑　annular erythema
环形卡环/環狀扣　circumferential clasp
环形溃疡/環狀潰瘍　annular ulcer
环形破裂/環形破裂　loop fracture
环形韧带/環形韌帶　ring ligament
环形肉芽肿/環形肉芽腫　granuloma annulare eruption
环形烧伤/環形燒傷　circumferential burn
环形胎盘/環狀胎盤　annular placenta
环形泰勒虫/環狀泰勒蟲　Theileria annulata
环形疹/環形疹　ringed eruption
环型/環型　ring form
环性精神病/環性精神病　cycloid psychosis

环咽部/環咽部　cricopharyngeal part
环咽弛缓不能综合征/環狀軟骨與咽弛緩不能症候群　cricopharyngeal achalasia syndrome
环咽的/環狀軟骨與咽的　cricopharyngeal
环咽肌/環咽肌　cricopharyngeal muscle
环咽肌切开术/環咽肌切開術　cricopharyngeal myotomy
环咽憩室/環咽憩室　cricopharyngeal diverticulum
环咽憩室切除术/環咽憩室切除術　cricopharyngeal diverticulectomy
环咽韧带/環咽韌帶　cricopharyngeal ligament
环咽失弛缓症/環咽失弛緩症　cricopharyngeal achalasia
环氧丙烯酸盐/環氧丙烯酸鹽　epoxy acrylates
环氧化合物/環氧化合物　epoxy compound
环氧化酶/環氧化酶　cyclo-oxygenase
环氧化酶抑制剂/環氧化酶抑制劑　cyclo-oxygenase inhibitor
环氧化物/環氧化物　epoxide
环氧化物水解酶/環氧化物水解酶　epoxide hydrolase
环氧化物水解酶类/環氧化物水解酶類　epoxide hydrolases
环氧聚合物树脂/環氧聚合物樹脂　epoxy
环氧-1,2-氯-3-丙烷/環氧-1,2-氯-3-丙烷　epichloronydrin
环氧乳醇/環氧乳醇　dianhydrogalactitol
环氧树脂/環氧樹脂　epoxy resin
环氧乙烷/環氧乙烷　ethylene oxide
环 AMP 依赖性蛋白激酶类/環 AMP 依賴性蛋白激酶類　cyclic AMP-dependent protein kinases
环 GMP 依赖性蛋白激酶类/環 GMP 依賴性蛋白激酶類　cyclic GMP-dependent protein kinases
环乙巴妥/環乙烯巴比妥　methexenyl
环异构酶/環異構酶　cycloisomerase
环羽肌/環羽肌　circumpennate muscle
环运行/環運行　inscription of loop
环扎综合征/環扎症候群　encircling syndrome
环指/環指　ring finger
环转节律/馬戲狀節律,馬戲狀運動　circus rhythm
环状氨基酸类/環狀胺基酸類　cyclic amino acids
环状暗点/環狀暗點　annular scotoma
环状瘢痕挛缩/環狀瘢痕攣縮　circumferential cicatricial contracture
环状襞/環狀皺襞　circular fold
环状扁平苔藓/環狀扁平苔藓　annular lichen planus
环状处女膜/環狀處女膜　annular hymen
环状丛/環狀叢　annular plexus

环状的/環狀的　annular
环状感觉缺失/循環式麻醉　circular anesthesia
环状骨/環狀骨　orbicular bone
环状关节面/關節環狀面　articular circumference
环状龟头炎/環狀龜頭炎　balanitis circinata
环状角膜炎/環狀角膜炎　annular keratitis
环状角质层分解/環狀角質層分解　ringed keratolysis
环状睫/環狀睫　cilium circinatum
环状糠疹/連圈狀糠疹　pityriasis circinata
环状溃疡/環狀潰瘍　annular ulcer
环状狼疮/環狀狼瘡　lupus annularis
环状梅毒疹/環狀梅毒疹　syphilid annularis
环状糜烂性龟头包皮炎/環狀糜爛性龜頭包皮炎　balanoposthitis erosiva circinata
环状糜烂性龟头炎/環狀糜爛性龜頭炎　circinate erosive balanitis
环状染色体/環形染色體　ring chromosome
环状韧带/環狀韌帶　orbicular ligament
环状软骨/環狀軟骨　cricoid cartilage
环状软骨板/環狀軟骨板　lamina of cricoid cartilage
环状软骨弓/環狀軟骨弓　arch of cricoid cartilage
环状软骨气管切开术/環狀軟骨式氣管切開術　cricotracheotomy
环状软骨气管韧带/環氣管韌帶　cricotracheal ligament
环状软骨切除术/環狀軟骨切除術　cricoidectomy
环状软骨切开术/環狀軟骨切開術　cricotomy
环状软骨食管腱/環狀軟骨食管腱　cricoesophageal tendon
环状软骨痛/環狀軟骨痛　cricoidynia
环状软骨咽韧带/環狀軟骨咽韌帶　cricopharyngeal ligament
环状疝/環狀疝　annular hernia
环状肾/圓圈狀腎　doughnut kidney
环状弹力纤维松解性肉芽肿/環狀彈力纖維分解性肉芽腫　annular elastolytic granuloma
环状秃发/環狀秃髮　alopecia orbicularis
环状突/環狀突　annular apophysis
环状萎缩/環狀萎縮　gyrate atrophy
环状萎缩性斑块/環狀萎縮性斑塊　annular atrophic plaque
环状血栓/環狀血栓　annular thrombus
环状雅司病/環狀雅司病　circinate yaws
环状痒疹/環型癢疹　prurigo annularis
环状胰腺/環狀胰　annular pancreas
环状银屑病/環狀牛皮癬　psoriasis annulata
环状运动/環狀運動　circling

环状脂肪萎缩/環狀脂肪萎縮　lipoatrophia annularis
环状子宫托/環餅狀子宫托　doughnut pessary
环状阻塞/環狀阻塞　ring block
环钻/環錐法　trephinement
环钻术/鑽刺　terebration
环钻者/環鋸術士,環錐術士　trephiner
环佐辛/環佐辛　cyclazocine
寰齿后关节/寰齒後關節　posterior atlantodentale joint
寰齿前关节/寰齒前關節　anterior atlantodentale joint
寰枢侧关节/寰樞側關節　lateral atlantoaxial articulation
寰枢关节/寰樞關節,環椎-樞椎關節　atlanto-axial joint
寰枢关节脱位/寰樞椎脱位　atlantoaxial dislocation
寰枢外侧关节/寰樞外側關節　lateral atlantoaxial joint
寰枢正中关节/寰樞正中關節　median atlantoaxial joint, medial atlantoaxial articulation
寰枕关节/寰枕關節　atlantooccipital joint, atlantooccipital articulation
寰枕后膜/寰枕後膜　posterior atlantooccipital membrane
寰枕后韧带/寰枕後韌帶　posterior atlantooccipital ligament
寰枕前膜/寰枕前膜　anterior atlantooccipital membrane
寰枕外侧韧带/寰枕外側韌帶　lateral atlantooccipital ligament
寰椎/寰椎　atlas
寰椎侧块/寰椎側塊　lateral mass of atlas
寰椎横韧带/寰椎橫韌帶　transvers ligament of atlas
寰椎后弓/寰椎後弓　posterior arch of atlas
寰椎后结节/寰椎後結節　posterior tubercle of atlas
寰椎破裂性骨折/Jefferson氏骨折　Jefferson fracture
寰椎前弓/寰椎前[側]弓　anterior arch of atlas
寰椎前结节/寰椎前結節　anterior tubercle of atlas
寰椎上关节面/寰椎上關節面　superior articular surface of atlas
寰椎十字韧带/寰椎十字韌帶　cruciform ligament of atlas, cruciate ligament of atlas
寰椎下关节面/寰椎下關節面　inferior articular surface of atlas
缓冲/緩衝　buffer
缓冲的/緩衝的　buffered
缓冲对/緩衝對　buffer pair

缓冲剂/緩衝劑　buffer
缓冲碱/緩衝鹼　buffer base
缓冲疗法/緩衝療法　buffer therapy
缓冲区/緩衝區　buffer area
缓冲溶液/緩衝[溶]液　buffer solution
缓冲神经/緩衝神經　buffer nerve
缓冲物质/緩衝物質　buffer substance
缓冲系统/緩衝系[統]　buffer system
缓冲盐溶液/緩衝鹽溶液　buffer salt solution
缓冲值/緩衝值　buffer value
缓冲作用/緩衝作用　buffer action
缓方/緩方　gentle prescription
缓和剂/緩和劑　alleviator
缓激肽/[遲]緩激肽　bradykinin
缓激肽拮抗药/緩激肽拮抗藥　bradykinin antagonist
缓激肽受体/緩激肽受體　bradykinin receptor
缓激肽B1受体/緩激肽B1受體　bradykinin B1 receptor
缓激肽B2受体/緩激肽B2受體　bradykinin B2 receptor
缓解/緩解,救助　relief
缓解期/緩解期　catabasis
缓解诱导/緩解誘導　remission induction
缓脉/緩脈　moderate pulse
缓慢摆动/運動徐緩性擺動　bradykinetic oscillation
缓慢谵妄/緩慢譫妄　low delirium
缓释制剂/延釋製劑　sustained release preparation
缓缩肌/緩縮肌　sluggish muscle
缓则治本/緩則治本　radical treatment in chronic case
幻触/幻觸　tactile hallucination
幻感觉/幻感覺　phantom sensation
幻觉/幻覺　hallucination
幻觉妄想状态/幻覺妄想狀態　hallucinatory paranoid state
幻觉性/幻覺的　hallucinatory
幻觉性神经痛/幻覺性神經痛　hallucinatory neuralgia
幻觉性牙痛/幻覺性牙痛　phantom odontalgia
幻觉症/幻覺病　hallucinosis
幻视/幻視　visual hallucination
幻视器/視網膜檢影鏡,視網膜檢影器　fantascope
幻听/幻聽　auditory hallucination
幻痛/幻痛　ghost pain
幻味/幻味　gustatory hallucination
幻想/幻想　fantasy
幻想性谎言癖/狂想謊語症　pseudologia fantastica
幻像/幻象,幻覺　phantom

幻像学/幻視學　phantasmatology
幻嗅/幻嗅　olfactory hallucination
幻影棘慢复合波/幻影棘慢複合波　phantom spike and slow wave complex
幻影细胞/幻影細胞,幽靈細胞　shadow cell
幻肢/幻想肢,想像肢　phantom limb
幻肢痛/幻肢痛,假肢痛　phantom limb pain
换瓣术后血栓形成/換瓣術後血栓形成　post-valve-replacement thrombosis
换能器/轉導物　transducer
换气/換氣　ventilation
换气比值/換氣比值　respiratory exchange ratio
换气过度/換氣過度　overventilation
换气通风/換氣通風　perflation ventilation
换位/互换位置　transposition
换位行为/轉移行爲　displacement behavior
换窝异亲抚养试验/換窩異親撫養試驗　litters cross fostering study
换血/換血　exsanguination transfusion
唤醒试验/喚醒試驗　awaken test
患病率/患病率　prevalence
患病率调查/患病率調查　prevalence survey
患不治之症者/患不治之症者　incurable
患者分级医疗/患者分級醫療　progressive patient care
患者拒绝治疗/患者拒絕治療　treatment refusal
肓门/肓門　huangmen, BL51
肓俞/肓俞　huangshu, KI16
慌张步态/急促步式,急步　festination
黄/黄　yellow
黄柏/黄柏　amur cork-tree
黄斑/黄斑　macula lutea
黄斑变性/黄斑變性　degeneration of macula
黄斑病变/斑狀丘疹　maculopathy
黄斑发育不全/黄斑發育不全　aplasia of macula
黄斑光应力试验/黄斑光應力試驗　macular photostress test
黄斑回避/黄斑回避　sparing of macula
黄斑及中央小凹/黄斑及中央小凹　macula lutea and central fovea
黄斑裂孔/黄斑裂孔　macular hole
黄斑瘤/黄斑瘤　xanthelasma
黄斑盘状脱离/黄斑盤狀脫離　disciform macular detachment
黄斑缺损/黄斑缺損　macular coloboma
黄斑上小动脉/黄斑上小動脈　superior macular arteriole
黄斑上小静脉/黄斑上小靜脈　superior macular venule
黄斑下小动脉/黄斑下小動脈　inferior macular arteriole
黄斑下小静脉/黄斑下小靜脈　inferior macular venule
黄斑小动脉/黄斑小動脈　corkscrew artery
黄斑异位/黄斑異位　heterotopy of macula
黄斑皱褶/黄斑皺褶　macular pucker
黄变/黄變症　xanthochromia
黄变的/黄病變的　xanthochromic
黄病毒/黄病毒　flavivirus
黄病毒感染/黄病毒感染　flavivirus infection
黄病毒科感染/黄病毒科感染　Flaviviridae infection
黄常山硷/黄常山鹼　dichroine
黄带/黄帶　yellow vaginal discharge
黄带[病]/黄帶[病],黄帶下　yellowish vaginal discharge, yellow vaginal discharge
黄带·湿毒蕴结证/黄帶·濕毒蘊結證　yellow vaginal discharge with pattern of accumulation and binding of damp-poison
黄带·湿热下注证/黄帶·濕熱下注證　yellow vaginal discharge with pattern of downward diffusion of damp-heat
黄疸/黄疸　icterus
黄疸病/黄疸病　yellow disease
黄疸弛张疟/膽性弛張瘧　bilious remittent malaria
黄疸的/黄疸的　icteric
黄疸性肺炎/黄疸性肺炎,膽型肺炎　bilious pneumonia
黄疸性肝炎/黄疸型肝炎　icterepatitis
黄疸性钩端螺旋体病/黄疸性鉤端螺旋體病　icteric leptospirosis
黄疸血红蛋白尿/黄疸血紅素尿　icterohemoglobinuria
黄疸血尿/黄疸血尿,黑水熱　icterohematuria
黄帝/黄帝　Huangdi, Yellow Emperor
黄帝内经/黄帝内經　Inner Canon of Huangdi, Huangdi Neijing
黄帝内经太素/黄帝内經太素　Grand Simplicity of Inner Canon of Huangdi, Huangdi Neijing Taisu
黄碘化亚汞/黄色碘化亞汞　hydrargyri iodidum flavum
黄蝶呤/黄喋呤　xanthopterin
黄耳伤寒/黄耳傷寒　cold-attack due to purulent ear, otogenic intracranial infection
黄耳伤寒·热入营血证/黄耳傷寒·熱入營血證　cold-attack due to purulent ear with pattern of heat entering nutrient-blood

黄耳伤寒·热盛动风证/黄耳傷寒·熱盛動風證 cold-attack due to purulent ear with pattern of heat exuberance stirring wind
黄耳伤寒·热陷心包证/黄耳傷寒·熱陷心包證 cold-attack due to purulent ear with pattern of heat sinking into pericardium
黄风内障/黄風內障 yellow wind glaucoma
黄蜂毒液类/黃蜂毒液類 wasp venoms
黄[蜂]蜡/黃蠟 unbleached beeswax
黄蜂螫伤/黄蜂螫傷 wasp sting
黄苷酸/黄核苷酸，黄嘌呤酸 xanthylic acid
黄骨髓/黃骨髓,脂髓 yellow bone marrow, fat marrow
黄瓜痈/黄瓜癰 paravertebral abscess
黄光油溶红/黄光油溶紅 cerasine
黄胱氨酸/黃胱胺酸 xanthocystine
黄汗[病]/黄汗 yellowish sweating
黄红皮肤/黃紅膚症 xanthoerythrodermia
黄黄质/黄花色素 flavoxanthin
黄昏幻觉/黃昏幻覺 vesperal hallucination
黄家/黄家 person suffering from jaundice
黄甲综合征/黄甲症候群 yellow nails syndrome
黄精/黄精 solomonseal rhizome
黄葵油/黃葵油 ambrette oil
黄蓝色盲/黃藍色盲 yellow-blue blindness
黄连/黄連 golden thread
黄连解毒汤/黃連解毒湯 huanglian jiedu decoction
黄连属/黃連屬 Coptis
黄瘤病/黄瘤病 xanthomatosis
黄绿青霉素/黄毒素 citreoviridin
黄麻/黄麻 jute
黄毛舌/黄毛舌 yellow hairy tongue
黄酶[类]/黃色酵素 yellow enzymes
黄绵马酸/黄綿馬酸 flavaspidic acid
黄嘌呤/黄嘌呤 xanthine
黄嘌呤类/黄嘌呤類 xanthines
黄嘌呤尿/黄嘌呤尿 xanthinuria
黄嘌呤脱氢酶/黄嘌呤去氫酶,黄嘌呤脫氫酵素 xanthine dehydrogenase
黄嘌呤氧化酶/黄嘌呤氧化酶,黄嘌呤氧化酵素 xanthine oxidase
黄嘌呤氧化酶缺乏/黄嘌呤氧化酶缺乏 xanthine oxidase deficiency
黄期过短/黄期過短 short luteal phase
黄芪/黄芪 astragalus membranaceus, milkvetch root
黄芪胶/黄芪膠 gum tragacanth
黄芩/黄芩 baical skullcap root
黄曲霉毒素/黄麴毒素 aflatoxin
黄曲霉[毒素]中毒/黄麴毒素中毒 aflatoxicosis
黄曲霉菌/黃麴菌 Aspergillus flavus
黄热病/黃熱病 yellow fever
黄热病毒/黄熱病病毒 yellow fever virus
黄热病毒质/黄熱病毒素 amaril
黄热病疫苗/黄熱病疫苗 yellow fever vaccine
黄仁/黄仁 iris
黄韧带/黄韌帶 ligamenta flava
黄肉芽肿/黄肉芽腫 xanthogranuloma
黄肉芽肿性肾盂肾炎/黄肉芽腫性腎盂腎炎 xanthogranulomatous pyelonephritis
黄色棒状杆菌/黄色棒狀桿菌 corynebacterium flavidum
黄色蛋白/黄蛋白質 xanthoprotein
黄色蛋白酸/黄蛋白酸 xanthoproteic acid
黄色蛋白[质]反应/黄蛋白反應 xanthoproteic reaction
黄色肝样变/黄色肝樣變 yellow hepatization
黄色幻视/黄色幻視,黄光幻視 xanthophose
黄[色]瘤/黄瘤,黄疣 xanthoma
黄色瘤细胞/黄瘤細胞 xanthoma cell
黄色盲/黄色盲 yellow blindness
黄[色]肉芽肿病/黄色肉芽腫症 xanthogranulomatosis
黄色肉芽肿性胆囊炎/黄色肉芽腫性膽囊炎 xanthogranulomatous cholecystitis
黄色素细胞/脂色素細胞 lipophore
黄色萎缩/黄色萎縮 yellow atrophy
黄色细胞/黄色細胞 xanthocyte
黄色正铁血红素/黄色正鐵血紅素 xanthematin
黄珊瑚精/黄珊瑚精 yellow corallin
黄蓍胶/西黃蓍膠,膠黃蓍樹膠 tragacanth
黄视症/黄視症,黄色視覺,視物顯黄症 xanthopsia
黄鼠李苷/鼠李黄素 xanthorhamnin
黄水疮/黄水瘡,膿皰症 impetigo, yellow fluid ulcers
黄水疮·脾虚湿困证/黄水瘡·脾虛濕困證 impetigo with pattern of spleen deficiency and dampness retention
黄水疮·暑湿热蕴证/黄水瘡·暑濕熱蘊證 impetigo with pattern of summerheat-dampness heat amassment
黄素/黄[色]素 flavin
黄素单核苷酸/黄素單核苷酸 flavin mononucleotide
黄素蛋白/黄色素蛋白 flavoprotein
黄素类/黄素類 flavins
黄素腺嘌呤二核苷酸/黄素腺嘌呤二核苷酸 flavin-

adenine dinucleotide
黄素氧还蛋白/黄素氧還蛋白　flavodoxin
黄髓/黄骨髓　yellow marrow
黄苔/黄苔　yellow fur
黄体/黄體　corpus luteum
黄体保持/黄體保持　corpus luteum maintenance
黄体的/黄體的　luteal
黄体功能不足/黄體功能不足　inadequate luteal function
黄体化/黄體[素]化　luteinization
黄体化过度/黄體化過度　hyperluteinization
黄体激素类/黄體激素類　corpus luteum hormones
黄体瘤/黄體瘤　luteoma
黄体期/黄體期　luteal phase
黄体期缺乏/黄體期缺乏　luteal phase deficiency
黄体切除术/黄體切除術　luteectomy
黄体溶解/黄體分解　luteolysis
黄体溶解剂/黄體溶解劑　luteolytic agent
黄体素细胞/黄體素細胞　lutein cell
黄体酮/黄體酮　progesterone
黄体酮试验/黄體酮試驗　progesterone test
黄体细胞/黄體細胞　luteal cell, lutein cell
黄铜/黄銅　brass
黄铜匠病/黄銅匠病　brass-founder disease
黄铜色小体/黄銅色紅血球,黄銅小體　brassy body
黄铜屑眼炎/黄銅眼炎,黄銅眼病　chalcitis
黄铜铸工寒战/鋅寒顫　spelter shakes
黄酮/黄酮　flavone
黄酮醇/黄酮醇　flavonol
黄酮苷/黄酮苷　flavonoid glycoside
黄酮呱酯/黄酮呱酯　flavoxate
黄酮类/黄酮類　flavonoid, flavones
黄头孢霉/黄頭孢黴　Cephalosporium chrysogenum
黄土汤/黄土湯　huangtu decoction
黄烷/黄烷　flavane
黄烷类/黄烷類　flavanoid
黄烷酮/黄烷酮　flavanone
黄烷酮醇/黄烷酮醇　flavanonol
黄烷酮类/黄烷酮類　flavanones
黄癣/黄癬　tinea favosa
黄癣痂/黄癬痂　scutulum
黄癣菌/黄癬菌　Achorion
黄癣毛癣菌/黄癬毛癬菌　Trichophyton favosa
黄癣疹/黄癬過敏性皮疹　favid
黄癣状的/黄癬狀的　favaginous
黄药子/黄藥子　air potato
黄叶素/黄葉素　xanthophylls
黄液上冲/黄液上冲　hypopyon, upward rushing of yellow fluid
黄液上冲·脾胃积热证/黄液上冲·脾胃積熱證　upward rushing of yellow fluid with pattern of heat accumulation in spleen-stomach
黄液上冲·阴虚火旺证/黄液上冲·陰虚火旺證　upward rushing of yellow fluid with pattern of yin deficiency and fire effulgence
黄油/黄油,乳酪　butter
黄油样粪/黄油樣糞　butter stool
黄油样囊肿/[乳]酪狀囊腫　butter cyst
黄油样肿胀/乳酪狀腫　butyroid tumor
黄油障/黄油障　pinguecula
黄原酸盐/黄嘌呤酸鹽　xanthate
黄樟脑/黄樟腦　safrole
黄樟烯/黄梓烯　safrene
煌黄/煌黄　brilliant yellow
磺胺/磺醯胺　sulfonamide
磺胺苯吡唑/磺胺苯吡唑　sulfaphenazole
磺胺吡啶/磺胺吡啶　sulfapyridine
磺胺薄膜/磺胺藥膜　sulfa film
磺胺醋酰/乙醯磺胺　sulfacetamide
磺胺胆/磺胺劑膽汁症　sulfonamidocholia
磺胺地托辛/磺胺二甲氧基噻啶　sulfadimethoxine
磺胺丁脲/磺胺丁尿素　carbutamide
磺胺多辛/周效磺胺　sulfadoxine
磺胺噁唑/磺胺噁唑　sulfamoxole
磺胺二甲嘧啶/磺胺二甲基嘧啶　sulfamethazine
磺胺化合物/磺醯胺化合物　sulfonamides compound
磺胺剂性无尿/磺胺劑性無尿　sulfanuria
磺胺甲基异噁唑/磺胺甲異噁唑　sulfamethoxazole
磺胺甲基嘧啶/磺胺甲基嘧啶　sulfamerazine
磺胺甲噻二唑/磺胺甲基嘧二唑　sulfamethizole
磺胺甲氧嗪/磺胺甲氧基噠嗪　sulphamethoxypyridazine
磺胺间甲氧嘧啶/磺胺間甲氧嘧啶　sulfamonomethoxine
磺胺喹噁啉/磺胺喹噁啉　sulfaquinoxaline
磺胺类药/磺胺類藥　sulfonamides
磺胺林/磺胺林　sulfalene
磺胺氯达嗪/磺胺氯噠嗪　sulfachlorpyridazine
磺胺米隆/磺胺米隆　mafenide
磺胺脒/磺胺胍　sulfaguanidine
磺胺嘧啶/磺胺嘧啶　sulfadiazine
磺胺嘧啶银/磺胺嘧啶銀　silver sulphadiazine
磺胺尿/磺胺尿　sulfonamiduria
磺胺噻唑/磺胺噻唑　norsulfazole
磺胺噻唑类/磺胺噻唑類　sulfathiazoles
磺胺索嘧啶/磺胺異二甲嘧啶　sulfisomidine

磺胺血/磺胺劑血症　sulfonamidemia
磺胺药/磺胺類藥物　sulfa drug
磺胺药肾病/磺胺藥腎病　sulphonamide nephropathy
磺胺乙二唑/磺胺乙基嘧二唑　sulfaethidole
磺胺异噁唑/磺胺異噁唑　sulfafurazole
磺胺[中毒]性甲状腺肿/磺胺中毒性甲狀腺腫　sulfonamide goiter
磺苯酯/碘酚十一烯酸乙酯　iophendylate
磺吡酮/苯磺唑酮　sulfinpyrazone
磺苄西林/磺苄西林　sulbenicillin
磺化油/磺化油　sulphonated oil
磺基/磺基　sulfone
磺基丙氨酸/磺基丙胺酸　cysteic acid
磺基琥珀酸二辛酯/磺基琥珀酸二辛酸　dioctyl sulfosuccinic acid
磺基水杨酸/磺基水楊酸　salicylsulfonic acid
磺基转移酶类/磺基轉移酶類　sulfotransferases
磺脲类/磺脲類　sulphonylureas
磺酸/磺酸,硫代酸　sulfoacid
磺酸基/磺基,磺族　sulfonic group
磺酸甲酯/磺酸甲酯　methyl sulfonate
磺酸类/磺酸類　sulfonic acids
磺酸萘酚/萘酚磺酸　naphtholsulfonic acid
磺酸盐/磺酸鹽　sulfosalt
磺酰脲化合物/磺醯脲化合物　sulfonylurea compound
磺酰脲类/磺醯尿素　sulfonylurea
磺溴酞/磺溴酞　sulfobromophthalein
磺溴酞钠试验/磺溴酞鈉試驗　bromsulphalein test
磺乙酰胺钠/磺乙醯胺鈉　sodium sulfacetamide
恍惚/恍惚　absent-mindedness
灰被/灰被　indusium griseum
灰侧耳菌素/灰側耳素　pleurotin
灰尘感染/塵埃傳染　dust infection
灰的/灰色的　ashy
灰分/灰分　ash
灰分测定/灰分測定　determination of ash
灰黄霉素/灰黃黴素　griseofulvin
灰交通支/灰交通支　grey communicating branch
灰结节/灰結節　tuber cinereum
灰结节支/灰結節支　branch of tuber cinereum
灰烬/灰燼　ash
灰绿曲霉/淡藍色麴菌　Aspergillus glaucus
灰泥/灰泥　plaster
灰泥角化病/灰泥角化病　stucco keratosis
灰色变性/灰色變性　gray degeneration
灰色皮病/灰色皮膚病　ashy dermatosis
灰色萎缩/灰色萎縮　gray atrophy
灰苔/灰苔　gray fur
灰像/灰像　spodogram
灰小结节/灰小結節　tuberculum cinereum
灰指甲/灰指甲,甲癬　onychomycosis, tinea unguium
灰趾甲/甲黴菌病,甲癬　tinea unguium
灰质/灰質　gray matter, gray substance
灰质后连合/灰質後連合　posterior gray commissure
灰质胶质/灰質膠質　gelatinous substance of gray substance
灰质前连合/灰質前連合,前灰[質]連合　anterior gray commissure
灰质柱/灰質柱　gray column
挥鞭伤/揮鞭傷　whiplash injury
挥发器/揮發器　volatilizer
挥发性脂肪酸类/揮發性脂肪酸類　volatile fatty acids
挥发油/揮發油　volatile oil, distilled oil
挥发油测定/揮發油測定　determination of volatile oil
挥发油测定器/揮發油測定器　volatile oil determination apparatus
挥发油类/揮發油類　volatile oils
挥发作用/揮發作用　volatilization
恢复/恢復,復原　recovery, restoration
恢复期/恢復期　convalescence
恢复期病人/恢復者　convalescent
恢复期护养/恢復期護養　aftercare
恢复期膳食/恢復期飲食　convalescent diet
恢复期血清/恢復期血清　convalescence serum
恢复体力药/強壯劑　antasthenic
回避行为/迴避行爲　abient behavior
回避学习/回避學習　avoidance learning
回波搏动/回波搏動　echo beat
回波描记术/回聲波描記術　echography
回波平面成像/回波平面成像　echo-planar imaging
回肠/迴腸　ileum
回肠动脉/迴腸動脈　ileal artery
回肠缝术/迴腸縫合術　ileorrhaphy
回肠肛管吻合术/迴腸肛管吻合術　ileoanal anastomosis
回肠横结肠吻合术/迴腸橫結腸造口吻合術　ileotransversostomy
回肠回肠吻合术/迴腸造口吻合術　ileoileostomy
回肠疾病/迴腸疾病　ileal disease
回肠结肠的/迴結腸的　ileocolic
回肠结肠动脉/迴結腸動脈　ileocolic artery
回肠结肠静脉/迴結腸靜脈　ileocolic vein

回肠结肠切开术/迴結腸切開術 ileocolotomy
回肠结肠吻合术/迴結腸造口吻合術 ileocolostomy
回肠结肠炎/迴結腸炎 ileocolitis
回肠静脉/迴腸靜脈 ileal vein
回肠阑尾窝疝/迴腸闌尾窩疝 ileoappendicular hernia
回肠盲肠吻合术/迴盲腸吻合術 ileocecostomy
回肠纽结/迴腸紐結 ileal kink
回肠膀胱成形术/迴腸膀胱成形術 ileocystoplasty
回肠膀胱扩大术/迴腸膀胱擴大術 ileum augmentation cystoplasty
回肠膀胱尿流改道术/迴腸膀胱尿流改道術 ileal conduit diversion
回肠膀胱术/迴腸膀胱術 ileal conduit
回肠憩室/迴腸憩室 ileal diverticulum
回肠切除术/迴腸切除術 ileectomy
回肠切开术/迴腸切開術 ileotomy
回肠系膜/迴腸繫膜 mesoileum
回肠炎/迴腸炎 ileitis
回肠乙状结肠吻合术/迴腸乙狀結腸造口吻合術 ileosigmoidostomy
回肠造口术/迴腸造口術 ileostomy
回肠造口周围湿疹/迴腸造口周圍濕疹 circumileostomy eczema
回肠支/迴腸支 ileal branch
回肠直肠吻合术/迴腸直腸造口吻合術 ileoproctostomy
回肠肿瘤/迴腸腫瘤 ileal neoplasm
回返绷带/迴返繃帶 recurrent bandage
回复变株/回復[突]變株 reverse mutant, revertant
回复的/回復的 redux
回复体/回復體 revertant
回复突变/回復突變 reverse mutation, back mutation
回顾性道德评判/回顧性道德評判 retrospective moral judgment
回顾性研究/回顧性研究 retrospective study
回归分析/回歸分析 regression analysis
回归热/回歸熱 recurrent fever
回归热淋巴细胞瘤/回歸熱淋巴細胞瘤 Borrelia lymphocytoma
回归热密螺旋体/回歸熱[密]螺旋體 Treponema recurrentis
回归热疏螺旋体/回歸熱螺旋體 Borrelia recurrentis
回归系数/回歸係數 regression coefficient
回结肠襞/迴結腸皺襞 ileocolic fold
回结肠丛/迴結腸叢 ileocolic plexus
回结肠淋巴结/迴結腸淋巴結 ileocolic lymph node

回力充填器/回力充填器 back-action plugger
回力卡环/回力卡環 back-action clasp
回流/回流,逆流 backflow, reflux
回盲瓣/迴盲瓣 ileocecal valve
回盲瓣口/迴盲瓣口 orifice of ileocecal valve
回盲瓣上唇/迴盲瓣上唇 upper lip of ileocecal valve
回盲瓣系带/迴盲瓣繫帶 frenulum of ileocecal valve
回盲瓣下唇/迴盲瓣下唇 lower lip of ileocecal valve
回盲瓣炎/迴盲瓣炎 typhlodicliditis
回盲襞/迴盲皺襞,迴腸盲腸皺襞 ileocecal fold
回盲部结核/迴盲部結核 ileocecal tuberculosis
回盲肠皮肤尿流改道术/迴盲腸皮膚尿流改道術 ileocecal cutaneous diversion
回盲口/迴盲口 ileocecal orifice
回盲乳头/迴盲乳頭 ileocecal papilla
回盲上襞/迴盲上襞 plica ileocaecalis cranialis
回盲上隐窝/迴盲上隱窩 superior ileocecal recess
回盲下隐窝/迴盲下隱窩 inferior ileocecal recess
回盲隐窝/迴盲陷凹 ileocecal pouch
回乳/回乳 terminating lactation
回声/回聲 echo
回声定位/回聲測定 echolocation
回声感觉/回聲幻聽 echoacousia
回声征/叩診時之回響 echo sign
回收/回收率 recovery
回缩/回縮,縮回 rebound, retraction
回缩睾丸/回縮睾丸 retracted testis
回缩现象/何-史二氏現象,回躍現象 Holmes-Stewart phenomenon
回旋长肌/迴旋長肌 long rotator muscle
回旋短肌/迴旋短肌 musculi rotatores breves
回旋肌/迴旋肌,迴轉肌 rotatores, rotator muscle, musculi rotatores
回旋加速器/原子核撞擊機 cyclotron
回旋灸/迴旋灸 revolving moxibustion
回旋棱镜/迴旋棱鏡 rotary prism
回旋套/迴旋套 rotator cuff
回旋现象/迴旋現象 Yoyo phenomenon
回旋形线状鱼鳞病/迴旋形線狀魚鱗病 ichthyosis linearis circumflexa
回旋状/迴旋狀 gyrata
回旋状的/迴旋狀的 gyratus
回旋状牛皮癣/迴旋狀牛皮癬 psoriasis gyrata
回阳[救逆]/回陽救逆 restoring yang and rescuing patient from collapse
回阳救逆剂/回陽救逆劑 formula for restoring yang and rescuing patient from collapse
回阳生肌/回陽生肌 restoring yang and promoting

granulation
回忆性神经痛/追憶性神經痛　reminiscent neuralgia
回忆应答/記憶反應　anamnestic response
回音平面影像/回音平面影像　echo-planar imaging
回音延迟时间/回音延遲時間　echo delay time
回状头皮/迴狀頭皮　cutis verticis gyrata
茴芹苦素/苦芹菜素　pimpinellin
茴三硫/茴三硫　anethole trithione
茴香/茴香　fennel sweet
茴香橘核丸/茴香橘核丸　huixiang juhe pills
茴香霉素/茴香黴素　anisomycin
茴香醚类/茴香醚類　anisoles
茴香醛/洋茴香醛　anisic aldehyde
茴香酸盐/洋茴香酸鹽　anisate
茴香酰甘氨酸/茴香醯甘胺酸　anisuric acid
蛔虫/蛔蟲　ascaris
蛔虫病/蛔蟲病　ascariasis
蛔虫病·虫积肠道证/蛔蟲病·蟲積腸道證　ascariasis with pattern of accumulation of worms in intestine
蛔虫病·脾胃气虚证/蛔蟲病·脾胃氣虛證　ascariasis with pattern of qi deficiency of spleen and stomach
蛔虫感染/蛔蟲感染　roundworm infection
蛔虫目感染/蛔目感染　Ascaridida infection
蛔厥/蛔厥　cold limbs pattern due to ascariasis, syncope due to ascariasis
毁灭效应/毀滅效應　shatter effect
毁容/毀容　disfigurement of face
毁损伤/毀損傷　smashed wound
毁胎术/毀胎術　destructive operation
毁形的/毀形的　mutilans
毁形性鼻咽炎/毀形性鼻咽炎　rhinopharyngitis mutilans
汇合的/融合的　confluent
会聚的/會聚的,集合的　convergent
会聚射线/集合光線,會光線　convergent ray
会聚性透镜/會聚性透鏡　converging meniscus
会聚性眼球震颤/會聚性眼球震顫　convergent nystagmus
会厌/會厭　epiglottis
会厌垫/會厭墊　cushion of the epiglottis
会厌谷/會厭溪　epiglottic vallecula
会厌结节/會厭結節　tubercle of epiglottis
会厌切除[术]/會厭切除術　epiglottectomy
会厌软骨/會厭軟骨　epiglottic cartilage
会厌软骨茎/會厭軟骨莖　stalk of epiglottis
会厌软骨前脂体/會厭軟骨前脂體　preepiglottic adipose body
会厌炎/會厭炎　epiglottitis

会厌痈/會厭癰　epiglottic abscess
会阳/會陽　huiyang, BL35
会阴/會陰　①perineum ②huiyin RN1
会阴部烧伤/會陰部燒傷　burn of perineal region
会阴部阻滞/陰部神經阻斷麻醉　pudendal block
会阴成形术/會陰造形術,會陰修補術　perineoplasty
会阴的/會陰的　perineal
会阴点/會陰點　perineum point
会阴动脉/會陰動脈　perineal artery
会阴动脉阴唇后支/會陰動脈陰唇後支　posterior labial branch of perineal artery
会阴动脉阴囊后支/會陰動脈陰囊後支　posterior scrotal branch of perineal artery
会阴缝术/會陰縫合術　perineorrhaphy
会阴缝/會陰縫　perineal raphe
会阴肛门成形术/會陰肛門成形術　perineal anoplasty
会阴横动脉/會陰橫動脈　transverse perineal artery
会阴横韧带/會陰橫韌帶　transverse ligament of perineum, transverse perineal ligament
会阴肌/會陰肌　perineal muscle, musculi perinei
会阴痉挛/會陰痙攣,陰道痛　perineal spasm
会阴裂伤/會陰裂傷　perineal laceration
会阴瘘/會陰瘻　perineal fistula
会阴美容术/會陰美容術　aesthetic perineum surgery
会阴尿道下裂/會陰尿道下裂　perineal hypospadia
会阴浅横肌/會陰淺橫肌　superficial transverse muscle of perineum, musculus transversus perinei superficialis
会阴浅[间]隙/會陰淺[間]隙　superficial perineal space
会阴浅筋膜/會陰淺筋膜　superficial fascia of perineum
会阴浅隙/會陰淺隙　superficial perineal space
会阴切开术/會陰切開術　episiotomy
会阴曲/會陰曲　perineal flexure
会阴人字形绷带/Hueter氏繃帶　Hueter bandage
会阴疝/會陰疝,會陰赫尼亞　perineal hernia
会阴深横肌/會陰深橫肌　deep transverse muscle of perineum
会阴深[间]隙/會陰深[間]隙　deep perineal space
会阴神经/會陰神經　perineal nerve
会阴神经肌支/會陰神經肌支　muscular branch of perineal nerve
会阴收缩力计/陰道周圍肌力計　perineometer
会阴下降综合征/會陰下降症候群　descending perineum syndrome
会阴型尿道下裂/會陰部尿道下裂　perineal

hypospadias
会阴修复术/會陰修復術 perineal repair
会阴阴道裂伤/會陰陰道裂傷 colpoperineal laceration
会阴阴道瘘/會陰陰道瘻 perinovaginal fistula
会阴粘连/會陰粘連 perineal adhesion
会阴正中切开术/會陰正中切開術 median episiotomy
会阴支/會陰支 perineal branch
会阴中心腱/會陰中心腱 perineal central tendon
会阴综合征/會陰症候群 perineal syndrome
会诊医师/會診醫師 consulting staff
会宗/會宗 huizong, SJ7
绘画疗法/繪畫療法 painting therapy
绘图模拟/繪圖模擬 paint simulation
彗星试验/彗星試驗 comet assay
彗星细胞/尾狀細胞 caudate cell
彗星样细胞/彗星樣細胞 cometal cell
秽亵行为/穢褻行爲 copropraxia
秽亵症/穢語症,穢褻言語 eschrolalia
惠勒手术/惠勒手術 Wheeler technique
惠民和济局/惠民和濟所 People's Welfare Pharmacies
惠民局/惠民局 Medical Institute of Benevolence
惠普尔病/惠普爾病 Whipple disease
惠普尔三联征/惠普爾三聯徵 Whipple triad
惠特病/Whytt 氏病 Whytt disease
喙肱肌/喙肱肌 coracobrachialis
喙肱肌囊/喙肱肌囊 coracobrachial bursa
喙肱韧带/喙肱韌帶 coracohumeral ligament
喙肩韧带/喙肩韌帶 coracoacromial ligament
喙囊韧带/喙囊韌帶 coracocapsular ligament
喙锁韧带/喙鎖韌帶 coracoclavicular ligament
喙锁韧带粗隆/喙鎖韌帶粗隆 tuberosity for coracoclavicular ligament
喙突/喙突 coracoid process
喙突后注射法/喙突後注射法 posterior coronoid process injection
喙突尖点/喙突尖點 coronion
喙突下脱臼/突下肩關節脱位 subcoracoid dislocation
喙突炎/喙突炎 coracoiditis
喙形头[畸胎]/喙形頭 coccycephalus
昏厥/昏厥 fainting, syncope
昏迷/昏迷 coma
昏迷性疟/昏迷性瘧 malaria comatosa
昏睡病/昏睡病 sleeping sickness
婚后梅毒/婚後梅毒 postmarital syphilis
婚后弱视/婚後弱視 postmarital amblyopia
婚前检查/婚前檢查 premarital examinations
婚外关系/婚外關係 extramarital relation
婚姻/婚姻 marriage
婚姻疗法/婚姻療法 marital therapy
婚姻率/婚姻率,結婚率 nuptiality
婚姻状况/婚姻狀況 marital status
婚育史/婚育史 history of marriage, pregnancy and delivery
浑浊化/渾濁化 opacification
魂/魂 soul
魂门/魂門 hunmen, BL47
混叠效应/混疊效應 aliasing effect
混合/混合 mixing, compounding
混合白细胞反应/混合白血球反應 mixed leukocyte reaction
混合充血/混合充血 mixed congestion
混合传导感音神经性听觉丧失/混合傳導感音神經性聽覺喪失 mixed conductive-sensorineural hearing loss
混合醇中毒/混合酒精中毒 polyalcoholism
混合大疱病/混合型水疱病 mixed bullous disease
混合的/混合的 mixed
混合发声/融合音節 confluent articulation
混合感染/混合傳染 mixed infection
混合功能氧化酶类/混合功能氧化酶類 mixed function oxygenases
混合固定相/混合固定相 mixed stationary phase
混合机/混合機 mixer
混合集落生成单位/混合集落形成單位 CFU-MIX, mixed colony-forming unit
混合痉挛/混合痙攣 mixed spasm
混合静脉血/混合靜脈血 mixed venous blood
混合静脉血氧张力/混合靜脈血氧張力 mixed venous blood oxygen tension
混合抗球蛋白反应/混合抗球蛋白反應 mixed antiglobulin reaction
混合冷球蛋白病/混合低温球蛋白疾病 mixed cryoglobulin disease
混合淋巴细胞反应/混合淋巴細胞反應,混合白血球反應 mixed lymphocyte reaction
混合淋巴细胞培养/混合淋巴球培養 mixed lymphocyte culture
混合淋巴细胞培养试验/混合淋巴细胞培養試驗 mixed lymphocyte culture test
混合瘤/混合瘤 mixed tumor
混合麻醉/混合麻醉法 mixed anesthesia
混合脉动/混合脈動 mixed beat

混合免疫/混合免疫　mixed immunity
混合囊肿/混合囊腫　hybrid cyst
混合内障/整體内障　general cataract
混合凝集反应/混合凝集反應　mixed agglutination reaction
混合散光/混合性散光,遠近視散光　mixed astigmatism
混合膳食/混合飲食　mixed diet
混合神经/混合神經　mixed nerve
混合突触/混合突觸　mixed synapse
混合喂养/混合餵養　mixed feeding
混合物/混合物　mixture
混合物设计统计技术/混合設計統計技術　mixture design statistic technique
混合细胞白血病/混合細胞白血病　mixed-cell leukemia
混合细胞淋巴瘤/混合細胞淋巴瘤　mixed-cell lymphoma
混合下疳/混合下疳　mixed chancre
混合腺/混合腺　mixed gland
混合腺泡/混合腺泡　mixed acinus
混合型卟啉病/斑駁吡咯紫質沈著病　porphyria variegata
混合型𬌗/混合型𬌗　mixed type occlusion
混合型卡环/混合型卡環　combination clasp
混合型鞘膜积液/混合型鞘膜積液　combination hydrocele
混合型切平面/混合型切平面　combination incisal plane
混合型青光眼/混合型青光眼　mixed glaucoma
混合型肾小管性酸中毒/混合型腎小管性酸中毒　mixed renal tubular acidosis
混合性白血病/混合性白血病　mixed leukemia
混合性鼻音/混合性鼻音　mixed rhinolalia
混合性关节炎/混合性關節炎　mixed arthritis
混合性结缔组织病/混合結締組織疾病　mixed connective tissue disease
混合性结石/混合性結石　mixed stone
混合性近视/混合性近視　mixed myopia
混合性精神病/複精神病,混合精神病　compound insanity
混合性淋巴管瘤/混合性淋巴管瘤　mixed lymphangioma
混合性聋/混合性聾　mixed deafness
混合性皮肤/混合性皮膚　mixed skin
混合性肾上腺病/混合性腎上腺病　mixed adrenal disease
混合性失语/複合性失語症　mixed aphasia
混合性睡眠呼吸暂停/混合性睡眠呼吸暫停　mixed sleep apnea
混合性酸碱平衡失调/混合性酸鹼平衡失調　mixed acid-base balance disorder
混合性通气障碍/混合性通氣障礙　mixed ventilatory disorder
混合性性腺发育不全/混合性性腺發育不全　mixed gonadal dysgenesis
混合性血管瘤/混合性血管瘤　mixed hemangioma
混合性牙瘤/複合性牙瘤　complex odontoma
混合性痔/混合性痔　combined hemorrhoid
混合[性]转位/混合[性]轉位　mixed rotation
混合性左位心/混合型左位心　mixed levocardia
混合血清/混合血清　pooled serum
混合血栓/混合性血栓　mixed thrombus
混合牙列/混合牙　mixed dentition
混合遗传/融合遺傳　blending inheritance
混合痔/混合[性]痔　mixed hemorrhoid
混合痣/混合痣　compound nevus
混睛障/混睛障　mixed nebula, stromal keratitis
混睛障·肝胆热毒证/混睛障·肝膽熱毒證　murky-eye nebula with pattern of heat-toxin in liver and gallbladder
混睛障·脾气虚证/混睛障·脾氣虛證　murky-eye nebula with spleen qi deficiency pattern
混睛障·湿热上攻证/混睛障·濕熱上攻證　murky-eye nebula with pattern of dampness-heat attacking upward
混睛障·阴虚火旺证/混睛障·陰虛火旺證　murky-eye nebula with pattern of yin deficiency and fire effulgence
混乱圈/迷亂環　circle of confusion
混乱型精神分裂症/無組織型精神分裂症　disorganized schizophrenia
混色/混色　mixing color
混涎作用/混涎[作用]　insalivation
混淆/假像　aliasing
混淆品/摻假品　adulterant
混淆色/混[淆]色　confusion colors
混悬度测定器/混懸液檢定器　suspensiometer
混悬型颗粒剂/懸液型顆粒劑　suspension granule
混悬型气雾剂/懸液型氣化霧劑　suspension aerosol
混杂因素/混雜因素　confounding factor
混浊尿/霧狀尿　nebulous urine
混浊肿胀/混濁腫脹　cloudy swelling
豁痰息风/豁痰息風　eliminating phlegm and checking wind, eliminating phlegm for calming endogenous wind

活瓣性气胸/活門狀氣胸　valvular pneumothorax
活病毒/活病毒　live virus
活动的/活動的　active
活动[度]/活動[度]　activity
活动过强/活動過強　superactivity
活动幻镜/連續活動鏡，活動畫鏡　zoetrope
活动夹/活動夾板，治療夾　ambulatory splint, therapeutic splint
活动减退/活動過少，活動性不足　hypoactivity
活动结肠/活動性結腸　mobile colon
活动连接体/活動連接體　nonrigid connector
活动盲肠/活動盲腸　mobile cecum
活动模式/動作範型　action pattern
活动平板训练/活動平板訓練　treadmill training
活动[X射线]滤线栅/X光活動濾線柵　moving grid
活动性肺结核检出率/活動性肺結核檢出率　detection rate of active pulmonary tuberculosis
活动性肝炎/活動性肝炎　active hepatitis
活动性夹板/活動性夾板　live splint
活动性肉瘤性增生/活動性肉瘤性增生　active sarcomatous proliferation
活动训练[疗]法/活動訓練療法　ponesiatrics
活动影片查看器/立體活動檢視器　stereophoroscope
活动周期/活動週期　activity cycle
活动状态/活動狀態　active state
活动锥虫/羊錐蟲　Trypanosoma caprae
活化/活化　activation, activating
活化白细胞黏附分子/活化白細胞黏附分子　activated-leukocyte cell adhesion molecule
活化蛋白C抵抗/活化蛋白C抵抗　activated protein C resistance
活化分析/活化分析　activation analysis
活化剂/活化劑　activator
活化巨噬细胞/活化巨噬細胞　activated macrophage
活化淋巴细胞/活化淋巴細胞　activated lymphocyte
活化酶/活化酵素　activating enzyme
活化能/活化能　activation energy
活化杀伤单核细胞/啟動殺傷單核細胞　activated killer monocyte
活化污泥池/活化汙泥地　activated sludge tank
活化物/活化劑　activator
活化[状]态/活化狀態　activated state
活套疗法/活套療法　emotional therapy corresponding to five elements
活体部分肝移植/活體部分肝移植　partial living liver transplantation
活体非亲属供者/活體非親屬供者　living unrelated donor
活体供者/活體供者　living donor
活[体]膜透析/活膜滲析　vividialysis
活体亲属供者/活體親屬供者　living related donor
活体亲属脾移植/活體親屬脾移植　living related splenic transplantation
活体亲属肾移植/活體親屬腎移植　living related renal transplantation
活体染剂/活體染劑　vital dye
活体移植/活體移植　viable transplantation
活性/活性　activity
活性部位/活性部位　active site
活性成分/活性成分　active constituent
活性氮/活性氮　reactive nitrogen species
活性肽/生物活性肽　bioactive peptide
活性肽药物/活性肽藥物　active peptide drug
活性炭/活性炭　activated charcoal
活性污泥/促動糞泥　activated sludge
活性污水/活化汙水　activated sewage
活性物质/活性物質　active substance
活性血清/活性血清　active serum
活性中心/活性中心　active center
活血化瘀/活血化瘀　activating blood circulation to dissipate blood stasis, promoting blood circulation for removing blood stasis
活血化瘀法/活血化瘀法　activating blood and resolving stasis
活血剂/活血劑　blood-activating formula
活血解毒/活血解毒　promoting blood circulation and detoxication
活血去腐/活血去腐　promoting blood circulation and eliminating necrosis
活血调经/活血調經　promoting blood circulation for regulating menstruation
活血通络/活血通絡　promoting blood circulation for removing obstruction in collaterals
活血止痛散/活血止痛散　huoxue zhitong powder
活跃期/活躍期　active phase
活跃期宫口扩张停滞/活躍期宮口擴張停滯　protracted active phase dilatation
活跃期停滞/活躍期停滯　protracted active phase
活跃期延长/活躍期延長　prolonged active phase
活跃锥虫/活潑錐蟲　Trypanosoma vivax
活质体/活動質　energid
活组织分光度测量术/生體分光計檢視法　biospectrometry
活组织分光镜检查/生體分光鏡檢查法　biospectroscopy
活组织检查/活體組織切片檢查　biopsy

活组织显微镜/活體組織顯微鏡　biomicroscope
活组织显微镜检查/活體組織檢視法　biomicroscopy
火/火　fire
火斑疮/火斑瘡　fire dermatitis
火闭/火閉　fire block
火赤疮/火赤瘡，皰疹性皮膚炎　red-fire sore, red-fire ulcers, dermatitis herpetiformis
火毒证/火毒證　fire-toxicity pattern
火疳/火疳　fire gan, fire malnutrition of eye, episcleritis
火疳·肺经郁火证/火疳·肺經鬱火證　fire gan with pattern of fire stagnation in lung channel
火疳·肺阴虚证/火疳·肺陰虛證　fire gan with lung yin deficiency pattern
火疳·风湿热邪证/火疳·風濕熱邪證　fire gan with wind-dampness heat pattern
火疳·火毒蕴结证/火疳·火毒蘊結證　fire gan with fire-toxin amassment pattern
火罐法/火罐法　fire cupping
火耗气伤阴/火耗氣傷陰　fire consuming qi and injuring yin
火候/火候　optimal fire
火克金/火克金　fire restricting metal
火烙疗法/火烙療法　cauterization therapy
火麻仁/火麻仁　hemp seed
火棉/火棉　celloidin
火棉胶/火棉膠　cuticle liquid
火棉胶敷裹/火棉膠敷裹　collodion dressing
火棉胶剂/火棉膠劑　collodion
火棉胶切片/火棉膠切片　celloidin section
火棉胶[样]婴儿/火棉膠[樣]嬰兒　collodion baby
火逆/火逆　mistreatment by warming therapy, fire reversal
火器伤/火器傷　firearm wound
火山口样溃疡/火山口狀潰瘍　crateriform ulcer
火山口状切除术/火山口狀切除法　craterization
火山样病灶/火山樣病灶　volcano lesion
火珊瑚/火珊瑚　fire coral
火生土/火生土　fire generating earth
火石玻璃/火石玻璃　flint glass
火陷/火陷　fire inward collapse
火邪/火邪　fire pathogen
火形人/火形人　fire-phase person
火性炎上/火性炎上　characteristic of fire being flaring up
火焰/火焰　flame
火焰离子化/火焰離子化　flame ionization
火焰烧伤/火焰燒傷　flame burn
火焰图样/火焰圖樣　flame figure
火焰抑制剂/火焰抑制劑　flame retardant
火焰状出血/火焰狀出血　flame-shaped hemorrhage
火焰状出血点/火焰狀斑　flame spot
火蚁/火蟻　fire ant
火蚁属/火蟻屬　Solenopsis
火易扰心/火易擾心　fire being likely to disturb heart
火易生风动血/火易生風動血　fire being likely to cause convulsion and bleeding
火郁/火鬱　fire stagnation
火曰炎上/火曰炎上　fire characterized by flaring up
火针烙法/火針烙法　cauterization with heated needle
火针疗法/火針療法　fire needle therapy, puncturing point with hot-red needle
火针术/火針術，熱刺術　caloripuncture
火证/火證　fire pattern
火中/火中　fire parapoplexy
获得耐受[性]/獲得性耐力　acquired tolerance
获得性鼻畸形/獲得性鼻畸形　acquired nose deformities
获得性迟发性皮肤卟啉病/獲得性遲發性皮膚卟啉病　acquired porphyria cutanea tarda
获得性大疱性表皮松解[症]/獲得性大皰性表皮鬆解[症]　epidermolysis bullosa acquisita
获得性耳畸形/獲得性耳畸形　acquired ear deformities
获得性反应性穿通性皮病/後天性反應性穿通性皮膚病　acquired reactive perforating dermatosis
获得性骨肥大综合征/獲得性骨肥大症候群　acquired hyperostosis syndrome
获得性关节畸形/獲得性關節畸形　acquired joint deformity
获得性过敏/後天性過敏　acquired anaphylaxis
获得性褐黄病/後天性赭色病　acquired ochronosis
获得性黑素减少病/後天性黑色素減少症　acquired hypomelanosis
获得性甲周纤维角化瘤/後天性甲周圍纖維角化瘤　acquired periungual fibrokeratoma
获得性甲状腺功能减退症/後天[的]甲狀腺功能減退症　acquired hypothyroidism
获得性角皮症/後天[的]角皮病　acquired keratoderma
获得性局限性多毛症/後天性限界性多毛症　acquired circumscribed hypertrichosis
获得性巨结肠/後天性巨結腸　acquired megacolon
获得性淋巴管瘤/獲得性淋巴管瘤　acquired

lymphangioma
获得性免疫/獲得性免疫,後天性免疫　acquired immunity
获得性免疫缺陷/後天免疫性缺乏　acquired immunodeficiency
获得性免疫缺陷综合征/愛滋病,後天性免疫不全症候群　acquired immunodeficiency syndrome
获得性耐药/獲得性耐藥　acquired drug resistance
获得性全身多毛症/後天性全身多毛症　acquired universal hypertrichosis
获得性手畸形/獲得性手畸形　acquired hand deformities
获得性纤维角化瘤/獲得性纖維角化瘤　acquired fibrokeratoma
获得性锌缺乏/後天性鋅缺乏　acquired zinc deficiency
获得性遗传/獲得性特徵之遺傳　homotropic inheritance
获得性鱼鳞病/獲得性魚鱗病　acquired ichthyosis
获得性阅读障碍/獲得性閱讀障礙　acquired dyslexia
获得性指纤维角化瘤/後天性指纖維角化瘤　acquired digital fibrokeratoma
获得性趾纤维角化瘤/後天性趾纖維角化瘤　acquired digital fibrokeratoma
获得性状/後天特性　acquired character
获得性自体免疫病毒感染性瘙痒性丘皮疹/後天性自體免疫缺乏症患者之搔癢性丘疹性皮疹　papular pruritic eruption in HIV infection
获得性自体免疫病毒感染性顽固性红色脱皮症/後天性自體免疫缺乏症候群患者的頑固性紅色脫皮症　recalcitrant erythematous desquamating disorder in HIV infection
获得性足畸形/獲得性足畸形　acquired foot deformities
获能/獲能作用　capacitation
霍茨手术/霍茨手術　Hotz operation
霍达腊氏病/霍達氏病　Hodara disease
霍尔病/Hall 氏病　Hall disease
霍尔伯格效应/哈伯格氏效應　Hallberg effect
霍尔茨曼墨迹测验/霍耳茨曼墨跡測驗　Holtzman inkblot test
霍尔帕克冷热试验/霍爾派克冷熱試驗　Hallpike caloric test
霍尔思手术/霍司氏手術　Holth operation
霍尔斯特德疝修补术/霍爾斯特德疝修補術　Halsted herniorrhaphy
霍尔特心电动态监测仪/Holter 氏心電圖記錄器, Holter 氏心電圖記錄儀　Holter monitor
霍尔兹克尼希特胃/霍奈氏胃　Holzknecht stomach
霍法-洛兰茨手术/霍-洛二氏手術　Hoffa-Lorenz operation
霍夫鲍尔细胞/霍夫鮑爾細胞　Hofbauer cell
霍夫曼管/Hoffmann 氏管　Hoffmann duct
霍夫曼肌萎缩/Hoffmann 氏萎縮　Hoffmann atrophy
霍夫曼征/霍夫曼徵　Hoffmann sign
霍金夹/Hodgen 氏夾板　Hodgen splint
霍利保持器/霍利保持器　Hawley retainer
霍利迪连结体解离酶类/霍利迪連結體解離酶類　Holliday junction resolvases
霍乱/霍亂　cholera
霍乱毒素/霍亂毒素　cholera toxin
霍乱杆菌/霍亂桿菌　Bacillus cholerae
霍乱[弧菌]嗜菌体/噬霍亂菌體,霍亂噬菌體　choleraphage
霍乱菌苗/霍亂菌苗　cholera vaccine
霍乱面容/霍亂面容　cholera face
霍乱嘶哑声/霍亂嘎聲,霍亂語聲　vox cholerica
霍乱型疟/霍亂型瘧　choleraic malaria
霍乱样腹泻/霍亂樣腹瀉　choleraic diarrhea
霍乱预防接种/霍亂預防接種　cholerization
霍乱躁狂[症]/霍亂躁狂　choleromania
霍乱转筋/霍亂轉筋　cholera with muscular spasm
霍乱状病/霍亂狀病　choleraic disease
霍洛卡因/霍洛卡因,芬那卡因　holocaine
霍姆斯-阿迪/Holmes-Adie 氏症候群　Holmes-Adie syndrome
霍姆斯变性/霍姆氏變性　Holmes degeneration
霍纳肌/Horner 氏肌　Horner muscle
霍纳上睑下垂/Horner 氏上瞼下垂　Horner ptosis
霍纳综合征/霍納症候群　Horner syndrome
霍佩-赛勒试验/霍-史二氏試驗　Hoppe-Seyler test
霍普金斯-科尔试验/霍-柯二氏試驗　Hopkins-Cole test
霍普曼乳头状瘤/Hopmann 氏乳頭狀瘤　Hopmann papilloma
霍奇金病/霍奇金病　Hodgkin disease
霍奇金淋巴瘤/Hodgkin 氏淋巴瘤,何傑金氏淋巴瘤　Hodgkin lymphoma
霍奇金细胞/Hodgkin 氏細胞　Hodgkin cell
霍维斯静脉丛/哈威斯氏叢　Hovius plexus
霍伊泽膜/霍伊塞氏膜,胚外體腔膜　Heuser membrane
藿胆丸/藿膽丸　huodan pills
藿香正气散/藿香正氣散　huoxiang zhengqi powder

J

击打法/擊打法 striking manipulation
饥不欲食/飢不欲食 hunger without desire to eat
饥饿疗法/飢餓療法 hunger cure
饥饿热/饑饉熱 famine fever
饥饿性精神病/飢餓性精神病 famine psychosis
饥饿性水肿/飢腫 hunger swelling
饥饿性酸毒症/飢餓性酸血症 starvation acidosis
饥饿性萎缩/飢餓性萎縮 inanition atrophy
饥饿性虚损/餓癆 limophthisis
饥饿性谵妄/飢餓性譫妄 inanition delirium
饥饿终期反应/飢餓終期反應 zed reaction
饥荒/饑荒 famine
饥尿[症]/饑溲症 opsiuria
机车后座骨折/機車後座骨折，股骨下端骨折 pillion fracture
机构间关系/機構間關係 interinstitutional relations
机化/機化 organization
机化性肺炎/機化性肺炎 organized pneumonia
机化血栓/機化血栓 organized thrombus
机会性感染/伺機傳染 opportunistic infection
机理/機理 mechanism
机能整体性/機能整體論 holism
机器样杂音/機械性雜音 machinery murmur
机体性病毒/機體性病毒 organized virus
机头/機頭 handpiece
机头颈部/機頭頸部 cervix handpiece
机械瓣/機械瓣 mechanical prosthetic valve
机械[刺激]应激性/機械應激性 mechanical irritability
机械辅助器/機械性輔助器 mechanical assist device
机械感受器/機械感受器 mechanoreceptor
机械过滤池/機械濾器 mechanical filter
机械论者/機械論者 mechanist
机械通气/機械換氣法 mechanical ventilation
机械通气机/機械通氣機 mechanical ventilator
机械性肠梗阻/機械性腸梗阻 mechanical intestinal obstruction
机械[性刺激]感受器/機械受器 mechanicoreceptor
机械性痤疮/機械性痤瘡 acne mechanica
机械性的/機械的,力學的 mechanical
机械性黄疸/機械性黃疸 mechanical jaundice
机械性咳/機械性欬嗽 mechanical cough
机械性尿路梗阻/機械性尿路梗阻 mechanical obstruction of urinary tract
机械性上睑下垂/機械性上瞼下垂 mechanical ptosis
机械[性损]伤/機械[性損]傷 mechanical injury
机械性痛经/機械性痛經 mechanical dysmenorrhea
机械性秃/機械性秃 alopecia mechanica
机械性眩晕/機械性眩暈 mechanical vertigo
机械性血栓/機械性血栓 mechanical thrombus
机械性眼外伤/機械性眼外傷 mechanical ocular injury
机械性止血物/機械性止血劑 mechanical styptic
机械性紫癜/機械性紫瘢 mechanical purpura
机械震颤按摩/震顫按摩法 tremolo massage
肌/肌 muscle
肌氨酸/肌胺酸 sarcosine
肌氨酸血症/高肌胺酸血症 sarcosinemia
肌胺/肌胺 musculamine
肌瓣/肌瓣 muscle flap
肌痹/肌痺 dermatomyositis, muscle bi, muscle bi-disease
肌痹·肝肾阴虚证/肌痺·肝腎陰虛證 dermatomyositis with liver-kidney yin deficiency pattern
肌痹·寒湿闭阻证/肌痺·寒濕閉阻證 dermatomyositis with cold-dampness blockage pattern
肌痹·脾气虚证/肌痺·脾氣虛證 dermatomyositis with spleen qi deficiency pattern
肌痹·脾肾阳虚证/肌痺·脾腎陽虛證 dermatomyositis with spleen-kidney yang deficiency pattern
肌痹·脾虚湿困证/肌痺·脾虛濕困證 muscle bi with pattern of damp retention due to spleen deficiency
肌痹·热毒炽盛证/肌痺·熱毒熾盛證 dermatomyositis with blazing heat-toxin pattern
肌痹·湿热瘀阻证/肌痺·濕熱瘀阻證 muscle bi with pattern of blockade of damp-heat and static blood

肌痹·湿热蕴结证/肌痺·濕熱蘊結證 dermatomyositis with dampness-heat amassment pattern
肌痹·阴虚内热证/肌痺·陰虛内熱證 muscle bi with pattern of internal heat due to yin deficiency
肌变性/肌變性 myodegeneration
肌病/肌病 myopathy
肌病性脊柱侧凸/肌病性脊柱側彎 myopathic scoliosis
肌病性痉挛/肌病性痙攣 myopathic spasm
肌病性面容/肌病面容 myopathic face
肌病性萎缩/肌病性萎縮 myopathic atrophy
肌部/肌部 muscular part
肌[部分]切除术/肌切除術 myectomy
肌部室间隔缺损/肌部室間隔缺損 muscular ventricular septal defect
肌层/肌層 muscular layer
肌颤搐/肌顫動 myopalmus
肌沉淀素/肌沈澱素 musculoprecipitin
肌成分/肌成分 sarcous element
肌成纤维细胞/成肌纖維細胞 myofibroblast
肌成形术/肌整形術 myoplasty
肌弛缓/肌弛緩,肌緊張缺失,肌無緊張 amyotonia
肌醇/肌醇 inositol
肌醇-1-磷酸合酶/肌醇-1-磷酸合酶 myo-inositol-1-phosphate synthase
肌醇磷酸类/肌醇磷酸類 inositol phosphates
肌醇尿/肌醇尿 inosituria
肌醇三磷酸/三磷酸肌醇 inositol triphosphate
肌蛋白轻链/肌蛋白輕鏈 myosin light chain
肌蛋白[质]/肌蛋白 myoprotein
肌蛋白质类/肌蛋白質類 muscle proteins
肌蛋白重链/肌蛋白重鏈 myosin heavy chain
肌蛋白重链基因/肌蛋白重鏈基因 myosin heavy chain gene
肌电波描记法/肌電波描記法 rheotachygraphy
肌电堆/肌電堆 muscular pile
肌电描记术/肌電描記法,肌電圖測定 electromyography
肌电生物回馈疗法/肌電生物回饋療法 electromyographic biofeedback therapy
肌电图/肌電圖 electromyogram, EMG
肌电图描记器/肌電圖描記器 electromyograph
肌动波/肌動波 curve muscle
肌动蛋白/肌動蛋白 actin
肌动蛋白类/肌動蛋白類 actins
肌动反应延缓/肌反應推遲 myautonomy
肌动觉测量器/動覺測定計 kinesi-esthesiometer

肌动力描记器/肌動力描記器 ergodynamograph
肌动力学/肌動力學 myodynamics
肌动描记器/肌動描記器 myograph
肌动描记术/肌動描記法 myography
肌动[描记]图/肌動[描記]波 myogram
肌动球蛋白/肌動球蛋白,肌動肌凝蛋白 actomyosin
肌毒/肌毒 muscle poison
肌断裂/肌破裂 myorrhexis
肌乏力性神经衰弱/肌神經衰弱 myoneurasthenia
肌反射/肌反射 muscular reflex
肌范型/肌範型 muscle pattern
肌肥大/肌肥大 muscular hypertrophy
肌分离/肌分離 myodiastasis
肌风湿病/肌風濕病 muscular rheumatism
肌蜂窝[组]织炎/肌蜂窝組織炎 myocellulitis
肌缝术/肌縫合術 myorrhaphy
肌肤甲错/肌膚甲錯 squamous and dry skin
肌腹/肌腹 muscle belly, belly muscle
肌钙蛋白/肌鈣蛋白 troponin
肌肝脑眼侏儒症/肌肝腦眼侏儒症 mulibrey nanism
肌苷/肌核苷 inosine
肌苷二磷酸/肌苷二磷酸 inosine diphosphate
肌苷核苷酸类/肌苷核苷酸類 inosine nucleotides
肌苷三磷酸/肌苷三磷酸 inosine triphosphate
肌苷一磷酸/肌苷一磷酸 inosine monophosphate
肌酐清除率/肌酐清除率 creatinine clearance rate
肌感受器/肌受器 myoceptor
肌膈动脉/肌膈動脈 musculophrenic artery
肌膈静脉/肌膈靜脈 musculophrenic vein
肌功能矫治器/肌功能矯治器 myofunctional appliance
肌功能疗法/肌功能療法 myofunctional therapy
肌骨骼疾病/肌骨骼疾病 musculoskeletal disease
肌骨化/肌組織骨化 sarcostosis
肌骨瘤/肌骨瘤 myosteoma
肌管/肌管 myotube
肌管性肌病/肌管性肌病 myotubular myopathy
肌黑变病/肌黑變病 myomelanosis
肌红蛋白/肌血球素 myoglobin
肌红蛋白尿/肌血球素尿 myoglobinuria
肌滑车/肌滑車 muscular trochlea
肌坏死/肌壞死 myonecrosis
肌机能不全/肌官能不全 muscular insufficiency
肌基质/肌基質 myostroma
肌基质蛋白/肌基質蛋白 myostromin
肌激酶/肌活動酵素,肌激素 myokinase
肌疾病/肌疾病 muscular disease

肌集钙蛋白/肌集鈣蛋白　calsequestrin
肌间的/肌間的　intermuscular
肌间神经丛/肌間神經叢　myenteric nervous plexus
肌间线蛋白/肌間線蛋白　desmin
肌间质细胞/肌胚細胞,肌母細胞　sarcoplast
肌监控仪/肌監控儀　myo-monitor
肌碱/肌鹼　myokinin
肌腱/肌腱　muscle tendon, tendon of muscle
肌腱成形术/腱造形術,補腱術　tenoplasty
肌腱固定术/腱固定術　tenodesis
肌腱皮瓣/肌腱皮瓣　teno-cutaneous flap
肌腱烧伤/肌腱燒傷　burn of tendon
肌腱松解术/腱鬆解術　tenolysis
肌腱延长术/肌腱延長術　tendon lengthening
肌腱炎/肌腱炎　myotenositis
肌腱移植/腱移植法　tendon transplantation
肌腱移植物/腱移植物　tendon graft
肌腱粘连/肌腱粘連　adhesion of tendon
肌腱转位术/肌腱轉位術　tendon transposition
肌浆/肌漿　plasma muscle
肌浆凝块/肌血塊　muscle clot
肌浆球蛋白/肌凝蛋白質,肌球素　myosin
肌浆球蛋白尿/肌凝蛋白尿症　myosinuria
肌浆[球蛋白]纤维蛋白/肌凝蛋白纖維素　myosin fibrin
肌浆网/肌漿網　sarcoplasmic reticulum
肌僵硬/肌強硬　muscle rigidity
肌胶质/肌膠質纖維　border fibrils
肌感觉/肌覺　muscular sense
肌节间槽/肌節間槽　intersomitic furrow
肌节间沟/肌節間溝　intersomitic groove
肌节腔/肌節腔　myocoel
肌结节病/肌肉肉瘤病　muscular sarcoidosis
肌筋膜/肌筋膜　muscular fasciae
肌筋膜疼痛综合征/肌筋膜疼痛症候群　myofascial pain syndrome
肌筋膜炎/肌筋膜炎　myofascitis
肌紧张/肌緊張　muscular tension
肌紧张的/肌強直病的　myotonic
肌紧张分裂/肌緊張分裂　schizotonia
肌痉挛/肌痙攣　myospasm
肌痉挛病/肌抽搐　myospasmia
肌痉挛状态/肌痙攣狀態　muscle spasticity
肌静脉/肌靜脈　muscular vein
肌局部缺血/肌[局部]缺血　myoischemia
肌觉过敏/肌感覺過敏　muscular hyperesthesia
肌觉缺失/肌覺缺失　muscular anesthesia
肌蜡样变性/肌蠟樣變性　myocerosis

肌力/肌力　muscular strength
肌力测定/肌力測定　muscle strength test
肌力测量器/肌力計　myosthenometer
肌力描记器/肌力描記器,動力描記器　dynamograph
肌磷酸化酶/肌磷酸化酶　myophosphorylase
肌瘤/肌瘤　myoma
肌瘤切除术/肌瘤切除術　myomatectomy
肌瘤切开术/肌瘤切開術　myomotomy
肌瘤子宫切除术/子宫肌瘤切除術　myomohysterectomy
肌螺旋神经/肌螺旋神經　musculospiral nerve
肌螺旋神经沟/肌螺旋神經溝　musculospiral groove
肌命名法/肌命名法　myonymy
肌膜/肌[纖維]膜　sarcolemma
肌膜下池/肌膜下池　subsarcolemmal cisterna
肌耐力/肌耐力　muscular endurance
肌内的/肌内的　intramuscular
肌内膜/肌内膜　endomysium
肌内皮连接/肌内皮連接　myoendothelial junction
肌能修整/肌能修整　muscle trimming
肌衄/肌衄　sweat pore bleeding
肌皮瓣/肌皮片　musculocutaneous flap
肌皮动脉/肌皮動脈　musculocutaneous artery
肌皮神经/肌皮神經　musculocutaneous nerve
[肌皮神经]肌支/[肌皮神經]肌支　muscular branch of musculocutaneous nerve
肌疲劳/肌疲勞　muscle fatigue
肌腔隙/肌腔隙　lacuna musculorum, iliac canal
肌强直/肌強直　myotonia
肌强直电位/肌強直電位　myotonic potential
肌强直反应/肌強直性反應　myotonic reaction
肌强直失调症/肌強直失調症　myotonic disorder
肌强直性白内障/肌強直性白内障　myotonic cataract
肌强直性萎缩/肌強直性萎縮　myotonic atrophy
肌鞘/肌鞘　sheath muscle
肌切开术/肌切開術　myotomy
肌球蛋白/肌球蛋白　myoglobulin
肌球蛋白类/肌球蛋白類　myosins
肌球蛋白尿/肌球蛋白尿　myoglobulinuria
肌球蛋白轻链/肌球蛋白輕鏈　myosin light chain
肌球蛋白轻链激酶/肌球蛋白輕鏈激酶　myosin-light-chain kinase
肌球蛋白轻链磷酸酶/肌球蛋白輕鏈磷酸酶　myosin-light-chain phosphatase
肌球蛋白亚碎片/肌球蛋白亞碎片　myosin subfragment

肌球蛋白重链/肌球蛋白重鏈 myosin heavy chain
肌去神经法/肌去神經法 muscle denervation
肌缺血性萎缩/缺血性肌萎縮 ischemic muscular atrophy
肌溶解/肌細胞分解,肌崩解 myolysis
肌[肉]/肌[肉] muscle
肌[肉]的/肌[肉]的 muscular
肌肉短滞/肌肉短滯 brachystasis
肌肉发育/肌肉發育 muscle development
肌[肉]发育不良/肌肉發育不全,肌肉形成不全 amyoplasia
肌[肉感]觉/肌肉感覺 myesthesia
肌肉骨骼发育/肌肉骨骼發育 musculoskeletal development
肌肉骨骼畸形/肌肉骨骼畸形 musculoskeletal abnormality
肌肉骨骼平衡/肌肉骨骼平衡 musculoskeletal equilibrium
肌肉骨骼生理过程/肌肉骨骼生理過程 musculoskeletal physiologic process
肌肉骨骼生理现象/肌肉骨骼生理現象 musculoskeletal physiologic phenomena
肌肉骨骼生理学/肌肉骨骼生理學 musculoskeletal physiology
肌肉骨骼手法/肌肉骨骼手法 musculoskeletal manipulation
肌肉骨骼系统/肌肉骨骼系統 musculoskeletal system
肌肉磷酸果糖激酶缺乏/肌肉磷酸果糖酶缺乏 muscle phosphofructokinase deficiency
肌肉磷酸酶缺乏/肌肉磷酸酶缺乏 muscle phosphorylase deficiency
肌肉瘤/肌肉瘤 myosarcoma
肌肉漏斗/肌肉漏斗 muscular funnel
肌肉牵拉/肌肉牽拉 pull
肌肉强烈收缩力/肌肉強烈收縮力 forced myotasis
肌肉软/肌肉軟 flaccidity of muscle
肌肉收缩质促解物/激肌質 apheter
肌肉松弛药/肌肉鬆弛藥,肌肉弛緩劑 muscle relaxant
肌肉萎缩/肌肉萎縮 muscular atrophy
肌肉萎缩的/肌萎縮的 amyotrophic
肌肉位/肌肉位 muscular position
肌肉系统/肌系,肌群 musculature
肌肉移植/肌肉移植 muscle transplantation
肌肉周围丛/肌肉周圍叢 perimuscular plexus
肌肉主动脉下部狭窄/肌肉性主動脈下部狹窄 muscular subaortic stenosis
肌肉注射/肌肉注射 intramuscular injection
肌肉组织/肌樣組織 myoideum
肌乳酸/肌乳酸 sarcolactic acid
肌乳酸盐/肌乳酸鹽 sarcolactate
肌软化/肌肉鬆軟 malacosarcosis
肌三角/肌三角 muscular triangle
肌色素/肌色素 myochrome
肌上皮/肌上皮組織 myoepithelium
肌上皮癌/肌上皮癌 myoepithelial carcinoma
肌上皮岛/肌上皮島 myoepithelial island
肌上皮的/肌上皮的 myoepithelial
肌上皮瘤/肌上皮瘤 myoepithelioma
肌上皮细胞/肌上皮細胞 myoepithelial cell
肌伸张/肌伸張 myotasis
肌伸张应激性/肌伸張應激性 myotatic irritability
肌神经传导缺失/肌肉無神經分布 adromia
肌神经接点/肌神經結合 myoneural junction
肌神经痛/肌神經痛 myoneuralgia
肌神经细胞/肌神經細胞 myoneure
肌式肾固定术/肌式腎固定術,游動腎固定術 myonephropexy
肌收缩/肌收縮 muscle contraction
肌收缩计/肌動計 myocinesimeter
肌收缩力/肌收縮力,肌收縮性 myotility
肌收缩原/肌收縮原,肌纖維原 inogen
肌束/肌束 fasciculus muscle
肌束变性/肌束變性 fascicular degeneration
肌束颤搐/肌束牽搊 fascicular twitching
肌束膜/肌束膜 perimysium
肌束膀胱/肌束膀胱 fasciculated bladder
肌束震颤/肌纖維自發性收縮 fasciculation
肌丝/肌絲 myofilament
肌丝滑动学说/肌絲滑動學説,滑行細絲學説 sliding filament hypothesis
肌松弛/肌鬆弛 muscle relaxation
肌酸/肌酸 creatine
肌酸酐/肌胺酸酐 creatinine
肌酸酐廓清率/肌胺酸酐廓清力 creatinine clearance
肌酸酐廓清试验/肌胺酸酐清除試驗 creatinine clearance test
肌酸酐酶/肌胺酸酐酵素 creatininase
肌酸激酶/肌胺酸活化酵素,肌胺酸激酶 creatine kinase
肌酸磷酸/磷酸肌胺酸 creatine phosphate
肌酸磷酸激酶/肌酸磷酸激酶 creatine phosphokinase
肌酸酶/肌胺酸酵素 creatinase
肌酸尿/肌胺酸尿 creatinuria

肌酸血/肌胺酸血症　creatinemia
肌梭/肌梭　muscle spindles
肌梭运动[神经]的[纤维]/肌梭運動的　fusimotor
肌肽/肌肽　carnosine
肌肽酶/肌肽酶　carnosinase
肌肽尿/肌肽尿　carnosinuria
肌肽血/肌肽血　carnosinemia
肌痛/肌痛　myalgia
肌痛性痉挛/肌痛性痙攣　muscle cramp
肌痛性衰弱/肌痛性無力　myalgic asthenia
肌头/肌頭　head of muscle
肌突/肌突　muscular process
肌突出/肌赫尼亞,肌膨出　myocele
肌外膜/肌外膜　epimysium
肌萎缩/肌萎縮　amyotrophia
肌萎缩性[脊髓]侧索硬化/肌萎縮性脊髓側索硬化　amyotrophic lateral sclerosis
肌卫星细胞/肌衛星細胞　muscle satellite cell
肌无力/肌無力　muscle weakness, myasthenia
肌无力测量计/肌無力計　asthenometer
肌无力面容/肌無力面　myasthenic face
肌无力性反应/肌無力性反應　myasthenic reaction
肌细胞/肌細胞　muscle cell
肌细胞瘤/肌細胞瘤　myocytoma
肌细胞收缩线/肌細胞收縮線　inotagma
肌下囊/肌下囊　submuscular bursa
肌下植入/肌下植入　submuscular implantation
肌纤维/肌纖維　muscle fiber
肌纤维变性/肌纖維變性　myofibrosis
肌纤维颤搐/肌纖維顫動　myokymia
肌纤维瘤/肌纖維瘤　myofibroma
肌纤维鞘炎/肌纖維鞘炎　myofibrositis
肌[纤维]素/肌纖維素　myolin
肌纤维性肌阵挛/肌陣攣病　fibrillary chorea
肌纤维震颤/纖維顫動　fibrillation
肌线粒体/肌線粒體　muscle mitochondria
肌腺苷磷酸/肌磷酸腺苷酸　muscle adenosine phosphoric acid
肌小板/肌小板　sarcous disc
[肌小板]暗板/[肌小板]暗板　dark disc
肌细胞生成素/肌形成蛋白　myogenin
肌形成调节因子/肌形成調節因子　myogenic regulatory factor
肌型磷酸果糖激酶/肌型磷酸果糖激酶　muscle type phosphofructokinase
肌型糖原磷酸化酶/肌型糖原磷酸化酶　muscle form glycogen phosphorylase
肌性动脉/肌動脈　muscular artery

肌性防御/肌性防衛　muscular defense
肌性骨联接/肌性骨結合,肌性骨聯合　syssarcosis
肌性视疲劳/肌性眼力疲勞　muscular asthenopia
肌性室间隔缺损/肌性室間隔缺陷　muscular septal defect
肌性消化不良/肌性消化不良　muscular dyspepsia
肌性斜颈/肌性斜頸　myogenic torticollis
肌学/肌學　myology
肌咽鼓管/肌咽鼓管　musculotubal canal
肌咽鼓管隔/肌咽鼓管隔　septum of musculotubal canal
肌炎/肌炎　myositis
肌样的/肌樣的　myoid
肌样细胞/肌樣細胞　myoid cell
肌移植功能重建术/肌移植功能重建術　functional rebuilding by muscle grafting
肌移植术/肌移植術　muscle grafting
肌移植物/肌[肉]移植物　muscle graft
肌音/肌音　myocrismus
肌音描记法/肌音描記法　phonomyography
肌音听测器/肌肉擴音器　miophone
肌音图/肌音描記像　phonomyogram
肌营养/肌營養　myotrophy
肌营养不良/肌營養不良　muscular dystrophy
肌营养不良蛋白/肌營養不良蛋白　dystrophin
肌营养不良蛋白聚糖类/肌營養不良蛋白聚糖類　dystroglycans
肌营养不良蛋白相关蛋白复合物/肌營養不良蛋白相關蛋白複合物　dystrophin-associated protein complex
肌营养不良蛋白相关蛋白质类/肌營養不良蛋白相關蛋白質類　dystrophin-associated proteins
肌应激性/肌應激性　muscular irritability
肌硬化/肌硬化　myosclerosis
肌硬结/肌凝塊,肌結塊　myogelosis
肌原肉瘤/肌原肉瘤　myogenic sarcoma
肌原细胞/肌原細胞　myogenous cell
肌原纤维/肌原纖維　myofibril
肌原纤维蛋白/微纖維蛋白　fibrillin
肌[原纤维]节/肌節　sarcomere
肌[原]性的/肌原的　myogenic
肌[原]性紧张/肌性緊張　myogenic tonus
肌[原]性上睑下垂/肌[原]性上瞼下垂　myogenic ptosis
肌运动/肌運動,肌移動　myokinesis
肌杂音/肌雜音　muscle murmur
肌粘连/肌黏合　myosynizesis
肌张力/肌張力　muscle tonus

肌张力测量器/肌張力計　myotonometer
肌张力过低/肌張力過低　muscle hypotonia
肌张力过度/肌張力過強　hypermyotonia
肌张力减低/肌張力不足,肌緊張過弱　hypomyotonia
肌张力障碍/肌緊張異常　dysmyotonia
肌阵挛/肌陣攣病　myoclonus
肌阵挛发作/肌陣攣發作　myoclonic seizure
肌阵挛性癫痫/肌陣攣性癲癇　myoclonic epilepsies
肌阵挛性小脑性协同失调/肌陣攣性小腦性協同失調　myoclonic cerebellar dyssynergia
肌震颤/肌震顫,肌静止不能　amyostasia
肌震颤的/肌震顫的　amyostatic
肌震颤性综合征/肌震顫性症候群　amyostatic syndrome
肌震颤运动型/肌震顫型　amyostatic-kinetic type
肌支/肌支　muscular branch
肌脂肪变性/肌脂肪變性　myodemia
肌脂瘤/肌脂瘤　myolipoma
肌质/肌質,肌漿　muscular substance, sarcoplasm
肌质网/肌質網　sarcoplasmic reticulum
肌肿瘤/肌腫瘤　muscle neoplasm
肌周皮细胞瘤/肌周皮細胞瘤　myopericytoma
肌周炎/肌周圍炎　perimyositis
肌转移功能重建术/肌轉移功能重建術　functional rebuilding by muscle transfer
肌自发收缩性/肌本質收縮性　idiomuscular contractility
肌组织/肌組織　muscular tissue, muscle tissue
肌组织肿瘤/肌組織腫瘤　muscle tissue neoplasm
鸡白喉病毒/雞白喉病毒　fowl diphtheria virus
鸡白痢菌素/雞白痢疾桿菌素　pullorin
鸡白血病病毒/雞白血病病毒　fowl leukosis virus
鸡蛋花素/雞蛋花素　plumericin
鸡骨草/雞骨草　canton love-pea vine
鸡冠/雞冠　crista galli
鸡冠花/雞冠花　cockcomb inflorescence
鸡冠蚬肉/雞冠蜆肉　cockscomb-like ecphyma on eyelid
鸡冠癣/雞冠癬　comb disease
鸡冠翼/雞冠翼　ala of crista galli
鸡冠痔/雞冠痔　anal skin tag
鸡冠狀溃疡/雞冠狀潰瘍　cocks-comb ulcer
鸡蛔虫病/雞蛔蟲病　ascaridiasis
鸡螺旋体病/雞螺旋體病　fowl spirochetosis
鸡鸣状鼾息/雞鳴鼾狀　hen-cluck stertor
鸡内金/雞內金　inner membrane of chicken gizzard
鸡疟/雞瘧　avian malaria

鸡胚/雞胚　chick embryo
鸡胚抗原/雞胚抗原　chick embryo antigen
鸡皮刺螨/雞螨　chicken mite
鸡沙门氏菌病/雞沙門氏菌病　pullorum disease
鸡尾酒疗法/雞尾酒療法　cocktail therapy
鸡尾酒性紫癜/雞尾酒性紫癜　cocktail purpura
鸡瘟病毒/雞瘟病毒　fowl plague virus
鸡新城疫结膜炎病毒/Newcastle 雞瘟結膜炎病毒　Newcastle disease conjunctivitis virus
鸡胸/雞胸　pigeon chest, pigeon breast
鸡血清/雞血清　chicken serum
鸡血藤/雞血藤　suberect spatholobus stem
鸡眼/雞眼,釘胼　clavus
鸡虱虫/雞虱蟲　poultry mite
奇结节/奇結節,單結節　tuberculum impar
奇静脉/奇靜脈　azygos vein, vena azygos
奇静脉弓/奇靜脈弓　arch of azygos vein
奇静脉弓淋巴结/奇靜脈弓淋巴結　lymph node of azygos arch
奇静脉原理/奇靜脈原理　azygos principle
奇静脉造影术/奇靜脈 X 光攝影術　azygography
奇静脉造影照片/奇靜脈 X 光像　azygogram
奇神经节/奇神經節,尾神經節　ganglion impar
积存胰岛素/積存胰島素　depot insulin
积分仪/積分儀　integrator
积粉苔/積粉苔　powder-like fur
积极共生/建設性共生　constructive symbiosis
积精全神/積精全神　cultivating mental faculties
积聚/積聚　amassment and accumulation, abdominal mass
积聚·肝气郁结证/積聚·肝氣鬱結證　amassment and accumulation with pattern of liver qi depression
积聚·食滞痰阻证/積聚·食滯痰阻證　amassment and accumulation with pattern of food stagnation and phlegm blockade
积脓/積膿,蓄膿　empyema
积气[症]/積氣[病]　pneumatosis
积水性脊髓膜突出/積水性脊髓膜突出　hydromyelocele
积水性脑膜脑膨出/積水性腦膜腦膨出　meningohydroencephalocele
积水性脑膜突出/積水性腦膜突出,腦膜水囊膨出　hydromeningocele
积水性脑脑膜突出/積水性腦腦膜膨出　hydrencephalomeningocele
积水性脑突出/積水性腦膨出　encephalocystocele
积水性腮腺炎/積水性腮腺炎　hydroparotitis
积水性无脑畸形/積水性無腦症　hydranencephaly

积水性小头/積水性小頭　hydromicrocephaly
积水性心包炎/積水性心包炎　hydropericarditis
积水性阴囊疝/積水性陰囊疝　hydroscheocele
积雪草苷/積雪草苷　asiaticoside
积证/積證　amassment disease
积滞/不消化,消化不良　indigestion
积滞·脾虚夹积证/積滯·脾虛夾積證　indigestion with pattern of malnutrition due to spleen deficiency
积滞·乳食积滞证/積滯·乳食積滯證　indigestion with pattern of milk and food stagnation
姬螨皮炎/姬蟎皮炎　Cheyletiella dermatitis
基/基部　basement
基板/基板　basal plate, placode
基本的/元素的,初級的　elementary
基本粒子/基本粒子　elementary particle
基本粒子相互作用/基本粒子相互作用　elementary particle interaction
基本培养基/基本培養基　minimal medium, MM
基本日常生活活动功能/基本的日常生活活動功能　basic activities of daily living
基本组织学/基本組織學,普通組織學　general histology
基础/基礎　base
基础创伤生命支持/基礎創傷生命支持　basic trauma life support
基础代谢/基礎代謝　basal metabolism
基础代谢测量法/基礎代謝測定法　metabolimetry
基础代谢计/基礎代謝計　metabolimeter
基础代谢率/基礎代謝率　basal metabolic rate
基础护理/初級照護　primary care service
基础麻醉/基礎麻醉　basic anesthesia
基础免疫学/基礎免疫學　basic immunology
基础神经丛/基礎神經叢　fundamental plexus
基础生命支持/基礎生命支持　basic life support
基础酸排出量/基礎酸排出量　basal acid output
基础体温/基礎體溫　basal body temperature
基础医学/基礎醫學　preclinical medicine
基础饮食/基礎飲食　basal diet
基础油/基礎油　base oil
[基]底/基底　base
基底部/基底部　basilar part
基底材料/背材　backing material
基底层/基底層,生長層　basal lamina, stratum basale
基底丛/基底叢　plexus basilaris
基底的/底的　based
基底动脉/基底動脈　basilar artery
基底动脉瘤/基底動脈瘤　basilar artery aneurysm

基底缝/底缝　basilar suture
基底沟/基底溝　basilar sulcus
基[底]骨/基骨　basal bone
基底冠矢轴/基底囟軸　basibregmatic axis
基底核/基底核　basal nucleus
基底浆质膜/基底漿質膜　basal plasma membrane
基底静脉/基底靜脈　basal vein, vena basalis
基底静脉丛/基底靜脈叢,腦底靜脈叢　basilar venous plexus
基底颗粒细胞/基底顆粒細胞　basal granulated cell
基底鳞状癌/基底鱗狀癌　basosquamous carcinoma
基底鳞状细胞癌/基底鱗狀細胞癌　basosquamous cell carcinoma
基底鳞状细胞棘皮瘤/基底鱗狀細胞棘皮瘤　basosquamous cell acanthoma
基底鳞状细胞上皮瘤/基底鱗狀細胞上皮瘤　basal squamous cell epithelioma
基底颅骨骨折/基底顱骨骨折　basilar skull fracture
基底面/基底面　basal surface
基底膜/基底膜　basilar membrane
基底膜带/基底膜區　basement membrane zone
基底膜抗原/基底膜抗原　basement membrane antigen
基底神经节/基底神經節　basal ganglia, basal ganglion
基底神经节疾病/基底神經節疾病　basal ganglia disease
基底室/基底室　basal compartment
基底外侧部/基底外側部　basolateral part
基底纹/基底紋　basal striation
基底细胞/基底細胞　basal cell
基底细胞癌/基底細胞癌　basal cell carcinoma
基底细胞瘤/基底細胞瘤　basalioma
基底细胞乳头状瘤/基底細胞乳突瘤　basal cell papilloma
基底细胞上皮瘤/基底細胞上皮瘤　basal cell epithelioma
基底细胞腺癌/基底細胞腺癌　basal cell adenocarcinoma
基底细胞腺瘤/基底細胞腺瘤　basal cell adenoma
基底细胞型成釉细胞瘤/基底細胞型成釉細胞瘤　basal cell type ameloblastoma
基底细胞样毛囊错构瘤/基底細胞樣毛囊錯構瘤　basaloid follicular hamartoma
基底细胞增生/基底細胞增生　basal cell hyperplasia
基底细胞痣/基底細胞痣,基底細胞母斑　basal cell nevus
基底细胞痣综合征/基底細胞痣症候群　basal cell

nevus syndrome
基底细胞肿瘤/基底細胞腫瘤 basal cell neoplasms
基底纤维/基底纖維 basilar fibers
基底纤维软骨/基底纖維軟骨 basal fibrocartilage
基嵴/扣帶 basal ridge
基金募集/基金募集 fund raising
基勒病/基勒病 Kyrle disease
基利安憩室/基利安憩室 Killian diverticulum
基利安切口/基利安切口 Killian incision
基膜/基膜 basement membrane
基频吸收带/基頻吸收帶 basic frequency absorption band
基强度/基電流 rheobase
基思低离子饮食/Keith 氏低鈉飲食 Keith low ionic diet
基态/基態 ground state
基体/基體 basal body
基团/基團 group
基蜕膜/基蜕膜 subplacenta
基托成形器/基托成形器 base-former
基托蜡片/基托蠟片 base plate wax
基线分离峰/基線分離峰 baseline resolved peak
基牙定位器/支柱牙定位器 abutment locater
基牙夹/支柱牙固定裝置 abutment splint
基因/基因 gene
基因表达/基因表達 gene expression
基因表达谱/基因表達譜 gene expression profiling
基因表达调控/基因表達調控 gene expression regulation
基因操作/基因操作 genetic manipulation
基因沉默/基因沈默 gene silencing
基因成分/基因成分 gene component
基因重排/基因重排 gene rearrangement
基因簇/基因簇 gene cluster
基因的/基因的 genetic
基因定位/基因定位 gene mapping
基因多效性/基因多效性 gene pleiotropism
基因复制/基因複製 gene duplication
基因工程/基因工程 genetic engineering
基因工程抗生素/基因工程抗生素 gene engineered antibiotic
基因固定/基因固定 fixation of gene
基因激活/基因活性化 gene activation
基因剂量/基因劑量 gene dosage
基因家族/基因家族 gene family
基因间 DNA/基因間 DNA intergenic DNA
基因间序列/基因間序列 intergenic sequence
基因拷贝/基因拷貝 gene copy

基因克隆/基因選殖 genetic cloning
基因库/基因庫 gene bank, gene pool
基因扩增/基因擴增 gene amplification
基因理论与原则/基因原理與原則 genetic theory and principle
基因疗法/基因療法 gene therapy
基因流动/基因流動 gene flow
基因内互补/基因內互補作用 interallelic complementation
基因频率/基因頻率 gene frequency
基因平衡/基因平衡 genic balance
基因缺失/基因缺失 gene deletion
基因融合/基因融合 gene fusion
基因顺序/基因順序 gene order
基因探针/基因探針 gene probe
基因突变/基因突變 gene mutation
基因图谱/基因圖譜比對 gene mapping
基因文库/基因[文]庫 gene library
基因型/基因型 genotype
基因性角膜退化/基因性角膜退化 corneal dystrophia
基因修饰动物/基因修飾動物 genetically modified animal
基因修饰生物/基因修飾生物 genetically modified organism
基因修饰食品/基因修飾食品 genetically modified food
基因修饰植物/基因修飾植物 genetically modified plant
基因诊断/基因診斷 gene diagnosis
基因转变/基因轉變 gene conversion
基因转移/基因轉移 gene transfer
基因转移技术/基因轉移技術 gene transfer technique
基因咨询/基因諮詢 genetic counsel
基因组/基因組 genome
基因组 DNA/基因組 DNA genomic DNA
基因组不稳定性/基因組不穩定性 genomic instability
基因组成分/基因組成分 genome component
基因组岛/基因組島 genomic island
基因组探针/基因組探針 genomic probe
基因组突变/基因組突變 genomic mutation
基因组文库/基因組文庫 genomic library
基因组学/基因組學 genomics
基因组印迹/基因組印跡 genomic imprinting
基因作用/基因作用 gene action
基因座连锁分析/基因座連鎖分析 locus linkage

analysis
基因座调控区/基因座調控區　locus control region
基源鉴定/基源鑒定　identification of origin
基质/基質　matrix
基质的/基質的　stromal
基质结石/基質結石　matrix calculus
基质金属蛋白酶类/基質金屬蛋白酶類　matrix metalloproteinases
基质启动学说/基質啟動學說　theory of matrix initiation
基质溶解/基質溶解　stromatolysis
基质深[层]丛/深間質神經叢　deep stroma plexus
基质细胞/基質細胞　matrix cell, stroma cell
基质纤维蛋白/基質纖維素,間質纖維素　stroma fibrin
基质性角膜炎/間質性角膜炎　interstitial keratitis
基质性子宫内膜异位/基質性子宮內膜異位　stromal adenomyosis
畸胎/畸胎　monster
畸胎癌/畸胎癌　teratocarcinoma
畸胎毁除术/畸胎消毁　monstricide
畸胎瘤/畸胎瘤　teratoma
畸胎瘤发生/畸胎癌形成　teratocarcinogenesis
畸胎形囊肿/畸胎形囊腫　teratoid cyst
畸胎学/畸胎學　teratology
畸胎样的/畸胎狀的　teratoid
畸胎样瘤/畸胎[樣]瘤　teratoblastoma
畸细胞皮纤维瘤/畸細胞皮纖維瘤　dermatofibroma with monster cells
畸形/畸形　malformation
畸形的/變形的　dysmorphic
畸形发生/畸形發生,畸胎發生　teratogenesis
畸形精子[症]/畸形精子症　teratospermia
畸形恐怖/醜形恐怖症　dysmorphophobia
畸形谱/畸形譜　spectrum of defect
畸形舌侧尖/畸形舌側尖　talon cusp
畸形舌侧窝/畸形舌側窩　invaginated lingual fossa
畸形手/畸形手　clubhand
畸形学/畸形學　teratology
畸形易发性/畸形易發性　susceptibility to teratogenesis
畸形愈合/畸形愈合　malunion
畸形指甲/畸形指甲　malformed nail
畸形趾甲/畸形趾甲　malformed nail
畸形综合征/畸形症候群　malformation syndrome
畸形足/畸形足　clubfoot, club foot, reel foot
畸形足者/畸足者　taliped
箕门/箕門　jimen, SP11

稽留流产/過期流產,死胎不出　missed abortion
稽留热/稽留熱　continued fever
激动/激動　agonism
激动剂/激動劑　agonist
激动状态/激動狀態　affective state
激发变异/激發變異　impressed variation
激发试验/激發試驗　rechallenge
激发态/激發態　excited state
激发性华氏反应/激發性威瑟曼氏反應　provocative Wassermann reaction
激发性伤寒/激發性傷寒　provocation typhoid
激发性饮食/激發性飲食　provocative diet
激发眼/刺激眼　exciting eye
激发诊断/激發診斷　provocative diagnosis
激发状态/興奮狀態　excited state
激光/雷射　laser
激光多普勒流量测定/雷射多普勒流量測定　laser-doppler flowmetry
激光光凝术/雷射光凝術　laser photocoagulation
激光虹膜切开术/雷射虹膜切開術　laser iridotomy
激光角膜切削术/雷射角膜切削術　laser keratectomy
激光解吸质谱法/雷射脫附質譜法　laser desorption mass spectrometry, LDMS
激光疗法/雷射療法　laser therapy
激光毛发移植[术]/雷射毛髮移植[術]　laser hair transplantation
激光凝固术/雷射凝固術　laser coagulation
激光切割手术/雷射切割手術　incisional laser surgery
激光扫描/雷射掃描　laser scanning
激光扫描共聚焦显微镜/雷射掃描共聚焦顯微鏡　laser scanning confocal microscope, LSCM
激光扫描检眼镜/雷射掃描檢眼鏡　scanning laser ophthalmoscope
激光扫描细胞术/雷射掃描細胞術　laser scanning cytometry
激光伤/雷射傷　laser injury
激光手术/雷射手術　laser surgery
激光[手术]刀/雷射[手術]刀　laser scalpel
激光碎石术/雷射碎石術　laser lithotripsy
激光显微镜/激光顯微鏡,雷射顯微鏡　laser microscope
激光消融[术]/雷射消融[術]　laser ablation
激光小梁成形术/雷射小梁成形術　laser trabeculoplasty
激光小梁刺激术/雷射小梁刺激術　laser trabeculostimulation

激光血管成形术/雷射血管成形術 laser angioplasty
激光荧光诊断技术/雷射螢光診斷技術 laser fluorescent diagnostic technique
激光原位角膜磨削术/雷射原位角膜磨鑲術 laser in situ keratomileusis
激光治疗仪/雷射治療儀 laser therapeutic apparatus
激活/激活,活化 activation
激活剂前体/前促動劑,前活酶 proactivator
激活抗原/啟動抗原 activation antigen
激酶/激酶,活化酵素 kinase
激泌素/激泌素 crinin
激怒/激怒 irritate
激惹心境/激惹心境 irritable mood
激素/激素 hormone
激素的/激素的 hormonal
激素补充治疗/激素補充治療 hormone-replacement therapy
激素反应元件/激素反應元件 hormone response element
激素过多症/激素過多症 hormonosis
激素拮抗药/激素拮抗藥 hormone antagonist
激素抗肿瘤药/激素抗腫瘤藥 hormonal antineoplastic agent
激素类/激素類 hormones
激素免疫测定/激素免疫測定 hormone immunoassay
激素取代治疗/激素取代治療 hormone-replacement therapy
激素缺乏/激素缺少 hormonoprivia
激素生成/激素生成 hormonogenesis
激素受体/激素受體 hormone receptor
激素替代疗法/激素替代療法 hormone replacement therapy
激素血/激素血 hemocrinia
激素依赖性皮炎/激素依賴性皮炎 steroid-dependent dermatitis
激素依赖性肿瘤/激素依賴性腫瘤 hormone-dependent neoplasm
激肽/激肽 kinin
激肽释放酶类/激肽釋放酶類 kallikreins
激肽原/激肽原 kininogen
激肽原类/激肽原類 kininogens
激糖素/激糖素 glucokinin
激育素/激育素 tocokinin
激越性痴呆/激越性精神分裂症 dementia agitata
激越性抑郁[症]/激昂性抑鬱 agitated depression
激越性忧郁症/騷動性憂鬱症 agitated melancholia
吉本阴囊水肿/Gibbon氏陰囊水腫 Gibbon hydrocele
吉伯纳韧带/Gimbernat氏韌帶 Gimbernat ligament
吉伯索尼氏圆虫/吉伯索尼氏圓蟲 Strongylus gibsoni
吉布尼绷带/Gibney氏繃帶 Gibney bandage
吉布森夹/Gibson氏夾板 Gibson splint
吉布森杂音/吉布森氏雜音 Gibson murmur
吉尔伯特病/吉伯特病 Gilbert disease
吉尔伯特综合征/吉伯特症候群 Gilbert syndrome
吉尔默夹/Gilmer氏夾板 Gilmer splint
吉尔森溶液/Gilson氏溶液 Gilson solution
吉尔森液/Gilson氏液 Gilson fluid
吉法酯/吉法酯 Gefarnate
吉非贝齐/吉非貝琪 Gemfibrozil
吉-赫-霍综合征/Gee-Herter-Heubner三氏症候群 Gee-Herter-Heubner syndrome
吉姆萨染色/吉姆薩染色 Giemsa staining
吉姆萨显带/吉姆薩顯帶 Giemsa banding
吉普车病/吉普車病 jeep disease
吉他林/吉他林 gitalin
吉他霉素/北里黴素,柱晶白黴素 kitasamycin
吉他乳头/吉他乳頭 guitar nipple
吉特克/馬錢子毒 tjettek
吉田肉瘤/吉田肉瘤 Yoshida sarcoma
吉托吉宁/吉托吉寧 gitogenin
吉托宁/吉托寧 gitonin
级联反应/級聯反應 cascade reaction
极侧咬合/極側咬合 extreme lateral occlusion
极的/極的,端的 polar
极低出生体重婴儿/極低出生體重嬰兒 very low birth weight infant
极地贫血/極地貧血 polar anemia
极垫/極墊 polar cushion
极度矮小/極度矮小 hypernanosoma
极端微生物/極端微生物 extreme microorganism
极辐射/極輻射 polar radiation
极化/極化 polarization
极谱法/偏極描記法 polarography
极谱图/極化圖 polarogram
极泉/極泉 jiquan, HT1
极隧射线/陽極射線 canal ray
极体/極體 polar body
极晚期抗原受体/甚晚抗原受體 very late antigen receptor
极微的/最小的 minimal
极细胞/極細胞 polar cell
极细粉/細撒粉 impalpable powder
极性/極性 polarity

极性发育不全/兩極性發育不全　polar hypogenesis
极性分子/極性分子　polar molecule
极性键/極性鍵　polar bond
极性成胶质细胞瘤/極性膠質母細胞瘤　spongioblastoma polare
极性增生/兩極性增殖　polar hyperplasia
即刻记忆/短暫性記憶　immediate memory
即刻义齿/即刻義齒，臨時假牙　immediate denture
即时的/即時的　immediate
即早基因/即早基因　immediate-early gene
急冲脉/急沖狀脈　jerky pulse
急冲状呼吸/急衝式呼吸　jerky respiration
急促动作/急促動作　mication
急方/急方　drastic prescription
急腹症/急腹症　acute abdomen
急喉痹/急喉痺　acute pharyngitis, acute throat obstruction
急喉风/急喉風　acute laryngeal infection, acute throat wind
急喉风·风热外袭证/急喉風·風熱外襲證　acute throat wind with pattern of external assault by wind-heat
急喉风·热毒熏蒸证/急喉風·熱毒薰蒸證　acute throat wind with heat-toxin fumigating pattern
急喉风·痰浊凝聚证/急喉風·痰濁凝聚證　acute throat wind with pattern of phlegm-turbidity coagulation and aggregation
急喉喑/急喉喑　acute hoarseness
急喉瘖/急喉瘖　acute hoarseness disease
急黄/急黃　fulminant jaundice
急黄·热毒炽盛证/急黃·熱毒熾盛證　fulminant jaundice with pattern of blazing heat-toxin
急黄·热毒内陷证/急黃·熱毒内陷證　fulminant jaundice with pattern of interior invasion of heat-toxin
急进性高血压/惡性高血壓　accelerated hypertension
急进性肾小球肾炎/急進性腎小球腎炎　rapidly progressive glomerulonephritis
急惊风/急驚風　acute infantile convulsion
急惊风·风热发搐证/急驚風·風熱發搐證　acute infantile convulsion due to wind-heat
急惊风·惊恐惊风证/急驚風·驚恐驚風證　acute infantile convulsion due to fright
急惊风·湿热疫毒证/急驚風·濕熱疫毒證　acute infantile convulsion with pattern of damp-heat and pestilent toxin
急惊风·暑热发搐证/急驚風·暑熱發搐證　acute infantile convulsion due to hot-summerheat
急惊风·痰食惊风证/急驚風·痰食驚風證　acute infantile convulsion due to phlegm-food
急惊风·温热疫毒证/急驚風·溫熱疫毒證　acute infantile convulsion with pattern of warm-heat and pestilent toxin
急救/急救[法]　the first aid
急救半径/急救半徑　rescuing radius
急救技师/急救技師　emergency medical technician
急救入院者/急救入院者　casual
急救网络/急救網路　emergency network
急救医疗标签/急救醫療標簽　emergency medical tag
急救医疗服务/急救醫療服務　emergency medical service
急救医疗服务通信系统/急救醫療服務通信系統　emergency medical service communication system
急救医士/急救醫士　paramedic
急救医学/急救醫學　emergency medicine
急救员/急救員　emergency medical service technician
急救中心/急救中心　emergency center
急脉/急脈　jimai, LR12
急迫性失禁/急迫性失禁　urgency incontinence
急乳蛾/急乳蛾，急性扁桃體炎　acute nippled moth, acute tonsillitis
急跳运动/急跳運動　jerky exercise
急相蛋白质类/急相蛋白質類　acute-phase proteins
急相反应/急相反應　acute-phase reaction
急效应区/急性效應區　acute effect zone
急性/急性　acute
急性白血病/急性白血病　acute leukemia
急性暴发性脑膜炎球菌血症/急性暴發性腦膜炎球菌血症　acute fulminating meningococcemia
急性闭塞性细支气管炎/急性阻塞性細支氣管炎　acute obliterating bronchiolitis
急性病/急性病　acute disease
急性播散性扁平苔藓/急性播散性扁平苔蘚　acute disseminated lichen planus
急性播散性脑脊髓炎/急性播散性腦脊髓炎，傳染病後腦炎　acute disseminated encephalomyelitis
急性卟啉症/急性紫質沈著病　acute porphyria
急性肠系膜淋巴结炎/急性腸繫膜淋巴結炎　acute mesenteric lymphadenitis
急性充血性心力衰竭/急性鬱血性心衰竭　acute congestive heart failure
急性出血/急性失血　acute bleeding
急性出血性结膜炎/急性出血性結膜炎　acute hemorrhagic conjunctivitis

急性出血性脑白质炎/急性出血性腦白質炎 acute hemorrhagic leukoencephalitis

急性出血性胰腺炎/急性出血性胰炎 acute hemorrhagic pancreatitis

急性传染性肝炎/急性傳染性肝炎 acute infectious hepatitis

急性传染性紫癜/急性傳染性紫瘢病 purpura infectiosa acuta

急性痤疮/急性痤瘡 acute acne

急性单核细胞白血病/急性單核細胞白血病 acute monocytic leukemia

急性胆囊炎/急性膽囊炎 acute cholecystitis

急性的/急性的 acutus

急性痘疮样类银屑病/急性痘瘡樣類乾癬 parapsoriasis varioliformis acuta

急性痘疮样脓疱病/急性牛痘狀膿疱病 pustulosis varioliformis acuta

急性痘疮样苔藓性类银屑病/急性痘瘡樣苔蘚性類乾癬 parapsoriasis lichenoides et varioliformis acuta

急性毒效应区/急性毒效應區 acute toxic effect zone

急性毒性/急性毒性 acute toxicity

急性毒性试验/急性毒性試驗 acute toxicity test

急性多发性龈脓肿/急性多發性齦膿腫 acute multiple gingival abscess

急性发热性感染性黄疸/急性發熱傳染性黃疸 acute febrile infectious jaundice

急性发热性聚合性痤疮/急性發熱性團聚性痤瘡 acute febrile conglobate acne

急性发热性嗜中性[细胞]皮肤病/急性發熱性嗜中性[細胞]皮膚病 acute febrile neutrophilic dermatosis

急性泛发性扁平苔藓/急性泛發性扁平苔蘚 acute widespread lichen planus

急性泛发性脓疱病/急性泛發性膿疱症 pustulosis acuta generalisata

急性放射[性]综合征/急性放射性症候群 acute radiation syndrome

急性非过敏性荨麻疹/急性非過敏性蕁麻疹 acute nonallergic urticaria

急性非淋巴细胞白血病/急性非淋巴細胞白血病 acute nonlymphocytic leukemia

急性非少尿型肾[功能]衰竭/急性非少尿型腎[功能]衰竭 acute nonoliguric renal failure

急性非特异性心包炎/急性非特異性心包炎 acute nonspecific pericarditis

急性非特异性龈炎/急性非特異性齦炎 acute nonspecific gingivitis

急性风湿性关节炎/急性風濕性關節炎 acute rheumatic arthritis

急性腐蚀性食管炎/急性腐蝕性食管炎 acute corrosive esophagitis

急性附骨疽/急性附骨疽 acute bone-attaching abscess, acute suppurative osteomyelitis

急性腹水/急性腹水 acute ascites

急性腹泻/急性腹瀉 acute diarrhea

急性肝功能衰竭/急性肝功能衰竭 acute liver failure

急性感染后肾小球肾炎/急性感染後腎小球腎炎 acute postinfectious glomerulonephritis

急性感染性胃肠炎/急性傳染性胃腸炎 acute infectious gastroenteritis

急性干细胞白血病/急性幹細胞白血病 acute stem cell leukemia

急性高空病/急性高空病 acute altitude sickness

急性高尿酸血症的/急性高尿酸血症的 acute-hyperuricemic

急性梗阻性化脓性胆管炎/急性梗阻性化膿性膽管炎 acute obstructive suppurative cholangitis

急性骨炎/急性骨炎 acute osteitis

急性关节炎/急性關節炎 acute arthritis

急性冠状动脉供血不足/急性冠狀動脈供血不足 acute coronary insufficiency

急性喉气管炎/急性喉氣管炎 acute laryngotracheitis

急性喉气管支气管炎/急性喉氣管支氣管炎 acute laryngotracheobronchitis

急性呼吸窘迫综合征/急性呼吸窘迫症候群 acute respiratory distress syndrome

急性化脓性扁桃腺炎/急性化膿性扁桃腺炎 acute suppurative tonsillitis

急性化脓性骨髓炎/急性化膿性骨髓炎 acute suppurative osteomyelitis

急性化脓性骨髓炎·风温内扰证/急性化膿性骨髓炎·風溫內擾證 acute suppurative osteomyelitis with pattern of wind-warm disturbing inward

急性化脓性骨髓炎·三焦热盛证/急性化膿性骨髓炎·三焦熱盛證 acute suppurative osteomyelitis with pattern of heat exuberance in sanjiao

急性化脓性骨髓炎·营血两燔证/急性化膿性骨髓炎·營血兩燔證 acute suppurative osteomyelitis with pattern of flaming of nutrient-blood phases

急性化脓性滑囊炎/急性化膿滑囊炎 acute suppurative synovitis

急性化脓性腱鞘炎/急性化膿腱鞘炎 tenosynovitis

acuta purulenta
急性化脓性肾炎/急性膿性腎炎 acute suppurative nephritis
急性化脓性牙髓炎/急性化膿性牙髓炎 acute suppurative pulpitis
急性坏死溃疡性[齿]龈炎/急性壞死潰瘍性[齒]齦炎 acute necrotizing ulcerative gingivitis
急性坏死性齿龈炎/急性壞死性齒齦炎 acute necrotizing gingivitis
急性坏死性胰腺炎/急性壞死性胰腺炎 acute necrotizing pancreatitis
急性幻觉性妄想狂/急性幻覺性妄想狂 acute hallucinatory paranoia
急性幻觉性躁狂/急性幻覺性躁狂 acute hallucinatory mania
急性黄色肝萎缩/急性黃色性肝萎縮 hepatodystrophy
急性黄色萎缩/急性黃色萎縮 acute yellow atrophy
急性脊髓侧角灰质炎/急性脊髓側灰質炎 acute lateral poliomyelitis
急性脊髓膜炎/急性脊髓膜炎 acute spinal meningitis
急性脊髓前角灰质炎/急性脊髓前灰白質炎 acute anterior poliomyelitis
急性脊髓炎/急性脊髓炎 acute myelitis
急性甲状腺肿/急性甲狀腺腫 acute goiter
急性间歇性卟啉病/急性間歇性吡咯紫質沈著病 acute intermittent porphyria
急性间质性肺炎/急性間質性肺炎 acute interstitial pneumonia
急性间质性肾炎/急性間質性腎炎 acute interstitial nephritis
急性间质性胰腺炎/急性間質性胰腺炎 acute interstitial pancreatitis
急性浆细胞白血病/急性漿細胞白血病 acute plasma cell leukemia
急性浆液性牙髓炎/急性漿液性牙髓炎 acute serous pulpitis
急性结肠炎/急性結腸炎 acute colitis
急性精神错乱状态/急性意識模糊狀態 acute confusional state
急性酒精中毒/急性酒精中毒 acute alcoholism
急性卡他性鼻炎/急性卡他性鼻炎 acute catarrhal rhinitis
急性卡他性扁桃体炎/急性卡他性扁桃腺炎 acute catarrhal tonsillitis
急性卡他性喉炎/急性卡他性喉炎 acute catarrhal laryngitis
急性卡他性阑尾炎/急性卡他性闌尾炎 acute catarrhal appendicitis
急性卡他性中耳炎/急性卡他性中耳炎 otitis media catarrhalis acuta
急性阑尾炎/急性闌尾炎 acute appendicitis
急性狼疮/急性狼瘡 acute lupus
急性粒细胞白血病/急性粒細胞白血病 acute myeloblastic leukemia
急性链球菌感染后肾小球肾炎/急性鏈球菌感染後腎小球腎炎 acute poststreptococcal glomerulonephritis
急性链球菌性肾小球肾炎/急性鏈球菌性腎絲球腎炎 acute streptococcal glomerulonephritis
急性链球菌性龈口炎/急性鏈球菌性齦口炎 acute streptococcal gingvostomatitis
急性良性成淋巴细胞增多[症]/急性良性淋巴胚細胞過多病 acute benign lymphoblastosis
急性良性心包炎/急性良性心包膜炎 acute benign pericarditis
急性淋巴细胞白血病/急性淋巴細胞白血病 acute lymphoblastic leukemia
急性滤泡性扁桃体炎/急性濾泡性扁桃腺炎 acute follicular tonsillitis
急性毛囊炎/急性毛囊炎 acute folliculitis
急性弥漫性腹膜炎/急性彌漫性腹膜炎 acute diffuse peritonitis
急性弥漫性阑尾炎/急性彌漫性闌尾炎 acute diffuse appendicitis
急性脑膜炎/急性腦膜炎 acute cerebral meningitis
急性脑肿胀/急性腦腫脹 acute brain swelling
急性脑综合征/急性腦症候群 acute brain syndrome
急性尿酸盐肾病/急性尿酸鹽腎病 acute urate nephropathy
急性女阴溃疡/急性女陰潰瘍 ulcus vulvae acutum
急性排斥反应/急性排斥 acute rejection
急性疱疹性女阴阴道炎/急性皰疹性女陰陰道炎 acute herpetic vulvovaginitis
急性盆腔炎/急性盆腔炎 acute pelvic inflammatory disease
急性盆腔炎·热毒壅盛证/急性盆腔炎·熱毒壅盛證 acute pelvic inflammatory disease with exuberance of heat-toxin
急性盆腔炎·湿热[蕴结]证/急性盆腔炎·濕熱[蘊結]證 acute pelvic inflammatory disease with pattern of accumulation and binding of damp-heat
急性砒霜中毒/急性砒霜中毒 acute arsenic poisoning
急性皮炎/急性皮膚炎 acute dermatitis

急性脾肿瘤/急性脾腫瘤 acute splenic tumor
急性期蛋白/急性期蛋白 acute phase protein
急性前角神经细胞炎/急性前角神經細胞炎 acute anterior celluloneuritis
急性浅表性龟头炎/急性表淺性龜頭炎 acute superficial balanitis
急性浅表性毛囊炎/急性表淺性毛囊炎 acute superficial folliculitis
急性热病性多神经炎/庫-蘭二氏麻痺，蘭德里氏麻痺 Kussmaul-Landry paralysis
急性色素上皮炎/急性色素上皮炎 acute pigment epithelitis
急性上行性麻痹/急性上行性麻痺 acute ascending paralysis
急性少尿型肾[功能]衰竭/急性少尿型腎[功能]衰竭 acute oliguric renal failure
急性砷剂皮炎/急性砷劑皮膚炎 acute arsenical dermatitis
急性肾病/急性腎病 acute nephrosis
急性肾功能衰竭/急性腎功能衰竭 acute kidney failure
急性肾机能不全/急性腎機能不全 acute renal insufficiency
急性肾乳头坏死/急性腎乳頭壞死 acute renal papillary necrosis
急性肾损伤/急性腎損傷 acute kidney injury
急性肾小管坏死/急性腎小管壞死 acute kidney tubular necrosis
急性肾小球肾炎/急性腎小球腎炎 acute glomerulonephritis
急性肾炎/急性腎炎 acute nephritis
急性湿疹/急性濕疹 acute eczema
急性实质性肝炎/急性實質性肝炎 acute parenchymatous hepatitis
急性视网膜坏死/急性視網膜壞死 acute retinal necrosis
急性视网膜坏死综合征/急性視網膜壞死症候群 acute retinal necrosis syndrome
急性水肿性胰腺炎/急性水腫性胰腺炎 acute edematous pancreatitis
急性粟粒性肺炎/急性粟粒性肺炎 acute miliary pneumonitis
急性粟粒性皮肤结核/急性粟粒性皮膚結核 acute miliary tuberculosis of the skin
急性苔藓痘疮样糠疹/急性苔癬痘狀糠疹 pityriasis lichenoides et varioliformis acuta
急性苔藓样糠疹/急性苔藓樣糠疹 pityriasis lichenoides acuta

急性痛风性关节炎/急性痛風性關節炎 acute gouty arthritis
急性透析/急性透析 acute dialysis
急性脱髓鞘病/急性髓鞘脱失病 acute demyelinating disease
急性未定型白血病/急性未定型白血病 acute unclassified leukemia
急性未分化细胞白血病/急性未分化細胞白血病 acute undifferentiated cell leukemia
急性胃肠炎/急性腸胃炎 acute gastroenteritis
急性胃扩张/急性胃擴張 acute dilatation of stomach
急性细胞性排斥反应/急性細胞排斥反應 acute cellular rejection
急性细菌性心肌炎/急性細菌性心肌炎 acute bacterial myocarditis
急性夏令腹泻/急性夏令腹瀉 acute summer diarrhea
急性纤维蛋白性心包炎/急性纖維性心包膜炎 acute fibrinous pericarditis
急性涎腺炎/急性涎腺炎 acute salivary adenitis
急性陷窝性扁桃体炎/急性陷窩性扁桃體炎 acute lacunar tonsillitis
急性小管性排斥反应/急性小管性排斥反應 acute tubular rejection
急性心肌梗死/急性心肌梗塞 acute myocardial infarction
急性血管神经性水肿/急性血管神經性水腫 acute circumscribed edema
急性血管性排斥反应/急性血管性排斥反應 acute vascular rejection
急性血管性紫癜/急性血管性紫瘢病 acute vascular purpura
急性血吸虫病/急性血吸蟲病 acute schistosomiasis
急性荨麻疹/急性蕁麻疹 acute hives
急性压塞三征/急性心臟受壓迫之三徵 acute compression triad
急性延髓灰质炎/急性延髓灰質炎 acute bulbar poliomyelitis
急性炎/急性炎 acute inflammation
急性腰扭伤/急性腰扭傷 acute lumbar muscle sprain, acute lumbar sprain
急性腰扭伤·气滞证/急性腰扭傷·氣滯證 acute lumbar sprain with qi stagnation pattern
急性腰扭伤·血瘀证/急性腰扭傷·血瘀證 acute lumbar sprain with blood stasis pattern
急性抑郁[症]/急性抑鬱[症] acute depression
急性应激性溃疡/急性應激性潰瘍 acute stress ulcer

急性阈剂量/急性閾劑量　acute threshold dose
急性阈浓度/急性閾濃度　acute threshold concentration
急性暂时性髋关节滑膜炎/急性暫時性髖關節滑膜炎　acute transient synovitis of hip
急性早幼粒细胞白血病/急性早幼粒細胞白血病　acute promyelocytic leukemia
急性造血停滞/急性造血停滯　acute arrest of hemopoiesis
急性躁狂/急性躁狂　acute mania
急性支气管炎/急性支氣管炎　acute bronchitis
急性中耳炎/急性中耳炎　acute middle ear catarrh
急性中毒/急性中毒　acute intoxication, acute poisoning
急性中毒性脑炎/急性中毒性腦炎　acute toxic encephalitis
急性重型肝炎/急性重型肝炎　acute severe hepatitis
急性子/急性子　garden balsam seed
急性子痈/急性子癰　acute epididymitis and orchitis, acute testicular abscess
急性自发水肿/急性自發性水腫　acute essential edema
急性组织细胞白血病/急性組織細胞白血病　acute histocytic leukemia
急性左心室衰竭/急性左心室衰竭　acute left ventricular failure
急躁性错写/躁急錯寫症　agitographia
急躁性错语/躁急錯語症　agitolalia
急躁谵妄/急躁譫妄　Bell delirium
急则治标/急則治標　symptomatic treatment in acute condition
急诊处理/急救療法　emergency treatment
急诊肝移植/急診肝移植　emergency liver transplantation
急诊空运中心/急診空運中心　airborne emergency medical center
急诊心脏病监护治疗病房/急診心臟病監護治療病房　emergency cardiac care unit
急诊医疗/急診照顧　emergency care
急诊医疗体系/急診醫療體系　emergency medical service system
急症/急症　emergencies
急症护理/急症護理　emergency nursing
急支糖浆/急支糖漿　jizhi syrup
疾病/疾[病]　disease
疾病报告/疾病報告　disease report
疾病暴发流行/疾病暴發流行　disease outbreak
疾病传播/疾病傳播　disease transmission

疾病地理学/病理地學　nosochthonography
疾病毒素/疾病毒素　nosotoxin
疾病恶化/疾病惡化　disease progression
疾病遏制/疾病遏制　arrest of disease
疾病分类法/疾病分類法　nosonomy
疾病分类学/疾病分類學　nosology
疾病管理/疾病管理　disease management
疾病鉴诊器用法/疾病鑒診器用法　logoscopy
疾病鉴诊图/病情説明圖表,病況記録説明圖　logogram
疾病恐怖者/懼病恐懼者　nosophobe
疾病媒介/疾病媒介　disease vector
疾病平行现象/疾病平行現象　parallelism of disease
疾病适应性/疾病適應性　pathophilia
疾病特征/疾病特徵　disease attribute
[疾病]突发反应/病發反應　flare-up reaction
疾病消除/疾病消除　patholysis
疾病严重程度量表/疾病嚴重程度量表　severity of illness scale
疾病严重程度指数/疾病嚴重程度指數　severity of illness index
疾病遗传易感性/疾病遺傳易感性　genetic predisposition to disease
疾病易感性/疾病易感性　disease susceptibility
疾病影响状态调查/疾病影響狀態調查　sickness impact profile
疾病贮主/疾病貯主　disease reservoirs
[疾]病[状]态/疾病狀態　morbid state
疾患/病變　affection
疾脉/疾脈　swift pulse
疾医/疾醫　general medicine
棘阿米巴病/棘阿米巴病　acanthamebiasis
棘阿米巴角膜炎/棘阿米巴角膜炎　acanthamoeba keratitis
棘波/棘波　spike wave
棘层/棘[細胞]層,棘狀層　stratum spinosum
棘层肥厚/棘層肥厚病　acanthosis
棘层生成的/棘層生成的　acanthogenic
棘层松解的/皮膚棘層鬆解的　acantholytic
棘层松解细胞/棘層鬆解細胞　acantholytic cell
棘层松解性棘皮瘤/棘層鬆解性棘皮瘤　acantholytic acanthoma
棘层松解性角化不良/棘層鬆解性角化不良　acantholytic dyskeratosis
棘层松解性疱疹样皮炎/棘層鬆解性皰疹樣皮膚炎　acantholytic herpetiform dermatitis
棘唇虫病/棘唇蟲病　acanthocheilonemiasis
棘唇属感染/棘唇屬感染　*Dipetalonema* infection

棘唇丝虫属/棘唇絲蟲屬　Acanthocheilonema
棘红细胞/棘紅細胞　acanthocyte
棘肌/棘肌　spinalis, musculus spinalis
棘间肌/棘間肌　interspinale, interspinal muscle
棘间平面/棘間平面　interspinous plane
棘间韧带/棘間韌帶　interspinous ligament
棘孔/棘孔　foramen spinosum
棘口吸虫病/棘口吸蟲病　echinostomiasis
棘口吸虫属/棘口吸蟲類　Fascioletta
棘肋肌/棘肋肌　spinocostalis
棘慢复合波/棘慢複合波　spike and slow wave complex
棘皮层增殖/棘皮層增殖　hyperacanthosis
棘皮动物/棘皮動物　echinoderm
棘皮动物门/棘皮動物門　Echinodermata
棘皮瘤/棘皮瘤　acanthoma
棘皮瘤型成釉细胞瘤/棘皮瘤型成釉細胞瘤　acanthomatous type of ameloblastoma
棘器/棘器　spine apparatus
棘球囊尿/包蟲囊尿　hydatiduria
棘球囊切开引流术/包蟲囊造口引流術　hydatidostomy
棘球绦虫/棘球條蟲　caseworm
棘球蚴病/包蟲病　echinococciasis
棘上肌/棘上肌　supraspinatus
棘上筋膜/棘上腱膜　supraspinous aponeurosis
棘上韧带/棘上韌帶　supraspinal ligament
棘头虫/棘頭蟲　spiny headed worm
棘头虫病/棘頭蟲病　acanthocephaliasis
棘突/棘突　spinous process
棘突平面/棘突平面　spinous plane
棘细胞/棘細胞　heckle cell
棘[细胞]层/棘細胞層　prickle cell layer
棘隙吸虫病/棘隙吸蟲病　echinochasmiasis
棘下肌/棘下肌　musculus infraspinatus
棘状的/棘狀的,似刺的　acanthoid
棘状红细胞增多/棘狀紅細胞增多　echinocytosis
棘状外瓶霉/棘狀外瓶黴　exophiala spinifera
棘状细胞/棘狀細胞　spinous cell
集合/集合　aggregation
集合度计/集合度計　aggregometer
集合范围/集合範圍　range of convergence
集合幅度/會聚幅度　amplitude of convergence
集合管/集合小管　collecting duct
集合过度/集合過度　convergence excess
集合近点/集合近點　near point of convergence
集合静脉/集合静脈　collecting vein
集合淋巴管/集合淋巴管　collecting lymphatic vessel
集合淋巴滤泡/集合淋巴濾泡　aggregated lymphatic follicle
集合淋巴小结/集合淋巴小結　aggregated lymphoid nodule
集合麻痹/集合麻痺　convergence paralysis
集合肾小管/集合腎小管　collecting kidney tubule
集合小管/集合[小]管　collecting tubule
[集合小管]闰细胞/[集合小管]閏細胞　intercalated cell
[集合小管]主细胞/[集合小管]主細胞　principal cell
集合行为/集體行爲　collective behavior
集合性天花/凝聚痘　coherent smallpox
集合远点/集合遠點　far point of convergence
集结淋巴结/集結淋巴結　aggregated lymph node
集落/集落,菌落　colony
集落刺激因子/群落刺激因子　colony-stimulating factor
集落刺激因子受体/集落刺激因子受體　colony-stimulating factor receptor
集落生成单位/菌落形成單位,集落形成單位　colony-forming unit, CFU
集落形成单位测定/集落形成單位測定　colony-forming units assay
集群行为/集群行爲　mass behavior
集散性眼球震颤/分開性眼球震顫　disjunctive nystagmus
集体胸部检查/集體胸部檢查　mass chest examination
集体意识/集體意識　collective consciousness
集体助听器/集體助聽器　group hearing aid
集中进化/集合性進化　convergent evolution
集中式医院服务/集中式醫院服務　centralized hospital service
蒺藜/蒺藜　puncturevine caltrop fruit
蒺藜苜蓿/蒺藜苜蓿　Medicago truncatula
蒺藜中毒/蒺藜中毒　tribulosis
嵴/嵴　ridge
嵴帽沉石病/嵴帽結石　cupulolithiasis
嵴帽敏度测量[法]/嵴帽頂反應測量法　cupulometry
嵴上平面/嵴上平面　supracristal plane
嵴数/嵴數　ridge count
嫉妒妄想/嫉妒妄想　delusion of jealousy
几何容量/幾何容量　geometric capacity
几何图形样/幾何圖形樣　geomatrica
几何图形样坏疽/幾何圖形樣壞疽　phagedena geomatrica

几何异构/幾何異構　geometrical isomerism
几内亚虫/幾内亞蟲　Guinea worm
几内亚龙线虫病/幾内亞蟲病　Guinea worm disease
己胺/己基胺　caproylamine
己醇类/己醇類　hexanols
己二胺/六次甲基二胺　hexamethylendiamine
己二酸/己二酸　adipic acid
己二烯雌酚/己二烯雌酚　dienestrol
己基/己基　hexyl
己基巴比妥钠/己基巴比妥鈉　hexethal sodium
己聚糖/己聚糖　hexosan
己内酰胺/己内醯胺　caprolactam
己酸/己酸　hexanoate
己酸类/己酸類　hexanoic acids
己酸盐/己酸鹽　caproate
己糖/己糖　hexose
己糖胺类/己糖胺類　hexosamines
己糖胺酶类/己糖胺酶類　hexosaminidases
己糖二磷酸盐类/己糖二磷酸鹽類　hexosediphosphates
己糖基转移酶类/己糖基轉移酶類　hexosyltransferases
己糖激酶/己糖激酶　hexokinase
己糖类/己糖類　hexoses
己糖[磷酸]激酶/異磷酸鹽酵素　heterophosphatase
己糖磷酸盐类/己糖磷酸鹽類　hexosephosphates
己糖醛酸/己糖醛酸　hexuronic acid
己糖脎/己糖脎　hexosazone
己糖酸/己糖酸　hexonic acid
己糖脱氢酶/己糖脱氫酶　hexose dehydrogenase
己糖转移酶/[己糖]轉移酶　transhexosylase
己酮可可碱/己酮可哥鹼　pentoxifylline
己酮类/己酮類　hexanones
己酮酸/己酮酸　ketocaproic acid
己酮糖/己酮醣　ketohexose
己酮糖酸/己酮醣酸　ketohexonic acid
己烷/己烷　hexane
己烷雌酚/己烷雌酚　hexestrol
己烷磺酸钠/己烷磺酸鈉　sodium hexanesulfonate
己烷类/己烷類　hexanes
己酰基/己醯基　caproyl
挤夹式带环/夾捏帶環　pinch band
挤夹式固位带环/夾捏接合帶環　pinch attachment band
挤奶工结节/擠奶員結節　milker nodule
挤乳工痉挛/擠乳工痙攣　milker spasm
挤压伤/擠壓傷　crush injury
挤压性肾炎/擠壓性腎炎　crush nephritis

挤压综合征/壓擊症候群　crush pattern, crush syndrome
脊背静脉/脊背静脈　dorsispinal vein
脊顶/脊上脊　crest of ridge
脊肌征/脊柱性徵象　spinal sign
脊静脉/脊静脈　spinal vein
脊膜脊髓膨出/脊髓脊髓膜膨出　meningomyelocele
脊膜脊髓神经根炎/脊髓膜脊髓根炎　meningomyeloradiculitis
脊膜脊髓炎/脊膜脊髓炎　meningomyelitis
脊膜瘤/脊膜瘤　spinal meningioma
脊膜炎/脊髓膜炎　spinal meningitis
脊上型室间隔缺损/脊上型室間隔缺損　supracristal ventricular septal defect
脊神经/脊神經　spinal nerve
脊神经丛/脊神經叢　plexus of spinal nerve
脊神经干/脊神經幹　trunk of spinal nerve
脊神经根/脊神經根　spinal nerve root
脊神经根切断术/脊神經根切斷術　rhizotomy
脊神经根丝/脊神經根絲　rootlets of spinal nerve
脊神经沟/脊神經溝　sulcus for spinal nerve
脊神经后根/脊神經後根　posterior root of spinal nerve
脊神经后根切断术/脊神經後根切斷術　spinal posterior rhizotomy
脊神经后支/脊神經後支　posterior branch of spinal nerve
脊神经脊膜支/脊神經脊膜支　meningeal branch of spinal nerve
脊神经交通支/脊神經交通支　communicating branch of spinal nerve
脊神经节/脊神經節　spinal ganglion, spinal ganglia
脊神经麻痹性脊髓灰质炎/脊神經麻痺性脊髓灰質炎,急性脊髓侧灰質炎　spinal paralytic poliomyelitis
脊神经前根/脊神經前根　anterior root of spinal nerve
脊神经前根切断术/脊神經前根切斷術　anterior rhizotomy
脊神经前支/脊神經前支　anterior branch of spinal nerve
脊髓/脊髓　spinal cord, spinal marrow
脊髓白质/脊髓白質　white matter of spinal cord
脊髓白质病/脊髓白質病　leukomyelopathy
脊髓白质炎/脊髓白質炎　leukomyelitis
脊髓病/脊髓病　myelopathy
脊髓病变/脊髓病變　myeleterosis
脊髓病变性肌萎缩/脊髓病變性肌萎縮　myelopathic

muscular atrophy
脊髓病性斑/脊髓病斑　taches spinale
脊髓病性膀胱/脊髓病性膀胱　cord bladder
脊髓侧角/脊髓側角　lateral horn of spinal cord
脊髓侧索及前角综合征/脊髓側索及前角症候群　lateral cord and associated anterior cornual syndrome
脊髓出血/脊髓出血　hematomyelia
脊髓挫伤/脊髓挫傷　contusion of spinal cord
脊髓切开刀/脊髓刀　myelotome
脊髓倒经/脊髓倒經　myelomenia
脊髓电[流]图/脊髓電圖　electrospinogram
脊髓电描记术/脊髓電圖學　electromyelography
脊髓顶盖的/脊髓與四疊體的　spinotectal
脊髓顶盖束/脊髓四疊板徑　spinotectal tract
脊髓[动脉]栓塞/脊髓栓塞　spinal embolism
脊髓段动脉/脊髓段動脈　segmental medullary artery
脊髓多神经炎/脊髓多神經炎　myeloneuritis
脊髓发育不良/脊髓發育不良　myelodysplasia
脊髓发育不全/脊髓發育不全　myelatelia
脊髓肥大/脊髓肥大　myelauxe
脊髓橄榄束/橄欖脊髓徑,脊髓橄欖徑　spino-olivary tract
脊髓根/脊髓根　spinal root
脊髓共济失调/脊髓性失調症　spinal ataxia
脊髓后侧索综合征/脊髓後外索症候群　posterolateral syndrome
脊髓后动脉/脊髓後動脈　posterior spinal artery
脊髓后副正中沟/脊髓後副正中溝　suicus intermedius posterior medullae spinalis
脊髓后角/脊髓後角　posterior horn of spinal cord
脊髓后静脉/脊髓後静脈　posterior spinal vein
脊髓后内侧核/脊髓後内側核　posteromedial nucleus of spinal cord
脊髓后索综合征/脊髓後索症候群　posterior cord syndrome
脊髓后外侧沟/脊髓後外側溝　posterolateral sulcus of spinal cord, sulcus lateralis posterior medullae spinalis
脊髓后外侧核/脊髓後外側核　posterolateral nucleus of spinal cord
脊髓后外侧后核/脊髓後外側後核　retroposterolateral nucleus of spinal cord
脊髓后外侧静脉/脊髓後外側静脈　posterolateral spinal vein
脊髓后正中隔/脊髓後正中隔　posterior median septum of spinal cord
脊髓后正中沟/脊髓後正中溝　posterior median sulcus of spinal cord
脊髓后中间沟/脊髓後中間溝　posteror intermediate sulcus of spinal cord
脊髓后中央灰质综合征/脊髓灰質中後部症候群　centroposterior syndrome
脊髓灰质/脊髓灰質　gray matter of spinal cord, gray substance of spinal cord
脊髓灰质病/脊髓灰質病　poliomyelopathy
脊髓灰质角炎/脊髓灰質角炎　cornual myelitis
脊髓灰质炎/脊髓灰質炎　poliomyelitis
脊髓灰质炎病毒/脊髓灰質炎病毒　poliomyelitis virus
脊髓灰质炎病毒疫苗/脊髓灰質炎病毒疫苗　poliovirus vaccine
脊髓灰质炎后综合征/脊髓灰質炎後症候群　post poliomyelitis syndrome
脊髓灰质原节/脊髓灰質節　polioneuromere
脊髓灰质综合征/脊髓灰質症候群　gray spinal syndrome
脊髓肌的/脊髓與肌的　spinomuscular
脊髓肌束/脊髓肌徑　spinomuscular tract
脊髓积水空洞症/積水空洞症　hydrosyringomyelia
脊髓疾病/脊髓疾病　disease of spinal cord
脊髓脊膜膨出/脊髓脊膜膨出　meningomyelocele
脊髓脊膜炎/脊髓脊膜炎　myelomeningitis
脊髓胶质/脊髓膠質　gelatinous substance of spinal cord
脊髓角/脊髓角　cornua of spinal cord
脊髓[节]段/脊髓節[段],脊節　spinal segment, segment of spinal cord
脊髓节段综合征/脊髓節段症候群　segmentary syndrome
脊髓结核瘤/脊髓結核瘤　spinal cord tuberculoma
脊髓空洞症/脊髓空洞症　syringomyelia
脊髓空洞症性感觉分离/脊髓空洞性感覺變異　syringomyelic dissociation
脊髓空洞综合征/脊髓空洞症候群　central cord syndrome
脊髓孔/脊髓孔　myelopore
脊髓痨/脊髓痨　tabes dorsalis
脊髓痨的/脊髓痨的　tabetic
脊髓痨性耳痛/脊髓痨性耳痛　tabetic otalgia
脊髓痨性感觉分离/脊髓痨性感覺變異　tabetic dissociation
脊髓痨性骨关节病/脊髓痨性骨關節病　tabetic osteoarthropathy
脊髓痨性关节病/脊髓痨關節病　tabetic arthropathy

脊髓痨性面具感/哈欽生氏脊髓癆面貌　tabetic mask
脊髓痨性足病/脊髓癆性足病　tabetic foot
脊髓疗法/脊髓療法　medullotherapy
脊髓裂/脊髓裂　myeloschisis
脊髓裂伤/脊髓裂傷　laceration of spinal cord
脊髓麻醉/脊髓麻醉　medullary narcosis
脊髓梅毒/脊髓梅毒　myelosyphilis
脊髓梅毒瘤/脊髓梅毒瘤　spinal cord syphiloma
脊髓膜中央管突出/脊髓膜中央管膨出　syringomeningocele
脊髓囊肿/脊髓管囊腫　myelocyst
脊髓内脂肪瘤/脊髓内脂肪瘤　intramedullary lipoma
脊髓脓肿/脊髓膿腫　spinal cord abscess
脊髓偏侧损伤/單側損害，半側損害　hemilesion
[脊髓]偏侧综合征/單側症候群　hemisyndrome
脊髓前侧索硬化/前側索硬化　anterolateral sclerosis
脊髓前侧索综合征/脊髓前側索症候群　anterolateral syndrome
脊髓[前侧柱]切断术/脊索切開術　chordotomy
脊髓前动脉/脊髓前動脈　anterior spinal artery
脊髓前副正中沟/脊髓前副正中溝　sulcus intermedius anterior medullae spinalis
脊髓前角/[脊髓]前角　ventricornu
脊髓前角综合征/脊髓前角症候群　anterior cornual syndrome
脊髓前静脉/脊髓前靜脈　anterior spinal vein
脊髓前连合切断术/脊髓前連合切斷術　anterior commissurotomy of spinal cord
脊髓前内侧核/脊髓前内側核　anteromedial nucleus of spinal cord
[脊髓]前索综合征/前索帶症候群　anterior cord syndrome
脊髓前外侧沟/脊髓前外側溝　anterolateral sulcus of spinal cord, anterolateral groove of spinal cord
脊髓前外侧核/脊髓前外側核　anterolateral nucleus of spinal cord
脊髓前外侧静脉/脊髓前外側靜脈　anterolateral spinal vein
脊髓前外侧束切断术/脊髓前外側束切斷術　anteriolateral cordotomy
脊髓前正中沟/脊髓前正中溝　anterior paramedian groove of spinal cord
脊髓前正中裂[隙]/脊髓前正中裂[隙]　anterior median fissure of spinal cord
脊髓切开术/脊神經切斷術　myelotomy
脊髓丘脑侧束/脊髓丘腦側徑　lateral spinothalamic tract
脊髓丘脑的/脊髓與丘腦的　spinothalamic
脊髓丘脑腹侧束/腹側脊髓丘腦徑　ventral spinothalamic tract
脊髓丘脑前束/脊髓丘腦前束，前脊髓丘腦徑　anterior spinothalamic tract
脊髓丘脑束/脊髓丘腦徑　spinothalamic tract
脊髓丘系/脊髓丘徑　spinal lemniscus
脊髓缺血/脊髓缺血　spinal cord ischemia
脊髓软化/脊髓軟化　myelomalacia
脊髓三叉神经核/脊髓三叉神經核　spinal trigeminal nucleus
脊髓闪烁图/脊髓閃爍圖　myeloscintogram
脊髓神经根病/脊髓脊神經根病　myeloradiculopathy
脊髓神经根发育异常/脊髓脊神經根發育不良　myeloradiculodysplasia
脊髓神经[后]根炎/脊髓神經後根炎　myeloradiculitis
脊髓神经性肌萎缩/脊髓神經萎縮　spinoneural atrophy
脊髓生殖中枢/生殖脊髓中樞　genital center
脊髓视神经病/脊髓視神經病　myelo-opticoneuropathy
脊髓室/脊髓室　ventricle of cord
脊髓受压/脊髓受壓　compression of spinal cord
脊髓束间束变性/脊髓束間束變性　comma degeneration
脊髓栓系综合征/脊髓栓系症候群　tethered cord syndrome
脊髓损伤/脊髓損傷　spinal cord injury
脊髓索切断术/脊髓索切斷術　cordotomy
脊髓索炎/脊髓索炎　funicular myelitis
脊髓痛/脊髓痛　myelalgia
脊髓突出/脊髓膨出　myelocele
脊髓网状结构/脊髓網狀結構　reticular formation of spinal cord
脊髓网状束/脊髓網狀徑　spinoreticular tract
脊髓萎缩/脊髓萎縮　amyelotrophy
脊髓纤维束/脊髓纖維徑　fiber tract of spinal cord
脊髓小脑变性/脊髓小腦變性　spinocerebellar degeneration
脊髓小脑的/脊髓與小腦的　spinocerebellar
脊髓小脑腹侧束/前脊髓小腦徑　anterior spinocerebellar tract
脊髓小脑共济失调/脊髓小腦共濟失調　spinocerebellar ataxias
脊髓小脑后束/脊髓小腦後徑　posterior spinocerebellar tract
脊髓小脑前束/脊髓小腦前束，脊髓小腦前徑

anterior spinocerebellar tract, tractus spinocerebellaris anterior
脊髓小脑束/脊髓小腦束 spinocerebellar tract
脊髓小脑性共济失调/脊髓小腦性失調症 spinocerebellar ataxia
脊髓兴奋药/脊髓興奮藥 spinant
脊髓型颈椎病/頸部脊椎脊髓病 cervical spondylotic myelopathy
脊髓性肌萎缩/脊髓性肌萎縮, Duchenne-Aran 二氏肌萎縮 spinal muscular atrophy, Duchenne-Aran muscular atrophy
脊髓性偏身麻木/脊髓性單側麻木 spinal hemianesthesia
脊髓性神经衰弱/脊髓性神經衰弱 myelasthenia
脊髓胸段/胸脊髓 thoracic spinal cord
脊髓休克/脊髓休克 spinal shock
脊髓血管畸形自发栓塞症/Foix-Alajouanine 二氏病 Foix-Alajouanine disease
脊髓血管疾病/脊髓血管疾病 spinal cord vascular disease
脊髓压迫症/脊髓壓迫症 spinal cord compression
脊髓炎/脊髓炎 myelitis
脊髓液/脊髓液 spinal fluid
脊[髓]液血色症/脊液紅變 erythrochromia
脊髓诱导/脊髓誘導 spinal induction
脊髓诱发电位/脊髓誘發電位 spinal evoked potential
脊髓圆锥/脊髓圓錐 conus medullaris, terminal cone of spinal cord
脊髓运动神经元/脊髓神經肌肉運動單位 dynamoneure
脊髓造影术/脊髓 X 光攝影術 myelography
脊髓真菌性肉芽肿/脊髓真菌性肉芽腫 mycotic granuloma of spinal cord
脊髓震荡/脊髓震蕩 concussion of spinal cord
脊髓[直]流电疗法/脊髓電療法 spinogalvanization
脊髓质性膀胱/弦張性膀胱 string bladder
脊髓中间带/脊髓中間帶 intermediate zone of spinal cord
脊髓中央管/脊髓中央管 central canal of spinal cord
脊髓中央管扩张/脊髓中央管擴張 syringomyelus
脊髓中央管突出/脊髓中央管膨出 syringomyelocele
脊髓中央核/脊髓中央核 central nucleus of spinal cord
脊髓肿瘤/脊髓腫瘤 spinal cord neoplasm
脊髓周造影术/脊髓膜 X 光攝影法 perimyelography
脊髓蛛网膜/脊髓蛛網膜, 脊蜘蛛膜 spinal arachnoid mater, arachnoid of spinal cord
脊髓蛛网膜下[腔]阻滞/脊髓蜘蛛網膜下腔阻斷 spinal subarachnoid block
脊髓蛛网膜炎/脊髓蛛網膜炎 arachnoiditis of spinal cord
脊髓注射/脊髓注射 spinal injection
脊髓纵裂/脊髓縱裂 diastematomyelia
脊髓纵裂畸形/雙脊髓畸形 diplomyelia
脊髓纵切开术/脊髓縱切開術 commissural myelotomy
脊髓阻滞/脊髓阻斷 spinal block
脊索/脊索 notochord
脊索动物/脊索動物 chordate
脊索动物门/脊索動物門 Chordata
脊索骨骼/脊索骨骼 chordoskeleton
脊索裂畸形/脊索裂畸形 split notochord deformity
脊索瘤/脊索瘤 chordoma
脊索颅端/脊索頭端 cephalostyle
脊索膜/脊索膜 perichord
脊索形成/脊索形成, 脊索生成 notogenesis
脊痛/脊痛 spinalgia
脊尾麻醉/脊尾麻醉法 caudal anesthesia
脊下型室间隔缺损/脊下型室間隔缺損 infracristal ventricular septal defect
脊线/脊線 ridge line
脊液压系数/髓壓比 spinal quotient
脊支/脊支 spinal branch
脊中/脊中 jizhong, DU6
脊柱/脊柱 vertebral column, back bone
脊柱不全裂/部分脊柱側裂 mesorachischisis
脊柱部/脊柱部 vertebral part
脊柱侧凸/脊柱側凸, 脊柱側彎 scoliosis
脊柱侧凸[测量]计/脊柱側凸彎度計 scoliosometer
脊柱侧凸矫正器/脊柱側彎矯正器 scoliotone
脊柱侧凸症/脊柱側凸症 scoliosis
脊柱的/脊[柱]的 spinal
脊柱骶曲/脊柱骶曲 sacral curvature of vertebral column
脊柱骨折/脊柱骨折 fracture of spine
脊柱骨赘病/脊柱骨贅病 spinal osteophytosis
脊柱后凸/脊柱後凸 kyphosis, hump back
脊柱后凸侧弯/脊柱後側凸 kyphoscoliosis
脊柱疾病/脊柱疾病 spinal diseases
脊柱结核/脊椎結核 spinal tuberculosis
脊柱颈曲/脊柱頸曲 cervical curvature of vertebral column
脊柱静脉/脊柱靜脈 veins of vertebral column
脊柱联胎/脊柱連胎 spondylodymus

脊柱联胎畸形/脊柱連胎畸形　spondylodidymia
脊柱裂/脊柱裂　rachischisis, hydrocele spinalis
脊柱描记器/脊柱描記器　rachigraph
脊柱扭转测量器/脊柱扭轉度計　torsionometer
脊柱旁的/脊柱旁的　paravertebral
脊柱旁骨膜外胸廓成形术/脊柱旁骨膜外胸廓成形術　paravertebral extraperiosteal thoracoplasty
脊柱旁线/脊柱[旁]線　paravertebral line
脊柱旁胸廓成形术/脊柱旁胸廓成形術　paravertebral thoracoplasty
脊柱旁阻滞/脊柱旁阻斷麻醉　paravertebral block
脊柱器质性侧凸/器質性脊柱側彎　organic scoliosis
脊柱前侧凸/脊柱前側凸　lordoscoliosis
脊柱前凸过度/脊柱過度前凸或彎　hyperlordosis
脊柱强直/[風濕性]脊椎僵直　poker spine
脊柱区/脊部　vertebral region
脊柱全裂/脊柱全裂　holorachischisis
脊柱融合术/脊柱融合術, 脊柱湊合術　spondylosyndesis
脊柱损伤/脊柱損傷　spinal injury
脊柱凸度测量法/脊柱側彎計　scoliosiometry
脊柱推拿/脊柱推拿　spinal manipulation
脊柱外静脉/脊柱外靜脈　external vertebral column vein
脊柱弯度计/脊柱彎度計　rachiometer
脊柱弯曲/脊柱彎曲　spinal curvature
脊柱线/椎骨線　vertebral line
脊柱小关节综合征/脊柱小關節症候群　facet syndrome
脊柱胸曲/脊柱胸曲　thoracic curvature of vertebral column
脊柱炎/脊椎炎　spondylitis
脊柱腰曲/脊柱腰曲　lumbar curvature of vertebral column
脊柱征/脊骨徵象　spine sign
[脊柱]椎间孔/[脊柱]椎間孔　intervertebral foramen
脊椎穿刺/脊椎穿刺術　spinal puncture
脊椎穿刺针/脊椎穿刺針, 腰椎穿刺針　spinal needle
脊椎的/脊椎的, 椎骨的　vertebral
脊椎动物/脊椎動物　vertebrate
脊椎动物病毒/脊椎動物病毒　vertebrate virus
脊椎动物光感受器/脊椎動物光感受器　vertebrate photoreceptor
脊椎干骺端发育不良/脊椎骨端發育不全　spondyloepimetaphyseal dysplasia
脊椎沟/椎溝　vertebral groove
脊椎骨骺发育不良/脊椎骨骺鈣化缺陷　spondyloepiphyseal dysplasia
脊椎骨软骨病/脊椎骨軟骨病　vertebral osteochondrosis
脊椎关节疾病/脊椎關節疾病　spondyloarthropathy
[脊]椎关节强硬/椎關節粘連, 椎關節病　spondylosis
脊椎关节炎/脊椎關節炎　vertebral arthritis
脊椎滑脱/脊骨脫離　spondylolysis
脊椎化脓/脊椎化膿　spondylopyosis
脊椎结核/脊椎結核　tuberculosis of spine
脊椎疗法/脊椎療法　spondylotherapy
脊椎麻醉/脊髓麻醉法　spinal anesthesia
脊椎[膜]穿刺/椎管穿刺術　thecal puncture
脊椎旁神经麻醉/脊柱旁麻醉法　paravertebral anesthesia
脊椎前移/脊椎前移　spondylolisthesis
脊椎融合术/脊椎融合術　spondylodesis
脊椎软化/脊椎軟化　spondylomalacia
脊椎痛/脊椎痛　spondylalgia
脊椎脱位/脊椎脱位　vertebral dislocation
脊椎下移/椎骨下移症　spondylizema
脊椎指压治疗师/按脊師　chiropractor
脊椎肿瘤/脊椎腫瘤　spinal neoplasm
脊椎阻滞/脊椎阻斷　vertebral block
麂革样皮肤/麂皮樣皮膚　wash-leather skin
计划/計劃　plan
计划生育服务/計劃生育服務　family planning service
计划生育政策/計劃生育政策　family planning policy
计量阀门/定量閥　metering valve
计数/計數　counting
计数池/計數池　counting cell
计数器/計數器　counter
计算不能/計算不能　anarithmia
计算的/計算的　computed
计算机/電腦　computer
计算机断层扫描/電腦斷層掃描　computed tomographic scan
计算机辅助放射疗法/電腦輔助放射療法　computer-assisted radiotherapy
计算机辅助放射摄影影像解释/電腦輔助放射攝影影像解釋　computer-assisted radiographic image interpretation
计算机辅助放射治疗计划/電腦輔助放射治療計劃　computer-assisted radiotherapy planning
计算机辅助外科手术/電腦輔助外科手術　computer-assisted surgery

计算机辅助药物分析/電腦輔助藥物分析 computational pharmaceutical analysis, computer-aided pharmaceutical analysis
计算机辅助药物疗法/電腦輔助藥物療法 computer-assisted drug therapy
计算机辅助药物设计/電腦輔助藥物設計 computer-aided drug design
计算机辅助诊断/電腦輔助診斷 computer-assisted diagnosis
计算机辅助治疗/電腦輔助治療 computer-assisted therapy
计算机化病案系统/電腦化病案系統 computerized medical records system
计算机控制发酵罐/電腦控制發酵槽 computer controlled fermenter
计算机体层摄影/電腦斷層掃描 computerized tomography, CT
计算机体层摄影结肠检查/電腦體層攝影結腸檢查 computed tomographic colonography
计算机图形学/電腦圖形學 computer graphics
计算生物学/計算生物學 computational biology
记波术/波動描記法 kymography
记波[纹]器/描波器,波動描記器 cymograph
记波[纹]图/記錄圖 kymogram
记存模型/記存模型 record model
记录/記錄 record
记录连结/記錄連結 record-linkage
记录连结性研究/記錄連結性研究 record-linkage study
记时脉搏描记器/記時脈波計 chronosphygmograph
记时器/記時標志 time marker
记忆保持力/記憶保持力 retention
记忆错误/記憶錯誤,記憶失常 paramnesia
记忆[力]/記憶 memory
记忆[力]减退/記憶減退 hypomnesis
记忆缺损/記憶力不足 retention defect
记忆B细胞/記憶B細胞 memory B cell
记忆T细胞/記憶T細胞 memory T cell
记忆细胞/記憶細胞 memory cell
记忆影像/記憶像 memory image
记忆障碍/記憶障礙 memory disorder
记忆障碍的/記憶障礙的 dysmnesic
记载生物学/記載生物學 biophysiography
技工室染色/技工室染色 laboratory staining
技工心理学/勞工心理學,勞動心理學 technopsychology
技术性护理设施/技術性護理設施 skilled nursing facility

季铵化合物/四級銨化合物 quaternary ammonium compound
季德胜蛇药片/季德勝蛇藥片 jidesheng sheyao tablets
季节性情感障碍/季節性情感障礙 seasonal affective disorder
季肋区/季肋部 hypochondriac region
季戊四醇/季戊四醇 pentaerythritol
剂量/劑量 dose, dosage
剂量率/劑量率 dose rate
剂量调整/劑量調定 dose titration
剂量无关型不良反应/劑量無關性藥物不良反應 dose-independent ADR
剂量相关型不良反应/劑量依賴性藥物不良反應 dose-dependent ADR
剂量效应关系/劑量效應關係 dose-effect relationship
剂量效应曲线/劑量效應曲線 dose effect curve
剂量制/劑量制 dosimetric system
剂型/劑型 preparation, dosage form
剂型设计/劑型設計 dosage form design
济川煎/濟川煎 jichuan decoction
济生肾气丸/濟生腎氣丸 jisheng shenqi pills
济阴纲目/濟陰綱目 Outline for Women's Diseases
继承牙/繼承牙 successor
继承牙板/繼承牙板 successional dental lamina
继代培养/繼代培養 subculture
继发闭经/繼發性閉經 secondary amenorrhea
继发变应原/繼發變應原 secondary allergen
继发病/續發病 secondary disease
继发不孕[症]/繼發不孕[症] secondary infertility
继发腭/繼發腭,後起性腭 secondary palate
继发反应/續發反應 secondary reaction
继发肥大性骨关节病/繼發肥大性骨關節病 secondary hypertrophic osteoarthropathy
继发骨/續發骨 secondary bone
继发畸形/繼發畸形 secondary deformity
继发孔型房间隔缺损/繼發心房中隔缺陷 ostium secundum defect
继发囊肿/次囊腫 secondary cyst
继发龋/繼發齲 recurrent caries
继发伤道/繼發傷道 secondary wound tract
继发效应/續發作用 secondary effect
继发性癌/繼發性癌,轉移性癌 secondary carcinoma
继发性瘢痕挛缩/繼發性瘢痕攣縮 extrinsic cicatricial contracture
继发性出血/續發性出血 secondary hemorrhage
继发性动脉瘤/續發性動脈瘤 secondary aneurysm

继发性肥大性骨炎/續發性肥大性骨炎 secondary hypertrophic osteitis
继发性肺结核病/繼發性肺結核病 secondary pulmonary tuberculosis
继发性肺炎/續發性肺炎 secondary pneumonia
继发[性]感染/續發性傳染 secondary infection
继发性高血压/繼發性高血壓 secondary hypertension
继发性骨折/續發性骨折 secondary fracture
继发性红细胞增多/續發性紅血球增多症 secondary polycythemia
继发性甲状旁腺功能亢进症/繼發性甲狀旁腺功能亢進症 secondary hyperparathyroidism
继发性甲状腺功能亢进/續發性甲狀腺機能亢進 secondary hyperthyrodidsm
继发性巨结肠/繼發性巨結腸 secondary megacolon
继发性淋巴水肿/繼發性淋巴水腫 secondary lymphedema
继发性免疫缺陷/繼發性免疫缺陷 secondary immunodeficiency
继发性黏液水肿/續發性黏液水腫 secondary myxedema
继发性帕金森病/繼發性帕金森病 secondary Parkinson disease
继发性皮损/繼發性皮損 secondary lesion
继发性偏斜/繼發偏斜 secondary deviation
继发性贫血/繼發性貧血 secondary anemia
继发性青光眼/續發性青光眼 secondary glaucoma
继发性醛固酮症/繼發性醛固酮症 secondary aldosteronism
继发[性损]伤/繼發[性損]傷 secondary injury
继发性痛风/續發性痛風 secondary gout
继发性痛经/續發性痛經 secondary dysmenorrhea
继发性妄想/次發性妄想 secondary delusion
继发性污染/繼發性汙染 secondary contamination
继发性心肌病/次發性心肌病 secondary cardiomyopathy
继发性血小板减少紫癜/續發性血小板減少紫癜病 secondary thrombocytopenic purpura
继发性牙本质/次生牙質 secondary dentin
继发性阳痿/續發性陽痿 secondary impotence
继发性粘连/繼發性粘連 secondary adhesion
继发原发性肿瘤/繼發原發性腫瘤 the second primary neoplasm
继发作用/繼發作用 secondary action
继续教育/繼續教育 continuing education
继续医学教育/醫學繼續教育 continuing medical education
继续长出/繼續長出 continuous eruption
继续治疗阶段/繼續治療階段 continuation phase of treatment
寄螨目/恙蟲目 Parasitiformes
寄生/寄生 parasitize
寄生虫/寄生物,寄生體 parasite
寄生虫包囊/寄生性囊腫 parasitic cyst
寄生虫病/寄生蟲病 parasitosis
寄生虫病妄想症/寄生蟲病妄想症 delusions of parasitosis
寄生虫虫卵计数/寄生蟲蟲卵計數 parasite egg count
寄生虫的/寄生蟲的,寄生性的 parasitic
寄生虫感染/寄生蟲感染 parasitic infection
寄生虫恐怖症/寄生蟲恐懼症 parasitophobia
寄生虫敏感性试验/寄生蟲敏感性試驗 parasitic sensitivity test
寄生虫肾病/寄生蟲腎病 parasitic nephropathy
寄生虫栓/寄生蟲凝栓 parasitic thrombus
寄生虫栓塞/寄生蟲栓塞 parasitic embolism
寄生虫栓子/寄生物栓子 parasitic embolus
寄生虫妄想症/寄生蟲妄想症 parasitosis delusion
寄生虫性肠疾病/寄生蟲性腸疾病 parasitic intestinal disease
寄生虫性肺疾病/寄生蟲性肺疾病 parasitic lung disease
寄生虫性腹泻/寄生蟲性腹瀉 parasitic diarrhea
寄生虫性肝疾病/寄生蟲性肝疾病 parasitic liver disease
寄生虫性睑炎/寄生蟲性瞼炎 blepharitis parasitica
寄生虫性阑尾炎/寄生蟲性闌尾炎 verminous appendicitis
寄生虫性脓疱病/寄生性膿皰病 impetigo parasitaria
寄生虫性皮肤疾病/寄生蟲性皮膚疾病 parasitic skin disease
寄生虫性前列腺炎/寄生蟲性前列腺炎 parasitic prostatitis
寄生虫性妊娠并发症/寄生蟲性妊娠并發症 parasitic pregnancy complication
寄生虫性湿疹/寄生蟲性濕疹 eczema parasiticum
寄生虫性心肌炎/寄生蟲性心肌炎 parasitic myocarditis
寄生虫性眼感染/寄生蟲性眼感染 parasitic eye infection
寄生虫学/寄生蟲學 parasitology
寄生虫血症/寄生物血症 parasitemia
寄生动物/動物寄生蟲 zooparasite

寄生畸胎/寄生畸胎，畸胎狀寄生物　parasitic monster, teratoid parasite
寄生目/寄生蟲目　Parasita
寄生曲菌/寄生麴菌　Aspergillus parasiticus
寄生胎/寄生胎　parasitus, parasitic fetus
寄生物感染/寄生物感染　parasitization
寄生物性阉/寄生物性閹割　parasitic castration
寄生性耳炎/寄生性耳炎　parasitic otitis
寄生性色素缺乏/寄生性無色素症　achromia parasitica
寄生性须疮/寄生性鬚瘡　parasitic sycosis
寄生植物/寄生植物　phytoparasite
寄生植物性感染/寄生植物性感染　phytogenic infection
寄托医疗设施/寄託醫療設施　residential facility
寄托治疗/寄託治療　residential treatment
绩效/績效　performance
加贝酯/加貝酯　gabexate
加成的/加成的　additive
加成化合物/加成化合物　addition compound
加德纳-布朗试验/加-布二氏試驗　Gardiner-Brown test
加德纳综合征/加德纳症候群　Gardner syndrome
加顿伤寒病饮食/Garton 氏飲食　Garton diet
加尔桑综合征/加桑症候群　Garcin syndrome
加夫基表/加夫基氏表　Gaffky scale
加辅料炒/加輔料炒　fried with adjuvant material
加盖术/棚架手術　shelf operation
加工/加工　processing
加工乳/改變乳　modified milk
加工信号/加工信號　processing signal
加宫之人/加宫之人　atypical earth-phase person, more optimistic
加固用绷带/加固用繃帶　impregnated bandage
加合物/加合物　adduct
加和性/加成性　additivity
加减葳蕤汤/加減葳蕤湯　jiajian weirui decoction
加聚物/加分子聚合物　addition polymer
加拉碘铵/加拉碘銨　gallamine
加兰他敏/加蘭他敏　galantamine
加兰肽/加蘭肽　galanin
加勒比海黑人儿童面疹/加勒比海黑人兒童面疹　facial Afro-Caribbean childhood eruption
加力带环/增力帶環　reinforced band
加立新/[类]糊精物质　gallisin
加利福尼亚脑炎/加利福尼亞腦炎　California encephalitis
加利福尼亚脑炎病毒/加利福尼亞腦炎病毒　California encephalitis virus
加利·马伊尼尼试验/加曼尼氏試驗　Galli Mainini test
加利移植物/蓋利移植物　Gallie transplant
加帽位点/加帽位點　cap site
加姆基敷料/蓋吉氏敷料　Gamgee tissue
加拿大松脂/加拿大松脂　Canada pitch
加强创伤生命支持/加強創傷生命支持　advanced trauma life support
加强剂量/加強劑量　booster dose
加强免疫接种/加強免疫接種　secondary immunization
加强生命支持/加強生命支持　advanced life support
加强通气/加強通氣　augmented ventilation
加强心脏生命支持/加強心臟生命支持　advanced cardiac life support
加强治疗室/加護病房　intensive therapy room
加强注射/激發注射　booster injection
加权因子/加權因子　weighter factor
加权直线回归/加權直線回歸　weighted linear regression
加热沉淀素/加熱沈澱素　coctoprecipitin
加热蛋白/加熱過蛋白質　coctoprotein
加热免疫原/加熱免疫原　cocto-immunogen
加热贮槽进样器/加熱貯槽進樣器　heatable reservoir inlet
加塞管/加塞利氏管　Gasserian duct
加塞综合征/Gasser 氏症候群　Gasser syndrome
加氏计数法/卡夫基氏度標　Gaffky scale
加速/加速　accelerate
加速的/加速的　accelerated
加速度/加速度　acceleration
加速反应/加速反應　accelerated response
加速房室结合节律/加速性房室結合心律　accelerated atrioventricular junctional rhythm
加速神经/加速神經　accelerator nerve
加速性房室结传导/加速性房室結傳導　enhanced atrioventricular nodal conduction
加速性交接区心律/加速性交接區心律　accelerated junctional rhythm
加速性排斥反应/加速性排斥反應　accelerated rejection
加速性室性自主节律/加速心室本身節律　accelerated idioventricular rhythm
加速性[损]伤/加速性[損]傷　acceleration injury
加特纳管/加特納管　Gartnerian duct
加甜剂/加甜味劑　edulcorant
加瓦尔肌/Gavard 氏肌　Gavard muscle

加性基因/加性基因　additive gene
加压/壓迫　compression
加压包扎法/壓力敷料　pressure dressing
加压包扎止血法/加壓包扎止血法　compression bandage hemostatic method
加压催产素/加壓催產素　vasotocin
加压钢板固定[术]/加壓鋼板固定[術]　compression plating
加压灌注/加壓灌注　enhancing perfusion
加压过滤/加壓過濾　pressure filtration
加压疗法/加壓療法　compression therapy
加压麻醉/壓迫麻醉法　pressure anesthesia
加压神经/昇壓神經　pressor nerve
加压素/[血管]昇壓素　vasopressin
加压袜/加壓襪子　compression stocking
加压印模/壓迫塑型　compression molding
加亚尔综合征/Gailliard氏症候群　Gailliard syndrome
加氧酶/加氧酶　oxygenase
加药配液/加藥配液　admixture
加重杂音/加重雜音　accentuated murmur
夹板/夾板　splint
夹板骨/夾板骨　splenial bone
夹板固定疗法/夾板固定療法　splint-fixing therapy
夹板卡环/夾板卡環　splint clasp
夹肠器/夾腸器　splanchnotribe
夹持进针法/夾持進針法　fingers-squeezed-needle inserting
夹发试验/夾髮試驗　pinch-pulling test
夹合/夾具縫術　clamp suture
夹合缝/夾合縫,夾合連接,溝縫　schindylesys, wedge-and-groove suture
夹肌/夾肌　splenius
夹挤分骨/夾擠分骨　bone-separation by pinching-squeezing manipulation
夹脊/夾脊　jiaji, EX-B2
夹具/夾　clamp
夹圈/夾環　clamp band
夹入照射/夾入照射　sandwich irradiation
夹心技术/夾心技術　sandwich technique
夹心杂交/夾心雜交　sandwich hybridization
夹指试验/夾指試驗　clipping paper test
夹竹桃麻素/加拿大麻素　apocynin
夹竹桃中毒/夾竹桃中毒　oleander poisoning, oleandrism
痂/痂　crust, scab
痂性湿疹/痂性濕疹　eczema crustosum
痂疹/痂疹　crustaceous eruption

家尘螨/家塵螨　house-dust mite
[家畜]前胸/家畜之前胸　brisket
家畜硒中毒/鹼質病　alkali disease
家畜消化不良症/家畜消化不良症　hooves
家禽白喉/家禽白喉　avian diphtheria
家禽产品/家禽產品　poultry product
家禽疾病/家禽疾病　poultry disease
家禽伤寒/家禽傷寒病　fowl typhoid
家鼠螨/家鼠螨　house mouse mite
家庭/家庭　family
家庭保健/居家照護　home care
家庭保健机构/家庭保健機構　home care agency
家庭保健助手/家庭保健助手　home health aide
家庭暴力/家庭暴力　family violence
家庭冲突/家庭衝突　family conflict
家庭出诊/出診　house call
家庭档案/家庭檔案　family folder
家[庭]访[视]/家庭訪視　home visit
家庭分娩/家庭分娩　home childbirth
家庭抚养子女补助/家庭撫養子女補助　aid to families with dependent children
家庭功能/家庭功能　family function
家庭关系/家庭關係　family relation
家庭护理/家庭護理　family nursing
家庭结构/家庭結構　family structure
家庭类型/家户類型,家户形式　household type
家庭内资源/家庭内資源　intra-familial resource
家庭评估/家庭評估　family assessment
家庭取向/家庭取向　family-oriented
家庭圈/家庭圈　family circle
家庭全胃肠外营养/家庭全胃腸外營養　home total parenteral nutrition
家庭生活周期/家庭生活週期　family life cycle
家庭事故/家庭事故　home accident
家庭输注疗法/家庭輸注療法　home infusion therapy
家庭托儿及病人照管/家庭託兒及病人照管　foster home care
家庭危机/家庭危機　family crisis
家庭卫生/家庭衛生　family health
家庭胃肠外营养/家庭胃腸外營養　home parenteral nutrition
家庭心理疗法/家庭心理療法　family therapy
家庭血液透析/家庭血液透析　home hemodialysis
家庭医疗保健服务/家庭醫療保健服務　home care service
家庭医师/家庭醫師　family doctor
家庭医学/家庭醫學　domestic medicine, family

medicine
家庭咨询/家庭會談　family counseling
家庭资源/家庭資源　family resource
家务/家庭工作　house work
家养动物/家養動物　domestic animal
家蝇/家蠅　house flies
家用治疗牙科装置/家用治療牙科裝置　home care dental device
家族/家族　kindred
家族的/家族的　familial
家族史/家族病史　family history
家族图/家族圖　genogram
家族外的/家族外的　extra-familial
家族外资源/家族外資源　extra-familial resource
家族性部分脂肪营养不良/家族性部分脂肪營養不良　familial partial lipodystrophy
家族性肠息肉病/家族性腸息肉病　familial intestinal polyposis
家族性低磷性骨疾病/家族性低磷酸骨疾病　familial hypophosphatemic bone disease
家族性低磷血症/家族性低磷酸鹽血症　familial hypophosphatemia
家族性地中海热/家族性地中海熱　familial Mediterranean fever
家族性淀粉样变/家族性澱粉樣變　familial amyloidosis
家族性淀粉样神经病/家族性澱粉樣神經病　familial amyloid neuropathy
家族性动脉粥样硬化/家族性動脈粥樣硬化　familial atherosclerosis
家族性多发性毛细管扩张/家族多發性毛細血管擴張　familial multiple telangiectasia
家族性多发性内分泌功能障碍/家族性多發性内分泌功能失調　familial multiple endocrine dysfunction
家族性非典型痣-恶性黑色素瘤综合征/家族性非典型痣-惡性黑色素瘤症候群　Fanconi
家族性非溶血性黄疸/家族非溶血性黄疸　familial non-hemolytic jaundice
家族性肺间质纤维化/家族性肺間質纖維化　familial pulmonary interstitial fibrosis
家族性肝炎/家族性肝炎　familial hepatitis
家族性高胆固醇血症/家族性高膽固醇血症　familial hypercholesterolemia
家族性高甘油三酯血症/家族性高三酸甘油脂血症　familial hypertriglyceridemia
家族性高密度脂蛋白缺乏/家族性高密度脂蛋白缺乏症　familial high density lipoprotein deficiency
家族性高α脂蛋白血症/家族性高α脂蛋白血症　familial hyper alpha lipoproteinemia
家族性高脂蛋白症第三型/家族性高脂蛋白症第三型　familial hyperlipoproteinemia type Ⅲ
家族性共济运动失调/家族性共濟運動失調　family ataxia
家族性混合性高脂血症/家族性混合性高脂血症　familial combined hyperlipidemia
家族性疾病/家族性疾病　familial disorder
家族性脊髓肌萎缩/家族性脊髓肌萎縮症　familial spinal muscular atrophy
家族性甲状腺肿/家族性甲狀腺腫　familial goiter
家族性胶样变性/家族性膠狀變性　familial colloid degeneration
家族性角化不良性黑头粉刺/家族性角化不良性粉刺　familial dyskeratotic comedone
家族性结肠息肉病/家族性結腸息肉病　familial polyposis coli
家族性进行性色素沉着/家族性進行性色素沈著　familial progressive hyperpigmentation
家族性巨颌症/颌骨增大症　cherubism
家族性抗维生素D佝偻病/家族性抗維生素D佝僂病　familial vitamin D resistant ricket
家族性颏骨纤维化发育不良/家族性頦骨纖維化發育不全　familial fibrous dysplasia of the jaw
家族性连续性脱皮综合征/家族性連續性脫皮症候群　familial continual skin peeling syndrome
家族性良性慢性天疱疮/家族良性慢性天疱瘡　familial benign chronic pemphigus
家族性良性天疱疮/家族性良性天疱瘡　familial benign pemphigus
家族性良性血尿/家族性良性血尿　benign familial hematuria
家族性卵磷脂胆固醇酰基转移酶缺乏症/家族性卵磷脂膽固醇醯基轉移酶缺乏症　familial lecithin cholesterol acyltransferase deficiency
家族性脑淀粉样血管病变/家族性腦澱粉樣血管病變　familial cerebral amyloid angiopathy
家族性脑中叶硬化/家族性腦中葉硬化　aplasia axialis extracorticalis congenita
家族性黏液血管纤维瘤/家族性黏液血管纖維瘤　familial myxovascular fibroma
家族性皮肤胶原瘤/家族性皮膚膠原瘤　familial cutaneous collagenoma
家族性醛固酮缺乏/家族性醛固酮缺乏　familial aldosterone deficiency
家族性色素性紫癜疹/家族性色素沈著性紫癜疹　familial pigmented purpuric eruption

家族性身材矮小/家族性身材矮小　familial short stature
家族性肾炎/家族性腎炎　familial nephritis
家族性噬血细胞性/家族性吞噬血色素性　familial hemophagocytic
家族性双侧巨细胞瘤/家族性兩側巨細胞瘤　familial bilateral giant cell tumor
家族性网状组织细胞增多症/家族性組織細胞網狀增生症　familial histiocytic reticulosis
家族性无胆尿性黄疸/家族性無膽尿性黃疸　familial acholuric jaundice
家族性下颌-肢端发育不全/家族性下頜骨與肢端發育異常　familial mandibulo-acral dysplasia
家族性心脏和上肢异常综合征/Holt-Oram 二氏症候群　Holt-Oram syndrome
家族性婴儿黑矇症/家族性嬰兒黑矇症　infantile amaurotic familial disease
家族性载脂蛋白 c Ⅱ 缺乏症/家族性載脂蛋白 c Ⅱ 缺乏症　familial apolipoprotein c Ⅱ deficiency
家族性脂蛋白脂酶缺乏症/家族性脂蛋白脂酶缺乏症　familial lipoprotein lipase deficiency
家族性脂肪诱发性高甘油三酯血症/家族性脂致性高三酸甘油酯血症　familial fat-induced hypertriglyceridemia
家族性指骨关节病/家族性指骨關節病　familial osteoarthropathy of finger
家族性中叶性硬化/家族性中葉硬化症，佩-莫二氏病　Pelizaeus-Merzbacher disease
家族性自主神经功能异常/家族性自主神經機能異常　familial autonomic dysfunction
家族性组织细胞性皮肤关节炎/家族性組織細胞皮膚關節炎　familial histiocytic dermatoarthritis
家族周期性麻痹/家族週期性麻痺　familial periodic paralysis
嘉祐本草/嘉祐本草　Jiayou Bencao
镓/鎵　gallium
镓放射性同位素/鎵放射性同位素　gallium radioisotope
镓摄影机/鎵攝影機　gallium camera
镓同位素/鎵同位素　gallium isotope
荚豆二糖/蠶豆糖　vicianose
荚壳样脱屑/莢殼樣脫屑　siliquose desquamation
荚膜多糖/莢膜菌多醣體　capsular polysaccharide
荚膜反应/莢膜反應　capsular reaction
荚膜抗原/莢膜抗原　capsular antigen
荚膜肿胀反应/莢膜膨大反應　quellung reaction
荚膜组织胞浆菌/莢膜組織漿菌　histoplasma capsulatum
荚膜组织胞浆菌荚膜变种/莢膜組織胞漿菌莢膜變種　histoplasma capsulatum var. capsulatum
荚膜组织胞浆菌试验/組織漿菌素試驗　histoplasmin test
颊/頰　cheek, bucca
颊阿米巴/頰阿米巴　Amoeba buccalis
颊白斑病/頰白斑病　leukoplakia buccalis
颊板区/頰板區　buccal shelf area
颊部投药/頰部投藥　buccal administration
颊侧翼缘/頰側凸緣　buccal flange
颊侧龈/頰面齦　buccal gingiva
颊车/頰車　jiache, ST6
颊车痈/頰車癰　Jiache abscess
颊成形术/頰成形術　melonoplasty
颊的/頰的　buccal
颊动脉/頰動脈　buccal artery
颊耳畸形/頰耳畸形　melotia
颊反射现象/頰現象　cheek phenomenon
颊㿗/齒頰側咬合　buccal occlusion
颊肌/頰肌　buccinator, buccinator muscle
颊肌淋巴结/頰肌淋巴結　buccal lymph node
颊间隙/頰間隙　buccal space
颊颈脊/齒頸頰脊　buccocervical ridge
颊裂/裂頰　cleft cheek
颊瘤/頰瘤　meloncus
颊螺旋体/頰螺旋體　treponema buccale
颊面/頰面　buccal surface
颊面管/頰面管　buccal tube
颊面修复/頰面復位　buccal restoration
颊黏膜/頰黏膜　buccal mucosa
颊黏膜白斑[病]/頰黏膜白斑病　psoriasis buccalis
颊黏膜襞/黏膜頰皺襞　mucobuccal fold
颊黏膜结核/頰黏膜結核　tuberculosis of buccal mucosa
颊区/頰部　buccal region
颊舌咽炎/頰舌咽炎　buccoglossopharyngitis
颊神经/頰神經　buccal nerve
颊神经管/頰神經管　bucconeural duct
颊系带/頰繫帶　buccal frenum
颊线/頰線　cheek line
颊腺/頰腺　buccal gland
颊向错位/[牙齿]向頰移位　buccoversion
颊向移位/向頰移位　buccoplacement
颊向阻生/頰向阻生　buccoangular impaction
颊咽部/頰咽部　buccopharyngeal part
颊咽肌/頰咽肌　buccopharyngeal muscle
颊咽筋膜/頰咽筋膜　buccopharyngeal fascia
颊支/頰支　buccal branch

颊脂垫/頰脂墊　buccal pad
颊脂体/頰脂體　buccal fat pad
甲氨蝶呤/胺基甲基葉酸　methotrexate
甲氨基酚皮炎/甲胺基酚皮炎　metol dermatitis
甲胺/甲胺　methylamine
甲板/甲板　nail plate
甲拌磷/甲拌磷　phorate
甲苯/甲苯　methylbenzene
甲苯胺类/甲苯胺類　toluidines
甲苯比妥/甲基巴比特魯　mephobarbital
甲苯丙醇/美安生　myanesin
甲苯达唑/甲苯噠唑　mebendazole
甲苯二酸/甲基間苯二酸　xylidic acid
甲[苯]酚/甲酚　cresol
甲苯磺吡胺/甲苯磺吡咯烷羧醯胺　tolpyrramide
甲苯磺丁脲/甲苯磺丁脲　tolbutamide
甲苯磺酰胺/甲苯磺醯胺　toluenesulfonamide
甲苯磺酰化合物/甲苯磺醯化合物　tosyl compound
甲苯磺酰精氨酸甲酯/甲苯磺醯精氨酸甲酯
　tosylarginine methyl ester
甲苯磺酰赖氨酰氯甲酮/甲苯磺醯賴氨醯氯甲酮
　tosyl lysine chloromethyl ketone
甲苯基/甲苯基　tolyl
甲苯酮/甲苯酮　methylphenyl ketone
甲苯酰基/甲苯甲醯基　toluyl
甲苯蒸馏法/甲苯蒸餾法　toluene distillation method
甲吡酮试验/甲吡酮試驗　metyrapone test
甲襞/甲褶　nail fold
甲变色/甲變色　nail discoloration
甲髌骨综合征/甲髕骨症候群　nail-patella syndrome
甲丙氨酯/甲丙胺酯　meprobamate
甲病/[爪]甲病　onychopathy
甲病毒感染/甲病毒感染　alphavirus infection
甲剥离/甲松動,甲分開　onycholysis
甲部脉搏/爪甲脈搏　nail pulse
甲虫/甲蟲　beetle
甲虫皮炎/甲蟲皮膚炎　beetle dermatitis
甲床/甲床,爪床　nail bed
甲床表皮囊肿/甲床表皮囊腫　epidermal cysts of
　nail bed
甲床沟/甲床溝　sulcus matricis unguis
甲床角化/甲床角化　onychophosis
甲床细胞瘤/甲床細胞瘤　pilomatrixoma
甲床炎/甲床炎,爪床炎　onychia
甲醇/甲醇　methanol
甲醇分解/甲醇分解　methanolysis
甲地高辛/甲基地高辛　medigoxin
甲地嗪/甲吡咯烷基吩噻嗪　methdilazine

甲地孕酮/甲地孕酮　megestrol
甲地孕酮乙酸盐/醋酸甲地孕酮,甲羟孕二烯二酮醋
　酸鹽　megestrol acetate
甲二磺酸/甲二磺酸　methionic acid
甲发育不良/指甲發育不良,趾甲發育不良
　onychodysplasia
甲泛葡胺/甲泛葡胺　metrizamide
甲泛影酸盐/甲泛影酸鹽　metrizoate
甲肥厚/[爪]甲肥大　onychauxis
甲酚/甲酚　cresol
甲酚类/甲酚類　cresols
甲酚品红/甲酚品紅　kresofuchsin
甲酚酞/甲酚酞　cresolphthalein
甲酚皂溶液/皂化甲酚溶液　saponated cresol solution
甲酚紫/甲酚紫　cresyl violet
甲砜霉素/甲碸黴素　thiamphenicol
甲氟喹/甲氟喹　mefloquine
甲基睾酮/甲基睾丸酮　methyltestosterone
甲根/甲根,爪根　nail root
甲沟/甲[床]溝　nail groove
甲沟脓炎/甲溝膿腫　pyonychia
甲沟炎/甲溝炎　paronychia
甲哌卡因/甲哌卡因　mepivacaine
甲关节面/甲關節面　thyroid articular surface
甲冠/甲冠　jacket crown
甲郭/甲郭　nail fold
甲琥胺/甲琥胺　methsuximide
甲磺酸甲酯/甲磺酸甲酯　methyl methanesulfonate
甲磺酸盐类/甲磺酸鹽類　mesylates
甲磺酸乙酯/甲磺酸乙酯　ethyl methanesulfonate
甲会厌肌/甲會厭肌　musculus thyroepiglotticus
甲基/甲基　methyl
甲基氨基酸/甲胺基酸　methylamino acid
甲基半乳糖苷类/甲基半乳糖苷類　methyl
　galactosides
甲[基]胞嘧啶/甲基胞核嘧啶　methylcytosine
甲[基]苯丙胺/甲基安非他命　methamphetamine
甲[基]苯肼/甲苯肼　methylphenylhydrazine
甲[基]吡啶/甲吡啶　methylpyridine
甲基吡啶类/甲基吡啶類　picolines
甲基丙二酸/甲基丙二酸　methylmalonic acid
甲基丙二酸单酰 CoA 变位酶/甲基丙二酸單醯 CoA
　變位酶　methylmalonyl-CoA mutase
甲基丙二酸尿症/甲醛巴比妥酸性尿
　methylmalonic aciduria
甲基丙二酰 CoA 脱羧酶/甲基丙二醯 CoA 脱羧酶
　methylmalonyl-CoA decarboxylase
甲基丙烯酸/甲基丙烯酸　methacrylic acid

甲基丙烯酸共聚物液/甲基丙烯酸共聚物液 methacrylic acid copolymer solution
甲基丙烯酸甲酯/甲基丙烯酸甲酯 methyl methacrylate
甲基丙烯酸甲酯类/甲基丙烯酸甲酯類 methyl methacrylates
甲基丙烯酸甲酯树脂/甲基丙烯酸甲酯樹脂 polymethyl methacrylate resin
甲基丙烯酸羟乙酯共聚物液/甲基丙烯酸羥乙酯共聚物液 hydroxyethyl methacrylate copolymer solution
甲基丙烯酸树脂/甲基丙烯酸樹脂 methacrylate
甲基丙烯酸烷酯/甲基丙烯酸烷酯 alkyl methacrylate
甲基丙烯酸盐/甲基丙烯酸鹽 methacrylates
甲基丙烯酸乙酯/甲基丙烯酸乙酯 ethyl methacrylate
甲基胆蒽/甲基膽蒽 methylcholanthrene
甲基对硫磷/甲基對硫磷 methyl parathion
甲基多巴/甲基多巴 aldomet
α-甲基多巴/α-甲基多巴 alpha-methyldopa
甲基二甲氨基偶氮苯/甲基二甲胺基偶氮苯 methyl dimethyl aminoazobenzene
甲基二氯胂/氯化甲胂 methyldichlorarsin
甲基甘露糖苷类/甲基甘露糖苷類 methylmannosides
甲基汞化合物/甲基汞化合物 insurance claim reporting
甲基胍/甲基胍 methylguanidine
甲基化/甲烷化,加甲基作用 methylation
甲基黄嘌呤/甲基黄嘌呤 methylxanthine
甲基肼类/甲基肼類 methylhydrazines
甲[基]喹啉/甲喹啉 methylquinoline
甲基酪氨酸类/甲基酪胺酸類 methyltyrosines
甲基硫代肌苷/甲基硫代肌苷 methylthioinosine
甲基硫酸新斯的明/甲基硫酸新斯弟格明 neostigmine methylsulfate
甲基绿/甲基緑 methyl green
甲基麦角新碱/甲基麥角新鹼 methylergonovine
甲[基]嘌呤/甲基嘌呤 methylpurine
甲基葡糖苷类/甲基葡糖苷類 methylglucosides
甲基葡萄糖胺茶碱/甲基葡萄糖胺茶鹼 theophylline methylglucamine
甲基炔诺酮/甲基炔諾酮 norgestrel
甲基胂酸/甲砷酸 methyl-arsinic acid
甲[基]胂酸盐/甲基次胂酸鹽 methylarsinate
甲基水杨酸/甲酚酸 cresotic acid
甲基糖苷类/甲基糖苷類 methylglycosides

甲基戊聚糖/甲基聚合戊糖 methyl pentosan
甲基戊炔醇/甲基戊炔醇 methylparafynol
甲基纤维素/甲基纖維素 methylcellulose
甲基亚硝脲/甲基亞硝脲 methylnitrosourea
甲基氧化偶氮甲醇醋酸酯/甲基氧化偶氮甲醇醋酸酯 methylazoxymethanol acetate
甲基异吡唑/甲基異吡唑 methylglyoxalidin
甲基正丁酮/甲基正丁酮 methyl n-butyl ketone
甲基转移酶/甲基轉移酶 methyltransferase
甲基组氨酸类/甲基組胺酸類 methylhistidines
甲基组胺类/甲基組胺類 methylhistamines
甲壳质/甲殼質 chitin
甲喹酮/安眠酮 methaqualone
甲廓/[爪]甲廓 nail wall
甲硫氨酸/甲硫胺酸 methionine
甲硫氨酸tRNA连接酶/甲硫胺酸tRNA連接酶 methionine-tRNA ligase
甲硫氨酸脑啡肽/甲硫胺酸腦啡肽 methionine enkephalin
甲硫氨酸腺苷转移酶/甲硫胺酸腺苷轉移酶 methionine adenosyltransferase
甲硫醇/甲硫醇 methylmercaptan
甲硫米胺/甲硫米胺 metiamide
甲硫替平/甲硫替平 methiothepin
甲硫氧嘧啶/甲基硫尿嘧啶 methylthiouracil
甲氯芬那酸/甲氯滅酸 meclofenamic acid
甲氯芬酯/氯酯醒,對氯苯氧基醋酸甲胺基乙酯 meclofenoxate
甲氯噻嗪/甲氯噻嗪 methyclothiazide
甲麦角林/麥角苄林 metergoline
甲醚类/甲醚類 methyl ethers
甲灭酸/甲滅酸 mefenamic acid
甲母质/甲母質 nail matrix
甲脲化合物/甲脲化合物 methylurea compound
甲胬肉/翼狀爪甲 pterygium unguis
甲泼尼龙/甲基去氢氧化可的松 methylprednisolone
甲泼尼龙琥珀酸酯/甲潑尼龍琥珀酸酯 methylprednisolone hemisuccinate
甲羟戊二酸单酰CoA裂解酶/羥甲戊二酸輔酶甲溶酶 hydroxymethylglutaryl-CoA lyase
甲羟戊酸/羥基戊酸 mevalonic acid
甲羟孕酮/甲羥孕酮 medroxyprogesterone
甲羟孕酮17-乙酸酯/甲羥孕酮17-乙酸酯 medroxyprogesterone 17-acetate
甲切除术/[爪]甲切除術 onychectomy
甲切开术/爪甲切開術 onychotomy
甲氰吡酮/米力农 milrinone
甲巯丙脯酸肾图/甲巯丙脯酸腎圖 captopril

renogram
甲巯咪唑/甲巰咪唑 methimazole
甲醛/甲醛 formaldehyde
甲醛肠线/蟻醛制腸線 formaldehyde catgut
甲醛滴定[法]/甲醛滴定[法] formol titration
甲醛甲酚合剂/甲醛甲酚 formocresol
甲醛类毒素/蟻醛類毒素 formol toxoid
甲醛煤酚/甲醛煤酚合劑 formocresol
甲醛凝胶试验/蟻醛液凝膠試驗 formol-gel test
甲醛-浓硫酸试液/甲醛-濃硫酸試液 marquis test solution
甲醛溶液/甲醛液 formaldehyde solution
甲醛释放剂/甲醛釋放劑 formaldehyde releaser
甲醛树脂/甲醛樹脂 formaldehyde resin
甲醛溴化铵固定/甲醛溴化銨固定 formalin-ammonium bromide fixing
甲醛溴化铵固定液/甲醛溴化銨固定液 formalin-ammonium bromide fixing fluid
甲醛诱发荧光法/甲醛誘導螢光法 formaldehyde induced fluorescence method
甲缺如/甲缺如 anonychia
甲软化/爪甲軟化,指甲軟化 onychomalacia
甲色素沉着/指甲色素沈著,趾甲色素沈著 nail pigmentation
甲上皮/甲表皮,爪甲緣層 eponychium
甲杓肌/甲杓肌 thyroarytenoid
甲舌骨肌/甲舌骨肌 musculus thyrohyoideus
甲松离/爪甲鬆開 onychoschizia
甲酸类/甲酸類 formic acids
甲酸生成酶/甲醛生成酶 formilase
甲酸-四氢叶酸连接酶/甲酸-四氫葉酸連接酶 formate-tetrahydrofolate ligase
甲酸脱氢酶/甲酸脱氫酶 formate dehydrogenase
甲酸脱氢酶类/甲酸脱氫酶類 formate dehydrogenases
甲酸盐类/甲酸鹽類 formates
甲酸乙酯/蟻酸乙酯 formic ether
甲酸酯类/甲酸酯類 formic acid esters
甲胎蛋白/甲型胎兒蛋白 alpha-fetoprotein
甲胎蛋白测定/甲型胎兒蛋白測定 alpha-fetoprotein determination
甲糖精/甲糖精 sugarin
甲体/爪甲體 nail body
甲脱落/爪甲脱落 onychoptosis
甲弯曲/甲彎曲 onychogryphosis
甲烷/甲烷 methane
甲烷氯氟碳/甲烷氯氟碳 methane chlorofluorocarbons
甲烷四氢叶酸环水解酶/甲烷四氫葉酸環水解酶 methenyltetrahydrofolate cyclohydrolase
甲萎缩/甲萎縮 nail atrophy
甲烯蓝/甲烯藍 methylene blue
甲烯土霉素/甲烯土黴素 methacycline
甲下表皮样包涵体/甲下表皮樣包涵體 subungual epidermoid inclusion
甲下黑[色]素瘤/甲下黑素瘤 subungual melanoma
甲下角化症/甲下角化症 subungual keratosis
甲下皮/甲床,爪下層 hyponychium
甲下色素痣/甲下色素痣 subungual nevus
甲下外生骨疣/甲下外生骨疣 subungual exostosis
甲下血管球瘤/甲下血管球瘤 subungual glomus tumor
甲下血肿/甲下血腫 subungual hematoma
甲下瘀斑/甲下瘀斑 hyponychon
甲酰胺/甲醯胺 formamide
甲酰胺类/甲醯胺類 formamides
甲酰蝶呤氨基甲酸/甲醯喋呤胺基甲酸 formylpteroic acid
甲酰基/甲醯基 formyl
甲酰[基]卟啉/甲醯卟啉 formylporphyrin
甲酰脲[基]草酸/甲醯尿素草酸 formyloxaluric acid
甲酰四氢叶酸盐类/甲醯四氫葉酸鹽類 formyltetrahydrofolates
甲酰肽受体/甲醯肽受體 formyl peptide receptor
甲硝基亚硝胍/甲硝基亞硝胍 methylnitronitrosoguanidine
甲硝唑/滅滴靈 metronidazole
甲小皮/甲小皮 nail cuticle
甲型半乳糖苷酶缺乏/甲型半乳糖苷酶缺乏 α-galactosidase deficiency
甲型[病毒性]肝炎/甲型[病毒性]肝炎 viral hepatitis type A, hepatitis A
甲型干扰素/甲型干擾素 interferon alpha
甲型肝炎病毒/甲型肝炎病毒 hepatitis A virus
甲型肝炎抗体/甲型肝炎抗體 hepatitis A antibody
甲型肝炎抗原/甲型肝炎抗原 hepatitis A antigen
甲型肝炎疫苗/甲型肝炎疫苗 hepatitis A vaccine
甲型肌动蛋白/甲型肌動蛋白 alpha actin
甲癣/甲黴菌病 onychomycosis
甲咽部/甲咽部 thyropharyngeal part
甲咽管/甲狀咽管 thyropharyngeal duct
甲氧苯青霉素/二甲氧基苯青黴素 methicillin
甲氧苯青霉素抗药性/甲氧西林抗藥性 methicillin resistance
甲氧苄啶/三甲氧苄胺嘧啶 trimethoprim
甲氧苄啶磺胺甲异噁唑合剂/甲氧苄啶磺胺甲異噁唑合劑 trimethoprim-sulfamethoxazole

甲氧苄啶抗药性/甲氧苄啶抗藥性 trimethoprim resistance combination
甲氧氟烷/甲氧氟烷 methoxyflurane
甲氧基/甲氧基 methoxyl
甲氧基二甲色胺类/甲氧基二甲色胺類 methoxydimethyltryptamines
3-甲氧基肾上腺素/甲氧基肾上腺素 metanephrine
甲氧基乙醇/甲氧基乙醇 methoxyethanol
甲氧氯/甲氧氯 methoxychlor
甲氧氯普胺/甲氧氯普胺 metoclopramide
甲氧明/甲氧明 methoxamine
甲氧萘基二甲戊酸/甲氧萘基二甲戊酸 methallenestril
甲氧普烯/烯蟲酯 methoprene
甲氧沙林/甲氧沙林 methoxsalen
甲乙基戊酰胺/甲乙基戊醯胺 valnoctamide
甲缘逆剥/甲刺 hang nail
甲臘/甲臘 formazan
甲折断/[爪]甲破折 onychoclasis
甲褶/[爪]甲皺襞 nail fold
甲指失养-耳聋综合征/甲指失養-耳聾症候群 nail dystrophy-deafness syndrome
甲中部营养不良/甲中部营養不良 median nail dystrophy
甲种球蛋白类/甲種球蛋白類 alpha-globulins
甲周的/指甲周圍的,趾甲周圍的 periungual
甲周膜/甲周膜 perionychium, perionyx
甲状会厌韧带/甲狀會厭韌帶 thyroepiglottic ligament
甲状颈干/甲狀頸幹 thyrocervical trunk
甲状颈管/甲狀頸管 thyrocervical duct
甲状旁腺/甲狀旁腺,副甲狀腺 parathyroid, parathyroid gland
甲状旁腺病/副甲狀腺病變 parathyropathy
甲状旁腺功能减退/副甲狀腺機能不足 hypoparathyreosis
甲状旁腺功能减退症/低甲狀旁腺功能症 hypoparathyroidism
甲状旁腺功能亢进症/副甲狀腺機能過旺 hyperparathyroidism
甲状旁腺功能缺失/副甲狀腺機能缺失 aparathyroidism
甲状旁腺[激]素/副甲狀腺素 parathormone
甲状旁腺激素受体/副甲狀腺激素受體 parathyroid hormone receptor
甲状旁腺激素相关蛋白质/副甲狀腺激素相關蛋白質 parathyroid hormone-related protein
甲状旁腺疾病/甲狀旁腺疾病,副甲狀腺疾病 parathyroid disease
甲状旁腺浸膏/副甲狀腺浸質 parathyroid extract
甲状旁腺瘤/副甲狀腺瘤 parathyroidoma
甲状旁腺片移植/副甲狀腺片移植 parathyroid slices transplantation
甲状旁腺切除术/副甲狀腺切除術 parathyroidectomy
甲状旁腺缺乏性手足搐搦/副甲狀腺缺乏性肢搦病 parathyroid tetany
甲状旁腺缺失状态/副甲狀腺缺失症 parathyroprivia
甲状旁腺溶液/副甲狀腺溶液 parathyroid solution
甲状旁腺素/副甲狀腺激素 parathyroid hormone
甲状旁腺素不敏感症/副甲狀腺素不敏感症 parathyroid hormone insensitivity
甲状旁腺素试验/副甲狀腺素試驗 parathyroid hormone infusion test
甲状旁腺损伤/副甲狀腺損傷 parathyroid injury
甲状旁腺性骨炎/副甲狀腺性骨炎 parathyroid osteitis
甲状旁腺移植/副甲狀腺移植 parathyroid transplantation
甲状旁腺原基/甲狀旁腺原基,副甲狀腺原基 primordium of parathyroid gland
甲状旁腺中毒症/副甲狀腺毒症 parathyrotoxicosis
甲状旁腺肿/副甲狀腺腫 parastruma
甲状旁腺肿瘤/副甲狀腺腫瘤 parathyroid neoplasms
甲状旁腺注射/副甲狀腺注射劑 parathyroid injection
甲状软骨/甲狀軟骨 thyroid cartilage
甲状软骨成形术/甲狀軟骨成形術 thyroplasty
甲状软骨刀/甲狀軟骨刀 thyrotome
甲状软骨分裂术/甲狀軟骨造裂術,甲狀軟骨造口術 thyrofissure
甲状软骨孔/甲狀軟骨孔 thyroid foramen
甲状软骨切开术/甲狀軟骨切開術 thyrochondrotomy
甲状软骨上角/甲狀軟骨上角 superior cornu of thyroid cartilage
甲状软骨上切迹/甲狀軟骨上切跡 superior thyroid notch, superior thyroid incisure
甲状软骨下角/甲狀軟骨下角 inferior cornu of thyroid cartilage
甲状软骨下切迹/甲狀軟骨下切跡 inferior thyroid notch, inferior thyroid incisure
甲状软骨斜线/甲狀軟骨斜線 oblique line of

thyroid cartilage
甲状上动脉/上甲狀腺動脈　superior thyroid artery
甲状舌骨肌/甲[狀]舌骨肌　thyrohyoid muscle
甲状舌骨肌支/甲狀舌骨肌支　thyrohyoid branch
甲状舌骨膜/甲狀舌骨膜　thyrohyoid membrane
甲状舌骨韧带/甲狀舌骨韌帶　thyrohyoid ligament
甲状舌骨外侧韧带/甲狀舌骨外側韌帶　lateral thyrohyoid ligament
甲状舌骨正中韧带/甲狀舌骨正中韌帶　median thyrohyoid ligament
甲状舌管/甲狀[腺]舌管　thyroglossal duct
甲状舌[管]的/甲狀腺與舌的　thyroglossal
甲状舌管窦[道]/甲狀舌管竇[道]　thyroglossal sinus
甲状舌管瘘/甲狀腺舌管瘘　thyroglossal fistula
甲状舌管囊肿/甲狀[腺]舌管囊腫　thyroglossal cyst
甲状下结节/甲狀下結節　inferior thyroid tubercle
甲状腺/甲狀腺　thyroid gland, thyroid
甲状腺癌/甲狀腺癌　carcinoma of thyroid
甲状腺杵状指/甲狀腺杵狀指　thyroid acropachy
甲状腺次全切除术/甲狀腺次全切除術　subtotal thyroidectomy
甲状腺刺激免疫球蛋白类/甲狀腺刺激免疫球蛋白類　thyroid-stimulating immunoglobulins
甲状腺毒素/甲狀腺毒素　thyroidotoxin
甲状腺毒性的/甲狀腺毒的　thyrotoxic
甲状腺毒性肌病/甲狀腺機能亢進性肌病　thyrotoxic myopathy
甲状腺毒性心脏病/甲狀腺中毒心臟病　thyrocardiac disease
甲状腺毒症/甲狀腺[中]毒症　thyrotoxicosis
甲状腺发育不全/甲狀腺發育不全　thyroaplasia
甲状腺分泌减少/[潛伏性]甲狀腺機能不足　thyropenia
甲状腺功能病/甲狀腺官能病　thyrosis
甲状腺功能病患者/甲狀腺體質者　thyrotrope
甲状腺功能减退的/甲狀腺機能不足的　hypothyroid
甲状腺功能减退心脏病/甲狀腺功能減退心臟病　hypothyroid heart disease
甲状腺功能减退性肥胖/甲狀腺官能不足性肥胖　hypothyroid obesity
甲状腺功能减退[症]/甲狀腺機能不足　hypothyroidism
甲状腺功能亢进的/甲狀腺機能亢進的　hyperthyroid
甲状腺功能亢进体型者/甲狀腺機能亢進傾向者　hyperontomorph
甲状腺[功能亢进]性精神病/甲狀腺性精神錯亂　thyroidomania
甲状腺功能亢进[症]/甲狀腺機能亢進[症]　hyperthyroidism
甲状腺功能缺失[症]/甲狀腺機能缺失　dethyroidism
甲状腺功能试验/甲狀腺機能試驗　thyroid function test
甲状腺功能障碍/甲狀腺機能障礙　dysthyreosis
甲状腺功能障碍性幼稚型/甲狀腺官能不足性幼稚型　dysthyroidal infantilism
甲状腺功能正常/甲狀腺官能正常　euthyroidism
甲状腺管皮样囊肿/甲狀腺管皮樣囊腫　thyroid dermoid
甲状腺核白蛋白/甲狀腺核蛋白素　thyronucleoalbumin
甲状腺基质/甲狀腺基質　stroma of thyroid gland
甲状腺激素抵抗综合征/甲狀腺激素抵抗症候群　thyroid hormone resistance syndrome
甲状腺激素结合球蛋白异常症/甲狀腺激素結合球蛋白異常症　thyroid hormone-binding globulin abnormality
甲状腺激素类/甲狀腺激素類　thyroid hormones
甲状腺激素受体/甲狀腺激素受體　thyroid hormone receptor
甲状腺疾病/甲狀腺疾病　thyroid disease
甲状腺剂疗法/甲狀腺劑療法　thyroidotherapy
甲状腺甲状旁腺切除术/甲狀腺副甲狀腺切除術　thyroparathyroidectomy
甲状腺胶体/甲狀腺膠體　thyroid colloid
甲状腺胶样腺瘤/膠性腺瘤　adenoma gelatinosum
甲状腺胶质/甲狀腺膠質　thyrocolloid
甲状腺结节/甲狀腺結節　thyroid nodule
甲状腺抗体/甲狀腺抗體　thyroid antibody
甲状腺淋巴结/甲狀腺淋巴結　thyroid lymph node
甲状腺瘤/甲狀腺瘤　thyroid tumor
甲状腺滤泡/甲狀腺胞　thyroid follicle
[甲状腺]滤泡旁细胞/濾泡旁細胞　parafollicular cell
[甲状腺]滤泡上皮细胞/濾泡上皮細胞　follicular epithelial cell
甲状腺囊肿/甲狀腺囊腫　thyroid cyst
甲状腺内固定术/甲狀腺內固定術　endothyropexy
甲状腺片/甲狀腺片　thyroid tablet
甲状腺奇静脉丛/甲狀腺奇靜脈叢　unpaired thyroid venous plexus
甲状腺憩室/甲狀腺憩室　thyroid diverticulum
甲状腺鞘/甲狀腺鞘　sheath of thyroid gland
甲状腺切除后黏液水肿/甲狀腺缺失性惡病質

operative myxedema
甲状腺切除术/甲狀腺切除術 thyroidectomy
甲状腺切开术/甲狀腺切開術 thyroidotomy
甲状腺球蛋白/甲狀腺球蛋白 thyroglobulin
甲状腺全切除术/甲狀腺全切除術 total thyroidectomy
甲状腺扫描/甲狀腺掃描 thyroid scintiscan
甲状腺上动脉/甲狀腺上動脈 superior thyroid artery
甲状腺上动脉后腺支/甲狀腺上動脈後腺支 posterior glandular branch of superior thyroid artery
甲状腺上动脉前腺支/甲狀腺上動脈前腺支 anterior glandular branch of superior thyroid artery
[甲状腺上动脉]胸锁乳突肌支/[甲狀腺上動脈]胸鎖乳突肌支 sternocleidomastoid branch
甲状腺上结节/甲狀上結節 superior thyroid tubercle
甲状腺上静脉/甲狀腺上静脈 superior thyroid vein
甲状[腺]舌管囊肿/甲狀舌管囊腫 thyroglossal duct cyst
甲状腺摄碘率/甲狀腺攝碘率 thyroid iodine uptake
甲状腺神经性营养不良/甲狀腺神經性營養不良 thyroneural dystrophy
甲状腺素/甲狀腺素 thyroxine
甲状腺素结合蛋白质类/甲狀腺素結合蛋白質類 thyroxine-binding proteins
甲状腺素钠/甲狀腺素鈉 thyroxine sodium
甲状腺素休克/甲狀腺素休克 thyroxine shock
甲状腺素血[症]/甲狀腺素血症 thyroxinemia
甲状腺髓样癌/甲狀腺髓樣癌 medullary thyroid carcinoma
甲状腺提肌/甲狀腺提肌,提甲狀腺肌 levator glandulae thyroideae, levator muscle of thyroid gland
甲状腺外固定术/甲狀腺外固定術 exothyroidopexy
甲状腺危象/甲狀腺危象 thyroid crisis
甲状腺细胞肿瘤/甲促素細胞瘤 thyrotrope tumor
甲状腺峡/甲狀腺峽 isthmus of thyroid gland
甲状腺下丛/甲狀腺下叢 plexus thyreoideps inferior
甲状腺下动脉/甲狀腺下動脈 inferior thyroid artery
[甲状腺下动脉]脊支/[甲狀腺下動脈]脊支 spinal branch
甲状腺下静脉/甲狀腺下静脈 inferior thyroid vein
甲状腺腺瘤/甲狀腺腺瘤 thyroid adenoma
甲状腺性恶病质/甲狀腺性惡病質 thyroid cachexia
甲状腺性心炎/甲狀腺性心肌炎 thyrocarditis
甲状腺悬韧带/甲狀腺懸韌帶 suspensory ligament of thyroid gland

甲状腺炎/甲狀腺炎 thyroiditis
甲状腺移植物/甲狀腺移植物 thyroid graft
甲状腺抑制试验/甲狀腺抑制試驗 thyroid suppression test
甲状腺右叶/甲狀腺右葉 right lobe of thyroid gland
甲状腺原氨酸类/甲狀腺原胺酸類 thyronines
甲状腺制剂疗法/甲狀腺療法 thyroid treatment
甲状腺中静脉/甲狀腺中静脈 middle thyroid vein
甲状腺肿/甲狀腺腫 goitre
甲状腺肿-耳聋综合征/彭德萊症候群 Pendred syndrome
甲状腺肿瘤/甲狀腺腫瘤 thyroid neoplasm
甲状腺肿切除术/甲狀腺腫切除術 strumectomy
甲状腺肿周炎/甲狀腺腫周圍炎 peristrumitis
甲状腺锥体叶/甲狀腺錐體葉,拉路埃特氏錐體 pyramid of thyroid
甲状腺阻塞/甲狀腺阻塞 thyremphraxis
甲状腺最下动脉/甲狀腺最下動脈 lowest thyroid artery
甲状腺左叶/甲狀腺左葉 left lobe of thyroid gland
甲状咽肌/甲狀咽肌 thyropharyngeal muscle
甲子/甲子 sixty-year cycle
甲纵沟/甲縱溝 longitudinal furrow of nail
甲纵裂/甲縱裂 longitudinal split of nail
岬/岬 promontory
岬毒素/隱翅蟲毒素 pederin
岬沟/岬溝 sulcus of promontory
岬下托/岬下腳 subiculum of promontory
贾第虫病/梨形蟲病 giardiasis
贾金斯冠状动脉导管/賈金斯冠狀動脈導管 Judkins coronary catheter
贾金斯技术/Judkins氏技術 Judkins technique
贾柯米尼带/Giacomini氏帶 Giacomini band
贾-利病/Jaffe-Lichtenstein二氏病 Jaffe-Lichtenstein disease
钾/鉀 potassium
钾放射性同位素/鉀放射性同位素 potassium radioisotope
钾化合物/鉀化合物 potassium compound
钾碱/鉀鹽 potash
钾镁天冬氨酸/鉀鎂天冬胺酸 potassium magnesium aspartate
钾氢反向转运物/鉀氫反向轉運物 potassium-hydrogen antiporter
钾缺乏/鉀缺乏 potassium deficiency
钾通道/鉀通道 potassium channel
钾通道阻滞剂/鉀通道阻滯劑 potassium channel blocker

钾同位素/鉀同位素　potassium isotope
假阿洪病/假自發性斷趾　pseudoainhum
假癌性增生/假性癌性增生　pseudocarcinomatous hyperplasia
假白斑病外阴炎/假白斑病女陰炎　pseudoleukoplakic vulvitis
假白喉/假白喉　pseudodiphtheria
假白喉棒状杆菌/假白喉棒狀桿菌　corynebacterium commune
假白喉杆菌/假白喉桿菌　Corynebacterium pseudodiphthericum
假[斑疹]伤寒/假性斑疹傷寒　pseudotyphus
假瓣膜/假瓣膜　pseudovalve
假表皮脱落/假表皮脱落　pseudoexfoliation
假波动/假波動　pseudofluctuation
假波特病/假性 Pott 氏病　pseudo-Pott disease
假卟啉病/假性紫質病　pseudoporphyria
假糙皮病/假性糙皮病，假玉蜀黍病　pseudopellagra
假痴呆/假癡呆　pseudodementia
假卒中/假中風，類中風　pseudoapoplexy
假单胞菌感染/假單胞菌感染　pseudomonas infection
假单胞菌属/假單胞菌屬　*Pseudomonas*
假单胞菌属噬菌体/假單胞菌屬噬菌體　*Pseudomonas* phage
假单极神经元/假單極神經元，僞單極神經元　pseudounipolar neuron
假单极神经元中枢支/假單極神經元中樞支　central branch of pseudounipolar neuron
假单极神经元周围支/假單極神經元周圍支　peripheral branch of pseudounipolar neuron
假胆囊炎/假性膽囊炎　pseudocholecystitis
假胆脂瘤/假性膽脂醇瘤　pseudocholesteatoma
假的/假的　spurious
假低钠血/假低鈉血症　pseudohyponatremia
假动脉干/僞軀幹動脈　pseudotruncus arteriosus
假动脉瘤/假動脈瘤　pseudoaneurysm, spurious aneurysm
假毒毛旋花子苷/僞毒毛旋花素　pseudostrophanthin
假多毛[症]/假多胎毛症　pseudohypertrichosis
假恶性[病]/假惡性病　pseudomalignancy
假耳/假耳　auricle prosthesis
假二倍体/假二倍體　pseudodiploid
假放线菌病/假放線菌病　pseudactinomycosis
假肥大/假肥大　pseudohypertrophy
假肥大的/假肥大的　pseudohypertrophic
假肥大性肌麻痹/假肥大性肌肉麻痺　pseudohypertrophic muscular paralysis
假肥大性肌营养不良/假肥大性肌營養不良　pseudohypertrophic muscular dystrophy
假肥大性营养不良/假肥大性營養不良　pseudohypertrophic dystrophy
假肺炎/假肺炎　pseudopneumonia
假风湿病/假風濕病　pseudorheumatism
假缝/骨與骨間之假縫　bastard suture
假复层纤毛柱状上皮/假複層纖毛柱狀上皮　pseudostratified ciliated columnar epithelium
假复层柱状上皮/假複層柱狀上皮　pseudostratified columnar epithelium
假腹膜炎/假腹膜炎　peritonism
假甘松香/假甘松　false spikenard
假[肝]硬变/假[性肝]硬變　pseudocirrhosis
假格鲁布/胸腺性氣喘,假嘶吼　pseudocroup
假隔/假隔　spurious septum
假根/假根　rhizoid
假梗阻/假阻塞　pseudo-obstruction
假骨折/假性骨折　pseudofracture
假关节/假關節　pseudarthrosis
假关节活动/假關節活動　movement of false joint
假关节形成/假關節形成　pseudoarticulation formation
假管型/假管型　pseudocast
假果糖/僞果糖　pseudofructose
假过敏反应/假過敏反應　pseudoallergic reaction
假过敏性的/假過敏性的　pseudoanaphylactic
假褐黄病/假性赭色病　pseudo-ochronosis
假黑变病/假黑變病　pseudomelanosis
假黑素瘤/假性黑色素瘤　pseudomelanoma
假虹膜缺损/假虹膜缺損　pseudocoloboma
假喉音/假聲　pseudovoice
假骺/假骨骺　pseudoepiphysis
假黄疸/假黃疸　pseudoicterus
假黄瘤/假黃瘤　pseudoxanthoma
假黄嘌呤/僞黃嘌呤　pseudoxanthine
假黄色瘤细胞/假黃瘤細胞　pseudoxanthoma cell
假黄体/假黃體　pseudo-corpus luteum
假脊髓灰质炎/假脊髓灰質炎　pseudopoliomyelitis
假脊髓痨/假脊髓痨　peripheral tabes
假寄生物/假寄生物　pseudoparasite
假甲状腺功能减退/假性甲狀腺機能減退　pseudohypothyroidism
假减数分裂/假性減數分裂　pseudoreduction
假胶体/僞膠體　pseudocolloid
假胶质瘤/假神經膠質瘤　pseudoglioma
假角蛋白/假性角蛋白　false keratin
假拮抗肌/假拮抗肌　pseudoantagonist

假结肠袋/假結腸袋　pseudohaustration
假结核棒状杆菌/假結核棒狀桿菌　Corynebacterium pseudotuberculosis
假结核病/假結核病　pseudotuberculosis
假结核结节/假結核結節　pseudotubercle
假结核瘤/假結核瘤　pseudotuberculoma
假结石病/假結石病　pseudolithiasis
假截瘫/假截癱　pseudoparaplegia
假借针药/假藉針藥　placebo with acupuncture therapy
假荆芥内酯/假荆芥内酯　nepetalactone
假晶状体/假晶狀體病　pseudophakia
假巨结肠/假性巨結腸　pseudomegacolon
假菌胶团/假菌膠團　pseudozooglea
假菌丝/假菌絲　pseudohyphae
假咯血/假欬血　pseudohemoptysis
假空泡/假空泡　pseudovacuole
假孔/假孔　pseudostoma
假哭综合征/假哭性症候群,味覺性流淚　crocodile tears syndrome
假狂犬病病毒/假狂犬病病毒　pseudorabies virus
假阑尾炎/假闌尾炎　pseudoappendicitis
假痨病/假痨病　pseudophthisis
假肋/假肋,弓肋　false rib
假离子/假離子　pseudoion
假痢疾/假痢疾　pseudodysentery
假莨菪碱/偽莨菪素　pseudohyoscyamine
假两性畸形/假性兩性畸形,假性半陰陽人　false hermaphroditism, pseudohermaphroditism
假两性同体/假兩性同體,假雌雄同體,假兩性畸形　false hermaphroditism
假临产/假产　false labor
假淋巴瘤/假淋巴瘤　pseudolymphoma
假淋巴细胞性脉络丛脑膜炎病毒/假淋巴細胞性脈絡叢腦膜炎病毒　pseudolymphocytic choriomeningitis virus
假磷酸酶过少[症]/假性磷酸脂酶過少　pseudohypophosphatasia
假流涎/假性流涎症　pseudoptyalism
假瘤/假瘤　pseudoneoplasm
假卵/假卵　pseudo-ovum
假麻痹性重症肌无力/假癱性重肌無力症　myasthenia gravis pseudoparalytica
假麻黄碱/偽麻黄素　pseudoephedrine
假麻醉[状态]/假性麻醉　pseudonarcotism
假毛囊炎/假性毛囊炎　pseudofolliculitis
假霉菌病/假黴菌病　pseudomycosis
假膜/假膜　pseudomembrane

假膜的/假膜性的　pseudomembranous
假膜性鼻炎/假膜性鼻炎　pseudomembranous rhinitis
假膜性结肠炎/假膜性結腸炎　pseudomembranous colitis
假膜性结膜炎/假膜性結膜炎　pseudomembranous conjunctivitis
假膜性淋巴/浮膜性淋巴　croupous lymph
假膜性痛经/假膜性痛經　dysmenorrhea pseudomembranosa
假膜性胃炎/假膜性胃炎　pseudomembranous gastritis
假膜性炎/假膜性炎　pseudomembranous inflammation
假膜性咽峡炎/假膜性咽喉炎　pseudomembranous angina
假脑积水/假性水腦　pseudohydrocephalus
假脑畸胎/假腦畸胎　pseudencephalus
假脑瘤/假性腦瘤　pseudotumor cerebri
假黏蛋白/假黏蛋白　pseudomucin
假黏蛋白的/假黏蛋白的　pseudomucinous
假黏液瘤/假性液瘤　pseudomyxoma
假黏液性囊腺瘤/假黏液性囊腺瘤　pseudomucinous cystadenoma
假念珠形发/假性念珠形毛髮　pseudomonilethrix
假尿毒症/假尿毒症　pseudouremia
假尿苷/假尿嘧啶核苷　pseudouridine
假牛痘病毒/假牛痘病毒　pseudocowpox virus
假怒/假憤怒　sham rage
假皮萎缩/假性皮膚萎縮症　pseudoatrophoderma
假贫血/假貧血　pseudoanemia
假破伤风/假破傷風　pseudotetanus
假葡萄糖脎/偽葡萄糖脎　pseudoglucosazone
假蹼形成/假蹼形成　interdigital web formation
假气肿/假肺氣腫　pseudoemphysema
假憩室/假憩室　pseudodiverticulum
假青春期/假性青春期　pseudopuberty
假染色体/假染色體　batonet
假热带念珠菌/假熱帶念珠菌　Candida pseudotropicalis
假韧带/假韌帶　false ligament
假妊娠/假妊娠,假懷孕　false pregnancy
假溶液/偽溶液　pseudosolution
假蠕虫/假蠕蟲　pseudohelminth
假乳房/假乳房　pseudomamma
假乳头/假乳頭　pseudopapilla
假色汗[症]/假性色汗症　pseudochromidrosis
假沙利度胺综合征/假性沙立竇邁症候群

pseudothalidomide syndrome
假沙眼/假沙眼 pseudotrachoma
假疝/假疝 false hernia
假伤寒/假傷寒 pseudotyphoid
假伤寒性脑膜炎/假傷寒性腦膜炎 pseudotyphoid meningitis
假上皮瘤样增生/假上皮細胞瘤性增生 pseudoepitheliomatous hyperplasia
假设同意/假設同意 presumed consent
假神/假神 false vitality
假神经节/假神經節 pseudoganglion
假神经瘤/假神經瘤 pseudoneuroma
假肾盂积水/假性腎水腫 pseudohydronephrosis
假生脓性肉芽肿/假性化膿性肉芽腫 pseudopyogenic granuloma
假声门/假聲門 pseudoglottis
假视神经乳头水肿/假視乳頭水腫 pseudopapilledema
假视神经炎/假性視神經炎 pseudoneuritis
假视网膜像/假視象 pseudo-optogram
假水肿/假水腫 pseudoedema
假饲/假餵法 sham feeding
假髓石/假髓石 false denticle
假缩窄/假縮窄 pseudocoarctation
假胎块/假胎塊 false mole
假胎盘/假胎盤 placenta spuria
假弹性纤维假黄瘤/假彈性纖維假黃瘤 pseudo-pseudoxanthoma elasticum
假体/假體 prosthesis
假体安装/假體安裝 prosthesis fitting
假体的/人工的 prosthetic
假体腔/假體腔 pseudocoelom
假体腔动物/假胚腔動物 pseudocoelomate
假体设计/假體設計 prosthesis design
假体失效/假體失效 prosthesis failure
假体相关感染/假體相關感染 prosthesis-related infection
假体植入/假體植入 prosthesis implantation
假体置换/假體置換 prosthetic replacement
假体着色/假體著色 prosthesis coloring
假通道/假通道 false channel
假吐/假吐 pseudovomiting
假托品/偽莨菪鹼 pseudotropine
假脱臼/假脱臼 pseudoluxation
假无头畸胎/假無頭畸胎 pseudoacephalus
假无牙/假性無齒 pseudoanodontia
假息肉/假息肉 pseudopolyp
假息肉病/假息肉症 pseudopolyposis

假狭心症/假狹心症 pseudo-angina
假下疳/假下疳 pseudochancre
假腺期/假腺期 pseudoglandular period
假腺样鳞状细胞癌/假腺樣鱗狀細胞癌 pseudoglandular squamous cell carcinoma
假心绞痛/假性心絞痛 pseudangina
假猩红热/假猩紅熱 pseudoscarlatina
假性/假性 pseudo
假[性]斑秃/假性簇狀禿髮 pseudopelade
假[性]变态反应/假過敏性反應 pseudoallergic reaction
假性毒性甲状腺肿/類巴塞杜氏病 basedoid
假[性]发绀/假性發紺 false cyanosis
假[性]肥大/假[性]肥大 pseudohypertrophy
假[性]肥大性肌萎缩/假肥大性肌肉萎縮 pseudohypertrophic muscular atrophy
假[性]分娩阵痛/假[性]分娩陣痛,假性陣痛 false labor pain
假[性]感染性直肠炎/假性感染性直腸炎 pseudoinfectious proctitis
假[性]共济失调/假性運動失調 pseudoataxia
假[性]骨软化/假軟骨病 pseudo-osteomalacia
假[性]关节/假性關節 false articulation
假[性]关节强硬/假性關節粘連 pseudankylosis
假[性]关节炎/幻性關節炎,癔病性關節炎 pseudarthritis
假[性]黑棘皮病/假性黑色棘皮症 pseudoacanthosis nigrican
假[性]红细胞过多症/假性紅血球過多症 spurious polycythemia
假[性]红细胞增多/假紅血球增多症 pseudopolycythemia
假[性]幻觉/假幻覺 pseudohallucination
假[性]黄斑/假[性]黃斑 pseudomacula
假[性]肌肥大/肌假肥大,假肥大性麻痺 muscular pseudohypertrophy
假[性]肌强直/假性肌強直 pseudomyotonia
假[性]棘皮症/假棘皮症 pseudoacanthosis
假[性]寄生物/假性寄生物 spurious parasite
假性甲状旁腺功能减退症/假性副甲狀腺機能不足 pseudohypoparathyroidism
假性假种皮/擬假種皮 arillode
假[性]浆细胞/假性漿細胞 pseudoplasma cell
假[性]结肠梗阻/假性結腸阻塞 false colonic obstruction
假[性]结核疹/假性結核疹 pseudotuberculide
假[性]近视/假性近視 pseudomyopia
假[性]卡波西肉瘤/假性卡波西肉瘤 pseudo-Kaposi

sarcoma
假[性]狂犬病/假性狂犬病　pseudorabies
假[性]狂犬病疫苗/假性狂犬病疫苗　pseudorabies vaccine
假[性]眶距过宽/假性眶距過寬　false orbital hypertelorism
假[性]淋巴瘤状毛囊炎/假性淋巴瘤狀毛囊炎　pseudolymphomatous folliculitis
假[性]淋巴瘤综合征/假性淋巴瘤症候群　pseudolymphoma syndrome
假[性]瘤/假[性]瘤,虚瘤　false tumor, phantom tumor
假[性]麻痹/假性麻痺　pseudoparalysis
假性[男子]女性型乳房/假性男子女乳化　pseudogynecomastia
假[性]囊肿/假性囊腫　false cyst
假[性]脑膜膨出/假性腦脊髓膜膨出　spurious meningocele
假[性]脑膜炎/虛性腦膜炎　meningism
假[性]脑膨出/假性腦膨出　pseudocephalocele
假[性]黏液囊肿/假性黏液囊腫　pseudomucinous cyst
假[性]尿失禁/假失禁　false incontinence
假[性]气肿/假性氣腫　false emphysema
假[性]全身麻痹/假麻痺狂　pseudoparesis
假[性]醛固酮减少症/假性醛固酮缺乏　pseudohypoaldosteronism
假[性]醛固酮增多症/假性醛固酮增多症　pseudohyperaldosteronism
假[性]融合脉动/假性融合脈動　pseudofusion beats
假性肉瘤/假性肉瘤　pseudosarcoma
假[性]软骨发育不良/假性軟骨發育不全　pseudoachondroplastic dysplasia
假[性]上睑下垂/假上瞼下垂　false ptosis
假[性]失写/寫義缺失　pseudographia
假[性]失写[症]/假失寫症　pseudagraphia
假[性]噬神经细胞现象/假性神經細胞吞噬作用　pseudoneuronophagia
假[性]手足徐动症/假性指痙病,假性趾痙病　pseudoathetosis
假[性]通道/假路,歧路　false passage
假[性]同形异质现象/假性 Kobner 氏現象　pseudo-Kobner phenomenon
假[性]痛风/假痛風　pseudogout
假[性]外隐斜视/假外轉隱斜眼　pseudoexophoria
假[性]舞蹈病/假舞蹈病　pseudochorea
假[性]下颌前突/假凸頷[畸型]　pseudoprognathism
假[性]纤毛/假性纖毛　pseudocilia

假[性]腺样鳞状细胞癌/假性腺樣鱗狀細胞癌　pseudoglandular squamous cell carcinoma
假[性]小头者/假腦小症　pseudomicrocephalus
假[性]斜视/假性斜視　pseudostrabismus
假[性]性早熟/假性性早熟　pseudo-precocious puberty
假[性]血尿/假性血尿　false hematuria
假[性]延髓麻痹/假性延髓性癱瘓,假性球麻痺　pseudobulbar palsy
假[性]翼状胬肉/假翼狀胬肉,假視翼　pseudopterygium
假[性]肿瘤/假瘤,虚瘤　pseudotumor
假[性]子宫内膜炎/假性子宮內膜炎　pseudoendometritis
假[性]足分支菌病/假足分支菌病　pseudomycetoma
假血凝反应/假性血球凝集　pseudohemagglutination
假血友病/假血友病　pseudohemophilia
假牙/假牙,義齒　denture
假牙关紧闭/假性牙關閉鎖　pseudotrismus
假牙修复学家/假牙修復專家,假牙贗復學家　prosthodontist
假眼球震颤/假性眼球震顫　pseudonystagmus
假阳性反应/假陽性反應　false positive reaction
假叶目/類葉目　pseudophyllidea
假胰高血糖素瘤综合征/假昇糖素瘤症候群　pseudoglucagonoma syndrome
假遗传/假遺傳　paraheredity
假异花[青]色苷/僞異花色苷　pseudocyanin
假异位/假性位置異常　pseudoheterotopia
假阴囊/假陰囊　pseudoscrotum
假阴性反应/假陰性反應　false negative reaction
假荧光/假螢光　pseudofluorescence
假硬化病/假性硬皮病　pseudosclerema
假硬化症/假性硬化　pseudosclerosis
假硬皮病/假性硬皮症　pseudoscleroderma
假右位心/假性右位心　pseudodextrocardia
假愈期/假愈期　latent phase
假圆柱状体/假圓柱樣體　pseudocylindroid
假月经/假行經　pseudomenstruation
假孕/假孕　pseudocyesis, false pregnancy
假杂种/假雜種　false hybrid
假阵痛/假性陣痛　false pain
假震颤/假震顫　pseudothrill
假震颤[性]麻痹/假性震顫麻痺　pseudoparalysis agitan
假支气管扩张/假性支氣管擴張症　pseudobronchiectasis
假肢/假肢,人工肢　artificial limb

假指成形术/假指節形成法　phalangization
假趾成形术/假趾節形成法　phalangization
假种皮/假種皮,子衣　aril
假椎/假椎　false vertebrae
驾驶盘[损]伤/駕駛盤傷,駕駛盤損害　steering-wheel injury
驾驶人骨折/駕駛人骨折　chauffeur fracture
驾驶人足/駕駛人足　chauffeur foot
架火法/架火法　alcohol fire-separated cupping, fire throwing method
嫁接性精神分裂症/嫁接性精神分裂症,嫁接性思覺失調症　engrafted schizophrenia
嫁接性青春期痴呆/嫁接性青春期癡呆　pfropfhebephrenia
尖/[瓣]尖　apex, cusp
尖波/尖波　sharp wave
尖顶/尖頂　apex of cuspis
尖端/尖　tip
尖端扭转型室性心动过速/尖端扭轉型室性心動過速　torsade de pointes
尖段/尖段　apical segment
尖段支气管/尖段支氣管　apical segmental bronchus
尖耳轮耳/猩猩耳　satyr ear
尖圭湿疣/尖圭濕疣　condyloma papilloma
尖后段/尖後段　apicoposterior segment
尖后段支气管/尖後段支氣管　apicoposterior segmental bronchus
尖后支/尖後支　apicoposterior branch
尖芽孢镰刀菌/尖孢鐮刀菌,尖鐮孢子菌　Fusarium oxysporum
尖淋巴结/尖淋巴結　apical lymph node
尖颅多指并指[畸形]/尖頭多指并指畸形　acrocephalopolysyndactyly
尖颅多趾并趾[畸形]/尖頭多趾并趾畸形　acrocephalopolysyndactyly
尖慢复合波/尖慢複合波　sharp and slow wave complex
尖平面/尖平面　cusp-plane
尖锐湿疣/尖形濕疣　condyloma acuminatum
尖锐显疣/花菜狀瘤　cauliflower excrescence
尖头[畸形]/尖頭畸形　acrocephaly
尖头脑积水/尖頭水腦　oxyhydrocephalus
尖头湿疣/尖頭濕疣　verruca venereal
尖牙/犬齒　canine tooth, cuspid
尖牙保护殆/尖牙保護殆　cuspid-protected occlusion
尖牙卡环/尖牙卡環　cuspid clasp
尖牙隆起/犬齒隆起,犬齒隆凸　canine eminence
尖牙窝/犬齒窩　canine fossa

尖音/聲音尖銳,尖聲　oxyphonia
尖支/尖支　apical branch
坚持服药率/堅持服藥率　compliance rate
坚果/堅果　nut
坚果过敏/堅果過敏　nut hypersensitivity
坚牢绿FCF/堅牢綠FCF　fast green FCF
间氨基苯酚/間胺苯酚　m-aminophenol
间板/間板　intermediate lamella
间苯二酚/間苯二酚　resorcin
间苯甲酰二乙胺/間苯甲醯二乙胺　diethyltoluamide
间苯三酚/間苯三酚　phloroglucinol
间苯三酚试验/間苯三酚試驗　phloroglucin test
间变/間變　anaplasia
间变性的/退行性變化的　anaplastic
间[充]质/間[充]質　desmohemoblast, mesenchyme
间[充]质上皮/間葉上皮　mesenchymal epithelium
间充质细胞/間質細胞　mesenchymal cell
间动电疗法/間動電療法　diadynamic electrotherapy
间骨板/間骨板　interstitial lamella
间甲酚/間甲酚　metacresol
间介中胚层/間介中[胚]層,中間中胚層　intermediate mesoderm
间距过远/距離過遠症,過距症　hypertelorism
间脑/間腦　diencephalon
间脑病/間腦病　diencephalosis
间脑静脉/間腦靜脈　vein of diencephalon
间皮/間皮　mesothelium
间皮的/間皮的　mesothelial
间皮瘤/間皮瘤　mesothelioma
间皮细胞/間皮細胞　mesothelial cell
间皮性髓质瘤/間皮性髓質瘤　mesothelial hyloma
间皮肿瘤/間皮腫瘤　mesothelial neoplasm
间期/間期　interval
Q-T间期/Q-T間期　Q-T interval
间期手术/間期手術　interval operation
间期细胞遗传学/間期細胞遺傳學　interphase cytogenetics
间羟胺/間羥胺　metaraminol
间日疟/間日瘧　tertian malaria, vivax malaria
间日疟原虫/間日瘧原蟲　Plasmodium vivax
间日热/間日熱　tertian
间使/間使　jianshi, PC5
间室性坏死/間室性壞死　compartmental necrosis
间体/間體　mesosome
间位/間位　interposition
间位核/間質核　interstitial nucleus
间型霉素/間型黴素　formycins
间叶/間葉　mesenchyme

间叶的/間葉的　mesenchymal
间叶瘤/間葉瘤　mesenchymoma
间叶性髓质瘤/間葉性髓質瘤　mesenchymal hyloma
间质/間質　interstitial substance
间质板/間質板　interstitial disc
间质病/間質病　interstitial disease
间质干细胞/間質幹細胞　mesenchymal stem cell
间质干细胞移植/間質幹細胞移植　mesenchymal stem cell transplantation
间质内照射/組織間隙照射　interstitial irradiation
间质生长/介於中間的生長　interstitial growth
间质腺/間介腺　interstitial gland
间质性肺疾病/間質性肺疾病　interstitial lung disease
间质性肺炎/間質性肺炎　interstitial pneumonia
间质性膀胱炎/間質性膀胱炎　interstitial cystitis
间质性乳腺炎/間質性乳腺炎　interstitial mastitis
间质性软骨肉瘤/間質性軟骨肉瘤　mesenchymal chondrosarcoma
间质性神经炎/間質性神經炎　interstitial neuritis
间质性肾炎/間質性腎炎　interstitial nephritis
间质性视神经炎/間質性視神經炎　interstitial optic neuritis
间质性胃炎/間質性胃炎　interstitial gastritis
间质性炎/間質炎［症］　interstitial inflammation
间质液/組織間隙液　interstitial fluid
间质植入/間質植入　interstitial implantation
间质组织/間質組織　interstitial tissue
间质组织移行错误/間質組織移行錯誤　mesenchymal tissue migration error
肩/肩　shoulder
肩部筋伤/肩部筋傷　injury of shoulder fascia
肩部叩响/肩帶響　shoulder-strap resonance
肩峰/肩峰　acromion, shoulder peak
肩峰凹窝/肩峰凹窩　acromial dimple
肩峰成形术/肩峰成形術　acromioplasty
肩峰的/肩峰的　acromial
肩峰点/肩峰點　acromion point
肩峰端/肩峰端　acromial end
肩峰-肱骨的/肩峰與肱骨的　acromio-humeral
肩峰骨/肩峰骨　acromial bone
肩峰骨折/肩峰骨折　acromial fracture
肩峰关节面/肩峰關節面　articular facet of acromion
肩峰角/肩峰角　acromial angle
肩峰皮下囊/肩峰皮下囊　subcutaneous acromial bursa
肩峰-锁骨的/肩峰與鎖骨的　acromio-clavicular
肩峰锁骨关节/肩峰鎖骨關節　acromioclavicular articulation
肩峰网/肩峰網　acromial rete
肩峰下滑囊炎/肩峰下滑［液］囊炎　subacromial bursitis
肩峰下滑液囊炎/Duplay 氏症候群　Duplay syndrome
肩峰下囊/肩峰下囊　deltoid bursa
肩峰胸静脉/肩峰胸靜脈　acromiothoracic vein
肩峰支/肩峰支　acromial branch
肩骨折/肩骨折　shoulder fracture
肩关节/肩關節　shoulder joint
肩关节后脱位/肱骨頭向後脫位　posterior shoulder dislocation
肩关节结核/肩關節結核　tuberculosis of shoulder joint
肩关节前脱位/肱骨頭向前脫位　anterior shoulder dislocation
肩［关节］痛风/肩［關節］痛風　omagra
肩关节脱位/肩關節脫位　scapular dislocation, shoulder dislocation
肩关节炎/肩關節炎　omarthritis
肩关节周围炎/肩關節周圍炎　periarthritis of shoulder
肩关节周围炎•风寒湿阻证/肩關節周圍炎•風寒濕阻證　periarthritis of shoulder with wind-cold-dampness obstruction pattern
肩关节周围炎•气血两虚证/肩關節周圍炎•氣血兩虛證　periarthritis of shoulder with qi-blood deficiency pattern
肩关节周围炎•血瘀气滞证/肩關節周圍炎•血瘀氣滯證　periarthritis of shoulder with pattern of blood stasis and qi stagnation
肩后位/肩产式向後先露　scapuloposterior
肩喙韧带/肩喙韌帶　acromiocoracoid ligament
肩胛/肩胛　shoulder blade scapula
肩胛背动脉/肩胛背動脈　dorsal scapular artery
肩胛背静脉/肩胛背靜脈　dorsal scapular vein
肩胛背面/肩胛背面　dorsal surface of scapula
肩胛背神经/肩胛背神經　dorsal scapular nerve, dorsal digital nerve scapula
肩胛带综合征/肩胛帶症候群　shoulder girdle syndrome
肩胛冈/肩胛岡　spine of scapula
肩胛肱骨的/肩胛與肱骨的　scapulohumeral
肩胛肱骨黏液囊炎/肩胛與肱骨黏液囊炎　scapulohumeral bursitis
肩胛沟/肩胛溝　scapular groove
肩胛［骨］/肩胛［骨］　shoulder-blade, scapula, blade

bone
肩胛骨背侧面/肩胛骨背側面　dorsal surface of scapula
肩胛骨骨折/肩胛骨骨折　fracture of scapula, scapula fracture
肩胛骨关节盂/肩胛骨關節盂　glenoid cavity of scapula
肩胛[骨]后面/肩胛後面　posterior surface of scapula
肩胛骨喙突/肩胛骨喙突　coracoid process of scapula
肩胛[骨]肋面/肩胛骨肋骨面　costal surface of scapula, facies costalis scapulae
肩胛骨上部/肩胛骨上部　prescapula
肩胛骨上角/肩胛骨上角　superior angle of scapula
肩胛骨外侧角/肩胛骨外側角　lateral angle of scapula
肩胛骨下角/肩胛骨下角　inferior angle of scapula
肩胛骨下角点/肩胛骨下角點　angulus inferior scapulae point
肩胛固定术/肩胛固定術　scapulopexy
肩胛横动脉/肩胛橫動脈　transverse scapular artery
肩胛后动脉/肩胛後動脈　posterior scapular artery
肩胛喙突韧带/肩胛喙突韌帶　coracoid ligament of scapula
肩胛颈/肩胛頸　neck of scapula
肩胛切除术/肩胛切除術　scapulectomy
肩胛切迹/肩胛切跡　scapular notch
肩胛区/肩胛部　scapular region
肩胛上动脉/肩胛上動脈　suprascapular artery
肩胛上横韧带/肩胛上橫韌帶　superior transverse scapular ligament
肩胛上静脉/肩胛上靜脈　suprascapular vein
肩胛上神经/肩胛上神經　suprascapular nerve
肩胛舌骨肌/肩胛舌骨肌　omohyoid
肩胛舌骨肌气管三角/肩胛舌骨肌氣管三角　omotracheal triangle
肩胛舌骨肌上腹/肩胛舌骨肌上腹　superior belly of omohyoid
肩胛舌骨肌锁骨三角/肩胛舌骨肌鎖骨三角　omaoclavicular triangle
肩胛舌骨肌下腹/肩胛舌骨肌下腹　inferior belly of omohyoid
肩胛舌骨肌斜方肌三角/肩胛舌骨肌斜方肌三角　trigonum omotrapezium
肩胛提肌/提肩胛肌　levator muscle of scapula, musculus levator scapulae
肩[胛]痛/肩胛部痛　scapulodynia
肩胛外侧髁/肩胛外側髁　condyle of scapula
肩胛下动脉/肩胛下動脈　subscapular artery
肩胛下横韧带/肩胛下橫韌帶　inferior transverse scapular ligament
肩胛下肌/肩胛下肌　subscapularis, musculus subscapularis
肩胛下肌腱下囊/肩胛下肌腱下囊　subtendinous bursa of subscapularis
肩胛下肌囊/肩胛下肌囊　bursa musculi subscapularis
肩胛下静脉/肩胛下靜脈　subscapular vein
肩胛下淋巴结/肩胛下淋巴結　subscapular lymph node
肩胛下区/肩胛下部　infrascapular region
肩胛下神经/肩胛下神經　subscapular nerve
肩胛下窝/肩胛下凹　subscapular fossa
肩胛下支/肩胛下支　subscapular branch
肩胛线/肩胛線　scapular line
肩胛悬带/肩胛懸帶　scapulary
肩井/肩井　jianjing, GB21
肩疽/肩疽　shoulder carbuncle
肩宽/肩寬　shoulder breadth
肩髎/肩髎　jianliao, SJ14
肩难产/肩難產　shoulder dystocia
肩扭伤/肩扭傷　stubbed shoulder
肩前位/肩产式向前先露　scapuloanterior
肩-手综合征/肩手症候群　shoulder-hand syndrome
肩锁关节/肩鎖關節　acromioclavicular joint
肩锁关节板/肩鎖關節盤　acromioclavicular disc
肩锁关节脱位/肩鎖關節脱位　acromioclavicular dislocation
肩锁韧带/肩鎖韌帶　acromioclavicular ligament
肩痛/肩痛　shoulder pain
肩脱位/肩脱位　shoulder dislocation
肩外俞/肩外俞　jianwaishu, SI14
肩息/肩息　raised-shoulder breathing
肩下垂/肩下垂　drop shoulder
肩先露/肩产式　shoulder presentation
肩袖断裂/肩袖斷裂　shoulder rotator cuff rupture
肩袖损伤/肩袖損傷,迴旋肌套損傷　rotator cuff injury, shoulder rotator cuff injury
肩盂韧带/肩胛岡與關節盂韌帶　spinoglenoid ligament
肩髃/肩髃　jianyu, LI15
肩贞/肩貞　jianzhen, SI9
肩中俞/肩中俞　jianzhongshu, SI15
肩周炎/肩周炎　periarthritis humeroscapularis
肩撞击综合征/肩撞擊症候群　shoulder impingement syndrome

艰难梭状芽孢杆菌/困难梭状芽孢桿菌　Clostridium difficile
监测导联/監測導聯　monitoring lead
监测检查/監測檢查　monitoring test
监测仪/監視器　monitor
监督/監督，監視　supervision, surveillance
监督护理/監督護理　supervisory nursing
监护/監護　custodial care
监禁反应/監禁反應　imprisonment reaction
监禁性精神病/拘禁精神病，監獄精神病　prison psychosis
兼嗜性的/雙染性的　amphophilic
兼向性病毒/兼向性病毒　amphotropic virus
兼性表面活性剂/酸鹼兼性劑　amphoterics
兼性寄生物/兼性寄生物　facultative parasite
缄默性躁狂/不活動性躁狂，無效性躁狂　unproductive mania
缄默症/緘默症　mutism
煎剂/煎劑　decoction
茧唇/繭唇　lip cancer
茧唇·脾胃实热证/繭唇·脾胃實熱證　lip cancer with pattern of excessive heat in spleen and stomach
茧唇·心脾火毒证/繭唇·心脾火毒證　lip cancer with pattern of fire-toxin in heart and spleen
茧唇·阴虚火旺证/繭唇·陰虛火旺證　lip cancer with pattern of yin deficiency and fire effulgence
茧蜜/繭蜜　trehala
茧式敷料/火棉膠紗布敷料　cocoon dressing
检测限/可檢測性　detectability
检查/檢查，診察　examination
检弹探子/槍彈探子，子彈探針　bullet probe
检定菌/試驗菌　test organism
检镜片计/檢鏡片計　lensometer
检漏试验/檢漏試驗，測漏試驗　leak test, leak testing
检尿判病/檢尿判病規範　urocriterion
检尿诊病法/檢查尿診病法　urocrisia
检尸温度计/死溫表　thanatometer
检牙镜/口內視鏡　odontoscope
检眼镜/檢眼鏡　ophthalmoscope
检眼镜检查/檢眼鏡用法　ophthalmoscopy
检眼镜诊断法/檢眼鏡診斷法　medical ophthalmoscopy
检眼屈光镜/屈光檢眼鏡　ophthalmometroscope
F-检验/F-檢驗　F-test
检疫/檢疫　quarantine
检音导管/傳音導管　phonocatheter
检影镜/視網膜檢影器　skiascope
减病药/代用藥　supersedent
减充血剂/解除充血劑　decongestant
减滴质/減滴質　miostagmin
减毒病毒/減弱病毒　attenuated virus
减毒的/減弱的　attenuated
减毒活结核菌素/減毒活性核菌素　vital tuberculin
减毒接种/弱毒免疫　jennerization
减毒性结核/弱毒性結核　attenuated tuberculosis
减毒疫苗/減毒疫苗　attenuated vaccine
减肥药/減肥藥　anti-obesity agent
减缓心率药/減緩心率藥　bradycardiac drug
减量调节/減量調節　down regulation
减慢心率药/心搏減緩劑　bradycardiac
减尿氯药/尿氯減少劑　dechlorurant
减尿氯[作用]/減少尿氯排洩法　dechloruration
减轻/減輕　abatement
减少蠕动药/減少蠕動藥　antiperistaltic
减湿器/濕度減低器　dehumidifier
减食疗法/減食療法　slimming
减食欲剂/減食欲劑，食欲控制劑　anorexiant
减数分裂/減數分裂　meiosis
减数分裂后期/減數分裂後期　postmeiotic phase
减数分裂期/減數分裂期　reduction division phase
减数分裂前期/減數分裂前期　meiotic prophase
减数萎缩/數量萎縮　numeric atrophy
减速期/減速期　deceleration phase
减速期延长/減速期延長　prolonged deceleration phase
减速性[损]伤/減速性[損]傷　deceleration injury
减速依赖性心脏传导阻滞/減速依賴性心臟傳導阻斷　deceleration-dependent heart block
减体积肺移植/減體積肺移植　reduced-size lung transplantation
减体积肝移植/減體積肝移植　reduced-size liver transplantation
减效基因/遺漏基因　leaky gene
减压病/減壓病　decompression disease
减压曲线/減壓曲線　decreasing pressure curve
减压性[损]伤/減壓損傷，減壓病　decompression injury
减荧光物/減螢光質　bathoflore
减影技术/減影技術　subtraction technique
减张缝合/減壓縫法　tension suture
减张剂/減張劑　introfier
减张切口/減張切口　relaxation incision
减脂[术]/減脂[術]　defatting
减重膳食/減重膳食　reducing diet

剪刀式步态/剪刀式步態　scissor gait
剪动/剪式運動　scissors movement
剪接/剪接　splicing
剪接体/剪接體　spliceosome
剪切率/剪切率　shear rate
剪切黏度/切面黏度　shear viscosity
剪切启动因子/剪切啟動因子　cleavage stimulation factor
剪式探针/剪刀探針　scissors probe
剪式振动/剪式振動　scissoring vibration
剪形腿/剪形腿　scissor leg
睑板/瞼板　tarsal plate
睑板结膜瓣/瞼板結膜瓣　tarso-conjunctival flap
睑板瘤/瞼板瘤　tarsophyma
睑板膜/瞼板膜　tarsal membrane
睑板切开术/瞼板切開術　tarsotomy
睑板软化/瞼板軟化　tarsomalacia
睑板上凹陷[畸形]/瞼板上凹陷[畸形]　supratarsal depression
睑板腺/瞼[板]腺　tarsal gland
睑板腺癌/瞼板腺癌　carcinoma of meibomian gland
睑板腺痤疮/瞼痤瘡　acne tarsi
睑板腺囊肿/瞼板腺囊腫　tarsal cyst
睑板腺囊肿刮匙/瞼板腺囊腫刮匙　chalazion curet
睑板腺囊肿夹/瞼板腺囊腫夾　chalazion forcep
睑板腺炎/瞼板腺炎　blepharitis glandularis
睑板腺阻塞/瞼板腺阻塞　obstruction of tarsal gland
睑鼻襞/瞼鼻皺襞　palpebronasal fold
睑部/瞼部　palpebral part
睑的/瞼的　palpebral
睑肥厚/瞼肥厚　blepharopachynsis
睑粉瘤/瞼粥狀瘤　blepharoatheroma
睑缝合术/瞼縫合術　blepharorrhaphy
睑后面/瞼後面　posterior surface of eyelid
睑后缘/瞼後緣　posterior palpebral edge
睑黄斑瘤/瞼黃斑瘤　palpebral xanthelasma
睑夹/瞼夾　lid clamp
睑角炎/瞼角炎　blepharitis angularis
睑结膜/[眼]瞼結膜　palpebral conjunctiva
睑结膜炎/瞼結[合]膜炎，瞼內面炎　blepharitis internus, blepharoconjunctivitis
睑静脉/瞼靜脉　palpebral vein
睑静脉曲张/瞼靜脉曲張　varicoblepharon
睑裂/瞼裂，瞼缺損，眼瞼間裂隙　palpebral fissure, coloboma of eyelid, fissura palpebrae
睑裂高/瞼裂高　palpebral fissure height
睑裂宽/瞼裂寬　palpebral fissure breadth
睑裂扩大/瞼分離，閉眼不全　blepharodiastasis

睑裂倾斜度/瞼裂傾斜度　inclination of palpebral fissure
睑裂狭小/瞼口狹小　blepharophimosis
睑裂下斜/瞼裂下斜　antimongoloid slant of palpebral fissure
睑瘤/瞼瘤，瞼腫，眼贅疣　blepharoncus, blepharophyma
睑眉成形术/瞼眉造形術　blepharophryplasty
睑摩擦法/磨瞼療法　blepharoxysis
睑内侧动脉/瞼内側動脈　medial palpebral artery
睑内侧连合/内瞼連合　medial palpebral commissure
睑内侧韧带/瞼内側韌帶　medial palpebral ligament
[睑]内翻/[瞼]内翻，使起内翻，内轉瞼　entropionize, blepharelosis
睑内翻夹/瞼内翻鉗　entropion forcep
睑内翻矫正术/瞼内翻矯正術　correction of entropion
睑内结石/瞼内結石，結合膜石形成　conjunctival lithiasis
睑脓溢/瞼膿漏，化膿性眼瞼炎　blepharopyorrhea
睑皮松垂成形术/瞼皮鬆垂成形術　blepharochalasis plasty
睑皮松垂症/眼瞼鬆垂　dermatolysis palpebrarum
睑皮脂/眼脂　lema
睑前面/瞼前面　anterior surface of eyelid
睑前缘/瞼前緣　anterior palpebral edge
睑切除术/瞼切除術　blepharectomy
睑球后粘连/瞼球後粘連　posterior symblepharon
睑球前粘连/瞼球前粘連　anterior symblepharon
睑球全粘连/瞼球完全粘連　total symblepharon
睑球粘连/瞼球粘連　symblepharon
睑缺损/瞼缺損　eyelid coloboma
睑韧带/瞼韌帶　palpebral ligament
睑虱病/睫蝨病　pediculosis palpebrarum
睑水肿/瞼水腫，眼瞼積水　hydroblepharon
睑外侧动脉/瞼外側動脈　lateral palpebral artery
睑外侧缝/瞼外側縫　lateral palpebral raphe
睑外侧连合/外瞼連合　lateral palpebral commissure
睑外侧韧带/瞼外側韌帶　lateral palpebral ligament
睑外翻矫正术/瞼外翻矯正術　correction of ectropion
睑弦/瞼弦，瞼緣　palpebral margin
睑弦赤烂/瞼弦赤爛　ulcerous eyelid margin, marginal blepharitis
睑弦赤烂·风热袭表证/瞼弦赤爛·風熱襲表證　ulcerous eyelid margin with pattern of wind-heat assaulting exterior
睑弦赤烂·湿热壅盛证/瞼弦赤爛·濕熱壅盛證

ulcerous eyelid margin with pattern of dampness-heat congestion and excessiveness
睑弦赤烂·心火上炎证/瞼弦赤爛·心火上炎證　ulcerous eyelid margin with pattern of heart-fire flaring upward
睑腺炎/瞼腺炎,麥粒腫　stye
睑性眼疲劳/瞼板性眼力疲勞　tarsal asthenopia
睑黡/瞼黡　dark eye circle
睑硬结/瞼硬結　scleriasis
[睑]缘成形术/邊緣修補術,邊緣造形術　marginoplasty
睑缘缝合术/瞼緣縫合術　tarsorrhaphy
睑缘腺/瞼緣腺　Zeis gland
睑缘炎/瞼緣炎　blepharitis ciliaris
睑缘粘连/瞼緣粘連　ankyloblepharon
睑粘连/瞼粘連,上下瞼粘合　blepharosynechia
睑阵挛/瞼陣攣　blepharoclonus
睑支/瞼支　palpebral branch
睑赘皮/瞼贅皮,内眥贅皮　epiblepharon
简单并指/單純并指畸形　simple syndactyly
简单并趾/單純并趾畸形　simple syndactyly
简单部分发作/簡單部分發作　simple partial seizure
简单的/單純的　simple
简单𬌗架/簡單𬌗架　simple articulator
简单支抗/簡單支抗　simple anchorage
简弓/簡弓　simple arch
简化眼/簡化眼　reduced eye
简略损伤量表/簡略損傷量表　abbreviated injury scale
简明精神病状态评定量表/簡明精神病狀態評定量表　brief psychiatric rating scale
简易呼吸机/簡易呼吸機　simple respirator
碱/鹼　base, alkali
碱白蛋白/鹼性白蛋白　alkali albumin
碱潮/鹼潮　alkaline tide
碱储量/鹼儲量　alkali reserve
碱定量法/鹼定量法　alkalimetry
碱度/鹼度　alkalinity
碱过剩/鹼過量　base excess
碱化/鹼化　alkalizing
碱化剂/鹼化劑　alkalizer
碱化[作用]/鹼化,使成鹼性　alkalinization
碱基错配/鹼基錯配　base pair mismatch
碱基堆积/鹼基堆積　base stacking
碱基对/鹼基對　base pair, BP
碱基核蛋白/鹼基核蛋白　basic nuclear protein
碱基配对/鹼基配對　base pairing
碱基序列/鹼基序列　base sequence

碱基置换/鹼基置換　base substitution
碱基组成/鹼基組成　base composition
碱金属/鹼金屬　Alkalies
碱疗法/鹼療法　alkalitherapy
碱尿/鹼尿　alkalinuria
碱烧伤/鹼燒傷　alkali burn
碱石灰/蘇打石灰　soda lime
碱式醋酸铝溶液/次醋酸鋁溶液　aluminum subacetate solution
碱式醋酸铅溶液/次醋酸鉛溶液　lead subacetate solution
碱式硫酸铁溶液/亞硫酸鐵　ferric subsulfate solution
碱式水扬酸铋/次水楊酸鉍　bismuth subsalicylate
碱性/鹼性　alkaline
碱性氨基酸类/鹼性胺基酸類　basic amino acids
碱性氨基酸转运系统/鹼性胺基酸轉運系統　basic amino acid transport system
碱性成纤维细胞生长因子/鹼性纖維母細胞生長因子　basic fibroblast growth factor
碱性醋酸铅溶液/鹽基性醋酸鉛溶液　basic lead acetate solution
碱性反流性胃炎/鹼性反流性胃炎　alkaline reflux gastritis
碱性反应/鹼性反應　alkaline reaction
碱性刚果红染剂/鹼性剛果紅染劑　alkaline Congo red stain
碱性枸橼酸铵溶液/鹼性檸檬酸銨溶液　alkaline ammonium citrate solution
碱性过度/鹼過度,過鹼性　hyperalkalescence
碱性痂块膀胱炎/鹼性痂塊膀胱炎　alkaline incrusted cystitis
碱性结核菌素/鹼結核菌素,T. A.結核菌素　alkaline tuberculin
碱性磷酸酶/鹼性磷酸酶　alkaline phosphatase
碱性磷酸钠铝/鹼性磷酸鋁鈉　alkaline sodium phosphate
碱性硫化物/鹼性硫化物　alkaline sulfide
碱性硫酸盐/鹼式硫酸鹽　basic sulfate
碱性品红/鹼基性複紅　basic fuchsin
碱性染剂/鹼基性染料,鹼基性色料　basic dye, basic stain
碱性溶液/鹼性溶液　alkaline solution
碱性蕊香红/鹼性蕊香紅　rhodamine
碱性食品/鹼性食品　basic food
碱性消化不良/鹼性消化不良　alkaline dyspepsia
碱性盐/鹼式鹽,鹼基性鹽　basic salt
碱性饮食/鹼性飲食　basic diet

碱性浴/鹼性浴　alkaline bath
碱性正铁血红素/鹼性正鐵血紅素　alkali haematin
碱血[症]/鹼血症　alkalemia
碱液/灰汁　lye
碱中毒/鹼中毒　alkali intoxication, alkaline intoxication
碱中毒综合征/鹼中毒症候群　syndrome of alkalosis
见红/見紅　bloody show
见血封喉/見血封喉　Bohun upas
间断缝合/間斷縫法　interrupted suture
间断夹/間斷夾　interrupted splint
间断浆肌层缝合/間斷漿肌層縫合　interrupted seromuscular suture
间断性呼吸/間斷呼吸　interrupted respiration
间隔/分割空间　compartment
间隔分支阻滞/間隔分支阻滯　septal fascicular block
间隔区/間隔器　spacer
间接保持/間接保持　indirect retention
间接暴力/間接暴力　indirect violence, indirect force
间接冲洗法/間接注洗法　mediate irrigation
间接触染/間接觸染　mediate contagion
间接传染/間接傳染　indirect infection
间接刺激/間接刺激　indirect stimulation
间接催吐药/間接催吐藥　indirect emetic
间接的/間接的　indirect, mediate
间接范本假说/間接範本假說　indirect template hypothesis
间接复合伤/間接複合傷　combined indirect injury
间接盖髓术/間接蓋髓術　indirect pulp capping
间接骨折/間接骨折　indirect fracture
间接固位体/間接保持器　indirect retainer
间接喉镜检查[法]/間接喉鏡檢查　indirect laryngoscopy
间接呼吸/間接呼吸　indirect respiration
间接检眼镜/間接檢眼鏡　indirect ophthalmoscope
间接叩诊/間接叩診　indirect percussion
间接量热法/間接測熱法　indirect calorimetry
间接皮瓣/間接皮瓣　indirect skin flap
间接切口/間接切口　indirect incision
间接输血法/間接轉血法　indirect transfusion, mediate transfusion
间接胎盘X射线造影术/間接胎盤X光攝影術　indirect placentography
间接听诊/間接聽診法　mediate auscultation
间接血凝试验/間接血凝試驗　indirect hemagglutination test
间接荧光抗体技术/間接螢光抗體技術　indirect fluorescent antibody technique
间接诱变物/間接突變物　indirect acting mutagen
间接杂音/間接雜音　indirect murmur
间接照明法/間接照明法　indirect illumination
间接症状/間接症狀　indirect symptom
间接致癌物/間接致癌物　indirect acting carcinogen
间接转移/間接轉移　indirect transfer
间接作用/間接作用　indirect action
间隙/間隙　space
间隙保持/間隙保持　space maintenance
间隙卡环/間隙卡環　embrasure clasp
间歇负压通气/間歇負壓通氣　intermittent negative pressure ventilation
间歇疗法/間歇療法　intermittent treatment
间歇脉/間歇脈　intermittent pulse
间歇疟/間歇瘧　intermittent malaria
间歇强制通气/間歇強制通氣　intermittent mandatory ventilation
间歇热/間歇熱　intermittent fever
间歇沙滤池/間歇性砂礫濾器　intermittent sand filter
间歇式透析/間歇性透析　intermittent dialysis
间歇性跛行/間歇跛　intermittent claudication
间歇性蛋白尿/間歇性蛋白尿　intermittent proteinuria
间歇性导尿术/間歇性導尿術　intermittent catheterization
间歇性腹膜透析/間歇性腹膜透析　intermittent peritoneal dialysis
间歇性关节积水/間歇性關節積水　intermittent hydrarthrosis
间歇性关节痛/間歇性關節痛　intermittent arthralgia
间歇性加压呼吸/間歇正壓呼吸　intermittent positive pressure breathing
间歇性痉挛/間歇性痙攣　intermittent cramp
间歇性排尿/斷續排尿　stuttering urination
间歇性气体压缩装置/間歇性氣體壓縮裝置　intermittent pneumatic compression device
间歇性失禁/間歇性失禁　intermittent incontinence
间歇性斜视/間歇性斜視　intermittent strabismus
间歇性眼球突出/間歇性眼球突出　intermittent exophthalmos
间歇性眼球震颤/間歇性眼球震顫　intermittent nystagmus
间歇性运动障碍/間歇性運動障礙　intermittent dyskinesia
间歇性主动脉血流阻断/間歇性主動脈血流阻斷

intermittent aortic occlusion
间歇正压通气/間歇正壓通氣　intermittent positive pressure ventilation
建里/建里　jianli, RN11
建立细胞系/已建立之細胞系　established cell line
建筑材料/建築材料　construction materials
建筑规程/建築規程　building code
建筑物出入口/建築物出入口　architectural accessibility
建筑学/建築學　architecture
剑霉酸/劍黴酸　gladiolic acid
剑鞘形气管/鞘套狀氣管　scabbard trachea
剑突/劍突　xiphoid process
剑突联胎/劍突連胎　xiphopagus
剑突联胎切分术/劍突連胎分割術　xiphopagotomy
剑突摩擦音/劍突碎裂音　xiphisternal crunching sound
剑突脐联体/劍突臍聯體　xiphomphalopagus
剑突韧带/肋軟骨劍突韌帶　chondroxiphoid ligament
剑突痛/劍突痛　xiphodynia
剑突炎/劍突炎　xiphoiditis
剑胸结合/劍胸結合　xiphisternal synchondrosis
健肠药/健腸藥　intestinal tonic
健康保健/健康照護　health care
健康保险/健康保險　health insurance
健康城市/健康城市　healthy city
健康促进/健康促進　health promotion
健康促进学校/健康促進學校　health promoting school
健康促进医院/健康促進醫院　health promoting hospital
健康的/健康的，健全的　healthy
健康调查/健康調查　health survey
健康工人效应/健康工人效應　healthy worker effect
健康管理/醫務管理　healthcare management
健康计划/健康計劃　health planning
健康家庭/健康家庭　healthy family
健康教育/健康教育　health education
健康教育者/健康教育者　health educator
健康老龄化/健康老齡化　successful aging
健康态度/健康態度　attitude to health
健康体适能/健康體適能　health related physical fitness
健康维护组织/健康維護組織　health maintenance organization
健康相关生活质量/健康相關生活品質　health-related quality of life
健康信念/健康信念　health belief
健康信念模式/健康信念模式　health belief model
健康行为/健康行爲　health behavior
健康预期寿命/健康預期壽命　active life expectancy
健康状况/健康狀況　health status
健康状况指标/健康狀況指標　health status indicator
健美操/健身體操　calisthenics
健脾化湿/健脾化濕　invigorating spleen for eliminating dampness
健脾利水/健脾利水　invigorating spleen for diuresis
健脾驱虫/健脾驅蟲　invigorating spleen for expelling intestinal parasites
健身训练/健身訓練　fitness training
健身中心/健身中心　fitness center
健神经药/健補神經劑　neurotonic
健忘[病]/健忘[症]　amnesia
健忘·肝气郁结证/健忘·肝氣鬱結證　amnesia with pattern of liver qi depression
健忘·年老神衰证/健忘·年老神衰證　amnesia with pattern of senile neurasthenia
健忘·肾精亏虚证/健忘·腎精虧虛證　amnesia with pattern of kidney essence insufficiency
健忘·痰瘀闭阻证/健忘·痰瘀閉阻證　amnesia with pattern of blockade of phlegm and static blood
健忘·痰浊上扰证/健忘·痰濁上擾證　amnesia with pattern of upward disturbance of phlegm-turbidity
健忘·心脾两虚证/健忘·心脾兩虛證　amnesia with pattern of heart-spleen deficiency
健忘·心肾不交证/健忘·心腎不交證　amnesia with pattern of incoordination between heart and kidney
健忘虚谈综合征/健忘虛談症候群　amnestic-confabulatory
健忘·血瘀闭阻证/健忘·血瘀閉阻證　amnesia with pattern of blockade of blood stasis
健胃/健胃　invigorating the stomach
健胃药/健胃藥　stomachic, stomachic tonic
渐进抗阻运动/漸進抗阻運動　progressive resistant exercise
渐进性坏死/漸進性壞死　necrobiosis
渐进性坏死疾患/漸進性壞死疾患　necrobiotic disorder
渐进性坏死性黄肉芽肿/壞死性黃肉芽腫　necrobiotic xanthogranuloma
渐强性睡眠/漸強性睡眠　crescendo sleep
渐强杂音/漸強雜音　crescendo murmur
践底趾/踐底趾　undertoe
腱/腱　tendon

腱包膜/腱包膜　peritendon
腱成形术/腱造形術　tendinoplasty
腱刀/腱刀　tendotome
腱的/肌腱的　tendinous
腱反射/腱反射　tendon reflex
腱反应/腱反應　tendon jerk
腱缝术/腱縫合術　tendinosuture
腱感受器/腱受器　tenoreceptor
腱弓/腱弓　tendinous arch
腱骨化/腱骨化　tenonostosis
腱划/腱劃　tendinous intersection
腱滑膜鞘/腱滑膜鞘　synovial sheath of tendon
腱黄[色]瘤/腱性黄瘤　xanthoma tendinosum
腱肌成形术/腱肌造形術　tenomyoplasty
腱间结合/腱間結合　intertendinous connection
腱交叉/腱交叉　tendinous chiasma
腱结合/腱結合　tendinous junction
腱瘤/腱瘤　tenontophyma
腱论/腱論　tenontography
腱膜/腱膜　aponeurosis
腱膜刀/腱膜刀　aponeurotome
腱膜的/腱膜的　aponeurotic
腱膜切除术/腱膜切除術　aponeurectomy
腱膜切开术/腱膜切開術　aponeurotomy
腱膜下间隙/腱膜下間隙　subaponeurotic space
腱膜纤维瘤/腱膜纖維瘤　aponeurotic fibroma
腱膜学/腱膜學　aponeurology
腱膜炎/腱膜炎　aponeurositis
腱内膜/肌腱内膜　endotendineum
腱黏液鞘/腱黏液鞘　mucous sheath of tendon
腱纽/腱紐　vincula tendinum
腱旁组织/腱隙組織　paratenon
腱鞘/腱鞘,腱外衣,腱外膜　tendinous sheath, epitenon
腱鞘瘭疽/腱鞘瘭疽　thecal whitlow
腱鞘滑膜憩室/腱鞘滑膜憩室　ganglion diverticulum
腱鞘囊肿/腱鞘囊腫,包鞘囊腫　thecal cyst, ganglion cyst, weeping sinew
腱鞘囊肿造口术/腱鞘囊腫造口術　ganglionostomy
腱鞘切除术/腱鞘切除術　tenosynovectomy
腱鞘狭窄/腱鞘狹窄　thecostegnosis
腱鞘纤维瘤/腱鞘纖維瘤　fibroma of tendon sheath
腱鞘炎/腱鞘炎　tendinous synovitis, tenosynovitis
腱鞘炎·风寒证/腱鞘炎·風寒證　tenosynovitis with wind-cold pattern
腱鞘炎·血瘀证/腱鞘炎·血瘀證　tenosynovitis with blood stasis pattern
腱鞘肿/腱鞘腫脹　onkinocele
腱切除术/腱[鞘]切除術　tenectomy
腱切断/腱切斷　tenotomize
腱切断术/腱切斷術　tendotomy
腱束/腱束　tendon bundle
腱束膜/腱鞘　peritendineum
腱撕裂/肌腱曳傷　pulled tendon
腱损伤/腱損傷　tendon injury
腱梭/腱梭　tendon spindle
腱索/腱索　chordae tendineae
腱索断裂/腱索斷裂　rupture of chordae tendineae
腱索缩短术/腱索縮短術　shortening of chordae tendineae
腱索心内膜炎/腱索心内膜炎　endocarditis chordalis
腱索延长术/腱索延長術　lengthening of chordae tendineae
腱索移位术/腱索移位術　transposition of chordae tendineae
腱糖蛋白/腱糖蛋白　tenascin
腱跳动/腱跳動　subsultus tendinum
腱痛/腱痛　teinodynia
腱痛风/腱痛風,痛風性腱病　tenontagra
腱外膜/腱[纖維]鞘　epitendineum
腱系膜/腱間膜　mesotendineum
腱细胞/肌腱細胞　tendon cell
腱下囊/腱下囊　subtendinous bursa
腱纤维/腱纖維　tendon fiber
腱性联接/腱性連合　syntenosis
腱学/腱學　tenontology
腱炎/腱炎　tendinitis
腱转移术/腱轉移術　tendon transfer
腱赘/腱贅　tenophyte
溅射现象/濺射現象　sputtering phenomenon
鉴别标识/鑑別標志　identification marker
鉴别培养基/鑑別培養基　differential medium
鉴别皮肤反应/鑑別性皮膚反應　differential cutireaction
鉴别染色法/鑑別染色法　differential staining
鉴别诊断/鑑別診斷　differential diagnosis
鉴定/鑑定,鑑別　identification
键长/鍵長　bond length
键合/連結,鍵結　linkage
键角/鍵角　bond angle
箭毒/箭毒　curare
箭毒化/箭毒中毒作用　curarization
箭毒碱/箭毒素　curarine
箭毒蛙碱/蛙毒素　batrachotoxin
箭毒样[神经]阻断剂/箭毒樣神經阻斷劑　curaremimetic

箭鱼精蛋白/箭魚精蛋白　xiphin
江湖药/江湖藥　street drug
江湖医术/江湖醫術　quack medicine
江内斯科脊髓麻醉/Jonnesco 氏脊髓麻醉　Jonnesco spinal anesthesia
江珧柱蛋白/江珧柱蛋白　pinnaglobin
将军之官/將軍之官　liver as the general organ
姜半夏/姜半夏　ginger processed pinellia tuber
姜黄/薑黄　turmeric
姜黄[试]纸/薑黄紙　turmeric paper
姜黄素/薑黄素　curcumin
姜酒中毒性多神经炎/薑酒中毒性多神經炎　jamaica ginger polyneuritis
姜片虫病/薑片蟲病　fasciolopsiasis
姜汁制/薑汁制　stir-frying with ginger juice
豇豆球蛋白/豇豆蛋白　vignin
浆果/漿果　berry
浆果薯蓣属/漿果薯蕷　Tamus
浆果细胞/漿果細胞　berry cell
浆果状动脉瘤/漿果狀動脈瘤　berry aneurysm
浆酶原细胞/漿酶原細胞　serozymogenic cell
浆膜/漿膜　serous membrane
浆膜结核/漿膜結核　tuberculosis of serous membranes
浆膜囊/漿液囊　serous sac
浆膜黏蛋白/漿膜黏蛋白　serosamucin
浆膜腔/漿膜腔　serous cavity
浆膜下层/漿膜下層,漿膜下組織　subserosa
浆膜下丛/漿膜下神經叢　subserous plexus
浆膜下的/漿膜下的　subserous
浆膜下[肌]层/漿膜下[肌]層　subserous layer
浆膜下麻醉/漿膜下麻醉　subserous anesthesia
浆膜下组织/漿膜下組織　adventitious coat of uterine tube
浆膜心包/心包漿膜層　serous pericardium
浆膜炎/漿膜炎　serositis
浆母细胞/漿母細胞　plasmablast
浆黏液细胞/漿黏液細胞　seromucous cell
浆细胞/漿細胞　plasma cell
浆细胞白血病/漿細胞白血病　plasmacytic leukemia
浆细胞肝炎/血漿細胞肝炎　plasma cell hepatitis
浆细胞龟头炎/漿細胞龜頭炎　plasma cell balanitis
浆细胞淋巴瘤/漿細胞淋巴瘤　plasmacytic lymphoma
浆细胞瘤/漿細胞瘤　plasmacytoma
浆细胞肉芽肿/漿細胞肉芽腫　plasma cell granuloma
浆细胞性白血病样反应/漿細胞性白血病樣反應　plasmacytic leukemoid reaction
浆细胞性唇炎/漿細胞口唇炎　plasma cell cheilitis
浆细胞性龟头炎/漿細胞性龜頭炎　plasma cell balanitis
浆细胞性开口部位黏膜炎/漿細胞性開口部位黏膜炎　plasma cell orificial mucositis
浆细胞性乳腺炎/漿細胞性乳腺炎　plasma cell mastitis
浆细胞性外阴炎/漿細胞女陰炎　plasma cell vulvitis
浆细胞性网状细胞增多症/漿細胞性網狀細胞增多症　plasmacytic reticulosis
浆细胞龈炎/漿細胞齦炎　plasma cell gingivitis
浆细胞增多[症]/漿細胞增多　plasmacytosis
浆液/漿液　serous fluid
浆液半月/漿液半月　serous demilune
浆液恶露/漿性惡露　lochia serosa
浆液囊腺癌/漿液囊腺癌　serous cystadenocarcinoma
浆液囊腺瘤/漿液性囊腺瘤　serous cystadenoma
浆液囊肿/漿液囊腫　serous cyst
浆液黏液性的/漿黏液性的　seromucous
浆液气胸/漿液氣胸　pneumoserothorax
浆液细胞/漿液細胞　serous cell
浆液纤维蛋白性的/漿液纖維蛋白的　serofibrinous
浆液纤维蛋白性心包炎/漿液纖維素性心包炎　serofibrinous pericarditis
浆液腺/漿液腺　serous gland
浆液腺泡/漿液腺泡　serous acinus
浆液性/漿液性　serosity
浆液性肠炎/漿性腸炎　lymphenteritis
浆液性出血/漿液性出血　serous hemorrhage
浆液[性]的/漿液性的　serous
浆液性恶露/漿液性惡露　serous lochia
浆液性腹膜炎/漿液性腹膜炎　serous peritonitis
浆液性肝病/漿液性肝障礙　serous hepatosis
浆液性根尖周炎/漿液性根尖周炎　serous periapical periodontitis
浆液性虹膜炎/漿液性虹膜炎　aquocapsulitis
浆液性滑膜炎/漿液性滑膜炎　serous synovitis
浆液性脑膜炎/漿液性腦膜炎　meningitis serosa
浆液性脓/漿液性膿　seropus
浆液性渗出/漿性滲出液　serous effusion
浆液性萎缩/漿液性萎縮　serous atrophy
浆液性心包炎/漿液性心包炎　pericarditis serous
浆液性炎/漿液性炎,漿注性炎症　serous inflammation
浆液性咽峡炎/漿液性咽峽炎　serous angina
浆液性中耳炎/漿液性中耳炎　otitis media serosa
浆液血性恶露/漿液血性惡露　lochia serosanguinea

浆液组织形成性炎/漿液成形性炎症　seroplastic inflammation
僵蚕/僵蠶　stiff silkworm
僵人综合征/僵人症候群　stiff man syndrome
僵硬/堅硬度　stiffness
僵直皮肤综合征/僵直皮膚症候群,先天性肌膜失養　stiff-skin syndrome
僵住症/倔強症,强直性昏厥　catalepsy
僵住症患者/倔強症患者　cataleptic
缰/繮　Habenula(拉)
缰核/繮核　habenular nucleus
缰核脚间束/繮核腳間束　habenulointerpeduncular tract
缰核束/繮徑　habenular tract
缰连合/繮連合　habenular commissure
缰脑脚间束/繮腳徑　habenulopeduncular tract
缰内侧核/繮內側核　medial habenular nucleus
缰三角/繮三角　habenular trigone
缰外侧核/繮外側核　lateral habenular nucleus
桨状手板/蹼型手板　paddle-shaped hand plate
桨状足板/蹼型足板　paddle-shaped foot plate
降鼻中隔肌/降鼻中隔肌　musculus depressor septi nasi
降部/降部　descending part
降低胆固醇活性/降低膽固醇活性　cholesterol-lowering activity
降低胆固醇物质/降低膽固醇物質　cholesterol-lowering substance
降低风险行为/降低風險行爲　risk reduction behavior
降钙素/抑鈣素　calcitonin
降钙素基因相关肽/抑鈣素基因系肽　calcitonin gene-related peptide
降钙素基因相关肽受体/抑鈣素基因系肽受體　calcitonin gene-related peptide receptor
降钙素受体/抑鈣素受體　calcitonin receptor
降钾剂/降鉀劑　hypokalemic
降结肠/降結腸　descending colon
降结肠系膜/降結腸繫膜　mesentery of descending part of colon
降结肠周炎/降結腸周圍炎　pericolitis sinistra
降解/降解　degradation
降口角肌/降口角肌　depressor anguli oris, depressor muscle of angle of mouth
降落伞式二尖瓣/降落傘式二尖瓣　parachute mitral valve
降眉肌/降眉肌　musculus depressor supercilii
降眉间肌/降眉間肌　procerus, musculus procerus
降脑胺药/降腦胺藥　brain amine depleter
降气剂/降氣劑　formula for descending qi
降温/使清涼　cooling
降温神经/降溫神經　frigorific nerve
降下唇肌/降下唇肌,下唇掣肌　depressor labii inferioris, depressor muscle of lower lip
降线二波/降線重搏波　catadicrotic wave
降线二波脉[现象]/降線重搏脈,降線重脈搏,降線複搏脈　catadicrotism, catadicrotic pulse
降线三波脉[现象]/降線三搏脈　catatricrotism
降线一波脉[现象]/小隆狀態,降線小隆波　catacrotism, catacrotic wave
降香/降香　rosewood
降血糖药/降血糖藥　hypoglycemic, hypoglycemic agent
降血压药/降血壓藥　hypotensor
降血脂药/降血脂藥　hypolipidemic, antilipemic agent
降压物质/降壓物質　depressor substance
降压物质检查法/降壓物質檢查法　test of depressor substance
降支/降支　descending branch
降主动脉/降主動脈　descending aorta
绛舌/絳舌　deep red tongue
酱汁状痰/醬汁狀痰　prune-juice sputum
交臂皮瓣/交臂皮瓣　cross arm skin flap
交叉/交叉　cross
交叉步态/八字步式　cross-legged progression
交叉池/交叉池　chiasmatic cistern
交叉唇瓣/交叉唇瓣　cross lip flap
交叉端化/交叉端化　terminalization of chiasma
交叉反应/交叉反應　cross reaction
交叉反应抗原/交叉反應抗原　cross reacting antigen
交叉感染/交互傳染,相互傳染　cross infection
交叉感知受体/交叉感知受體　receptor cross-talk
交叉沟/交叉溝　chiasmatic groove
交叉灌注/交叉灌注　cross perfusion
交叉肌/交叉肌　cruciate muscle
交叉睑瓣/交叉瞼瓣　eyelid switch flap
交叉耐受[性]/交叉耐受[性]　cross tolerance
交叉凝集[反应]/交互凝集,類屬凝集　cross agglutination
交叉凝集素/交互凝素　cross agglutinin
交叉配血/交互配合法　cross matching
交叉偏利/交叉偏側　crossed laterality
交叉启动/交叉啟動　cross-priming
交叉前沟/交叉前溝　sulcus prechiasmaticus
交叉桥/交叉橋　cross-bridge

交叉设计/交叉設計　cross-over design
交叉栓塞/對側栓塞　crossed embolism
交叉污染/交叉汙染　cross-contamination
交叉吸收[试验]/交叉吸收[試驗]　cross absorption test
交叉心/交叉心　crisscross heart
交叉性反射/交叉性反射　crossed jerk
交叉性复视/交叉性複視　crossed diplopia
交叉性感觉缺失/對側感覺缺失　crossed anesthesia
交叉性麻痹/交叉性麻痺　transverse palsy
交叉性偏侧感觉缺失/交叉性單側麻木　alternate hemianesthesia
交叉性弱视/交叉性弱視　crossed amblyopia
交叉性瘫痪/交叉性癱瘓　crossed paralysis
交叉性转移/交叉性轉移　crossed metastasis
交叉循环/交叉循環　cross circulation
交叉遗传/[異性]交叉遺傳　crisscross inheritance
交叉异位肾/交叉異位腎　crossed ectopic kidney
交叉扎法/交織性結扎　interlacing ligature
交叉柱镜/交叉柱鏡　crossed cylinder lens
交叉锥体束/錐體交叉徑　crossed pyramidal tract
交错突细胞/交錯性網織細胞　interdigitating cell
交感/交感　jiaogan, AH6a, sympathetic
交感成神经细胞/交感神經原細胞,交感神經母細胞　sympathetic neuroblast
交感的/交感的　sympathic
交感干/交感幹　sympathetic trunk
交感干神经节/交感幹神經節　ganglia of sympathetic trunk
交感根/交感根　sympathetic root
交感神经/交感神經　sympathetic nerve
交感神经的/交感神經的　sympathetic
交感[神经]干/交感神經索　ganglionated cord
交感神经节/交感神經節　sympathetic ganglion, sympathetic ganglia
交感神经节切除术/交感神經節切除術　gangliosympathectomy
交感神经链/交感神經鏈　sympathetic chain
交感神经切除术/交感神經切除術　sympathectomy
交感神经手术/交感神經手術　operation on sympathetic nervous system
交感神经系统/交感神經系統　sympathetic system
交感神经系统病/交感神經[系]病　sympathicopathy
交感神经细胞/交感神經細胞　sympathetic cell
交感神经型颈椎病/交感神經型頸椎病　sympathetic type of cervical spondylosis
交感神经性上睑下垂/交感神經性垂瞼　ptosis sympathica
交感神经性涎/交感神經性腺涎　sympathetic saliva
交感神经压轧术/交感神經壓碎術　sympathicotripsy
交感神经原细胞/交感神經胚細胞　sympathogonium
交感神经张力过敏/交感神經系興奮性過強　hypersympathicotonus
交感神经张力减退/交感神經系興奮性過弱　hyposympathicotonus
交感神经支配/交感神經支配　sympathetic innervation
交感神经阻滞/交感神經阻斷麻醉　sympathetic block
交感神经阻滞药/交感神經阻斷藥　sympatholytic
交感嗜铬的/交感神經嗜鉻細胞的　sympathochromaffin
交感嗜铬细胞/交感神經嗜鉻細胞　sympathochromaffin cell
交感性刺激/交感性刺激　sympathetic irritation
交感性虹膜麻痹/交感性虹膜麻痺　sympathetic iridoplegia
交感性脑膜炎/交感性腦膜炎　meningitis sympathica
交感性萎缩/交感性萎縮　sympathetic atrophy
交感性眼炎/共感性眼炎　sympathetic ophthalmia
交感眼/共炎眼　sympathizing eye
交媾不能/交媾不能　impotentia coeundi
交骨/交骨　pubic symphysis, pubis bone
交合盘/交合盤　copulatory disc
交互催化/交互催化,對偶催化　allelocatalysis
交互的/交互的,相互的　reciprocal
交互分析/交互分析　transactional analysis
交互神经支配/交互神經支配　reciprocal innervation
交互输血/交互輸血法　reciprocal transfusion
交互突触/交互突觸　reciprocal synapse
交互抑制/相互抑制　reciprocal inhibition
交互证实/交互確效　cross-validation
交互支抗/交互支抗　reciprocal anchorage
交互作用/交互作用　interaction
交互作用节律/交互作用節律　reciprocating rhythm
交换器/交換器　exchanger
交换输血法/交換輸血　exsanguinotransfusion
交会穴/交會穴　crossing point
交货/交貨　consignment delivery
交接出血/交接出血　postcoital bleeding
交接处逸搏心律/房室結性逸脫節律　junctional escape rhythm
交接区心律/節律房室結合點,結合節律　junctional rhythm
交接区性心动过速/房室結性心搏快速　junctional

tachycardia
交界分离术后综合征/後聯合切開症候群 postcommissurotomy syndrome
交界瘤/交界瘤 borderline tumor
交界型大疱性表皮松解[症]/交界型大皰性表皮鬆解[症] junctional epidermolysis bullosa
交界痣/交界痣 junctional nevus
交联试剂/交聯試劑 cross-linking reagent
交联学说/交聯學說 cross linkage theory
交联助听器/交聯助聽器 contralateral routing of signals aid
交流障碍/交流障礙 communication disorder
交配/交合,交媾 copulation
交配型/交配型 mating type
交沙霉素/交沙黴素 josamycin
交替/交替 alternant
交替的/交替性 alternate
交替激活途径/替代啟動途徑 alternative activation pathway
交替冷热试验/交替冷熱試驗 alternate hot and cold caloric test
交替脉/交替脈,交互脈 pulsus alternans
交替宿主/交替宿主 alternate host
交替型精神病/交替性精神病 alternating psychosis
交替[性]的/交替[性]的,替代的 alternative
交替性瘫痪/交替性癱瘓 alternate hemiplegia
交替性瞳孔开大/交替性散瞳,跳躍性散瞳 alternating mydriasis
交替性斜视/交替性斜視 alternating strabismus
交替遗传/交互遺傳 alternative inheritance
交替遮盖试验/交替遮蓋試驗 alternative cover test
交通的/交通的 communicans
交通动脉/穿通動脈 perforating artery
交通工具损伤/交通損傷 traffic injury
交通后部/交通後部 postcommunicating part
交通静脉/穿通靜脈 perforating vein
交通前部/交通前部 precommunicating part
交通事故/交通事故 traffic accident
交通[事故]伤/交通[事故]傷 traffic accident injury
交通事故医学/交通事故醫學 traffic medicine
交通心肾/交通心腎 restoring normal coordination between heart and kidney, treating incoordination between heart and kidney
交通性脑积水/交通性水腦 communicating hydrocephalus
交通性鞘膜积液/交通性水囊 communicating hydrocele
交通噪声/交通雜訊 transportation noise

交通支/交通支 communicating branch
交腿皮瓣/交腿皮瓣 cross leg skin flap
交腿性麻痹/架腿麻痺 crossed leg palsy
交信/交信 jiaoxin, KI8
郊区卫生/郊區衛生 suburban health
郊区卫生服务/郊區衛生服務 suburban health service
胶孢子虫的/膠孢子囊的 psorospermial
胶孢子虫囊肿/膠孢子蟲囊腫 psorospermial cyst
胶布/膠布 adhesive tape
胶布绷带/可黏性繃帶 adhesive bandage
胶布帽/膠布帽 adhesive tape cap
胶布皮炎/膠布皮膚炎 adhesive tape dermatitis
胶冻剂/凍膠 jelly
胶耳/膠耳 glue ear
胶工溃疡病/膠工潰瘍病,Chiclero 氏潰瘍 Chiclero ulcer
胶固素/膠固素 conglutinin
胶剂/膠劑 colloids
胶浆剂/膠漿劑 mucilloid
胶酵母/明膠酵母菌 saccharomyces glutinis
胶粒/膠體粒子 colloidal particle
胶霉毒素/膠毒素 gliotoxin
胶囊[剂]/膠囊[劑] capsule
胶黏剂/黏著物 adhesive
胶黏剂皮炎/膠黏劑皮膚炎 adhesive dermatitis
胶凝力计/膠凝力計 gelometer
胶[凝状]态/膠態 colloidal state
胶凝作用/凝膠作用,凝膠化 gelation, pectization
胶片辐射剂量测定法/膠片輻射劑量測定法 film dosimetry
胶溶[作用]/消膠作用 peptization
胶乳/膠乳 latex
胶乳过敏症/膠乳過敏症 latex hypersensitivity
胶乳结合试验/膠乳結合試驗 latex fixation test
胶束/膠粒 micelle
胶束电动毛细管色谱法/膠束電動毛細管色譜法 micellar electrokinetic capillary chromatography
胶束动电毛细管色谱法/微膠束電動毛細管層析法 micellar electrokinetic capillary chromatography, MECC
胶束色谱法/微膠束層析法 micellar chromatography
胶束增敏荧光分析法/微膠束增敏螢光分析法 micellar enhanced spectrofluorometric method
胶态硫/膠狀硫 colloidal sulfur
胶态液体/膠質溶液 colloidal solution
胶体/膠體,膠質 colloid

胶体化学/膠體化學　collochemistry
胶体金/膠體金　gold colloid, colloidal gold
胶体膜平衡/膠體膜平衡　colloid equilibrium
胶体磨/膠體磨　colloid mill
胶体平衡障碍性休克/膠質平衡障礙性休克　colloidoclastic shock
胶体溶液/膠體溶液　colloidal solution
胶体渗透压/膠體滲透壓　colloid osmotic pressure
胶体吞噬/膠質吞噬　colloidophagy
胶体硒/膠體硒　electroselenium
胶体性猝衰/膠質平衡障礙　colloidoclasia
胶体性休克/膠質性休克　colloid shock
胶体悬液/懸膠體　suspension colloid
胶性电解质/膠質電解質　colloidal electrolyte
胶样变性/膠狀變性　colloid degeneration
胶样甲状腺肿/膠性甲狀腺腫　colloid goiter
胶样假性粟丘疹/膠樣假粟丘疹　colloid pseudomilium
胶样角化/膠樣角化　colloid keratosis
胶样囊肿/膠[質]狀囊腫　colloid cyst
胶样粟丘疹/膠樣粟丘疹　colloid milium
胶样小体/膠樣小體　colloid body
胶原/膠原,成膠質　collagen
胶原病/膠原病　collagen disease
胶原沉积/膠原沈積　collagen deposition
胶原重组/膠原重組　collagen recombination
胶原缝线/膠原縫線　collagen suture
胶原紧缩/膠原緊縮　collagen shrinkage
胶原浸充移植物/膠原浸充移植物　collagen impregnated graft
胶原均质化/膠原均質化　homogenization of collagen
胶原瘤/膠原瘤　collagenoma
胶原酶/成膠質酵素,膠原酵素　collagenase
胶原凝素类/膠凝素類　collectins
胶原溶解/膠原溶解　collagenolysis
胶原生成/膠原生成　collagenation
胶原受体/膠原受體　collagen receptor
胶原细胞/膠原細胞　collagenocyte
胶原纤维/膠原纖維　collagen fiber
胶原纤维瘤/膠原性纖維瘤　collagenous fibroma
胶原性疾病/膠原性疾病　collagenosis
胶原性结肠炎/膠原性結腸炎　collagenous colitis
胶原性类晶体/膠原性類晶體　collagenous crystalloids
胶原性小球症/膠原性小球症　collagenous spherulosis
胶原血管病/膠原血管疾病　collagen vascular disease
胶原抑制药/膠原抑制藥　collagen inhibitor
胶原原纤维/膠原原纖維　collagen fibril
胶原植入物/膠原植入物　collagen implant
胶原注射/膠原注射　collagen injection
胶质/膠質　colloid substance
胶质尘肺病/膠質塵肺症　collagenous pneumoconiosis
胶质界膜/[神經]膠質界膜　glial limiting membrane
胶质母细胞瘤/神經膠母細胞瘤　glioblastoma
胶质丝/膠質絲　glial filament
胶质素/膠質素　collastin
胶质细胞成熟因子/膠質細胞成熟因子　glia maturation factor
胶质小体/膠質小體　colloid body
胶质原纤维/膠質原纖維　glial fibril
胶状癌/膠狀癌　carcinoma gelatinosum
胶状的/膠狀的　colloidal
胶状骨髓/膠狀骨髓　gelatinous bone marrow
胶状瘤/膠狀瘤　colloid tumor
胶状黏液瘤/膠狀黏液瘤　myxoma gelatinosum
胶状质/膠狀質　substantia gelatinosa, gelatinosa
胶着性糖蛋白缺乏症/膠著性糖蛋白缺乏症　adhesive glycoprotein deficiency
椒疮/椒瘡　prickly-ash-like sore, trachoma
椒疮·风热客睑证/椒瘡·風熱客瞼證　prickly-ash-like sore with pattern of wind-heat lodging in eyelid
椒疮·脾胃湿热证/椒瘡·脾胃濕熱證　prickly-ash-like sore with pattern of dampness-heat in spleen and stomach
椒疮·血热瘀滞证/椒瘡·血熱瘀滯證　prickly-ash-like sore with pattern of blood-heat stasis and stagnation
焦点/焦點　focal spot
焦点距离/焦點距離,焦距　focal distance, focal length
焦点黏着/焦點粘著　focal adhesion
焦点型透镜/焦點型透鏡　punktal lens
焦点照明/焦點照明　focal illumination
焦耳效应/焦耳效應　joule effect
焦谷氨酸水解酶/焦穀胺酸水解酶　pyroglutamate hydrolase
焦谷氨酸肽酶/焦穀胺酸肽酶　pyroglutamyl-peptidase
焦糊精/焦糊精　pyrodextrin
焦痂/焦痂　eschar
焦痂切除术/焦痂切除術　escharectomy
焦痂切开术/焦痂切開術　escharotomy
焦痂下抗生素灌注治疗/焦痂下抗生素灌注治療

subeschar antibiotic infusion therapy
焦痂下细菌计数/焦痂下細菌計數　subeschar bacterial count
焦痂性冻疮/焦痂性凍瘡　escharotic frostbite
焦痂自溶/焦痂自溶　autolysis of eschar
焦间距/焦間距　focal interval
焦磷酸/焦磷酸　pyrophosphoric acid
焦磷酸钙/焦磷酸鈣　calcium pyrophosphate
焦磷酸钙沉积症/焦磷酸鈣沈積症　calcium pyrophosphate deposition disease
焦磷酸硫胺素/焦磷酸硫胺素　thiamin pyrophosphate
焦磷酸酶/焦磷酸酶　pyrophosphatase
焦磷酸钠/焦磷酸鈉　sodium pyrophosphate
焦磷酸盐/焦磷酸鹽　pyrophosphate
焦虑/焦慮　anxiety
焦虑不安/精神激動　agitation
焦虑不安的/精神激動的　agitated
焦虑发作/焦慮發作　anxiety attack
焦虑紧张状态/焦慮緊張狀態　anxiety tension state
焦虑性精神病/焦慮性精神病　anxiety psychosis
焦虑性神经症/焦慮性神經病　anxiety neurosis
焦虑性抑郁[症]/焦慮性抑鬱[症]　anxious depression
焦虑性癔病/焦慮性癔病　anxiety hysteria
焦虑性谵妄/焦慮譫妄　anxious delirium
焦虑与忧郁混合障碍/焦慮與憂鬱混合障礙　mixed anxiety and depression disorder
焦虑状态/焦慮狀態　anxious state
焦虑综合征/焦慮症候群　anxiety syndrome
焦没食子酚/焦性没食子酚　pyrogallol
焦木酸/焦木酸,木醋酸　pyroligneous acid
焦硼酸/焦硼酸　pyroboric acid
焦硼酸盐/焦硼酸鹽　pyroborate
焦砷酸/焦砷酸　pyroarsenic acid
焦炭/熟煤,焦煤　coke
焦碳酸二乙酯/焦碳酸二乙酯　diethyl pyrocarbonate
焦糖/焦糖　caramel
焦土霉素/焦土黴素　showdomycin
焦亚硫酸钠/焦亞硫酸鈉　sodium pyrosulfite
焦油/焦油　tar
焦油癌/焦油癌　tar carcinoma
焦油角化病/焦油角化症　tar keratosis
焦油冷浸剂/焦油冷浸劑　tar-water
焦油性黑变病/焦油黑變病　tar melanosis
嚼肌肥大/嚼肌肥大　masseteric hypertrophy
嚼肌间隙/嚼肌間隙　masseteric space
嚼咀咬合面/嚼咀咬合面　working occlusal surface

嚼力计/嚼力計,咀嚼力測驗器　phagodynamometer
角/角　angle, horn
角部/角部　angular part
角层分离/角質分離　deciduous skin
角层下的/角質層下的　subcorneal
角层下脓疱性皮肤病/角質層下膿疹性皮膚病　subcorneal pustular dermatosis
角叉菜/鹿角菜　carrageen
角叉菜胶/鹿角菜膠　carrageenan
角蛋白/角蛋白　ceratin
角蛋白酶/角蛋白酵素　keratinase
角蛋白细胞/角蛋白細胞　keratinocyte
角蛋白小体/角蛋白顆粒　keratinosome
角的/角的　angular
角动/角動　angular movement
角弓反张/角弓反張　opisthotonus, opisthotonos
角巩膜/角鞏膜　corneosclera
角巩膜表层炎/慢性角膜鞏膜炎　epicorneascleritis
角巩膜割烙术/角鞏膜割烙術　cutting and cauterizing therapy for sclera and cornea
角化/角化　cornification, keratinization
角化癌/角化癌　cancroid
角化病/角化病,角質層病　keratosis
角化病的/角化病的　keratotic
角化不良/角化不良　dyskeratosis
角化不良瘤/角化不良瘤　dyskeratoma
角化不良症/角化不全症　dyskeratosis
角化不全/角質化不全　parakeratosis
角化不全的/角化不全的　parakeratotic
角化不全细胞/角化不全的細胞　parakeratotic cell
角化复层扁平上皮/角化複層扁平上皮　keratinized stratified squamous epithelium
角化过度/角化病,角化過度症　hyperkeratosis
角化棘皮瘤/角質棘皮瘤　keratoacanthoma
角化囊肿/角質囊腫　keratocyst
角化性痤疮/角化性痤瘡　acne cornea
角化珠/角化珠　horny pearl
角化[作用]/角化[作用]　cutinization
角环肌/角環肌　ceratocricoid, ceratocricoid muscle
角环韧带/角環韌帶　ceratocricoid ligament
角回/角迴　angular gyrus
角回动脉/角迴動脈　artery of angular gyrus
角回综合征/角迴症候群　angular gyrus syndrome
角棘/角棘　alar spine
角结膜炎/角膜結膜炎　keratoconjunctivitis
角孔径/孔徑角　angle of aperture
角膜/角膜　cornea
角膜白斑/角膜白斑　keratoleukoma

角膜斑/角膜斑點 epicauma
角膜斑翳/角膜斑翳 corneal macula
角膜病/角膜病 ceratonosus
角膜病变/角膜病變 keratopathy
角膜薄翳/角膜薄翳 corneal nebula
角膜[部分]切除术/角膜切除術 kerectomy
角膜擦伤/角膜擦傷 corneal abrasion
角膜测厚仪/角膜測厚儀 corneal pachymeter
角膜穿刺/角膜穿刺 keratonyxis
角膜穿刺术/角膜穿刺放液術 keratocentesis
角膜穿孔/角膜穿孔 perforation of cornea
角膜穿孔伤/角膜穿孔傷 corneal perforating injury
角膜穿孔性虹膜脱出/膜傍性虹膜膨出 myiocephalon
角膜带状变性/角膜帶狀變性 bandshaped degeneration of cornea
角膜刀/角膜刀 keratome
角膜的/角膜的 corneal
角膜地形图/角膜地形圖 corneal topography
角膜点状变性/點狀角膜 cornea guttata
角膜顶/角膜頂 vertex of cornea
角膜反光点法/角膜反光點法 corneal reflection method
角膜放大镜/角膜放大鏡 corneal loupe
角膜钙化/角膜鈣化 corneal calcification
角膜巩膜环钻术/角膜鞏膜環鑽術 corneoscleral trephining
角膜巩膜炎/角膜鞏膜炎 keratoscleritis
角膜虹膜睫状体炎/角膜虹膜睫狀體炎 keratoiridocyclitis
角膜虹膜镜/角膜虹膜鏡 keratoiridoscope
角膜虹膜炎/角膜虹膜炎 corneoiritis
角膜后沉着物/角膜後沈著物 keratic precipitates
[角膜]后界层/後界膜,後彈性層[角膜] posterior limiting lamina
角膜后面/角膜後面 posterior surface of cornea
角膜后弹力层/角膜後彈力層,角膜内附層 entocornea
角膜后[弹性]层突出/角膜最内層膨出 keratocele
角膜坏死/角膜壞死 corneal necrosis
角膜环形脓肿/角膜環形膿腫 ring abscess of cornea
角膜环钻/角膜環鑽 corneal trephine
角膜混浊/角膜混濁 corneal opacity
角膜基质/角膜基質 corneal stroma
角膜疾病/角膜疾病 corneal disease
角膜剪/角膜剪 corneal scissor
角膜睑粘连/角膜瞼粘連 corneoblepharon
角膜接触镜/角膜接觸鏡 corneal contact lens
角膜浸润/角膜浸潤 corneal infiltration
角膜镜/角膜鏡 keratoscope
角膜镜检查/角膜鏡檢查術 keratoscopy
角膜溃疡/角膜潰瘍 corneal ulcer
角膜隆凸/角膜隆凸 corneal torus
角膜瘘/角膜瘘管 fistula corneae
角膜迷芽瘤/角膜迷芽瘤 choristoma of cornea
角膜糜烂/角膜糜爛 corneal erosion
角膜磨削术/角膜磨削術 keratomileusis
角膜内皮/角膜内皮 corneal endothelium
角膜内皮显微镜/角膜内皮顯微鏡 specular microscope
角膜镊/角膜鑷 corneal forcep
角膜膨隆/角膜膨隆 corneal ectasia
角膜破裂/角膜破裂 corneal rupture
角膜葡萄肿/角膜葡萄腫 corneal staphyloma
[角膜]前界层/前界膜,前彈性層[角膜] anterior limiting lamina
角膜前面/角膜前面 anterior surface of cornea
角膜浅凹/角膜靠顳部凹陷 dellen of cornea
角膜切开术/角膜切開術 keratotomy
[角膜]青年环/角膜幼年環 arcus juvenilis
角膜曲率/角膜曲率 corneal curvature
角膜曲率半径/角膜曲率半徑 corneal curvature radius
角膜染色术/角膜染色術 corneal tattooing
角膜软化[症]/角膜軟化 keratomalacia
角膜散光计/角膜彎度計 keratometer
角膜上皮/角膜上皮 corneal epithelium
角膜上皮擦伤/角膜上皮擦傷 abrasio corneae
角膜上皮内上皮癌/角膜上皮内上皮癌 intraepithelial neoplasm of cornea
角膜试验/角膜試驗 corneal test
角膜水肿/角膜水腫 corneal edema
角膜痛/角膜痛 keratalgia
角膜透镜/角膜透鏡 corneal lens
角膜细胞/角膜細胞 corneal cell
角膜小面/角膜小面 corneal facet
角膜新生血管化/角膜新生血管化 corneal neovascularization
角膜血沉着/角膜鬱血 keratohemia
角膜血染/角膜血染 blood staining of cornea
角膜炎/角膜炎 keratitis
角膜移植/角膜移植 corneal transplantation
角膜移植片/角膜移植物 corneal graft
角膜移植术/角膜成形術,角膜修補術 keratoplasty, epikeratophakia

角膜异物/角膜異物　corneal foreign body
角膜翳擦除法/角膜翳擦除法　apotripsis
角膜营养不良/角膜營養不良　corneal dystrophy
角膜缘/角膜緣　corneal limbus, limbus corneae, limbus
角膜缘溃疡/角膜緣潰瘍　argema
角膜真菌病/角膜真菌病　mycotic keratitis
角膜脂肪性营养不良/角膜脂肪變性營養不良　dystrophia adiposa corneae
角膜周围充血/角膜周圍充血　circumcorneal injection
角膜周[围]的/角膜周圍的　circumcorneal
角膜贮存/角膜貯存　corneal storage
角膜子午线/角膜子午線　meridian of cornea
角母蛋白/角母蛋白　eleidin
角切迹/角切跡　angular incisure
角鲨烷/鯊烷　squalane
角鲨烯/鯊烯　squalene
角孙/角孫　jiaosun, SJ20
角窝上/角窩上　jiaowoshang, superior triangular fossa, TF1
角窝中/角窩中　jiaowozhong, middle triangular fossa, TF3
角咽肌/角咽肌　chondropharyngeal muscle
角衣片/角質錠, 類角蛋白　keratinoid
角蝇/角蠅　horn fly
角疣/角疣　horny wart
角质层/角質層　cuticle, corneum, stratum corneum
角质层分离/角質層分離　keratolysis
角质层分离剂/溶角藥, 角質溶解藥　keratolytic
角质带/角質帶　horny band
角质蛋白/角[質]蛋白　keratoprotein
角质的/角質的　horny
角[质]化/角質變性, 角變, 角化　cornification
角质溶解药/角質溶解藥　keratolytic agents
角质软化剂/去角質藥　keratolytic
角质生成/角質生成　keratogenesis
角质栓/角質栓　horn plug
角质细胞/角質細胞　horny cell
角质形成细胞/角質[形成]細胞　keratinocyte
角质样的/角質狀的　keratoid
角质痣/角質痣　nevus corneum
角质状变性/角質狀變性　keratoid degeneration
角珠/角珠　horn pearl
绞棒帆布止血带/絞扼式止血帶　garrote tourniquet
绞扼止血器/絞扼止血器　garrot
绞股兰总苷片/絞股蘭總苷片　jiaogulan total glucoside tablets

绞痛/絞痛　colic, colicky pain, griping pain
绞痛病/絞痛病　anginosis
绞痛病的/絞痛病的　anginose
绞痛麻痹/絞痛麻痺　colicoplegia
绞线/絞線　strepsinema
绞线期/絞線期　strepsitene
绞窄的/絞扼的, 絞勒的　strangulated
绞窄性肠梗阻/絞窄性腸梗阻　strangulated intestinal obstruction
绞窄性疝/絞扼性疝, 絞勒性赫尼亞　strangulated hernia
绞窄性牙髓息肉/絞窄性牙髓息肉　strangulated hernia of pulp
绞窄性痔/絞窄性痔　strangulated hemorrhoid
绞状体综合征/絞狀體症候群　syndrome of corpus striatum
铰链区/鉸鏈區　hinge region
铰链式面弓/牙科鉸鏈式面弓　hinge-bow
铰链位/鉸鏈位置　hinge position
铰链运动/鉸鏈式運動　hinge movement
铰链轴/樞紐軸　hinge axis
铰链轴点/鉸鏈軸點　hinge axis point
铰链轴型𬌗/鉸鏈軸型𬌗　hinge axis type occlusion
矫视三棱镜/遠距雙眼儀　telebinocular
矫味药/矯味藥　corrigent
矫形的/矯形的　orthopedic
矫形法/歪扭部之整直法, 伸直法　orthosis
矫形力/矯形力　orthopedic force
矫形疗法/矯形療法　orthotherapy
矫形术/矯形術, 畸形矯正術　orthomorphia
矫形外科固定装置/矯形外科固定裝置　orthopedic fixation device
矫形外科护理/矯形外科護理　orthopedic nursing
矫形外科器材/矯形外科器材　orthopedic equipment
矫形外科手术/矯形外科手術　orthopedic procedure
矫形外科学/骨科矯形學　orthopedics
矫形外科医师/骨科矯形醫師　orthopedist
矫形鞋/矯形鞋　orthopedic shoe
矫正不足/矯正不足　undercorrection
矫正固位器/矯正固位器　positioner
矫正过度/矯正過度, 過度矯正　overcorrection
矫正镜片/矯正鏡片　correcting lens
矫正器修配者/矯正學家　orthetist
矫正屈光不正/折光異常之矯正　correction of refractive error
矫正散光透镜/矯正散光透鏡　anastigmatic lens
矫正视力/矯正視力　corrected vision
矫正型大动脉转位/矯正型大動脈轉位　corrected

transposition of great artery
矫正学/矯正學 orthetics
矫正运动/矯治運動,矯治操練 corrective exercise
矫正正畸学/矯正正畸學 corrective orthodontics
矫正装置/矯正裝置 orthotic device
矫治器/矯治器 appliance
脚/腳 feet
脚的/腳的 crural
脚底/枕骨底部,底骨 basilar bone
脚间池/[腦]腳間池 interpeduncular cistern
脚间核/腳間核 interpeduncular nucleus
脚间窝/腳間窩 interpeduncular fossa
脚间纤维/[腦]腳間纖維 intercrural fiber
脚力测定器/足力計 pedodynamometer
脚气病/腳氣[病],衰弱足 beriberi, weak foot, perneiras
脚气[病]心/腳氣病心臟 beriberi heart
脚气冲心/腳氣衝心 beriberi involving heart, disease of weak foot affecting heart
脚桥被盖网状核/腳橋被蓋網狀核 pedunculopontine reticular tegmental nucleus
脚拳不展/腳拳不展 inextensible toes
脚湿气/腳濕氣,足癬,腳癬 tinea pedis
脚湿气·湿热下注证/腳濕氣·濕熱下注證 tinea pedis with pattern of dampness-heat diffusing downward
脚湿气·血虚风燥证/腳濕氣·血虛風燥證 tinea pedis with pattern of wind-dryness due to blood deficiency
脚踏车测力器/腳踏車測力器 bicycle ergometry
脚癣/腳癬 Hong Kong foot
脚趾静脉/腳趾靜脈 digital vein
搅拌轴转速/攪拌軸轉速 agitator shaft speed
搅家狂/家庭勃溪癖,擾家癖 ecomania
校正/校正 calibration
校正集/校正集 calibration set
较小的/小的,少量的 minor
教学医院/教學醫院 teaching hospital
教养院儿童/教養院兒童 institutionalized child
教育程度/教育程度 educational status
教育技术/教育技術 educational technology
教育康复/教育康復 educational rehabilitation
教育模型/教育模型 educational model
教育心理学/教育心理學 educational psychology
酵母/酵母 yeast
酵母氨酸脱氢酶类/酵母胺酸脫氫酶類 saccharopine dehydrogenases
酵母成分压出[法]/酵母成分壓出[法] zymasis

酵母蛋白酶/內胰蛋白酶 endotrypsin
酵母多糖/酵母多醣 zymosan
酵母己糖磷酸/酵母磷酸鹽 zymophosphate
酵母菌脑膜炎/酵母菌腦膜炎 yeast meningitis
酵母菌性脑膜炎/酵母性腦膜炎 torula meningitis
酵母溶解[现象]/酵母菌分解 saccharomycetolysis
酵母属/酵母屬 Saccharomyces
酵素/酵素 ferment
阶段/階段 stage
阶段性排列原理/階段性排列原理 phased array principle
阶梯状缝合/階梯狀縫合 stepping suture
疖/癤 boil, furuncle
疖病/癤病 furunculosis, furuncle disease
疖病·湿热蕴结证/癤病·濕熱蘊結證 furunculosis with dampness-heat amassment pattern
疖病素质/癤病素質 furuncular diathesis
疖病·正虚毒结证/癤病·正虛毒結證 furunculosis with pattern of healthy qi deficiency and toxin accumulation
疖的/癤的 furuncular
疖·热毒蕴结证/癤·熱毒蘊結證 furuncle with heat-toxin amassment pattern
疖·暑湿蕴结证/癤·暑濕蘊結證 furuncle with summerheat-dampness amassment pattern
疖性外耳炎/癤性外耳炎 otitis externa furunculosa
疖样的/癤狀的 furunculoid
疖·正虚邪恋证/癤·正虛邪戀證 furuncle with pattern of healthy qi deficiency and lingering pathogen
接触/接觸 contact
接触癌/接觸癌 contact cancer
接触变应性光皮炎/接觸變應性光皮炎 contact allergic photodermatitis
接触部分离/接觸部分開 solution of contiguity
[接]触[传]染的/接觸傳染的 contagious
接触传染性结核菌素/接觸傳染性結核菌素 tuberculin contagious
接触传染性无乳/傳染性無乳 contagious agalactia
接触点/接觸點 contact point
接触感受器/受觸器 tangoreceptor
接触光毒性皮炎/接觸光毒性皮炎 contact phototoxic dermatitis
接触环/接觸環 contact ring
接触角/接觸角 contact angle
接触镜/隱形眼鏡 contact lens
接触镜片/接觸眼鏡,直接眼鏡 contact glasses
接触镜溶液/接觸鏡溶液 contact lens solution

接触镜学/隱形眼鏡學　contactology
接触冷冻法/接觸冷凍法　contact freezing
接触酶/接觸酶　contact substance
接触面/接觸面　contact surface
接触脑脊液神经元/接觸腦脊液神經元　cerebrospinal fluid-contacting neuron
接触区/接觸區　contingent area, contact area
接触烧伤/接觸燒傷　contact burn
接触试验/接觸試驗　contact test
接触物/接觸物　contactant
接触性变态反应/接觸性過敏　contact allergy
接触性传染病/接觸傳染病　contagious disease
接触性唇炎/接觸性唇炎　contact cheilitis
接触性痤疮/接觸性痤瘡　contact acne
接触性毒性口炎/接觸性口角炎　contact stomatitis
接触[性]感染/接觸傳染　contact infection
接触性阑尾炎/波及性闌尾炎　appendicitis by contiguity
接触性皮炎/接觸性皮膚炎　contact dermatitis
接触性转移/接觸性轉移　contact metastasis
接触异性欲/接觸異性欲　contrectation
接触抑制/接觸抑制　contact inhibition
接触应激性/接觸應激性　tactile irritability
接触照明/接觸照明　contact illumination
接触者追踪/接觸者追蹤　contact tracing
接骨板/接骨板　blade plate
接骨木/接骨木　elder
接骨木果/接骨木果　elder berry
接骨续筋/接骨續筋　reunion of fractured tendon and bone
接骨者/接骨師　bone setter
接合孢子/接合孢子　zygosperm
接[合]处/接合處　junction
接合的/接合的,結合的　junctional
接合骨/接合骨　zeugopodium
接合后体/接合後體　exconjugant
接合夹/接合夾　coaptation splint
接合菌病/接合菌病　zygomycosis
接合配子/接合配子　zygosphere
接合器/接合器　adapter
接合[神经]细胞/接合神經細胞　zygoneure
接合胎盘/接合胎盤　placenta conjugata
接合性/接合性　zygosity
接近的/近端的,近侧的　proximal
接近行为/趨近行為　adient behavior
接近淹溺/接近淹溺　near drowning
接连性脱位/接連性脱位　consecutive dislocation
接龙试验/接龍試驗　trail making test

接目镜/接目鏡,眼透鏡　ocular lens
接纳体/接納體,受體　acceptor
接头传导/接合性傳導　synaptic conduction
接种并发症/種痘并發症　vaccination complication
接种刀/種痘針　vaccinostyle
接种红晕/接種紅暈　vaccinal areola
接种后的/接種疫苗後的　postvaccinal
接种后肝炎/接種疫苗後肝炎　postvaccinal hepatitis
接种后脊髓灰质炎/接種疫苗後脊髓灰質炎　postinoculation poliomyelitis
接种后脊髓炎/接種疫苗後脊髓炎　postvaccinal myelitis
接种后结核菌素阳转率/接種疫苗後結核菌素陽轉率　postvaccinal tuberculin positive conversion rate
接种后天花/接種後天花　variola inoculata
接种量/接種量　inoculum size
接种疟/接種瘧　inoculated malaria
接种试验/接種試驗　inoculation test
接种性脊髓炎/種痘後脊髓炎　myelitis vaccinia
接种性水痘/接種性水痘　varicella inoculata
接种疫苗/接種　vaccinate
接种针/接種針　vaccination needle
节孢子/節孢子　gangliospore
节的/節的,段的　segmental
节点/節點　node
节段小肠移植/節段小腸移植　segmental small intestine transplantation
节段性肠扩张/節段性腸擴張　segmental dilatation of intestine
节段性阑尾炎/片段性闌尾炎　segmental appendicitis
节段性神经纤维瘤病/分節性神經纖維瘤病　segmental neurofibromatosis
节段性肾发育不良/節段性腎發育不良　segmental dysplasia of kidney
节段性透明变性样血管炎/分節性透明樣血管炎　segmental hyalinizing vasculitis
节段胰腺移植/節段胰腺移植　segmental pancreas transplantation
节后副交感神经纤维/節後副交感神經纖維　postganglionic parasympathetic fiber
节后交感神经纤维/節後交感神經纖維　postganglionic sympathetic fiber
节后[神经]纤维/節後[神經]纖維　postganglionic neurofiber, postganglionic fiber
节后神经元/節後神經元　postganglionic neuron
节后自主神经纤维/節後自主神經纖維　postganglionic autonomic fiber

节间动脉/節間動脈　intersegmental artery
节间支/節間支　interganglionic branch
节律/節律　rhythm
α-节律/α-節律　alpha rhythm
δ-节律/δ-節律　delta rhythm
节律性/節律性,週期性　rhythmicity
节律性抽搐/節律性抽搐　krauomania
节律性呼吸/節律性呼吸　rhythmic respiration
节律性眼球震颤/夏-史二氏眼球震顫　Cheyne-Stokes nystagmus
节律性运动/節律性運動　rhythmic exercise
节律运动障碍/節律動作不能　arrhythmokinesis
节律障碍/節律異常,心律不整　dysrhythmia
节旁体/副神經節　paraganglion
节前神经元/節前神經元　preganglionic neuron
节前纤维/節前[神經]纖維　preganglionic fiber
节前自主神经纤维/節前自主神經纖維　preganglionic autonomic fiber
节饮疗法/節飲療法,口渴療法　thirst cure
节肢动物/節肢動物　arthropod
节肢动物叮咬/節肢動物叮咬　arthropod bite
节肢动物毒液类/節肢動物毒液類　arthropod venoms
节肢动物媒介/節肢動物媒介　arthropod vector
节肢动物门/節肢動物類,節足動物類　Arthropoda
节肢动物皮肤病/節肢動物皮膚病　arthropod dermatosis
节[制生]育/節育法　oligogenics
节制索/調節帶　moderator band
节柱/節柱　segmented column, striated column
节足动物媒介病毒/節足動物媒介病毒　arbovirus
杰克逊癫痫/傑克遜癲癇　Jackson epilepsy
杰克逊植皮术/傑克遜植皮術　Jackson skin grafting method
杰克逊综合征/傑克遜症候群　Jackson syndrome
杰利内克征/Jellinek 氏徵象　Jellinek sign
拮抗/拮抗　antagonism, clashing
拮抗共生/拮抗性共生　enantiobiosis
拮抗肌/拮抗肌　antagonistic muscle
拮抗剂/拮抗劑,抗拮劑　antagonist
拮抗性共生/對抗性共生　antagonistic symbiosis
拮抗作用/拮抗作用　antagonism
洁齿剂/潔齒劑　dentifrice
洁净区/潔淨區,清淨區　clean area
洁霉素/林肯黴素　lincomycin
洁牙饮食/潔牙飲食　detergent diet
洁治器/刮牙器　scaler
洁治术/潔治術　oral prophylaxis

结/結[節]　node
结瘢/結瘢,收瘢　synulosis
结瘢剂/收瘢藥,結瘢藥　cicatrizant
结瘢药/收瘢藥　synulotic
结肠/結腸　colon
结肠阿米巴/結腸阿米巴　Amoeba coli
结肠癌/結腸癌　cancer of colon
结肠癌杜克斯分类法/結腸癌杜克斯分類法　Dukes classification for colon cancer
结肠半月襞/結腸半月皺襞　semilunar fold of colon
结肠瓣闭锁不全/迴盲瓣閉鎖不全　ileocecal incompetence
结肠病/結腸病　colonopathy
结肠部分切除术/結腸部分切除術　hemicolectomy
结肠出血/結腸出血　colonorrhagia
结肠穿刺术/結腸穿刺術　colipuncture
结肠穿孔/結腸穿孔　colonic perforation
结肠次全切除术/結腸次全切除術　subtotal colectomy
结肠带/結腸帶　colic band, taeniae of colon
结肠袋/結腸袋　haustrum of colon, haustra of colon
结肠袋分节运动/結腸袋分節運動　haustral segmentation
结肠的/結腸的　colonic
结肠非特异性溃疡/結腸非特異性潰瘍　nonspecific ulcer of colon
结肠缝合术/結腸縫合術　colorrhaphy
结肠腹膜炎/結腸腹膜炎　exocolitis
结肠肝固定术/結腸肝臟固定術　colohepatopexy
结肠孤立性溃疡/結腸孤立性潰瘍　colonic solitary ulcer
结肠固定切开术/結腸固定切開術　colopexotomy
结肠固定术/結腸固定術　colofixation
结肠黑色素沉着病/結腸黑變病　melanosis coli
结肠后胃空肠吻合术/結腸後胃空腸吻合術　retrocolic gastrojejunostomy
结肠回肠的/結腸與迴腸的　coloileal
结肠回肠瘘/結腸迴腸瘻管　coloileal fistula
结肠活动测定器/結腸活動計　colometrometer
结肠疾病/結腸疾病　colonic disease
结肠假性梗阻/結腸假性梗阻　colonic pseudo-obstruction
结肠浆膜炎/結腸漿膜炎　serocolitis
结肠结肠吻合术/結腸結腸吻合術　cococolostomy
结肠结核/結腸結核　tuberculosis of colon
结肠镜/結腸鏡　colonoscope
结肠镜检查/結腸鏡檢法　colonoscopy
结肠扩张/結腸擴張　ectocolon

结肠瘘/結腸瘻管　colonic fistula
结肠麻醉/結腸麻醉法　colonic anesthesia
结肠盲肠吻合术/結腸盲腸吻合術　colocecostomy
结肠面/結腸面　colic surface
结肠黏膜炎/結腸黏膜炎　endocolitis
结肠旁沟/結腸旁溝　paracolic sulci
结肠旁淋巴结/結腸旁淋巴結　paracolic lymph node
结肠膀胱的/結腸膀胱的　colovesical
结肠膀胱瘘/結腸膀胱瘻　colovesical fistula
结肠皮肤的/結腸[與]皮膚的　colocutaneous
结肠皮肤瘘/結腸[與]皮膚瘻管　colocutaneous fistula
结肠憩室/結腸憩室　colon diverticulum
结肠憩室病/結腸憩室病　colonic diverticulosis
结肠憩室炎/結腸憩室炎　colonic diverticulitis
结肠前带/結腸前帶　anterior band of colon
结肠前韧带/結腸前韌帶　anterior ligament of colon
结肠前胃空肠吻合术/結腸前胃空腸吻合術　antecolonic gastrojejunostomy
结肠强直/鉛管結腸　lead-pipe colon
结肠切除术/結腸切除術　colectomy
结肠切开术/結腸切開術　colotomy
结肠缺血/結腸缺血　colonic ischemia
结肠松解术/結腸鬆解術　cololysis
结肠痛/結腸痛　colonalgia
结肠无力/結腸無力　colonic inertia
结肠息肉/結腸息肉　colonic polyp
结肠息肉病/結腸息肉病　colonic polyposis
结肠系膜/結腸繫膜　mesocolon
结肠系膜带/結腸繫膜帶　mesocolic band
结肠系膜的/結腸繫膜的　mesocolic
结肠系膜固定术/結腸繫膜固定術　mesocolopexy
结肠系膜架/結腸繫膜架　mesocolic shelf
结肠系膜淋巴结/結腸繫膜淋巴結　mesocolic lymph node
结肠系膜疝/結腸繫膜疝　mesocolic hernia
结肠系膜折术/結腸繫膜折疊術　mesocoloplication
结肠下垂/結腸下垂　coloptosis
结肠下区/結腸下區　infracolic compartment
结肠纤维镜/結腸纖維鏡　fibercolonoscope
结肠腺瘤/結腸腺瘤　adenoma of colon
结肠小袋[纤毛]虫/大腸纖毛蟲　Balantidium coli
结肠型伤寒/結腸型傷寒　colotyphoid
结肠性消化不良/結腸性消化不良　colon dyspepsia
结肠压迹/結腸壓跡　colic impression
结肠炎/結腸炎　colitis
结肠乙状结肠吻合术/結腸乙狀結腸吻合術　colosigmoidostomy
结肠阴道的/結腸陰道的　colovaginal
结肠阴道瘘/結腸陰道瘻管　colovaginal fistula
结肠右曲/結腸右曲　right colic flexure, hepatic flexure of colon
结肠缘动脉/結腸緣動脈　colic marginal artery
结肠造口术/結腸造口術，結腸造瘻術　colostomy
结肠折叠术/結腸折疊術　coliplication
结肠支/結腸支　colic branch
结肠直肠/結腸直腸　colorectum
结肠直肠切除术/結腸直腸切除術　coloproctectomy
结肠直肠吻合术/結腸直腸吻合術　coloproctostomy
结肠直肠炎/結腸直腸炎　coloproctitis
结肠肿瘤/結腸腫瘤　colonic neoplasm
结肠周的/結腸周圍的　pericolic
结肠周膜综合征/結腸周圍膜症候群　pericolic-membrane syndrome
结肠周炎/結腸外層炎　paracolitis
结肠自由带/結腸自由帶　free band of colon
结肠纵肌纤维带/結腸縱腺纖維帶　longitudinal band of colon
结肠左曲/結腸左曲　left colic flexure, left flexure of colon
结的/結[節]的　nodal
结缔组织/結締組織　connective tissue
结缔组织病/結締組織病　connective-tissue disease
结缔组织黏液瘤/結締組織瘤　connective-tissue myxoma
结缔组织生成/纖維組織發生　desmoplasia
结缔组织细胞/結締組織細胞　connective tissue cell
结缔组织细胞增生/結締組織細胞增多　phorocytosis
结缔组织纤维发生/結締組織微纖維生成　fibrocytogenesis
结缔组织学说/結締組織學説　connective tissue theory
结缔组织增生纤维瘤/引起粘連之纖維瘤　desmoplastic fibroma
结缔组织增生性恶性黑色素瘤/結締組織增生性惡性黑色素瘤　desmoplastic malignant melanoma
结缔组织增生性毛发上皮瘤/結締組織增生性毛囊上皮瘤　desmoplastic trichoepithelioma
结缔组织增生性亲神经性黑色素瘤/結締組織增生性親神經性黑色素瘤　desmoplastic-neurotropic melanoma
结缔组织增生性痣/結締組織增生性母斑　desmoplastic nevus
结缔组织痣/結締組織痣　connective tissue nevus
结缔组织肿瘤/結締纖瘤　desmoneoplasm

结冻试验/冷凍試驗 freezing test
结构/結構 structure
结构基因/結構基因 structural gene
结构畸变/結構畸變 structural aberration
[结构]类似物/結構類似物 analog
结构模型/結構模型 structural model
结构式/結構式 structural formula
结构性鼻炎/結構性鼻炎 structural rhinitis
结构性脊柱侧凸/結構性脊柱側彎 structural scoliosis
结构性失用[症]/結構性失用[症] constructional apraxia
结构异构/結構同質異構 structural isomerism
结果可重复性/結果可重複性 reproducibility of result
结果评价/結果評價 outcome assessment
结合/連結 bond
结合臂交叉/上小腦腳交叉 decussation of superior cerebellar peduncles
结合臂静脉/結合臂静脈 vein of the brachium conjunctivum
结合部位/結合部位 binding site
结合常数/結合常數 binding constant
结合簇/結合群,結納群 haptophore
结合反应/結合反應 fixation reaction
结合抗原/結合抗原 conjugated antigen
结合力/連結力 couple-force
结合囊肿/結合囊腫 junctional cyst
结合上皮/關節上皮 junctional epithelium
结合水/結合水 bound water
结合物/結合物 conjugate
结合性痤疮/結合性痤瘡 concrete acne
结合牙/結合牙 concrescence of tooth
结合药物/結合藥物 bound drug
结合疫苗/結合疫苗 conjugate vaccine
结合质/結合質 cement substance
结核/結核[病],癆病 tuberculosis, nodule
结核病爆发流行/結核病爆發流行 fulminating epidemic of tuberculosis
结核病病死率/結核病病死率 tuberculosis fatality rate
结核病登记率/結核病登記率 tuberculosis case registration rate
结核病发病率/結核病發病率 incidence of tuberculosis
结核病感染率/結核病感染率 tuberculosis infection rate
结核病化学药物治疗/結核病化學藥物治療 chemotherapy of tuberculosis
结核病患病率/結核病患病率 prevalence rate of tuberculosis
结核病监测/結核病監測 tuberculosis surveillance
结核病控制/結核病控制 tuberculosis control
结核病疗养院/結核病療養院 sanatorium for tuberculosis
结核病流行病学抽样调查/結核病流行病學抽樣調查 tuberculosis epidemiological random sampling survey
结核病年感染率/結核病年感染率 tuberculosis annual infection rate
结核病死亡率/結核病死亡率 tuberculosis mortality rate
结核病新登记率/結核病新登記率 tuberculosis new case registration rate
结核病学会/結核病學會 tuberculosis society
结核[病]样的/結核節狀的 tuberculoid
结核的/結核的,結節的 tubercular
结核分枝杆菌/結核桿菌 Mycobacterium tuberculosis
结核杆菌蜡质/結核菌蠟 tubercle bacillus wax
结核过敏现象/結核過敏現象 tuberculous allergic phenomenon
结核[结]节/結節,結核 tubercle
结核[结]节炎/結核[節]炎 tuberculitis
结核浸润/結核性浸潤 tuberculous infiltration
结核菌醇/結核桿菌蠟醇 phthiocerol
结核菌蛋白/結核菌蛋白質 tuberculoprotein
结核菌蜡/結核菌浸劑 tuberculase
结核菌类/結核菌類 tuberculomyces
结核菌苗/結核菌苗 tuberculosis vaccine
结核菌素/結核菌素 tuberculin
结核菌素斑贴试验/結核菌素膠布試驗 tuberculin patch test
结核菌素迟发超敏反应/結核菌素遲發超敏反應 tuberculin delayed hypersensitivity
结核菌素纯蛋白衍生物/結核菌素之純化蛋白質衍生物 purified protein derivate of tuberculin
结核菌素单位/結核菌素單位 tuberculin unit
结核菌素反应/結核菌素反應 tuberculin reaction
结核菌素疗法/結核菌素療法 tuberculinotherapy
结核菌素皮内试验/馬滔氏試驗 Mantoux test
结核菌素试验/結核菌素試驗 tuberculin test
结核菌素效价试验/結核菌素效價試驗 tuberculin titer test
结核菌调理指数/結核菌調理指數 tuberculo-opsonic index

结核菌抑制/抑制結核菌生長　tuberculostatic
结核瘤/結核瘤　tuberculoma
结核性鼻炎/結核性鼻炎　tuberculous rhinitis
结核性痤疮/結核病性痤瘡　acne scrofulosorum
结核性骶髂关节炎/結核性骶髂關節炎　tuberculous sacroiliitis
结核性多浆膜炎/結核性多漿膜炎　tuberculous polyserositis
结核性肺炎/結核性肺炎　tuberculous pneumonia
结核性风湿病/結核性風濕病　tuberculous rheumatism
结核性腹膜炎/結核性腹膜炎　tuberculous peritonitis
结核性腹泻/結核性腹瀉　tubercular diarrhea
结核性肛门周围脓肿/結核性肛門周圍膿腫　tuberculous perianal abscess
结核性宫颈炎/結核性宮頸炎　tuberculous cervicitis
结核性巩膜炎/結核性鞏膜炎　tuberculous scleritis
结核性骨干炎/結核性骨幹炎　tuberculous diaphysitis
结核性骨髓炎/結核性骨髓炎　tuberculous osteomyelitis
结核性骨炎/結核性骨炎　tuberculous osteitis
结核性关节炎/結核性關節炎　tuberculous arthritis
结核性滑膜炎/結核性滑膜炎　tuberculous synovitis
结核性脊椎病/結核性脊椎病　tuberculous spondylosis
结核性脊椎炎/結核性脊椎炎　tuberculous spondylitis
结核性腱鞘炎/結核性腱鞘炎　tuberculous tenosynovitis
结核性结节性红斑/結核性結節性紅斑　tuberculous erythema nodosum
结核性结节性静脉炎/結核性結節性静脉炎　phlebitis nodosa tuberculosa
结核性空洞开放性愈合/結核性空洞開放性愈合　open healing of tuberculous cavity
结核性髋关节炎/結核性髖關節炎　tuberculous coxitis
结核性溃疡/結核性潰瘍　tuberculous ulcer
结核性泪囊炎/結核性淚囊炎　tuberculous dacryocystitis
结核性淋巴结炎/結核性淋巴腺炎　tuberculous lymphadenitis
结核性脓胸/結核性蓄膿　tuberculous empyema
结核性脓肿/結核性膿腫　scrofulous abscess
结核性葡萄膜炎/結核病性葡萄膜炎　tuberculous uveitis
结核性气管炎/結核性氣管炎　tuberculous tracheitis
结核性乳突炎/結核性乳突炎　tuberculous mastoiditis
结核性肾炎/結核性腎炎　tuberculous nephritis
结核性肾盂肾炎/結核性腎盂腎炎　tuberculous pyelonephritis
结核性肾盂炎/結核性腎盂炎　tuberculous pyelitis
结核性输卵管炎/結核性輸卵管炎　tuberculous salpingitis
结核性树胶肿/結核腫　tuberculous gumma
结核性下疳/結核性下疳　tuberculous chancre
结核性心包炎/結核性心包炎　tuberculous pericarditis
结核性心肌炎/結核性心肌炎　tuberculous myocarditis
结核性胸膜炎/結核性胸膜炎　tuberculous pleuritis
结核性胸腔积液/結核性胸腔積液　tuberculous pleural effusion
结核性眼内炎/結核性眼内炎　tuberculous endophthalmitis
结核性支气管扩张/結核性支氣管擴張　tuberculous bronchiectasis
结核性支气管狭窄/結核性支氣管狹窄　tuberculous bronchostenosis
结核性指炎/結核性指炎　tuberculous dactylitis
结核性趾炎/結核性趾炎　tuberculous dactylitis
结核性中耳炎/結核性中耳炎　tuberculous otitis media
结核样麻风/結核樣麻風　tuberculoid leprosy
结核疹/結核疹　tuberculid
结痂的/結痂的　crustosus
结痂性角化不全/蠣殼狀角化不全　parakeratosis ostracea
结痂性疥疮/結痂性疥瘡　crusted scabies
结痂性狼疮/結痂性狼瘡　crustosus lupus
结痂性膀胱炎/結痂性膀胱炎　incrusted cystitis
结痂性皮脂漏/結痂性皮脂漏　seborrhea concrete
结间部/結間節　internode
结间束/結間束　internodal tract
结间体/神經結間，節間　internode
结间通道/結間通道　internodal pathway
结节/結節，[小]結　①nodule ②jiejie, HX8
结节的/結狀　nodose
结节核/結節核　tuberal nucleus
结节红斑/結節紅斑　erythema nodosa
结节间沟/結節間溝　intertubercular sulcus
结节间腱鞘/結節間腱鞘　intertubercular tendinous sheath

结节间平面/結節間平面　transtubercular plane
结节溃疡性梅毒疹/結節潰瘍性梅毒疹　nodulo-ulcerative syphilid
结节狼疮/結節狼瘡　lupus nodosus
结节漏斗束/結節漏斗束　tuberoinfundibular tract
结节梅毒疹/結節梅毒疹　syphilid nodosa
结节囊肿性痤疮/結節囊腫性痤瘡　acne nodulocystica
结节丘疹性黄瘤/結節丘疹性黃瘤　tuberous papular xanthoma
结节区/結節部　tuberal region
结节萎缩性皮肤淀粉样变/結節萎縮性皮膚澱粉樣變性症　amyloidosis cutis nodularis et atrophicans
结节细胞/結節細胞　nodal cell
结节线虫病/結節線蟲病　oesophagostomiasis
结节形成/結節病　tuberosis
结节型皮肤利什曼病/結節型皮膚利什曼病　qcepo
结节性/結節　nodosa
结节性白斑/結節性白斑　nodular leukoplakia
结节性表皮下纤维变性/結節性表皮下纖維變性　nodular subepidermal fibrosis
结节性脆发病/結節性斷髮症　clastothrix
结节性痤疮/結節性痤瘡　acne tuberata
结节性的/[有]結節的，粗隆的　nodular, tuberous
结节性动脉周围炎/結節性動脈外層炎　periarteritis nodosa
结节性多动脉炎/結節性多動脈炎　polyarteritis nodosa
结节性恶性黑[色]素瘤/結節性惡性黑[色]素瘤　nodular malignant melanoma
结节性非化脓性脂膜炎/結節性非化膿性脂層炎　nodular nonsuppurative panniculitis
结节性关节炎/結節性關節炎　arthritis nodosa
结节性汗腺瘤/結節性汗腺瘤　nodular hidradenoma
结节性红斑/結節性紅斑　erythema nodosum
结节性黄[色]瘤/結節性黃色瘤　tuberous xanthoma
结节性甲状腺肿/結節性甲狀腺腫　nodular goiter
结节性腱鞘炎/結節性腱鞘炎　nodular tenosynovitis
结节性疥疮/結節性疥瘡　nodular scabies
结节性筋膜炎/結節性筋膜炎，增生性筋膜炎　nodular fasciitis
结节性类天疱疮/結節性類天皰瘡　pemphigoid nodularis
结节性马皮疽/結節性馬皮疽　button farcy
结节性毛发/結節性毛髮　nodose hair
结节性毛发菌病/結節性毛癬　trichomycosis nodularis
结节性梅毒疹/結節性梅毒疹　nodular syphilide

结节性[脑]硬化/結節性硬化病　epiloia
结节性黏液水肿/結狀黏液水腫　nodular myxedema
结节性皮癌/塊狀癌　carcinoma tuberosum
结节性前巩膜炎/結節性前鞏膜炎　nodular anterior scleritis
结节性丘疹样黏蛋白增多症/結節性丘疹樣黏液素病　papulonodular mucinosis
结节性全动脉炎/結節性全動脈炎　panarteritis nodosa
结节性声带炎/聲帶粒腫　trachoma of vocal band
结节性弹性样组织变性/結節性彈性樣組織變性　nodular elastoidosis
结节性弹性组织变性/結節性彈性組織變性　nodular elastosis
结节性纤维肌炎/結節性纖維肌炎　nodular fibromyositis
结节性血管炎/結節性脈管炎　nodular vasculitis
结节性荨麻疹/結節性蕁麻疹　urticaria tuberosa
结节性痒疹/結節性癢疹　nodular prurigo
结节性移行性脂膜炎/結節性遊走性脂層炎　nodular migratory panniculitis
结节性硬化症/結節性硬化　tuberous sclerosis
结节性脂肪坏死/結節性脂肪壞死　nodular fat necrosis
结节疹/結節疹　tubercular eruption
结节状的/有結節的，粗隆的　tuberose
结节状瘤/結節狀瘤　tuberous tumor
结节纵静脉/結節縱靜脈　longitudinal tuberal vein
结晶/結晶，晶體　crystal
结晶的/晶狀的　crystalline
结晶度/結晶性　crystallinity
结晶罐/結晶槽　crystallizer
结晶囊/結晶囊　crystal sac
结晶尿/晶[體]尿症　crystalluria
结晶尿汗症/晶狀尿汗症，尿晶汗症　urhidrosis crystallina
结晶水/結晶水　water of crystallization
结晶细度/結晶細度　crystal fineness
结晶性石蕊红素/紅色石蕊素　erythrolitmin
结晶胰岛素/結晶性胰島素　crystalline insulin
结晶紫/結晶紫　crystal violet
结晶紫溶液/結晶紫溶液　crystal violet solution
结晶紫疫苗/結晶紫疫苗　crystal violet vaccine
结连舌/舌粘連，結舌，舌繫帶短縮　ankyloglossia, tie up tongue
结脉/結脈　irregularly intermittent pulse
结膜/結[合]膜　conjunctiva
结膜半月皱襞/結膜半月皺襞　conjunctival

semilunar fold
结膜瓣/結膜瓣 conjunctival flap
结膜鼻腔吻合术/結膜鼻腔吻合術 conjunctivorhinostomy
结膜成形术/結膜成形術 conjunctiviplasty
结膜充血/結膜充血 conjunctival congestion
结膜分泌物/結膜分泌物 conjunctival secretion
结膜干燥症/結膜乾燥症 xerosis of conjunctiva
结膜刮匙/結合膜刮器 ophthalmoxyster
结膜黑变病/結膜黑變病 melanosis of conjunctiva
结膜后内侧动脉/結合膜後内側動脈 medial posterior conjunctival artery
结膜后外侧动脉/結合膜後外側動脈 lateral posterior conjunctival artery
结膜环/結膜環 conjunctival ring
结膜黄斑/瞼裂斑 pinguecula
结膜疾病/結膜疾病 conjunctival disease
结膜结核/結膜結核 tuberculosis of conjunctiva
结膜结石/結膜結石 conjunctival concretion
结膜静脉/結合膜靜脈 conjunctival vein
结膜静脉曲张/眼結膜靜脈曲張 cirsophthalmia
结膜泪囊吻合术/結膜淚囊吻合術 conjunctivodacryocystostomy
结膜瘤/結膜瘤 conjunctivoma
结膜滤泡症/結膜濾泡症 conjunctival folliculosis
结膜囊/結[合]膜囊 conjunctival sac
结膜囊冲洗法/結膜囊沖洗法 irrigation of conjunctival sac
结膜皮样囊肿/結膜皮樣囊腫 dermoid cyst of conjunctiva
结膜皮脂瘤/結膜皮脂瘤 dermolipoma of conjunctiva
结膜前垂/先天翼狀贅肉 epitarsus
结膜前动脉/結合膜前動脈 anterior conjunctival artery
结膜切除术/結膜切除術 logadectomy
结膜蛆病/蛆結膜炎 larval conjunctivitis
结膜肉芽肿/結膜肉芽腫 conjunctival granuloma
结膜乳头[状]瘤/結膜乳頭[狀]瘤 papilloma of conjunctiva
结膜色素沉着/結膜色素沈著 pigmentation of conjunctiva
结膜色素痣/結膜色素痣 pigmented nervus of conjunctiva
结膜上皮/結膜上皮 conjunctival epithelium
结膜上皮癌/結膜上皮癌 epithelioma of conjunctiva
结膜上穹/結膜上穹 superior conjunctival fornix
结膜水肿/結合膜水腫 chemosis
结膜水肿的/結合膜水腫的 chemotic
结膜天疱疮/結膜天皰瘡 pemphigus of conjunctiva
结膜铁质沉着/結合膜鐵質沈著 siderosis conjunctivae
结膜下出血/結膜下出血 subconjunctival hemorrhage
结膜下的/結膜下的 subconjunctival
结膜下穹/結膜下穹 inferior conjunctival fornix
结膜下注射/結膜下注射 subconjunctival injection
结膜腺/結膜腺 conjunctival gland
结膜血管瘤/結膜血管瘤 conjunctival angioma
结膜炎/結膜炎 conjunctivitis
结膜移植片/結膜移植片 conjunctival graft
结膜移植术/結膜移植術 transplantation of conjunctiva
结膜银沉着症/結膜銀沈著症 argyrosis of conjunctiva
结膜遮盖角膜术/結膜覆蓋被切除的角膜前部 keratoleptynsis
结膜褶/結合膜皺襞 conjunctival fold
结膜肿瘤/結膜腫瘤 conjunctival neoplasms
结石/結石 calculus
结石病/結石病 lithiasis
结石测定器/測石器 lithometer
结石排出/結石排除 lithecbole
结石溶解/溶石 litholysis
结石性的/結石性的 calculous
结石性肾盂肾炎/結石性腎盂腎炎 pyelonephritis calculosa
结石性肾盂炎/結石性腎盂炎 calculous pyelitis
结石性无尿/結石性無尿 calculous anuria
结石性哮喘/結石性氣喘 stone asthma
结石性胰腺炎/結石性胰[腺]炎 calcareous pancreatitis
结石学/結石病學 lithology
结石钻孔术/鑿石術 lithotresis
结实的/結實的 beefy
结性节律/結性節律 nodal rhythm
结性心动过缓/結性心搏徐緩 nodal bradycardia
结性心律不齐/結性心律不整 nodal arrhythmia
结胸变证/結胸變證 deteriorated case of chest binding pattern
结胸证/結胸證 chest binding pattern
结扎/結扎 ligate
结扎法/結扎法 ligation method
结扎疗法/結扎療法 ligating therapy
结扎术/結扎術 ligation
结扎丝/結扎絲 ligature wire

结扎丝切断钳/縛線刀　ligature cutter
结扎针/結扎針,縛線針　ligature needle
结扎征/結扎徵象,緊縛徵象　ligature sign
结直肠外科手术/結直腸外科手術　colorectal surgery
结直肠肿瘤/結直腸腫瘤　colorectal neoplasm
结状神经节/結狀神經節,迷走神經下節　nodose ganglion
桔梗/桔梗　platycodon root
捷列斯尼茨基液/Tellyesniczky 氏液　Tellyesniczky fluid
睫的/睫狀體的,纖毛的　ciliary
睫后长动脉/睫後長動脈　long posterior ciliary artery
睫后短动脉/睫後短動脈　short posterior ciliary artery
睫毛/睫　cilium, eyelash
睫毛电解术/睫毛電解術　electrolysis of eye lash
睫毛镊/拔睫鑷　ciliary forcep
睫毛脱落/睫毛脱落　madarosis
睫毛腺/睫腺,Mall 氏腺　ciliary gland, Moll gland
睫毛移植[术]/睫毛移植[術]　eyelashes grafting
睫毛再造术/睫毛再造術　eyelashes reconstruction
睫前动脉/睫前動脈　anterior ciliary artery
睫前静脉/睫前靜脈　anterior ciliary vein
睫区镜/睫狀體鏡　ciliariscope
睫癣/睫癬　tinea ciliorum
睫状襞/睫狀褶　ciliary fold
睫状长动脉/睫狀長動脈　long ciliary artery
睫状长神经/睫狀長神經,長睫神經　long ciliary nerve
睫状充血/睫狀充血　ciliary congestion
睫状动脉/睫狀動脈　ciliary artery
睫状短神经/睫狀短神經　short ciliary nerve
睫状冠/睫狀冠　ciliary crown
睫状后长动脉/睫狀後長動脈　long posterior ciliary artery
睫状环/睫狀環　ciliary ring
睫状肌/睫狀肌　ciliary muscle, ciliaris
睫状肌不全麻痹/睫狀肌不全麻痺　cycloparesis
睫状肌刀/睫狀體刀　cyclotome
睫状肌辐射状纤维/睫狀肌輻射狀纖維　radiate fiber of ciliary muscle
睫状肌环形纤维/睫狀肌環形纖維　circular fiber of ciliary muscle
睫状肌经线纤维/睫狀肌經線纖維　meridional fiber of ciliary muscle
睫状肌麻痹/睫狀肌麻痺　cycloplegia
睫状肌麻痹剂/睫狀肌麻痺劑　cycloplegic
睫状肌切开术/睫狀肌切開術,睫狀體切開術　cyclicotomy
睫状肌屈光度/睫狀肌折光力　myodiopter
睫状前动脉/睫狀前動脈　anterior ciliary artery
睫状前静脉/睫狀前靜脈　anterior ciliary vein
睫状神经节/睫狀神經節,睫狀神經結　ciliary ganglion
睫状神经节丛/睫狀神經節叢　ciliary ganglionic plexus
睫状神经节副交感根/睫狀神經節副交感根　parasympathetic root of ciliary ganglion
睫状神经节感觉根/睫結感覺根　sensory root of ciliary ganglion
睫状神经节交感根/睫狀神經節交感根　sympathetic root of ciliary ganglion
睫状神经节交通支/睫狀神經節交通支　communicating branch with ciliary ganglion
睫状神经切断术/睫狀神經切斷術　ciliotomy
睫状神经痛/睫狀神經痛　ciliary neuralgia
睫状神经营养因子/睫狀神經營養因子　ciliary neurotrophic factor
睫状神经营养因子受体/睫狀神經營養因子受體　ciliary neurotrophic factor receptor
睫状体/睫狀體　ciliary body
睫状体电解术/睫狀體電解術　cycloelectrolysis
睫状体分离术/睫狀體分離術　cyclodialysis
睫状体基底层/睫狀體基底層　basal lamina of ciliary body
睫状体角膜炎/睫狀體色膜炎　cycloceratitis
睫状体结核/睫狀體結核　tuberculosis of ciliary body
睫状体冷冻疗法/睫狀體冷凍療法　cyclocryotherapy
睫状体冷凝术/睫狀體冷凝術　cyclocryosurgery
睫状体脉络膜炎/睫狀體脈絡膜炎　cyclochoroiditis
睫状体贫血术/睫狀體貧血術　cycloanemization
睫状体葡萄肿/睫狀體葡萄腫　ciliary staphyloma
睫状体切除术/睫狀體切除術,瞼緣切除術　cyclectomy
睫状体切开术/睫狀體切開術　ciliarotomy
睫状体区/睫狀[體]部　ciliary region
睫状体韧带/睫狀體韌帶　ciliary ligament
睫状[体]上皮/睫狀[體]上皮　ciliary epithelium
睫状体透热疗法/睫狀體透熱凝固法　cyclodiathermy
睫状体炎/睫狀體炎　cyclitis
睫状突/睫狀突　ciliary process
睫状小带/睫[狀小]帶　zonula ciliaris
睫状小带切开术/睫狀小帶切開術　zonulotomy

睫状小带松解法/睫狀小帶溶解　zonulolysis
睫状小带炎/睫狀小帶炎　zonulitis
睫状缘/睫狀緣　ciliary margin
睫状中纬线纤维/睫狀中緯線纖維　cilioequatorial fiber
截断/截斷　chopping
截断的/遮斷的　interceptive
截断伤/截斷傷　amputation injury
截断性溃疡/截斷性潰瘍　amputating ulcer
截根术/截根術　root amputation
截骨术/截骨術,骨切開術　osteotomy
截面密度/截面密度　sectional density
截囊刀/截囊刀　cystotome
截石位/截石位　lithotomy position
截瘫/截癱,下身麻痹　paraplegia
截形伪端盘吸虫/平頂假雙口吸蟲　Pseudamphistomum truncatum
截肢残端/截肢殘端　amputation stump
截肢术/截斷術　amputation
截肢性神经瘤/截肢性神經瘤　amputation neuroma
截肢者/截肢者　amputees
姐妹染色[单]体交换/姐妹染色[單]體交換　sister chromatid exchange, SCE
解表法/解表法　relieving exterior method
解表剂/解表劑　exterior-relieving formula
解表清里剂/解表清裡劑　formula for relieving exterior and clearing interior
解表通里剂/解表通裡劑　formula for relieving exterior and catharsis
解表温里剂/解表溫裡劑　formula for relieving exterior and warming interior
解除催眠状态/解除催眠　dehypnotize
解除吸附/解除吸附,去除吸附　desorb
解胨的/解腖的　peptolytic
解毒/解毒,脱毒　detoxication
解毒护阴/解毒護陰　removing toxicity for protecting yin
解毒化瘢/解毒化瘢　removing toxicity substance and resolving macula
解毒息风/解毒息風　removing toxicity substance and calming endogenous wind
解毒消痈/解毒消癰　removing toxicity for eliminating carbuncles
解毒消肿/解毒消腫　removing toxicity for detumescence
解毒药/解毒藥,解毒劑　antidote, antidote
解肌清热/解肌清熱　expelling pathogenic factors from muscles for clearing heat

解碱药/解鹼藥　antalkaline
解痉素/解痙素　adiphenine
解痉药/解痙藥　antispasmodic, spasmolytic
解痉[作用]/解痙作用　spasmolysis
解聚[合]/去聚合化　depolymerize
解聚[作用]/解聚合[作用],去聚合[作用]　depolymerization
解离/解離　dissociation
解离组织/解離組織　disintegrated tissue
解链温度/融解溫度　melting temperature
解磷定化合物/解磷定化合物　pralidoxime compound
解颅/解顱　hydrocephalus due to nonclosure of fontanel, metopism
解颅·脾虚水泛证/解顱·脾虛水泛證　metopism with pattern of water overflowing due to spleen deficiency
解颅·热毒壅滞证/解顱·熱毒壅滯證　metopism with pattern of congestion and stagnation of heat-toxin
解颅·肾气虚证/解顱·腎氣虛證　metopism with pattern of kidney qi deficiency
解颅·肾虚肝旺证/解顱·腎虛肝旺證　metopism with pattern of spleen deficiency and liver hyperactivity
解脲支原体/解脲支原體　ureaplasma urealyticum
解偶联剂/解偶聯劑　uncoupling agent
解剖/解剖　anatomise
解剖成分/解剖成分　anatomic element
解剖的/解剖的　anatomic
解剖根/解剖根　anatomical root
解剖冠/解剖冠　anatomical crown
解剖颈/解剖頸　anatomical neck
解剖镜/解剖透鏡　anatomical lens
解剖式牙/解剖式牙　anatomic tooth
解剖位置/解剖模型姿勢　anatomical position
解剖无效腔/解剖死腔　anatomical dead space
解剖性咬合/齒正位咬合　anatomic occlusion
解剖学/解剖學　anatomy
解剖学病理状态/解剖學病理狀態　anatomical pathological condition
解剖学肛管/解剖學肛管　anatomic anal canal
解剖学各论/解剖學各論　special anatomy
解剖学灌注/解剖學注射　anatomical injection
解剖学家/解剖學家　anatomist
解剖学名词/解剖學名詞　nomina anatomica
解剖学模型/解剖學模型　anatomic model
解剖学术语/解剖學術語　anatomical term

解剖学姿势/解剖體位　anatomical position
解剖学总论/解剖學總論　general anatomy
解剖医学/解剖醫學　anatomic medicine
解剖疣/解剖疣　anatomic wart
解剖针/解剖針　dissecting needle
解热药/解熱藥　antipyretic, antifebrile
解热镇痛药/解熱鎮痛藥　antipyretic analgesic
解蛇毒剂/治蛇咬藥　antiophidica
解蛇毒素/解蛇毒素　tyresin
解砷毒药/砷中毒解藥　antidote against arsenic
解酸剂/制酸劑　antacid
解体细胞/解體細胞　disintegrated cell
解酮[作用]/酮分解　ketolysis
解吸附作用/去吸附作用　desorption
解溪/解溪　jiexi, ST41
解压/減壓　decompression
解疑释惑[疗法]/解疑釋惑[療法]　answer by setting straight
解郁安神/解鬱安神　relieving stagnation and tranquilizing the mind, resolving stagnation for tranquilization
解脂酶/脂解酶　fat-splitting enzyme
介电常数/介電常數　dielectric constant
介入性超声检查/介入性超聲檢查　interventional ultrasonography
介入性放射摄影术/介入性放射攝影術　interventional radiography
介入性放射学/介入性放射學　interventional radiology
介入治疗/介入治療　interventional therapy
介体/介體　desmon
介体试纸/介體試紙　amboceptor paper
介体原/介體抗原　amboceptorgen
介质/介質　mediator, media
介质耗竭/介質耗盡　mediator exhaustion
介质排空/介質排空　mediator depletion
介子/介子　meson
戒断/戒斷,脱癮　withdrawal
戒断反应/禁斷反應　abstinence reaction
戒断症状/禁斷症狀　abstinence syndrome
戒断综合征/戒斷症候群　withdrawal syndrome
戒酒性发作/戒酒性發作　alcohol withdrawal seizure
戒酒性谵妄/戒酒性譫妄　alcohol withdrawal delirium
戒酒药/戒酒藥　alcohol deterrent
戒烟/戒煙　smoking cessation
戒瘾/忌,戒,斷除　abstinence
芥酸类/芥酸類　erucic acids

芥子/芥子,芥屬　sinapis, mustard seed
芥子化合物/芥子化合物　mustard compound
芥子泥罨/芥末糊劑　mustard poultice
芥子气/芥子氣　mustard gas
芥子气烧伤/芥子氣燒傷　mustard gas burn
芥子植物/芥子植物　mustard plant
界板/界板　limiting plate
界沟/界溝　sulcus terminalis, terminal sulcus, sulcus limitans
界嵴/界嵴　crista terminalis
界面表面张力/分界面張力　interfacial surface tension
界面的/分界面的　interfacial
界面张力/界面張力　interfacial tension
界线/界線　terminal line
疥疮/疥瘡,疥[癬]　scabies
疥螨病/疥蟲病　sarcoptic acariasis
疥螨属/疥蟎屬　Sarcoptes
疥状肠变化/乾癬狀腸炎　psorenteritis
斤/斤　jin
今今尼亚病/吉吉尼亞病　jhin jhinia
金/金　metal
金胺/槐黄　auramine
金胺O/金胺O　auramine O
金伯克-亚当森点/金-亞二氏點　Kienbock-Adamson point
金沉着性皮变色/金皮症　chrysoderma
金疮肿科/金瘡腫科　department of sores and wounds
金创痉/金創痙　traumatic tetanus
金瓷修复体/金瓷修復體　metal ceramic prosthesis
金德勒综合征/Kindler氏症候群　Kindler syndrome
金垫/金墊　gold cushion
金放射性同位素/金放射性同位素　gold radioisotope
金沸草/金沸草　inula herb
金沸草散/金沸草散　jinfeicao powder
金疳/金疳　metal gan, golden malnutrition of eye, phlyctenular conjunctivitis
金疳·肺经燥热证/金疳·肺經燥熱證　metal gan with pattern of dryness-heat in lung channel
金疳·脾肺气虚证/金疳·脾肺氣虛證　metal gan with spleen-lung qi deficiency pattern
金刚砂/金剛砂　carborundum
金刚砂轮/矽碳輪　carborundum wheel
金刚砂钻/金剛砂鑽　diamond bur
金刚烷/金剛烷　adamantane
金刚烷胺/金剛烷胺,三環癸烷胺　amantadine
金刚乙胺/金剛烷乙胺　rimantadine

金刚钻刀/金剛鑽刀　diamond knife
金果榄/金果欖　tinospora root
金合金/金合金　gold alloy
金衡制/金衡制　troy weight
金花内障/金花内障　complicated cataract induced by uveitis, golden flower cataract
金化合物/金化合物　gold compound
金黄色葡萄球菌/金黃色葡萄球菌　S. aureus
金黄色葡萄球菌感染/金黃色葡萄球菌感染　staphylococcus aureus infection
金黄色苔藓/金黃色苔蘚　lichen aureus
金鸡纳反应/金雞納反應　cinchonism
金鸡纳皮/金雞納皮　cinchona bark
金鸡纳生物碱类/金雞納生物鹼類　cinchona alkaloids
金鸡纳树皮/金雞納樹皮　cinchona
金鸡纳中毒/金雞納中毒　cinchonism
金剂性皮肤变色/金劑性皮膚變色　aurochromoderma
金剂疹/金疹　aurid
金津/金津　jinjin, EX-HN12
金津玉液/金津玉液　Jinjin and Yuye
金精三羧酸/金精三羧酸　aurintricarboxylic acid
金克木/金克木　metal restricting wood
金匮钩玄/金匱鉤玄　An Elucidation of the Golden Chamber
金匮要略/金匱要略[方論]　Synopsis of Golden Chamber
金疗法/金劑療法　aurotherapy
金铃子散/金鈴子散　jinlingzi powder
金硫丁二钠/金硫基丁二酸鈉　sodium aurothiomalate
金鲈类/金鱸類　perches
金轮菌素/金輪菌素　aurovertin
金缕梅糖/金縷酶糖　hamamelose
金霉素/金黴素,氯四環素　chlortetracycline
金门/金門　jinmen, BL63
金礞石/金礞石　micaschist
金诺芬/金諾芬　auranofin
金破不鸣/金破不鳴　broken metal failing to sound, damaged lung not functioning normally
金普顿-布朗管/金-布二氏管　Kimpton-Brown tube
金钱白花蛇/金錢白花蛇　coin-like white-banded snake
金钱草/金錢草　christina loosestrife
金荞麦/金蕎麥　golden buckwheat rhizome
金雀花/金雀花　scoparius
金雀花素/金雀花素　scoparin
金雀花中毒/金雀花中毒　broom poisoning
金渗散/金渗散　chrysophoresis
金生水/金生水　metal generating water
金石中毒/金石中毒　metallic poisoning
金实不鸣/金實不鳴　muffled metal failing to sound, obstructed lung not functioning normally
金氏单位/金氏單位　King unit
金属/金屬　metal
金属背牙/金屬背牙　metal backing tooth
金属边料/金屬片　scissel
金属卟啉/卟啉金屬鹽　metalloporphyrin
金属沉积/金屬沈著　metallic deposition
金属[触]觉/金屬觸覺,金屬樣的感覺　metallesthesia
金属蛋白酶类/金屬蛋白酶類　metalloproteases
金属蛋白质类/金屬蛋白質類　metalloproteins
金属的/金屬的　metallic
金属丁当音/金屬叮噹音　metallic tinkle
金属反应检查法/金屬作用測定法　metalloscopy
金属黄素蛋白/金屬黃素蛋白　metalloflavoprotein
金属基托/金屬基托　metal base
金属加固环/金屬加固環　ferrule
金属烤瓷合金/金屬烤瓷合金　metal ceramic alloy
金属疗法/金屬療法　metallotherapy
金属硫蛋白/金屬硫蛋白　metallothionein
金属磨带/金屬磨帶　metal tap
金属内肽酶类/金屬内肽酶類　metalloendopeptidases
金属牵引器疗法/金屬牵引器法　tractoration
金属丝/金屬線　wire
金属陶瓷/金屬陶瓷　ceramic metal
金属外肽酶类/金屬外肽酶類　metalloexopeptidases
金属性变色/金屬性變色　metallic discoloration
金属性回声/金屬性回響　metallic echo
金属性杂音/金屬性雜音　metallic murmur
金属烟尘热/金屬蒸氣熱　metal fume fever
金属异物探测器/金屬探測器　boloscope
金属支架/金屬架　metal rack
金丝雀痘/金絲雀痘　canarypox
金丝雀痘病毒/金絲雀痘病毒　canarypox virus
金斯利夹/Kingsley氏夾板　Kingsley splint
金酸/金酸　auric acid
金锁固精丸/金鎖固精丸　jinsuo gujing pills
金同位素/金同位素　gold isotope
金形[之]人/金形[之]人　metal-phase person
金银花/金銀花　honeysuckle, honeysuckle bud and flower
金银花露/金銀花露　jinyinhua distillate

金樱子/金櫻子 cherokee rose fruit
金蝇属/金蠅屬 Chrysomyia
金油疗法/金油療法 oleochrysotherapy
金元四家/金元四家 four scholastic sects of Jin-Yuan dynasties
金曰从革/金曰從革 metal characterized by clearing and changing
金盏花/金盞花 marigold
金盏花抽提液/金盞花抽提液 calendula extract
金盏花属/金盞花屬 Calendula
金针拨障疗法/金針撥障療法 cataractopiesis with metal needle therapy, method of removing cataract with metal needle
金质沉着病/金質沈著病 chrysiasis
金字塔形的/錐體的, 錐狀的 pyramidal
津/津 clear fluid
津枯血燥/津枯血燥 depletion of fluid causing blood dryness
津亏热结证/津虧熱結證 pattern of deficiency of fluid and accumulated heat
津气亏虚证/津氣虧虛證 pattern of deficiency of fluid and qi
津脱/津脫 clear fluid depletion
津血同源/津血同源 homogeny of clear fluid and blood
津液/液體 fluid
津液亏虚证/津液虧虛證 pattern of deficiency of fluid
津泽不协调现象/秦塞氏不協調現象 Zinsser inconsistency
筋/筋, 腱 tendon and ligament, soft tissue, tendon
筋痹/筋痺, 肌風濕病 muscular rheumatism, tendon bi
筋粗/筋粗 hypertrophy of tendon and muscle
筋断/筋斷, 筋傷斷裂 laceration of muscle and tendon, tendon ruptured
筋断伤/筋斷傷 fragmentation of muscle and tendon
筋骨并重/筋骨并重 pay equal attention to bone and flesh
筋瘤/筋瘤 nodular varicosity, tendon tumor
筋瘤·寒湿凝聚证/筋瘤·寒濕凝聚證 tendon tumor with pattern of cold-dampness congelation and aggregation
筋瘤·劳倦伤气证/筋瘤·勞倦傷氣證 tendon tumor with overstrain injuring qi pattern
筋瘤·血瘀气滞证/筋瘤·血瘀氣滯證 tendon tumor with pattern of blood stasis and qi stagnation
筋挛/筋攣 muscular cramp

筋膜/筋膜 fascia
筋膜瓣/筋膜瓣 fascial flap
筋膜成形术/筋膜成形術 fasciaplasty
筋膜带移植肛门括约肌成形术/筋膜帶移植肛門括約肌成形術 fascial string grafting and anal sphincteroplasty
筋膜的/筋膜的 fascial
筋膜蒂皮瓣/筋膜蒂皮瓣 fascial pedicle skin flap
筋膜吊带/筋膜吊帶 fascia sling
筋膜缝术/筋膜縫合術 fasciorrhaphy
筋膜骨化增生/筋膜骨化增生 hyperplasia fascialis ossificans
筋膜固定术/筋膜腱縫合術 fasciodesis
筋膜间隔区综合征/筋膜間隔區綜合徵 pattern of aponeurotic space
筋膜间隔综合征/筋膜間隔症候群 compartment syndrome
筋膜间隙充气造影照片/筋膜充氣照片 pneumofasciogram
筋膜皮瓣/筋膜皮瓣 fascio-cutaneous flap
筋膜切除术/筋膜切除術, 肌膜切除術 fasciectomy
筋膜切开术/筋膜切開術, 肌膜切開術 fasciotomy
筋膜疝/筋膜疝 fascial hernia
筋膜上的/筋膜上的 epifascial
筋膜上注射/筋膜上注射 epifascial injection
筋膜条抽取器/筋膜條抽取器 fascia stripper
筋膜条悬吊术/筋膜條懸吊術 fascial sling suspension
筋膜下囊/筋膜下囊 subfascial bursa
筋膜炎/筋膜炎 fasciitis
筋膜移植/筋膜移植 fascial transplantation
筋膜移植术/筋膜移植術 fascia grafting
筋膜移植物/筋膜移植物 fascia graft
筋膜造影片/筋膜 X 光片 fasciagram
筋膜造影术/筋膜 X 光攝影術 fasciagraphy
筋强/筋強 muscular rigidity
筋疝/筋疝 penitis, varicocele
筋伤/筋傷, 腱損傷 injury of tendons, tendon injury
筋伤病机/筋傷病機 pathogenesis of injury of muscle and tendon
筋缩/筋縮 ①muscle and tendon crispation ②jinsuo, DU8
筋惕肉瞤/筋惕肉瞤 muscular twitching and cramp
筋未断伤/筋未斷傷 laceration of muscle and tendon
筋之府/筋之府 house of tendons
筋转/筋轉 myospasm
紧凑的/致密的 compact
紧喉风/緊喉風 fulminant throat wind

紧急/緊急,急迫 urgency
紧急反应/警告反應 alarm reaction
紧急救援/緊急救援 emergency relief
紧急心脏起搏/緊急心臟起搏 emergency cardiac pacing
紧急照护/急性照護 acute care
紧脉/緊脈 tight pulse
紧密连接/緊密結合 tight junction
紧皮的/緊皮的,硬皮的 bound skin
紧迫流产/危迫流産 imminent abortion
紧迫性红细胞过多/緊迫性紅血球過多症 stress erythrocytosis
紧窄性充血法/收縮性充血 constriction hyperemia
紧张部/緊張部 tense part
紧张过度/過度緊張 overstress
紧张型精神分裂症/緊張型精神分裂症 catatonic schizophrenia
紧张性木僵/緊張性木僵 catatonic stupor
紧张性瞳孔/強直性瞳孔 tonic pupil
紧张性头痛/緊張性頭痛 tension headache
紧张性兴奋/僵直型興奮 catatonic excitement
紧张症/緊張症 catatonia
紧张症患者/緊張症患者 catatonic
堇色毛癣菌/紫色毛癬菌 Trichophyton violaceum
锦灯笼/錦燈籠 franchet groundcherry fruit
锦葵/錦葵 mallow
进程/進程 process
进化/進化 evolution
进化论/進化論 evolutionism
进化遗传学/進化遺傳學 evolutionary genetics
进食/進食 eating
进食障碍/進食障礙 eating disorder
进行性/進行的 progressive
进行性斑状色素过少症/進行性斑狀色素過少症 progressive macular hypopigmentation
进行性半侧舌萎缩/進行性偏側舌萎縮 progressive lingual hemiatrophy
进行性苍白球变性/進行性蒼白球變性 progressive pallidal degeneration
进行性单侧面萎缩症/進行性單側面萎縮症 progressive facial hemiatrophy
进行性豆状核变性/進行性豆狀核變性 progressive lenticular degeneration
进行性多发性透明性浆膜炎/進行性多漿膜炎 progressive multiple hyaloserositis
进行性多灶性脑白质病/進行性多灶性腦白質病 progressive multifocal leukoencephalopathy
进行性肥大间质性神经病/進行性間質增生性神經病變 progressive hypertrophic interstitial neuropathy
进行性复发性皮肤纤维瘤/進行性復發型皮膚纖維瘤 progressive recurring dermatofibroma
进行性骨化错生/進行性骨化錯生 progressive osseous heteroplasia
进行性骨化性肌炎/進行性骨化性肌炎 progressive ossifying myositis
进行性核上麻痹/進行性核上麻痺 progressive supranuclear palsy
进行性肌萎缩/進行性肌萎縮,消耗性癱瘓 wasting palsy
进行性肌营养不良/進行性肌營養不良 progressive muscular dystrophy
进行性肌阵挛性癫痫/進行性肌陣攣性癲癇 progressive myoclonic epilepsy
进行性脊髓性肌萎缩/進行性脊髓性肌萎縮 progressive spinal muscular atrophy
进行性脊椎前凸步行困难/進行性脊椎前凸步行困難 dyspepsia lordotica progressiva
进行性结节性组织细胞瘤/進行性結節性組織細胞瘤 progressive nodular histiocytoma
进行性精神分裂症/進行型思覺失調症 process schizophrenia
进行性麻痹/進行性肌萎縮 creeping palsy
进行性面偏侧萎缩[症]/進行性單側顔面萎縮 progressive unilateral facial atrophy
进行性面萎缩/進行性顔面萎縮 progressive facial atrophy
进行性[脑]卒中/進行性[腦]卒中 progressive stroke
进行性牛痘/進行性牛痘 progressive vaccinia
进行性扭转痉挛/進行性扭轉痙攣,變形性肌緊張不足 progressive torsion spasm
进行性皮质下脑病/進行性皮質下腦病 progressive subcortical encephalopathy
进行性色素性皮肤病/進行性色素皮膚病 progressive pigmentary dermatosis
进行性色素性紫癜/進行性色素性紫癜 prupura progressive pigmentosa
进行性色素性紫癜性皮肤病/進行性色素性紫癜樣皮膚病 progressive pigmented purpuric dermatosis
进行性筛状及带状疱疹样色素过度沉着症/進行性篩狀及帶狀皰疹樣色素過度沈著症 progressive cribriform and zosterform hyperpigmentation
进行性神经[病]性肌萎缩/馬-托二氏病 Marie-Tooth disease
进行性神经肌肉萎缩/進行性神經肌萎縮

progressive neuromuscular atrophy
进行性神经性腓骨肌萎缩/進行性神經病變腓骨肌萎縮　progressive neuropathic peroneal muscular atrophy
进行性水疱性表皮松解症/進行性水皰性表皮鬆解症　epidermolysis bullosa progressiva
进行性特发性皮肤萎缩/進行性特發性皮膚萎縮　atrophia cutis idiopathica progressiva
进行性系统性硬化病/進行性全身硬化　progressive systemic sclerosis
进行性延髓麻痹/進行性延髓性麻痺　progressive bulbar palsy
进行性翼状胬肉/進行性翼狀胬肉　progressive pterygium
进行性掌跖角皮病/進行性掌蹠角化症　progressive palmoplantar keratoderma
进行性肢端黑变病/進行性肢端黑變症　acromelanosis progressiva
进行性脂肪萎缩/進行性脂肪萎縮症　progressive lipoatrophy
进行性脂肪营养不良/進行性脂質營養不良　progressive lipodystrophy
进行性脂瘤性巨大发育/進行性脂瘤性巨體發育異常　macrodystrophia lipomatosa progressiva
进行性锥体苍白球变性/進行性錐體蒼白球變性　progressive pyramidopallidal degeneration
进样阀/進樣閥　injection valve
进样隔膜胶垫/進樣隔膜膠墊　injecting septum
进针法/進針法　method of needle insertion
近部取穴/近部取穴　neighboring point selection
近侧/近側　proximal
近侧面/近側面　proximate surface
近侧血块/近側血塊　proximal clot
近侧中心粒/近側中心粒,近側中心區　proximal centriole
近程增益/近程增益　near area gain
近等裂/對等分裂　adequal cleavage
近点/近點　near point
近端点着丝粒染色体/中央節近末端染色體　acrocentric chromosome
近端肾小管/近端腎小管　proximal kidney tubule
近端肾小管性酸中毒/近端腎小管性酸中毒　proximal renal tubular acidosis
近端小管/近端小管　proximal tubule
近端着丝的/中央節近末端的　acrocentric
近复视像/同側性複像　homonymous image
近红外线疗法/近紅外線療法　near-infrared therapy
近红外线谱学/近紅外線譜學　near-infrared spectroscopy
近交系数/近交係數　coefficient of inbreeding
近节指骨/近側指節骨　proximal phalanx
近节趾骨/近側趾節骨　proximal phalanx
近距离放射疗法/近距放射線療法　brachytherapy
近距碰撞/近距碰撞　near mass collision
近皮质的/近皮質的　juxtacortical
近皮质骨肉瘤/近皮質骨肉瘤　juxtacortical osteosarcoma
近平滑假丝酵母/近平滑念珠菌　Candida parapsilosis
近腔室/近腔室　abluminal compartment
近亲/血親　consanguinity
近亲繁殖/近親交配　inbreeding
近亲结婚/近親結婚,近親婚姻,血親結婚　consanguineous marriage
近亲系数/近親係數,近交係數　coefficient of consanguinity
近肾小球的/近腎絲球的　juxtaglomerular
近[肾小]球细胞/近腎絲球細胞　juxtaglomerular cell
近似致死剂量/近似致死劑量　approximate lethal dose, ALD
近事遗忘/近事遺忘,逆行性健妄　ecmnesia
近视/近視　myopia
近视·肝肾两虚证/近視·肝腎兩虛證　myopia with liver-kidney deficiency pattern
近视角膜磨削术/近視角膜磨削術　myopia keratomileusis
近视力/视近力　near vision
近视力检查[法]/近視力檢查[法]　examination of near vision, near vision test
近视·脾气虚证/近視·脾氣虛證　myopia with spleen qi deficiency pattern
近视散光/近視散光　myopic astigmatism
近视·心阳虚证/近視·心陽虛證　myopia with heart yang deficiency pattern
近视者/近視者　myope
近锁骨念珠状线/近鎖骨念珠狀線　juxta-clavicular beaded line
近血/近血　proximal bleeding, nearby anal bleeding
近因/近因　proximate cause
近阈刺激物/近閾刺激　liminal stimulus
近中唇[侧]的/内側[及]唇側的　mesiolabial
近中唇[侧]切缘的/内側唇側及切緣側的　mesiolabioincisal
近中的/近中的,正中的　mesial
近中𬌗/[齒]内側咬合　mesial occlusion

近中牙合面的/内側[及]咬合面的 mesio-occlusal
近中牙合远側的/内側咬合側及遠側的 mesio-occlusodistal
近中頰[側]的/内側[與]頰側的 mesiobuccal
近中頰牙合面的/内側頰側及咬合面的 mesiobucco-occlusal
近中頰髓的/内側、頰側及髓側的 mesiobuccopulpal
近中面/近中面 mesial surface
近中切[缘]远側的/近中切緣遠側的 mesioincisodistal
近中傾斜/近中傾斜 mesioclination
近中舌側的/内側[與]舌側的 mesiolingual
近中舌側牙合面的/内側、舌側及咬合側的 mesiolinguo-occlusal
近中舌[側]切緣的/内側舌側及切緣側的 mesiolinguoincisal
近中舌[側]髓的/内側舌側及髓側的 mesiolinguopulpal
近中髓唇的/内側、髓側及唇側面的 mesiopulpolabial
近中髓舌的/内側髓側及舌側的 mesiopulpolingual
近中向位/近中向位 mesioversion
近中[向]阻生/近中[向]阻生 mesioangular impaction
近中心的/近中心的 paracentral
近中齦的/齒之近心側及齦側的 mesiogingival
近中远側的/内側與遠側的 mesiodistal
近子宫頸膀胱[阴道]瘘/近子宫頸膀胱陰道瘻管 juxtacervicovesical fistula
近紫外线/近紫外綫 near ultraviolet
浸出工艺/抽提技術 extract technology
浸出物测定/抽提物測定 determination of extractive
浸膏剂/萃取 extract
浸剂沉淀物/浸劑沈澱物 apothem
浸没透镜/浸漬鏡，油浸鏡 immersion lens
浸没物镜/油浸接物鏡 immersion objective
浸泡手/浸泡手 immersion hand
浸泡足/浸潤足 immersion foot
浸入折射计/浸入式折射計 immersion refractometer
浸软/浸軟 maceration
浸润/浸潤 immersion
浸润麻醉/浸潤麻醉法 infiltration anesthesia
浸润型肺结核/浸潤型肺結核 infiltrative pulmonary tuberculosis
浸润性成骨细胞瘤/侵襲性骨母細胞瘤 aggressive osteoblastoma
浸洗疗法/浸洗療法 immersion and wash therapy

浸淫疮/浸淫瘡 general effused eczema
浸浴/浸浴 bathing
浸浴疗法/浸浴療法 immersion therapy
浸渍/浸漬 maceration
浸渍器/浸漬器 macerator
禁闭心/包臟心 encased heart
禁汗/禁汗 contraindication for diaphoresis
禁忌克隆/禁忌克隆 forbidden clone
禁忌症/禁忌症，禁忌徵象 contraindication
禁科/禁科 department of incantation
禁利小便/禁利小便 contraindication for diuresis
禁食/禁食 absolute diet
禁水/禁水 water deprivation
禁水试验/禁水試驗 water deprivation test
禁下/禁下 contraindication for catharsis
禁咒/禁咒 incantation
禁咒疗法/禁咒療法 incantation therapy
噤口痢/噤口痢 anorectic dysentery
茎/莖 peduncle
茎乳动脉/莖乳動脈 stylomastoid artery
茎乳孔/莖乳[突]孔 stylomastoid foramen
茎乳突静脉/莖乳突靜脈 stylomastoid vein
茎突/莖突 styloid process
茎突点/莖突點 stylion
茎突过长/莖突過長 elongated styloid process
茎突鞘/鞘突 sheath of styloid process
茎突舌骨肌/莖突舌骨肌 stylohyoid
茎突舌骨肌支/莖突舌骨肌支 stylohyoid branch
茎突舌骨韧带/莖突舌骨韌帶 stylohyoid ligament
茎突舌骨神经/莖突舌骨神經 stylohyoid nerve
茎突舌肌/莖突舌肌 musculus styloglossus
茎突凸/莖凸 styloid prominence
茎突下颌韧带/莖突下頜韌帶 stylomandibular ligament
茎突咽肌/莖突咽肌 musculus stylopharyngeus
茎突咽肌神经/莖突咽肌神經 stylopharyngeal nerve
茎突咽肌支/莖突咽肌支 stylopharyngeal branch
茎突炎/莖突炎 styloiditis
茎状骨赘/莖狀骨贅 stylosteophyte
[京]大戟/[京]大戟 Peking euphorbia root
京骨/京骨 jinggu, BL64
京门/京門 jingmen, GB25
京师药物院/京師藥物院，廣惠司 Capital Medical Institute
京万红/京萬紅 jingwanhong soft plaster
经鼻/經鼻 per nasal
经鼻垂体切除术/經鼻垂體切除術 transnasal hypophysectomy

经鼻盲探气管内插管/經鼻盲探氣管内插管 blind nasotracheal intubation
经鼻气管内插管/經鼻氣管内插管 nasotracheal intubation
经鼻入路/經鼻入路 transnasal approach
经闭/月經停滯,月經留滯 menischesis
经别/經别 branched channel
经侧裂入路/經側裂入路 transsylvian approach
经侧脑室三角区入路/經側腦室三角區入路 transtrigone lateral ventricle approach
经产/經産 multiparity
经产妇/經産婦 multipara
经潮期/經潮期,來經期 menacme
经大脑半球间入路/經大腦半球間入路 transinterhemispheric approach
经骶骨的/經骶骨的 transsacral
经骶管阻滞/經骶管阻滯,經骶麻醉法 transsacral block
经骶麻醉/經骶麻醉法 transsacral anesthesia
经典补体途径/經典補體途徑 classical complement pathway
经典条件反射/經典條件反射 classical conditioning
经蝶窦入路/經蝶竇入路 transsphenoidal approach
经断复来/經斷復來 postmenopausal menstruation, vaginal bleeding after menopause
经断复来·脾虚肝郁证/經斷復來·脾虛肝鬱證 vaginal bleeding after menopause with pattern of spleen deficiency and liver depression
经断复来·气虚证/經斷復來·氣虛證 vaginal bleeding after menopause with qi deficiency pattern
经断复来·湿毒瘀结证/經斷復來·濕毒瘀結證 vaginal bleeding after menopause with pattern of intermingling of damp-poison-static blood
经断复来·阴虚火旺证/經斷復來·陰虛火旺證 vaginal bleeding after menopause with pattern of exuberant fire due to yin deficiency
经额叶脑室入路/經額葉側腦室入路 transfrontal lateral ventricle approach
经方/經方 classical prescriptions
经房间隔左心导管检查/經房間隔左心導管檢查 transseptal left heart catheterization
经腹骶直肠切除术/經腹骶直腸切除術 anterior resection
经腹肾切除术/腹[前]式腎切除術 abdominal nephrectomy
经腹肾切开术/腹式腎切開術 abdominal nephrotomy
经腹直肌切口/經腹直肌切口 transrectal incision
经肝括约肌切开术/經肝括約肌切開術 transhepatic sphincterotomy
经股静脉插管/經股靜脈插管 transfemoral catheterization of femoral vein
经后期/經後期 postmenstrua, post menstrual period
经回肠膀胱逆行输尿管造影[术]/經迴腸膀胱逆行輸尿管造影[術] retrograde ileocystoureterography
经会阴活检/經會陰活檢 transperineal biopsy
经会阴膀胱切开术/下部式膀胱切開術,會陰式膀胱切開術 hypocystotomy
经会阴前列腺切除术/會陰式前列腺切除術 perineal prostatectomy
经会阴前列腺全切除术/經會陰前列腺全切除術 total perineal prostatectomy
经会阴切石术/會陰式截石術 perineal lithotomy
经济疗法/經濟療法 economic cure
经间期/經間期 intermenstrual period
经间[期]出血/經間[期]出血 intermenstrual bleeding
经间期出血·脾气虚证/經間期出血·脾氣虛證 intermenstrual bleeding with pattern of spleen qi deficiency
经间期出血·肾阴虚证/經間期出血·腎陰虛證 intermenstrual bleeding with pattern of kidney yin deficiency
经间期出血·湿热[蕴结]证/經間期出血·濕熱[蕴結]證 intermenstrual bleeding with pattern of accumulation and binding of damp-heat
经间期出血·血瘀证/經間期出血·血瘀證 intermenstrual bleeding with blood stasis pattern
经间期痛经/經間期痛經 dysmenorrhea intermenstrualis
经间痛/經間痛 intermenstrual pain
经筋/經筋 aponeurotic system
经尽/經盡 disease of one channel without transmission
经颈骨折/頸横骨折 transcervical fracture
经颈静脉胆管造影[术]/經頸靜脈膽管造影[術] transjugular cholangiography
经颈静脉肝内门体分流术/經頸靜脈肝内門體分流術 transjugular intrahepatic portasystemic shunt
经静脉起搏/經靜脈起搏 transvenous pacing
经静脉起搏器/經靜脈起搏器 transvenous pacemaker
经绝期精神病/更年期精神病 climacteric psychosis
经髁的/經髁的 transcondylar

经髁骨折/齊髁骨折　transcondylar fracture
经口/經口　per os
经口鼻蝶窦入路/經口鼻蝶竇入路　transoro-nasosphenoidal approach
经口胆管镜检查[术]/經口膽管鏡檢查[術]　peroral cholangioscopy
经口的/經口的　peroral
经口感染/經口傳染　peroral infection
经口明视插管/經口明視插管　direct vision orotracheal intubation
经口气管内插法/經口氣管内插法　ortracheal intubation
经口入路/經口入路　transoral approach
经眶入路/經眶入路　transorbital approach
经量/經量　menstrual volume
经卵巢的/經卵巢的　transovarian
经卵巢感染/經卵巢感染　transovarian infection
经络/經絡　channel, meridians
经络辨证/經絡辨證　pattern identification of channel theory
经络现象/經絡現象　channel phenomenon, meridian phenomenon
经络学/經絡學　subject of channel and collateral, subject of meridian and collateral
经络学说/經絡學說　channel theory
经络诊断/經絡診斷　channel diagnostics, meridian diagnostics
经脉/經脈　channel
经脉反应/經脈反應　meridian and acupoint
经脉循行/經脈循行　running course of channel, running course of meridian
经迷路入路/經迷路入路　translabyrinthine approach
经内听道入路/經内聽道入路　transmeatal approach
经尿道活检/經尿道活檢　transurethral biopsy
经尿道尿道瓣膜切除术/經尿道尿道瓣膜切除術　transurethral resection of urethral valve
经尿道膀胱颈切开术/經尿道膀胱頸切開術　transurethral vesical neck incision
经尿道膀胱肿瘤切除术/經尿道膀胱腫瘤切除術　transurethral resection of bladder tumor
经尿道前列腺切除[术]/經尿道前列腺切除[術]　transurethral prostatic resection
经尿道前列腺切除术/經尿道前列腺切除術　transurethral resection of prostate
经尿道前列腺切除综合征/經尿道前列腺切除症候群　transurethral prostatic resection syndrome
经尿道前列腺切开[术]/經尿道前列腺切開[術]　transurethral incision of prostate

经尿道切除术/經尿道切除術　transurethral resection
经尿道输尿管肾盂镜检查术/經尿道輸尿管腎盂鏡檢查術　transurethral ureteropyeloscopy
经尿道外括约肌切开术/經尿道外括約肌切開術　transurethral sphincterotomy
经皮层的/皮質間的　transcortical
经皮层失语症/皮質間性失語症　transcortical aphasia
经皮的/經皮的,皮内的,透皮的　endermatic, percutaneous
经皮二氧化碳监测/經皮二氧化碳監測　percutaneous carbon dioxide monitoring
经皮肤感染/經皮膚傳染　percutaneous infection
经皮管内/經皮管内　percutaneous transluminal
经皮经肝胆管镜检查[术]/經皮經肝膽管鏡檢查[術]　percutaneous transhepatic cholangioscopy
经皮经肝胆管造影[术]/經皮穿肝X光膽管攝影術　percutaneous transhepatic cholangiography
经皮经肝胆囊镜检查[术]/經皮經肝膽囊鏡檢查[術]　percutaneous transhepatic cholecystoscopy
经皮经肝栓塞/經皮經肝栓塞　percutaneous transhepatic embolization
经皮内镜胃造瘘[术]/經皮内鏡胃造瘻[術]　percutaneous endoscopic gastrostomy
经皮膀胱造口术/經皮膀胱造口術　percutaneous cystostomy
经皮起搏器/經皮起搏器　percutaneous pacemaker
经皮腔内斑块旋切术/動脈粥樣硬化切除術　atherectomy
经皮腔内冠状动脉成形术/經皮腔内冠狀動脈成形術　percutaneous transluminal coronary angioplasty
经皮腔内球囊瓣膜成形术/經皮腔内球囊瓣膜成形術　percutaneous transluminal balloon valvuloplasty
经皮腔内球囊二尖瓣成形术/經皮腔内球囊二尖瓣成形術　percutaneous transluminal balloon mitral valvuloplasty
经皮腔内球囊肺动脉瓣成形术/經皮腔内球囊肺動脈瓣成形術　percutaneous transluminal balloon pulmonary valvuloplasty
经皮腔内球囊扩张静脉狭窄/經皮腔内球囊擴張静脈狹窄　percutaneous transluminal balloon dilatation of venous stenosis
经皮腔内球囊三尖瓣成形术/經皮腔内球囊三尖瓣成形術　percutaneous transluminal balloon tricuspid valvuloplasty
经皮腔内球囊主动脉瓣成形术/經皮腔内球囊主動脈瓣成形術　percutaneous transluminal balloon

aortic valvuloplasty
经皮腔内肾动脉成形术/經皮腔內腎動脈成形術 percutaneous transluminal renal angioplasty
经皮腔内血管成形术/經皮腔內血管成形術 percutaneous transluminal angioplasty
经皮腔内周围动脉成形术/經皮腔內周圍動脈成形術 percutaneous peripheral artery angioplasty
经皮神经电刺激/經皮神經電刺激 transcutaneous electric nerve stimulation
经皮肾动脉造影[术]/經皮腎動脈造影[術] Seldinger technique of renal arteriography
经皮肾镜取石术/經皮腎鏡取石術 percutaneous nephrolithotomy
经皮肾造口术/經皮腎造口術 percutaneous nephrostomy
经皮吸收/經皮吸收作用 percutaneous absorption
经皮吸收剂/經皮吸收劑 transdermic absorbent
经皮血气监测/經皮血氣監測 transcutaneous blood gas monitoring
经皮氧监测/經皮氧監測 percutaneous oxygen monitoring
经皮针刺肺活检/經皮針刺肺活檢 percutaneous needle lung biopsy
经皮质感觉性失语[症]/經皮質感覺性失語[症] transcortical sensory aphasia
经皮质切骨术/經皮質切開骨術 corticalosteotomy
经皮质性运用不能/皮質間性失用症 transcortical apraxia
经皮质运动性失语[症]/經皮質運動性失語[症] transcortical motor aphasia
经皮椎间盘切除术/經皮椎間盤切除術 percutaneous diskectomy
经胼胝体入路/經胼胝體入路 transcallosal approach
经期白带/月經性白帶，週期性白帶 menstrual leukorrhea
经期毒素/經期毒物 menotoxin
经期绞痛/月經絞痛 menstrual colic
经期精神病/經期精神病 menstrual psychosis
经期目病/經期目病 menstrual eye disease
经期前虹膜炎/經期虹膜炎 iritis catamenialis
经期前中毒/經期前中毒 premenstrual intoxication
经期蜕膜/月經蛻膜 menstrual decidua
经期延长/經期延長 menostaxis, bradymenorrhea
经期延长·气不摄血证/經期延長·氣不攝血證 menostaxis with pattern of failure of qi to keep blood
经期延长·湿热[蕴结]证/經期延長·濕熱[蘊結]證 menostaxis with pattern of accumulation and binding of damp-heat
经期延长·血瘀证/經期延長·血瘀證 menostaxis with blood stasis pattern
经期延长·阴虚血热证/經期延長·陰虛血熱證 menostaxis with pattern of blood heat due to yin deficiency
经期中毒/經期中毒 menstrual intoxication
经期中毒的/經期毒物的 menotoxic
经气/經氣 channel qi
经气管多普勒心输出量监测/經氣管都卜勒心輸出量監測 transtracheal Doppler cardiac output monitoring
经前紧张征/經前緊張徵 premenstrual tension syndrome
经前期/經前期 premenstrual period, premenstrual phase
经前期紧张/月經前緊張 premenstrual tension
经前期综合征/經前期症候群 premenstrual syndrome
经前失眠/經前失眠 premenstrual insomnia
经渠/經渠 jingqu, LU8
经颧颞入路/經顴顳入路 transzygomatic temporal approach
经色/經色 menstrual color
经筛蝶窦入路/經篩蝶竇入路 transethmoid sphenoidal approach
经食管超声心动描记术/經食管超聲心動描記術 transesophageal echocardiography
经史证类备急本草/經史證類備急本草 Classified Materia Medica from Historical Classics for Emergency
经手感染/經手傳染 hand-borne infection
经手术牙长出/經手術牙長出 surgical eruption
经胎盘的/經[由]胎盤的 diaplacental
经胎盘感染/經胎盤傳染 diaplacental infection
经外[奇]穴/經外[奇]穴 extra ordinary point, extra point
经线/經線子午線 meridian
经线裂/經面分裂 meridional cleavage
经线纤维/經線纖維 meridional fiber
经小脑幕入路/經小腦幕入路 transtentorial approach
经行不寐/經行不寐 premenstrual insomnia
经行发热/經行發熱 menstrual fever
经行发热·肝肾阴虚证/經行發熱·肝腎陰虛證 menstrual fever with pattern of liver-kidney yin deficiency
经行发热·肝郁化火证/經行發熱·肝鬱化火證

menstrual fever with pattern of liver depression transforming into fire

经行发热·气血两虚证/經行發熱·氣血兩虛證 menstrual fever with pattern of deficiency of both qi and blood

经行发热·瘀热阻滞证/經行發熱·瘀熱阻滯證 menstrual fever with pattern of blockade of static blood and heat

经行风疹块/經行風疹塊 menstrual urticaria, rubella during menstruation

经行风疹块·风热证/經行風疹塊·風熱證 menstrual urticaria with wind-heat pattern

经行风疹块·血虚证/經行風疹塊·血虛證 menstrual urticaria with blood deficiency pattern

经行浮肿/經行浮腫, 月经期水腫 edema during menstruation, menstrual edema

经行浮肿·脾肾阳虚证/經行浮腫·脾腎陽虛證 menstrual edema with pattern of yang deficiency of spleen and kidney

经行浮肿·气滞湿阻证/經行浮腫·氣滯濕阻證 menstrual edema with pattern of qi stagnation and damp retention

经行浮肿·气滞血瘀证/經行浮腫·氣滯血瘀證 menstrual edema with pattern of qi stagnation and blood stasis

经行口糜/經行口糜 menstrual aphtha, oral aphthae during menstruation

经行口糜·胃火炽盛证/經行口糜·胃火熾盛證 menstrual aphtha with pattern of blazing stomach fire

经行口糜·阴虚火旺证/經行口糜·陰虛火旺證 menstrual aphtha with pattern of exuberant fire due to yin deficiency

经行情志异常/經行情志異常 emotional disorders during menstruation, menstrual mental disorders, moody state during menstruation

经行情志异常·肝气郁结证/經行情志異常·肝氣鬱結證 menstrual mental disorder with pattern of liver qi depression

经行情志异常·痰火扰神证/經行情志異常·痰火擾神證 menstrual mental disorder with pattern of phlegm-fire disturbing spirit

经行情志异常·心血虚证/經行情志異常·心血虛證 menstrual mental disorder with pattern of heart blood deficiency

经行乳房胀痛/經行乳房脹痛 distending pain of breasts during menstruation, menstrual distending pain of breasts

经行乳房胀痛·肝气郁结证/經行乳房脹痛·肝氣鬱結證 menstrual distending pain of breast with pattern of liver qi depression

经行乳房胀痛·肝肾阴虚证/經行乳房脹痛·肝腎陰虛證 menstrual distending pain of breast with pattern of liver-kidney yin deficiency

经行身痛/經行身痛 general aching during menstruation, menstrual body pain

经行身痛·寒湿凝滞证/經行身痛·寒濕凝滯證 menstrual body pain with pattern of stagnation and congelation of cold-damp

经行身痛·血虚证/經行身痛·血虛證 menstrual body pain with blood deficiency pattern

经行身痛·血瘀证/經行身痛·血瘀證 menstrual body pain with blood stasis pattern

经行头痛/經行頭痛 menstrual headache

经行头痛·肝火旺盛证/經行頭痛·肝火旺盛證 menstrual headache with pattern of liver fire exuberance

经行头痛·痰湿阻滞证/經行頭痛·痰濕阻滯證 menstrual headache with pattern of stagnation and blockade of phlegm-damp

经行头痛·血虚证/經行頭痛·血虛證 menstrual headache with blood deficiency pattern

经行头痛·血瘀证/經行頭痛·血瘀證 menstrual headache with blood stasis pattern

经行头痛·阴虚阳亢证/經行頭痛·陰虛陽亢證 menstrual headache with pattern of yang hyperactivity and yin deficiency

经行吐衄/經行吐衄 hematemesis and/or epistaxis during menstruation

经行吐衄·肺肾阴虚证/經行吐衄·肺腎陰虛證 menstrual hematemesis and/or epistaxis with pattern of yin deficiency of lung and kidney

经行吐衄·肝经郁火证/經行吐衄·肝經鬱火證 menstrual hematemesis and/or epistaxis with pattern of fire stagnating in Liver Channel

经行吐衄·胃火炽盛证/經行吐衄·胃火熾盛證 menstrual hematemesis and/or epistaxis with pattern of blazing stomach fire

经行泄泻/經行洩瀉 diarrhea during menstruation, menstrual diarrhea

经行泄泻·肝郁脾虚证/經行洩瀉·肝鬱脾虛證 menstrual diarrhea with pattern of liver qi depression and spleen deficiency

经行泄泻·脾气虚证/經行洩瀉·脾氣虛證 menstrual diarrhea with pattern of spleen qi deficiency

经行泄泻·肾阳虚证/經行洩瀉·腎陽虛證 menstrual diarrhea with pattern of kidney yang deficiency
经行眩晕/經行眩暈 dizziness during menstruation, menstrual vertigo
经行眩晕·气血两虚证/經行眩暈·氣血兩虛證 menstrual vertigo with pattern of deficiency of both qi and blood
经行眩晕·痰浊上扰证/經行眩暈·痰濁上擾證 menstrual vertigo with pattern of upward disturbance of phlegm-turbidity
经行眩晕·阴虚阳亢证/經行眩暈·陰虛陽亢證 menstrual vertigo with pattern of yang hyperactivity and yin deficiency
经胸肝切开术/經胸肝切開術 transthoracic hepatotomy
经胸起搏/經胸起搏 transthoracic pacing
经穴/經穴 channel point, meridian point
经血/經血 menstrual blood
经血潴留/經血瀦留 retention of menses
经眼眶白质切断术/經眶額葉白質切除術 transorbital leukotomy
经验风险/經驗風險 empiric risk
经验护士/護理佐理員 practical nurse
经验医学/經驗醫學 empirical medicine
经腰部主动脉造影/經腰主動脈 X 光攝影術 translumbar aortography
经腰肾切除术/腰式腎切除術 lumbar nephrectomy
经腰肾切开术/腰式腎切開術 lumbar nephrotomy
经阴道切石术/陰道式[膀胱]截石術 vaginal lithotomy
经支气管肺活组织检查/經支氣管肺活檢 transbronchial lung biopsy
经直肠/經直腸 per rectum
经直肠活检/經直腸活檢 transrectal biopsy
经直肠膀胱套针/經直腸膀胱套針 rectal trocar
经质/經質 menstrual property
经转子切骨术/粗隆處截骨術 transtrochanteric osteotomy
经子宫颈的/經頸的 transcervical
荆芥/荆芥 fineleaf schizonepeta herb
惊/驚 fright
惊怖/驚怖 feeling fright and fear
惊风/驚風 infantile convulsion
惊骇/驚駭 feeling fear and worry
惊悸/驚悸 fright palpitation, palpitation due to fright, palpitation due to alarm
惊惧状态/驚懼狀態 phobic state

惊厥/驚厥 convulsion
惊厥疗法/驚厥療法 convulsive therapy
惊厥型疟/驚厥型瘧 eclamptic malaria
惊厥性/驚厥性 convulsibility
惊厥性的/抽搐的,痉挛的 convulsive
惊厥性谵妄/子癇癎性譫妄 delirium eclampticum
惊厥性震颤/驚厥性震顫 convulsive tremor
惊厥药/驚厥藥 convulsants
惊恐/驚懼 panic
惊恐病/驚恐病 panic disorder
惊恐发作/驚恐發作 panic attack
惊恐疗法/驚恐療法 frightening therapy
惊恐伤肾/驚恐傷腎 fear impairing kidney
惊恐性失语/感動性失語症 pathematic aphasia
惊狂/驚狂 mania
惊伤/驚傷 impairment due to fright
惊吓/驚嚇 fright
惊吓反射/驚嚇反射 startle reflex
惊吓反应/驚嚇反應 startle reaction
惊痫/驚癎 epilepsy induced by fright
惊醒性休克/驚醒性休克 hypnoclastic shock
惊郁/驚鬱 stagnation pattern caused by fright
惊则气乱/驚則氣亂 fright causing disorder of qi, fright leading to qi turbulence
惊者平之/驚者平之 driving away fears and calming the mind
惊震内障/驚震內障 traumatic cataract
惊震内障·毒邪侵袭证/驚震內障·毒邪侵襲證 traumatic cataract with toxin invasion pattern
惊震内障·血瘀气滞证/驚震內障·血瘀氣滯證 traumatic cataract with pattern of blood stasis and qi stagnation
惊中/驚中 stroke due to fright
晶格假说/格子假說 lattice hypothesis
晶核/晶核 crystal nucleus
晶化智力/晶化智力 crystallized intelligence
晶癖/晶癖 crystal habit
晶体蛋白质类/晶體蛋白質類 crystallins
晶体溶液/晶體溶液 crystalloid solution
晶体渗透压/晶體滲透壓 crystalloid osmotic pressure
晶体心脏停搏液/晶體心臟停搏液 crystalloid cardioplegic solution
晶体性关节炎/晶體性關節炎 crystal-induced arthritis
晶体性肾病/晶體性腎病 crystalline nephropathy
晶体学/結晶學,結晶論 crystallography
晶体血液稀释/晶體血液稀釋 crystalloid

hemodilution
晶纤维/結晶纖維　crystal fiber
晶形/晶型　crystal form
晶珠/晶珠,水晶珠光,水晶珍珠　crystal pearl
晶状体/晶狀體　lens, crystalline lens, lentis
晶状体凹/晶狀體凹　lens pit
晶状体半径/晶狀體放線　radius of lens
晶状体半脱位/晶體半脫位　lens subluxation
晶状体不全脱位/晶體半脫位　subluxation of lens
晶状体匙/晶狀體匙　lens scoop
晶状体的/晶狀體的,透鏡的　lenticular
晶状体粉碎器/晶狀體粉碎器　phacofragmentor
晶状体粉碎术/晶狀體粉碎術　phacofragmentation
晶状体辐射/晶狀體輻射線　radii of lens
晶状体过敏性眼内炎/晶狀體蛋白過敏性眼內炎
　　endophthalmitis phaco-allergica
晶状体过敏症/晶狀體蛋白過敏性
　　phacoanaphylaxis
晶状体核/晶[狀]體核　lens nucleus, crystalline lens nucleus
晶状体后的/晶狀體後的　retrolental
晶状体后极/晶狀體後極　posterior pole of lens
晶状体后面/晶狀體後面　posterior surface of lens
晶状体后纤维增生症/晶[狀]體後纖維增生症
　　retrolental fibroplasia
晶状体环/晶狀體環　lens whorl
晶状体混浊/晶狀體混濁　phacoscotasmus
晶状体[基]板/晶[狀]體基板　lens placode
晶状体疾病/晶[狀]體疾病　lens disease
晶状体镜/晶狀體鏡,晶狀體檢查器　phacoidoscope
晶状体镜检查/晶狀體鏡檢法　phacoscopy
晶状体瘤/晶狀體瘤,視網膜瘤　phacoma
晶状体酶/晶狀體酵素　phacozymase
晶状体囊/晶[狀]體囊　lens capsule, crystalline lens capsule
晶状体囊[部分]切除术/晶狀體囊切除術
　　phacocystectomy
晶状体囊刀/晶狀體囊刀　cystitome
晶状体囊镊/晶狀體囊鑷　lens capsule forcep
晶状体囊切开术/晶狀體囊切開術　capsulotomy
晶状体囊炎/晶[狀]體囊炎　capsitis
晶状体泡/晶[狀]體泡　lens vesicle
晶状体皮层/晶體皮層　crystalline lens cortex
晶状体皮质/晶體皮質　cortex of lens, cortical substance of lens
晶状体脐状凹陷/晶狀體臍狀凹陷　umbilication of lens
晶状体前极/晶狀體前極　anterior pole of lens
晶状体前面/晶狀體前面　anterior surface of lens
晶状体切除术/晶狀體摘除術　lentectomy
晶状体切割术/晶狀體去除術　lensectomy
晶状体曲率/晶狀體彎度,晶狀體凸度　curvature of lens
晶状体全脱位/晶狀體全脫位　complete luxation of lens
晶状体缺损/晶狀體缺損　coloboma of lens
晶状体溶素/晶狀體溶素　phacolysin
晶状体乳化器/晶狀體乳化器　phacoemulsifier
晶状体色粒/晶狀體色粒　particles lens
晶状体上皮/晶狀體上皮　lens epithelium, epithelium of lens
晶状体套圈/晶狀體套圈　lens loop
晶状体透热摘出器/晶狀體透熱摘出器
　　electrodiaphake
晶状体突出/晶狀體膨出　phacocele
晶状体脱位/晶狀體脫位　luxation of lens
晶状体涡/晶狀體渦　nuclear arc
晶状体吸盘/晶狀體吸除器　erysiphake
晶状体纤维/晶狀體纖維　lens fiber
晶状体性青光眼/晶狀體青光眼　phacoglaucoma
晶状体性散光/晶狀體性散光　lenticular astigmatism
晶状体悬[韧]带/晶狀體懸韌帶　suspensory ligament of lens
晶状体炎/晶狀體炎　crystallitis
晶状体移位/晶狀體移位　phacometachoresis
晶状体异位/晶狀體異位　ectopia lentis
晶状体硬化/晶狀體硬化,硬內障　phacosclerosis
晶状体游动/晶狀體遊動,遊走性晶狀體
　　phacoplanesis
晶状体原基/晶狀體始基　lens rudiment
晶状体再生/晶狀體再生　phacopalingenesis
晶状体摘出术/晶狀體摘出術　extraction of lens
晶状体针拨术/晶狀體針撥術　couching of lens
晶状体针吸术/晶狀體吸除法　phacoerysis
晶状体质/晶狀體質　substance of lens, parenchyma of lens
晶状体中纬线/晶狀體中緯線　equator of crystalline lens
晶状体轴/晶狀體軸　axis of lens
腈/腈　nitrile
腈水解酶/腈分解酵素　nitrilase
睛明/睛明　jingming, BL1
精/精　essence, semen
精氨琥珀酸尿症/精胺琥珀酸尿症　argininosuccinic aciduria

精氨基琥珀酸/精胺基琥珀酸，精胺酸琥珀酸 argininosuccinic acid

精氨基琥珀酸合酶/精胺基琥珀酸合成酶 argininosuccinate synthase

精氨基琥珀酸裂合酶/精胺基琥珀酸裂解酶 argininosuccinate lyase

精氨[基]琥珀酸酶/精胺琥珀酸酶 argininosuccinase

精氨基琥珀酸血/精胺基琥珀酸血 argininosuccinic acidemia

精氨基琥珀酸盐/精胺基琥珀酸鹽 argininosuccinate

精氨酸/精胺酸 arginine

精氨酸激酶/精胺酸激酶 arginine kinase

精氨酸 tRNA 连接酶/精胺酸 tRNA 連接酶 arginine-tRNA ligase

精氨酸酶/精胺酸酶 arginase

精氨酸酶缺乏症/精胺酸酶缺乏症 arginase deficiency

精氨酸血管加压素/精胺酸血管加壓素 arginine vasopressin

精胺/精素 spermine

精胺合酶/精胺合酶 spermine synthase

精薄/精薄 thin sperm

精蛋白钙胰岛素/精蛋白鈣胰島素 protamine calcium insulin

精蛋白锌胰岛素/[魚]精蛋白鋅胰島素 protamine zinc insulin

精蛋白胰岛素/[魚]精蛋白胰島素 protamine insulin

精阜/精阜 seminal colliculus

精阜切除术/精阜切除術 colliculectomy

精阜炎/精阜炎 verumontanitis

精管/精管 seminal duct

精管石/精管石 spermolith

精浆/精漿 seminal plasma

精浆蛋白质类/精漿蛋白質類 seminal plasma proteins

精冷/精冷 cold sperm

精力/精力 energy

精癃/精癃 hypertrophy of prostate, prostatic hypertrophy

精癃·气滞血瘀证/精癃·氣滯血瘀證 prostatic hypertrophy with pattern of qi stagnation and blood stasis

精癃·肾阳虚证/精癃·腎陽虛證 prostatic hypertrophy with kidney yang deficiency pattern

精癃·肾阴虚证/精癃·腎陰虛證 prostatic hypertrophy with kidney yin deficiency pattern

精癃·湿热下注证/精癃·濕熱下注證 prostatic hypertrophy with pattern of dampness-heat diffusing downward

精癃·中气下陷证/精癃·中氣下陷證 prostatic hypertrophy with pattern of sinking of middle-qi

精卵质膜融合/精卵質膜融合 sperm-oocyte membrane fusion

精密附着体/精確附著 precision attachment

精密天平/精密天平 precision balance

精密支托/精密支托 precision rest

精明之府/精明之府 house of intelligence

精母细胞/精母細胞 spermatocyte

精母细胞单位/精母細胞單位 spermatocyte unit

精母细胞发生/精母細胞發生，精母細胞生成 spermatocytogenesis

精囊/精囊 seminal vesicle

精囊癌/精囊癌 carcinoma of seminal vesicle

精囊丛/精囊叢 plexus glandulae vesiculosae

精囊放线菌病/精囊放線菌病 actinomycosis of seminal vesicle

精囊分泌蛋白质类/精囊分泌蛋白質類 seminal vesicle secretory proteins

精囊管/精囊管 duct of seminal vesicle

精囊积脓/精囊積膿 pyovesiculosis

精囊结核/精囊結核 tuberculosis of seminal vesicle

精囊结石/精囊結石 calculus of seminal vesicle

精囊梅毒/精囊梅毒 syphilis of seminal vesicle

精囊囊肿/精囊囊腫 cyst of seminal vesicle

精囊排泄管/精囊排洩管 ductus excretorius vesiculae seminalis

精囊切除术/精囊切除術 seminal vesiculectomy

精囊切开术/精囊切開術 spermatocystotomy

精囊[X射线]造影术/精囊 X 光攝影術 vesiculography

精囊[腺]/[儲]精囊 seminal vesicle

精囊腺癌/精囊腺癌 adenocarcinoma of seminal vesicle

精囊炎/精囊炎 seminal vesiculitis, cystospermitis

精囊炎·脾肾两虚证/精囊炎·脾腎兩虛證 cystospermitis with spleen-kidney deficiency pattern

精囊炎·湿热下注证/精囊炎·濕熱下注證 cystospermitis with pattern of dampness-heat diffusing downward

精囊炎·阴虚火旺证/精囊炎·陰虛火旺證 cystospermitis with pattern of yin deficiency and fire effulgence

精囊炎·瘀血阻滞证/精囊炎·瘀血阻滯證 cystospermitis with pattern of static blood obstruction and stagnation

精囊造影[术]/精囊造影[術]　seminal vesiculography
精囊造影照片/精囊 X 光像　vesiculogram
精囊肿瘤/精囊腫瘤　tumor of seminal vesicle
精囊周炎/精囊周圍炎　perivesiculitis
精凝/精凝　coagulated sperm, sperm agglutination
精气/精氣　essential qi
精气夺/精氣奪　consumption of vital essence
精气亏虚证/精氣虧虛證　pattern of deficiency of vital essence
精气神/精氣神　essence, qi and spirit
精窍/精竅　external orifice of male urethra, seminal orifice
精清/精清　dilute semen
精曲小管/精曲小管　contorted seminiferous tubules
精确定位/精確定位　pinpoint
精少/精少　oligospermia, scant sperm
精神/精神　spirit
精神安定药/精神安定藥　neuroleptic
精神崩溃/精神崩潰　psychorrhexis
精神变态者/精神變態者　psychopathic
精神病/精神病　psychosis
精神病保险/精神病保險　psychiatric insurance
精神病辩护/精神病辯護　insanity defense
精神病发作/精神病發作　attack of insanity
精神病房/精神病房　psychopathic ward
精神病护理学/精神病護理學　psychiatric nursing
精神病护理员/精神病護理員　psychiatric aide
精神病患者/精神病患者　psychotic
精神病急诊室/精神病急診室　psychiatric emergency service
精神病集体治疗/精神病集體治療　therapeutic community
精神病理学/精神病理學,變態心理學　psychopathology
精神病躯体疗法/精神病軀體療法　psychiatric somatic therapy
精神病人/精神病人　mentally ill person
精神病人强制住院/精神病人強制住院　commitment of mentally ill
精神病社会工作/精神病社會工作　psychiatric social work
精神病体质/精神病體質　psychopathic constitution
精神病体质状态/體質性精神病狀態　constitutional psychopathic state
精神病性情感障碍/精神病性情感障礙　psychotic affective disorder
精神病性[血清]反应/精神病反應　psychoreaction

精神病学/精神病學　mental medicine
精神病学的/精神病學的　psychiatric
精神病学家/精神病學家　psychiatrist
精神[病]药理学/精神藥理劑　psychopharmacological
精神病医院/精神病醫院　psychiatric hospital
精神病状态评定量表/精神病狀態評定量表　psychiatric status rating scale
精神残疾/精神殘疾　mental handicap
精神创伤/心理損傷,精神性創傷　psychic trauma
精神错乱/精神迷亂,精神障礙　mental aberration, amentia
精神的/精神的　mental, psychic, psychical
精神动力学/精神動力學　psychodynamics
精神发育迟滞/精神遲延　mental retardation
精神发作/精神發作　psycholeptic episode
精神分裂型人格障碍/精神分裂型人格障礙　schizotypal personality disorder
精神分裂样谵妄/思覺失調樣譫妄　delirium schizophrenoide
精神分裂症/精神分裂症,思覺失調症　schizophrenia
精神分裂症患者/精神分裂症患者　schizophrenic
精神分裂症心理学/精神分裂症心理學　schizophrenic psychology
精神分裂症样精神病/精神分裂症樣精神病　schizophreniform psychosis
精神分裂症语言/精神分裂症語言　schizophrenic language
精神分析/精神分析　psychoanalysis
精神分析理论/精神分析理論　psychoanalytic theory
精神分析疗法/精神分析療法　psychoanalytic therapy
精神分析学家/心理分析學家　psychoanalyst
精神分析学解释/精神分析學解釋　psychoanalytic interpretation
精神分析治疗/精神分析治療　abreactive therapy
精神感觉性失语/精神感覺性失語症　psychosensory aphasia
精神过敏/精神過敏　psychic anaphylaxis
精神过旺/精神活動過旺　overproductivity
精神化学/精神化學　psychochemistry
精神活动过度/精神活動過強　hypernoia
精神活泼/精神活潑　prothymia
精神疾病/精神性疾病　psychiatric disease
精神记时法/心理測時法　mental chronometry
精神检查/精神檢查　psychiatric interview
精神结构/精神結構　mental apparatus
精神决定论/精神決定論　psychic determinism

精神内守/精神内守　keeping essence and spirit in the interior
精神能力/精神能力　mental competency
精神皮肤的/精神性皮膚的　psychocutaneous
精神疲劳/精神疲勞　mental fatigue
精神神经[功能]病/精神神經病,精神性神經官能病　psychoneurosis
精神神经[功能]病患者/精神神經病患者　psychoneurotic
精神神经免疫学/精神神經免疫學　psychoneuroimmunology
精神伤害/精神扼殺　menticide
精神声学/心理聲學　psychoacoustics
精神失调/精神失調　psychataxia
精神疏泄/精神發洩　abreaction
精神衰弱/精神衰弱　psychasthenia
精神衰弱者/精神衰弱者　psychasthene
精神特征/精神特徵　psychic stigma
精神痛苦/精神痛苦　mental distress, soul pain
精神外科手术/精神病外科學　psychosurgery
精神卫生/精神衛生　mental health
精神卫生服务/精神衛生服務　mental health service
精神卫生协会/精神衛生協會　mental health association
精神物理学/精神物理學　psychophysics
精神现象/心理現象　psychological phenomenon
精神现状检查/精神現狀檢查　present state examination
精神兴奋过度/精神過度興奮症　hyperphrenia
精神兴奋药/精神興奮藥,精神興奮劑　psychostimulant, psychoanaleptic
精神性闭经/精神性閉經　psychogenic amenorrhea
精神性便秘/精神性便秘　psychogenic constipation
精神性的/精神原的　psychogenic
精神性多汗症/情緒性多汗症　emotional hyperhidrosis
精神性感觉的/精神感覺的　psychosensory
精神性感觉缺失/精神性感覺缺失　mental anesthesia
精神性盲/精神性盲　mind blindness
精神性排尿困难/精神性排尿困難　psychic dysuria
精神性皮肤疾病/精神性皮膚疾病　psychocutaneous disorder
精神性瘙痒症/精神性搔癢症　psychogenic pruritus
精神性书写不能/精神性書寫不能　mental agraphia
精神性疼痛/精神性疼痛　psychogenic pain
精神性痛/精神[性]痛　mind pain
精神性消化不良/精神性消化不良　psychic indigestion
精神性性交困难/精神性交媾困難　psychologic dyspareunia
精神性休克/精神性休克　mental shock
精神性眩晕/精神性眩暈　psychogenic vertigo
精神性阳痿/精神性陽痿　psychic impotence
精神性阴道痉挛/精神性陰道痙攣　mental vaginismus
精神性执拗/精神性執拗　psychic possession
精神性紫癜/心理性紫癜病　psychogenic purpura
精神休克/精神休克　psychic shock
精神修养/精神修養　spiritual health care
精神药理学/精神藥理學　psychopharmacology
精神药物/精神藥物　psychotropic drug
精神医学/精神醫學　psychiatric medicine
精神依赖/心理性依賴　psychological dependence
精神抑郁/精神抑鬱　mental depression, psychical depression
精神抑制药/精神抑制藥,抗精神病藥,精神鬆弛藥　antipsychotic, psycholeptic
精神因素/精神性因素　mental factor
精神[因素]性假妊娠/癔病性妊娠　hysteric pregnancy
精神运动/精神運動性的　psychomotor
精神运动型癫痫/精神運動性癲癇　psychomotor epilepsy
精神运动性幻觉/精神運動性幻覺　psychomotor hallucination
精神运动性激动/精神運動性激動　psychomotor agitation
精神运动性兴奋/精神運動性興奮　psychomotor excitement
精神运动性行为/精神運動性行為　psychomotor performance
精神运动性抑制/精神運動性抑制　psychomotor inhibition
精神运动性障碍/精神運動性障礙　psychomotor disorder
精神障碍/精神障礙　mental disorder
精神镇静[法]/精神鎮靜法　psychosedation
精神镇静药/精神鎮靜藥　psychosedative
精神正常/精神生活正常,精神反應性正常　orthophrenia
精神治疗/精神療法　mental healing
精神治疗药物/精神治療藥物　psychotropic drug
精神状态/精神狀態　mental status
精神状态检查表/精神狀態檢查表　mental status schedule

精神作用/精神作用　mentation
精室/精室　essence chamber
精索/精索　spermatic cord
精索癌/精索癌　carcinoma of spermatic cord
精索被膜/精索被膜　tunicae of spermatic cord
精索[部分]切除术/精索切除術　spermectomy
精索丛/精索叢　spermatic plexus
精索附睾丝虫病/精索附睾絲蟲病　filariasis of funiculoepididymis
精索固定术/精索固定術　funiculopexy
精索静脉/精索静脈　spermatic vein
精索静脉曲张/精索静脈曲張　varicocele
精索静脉曲张切除术/精索静脈腫切除術　varicocelectomy
精索静脉曲张水囊肿/水囊静脈瘤　hydrocirsocele
精索内动脉/精索内動脈　internal spermatic artery
精索内筋膜/精索内筋膜, 漏斗狀筋膜　internal spermatic fascia
精索扭转/精索扭轉　spermatic cord torsion
精索皮样囊肿/精索皮樣囊腫　dermoid cyst of spermatic cord
精索鞘膜积液/精索水囊　hydrocele of the spermatic cord
精索肉瘤/精索肉瘤　sarcoma of spermatic cord
精索神经痛/精索神經痛　spermoneuralgia
精索水囊肿/精索水囊腫　spermatic hydrocele
精索水肿/精索水腫　mumu
精索突出/精索突出, 精索疝　funicular hernia
精索外筋膜/精索外筋膜　external spermatic fascia
精索外神经/精索外神經　external spermatic nerve
精索纤维瘤/精索纖維瘤　fibroma of spermatic cord
精索炎/精索炎　funiculitis
精索脂肪瘤/精索脂肪瘤　lipoma of spermatic cord
精索肿瘤/精索腫瘤　tumor of spermatic cord
精索周围组织炎/精索周圍炎　perispermatitis
精脱/精脱　depletion of essence
精微测量器/精微測量器　acribometer
精细胞/精細胞　sperm cell
精细胞球/精細胞球　spermosphere
精细感觉/精微感覺　epicritic sensibility
精血同源/精血同源　homogeny of essence and blood
精液/精液　semen fluid, semen
精液保存/精液保存　semen preservation
精液的/精[液]的　seminal
精液分泌抑制/精液分泌抑制　spermatoschesis
精液结晶/精液結晶　sperm crystal
精液瘘/精[液]瘻　spermatic fistula
精液囊肿/精液囊腫　seminal cyst
精液囊肿切除术/精液囊腫切除術　spermatocelectomy
精液尿/精尿症　semenuria
精液凝固酶/前列腺酵素　vesiculase
精液微粒/精液微粒　spermatomicron
精液纤维蛋白溶酶/精液溶纖維蛋白酵素　seminal fibrinolysin
精液学/精液學　semenology
精液学家/精液學家　seminologist
精液受阻/精液阻塞　spermatemphraxis
精油/精油　essential oil
精原干细胞/幹精原細胞　primitive spermatogonium, stem spermatogonium
精原细胞/精原細胞, 精祖細胞　spermatogonium
精原细胞瘤/精細胞瘤, 生殖細胞瘤　seminoma
精源论者/精原論者　animalculist
精直小管/精直小管　straight seminiferous tubule
精制结核菌素/漂淨結核菌素　purified tuberculin
精制可卡因/精製可卡因　crack cocaine
精制棉/精製棉　purified cotton
精细胞原生质/精細胞原漿　spermoplasm
精浊/精濁　turbid sperm, chronic prostatitis, turbid semen
精浊·气滞血瘀证/精濁·氣滯血瘀證　turbid sperm with pattern of qi stagnation and blood stasis
精浊·肾阳虚证/精濁·腎陽虛證　turbid sperm with kidney yang deficiency pattern
精浊·湿热蕴结证/精濁·濕熱蘊結證　turbid sperm with dampness-heat amassment pattern
精浊·阴虚火旺证/精濁·陰虛火旺證　turbid sperm with pattern of yin deficiency and fire effulgence
精子/精子　sperm, spermatozoon
精子成熟/精子成熟　sperm maturation
[精子]穿孔蛋白/穿孔素　perforin
精子穿卵试验/精子穿卵試驗　egg penetration test
精子穿入/精子入卵　sperm penetration
精子毒素/精子毒素　spermotoxin
精子发生/精子發生, 精子形成　spermatogenesis
精子发生的/產生精液的　spermatogenic
精子发生图/精子發生圖　spermiogram
精子核酸/精核酸　spermanucleic acid
精子活力不足/精子活力不足, 精子無力　asthenospermia
精子获能/精子獲能　sperm capacitation
精子计数/精子計數　sperm count
精子库/精子庫　sperm bank
[精子]连接段/連結部　connecting piece
精子卵子相互作用/精子卵子相互作用　sperm-

ovum interaction
精子能动性/精子能動性　sperm motility
精子凝集/精子凝集　sperm agglutination
精子排放/精子排放，精子放出　spermiation
精子缺乏症/精子缺乏症　azoospermatism, azoospermia
精子溶解/精子溶解　spermatolysis
精子溶素/溶精子素　spermatolysin
精子生成阻滞药/精子生成阻滯藥　spermatogenesis-blocking agent
精子释出/放精　spermiation
精子贴附/精子貼附　sperm binding
精子头/精子頭　sperm head
[精子头]赤道段/[精子頭]赤道段　equatorial segment
精子尾/精子尾　sperm tail
[精子]小头/小頭　capitulum
精子形成/精子形成　spermiogenesis
精子制动药/精子制動藥　sperm immobilizing agent
精子中段/精子中段　sperm midpiece
精子转运/精子轉運　sperm transport
精子着色/精液著色症　chromospermism
鲸醇/鯨油醇　kitol
鲸蜡醇/鯨蠟醇　cetanol
鲸蜡醇十六酸酯/棕櫚酸鯨蠟酯　cetyl palmitate
鲸蜡基/十六烷基　cetyl
鲸蜡硬脂醇/鯨蠟硬脂醇　cetostearyl alcohol
井疽/井疽　precardial abscess
井[穴]/井穴　jing-well point
肼苯哒嗪/聯胺嗪，肼酞嗪　hydralazine
肼类/肼類　hydrazines
颈/頸　neck
颈百劳/頸百勞　jingbailao, EX-HN15
颈瘢痕挛缩/頸瘢痕攣縮　cervical cicatricial contracture
颈半棘肌/頸半棘肌　musculus semispinalis cervicis
颈背的/頸背的　cervicodorsal
颈背突/頸背突　hump
颈臂丛/頸臂叢　plexus cervicobrachialis
颈臂丛综合征/頸臂症候群　cervicobrachial syndrome
颈臂的/頸與臂的　cervicobrachial
颈臂神经痛/頸與臂神經痛　cervicobrachial neuralgia
颈臂痛/頸臂痛　cervicobrachialgia
颈病学/頸病學　trachelology
颈病学家/頸病專家　trachelologist
颈部/頸部　cervical part
颈部白斑病/頸白斑病　leukoderma colli

颈部耳状附件/頸部耳狀附件　cervical auricle
颈部横突间后肌/頸部橫突間後肌　musculi intertransversarii posteriores cervicis
颈部环形脂瘤/頸環狀脂瘤　lipoma annulare colli
颈[部]肌节/頸[部]肌節　cervical myotome
颈部脊髓病/頸部脊髓病變　cervical myelopathy
颈部假性皮萎缩/頸部假皮萎病　pseudoatrophoderma colli
颈部块状切除术/根本的頸部切除開刀　block dissection of the neck
颈部梅毒白斑病/花柳頸圈　collar of Venus
颈部囊肿/頸部囊腫　cervical cyst
颈[部]膨大/頸膨大部　cervical enlargement
颈部切诊/頸部切診　palpation of neck
[颈部]鳃瘘/頸瘻管　cervical fistula
颈部烧伤/頸部燒傷　burn of neck region
颈部湿疹/頸部濕疹　eczema nuchae
颈部食管胃吻合术/頸部食管胃吻合術　cervical esophagogastrostomy
颈部水囊瘤/頸水瘤　hygroma colli
颈部损伤/頸部損傷　neck injury
颈部透明带检查/頸部透明帶檢查　nuchal translucency measurement
颈部纤维瘤病/頸部纖維瘤病　fibromatosis colli
颈部腺肿大/頸淋巴腺腫大　deradenoncus
颈部胸腺囊肿/頸部胸腺囊腫　cervical thymic cyst
颈长肌/頸長肌　longus colli
颈成形术/頸成形術　cervicoplasty
颈丛/頸叢　cervical plexus, plexus cervicalis
颈导管积水/頸水囊　hydrocele of neck
颈的/頸的　cervicalis
颈点/頸點　cervicale
颈动脉/頸動脈　carotid
颈动脉壁/頸動脈壁　carotid wall
颈动脉搏动/頸動脈脈搏　carotid pulse
颈动脉杈/頸動脈杈　carotid bifurcation
颈动脉-蝶骨床突韧带/頸動脈與蝶骨床突韌帶　carotico-clinoid ligament
颈动脉窦/頸動脈竇　carotid sinus
颈动脉窦支/頸動脈竇支　carotid sinus branch
颈动脉窦综合征/頸動脈竇症候群　carotid sinus syndrome
颈动脉沟/頸動脈溝　carotid sulcus
颈动脉管/頸動脈管　carotid canal
颈动脉海绵窦瘘/頸動脈海綿竇瘻　carotid-cavernous sinus fistula
颈动脉海绵窦瘘管/頸動脈海綿竇瘻管　carotid-cavernous fistula

颈动脉疾病/頸動脈疾病　carotid artery disease
颈动脉结节/頸動脈結節　carotid tubercle
颈动脉结扎术/頸動脈結扎術　carotid artery ligation
颈动脉孔/頸動脈孔　carotid foramen
颈动脉瘤/頸動脈瘤　aneurysm of carotid artery
颈动脉内的/頸動脈内的　intracarotid
颈动脉内膜切除术/頸動脈内膜切除術　carotid endarterectomy
颈动脉内综合征/頸動脈内症候群　intracarotid syndrome
颈动脉鞘/頸動脈鞘　carotid sheath
颈动脉三角/頸動脈三角　carotid triangle, carotid trigone
颈动脉神经节/頸動脈神經節　carotid ganglion
颈动脉损伤/頸動脈損傷　carotid artery injury
颈动脉体/頸動脈體,頸動脈球　carotid body
颈动脉体化学感受器瘤/頸動脈體化學感受器瘤　chemodectoma of carotid body
颈动脉体瘤/頸動脈體腫　carotid body tumor
颈动脉痛/頸動脈痛　carotidynia
颈动脉狭窄/頸動脈狭窄　carotid stenosis
颈动脉小球/頸動脈球　carotid glomus
颈动脉血栓切除术/頸動脈血栓切除術　carotid thrombectomy
颈动脉血栓形成/頸動脈血栓形成　carotid artery thrombosis
颈动脉植片修补术/頸動脈植片修補術　patch grafting of carotid artery
颈窦/頸竇　cervical sinus
颈段/頸段　cervical segment
颈耳窦道/頸耳竇道　cervical aural sinus
颈耳瘘管/頸耳瘻管　cervical aural fistula
颈耳囊肿/頸耳囊腫　cervical aural cyst
颈干/頸[淋巴]幹　jugular trunk
颈根外侧点/頸根外側點　lateral neck root point
颈骨/頸椎　cervical vertebra
颈鼓动脉/頸鼓動脈　caroticotympanic artery
颈鼓神经/内頸動脈鼓室神經　caroticotympanic nerve
颈鼓小管/頸鼓小管　caroticotympanic canaliculi
颈管消失/頸管消失　effacement of cervix
颈横动脉/頸橫動脈　transverse cervical artery
颈横动脉降支/頸橫動脈降支　descending branch of transverse cervical artery
颈横动脉浅支/頸橫動脈淺支　superficial branch of transverse cervical artery
颈横动脉深支/頸橫動脈深支　deep branch of transverse cervical artery
颈横动脉升支/頸橫動脈昇支　ascending branch of transverse cervical artery
颈横静脉/頸橫靜脈　transverse cervical vein
颈横神经/頸橫神經　transverse nerve of neck
颈横神经上支/頸橫神經上支　superior branch of transverse nerve of neck
颈横神经下支/頸橫神經下支　inferior branch of transverse nerve of neck
颈横突间后肌内侧部/頸橫突間後肌内側部　medial part of intertransversarii posteriores cervicis
颈横突间后肌外侧部/頸橫突間後肌外側部　lateral part of intertransversarii posteriores cervicis
颈横突间前肌/頸部橫突間前肌　intertransversarii anteriores cervicis
颈后倾/頸後傾　retrocollis
颈后区/頸後部　posterior region of neck
颈后屈痉挛/頸後痙攣　retrocollic spasm
颈后韧带/頸後韌帶　ligament nuchae
颈后三角/頸後三角　posterior triangle of neck
颈后神经丛/頸後叢　posterior cervical plexus
颈后纤维软骨性假瘤/後頸纖維軟骨性假瘤　nuchal fibrocartilaginous pseudotumor
颈回旋肌/頸迴旋肌　rotatores cervicis, musculi rotatores cervicis
颈肌/頸[部諸]肌　muscle of neck
颈肌扭伤/頸肌扭傷　sprain of neck muscle
颈肌炎/頸肌炎　trachelomyitis
颈颅底韧带/頸基底韌帶　cervicobasilar ligament
颈棘肌/項棘肌　spinalis cervicis
颈棘间肌/頸部棘間肌　inter spinale cervicis
颈夹肌/頸夾肌　splenius cervicis, musculus splenius cervicis
颈交感神经[节]切除术/頸交感神經[節]切除術　cervical sympathectomy
颈筋膜/頸筋膜　cervical fascia
颈筋膜气管前层/頸筋膜氣管前層　pretracheal layer of cervical fascia
颈筋膜浅层/頸筋膜淺層　superficial layer of cervical fascia
颈筋膜椎前层/頸筋膜椎前層　prevertebral layer of cervical fascia
颈静脉/頸靜脈　jugular vein
颈静脉壁/頸靜脈壁　jugular wall
颈静脉搏动/頸靜脈搏動　jugular venous pulse
颈静脉的/頸靜脈的　jugular
颈静脉弓/頸靜脈弓　jugular venous arch
颈静脉结节/頸靜脈結節,頸靜脈隆凸　jugular tubercle, jugular eminence

颈静脉孔/頸静脈孔　jugular foramen
颈静脉孔内突/頸静脈間突　intrajugular process
颈静脉孔综合征/頸静脈孔症候群，威内氏症候群　jugular foramen syndrome
颈静脉扩张/頸静脈擴張　jugular phlebectasia
颈静脉淋巴丛/頸静脈淋巴叢　jugular plexus
颈静脉淋巴结/頸静脈淋巴結，頸腺　jugular gland
颈静脉切迹/頸静脈切跡　jugular notch
颈静脉球/頸静脈球　glomus jugulare
颈静脉球瘤/頸静脈球瘤　glomus jugulare tumor
颈静脉上球/頸静脈上球　superior bulb of internal jugular vein
颈静脉神经/頸静脈神經　jugular nerve
颈静脉神经节/頸静脈神經節　jugular ganglion
颈静脉突/頸静脈突　jugular process
颈静脉窝/頸静脈窝　jugular fossa
颈静脉下球/頸静脈下球　inferior bulb of internal jugular vein
颈静脉征/頸静脈徵象，奎肯特氏徵象　jugular sign
颈颏角/頸頦角　cervico-mental angle
颈阔肌/頸闊肌　tetragonus
颈阔肌悬韧带/頸闊肌懸韌帶　suspensory platysma ligament
颈肋/頸肋　cervical rib
颈肋综合征/頸肋症候群　cervical rib syndrome
颈裂畸胎/頸裂［畸胎］　schistotrachelus
颈淋巴结清扫术/頸淋巴結清掃術　neck dissection
颈淋巴结炎/頸淋巴腺炎　cervical adenitis
颈淋巴囊/頸淋巴囊　jugular lymph sac
颈面放线菌病/頸面放線菌病　cervicofacial actinomycosis
颈脑畸胎/頸腦畸胎　derencephalus
颈内动脉/頸内動脈　internal carotid artery
颈内动脉丛/頸内動脈叢　internal carotid plexus, plexus caroticus internus
颈内动脉大脑部/頸内動脈大腦部　cerebral part of internal carotid artery
颈内动脉海绵窦部/頸内動脈海綿竇部　cavernous part of internal carotid artery
颈内动脉海绵窦瘘/頸内動脈海綿竇瘻　carotid-cavernous fistula
颈内动脉颈部/頸内動脈頸部　cervical part of internal carotid artery
颈内动脉静脉丛/頸内動脈静脈叢　internal carotid venous plexus
颈内动脉脑膜支/頸内動脈腦膜支　meningeal branch of internal carotid artery
颈内动脉神经/頸内動脈神經　internal carotid nerve
颈内动脉斜坡支/頸内動脈斜坡支　clival branch of internal carotid artery
颈内动脉岩部/頸内動脈岩部　petrosal part of internal carotid artery
颈内静脉/頸内静脈　internal jugular vein
颈内静脉二腹肌淋巴结/頸内静脈二腹肌淋巴結　jugulodigastric lymph node
颈内静脉肩胛舌骨肌淋巴结/頸内静脈肩胛舌骨肌淋巴結　juguloomohyoid lymph node
颈内静脉前淋巴结/頸内静脈前淋巴結　anterior jugular lymph node
颈内静脉神经/頸内静脈神經　internal jugular nerve
颈内静脉外侧淋巴结/頸内静脈外側淋巴結　lateral jugular lymph node
颈襻/頸襻　ansa cervicalis
颈襻上根/頸襻上根　superior root of ansa cervicalis
颈襻下根/頸襻下根　inferior root of ansa cervicalis
颈膨大/頸膨大　cervical enlargement
颈髂肋肌/頸髂肋肌　iliocostalis cervicis
颈前静脉/頸前静脈　anterior jugular vein
颈前淋巴结/頸前淋巴結　anterior cervical lymph node
颈前浅淋巴结/頸前淺淋巴結　superficial anterior cervical lymph node
颈前区/頸前部　anterior region of neck
颈前韧带/頸前韌帶　anterior cervical ligament
颈前三角/頸前三角　anterior triangle of neck
颈前深淋巴结/頸前深淋巴結　deep anterior cervical lymph node
颈强直/頸强直　cervical rigidity
颈曲/頸曲　cervical curvature, cervical flexure
颈圈/頸圈　collar
颈圈冠/頸圈狀齒冠　collar crown
颈上侧心神经/頸上側心神經　superior cervical cardiac nerve
颈上神经/頸上神經　superior cervical nerve
颈上神经节/頸上神經節　superior cervical ganglion
颈上心神经/頸上心神經　superior cervical cardiac nerve
颈上心支/頸上心支　superior cervical cardiac branch
颈深动脉/頸深動脈　deep cervical artery
颈深静脉/頸深静脈　deep cervical vein
颈神经/頸神經　cervical nerve
颈神经［根］综合征/頸部症候群　cervical syndrome
颈神经后支/頸神經後支　posterior branch of cervical nerve
颈神经后支内侧支/頸神經後支内側支　medial branch of posterior branch of cervical nerve

颈神经后支外侧支/頸神經後支外側支 lateral branch of posterior branch of cervical nerve
颈神经前支/頸神經前支 anterior branch of cervical nerve
颈升动脉/頸昇動脈 ascending cervical artery
颈髓炎/頸髓炎 cervical myelitis
颈痛/頸痛 neck pain
颈痛风/頸痛風 trachelagra
颈托/頸托 neck support
颈外侧核/頸外側核 lateral cervical nucleus
颈外侧淋巴结/頸外側淋巴結 lateral cervical lymph node
颈外侧囊肿/侧部頸囊腫,侧頸囊[腫] lateral cervical cyst
颈外侧浅淋巴结/頸外側淺淋巴結 superficial lateral cervical lymph node
颈外侧区/頸外側部 lateral region of neck
颈外侧韧带/外側頸韌帶 lateral cervical ligament
颈外侧上深淋巴结/頸外側上深淋巴結 superior deep lateral cervical lymph node
颈外侧深淋巴结/頸外側深淋巴結 deep lateral cervical lymph node
颈外侧下深淋巴结/頸外側下深淋巴結 inferior deep lateral cervical lymph node
颈外动脉/頸外動脈 external carotid artery
颈外动脉丛/頸外動脈叢 external carotid plexus
颈外动脉神经/頸外動脈神經 external carotid nerve
颈外动脉神经丛/外頸動脈神經叢 external carotid plexus
颈外静脉/頸外靜脈 external jugular vein
颈弯曲/頸部彎曲 cervical curve
颈位心/頸位心 cervical heart
颈窝点/頸窩點 fossa jugularis point
颈下神经节/頸下神經節 inferior cervical ganglion
颈下心神经/頸下心神經 inferior cervical cardiac nerve
颈下心支/頸下心支 inferior cervical cardiac branch
颈下行神经/頸下行神經 descending cervical nerve
颈性眩晕/頸源性眩暈 cervical vertigo
颈胸神经节/頸胸神經節 cervicothoracic ganglion
颈颜面的/頸面的 cervicofacial
颈硬/頸硬 stiff neck
颈痈/頸癰 acute pyogenic lymphadenitis of neck, cervical abscess, cervical carbuncle
颈痈·风热痰毒证/頸癰·風熱痰毒證 cervical abscess with pattern of wind-heat and phlegm-toxin
颈痈·气虚邪恋证/頸癰·氣虛邪戀證 cervical abscess with pattern of qi deficiency and lingering pathogen
颈痈·气郁化火证/頸癰·氣鬱化火證 cervical abscess with pattern of stagnated qi transforming into fire
颈痈·胃热壅盛证/頸癰·胃熱壅盛證 cervical abscess with pattern of stomach heat congestion and excessiveness
颈枕部神经痛/頸枕神經痛 cervico-occipital neuralgia
颈支/頸支 cervical branch
颈支抗/頸支抗 cervical anchorage
颈中神经节/頸中神經節 middle cervical ganglion
颈中心神经/頸中心神經 middle cervical cardiac nerve
颈主动脉/頸主動脈 princeps cervicis artery
颈椎/頸椎 cervical vertebrae, jingzhui
颈椎病/頸椎病 cervical spondylosis
颈椎病·风寒湿阻证/頸椎病·風寒濕阻證 cervical spondylosis with wind-cold-dampness obstruction pattern
颈椎病·肝肾亏虚证/頸椎病·肝腎虧虛證 cervical spondylosis with liver-kidney deficiency pattern
颈椎病·气血两虚证/頸椎病·氣血兩虛證 cervical spondylosis with qi-blood deficiency pattern
颈椎病·痰湿阻络证/頸椎病·痰濕阻絡證 cervical spondylosis with pattern of phlegm-dampness obstructing collateral
颈椎病·血瘀气滞证/頸椎病·血瘀氣滯證 cervical spondylosis with pattern of blood stasis and qi stagnation
颈椎飞鞭损伤/頸椎飛鞭損傷 whiplash injury
颈椎骨折/頸椎骨折 cervical fracture, fracture of cervical vertebrae
颈椎骨折与脱位/頸椎骨折與脫位 cervical fracture and dislocation
颈椎后凸/頸椎後彎 trachelocyrtosis
颈椎间盘突出症/頸椎間盤突出症 herniation of cervical disc
颈椎间盘综合征/頸椎間盤症候群 cervical disc syndrome
颈椎脑突出/頸椎腦膨出 derencephalocele
颈椎融合术/頸脊髓融合術,頸脊椎融合術 cervical spinal fusion
颈椎小关节错缝/頸椎小關節錯縫 dislocation of small joint of cervical vertebrae
颈总动脉/頸總動脈 common carotid artery, cephalic artery
颈总动脉丛/頸總動脈叢 common carotid plexus

颈总动脉神经丛/總頸動脈神經叢　plexus caroticus communis
颈最长肌/頸最長肌　longissimus cervicis
径向力/徑向力　radial force
净度/淨度　refined degree
净化/淨化,去汗染法　decontamination
净化水/淨化水　purified water
净司他丁/淨司他丁　zinostatin
净制/淨制　cleansing
胫/脛[部]　anticnemion
胫侧/脛側　tibial
胫侧副韧带/脛側副韌帶　tibial collateral ligament
胫侧骨/蹠脛骨　tibiale
胫侧跖骨点/脛側蹠骨點　metatarsale tibiale
胫动脉/脛動脈　tibial artery
胫腓骨干双骨折/脛腓骨幹雙骨折　fracture of shaft of tibia and fibula, tibiofibular shaft fracture
胫腓关节/脛腓關節,脛骨腓骨關節　tibiofibular joint, tibiofibular articulation
胫腓横韧带/脛腓橫韌帶　transverse tibiofibular ligament
胫腓后韧带/脛腓後韌帶　posterior tibiofibular ligament
胫腓连结/脛腓韌帶聯合　tibiofibular syndesmosis
胫腓前韧带/脛腓前韌帶　anterior tibiofibular ligament
胫腓韧带/脛腓韌帶　tibiofibular ligament
胫跟部/脛跟部　tibiocalcaneal part
胫骨/脛骨　tibia, shank bone
胫骨半月板/脛骨半月板　tibial menisci
胫骨粗隆/脛骨粗隆　tibial tuberosity, tuberosity of tibia
胫骨粗隆骨软骨病/脛骨粗隆骨軟骨病　Osgood-Schlatter disease
胫骨粗隆皮下囊/脛骨粗隆皮下囊　subcutaneous bursa of tibial tuberosity
胫骨干骨折/脛骨幹骨折　tibia shaft fracture
胫骨骨间缘/脛骨骨間緣　interosseous border of tibia
胫骨骨折/脛骨骨折　tibial fracture
胫骨后肌/脛骨後肌　tibialis posterior, musculus tibialis posterior
胫骨后肌沟/脛骨後肌溝　groove for tibialis posticus muscle
胫骨后肌腱鞘/脛骨後肌腱鞘　tendinous sheath of tibialis posterior
胫骨后静脉/脛骨後靜脈　venae tibiales posterior
胫骨后面/脛骨後面　posterior surface of tibia
胫骨髁状面/脛骨髁狀面　condyloid surface of tibia
胫骨肌/脛骨肌　tibialis
胫骨假关节/脛骨假關節　tibial pseudarthrosis
胫骨髁骨折/脛骨髁骨折　fracture of tibial malleolus, tibia condyle fracture
胫骨内侧髁/脛骨內側髁　medial condyle of tibia
胫骨内侧面/脛骨內側面　medial surface of tibia
胫骨内侧缘/脛骨內側緣　medial border of tibia
胫骨内翻/脛内翻　tibia vara
胫骨坪/脛骨高丘,脛骨岡　tibial plateau
胫骨前肌/脛骨前肌　tibialis anterior
胫骨前肌腱鞘/脛骨前肌腱鞘　tendinous sheath of tibialis anterior
胫骨前肌腱下囊/脛骨前肌腱下囊　subtendinous bursa of tibialis anterior
胫骨前皮疹热/脛前熱　pretibial fever
胫骨前下点/脛骨前下點　anterior distal end of tibia point
胫骨前缘/脛骨前緣　anterior border of tibia
胫骨上点/脛側跗骨　tibiale
胫骨上关节面/脛骨的上關節面　superior articular surface of tibia, superior articular facet of tibia
胫骨体/脛骨體　shaft of tibia
胫骨痛/脛骨痛　tibialgia
胫骨外侧髁/脛骨外側髁　lateral condyle of tibia
胫骨外侧面/脛骨外側面　lateral surface of tibia
胫骨外翻/脛外翻　valga tibia
胫骨下关节面/脛骨下關節面　inferior articular surface of tibia
胫骨炎/脛骨炎　cnemitis
胫骨滋养动脉/脛骨滋養動脈　tibial nutrient artery, nutrient artery of the tibia
胫后动脉/脛後動脈　posterior tibial artery
[胫后动脉]跟内侧支/[脛後動脈]跟内側支　medial calcaneal branch
胫后返动脉/脛後返動脈　posterior tibial recurrent artery
胫后肌腱功能障碍/脛後肌腱功能障礙　posterior tibial tendon dysfunction
胫后静脉/脛後靜脈　posterior tibial vein
胫后淋巴结/脛後淋巴結　posterior tibial lymph node
胫后神经/脛後神經　posterior tibial nerve
胫肌征/脛肌徵象　tibialis sign
胫疽/脛疽　shank abscess, suppurative osteomyelitis of tibia
胫距后部/脛距後部　posterior tibiotalar part
胫距前部/脛距前部　anterior tibiotalar part

胫前斑/脛部斑　shin spots
胫前的/脛前的　pretibial
胫前动脉/脛前動脈　anterior tibial artery
胫前返动脉/脛前返動脈　anterior tibial recurrent artery
胫前分隔综合征/前脛骨間隔症候群　anterior tibial compartment syndrome
胫前肌间隔综合征/脛前肌間隔症候群　anterior compartment syndrome
胫前肌瘫痪步态/脛前肌癱瘓步態　tabbing gait
胫前肌征/前脛骨徵象　anterior tibial sign
胫前静脉/脛前静脈　anterior tibial vein, venae tibiales anteriores
胫前淋巴结/脛前淋巴結　anterior tibial lymph node
胫前黏液囊炎/脛前黏液囊炎　pretibial bursitis
胫前黏液[性]水肿/脛前黏液水腫　pretibial myxoedema
胫前色素斑/脛前色素斑　pigmented pretibial patch
胫前神经/脛前神經　anterior tibial nerve
胫前着色斑/脛前著色斑　pigmented pretibial patch
胫前综合征/前脛骨症候群　anterior tibial syndrome
胫神经/脛神經　tibial nerve
胫神经病/脛神經病　tibial neuropathy
胫神经肌支/脛神經肌支　muscular branch of tibial nerve
胫舟部/脛舟部　tibionavicular part
痉病/痙病　convulsive disease
痉病·肝经热盛证/痙病·肝經熱盛證　convulsive disease with pattern of exuberant heat in Liver Channel
痉病·气血两虚证/痙病·氣血兩虛證　convulsive disease with pattern of deficiency of both qi and blood
痉病·热甚发痉证/痙病·熱甚發痙證　convulsive disease due to hyperpyrexia
痉病·痰浊阻滞证/痙病·痰濁阻滯證　convulsive disease with pattern of blockade of phlegm-turbidity
痉病·温热致痉证/痙病·溫熱致痙證　convulsive disease due to warm-heat pathogens
痉病·邪壅经络证/痙病·邪壅經絡證　convulsive disease with pattern of pathogen congesting channels and collaterals
痉病·心营热盛证/痙病·心營熱盛證　convulsive disease with pattern of exuberant heat in heart-nutrient phase
痉病·阳明热盛证/痙病·陽明熱盛證　convulsive disease with pattern of exuberant heat in Yangming
痉病·阴虚动风证/痙病·陰虛動風證　convulsive disease with pattern of wind stirring due to yin deficiency
痉病·阴血不足证/痙病·陰血不足證　convulsive disease with pattern of yin blood insufficiency
痉病·瘀血内阻证/痙病·瘀血内阻證　convulsive disease with pattern of internal blockade of static blood
痉厥/痙厥　coma with convulsion, syncope with convulsion
痉挛/痙攣　spasmus
痉挛步态/痙攣性步態　spastic gait
痉挛的/痙攣的　spasmodic
痉挛体质/痙攣體質　spasmodic diathesis
痉挛性便秘/痙攣性便秘　spastic constipation
痉挛性肠梗阻/痙攣性腸梗阻　spastic intestinal obstruction
痉挛性呃逆/痙攣性呃逆　spasmolygmus
痉挛性肛部痛/暫時性肛門痛　proctalgia fugax
痉挛性共济失调/痙攣性失調症　spasmodic ataxia
痉挛性共济失调步态/痙攣性共濟失調步態　spastic ataxic gait
痉挛性构语障碍/痙攣性口吃　spastic dysarthria
痉挛性喉炎/喘鳴性喉痙攣　spasmodic laryngitis
痉挛性呼吸困难/痙攣性呼吸困難　spasmodyspnea
痉挛性睑抽动/瞼搦,痙攣性瞼顫　cillo
痉挛性睑内翻/痙攣性瞼內翻　spastic entropion
痉挛性睑外翻/痙攣性瞼外翻　spastic ectropion
痉挛性结肠憩室病/痙攣性結腸憩室病　spastic colon diverticulosis
痉挛性结肠炎/痙攣性結腸炎　spastic colitis
痉挛性咳/痙攣性欬　spasmodic cough
痉挛性联带运动/痙攣性聯帶運動　spastic synkinesia
痉挛性尿闭/痙攣性尿閉　ischuria spastica
痉挛性排尿困难/痙攣性排尿困難　spastic dysuria
痉挛性膀胱/痙攣性膀胱　spastic bladder
痉挛性喷嚏/痙攣性噴嚏　ptarmus
痉挛性偏瘫/痙攣性偏癱　spastic hemiplegia
痉挛性气喘/痙攣性氣喘　spasmodic asthma
痉挛性轻截瘫/痙攣性輕截癱　spastic paraparesis
痉挛性失声/痙攣性失音　spastic aphonia
痉挛性失语/發音不能,發音肌痙攣性失語症　aphthongia
痉挛性双瘫/痙攣性兩側麻痹　spastic diplegia
痉挛性瘫痪/痙攣性麻痹　spastic paralysis
痉挛性痛经/痙攣性痛經　spasmodic dysmenorrhea
痉挛性吞咽困难/痙攣性咽物困難　dysphagia spastica

痉挛性狭窄/痙攣性狹窄　spastic stenosis
痉挛性狭窄环/挾縮環,收縮環　constriction ring
痉挛性斜颈/痙攣性斜頸　spasmodic torticollis
痉挛学/痙攣學,痙攣論　spasmology
痉挛状态/痙攣狀態,痙攣性　spasticity
痉跳病/痙跳病,跳躍病　jumping disease, saltatory spasm
痉笑/痙笑　cynic spasm, risus sardonicus
痉语症/痙語症　logospasm
竞争行为/競爭行爲　competitive behavior
竞争性拮抗/競爭性拮抗　competitive antagonism
竞争性结合/競爭性結合　competitive binding
竞争性投标/競爭性投標　competitive bidding
竞争性医疗计划/競爭性醫療計劃　competitive medical plan
竞争性抑制/競爭性抑制　competitive inhibition
竞争性抑制剂/競爭抑制物,競爭抑制劑　competitive inhibitor
敬礼状痉挛/敬禮狀痙攣　salaam spasm
静磁场疗法/靜磁場療法　static magnetic field therapy
静电刺激性味觉/靜電味覺　franklinic taste
静电疗法/靜電療法　electrostatic field therapy
静电喷雾/靜電噴霧　electrostatic spray
静电势/靜電勢　electrostatic potential
静电学/靜電學　electrostatics
静功/靜功　static qigong, still qigong
静力进样/靜力進樣　hydrostatic injection
静力性运动/靜態運動　static exercise
静力悬吊/靜力懸吊　static suspension
静力学/靜力學　statics
静脉/靜脈　vein
静脉瓣/靜脈瓣　venous valve
静脉瓣窦/靜脈瓣竇　sinus of the valve
静脉瓣骨化/靜脈瓣骨化病　diclidostosis
静脉闭塞性病/靜脈閉塞性病　venoocclusive disease
静脉壁无力/靜脈無力　phlebasthenia
静脉搏动描记器/靜脈搏描記器　phlebograph
静脉插管输液/靜脈插管輸液　intravenous cannula infusion
静脉插管[术]/靜脈插管[術]　venous cannulation
静脉成形术/靜脈成形術,靜脈造形術　phleboplasty
静脉抽出术/靜脈摘除術　phlebexairesis
静脉出血/靜脈出血　venous hemorrhage
静脉穿刺术/靜脈穿刺術　venepuncture
静脉丛/靜脈叢　venous plexus
静脉胆管造影[术]/靜脈膽管造影[術]　intravenous cholangiography

静脉胆囊造影[术]/靜脈膽囊造影[術]　intravenous cholecystography
静脉导管/靜脈導管　venous duct, ductus venosus
静脉导管插入/靜脈導管插入　venous catheterization
静脉的/靜脈的　venous
静脉滴注[法]/靜脈點滴,靜脈滴注　intravenous drip
静脉滴注麻醉/靜脈滴注麻醉法　infusion anesthesia
静脉动脉化皮瓣/靜脈動脈化皮瓣　venous arterialized skin flap
静脉动脉化游离皮瓣/靜脈動脈化游離皮瓣　venous arterialized free skin flap
静脉窦/靜脈竇　venous sinus, sinus venosus
静脉窦螺旋系统/靜脈竇螺旋系　sinospiral system
静脉窦血栓形成/靜脈竇血栓形成　thrombosis of venous sinus
静脉窦综合征/靜脈竇症候群　sinus venosus syndrome
静脉发育不全/靜脈發育不全　hypovenosity
静脉缝术/靜脈縫術　phleborrhaphy
静脉梗阻/靜脈血管阻塞　phlebemphraxis
静脉功能不全/靜脈機能不全　venous insufficiency
静脉沟/靜脈溝　venous groove
静脉固定术/靜脈固定術　phlebopexy
静脉哼鸣/靜脈唔聲　venous hum
静脉湖/靜脈腔隙　venous lake
静脉回流/靜脈回流　venous return
静脉回流管路/靜脈回流管路　venous return line
静脉间结节/靜脈間結節　intervenous tubercle
静脉静脉吻合术/靜脈間造口吻合術　phlebophlebostomy
静脉局部麻醉/靜脈局部麻醉　intravenous regional anesthesia
静脉扩张/靜脈擴張　phlebectasia
[静脉]扩张性血栓形成/擴張性血栓形成　dilatation thrombosis
静脉瘤/靜脈瘤　phlebangioma
静脉麻醉[法]/靜脈麻醉法　vein anesthesia
静脉麻醉药/靜脈麻醉藥　intravenous anesthetic
静脉毛细血管/靜脈微血管　venous capillary
静脉描记法/靜脈 X 光攝影法　venography
静脉囊状瘤/靜脈囊狀瘤　venous aneurysm
静脉内非典型血管增生/靜脈內異常性血管增生　intravenous atypical vascular proliferation
静脉内免疫球蛋白类/靜脈內免疫球蛋白類　intravenous immunoglobulins
静脉内膜炎/靜脈內膜炎　endophlebitis
静脉内输液复苏术/靜脈內輸液復甦術　intravenous

fluid resuscitation
静脉内输注/静脈內輸注　intravenous infusion
静脉内饲法/靜脈輸液營養　intravenous feeding
静脉内物质滥用/靜脈內物質濫用　intravenous substance abuse
静脉内氧合/靜脈內氧合　intravenous oxygenation
静脉内注射/靜脈內注射　intravenous injection
静脉怒张/靜脈怒張　venous engorgement
静脉皮瓣/靜脈皮瓣　venous skin flap
静脉破裂/靜脈破裂　phleborrhexis
静脉前淋巴结/靜脈前淋巴結　prevenal lymph node
静脉切除术/靜脈切除術　phlebectomy
静脉切开/靜脈切開術　venotomy
静脉切开刀/靜脈刀　phlebotome
静脉切开[放血]术/靜脈穿刺放血法　venesection
静脉切开术/靜脈切開術　venous cutdown
静脉曲张/靜脈曲張　varicosis
静脉曲张性动脉瘤/動靜脈交通瘤　varicose aneurysm
静脉曲张[性]溃疡/靜脈曲張性潰瘍　varicose ulcer
静脉韧带/靜脈韌帶　venous ligament, venous ligamentum, ligamentum venosum
静脉韧带裂/靜脈韌帶裂　fissure for ligamentum venosum
静脉韧带裂隙/靜脈韌帶裂隙　fissura ligamenti venosi
静脉X射线电影照相术/靜脈X光活動攝影術　cinephlebography
静脉石病/靜脈結石病　phlebolithiasis
静脉收缩药/靜脈收縮藥　venopressor
静脉输入营养液/靜脈高營養　intravenous hyperalimentation
静脉输血/靜脈輸血法　venous transfusion
静脉输液法/靜脈注射法　phleboclysis
静脉输注/靜脈灌注　venoclysis
静脉痛/靜脈痛　phlebalgia
静脉网/靜脈網　venous rete, venous network
静脉吸收/靜脈吸收　venous absorption
静脉狭窄/靜脈狹窄　phlebostenosis
静脉纤维变性/靜脈纖維變性　phlebofibrosis
静脉性跛行/靜脈性跛　venous claudication
静脉性溃疡/靜脈性潰瘍,靜脈曲張性潰瘍　venous ulcer
静脉性湿疹/靜脈性濕疹　venous eczema
静脉性水肿/靜脈性水腫　venous edema
静脉性小腿溃疡/靜脈性小腿潰瘍　venous ulceration of leg
静脉性心系膜/靜脈心繫膜　venous mesocardium
静脉学/靜脈學　phlebology
静脉血/靜脈血　venous blood
静脉血掺杂/靜脈血摻雜　venous admixture
静脉血动脉化/靜脈血動脈化　arterialization of venous blood
静脉血凝固/靜脈血凝固　thromballosis
静脉血平衡性肺泡气/靜脈血平衡性肺泡氣　venous alveolar air
静脉血栓形成/靜脈血栓病,靜脈栓塞　venous thrombosis
静脉血压计/靜脈血壓計　phlebomanometer
静脉压/靜脈血壓　venous pressure
静脉压检查法/靜脈血壓檢查法　phlebopiezometry
静脉炎/靜脈炎　phlebitis
静脉炎的/靜脈炎的　phlebitic
静脉炎后皮下组织钙化/靜脈炎後皮下組織鈣化　postphlebitis subcutaneous calcinosis
静脉炎后综合征/靜脈炎後症候群　postphlebitic syndrome
静脉移植/靜脈移植　vein transplantation
静脉硬化/靜脈硬化　phlebosclerosis
静脉硬化法/靜脈曲張之硬化療法　phlebosclerosation
静脉游离皮瓣/靜脈游離皮瓣　venous free skin flap
静脉淤滞/靜脈停滯　venous stasis
静脉杂音/靜脈雜音　venous murmur
静脉造影术/靜脈搏描記法,靜脈X光攝影法　phlebography
静脉征/靜脈病徵　vein sign
静脉止血法/靜脈止血法　phlebostasis
静脉中层炎/靜脈中膜炎　mesophlebitis
静脉周围炎/靜脈外膜炎,靜脈周膜炎　periphlebitis
静脉贮血器/靜脈貯血器　venous reservoir
静脉注射/靜脈注射　intravenous injection
静脉[注射]麻醉[法]/靜脈注射麻醉[法]　phlebanesthesia
静脉注射明胶溶液/靜脈專用膠溶液　special intravenous gelatin solution
静脉注射肾盂摄影/靜脈腎盂攝影術　intravenous pyelography
静脉注射用脂肪乳剂/靜脈注射用脂肪乳劑　intravenous fat emulsions
静区/靜區　silent area
静态暗间隙/靜態暗間隙　static dark space
静态定量视野计/靜態定量視野計　static quantitative perimeter
静态肺顺应性/靜態肺順應性　static lung compliance

静态检影[法]	静態檢影[法]	static retinoscopy
静态屈光	静態屈光	static refraction
静态人口学	静態人口統計學	static demography
静态视野计	静態視野計	static perimeter
静态医学	静態療法	static medicine
静态影像装置	静態影像裝置	static imaging device
静态症状	静態症狀	passive symptom
静位的	静止的	static
静位觉	静力覺	static sense
静息电位	休止電位,静電位	resting potential
静息能量消耗	静息能量消耗	rest energy expenditure
静息相	休止時期	resting phase
静息心排出量	静息心排出量	resting cardiac output
静纤毛	静纖毛	stereocilium
静性坏死	静性壞死	quiet necrosis
静止	静止	still
静止负重相	静止負重相	stance phase
静止滤线栅	静止濾線柵	stationary grid
静止期脱发	毛囊静止期脱髮	telogen effluvium
静止龋	休止齲	arrested caries
静止痛	静止痛	rest pain
静止型全身麻痹	静止型麻痺性癡呆	stationary paresis
静止性共济失调	静止時運動失調	static ataxia
静止性脊柱侧凸	静止性脊柱側彎	static scoliosis
静止性牙周炎	静止性牙周炎	arrested periodontitis
静止性震颤	静止性震顫	static tremor
静坐不能	静坐不能	akathisia
境界带	葛蘭茲區域	Grenz zone
境遇	處境,地位	situation
境遇性焦虑	環境恐懼	situation anxiety
境遇性精神病	境遇性精神病	situational psychosis
镜	鏡	mirror
镜面区	明鏡區	mirror area
镜面舌	鏡面舌	mirror-like tongue
镜面式视轴测定器	鏡面式視軸計	mirror haploscope
镜面试验	鏡子試驗	mirror test
镜片	鏡片	ophthalmic lens
镜片光心	鏡片光心	optical center of lens
镜片中心	鏡片中心	center of lens
镜下血尿	顯微血尿	microscopic hematuria
镜像异构现象	鏡像體	enantiomorphism
镜像手	鏡像手	mirror hand
镜像书写	書寫顛倒,反寫	mirror writing
镜轴计	透鏡軸線計	axonometer
炅则气泄	炅則氣洩	overheat causing qi leakage
窘迫	窘迫,困苦	distress
纠发病	糾髮病	plica polonica
鸠尾	鳩尾	jiuwei, RN15
鸠尾峡	鳩尾峽	dovetail form isthmus
鸠尾形	鳩尾形	dovetail form
九产妇	九[次]産婦	nonipara
九刺	九刺	nine techniques of needling
九分法	九分法	rule of nine
九华膏	九華膏	jiuhua plaster
九里香	九里香	murraya jasminorage
九梦	九夢	nine types of dream
九气感疾更相为治衍	九氣感疾更相爲治衍	Treatise on Emotional Therapy
九气论	九氣論	nine causes of qi disorder
九窍	九竅	nine orifices
九日红斑	九日紅斑	the ninth-day erythema
九肽	九肽	nonapeptide
九味羌活汤	九味羌活湯	jiuwei qianghuo decoction
九仙散	九仙散	jiuxian powder
九香虫	九香蟲	stink-bug
九旬老人	九旬老人	nonagenarian
九针	九針	nine classical needles
九针论	九針論	Treatise on Nine Kinds of Needles
久汗	久汗	lingering sweating
久咳	久欬	chronic cough
久痢	久痢	chronic dysentery
久聋	久聾	chronic deafness
久疟	久瘧,慢性瘧	chronic malaria
久卧结石	久臥者結石	decubitus calculus
久卧性皮炎	臥床皮膚炎	decubitus dermatitis
久效磷	久效磷	monocrotophos
久泻	久瀉,慢性腹瀉	chronic diarrhea
久泻·脾虚证	久瀉·脾虛證	chronic diarrhea with spleen deficiency pattern
久泻·肾虚证	久瀉·腎虛證	chronic diarrhea with kidney deficiency pattern
久泻·阴虚证	久瀉·陰虛證	chronic diarrhea with yin deficiency pattern
久喑	久喑	lingering dysphonia
久远记忆	久遠記憶	remote memory
灸法	灸法	moxibustion
灸剂	灸劑	moxibustion formula
灸禁	灸禁	moxibustion contraindications
韭菜子	韭菜子	tuber onion seed
酒悖	酒悖	mis-action due to wine
酒病	酒精中毒	alcoholism
酒疸	酒疸	alcoholic jaundice
酒毒性多神经炎	酒癮者多神經炎	polyneuritis

potatorum
酒毒性共济失调/酒毒性失調症　alcoholic ataxia
酒毒性精神病/酒毒性精神病　alcoholic psychosis
酒毒性脑膜炎/酒精性腦膜炎　alcoholic meningitis
酒毒性神经炎/酒毒性神經炎　alcoholic neuritis
酒炖/酒燉　stewing with wine
酒风/酒風　alcoholic wind
酒臌/酒臌　alcoholic tympanites
酒红斑/酒紅斑　wine erythema
酒红色痣/酒紅色母斑　port wine stain
酒积/酒積　alcoholic food amassment
酒积便血/酒積便血　alcoholic hematochezia
酒剂/酒劑　wine
酒瘕/酒瘕　alcoholic abdominal mass
酒煎/酒煎　decoct with wine
酒禁/酒禁　alcoholic tremor
酒精可溶性抗原/酒精可溶性抗原　alcoholic-soluble antigen
酒精滥用/酒精濫用　alcohol abuse
酒精相关性障碍/酒精相關性障礙　alcohol-related disorder
酒精性肝疾病/酒精性肝疾病　alcoholic liver disease
酒精性肝炎/酒精性肝炎　alcoholic hepatitis
酒精性肝硬化/酒精性肝硬變　alcoholic cirrhosis
酒精性高脂血症/酒精性高脂血症　alcoholic hyperlipemia
酒精性红斑/酒精性紅斑　alcohlic erythema
酒精性脑障碍/酒精性腦障礙　alcoholic brain disorder
酒精性神经病/酒精性神經病變　alcoholic neuropathy
酒精性心肌病/酒精性心肌病　alcoholic cardiomyopathy
酒精性胰腺炎/酒精性胰腺炎　alcoholic pancreatitis
酒精性遗忘症/酒精健忘障礙　alcohol amnestic disorder
酒精性饮料/酒精性飲料　alcoholic beverage
酒精性谵妄/酒精性譫妄　alcoholic delirium
酒精性脂肪肝/酒精性脂肪肝　alcoholic fatty liver
酒精诱发性障碍/酒精誘發性障礙　alcohol-induced disorder
酒精制剂/酒精製劑　alcoholica
酒精中毒/酒精中毒　alcoholism
酒精中毒昏迷/醉酒昏迷,酒毒性昏迷　alcoholic coma
酒精中毒性精神病/酒精中毒性精神病　alcoholic psychois
酒精中毒性弱视/酒精中毒性弱視　alcohol amblyopia
酒厥/酒厥　syncope due to excessive drinking, alcoholism syncope, syncope due to immoderate drinking
酒渴/酒渴　alcoholic thirst
酒客/酒徒　drinker
酒狂/酒狂,酒癖　methilepsia
酒石/酒石　tartar
酒石黄/酒石黃　tartrazine
酒石酸/酒石酸　tartaric acid
酒石酸麦角胺/酒石酸麥角胺　ergotamine tartrate
酒石酸钠盐/酒石酸鈉鹽　sodiotartrate
酒石酸锑钾/酒石酸銻鉀　antimony potassium tartrate
酒石酸锑钠/酒石酸銻鈉　antimony sodium tartrate
酒石酸五吡咯烷/酒石酸五吡咯烷　pentolinium tartrate
酒石酸性肾炎/酒石酸性腎炎　tartrate nephritis
酒石酸盐/酒石酸鹽　tartrate
酒石酸盐类/酒石酸鹽類　tartrates
酒石症/酒石病　tartaric disease
酒痰/酒痰　alcoholic phlegm
酒徒谵妄/酒徒譫妄　drinkers delirium
酒泄/酒洩　alcoholic diarrhea
酒氧化酶/酸酒酵素,酒敗酵素　enoxidase
酒渣鼻/酒渣鼻　brandy nose, acne rosacea, rosacea
酒渣鼻·肺胃热盛证/酒渣鼻·肺胃熱盛證　brandy nose with pattern of heat exuberance in lung and stomach
酒渣鼻角膜炎/酒糟鼻角膜炎　acne rosacea keratitis
酒渣鼻·气滞血瘀证/酒渣鼻·氣滯血瘀證　brandy nose with pattern of qi stagnation and blood stasis
酒渣鼻切割术/酒渣鼻切割術　rosacea cutting
酒渣鼻·湿热毒蕴证/酒渣鼻·濕熱毒蘊證　brandy nose with pattern of dampness-heat toxin amassment
酒渣鼻性痤疮/酒渣性痤瘡　acne rosacea
酒渣鼻样结核疹/酒渣樣結核疹　rosacea-like tuberculid
酒渣鼻样皮炎/酒渣樣皮膚炎　rosacea-like dermatitis
酒渣性眼病变/酒渣性眼病變　ophthalmic rosacea
酒渣样三期梅毒/酒渣樣三期梅毒　rosacea-like tertiary syphilis
酒胀/酒脹　alcoholic distention
酒蒸/酒蒸　steaming with wine
酒制/酒制　processing with wine
酒炙/酒炙　stir-frying with wine

酒渍/酒漬　macerate in wine
酒醉步态/酒醉步態　drunken gait
酒醉测定器/醉酒檢出器　drunkometer
旧大陆沙粒病毒/舊大陸沙粒病毒　old world arenavirus
旧结核菌素/舊結核菌素　old tuberculin
旧皮质/舊［大腦］皮質，原腦皮層　paleocortex, palaeopallium
旧纹状体的/舊紋狀體的　paleostriatal
旧纹状体综合征/舊紋狀體症候群　paleostriatal syndrome
旧小脑/古小腦　paleocerebellum
枢［状］形成/樞狀構造　coffin formation
救护车/救護車　ambulance
救护飞机/救護飛機　air ambulance
救护站/救護站　first aid station
救荒本草/救荒本草　Materia Medica for Famines
救急稀涎散/救急稀涎散　jiuji xixian powder
厩螫蝇/［廐］螫蠅　Stomoxys calcitrans
厩蝇/廐蠅　stable fly
居经/居經　quarterly menstruation
居髎/居髎　juliao, GB29
居留细胞/不遊走細胞　residential cell
居维叶管/Cuvier 氏管　ducts of Cuvier
居西切道描记器/吉西切道描記器　Gysi incisive path maker
居住流动性/居住流動性　residential mobility
居住特征/居住特徵　residence characteristics
疽/疽　ju, carbuncle and abscess, deep-rooted carbuncle
疽毒内陷/疽毒內陷　inward collapse of carbuncle toxin
鞠躬状抽搐/鞠躬狀抽搐　bowing tic
局部白化病/局部白化病　localized albinism, partial albinism
局部病/局部病　local disease
局部肠梗阻/局部的腸阻塞　regional ileus
局部抽搐/局部抽搐　local tic
局部刺激状态/局部刺激狀態　local excitatory state
局部的/局部的　regional
局部发绀/局部發紺　local cyanosis
局部反应/局部反應　local reaction
局部防卫法/局部防禦作用　topophylaxis
局部分化/區域分化　regional differentiation
局部感觉迟钝/局部感覺遲鈍　topodysesthesia
局部感觉异常/局部感覺異常　topoparesthesia
局部感染/局部感染　local infection
局部灌注/局部灌注　regional perfusion

局部过敏反应/局部過敏性　local anaphylaxis
局部坏死/局部死亡　local death
局部肌张力障碍/局部肌肉緊張不足　focal dystonia
局部结节性滑膜炎/局部結節性滑膜炎　localized nodular synovitis
局部解剖学/局部解剖學　regional anatomy
局部浸润麻醉/局部浸潤麻醉　local infiltration anesthesia
局部痉挛/局部痙攣　idiospasm
局部局麻/局部麻醉　regional block
局部菌苗疗法/局部疫苗療法　topovaccinotherapy
局部抗感染药/局部抗感染藥　local anti-infective agent
局部抗菌治疗/局部抗菌治療　topical antibacterial therapy
局部抗真菌治疗/局部抗真菌治療　topical antifungal therapy
局部叩击痛/局部叩擊痛　local percussion pain
局部淋巴结/局部淋巴結　regional lymph node
局部淋巴结试验/局部淋巴結試驗　local lymph node assay
局部麻醉/局部麻醉法　local anesthesia
局部麻醉药/局部麻醉藥　local anesthetic
局部面颊真皮发育不良/局部臉頰真皮發育異常　focal facial dermal dysplasia
局部皮瓣/局部皮瓣　local skin flap
局部取穴/局部取穴　local point selection
局部缺血/局部窒息　local asphyxia
局部失调/局限性障礙　localized disturbance
局部视网膜电图/局部視網膜電圖　local electroretinogram
局部损害/局部性病灶　local lesion
局部痛/局部［精神］痛　topalgia
局部投药/局部投藥　topical administration
局部秃发/局部性秃髮　alopecia localis
局部推进皮瓣移植术/局部推進皮瓣移植術　local advancement skin flap grafting
局部退化/局部退化　regional degeneration
局部温度［感］觉测量器/局部溫度計　topothermesthesiometer
局部兴奋剂/局部刺激藥　local stimulant
局部旋转皮瓣移植术/局部旋轉皮瓣移植術　local rotation skin flap grafting
局部旋转推进皮瓣移植术/局部旋轉推進皮瓣移植術　local advancement and rotation flap transplantation
局部血流/局部血流　regional blood flow
局部义齿/部分假牙　partial denture

局部原因/局部原因　local cause
局部真皮发育不良/局部真皮發育異常　focal dermal dysplasia
局部症状/局部症狀　local symptom
局部肿瘤复发/局部腫瘤復發　local neoplasm recurrence
局部阻滞麻醉/區域性阻斷麻醉　field block
局部作用/局部作用　local action
局方发挥/局方發揮　Elaboration of Bureau Prescription
局限的/局限的　circumscribed
局限化/局部化　localization
局限型癫痫/局部性癲癇，病灶性癲癇　focal epilepsy
局限性癌前期黑变病/局限性癌前期黑變症　circumscribed precancerous melanosis
局限性剥脱性舌炎/小區域脱落性舌炎　glossitis areata exfoliativa
局限性肠炎/局限性腸炎　regional enteritis
局限性动脉瘤/限界性動脈瘤　circumscribed aneurysm
局限性腹膜炎/局部性腹膜炎　localized peritonitis
局限性钙沉着/限界性鈣質沈著症　calcinosis circumscripta
局限性坏疽/局限性壞疽　circumscribed gangrene
局限性结节状增生/局限性結節狀增生　focal nodular hyperplasia
局限性淋巴管瘤/限界性淋巴管瘤　lymphangioma circumscriptum
局限性毛细管扩张/局限性皮膚毛細管擴張　papillary ectasia
局限性囊状骨炎/限界性囊狀骨炎　osteitis cystica localisata
局限性黏液水肿/局限性黏液水腫　circumscribed myxedema
局限性脓肿/有包壁的膿腫　circumscribed abscess
局限性皮肤结核/局限性皮膚結核　localized forms tuberculosis of skin
局限性皮肤水肿/局限性皮膚水腫　oedema cutis circumscriptum
局限性浅表性萎缩硬皮病/限界性表淺性萎縮硬皮病　atrophoscleroderma superficialis circumscripta
局限性神经纤维瘤/局限性神經纖維瘤　localized neurofibroma
局限性神经性皮炎/局限性神經皮膚炎　circumscribed neurodermatitis
局限性脱发/局限性禿髮　alopecia circumscripta
局限性外耳炎/局限性外耳炎　otitis externa circumscripta
局限性涡纹样胶原瘤/局限性渦紋樣膠原瘤　circumscribed storiform collagenoma
局限性纤维性骨炎/局限性[囊狀]纖維性骨炎　osteitis fibrosa circumscripta
局限性心包炎/局限性心包炎　localized pericarditis
局限性血管角化瘤/局限性血管角化瘤　angiokeratoma circumscriptum
局限性硬皮病/局限性硬皮病　limited scleroderma, scleroderma circumscriptum
局限性掌跖角化病/局限性掌蹠角化病　keratosis palmoplantaris circumscripta
局限性脂肪萎缩/局限性脂肪萎縮　localized lipoatrophy
局限[性]阻塞性肺气肿/局限[性]阻塞性肺氣腫　local obstructive pulmonary emphysema
局限转导/限制性傳導　restricted transduction
局灶性黑变[症]/局灶性黑變[症]　focal melanosis
局灶性坏死/局限性壞死　focal necrosis
局灶性坏死性肾小球肾炎/局灶性壞死性腎小球腎炎　focal necrotic glomerulonephritis
局灶性脊髓病/局部脊髓病變　focal myelopathy
局灶性脊髓炎/局灶性脊髓炎　focal myelitis
局灶性节段性肾小球肾炎/局灶性節段性腎小球腎炎　focal segmental glomerulonephritis
局灶性皮肤发育不全/局灶性皮膚發育不全　focal dermal hypoplasia
局灶性皮肤棘层松解性角化不良/局部棘層鬆解性角化異常　focal acantholytic dyskeratosis
局灶性上皮增生/局灶性上皮增生　focal epithelial hyperplasia
局灶性肾小球肾炎/局灶性腎絲球腎炎　focal glomerulonephritis
局灶性肾炎/局灶性腎炎　focal nephritis
局灶性炎/病灶性炎症　focal inflammation
局灶性硬化性肾小球肾炎/局灶性硬化性腎小球腎炎　focal sclerotic glomerulonephritis
局灶性增生性肾小球肾炎/局灶性增生性腎小球腎炎　focal proliferative glomerulonephritis
局灶性肢端角化过度/局部肢端過度角化症　focal acral hyperkeratosis
局质分泌/局[部]泌　merocrine
局质分泌腺/局泌腺　merocrine gland
桔皮状征/橘皮微象　orange-peel sign
桔青霉/桔青黴菌　Penicillium citrinum
菊粉/菊粉　dahlin
菊粉清除率/菊粉清除率　inulin clearance rate
菊蒿/菊蒿　Tanacetum parthenium

菊花/菊花　chrysanthemum flower
菊花心/菊花心　radial striations
菊苣/菊苣　chicory
菊科/菊科　Compositae
菊科植物性皮炎/菊科皮膚炎　Compositae dermatitis
菊糖/菊糖　inulin
橘核/橘核　tangerine seed
橘核丸/橘核丸　juhe pills
橘红/橘紅　red tangerine peel
橘红丸/橘紅丸　juhong pills
橘霉素/檸檬色黴素　citrinin
橘皮竹茹汤/橘皮竹茹湯　jupi zhuru decoction
咀嚼/[咀]嚼　mastication
咀嚼不能/無法咀嚼　amasesis
咀嚼肌/咀嚼肌　masticatory muscle
咀嚼肌痉挛/嚼肌痙攣　masticatory spasm
咀嚼剂/咀嚼劑　masticatory
咀嚼黏膜/咀嚼黏膜　masticatory mucosa
咀嚼片剂/咀嚼錠　chewable tablet
咀嚼生理学/咀嚼生理學　masticatory physiology
咀嚼系统/咀嚼系統　masticatory system
咀嚼效能/咀嚼效能　masticatory efficiency
咀嚼型/咀嚼型　masticatory pattern
咀嚼循环/咀嚼循環　masticatory cycle
咀嚼用/咀嚼用　chewing
咀嚼运动/咀嚼運動　masticatory movement
沮丧的/凹陷的　depressed
枸橼/枸櫞　citron
枸橼磷酸盐/檸檬磷酸鹽　citrophosphate
枸橼酸铋钾/枸櫞酸鉍鉀　bismuth potassium citrate
枸橼酸二氢胆碱/雙氫檸檬酸膽素　choline dihydrogen citrate
枸橼酸氯森/枸櫞酸氯森　chlorothen citrate
枸橼酸钠/檸檬酸鈉　sodium citrate
枸橼酸钠血浆/加檸檬酸鹽血漿　citrated plasma
枸橼酸铁胆碱/膽素鐵質　ferrocholinate
枸橼酸铜/檸檬酸銅　copper citrate
枸橼酸盐/檸檬酸鹽　citrate
矩形充填器/方型填壓器　parallelogram condenser
P矩阵法/P-矩陣法　P-matrix method
举按寻/舉按尋　pressing and searching, touching
举痛论篇/舉痛論篇　Discussion on Pain
巨斑刺蛾/巨斑刺蛾　Automeris io
巨鼻/巨鼻[畸形]　macrorhinia
巨臂/巨臂[畸形],長臂畸形　macrobrachia
巨并指/巨指粘連畸形　megalosyndactyly
巨并趾/巨趾粘連畸形　megalosyndactyly

巨肠/巨腸症　enteromegalia
巨成白细胞/巨母白血球,巨胚白血球　macroleukoblast
巨成红细胞/巨胚紅血球,巨母紅血球　macroblast
巨成髓细胞/巨骨髓母細胞,巨骨髓胚細胞　macromyeloblast
巨唇/巨唇[畸形]　macrolabia
巨大的/巨人　giant
巨大儿/巨嬰　giant baby
巨大肥厚性胃炎/巨大肥厚性胃炎　giant hypertrophy gastritis
巨大骨盆/巨大骨盆　giant pelvis
巨大尖锐湿疣/巨大尖銳濕疣　giant condyloma acuminatum
巨大皮肤透明变性/大塊性皮膚透明變性　massive cutaneous hyalinosis
巨大色素痣/巨大色素痣　giant pigmented nevus
巨大肾积水/巨大腎積水　giant hydronephrosis
巨大湿疣/巨大濕疣　giant condyloma
巨大胎儿/巨大胎兒　fetal macrosomia
巨大血小板/巨型血小板　giant platelet
巨大运动单位动作电位/巨大運動單位動作電位　giant motor unit action potential
巨大皱襞/巨大皺襞　giant fold
巨单核细胞/巨單核血球　macromonocyte
巨淀粉酶血症/巨澱粉酶血症　macroamylasemia
巨耳畸形/巨耳[畸形]　macrotia
巨杆菌素/巨桿菌素　megacin
巨睾前殖吸虫/巨睾前殖吸蟲　prosthogonimus macrorchis
巨骨/巨骨　jugu, LI16
巨核细胞/巨核細胞　megakaryocyte
巨核细胞白血病/巨核細胞性白血病　megakaryocytic leukemia
巨核细胞集落生成单位/巨核細胞集落形成單位　colony-forming unit-megakaryocyte, CFU-Meg
巨核细胞增多症/巨核細胞血症　megakaryocytosis
巨颌[症]/巨頜[畸形]　macrognathia
巨红细胞/巨紅血球　megalocyte
巨红细胞溶解酶/巨紅血球溶解酵素　macrocytase
巨红细胞症/巨紅血球症　megalocytosis
巨睑/巨瞼[畸形]　macroblepharia
巨角膜/巨角膜　macrocornea
巨结肠/巨結腸　megacolon
巨结肠根治术/巨結腸根治術　definitive operation for Hirschsprung disease
巨颏/巨頦症　macrogenia
巨口/巨口[畸形]　macrostomia

巨口双腔吸虫/巨口雙腔吸蟲　dicrocoelium macrostomum
巨眶的/巨眶的　megaseme
巨粒嗜曙红白细胞/大形嗜酸白血球,粗粒嗜伊红白血球　megoxyphil
巨髎/巨髎　juliao, ST3
巨淋巴结增生/巨淋巴結增生　giant lymph node hyperplasia
巨颅/巨顱　macrocrania
巨滤泡性淋巴瘤/巨濾胞性淋巴瘤,布-希二氏病　Brill-Symmers disease
巨盲肠/巨盲腸　megacecum
巨面/巨面[畸形]　macroprosopia
巨囊/巨囊[腫]　macrocyst
巨脑/巨腦[畸形]　macrencephalia
巨脑回/巨腦迴,巨迴畸形　macrogyria
巨尿道/巨尿道　megalourethra
巨前髓细胞/巨前骨髓細胞　macropromyelocyte
巨球蛋白/大球蛋白　macroglobulin
巨球蛋白血[症]/大球蛋白血症　macroglobulinemia
巨球蛋白血症肾病/巨球蛋白血症腎病　macroglobulinemic nephropathy
巨球蛋白血症性紫癜/巨球蛋白血症性紫瘢症　purpura macroglobulinemia
巨曲霉/巨麴黴　Aspergillus giganteus
巨阙/巨闕　juque, RN14
巨染色体/巨染色體　giant chromosome
巨人症/巨人症,巨大畸形　gigantism
巨乳房/巨乳房,乳房過大　gigantomastia, macromastia
巨乳头性结膜炎/巨乳頭性結膜炎　macropapillary conjunctivitis
巨色素粒/巨大色素顆粒　giant pigment granules
巨舌/巨舌[畸形]　macroglossia
巨肾盏/巨腎盞　megacalyx
巨生殖器/巨生殖器巨體[畸形]　macrogenitosomia
巨十二指肠/巨十二指腸　megaduodenum
巨嗜酸细胞/大形嗜酸白血球　megoxycyte
巨噬细胞/巨噬細胞　macrophage
巨噬细胞活化/巨噬細胞活化　macrophage activation
巨噬细胞活化因子/巨噬細胞活化因子　macrophage activating factor
巨噬细胞集落刺激因子/巨噬細胞集落刺激因子　macrophage colony-stimulating factor
巨噬细胞集落刺激因子受体/巨噬細胞集落刺激因子受體　macrophage colony-stimulating factor receptor
巨噬细胞启动因子/巨噬細胞啟動因子　macrophage-activating factor
巨噬细胞趋化因子/巨噬細胞趨化因子　macrophage chemotactic factor
巨噬细胞细胞毒因子/巨噬細胞細胞毒因子　macrophage cytotoxic factor
巨噬细胞炎性蛋白质类/巨噬細胞炎性蛋白質類　macrophage inflammatory proteins
巨噬细胞移动试验/巨噬細胞移動試驗　macrophage migration test
巨噬细胞移动抑制因子/巨噬細胞移動抑制因子　macrophage migration inhibition factor
巨手/巨手[畸形]　cheiromegaly
巨输尿管/巨輸尿管　megaloureter
巨头/巨頭[畸形]　megacephaly
巨头症/巨頭[症]　cephalonia
巨腿/巨腿[畸形]　macroscelia
巨胃/巨胃　gastromegaly
巨吻棘头虫病/巨吻棘頭蟲病　macracanthorhynchiasis
巨细胞/巨細胞　giant cell
巨细胞癌/巨細胞癌　carcinoma giant-celled
巨细胞包涵体病/巨細胞包涵體病　cytomegalic inclusion disease
巨细胞包涵体病病毒/巨細胞包涵體病病毒　cytomegalic inclusion disease virus
巨细胞病毒/巨細胞病毒　cytomegalovirus
巨细胞病毒感染/巨細胞病毒感染　cytomegalovirus infection
巨细胞病毒尿/巨細胞病毒尿症　cytomegaloviruria
巨细胞病毒视网膜炎/巨細胞病毒視網膜炎　cytomegalovirus retinitis
巨细胞病毒性单核白细胞增多症/巨細胞病毒性單核白血球增多症　cytomegalovirus mononucleosis
巨细胞病毒疫苗/巨細胞病毒疫苗　cytomegalovirus vaccine
巨细胞的/巨細胞的　cytomegalic
巨细胞动脉炎/巨[大]細胞動脈炎　giant-cell arteritis
巨细胞胶原纤维瘤/巨大細胞膠原纖維瘤　giant collagenoma
巨细胞瘤/巨細胞瘤　giant cell tumor
巨细胞肉芽肿/巨細胞肉芽腫　giant cell granuloma
巨细胞苔藓样皮炎/巨大細胞苔藓樣皮膚炎　giant cell lichenoid dermatitis
巨细胞透明血管病/巨細胞透明血管病　giant cell hyaline angiopathy
巨细胞网状核/巨細胞網狀核　gigantocellular

reticular nucleus
巨细胞性肺炎/巨細胞性肺炎　giant cell pneumonia
巨细胞性肝炎/巨細胞性肝炎　neonatal giant cell hepatitis
巨细胞性牙龈瘤/巨大細胞齦瘤　giant cell epulis
巨细胞血管母细胞瘤/巨大細胞血管母細胞瘤　giant cell angioblastoma
巨隙前牙/女巫牙　hag teeth
巨小腿/巨小腿　macrocnemia
巨心畸胎/巨心畸胎　macrocardius
巨血小板/巨血小板，大血小板　megaloplastocyte
巨血小板综合征/伯-梭二氏症候群　Bernard-Soulier syndrome
巨牙/巨牙症,巨齒[畸形]　macrodontia, macrotooth
巨眼/巨眼[畸形]　macrophthalmia
巨阴蒂/巨陰蒂　macroclitoris
巨阴茎/巨陰莖,巨陽　megalopenis
巨幼红细胞/巨幼紅細胞　megaloblasts
巨幼细胞性贫血/巨胚紅血球貧血　megaloblastic anemia
巨圆锥体状肌病/大錐狀顆粒肌病　megaconial myopathy
巨肢/巨肢[畸形]　macromelia
巨肢者/巨肢者　macromelus
巨指/巨指症　dactylomegaly
巨指畸形/巨指畸形　macrodactylia
巨指甲/巨[指]甲　macronychia, magalonychia
巨指偏侧肥大及结缔组织痣/巨指偏侧肥大及結締組織痣　macrodactyly hemihypertrophy and connective tissue nevus
巨趾/巨趾症　dactylomegaly
巨趾畸形/巨趾畸形　macrodactylia
巨趾甲/巨[趾]甲　macronychia, magalonychia
巨趾偏侧肥大及结缔组织痣/巨趾偏侧肥大及結締組織痣　macrodactyly hemihypertrophy and connective tissue nevus
巨痣/巨痣　giant nevus
巨锥体细胞/大錐狀細胞　giant pyramidal cell
巨足/巨足　megalopodia
拒苏丹单位/厭蘇丹單位　sudanophobic unit
具二尖头的/雙尖　bicuspidatus
具角的/有角的　corniculate
具体思维/具體思想　concretism
具纤毛的/有纖毛的　ciliated
具象思维/具象思維　concrete thinking
具遗觉能力者/直觀像持有者　eidetic
具缘纹孔/具緣紋孔　bordered pit
剧毒性/劇毒性　hypertoxicity
剧渴/劇渴　anadipsia
剧烈口吃/劇烈口吃　hottentotism
剧痛/劇痛　severe pain, throe
剧吐/劇吐　hyperemesis
剧痒疹/劇癢疹　prurigo ferox
距的/距狀的　calcarine
距腓后韧带/距腓後韌帶　posterior talofibular ligament
距腓前韧带/距腓前韌帶　anterior talofibular ligament
距跟骨间韧带/距跟骨間韌帶　interosseous talocalcaneal ligament
距跟后韧带/距跟後韌帶　posterior talocalcaneal ligament
距跟内侧韧带/距跟内側韌帶　medial talocalcaneal ligament
距跟前韧带/距跟前韌帶　anterior talocalcaneal ligament
距跟韧带/距跟韌帶　talocalcaneal ligament
距跟外侧韧带/距跟外側韌帶　lateral talocalcaneal ligament
距跟舟关节/距跟舟關節　talocalcaneonavicular joint, talocalcaneonavicular articulation
距骨/距骨　talus
距骨沟/距骨溝　sulcus of talus
距骨骨折/距骨骨折　fracture of talus, talus fracture
距骨后突/距骨後突　posterior process of talus
距骨后突内侧结节/距骨後突内側結節　medial tubercle of posterior process of talus
距骨后突外侧结节/距骨後突外側結節　lateral tubercle of posterior process of talus
距骨滑车/距骨滑車　trochlea of talus
距骨颈/距骨頸　neck of talus
距骨内踝面/距骨内踝面　medial malleolar facet of talus
距骨切除术/距骨切除術　astragalectomy
距骨上面/距骨上面　superior surface of talus
距骨体/距骨體　body of talus
距骨头/距骨頭　head of talus
距骨脱位/距骨脱位　dislocation of talus, talus dislocation
距骨外侧突/距骨外側突　lateral process of talus
距骨外踝面/距骨外踝面　lateral malleolar facet of talus
距骨下脱位/距骨下脱位　subastragalar dislocation
距骨舟关节面/距骨舟關節面　navicular articular surface of talus
距骨周围脱位/距骨周圍脱位　peritalus dislocation

距骺突骨折/Shepherd 氏骨折　Shepherd fracture
距离/距離　distance
距离感受器/距離感受器　distance receptor
距离像差/距離偏差　distantial aberration
距离知觉/距離知覺　distance perception
距上骨/距上骨　supratalus bone
距下关节/距下關節　subtalar joint
距小腿关节/距骨小腿關節　talocrural joint
距小腿后区/距小腿後部　posterior talocrural region
距小腿前区/距小腿前部　anterior talocrural region
距舟背侧韧带/距舟背側韌帶　talonavicular dorsal ligament
距舟骨/距舟骨　astragaloscaphoid bone
距舟关节/距舟關節　talonavicular articulation
距舟韧带/距舟韌帶　talonavicular ligament
距状沟/距狀溝　calcarine sulcus
距状沟支/距狀支　calcarine branch
距状后静脉/距狀後静脈　posterior calcarine vein
距状裂/距狀裂隙　fissura calcarina
距状裂皮质/距狀裂皮質　calcarine cortex
距状前静脉/距狀前静脈　anterior calcarine vein
惧梦/懼夢　fearful dream
锯齿扫描/鋸齒掃描　zigzag scanning
锯齿状处女膜/齒狀處女膜　denticular hymen
锯齿状骨折/鋸齒狀骨折　indentation fracture
锯齿状切口/鋸齒狀切口　zigzag incision
锯肌/鋸肌　serratus
锯状缝/鋸狀縫　serrate suture
锯状缘/鋸齒緣　ora serrata
聚氨基甲酸酯类/聚氨基甲酸酯類　polyurethanes
聚氨酯卡套/聚氨酯卡套　polyurethane ferrule
聚胺类/聚胺類　polyamines
聚半乳糖醛酸酶/聚半乳糖醛酸苷酶　polygalacturonase
聚胞苷酸类/聚胞苷酸類　poly C
聚苯乙烯/聚苯乙烯　polystyrenes
聚苯乙烯薄膜/聚苯乙烯薄膜　polystyrene film
聚苯乙烯凝胶/聚苯乙烯凝膠　polystyrene gel
聚丙烯类/聚丙烯類　polypropylenes
聚丙烯酰胺凝胶/聚丙烯醯胺凝膠　polyacrylamide gel
聚丙烯酰胺凝胶电泳/聚丙烯醯胺凝膠電泳　polyacrylamide gel electrophoresis
聚醋酸乙烯酯/聚醋酸乙烯酯　polyvinyl acetate
聚电解质/聚電解質　polyelectrolyte
聚对苯二甲酸乙酯类/聚對苯二甲酸乙酯類　polyethylene terephthalates
聚二噁烷酮/聚二噁烷酮　polydioxanone

聚泛素/聚泛素　polyubiquitin
聚光镜/聚光透鏡　condensing lens
聚光[X射线]滤线栅/X光聚光濾線柵　focused grid
聚硅酮类/聚矽酮類　silicones
聚酐类/聚酐類　polyanhydrides
RNA 聚合酶/核糖核酸聚合酶　RNA polymerase
聚合酶链反应/聚合酶鏈反應　polymerase chain reaction, PCR
聚合免疫球蛋白受体/聚合免疫球蛋白受體　polymeric immunoglobulin receptor
聚合物/聚合物　polymer
聚合现象/聚合現象　polymerism
聚合性痤疮/聚集性痤瘡　acne conglobata
聚合[作用]/聚合[作用]　polymerization
聚核苷酸类/聚核苷酸類　polynucleotides
聚核苷酸连接酶类/聚核苷酸連接酶類　polynucleotide ligases
聚核苷酸 5'-羟基激酶/聚核苷酸 5'-羥基激酶　polynucleotide 5'-hydroxyl-kinase
聚肌胞苷酸/聚肌胞苷酸　poly I-C
聚肌苷酸类/聚肌苷酸類　poly I
聚集/聚集　aggregation
聚集棒杆菌/扁闊棒狀桿菌　corynebacterium fascians
聚集蛋白/聚集蛋白　agrin
聚集性胶样弹力纤维变性/聚集性膠樣彈力纖維變性　elastosis colloidalis conglomerata
聚甲基丙烯酸类/聚甲基丙烯酸類　polymethacrylic acids
聚甲基异丁烯酸/聚甲基異丁烯酸　polymethyl methacrylate
聚赖氨酸/聚離胺酸　polylysine
聚类分析/聚類分析　cluster analysis
聚氯醛糖/副氯醛醣　parachloralose
聚氯乙烯/聚氯化乙烯　polyvinyl chloride
聚醚类抗生素/聚醚類抗生素　polyether antibiotics
聚醚橡胶印模材料/聚醚橡膠印模材料　polyether rubber impression material
聚明胶肽/聚明膠肽　polygeline
聚鸟苷酸类/聚鳥苷酸類　poly G
聚尿苷酸类/聚尿苷酸類　poly U
聚泉/聚泉　juquan, EX-HN10
聚山梨醇酯类/聚山梨醇酯類　polysorbates
聚四氟乙烯/聚四氟乙烯　polytetrafluoroethylene
聚羧酸盐黏固剂/聚羧酸鹽黏固劑　polycarboxylate cement
聚酮合成酶类/聚酮合成酶類　polyketide synthases
聚脱氧核糖核酸类/聚去氧糖核酸類

polydeoxyribonucleotides
聚脱氧腺苷酸-脱氧胸苷酸类/聚去氧腺苷酸-去氧胸苷酸類　poly dA-dT
聚维酮/聚維酮　povidone
聚维酮碘/優碘　povidone-iodine
聚烯类/聚烯類　polyenes
聚腺苷二磷酸酯核糖/聚腺苷二磷酸酯核糖　poly adenosine diphosphate ribose
聚腺苷酸类/多腺苷酸　poly A
聚腺尿苷酸类/聚腺尿苷酸類　poly A-U
聚星障/聚星障　clustered-star nebula, herpes simplex keratitis, starred nebula
聚星障·风热犯目证/聚星障·風熱犯目證　clustered-star nebula with pattern of wind-heat assailing eye
聚星障·肝胆实热证/聚星障·肝膽實熱證　clustered-star nebula with pattern of liver-gallbladder excessive heat
聚星障·湿热蕴蒸证/聚星障·濕熱蘊蒸證　clustered-star nebula with pattern of dampness-heat amassing and steaming
聚星障·正虚邪恋证/聚星障·正虛邪戀證　clustered-star nebula with pattern of healthy qi deficiency and lingering pathogen
聚胸苷酸类/聚胸苷酸類　poly T
聚阳离子/聚陽離子　polycation
聚氧乙烯月桂醚硫酸酯铵液/聚氧乙烯月桂醚硫酸酯銨液　ammonium polyoxyethylene lauryl ether sulfate solution
聚乙醇酸/聚乙醇酸　polyglycolic acid
聚乙二醇/聚乙烯二醇　macrogol
聚乙酸乙烯酯/聚醋酸乙烯　polyvinyl acetate
聚乙烯/聚乙烯　polyethylene
聚乙烯薄膜封包法/聚乙烯薄膜封包法　saran wrap
聚[乙]烯吡[咯烷]酮/聚乙烯一氮五圜酮　polyvinyl pyrrolidone
聚乙烯二醇类/聚乙烯二醇類　polyethylene glycols
聚乙烯亚胺/聚乙烯亞胺　polyethyleneimine
聚乙烯醇/聚乙烯醇　polyvinyl alcohol
聚异戊烯磷酸单糖类/聚異戊烯磷酸單糖類　polyisoprenyl phosphate monosaccharides
聚异戊烯磷酸寡聚糖类/聚異戊烯磷酸寡聚糖類　polyisoprenyl phosphate oligosaccharides
聚异戊烯磷酸糖类/聚異戊烯磷酸糖類　polyisoprenyl phosphate sugars
聚异戊烯磷酸盐类/聚異戊烯磷酸鹽類　polyisoprenyl phosphates
聚阴离子/聚陰離子　polyanion

聚证/蓄積病　accumulation disease
聚脂/聚脂　polyester
聚脂屏网式滤器/聚脂屏網式濾器　polyester screen filter
蠲痹汤/蠲痺湯　juanbi decoction
卷绷带器/纏繃帶器　bandage winder
卷耳/卷耳　scroll ear
卷睫夹/睫毛夾　eyelash curler
卷曲螺旋/卷曲螺旋　coiled coil
卷曲霉素硫酸盐/卷麴黴素硫酸鹽　capreomycin sulfate
卷筒式硅胶膜式氧合器/卷筒式矽膠膜式氧合器　coiled silicone membrane oxygenator
卷尾猴/卷尾猴　sapajou
卷须霉素/纏黴素　capreomycin
卷旋状的/螺旋形的　helicoid
狷者/狷者　person with low ambition
绢云母/絹雲母　sericite
决策规则/決策規則　decision rule
决明子/決明子　cassia seed
决疑法/決疑法　casuistry
觉醒/覺醒　arousal
觉醒状态/覺醒狀態　waking state
觉知/覺知　awareness
绝对暗点/絕對暗點　absolute scotoma
绝对变性反应/絕對變性反應　reaction of absolute degeneration
绝对病原菌/絕對病原菌　absolute pathogen
绝对不应期/絕對反拗期　absolute refractory period
绝对的/絕對的　absolute
绝对构型/絕對構型　absolute configuration
绝对骨导/絕對骨導　absolute bone conduction
绝对红细胞增多症/絕對紅血球增多症　absolute polycythemia
绝对零度/絕對零度　absolute zero
绝对期青光眼/絕對期青光眼　absolute glaucoma
绝对区/絕對區　absolute field
绝对生物利用度/絕對生體可用率　absolute bioavailability
绝对生长/絕對生長　absolute growth
绝对湿度/絕對濕度　absolute humidity
绝对视野/絕對視野　absolute visual field
绝对素食者/絕對素食者　vegan
绝对素食主义/絕對素食主義　veganism
绝对性白细胞增多/絕對性白血球增多　absolute leukocytosis
绝对远视/絕對遠視　absolute hypermetropia
绝对致死量/絕對致死劑量　absolute lethal dose

绝对致死浓度/絕對致死濃度 absolute lethal concentration
绝对浊叩响/絕對濁叩響 absolutely dull percussion resonance
绝汗/絕汗 sweating of dying
绝经/經絕,停經 menopause, change of life
绝经妇女骨质疏松症/絕經婦女骨質疏鬆症 postmenopausal osteoporosis
绝经妇女骨质疏松症·脾肾气虚证/絕經婦女骨質疏鬆症·脾腎氣虛證 postmenopausal osteoporosis with pattern of qi deficiency of spleen and kidney
绝经妇女骨质疏松症·肾精亏虚证/絕經婦女骨質疏鬆症·腎精虧虛證 postmenopausal osteoporosis with pattern of kidney essence insufficiency
绝经妇女骨质疏松症·阴虚内热证/絕經婦女骨質疏鬆症·陰虛內熱證 postmenopausal osteoporosis with pattern of internal heat due to yin deficiency
绝经妇女骨质疏松症·阴阳两虚证/絕經婦女骨質疏鬆症·陰陽兩虛證 postmenopausal osteoporosis with pattern of deficiency of both yin and yang
绝经后骨质疏松/絕經後骨質疏鬆 postmenopausal osteoporosis
绝经后期/絕經後期 postmenopause
绝经后萎缩/停經後萎縮 postmenopausal atrophy
绝经后综合征/停經症候群 postmenopause syndrome
绝经期/絕經期,斷經期 menopause
绝经期妇女/絕經期婦女 menopausal woman
绝经期关节炎/經絕期關節炎 menopausal arthritis
绝经期皮肤角化病/絕經期皮膚角化病,停經期角皮病 climacteric keratoderma
绝经期综合征/絕經期症候群 menopausal syndrome
绝经前后诸证/絕經前後諸證 menopausal disorders, perimenopausal disorders
绝经前后诸证·肾阳虚证/絕經前後諸證·腎陽虛證 perimenopausal disorders with pattern of kidney yang deficiency
绝经前后诸证·肾阴虚证/絕經前後諸證·腎陰虛證 perimenopausal disorders with pattern of kidney yin deficiency
绝经前后诸证·肾阴阳两虚证/絕經前後諸證·腎陰陽兩虛證 perimenopausal disorders with pattern of deficiency of both kidney yin and kidney yang
绝经前后诸证·心脾两虚证/絕經前後諸證·心脾兩虛證 perimenopausal disorders with pattern of heart-spleen deficiency
绝经前后诸证·心肾不交证 perimenopausal disorders with pattern of incoordination between heart and kidney
绝经前期/絕經前期 premenopause
绝缘体/絕緣體 insulator
绝缘子组件/絕緣子元件 insulator elements
掘壕掩埋法/掘壕掩埋法 trenching
掘穴/掘穴 burrowing
厥气/厥氣 adverse flow of qi
厥热胜复/厥熱勝複 alternate cold and heat
厥心痛/厥心痛 precordial pain with cold limbs, true heart pain with cold limbs
厥阴病证/厥陰病證 Jueyin disease, Jueyin pattern
厥阴寒厥证/厥陰寒厥證 cold syncope pattern of Jueyin
厥阴寒利/厥陰寒利 Jueyin disease with cold diarrhea
厥阴寒证/厥陰寒證 Jueyin disease with cold pattern
厥阴蛔厥证/厥陰蛔厥證 pattern of syncope due to ascariasis of Jueyin
厥阴热厥证/厥陰熱厥證 heat syncope pattern of Jueyin
厥阴热利/厥陰熱利 Jueyin disease with heat diarrhea
厥阴热证/厥陰熱證 Jueyin disease with heat pattern
厥阴伤寒/厥陰傷寒 Jueyin disease with cold damage
厥阴俞/厥陰俞 jueyinshu, BL14
厥阴头痛/厥陰頭痛 Jueyin disease with headache
厥阴中风/厥陰中風 Jueyin disease with wind affection
厥证/厥證,暈厥 syncope
蕨类植物/蕨類植物 ferns
蕨样变/蕨變現象 ferning
军刀状胫/軍刀狀[小]脛 saber shin
军刀状胫骨/軍刀狀脛骨 saber tibia
军队卫生/軍隊衛生 military hygiene
军队医院/軍隊醫院 military hospital
军事护理/軍事護理 military nursing
军事精神病学/軍事精神病學 military psychiatry
军事心理学/軍事心理學 military psychology
军事牙科学/軍事牙科學 military dentistry
军事医学/戰爭醫學 war medicine
军团病/軍團病 legionnaires disease
军用毒气/軍用毒氣 war gas
均等分裂/均等分裂 homeokinesis
均等分裂期/均等分裂期 equational division phase

均等联体双胎/均等聯體雙胎　equal conjoined twins
均等卵裂/等裂　equal cleavage
均等兴奋性/均等興奮性　isobolism
均分[剂]量/均分劑量　divided dose
均衡膳食/均衡飲食　balanced diet
均衡状态/均衡狀態　state of equalisation
均黄卵/均黃卵　isolecithal ovum
均聚合物/同質聚合體,同聚物　homopolymer
均染区/均質染色區　homogeneously staining region
均相反应/均相反應　homogeneous reaction
均相液体药剂/均相液體製劑　homogeneous liquid preparation
均小骨盆/均小骨盆　generally contracted pelvis
均匀辐射/均勻輻射　homogeneous radiation
均匀系/均質系　homogeneous system
均质膜/均質膜　homogeneous membrane
均质性白斑/均質性白斑　homogeneous leukoplakia
均质性抗体/均質性抗體　homogeneous antibody
君火/君火　sovereign fire
君药/君藥　sovereign drug
君主之官/君主之官　heart as the monarch organ
菌斑控制/菌斑控制　plaque control
菌斑试验/菌斑試驗　plaque assay
菌斑显示剂/菌斑顯示劑　plaque disclosing agent
菌斑指数/菌斑指數　plaque index
菌根/菌根　mycorrhizae
菌核/菌絲塊,菌絲團　sclerotium
菌胶团/菌膠團　zoogloea
菌落原位杂交/菌落原位雜交　in situ colony hybridization
菌毛蛋白质类/菌毛蛋白質類　fimbriae proteins
菌苗/菌苗,細菌疫苗　bacterial vaccine
菌黏素/菌黏素　glischrin
菌黏素尿/黏素尿　glischruria
菌群改变/菌種改變　bacterial flora alternation
菌群失调性肠炎/菌群失調性腸炎　flora imbalance enteritis
菌丝/菌絲　hypha
菌丝生长阶段/菌絲成長期　vegetative stage
菌丝体/菌絲體　mycelium
菌体凝集素/菌體凝集素　somatic agglutinin
菌体浓度/細胞濃度　cell concentration
菌体生长控制/菌體生長控制　cell growth control
菌体肿胀/菌體膨大　volumination
菌团/菌團　cenobium
菌细胞/細菌細胞　bacterial cell
菌血性败血病/菌血症性敗血病　bacteremic septicemia
菌血症/細菌血症　bacteremia
菌样瘤/菌樣瘤　fungating tumor
菌种鉴别/菌種鑒別　strain identification
菌种选育/菌種改良　strain improvement
菌紫素/菌[體]紫質　bacteriopurpurin
皲裂/皸裂　chap, rhagades
皲裂疮/皸裂[瘡]　rhagades
皲裂状的/皸裂狀的　rhagadiform
峻泻药/峻下藥　drastic purgative

K

咖啡尿酸/咖啡尿酸　caffuric acid
咖啡尿质/尿啡质　coffeurin
咖啡牛奶斑/咖啡牛奶斑　cafe au lait macule
咖啡牛奶色[素]斑/咖啡牛奶點　cafe au lait spot
咖啡鞣酸/咖啡鞣酸　caffetannic acid
咖啡乳斑/咖啡乳斑　cafe-au-lait spot
咖啡酸类/咖啡酸類　caffeic acids
咖啡因/咖啡因　caffeine
卡巴多司/卡巴多司　carbadox
卡巴胂/卡巴胂,對尿素基苯胂酸　aminarsone
卡比多巴/卡比多巴　carbidopa
卡比马唑/卡比馬唑　carbimazole
卡波金/碳氧混合氣　carbogen
卡波醌/卡波醌　carbazilquinone
卡波罗孟/卡波羅孟　chromonar
卡波前列素/卡波前列素　carboprost
卡波西肉瘤/卡波西肉瘤　Kaposi sarcoma
卡波西水痘样疹/卡波西水痘樣疹　Kaposi varicelliform eruption
卡伯囊肿/Cowper 氏腺囊腫　Cowper cyst
卡伯特夹板/Cabot 氏夾板　Cabot splint
卡铂/卡鉑　Carboplatin
卡茨公式/卡茨氏公式　Katz formula
卡嗒音/滴答狀水泡音　clicking rale
卡嗒音气胸/滴答聲氣胸　clicking pneumothorax
卡-达溶液/Carrel-Dakin 二氏溶液　Carrel-Dakin solution
卡恩试验/坎恩氏試驗　Kahn test
卡尔鲍姆病/Kahlbaum 氏病　Kahlbaum disease
卡尔达尼韧带/Caldani 氏韌帶　Caldani ligament
卡尔卡索恩韧带/Carcassonne 韌帶　Carcassonne ligament
卡尔曼滤波法/卡爾曼濾波法　Kalman filtering method
卡尔曼增益/卡爾曼增益　Kalman gain
卡尔曼综合征/卡爾曼症候群　Kallman syndrome
卡[尔默特]氏锥虫/卡梅特氏錐蟲　Trypanosoma calmetii
卡尔庞捷环/卡爾龐捷環　Carpentier ring
卡尔-普赖斯试验/卡-普二氏試驗　Carr-Price test
卡方分布/卡方分布　chi-square distribution
卡方检验/卡方檢驗　chi-square test, χ^2 test
卡非西林/卡非西林　carfecillin
卡芬太尼/卡芬太尼　carfentanil
卡哈特切迹/卡哈特切跡　Carhart notch
卡痕率/卡痕率　BCG scar rate
卡红/胭脂紅,洋紅　carmine
卡红明矾染液/胭脂紅明礬染液　carmalum
卡红溶液/卡紅溶液　carmine solution
卡环/托環　clasp
卡环臂/卡環臂　arm of clasp
卡环固位/卡環固位　clasp retention
卡环体/卡環體　body of clasp
卡环托牙/托環假牙　clasp denture
卡介苗/卡介苗,卡梅特氏疫苗　BCG vaccine
卡介苗覆盖率/卡介苗覆蓋率　BCG coverage rate
卡介苗接种/卡介苗接種　BCG vaccination
卡介苗接种保护率/卡介苗接種保護率　protective rate of BCG vaccination
卡介苗接种率/卡介苗接種率　BCG vaccination rate
卡拉巴水肿/Calabar 水腫　Calabar edema
卡拉巴丝虫性肿块/Calabar 氏隆起　Calabar swelling
卡拉巴肿/Calabar 腫　Calabar swelling
卡拉米芬/卡拉米芬　caramiphen
卡拉爪/卡拉爪　kalagua
卡莱尔-达金疗法/卡-達二氏療法　Carrel-Dakin treatment
卡莱尔-达金液/卡-達二氏液　Carrel-Dakin fluid
卡雷尔饮食/卡瑞爾氏飲食　Karell diet
卡立普多/卡立普多　Carisoprodol
卡律蝎毒素/蠍毒素　Charybdotoxin
卡伦征/Cullen 氏徵象　Cullen sign
卡罗综合征/卡羅氏症候群　Karroo syndrome
卡洛疗法/卡洛氏療法　Calot treatment
卡马西平/卡馬西平　Carbamazepine
卡莫司汀/雙氯乙基亞硝脲　Carmustine
卡那霉素/卡那黴素　kanamycin
卡那霉素激酶/卡那黴素激酶　kanamycin kinase
卡那霉素抗药性/卡那黴素抗藥性　kanamycin resistance
卡纳万病/卡納萬病　Canavan disease

卡内韦尔托手夹/Kanavel 氏撑起夹板　Kanavel cock-up splint
卡诺夫斯基能力状态/卡諾夫斯基能力狀態　Karnofsky performance status
卡[皮斯特兰]氏疟原虫/鳥瘧蟲　Plasmodium capistrani
卡普德蓬综合征/遺傳性牙[本]質生長不全,卡普德龐特氏症候群　Capdepont syndrome
卡普格拉综合征/Capgras 症候群　Capgras syndrome
卡柔比星/卡柔比星　Carubicin
卡塞尔肌/Casser 氏肌　Casser muscle
卡赛病/卡賽病　kasai
卡氏肺囊虫/卡氏肺囊蟲　Pneumocystis carinii
卡氏棘阿米巴/卡氏棘阿米巴　Acanthamoeba castellanii
卡氏征/Carvallo 氏徵象　Carvallo sign
卡氏枝孢霉/卡氏枝孢黴　Cladosporium carrionii
卡斯凯米丁/古柯米定　cuscamidine
卡斯凯明/古柯明　cuscamine
卡斯太拉尼涂剂/Castellani 氏塗劑　Castellani paint
卡斯特细胞/Custer 氏細胞　Custer cell
卡他/多分泌性　catarrh
卡他性鼻炎/卡他性鼻炎　rhinitis catarrhalis
卡他性[的]/黏膜炎的　catarrhal
卡他性腹泻/多泌性腹瀉　catarrhal diarrhea
卡他性黄疸/多泌性黃疸　catarrhal jaundice
卡他性角膜溃疡/卡他性角膜潰瘍　catarrhal corneal ulcer
卡他性胃肠炎/卡他性胃腸炎　gastroenteritis catarrhalis
卡他性胃炎/卡他性胃炎　catarrhal gastritis
卡他性消化不良/卡他性消化不良　catarrhal dyspepsia
卡他性哮喘/多泌性氣喘　catarrhal asthma
卡他性咽炎/多泌性咽喉炎　catarrhal pharyngitis
卡他性炎/黏膜性炎症　catarrhal inflammation
卡塔格纳三联征/卡塔格納三聯徵　Kartagener triad
卡塔格纳综合征/卡塔格納症候群　Kartagener syndrome
卡套/卡套　ferrule
卡特鼻内夹/Carter 氏鼻內夾板　Carter intranasal splint
卡替卡因/卡替卡因　carticaine
卡替洛尔/卡替洛爾　carteolol
卡托普利/硫甲丙脯酸　captopril
卡瓦根/卡瓦根　kava
卡希谷病毒/克席山谷病毒　Cache Valley virus
卡溴脲/溴二甲基乙醯脲　carbromal
卡因/卡因　caine
卡扎尔金氯化汞溶液/Cajal 氏金氯化汞溶液　Cajal gold-sublimate solution
卡扎尔细胞/Cajal 氏細胞　Cajal cell
卡唑类/卡唑類　carbazoles
咔啉类/咔啉類　carbolines
咯脓/欬膿　pyoptysis
咯血[病]/咯血[病],欬血　hemoptysis
咯血·肝火犯肺证/咯血·肝火犯肺證　hemoptysis with pattern of liver fire invading lung
咯血·气虚血瘀证/咯血·氣虛血瘀證　hemoptysis with pattern of qi deficiency and blood stasis
咯血·痰热壅肺证/咯血·痰熱壅肺證　hemoptysis with pattern of phlegm-heat congesting lung
咯血·阴虚肺热证/咯血·陰虛肺熱證　hemoptysis with pattern of yin deficiency and lung heat
咯血·燥热伤肺证/咯血·燥熱傷肺證　hemoptysis with pattern of dryness-heat injuring lung
开瓣音/開瓣音　opening snap
开宝本草/開寶本草　Kaibao Bencao
开窗术/開窗手術　windowing
开大肌/開大肌　dilator, dilatator
开导式情感心理疗法/開導式情感心理療法　rational-emotive psychotherapy
开放部/開放部　patent part
开放点滴法/開放點滴法　open drop method
开放读码框架/開放讀碼框架　open reading frames
开放敷裹/開放敷料　air dressing
开放皮瓣/開放皮瓣　open skin flap
开放伤/開放傷　open injury
开放式麻醉/開放麻醉法　open anesthesia
开放试验/開放試驗　open trial
开放性鼻音/開放性鼻音　open rhinolalia
开放性创伤/開放性創傷　open wound
开放性骨折/開放性骨折　open fracture
开放性结核/開放性結核　open tuberculosis
开放性颅骨骨折/開放性顱骨骨折　open fracture of skull
开放性颅脑损伤/開放性顱腦損傷　open craniocerebral injury
开放性脑创伤清创术/開放性腦創傷清創術　debridement of open wound of brain
开放性气胸/開放性氣胸　open pneumothorax
开放性手术/開放手術　open operation
开放性脱位/肌肉裂開脫位　open dislocation
开放循环学说/開放循環學說　open circulation theory

开放引流[术]/開放洩液法　open drainage
开放装置/開放裝置　open system
开关基因/開關基因　switch gene
开合夹板/閉合夾板　flange splint
开𬌗/開式咬合　open bite
开𬌗畸形/開𬌗畸形　open bite deformity
开阖补泻/開闔補瀉　reinforcing and reducing method by keeping hole opened or closed
开环甾类化合物/開環甾類化合物　secosteroid
开睑器/開瞼器　eye speculum
开角型青光眼/開角型青光眼　openangle glaucoma
开孔绷带/開孔繃帶　fenestrated bandage
开孔敷布/窗狀壓布　fenestrated compress
开口期阵痛/分娩第一期之疼痛　dilating pain
开口印模/開口印模　open-mouth impression
开乐散/開樂散　dicofol
开链/開鏈　open chain
开裂/裂開　dehiscence
开颅器/頭顱切開器,破顱器　craniotome
开面冠/有窗金牙冠,被層牙冠　window crown
开窍法/開竅法　inducing resuscitation method, resuscitation inducing therapy
开窍剂/開竅劑　formula for resuscitation
开窍醒神/開竅醒神　inducing resuscitation
开胃剂/開胃藥,食慾促進藥　appetizer
开胃早餐/開胃早餐　breakfast appetite
开胸肺活检/開胸肺活檢　open lung biopsy
开胸顺气丸/開胸順氣丸　kaixiong shunqi pills
开胸探查术/開胸探查術　exploratory thoracotomy
开胸心脏按压/開胸心臟按壓　open chest cardiac massage
开业护理/開業護理　practical nursing
开业护士/開業護士　nurse practitioners
开业医师诊疗工作准则/開業醫師診療工作準則　practice guidelines
开业诊室护理/開業診室護理　office nursing
开音/開音　easing voice, sound producing
开之以其苦/開之以其苦　gentle persuasion to be broad-minded
揩齿/揩齒　wiping tooth
凯-布夹/Keller-Blake 二氏夾板　Keller-Blake splint
凯尔尼格征/凱爾尼格徵　Kernig sign
凯拉特增殖性红斑/Queyrat 氏增殖性紅斑　Queyrat erythroplasia
凯拉增生性红斑/克雷特氏紅斑瘤　erythroplasia of Queyrat
凯林/二甲氧基甲基呋喃黄素酮　Khellin
凯撒痛风病饮食/Caesar 氏痛風病飲食　Caesar diet
凯松病/潛水夫病,減壓病　Caisson disease
凯泽病/Kayser 氏病　Kayser disease
凯泽-弗莱舍环/卡-弗二氏環　Kayser-Fleischer ring
凯泽林溶液/Kaiserling 氏溶液　Kaiserling solution
铠甲癌/鎧甲狀癌　jacket cancer
龛影/壁龕徵象　niche sign
堪萨斯/堪薩斯　Kansas
堪萨斯分枝杆菌/堪薩斯分枝桿菌　Mycobacterium kansasii
堪萨斯分枝杆菌纯蛋白衍生物/堪薩斯分枝桿菌純蛋白衍生物　PPD of Mycobacterium kansasii
堪萨斯分枝杆菌肺病/堪薩斯分枝桿菌肺病　pulmonary disease due to Mycobacterium kansasii
堪萨斯杆菌素/康沙辛　kansasiin
坎苯达唑/坎苯達唑　cambendazole
坎离砂/坎離砂　kanlisha, kanlisha coarse sand granules
坎利酸钾/坎利酸鉀　canrenoate potassium
坎利酮/坎利酮　canrenone
坎那丁/金印草黃素　xanthpuccine
坎宁安蚀斑技术/坎甯安蝕斑技術　Cunningham plaque technique
坎珀尔韧带/Camper 氏韌帶　Camper ligament
坎氏酵母/坎特里埃氏酵母菌　Saccharomyces cantliei
坎塔尼饮食/Cantani 飲食　Cantani diet
坎特尔管/卡達氏管　Cantor tube
坎图综合征/Cantu 氏症候群　Cantu syndrome
砍伤/砍傷　chopped wound
莰烯/莰烯　camphene
康迪液/Condy 氏液　Condy fluid
康复/復健,機能回復　rehabilitation
康复方案/康復方案　rehabilitation scheme
康复工程/康復工程　rehabilitation engineering
康复护理/康復護理　rehabilitation nursing
康复评定/康復評定　rehabilitation evaluation
康复评估/康復評估　rehabilitation assessment
康复心理学/康復心理學　rehabilitation psychology
康复医学/康復醫學　rehabilitation medicine
康复医院/康復醫院　convalescent hospital
康复中心/康復中心　rehabilitation center
康复咨询/康復諮詢　rehabilitation counselling
康纳-艾伦单位/康-艾二氏單位　Corner-Allen unit
康纳-艾伦试验/康-艾二氏試驗　Corner-Allen test
康纳塞子/Corner 氏塞子　Corner tampon
康奈尔医学指数/康乃爾醫學指數　Cornell medical index
康南德心脏导管/Cournand 氏心導管　Cournand

cardiac catheter
康宁麻醉/Corning 氏麻醉　Corning anesthesia
康普顿效应/卡帕登氏效應　Compton effect
康氏立克次体/康氏立克次體　Rickettsia conorii
康斯尔曼细胞/Councilman 氏細胞　Councilman cell
糠秕孢子菌毛囊炎/皮屑芽孢菌毛囊炎
　　pityrosporum folliculitis
糠秕性脱发/糠秕性禿髮　alopecia pityroides capillitii
糠敷料/糠敷料　bavarian dressing
糠醛/糠醛　furaldehyde
糠样脱屑/糠樣脱屑　furfuraceous desquamation
糠浴/糠浴　bran bath
糠疹/糠疹,蛇皮癣　pityriasis
糠状的/糠狀的　branny, furfuraceous
糠状皮肤真菌病/皮屑皮膚黴菌病　dermatomycosis
　　furfuracea
糠状秃发/糠狀禿髮　alopecia furfuracea
亢害承制/亢害承制　restraining excessiveness to
　　acquire harmony
抗阿米巴药/抗阿米巴藥　anti-amebic
抗癌药/抗癌劑　anticarcinogen
抗艾滋病药/抗艾滋病藥　anti-acquired
　　immunodeficiency syndrome drug, anti-AIDS drug
抗巴豆毒素/抗巴豆毒素　anticrotin
抗白蛋白/抗蛋白素　antialbumin
抗白发维生素/抗白髮維生素　anticanitic vitamin
抗白喉球蛋白/抗白喉球蛋白　antidiphtheritic
　　globulin
抗百日咳血清/抗百日欬血清　antipertussis serum
抗蓖麻毒蛋白/抗蓖麻毒素　antiricin
抗扁蠕虫药/抗扁蠕蟲藥　antiplatyhelmintic agents
抗变态反应药/抗變態反應藥,抗過敏反應藥　anti-
　　allergic drug
抗变性 DNA 抗体/抗變性 DNA 抗體　anti-
　　denatured DNA antibody
抗病毒免疫/抗病毒免疫力　antiviral immunity
抗病毒模型/抗病毒模式　antiviral model
抗病毒药/抗病毒藥　antiviral drug
抗病原物质/殺病原藥　antipathogen
抗补体/抗補體　anticomplement
抗补体试验/抗補體試驗　anticomplement test
抗补体血清/抗補體血清　anticomplementary serum
抗不育维生素/抗不孕症維生素　antisterility vitamin
抗糙皮病维生素/抗糙皮症維生素　antipellagra
　　vitamin
抗蟾蜍溶血素/蟾蜍毒抗毒素　antiphrynolysin
抗[肠胃]气胀药/抗氣脹藥　antiflatulent
抗超重飞行衣/重力服　gravity suits

抗沉淀素/抗沈澱素　antiprecipitin
抗充血性心功能不全药/抗充血性心衰竭
　　anticongestive-heart-failure drug
抗出血维生素/抗出血維生素　antihemorrhagic
　　vitamin
抗出血药/抗出血藥　antihemorrhagic
抗雌激素类/抗雌激素　anti-estrogens
抗刺槐毒素/刺槐毒素抗毒素　antirobin
抗刺激剂/抗刺激藥　counterirritant
抗促性腺激素类/抗促性腺激素　antigonadotrophins
抗痤疮药/抗痤瘡藥　anti-acne drug
抗代谢[产]物/競争性對抗劑　competitive
　　antagonist
抗代谢物/抗代謝産物　metabolic antagonist,
　　antimetabolite
抗代谢药/抗代謝藥　antimetabolite
抗单链 DNA 抗体/抗單鏈 DNA 抗體　anti-ssDNA
　　antibody
抗胆固醇血药/抗膽固醇血症藥　anticholesteremic
抗胆碱能药/抗膽素能藥　anticholinergic
抗胆碱能药综合征/抗副交感神經症候群
　　anticholinergic syndrome
抗胆碱药/抗膽鹼藥　anticholinergic
抗胆碱酯酶/抗膽鹼酯酶　anticholinesterase
抗胆碱酯酶药/抗膽鹼酯酶藥　anticholinesterase
　　drug
抗胆结石药/抗膽結石藥　anticholelithogenic
抗蛋白酶/抗蛋白酵素　antiprotease
抗低血压药/抗低血壓藥　antihypotensive
抗滴虫药/抗滴蟲藥　antitrichomonal drug
抗癫痫药/抗癲癇藥,鎮癲癇劑　antiepileptic
抗淀粉酶/抗澱粉酵素　antiamylase
抗淀粉[水解]酶/抗澱粉水解酵素,抗澱粉酶
　　antidiastase
抗动脉粥样硬化药/抗動脈粥樣硬化藥
　　antiatherosclerotic
抗冻蛋白/抗凍蛋白　antifreeze protein
抗毒剂/抗毒劑,解毒性毒物　counterpoison
抗毒素/抗毒素　antitoxin
抗毒素单位/抗毒素單位　antitoxic unit
抗毒素类/抗毒素類　antitoxins
抗毒素免疫/抗毒免疫性,毒素免疫性　antitoxic
　　immunity
抗毒素球蛋白/抗毒素性球蛋白　antitoxic globulin
抗毒素原/抗毒素原　antitoxigen
抗毒蕈碱药/抗蕈鹼藥　antimuscarinic drug
抗独特型抗体/抗獨特型抗體　antiidiotype antibody
抗多种药物性结核/抗多種藥物性結核　multidrug-

resistant tuberculosis
抗恶病质药/治惡病質藥 anticachectic
抗恶性细胞增生的/抗增生的 antiproliferative
抗[防]卫力毁灭/抗防衛反應 anticataphylaxis
抗[防]卫力毁灭剂/抗防衛反應劑 anticataphylactic
抗非组蛋白抗体/抗非組蛋白抗體 anti-nonhistone antibody
抗肥胖药/抗肥胖藥 antiadipositas drug
抗肺炎球菌血清/抗肺炎球菌血清 antipneumococcus serum
抗分泌药/抗分泌藥 antisecretory drug
抗分生霉素/抗分生黴素劑 antimeristem
抗分支杆菌药/抗分支桿菌藥 antimycobacterial drug
抗风湿药/抗風濕藥 antirheumatic agent
抗辐射性/抗輻射性 radioresistance
抗辐射药/抗輻射藥 antiradiation drug
抗腐蚀剂/抗腐蝕劑 anticorrosin
抗副交感神经药/抗副交感神經藥 parasympatholytic
抗干癣剂/抗乾癬劑 antipsoriatic
抗干眼病维生素/抗乾眼維生素 antixerophthalmic vitamin
抗肝血清/抗肝血清 antihepatic serum
抗肝炎药/抗肝炎藥 antihepatitis drug
抗感染维生素/抗感染維生素 anti-infection vitamin
抗感染药/抗感染藥 anti-infective, anti-infective agent
抗高苯丙氨酸药/抗高苯丙氨酸藥 antihyperphenylalaninemic
抗高胆固醇血药/抗血膽固醇過多劑 antihypercholesterolemic
抗高胆固醇药/抗高膽固醇藥 antihypercholesterolemic
抗高血氨药/抗高血氨藥 antihyperammonemic
抗高血糖药/抗高血糖藥,抗血糖過高藥 antihyperglycemic
抗高血压剂/降血壓劑 antihypertensive agent
抗高血压药/抗高血壓藥 antihypertensive, antihypertensive agents
抗高血脂药/抗高血脂藥 antihyperlipidemic, antilipemic
抗高脂蛋白药/抗高脂蛋白藥 antihyperlipoproteinemic
抗攻击素/抗攻擊素 antiaggressin
抗佝偻病维生素/抗佝僂病維生素 antirachitic vitamin
抗骨增生丸/抗骨增生丸 kanggu zengsheng pills

抗骨质疏松药/抗骨質疏鬆藥 anti-osteoporotic
抗关节炎药/抗關節炎藥 anti-arthritic
抗过敏素/抗過敏素 antianaphylactin
抗过敏[性]/抗過敏性 ananaphylaxis
抗核抗体/抗核抗體 antinuclear antibody
抗核抗体免疫荧光试验/抗核抗體免疫螢光試驗 antinuclear antibody immunofluorescent test
抗核抗体试验/抗核抗體試驗 antinuclear antibody test
抗核仁抗体/抗核仁抗體 anti-nucleolar antibody
抗核因子试验/抗核因數試驗 ANT test
抗黑热病药/抗黑熱病藥 anti-kala-azar drug
抗红细胞增生药/抗紅血球增生藥 antipolycythemic
抗坏血病维生素/抗壞血病維生素 antiscorbutic vitamin
抗坏血病药/壞血病治劑 antiscorbutic
抗坏血酸/抗壞血酸 ascorbic acid
抗坏血酸钠/抗壞血酸鈉 sodium ascorbate
抗坏血酸尿/抗壞血酸尿 ascorburia
抗坏血酸缺乏/抗壞血酸缺乏 ascorbic acid deficiency
抗坏血酸血/抗壞血酸血症 ascorbemia
抗坏血酸盐/抗壞血酸鹽 ascorbate
抗坏血酸氧化酶/抗壞血酸氧化酶 ascorbate oxidase
抗坏血酸硬脂酸酯/硬酯酸抗壞血酯 ascorbyl stearate
抗坏血酸棕榈酸盐/四異棕櫚酸抗壞血酯 ascorbyl tetraisopalmitate
抗坏血酸棕榈酸酯/抗壞血酸棕櫚酸酯 ascorbyl palmitate
抗环酸/抗環酸 anticyclic acid
抗霍乱菌素/抗霍亂菌素 anticholerin
抗霍乱血清/抗霍亂血清 anticholera serum
抗肌内膜抗体/抗肌内膜抗體 anti-endomystral antibody
抗基弯曲/抗基彎曲 anchor bend
抗激素/抗激素 antihormone
抗寄生虫免疫/抗寄生蟲免疫 antiparasitic immunity
抗寄生虫模型/抗寄生蟲模式 antiparasitic model
抗寄生虫药/抗寄生蟲藥 antiparasitic agent
抗甲氧西林金黄色葡萄球菌/二甲氧苯青黴素金色葡萄球菌,二甲氧苯西林的金黄色葡萄球菌 methicillin resistant staphylococcus aureus, MRSA
抗甲状腺球蛋白抗体/抗甲狀腺球蛋白抗體 antithyroglobulin antibody
抗甲状腺药/抗甲狀腺藥 antithyroid agent

抗剪切强度/抗剪切強度　shear strength
抗箭毒药/抗箭毒劑　anticurare
抗交感神经药/抗交感神經藥　sympatholytic
抗胶原酶/抗膠原酶質,抗膠原酶素　anticollagenase
抗焦虑药/抗焦慮藥　anxiolytic, anti-anxiety agent
抗焦虑镇静药/抗焦慮鎮靜藥　anxiolytic sedative
抗角质化剂/抗角質化劑　antikeratinizing agent
抗脚气病维生素/硫胺　antiberiberic vitamin
抗结核菌素/抗結核菌素　antituberculin
抗结核抗生素类/抗結核抗生素類　antitubercular antibiotics
抗结核血清/抗結核病血清　antitubercle serum
抗结核药/抗結核藥　antituberculotic
抗结剂/抗結塊劑　anticaking agent
抗解毒药/抗解毒劑　antiantidote
抗疥药/抗疥藥　antiscabietic
抗惊厥药/抗驚厥藥,抗痙攣藥　anticonvulsant
抗惊厥药肾病/抗驚厥藥腎病　anticonvulsants nephropathy
抗惊药/抗痙攣劑　anticonvulsant
抗精神病药/抗精神病藥,精神抑制藥　antipsychotic agent
抗精神分裂症药/抗精神分裂症藥　antischizophrinic
抗精子毒素/抗精子毒素　antispermotoxin
抗精子发生药/抗精子發生藥　antispermatogenic agent
抗静脉曲张药/抗靜脈曲張藥　antivaricose drug
抗局部缺血药/抗局部缺血藥　antiischemic
抗具窍蝮蛇血清/抗具竅蝮蛇毒血清　antibothropic serum
抗菌的/抗細菌的　antibacterial
抗菌防腐药/抗菌防腐藥　antiseptic
抗菌活性/抗菌活性　antibacterial activity
抗菌剂/抗菌劑　antibacterial agent
抗菌免疫/细菌免疫性,抗菌免疫性　antibacterial immunity
抗菌模型/抗菌模式　antimicrobial model
抗菌谱/抗菌譜　antimicrobial spectrum
抗菌酸剂/抗菌酸劑　aseptic acid
抗菌型/抗菌型　antimicrobial form
抗菌性药皂/抗菌性皂　antibacterial soap
抗菌药/抗菌藥　antibacterial agent
抗抗毒素/抗抗毒素　antiantitoxin
抗抗体/抗抗體　antiantibody
抗 DNA 抗体/抗 DNA 抗體　anti-DNA antibody
抗狂犬病毒质/抗狂犬病毒質　antivirulin
抗狂犬病血清/抗狂犬病血清　rabies antiserum
抗溃疡病药/抗潰瘍病藥　anti-ulcer agent

抗酪氨酸酶/酪氨酸酶抗酶　antityrosinase
抗酪蛋白血清/酪蛋白血清　caseoserum
抗类风湿药/抗類風濕藥　antirheumatoid drug
抗类脂[物质]/抗類脂質　antilipoid
抗力/抗力　resistance force
抗力桥基/抗力支樘　resistance abutment
抗力形/抗力形　resistance form
抗立克次体药/抗立克次體藥　antirickettsial
抗利尿激素/抗利尿激素,血管加壓素　antidiuretic hormone
抗利尿激素分泌过多综合征/抗利尿激素分泌不當症候群　syndrome of inappropriate antidiuretic hormone
抗利尿激素分泌失调综合征/抗利尿激素分泌失調症候群　syndrome of inappropriate ADH secretion
抗利尿药/抗利尿藥　antidiuretic
抗利什曼虫药/抗利什曼氏原蟲藥　antileishmanial
抗痢疾药/抗痢疾藥,止痢藥　antidysenteric
抗痢剂/抗慢性瀉痢劑　antidysentericum
抗镰状细胞贫血药/抗鐮狀細胞貧血藥　antisickling agent
抗链[球菌]激酶/鏈球菌激酶抑制物　antistreptokinase
抗链球菌溶血素/鏈球菌毒素抑制劑　antistreptolysin
抗链球菌溶血素 O/O 型抗鏈球菌分解素　antistreptolysin O
抗链球菌溶血素效价/抗鏈球菌溶血素效價　ASO titer
抗链球菌血清/抗鏈球菌血清　antistreptococcus serum
抗淋巴细胞球蛋白/抗淋巴球球蛋白　antilymphocyte globulin
抗淋巴细胞血清/抗淋巴球血清　antilymphocyte serum
抗磷脂抗体/抗磷脂抗體　antiphospholipid antibody
抗磷脂综合征/抗磷脂質症候群　antiphospholipid syndrome
抗卵蛋白血清/抗卵蛋白性血清,卵白蛋白抗血清　ovoserum
抗密螺旋体抗体/抗螺旋體抗體　antitreponemal antibody
抗麻痹性痴呆剂/治輕癱劑　contraparetic
抗麻痹药/抗麻痹藥　antiparalytic
抗麻风[病]药/抗麻風藥,抗麻風劑　antileprosy drug, antileprotic
抗毛滴虫药/殺滴蟲劑　antitrichomonal
抗梅毒血清/抗梅毒血清　syphitoxin

抗梅毒药/抗梅毒藥,抗梅毒劑　antisyphilitic, antiluetic
抗酶/抗酶　antienzyme
抗霉菌剂/抗黴菌劑　antimycotics
抗霉素 A/抗黴素 A　antimycin A
抗密螺旋体药/抗密螺旋體藥　antitreponemal agent
抗眠药/防止睡眠藥　antihypnotic
抗免疫物质/抗免疫體　anti-immune substance
抗脑膜炎球菌血清/抗腦膜炎球菌血清　antimeningococcus serum
抗内毒素/内毒素抗體　antiendotoxin
抗逆转录病毒药/抗逆轉錄病毒藥　anti-retroviral agent
抗尿激酶/抗尿激酶　antiurokinase
抗尿结石药/抗尿路結石藥　anti-urolithic
抗凝枸橼酸葡萄糖溶液/抗凝血酸檸檬酸葡萄糖溶液　anticoagulant acid citrate dextrose solution
抗凝集素/抗凝[集]素　antiagglutinin
抗 Rh 凝集素/抗恆河猴凝素,抗 Rh 凝素　anti-Rh agglutinin
抗凝剂拮抗剂/抗凝劑拮抗劑　anticoagulant antagonist
抗凝乳酶/抗凝酪酵素　antichymosin
抗凝[血]剂/制凝藥,阻凝藥　anticoagulant
抗凝[血]疗法/抗凝血治療,抑制凝血療法　anticoagulant therapy
抗凝血酶/抗凝血酵素　antithrombin
抗凝血酶Ⅲ/抗凝血酶Ⅲ　antithrombin Ⅲ
抗凝血酶Ⅲ缺乏/抗凝血酶Ⅲ缺乏　antithrombin Ⅲ deficiency
抗凝血酶原/抗凝血酶原　antiprothrombin
抗凝血素/抗凝固酵素　anticoagulin
抗凝血药/抗凝血藥　anticoagulant
抗凝药/抗凝藥　anticoagulant
抗疟[疾]药/抗瘧疾藥　antimalarial drug
抗排斥治疗/抗排斥治療　antirejection therapy
抗配子体/抵抗配子細胞　antigametocyte
抗皮脂溢药/抗皮脂溢藥　antiseborrheic
抗疲倦毒素/抗疲勞毒素物,疲勞毒抑制素　antikenotoxin
抗偏头痛药/抗偏頭痛藥　antimigraine
抗贫血物质/抗貧血成分　hematinic principle
抗贫血药/抗貧血藥　anti-anemic
抗破伤风溶血[毒]素/抗破傷風溶血素　antitetanolysin
抗葡萄球菌[溶血]素/抗葡萄球菌溶血素　antistaphylohemolysin
抗葡萄球菌血清/抗葡萄球菌血清　antistaphylococcus serum
抗前列腺素/抗前列腺素　antiprostaglandin
抗侵袭素/抗侵襲素　anti-invasin
抗亲脂性/抗親脂　antilipotropism
抗球虫药/抗球蟲藥　anticoccidial drug
抗球蛋白/抗球蛋白素　antiglobulin
抗球蛋白反应/抗球蛋白反應　antiglobulin reaction
抗球蛋白试验/抗球蛋白試驗　antiglobulin test
抗球蛋白消耗试验/抗球蛋白消耗試驗　antiglobulin consumption test
抗醛缩酶/酵己糖酶抗酶　antizymohexase
抗溶素/抗溶素　antilysin
抗溶素作用/抗溶素作用　antilysis
抗溶细胞素/抗溶細胞素　anticytolysin
抗溶血素/抗溶血素,抗溶紅血球素　antihemolysin
抗肉瘤血清/抗肉瘤血清　antisarcomatous serum
抗蠕虫药/抗蠕蟲藥　anthelmintics
抗蠕霉素/抗蠕蟲黴素　anthelmycin
抗乳糖酶/抗乳糖酵素　antilactase
抗乳血清/抗乳血清　antilactoserum
抗伤寒血清/抗傷寒血清　antityphoid serum
抗蛇毒素/抗蛇毒素　antivenin
抗蛇毒素类/抗蛇毒素類　antivenins
抗蛇毒血清/抗蛇毒血清　antivenomous serum, snake antivenin
抗蛇毒疫苗/蝮蛇素疫苗　echidnovaccine
抗砷素/抗砷素,抗砒素　antiarsenin
抗神经毒素/抗神經毒素　antineurotoxin
抗神经炎维生素/抗神經炎維生素　antineuritic vitamin
抗α-肾上腺素能药/抗α-腎上腺素能藥　alphalytic
抗肾上腺素药/抗腎上腺素藥　antiadrenergic
抗肾小球基膜疾病/抗腎小球基膜疾病　anti-glomerular basement membrane disease
抗肾小球基膜型肾小球肾炎/抗腎小球基膜型腎小球腎炎　antiglomerular basement membrane glomerulonephritis
抗生蛋白链菌素/抗生蛋白鏈菌素　streptavidin
抗生素/抗生素　antibiotic
抗生素后效应/抗生素後效應　post antibiotic effect
抗生素性接触性皮炎/抗生素接觸性皮膚炎　antibiotic contact dermatitis
抗生素预防/抗生素預防　antibiotic prophylaxis
抗生酮/减酮劑,減酮質　antiketogen
抗生酮膳食/抗生酮飲食　antiketogenic diet
抗生酮质/抗生酮質　antiketogenic substance
抗生酮作用/減除酮體作用　antiketogenesis
抗生物素/抗生物素　antibiotin

抗生物素蛋白/抗生物素蛋白,卵白素　avidin
抗生物素蛋白-生物素-过氧化物酶复合物法/抗生物素蛋白-生物素-過氧化酶複合物法　ABC method, avidin-biotin-peroxidase complex method
抗生作用/抗生[现象]　antibiosis
抗失重措施/抗失重措施　weightlessness countermeasure
抗湿疹药/抗濕疹藥　antieczematic
抗嗜眠药/阻止睡眠藥　antilethargic
抗噬菌体变株/抗噬菌病毒體變株　antiphage mutant
抗受精素/抗受精素　anti-fertilizin
抗鼠疫血清/抗鼠疫血清　antiplague serum
抗双股DNA抗体试验/抗雙股DNA抗體試驗　anti-double-stranded DNA antibody test
抗双链DNA抗体/抗雙鏈DNA抗體　anti-dsDNA antibody
抗丝虫药/抗絲蟲藥　antifilarial drug
抗酸剂/抗酸劑　antacid
抗酸染色法/抗酸染色法　acid-fast staining method
抗酸药/制酸藥　antacid
抗糖尿病发生药/防止糖尿病發生藥　antidiabetogenic
抗糖尿病药/抗糖尿病藥,治糖尿病藥　antidiabetic
抗糖尿膳食/抗糖尿飲食　antidiabetic diet
抗绦虫药/抗條蟲藥　antitapeworm drug
抗体/抗體　antibody
抗体半衰期/抗體半衰期　antibody half life
抗体多样性/抗體多樣性　antibody diversity
抗体过剩/抗體過剩　antibody excess
抗体结合部位/抗體結合部位　antibody binding site
抗体亲和力/抗體親和力　antibody affinity
抗体轻链/抗體輕鏈　light chain of antibody
抗体生成/抗體形成　antibody formation
抗体生成细胞/抗體生成細胞　antibody-producing cell
抗体特异性/抗體特異性　antibody specificity
抗体吸收试验/抗體吸收試驗　antibody absorption test
抗体一元论/抗體一元學說　unitarian hypothesis
抗体依赖细胞细胞毒性/抗體依賴細胞細胞毒性　antibody-dependent cell cytotoxicity
抗体依赖性促进作用/抗體依賴性促進作用　antibody-dependent enhancement
抗体异质性/抗體異質性　antibody heterogeneity
抗体重链/抗體重鏈　heavy chain of antibody
抗调理素/抗調理素　antiopsonin
抗同效维生素/抗擬維生素,抗擬維他命　antivitamer
抗同种溶素/抗同屬溶素　anti-isolysin
抗铜绿假单胞菌高免疫球蛋白/抗銅綠假單胞菌高免疫球蛋白　antipseudomonas aeruginosa hyperimmune globulin
抗痛风药/抗痛風藥　gout suppressants
抗吞噬素/抗吞噬素,抗噬菌素　antiphagin
抗吞噬血清/抗噬細胞血清　antiphagocytic serum
抗微管蛋白剂/抗微管蛋白劑　antitubulin agent
抗微生物的/抗微生物的　antimicrobial
抗微生物阳离子肽类/抗微生物陽離子肽類　antimicrobial cationic peptides
抗微生物药/抗微生物藥　antimicrobial drug
抗维生素/抗維生素,抗維他命　antivitamin
抗维生素D佝偻病/抗維生素D佝僂病　vitamin D resistant rickets
抗[胃肠]气胀药/抗[胃腸]脹氣藥　antiflatulent
抗胃蛋白酶/抗胃蛋白酶,抗胃液素　antipepsin
抗细胞毒素/抗細胞毒素　anticytotoxin
抗细胞间质抗体/抗細胞間質抗體　anti-intercellular substance antibody
抗纤维蛋白/抗纖維蛋白　antifibrin
抗纤维蛋白溶解药/抗纖維蛋白溶解藥　antifibrinolytic agent
抗纤维蛋白溶酶/胞漿素抑制素　antiplasmin
抗线虫药/抗線蟲藥　antinematodal agent
抗线粒体抗体试验/抗線粒體抗體試驗　antimitochondrial antibody test
抗哮喘药/抗哮喘藥　anti-asthmatic agent
抗心动过缓药/抗心搏過緩藥　antibradycardiac drug
抗心动过速起搏器/抗心動過速起搏器　antitachycardia pacemaker
抗心绞痛药/抗心絞痛藥　anti-anginal drug
抗心磷脂综合征/抗牛心脂素症候群　anticardiolipin syndrome
抗心律不齐剂/抗心律不整劑　antiarrhythmics
抗心律失常药/抗心律失常藥,抗心律不整藥　anti-arrhythmic, anti-arrhythmia agent
抗[心脏]纤维性颤动药/心臟纖維性顫動抑制劑　antifibrillatory
抗心脂抗体/抗心脂抗體　anticardiolipin antibody
抗兴奋药/抗刺激劑　contrastimulus
抗性质粒/阻抗性質體　resistance plasmid
抗胸腺细胞球蛋白/抗胸腺細胞球蛋白　antithymocyte globulin
抗胸腺细胞血清/抗胸腺細胞血清　antithymocyte serum
抗雄激素类/抗雄激素類　anti-androgens

抗雄激素[物质]/抗雄性激素　antiandrogen
抗休克裤/抗休克褲　military antishock trousers
抗休克药/抗休克藥　antishock drug
抗眩测量器/炫目測定計　glarometer
抗眩晕药/抗眩暈藥　antivertigo drug
抗血凝素/抗血球凝集素　antihemagglutinin
抗血清/抗血清　antisera
抗血清过敏反应/抗血清過敏性　antiserum anaphylaxis
抗血栓药/抗血栓藥　antithrombotic
抗血栓治疗/抗凝血療法　antithrombotic therapy
抗血吸虫药/抗血吸蟲藥　antischistosomal drug
抗血小板的/抗血小板的　antiplatelet
抗血小板剂/抗血小板劑　antiplatelet agent
抗血小板聚集药/抗血小板凝集藥　platelet aggregation inhibitor
抗血小板血清/抗血小板血清　antiplatelet serum
抗血友病球蛋白/抗血友病球蛋白　antihemophilic globulin
抗血友病性人类血浆/抗血友病性人類血漿　antihemophilic human plasma
抗血友病药/抗血友病藥,抗血友病劑　antihemophilic
抗血酯药/抗血脂藥　antilipemic
抗压强度/抗壓強度　compressive strength
抗炎药/抗發炎藥　antiinflammatory drug
抗氧化剂/抗氧化劑　antioxidant
抗氧化酶/抗氧化酶素　antioxidase
抗药性/抗藥性　resistance, drug resistance
抗药性质粒/抗藥性質粒　R plasmid
抗胰蛋白酶/抗胰蛋白酵素　antitrypsin
抗胰蛋白酶试验/抗胰蛋白酵素試驗　antitrypsin test
抗胰蛋白酶指数/抗蛋白分解指數　antitryptic index
抗胰岛素/抗胰島素　anti-insulin
抗胰血清/抗胰血清　antipancreatic serum
抗胰[脂]酶/抗胰脂酵素　antisteapsin
抗乙二醛酶/抗乙醛酵素　antiglyoxalase
抗异物功能/異物反應功能　antixenic function
抗异种溶素/抗異溶素　antiheterolysin
抗抑郁药/抗抑鬱藥　antidepressant
抗癔病药/癔病藥　anthysteric
抗银屑病药/抗銀屑病藥,抗牛皮癬藥　antipsoriatic
抗疣疗法/抗疣療法　antiwart therapy
抗有丝分裂的/抗有絲分裂的　antimitotic
抗[有丝]裂剂/抗有絲分裂劑　antimitotic agent
抗诱变药/抗誘變藥　antimutagenic agent
抗原/抗原　antigen

抗原变异/抗原變異　antigenic variation
抗原呈递/抗原呈現　antigen presentation
抗原呈递细胞/抗原呈遞細胞　antigen presenting cell
抗原虫药/抗原蟲藥　antiprotozoal drug
抗原单位/抗原單位　antigen unit
抗原过剩/抗原過剩　antigen excess
抗原加工/抗原加工　antigen processing
抗原结构/抗原構造　antigenic structure
抗原竞争/抗原競爭　antigenic competition
抗原决定簇/抗原決定簇　antigenic determinant
抗原-抗体反应/抗原-抗體反應　antigen-antibody reaction
抗原抗体复合物/抗原抗體複合物　antigen-antibody complex
抗原扩散常数/抗原擴散常數　antigen diffusion constant
抗原疗法/抗原療法　antigen treatment
抗原缺失/抗原缺失　antigenic deletion
抗原生动物剂/殺原蟲劑,制原蟲劑　antiprotozoal
抗原识别/抗原識別　antigen recognition
抗原受体/抗原受體　antigen receptor
抗原调整/抗原調節　antigenic modulation
[抗原]限制位/抗原識別位　agretope
抗原性/抗原力　antigenicity
抗原性逆转/抗原逆轉　antigenic reversion
抗原血症/抗原血　antigenemia
抗原转换/抗原轉換　antigenic diversion
抗运动障碍药/抗運動障礙藥　anti-dyskinesia agent
抗躁狂药/抗躁狂[症]藥　antimanic agent
抗真菌抗生素类/抗真菌抗生素類　antifungal antibiotics
抗真菌药/抗真菌藥　antifungal drug
抗真菌制剂/抗真菌製劑　antifungal preparation
抗震颤麻痹药/抗震顫麻痺藥,抗帕金森氏症藥　antiparkinsonian drug
抗症状疗法/對症療法　heterotherapy
抗脂肪肝药/抗脂肪肝藥　lipotropic drug
抗脂肪酶/抗脂肪酵素　antilipase
抗脂溢药/抗脂溢藥　antiseborrhoic
抗酯酶/抗解酯酶劑　antiesterase
抗致癌药/抗致癌藥　anticarcinogenic agent
抗致敏物质/抗介體　antisensitizer
抗致敏药/抗致敏藥　antisensitizer
抗中心粒抗体/抗中心粒抗體　anticentriole antibody
抗中性白细胞胞质抗体/抗中性白細胞胞質抗體　antineutrophil cytoplasmic antibody
抗中性白细胞减少药/抗中性白細胞減少藥

antineutropenic
抗肿瘤活性/抗腫瘤活性　anti-tumor activity
抗肿瘤抗代谢药/抗腫瘤抗代謝藥　antineoplastic antimetabolite
抗肿瘤抗生素类/抗腫瘤抗生素類　antineoplastic antibiotics
抗肿瘤联合化疗方案/抗腫瘤聯合化療方案　antineoplastic combined chemotherapy protocol
抗肿瘤模型/抗腫瘤模式　antitumor model
抗肿瘤药/抗［恶性］腫瘤藥　antineoplastic agent
抗肿瘤药物筛选试验/抗腫瘤藥物篩選試驗　antitumor drug screening assay
抗重力/抗重力　antigravity
抗重力肌/抗重力肌　antigravity muscle
抗重症肌无力药/抗重症肌無力藥　antimyasthenic
抗皱/除皺　antiwrinkling
抗蛛毒溶血素/抗蛛毒溶血素　antiarachnolysin
抗锥体虫药/治錐蟲病藥　antitrypanosomal
抗着丝点抗体/抗著絲點抗體　anti-centromere antibody
抗自溶素/抗自溶素　antiautolysin
抗阻运动/抗阻運動　resistant exercise
抗组胺/抗組纖胺　antihistamine
抗组胺药/抗組纖胺藥，抗組纖胺劑　antihistaminic
抗组蛋白抗体/抗組蛋白抗體　anti-histone antibody
抗组织型/抗組織型　antitissue form
考德威尔-路克手术/卡-路二氏手術　Caldwell-Luc operation
考来替泊/考來替泊　Colestipol
考来烯胺/消膽銨　Cholestyramine
考珀韧带/Cowper 氏韌帶　Cowper ligament
烤瓷熔附金属修复体/烤瓷熔附金屬修復體　porcelain-fused-to-metal restoration
靠背/病床靠背　back rest
靠角/靠角　rest angle
靠近的/毗連的　adjacent
苛性碱/苛性鹼　caustic alkali
苛性碱烧伤/苛性鹼燒傷　caustic alkali burn
苛性钠/氫氧化鈉　caustic soda
柯蒂斯病/Curtis 氏病　Curtis disease
柯尔蒂细胞/Corti 氏細胞　cell of Corti
柯赫尔处置/柯克爾氏法　kocherization
柯赫尔扩张性溃疡/Kocher 氏擴張性潰瘍　Kocher dilatation ulcer
柯克兰病/Kirkland 氏病　Kirkland disease
柯里因/柯里因　coriin
柯立尔束/Collier 氏束　Collier tract
柯林溃疡/Curling 氏潰瘍　Curling ulcer

柯普气喘/Kopp 氏氣喘　Kopp asthma
柯萨奇病毒/Coxsackie 病毒　Coxsackie virus
柯萨奇病毒感染/柯薩奇病毒感染　Coxsackie virus infection
柯替杆内层/克提氏桿內層　stege
柯桠素/柯椏素，驅蟲豆素　chrysarobin
科病毒/Coe 病毒　Coe virus
科伯试剂/科伯試劑　Kober reagent
科伯试验/克伯氏試驗　Kober test
科布综合征/科布症候群　Cobb syndrome
科恩海姆动脉/Cohnheim 氏動脈　Cohnheim artery
科恩溶液/Cohn 氏溶液　Cohn solution
科尔夫纤维/科爾夫纖維　Korff fiber
科尔劳施屈曲/科爾勞施屈曲　Kohlrausch bend
科尔曼-谢弗饮食/Coleman-Shaffer 氏飲食　Coleman-Shaffer diet
科尔萨科夫精神病/Korsakoff 氏精神病　Korsakoff psychosis
科尔萨科夫综合征/Korsakoff 氏症候群　Korsakoff syndrome
科菲-亨伯疗法/柯-赫二氏療法　Coffey-Humber treatment
科根病/Cogan 氏病　Cogan disease
科赫尔综合征/Kocher 氏症候群　Kocher syndrome
科赫囊袋/科赫囊袋　Koch pouch
科赫三角/科赫三角　Koch triangle
科赫现象/科赫現象　Koch phenomenon
科卡浸出液/Coca 氏浸出液　Coca extracting fluid
科凯恩综合征/Cockayne 氏症候群　Cockayne syndrome
科克尔骨折/科克爾骨折　Kocher fracture
科克尔切口/科克爾切口　Kocher incision
科克尔手法/科克爾手法　Kocher maneuver
科拉尼听诊法/柯蘭尼氏叩診　Koranyi percussion
科-劳综合征/Coffin-Lowry 氏症候群　Coffin-Lowry syndrome
科莱-西卡尔综合征/克雷氏症候群，克-西二氏症候群　Collet-Sicard syndrome
科莱综合征/Collet 氏症候群　Collet syndrome
科里病/Cori 氏病　Cori disease
科里根肺炎/Corrigan 氏肺炎　Corrigan pneumonia
科利普单位/克立普單位　Collip unit
科利斯骨折/科萊氏骨折　Colles fracture
科利斯手术/科利斯手術　Collis technique
科隆纳手术/科隆納手術　Colonna operation
科罗拉多蜱传热/科羅拉多壁蝨熱　Colorado tick fever
科罗拉多蜱传热病毒/科羅拉多壁蝨熱病毒

Colorado tick fever virus
科罗特科夫音/克羅科氏音　Korotkoff sound
科佩沙尔溶液/Koppeschaar 氏溶液　Koppeschaar solution
科热夫尼科夫病/Kozhevnikov 氏病　Kozhevnikov disease
科萨科夫综合征/科薩科夫症候群　Korsakoff syndrome
科萨努尔丛林病病毒/Kyasanur 森林病病毒　Kyasanur Forest disease virus
科萨努尔森林病/凱撒納叢林病　Kyasanur forest disease
科施维茨管/Coschwitz 氏管　Coschwitz duct
科氏斑/科氏斑　Koplik spot
科斯滕综合征/科斯滕症候群　Costen syndrome
科-斯综合征/Coffin-Siris 氏症候群　Coffin-Siris syndrome
科瓦茨滞留指数/科瓦茨保留指數　Kovats retention index
科维萨尔病/Corvisart 氏病　Corvisart disease
颏/頦　chin
颏部美学/頦部美學　chin aesthetics
颏成形术/頦成形術,頦造形術,補頦術　genioplasty
颏唇沟/頦唇溝　mentolabial furrow
颏点/頦穴　mental point
颏动脉/頦動脈　mental artery
颏兜/頦兜　chincap
颏横肌/頦橫肌　musculus transversus menti
颏横位/胎兒頦橫位　mentotransverse
颏后点/頦後點　genion
颏后位/頦向後　mentoposterior
颏肌/頦肌　mentalis
颏棘/頦棘　mental spine
颏棘点/頦棘點　genion
颏结节/頦結節　mental tubercle
颏颈挛缩/頦頸攣縮　mental cervical contracture
颏颈粘连/頦頸粘連　mental cervical adhesion
颏孔/頦孔　mental foramen
颏孔点/頦孔點,頦結節　mentale
颏隆凸/頦隆凸　mental protuberance
颏前点/頦前點　pogonion
颏前位/頦向前　mentoanterior
颏区/頦部　mental region
颏上点/頦上點　supramentale
颏舌骨肌/頦舌骨肌　geniohyoid, musculus geniohyoideus
颏舌肌/頦舌肌　genioglossus muscle
颏神经/頦神經　mental nerve

颏神经唇支/頦神經唇支　labial branch of mental nerve
颏神经颏支/頦神經頦支　mental branch of mental nerve
颏神经牙龈支/頦神經牙齦支　gingival branch of mental nerve
颏缩小成形术/頦缩小成形術　reductive genioplasty
颏突度/頦突度　chin projection
颏下的/頦下的　submental
颏下点/頦下點　gnathion
颏下动脉/頦下動脈　submental artery
颏下间隙/頦下間隙　submental space
颏下静脉/頦下靜脈　submental vein
颏下淋巴结/頦下淋巴結　submental lymph node
颏下瘘/頦下瘻　submental fistula
颏下三角/頦下三角　submental triangle
颏下脂肪切除术/頦下脂肪切除術　submental lipectomy
颏胸挛缩/頦胸攣縮　mental sternal contracture
颏胸粘连/頦胸粘連　mental sternal adhesion
颏痈/頦癰　chin abscess
颏支/頦支　mental branches
颗粒变性/粒狀變性　granular degeneration
颗粒丙酸杆菌/顆粒丙酸桿菌　Propionibacterium granulosum
颗粒层/顆粒層　granular layer
颗粒层增厚/顆粒層增厚　hypergranulosis
颗粒管型/顆粒管型　granular cast
颗粒黄体细胞/黃體顆粒細胞　granulosa lutein cell
颗粒机/顆粒機　granulator
颗粒剂/顆粒[劑]　granule
颗粒囊泡/顆粒囊泡　granular vesicle
颗粒[体]/顆粒　granule
颗粒细胞/顆粒細胞　granular cell
颗粒细胞瘤/顆粒細胞瘤　granular cell tumor
颗粒细胞神经鞘瘤/顆粒細胞神經鞘瘤　granular cell schwannoma
颗粒细胞型成釉细胞瘤/顆粒細胞型成釉細胞瘤　granular cell type ameloblastoma
颗粒细度/顆粒細度　fineness of the particles
颗粒小凹/顆粒小凹　granular foveola
颗粒型/微粒型態　particulate pattern
颗粒型巨核细胞/顆粒型巨核細胞　granular megakaryocyte
颗粒[性]的/粒狀的　granular
颗粒性骨折/顆粒性骨折　granular fracture
颗粒性抗原/顆粒性抗原　particulate antigen
颗粒性输尿管炎/顆粒性輸尿管炎　ureteritis

granulosa
颗粒性微栓子/顆粒性微栓子 particulate microemboli
颗粒状移植皮片/小移植物 pinch graft
颗粒锥虫/顆粒錐蟲 Trypanosoma granulosum
髁/髁 condyle
髁鼻平面/鼻根穴後髁平面 nasion-postcondylare plane
髁部导静脉/髁部導靜脈 vena emissaria condylaris
髁槽/髁槽 condylar slot
髁侧方指标刻度/髁側方指標刻度 calibration for lateral adjustment
髁导/髁導子 condylar guidance
髁导静脉/髁[部]導靜脈 condylar emissary vein
髁导斜度/髁導斜度 condylar guidance inclination
髁道/髁徑 condyle path
髁道斜度/髁道斜度 condyle path inclination
髁的/髁的 condylar
髁杆/髁杆 condylar shaft
髁骨折/髁骨折 condylar fracture
髁关节/髁關節 condylar articulation
髁管/髁管 condylar canal
髁后孔/髁後孔 posterior condyloid foramen
髁环/髁環 condylar ring
髁间后区/髁間後區 posterior intercondylar area
髁间隆起/髁間隆起 intercondylar eminence
髁间内侧结节/髁間内側結節 medial intercondylar tubercle
髁间前区/髁間前區 anterior intercondylar area
髁间切迹/髁間切跡 intercondylar notch
髁间外侧结节/髁間外側結節 lateral intercondylar tubercle
髁间窝/髁間窝 intercondylar fossa
髁间线/髁間線 intercondylar line
髁间 T 形骨折/髁間 T 形骨折 intercondylar T fracture
髁间 Y 形骨折/髁間 Y 形骨折 intercondylar Y fracture
髁梁/髁梁 sliding condyle rod
髁前伸指标刻度/髁前伸指標刻度 calibration for horizontal adjustment
髁切除术/髁切除術,骨髁截除術 condylectomy
髁球/髁球 condylar ball
髁上骨折/髁上骨折 supracondylar fracture
髁上突/髁上突 supracondylar process
髁突/髁突 condylar process
髁突间距离/髁突間距離 intercondylar distance
髁突内点/髁突內點 condylion mediale

髁突外点/髁突外點 condylion laterale
髁突下截骨术/髁突下截骨術 subcondylar osteotomy
髁突运动/髁突運動 condyle movement
髁脱位/髁脱位 condyle dislocation
髁窝/髁窝,髁凹 condylar fossa
髁柱/髁柱 condylar post
髁状关节/髁狀關節 condyloid articulation
髁状突外点/頜髁穴 condylion
髁状突植体/髁狀突植體 condylar implant
壳多糖合酶/殼多醣合酶 chitin synthase
壳多糖酶/甲殼素酵素,殼質酶 chitinase
壳二糖/甲殼乙糖 chitobiose
壳冠/殼冠 shell crown
壳核出血/殼核出血 putamen hemorrhage
壳聚糖/聚甲殼糖 chitosan
壳三糖/甲殼丙糖 chitotriose
壳体/殼體,衣殼 capsid
壳形甲综合征/殼形甲症候群 shell-nail syndrome
壳脂蛋白/皮菌素 cuticulin
壳状牙/殼齒 shell tooth
咳黑痰/欬黑痰 melanoptysis
咳后回吸声/嗽後吸聲 post-tussive suction
咳皿/欬嗽平碟 cough plate
咳逆倚息/欬逆倚息 coughing and dyspnea in semireclining position
咳嗽/欬[嗽] cough
咳嗽平板培养基/欬嗽平板培養基 cough plates
咳嗽性肺压缩/欬嗽性肺壓縮 tussive squeeze
咳嗽性震颤/欬嗽震顫 tussive fremitus
咳嗽晕厥/欬嗽性昏厥 cough syncope
咳嗽综合征/欬嗽症候群 cough syndrome
咳痰/欬痰 expectoration, coughing of phlegm
咳血/欬血 hemoptysis
咳血方/欬血方 kexue formula
咳音/欬響 cough resonance
可变区/可變區 variable region
可变区群/可變區群 variable region group
可变区亚群/可變區亞群 variable region subgroup
可变行为/可改變的行爲 variable behavior
可变性系数/變異係數 coefficient of variability
可变性掌跖角皮病/變化性掌蹠角皮症 variable palmoplantar keratoderma
可拆线连续皮内缝合/可拆線連續皮内縫合 removable continuous intradermal suture
可程控起搏器/可程式控制起搏器 programmable pacemaker
可触知的/可觸知的,可觸到的 palpable

可传播的/可傳播的,可傳染的　transmissible
可待因/可待因　codeine
可的松/可的松　cortisone
可的松还原酶/可的松還原酶　cortisone reductase
可动骨缝/可動骨縫　scolopsia
可动黏膜/可活動黏膜　movable type mucosa
可动牙科治疗台/可動牙科治療檯　mobile dental cart unit
可反转的/可逆的　reversible
可复位的/可回復的,可還原的　reducible
可复性疝/可復性疝　reducible hernia
可呼吸的/適於呼吸的　respirable
可见光疗法/可見光療法　visible light therapy
[可]接合质粒/接合質體　conjugative plasmid
可接种性/接種可能性　inoculability
可近性/可近性　accessibility
可浸出的核抗原/可抽提之核抗原　extractable nuclear antigen
可卡因/可卡因,古柯鹼　cocaine
可卡因麻醉法/可卡因麻醉法　cocainization
可卡因相关性障碍/可卡因相關性障礙　cocaine-related disorders
可卡因谵妄/古柯鹼譫妄　cocaine delirium
可靠度/可靠性,安全性　reliability
可可/可哥豆　cacao
可可豆乳酪/可哥豆乳酪　cacao butter
可可碱/可哥鹼　theobromine
可控涡流离心泵/可控渦流離心泵　controlled vortex centrifugal pump
可控性回肠膀胱术/可控性迴腸膀胱術　continent ileal reservoir
可控性人工膀胱/可控性人工膀胱　continent urinary reservoir
可乐定/可樂定　clonidine
可逆胶体/可逆性膠質　reversible colloid
可逆效应/可逆效應　reversible effect
可逆性/可逆性　reversibility
可逆性竞争性拮抗/可逆性競爭性拮抗　reversible competitive antagonism
可逆性脑缺血发作/可逆性腦缺血發作　reversible ischemic attack
可逆性休克/可逆性休克　reversible shock
可凝集物质/可凝集物,可凝物質　agglutinable substance
可染性/可染性,著色性　tingibility
可溶化结扎线/可溶性結扎線　soluble ligature
可溶性淀粉/可溶性澱粉,澱粉顆粒糖　amidulin
可溶性复合物/可溶性複合物　soluble complex

可溶性抗原/可溶性抗原　soluble antigen
可湿性/可濕性　wettability
可视光自体动作/可視光自體動作　visible light autokinesis
可手术性/可手術性　operability
可水解鞣质/可水解鞣質　hydrolysable tannin
可塑状态/可塑狀態　plastic state
可替宁/可替寧　cotinine
可调式[牙]带环/可調性帶環　adjustable band
可调整连接器/調整性連接器　adjustable articulator
可调[整性]安抗带环/可調性錨圈　adjustable anchor band
可听域/可聽範圍　range of audibility
可托多松/可托多松　cortodoxone
可吸收衬垫/可吸收襯墊　absorbent pads
可吸收缝线/吸收縫線　absorbable suture
可吸收纱布/吸收紗布　absorbable gauze
可吸收性植入物/可吸收性植入物　absorbable implant
可消化性/可消化性,消化度　digestibility
可行性研究/可行性研究　feasibility studies
可压性/可壓性　compressibility
可预报不良反应/可預期藥物不良反應　predictable ADR
可摘矫治器/活動矯正器　removable appliance
可摘局部义齿/可摘局部義齒　removable partial denture
可摘局部义齿修复学/可摘局部義齒修復學　removable partial prosthodontics
可摘式正畸矫正器/可摘式正畸矯正器　removable orthodontic appliances
可摘义齿修复学/可摘義齒修復學　removable prosthodontics
渴/口[渴]　thirst
渴不欲饮/渴不欲飲　thirst without desire to drink
渴感倒错/異樣渴　paradipsia
渴感过少/渴感缺失　oligodipsia
渴感减退/渴感減退　hypodipsia
渴感正常/渴感正常　eudipsia
克/公克　gram
克-鲍综合征/Cruveilhier-Baumgarten 二氏症候群　Cruveilhier-Baumgarten syndrome
克-伯-霍综合征/Claude-Bernard-Horner 三氏症候群　Claude-Bernard-Horner syndrome
克分子溶液/克分子溶液　gram molecular solution
克-哈综合征/Clarke-Hadfield 二氏症候群　Clarke-Hadfield syndrome
克-坎复合征/克-坎二氏症候群　Clerambault-

Kandinsky complex
克拉伯病/克拉伯病　Krabbe disease
克拉伯综合征/Krabbe 氏症候群　Krabbe syndrome
克拉多韧带/Clado 氏韌帶　Clado ligament
克拉克-科利普法/克-科二式法　Clark-Collip method
克拉克溶液/Clark 氏溶液　Clark solution
克拉克氏溃疡/Clarke 氏潰瘍　Clarke ulcer
克拉克细胞/Clarke 氏細胞　Clarke cell
克拉拉细胞/克氏細胞,支氣管無纖毛分泌細胞　Clara cell
克拉霉素/克拉黴素　Clarithromycin
克拉屈滨/克利屈濱　Cladribine
克拉维酸/克拉維酸　clavulanic acid
克腊托姆/克臘托姆　kratom
克莱恩-莱文综合征/克-勒二氏症候群　Kleine-Levin syndrome
克兰德尔综合征/Crandall 氏症候群　Crandall syndrome
克兰顿肌/Crampton 氏肌　Crampton muscle
克兰费尔特综合征/克氏症候群　Klinefelter syndrome
克朗德尔征/克朗德爾徵　Kerandel sign
克劳迪乌斯细胞/克勞氏細胞,錐狀細胞　Claudius cell
克劳泽骨/髖骨　Krause bone
克劳泽韧带/Krause 氏韌帶,會陰橫韌帶　Krause ligament
克劳泽-瓦尔夫移植片/克-沃二氏移植物,全層皮移植物　Krause-Wolfe graft
克劳泽终球/克勞澤終球　Krause end bulb
克雷伯菌感染/克雷伯菌感染　Klebsiella infections
克雷奇默体型/克希默氏體型　Kretschmer types
克离子/克離子　gram ion
克里格勒-纳贾尔综合征/Crigler-Najar 二氏症候群　Crigler-Najjar syndrome
克里米亚出血热/克里米亞出血熱　Crimean hemorrhagic fever
克里米亚-刚果出血热病毒/克里米亞-剛果出血熱病毒　Crimean-Congo hemorrhagic fever virus
克里萨贝病/Krishaber 氏病　Krishaber disease
克里斯马斯病/Chirstmas 氏病,乙型血友病　Christmas disease
克里斯普动脉瘤/Crisp 氏動脈瘤　Crisp aneurysm
克里斯琴综合征/Christian 氏症候群　Christian syndrome
克里斯坦森现象/克里斯坦森现象　Christensen phenomenon

克-里综合征/Clough-Richter 二氏症候群　Clough-Richter syndrome
克利佩尔-费尔综合征/克-費二氏症候群　Klippel-Feil syndrome
克林霉素/氯去氧林肯黴素　Clindamycin
克隆/基因轉殖　clone, cloning
克隆流产假说/克隆流產假說　clonal abortion hypothesis
克隆普克-德热里纳综合征/Klumpke-Déjerine 二氏症候群　Klumpke-Déjerine syndrome
克隆清除/克隆清除　Clonal deletion
克隆无能/克隆無能　Clonal anergy
克隆细胞/克隆細胞　Clone cell
克隆选择学说/克隆選擇學說　clonal selection theory
克鲁克斯暗区/克鲁克氏暗區　Crookes space
克鲁克斯管/克鲁克氏管　Crookes tube
克鲁斯念珠菌/克鲁斯念珠菌　Candida krusei
克鲁宗综合征/克鲁宗症候群　Crouzon syndrome
克仑特罗/克侖特羅　Clenbuterol
克伦佩雷尔病/Klemperer 氏病　Klemperer disease
克罗恩病/Crohn 氏症　Crohn disease
克罗扎矫治器/克羅扎矯治器　Crozat appliance
克洛德综合征/Claude 氏症候群　Claude syndrome
克洛凯韧带/Cloquet 氏韌帶　Cloquet ligament
克洛凯疝/Cloquet 氏疝氣　Cloquet hernia
克吕韦耶丛/Cruveilhier 氏叢　Cruveilhier plexus
克吕韦耶韧带/Cruveilhier 氏韌帶　Cruveilhier ligaments
克吕韦耶萎缩[病]/Cruveilhier 氏萎縮　Cruveilhier atrophy
克麦克尔冠/卡麥克氏冠　Carmichael crown
克霉唑/氯三苯甲咪唑　Clotrimazole
克普结节/克普結節　Koeppe nodule
克山病/克山病　Keshan disease
克氏针/基爾納氏鋼絲　Kirschner wire
克斯-别赫捷列夫层/凱-貝二氏層　Kaes-Bekhterev layer
克-亚综合征/克-亞症候群　Creutzfeldt-Jakob syndrome
刻板/刻板　stereotyping
刻板动作/刻板動作　stereotypic act
刻板行为/刻板行爲　stereotypic behavior
刻板言语/重複言語　stereotypy of speech
刻板运动障碍/刻板運動障礙　stereotypic movement disorder
客观测听[法]/客觀測聽[法]　objective audiometry
客观的/客觀的　objective

客观精神生物学/精神作用學，客觀心理生物學 ergasiology
客观症状/客觀症状 objective symptom
客气/客氣 guest climatic qi
客色/客色 visiting complexion
客体依恋/客體依戀 object attachment
客忤/客忤 sudden frightening in infant
客邪/客邪 visiting pathogen
客运/客運 guest evolutive phase
客主加临/客主加臨 guest climatic qi adding to fixed host qi
氪放射性同位素/氪放射性同位素 krypton radioisotope
肯定携带者/肯定攜帶者 obligatory carrier
肯尼迪分类法/甘迺迪分類法 Kennedy classification
肯尼迪综合征/Kennedy 氏症候群 Kennedy syndrome
肯尼亚斑疹热/肯亞熱 Kenya fever
肯普纳饮食/Kempner 氏飲食 Kempner diet
肯特束/肯特束 bundle of Kent
坑气/坑氣，礦坑毒氣 damp
空凹外翻足/空凹外翻足 cavovalgus
空肠/空腸 jejunum, jejuni
空肠的/空腸的 jejunal
空肠动脉/空腸動脈 jejunal artery
空肠缝术/空腸縫合術 jejunorrhaphy
空肠回肠旁路术/空腸迴腸旁路術 jejunoileal bypass
空肠回肠吻合术/空迴腸吻合術 jejunoileostomy
空肠回肠炎/空迴腸炎 jejunoileitis
空肠疾病/空腸疾病 jejunal disease
空肠间置代胆道术/空腸間置代膽道術 choledochoplasty by jejunal interposition
空肠结肠瘘/空腸結腸瘻管 jejunocolic fistula
空肠结肠吻合术/空結腸吻合術 jejunocolostomy
空肠静脉/空腸靜脈 jejunal vein
空肠静脉分支/空腸靜脈分支 branch of jejunal vein
空肠空肠吻合术/空腸空腸吻合術 jejunojejunostomy
空肠盲肠吻合术/空盲腸吻合術 jejunocecostomy
空肠切除术/空腸切除術 jejunectomy
空肠切开术/空腸切開術 jejunotomy
空肠弯曲杆菌/空腸彎曲桿菌 Campylobacter jejuni
空肠系膜/空腸繫膜 mesojejunum
空肠炎/空腸炎 jejunitis
空肠移植/空腸移植 jejunum transplantation
空肠造口术/空腸造口術 jejunostomy
空肠肿瘤/空腸腫瘤 jejunal neoplasms

空肠周围炎/空腸周圍炎 perijejunitis
空肠综合征/空腸症候群 jejunal syndrome
空蝶鞍综合征/空蝶鞍症候群 empty sella syndrome
空洞呼吸音/空洞呼吸音 cavernous respiration
空洞形成/成洞，腔洞形成 cavitation
空洞性肺结核/空洞性肺結核 cavitary pulmonary tuberculosis
空洞性脊髓突出/空洞性脊髓膨出 syringocele
空洞性脊髓炎/空洞性脊髓炎 cavitary myelitis
空洞音/空洞水泡音 cavernous rale
空洞语音/空甕音，空洞音 amphoric voice
空腹服/空腹服 administered at empty stomach
空腹痛/飢痛 hunger pain
空架夹/空架夾 skeleton splint
空间/空間 space
空间对比敏感度/空間對比敏感度 spatial contrast sensitivity
空间呼吸音/空洞呼吸 Austin Flint respiration
空间觉/空間覺 sense of space
空间脉冲长度/空間脈衝長度 spatial pulse length
空间谱带展宽/空間譜帶展寬 band broading in space
空间效应/空間效應 steric effect
空间心电向量描记法/立體向量心電圖 spatial vectocardiography
空间行为/空間行爲 spatial behavior
空间知觉/空間知覺 space perception
空泡/空泡 vacuoles
空泡变性/空泡變性 vacuolar degeneration
空泡病毒/空泡形成病毒 vacuolating virus
空泡的/空泡的 vacuolar
空泡细胞/空泡細胞 physaliferous cell
空泡形成/空泡形成，空泡狀態 vacuolation
空泡性脊髓病/空泡性脊髓病 vacuolar myelopathy
空泡性肾变病/空泡性腎病變 vacuolar nephrosis
空泡质子转运 ATP 酶/空泡質子轉運 ATP 酶 vacuolar proton-translocating ATPase
空疱天花/長莢狀天花 variola siliquosa
空气/[空]氣 air
空气按摩/空氣按摩 pneumatic massage
空气传播的/空氣傳播的 airborne
空气传染/空氣傳染 airborne infection
空气纯度测定器/氣濁計 cacaerometer
空气纯度测定仪/氣體分析器，空氣純度測定器 eudiometer
空气的/空氣的 aerial
空气电离/空氣電離 air ionization
空气过滤器/空氣過濾器 air filter

空气饥/空氣饑　air hunger
空气冷却力计/空氣冷卻力計　comfimeter
空气离子化疗法/電荷化噴霧吸入療法　aeroionotherapy
空气量/空氣量　air dose
空气疗法/空氣療法　aerotherapy
空气流动/空氣流動　air movement
空气栓塞/氣泡栓塞　air embolism
空气调节/空氣調節　air conditioning
空气微生物学/空氣微生物學　air microbiology
空气污染/空氣汙染　air pollution
空气污染物/空氣汙染物　air pollutant
空气消毒气雾剂/空氣消毒氣化噴霧劑　air-disinfectant aerosol
空气有机质测定计/空氣汙度計　sepsometer
空气振荡/空氣震荡　air concussion
空气滞留/空氣滯留　air trapping
空气阻滞/氣阻斷　air block
空调机/空調器　air conditioner
空痛/空痛　empty pain
空瓮呼吸音/空甕呼吸音　amphoric respiration
空瓮性/叩诊或听诊时听到的空甕聲　amphoricity
空瓮性呼吸音/空甕雜音　amphoric murmur
空瓮性回声/空甕性回響　amphoric echo
空瓮性语音/空甕語聲　amphoriloquy
空瓮音/空甕音，空甕響　amphoric resonance
空匣叩响/木板箱響　bandbox resonance
空匣音/空洞音　box-note
空想癖/空想癖　dereism
空想性视错觉/空想性錯視　pareidolia
空心针/空心針　hollow needle
空虚近视/空虛近視　empty myopia
孔/孔　aperture, foramen
孔蛋白类/孔蛋白類　porins
孔道狭窄/管孔狹小　arctation
孔洞脑/孔洞腦［畸形］，腦穿通畸形　porencephaly
孔恩液/Cohn 氏液　Cohn liquid
孔隔/孔隔　pore diaphragm
孔沟/孔溝　pit canal
孔口/孔口　orifice
孔隙率/孔隙度　porosity
孔状骨折/鈕孔狀骨折　buttonhole fracture
孔最/孔最　kongzui, LU6
恐/恐　fear
恐怖症/恐懼［症］　phobia
恐高症/懼高症　acrophobia
恐惧/恐懼，恐怖　fear
恐惧性唾液分泌抑制/乾恐懼症　xerophobia

恐恐怖症/恐懼恐懼症　phobophobia
恐伤肾/恐傷腎　fear impairing the kidney
恐胜法/恐勝法　frightening therapy
恐胜喜/恐勝喜　frightening to control overjoy
恐水症/水恐懼症,恐水症　hydrophobia, aquaphobia
恐为肾志/恐爲腎志　kidney being associated with fear
恐郁/恐鬱　stagnation pattern caused by fear
恐则气下/恐則氣下　fear causing qi sinking, fear leading to qi sinking
恐中/恐中　stroke due to terror
空白幻觉/空白幻覺　blank hallucination
空隙性遗忘/空隙性健忘　lacunar amnesia
控释制剂/控釋製劑　controlled release preparation
控涎丹/控涎丹　drool controlling pill, kongxian pill
控制/控制　control
控制联想/制限聯想　controlled associations
控制论/聯絡管制學　cybernetics
控制生物危害物扩散/控制生物危害物擴散　containment of biohazards
控制式通气/控制式通氣　control mode ventilation
控制式引流/控制式引流,紗布引流　controlled drain
控制通气/控制通氣　controlled ventilation
控制物质法/控制物質法　controlled substances act
控制性膈呼吸/控制性膈呼吸　controlled diaphragmatic respiration
控制性降压/控制性低血壓　controlled hypotension
芤脉/芤脈　hollow pulse
口/口　mouth, kou
口凹/口凹,口管，口道　stomodeum
口白斑病/口白斑病　leukoplakia oris
口板/口板　oral plate
口鼻的/口鼻的　oronasal
口鼻呼吸/口鼻呼吸　oronasal breathing
口鼻瘘/口鼻瘻管　oronasal fistula
口闭锁/口閉鎖　atresia oris
口部厚皮病/口部厚皮病　pachydermia orlis
口部皮结核/口部皮結核　orifical tuberculosis
口吃/口吃　dysarthria literalis, stuttering
口齿病/口齒病　disease of mouth and teeth
口齿科/口齒科　department of dentistry and stomatology
口臭/口臭　bad breath, halitosis
口臭·脾胃蕴热证/口臭·脾胃蘊熱證　halitosis with pattern of spleen-stomach amassing heat
口臭·食滞胃肠证/口臭·食滯胃腸證　halitosis with pattern of food stagnation in stomach and intestine
口臭·胃火炽盛证/口臭·胃火熾盛證　halitosis with

blazing stomach fire pattern

口臭·虚火郁结证/口臭·虛火鬱結證　halitosis with deficiency-fire stagnation pattern

口臭[症]/口臭症　ozostomia

口出血/口出血　stomatorrhagia

口疮/口瘡　oral sore, aphtha

口疮病/口瘡病　aphthosis

口疮·肝郁蕴热证/口瘡·肝鬱蘊熱證　oral sore with pattern of liver depression and heat amassment

口疮·脾虚湿困证/口瘡·脾虛濕困證　oral sore with pattern of spleen deficiency and dampness retention

口疮·气血两虚证/口瘡·氣血兩虛證　oral sore with qi-blood deficiency pattern

口疮热/口瘡熱　aphthous fever

口疮·心火上炎证/口瘡·心火上炎證　oral sore with pattern of heart-fire flaring upward

口疮·心脾积热证/口瘡·心脾積熱證　oral sore with pattern of heart-spleen heat accumulation

口疮性口炎/口瘡性口角炎　aphthous stomatitis

口疮性咽炎/口瘡性咽炎　aphthous pharyngitis

口疮性龈炎/口瘡性齦炎　aphthous ulitis

口疮样/口瘡樣　aphthous-like

口疮样疹/擬口瘡　aphthoid

口疮·阴虚火旺证/口瘡·陰虛火旺證　oral sore with pattern of yin deficiency and fire effulgence

口唇/口唇　oral lip

口唇闭锁/口唇閉鎖　oral phimosis

口唇颤动/口唇顫動　tremor of lips

口唇淡白/口唇淡白　pale lip

口唇红肿/口唇紅腫　reddened and swollen lip

口唇焦裂/口唇焦裂　dry and withered lip

口唇青紫/口唇青紫　cyanotic lip

口淡/口淡　tastelessness

口底/口[腔]底　floor of mouth, mouth floor

口点/口點　orale

口对鼻呼气/口對鼻呼氣　mouth to nose respiration

口对口吹气法/口對口吹氣法　mouth to mouth insufflation

口对口复苏法/口對口復甦　transanimation

口对口呼气/口對口呼氣　mouth to mouth respiration

口发育不全/口發育不全　atelostomia

口飞沫/口沫　spray mouth

口服避孕药/口服避孕藥　oral contraceptive

口服补液盐/口服補液鹽　oral rehydration salt

口服胆囊造影[术]/口服膽囊造影[術]　oral cholecystography

口服法尿路造影术/經口尿道攝影術　oral urography

口服脊髓灰质炎病毒疫苗/口服脊髓灰質炎病毒疫苗　oral poliovirus vaccine

口服降血糖药/口服降血糖藥　oral hypoglycemic

口服抗菌素/口服抗生素　oral antibiotic

口服葡萄糖耐量试验/口服葡萄糖耐量試驗　oral glucose tolerance test

口服投药/口服投藥　oral administration

口服吸收度/口服吸收度　oral absorbability

口服液/口服液　oral liquid

口服胰岛素/口服胰島素, 内服胰島素　oral insulin, peroral insulin

口干/口乾　dry mouth

口干燥/謝格連氏病　dry mouth

口疳/口疳　oral gan disease

口沟/口溝　oral groove

口含棒/口含棒　mouthstick

口含片剂/口腔錠　buccal tablet

口禾髎/口禾髎　kouheliao, LI19

口颌的/口頜的　oromaxillary

口颌疾病/口頜疾病　stomatognathic disease

口颌系统/口頜系統, 咀嚼系統　stomatognathic system

口颌系统畸形/口頜系統畸形　stomatognathic system abnormality

口黑色素斑/口腔黑色素斑　oral melanotic macule

口后点/口後點　staphylion

口厚皮病/口厚皮病　pachyderma oralis, pachyderma oris

口呼吸/張口呼吸　buccal respiration

口呼吸相关牙龈炎/口呼吸相關牙齦炎　mouth-breathing-related gingivitis

口角/口角　angle of mouth

口角唇炎/口角唇炎　angular cheilitis

口角干裂/口角乾裂　angular cheilosis

口角结节性寄生虫病/口角結節性寄生蟲病　button disease

口角开大术/口角開大術　commissurotomy

口角瘘/口角瘻　angular fistula

口角提肌/口角提肌, 口角舉肌　levator anguli oris

口角线/口角線　line of angulus oris

口角炎/口角炎　angular stomatitis

口噤/口噤　lockjaw

口镜/口鏡　dental mirror

口渴/[口]渴　dipsia, thirst, hydrodipsia

口苦/口苦　bitter taste in mouth

口溃疡/口潰瘍　canker

口括约肌/口括約肌　oral sphincter

口裂/口裂,裂口畸形　oral fissure, orifice of mouth
口裂点/口裂點　stomion
口裂宽/口裂寬　breadth of oral fissure
口轮匝肌/口輪匝肌　orbicularis oris, musculus orbicularis oris
口轮匝肌唇部/口輪匝肌唇部　labial part of orbicularis oris
口轮匝肌缘部/口輪匝肌緣部　marginal part of orbicularis oris
口麻/口麻　numbness in mouth
口霉菌病/口黴菌病　stomatomycosis
口糜/口糜　aphthous stomatitis, aphtha, coccigenic stomatitis
口糜·脾胃气虚证/口糜·脾胃氣虛證　aphthous stomatitis with spleen-stomach qi deficiency pattern
口糜·心脾积热证/口糜·心脾積熱證　aphthous stomatitis with pattern of heart-spleen heat accumulation
口糜·阴虚火旺证/口糜·陰虛火旺證　aphthous stomatitis with pattern of yin deficiency and fire effulgence
口面的/口與[顏]面的　orifical
口面复合体/口顏複合體　orofacial complex
口面角/口面角　orofacial angle
口面区/口面區　orofacial region
口面肉芽肿病/口面肉芽腫病　orofacial granulomatosis
口面运动障碍/口面運動障礙　orofacial dyskinesia
口面指/口面指　orofaciodigital
口面指综合征/口面指症候群　orofaciodigital syndrome
口面趾/口面趾　orofaciodigital
口面趾综合征/口面趾症候群　orofaciodigital syndrome
口内的/口内的　intraoral
口内弓/口内弓　inner bow
口内检查/口内的檢查　intraoral examination
口内胶片/口内軟片　intraoral film
口内抗基/口内錨定　intraoral anchorage
口内髁下骨切开术/口腔内髁下骨切開術　intraoral subcondylar osteotomy
口内鳞状细胞癌/口腔内鱗狀細胞癌　intraoral squamous carcinoma
口内流电效应/口内流電效應　intraoral electrogalvanism
口内麻醉/口内麻醉　intraoral anaesthesia
口内描绘器/口内描繪器　intraoral tracing device
口内描记法/口内描記法　intraoral tracing
口内描记器/口内描記器　intraoral tracer
口内囊袋/口内囊袋　intraoral pocket
口内射线照相检查/口内放射線檢查　intraoral radiographic examination
口内升支截骨术/口内昇支截骨術　intraoral ramus osteotomy
口内升支矢状劈开术/口内昇支矢狀劈開術　intraoral sagittal split ramus osteotomy
口内矢面切骨术/口内矢面切骨術　intraoral sagittal osteotomy
口内透照灯/口腔燈　mouth lamp
口内下颌升支垂直切骨术/口内下頜支垂直截骨術　intraoral vertical ramus osteotomy
口内牙科植入物/口内牙科植體　intraoral dental implant
口内照片/口内照片　intraoral photograph
口内支抗/口内支抗　intraoral anchorage
口黏腻/口黏膩　sticky and greasy in mouth
口僻[病]/口僻[病]　wry mouth
口破/口破　adult thrush
口期施虐欲/口式施虐淫　oral sadism
口腔/口腔　oral cavity
口腔白斑/口腔白斑　oral leukoplakia
口腔白色水肿/口腔白色水腫　oral leukoedema
口腔保护剂/口腔保護劑　oral screen
口腔扁平苔藓/口腔扁平苔癬　oral lichen planus
口腔表现/口腔表現　oral manifestations
口[腔]病/口腔病　stomatopathy, oral disorder, oral disease
口腔病理学/口腔病理學　oral pathology
口腔病灶/口腔病灶　oral focus
口腔病灶感染/口腔病灶感染　oral focal infection
口腔病治疗学/口腔疾病療法　stomatologic therapeutics
口腔部切诊/口腔部切診　palpation of oral cavity
口腔部闻诊/口腔部聞診　auscultation and olfaction of oral cavity
口腔材料学/口腔材料學　science of dental materials
口腔菜花样乳头状瘤病/口腔菜花樣乳頭狀瘤病　oral florid papillomatosis
口腔插管法/口腔插管法　oral intubation
口腔齿龈沟上皮/口腔齒齦溝上皮　oral sulcular epithelium
口腔出血/口腔出血　oral hemorrhage
口腔吹药法/口腔吹藥法　insufflation therapy for oral cavity disease
口腔刺割法/口腔刺割法　puncture-cut method for oral cavity disease

口腔法医学/牙科法醫學　forensic dentistry
口腔防护器/口腔防護器　mouth protector
口腔放射学/口腔放射學，牙科放射學　oral radiology
口腔敷贴法/口腔敷貼法　plastering therapy for oral cavity disease
口腔干燥/口腔乾燥，口乾燥病　xerostomia
口腔感染控制/口腔感染控制　dental infection control
口腔隔/口腔膈　oral diaphragm
口腔公共卫生/口腔公共衛生　oral public health
口腔含漱法/口腔含漱法　rinsing method for oral cavity disease
口腔颌面解剖学/口腔頜面解剖學　oral and maxillofacial anatomy
口腔颌面外科学/口腔、上頜與面外科　oral and maxillofacial surgery
口腔环境/口腔環境　oral environment
口腔活动行为/口腔運動行為　oral motor behavior
口腔畸形/口腔畸形　mouth abnormality
口腔急诊学/口腔急診學　dental emergency
口腔疾病/口腔疾病　oral disease
口腔矫形修复/彌補物整復　prosthetic restoration
口腔[结构]软化/口軟化　stomatomalacia
口腔结核/口腔結核　oral tuberculosis
口腔解剖学/口腔解剖學　oral anatomy
口腔镜/齒[科反光]鏡　dental reflector
口腔菌丛/口腔細菌叢　oral flora
口腔康复/口腔機能恢復　oral rehabilitation
口腔溃疡/口腔潰瘍　oral ulcer
口腔淋巴上皮囊肿/口腔淋巴上皮囊腫　oral lymphoepithelial cyst
口腔瘘/口腔瘻　oral fistula
口腔伦理学/口腔倫理學　oral ethics
口腔论/口論　stomatography
口腔螺旋体/口腔螺旋體　Borrelia buccalis
口腔麻醉学/口腔麻醉學　oral anesthesiology
口腔毛滴虫/頰滴蟲　Trichomonas buccalis
口腔毛状黏膜白斑病/口腔絨毛狀白斑病　oral hairy leukoplakia
口腔美容学/美容牙科學　esthetic dentistry
口腔面/口腔面　oral surface
口腔黏膜/口腔黏膜　mucous membrane of mouth, oral mucosa, oral mucous membrane
口腔黏膜发疹性卫星状血管瘤/口腔黏膜發疹性衛星狀血管瘤　eruptive satellite angiomas of the oral mucosa
口腔黏膜黑斑[症]/口腔黑斑[症]　oral melanoplakia
口腔黏膜红斑/口腔紅斑　oral erythroplakia
口腔黏膜坏死性溃疡/口腔黏膜壞死性潰瘍　ulcus necroticum mucosae oris
口腔黏膜疾病/口腔黏膜疾病　oral mucosa disorder
口腔黏膜良性角化过度/口腔黏膜良性角化過度　benign hyperkeratosis of oral mucosa
口腔黏膜下纤维化/口腔黏膜下纖維化　oral submucosa fibrosis
口腔念珠菌病/口腔念珠菌病　oral moniliasis
口腔脓毒病/口腔性敗血病　oral sepsis
口腔胚胎学/口腔胚胎學　oral embryology
口腔前庭/口腔前庭　oral vestibule, vestibule of mouth
口腔褥疮/口腔褥瘡　decubitus ulcer of mouth
口腔上颌窦瘘/口腔上頜竇瘻　oroantral fistula
口腔上皮/口腔上皮　oral epithelium
口腔上皮痣/口腔上皮痣　oral epithelial nevi
口腔烧伤/口腔燒傷　burn of oral cavity
口腔生理学/口腔生理學　oral physiology
口腔生态学/口腔生態學　ecology of oral cavity
口腔听诊器/口腔聽診器，乳突診察器　pneumatoscope
口腔筒线虫病/口腔圓絲蟲病　gongylonemiasis of the mouth
口[腔]痛/口痛　stomalgia
口腔脱屑/口腔脫屑　oral desquamation
口腔外科手术/口腔外科手術　oral surgical procedure
口腔卫生/口腔衛生　mouth hygiene
口腔卫生调查/口腔健康調查　oral health survey
口腔卫生委员会/口腔衛生委員會　board of oral health
口腔卫生指数/口腔衛生指數　oral hygiene index
口腔卫生专家/口腔衛生專家　oral hygienist
口腔温度计/口腔溫度計　oral thermometer
口腔吸入器/口腔吸入器，口腔吸入劑　oral inhaler
口腔吸引器/口腔抽吸器　oral evacuator
口腔习惯/口腔習慣　oral habit
口腔腺/口腔腺　gland of oral cavity, oral gland
口腔消化/口腔消化　oral digestion
口腔修复美学/口腔修復美學　oral prosthetic aesthetics
口腔修复学/補牙學，齒復學　prosthetic dentistry
口腔修复牙制备/口腔修復牙製備　prosthodontic tooth preparation
口腔学/口腔[衛生]學　oralogy
口腔学家/口腔學家　stomatologist

口腔学研究/口腔學研究　dental research
口腔医疗质量评定/口腔醫療品質評定　dental audit
口腔医学/口腔醫學,牙科學　oral medicine
口腔医学美学/口腔醫學美學　stomatological medical aesthetics
口腔异常/口腔異常　oral anomaly
口腔异位性胃肠囊肿/口腔異位性胃腸囊腫　heterotopic oral gastrointestinal cyst
口腔预备/口腔準備　mouth preparation
口腔诊断/口腔診斷　oral diagnosis
口腔振动器/口腔振動器　oral vibrator
口腔正畸点焊机/口腔正畸點焊機　orthodontic spot welder
口腔正畸美学/口腔正畸美學　orthodontic aesthetics
口腔支原体/口支原菌,咽黴漿菌　mycoplasma orale
口腔植入物/口內植體　oral implant
口腔植入学家/口腔植體專科醫師　oral implantologist
口腔肿瘤/口腔腫瘤　mouth neoplasm
口腔种植学/口腔種植學　oral implantology
口腔灼烧/口腔灼燒　burning mouth
口腔灼痛综合征/口腔灼痛症候群　burning-mouth syndrome
口腔组织/口腔組織　oral tissues
口腔组织学/口腔組織學　oral histology
口区/口部　oral region
口软/口軟　flaccidity of mastication
口上颌窦瘘/口上頜竇瘺　oromaxillary fistula
口舌的/口舌的　orolingual
口舌感觉异常/口舌感覺異常　orolingual paresthesia
口舌痰包/口舌痰包　phlegmatic mass in mouth and tongue
口舌炎/口舌炎　stomatoglossitis
口声试验/口聲試驗　live-voice test
口手联带运动/口手連帶運動,桑德斯氏徵狀　mouth-and-hand synkinesis
口诉言词评分法/口訴言詞評分法　verbal rating scale
口酸/口酸　sour taste in mouth
口蹄疫/足病　foot-and-mouth disease
口蹄疫病毒/口蹄疫病毒　FMD virus
口甜/口甜　sweet taste in mouth
口头契约/口頭契約　express contract
口头同意/口頭同意　express consent
口外安抗/口外錨定　extraoral anchorage
口外的/口外的　extraoral
口外环口放射摄影/口外環口放射攝影　external oral annulus radiography
口外矫形力/口外矯形力　extraoral orthopedic force
口外瘘管/口外瘺管　extraoral fistula
口外麻醉/口外麻醉　extraoral anesthesia
口外描绘及装置/口外描繪及裝置　extraoral tracing and device
口外描记法/口外描記　extraoral tracing
口外描记器/口外描記器　extraoral tracer
口外牵引器/口外牽引器　extraoral traction appliance
口外牵引装置/口外牽引裝置　extraoral traction appliance
口外[X射线]胶片/口外膠片　extraoral film
口外X射线照相检查/口外放射線檢查　extraoral radiographic examination
口外喂养/非經口哺養法　extrabuccal feeding
口外下颌支垂直截骨术/口外下頜支垂直截骨術　extraoral vertical ramus osteotomy
口外C型截骨术/口外C型截骨術　extraoral C osteotomy
口外影像/口外影像　extraoral photograph
口外支抗/口外支抗　extraoral anchorage
口外装置/口外裝置　extraoral applicance
口吻疮/口吻瘡　labial commissure sore
口吻疮·脾胃湿热证/口吻瘡·脾胃濕熱證　labial commissure sore with pattern of dampness-heat in spleen and stomach
口吻疮·脾虚湿困证/口吻瘡·脾虛濕困證　labial commissure sore with pattern of spleen deficiency and dampness retention
口吻疮·燥邪外侵证/口吻瘡·燥邪外侵證　labial commissure sore with pattern of external invasion by dryness
口狭窄/口狹窄,狹口　stenostomia
口-下颌-耳三联征/口頜耳徵　oral-mandibular-auricular triad
口咸/口咸　salty taste in mouth
口腺瘤病/口的腺瘤病　adenomatosis oris
口形红细胞增多/裂口紅血球症　stomatocytosis
口咽/口咽　oral part of pharynx, oropharynx
口咽膜/口咽膜　oropharyngeal membrane
口咽峡/[口]咽峽　oropharyngeal isthmus
口咽肿瘤/口咽腫瘤　oropharyngeal neoplasm
口炎/口炎　stomatitis
口炎清颗粒/口炎清顆粒　kouyanqing granule
口炎性腹泻/口炎性腹瀉,熱帶口瘡　sprue, sprue diarrhea
口眼裂/口眼裂　oro-ocular facial cleft
口眼喎斜/口眼喎斜　wry eye and mouth

口欲期/口腔期　oral stage
口缘的/口腔周围　peristomal
口缘中胚层/中胚葉口周圍層　peristomal mesoderm
口源性感染/口原性感染　stomatogenous infection
口-指-面骨发育不全/口指面骨發育不全症　orodigitofacial dysostosis
口-指-面骨综合征/指口臉症候群　orodigitofacial syndrome
口指数/口指數　oral index
口中和/口中和　normal sensation in mouth
口中生疮/口中生瘡　sore in mouth
口周白斑/口圍白斑　perioral leukoderma
口周瘢痕挛缩/口周瘢痕攣縮　perioral cicatricial contracture
口周苍白/口周圍蒼白　perioral pallor
口周苍白圈/口周蒼白圈　circumoral pallor
口周刺激性皮炎/口腔周圍之刺激性皮膚炎　peristomal irritant contact dermatitis
口周的/口周的,口圍　perioral
口周皮炎/口周皮炎　perioral dermatitis
口周雀斑样痣病/口圍小痣症　periorificial lentiginosis
口周围区域/口圍區域　perioral area
口周皱纹/口周皺紋　perioral aging line
口周着色斑病综合征/口圍色素沈著症候群　periorificial lentiginosis syndrome
口灼伤综合征/口灼傷症候群　burning mouth syndrome
叩齿/叩齒　clicking tooth
叩触试验/叩觸試驗　percussion test
叩打法/叩打法　tapping manipulation
叩喉听诊法/叩喉聽音法　plegaphonia
叩击按摩法/叩擊按摩法　beating percussion massage
叩击波/叩波　percussion wave
叩听诊法/聽叩診器療法　phonacoscopy
叩听诊器/聽叩診器　auscultoplectrum
叩响/叩響　percussion resonance
叩诊/叩診[法]　percussion
叩诊槌/叩診槌　plessor, percussion hammer
叩诊咳/叩診欬　tapotage
叩诊器/叩診器　percussor
扣带沟/扣帶溝　cingulate sulcus
扣带回/扣帶迴　cingulate gyrus
扣带回切开术/扣帶迴切除　cingulotomy
扣带回峡/扣帶迴峽　isthmus of cingulate gyrus
扣带支/扣帶支　cingular branch
枯草杆菌蛋白酶/枯草桿菌蛋白酶　subtilisin

枯草菌素/枯草菌素　subtilin
枯草热/乾草熱,花粉熱　hay fever
枯草热性结膜炎/枯草熱性結膜炎　hay fever conjunctivitis
枯草哮喘/乾草氣喘　hay asthma
枯骨状手/枯骨狀手　main en squelette
枯舌/枯舌　withered tongue
枯萎癌/萎縮癌　withering cancer
枯萎期/枯萎期　withering period
枯痔法/枯痔法　hemorrhoid sclerosing and necrotizing method
哭泣/哭泣　weep
苦/苦　bitter
苦艾/苦艾　absinthium
苦艾酒/苦艾酒　absinthe
苦艾油/苦艾油　absinthe oil
苦橙皮/苦橙皮　bitter orange peel
苦橙皮提取物/苦橙皮萃取　bitter orange peel extract
苦根/苦根,龍膽根　bitter root
苦楝/[苦]楝　azedarach
苦楝皮/苦楝皮　Sichuan chinaberry bark
苦硫酸/苦硫酸　picrosulfuric acid
苦马豆素/苦馬豆素　swainsonine
苦木素类/苦木素類　quassins
苦皮/苦味皮,洪都拉司樹皮　cascara amarga
苦参/苦參　lightyellow sophora root
苦苏属/苦蘇屬　*Brayera*
苦味素/苦味素　bitter principle
苦味酸/苦味酸　picric acid
苦味酸苯胺黑/苦味酸苯胺黑　picronigrosin
苦味酸性黄疸/苦味酸性黃疸　picric acid jaundice
苦味酸盐类/苦味酸鹽類　picrates
苦味酸银/苦味酸銀　silver picrate
苦味异常/苦味異常,病理性苦味覺　picrogeusia
苦味质/苦味質　amaroid
苦温燥湿/苦溫燥濕　dispelling dampness with bitter and warm-natured drugs
苦杏仁苷/苦杏仁素　amygdalin
苦杏仁苷酶/杏糖酵素,杏糖酶　amygdalase
苦杏仁酶/苦杏仁酵素　emulsin, synaptase
苦杏仁糖/[苦]杏糖　amygdalose
库柏内尔征/庫柏納氏徵象　Coopernail sign
库柏韧带/Cooper氏韌帶　Cooper ligament
库尔洛夫体/Kurloff氏小體　Kurloff body
库尔曼智力测验/庫爾曼氏試驗　Kuhlmann test
库尔奇茨基细胞/庫爾奇茨基細胞　Kultschitzky cell
库房/庫房　kufang, ST14

库房现象/庫房現象　depot phenomenon
库夫斯病/庫夫氏病　Kufs disease
库检索/[資料]庫搜索　library searching
库-金呼吸/Kussmaul-Kien 二氏呼吸　Kussmaul-Kien respiration
库腊普病/庫臘普病　courap
库勒压力栓钉系列/庫勒壓力栓釘系列　Kurer press stud system
库雷里公式/柯雷里公式　Curreri formula
库利奇管/庫立吉氏球管　Coolidge tube
库马磷/庫馬磷　coumaphos
库马霉素/香豆黴素　coumamycin
库蠓属/糠蚊屬　Culicoides
库姆斯抗人球蛋白试验/Coombs 氏試驗　Coombs test
库珀疝/Cooper 氏疝　Cooper hernia
库珀腺管/尿道球腺管　cowperian duct
库普费尔细胞/Kupffer 氏細胞　Kupffer cell
库普弗细胞/庫普弗細胞　Kupffer cell
库斯毛尔呼吸/Kussmaul 氏呼吸　Kussmaul respiration
库斯毛尔失语/Kussmaul 氏失語症　Kussmaul aphasia
库斯毛尔征/Kussmaul 氏徵象　Kussmaul sign
库瓦西耶-泰里耶综合征/科-特二氏症候群　Courvoisier-Terrier syndrome
库瓦西耶征/庫瓦西耶徵　Courvoisier sign
库蚊属/家蚊屬　Culex
库欣病/庫欣病　Cushing disease
库欣溃疡/Cushing 氏潰瘍　Cushing ulcer
库欣现象/庫欣現象　Cushing phenomenon
库欣综合征/庫欣症候群　Cushing syndrome
夸大/誇大　grandeur
夸大狂/誇大狂,誇大妄想　megalomania
夸大狂者/誇大狂者,狂妄者　megalomaniac
夸大妄想/誇大妄想　delusion of grandeur
夸大妄想性谵妄/誇大妄想性譫妄　macromaniacal delirium
胯腹痈/胯腹癰　inguinal abscess, acute inguinal pyogenic carbuncle, acute pyogenic inguinal lymphadenitis
胯腹痈·湿热蕴结证/胯腹癰·濕熱蘊結證　inguinal abscess with dampness-heat amassment pattern
跨界射线/限界射線　grenz ray
跨立病/跨立病　quebrabunda
跨膜压/跨膜壓　transmembrane pressure
跨文化护理/跨文化護理　transcultural nursing
跨文化精神病学/跨文化精神病學　transcultural psychiatry
跨阈步态/跨閾步態　steppage gait
块/塊　piece, block
快波睡眠/快波睡眠　fast wave sleep
快感减少/快感減少,興致減少　hyphedonia
快感缺乏/快感缺乏,興趣缺乏　anhedonia
快感学/快樂論　hedonics
快乐-痛苦原则/精神興奮主義　pleasure-pain principle
快速胆固醇反应/急促膽脂反應,快速膽脂醇反應　citochol reaction
快速胆固醇试验/急促膽脂反應　citochol test
快速发生/胚胎發育初期過速　tachygenesis
快速傅里叶变换/快速傅立葉變換　fast Fourier transform
快速降温/快速降溫　fast cooling
快速进行性牙周炎/快速進行性牙周炎　rapidly progressive periodontitis
快速免疫/急速免疫　tachyphylaxis
快速耐受/急速耐藥性　tachyphylaxis
快速软组织扩张术/快速軟組織擴張術　rapid soft tissue expansion
快速生长/快速生長,局部快速發育　tachyauxesis
快速消毒法/瞬間消毒法　flash method
快速性心律不齐/過速性心律不整　tachyarrhythmia
快速血浆反应素试验/梅毒快速血漿反應素試驗　rapid plasma reagin test
快速血糖过多/快速血糖過多　oxyhyperglycemia
快速循环型情感障碍/快速循環型情感障礙　rapid cycling affective disorder
快速眼[运]动睡眠/快速眼球轉動睡眠,快速眼運動睡眠　rapid eye movement sleep, REM sleep
快速中子束/快速中子束　fast neutron beams
快缩肌/快縮肌　quick muscle
快缩肌纤维/快縮肌纖維　fast-twitch muscle fibers
宽度/寬度　breadth
宽拇指-姆趾综合征/寬拇指-腳拇趾症候群　broad thumb-hallux syndrome
宽频光源/寬頻光源　broad band light source
宽叶熏衣草油/歐洲薰衣草油　oil of spike
髋/髖　hip, kuan
髋部分切除术/髖部分切除術　ischiectomy
髋股痛/股髖痛　merocoxalgia
髋骨/髖骨　hip bone, haunch bone, os coxae
髋骨关节炎/髖骨關節炎　hip osteoarthritis
髋骨往下脱位/髖骨往下脱位　obturator dislocation
髋骨先天性脱位/髖骨先天性脱位　congenital dislocation of the hip

髋骨向后脱位/髋骨脱位傷及坐骨神經　sciatic dislocation
髋骨[穴]/髖骨[穴]　kuangu, EX-LE1
髋骨折/髖骨折　hip fracture
髋关节/髖關節　hip joint, articulation of hip
髋关节病/髖關節病　coxarthropathy
髋关节结核/髖關節結核　coxotuberculosis
髋[关节]轮匝肌带/輪匝帶　zonular band
髋关节切开术/髖關節切開術　coxotomy
髋关节屈曲挛缩试验/髖關節屈曲攣縮試驗　Thomas sign
髋关节脱位/髖關節脱位　hip dislocation, dislocation of hip joint
髋关节炎/髖關節炎　coxitis
髋关节炎性脊柱侧凸/髖關節炎性脊柱側彎　coxitic scoliosis
髋关节一过性滑膜炎/髖關節一過性滑膜炎　transient synovitis of hip joint
髋关节盂缘/髖臼韌帶　cotyloid ligament
髋关节真菌病/髖關節黴菌病　coxarthrocace
髋关节周炎/髖關節周圍炎　pericoxitis
髋假体/髖假體　hip prosthesis
髋臼/髖臼　acetabulum, cotyloid bone
髋臼成形术/髖臼成形術　acetabuloplasty
髋臼唇/髖臼唇　acetabular labrum
髋臼的/髖臼的　acetabular
髋臼动脉/髖臼動脈　acetabular artery
髋臼发育不良/髖臼發育不良　acetabular dysplasia
髋臼骨/髖臼骨　acetabular bone
髋臼横韧带/髖臼橫韌帶　transverse acetabular ligament
髋臼切除术/髖臼切除術　acetabulectomy
髋臼切迹/髖臼切跡　acetabular notch
髋臼上沟/髖臼上溝　supraacetabular groove
髋臼窝/髖臼凹　acetabular fossa
髋臼缘/髖臼緣　margin of acetabulum
髋臼月状面/髖月狀面　facies lunata acetabuli
髋臼支/髖臼支　acetabular branch
髋挛缩/髖攣縮　hip contracture
髋内翻/髖內翻　coxa vara
髋损伤/髖損傷　hip injury
髋痛/髖部痛　coxodynia
髋脱位/髖脱位　hip dislocation
髋外翻/髖外翻　coxa valga
髋增大/大髖　coxa magna
款冬/款冬　coltsfoot
款冬花/款冬花　common coltsfoot flower
狂暴性狂犬病/狂暴性狂犬病　furious rabies

狂暴性谵妄/狂暴性譫妄　delirium furibundum
狂病/狂病,躁狂性精神病　mania, manic psychosis
狂病·肝火发狂证/狂病·肝火發狂證　manic psychosis due to liver fire
狂病·火盛伤阴证/狂病·火盛傷陰證　manic psychosis with pattern of blazing fire injuring yin
狂病·气血瘀滞证/狂病·氣血瘀滯證　manic psychosis with pattern of qi stagnation and blood stasis
狂病·痰火扰神证/狂病·痰火擾神證　manic psychosis with pattern of phlegm-fire disturbing spirit
狂病·痰热瘀结证/狂病·痰熱瘀結證　manic psychosis with pattern of binding of phlegm-heat and static blood
狂病·心肾不交证/狂病·心腎不交證　manic psychosis with pattern of incoordination between heart and kidney
狂病·阴虚火旺证/狂病·陰虛火旺證　manic psychosis with pattern of exuberant fire due to yin deficiency
狂病·瘀血阻窍证/狂病·瘀血阻竅證　manic psychosis with pattern of static blood blocking orifices
狂狷/狂狷　arrogant and prudent
狂乱/暴怒,精神錯亂　corybantiasm
狂怒的/狂亂的,憤怒的　furibund
狂犬病/狂犬病　rabies
狂犬病病毒/狂犬[病]病毒　rabies virus
狂犬病固定毒株/狂犬病固定病毒　rabies fixed virus
狂犬病恐怖/狂犬病恐懼症　lyssophobia
狂犬病疫苗/狂犬病疫苗　rabies vaccine
狂言[乱语]/狂言[亂語]　ravings
狂蝇蛆病/狂蠅蛆病　estriasis
狂越/狂越　madness
狂者/狂者　arrogant person
矿工斑纹/礦工斑紋　colliers stripe
矿工病/礦工病　miner disease
矿工气喘/礦工氣喘　miners asthma
矿工性眼球震颤/礦工性眼球震顫　miner nystagmus
矿泉疗法/礦泉療法　crenotherapy
矿泉疗养学/礦泉療學　crenology
矿物燃料/礦物燃料　fossil fuel
矿物盐类/礦物鹽類　mineral salts
矿物药物学/礦質藥學　pharmaco-oryctology
矿物质/礦物質　mineral

矿物质纤维/礦物質纖維　mineral fiber
矿盐滤除率/礦物排除係數　coefficient of demineralization
矿脂/軟石蠟,凡士林　petrolatum
矿质过多/礦質過多　hypermineralization
矿质过少/礦質過少,礦質不足　hypomineralization
矿质皮质激素类/礦質皮質激素　mineral corticoids
矿质皮质激素类拮抗药/鹽質皮質激素類拮抗藥　mineral corticoid antagonists
框架区/框架區　framework region
眶/眶　orbit
眶板/眶板　orbital plate
眶部/眶部　orbital part
眶[部]肌节/眶[部]肌節　orbital myotome
眶部联胎/眶連胎　orbitopagus
眶底爆裂性骨折/眶底爆裂性骨折　blowout fracture of orbital floor
眶底综合征/眶底症候群　orbital floor syndrome
眶蝶骨/眶蝶骨　orbitosphenoidal bone
眶额后静脉/眶額後静脈　posterior orbitofrontal vein
眶额前静脉/眶額前静脈　anterior orbitofrontal vein
眶隔/眶隔　orbital septum
眶沟/眶溝　orbital sulcus
眶骨骨膜炎/眶骨骨膜炎　orbital osteoperiostitis
眶骨膜/眶骨膜　periorbita
眶骨膜炎/眶骨膜炎　periorbititis
眶骨折/眶骨折　orbital fracture
眶横纹肌肉瘤/眼眶横紋肌肉瘤　orbital rhabdomyosarcoma
眶回/眶迴　orbital gyrus
眶肌/[眼]眶肌　orbital muscle
眶疾病/眶疾病　orbital disease
眶假瘤/眼窩假瘤　orbital pseudotumor
眶尖综合征/眶尖症候群　orbital apex syndrome
眶间角/眼眶軸線夾角　biorbital angle
眶筋膜/眶筋膜　orbital fasciae
眶距过宽/眶距過寬,兩眼距離過遠　orbital hypertelorism
眶距过窄/眶距過窄,兩眼距離過近　orbital hypotelorism
眶口/眶口　orbital aperture, orbital opening
眶隆起/眶隆凸　orbital eminence, orbital tubercle
眶颅/眶顱　orbitocranium
眶颅管/前顱管　anterior ethmoid canal
眶面/眶面　orbital surface
眶内侧壁/眶內側壁　medial wall of orbit
眶内侧缘/眶內側緣　medial orbital margin
眶内脑膜瘤/眶內腦膜瘤　intraorbital meningioma
眶内容摘除术/眶內容摘除術　evisceration of orbit
眶内异物/眶內異物　intraorbital foreign body
眶内缘点/眶內緣點　dakryon
眶切开术/眶切開術　orbitotomy
眶球粘连/眶球粘連　syncanthus
眶筛管/後篩管　posterior ethmoid canal
眶上壁/眶上壁　superior orbital wall
眶上的/眶上的　supraorbital
眶上动脉/眶上動脈　supraorbital artery
眶上静脉/眶上静脈　supraorbital vein
眶上孔/眶上孔　supraorbital foramen
眶上裂/眶上裂　superior orbital fissure, fissura orbitalis superior
眶上裂综合征/眶上裂症候群　superior orbital fissure syndrome
眶上切迹/眶上切跡　supraorbital incisure, supraorbital notch
眶上神经/眶上神經　supraorbital nerve
眶上神经痛/眶上神經痛　supraorbital neuralgia
眶上索/眶上索　supraorbital band
眶上缘/眶上緣　supraorbital margin
眶神经/眼眶神經　orbital nerve
眶突/眶突　orbital process
眶外侧壁/眶外側壁　lateral wall of orbit
眶外侧壁切开术/眶外側壁切開術　lateral orbitotomy
眶外侧缘/眶外側緣　lateral orbital margin
眶外缘点/眶外緣點　ektokonchion
眶下壁/眶下壁　inferior orbital wall
眶下丛/眶下叢　plexus infraorbitalis
眶下的/眶下的　infraorbital
眶下动脉/眶下動脈　infraorbital artery
眶下缝/眶下縫　infraorbital suture
眶下沟/眶下溝　infraorbital groove
眶下管/眶下管　infraorbital canal
眶下间隙/眶下間隙　infraorbital space
眶下孔/眶下孔　infraorbital foramen
眶下孔[管]注射法/眶下孔[管]注射法　infraorbital foramen canal injection
眶下裂/眶下裂　inferior orbital fissure, fissura orbitalis inferior
眶下裂后方注射法/眶下裂後方注射法　posterior infraorbital fissure injection
眶下区/眶下部　infraorbital region
眶下神经/眶下神經　infraorbital nerve
眶下神经鼻内支/眶下神經鼻內支　internal nasal branches of infraorbital nerve
眶下神经鼻外支/眶下神經鼻外支　external nasal

branches of infraorbital nerve
眶下神经上唇支/眶下神經上唇支　superior labial branches of infraorbital nerve
眶下神经下睑支/眶下神經下瞼支　inferior palpebral branches of infraorbital nerve
眶下缘/眶下緣　infraorbital margin
眶下缘点/眶最下點　orbitale
眶压测量法/眼球後移測量法　orbitonometry
眶压计/眼球後移計　orbitonometer
眶缘/眶緣　orbital margin
眶支/眶支　orbital branch
眶脂肪突出/眶脂肪突出　protrusion of intraorbital fat
眶脂体/眶脂體　adipose body of orbit
眶肿瘤/眶腫瘤　orbital neoplasm
眶周的/眼眶周圍　periorbital
眶周黑变病/眼眶周圍黑變症　periorbital melanosis
眶周色素沉着/眶周色素沈著　periorbital hyperpigmentation
眶轴计/眶軸計　orbitostat
盔甲状癌/鎧甲狀癌　carcinoma en cuirasse
盔甲样的/盔甲樣的　armorlike
窥视色情癖/窺體欲　scopophilia
窥阴癖/窺陰色情，窺淫狂　voyeurism
奎尔万骨折/Quervain 氏骨折　Quervain fracture
奎吉拉病/奎吉拉病　quigila
奎克试验/奎克氏試驗　Quick test
奎肯施泰特试验/奎肯施泰特試驗　Queckenstedt test
奎纳克林/奎納克林　quinacrine
奎纳克林氮芥/奎納克林氮芥　quinacrine mustard
奎尼丁/奎尼丁　quinidine
奎尼酸/[金]雞納酸　quinic acid
奎宁/奎寧　quinine
奎宁标准规定/奎寧標準測定法　quinometry
奎宁环类/奎寧環類　quinuclidines
奎宁绿脂/奎寧綠脂　thalleioquin
奎宁酸/奎寧酸　quininic acid
奎宁中毒性弱视/奎寧毒性弱視　quinine amblyopia
奎鞣酸/金雞納鞣酸　quinotannic acid
奎孕酮/孕酮環戊烯醇　quingestrone
葵花油/葵花油　sunflower oil
葵花籽饼/向日葵子油粕　sunflower seed cake
葵花籽油/向日葵子油　sunflower seed oil
喹吡罗/喹吡羅　quinpirole
喹噁啉类/喹噁啉類　quinoxalines
喹呱嗪/喹呱嗪　quipazine
喹啉/喹啉　quinoline

喹啉生物碱/喹啉生物鹼　quinoline alkaloid
喹啉酸/喹啉酸　quinolinic acid
喹啉鎓化合物/喹啉鎓化合物　quinolinium compound
喹哪啶类/喹哪啶類　quinaldines
喹哪啶酸/喹啉甲酸　quinaldinic acid
喹诺酮/喹啉酮　quinolone
喹诺酮类/喹啉酮類　quinolones
喹嗪类/喹嗪類　quinolizines
喹嗪生物碱/喹啉聯啶生物鹼　quinolizidine alkaloid
喹唑啉类/喹唑啉類　quinazolines
喹唑啉生物碱/喹唑啉生物鹼　quinazoline alkaloid
蝰蛇毒液类/蝰蛇毒液類　viper venoms
溃烂型皮肤利什曼病/潰瘍型皮膚利什曼病　tiacarana
溃烂性痤疮/潰瘍性痤瘡　acne exulcerans
溃蚀密螺旋体/蝕瘡螺旋體　Treponema phagedenis
溃疡/潰瘍　ulcer, ulcerans
溃疡残毁性血管瘤病/潰瘍殘毀性血管瘤病　ulceromutilating hemangiomatosis
溃疡残毁性肢端病/肢端殘毀性潰瘍　ulceromutilating acropathy
溃疡分枝杆菌/潰瘍分枝桿菌　Mycobacterium ulcerans
溃疡坏死的/潰瘍壞死的　ulceronecrotic
溃疡假膜性口炎/潰瘍膜性口炎　ulceromembranous stomatitis
溃疡假膜性牙龈炎/潰瘍假膜性齦炎　ulceromembranous gingivitis
[溃疡]结痂性肾盂炎/黏附性腎盂炎　encrusted pyelitis
溃疡膜性[的]/潰瘍性及膜性的　ulceromembranous
溃疡肉芽肿/潰瘍肉芽腫　ulcerogranuloma
溃疡形成/潰瘍[形成]　elcosis
溃疡[型]皮肤利什曼病/皮膚之潰瘍型利什曼病　juccuya
溃疡性/潰瘍性　ulcerative
溃疡性扁平苔藓/潰瘍性扁平苔藓　ulcerative lichen planus
溃疡性睑缘炎/潰瘍性瞼緣炎　ulcerative blepharitis
溃疡性结肠炎/潰瘍性結腸炎　ulcerative colitis
溃疡性结核/潰瘍性結核　tuberculosis ulcerosa
溃疡性口炎/潰瘍性口炎　ulcerative stomatitis
溃疡性狼疮/潰蝕性狼瘡　lupus exedens
溃疡性皮肤结核/潰瘍性皮膚結核　tuberculosis cutis ulcerosa
溃疡性胃炎/潰瘍性胃炎　gastritis ulcerosa
溃疡性心内膜炎/潰瘍性心內膜炎　ulcerative

溃疡性心内膜炎/潰瘍性心內膜炎 ulcerative endocarditis
溃疡性咽峡炎/潰瘍性咽峽炎 angina ulcerosa
溃疡学/潰瘍學 helcology
溃疡作痒/潰瘍作癢 itching due to ulcer
昆巴病毒/肯巴病毒 Kumba virus
昆布/昆布 kelp
昆虫/昆蟲 insect
昆虫病毒/昆蟲病毒 insect virus
昆虫蛋白质类/昆蟲蛋白質類 insect proteins
昆虫基因/昆蟲基因 insect gene
昆虫激素类/昆蟲激素類 insect hormones
昆虫媒介/昆蟲媒介 insect vector
昆虫学/昆蟲學 entomology
昆克脉搏/Quincke 氏脈搏 Quincke pulse
昆克脑膜炎/Quincke 氏腦膜炎 Quincke meningitis
昆克水肿/Quincke 氏水腫,血管神經性水腫 Quincke edema
昆克征/Quincke 氏徵象 Quincke sign
昆仑/昆侖 kunlun, BL60
昆士兰蜱传斑疹伤寒/昆士蘭蜱傳斑疹傷寒 Queensland tickborne typhus
醌醇/氫醌 hydroquinol
醌还原酶类/醌還原酶類 quinone reductases
醌类/醌類 quinones
扩创引流/擴創引流 debridement and drainage
扩大/擴大 dilation
扩大的肾盂切开取石术/擴大的腎盂切開取石術 extended pyelolithotomy
扩大根治性乳房切除术/擴大性徹底根除之乳房切除術 extended radical mastectomy
扩弓螺旋器/擴弓螺旋器 expansion screw
扩散/擴散 diffusion
扩散盒/擴散盒 diffusion chamber
扩散系数/擴散係數 diffusion coefficient
扩散性皮质抑制/擴散性皮質抑制 spreading cortical depression
扩散与集中/擴散與集中 irradiation and concentration
扩音听诊器/擴音聽診器 auscultoscope
扩增/放大,擴大 amplification
扩张/擴張 dilate
扩张剂/擴張劑 dilator
扩张器/擴張器 dilator
扩张探条/擴張探條 dilating bougie
扩张纹/擴張紋 striae distensae
扩张型心肌病/擴張型心肌病 dilated cardiomyopathy
扩张性搏动/擴張性搏動 expansile pulsation
扩张性动脉瘤/擴張性動脈瘤 ectatic aneurysm
扩张性肺气肿/肺泡擴張性氣腫 ectatic emphysema
扩张[性]囊肿/擴張囊腫 dilatation cyst
括约肌/括約肌 sphincter, musculus sphincter
括约肌测压/括約肌測壓 sphincterometry
括约肌成形术/括約肌造形術 sphincteroplasty
括约肌弛缓不能/括約肌弛緩不能 sphincteral achalasia
括约肌切除术/括約肌切除術 sphincterectomy
括约肌切开器/括約肌刀 sphincterotome
括约肌切开术/括約肌切斷術 sphincterotomy
括约肌外瘘/括約肌外瘻 extrasphincteric fistula
括约肌炎/括約肌炎 sphincteritis
蛞蝓阿米巴/蛞蝓阿米巴 Amoeba limax
阔颌面容/闊頜狀態 eurygnathism
阔节裂头绦虫/廣節裂頭條蟲 diphyllobothrium latum
阔节裂头绦虫病/闊節裂頭條蟲病 diphyllobothriasis latum
阔筋膜/闊筋膜 fascia lata
阔筋膜张肌/闊筋膜張肌 musculus tensor fasciae latae
阔面/闊面,扁面 platyopia
阔盘吸虫病/闊盤吸蟲病 eurytremiasis
阔韧带/闊韌帶 broad ligament
阔韧带囊肿/闊韌帶囊腫 cyst of broad ligament
阔韧带内妊娠/韌帶內妊娠 intraligamentary pregnancy
阔韧带脓肿/闊韌帶膿腫 broad ligament abscess
阔韧带妊娠/闊韌帶妊娠 broad ligament pregnancy
阔眼裂/大眼,大眶 euryopia
阔跖足/闊蹠足 broad foot
阔足/擴散足 spread foot
廓清/廓清作用 clearance

L

拉埃内克肝硬化/拉埃內克肝硬化　Laennec cirrhosis
拉巴拉克溶液/Labarraque 氏溶液　Labarraque solution
拉贝洛尔/拉貝洛爾　Labetalol
拉德手术/拉德手術　Ladd operation
拉尔逊-约翰逊病/拉-强二氏病　Larsen-Johansson disease
拉封/拉封　pull-seal
拉福拉病/拉福拉病　Lafora disease
拉吉细胞/Raji 氏細胞　Raji cell
拉克塔西丁/含乳酸[食品]保存剂　lactacidin
拉雷绷带/Larrey 氏繃帶　Larrey bandage
拉伦侏儒症/拉倫侏儒症　Laron dwarfism
拉曼光谱分析/拉曼光譜分析　Raman spectrum analysis
拉曼效应/拉曼效應　Raman effect
拉米夫定/拉米夫定　lamivudine
拉姆齐·亨特综合征/拉姆齊·亨特症候群　Ramsay Hunt syndrome
拉尼镍/拉尼鎳　Raney nickel
拉诺辛/拉諾辛　lanoxin
拉普拉斯定律/Laplace 氏定律　Laplace law
拉普兰消化不良/消化不良症　ullem
拉塞尔小体/Russell 小體　Russell body
拉塞格征/拉塞格徵　Lasegue sign
拉沙病毒/拉沙病毒　Lassa virus
拉沙里菌素/拉沙洛西　Lasalocid
拉沙热/拉沙熱　lassa fever
拉伸强度/牵引韌力　tensile strength
拉斯穆森动脉瘤/Rasmussen 氏動脈瘤　Rasmussen aneurysm
拉斯泰利手术/拉斯泰利手術　Rastelli operation
拉特克管/拉克氏管　Rathke duct
拉特克囊/拉克氏囊,脊椎動物胚胎外胚層盲管　Rathke pouch
拉特克囊肿/拉克氏囊腫　Rathke cyst, Rathke pouch cyst
拉氧头孢/拉氧頭孢　Moxalactam
拉耶病/Rayer 氏病　Rayer disease
腊肠样手/浮脹手,水腫手　main succulente
腊肠中毒/臘腸中毒　allantiasis
腊肠状腹块/臈卷　iliac roll
蜡/蠟　wax
蜡布/蠟布　cerecloth
蜡成型术/蠟造模型術　ceroplasty
蜡刀/蠟刀　wax spatula
蜡痕法/咬合蠟痕　wax bite
蜡疗法/蠟療法　wax therapy
蜡模拟/蠟模擬　wax simulation
蜡膜/蠟膜　wax mask
蜡目/蠟目　eyelid myiasis, waxy eye
蜡酸/蠟酸　cerotic acid
蜡丸/蠟丸　wax pill
蜡型/蠟型　wax form
蜡型制作/蠟模形成　waxing
蜡[样变]瘤/蠟樣變瘤　ceroma
蜡样变性/蠟樣變性　waxy degeneration
蜡样的/蠟樣的,蠟狀的　waxy
蜡样管型/蠟狀圓柱　waxy cast
蜡样坏死/蠟樣壞死　waxy necrosis
蜡样皮脂溢/蠟性皮脂漏　seborrhea cerea
蜡样屈曲/蠟樣屈曲　waxy flexibility
蜡样色素/蠟樣色素　ceroid pigment
蜡样物质/蠟樣物質　ceroidlike material
蜡样脂贮积病/蠟狀儲積症　ceroid storage disease
蜡状皮肤和僵直关节/臈狀皮膚和僵直關節　waxy skin and stiff joint
辣根菜/壞血病草　Cochlearia officinalis
辣根过氧化物酶/辣根過氧化物酶　horseradish peroxidase, HRP
辣椒/辣椒　capsicum
辣椒酊/番椒酊　capsicum tincture
辣椒粉/辣椒粉　cayenne pepper
辣椒粉斑/辣椒粉斑　cayenne pepper spot
辣椒辣素/辣椒辣素　capsaicin
辣椒酸/辣椒酸　capsic acid
辣木子油酸/二十二烷酸　behenic acid
来回摩擦音/來回擦音　to-and-fro sound
来苏糖/來蘇糖　lyxose
来苏糖酸/來蘇糖酸　lyxonic acid
来源/[來]源　source

莱昂病毒/Leon 病毒　Leon virus
莱昂化作用/里昂化作用　lyonization
莱昂假说/里昂假說　Lyon hypothesis
莱奥糖/萊奧糖　laiose
莱伯病/萊伯病　Leber disease
莱登共济失调/Leyden 氏失調症　Leyden ataxia
莱迪希管/Leydig 氏管　Leydig duct
莱迪希细胞/Leydig 氏間質細胞　Leydig cell
莱迪希细胞瘤/睾丸間質細胞瘤　Leydig cell tumor
莱恩带/Lane 氏帶　Lane band
莱恩[接骨]板/蘭氏板　Lane plate
莱恩纽结/Lane 氏帶　Lane band
莱尔病/Lyell 氏病　Lyell disease
莱尔米特征/賴爾米特徵　Lhermitte sign
莱菔子/萊菔子　radish seed
莱加尔试验/萊加爾試驗　Legal test
莱里征/萊里徵　Leri sign
莱-麦综合征/Lhermitte-McAlpine 二氏症候群　Lhermitte-McAlpine syndrome
莱姆病/萊姆氏病　Lyme disease
莱姆病菌苗/萊姆病菌苗　Lyme disease vaccine
莱姆关节炎/萊姆關節炎　Lyme arthritis
莱穆瓦耶综合征/萊穆瓦耶症候群　Lermoyez syndrome
莱施-奈恩综合征/萊施-奈恩症候群　Lesch-Nyhan syndrome
莱氏病/Lain 氏病　Lain disease
莱特蛋白补体结合试验/Reiter 氏蛋白補體結合試驗　Reiter protein complement-fixation test
莱特尔综合征/Reiter 氏症候群　Reiter syndrome
莱特雷尔-西韦病/勒-賽二氏病　Letterer-Siwe disease
莱特伍德综合征/Lightwood 氏症候群　Lightwood syndrome
莱维综合征/Levi 氏症候群　Levi syndrome
赖氨酸/賴胺酸　lysine
赖氨酸丙氨酸/賴胺酸丙氨酸　Lysinoalanine
赖氨酸 tRNA 连接酶/賴胺酸 tRNA 連接酶　lysine-tRNA ligase
赖氨酸升压素/賴胺酸昇壓素　lysine vasopressin
赖氨酸羧肽酶/賴胺酸羧肽酶　lysine carboxypeptidase
赖氨酰氧化酶/賴胺醯氧化酶　lysyl oxidase
赖-戴综合征/Riley-Day 二氏症候群　Riley-Day syndrome
赖尔带/Reil 氏帶　band of Reil
赖芬斯坦综合征/賴芬斯坦症候群　Reifenstein syndrome
赖甲环素/賴甲四環素　lymecycline
赖诺普利/賴諾普利　Lisinopril
赖特染剂/賴特染劑　Wright stain
赖特综合征/Wright 氏症候群　Wright syndrome
赖希曼病/Reichmann 氏病　Reichmann disease
赖歇尔泄殖腔管/Reichel 氏洩殖腔管　Reichel cloacal duct
赖歇特瘢痕/Reichert 氏瘢　Reichert scar
赖歇特软骨/賴歇特軟骨　Reichert cartilage
赖药菌/賴藥菌　drug dependent organism
赖因克晶体/賴因克晶體　crystal of Reinke
兰伯贾第虫/腸梨形蟲　Giardia lamblia
兰[伯]氏鞭毛虫病/蘭伯氏鞭毛蟲病　lambliasis
兰德里瘫痪/Landry 氏癱瘓　Landry palsy
兰德里综合征/Landry 氏症候群　Landry syndrome
兰格肌/Langer 氏肌　Langer muscle
兰格溶液/Lange 氏溶液　Lange solution
兰吉尔绷带/Langier 氏繃帶　Langier bandage
兰开斯特屏/蘭開斯特屏　Lancaster screen
兰利神经/Langley 氏神經　Langley nerve
兰尼碱/蘭尼鹼　ryanodine
兰尼碱受体钙释放通道/蘭尼鹼受體鈣釋放通道　ryanodine receptor calcium release channel
兰室秘藏/蘭室秘藏　Secret Book of Orchid Chamber
兰斯菲尔德分类/蘭菲德氏分類法　lancefield classification
兰西神经/Lancisi 氏神經　nerve of Lancisi
阑尾/蘭尾　①vermiform appendix, appendix vermiformis ②lanwei
阑尾残端/蘭尾殘端　appendiceal stump
阑尾的/蘭尾的　appendiceal
阑尾动脉/蘭尾動脈　appendicular artery
阑尾粪石/蘭尾糞石　appendiceal fecalith
阑尾积水/蘭尾積水　hydroappendix
阑尾集合淋巴滤泡/蘭尾集合淋巴濾泡　aggregated lymphatic follicle of vermiform appendix
阑尾绞痛/蘭尾絞痛　appendicular colic
阑尾静脉/蘭尾靜脈　appendicular vein
阑尾口/蘭尾口　orifice of vermiform appendix, opening of vermiform appendix
阑尾淋巴结/蘭尾淋巴結　appendicular lymph node
阑尾盲肠吻合术/蘭尾盲腸造口吻合術　appendicocecostomy
阑尾黏膜炎/蘭尾黏膜炎,卡他性蘭尾炎　endoappendicitis
阑尾黏液囊肿/蘭尾黏液囊腫　appendiceal mucocele
阑尾脓肿/蘭尾膿腫　appendiceal abscess

阑尾旁炎/闌尾旁組織炎,蚓突旁炎 para-appendicitis
阑尾切除术/闌尾切除術 appendectomy
阑尾疝/闌尾疝氣 appendicocele
阑尾[X射线]造影术/闌尾X光攝影術 vermography
阑尾石病/闌尾結石病 appendicolithiasis
阑尾输尿管成形术/闌尾輸尿管成形術 appendix ureteroplasty
阑尾系膜/闌尾繫膜 mesoappendix
阑尾系膜炎/闌尾繫膜炎 mesoappendicitis
阑尾性胃痛/闌尾性胃痛 appendicular gastralgia
阑尾性消化不良/闌尾性消化不良 appendicular dyspepsia
阑尾[穴]/闌尾[穴] lanwei, EX-LE7
阑尾炎/闌尾炎 appendicitis
阑尾造口术/闌尾造口術,闌尾造瘻術 appendicostomy
阑尾粘连分离术/闌尾鬆解術,闌尾分離術 appendicolysis
阑尾肿瘤/闌尾腫瘤 appendiceal neoplasms
阑尾周围脓肿/闌尾周圍膿腫 periappendiceal abscess
阑尾周炎/闌尾周圍炎 periappendicitis
蓝斑/藍斑 locus coeruleus
蓝斑核/藍斑核 nucleus ceruleus
蓝斑下核/藍斑下核 subceruleus nucleus
蓝鼻病/藍鼻病 blue nose disease
蓝刺头属植物/藍刺頭屬植物 Echinops plant
蓝顶囊肿/藍頂囊腫 blue-dome cyst
蓝盾会/藍盾會 blue shield
蓝盾医疗保险/[美國]藍盾醫療門診保險 blue shield movement
蓝巩膜/藍鞏膜 blue sclerae
蓝巩膜综合征/藍鞏膜症候群 blue-sclera syndrome
蓝鼓膜/藍鼓膜 blue drum
蓝光幻视/藍光幻視 cyanophose
蓝黄色盲/藍黃色盲 blue-yellow blindness
蓝脊章鱼/藍脊章魚 blue-ridged octopus
蓝甲/藍甲 blue nails
蓝绿藻/藍綠藻 blue-green algae
蓝莓松饼状病灶/藍莓松餅狀病灶 blueberry muffin lesions
蓝脓/藍[色]膿 blue pus
蓝色病/嬰兒發紺病 blue disease
蓝色巩膜/青色鞏膜 blue sclera
蓝色黑色素瘤/藍色黑色素瘤 blue melanoma
蓝色犁头霉/藍色犁頭黴 Absidia coerulea
蓝色盲/第三原色色盲 tritanopsia
蓝色皮片/藍色皮片 blue graft
蓝色弱/藍色弱 tritanomalia
蓝色水肿/藍色水腫 blue edema
蓝色橡皮疱样痣/藍色橡皮皰樣痣 blue rubber bleb nevus
蓝色橡皮球痣综合征/藍色橡皮球痣症候群 blue rubber bleb nevus syndrome
蓝舌病/藍舌病 bluetongue
蓝舌病毒/藍舌病毒 bluetongue virus
蓝神经痣/藍色神經樣痣 blue neuronevus
蓝十字会/藍十字會 blue cross
蓝视症/青幻視,藍幻視 cyanopsia
蓝曙红/藍伊紅 safrosin
蓝辛病毒/藍辛病毒 Lansing virus
蓝移/藍移 blue shift
蓝趾综合征/藍色腳趾症候群 blue toe syndrome
蓝痣/藍痣 blue nevus
蓝紫光疗法/藍紫光療法 blue and violet light therapy
篮细胞/籃狀細胞 basket cell
榄香脂/欖香脂 elemi
烂疔/爛疔 gas gangrene
烂疔·毒入营血证/爛疔·毒入營血證 gas gangrene with pattern of toxin entering nutrient-blood phases
烂疔·湿火炽盛证/爛疔·濕火熾盛證 gas gangrene with blazing dampness-fire pattern
烂喉丹痧/爛喉丹痧,猩紅熱 scarlatina, scarlet fever
烂喉丹痧·毒燔气营证/爛喉丹痧·毒燔氣營證 scarlet fever with pattern of toxin pervading both qi and nutrient phases
烂喉丹痧·毒侵肺卫证/爛喉丹痧·毒侵肺衛證 scarlet fever with pattern of toxin invading lung-defense phase
烂喉丹痧·毒壅气分证/爛喉丹痧·毒壅氣分證 scarlet fever with pattern of toxin congesting qi phase
烂喉丹痧·余邪伤阴证/爛喉丹痧·餘邪傷陰證 scarlet fever with pattern of yin injury by lingering pathogen
滥用/濫用 abuse
郎飞结/郎飛結 Ranvier node
郎飞细胞/Ranvier氏細胞 Ranvier cell
狼疮/狼瘡 lupus
狼疮带/狼瘡帶 lupus band
狼疮抗凝物/狼瘡抗凝物,狼瘡抑制劑 lupus anticoagulant

狼疮脑病/狼瘡腦病　lupus encephalopathy
狼疮凝固抑制物/狼瘡凝固抑制物　lupus coagulation inhibitor
狼疮肾炎/狼瘡性腎炎　lupus nephritis
狼疮性肾小球性肾炎/狼瘡腎絲球腎炎　lupus glomerulonephritis
狼疮样痤疮/狼瘡樣痤瘡　lupoid acne
狼疮样肝炎/類狼瘡性肝炎　lupoid hepatitis
狼疮样溃疡/類狼瘡潰瘍　lupoid ulcer
狼疮样腺瘤/狼瘡狀腺瘤　lupiform adenoma
狼疮样须疮/狼瘡狀鬚瘡　lupoid sycosis
狼疮样综合征/類狼瘡症候群　lupus-like syndrome
狼疮抑制剂/狼瘡抑制劑　lupus inhibitor
狼疮状的/狼瘡狀的　lupiform
狼毒中毒/狼毒中毒　stellerae poisoning
狼蛛/塔蘭登毒蛛　tarantula
朗伯/朗伯　Lambert
朗杜齐病/Landouzy 氏疾病　Landouzy disease
朗杜齐-格拉塞定律/蘭-格二氏定律　Landouzy-Grasset law
朗杜齐紫癜/Landouzy 氏紫癜病　Landouzy purpura
朗多环形视力表/朗多環形視力表　Landolt chart
朗格汉斯细胞/蘭格漢[氏]細胞　Langerhans cell
朗格溶液/Lang 氏溶液　Lang solution
朗格液/Lang 氏液　Lang fluid
朗汉斯巨细胞/朗漢斯巨細胞　Langhans giant cell
劳复/勞復　recurrence caused by overexertion
劳宫/勞宮　laogong, PC8
劳倦/勞倦,過勞　overstrain
劳拉西泮/蘿拉西泮　Lorazepam
劳力性呼吸困难/用力性呼吸困難　exertional dyspnea
劳痢/勞痢　phthisic dysentery
劳淋/勞淋　overstrain strangury, stranguria due to overstrain
劳伦斯-比德尔综合征/洛-比二氏症候群　Laurence-Biedl syndrome
劳伦斯-穆恩-比德尔综合征/勞-莫-比三氏症候群　Laurence-Moon-Biedl syndrome
劳伦斯-穆恩综合征/勞倫斯-穆恩症候群　Laurence-Moon syndrome
劳疟/勞瘧　overstrain malaria
劳-赛综合征/Lawrence-Seip 氏症候群,脂肪萎縮性糖尿病症候群　Lawrence-Seip syndrome
劳氏肉瘤病毒/Rous 氏肉瘤病毒　Rous sarcoma virus
劳斯肉瘤/勞斯肉瘤　Rous sarcoma
劳斯相关病毒/勞斯肉瘤相關病毒　Rous-associated virus
劳嗽/勞嗽　overstrain cough
劳损/勞損　chronic strain
劳则气耗/勞則氣耗　overexertion leading to qi consumption
牢脉/牢脈　firm pulse
痨病/癆病　consumptive disease, phthisis
痨病型/肺癆型　phthisic type
痨病性潮红/癆病性潮紅　hectic flush
痨病治疗/癆病治療　phthisiotherapeutics
老鹳草/老鸛草　common heron's bill herb, wilford granesbill herb
老化/陳化　aging
老化皮肤/老化皮膚　aging skin
老龄化指数/老齡化指數　index of aging
老年/老年　advanced age
老年斑/老年棕斑　senile lentigines
老年扁平疣/老年扁平疣　verruca plana senilis
老年肺气肿/老年肺氣腫　jenner emphysema
老年粉刺/老年性粉刺　senile comedones
老年抚养率/老年撫養率　aged dependency ratio
老年骨折/老年骨折　senile fracture
老年黑皮病/老年性黑皮病　senile melanoderma
老年护理学/老年護理學　geriatric nursing
老年化/衰老,老邁　senescence
老年环/老人環,老人弓　arcus senilis
老年角化[病]/老年角化病　senile keratosis
老年精神病学/老年精神病學　geriatric psychiatry
老年口腔医学/老人牙科學,老年牙醫學　gerodontics
老年聋/老年聾　senile deafness
老年皮肤萎缩/老年皮膚萎縮　atrophia cutis senilis
老年皮脂腺痣/老年性皮脂腺痣　senile sebaceous gland nevus
老年[期]精神病/老年精神病　senile psychosis
老年前期/老年前期,將老期　presenium
老年前期精神病/老年前期精神病,早老性精神病　presenile psychosis
老年前期萎缩/老年前期萎縮　presenile atrophy
老年人/老年人　elderly
老年人保健服务/老年人保健服務　health services for the aged
老年人口比例/老年人口比例　proportion of aged population
老年人身心健康评价/老年人身心健康評價　geriatric assessment
老年人牙科医疗/老年人牙科醫療　dental care for aged

老年神经外科[学]/老年神經外科[學] geriatric neurosurgery
老年脱发/老年秃髮 alopecia senilis
老年心脏病/老年心臟病 presbycardia
老年性/老年的,老人的 senile
老年性白内障/老年内障 senile cataract
老年性黄斑变性/老年性黃斑變性 senile macular degeneration
老年性睑外翻/老年性瞼外翻 senile ectropion
老年性精神障碍/老年癡呆,老憒 presbyophrenia
老年性静脉扩张/老年性靜脈擴張 senile phlebectasia
老年性聋/老年性聾 presbycusis
老年性皮脂腺增生/老年性皮脂腺增生 senile sebaceous hyperplasia
老年性雀斑/老年性雀斑 age freckles
老年性雀斑样痣/老人斑 lentigo senilis
老年[性]瘙痒/老年搔癢症 pruritus senilis
老年性上睑松垂/老年性上瞼鬆垂 senile blepharochalasis of upper eyelid
老年性肾硬化/老年性腎硬化 senile nephrosclerosis
老年性食管/食道老化,食道退化 presbyesophagus
老年性退化/老年性退化 senile involution
老年性萎缩/老年萎縮 senile atrophy
老年性消瘦/老年性消瘦 geromarasmus
老年性血管瘤/老年性血管瘤 senile angioma
老年性阴道炎/老年性陰道炎 senile vaginitis
老年性谵妄/老年譫妄 senile delirium
老年性震颤/老年性震顫 senile tremor
老年性紫癜/老年紫癜病 purpura senilis
老年学/老人科學 gerontology
老年牙科学/老年牙科 geriatric dentistry
老年牙医/老人牙科醫師 geriodontist
老年药理学/老年藥理學 gerontopharmacology
老年药学/老年藥學 geriatric pharmacy
老年医学/老年醫學 geriatric medicine
老年医学的/老年醫學的,老年病學的 geriatric
老年疣/老年性疣 senile wart
老年状皮肤/老年狀皮膚 geroderma
老年综合征/老年症候群 geriatric syndrome
老人护理/老人照護 elderly care
老人疗养院/老人療養院 homes for the aged
老人疣/老人疣 verruca senilis
老人之家/老人之家 nursing home
老舌/老舌 tough tongue
老视/遠視,老花眼 presbyopia
老视者/老花眼者 presbyope
老眼晕/老眼暈 senile halo

铑/銠 rhodium
烙除法/烙除法 igniextirpation
烙[铁]术/烙[鐵]術 technocausis
烙针/烙針 cautery needle
落枕/落枕 stiff neck
落枕·风寒侵袭证/落枕·風寒侵襲證 stiff neck with wind-cold invasion pattern
落枕·血瘀气滞证/落枕·血瘀氣滯證 stiff neck with pattern of blood stasis and qi stagnation
酪氨酸/酪胺[基]酸 tyrosine
酪氨酸代谢病/酪胺基酸病 tyrosinosis
酪氨酸单氧化酶/酪胺酸單氧化酶 tyrosine 3-monooxygenase
酪氨酸酚裂合酶/酪胺酸酚裂合酶 tyrosine phenol-lyase
酪氨酸 tRNA 连接酶/酪胺酸 tRNA 連接酶 tyrosine-tRNA ligase
酪氨酸磷酸化抑制剂/酸胺磷酸化抑制劑 tyrphostin
酪氨酸酶/酪胺基酸酶 tyrosinase
酪氨酸尿症/酪胺基酸尿症 tyrosinuria
酪氨酸脱羧酶/酪胺酸脫羧酶 tyrosine decarboxylase
酪氨酸血症/酪胺酸血症 tyrosinemia
酪氨酸转氨酶/酪胺酸轉胺基酶 tyrosine transaminase
酪氨酰基尿/氧苯胺丙酸尿症 tyrosyluria
酪胺/酪胺 tyramine
酪胺试验/酪胺試驗 tyramine test
酪蛋白/酪蛋白 casein
酪[蛋白]胨/乳酪腖 casein peptone
酪蛋白钙/酪蛋白酸鈣 calcium caseinate
酪蛋白激酶类/酪蛋白激酶類 casein kinases
酪蛋白类/酪蛋白類 caseins
酪蛋白酶/酪蛋白酶 casease
酪蛋白所致/酪蛋白引起的 casein-induced
酪蛋白样白蛋白/酪蛋白樣白蛋白 caseiniform albumin
酪蛋白原/酪蛋白原,乾酪素原 caseinogen
酪蛋白原酸盐/酪蛋白原酸鹽 caseinogenate
酪蜜/奶油蜜 butyromel
乐果/樂果 dimethoate
勒奥伊综合征/Leroy 氏症候群,脂質黏多醣代謝障礙症 Leroy syndrome
勒夫特病/Luft 氏病 Luft disease
勒福截骨术/勒福截骨術 Le Fort osteotomy
勒福I型骨折/勒福I型骨折 Le Fort fracture
勒福I型截骨术/勒福I型截骨術 Le Fort osteotomy

勒加尔病/Legal 氏病　Legal disease
勒里什压迫/Leriche 氏壓迫　Leriche compression
勒内格尔病/勒內格爾病　Lenegre disease
勒尼奥残余胞质/勒尼奧殘餘胞質　residual cytoplasm of Regnaud
勒斯克综合征/Leschke 氏症候群　Leschke syndrome
勒韦病/Lowe 氏病　Lowe disease
勒韦综合征/Lowe 氏症候群　Lowe syndrome
勒伊斯肌/Ruysch 氏肌　Ruysch muscle
雷夫叙姆病/雷夫叙姆病　Refsum disease
雷夫叙姆综合征/雷夫叙姆症候群,Refsum 氏症候群　Refsum syndrome
雷复尼特/雷複尼特　Rafoxanide
雷公炮炙论/雷公炮製論　Master Lei's Discourse on Drug Processing, Leigong Paozhilun
雷公藤多苷/雷公藤多苷　Tripterygium Glycosides
雷公藤片/雷公藤片　leigongteng tablet
雷公藤中毒/雷公藤中毒　Tripterygium wilfordii poisoning
雷火神针/雷火神針　thunder-fire miraculous moxa roll
雷克林豪森病/Recklinghausen 氏病　Recklinghausen disease
雷氯必利/雷氯必利　raclopride
雷洛昔芬/雷洛昔芬　raloxifene
雷马克带/Remak 氏帶　band of Remak
雷蒙·塞斯唐综合征/雷蒙·塞斯唐症候群　Raymond Cestan syndrome
雷米尔病/Lemierre 氏病　Lemierre disease
雷米普利/雷米普利　Ramipril
雷尼替丁/雷尼替丁　Ranitidine
雷诺病/Raynaud 氏病　Raynaud disease
雷诺现象/Raynaud 氏現象　Raynaud phenomenon
雷丘斯细胞/Retzius 氏細胞　cell of Retzius
雷-塞综合征/Raymond-Cestan 二氏症候群　Raymond-Cestan syndrome
雷氏铵/雷氏銨　ammonium reineckate
雷氏盐/雷氏鹽　Reinecke salt
雷琐辛类/雷瑣辛類　resorcinols
雷头风/雷頭風　thunder headache
雷丸/雷丸　thunder ball
雷维尔丹移植物/Reverdin 氏移植物　Reverdin graft
雷维尔丹针/Reverdin 氏針　Reverdin needle
雷蚴/雷蚴　rediae
镭/鐳　radium
镭插入器/鐳插入器,鐳錠儀　radiode
镭管/鐳管　radium cell

镭疗法/鐳療法,居里療法　Curie therapy
镭疗器/鐳療器　radioactor
镭透照镜/鐳透照鏡　radiodiaphane
镭性坏死/鐳性壞死　radium necrosis
镭针/鐳針　radium needle
累积创伤/累積創傷　cumulative trauma disorder
累积反射/累積反射　integrated reflection
蕾状磨牙/蕾狀臼齒　bud molar
蕾状期/蕾狀期　bud stage
蕾状牙/蕾狀牙　bud tooth
肋/肋　rib, costa
肋臂综合征/肋臂症候群　costobrachial syndrome
肋部/肋部　costal part
肋长提肌/提肋長肌　musculi levatores costarum longi
肋短提肌/提肋短肌　levatores costarum breves
肋膈隐窝/肋膈隱窩　costodiaphragmatic recess
肋弓/肋弓　costal arch, arch of ribs
肋弓角/胸廓切跡　thoracic incisure
肋沟/肋溝　costal groove, costal sulcus
肋骨/肋骨　costal bone
肋骨底的/肋骨底的　rib-basal
肋骨肺固定术/肋骨肺固定術　costopneumopexy
肋骨分叉-基底细胞痣-颌骨囊肿综合征/分歧肋骨基底細胞痣頜囊腫症候群　bifid rib-basal cell nevus-jaw cyst syndrome
肋骨沟/肋骨溝　sulucs costae
肋骨骨膜剥脱术/肋骨骨膜剝脫術　periosteal stripping of rib
肋骨骨折/肋骨骨折　rib fracture, costal fracture
肋骨横突切除术/肋骨及橫突切除術　costotransversectomy
肋骨颈外韧带/肋骨頸外韌帶　external ligament of neck of rib
肋骨[肋]软骨的/肋與其軟骨的　costochondral
肋骨劈裂移植颅成形术/肋骨劈裂移植顱成形術　split-rib cranioplasty
肋骨劈裂移植术/肋骨劈裂移植術　split-rib grafting
肋骨切除术/肋骨切除術　costatectomy
肋骨切开术/肋骨切斷術　costotomy
肋骨特征/肋骨特徵　costal stigma
肋骨体/肋骨幹　shaft of rib
肋骨痛/肋痛　costalgia
肋骨头前韧带/肋骨頭前韌帶　anterior ligament of head of rib
肋骨头小嵴/肋骨小頭嵴,肋骨頭三角狀隆凸　cuneiform eminence of head of rib
肋骨外翻胸骨成形术/肋骨外翻胸骨成形術

costoversion thoracoplasty
肋骨纤维性发育不良/肋骨纖維性發育不良 fibrous dysplasia of rib
肋骨胸骨成形术/肋骨胸骨成形術 costosternoplasty
肋横突关节/肋橫突關節 costotransverse joint, costotransverse articulation
肋横突后韧带/肋橫突後韌帶 posterior costotransverse ligament
肋横突孔/肋橫突孔 costotransverse foramen
肋横突韧带/肋橫突韌帶 costotransverse ligament
肋横突上韧带/肋橫突上韌帶 superior costotransverse ligament
肋横突外侧韧带/肋橫突外韌帶，外側肋橫突韌帶 lateral costotransverse ligament
肋后吻合/肋後吻合 postcostal anastomosis
肋喙韧带/肋喙韌帶 costocoracoid ligament
肋间臂神经/肋間臂神經 intercostobrachial nerve
肋间[的]/肋間的 intercostal
肋间后动脉/肋間後動脈 posterior intercostal artery
肋间后动脉背侧支/肋間後動脈背側支 dorsal branch of posterior intercostal artery
肋间后动脉脊支/肋間後動脈脊支 spinal branch of posterior intercostal artery
肋间后动脉乳房外侧支/肋間後動脈乳房外側支 lateral mammary branch of posterior intercostal artery
肋间后静脉/肋間後靜脈，後肋間靜脈 posterior intercostal vein, venae intercostales posterior
肋间后淋巴结/肋間後淋巴結 posterior intercostal lymph node
肋间肌/肋間肌 intercostal muscle
肋间淋巴结/肋間淋巴結 intercostal lymph node
肋间内肌/肋間內肌 internal intercostal muscle
肋间内膜/肋間內膜 internal intercostal membrane
肋间前动脉/肋間前動脈 anterior intercostal artery
肋间前静脉/前肋間靜脈 anterior intercostal veins, venae intercostales anterior
肋间前淋巴结/肋間前淋巴結 anterior intercostal lymph node
肋间前支/肋間前支 anterior intercostal branch
肋间韧带/肋間韌帶 intercostal ligament
肋间神经/肋間神經 intercostal nerve
肋间神经前皮支/肋間神經前皮支 anterior cutaneous branch of intercostal nerve
肋间神经痛/肋間神經痛 intercostal neuralgia
肋间神经外侧皮支/肋間神經外側皮支 lateral cutaneous branch of intercostal nerve
肋间神经阻滞术/肋間神經阻滯術 intercostal nerve block
肋间外肌/肋間外肌 external intercostal muscle
肋间外膜/肋間外膜 external intercostal membrane
肋间外韧带/外肋間韌帶 external intercostal ligament
肋间隙/肋間隙 intercostal space
肋间型霉素/肋間型黴素 coformycin
肋间引流术/肋間引流術 intercostal drainage
肋间中间淋巴结/肋間中間淋巴結 intermediate intercostal lymph node
肋间最内肌/肋間最內肌 musculi intercostales intimi
肋间最上动脉/最上肋間動脈 supreme intercostal artery, highest intercostal artery
肋间最上静脉/最上肋間靜脈 highest intercostal vein, vena intercostalis suprema
肋剑突韧带/肋劍突韌帶 costoxiphoid ligament
肋角/肋角 costal angle, angle of rib
肋结肠韧带/肋結腸韌帶 costocolic ligament
肋结节/肋結節 costal tubercle
肋结节关节面/肋結節關節面 articular facet of costal tubercle
肋结节韧带/肋結節韌帶 ligament of tubercle of rib
肋颈/肋頸 costal neck
肋颈干/肋頸幹 costocervical trunk
肋颈嵴/肋頸嵴 crest of costal neck
肋颈韧带/肋骨頸韌帶 ligament of neck of rib
肋疽/肋疽 tuberculosis of costal region
肋面/肋面 costal surface
肋切迹/肋骨切跡 costal notch
肋软骨/肋軟骨 costal cartilage, cartilaginous extremity of rib
肋软骨发育不全/肋軟骨發育不全 achondroplasia of rib
肋软骨间关节/肋軟骨間關節 interchondral articulation of ribs
肋软骨连结/肋軟骨連接 costochondral joint
肋软骨切断术/肋軟骨切斷術 costal chondrotomy
肋软骨松动变形/鬆動的肋軟骨 slipping rib cartilage
肋软骨炎/肋軟骨炎 costochondritis
肋软骨综合征/肋軟骨症候群 costochondral syndrome
肋式呼吸/肋式呼吸 costal respiration
肋锁的/肋與其鎖骨的 costoclavicular
肋锁韧带/肋鎖韌帶 costoclavicular ligament
肋锁韧带压迹/肋鎖韌帶壓痕 impression for

costoclavicular ligament
肋锁综合征/肋與鎖骨症候群　costoclavicular syndrome
肋提肌/提肋肌　levator muscle of ribs
肋体/肋骨體　shaft of rib
肋头/肋頭　costal head
肋头辐状韧带/肋頭輻射韌帶　radiate ligament of costal head
肋头关节/肋頭關節　joint of costal head, articulation of head of rib
肋头关节面/肋頭關節面　articular facet of costal head
肋头关节内韧带/肋頭關節內韌帶　intraarticular ligament of costal head
肋头嵴/肋頭嵴　crest of costal head
肋突/肋突　costal process
肋外侧支/肋外側支　lateral costal branch
肋下动脉/肋下動脈　subcostal artery
肋下动脉背侧支/肋下動脈背側支　dorsal branch of subcostal artery
肋下动脉脊支/肋下動脈脊支　spinal branch of subcostal artery
肋下沟/肋下溝　subcostal groove
肋下肌/肋下肌　subcostale
肋下静脉/肋下靜脈　subcostal vein
肋下平面/肋下平面　subcostal plane
肋下神经/肋下神經　subcostal nerve
肋小头辐状韧带/肋小頭輻狀韌帶　radiate ligament of rib
肋心包韧带/肋心包膜韌帶　costopericardiac ligament
肋胸骨韧带/肋胸骨韌帶　costosternal ligament
肋胸膜/肋胸膜　costal pleura, costal part
肋腋静脉/肋腋靜脈　costoaxillary vein
肋中央韧带/肋中央韌帶　costocentral ligament
肋椎关节/肋椎關節　costovertebral joint, costocentral articulation
肋椎韧带/肋椎韌帶　costovertebral ligament
肋纵隔隐窝/肋縱隔隱窩　costomediastinal recess
泪/淚　tear
泪鼻甲缝/淚甲縫　lacrimoconchal suture
泪襞/鼻淚管皺襞　lacrimal fold
泪部/淚部　lacrimal part
泪道/淚道　lacrimal passage
泪道冲洗/淚道沖洗　irrigation of lacrimal passage
泪道探通术/淚道探通術　probing of lacrimal passage
泪道探针/淚道探針　lacrimal probe
泪道狭窄/淚道狹窄　stenosis of lacrimal passage
泪道阻塞/淚道阻塞　obstruction of lacrimal passage
泪点/淚點　lacrimal punctum, dacryon
泪点扩张器/淚點擴張器　punctum dilator
泪点扩张术/淚點擴張術　dilatation of lacrimal puncta
泪点外翻/淚點外翻　eversion of lacrimal punctum
泪点狭窄/淚點狹窄　stenosis of lacrimal punctum
泪点阻塞/淚點阻塞　obstruction of lacrimal punctum
泪阜/淚阜　lacrimal caruncle
泪阜生毛症/淚阜生睫病　trichosis carunculae
泪沟/淚溝　lacrimal sulcus, lacrimal groove
泪骨/淚骨　lacrimal bone, os lacrimale
泪骨沟/淚骨溝　groove of lacrimal bone
泪骨钩/淚骨鉤　lacrimal hamulus
泪骨筛房/淚骨篩房　lacrimoethmold cell
泪管/淚管　lacrimal duct
泪管闭塞/淚管閉塞　dacryagogatresia
泪管剪/淚管剪　canalicular scissors
泪管泪囊吻合术/淚管淚囊吻合術　canaliculodacryocystostomy
泪管黏液溢/淚囊黏液漏　dacryoblennorrhea
泪管狭窄/淚管狹窄　dacryostenosis
泪管炎/淚管炎　dacryosolenitis
泪管肿大/淚管瘤，淚囊瘤　dacryoma
泪河/淚河　lacrimal river
泪后嵴/淚後嵴　posterior lacrimal crest
泪湖/淚湖　lacrimal lacus, lacrimal bay
泪膜破裂时间/淚膜破裂時間　breakup time of tear film
泪囊/淚囊　lacrimal sac
泪囊鼻腔切开术/淚囊鼻腔切開術　dacryocystorhinotomy
泪囊鼻腔吻合术/淚囊鼻腔造瘺術　dacryocystorhinostomy
泪囊刀/淚囊[切開]刀　dacryocystitome, dacryocystotome
泪[囊或管结]石病/淚石病　dacryolithiasis
泪囊扩张/淚囊擴張　dacryocystectasia
泪囊泪管切开术/淚囊淚管切開術　dacryocystosyringotomy
泪囊瘘/淚囊瘺　lacrimal sac fistula
泪囊黏液囊肿/淚囊黏液囊腫　mucocele of lacrimal sac
泪囊牵开器/淚囊牽開器　lacrimal sac retractor
泪囊切除术/淚囊壁切除術　dacryocystectomy
泪囊切开术/淚囊切開術　dacryocystotomy

泪囊穹/淚囊穹窿　fornix of lacrimal sac
泪囊筛窦吻合术/淚囊篩竇吻合術　dacryocystoethmoidotomy
泪囊痛/淚囊痛　dacrycystalgia
泪囊突出/淚囊膨出　dacryocele
泪囊脱垂/淚囊脱垂　dacryocystoptosis
泪囊窝/淚囊凹　fossa for lacrimal sac
泪囊狭窄/淚囊狹窄　dacryocystostenosis
泪囊炎/淚囊炎　dacryocystitis
泪囊造口术/淚囊造口術　dacryocystostomy
泪囊造影[术]/淚囊造影術　dacryocystography
泪器/淚器　lacrimal apparatus
泪器化脓/淚器化膿　dacryopyosis
泪器疾病/淚器疾病　lacrimal apparatus disease
泪器溃疡/淚器潰瘍　dacryelcosis
泪器切开术/淚器切開術　lacrimotomy
泪器阻塞/淚器阻塞　lacrimal duct obstruction
泪前嵴/淚前嵴　anterior lacrimal crest
泪窍/淚竅　tear orifice, lachrymal punctum, lacrimal punctum
泪切迹/淚切跡　lacrimal notch
泪泉/淚泉　lachrymal spring
泪乳头/淚乳頭　lacrimal papilla
泪上颌缝/淚頜縫　lacrimomaxillary suture
泪突/淚突　lacrimal process
泪腺/淚腺　lacrimal gland
泪腺动脉/淚腺動脈　lacrimal artery
泪腺动脉吻合支/淚腺動脈吻合支　anastomotic branch with lacrimal artery
泪腺管切断术/淚腺管切斷術　lacrimal gland ducts division
泪腺核/淚腺核　lacrimal nucleus
泪腺混合瘤/淚腺混合瘤　mixed tumor of lacrimal gland
泪腺睑部/淚腺瞼部　palpebral part of lacrimal gland, palpebral process
泪腺结核/淚腺結核　tuberculosis of lacrimal gland
泪腺静脉/淚腺靜脈　lacrimal vein
泪腺眶部/淚腺眶部　orbital part of lacrimal gland
泪腺瘘/淚腺瘻　fistula of lacrimal gland
泪[腺]酶/淚腺酶　lacrimase
泪腺囊肿/淚腺囊腫　cyst of lacrimal gland
泪腺排泄小管/淚腺排洩小管　excretory ductule of lacrimal gland
泪腺切除术/淚腺切除術　dacryoadenectomy
泪腺神经/淚腺神經　lacrimal nerve
泪[腺]石/淚石　dacryolith
泪腺痛/淚腺痛　dacryadenalgia

泪腺脱垂/淚腺脱垂　dislocation of lacrimal gland
泪腺窝/淚腺窩　fossa for lacrimal gland
泪腺炎/淚腺炎　dacryoadenitis
泪腺异位/淚腺異位　ectopia of lacrimal gland
泪腺圆柱瘤/淚腺圓柱瘤　cylindroma of lacrimal gland
泪小管/淚小管　lacrimal ductule, lacrimal canal
泪小管插管术/淚小管插管術　canaliculus intubation
泪小管成形术/淚小管成形術　canaliculoplasty
泪小管刀/鼻淚管刀　canalicular knife
泪小管壶腹/淚管壺腹　ampulla of lacrimal ductule
泪小管切开术/淚小管切開術　canaliculotomy
泪小管撕裂/淚小管撕裂　laceration of canaliculus
泪小管狭窄/淚小管狹窄　stenosis of lacrimal canaliculus
泪小管炎/淚小管發炎　canaliculitis
泪小管注射器/淚小管注射器　dacryosyringe
泪小管阻塞/淚小管阻塞　obstruction of lacrimal canaliculus
泪液分泌异常/淚液分泌異常　lacrimal secretion anomaly
泪溢/淚溢,淚漏　epiphora
泪溢出/淚溢流　overflow of tears
泪缘/淚骨緣　lacrimal margin
类阿片受体拮抗药/類阿片受體拮抗藥　opioid receptor antagonist
类癌/類癌　carcinoid
类癌瘤/類癌腫瘤　carcinoid tumor
类癌心脏病/類癌引起心臟疾病　carcinoid heart disease
类癌综合征/類癌症候群　carcinoid syndrome
类白蛋白/類蛋白素　albuminoid
类白喉感染/類白喉感染　diphtheroid infection
类白血病的/白血病樣的　leukemoid
类百日咳综合征/類百日欬症候群　pertussislike syndrome
类孢子虫/類孢子蟲　sporozooid
类孢子丝菌症淋巴管炎/類孢子絲菌症淋巴腺炎　sporotrichoid lymphangitis
类鼻疽/類鼻疽　melioidosis
类鼻疽杆菌/類鼻疽桿菌　pseudomonas pseudomallei
类变形性骨炎/類變形性骨炎　pagetoid osteitis
类变应原/類變應原　allergoid
类别试剂/通用試劑,一般試劑　general reagent
类病毒/類病毒　viroids
类补体/類補體,變性補體　complementoid
类糙皮病/類癩皮病　pellagroid
类沉淀素/變性沈澱素,失能沈澱素　precipitoid

类催眠状态/類催眠狀態　hypnoidic state
类丹毒/類丹毒　erysipeloid
类蛋白质/類蛋白質　proteinoid
类胨/類腖　peptonoid
类毒素/類毒素,變性毒素　toxoid
类毒素反应/減毒素反應　anatoxin reaction
类毒素抗毒素絮片/類毒素抗毒素絮狀物　toxoid-antitoxin floccule
类毒素-抗类毒素/類毒素與抗類毒素合劑　toxoid-antitoxoid
类毒素类/類毒素類　toxoids
类肺炎/副肺炎　parapneumonia
类风湿尘肺/類風濕塵肺　caplan syndrome
类风湿结节/類風濕結節　rheumatoid nodule
类风湿性尘肺症/類風濕性塵肺症　rheumatoid pneumoconiosis
类风湿性肺病/類風濕性肺疾　rheumatoid lung disease
类风湿[性]关节炎/類風濕性關節炎　rheumatoid arthritis
类风湿血管炎/類風濕性血管炎　rheumatoid vasculitis
类风湿因子/類風濕因數　rheumatoid factor
类肝素/類肝素　heparinoid
类肝素类/類肝素類　heparinoids
类肝素硫酸盐/類肝素硫酸鹽　heparitin sulfate
类咕啉类/類咕啉類　corrinoids
类骨质/類骨質,骨樣的　osteoid
类固醇/類固醇　steroid
类固醇分泌细胞/類固醇分泌細胞　steroid-secretory cell
类固醇高脂血症/類固醇高脂血症　steroidogenic hyperlipidemia
类固醇后脂膜炎/類固醇後脂層炎　poststeroid panniculitis
类固醇溃疡/類固醇性潰瘍　steroid ulcer
类固醇21-羟化酶/類固醇21-羥化酶　steroid 21-hydroxylase
类固醇受体/類固醇受體　steroid receptor
类固醇停药综合征/類固醇停藥症候群　steroid withdrawal syndrome
类胡萝卜素类/類胡蘿蔔素類　carotenoids
类花生酸/類花生酸　eicosanoid
类花生酸受体/類花生酸受體　eicosanoid receptor
类黄瘤/類黄斑瘤　xanthelasmoidea
类黄体素/類黄體素　luteoid
类黄酮物质/類黄酮物質　flavonoids
类霍乱病/副霍亂　paracholera

类基底细胞/基底樣細胞　basaloid cell
类激素/類激素　anahormone
类浆/類漿　plasmoid
类结核菌素/改良型結核菌素　tuberculoidin
类经/類經　Classified Canon
类晶体/類晶體　crystalloid
类酒石酸/副酒石酸　paratartaric acid
类髋关节痛/髋旁痛　paracoxalgia
类狼疮/類狼瘡　lupoid
类落矶山热/類落磯山熱　Tobia fever
类酶/類酵素　fermentoid
类囊体/類囊體　thylakoid
类囊肿/類囊腫　cystoid
类脑积水/假水腦,擬水腦　hydrocephaloid
类内毒素/類內毒素　endotoxoid
类黏蛋白/黏液樣的　mucoid
类黏蛋白变性/黏液膠質樣變性　mucinoid degeneration
类尿胆素/似尿膽質素,尿膽質樣素　urobilinoiden
类凝集素反应/類凝集素反應　agglutinoid reaction
类皮肤肿瘤/類皮膚腫瘤　paracutaneous neoplasm
类皮质激素/腎上腺類皮質素　corticoid
类偏执狂的/妄想狂樣的　paranoid
类器官/類器官　organoids
类青春期痴呆/類青春期癡呆　heboidophrenia
类球孢子菌病/副球黴菌病　paracoccidioidomycosis
类曲细精管卵巢腺瘤/類睾丸管卵巢腺瘤　adenoma ovarii testiculare
类人猿/類人猿　anthropoid
类人猿型/類人猿型　anthropoid type
类肉瘤/類肉瘤的　sarcoid
类肉芽肿/亞型肉芽腫　paragranuloma
类沙眼/類沙眼　paratrachoma
类上皮癌/類上皮癌　carcinoma epithelioides
类上皮细胞组织细胞瘤/上皮樣細胞組織細胞瘤　epithelioid cell histiocytoma
类神经兴奋剂/類神經興奮劑　neuromimetic
类[肾上腺]髓质素/類髓質　medulloid
类视黄醇X受体/維他命A酸X接受器　retinoid X receptor
类嘶音性呼吸音/類嘶音性呼吸音　subsibilant respiration
类似株/類似株　pleiston
类髓磷脂/類髓鞘質素　myeloidin
类肽类/類肽類　peptoids
类天花/[輕痘]類天花　alastrim
类天花病毒/類天花病毒　alastrim virus
类天花水痘/類天花水痘　varioloid varicella

类天疱疮/類天皰瘡　pemphigoid
类天疱疮综合征/類天皰瘡症候群　pemphigoid syndrome
类同品/類似藥　allied drug
类维生素 A/類維生素 A　retinoid
类维生素缺乏病/亞維生素缺乏病　paravitaminosis
类无睾/類閹人,類宦者　eunuchoid
类无睾者语音/閹人聲　eunuchoid voice
类纤维蛋白/類纖維素,擬纖維蛋白　fibrinoid
类星形念珠菌/類星狀念珠菌　candida stellatoidea
类型/[類]型　type
类牙骨质/類齒堊質　cementoid
类牙关紧闭/類牙關緊閉　trismoid
类阉者巨人症/閹性巨體,無睾性巨人症　eunuchoid gigantism
类药品/類藥品　quasi drug
A 类药品不良反应/A 類藥物不良反應　adverse drug reaction type A
B 类药品不良反应/B 類藥物不良反應　adverse drug reaction type B
类胰蛋白酶/類胰蛋白酶　tryptase
类胰岛素/擬胰島素　para-insulin
类银屑病/亞牛皮癬　parapsoriasis
类尤文氏牙釉质瘤/類 Ewing 氏牙釉質瘤　ewinglike adamantinoma
类圆线虫病/類圓線蟲病　strongyloidiasis
类肢端肥大症/擬肢端肥大病　acromegaloidism
类脂/類脂質　lipoid
类脂蛋白质沉积症/脂質蛋白質症　lipoidproteinosis
类脂铁质沉积症/脂鐵質沈著病　lipoidsiderosis
类脂性肾病/脂質性腎病　lipoid nephrosis
类脂性痛风/類脂性痛風　lipoid gout
类脂质蛋白沉积症/類脂質蛋白沈積症　lipoid proteinosis
类脂组织增生/類脂質性增殖　lipoid hyperplasia
类肿瘤综合征/類腫瘤症候群　paraneoplastic syndrome
类中风/類中風　parapoplexy
类中风性的/中風狀的　apoplectiform
棱晶/棱晶,方晶　prism
棱镜底/棱鏡底　base of prism
棱镜底向内/棱鏡底向內　base of prism in
棱镜底向上/棱鏡底向上　base of prism up
棱镜底向外/棱鏡底向外　base of prism out
棱镜度/棱鏡度數　prism degree
棱镜尖/棱鏡尖　apex of prism
棱镜矫视器/眼球震顫矯正器　kratometer
棱镜片/棱鏡片　prismatic lens

棱球镜/棱球面透鏡　prismosphere
棱形骨/棱形骨,小多角骨　trapezoid bone
棱形韧带/棱形韌帶,斜方韌帶　trapezoid ligament
棱状巨尿道/棱狀巨尿道　fusiform megalourethra
冷藏精液/冷藏精液　cryopreserved semen
冷藏胚胎/冷藏胚胎　cryopreserved embryo
冷藏组织移植物/冷藏組織移植物　refrigerated tissue graft
冷场发射/冷場發射　cold field emission
冷超敏性/冷超敏性　cold hypersensitivity
冷沉[淀]比容/冷沈比容　cryocrit
冷沉[淀]蛋白/冷凝蛋白　cryoprotein
冷沉淀物/冷沈澱物,降溫沈澱物　cryoprecipitate
冷沉[淀]性/冷沈澱性　cryoprecipitability
冷除法/冷除法　cold division
冷点/冷覺點,冷區　cold spot
冷冻/冰凍　freezing
冷冻保护剂/冷凍保護劑　cryoprotective agent
冷冻超薄切片术/冷凍超薄切片術　cryoultramicrotomy
冷冻断裂/冷凍斷裂　freeze fracturing
冷冻断裂复型/冷凍斷裂復型　freeze fracture replica
冷冻干燥/冷凍乾燥　freeze drying, lyophilization
冷冻干燥法组织贮存/冷凍乾燥法組織貯存　tissue storage by freezing and drying
冷冻干燥皮/冷凍乾燥皮　lyophilized skin
冷冻干燥制品/冷凍乾燥製品　freeze-dried product
冷冻割断/冷凍割斷,冷凍撕裂　freeze cleave, freeze cracking
冷冻剂/冷凍劑　cryogen
冷冻剂量/冷凍劑量　cryodose
冷冻疗法/冷[凍]療法　cryotherapy
冷冻麻醉/冷凍麻醉　anesthesia by freezing
冷冻美容疗法/冷凍美容療法　cosmetic cryotherapy
冷冻[内障]摘出术/冷取內障法　cryoextraction
冷冻凝固/冷凍凝固　cryocoagulation
冷冻切片/冷凍切片　frozen section
冷冻切片机/冰凍切片機　freezing microtome
冷冻取代/冷凍取代　freeze substitution
冷冻时间/冷凍時間　cooling time
冷冻食品/冷凍食品　frozen food
冷冻蚀刻/冷凍蝕刻　freeze etching
冷冻蚀刻复型/冷凍蝕刻復型　freeze etch replica
冷冻蚀刻技术/冷凍蝕刻技術　freeze-etching technique
冷冻睡眠法/冰凍睡眠法　frozen sleep
冷冻损伤/冷凍損傷　cryolesion
冷冻外科手术/冷凍手術法　cryosurgery

冷冻消融[术]/冷凍剝離法　cryoablation
冷冻眼科学/冷凍眼科學　cryoophthalmology
冷冻摘出器/冷取內障器　cryoextractor
冷冻止血/冷凍止血　cryohemostasis
冷冻治疗器/冷凍治療器　cryosurgical engineering
冷冻[作用]/冷凍[作用]　refrigeration
冷反射性荨麻疹/冷反射性蕁麻疹　cold reflex urticaria
冷敷[法]/冷敷法,冷壓布　cold compress
冷服/冷服　administered cold
冷灌法/冷式充填法　cold filling
冷裹法/冷濕布裹法　cold pack
冷汗/冷汗　cold sweating
冷红斑/冷因性紅斑　cold erythema
冷浸剂/冷浸劑　cold infusion
冷觉/冷覺　sense of cold
冷觉缺失/冷覺缺失　arrhigosis
冷勒除器/冷圈刃　cold snare
冷泪/冷淚　cold lacrimation, cold tear, epiphora
冷疗法/冷療法　cold therapy
冷庐医话/冷廬醫話　Medical Talks in a Quiet House
冷秘/冷秘　cold constipation
冷凝集[反应]/冷凝集　cold agglutination
冷凝集试验/冷凝集試驗　cold agglutination test
冷凝集素/冷凝集素　cold agglutinin
冷凝器/冷凝器　condenser
冷凝缩/冷凝縮　cryocondensation
冷气疗法/冷氣療法　cryoaerotherapy
冷球蛋白/冷凝球蛋白　cryoglobulin
冷球蛋白血症/冷凝球蛋白血症　cryoglobulinemia
冷球蛋白血症紫癜/冷球蛋白血症紫癜　purpura cryoglobulinemia
冷缺血时间/冷缺血時間　cold ischemia time
冷却麻醉法/冷卻麻醉法　refrigeration anesthesia
冷却器/冷卻器　cooler
冷却溶解/冷熱溶解　hot-cold lysis
冷却速度/冷卻速率　rate of cooling
冷热交替浴/冷熱交替浴　contrast bath
冷热交替直喷浴/蘇格蘭式沖洗　Scotch douche
冷热空气试验/冷熱空氣試驗　air caloric test
冷热试验/熱量試驗　caloric test
冷热水试验/冷熱水試驗　water caloric test
冷溶血素/冷溶血素　cold hemolysin
冷伤/冷傷　cold injury
冷霜/冷霜　cold cream
冷水浴/冷[水]浴　cold bath
冷痛/冷痛,寒濕痛　crymodynia, cold pain

冷痛觉/冷痛　cryalgesia
冷哮/冷哮　cold wheezing
冷心脏停搏[法]/冷心臟停搏[法]　cold cardioplegia
冷心脏停搏液/冷心臟停搏液　cold cardioplegic solution
冷血凝素/冷血球凝集素　cold hemagglutinin
冷瘴/冷瘴　algid miasma
冷柱头进样器/冷管柱進樣器　cold on-column injector
厘泊/厘泊　centipoise
厘弧度/厘弧度　centrad
厘米波疗法/厘米波療法　centimeter wave therapy
厘摩/厘摩　centimorgan
离床活动/離床活動　ambulation
离断术/切斷術　division
离婚/離婚　divorce
离魂症/離魂症　dispersed soul, hallucination
离家潜逃行为/離家潛逃行爲　runaway behavior
离解麻醉药/離解麻醉藥　dissociative anesthetics
离经脉/離經脈　abnormal frequency pulse, middle finger pulsation during labor
离口的/離口的　aboard
离神经电流/離神經電流　abneural current
离体/離體　exsomatize
离体灌注/離體灌注　ex vivo perfusion
离体活体染色/超體體染法,體外活體染法　supravital staining
离小脑的/離小腦的　cerebellofugal
离心泵/離心泵　centrifugal pump
离心的/離心的　centrifugal
离心法/離心沈澱法　centrifugation
离心机/離心機　centrifuge
离心式细胞清洗器/離心式細胞清洗器　centrifugal cell washer
离心收缩/離心收縮　eccentric contraction
离心性[骨]软骨发育不良/離心性骨軟骨發育不良　eccentrochondroplasia
离心性环状红斑/離心性環狀紅斑　erythema annulare centrifugum
离心铸造机/離心鑄造機　centrifugal casting machine
离子/離子　ion
离子泵/離子泵　ion pump
离子蛋白/離子蛋白　ion-protein
离子-分子复合物/離子-分子複合物　ion-molecule complex
离子化基团/游離質,離子化物　ionogen
离子计/離子計　ionometer

离子键/離子鍵　ionic bond
离子交换/離子交換　ion exchange
离子交换膜/離子交換膜　ion exchange membrane
离子交换色谱法/離子交換層析法　ion exchange chromatography
离子交换树脂/離子交換樹脂　ion exchange resin
离子交换纤维素/離子交換纖維素　ion-exchange cellulose
离子霉素/離子黴素　ionomycin
离子浓度/離子濃度　ionic concentration
离子强度/離子強度　ionic strength
离子通道/離子通道　ion channel
离子透入法/離子透入法　iontophoresis
离子透药疗法/電離子藥療法，離子化學給藥法　ionic medication
离子选择电极/離子選擇電極　ion-selective electrode
离子移动/離子移動　migration of ion
离子抑制/離子抑制　ion suppress
离子载体/離子載體　ionophore
离子转运/離子轉運　ion transport
梨形的/梨形的　piriform
梨形四膜虫/梨形四膜蟲　Tetrahymena pyriformis
梨形瞳孔/梨形瞳孔　pear-shaped pupil
梨形胸/梨狀胸　pyriform thorax
梨状腹综合征/梨狀腹症候群　prune belly syndrome
梨状肌/梨狀肌　piriformis, musculus piriformis
梨状肌紧张试验/梨狀肌緊張試驗　piriformis tension test
梨状肌囊/梨狀肌囊　bursa of piriformis
梨状肌神经/梨狀肌神經　nerve to piriformis
梨状肌下孔/梨狀肌下孔　infrapiriform foramen
梨状肌综合征/梨狀肌症候群　pyriformis syndrome
梨状肌综合征·风寒湿阻证/梨狀肌症候群·風寒濕阻證　piriformis syndrome with wind-cold-dampness obstruction pattern
梨状肌综合征·肝肾亏虚证/梨狀肌症候群·肝腎虧虛證　piriformis syndrome with liver-kidney deficiency pattern
梨状肌综合征·湿热阻络证/梨狀肌症候群·濕熱阻絡證　piriformis syndrome with pattern of dampness-heat obstructing collateral
梨状肌综合征·血瘀气滞证/梨狀肌症候群·血瘀氣滯證　piriformis syndrome with pattern of blood stasis and qi stagnation
梨状孔/梨狀孔　piriform aperture
梨状细胞层/梨狀細胞層　piriform cell layer
梨状心/梨狀心　pear-shaped heart
梨状叶/梨狀區　pyriform area

梨状隐窝/梨狀隱窩　piriform recess
犁鼻器/犁鼻器　vomeronasal organ
犁鼻软骨/犁鼻軟骨　vomeronasal cartilage
犁骨/犁骨　vomer
犁骨鼻后孔嵴/犁骨鼻後孔嵴　vomerochoanal crest
犁骨沟/犁骨溝　vomerine groove
犁骨黏膜瓣/犁骨黏膜瓣　vomer mucosal flap
犁骨楔状部/犁骨楔狀部　cuneiform part of vomer
犁骨翼/犁骨翼　ala of vomer
犁鞘沟/犁鞘溝　vomerovaginal sulcus
犁鞘管/犁鞘管　vomerovaginal canal
犁头霉属/犁頭黴屬　*Absidia*
犁嘴管/犁嘴管　vomerorostral canal
罹病癖/罹病癖　nosophilia
藜草/白藜　Chenopodium album
藜芦次碱/藜蘆次鹼　veratroidine
藜芦碱/藜蘆定鹼　veratridine
藜芦生物碱类/藜蘆生物鹼類　veratrum alkaloids
藜芦中毒/藜蘆中毒　veratrum poisoning
藜麦/奎奴亞藜　Chenopodium quinoa
黧黑斑/黧黑斑，[黄]褐斑　brownish black macula, chloasma
黧黑斑·肝气郁结证/黧黑斑·肝氣鬱結證　brownish black macula with liver qi stagnation pattern
黧黑斑·肝肾两虚证/黧黑斑·肝腎兩虛證　brownish black macula with liver-kidney deficiency pattern
黧黑斑·脾虚湿困证/黧黑斑·脾虛濕困證　brownish black macula with pattern of spleen deficiency and dampness retention
黧黑斑·气滞血瘀证/黧黑斑·氣滯血瘀證　brownish black macula with pattern of qi stagnation and blood stasis
李当之药录/李當之藥錄　Li Dangzhi Yaolu
李痘病毒/李痘病毒　Plum Pox Virus
李杲/李杲　Li Gao
李时珍/李時珍　Li Shizhen
李-斯细胞/Reed-Sternberg 二氏細胞　Reed-Sternberg cell
里-埃溶液/Rees-Ecker 二氏溶液　Rees-Ecker solution
里奥郎肌/Riolan 氏肌　Riolan muscle
里病出表/裡病出表　interior disease involving exterior
里布尔绷带/Ribble 氏繃帶　Ribble bandage
里德二尖瓣瓣环成形术/里德二尖瓣瓣環成形術　Reed mitral annuloplasty
里德-斯特恩伯格细胞/里德-斯特恩伯格細胞　Reed-Sternberg cells

里德细胞/Rieder 氏細胞　Rieder cell
里德细胞性白血病/Rieder 氏細胞白血病　Rieder cell leukemia
里厄疝/Rieux 氏疝　Rieux hernia
里尔黑变病/Riehl 氏黑變症　Riehl melanosis
里寒/裡寒　interior cold
里寒证/裡寒證　interior cold pattern
里喉痈/裡喉癰，咽後癰，咽後膿腫　retropharyngeal abscess
里急/裡急　abdominal pain
里急后重/裡急後重，後墜　tenesmus
里加病/裡加病　Riga disease
里热/裡熱　interior heat
里热证/裡熱證　interior heat pattern
里实/裡實　interior excess
[里]实证/[裡]實證　interior excess pattern
里斯取皮机/里斯取皮機　Reese dermatome
里-托病/Ribas-Torres 二氏病　Ribas-Torres disease
里维努斯管/Rivinus 氏管，舌下腺導管　ducts of Rivinus
里希特疝/Richter 氏疝　Richter hernia
里歇绷带/Richet 氏繃帶　Richet bandage
里歇动脉瘤/Richet 氏動脈瘤　Richet aneurysm
里虚/裡虛　interior deficiency
[里]虚证/[裡]虛證　interior deficiency pattern
里证/裡證　interior pattern
理发师/理髮師　hairdresser
理发师外科医师/理髮師外科醫師　barber surgeon
理法方药/理法方藥　principle-method-recipe-medicines
理化鉴定/理化鑒定　physical and chemical identification
理解力/理解力　comprehension
理筋手法/理筋手法　therapeutic manipulation for injured soft tissue
理论/理論，假說　theory
理论模型/理論模型　theoretical model
理气/理氣　regulating qi
理气法/理氣法　qi-regulating method
理气和胃/理氣和胃　regulating qi for harmonizing stomach
理气化痰/理氣化痰　regulating qi for eliminating phlegm
理气剂/理氣劑　qi-regulating formula
理气健脾/理氣健脾　regulating qi for strengthening spleen
理气行滞/理氣行滯　regulating qi for activating stagnation
理气止痛/理氣止痛　regulating qi for relieving pain
理想𬌗/齒理想咬合　ideal occlusion
理想弓/理想弓　ideal arch
理想精神/理想精神[內容]　anagoge
理想牙排列/理想牙排列　ideal tooth alignment
理想正常𬌗/理想正常𬌗　ideal normal occlusion
理性筛选/合理篩選　rational screening
理血/理血　regulating blood condition
理血法/理血法　regulating blood method
理血剂/理血劑　blood-regulating formula
理瀹骈文/理瀹駢文　Rhymed Discourse for Topical Remedies
理中/理中　regulating middle jiao
理中汤/理中湯　lizhong decoction
锂/鋰　lithium
锂化合物/鋰化合物　lithium compound
锂卡红/鋰洋紅　lithium carmine
锂肾病/鋰腎病　lithium nephropathy
鲤精蛋白甲/鯉毒素　cyprinin
鲤鱼类/鯉魚類　carps
蠡沟/蠡溝　ligou, LR5
力/力　force
力量/力量　strength
力量频率关系/力量頻率關係　force-frequency relation
力量速度关系/力量速度關係　force-velocity relation
力偶/力偶　couples
力偶比/力偶比　couple-force ratio
力偶观念/力偶觀念　force-couple concept
力向/力向　line of force
力与应力/力與應力　force and stress
历史/史　history
厉兑/厲兌　lidui, ST45
厉疽/厲疽　carbuncle on lateral aspect of foot
立迟/立遲　retardation in standing
立方上皮/立方上皮，骰形上皮　cubical epithelium
立方[形]细胞/立方細胞　cuboid cell
立夫特山谷热病毒/立夫特山谷熱病毒　Rift Valley fever virus
立高/立高　standing height
立肌/豎肌，豎起者　arrector
立克次体病/立克次體病　rickettsiosis
立克次体的/立克次體的　rickettsial
立克次体痘/立克次體痘　rickettsial pox
立克次体肺炎/立克次體肺炎　rickettsial pneumonia
立克次体菌苗/立克次體菌苗　rickettsial vaccine
立克次体科感染/立克次體科感染　rickettsiaceae infection

立克次体心肌炎/立克次體性心肌炎　rickettsial myocarditis
立克次体性脑膜炎/立克次體性腦膜炎　rickettsial meningitis
立毛反射/立毛反射，豎毛現象　trichographism
立毛肌/立毛肌　arrector muscle of hair
立毛神经/立毛神經　pilomotor nerves
立氏立克次体/立氏立克次體　Rickettsia rickettsii
立体定位技术/立體定位技術　stereotaxic technique
立体定向脊髓束切断术/立體定向脊髓束切斷術　stereotaxic cordotomy
立体定向手术/趨異體外科　stereotactic surgery
立体定向仪/立體定向儀　stereotactic apparatus
立体动态干扰电疗法/立體動態干擾電療法　stereodynamic interferential electrotherapy
立体化学/立體化學　stereochemistry
立体镜/實體鏡　stereoscope
立体镜检查[法]/實體鏡檢查　stereoscopy
立体觉缺失/實體感覺缺失　stereoanesthesia
立体X射线照相术/實體X射線攝影術　stereoradiography
立体X射线正影器/X光實體攝影器　orthostereoscope
立体视觉/實體視覺　stereoscopic vision
立体视野计/立體視野計　stereocampimeter
立体显微照片/立體顯微照片　stereophotomicrograph
立体选择合成/立體選擇合成　stereoselective synthesis
立体选择性/立體專一性　stereoselectivity
立体异构[现象]/立體異構　stereoisomerism
立体[隐]斜视矫正器/立體隱斜視矯正器　stereophorometer
立体荧光电影照相术/立體活動性螢光屏攝影術　stereocinefluorography
立体照相术/立體照相法　stereophotography
立位舞蹈病/起立時舞蹈病　orthochorea
丽丝胺绿染料/麗絲胺綠染料　Lissamine Green Dyes
利奥前列素/利奧前列素　rioprostil
利巴韦林/三氮唑核苷　ribavirin
利比希试验/利比氏試驗　Liebig test
利弊权衡/利弊權衡　benefit-risk balance
利伯曼试验/利伯曼試驗　Liebermann test
利胆排石片/利膽排石片　lidan paishi tablet
利胆药/利膽藥　cholagogic
利德尔综合征/利德爾症候群　Liddle syndrome
利多氟嗪/利多氟嗪　lidoflazine

利多卡因/利多卡因　lidocaine
利福布汀/利福布汀　Rifabutin
利福霉素/利福黴素　rifamycin
利福平/利福平　rifampicin
利谷隆/利谷隆　linuron
利害冲突/利害衝突　conflict of interest
利鲁唑/利蘆噻唑　riluzole
利钠因子/利鈉因數　natriuretic factor
利奈孕酮/利奈孕酮　lynestrenol
利尿/利尿　diuresis
利尿钠肽/利鈉尿勝肽　natriuretic peptide
利尿排钠激素/促尿鈉排洩激素　natriuretic hormone
利尿肾图/利尿腎圖　furosemide renography
利尿酸钠/利尿酸鈉　ethacrynate sodium
利尿药/利尿藥　diuretic
利培酮/利哌立酮　risperidone
利普曼失用症/Liepmann氏失用症　Liepmann apraxia
利普许茨细胞/Lipschütz氏細胞　Lipschütz cell
利-萨综合征/Libman-Sacks二氏症候群　Libman-Sacks syndrome
利舍平/蛇根素　serpasil
利什曼斑/利什曼斑　leishmanoid
利什曼病/利什曼病　leishmaniasis
利什曼结节/利什曼皮節　leishmanid
利什曼素皮肤试验/利什曼素皮膚試驗　Montenegro test
利什特海姆失语/Lichtheim氏失語症　Lichtheim aphasia
利什特海姆综合征/Lichtheim氏症候群　Lichtheim syndrome
利氏病/賴氏症候群　Leigh disease
利水祛湿法/利水祛濕法　promoting urination and eliminating dampness
利水渗湿剂/利水滲濕劑　formula for diuresis and diffusing dampness
利水消肿/利水消腫　inducing diuresis for removing edema
利斯顿夹/Liston氏夾板　Liston splint
利斯弗朗韧带/Lisfranc氏韌帶　Lisfranc ligament
利斯弗朗脱位/Lisfranc氏脫位　Lisfranc dislocation
利斯特敷料/利斯特氏敷料　Lister dressing
利斯特菌病/利斯特氏菌病　listeriosis
利斯特菌感染/利斯特氏菌感染　Listeria infections
利斯特菌性脑膜炎/利斯特氏性腦膜炎　Listeria meningitis
利坦色林/利坦色林　Ritanserin

利特尔区/利特爾區　Little area
利特雷疝/Littre氏疝　Littre hernia
利托纳韦/利托納韋　Ritonavir
利沃辛/利沃辛　levosin
利希特海姆测验/李克席試驗　Lichtheim test
利咽/利咽　relieving sore throat, relieving throat disorder
利用/利用　utilization
沥青/瀝青　asphalt, pitch
沥青工人癌/瀝青工人癌　pitchworkers cancer
沥青皮炎/瀝青皮炎　asphalt dermatitis
沥青烧伤/瀝青燒傷　bitumen burn
沥青疣/瀝青疣　pitch wart
疠气/癘氣　pestilential qi
荔枝核/荔枝核　lychee seed
栗色棒状杆菌/粟色棒狀桿菌　corynebacterium helvolum
蛎壳疮/蠣殼瘡　rupia
蛎壳疮状的/蠣殼瘡狀的　oyster-shaped
蛎壳状银屑病/蠣殼狀乾癬　psoriasis ostracea
粒层/〔顆〕粒層　stratum granulosum
粒层黄体[素]细胞/粒層黃體素細胞　granulosa lutein cell
粒层细胞/粒層細胞　granulosa cell
粒层细胞癌/粒層細胞癌　granulosa cell carcinoma
粒层细胞瘤/粒層細胞瘤　granulosa tumor
粒单核细胞白血病/骨髓單核球白血病　myelomonocytic leukemia
粒度分布/粒徑分布　particle size distribution
粒密度/顆粒密度　granule density
粒细胞/粒細胞　granulocytes
粒细胞白血病/顆粒細胞性白血病,骨髓細胞性白血病　granulocytic leukemia
粒细胞沉积/粒細胞沈積　granulocyte deposition
粒细胞-单核细胞集落生成单位/粒細胞-單核細胞集落形成單位　colony-forming unit-granulocyte and monocyte, CFU-GM
粒细胞发生/顆粒球生成　granulocytopoiesis
粒细胞过少症/粒性白血球減少症　hypogranulocytosis
粒细胞集落刺激因子/粒細胞集落刺激因數　granulocyte colony-stimulating factor
粒细胞集落刺激因子受体/粒細胞集落刺激因數受體　granulocyte colony-stimulating factor receptor
粒细胞巨噬细胞集落刺激因子/粒細胞巨噬細胞集落刺激因數　granulocyte-macrophage colony-stimulating factor
粒细胞巨噬细胞集落刺激因子受体/粒細胞巨噬細胞集落刺激因數受體　granulocyte-macrophage colony-stimulating factor receptor
粒细胞前体细胞/粒細胞前體細胞　granulocyte precursor cell
粒细胞缺乏/粒細胞缺乏　agranulocytosis
粒细胞缺乏性贫血/顆粒性白血球缺乏性貧血　agranulocytic anemia
粒细胞缺乏症/顆粒性白血球缺乏性咽峽炎　agranulocytic angina
粒细胞肉瘤/粒細胞肉瘤　granulocytic sarcoma
粒细胞增多/粒細胞增多　granulocytosis
粒腺体/粒腺體　mitochondria
粒状皮层/顆粒皮質　koniocortex
粒状皮质/粒狀皮質　granular cortex
粒状肾炎/粒狀腎炎　granular nephritis
粒状嗜曙红白细胞/粒狀嗜伊紅白血球　granular eosinophil leukocyte
粒子大小/粒子大小　particle size
粒子加速器/粒子加速器　particle accelerator
粒子束/粒子束　particle beam
粒子形态/粒子形態　particle shape
粒子诱导质谱法/粒子誘導質譜法　particle induced mass spectrometry
痢疾/痢疾　dysenteria, dysentery
痢疾后综合征/痢疾後症候群　postdysenteric syndrome
痢疾型疟/痢疾型瘧　dysenteric malaria
痢疾性关节炎/痢疾性關節炎　dysenteric arthritis
痢疾样腹泻/痢疾性腹瀉　dysenteric diarrhea
痢疾志贺菌/痢疾桿菌　Shigella dysenteriae
连冠牙瘤/牙冠瘤　coronal odontoma
连贯表意不能/連續言語不能　acataphasia
连合凹/連合凹　commissural pit
连合部缝合术/連合帶縫合術　commissurorrhaphy
连合的/連合的　commissural
连合管/連合管　ductus reuniens
连合核/連合核　commissural nucleus
连合尖/連合尖　commissural cusps
连合间线/連合間線　intercommissural line
连合细胞/連合細胞　commissural cell
连合下器/連合下器[官]　subcommissural organ, SCO
连合纤维/連合纖維　commissural fiber
连合性失语/接合處性失語症　commissural aphasia
连颌畸形/連頜畸形　syngnathia
连枷/連枷　flail
连枷胸/連枷胸　flail chest
连枷状关节/連枷關節　flail joint

连接/連接 conjunction, linkage
连接不良/連接不良 faulty union
连接不全性骨折/連接不全性骨折 malunited fracture
连接不正/連接不正，連接不良 vicious union
连接错位骨折/連接錯位骨折 malunited fracture
连接蛋白类/連接蛋白類 connexins
连接复合体/連接複合體 junctional complex
连接共生/連體性共生 conjunctive symbiosis
连接函数/連接函數 connectivity function
连接活动/接合處活性 junctional activity
连接酶/連接酶 ligase
连接酶链反应/連接酶鏈反應 ligase chain reaction
连接体/連接體 connector
连接物/接合物 connective
连接子/連接子 connexon
连结核/連結核 reuniens nucleus
连结性牙骨小体/粘連性牙骨質贅，附著性牙骨質贅 adherent cementicle
连朴饮/連朴飲 lianpo drink
连钱草/連錢草 longtube ground ivy herb
连翘/連翹 weeping forsythia capsule
连舌/連舌 ankyloglossia, tongue-tie
连丝核中性白细胞/有絲嗜中性白血球 filamented neutrophil
连四硫酸/四硫酸 tetrathionic acid
连锁不平衡/連鎖不平衡 linkage disequilibrium
连锁分析/連鎖分析 linkage analysis
连锁缝合/連鎖縫合 continuous lock suture
连锁群/連鎖群 linkage group
连锁图/連鎖遺傳圖 linkage map
连锁相/連鎖相 linkage phase
X连锁智力缺乏/X連鎖智力不足 X-linked mental deficiency
连续变异/連續變異 continuous variation
连续补料/連續補料 continuous feeding
连续Z成形术/連續Z成形術 continuous Z-plasty
连续冲洗法/連續注洗法 continuous irrigation
连续传代/系列性轉種 serial passage
连续的/連續的 continuous
连续动静脉血液滤过/連續動靜脈血液濾過 continuous arteriovenous hemofiltration
连续发酵/連續發酵 continuous fermentation
连续反应/連續反應 successive reaction
连续缝合/連續縫法 continuous suture
连续杆固位体/連貫棒保持器 continuous bar retainer
连续感染/連續傳染 consecutive infection

连续横褥式缝合/連續橫褥式縫合 continuous transverse mattress suture
连续浆肌层缝合/連續漿肌層縫合 continuous seromuscular suture
连续浆肌层内翻缝合/連續漿肌層內翻縫合 cushing suture
连续接种法/連續接種法 vaccinization
连续卡环/連續卡環 continuous clasp
连续毛细血管/連續毛細管 continuous capillary
连续谱/連續光譜 continuous spectrum
连续气道正压通气/連續氣道正壓通氣 continuous positive airway pressure
连续切片/連續切片 serial section
连续全层内翻缝合/連續全層內翻縫合 continuous full layer inverting suture
连续[实体]照片投影检查/X射線連續檢法 serioscopy
连续丝/連續纖維 continuous fibers
连续体分开/連續體分開 solution of continuity
连续突触/連續突觸 serial synapse
连续小环结扎术/連續環狀栓結術 continuous loop wiring
连续性/連續性 continuity
连续性动脉瘤/連續性動脈瘤 consecutive aneurysm
连续性肌肉活动综合征/連續性肌肉活動症候群 continuous muscle activity syndrome
连续性接合/創口或骨折之連續性接合 synthesis of continuity
连续性杂音/連續性雜音 continuous murmur
连续性肢端皮炎/連續性肢皮炎 acrodermatitis continua
连续循环腹膜透析/連續性循環式腹膜透析 continuous cycling peritoneal dialysis
连续展开/連續展開 continuous development
连续症状/連續症狀 consecutive symptom
连指手套状并指/連指手套狀並指 mitten deformity
帘珠喉痹/簾珠喉痺 beaded throat obstruction, chronic hypertrophic pharyngitis
莲房/蓮房 lotus receptacle
莲须/蓮鬚 lotus stamen
莲叶桐萜醛/蓮葉桐萜醛 hyrtenal
莲子/蓮子 lotus seed
莲子心/蓮子心 lotus plumule
联苯胺/聯苯胺 benzidine
联苯胺过氧化酶试验/聯苯胺過氧化酵素試驗 benzidine peroxidase test
联苯胺试剂/聯苯胺試劑 benzidine reagent
联苯胺试验/聯苯胺試驗 benzidine test

联苯化合物/聯苯化合物　biphenyl compound
联苯基/聯苯基　xenyl
联苯双酯/聯苯雙酯　bifendate
联苄类/聯苄類　bibenzyls
联带运动/聯帶運動　synkinesia
联[二]苯/聯苯　biphenyl
联二脲/聯二脲　hydrazo dicarbonamide
联合/聯合　symphysis
联合部/聯合部　copula
联合的/聯合的,伴随的　associated
联合概率/聯合概率　joint probability
联合胶体/聯合膠體　association colloid
联合卡环/聯合卡環　combined clasp
联合开业/聯合開業　group practice
联合开业医院/聯合開業醫院　group practice hospital
联合开业诊疗/聯合開業診療　partnership practice
联合免疫缺陷病/多種免疫功能不全疾病　combined immunodeficiency disease
联合免疫缺陷综合征/聯結性免疫缺乏症候群　combined immunodeficiency syndrome
联合目录/聯合目錄　union catalog
联合妊娠/混合妊娠　combined pregnancy
联合神经/聯合神經　association nerve
联合神经中枢/聯合神經中樞　association nerve center
联合束/聯合束　association bundle
联合突/介體,聯桁　copula
联合系统病/合并性系統病　combined system disease
联合性痉挛/關聯性痙攣　associated spasm
联合性麻痹/關聯性麻痹　associated paralysis
联合性自动控制/聯合自動調節　associative automatic control
联合药物疗法/聯合藥物療法　combination drug therapy
联合医疗/集團醫學　group medicine
联合疫苗/聯合疫苗　combined vaccines
联合印模/聯合印模　combined impression
联合用药/藥物并用　drug combination
联合游离皮瓣/聯合游離皮瓣　combined free skin flap
联合运动/聯合運動　associated movement
联合支持/聯合支持　combination support
联合支持式/聯合支持式　mixed-borne type
联合转胎位术/混合轉向術　combined version
联茴香胺/二茴香胺　dianisidine
联会/聯會　synapsis

联会复合体/聯會複合體　synaptonemal complex
联接器/連接器　articulator
联接头/聯接頭　union
联结的/聯結的　linked
联结节律/聯結節律　coupled rhythm
联结器/聯結器　coupler
联觉/牽連感覺,連帶感覺　synesthesia
联络精神病学/聯絡精神病學　liaison psychiatry
联络[神经]束/聯合徑　association tract
联络神经元/聯絡神經元,聯合神經元　association neuron
联络纤维/聯絡纖維　association fibers
联络性失语/聯合性失語症　associative aphasia
联三苯化合物/聯三苯化合物　terphenyl compounds
联胎/暹羅雙胎,連體嬰　siamese twins
联胎自养体/連胎自養體　autosite
联体生活/連體生活　parabiosis
联体双生/聯體雙生　conjoined twins
联体双胎/雙畸胎,聯胎　conjoined twins
联想/聯想　association of ideas
联想测验/聯想試驗法　association test
联想反应/隨伴性反應　associative reaction
联想学习/聯想學習　association learning
联想中枢部/大腦之思想域　phronema
联想阻隔/心理分裂　sejunction
联硝氯酚/聯硝氯酚　niclofolan
联用麻醉药/聯用麻醉藥　combined anesthetics
廉泉/廉泉　lianquan, RN23
刿洗法/刿洗法　pricking/scraping-washing therapy
臁疮/臁瘡,深膿皰　chronic shank ulcer, ecthyma
臁疮·脾虚湿困证/臁瘡·脾虛濕困證　chronic shank ulcer with pattern of spleen deficiency and dampness retention
臁疮·气虚血瘀证/臁瘡·氣虛血瘀證　chronic shank ulcer with pattern of qi deficiency and blood stasis
臁疮·湿热下注证/臁瘡·濕熱下注證　chronic shank ulcer with pattern of dampness-heat diffusing downward
镰/鐮　falx
镰孢菌酸/鐮刀菌酸　fusaric acid
镰孢[霉]属/梭菌屬　*Fusarium*
镰刀菌病/馬鐮刀菌病　fusaridiosis
镰刀菌中毒[症]/鐮刀菌中毒症　fusariotoxicosis
镰形洁治器/鐮狀刮牙器　sickle scaler
镰状/鐮狀　falciform
镰状处女膜/鐮狀處女膜　falciform hymen
镰状红细胞血红蛋白C病/鐮狀紅血球血紅素C病　sickle cell-hemoglobin C disease

镰状红细胞血红蛋白 D 病/鐮狀紅血球血紅素 D 病 sickle cell-hemoglobin D disease
镰状皮瓣/鐮狀皮瓣 sickle skin flap
镰状韧带/鐮狀韌帶 falciform ligament
镰状体/鐮狀體 falciform body
镰状头孢子菌/鐮刀狀頭孢黴 Cephalosporium falciforme
镰状突/鐮狀突 falciform process
镰状细胞/鐮狀細胞 drepanocyte
镰状细胞病/鐮狀細胞病 drepanocytosis
镰状细胞贫血肾病/鐮狀細胞貧血腎病 kidney disease in sickle cell anemia
镰状细胞贫血症/鐮狀細胞貧血症,鐮狀細胞性貧血 sicklemia
镰状细胞肾病/鐮狀細胞腎病 sickle cell nephropathy
镰状细胞性贫血/鐮狀細胞性貧血 sickle cell anemia
镰状细胞性状/鐮狀細胞特質 sickle cell trait
镰状血红蛋白/鐮狀血紅素 sickle hemoglobin
镰状缘/鐮緣 falciform margin
镰状缘上角/鐮狀緣上角 superior cornu of falciform margin
镰状缘下角/鐮狀緣下角 inferior cornu of falciform margin
镰状支顶孢菌/鐮刀狀支頂孢黴,鐮刀狀頭孢黴 Acremonium falciforme
敛疮止痛/斂瘡止痛 healing sore and relieving pain
敛肺止咳/斂肺止欬 astringing lung for relieving cough
敛肺止咳剂/斂肺止欬劑 formula for astringing lung for relieving cough
敛阴/斂陰 astringing yin
敛阴固表/斂陰固表 astringing yin and consolidation of exterior
脸红/臉紅 blush
练功反应/練功反應 possible reactions to qigong practice
练功疗法/練功療法 functional exercise
练肌器/肌力練習機 ergostat
练音体操/練音體操 vocal gymnastics
炼丹派医学/煉丹派醫學 hermetic medicine
炼丹术/煉丹術 alchemy
炼己/煉己 refine oneself
炼乳/煉乳 condensed milk
恋父情结/愛雷特氏情結 Electra complex
恋母情结/戀母情結 Oedipus complex
恋尸癖/戀屍癖 necrophilia
恋丝织物[色情]癖/織物愛,戀綢癖 hyphephilia
恋童癖/戀童癖 paedophilia
恋童色情/戀女癖,幼女色情 pederosis
恋物癖/戀物癖 fetishism
链/鏈 chain
J 链/J 鏈 J chain
链道酶/鏈道酶 streptodornase
链格孢属/交替菌屬 Alternaria
链格孢中毒/鏈格孢中毒 alternariatoxicosis
链黑霉素/鏈黴黑素 streptonigrin
链激酶/鏈球菌激酶,鏈球菌活動酶 streptokinase
链激酶-链道酶/鏈激酶-鏈道酶 streptokinase-streptodornase
链霉胺/鏈[黴]胺 streptamine
链霉蛋白酶/鏈黴蛋白酶 pronase
链霉二糖胺/鏈黴二糖胺 streptobiosamine
链霉胍/鏈[黴]胺基酸 streptidine
链霉菌/鏈黴菌 streptomycete
链霉菌病/線菌病 streptomycosis
链霉菌属/鏈黴菌屬 Streptomyces
链霉素/鏈黴素 streptomycin
链霉素 B/鏈黴素 B streptomycin B
链霉素硫酸盐/硫酸鏈黴素 streptomycin sulfate
链脲菌素/鏈脲菌素 streptozocin
链[球]杆菌属/鏈桿菌屬 Streptobacillus
链球菌败血病/鏈球菌敗血病 streptosepticemia
链球菌的/鏈球菌的 streptococcal
链球菌感染/鏈球菌感染 streptococcal infection
链球菌菌苗/鏈球菌菌苗 streptococcal vaccine
链球菌菌血症/鏈球菌血症 strepticemia
链球菌溶血素/鏈球菌溶血素 streptohemolysin
链球菌溶血素类/鏈球菌溶血素類 streptolysins
链[球菌]杀白细胞素/鏈球菌殺白血球素 streptoleukocidin
链球菌噬菌体/鏈球菌噬菌體 streptococcus phage
链球菌属/鏈球菌屬 Streptococcus
链球菌性咽峡炎/鏈球菌性咽喉炎 streptococcus angina
链球菌性龈炎/鏈球菌性齦炎 streptococcal gingivitis
链球菌性肢端皮炎/鏈球菌性肢端皮炎 streptococcus acrodermatitis
链丝菌病/鏈絲菌病 streptothricosis
链丝菌素/鏈絲菌素 streptothricin
链烷/烷屬烴,烷屬碳化氫 alkane
链烷磺酸/鏈烷磺酸 alkanesulfonic acid
链烷磺酸盐类/鏈烷磺酸鹽類 alkanesulfonates
链尾线虫病/鏈尾線蟲病 streptocerciasis

链烯/烯屬烴 alkene
链形多头绦虫/犬多頭條蟲 Multiceps serialis
链阳菌素 A/鏈陽菌素 A streptogramin A
链阳菌素 B/鏈陽菌素 B streptogramin B
链阳菌素类/鏈陽菌素類 streptogramins
链阳菌素 A 组/鏈陽菌素 A 組 streptogramin group A
链阳菌素 B 组/鏈陽菌素 B 組 streptogramin group B
良附丸/良附丸 liangfu pills
良性斑块皮肤病/良性板塊皮膚病 benign plaque dermatosis
良性斑块状类银屑病/良性板塊狀類乾癬 parapsoriasis en plaques benign type
良性斑疹伤寒/良性斑疹傷寒，布利爾氏病 benign typhus
良性成牙骨质细胞瘤/良性成牙骨質細胞瘤 benign cementoblastoma
良性刺激/良性刺激 optimal stimulation
良性单克隆丙种球蛋白病/良性單克隆丙種球蛋白病 benign monoclonal gammopathy
良性的/良性的 benign
良性对称性脂肪过多症/良性對稱性脂肪瘤病 benign symmetric lipomatosis
良性附属器肿瘤/良性附屬器腫瘤 benign appendage tumor
良性钙化上皮瘤/良性鈣化上皮瘤 benign calcifying epithelioma
良性感受器/有益受體 beneceptor
良性高血压/良性高血壓 benign hypertension
良性黑棘皮病/良性黑棘皮病 benign acanthosis nigricans
良性红细胞增多症/良性紅血球增多症 benign polycythemia
良性积脓/良性積膿 benign empyema
良性家族性慢性天疱疮/良性家族性慢性天皰瘡 benign familial chronic pemphigus
良性家族性天疱疮/良性家族性天皰瘡 benign familial pemphigus
良性间日疟/良性間日瘧 benign tertian malaria
良性淋巴管性丘疹/良性淋巴管性丘疹 benign lymphangiomatous papule
良性淋巴上皮病变/良性淋巴上皮病變 benign lymphoepithelial lesion
良性淋巴细胞性脑膜炎/良性淋巴球性腦膜炎 benign lymphocytic meningitis
良性鳞状角化病/良性鱗狀角化症 benign squamous keratosis

良性瘤/良性瘤 benign tumor
良性颅内高血压/良性顱內高血壓 benign intracranial hypertension
良性囊性畸胎瘤/良性囊狀畸胎瘤 benign cystic teratoma
良性囊状上皮瘤/良性囊狀上皮瘤 benign cystic epithelioma
良性黏膜类天疱疮/良性黏膜樣類天皰瘡 benign mucosal pemphigoid
良性黏膜天疱疮/良性黏膜天皰瘡 benign mucous membrane pemphigus
良性疟/良性瘧 benign malaria
良性皮肤病性淋巴腺病变/良性皮膚病性淋巴腺病變 benign dermatopathic lymphadenopathy
良性皮肤结节性多动脉炎/良性皮膚結節性多動脈炎 benign cutaneous polyarteritis nodosa
良性前列腺增生/良性前列腺增生 benign prostatic hyperplasia
良性丘疹性棘层松解性皮肤病/良性丘疹性棘層鬆解皮膚病 benign papular acantholytic dermatosis
良性肾硬化/良性腎硬化 benign nephrosclerosis
良性苔藓样角化病/良性苔蘚樣角化症 benign lichenoid keratosis
良性天花/良性天花 variola benigna
良性天疱疮/良性天皰瘡 benign pemphigus
良性头部组织细胞增多症/良性頭部組織細胞增生症 benign cephalic histiocytosis
良性网状组织细胞增多症/良性網狀組織細胞增多症 benign reticulohistiocytosis
良性心内膜炎/良性心內膜炎 endocarditis benigna
良性新生儿癫痫/良性新生兒癲癇 benign neonatal epilepsy
良性型/良性型 benign form
良性血管内皮瘤/良性血管內皮瘤 benign hemangioendothelioma
良性移行性舌炎/良性移行性舌炎 benign migratory glossitis
良性幼年黑素瘤/良性青年性黑色素瘤 benign juvenile melanoma
良性阵发性眩晕/良性陣發性眩暈 benign paroxysmal vertigo
良性阵发性眼震/良性陣發性眼震 benign paroxysmal nystagmus
良性脂肪母细胞瘤/良性脂母細胞瘤 benign lipoblastoma
良性转移性甲状腺肿/良性轉移性甲狀腺腫 benign metastasizing goiter
莨菪/莨菪 henbane

莨菪根/莨菪根　insane root
莨菪碱中毒性舞蹈病/東莨菪鹼中毒性舞蹈病　hyoscine chorea
莨菪烷/莨菪烷　tropane
莨菪烷生物碱/莨菪烷生物鹼　tropane alkaloid
莨菪中毒/莨菪中毒　henbane poisoning
凉/涼　cool
凉膈散/涼膈散　liangge powder
凉开剂/涼開劑　cold formula for resuscitation
凉血/涼血　cooling blood
凉血化瘢/涼血化瘢　cooling blood for resolving macula
凉血明目/涼血明目　cooling blood to brighten eye
凉血明目法/涼血明目法　method of cooling blood to brighten eye
凉血息风/涼血息風　cooling blood for calming endogenous wind
凉血止血/涼血止血　cooling blood and arresting blood
凉血止血法/涼血止血法　method of cooling blood and arresting blood
凉燥/燥涼　cool dryness
凉燥证/涼燥證　cold-dryness pattern
梁门/梁門　liangmen, ST21
梁丘/梁丘　liangqiu, ST34
量鼻器/量鼻器,鼻腔計　rhinometer
量热法/熱量測定法,測熱法　calorimetry
量听望联[合]诊法/量、聽、視聯合診療法　metrechoscopy
两/兩　liang
两[边]凹/兩面凹陷　amphicelous
两侧错觉/兩側錯覺　synchiria
两侧对称/兩側對稱　bilateral symmetry
两侧痉挛/兩側痙攣　paraspasm
两侧听觉丧失/兩側聽覺喪失　bilateral hearing loss
两处骨折/兩處骨折　double fracture
两触点区别阈/二點識別閾　limen of twoness
两点辨别觉/兩點辨別　two-point discrimination
两度性熟/兩次性成熟　dissogeny
两分的/兩分的,兩歧的　hecatomeric
两感/兩感　cold attack on paired channels
两极倒转术/兩端式轉向術　bipolar version
两极囊胚/兩極囊胚　amphiblastula
两极[神经]细胞/雙極神經細胞　bipolar nerve cell
两极原肠胚/兩極[原]腸胚　amphigastrula
两极扎法/極性結扎,兩端結扎　pole ligation
两脚规式步行夹板/兩腳規式步行夾板　walking-calliper splint
两脚规式夹/兩腳規式夾　caliper splint
两阶段化学治疗/兩階段化學治療　two phases chemotherapy
两裂的/兩裂的,分歧的　bifid
两面针/兩面針　shinyleaf pricklyash root
两囊型疝/雙囊疝　hernia en bissac
两栖动物蛋白质/兩棲動物蛋白質　amphibian protein
两栖动物毒液/兩棲動物毒液　amphibian venom
两栖类/兩棲類　amphibians
两歧/兩歧　bifurcation of uterus, uterine tubes and ovaries
两歧桑葚胚/兩歧桑葚體　amphimorula
两歧性分子/兩歧性分子　amphipath
两腔心/兩腔心　bilocular heart
两亲的/兩性的　amphiphilic
两染细胞/兩染細胞　amphochromatophil
两染性/複染性　dichromophilism
两手不利/雙手均不能　ambilevosity
两手撮空/兩手撮空　groping in the air
两手同利/雙手同能　ambidextrality
两物体密接/兩物體密接　buttner
两向传导/兩向傳導　duplex transmission
两向发育/兩向發育　dichogeny
两相滴定/兩相滴定　diphasic titration
两胁胀满/兩脅脹滿　fullness in chest and abdominal
两胁胀痛/兩脅脹痛　pain and fullness in chest and abdominal
两型[状态]/兩型并存　amphitypy
两性电解质/兩性電解質　ampholyte
两性电解质合剂/兩性電解質合劑　ampholyte mixture
两性肌酸/兩性肌酸　amphicreatine
两性肌酸酐/兩性肌酸酐　amphicreatinine
两性畸形/兩性畸形　hermaphroditism
两性离子/兩性離子　zwitterion
两性霉素 B/兩性黴素 B　amphotericin B
两性[生殖]腺共存/兩性[生殖腺]共存,真兩性畸形　amphigonadism
两性同体/兩性同體,雌雄同體,兩性畸形　hermaphroditism
两性性欲/兩性性欲　bisexual libido
两性选择/兩性選擇　ampheclexis
两眼不等视/兩眼不等視,異視　heteropsia
两眼复视/兩眼複視　amphodiplopia
两眼虹膜异色/色彩非對稱　chromatic asymmetry
两眼视差/兩眼視差　binocular parallax
两眼视力不等/兩眼視力不等　anisopia

两眼视线等平/兩眼視線等平　isophoria
两眼调节参差/兩眼調節力不等　anisoaccommodation
两音听诊器/兩音聽診器　diechoscope
两指并指/單一并指畸形　single syndactyly
两指畸形/二指畸形　didactylism
两趾并趾/單一并趾畸形　single syndactyly
两趾畸形/二趾畸形　didactylism
亮氨酸/白胺酸　leucine
亮氨酸-2-丙氨酸脑啡肽/亮胺酸-2-丙氨酸腦啡肽　leucine-2-alanine enkephalin
亮氨酸拉链/亮胺酸拉鏈　leucine zipper
亮氨酸 tRNA 连接酶/亮胺酸 tRNA 連接酶　leucine-tRNA ligase
亮氨酸脑啡肽/亮胺酸腦啡肽　leucine enkephalin
亮氨酸尿/白胺酸尿症　leucinuria
亮氨酸乙酯/白胺酸乙酯　leucinethylester
亮氨酰-β-萘氨酶/亮胺醯-β-萘胺酶　leucyl-β-naphthylamidase
亮丙瑞林/亮丙瑞林　leuprolide
亮度测定法/光度測法　photometry
亮度适应计/暗光適應力計　biophotometer
亮肽素/亮肽菌素　leupeptin
亮酰氨肽酶/亮胺醯胺肽酶　leucyl aminopeptidase
量化构效关系/量化構效關係　quantitative structure-activity relationship
量子常数/量子常數　quantum constant
量子单位/量子單位　quantum unit
量子点/量子點　quantum dot
量子化学/量子化學　quantum chemistry
量子论/量子論,量子[學]説　quantum theory
量子药理学/量子藥理學　quantum pharmacology
疗效性化妆品/療效性化妝品　therapeutic cosmetic
疗养美容/療養美容　recuperating aesthetics
疗养所/療養所　halfway houses
疗养院/療養院,休養地　sanatorium
撩痒/搔癢　tickling
燎/燎　burning
钌放射性同位素/釕放射性同位素　ruthenium radioisotope
钌红/釕紅　ruthenium red
钌化合物/釕化合物　ruthenium compound
列夫病/列夫病　Lev disease
列缺/列缺　lieque, LU7
劣生/成長異常　cacogenesis
劣药/劣藥　drug of inferior
烈性噬菌体/烈性噬菌體　virulent phage
掠伤/不全脱骱　luxatio imperfecta

猎蝽科/獵蝽科　reduviidae
猎枪弹伤/獵槍彈傷　shotgun wound
裂/裂［縫］　cleft
裂点簇区/裂點簇區　breakpoint cluster region
裂额露脑畸胎/裂額露腦畸形　proencephalus
裂腭外侧粘连综合征/裂腭外側粘連症候群　cleft palate lateral synechia syndrome
裂发［症］/頭髮分歧　trichoschisis
裂缝骨折/裂縫骨折,坼裂骨折　fissured fracture
裂缝舌/溝裂舌　fissured tongue
裂谷热/裂谷熱　rift valley fever
裂合酶/裂解酵素　lyase
裂环马钱素色胺生物碱类/裂環馬錢素色胺生物鹼類　secologanin tryptamine alkaloids
裂环烯醚萜/裂環烯醚萜　secoiridoid
裂环烯醚萜苷/裂環烯醚萜苷　secoiridoid glycoside
裂解/裂解,裂開　cleavage
裂开性溃疡/裂開性潰瘍　fissured ulcer
裂孔/裂孔　hiatus, slit pore
裂孔的/裂孔的　hiatal
裂孔隔膜/裂孔隔膜　slit diaphragm
裂孔旁横膈疝/裂孔旁橫膈疝　parahiatal diaphragmatic hernia
裂口红细胞/裂口紅血球　stomatocyte
裂榄树胶/裂欖樹膠　tacamahac
裂模法/分裂模型法　split cast method
裂脑综合征/裂腦症候群　split-brain syndrome
裂片形出血/指甲下之線狀出血,趾甲下之線狀出血　splinter hemorrhage
裂［齲］洞/齒裂齲齒腔洞　fissure cavity
裂手/裂手　cleft hand
裂体吸虫性脓肿/血吸蟲性膿腫　bilharziasis abscess
裂痛/裂痛　tearing pain
裂头绦虫病/裂頭蟲病　diphyllobothriasis
裂头［绦虫］属/裂頭蟲屬　*Diphyllobothrium*
裂头蚴病/裂頭蚴病　sparganosis
裂纹舌/裂紋舌　fissured tongue
裂纹性湿疹/裂性濕疹　crackled eczema
裂纹状红斑/裂紋狀紅斑　erythema craquele
裂细胞症/裂血球症　schistocytosis
裂隙灯/裂隙燈　slit-lamp
裂隙灯检查[法]/裂隙燈檢查[法]　slitlamp examination
裂隙灯显微镜/裂隙燈顯微鏡　slitlamp microscope
裂隙灯照相[术]/裂隙燈照相[術]　slitlamp photography
裂隙片/裂隙片　stenopeic disk
裂隙羊膜/裂隙羊膜　schizamnion

裂隙性肉芽肿/裂口肉芽腫　granuloma fissuratum
裂殖菌纲/裂殖菌綱　Schizomycetes
裂殖前体/裂殖前體,瘧蟲之節裂前體　presegmenter
裂殖生殖/分裂生殖,無性生殖　agamocytogeny
裂殖体/分裂體,無性生殖體　agamont
裂殖藻纲/裂殖藻綱　Schizophyceae
裂殖周期/裂殖週期　schizogenic cycle
裂殖子表面蛋白质/裂殖子表面蛋白質　merozoite surface protein
裂足/裂足　cleft foot
裂钻/裂鑽　fissure bur
邻-氨基苯酚/鄰胺苯酚　o-aminophenol
邻氨基苯甲酸/鄰胺苯甲酸　anthranilic acid
邻氨基苯甲酸合酶/鄰胺苯甲酸合酶　anthranilate synthase
邻氨基苯甲酸磷酸核糖基转移酶/鄰胺基苯甲酸磷酸核糖基轉移酶　anthranilate phosphoribosyltransferase
邻苯二甲酸酐/鄰苯二甲酸酐　phthalic anhydride
邻苯甲二酸二丁酯/鄰苯二酸二丁酯　dibutyl phthalate
邻唇的/齒之近側及唇側的　proximolabial
邻二氮杂菲/鄰二氮雜菲　orthophenanthrolene
邻二氯苯/鄰位二氯苯　orthodichlorobenzene
邻酚酶/鄰位酚分解酵素　orthophenolase
邻颊的/齒之近側及頰側的　proximobuccal
邻甲酚/鄰位甲酚　orthocresol
邻甲酚酞/鄰位甲酚酞　orthocresol phthalein
邻甲基苯胺试验/正甲苯胺試驗　orthotoluidine test
邻接面/鄰接面　approximal surface
邻接性蔓延/接觸性蔓延　extension per contiguitatem
邻近取穴/鄰近取穴　nearby point selection
邻面沟/近側溝　proximal groove
邻面接触/近側接觸　proximal contact
邻面[齲]洞/近側面齲齒腔洞　proximal cavity
邻面轴沟/鄰面軸溝　axial proximal groove
邻耦/鄰耦　vicinal coupling
邻舌的/齒之近側及舌側的　proximolingual
邻酮醛糖/糖醛酮　osone
邻位交叉构象/鄰位交叉構象　gauche conformation
邻位皮瓣/鄰位皮瓣　adjacent skin flap
邻乙基[苯]酚/鄰乙基[苯]酚　phlorol
邻指皮瓣/鄰指皮瓣　cross finger skin flap
林白泵/林德白氏泵　Lindbergh pump
林道-[冯]希佩尔病/林道希培氏病　Lindau-von Hippel disease
林德弗莱施细胞/Rindfleisch 氏細胞　Rindfleisch cell
林-蒂溶液/Ringer-Tyrode 二氏溶液　Ringer-Tyrode solution
林格[溶]液/Ringer 氏液　Ringer solution
林-洛溶液/Ringer-Locke 二氏溶液　Ringer-Locke solution
林内试验/林納試驗　Rinne test
临产/臨產　in labor
临产轻瘫/臨產輕癱　parturient paresis
临床病理学/臨床病理學　clinical pathology
临床单位/臨床單位　clinical unit
临床的/臨床的　clinical
临床毒理学/臨床毒理學　clinical toxicology
临床对照试验/臨床對照試驗　controlled clinical trial
临床方案/臨床方案　clinical protocol
临床分光镜检查/臨床分光鏡檢查　clinical spectroscopy
临床根/臨床根　clinical root
临床工作能力/臨床工作能力　clinical competence
临床沟通/臨床溝通　clinical communication
临床冠/臨床冠　Corona clinica
临床护理研究/臨床護理研究　clinical nursing research
临床护理医生/臨床護理醫生　nurse clinician
临床化学/臨床化學　clinical chemistry
临床化学试验/臨床化學試驗　clinical chemistry test
临床记录/臨床表記法　clinography
临床解剖学/臨牀解剖學　clinical anatomy
临床决策支持系统/臨床決策支援系統　clinical decision support system
临床路径/臨床路徑　critical pathway
临床伦理学/臨床倫理學　clinical ethics
临床伦理学委员会/臨床倫理學委員會　clinical ethics committee
临床麻醉/臨床麻醉　clinical anesthesia
临床免疫学/臨床免疫學　clinical immunology
临床明显脱位/臨床明顯脱位　frank dislocation
临床前期的/症狀出現前的　preclinical
临床前药物评价/臨床前藥物評價　preclinical drug evaluation
临床肾结核/臨床腎結核　clinical renal tuberculosis
临床实习/臨床實習　clinical clerkship
临床实验室技术/臨床實驗室技術　clinical laboratory technique
临床实验室信息系统/臨床實驗室資訊系統　clinical laboratory information system
临床试验/臨床試驗　clinical trial

临床试验规范/優良臨床實驗規範 good clinical practice, GCP
临床试验数据监测委员会/臨床試驗資料監測委員會 clinical trials data monitoring committee
临床试用新药申请/臨床試用新藥申請 investigational new drug application
临床试用药物/臨床試用藥物 investigational drug
临床死亡/臨床死亡 clinical death
临床显微镜检查/臨床顯微鏡檢查 clinical microscopy
临床心理学/臨床心理學 clinical psychology
临床性流感/臨床性流行性感冒 clinical influenza
临床牙根/臨床牙根 clinical root of tooth
临床牙冠/臨床牙冠 clinical crown of tooth
临床研究性治疗/臨床研究性治療 investigational therapy
临床药理学/臨床藥理學 clinical pharmacology
临床药学/臨床藥學 clinical pharmacy
临床药学信息系统/臨床藥學資訊系統 clinical pharmacy information system
临床医学/臨床醫學 clinical medicine
临床遗传学/臨床遺傳學 clinical genetics
临床诊断/臨床診斷 clinical diagnosis
临床指标/臨床指標 clinical indicator
临床总体印象量表/臨床總體印象量表 clinical global impression scale
临界的/臨界的 critical
临界点/臨界點 critical point
临界胶团浓度/臨界微膠束濃度 critical micelle concentration
临界区域/臨界區域 critical region
临界容积学说/臨界容積學說 critical volume theory
临界闪烁融合频率/臨界閃光頻率 critical flicker fusion frequency
临界温度/臨界溫度 critical temperature
临界相对湿度/臨界相對濕度 critical relative humidity
临界性高血压/底線性高血壓 borderline hypertension
临界照明/臨界照明 critical illumination
临时的/暫時的 provisional
临时敷裹/臨時包扎 temporary dressing
临时结扎线/暫時結扎 provisional ligature
临时皮质/暫時性皮質 provisional cortex
临睡服/臨睡服 administered before bed time
临证指南医案/臨證指南醫案 Case Records as a Guide to Clinical Practice, Guide to Clinical Practice with Medical Records

临终病人/臨終病人 terminally ill patient
临终关怀/安寧療護 hospice
临终关怀医疗/臨終關懷醫療 hospice care
临终关怀医院/臨終關懷醫院 hospice
临终照料/臨終照料 terminal care
淋巴/淋巴 lymph
淋巴棒状杆菌/淋巴棒狀桿菌 corynebacterium lymphophilum
淋巴导管/淋巴[導]管 lymphatic duct
淋巴道/淋巴道 lymph tract
淋巴的/淋巴的 lymphatic
淋巴毒素/淋巴毒素 lymphotoxin
淋巴干/淋巴幹 lymphatic trunk
淋巴管/淋巴管 lymphatic vessel, lymphatic duct
淋巴管瓣/淋巴管瓣 lymphatic valve
淋巴管成形术/淋巴管形成術 lymphangioplasty
淋巴管丛/淋巴管叢 lymphatic plexus
淋巴管肌瘤/淋巴管肌瘤 lymphangiomyoma
淋巴管畸形/淋巴管畸形 lymphatic abnormality
淋巴管静脉炎/淋巴管靜脈炎 lymphangiophlebitis
淋巴管扩张/淋巴管擴張 lymphangiectasis
淋巴管瘤/淋巴管瘤 lymphangioma
淋巴管瘤病/淋巴管瘤病 lymphangiomatosis
淋巴管瘤病性象皮病/淋巴管瘤病性象皮病 elephantiasis lymphangiomatosis
淋巴管马皮疽/鼻疽管 farcy pipe
淋巴管内淋巴/淋巴管內淋巴 intravascular lymph
淋巴管内皮/淋巴管內皮 lymphatic endothelium
淋巴管内皮瘤/淋巴管內皮瘤 lymphangioendothelioma
淋巴管内注射/淋巴管內注射 intralymphatic injection
淋巴管切除术/淋巴管切除術 lymphangiectomy
淋巴管切开术/淋巴管切開術 hydrangiotomy
淋巴管曲张/淋巴管曲張 lymph varix
淋巴管肉瘤/淋巴管肉瘤 lymphangiosarcoma
淋巴管生成/淋巴管生成 lymphangiogenesis
淋巴管栓塞/淋巴管栓塞 lymph embolism
淋巴管栓塞症/淋巴管栓塞症 lymphangiothrombosis
淋巴管纤维瘤/淋巴管纖維瘤 lymphangiofibroma
淋巴管学/淋巴管學 hydrangiology
淋巴管炎/淋巴管炎 lymphangitis
淋巴管移植术/淋巴管移植術 lymphatic vessel grafting
淋巴管造口术/淋巴管造口術 lymphaticostomy
淋巴管造影[术]/淋巴管X光攝影術 lymphangiography

淋巴管[造影]照片/淋巴管 X 射線照片 lymphangiogram
淋巴管痣/淋巴管痣 nevus lymphaticus
淋巴管周炎/淋巴管周圍炎 perilymphangitis
淋巴管注射/淋巴管注射 intralymphatic injection
淋巴管组织瘤/淋巴管組織瘤 lymphatic vessel tumor
淋巴激素活化细胞/淋巴激素活化細胞 lymphokine activated cell
淋巴浆/淋巴漿 lymph plasma
淋巴结/淋巴結 lymph node
淋巴结病/淋巴腺病 lymphadenopathy
淋巴结结核/淋巴結結核 lymph node tuberculosis
淋巴结静脉吻合术/淋巴結静脈吻合術 lymph node-venous anastomosis
淋巴结门/淋巴結門 hilum of lymph gland
淋巴结囊肿/淋巴腺囊腫 adenolymphocele
淋巴结脓肿/淋巴腺膿腫 glandular abscess
淋巴结切除术/淋巴結切除術 lymph node excision
淋巴结切开术/淋巴結切開術 lymphadenotomy
淋巴结炎/淋巴腺炎 lymphadenitis
淋巴结样的/淋巴腺樣的 lymphadenoid
淋巴结样甲状腺肿/淋巴腺樣甲狀腺腫 lymphadenoid goiter
淋巴结造影术/淋巴腺攝影術 lymphadenography
淋巴结造影照片/淋巴腺 X 射線圖 lymphadenogram
淋巴结增大/淋巴腺曲張 lymphadenovarix
淋巴结肿块/瘰癧 pleiades
淋巴结周炎/淋巴腺周圍炎 perilymphadenitis
淋巴静脉分流术/淋巴静脈分流術 lymphatico-venous shunt
淋巴静脉吻合术/淋巴静脈吻合術 lymphatico-venous anastomosis
淋巴瘤/淋巴瘤 lymphoma
淋巴瘤病/淋巴瘤病 lymphomatosis
淋巴瘤前期疹/淋巴瘤前期疹 prelymphomatous eruption
淋巴瘤细胞白血病/淋巴瘤細胞白血病 lymphoma cell leukemia
淋巴瘤性甲状腺肿/淋巴瘤性甲狀腺腫 struma lymphomatosa
淋巴瘤性乳头状囊腺瘤/淋巴瘤性乳頭狀囊腺瘤 papillary cystadenoma lymphomatosum
淋巴瘤性咽峡炎/淋巴瘤性咽峡炎 angina lymphomatosa
淋巴瘤样的/淋巴瘤樣的 lymphomatoid
淋巴瘤样丘疹病/淋巴瘤樣丘疹病 lymphomatoid papulosis
淋巴瘤样肉芽肿病/淋巴瘤樣肉芽腫病 lymphomatoid granulomatosis
淋巴瘘/淋巴瘻 lymphatic fistula
淋巴滤泡病/淋巴濾泡症 lymphofolliculosis
淋巴滤泡性膀胱炎/淋巴濾泡性膀胱炎 lymphofollicular cystitis
淋巴母细胞/淋巴胚細胞，母淋巴球 lymphoblast
淋巴囊/淋巴囊 lymph sac
淋巴囊肿/淋巴囊腫 lymphocele
淋巴黏液瘤/淋巴黏液瘤 lymphomyxoma
淋巴尿/淋巴尿 lymphuria
淋巴器官/淋巴器官 lymphatic organ, lymphoid organ
淋巴腔/淋巴腔 geode
淋巴去除术/淋巴去除術 lymphopheresis
淋巴肉瘤/淋巴肉瘤 lymphatic sarcoma
淋巴肉瘤病/淋巴肉瘤症 lymphosarcomatosis
淋巴肉瘤细胞性白血病/淋巴肉瘤細胞白血病 leukolymphosarcoma
淋巴肉芽肿/惡性淋巴肉芽腫 lymphogranuloma
淋巴上皮瘤/淋巴上皮瘤 lymphoepithelioma
淋巴上皮瘤样癌/淋巴上皮瘤樣表皮癌 lymphoepithelioma-like carcinoma
淋巴-上皮小结/淋巴-上皮小結 lympho-epithelial nodule
淋巴-上皮组织/淋巴-上皮組織 lympho-epithelial tissue
淋巴生成/淋巴生成 lymphization
淋巴树突细胞/淋巴樹突細胞 lymphoid dendritic cell
淋巴水肿/淋巴水腫 lymphoedema
淋巴水肿性气压疗法/淋巴水腫之氣壓壓迫療法 pneumatic compression therapy in lymphoedema
淋巴体质/淋巴體質 lymphatic constitution
淋巴[体质]性幼稚型/淋巴體質性幼稚型 lymphatic infantilism
淋巴网状内皮细胞增生[症]/淋巴網狀內皮細胞增生 lymphoreticulosis
淋巴网状系统/淋巴網狀細胞系 lymphoreticular system
淋巴吸收/淋巴管吸收 lymphatic absorption
淋巴系闪烁造影[术]/淋巴系閃爍造影[術] lymphoscintigraphy
淋巴系统/淋巴系統 lymphatic system
淋巴系统疾病/淋巴系統疾病 lymphatic disease
淋巴系造影术/淋巴系造影術，淋巴腺攝影術 lymphangioadenography

淋巴系[造影]照片/淋巴管 X 光線圖　lymphogram
淋巴细胞/淋巴細胞,淋巴球　lymph cell, lymphocyte
T 淋巴细胞/T 淋巴球　T lymphocytes
淋巴细胞白血病/淋巴球性白血病　lymphocytic leukemia
淋巴细胞的/淋巴球的　lymphocytic
淋巴细胞毒素/淋巴球毒素　lymphocytotoxin
淋巴细胞发生/淋巴細胞發生　lymphcytopoiesis
淋巴细胞功能相关抗原/淋巴細胞功能相關抗原　lymphocyte function-associated antigen
淋巴细胞归巢受体/淋巴細胞歸巢受體　lymphocyte homing receptor
淋巴细胞恢复疹/淋巴球恢復疹　eruption of lymphocyte recovery
淋巴细胞活化/淋巴細胞活化　lymphocyte activation
淋巴细胞集积/淋巴集積　lymphorrhage
淋巴细胞计数/淋巴細胞計數　lymphocyte count
淋巴细胞减少/淋巴球減少症　lymphopenia
淋巴细胞减少性胸腺发育不良/少淋巴球性胸腺發育不良　lymphopenic thymic dysplasia
淋巴细胞决定簇/淋巴細胞決定簇　lymphocyte determinant
淋巴细胞瘤/淋巴細胞瘤　lymphocytoma
淋巴细胞破裂/淋巴球破裂　lymphocytorrhexis
淋巴细胞趋向性/趨淋巴球性　lymphotaxis
淋巴细胞去除术/淋巴細胞去除術　lymphocyte depletion
淋巴细胞缺乏/淋巴球缺乏　alymphocytosis
淋巴细胞生成/淋巴細胞造成　lymphopoiesis
淋巴细胞生长酸/淋巴細胞生長酸　lymphokentric acid
淋巴细胞输注/淋巴細胞輸注　lymphocyte transfusion
淋巴细胞吞噬症/淋巴球吞噬症　lymphophagocytosis
淋巴细胞协同作用/淋巴細胞協同作用　lymphocyte cooperation
淋巴[细胞]性多能干细胞/淋巴[細胞]性多能幹細胞　bipotential lymphoid-restricted stem cell
淋巴细胞性甲状腺炎/淋巴細胞性甲狀腺炎　lymphocytic thyroiditis
淋巴细胞性甲状腺肿/Hashimoto 氏甲狀腺腫　Hashimoto goiter
淋巴细胞性结肠炎/淋巴細胞性結腸炎　lymphocytic colitis
淋巴细胞性泪腺涎腺慢性肿大综合征/Mikulicz 氏症候群　Mikulicz syndrome
淋巴细胞性类白血病反应/淋巴球性白血病樣反應　lymphocytic leukemoid reaction
淋巴细胞性脉络丛脑膜炎/淋巴細胞性脈絡叢腦膜炎　lymphocytic choriomeningitis
淋巴细胞性脉络丛脑膜炎病毒/淋巴細胞性脈絡叢腦膜炎病毒　LCM virus
淋巴细胞性脑膜炎/淋巴球性腦膜炎　lymphocytic meningitis
淋巴细胞亚群/淋巴細胞亞群　lymphocyte subset
淋巴细胞隐病毒/淋巴細胞隱病毒　lymphocryptovirus
淋巴细胞再循环/淋巴細胞再循環　lymphocyte recirculation
淋巴细胞再循环库/淋巴細胞再循環庫　lymphocyte recirculating pool
淋巴细胞增多/淋巴球增多症　lymphocytosis
淋巴细胞增生性疾病/淋巴細胞增生性疾病　lymphoproliferative disease
淋巴细胞增生综合征/淋巴球增生症候群　lymphoproliferative syndrome
淋巴细胞转化/淋巴細胞變性　lymphocyte transformation
淋巴细胞组织增生/淋巴球組織增生病　lymphoid leukosis
淋巴腺病相关病毒/淋巴腺病相關病毒　lymphadenopathy associated virus
淋巴腺瘤/淋巴腺瘤　lymphadenoma
淋巴腺瘤细胞/淋巴腺瘤細胞　lymphadenoma cell
淋巴腺皮质/淋巴腺皮質　cortical substance of lymph node
淋巴腺鼠疫/淋巴腺鼠疫　bubonic plaque
淋巴小结/淋巴小結　lymphatic nodule, lymphoid follicle
淋巴心/淋巴心　lymph heart
淋巴性恶病质/淋巴性惡病質　lymphatic cachexia
淋巴性假白血病/淋巴性假白血病　pseudoleukemia lymphatica
淋巴性水疱/淋巴性水皰　lymphatic bulla
淋巴性水肿/淋巴性水腫　lymphatic edema
淋巴性咽峡炎/淋巴性咽峽炎　lymphatic angina
淋巴学/淋巴學　lymphatology
淋巴循环/淋巴循環　lymph circulation
淋巴样的/類淋巴的　lymphoid
淋巴样细胞/淋巴樣細胞　lymphoid cell
淋巴液缺乏/淋巴液缺乏　alymphia
淋巴液性溃疡/淋巴液性潰瘍　lymphatic ulcer
淋巴溢/淋巴液漏　lymphorrhea
淋巴因子/淋巴因子　lymphokine

淋巴因子启动杀伤细胞/淋巴因數啟動殺傷細胞 lymphokine-activated killer cell
淋巴郁积性血管病变/淋巴鬱積性血管病變 lymphostatic vasculopathy
淋巴源结核/淋巴源結核 lymphogenous tuberculosis
淋巴照射/淋巴照射 lymphatic irradiation
淋巴转移/淋巴轉移 lymphatic metastasis
淋巴阻塞性尘肺/淋巴阻塞性塵肺 coniolymphstasis
淋巴阻塞性溃疡/淋巴阻塞性潰瘍 lymph obstructive ulcer
淋巴组织/淋巴組織 lymphoid tissue, lymphatic tissue
淋巴[组织]发育不全/淋巴組織發育不全 alymphoplasia
淋巴组织发育障碍/淋巴組織發育障礙 lymphotism
淋巴[组织]瘤/淋巴腺瘤 lymphadenoma
淋巴[组织]瘤的/淋巴瘤的 lymphomatous
淋巴组织切除术/淋巴組織切除術 lymphoidectomy
淋巴组织溶素/淋巴組織溶素 lymphatolysin
淋巴组织细胞增多症/淋巴組織細胞增生症 lymphohistiocytosis
淋巴组织性白细胞生成/淋巴腺白血球增生 lymphadenoleukopoiesis
淋巴组织增生[病]/淋巴組織增殖病 lymphadenosis
淋巴组织增生的/淋巴球增生的 lymphoproliferative
淋巴组织增殖性疾病/淋巴組織增殖性疾病 lymphoproliferative disorder
磷/磷 phosphorus
磷氨基酸类/磷氨基酸類 phosphoamino acids
磷胺/磷胺 phosphamidon
磷苯二甲酸二甲酯/磷苯二酸二甲酯 dimethylphthalate
磷壁酸类/磷壁酸類 teichoic acids
磷代谢/磷代謝 phosphorus metabolism
磷代谢紊乱/磷代謝紊亂 disorders of phosphorus metabolism
磷代谢障碍/磷代謝障礙 phosphorus metabolism disorder
磷蛋白/磷蛋白 phosphoprotein
磷蛋白磷酸酶/磷蛋白磷酸酶 phosphoprotein phosphatase
磷蛋白质/磷蛋白質 phosphoprotein
磷毒性坏死/磷毒性壞死 phosphonecrosis
磷放射性同位素/磷放射性同位素 phosphorus radioisotope
磷光计/磷光計 phosphoroscope
磷光性汗/磷光性汗 phosphorescent sweat
磷化合物/磷化合物 phosphorus compound
磷化氢类/磷化氫類 phosphines
磷化石灰/磷石灰 calcarea phosphorica
磷化物/磷化物 phosphide
磷灰石/磷灰石 apatite
磷霉素/磷黴素 fosfomycin
磷钼酸/磷鉬酸 phosphomolybdic acid
磷钼酸试剂/磷鉬酸試劑 sonnenschein reagent
磷尿症/磷尿症 phosphoruria
磷缺乏症/磷缺乏症 phosphate deficiency
磷肉酸/磷肉酸 phosphocarnic acid
磷烧伤/磷燒傷 phosphorus burn
磷尸碱/磷屍鹼,磷腐鹼 phosphoptomaine
磷酸/磷酸 phosphoric acid
磷酸吡哆醛/磷酸吡哆醛 pyridoxal phosphate
磷酸丙酮酸水合酶/磷酸丙酮酸水合酶 phosphopyruvate hydratase
磷酸单酯酶/磷酸單酯酶 phosphomonoesterase
磷酸单酯水解酶类/磷酸單酯水解酶類 phosphoric monoester hydrolases
磷酸二钙/磷酸二鈣 dicalcium phosphate
磷酸二氧林/磷酸甲基高罌粟鹼 dioxyline phosphate
磷酸二酯酶/磷酸二酯酶 phosphodiesterase
磷酸二酯酶抑制药/磷酸二酯酶抑制劑 phosphodiesterase inhibitor
磷酸二酯水解酶类/磷酸二酯水解酶類 phosphoric diester hydrolases
磷酸分解[作用]/磷酸分解 phosphorolysis
磷酸钙/磷酸鈣,鈣磷酸鹽 calcium phosphate
磷酸钙结石/磷酸鈣結石 calcium phosphate stone
磷酸钙类/磷酸鈣類 calcium phosphates
磷酸甘油酸/磷酸甘油酸 phosphoglyceric acid
磷酸甘油酸酯变位酶/磷酸甘油酸鹽變位酶 phosphoglycerate mutase
磷酸甘油酸酯激酶/磷酸甘油酸鹽啟動酶,磷酸甘油脂活化酵素 phosphoglycerate kinase
磷酸胍/磷酸胍 phosphoguanidine
磷酸硅黏固剂/磷酸矽黏固劑 silicate phosphate cement
磷酸果糖激酶/磷酸果糖啟動酶 phosphofructokinase
磷酸果糖醛缩酶/磷酸果糖醛縮酶 phosphofructose aldolase
磷酸核糖胺/磷酸核糖胺 phosphoribosylamine
磷酸核糖激酶/磷酸核糖啟動酶 phosphoribokinase
磷酸核糖焦磷酸/磷酸核糖焦磷酸 phosphoribosyl pyrophosphate
磷酸核糖焦磷酸激酶/磷酸核糖焦磷酸激酶 ribose-

phosphate pyrophosphokinase
磷酸化硫胺素/磷酸化硫胺素 phosphorylated thiamin
磷酸化酶/磷酸化酵素 phosphorylating enzyme
磷酸化酶激酶/磷酸化酶啟動酶 phosphorylase kinase
磷酸化酶磷酸酶/磷酸化酶磷酸酶 phosphorylase phosphatase
磷酸肌醇/磷酸肌醇 phosphoinositide
磷酸己糖激酶/磷酸己糖激酶 phosphohexokinase
磷酸己糖酶/己糖磷酸酯酶 hexosephatase
磷酸己糖酯/磷酸己糖酯 hexosephosphoric ester
磷酸结合蛋白质类/磷酸結合蛋白質類 phosphate-binding proteins
磷酸精氨酸/磷鮭卵酸,磷酸精胺酸 phosphoarginine
磷酸精胺/精素磷酸鹽 spermine phosphate
磷酸聚根皮素/多根皮素磷酸鹽 polyphloretin phosphate
磷酸可待因/磷酸可待因 codeine phosphate
磷酸酪氨酸/磷酸酪胺酸 phosphotyrosine
磷酸类/磷酸類 phosphoric acids
磷酸铝凝胶/磷酸鋁凝膠,磷酸鋁乳膠體 aluminum phosphate gel
磷酸氯喹/磷酸氯喹 chloroquine phosphate
磷酸酶试验/磷酸[酯]酶試驗 phosphatase test
磷酸镁铵结石/磷酸鎂銨結石 magnesium ammonium phosphate calculus
磷酸钠溶液/磷酸鈉溶液 sodium phosphate solution
磷酸葡糖激酶/磷酸葡萄糖啟動酶 phosphoglucokinase
磷酸葡糖脱氢酶/磷酸葡糖脱氫酶 phosphogluconate dehydrogenase
磷酸葡萄糖异构酶/磷酸葡萄糖異構酶 phosphoglucose isomerase
磷酸氢二钾/磷酸鉀 dipotassium phosphate
磷酸球蛋白/磷球蛋白 phosphoglobulin
磷酸三甲酚酯类/磷酸三甲酚酯類 tritolyl phosphates
磷酸三酯水解酶类/磷三酯水解酶類 phosphoric triester hydrolases
磷酸丝氨酸/磷酸絲胺酸 phosphoserine
磷酸苏氨酸/磷酸蘇氨酸 phosphothreonine
磷酸酮醇酶/磷酸酮醇酶 phosphoketolase
磷酸烯醇丙酮酸/磷酸烯醇丙酮酸鹽 phosphoenolpyruvate
磷酸烯醇丙酮酸羧基酶/磷酸烯醇丙酮酸羧基酶 phosphoenolpyruvate carboxylase
磷酸烯醇丙酮酸羧激酶/磷酸烯醇丙酮酸羧激酶 phosphoenolpyruvate carboxykinase
磷酸烯醇丙酮酸糖磷酸转移酶系统/磷酸烯醇丙酮酸糖磷酸轉移酶系統 phosphoenolpyruvate sugar phosphotransferase system
磷酸腺苷酰硫酸/磷酸腺苷磷醯硫酸 phosphoadenosine phosphosulfate
磷酸锌黏固剂/磷酸鋅黏固劑 zinc phosphate cement
磷酸盐/磷酸鹽 phosphate
磷酸盐沉着/磷酸鹽沈積 phosphatoptosis
磷酸盐缓冲液/磷酸鹽緩衝系統 phosphate buffer
磷酸盐类/磷酸鹽類 phosphates
磷酸盐尿/磷酸鹽尿 phosphaturia
磷酸盐血/磷酸鹽血症 phosphatemia
磷酸乙酰基转移酶/磷酸乙醯基轉移酶 phosphate acetyltransferase
磷酸月桂酯钠/磷酸月桂酯鈉 sodium lauryl phosphate
磷酸酯类/磷酸酯類 phosphoric acid esters
磷酸[酯]酶/磷酸[酯]酶 phosphatase
磷酸酯酶过多/高磷酸酶症 hyperphosphatasia
磷酸转移酶类/磷酸轉移酶類 phosphotransferases
磷酸转运蛋白质类/磷酸轉運蛋白質類 phosphate transport proteins
磷酸组胺/磷酸組織胺 histamine phosphate
磷肽类/磷肽類 phosphopeptides
磷碳酸钙/磷碳酸鈣 dahllite
磷糖/磷糖類 phosphosugar
磷糖蛋白/磷糖蛋白 phosphoglucoprotein
磷同位素/磷同位素 phosphorus isotope
磷钨酸/磷鎢酸 phosphotungstic acid
磷酰胺氮芥类/磷酸醯胺氮芥類 phosphoramide mustards
磷酰胺酶/磷醯胺酶 phosphoamidase
磷酰胆碱/磷酸膽鹼 phosphorylcholine
磷酰化/磷酸化作用 phosphorylation
磷酰[基]/磷基 phosphoryl
磷酰精氨酸/鮭卵酸磷酸鹽,磷鮭卵酸 arginine phosphate
磷氧裂合酶类/磷氧裂合酶類 phosphorus-oxygen lyases
磷氧酸黏固粉/磷氧酸黏固粉 oxyphosphate cement
磷脂/磷脂 phospholipid, phosphatide
磷脂沉积症/磷脂質代謝症 phosphatide lipoidosis
磷脂类/磷脂類 phospholipids
磷脂酶/磷脂酶 phospholipase
磷脂醚类/磷脂醚類 phospholipid ethers

磷脂酸/磷脂酸 phosphatidic acid
磷脂酸磷酸酶/磷脂酸磷酸酯酶 phosphatidate phosphatase
磷脂酰胆碱类/磷脂醯膽鹼類 phosphatidylcholines
磷脂酰胆碱-甾醇 o-酰基转移酶/磷脂醯膽鹼-甾醇 o-醯基轉移酶 phosphatidylcholine-sterol o-acyltransferase
磷脂酰甘油类/磷脂醯甘油類 phosphatidylglycerols
磷脂酰肌醇/磷脂醯肌醇 phosphatidylinositol
磷脂酰肌醇二酰甘油裂合酶/磷脂醯肌醇二醯甘油裂合酶 phosphatidylinositol diacylglycerol-lyase
磷脂酰肌醇磷酸盐类/磷脂醯肌醇磷酸鹽類 phosphatidylinositol phosphates
磷脂酰丝氨酸/磷脂醯絲胺酸 phosphatidylserine
磷脂酰乙醇胺/磷脂醯乙醇胺 phosphatidylethanolamine
磷脂酰乙醇胺结合蛋白质/磷脂醯乙醇胺結合蛋白質 phosphatidylethanolamine binding protein
磷脂血/磷脂血症 phospholipidemia
磷脂转移蛋白质类/磷脂轉移蛋白質類 phospholipid transfer proteins
鳞部/鱗部 squamous part
鳞顶缝/鱗頂縫 squamosoparietal suture
鳞缝/鱗縫 squamous suture
鳞鼓裂/鱗鼓裂 squamotympanic fissure
鳞乳突缝/鱗乳突縫 squamosomastoid suture
鳞石英/鱗石英 tridymite
鳞屑/鱗屑 scale
鳞屑性睑炎/鱗屑性瞼炎 blepharitis squamosa
鳞屑性丘疹样梅毒疹/鱗屑性丘疹樣梅毒疹 papulosquamous syphilide
鳞屑性湿疹/鱗屑性濕疹 eczema squamosum
鳞屑疹/鱗屑疹 scaly eruption
鳞癣/魚鱗癬 ichthyosis
鳞癣状的/魚鱗癬狀的 ichthyosiform
鳞缘/鱗緣 squamosal border, squamosal margin
鳞枕骨/枕骨鱗 squamo-occipital bone
鳞状癌/鱗狀[細胞]癌 squamous carcinoma
鳞状的/鱗屑狀的 scaly
鳞状缝/鱗狀縫 squamous suture
鳞状骨/鱗狀骨 squamosal
鳞状毛囊角化病/鱗狀毛囊角化病 squamous follicular keratosis
鳞状毛壅症/鱗狀毛壅症 trichostasis squamosa
鳞状乳头状瘤/鱗狀乳突狀瘤 squamous papilloma
鳞状上皮/鱗狀上皮 squamous epithelium
鳞状上皮瘤/鱗狀上皮瘤 squamous epithelioma
鳞状[上皮]细胞/鱗狀細胞 squamous cell
鳞状[上皮]细胞乳头[状]瘤/鱗狀上皮細胞乳頭狀瘤 squamous cell papilloma
鳞状细胞癌/鱗狀細胞癌 squamous cell carcinoma
鳞状[细胞]化/鱗狀細胞化 squamatization
鳞状细胞乳头状瘤/鱗狀細胞乳頭狀瘤 squamous cell papilloma
鳞状细胞上皮瘤/鱗狀細胞上皮瘤 squamous cell epithelioma
鳞状细胞肿瘤/鱗狀細胞腫瘤 squamous cell neoplasm
鳞状细胞珠/鱗狀細胞珠 squamous pearl
鳞状漩涡角化/鱗狀漩渦角化 squamous eddies
鳞状牙源性肿瘤/鱗狀牙源性腫瘤 squamous odontogenic tumor
淋病/淋病 gonorrhoea
淋病抗毒素/淋病抗毒素 gonorrhea antitoxin
淋病奈瑟球菌/淋病雙球菌 Neisseria gonorrhoeae
淋病性关节痛/淋病性關節痛 gonorrheal arthralgia
淋病性关节炎/淋病性關節炎 urethral arthritis
淋病性龟头炎/淋性陰莖頭炎 balanoblennorrhea
淋病性滑膜炎/淋病性滑膜炎 gonorrheal synovitis
淋病性腱鞘炎/淋菌性腱鞘炎 gonococcic tenosynovitis
淋病性角化病/淋病性角化病 gonorrheal keratosis
淋病性尿道炎/淋病性尿道炎 gonorrheal urethritis
淋病性肿胀/淋病性腫脹 blennorrhagic swelling
淋病学/淋病學 neisseriology
淋病疣/淋病疣 gonorrheal wart
淋菌性尿道炎/淋菌性尿道炎 gonococcal urethritis
淋菌性前列腺炎/淋菌性前列腺炎 gonococcal prostatitis
淋球菌的/淋球菌的 gonococcal
淋球菌性结膜炎/淋球菌性結膜炎 gonococcal conjunctivitis
淋球菌性皮炎/淋球菌性皮炎 gonococcal dermatitis
淋润/淋潤 showering moistening
淋证/淋證,痛性尿淋瀝 stranguria, strangury
膦甲酸/膦甲酸 foscarnet
膦酸类/膦酸類 phosphonic acids
膦酸乙酸/膦酸乙酸 phosphonoacetic acid
灵道/靈道 lingdao, HT4
灵龟八法/靈龜八法 eight methods of intelligent turtle
灵机记性/靈機記性 psychological activity
灵机记性在脑说/靈機記性在腦説 theory of psychological activity associated with the brain
灵菌红素/靈菌紅素 prodigiosin
灵兰秘典论篇/靈蘭秘典論篇 Ling Lan's Treatise

on Misteries
灵枢经/靈樞經　Lingshu Jing, Miraculous Pivot
灵台/靈臺　lingtai, DU10
灵墟/靈墟　lingxu, KI24
灵长类疾病/靈長類疾病　primate disease
灵长类嗜T淋巴细胞病毒/靈長類嗜T淋巴細胞病毒　primate T-lymphotropic virus
灵长目/靈長類　primates
灵芝/靈芝　glossy ganoderma
苓桂术甘汤/苓桂朮甘湯　linggui zhugan decoction
铃蟾肽/鈴蟾素　bombesin
铃蟾肽受体/鈴蟾肽受體　bombesin receptor
铃兰氨酸/鈴蘭氨酸　azetidine-2-carboxylic acid
凌霄花/凌霄花　trumpet-creeper flower
菱唇/菱腦唇　rhombic lip
菱脑/菱腦　rhombencephalon
菱脑沟/菱腦溝　rhombic groove
菱脑节/菱腦原節,腦節　neuromere, rhombomere
菱脑峡/菱腦峽　rhombencephalic isthmus
菱形核/菱形核　rhomboidal nucleus
菱形皮瓣/菱形皮瓣　rhomboid skin flap
菱形皮肤/菱形皮膚　cutis rhomboidalis
菱形韧带/菱形韌帶　rhomboid ligament
菱形吻合[术]/菱形吻合[術]　diamond shaped anastomosis
菱形窝/菱形窩　rhomboid fossa
菱形窝界沟/菱形窩界溝　sulcus limitans of rhomboid fossa
菱形窝内侧隆起/菱形窩内側隆凸　terete eminence
菱形窝上凹/菱形窩上凹　superior fovea of rhomboid fossa
菱形窝正中沟/菱形窩正中溝　median sulcus of rhomboid fossa
菱形胸/菱形胸,四面體胸　tetrahedron chest
羚角钩藤汤/羚角鉤藤湯　lingjiao gouteng decoction
羚羊角/羚羊角　antelope horn
零级动力学/零級動力學　zero order kinetics
岭回归/嶺回歸　ridge regression
领鞭虫/領鞭蟲　choanoflagellate
领会障碍/領會障礙　disturbance of apprehension
领夹/領夾　collar splint
另煎/另煎　decocted separately
刘涓子鬼遗方/劉涓子鬼遺方　Liu Juanzi's Remedies Bequeathed by Ghosts
刘完素/劉完素　Liu Wansu
留罐/留罐　cup retaining, retaining cup
留钾利尿药/留鉀利尿劑　potassium-sparing diuretic
留饮/留飲　prolonged fluid retention
留针/留針　retention of needle
留置导管/留置導管　indwelling catheter
流产/流産　embryotocia
流产胎/流産兒　abortus
流产菌素/流産素　abortin
流产申请人/流産申請人　abortion applicant
流产胎儿/流産胎兒　aborted fetus
流程/程式,步驟　procedure
流程图/流程圖　flow chart, flow sheet
流出道补片术/流出道補片術　outflow tract patching
流电病变/流電病變　galvanism
流电刺激/流電刺激　galvanic shock
流电试验/流電試驗　galvanic test
流电应激性/化學應激性　galvanic irritability
流[动]/流動　flux
流动吸收池/流動貯液槽　flow cell, flow cuvette
流动性/流動性　fluidity
流动注射分析/流動注射分析　flow injection analysis
流感病毒/流行性感冒病毒　influenza virus
流感病毒A型/流感病毒A型　influenza A virus
流感病毒血凝素糖蛋白类/流感病毒血凝素糖蛋白類　influenza virus hemagglutinin glycoproteins
流感病毒疫苗/流行感冒病毒疫苗　influenza virus vaccine
流感脑炎/流感腦炎,流行性腦炎　influenzal encephalitis
流感疫苗/流感疫苗　influenza vaccine
流化床包衣/流化床著衣　fluidized bed coating
流化床制粒/流動床造粒　fluidized bed granulation
流火/流火　shank erysipelas
流火·火毒内陷证/流火·火毒内陷證　shank erysipelas with pattern of fire-toxin sinking inward
流火·湿热化火证/流火·濕熱化火證　shank erysipelas with pattern of dampness-heat transforming into fire
流金凌木/流金凌木　flowing metal invading wood, pseudopterygium
流浸膏/流浸膏　fluid extract
流浸膏剂/流浸膏劑　liquid extract
流浪者病/遊民病　vagabond disease
流泪/流淚　lacrimation
流泪[病]/流淚[病]　dacryorrhea, lacrimation disease
流泪·肺虚风袭证/流淚·肺虚風襲證　lacrimation with pattern of lung deficiency and wind invasion
流泪·肝肾两虚证/流淚·肝腎兩虚證　lacrimation with liver-kidney deficiency pattern

流泪·气血两虚证/流淚·氣血兩虛證 lacrimation with qi-blood deficiency pattern
流量/流量 flow rate
流量计/流量計 flowmeter
流能磨/流能磨 fluid energy mill
流皮漏/流皮漏 lupus vulgaris, spreading skin ulcer
流皮漏·气血两虚证/流皮漏·氣血兩虛證 spreading skin ulcer with qi-blood deficiency pattern
流皮漏·痰热瘀阻证/流皮漏·痰熱瘀阻證 spreading skin ulcer with pattern of phlegm-heat stasis and obstruction
流皮漏·阴虚内热证/流皮漏·陰虛內熱證 spreading skin ulcer with pattern of yin deficiency and internal heat
流入式通风系统/充實通氣法 plenum system
流食/流質飲食 fluid diet
流式细胞术/流式細胞術 flow cytometry
流式细胞仪/流式細胞儀 flow cytometer
流速/流速 flow rate
流速程序高效液相色谱法/流速程控高效液相層析法 flow programming high performance liquid chromatography
流痰/流痰 flowing phlegm, chronic suppurative abscess of bones and joints, tuberculosis of bone and joint
流痰·肝肾两虚证/流痰·肝腎兩虛證 flowing phlegm with liver-kidney deficiency pattern
流痰·气血两虚证/流痰·氣血兩虛證 flowing phlegm with qi-blood deficiency pattern
流痰·阳虚痰凝证/流痰·陽虛痰凝證 flowing phlegm with pattern of yang deficiency and phlegm coagulation
流痰·阴虚内热证/流痰·陰虛內熱證 flowing phlegm with pattern of yin deficiency and internal heat
流体动力学/流體動力學 hydrodynamics
流体静力压/流體靜壓 hydrostatic pressure
流通蒸汽灭菌/流通蒸汽滅菌 flowing steam sterilization
流涎/流涎 sialorrhea, salivation
流涎症/流涎症 ptyalism
流行病发生/流行病形成 epidemiogenesis
流行病特征/流行[病]特徵 genius epidemicus
流行病学/流行病學 epidemiology
流行病学方法/流行病學方法 epidemiologic method
流行病学计量/流行病學計量 epidemiologic measurement
流行病学家/流行病學專家 epidemiologist
流行病学研究/流行病學研究 epidemiologic study
流行病学研究设计/流行病學研究設計 epidemiologic research design
流行病学研究特征/流行病學研究特徵 epidemiologic study characteristics
流行病学因素/流行病學因素 epidemiologic factor
流行性/流行性,流行狀態 epidemicity
流行性斑疹伤寒/流行性斑疹傷寒 epidemic typhus fever
流行性剥脱性皮炎/流行性剝落性皮膚炎 epidemic exfoliative dermatitis
流行性出血病/流行性出血性病 epidemic hemorrhagic disease
流行性出血病病毒/流行性出血病病毒 epizootic hemorrhagic disease virus
流行性痤疮/流行性痤瘡 epidemic acne
流行性呃逆/流行性呃逆 epidemic hiccough
流行性肝炎/流行性肝炎 epidemic hepatitis
流行性感冒/流行[性]感冒 epidemic influenza, influenza
流行性感冒关节炎/流行性感冒關節炎 influenzal arthritis
流行性关节炎性红斑/流行性關節炎性紅斑 epidemic arthritic erythema
流行性坏疽性直肠炎/流行性壞疽性直腸炎 epidemic gangrenous proctitis
流行性黄疸/流行性黃疸 epidemic jaundice
流行性霍乱/流行性霍亂 epidemic cholera
流行性甲型脑炎/流行性甲型腦炎 epidemic encephalitis type A
流行性角膜结膜炎病毒/流行性角膜結膜炎病毒 epidemic keratoconjunctivitis virus
流行性卡他性黄疸/流行性卡他性黃疸 epidemic catarrhal jaundice
流行性痢疾/流行性痢疾 epidemic dysentery
流行性脑脊髓膜炎/流行性腦脊髓膜炎 epidemic cerebrospinal meningitis
流行性脑炎/流行性腦炎 epidemic encephalitis
流行性脑炎病毒/流行性腦炎病毒 epidemic encephalitis virus
流行性牛肺炎/流行性牛肺炎 enzootic pneumonia of calves
流行性腮腺炎/流行性腮腺炎 epidemic parotitis
流行性腮腺炎性脑膜炎/流行性腮腺炎腦膜炎 mumps meningitis
流行性神经肌无力/流行性神經肌無力 epidemic neuromyasthenia
流行性虱传斑疹伤寒/流行性蝨傳斑疹傷寒

epidemic louse-borne typhus
流行性水肿/流行性水腫　epidemic dropsy
流行性胸膜痛/流行性胸膜痛　epidemic pleurodynia
流行性荨麻疹/流行性蕁麻疹　epidemic urticaria
流行性乙型脑炎/流行性乙型腦炎　epidemic encephalitis type B
流行性乙型脑炎病毒/日本 B 型腦炎病毒　Japanese B encephalitis virus
流行性中毒综合征/流行性毒性症候群　toxic epidemic syndrome
流饮/流飲　flowing fluid retention
流质膳[饮]食/流質食物　liquid diet
流注/流注　deep multiple abscess, gravitational abscess
流注性脓肿/重力性膿瘍　gravitation abscess
琉璃苣/琉璃苣　borage
硫氨基酸类/硫氨基酸類　sulfur amino acids
硫胺素/硫胺素　aneurine
硫胺素焦磷酸激酶/硫胺素焦磷酸激酶　thiamine pyrophosphokinase
硫胺素焦磷酸酶/硫胺素焦磷酸酶　thiamine pyrophosphatase
硫胺素焦磷酸盐/硫胺素焦磷酸鹽　thiamine pyrophosphate
硫胺素磷酸盐/硫胺素磷酸鹽　thiamine monophosphate
硫胺素酶/硫胺酶　thiaminase
硫胺素缺乏/硫胺素缺乏　thiamine deficiency
硫胺素三磷酸盐/硫胺素三磷酸鹽　thiamine triphosphate
硫巴比妥酸/硫巴比妥酸　thiobarbituric acid
硫巴比妥酸反应物/硫巴比妥酸反應物　thiobarbituric acid reactive substance
硫巴比妥酸盐类/硫巴比妥酸鹽　thiobarbiturates
硫半乳糖苷类/硫半乳糖苷類　thiogalactosides
硫贲妥钠/戊硫巴比妥　thiopentone
硫必利/泰必利　tiapride
硫醇/硫醇　mercaptan
硫醇尿酸/硫醇尿酸　mercapturic acid
硫醇盐/硫醇鹽　mercaptide
硫醇乙酸铵液/硫醇乙酸銨液　ammonium sulphate solution
硫代氨基甲酸酯类/硫代氨基甲酸酯類　thiocarbamates
硫代醋酸/硫代醋酸　thiuretic acid
硫代丁二酸二辛钙/硫醯丁二酸二辛鈣　dioctyl calcium sulfosuccinate
硫代丁二酸二辛钠/多庫酯鈉　dioctyl sodium sulfosuccinate
硫代核苷类/硫代核苷類　thionucleosides
硫代核苷酸类/硫代核苷酸類　thionucleotides
硫代磺酸类/硫代磺酸類　thiosulfonic acids
硫代肌苷/硫代肌苷　thioinosine
硫代磷酸酯类/硫代磷酸酯類　thiophosphoric acid esters
硫代硫酸金钠/硫代硫酸金鈉　gold sodium thiosulfate
硫代硫酸硫基转移酶/硫代硫酸硫基轉移酶　thiosulfate sulfurtransferase
硫代硫酸钠/硫代硫酸鈉　sodium thiosulfate
硫代硫酸盐/硫代硫酸鹽　thiosulfate
硫代苹果酸金钠/硫代蘋果酸金鈉　gold sodium thiomalate
硫代苹果酸锑锂/硫代蘋果酸銻鋰　antimony lithium thiomalate
硫代苹果酸盐类/硫代蘋果酸鹽類　thiomalates
硫代水杨酸/硫代水楊酸,硫柳酸　thiosalicylic acid
硫代糖苷类/硫代糖苷類　thioglycosides
硫代酰胺类/硫代醯胺類　thioamides
硫代亚砷酸盐/硫亞砷酸鹽　thioarsenite
硫代乙酰胺/硫代乙醯胺　thioacetamide
硫丹/硫丹　endosulfan
硫胆碱/硫膽鹼　thiocholine
硫蛋白/硫蛋白　sulfoprotein
硫碘疗法/硫碘療法　thiodotherapy
硫蒽酮/硫蒽酮　lucanthone
硫凡士精/凡士精硫磺軟膏　sulfur vasogen
硫放射性同位素/硫放射性同位素　sulfur radioisotope
硫苷/硫苷　thioglycoside
硫固定/硫固定,定硫力　thiopexy
硫华/硫華　flower of sulfur
硫化/硫化　sulfurize
硫化镉/硫化鎘　cadmium sulfide
硫化合物/硫化合物　sulfur compound
硫化氢/硫化氫,氫硫酸　hydrogen sulfide
硫化氢尿/硫化氫尿　hydrothionuria
硫化氢血/硫化氫血症　hydrothionemia
硫化氢浴/硫化氫浴　hydrogen sulfide bath
硫化物/硫化物　sulfide
硫化硒/硫化硒　selenium sulfide
硫磺/硫磺　sulfur
硫磺颗粒/硫磺顆粒　sulphur granule
硫[磺]色肝/硫磺肝　brimstone liver
硫磺浴/硫磺浴　sulfur bath
硫磺中毒/硫磺中毒　sulfur poisoning

硫基转移酶类/硫基轉移酶類　sulfurtransferases
硫金代葡萄糖/金硫葡萄糖　aurothioglucose
硫堇/硫堇　thionin
硫康唑/硫康唑　sulconazole
硫醚嗪/硫醚嗪　thioridazine
硫链丝菌肽/硫鏈絲菌素　thiostrepton
硫硫键异构酶类/硫硫鍵異構酶類　sulfur-sulfur bond isomerases
硫柳汞/硫柳汞　thimerosal
硫六氟化物/硫六氟化物　sulfur hexafluoride
硫氯酚/雙硫酚醇　bithionol
硫醚/硫醚　thioether
硫黏蛋白/硫黏蛋白　sulfomucin
硫鸟嘌呤/硫鳥嘌呤　thioguanine
硫尿核苷/硫尿核苷　thiouridine
硫脲/硫脲　thiourea
硫脲嘧啶/硫尿嘧啶,硫二羟嘧啶　thiouracil
硫脲[中毒]性甲状腺肿/硫脲中毒性甲狀腺腫　thiourylene goiter
硫配糖体/硫代葡糖酸鹽類　glucosinolates
硫葡糖/硫葡萄糖　thioglucose
硫葡糖苷类/硫葡糖苷類　thioglucosides
硫普罗宁/硫普羅寧　thiopronine
硫氰化物中毒性甲状腺肿/硫氰化物中毒性甲狀腺腫　thiocyanate goiter
硫氰酸钾/硫氰酸鉀　potassium thiocyanate
硫氰酸盐/硫氰酸鹽　thiocyanate
硫氰乙酸异冰片酯/硫氰醋酸異龍腦　isobornyl thiocyanoacetate
硫醛/硫醛　sulfaldehyde
硫缺乏症/硫缺乏,缺硫病　asulfurosis
硫色素反应/硫色素反應　thiochrome reaction
硫胂凡纳明/硫阿斯凡鈉明　sulfarsphenamine
硫试验/硫試驗　sulfur test
硫酸/硫酸　oil of vitriol
硫酸2-氨-5-硝苯酚/硫酸2-胺-5-硝苯酚　2-amino-5-nitrophenol sulfate
硫酸铵/硫酸銨　ammonium sulfate
硫酸铵分级分离/硫酸銨分離法　ammonium sulfate fractionation
硫酸钡/硫酸鋇　barium sulfate
硫酸苯胺/硫酸苯胺　aniline sulfate
硫酸长春碱/硫酸長春花鹼　vinblastine sulfate
硫酸对氨苯酚/硫酸對胺苯酚　p-aminophenol sulfate
硫酸多黏菌素B/硫酸多黏菌素B　polymyxin B sulfate
硫酸二甲酯/硫酸二甲酯,二甲基硫酸　dimethyl sulfate
硫酸反苯环丙胺/硫酸反苯環丙胺　tranylcypromine sulfate
硫酸钙/硫酸鈣　calcium sulfate
硫酸间氨苯酚/硫酸間胺苯酚　m-aminophenol sulfate
硫酸角质素/硫酸角質素　keratan sulfate
硫酸结合作用/硫酸結合作用　sulfoconjugation
硫酸金鸡纳啶/硫酸辛柯尼定　cinchonidine sulfate
硫酸金雀花碱/硫酸金雀花素　sparteine sulfate
硫酸可待因/硫酸可待因　codeine sulfate
硫酸奎尼丁/硫酸奎尼丁　quinidine sulfate
硫酸奎宁/硫酸奎寧　quinine sulfate
硫酸类/硫酸類　sulfuric acids
硫酸邻氨苯酚/硫酸鄰胺苯酚　o-aminophenol sulfate
硫酸邻氯对苯二氨/硫酸鄰氯對苯二胺　o-chloro-p-phenylenediamine sulfate
硫酸麻黄碱/硫酸麻黄素　ephedrine sulfate
硫酸麻黄素溶液/硫酸麻黄素溶液　ephedrine sulfate solution
硫酸吗啡/硫酸嗎啡　morphine sulfate
硫酸镁/硫酸鎂　magnesium sulfate
硫酸钠/硫酸鈉　sodium sulfate
硫酸皮肤素/硫酸皮膚素　dermatan sulfate
硫酸葡聚糖/硫酸葡聚糖　dextran sulfate
硫酸溶胶/硫酸溶膠體　sulfosol
硫酸软骨素/硫酸軟骨素　chondroitin sulfate
硫酸软骨素钠/硫酸軟骨素鈉　sodium chondroitin sulfate
硫酸弱金鸡纳碱/硫酸金雞納素　cinchonine sulfate
硫酸烧伤/硫酸燒傷　sulfuric acid burn
硫酸双丁妥林/硫酸雙丁妥林　dibutoline sulfate
硫酸[双分]解/加硫酸分解　sulfolysis
硫酸铜/硫酸銅　copper sulfate
硫酸脱氢表雄酮/硫酸脱氫表雄酮　dehydroepiandrosterone sulfate
硫酸戊聚糖聚酯/硫酸戊聚糖聚酯　pentosan sulfuric polyester
硫酸腺苷酰转移酶/硫酸腺苷醯轉移酶　sulfate adenylyltransferase
硫酸锌/硫酸鋅　zinc sulfate
硫酸新霉素软膏/硫酸新黴素軟膏　neomycin sulfate ointment
硫酸亚铊/硫酸鉈　thallium sulfate
硫酸亚铁/硫酸亞鐵　ferrous sulfate
硫酸盐/硫酸鹽　sulfate
硫酸盐血症/硫酸鹽血症　sulfatemia

硫酸吲哚酚/氧吲哚硫酸盐,氧靛基质硫酸盐 indoxyl-sulfate
硫酸罂粟碱/硫酸罌粟鹼 papaverine sulfate
硫酸鱼精蛋白注射液/硫酸魚精蛋白注射液 protamine sulfate injection
硫酸月桂酯铵/硫酸月桂酯銨 ammonium lauryl sulfate
硫酸酯类/硫酸酯類 sulfuric acid esters
硫酸酯酶/硫酸鹽酵素 sulfatase
硫酸酯酶缺乏/硫酸酯酶缺乏病 sulfatase deficiency
硫酸中毒/硫酸中毒 sulfoxism
硫糖铝/硫糖鋁 sucralfate
硫同位素/硫同位素 sulfur isotope
硫酮类/硫酮類 thiones
硫戊巴比妥/硫戊巴比妥 thiamylal
硫辛酸/硫辛酸 thioctic acid
硫血红蛋白/硫血紅素,硫紅血球素 sulfhemoglobin
硫血红蛋白血症/硫血紅素血症 sulfhemoglobinemia
硫血[症]/硫血症 thiemia
硫氧化物类/硫氧化物類 sulfur oxides
硫氧还蛋白/硫氧還蛋白 thioredoxin
硫氧还蛋白还原酶/硫氧還蛋白還原酶 thioredoxin reductase
硫乙拉嗪/乙硫匹拉嗪 thiethylperazine
硫酯水解酶类/硫酯水解酶類 thioester hydrolases
硫族元素/硫族元素 chalcogen
硫族转移酶类/硫族轉移酶類 sulfur group transferases
硫唑嘌呤/硫唑嘌呤 imuran
瘤/瘤 tumor
瘤巨细胞/瘤巨細胞 tumor giant cell
瘤胃/瘤胃 rumen
瘤形成/瘤形成 neoplasia
瘤型麻风/瘤性麻風,結節性麻風 lepromatous leprosy
瘤性骨折/腫瘤性骨折 neoplastic fracture
瘤性增生/腫瘤性增生 neoplastic hyperplasia
瘤蝇属/瘤蠅屬 Cordylobia
瘤组织钳/腫瘤切除器 kelectome
柳氮磺胺吡啶/柳氮磺胺嘧啶 azulfidine
柳黑苷/柳皮苷 salinigrin
柳枝状骨折/柳枝狀骨折 willow fracture
六倍体/六倍體 hexaploid
六倍性/六倍性 hexaploidy
六鞭毛虫病/六鞭蟲病 hexamitiasis
六尘/六塵 six dust
六重峰/六重峰 sextet

六出花属/百合水仙屬 Alstroemeria
六腑/六腑 six fu-viscera
六腑咳/六腑欬 six fu-viscera cough
六根/六根 six roots
六合定中丸/六合定中丸 liuhe dingzhong pill
六合维生素/六種維生素劑 hexavitamin
六甲胺化合物/六甲胺化合物 hexamethonium compound
六甲铵/六烴季銨 hexamethonium
六甲磷酰胺/六甲磷醯胺 hempa
六甲蜜胺/六甲蜜胺 altretamine
六角立方晶体系统/六角立方晶體系統 hexagonal crystal system
六经辨证/六經辨證 pattern identification of six channels theory
六君子丸/六君子丸 liujunzi pill
六氯苯/六氯苯 hexachlorobenzene
六氯酚/六氯酚 hexachlorophene
γ-六氯化苯/六氯丙苯 gamma benzene hexachloride
六梦/六夢 six types of dream
六气/六氣 six climatic factors
六氢脱氧麻黄碱/六氫脫氧麻黃鹼 propylhexedrine
六氢异烟酸类/異六氫煙酸類 isonipecotic acids
六神丸/六神丸 liushen pill
六识/六識 six cognition
六水合铝/六水合鋁 aluminium hexahydrate
六岁磨牙/六歲大臼齒 the sixth-year molar
六烃季铵烟酸酯/六烴季銨煙酸酯 hexonate
六味地黄丸/六味地黃丸 liuwei dihuang pill
六烯类/六烯類 hexaenes
六硝酸甘露醇/六硝酸甘露醇 mannitol hexanitrate
六一散/六一散 liuyi powder
六淫/六淫 six climatic exopathogens
六郁/六鬱 six stagnation diseases, six types of stagnation pattern
六元正纪大论篇/六元正紀大論篇 Treatise on Stagnancy and Depression
六指畸形/六指畸形 hexadactylia
六趾畸形/六趾畸形 hexadactylia
龙贝格病/Romberg 氏病 Romberg disease
龙贝格痉挛/Romberg 氏痙攣 Romberg spasm
龙贝格征/龍貝格徵 Romberg sign
龙葱/龍蔥 Longcong
龙胆/龍膽 Chinese gentian
龙胆苦苷/龍膽苦苷 gentiopicrin
龙胆鞣酸/龍膽鞣酸 gentiotannic acid
龙胆三糖/龍膽[三]糖 gentianose

龙胆酸盐/龍膽酸鹽　gentisate
龙胆泻肝汤/龍膽瀉肝湯　longdan xiegan decoction
龙胆紫/龍膽紫,結晶紫　gentian violet
龙胆紫溶液/龍膽紫染液　gentian violet solution
龙骨/龍骨　bone fossil of big mammal
龙舌兰汁/龍舌蘭汁　aguamiel
龙虾肌碱/龍蝦肌鹼　homarine
龙虾钳状手/龍蝦鉗狀手　lobster hand
龙涎香/龍涎香　Ambergris
龙形肾盂造影照片/龍形腎盂攝影照片　dragon pyelogram
龙须瘟/龍鬚瘟　dragon beard pestilence
龙牙草/龍牙草　agrimony
龙眼肉/龍眼肉　longan aril
龙爪鳌豆球蛋白/絲絨豆球蛋白　stizolobin
聋/聾[症],聽覺缺失　deafness
聋点/聾點　deaf spot
聋哑/聾啞[症]　deaf-mutism
聋哑教练法/教授唇語　demutization
聋哑人/聾啞者　deaf-mute
聋哑症/聾啞病　alalia cophica
笼形[化合]物/籠形化合物　clathrate
笼状种植体/籠狀種植體　cage implant
隆鼻术/隆鼻術　augmentation rhinoplasty
隆颏术/隆頦術　chin augmentation
隆隆样杂音/隆隆樣雜音　rumbling murmur
隆起性病变/隆起性病變　protrusion lesion
隆凸/隆凸　protuberantia
隆凸成形术/隆凸成形術　carinoplasty
隆凸的/隆凸狀的　carinate
隆凸骨折/隆凸骨折　torus fracture
隆凸切除术/隆凸切除術　carina resection
隆凸性皮肤纤维肉瘤/隆凸性皮膚纖維肉瘤　dermatofibrosarcoma protuberans
隆凸性色素痣/隆凸性色素母斑　protuberant nevus
隆凸状腹/隆凸狀腹　carinate abdomen
隆椎/隆椎,第七頸椎　vertebra prominens, prominent vertebra
癃闭/癃閉,蓄尿,尿滯留　dribbling and retention of urine, retention of urine
癃闭・肺热壅盛证/癃閉・肺熱壅盛證　dribbling and retention of urine with pattern of exuberance of lung heat
癃闭・肝气郁结证/癃閉・肝氣鬱結證　dribbling and retention of urine with pattern of liver qi depression
癃闭・膀胱湿热证/癃閉・膀胱濕熱證　dribbling and retention of urine with pattern of damp-heat in bladder
癃闭・肾气虚证/癃閉・腎氣虛證　dribbling and retention of urine with pattern of kidney qi deficiency
癃闭・肾阳衰微证/癃閉・腎陽衰微證　dribbling and retention of urine with pattern of kidney yang exhaustion
癃闭・肾阴虚证/癃閉・腎陰虛證　dribbling and retention of urine with pattern of kidney yin deficiency
癃闭・湿热下注证/癃閉・濕熱下注證　dribbling and retention of urine with pattern of downward diffusion of damp-heat
癃闭・瘀浊阻塞证/癃閉・瘀濁阻塞證　dribbling and retention of urine with pattern of blockade of static blood and turbidity
癃闭・中气下陷证/癃閉・中氣下陷證　dribbling and retention of urine with pattern of middle qi collapse
蒌叶/蔞葉　Piper betle
蝼蛄疖/螻蛄癤　folliculitis abscedens et suffodiens, mole cricket furuncle
蝼蛄疖・风热上攻证/螻蛄癤・風熱上攻證　mole cricket furuncle with pattern of wind-heat attacking upward
蝼蛄疖・暑湿蕴结证/螻蛄癤・暑濕蘊結證　mole cricket furuncle with summerheat-dampness amassment pattern
蝼蛄疖・正虚毒结证/螻蛄癤・正虛毒結證　mole cricket furuncle with pattern of healthy qi deficiency and toxin accumulation
瘘/瘻[管]　fistula
瘘管/瘻管　fistula
瘘管刀/瘻管刀　fistulatome
瘘管切除术/瘻管切除術　fistulectomy
瘘管切开术/瘻管切開術　fistulotomy
瘘管试验/瘻管試驗　fistula test
瘘管形成/瘻管形成,成瘻　fistulization
瘘性溃疡/瘻性潰瘍　fistulous ulcer
漏出液/漏出液,漏出物　transudate
漏斗/漏斗　infundibulum, funnel
漏斗部闭锁/漏斗部閉鎖　infundibular atresia
漏斗部角化症/漏斗部角化症　funnel keratosis
漏斗部腺瘤/漏斗部腺瘤　infundibular adenoma
漏斗干/漏斗幹,漏斗柄　infundibular stem
漏斗骨盆/漏斗骨盆　funnel shaped pelvis
漏斗腱/漏斗腱　infundibular tendon
漏斗体/漏斗體　infundibular body
漏斗形处女膜/漏斗狀處女膜　infundibuliform hymen

漏斗胸矫正术/漏斗胸矯正術　corrective operation of pectus excavatum
漏斗引流术/漏斗引流法　funnel drainage
漏斗隐窝/漏斗隱窩　infundibular recess
漏斗状的/漏斗狀的　crateriform, infundibuliform
漏斗状肛门/漏斗狀肛門　infundibuliform anus
漏斗[状]胸/漏斗胸　funnel chest
漏谷/漏谷　lougu, SP7
漏睛/漏睛,淚囊炎　leaking eye, chronic dacryocystitis, dacryocystitis
漏睛疮/漏睛瘡　acute dacryocystitis, leaking eye sore
漏睛疮·风热上攻证/漏睛瘡·風熱上攻證　leaking eye sore with pattern of wind-heat attacking upward
漏睛疮·热毒炽盛证/漏睛瘡·熱毒熾盛證　leaking eye sore with blazing heat-toxin pattern
漏睛·风热停留证/漏睛·風熱停留證　leaking eye with wind-heat lingering pattern
漏睛·心脾湿热证/漏睛·心脾濕熱證　leaking eye with pattern of dampness-heat in heart and spleen
漏睛·正虚邪恋证/漏睛·正虛邪戀證　leaking eye with pattern of healthy qi deficiency and lingering pathogen
漏芦/漏蘆　uniflower swisscentaury root
漏尿/漏尿　leakage of urine
漏下/漏下　metrostaxis
卢茨慢性多形性痒疹/露茲型慢性多型性癢疹　prurigo chronica multiformis of Lutz
卢克手术/盧克手術　Luque technique
卢肯带环/Luken 氏帶環　Luken band
卢-皮综合征/Lubarsch-Pick 二氏症候群　Lubarsch-Pick syndrome
卢瑟福综合征/Rutherford 氏症候群　Rutherford syndrome
卢施卡扁桃体/Luschka 氏扁桃腺　Luschka tonsil
卢施卡韧带/Luschka 氏韌帶　Luschka ligament
卢滕巴赫综合征/Lutembacher 氏症候群　Lutembacher syndrome
芦丁/蘆丁　rutin
芦根/蘆根　reed rhizome
芦荟/蘆薈　aloe
芦荟黄质/黄精素,蘆薈黄嘌呤　aloxanthin
芦荟泻素/蘆薈大黄苷　aloe-emodin
芦笋/蘆筍　asparagus
芦他霉素/蘆他徽素　rutamycin
芦竹碱/蘆竹鹼　donaxine
炉甘石/爐甘石　calamine
炉甘石洗剂/爐甘石洗劑　calamine lotion

鸬鹚瘟/鸕鶿瘟　cormorant-like pestilence
颅/顱　cranium, skull
颅背侧锯肌/顱背側鋸肌　musculus serratus dorsalis cranialis
颅病/顱病,頭病　craniopathy
颅不全畸胎/腦壓出畸胎　thlipsencephalus
颅部脑膜膨出/腦膜膨出　craniomeningocele
颅槽指数/基底指數　basilar index
颅侧/頭側　cranial
颅侧点/顱側點　euryon
颅测量器/測顱器,量顱器　craniometer
颅长高指数/顱高指數　altitudinal index
颅长阔指数/頭顱的長闊指數　length-breadth index
颅穿刺术/顱穿刺術　craniopuncture
颅垂体部黄瘤/腦垂體黄瘤　craniohypophyseal xanthoma
颅底/顱底　skull base
颅底点/顱底點,底穴　basion, endobasion
颅底骨折/顱底骨折　basal skull fracture
颅底内面/顱底內面　internal surface of base of skull
颅底外面/顱底外面,顱底外部　external surface of base of skull
颅底性眼肌麻痹/腦底性眼肌麻痺　basal ophthalmoplegia
颅[底]咽管/顱咽管,咽底管　basipharyngeal canal, craniopharyngeal canal
颅底肿瘤/顱底腫瘤　skull base neoplasm
颅底蛛网膜炎/顱底蜘蛛膜炎　basiarachnitis
颅顶/顱頂,頭頂　skull cap
颅顶骨多孔[畸形]/胎兒顱頂部骨骼發育缺失　craniofenestria
颅顶骨内面凹陷/顱骨陷窩　craniolacunia
颅顶肌/顱頂肌　epicranius, epicranial muscle
颅动脉炎/顱動脈炎　cranial arteritis
颅窦/顱竇　cranial sinus
颅耳间沟/顱耳間溝　cranioauricular sulcus
颅耳角/顱耳角　cranioauricular angle
颅缝/顱縫　cranial suture
颅缝重建术/顱縫重建術　reconstruction of cranial suture
颅缝[先天]骨化/顱縫先天骨化　craniostosis
颅缝早闭-桡骨发育不良综合征/顱縫線封閉過早及橈骨發育不全症候群　craniosynostosis-radial aplasia syndrome
颅盖/顱蓋　calvarium
颅骨/顱骨　bone of cranium
颅骨凹陷骨折/顱骨凹陷骨折　depressed fracture of skull

颅骨凹陷骨折整复术/顱骨凹陷骨折整復術 elevation of depressed fracture of skull
颅[骨]成形术/頭顱造形術，頭顱成形術 cranioplasty
颅骨顶/顱骨頂 vertex of bony cranium
颅骨分层/顱骨分層 tablature
颅骨粉碎骨折/顱骨粉碎骨折 comminuted fracture of skull
颅[骨]缝早闭/顱縫早閉，顱縫線封閉過早 craniosynostosis
颅骨干骺端发育不良/顱骨生長過大及骨骺端硬化 craniometaphysial dysplasia
颅骨骨干发育不良/顱骨增厚硬化 craniodiaphysial dysplasia
颅骨骨瘤/顱骨骨瘤 osteoma of skull
颅骨骨盆牵引器/顱骨骨盆牽引器 halopelvic distraction apparatus
颅骨骨髓炎/顱骨骨髓炎 osteomyelitis of skull
颅骨骨折/顱骨骨折 cranial fracture
颅骨骨折内陷/顱骨陷落骨折 enthlasis
颅骨海绵状血管瘤/顱骨海綿狀血管瘤 cavernous hemangioma of skull
颅骨环锯术/穿顱術，頭顱環錐術 cephalotrypesis
颅骨环钻术/顱骨環鑽術 trephination of skull
颅骨剪/顱骨剪 craniotomy scissor
颅骨隆凸畸形/枕骨前屈畸形 convexobasia
颅骨面骨分离/顱骨面骨分離 craniofacial dysjunction
颅骨膜/顱骨膜，頭骨膜 pericranium
颅骨膜分离器/顱骨膜分離器 separatorium
颅骨膜血窦/顱蓋瘤 sinus pericranii
颅骨膜炎/顱骨膜炎 pericranitis
颅骨牵引钳/顱骨牽引鉗 crutchfield tong
颅骨牵引术/顱骨牽引術 skull traction
颅骨切除术/顱骨切除術 craniectomy
颅骨切开术/頭顱切開術，破顱術 craniotomy
颅骨缺损/顱骨缺損 defect of skull
颅骨软化/顱骨軟化 craniotabes
颅骨烧伤/顱骨燒傷 burn of cranium
颅骨生长性骨折/顱骨生長性骨折 growing fracture of skull
颅骨嗜酸细胞肉芽肿/顱骨嗜酸細胞肉芽腫 eosinophilic granuloma of skull
颅骨手术/顱骨手術 skull operation
颅骨死骨摘除术/顱骨死骨摘除術 cranial sequestrectomy
颅骨松解术/顱骨鬆解術 craniolysis
颅骨锁骨发育不良/鎖骨顱骨發育不良 cleidocranial dysostosis
颅骨纤维性结构不良/顱骨纖維性結構不良 fibrous dysplasia of skull
颅骨线形骨折/顱骨線形骨折 linear fracture of skull
颅骨学/顱骨學 craniology
颅骨炎/顱骨炎 cranitis
颅骨硬化/顱骨硬化 craniosclerosis
颅骨肿瘤/顱骨腫瘤 skull neoplasm
颅骨钻孔术/顱骨鑽孔術 burr hole of skull
颅颌紊乱症/顱下頜骨病症 craniomandibular disorder
颅后点/顱後點，後頭穴 opisthion
颅后窝/顱後窩 posterior cranial fossa
颅后窝先天异常合并婴儿型血管瘤/後腦窩先天異常合并嬰兒型血管瘤 posterior fossa anomalies associated with infantile hemangioma
颅脊柱裂/顱脊柱裂 craniorachischisis
颅颊的/顱與頰的 craniobuccal
颅颊囊肿/顱頰囊腫 craniobuccal cyst
颅甲角/顱甲角 cranioconchal angle
颅节/顱骨分段 cranial segment
颅结合/顱軟骨結合 cranial synchondrosis, synchondrosis of cranium
颅颈交界处脑膜瘤/顱頸交界處腦膜瘤 meningioma of craniocervical junction
颅叩听诊法/頭顱聽診法 craniotonoscopy
颅阔点/闊穴 euryon
颅联体/顱部連胎，頭部連胎 craniopagus
颅梁/顱梁 trabecula cranium
颅裂[畸形]/裂顱[畸形] cranioschisis
颅面成形术/顱面成形術 craniofacioplasty
颅面骨发育不全/顱骨面骨成骨不全 craniofacial dysostosis
颅面[骨]畸形/顱面骨畸形 craniofacial abnormality
颅面联合进路/顱面聯合進路 combined craniofacial approach
颅面裂/顱面裂 craniofacial cleft
颅面形态/顱面形態 craniofacial shape
颅鸣/顱鳴 cranial tinnitus
颅脑不全畸胎/缺腦畸胎 nosencephalus
颅脑局部解剖学/頭顱局部解剖學 craniotopography
颅脑手术/顱腦手術 craniocerebral operation
颅脑损伤/顱腦損傷 craniocerebral injury
颅脑损伤手术/顱腦損傷手術 operation of craniocerebral injury
颅脑先天性畸形/顱腦先天性畸形 congenital

deformity of cranium and brain
颅脑照射/顱腦照射　cranial irradiation
颅内部/顱內部　intracranial part
颅内出血/顱內出血　intracranial hemorrhage
颅内创伤性动脉瘤/顱內創傷性動脈瘤　intracranial traumatic aneurysm
颅内的/顱內的　intracranial
颅内低压/顱內壓力減低　intracranial hypotension
颅内动静脉畸形/顱內動靜脈畸形　intracranial arteriovenous malformation
颅内动静脉畸形切除术/顱內動靜脈畸形切除術　excision of intracranial AVM
颅内动脉疾病/顱內動脈疾病　intracranial arterial disease
颅内动脉瘤/顱內動脈瘤　intracranial aneurysm
颅内动脉瘤包裹术/顱內動脈瘤包裹術　wrapping of intracranial aneurysm
颅内动脉瘤孤立术/顱內動脈瘤孤立術　trapping of intracranial aneurysm
颅内动脉瘤夹闭术/顱內動脈瘤夾閉術　clipping of intracranial aneurysm
颅内动脉瘤结扎术/顱內動脈瘤結扎術　ligation of intracranial aneurysm
颅内动脉瘤球囊栓塞术/顱內動脈瘤球囊栓塞術　balloon embolization of intracranial aneurysm
颅内动脉瘤手术/顱內動脈瘤手術　operation for intracranial aneurysm
颅内动脉硬化/顱內動脈硬化　intracranial arteriosclerosis
颅内动脉硬化性动脉瘤/顱內動脈硬化性動脈瘤　intracranial arteriosclerotic aneurysm
颅内窦血栓形成/顱內竇血栓形成　intracranial sinus thrombosis
颅内感染/顱內感染　intracranial infection
颅内感染性动脉瘤/顱內感染性動脈瘤　intracranial infected aneurysm
颅内高压/顱內高壓　intracranial hypertension
颅内骨肥大/顱內骨肥大　endocraniosis
颅内海绵状血管瘤/顱內海綿狀血管瘤　intracranial cavernous hemangioma
颅内寄生虫病/顱內寄生蟲病　intracranial parasitosis
颅内夹层动脉瘤/顱內夾層動脈瘤　intracranial dissecting aneurysm
颅内假性动脉瘤/顱內假性動脈瘤　intracranial false aneurysm
颅内结核瘤/顱內結核瘤　intracranial tuberculoma
颅内静脉畸形/顱內靜脈畸形　intracranial venous malformation
颅内静脉血栓形成/顱內靜脈血栓形成　intracranial venous thrombosis
颅内联胎畸胎/主胎顱內畸型寄生胎　encranius
颅内毛细管扩张[症]/顱內毛細管擴張[症]　intracranial telangiestasia
颅内皮样的/顱內皮囊瘤　intracranial dermoid
颅内栓塞/顱內栓塞　intracranial embolism
颅内先天性动脉瘤/顱內先天性動脈瘤　intracranial congenital aneurysm
颅内血管畸形/顱內血管畸形　intracranial vascular malformation
颅内血管痉挛/顱內血管痙攣　intracranial vasospasm
颅内血栓形成/顱內血栓形成　intracranial thrombosis
颅内血肿清除术/顱內血腫清除術　evacuation of intracranial hematoma
颅内循环/顱內循環　intracranial circulation
颅内压/顱內壓力　intracranial pressure
颅内压增高/顱內壓增高　increased intracranial pressure
颅内异物/顱內異物　intracranial foreign body
颅内痈/顱內癰　intracranial abscess
颅内肿瘤手术/顱內腫瘤手術　operation of intracranial tumor
颅内注气/顱內灌氣法　cranial insufflation
颅内转移瘤/顱內轉移瘤　intracranial metastatic tumor
颅前窝/顱前窩　anterior cranial fossa
颅腔/顱腔　cranial cavity
颅腔积气/顱腔積氣　pneumocephalus
颅侵蚀/顱骨因瘤壓迫而破壞　autotrepanation
颅神经手术/顱神經手術　operation for cranial nerve
颅外的/顱外的　extracranial
颅外纤维肌性发育不良/顱外纖維肌性發育不全　extracranial fibromuscular dysplasia
颅位保持器/顱位保持器,支顱器　craniophore
颅息/顱息　luxi, SJ19
颅狭[窄]症/頭顱縮小　craniostenosis
颅相学/顱相術,腦理學　phrenology
颅囟/顱囟　cranial fontanell
颅形论/顱形論,顱骨論　craniography
颅形描记器/顱骨描記器　craniograph
颅咽的/顱與咽的　craniopharyngeal
颅咽管瘤/顱咽管瘤　craniopharyngioma, craniopharyngeal duct tumor
颅指数/頭顱指數　cephalic index

颅中窝/顱中凹 middle cranial fossa
颅中窝脑膜瘤/顱中窩腦膜瘤 meningioma of middle cranial fossa
颅周切开术/頭顱環切術 craniamphitomy
颅椎关节/顱椎關節 craniovertebral articulation
颅纵裂/顱裂 diastematocrania
鲈精蛋白/鱸魚精蛋白 percine
卤芬酯/鹵芬酯 halofenate
卤化/加鹵作用 halogenation
卤化烃类/鹵化烴類 halogenated hydrocarbons
卤化物/鹵化物 halide
卤化物皮疹/鹵化物皮疹 halodermia
卤素痤疮/鹵素痤瘡 halogen acne
卤素化芳香族碳氢化合物/鹵素化芳香族碳氫化合物 halogenated aromatic hydrocarbon
卤素类/鹵素類 halogens
鲁宾斯坦-泰比综合征/Rubinstein-Taybi 氏症候群 Rubinstein-Taybi syndrome
鲁宾逊病/Robinson 氏病 Robinson disease
鲁德综合征/Rud 氏症候群 Rud syndrome
鲁菲尼小体/鲁菲尼小體 Ruffini corpuscle
鲁格溶液/Ruge 氏溶液 Ruge solution
鲁米诺/魯米諾 luminol
鲁热肌/Rouget 氏肌 Rouget muscle
鲁热细胞/Rouget 氏細胞 Rouget cell
鲁斯科尼肛门/Rusconi 肛門 anus of Rusconi
鲁斯霉素/魯斯黴素 Lucensomycin
鲁斯特综合征/Rust 氏症候群 Rust syndrome
鲁特维咽峡炎/Ludovici 氏咽峽炎 angina Ludovici
鲁瓦卡巴-米赫尔-史密斯综合征/Ruvalcaba-Myhre-Smith 三氏症候群 Ruvalcaba-Myhre-Smith syndrome
鲁西-莱维病/Roussy-Lévy 二氏病 Roussy-Lévy disease
陆以湉/陸以湉 Lu Yitian
鹿角/鹿角 antler, deer horn
鹿角菜/鹿角菜 carrageen
鹿角胶/鹿角膠 deer-horn glue
鹿角霜/鹿角霜 degelatined deer-horn
鹿角形石/鹿角狀石 staghorn stone
鹿茸/鹿茸 pilose antler
鹿衔草/鹿衔草 pyrola herb
路-巴综合征/Louis-Bar 氏症候群,共濟失調-微血管擴張症候群 Louis-Bar syndrome
路布杜普/表示心臟之第一及第二心音 lubb-dupp
路德维希咽峡炎/路特維氏咽峽炎 Ludwig's angina
路径/路徑 pathway
路路通/路路通 beautiful sweetgum fruit
路西奥现象/Lucio 氏現象 Lucio phenomenon
路易斯安那病毒/Louisiana 病毒 Louisiana virus
路易斯-巴尔病/Louis-Bar 二氏病 Louis-Bar disease
辘轳肩病/轆轤肩病 tackle shoulder
辘轳转关/轆轤轉關 nystagmus, pulley eye
露剂/露劑 distillate formula
露脑[畸形]/露腦畸形 exencephaly
露脑畸胎/露腦畸胎 exencephalon
露髓/露髓 pulp exposure
露阴癖/露陰癖,陰部顯露欲 exhibitionism
露龈笑/露齦笑 gummy smile
露脏畸形/露臟畸形 celosomia
吕戈尔溶液/Lugol 氏溶液,濃碘溶液 Lugol solution
捋顺法/捋順法 back-and-forth pushing manipulation, twisting to order manipulation
旅行病/旅行病 travel sickness
旅行性腹泻/旅行者腹瀉 traveler diarrhea
旅行[者]医学/旅遊醫學 emporiatrics
铝/鋁 aluminium
铝衬液/鋁襯液 aluminum lining liquid
铝瓷冠/鋁瓷冠 alumina porcelain crown
铝粉/鋁粉 aluminium powder
铝化合物/鋁化合物 aluminum compound
铝镁合金中毒/鎂鋁合金中毒 dural poisoning
铝皮炎/鋁皮膚炎 aluminium dermatitis
铝肉芽肿/鋁肉芽腫 aluminium granuloma
铝钨合金/鎢鋁合金 partinium
铝相关性肾性骨营养不良/鋁相關性腎性骨營養不良 aluminum associated renal osteodystrophy
律动性眼球震颤/律動性眼球震顫 rhythmical nystagmus
虑/[焦]慮 anxiety, thought
绿薄荷/綠薄荷 spearmint
绿薄荷酊/綠薄荷酊 spearmint spirit
绿薄荷油/綠薄荷油 spearmint oil
绿蟾蜍精/綠藜蘆蟾蜍腺素 viridobufagin
绿风内障/綠風內障 acute angle-closure glaucoma, green wind glaucoma
绿风内障·风火攻目证/綠風內障·風火攻目證 green wind glaucoma with pattern of wind-fire attacking eye
绿风内障·肝郁化火证/綠風內障·肝鬱化火證 green wind glaucoma with pattern of liver depression transforming into fire
绿风内障·痰火郁结证/綠風內障·痰火鬱結證 green wind glaucoma with phlegm-fire stagnation pattern

绿风内障•阴虚阳亢证/綠風內障•陰虛陽亢證 green wind glaucoma with pattern of yin deficiency and yang hyperactivity
绿枸橼酸铁/綠色檸檬酸鐵 iron citrate green
绿过氧化物酶/綠過氧化酶 verdoperoxidase
绿甲/綠甲 green nail
绿甲综合征/綠甲症候群 green nail syndrome
绿胶霉素/綠膠黴素 viridin
绿藜芦/綠藜蘆,美藜蘆 American hellebore
绿藜芦全碱/綠藜蘆全鹼 cryptenamine
绿盲/綠色盲 green blindness
绿脓菌病/綠膿菌感染症 pyocyanosis
绿脓菌蛋白质/綠膿桿菌蛋白質 pyocyanic protein
绿脓菌的/綠膿菌的 pyocyanic
绿脓菌感染/綠膿桿菌感染 pyocyanic infection
绿脓菌红素/綠膿紅素 pyorubin
绿脓菌酶/綠膿酵素 pyocyanase
绿脓菌酶蛋白溶菌素/綠膿菌酶蛋白溶菌素 pyocyanase proteidin
绿脓[菌]素/綠膿素 pyocyanin
绿脓色素/綠膿色素,膿綠質 cyopin
绿色癌/綠色癌 green cancer
绿色白血病/綠色白血病 chloroleukemia
绿色成红细胞[细胞]瘤/綠色瘤與紅血球母細胞瘤 chloroerythroblastoma
绿色腹泻/綠色腹瀉 green diarrhea
绿色骨髓瘤/綠色骨髓瘤 chloromyeloma
绿色黄疸/綠色黃疸 green jaundice
绿色觉异常者/綠色色盲患者 deutan
绿色瘤/綠色瘤 chloroma
绿色盲/第二原色盲,綠色色盲 deuteranopsia
绿色[肉]瘤/綠色肉瘤 chloromatous sarcoma
绿色弱视/第二原色異常 deuteranomalopia
绿色荧光蛋白质类/綠色螢光蛋白質類 green fluorescent proteins
绿色组织/葉綠組織 chlorenchyma
绿视症/綠視症,綠幻視 chloropsia
绿苔/綠苔 green fur
绿头苍蝇/綠頭蒼蠅 blowfly
绿蝇属/綠蠅屬 Lucilia
绿原酸/綠原酸 chlorogenic acid
绿藻类/綠藻類 green algae
绿珠蛋白尿/膽綠蛋白尿 verdoglobinuria
葎草酮/葎草酮 humulone
氯/氯 chlorine
氯胺 T 滴定法/氯胺 T 滴定法 chloramine-T titration
氯胺类/氯胺類 chloramines
氯胺酮/氯胺酮 ketamine
氯贝丁酯/對氯苯氧異丁酸乙酯 clofibrate
氯贝酸/氯貝酸 clofibric acid
氯倍他索/氯倍他索 clobetasol
氯苯/氯苯 chlorobenzene
氯苯吡胺/氯菲安明 chlorpheniramine
氯苯噁唑胺/氯苯噁唑胺 zoxazolamine
氯苯甘醚/氯苯甘醚 chlorphenesin
氯苯胍/羅貝胍 robenidine
氯苯甲脒/氯苯甲脒 chlorphenamidine
氯苯甲酸/氯苯甲酸 chlorobenzoate
氯苯类/氯苯類 chlorobenzenes
氯苯那敏/氯苯那敏 chlorphenamine
氯苄烷铵/氯化卞二甲烴銨 benzalkonium chloride
氯丙嗪/氯丙嗪 chloropromazine
氯丙嗪皮炎/氯丙嗪皮炎 chlorpromazine dermatitis
氯铂酸/氯鉑酸 chloroplatinic acid
氯醇类/氯醇類 chlorohydrins
氯醋甲胆碱/氯醋甲膽鹼 methacholine chloride
氯痤疮/氯痤瘡 chlorine acne
氯丹/氯丹 chlordan
氯氮平/氯氮平 clozapine
氯氮血症性肾炎/氯氮血症性腎炎 chloro-azotemic nephritis
氯氮䓬/氯二氮平 chlordiazepoxide
氯碘羟喹/氯碘羥喹 clioquinol
氯丁二烯/氯丁二烯 chloroprene
氯丁橡胶/氯丁[二烯]橡膠 neoprene
氯定量法/氯定量法 chlorometry
氯二甲苯酚/氯二甲酚 chloroxylenol
氯法齐明/氯法齊明 clofazimine
氯仿/氯仿,三氯甲烷 chloroform
氯仿麻醉/氯仿麻醉 chloroform anesthesia
氯仿牙胶/氯仿乳膠 chloropercha
氯芬磷/氯芬磷 chlorfenvinphos
氯酚类/氯酚類 chlorophenols
氯氟碳类/氯氟碳類 chlorofluorocarbons
氯汞苯甲酸盐类/氯汞苯甲酸鹽類 chloromercuribenzoates
氯汞君/氯汞君 chlormerodrin
氯胍/氯胍 chloroguanide
氯化氨甲酰胆碱/氯化胺甲醯膽鹼 carbamylcholine chloride
氯化铵/氯化銨 ammonium chloride
氯化铵负荷试验/氯化銨負荷試驗 ammonium chloride loading test
氯化钯液/氯鈀液 chlorpalladium fluid
氯化苯[甲烃]铵溶液/氯化苯銨溶液 benzalkonium

chloride solution
氯化苄乙氧铵/氯化苯松寧 benzethonium chloride
氯化铂/氯化鉑 platinum chloride
氯化胆碱/氯化膽素 choline chloride
氯化碘/氯化碘 iodine chloride
氯化二苯胺胂/氯化二苯胺胂 adamsite
氯化钙/氯化鈣 calcium chloride
氯化镉/氯化鎘 cadmium chloride
氯化汞铵/氯化汞銨 alembroth
氯化合物/氯化合物 chlorine compound
氯化甲基玫瑰苯胺溶液/氯化甲基玫瑰色素溶液 methylrosaniline chloride solution
氯化钾/氯化鉀 potassium chloride
氯化鲸蜡三甲铵/氯化鯨蠟三甲銨 cetyl trimethyl ammonium chloride
氯化可他宁/氯化可他寧 cotarnine chloride
氯化锂/氯化鋰 lithium chloride
氯化铝/氯化鋁 aluminium chloride
氯化氯异吲哚铵/氯化氯異吲哚銨 chlorisondamine chloride
氯化镁/氯化鎂 magnesium chloride
氯化钠/氯化鈉 sodium chloride
氯化钠溶液/氯化鈉溶液 sodium chloride solution
氯化钠注射液/氯化鈉注射液 sodium chloride injection
氯化铅/氯化鉛 lead chloride
氯化砷溶液/氯化砷溶液,亞砷酸溶液 arsenic chloride solution
氯化十六烷吡啶/氯化鯨蠟吡啶 cetylpyridinium chloride
氯化石蜡/含氯石蠟 chlorinated paraffin
氯化铁/[三]氯化鐵 ferric chloride
氯化铁溶液/氯化鐵溶液 ferric chloride solution
氯化铁试验/氯化鐵試驗 ferric chloride test
氯化烃/氯化烴 chlorinated hydrocarbon
氯化烃类/氯化烴類 chlorinated hydrocarbons
氯化烷三甲铵/氯化烷三甲銨 alkyltrimethylammonium chloride
氯化物/氯化物 chloride
氯化物定量器/氯化物定量器 chloridimeter
氯化物过多/體內氯化物過多 hyperchloruration
氯化物过氧化物酶/氯化物過氧化物酶 chloride peroxidase
氯化物停滞/氯化物停滯 chloride retention
氯化物通道/氯化物通道 chloride channel
氯化锌/鋅酪 butter of zinc
氯化血红素/氯化血紅素 hemin
氯化乙基汞/氯化乙基汞 ethylmercuric chloride

氯化银电极/氯化銀電極 silver chloride electrode
氯化甾类/氯化甾類 chlorinated steroids
氯化重碳酸反向转运物/氯化重碳酸反向轉運物 chloride-bicarbonate antiporter
氯磺丙脲/氯苯磺丙脲 chlorpropamide
氯磺酸/氯磺酸 chlorosulfonic acid
氯吉兰/氯吉蘭 clorgyline
氯己定/洛赫西定 chlorhexidine
氯甲酚/氯甲苯酚 chlorocresol
氯甲酸甲酯/氯甲酸甲酯 methylchloroformate
氯甲烷/氯[化]甲烷 methyl chloride
氯结合/氯結合,氯定著 chloropexia
氯解磷定/氯解磷定 pralidoxime chloride
氯金酸/氯金酸 chlorauric acid
氯喹/氯喹 aralen
氯喹啉醇类/氯喹啉醇類 chloroquinolinols
氯喹那多/氯喹那多 chlorquinaldol
氯醌/氯醌 chloranil
氯雷他定/氯雷他定 loratadine
氯离子/氯離子 chloridion
氯[离子]转移/氯化物更换 chloride shift
氯膦酸/氯膦酸 clodronic acid
氯马斯汀/氯馬斯汀 clemastine
氯霉素/氯黴素,氯絲菌素 chloramphenicol
氯霉素抗药性/氯黴素抗藥性 chloramphenicol resistance
氯霉素眼膏/氯黴素眼用軟膏 chloramphenicol ophthalmic ointment
氯霉素 o-乙酰转移酶/氯黴素 o-乙醯轉移酶 chloramphenicol o-acetyltransferase
氯美噻唑/氯美噻唑 chlormethiazole
氯美扎酮/氯美扎酮 chlormezanone
氯米芬/氯米芬 clomiphene
氯米帕明/氯米帕明 clomipramine
氯萘/氯萘 chloronaphthalene
氯蜡痤疮/氯蠟痤瘡 halowax acne
氯蜡皮炎/氯蠟皮炎,氯蠟痤瘡 halowax dermatitis
氯尼辛/氯尼辛 clonixin
氯尿[症]/氯尿症 chloriduria
氯帕胺/利尿降壓藥 clopamide
氯哌噻吨/氯呱噻噸 clopenthixol
氯普芬/氯普芬 chlorpropham
氯普鲁卡因/氯普魯卡因 chloroprocaine
氯普鲁卡因青霉素 O/氯普魯卡因青黴素 O chloroprocaine penicillin O
氯普噻吨/氯普噻噸 chlorprothixene
氯芪酚试验/氯芪酚試驗 clomiphene test
氯前列醇/氯前列醇 cloprostenol

氯羟吡啶/氯吡多　clopidol
氯醛/氯醛　chloral
氯醛卡红/胭脂红氯醛　chloral carmine
氯醛糖/氯醛醣　chloralose
氯醛瘾/氯醛瘾　chloralism
氯醛樟脑/氯醛樟腦　chloral camphor
氯噻嗪/氯磺噻唑　chlorothiazide
氯噻酮/氯薩利酮　chlorthalidone
氯麝酚/氯麝香草酚　chlorothymol
氯水合铝/氯水合鋁　aluminum chloride hydrate
氯酸盐/氯酸鹽　chlorate
氯铁胆绿素/綠血晶質　verdohemin
氯烯雌醚/氯烯雌醚　chlorotrianisene
氯硝柳胺/二氯硝基水楊醯胺　niclosamide
氯硝西泮/氯硝西泮　clonazepam
氯氧化物/氧氯化物　oxychloride
氯乙酸/氯醋酸,氯乙醯酸　chloracetic acid
氯乙烷/氯[化]乙烷　ethyl chloride
氯乙烷麻醉/氯乙烷麻醉　ethyl chloride anesthesia
氯乙烯/氯化乙烯　vinyl chloride
氯唑沙宗/氯唑沙宗　chlorzoxazone
氯唑西林/氯灑西林,鄰氯青黴素　cloxacillin
滤棒/濾棒　filter candle, filter stick
滤饼/濾餅　filter cake
滤[出]液/濾液　filtrate
滤过分数/濾過分數　filtration fraction
滤过钠排泄分数/濾過鈉排洩分數　fractional excretion of filtrated sodium
滤过屏障/濾過屏障　filtration barrier
滤过术/濾過術　filtering operation
滤过外科手术/濾過外科手術　filtering surgery
滤过性病毒/濾過性病毒　filterable virus
滤囊泡膜细胞增殖/濾泡膜細胞增殖　hyperthecosis
滤泡刺激素/濾泡刺激素　FSH
滤泡的/濾泡的　follicular
滤泡间的/濾泡間的　interfollicular
滤泡间细胞/甲狀腺濾泡間細胞　interfollicular cell
滤泡囊肿/濾泡囊腫　follicular cyst
滤泡旁的/濾泡旁的　parafollicular
滤泡树突细胞/濾泡樹突細胞　follicular dendritic cell
滤泡素过多/濾泡素過多症　hyperfolliculinism
滤泡小斑/濾泡斑　follicular stigma
滤泡型成釉细胞瘤/濾泡型成釉細胞瘤　follicular ameloblastoma
滤泡型淋巴瘤/濾泡性淋巴瘤　follicular lymphoma
滤泡性扁桃体炎/斑點狀咽炎,濾泡性扁桃腺炎　spotted sore throat

滤泡性窦炎/濾泡性竇炎　follicular sinusitis
滤泡性黄体素细胞/濾泡性黃體素細胞　follicular lutein cell
滤泡性甲状腺癌/濾泡性甲狀腺癌　follicular thyroid carcinoma
滤泡性甲状腺肿/濾泡性甲狀腺腫　follicular goiter
滤泡性结肠炎/濾泡性結腸炎　follicular colitis
滤泡性结膜炎/濾泡性結膜炎　follicular conjunctivitis
滤泡性溃疡/濾胞性潰瘍　follicular ulcer
滤泡性膀胱炎/濾泡性膀胱炎　follicular cystitis
滤泡性腺癌/濾泡腺癌　follicular adenocarcinoma
滤泡性咽峡炎/濾泡性咽峡炎　follicular angina
滤泡液/濾泡液　liquor folliculi
滤泡增生/濾泡增生　follicular hyperplasia
滤泡周的/濾泡周圍的　perifollicular
滤片/濾片　filter disc
滤器/濾器　filter
滤筒/濾筒　filtering cartridge
滤液结核菌素/濾液結核菌素　tuberculin filtrate
滤纸/濾紙　filter paper
滤纸试验/濾紙試驗　filter-paper test
李果藤/欒果藤　mitchella
孪生/雙生子,雙胎　twins
孪生精神病/孿生性精神病　folie gemellaire
挛缩/攣縮　contracture
挛缩素质/攣縮素質,痙攣體質　contractural diathesis
挛缩性瘢痕/攣縮性瘢痕　contracted scar
挛缩性抽搐疾病/攣縮性抽搐疾病　convulsive tic disease
挛缩足/收縮足　contracted foot
卵/卵　egg
卵[白]沉淀素/卵沈澱素　ovoprecipitin
卵白蛋白/卵白蛋白,卵蛋白素　ovalbumin
卵白素-生物素-过氧化酶复合体/卵白素-生物素-過氧化酶複合體　avidin-biotin-peroxidase complex
卵白综合征/卵白症候群　egg-white syndrome
卵孢子/卵孢子　oospore
卵巢/卵巢　ovary
卵巢癌/卵巢癌　ovary carcinoma
卵巢白斑/卵巢白斑　white scar of ovary
卵巢病/卵巢病　oophoropathy
卵巢不发生/卵巢未發生,卵巢未形成,卵巢不發育　ovarian agenesis
卵巢成形术/卵巢造形術　oophoroplasty
卵巢穿刺术/卵巢穿刺術　ovariocentesis
卵巢丛/卵巢叢　ovarian plexus

卵巢[大]出血/卵巢出血　oophorrhagia
卵巢动脉/卵巢動脈　ovarian artery
卵巢动脉输卵管支/卵巢動脈輸卵管支　tubal branch of ovarian artery
卵巢动脉输尿管支/卵巢動脈輸尿管支　ureteric branch of ovarian artery
卵巢独立缘/卵巢獨立緣　free border of ovary
卵巢发育不全/卵巢發育不全,卵巢發育不良　ovarian dysgenesis, ovarian hypoplasia
卵巢缝合术/卵巢縫合術　ovariorrhaphy
卵巢功能减退/卵巢機能不足　hypo-ovarianism
卵巢功能亢进/卵巢發育過度　hyperovaria
卵巢功能试验/卵巢功能試驗　ovarian function test
卵巢功能早衰/卵巢功能早衰　premature ovarian failure
卵巢固定术/卵巢固定術,子宮附件固定術　oophoropexy
卵巢固有韧带/卵巢固有韌帶　proper ligament of ovary
卵巢冠/卵巢冠　epoophoron
卵巢冠管/卵巢冠管　duct of epoophoron
卵巢冠横管/Kobelt氏管　duct of Kobelt
卵巢冠囊肿/卵巢冠囊腫　parovarian cyst
卵巢冠囊状附件/卵巢冠囊狀附件　vesicular appendix of epoophoron
卵巢冠切除术/卵巢冠切除術　epoophorectomy
卵巢冠炎/卵巢冠炎　parovaritis
卵巢过度刺激综合征/卵巢過度刺激症候群　ovarian hyperstimulation syndrome
卵巢积脓/卵巢積膿,卵巢膿腫　pyo-ovarium
卵巢积水/卵巢積水　hydrovarium
卵巢基质增生/卵巢基質增生　ovarian stromal hyperplasia
卵巢畸胎瘤/卵巢畸胎瘤　ovarian teratoma
卵巢疾病/卵巢疾病　ovarian disease
卵巢甲状腺肿/甲狀腺腫狀卵巢瘤　struma ovarii
卵巢绞痛/卵巢絞痛　ovarian colic
卵巢结核/卵巢結核　ovarian tuberculosis
卵巢精原细胞瘤/卵細胞瘤　ovarian seminoma
卵巢静脉曲张/卵巢靜脈曲張　ovarian varicocele
卵巢静脉综合征/卵巢靜脈症候群　ovarian vein syndrome
卵巢瘤/卵巢瘤　oophoroma
卵巢门/卵巢門　hilum of ovary
卵巢门间质细胞/卵巢門間質細胞　hilus interstitial cell
[卵巢]门细胞/卵巢門細胞　hilus cell
卵巢囊肿/卵巢囊腫　oophoritic cyst

卵巢囊肿切除术/卵巢囊腫切除術　enucleation of ovarian cyst
卵巢囊肿形成/卵巢囊腫形成　oophorocystosis
卵巢[囊肿]造口[引流]术/卵巢造口術　oophorostomy
卵巢内侧面/卵巢內側面　medial surface of ovary
卵巢旁体/卵巢旁體　paroophoron
卵巢皮质/卵巢皮質　cortex of ovary, ovary cortex, ovarian cortex
卵巢破裂/卵巢破裂　ovariorrhexis
卵巢切除/卵巢切除　oophorectomize
卵巢切除术/卵巢切除術　ovariectomy
卵巢切开术/卵巢[瘤]切除術　ovariotomy
卵巢切开探查术/卵巢切開探查術　incision and exploration of ovary
卵巢韧带/卵巢韌帶　ovarian ligament
卵巢妊娠/卵巢妊娠　ovarian pregnancy
卵巢伞/卵巢傘,輸卵管之傘端　ovarian fimbria, fimbriated extremity of fallopian tube
卵巢神经痛/卵巢神經痛　ovarian neuralgia
卵巢输卵管端/卵巢輸卵管端　tubal extremity of ovary
卵巢输卵管炎/卵巢輸卵管炎　oophorosalpingitis
卵巢输卵管周炎/卵巢輸卵管周圍炎　perioophorosalpingitis
卵巢髓质/卵巢髓質　medulla of ovary, ovarian medulla
卵巢痛/卵巢痛　oophoralgia
卵巢突出/卵巢突出,卵巢疝　ovarian hernia
卵巢外侧面/卵巢外側面　lateral surface of ovary
卵巢网/卵巢網　rete ovarium
卵巢网囊肿/卵巢網囊腫　cyst of rete ovarii
卵巢网腺瘤/卵巢網腺瘤　adenoma of ovary rete
卵巢窝/卵巢窩　ovarian fossa
卵巢系膜/卵巢繫膜　mesovarium, mesoarium
卵巢系膜缘/卵巢繫膜緣　mesovarian border of ovary
卵巢纤维上皮瘤/伯瑞那氏瘤　Brenner tumor
卵巢楔形切除术/卵巢楔形切除術　wedge resection of ovary
卵巢性闭经/卵巢性停經　ovarian amenorrhea
卵巢性痛经/卵巢性痛經　ovarian dysmenorrhea
卵巢性消化不良/卵巢病性消化不良　ovarian dyspepsia
卵巢悬韧带/卵巢懸韌帶　suspensory ligament of ovary
卵巢炎/卵巢炎　oophoritis
卵巢移植/卵巢移植　ovary transplantation

卵巢移植术/卵巢移植術　transplantation of ovary
卵巢移植物/卵巢移植物　ovarian graft
卵巢支/卵巢支　ovarian branch
卵巢制剂疗法/卵巢治療法　ootherapy
卵巢肿瘤/卵巢腫瘤　ovarian tumor
卵巢周期/卵巢週期　ovarian cycle
卵巢周炎/卵巢周圍炎　perioophoritis
卵巢子宫端/卵巢子宮端　uterine extremity of ovary
卵巢子宫切除术/卵巢子宮切除術　oophorohysterectomy
卵巢组织移植/卵巢組織移植　ovarian tissue transplantation
卵蛋白质类/卵蛋白質類　egg proteins
卵分裂期/卵分裂期　ovum cleavage stage
卵冠丘复合体/卵冠丘複合體　oocyte corona cumulus complex, OCCC
卵核分裂/卵核分裂　ookinesis, oocinesia
卵黄/卵黄　yolk
卵黄板/卵黄板　vitelline disc
卵黄肠的/卵黄與腸的　vitellointestinal
卵黄肠管/卵黄腸管　vitellointestinal duct, vitellointestinal duct
卵黄肠管囊肿/卵黄腸管囊腫　vitellointestinal cyst
卵黄蛋白原类/卵黄蛋白原類　vitellogenins
卵黄的/卵黄的　vitelline
卵黄蒂/卵黄蒂　yolk stalk
卵黄动脉/卵黄動脈　vitelline artery
卵黄发生/卵黄生成,卵黄合成　vitellogenesis
卵黄高磷蛋白/卵黄高磷蛋白　phosvitin
卵黄管/卵黄管　vitelline duct
卵黄管囊肿/卵黄管囊腫　vitelline cyst
卵黄静脉/卵黄靜脈　vitelline vein
卵黄磷蛋白/卵黄素　ovovitellin
卵黄磷蛋白质类/卵黄磷蛋白質類　vitellins
卵黄囊/卵黄囊　yolk sac
卵黄囊癌/卵黄囊癌　yolk sac carcinoma
卵黄囊抗原/卵黄囊抗原　yolk sac antigen
卵黄囊胎盘/卵黄囊胎盤　yolk sac placenta
卵黄栓/卵黄栓子　yolk plug
卵黄素/卵黄素　lututrin
卵黄体/卵黄體　vitelline body
卵黄细胞/卵黄細胞　yolk cell
卵黄腺/卵黄腺　vitellarium
卵黄悬胶液/卵黄懸膠液　lecithovitellin
卵黄循环/卵黄循環　vitelline circulation
卵黄油/卵黄油　egg yolk oil
卵黄状黄斑变性/卵黄狀黄斑變性　vitelliform macular degeneration
卵黄状黄斑营养不良/卵黄囊狀黄斑失養症　vitelliform macular dystrophy
卵黄状痰/卵黄狀痰　egg yolk sputum
卵壳/卵殼　egg shell
卵壳黄素/卵[殼]黄質　ooxanthine
卵类黏蛋白/卵擬黏蛋白　ovomucoid
卵裂/卵裂　cleavage
卵裂纺锤体/分裂紡錘體　cleavage spindle
卵裂沟/卵裂溝,分裂溝　cleavage furrow
卵裂面/卵裂面　cleavage plane
卵裂球/卵裂球,分裂球　blastomere
卵裂型/卵裂型　cleavage pattern
卵磷脂/卵磷脂　egg yolk lecithin
卵磷脂白蛋白/卵磷脂蛋白素　lecithalbumin
卵磷脂蛋白/卵磷脂蛋白質類　lecithoprotein
卵磷脂酶/[卵]磷脂酶　lecithinase
卵磷脂酰基转移酶缺乏症/卵磷脂醯基轉移酶缺乏症　lecithin acyltransferase deficiency
卵磷脂血症/卵磷脂血症　lecithinemia
卵磷脂与鞘磷脂比值/卵磷脂與鞘磷脂比值　lecithin sphingomyelin ratio
卵模[腔]/吸蟲之卵囊　ootype
卵膜水/卵膜積水　hydroperion
卵母细胞/卵母細胞　egg mother cell, oocyte
卵母细胞成熟抑制物/卵母細胞成熟抑制物　oocyte maturation inhibitor
卵母细胞移植/卵母細胞移植　oocyte donation
卵囊率/卵囊率　oocyst rate
卵囊泡膜细胞/卵囊泡膜細胞　theca-cell
卵黏蛋白/卵黏蛋白　ovomucin
卵泡/卵泡　ovarian follicle
卵泡斑/卵泡斑　follicular stigma
卵泡闭锁/卵泡閉鎖　atresia folliculi
卵泡刺激素/卵泡刺激素　follicle stimulating hormone
卵泡瘤/卵泡瘤　folliculoma
卵泡膜/卵泡膜,卵囊膜　follicular theca
卵泡膜黄体囊肿/黄體内膜性囊腫　theca lutein cyst
卵泡膜黄体细胞/卵泡膜黄體細胞　theca lutein cell
卵泡膜内层/卵泡膜内層,卵泡内膜　theca interna
卵泡膜外层/卵泡膜外層,外泡膜　theca externa
[卵泡]膜细胞/濾泡膜細胞　theca cell
卵泡膜细胞瘤/卵囊膜[細胞]瘤　thecoma
卵泡膜细胞增生症/卵囊膜瘤症　thecomatosis
卵泡期/卵泡期　follicular phase
卵泡腔/濾泡腔　follicular antrum, follicular cavity
卵泡上皮/濾泡上皮　follicular epithelium
卵泡细胞/濾泡細胞　follicle cell, follicular cell

卵泡选择/卵泡選擇　selection of follicle
卵泡液/卵泡液　ovarian follicular fluid
卵泡抑素/卵泡抑素　follistatin
卵泡抑素相关蛋白质类/卵泡抑素相關蛋白質類　follistatin-related proteins
卵泡征集/卵泡徵集　recruitment of follicle
卵皮质/卵皮質　cortical ooplasm
卵丘/卵丘　discus proligerus
卵球蛋白/卵球蛋白　ovoglobulin
卵生/产卵性,卵生性　oviparity
卵生体/卵生體　oozooid
卵胎生/卵胎生　ovoviviparity
卵体/卵體　oophyte
卵细胞/卵細胞　egg cell
卵[细胞]膜/卵黄膜　oolemma
卵[细胞]质/卵質　ooplasm, ovoplasm
卵形红细胞/卵圓紅血球　ovalocyte
卵形红细胞症/卵圓紅血球症　ovalocytosis
卵形疟原虫/卵形瘧蟲　plasmodium ovale
卵形[疟原虫]疟/卵圓瘧原蟲病　ovale malaria
卵形头者/卵形頭者　oocephalus
卵原论者/卵原論者　ovist
卵原细胞/卵原細胞　oogonia, oogonium
卵圆窗/卵圓窗　oval window
卵圆孔/卵圓孔　foramen ovale
卵圆孔瓣/卵圓孔瓣　valve of foramen ovale
卵圆孔静脉从/卵圓孔靜脈叢　venous plexus of foramen ovale
卵圆孔未闭/卵圓孔未閉　patent oval foramen, patent foramen ovale
卵圆孔注射法/卵圓孔注射法　oval foramen injection
卵圆窝/卵圓窩　fossa ovalis
卵圆窝缘/卵圓窩緣　limbus fossae ovalis
卵[圆]形的/卵圓形的　ovate
卵圆形糠秕孢子菌/橢圓形皮屑芽孢菌　pityrosporum ovale
卵圆状红细胞性贫血/卵圓紅血球性貧血　ovalocytary anemia
卵植入期出血/植入性出血　implantation bleeding
卵中心体/卵中心體　oocenter
卵周隙/卵周隙,圍卵腔　perivitelline space
卵周隙液/卵周隙液　perivitelline liquid
卵[子]/卵[子]　ovum
卵[子]发生/卵子發生,卵之生成　ovigenesis, oogenesis
卵子瘟/卵子瘟　mumps orchitis
卵子瘟·瘟毒下注证/卵子瘟·瘟毒下注證　mumps orchitis with pattern of epidemic toxin diffusing downward
卵子转运/卵子轉運　ovum transport
乱搏心/亂搏心　chaotic heart
乱伦/亂倫,近親通姦　incest
乱杂性失语/雜亂失語症　jargonaphasia
乱杂语/亂雜,亂語　jargon
伦哈茨胃溃疡饮食/Lenhartz氏胃潰瘍飲食　Lenhartz diet
伦理的/倫理的　ethical
伦纳特淋巴瘤/Lennert氏淋巴瘤　Lennert lymphoma
伦琴/倫琴　Röntgen
伦琴辐射/倫琴放射線　Röntgen radiation
伦琴射线/倫琴射線,X射線　Röntgen ray
伦琴线强度/X射線強度　intensity of Röntgen ray
轮1/輪1　helix 1
轮2/輪2　helix 2
轮3/輪3　helix 3
轮4/輪4　helix 4
轮虫纲/輪蟲綱　Rotifera
轮箍术/縛扎法　tiring
轮廓乳头/輪廓乳頭　vallate papilla, circumvallate papilla
轮廓胎盘/輪廓胎盤　circumvallate placenta
轮廓线/外廓線　contour line
轮廓性湿疹/輪廓性濕疹　eczema marginatum
轮替动作不能/輪替動作不能　adiadochokinesia
轮替动作困难/輪替運動障礙　dysdiadochokinesia
轮替运动/輪替運動　diadochokinesis
轮替运动障碍/輪替運動錯亂　dysdiadochocinesia
轮烷类/輪烷類　rotaxanes
轮细胞/輪細胞　wheel cell
轮椅/輪椅　wheel chair
轮匝带/輪匝帶　zona orbicularis
轮匝肌/輪匝肌　orbicular muscle, musculus orbicularis
轮转切片机/旋轉式切片機　rotary microtome
轮状病毒感染/輪狀病毒感染　rotavirus infection
轮状病毒疫苗/輪狀病毒疫苗　rotavirus vaccine
轮状的/輪廓狀的　circumvallate
轮状脓疱病/環狀膿皰病,圓形膿皰病　impetigo circinata
轮状乳突/輪廓狀乳突　circumvallate papillae
轮状胎盘/城廓狀胎盤,輪廓狀胎盤　placenta circumvallata
论情志三郁证治/論情志三鬱證治　Treatise on Three Types of Stagnancy

论勇/論勇　Treatise on Bravery
罗阿丝虫病/羅阿絲蟲病　loaiasis
罗-比细胞/Rohon-Beard 二氏細胞　Rohon-Beard cell
罗伯特韧带/Robert 氏韌帶　Robert ligament
罗伯逊易位/羅伯遜易位　robertsonian translocation
罗布麻属/羅布麻屬　Apocynum
罗布麻叶/羅布麻葉　dogbane leaf
罗德西亚锥虫/羅德西亞錐蟲　Trypanosoma rhodesiense
罗尔沙赫氏试验/羅爾沙赫氏試驗　Rorschach test
罗夫辛征/羅夫辛徵　Rovsing sign
罗汉果/羅漢果　grosvenor momordica fruit
罗红霉素/羅紅黴素　roxithromycin
罗基坦斯基疝/Rokitansky 氏疝　Rokitansky hernia
罗杰病/羅格氏病　maladie de Roger
罗杰杂音/Roger 氏雜音　bruit de Roger
罗杰综合征/Roger 氏症候群　Roger syndrome
罗库溴铵/羅庫溴銨　rocuronium
罗兰多骨折/羅蘭多骨折　Rolando fracture
罗蓝核/羅勒核　Roller nucleus
罗朗多细胞/Rolando 氏細胞　Rolando cell
罗利环素/羅利環素　Rolitetracycline
罗利耶[日光紫外线]照射/Rollier 氏輻射療法　Rollier radiation
罗马诺-沃德综合征/Romano-Ward 症候群　Romano-Ward syndrome
罗哌卡因/羅哌卡因　ropivacaine
罗齐耶病/Rauzier 氏病　Rauzier disease
罗森巴赫类丹毒/Rosenbach 氏類丹毒　erysipeloid of Rosenbach
罗森巴赫综合征/Rosenbach 氏症候群　Rosenbach syndrome
罗森塔尔静脉/Rosenthal 氏靜脈　Rosenthal vein
罗沙胂/羅沙胂　roxarsone
罗斯河病毒/羅斯河病毒　Ross River virus
罗斯曼液/Rossman 氏液　Rossman fluid
罗斯综合征/Ross 氏症候群　Ross syndrome
罗索利莫征/羅梭利莫徵　Rossolimo sign
罗特蒙德综合征/Rothmund 氏症候群　Rothmund syndrome
罗托综合征/羅托症候群　Rotor syndrome
罗威综合征/Rowell 氏症候群　Rowell syndrome
罗硝唑/羅硝唑　Ronidazole
罗泽针/Roser 氏針　Roser needle
萝卜/蘿蔔　radish
萝芙木碱/蘿芙木鹼　rauwolfia
啰音/囉音　rale
逻辑倒错性思维/邏輯倒錯性思維　paralogic thinking
螺蛋白酶/蝸蛋白酶　helicopepsin
螺杆菌感染/螺桿菌感染　helicobacter infection
螺环化合物/螺環化合物　spiro compound
螺菌溶解/螺旋菌溶解　spirillolysis
螺菌血症/螺旋菌血症　spirillemia
螺内酯/螺内脂,安體舒通　spironolactone
螺哌隆/螺哌隆　spiperone
螺糖蛋白/蝸糖蛋白質　helicoprotein
螺纹管/螺紋管　corrugated tubing
螺线管/螺旋管　solenoid
α 螺旋/α 螺旋　α-helix
螺旋板/螺旋板　spiral lamina
螺旋板钩/螺旋板鉤　hamulus of spiral lamina
螺旋绷带/螺旋繃帶　spiral bandage
螺旋襞/螺旋皺襞　spiral fold
螺旋虫感染/螺旋蟲感染　screw worm infection
螺旋动脉/螺旋[狀]動脈　helicine artery, spiral artery
螺旋反转绷带/螺旋反轉繃帶　spiral reversed bandage
螺旋沟/螺旋溝　spiral groove
螺旋骨折/螺旋骨折　helicoid fracture
螺旋-环-螺旋构型/螺旋-環-螺旋構型　helix-loop-helix motif
螺旋结构/螺旋結構　helical structure
螺旋菌鼠咬热/螺旋菌鼠咬熱　Spirillum minus rat-bite fever
螺[旋]菌性痢疾/螺旋菌痢疾　spirillar dysentery
螺旋孔列/螺旋孔徑　foraminous spiral tract
螺旋隆凸/螺旋隆凸　spiral prominence
螺旋霉素/螺旋黴素　spiramycin
螺旋器/螺旋器　spiral organ, spiral organ of Corti
[螺旋器]网状膜/[螺旋器]網狀膜　reticular membrane
螺旋韧带/螺旋韌帶　spiral ligament
螺旋塞子/螺旋塞子　screw tampon
螺旋神经节/螺旋神經節　spiral ganglion
螺旋式扫描/螺旋式掃描　spiral scanning
螺旋体/螺旋體　spirochete
螺旋体病/螺旋體病　spirochetosis
螺旋体传染性皮肤病/螺旋體傳染性皮膚病　Spirochete infectious skin disease
螺旋体的/螺旋體的　spirochetal
螺旋体感染/螺旋體感染　spirochetal infection
螺旋体尿/螺旋體尿　spirocheturia
螺旋体溶解[作用]/螺旋體溶解　spirochetolysis
螺旋体属/螺旋體屬　Treponema

螺旋体性黄疸/螺旋體性黄疸　leptospiral jaundice
螺旋体血症/螺旋體血症　spirochetemia
螺旋纤维细胞/螺旋纖維細胞　spiral fiber cell
螺旋小体/螺旋小體　coiled body
螺旋形缝合针/螺旋形縫合針　helicoid suture needle
螺旋形骨折/螺旋形骨折　spiral fracture
螺旋蝇/螺旋蠅　screw worm
螺旋缘/螺旋緣　spiral limbus
螺旋正牙器/螺旋正牙器　jackscrew
螺旋支/螺旋支　spiral branch
螺旋止血带/螺旋止血帶　screw tourniquet
螺旋种植体/螺旋種植體　spiral-shafted implant
螺旋-转角-螺旋构型/螺旋-轉角-螺旋構型　helix-turn-helix motif
螺旋状/螺旋狀　spiral
螺旋状管/螺旋狀管　spiraled duct
螺旋状视野/螺旋狀視野　spiral visual field
螺旋甾烷/螺旋甾烷　spirostane
螺甾烷类/螺甾烷類　spirostans
裸淋巴细胞/裸淋巴細胞　null lymphocyte
裸淋巴细胞综合征/裸淋巴球症候群　bare lymphocyte syndrome
裸露的/裸露的　denuded, naked
裸区/裸區　bare area of liver
裸体恐怖/裸體恐懼症　nudophobia
裸细胞/裸細胞　naked cell
裸细胞白血病/裸細胞白血病　null-cell leukemia
裸眼视力/裸眼視力　naked vision
裸子植物/裸子植物　gymnospermae
瘰疬/瘰癧,頸部淋巴結核　cervical scrofula, scrofula
瘰疬的/瘰癧的　scrofulous
瘰疬·肺肾阴虚证/瘰癧·肺腎陰虛證　cervical scrofula with lung-kidney yin deficiency pattern
瘰疬分枝杆菌/瘰癧分枝桿菌　Mycobacterium scrofulaceum
瘰疬分枝杆菌纯蛋白衍生物/瘰癧分枝桿菌純蛋白衍生物　PPD of Mycobacterium scrofulaceum
瘰疬分枝杆菌肺病/瘰癧分枝桿菌肺病　pulmonary disease due to Mycobacterium scrofulaceum
瘰疬·气血两虚证/瘰癧·氣血兩虛證　cervical scrofula with qi-blood deficiency pattern
瘰疬·气滞痰凝证/瘰癧·氣滯痰凝證　cervical scrofula with pattern of qi stagnation and phlegm coagulation
瘰疬性苔藓/瘰癧性苔蘚　lichen scrofulosorum
瘰疬性眼炎/腺病質性眼炎　scrofulous ophthalmia
瘰疬·阴虚火旺证/瘰癧·陰虛火旺證　cervical scrofula with pattern of yin deficiency and fire effulgence
洛布斯坦癌/Lobstein 氏癌　Lobstein cancer
洛伐他汀/洛伐他汀　lovastatin
洛非帕明/洛非帕明　lofepramine
洛芬太尼/洛芬太尼　lofentanil
洛呱丁胺/洛呱丁胺　loperamide
洛苛草中毒/洛苛草中毒,瘋草病　locoism
洛克柠檬酸溶液/Locke 氏檸檬酸溶液　Locke citrate solution
洛克[溶]液/Locke 氏溶液　Locke solution
洛克伍德韧带/Lockwood 氏韌帶　Lockwood ligament
洛兰茨截骨术/洛倫茨截骨術　Lorenz osteotomy
洛里加病/Loriga 氏病　Loriga disease
洛-林溶液/Locke-Ringer 二氏溶液　Locke-Ringer solution
洛莫司汀/洛莫司汀　Lomustine
洛沙平/洛沙平　Loxapine
洛沙坦/洛沙坦　Losartan
洛威特细胞/Loevit 氏細胞　Loevit cell
洛温塔尔束/Lowenthal 氏徑　Lowenthal tract
骆驼痘/駱駝痘　camelpox
骆驼痘病毒/駱駝痘病毒　camelpox virus
络合剂/錯合劑,複合劑　complexant, complexing agent
络合物/複合物　complex
络脉/絡脈　collateral
络却/絡卻　luoque, BL8
络伤出血证/絡傷出血證　pattern of bleeding due to collateral injury
络石藤/絡石藤　Chinese starjasmine stem
络穴/絡穴　luo-connecting point
落槌叩诊/落叩法　drop percussion
落基山斑疹热/洛磯山斑疹熱　Rocky Mountain spotted fever
落皮层/落皮層　rhytidome
落球黏度计/落球式黏度計　falling sphere viscometer
落蕈酸/落葉松蕈酸　agaricic acid
落叶松酸/落葉松酸　laricic acid
落叶型天疱疮/葉狀天皰瘡　pemphigus foliaceus
落叶性天疱疮抗原/落葉性天皰瘡抗原　pemphigus foliaceus antigen

M

麻痹/麻痺 palsy, paralysis, paralyze
麻痹性肠梗阻/麻痺性腸阻塞 paralytic ileus
麻痹性痴呆/麻痺性癡呆 general paresis of insane
麻痹性痴呆公式/麻痺定則 paretic formula
麻痹性的/癱瘓的, 麻痺的 paralytic
麻痹性分泌/麻痺性分泌 paralytic secretion
麻痹性畸形足/癱瘓性畸形足 paralytic club foot
麻痹性脊柱侧凸/麻痺性脊柱側彎 paralytic scoliosis
麻痹性睑外翻/麻痺性瞼外翻 paralytic ectropion
麻痹性狂犬病/麻痺性狂犬病 paralytic rabies
麻痹性[尿]失禁/麻痺性失禁 paralytic incontinence
麻痹性膀胱/麻痺性膀胱 paralytic bladder
麻痹性上睑下垂/麻痺性上瞼下垂 paralytic ptosis
麻痹性吞咽困难/麻痺性吞嚥困難 dysphagia paralytica
麻痹性舞蹈病/軟舞蹈病 chorea mollis
麻痹性斜视/麻痺性斜視 paralytic strabismus
麻痹性休克/麻痺性休克 paralytic shock
麻痹性眩晕/麻痺性眩暈 paralytic vertigo
麻痹胸/麻痺胸 paralytic thorax
麻刺感/刺感, 刺痛 tingling
麻毒/麻毒 toxic pathogen causing measles
麻沸散/麻沸散 powder for anesthesia
麻风/麻風 leprosy
麻风病/Hansen 氏病 lepriasis
麻风病人/麻風病人 leper
麻风病院/麻風病院 leper colony
麻风的/麻風的 leprotic, leprous
麻风结节/麻風瘤 leproma
麻风结节性红斑/麻風性結節性紅斑 erythema nodosum leprosum
麻风菌素/麻風結節素, 麻風菌素 lepromin
麻风菌素反应/麻風素反應 lepromin reaction
麻风细胞/麻風細胞 lepra cell
麻风性溃疡/麻風潰瘍 leprous ulcer
麻风性葡萄膜炎/麻風性葡萄膜炎 leprotic uveitis
麻风性脱发/麻風性禿髮 alopecia leprotica
麻风学/麻風學 leprology
麻风学家/麻風專家 leprologist
麻风抑制药/麻風抑制藥 leprostatic agent

麻黄/麻黄 ephedra sinica, ephedra
麻黄根/麻黄根 ephedra root
麻黄碱/麻黄素 ephedrine
麻黄属/麻黄屬 *Ephedra*
麻黄汤/麻黄湯 mahuang decoction
麻黄杏仁甘草石膏汤/麻黄杏仁甘草石膏湯 mahuang xingren gancao shigao decoction
麻卡因/麻卡因 marcaine
麻立病/跳躍病 mali-mali
麻木/麻木, 無感覺 numbness
麻油/麻油 sesame oil
麻疹/麻疹 rubeola, measles
麻疹病毒/麻疹病毒 measles virus
麻疹病毒感染/麻疹病毒感染 morbillivirus infection
麻疹·毒陷心肝证/麻疹·毒陷心肝證 measles with pattern of toxin invading heart and liver
麻疹·肺胃热盛证/麻疹·肺胃熱盛證 measles with pattern of exuberant heat in lung and stomach
麻疹·逆证/麻疹·逆證 unfavorable case of measles
麻疹-腮腺炎-风疹疫苗/麻疹-腮腺炎-風疹疫苗 measles-mumps-rubella vaccine
麻疹·顺证/麻疹·順證 case of measles with favorable prognosis
麻疹·邪毒闭肺证/麻疹·邪毒閉肺證 measles with pattern of lung blocked by pathogenic toxin
麻疹·邪毒攻喉证/麻疹·邪毒攻喉證 measles with pattern of pathogenic toxin attacking throat
麻疹·邪犯肺卫证/麻疹·邪犯肺衛證 measles with pattern of pathogen invading lung-defense phase
麻疹·邪退阴伤证/麻疹·邪退陰傷證 measles with pattern of yin injury after pathogen subsidence
麻疹性角膜炎/麻疹性角膜炎 measles keratitis
麻疹样的/麻疹樣的 morbilliform
麻疹样红斑/麻疹狀紅斑 erythema morbilliforme
麻疹样皮疹/麻疹樣皮疹 morbilliform eruption
麻疹疫苗/麻疹疫苗 measles vaccine
麻子仁丸/麻子仁丸 maziren pill
麻醉/麻醉 anesthesia
麻醉催眠术/麻醉催眠術 anesthetic hypnosis
麻醉法/麻醉法 anesthetization
麻醉分析/麻醉分析 narcotic analysis

麻醉后护理/麻醉後護理 postanesthesia nursing
麻醉后麻痹/麻醉後麻痺 anesthesia paralysis
麻醉恢复期/麻醉恢復期 anesthesia recovery period
麻醉机/麻醉機 anesthetic machine
麻醉功能基/麻醉功能基 anesthesiophore
麻醉记录/麻醉記錄 anesthetic record
麻醉剂/麻醉劑 anesthetic
麻醉剂量调节器/麻醉藥計量器 anesthetometer
麻醉品/麻醉品 narcotics
麻醉品拮抗药/麻醉品拮抗藥 narcotic antagonist
麻醉期痉挛/麻醉期痙攣 anesthetospasm
麻醉前病情评估/麻醉前病情評估 preanesthetic evaluation
麻醉前用药/麻醉前用藥 preanesthetic medication, premedication
麻醉前准备/麻醉前準備 preanesthetic preparation
麻醉强度/麻醉強度 anesthetic potency
麻醉深度/麻醉深度 depth of anesthesia
麻醉手术护士/麻醉手術護士 nurse anesthetist
麻醉疗法/麻醉睡眠療法 narcotherapy
麻醉危险性/麻醉危險性 anesthesia risk
麻醉维持/麻醉維持 maintenance of anesthesia
麻醉性昏睡/昏糊 narcoma
麻醉性镇痛药/麻醉性鎮痛藥 narcotic analgesic, narcosis analgesic
麻醉性阻断/麻醉性阻斷 anesthetic block
麻醉学/麻醉學 anesthesiology
麻醉学家/麻醉學家 anesthesiologist
麻醉药/麻醉藥,麻醉劑 anesthetic
麻醉药浓度/麻醉藥濃度 anesthetic concentration
麻醉药品/麻醉藥品 narcotic
麻醉药阻断/麻醉藥阻斷 methadone block
麻醉用乙烯/麻醉用乙烯 aethylenum pro narcosi
麻醉诱导/麻醉誘導 induction of anesthesia
麻醉佐剂/麻醉佐劑 anesthesia adjuvant
麻醉作用/麻醉作用 anesthetic action
马鞍菌酸/馬鞍[菌]酸 helvellic acid
马鞍形头/馬鞍形頭 saddle head
马鼻疽/馬鼻疽 farcy
马鞭草/馬鞭草 verbena, European verbena herb
马鞭草烯醇/馬鞭草烯醇 verbenol
马鞭草烯酮/馬鞭草烯酮 verbenone
马勃/馬勃 puff-ball
马齿苋/馬齒莧 purslane herb
马传染性贫血病毒/馬傳染性貧血病毒 equine infectious anemia virus
马促性腺素类/馬促性腺素類 equine gonadotropins
马达加斯加海芒果素/馬達加斯加海芒果素 tanghin
马-戴电池/Marie-Davy 氏電池 Marie-Davy cell
马刀侠瘿/馬刀俠瘿 axillary, chest and hypochondrium tuberculosis
马的/馬的 equine
马德隆病/Madelung 氏病 Madelung disease
马德隆畸形/馬德隆畸形 Madelung deformity
马丁绷带/Martin 氏繃帶 Martin bandage
马丁病/Martin 氏病 Martin disease
马丁诺蒂细胞/Martinotti 氏細胞 Martinotti cell
马动脉炎病毒/馬動脈炎病毒 equine arteritis virus
马兜铃/馬兜鈴 dutohmanspipe fruit
马兜铃素/馬兜鈴素 aristin
马兜铃酸/馬兜鈴酸 aristolochic acid
马兜铃酸肾病/馬兜鈴酸腎病 aristolochic acid nephropathy
马痘/馬痘 horsepox
马痘病毒/馬痘病毒 horsepox virus
马杜拉分枝菌病/馬杜拉真菌病 Maduromycosis
马杜拉足/Madura 氏足 Madura foot
马多克斯杆/麥達克斯杆 Maddox rod
马多克斯杆试验/麥達克斯杆試驗 Maddox rod test
马多克斯棱镜/麥達克斯氏棱鏡 Maddox prism
马多克斯翼/馬多克斯翼 Maddox wing
马尔堡病/馬伯格病 Marburg disease
马尔堡病毒病/馬伯格病毒病 Marburg virus disease
马尔盖涅骨盆骨折/瑪律蓋涅骨盆骨折 Malgaigne fracture of pelvis
马尔基小球/瑪律基小球 Marchi ball
马尔基亚法瓦-比尼亚米病/馬-比二氏病 Marchiafava-Bignami disease
马尔内夫青霉/瑪律尼菲青黴 Penicillium marneffei
马尔内夫青霉病/瑪律尼菲青黴病 Penicilliosis marneffei
马尔皮基细胞/角質細胞 Malpighian cell
马尔萨斯人口论/馬塞士氏主義 malthusianism
马尔尚细胞/Marchand 氏細胞 Marchand cell
马凡综合征/馬凡症候群 Marfan syndrome
马粪甾醇/馬糞[硬]脂醇 hippocoprosterol
马疯木/毒番石榴 manchineel
马富奇综合征/Maffucci 氏症候群 Maffucci syndrome
马格第溶液/Magendies 氏溶液 Magendies solution
马格努森夹/Magnuson 氏夾板 Magnuson splint
马哈马里/馬哈馬里 mahamari
马海姆纤维/馬海姆纖維 Mahaim fiber
马赫病/Maher 氏病 Maher disease

马赫特试验/馬克特氏試驗　Macht test
马黑[色]素/馬黑色素,馬黑質　hippomelanin
马吉尔带环/Magill 氏帶環　Magill band
马尖尾线虫/馬尖尾線蟲　Oxyuris equi
马交媾病/馬交媾病　covering disease
马接触传染性胸膜肺炎病毒/馬接觸傳染性胸膜肺炎病毒　equine contagious pleuropneumonia virus
马颈盘尾丝虫/馬頸蟠尾絲蟲　Onchocerca cervicalis
马驹嗜睡病/駒昏睡病　sleepy foal disease
马口异位/馬口異位　hypospadias
马奎斯试验/馬奎斯試驗　Marquis test
马拉巴尔溃疡/Malabar 潰瘍　Malabar ulcer
马拉硫磷/馬拉硫磷　Malathion
马来酰/馬來酰　Maleic hydrazide
马来丝虫/馬來絲蟲　Wuchereria malayi
马来丝虫病/馬來絲蟲病　filariasis malayi
马来酸酐类/馬來酸酐類　maleic anhydrides
马来酸麦角新碱/順丁烯二酸麥角新鹼　ergonovine maleate
马来酸盐类/馬來酸鹽類　maleates
马来酰亚胺类/馬來醯亞胺類　maleimides
马[莱尔布]钙化上皮瘤/Malherbe 氏鈣化上皮瘤　calcifying epithelioma of Malherbe
马雷克病/Marek 氏病　Marek disease
马雷克病病毒/Marek 氏病病毒　Marek disease virus
马里昂病/Marion 氏病　Marion disease
马里共济失调/Marie 氏運動失調症　Marie ataxia
马里兰[固定]桥/馬里蘭[固定]橋　Maryland fixed bridge
马里综合征/Marie 氏症候群　Marie syndrome
马林综合征/Malin 氏症候群　Malin syndrome
马铃薯/馬鈴薯　potato
马铃薯疗法/馬鈴薯療法　potato cure
马铃薯磷酸化酶/馬鈴薯磷酸化酶　potato phosphorylase
马铃薯球蛋白/馬鈴薯球蛋白　tuberin
马铃薯样瘤/頸動脈體瘤　potato tumor
马铃薯状癌/馬鈴薯狀癌　solanoid cancer
马铃薯状的/馬鈴薯狀的　solanoid
马流产病毒/馬流产病毒　equine abortion virus
马流感病毒/馬流行性感冒病毒　equine influenza virus
马流行性感冒/馬流行性感冒　equine influenza, horse influenza
马-罗综合征/Marie-Robinson 二氏症候群　Marie-Robinson syndrome
马洛里-魏斯综合征/Mallory-Weiss 二氏症候群　Mallory-Weiss syndrome
马洛里小体/馬婁里小體　Mallory body
马毛癣菌/馬毛癬菌　Trichophyton equinum
马-米病/Marchiafava-Micheli 二氏病　Marchiafava-Micheli disease
马-米综合征/Marchiafava-Micheli 二氏症候群　Marchiafava-Micheli syndrome
马萘雌酮/馬萘雌酮　equilenin
马脑脊髓炎病毒/馬脑脊髓炎病毒　equine encephalomyelitis virus
马普替林/馬普替林　Maprotiline
马奇病/March 氏病　March disease
马钱子/馬錢子,番木鱉　nux-vomica
马钱子酊/番木鱉酊　nux vomica tincture
马钱子中毒/馬錢子中毒　strychnine poisoning
马瑞尼蚝绿/馬雷林　marennin
马若兰溃疡/Marjolin 氏潰瘍　Marjolin ulcer
马萨病/Massai 氏病　Massai disease
马森假血管肉瘤/Masson 氏假血管肉瘤　Masson pseudoangiosarcoma
马杉肾炎/馬杉腎炎　Masugi nephritis
马氏小管/馬氏小管　Malpighian tubule
马丝虫/馬絲蟲　Filaria equina
马斯塔德手术/馬斯塔德手術　Mustard operation
马斯特二级梯运动试验/馬斯特二級梯運動試驗　Master two-step exercise test
马塔斯带/Matas 氏帶　Matas band
马塔斯手术/Matas 氏手術　Matas operation
马蹄/馬蹄鐵　horseshoe
马蹄冠/蹄冠　coronet
马蹄内翻足/馬蹄内翻足　talipes equinovarus
马蹄肾/馬蹄形腎[臟]　horseshoe kidney
马蹄外翻足/馬蹄外翻足　talipes equinovalgus
马蹄形[肛门]瘘/肛門蹄鐵狀瘺　horseshoe fistula
马蹄形夹板/蹄鐵狀夾板　horseshoe splint
马蹄形裂孔/馬蹄形裂孔　horseshoe hole
马蹄形切口/馬蹄形切口　horseshoe incision
马蹄形肾/[馬]蹄鐵形腎　horseshoe kidney
马蹄形胎盘/蹄鐵狀胎盤　horseshoe placenta
马蹄形止血带/蹄鐵形止血帶　horseshoe tourniquet
马蹄状足/緊張足　taut foot
马蹄足/馬蹄足　equinus
马蹄足畸形/馬蹄足變形　equinus deformity
马天花/馬天花　variola equina
马桶座圈皮炎/馬桶皮膚炎　toilet seat dermatitis
马托雷尔溃疡/Martorell 氏潰瘍　Martorell ulcer
马尾/馬尾　cauda equina
马尾损伤/馬尾損傷　injury of cauda equina

马尾综合征/馬尾症候群　syndrome of cauda equina
马西叶髂胫韧带/Maissiat 氏髂脛韌帶　iliotibial ligament of Maissiat
马烯雌酮/馬烯雌酮　equilin
马歇尔静脉/Marshall 氏斜靜脈,左心房斜静脉　Marshall oblique vein
马谢单位/馬凱單位　Mache unit
马亚罗病毒/馬亞羅病毒　Mayaro virus
马疫/馬疫　horse sickness
马吲哚/馬吲哚　mazindol
马应龙麝香痔疮膏/馬應龍麝香痔瘡膏　mayinglong shexiang zhichuang ointment
马蝇/馬蠅　horse botfly
马圆线虫/馬圓蟲　palisade worm
马圆线虫感染/馬圓線蟲感染　equine strongyle infection
马源性哮喘/馬原性氣喘　horse asthma
马约基病/Majocchi 氏病　Majocchi disease
马约基肉芽肿/Majocchi 氏肉芽腫　Majocchi granuloma
马约基紫癜/Majocchi 氏紫癜　Majocchi purpura
马锥虫/馬錐蟲　Trypanosoma equinum
马锥虫病/馬媾疫,馬花柳病,馬性病　dourine
马鬃除鲠器/馬鬃捕鯁器　bristle probang
马鬃丝虫/馬[腹腔]絲蟲　Setaria equina
吗多明/嗎多明　Molsidomine
吗啡/嗎啡　Morphine
吗啡断瘾状态/嗎啡斷癮狀態,嗎啡禁斷　amorphinism
吗啡脱瘾法/除嗎啡癮法,嗎啡戒除法　demorphinization
吗啡烷类/嗎啡烷類　morphinans
吗啡烷生物碱/嗎啡烷生物鹼　morphinane alkaloid
吗啡衍生物/嗎啡衍生物　morphine derivative
吗啡依赖/嗎啡依賴　morphine dependence
吗啉类/嗎啉類　morpholines
吗氯贝胺/嗎氯貝胺　moclobemide
蚂蝗咬伤/螞蝗咬傷　leech sting
埋藏的/包埋的　embedded
埋藏缝术/[組織]埋植法　encatarrhaphy
埋藏式自动复律除颤器/埋藏式自動復律除顫器　implantable automatic cardiovertor defibrillator
埋伏牙/埋伏牙　embedded tooth
埋入性扁桃体/埋入性扁桃腺　buried tonsil
埋线法重睑成形术/埋線法重瞼成形術　doubling eyelid operation by buried suture method
迈博姆囊肿/瞼板腺囊腫　meibomian cyst
迈尔/熱量單位　Mayer

迈尔试剂/碘化汞鉀試劑　Mayer reagent
迈尔斯手术/邁爾斯手術　Miles operation
迈克尔森干涉仪/邁克爾遜干涉儀　Michelson interferometer
迈-墨饮食/Minot-Murphy 二氏飲食　Minot-Murphy diet
迈内特基底核/邁內特基底核　basal nucleus of Meynert
迈内特细胞/Meynert 氏細胞　Meynert cell
迈氏唇鞭毛虫/邁氏唇鞭蟲　Chilomastix mesnili
迈松纳夫绷带/Maisonneuve 氏繃帶　Maisonneuve bandage
迈耶病/Meyer 氏病　Meyer disease
迈耶蛋白/Mayer 氏白蛋白　Mayer albumin
迈耶森痣/Meyerson 氏母斑　Meyerson nevus
迈耶征/邁耶徵　Mayer sign
麦醇溶蛋白/麥膠蛋白　gliadin
麦蛋白/麥蛋白　aleuronat
麦地那龙线虫/麥迪那蟲,幾内亞蟲　Dracunculus medinensis
麦冬/麥冬　dwarf lilyturf tuber
麦粉[蛋白]样粒/麵粉蛋白樣顆粒　aleuronoid granule
麦格尼毛癣菌/麥格尼毛癬菌　Trichophyton meginii
麦吉夹/McGee 氏夾板　McGee splint
麦角/麥角　ergot
麦角胺/麥角胺　ergotamine
麦角胺咖啡因/麥角胺咖啡因　ergotamine and caffeine
麦角毒碱/麥角毒素　ergotoxine
麦角固醇/麥角[硬]脂醇　ergosterol
麦角红质/麥角紅色素　sclererythrin
麦角碱酸/麥角鹼酸　ergotinic acid
麦角痉挛碱/生痙素　spasmotin
麦角菌中毒/麥角菌中毒　ergotoxicosis
麦角卡里碱/麥角隱亭鹼　ergocryptine
麦角苦碱/麥角苦鹼　picrosclerotine
麦角林类/麥角林類　ergolines
麦角硫因/麥硫因　ergothioneine
麦角生物碱类/麥角生物鹼類　ergot alkaloids
麦角酸/麥角酸　lysergic acid
麦角酸二乙胺/麥角酸二乙胺　lysergic acid diethylamide
麦角新碱/麥角新素　ergometrine
麦角溴烟酯/尼麥角林　nicergoline
麦角乙脲/利舒脲　lisuride
麦角硬酸/麥角硬酸　sclerotinic acid
麦角中毒/麥角中毒　ergotism

麦卡德尔病/McArdle 氏病,第五型肝糖贮积症 McArdle disease
麦卡利关节盂韧带/肱骨關節盂韌帶,Macalister 氏關節盂韌帶 glenoid ligament of Macalister
麦考尔龈缘突/麥考爾齦緣突 McCall festoon
麦克伯尼点/麥克伯尼點 McBurney point
麦克伯尼切口/麥克伯尼切口 McBurney incision
麦克金-怀特征/麥-懷二氏徵象 McGinn-White sign
麦克莱恩-马克斯韦尔病/馬-麥二氏病 MacLean-Maxwell disease
麦克雷诺兹相常数/麥克雷諾相常數 McReynolds phase constant
麦克斯韦/馬士威 Maxwell
麦克维疝修补术/麥克維疝修補術 McVay herniorrhaphy
麦克尤恩征/麥克尤恩徵 MacEwen sign
麦肯齐病/Mackenzie 氏病 Mackenzie disease
麦肯齐综合征/Mackenzie 氏症候群 Mackenzie syndrome
麦夸里试验/馬奎里氏試驗 MacQuarrie test
麦粒灸/麥粒灸 moxibustion with seed-sized moxa cone
麦粒软骨/麥粒軟骨 triticeal cartilage
麦粒形痤疮/麥粒形痤瘡 acne hordeoiaris
麦门冬汤/麥門冬湯 maimendong decoction
麦胚核酸/麥胚核酸 triticonucleic acid
麦胚凝集素-辣根过氧化物酶轭合物/麥胚凝集素-辣根過氧化物酶軛合物 Wheat Germ Agglutinin-Horseradish Peroxidase Conjugate
麦胚凝集素类/麥胚凝集素類 wheat germ agglutinins
麦氏插管钳/麥氏插管鉗 Magill intubating forcep
麦氏重排/麥氏重排 McLafferty rearrangement
麦氏恶丝虫/麥氏惡絲蟲 Dirofilaria magalhaesi
麦氏喉镜/麥氏喉鏡 Machintosh laryngoscope
麦氏征/麥克莫雷氏徵象 McMurray sign
麦司卡林/南美仙人掌毒鹼 mescaline
麦斯纳小体/Meissner 氏小體 Meissner corpuscle
麦仙翁/毒莠草 Agrostemma githago
麦芽/麥芽 germinated barley
麦芽酚反应/麥芽酚反應 maltol reaction
麦芽黄素/麥芽黃素 maltoflavin
麦芽浸质溶液/麥芽浸質溶液 malt extract solution
麦芽三糖/麥芽三醣 maltotriose
麦芽糖/麥芽糖 maltose
麦芽糖醇/麥芽醇 maltol
麦芽[糖]苷/麥芽糖苷 maltoside
麦芽[糖]糊精/麥芽[糖]糊精 maltodextrin
麦芽糖酶/麥芽糖酵素 maltase
麦芽糖尿/麥芽糖尿症 maltosuria
麦芽糖脎/麥芽糖脎 maltosazone
麦芽氧化酶/大麥氧化酶 spermase
麦芽汁/啤酒麥芽汁 beerwort
脉/脈 vessel
脉痹/脈痺 vessel bi, vessel bi-disease
脉波/脈[搏]波 pulse wave
脉波后间期/心脈後期 postsphygmic interval
脉波前间期/心脈前期 presphygmic interval
脉搏查看器/脈搏計,脈鏡 sphygmoscope
脉搏动/脈搏動 pulse beat
脉搏短绌/脈搏短缺,脈缺落 pulse deficit
脉搏计/脈搏計 sphygmometer
脉搏检查/脈搏計檢法 sphygmoscopy
脉搏节律/脈搏節律 pulse rhythm
脉搏力计/脈搏動力計 sphygmodynamometer
脉搏率/脈率 pulse rate
脉搏描记法/脈搏描記法,脈波計用法 sphygmography
脉搏容量/脈搏容量 pulse volume
脉搏体积描记器/脈波容積描記器 sphygmoplethysmograph
脉搏徐缓/脈搏徐緩 bradysphygmia
脉搏氧饱和度仪/脈搏氧飽和度儀 pulse oximeter
脉搏自动描记器/脈搏自動脈波計 sphygmochronograph
脉冲场凝胶电泳/脈衝場凝膠電泳 pulsed field gel electrophoresis
脉冲超短波疗法/脈衝超短波療法 pulsed ultrashort wave therapy
脉冲磁场疗法/脈衝磁場療法 pulsed magnetic field therapy
脉冲短波疗法/脈衝短波療法 pulsed short wave therapy
脉冲多普勒超声心动描记术/脈衝都卜勒超聲心動描記術 pulsed Doppler echocardiography
脉冲发生器/脈衝發生器 pulse generator
脉冲幅度/脈衝幅度 pulse amplitude
脉冲辐射分解/脈衝輻射分解 pulse radiolysis
脉冲宽度/脈衝寬度 pulse width
脉冲类型/脈衝類型 pulse pattern
脉冲频率/脈衝頻率 pulse frequency
脉冲式分泌/脈衝式分泌 pulsatile secretion
脉岛数/脈島數 vein islet number
脉管壁血管/脈管壁血管,血管滋養管 vascular vessel
脉管丛/脈管叢 vascular plexuses

脉管弓突起/胸前骨凸　hemapophysis
脉管神经/脈管神經　vascular nerve
脉管渗透异常/血管渗透性異常　dysoria
脉管痛/脈管痛　vasalgia
脉管系统/血管分布　vasculature
脉管学/脈管學，血管學　angiology
脉管炎/脉管炎　angiitis
脉管组织/脈管組織　vasalium
脉经/脈經　Mai Jing
脉静/脈靜　tranquil pulse
脉律不齐/不整脈　arrhythmia of pulse
脉络丛/脈絡叢　choroid plexus
脉络丛后内侧支/脈絡叢後内側支　posterior medial choroidal branch
脉络丛后外侧支/脈絡叢後外側支　posterior lateral choroidal branch
脉络丛脑膜炎/脈絡叢腦膜炎　choriomeningitis
脉络丛前动脉/脈絡膜前動脈　anterior choroidal artery
脉络丛乳头[状]瘤/脈絡叢乳頭狀瘤　papilloma choroideum
脉络丛上静脉/脈絡叢上靜脈　superior choroid vein
脉络丛下静脉/脈絡叢下靜脈　inferior choroid vein
脉络丛肿瘤/脈絡叢腫瘤　choroid plexus neoplasm
脉络带/脈絡帶　tenia choroidea
脉络裂/脈絡裂　choroid fissure
脉络膜/脈絡膜　choroid
脉络膜病/脈絡膜病　choroidopathy
脉络膜出血/脈絡膜出血　choroid hemorrhage
脉络膜丛乳头状瘤/脈絡膜叢乳頭狀瘤　choroid plexus papilloma
脉络膜动脉丛/脈絡膜動脈叢　plexus arteriae choroidea
脉络膜动脉硬化/脈絡膜動脈硬化　choroidal arteriosclerosis
脉络膜孤立结核/脈絡膜孤立結核　tuberculosis solitaria choroidea
脉络膜骨瘤/脈絡膜骨瘤　choroidal osteoma
脉络膜黑色素瘤/脈絡膜黑色素瘤　melanoma of choroid
脉络膜虹膜炎/脈絡膜虹膜炎　choroidoiritis
脉络膜基底层/脈絡膜基底層　basal lamina of choroid
脉络膜疾病/脈絡膜疾病　choroid disease
脉络膜睫状体炎/脈絡膜睫狀體炎　choroidocyclitis
脉络膜静脉/脈絡膜靜脈　choroid vein
脉络膜裂/脈絡膜裂，脈絡膜隙　choroid fissure
脉络膜裂隙/脈絡膜裂隙　fissura choroidea

脉络膜毛细血管层/脈絡膜血管層　choriocapillary layer
脉络膜膨出/脈絡膜膨出　choriocele
脉络膜切除术/脈絡膜切除術　choroidectomy
脉络膜缺损/脈絡膜缺損　coloboma of choroid
脉络膜上层/脈絡膜上層　suprachoroid lamina
脉络膜视网膜病/脈絡膜視網膜病　chorioretinopathy
脉络膜视网膜炎/脈絡膜視網膜炎　chorioretinitis
脉络膜粟粒结核/脈絡膜粟粒結核　tuberculosis miliaria choroidea
脉络膜脱离/脈絡膜脱離　detachment of choroid
脉络膜新生血管化/脈絡膜新生血管化　choroidal neovascularization
[脉络膜]血管层/[脈絡膜]血管層　vessel layer
脉络膜血管瘤/脈絡膜血管瘤　choroidal angioma
脉络膜炎/脈絡膜炎　choroiditis
脉络[膜]中层/脈絡膜中層　mesochoroidea
脉络膜肿瘤/脈絡膜腫瘤　choroid neoplasm
脉络膜周间隙/脈絡膜周間隙　perichoroidal space
脉络组织/脈絡組織　tela choroidea
脉能测量器/脈能計　energometer
脉能描记法/脈力計檢法　sphygmobolometry
脉能描记器/脈力計　sphygmobolometer
脉逆四时/脈逆四時　incongruence of pulse with four seasons
脉象/脈象　pulse manifestation
脉压/脈[搏]壓　pulse pressure
脉要精微论篇/脈要精微論篇　Treatise on Pulse Diagnosis
脉音听诊器/脈音器　sphygmophone
脉应四时/脈應四時　congruence of pulse with four seasons
脉诊/脈診　pulse taking examination
脉症合参/脈症合參　comprehensive analysis of both pulse manifestation and symptoms
唛酚生/唛酚生,甲苯丙醇　cresoxydiol
满山红/滿山紅　dahurian rhododendron leaf
满月脸/月形臉　moon face
满足感/滿足感　satiety response
满足欲望行为/滿欲行爲　appetitive behavior
螨/蟎　Acari
螨病/蟎病,恙蟲病,疥蟲病　acariasis
螨感染/蟎感染　mite infestation
螨恐怖症/恙蟲恐懼症,疥癬恐懼症　acarophobia
螨目/蟎目　Acarina
螨皮炎/蟎蟲皮膚炎　acarodermatitis
曼-博尔曼瘘/馬-波二氏腸瘻　Mann-Bollman fistula

曼彻斯特手术/曼徹斯特手術　Manchester operation
曼德林试剂/曼德林試劑　Mandelin reagent
曼德森综合征/Mendelsohn氏症候群　Mendelsohn syndrome
曼尼期碱类/曼尼期鹼類　mannich bases
曼森病/Manson氏病　Manson disease
曼森溶液/Manson氏溶液　Manson solution
曼氏尖旋尾线虫/曼氏尖旋尾線蟲　Oxyspirura mansoni
曼氏裂头绦虫病/曼氏裂頭條蟲病　bothriocephaliasis mansoni
曼氏裂头蚴病/曼氏裂頭蚴病　sparganosis mansoni
曼氏丝虫病/曼森線蟲病　Mansonelliasis
曼氏血吸虫/曼森氏血吸蟲　Schistosoma mansoni
曼氏血吸虫病/曼森氏血吸蟲病　Schistosomiasis mansoni
曼陀罗/曼陀羅　Datura stramonium
曼陀罗中毒/曼陀羅中毒　stramonium poisoning
曼-威廉森溃疡/曼-威二氏潰瘍　Mann-Williamson ulcer
蔓茎毒毛旋花子苷配基/蔓莖毒毛旋花子苷雜質　sarmentogenin
蔓茎毒毛旋花子糖/蔓莖毒毛旋花子配糖體　sarmentose
蔓荆子/蔓荊子　shrub chastetree fruit
蔓延性溃疡/蔓延性潰瘍　spreading ulcer
蔓状动脉瘤/蔓狀動脈瘤　racemose aneurysm
蔓状动脉血管瘤/串狀花樣動脈血管瘤　angioma arteriale racemosum
蔓状[静脉]丛/蔓狀叢　pampiniform plexus
蔓状胎盘/蜿蜒狀胎盤　cirsoid placenta
蔓状血管瘤/蔓狀血管瘤　cirsoid hemangioma
漫反射/漫反射　diffuse reflectance
漫游症/漫遊症　wandering
慢病毒/慢病毒　slow virus
慢病毒感染/慢病毒感染　lentivirus infection
慢病毒疾病/慢病毒疾病　slow virus disease
慢反应物质A/慢反應物質A　slow reacting substance A
慢喉痹/慢喉痺　chronic pharyngitis, chronic throat obstruction
慢喉瘖/慢喉瘖　chronic hoarseness disease
慢惊风/慢驚風　chronic infantile convulsion
慢惊风·脾肾阳虚证/慢驚風·脾腎陽虛證　chronic infantile convulsion with pattern of yang deficiency of spleen and kidney
慢惊风·脾虚肝旺证/慢驚風·脾虛肝旺證　chronic infantile convulsion with pattern of spleen deficiency and liver hyperactivity
慢惊风·气血两虚证/慢驚風·氣血兩虛證　chronic infantile convulsion with pattern of deficiency of both qi and blood
慢惊风·阴虚动风证/慢驚風·陰虛動風證　chronic infantile convulsion with pattern of wind stirring due to yin deficiency
慢跑者脚趾/慢跑者腳趾　jogger toe
慢乳蛾/慢乳蛾　chronic nippled moth
慢沙滤池/慢沙濾器　slow sand filter
慢食癖/吞食徐緩　bradyphagia
慢缩肌纤维/慢縮肌纖維　slow-twitch muscle fiber
慢性/慢性　chronica
慢性鼻咽炎/慢性鼻咽炎,鼻後卡他　postnasal catarrh
慢性闭锁性牙髓炎/慢性閉鎖性牙髓炎　chronic closed pulpitis
慢性扁桃体炎/慢性扁桃體炎　chronic tonsillitis
慢性病/慢性病　chronic disease
慢性病医院/慢性病醫院　chronic disease hospital
慢性病照护模式/慢性病照護模式　chronic illness care model
慢性出血性绒毛状滑膜炎/慢性出血性絨毛狀滑膜炎　chronic hemorrhagic villous synovitis
慢性穿孔性增生/慢性穿孔性增生　chronic perforating hyperplasia
慢性穿透性溃疡/慢性穿透性潰瘍　chronic undermining ulcer
慢性穿凿性窦道性溃疡/慢性穿鑿性竇道性潰瘍　chronic undermining burrowing ulcer
慢性传染性关节炎/慢性傳染性關節炎　chronic infectious arthritis
慢性传染源/慢性傳染源　chronic source of infection
慢性醇中毒/慢性酒精中毒　chronic alcoholism
慢性单纯性苔藓/Vidal病　Vidal disease
慢性单纯性咽炎/慢性單純性咽炎　chronic simple pharyngitis
慢性单核细胞增多[症]/慢性單核白血球增多症　chronic mononucleosis
慢性低补体性肾小球肾炎/慢性補體結合不足性腎絲球腎炎　chronic hypocomplementemic glomerulonephritis
慢性地方性氟中毒/慢性地方性牙氟中毒　chronic endemic fluorosis
慢性痘疮样糠疹/慢性痘瘡樣糠疹　pityriasis varioliformis chronica
慢性毒效应区/慢性毒效應區　chronic toxic effect zone

慢性毒性/慢性毒性 chronic toxicity
慢性毒性试验/慢性毒性試驗 chronic toxicity test
慢性多关节滑膜炎/慢性絨毛狀多關節炎 chronic villous polyarthritis
慢性耳轮结节性软骨皮炎/慢性耳輪結節性軟骨皮膚炎 chondrodermatitis nodularis helicis chronica
慢性非化脓性骨炎/慢性非化膿性骨炎 chronic nonsuppurative osteitis
慢性非化脓性破坏性胆管炎/慢性非化膿性破壞性膽管炎 chronic nonsuppurative destructive cholangitis
慢性肥大性心肌炎/慢性肥大性心肌炎 chronic hypertrophic myocarditis
慢性肥厚性喉炎/慢性肥厚性喉炎 chronic hypertrophic laryngitis
慢性肥厚性咽炎/慢性肥厚性咽炎 chronic hypertrophic pharyngitis
慢性肺泡换气不足/慢性肺泡換氣不足 chronic alveolar hypoventilation
慢性风湿性关节病/慢性關節性風濕病 chronic articular rheumatism
慢性风湿性心脏病/慢性風濕性心臟病 chronic rheumatic heart disease
慢性附骨疽/慢性附骨疽 chronic bone-attaching abscess, chronic suppurative osteomyelitis
慢性复发性丹毒/慢性復發性丹毒 chronic recurrent erysipelas
慢性腹泻/慢性腹瀉 chronic diarrhea
慢性肝炎/慢性肝炎 chronic hepatitis
慢性感染性胆管炎/遷延性膽管炎，無膽石性慢性傳染性膽管炎 cholangitis lenta
慢性感染性脱髓鞘性多发性神经根性神经病/慢性感染性脫髓鞘性多發性神經根性神經病 chronic inflammatory demyelinating polyradiculoneuropathy
慢性高空病/慢性高空病 chronic altitude sickness
慢性骨髓炎/慢性骨髓炎 chronic suppurative osteomyelitis
慢性骨髓炎·气血两虚证/慢性骨髓炎·氣血兩虛證 chronic suppurative osteomyelitis with qi-blood deficiency pattern
慢性骨髓炎·湿热邪滞证/慢性骨髓炎·濕熱邪滯證 chronic suppurative osteomyelitis with dampness-heat stagnation pattern
慢性骨炎/慢性骨炎 chronic osteitis
慢性关节炎/慢性關節炎 chronic arthritis
慢性光化性皮炎/慢性光化性皮炎 farmer skin
慢性光线性皮炎/慢性光線性皮炎 chronic actinic dermatitis
慢性过度换气综合征/慢性過度換氣症候群 chronic hyperventilation syndrome
慢性过敏反应/慢性過敏性反應 chronic anaphylaxis
慢性化脓性滑膜炎/慢性化膿性滑膜炎 chronic purulent synovitis
慢性化脓性肾炎/慢性化膿性腎炎 chronic suppurative nephritis
慢性活动性肝炎/慢性活動性肝炎 chronic active hepatitis
慢性脊髓性肌萎缩/慢性脊髓性肌萎縮 chronic spinal muscular atrophy
慢性脊髓炎/慢性脊髓炎 chronic myelitis
慢性甲状腺炎/慢性甲狀腺炎 chronic thyroiditis
慢性间歇热/佩-埃二氏症狀 Pel-Ebstein symptom
慢性间质性肝炎/慢性間質性肝炎 chronic interstitial hepatits
慢性间质性肾炎/慢性間質性腎炎 chronic interstitial nephritis
慢性间质性输卵管炎/慢性間質性輸卵管炎 chronic interstitial salpingitis
慢性浆性滑膜炎/慢性漿性滑膜炎 chronic serous synovitis
慢性浆液性腱鞘炎/慢性漿液性腱鞘炎 tenosynovitis serosa chronica
慢性结节性耳轮软骨皮炎/慢性結節性耳輪軟骨皮炎 chondrodermatitis nodularis chronica helicis
慢性结膜炎/慢性結膜炎 chronic conjunctivitis
慢性进行性多发性硬化/慢性進行性多發性硬化 chronic progressive multiple sclerosis
慢性进行性脊髓病/慢性進行性脊髓病 chronic progressive myelopathy
慢性进行性外侧眼肌麻痹/慢性進行性外側眼肌麻痺 chronic progressive external ophthalmoplegia
慢性酒精中毒性谵妄/慢性酒毒性譫妄 chronic alcoholic delirium
慢性卡他性鼻炎/慢性卡他性鼻炎 chronic catarrhal rhinitis
慢性卡他性喉炎/慢性卡他性喉炎 chronic catarrhal laryngitis
慢性卡他性中耳炎/慢性卡他性中耳炎 otitis media catarrhalis chronica
慢性溃疡/慢性潰瘍 chronic ulcer
慢性溃疡性牙髓炎/慢性潰瘍性牙髓炎 chronic ulcerative pulpitis
慢性阑尾炎/慢性闌尾炎 chronic appendicitis
慢性粒细胞白血病/慢性粒細胞白血病 chronic myelocytic leukemia, chronic granulocytic leukemia
慢性粒细胞白血病急变/慢性粒細胞白血病急變

acute transformation of chronic myelocytic leukemia

慢性粒细胞白血病原始细胞危象/慢性粒細胞白血病原始細胞危象　blast crisis of chronic myelocytic leukemia

慢性淋巴管炎/慢性淋巴管炎　chronic lymphangitis

慢性淋巴细胞白血病/慢性淋巴細胞白血病　chronic lymphocytic leukemia

慢性淋巴细胞性甲状腺炎/慢性淋巴腺性甲狀腺炎　chronic lymphocytic thyroiditis

慢性磷中毒/慢性磷中毒　phosphorism

慢性弥漫性肾炎/慢性彌漫性腎炎　chronic diffuse nephritis

慢性脑膜炎球菌败血症/慢性腦膜炎球菌敗血症　chronic meningococcemia

慢性脑损害/慢性腦損害　chronic brain damage

慢性脑损伤/慢性腦損傷　chronic brain injury

慢性黏膜皮肤念珠菌病/慢性黏膜皮膚念珠菌病　chronic mucocutaneous candidiasis

慢性脓毒病/慢性膿毒症，緩慢性敗血病　chroniosepsis

慢性疟/慢性瘧　malaria chronica

慢性排斥反应/慢性排斥反應　chronic rejection

慢性排菌者/慢性排菌者　chronic excreter

慢性盆腔炎/慢性盆腔炎　chronic pelvic inflammatory disease

慢性盆腔炎·寒湿凝滞证/慢性盆腔炎·寒濕凝滯證　chronic pelvic inflammatory disease with pattern of stagnation and congelation of cold-dampness

慢性盆腔炎·气虚血瘀证/慢性盆腔炎·氣虛血瘀證　chronic pelvic inflammatory disease with pattern of qi deficiency and blood stasis

慢性盆腔炎·气滞血瘀证/慢性盆腔炎·氣滯血瘀證　chronic pelvic inflammatory disease with pattern of qi stagnation and blood stasis

慢性盆腔炎·湿热[蕴结]证/慢性盆腔炎·濕熱[蘊結]證　chronic pelvic inflammatory disease with pattern of accumulation and binding of dampness-heat

慢性砒霜中毒/慢性砒霜中毒　chronic arsenic poisoning

慢性皮质下脑炎/慢性皮質下腦炎　chronic subcortical encephalitis

慢性疲劳综合征/慢性疲勞症候群　chronic fatigue syndrome

慢性脾肿大性红细胞增多病/慢性脾腫大性紅血球增多症　chronic splenomegalic polycythemia

慢性前列腺纤维化/慢性前列腺纖維化　chronic fibrosis of prostate

慢性潜行性穿掘性溃疡/慢性潛行性穿掘性潰瘍　chronic undermining burrowing ulcer

慢性浅层鳞状皮炎/慢性表淺性鱗屑性皮膚炎　chronic superficial scaly dermatitis

慢性侵袭性甲状腺炎/慢性侵襲性甲狀腺炎　chronic invasive thyroiditis

慢性绒毛性关节炎/慢性絨毛狀關節炎　chronic villous arthritis

慢性肉芽肿病/慢性肉芽腫疾病　chronic granulomatous disease

慢性乳腺病/慢性乳腺病　chronic mastopathy

慢性色素沉着性紫癜/慢性色素性紫瘢症　purpura pigmentosa chronica

慢性砷中毒/慢性砷中毒　chronic arsenism

慢性肾病/慢性腎病變　chronic nephrosis

慢性肾功能不全/慢性腎機能不全　chronic renal insufficiency

慢性肾功能衰竭/慢性腎功能衰竭　chronic kidney failure

慢性肾小球肾炎/慢性腎小球腎炎　chronic glomerulonephritis

慢性肾炎/慢性腎炎　chronic nephritis

慢性湿疹/慢性濕疹　chronic eczema

慢性髓细胞单核细胞性白血病/慢性骨髓單核球性白血病　chronic myelomonocytic leukemia

慢性苔藓[样]糠疹/慢性苔蘚樣糠疹　chronic lichenoid pityriasis

慢性特发肥大性骨关节病/慢性特發肥大性骨關節病　chronic idiopathic hypertrophic osteoarthropathy

慢性特发性黄疸/慢性特發性黃疸　chronic idiopathic jaundice

慢性特发性黄瘤病/慢性特發性黃瘤病　chronic idiopathic xanthomatosis

慢性特发性组织细胞增多症/慢性特發性組織細胞增多症　Hand-Schüller-Christian disease

慢性透析/慢性透析　chronic dialysis

慢性萎缩性多软骨炎/慢性萎縮性多發性軟骨炎　chronic atrophic polychondritis

慢性萎缩性肢端皮炎/慢性萎縮性肢端皮炎　acrodermatitis chronica atrophicans

慢性无胆色素尿性黄疸/慢性無膽色素尿性黃疸　chronic acholuric jaundice

慢性吸收性关节炎/慢性吸收性關節炎　chronic absorptive arthritis

慢性纤维空洞型肺结核/慢性纖維空洞型肺結核　chronic fibrocavernous pulmonary tuberculosis

慢性纤维性甲状腺炎/慢性纖維性甲狀腺炎

chronic fibrous thyroiditis
慢性纤维性乳腺炎/慢性纖維性乳腺炎 mastitis chronica fibrosa
慢性消耗性疾病/慢性消耗性疾病 chronic wasting disease
慢性心肌炎/慢性心肌炎 chronic myocarditis
慢性心内膜炎/慢性心內膜炎 chronic endocarditis
慢性锌中毒/慢性鋅中毒 zincalism
慢性休止期脱发/慢性休止期脫髮 chronic telogen effluvium
慢性血行播散型肺结核/慢性血行播散型肺結核 chronic hematogenous pulmonary tuberculosis
慢性血吸虫病/慢性血吸蟲病 chronic schistosomiasis
慢性荨麻疹/慢性蕁麻疹 chronic urticaria, urticaria chronica
慢性牙槽骨髓炎/慢性齒槽骨髓炎 chronic alveolar osteomyelitis
慢性炎/慢性炎症 chronic inflammation
慢性抑郁[症]/慢性抑鬱[症] chronic depression
慢性游走性红斑/慢性遊走紅斑 erythema chronicum migrans
慢性阈剂量/慢性閾劑量 chronic threshold dose
慢性阈浓度/慢性閾濃度 chronic threshold concentration
慢性躁狂/慢性躁狂 chronic mania
慢性增生性腹膜炎/慢性增生性腹膜炎 chronic proliferative peritonitis
慢性增生性牙髓炎/慢性增生性牙髓炎 chronic hyperplastic pulpitis
慢性增殖性输卵管炎/慢性增殖性輸卵管炎 chronic vegetating salpingitis
慢性支气管炎/慢性支氣管炎 chronic bronchitis
慢性肢端皮炎/慢性肢端皮膚炎 chronic acral dermatitis
慢性植体抗宿主病/慢性植體抗宿主病 chronic graft-versus-host disease
慢性重型肝炎/慢性重型肝炎 chronic severe hepatitis
慢性主动脉髂动脉阻塞/慢性主動脈髂動脈阻塞 chronic aortoiliac obstruction
慢性子痫/慢性子癇 chronic epididymitis and orchitis, chronic testicular abscess
慢性阻塞性肺病/慢性阻塞性肺病 chronic obstructive lung disease
慢性阻塞性肺疾病/慢性阻塞性肺疾患 chronic obstructive pulmonary disease
芒刺舌/芒刺舌 prickly tongue
芒果状趾/芒果狀趾 mango toe
芒罗微脓肿/孟洛微膿瘍 Munro microabscess
芒硝/芒硝 crystallized sodium sulfate
芒针疗法/芒針療法 elongated needle therapy
盲/盲,失明 blindness
盲肠/盲腸 cecum
盲肠襞/盲腸皺襞 cecal fold
盲肠缝合术/盲腸縫合術 cecorrhaphy
盲肠固定术/盲腸固定術 cecofixation
盲肠后的/盲腸後的 retrocecal
盲肠后动脉/盲腸後動脈 posterior cecal artery
盲肠后淋巴结/盲腸後淋巴結 retrocecal lymph node
盲肠后疝/盲腸後疝 retrocecal hernia
盲肠后位阑尾/盲腸後位闌尾 retrocecal appendix
盲肠后隐窝/迴盲後隱窩 retrocecal recess
盲肠疾病/盲腸疾病 cecal disease
盲[肠]结肠/盲結腸 cecocolon
盲肠结肠固定术/盲腸結腸固定術 cecocolopexy
盲肠结肠吻合术/盲腸結腸造口吻合術 cecocolostomy
盲肠结肠炎/盲結腸炎 typhlocolitis
盲肠脓肿/盲腸膿腫 typhloempyema
盲肠旁炎/盲腸旁組織炎 paratyphlitis
盲肠膀胱扩大术/盲腸膀胱擴大術 cecum augmentation cystoplasty
盲肠膨胀/盲腸膨脹 typhlectasis
盲肠憩室/盲腸憩室 cecal diverticulum
盲肠前动脉/盲腸前動脈 anterior cecal artery
盲肠前淋巴结/盲腸前淋巴結 prececal lymph node
盲肠切除术/盲腸切除術 cecectomy
盲肠切开术/盲腸切開術 cecotomy
盲肠疝/盲腸疝 cecal hernia
盲肠石病/盲腸石病 typhlolithiasis
盲肠输尿管吻合术/盲腸輸尿管造口吻合術 typhloureterostomy
盲肠系膜/盲腸繫膜 mesocecum
盲肠狭窄/盲腸狹窄 typhlostenosis
盲肠下垂/盲腸下垂 typhloptosis
盲肠血管襞/盲腸血管皺襞 vascular cecal fold
盲肠炎/盲腸炎 typhlitis
盲肠乙状结肠造口吻合术/盲腸乙狀結腸造口吻合術 cecosigmoidostomy
盲肠造口术/盲腸造口術 cecostomy
盲肠折[叠]术/盲腸折疊手術 cecoplication
盲肠肿瘤/盲腸腫瘤 cecal neoplasm
盲肠周围炎/盲腸周圍炎 pericecitis
盲点/盲點 blind spot

盲端异位输尿管膨出/盲端異位輸尿管膨出　blind ectopic ureterocele
盲法线锯髁突截开术/盲法線鋸髁突截開術　blind Gigli saw condylotomy
盲孔/盲孔　foramen cecum
盲襻综合征/盲襻症候群　blind loop syndrome
盲人点字法/盲人點字法　braille
盲学/盲學　typhlology
莽草毒素/莽草毒素　sikimitoxin
莽草素/莽草素　shikimene
莽草酸/莽草酸　shikimic acid
莽草酸途径/莽草酸途徑　shikimic acid pathway
猫喘样震颤/貓咕狀震顫　purring tremor
猫耳/貓耳　cat ear
猫耳螨/貓節痂蟎　notoedres cati
猫耳状皱襞/貓耳狀皺襞　cat ear like skin fold
猫感染性肠炎病毒/貓傳染性腸炎病毒　feline infectious enteritis virus
猫鼾状杂音/貓咕狀雜音　purring murmur
猫叫综合征/貓叫症候群　cri du chat syndrome
猫哭综合征/貓哭症候群　cat cry syndrome
猫毛/貓毛　cat hair
猫免疫缺陷性病毒/貓免疫缺陷性病毒　feline immunodeficiency virus
猫眼疮/貓眼瘡,多形性紅斑　cat eye sore, erythema multiforme
猫眼疮·寒湿阻络证/貓眼瘡·寒濕阻絡證　cat eye sore with pattern of cold-dampness obstructing collateral
猫眼疮·火毒炽盛证/貓眼瘡·火毒熾盛證　cat eye sore with blazing fire-toxin pattern
猫眼疮·湿热蕴结证/貓眼瘡·濕熱蘊結證　cat eye sore with dampness-heat amassment pattern
猫眼样细睑裂/貓眼樣細瞼裂　aeluropsis
猫眼综合征/貓眼症候群　cat eye syndrome
猫咬病/貓咬病　cat-bite disease
猫爪草/貓爪草　Cat's Claw, catclaw buttercup root
猫[栉首]蚤/貓蚤　cat flea
猫抓病/貓抓病　cat scratch disease
猫抓热/貓抓熱　cat scratch fever
毛/毛　pili
毛孢子菌病/毛髮芽孢菌病　trichosporosis
毛玻璃/毛玻璃　ground glass
毛虫/毛蟲　caterpillar
毛虫皮炎/毛蟲皮膚炎　caterpillar dermatitis
毛虫症/毛蟲症　erucism
毛悴色夭/毛悴色夭　withered skin and hair
毛滴虫/滴蟲,梨形蟲　trichomonad

毛地黄/毛地黃　digitalis
毛地黄毒苷/毛地黃毒苷　digitoxin
毛地黄毒素糖/毛地黃毒糖　digitoxose
毛地黄糖/毛地黃糖　digitalose
毛地黄皂苷反应/洋地黃皂苷反應　digitonin reaction
毛地黄皂苷配基/毛地黃皂素　digitogenin
毛发/毛髮　hair
毛发-鼻-指综合征/毛髮-鼻-指骨症候群　tricho-rhino-phalangeal syndrome
毛发-鼻-趾综合征/毛髮-鼻-趾骨症候群　tricho-rhino-phalangeal syndrome
毛发错构瘤/毛髮錯構瘤　pilar hamartoma
毛发低硫营养不良/毛髮低硫營養不良　trichothiodystrophy
毛发端分裂/毛髮端分裂　schizotrichia
毛发复合癌/毛髮複合癌　pilar complex carcinoma
毛发[感]觉/毛髮感覺　trichesthesia
毛发感觉测量器/毛髮感覺計　trichoesthesiometer
毛发感觉缺失/缺乏毛髮感覺　trichoanesthesia
毛发红糠疹/毛髮紅糠疹　pityriasis rubra pilaris
毛发环曲/環毛　pili annulati
毛发基质癌/毛髮基質癌　pilomatrix carcinoma
毛发疾病/毛髮疾病　hair disease
毛发痂性角化不全/堆痂性角化不全　parakeratosis scutularis
毛发检查/檢視毛髮　trichoscopy
毛发囊肿/毛髮囊腫　pilar cyst
毛发皮屑/毛髮皮屑　dander
毛发球状变形/氣泡狀毛髮畸型　bubble hair deformity
毛发去除/毛髮去除　hair removal
毛发缺乏/無毛症　atrichia
毛发软化/毛髮軟化　trichomalacia
毛发色素缺乏/毛髮無色症　achromotrichia
毛发上皮瘤/毛髮上皮瘤　trichoepithelioma
毛发神经嵴性错构瘤/毛髮神經嵴性錯構瘤　pilar neurocristic hamartoma
毛发生长周期/毛髮生長週期　growth cycle of hair
毛发湿度计/毛髮濕度計　hair hygrometer
毛发苔藓/毛髮苔藓　lichen pilaris
毛发铁色素/毛髮鐵質素　trichosiderin
毛发脱落/毛髮脫落　loss of hair
毛发腺瘤/毛髮腺瘤　trichoadenoma
毛发型基底细胞上皮瘤/毛髮形基底細胞上皮瘤　pilar type of basal cell epithelioma
毛[发]癣菌病/髮癬[菌病]　trichophytosis
毛[发]癣菌素试验/髮癬菌素試法　trichophytin test

毛发学/毛髮學　pilology trichology
毛发颜色/毛髮顏色　hair color
毛发-眼-皮肤-椎骨综合征/毛髮-眼-皮-脊椎骨症候群　tricho-oculo-dermo-vertebral syndrome
毛发移植[术]/毛髮移植[術]　hair grafting
毛[发]异色/毛髮異色　heterotrichosis
毛发真菌病/毛髮真菌病，髮癬菌病　trichomycosis
毛发周期/毛髮週期　hair cycle
毛发周[围]的/毛髮周圍的　peripilar
毛[发]着色/毛髮著色症　chromotrichia
毛[发]着色不足/髮色素過少　hypochromotrichia
毛干/毛幹　hair shaft cortex, hair shaft
毛根/毛根　hair root
毛根黑点病/毛根黑點病　trichostasis spinulosa
毛根鞘瘤/毛根鞘瘤　trichilemmoma
毛根鞘囊肿/毛根鞘囊腫　trichilemmal cyst
毛根鞘小皮/根鞘表皮，毛囊表皮　cuticle of root sheath
毛茛科/毛茛科　Ranunculaceae
毛管发育/毛管之發育　hair canal development
毛果芸香碱/毛果芸香鹼，毛果芸香素　pilocarpine
毛-汗管-皮脂腺痣/毛囊汗管皮脂腺痣　pilo-syringo-sebaceous nevus
毛花苷类/毛花苷類　lanatosides
毛花洋地黄苷 C/毛地黄苷 C　lanatoside C
毛基质/毛髮基質，毛髮母質　hair matrix
毛际/毛際　mons pubis
毛交叉/毛交叉　hair cruces
毛菌纲/毛髮菌類，髮癬菌類　Trichomycetes
毛壳[菌]属/毛殼菌屬　*Chaetomium*
毛孔扩大/毛孔擴大　patulous follicle orifice
毛孔瘤/毛孔瘤　poroma folliculum
毛孔收缩面膜/毛孔收縮面膜　pore reducer mask
毛孔透药疗法/毛孔透藥療法　poropathy
毛类圆线虫病/毛圓線總科病　trichostrongyloidiasis
毛领征/毛領表徵　hair collar sign
毛流/毛浪　hair stream
毛霉蛋白/黴蛋白　mucorin
毛霉菌病/白黴菌病　mucormycosis
毛蠓科/蛾蚋科　Psychodidae
毛母质/毛母質　hair matrix
毛母质瘤/鈣化上皮瘤　pilomatricoma
毛囊/毛囊　hair follicle
毛囊闭塞三联症/毛囊阻塞三疊症　follicular occlusion triad
毛囊扁平苔藓/毛囊扁平苔蘚　follicular lichen planus
毛囊刺/毛囊刺　follicular spicule

毛囊感受器/毛囊感受器　hair-follicle receptor
毛囊汗管皮脂腺/毛囊汗管皮脂腺　pilo-syringo-sebaceous
毛囊和毛囊旁角化过度病/毛囊及毛囊周圍角化過度　hyperkeratosis follicularis et parafollicularis
毛囊角化病/毛囊角化病　keratosis follicularis
毛囊角化不良/毛囊角化不良　dyskeratosis follicularis
毛囊抗原/毛囊抗原　hair-follicle antigen
毛囊扩大/毛囊擴大　patulous follicle
毛囊瘤/毛囊瘤　follicular tumor
毛囊漏斗部炎/毛囊漏斗部炎　infundibulofolliculitis
毛囊漏斗肿瘤/毛囊漏斗腫瘤　tumor of the follicular infundibulum
毛囊母细胞瘤/毛囊母細胞瘤　trichoblastoma
毛囊脓疱病/毛囊膿皰病　impetigo follicularis
毛[囊]皮脂单位/毛囊與皮脂腺單位　pilosebaceous unit
毛[囊]皮脂腺的/毛囊與皮脂腺的　pilosebaceous
毛囊皮脂腺囊性错构瘤/毛囊皮脂腺囊狀錯構瘤　folliculosebaceous cystic hamartoma
毛囊皮脂腺黏蛋白累积病/毛囊皮脂腺黏蛋白累積病　follicular mucinosis
毛囊皮脂腺器/毛囊及皮脂腺結構　pilosebaceous apparatus
毛囊蠕[形]螨/毛囊蠕形蟲　demodex folliculorum
毛囊虱/毛囊蝨　follicle mite
毛囊性糠疹/毛孔性糠疹　pityriasis folliculorum
毛囊性梅毒疹/毛囊性梅毒疹　syphilid follicularis
毛囊性脓痂疹/毛囊性膿痂疹　follicular impetigo of Bockhart
毛囊性皮肤萎缩/毛囊性皮膚萎縮　follicular atrophoderma
毛囊性皮肤萎缩和基底细胞癌/毛囊萎縮性真皮與基底細胞癌　follicular atrophoderma and basal cell carcinoma
毛囊性上皮癌/毛囊性上皮癌　follicular carcinoma
毛囊性银屑病/毛囊性乾癬　psoriasis follicularis
毛囊炎/毛囊炎　folliculitis
毛囊炎性秃发/毛囊炎性禿髮　alopecia follicularis
毛囊炎性脱发/禿性毛囊炎　folliculitis decalvans
毛囊恙虫/毛囊恙蟲　face mite
毛囊痣/毛囊痣，毛囊母斑　hair-follicle nevus
毛囊周角化病/毛囊周角化病　perifollicular keratosis
毛囊周围斑状萎缩症/毛囊周圍斑狀萎縮症　perifollicular macular atrophy
毛囊周围肉芽肿/毛囊周圍肉芽腫　perifollicular

granuloma
毛囊周围弹性纤维溶解症/毛囊周圍彈性纖維溶解症　perifollicular elastosis
毛囊周围萎缩症/毛囊周圍萎縮症　perifollicular atrophy
毛囊周围纤维瘤/毛囊周圍纖維瘤　perifollicular fibroma
毛囊周炎/毛囊周圍炎　perifolliculitis
毛囊状鱼鳞癣/毛囊狀魚鱗癬　ichthyosis follicularis
毛囊阻塞四叠症/毛囊阻塞四疊症　follicular occlusion tetrad
毛内癣菌感染/毛内癬菌感染　endothrix infection
毛尿症/毛尿症　pilimictio
毛盘瘤/毛盤瘤　trichodiscoma
毛胚芽/毛胚芽　hair germ
毛皮脂腺囊肿/毛囊與皮脂腺囊腫　pilosebaceous cyst
毛平滑肌瘤/毛平滑肌瘤　piloleiomyomas
毛鞘棘皮瘤/毛鞘棘皮瘤　pilar sheath acanthoma
毛球/毛球　bulb of hair, hair bulb
毛乳头/毛乳頭　hair papilla
毛舌/毛舌　hairy tongue
毛石/毛石　trichobezoar
毛首鞭虫/毛首鞭蟲　Trichuris trichiura
毛毯甲虫皮炎/地毯甲蟲皮膚炎　carpet beetle dermatitis
毛特纳细胞/Mauthner 氏細胞　Mauthner cell
毛透明蛋白/毛透明蛋白,毛透明質　trichohyalin
毛外根鞘癌/外毛根鞘癌　trichilemmocarcinoma
毛外霉菌/毛外黴菌　ectothrix fungi
毛涡/毛渦　hair whirlpool
毛细胞/毛細胞,髮細胞　bristle cell, hair cell
毛细胆管/毛細膽管　cholangiole
毛细管/毛細管　capillary
毛细管病/毛細管病　capillaropathy
毛细管电泳/毛細管電泳　capillary electrophoresis, CE
毛细管激素/毛細管内分泌素　capillary hormone
毛细管间性肾小球硬化症/基-威二氏症候群　Kimmelstiel-Wilson syndrome
毛细管扩张/毛細管擴張　telangiectasia
毛细管扩张性狼疮疹/血管類狼瘡　angiolupoid
毛细管扩张性肉瘤/毛細管擴張性肉瘤　telangiectatic sarcoma
毛细管扩张性血管瘤/毛細管擴張性血管瘤　telangiectatic angioma
毛细管熔点测定/毛細管熔點測定　capillary melting point determination

毛细管水/毛細管水　capillary water
毛细管显微镜检查/毛細管之顯微鏡檢　capillaroscopy
毛细管型膜式氧合器/毛細管型膜式氧合器　capillary membrane oxygenator
毛细管血行正常/毛細管血行正常　eudiemorrhysis
毛细管炎/毛細管炎　capillaritis
毛细管周的/毛細管周的　pericapillary
毛细管作用力/毛細管作用力　capillary force
毛细淋巴管/毛細淋巴管,淋巴毛細管　lymphatic capillary, lymph capillary
毛细淋巴管扩张/毛細淋巴管擴張　telangiectasia lymphatica
毛细淋巴管瘤/毛細淋巴管瘤　capillary lymphangioma
毛细淋巴管网/毛細淋巴管網　lymphatic capillary net
毛细吸引/毛細管吸引作用　capillary attraction
毛细线虫病/毛細線蟲病　capillariasis
毛细血管/毛細血管　capillaries, blood capillary
毛细血管搏动/毛細管搏動　capillary pulsation
毛细血管出血/微血管出血,滲血　capillary hemorrhage
毛细血管床/毛細管床　capillary bed
毛细血管丛/微血管叢　capillary plexus
毛细血管脆性/毛細管脆弱,微血管脆性　capillary fragility
毛细血管动脉瘤/微血管動脈瘤　capillary aneurysm
毛细血管后微静脉/毛細血管後微靜脈　postcapillary venule
毛细血管间肾小球硬化症/毛細管間糖尿病性腎絲球病變　intercapillary glomerulosclerosis
毛细血管扩张/毛細血管擴張　telangiectasis
毛细血管扩张性癌/毛細管擴張癌　carcinoma telangiectaticum
毛细血管扩张性痤疮/微血管擴張性痤瘡　acne telangiectodes
毛细血管扩张性的/毛細管擴張性的　telangiectodes
毛细血管扩张性骨肉瘤/骨毛細血管擴張病　osteotelangiectasia
毛细血管扩张性环状紫癜/毛細管擴張性環狀紫瘢病　purpura annularis telangiectodes
毛细血管扩张性肉芽肿/毛細管擴張性肉芽腫　granuloma telangiectaticum
毛细血管扩张性神经胶质瘤/毛細管擴張性神經膠瘤　telangiectatic glioma
毛细血管扩张性象皮病/毛細管擴張性象皮病　elephantiasis telangiectodes

毛细血管扩张性脂肪瘤/毛細管擴張性脂瘤 lipoma telangiectodes
毛细血管扩张样癌/微血管擴張樣癌 carcinoma telangiectodes
毛细血管瘤/毛細血管瘤,焰色痣 capillary hemangioma
毛细血管脉搏/微血管脈搏 capillary pulse
毛细血管内增生性肾小球肾炎/毛細血管內增生性腎小球腎炎 endocapillary proliferative glomerulonephritis
毛细血管襻/毛細血管圈 capillary loop
毛细血管前括约肌/微血管前括約肌,前毛細血管括約肌 precapillary sphincter
毛细血管前微动脉/毛細管前微動脈 precapillary arteriole
毛细血管渗漏综合征/毛細血管滲漏症候群 capillary leak syndrome
毛细血管调节/毛細管調節作用 capillary regulation
毛细血管通透性/毛細血管滲透性 capillary permeability
毛细血管通透性增强因子/毛細血管通透性增強因數 capillary permeability increasing factor
毛细血管外肾小球肾炎/毛細血管外腎小球腎炎 extracapillary glomerulonephritis
毛细血管外增生性肾小球肾炎/毛細血管外增生性腎小球腎炎 extracapillary proliferative glomerulonephritis
毛细血管网/微血管網 capillary network
毛细血管无灌注/毛細血管無灌注 capillary nonperfusion
毛细血管显微镜/毛細血管顯微鏡 angioscope
毛细血管显微术/微血管顯微性檢查 capillary microscopy
毛细血管血/毛細血管血 capillary blood
毛细[血]管循环/微血管循環 capillary circulation
毛细血管止血药/微血管止血藥 capillary hemostatic
毛细血管痣/微血管痣 capillary nevus
毛细血管周围细胞/微血管周圍細胞 pericapillary cell
毛细血管阻力/毛細管抵抗力 capillary resistance
毛细支气管炎/毛細支氣管炎 capillary bronchitis
毛细作用/毛細作用 capillarity
毛线虫病/毛線蟲病 trichonematosis
毛小皮/毛小皮 hair cuticle
毛癣菌属/毛癬菌屬 Trichophyton
毛癣菌性肉芽肿/髮癬菌肉芽腫 trichophytic granuloma
毛癣菌疹/髮癬菌疹 trichophytid
毛芽/毛芽,毛胚 hair bud
毛原细胞/生毛細胞 trichogen cell
毛原性附属器瘤/毛源性附屬器瘤 trichogenic adnexal tumour
毛圆线虫病/毛狀圓蟲病 trichostrongyliasis
毛植物粪石/毛糞石,毛團 trichophytobezoar
毛痣/毛痣 nevus pilosus
毛状白斑/毛狀白斑 hairy leukoplakia
矛盾性杂音/矛盾性雜音 paradox murmur
矛盾意向/矛盾情緒 ambivalence
锚蛋白复制/錨蛋白複製 ankyrin repeat
锚蛋白类/錨蛋白類 ankyrins
锚定 PCR/錨定 PCR anchor PCR
锚状骨内种植体/錨狀骨內種植體 anchor endosteal implant
锚状夹板/錨式夾板 anchor splint
冒暑/冒暑 summerheat affection
帽/帽 cap
帽化/帽化 capping
帽式绷带/帽式繃帶 capeline bandage
帽章状梅毒疹/帽章狀梅毒疹 cockade syphilid
帽章状痣/帽章狀痣 cockade nevus
帽章状紫癜/帽章狀紫瘢 cockade purpura
帽状腱膜/帽狀腱膜 galea aponeurotica
帽状腱膜下出血/帽狀腱膜下出血 subgaleal hemorrhage
帽状腱膜下的/帽狀腱膜下的 subgaleal
帽状期/帽狀期 cap stage
瞀昧/瞀昧 restlessness with foggy head
瞀闷/瞀悶 unconsciousness and irritability
玫瑰斑/玫瑰斑 rose spot
玫瑰红/玫瑰紅 rose bengal
玫瑰花/玫瑰花 rose flower
玫瑰花结/玫瑰花狀 rosette
玫瑰花结形成/玫瑰花結形成 rosette formation
玫瑰糠疹/玫瑰色糠疹 pityriasis rosea
玫瑰树碱类/玫瑰樹鹼類 ellipticines
玫瑰疹/玫瑰疹 roseolar rash
眉部瘢痕性红斑/眉毛瘢痕性紅斑 ulerythema ophryogenes
眉冲/眉沖 meichong, BL3
眉疔/眉疔 ding of eyebrow, furuncle on eyebrow
眉弓/眉弓 superciliary arch
眉间/眉間,印堂 glabella
眉间中点/眉間中點 ophryon
眉间皱纹/眉間皺紋 glabellar frown line
眉痉挛/眉痙攣 ophryosis

眉棱骨/眉棱骨　supraorbital bone
眉棱骨痛/眉棱骨痛　pain in supraorbital bone, supraorbital neuralgia
眉棱骨痛·风热上扰证/眉棱骨痛·風熱上擾證　pain in supraorbital bone with pattern of wind-heat disturbing upward
眉棱骨痛·风痰上扰证/眉棱骨痛·風痰上擾證　pain in supraorbital bone with pattern of wind-phlegm disturbing upward
眉棱骨痛·肝火上炎证/眉棱骨痛·肝火上炎證　pain in supraorbital bone with pattern of liver fire flaring upward
眉棱骨痛·肝血虚证/眉棱骨痛·肝血虛證　pain in supraorbital bone with liver blood deficiency pattern
眉恋疮/眉戀瘡　eyebrow eczema
眉毛/眉[毛]　eyebrow
眉毛移植[术]/眉毛移植[術]　eyebrow grafting
眉缺损/眉缺損　defect of eyebrow
眉提升术/眉提昇術　eyebrow lifting
眉下垂/眉下垂　ptosis of eyebrow
眉心疽/眉心疽　glabellar carbuncle
眉异色/眉異色　heterotrichosis superciliorum
眉再造术/眉再造術　eyebrow reconstruction
梅奥静脉/Mayo 氏静脈　Mayo vein
梅奥手术/Mayo 氏手術,臍疝修補術　Mayo operation
梅-贝病/Meyer-Betz 二氏病　Meyer-Betz disease
梅毒/梅毒　syphilis, lues venerea
梅毒·毒结筋骨证/梅毒·毒結筋骨證　syphilis with pattern of toxin accumulated in tendon and bone
梅毒·肝经湿热证/梅毒·肝經濕熱證　syphilis with pattern of dampness-heat in liver channel
梅毒·肝肾两虚证/梅毒·肝腎兩虛證　syphilis with liver-kidney deficiency pattern
梅毒患者/梅毒患者　syphilitic
梅毒菌素/梅毒菌素　luetin
梅毒恐怖/梅毒恐懼症　syphilomania
梅毒瘤的/梅毒腫的　gummatous
梅毒瘤性骨炎/梅[毒]性骨炎　gummatous osteitis
梅毒瘤性溃疡/梅[毒]性潰瘍　gummatous ulcer
梅毒瘤状的/梅毒瘤狀的,梅毒腫的　gummy
梅毒螺旋体素/巴里定　pallidin
梅毒螺旋体血液凝集试验/梅毒螺旋體血液凝集試驗　TP hemagglutination test
梅毒瓦[塞尔曼]氏反应/梅毒 Wassermann 氏反應　Wassermann reaction for syphilis
梅毒·心肾两虚证/梅毒·心腎兩虛證　syphilis with heart-kidney deficiency pattern
梅毒性鼻炎/梅毒性鼻炎　syphilitic rhinitis
梅毒性痤疮/梅毒性痤瘡　acne syphilitica
梅毒性动脉瘤/梅毒性動脈瘤　syphilitic aneurysm
梅毒性骨炎/梅毒性骨炎　syphilitic osteitis
梅毒性关节炎/梅毒性關節炎　syphilitic arthritis
梅毒性冠状动脉口狭窄/梅毒性冠狀動脈口狹窄　syphilitic coronary ostial stenosis
梅毒性喉炎/梅毒性喉炎　syphilitic laryngitis
梅毒性滑膜炎/梅毒性滑膜炎　syphilitic synovitis
梅毒性脊髓病/梅毒性脊髓病,脊髓梅毒　myelosyphilosis
梅毒性脊髓病性肌萎缩/梅毒脊髓性肌萎縮　syphilitic spinal muscular atrophy
梅毒性脊髓炎/梅毒性脊髓炎　syphilitic myelitis
梅毒性结节/梅毒性松石,梅毒結節　tophus syphiliticus
梅毒性精神病/梅毒性精神病　syphilopsychosis
梅毒性溃疡/梅毒性潰瘍　syphilitic ulcer
梅毒性玫瑰疹/梅毒性玫瑰疹　roseola syphilitica
梅毒性脑膜炎/梅毒性腦膜炎　gummatous meningitis
梅毒性脓疮/梅毒性膿瘍　gummatous abscess
梅毒性脓疱病/梅毒性膿皰病　impetigo syphilitica
梅毒性葡萄膜炎/梅毒性葡萄膜炎　syphilitic uveitis
梅毒性肾炎/梅毒性腎炎　syphilitic nephritis
梅毒性天疱疮/梅毒性天皰瘡　pemphigus syphiliticus
梅毒性脱发/梅毒性禿髮　alopecia syphilitica
梅毒性胃炎/梅毒性胃炎　syphilitic gastritis
梅毒性下疳/梅毒性下疳　syphilitic chancre
梅毒性心肌树胶样肿/梅毒性心肌樹膠樣腫　syphilitic gumma of myocardium
梅毒性肿块/梅毒性贅疣　syphilophyma
梅毒性主动脉炎/梅毒性主動脈炎　syphilitic aortitis
梅毒血清试验/梅毒血清試驗　serological test for syphilis
梅毒血清诊断/梅毒血清診斷　syphilis serodiagnosis
梅毒疹/梅毒疹　syphilide
梅尔策麻醉法/Meltzer 氏麻醉法　Meltzer anesthesia
梅格斯综合征/Meigs 氏症候群　Meigs syndrome
梅核气/梅核氣,臆球症　globus hystericus, plum-stone qi
梅核气·肝气郁结证/梅核氣·肝氣鬱結證　plum-stone qi with liver qi stagnation pattern
梅核气·痰气互结证/梅核氣·痰氣互結證　plum-stone qi with pattern of intermingled phlegm and qi
梅花针/梅花針　plum-blossom needle
梅克尔触盘/梅克爾氏觸盤　Merckel tactile disc

梅克尔带/Meckel氏帶　Meckel band
梅克尔肌/Merkel氏肌　Merkel muscle
梅克尔憩室/米克爾憩室,迴腸卵黄管憩室,Meckel氏盲管　Meckel diverticulum
梅克尔软骨/美克耳氏軟骨,第一鰓弓軟骨　Meckel cartilage
梅克尔细胞/梅克爾細胞　Merkel cell
梅－克照射/Medinger-Craver二氏照射　Medinger-Craver irradiation
梅勒达病/Meleda島病　Meleda disease
梅勒尼溃疡/Meleney氏潰瘍　Meleney ulcer
梅勒尼协同性坏疽/梅勒尼協同性壞疽　Meleney synergistic gangrene
梅-雷细胞/Merkel-Ranvier二氏細胞　Merkel-Ranvier cell
梅-罗综合征/梅-羅症候群　Melkersson-Rosenthal syndrome
梅内特里耶病/梅内特里耶病　Menetrier disease
梅尼埃病/梅尼埃病　Meniere disease
梅尼埃病样多发性脑神经炎/大腦耳性眩暈病狀多神經炎　polyneuritis cerebralis menieriformis
梅齐尼试验/馬利尼試驗　Mazzini test
梅热耶夫斯基效应/米若斯基氏效應　Mierzejewski effect
梅森夹板/Mason氏夾板　Mason splint
梅耶尔-施维克拉特综合征/Meyer-Schwicherath氏症候群　Meyer-Schwicherath syndrome
湄公血吸虫病/湄公血吸蟲病　schistosomiasis mekongi
媒介/媒介　medium
媒介过程/媒傳　vection
煤焦油/煤焦油　pix carbonis
煤焦油溶液/煤焦油溶液　coal tar solution
煤焦油烧伤/煤焦油燒傷　coal tar burn
煤矿工肺病/煤礦工肺病　coal-miner lung
煤[气]焦油/煤氣焦油,瓦斯焦油　gas tar
煤气中毒/煤氣中毒　carbon monoxide poisoning
煤烟癌/煙囱工人癌　soot cancer
煤油乳剂/煤油乳劑　kerosene emulsion
酶/酶,酵素　enzyme
酶标记/酶標記　enzyme labelling
酶标记探针/酶標記探針　enzyme labelled probe
酶[不全]病/酶不全病　enzymopathy
酶重活化剂/酶再啟動劑　enzyme reactivator
酶促反应/酶促反應　enzymatic reaction
酶催化/酶催化　enzyme catalysis
酶[催化]合成/酶[催化]合成　enzymic synthesis
酶蛋白/酵素蛋白質　zymoprotein

酶电极/酶電極　enzyme electrode
酶多种免疫测定技术/酶多種免疫測定技術　enzyme multiplied immunoassay technique
酶法拆分/酶法拆分　enzymatic resolution
酶化学/酶化學　zymochemistry
酶活性/酶活性　enzymatic activity
酶激活/酶啟動　enzyme activation
酶激活药/酶激活藥　enzyme activator
酶降解性皮炎/酵素分解性皮膚炎　enzyme degradation dermatitis
酶解肌球蛋白/酶解肌凝蛋白　meromyosin
酶解[作用]/酶[分]解作用　enzymolysis, zymolysis
酶类药物/酶類藥物　enzyme drug
酶联免疫吸附测定/酶聯免疫吸附測定,酵素免疫吸附法　enzyme-linked immunosorbent assay, ELISA
酶免疫电泳/酶免疫電泳　enzymoimmunoelectrophoresis
酶免疫分析/酶免疫分析法　enzyme immunoassay, EIA
酶尿/酵素尿　enzymuria
酶平衡/酵素平衡　enzyme balance
酶前体/酶前體　enzyme precursor
酶缺乏/酵素缺乏　azymia
酶溶痂术/酶溶痂術　enzymatic debridement
酶生成[作用]/酵素生成,酵素產生　zymogenesis
酶试验/酶試驗　enzyme test
酶稳定性/酶穩定性　enzyme stability
酶性坏死/酵素性壞死　enzymatic necrosis
酶性血栓形成/酵素性血栓形成　ferment thrombosis
酶性脂膜炎/酵素性脂層炎　enzyme panniculitis
酶学/發酵學　zymetology
酶学基因表达调控/酶學基因表達調控　enzymologic gene expression regulation
酶血症/酵[素]血　fermentemia
酶抑制剂/酶抑制劑　enzyme inhibitor
酶抑制相互作用/酶抑制交互作用　enzyme inhibiting interaction
酶抑制药/酶抑制藥　enzyme inhibitor
酶抑制作用/酶抑制作用,酵素壓制　enzyme inhibition
酶诱导/酶誘導性作用,酵素性誘導　enzyme induction
酶诱导相互作用/酶誘導交互作用　enzyme inducing interaction
酶原/酶原,酵素原　proenzyme, zymogen
酶原粒/酶原粒　zymogen granule

酶原细胞/产酶细胞　zymogenic cell
酶自杀底物/自殺型酶受質　suicide substrate of enzyme
霉变/黴變　milden and rot
霉疮秘录/黴瘡秘録　Secret Record for Syphilis
霉酚酸/黴酚酸　mycophenolic acid
霉酱苔/黴醬苔　berry-sauce fur
霉菌病/黴菌病　mycosis
霉菌病肉芽肿/黴菌病肉芽腫　mycotic granulomas
霉菌的/黴菌的　fungous, mycotic
霉菌毒素/黴菌毒素　mycotic toxin
霉菌毒素接种/黴菌毒素接種法　mycotoxinization
霉菌感染/黴菌感染　fungal infection
霉菌过敏/黴菌過敏　mycotic allergy
霉菌性动脉瘤/菌病性動脈瘤　mycotic aneurysm
霉菌性关节炎/黴菌性關節炎　arthritis fungosa
霉菌性滑膜炎/黴菌性滑膜炎　fungous synovitis
霉菌性口炎/黴菌性口炎,鵝口瘡　mycotic stomatitis
霉菌性溃疡/黴菌性潰瘍　mycotic ulcer
霉菌性胃炎/黴菌性胃炎　mycotic gastritis
霉菌性须疮/黴菌鬚癬,真菌鬚癬　mycotic sycosis
霉菌血症/黴菌血症　mycethemia
霉菌样支原体/絲狀黴漿菌　Mycoplasma mycoides
霉菌制阻/黴菌受抑制,制菌作用　mycostasis
每搏输出量/心動容量,心動排出量　stroke volume
每搏作功/每搏作功　stroke work
每搏作功指数/每搏作功指數　stroke work index
每分通气量/每分通氣量　minute ventilation volume
每分钟手控通气/每分鐘手控通氣　manual minute ventilation
每年实际死亡率/年實際死亡率　annual actual mortality
每日允许摄入量/每日允許攝入量,每日允許攝取量　acceptable daily intake, ADI
美贝维林/美貝維林　mebeverine
美雌醇/美雌醇　mestranol
美达西泮/美達西泮　medazepam
美登素/美坦辛　maytansine
美椴木/美椴木　basswood
美法仑/左旋溶肉瘤素　melphalan
美发用品/美髮用品　hair preparation
美芬丁胺/美芬丁胺　mephentermine
美芬妥英/美芬妥英　mephenytoin
美芬新/美芬新　mephenesin
美夫西特/强速尿靈　mefruside
美睾酮/甲二氫睾酮　mesterolone
美格鲁托/美格魯托　meglutol
美卡拉明/四甲基樟烷胺　mecamylamine
美金刚/美金剛　memantine
美克洛嗪/美克利淨　meclizine
美拉德反应/美拉德反應　Maillard reaction
美拉胂醇/美拉胂醇　melarsoprol
美利曲辛/四甲基蒽丙胺　melitracen
美洛西林/美洛西林　mezlocillin
美诺立尔/美諾立爾　menogaril
美帕曲星/美帕曲星　mepartricin
美普他酚/美普他酚　meptazinol
美曲勃龙/美曲勃龍　metribolone
美屈孕酮/二甲脱氢孕酮　medrogestone
美容按摩/美容按摩　cosmetic massage
美容保健/美容保健　aesthetic health care
美容护理/美容護理　aesthetic nursing
美容技术/美容技術　cosmetic technique
美容就医者/美容就醫者　aesthetic seeking patient
美容内科学/美容內科學　aesthetic internal medicine
美容皮肤科学/美容皮膚科學　cosmetic dermatology
美容皮肤外科学/美容皮膚外科學　cosmetic dermatosurgery
美容术/美容術　cosmesis
美容外科学/美容外科學　aesthetic surgery
美容心理学/美容心理學　cosmetic psychology
美容性文身/美容性文身　cosmetic tattoo
美容学/美容學　cosmetology
美容业/美容業　beauty culture
美容医学/美容醫學　aesthetic medicine
美容医学心理学/美容醫學心理學　cosmetic medical psychology
美容院/美容院　beauty parlor
美沙吡啉/美沙吡啉　methapyrilene
美沙酮/美沙酮　methadone
美司钠/美司鈉　mesna
美索巴莫/美索巴莫　methocarbamol
美索达嗪/美索達嗪　mesoridazine
美替拉酮/美替拉酮　metyrapone
美替洛尔/美替洛爾　metipranolol
美替诺龙/甲基雄烯醇酮　methenolone
美替沙腙/甲基吲哚二酮縮胺硫尿素　methisazone
美托拉宗/美托拉宗　metolazone
美托洛尔/美托洛爾　metoprolol
美托咪啶/美托咪啶　medetomidine
美维库铵/美維庫銨　mivacurium
美西律/美西律　mexiletine
美西麦角/羥甲丙基甲麥角醯胺　methysergide
美线/美線　aesthetic line
美雄醇/美雄醇　methandriol
美溴沙仑/美溴沙侖　metabromsalan

美学参数/美學參數　aesthetic parameter
美学的/美學的　aesthetic
美学平面/美學平面　aesthetic plane
美学评价/美學評價　aesthetic evaluation
美学修复/美學修復　aesthetic repair
美学牙医学/美學牙醫學　aesthetic dentistry
美学诊断/美學診斷　aesthetic diagnosis
美学诊断蜡型/美學診斷蠟型　aesthetic diagnostic wax-up
美学治疗计划/美學治療計劃　aesthetic treatment plan
美洲板口线虫/美洲板口線蟲　Necator americanus
美洲出血热/美洲出血熱　American hemorrhagic fever
美洲毒蜘蛛/美洲毒蜘蛛　Eurypelma hentzii
美洲钝眼蜱/美洲鈍眼蜱　Amblyomma americanum
美洲钩虫/美洲鉤蟲　Ancylostoma americanum
美洲钩虫病/美洲鉤蟲病　ancylostomiasis americanus
美洲利什曼病/美洲利什曼病　American leishmaniasis
美洲内脏利什曼病/美洲內臟利什曼病　American visceral leishmaniasis
美洲犬蜱/美洲犬蜱　American dog tick
美洲 Burkitt 氏淋巴瘤/美洲 Burkitt 氏淋巴瘤　American Burkitt lymphoma
美洲锥虫/美洲錐蟲　Trypanosoma americanum
美洲锥虫病/美洲錐蟲病　American trypanosomosis
镁/鎂　magnesium
镁代谢紊乱/鎂代謝紊亂　disorder of magnesium metabolism
镁化合物/鎂化合物　magnesium compounds
镁麻醉/鎂麻醉　magnesium anesthesia
镁缺乏/鎂缺乏　magnesium deficiency
镁乳[浆]/鎂乳　magnesia magma
镁硝酸试验/硝酸鎂試驗　magnesionitric test
袂康酸/罌粟酸,鴉片酸　meconic acid
袂康酸盐/罌粟酸鹽　meconate
门/門　hilus
门齿骨/門齒骨　os incisivum
门齿管/門齒管,門牙管　incisive duct
门齿肌/門牙肌　incisive muscle
门齿孔/門牙孔　incisive foramen
门齿内陷/門齒內陷　incisor intrusion
门齿排列/門齒排列　incisor alignment
门齿切面/門齒切面　incisal surface
门冬氨酸氨基转移酶/天門冬胺酸轉胺酶　aspartate aminotransferase
门戈病毒/門戈病毒　Mengo virus
门戈脑脊髓炎/門戈腦脊髓炎　Mengo encephalomyelitis
门管区/門管區　portal area
门管小叶/門管小葉　portal lobule
门管周组织间隙/門管周組織間隙　periportal tissue space
门静脉/門靜脈　vena portae
门静脉高血压/門靜脈性高血壓　portal hypertension
门静脉扩张/門靜脈擴張　pylephlebectasis
门静脉血栓静脉炎/門靜脈血栓靜脈炎　pylethrombophlebitis
门静脉血栓形成/門靜脈血栓形成　portal thrombosis
门静脉循环/門靜脈循環　portal circulation
门静脉压/門靜脈壓　portal pressure
门静脉炎/門靜脈炎　pylephlebitis
门静脉造影术/門靜脈 X 光攝影術　portography
门静脉造影照片/門靜脈 X 光像　portogram
门静脉周的/門靜脈周圍的　periportal
门静脉周围癌/門靜脈周圍癌　carcinoma periportal
门静脉周围炎/門靜脈周圍炎　peripylephlebitis
门静脉阻塞/門靜脈阻塞　portal block
门克斯病/門克斯病　Menkes disease
门控血池显像/門控血池顯像　gated blood-pool imaging
门罗-里希特线/孟-李二氏線　Monro-Richter line
门脉系统/門靜脈系統　portal system
门脉性肝硬化/門[靜]脈性肝硬變　portal cirrhosis
门脉循环/[肝]門靜脈循環　portal circulation
门脉周癌/肝門靜脈周圍癌　periportal carcinoma
门脉周肝硬变/門脈周圍性肝硬變　periportal cirrhosis
门腔静脉[吻合]分流术/門腔靜脈分流術,上腔靜脈分流術　portacaval shunt
门体脑病/門體腦病　portosystemic encephalopathy
门诊病人/門診病人　outpatient
门诊部/門診[部]　ambulant clinic
门诊精神分裂症/有行動力之思覺失調症,有行動力之精神分裂症　ambulatory schizophrenia
门诊外科手术/門診外科手術　ambulatory surgical procedure
门诊医疗/門診醫療　ambulatory care
门诊医疗设施/門診醫療設施　ambulatory care facility
门诊医疗信息系统/門診醫療資訊系統　ambulatory care information system
门诊咨询/門診諮商　office counseling

闷瞀/悶瞀　restlessness and blurred vision
闷痛/悶痛　stuffy pain
虻叮咬/虻叮傷　tabanidae bite
萌出节律/萌出節律　eruption rhythm
萌出期囊肿/萌出期囊腫　eruption cyst
萌发期/萌發期　germination period
萌牙困难/萌牙困難　teething trouble
萌芽/萌芽,生芽　germination
萌芽的/萌芽的　germinative
蒙道尔病/Mondor 氏病　Mondor disease
蒙克病/Munk 氏病　Munk disease
蒙森殆球面学说/蒙森殆球面學說　Monson spherical theory of occlusion
蒙特吉亚骨折脱位/蒙泰賈骨折脫位　Monteggia fracture dislocation
蒙特吉亚脱位/Monteggia 氏脫位　Monteggia dislocation
蒙特卡罗法/蒙特卡羅法　Monte Carlo method
蒙脱石/蒙脱石　smectite
蒙脱土/微晶高嶺土　montmorillonite clay
朦胧/朦朧　twilight
朦胧麻醉/朦朧麻醉　twilight anesthesia
朦胧睡眠/朦朧睡態,半麻醉狀態　twilight sleep
朦胧状态/朦朧狀態　twilight state
朦昧/朦昧　unconsciouness
礞石滚痰丸/礞石滚痰丸　Pill of Chlorite-Schist for Expelling Phlegm, mengshi guntan pills
蒙古人/蒙古人　Mongolian
蒙古褶/蒙古褶　Mongoloid fold
猛兽伤/猛獸傷　preyer injury
锰/錳　manganese
锰化合物/錳化合物　manganese compound
锰酸/錳酸　manganic acid
锰酸盐/錳酸鹽　manganate
锰中毒/錳中毒　manganese poisoning
蠓科/蠓科　Ceratopogonidae
蠓皮炎/蠓皮炎　heleidae dermatitis
孟德尔比率/孟德爾比率　Mendelian rate
孟德尔式性状/孟德爾氏遺傳特性　Mendelian character
孟德尔遗传/孟德爾式遺傳　Mendelian inheritance
孟德尔遗传学说/孟德爾氏遺傳學說　Mendelism
孟诜/孟詵　Meng Shen
梦/夢　dream
梦交[病]/夢交[病]　sexual intercourse in dream, wet dream
梦交·心脾两虚证/夢交·心脾兩虛證　wet dream with pattern of heart-spleen deficiency
梦交·阴虚火旺证/夢交·陰虛火旺證　wet dream with pattern of exuberant fire due to yin deficiency
梦境/夢境　dreamland
梦联想/夢聯想　dream association
梦失精/夢失精　nocturnal emission
梦态分析/夢態精神分析　oneiroanalysis
梦行者/夢遊者　somnambulator
梦行[症]/夢遊症　noctambulation
梦醒状谵妄/夢醒狀譫妄　oneirism delirium
梦魇/夢魘　nightmare
梦样状态/夢樣狀態　oneiroid state
梦遗[精]/夢遺,夢洩　oneirogmus, nocturnal emission
梦呓者/夢囈者　somniloquist
梦游/夢遊　sleep walking, somnambulism
咪达唑仑/咪達唑侖　midazolam
咪多卡/咪多卡　imidocarb
咪康唑/咪康唑　miconazole
咪拉地尔/咪拉地爾　mibefradil
咪噻吩/曲美芬　trimethaphan
咪唑克生/咪唑克生　idazoxan
咪唑类/咪唑類　imidazoles
咪唑啉啶类/咪唑啉啶類　imidazolidines
咪唑啉类/咪唑啉類　imidazolines
咪唑生物碱/咪唑生物鹼　imidazole alkaloid
弥补性牙质/補性牙質　tertiary dentin
弥漫的/彌漫的,擴散的　diffuse
弥漫对称性硬皮病/彌漫性對稱性硬皮病　diffuse symmetrical scleroderma
弥漫型淋巴瘤/彌漫性淋巴瘤　diffuse lymphoma
弥漫性动脉瘤/彌漫性動脈瘤　diffuse aneurysm
弥漫性肺间质纤维化/彌漫性肺間質纖維化　diffuse interstitial pulmonary fibrosis
弥漫性肺泡损伤综合征/彌漫性肺泡損傷症候群　diffuse alveolar damage syndrome
弥漫性腹膜炎/彌漫性腹膜炎　diffuse peritonitis
弥漫性钙化变性/彌漫性鈣化變性　diffuse calcific degeneration
弥漫性脊髓病/彌漫性脊髓病　diffuse myelopathy
弥漫性脊髓炎/彌漫性脊髓炎　diffuse myelitis
弥漫性甲状腺肿/彌散性甲狀腺腫　diffuse goiter
弥漫性腱鞘囊肿/彌漫性腱鞘囊腫　diffuse ganglion
弥漫性筋膜炎/彌漫性筋膜炎　diffuse fasciitis
弥漫性[精索]水囊肿/彌漫性水囊腫　diffused hydrocele
弥漫性蜡样脾/彌漫性蠟狀脾　diffuse waxy spleen
弥漫性皮肤利什曼病/彌漫性皮膚利什曼病　diffuse cutaneous leishmaniasis

弥漫性平滑肌错构瘤/彌漫性平滑肌錯構瘤 diffuse smooth muscle hamartoma
弥漫性前巩膜炎/彌漫性前鞏膜炎 diffuse anterior scleritis
弥漫性躯体性血管角化瘤/彌漫性軀幹血管角化瘤 angiokeratoma corporis diffusum
弥漫性缺氧/彌漫性缺氧 diffuse hypoxemia
弥漫性乳头状瘤/彌漫性乳頭狀瘤 papilloma diffusum
弥漫性上皮瘤/彌漫性上皮瘤 diffuse epithelioma
弥漫性神经胶质增生/擴散性神經膠質增殖病 diffuse gliosis
弥漫性肾炎/彌漫性腎炎 diffuse nephritis
弥漫性食管痉挛/彌漫性食道痙攣 diffuse esophageal spasm
弥漫性特发性骨骼骨肥厚/彌漫性特發性骨骼骨肥厚 diffuse idiopathic skeletal hyperostosis
弥漫性特发性间质骨肥大症/彌漫性特發性間質骨肥大症 diffuse idiopathic interstitial hyperostosis
弥漫性特发性皮肤萎缩/彌漫性特發性皮膚萎縮 atrophia cutis idiopathica diffusa
弥漫性外耳道炎/散布性外耳炎 otitis externa diffusa
弥漫性萎缩/彌漫性萎縮 diffuse atrophy
弥漫性心内膜炎/彌漫性心內膜炎 endocarditis diffusa
弥漫性新生儿血管瘤病/彌漫性新生兒血管瘤病 diffuse neonatal hemangiomatosis
弥漫性血管内凝血/廣泛性血管内凝固 disseminated intravascular coagulation
弥漫性炎/彌漫性炎症 diffuse inflammation
弥漫性营养不良/彌漫性營養不良 dystrophia diffusa
弥漫性硬化骨髓炎/彌漫性硬化骨髓炎 diffuse sclerosing osteomyelitis
弥漫性轴索损伤/彌漫性軸索損傷 diffuse axonal injury
弥漫[性]阻塞性肺气肿/彌漫[性]阻塞性肺氣腫 diffuse obstructive pulmonary emphysema
弥漫增生性肾小球肾炎/彌漫增生性腎小球腎炎 diffuse proliferative glomerulonephritis
弥散磁共振成像/彌散磁振成像 diffusion magnetic resonance imaging
弥散光/彌散光 diffused light
弥散光线照明法/彌散光線照明法 diffuse illumination
弥散节细胞/彌散節細胞 diffuse ganglion cell
弥散菌落/扁平菌叢 effuse colony

弥散量/彌散量 diffusing capacity
弥散淋巴组织/彌散淋巴組織 diffuse lymphoid tissue
弥散圈/彌散圈 circle of diffusion
弥散神经内分泌系统/彌散神經內分泌系統 diffuse neuroendocrine system
弥散性间质性肺纤维化/哈-李二氏症候群 Hamman-Rich syndrome
弥散性血管内凝血/彌散性血管内凝血 disseminated intravascular coagulation
弥散性血管内凝血病/彌漫性血管内凝血功能障礙 disseminated intravascular coagulopathy
弥散性硬皮病/彌漫性硬皮病 diffuse scleroderma
弥散障碍/彌散障礙 diffusion disorder
迷迭香/迷迭香 rosemary
迷宫术/迷宮術 maze operation
迷宫学习/迷宮學習 maze learning
迷管/迷管 aberrant duct
迷行束/迷束 aberrant bundle
迷路/迷路 labyrinth
迷路壁/迷路壁 labyrinthine wall
迷路的/迷路的 labyrinthine
迷路动脉/迷路動脈 labyrinthine artery, artery of labyrinth
迷路感觉/迷路感覺 labyrinthine sense
迷路积水/迷路積水 hydrolabyrinth
迷路疾病/迷路疾病 labyrinth disease
迷路结核/迷路結核 tuberculosis of labyrinth
迷路静脉/迷路靜脈 labyrinthine vein, vein of labyrinth
迷路开窗术/迷路開窗術 labyrinth fenestration
迷路切除术/迷路切除術 labyrinthectomy
迷路切开术/迷路切開術 labyrinthotomy
迷路胎盘/迷路胎盤 labyrinthine placenta
迷路系统/迷路系統 labyrinthine system
迷路性共济失调/前庭性運動失調 labyrinthine ataxia
迷路性眩晕/迷路性眩暈 labyrinthine vertigo
迷路炎/迷路炎 labyrinthitis
迷路液/迷路液 labyrinthine fluid
迷路震荡/耳迷路蕩傷 concussion of the labyrinth
迷路支援细胞/迷路支援細胞 labyrinth supporting cell
迷路周炎/迷路周圍炎 perilabyrinthitis
迷路周组织/迷路周圍組織 perilabyrinth
迷芽瘤/迷芽瘤 choristoma
迷走动脉/迷動脈 aberrant artery
迷走副神经/迷走副神經 vagal accessory nerve

迷走副神经综合征/迷走副神經症候群　vago-accessory syndrome
迷走神经/迷走神經　vagus nerve
迷走神经背侧运动核/迷走神經運動背核　dorsal motor nucleus of vagus nerve
迷走神经背核/迷走神經背核　dorsal nucleus of vagus nerve
迷走神经电[流]图/迷走神經電圖　electrovagogram
迷走神经耳支/迷走神經耳支　auricular branch of vagus nerve
迷走神经耳支交通支/迷走神經耳支交通支　communicating branch with auricular branch of vagus nerve
迷走神经肺丛/迷走神經肺叢　pulmonary plexus of vagus nerve
迷走神经后干/迷走神經後幹　posterior vagal trunk
迷走神经疾病/迷走神經疾病　vagus nerve disease
迷走神经交通支/迷走神經交通支　communicating branch with vagus nerve
迷走[神经]紧张素/迷走神經緊張素　vagotonin
迷走神经颈上心支/迷走神經頸上心支　superior cervical cardiac branch of vagus nerve
迷走神经颈下心支/迷走神經頸下心支　inferior cervical cardiac branch of vagus nerve
迷走神经脑膜支/迷走神經腦膜支　meningeal branch of vagus nerve
迷走神经前干/迷走神經前幹　anterior vagal trunk
迷走神经切断术/迷走神經切斷術　vagotomy
迷走神经三角/迷走神經三角　vagal triangle, trigone of vagus nerve
迷走神经上神经节/迷走神經上神經節　superior ganglion of vagus nerve
迷走神经舌咽神经交通支/迷走神經舌咽神經交通支　communicating branch of vagus nerve with glossopharyngeal nerve
迷走神经食管丛/迷走神經食管叢　esophageal plexus of vagus nerve
迷走神经食管支/迷走神經食管支　esophageal branch of vagus nerve
迷走神经[食管支]松解术/迷走神經鬆解術　vagolysis
迷走神经下神经节/迷走神經下神經節　inferior ganglion of vagus nerve
迷走神经心上支/迷走神經心上支　supreme cardiac nerve
迷走神经性发作/迷走神經性發作　vagal attack
迷走神经性肺炎/迷走神經性肺炎　vagus pneumonia
迷走神经性节律不齐/迷走神經性節律不齊　vagal arrhythmia
迷走神经性脉搏/迷走神經性脈搏　vagus pulse
迷走神经性心动过缓/迷走神經性心搏徐緩　vagal bradycardia
迷走神经性心律不齐/迷走神經性心律不整　phasic sinus arrhythmia
迷走神经胸心支/迷走神經胸心支　thoracic cardiac branch of vagus nerve
迷走神经咽丛/迷走神經咽叢　pharyngeal plexus of vagus nerve
迷走神经咽支/迷走神經咽支　pharyngeal branch of vagus nerve
迷走神经支气管支/迷走神經支氣管支　bronchial branch of vagus nerve
迷走神经阻滞麻醉/迷走神經阻斷麻醉　vagal block
迷走性甲状腺肿/迷走性甲狀腺腫大　aberrant goiter
迷走右锁骨下动脉/迷走右鎖骨下動脈　aberrant right subclavian artery
迷走左肺动脉/迷走左肺動脈　aberrant left pulmonary artery
猕猴耳/獼猴耳　macacus ear
猕因子/Rh 因數　Rh factor
醚床/醚床　ether bed
醚化/醚化　etherification
醚类/醚類　ethers
醚氯仿混合液麻醉/醚氯仿混合液麻醉　chloroform ether mixture anesthesia
醚麻醉/醚麻醉法　etherization
醚溶性浸出物/乙醚抽提物　ether-soluble extractive
醚溶性酸性物/醚溶性酸性物　ether-soluble acidic matter
醚试验/乙醚試驗　ether test
醚吸入器/醚吸器　ether inhaler
醚性溶液/醚溶液　ethereal solution
糜蛋白酶/糜蛋白酶,胰凝乳蛋白酶　chymotrypsin
糜蛋白酶原/胰凝乳蛋白酶原　chymotrypsinogen
糜烂/糜爛[腐蝕]　erosion
糜烂性白斑/糜爛性白斑　erosive leukoplakia
糜烂性包皮龟头炎/糜爛性包皮龜頭炎　erosive balanoposthitis
糜烂性龟头炎/糜爛性龜頭炎　balanitis erosiva
糜烂性女阴阴道炎/糜爛性女陰陰道炎　erosive vulvovaginitis
糜烂性外阴炎/糜爛性女陰炎　erosive vulvitis
糜烂性胃炎/糜爛性胃炎　erosive gastritis
糜烂性咽峡炎/糜爛性咽峽炎　pultaceous angina

米/公尺　meter
米安色林/米安色林　mianserin
米贝利汗孔角化症/Mibelli 氏汗孔角化症　Mibelli porokeratosis
米贝利血管角化瘤/米貝利血管角化瘤　angiokeratoma of Mibelli
米德尔多夫夹板/Middeldorpf 氏夾板　Middeldorpf splint
米多君/米多君　midodrine
米尔克甲/Muehrcke 氏甲　Muehrcke nail
米尔克曼综合征/Milkman 氏症候群　Milkman syndrome
米尔罗伊病/Milroy 氏病　Milroy disease
米尔罗伊-米杰营养性水肿/Milroy-Meige 氏營養性浮腫　Milroy-Meige trophic edema
米尔罗伊水肿/Milroy 氏水腫　Milroy edema
米尔斯-赖因克现象/米-雷二氏現象　Mills-Reincke phenomenon
米非司酮/米非司酮　mifepristone
米泔水样便/米泔水樣便　ricewater stool
米-古综合征/Millard-Gubler 二氏症候群　Millard-Gubler syndrome
米谷蛋白/米膠蛋白　oryzenin
米酵菌酸/米酵菌酸　bongkrekic acid
米卡霉素/米卡黴素　mikamycin
米库利奇病/米庫利奇病　Mikulicz disease
米库利奇口疮/Mikulicz 氏口瘡　Mikulicz aphtha
米库利奇溃疡/Mikulicz 氏潰瘍　Mikulicz ulcer
米库利奇细胞/Mikulicz 氏細胞　Mikulicz cell
米库利兹结肠造口术/米庫里茲結腸造口術　Mikulicz colostomy
米库利兹综合征/米庫里茲症候群　Mikulicz syndrome
米拉哮喘/Millar 氏氣喘　Millar asthma
米勒-艾波特管/米-亞二氏管　Miller-Abbott tube
米勒·费希尔综合征/米勒·費希爾症候群　Miller Fisher syndrome
米勒管/Müller 氏管　duct of Müller
米勒管囊肿/Müller 氏囊腫　Müllerian cyst
米勒混合瘤/苗勒混合瘤　Müllerian mixed tumor
米勒链球菌群/米勒鏈球菌群　Streptococcus Milleri group
米利安白色萎缩/米利安白色萎縮　Milian white atrophy
米利安红斑/Milian 氏紅斑　Milian erythema
米利安综合征/Milian 氏症候群　Milian syndrome
米隆溶液/Millon 氏溶液　Millon solution
米诺地尔/米諾西定　Minoxidil
米诺环素/米諾四環素　Minocycline
米诺特-墨菲饮食疗法/麥-莫二氏飲食療法　Minot-Murphy diet treatment
米帕林/阿滌平　atabrine
米-千克-秒制/公尺公斤秒制　meter-kilogram-second system
米切尔疗法/米契爾氏療法　Mitchell treatment
米切尔液/Mitchell 氏液　Mitchell fluid
米曲霉/米麴黴菌　Aspergillus oryzae
米曲霉酶/米麴菌酶　asperkinase
米曲纤溶酶/米麴纖維溶解蛋白酶　brinolase
米舍唇炎/Miescher 氏唇炎　Miescher cheilitis
米舍尔肉芽肿/Miescher 氏肉芽腫　Miescher granuloma
米食/米食　rice diet
米斯廷/米斯廷　mystin
米斯线/米斯線, 條痕　Mees line
米索前列醇/米索前列醇　Misoprostol
米索硝唑/米索硝唑　Misonidazole
米汤样便/米湯狀糞便　rice-water stool
米吐尔/米吐爾　metol
米托蒽醌/米托蒽醌　mitoxantrone
米托胍腙/米托胍腙　mitoguazone
米托坦/米托坦　mitotane
米夏埃利斯菱形区/米夏埃利斯氏菱形區　Michaelis rhomboid
脒/脒　Amidine
脒基转移酶类/脒基轉移酶類　amidinotransferases
脒裂解酶/脒裂解酶　amidine-lyase
觅食反射/覓食反射　rooting reflex
泌汗神经/制汗神經　sudomotor nerve
泌尿道/尿路　urinary tract
泌尿道感染/泌尿道感染　urinary tract infection
泌尿道生理学/泌尿道生理學　urinary tract physiology
泌尿科学/泌尿科學　urology
泌尿科诊断技术/泌尿科診斷技術　urological diagnostic technique
泌尿器官/泌尿器官　urinary organ
泌尿生殖道/尿生殖管　urogenital duct
泌尿生殖道瘘/泌尿生殖道瘻　urogenital fistula
泌尿生殖窦/泌尿生殖竇　urogenital sinus
泌尿生殖膈/泌尿生殖器膈　urogenital diaphragm
泌尿生殖膈膜/泌尿生殖膈膜　diaphragma urogenitale
泌尿生殖器/泌尿生殖器　genitourinary apparatus
泌尿生殖器膈膜肌/泌尿生殖器膈膜肌　muscle of urogenital diaphragm

泌尿生殖器淋病/尿道生殖器淋病　urogenital gonorrhea
泌尿生殖器外伤/泌尿生殖器外傷　genitourinary trauma
泌尿生殖外科手术/泌尿生殖外科手術　urogenital surgical procedure
泌尿生殖系变应性疾病/泌尿生殖系變應性疾病　allergic disease of genitourinary system
泌尿生殖系滴虫病/泌尿生殖系滴蟲病　trichomoniasis of genitourinary system
泌尿生殖系寄生虫病/泌尿生殖系寄生蟲病　parasitosis of genitourinary system
泌尿生殖系结核病/生殖泌尿道結核病　genitourinary tuberculosis
泌尿生殖系软斑病/泌尿生殖系軟斑病　malakoplakia of genitourinary system
泌尿生殖系统/泌尿生殖系統　urogenital system
泌尿生殖系统腹膜/泌尿生殖系統腹膜　urogenital peritoneum
泌尿生殖系统畸形/泌尿生殖系統畸形　urogenital abnormality
泌尿[生殖]系统记波照相术/泌尿生殖描波法　urokymography
泌尿生殖系统结核/泌尿生殖系統結核　tuberculosis of genitourinary system
泌尿生殖系统肿瘤/泌尿生殖系統腫瘤　urogenital neoplasm
泌尿生殖系血吸虫病/泌尿生殖系血吸蟲病　genitourinary schistosomiasis
泌尿外科检查/泌尿外科檢查　urologic examination
泌尿外科手术/泌尿外科手術　urologic surgical procedure
泌尿系表现/泌尿系表現　urological manifestation
泌尿系疾病/泌尿系疾病　urologic disease
泌尿系抗感染药/泌尿系抗感染藥　urinary anti-infective agent
泌尿系抗体包被细菌试验/泌尿系抗體包被細菌試驗　urinary antibody-coated bacteria test
泌尿系统/泌尿系統　urinary system
泌尿系异物/泌尿系異物　foreign body in urinary system
泌尿系肿瘤/泌尿系腫瘤　urologic neoplasm
泌尿系子宫内膜异位症/泌尿系子宮内膜異位症　endometriosis of urinary system
泌尿小管/細腎管，細尿管　uriniferous tubule
泌乳/泌乳　lactation
泌乳过多/多乳症，乳汁過多　polygalactia
泌乳细胞/輸乳細胞　lactiferous cell
泌乳障碍/泌乳障礙　lactation disorder
泌色作用/泌色作用,色素泌洩作用　chromocrinia
泌酸的/泌酸的　oxyntic
泌酸细胞/泌酸細胞　oxyntic cell
秘传眼科龙木论/秘傳眼科龍木論　Nagarjuna's Ophthalmology Secretly Handed Down
秘方/秘方　secret recipe, nostrums
密斑/密斑　dense patch
密度/密度　density
密度分析/密度分析　densimetric analysis
密度计/密度計　densimeter
密度天平/密度天平　density balance
密集恐惧症/密集恐懼症　trypophobia
密接阵发性咳/小槍似欬嗽　minute gun cough
密螺旋体/密螺旋體　treponeme
密螺旋体病/[密]螺旋體病　treponematosis
密螺旋体感染/密螺旋體感染　treponemal infection
密螺旋体抗原试验/螺旋體抗原試驗　treponemal antigen test
密螺旋体属/螺旋體屬　*Treponema*
密螺旋体制动试验/密螺旋體制動試驗　treponemal immobilization test
密码/密碼　code
密码兼并/密碼兼并　code degeneracy
密码子/密碼子　codon
密蒙花/密蒙花　pale butterflybush flower
密施病/米斯病　Mish disease
密体/密體　dense body
密旋霉素/密旋黴素　pactamycin
密质骨/密質骨　compact bone
密质骨瘤/密質骨瘤，骨質骨瘤　compact osteoma
嘧啶/嘧啶　pyrimidine
嘧啶二聚物/嘧啶二聚物　pyrimidine dimers
嘧啶核苷酸类/嘧啶核苷酸類　pyrimidine nucleotides
嘧啶类/嘧啶類　pyrimidines
嘧啶酮类/嘧啶酮類　pyrimidinones
蜜二糖/蜜二糖　melibiose
蜜蜂/蜜蜂　bee
蜜蜂毒[液]/蜜蜂毒　meltittin venom
蜜蜂花/香蜂草　melissa
蜜柑霉素/蜜柑黴素　mikamycin
蜜剂/蜜劑　mellitum
蜜丸/蜜丸　honeyed pill
蜜制/蜜制　stir-frying with honey
绵马贯众/綿馬貫眾　male fern rhizome
绵马鞣酸/綿馬鞣酸　filicitannic acid
绵马酸/綿馬酸　filicic acid

绵马油/綿馬油　oil of male fern
绵马油树脂/綿馬油樹脂　aspidium oleoresin
绵羊肺腺瘤逆转录病毒/綿羊肺腺瘤逆轉錄病毒　Jaagsiekte sheep retrovirus
绵羊脱髓鞘性脑白质炎/綿羊脱髓鞘性腦白質炎　visna
绵羊夏氏线虫/綿羊夏氏線蟲　Chabertia ovina
棉尘肺/棉屑沈著病　byssinosis
棉尘性哮喘/棉絮性氣喘　cotton-dust asthma
棉酚/棉酚　gossypol
棉缝线/棉縫線　cotton suture
棉根皮/棉根皮　cortex gossypii radicis
棉卷/棉卷　cotton roll
棉卷口炎/棉卷口炎　cotton roll stomatitis
棉塞/棉塞　tampon
棉塞支托法/棉塞支托法　columning
棉尾兔乳头瘤病毒/棉尾兔乳頭瘤病毒　Cottontail rabbit papillomavirus
棉纤维/棉纖維　cotton fiber
棉纤维素/棉纖維素　gossypin
棉籽/棉籽　cottonseed
棉籽糖/棉籽糖　raffinose
棉籽糖酶/棉籽糖酶　raffinase
棉籽油/棉籽油　cottonseed oil
棉籽油脂酸甘油酯/棉籽油脂酸甘油酯　cottonseed glyceride
免费医疗/免費醫療　uncompensated care
免疫/免疫　immunity
免疫表型/免疫表型　immunophenotyping
免疫病理学/免疫病理學　immunopathology
免疫测定/免疫測定　immunoassay
免疫沉淀法/免疫沈澱　immunoprecipitation
免疫磁化分离/免疫磁化分離　immunomagnetic separation
免疫刺激药/免疫刺激藥　immunostimulant
免疫催化作用/免疫催化作用　immunecatalysis
免疫蛋白/免疫蛋白　immune protein
免疫电镜法/免疫電鏡法　immunoelectron microscopic method
免疫电镜术/免疫電子顯微鏡術　immunoelectron microscopy
免疫电吸附[法]/免疫電吸附　immunoelectron adsorption
免疫电泳/免疫電泳　immunoelectrophoresis
免疫电子显微镜检查/免疫電子顯微鏡檢查　immunoelectron microscopy
免疫毒理学/免疫毒理學　immunotoxicology
免疫毒素/免疫毒素,抗毒素　immunotoxin
免疫法/免疫法　immunization
免疫反应/免疫反應　immunological reaction
免疫反应型/免疫反應型　immunological pattern
免疫防御/免疫防禦　immune defence
免疫放射分析/免疫放射分析　immunoradiometric assay
免疫复合物/免疫複合體　immune complex
免疫复合物病/免疫複合物病　immune complex disease
免疫复合物沉着病/免疫沈著病　immune deposit disease
免疫复合物[疾]病/免疫複合體病　immune complex disease
免疫复合物肾小球肾炎/免疫複合物腎小球腎炎　immune complex glomerulonephritis
免疫隔离室/免疫隔離室　immunoseparation room
免疫过滤[法]/免疫濾過法　immunofiltration
免疫过氧化酶/免疫過氧化酶　immunoperoxidase
免疫过氧化酶技术/免疫過氧化酶技術　immunoperoxidase technique
免疫核糖核酸/免疫核糖核酸　immune ribonucleic acid
免疫化学/免疫化學　immunochemistry
免疫活化细胞/免疫活化細胞　immunologically activated cell
免疫活性/免疫能力　immunocompetence
免疫活性的/免疫活性的　immunocompetent
免疫活性细胞/免疫活性細胞,免疫機能健全之細胞　immunocompetent cell, immunologically competent cell
免疫记忆/免疫性記憶　immunologic memory
免疫剂量/免疫劑量,致免疫反應抗原劑量　immunizing dose
免疫剂量效应关系/免疫劑量效應關係　immunologic dose-response relationship
免疫监视/免疫監測　immune surveillance
免疫监视假说/免疫監視假説　immunologic surveillance hypothesis
免疫减弱宿主/免疫減弱宿主　immunocompromised host
免疫胶固素/免疫凝集素　immunoconglutinin
免疫接种程序表/免疫接種程式表　immunization schedule
免疫接种规划/免疫接種規劃　immunization program
免疫结合剂/免疫結合劑　immunoconjugator
免疫金法/免疫金法　immunogold method
免疫金染色法/免疫金染色法　immunogold staining

免疫金银染色法/免疫金銀染色法 immunogoldsilver staining
免疫抗体/免疫抗體 immune antibody
免疫扩散/免疫擴散 immunodiffusion
免疫疗法/免疫療法 immunotherapy
免疫帽形成/免疫帽形成 immunologic capping
免疫媒介疾病/免疫媒介疾病 immune-mediated disease
免疫酶法/免疫酶法 immunoenzyme method
免疫酶技术/免疫酶技術 immunoenzyme technique
免疫耐受/免疫耐受 immune tolerance
免疫耐受[性]/免疫耐受性 immunological tolerance
免疫凝集素/免疫凝[集]素 immune agglutinin
免疫排斥[反应]/免疫排斥[反應] immunologic rejection
免疫屏障/免疫屏障 immunologic barrier
免疫潜能/免疫潜能 immunological competence
免疫球蛋白/免疫球蛋白 immune globulin
免疫球蛋白个体基因型/免疫球蛋白個體基因型 immunoglobulin idiotype
免疫球蛋白 M 过多综合征/免疫球蛋白 M 過多症候群 hyper IgM syndrome
免疫球蛋白基因/免疫球蛋白基因 immunoglobulin gene
免疫球蛋白结合区/免疫球蛋白結合區 immunoglobulin joining region
免疫球蛋白开关区/免疫球蛋白開關區 immunoglobulin switch region
免疫球蛋白可变区/免疫球蛋白可變區 immunoglobulin variable region
免疫球蛋白类/免疫球蛋白類 immunoglobulins
免疫球蛋白类别/免疫球蛋白類別 immunoglobulin class
免疫球蛋白类别转换/免疫球蛋白類別轉換 immunoglobulin class switching
免疫球蛋白轻链基因/免疫球蛋白輕鏈基因 immunoglobulin light chain gene
免疫球蛋白受体/免疫球蛋白受體 immunoglobulin receptor
免疫球蛋白碎片/免疫球蛋白碎片 immunoglobulin fragment
免疫球蛋白体细胞高突变/免疫球蛋白體細胞高突變 immunoglobulin somatic hypermutation
免疫球蛋白同型/免疫球蛋白同型 immunoglobulin isotype
免疫球蛋白同种异型/免疫球蛋白同種異型 immunoglobulin allotype
免疫球蛋白亚类/免疫球蛋白亞類 immunoglobulin subclass
免疫球蛋白异常血症/異常免疫球蛋白血症 dysimmunoglobulinemia
免疫球蛋白重链基因/免疫球蛋白重鏈基因 immunoglobulin heavy chain gene
免疫缺乏综合征/免疫缺乏症候群 immunologic deficiency syndrome
免疫缺陷/免疫缺陷,免疫缺乏 immune deficiency, immunodeficiency
免疫缺陷病/免疫力不全病 immunodeficiency disease
免疫缺陷病毒感染/免疫不全病毒感染 immunodeficiency virus infection
免疫缺陷综合征/免疫缺陷症候群 immunologic deficiency syndrome
免疫溶菌作用/免疫溶菌作用 immune bacteriolysis
免疫溶血[反应]/免疫性溶血 immune hemolysis
免疫溶血素/免疫性溶血素 immune hemolysin
免疫溶血性贫血/免疫性溶血性貧血 immunohemolytic anemia
免疫-神经-内分泌网络/免疫-神經-内分泌網路 immune-neuroendocrine network
免疫生理学/免疫生理學 immunophysiology
免疫生物学/免疫生物學 immunobiology
免疫受体/免疫受體 immunologic receptor
免疫输血法/免疫輸血法 immunotransfusion
免疫衰老/免疫衰老 immunosenescence
免疫特惠器官/免疫特惠器官 immunologically privileged organ
免疫特惠区/免疫特惠區 immunologically privileged site
免疫调变剂/免疫調變劑 immunomodulating agent
免疫调节/免疫調節 immunoloregulation
免疫调节药/免疫調節藥 immunomodulator
免疫调理素/免疫調理素 immune opsonin
免疫铁蛋白/免疫鐵蛋白 immunoferritin
免疫铁蛋白技术/免疫鐵蛋白技術 immunoferritin technique
免疫脱敏法/免疫脱敏法 immunologic desensitization
免疫网络/免疫網路 immunological network
免疫网络学说/免疫網路學説 immunologic network theory
免疫无应答[性]/免疫無應答[性] immunological unresponsiveness
免疫物质/免疫質 immune substance
免疫吸附技术/免疫吸附技術 immunosorbent technique

免疫吸附剂/免疫吸附劑 immunoadsorbent
免疫系统/免疫系統 immune system
免疫系统疾病/免疫系統疾病 immune system disease
免疫细胞/免疫細胞 immunocyte
免疫细胞毒性/免疫細胞毒性 immunologic cytotoxicity
免疫细胞毒性试验/免疫細胞毒性試驗 immunologic cytotoxicity test
免疫细胞化学/免疫細胞化學 immunocytochemistry
免疫细胞化学技术/免疫細胞［組織］化學技術 immunocytochemical technique
免疫细胞粘连/免疫細胞粘連 immunocytoadherence
免疫显性表位/免疫顯性表位 immunodominant epitope
免疫相关抗原/免疫相關抗原 immune associated antigen
免疫性不孕/免疫性不孕 immune infertility
免疫性消失/無免疫性 disimmunity
免疫性血小板减少性紫癜/免疫性血小板減少性紫癜 immunologic thrombocytopenic purpura
免疫性血小板减少症/免疫性血小板減少症 immune thrombocytopenia
免疫选择［法］/免疫選擇 immunoselection
免疫学/免疫學 immunology
免疫学避孕/免疫學避孕 immunologic contraception
免疫学技术/免疫學技術 immunologic technique
免疫学家/免疫學家 immunologist
免疫学监测/免疫學監測 immunologic monitoring
免疫学监视/免疫學監視 immunologic surveillance
免疫学模型/免疫學模型 immunological model
免疫学妊娠试验/免疫學妊娠試驗 immunologic pregnancy test
免疫学试验/免疫學試驗 immunologic test
免疫血清/免疫血清 immune sera
免疫血清球蛋白/免疫血清球蛋白 immune serum globulin
免疫血液学/免疫血液學 immunohematology
免疫压抑/免疫壓抑 immunodepression
免疫药理学/免疫藥理學 immunopharmacology
免疫遗传分型/免疫遺傳分型 immunogenotyping
免疫遗传学/免疫遺傳學 immunogenetics
免疫异常/免疫異常 dysimmunity
免疫抑制/免疫抑制 immunosuppression
免疫抑制剂/免疫抑制劑 immunosuppressant
免疫抑制药/免疫抑制藥 immunosuppressant
免疫抑制因子/免疫抑制因數 immunologic suppressor factor
免疫抑制治疗/免疫抑制治療 immunosuppressive therapy
免疫因子/免疫因數 immunologic factor
免疫印迹/免疫墨點 immunoblotting
免疫印迹法/免疫印跡法 immunoblotting
免疫荧光［法］/免疫螢光法 immunofluorescence method
免疫萤光技术/免疫螢光技術 immunofluorescence technique
免疫应答/免疫應答 immunological response
免疫应答基因/免疫反應基因 immune response gene
免疫预防/免疫預防 immunoprophylaxis
免疫原/免疫原 immunogen
免疫原性/免疫原性 immunogenicity
免疫增强剂/免疫增強劑 immunopotentiator
免疫增生性疾病/免疫增生性疾病 immunoproliferative disorder
免疫增生性小肠病/免疫增生性小腸病 immunoproliferative small intestinal disease
免疫增生障碍/免疫增生障礙 immunoproliferative disorder
免疫粘连/免疫黏著 immune adherence
免疫粘连反应/免疫黏著反應 immune adherence reaction
免疫者/免疫者 immune
免疫诊断/免疫診斷 immunologic diagnosis
免疫诊断学/免疫診斷學 immunodiagnostics
免疫自身稳定/免疫恆定性 immunologic homeostasis
免疫组织化学/免疫組織化學 immunohistochemistry
免疫佐剂/免疫佐劑，免疫佐藥 immunologic adjuvant
免疫佐药/免疫佐藥，免疫佐劑 immunological adjuvant
勉力呼吸/勉力呼吸 labored respiration
娩出/娩出 expulsion
娩出期阵痛/娩出期陣痛 expulsive pain
面/面 face
面包师湿疹/麵包師濕疹 bakers eczema
面包师痒病/麵包師癢病 bakers itch
面臂偏瘫/面臂偏癱 faciobrachial hemiplegia
面部/面［容］ face
面部表情/面部表情 facial expression
面部播散性粟粒状狼疮/面部播散性粟粒狀狼瘡 lupus miliaria disseminatus faciei

面部不对称/面部不對稱　facial asymmetry
面部侧貌/面部側貌　facial profile
面部除皱术/面部除皺術　face rhytidectomy
面部单侧痉挛/面部單側痙攣　hemifacial spasm
面部单侧萎缩/面部單側萎縮　facial hemiatrophy
面部的/面[部]的,颜面的　facial
面部对称性网状皮肤萎缩/顏面對稱性網狀皮萎病　atrophoderma reticulata symmetrica faciei
面部二等分比例/面部二等分比例　facial two equal division ratio
面部干性糠疹/顏面乾性糠疹　pityriasis sicca faciei
面部[感觉]测距能力/面視覺　facial vision
面部红色毛发角化病/面部紅色毛髮角化病　keratosis pilaris rubra faciei
面部肌肉/面部肌肉　facial muscle
面部狼疮/面部狼瘡　lupus facialis
面部老化/面部老化　aging face
面部联动/面部聯動　facial syncinesis
面部联胎/面連胎　prosopopagus
面部毛囊红斑黑变病/面部毛囊紅斑黑變病　erythromelanosis follicularis faciei
面部美学分区/面部美學分區　aesthetic unit of face
面部脓皮病/面部膿皮病　pyoderma faciale
面部皮肤病/面部皮膚病　facial dermatosis
面部皮肤韧带/面部皮膚韌帶　facial cutaneous ligament
面部平面/面部平面　facial plane
面部肉芽肿/面部肉芽腫　granuloma faciei
面部三等分比例/面部三等分比例　facial three equal division ratio
面部烧伤/面部燒傷　burn of face
面部神经痛/面部神經痛　prosoponeuralgia
面部湿疹/顏面濕疹　eczema faciei
面部损伤/面部損傷　facial injury
面部疼痛/面部疼痛　facial pain
面部条纹矫正/面部條紋矯正　facial line correction
面部知觉/面部知覺　facial perception
面部中央的/面部中央的　centrofacial
面部肿瘤/面部腫瘤　facial neoplasm
面成形术/面造形術,面整形術　facioplasty
面动脉/[顏]面動脈　facial artery
面动脉腺支/面動脈腺支　glandular branch of facial artery
面-耳-脊椎的/顏-耳-脊椎的　facioauriculovertebral
面-耳-脊椎发育异常综合征/顏-耳-脊椎發育異常症候群　facial-auriculovertebral dysplasia syndrome
面粉/麵粉　flour
面粉谷胶测定器/穀粉測量計　farinometer
面粉螨虫/麵粉螨蟲　Tyroglyphus farinae
面风/面風　facial wind disease
面高/面高　face height
面弓/面弓　face bow
面弓记录/面弓記錄　face-bow record
面垢/面垢　dirty face
面骨/面部骨,顏面骨　facial bone, ossa faciei
面横动脉/面橫動脈　transverse facial artery
面横静脉/面橫靜脈　facial transverse vein, transverse facial vein
面横裂/橫裂面[畸形]　transverse facial cleft, horizontal facial cleft
面后静脉/面後靜脈　posterior facial vein
面肌/面肌　facial muscle
面肌抽搐/面肌抽搐　convulsive tic
面肌抽搐射频热凝固术/面肌抽搐射頻熱凝術　radiofrequency thermocoagulation for facial tic
面肌痉挛/面肌痙攣　prosopospasm
面基的/面根的　basifacial
面基轴/面根軸　basifacial axis
面颊/面頰　cheek
面肩臂萎缩/面肩臂萎縮　facioscapulohumeral atrophy
面肩肱型肌营养不良/面肩肱型肌營養不良　facioscapulohumeral muscular dystrophy
面肩肱型营养不良/臉肩胛肱骨失養症　facioscapulohumeral dystrophy
面颈部毛囊性红斑黑变病/面頸部毛囊性紅斑黑變病　erythromelanosis follicularis of face and neck
面颈除皱术/面頸除皺術　faciocervical rhytidectomy
面痉挛/面痙攣　facial spasm
面静脉/面靜脈　facial vein
面裂/裂面[畸胎]　facial cleft
面裂畸胎/面裂畸胎　schistoprosopus
面裂囊肿/面裂囊腫　facial cleft cyst
面淋巴结/面淋巴結　facial lymph node
面颅/面顱　facial cranium
面颅骨/面顱骨　bone of facial cranium
面膜/面膜　face pack
面平衡/面平衡　face balance
面前静脉/面前靜脈　anterior facial vein
面容/面容　face
面容憔悴/面容憔悴　scythropasmus
面容失认症/面部認識不能　prosopagnosia
面容诊断法/面容診病法,觀貌診斷法　physiognosis
面三角/面三角　facial triangle
面色/面色　complexion
面色白/面色白　pale complexion

面色苍白/面色蒼白　pale complexion
面色淡白/面色淡白　pale white complexion
面色红/面色紅　red complexion
面色晄白/面色晄白　pallid complexion
面色晦暗/面色晦暗　dim complexion
面色黧黑/面色黧黑　darkish complexion
面色青/面色青　greenish complexion
面色萎黄/面色萎黄　sallow complexion
面纱细胞/面紗細胞　veiled cell
面上部慢性红斑性水肿/上顏面慢性紅斑性水腫　chronic erythematous edema of the upper face
面深静脉/面深靜脈　deep facial vein
面神经/面神經　facial nerve, nervus facialis
面神经丛/顏面神經叢　facial plexus
面神经根/面神經根　facial root
面神经管/面神經管　canal for facial nerve, facial canal
面神经管凸/面神經管凸　prominence of facial canal
面神经管膝/面神經管膝　geniculum of facial canal
面神经核/面神經核　nucleus of facial nerve
面神经疾病/面神經疾病　facial nerve disease
面神经减压术/面神經減壓術　facial nerve decompression
面神经交通支/面神經交通支　communicating branch with facial nerve
面神经麻痹/面神經麻痺　facial paralysis
面[神经]麻木/面神經性感覺缺失　facial anesthesia
面[神经]丘/面[神經]丘　facial colliculus
面神经区/面神經區　area of facial nerve
面神经舌咽神经交通支/面神經舌咽神經交通支　communicating branch of facial nerve with glossopharyngeal nerve
面神经舌支/面神經舌支　lingual branch of facial nerve
面神经损伤/面神經損傷　facial nerve injury
面神经痛/面神經痛　facial neuralgia
面神经吻合术/面神經吻合術　facial nerve anastomosis
面神经膝/面神經膝　genu of facial nerve, geniculum of facial nerve
面神经中间神经/面神經中間神經　intermedial nerve of facial nerve
面生长型/面生長型　face growth pattern
面瘫/面癱　facial palsy
面头痛/顏面頭痛　faciocephalalgia
面团感/麵團感　doughy sensation
面萎缩/[進行性]顏面萎縮　facial atrophy
面先露/面產式　face presentation
面斜裂/斜裂面[畸形],臉斜裂　oblique facial cleft
面形/面形　face form
面形测定器/面形測定器　profilometer
面形美/面形美　beauty of face form
面型/面型　face type
面胸骨联胎畸形/面胸骨連胎畸形　prosoposternodymia
面胸联胎/面胸連胎　prosopothoracopagus
面癣/顏面癬　tinea faciei
面游风/面游風,[皮]脂溢性皮炎　facial wandering wind, facial seborrheic dermatitis, seborrheic dermatitis
面游风·风热血燥证/面游風·風熱血燥證　facial wandering wind with pattern of wind-heat and blood dryness
面游风·脾胃湿热证/面游風·脾胃濕熱證　facial wandering wind with pattern of dampness-heat in stomach and spleen
面罩/面罩　face mask
面罩给氧/面罩給氧　mask oxygen inhalation
面罩活瓣呼吸装置/面罩活瓣呼吸裝置　bag valve mask respiration unit
面征/面徵象　facial sign
面正中裂/面正中裂　median facial cleft
面直径测量器/臉徑測定計　faceometer
面、指、生殖器发育不良/面、指、生殖器發育不全　faciodigitogenital dysplasia
面中部/中顏面　midface
面中部发育不良/面中部發育不良　midfacial hypoplasia
面中部发育不足/中顏面不足,中臉部發育不足　midface deficiency
面中部发育过度/中顏面發育過剩　midface excess
面中部骨折/中顏面骨折　midfacial fracture
面中部畸形/中顏面畸形　midface deformity
面中部前突/中顏面前突　midface protrusion
面中部色素性红斑/顏面中部色素性紅變症　erythrosis pigmentosa mediofacialis
面中线/面中線　facial midline
面总静脉/面總靜脈　common facial vein
描记装置/描記裝置　tracing device
描界器/測外形器　diagraph
描述胚胎学/描述胚胎學　descriptive embryology
描述性精神病学/檢證精神病學　descriptive psychiatry
眇目/眇目　monocular blindness and mono microphthalmia
缪希雍/繆希雍　Miao Xiyong

灭癌[细胞]的/滅癌的　cancericidal
灭活脊髓灰质炎病毒疫苗/滅活脊髓灰質炎病毒疫苗　inactivated poliovirus vaccine
灭活血清/滅能血清,失活性血清　inactivated serum
灭活眼镜蛇毒/滅活眼鏡蛇毒　anacobra
灭活疫苗/滅活疫苗,去活性疫苗　inactivated vaccine
灭火系统/滅火系統　fire extinguishing system
灭菌/滅菌　sterilization
灭菌混悬剂/無菌懸液劑　sterile suspension
灭[昆]虫法/昆蟲撲滅法　disinsection
灭卵药/滅卵藥　ovicide
灭虱剂/殺蝨劑　lousicide
灭虱器/除蝨器　delouser
灭虱药/滅蝨藥　pediculicide
灭鼠剂/殺鼠劑　rodenticide
灭蚁灵/滅蟻靈　mirex
灭蚴药/滅蚴藥　lenticide
灭蚤药/殺蚤藥,殺蚤物　pulicicide
灭藻剂/滅藻劑　algicide
民间医药/民間醫藥　folk medicine
敏感菌/敏感菌　sensitive organism
敏感性/敏感性　sensitivity
敏感性皮肤/敏感性皮膚　sensitive skin
敏感性训练组/敏感性訓練組　sensitivity training group
敏锐/銳敏　acuity
名花风/名花風　anthomaniac
名医别录/名醫別録　Mingyi Bielu
名医类案/名醫類案　Classified Case Records of Famous Physicians, Classified Case Records of Celebrated Physicians
明板/I板　isotropic disk
明党参/明黨參　medicinal changium root
明煅/明煅　calcining openly
明矾/[明]礬　alum
明矾[沉淀]类毒素/明礬類毒素　alum toxoid
明矾化合物/明礬化合物　alum compound
明矾乳/明礬乳　alum curd
明胶/明膠　gelatin
明胶海绵/明膠海綿,止血膠棉　gelatin sponge, gelfoam
明胶基质植入物/明膠基質植入物　gelatin matrix implant
明胶酶类/明膠酶類　gelatinases
明胶性腹水/明膠性腹水　gelatinous ascites
明胶注射液/明膠注射劑　gelatin injection
明科夫斯基-肖法尔综合征/Minkowski-Chauffard 二氏症候群　Minkowski-Chauffard syndrome
明亮细胞丘疹病/明亮細胞丘疹病　clear cell papulosis
明目/明目　improving eyesight
明目地黄丸/明目地黄丸　mingmu dihuang pills
明目上清丸/明目上清丸　mingmu shangqing pill
明视觉/明光視力　photopic vision
明视视网膜电图/明視視網膜電圖　photopic electroretinogram
明适应/明適應　light adaptation
明堂/明堂　①acupoint chart ②nose
明堂图/明堂圖　acupuncture and moxibustion chart
明希豪森综合征/Münchhausen 氏症候群　Münchhausen syndrome
鸣天鼓/鳴天鼓　occipital-knocking therapy
命关/命關　life pass
命令/命令　imperative
命门/命門　①vital gate ②mingmen, DU4
命门火衰/命門火衰　decline of vital gate fire
命门火衰证/命門火衰證　pattern of decline of vital gate fire
命门之火/命門之火　vital gate fire
命名性失语[症]/難名性失語症　nominal aphasia
命名障碍/舉名不能　anomia
模仿表情/模仿性表情,模仿性擬態　echomimia
模仿病/模仿病,擬病,伴病　neuromimesis, pathomimesis
模仿病态/模仿病態　echopathy
模仿的/表情的　mimetic
模仿动作/模仿動作,模仿運用　echopraxia
模仿过分/模仿過甚　macromimia
模仿书写/模仿書寫　echographia
模仿行为/模仿行爲　imitative behavior
模仿性联带运动/模仿性聯帶運動　imitative synkinesia
模仿言语/模仿言語　echo speech
模糊/模糊　haziness
模拟计算机/類比電腦　analog computer
模拟数字转换/類比數位轉換　analog-digital conversion
模式/模式　pattern
模式识别/模式識別　pattern recognition
模式种/典型種　type species
模型材料/模型材料　modeling material
模型分析/模型分析　model analysis
模型化与参数估计/模型化與參數估計　modeling and parameter estimation
模型解剖学/造形解剖學　plastic anatomy

模型修整机/模型修整器　model trimmer
模型眼/模型眼　schematic eye
模型振荡器/模型振盪器　model vibrator
模制片/模製錠[劑]　molded tablet
膜/膜　membrane
Z膜/Z膜　Z membrane
膜板/膜板　membranous lamina
膜半规管/膜質半規管　membranous semicircular duct, membranous semicircular canal
[膜半规管]固有膜/[膜半規管]固有膜　proper membrane of semicircular duct
膜被颗粒/膜被顆粒,角質小體　membrane-coating granule
膜壁/膜壁　membranous wall
膜部/膜部　membranous part
膜部尿道/膜性尿道　membranous urethra
膜部胚盘/外位胚層　extraembryonic blastoderm
膜部室间隔缺损/膜部室間隔缺損　membranous ventricular septal defect
膜翅目/膜翅類　Hymenoptera
膜翅[目]昆虫/膜翅[目]昆蟲　hymenopteran
膜蛋白/膜蛋白　membranin
膜蛋白质类/膜蛋白質類　membrane proteins
膜电位/膜電位　membrane potential
膜毒理学/膜毒理學　membrane toxicology
膜法/膜法　film method
膜过滤/膜過濾　membrane filtration
膜壶腹/膜壺腹　membranous ampullae
膜黄体细胞/濾泡膜黃體細胞　theca lutein cell
Z膜基质/Z膜基質　Z membrane matrix
膜间部/膜間部　intermembranous part
膜脚/膜腳　membranous crura
膜抗体/膜抗體　membrane antibody
膜抗原/膜抗原　membrane antigen
膜抗原受体/膜抗原受體　membrane antigen receptor
膜壳绦虫病/包膜蟲病　hymenolepiasis
膜孔电析/膜孔電析　electrostenolysis
膜流动性/膜流動性　membrane fluidity
膜颅/膜顱　desmocranium
膜滤器/膜濾器　membrane filter
膜螺旋板/膜螺旋板　membranous spiral lamina
膜迷路/膜迷路　membranous labyrinth
膜免疫荧光技术/膜免疫螢光技術　membrane immunofluorescence technique
膜内成骨/膜內骨化　intramembranous ossification
膜盘/膜盤　membranous disc
膜泡运输蛋白质类/膜泡運輸蛋白質類　vesicular transport proteins
膜泡运输衔接蛋白质类/膜泡運輸銜接蛋白質類　vesicular transport adaptor proteins
膜膨胀学说/膜膨脹學說　membrane expansion theory
膜片尿/膜片尿[症]　meninguria
膜片钳术/膜片鉗術　patch-clamp technique
膜切除术/膜切除術　membranectomy
膜融合/膜融合　membrane fusion
膜式氧合器/膜式氧合器　membrane oxygenator
膜糖蛋白类/膜糖蛋白類　membrane glycoproteins
膜通透性/膜通透性　membrane permeability
膜微区/膜微區　membrane microdomain
膜细胞淋巴瘤/膜細胞淋巴瘤　mantle-cell lymphoma
膜性白内障/膜性白內障　membranous cataract
膜性半规管/膜性半規管　membranous semicircular canal
膜性鼻炎/膜性鼻炎　membranous rhinitis
膜性闭锁肛/膜性閉鎖肛　membranous atresia of anus
膜性的/膜性的　membranaceous
膜性骨/膜性骨　membrane bone
膜性喉炎/膜性喉炎　membranous laryngitis
膜性结肠炎/膜性結腸炎　membranous colitis
膜性结肠周炎/膜性結腸周圍炎　membranous pericolitis
膜性尿道括约肌/膜狀尿道括約肌　sphincter muscle of membranous urethra
膜性肾病/膜性腎病　membranous nephropathy
膜性肾小球肾炎/膜性腎絲球腎炎　membranous glomerulonephritis
膜性室间隔缺损/膜性室間隔缺陷　membranous septal defect
膜性脱屑/膜性脱屑　membranous desquamation
膜性胃炎/膜性胃炎　membranaceous gastritis
膜性咽峡炎/假膜性咽喉炎,膜性喉炎　angina membranacea
膜性[样]月经/膜性月經　membranous menstruation
膜性子宫内膜炎/膜性子宮内膜炎　membranous endometritis
膜学/膜學　hymenology
膜样痛经/膜剝落性痛經　membranous dysmenorrhea
膜原/膜原　interpleuro-diaphragmatic space
膜增生性肾小球肾炎/膜增生性腎小球腎炎　membranoproliferative glomerulonephritis
膜脂质类/膜脂質類　membrane lipids

膜转运蛋白质类/膜轉運蛋白質類　membrane transport proteins
膜状的/膜的　membranous
膜状胎盘/膜狀胎盤　placenta membranacea
膜状脂肪营养不良/膜性脂肪營養不良　membranous lipodystrophy
摩擦/摩擦　rubbing
摩擦[发]光/摩擦光　triboluminescence
摩擦癖/摩擦色情,摩擦欲　frotteurism
摩擦性震颤/摩擦震顫　friction fremitus
摩擦音/摩擦音　friction rub
摩擦淫者/摩擦欲者　frotteur
摩擦杂音/摩擦雜音　attrition murmur
摩动关节/摩動關節,滑動關節　arthrodia
摩动诊法/觸摸診法　psauoscopy
摩尔混液/克分子溶液,容積克分子溶液　molar solution
摩尔[量]/摩爾　mole
摩尔溶液/重量克分子溶液　molal solution
摩法/摩法　rubbing manipulation
摩[根]/摩根　Morgan
磨刀工病/磨刀工病　knife-grinder disease
磨光面/磨光面　polished surface
磨光器/磨光器　burnisher
磨光条/磨帶　polishing strip
磨光用橡皮杯/磨光用橡皮杯　polishing rubber cup
磨光钻/磨光鑽　finishing bur
磨耗/耗損,消磨　detrition
磨耗小平面/磨耗小平面　facet in dental wear
磨碎/磨碎　confrication
磨铁工病/磨鐵工病　steel-grinder disease
磨牙/磨牙,[大]白齒　molar, mylodus, grinding of teeth
磨牙半切术/磨牙半切術　hemisection of molar
磨牙后三角/磨牙後三角　retromolar triangle
磨牙后腺/磨牙後腺　retromolar gland
磨牙旁额外牙/副白齒,旁白齒　paramolar
磨牙癖/神經質性磨牙癖　bruxomania
磨牙声/磨牙聲　dentium stridor
磨牙腺/磨牙腺,白齒腺　molar gland
磨牙形的/大白齒狀　molariform
磨牙症/磨牙癖　bruxism
蘑菇肺/蘑菇肺　mushroom worker disease
末次月经/末次月經　last menstrual period
末端重复序列/末端重複序列　terminal repeat sequence
末端的/終端的,末期的　terminal
末端分析/末端分析　terminal analysis, end-group analysis
末端铰链位/末端鉸鏈位　terminal hinge position
末端切断钳/末端切斷鉗　distal cutter
末端吸收/末端吸收　end absorption
末端与末端/末端與末端　end-to-end
末端扎法/終端結扎　terminal ligature
末端种植体/末端種植體　terminal implant
末端转移酶端粒/末端轉移酶端粒　telomerase
末段/終端,末節　end-piece
末节指骨/第三指節骨　phalangette
末节指骨下垂/第三指節下垂　drop phalangette
末节趾骨/第三趾節骨　phalangette
末节趾骨下垂/第三趾節下垂　drop phalangette
末脑/末腦　myelencephalon
末期/末期　telophase
末期感染/末期感染　terminal infection
末期核变/子核再生　katachromasis
末期水肿/末期水腫　terminal edema
末期心包炎/末期心包炎　terminal pericarditis
末期心内膜炎/末期心内膜炎　terminal endocarditis
末梢刺激/末梢刺激　peripheral stimulation
末梢感觉缺失/末端感覺缺失　terminal anesthesia
末梢神经/末梢神經　peripheral nerve
末梢神经鞘瘤/周邊神經鞘瘤　peripheral nerve sheath tumor
末梢性循环衰竭/末梢性循環衰竭　peripheral circulatory failure
末梢血管疾病/末梢血管疾病　peripheral vascular disorder
末梢循环/末稍循環　peripheral circulation
没食子/没食子　Aleppo gall
没食子苯乙酮/没食子苯乙酮　gallacetophenone
没食子单宁/没食子鞣質　gallotannin
没食子鞣酸/没食子鞣酸　gallotannic acid
没食子酸/没食子酸　gallic acid
没食子酸丙酯/丙基没食子醯鹽　propyl gallate
没药/没藥　myrrh
没药醇/没藥醇　bisabolol
莫顿咳嗽/Morton氏欬嗽　Morton cough
莫顿神经瘤/Morton氏神經瘤　Morton neuroma
莫顿神经痛/Morton氏神經痛　Morton neuralgia
莫顿液/Morton氏液　Morton fluid
莫顿趾/Morton氏趾　Morton toe
莫顿综合征/Morton氏症候群　Morton syndrome
莫顿足/Morton氏足　Morton foot
莫尔基奥综合征/Morquio氏症候群　Morquio syndrome
莫尔加尼-斯图尔特-莫里尔综合征/Morgagni-

Stewart-Morel 三氏症候群　Morgagni-Stewart-Morel syndrome
莫尔加尼脱垂/Morgagni 氏脱出　Morgagni prolapse
莫尔万综合征/Morvan 氏症候群　Morvan syndrome
莫尔腺/Moll 氏腺體　gland of Moll, Moll gland
莫尔综合征/Mohr 氏症候群　Mohr syndrome
莫菲姆/莫菲姆　morpheme
莫呱达醇/莫呱達醇　Mopidamol
莫-海饮食/Moro-Heisler 二氏飲食　Moro-Heisler diet
莫基奥综合征/莫基奥症候群　Morquio syndrome
莫拉菌科感染/莫拉菌科感染　Moraxellaceae infection
莫拉雷脑[脊]膜炎/Mollaret 氏腦膜炎　Mollaret meningitis
莫朗足/Morand 氏足　Morand foot
莫雷尔耳/Morel 氏耳　Morel ear
莫雷尔综合征/Morel 氏症候群　Morel syndrome
莫雷西嗪/莫雷西嗪　Moricizine
莫里茨反应/莫里茲反應　Moritz reaction
莫利希试验/莫里斯試驗　Molisch test
莫仑太尔/莫侖太爾　Morantel
莫罗反射/莫羅反射　Moro reflex
莫罗紧抱反射/擁抱反射　Moro embrace reflex
莫洛尼实验/莫洛尼氏試驗　Moloney test
莫洛试验/Moro 氏試驗　Moro test
臭纳科夫综合征/Monakow 氏症候群　Monakow syndrome
莫能菌素/莫能星　Monensin
莫匹罗星/莫匹羅星　Mupirocin
莫塞尔细胞/Mooser 氏細胞　Mooser cell
莫氏板/莫氏板　Moe plate
莫斯综合征/Mosse 氏症候群　Mosse syndrome
莫泰手术/莫泰手術　Motais operation
莫提默病/Mortimer 氏病　Mortimer disease
莫西赛利/莫西賽利　Moxisylyte
莫泽尔病/Mozer 氏病　Mozer disease
莫唑胺/莫唑胺　Muzolimine
墨菲钮/穆菲鈕　Murphy button
墨菲征/墨菲徵　Murphy sign
墨旱莲/墨旱蓮　yerbadetajo herb
墨迹测验/墨跡測驗　ink blot test
墨累山谷脑炎/莫瑞山谷腦炎　Murray Valley encephalitis
墨累山谷脑炎病毒/莫瑞山谷腦炎病毒　Murray Valley Encephalitis Virus
墨西哥薯蓣/墨西哥薯蕷　Dioscorea mexicana
默基森-佩尔-埃布斯坦热/穆-佩-埃三氏熱　Murchison-Pel-Ebstein fever
默克尔细胞/默克爾細胞　Merkel cell
默勒-巴洛病/莫-巴二氏病　Moeller-Barlow disease
默勒舌炎/默勒舌炎　Moeller glossitis
默塞堡三征/墨塞堡三徵　Merseburg triad
默-桑综合征/Murchison-Sanderson 二氏症候群　Murchison-Sanderson syndrome
磨坊工气喘/磨坊工人氣喘　millers asthma
磨片/磨片　ground section
貘状口/貘嘴　tapir mouth
模板/模板,樣本　template
模具/模具　die
模具持续压迫阴道形成术/模具持續壓迫陰道形成術　construction of vagina by continuous pressure with stent
母病及子/母病及子　illness of mother viscera affecting the child
母瘤/母瘤　parent tumor
母囊/母囊腫　mother cyst
母气/母氣　mother qi
母亲/母親　mother
母亲暴露/母親暴露　maternal exposure
母亲福利/母親福利　maternal welfare
母亲年龄/母親年齡　maternal age
母亲年龄效应/母親年齡效應　maternal age effect
母亲胎儿关系/母親胎兒關係　maternal-fetal relation
母亲行为/母親行爲　maternal behavior
母乳喂养/母乳餵養,人乳哺養　breast feeding
母乳性黄疸/母乳性黃疸　breast milk jaundice
母体苯丙酮尿症/母體苯丙酮尿症　maternal phenylketonuria
母体化合物/母體化合物　parent compound
母体获得性免疫/母體獲得性免疫　maternally-acquired immunity
母体面娩出式/母體面娩出式　Duncan mechanism
母体胎儿间交换/母體胎兒間交換　maternal-fetal exchange
母系遗传/母系遺傳　maternal inheritance
母细胞/母細胞　mother cell
母性本能/母性本能　mother instinct
母性表型/母[性表]型,偏母表現型　matromorph
母血疗法/母血注射療法　maternohemotherapy
母羊产乳热/母羊產乳熱　lambing sickness
母液/母液　mother liquor
母婴护理/母嬰護理　maternal-child nursing
母婴同室/母嬰同室　rooming-in care
母疣/母疣　mother wart

母子关系/母子關係　mother-child relation
牡丹皮/牡丹皮　tree peony root bark
牡荆叶/牡荊葉　hempleaf negundo chastetree leaf
牡蛎散/牡蠣散　oyster powder
牡蛎甾醇/蠣[硬]脂醇　ostreasterol
牡蛎状卵巢/蠣狀卵巢　oyster ovary
牡牛颈/牡牛頸　bull neck
拇长屈肌/屈拇長肌　flexor pollicis longus
拇长屈肌腱鞘/屈拇長肌腱鞘　tendinous sheath of flexor pollicis longus
拇长伸肌/伸拇[指]長肌　long extensor muscle of thumb
拇长伸肌腱鞘/伸拇長肌腱鞘　tendinous sheath of extensor pollicis longus
拇长展肌/外展拇[指]長肌　long abductor muscle of thumb
拇长展肌和拇短伸肌腱鞘/外展拇長肌及伸拇短肌腱鞘　tendinous sheath of abductor longus and extensor brevis pollicis
拇短屈肌/屈拇短肌　musculus flexor pollicis brevis
拇短屈肌浅头/拇短屈肌淺頭　superficial head of flexor pollicis brevis
拇短屈肌深头/拇短屈肌深頭　deep head of flexor pollicis brevis
拇短伸肌/伸拇[指]短肌　musculus extensor pollicis brevis
拇短展肌/外展拇短肌　abductor pollicis brevis
拇收肌/内收拇肌　adductor pollicis
拇收肌横头/拇收肌横頭　transverse head of adductor pollicis
拇收肌后间隙/拇收肌後間隙　posterior space of abductor pollicis
拇收肌筋膜/拇收肌筋膜　fascia of abductor pollicis
拇收肌鞘/拇收肌鞘　compartment of abductor pollicis
拇收肌斜头/拇收肌斜頭　oblique head of adductor pollicis
拇外翻/拇外翻　pollex valgus
拇指/拇指　thumb
拇指对掌/拇指對掌　palmar opposition of thumb
拇[指]对掌肌/拇指對掌肌　musculus opponens pollicis
拇指对指/拇指對指　digital opposition of thumb
拇指功能重建术/拇指功能重建術　functional reconstruction of thumb
拇指化[术]/拇指重置術　pollicization
拇指内收/拇指内收　adduction of thumb
拇指内收畸形/拇指内收畸形　adduction deformity of thumb
拇指桡侧外展/拇指橈側外展　radial abduction of thumb
拇指同身寸/拇指同身寸　proportional unit of thumb, thumb cun
拇指腕掌关节/拇指腕掌關節　carpometacarpal joint of thumb
拇指再造术/拇指再造術　reconstruction of thumb
拇指掌侧外展/拇指掌側外展　palmar abduction of thumb
拇主要动脉/拇主要動脈　principal artery of thumb
姆崩毒/姆崩毒　mbundu
𧿹背外侧神经/𧿹背外側神經　dorsal lateral nerve of great toe
𧿹长屈肌/屈[𧿹]長肌　flexor hallucis longus
𧿹长屈肌腱沟/𧿹長屈肌腱溝　sulcus for tendon of flexor hallucis longus
𧿹长伸肌/伸𧿹長肌　extensor hallucis longus
𧿹短屈肌/屈𧿹肌　flexor hallucis brevis
𧿹囊肿/𧿹囊腫　parent cyst
𧿹外翻/𧿹外翻　hallux valgus
𧿹展肌/𧿹展肌，外展𧿹肌　abductor hallucis, abductor muscle of great toe
𧿹趾/𧿹趾　great toe, hallux
𧿹[趾]短屈肌/屈[𧿹趾]短肌　musculus flexor hallucis brevis, short flexor muscle of great toe
𧿹[趾]短伸肌/伸𧿹[趾]短肌　musculus extensor hallucis brevis
𧿹趾滑[膜]囊炎/𧿹趾滑[膜]囊炎　synovitis of great toe, bunion
𧿹[趾]伸肌/伸𧿹[趾]肌　long extensor muscle of great toe
𧿹[趾]长屈肌/屈𧿹[趾]長肌　long flexor muscle of great toe
𧿹[趾]长伸肌/伸𧿹[趾]長肌　musculus extensor hallucis longus
𧿹趾外翻/𧿹趾外翻　hallux valgus
木板样的/木板樣的　boardlike
木薄壁细胞/木薄壁細胞　xylem parenchyma
木鳖子/木鱉子　cochinchina momordica seed
木村网状肢端色素沉着/木村網狀肢端色素沈著　reticular acropigmentation of Kitamura
木酚素类/木酚素類　lignans
木工疗法/木工療法　carpentry therapy
木瓜蛋白酶/木瓜蛋白酶素　papain
木瓜凝乳蛋白酶/木瓜凝乳蛋白酶　chymopapain
木瓜丸/木瓜丸　mugua pills
木蝴蝶/木蝴蝶　Indian trumpetflower seed

木夹板/木夾板　wood splint
木间韧皮部/木間韌皮部　interxylary phloem
木僵/木僵　stupor
木僵性忧郁症/木僵性憂鬱病　stuporous melancholia
木僵状凝固反应/木僵狀凝固反應　cataleptic freezing reaction
木僵状态/木僵狀態　stuporous state
木槿花萃取液/木槿花萃取液　althea extract
木聚糖类/木聚糖類　xylans
木克土/木克土　wood restricting earth
木兰属/木蘭屬　Magnolia
木霉菌素/木黴素　trichodermin
木乃伊样裹身/木乃伊式拘束法　mummying
木偶式感觉缺失/木偶式感覺缺失　doll head anesthesia
木舌/木舌　rigid swollen tongue, wooden tongue
木射线/木射線　xylem ray
木生火/木火刑金　wood generating fire
木薯淀粉/木薯澱粉　tapioca
木栓/木栓　cork, phellem
木栓石细胞/木栓石細胞　cork stone cell
木栓素/木栓素　suberin
木栓烷/木栓烷　friedelane
木髓火棉/木纖維膠　photoxylin
木糖/木糖　xylose
木糖醇/木糖醇　xylitol
木糖醇脱氢酶缺乏症/木糖醇脱氫酶缺乏症　xylitol dehydrogenase deficiency
木糖苷/木糖苷　xyloside
木糖苷酶类/木糖苷酶類　xylosidases
木糖尿/木[膠]糖尿　xylosuria
木糖酸/木質酸　xylonic acid
木通/木通　akebia stem
木酮糖/木酮醣　xylulose
木酮糖尿/木酮醣尿　xyloketosuria
木犀草/木犀草　reseda
木犀草素/木犀草素　luteolin
木纤维/木纖維　wood fiber
木香/木香　common aucklandia root
木香槟榔丸/木香檳榔丸　muxiang binlang pill
木香顺气丸/木香順氣丸　muxiang shunqi pill
木鞋状心/木鞋狀心　sabot heart
木形人/木形人　wood-phase person
木性叩响/木性叩響　wooden percussion resonance
木样蜂窝组织炎/木樣蜂窩組織炎　ligneous phlegmon
木异物肉芽肿/木異物肉芽腫　wood foreign body granuloma
木郁达之/木鬱達之　promoting flow of liver qi when it is stagnated
木郁化风/木鬱化風　stagnated liver qi transforming into wind
木郁化火/木鬱化火　stagnated liver qi transforming into fire
木曰曲直/木曰曲直　wood characterized by bending and straightening
木贼/木賊　common scouring rush herb
木脂内酯/木脂内酯　lignanolide
木脂体/木脂體　lignan
木纸浆/木漿　wood pulp
木质部/木質部　xylem
木[质]疗法/按木療法，木質療法　xylotherapy
木质瘤/木瘤，樹瘦　xyloma
木质素/木素　lignin
木状的/木狀的　ligneous
目/目，眼　eye
目闭不开/目閉不開　inability to open eye
目标射线/定向光線　direction ray
目标因子分析/目標因子分析　target factor analysis
目不瞑/目不瞑　inability to close eye
目眵/目眵　epiphora
目赤/目赤　conjunctival hyperemia, red eye
目赤如鸠眼/目赤如鳩眼　Behcet's disease, red eye as turtle-dove
目窗/目窗　muchuang, GB16
目昏/目昏　blurred vision, cloudy vision
目镜测微尺/目鏡測微尺，目鏡顯微量尺　ocular micrometer
目窠/眼眶，眼窝　eye socket
目盲/目盲　blindness
目内眦/[目]内眥　inner canthus
目偏视/目偏視　squint, strabismus
目偏视·风痰阻络证/目偏視·風痰阻絡證　squint with pattern of wind-phlegm obstructing collateral
目偏视·风邪中络证/目偏視·風邪中絡證　squint with pattern of wind striking collateral
目偏视·脾气虚证/目偏視·脾氣虛證　squint with spleen qi deficiency pattern
目偏视·气滞血瘀证/目偏視·氣滯血瘀證　squint with pattern of qi stagnation and blood stasis
目涩/目澀　dry and uncomfortable eye, dry eye
目痛/目痛　eye pain, pain of eye
目外眦/目外眥，目銳眥　outer canthus
目妄见/目妄見　heteroptics, vision trouble
目系/目系　eye connector

目下陷/目下陷　collapsed eye, sunken eye
目眩/眩暈,頭風　dizziness
目痒[病]/目癢　eye itching, itching of eye
目蝇/目蠅　eye fly
目晕/目暈　arcus senilis, halo vision
目劄/目劄　frequent blinking, frequent nictitation
目劄·肺阴虚证/目劄·肺陰虛證　frequent blinking with lung yin deficiency pattern
目劄·脾虚肝旺证/目劄·脾虛肝旺證　frequent blinking with pattern of spleen deficiency and liver hyperactivity
目珠管/目珠管　follicle on white of the eye
沐浴疗法/沐浴療法　loutrotherapy
沐浴油/沐浴油　bath oil
苜蓿花叶病毒/苜蓿花葉病病毒　Alfalfa mosaic virus
牧师心理治疗/牧師心理治療　pastoral care
钼酸/鉬酸　molybdic acid
钼酸铵-浓硫酸试液/鉬酸銨-濃硫酸試液　Frohde test solution
钼酸盐/鉬酸鹽　molybdate
募穴/募穴　front-mu point
幕面/幕面　tentorial surface
幕切迹/幕切跡　tentorial incisure

幕上入路/幕上入路　supratentorial approach
幕上肿瘤/幕上腫瘤　supratentorial neoplasm
幕下肿瘤/幕下腫瘤　infratentorial neoplasm
慕男狂/慕男狂,女子淫狂　nymphomania
慕男狂者/女子淫狂者,女子淫狂的　nymphomaniac
暮食朝吐/暮食朝吐　vomit in the morning what eaten last night
穆尔骨折/Moore 氏骨折　Moore fracture
穆尔黑德[金属]异物探索器/穆赫德氏金屬異物探索器　Moorhead foreign body locator
穆尔加尼白内障/莫爾加尼白內障　Morgagni cataract
穆尔培养液/Moore 氏溶液　Moore solution
穆尔斯洁治器/莫爾斯潔治器　Morse scaler
穆尔综合征/Moore 氏症候群　Moore syndrome
穆哈-哈伯曼病/Mucha-Habermann 二氏病　Mucha-Habermann disease
穆赫-霍尔兹曼反应/穆-霍二氏反應　Much-Holzmann reaction
穆瑞-威廉斯疣/穆瑞-威廉斯疣　Murray Williams wart
穆斯堡尔谱学/穆斯堡爾譜學　Mossbauer spectroscopy

N

拿法/拿法　grasping manipulation
那法瑞林/那法瑞林　nafarelin
那可丁/那可汀　noscapine
纳博特囊肿/Naboth 氏囊腫,子宮頸腺囊腫　Naboth cyst
纳布啡/納布啡　nalbuphine
纳呆/厭食症　anorexia
纳单位/纖單位,毫微單位　nanounit
纳多洛尔/納多洛爾　Nadolol
纳尔逊综合征/奈爾森氏症候群　nelson syndrome
纳夫齐格综合征/Naffziger 氏症候群　Naffziger syndrome
纳格勒效应/納爾森氏效應　Nagler effect
纳谷不香/納谷不香　poor appetite
纳归虫病/内格里阿米巴原蟲感染　naegleriasis
纳甲法/納甲法　heavenly stem-prescription of point selection
纳洛酮/丙烯基二氫羥嗎啡酮　naloxone
纳米管/納米管　nanotube
纳米技术/納米技術　nanotechnology
纳米结构/納米結構　nanostructure
纳米粒/毫微粒,奈米粒　nanoparticle
纳帕因/納帕因　naepaine
纳屈肝素/納屈肝素　nadroparin
纳曲酮/納曲酮　naltrexone
纳热奥特根神经/Nageotte 氏根神經　Nageotte radicular nerve
纳热奥特细胞/Nageotte 氏細胞　Nageotte cell
纳他霉素/納他黴素　natamycin
纳子法/納子法　earthly branch-prescription of point selection
钠/鈉　sodium
钠放射性同位素/鈉放射性同位素　sodium radioisotope
钠负荷试验/鈉負荷試驗　sodium loading test
钠钙交换蛋白/鈉鈣交換蛋白　sodium-calcium exchanger
钠过多性水肿/鹽性水腫　salt edema
钠化合物/鈉化合物　sodium compound
钠钾氯化物协同转运子/鈉鉀氯化物協同轉運子　sodium-potassium-chloride symporter
钠钾腺苷三磷酸酶/鈉鉀腺苷三磷酸酶　sodium-potassium-ATPase
钠酪蛋白/鈉酪蛋白　nutrose
钠尿排泄/鈉尿排洩　natriuresis
钠排泄分数/鈉排洩分數　fractional excretion of sodium
钠氢反向转运物/鈉氫反向轉運物　sodium-hydrogen antiporter
钠缺乏症/鈉缺乏　sodium deficiency
钠通道/鈉通道　sodium channel
钠通道阻滞剂/鈉通道阻滯劑　sodium channel blocker
钠同位素/鈉同位素　sodium isotope
钠消耗/鈉消耗　sodium waste
钠血[症]/鈉血症　natremia
钠依赖有机阴离子转运子/鈉依賴有機陰離子轉運子　sodium-dependent organic anion transporter
钠重碳酸盐协同转运子/鈉重碳酸鹽協同轉運子　sodium-bicarbonate symporter
奶蓟/奶薊　milk thistle
奶麻/嬰兒玫瑰疹　roseola infantum
奶麻·邪透肌肤证/奶麻·邪透肌膚證　roseola infantum with pattern of pathogen diffusing into muscle and skin
奶麻·邪郁肺胃证/奶麻·邪鬱肺胃證　roseola infantum with pattern of pathogen stagnated in lung and stomach
奶排出/奶排出　milk ejection
奶瓶/哺乳瓶,餵奶瓶　nursing bottle
奶癣/嬰兒濕疹　infantile eczema
奶癣·风热留恋证/奶癬·風熱留戀證　infantile eczema with pattern of lingering wind-heat
奶癣·湿热浸淫证/奶癬·濕熱浸淫證　infantile eczema with pattern of inundated dampness-heat
奶癣·血虚风燥证/奶癬·血虛風燥證　infantile eczema with pattern of blood deficiency and wind-dryness
奶油餐/牛油餐　butter meal
奶油样菌落/酪狀菌落　butyrous colony
奶脂计/乳酪計　lactoscope
奈多罗米/奈多羅米　nedocromil

奈非那韦/奈芬納韋　nelfinavir
奈瑟-德林现象/納-杜二氏現象　Neisser-Doering phenomenon
奈瑟菌属/Neisseria 氏球菌屬　*Neisseria*
奈瑟球菌科感染/奈瑟球菌科感染　Neisseriaceae infection
奈氏试剂处理法/奈斯勒氏處置　Nesslerization
奈替米星/奈替米星　netilmicin
奈韦拉平/奈韋拉平　nevirapine
耐促性腺激素性卵巢综合征/耐促性腺激素性卵巢症候群　gonadotropin resistant ovarian syndrome
耐高温包埋材料/耐高溫包埋材料　refractory investment
耐高温模型/耐高溫模型　refractory cast
耐碱性/鹼耐受力　alkali tolerance
耐力运动/耐力運動　endurance exercise
耐量/耐量　tolerance
耐量试验/耐力試驗　tolerance test
耐热小体/耐熱體　thermostabile body
耐热性 DNA 聚合酶/耐熱性 DNA 聚合酶　taq DNA polymerase
耐受/耐受　tolerance
耐受原/耐受原　tolerogen
耐酸纤维/耐酸纖維　oxytalan
耐酸纤维溶解/耐酸纖維溶解　oxytalanolysis
耐盐的/耐鹽的　haloduric
耐用性/耐用性　ruggedness
耐用医疗设备/耐用醫療設備　durable medical equipment
萘醋酸类/萘醋酸類　naphthalene acetic acids
萘啶类/萘啶類　naphthyridines
萘啶酸/萘啶酸　nalidixic acid
萘酚/萘酚　naphthol
萘酚化物/萘酚化物　naphtholate
萘酚类/萘酚類　naphthols
萘酚平/萘酚平　nafenopin
萘酚中毒/萘酚中毒　naphtholism
萘夫西林/萘夫西林　nafcillin
萘呋胺/萘呋胺　nafronyl
萘福泮/萘福泮　nefopam
萘福昔定/萘福昔定　nafoxidine
萘磺酸盐类/萘磺酸鹽類　naphthalenesulfonates
萘基/萘基　naphthyl
萘甲酸帕马喹/萘甲酸帕馬喹　pamaquine naphthoate
萘甲唑啉/萘唑啉　naphazoline
萘醌类/萘醌類　naphthoquinones
萘类/萘類　naphthalenes

萘普生/萘普生　naproxen
萘性内障/萘内障　naphthalinic cataract
萘乙酮/萘乙酮　acetonaphthone
萘乙烯吡啶/萘乙烯吡啶　naphthylvinylpyridine
男护士/男護士　male nurse
男假两性畸形/男假兩性畸形　male pseudohermaphroditism
男科学/男性科學　andrology
男尿道/男尿道　male urethra
男胚瘤/男胚瘤,睾丸瘤　testiculoma
男人/男人　man
男乳房/男乳房　male breast
男型/男型　android type
男性/男性,雄性　male
男性避孕药/男性避孕藥　contraceptive for male
男性病/男性病　andropathy
男性不育/男性不育　male infertility
男性不育·肝气郁结证/男性不育·肝氣鬱結證　male infertility with liver qi stagnation pattern
男性不育·气血两虚证/男性不育·氣血兩虛證　male infertility with qi-blood deficiency pattern
男性不育·肾阳虚证/男性不育·腎陽虛證　male infertility with kidney yang deficiency pattern
男性不育·肾阴虚证/男性不育·腎陰虛證　male infertility with kidney yin deficiency pattern
男性不育·湿热下注证/男性不育·濕熱下注證　male infertility with pattern of dampness-heat diffusing downward
男性不育·痰热蕴结证/男性不育·痰熱蘊結證　male infertility with phlegm-heat amassment pattern
男性更年期/男性更年期　andropause
男性化/女子之男性化,男化　virilism
男性化瘤/男性化瘤,雄性化瘤　virilizing tumor
男性化卵巢瘤/男性化卵巢瘤　virilizing ovarian tumor
男性化肾上腺瘤/男性化腎上腺瘤　virilizing adrenal tumor
男性化综合征/男性化症候群　virilizing syndrome
男性假两性体/男性假陰陽人　male pseudohermaphrodite
男性假两性同体/男性假兩性同體,男性假兩性畸形　male pseudohermaphroditism
男性泌尿生殖系放线菌病/男性泌尿生殖系放線菌病　actinomycosis of male genitourinary system
男性泌尿生殖系结核/男性泌尿生殖系結核　tuberculosis of male genitourinary system
男性泌尿生殖系梅毒/男性泌尿生殖系梅毒

syphilis of male urogenital system
男性泌尿外科手术/男性泌尿外科手術　male urologic surgical procedure
男性内生殖器/男性内生殖器　male internal genital organ
男性尿道/男性尿道　male urethra
男性女声/假聲,尖聲　falsetto
男性乳房/男性乳房　mamma masculina
男性乳腺肿瘤/男性乳腺腫瘤　male breast neoplasm
男性生殖器/男性生殖器　male genitalia
男性生殖器疾病/男性生殖器疾病　male genital disease
男性生殖器结核/男性生殖器結核　male genital tuberculosis
男性生殖器肿瘤/男性生殖器腫瘤　male genital neoplasm
男性生殖系统/雄性生殖系統　male reproductive system
男性同性恋/同性戀男性　homosexual male
男性外生殖器官/男性外生殖器官　external genital organ of male
男性细胞瘤/[卵巢]男胚瘤　arrhenoblastoma
男性型脱发/雄性禿　male-pattern alopecia
男性性功能障碍/男性性功能障礙　male sexual dysfunction
男性性腺功能减退症/男性性腺功能減退症　male hypogonadism
男性征丧失/男性性徵喪失　demasculinization
男用避孕器械/男用避孕器械　male contraceptive device
男用避孕药/男用避孕藥　male contraceptive agent
男用致育药/男用致育藥　male fertility agent
男征发生/男性徵象發生,男性化　masculation
男子泌乳/男子乳房溢乳　androgalactozemia
男子女性型乳房/迴饋男子女乳症　refeeding gynecomastia
男子乳腺发育/男子乳腺發育　gynecomastia
南方钩端螺旋体/澳洲螺旋體　Leptospira australis
南非壁虱咬热/南非蜱咬熱　South African tick-bite fever
南非野葛素/毒葛素　hyenanchin
南极绦虫/南極條蟲　Taenia antarctica
南美鸡蛋花/南美雞蛋花　sucuuba
南美犰狳/南美犰狳　armadillo
南美庭菖蒲/南美庭菖蒲　Sisyrinchium galaxioides
南美芽生菌病/南美芽生菌病　South American blastomycosis
南美云实荚/南美雲實荚　divi-divi

南美洲锥虫结节/美洲錐蟲腫　chagoma
南美锥虫病/南美錐蟲病　South American trypanosomiasis
南欧斑疹热/浦東熱　boutonneuse
南欧嗜眠性脑炎/南歐嗜眠性腦炎,嗜眠性腦炎　nona
南沙参/南沙參　fourleaf ladybell root
南斯剩余间隙/南斯剩餘間隙　Nance leeway space
南洋玉兰/南洋玉蘭　Talauma elegans
难产/難產,生產困難　dystocia, difficult delivery
难产·气血两虚证/難產·氣血兩虛證　difficult delivery with pattern of deficiency of both qi and blood
难产·气滞血瘀证/難產·氣滯血瘀證　difficult delivery with pattern of qi stagnation and blood stasis
难复性疝/難復性疝　irreducible hernia
难经/難經　Classic of Questioning
难控制性呕吐/難抑制性嘔吐　incoercible vomiting
难免流产/無可避免的流產　inevitable abortion
难免性出血/難免性出血　unavoidable hemorrhage
难染性/難染性　chromophobia
难治的/難治的,頑固的　intractable
难治性贫血/難治性貧血　refractory anemia
喃氟啶/喃氟啶　tegafur
赧颜症/赧顏症　erythromania
囊/囊　capsule
囊胞/胚胞　blastocyst
囊壁/膠囊壁　capsule wall
囊变性纤维瘤/囊腫性纖維瘤,纖維囊腫　fibrocyst
囊部/囊部　diverticular part
囊材/膠囊壁材質　capsule wall material
囊虫/囊蟲　cyst worm
囊虫病/囊[尾幼]蟲病　cysticercosis
囊虫病·虫痰互结证/囊蟲病·蟲痰互結證　cysticercosis with pattern of entwining of worm and phlegm
囊虫病·侵脑证/囊蟲病·侵腦證　cysticercosis involving brain
囊的/囊的　capsular
囊瘤/囊瘤　cystoma
囊瘤炎/囊瘤炎　cystomatitis
囊内的/囊内的　intracapsular
囊内韧带/囊内韌帶　intracapsular ligament
囊内乳头[状]瘤/囊内乳頭狀瘤　intracystic papilloma
囊胚/囊胚,胚囊　blastula
囊胚发育图/胚育圖　fate map

囊胚基质/囊胚基[質] blastostroma
囊胚期/囊胚期 blastula stage
囊胚腔/囊胚腔 blastocoele
囊胚腔液/囊胚腔液，胚液 blastochyle
囊胚形成/囊胚形成 blastulation
囊鞘间隙/囊鞘間隙 space between capsule and sheath
囊切开术/[精]囊切開術 vesiculotomy
囊韧带/囊韌帶 capsular ligament
囊外韧带/囊外韌帶 extracapsular ligament
囊尾蚴/囊尾蚴，囊蟲 cysticercus
囊细胞/囊細胞 bladder cell
囊腺癌/囊腺癌 cystadenocarcinoma
囊腺瘤/囊[狀]腺瘤 cystadenoma, cystic adenoma
囊心/膠囊核 capsule core
囊形/囊形 cystic form
囊性白内障/囊内障，被膜内障 capsular cataract
囊性变[性]/囊腫變性 cystic degeneration
囊性成釉细胞瘤/囊性成釉細胞瘤 cystic ameloblastoma
囊性痤疮/囊狀痤瘡 acne cystica
囊性腹水/囊性腹水 ascites saccatus
囊性甲状腺肿/囊狀甲狀腺腫 cystic goiter
囊性间皮瘤/囊性間皮瘤 cystic mesothelioma
囊性淋巴管瘤/囊性淋巴管瘤 lymphangioma cysticum
囊性瘤/囊狀腫瘤 cystic tumor
囊性黏液瘤/囊性黏液瘤 cystic myxoma
囊性尿道炎/囊性尿道炎 urethritis cystica
囊性膀胱炎钙质沉着/囊性膀胱炎鈣質沈著 cystitis cystica calcinosa
囊性肉瘤/囊肉瘤 cystosarcoma
囊性乳头状瘤/囊性乳頭狀瘤 cystic papilloma
囊性上皮瘤/囊性上皮瘤 cystoepithelioma
囊性肾盂炎/囊狀腎盂炎 pyelitis cystica
囊性输尿管炎/囊性輸尿管炎 ureteritis cystica
囊性纤维化/囊性纖維變性 cystic fibrosis
囊性纤维化跨膜传导调节因子/囊性纖維化跨膜傳導調節因數 cystic fibrosis transmembrane conductance regulator
囊性纤维瘤/囊性纖維瘤 cystofibroma
囊性腺瘤样畸形/囊性腺瘤樣畸形 cystic adenomatoid malformation
囊性腺样棘皮瘤/囊性腺樣棘皮瘤 acanthoma adenoides cysticum
囊性腺样上皮瘤/囊性腺狀上皮瘤 epithelioma adenoides cysticum
囊性增生病/囊狀增生 cystic hyperplasia
囊炎/[精]囊炎 vesiculitis
囊样变性/囊性化生 cystoid degeneration
囊样含毛的/囊狀含毛的 pilocystic
囊样黄斑变性/囊樣黃斑變性 cystoid degeneration of macula
囊样黄斑水肿/囊樣黃斑水腫 cystoid macular edema
囊痈/囊癰 scrotal abscess
囊痈·肝肾阴虚证/囊癰·肝腎陰虛證 scrotal abscess with liver-kidney yin deficiency pattern
囊痈·湿热下注证/囊癰·濕熱下注證 scrotal abscess with pattern of dampness-heat diffusing downward
囊支/囊支 capsular branch
囊肿/囊腫 cyst
囊肿黄素/囊腫黃質 cystolutein
囊肿性痤疮/囊性痤瘡 cystic acne
囊肿性动脉瘤/囊腫性動脈瘤 cystogenic aneurysm
囊肿性脊柱裂/囊腫性脊柱裂 spina bifida cystica
囊肿性视网膜血管瘤/血管晶狀體瘤形成 angiophakomatosis
囊肿液/囊腫液 cyst fluid
囊肿硬化/囊腫硬化 cystosclerosis
囊周膜/囊膜，囊衣 pericystium
囊状癌/囊狀癌 cystic cancer
囊状产色霉菌病/囊狀産色黴菌病 cystic chromomycosis
囊状肠重复畸形/囊狀腸重複畸形 cystic intestinal duplication
囊状[的]/囊狀的，胞狀的 vesicular, saccular
囊状动脉瘤/囊狀動脈瘤 sacculated aneurysm
囊状附件/囊狀附件 vesicular appendage
囊状骨纤维瘤病/囊狀骨纖維瘤病 cystic osteofibromatosis
囊状畸胎瘤/囊狀畸胎瘤 cystic teratoma
囊状卵泡/囊狀卵泡 vesicular follicle
囊状脑畸胎/囊腦畸胎 cystencephalus
囊状平库斯纤维上皮瘤/囊狀的比庫斯纖維上皮瘤 cystic fibroepithelioma of Pinkus
囊状韧带/囊狀韌帶 sacciform ligament
囊状息肉/囊狀息肉 hydatid polyp
囊状限局性浆液性脑膜炎/囊胞限局性漿液性腦膜炎 meningitis serosa circumscripta cystica
囊状眼/囊狀眼 cystic eye
囊状隐窝/囊狀隱窩 sacciform recess
蛲虫病/蟯蟲病 enterobiasis, oxyuriasis
脑/腦 brain
脑白质/腦白質 alba

脑白质病/腦白質病　leukoencephalopathy
脑白质切断器/腦白質切除器　leukotome
脑白质切断术/額葉白質切除術　leukotomy
脑白质疏松/腦白質疏鬆症　leukoaraiosis
脑白质营养不良/腦白質障礙症　leukodystrophy
脑瘢痕/腦瘢痕　brain cicatrix
脑半球间裂/腦間裂隙　intercerebral fissure
脑本身的/腦本質的　idiophrenic
脑表层炎/腦表層炎　periencephalitis
脑病/腦病　encephalopathia
脑病划痕/腦病劃痕,腦膜炎劃痕　meningeal streak
脑病性精神病/腦病性精神病　idiophrenic psychosis
脑病性木僵/腦病性木僵　encephalonarcosis
脑不全[畸形]/腦不全畸形　parencephalia
脑部杂音/腦部雜音　brain murmur
脑层/腦層　cerebral layer
脑超声描记术/超音波腦檢查[法]
    echoencephalography
脑出血/腦出血　encephalorrhagia
脑穿刺术/腦穿刺　encephalopuncture
脑穿通畸形/腦穿通畸形　porencephaly
脑穿通性囊肿/腦穿通性囊腫　porencephalic cyst
脑垂体/腦垂體　hypophysis
脑垂体分泌过多性巨人症/垂體亢進巨大畸形
    hyperpituitary gigantism
脑垂体激素与皮脂腺活性/腦下垂體荷爾蒙與皮脂
    腺活性　pituitary hormone and sebaceous gland
    activity
脑垂体移植/腦垂體移植　pituitary transplantation
脑垂体肿/腦垂體腫　pituitary goiter
脑磁波描记器/腦磁波描記器
    magnetoencephalograph
脑磁波描记术/腦磁波描記術
    magnetoencephalography
脑挫伤/腦挫傷　contusion of brain
脑代谢改善药/腦代謝改善藥　nootropic agent
脑刀/腦[解剖]刀　encephalotome
脑的/腦的　encephalic
脑底静脉环/腦底静脈環　cerebral basal venous
    circle
脑底神经胶质增生/腦底神經膠質增殖病　basilar
    gliosis
脑底异常血管网病/模亞模亞病　moyamoya disease
脑底引流法/底部蛛網膜下腔引流法　basal drainage
脑电描记器/腦電描記器,腦電圖儀,腦波儀
    electroencephalograph
脑电描记术/腦電描記法,腦電圖測定
    electroencephalography
脑电图/腦電圖,腦電像,腦波圖
    electroencephalogram
脑淀粉样血管病/腦澱粉樣血管病　cerebral amyloid
    angiopathy
脑定点切开器/腦定點切開器　stereoencephalotome
脑定点切开术/腦定點切開術　stereoencephalotomy
脑动脉疾病/腦動脈疾病　cerebral arterial disease
脑动脉硬化/腦動脈硬化　cerebral arteriosclerosis
脑动脉造影术/腦動脈攝影術　encephalo-
    arteriography
脑发生不良/終腦發生不全　cerebral dysplasia
脑发育异常/先天性腦畸形　encephalodysplasia
脑啡肽类/腦啡肽類　enkephalins
脑啡肽酶/腦啡肽酶　neprilysin
脑肥大/腦肥大　encephalauxe
脑肝肾综合征/腦、肝與腎症候群
    cerebrohepatorenal syndrome
脑苷脂/腦糖苷　cerebroside
脑苷脂硫酸酯酶/腦苷脂硫酸酯酶　cerebroside
    sulfatase
脑苷脂硫酸酯酶缺乏/腦苷酯硫酸酯酶缺乏
    cerebroside sulfatase deficiency
脑苷脂贮积病/腦糖苷沈著病　cerebrosidosis
脑干/腦幹　brainstem
脑干梗死/腦幹梗塞　brainstem infarction
脑干静脉/腦幹静脈　vein of encephalic trunk, vein
    of brainstem
脑干损伤/腦幹損傷　brainstem injury
脑干听觉区移植/腦幹聽覺區移植　auditory
    brainstem implantation
脑干听觉区移植物/腦幹聽覺區移植物　auditory
    brainstem implant
脑干听觉诱发电位/腦幹聽覺誘發電位　brainstem
    auditory evoked potential
脑干网状结构/腦幹網狀構造　reticular formation of
    brainstem
脑干肿瘤/腦幹腫瘤　brainstem neoplasm
脑根/腦根　cranial root
脑梗死/[大]腦梗塞　brain infarction, cerebral
    infarction
脑弓形虫病/腦弓形蟲病　cerebral toxoplasmosis
脑功能障碍/腦機能障礙　brain disorder
脑灌注/腦灌注　cerebral perfusion
脑过小/腦小[畸形],小腦　microencephaly,
    micrencephalon
脑户/腦户　①door of brain ②naohu, DU17
脑化学/腦化學　brain chemistry

脑坏疽/腦壞疽 encephalosepsis
脑黄斑变性/大腦黃斑變性 cerebromacular degeneration
脑灰质/腦外灰質 ectocinerea
脑灰质病/腦灰質病 polioencephalopathy
脑灰质[厚度]测量计/腦灰質厚度計 tephrylometer
脑灰质炎/腦灰質炎 polioencephalitis
脑回/腦迴 gyri
脑回波描记器/超音波腦檢查計 echoencephalograph
脑回波图/超音波腦檢查圖 echoencephalogram
脑回裂[畸形]/裂腦迴 schizogyria
脑回萎缩/腦迴萎縮 convolutional atrophy
脑回萎小/腦迴萎小 ischogyria
脑回压迹/腦迴壓跡 impression for cerebral gyri
脑活动力缺失性反应/腦機能障礙性反應 anergastic reaction
脑活组织检查/腦活檢 biopsy of brain
脑积水/腦積水,水腦 hydrocephalus
脑积水喊叫/水腦喊叫 hydrocephalic cry
脑疾病/腦疾病 brain disease
脑[脊]膜/腦[脊]膜 meninges
脑[脊]膜病/腦脊髓膜病 meningopathy
脑[脊]膜出血/腦脊髓膜出血 meningorrhagia
脑[脊]膜缝合术/腦脊髓膜縫合術 meningeorrhaphy
脑[脊]膜瘤/[外]腦膜瘤,硬腦膜瘤 exothelioma
脑[脊]膜脑脊髓病/腦膜腦病 meningoencephalomyelopathy
脑[脊]膜脑脊髓炎/腦膜腦脊髓炎 meningoencephalomyelitis
脑[脊]膜膨出/腦[脊]膜膨出 meningocele
脑[脊]膜膨出修补术/腦[脊]膜膨出修補術 repair of spinal meningocele
脑[脊]膜神经根炎/腦膜神經根炎 meningoradiculitis
脑[脊]膜外的/腦膜外的 extrameningeal
脑脊膜炎/腦脊髓膜炎 cerebrospinal meningitis
脑脊髓病/腦脊髓病 encephalomyelopathy
脑脊髓刺毁法/腦脊髓刺毀法 pithing
脑脊髓的/腦脊髓的 cerebrospinal
脑脊髓灰质脑脊膜炎/腦脊髓灰質腦脊髓膜炎 polioencephalomeningomyelitis
脑脊髓灰质炎/腦脊髓灰質炎 polioencephalomyelitis
脑脊髓脊神经根病/腦脊髓神經根病 encephalomyeloradiculopathy
脑脊髓脊神经根炎/腦脊髓神經根炎 encephalomyeloradiculitis
脑脊髓节/腦脊髓節 zoonite
脑脊髓空洞症/腦脊髓空洞症 syringoencephalomyelia
脑脊髓梅毒/腦脊髓梅毒 cerebrospinal syphilis
脑脊髓膜热/腦脊髓膜熱 cerebrospinal fever
脑脊髓膨出/腦脊髓膨出 encephalomyelocele
脑脊髓神经病/腦脊髓神經病 encephalomyeloneuropathy
脑脊髓炎/腦脊髓炎 encephalomyelitis
脑脊髓药/腦脊髓藥 cerebrospinant
脑脊髓液蛋白质类/腦脊髓液蛋白質類 cerebrospinal fluid proteins
脑脊髓液分流术/腦脊髓液分流術 cerebrospinal fluid shunt
脑脊髓液压/腦脊髓液壓 cerebrospinal fluid pressure
脑脊髓液阻断/腦脊髓液阻斷 cerebrospinal-fluid block
脑脊液/腦脊髓液 cerebrospinal fluid, CSF
脑脊液白蛋白定量器/腦脊液白蛋白定量器 rachialbuminimeter
脑脊液鼻漏/腦脊液性鼻漏 cerebrospinal fluid rhinorrhea
脑脊液耳漏/腦脊液耳漏 cerebrospinal fluid otorrhea
[脑脊液]分隔综合征/腦脊液分隔症候群 loculation syndrome
脑脊液[淋巴]细胞增多/腦脊液內淋巴細胞增多 pleocytosis
脑脊液-脑屏障/腦脊液-腦屏障 CSF-brain barrier, CBB
脑脊液凝固/廣泛性凝固 massive coagulation
脑脊液糖分过多/腦脊髓液含糖過多 hyperglycorrhachia
脑脊液糖分过少/腦脊髓液糖過少 hypoglycorrhachia
脑脊液压/腦脊髓液壓力 cerebrospinal pressure
脑脊液氧化酶/腦脊髓酵素 cerebrospinase
脑寄虫病/腦寄蟲病 cerebral parasitosis
脑减压术/腦減壓術 decompression of brain
脑腱的/腦肌腱的 cerebrotendinous
脑腱性黄瘤病/腦肌鍵黄瘤病 cerebrotendinous xanthomatosis
脑降温装置/腦降温裝置 brain cooling system
脑脚横束/大腦腳橫徑 transverse peduncular tract
脑节/腦胚節 encephalomere
脑结核/大腦性結核病 cerebral tuberculosis

脑结核瘤/腦結核瘤　brain tuberculoma
脑静脉/腦靜脈　cerebral vein
脑静脉综合征/Rolando 氏静脈症候群　rolandic vein syndrome
脑疽/腦疽　carbuncle in nape, nape carbuncle
脑空/腦空　naokong, GB19
脑空洞病/腦空洞病　cerebral porosis
脑空洞症/腦空洞症　syringoencephalia
脑、肋骨与下颌骨综合征/腦、肋骨與下頜骨症候群　cerebrocostomandibular syndrome
脑立清丸/腦立清丸　naoliqing pill
脑立体定向活检/腦立體定向活檢　stereotactic biopsy of brain
脑利钠肽/腦利鈉肽　brain natriuretic peptide
脑裂伤/腦裂傷　laceration of brain
脑磷脂/腦磷脂　cephalin
脑磷脂胆固醇絮状试验/腦磷膽固醇凝絮試驗　cephalin-cholesterol flocculation test
脑磷脂磷酸/腦磷酸　kephalophosphoric acid
脑硫脂病/硫脂累積病　sulfatidosis
脑瘤/腦瘤　cerebroma
脑瘤·风毒上扰证/腦瘤·風毒上擾證　cerebroma with pattern of wind-poison disturbing upward
脑瘤·痰瘀阻窍证/腦瘤·痰瘀阻竅證　cerebroma with pattern of phlegm and static blood blocking orifice
脑瘤·阴虚动风证/腦瘤·陰虛動風證　cerebroma with pattern of wind stirring due to yin deficiency
脑颅/腦顱,神經顱　cerebral cranium
脑颅骨/腦顱骨　bone of cerebral cranium
脑颅皮脂肪瘤病/腦顱皮脂肪瘤病　encephalocraniocutaneous lipomatosis
脑络痹/腦絡痹　brain collateral bi, brain collateral painful impediment
脑律动/腦律動,自動精神性節律　autopsychorhythmia
脑毛霉菌病/大腦白黴菌病　cerebral mucormycosis
脑梅毒瘤/腦梅毒瘤　brain syphiloma
脑面血管瘤病/腦面血管瘤病　encephalofacial angiomatosis
脑鸣/腦鳴　noise in the head, buzzing in brain, intracranial tinnitus
脑膜白血病/腦膜白血病　meningeal leukemia
脑膜动脉/腦膜動脈　meningeal artery
脑膜动脉炎/腦脊髓膜動脈炎　meningoarteritis
脑膜返支/腦膜返支　recurrent meningeal branch
脑膜肺炎/腦膜肺炎　meningopneumonitis
脑膜肺炎病毒/腦膜肺炎病毒　meningopneumonitis virus
脑膜副动脉/腦膜副動脈　accessory meningeal artery
脑膜副支/腦膜副支　accessory meningeal branch
脑膜后动脉/腦膜後動脈　posterior meningeal artery
脑膜结核/腦膜結核　meningeal tuberculosis
脑膜静脉/腦膜靜脈　meningeal vein
脑膜瘤/腦膜瘤　meningioma
脑膜脑膨出/腦膜腦膨出　meningoencephalocele
脑膜脑炎/膜腦炎　meningoencephalitis
脑膜膨出/腦脊髓膜膨出　meningocele
脑膜前动脉/腦膜前動脈　anterior meningeal artery
脑膜前支/腦膜前支　anterior meningeal branch
脑膜软化/腦膜軟化　meningomalacia
脑膜神经/腦膜神經　meningeal nerve
脑膜神经梅毒/腦膜性神經梅毒　meningeal neurosyphilis
脑膜性阻断/腦膜性阻斷　meningeal block
脑膜血管神经梅毒/腦膜血管性神經梅毒　meningovascular neurosyphilis
脑膜炎/腦膜炎　cerebral meningitis
脑膜炎球菌/腦膜炎球菌　meningococci
脑膜炎球菌毒素/腦膜炎球菌毒素　meningococcal toxin
脑膜炎球菌素/腦膜炎球菌素　meningococcin
脑膜炎球菌性脑膜炎/腦膜炎球菌性腦膜炎　meningococcal meningitis
脑膜炎球菌血症/腦膜炎球菌血症　meningococcemia
脑膜炎双球菌病/腦膜炎雙球菌病　meningococcosis
脑膜炎双球菌感染/腦膜炎雙球菌感染　meningococcal infection
脑膜炎双球菌菌苗/腦膜炎雙球菌菌苗　meningococcal vaccine
脑膜炎性呼吸/腦膜炎性呼吸　meningitic respiration
脑膜造影术/腦表層 X 光攝影法　periencephalography
脑膜支/腦膜支　meningeal branch
脑膜支交通支/腦膜支交通支　communicating branch with meningeal branch
脑膜中动脉/腦膜中動脈　middle meningeal artery
脑膜中动脉顶支/腦膜中動脈頂支　parietal branch of middle meningeal artery
脑膜中动脉额支/腦膜中動脈額支　frontal branch of middle meningeal artery
脑膜中动脉沟/腦膜中動脈溝　sulcus for middle meningeal artery
脑膜中动脉眶支/腦膜中動脈眶支　orbital branch of middle meningeal artery

脑膜中动脉吻合支/腦膜中動脈吻合支　anastomotic branch with middle meningeal artery
脑膜中静脉/腦膜中靜脈　middle meningeal vein
脑膜肿瘤/腦膜腫瘤　meningeal neoplasm
脑膜周围感染/腦膜周圍感染　perimeningeal infection
脑膜[组织]细胞/腦膜[組織]細胞　meningocyte
脑幕的/天幕　tentorium
脑幕疝/腦幕疝　tentorial hernia
脑脑膜病/腦膜病　encephalomeningopathy
脑脑膜膨出/腦腦膜膨出　encephalomeningocele
脑脑膜炎/腦腦膜炎　cerebromeningitis
脑内血肿/腦內血腫　intracerebral hematoma
脑内异物摘除术/腦內異物摘除術　removal of foreign body in brain
脑脓肿/腦膿腫　brain abscess
脑脓肿抽吸术/腦膿腫抽吸術　aspiration of brain abscess
脑脓肿切除术/腦膿腫切除術　excision of brain abscess
脑脓肿手术/腦膿腫手術　brain abscess operation
脑脓肿引流术/腦膿腫引流術　drainage of brain abscess
脑旁体/腦上旁突體，腦副體　paraphysis
脑泡/胚胎腦囊　brain bladder
脑膨出/腦[質]膨出　cenencephalocele
脑皮层电图/腦皮質電圖　electrocorticogram
脑皮层电图学/腦皮質電圖學　electrocorticography
脑皮层脑膜炎/腦表層腦膜炎　periencephalomeningitis
脑皮层切除术/皮質切除術　corticectomy
脑皮层[神经]纤维结构/腦皮層纖維結構　myeloarchitecture
脑屏障/腦障　brain barrier
脑破伤风/腦破傷風　cerebral tetanus
脑器质性精神障碍/腦器質性精神障礙　organic mental disorder
脑器质性行为障碍/腦器質性行爲障礙　organic behavior disorder
脑器质性谵妄/腦器質性譫妄　organic delirium
脑桥/橋腦　pons
脑桥被盖部/腦橋被蓋部　tegmentum of pons
脑桥被盖网状核/腦橋被蓋網狀核　tegmentoreticular nucleus of pons
脑桥臂/橋腦臂　pontibrachium
脑桥出血/橋腦出血　pontine hemorrhage
脑桥动脉/腦橋動脈　pontine artery
脑桥核/腦橋核　pontine nucleus
脑桥核障碍/橋腦核障礙　cerebelloparenchymal disorder
脑桥横行纤维/腦橋橫行纖維　transverse fiber of pons
脑桥基底部/腦橋基底部　basilar part of pons
脑桥基底沟/腦橋基底溝　basilar sulcus of pons
脑桥脊髓束/橋腦脊徑　pontospinal tract
脑桥脚被盖核/腦橋腳被蓋核　pedunculopontine tegmental nucleus
脑桥静脉/腦橋靜脈，橋腦靜脈　vein of pons
脑桥空洞症/橋腦空洞病　syringopontia
脑桥良性肥大/腦橋良性肥大　benign hypertrophy of the pons
脑桥前外侧静脉/腦橋前外側靜脈　anterolateral pontine vein
脑桥前正中静脉/腦橋前正中靜脈　anteromedian pontine vein
脑桥曲/橋腦曲　pontine flexure
脑桥上横静脉/腦橋上橫靜脈　superior transverse pontine vein
脑桥束性眼肌麻痹/束性眼肌癱瘓　fascicular ophthalmoplegia
脑桥外侧静脉/腦橋外側靜脈　lateral pontine vein
脑桥网状脊髓束/腦橋網狀脊髓徑　pontoreticulospinal tract
脑桥尾侧网状核/腦橋尾側網狀核　caudal pontine reticular nucleus
脑桥下横静脉/腦橋下橫靜脈　inferior transverse pontine vein
脑桥小脑的/橋腦與小腦的　pontocerebellar
脑桥小脑三角/腦橋小腦三角　pontocerebellar trigone
脑桥小脑束/橋腦小腦徑　pontocerebellar tract
脑桥小脑纤维/腦橋小腦纖維　pontocerebellar fiber
脑桥性偏身麻木/橋腦性單側麻木　mesocephalic hemianesthesia
脑桥延髓/橋腦與延髓　pons-oblongata
脑桥延髓空洞症/橋腦延髓空洞病　pontobulbia
脑桥中部髓鞘溶解/中心性腦橋髓鞘破壞　central pontine myelinolysis
脑桥中缝/腦橋中縫　pontine raphe
脑桥中缝核/腦橋中縫核　rapheal nucleus of pons
脑桥中脑前静脉/腦橋中腦前靜脈　anterior pontomesencephalic vein
脑桥综合征/橋腦症候群　pontine syndrome
脑桥嘴侧网状核/腦橋嘴側網狀核　rostral pontine reticular nucleus
脑切开术/腦切開術　encephalotomy

脑切开[造口]术/腦切開造口術　cerebrostomy
脑缺血/腦缺血　brain ischemia
脑缺氧/腦缺氧　brain hypoxia
脑缺氧缺血/腦缺氧缺血　brain hypoxia-ischemia
脑软化/腦軟化　cerebral malacia
脑三叉神经区血管瘤病/大腦三叉神經性血管瘤病　encephalotrigeminal angiomatosis
脑三叉神经血管综合征/腦三叉神經血管症候群　encephalotrigeminal vascular syndrome
脑三叉神经综合征/腦三叉神經症候群　encephalotrigeminal syndrome
脑砂/腦砂　brain sand
脑疝/腦疝　cerebral hernia, hernia cerebri
脑神经/腦神經　cranial nerve, cerebral nerve
脑神经核/腦神經核　nucleus of cranial nerve
脑神经核发育不全/腦神經核發育不全　nuclear dysplasia
脑神经疾病/顱神經疾病　cranial nerve disease
脑神经节/腦神經節　cranial ganglion
脑神经损伤/顱神經損傷　cranial nerve injury
脑神经痛/腦神經痛　cranial neuralgia
脑神经中央径/腦神經中央徑　central tract of cranial nerve
脑神经肿瘤/顱神經腫瘤　cranial nerve neoplasm
脑神说/腦神説　theory of brain governing mental activity
脑石/腦[結]石　encephalolith
脑室/腦室　cerebral ventricle
脑室充气造影术/腦充氣Ｘ光攝影法　cerebral pneumography
脑室穿刺/腦室穿刺術　ventricular puncture
脑室腹膜分流术/腦室腹膜分流術　ventriculoperitoneal shunt
脑室梗阻/腦室梗阻　ventricular block
[脑]室管膜周围脊髓炎/室管膜周圍脊髓炎　periependymal myelitis
脑室积脓/腦室積膿　pyocephalus
脑室静脉分流术/腦室静脈分流　ventriculovenous shunt
脑室静脉造口[引流]术/腦室静脈造口引流術　ventriculovenostomy
脑室镜/腦室鏡　ventriculoscope
脑室镜检查/腦室鏡檢法　ventriculoscopy
脑室瘘/腦室瘻　ventriculostium
脑室脑池分流术/腦室腦池分流　ventriculocisternal shunt
脑室脑池造口[引流]术/腦室腦池吻合術　ventriculocisternostomy

脑室内出血/腦室内出血　intraventricular hemorrhage
脑室内脑膜瘤/腦室内腦膜瘤　intraventricular meningioma
脑室内注射/腦室内注射　intraventricular injection
脑室心房分流术/腦室動脈分流　ventriculoatrial shunt
脑室心房造口[引流]术/腦水導心術,腦室心房造口引流術　ventriculoatriostomy
脑室胸腔分流术/腦室胸膜分流　ventriculopleural shunt
脑室压测量法/腦室容積或壓力測定法　ventriculometry
脑室炎/腦室炎　ventriculitis
脑室液/腦室液　ventricular fluid
脑室造口术/腦室造口術　ventriculostomy
脑室造影术/腦室造影術　cerebral ventriculography
脑室肿瘤/腦室腫瘤　cerebral ventricle neoplasm
脑室周围白质软化病/腦室周圍白質軟化病　periventricular leukomalacia
脑室周系统/腦室周系統　periventricular system
脑受压/腦受壓　compression of brain
脑栓塞/腦栓塞　cerebral embolism
脑水肿/腦水腫　brain edema
脑死亡/腦死亡　brain death
脑髓/腦髓　brain marrow
脑髓动脉/腦髓動脈　medullary artery of brain
脑髓苷/腦髓苷　encephalin
脑髓说/腦髓説　theory of brain marrow
脑髓消/腦髓消　brain marrow consumption
脑损伤/腦損傷　brain injury
脑损伤后昏迷/腦損傷後昏迷　post-head injury coma
脑图/腦圖　brain mapping
脑[外伤或病态]性休克/腦休克　cerebral shock
脑萎缩/腦萎縮　brain atrophy
脑细胞移植/腦細胞移植　brain cell transplantation
脑心肌炎/腦心肌炎　encephalomyocarditis
脑心肌炎病毒/腦及心肌炎病毒　encephalomyocarditis virus
脑心脏的/腦與心的　cerebrocardiac
脑心综合征/腦與心症候群　cerebrocardiac syndrome
脑形成/腦形成　encephalization
脑形的/腦狀的　cerebriform
脑形先天性痣/腦回樣先天性痣　cerebriform congenital nevus
脑型肺炎/腦型肺炎　cerebral pneumonia

脑型疟疾/腦型瘧 cerebral malaria
脑型糖原磷酸化酶/腦型糖原磷酸化酶 brain form glycogen phosphorylase
脑性黑矇/腦性黑矇 cerebral amaurosis
脑性巨人症/大腦巨大畸形 cerebral gigantism
脑性两侧共济失调/大腦性雙側共濟失調 cerebral diataxia
脑性呕吐/腦性嘔吐 cerebral vomiting
脑性偏瘫/大腦性半身不遂,大腦性偏癱 cerebral hemiplegia
脑性瘫痪/大腦性癱瘓,腦性麻痺 cerebral palsy
脑性眩晕/腦性眩暈 encephalic vertigo
脑性子痫/腦性子癇症 cerebral eclampsia
脑学/腦學,大腦論 cerebrology
脑血管病/腦血管疾病 cerebral vascular disease
脑血管重建术/腦血管重建術 cerebral revascularization
脑血管的/腦血管的 cerebrovascular
脑血管基底神经节出血/腦血管基底神經節出血 basal ganglia hemorrhage
脑血管基底神经节疾病/腦血管基底神經節疾病 basal ganglia cerebrovascular disease
脑血管疾病手术/腦血管疾病手術 operation for cerebrovascular disease
脑血管扩张药/腦血管擴張藥 cerebral vasodilator
脑血管缺血/腦血管缺血 cerebrovascular ischemia
脑血管损伤/腦血管損傷 cerebrovascular trauma
脑血管性痴呆/腦血管性癡呆 cerebral vascular dementia
脑血管循环/腦血管循環 cerebrovascular circulation
脑血管意外/腦血管意外,腦血管病變,腦血管意外病變 cerebrovascular accident
脑血管造影术/腦血管造影術 cerebral angiography
脑血管障碍/腦血管障礙 cerebrovascular disorder
脑血栓形成/腦血栓形成,腦栓塞 cerebral thrombosis
脑炎/腦炎 encephalitis
脑炎病毒/腦炎病毒 encephalitis virus
脑炎后帕金森病/腦炎後帕金森病 postencephalitic parkinson disease
脑颜面血管瘤病/腦顏面血管瘤病 encephalo-facial angiomatosis
脑眼发育不全/腦性眼球發育不良 encephalo-ophthalmic dysplasia
脑样癌/腦樣癌,腦狀癌 myelomyces
脑叶切除术/腦葉切除術 lobectomy of brain
脑叶神经胶质增生/腦葉神經膠質增殖病 lobar gliosis
脑叶萎缩/腦葉萎縮 lobar atrophy
脑叶硬化/腦葉硬化,腦回萎縮 lobar sclerosis
脑硬化/腦硬化 cerebrosclerosis
脑域测定器/腦域測定器,腦部位測算器 encephalometer
脑源性神经营养因子/腦源性神經營養因數 brain-derived neurotrophic factor
脑甾醇/腦[硬]脂醇 phrenosterol
脑照相术/腦攝影術,腦X光檢查法 encephalography
脑真菌性肉芽肿/腦真菌性肉芽腫 mycotic granuloma of brain
脑震荡/腦震盪 brain concussion
脑震荡后综合征/腦震盪後症候群 post-concussion syndrome
脑震荡性失明/震盪性盲 concussion blindness
脑震伤/腦震傷 brain concussion
脑脂尘/髓塵質 myelocone
脑中隔/腦中隔 septum of brain
脑肿瘤/腦腫瘤 brain neoplasm
脑蛛网膜/腦蜘蛛膜 cerebral arachnoid mater, arachnoid of brain
脑蛛网膜炎/腦蛛網膜炎 arachnoiditis of brain
脑主神明/腦主神明 brain governing mental activity
脑主神明论/腦主神明論 theory of brain governing mental activity
脑状癌/腦狀癌 cerebriform cancer
脑紫癜/腦紫癜病 brain purpura
脑组织移植/腦組織移植 brain transplantation, brain tissue transplantation
瑙海姆疗法/瑙海姆溫泉療法 Nauheim treatment
瑙海姆浴/瑙海姆浴 Nauheim bath
瑙宁-明科夫斯基法/納-米二氏法 Naunyn-Minkowski method
臑会/臑會 naohui, SJ13
臑俞/臑俞 naoshu, SI10
内阿米巴病/内阿米巴病 entamoebiasis
内板/内板 inner plate
内孢子/内孢子 endospore
内孢子膜/内芽孢膜,孢子内皮 endosporium
内鼻/内鼻 neibi, internal nose, TG4
内闭外脱/内閉外脱 inner blocking causing collapse
内标物/内部標準物質 internal standard substance
内表皮/内表皮 endocuticle
内病性皮疹/皮徵 dermadrome
内补黄芪汤/内補黄芪湯 neibu huangqi decoction
内捕食者/内捕食者 endopredator
内部/内部 interior

内部感觉/內部感覺，内界感覺，主觀的感覺 internal sensation, internal sense
内藏式𬌗支持物/內藏式咬合支持物 internal occlusal rest
内侧/內側 medial
内侧半月板/內側半月板 medial meniscus
内侧背核/內側背核 mediodorsal nucleus
内侧鼻突/內側鼻突 median nasal prominence, median nasal process
内侧壁/內側壁 medial wall
内侧部/內側部 medial part
内侧苍白球/內側蒼白球 medial globus pallidus
内侧唇/內側唇 medial lip
内侧底段/內側底段 medial basal segment
内侧底段支气管/內側底段支氣管 medial basal segmental bronchus
内侧底支/內側底支 medial basal branch
内侧段/內側段 medial segment
内侧段动脉/內側段動脈 medial segmental artery
内侧段支气管/內側段支氣管 medial segmental bronchus
内侧副橄榄核/內側副橄欖核 medial accessory olivary nucleus
内侧根/內側根 medial root
内侧弓状韧带/內側弓狀韌帶 medial arcuate ligament
内侧腘绳肌腱/膕內側腱 inner hamstring
内侧核群/內側核群 medial nuclear group
内侧嵴/內側嵴 medial crest
内侧脚/內側腳 medial crus
内侧结节/內側結節 medial tubercle
内侧髁/內側髁 medial condyle
内侧髁上嵴/內側髁上嵴 medial supracondylar ridge
内侧髁上线/內側髁上線 medial supracondylar line
内侧隆起/內側隆起 medial eminence
内侧面/內側面 medial surface
内侧皮支/內側皮支 medial cutaneous branch
内侧丘系/內側丘系 medial lemniscus
内侧丘系交叉/內側丘系交叉 decussation of medial lemniscus
内侧韧带/內側韌帶 medial ligament
内侧软骨板/內側軟骨板 medial cartilaginous lamina
内侧舌侧沟/內側舌側溝 mesiolingual groove
内侧束/內側束 medial cord
内侧髓板/內側髓板 medial medullary lamina
内侧锁骨上神经/內側鎖骨上神經 medial supraclavicular nerve

内侧头/內側頭 medial head
内侧膝状体/內側膝狀體 medial geniculate body
内侧膝状体核/內側膝狀體核 medial geniculate nucleus
内侧楔骨/內側楔骨 medial cuneiform bone, os cuneiforme mediale
内侧斜面/内斜面 internal bevel
内侧嗅回/內側嗅迴 medial olfactory gyrus
内侧嗅纹/內側嗅紋 medial olfactory stria
内侧缘/內側緣 medial border, medial margin
内侧缘静脉/內側緣靜脈 medial marginal vein
内侧支/內側支 medial branch
内侧肘后肌/內側肘後肌 medial anconeus muscle
内侧纵束/內側縱束 medial longitudinal fasciculus, longitudinal medial bundle
内侧纵纹/內側縱紋 medial longitudinal stria
内层软脑[脊]膜炎/軟腦膜內層炎，軟膜炎 leptomeningitis interna
内冲式冷却骨钻/內沖式冷卻骨鑽 internally cooled drill
内出血/內出血 internal hemorrhage
内唇/內唇 inner lip
内错位/内突 mediotrusion
内丹功法/內丹功法 internal elixir qigong
内蒂核/內蒂核 entopeduncular nucleus
内电渗/內電滲 electroendosmosis
内[电]阻/內電阻 essential resistance
内动脉瘤/內動脈瘤 internal aneurysm
内毒素/內毒素 endotoxin
内毒素的/內毒素的 endotoxic
内毒素休克/內毒性休克 endotoxic shock
内毒素血症/內毒素血症 endotoxemia
内多倍体/核內多套染色體 endopolyploid
内耳/內耳 internal ear
内耳道/內耳道 internal acoustic meatus
内耳道垂直嵴/內耳道垂直嵴 vertical crest of internal acoustic meatus
内耳道底/內耳道底 fundus of internal acoustic meatus
内耳道底前庭上区/內耳道底前庭上區 superior vestibular area of fundus of internal acoustic meatus
内耳道底前庭下区/內耳道底前庭下區 inferior vestibular area of fundus of internal acoustic meatus
内耳门/內耳門 internal acoustic pore
内耳炎/內耳炎 otitis interna
内发丹毒/內發丹毒 endogenous erysipelas
内翻的/内翻[的] varus
内翻缝合/反轉縫合術 inverting suture

内翻乳头状瘤/内翻乳頭狀瘤　inverted papilloma
内翻性导管乳头状瘤/内翻性導管乳頭狀瘤　inverted ductal papilloma
内翻性毛囊角化病/内翻性毛囊角化病　inverted follicular keratosis
内翻足/内偏足　varus foot
内烦/内煩　vexing heat in the chest
内防御力/自體抗毒作用　endophylaxination
内啡肽/腦内啡　endorphine
内分泌/内分泌　endocrine
内分泌变[态反]应/内分泌性過敏　endocrine allergy
内分泌病/内分泌[腺]病　endocrinopathy
内分泌病患者/内分泌病患者　endocrinopath
内分泌功能试验/内分泌功能試驗　endocrine function test
内分泌功能紊乱/内分泌機能障礙　endocrine dysfunction
内分泌浸润性突眼/内分泌浸潤性突眼　endocrine infiltrative exophthalmos
内分泌疗法/内分泌療法　incretotherapy
内分泌平衡/内分泌平衡　endocrine balance
内分泌失调性鼻炎/内分泌失調性鼻炎　dyscrinic rhinitis
内分泌外科手术/内分泌外科手術　endocrine surgical procedure
内分泌系统/内分泌系統　endocrine system
内分泌系统疾病/内分泌系統疾病　endocrine system disease
内分泌系统结核/内分泌系統結核　endocrine tuberculosis
内分泌细胞/内分泌細胞　endocrine cell
内分泌腺/内分泌腺　endocrine gland
内分泌腺体/内分泌腺體　endocrine gland
内分泌腺移植/内分泌腺移植　transplantation of endocrine gland
内分泌腺源性血管内皮生长因子/内分泌腺源性血管内皮生長因子　endocrine-gland-derived vascular endothelial growth factor
内分泌腺障碍性综合征/内分泌腺障礙性症候群　dysglandular syndrome
内分泌腺肿瘤/内分泌腫瘤　endocrine neoplasia
内分泌性骨疾病/内分泌性骨疾病　endocrine bone disease
内分泌性骨折/内分泌性骨折　endocrine fracture
内分泌性类肉瘤病/内分泌性類肉瘤病　endocrine sarcoidosis
内分泌性突眼/内分泌性眼球凸出　endocrine exophthalmos

内分泌性萎缩/内分泌性萎縮　endocrine atrophy
内分泌性血管[舒缩]障碍/内分泌性血管障礙　angiocrinosis
内分泌性阳痿/内分泌性陽痿　endocrinologic impotence
内分泌学/内分泌學　endocrinology
内分泌异常/内分泌異常　cryptorrhea
内分泌障碍/内分泌障礙　dyshormonism
内分泌障碍性精神病/内分泌障礙性精神病　dysglandular psychosis
内分泌诊断技术/内分泌診斷技術　endocrine diagnostic technique
内分泌质/内分泌質　autacoid substance
内分泌综合征/内分泌症候群　endocrine syndrome
内分生孢菌中毒症/内分生孢菌中毒症　endoconidiotoxicosis
内风/内風　endogenous wind
内服菌苗法/疫苗口服法　endovaccination
内服液体药剂/内服液體製劑　oral liquid preparation
内附肌/内部肌　intrinsic muscle
内附着体/内部固定法　internal attachment
内感受器/内感器　interoceptor
内感受性幻觉/内感性幻覺　enteroceptive hallucination
内格利培养液/Naegeli氏溶液　Naegeli solution
内根鞘小皮/内根鞘小皮　cuticle of internal root sheath
内弓状纤维/内弓狀纖維,内弧纖維　internal arcuate fiber
内巩膜沟/内鞏膜溝　internal scleral sulcus
内共生体/内共生生物　endosymbiont
内共生[现象]/内共生現象　endosymbiosis
内骨骼/内骨骼　endoskeleton
内骨折固定术/内骨折固定術　internal fracture fixation
内固定/内[部]固定　internal fixation
内固定器/内固定器　internal fixator
内关/内關　neiguan, PC6
内关节/内關節　intrinsic articulation
内关节盂平面/内關節盂平面　entoglenoid plane
内果皮/内果皮　endocarp
内含肽类/内含肽類　inteins
内含子/内含子　intron
内函韧皮部/内函韌皮部　included phloem
内寒/内寒　endogenous cold
内颌/内頜　endognathion
内颌点/中頜點　mesognathion

内呼吸/内呼吸　internal respiration
内踝/内踝　medial malleolus, inner malleolus
内踝点/内踝點　medial malleolus point
内踝沟/内踝溝　medial malleolar sulcus
内踝骨折/内踝骨折　fracture of medial malleolus
内踝关节面/内踝關節面　articular facet of medial malleolus
内踝尖[穴]/内踝尖[穴]　neihuaijian, EX-LE8
内踝面/内踝面　medial malleolar facet
内踝皮下囊/内踝皮下囊　subcutaneous bursa of medial malleolus
内踝前动脉/前内踝動脈　medial anterior malleolar artery
内踝网/内踝網　medial malleolar rete
内踝支/内踝支　medial malleolar branch
内环骨板/内環骨板　inner circumferential lamella
内环境稳定/内環境穩定　homeostasis
内基因子/内基因子　endogenote
内寄生物/内寄生物　entorganism
内寄生物病/内寄生蟲病　entozootic disease
内监护/内監護　internal electronic monitoring
内假体/内假體　endoprosthesis
内睑腺炎/内瞼腺炎　internal hordeolum
内颈动脉鼓室支/内頸動脈鼓室支　caroticotympanic artery
内颈动脉神经丛/内頸動脈神經叢　plexus caroticus internus
内景/内景　internal sight
内镜/内腔鏡，内診鏡，内視鏡　endoscope
内镜超声检查[术]/内視鏡超音波檢查法　endoscopic ultrasonography
内镜胆管引流[术]/内鏡膽管引流[術]　endoscopic biliary drainage
内镜复位[术]/内鏡復位[術]　endoscopic reduction
内镜检查/内腔鏡檢法　endoscopy
内镜经胸交感神经切除术/内視鏡經胸交感神經切除術　endoscopic transthoracic sympathectomy
内镜括约肌切开术/内窥鏡括約肌切開術　endoscopic sphincterotomy
内镜[面部]除皱术/内窥鏡[面部]除皺術　endoscopic face rhytidectomy
内镜逆行胰胆管造影术/内視鏡逆行性膽胰顯影術　endoscopic retrograde cholangiopancreatography
内镜黏膜下肿瘤切除[术]/内鏡黏膜下腫瘤切除[術]　endoscopic enucleation of submucosal tumor
内镜取石[术]/内鏡取石[術]　endoscopic stone extraction technique
内镜碎石[术]/内鏡碎石[術]　endoscopic lithotripsy

内镜胰管引流[术]/内鏡胰管引流[術]　endoscopic drainage of pancreatic duct
内镜止血/内窺鏡止血　endoscopic hemostasis
内镜治疗[术]/内鏡治療[術]　therapeutic endoscopy
内镜注射治疗[术]/内鏡注射治療[術]　endoscopic injection therapy
内聚的/内聚性的　cohesive
内聚力/内聚力　cohesion
内科病/内科疾病　internal disease
内科病理学/内科病理學　internal pathology
内科学/内科學,内科　internal medicine
内科医师/内科醫生　internist
内[颗]粒层/内[顆]粒層　internal granular layer
内[颗]粒层纹/内[顆]粒層紋　stria of internal granular layer
内括约肌重建术/内括約肌重建術　internal sphincter reconstruction
内括约肌后切术/内括約肌後切術　Thomas procedure
内拉东脱位/Nelaton 氏脱位　Nelaton dislocation
内臁疮/内臁瘡　medial shank ulcer
内淋巴/内淋巴　endolymph
内淋巴分流术/内淋巴分流術　endolymphatic shunt
内淋巴管/内淋巴管　endolymphatic duct
内淋巴积液/内淋巴水腫　endolymphatic hydrops
内淋巴囊/内淋巴囊　endolymphatic sac
内淋巴囊减压术/内淋巴囊減壓術　endolymphatic sac decompression
内淋巴蛛网膜下腔分流术/内淋巴蛛網膜下腔分流術　endolymphatic subarachnoid shunt
内瘘/内部瘻管　internal fistula
内罗毕病/奈洛比病　Nairobi disease
内罗毕绵羊病病毒/奈洛比綿羊病病毒　Nairobi sheep disease virus
内罗毕疾病/奈洛比羊病　Nairobi sheep disease
内螺旋沟/内螺旋溝　inner spiral sulcus
内[毛]根鞘/内根鞘　inner root sheath, internal root sheath
内毛细胞/内毛細胞　inner hair cell
内面/内面　internal surface
内膜/内膜　intima
内膜垫/内膜墊　intima cushion
内膜纤维化/内膜纖維化　intimal fibrosis
内膜源性收缩因子/内膜源性收縮因數　endothelium-derived contracting factor
内膜源性舒张因子/内膜源性舒張因數　endothelium-derived relaxing factor
内膜锥/内膜錐　theca interna cone

内摩擦/內摩擦　internal friction
内囊/內囊　internal capsule
内囊出血/內囊出血　internal capsule hemorrhage
内囊后肢/內囊後肢　posterior limb of internal capsule
内囊前肢/內囊前肢　anterior limb of internal capsule
内囊膝/內囊膝　genu of internal capsule
内囊性偏瘫/內囊性偏癱　capsular hemiplegia
内囊血栓形成综合征/內囊血栓形成性症候群　capsular thrombosis syndrome
内囊支/內囊支　branch of internal capsule
内脑[脊]膜/內腦[脊]膜,脑内膜　endomeninx
内胚层/內胚層　endoderm
内胚层窦瘤/內胚層竇瘤　endodermal sinus tumor
内胚层沟/內胚層溝　endodermic groove
内胚层裂球/内分裂球　entomere
内胚层体型/內胚層型　endomorphy
内胚层体型者/內胚層型者　endomorph
内胚层性泄殖腔/內胚層洩殖腔　entodermal cloaca
内[胚层原]中胚层/內中胚層　endomesoderm
内皮/內皮　endothelium
内皮癌/內皮細胞癌　endothelial cancer
内皮白细胞附着分子-1/內皮白血球附著分子-1　endothelial leucocyte adhesion molecule-1
内皮层/內皮層　endodermis
内皮毒素/皮素　endotheliotoxin
内皮化/內皮化,血管内皮修補　endothelialization
内皮瘤/內皮[細胞]瘤　endothelioma
内皮瘤病/內皮瘤病　endotheliomatosis
内皮囊肿/內皮囊腫　endothelial cyst
内皮绒毛膜胎盘/內皮絨毛膜胎盤　endotheliochorial placenta
内皮溶素/溶內皮素　endotheliolysin
内皮肉瘤/內皮肉瘤　endotheliosarcoma
内皮生长因子/內皮生長因數　endothelial growth factor
内皮素/內皮素　endothelin
内皮素A受体/內皮素A受體　endothelin A receptor
内皮素B受体/內皮素B受體　endothelin B receptor
内皮缩血管肽受体/內皮縮血管肽受體　endothelin receptor
内皮系膜性肾小球肾炎/內皮繫膜性腎小球腎炎　endotheliomesangial glomerulonephritis
内皮细胞/內皮細胞　endothelial cell
内皮[细胞]性骨髓瘤/內皮細胞性骨髓瘤　endothelial myeloma
内皮细胞增多/內皮細胞增多症　endotheliocytosis
内皮细胞增生/內皮細胞增生　endothelial hyperplasia
内皮下层/內皮下層　subendothelial layer
内皮下膜/內皮下膜　subendothelium
内皮性白细胞/內皮性白血球　endothelial leukocyte
内皮炎/內皮炎　endotheliitis
内皮衍生舒缓因子/內皮衍生放鬆因數　endothelium-derived relaxing factor
内皮样型/內皮樣型　endothelioid habit
内皮依赖性松弛因子/內皮依賴性鬆弛因數　endothelium-dependent relaxing factor
内皮抑素类/內皮抑素類　endostatins
内皮增生/內皮增生症　endotheliosis
内嵌毛/內嵌毛　pili incarnati
内嵌植皮术/內嵌植皮術　inlay skin grafting
内腔容积测定法/腔容量測定法,測腔量法　endometry
内切核酸酶/內切核酸酶　endonuclease
内切核糖核酸酶类/內切核糖核酸酶類　endoribonucleases
内切脱氧核糖核酸酶类/內切去氧核糖核酸酶類　endodeoxyribonucleases
内求诸己/內求諸己　look inside for oneself
内区上皮/內區上皮　inner zone epithelium
内驱力/內驅力　drive
内屈/內曲,內彎　introflexion
内热/內熱　endogenous heat
内融合/核内混合　endomixis
内疝/内赫尼亞,內疝氣　entocele
内伤/內傷　internal damage
内伤发热/內傷發熱　endogenous fever, fever due to internal injury
内伤发热·肝气郁结证/內傷發熱·肝氣鬱結證　endogenous fever with pattern of liver qi depression
内伤发热·气虚证/內傷發熱·氣虛證　endogenous fever with qi deficiency pattern
内伤发热·伤酒证/內傷發熱·傷酒證　endogenous fever with alcoholism pattern
内伤发热·湿阻证/內傷發熱·濕阻證　endogenous fever with dampness retention pattern
内伤发热·痰积证/內傷發熱·痰積證　endogenous fever with pattern of phlegm accumulation
内伤发热·痰湿证/內傷發熱·痰濕證　endogenous fever with phlegm-damp pattern
内伤发热·血虚证/內傷發熱·血虛證　endogenous fever with blood deficiency pattern
内伤发热·血瘀证/內傷發熱·血瘀證　endogenous

fever with blood stasis pattern
内伤发热·阳虚证/內傷發熱·陽虛證 endogenous fever with yang deficiency pattern
内伤发热·阴虚证/內傷發熱·陰虛證 endogenous fever with yin deficiency pattern
内伤咳嗽/內傷欬嗽 endogenous cough
内伤咳嗽·肺热证/內傷欬嗽·肺熱證 endogenous cough with lung heat pattern
内伤咳嗽·肝火犯肺证/內傷欬嗽·肝火犯肺證 endogenous cough with pattern of liver fire invading lung
内伤咳嗽·气虚证/內傷欬嗽·氣虛證 endogenous cough with qi deficiency pattern
内伤咳嗽·痰热证/內傷欬嗽·痰熱證 endogenous cough with phlegm-heat pattern
内伤咳嗽·痰湿证/內傷欬嗽·痰濕證 endogenous cough with phlegm-dampness pattern
内伤咳嗽·阳虚证/內傷欬嗽·陽虛證 endogenous cough with yang deficiency pattern
内伤咳嗽·阴虚证/內傷欬嗽·陰虛證 endogenous cough with yin deficiency pattern
内伤痰饮眩晕/內傷痰飲眩暈 vertigo with pattern of endogenous phlegm-fluid
内伤头痛/內傷頭痛 endogenous headache
内伤泄泻/內傷洩瀉 endogenous diarrhea
内伤眩晕/內傷眩暈 endogenous vertigo
内伤眩晕·气虚证/內傷眩暈·氣虛證 endogenous vertigo with qi deficiency pattern
内伤眩晕·气血两虚证/內傷眩暈·氣血兩虛證 endogenous vertigo with pattern of deficiency of both qi and blood
内伤眩晕·血虚证/內傷眩暈·血虛證 endogenous vertigo with blood deficiency pattern
内上段静脉/內上段靜脈 internal superior segment
内上髁/內上髁 medial epicondyle
内肾小球/內腎小球 internal glomerulus
内渗/內滲,透膜渗入 endosmosis
内渗当量/內滲當量 endosmotic equivalent
内渗压测定器/內滲計 endosmometer
内生的/內生的 endogenous
内生骨疣/內生骨疣 entostosis
内生肌酐清除率/內生肌酐清除率 endogenous creatinine clearance rate
内生囊/內生囊 endogenous cyst
内生软骨瘤/內生軟骨瘤 enchondroma
内生软骨瘤病/內生軟骨瘤病 enchondromatosis
内生软骨瘤的/[內生]軟骨瘤的 enchondromatous
[内生]软骨黏液瘤/[內生]軟骨黏液瘤 enchondromatous myxoma
内生软骨肉瘤/內生軟骨肉瘤 enchondrosarcoma
内生性动脉瘤/內生性動脈瘤 endogenous aneurysm
内生性生长/內生性生長 endophytic growth
内生性氧合/內生性氧合 endogenous oxygenation
内生殖器/內生殖器 internal genitals
内湿/內濕 endogenous dampness
内氏放线菌/Naeslundii 氏放線菌 Actinomyces Naeslundii
内氏小体/奈格利氏小體 Negri body
内视/內視 inward reflection
内视视觉/內視視覺 entoptic vision
内视现象/內視現象 entopic phenomenon
内收肌/內收肌 adductor, adductor muscle
内收[踇]趾肌/內收[踇]肌 adductor hallucis
内收内翻跖/內收內翻蹠,歪腳 metatarsus adductovarus, skewfoot
内收[作用]/內收作用 adduction
内斯勒溶液/Nessler 氏溶液 Nessler solution
内髓板/內髓板 internal medullary lamina
内隧道/內隧道,內坑道 inner tunnel
内缩松脱/內縮鬆脫 intrusive luxation
内肽酶/內勝肽酶 endopeptidase
内弹性膜/內彈性膜 internal elastic lamina, internal elastic membrane
内听道/內聽道 internal auditory meatus
内听道孔/內聽道孔 internal acoustic meatus foramen
内听诊/內聽診法 endoauscultation
内庭/內庭 neiting, ST44
内脱位骨生成/內脫位骨生成 distraction osteogenesis
内外兼治/內外兼治 principle of combined internal and external treatment
内外异性畸形/內外不符性半陰陽 transverse hermaphroditism
内吸渗/內吸滲 insorption
内吸收/內吸收 internal absorption
内膝眼/內膝眼 neixiyan, EX-LE4
内细胞群/內細胞群 inner cell mass
内细胞团/內細胞團 inner cell mass
内下段静脉/內下段靜脈 internal inferior segment vein
内下隐斜视/內下隱斜視 esocataphoria
内酰胺/內醯胺 lactam
β-内酰胺聚合物/β-內醯胺聚合物 β-lactam polymer
β-内酰胺类抗生素/β-內醯胺類抗生素 β-lactam

antibiotics
β-内酰胺酶抑制药/β-内醯胺酶抑制藥　β-lactamase inhibitor
内酰亚胺/内醯亞胺　lactim
内陷/内陷　inward sinking, organ failure
内陷·脾肾阳衰证/内陷·脾腎陽衰證　organ failure with spleen-kidney yang declining pattern
内陷·邪盛热极证/内陷·邪盛熱極證　organ failure with pattern of pathogen excessiveness and heat extremity
内陷·阴伤胃败证/内陷·陰傷胃敗證　organ failure with pattern of yin injury and stomach declining
内陷·正虚邪盛证/内陷·正虚邪盛證　organ failure with pattern of healthy qi deficiency and pathogen excessiveness
内向投射/内向投射　introjection
内向性龋/内部齲蛀　internal caries
内向性思维/内向性思維　autistic thinking
内向整流钾通道/内向整流鉀通道　inwardly rectifying potassium channel
内消瘰疬丸/内消瘰癧丸　neixiao luoli pill
内消旋化合物/内消旋化合物　meso compound
内斜脊/内斜脊　internal oblique ridge
内斜视/内斜視　esotropia
内嗅皮层/内嗅皮層　entorhinal cortex
内嗅区/内嗅區　entorhinal area
内旋肌/内扭肌　intorter
内旋转/内旋轉　internal rotation
内旋转斜视/内轉定斜眼　incyclotropia
内旋转隐斜/内轉動斜眼　incyclophoria
内压性憩室/内壓性憩室　pressure diverticulum
内压性疝/壓出性疝　pulsion hernia
内芽性增殖/肉芽增殖　endodyogeny
内眼检查[法]/内眼檢查[法]　examination of internal eye
内移行/内移行　internal transmigration
内因/内因　internal cause
内因败血病/内因性敗血病　endosepsis
内因素/内因數　intrinsic factor
内因性凝血/内因性凝血　intrinsic coagulation
内因性物种形成/内因性物種形成　intrinsic speciation
内因性抑郁/内生性抑鬱　endogenous depression
内隐静脉/内隱静脈　internal saphenous vein
内隐斜/内轉隱斜視　esophoria
内迎香/内迎香　neiyingxiang, EX-HN9
内影像/内影像　internal image
内痈/内癰　internal abscess

内用法/内用　internal application
内釉上皮/内釉上皮　inner enamel epithelium
内郁/内鬱　interior stagnation pattern
内原细胞/内原細胞　endogenous cell
内源代谢/内生性代謝　endogenous metabolism
内源基因/内源基因　endogenous gene
内源性大麻酚类/内源性大麻酚類　endocannabinoids
内源性感染/内生性傳染　endogenous infection
内源性感染再燃/内源性感染再燃　endogenous reinfection
内源性高三酸甘油脂血症/内生性高三酸甘油脂血症　endogenous hypertriglyceridemia
内源性类脂性肺炎/内源性類脂性肺炎　endogenous lipoid pneumonia
内源性逆转录病毒/内源性逆轉錄病毒　endogenous retrovirus
内源性染色/内源性染色　intrinsic staining
内源性睡眠障碍/内源性睡眠障礙　intrinsic sleep disorder
内源性哮喘/内因性氣喘　intrinsic asthma
内源性正压呼吸/内源性正壓呼吸　intrinsic positive-pressure respiration
内在光感/内在光感　intrinsic light
内在化/内在化　internalization
内在活性/固有[内在]活性　intrinsic activity
内在偏转/内部偏向傳導　intrinsic deflection
内在神经/内在神經　intrinsic nerve
内在途径/内在路徑　intrinsic pathway
内在性骨炎/内在性骨炎　osteitis interna
内在性子宫内膜异位症/子宮肌腺症　adenomyosis
内脏/内臟　viscera
内脏病/内臟病　splanchnopathy
内脏病原说/内臟病原説　visceralism
内脏不全[畸形]/内臟發育畸形　perosplanchnia
内脏传入神经/内臟傳入神經　visceral afferent nerve
内脏错位/内臟錯位　transposition of viscera
内脏大神经/内臟大神經　greater splanchnic nerve
内脏的/内臟的　splanchnic
内脏反位/内臟位置逆轉　situs inversus viscerum
内脏肥大/臟器肥大　visceromegaly
内脏风湿病/内臟風濕病　visceral rheumatism
内脏感觉/内臟感覺　splanchnesthesia
内脏感觉缺失/内臟感覺缺失　visceral anesthesia
内脏感觉神经/内臟感覺神經　visceral sensory nerve
内脏感觉异常/内臟感覺異常　visceral paresthesia
内脏感觉组元/内臟感覺組元　splanchnic sensory

内脏骨骼/內臟骨骼 splanchnoskeleton
内脏骨突/內臟骨突 splanchnapophysis
内脏过小/內臟過小 splanchnomicria
内脏机制/內臟機構 splanchnic mechanism
内脏肌/內臟肌 visceral muscle
内脏解剖论/內臟解剖論 splanchnography
内脏镜检查/腹臟鏡檢法 organoscopy
内脏利什曼病/內臟型利什曼病,黑熱病 visceral leishmaniasis
内脏麻醉/內臟麻醉法 splanchnic anesthesia
内脏逆位/內臟逆位,內臟反向 situs inversus viscerum
内脏皮肤型棕斜蛛咬中毒/內臟皮膚型棕蜘蛛中毒 viscerocutaneous loxoscelism
内脏腔/臟腑腔 splanchnic cavity
内脏强健型性格/內臟強健型性格 viscerotonia
内脏伤/內臟損傷 visceral injury
内脏烧伤/內臟燒傷 visceral burn
内脏神经/內臟神經 visceral nerve
内脏神经节/內臟神經結 visceral ganglion
内脏神经切除术/內臟神經切除術 splanchnicectomy
内脏神经切断术/內臟神經切斷術 splanchnicotomy
内脏神经痛/內臟神經痛 visceral neuralgia
内脏神经系统/內臟神經系統 visceral nervous system
内脏神经纤维/內臟神經纖維 visceral nerve fiber
内脏[神经]阻滞/內臟神經阻斷 splanchnic block
内脏石/內臟石 splanchnolith
内脏痛/內臟痛 visceral pain
内脏透照法/內臟鏡檢查 splanchnoscopy
内脏下垂/內臟下垂 splanchnoptosis
内脏小神经/內臟小神經 lesser splanchnic nerve
内脏性幻觉/內臟性幻覺 visceral hallucination
内脏性痛风/內臟痛風 visceral gout
内脏学/內臟學 splanchnology
内脏循环/內臟循環 splanchnic circulation
内脏异位/內臟異位 heterotaxy
内脏硬化/內臟硬化 splanchnosclerosis
内脏游离部/內臟隔離部 exclave
内脏幼虫移行症/內臟幼蟲移行症 visceral larva migrans
内脏运动神经/內臟運動神經 visceral motor nerve
内脏运动组元/內臟運動組元 splanchnic motor component
内脏正常/內臟正常 eusplanchnia
内脏周围炎/臟腑周圍炎 perisplanchnitis
内脏最下神经/內臟最下神經 lowest splanchnic nerve
内脏最小神经/內臟最小神經 least splanchnic nerve
内燥/內燥 endogenous dryness
内燥证/內燥證 pattern of endogenous dryness
内障/內障 internal ophthalmopathy
内障刀/白內障刀 cataract knife
内障压下术/內障撥下摘除法 cataractopiesis
内障针/內障針 cataract needle
内折/內折 infolding
内证/內證 interior pattern
内支/內支 internal branch
内直肌/內直肌 medial rectus, medial rectus muscle
内指细胞/內指[狀]細胞 inner phalangeal cell
内酯类/內酯類 lactones
内质体/內質體 endoplast
内质网/內質網 endoplasmic reticulum
内质网池内 A 粒子基因/內質網池內 A 粒子基因 intracisternal A-particle gene
内治法/內治法 internal treatment
内痔/內痔 internal hemorrhoid
内痔·风伤肠络证/內痔·風傷腸絡證 internal hemorrhoid with pattern of wind injuring intestine collateral
内痔·脾虚气陷证/內痔·脾虛氣陷證 internal hemorrhoid with pattern of spleen deficiency and qi sinking
内痔·气滞血瘀证/內痔·氣滯血瘀證 internal hemorrhoid with pattern of qi stagnation and blood stasis
内痔·湿热下注证/內痔·濕熱下注證 internal hemorrhoid with pattern of dampness-heat diffusing downward
内中胚层细胞/內中胚層細胞 endo-mesoderm cell
内终接线/內終接線 internal finishing line
内柱细胞/內柱細胞 inner pillar cell
内转肌/內轉肌 invertor
内转胎位术/內轉向術 internal version
内锥体层纹/內錐體層紋 stria of internal pyramidal layer
内锥体[细胞]层/內錐體[細胞]層 internal pyramidal layer
内锥体[细胞]层纹/內錐體[細胞]層紋 stria of internal pyramidal layer
内着色/內著色 intrinsic coloring
内眦/內眥,眼鼻角 medial angle of eye
内眦动脉/內眥動脈 angular artery
内眦间距/內眥間距 inner canthic diameter

内眦静脉/内眥静脈　angular vein
内眦距过宽/遠距眼角　telecanthus
内眦脓肿穿破/内側眥部穿孔性膿瘍　egilops
内眦赘皮/内眥贅皮　epicanthus
内眦赘皮矫正术/内眥贅皮矯正術　epicanthal plasty
嫩舌/嫩舌　tender tongue
能动的/能動的　motile
能动细胞/能動細胞　locomotive cell
能力/能力　ability
能量传递/能量傳遞　energy transfer
能量代谢/能量代謝　energy metabolism
能量过滤透射电子显微镜检查/能量過濾透射電子顯微鏡檢查　energy-filtering transmission electron microscopy
能量平衡/能量平衡　energy balance
能量摄取/能量攝取　energy intake
能量外转换/能量外轉換　external conversion of energy
能收缩的/能收縮的　contractile
能斯特灯/能斯特燈　Nernst glower
能走动的/能走動的　ambulatory
尼埃尔间隙/紐耳氏間隙　Nuel space
尼尔-穆塞反应/尼-莫二氏反應　Neill-Mooser reaction
尼尔-穆塞体/尼-莫二氏體　Neill-Mooser body
尼氟灭酸/尼氟滅酸　Niflumic Acid
尼古丁/尼古丁　nicotina
尼古丁胶姆糖/煙鹼口香糖　nicotine gum
尼卡地平/尼卡地平　nicardipine
尼科尔棱镜/尼科爾氏棱鏡　Nicol prism
尼科尔斯基征/尼科利斯基徵　Nikolsky sign
尼可地尔/尼可地爾　nicorandil
尼可刹米/尼可刹米　nikethamide
尼克酸/煙鹼酸　niacin
尼立达唑/尼立達唑　niridazole
尼曼病/Niemann 氏病　Niemann disease
尼曼-皮克病/尼曼-匹克症　Niemann-Pick disease
尼曼-皮克细胞/Niemann-Pick 二氏細胞　Niemann-Pick cell
尼莫地平/尼莫地平　nimodipine
尼莫司汀/尼莫司汀　nimustine
尼莫唑/尼莫唑　nimorazole
尼群地平/尼群地平　nitrendipine
尼日利亚菌素/奈及利亞菌素　nigericin
尼氏染色/尼氏染色　Nissl staining
尼氏染色法/尼氏染色法　Nissl staining method
尼氏体/尼斯小體　Nissl body
尼索地平/尼索地平　nisoldipine
尼扎替丁/尼扎替丁　nizatidine
呢喃谵妄/呢喃譫妄　delirium mussitans
泥疗法/泥療法　mud therapy
泥螺/泥螺　bullacta
泥螺光敏性皮炎/泥螺光敏性皮膚炎　bullactophotodermatitis
泥螺日光性皮炎/泥螺日光性皮膚炎　bullacta-solar dermatitis
泥浴/泥浴　mud bath
泥浴疗法/泥浴療法　illutation
鲵精蛋白/梭魚精蛋白　esocine
拟胆碱药/擬膽鹼[能]藥　cholinomimetic
拟胆碱酯酶/假膽鹼酯酶　pseudocholinesterase
拟等位基因/假對偶基因　pseudoallele
拟等位性/假等位性　pseudoallelism
拟多巴胺药/多巴胺能藥　dopaminergic
拟副交感神经药/擬副交感神經藥　parasympathomimetic
拟杆菌感染/擬桿菌感染　bacteroides infection
拟杆菌科感染/擬桿菌科感染　Bacteroidaceae infection
拟杆菌属/類桿菌屬　*Bacteroides*
拟谷盗甲虫/碾粉蟲　meal worm
拟基因/擬基因　pseudogene
拟基因型/擬基因型　genocopy
拟甲状腺素药/擬甲狀腺素藥　thyromimetic
拟交感神经兴奋活性/擬交感神經興奮活性　sympathomimetic activity
拟交感神经药/擬交感神經藥　sympathomimetic
拟交感兴奋胺/擬交感神經作用胺　sympathomimetic amine
拟角蛋白/類角質素　pseudokeratin
拟南芥蛋白质类/擬南芥蛋白質類　arabidopsis proteins
拟青霉属/擬青黴　*Paecilomyces*
拟染色体/類染色體　chromatoid
拟α-肾上腺素能药/擬α-腎上腺素能藥　alphamimetic
拟脂质浮肿病/類油質浮腫　pathomimic elaiopathy
逆传/逆傳　reverse transmission
逆传心包/逆傳心包　reversed transmission to pericardium, reverse transmission to the pericardium
逆传心包证/逆傳心包證　pattern of reverse transmission to the pericardium
逆动/逆動　against movement
逆规性散光/逆規性散光　astigmatism against rule
逆流/逆流,反流　countercurrent

逆蠕动/逆蠕動,抗蠕動 antiperistalsis
逆蠕动吻合[术]/反蠕動向吻合術 antiperistaltic anastomosis
逆向变性/逆向變性 retrograde degeneration
逆向传导/逆向傳導 antidromic conduction
逆向学习/逆向學習 reversal learning
逆向运行/反向運動,對抗運動 antikinesis
逆向轴突运输/逆行軸突運輸 retrograde axonal transport
逆行变性/退行性變性 retrograde degeneration
逆行搏动/逆行搏動 retrograde beat
逆行插管法/逆行插管法 retrocatheterism
逆行充填/逆行充填 retrograde obturation
逆行充盈/逆行充盈 retrograde filling
逆行导引插管/逆行導引插管 retrograde intubation
逆行岛状皮瓣/逆行島狀皮瓣 reverse island skin flap
逆行的/逆向的 antidromic
逆行尿道造影[术]/逆行尿道造影[術] retrograde urethrography
逆行膀胱造影[术]/逆行膀胱造影[術] retrograde cystography
逆行疝/逆行性疝 retrograde hernia
逆行射精/逆行射精 retrograde ejaculation
逆行肾盂造影[术]/逆行腎盂造影[術] retrograde pyelography
逆行栓塞/逆行性栓塞 retrograde embolism
逆行[性]感染/逆行性感染 retrograde infection
逆行性嵌顿疝/逆行性嵌頓疝 retrograde incarcerated hernia
逆行性龋/倒行性龋蚀 backward caries
逆行性疝/逆行性疝,W字型疝 W hernia
逆行性心脏停搏液灌注/逆行性心臟停搏液灌注 retrograde perfusion of cardioplegic solution
逆行性牙髓炎/逆行性牙髓炎 ascending pulpitis
逆行性遗忘/逆行性遺忘 retrograde amnesia
逆行性月经/經血倒流 retrograde menstruation
逆行性阻滞/逆行性傳導阻滯 retrograde block
逆行月经/返流性月經 regurgitant menstruation
逆行主动脉造影[术]/逆行性主動脈造影術 retrograde aortography
逆行转移/逆理性轉移,退行性轉移 paradoxical metastasis
逆移情/逆移情 countertransference
逆引导尿管插入术/逆引導尿管插入術 retrourethral catheterization
逆证/逆證 deteriorative pattern, pattern with unfavorable prognosis
逆治/逆治 counteractive treatment
逆转/逆轉,倒轉 reverse
逆转过敏反应/可逆過敏性 reverse anaphylaxis
逆转录病毒/反轉錄病毒 retrovirus
逆转录病毒科蛋白质类/逆轉錄病毒科蛋白質類 retroviridae proteins
逆转录病毒科感染/逆轉錄病毒科感染 retroviridae infection
逆转录聚合酶链反应/逆轉錄聚合酶鏈反應 reverse transcriptase polymerase chain reaction
逆[转]录酶/逆[轉]錄酶 reverse transcriptase
逆转录酶抑制剂/逆轉錄酶抑制劑 reverse transcriptase inhibitor
逆转录作用/逆轉錄 reverse transcription
逆转三碘甲状腺原氨酸/逆轉三碘甲狀腺原氨酸 reverse triiodothyronine
匿名的/無名的 anonymous
腻苔/膩苔 greasy fur
溺水/沈溺 drowning
溺水肺/溺水肺 drowned lung
年龄/年齡 age
年龄分布/年齡分布 age distribution
年龄相一致的/年齡相符的 age-matched
年龄因素/年齡因素 age factor
年龄中位数/年齡中位數 median age
年龄组/年齡組 age group
鲇毒痉挛素/鯰痙攣素 plotospasmin
鲇毒溶血素/鯰溶血素 plotolysin
黏稠菌落/黏液狀菌落 M colony
黏稠物阻塞症/膠稠性黏液病 mucoviscidosis
黏蛋白/黏液素 mucin
黏蛋白沉积症/黏液素病,黏蛋白病 mucinosis
黏蛋白累积病/黏蛋白累積病 mucinoses
黏蛋白膜/黏蛋白膜 mucolemma
黏蛋白尿/黏液素尿 mucinuria
黏蛋白性脱发/黏液性秃 alopecia mucinosis
黏蛋白性小汗腺癌/黏液蛋白小汗腺癌 mucinous eccrine carcinoma
黏蛋白原/黏液素原 mucigen
黏蛋白质类/黏蛋白質類 mucoproteins
黏度/黏[滯]性,黏稠性 viscosity
黏度测量法/黏滯性測定法 viscosimetry
黏度计/黏度計 viscometer
黏多糖/黏多醣 mucopolysaccharide
黏多糖类药物/黏多醣類藥物 mucopolysaccharide drug
黏多糖酶/黏液素酶 mucase
黏多糖尿/黏多醣尿 mucopolysachariduria

黏多糖贮积病/黏多醣貯積症 mucopolysaccharidosis
黏多糖贮积症/黏多醣累積病 mucopolysaccharidoses
黏附/黏附 sticking, adhesion
黏附细胞/黏附細胞 adherent cell
黏合/黏合 bonding
黏合剂/黏合劑 binder
黏合剂敷料/黏固粉敷料 cement dressing
黏合质/接合素 cementin
黏合作用/黏合法 cementation
黏浆液细胞/黏液蛋白性細胞 mucoalbuminous cell
黏结固定桥/黏結固定橋 adhesion fixed bridge
黏均分子量/黏度平均分子量 viscosity-average molar mass, viscosity-average molecular weight
黏菌/黏質真菌 slime fungus
黏菌虫类/黏菌類 mycetozoa
黏菌素/黏菌素 colistin
黏蜡/黏蠟 sticky wax
黏粒/黏粒 cosmid
黏膜/黏膜 mucous membrane, mucosa
黏膜白斑病/黏膜白斑病 leukokeratosis
黏膜白色海绵状痣/黏膜白色海綿狀痣 nevus spongiosus albus mucosae
黏膜瓣/黏膜瓣 mucosal flap
黏膜襞/黏膜皺襞 mucous fold
黏膜病病毒/黏膜病病毒 mucosal disease virus
黏膜剥离术/除黏膜法 demucosation
黏膜不平/黏膜不平 uneven mucosa
黏膜层疝/黏膜層疝 tunicary hernia
黏膜肥厚/黏膜異常增厚 pachymucosa
黏膜骨瘤/黏膜骨瘤 osteoma mucosae
黏膜骨膜瓣/黏膜骨膜瓣 mucoperiosteum flap
黏膜黑变病/黏膜的黑變症 mucosal melanosis
黏膜黑[色]素瘤/黏膜性黑色瘤 mucosal melanoma
黏膜红白斑/黏膜紅白斑 erythroleukoplakia
黏膜红斑病/黏膜紅斑 erythroplakia
黏膜毁除术/黏膜摧毀法 mucoclasis
黏膜肌层/黏膜肌層 muscularis mucosae
黏膜狼疮/黏膜狼瘡 lupus mucosae
黏膜类天疱疮/黏膜的天皰瘡樣 mucous membrane pemphigoid
黏膜良性淋巴组织增生病/黏膜良性淋巴組織增生病 benign lymphadenosis of mucosa
黏膜霉菌病/黏膜黴菌病 mucomycosis
黏膜密螺旋体/黏膜螺旋體 Treponema mucosum
黏膜免疫/黏膜免疫 mucosal immunity
黏膜内种植术/黏膜內種植術 intramucosal implantation
黏膜皮肤的/黏膜與皮膚的 mucocutaneous
黏膜皮肤利什曼病/黏膜皮膚利什曼病 mucocutaneous leishmaniasis
黏膜皮肤连接/黏膜皮膚連接 mucocutaneous junction
黏膜皮肤淋巴结综合征/黏膜皮膚淋巴結症候群 mucocutaneous lymph node syndrome
黏膜皮肤痔/黏膜皮膚痔 mucocutaneous hemorrhoid
黏膜桥/黏膜橋 mucosal bridge
黏膜切除术/黏膜切除術 mucosectomy
黏膜缺乏光泽/黏膜缺乏光澤 lack of mucosal luster
黏膜神经瘤综合征/黏膜神經瘤症候群 mucosal neuroma syndrome
黏膜脱垂/黏膜脫垂 prolapse of mucosa
黏膜下层/黏膜下層 submucosa
黏膜下丛/黏膜下叢 submucous plexus
黏膜下[肌]层/粘膜下[肌]層 submucous layer
黏膜下浸润麻醉/黏膜下浸潤麻醉 submucous infiltration anesthesia
黏膜下溃疡/黏膜下潰瘍 submucous ulcer
黏膜下麻醉/黏膜下麻醉 submucous anesthesia
黏膜下膜/黏膜下[組織]膜 submucous membrane
黏膜下前庭成形术/黏膜下前庭成形術 submucosal vestibuloplasty
黏膜下神经丛/黏膜下神經叢 submucosal nervous plexus
黏膜下纤维化/黏膜下纖維化 submucous fibrosis
黏膜下种植体/黏膜下種植體 submucosal implant
黏膜纤毛清除/黏膜纖毛清除 mucociliary clearance
黏膜相关淋巴样组织淋巴瘤/黏膜相關淋巴樣組織淋巴瘤 mucosa-associated lymphoid tissue lymphoma
黏膜性骨膜/黏膜性骨膜，骨黏膜 mucoperiosteum
黏膜性咽炎/黏膜性咽炎 angina catarrhails
黏膜牙龈界/齒齦黏膜結合 mucogingival junction
黏膜炎/黏膜炎 mucositis
黏膜移植/黏膜移植 mucosa transplantation
黏膜移植术/黏膜移植術 mucosa grafting
黏膜移植物/黏膜移植物 mucosa graft
黏膜用气雾剂/黏膜用氣化噴霧劑 mucosa aerosol
黏膜疹/黏膜疹 enanthem
黏膜支援/黏膜支援 mucosa support
黏膜支援式/黏膜支援式 mucosa-borne type
黏膜皱襞杵状肥大/黏膜皺襞杵狀肥大 clubbing of mucosal fold

黏膜皱襞前端变细/黏膜皺襞前端變細　tapering of mucosal fold
黏膜皱襞中断/黏膜皺襞中斷　abrupt ending of mucosal fold
黏腻苔/黏膩苔　sticky greasy fur
黏球蛋白/黏液球蛋白　mucoglobulin
黏弹性/黏彈性　viscoelasticity
黏性绷带/黏性繃帶　cohesive bandage
黏性末端/黏性末端　cohesive end
黏性凝胶/黏膠體　viscogel
黏性吸收性敷料/可黏吸收性敷料　adhesive absorbent dressing
黏液/黏液　mucilage, mucus
黏液癌/黏液[性]癌　carcinoma mucosum
黏液变细胞/黏液變性細胞,黏液樣細胞　mucocyte
黏液变性/黏液變性　mucinous degeneration
黏液表皮样癌/黏液表皮樣癌　mucoepidermoid carcinoma
黏液表皮样的/黏液性表皮樣的　mucoepidermoid
黏液表皮样瘤/黏液性上皮瘤　mucoepidermoid tumor
黏液病毒/黏液病毒　myxovirus
黏液的/[分泌]黏液的　mucous
黏液分解酶/黏液分解酵素　mucolytic enzyme
黏液分泌过多/黏液分泌過多,多黏液症　polyblennia
黏液[分泌]减少/黏液過少　hypomyxia
黏液分泌缺乏/缺乏黏液分泌　amyxorrhea
黏液[分泌]神经功能病/黏液分泌神經官能病　myxoneurosis
黏液化/黏液化,黏液變性　mucification
黏液肌瘤/黏液肌瘤　myxomyoma
黏液浆液性的/黏液漿液性的　mucoalbuminous
黏液[结缔]组织/黏液結締組織　mucous connective tissue
黏液菌孢子丝/黏液菌孢子絲　capillitium
黏液抗体/黏膜抗體　mucoantibody
黏液链球菌性耳炎/黏液球菌性耳炎　mucosis otitis
黏液瘤/黏液瘤　myxoma
黏液瘤病毒/黏液瘤病毒　myxoma virus
黏液瘤性脂肪瘤/黏液瘤性脂瘤　lipoma myxomatodes
黏液瘤样癌/黏液性癌　carcinoma myxomatodes
黏液膜性结肠炎/黏液性結腸炎　myxomembranous colitis
黏液囊/黏液囊　bursa
黏液囊病/黏液囊病　bursopathy
黏液囊切除术/黏液囊切除術　bursectomy

黏液囊切开术/黏液囊切開術　bursotomy
黏液囊石/黏液囊石　bursolith
黏液囊腺癌/黏液囊腺癌　mucinous cystadenocarcinoma
黏液囊腺瘤/黏液性囊腺瘤　mucinous cystadenoma
黏液囊肿/黏液囊腫　myxoid cyst
黏液内皮瘤/黏液內皮瘤　myxoendothelioma
黏液尿/黏液尿　blennuria
黏液脓性的/黏液樣膿的　mucopurulent
黏液呕吐/黏液嘔吐　blennemesis
黏液排泄/黏液排洩　myxiosis
黏液球囊性阑尾炎/黏液球囊性闌尾炎　appendicitis myxoglobulosis
黏液球囊肿/黏液球囊腫,闌尾黏液囊腫　myxoglobulosis
黏液缺乏/黏液缺乏　amyxia
黏液溶解药/黏液溶解藥　mucolytic
黏液肉瘤/黏液肉瘤,肉黏液瘤　myxoma sarcomatosum
黏液乳头瘤/黏液乳頭狀瘤　myxopapilloma
黏液软骨/黏液軟骨　mucocartilage
黏液软骨瘤/黏液軟骨瘤　myxochondroma
黏液软骨肉瘤/黏液軟骨肉瘤　myxochondrosarcoma
黏液软骨纤维肉瘤/黏液軟骨纖維肉瘤　myxochondrofibrosarcoma
黏液塞/黏液栓子　mucous plug
黏液神经胶质瘤/黏液神經膠質瘤　myxoglioma
黏液生成/黏液生成　myxopoiesis
黏液水肿/黏液水腫　oedema mucosum
黏液水肿性白痴/黏液水腫性白癡　myxidiocy
黏液水肿性苔藓/黏液水腫性苔蘚　lichen myxedematosus
黏液酸试验/黏液酸試驗　mucic acid test
黏液细胞/黏液細胞　mucilage cell
黏液细胞癌/黏液細胞癌　carcinoma mucocellulare
黏液纤维瘤/黏液纖維瘤　myxofibroma
黏液纤维肉瘤/黏液纖維肉瘤　myxofibrosarcoma
黏液腺/黏液腺　mucous gland
黏液腺癌/黏液腺癌　mucinous adenocarcinoma
黏液[腺]管炎/黏液管炎　myxangitis
黏液腺瘤/黏液腺瘤　myxadenoma
黏液腺囊肿/黏液腺囊腫　cyst of mucous gland
黏液腺泡/黏液[性]腺胞　mucous acinus
黏液腺炎/黏液腺炎　blennadenitis
黏液性肠炎/黏液性腸炎　mucoenteritis
黏液性粪/黏液性糞　mucous stool
黏液性啰音/黏液水泡音　mucous rale
黏液性脓/黏[液]膿　mucopus

黏液性水肿/黏液水腫　solid edema
黏液性水肿昏迷/黏液性水腫昏迷　myxedema coma
黏液性水肿心/黏液性水腫心　myxedema heart
黏液性增生/黏液性增生　myxomatous proliferation
黏液性脂肪瘤/黏液性脂肪瘤　myxolipoma
黏液样变性/黏液樣變性　mucoid degeneration
黏液样便/黏液樣便　mucoid stool
黏液样浆液性/黏液樣漿液性　mucoserous
黏液样浆液性细胞/黏液樣漿液性細胞　mucoserous cell
黏液[样]囊瘤/黏液囊瘤　myxocystoma
黏液样囊肿/黏液樣囊腫　mucoid cyst
黏液样曲霉/黏液狀麴菌　Aspergillus mucoroides
黏液样脂肪肉瘤/黏液樣脂肪肉瘤　myxoid liposarcoma
黏液溢/黏液漏,黏液溢出　myxorrhea
黏液溢出的/黏液過多的　blennorrhagic
黏液真杆菌/黏液真桿菌　Eubacterium limosum
黏液脂瘤/脂黏液瘤　lipomyxoma
黏液制止法/黏液遏制　blennostasis
黏脂质/黏脂質　mucolipid
黏脂[贮积]病/黏脂貯積病　mucolipidosis
黏脂贮积症Ⅱ型/黏脂貯積症Ⅱ型　mucolipidosis type Ⅱ
黏质发酵/黏滯性發酵　viscous fermentation
黏滞系数/黏度係數　coefficient of viscosity
黏滞性过高/黏滯性過高,黏性過大　hyperviscosity
黏着连接/黏著連接　adherens junction
黏着性/黏著性　cohesiveness, adhesiveness
黏着液/黏著液　adhering liquid
捻发音/撚髮音,碎裂音　crepitation
捻法/撚法　holding-twisting manipulation
捻颈瘟/撚頸瘟　neck-twisted-like pestilence
捻皮癣/擦身癣,摸皮癣　dermatothlasia
捻丸样震颤/撚丸樣震顫　pill rolling tremor
捻衣摸床/撚衣摸床　floccilation
捻转/撚轉　twirling of needle
捻转补泻/撚轉補瀉　reinforcing-reducing method by twirling
捻转血矛线虫/扭旋血線蟲　Haemonchus contortus
碾槽/碾槽　mill groove
碾挫伤/碾挫傷　grinding contusion
碾压伤/碾壓傷　mangled injury
念珠菌病/念珠菌病　candidosis
念珠菌尿/念珠菌尿症　candiduria
念珠菌膀胱炎/念珠菌膀胱炎　Candida cystitis
念珠菌肉芽肿/念珠菌性肉芽腫　Candida granuloma
念珠菌属/念珠菌屬　Candida
念珠菌性对磨疹/念珠菌性對磨疹　Candida intertrigo
念珠菌性龟头炎/念珠菌性龜頭炎　Candida balanitis
念珠菌性甲沟炎/念珠菌性甲溝炎　Candida paronychia
念珠菌性甲癣/念珠菌性甲癬　Candida onychomycosis
念珠菌性女阴阴道炎/念珠菌性女陰陰道炎　Candida vulvovaginitis
念珠菌血[症]/念珠菌血病　candidemia
念珠菌阴道炎/念珠菌陰道炎　candidal vaginitis
念珠菌疹/念珠菌疹　candidide
念珠样的/念珠樣的　beadlike
念珠状错构瘤/念珠狀錯構瘤　moniliform hamartoma
念珠状发/念珠狀髮　beaded hair
念珠状红苔藓/念珠狀紅色苔蘚　lichen ruber moniliformis
念珠状链杆菌/念珠狀鏈桿菌　Streptobacillus moniliformis
念珠状[神经]纤维/曲張纖維　varicose fiber
酿酒酵母蛋白质类/釀酒酵母蛋白質類　saccharomyces cerevisiae proteins
酿酶复体/釀酶複體　zymase complex
鸟/鳥,禽　bird
鸟氨酸/鳥胺基酸　ornithine
鸟氨酸氨甲酰转移酶/鳥胺酸甲胺醯基轉移酶　ornithine carbamoyltransferase
鸟氨酸氨甲酰转移酶缺乏症/鳥胺酸甲胺醯基轉移酶缺乏症　ornithine carbamoyltransferase deficiency disease
鸟氨酸加压素/鳥氨酸昇壓素　ornipressin
鸟氨酸脱羧酶/鳥胺酸脫羧酶　ornithine decarboxylase
鸟氨酸脱羧酶抑制药/鳥胺酸脫羧酶抑制藥　ornithine decarboxylase inhibitor
鸟氨酸循环/鳥胺酸循環　ornithine cycle
鸟氨酸-氧-酸转氨酶/鳥胺酸-氧-酸轉胺酶　ornithine-oxo-acid transaminase
鸟巢式腔静脉过滤网/鳥巢式腔靜脈過濾網　bird nest vena caval filter
鸟传染性喉气管炎病毒/鳥傳染性喉氣管炎病毒　avian infectious laryngotracheitis virus
鸟蛋白质类/鳥蛋白質類　avian proteins
鸟等孢子球虫/鳥類同形孢子蟲　Isospora lacazei
鸟苷/鳥苷　guanosine
鸟苷二磷酸/鳥苷二磷酸　guanosine diphosphate
鸟苷二磷酸甘露糖/鳥苷二磷酸甘露糖　guanosine

diphosphate mannose
鸟苷二磷酸糖类/鳥苷二磷酸糖類　guanosine diphosphate sugars
鸟苷二磷酸岩藻糖/鳥苷二磷酸岩藻糖　guanosine diphosphate fucose
鸟苷三磷酸/鳥苷三磷酸　guanosine triphosphate
鸟苷四磷酸/鳥苷四磷酸　guanosine tetraphosphate
鸟苷酸环化酶/鳥苷酸環化酶　guanylate cyclase
鸟苷五磷酸/鳥苷五磷酸　guanosine pentaphosphate
鸟苷酰硫脲/鳥苷醯硫脲　guanylthiourea
鸟苷酰亚氨二磷酸/鳥苷醯亞胺二磷酸　guanylyl imidodiphosphate
鸟尿酸/鳥尿酸　ornithuric acid
鸟嘌呤/鳥嘌呤　guanine
鸟嘌呤核苷酸交换因子类/鳥嘌呤核苷酸交換因數類　guanine nucleotide exchange factors
鸟嘌呤核苷酸接合蛋白/鳥嘌呤核苷酸接合蛋白　guanine-nucleotide-binding protein
鸟嘌呤核苷酸类/鳥嘌呤核苷酸類　guanine nucleotides
鸟嘌呤核苷酸释放因子/鳥嘌呤核苷酸釋放因數　guanine nucleotide-releasing factor
鸟嘌呤核苷酸调节蛋白/鳥嘌呤核苷酸調節蛋白　guanine nucleotide regulatory protein
鸟嘌呤核苷酸游离阻滞剂/鳥嘌呤核苷酸游離阻滯劑　guanine nucleotide dissociation inhibitor
鸟嘌呤脱氨酶/鳥嘌呤去胺酶　guanine deaminase
鸟嘌呤细胞/鳥嘌呤細胞　guanine cell
鸟嘌呤性痛风/鳥嘌呤性痛風　guanine gout
鸟嘌呤一磷酸/鳥嘌呤單磷酸　guanine monophosphate
鸟头状侏儒症/鳥頭狀侏儒症　bird-headed dwarfism
鸟状臂/鳥臂　bird arm
鸟状脸/鳥面　bird-face
鸟状腿/鳥腿　bird-leg
尿/尿,小便　urina
尿白蛋白/尿白蛋白　urinary albumin
尿崩/尿崩　profuse urination
尿崩症/尿崩症　insipi-dus
尿比重测量法/尿比重測定法　urinometry
尿比重计/尿比重計　urinometer
尿闭/尿閉,尿液閉止　ischuria
尿变碱性反应/尿反應　uro-reaction
尿冰点测定法/尿冰點測定法　urinocryoscopy
尿丙酮定量器/丙酮尿定量器　acetonumerator
尿卟啉/尿卟啉,尿紫質　uroporphyrin
尿卟啉[过多]症/尿卟啉過多症　uroporphyria
尿卟啉原Ⅲ合成酶/尿卟啉原Ⅲ合成酶　uroporphyrinogen Ⅲ synthetase
尿卟啉原类/尿卟啉原類　uroporphyrinogens
尿卟啉原脱羧酶/尿卟啉原脱羧酶　uroporphyrinogen decarboxylase
尿布/尿布　diaper, napkin
尿布皮炎/尿布皮炎　diaper dermatitis
尿布疹/尿布疹　diaper rash
尿肠/胎兒之尿腸　urogaster
尿沉淀/尿沈澱,尿[沈]渣　urinary sediment
尿臭/尿臭　urinary smell
尿次[数]减少/排尿次數過少　oligakisuria
尿次[数]正常/尿數正常　orthuria
尿胆素/尿膽素,尿膽質　urobilin
尿胆素络合物/尿膽素複體　urobilin complex
尿胆素尿/尿膽素尿,尿膽質尿症　urobilinuria
尿胆素性黄疸/尿膽質性黄疸　urobilin jaundice
尿胆素原/尿膽素原,尿膽質原　urobilinogen
尿胆素原尿/尿膽素原尿,尿膽質原尿症　urobilinogenuria
尿胆素原血/尿膽素原血,尿膽質原血症　urobilinogenemia
尿氮减少/尿氮減少　hypazoturia
尿道/尿道　urethra
尿道癌/尿道癌　carcinoma of urethra
尿道白斑病/尿道白斑病　leukoplakia urethralis
尿道瓣膜/尿道瓣膜　urethral valve
尿道逼尿肌/尿道逼尿肌　compressor of urethra
尿道闭合压力图/尿道閉合壓力圖　urethral closure pressure profile
尿道闭锁/尿道閉鎖　atresia urethralis
尿道测量器/尿道計　urethrometer
尿道成形术/尿道成形術,尿道造形術　urethroplasty
尿道出血/尿道出血　urethrorrhagia
尿道刀/尿道刀　urethrotome
尿道的/尿道的　urethral
尿道动脉/尿道動脈　urethral artery
尿道发育不全/尿道發育不全　hypoplastic urethra
尿道肛/尿道肛　anus urethralis
尿道梗阻/尿道梗阻　urethral obstruction
尿道沟/[胚胎]尿道溝　urethral groove
尿道固定术/尿道固定術　urethropexy
尿道海绵体/尿道海綿體　cavernous body of urethra
尿道海绵体白膜/尿道海綿體白膜　albuginea of urethra cavernous body
尿道海绵体部/尿道海綿體部　cavernous part of urethra
尿道海绵体腔/尿道海綿體腔　caverns of urethra cavernous body

尿道海绵体小梁/尿道海綿體小梁　trabecula of penis cavernous body
尿道会师手术/尿道會師手術　reconstruction of ruptured urethra by Bank method
尿道畸形/尿道畸形　deformity of urethra
尿道疾病/尿道疾病　urethral disease
尿道嵴/尿道嵴　urethral ridge, urethral crest
尿道尖锐湿疣/尿道尖銳濕疣　condylomata acuminata of urethra
尿道结核/尿道結核　tuberculosis of urethra
尿道结石/尿道結石　calculus of urethra
尿道精囊差别回流/尿道精囊分道回流　urethro vesiculo-differential reflux
尿道痉挛/尿道痙攣　urethrism
尿道镜/尿道鏡　urethroscope
尿道镜检查术/尿道鏡檢法　urethroscopy
尿道口/尿道口　urinary meatus
尿道口成形术/尿道口成形術　urethral meatoplasty
尿道口刀/尿道口切開刀　meatome
尿道口缝合术/尿道縫合術　meatorrhaphy
尿道口计/測尿道器　meatometer
尿道口镜检查/尿道鏡檢查　meatoscopy
尿道口黏液囊肿/尿道口黏液囊腫　Tyson cyst
尿道口前移阴茎头成形术/尿道口前移陰莖頭成形術　meatal advancement and glandular plasty
尿道口切开术/尿道口切開術　urethral meatotomy
尿道口狭窄/尿道口狹窄　meatal stenosis
尿道口血管瘤/尿道口血管瘤　angioma of urethral meatus
尿道扩张/尿道擴張　urethral sounding
尿道扩张器/尿道擴張器　divulsor
尿道扩张取石术/尿道擴大取石術　lithectasy
尿道括约肌/尿道括約肌　sphincter of urethra, musculus sphincter urethrae
尿道括约肌横纤维/尿道橫肌　transversourethralis
尿道括约肌肌电图/尿道括約肌肌電圖　urethral sphincter electromyogram
尿道括约肌压力测定/尿道括約肌測壓　urethrosphincterometry
尿道淋病/尿道淋病　urethral gonorrhea
尿道瘘/尿道瘻　urethral fistula
尿道面/尿道面　urethral surface
尿道膜部/尿道膜部　membranous part of urethra
尿道内径描记器/尿道口徑記錄器　urethrograph
尿道内口/尿道内口　internal urethral orifice, internal orifice of urethra
尿道内括约肌/尿道內括約肌　internal sphincter muscle of urethra
尿道内切开术/尿道内切開術　internal urethrotomy
尿道黏膜脱垂/尿道黏膜脱垂　prolapse of urethra
尿道脓溢/尿道膿漏　urethroblennorrhea
尿道旁管/尿道旁[導]管　paraurethral canal, paraurethral duct
尿道旁裂/尿道旁裂　paraspadias
尿道膀胱的/尿道與膀胱的　urethrovesical
尿道膀胱固定术/尿道膀胱固定術　urethrocystopexy
尿道膀胱三角炎/尿道膀胱三角炎　urethrotrigonitis
尿道膀胱X射线照片/尿道膀胱X光相片　urethrocystogram
尿道膀胱吻合[术]/尿道膀胱吻合[術]　urethrovesical anastomosis
尿道膀胱悬吊术/尿道膀胱懸吊術　Marshall-Marchetti-Kranz procedure
尿道膀胱炎/尿道膀胱炎,膀胱尿道炎　urethrocystitis
尿道膀胱造影[术]/尿道膀胱X射線攝影術　urethrocystography
尿道膨出/尿道膨出,尿道憩室　urethrocele
尿道皮肤瘘/尿道皮膚瘻　urethrocutaneous fistula
尿道憩室/尿道憩室　urethral diverticulum
尿道前移术/尿道前移術　urethral advancement
尿道切除术/尿道切除術　urethrectomy
尿道切开术/尿道切開術　urethrotomy
尿道球/尿道球　bulb of urethra
尿道球动脉/尿道球動脈　urethral bulbar artery
尿道球静脉/尿道球靜脈　urethral bulbar vein
尿道球腺/尿道球腺　bulbourethral gland
尿道球腺导管/尿道球腺導管　duct of bulbourethral gland
尿道球腺疾病/尿道球腺疾病　diseases of Cowper gland
尿道球腺结核/尿道球腺結核　tuberculosis of Cowper gland
尿道球腺囊肿/尿道球腺囊腫　cyst of Cowper gland
尿道球腺脓肿/尿道球腺膿腫　abscess of Cowper gland
尿道球腺腺癌/尿道球腺腺癌　adenocarcinoma of bulbourethral gland
尿道球腺炎/尿道球腺炎　cowperitis
尿道球腺肿瘤/尿道球腺腫瘤　tumor of Cowper gland
尿道球炎/尿道球炎　bulbitis
尿道肉阜/尿道肉阜　urethral caruncle
尿道上裂/尿道上裂　epispadia
尿道上裂者/尿道上裂者　epispadiac

尿道上皮/尿道上皮　urothelium
尿道渗血/尿道滲血　urethrostaxis
尿道丝状探子/尿道絲狀探子　urethral filiform
尿道损伤/尿道損傷　urethral injury
尿道抬举试验/尿道抬舉試驗　Marshall-Marchetti test
尿道探子/尿道探子　urethral sound
尿道痛/尿道痛　urethralgia
尿道外口/尿道外口　external orifice of urethra
尿道外口炎/外尿道口炎　urethritis orificii externi
尿道外括约肌/尿道外括約肌　external sphincter muscle of urethra
尿道外切开术/尿道外切開術　external urethrotomy
尿道息肉/尿道息肉　polyp of urethra
尿道狭窄/尿道狹窄　urethral stricture
尿道狭窄扩张术/尿道狹窄擴張術　dilatation of urethral stricture
尿道下裂/尿道下裂　hypospadia
尿道下裂者/尿道下裂患者　hypospadiac
尿道陷窝/尿道陷窩　urethral lacuna
尿道腺/尿道腺　urethral gland
尿道腺癌/尿道腺癌　adenocarcinoma of urethra
尿道腺瘤/尿道腺瘤　adenoma of urethra
尿道腺炎/尿道腺炎　littritis
尿道性血尿/尿道性血尿　urethral hematuria
尿道血管瘤/尿道血管瘤　hemangioma of urethra
尿道压肌/Jarjavay 氏肌　Jarjavay muscle
尿道炎/尿道炎　urethritis
尿道液溢/尿道[液]漏　urethrorrhea
尿道异物/尿道異物　foreign body in urethra
尿道阴道的/尿道與陰道的　urethrovaginal
尿道阴道隔/尿道陰道隔　urethrovaginal septum
尿道阴道括约肌/尿道陰道括約肌　urethrovaginal sphincter
尿道阴道瘘/尿道陰道瘻　urethrovaginal fistula
尿道造口术/尿道造口術　urethrostomy
尿道造影[术]/尿道攝影術　urethrography
尿道折叠术/尿道折疊術　plication operation of urethra
尿道直肠瘘/尿道直腸瘻　urethrorectal fistula
尿道肿瘤/尿道腫瘤　tumor of urethra
尿道舟状窝/尿道舟狀窩　navicular fossa of urethra
尿道周的/尿道周圍的　periurethral
尿道周围蜂窝组织炎/尿道周圍蜂窩組織炎　periurethral phlegmon
尿道周围脓肿/尿道周膿腫　periurethral abscess
尿道周炎/尿道周圍炎　periurethritis
尿道注入法/尿道注入法　urethral injection

尿道综合征/尿道症候群　urethral syndrome
尿道阻塞/尿道阻塞　urethral obstruction
尿靛蓝/尿青質,尿靛質　cyanurin
尿靛石/靛基石　indigo calculus
尿毒素/尿毒素　urotoxin
尿毒素单位/尿毒質單位　urotoxic unit
尿毒性/尿毒性,尿毒力　urotoxicity
尿毒性黑矇/尿毒性黑矇　uremic amaurosis
尿毒性瘙痒[症]/尿毒性搔癢[症]　uremic pruritus
尿毒性肾髓质囊肿病/尿毒性腎髓質囊腫病　uremic medullary cystic disease
尿毒症/尿毒[血]症　uremia
尿毒症肺/尿毒症肺　uremic lung
尿毒症肺炎/尿毒症肺炎　uremic pneumonia
尿毒症高脂血症/尿毒症高脂血症　uremic hyperlipemia
尿毒症昏迷/尿毒症昏迷　uremic coma
尿毒症结肠炎/尿毒症結腸炎　uremic colitis
尿毒症脑病/尿毒症腦病　uremic encephalopathy
尿毒症心包炎/尿毒性心包炎　uremic pericarditis
尿毒症心肌病/尿毒症心肌病　uremic myocardiopathy
尿毒症性呼吸困难/尿毒性呼吸困難　uremic dyspnea
尿毒症性甲状旁腺功能亢进/尿毒症性甲狀旁腺功能亢進　uremic hyperparathyroidism
尿毒症性惊厥/尿毒症性抽搐　uremic convulsion
尿毒症谵妄/尿毒性譫妄　delirium uraemicum
尿毒症周围神经病变/尿毒症周圍神經病變　uremic peripheral neuropathy
尿芳香碱/尿香質　aromine
尿绯质原/尿緋質原　uroroseinogen
尿分光色素/尿影色素　urospectrin
尿分析/尿分析法　urinalysis
尿苷/尿[嘧啶]核苷　uridine
尿苷二磷酸/尿核苷雙磷酸鹽,雙磷酸尿核苷　uridine diphosphate
尿苷二磷酸半乳糖/尿核苷雙磷酸半乳糖　uridine diphosphate galactose
尿苷二磷酸木糖/尿苷二磷酸木糖　uridine diphosphate xylose
尿苷二磷酸葡糖/尿核苷二磷酸葡萄糖　uridine diphosphate glucose
尿苷二磷酸葡糖醛酸/尿苷二磷酸葡糖醛酸　uridine diphosphate glucuronic acid
尿苷二磷酸葡糖脱氢酶/尿苷二磷酸葡糖脱氫酶　uridine diphosphate glucose dehydrogenase
尿苷二磷酸糖类/尿苷二磷酸糖類　uridine

diphosphate sugars
尿苷二磷酸 N-乙酰氨基半乳糖/尿苷二磷酸 N-乙醯氨基半乳糖　uridine diphosphate N-acetylgalactosamine
尿苷二磷酸 N-乙酰氨基葡萄糖/尿苷二磷酸 N-乙醯氨基葡萄糖　uridine diphosphate N-acetylglucosamine
尿苷二磷酸 N-乙酰胞壁酸/尿苷二磷酸 N-乙醯胞壁酸　uridine diphosphate N-acetylmuramic acid
尿苷激酶/尿苷激酶　uridine kinase
尿苷-磷酸/尿核苷單磷酸鹽,尿苷酸　uridine monophosphate
尿苷磷酸化酶/尿苷磷酸化酶　uridine phosphorylase
尿苷三磷酸/尿核苷三磷酸鹽,三磷酸尿核苷　uridine triphosphate
尿过少/尿減少　uropenia
尿汗症/尿[質]汗症　urhidrosis
尿黑素/尿黑素,尿黑質　uromelanin
尿黑酸/尿黑酸,龍膽酸　homogentisic acid
尿黑酸尿/奪鹼質尿,黑尿病　alkaptonuria
尿黑酸尿症/尿黑酸尿症　alcaptonuria
尿黑质/尿黑質　melanurin
尿红素/尿緋質　nephrorosein
尿红正铁血红素/尿紅血基質　urorubrohematin
尿红质/尿紅質　urorubin
尿红质原/尿紅質原　urorubinogen
尿后余沥/尿後餘瀝　dribble of urine
尿黄[色]素/尿[卵]黄質　urolutein
尿灰质/尿灰質　urophein
尿激酶/尿激酶　urokinase
尿激酶纤维蛋白溶酶原激活剂/尿激酶血漿蛋白原活化劑　urokinase plasminogen activator
尿激酶原/前尿激酶　prourokinase
尿极/尿極　urinary pole
尿急/尿急　urgent micturition
尿钾排泄/鉀尿　kaliuresis
尿钾排泄药/尿鉀排洩藥　kaliuretic
尿检查/尿檢視法,檢尿法　uronoscopy
尿焦质/尿焦質,尿瀝青質　uropittin
尿紧张素类/尿緊張素類　urotensins
尿浸润/尿液滲漏　urecchysis
尿刊酸/尿犬酸　urocanic acid
尿刊酸酶/尿犬酸酶　urocanase
尿刊酸水合酶/尿犬酸酯水合酶　urocanate hydratase
尿刊酸酯/尿犬酸酯　urocanate
尿蓝母定量器/靛青質計,尿靛素計　indicanmeter
尿蓝母脑脊液/靛苷脊液症,靛青質脊液症　indicanorachia
尿蓝母尿/靛青質尿　indicanuria
尿蓝母血/靛青質血症　indicanemia
尿蓝质/尿藍質,尿綠質　urocyanin
尿蓝质原/尿藍質原　urocyanogen
尿粒形阿米巴/成粒尿阿米巴　Amoeba urinae granulata
尿亮酸/尿白胺酸　uroleucic acid
尿量/尿量　urine volume
尿磷定量器/尿磷定量器　urophosphometer
尿磷[酸盐]排泄/磷排洩　phosphuresis
尿流动力学/尿動力學　urodynamics
尿流动力学检查/尿流動力學檢查　urodynamic study
尿流分叉/尿流分叉　bifurcation of urination
尿流改道术/尿流改道術　diversion of urine
尿流率测定/尿流率測定　uroflometry
尿流中断/尿流中斷　interruption of urinary stream
尿硫蝶呤/尿蝶翅色質　uropterin
尿瘘/尿瘻　urinary fistula
尿路病变/尿路病,泌尿器病　uropathy
尿路病原体/泌尿道致病菌　uropathogen
尿路刺激征/尿路刺激徵　urinary irritation symptom
尿路感染/尿路感染　urinary tract infection
尿路梗阻/尿路阻塞　urinary obstruction
尿路结石/尿路結石　urinary calculi
尿路结石症/尿石病,尿石形成　urolithiasis
尿路溃疡/尿路潰瘍,泌尿器潰瘍　urelcosis
尿路念珠菌病/尿路念珠菌病　urinary moniliasis
尿路上皮肿瘤/尿路上皮腫瘤　urothelial tumor
尿路 X 射线电影照相术/尿路 X 光活動攝影術　cineurography
尿路造影术/尿道[X 射線]攝影術　urography
尿路[造影]照片/尿道 X 光像,尿道 X 光相片　urogram
尿氯过多/尿氯增多　pleiochloruria
尿氯排泄/氯尿症,氯化物尿　chloruresis
尿氯酸/尿氯醛酸　urochloralic acid
尿滤泡素过多/尿内濾泡素過高　hyperfolliculinuria
尿嘧啶/尿嘧啶　uracil
尿嘧啶氮芥/尿嘧啶氮芥　uracil mustard
尿嘧啶核苷酸类/尿嘧啶核苷酸類　uracil nucleotides
尿末滴沥/尿末滴瀝　terminal dribbling
尿囊/尿囊　allantois, allantoic bladder
尿囊柄/尿囊管　allantoic duct
尿囊蒂/尿囊蒂　allantoic stalk
尿囊动脉/尿囊動脈　allantoic artery

尿囊毒/尿囊毒質　allantotoxicon
尿囊寄生物/尿囊寄生胎　allantoic parasite
尿囊静脉/尿囊静脈　allantoic veins
尿囊囊肿/尿囊囊腫　allantoic cyst
尿囊憩室/尿囊憩室　allantoic diverticulum
尿囊腔/尿囊腔　allantoic cavity
尿囊绒[毛]膜/尿囊絨毛膜　allantochorion
尿囊生成/尿囊形成　allantogenesis
尿囊素/尿囊素,尿膜素　allantoin
尿囊素酶/尿囊素酶　allantoinase
尿囊素尿/尿囊素尿　allantoinuria
尿囊酸/尿囊酸　allantoic acid
尿囊酸酶/尿囊素轉變質　allantoicase
尿囊胎盘/尿囊胎盤　placenta allantoidea
尿囊循环/尿囊循環　allantoic circulation
尿囊液/尿囊液　allantoic fluid
尿[内]尿囊素过多/尿内尿囊素過多症　hyperallantoinuria
尿[内]尿酸正常/尿中尿酸正常　normouricuria
尿黏液样物/尿擬黏蛋白　urine-mucoid
尿脓/尿膿　purulent urine
尿脓毒素/尿敗血素　urosepsin
尿脓毒症/尿敗血病　urosepsis
尿排出量/尿排出量　urinary output
尿排泄[率]均匀/尿排洩率均匀　homaluria
尿频/尿頻,排尿頻繁　frequent micturition
尿塞通片/尿塞通片　niaosaitong tablet
尿色情/尿色情,尿性淫亂,尿性淫樂　urolagnia
尿沙/尿沙　urocheras
尿渗透压/尿滲透壓　osmotic pressure of urine
尿生成/生尿,泌尿　uropoiesis
尿生殖板/尿生殖板　urogenital plate
尿[生]殖窦/尿[生]殖竇,泌尿生殖竇　urogenital sinus
尿[生]殖窦括约肌/尿[生]殖竇括约肌　urogenital sinus sphincter
尿生殖膈/尿生殖膈　urogenital diaphragm
尿生殖膈上筋膜/尿生殖膈上筋膜　superior fascia of urogenital diaphragm
尿生殖膈下筋膜/尿生殖膈下筋膜　inferior fascia of urogenital diaphragm, ischioprostatic fascia
尿生殖沟/泌尿生殖溝　urogenital groove
尿生殖嵴/尿生殖嵴　urogenital ridge
尿生殖[嵴]系膜/尿生殖[嵴]繫膜　urogenital mesentery
尿生殖孔/尿生殖孔,洩殖孔　urogenital opening
尿[生]殖膜/尿[生]殖膜,泌尿生殖膜　urogenital membrane

尿生殖区/尿生殖部　urogenital region
尿生殖褶/泌尿生殖褶　urogenital fold
尿失禁/小便失禁　urinary incontinence
尿石/尿石　urolith
尿石学/尿石學　urolithology
尿食盐排泄/鹽尿　saluresis
尿素/尿素　urea
尿素分解/尿素分解　ureolysis
尿素酶/尿素酶,脲酵素　urease
尿素清除率/尿素清除率　urea clearance rate
尿素试验/尿素試驗　urea test
尿素霜/尿素霜　urea frost
尿素水解酶类/尿素水解酶類　ureohydrolases
尿素循环/尿素循環　urea cycle
尿素循环障碍/尿素循環障礙　urea cycle disorder
尿酸/尿酸　uric acid
尿酸胆汁[症]/尿酸膽症　uricocholia
尿酸度测定器/尿液酸度計　uroacidimeter
尿酸分解[作用]/尿酸分解　uricolysis
尿酸酶/[解]尿酸酵素　uricase
尿酸尿/尿酸尿症　uricaciduria
尿酸生成/尿酸生成　uricopoiesis
尿酸素质/尿酸體質　uric acid diathesis
尿酸性关节炎/尿酸性關節炎,痛風性關節炎　uratic arthritis
尿酸血症/尿酸血症　uricacidemia
尿酸盐/尿酸鹽　lithate
尿酸盐沉着性结膜炎/尿酸鹽沈著性結膜炎　uratic conjunctivitis
尿酸盐结晶/尿酸鹽結晶　urate crystal
尿酸盐性变性/尿酸鹽性變性　uratic degeneration
尿酸盐血/尿酸鹽血症　uratemia
尿酸氧化酶/尿酸鹽氧化酶　urate oxidase
尿酸乙胺/尿酸乙胺　ethylamine urate
尿酸骤增/尿酸驟增　uric acid shower
尿酸转化酶/尿酸轉化酵素　uricolytic enzyme
尿糖测定法/尿糖檢法,尿糖定量法　urosaccharometry
尿糖过多/尿糖過多　hyperglycosuria
尿糖计/測尿糖計　diabetograph
尿铁酸/尿鐵酸　uroferric acid
尿铜排泄/銅尿排洩　cupruresis
尿痛/尿痛　pain in urination
尿外渗/尿外滲　urinary extravasation
尿[外渗性]脓肿/尿外滲性膿腫　urinary abscess
尿胃蛋白酶/尿胃液素　uropepsin
尿胃蛋白酶原/尿胃蛋白酶原　uropepsinogen
尿细胞学/尿細胞學　urinary cytology

尿性腹水/尿性腹水　urinary ascites
尿性囊肿/尿性囊腫　urinoma
尿性消化不良/尿性消化不良　urinaria dyspepsia
尿性质不良/尿質不良　uracrasia
尿性肿胀/尿腫　uroncus
尿血[病]/尿血[病],血尿[症]　hematuria
尿血卟啉/尿血卟啉,尿血紫質　urohematoporphyrin
尿血管紧张素/尿增血壓素　urohypertensin
尿血·脾不统血证/尿血·脾不統血證　hematuria with pattern of failure of spleen to control blood
尿血·肾气不固证/尿血·腎氣不固證　hematuria with pattern of unconsolidated kidney qi
尿血无机盐指数/血腎鹽類指數　hemorenal salt index
尿血·下焦热盛证/尿血·下焦熱盛證　hematuria with pattern of heat exuberant in lower jiao
尿血·下焦湿热证/尿血·下焦濕熱證　hematuria with pattern of damp-heat in lower jiao
尿血·阴虚火旺证/尿血·陰虛火旺證　hematuria with pattern of exuberant fire due to yin deficiency
尿药浓度/尿藥濃度　urine drug level
尿液分段检查/尿液分段檢查　fractional examination of urine
尿[液]囊肿/尿液囊腫　urinary cyst
尿液性水肿/尿液[性水]腫　uredema
尿源性肾盂肾炎/尿源性腎盂腎炎　urogenous pyelonephritis
尿源性肾盂炎/尿源性腎盂炎　urogenous pyelitis
尿[诊断]检查/檢尿法　uroscopy
尿诊断学/尿診學　urosemiology
尿脂石/尿脂石　urostealith
尿直肠隔/泌尿直腸隔　urorectal septum
尿中砂石/尿中砂石　sandy urine
尿潴留/尿瀦留　urinary retention
尿浊[病]/尿濁[病]　turbid urine
尿浊·脾虚气陷证/尿濁·脾虛氣陷證　turbid urine with pattern of qi collapse and spleen deficiency
尿浊·肾阳衰微证/尿濁·腎陽衰微證　turbid urine with pattern of kidney yang exhaustion
尿浊·肾阴虚证/尿濁·腎陰虛證　turbid urine with pattern of kidney yin deficiency
尿浊·湿热下注证/尿濁·濕熱下注證　turbid urine with pattern of downward diffusion of damp-heat
尿浊·湿热[蕴结]证/尿濁·濕熱[蘊結]證　turbid urine with pattern of accumulation and binding of damp-heat
尿着色合剂/尿著色劑　cystochrome
尿紫褐血红质/尿棕羥高鐵血紅素　urofuscohematin
尿[紫]褐质/尿棕質,尿褐質　urofuscin
尿紫素尿/尿紫質尿　purpurinuria
脲/脲　carbamide
脲苯甲酸/脲基苯甲酸　uraminobenzoic acid
脲合四氧嘧啶酸/脲合四氧嘧啶酸　alluranic acid
脲基甲酸/脲基甲酸　allophanic acid
脲基甲酸水解酶/脲基甲酸水解酶　allophanate hydrolase
脲牛磺酸/脲牛磺酸　uraminotauric acid
脲浓缩试验/尿素濃度試驗　urea concentration test
脲乙醛酸/脲乙醛酸　allanic acid
脲乙酸/内醯脲酸　hydantoic acid
脲原体属感染/脲原體屬感染　ureaplasma infection
溺孔/溺孔　external orifice of urethra, urethral orifice
溺窍/溺竅　external orifice of male urethra, seminal orifice
捏法/捏法　pinching manipulation
捏积/捏積　chiropractic
捏脊/捏脊,按脊術　chiropractic, spinal pinching
捏脊手法/捏脊手法　chiropractic manipulation
捏丸样震颤/滾丸震顫　pill-rolling tremor
捏小腿三头肌试验/捏小腿三頭肌試驗　Thompson test
啮齿动物/齧齒動物　rodent
啮齿动物疾病/齧齒動物疾病　rodent disease
啮齿动物控制/齧齒動物控制　rodent control
啮唇癖/齧唇癖　cheilophagia
啮舌/齧舌　tongue biting
啮蚀艾肯菌/嚙蝕 Eikenella 氏菌　Eikenella corrodens
镊[子]/鑷子　forceps
镍铬合金/鎳鉻合金　nichrome
镍铬线圈/鎳鉻線圈　nichrome coil
镍皮炎/鎳皮炎　nickel dermatitis
镍钛/鎳鈦　nickel-titanium
镍疹/鎳疹　nickel rash
颞/顳　nie, AT 2, temple
颞半侧视网膜/視網膜顳部　temporal retina
颞部除皱术/顳部除皺術　temporal rhytidectomy
颞[部]的/顳的　temporal
颞部入路/顳部入路　temporal approach
颞侧偏盲/顳側偏盲　temporal hemianopsia
颞顶的/顳骨與頂骨的　temporoparietal
颞顶肌/顳頂肌　musculus temporoparietalis
颞顶性失语/顳葉頂葉性失語症　temporoparietal aphasia
颞动脉/顳動脈　temporal artery

颞动脉炎/顳動脈炎 temporal arteritis
颞额的/顳與額骨的 temporofrontal
颞额颧点/顳額顴點 frontomalare temporale
颞额束/顳額徑 temporofrontal tract
颞骨/顳骨 temporal bone
颞骨大脑面/顳骨大腦面 cerebral surface of temporal bone
颞骨鼓部/鼓骨,鼓板 tympanic bone
颞骨关节面/顳骨關節面 articular surface of temporal bone
颞骨茎突/顳骨莖突 styloid process of temporal bone
颞骨颧突/顳骨顴突 zygomatic process of temporal bone
颞骨乳突/顳骨乳突 mastoid process of temporal bone
颞骨乳突切迹/顳骨乳突切跡 incisura mastoidea ossis temporalis
颞骨下颌关节/顳骨下頜關節 temporomandibular articulation
颞骨下颌关节静脉/顳骨下頜關節靜脈 temporomandibular articular vein
颞骨下颌关节综合征/顳骨下頜關節症候群 temporomandibular joint syndrome
颞骨岩部/顳骨岩部 petrous part of temporal bone, petrosal bone
颞骨乙状窦沟/顳骨乙狀竇溝 sulcus sinus sigmoidei ossis temporalis
颞骨乙状沟/顳骨乙狀溝 sigmoid groove of temporal bone
颞骨枕缘/顳骨枕緣 occipital margin of temporal bone
颞颌关节脱位/顳[下]頜關節脫位 dislocation of temporomandibular joint, temporomandibular dislocation
颞颌关节紊乱症/顳下頜關節紊亂 disorders of temporomandibular joint
颞横沟/顳橫溝 transverse temporal sulci
颞横回/顳橫迴 transverse temporal gyri
颞后板障静脉/顳後板障靜脈 posterior temporal diploic vein
颞后线/顳後線 posterior temporal line
颞肌/顳肌 temporalis, musculus temporalis
颞肌嵴/顳肌嵴 temporal crest
颞极/顳極 temporal pole
颞间隙/顳間隙 temporal space
颞筋膜/顳筋膜 temporal fascia
颞筋膜浅层/顳筋膜淺層 superficial layer of temporal fascia
颞筋膜深层/顳筋膜深層 deep layer of temporal fascia
颞鳞/顳鱗,顳骨鱗部 temporal squama
颞面/顳面 temporal surface
颞皮下神经/顳皮下神經 subcutaneous temporal nerve
颞前板障静脉/顳前板障靜脈 anterior temporal diploic vein
颞前线/顳前線 anterior temporal line, MS10
颞浅动脉/顳淺動脈 superficial temporal artery
[颞浅动脉]额支/[顳淺動脈]額支 frontal branch
颞浅筋膜/顳淺筋膜 superficial temporal fascia
颞浅静脉/顳淺靜脈 superficial temporal vein
颞浅神经/淺顳神經 superficial temporal nerve
颞浅脂肪垫/顳淺脂肪墊 superficial temporal fat pad
颞桥的/顳葉與橋腦的 temporopontine
颞桥束/顳葉橋腦徑 temporopontine tract
颞区/顳部 temporal region
颞颧缝/顳顴縫 temporozygomatic suture
颞颧神经/顳顴神經 temporomalar nerve
颞上沟/顳上溝 superior temporal sulcus
颞上颌关节/顳上頜關節 temporomaxillary articulation
颞上回/顳上迴 superior temporal gyrus
颞上区/顳上區 superior temporal area
颞深后动脉/顳深後動脈 posterior deep temporal artery
颞深筋膜/顳深筋膜 deep temporal fascia
颞深筋膜浅层/顳深筋膜淺層 superficial layer of deep temporal fascia
颞深筋膜深层/顳深筋膜深層 deep layer of deep temporal fascia
颞深静脉/顳深靜脈 deep temporal vein
颞深前动脉/顳深前動脈 anterior deep temporal artery
颞深神经/顳深神經 deep temporal nerve
颞深脂肪垫/顳深脂肪墊 deep temporal fat pad
颞突/顳突 temporal process
颞窝/顳凹 temporal fossa
颞下点/顳下點 infratemporale
颞下沟/顳下溝 inferior temporal sulcus
颞下颌的/顳骨與下頜的 temporomandibular
颞下颌关节/顳下頜關節 temporomandibular joint, maxillary articulation
颞下颌关节侧位体层片/顳下頜關節側位體層片 lateral tomogram of TMJ

颞下颌关节[功能]紊乱综合征/顎下頜關節[功能]紊亂症候群　temporomandibular joint disturbance syndrome
颞下颌关节紧张综合征/顎下頜關節緊張症候群　TMJ stress syndrome
颞下颌关节静脉/顎下頜關節靜脈　articular vein
颞下颌关节内侧韧带/顎下頜關節內側韌帶　lateral ligament of internal temporomandibular joint
颞下颌关节盘/顎下頜關節盤　articular disc of temporomandibular joint, temporomandibular joint disk
颞下颌关节前脱位/顎下頜關節前脫位　anterior dislocation of TMJ
颞下颌关节炎/顎下頜關節炎　hyposiagonarthritis
颞下颌关节造影术/顎下頜關節造影術　TMJ arthrography
颞下颌关节障碍/顎下頜關節障礙　temporomandibular joint disorders
颞下颌关节综合征/Costen 氏症候群　Costen syndrome
颞下颌内侧韧带/顎下頜內側韌帶　medial temporomandibular ligament
颞下颌外侧韧带/顎下頜外側韌帶　lateral temporomandibular ligament
颞下回/顎下迴　inferior temporal gyrus
颞下嵴/顎下嵴　infratemporal crest
颞下间隙/顎下間隙　infratemporal space
颞下减压术/顎下減壓法　subtemporal decompression
颞下面/顎下面　infratemporal surface
颞下区/顎下區　inferior temporal area
颞下入路/顎下入路　subtemporal approach
颞下窝/顎下凹　infratemporal fossa
颞下窝入路/顎下窝入路　infratemporal approach
颞下窝综合征/顎下窝症候群　infratemporal fossa syndrome
颞线/顎線　temporal line
颞小脑的/顎小腦束的　temporocerebellar
颞小脑束/顎葉小腦徑　temporocerebellar tract
颞叶/顎葉　temporal lobe
颞叶岛盖/顎蓋　temporal operculum
颞叶癫痫/顎葉癫癇　temporal lobe epilepsy
颞叶后动脉/顎後動脈　posterior temporal artery
颞叶后支/顎後支　posterior temporal branch
颞叶前动脉/顎前動脈　anterior temporal artery
颞叶前支/顎前支　anterior temporal branch
颞叶晕厥/顎葉暈厥　temporal lobe syncope
颞叶中动脉/顎中動脈　middle temporal artery
颞叶中间支/顎中間支　intermediate temporal branch
颞支/顎支　temporal branch
颞中动脉/顎中動脈,中顎動脈　middle temporal artery
颞中动脉沟/顎中動脈溝,中顎動脈溝　sulcus for middle temporal artery, groove for middle temporal artery
颞中回/顎中迴　middle temporal gyrus
颞中筋膜/顎中筋膜　middle temporal fascia
颞中静脉/顎中靜脈　middle temporal vein
颞中区/顎中區　middle temporal area
颞中央回束/顎葉中央回徑　temporocentral tract
颞中央束的/顎中央束的　temporocentral
宁神静志/寧神靜志　calming the mind
宁心开窍/寧心開竅　calming heart for resuscitation, relieving mental stress and inducing resuscitation
宁心顺气/寧心順氣　relieving mental stress and checking adverse flow of qi, relieving mental stress and regulating qi flow
柠康酐类/檸康酐類　citraconic anhydrides
柠檬酊/檸檬劑,檸檬皮酊　lemon tincture
柠檬苦素类/檸檬苦素類　limonins
柠檬皮/檸檬皮　lemon peel
柠檬酸/檸檬酸,枸櫞酸　citric acid
柠檬酸铋铵/檸檬酸鉍銨　bismuth and ammonium citrate
柠檬酸钙/檸檬酸鈣,枸櫞酸鈣　calcium citrate
柠檬酸钾/檸檬酸鉀,枸櫞酸鉀　potassium citrate
柠檬酸镁溶液/檸檬酸鎂溶液　magnesium citrate solution
柠檬酸脱氢酶/枸櫞酸脫氫酶　citric dehydrogenase
柠檬酸循环/檸檬酸循環,三羧酸循環　citric acid cycle
柠檬酸盐类/檸檬酸鹽類　citrates
凝点/凝固點　congealing point
凝固/凝固,凝血　coagulation
凝固白蛋白/凝固白蛋白　coagulated albumin
凝固带/凝固帶　coagulation band
凝固蛋白紊乱/凝固蛋白紊亂　coagulation protein disorder
凝固蛋白质/凝固蛋白質　coagulated protein
凝固反应/凝固反應　coagulation reaction
凝固酶/凝固酶　coagulase
凝固汽油烧伤/凝固汽油燒傷　napalm burn
凝固[乳]酪蛋白/乳酪凝塊,乳酥　tyrein
凝固时间/凝固時間　clotting time
凝固试验/凝固試驗　coagulation test

凝固性/凝性,凝固力　coagulability
凝固性过低/低凝固性　hypocoagulability
凝固性坏死/凝固性壞死　coagulation necrosis
凝固性注射/凝固性注射　coagulation injection
凝固作用/凝結　coagulation
凝集/凝集　agglutination, clumping
凝集反应/凝集作用反應　agglutination reaction
凝集反应镜/凝集檢視鏡　agglutinoscope
凝集反应器/凝集試驗器　agglutometer
凝集反应效价/凝集價　agglutination titer
凝集试验/凝集試驗　agglutination test
凝集素/凝集素　agglutinin
凝集素吸收/凝集素吸收　agglutinin absorption
凝集物质/凝集物質,凝集素　agglutinating substance
凝集性血栓/凝集性血栓　agglutinative thrombus
凝集抑制试验/凝集抑制試驗　agglutination inhibition test
凝集因子/凝集因數　clumping factor
凝集原/凝[集]原　agglutinogen
凝胶/凝膠　gel
凝胶的/膠性的　gelatinous
凝胶电泳/凝膠電泳　gel electrophoresis
凝胶硅/凝膠矽　silicone gel
凝胶过滤/凝膠過濾　gel filtration
凝胶剂/凝膠劑　gel
凝胶扩散/凝膠擴散　gel diffusion
凝胶扩散试验/凝膠擴散試驗　gel diffusion test
凝胶类/凝膠類　gels
凝胶色谱法/凝膠色譜法　gel chromatography
凝胶试验/膠質試驗　gel test
凝结物/凝結物　concretion
凝聚/凝聚,共聚　condensation, coacervation
凝聚性/凝聚性　cohesiveness
凝膜/凝膜　haptogen membrane
凝乳/乳凝塊　ziega
凝乳发酵/乾酪性發酵　caseous fermentation
凝乳酶/凝乳酶,凝固酵素　clotting enzyme, curdling enzyme
凝乳酶原/凝乳酶原,凝酪酶原　chymosinogen
凝乳样脓/乳塊狀膿　curdy pus
凝神/凝神　focusing one's attention
凝视瘫痪/凝視癱瘓　gaze paralysis
凝视性眼球震颤/凝視性眼球震顫　fixation nystagmus
凝缩/凝縮　condensation
凝血/血凝固　blood coagulation
凝血病/凝血病變　coagulopathy

凝血功能试验/凝血功能試驗　coagulation function test
凝血激酶/凝血激酶,凝血激素　thrombocinase
凝血级联系统/凝血級聯系統　coagulation cascade system
凝血块/滯血　sludged blood
凝血块变态/血小板性變形　platelet metamorphosis
凝血块肾盂切开取石术/凝血塊腎盂切開取石術　coagulum pyelolithotomy
凝血酶/凝固酵素,凝血酵素,纖維蛋白酵素　coagulating enzyme, thrombin
凝血酶敏感蛋白类/凝血酶敏感蛋白類　thrombospondins
凝血酶时间/凝血酶時間　thrombin time
凝血酶受体/凝血酶受體　thrombin receptor
凝血酶原/凝血酶原　prothrombin
凝血酶原 A/前凝血酶 A　fraction A prothrombin
凝血酶原 B/前凝血酶 B　fraction B prothrombin
凝血酶原激活剂/凝血酵素原活化質　prothrombin activator
凝血酶原减少[症]/前凝血酵素減少症　prothrombinopenia
凝血酶原缺乏[症]/凝血酶原缺乏[症]　prothrombin deficiency
凝血酶原时间/凝血酶原時間,前凝血酵素時間　prothrombin time
凝血酶原抑制药/凝血酶原抑制藥　prothrombin inhibitor
凝血时间图/凝固圖　coagulogram
凝血试验/血栓形成測驗　thrombotest
凝血弹性描记法/血小板強度測定法　thromboelastography
凝血弹性描记器/血小板強度器　thromboelastograph
凝血弹性[描记]图/血小板強度圖　thromboelastogram
凝血性血栓形成/凝血性血栓形成　coagulation thrombosis
凝血药/凝血藥　coagulant
凝血因子/凝血因子,凝血因數　blood coagulation factor, coagulation factor
凝血因子Ⅻ/哈格曼因數,第十二凝血因數　Hageman factor
凝血因子类/凝血因子類　blood clotting factors
凝血脂素 A2/凝血脂素 A2　thromboxane A2
凝血脂素 B2/凝血脂素 B2　thromboxane B2
凝血致活酶/血栓形成質,凝血質,凝血激素　thromboplastin

凝脂翳/凝脂翳　congealed-fat nebula, bacterial keratitis
凝脂翳·肝经风热证/凝脂翳·肝經風熱證　congealed-fat nebula with pattern of wind-heat in liver channel
凝脂翳·气阴两虚证/凝脂翳·氣陰兩虛證　congealed-fat nebula with qi-yin deficiency pattern
凝脂翳·热盛腑实证/凝脂翳·熱盛腑實證　congealed-fat nebula with pattern of heat exuberance in fu
拧捏性紫癜/撐捏性紫癜　pinch purpura
拧痛/撐痛　gripping pain
拧转止血带/撐轉止血帶　screwing tourniquet
牛白喉/犢白喉　calf diphtheria
牛白血病病毒/牛白血病病毒　bovine leukemia virus
牛棒状杆菌/牛棒狀桿菌　corynebacterium bovis
牛蒡/牛蒡　burdock
牛蒡子/牛蒡子　great burdock achene
牛病毒性腹泻病毒类/牛病毒性腹瀉病毒類　bovine viral diarrhea viruses
牛病毒性腹泻-黏膜病/牛病毒性腹瀉-黏膜病　bovine virus diarrhea-mucosal disease
牛布鲁杆菌病/牛布魯桿菌病　bovine brucellosis
牛肠道孤病毒/牛腸道孤病毒　ECBO virus
牛出血综合征/牛出血症候群　bovine hemorrhagic syndrome
牛传染性鼻气管炎/牛傳性鼻氣管炎　infectious bovine rhinotracheitis
牛带绦虫病/牛條蟲病　taeniasis bovis
牛胆汁/牛膽汁　fel bovis
牛痘/牛痘,牛天花病　vaccinia
牛痘病毒/牛痘病毒　cowpox virus
牛痘免疫球蛋白/牛痘免疫球蛋白　vaccinia immune globulin
牛痘苗/牛痘苗　variolovaccine
牛痘苗素/牛痘苗素　vaccinin
牛痘苗制造者/畜養痘牛者　vacciniculturist
牛痘性角膜炎/牛痘性角膜炎　vaccinial keratitis
牛痘性结膜炎/牛痘性結膜炎　vaccinal conjunctivitis
牛痘性蔷薇疹/牛痘性薔薇疹　roseola vaccinia
牛痘样水疱症/牛痘狀水皰病　hydroa vacciniforme
牛顿流体/牛頓流體　Newtonian fluid
牛杆菌性肾盂肾炎/牛桿菌性腎盂腎炎　pyelonephritis bacillosa bovum
牛海绵状脑病/牛海綿狀腦病　bovine spongiform encephalopathy
牛黄/牛黄　bezoar
牛黄抱龙丸/牛黃抱龍丸　niuhuang baolong pill

牛黄降压胶囊/牛黃降壓膠囊　niuhuang jiangya capsule
牛黄解毒片/牛黃解毒片　niuhuang jiedu tablet
牛黄清心丸/牛黃清心丸　niuhuang qingxin pill
牛黄上清丸/牛黃上清丸　niuhuang shangqing pill
牛黄蛇胆川贝液/牛黃蛇膽川貝液　niuhuang shedan chuanbei mixture
牛黄至宝丸/牛黃至寶丸　niuhuang zhibao pill
牛磺胆酸/牛膽酸　taurocholic acid
牛磺胆酸排出过多/牛膽酸排洩量增多　taurocholaneresis
牛磺胆酸生成/牛膽酸生成　taurocholanopoiesis
牛磺胆酸血/牛膽酸血症　taurocholemia
牛磺胆酸盐/牛膽酸鹽　taurocholate
牛磺鹅脱氧胆酸/牛磺鵝去氧膽酸　taurochenodeoxycholic acid
牛磺石胆酸/牛磺石膽酸　taurolithocholic acid
牛磺酸/牛磺酸　taurine
牛磺脱氧胆酸/牛磺去氧膽酸　taurodeoxycholic acid
牛磺酰酸/牛磺醯酸　taurylic acid
牛胶体/牛膠　bovine colloid
牛角形钳/牛角鉗　cowhorn forceps
牛结核/牛結核　bovine tuberculosis
牛结核病/牛結核病　pearl disease
牛津单位/牛津單位　Oxford unit
[牛马]玉米杆病/牛馬玉薯黍莖病　cornstalk disease
牛疟/牛瘧　bovine malaria
牛皮癣/牛皮癣　cattle-skin lichen, neurodermatitis
牛皮癣·风湿蕴肤证/牛皮癣·風濕蘊膚證　cattle-skin lichen with pattern of wind-dampness amassing in skin
牛皮癣·肝郁化火证/牛皮癣·肝鬱化火證　cattle-skin lichen with pattern of liver depression transforming into fire
牛皮癣关节炎/牛皮癣關節炎　psoriatic arthritis
牛皮癣患者/牛皮癣患者　psoriatic
牛皮癣性关节病/乾癣性關節病　arthropathia psoriatica
牛皮癣·血虚风燥证/牛皮癣·血虛風燥證　cattle-skin lichen with pattern of wind-dryness due to blood deficiency
牛皮癣状/乾癣樣　psoriasiform
牛丘疹口炎病毒/牛丘疹性口瘡病毒　bovine papular stomatitis virus
牛缺铜病/牛缺銅病　falling disease
牛肉绦虫/牛肉條蟲,無鉤條蟲　Taenia saginata
牛乳头状瘤病病毒/牛乳頭狀瘤病病毒　bovine papillomatosis virus

牛瘟病毒/牛瘟病毒　rinderpest virus
牛膝/牛膝　twotoothed achyranthes root
牛膝草/牛膝草　hyssop
牛心包瓣/牛心包瓣　bovine pericardium valve
牛型放线菌/牛型放線菌　Actinomyces bovis
牛血清白蛋白/牛血清白蛋白　bovine serum albumin
牛眼肩/牛眼肩　bull's-eye shoulder
牛样眼/牛樣眼　bull eye
牛蝇蛆病/牛蠅蛆病　botfly myiasis
牛疣/牛疣　cattle wart
牛脂/牛脂　tallow
牛脂脂肪酸/牛脂脂肪酸　tallow fatty acid
扭秤/扭轉天平　torsion balance
扭发/扭卷毛　twisted hair
扭颈试验/扭頸試驗　neck torsion test
扭曲鼻/扭曲鼻　crooked nose
扭曲物/扭曲之物　distortor
扭曲振动/扭曲振動　twisting vibration
扭伤/扭傷　sprain
扭伤骨折/扭傷骨折,扭挫骨折　sprain fracture
扭体露脏畸胎/扭體畸胎　strophosomus
扭头畸胎/扭頭畸胎　strophocephalus
扭头[畸形]/扭頭畸形　strophocephaly
扭转/扭轉　torsion
扭转暴力/扭轉暴力　rotation force
扭转错位/扭轉[異]位　torsiversion
扭转度计/扭轉度計　torsiometer
扭转发/扭曲髮,扭曲毛　pili torti
扭转骨折/扭轉骨折　torsion fracture
扭转𬌗/扭轉咬合位　torso-occlusion
扭转角/扭轉角　torsion angle
扭转痉挛/扭轉痙攣　torsion spasm
扭转毛细线虫/扭轉毛體線蟲　Trichosoma contortum
扭转性肌张力障碍/扭轉性肌張力障礙　torsion dysmyotonia
纽蛋白/紐蛋白　vinculin
纽菲尔德钉/紐費德氏釘　Neufeld nail
纽结/扭結　kink
纽结发/扭結髮　kinking hair
纽卡斯尔抑郁诊断量表/紐卡斯爾抑鬱診斷量表　Newcastle diagnostic scale for depression
纽形动物/紐形動物　nemertean
钮孔/鈕孔　buttonhole
钮孔状畸形/鈕孔狀畸形　button hole deformity
钮孔状僧帽瓣狭窄/鈕孔狀僧帽瓣狹窄　buttonhole mitral stenosis
钮扣形缝合/鈕縫　button suture
钮扣状畸形/鈕扣狀畸形　boutonniere deformity
钮式烙器/鈕狀烙器　button cautery
钮式引流法/腹膜鈕管引流　button drainage
钮状坏血病/鈕狀物壞血病　button scurvy
农民肺/農民肺　farmer lung
农内-米尔罗伊-梅热综合征/諾-米-邁三氏症候群,米羅伊氏病　Nonne-Milroy-Meige syndrome
农内综合征/Nonne 氏症候群　Nonne syndrome
农药残留量/農藥殘留量　pesticide residue
农药增效剂/農藥增效劑　pesticide synergist
农业/農業　agriculture
农业的/農業的　agricultural
农业工人疾病/農業工人疾病　agricultural workers' disease
农业职业性皮肤病/農業職業性皮膚病　agricultural occupational dermatosis
农用抗生素/農用抗生素　agricultural antibiotic
浓氨溶液/強氨溶液　strong ammonia solution
浓氨水/強氨水　stronger ammonia water
浓碘酊/強力碘酊　strong iodine tincture
浓碘溶液/強碘溶液　strong iodine solution
浓度/濃度　concentration
浓度比率/濃度比率　concentration ratio
浓度-时间曲线/濃度-時間曲線　concentration-time curve
浓氢氧化铵溶液/強氫氧化銨溶液　stronger ammonium hydroxide solution
浓缩法/濃集法　concentration method
浓缩肝/肝濃縮劑　liver concentrate
浓缩煎剂/濃縮煎劑　concentrated decoction
浓缩试验/濃縮試驗　concentration test
浓缩丸/濃縮丸　concentrated pill
浓缩维生素/維生素濃縮劑　vitamin concentrate
浓缩血/脫水血　deshydremia
浓痰/膿性痰　purulent sputum
脓/膿　pus
脓胞素/膿胞素　pyosin
脓毒素血[症]/膿毒血症　pyotoxinemia
脓毒性的/敗血病的　septic
脓毒性感染/敗血病,敗血性感染　septic infection
脓毒性梗死/膿毒性梗死　septic infarct
脓毒性关节炎/膿毒性關節炎　septic arthritis
脓毒性坏死/敗血性壞死　septic necrosis
脓毒性静脉炎/膿毒性靜脈炎,敗血性靜脈炎　septophlebitis
脓毒性类酶/敗血病類酵素　septicozymoid
脓毒性伤口/染毒創傷　septic wound

脓毒性视网膜炎/敗血性視網膜炎　septic retinitis
脓毒性栓塞/膿毒性栓塞　pyemic embolism
脓毒性心内膜炎/敗血性心内膜炎　septic endocarditis
脓毒性休克/敗血病性休克　septic shock
脓毒性咽峡炎/膿毒性咽峽炎　septic angina
脓毒性子宫炎/敗血性子宫炎　septimetritis
脓毒症/膿毒病　sepsis
脓毒症的/膿毒症的　pyemic
脓毒中毒/敗血症　septic intoxication
脓耳/膿耳　purulent ear, suppurative otitis media
脓耳变证/膿耳變證　deteriorated case of purulent ear
脓耳·风热外袭证/膿耳·風熱外襲證　purulent ear with pattern of external assault by wind-heat
脓耳·肝胆火盛证/膿耳·肝膽火盛證　purulent ear with pattern of liver-gallbladder fire excessiveness
脓耳口眼㖞斜/膿耳口眼㖞斜　facial hemiparalysis due to purulent ear, purulent ear lead to wry mouth and eye
脓耳面瘫/膿耳面癱　facial paralysis due to purulent ear
脓耳面瘫·气虚毒滞证/膿耳面癱·氣虛毒滯證　facial paralysis due to purulent ear with pattern of qi deficiency and toxin stagnation
脓耳面瘫·热毒灼络证/膿耳面癱·熱毒灼絡證　facial paralysis due to purulent ear with pattern of heat-toxin scorching collateral
脓耳·脾虚湿困证/膿耳·脾虛濕困證　purulent ear with pattern of spleen deficiency and dampness retention
脓耳·肾元亏损证/膿耳·腎元虧損證　purulent ear with kidney origin depletion pattern
脓耳眩晕/膿耳眩暈　vertigo due to purulent ear
脓耳眩晕·肝胆湿热证/膿耳眩暈·肝膽濕熱證　vertigo due to purulent ear with pattern of dampness-heat in liver and gallbladder
脓耳眩晕·脾虚湿困证/膿耳眩暈·脾虛濕困證　vertigo due to purulent ear with pattern of spleen deficiency and dampness retention
脓耳眩晕·肾元亏损证/膿耳眩暈·腎元虧損證　vertigo due to purulent ear with kidney origin depletion pattern
脓精/膿精　purulent sperm, pyospermia
脓菌素类/膿菌素類　pyocins
脓窠疮/膿窠瘡　pus hole sore
脓扩散/膿液移動,膿液遷移　pyoplania
脓泪溢/膿淚溢　dacryopyorrhea

脓漏眼/膿漏眼　gonococcal conjunctivitis
脓漏眼·火毒炽盛证/膿漏眼·火毒熾盛證　gonococcal conjunctivitis with blazing fire-toxin pattern
脓漏眼·气血两燔证/膿漏眼·氣血兩燔證　gonococcal conjunctivitis with pattern of flaming of qi-blood
脓尿/膿尿[症]　pyuria
脓疱/膿皰　pustule
脓疱病/膿皰病　impetigo
脓疱形成/膿皰形成　pustulation
脓疱性痤疮/膿皰性痤瘡　acne pustulosa, pustular acne
脓疱性冻疮/膿皰性凍瘡　pustular chilblain
脓疱性痱/膿皰性痱　miliaria pustulosa
脓疱性黑变症/膿皰性黑變症　pustular melanosis
脓疱性环状牛皮癣/環狀膿皰型乾癬　annular pustular psoriasis
脓疱性角化不全/膿皰性角化不全　parakeratosis pustulosa
脓疱性狼疮/膿皰性狼瘡　lupus impetigizosus
脓疱性毛囊周围炎/膿皰性毛囊周圍炎　pustular perifolliculitis
脓疱性梅毒疹/膿皰性梅毒疹　pustular syphilide
脓疱性皮肤病/膿皰性皮膚病　pustular dermatosis
脓疱性丘疹/膿皰性丘疹　papulopustule
脓疱性妊娠疱疹/膿皰性妊娠皰疹　pustular herpes gestationis
脓疱性湿疹/膿皰性濕疹　eczema pustulosum
脓疱性水痘/膿皰性水痘　pustular varicella
脓疱性粟粒疹/膿皰性汗疹　pustular miliaria
脓疱性细菌疹/膿性細菌疹　pustular bacterid
脓疱性心内膜炎/膿皰性心内膜炎　pustular endocarditis
脓疱性血管炎/膿皰性血管炎　pustular vasculitis
脓疱性药物疹/膿皰性藥物疹　pustular drug eruptions
脓疱性银屑病/膿皰性乾癬　psoriasis pustulosa
脓疱性肢端皮炎/膿皰性肢端皮膚炎　pustular acrodermatitis
脓疱疹/積膿皰疹　pustular eruption
脓疱症/膿皰症　pustulosis
脓皮病/膿皮病,膿性皮膚病　pyoderma
脓脐/膿臍　pyoumbilicus
脓气腹/膿氣腹　pyopneumoperitoneum
脓气囊肿/膿氣性囊腫,膿氣囊　pyopneumocyst
脓气心包/膿氣心包　pyopneumopericardium
脓气性胆囊炎/膿氣性膽囊炎

pyopneumocholecystitis
脓气性腹膜炎/膿氣性腹膜炎　pyopneumoperitonitis
脓气性肝炎/膿氣性肝炎　pyopneumohepatitis
脓气胸/膿氣胸　pyopneumothorax
脓丘疱疹/膿丘皰疹　papulopustule
脓肾/膿腎　pyonephrosis
脓细胞/膿細胞　pus cell
脓细胞培养/活膿培養法　biopyoculture
脓细胞素/膿素　pyogenin
脓性产后排出物/膿性産後排出物　lochia purulenta
脓性蛋白质/膿性蛋白質　pyogenic protein
脓性的/膿性的　purulent
脓性粪/膿糞　pyochezia
脓性腹膜炎/膿性腹膜炎　pyoperitonitis
脓性肝炎/膿性肝炎　purohepatitis
脓性感染/膿性感染　pyogenic infection
脓性肌炎/膿性肌炎　pyomyositis
脓性口炎/膿性口炎　pyostomatitis
脓性迷路炎/膿性耳迷路炎　pyolabyrinthitis
脓性肾石病/膿性腎石病　pyonephrolithiasis
脓性肾盂积水/化膿性腎盂積水, 化膿性腎水腫　pyohydronephrosis
脓性肾盂扩张/膿性腎盂擴張　pyopyelectasis
脓性渗出物/化膿性滲出物　purulent exudate
脓性输卵管卵巢炎/膿性輸卵管卵巢炎　pyosalpingo-oophoritis
脓性输卵管炎/膿性輸卵管炎　pyosalpingitis
脓性水肿/膿性水腫　purulent edema
脓性心包炎/心包蓄膿　empyema of pericardium
脓性血栓[性]动脉炎/化膿性血栓動脈炎　thromboarteritis purulenta
脓性眼炎/膿性眼炎, 眼膿漏　ophthalmoblennorrhea
脓性硬化/膿性硬化　pyosclerosis
脓性子宫炎/膿性子宮炎　pyometritis
脓胸/膿胸, 肋膜腔積膿　empyema of the chest, empyema pleurae
脓胸性脊柱侧凸/蓄膿性脊柱側彎　empyematic scoliosis
脓癣/膿癬　tinea kerion
脓血胸/膿血胸　pyohemothorax
脓血症/膿血症　pyemia
脓样物质/膿狀物質　pyoid
脓液/膿水, 腐液, 創液　ichor
脓液疗法/膿液療法　pyotherapy
脓液培养法/膿液培養法　pyoculture
脓液溢/膿[液]漏　pyoblennorrhea
脓溢/膿溢, 膿漏　pyorrhea
脓溢性角化病/膿漏性角化病　keratosis
blennorrhagica
脓肿/膿腫, 膿瘍　abscess
脓肿刀/膿腫刀　abscess lancet
脓肿性/膿腫性　abscedens
脓肿性腺性唇炎/膿瘍性腺性唇炎　cheilitis glandularis apostematosa
脓肿引流术/膿腫引流術　abscess drainage
弄舌/弄舌　frequent protruding and wagging tongue, frequent protrusion of tongue
弄胎/弄胎　trial labor
努恩单位/努恩單位　Noon unit
努克水囊/Nuck氏水囊　Nuck hydrocele
努力/努力, 奮發　nisus
努南综合征/努南症候群　Noonan syndrome
努伤失血/努傷失血　bleeding due to overstrain
胬肉/胬肉　luxuriant granulation
胬肉攀睛/胬肉攀睛　pterygium
胬肉攀睛·脾胃积热证/胬肉攀睛·脾胃積熱證　pterygium with pattern of heat accumulation in spleen-stomach
胬肉攀睛·心肺风热证/胬肉攀睛·心肺風熱證　pterygium with pattern of wind-heat in heart and lung
胬肉攀睛·阴虚火旺证/胬肉攀睛·陰虛火旺證　pterygium with pattern of yin deficiency and fire effulgence
怒/怒　anger
怒伤肝/怒傷肝　rage impairing the liver
怒胜法/怒勝法　frightening therapy
怒胜思/怒勝思　angering to relieve worry
怒为肝志/怒爲肝志　liver being associated with anger
怒郁/怒鬱　stagnation pattern caused by anger
怒则气上/怒則氣上　rage driving qi upward, rage leading to qi ascending
怒中/怒中　stroke due to anger
女导尿管/女用導[尿]管　female catheter
女假两性畸形/女假兩性畸形　female pseudohermaphroditism
女劳疸/女勞疸　sex jaundice
女尿道/女尿道　female urethra
女同性恋者/女同性戀者　lesbian
女性避孕药/女性避孕藥　contraceptive for female
女性不育/女性不育　female infertility
女性后天性尿道黏膜包涵囊肿/女性後天性尿道黏膜包涵囊腫　acquired inclusion cyst of urethral epithelium of female
女性化/女性化, 男子女化　feminization

女性化瘤/女性化瘤　feminzing tumor
女性化肾上腺瘤/女性化腎上腺瘤　feminizing adrenal tumor
女性化综合征/女性化症候群　feminizing syndrome
女性假两性畸形/女性假半陰陽　pseudarrhenia
女性假两性体/女性假陰陽人　female pseudohermaphrodite
女性假两性同体/女性假兩性同體，女性假兩性畸形　female pseudohermaphroditism
女性男声/女子男聲　androglossia
女性内生殖器/女性内生殖器　internal genital organ of female
女性内生殖器官/女性内生殖器官　organa genitalia feminina interna
女性尿道/女性尿道　female urethra
女性尿道囊肿/女性尿道囊腫　urethral cyst in female
女性尿道外口/女性尿道外口　external orifice of female urethra
女性尿道下裂/女性尿道下裂　female hypospadias
女性尿道纤维息肉/女性尿道纖維息肉　fibrous polyps of female urethra
女性尿道周瘘/女性尿道周瘻管　folliculovestibular fistula
女性尿失禁/女性尿失禁　female incontinence
女性生殖器/女性生殖器　female genitalia
女性生殖器官充气X射线[照]片/女性生殖器充氣X光照片　pneumogynogram
女性生殖器疾病/女性生殖器疾病　female genital disease
女性生殖器结核/女性生殖器結核　female genital tuberculosis
女性生殖器肿瘤/女性生殖器腫瘤　female genital neoplasm
女性生殖系统/女[性]生殖系統　female reproductive system
女性水囊肿/女性水囊腫　hydrocele feminae
女性特征型/女型　gynecoid type
女性同性恋/女子同性戀愛　female homosexuality
女性外生殖器/女性外生殖器　external genital organ of female
女性阴部切割术/陰蒂切開術　female circumcision
女性性激素因素/女性性激素因素　female sex hormonal factor
女牙医/女牙醫師　women dentist
女医师/女醫師　women physician
女阴/女陰　female pudendum, vulva
女阴白斑症/女陰白斑病　leukoplakia vulvae
女阴闭锁/外陰閉鎖　atresia vulvae
女阴成形术/女陰造形術　episioplasty
女阴的/女陰的　vulvar
女阴干皱/女陰乾皺　kraurosis vulvae
女阴会阴成形术/女陰會陰造形術　episioperineoplasty
女阴裂/外陰裂　pudendal cleft, vulval cleft
女阴湿疹/女陰濕疹　pudendum eczema
女阴蚀疮/女陰蝕瘡　esthiomene
女阴水囊肿/女陰水囊　hydrocele muliebris
女阴疼痛症/陰唇痛症　vulvodynia
女阴狭窄/女陰狹窄　episiostenosis
女阴炎/女陰炎　vulvitis
女阴阴道念珠菌病/外陰陰道念珠菌病　vulvovaginal candidiasis
女用避孕器械/女用避孕器械　female contraceptive device
女用避孕套/女用避孕套　female condom
女用避孕药/女用避孕藥　female contraceptive agent
女用致育药/女用致育藥　female fertility agent
女贞子/女貞子　glossy privet fruit
女子男征/色情男化，女子男化　viraginity
女子同性恋/女同性戀者　lesbian
衄血/衄血　bleeding from five aperture or subcutaneous tissue
暖肝煎/暖肝煎　nuangan decoction
暖肝散寒/暖肝散寒　warming liver for dispelling cold
暖宫散寒/暖宫散寒　warming uterus for dispelling cold, warming womb for dispelling cold
暖炉烧伤/火籃灼傷　kangri burn
疟点彩/瘧疾彩斑　malarial stippling
疟疾/瘧[疾]　malaria
疟疾恶病质/瘧疾惡病質　cachexia malarica
疟疾肾病/瘧疾腎病　malarial nephropathy
疟疾·暑热内郁证/瘧疾·暑熱內鬱證　malaria with pattern of internal retention of hot-summerheat
疟疾·暑湿内蕴证/瘧疾·暑濕內蘊證　malaria with pattern of internal retention of summerheat-damp
疟疾统计/瘧疾統計法　malariometry
疟疾·邪在少阳证/瘧疾·邪在少陽證　malaria with pattern of pathogen involving Shaoyang Channel
疟疾性心脏病/瘧疾性心臟病，心臟型瘧疾　cardiopaludism
疟疾学/瘧疾學　malariology
疟疾学家/瘧疾專家　malariologist
疟疾·疫毒侵袭证/瘧疾·疫毒侵襲證　malaria with pattern of epidemic toxin invasion

疟疾疫苗/瘧疾疫苗　malaria vaccines
疟疾·正虚邪恋证/瘧疾·正虛邪戀證　malaria with pattern of lingering pathogen due to vital qi deficiency
疟疾周期性/瘧疾之週期發作性　malarial periodicity
疟母/瘧母　malaria with abdominal mass
疟热疗法/瘧疾療法　impaludation
疟色素/瘧色素，瘧色質　malarial pigment
疟色素沉着/瘧色素沈著　malarial pigmentation
疟邪/瘧邪　malarial pathogen
疟性痢疾/瘧疾型痢疾　malarial dysentery
疟原虫/瘧原蟲　hematozoon of malaria
疟原虫的/瘧原蟲的　plasmodial
疟原虫色素/血蟲色素，瘧蟲色素　hemozoin
疟原虫性脑膜炎/瘧原蟲性腦膜炎　plasmodial meningitis
[疟原虫]依附型/瘧原蟲之飾紋型　accole form
虐待儿童/虐待兒童　child abuse
虐待老人/虐待老人　elder abuse
虐待配偶/虐待配偶　spouse abuse
挪威疥癣病/挪威型疥瘡　Norwegian scabies
诺尔道病/Nordau 氏症　Nordau disease
诺氟沙星/諾氟沙星　Norfloxacin
诺卡尔菌感染/諾卡爾菌感染　Nocardia infection
诺卡[放线]菌病/土壤絲菌病　nocardiasis
诺卡[放线]菌的/土壤絲菌的　nocardial
诺卡[放线]菌素/土壤絲菌素　nocardin
诺卡菌病/諾卡菌病　nocardiosis
诺卡菌素/諾卡菌素　nocardicin
诺卡氏菌性脓肿/土壤絲菌膿瘍　nocardial abscess
诺考达唑/諾考達唑　nocodazole
诺拉霉素/諾拉黴素　nogalamycin
诺龙/諾龍　nandrolone
诺-米病/Nonne-Milroy 二氏病　Nonne-Milroy disease
诺米芬辛/諾米芬辛　Nomifensine
诺氏疟原虫/猴瘧蟲　Plasmodium knowlesi
诺特纳格尔征/諾特納格爾徵　Nothnagel sign
诺特纳格尔综合征/Nothnagel 氏症候群　Nothnagel syndrome
诺沃克病毒/諾沃克病毒　Norwalk virus
诺沃克组病毒性胃肠炎/諾沃克組病毒性胃腸炎　Norwalk agents gastroenteritis
诺伍德手术/諾伍德手術　Norwood procedure
诺昔硫脲/諾昔硫脲　noxythiolin
诺伊鲍尔动脉/Neubauer 氏動脈　Neubauer artery
诺伊曼细胞/Neumann 氏細胞　Neumann cell
诺乙雄龙/諾乙龍　norethandrolone
诺孕烯酮/諾孕烯酮　norgestrienone

O

欧白芷酸/歐獨活酸,白芷酸　angelic acid
欧博克箭毒/非洲箭毒　onobaio
欧薄荷精/薄荷精　essence of peppermint
欧车前/洋車前子　Psyllium
欧夹竹桃苷/夾竹桃素　oleandrin
欧姆斯缔掌跖角化症/歐姆斯締掌蹠角化症　Olmsted palmoplantar keratoderma
欧茜草[根]/茜草[根]　madder
欧氏曼森线虫/寶馬凱氏絲蟲　Filaria demarquayi
欧氏丝虫病/歐氏絲蟲病　Ozzard filariasis
欧鼠李皮/歐鼠李皮　Frangula
欧洲芽生菌病/歐洲芽生黴菌病　European blastomycosis
欧洲油菜/歐洲油菜　Brassica napus
鸥翼切平面/鷗翼切平面　gull wing incisal plane
呕吐/嘔吐　vomiting
呕吐病/嘔吐病　vomiting sickness
呕吐中枢/嘔吐中樞　vomiting center
呕涎/吐涎症　sialemesis
呕血/嘔血,吐血　hematemesis
偶/偶　couple
偶氮苯/偶氮苯　azobenzene
偶氮蛋白/偶氮蛋白　azoprotein
偶氮化合物/偶氮化合物　azo compounds
偶氮磺胺/普浪多息　prontosil
偶氮类甾醇类/偶氮類甾醇類　azasteroids
偶氮染料/偶氮染料　azo dyes
偶氮染料皮肤病/偶氮染料皮膚病　azo-dyes dermatosis
偶氮色素/偶氮色素　azopigment
偶氮胂/偶氮胂　arsenazo
偶发/偶發　chance
偶发分枝杆菌/偶然分支桿菌　Mycobacterium fortuitum
偶发寄生物/偶發寄生物　accidental parasite
偶发疟/偶發瘧　incidental malaria
偶发事件/偶發事件　episode
偶发性精神病/偶發性精神病　accidental psychosis
偶发性杂音/偶發性雜音　accidental murmur
偶发组织/偶發組織　accidental tissue
偶方/偶方　even-ingredient prescriptions
偶极/偶極,雙極　dipole
偶极离子/偶極離子,兩性離子　dipolar ion
偶联反应/偶聯反應,偶合反應　coupled reaction
偶联间期/偶聯間期　coupling interval
偶然发现/偶然發現　incidental finding
偶胂苯/胂苯　arsenobenzene
偶生的/偶生的　adventitious
偶线期/偶線期　zygotene stage
藕节/藕節　lotus rhizome node

P

爬虫恐怖/爬蟲恐懼症　herpetophobia
爬虫类动物蛋白质类/爬蟲類動物蛋白質類　reptilian proteins
爬行的/爬行的　creeping
爬行动物/爬蟲類　reptiles
爬行运动/爬行運動　crawling exercise
帕尔奇手术/Partsch 氏手術　Partsch operation
帕基奥尼凹陷/Pacchionian 氏凹陷　Pacchionian depression
帕吉林/帕吉林　pargyline
帕杰特植皮刀/潘傑特氏植皮刀　Padgett dermatome
帕金森病/Parkinson 氏病,帕金森氏病　Parkinson disease
帕金森病的/Parkinson 氏病的　Parkinsonian
帕金森神经功能障碍/帕金森狀態,帕金森氏症候群　parkinsonism
帕金森障碍/帕金森障礙　Parkinsonian disorder
帕金森综合征/Parkinson 氏症候群　Parkinsonian syndrome
帕克希尔螺旋[夹]/巴克爾氏螺旋　Parkhill screw
帕克液/Parker 氏液　Parker fluid
帕库林/哥倫比亞箭毒　pakurin
帕拉米松/帕拉米松　paramethasone
帕勒姆带/Parham 氏帶　Parham band
帕里诺结膜炎/帕里諾結膜炎　Parinaud conjunctivitis
帕里诺眼淋巴结综合征/帕里諾眼睛腺體症候群　Parinaud oculoglandular syndrome
帕里诺综合征/Parinaud 氏症候群　Parinaud syndrome
帕立卡/帕立卡　parica
帕罗假性麻痹/Parrot 氏假性麻痺　Parrot pseudoparalysis
帕罗溃疡/Parrot 氏潰瘍　Parrot ulcer
帕罗西汀/帕羅西汀　paroxetine
帕罗杂音/Parrot 氏雜音　Parrot murmur
帕内特细胞/Paneth 氏細胞,班尼斯細胞　Paneth cell
帕佩兹回路/帕佩兹回路　Papez circle
帕奇尼小体/Pacini 氏小體　Pacini corpuscle

帕萨万特垫/Passavant 氏墊　Passavant cushion
帕萨万特脊/帕薩萬特脊　Passavant ridge
帕斯蒂亚线/Pastia 氏線　Pastia line
帕塔综合征/Patau 氏症候群　Patau syndrome
帕特南-达纳综合征/Putnam-Dana 二氏症候群　Putnam-Dana syndrome
拍打法/拍打法　clapping manipulation
拍击疗法/拍擊療法　patting-striking manipulation
拍击音/拍擊音　flapping sound
拍叩[诊]/擊叩法　slapping percussion
排氨代谢/氨代謝　ammonotelic metabolism
排便/排便,排糞　defecation
排便反射/排便反射　defecation reflex
排便节制/排便自製力　fecal continence
排便X射线摄影术/排便X線攝影術　defecography
排便训练/排便訓練　toilet training
排斥[反应]/排斥[反應]　rejection
排斥危象/排斥危象　rejection crisis
排出的/排出的　expulsive
排出器/抽吸器　evacuator
排除剂/瀉劑　eliminant
排除式饮食/排除式飲食　exclusion diet
排除障碍/排除障礙　elimination disorder
排毒剂/排毒藥　expellent
排空/排除,清空　evacuation
排卵/排卵　ovulation
排卵变态/排卵性變形　ovulational metamorphosis
排卵过少/排卵過少　oligo-ovulation
排卵监测/排卵監測　ovulation detection
排卵龄/排卵齡　ovulation age
排卵期出血/排卵期出血　ovulation bleeding
排卵期月经/排卵期月經　kleine regel
排卵痛/排卵期痛　ovulation pain
排卵性功能失调性子宫出血/排卵性功能失調性子宮出血　ovulatory dysfunctional uterine bleeding
排卵抑制/排卵抑制　ovulation inhibition
排卵诱导/排卵誘導　ovulation induction
排卵预测/排卵預測　ovulation prediction
排尿/排尿　micturition
排尿反射/排尿反射　micturition reflex
排尿感觉/排尿感覺,尿意　uresiesthesis

排尿过慢/排尿徐緩　bradyuria
排尿急遽/排尿急遽　precipitate micturition
排尿减少/排尿過少　hypouresis
排尿节制/排尿自製力　urinary continence
排尿恐怖/尿溺恐懼症,排尿恐懼症　urophobia
排尿困难/排尿困難　difficulty of urination
排尿里急后重/排尿性裡急後重,膀胱性裡急後重　vesical tenesmus
排尿频次/小便次數　frequency of micturition
排尿期膀胱测压/排尿期膀胱測壓　voiding cystometry
排尿期膀胱尿道造影[术]/排尿期膀胱尿道造影[術]　micturition urethrocystography
排尿素代谢/尿素代謝　ureotelic metabolism
排尿酸代谢/尿酸終末代謝　uricotelic metabolism
排尿酸[氮]代谢/尿酸排洩　uricotelism
排尿酸药/排尿酸藥　uricosuric
排尿痛/[排]尿痛　urodynia
排尿无力/排尿無力　acraturesis
排尿异常/排尿異常,排尿障礙　paruria
排尿犹豫/排尿猶豫　hesitancy in urination
排尿晕厥/排尿性暈厥　micturition syncope
排尿障碍/排尿障礙　urination disorder
排尿指数/排尿指數　micturition index
排尿中枢/排尿中樞　center micturition
排气/氣體排出法　exsufflation
排色[素]检胆[功能]法/膽管色素排洩機能檢查法　chromocholoscopy
排石颗粒/排石顆粒　paishi granule
排水性利尿药/逐水性利尿藥　hydragoguc diuretic
排痰性咳/痰性欬嗽　productive cough
排泄/排洩　excretion
排泄管/排洩管　excretory duct
排泄过多/排洩過多　hypereccrisia
排泄过少/排洩過少,排洩不足　hypoeccrisia
排泄剂/排洩促進劑　eccritic
排泄失禁/排洩失禁,抑留不能　acathexia
排泄物/排洩物,排出物　egesta
排泄物吸收/排洩物吸收　excremental absorption
排泄性尿道造影[术]/排洩性尿道造影[術]　excretory urethrography
排泄性膀胱造影[术]/排洩性膀胱造影[術]　excretory cystography
排泄药/排除藥　evacuant
排牙/排牙　tooth arrangement
哌醋甲酯/哌醋甲酯　methylphenidate
哌啶类/哌啶類　piperidines
哌啶生物碱/哌啶生物鹼　piperidine alkaloid

哌啶酮类/哌啶酮類　piperidones
哌腈米特/哌腈米特　pirinitramide
哌卡嗪/哌卡嗪　pecazine
哌克昔林/哌克昔林　perhexiline
哌库溴铵/哌庫溴銨　pipecuronium
哌仑西平/哌侖西平　pirenzepine
哌罗克生/哌羅克生　piperoxan
哌泊溴烷/哌泊溴烷　pipobroman
哌嗪类/哌嗪類　piperazines
哌替啶/度蘭汀　meperidine
哌唑嗪/哌唑嗪　prazosin
派尔夹/派爾氏夾　Payr clamp
派克兰公式/派克蘭公式　Parkland formula
派若宁/派羅寧　Pyronine
派生的/衍化的　derived
潘必啶/五甲吡啶　pempidine
潘科斯特综合征/Pancoast氏症候群　Pancoast syndrome
潘尼西丁/潘尼西丁　penicidin
潘托西/白血生　pentoxyl
攀登运动/攀登運動　climbing exercise
攀缘纤维/攀緣纖維,攀爬纖維　climbing fiber
盘尼西林/青黴素　penicillin
盘片式氧合器/碟片式氧合器　disc oxygenator
盘钳/盤鉗　disk forcep
盘尾丝虫病/蟠尾絲蟲病　onchocerciasis
盘尾丝虫瘤/蟠尾絲蟲病瘤　onchocercoma
盘尾丝虫皮炎/蟠尾絲蟲皮膚炎　onchodermatitis
盘尾丝虫属/蟠尾絲蟲屬　*Onchocerca*
盘形囊胚/盤狀囊胚　discoblastula
盘形原肠胚/盤狀原腸胚　discogastrula
盘状红斑狼疮/盤狀紅斑狼瘡　discoid lupus erythematosus
盘状黄斑变性/盤狀黃斑變性　disciform degeneration of macula
盘状黄斑的/盤型斑狀變性　disciform macular
盘状角膜炎/盤狀角膜炎　disciform keratitis
盘[状卵]裂/盤狀分裂　discoidal cleavage
盘状牛皮癣/盤狀牛皮癬　psoriasis discoidea
盘状乳房/盤狀乳房　discoid breast
盘状软骨/盤狀軟骨　discoid meniscus
盘状肾/盤狀腎　discoid kidney, disk kidney
盘状胎盘/盤狀胎盤　discoid placenta
蹒跚/蹣跚,搖擺　reel
蹒跚病/蹣跚病　silage disease
蹒跚步态/蹣跚步態,蹣跚步式　staggering gait, waddling gait, titubation
蹒跚者/步法蹣跚者,顛搖者　titubant

蟠管型透析器/蟠管型透析器　coil dialyser
蟠管状的/蟠管狀的　eiloid
蟠曲状瘤/蟠曲狀瘤　eiloid tumor
蟠蛇瘵/蟠蛇癧　coiled snake scrofula, pericervical scrofula
蟠尾丝虫结节/旅行性丹毒　coast erysipelas
判别分析/判别分析　discriminant analysis
判角之人/判角之人　atypical wood-phase person
泮加酸/葡萄醛酸之胺基衍化物　pangamic acid
泮库溴铵/泮庫溴銨　pancuronium
襻式结肠造口术/襻式結腸造口術　loop colostomy
彷徨[不安]感/彷徨[不安]感　anacatesthesia
庞蒂亚克热/龐蒂亞克熱　Pontiac fever
旁边/側　side
旁侧前置胎盘/旁側前置胎盤　placenta praevia lateralis
旁分泌/旁分泌　paracrine
旁分泌细胞交流/旁分泌細胞交流　paracrine communication
旁睾/旁睾　paradidymis
旁观者效应/旁觀者效應　bystander effect
旁巨细胞网状核/旁巨細胞網狀核　paragigantocellular reticular nucleus
旁路/旁路　bypass
旁路补体途径/補體恢復路徑　alternative complement pathway
旁路途径/旁路途徑　alternative pathway
旁栖的/旁棲的　paratenic
旁绒球/副絨球,旁絨球　paraflocculus
旁体/旁體　lateralis
旁嗅沟/旁嗅溝　parolfactory sulcus
旁正中沟/旁正中溝　paramedian sulcus
旁正中切口/側正中切開　paramedian incision
旁正中网状核/旁正中網狀核　paramedian reticular nucleus
旁正中小叶/旁正中小葉　paramedian lobule
旁中心暗点/中心旁暗點　paracentral scotoma
旁中心视力/旁中心視力　paracentral vision
旁角心注视/旁中心注視　paracentral fixation
旁中央动脉/旁中央動脈　paracentral artery
旁中央静脉/旁中央靜脈　paracentral vein
膀胱/膀胱,囊[泡]　①urinary bladder, bladder, vesico ②pangguang
膀胱癌/膀胱癌　bladder cancer
膀胱癌・肝肾阴虚证/膀胱癌・肝腎陰虛證　bladder cancer with pattern of liver-kidney yin deficiency
膀胱癌・脾肾气虚证/膀胱癌・脾腎氣虛證　bladder cancer with pattern of qi deficiency of spleen and kidney
膀胱癌・气阴两虚证/膀胱癌・氣陰兩虛證　bladder cancer with pattern of deficiency of both qi and yin
膀胱白斑病/膀胱白斑病　leukoplakia of bladder
膀胱逼尿肌/膀胱逼尿肌　detrusor of bladder
膀胱闭锁/膀胱閉鎖　atresia of bladder
膀胱部分切除术/膀胱部分切除術　partial cystectomy
膀胱测压/膀胱內壓測量法　cystometry
膀胱肠瘘/膀胱腸瘻　vesicointestinal fistula
膀胱肠疝/膀胱腸赫尼亞,膀胱腸脫垂　cystoenterocele
膀胱成形术/膀胱成形術,膀胱造形術　cystoplasty
膀胱耻骨韧带/膀胱恥骨韌帶　vesicopubic ligament
膀胱冲洗法/膀胱沖洗法　bladder washout method
膀胱充气造影[术]/膀胱充氣造影[術]　pneumography of bladder
膀胱出血/膀胱出血　cystirrhagia
膀胱垂/膀胱懸雍垂　vesical uvula
膀胱丛/膀胱叢　vesical plexus
膀胱挫伤/膀胱挫傷　contusion of bladder
膀胱大疱性水肿/膀胱泡性水腫　edema bullosum vesicae
膀胱的/膀胱的　vesical
膀胱底/膀胱底　fundus of bladder, infundibulum of urinary bladder
膀胱电位描记法/膀胱電測定　electrocystography
膀胱淀粉样变性/膀胱澱粉樣變性　amyloidosis of bladder
膀胱顶部/膀胱尖　summit of bladder
膀胱反射/膀胱反射　bladder reflex
膀胱缝合术/膀胱縫合術　cystorrhaphy
膀胱腹壁缝合术/膀胱腹壁縫合術　ventrocystorrhaphy
膀胱腹腔引流/膀胱腹腔引流　vesicocelomic drainage
膀胱肛门/膀胱肛門　anus vesicalis
膀胱固定术/膀胱固定術　cystopexy
膀胱灌洗术/膀胱内注射法　vesicoclysis
膀胱灌注/膀胱灌注　irrigation of bladder
膀胱过敏/膀胱過敏　cysterethism
膀胱横襞/膀胱橫皺襞　transverse vesical fold
膀胱后的/膀胱後的　retrovesical
膀胱后淋巴结/膀胱後淋巴結　postvesical lymph node
膀胱后疝/膀胱後疝　retrovesical hernia
膀胱坏疽/膀胱壞疽　gangrene of bladder
膀胱肌层/膀胱肌層　muscular layer of urinary

bladder
膀胱肌肥厚/膀胱肌肥厚　cysthypersarcosis
膀胱肌瘤/膀胱肌瘤　myoma of bladder
膀胱积脓/膀胱積膿　pyocystis
膀胱畸形/膀胱畸形　deformity of bladder
膀胱假性憩室/膀胱假性憩室　false diverticulum of bladder
膀胱间质瘤/膀胱間質瘤　mesenchymal tumor of bladder
膀胱绞痛/膀胱絞痛　cystic colic
膀胱结肠的/膀胱與結腸的　vesicocolic
膀胱结肠瘘/膀胱結腸瘻　vesicocolic fistula
膀胱结核/膀胱結核　tuberculosis of bladder
膀胱结石/膀胱石　vesical calculus
膀胱颈/膀胱頸　neck of bladder
膀胱颈切开术/膀胱頸切開術　cystauchenotomy
膀胱颈炎/膀胱頸炎　cystauchenitis
膀胱痉挛/膀胱痙攣　cystospasm
膀胱静脉/膀胱靜脈　vesical vein
膀胱静脉丛/膀胱靜脈叢　vesical venous plexus
膀胱静脉曲张/膀胱靜脈曲張　varix of bladder
膀胱镜/膀胱鏡　cystoscope
膀胱镜检查/膀胱鏡檢查　cystoscopy
膀胱镜检查的/膀胱鏡檢查的　cystoscopic
膀胱镜碎石术/碎石鏡碎石術　lithotriptoscopy
膀胱镜性溃疡/膀胱鏡性潰瘍　cystoscopic ulcer
膀胱口前腔/膀胱口前腔　prebladder
膀胱溃疡/膀胱潰瘍　cystelcosis
膀胱括约肌/膀胱括約肌　sphincter vesicae
膀胱括约肌成形术/膀胱括約肌成形術　cystosphincteroplasty
膀胱裂/膀胱裂　bladder cleft
膀胱裂体吸虫病/膀胱裂體吸蟲病　Egyptian hematuria
膀胱淋巴肉瘤/膀胱淋巴肉瘤　lymphosarcoma of bladder
膀胱鳞状细胞癌/膀胱鱗狀細胞癌　squamous cell carcinoma of bladder
膀胱瘘/膀胱瘻　vesical fistula
膀胱挛缩/膀胱攣縮　contracture of bladder
膀胱麻痹/膀胱麻痺　cystoparalysis
膀胱梅毒/膀胱梅毒　syphilis of bladder
膀胱面/膀胱面　vesical surface
膀胱内翻性乳头状瘤/膀胱内翻性乳頭狀瘤　inverted papilloma of bladder
膀胱内投药/膀胱内投藥　intravesical administration
膀胱内压测量器/膀胱容積壓力計　cystometer
膀胱内压[测量]图/膀胱壓力描記圖　cystometrogram
膀胱内压描记法/膀胱壓力描記法　cystometrography
膀胱内引流式胰腺移植/膀胱内引流式胰腺移植　bladder drainage pancreas transplantation
膀胱内照相术/膀胱攝影術　cystophotography
膀胱[黏膜]囊肿/膀胱囊腫　cystic cystitis
膀胱黏膜炎/膀胱[内膜]炎　endocystitis
膀胱尿道镜/膀胱尿道鏡　cystourethroscope
膀胱尿道突出/膀胱尿道赫尼亞,膀胱尿道膨出　cystourethrocele
膀胱尿道吻合术/膀胱尿道吻合術　vesicourethral anastomosis
膀胱尿道炎/膀胱尿道炎　cystourethritis
膀胱尿道造影照片/膀胱尿道 X 光像　cystourethrogram
膀胱尿道照相[术]/膀胱尿道照相術　cystourethrography
膀胱[尿潴留]性前列腺病态/膀胱性前列腺肥大症候群　vesical prostatism
膀胱旁淋巴结/膀胱旁淋巴結　paravesical lymph node
膀胱旁窝/膀胱旁窩　paravesical fossa
膀胱疱疹/膀胱皰疹　herpes of bladder
膀胱膨出/膀胱膨出,膀胱赫尼亞,膀胱脱垂　cystocele
膀胱皮肤瘘/膀胱皮瘻　vesicocutaneous fistula
膀胱皮肤造口术/膀胱皮膚造口術　cutaneous vesicostomy
膀胱平滑肌瘤/膀胱平滑肌瘤　leiomyoma of bladder
膀胱平滑肌肉瘤/膀胱平滑肌肉瘤　leiomyosarcoma of bladder
膀胱破裂/膀胱破裂　rupture of bladder
膀胱葡萄状肉瘤/膀胱葡萄狀肉瘤　botryoid sarcoma of bladder
膀胱脐韧带/膀胱臍韌帶　vesicoumbilical ligament
膀胱气化/膀胱氣化　functioning of bladder
膀胱憩室/膀胱憩室　diverticulum of bladder
膀胱憩室结石/膀胱憩室結石　calculus in diverticulum of bladder
膀胱憩室切除术/膀胱憩室切除術　vesical diverticulectomy
膀胱前列腺切除术/膀胱式前列腺切除術　cystoprostatectomy
膀胱前淋巴结/膀胱前淋巴結　prevesical lymph nodes
膀胱前疝/膀胱前疝　hernia antevesicalis
膀胱切除术/膀胱切除術　cystectomy

膀胱切[开取]石术/膀胱切開取石法 lithocystotomy
膀胱切开术/膀胱切開術 cystotomy
膀胱去神经超过敏试验/膀胱去神經超過敏試驗 denervation supersensitivity test of bladder
膀胱全切除术/膀胱全切除術 total cystectomy
膀胱缺如/膀胱缺如 agenesis of bladder
膀胱肉瘤/膀胱肉瘤 sarcoma of bladder
膀胱乳头状癌/膀胱乳頭狀癌 papillary carcinoma of bladder
膀胱乳头状瘤/膀胱乳頭狀瘤 papilloma of bladder
膀胱乳头状瘤病/膀胱乳頭狀瘤病 papillomatosis of bladder
膀胱三对比造影[术]/膀胱三對比造影[術] triple contrast cystography
膀胱三角/膀胱三角 trigone of bladder
膀胱三角及输尿管间嵴肥大/膀胱三角及輸尿管間脊肥大 hypertrophy of trigone and interureteric ridge
膀胱三角[区]切除术/膀胱三角切除術 trigonectomy
膀胱三角区炎/膀胱三角炎 trigonitis
膀胱三角区乙状结肠吻合术/膀胱三角區乙狀結腸吻合術 trigonosigmoidostomy
膀胱疝/膀胱疝 cystic hernia
膀胱上动脉/膀胱上動脈 superior vesical artery
膀胱上动脉输尿管支/膀胱上動脈輸尿管支 ureteric branch of superior vesical artery
膀胱上窝/膀胱上窩 supravesical fossa
膀胱上组织炎/膀胱上[組織]炎 epicystitis
膀胱神经痛/膀胱神經痛 cystoneuralgia
膀胱肾盂肾炎/膀胱腎盂腎炎 cystopyelonephritis
膀胱肾盂炎/膀胱腎盂炎 cystopyelitis
膀胱渗血/膀胱滲血 cystistaxis
膀胱湿热/膀胱濕熱 dampness-heat of bladder
膀胱湿热证/膀胱濕熱證 pattern of dampness-heat of bladder
膀胱石/膀胱結石 bladder stone
膀胱石病/膀胱石病 cystolithiasis
膀胱石[窥]镜/膀胱石鏡 lithoscope
膀胱石切除术/膀胱石切除術 cystolithectomy
膀胱嗜铬细胞瘤/膀胱嗜鉻細胞瘤 pheochromocytoma of bladder
膀胱输尿管反流/膀胱輸尿管逆流 vesicoureteral regurgitation
膀胱输尿管瘘/膀胱輸尿管瘻 vesicoureteral fistula
膀胱输尿管肾盂炎/膀胱輸尿管腎盂炎 cystoureteropyelitis
膀胱输尿管炎/膀胱輸尿管炎 cystoureteritis
膀胱输尿管移植术/膀胱輸尿管移植術 cohen operation
膀胱俞/膀胱俞 pangguangshu, BL28
膀胱双对比造影[术]/膀胱雙對比造影[術] double contrast cystography
膀胱碎石器/膀胱碎石器 lithomyl
膀胱碎石洗出术/膀胱碎石洗出術 vesical litholapaxy
膀胱损伤/膀胱損傷 injury of bladder
膀胱体/膀胱體 body of bladder
膀胱痛/膀胱痛 cystalgia
膀胱透照检查/膀胱腹部透照法 cystodiaphanoscopy
膀胱突出/膀胱突出，膀胱疝 vesical hernia
膀胱脱垂/膀胱脱垂 prolapse of bladder
膀胱外侧淋巴结/膀胱外側淋巴結 lateral vesical lymph node
膀胱外翻/膀胱外翻 bladder exstrophy
膀胱萎缩/膀胱萎縮 cystatrophia
膀胱下动脉/膀胱下動脈 inferior vesical artery
膀胱下动脉输尿管支/膀胱下動脈輸尿管支 ureteric branch of inferior vesical artery
膀胱腺癌/膀胱腺癌 adenocarcinoma of bladder
膀胱腺瘤/膀胱腺瘤 adenoma of bladder
膀胱小肠裂/膀胱小腸裂 vesicointestinal fissure
膀胱小梁形成/膀胱小梁形成 trabeculation of bladder
膀胱性血尿/膀胱性血尿 vesical hematuria
膀胱虚寒/膀胱虛寒 deficiency-cold of bladder
膀胱虚寒证/膀胱虛寒證 pattern of deficiency-cold of bladder
膀胱血管瘤/膀胱血管瘤 hemangioma of bladder
膀胱炎/膀胱炎 cystitis
膀胱移行细胞癌/膀胱移行細胞癌 transitional cell carcinoma of bladder
膀胱乙状结肠瘘/乙狀結腸膀胱瘻 sigmoidovesical fistula
膀胱乙状结肠吻合术/膀胱乙狀結腸造口吻合術 vesicosigmoidostomy
膀胱异位/膀胱異位 ectopia vesicae
膀胱异物/膀胱異物 foreign body in bladder
膀胱阴道的/膀胱與陰道的 vesico-vaginal
膀胱阴道瘘/膀胱陰道瘻 vesico-vaginal fistula
膀胱造口术/膀胱造口術，膀胱造瘻術 cystostomy
膀胱造影[术]/膀胱X光攝影術 cystography
膀胱增大/膀胱增大 cystauxe
膀胱真菌病/膀胱真菌病 mycosis of bladder
膀胱直肠瘘/膀胱直腸瘻 vesicorectal fistula

膀胱直肠造口吻合术／膀胱直腸造口吻合術
　　cystoproctostomy
膀胱指诊／膀胱觸診　vesical touch
膀胱肿瘤／膀胱腫瘤　tumor of bladder
膀胱周炎／膀胱旁組織炎　paracystitis
膀胱周组织／膀胱旁組織　paracystium
膀胱注射／膀胱注射　intravesical injection
膀胱子宫腹壁固定术／子宮膀胱固定術
　　hysterocystopexy
膀胱子宫颈的／膀胱與子宮頸的　vesicocervical
膀胱子宫颈瘘／膀胱子宮頸瘻　vesicocervical fistula
膀胱子宫颈阴道瘘／膀胱子宮頸陰道瘻　vesico-
　　cervico-vaginal fistula
膀胱子宫瘘／膀胱子宮瘻　vesicouterine fistula
膀胱子宫内膜异位症／膀胱子宮內膜異位症
　　endometriosis of bladder
膀胱子宫韧带／膀胱子宮韌帶　vesicouterine
　　ligament
膀胱子宫陷凹／膀胱子宮陷凹　vesicouterine pouch,
　　vesicouterine excavation
膀胱紫癜／膀胱紫癜　purpura of bladder, vesical
　　purpura
螃蟹／蟹　crab
胖大海／胖大海　boat-fruited sterculia seed
胖大舌／胖大舌　plump tongue
抛光轮／軟皮輪　buff wheel
抛射剂／推動劑，推進劑　propellent
抛物面聚光器／抛物線集光器，抛物線聚光器
　　paraboloid condenser
炮制／炮製　processing
炮炙／炮炙，修事　processing
跑步机／履帶跑步機　treadmill
跑步者臀／跑者臀　runner rump
泡膜[间质]细胞／泡膜[間質]細胞　theca interstitial
　　cell
泡膜细胞／泡膜細胞　theca cells
泡沫／泡沫　foam
泡沫气雾剂／泡沫型氣化噴霧劑　foam aerosol
泡沫试验／泡沫試驗　foam test, foam stability test
泡沫栓塞／泡沫栓塞　foam embolism
泡沫栓子／泡沫栓子　foam embolus
泡沫细胞／泡沫細胞　foam cell
泡沫性血栓形成／泡沫性血栓形成　foam thrombosis
泡沫[样]痰／泡沫性痰　frothy sputum
泡沫浴／泡沫浴，發泡浴　foam bath
泡泡树碱／泡泡樹鹼　asiminine
泡润／泡潤　soaking moistening
泡腾顿服剂／生泡飲料　effervescing draft

泡腾颗粒剂／發泡性顆粒　effervescent granule
泡腾片／發泡錠　effervescent tablet
泡腾片剂／發泡性錠　effervescent tablet
泡蛙肽／南美蛙皮肽　physalaemin
泡心细胞／泡心細胞　centroacinar cell
泡形棘皮瘤／泡形棘皮瘤　acanthoma alveolare
泡型包装／泡型包裝　blister package
泡性荨麻疹／水泡性蕁麻疹　urticaria vesiculosa
泡翼线虫病／泡翼蟲病　physalopteriasis
泡翼线虫属／狗泡翼蟲　*Physaloptera*
泡状腺／泡狀腺　acinar gland, alveolar gland
泡状腺瘤／泡狀腺瘤　adenoma acinosum
疱性角膜结膜炎／小皰性角膜結膜炎　phlyctenular
　　keratoconjunctivitis
疱性角膜炎／水皰性角膜炎　phlyctenular keratitis
疱性结膜炎／濕疹性結膜炎，小皰性結膜炎
　　phlyctenular conjunctivitis
疱性血管翳／皰性血管翳　phlyctenular pannus
疱性眼炎／小水皰性眼炎　phlyctenular ophthalmia
疱疹／大水皰　bleb
疱疹病毒／皰疹病毒　herpes virus
疱疹B病毒感染／B型皰疹病毒感染　herpes B virus
　　infection
疱疹病毒科感染／皰疹病毒科感染　herpesviridae
　　infection
疱疹病毒疫苗／皰疹病毒疫苗　herpes virus vaccines
疱疹的／皰疹的　herpetic
疱疹后神经痛／皰疹後神經痛　postherpetic neuralgia
疱疹脑炎／皰疹腦炎　herpesencephalitis
疱疹性角膜炎／皰疹性角膜炎　herpetic keratitis
疱疹性口炎／皰疹性口炎　herpetic stomatitis
疱疹性溃疡／皰疹性潰瘍　herpetic ulcer
疱疹性脑炎／皰疹性腦炎　herpes encephalitis
疱疹性湿疹／皰疹性濕疹　eczema herpeticum
疱疹性外阴阴道炎／皰疹性外陰陰道炎　herpetic
　　vulvovaginitis
疱疹性须疮／皰疹性鬚瘡　herpetic sycosis
疱疹性咽峡炎病毒／皰疹性咽峽炎病毒　herpangina
　　virus
疱疹性咽炎／皰疹性咽炎　pharyngitis herpetica
疱疹性龈口炎／皰疹性齦口炎　herpetic
　　gingivostomatitis
疱疹性龈炎／皰疹性牙齦炎　herpetic gingivitis
疱疹样／皰疹樣　herpetiformis
疱疹样阿弗他口炎／皰疹樣阿弗他口炎　herpetiform
　　aphthous stomatitis
疱疹样的／皰疹樣的　herpetiform
疱疹样溃疡／皰疹樣潰瘍　herpetiform ulceration

疱疹样脓疱病/皰疹狀膿皰病　impetigo herpetiformis
疱疹样皮炎/皰疹樣皮膚炎　dermatitis herpetiformis
疱疹样水疱性表皮松解症/皰疹樣水皰性表皮鬆解症　epidermolysis bullosa herpetiformis
疱疹样天疱疮/皰疹樣天皰瘡　pemphigus herpetiformis
疱疹样硬斑病/皰疹樣硬斑病　herpetiform morphea
胚壁/胚壁　germ wall
胚层/胚層　embryonic layer, germ layer
胚层反向/外在式原腸形成　entypy
胚带/胚帶　germinal band
胚的/胚[胎]的　embryonic
胚盾/胚盾　embryonic shield
胚反应能力/胚胎官能力　embryonic competence
胚极/胚極　embryonic pole
[胚]极滋养层/[胚]極滋養層　polar trophoblast
胚孔/胚孔　blastopore
胚孔唇/胚孔唇　blastopore lip
胚内体腔/胚內體腔　intraembryonic coelom
胚盘/胚盤　embryonic disc, germ disc
胚[盘]下腔/胚盤下腔　subgerminal cavity
胚泡/胚泡,囊胚　blastocyst
胚泡期/胚泡期　blastocyst stage
胚泡腔/胚泡腔　blastocyst cavity
胚泡形成/胚泡形成　blastocyst formation
胚区定位/胚葉位　germinal localization
胚乳/内胚乳　endosperm
胚神经弓/胚神經弓　neurochondrite
胚神经孔/胚神經孔　blastoneuropore
胚[胎]/胚[胎]　embryo
胚胎病/胚胎病　embryopathia
胚胎病理学/胚胎病理學　embryopathology
胚胎处置/胚胎處置　embryo disposition
胚胎的/胚胎的　embryonal
胚胎丢失/胚胎丟失　embryo loss
胚胎毒性/胚胎毒性　fetal toxicity
胚胎发生/胚胎發生　embryogenesis
胚胎发生研究/胚胎發生研究　research embryo creation
胚胎发育/胚胎發育　fetal development, embryonic development
胚胎发育不全/成胎雜亂　asyntaxia
胚胎发育观察器/胚胎發育觀察器　embryoscope
胚胎肝细胞移植/胚胎肝細胞移植　fetal hepatocyte transplantation
胚胎肝移植/胚胎肝移植　fetal liver transplantation
胚胎睾丸退化症/胚胎睾丸退化症　embryonic testicular regression
胚胎工程/胚胎工程　embryo engineering
胚胎化/胚胎化　embryonization
胚胎结构/胚胎結構　embryonic structure
胚胎决定/胚胎決定　embryonic determination
胚[胎]龄/胚[胎]齡　embryonic age
胚胎瘤/胚[胎]瘤,胚組織瘤　embryoma
胚胎描记法/胎兒描記法　embryography
胚胎描记器/胚胎描記器　embryograph
胚胎脑组织移植/胚胎腦組織移植　fetal brain tissue transplantation
胚胎培养/胚[胎]培養　embryo culture
胚胎培养技术/胚胎培養技術　embryo culture technique
胚[胎]期/胚[胎]期　embryonic period, embryonic stage
胚胎期发育不良/胚組織發育異常　dysembryoplasia
胚胎期形成的/胚胎期形成的　brephoplastic
胚胎器官移植/胚胎器官移植　fetal organ transplantation
胚胎切除术/胚胎切除術　embryectomy
胚胎融合/胚胎融合　embryo fusion
胚胎三毛滴虫/胚胎三毛滴蟲　Tritrichomonas foetus
胚胎肾移植/胚胎腎移植　fetal kidney transplantation
胚胎吸收/胚胎再吸收　fetal resorption
胚胎细胞/胚胎細胞　embryonal cell
胚胎型横纹肌肉瘤/胚胎橫紋肌肉瘤　embryonal rhabdomyosarcoma
胚胎性癌/胚胎性癌　embryonal carcinoma
胚胎性瘤/胚胎細胞瘤　embryonal tumor
胚胎胸骨带/胚胎胸骨帶　sternal band
胚胎学/胚胎學　embryology
胚胎学家/胚胎學家　embryologist
胚胎研究/胚胎研究　embryo research
胚胎移植/胚胎移植　embryo transfer
胚胎移植物/胚胎組織移植物　brephoplastic graft
胚胎营养/胎兒營養,胚胎滋養　embryotrophy
胚胎诱导/胚胎誘導　embryonic induction
胚胎植入/胚胎植入　embryo implantation
胚胎植入前/胚胎植入前　preimplantation
胚胎滞育/胚胎滯育　embryonic diapause
[胚胎]中间丛/胚胎中間叢　intermediate plexus
胚胎[中]毒/胚胎毒　embryotoxic
胚胎状态/胚胎狀態　embryoism
胚胎组织调控区/胚胎組織調控區　embryonic organizer

胚胎组织移植/胚胎組織移植　fetal tissue transplantation
胚体壁/胚體壁　somatopleure
胚外的/胚[體]外的　extraembryonic
胚外内胚层/胚外內胚層　extraembryonic endoderm
胚外体壁中胚层/胚外體壁中胚層　extraembryonic somatopleuric mesoderm
胚外体腔/胚外體腔　extraembryonic coelom
胚外体腔膜/胚外體腔膜　exocoelomic membrane
胚外外胚层/胚外外胚層　extraembryonic ectoderm
胚外脏壁中胚层/胚外臟壁中胚層　extraembryonic splanchnopleuric mesoderm
胚外中胚层/胚外中胚層　extraembryonic mesoderm
胚细胞/胚細胞,原細胞,始基細胞　elementary cell, primordial cell
胚细胞白血病/胚細胞白血病　blast cell leukemia
胚细胞变性/胚種變質　blastophthoria
胚细胞瘤/胚細胞瘤　blastocytoma
胚性传染/胚性傳染,胚芽感染　germinal infection
胚性畸胎瘤/胚性畸胎瘤　embryonal teratoma
胚性囊肿/胚性囊腫　embryonic cyst
胚循环/胚循環　embryonic circulation
胚芽春/胚芽春　germitrine
胚芽碱/吉梅林　germerine
胚芽碱乙酸盐类/胚芽鹼乙酸鹽類　germine acetates
胚芽血管瘤/胚芽血管瘤　gemmangioma
胚原浆/胚原漿　germogen
胚种的/胚的,生長的　germinal
胚[组织]瘤/胚組織瘤　embryoma
培哚普利/培哚普利　perindopril
培氟沙星/培氟沙星　pefloxacin
培高利特/培高利特　pergolide
培拉嗪/培拉嗪　perazine
培洛霉素/培洛黴素　peplomycin
培养/培養　culture
培养基/培養基　culture media, culture medium
培养集落生成单位/培養集落形成單位　colony forming unit culture, CFU-C
培养技术/培養技術　culture technique
培养扩散盒/培養擴散盒　culture diffusion chamber
培养皿/培養碟　culture dish
培养瓶/培養瓶　culture flask
培养特征/培養特徵　cultural characteristic
培养液/培養液　nutrient fluid
佩恩血清絮状反应/潘恩氏血清凝絮反應　Penn seroflocculation reaction
佩尔-埃布斯泰因病/佩-埃二氏病　Pel-Ebstein disease
佩尔特斯试验/佩爾特斯試驗　Perthes test
佩吉[特]病/佩吉特病,Paget 氏病　Paget disease
佩吉特细胞/Paget 氏細胞　Paget cell
佩吉特样网状细胞增多症/佩吉氏網狀細胞增多症　pagetoid reticulosis
佩凯管/Pecquet 氏管　duct of Pecquet
佩莱格利尼-施蒂达病/佩-史二氏病　Pellegrini-Stieda disease
佩兰/佩蘭　fortune eupatorium herb
佩兰素/蘭草浸質　eupatorin
佩雷尼溶液/Perenyi 氏溶液　Perenyi solution
佩利亚核/伯利爾氏核　Perlia nucleus
佩罗尼病/Peyronie 氏病　Peyronie disease
佩罗胸/Peyrot 氏胸　Peyrot thorax
佩珀综合征/Pepper 氏症候群　Pepper syndrome
佩特里平碟/北德利平碟　Petri plate
佩特里细菌培养皿/北德利氏培養皿,平皿　Petri dish
佩特伦饮食/Petren 氏飲食　Petren diet
佩特森综合征/Paterson 氏症候群　Paterson syndrome
佩特兹病/佩提斯氏病　Perthes disease
配对分析/配對分析　matched-pair analysis
配方乳/實驗室乳　laboratory milk
配方食品/配方食品　formulated food
配合液/配合液　matching fluid
配基/配合基　ligand
配景听力计/配景聽力計　peep-show audiometer
配偶/配偶　spouse
配偶肾移植/配偶腎移植　spouse renal transplantation
配体/配體　ligand
配位化合物/配位化合物　coordination compound
配伍/配伍　concerted application, synergy
配伍禁忌/配伍禁忌　incompatibility of drugs in prescription
配穴法/配穴法　points association, points combination
配药天平/配藥天平　dispensing balance
配制区/配製區　preparation area
配子/配子　gamete
配子发生/配子發生　gametogenesis
配子囊/配子囊,配子器官　gametangium
配子生殖/配子生殖　gamogony
配子输卵管内移植/配子輸卵管植入　gamete intrafallopian transfer, GIFT
配子输卵管内植入/配子輸卵管內植入　gamete intrafallopian transfer

配子体/配子體　gametophyte
配子体疗法/生殖體療法　gametocyte therapy
配子消失/配子消失　gametophagia
配子学家/配子學家，有性生殖學家　gametologist
配子样细胞/類配子細胞，類生殖細胞　gametoid cell
喷布洛尔/噴布洛爾　penbutolol
喷滤池/噴濾器　sprinkling filter
喷气烙术/氣焰燒灼術　gas cautery
喷砂机/噴砂機　sandblasting machine
喷射/射出　ejection
喷射冷冻法/噴射冷凍法　spraying freezing
喷射乳头/噴射狀乳頭　squirting papilla
喷射性喀喇音/射出卡嗒音　ejection click
喷射性呕吐/射出性嘔吐　projectile vomiting
喷射性收缩期杂音/射出性收縮期雜音　ejection systolic murmur
喷射性杂音/噴射性雜音　ejection murmur
喷射血流空洞化/噴射血流空洞化　cavitation of jet blood flow
喷射音/射出音　ejection sound
喷射注射/噴氣注射　jet injection
喷司他丁/噴司他丁　pentostatin
喷他佐辛/潘他唑新，鎮痛新　pentazocine
喷嚏/噴嚏　sneezing
喷嚏病/噴嚏病　apomyttosis
喷托维林/噴托維林　pentoxyverine
喷雾干燥/噴霧乾燥　spray drying
喷雾剂/噴霧　spray
喷雾疗法/噴霧療法　spraying therapy
喷雾麻醉/噴霧麻醉法　spraying anesthesia
喷雾器/噴霧器　nebulizer
喷液眼镜蛇/噴液眼鏡蛇　spitting cobra
盆壁筋膜/盆壁筋膜　parietal pelvic fascia
盆部/盆部，骨盆　pelvic part
盆底肌痉挛综合征/盆底肌痙攣綜合徵　pattern of pelvic floor muscle spasm, spastic pelvic floor pattern
盆底肌痉挛综合征·气滞血瘀证/盆底肌痙攣綜合徵·氣滯血瘀證　spastic pelvic floor pattern with pattern of qi stagnation and blood stasis
盆底肌痉挛综合征·湿热下注证/盆底肌痙攣綜合徵·濕熱下注證　spastic pelvic floor pattern with pattern of dampness-heat diffusing downward
盆底肌痉挛综合征·阴虚火旺证/盆底肌痙攣綜合徵·陰虛火旺證　spastic pelvic floor pattern with pattern of yin deficiency and fire effulgence
盆膈/盆膈　pelvic diaphragm, diaphragm of pelvis
盆膈上筋膜/盆膈上筋膜　superior fascia of pelvic diaphragm
盆膈下筋膜/盆膈下筋膜　inferior fascia of pelvic diaphragm
盆骨/盆骨　pelvic bone
盆筋膜/盆筋膜　pelvic fascia
盆筋膜腱弓/盆筋膜腱弓　tendinous arch of pelvic fascia
盆内脏神经/盆內臟神經　pelvic splanchnic nerves
盆腔/盆腔　cavitas pelvis, TF5
盆腔包虫病/盆腔包蟲病　pelvic echinococcosis
盆腔的/骨盆的，骨盤的　pelvic
盆腔动脉瘤/骨盆動脈瘤　pelvic aneurysm
盆腔蜂窝[组]织炎/骨盆蜂窩組織炎　pelvicellulitis
盆腔感染/盆腔感染　pelvic infection
盆腔横纹肌肉瘤/盆腔橫紋肌肉瘤　pelvic rhabdomyosarcoma
盆腔积血/骨盆血囊　pelvic hematocele
盆腔廓清术/骨盆內臟器剜除法　pelvic exenteration
盆腔脓肿/骨盆膿腫　pelvic abscess
盆腔器官固定术/骨盆器官固定術　pelvifixation
盆腔[器官]X射线照相术/骨盆 X 光攝影法　pelviography
盆腔疝/盆腔疝　hernia intrapelvica
盆腔肾/盆部腎　pelvic kidney
盆腔停滞/盆腔停滯　pelvic arrest
盆腔炎性疾病/骨盆腔發炎　pelvic inflammatory disease
盆腔瘀血综合征/盆腔瘀血症候群　pelvic congestion syndrome
盆腔肿瘤/盆腔腫瘤　pelvic neoplasm
盆腔子宫内膜异位症/盆腔子宮內膜異位症　endometriosis in pelvis cavity
盆腔子宫内膜异位症·寒凝血瘀证/盆腔子宮內膜異位症·寒凝血瘀證　endometriosis with pattern of cold congelation and blood stasis
盆腔子宫内膜异位症·气虚血瘀证/盆腔子宮內膜異位症·氣虛血瘀證　endometriosis with pattern of qi deficiency and blood stasis
盆腔子宫内膜异位症·气滞血瘀证/盆腔子宮內膜異位症·氣滯血瘀證　endometriosis with pattern of qi stagnation and blood stasis
盆腔子宫内膜异位症·热灼血瘀证/盆腔子宮內膜異位症·熱灼血瘀證　endometriosis with pattern of blazing heat and blood stasis
盆腔子宫内膜异位症·肾虚血瘀证/盆腔子宮內膜異位症·腎虛血瘀證　endometriosis with pattern of kidney deficiency and blood stasis
盆腔子宫内膜异位症·痰瘀互结证/盆腔子宮內膜異

位症•痰瘀互结证 endometriosis with pattern of intermingling of phlegm and static blood
盆神经节/盆神經節 pelvic ganglion
盆脏筋膜/盆臟筋膜 visceral pelvic fascia
烹调法/烹調法 cookery
彭罗斯引流管/潘洛斯氏引流管 Penrose drain
彭氏丝虫/彭亨絲蟲 Brugia pahangi
蓬发综合征/亂髮症候群 uncombable hair syndrome
蓬佩病/Pompe氏症 Pompe disease
蓬塞病/蓬塞病 Poncet disease
蓬塞综合征/蓬塞症候群 Poncet syndrome
硼/硼 boron
硼化合物/硼化合物 boron compound
硼化物/硼化物 boride
硼砂/硼酸鈉 sodium borate
硼水杨酸/硼水楊酸 borosalicylic acid
硼酸/硼酸 boric acid
硼酸苯酯/苯硼酸 borophenylic acid
硼酸甘油/硼酸甘油 boroglycerol
硼酸化物/硼酸化物 boronic acid
硼酸酒石/硼砂酒石 borated tartar
硼酸类/硼酸類 boric acids
硼酸柠檬酸/硼檸檬酸 borocitric acid
硼酸溶液/硼酸溶液 boric acid solution
硼酸盐/硼酸鹽 borate
硼烷/硼烷 borane
硼中毒/硼中毒 borism
硼中子俘获疗法/硼中子俘獲療法 boron neutron capture therapy
膨体聚四氟乙烯人造血管/膨體聚四氟乙烯人造血管 expanded polytetrafluoroethylene graft
膨胀/膨脹 distention
膨胀处溃疡/膨脹處潰瘍 distention ulcer
膨胀度/膨脹度 swelling degree
膨胀囊肿/膨脹囊腫 distension cyst
膨胀性/可舒張性 distensibility
膨胀性生长/膨脹性生長 expansive growth
碰撞/碰撞 collision
碰撞骨折/碰撞骨折,保險杆骨折 bumper fracture
碰撞瘤/碰撞性瘤 collision tumor
批/批 batch, lot
批号/批號 batch number
批记录/批次記錄 batch record
批准/批準 approbation
披裂突/杓狀隆起 arytenoid swelling
披膜病毒科感染/披膜病毒科感染 Togaviridae infection

砒霜中毒/砒霜中毒 arsenic poisoning
劈裂乳房瓣/劈裂乳房瓣 split breast flap
劈裂式肝移植/劈裂式肝移植 split liver transplantation
皮/皮 bark, peel
皮埃尔•罗班综合征/皮埃爾•羅班症候群 Pierre Robin syndrome
皮瓣/皮瓣 skin flap
皮瓣断蒂[术]/皮瓣斷蒂[術] skin flap pedicle division
皮瓣逆转设计法/皮瓣逆轉設計法 planning of skin flap in reverse
皮瓣舒平[术]/皮瓣舒平[術] skin flap flattening
皮瓣形成/皮瓣形成 formation of skin flap
皮瓣修薄[术]/皮瓣修薄[術] thinning of skin flap
皮瓣修整[术]/皮瓣修整[術] revision of skin flap
皮瓣训练/皮瓣訓練 conditioning of skin flap
皮瓣移植/皮瓣移植 skin flap transplantation
皮瓣移植术/皮瓣移植術 skin flap grafting
皮瓣转移/皮瓣轉移 transfer of skin flap
皮痹/皮痺,硬皮症 dermatosclerosis, scleroderma, skin numbness
皮痹•风湿闭阻证/皮痺•風濕閉阻證 dermatosclerosis with wind-dampness blockage pattern
皮痹•脾肺气虚证/皮痺•脾肺氣虛證 dermatosclerosis with spleen-lung qi deficiency pattern
皮痹•脾肾阳虚证/皮痺•脾腎陽虛證 dermatosclerosis with spleen-kidney yang deficiency pattern
皮痹•气血闭阻证/皮痺•氣血閉阻證 scleroderma with pattern of qi and blood blockade
皮痹•气滞血瘀证/皮痺•氣滯血瘀證 dermatosclerosis with pattern of qi stagnation and blood stasis
皮痹•肾阳衰微证/皮痺•腎陽衰微證 scleroderma with pattern of kidney yang exhaustion
皮部/皮部 dermal parts
皮层/皮層 cortex
皮层感觉性失语/皮層感覺性失語,顳葉頂葉性失語症 cortical sensory aphasia
皮层色素缺乏/皮層色素缺乏 cortical achromia
皮层下失读/皮質下性失讀症 subcortical alexia
皮层性失读/皮質性失讀症 cortical alexia
皮层运动区活动过度/皮質運動神經活力過強 hyperponesis
皮层运动区活动障碍/皮質運動區活動障礙

dysponesis
皮刺螨属/皮刺蟎屬 Dermanyssus
皮单位/微微單位 picounit
皮电反应/化電性皮膚反應 galvanic skin response
皮尔彻袋/比爾徹氏囊 Pilcher bag
皮尔茨-韦斯特法尔现象/比-維二氏現象 Piltz-Westphal phenomenon
皮尔凯试验/結核菌素皮膚試驗 Pirquet test
皮肥厚/厚皮病 pachyderma
皮肥厚病/慢性厚皮症 pachydermatosis
皮肤/皮膚 skin, cutis
皮肤阿米巴病/皮膚阿米巴病 cutaneous amebiasis
皮肤癌/皮膚癌 carcinoma cutis
皮肤白喉/皮膚白喉 diphtheria cutis
皮肤白血病/皮膚白血病 leukemia cutis
皮肤保存/皮膚保存 skin preservation
皮肤保护/皮膚保護 skin care
皮肤壁厚度/皮膚壁厚度 skinfold thickness
皮肤变黄/膽固醇皮膚沈著病 cholesteroderma
皮肤变形性滑液囊肿/皮膚變形性滑液囊腫 cutaneous metaplastic synovial cysts
皮肤表现/皮膚表現 skin manifestations
皮肤病/皮膚病 dermatopathy
皮肤病的/皮膚病的 dermatopathic
皮肤病关节炎/皮膚病關節炎 dermatoarthritis
皮肤病理学/皮膚病理學 dermatopathology
皮肤病疗法/皮膚病療法 dermatotherapy
皮肤病性淋巴腺炎/皮病性淋巴腺炎 dermatopathic lymphadenitis
皮肤病学/皮膚病學 dermatology
皮肤病遗传因素/皮膚疾患中之基因因素 genetic factors in skin disorders
皮肤病预防/皮膚感染預防 dermatophylaxis
皮肤剥脱综合征/皮膚脱皮症候群 peeling skin syndrome
皮肤-肠综合征合并口咽溃疡/皮膚-腸症候群合并口咽潰瘍 cutaneous-intestinal syndrome with oropharyngeal ulceration
皮肤呈浅黑色的/皮膚眼髮呈淺黑色的 brunette
皮肤橙色病/皮膚橙色病,橘色皮,胡蘿蔔素沈著 aurantiasis cutis, carotinosis, carotenemia
皮肤出血/皮膚出血 dermatorrhagia
皮肤刺激试验/皮膚刺激試驗 skin irritancy tests
皮肤胆固醇栓塞/皮膚膽固醇栓塞 cutaneous cholesterol embolism
皮肤导管瘤/真皮管狀瘤 dermal duct tumor
皮肤的/皮膚的 cutaneous
皮肤电阻计/皮膚抵抗測定器 dermometer

皮肤淀粉样变性/皮膚澱粉樣變性症 cutaneous amyloidosis
皮肤毒理学/皮膚毒理學 dermatoxicology
皮肤恶性混合瘤/皮膚惡性混合瘤 cutaneous malignant mixed tumor
皮肤腭口线虫病/皮膚領口蟲病 cutaneous gnathostomiasis
皮肤发红/皮膚發紅 rubeosis
皮肤发育不全/皮膚再生不全或不能,皮膚形成不全 aplasia cutis
皮肤反射/皮膚反射 skin reflex
皮肤反应/皮膚反應 cutireaction
皮肤非典型分枝杆菌感染/皮膚非典型分枝桿菌感染 atypical mycobacterial infection of the skin
皮肤肥大细胞增生症/皮膚肥大細胞增生症 cutaneous mastocytosis
皮肤肥厚/皮膚肥厚 dermatohypertrophia
皮肤肺综合征/皮膚肺症候群 skin-pulmonary syndrome
皮肤分裂涂片/皮膚分裂塗片 split skin smear
皮肤附件/皮膚附件 appendage of skin
皮肤附件癌/皮膚附件癌 skin appendage carcinoma
皮肤附件及间叶错构瘤/皮膚附件及間葉錯構瘤 cutaneous hamartoma of adnexa and mesenchyme
皮肤附属器/皮膚附屬器 cutaneous appendage
皮肤钙化/皮膚結石 cutaneous calculus
皮肤钙质沉着症/皮膚鈣鹽沈著症 calcinosis cutis
皮肤肝卟啉症/慢性肝吡咯紫質沈著病 cutaneous hepatic porphyria
皮肤感觉/皮膚感覺 dermal sense
皮肤梗死/皮膚梗塞 cutaneous infarction
皮肤钩/皮膚鉤 skin hook
皮肤骨化/皮膚骨化 cutaneous ossification
皮肤骨瘤/皮膚骨瘤 osteoma cutis
皮肤光老化/皮膚光老化 skin photoaging
皮肤过敏反应/皮膚的過敏反應 cutaneous anaphylaxis
皮肤过敏性结节性血管炎/皮膚過敏性結節性血管炎 cutaneous allergic nodular vasculitis
皮肤黑素细胞瘤/皮膚黑色素細胞瘤 dermal melanocytoma
皮肤红斑狼疮/皮膚紅斑狼瘡 cutaneous lupus erythematosus
皮肤红斑消退试验/猩紅熱疹之消退現象 extinction sign
皮肤呼吸/皮膚呼吸 cutaneous respiration
皮肤划痕现象/皮劃紋現象,劃皮現象 dermatographia

皮肤划痕现象的/皮膚劃痕的　dermographic
皮肤划痕症/劃皮現象　dermatographism
皮肤划纹现象/皮膚劃紋現象　dermographism
皮肤坏疽/皮膚壞疽　gangrene of skin
皮肤坏死毒素/細菌製造的皮膚毒素　dermotoxin
皮肤坏死性血管炎/皮膚壞死性血管炎　cutaneous necrotizing vasculitis
皮肤环状萎缩性斑块/皮膚環狀萎縮性斑塊　annular atrophic plaque of the skin
皮肤混合瘤/皮膚混合瘤,軟骨樣汗腺瘤　mixed tumor of skin
皮肤活组织检查/皮膚切片　skin biopsy
皮肤[或毛发]变色/色素異常　dyschromia
皮肤畸形/皮膚畸形　skin abnormality
皮肤疾病/皮膚疾病　skin disease
皮肤棘层松解/皮膚棘層鬆解　acantholysis
皮肤棘细胞层水肿的/海綿層的　spongiotic
皮肤脊索瘤/皮膚脊索瘤　chordoma cutis
皮肤寄生虫病/皮膚寄生蟲病　dermatozoiasis
皮肤假白血病/皮膚假白血病　pseudoleukemia cutis
皮肤假肉瘤性息肉/皮膚假肉瘤性息肉　cutaneous pseudosarcomatous polyp
皮肤假性淋巴瘤/皮膚假淋巴瘤　cutaneous pseudolymphoma
皮肤间叶错构瘤/皮膚間葉錯構瘤　cutaneous mesenchymal hamartoma
皮肤胶原性血管病变伴全身性毛细血管扩张/皮膚膠原性血管病變伴廣泛性微血管擴張　cutaneous collagenous vasculopathy with generalized telangiectasia
皮肤角化病/角皮病　keratodermia
皮肤角化囊肿/皮膚角質囊腫　cutaneous keratocyst
皮肤角质层/皮膚角質層　keratoderma
皮[肤]结核/皮膚結核,結核性皮膚病　tuberculoderm, cutaneous tuberculosis
皮肤结核菌素反应/畢爾凱氏反應　dermotuberculin reaction
皮肤结节性多动脉炎/皮膚結節性多動脈炎　cutaneous polyarteritis nodosa
皮肤紧张度计/皮膚緊張度計　neurotonometer
皮肤镜检查/皮膚鏡檢查　dermoscopy
皮肤局部性异样/皮膚局部性異樣　regional diversity of skin
皮肤巨细胞透明血管病/皮膚巨細胞透明質血管病變　cutaneous giant cell hyaline angiopathy
皮肤开窗术/皮膚開窗術　skin window technique
皮肤抗原/皮膚病抗原　dermatogen
皮肤科用药/皮膚科用藥　dermatologic agent

皮肤口炎/皮口炎　dermatostomatitis
皮肤溃疡/皮膚潰瘍　skin ulcer
皮肤利什曼病/皮膚利什曼病　Cochin China sore
皮肤粒细胞性肉瘤/皮膚顆粒球性肉瘤　cutaneous granulocytic sarcoma
皮肤良性淋巴组织增生/良性皮膚淋巴組織增殖病　lymphadenosis benigna cutis
皮肤淋巴管病/皮膚淋巴管病　lymphodermia
皮肤淋巴结病/皮膚淋巴腺病　dermatopathic lymphadenopathy
皮肤淋巴细胞浸润症/皮膚淋巴細胞浸潤症　lymphocytic infiltration of skin
皮肤淋巴细胞抗原/皮膚淋巴細胞抗原　cutaneous lymphocyte antigen
皮肤淋巴细胞瘤/皮膚淋巴細胞瘤　lymphocytoma cutis
皮肤淋巴腺瘤/皮膚[的]淋巴腺瘤　cutaneous lymphadenoma, lymphadenoma cutaneous
皮肤淋巴样组织增生/表皮淋巴增生　cutaneous lymphoid hyperplasia
皮肤毛细管破裂/皮膚微血管破裂　dermatorrhexis
皮肤毛细血管瘤/皮膚毛細血管瘤　capillary hemangioma of skin
皮肤梅毒/皮膚梅毒　cutaneous syphilis
皮肤膜/皮膚膜　cutaneous membrane
皮肤摩擦术/擦皮法,手術整平法　dermabrasion
皮肤男性化/皮膚男性化　cutaneous virilism
皮肤囊肿/皮膚囊腫　cutaneous cyst
皮肤脑脊[髓]膜血管瘤病/皮膚腦脊[髓]膜血管瘤病　cutaneous meningospinal angiomatosis
皮肤脑膜瘤/皮膚腦膜瘤　cutaneous meningioma
皮肤黏蛋白病/皮膚黏液素病　cutaneous mucinosis
皮肤黏膜[梅毒]疹复发/黏膜皮膚疹再發　mucocutaneous relapse
皮肤黏膜透明变性/皮膚黏膜透明變性　hyalinosis cutis et mucosae
皮肤黏液瘤/皮膚黏液瘤　cutaneous myxoma
皮肤黏液囊炎/皮膚黏液囊炎　dermosynovitis
皮肤黏液囊肿/皮膚黏液囊腫　cutaneous mucous cyst
皮肤黏液样成纤维细胞瘤/皮膚黏液樣纖維母細胞瘤　cutaneous myxoid fibroblastoma
皮肤黏液样囊肿/皮膚黏液樣囊腫　cutaneous myxoid cyst
皮肤念珠菌病/皮膚念珠菌病　candidiasis cutis
皮肤佩吉特细胞样错构瘤/皮膚 Paget 氏細胞樣錯構瘤　cutaneous hamartoma with pagetoid cells
皮肤皮脂缺乏/皮膚皮脂缺乏症　asteatosis cutis

皮肤[平滑]肌瘤/皮[膚平滑]肌瘤 dermatomyoma, leiomyoma cutis
皮肤牵引/皮膚牽引 skin traction
皮肤浅表脓肿/皮膚淺表膿腫 cutaneous abscess
皮肤肉瘤病/皮膚肉瘤病 sarcomatosis cutis
皮肤肉瘤样纤维瘤/皮膚肉瘤樣纖維瘤 sarcomatoid fibroma of skin
皮肤乳头/真皮乳頭 dermal papilla
皮肤乳头瘤病/皮膚乳頭狀瘤病 cutaneous papillomatosis
皮肤乳头状瘤/皮膚乳頭狀瘤 cutaneous tag, cutaneous papilloma
皮肤软骨角膜的/皮-軟骨-眼角膜症候群 dermo-chondro-corneal
皮肤软骨瘤/皮膚軟骨腫瘤 cutaneous cartilaginous tumor
皮肤色素/皮膚色素 skin pigment
皮肤色素沉着/皮膚色素沈著 skin pigmentation
皮肤砂样瘤/皮膚沙樣瘤 cutaneous psammoma
皮肤β射线伤/皮膚β射線傷 β ray skin injury
皮肤神经节细胞迷芽瘤/皮膚神經節細胞迷芽瘤 cutaneous ganglion cell choristoma
皮肤神经瘤/皮膚神經瘤 cutaneous neuroma
皮肤神经内分泌癌/皮膚神經內分泌癌 cutaneous neuroendocrine carcinoma
皮肤神经学/皮膚神經學 dermatoneurology
皮肤神经炎/皮膚神經炎 cutaneous neurosis
皮肤生理学/皮膚生理學 skin physiology
皮肤湿度/皮膚濕度 humidity of skin
皮肤湿度计/皮膚濕度計 dermohygrometer
皮肤试验/皮膚試驗 skin test
皮肤试验终点滴定法/皮膚試驗終點滴定法 skin test end-point titration
皮肤嗜碱性粒细胞超敏反应/皮膚嗜鹼性球高敏感性 cutaneous basophil hypersensitivity
皮肤嗜曙红细胞性淋巴滤泡症/皮膚嗜伊紅球性淋巴濾泡症 eosinophilic lymphofolliculosis of the skin
皮肤书写觉/皮膚書寫覺 graphesthesia
皮肤输卵管子宫内膜异位病/皮膚輸卵管子宮內膜異位症 cutaneous endosalpingiosis
皮肤衰老/皮膚衰老 skin aging
皮肤水肿/皮膚水腫 edematous skin
皮肤松弛症/皮膚鬆弛症,皮膚鬆垂症 cutis laxa
皮肤松垂/皮膚鬆垂,皮膚鬆弛 anetoderma, dermatocele
皮肤酸碱度/皮膚酸鹼度 acid-base scale of skin
皮肤髓外造血/皮膚髓外造血,皮膚髓外血球生成 cutaneous extramedullary hematopoiesis, extramedullary hemopoiesis of the skin
皮肤糖分过多/皮膚含糖過多 hyperglycodermia
皮肤替代品/皮膚替代品 skin substitutes
皮肤通透性/皮膚通透性 permeability of skin
皮肤投药/皮膚投藥 cutaneous administration
皮肤透明血管病/皮膚透明質血管病變 cutaneous hyaline angiopathy
皮肤透照镜/皮膚透視器 phaneroscope
皮肤蜕模病/皮膚蛻膜病 cutaneous deciduosis
皮肤网状细胞瘤/皮膚網狀細胞瘤 reticulocytoma cutis
皮肤微波损伤/皮膚微波損傷 cutaneous microwave injury
皮肤微生物/皮膚上的微生物 skin flora
皮肤萎缩/皮膚萎縮 paper skin
皮肤萎缩症/皮膚萎縮病 atrophoderma
皮肤温度/皮膚溫度 skin temperature
皮肤无反应/皮膚無反應 dermoanergy
皮肤吸收/皮膚吸收 cutaneous absorption
皮肤系统/外皮系統 integumentary system
皮肤B细胞淋巴瘤/皮膚B細胞淋巴瘤 cutaneous B cell lymphoma
皮肤T细胞淋巴瘤/皮膚T細胞淋巴瘤 cutaneous T cell lymphoma
皮肤纤毛囊肿/皮膚纖毛囊腫 cutaneous ciliated cyst
皮肤纤维变性/皮膚纖維症 dermatofibrosis
皮肤纤维瘤/皮纖維瘤 dermatofibroma
皮肤纤维肉瘤/皮纖維肉瘤 dermatofibrosarcoma
皮肤癣菌/皮癬菌 dermatophyte
皮肤癣菌试验培养基/皮癬菌試驗培養基 dermatophyte test medium
皮肤学的/皮膚學的 dermatological
皮肤血管内乳头状内皮增生症/皮膚血管內乳突狀內皮細胞增生 cutaneous intravascular papillary endothelial hyperplasia
皮肤血管外坏死性肉芽肿/皮膚血管外壞死性肉芽腫 cutaneous extravascular necrotizing granuloma
皮肤眼炎/皮眼炎 dermato-ophthalmitis
皮肤伴病/皮膚科學性伴病 dermatological pathomimicry
皮肤移行毛/皮膚移行毛 cutaneous pili migrans
皮肤移植/皮膚移植 skin transplantation
皮肤移植术/皮移植法,植皮術 skin grafting
皮肤异色病/皮膚異色病 poikiloderma
皮肤疫苗/皮膚疫苗 dermovaccine
皮肤隐球菌病/皮膚隱球菌病 cryptococcosis cutis

皮肤蝇蛆病/皮膚蠅蛆病　myiasis cutis
皮肤用气雾剂/皮膚用氣化噴霧劑　skin aerosol
皮肤幼虫移行症/皮膚幼蟲移行症　cutaneous larva migrans
皮肤早老形象/皮膚早老形象　cutaneous geromorphism
皮肤藻菌病/皮膚藻菌病　cutaneous phycomycosis
皮肤灶性黏蛋白沉积症/皮膚灶性黏蛋白沈積症　cutaneous focal mucinosis
皮肤针/皮膚針　cutaneous needle, dermal needle
皮肤针疗法/皮膚針療法　cutaneous needle therapy
皮肤真菌病/皮膚黴菌病　dermatomycosis
皮肤真菌素/皮黴素　dermatomycin
皮肤真性组织细胞性淋巴瘤/皮膚真性組織細胞性淋巴瘤　cutaneous genuine histiocytic lymphoma
皮肤脂度测定/皮膚脂度測定　grease assay of skin
皮肤脂肪切除术/皮膚脂肪切除術　dermolipectomy
皮肤指节韧带/皮膚指節韌帶　cutaneophalangeal ligament
皮肤致敏抗体/皮膚致敏抗體　skin sensitizing antibody
皮肤肿块/皮膚結塊　phyma
皮肤肿瘤/皮膚腫瘤　skin neoplasm
皮肤皱襞/皮膚皺襞　skin fold
皮肤猪囊尾蚴病/皮膚豬囊尾蚴病　cysticercosis cutis
皮肤转白试验/皮膚轉白試驗　blanching test
皮肤转移性淋巴炎/皮膚轉移性淋巴炎　cutaneous metastatic lymphangitis
皮肤转移性绒毛膜癌/皮膚轉移性絨毛膜癌　cutaneous metastatic choriocarcinoma
皮肤转移性腺癌/皮膚轉移性腺癌　cutaneous metastatic adenocarcinoma
皮肤着色症/皮膚著色病　chromopathy
皮肤子宫内膜异位［症］/皮膚子宫內膜異位症　cutaneous endometriosis
皮肤组织细胞增生病X/皮膚組織細胞增生症X　cutaneous histiocytosis X
皮革样胃/革囊狀胃　leather bottle stomach
皮沟/皮溝　groove of skin
皮骨/皮內骨　dermal bone
皮管/皮管　skin tube
皮海绵毒质/皮海綿毒質　suberitin
皮厚度计/皮下脂層測定器　adipometer
皮货商病/皮貨商病　fell-monger disease
皮肌/皮肌　cutaneous muscle
皮肌炎/皮肌炎　dermatomyositis
皮嵴/皮嵴　dermal ridge

皮浆植皮术/皮漿植皮術　skin pulp grafting
皮角/皮角　cornu cutaneum
皮节/皮節　dermatomere
皮结核/皮膚結核病　tuberculosis cutis
皮静脉/皮靜脈　cutaneous vein
皮卡尔迪-拉叙尤尔-格拉哈姆-利特尔综合征/Piccardi-Lassueur-Graham-Little 氏症候群　Piccardi-Lassueur-Graham-Little syndrome
皮克病/皮克病　Pick disease
皮克雷尔溶液/Pickrell 氏溶液　Pickrell solution
皮克脑回萎缩/Pick 氏腦回萎縮　Pick convolutional atrophy
皮克细胞/Pick 氏細胞　Pick cell
皮克综合征/Pick 氏症候群　Pick syndrome
皮库/皮庫　skin bank
皮瘘/皮瘻　cutaneous fistula
皮-罗综合征/Pierre-Robin 二氏症候群　Pierre-Robin syndrome
皮螨属/皮蟎屬　*Chorioptes*
皮毛/皮毛　skin and hair
皮内的/皮內的　intracutaneous
皮内反应/皮内反應,泰布提氏反應　endodermoreaction
皮内缝合/皮內縫合　intradermal suture
皮内结核菌素试验/皮內結核菌素試驗　intracutaneous tuberculin test
皮内试验/皮內試驗　intradermal test
皮内针疗法/皮內針療法　intradermal needle therapy
皮内注射/皮內注射　intradermal injection
皮内注射性肺炎/皮膚性肺炎　dermal pneumonia
皮片/皮片　free skin graft
皮片成网器/皮片成網器　skin graft mesher
皮片移植术/皮片移植術　free skin grafting
皮破肉损/皮破肉損　skin and muscle wound
皮区/皮節區　dermatomic area
皮上层/胎［表］皮外層　epitrichium
皮上结核菌素试验/經皮膚之結核素試驗　percutaneous tuberculin test
皮神经/皮神經　cutaneous nerve
皮神经的/神經與皮膚的　neurocutaneous
皮神经营养血管蒂岛状皮瓣/皮神經營養血管蒂島狀皮瓣　cutaneous nerve nutritional vessel pedicle island skin flap
皮水/皮水　skin edema
皮特金溶液/Pitkin 氏溶液　Pitkin solution
皮痛/皮痛症,皮膚神經分布失常　dermatalgia
皮萎缩/皮萎縮　atrophic skin
皮纹/皮紋　dermatoglyph

皮纹[线]/皮紋[線] skin line
皮纹学/手紋學 dermatoglyphics
皮下/皮下的 hypodermic
皮下部/皮下部 subcutaneous part
皮下层/皮下層 subcutaneous layer
皮下蒂皮瓣/皮下蒂皮瓣 subcutaneous pedicle skin flap
皮下多形性错构瘤/皮下多形性錯構瘤 pleomorphic hamartoma of the subcutis
皮下骨锯/史雷迪氏皮下鋸 subcutaneous saw
皮下骨折/皮下骨折 subcutaneous fracture
皮下环状肉芽肿/皮下環狀肉芽腫 subcutaneous granuloma annulare
皮下黄色肉芽肿症/皮下黃色肉芽腫症 subcutaneous xanthogranulomatosis
皮下结节/皮下結節 subcutaneous nodules
皮下结石[症]/皮下結石病 hypodermolithiasis
皮下囊/皮下囊 subcutaneous bursa
皮下捻发音/皮下撚髮音 subcutaneous crepitation
皮下脓肿/皮下膿腫 subcutaneous abscess
皮下气肿/皮下氣腫 subcutaneous emphysema
皮下切开术/皮下切開術 hypodermatomy
皮下乳房切除术/皮下乳房切除術 subcutaneous mastectomy
皮下三角区/皮下三角區 triangular subcutaneous area
皮下伤/皮下傷 subcutaneous injury
皮下射片/皮下注射用錠劑 hypodermic tablet
皮[下]石/皮膚石 skin stones
皮下输液[法]/皮下轉輸法 subcutaneous transfusion
皮下投药法/皮下用藥 dermenchysis
皮下荨麻疹/皮下蕁麻疹 subcutaneous urticaria
皮下蝇蛆病/皮下蠅蛆病 hypodermiasis
皮下脂肪/皮下脂肪 subcutaneous fat
皮下脂肪代谢障碍/部分性營養不良 partial lipodystrophy
皮下脂肪肉芽肿病/皮下脂肪肉芽腫症 lipogranulomatosis subcutanea
皮下脂肪萎缩/局部脂肪萎縮 partial lipoatrophy
皮下脂肉芽肿症/皮下脂肉芽腫症 subcutaneous lipogranulomatosis
皮下植入法/皮下植入法 hypodermic implantation
皮下注射/皮下注射 subcutaneous injection, hypodermic injection
皮下注射器/皮下注射器 hypodermic syringe
皮下注射用片剂/下皮錠 hypodermic tablet
皮下注射针/皮下注射針 hypodermic needle
皮下注水法/蒸餾水之皮下注射法 aquapuncture
皮下组织/皮下組織 subcutaneous tissue, subcutis, hypodermis
皮下组织真菌病/皮下組織真菌病 subcutaneous mycosis
皮屑抗原/皮屑抗原 dander antigen
皮癣菌疹/皮癬菌疹 dermatophytid
皮癣菌疹反应/皮癬菌疹反應 dermatophytid reaction
皮血管镜检查/皮血管鏡檢查 dermatoscopy
皮血管炎/皮血管炎 angiodermatitis
皮炎/皮膚炎 dermatitis
皮炎外瓶霉/皮炎外瓶黴 Exophiala dermatitides
皮痒螨病/皮恙蟲病 chorioptic acariasis
皮样癌/類皮腫性癌 dermoid cancer
皮样的/皮樣的 dermoid
皮样瘤/皮樣瘤 dermoid tumor
皮样囊肿/皮樣囊腫 dermoid cyst, cuticular cyst
皮样囊肿切除术/皮樣囊腫切除術 dermoidectomy
皮移植物/真皮移植物 dermal graft
皮蝇病/皮瘤蠅[寄生]病 dermatobiasis
皮蝇属/皮蠅屬 Dermatobia
皮真菌病/皮癬菌病 dermatophytosis
皮疹/皮疹 rash
皮疹消退/皮疹消退 deflorescence
皮支/皮支 cutaneous branch
皮支持带/皮支持帶 retaining band of skin
皮脂/皮脂 sebum
皮脂肪筋膜移植物/皮脂肪筋膜移植物 derma-fat-fascia graft
皮脂分泌不足/皮脂分泌不足 hyposteatosis
皮脂瘤/皮膚脂瘤 dermolipoma
皮脂毛囊瘤/皮脂腺髮毛囊瘤 sebaceous trichofolliculoma
皮脂囊瘤/皮脂腺囊瘤 steatocystoma
皮脂囊瘤病/多發性皮脂囊腫 sebocystomatosis
皮脂囊肿病/皮脂瘤病 steatomatosis
皮脂缺乏的/缺脂的 asteatotic
皮脂缺乏性皮炎/缺脂性皮膚炎 asteatotic dermatitis
皮脂缺乏性湿疹/皮脂缺乏性濕疹,乾裂性濕疹 asteatotic eczema
皮脂缺乏[症]/皮脂缺乏病,皮脂減少病 asteatosis
皮脂腺/皮脂腺 sebaceous gland
皮脂腺癌/皮脂腺癌 sebaceous carcinoma
皮脂腺错构瘤/皮脂腺錯構瘤 sebaceous gland hamartoma
皮脂腺管/皮脂腺管 sebaceous duct

皮脂腺疾病/皮脂腺疾病　sebaceous gland disease
皮脂腺狼疮/皮脂腺狼瘡　lupus sebaceus
皮脂腺淋巴腺瘤/皮脂腺淋巴腺瘤　sebaceous lymphadenoma
皮脂腺瘤/皮脂腺囊腫　sebaceous tumor
皮脂腺上皮瘤/皮脂腺上皮瘤　sebaceous epithelioma
皮脂腺腺瘤/皮脂腺［腺］瘤　sebaceous adenoma
皮脂腺增生/皮脂腺增生　sebaceous hyperplasia
皮脂腺痣/皮脂腺痣　sebaceous nevus
皮脂腺肿瘤/皮脂腺腫瘤　sebaceous gland neoplasm
皮脂性腺癌/皮脂性腺癌　sebaceous adenocarcinoma
皮脂溢/脂漏　seborrhea
皮脂溢的/皮脂漏的　seborrheic
皮脂障碍症/皮脂障礙　dyssebacea
皮质/皮質　cortex, cortical substance
皮质板/皮質板　cortical plate
皮质变性/皮質變性　cortical degeneration
皮质醇结合球蛋白异常/皮質醇結合球蛋白異常　abnormality of cortisol-binding globulin
皮质醇增多症/高皮質醇症，皮質醇過多症　hypercortisolism
皮质反应/皮質反應，皮層反應　cortical reaction
皮质感觉性失语/Wernicke 氏失語症　Wernicke aphasia
皮质核束/皮質核徑　corticonuclear tract
皮质核纤维/腦皮質核纖維　corticobulbar fiber
皮质红核束/皮質紅核徑　corticorubral tract
皮质脊髓侧束/皮質脊徑，大腦皮質脊髓外側徑　lateral corticospinal tract, tractus corticospinalis lateralis
皮质脊髓的/腦皮質與脊髓的　corticospinal
皮质脊髓前束/皮質脊側徑，皮質脊前徑　anterior corticospinal tract
皮质脊髓束/皮質脊［髓］徑　corticospinal tract, tractus corticospinalis
皮质精神性盲/皮質精神性盲　cortical psychic blindness
皮质颗粒/皮質顆粒，皮部顆粒　cortical granule
皮质类固醇/皮質類固醇　corticosteroid
皮质类固醇性痤疮/皮質類固醇痤瘡　corticosteroid acne
皮质类固醇性紫癜/皮質類固醇性紫癜　corticosteroid purpura
皮质盲/皮質盲　cortical blindness
皮质迷路/皮質迷路　cortical labyrinth
皮质脑桥的/腦皮質與橋腦的　corticopontine
皮质脑桥束/皮質橋腦徑　corticopontine tract
皮质内侧部/皮質内側部　corticomedial part
皮质内骨肉瘤/皮質内骨肉瘤　intracortical osteosarcoma
皮质丘脑的/腦皮質與丘腦的　corticothalamic
皮质丘脑束/皮質丘腦徑　corticothalamic tract
皮质素/皮質素　cortin
皮质素葡萄糖耐量试验/皮質素葡萄糖耐量試驗　cortisone glucose tolerance test
皮质素抑制试验/皮質素抑制試驗　cortisone suppression test
皮质同步化/皮質同步化　cortical synchronization
皮质酮/皮［質］硬脂酮　corticosterone
皮质网状束/皮質網狀束　corticoreticular tract
皮质纹状体的/皮質紋狀體的　corticostriate
皮质纹状体辐射线/皮質紋狀體輻射線　corticostriate radiation
皮质下/皮質下　①subcortex ②pizhixia, AT 4
皮质下出血/皮質下出血　subcortical hemorrhage
皮质下失语/皮質下性失語　subcortical aphasia
皮质腺瘤/皮脂腺瘤　cortical adenoma
皮质小脑束/皮質小腦徑　corticocerebellar tract
皮质性白内障/皮質性白內障　cortical cataract
皮质性失用症/皮質性失用症　cortical apraxia
皮质性失语症/皮質性失語症　cortical aphasia
皮质延髓的/大腦皮質與延髓的　corticobulbar
皮质延髓束/皮質延髓徑　corticobulbar tract
皮质运动前区综合征/皮質運動前區症候群　premotor syndrome
皮质运动区活动不足/皮質運動區活動不足　hypoponesis
皮质柱/皮質柱　column of cortex
皮赘/皮贅　skin tag
皮赘状多指/皮贅狀多指　rudimentary accessory digit
枇杷叶/枇杷葉　loquat leaf
铍/鈹　beryllium
铍肉芽肿/鈹肉芽腫　beryllium granuloma
铍针/鈹針　stiletto needle
铍中毒/鈹毒症　berylliosis
疲倦毒素/疲勞毒素　kenotoxin
疲劳/疲勞，衰竭，疲憊　exhaustion, fatigue
疲劳反应/疲勞反應　fatigue reaction
疲劳骨折/疲勞性骨折　fatigue fracture
疲劳描记器/痛覺描記器　ponograph
疲劳性痉挛/疲勞性痙攣　fatigue spasm
疲劳症/疲勞症　apocamnosis
疲劳状态/疲勞狀態　fatigue state
啤酒花/啤酒花　hop
啤酒酵母/啤酒酵母菌　*Saccharomyces exiguus*

啤酒心/啤酒心　beer heart
脾/脾［臟］　spleen
脾被膜炎/脾被膜炎，脾外膜炎　episplenitis
脾痹/脾痺　spleen bi
脾［表面］刺激法/脾刺激法　splenocleisis
脾病/脾病　lienopathy
脾不统血/脾不統血　spleen failing to manage blood
脾不统血证/脾不統血證　pattern of spleen failing to manage blood
脾藏意/脾藏意　spleen storing idea
脾藏营/脾藏營　spleen storing nutrients
脾测定法/測脾法　splenometry
脾充血/脾充血　splenemia
脾穿刺/脾穿刺術　splenic puncture
脾丛/脾叢　splenic plexus
脾大/脾大　splenomegaly
脾大性红细胞增多/巨脾性紅血球過多症　splenomegalic polycythemia
脾的/脾的　splenic
脾动脉/脾動脈　splenic artery
脾动脉瘤/脾動脈瘤　splenic artery aneurysm
脾动脉胰支/脾動脈胰支　pancreatic branch of splenic artery
脾毒素/脾毒素　lienotoxin
脾恶/脾惡　critical condition of spleen
脾肺气虚证/脾肺氣虛證　pattern of qi deficiency of spleen and lung
脾肝大/肝脾腫大　splenohepatomegalia
脾疳/脾疳　spleen gan disease
脾膈面/脾膈面　diaphragmatic surface of spleen
脾膈韧带/脾膈韌帶　lienophrenic ligament
脾梗塞/脾梗塞　splenic infarction
脾功能亢进/脾功能亢進　hypersplenism
脾功能正常/脾官能正常　eusplenia
脾骨髓性白血病/脾骨髓性白血病　lienomyelogenous leukemia
脾固定术/脾固定術　splenopexia
脾合胃/脾合胃　spleen being connected with stomach
脾后端/脾後端　posterior extremity of spleen
脾疾病/脾疾病　splenic disease
脾集落生成单位/脾細胞族形成單位　colony forming unit spleen, CFU-S
脾结肠面/脾結腸面　colic surface of spleen
脾结核/脾結核　splenic tuberculosis
脾惊/脾驚　convulsion due to spleen disorders
脾静脉/脾靜脈　splenic vein
脾开窍于口/脾開竅於口　spleen opening at mouth

脾溃疡/脾潰瘍　splenelcosis
脾淋巴结/脾淋巴結　splenic lymph node
脾瘤/脾瘤　splenoma
脾门/脾門　hilum of spleen, porta of spleen
脾门静脉造影术/脾門靜脈攝影術　splenoportography
脾囊肿/脾囊腫　splenic cyst
脾内血细胞蓄积/脾臟血球蓄積症　sissorexia
脾片移植/脾片移植　splenic slice transplantation
脾破裂/脾破裂　rupture of spleen
脾气/脾氣　spleen qi
脾气下陷/脾氣下陷　sinking of spleen qi
脾气虚/脾氣虛　spleen qi deficiency
脾气虚证/脾氣虛證　pattern of spleen qi deficiency
脾前端/脾前端　anterior extremity of spleen
脾切除术/脾切除術　splenectomy
脾切开术/脾切開術　splenotomy
脾曲综合征/脾曲症候群　splenic flexure syndrome
脾热病/脾熱病　spleen heat disease
脾肉芽肿病/脾肉芽腫病　splenogranulomatosis
脾软化/脾軟化　lienomalacia
脾疝/脾疝　lienocele
脾善/脾善　favorable condition of spleen
脾上缘/脾上緣　superior border of spleen
脾［神经］痛/脾痛　splenalgia
脾肾动脉吻合术/脾腎動脈吻合術　splenorenal arterial anastomosis
脾肾分流/脾腎分流　splenorenal shunt
脾肾固定术/脾腎固定術　splenorenopexy
脾肾静脉分流/脾腎靜脈分流　renal-splenic venous shunt
脾肾面/脾腎面　renal surface of spleen
脾肾韧带/脾腎韌帶　splenorenal ligament, lienorenal ligament
脾肾下垂/脾腎下垂　splenonephroptosis
脾肾阳虚/脾腎陽虛　spleen-kidney yang deficiency
脾肾阳虚证/脾腎陽虛證　pattern of spleen-kidney yang deficiency
脾失健运/脾失健運　dysfunction of spleen in transportation
脾俞/脾俞　pishu, BL20
脾水/脾水　spleen edema
脾水·脾胃气虚证/脾水·脾胃氣虛證　spleen edema with pattern of spleen-stomach qi deficiency
脾水·脾阳虚证/脾水·脾陽虛證　spleen edema with pattern of spleen yang deficiency
脾髓测压［法］/脾髓測壓［法］　splenic pulp manometry

脾髓细胞/脾髓細胞 pulpar cell
脾髓压/脾髓壓 splenic pulp pressure
脾髓增殖性脾大/脾腺瘤 splenadenoma
脾索/脾索 splenic cord
脾统血/脾統血 spleen controlling blood
脾外固定术/脾外側固定術 exosplenopexy
脾为后天之本/脾爲後天之本 spleen being acquired foundation
脾为生痰之源/脾爲生痰之源 spleen being source of phlegm
脾痿/脾痿 spleen flaccidity
脾胃辨证/脾胃辨證 pattern identification of spleen and stomach
脾胃不和证/脾胃不和證 pattern of incoordination between spleen and stomach
脾胃论/脾胃論 Treatise on the Spleen and Stomach
脾胃面/脾胃面 gastric surface of spleen
脾胃气虚证/脾胃氣虛證 pattern of spleen-stomach qi deficiency
脾胃湿热/脾胃濕熱 dampness-heat of spleen and stomach
脾胃湿热证/脾胃濕熱證 pattern of dampness-heat of spleen and stomach
脾胃虚寒/脾胃虛寒 deficiency-cold of spleen and stomach
脾胃虚寒证/脾胃虛寒證 pattern of deficiency-cold of spleen and stomach
脾胃虚弱/脾胃虛弱 deficiency of spleen and stomach
脾胃阴虚/脾胃陰虛 yin deficiency of spleen and stomach
脾胃阴虚证/脾胃陰虛證 pattern of yin deficiency of spleen and stomach
脾喜燥恶湿/脾喜燥惡濕 spleen liking dryness and disliking dampness
脾细胞/脾細胞 splenic cell
脾细胞移植/脾細胞移植 spleen cell transplantation
脾下端/脾尾 tail of spleen
脾下缘/脾下緣 interior border of spleen
脾小结/脾結 splenic follicle, splenic nodule
脾心痛/脾心痛 true heart pain with cold limbs caused by spleen disease
脾性白血病/脾性白血病 splenic leukemia
脾性贫血/脾性貧血 splenic anemia
脾修补术/脾縫合術 splenorrhaphy
脾虚不固证/脾虛不固證 pattern of loss of control due to spleen deficiency
脾虚气陷证/脾虛氣陷證 pattern of sinking of qi due to spleen deficiency
脾虚生风/脾虛生風 spleen deficiency causing wind
脾虚生痰/脾虛生痰 spleen deficiency generating phlegm
脾虚湿困/脾虛濕困 dampness stagnancy due to spleen deficiency
脾虚湿困证/脾虛濕困證 pattern of dampness stagnancy due to spleen deficiency
脾虚湿热证/脾虛濕熱證 pattern of dampness-heat due to spleen deficiency
脾虚食积证/脾虛食積證 pattern of food retention due to spleen deficiency
脾虚水泛证/脾虛水泛證 pattern of water diffusion due to spleen deficiency
脾虚痰湿证/脾虛痰濕證 pattern of phlegm-dampness due to spleen deficiency
脾虚证/脾虛證 pattern of spleen deficiency
脾[血]窦/脾[血]竇 splenic sinusoid
脾炎/脾炎 lienitis
脾炎黄疸/脾炎黃疸 splenicterus
脾阳/脾陽 spleen yang
脾阳虚/脾陽虛 spleen yang deficiency
脾阳虚水泛证/脾陽虛水泛證 pattern of water diffusion due to deficiency of spleen yang
脾阳虚证/脾陽虛證 pattern of deficiency of spleen yang
脾样变/脾樣變 splenification
脾样变性肺炎/脾變性肺炎 splenopneumonia
脾样结节/脾樣結節 splenoid gland
脾移植/脾移植 spleen transplantation
脾阴/脾陰 spleen yin
脾阴虚/脾陰虛 spleen yin deficiency
脾阴虚证/脾陰虛證 pattern of spleen yin deficiency
脾隐窝/脾隱窩 splenic recess
脾硬化/脾硬化 splenceratosis
脾[与]骨髓软化/脾骨髓軟化 splenomyelomalacia
脾郁/脾鬱 stagnancy pattern of spleen qi
脾约/脾約 spleen constipation
脾杂音/脾雜音 splenic souffle
脾脏面/脾臟面 visceral surface of spleen
脾脏学/脾臟學 splenology
脾[脏]自切除/自體脾臟消失 autosplenectomy
脾造影术/脾 X 光攝影法 lienography
脾支/脾支 splenic branch
脾志思/脾志思 spleen being assocoated with pensiveness
脾肿瘤/脾腫瘤 splenic neoplasm
脾肿指数/脾指數 spleen index

脾周炎/脾周圍炎,脾外膜炎　perisplenitis
脾主肌肉/脾主肌肉　spleen governing muscles
脾主升清/脾主昇清　spleen governing ascending clear
脾主四肢/脾主四肢　spleen governing limbs
脾主运化/脾主運化　spleen governing transportation and transformation
脾组织腹腔种植/腹腔內脾組織植入　peritoneal splenosis
脾组织植入/脾組織植入,脾功能過盛　splenosis
蜱病/蜱病　ixodiasis
蜱传斑疹伤寒/壁蝨性斑疹傷寒　tick typhus
蜱传病毒/壁蝨媒病毒　tick-borne virus
蜱传播疾病/蜱傳播疾病　tick-borne disease
蜱传脑炎/蜱傳腦炎　tick-borne encephalitis
蜱传脑炎病毒亚组/蜱傳腦炎病毒亞組　tick-borne encephalitis viruses
蜱叮咬/蜱叮咬　tick bite
蜱感染/蜱感染　tick infestation
蜱螫伤/壁蝨螫傷　tick sting
蜱性麻痹/壁蝨性麻痺　tick paralysis
蜱中毒/蜱中毒　tick toxicosis
匹氨西林/別戊氨苄西林　pivampicillin
匹克威克综合征/比克維氏症候群　Pickwickian syndrome
匹莫林/匹莫林　pemoline
匹莫齐特/匹莫齊特　pimozide
匹配/匹配　matching
痞根/痞根　pigen, EX-B4
痞满/痞滿　distention and fullness
痞满[病]/痞滿[病]　abdominal distention and fullness, distention and fullness
痞满·肝胃不和证/痞滿·肝胃不和證　abdominal distention and fullness with pattern of disharmony between liver and stomach
痞满·脾胃气虚证/痞滿·脾胃氣虛證　abdominal distention and fullness with pattern of qi deficiency of spleen and stomach
痞满·湿热中阻证/痞滿·濕熱中阻證　abdominal distention and fullness with pattern of damp-heat blocking middle jiao
痞满·痰湿中阻证/痞滿·痰濕中阻證　abdominal distention and fullness with pattern of phlegm-damp blocking middle jiao
痞满·胃阴虚证/痞滿·胃陰虛證　abdominal distention and fullness with pattern of stomach yin deficiency
痞满·邪热内陷证/痞滿·邪熱內陷證　abdominal distention and fullness with pattern of inward invasion of pathogenic heat
痞满·饮食停滞证/痞滿·飲食停滯證　abdominal distention and fullness with food stagnation pattern
痞气/痞氣　spleen amassment
屁/胃腸氣　flatus
偏侧变位/偏侧位　lateroposition
偏侧大脑皮层切除/單側大腦皮質切除法　hemidecortication
偏侧动脉瘤/偏侧動脈瘤　partial aneurysm
偏侧发育不全/單側發育不全,半部發育不全　hemihypoplasia
偏侧肥大/單側肥大　hemihypertrophy
偏侧感觉缺失/偏侧感覺缺失,單側麻木　hemianesthesia
偏侧隔/半[中]隔　hemiseptum
偏侧膈/單側橫膈　hemidiaphragm
偏侧骨盆切除术/單側骨盆切除術　hemipelvectomy
偏侧灰发[症]/單側白髮　hemicanities
偏侧甲状腺切除术/半甲狀腺切除術　hemistrumectomy
偏侧巨大发育/單側巨大發育　hemigigantism
偏侧颅骨切除术/偏侧顱骨切除術　hemicraniectomy
偏侧迷走神经紧张症/單側迷走神經過敏　hemivagotony
偏侧面萎缩/單側顏面萎縮　unilateral facial atrophy
偏侧缺肢畸形/單側肢不全畸形,偏身缺肢畸形　hemiectromelia
偏[侧]色盲/半侧色盲　hemiachromatopsia
偏侧伸展过度/單側伸展過度　hemihypermetria
偏侧神经衰弱/單側神經衰弱　hemineurasthenia
偏侧肾盂积脓/半腎盂積膿　hemipyonephrosis
偏侧手足徐动症/單側手足徐動症　hemiathetosis
偏侧痛/單側痛　hemialgia
偏侧头眼痛/偏侧頭眼痛　hemiopalgia
偏侧凸颌/偏侧凸頜　hemi-prognathism
偏侧萎缩/偏侧萎縮　hemiatrophy
偏侧无睾[丸]者/單側無睾丸者　hemitomias
偏侧无脑[畸形]/半侧無腦　hemianencephaly
偏侧下身麻痹/單側下身麻痺　hemiparaplegia
偏侧下身麻木/單側下半身麻木,單側下半身感覺缺失　hemiparanesthesia
偏侧协同不能/單側共濟不能　hemiasynergia
偏侧颜面萎缩/半面萎縮　hemifacial atrophy
偏侧震颤麻痹/單側震顫麻痺　hemiparkinsonism
偏侧椎板切除术/單側椎板切除術　hemilaminectomy
偏端丛毛菌类/偏端鞭毛菌類　lophotrichea

偏钒酸盐/偏釩酸鹽　metavanadate
偏肺病毒/變性肺病毒　metapneumovirus
偏共振去偶/偏共振去偶　off resonance decoupling
偏光显微镜/偏光顯微鏡　polarizing microscope
偏光仪/偏光鏡　polariscope
偏结核样型界线类麻风/偏結核樣型界線類麻風
　　borderline tuberculoid leprosy
偏历/偏歷　pianli, LI6
偏磷酸/偏磷酸　metaphosphoric acid
偏磷酸盐/偏磷酸鹽　metaphosphate
偏瘤型界线类麻风/偏瘤型界線類麻風　borderline
　　lepromatous leprosy
偏漏/偏漏　fistula of bulbar conjunctiva
偏盲/偏[側]盲　hemianopsia
偏盲性瞳孔反应/半盲瞳孔反應　hemiopic pupillary
　　reaction
偏身颤搐/偏身顫搐　hemiballismus
偏身出汗/偏身出汗,單側出汗　hemidiaphoresis
偏身癫痫/單側癲癇　hemiepilepsy
偏身多汗/單側多汗　hemihyperidrosis
偏身肥胖/單側肥胖　hemiobesity
偏身感觉过敏/單側感覺過敏　hemihyperesthesia
偏身感觉障碍/單側感覺異常　hemidysesthesia
偏身肌无力/單側肌無力　hemiamyosthenia
偏身麻木/半側身觸覺缺失　unilateral anesthesia
偏身品他病/半身螺旋體性皮膚病　hemipinta
偏身手足搐搦/單側強痙病,單側手足搐搦病
　　hemitetany
偏身痛觉减退/單側痛覺遲鈍　hemihypalgesia
偏身痛觉缺失/單側痛覺缺失　hemianalgesia
偏身舞蹈症/單側舞蹈病　hemichorea
偏身张力减退/單側肌張力不全,單側張力減退
　　hemihypotonia
偏身震颤/單側震顫　hemitremor
偏砷酸/偏砷酸　metarsenic acid
偏食/偏食　food preference
偏瘫/偏癱,半身不遂　hemiparalysis
偏瘫步态/偏癱性步態　hemiplegic gait
偏瘫的/偏癱的　hemiplegic
偏瘫型疟/偏癱型瘧　hemiplegic malaria
偏瘫性强直/偏癱性強硬　hemiplegic rigidity
偏头风[痛]/偏頭風[痛]　migraine
偏头痛/偏頭痛　migraine headache, migraine
偏头痛性脑梗死/偏頭痛性梗塞　migrainous
　　infarction
偏向/偏向,偏轉　deflection
偏斜/偏斜,偏離　deviation
偏心/偏心　decentration

偏心切断术/偏心截斷術　eccentric amputation
偏心性肥大/偏心性肥大　eccentric hypertrophy
偏心性萎缩/偏心性萎縮　eccentric atrophy
偏心性限界/偏心性限度　eccentric limitation
偏心植入/離心植入　eccentric implantation
偏振光/偏[極化]光　polarized light
偏振[光]显微镜/顯微偏光鏡　micropolariscope
偏振镜的/偏光鏡的　polariscopic
偏振显微镜检查/偏振顯微鏡檢查　polarization
　　microscopy
偏执狂/妄想狂　paranoia
偏执狂性精神病/妄想性精神病　paranoiac psychosis
偏执行为/偏執行爲　paranoid behavior
偏执型精神分裂症/妄想型精神分裂症　paranoid
　　schizophrenia
偏执型精神障碍/偏執型精神障礙　paranoid
　　disorders
偏执型人格障碍/偏執型人格障礙　paranoid
　　personality disorder
偏执性精神障碍/偏執性精神障礙　paranoid
　　disorder
偏执状态/偏執狀態　paranoid state
偏轴透镜/偏軸透鏡　decentered lens
偏转检眼镜/偏轉檢眼鏡　ghost ophthalmoscope
偏最小二乘法/偏最小平方法　partial least square
　　method
胼胝/胼胝　callus
胼胝垫/胼胝墊　callus pad
胼胝交叉径/胼胝體交叉徑　callosal crossed tract
胼胝体/胼胝體　corpus callosum
胼胝体背侧静脉/胼胝體背側靜脈　dorsal vein of
　　corpus callosum
胼胝体背侧支/胼胝體背側支　dorsal branch of
　　callosal body
胼胝体的/胼胝體的　callosal
胼胝体辐射/胼胝體輻射線,胼體放線　radiation of
　　corpus callosum
胼胝体辐射线额部/前鉗狀體　forceps anterior
胼胝体辐射线枕部/大鉗狀體　forceps major
胼胝体干/胼胝體幹　trunk of corpus callosum
胼胝体沟/胼胝體溝　callosal sulcus
胼胝体后静脉/胼胝體後靜脈　posterior vein of
　　callosum
胼胝体上池/胼胝體上池　supracallosal cistern
胼胝体上回/胼胝體上迴　supracallosal gyrus
胼胝体膝/胼胝體膝　genu of corpus callosum
胼胝体下区/胼體下區,旁嗅區　subcallosal area
胼胝体压部/胼胝體壓部　splenium of corpus

胼胝体缘动脉/胼胝體緣動脈 callosomarginal artery
胼胝体周池/胼胝體周池 Cisterna pericallosa
胼胝体综合征/胼胝體症候群 callosal syndrome
胼胝体嘴/胼胝體嘴 rostrum of corpus callosum
胼胝性溃疡/胼胝性潰瘍 callous ulcer
胼胝性湿疹/胼胝性濕疹 tylotic eczema
胼胝性心包炎/胼胝性心包炎 pericarditis callosa
胼胝状湿疹/胼胝樣濕疹 eczema tyloticum
片/片 slice, flake
片层体/片層體 lamellasome
片层状鱼鳞癣/片層狀魚鱗癬 lamellar ichthyosis
片段/片段 fragment
片剂/片劑 tablet
片剂包衣/錠劑著衣 tablet coating
片块状浸润/片狀浸潤 patchy infiltration
片形吸虫病/瓜仁蟲病 fascioliasis
漂浮的/浮動的 floating
漂浮物质/漂浮物質 floating substance
瓢虫科/瓢蟲科 Coccinellidae
漂白[的]/漂白的,褪色的 bleaching
漂白粉/漂白粉 bleaching powder
漂白粉液/漂白液 bleaching fluid
漂白面粉/漂白麵粉 bleaching flour
漂布工哮喘/漂布工氣喘 fullers asthma
嘌呤/嘌呤 purine
嘌呤氮/嘌呤體氮質 alloxuric nitrogen
嘌呤定量器/嘌呤計算器 purinometer
嘌呤核苷类/嘌呤核苷類 purine nucleosides
嘌呤核苷磷酸化酶/嘌呤核苷磷酸化酶 purine-nucleoside phosphorylase
嘌呤核苷酸类/嘌呤核苷酸類 purine nucleotides
嘌呤核酸酶/嘌呤核苷酸酶,嘌呤核酸酵素 purine nuclease
嘌呤碱尿/嘌呤體尿症 alloxuria
嘌呤类/嘌呤類 purines
嘌呤酶/嘌呤酵素 purinase
嘌呤霉素/嘌呤徽素 puromycin
嘌呤能受体/嘌呤能受體 purinergic receptor
嘌呤生物碱/嘌呤生物鹼 purine alkaloid
嘌呤血[症]/嘌呤血症 purinemia
漂亮新小杆线虫/漂亮新小杆線蟲 Caenorhabditis elegans
漂亮新小杆线虫蛋白质类/漂亮新小杆線蟲蛋白質類 caenorhabditis elegans protein
拼合软骨支架/拼合軟骨支架 open spaced cartilage frame
贫病救助员/貧病救助員 parabolus
贫齿目/無齒動物類 Edentata
贫穷妄想/貧窮妄想 delusion of poverty
贫血/貧血 anemia
贫血小板血浆/貧血小板血漿 platelet poor plasma, PPP
贫血性变性/貧血性變性 anemic degeneration
贫血性梗死/貧血性梗塞 anemic infarct
贫血性梗死形成/貧血性梗塞形成 anemic infarction
贫血性甲状腺肿/貧血性甲狀腺腫 anemic goiter
贫血性尿/貧血性尿 anemic urine
贫血性缺氧/貧血性缺氧 anemic hypoxemia
贫血性瘙痒症/貧血性搔癢症 pruritus of anemia
贫血性杂音/貧血性[心]雜音 anemic murmur, hemic murmur
贫血饮食/貧血飲食 anemia diet
贫血痣/貧血痣 nevus anaemicus
频服/頻服 taken frequently
频咳/頻欬 teasing cough
频率/頻率 frequency
频率反应式起搏器/頻率反應式起搏器 rate responsive pacemaker
频率依赖顺应性/頻率依賴順應性 frequency dependent compliance
频率依赖性阻滞/頻率依賴性阻滯 rate dependent block
频尿/頻尿 sychnuria
频细震颤/細小震顫 fine tremor
品茶员咳/品茶客欬嗽 tea taster cough
品红类染料/品紅類染料 rosaniline dyes
品他病/品他病 pinta
品他病患者/品他病患者 pintado
品他病密螺旋体/品他病螺旋體 Treponema carateum
品他疹/品他病疹 pintid
品胎/品胎 triplets
品脱/品脱 pint
品质/品質 quality
品质性状/品質性狀 qualitative trait
乒乓球样骨/乒乓球樣骨 pingpong bone
乒乓球样骨折/乒乓骨折 pingpong fracture
平凹透镜/平凹透鏡 planoconcave lens
平板电泳/平板電泳 disk electrophoresis
平板型透析器/平板型透析器 Kiil dialyser
平补平泻/平補平瀉 even reinforcing-reducing method
平喘药/平喘藥 anti-asthmatic

平刺/平刺 horizontal insertion of needle
平旦服/平旦服 take at dawn
平底乳钵/研磨器 muller
平方/平方 square
平方反比定律/反平方定律 inverse-square law
平缝/平縫 plane suture
平覆𬌗/水平咬合過度 horizontal overbite
平肝降逆/平肝降逆 suppressing hyperactive liver for descending adverse qi
平肝潜阳/平肝潛陽 calming the liver and suppressing exuberant liver yang, suppressing hyperactive liver and subsiding yang
平肝息风/平肝息風 calming the liver and checking wind, suppressing hyperactive liver for calming endogenous wind
平肝熄风/鎮肝熄風 calming the liver to stop the wind
平光镜片/平光鏡片 plano lens
平和的/輕的,温和的 mild
平衡/平衡 balance
平衡棒/平衡棒 halter
平衡不良性关节病/静止性關節病 static arthropathy
平衡侧/平衡側 balancing side
平衡常数/平衡常數 equilibrium constant
平衡多态性/平衡多態性 balanced polymorphism
平衡感觉/平衡感覺 equilibrium sense
平衡感觉障碍/平衡感覺障礙 equilibratory disorder
平衡𬌗/平衡關節 balanced articulation
平衡觉减退/平衡覺減弱,不量性 hypoequilibrium
平衡麻醉/協合麻醉法 balanced anesthesia
平衡器/平衡器 equilibrator
平衡溶液/平衡溶液 balanced solution
平衡失调/不平衡 dysequilibrium
平衡式心血管摄影术/平衡式心血管攝影術 equilibrium angiocardiography
平衡试验/平衡試驗 balance test
平衡手术/平衡[性]手術 equilibrating operation
平衡透析/平衡滲透 equilibrium dialysis
平衡牙𬌗/平衡牙𬌗 balanced dental occlusion
平衡盐溶液/平衡鹽溶液 balanced salt solution
平衡易位/平衡易位 balanced translocation
平衡运动/平衡運動 balance exercise
平衡状态/平衡狀態 state of equilibrium
平滑/平滑 smooth
平滑肌/平滑肌 smooth muscle
平滑肌成肌细胞/平滑肌成肌細胞 smooth muscle myoblast
平滑肌肌球蛋白/平滑肌肌球蛋白 smooth muscle myosin
平滑肌肌细胞/平滑肌肌細胞 smooth muscle myocyte
平滑肌瘤/平滑肌瘤 leiomyoma
平滑肌瘤病/平滑肌瘤病 leiomyomatosis
平滑肌肉瘤/平滑肌肉瘤 leiomyosarcoma
平滑肌无力/平滑肌無力 leiasthenia
平滑肌细胞/平滑肌細胞 smooth muscle cell
平滑肌纤维/平滑肌纖維 smooth muscle fiber
平滑肌纤维瘤/平滑肌纖維瘤 leiomyofibroma
平滑肌兴奋药/平滑肌興奮藥 smooth muscle stimulant
平滑肌张力障碍/平滑肌緊張不足 leiodystonia
平滑肌痣/平滑肌痣 smooth muscle nevi
平滑肌组织瘤/平滑肌組織瘤 smooth muscle tumor
平滑面龋/平滑面齲 smooth surface caries
平滑绒毛膜/平滑絨[毛]膜 chorion laeve
平滑疣/平滑疣 verruca glabra
平均表面径/平均表面積直徑 mean surface diameter
平均卡/平均卡 mean calorie
平均粒径/平均粒徑 mean diameter
平均量/平均劑量,一般劑量 average dose
平均容积径/平均容積徑 mean volume diameter
平均寿命/平均壽命 average life
平均温度/平均温度 mean temperature
平均预期寿命/平均預期壽命 average life expectancy
平叩法/平叩診 flat percussion
平库斯瘤/Pinkus氏腫瘤 Pinkus tumor
平库斯纤维上皮瘤/Pinkus纖維上皮細胞瘤 fibroepithelioma of Pinkus
平脉/平脈 normal pulse
平面/平面 plane
平面导板/平面導板 flat bite plate
平面定位障碍/遊走性運動病 planotopokinesia
平面[反光]镜/平面鏡 plane mirror
平面关节/平面關節 plane joint, plane articulation
平面检影镜/平面檢影鏡 plane retinoscope
平面镜片/平面鏡片 flat lens
平面视野计检查法/視野檢法 campimetry
平面摇摆振动/平面搖擺振動 rocking vibration
平皿培养[物]/碟中培養 plate culture
平胬药/平胬藥 luxuriant granulation minifying medicine
平气/平氣 normal climatic factor
平人/平人 healthy person

平台期/平臺期　plateau phase
平坦性病变/平坦性病變　flat lesion
平调寒热/平調寒熱　mildly regulating cold and heat
平凸透镜/平凸透鏡　planoconvex lens
平胃散/平胃散　pingwei powder
平稳视跟踪/平穩視跟蹤　smooth pursuit
平息/正常呼吸　normal respiration
平熄内风剂/平熄內風劑　formula for calming down internal wind
平行/平行　parallelism
平行测定/平行含量測定　parallel assay
平行联会/并列接合,平行接合　parasynapsis
平行[X射线]滤线栅/X光平行濾線柵　parallel grid
平行纤维/平行纖維　parallel fiber
平行线/平行線　parallel
平仰卧位/平仰臥位　horizontal position
平跖外翻足/平蹠外翻足　splayfoot
平足症/平足症　flat foot disease
评定量表/評定量表　rating scale
评估/評估,判断　assessment
评价研究/評價研究　evaluation study
苹果酱状结节/蘋果醬樣結節　apple jelly nodule
苹果酸合酶/蘋果酸合酶　malate synthase
苹果酸脱氢酶/蘋果酸脫氫酶　malic dehydrogenase
苹果酸盐/蘋果酸鹽　malate
屏尖/屏尖　pingjian, TG1P, apex of tragus
屏间后/屏間後　pingjianhou, AT11, posterior intertragal notch
屏间前/屏間前　pingjianqian, TG21, anterior intertragal notch
屏幕/屏　screen
屏障/屏障　barrier
屏障避孕/屏障避孕　barrier contraception
屏障滤器/屏障濾光片　barrier filter
屏状核/帶狀核　claustrum
瓶梗/瓶梗　phialide
瓶梗托/瓶梗托　phialophore
瓶饲/瓶哺養　bottle feeding
瓶状心/瓶狀心　flask-shaped heart
泼尼莫司汀/潑尼氮芥　prednimustine
泼尼松/強體松　prednisone
泼尼松龙/腎上腺皮質酮　prednisolone
珀迪液/Purdy氏液　Purdy fluid
珀蒂韧带/Petit氏韌帶　Petit ligament
破骨细胞/破骨細胞　osteoclast
破骨细胞瘤/破骨細胞瘤　osteoclastoma
破冠器/破冠器　crown slitter
破壶音/破壺響　cracked-pot resonance

破裂/破裂　rupture
破裂动脉瘤/破裂動脈瘤　ruptured aneurysm
破裂孔/破裂孔　lacerate foramen
破裂性出血/破裂性出血　rhexis hemorrhage
破裂序列征/破裂序列徵　disruptive sequence
破软骨细胞/毀軟骨細胞　chondroclast
破伤风/破傷風　tetanus
破伤风毒素/破傷風毒素　tetanus toxin
破伤风·风毒入里证/破傷風·風毒入裡證　tetanus with pattern of wind-toxin entering interior
破伤风·风毒在表证/破傷風·風毒在表證　tetanus with pattern of wind-toxin in exterior
破伤风痉挛/破傷風性痙攣　tetanic spasm
破伤风痉挛毒素/破傷風痙攣毒素　tetanospasmin
破伤风抗毒素/破傷風抗毒素　tetanus antitoxin
破伤风类毒素/破傷風類毒素　tetanus toxoid
破伤风菌溶血素/破傷風溶血素　tetanolysin
破伤风·阴虚邪留证/破傷風·陰虛邪留證　tetanus with pattern of yin deficiency and lingering pathogen
破髓鞘细胞/破髓鞘細胞　myeloclast
破碎强度/破碎強度　crushing strength
破脱肉/破脫肉　emaciation and anorexia
破牙骨质细胞/破牙細胞　cementoclast
破瘀散结/破瘀散結　drastically removing blood stasis and resolving static blood
破折细胞/破碎細胞　clasmatocyte
破折细胞增多/破碎細胞增多　clasmatocytosis
魄/魄　corporeal soul, inferior spirit
魄户/魄戶　pohu, BL42
魄门/肛門　anus
剖腹产/腹部分娩　abdominal delivery
剖腹肠切开术/剖腹式小腸切開術　celioenterotomy
剖腹肠造口术/腹式腸造口術　laparoenterostomy
剖腹胆囊造口术/腹式膽囊切除術　laparocholecystotomy
剖腹刀/剖腹刀,開腹刀　laparotome
剖腹肝切开术/腹式肝切開術　laparohepatotomy
剖腹回肠切开术/腹式迴腸切開術　laparoileotomy
剖腹结肠切开术/腹式結腸切開術　laparocolotomy
剖腹结肠造口术/腹式結腸造口術　laparocolostomy
剖腹卵巢切除术/腹式卵巢切除術　abdominal ovariotomy
剖腹盲肠切开术/腹式盲腸切開術　laparotyphlotomy
剖腹囊肿切除术/腹式囊腫切除術　laparocystectomy
剖腹膀胱切开术/剖腹膀胱切開術　cystidoceliotomy
剖腹脾切除术/腹式脾切除術　laparosplenectomy

剖腹脾切开术/腹式脾切開術　laparosplenotomy
剖腹肾切除术/腹式腎切除術　laparonephrectomy
剖腹手术癖/嗜剖腹症　laparotomaphilia
剖腹输卵管卵巢切除术/腹式輸卵管卵巢切除術　laparosalpingo-oophorectomy
剖腹输卵管切除术/剖腹式輸卵管切除術　celiosalpingectomy
剖腹输卵管切开术/剖腹式輸卵管切開術　celiosalpingotomy
剖腹术/剖腹術　celiotomy
剖腹探查术/剖腹探查術　exploratory laparotomy
剖腹胃镜检查法/腹式胃鏡檢查法　laparogastroscopy
剖腹胃切开术/剖腹式胃切開術　celiogastrotomy
剖腹胃造口术/腹式胃造口術　laparogastrostomy
剖腹阴道切开术/剖腹式陰道切開術　celiocolpotomy
剖腹治疝术/剖腹式疝切開術,疝剖腹術　herniolaparotomy
剖腹子宫肌瘤切除术/腹式子宮瘤切除術　celiomyomectomy
剖腹子宫卵巢切除术/腹式子宮卵巢切除術　laparohystero-oophorectomy
剖腹子宫切除术/剖腹式子宮切除術,帝王式子宮切除術　celiohysterectomy
剖腹子宫切开术/剖腹式子宮切開術　hysterolaparotomy
剖腹子宫输卵管卵巢切除术/腹式子宮輸卵管卵巢切除術　laparohysterosalpingo-oophorectomy
剖宫产后阴道分娩/剖腹産後陰道分娩　vaginal birth after cesarean
剖宫产术/剖腹産[術]　cesarean section
剖宫产子宫切除术/剖腹産子宮切除術　cesarean hysterectomy
剖尸创伤/剖屍創傷　dissection wound
扑动/撲動　flutter
扑动-纤颤[型]/撲動-纖顫[型]　flutter-fibrillation
扑米酮/撲米酮　primidone
扑面粉/蜜粉　face powder
扑灭司林/撲滅司林　permethrin
扑翼样震颤/撲翼樣震顫,撲翅狀震顫　asterixis, flapping tremor
铺片/鋪片　stretched preparation
铺砖状细胞/舖磚狀細胞　pavement cell
仆参/僕參　pucan, BL61
匍匐曲霉/匍匐麴菌　Aspergillus repens
匍匐枝/匍匐枝　stolon
匐行性角膜溃疡/匐行性角膜潰瘍　serpiginous corneal ulcer
匐行性溃疡/匐行性潰瘍　serpiginous ulcer
匐行血管瘤/匐行血管瘤　nevus lupus
脯氨酸/普羅林,脯胺酸　proline
脯氨酸二甲内盐/脯胺酸二甲内酸　stachydrine
脯氨酸血/脯胺酸血　prolinemia
脯氨酸氧化酶/脯胺酸氧化酶　proline oxidase
脯氨酸依赖性蛋白激酶类/脯胺酸依賴性蛋白激酶類　proline-directed protein kinases
脯氨肽酶/脯胺酸肽酶　prolidase
脯氨酰氨基酸[二肽]酶/普羅林酵素,脯胺酸酶　prolinase
葡甲胺/甲基葡胺　meglumine
葡聚糖类/葡聚糖類　glucans
葡聚糖酶/葡聚糖酶　dextranase
葡聚糖凝胶/葡萄聚糖凝膠　polydextran gel
葡糖氨基聚糖类/糖胺聚糖類　glycosaminoglycans
葡糖胺/葡萄糖胺　glucosamine
葡糖二酸/葡萄糖二酸　glucaric acid
葡糖苷酶/配糖酵素　glucosidase
葡糖苷酶抑制药/葡萄糖苷酶抑制藥　glucosidase inhibitor
葡糖苷酸/葡萄糖醛酸化合物　glucuronide
葡糖苷酰鞘氨醇类/葡糖苷醯鞘氨醇類　glucosylceramides
葡糖苷酰鞘氨醇酶/神經醯胺酶　glucosylceramidase
葡糖激酶/葡萄糖激酶　glucokinase
葡糖-1-磷酸/磷酸[葡萄]糖　glucose-1-phosphate
葡糖磷酸变位酶/磷酸葡萄糖變位酶　phosphoglucomutase
葡糖磷酸类/葡糖磷酸類　glucosephosphates
葡糖-6-磷酸酶/葡糖磷酸酯酶　glucose-6-phosphatase
葡糖磷酸脱氢酶/葡糖磷酸脱氫酶　glucosephosphate dehydrogenase
葡糖磷酸脱氢酶缺乏/葡糖磷酸脱氫酶缺乏　glucosephosphate dehydrogenase deficiency
葡糖-6-磷酸盐/葡糖-6-磷酸鹽　glucose-6-phosphate
葡糖-6-磷酸异构酶/葡糖-6-磷酸異構酶　glucose-6-phosphate isomerase
葡糖硫苷酶/芥子酵素,黑芥酵素　myrosin
葡糖耐量试验/葡萄糖耐量試驗　glucose tolerance test
葡糖耐受不良/葡糖耐受不良　glucose intolerance
葡糖脑苷脂酶缺乏/葡萄糖腦苷酶缺乏　glucocerebrosidase deficiency
葡糖醛酸/葡糖醛酸　glucuronic acid

葡糖醛酸基转移酶/葡萄糖醛酸内酯基轉移酶 glucuronosyltransferase
葡糖醛酸糖苷酶/葡糖醛酸糖苷酶 glucuronidase
葡糖酸盐类/葡糖酸鹽類 gluconates
葡糖脱氢酶/葡糖糖脱氫酶 glucose dehydrogenase
葡糖脱氢酶类/葡糖脱氫酶類 glucose dehydrogenases
葡糖转移酶类/葡糖轉移酶類 glucosyltransferases
葡萄孢霉菌病/葡萄黴菌病 botrytimycosis
葡萄孢属/葡黴菌屬 *Botrytis*
葡萄簇状横纹肌肉瘤/葡萄狀橫紋肌肉瘤 botryoid rhabdomyosarcoma
葡萄酒色痣/酒色斑,焰色痣 port-wine stain
葡[萄]聚糖/聚葡萄糖 glucosan
葡萄聚糖生成发酵/葡萄聚糖發酵 dextran fermentation
葡萄疗法/葡萄療法 ampelotherapy
葡萄膜/葡萄膜 uvea
葡萄膜大脑炎/葡萄膜大腦炎 uveoencephalitis
葡萄膜灌注/葡萄膜灌注 uveal infusion
葡萄膜疾病/葡萄膜疾病 uveal disease
葡萄膜脑膜脑炎综合征/葡萄膜腦膜腦炎症候群 uveomeningoencephalitic syndrome
葡萄膜腮腺结核/葡萄膜腮腺結核 uveoparotid tuberculosis
葡萄膜炎/葡萄膜炎 uveitis
葡萄膜肿瘤/葡萄膜腫瘤 uveal neoplasm
葡萄木二糖/葡萄木二糖 glucoxylose
葡萄球菌/葡萄球菌 staphylococcus
葡萄球菌蛋白/葡萄球菌蛋白 staphylococcal protein
葡萄球菌A蛋白/葡萄球菌蛋白A staphylococcal protein A
葡萄球菌的/葡萄球菌的 staphylococcal
葡萄球菌毒素/葡萄球菌毒素 staphylotoxin
葡萄球菌感染/葡萄球菌感染 staphylococcal infection
葡萄球菌菌苗/葡萄球菌菌苗 staphylococcal vaccine
葡萄球菌类毒素/葡萄球菌類毒素 staphylococcal toxoid
葡萄球菌凝固酶/葡萄球菌凝血酵素 staphylocoagulase
葡萄球菌皮肤感染/葡萄球菌皮膚感染 staphylococcal skin infection
葡萄球菌溶[血]素/葡萄球菌溶血素 staphylolysin
葡萄球菌杀白细胞素/葡萄球菌殺白血球素 staphyloleukocidin
葡萄球菌烧灼性皮肤综合征/葡萄球菌燒灼性皮膚症候群 staphylococcal scalded skin syndrome
葡萄球菌食物中毒/葡萄球菌食物中毒 staphylococcal food poisoning
葡萄球菌噬菌体/葡萄球菌噬菌體 staphylococcus phage
葡萄球菌属/葡萄球菌屬 *Staphylococcus spp.*
葡萄球菌调理指数/葡萄球菌調理指數 staphyloopsonic index
葡萄球菌性肺炎/葡萄球菌性肺炎 staphylococcal pneumonia
葡萄球菌性脓疱病/葡萄球菌性膿皰病 impetigo staphylococcic
葡萄球菌性皮肤化脓/葡萄球菌性皮膚化膿 staphyloderma
葡萄穗霉属/葡萄穗黴屬 *Stachybotrys*
葡萄胎/葡萄胎,水囊狀胎塊 hydatidiform mole
葡萄胎假妊娠/葡萄胎假妊娠 sarcohysteric pregnancy
葡萄胎妊娠/胎塊妊娠 molar pregnancy
葡萄糖/葡萄糖 glucose
葡萄糖代谢障碍/葡萄糖代謝障礙 glucose metabolism disorder
葡萄糖毒醛/葡萄糖毒醛 glucal
葡萄糖矾钠/葡萄糖矾鈉 glucosulfone sodium
葡萄糖基/葡萄糖基 glucosyl
葡萄糖基转移酶/葡萄糖基轉移酶 glucosyltransferase
葡萄糖碱/葡萄糖鹼,葡萄糖鹽基 glucosin
葡萄糖结合剂/葡萄糖結合劑 dextrate
葡萄糖6磷酸脱氢酶缺乏症/葡萄糖6磷酸去氫酶缺乏 G6PD deficiency
葡萄糖氯化钠/葡萄糖氯化鈉 glucose and sodium chloride
葡萄糖耐量/葡萄糖耐受性 glucose tolerance
葡[萄]糖脑苷脂/葡萄糖腦苷脂 glucocerebroside
葡萄糖钳制技术/葡萄糖鉗制技術 glucose clamp technique
葡[萄]糖醛酸酯/葡萄糖醛酸酯 glucuronate
葡萄糖乳酸盐循环/葡萄糖乳酸循環 glucose-lactate cycle
葡[萄]糖脎/葡萄糖脎 glucosazone
葡[萄]糖生成/葡萄糖生成 glucogenesis
葡[萄]糖酸/葡萄糖酸 gluconic acid
葡萄糖酸钙/葡萄糖酸鈣 calcium gluconate
葡萄糖酸氯己定/葡萄糖酸洛赫西定 chlorhexidine gluconate
葡萄糖酸钠/葡萄糖酸鈉 sodium gluconate
葡萄糖酸内酯/葡萄糖酸内酯 glucolactone

葡萄糖酸锑钠/葡萄糖酸銻鈉　sodium stibogluconate
葡萄糖酸亚铁/葡萄糖酸亞鐵　ferrous gluconate
葡萄糖酸盐/葡萄糖酸鹽　gluconate
葡萄糖 1-脱氢酶/葡萄糖 1-脱氫酶　glucose 1-dehydrogenase
葡[萄]糖型抗坏血酸/葡萄糖型抗壞血酸　glucoascorbic acid
葡萄糖氧化酶/葡萄糖氧化酶　glucose oxidase
葡萄糖胰岛素钾盐溶液/葡萄糖胰島素鉀鹽溶液　glucose-insulin-potassium salt solution
葡萄糖注射[液]/葡萄糖注射液　dextrose injection
葡萄牙僧帽水母/僧帽水母　Portuguese man-of-war
葡萄疫/葡萄疫　grape-like pestilence
葡萄吲哚苷酸/羥吲哚葡萄糖醛酸　indoxylglucuronic acid
葡萄痔/葡萄痔　thrombosed external hemorrhoid
葡萄痔·血热瘀滞证/葡萄痔·血熱瘀滯證　thrombosed external hemorrhoid with pattern of blood-heat stasis and stagnation
葡萄肿/葡萄腫　staphyloma
葡萄肿切除术/葡萄腫切除術,懸雍垂切斷術　staphylotomy
葡萄状的/葡萄狀的,蔓狀的　racemose
葡萄状菌病/葡萄狀黴菌病　botryomycosis
葡萄状菌肿/葡萄狀黴菌瘤　botryomycoma
葡萄状肉瘤/葡萄狀肉瘤　sarcoma botryoides
葡萄状细胞/葡萄狀細胞　grape cell
葡萄状腺瘤/葡萄狀腺瘤　adenoma racemosum
蒲公英/蒲公英　dandelion
蒲黄/蒲黄　cattail pollen
浦肯野细胞/Purkinje 氏細胞　Purkinje cell
浦肯野纤维/浦肯野纖維　Purkinje fiber
浦肯野转移/最強視力區之移動　Purkinje shift
普遍的/普遍的,全體的　universal
普遍化/普遍化　generalize
普查/普查　census
普尔切病/Purtscher 氏病　Purtscher disease
普尔-施勒辛格尔征/普-史二氏徵象,史雷辛氏徵象　Pool-Schlesinger sign
普伐他丁/普伐他丁　Pravastatin
普凡嫩施蒂尔切口/普芬南施蒂爾切口　Pfannenstiel incision
普济方/普濟方　Prescriptions for Universal Relief
普济消毒饮/普濟消毒飲　puji xiaodu drink
普卡霉素/普卡黴素　plicamycin
普拉洛尔/普拉洛爾　practolol
普拉马林/普拉馬林　prajmaline

普拉西泮/普拉西泮　prazepam
普劳特咽峡炎/Plaut 氏咽峽炎　Plaut angina
普勒茨试验/布羅茲氏試驗　Proetz test
普雷茨位/普雷茨位　Proetz position
普里斯尼茨冷湿压绷带/Priessnitz 氏繃帶,冷濕繃帶　Priessnitz bandage
普里沃菌属/普雷沃菌　prevotella
普林兹梅特尔心绞痛/Prinzmetal 氏心絞痛　Prinzmetal angina
普卢默-文森综合征/普-維二氏症候群　Plummer-Vinson syndrome
普鲁卡因/普魯卡因　procaine
普鲁卡因胺/普魯卡因胺　procainamide
普鲁卡因青霉素 G/普魯卡因青黴素 G,青黴素 G 普魯卡因　procaine penicillin G
普鲁马西丁/二胺二苯碸之醯基磺醯胺鈉　promacetin
普鲁士蓝反应/普魯士藍反應　Prussian blue reaction
普鲁脂芬/普魯脂芬　procetofen
普罗布考/普羅布可　probucol
普罗地芬/普羅地芬　proadifen
普罗菲歇综合征/Profichet 氏症候群　Profichet syndrome
普罗帕酮/普羅帕酮　propafenone
普罗替林/普羅替林　protriptyline
普美孕酮/普美孕酮　promegestone
普萘洛尔/普萘洛爾　propranolol
普尼拉明/普尼拉明　prenylamine
普帕尔韧带/Poupart 氏韌帶,腹股溝韌帶　Poupart ligament
普瑞特罗/普瑞特羅　prenalterol
普氏立克次体/普氏立克次體　Rickettsia prowazekii
普通感觉/普通感覺　cenesthesia
普通护理/一般護理　general duty nursing
普通护士/普通護理人員　general duty nurse
普通可变型免疫缺陷/普通可變型免疫缺陷　common variable immunodeficiency
普通膳食/全食,普通飲食　full diet
普通松焦油/木焦油　liquid pitch
普通外科学/普通外科　general surgery
普通医生/普通醫師,開業醫師　general practitioner
普通转录因子类/普通轉錄因數類　general transcription factors
谱编辑/譜編輯　spectral editing
谱系/血統,家系　lineage
谱线检索/光譜檢索　spec-finder

蹼/蹼　web
蹼颈/蹼頸　webbed neck
蹼指/蹼指,鸭掌状手指　palmature
蹼状/蹼狀的　webbed
蹼状瘢痕/蹼狀瘢痕　webbed scar
蹼状阴茎/蹼狀陰莖　webbed penis
蹼状趾/蹼狀趾　webbed toe
蹼足/蹼足　wed foot
瀑布超灌流技术/階段式超灌流技術　cascade superfusion technique
瀑布形胃/瀑布狀胃　cascade stomach
曝/曝　exposed in the sun

Q

七宝美髯丹／七寶美髯丹　qibao meiran mini-pills
七倍体／七倍體　heptaploid
七重峰／七重峰　septet
七恶／七惡　seven critical conditions
七方／七方　seven kinds of prescriptions
七氟醚／七氟醚　sevoflurane
七价元素／七價元素　heptad
七厘散／七厘散　qili powder
七氯／七氯　heptachlor
七氯环氧化物／七氯環氧化物　heptachlor epoxide
七窍／七竅　seven orifices
七情／七情　①seven relations ②seven emotions
七情内伤／七情内傷　injury from frustration of emotions
七情学说／七情學説　theory of seven emotions
七情郁证／七情鬱證　stagnation pattern due to emotional stress
七情中／七情中　stroke due to emotional stress
七日热／七日熱　akiyami
七伤／七傷　seven damages, seven kinds of impairment
七肽／七肽，庚肽　heptapeptide
七烯类／七烯類　heptaenes
七星针／七星針　seven-star needle
七旬老人／七旬老人　septuagenarian
七叶苷／七葉苷　esculin
七叶素／七葉樹素，馬栗素　escin
七指畸形／七指畸形　heptadactylia
七趾畸形／七趾畸形　heptadactylia
七制香附丸／七制香附丸　qizhi xiangfu pills
期／期　period
期待性神经功能病／期望性神經病　expectation neurosis
期门／期門　qimen, LR14
期前收缩／期前收縮，過早搏動　premature beat
期外收缩／期外收縮　extra systole
期限／期限　term
期中流血／期中流血　midcyclic bleeding
漆疮／漆瘡　contact dermatitis, lacquer sore
漆疮·风热蕴肤证／漆瘡·風熱蕴膚證　lacquer sore with pattern of wind-heat amassing in skin
漆疮·湿热毒蕴证／漆瘡·濕熱毒蕴證　lacquer sore with pattern of dampness-heat toxin amassment
漆［儿茶］酚／漆酚　urushiol
漆酶／漆酶　laccase
漆皮／黏漆皮　hornskin
漆树／漆樹　sumac
漆树科／漆樹科　Anacardiaceae
漆树皮炎／漆樹皮炎　toxicodendron dermatitis
漆树属／漆樹屬　*Rhus*
漆中毒／漆中毒　lacquer poisoning
齐墩果酸／齊墩果酸　oleanolic acid
齐墩果烷／齊墩果烷　oleanane
齐多夫定／齊多夫定　zidovudine
齐恩韧带／Zinn 氏韌帶　Zinn ligament
齐尔-尼尔森方法／紀依爾-聶爾森方法　Ziehl-Nielsen method
齐尔溶液／Ziehl 氏溶液　Ziehl solution
齐美定／齊美利定　zimeldine
齐默飞机式夹／Zimmer 飛機式夾板　Zimmer airplane splint
齐默夹／Zimmer 夾板　Zimmer splint
齐-尼染剂／濟-尼二氏染法　Ziehl-Neelsen stain
齐普科斯基-马勾利斯综合征／Ziprkowski-Margolis 氏症候群　Ziprkowski-Margolis syndrome
奇方／奇方　odd-ingredient prescription
奇恒之腑／奇恆之腑　extraordinary fu-viscera
奇经八脉／奇經八脈　Eight Extraordinary Channels, Eight Extraordinary Meridians
奇昆古尼亚病毒／奇肯格尼病毒　Chikungunya virus
奇昆古尼亚热／奇肯格尼熱　Chikungunya fever
奇脉／奇脈　pulsus paradoxus
奇泰利综合征／Citelli 氏症候群　Citelli syndrome
奇维尼尼韧带／Civinini 氏韌帶，翼棘韌帶　ligament of Civinini
奇叶／奇葉　azygos lobe
歧点酶／歧點酵素　branch point enzyme
歧化反应／歧化反應　dismutation reaction
歧化酶／歧化酶　dismutase
歧化［作用］／歧化　dismutation
祈祷者结节／祈禱者結節　prayer nodule
脐／臍　umbilicus, navel

脐部/臍部 umbilical part
脐部联胎/單臍連胎 monomphalus
脐部脐肠系膜管息肉/臍部腸繫膜導管息肉 umbilical omphalomesenteric duct polyp
脐插管/臍插管 umbilical catheterization
脐肠管异常/臍腸管異常 omphalomesenteric duct anomalies
脐肠瘘/臍腸瘻 omphaloenteric fistula
脐肠系膜的/臍腸繫膜的 omphalomesenteric
脐肠系膜动脉/臍腸繫膜動脈 omphalomesenteric artery
脐肠系膜管/臍腸繫膜管 omphalomesenteric duct
脐肠系膜静脉/臍腸繫膜靜脈 omphalomesenteric vein
脐出血/臍出血 omphalorrhagia
脐疮/臍瘡 umbilical eczema, umbilical sore
脐带/臍帶 umbilical cord
脐带边缘附着/臍帶邊緣附著 cord marginal insertion
脐带缠绕/臍帶纏繞 cord entanglement
脐带穿刺术/臍帶穿刺採血法 cordocentesis
脐带帆状附着/臍帶帆狀附著 cord velamentous insertion
脐带过长/臍帶過長 long cord
脐带过短/臍帶過短 short cord
脐带假结/臍帶假結 false knot of cord
脐带胶质/臍帶膠質 umbilical jelly, Wharton jelly
脐带囊肿/臍帶囊腫 cyst of cord
脐带扭转/臍帶扭轉 torsion of cord
脐带水肿/臍帶水腫 edema of cord
脐带脱垂/臍帶脫垂 umbilical prolapse
脐带系膜/臍帶繫帶 mesocord
脐带狭窄/臍帶狹窄 stricture of cord
脐带血/[胎兒]臍帶血 cord blood
脐带血肿/臍帶血腫 hematoma of cord
脐带杂音/臍帶雜音 funic souffle
脐带真结/臍帶真結 true knot of cord
脐点/臍點 omphalion, hilum
脐动脉/臍動脈 umbilical artery
[脐动脉]闭塞部/[臍動脈]閉塞部 occlusive part of umbilical artery
[脐动脉]开放部/[臍動脈]開放部 patent part of umbilical artery
脐风/臍風 tetanus neonatorum
脐风·经络闭阻证/臍風·經絡閉阻證 tetanus neonatorum with channel-collateral blockage pattern
脐风·邪毒中脏证/臍風·邪毒中臟證 tetanus neonatorum with pattern of pathogenic toxin attacking zang-viscera
脐敷裹/臍包扎 umbilical dressing
脐腹/臍腹 perinavel region
脐腹痛/臍腹痛 perinavel pain
脐肛/臍肛 umbilical anus
脐管/臍管 umbilical duct
脐环/臍環 umbilical ring
脐积水/臍積水 hydromphalus
脐静脉/臍靜脈 umbilical vein
脐静脉曲张/臍靜脈曲張 varicomphalus
脐静脉炎/臍靜脈炎 omphalophlebitis
脐溃疡/臍潰瘍 omphalelcosis
脐裂/臍裂 omphaloschisis
脐瘤/臍瘤 omphaloma
脐瘘/臍瘻 umbilical fistula
脐囊/臍囊 umbilical vesicle
脐囊液/臍囊液 vital fluid
脐内侧襞/臍內側皺襞 medial umbilical fold
脐内侧韧带/臍內側韌帶 medial umbilical ligament
脐尿窦/臍尿[管]竇 urachal sinus
脐尿管/臍尿管 urachus, urachal duct
脐尿管癌/臍尿管癌 carcinoma of urachus
脐尿管的/臍尿管的 urachal
脐尿管窦道/臍尿管竇道 sinus of urachus
脐尿管放线菌病/臍尿管放線菌病 actinomycosis of urachus
脐尿管积脓/臍尿管積膿 pyourachus
脐尿管疾病/臍尿管疾病 diseases of urachus
脐尿管结核/臍尿管結核 tuberculosis of urachus
脐尿管瘘/臍尿管瘻 fistula of urachus
脐尿管囊肿/臍尿管囊腫 urachal cyst
脐尿管憩室/臍尿管憩室 urachal diverticulum
脐尿管未闭/臍尿管未閉 patent of urachus
脐尿管窝/臍尿管窩 urachal fossa
脐尿管腺癌/臍尿管腺癌 urachal adenocarcinoma
脐尿管肿瘤/臍尿管腫瘤 tumor of urachus
脐脓肿/臍積膿 empyocele
脐旁疝/臍旁疝 para-umbilical hernia
脐膨出/臍膨出,臍疝 exomphalia
脐破裂/臍破裂 omphalorrhexis
脐腔/臍腔 umbilical coelom
脐切除术/臍切除術 omphalectomy
脐绒毛膜/臍絨毛膜 omphalochorion
脐肉瘤/臍肉腫 sarcomphalocele
脐疝/臍疝,臍赫尼亞 umbilical hernia
脐上疽/臍上疽 supra-umbilical carbuncle
脐上胸联胎/胸[部]連胎 thoracodelphus
脐湿/臍濕 umbilical dampness

脐石/臍石　omphalolith
脐突/臍突　umbilical hernia
脐外侧襞/臍外側皺襞　lateral umbilical fold
脐息肉/臍息肉　umbilical polyp
脐下悸动/臍下悸動　throbbing below umbilical region
脐形成/臍發生，臍發育　omphalogenesis
脐血/臍血　umbilical bleeding, umbilical blood disorder
脐血干细胞移植/臍血幹細胞移植　cord blood stem cell transplantation
脐血管联胎/臍血管連胎　allantoidoangiopagus
脐循环/臍循環　umbilical circulation
脐炎/臍炎　omphalitis
脐液溢/臍液漏　omphalorrhea
脐营养畸胎/臍營養畸胎　omphalosite
脐痈/臍癰　umbilical abscess, umbilical carbuncle
脐痈·脾气虚证/臍癰·脾氣虛證　umbilical abscess with spleen qi deficiency pattern
脐痈·湿热火毒证/臍癰·濕熱火毒證　umbilical abscess with pattern of dampness-heat and fire-toxin
脐正中襞/臍中皺襞　median umbilical fold
脐正中韧带/臍中韌帶　median umbilical ligament
脐肿/臍腫　umbilical swelling
脐周穿孔性弹性纤维假黄瘤/肚臍周圍穿孔性彈性纖維假黄瘤　periumbilical perforating pseudoxanthoma elasticum
脐周的/臍周圍的　periumbilical
脐周蜂窝[组]织炎/臍周蜂窩織炎　periumbilical cellulitis
脐周静脉曲张/蛇髮女妖頭樣静脈曲張　caput Medusae
脐周蔷薇花状结节/肚臍周圍薔薇花狀結節　periumbilical rosette
骑跨逆行/跨在血管分支上的栓塞　saddle retrograde
骑跨室中隔/跨位性心室中隔　overriding ventricular septum
骑马者骨/騎士骨　rider bone
棋盘花碱/棋盤花鹼　zygadenine
旗征/旗幟徵象　flag sign
蕲蛇/蕲蛇　long-nosed pit viper
鳍状肢芽/鰭狀肢芽　flipper-like limb bud
企图性精神病/企圖性精神病　purpose psychosis
杞菊地黄丸/杞菊地黄丸　qiju dihuang pills
启动素类/啟動素類　activins
启动素受体/啟動素受體　activin receptor
启动子/啟動子　promoter
启动子区/啟動區　promoter region
启示性梦/啟示性夢　clairvoyant dream
起搏刺激/起搏刺激　pacing stimulation
起搏电极/起搏電極　pacing electrode
起搏方式/起搏方式　mode of cardiac pacing
起搏器/起搏器，心臟調律器　pacemaker
起搏器功能障碍/起搏器功能障礙　pacemaker malfunction
起搏器皮炎/心律調節器所致皮膚炎　pacemaker dermatitis
起搏器相关性心动过速/起搏器相關性心動過速　pacemaker related tachycardia
起搏器综合征/起搏器症候群　pacemaker syndrome
起搏细胞/起搏細胞　pacemaker cell
起搏阈值/起搏閾值　pacing threshold
起搏周长/起搏周長　paced cycle length
起端/起端　origin
起核/起核　nucleus of origin
起立不能/起立不能　ananastasia
起立不能发作/起立不能性癲癇發作　astatic seizure
起立困难/起立困難　dysstasia
起脓疱剂/促膿藥　pustulant
起泡剂/發泡劑　foaming agent
[起泡沫的]肥皂水/起泡肥皂水　soapsuds
起疱/發泡，起泡　vesication
起疱剂/發泡藥，起泡劑　vesicant
起始核/起始核　nucleus of origin
起始密码子/起始密碼子　initiation codon, initiator codon
起始耐药/起始耐藥　initial drug resistance
起始向量/起始向量　initial vector
气/氣　①odour ②qi
气闭/氣閉　qi block
气闭证/氣閉證　qi block pattern
气病及血/氣病及血　qi disease involving blood
气不化津/氣不化津　failure of qi transforming fluid
气不摄血/氣不攝血　qi failing to control blood
气不摄血证/氣不攝血證　pattern of qi failing to control blood
气冲/氣沖　qichong, ST30
气传导/空氣傳導　air conduction
气传导率/氣傳導率　conductance
气喘纸/氣喘紙　asthma paper
气锤工病/氣錐病　pneumatic hammer disease
气单胞菌属/產氣單胞菌屬　Aeromonas
气道/氣道　airway
气道传导率/氣道傳導率　airway conductance

气道阻力/氣道阻力 airway resistance
气道阻塞/氣道阻塞 airway obstruction
气的/氣的,呼吸的 pneumatic
气垫/氣墊 airbag
气垫征/氣墊徵象 air-cushion sign
气动平衡/氣體平衡 air balance
气动取皮机/氣動取皮機 air-driven dermatome
气端/氣端 qiduan, EX-LE12
气短/喘息 panting
气分/氣分 qi phase
气分湿热证/氣分濕熱證 pattern of dampness-heat in qi phase
气分证/氣分證 qi phase pattern
气腹/氣腹 pneumoperitoneum
气杆菌属/產氣桿菌 Aerobacter
气功/氣功 qigong
气功疗法/氣功療法 qigong therapy
气功偏差/氣功偏差 qigong deviation
气骨导间距/氣骨傳導隙 air-bone gap
气鼓传导/氣鼓傳導 aerotympanic conduction
气臌/氣臌 qi tympanites
气关/氣關 qi pass
气管/氣管 ①trachea ②qiguan, CO16
气管比翼线虫/氣管翼線蟲 Syngamus trachea
气管闭锁/氣管閉鎖 tracheal atresia
气管部[心音]听诊/氣管聽診 tracheophonesis
气管成形术/氣管造形術 tracheoplasty
气管重建术/氣管重建術 reconstruction of trachea
气管出血/氣管出血 tracheorrhagia
气管穿刺投药法/氣管穿刺投藥法 tracheofistulization
气管刀/氣管刀 tracheotome
气管导管/氣管導管 endotracheal tube
气管的/氣管的 tracheal
气管堵塞球/氣管堵塞球 bronchial blocker
气管缝合术/氣管縫合術 tracheorrhaphy
气管喉切开术/氣管喉切開術 tracheolaryngotomy
气管呼吸音/氣管呼吸音 tracheal respiration
气管肌/氣管肌 tracheal muscle, musculus trachealis
气管疾病/氣管疾病 tracheal disease
气管颈部/氣管頸部 cervical part of trachea
气管静脉/氣管靜脈 tracheal vein
气管镜检查/氣管鏡檢 tracheoscopy
气管开窗术/氣管開窗術 fenestration of trachea
气管扩张/氣管擴張 tracheaectasy
气管裂/氣管裂 tracheoschisis
气管裂开术/氣管裂開術 tracheofissure

气管隆嵴/氣管隆凸 carina of trachea
气管隆凸/支氣管中隔 bronchial septum
气管瘘/氣管瘻 tracheal fistula
气管啰音/氣管水泡音 tracheal rale
气管内插管/氣管內插管法 endotracheal intubation
气管内吹入法/氣管內吹氣法 endotracheal insufflation
气管内的/氣管內的 endotracheal
气管内给药法/氣管內投藥法 intratracheal medication
气管内径路/氣管內徑路 intratracheal route
气管内麻醉/氣管內麻醉法 endotracheal anesthesia
气管黏膜/氣管黏膜 mucous membrane of trachea
气管黏膜疝样突出/氣管赫尼亞,氣管膨出 trachelocele
气管黏液表皮样癌/氣管黏液表皮樣癌 mucoepidermoid carcinoma of trachea
气管旁淋巴结/氣管旁淋巴結 paratracheal lymph node
气管蹼/氣管蹼 tracheal web
气管气疝/氣管氣囊腫 tracheoaerocele
气管憩室/氣管憩室 tracheal diverticulum
气管牵开器/氣管牽開器 trachea retractor
气管牵引感/氣管牽曳 tracheal tugging
气管前层/氣管前層 pretracheal layer
气管前动脉/氣管前動脈 anterior bronchial artery
气管前间隙/氣管前間隙 pretracheal space
气管前淋巴结/氣管前淋巴結 pretracheal lymph node
气管腔内T形管置入术/氣管腔內T形管置入術 intratracheal T tube insertion
气管切除及重建术/氣管切除及重建術 tracheal resection and reconstruction
气管切开插管/氣管切開術用管 tracheotomy tube
气管切开后狭窄/氣管切開後狹窄 post-tracheotomy stenosis
气管切开术/氣管切開術 tracheotomy
气管软骨/氣管軟骨 tracheal cartilage
气管软骨软化病/氣管軟骨軟化病 tracheal chondromalacia
气管软化/氣管軟骨軟化 tracheomalacia
气管塞子/氣管塞子 tracheal tampon
气管上皮/氣管上皮 tracheal epithelium
气管食管隔/氣管食道隔 tracheoesophageal septum
气管食管瘘/氣管食管瘻 tracheoesophageal fistula
气管食管褶/氣管食道褶 tracheoesophageal fold
气管痛/氣管痛 trachealgia
气管无名动脉瘘/氣管無名動脈瘻

tracheoinnominate artery fistula
气管狭窄/氣管狹窄　tracheal stenosis
气管腺/氣管腺　tracheal gland
气管腺样囊性癌/氣管腺樣囊性癌　adenoid cystic carcinoma of trachea
气管胸部/氣管胸部　thoracic part of trachea
气管袖状全肺切除术/氣管袖狀全肺切除術　tracheal sleeve pneumonectomy
气管[延续性]支气管/氣管性支氣管　tracheal bronchus
气管炎/氣管炎　tracheitis
气管炎性咽峡炎/氣管炎性咽峡炎　angina trachealis
气管异物/氣管異物　foreign body in trachea
气管音/氣管音，氣管聲　tracheophony
气管造口/氣管瘻口　tracheostoma
气管造口术/氣管造口術　tracheostomy
气管支/氣管支　tracheal branch
气管支气管瘢痕狭窄/氣管支氣管瘢痕狹窄　tracheobronchial cicatricial stricture
气管支气管的/氣管支氣管的　tracheobronchial
气管支气管扩大/氣管與支氣管膨大　tracheobronchomegaly
气管支气管沟/氣管支氣管溝　tracheobronchial groove
气管支气管结核/氣管與支氣管結核　tracheobronchial tuberculosis
气管支气管镜检查/氣管與支氣管鏡檢法　tracheobronchoscopy
气管支气管淋巴结/氣管支氣管淋巴結　tracheobronchial lymph nodes
气管支气管上淋巴结/氣管支氣管上淋巴結　superior tracheobronchial lymph nodes
气管支气管树/氣管與支氣管分支　tracheobronchial tree
气管支气管缩窄/氣管支氣管縮窄　stricture of trachea and bronchi
气管支气管下淋巴结/氣管支氣管下淋巴結　inferior tracheobronchial lymph nodes
气管支气管炎/氣管與支氣管炎　tracheobronchitis
气管支气管运动障碍/氣管支氣管運動障礙　tracheobronchial dyskinesia
气管肿瘤/氣管腫瘤　tracheal neoplasms
气海/氣海　qihai, RN6
气海俞/氣海俞　qihaishu, BL24
气候病/氣候病　climatic disease
气候病理学/氣候病理學　meteoropathology
气候的/氣候的　climatic
气候[对人体]影响图/氣候圖　climograph

气候疗法/氣候療法　climatotherapy
气候影响性[反应]/氣候影響反應　meteorotropism
气户/氣戶　qihu, ST13
气化无权/氣化無權　failure in qi transformation
气化[作用]/氣化　gasification
气机/氣機　qi movement
气机不利/氣機不利　disorder of qi movement
气积性消化不良/氣積性消化不良　gaseous dyspepsia
气脊髓造影术/脊髓充氣 X 光攝影法　pneumomyelography
气绞痛/氣絞痛　wind colic
气街/氣街　pathway of qi
气结血瘀积证/氣結血瘀積證　amassment disease with pattern of qi congelation and blood stasis
气疱脓毒病/氣疱敗血症　gas sepsis
气厥/氣厥　qi syncope, syncope due to disorder of qi
气厥·实证/氣厥·實證　qi syncope with excess pattern
气厥·虚证/氣厥·虛證　qi syncope with deficiency pattern
气孔/氣孔　stoma
气孔数/氣孔數　stomatal number
气孔指数/氣孔指數　stomatal index
气浪弹伤/氣浪彈傷　blast bomb wound
气立/氣立　establishment of general qi
气痢/氣痢　qi dysentery
气淋/氣淋　qi strangury, stranguria due to disturbance of qi
气流/氣流　airflow
气流型态/氣流型態　flow pattern
气瘤/氣瘤　qi tumor, tumor due to disorder of qi
气瘤·肺气失宣证/氣瘤·肺氣失宣證　qi tumor with pattern of lung qi failing in dispersing
气瘤·肝气郁结证/氣瘤·肝氣鬱結證　qi tumor with liver qi stagnation pattern
气瘤·脾虚痰凝证/氣瘤·脾虛痰凝證　qi tumor with pattern of spleen deficiency and phlegm coagulation
气瘤·气滞血瘀证/氣瘤·氣滯血瘀證　qi tumor with pattern of qi stagnation and blood stasis
气瘘/氣瘻　aerial fistula
气轮/氣輪　qi wheel
气醚麻醉/氣醚麻醉　gas-ether anesthesia
气秘/氣秘　qi constipation
气磨洞形器/噴砂磨齒機　airdent
气磨器/氣磨器　airbrasive
气囊/氣囊　air bladder
气囊扩张器/氣球擴張器　balloon dilator

气囊扩张术/血管氣球擴張術　balloon dilatation
气囊填塞/氣囊填塞　balloon tamponade
气囊血管成形术/氣囊血管成形術　balloon angioplasty
气[囊]肿/氣囊腫　aerocele
气囊阻塞/氣囊阻塞　balloon occlusion
气脑脊髓造影术/腦脊髓充氣X光攝影法　pneumoencephalomyelography
气脑脊髓[造影]照片/腦充氣脊髓X光照片　pneumoencephalomyelogram
气脑疗法/腦氣體療法　cerebral pneumatotherapy
气逆/氣逆　reversed flow of qi
气逆证/氣逆證　pattern of reversed flow of qi
气凝胶[体]/充氣膠體　aerogel
气脓胸/氣性膿胸　empyema gaseosum
气脓肿/氣腫性膿腫　emphysematous abscess
气泡/氣泡　bubble
气泡监测器/氣泡監測器　bubble monitor
气泡血症/氣泡血症　pompholyhemia
气泡浴/氣泡浴　bubble bath
气腔形成/氣腔形成　pneumatization
气腔型/氣腔型　air-chamber pattern
气球/氣球　balloon
气球瓣膜成形术/氣球瓣膜整型術　balloon valvuloplasty
气球病/氣球病　balloon sickness
气球反搏术/氣球反搏術　balloon counterpulsation
气球心导管术/氣球心導管術　balloon catheterization
气球血管成形术/氣球血管成形術　balloon angioplasty
气球样变性/[细胞]腫脹變性　ballooning degeneration
气球样囊肿/氣球樣囊腫　balloon cyst
气球样细胞/氣球樣細胞　balloon cell
气球状细胞痣/氣球狀細胞痣　balloon cell nevus
气溶胶/霧化滴　aerosol
气溶胶吸入疗法/霧狀吸入劑療法　aerosol therapy
气溶胶[治疗]学/霧化吸入治療學　aerosolology
气乳瘤/氣乳瘤　pneumogalactocele
气褥/氣褥,氣墊　air bed
气疝/氣疝　distention in abdomen and vulva due to angry
气上冲心/氣上冲心　qi rushing upward to heart
气舍/氣舍　qishe, ST11
气生菌丝体/空氣傳導菌絲體　aerial mycelium
气栓/氣栓,潛水夫病　aeroembolism
气水胸/氣水胸　pneumohydrothorax

气水浴/發泡浴　effervescent bath
气随血脱/氣隨血脱　qi desertion due to blood depletion
气随液脱/氣隨液脱　depletion of fluid involving qi desertion
气体比重测定法/氣體密度測定法　aerometry
气体代谢/氣體代謝　gaseous metabolism
气体定量法/氣體測尿素法　gasometric method
气体动力学/氣體動力學　aerodynamics
气体放电/氣體放電　gaseous discharge
气体净化器/氣體淨化器　gas purifier
气体静力学/氣體靜力學　aerostatics
气体扩张器/氣體擴張器　pneumatic dilator
气体离子/氣體離子　gaseous ion
气体疗法/氣體療法　pneumatotherapy
气体疗法室/氣體療法室　pneumatic cabinet
气体滤器/氣體濾器　gas filter
气体麻醉药/氣體麻醉藥　gas anesthetic
气体密度计/氣體密度測定器　dasymeter
气体浓度分数/氣體濃度分數　fraction concentration of gas
气体清除器/氣體清除器　gas scavengers
气体容积/氣體容積　gas volume
气体容量分析/氣體密度檢查法　manoscopy
气体微栓/氣體微栓　gaseous microemboli
气体吸收压力阶差/氣體吸收壓力階差　gas absorption pressure gradient
气体张力/氣體張力　gaseous tension
气体中毒/毒氣中毒　gas poisoning
气体注射/氣體注射　gaseous injection
气痛/氣痛　qi pain
气脱/氣脱　qi desertion
气脱证/氣脱證　pattern of qi desertion
气为血帅/氣爲血帥　qi being commander of blood
气味/氣味　odors
气味测量法/氣味測定法　odorimetry
气味论/氣味論　odorography
气味受体/有氣味性物質受體　odorant receptors
气味腺/氣味腺　scent glands, odoriferous gland
气雾剂/氣霧劑,霧化滴　aerosol
气雾喷射剂/氣霧噴射劑　aerosol propellant
气陷证/氣陷證　pattern of qi sinking
气相反应/氣相反應　gas phase reaction
气相色谱法/氣相層析法　gas chromatography
气相色谱-[傅里叶变换]红外光谱联用仪/氣相層析-[傅立葉變換]紅外線儀　gas chromatograph-Fourier transform infrared spectrophotometer, GC-FTIR

气小房/氣小房　pneumatic cell
气性腹膜炎/積氣性腹膜炎　pneumoperitonitis
气性坏疽/氣性壞疽　gas gangrene
气性坏疽抗毒素/氣疽抗毒素　gas gangrene antitoxin
气性碱中毒/氣體性鹼血症　gaseous alkalosis
气性膀胱炎/氣性膀胱炎　emphysematous cystitis
气性肾盂肾炎/氣性腎盂腎炎　emphysematous pyelonephritis
气性水肿/氣性水腫　gaseous edema
气性酸中毒/氣體性酸血症　gaseous acidosis
气胸/氣胸　pneumothorax
气[嗅]/氣[嗅]　odor, smell
气虚/氣虛　qi deficiency
气虚不摄/氣虛不攝　failure of keeping fluid due to qi deficiency
气虚发热证/氣虛發熱證　pattern of fever due to qi deficiency
气虚外感证/氣虛外感證　pattern of exogenous disease due to qi deficiency
气虚血瘀/氣虛血瘀　blood stasis due to qi deficiency
气虚血瘀证/氣虛血瘀證　pattern of blood stasis due to qi deficiency
气虚证/氣虛證　pattern of qi deficiency
气虚中满/氣虛中滿　flatulence caused by qi deficiency
气穴/氣穴　qixue, KI13
气血两燔/氣血兩燔　flaring heat in qi and blood phases
气血两燔证/氣血兩燔證　pattern of flaring heat in qi and blood phases
气血两虚证/氣血兩虛證　pattern of deficiency of both qi and blood
气血失调/氣血失調　disorder of qi and blood
气血衰竭/氣血衰竭　exhaustion of qi and blood
气血双补剂/氣血雙補劑　formula for benefiting both qi and blood
气血胸/氣血胸　pneumohemothorax
气血虚痹/氣血虛痺　arthralgia due to qi-blood deficiency, bi disease due to qi-blood deficiency
气压病/氣壓調適不良　dysbarism
气压测定法/氣壓測量法　barometry
气压计/氣壓計　barometer
气压伤/氣壓傷　barotrauma
气压式蒸馏水器/蒸氣壓式蒸餾水機　vapor compression still
气压损伤性鼻窦炎/氣壓創傷性鼻竇炎　barotraumatic sinusitis
气压损伤性中耳炎/氣壓性耳炎　barotitis
气压性眩晕/氣壓性眩暈　alternobaric vertigo
气压性中耳炎/氣壓性中耳炎　aviator ear
气压压迫/氣的壓迫　pneumatic compression
气压眼压计/氣壓眼壓計　pneumatic tonometer
气阴两虚/氣陰兩虛　deficiency of both qi and yin
气阴两虚证/氣陰兩虛證　pattern of deficiency of both qi and yin
气营两燔/氣營兩燔　flaring heat in qi and nutrient phases
气营两燔证/氣營兩燔證　pattern of flaring heat in qi and nutrient phases
气瘿/氣瘿　qi goiter, endemic goiter, simple goiter
气瘿·肝气郁结证/氣瘿·肝氣鬱結證　qi goiter with liver qi stagnation pattern
气瘿·肝郁肾虚证/氣瘿·肝鬱腎虛證　qi goiter with pattern of liver depression and kidney deficiency
气壅如痰/氣壅如痰　qi congestion like sputum
气郁/氣鬱　qi depression, qi stagnation
气郁化火/氣鬱化火　qi depression transforming into fire, stagnated qi transforming into fire
气郁化火证/氣鬱化火證　pattern of qi depression transforming into fire
气郁吐血/氣鬱吐血　hematemesis due to qi stagnation
气郁脘痛/氣鬱脘痛　stomachache due to qi stagnation
气郁胁痛/氣鬱脅痛　hypochondriac pain due to stagnation of qi
气郁眩晕/氣鬱眩暈　dizziness due to stagnation of qi
气胀术/氣脹[診]法　ballooning
气枕床/氣枕床　low air loss bed
气质/氣質　temperament, disposition
气痔/氣痔　varicoid external hemorrhoid
气滞/氣滯　qi stagnation
气滞耳窍证/氣滯耳竅證　pattern of qi stagnation in ear
气滞湿阻证/氣滯濕阻證　pattern of blockade of dampness due to qi stagnation
气滞痰凝咽喉证/氣滯痰凝咽喉證　pattern of qi stagnation and coagulated phlegm in throat
气滞胃痛颗粒/氣滯胃痛顆粒　qizhi weitong granules
气滞血瘀/氣滯血瘀　qi stagnation and blood stasis
气滞血瘀证/氣滯血瘀證　pattern of qi stagnation and blood stasis
气滞血阻积证/氣滯血阻積證　amassment disease with pattern of qi stagnation and blood blockade

气滞证/氣滯證　pattern of qi stagnation
气中/氣中　qi parapoplexy
气肿/氣腫　emphysema, qi swelling
气肿的/氣腫的　emphysematous
气肿性胆囊炎/氣腫性膽囊炎　emphysematous cholecystitis
气肿性肺大疱/氣腫性肺大皰　emphysematous bulla
气肿性呼吸困难/氣腫性呼吸困難　pneumatodyspnea
气肿性炭疽/氣腫性炭疽　emphysematous anthrax
气肿性阴道炎/氣腫性陰道炎　emphysematous vaginitis
气肿性子宫颈阴道炎/氣腫性子宮頸陰道炎　cervicocolpitis emphysematosa
气主煦之/氣主煦之　qi warming body
汽车事故医学/汽車事故醫學　automotive medicine
汽管装配工气喘/汽管裝配工氣喘　steam-fitters asthma
汽锅工病/汽鍋匠病　boiler-marker disease
汽油烧伤/汽油燒傷　petrol burn
契坦登饮食/Chittenden 氏飲食　Chittenden diet
契维茨层/契維茨氏層　Chievitz layer
器官/器官　organ
器官保存/器官保存　organ preservation
器官保存液/器官保存液　organ preservation solution
器官测量/器官測量　organ size
器官簇移植/器官簇移植　organ cluster transplantation
器官的/器官[的]　organic
器官毒理学/器官毒理學　organ toxicology
器官发生/器官發生　organogenesis
器官发生期/器官發生期　organogenetic period
器官发育障碍/器官發育障礙　dysorganoplasia
器官灌注/器官灌注　organ perfusion
器官巨大症/器官巨大　organomegaly
器官疗法/臟器療法　organotherapy
器官瘤/器官瘤　organoma
器官耐受量/器官耐受量　organ tolerance dose
器官培养/器官培養　organ culture
器官培养技术/器官培養技術　organ culture techniques
器官切取/器官切取　organ procurement
器官 X 射线照相术/器官 X 光攝影術　organography
器官特异性/器官特異性　organ specificity
器官特异性抗原/器官特異性抗原　organ specific antigen
器官系统损害/系统性病灶　systemic lesion

器官形成/器官形成　organofaction
器官形成区/器官形成區　organ forming area
器官型生长/器官型生長　organotypic growth
器官性发声不良/器官性發音不良　olophonia
器官学/器官學　organology
器官样的/器官樣的，類器官　organoid
器官样瘤/器官樣新生物　organoid neoplasm
器官移植/器官移植　organ transplantation
器官原基/器官原基　organ primordium
器官组织学/器官組織學　organ histology
器械/器械，裝置　apparatus
器械灭菌法/器械滅菌法　mechanical sterilization
器械体操/機械體操　mechanogymnastics
器械压迫法/器械壓法　instrumental compression
器质论者/器質病説者　organicist
器质性病/器質病，器官病　structural disease
器质性癫痫/器質性癲癇　organic epilepsy
器质性精神病/器質性精神病　organic psychosis
器质性盲/器質性盲　organic blindness
器质性脑病综合征/器質性腦病症候群　organic brain syndrome
器质性痛经/器質性痛經　organic dysmenorrhea
器质性头痛/器質性頭痛　organic headache
器质性狭窄/器質性狹窄　organic stenosis
器质性心脏病/器質性心臟病　organic heart disease
器质性眩晕/器質性眩暈　organic vertigo
器质性阳痿/器官性陽痿　organic impotence
器质性杂音/器質性雜音　organic murmur
憩室/憩室　diverticula
憩室病/憩室病　diverticulosis
憩室的/憩室的　diverticular
憩室固定术/憩室固定術　diverticulopexy
憩室前期/憩室前期　prediverticular stage
憩室切除术/憩室切除術　diverticulectomy
憩室疝/憩室疝　diverticular hernia
憩室[X射线]造影/憩室攝影　diverticulogram
憩室形成/憩室形成　diverticularization
憩室炎/憩室炎　diverticulitis
掐/捏，夾　pinch
恰菲埃里希体/沙費埃里希體　Ehrlichia chaffeensis
恰加斯-克鲁斯病/恰-克二氏病　Chagas-Cruz disease
髂部剑突联胎/髂胸聯嬰，劍突連胎　ilioxiphopagus
髂部联胎/腸骨連胎　ileadelphus
髂耻的/髂恥的　iliopubic
髂耻弓/髂恥弓　iliopectineal arch
髂耻隆起/髂恥隆起　iliopubic eminence
髂耻囊/髂恥囊　iliopectineal bursa

髂耻束/髂恥徑　iliopubic tract
髂耻窝/髂恥窩,髂恥三角　iliopectineal trigone
髂丛/髂叢　iliac plexuses, iliac plexus
髂粗隆/髂粗隆　iliac tuberosity
髂粗隆韧带/髂粗隆韌帶　iliotrochanteric ligament
髂骶长韧带/髂骶長韌帶　long iliosacral ligament
髂骶盆面/髂骶骨盆面　sacropelvic surface of the ilium
髂骶前韧带/髂骶前韌帶　anterior iliosacral ligament
髂动脉/髂動脈　iliac artery
髂动脉瘤/髂動脈瘤　iliac aneurysm
髂腹股沟淋巴结切除术/髂腹股溝淋巴結切除術　ilioinguinal lymphadenectomy
髂腹股沟神经/胯鼠蹊神經　ilioinguinal nerve
髂腹下神经/髂腹下神經　iliohypogastric nerve
髂腹下神经前皮支/髂腹下神經前皮支　anterior cutaneous branch of iliohypogastric nerve
髂腹下神经外侧皮支/髂腹下神經外側皮支　lateral cutaneous branch of iliohypogastric nerve
髂股成形术/髂股成形術　iliofemoroplasty
髂股的/髂股的　iliofemoral
髂股韧带/髂股韌帶　iliofemoral ligament
髂股皱/髂股皺褶　iliofemoral crease
髂骨/髂骨　ilium
髂骨耳状面/髂骨耳狀面　auricular surface of ilium
髂骨体/髂骨體　body of ilium
髂骨下部/髂骨下的　subilium
髂骨翼/髂骨翼　ala of ilium
髂骨致密性骨炎/髂骨致密性骨炎　osteitis condensans ilium
髂关节盂旁沟/腸關節盂旁溝　preauricular groove of ilium
髂后上棘/髂後上棘　posterior superior iliac spine
髂后上棘点/髂後上棘點　iliospinale posterius
髂后输尿管/髂動脈後輸尿管　retroiliac ureter
髂后下棘/髂後下棘　posterior inferior iliac spine
髂肌/髂肌　iliacus, iliac muscle
髂肌腱下囊/髂肌腱下囊　subtendinous bursa of iliacus
髂棘测量器/髂棘測量器　iliometer
髂棘间径/髂棘間徑　interspinal diameter
髂嵴/髂嵴　iliac crest
髂嵴点/髂嵴點　iliocristale
髂嵴间径/髂嵴間徑　intercrestal diameter
髂嵴内唇/髂嵴內唇　inner lip of iliac crest
髂嵴外唇/髂嵴外唇　outer lip of iliac crest
髂间淋巴结/髂間淋巴結　interiliac lymph node
髂结节/髂骨結節　tubercle of iliac crest
髂筋膜/髂筋膜　iliac fascia
髂筋膜下疝/髂筋膜下疝　hernia iliacosubfascialis
髂胫的/髂與脛骨的　iliotibial
髂胫骨束/Maissiat 氏帶　Maissiat band
髂胫束/髂脛束　iliotibial tract
髂胫束粗隆/髂脛束粗隆　tuberosity for iliotibial tract
髂胫束紧张试验/髂脛束緊張試驗　Ober's sign
髂静脉/髂静脈　iliac vein
髂肋肌/髂肋肌　iliocostalis, iliocostal muscle
髂淋巴结/髂淋巴結　iliac lymph node
髂淋巴囊/髂淋巴囊　iliac lymph sac
髂内动脉/髂內動脈　internal iliac artery
髂内动脉结扎术/髂內動脈結扎術　ligation of internal iliac artery
髂内静脉/髂內静脈　internal iliac vein
髂内淋巴结/髂內淋巴結　internal iliac lymph node
髂前动脉/髂前動脈　anterior iliac artery
髂前上棘/髂前上棘　anterior superior iliac spine
髂前上棘点/髂前上棘點　iliospinale anterius
髂前下棘/髂前下棘　anterior inferior iliac spine
髂式结肠切开术/髂式結腸切開術　iliocolotomy
髂外动脉/髂外動脈　external iliac artery
髂外静脉/髂外静脈　external iliac vein
髂外淋巴丛/髂外淋巴叢　plexus iliacus externus
髂外淋巴结/髂外淋巴結　external iliac lymph node
髂外内侧淋巴结/髂外內側淋巴結　medial external iliac lymph node
髂外外侧淋巴结/髂外外側淋巴結　lateral external iliac lymph node
髂外中间淋巴结/髂外中間淋巴結　intermediate external iliac lymph node
髂尾肌/髂尾肌　iliococcygeus
髂窝/髂窩　iliac fossa
髂窝流注/髂窩流注　deep multiple abscess of iliac fossa
髂窝流注·热毒炽盛证/髂窩流注·熱毒熾盛證　deep multiple abscess of iliac fossa with blazing heat-toxin pattern
髂窝流注·湿热蕴结证/髂窩流注·濕熱蘊結證　deep multiple abscess of iliac fossa with dampness-heat amassment pattern
髂窝脓肿/髂膿腫　iliac abscess
髂窝疝/髂窩疝　hernia intrailiaca
髂小肌/髂小肌　iliocapsularis muscle
髂胸联胎/髂胸連體嬰　iliothoracopagus
髂腰动脉/髂腰動脈　iliolumbar artery
髂腰动脉脊支/髂腰動脈脊支　spinal branch of

髂腰动脉/髂腰動脈 iliolumbar artery
髂腰动脉髂支/髂腰動脈髂支 iliac branch of iliolumbar artery
髂腰动脉腰支/髂腰動脈腰支 lumbar branch of iliolumbar artery
髂腰肌/髂腰肌 iliopsoas, iliopsoas muscle
髂腰静脉/髂腰静脉 iliolumbar vein
髂腰韧带/髂腰韌帶 iliolumbar ligament
髂支/髂支 iliac branch
髂总动脉/髂總動脈 common iliac artery
髂总静脉/髂總静脉 common iliac vein
髂总淋巴结/髂總淋巴結 common iliac lymph node
髂总内侧淋巴结/髂總内側淋巴結 medial common iliac lymph node
髂总外侧淋巴结/髂總外側淋巴結 lateral common iliac lymph node
髂总中间淋巴结/髂總中間淋巴結 intermediate common iliac lymph node
千柏鼻炎片/千柏鼻炎片 qianbai biyan tablets
千斤杖素/千斤杖素 flemingen
千金要方/千金要方 Qianjin Yao Fang
千金翼方/千金翼方 Qianjin Yi Fang
千金子/千金子 caper euphorbia seed
千里光病/千里光病,千里光屬植物中毒 senecio disease
千里光属植物/千里光屬植物 *Senecio*
千里光叶碱/劉寄奴素 senecifolin
千年健/千年健 obscured homalomena rhizome
千足虫/千足蟲 millipede
迁徙性钙化/轉移性石灰變性,轉移性石灰化 metastatic calcification
迁延放射/遷延輻射線 protraction radiation
迁延性扁桃体炎/遷延性扁桃腺炎 tonsillitis lenta
迁延性肺嗜酸细胞浸润症/遷延性肺嗜酸細胞浸潤症 prolonged pulmonary eosinophilia
迁延性肝炎/遷延性肝炎 persistent hepatitis
迁延性心内膜炎/漸進性心內膜炎 endocarditis lenta
迁移/遷移 migration
迁移瓣/跳躍皮片 jump flap
迁移的/移動的,遊走的 migratory
迁移皮瓣/遷移皮瓣 jump skin flap
迁移时间/遷移時間 migration time
迁移性静脉炎/遷移性静脉炎 migratory phlebitis
迁移移植片/跳躍性移植物 jump graft
牵拉痛/拉痛 dragging pain
牵拉性脱发/牽引性禿髮 traction alopecia
牵拉肘/牽引肘 pulled elbow

牵连观念/牽涉觀念 idea of reference
牵牛花综合征/牽牛花症候群 morning glory syndrome
牵牛子/牽牛子 kaladana, pharbitis seed
牵舌器/牽舌器 glossotilt
牵涉性[感觉]投射/牽涉性投射,感覺投射 eccentric projection
牵涉性痛/牽涉性痛 referred pain
牵伸运动/牽伸運動 stretch exercise
牵胎钩/牽胎器,牽胎術用鉗 embryulcus
牵引绷带/牽引繃帶 traction bandage
牵引绷带法/牽引繃帶法 traction bandaging
牵引感/牽曳 tugging
牵引钩/牽引鉤 hook
牵引夹板/牽引夾 traction splint
牵引疗法/牽引療法 traction therapy
牵引术/牽引 traction
牵引性动脉瘤/牽引性動脈瘤 traction aneurysm
牵张反射/牽張性反射 stretch reflex
牵正散/牽正散 qianzheng powder
铅笔头触痛/鉛筆壓痛 pencil tenderness
铅的/鉛的 saturnine
铅毒性黄疸/鉛毒性黄疸 saturnine jaundice
铅毒性口炎/鉛毒性口炎 lead stomatitis
铅毒性脑病/鉛毒性腦病 saturnine encephalopathy
铅毒性肾炎/鉛毒性腎炎 saturnine nephritis
铅放射性同位素/鉛放射性同位素 lead radioisotopes
铅管匠/鉛管匠 plumbers
铅管样强直/鉛管強硬 lead-pipe rigidity
铅疗法/鉛療法 plumbotherapy
铅色素/鉛色素 lead pigment
铅线/鉛線 halo saturninus
铅性紫质病/鉛性紫質病 plumboporphyria
铅中毒/鉛中毒 plumbism
铅中毒绞痛/鉛中毒絞痛 saturnine colic
铅[中]毒性关节痛/鉛毒關節痛 arthralgia saturnina
铅中毒[性]口臭/鉛中毒口臭,鉛味呼氣 lead breath, halitus saturninus
铅中毒性脑炎/鉛毒性大腦炎 saturnine cerebritis
铅中毒性痛风/鉛痛風 lead gout
荨麻/蕁麻 nettle
荨麻属/蕁麻屬 *Urtica*
前白蛋白/前白蛋白 prealbumin
前半规管/前半規管 anterior semicircular duct, ductus semicircularis anterior
前半抗原/前半抗原 prohapten
前半月瓣/前半月瓣 anterior semilunar valve

前背侧核/前背側核　anterodorsal nucleus
前鼻镜检查[法]/鼻前孔檢視法　anterior rhinoscopy
前鼻孔/前鼻孔　anterior naris
前壁/前壁　anterior wall
前壁心肌梗死/前端心肌梗塞　anterior myocardial infarction
前臂/前臂　forearm
前臂背侧皮神经/前臂背側皮神經　dorsal cutaneous nerve of forearm
前臂长/前臂長　forearm length
前臂分叉术/前臂分叉術　forearm splitting operation
前臂骨间背侧动脉/前臂骨間背側動脈　dorsal interosseous artery of forearm
前臂骨间膜/前臂骨間膜　interosseous membrane of forearm
前臂后骨筋膜鞘/前臂後骨筋膜鞘　posterior osseofascial compartment of forearm
前臂后皮神经/前臂後皮神經　posterior antebrachial cutaneous nerve
前臂后区/前臂後部　posterior antebrachial region
前臂筋膜/前臂筋膜　antebrachial fascia
前臂内侧肌间隔/前臂內側肌間隔　medial antebrachial intermuscular septum
前臂内侧皮神经/前臂內側皮神經　medial antebrachial cutaneous nerve, medial cutaneous nerve of forearm
前臂内侧皮神经后支/前臂內側皮神經後支　posterior branch of medial antebrachial cutaneous nerve
前臂内侧皮神经前支/前臂內側皮神經前支　anterior branch of medial antebrachial cutaneous nerve
前臂内侧缘/前臂內側緣　medial border of forearm
前臂盘状湿疹/前臂盤狀濕疹　forearms discoid eczema
前臂前侧骨间神经/前臂前側骨間神經　anterior interosseous nerve of forearm
前臂前骨筋膜鞘/前臂前骨筋膜鞘　anterior osseofascial compartment of forearm
前臂前区/前臂前部　anterior antebrachial region
前臂损伤/前臂損傷　forearm injury
前臂外侧肌间隔/前臂外側肌間隔　lateral antebrachial intermuscular septum
前臂外侧皮神经/前臂外側皮神經　lateral cutaneous nerve of forearm
前臂外侧缘/前臂外側緣　lateral border of forearm
前臂旋转计/旋前度計　pronometer
前臂游离皮瓣/前臂游離皮瓣　forearm free skin flap
前臂征/上臂徵象　forearm sign
前臂正中静脉/前臂正中靜脈　median antebrachial vein
前部/前部　anterior part
前部椎体间融合术/前介體融合術　anterior interbody fusion
前层/前層　anterior layer
前肠/前腸　foregut
前穿质/前穿質　anterior perforated substance
前穿质支/前篩質支　branch of anterior perforated substance
前床突/前床突　anterior clinoid process
前垂/前垂,凸出　proptosis
前唇/前唇　anterior lip
前次月经/前次月經　past menstrual period
前[促]胃液素/前胃激素,胃激素原　progastrin
前带/凝集前區　prozone
前单核细胞/前單核球　promonocyte
前蛋白转化酶类/前蛋白轉化酶類　proprotein convertases
前导/前導　anterior guidance
前底段/前底段　anterior basal segment
前底段支气管/前底段支氣管　anterior basal segmental bronchus
前底支/前底支　anterior basal branch
前骶丛/前骶叢　anterior sacral plexus
前电位/前電位　prepotential
前蝶骨/前蝶骨　presphenoidal bone
前顶/前頂　qianding, DU21
前顶间骨/前頂間骨　preinterparietal bone
前定位/前定位　prelocalization
前端/前端　anterior extremity
前端细胞/前子體　proter
前段/前段　anterior segment
前段动脉/前段動脈　anterior segmental artery
前段尿道炎/前段尿道炎　anterior urethritis
前段支气管/前段支氣管　anterior segmental bronchus
前额除皱术/前額除皺術　forehead rhytidectomy
前额的/額葉前部的　prefrontal
前额面喉切术/前額面喉切除術　anterior frontal laryngectomy
前额皮质/前額皮質　prefrontal cortex
前[额]囟/前[額]囟　anterior frontal fontanelle
前腭沟/前腭溝　anterior palatine groove
前房/前房,前室　anterior chamber
前房冲洗器/前房沖洗器　anterior chamber irrigator
前房出血/眼前房出血,眼前房積血　hyphema

前房穿刺术/前房穿刺術　paracentesis of anterior chamber
前房穿刺针/前房穿刺針　paracentesis needle
前房积脓性角膜炎/前房積膿性角膜炎　hypopyon keratitis
前房角/前房角　angle of anterior chamber
前房角成形术/前房角成形術　gonioplasty
前房角出血/前房角出血　goniohemorrhage
前房角发育不全/前房角發育不全　goniodysgenesis
前房角镜/前房角鏡　gonioscope
前房角镜检查/前房角鏡檢查　gonioscopy
前房角切开术/前房角切開術　goniotomy
前房角粘连/前房角粘連　goniosynechia
前分泌素/前分泌活素，分泌活素原　presecretin
前负荷/前負荷　preload
前负荷储量/前負荷儲量　preload reserve
前腹/前腹　anterior belly
前腹侧核/前腹側核　anteroventral nucleus
前概率/前概率　prior probability
前根/前根　anterior root
前根动脉/前根動脈　anterior radicular artery
前根静脉/前根靜脈　anterior root vein
前跟关节面/跟骨前關節面　anterior calcanean articular surface
前弓/前弓　anterior arch
前弓反张/前弓反張　episthotonos
前弓区/前弓區　anterior arch area
前巩膜葡萄肿/前鞏膜葡萄腫　anterior scleral staphyloma
前巩膜炎/前鞏膜炎　anterior scleritis
前谷/前谷　qiangu, SI2
前股/前股　anterior division
前骨壶腹/前骨壺腹　anterior bony ampulla
前骨间综合征/前骨間症候群　anterior interosseous syndrome
前骨性半规管/前骨性半規管　anterior osseous semicircular canal
前固有束/前固有束　anterior fasciculus proprius
前关节面/前關節面　anterior articular facet
前核/前核，原核　pronucleus
前核群/前核群　anterior nuclear group
前龀/齒前位咬合　anterior occlusion
前颌骨/前上頜骨　premaxillary bone
前黑[色]素体/前黑色素　premelanosome
前黑[色]素细胞/前黑色素細胞　premelanocyte
前黑色素小体/前黑色素小體　premelanosome
前后的/前後側的　anteroposterior
前后距面部发育不全/前後距面部發育不全　anteroposterior facial dysplasia
前后配穴法/前後配穴法　anterior-posterior points combination
前胡/前胡　hogfennel root
前壶腹神经/前壺腹神經　anterior ampullary nerve
前寰椎/前寰椎　proatlas
前激肽释放酶/前激肽釋放酶　prekallikrein
前极/前極　anterior pole
前极白内障/前極內障　anterior polar cataract
前脊髓动脉缺血综合征/前脊椎動脈症候群　anterior spinal artery syndrome
前加速因子/凝血第五因数　proaccelerin
前尖/前尖　anterior cusp
前降支/前降支　anterior descending branch
前交叉韧带/前交叉韌帶　anterior cruciate ligament
前交通动脉/前交通動脈　anterior communicating artery
前交通静脉/前交通靜脈　anterior communicating vein
前胶原/原膠原蛋白　procollagen
前胶原 N 内肽酶/前膠原 N 內肽酶　procollagen N-endopeptidase
前胶原脯氨酸二氧酶/溶膠原脯胺酸二氧酶　procollagen-proline dioxygenase
前角/前角　anterior horn
前角细胞/前角細胞　anterior horn cell
前脚/前腳　anterior crus
前结节/前結節　anterior tubercle
前界层/角膜前界　anterior limiting lamina
前距关节面/距骨前關節面　anterior talar articular surface
前锯肌/前鋸肌　serratus anterior, anterior serratus muscle
前锯肌粗隆/前鋸肌粗隆　tuberosity for serratus anterior
前肋横突韧带/前肋橫突韌帶　anterior costotransverse ligament
前类脂/前脂質，初脂質　prelipoid
前连合/前連合　anterior commissure
前连合喉切除术/前連合喉切除術　anterior commissure laryngectomy
前连合后部/前連合後部　posterior part of anterior commissure
前连合前部/前連合前部　anterior part of anterior commissure
前列地尔/前列地爾　alprostadil
前列环素合酶/前列腺環素合成酶　prostacyclin synthase

前列通片/前列通片　qianlietong tablets
前列腺/前列腺,攝護腺　prostate, prostatic gland
前列腺癌/前列腺癌　carcinoma of prostate
前列腺癌肉瘤/前列腺癌肉瘤　carcinosarcoma of prostate
前列腺按摩/前列腺按摩　massage of prostate
前列腺病/前列腺肥大症候群　prostatism
前列腺病态/前列腺病者心理變態　prostateria
前列腺部/前列腺部　prostatic part
前列腺测量器/前列腺測量器　prostatometer
前列腺丛/前列腺叢　prostatic plexus
前列腺导管/前列腺導管　prostatic duct
前列腺的/攝護腺的　prostatic
前列腺底/前列腺底　base of prostate
前列腺窦/前列腺竇　prostatic sinus
前列腺毒素/前列腺毒素　prostatotoxin
前列腺肥大/前列腺肥大　prostatauxe
前列腺分泌蛋白质类/前列腺分泌蛋白質類　prostatic secretory proteins
前列腺管/攝護腺管　duct of prostate gland
前列腺管内腺癌/前列腺管内腺癌　intraductal adenocarcinoma of prostate
前列腺后面/前列腺後面　posterior surface of prostate
前列腺环素/前列腺環素　prostacyclin
前列腺肌瘤切除术/前列腺肌瘤切除術　prostatomyomectomy
前列腺疾病/前列腺疾病　prostatic disease
前列腺尖/前列腺尖　apex of prostate
前列腺结核/前列腺結核　tuberculosis of prostate
前列腺结石/前列腺結石　calculus of prostate
前列腺筋膜/前列腺筋膜　prostatic fascia
前列腺精囊包虫病/前列腺精囊包蟲病　echinococcus disease of prostate and seminal vesicle
前列腺精囊切除术/前列腺與精囊切除術　prostaticovesiculectomy
前列腺精囊炎/前列腺精囊炎　prostatovesiculitis
前列腺静脉丛/前列腺静脈叢　prostatic venous plexus, Santorini venous plexus
前列腺静脉曲张/前列腺静脈曲張　prostatic pile
前列腺溃疡/前列腺潰瘍　prostatelcosis
前列腺冷冻术/前列腺冷凍術　cryosurgery of prostate
前列腺淋巴肉瘤/前列腺淋巴肉瘤　lymphosarcoma of prostate
前列腺梅毒/前列腺梅毒　syphilis of prostate
前列腺囊/前列腺囊　prostatic capsule, false spermatic vesicle
前列腺囊肿/前列腺囊腫　cyst of prostate
前列腺尿道/尿道前列腺部　prostatic urethra
前列腺凝结体/前列腺凝結體　prostatic concretion
前列腺脓肿/前列腺膿腫　abscess of prostate
前列腺膀胱切开术/前列腺膀胱切開術　prostatocystotomy
前列腺膀胱炎/前列腺膀胱炎　prostatocystitis
前列腺前面/前列腺前面　anterior surface of prostate
前列腺鞘/前列腺鞘　prostatic sheath
前列腺切除术/前列腺切除術　prostatectomy
前列腺切开术/前列腺切開術　prostatomy
前列腺肉瘤/前列腺肉瘤　sarcoma of prostate
前列腺上皮内瘤病/前列腺上皮内瘤病　prostatic intraepithelial neoplasia
前列腺 X 射线照相术/前列腺 X 光照相術　prostatography
前列腺石/前列腺石　prostatolith
前列腺石切除术/前列腺石切除術　prostatolithotomy
前列腺实质/攝護腺腺質　glandular substance of prostate
前列腺素/前列腺素　prostaglandin
前列腺素 E1/前列腺素 E1　Prostaglandin E1, PG E-1
前列腺素还原酶/前列腺素還原酶　prostaglandin reductase
前列腺素拮抗药/前列腺素拮抗藥　prostaglandin antagonist
前列腺素内过氧化物/前列腺素内過氧化物　prostaglandin endoperoxide
前列腺素受体/前列腺素受體　prostaglandin receptor
前列腺损伤/前列腺損傷　prostate injury
前列腺特异抗原/前列腺特異性抗原　prostate specific antigen
前列腺提肌/前列腺提肌,提前列腺肌　levator prostatae, levator muscle of prostate
前列腺痛/前列腺痛　prostatalgia
前列腺烷酸类/前列腺烷酸類　prostanoic acids
前列腺峡/前列腺峽　isthmus of prostate
前列腺下外侧面/前列腺下外側面　posteriolateral surface of prostate
前列腺腺癌/前列腺腺癌　adenocarcinoma of prostate
前列腺腺瘤/前列腺腺瘤　prostatic adenoma
前列腺小管/前列腺管　prostatic ductules
前列腺炎/前列腺炎,攝護腺炎　prostatitis

前列腺液溢/前列腺液溢　prostatorrhea
前列腺移行细胞癌/前列腺移行細胞癌　transitional cell carcinoma of prostate
前列腺右侧叶/前列腺右側葉　right lobe of prostate
前列腺增生/前列腺增生　prostatic hyperplasia
前列腺增生抑制药/前列腺增生抑制藥　prostate growth inhibitor
前列腺支/前列腺支　prostate branch
前列腺中叶/前列腺中葉　middle lobe of prostate
前列腺肿瘤/前列腺腫瘤　prostatic neoplasm
前列腺周炎/前列腺旁組織炎　extraprostatitis
前列腺子宫内膜样癌/前列腺子宮內膜樣癌　endometrioid carcinoma of prostate
前列腺左侧叶/前列腺左側葉　left lobe of prostate
前淋巴/前淋巴　prelymph
前淋巴细胞/前淋巴球　prolymphocyte
前B[淋巴]细胞/前B細胞　pre-B lymphocyte
前T[淋巴]细胞/前T[淋巴]細胞　pre-T lymphocyte
前颅窝/前顱窩　anterior cranial fossa
前毛细血管吻合/微血管前吻合　precapillary anastomosis
前酶原/前酵素原　prezymogen
前面/前面　anterior surface
前面轻叩/前面輕叩　front tap
前膜壶腹/前膜壺腹　anterior membranous ampulla
前磨牙/前臼齒　premolar
前囊白内障/前囊白內障　anterior capsular cataract
前脑/[胚胎]前腦　prosencephalon
前脑内侧束/前腦內側[神經]束　medial forebrain bundle
前脑腔/前腦腔　prosocele
前脑无裂畸形/前腦無裂畸形　holoprosencephaly
前内侧核/前內側核　anteromedial nucleus
前内侧面/前內側面　anteromedial surface
前内侧中央动脉/前內側中央動脈　anteromedial central artery
前尿道瓣膜/前尿道瓣　anterior urethral valve
前尿道淋病/前尿道淋病　anterior urethral gonorrhea
前尿道炎/尿道前端炎　preurethritis
前颞叶切除术/前顳葉切除術　anterior temporal lobectomy
前凝集带/前類凝集素區　proagglutinoid zone
前凝血质/促凝劑,凝血劑原　procoagulant
前皮支/前皮支　anterior cutaneous branch
前破裂孔/前破裂孔　anterior lacerate foramen
前葡萄膜炎/前葡萄膜炎　anterior uveitis

前期白斑/前期白斑　preleukoplakia
前期肝硬变/初[期肝]硬化　precirrhosis
前期牙本质/初齒質,原齒質,前齒質　predentin
前期牙质/前牙質　dentinoid
前期综合征/前期症候群　per-excitation syndrome
前气门亚目/前氣門亞目　Prostigmata
前腔/前腔　anterior cavity
前侵袭素/入侵素原　pro-invasin
前丘脑核/前丘腦核　anterior thalamic nucleus
前驱斑/先驅斑　herald patch
前驱麻醉药/麻醉前誘導藥　preanesthetic
前驱期/前驅期　prodromal period
前驱期近视/前驅性近視　prodromal myopia
前驱期青光眼/前驅期青光眼　glaucoma imminens
前驱[轻]鼠疫/前驅性鼠疫　premonitory plague
前驱糖尿病/糖尿病前期　prediabetes
前驱阵痛/前驅陣痛　permonitory pain
前屈/前傾,前曲　antexion
前染色体/初染色體　prochromosome
前绒毛/初絨毛膜,卵蛋白膜　prochorion
前乳头肌/前乳頭肌　anterior papillary muscle
前软骨/初軟骨,胎軟骨　precartilage
前软骨组织/前軟骨組織　protochondrial tissue
前筛窦/前篩竇　anterior ethmoidal sinus
前哨淋巴结/前哨淋巴結　sentinel node
前哨淋巴结活组织检查/前哨淋巴結活組織檢查　sentinel lymph node biopsy
前哨痔/前哨痔　sentinel pile
前摄抑制/前促動抑制　proactive inhibition
前伸关系/前伸關係　protrusive relation
前伸𬌗/前伸𬌗　protrusive occlusion
前伸记录/突出記錄　protrusive record
前伸髁导斜度/前伸髁導斜度　inclination of protrusive condylar guidance
前伸平衡/前伸平衡　protrusive balance
前伸平衡𬌗/前伸平衡𬌗　protrusive balanced occlusion
前伸运动/前伸移動　protrusive movement
前神经孔/前神經孔　anterior neuropore
前肾/胚胎原肾,胚胎前肾　forekidney
前肾管/前腎管　pronephric duct
前升支/前昇支　anterior ascending branch
前视内镜/前視內鏡　forward-viewing endoscope
前室间静脉/前室間靜脈　anterior interventricular vein
前室间支/前室間支　anterior interventricular branch
前嗜铬组织/前嗜鉻組織　prechromaffin tissue
前噬菌体/前噬菌體,原噬菌體　probacteriophage

前髓帆组织/上帆　epitela
前髓细胞/前髓細胞　promyelocyte
前索/前索　anterior funiculus
前体/前驱物　precursor
前庭/前庭　vestibul
前庭襞/前庭皺襞　vestibular fold
前庭测量[法]/前庭測量[法]　vestibulometry
前庭成形术/口前庭造形術　vestibuloplasty
前庭窗/前庭窗　fenestra vestibuli
前庭窗小窝/前庭窗小凹　fossula of fenestra vestibuli
前庭唇/前庭唇　vestibular lip
前庭大腺/前庭大腺,巴特林氏腺　greater vestibular gland, Bartholin gland
前庭大腺囊肿/前庭大腺囊腫　Bartholin cyst
前庭大腺囊肿切除术/前庭大腺囊腫切除術　excision of Bartholin gland cyst
前庭大腺囊肿造口术/前庭大腺囊腫造口術　marsupialization of Bartholin gland cyst
前庭大腺脓肿/前庭大腺膿腫　abscess of Bartholin gland
前庭大腺炎/巴特林氏腺炎　bartholinitis
前庭毒性/前庭毒性　vestibulotoxicity
前庭盾/前庭盾　vestibular shield
前庭耳蜗神经疾病/前庭耳蝸神經疾病　vestibulocochlear nerve diseases
前庭感觉/前庭感覺　vestibular sense
前庭肛门/前庭肛門　anus vestibularis
前庭功能试验/前庭功能試驗　vestibular function test
前庭共济失调/前庭性失調症　vestibular ataxia
前庭沟扩展术/前庭溝擴展術　vestibular extension
前庭管静脉/前庭管静脈　vena aqueductus vestibuli
前庭喉炎/前庭性喉炎　vestibular laryngitis
前庭疾病/前庭疾病　vestibular diseases
前庭嵴/前庭嵴　vestibular crest
前庭脊[髓]束/前庭脊[髓]徑　vestibulospinal tract
前庭脊椎的/前庭脊椎的　vestibulospinal
前庭阶/前庭階　vestibular scale
前庭静脉/前庭静脈　vestibular vein
前庭框架/前庭框架　vestibular frame
前庭裂/[喉]前庭裂　vestibular fissure
前庭盲端/前庭盲端　vestibular cecum
前庭毛细胞/前庭毛細胞　vestibular hair cell
前庭迷路/前庭迷路　vestibular labyrinth
前庭面/前庭面　vestibular surface
前庭膜/前庭膜　vestibular membrane
前庭内侧核/前庭内側核　medial vestibular nucleus

前庭球/前庭球　bulb of vestibule
前庭球动脉/前庭球動脈　vestibular bulbar artery
前庭球静脉/前庭球静脈　vestibular bulbar vein
前庭球体静脉/前庭球體静脈　vein of bulb of vestibule
前庭球中间部/前庭球中間部　intermediate part of bulb
前庭区/前庭區　vestibular area
前庭韧带/前庭韌帶　vestibular ligament
前庭上核/前庭上核　superior vestibular nucleus
前庭上区/前庭上區　superior vestibular area
前庭神经/前庭神經　vestibular nerve
前庭神经核/前庭神經核　vestibular nucleus
前庭神经脊束/前庭神經脊徑　spinal tract of vestibular nerve
前庭神经节/前庭神經節　vestibular ganglion
前庭神经节上部/前庭神經節上部　superior part of vestibular ganglion
前庭神经节下部/前庭神經節下部　inferior part of vestibular ganglion
前庭神经切除术/前庭神經切除術　vestibular neurectomy
前庭神经炎/前庭神經炎　vestibular neuritis
前庭水管/前庭水管　vestibular aqueduct
前庭水管静脉/前庭水管静脈　vein of vestibular aqueduct
前庭水管内口/前庭水管内口　internal aperture of vestibular aqueduct
前庭水管外口/前庭水管外口　external aperture of aqueduct of vestibule
前庭外侧核/前庭外側核　lateral vestibular nucleus
前庭蜗器/前庭蝸器,位聽器[官]　vestibulocochlear organ
前庭蜗神经/前庭耳蝸神經　vestibulocochlear nerve
前庭习服/前庭習服　vestibular habituation
前庭下核/前庭下核　inferior vestibular nucleus
前庭下区/前庭下區　inferior vestibular area
前庭下区单孔/前庭下區單孔　single foramen of inferior vestibular area
前庭小管静脉/前庭小管静脈　vein of aqueduct of vestibule
前庭小脑束/前庭小腦束　vestibulocerebellar tract
前庭小腺/前庭小腺　lesser vestibular gland
前庭性眩晕/前庭性眩暈　vestibular vertigo
前庭炎/前庭炎　vestibulitis
前庭眼反射/前庭眼反射　vestibuloocular reflex
前庭支/前庭支　vestibular branch
前庭锥体/前庭錐體　pyramid of vestibule

前透镜/前透鏡 frontal lens
前突/前突 anterior process
前蜕膜细胞/前蛻膜細胞 predecidual cell
前外侧的/前外側的 anterolateral
前外侧沟/前外側溝 anterolateral sulcus
前外侧核/前外側核 anterolateral nucleus
前外侧脊髓丘脑束/前外側脊髓丘腦束 anterolateral spinothalamic tract
前外侧开胸术/前外側開胸術 anterolateral thoracotomy
前外侧面/前外側面 anterolateral surface
前外侧皮质脊髓束/前外側皮質脊髓束 anterolateral corticospinal tract
前外侧囟/前外側囟 anterolateral fontanelle
前外侧中央动脉/前外側中央動脈 anterolateral central arteries
前外弓状纤维/前外弓狀纖維 anterior external arcuate fiber
前维生素/前維生素 previtamin
前位/向前變位,前移 anteposition
前B细胞白血病/前B細胞白血病 pre-B-cell leukemia
前腺支/前腺支 anterior glandular branch
前向性心力衰竭/前行性心衰竭 forward heart failure
前斜角肌/前斜角肌 scalenus anterior, anterior scalene muscle
前斜角肌结节/前斜角肌結節 scalene tubercle
前斜角肌综合征/前斜角肌症候群,Naffziger氏症候群 scalenus-anticus syndrome, Naffziger syndrome
前囟/前囟,大囟 anterior fontanelle, anterior fontanel, bregma
前囟测压计/前囟測壓計 anterior fontanel monometer
前囟穿刺术/前囟穿刺術 puncture of anterior fontanelle
前囟点/前囟點 bregma
前囟骨/前囟骨 bregmatic bone
前囟联胎畸形/前囟連胎 bregmatodymia
前胸壁浅表血栓性静脉炎/前胸壁淺表血栓性靜脈炎 superficial thrombophlebitis of anterior chest wall
前胸壁综合征/前胸壁症候群 anterior chest wall syndrome
前牙/前牙,前齒,門齒 anterior tooth
前牙暗间隙/前牙暗間隙 anterior tooth dark space
前牙本质/前齒質,初齒質,原齒質 predentin

前牙言语空隙/前牙言語空隙 anterior tooth speech space
前沿轨道/前沿軌道 frontier orbital
前羊水/前羊水 forewaters
前药/前驅藥,準藥 prodrug
前叶/前葉 anterior lobe
前叶垂体/前葉垂體 anterior pituitary gland
前移/移前 advance
前阴/前陰,外生殖器 external genitalia
前缘/前緣 anterior border
前瞻性研究/前瞻性研究 prospective study
前褶柱/前皺襞 anterior column of ruga
前正中沟/前正中溝 anteromedian groove
前正中裂/前正中裂 anterior median fissure
前正中线/前正中線 anterior median line
前支/前支 anterior branch
前脂肪细胞/前脂肪細胞 pre-adipocyte
前致癌物/前致癌物 procarcinogen
前置/向前變位 antelocation
前置肌瘤/前置肌瘤 myoma praevium
前置胎盘/前置胎盤 placenta praevia, placenta previa
前中期/前中期 prometaphase
前终静脉/前終靜脈 anterior terminal vein
前主静脉/前主靜脈 anterior cardinal vein, anterior cardinal veins
前柱/前柱 anterior column
前纵隔/前縱隔 anterior mediastinum, mediastinum anterius
前纵韧带/前縱韌帶 anterior longitudinal ligament
钱币形的/錢幣狀的 nummular
钱币形损害/錢幣形病灶 coin lesion
钱币征/錢幣徵象 coin sign
钱币状角膜炎/錢幣狀角膜炎 nummular keratitis
钱币状融合乳头状瘤病/錢幣狀融合乳頭狀瘤病 nummular confluent papillomatosis
钱币状湿疹/錢幣狀濕疹 eczema nummulare
钱币状痰/錢幣狀痰 nummular sputum
钱币状银屑病/錢幣狀牛皮癬 psoriasis nummularis
钱币状主动脉炎/錢幣狀主動脈炎 nummular aortitis
钱伯伦产钳/夏伯倫氏產鉗 Chamberlen forceps
钱德勒毡领夹板/Chandler氏氈頸圈夾板 Chandler felt collar splint
钱斯背夹板/Chance氏背夾板 Chance back splint
钳闭的/箝閉的 incarcerated
钳夹活检[术]/鉗夾活檢[術] forceps biopsy
钳取器/異物取除器 protractor

钳胎术/鉗胎術　embryulcia
钳形连接/連鉤連結　clamp connection
钳压法/鉗壓法　forcipressure
潜出血/隱出血　occult bleeding
潜伏癌/潛伏癌　latent cancer
潜伏病毒/潛伏型病毒　latent virus
潜伏的/潛伏的　latent
潜伏化/潛伏化　latentiation
潜伏梅毒/潛伏梅毒　latent syphilis
潜伏期/潛伏期　latent period
潜伏[性]变态反应/潛[伏]性過敏　latent allergy
潜伏性腹膜炎/静止腹膜炎　silent peritonitis
潜伏性黄疸/潛伏性黃疸　latent jaundice
潜伏性甲状腺功能亢进/潛伏性甲狀腺機能亢進　latent hyperthyrodidsm
潜伏性痛风/潛伏性痛風　latent gout
潜伏影像/潛像　latent image
潜涵聋/潛涵聾　caisson deafness
潜能的/潜在的,可能的　potential
潜热/潛熱　latent heat
潜神经胶质瘤/隱神經膠質瘤　cryptoglioma
潜水性腹震荡/腹部震蕩　hydraulic abdominal concussion
潜水医学/潛水醫學　submarine medicine
潜水员病/潛水夫病　caisson sickness
潜水员耳炎/潛水夫耳炎　diver ear
潜水员麻痹/潛水夫癱瘓　diver palsy
潜行剥离/潛行剝離　undermining dissection
潜行的/潛行性　undermined
潜行性龋/潛蝕性齲　undermining caries
潜性月经/潛性月經　latent menstruation
潜蓄脓/潛蓄膿　latent empyema
潜血/隱血　occult blood
潜阳息风/潛陽息風　subduing exuberant liver yang and checking wind
潜意识/潛意識　unconscious
潜意识显露/潛意識顯露　acting out
潜意识抑制/潛意識的抑制　freudian censor
潜隐内容/潛藏内容　latent content
潜隐体/潛隱體,隱種蟲　cryptozoite
潜隐型精神分裂症/潛伏型精神分裂症　latent schizophrenia
潜在的/潛在的　underlying
潜在损伤/潛在損傷　potential trauma
潜在性感染/潛伏性傳染　latent infection
潜在性手足搐搦/潛伏性肢搦病　latent tetany
潜在致癌物/潛在致癌原　potential carcinogen
潜蚤病/沙蚤病　dermatophilus disease

潜知觉/下知覺,潛意識　subception
浅表肌腱膜系统/淺表肌腱膜系統　superficial musculoaponeurotic system
浅表扩散性黑[色]素瘤/淺表擴散性黑[色]素瘤　superficial spreading melanoma
浅表肾单位/淺表腎單元　superficial nephron
浅表性基底细胞上皮瘤/淺表性基底細胞上皮瘤　superficial basal cell epithelioma
浅表性脓疱性毛囊炎/淺表性膿皰性毛囊炎　superficial pustular folliculitis
浅表性皮肤脂肪瘤痣/淺表性皮膚脂肪瘤痣　nevus lipomatosis cutaneous superficialis
浅表性胃炎/淺表性胃炎　superficial gastritis
浅表性肢端纤维黏液瘤/表淺性肢端纖維黏液瘤　superficial acral fibromyxoma
浅部/淺部　superficial part
浅部真菌病/淺部真菌病　superficial mycosis
浅层/[顳筋膜]淺層[板]　superficial lamella, superficial layer
浅层点状角膜炎/淺層點狀角膜炎　superficial punctate keratitis
浅[层]皮质/淺[層]皮質　peripheral cortex
浅层视网膜出血/淺層視網膜出血　superficial retinal hemorrhage
浅层支/淺層支　ramus superficialis
浅的/淺的　superficialis
浅二度烧伤/淺二度燒傷　superficial the second degree burn
浅肱动脉/淺肱動脈　superficial brachial artery
浅环内侧脚/淺環内側腳　medial crus of superficial inguinal ring
浅环外侧脚/淺環外側腳　lateral crus of superficial inguinal ring
浅筋膜/淺筋膜　superficial fascia
浅静脉/淺靜脈　superficial vein
浅静脉炎/淺靜脈炎　superficial phlebitis
浅蓝菌素/變藍菌素　cerulenin
浅淋巴管/淺淋巴管　superficial lymphatic vessel
浅淋巴结/淺淋巴結　superficial lymph node
浅脓疱性毛囊周炎/表淺膿皰性毛囊周圍炎　superficial pustular perifolliculitis
浅色的/淡染的,著色不足的　hypochromic
浅头/淺頭　superficial head
浅掌动脉弓/淺掌動脈弓　superficial palmar arterial arch
浅支/淺支　superficial branch
浅椎静脉/淺椎靜脈　superficial vertebral vein
芡莲丹/芡蓮丹　gordon eryale and lotus plumule

pill, qianlian pill
芡实/芡實 gordon euryale seed
茜草/茜草 India madder root
茜素/茜草素 alizarin
茜素亮紫3B/茜素亮紫3B alizarin brilliant violet 3B
茜素亮紫R/茜素亮紫R alizarin brilliant violet R
茜素青绿/茜素青綠 alizarin viridine
茜素试验/茜草素試驗 alizarin test
嵌杯病毒科感染/嵌杯病毒科感染 Caliciviridae infections
嵌插缝合/嵌插縫合 tongue-groove suture
嵌插骨折/嵌插骨折 impacted fracture
嵌顿包茎/嵌頓包莖,箝閉包莖 paraphimosis
嵌顿性疝/箝閉性疝[氣] incarcerated hernia
嵌顿痔/嵌頓痔 incarcerated hemorrhoid
嵌合/嵌合,釘狀關節 gomphosis, dentoalveolar joint, peg and socket joint
嵌合素蛋白质类/嵌合素蛋白質類 chimericin proteins
嵌合体/嵌合體 chimera
嵌合状态/嵌合體特質 chimerism
嵌甲/嵌甲 onychocryptosis
嵌入的/嵌入的 impacted
嵌入法/嵌入法 inlays
嵌入骨折/嵌入骨折 impaction fracture
嵌入剂/嵌入劑 intercalating agent
嵌入性胎盘/嵌入性胎盤 placenta increta
嵌入性牙周膜/嵌入性齒周膜 periodontium insertionis
嵌套基因/重叠基因 nested gene
嵌体/鑲體 inlay
嵌体固位体/嵌入固位體 inlay retainer
嵌体蜡/鑲補蠟 inlay wax
嵌体铸模蜡/嵌體鑄模蠟 inlay casting wax
羌活胜湿汤/羌活勝濕湯 qianghuo shengshi decoction
枪刺刀畸形/槍刺刀畸形 bayonet-like deformity
枪刺毛发/槍刺狀毛 bayonet hair
枪刺形腿/槍刺形腿 bayonet leg
枪弹擦伤/槍彈擦傷 bullet splash injury
枪[击创]伤/槍[擊創]傷 gunshot wound
枪状双腔吸虫/槍狀雙腔吸蟲,槍形吸蟲 Dicrocoelium dendriticum
腔/腔 cava
腔孢纲/腔菌綱 Coelomycetes
腔肠虫/腔腸蟲 cavitary
腔肠淀粉酶/海葵澱粉酶 actinodiastase
腔肠动物[的]/腔腸動物[的] cnidarian
腔肠动物毒液类/腔腸動物毒液類 cnidarian venoms
腔肠动物门/腔腸動物門 Coelenterata
腔道泌尿外科学/腔道泌尿外科學 endourology
腔静脉/腔靜脈 vena cava
腔静脉插管[术]/腔靜脈插管[術] cannulation of vena cava
腔静脉的/腔靜脈的 caval
腔静脉窦/腔靜脈竇 sinus venarum cavarum
腔静脉沟/腔靜脈溝 sulcus for vena cava
腔静脉后淋巴结/腔靜脈後淋巴結 postcaval lymph node
腔静脉后输尿管/腔靜脈後輸尿管 retrocaval ureter
腔静脉孔/腔靜脈孔 vena caval foramen, opening for vena cava
腔静脉滤器/腔靜脈濾器 vena cava filter
腔静脉前淋巴结/腔靜脈前淋巴結 precaval lymph node
腔静脉外侧淋巴结/腔靜脈外側淋巴結 lateral caval lymph node
腔静脉系膜/腔靜脈繫膜 caval mesentery
腔静脉炎/腔靜脈炎 cavitis
腔静脉照相术/腔靜脈攝影術 venacavography
腔口[皮肤]结核/腔口[皮膚]結核 orificial tuberculosis
腔口周围浆细胞增多综合征/腔口周圍漿細胞增多症候群 syndrome of circumorificial plasmacytosis
腔内放射[法]/腔内照射法 intracavitary irradiation
腔上囊/洩殖腔囊 cloacal bursa
腔上囊类同器官/洩殖腔囊類同器官 bursa equivalent
[腔上]囊依赖淋巴细胞/囊依存性淋巴球 bursa-dependent lymphocyte
腔隙的/腔隙的,陷窩的 lacunar
腔隙内侧淋巴结/腔隙內側淋巴結 medial lacunar lymph node
腔隙韧带/腔隙韌帶,陷窩韌帶 lacunar ligament
腔隙外侧淋巴结/腔隙外側淋巴結 lateral lacunar lymph node
腔隙中间淋巴结/腔隙中間淋巴結 intermediate lacunar lymph node
腔液音/液體動蕩聲 hydatism
蜣螂蛀/蜣螂蛀 dung beetle erosion, tuberculosis of finger joint
强安定药/強安定藥 major tranquilizer
强擦按摩法/強擦按摩法 rubbing massage
强二波脉[现象]/重脈搏過顯,雙脈搏過強

hyperdicrotism
强啡肽类/強啡肽類　dynorphins
强光眼炎/光照性眼炎,曝光眼炎　photophthalmia
强化分级表/強化分級表　reinforcement schedule
强化乳/加强乳　fortified milk
强化食品/強化食品　fortified food
强间/強間　qiangjian, DU18
强筋壮骨/強筋壯骨　strengthening tendons and bones
强力呼吸/強力呼吸　forced respiration
强闪光眼炎/強閃光眼炎　flash photo-ophthalmia
强心苷/強心苷　cardiac glycoside
强心苷元/強心苷元　cardiac aglycone
强心剂/強心劑　cardiocinetic
强心利尿药/強心性利尿藥　cardiac diuretic
强心药/強心藥　cardiotonic
强心甾/強心類固醇　cardenolide
强银蛋白质/強銀蛋白質　strong sliver protein
强荧光/強螢光　hyperfluorescence
强直/強直　rigidity
强直病/僵病　stiff sickness
强直测验计/強直測量計　tetanometer
强直发作/緊張性癲癇發作　tonic seizure
强直反射/強直性反射　tonic reflex
强直痉挛/強直性痙攣　tonic spasm
强直性步态/強直性步態　tetanic gait
强直性昏厥发作/強直性昏厥發作　cataleptic attack
强直性肌肉营养不良/強直性肌肉營養不良症　myotonic muscular dystrophy
强直性脊柱炎/強直性脊柱炎,關節粘連性脊椎炎　ankylosing spondylitis
强直性惊厥/強直性抽搐　tetanic convulsion
强直性瞳孔/瞳孔強直　stiff pupil
强直阵挛发作/強直陣攣發作　tonic clonic seizure
强直阵挛性癫痫/強直陣攣性癲癇　tonic-clonic epilepsy
强直阵挛性痉挛/強直陣攣性痙攣　tonic-clonic spasm
强直状不动反应/強直狀不動反應　tonic immobility response
强制搏动/強制搏動　forced beat
强制性痴笑/強笑　compulsive laughter
强制性体检/強制性體檢　mandatory testing
强中[病]/強中[病]　persistent erection
蔷薇色发癣菌/玫瑰色毛癬菌　Trichophyton rosaceum
蔷薇油/玫瑰花油　rose oil
蔷薇疹病毒感染/蔷薇疹病毒感染　Roseolovirus infection
羟胺/羥胺　hydroxylamine
羟苯丙酮/羥苯丙酮　hydroxypropiophenone
羟苯磺酸钙/羥苯磺酸鈣　calcium dobesilate
羟苯异丙胺/羥安非他命　hydroxyamphetamine
羟苄羟麻黄碱/利托君　ritodrine
羟布宗/羥布宗　oxyphenbutazone
羟雌酮类/羥雌酮類　hydroxyestrones
羟丁酸/羥丁酸　hydroxybutyric acid
羟丁酸钠/羥丁酸鈉　sodium oxybate
羟丁酸脱氢酶/羥丁酸脱氫酶　hydroxybutyrate dehydrogenase
β-羟丁酸脱氢酶/β羥丁酸脱氫酶　beta hydroxybutyric dehydrogenase
羟丁酸盐类/羥丁酸鹽類　hydroxybutyrates
羟多巴胺/羥多巴胺　oxidopamine
羟睾酮类/羥睾酮類　hydroxytestosterones
羟谷氨酸/羥基麩胺酸　hydroxyglutamic acid
羟钴胺/羥鈷胺　hydroxocobalamin
羟化苯甲酸汞类/羥化苯甲酸汞類　hydroxymercuribenzoates
羟化钙/羥化鈣　calcium hydroxide
羟化酶/羥基化酶　hydroxylase
羟化酶缺乏/水解酶缺乏症　hydroxylase deficiency
羟化四甲铵/四甲基氫氧化銨　tetramethylammonium hydroxide
羟化物类/羥化物類　hydroxides
羟基/羥基　hydroxyl
羟基胺/羥基胺　hydramine
羟基苯甲酸类/羥基苯甲酸類　hydroxybenzoic acids
羟基胆骨化醇类/羥基膽骨化醇類　hydroxycholecalciferols
羟基胆固醇类/羥基膽甾醇類　hydroxycholesterols
羟基蛋白酸/羥基蛋白酸　oxyproteinic acid
羟基多巴胺类/羥基多巴胺類　hydroxydopamines
羟基蒽醌/羥基蒽醌　hydroxyanthraquinone
羟基化/羥基化　hydroxylation
羟基喹啉类/羥喹啉類　hydroxyquinolines
羟基磷灰石类/羥基磷灰石類　hydroxyapatites
羟基硫胺/氧硫胺　oxythiamine
羟基脲/羥基尿素　hydroxyurea
羟基皮质甾醇类/羥基皮質甾醇類　hydroxycorticosteroids
羟基嘌呤/氧基嘌呤　oxypurine
羟基脯氨酸尿症/羥基脯胺酸尿症　hydroxyprolinuria
α羟基酸/阿爾發羥基酸　alpha hydroxy acid
羟基吲哚乙酸/羥基吲哚乙酸　hydroxyindoleacetic

羟基游离根/羥基游離根　hydrocyl radical
羟甲基胆色烷合酶/羥甲基膽色烷合酶　hydroxymethylbilane synthase
羟甲基戊二酰 CoA 合酶类/羥甲基戊二酸輔酶甲合成酶　hydroxymethylglutaryl-CoA synthase
羟甲基戊二酰基 CoA 还原酶抑制剂/羥甲基戊二醯基 CoA 還原酶抑制劑　hydroxymethylglutaryl-CoA reductase inhibitor
羟甲基吲哚/氧糞質基　skatoxyl
羟甲烯龙/羥甲烯龍　oxymetholone
羟甲香豆素/羥甲香豆素　hymecromone
羟甲雄二烯酮/羥甲雄二烯酮　methandrostenolone
羟甲亚甲孕酮/羥甲亞甲孕酮　melengestrol
羟甲唑啉/羥甲唑啉　oxymetazoline
羟可酮/14-羥基二氢可待因酮　oxycodone
羟喹啉/氧基喹啉　oxyquinoline
羟赖氨酸/羥基離胺酸, 羥基賴胺酸　hydroxylysine
羟类固醇/羥類固醇　hydroxysteroid
羟类固醇脱氢酶缺乏/羥類固醇去氫酶缺乏　hydroxysteroid dehydrogenase deficiency
羟磷灰石/羥磷灰石　calcium phosphate hydroxide
羟磷灰石结晶/氫氧磷灰石結晶　hydroxyapatite crystal
羟氯奎宁/羥氯奎寧　hydroxy chloroquine
羟氯喹/羥氯喹　hydroxychloroquine
羟氯柳苯胺/羥氯扎胺　oxyclozanide
羟吗啡酮/氧嗎啡酮　oxymorphone
羟萘甲酸/羥基萘甲酸　hydroxynaphthoic acid
羟脑苷脂/腦脂　cerebron
羟脯氨酸/羥基脯胺酸　hydroxyproline
羟前列腺素脱氢酶类/羥前列腺素脱氫酶類　hydroxyprostaglandin dehydrogenases
羟嗪/羥乙氧呱嗪　hydroxyzine
羟色胺/羥色胺　hydroxytryptamine
5-羟色胺能神经元/5-羥色胺能神經元　serotoninergic neuron
5-羟色胺受体拮抗药/5-羥色胺受體拮抗藥　serotonin receptor antagonist
羟色醇/羥色氨乙醇　hydroxytryptophol
羟酸类/羥酸類　hydroxy acids
羟肟酸类/羥銨酸　hydroxamic acids
羟缬氨酸/羥基纈胺酸　hydroxyvaline
羟乙磺酸/羥乙基磺酸　isethionic acid
羟乙磺酸羟芪脒/羥乙磺酸羥蔗脒, 羥二脒蔗羥乙磺酸鹽　hydroxystilbamidine isethionate
羟乙基/羥乙基　hydroxyethyl
羟乙基阿朴叩卜林/羥乙基阿朴叩卜林　hydroxyethylapocupreine
羟乙基阿朴奎宁/羥乙基阿朴奎寧　hydroxyethylapoquinine
羟乙基淀粉/羥乙基澱粉　hetastarch
羟乙基云香苷/羥乙基雲香甙　hydroxyethylrutoside
羟乙磷酸/羥乙磷酸　etidronic acid
羟乙烯聚合物钙钾/羥乙烯聚合物鈣鉀　calcium potassium carboxyvinylpolymer
羟乙酰胺基芴/羥乙醯胺基芴　hydroxyacetylaminofluorene
羟吲哚磺酸/氧吲哚磺酸　indoxylsulfonic acid
羟吲哚生物碱/羥吲哚生物鹼　oxindole alkaloid
羟吲哚酸/氧吲哚酸　indoxylic acid
羟硬脂酸/羥硬脂酸　hydroxystearate
羟硬脂酸胆固醇酯/羥硬脂酸膽固醇酯　cholesterol hydroxystearate
羟孕酮/羥基黃體素　hydroxyprogesterone
羟孕酮酯钠/羥孕二酮鈉　hydroxydione sodium
羟甾类/羥甾類　hydroxysteroids
羟甾类脱氢酶类/羥甾類脱氫酶類　hydroxysteroid dehydrogenases
羟值/羥價　hydroxyl value
羟自由基/羥自由基　hydroxyl radical
强迫沉思状态/強迫沈思狀態　obsessive ruminative state
强迫的/強迫的　compulsive
强迫动作/強迫行爲　compulsive act
强迫观念/強迫觀念　obsessive idea
强迫行为/強迫行爲　compulsive act
强迫型人格障碍/強迫型人格障礙　obsessive-compulsive personality disorder
强迫性对立观念/強迫性對立觀念　obsessive contradictory idea
强迫性核对/強迫性核對　compulsive checking
强迫性怀疑/強迫性懷疑　obsessive doubt
强迫性回忆/強迫性回憶　obsessive reminiscence
强迫性计数/強迫性計數　compulsive counting
强迫性精神病/強迫性精神病　compulsive insanity
强迫性恐怖/強迫性恐怖　obsessive phobias
强迫性清洁/強迫性清潔　compulsive cleaning
强迫性穷思竭虑/強迫性思想　obsessive rumination
强迫性人格障碍/強迫性人格障礙　compulsive personality disorder
强迫性神经功能症/強迫觀念性神經病　obsessional neurosis
强迫性神经症/強迫性神經症　obsessive-compulsive neurosis
强迫性[疼]痛/強迫性疼痛　imperative pain

强迫性习惯/強迫性習慣　compulsive habit
强迫性仪式动作/強迫性儀式動作　compulsive ritual
强迫性障碍/強迫性障礙　obsessive-compulsive disorder
强迫性震颤/強迫性震顫　forced tremor
强迫症/強迫症　obsessive compulsive disorder
强迫周期/強搏心週期　forced cycle
强迫状态/強迫狀態　obsessive state
乔布综合征/Job 氏症候群　Job syndrome
乔丹畸形/Jordan 氏異常　Jordan anomaly
荞麦中毒/蕎麥中毒　fagopyrism
桥本甲状腺炎/橋本氏甲狀腺炎　Hashimoto thyroiditis
桥本甲状腺炎伴甲状腺毒症/橋本甲狀腺炎伴甲狀腺毒症　Hashimoto toxicosis
桥池/橋池　pontine cistern
桥固位体/牙橋固位體,牙齒矯正器　bridge retainer
桥环杂环化合物/橋環雜環化合物　bridged-ring heterocyclic compound
桥基/橋基　abutment
桥基化合物/橋基化合物　bridged compound
桥基牙/牙橋　abutment tooth
桥接坏死/橋接壞死　bridging necrosis
桥跨现象/橋跨現象　bridging phenomenon
桥粒/橋粒,胞橋小體　desmosome
桥连抗生物素蛋白-生物素法/橋連抗生物素蛋白-生物素法　bridged avidin-biotin method, BAB method
桥体/橋體　pontic
桥形缺损/橋狀眼器官裂開　bridge coloboma
桥形石膏绷带/橋形石膏繃帶　interrupted plaster-of-paris
桥形移植物/橋狀移植物　bridge graft
桥形皱襞/橋形皺襞　bridging fold
桥延沟静脉/橋延溝静脈　vein of the pontomedullary sulcus
桥延体核/橋延體核　nucleus of pontobulbar body
桥状瘢痕/橋狀瘢痕　bridged scar
巧克力样囊肿/巧克力色卵巢囊腫　chocolate cyst
翘鼻/翹鼻　pug nose
鞘/鞘　sheath
鞘氨醇/神經鞘胺醇　sphingosine
鞘翅目/鞘翅目　Coleoptera
鞘杆菌属/莢膜樣菌屬　Calymmatobacterium
鞘间隙/鞘間隙　intervaginal space
鞘磷脂类/鞘磷脂類　sphingomyelin
鞘磷脂磷酸二酯酶/鞘磷脂磷酸二酯酶　sphingomyelin phosphodiesterase
鞘毛细血管/鞘毛細管　sheathed capillary
鞘膜积脓/膿囊,膿性囊腫　pyocele
鞘膜积液培养基/鞘膜積液培養基　hydrocele fluid media
鞘膜囊疝/鞘膜囊疝　hernia interna vaginalis testiculi
鞘膜内腹水/鞘膜內腹水　ascites vaginalis
鞘内注射/鞘內注射　intrathecal injection
鞘蕊花属/彩葉草屬　Coleus
鞘突/鞘狀突　vaginal process
鞘突存留/鞘突存留　persistent processus vaginalis
鞘突遗迹/鞘突遺跡　vestige of vaginal process
鞘脂激活蛋白质类/鞘脂啟動蛋白質類　sphingolipid activator proteins
鞘脂类/鞘脂類　sphingolipids
鞘脂类代谢障碍/鞘脂代謝障礙　sphingolipidosis
切/切[削]　cutting
切除/切除　ablate
切除垂体/切除腦下垂體　hypophysectomize
切除刀/切除器　exsector
切除动脉内膜/動脈內膜切除　endarterectomize
切除活组织检查/切除式活體組織切片檢查　excisional biopsy
切除甲状旁腺/副甲狀腺切除　parathyroidectomize
切除甲状腺/切除甲狀腺　thyroidectomize
切除交感神经/交感神經切除　sympathectomize
切除肾上腺/腎上腺切除　adrenalectomize
切除术/切除術,截除術　ectomy
切除性牙周膜新附着术/切除性牙周膜新附著術　excisional new attachment of periodontum
切除胸腺/胸腺切除　thymectomize
切导/切導子　incisal guidance
切导盘/切導盤　incisal guidance table
切导斜度/切導斜度　incisal guidance inclination
切导针/切導針　incisal guidance pin
切道/切道　incisal path
切道斜度/切道斜度　incisal path inclination
切端暴露/切端暴露　incisal display
切端沟/切端溝　incisal groove
切端轮廓/切端輪廓　incisal silhouette
切端外展隙/切端外展隙　incisal embrasure
切端支托/齒切面托　incisal rest
切断骨折/切除骨折　resecting fracture
切断锯/截斷術鋸,截肢鋸　amputating saw
切断伤/切斷傷　amputating wound
切割器械/切削器械　cutting instrument
切骨矫形器/彎骨矯直器　osteocamp
切迹/切跡,凹痕　notch

切迹状畸形/切跡狀畸形　notch deformity
切开/切開［术］　incision
切开法重睑成形术/切開法重瞼成形術　doubling eyelid operation by incision method
切开复位［术］/切開回復術　open reduction
切开疗法/切開療法　incising therapy, incision therapy
切开气管/切開氣管　tracheotomize
切开引流/切開引流　incision and drainage
切口瘢痕/切口瘢痕　incisional scar
切口疝/割口疝　incisional hernia
［切］块/切碎　chopping
切面/切面,切片　section
切面超声心动描记术/切面超聲心動描記術　crosssection echocardiography
切面回波描记术/切面回聲描記術　tomoechography
切面显像/切面顯像　crosssection imaging
［切］片/切片,切開　slicing, section
切片机/切片機　microtome
切片术/切片法　microtomy
切平面/切平面　incisal plane
切取活组织检查/切取活體組織切片檢查　incisional biopsy
切伤/割創傷　incised wound
切石刀/截石刀　lithotome
切石术者/截石者　lithotomist
切线伤/正切創傷　tangential wound
切线神经纤维/切線神經纖維　tangential nerve fibers
切削/切削　cutting
切削型汞齐合金/切削型汞齊合金　lathe-cut amalgam alloy
切削油/切削油　cutting oil
切斜面/切緣斜面　incisal bevel
切牙/門齒,切齒　incisor
切牙唇面的/門齒嘴唇面的　incisolabial
切［牙］道/門齒徑　incisor path
切牙的/門牙的　incisive
切牙缝/門齒縫　incisive suture
切牙骨下点/下棘點　subspinale
切牙管/門齒管　incisive canal
切牙管囊肿/門牙管囊腫　incisive canal cyst
切牙颌内缝终点/切牙頜內縫終點　orale
切牙孔/切牙孔　incisive foramina
切牙邻面的/門齒近側面的　incisoproximal
切牙乳头/門齒乳頭　incisive papilla
切牙舌面的/門齒舌頭面的　incisolingual
切牙窝/門齒窩　incisive fossa

切牙型/切牙型　secodont
切龈融合/切齦融合　incisal-gingival blend
切缘/切緣,門緣　incisal margin, incisal edge
切缘壁/切緣壁　incisal wall
切缘补强/切緣補強　incisal offset
切缘嵴/切緣嵴　incisal ridge
切缘结节/切緣結節　mamelon
切缘悬突/切緣懸突　incisal ledge
切蛭吸血法/吸血水蛭切開法　bdellotomy
茄碱/馬鈴薯毒,馬鈴薯素　solanine
茄生物碱类/茄生物鹼類　solanaceous alkaloids
茄属/茄屬　Solanum
切昆贡亚热/奇昆古尼亞熱　Chikungunya fever
切伦科夫辐射/凱倫科夫氏輻射　Cerenkov radiation
切诊/切診　palpation and pulse taking, pulse taking and palpation
怯士/怯士　coward
侵入门户/侵入口　portal of entry
侵入性感染/侵入性感染　invasive infection
侵蚀性癌/侵蝕性癌　rodent cancer
侵蚀性溃疡/侵蝕性潰瘍　carious ulcer
侵袭期/侵襲期　invasive stage
侵袭型纤维瘤病/攻擊性纖維瘤病　aggressive fibromatosis
侵袭性葡萄胎/侵襲性葡萄胎　invasive hydatidiform mole
侵袭性生长/侵襲性生長　invasive growth
侵袭性婴儿肌纤维瘤病/侵襲性嬰兒肌纖維瘤病　aggressive infantile myofibromatosis
侵袭性婴儿纤维瘤病/侵襲性嬰兒纖維瘤病　aggressive infantile fibromatosis
侵袭性肢端乳突腺瘤及腺癌/侵襲性肢端乳突腺瘤及腺癌　aggressive digital papillary adenoma and adenocarcinoma
亲病灶性/趨病性,親病性　pathotropism
亲代/親［世］代　parental generation
亲代病毒/親代病毒　parental virus
亲代染色体/親代染色體　parental chromosome
亲代谢性谷氨酸盐受体/親代謝性穀氨酸鹽受體　metabotropic glutamate receptor
亲毒素的/親毒素的　toxiphoric
亲肺性/親肺性　pneumotropism
亲肺性病毒/親肺炎病毒　pneumotropic virus
亲和标记法/親和標記法　affinity labeling
亲和力/親和力,親和性　affinity
亲和力标记物/親和力標記物　affinity label
亲和色谱法/親和色譜法　affinity chromatography
亲核物质/親核體　nucleophile

亲红细胞毒/血[液]毒　hemotropic poison
亲环素 A/親環素 A　cyclophilin A
亲环素类/親環素類　cyclophilins
亲菌质/親菌質　bacteriotropic substance
亲类脂抗体/趨脂性抗體　lipoidotropic antibody
亲螺菌性/親螺旋菌性　spirillotropism
亲免蛋白/嗜免疫劑　immunophilin
亲内脏性病毒/親內臟性病毒　viscerotropic virus
亲皮性病毒/親皮性病毒　dermotropic virus
亲器官剂/趨器官劑　organotrope
亲器官性/親器官性　organophilism
亲人及动物性真菌/親人及動物性真菌　anthropozoophilic fungus
亲人性真菌/親人性真菌　anthropophilic fungus
亲水基团/親水基團　hydrophilic group
亲水胶体/親水膠質　hydrophilic colloid
亲水亲油平衡/親水親油平衡　hydrophil-lipophil balance
亲水亲油平衡值/親水親油平衡值　hydrophile-lipophile balance value
亲水软膏/親水軟膏　hydrophilic ointment
亲水软性角膜接触镜/親水軟性角膜接觸鏡　hydrophilic soft corneal contact lens
亲水小管/親水小管　hydrophilic channel
亲水性/親水性　hydrophilicity
亲水[性]的/親水的　hydrophilic
亲水性接触镜/親水性接觸鏡　hydrophilic contact lens
亲水性物质/親水性物質　hydrophilic substance
亲调理素性/親調理素性　opsonophilia
亲同类性/趨同性,親類性　homotropism
亲同种细胞抗体/親同種細胞抗體　homocytotropic antibody
亲细胞抗体/親細胞抗體　cytotropic antibody
亲细胞性过敏反应/親細胞性過敏反應　cytotropic anaphylaxis
亲细胞性血清/親細胞性血清　cytotropic serum
亲氧性/應氧性,趨氧性　oxytropism
亲液的/親溶媒性,親液性　lyophilic
亲液胶体/親水膠體　lyophilic colloid
亲异种细胞抗体/親異種細胞抗體　heterocytotropic antibody
亲银性/嗜銀　argentaffin
亲油基团/親油基團　lipophilic group
亲缘系数/親緣係數　coefficient of relationship
亲脂体/親脂質　lipophil
亲株/親株　parent strain
亲子关系/親子關係　parent-child relation

芹菜/芹菜　celery
芹菜素/芹菜素　apigenin
芹菜早枯尾孢霉/芹菜尾孢菌　Cercospora apii
芩连清心丸/芩連清心丸　Skullcap and Coptis Pill for Clearing Heat from the Heart
秦艽/秦艽　largeleaf gentian root
秦皮/秦皮　cortex fraxini, ash bark
禽艾美球虫/家禽球孢子蟲　Eimeria tenella
禽白细胞增生病毒/鳥白血病病毒　avian leukosis virus
禽传染性支气管炎病毒/鳥傳染性支氣管炎病毒　avian infectious bronchitis virus
禽霍乱/家禽霍亂　fowl cholera
禽结核/禽結核　fowl tuberculosis
禽距/禽距　calcar avis
禽淋巴瘤病/禽類淋巴瘤病　avian lymphomatosis
禽螨/禽蟎　bird mite
禽脑脊髓炎病毒/鳥腦脊髓炎病毒　avian encephalomyelitis virus
禽脐炎/小鳥臍炎　omphalitis of bird
禽肉瘤/禽肉瘤　avian sarcoma
禽腺病毒 A 型/禽腺病毒 A 型　fowl adenovirus A
噙化/噙化　administered under tongue
噙化法/噙化法　method of melt-in-mouth
青斑/青斑　livedo
青斑血管炎/青斑血管炎　livedo vasculitis
青斑样皮炎/青斑狀皮膚炎　livedoid dermatitis
青草病/青草病　belyando sprue
青春/青春期,青年期　adolescence, puberty
青春期痴呆者/青春期癡呆者　hebephreniac
青春期痤疮/青年期痤瘡　adolescent acne
青春期发育/青春期發育　adolescent development
青春期妇女/青春期婦女　pubertal woman
青春期甲状腺肿/青年期甲狀腺腫　adolescent goiter
青春期精神病学/青春期精神病學　adolescent psychiatry
青春期咳/青春期欬　hebetic cough
青春期声音变调/發聲期音變化　paraphonia pubescentium
青春期前乳房发育/青春期前乳房發育　premature thelarche
青春期妊娠/青春期妊娠　teenage pregnancy
青春期心理学/青春期心理學　adolescent psychology
青春期行为/青春期行爲　adolescent behavior
青春期学/春機發動學,發身學　ephebology
青春期医学/青春期醫學　adolescent medicine
青春期龈炎/青春期齦炎　pubertal gingivitis
青春前期/發身前期,青春期前期　prepuberty

青春前期功能性去势综合征/青春前期機能性閹症候群　functional prepubertal castration syndrome
青春前期牙周炎/青春前期牙周炎　prepuberty periodontitis
青春型精神分裂症/青春型精神分裂症　hebephrenic schizophrenia
青黛/青黛　natural indigo
青黛散/青黛散　qingdai powder
青地霉酸/青地黴酸　terrestric acid
青风内障/青風内障　blue wind glaucoma
青风内障·肝气郁结证/青風内障·肝氣鬱結證　blue wind glaucoma with liver qi stagnation pattern
青风内障·肝肾两虚证/青風内障·肝腎兩虛證　blue wind glaucoma with liver-kidney deficiency pattern
青风内障·痰湿内停证/青風内障·痰濕内停證　blue wind glaucoma with pattern of phlegm-dampness internal retention
青风藤/青風藤　orientvine vine
青光眼/青光眼　glaucoma
青光眼斑/青光眼斑　glaucomatous fleck
青光眼杯/青光眼杯,青光眼凹　glaucomatous cup
青光眼激发试验/青光眼激發試驗　provocative test for glaucoma
青光眼盲/青光眼盲　glaucosis
青光眼型/青光眼體型　glaucomatous habit
青光眼性陷凹/青光眼性陷凹　glaucomatous excavation
青光眼引流植入物/青光眼引流植入物　glaucoma drainage implant
青光眼晕轮/青光眼暈　glaucomatous halo
青果/青果　Chinese white olive
青汗[症]/青汗症　blue sweat
青蒿/青蒿　Artemisia annua, sweet wormwood herb
青蒿鳖甲汤/青蒿鱉甲湯　qinghao biejia decoction
青蒿素类/青蒿素類　artemisinins
青筋腿/青筋腿　varicose vein of leg
青灵/青靈　qingling, HT2
青盲/青盲,藍色盲　blue blindness, optic atrophy
青盲·风痰上扰证/青盲·風痰上擾證　blue blindness with pattern of wind-phlegm disturbing upward
青盲·肝气郁结证/青盲·肝氣鬱結證　blue blindness with liver qi stagnation pattern
青盲·肝肾两虚证/青盲·肝腎兩虛證　blue blindness with liver-kidney deficiency pattern
青盲·脾虚湿困证/青盲·脾虛濕困證　blue blindness with pattern of spleen deficiency and dampness retention
青盲·气血两虚证/青盲·氣血兩虛證　blue blindness with qi-blood deficiency pattern
青霉胺/青黴胺　penicillamine
青霉胺性/青黴胺引起的　penicillamine-induced
青霉胺引起的萎缩/青黴胺引起的萎縮　penicillamine-induced atrophy
青霉胺诱发匐行性穿通性弹力纤维病/青黴胺引起的匐行性穿通性彈性纖維病　penicillamine-induced elastosis perforans serpiginosa
青霉病/青黴[素]病　penicilliosis
青霉醛/青黴醛　penilloaldehyde
青霉素/青黴素　penicillin
青霉素结合蛋白/青黴素結合蛋白　penicillin-binding protein
青霉素结合蛋白质类/青黴素結合蛋白質類　penicillin-binding proteins
青霉素抗药性/青黴素抗藥性　penicillin resistance
青霉素类/青黴素類　penicillins
青霉素酶/青黴素酶,青黴素酵素　penicillinase
青霉素污染的/青黴素汙染的　penicillin-contaminated
青霉素酰胺酶/青黴素醯胺酶　penicillin amidase
青霉酸/青黴酸　penicillic acid
青霉烷类/青黴烷類　penams
青霉烷酸/青黴烷酸　penicillanic acid
青霉烯类/青黴烯類　penems
青礞石/青礞石　chlorite schist
青木香/青木香　slender dutchmanspipe root
青年间歇性黄疸/青年型間歇性黄疸　icterus intermittens juvenilis
青年疣/青年疣　verruca juvenilis
青皮/青皮　immature tangerine peel
青少年/青少年　adolescent
青少年保健服务/青少年保健服務　adolescent health service
青少年的/青少年期的　juvenile
青少年佩吉特病/青少年期的Paget氏病　juvenile Paget disease
青少年期妊娠/青少年期妊娠　pregnancy in adolescence
青少年型青光眼/青少年型青光眼　juvenile glaucoma
青少年性黄肉芽肿/幼年型黄肉芽腫　juvenile xanthogranuloma
青少年牙周炎/幼年型牙周炎　juvenile periodontitis
青舌/青舌　blue tongue
青蛇毒/青蛇毒　acute thrombophlebitis
青蛇毒·肝郁证/青蛇毒·肝鬱證　superficial vein thrombus with liver depression pattern

青蛇毒·湿热证/青蛇毒·濕熱證 superficial vein thrombus with dampness-heat pattern
青蛇毒·血热瘀滞证/青蛇毒·血熱瘀滯證 superficial vein thrombus with pattern of blood-heat stasis and stagnation
青蛇毒·瘀阻脉络证/青蛇毒·瘀阻脈絡證 superficial vein thrombus with pattern of stasis obstructing vessels and collateral
青石棉/青石棉 crocidolite asbestos
青铜/青銅 bronze
青铜色皮病/青銅色病 bronzed disease
青铜色肝/青銅色肝 bronze liver
青铜婴儿综合征/青銅嬰兒症候群 bronze baby syndrome
青蛙皮肤/青蛙皮膚 frog skin
青葙子/青葙子 feather cockscomb seed
青叶胆/青葉膽 ile swertia herb
青枝骨折/青枝骨折,旁彎骨折 greenstick fracture
青肿/淤傷 bruise
青贮饲料工人病/青貯飼料工人病 silo filler disease
青紫斑/青黑斑 pelidnoma
青紫色黄疸/青紫色黄疸 blue jaundice
青紫色[素]杆菌/紫紺性产色桿菌 *Chromobacterium violaceum*
青紫色萎缩/發紺性萎縮 cyanotic atrophy
青紫[色]窒息/青黑色窒息 asphyxia livida
轻闭塞性扎法/輕阻塞性結扎 suboccluding ligature
轻擦按摩法/輕擦按摩法 frolement
轻触诊/輕觸診 light palpation
轻刺激/輕刺激 subexcite
轻度出血/輕度出血,微出血 hyporrhea
轻度肺结核/最微結核 minimal tuberculosis
轻度感染/輕度感染 low-grade infection
轻度精神障碍/輕度精神障礙 paraphora
轻[度]恐怖/輕恐懼症 paraphobia
轻度妊高征/輕度妊高徵 mild pregnancy-induced hypertension syndrome
轻度伤/輕度傷 mild injury
轻度烧伤/輕度燒傷 mild degree burn
轻度收敛/輕度收斂 hypostypsis
轻[度]炎症/輕度炎症,隱炎症 subinflammation
轻度抑郁[症]/輕性抑鬱[症] mild depression
轻度谵妄/輕譫妄,亞譫妄 subdelirium
轻度舟状头[畸形]/輕度舟狀頭畸形 subscaphocephaly
轻粉/輕粉 calomel
轻粉中毒/輕粉中毒 calomel poisoning
轻昏迷/半迷睡,半昏迷 semisopor

轻霍乱/輕霍亂 cholerine
轻剂/輕劑 light formula
轻截瘫/下身輕癱 paraparesis
轻精神病/部分精神障礙,單純精神障礙 meroergasia
轻链/輕鏈 light chain
轻链蛋白尿/輕鏈蛋白尿 light chain proteinuria
轻链可变区/輕鏈可變區 variable region of light chain
轻链型/輕鏈型 light chain type
轻链亚型/輕鏈亞型 light chain subtype
轻偏瘫/輕偏癱,單側輕癱 hemiparesis
轻氢/[輕]氫 light hydrogen
轻鼠疫/輕鼠疫,副鼠疫 parapestis
轻瘫/輕癱,不全麻痺 paresis
轻微脑功能障碍/微小腦機能障礙 minimal brain dysfunction
轻微神经痛/輕神經痛 minor neuralgia
轻泻药/輕瀉藥 laxative, aperient
轻型/輕型 mitis
轻型地中海贫血/輕型海洋型貧血 thalassemia minima, thalassemia minor
轻型天花/類天花 mild smallpox
轻型心绞痛/輕型心絞痛 angina minor
轻型猩红热/輕猩紅熱 scarlatinella
轻型痒疹/輕型癢疹 prurigo mitis
轻性精神病/輕性精神病 minor psychosis
轻忧郁症/輕憂鬱病 hypomelancholia
轻晕厥/輕度暈厥 eclysis
轻躁狂/輕躁狂 hypomania
轻躁狂者/輕躁狂者 hypomaniac
轻质液状石蜡/輕白礦物油,輕液石蠟 light white mineral oil
氢/氫 hydrogen
氢碘酸/氫碘酸 hydriodic acid
氢氟甲噻/氫氟甲噻 hydroflumethiazide
氢氟酸/氫氟酸 hydrofluoric acid
氢氟酸烧伤/氫氟酸燒傷 hydrofluoric acid burn
氢供体/供氫體 hydrogen donor
氢化胆红素/氫基膽紅素,氫膽紅質 hydrobilirubin
氢化可的松/氫化可的松,氫皮質酮 hydrocortisone
氢化可的松琥珀酸钠/丁二酸鈉氫皮質酮 hydrocortisone sodium succinate
氢化可力丁/氫基膠吡啶 hydrocollidine
氢化酶/氫化酶,放氫酶 hydrogenase
氢化萘胺/氫萘酚胺 hydronaphthylamine
氢化物/氫化物 hydride
氢化辛可尼丁/氫化辛可尼丁 hydrocinchonidine

氢化作用/氫化作用　hydrogenation
氢键/氫鍵　hydrogen bond
氢键合/氫鍵合　hydrogen bonding
氢解作用/氫分解作用　hydrogenolysis
氢可他酯/氫可的松二乙氨基醋酸酯,乙酸氢皮質酮胺　hydrocortamate
氢可酮/氫可酮　hydrocodone
氢醌类/氫醌類　hydroquinones
氢离子/氫離子　hydrion
氢离子比色计/離子比色計　ionocolorimeter
氢离子浓度/氫離子濃度　hydrogen ion concentration
氢裂合酶类/氫裂合酶類　hydro-lyases
氢硫化铵血/氫硫化銨血症　hydrothionammonemia
氢硫化物/硫氫酸鹽　sulfhydrate
氢氯化物/鹽酸鹽　hydrochloride
氢氯噻嗪/氫氯苯噻噠嗪　hydrochlorothiazide
氢吗啡酮/氫嗎啡酮　hydromorphone
氢密度/氫密度　hydrogen density
氢硼化物/氫硼化物　borohydrides
氢氰酸/氫氰酸　hydrocyanic acid
氢氰酸中毒/氫氰酸中毒　hydrocyanism
氢溴化物/氫溴化物　hydrobromide
氢溴酸/氫溴酸　hydrobromic acid
氢溴酸槟榔碱/氫溴酸檳榔素　arecoline hydrobromide
氢溴酸东莨菪碱/氫溴酸東莨菪素　scopolamine hydrobromide
氢溴酸后马托品/氫溴酸後馬托品　homatropine hydrobromide
氢溴酸奎宁/氫溴酸奎寧　quinine hydrobromide
氢溴酸莨宕碱/氫溴酸莨菪鹼　hyoscyamine hydrobromide
氢溴酸羟苯异丙胺/氫溴酸羥苯異丙胺,氫溴酸安非他命　hydroxyamphetamine hydrobromide
氢氧化铵/氫氧化銨　ammonium hydroxide
氢氧化钙/氫氧化鈣　calcium hydroxide
氢氧化钙溶液/氫氧化鈣溶液　calcium hydroxide solution
氢氧化钾/氫氧化鉀　caustic potash
氢氧化钾溶液/氫氧化鉀溶液　potassium hydroxide solution
氢氧化铝/氫氧化鋁　aluminium hydroxide
氢氧化铝凝胶/氫氧化鋁膠液　aluminum hydroxide gel, amphojel
氢氧化镁/氫氧化鎂　magnesium hydroxide
氢氧化镁铝/氫氧化鎂鋁　magaldrate
氢氧化钠/氫氧化鈉　sodium hydroxide
氢氧化钠烧伤/氫氧化鈉燒傷　sodium hydroxide burn
氢氧化铁/氫氧化鐵　ferric hydroxide
氢氧化物/氫氧化物　hydroxide
氢氧离子/氫氧離子　hydroxyl ion
氢氧磷灰石沉积于关节之疾病/氫氧磷灰石沈積於關節之疾病　hydroxyapatite disease
氢氧氯化铝/氫氧氯化鋁　aluminium chlorohydroxide
倾倒综合征/傾倒症候群　dumping syndrome
倾角计/斜角計　inclinometer
倾斜测定仪/手術檯傾度計　tiltometer
倾斜式碟瓣/傾斜式碟瓣　tilting-disk prosthetic valve
倾斜试验/傾斜試驗　tilt testing
倾斜台试验/傾斜檯試驗　tilt-table test
倾注培养/傾注培養法　pour plate method
清半夏/清半夏　alum processed pinellia tuber
清炒/清炒　simple stir-frying
清晨上睑下垂/清晨垂瞼,乍醒垂瞼　morning ptosis
清除/清除　butyroid, clear
清除率/清除率　clearance
清除酶/過氧化物清除酶　scavenger enzyme
清除系统/清除系統　scavenging system
清除细胞/清除細胞,吞噬細胞　scavenger cell
清创术/清創術　debridement
清淡饮食/溫和飲食　bland diet
清道夫/清道夫　scavenger
清法/清法　clearing method
清肺润燥/清肺潤燥　clearing lung-heat and moistening dryness
清肝明目/清肝明目　removing liver-fire for improving eyesight
清肝明目法/清肝明目法　clearing liver to brighten eye
清肝息风/清肝息風　clearing liver-fire for calming endogenous wind
清肝泻肺/清肝瀉肺　clearing liver-fire and purging lung
清肝泻火/清肝瀉火　clearing away liver fire, clearing liver-fire
清骨散/清骨散　qinggu powder
清化暑湿/清化暑濕　clearing summerheat and dissipating dampness
清洁/清潔,澄清　clearing
清洁剂/清潔劑　cleansing agent
清解余毒/清解餘毒　expelling remnant toxicity
清静无为/清靜無爲　quietism

清静养神/清静養神 banishing distractions to repose
清开灵口服液/清開靈口服液 qingkailing oral liquid
清开灵注射液/清開靈注射液 qingkailing injection
清冷渊/清冷淵 qinglengyuan, SJ11
清利三焦/清利三焦 clearing heat-dampness in sanjiao
清凉糊剂/清涼糊劑,清涼貼布 cooling paste
清凉剂/清涼劑 algefacient
清凉油/清涼油 qingliang oil
清亮囊泡/清亮囊泡 clear vesicle
清络饮/清絡飲 qingluo drink
清脑药/清腦藥 cephalocathartic
清气分热剂/清氣分熱劑 formula for clearing heat at qi level
清气化痰丸/清氣化痰丸 qingqi huatan pill
清窍不利/清竅不利 blocked clear orifice
清热除蒸/清熱除蒸 clearing hectic heat
清热导滞/清熱導滯 clearing heat and removing food stagnation
清[热]法/清[熱]法 clearing heat method, heat-clearing therapy
清热攻下/清熱攻下 clearing heat and purgation
清热化癍/清熱化癍 clearing heat for resolving macula
清热化痰/清熱化痰 clearing heat and dissipating phlegm
清热剂/清熱劑 heat-clearing formula
清热解毒/清熱解毒 clearing heat and removing toxicity
清热解毒剂/清熱解毒劑 formula for clearing heat and removing toxicity
清热解暑/清熱解暑 clearing summerheat
清热解暑剂/清熱解暑劑 formula for clearing heat and antisummerheat
清热开窍/清熱開竅 clearing heat for resuscitation, waking up patient from unconsciouness by clearing heat
清热利湿/清暑利濕 clearing heat and promoting diuresis
清热凉血/清熱涼血 clearing heat and cooling blood
清热排脓/清熱排膿 clearing heat and discharging pus
清热祛湿剂/清熱祛濕劑 formula for clearing heat and eliminating dampness
清热润燥/清熱潤燥 clearing heat and moistening dryness
清热生津/清熱生津 clearing heat and promoting fluid production
清热收涩药/清熱收澀藥 heat-clearing and astringent medicine
清热通淋/清熱通淋 clearing heat and freeing strangury
清热透疹/清熱透疹 clearing heat for promoting eruption
清热息风/清熱息風 clearing heat for calming endogenous wind
清热消肿/清熱消腫 clearing heat for detumescence
清热泻肺/清熱瀉肺 clearing heat and purging lung
清热泻火/清熱瀉火 clearing heat-fire
清润化痰剂/清潤化痰劑 formula for resolving phlegm with clear-moistening drugs
清暑益气/清暑益氣 clearing summerheat and benefiting qi
清暑益气汤/清暑益氣湯 qingshu yiqi decoction
清胃散/清胃散 qingwei powder
清胃泻热/清胃瀉熱 clearing stomach and purging heat
清瘟败毒散/清瘟敗毒散 qingwen baidu powder
清泻肠热/清瀉腸熱 clearing intestinal heat
清泻肝胆/清瀉肝膽 clearing away heat from the liver and gallbladder, purging liver and gallbladder
清泻里热/清瀉裡熱 clearing interior heat
清泻相火/清瀉相火 clearing ministerial fire
清泻虚热/清瀉虛熱 clearing deficiency-heat
清心[火]/清心[火] clearing heart fire
清心泻火/清心瀉火 clearing heart and purging fire
清醒插管/清醒插管 conscious intubation
清醒性镇静/清醒性鎮靜 conscious-sedation
清虚热剂/清虛熱劑 formula for clearing asthenic fever
清宣郁热/清宣鬱熱 clearing stagnated heat
清血法/清血法 hemocatharsis
清咽/清咽 clearing heat from throat
清咽丸/清咽丸 qingyan pill
清营凉血剂/清營涼血劑 formula for clearing nutrient level and cooling blood
清营汤/清營湯 qingying decoction
清营泻热/清營瀉熱 clearing heat in ying phase
清脏腑热剂/清臟腑熱劑 formula for clearing heat in viscerae
清燥救肺汤/清燥救肺湯 qingzao jiufei decoction
鲭组蛋白/鯖精組織蛋白 scombrone
情调/感覺緊張度 feeling tone
情感爆发/情感爆發 raptus
情感不协调/情感不協調 incongruity of affect
情感迟钝/情感遲鈍 emotional blunting

情感脆弱/情感脆弱　emotional fragility
情感淡漠/無情感,神情呆滯　apathy
情感倒错/不正常之情感　parathymia
情感低落性整体反应/心神活动不足　hypothymergasia
情感发育龄/情緒成熟年齡　emotional age
情感反常/情感倒錯　paramania
情感分裂型精神障碍/精神分裂感情型障礙　schizoaffective disorder
情感高涨/昂然自得,激揚　elation
情感过强/情感過度　hyperaffectivity
情感疾病/情感疾病　mood disorder
情感减退/情感減退　hypothymia
情感拟人说/情感似人類　anthropopathy
情感贫乏/感情缺乏　emotional poverty
情感性精神病/情感性精神病　affective psychosis
情感性痉挛/情感痙攣　affect spasm
情感性忧郁症/情感性憂鬱病　affective melancholia
情感依附性抑郁[症]/依賴性抑鬱　anaclitic depression
情感增盛/情感增盛,感情過強　hyperthymia
情感障碍/感情障礙,情感病　affective disorder, disturbance of affectivity
情感症状/情感症狀　affective symptom
情结指标/心理狀態指示器　complex indicator
情境疗法/情境療法,情志相勝療法　emotional therapy corresponding with five elements
情绪不稳/情緒不穩　emotional lability
情绪的/情緒的,情感的　emotional
情绪性白细胞增多/情感性白血球增多　emotional leukocytosis
情绪性潮红/情緒性潮紅　emotional flushing
情绪性黄疸/情感性黃疸　emotional jaundice
情绪性荨麻疹/情緒性蕁麻疹　emotional urticaria
情绪性掌跖多汗症/情緒性掌蹠多汗症　palmoplantar emotional hyperhidrosis
情绪障碍/情緒障礙　mood disorder
情绪阻断/情緒阻斷　affect block
情欲的/性慾的　erotic
情志/情志　emotion
情志病/情志病　emotional disease
情志相胜/情志相勝　mutual restraint between emotions
情志相胜疗法/情志相勝療法,情境療法　emotional therapy corresponding with five elements
氰氨化钙/氰氨化鈣　calcium cyanamide
氰胺/氰胺,無水尿素　cyanamide
氰丙烯酸盐类/氰丙烯酸鹽類　cyanoacrylates

氰醇/氰醇　cyanoalcohol
氰仿/氰仿　cyanoform
氰苷/氰苷　cyanogenic glycoside
氰红血蛋白/氰紅血球素,氰血紅質　cyanhemoglobin
氰化高铁血红素/氰血[黑]質　cyanhematin
氰化钾/氰化鉀　potassium cyanide
氰化钠/氰化鈉　sodium cyanide
氰化氢/氰化氫　hydrogen cyanide
氰化物/氰化物　cyanide
氰化物中毒性甲状腺肿/氰化物中毒性甲狀腺腫　cyanide goiter
氰化正铁肌红蛋白/氰變性肌球素　cyanmetmyoglobin
氰化正铁血红蛋白/氰變性血紅素,氰變性血紅質　cyanmethemoglobin
氰[基]苷/含氰苷類,含氰配糖體　cyanophoric glycoside
氰酸/氰酸　cyanic acid
氰酸盐/氰酸鹽　cyanate
氰铁酸/鐵氰酸　ferricyanic acid
氰酮/氰酮　cyanoketone
庆大霉素/慶大黴素　gentamycin
穷人痛风/貧人痛風　poor man gout
穹窿/穹窿　fornix
穹窿核糖核蛋白颗粒/穹窿核糖核蛋白顆粒　vault ribonucleoprotein particle
穹窿脚/穹窿腳　crus of fornix
穹窿结膜/穹窿結膜　fornical conjunctiva
穹窿静脉瘘/穹窿靜脈瘺　fornicovenous fistula
穹窿连合/穹窿連合　commissure of fornix
穹窿体/穹窿體　body of fornix
穹窿下器[官]/穹窿下器[官]　subfornical organ, SFO
穹窿柱/穹窿柱　column of fornix
琼斯鼻[骨折]夹板/Jones 氏鼻夾板　Jones nasal splint
琼脂/瓊脂　agar
琼脂块法/瓊脂塊法　agar block method
琼脂扩散法/瓊脂擴散法　agar diffusion method
琼脂酶/瓊脂酶　gelase
琼脂凝胶电泳/瓊脂凝膠電泳　agar gel electrophoresis
琼脂糖/瓊脂糖　agarose
琼脂糖凝胶/瓊脂糖凝膠　agarose gel
琼脂糖凝胶电泳/瓊脂糖凝膠電泳　agarose gel electrophoresis
琼脂糖色谱法/瓊脂糖色譜法　agarose

chromatography
琼脂印模材料/瓊脂印模材料　agar impression material
丘/丘　agger
丘脊型齿/丘脊牙型　bunolophodont
丘脑/丘腦　thalamus
丘脑背内侧核/丘腦背內側核　mediodorsal thalamic nucleus
丘脑背内侧核切开术/丘腦背內側核切開術　dorsomedial thalamotomy
丘脑出血/丘腦出血　thalamic hemorrhage
丘脑带/丘腦帶　thalamic tenia
丘脑的/丘腦的　thalamic
丘脑底部/丘腦下部　subthalamus
丘脑底核/丘腦下核　subthalamic nucleus
丘脑电图/丘腦電圖　electrothalamogram
丘脑豆状核部/丘腦豆狀核部　thalamolentiform part
丘脑辐射/丘腦輻射　thalamic radiation
丘脑腹侧核/丘腦腹側核　ventral thalamic nucleus
丘脑腹外侧核毁损术/丘腦腹外側核毀損術　ventrolateral thalamotomy
丘脑感觉过敏性感觉缺失/丘腦性感覺過敏性感覺缺失　thalamic hyperesthetic anesthesia
丘脑橄榄束/丘腦橄欖徑　thalamo-olivary tract
丘脑核/丘腦核　thalamic nucleus
丘脑后辐射/丘腦後輻射　posterior thalamic radiation
丘脑后核/丘腦後核　posterior thalamic nucleus
丘脑后静脉/丘腦後靜脈　posterior thalamic vein
丘脑化学破坏术/丘腦化學破壞術　chemothalamectomy
丘脑疾病/丘腦疾病　thalamic disease
丘脑间黏合/丘腦間黏合　interthalamic adhesion
丘脑内侧核群/丘腦內側核群　medial nuclear group of thalamus
丘脑内髓板/丘腦內髓板　internal medullary lamina of thalamus
丘脑颞叶辐射/丘腦顳葉輻射　thalamotemporal radiation
丘脑皮层束/丘腦皮質徑　thalamocortical tract
丘脑破坏法/丘腦破壞法　thalamectomy
丘脑前辐射/丘腦前輻射　anterior thalamic radiations
丘脑前核切开术/丘腦前核切開術　anterior thalamotomy
丘脑前核群/丘腦前核群　anterior nuclear group of thalamus
丘脑前结节/丘腦前結節　anterior thalamic tubercle

丘脑前静脉/丘腦前靜脈　anterior thalamic vein
丘脑切开术/丘腦切除術　thalamotomy
丘脑上静脉/丘腦上靜脈　superior thalamic vein
丘脑室旁核/丘腦室旁核　thalamic paraventricular nucleus
丘脑束/丘腦束　thalamic fasciculus
丘脑髓板内核/丘腦髓板內核　intralaminar thalamic nucleus
丘脑髓束/丘腦脊髓徑　thalamospinal tract
丘脑髓纹/丘腦髓紋　thalamic medullary stria
丘脑外侧核群/丘腦外側核群　lateral nuclear group of thalamus
丘脑外髓板/丘腦外髓板　external medullary lamina of thalamus
丘脑网状核/丘腦網狀核　thalamic reticular nucleus
丘脑纹状静脉/丘腦紋狀靜脈　thalamostriate vein
丘脑纹状体静脉/丘腦紋狀體靜脈　vena thalamostriata
丘脑下脚/丘腦下腳　inferior thalamic peduncle
丘脑下静脉/丘腦下靜脈　inferior thalamic vein
丘脑延髓束/丘腦延髓徑　thalamobulbar tract
丘脑枕/丘腦枕,丘腦後結節　pulvinar
丘脑枕束/丘腦枕徑　thalamo-occipital tract
丘脑支/丘腦支　thalamic branch
丘脑中线核群/丘腦中線核群　midline nuclear group of thalamus
丘脑中央辐射/丘腦中央輻射　central thalamic radiation
丘脑中央核/丘腦中央核　midline thalamic nucleus
丘脑综合征/丘腦感覺過敏性感覺缺失症候群　thalamic syndrome
丘疱疹/丘皰疹　papulovesicle
丘纹上静脉/丘紋上靜脈　superior thalamostriate vein
丘纹下静脉/丘紋下靜脈　inferior thalamostriate vein
丘系交叉/蹄系交叉　decussation of fillet
丘系三角/蹄系三角　trigonum lemnisci
丘墟/丘墟　qiuxu, GB40
丘型齿/丘齒型　bunodont
丘月型齿/丘月齒型　bunoselenodont
丘疹/丘疹　papular eruption, papule
丘疹病/丘疹病　papulosis
丘疹的/丘疹的　papular
丘疹坏死的/壞死性丘疹樣的　papulonecrotic
丘疹坏死性结核/丘狀壞死性結核疹　papulonecrotic tuberculosis
丘疹坏死性皮[肤]结核病/丘疹壞死性皮膚結核

tuberculosis cutis papulonecrotica
丘疹结节/結節性丘疹　papulonodule
丘疹结节的/結節性丘疹樣的　papulonodular
丘疹鳞屑的/鱗屑性丘疹樣　papulosquamous
丘疹鳞屑性梅毒疹/丘疹鱗屑性梅毒疹　papulosquamous syphilid
丘疹鳞屑性皮肤疾病/丘疹鱗屑性皮膚疾病　papulosquamous skin disease
丘疹脓疱梅毒疹/膿疱性丘疹樣梅毒疹　papulopustular syphilide
丘疹脓疱性的/膿疱性丘疹樣的，丘疹膿疱性的　papulopustular
丘疹脓疱性酒渣鼻/膿疱性丘疹樣酒渣　papulopustular rosacea
丘疹水疱性的/丘疹水皰性的，水皰性丘疹樣的　papulovesicular
丘疹形成/丘疹形成　papulation
丘疹性痤疮/丘疹性痤瘡　acne papulosa
丘疹性冻疮病/丘疹性凍瘡病　papular perniosis
丘疹性豆状梅毒疹/丘疹性豆狀梅毒疹　syphilid lenticularis papulosa
丘疹性红斑/丘疹性紅斑　erythema papulatum
丘疹性虹膜炎/丘疹性虹膜炎　iritis papulosa
丘疹性环状肉芽肿/丘疹性環狀肉芽腫　papular granuloma annulare
丘疹性黄瘤/丘疹性黄色瘤　papular xanthoma
丘疹性酒渣鼻/丘疹性酒渣　papular rosacea
丘疹性玫瑰糠疹/丘疹性玫瑰糠疹　papular pityriasis rosea
丘疹性梅毒疹/丘疹性梅毒疹　papular syphilide
丘疹性黏蛋白病/丘疹性黏液素病　papular mucinosis
丘疹性肉样瘤/丘疹性類肉瘤　papular sarcoid
丘疹性瘙痒性手套和短袜综合征/手腳部位搔癢性丘疹症候群　papular pruritic gloves and socks syndrome
丘疹性色素沉着/丘疹性色素沈著　papular pigmentation
丘疹性湿疹/丘疹性濕疹　eczema papulosum
丘疹性血管角化瘤/丘疹性血管角化瘤　papular angiokeratoma
丘疹性血管形成/丘疹性血管增生　papular angioplasia
丘疹性荨麻疹/丘疹狀蕁麻疹　urticaria papulosa
丘疹性肢端皮炎/丘疹性肢端皮膚炎　papular acrodermatitis
丘疹状黏液水肿/丘疹狀黏液水腫　papular myxedema

丘状坏死性结核/丘狀壞死性結核　tuberculosis papulonecrotica
秋令热钩端螺旋体/日本之秋令熱螺旋體　Leptospira autumnalis
秋水仙胺/脱乙醯甲基秋水仙鹼　demecolcine
秋水仙碱/秋水仙素　colchicine
秋水仙酸/秋水仙酸　colchicinic acid
秋燥/秋燥　autumn dryness, autumn-dryness disease
秋燥·肺胃阴伤证/秋燥·肺胃陰傷證　autumn dryness with pattern of injury of lung and stomach yin
秋燥·肺燥肠闭证/秋燥·肺燥腸閉證　autumn dryness with pattern of lung dryness and intestine blockade
秋燥·肺燥肠热络伤证/秋燥·肺燥腸熱絡傷證　autumn dryness with pattern of collaterals injury due to lung dryness and intestine heat
秋燥·邪犯肺卫证/秋燥·邪犯肺衛證　autumn dryness with pattern of pathogen invading lung-defense phase
秋燥·燥干清窍证/秋燥·燥乾清竅證　autumn dryness with pattern involving clear orifices
秋燥·燥热伤肺证/秋燥·燥熱傷肺證　autumn dryness with pattern of dryness-heat injuring lung
蚯蚓血红蛋白/蚯蚓血紅蛋白　hemerythrin
蚯蚓瘴/蚯蚓瘴　earthworm-like miasma
球/球　ball
球孢菌病/球孢菌病　coccidioidomycosis
球孢菌素/球孢子菌素　coccidioidin
球孢子菌病/球孢子菌病　coccidioidosis
球孢子菌的/球孢子菌的　coccidioidal
球孢子菌瘤/球孢子菌瘤　coccidioidoma
球孢子菌属/球孢子菌屬　*Coccidioides*
球孢子菌素试验/球黴菌素試驗　coccidioidin test
球孢子菌性肉芽肿/球孢子菌性肉芽腫　coccidioidal granuloma
球虫病/球蟲病　coccidiosis
球虫[的]/球蟲[的]　coccidian
球丛/球叢　bulbar plexus
球蛋白/球蛋白　globulin
β-球蛋白/乙型球蛋白　beta-globulin
β-球蛋白类/乙型球蛋白類　beta-globulins
球蛋白尿/球蛋白尿症　globulinuria
球蛋白血/球蛋白血病　globulinemia
球海绵体肌/球海綿體肌　bulbocavernosus muscle
球后/球後　qiuhou, EX-HN7
球后毛细血管/球後毛細血管　postglomerular capillary

球后十二指肠溃疡/球後十二指腸潰瘍　postbulbar duodenal ulcer
球后视神经炎/球後視神經炎　retrobulbar optic neuritis
球后肿瘤/球後腫瘤　retrobulbar tumor
球后注射/球後注射　retrobulbar injection
球嵴/球嵴　bulbar ridge
球间的/小球間的　interglobular
球结膜/[眼]結膜　bulbar conjunctiva
球结膜环状切除术/環狀球結膜切除術　peridectomy
球镜片/球面透鏡，球狀水晶體　spherical lens
球菌的/球菌的　coccal
球菌性甲床血管瘤病/球菌性甲床血管瘤病　coccal nail-bed angiomatosis
球菌性须疮/球菌性鬚瘡　coccogenic sycosis
球粒体/球粒體　spheroplast
球笼型机械瓣/球籠型機械瓣　ball-cage mechanical prosthetic valve
球螺旋系统/球螺旋系　bulbospiral system
球霉菌病/球黴菌病　coccidioidomycosis
球面[角]度/球面度　steradian
球面像差/屈光像差　dioptric aberration
球磨机/球磨機　ball mill
球囊/球囊，小囊　saccule
球囊斑/球囊斑　macula sacculi
球囊泵/球囊泵　balloon pump
球囊切开术/球囊切開術　sacculotomy
球囊神经/球囊神經　saccular nerve
球囊隐窝/球狀窩　spherical recess
球拟酵母病/串菌病　torulopsis
球拍式牵引夹/五弦琴狀牽引夾　banjo traction splint
球拍状甲/球拍狀甲　racket nail
球拍状胎盘/打球板狀胎盤　battledore placenta
球切除术/血管球切除術　glomectomy
球室襞/球室皺襞　bulboventricular fold
球室沟/球室溝　bulboventricular sulcus
球室襻/球室襻　bulboventricular loop
球头除鲠器/球頭捕鲠器　ball probang
球窝关节/球窩關節　ball and socket joint, ball-and-socket articulation
球细胞/球細胞　glomus cell
球形蛋白/球狀蛋白質　globular protein
球形的/球形的　globose
球形红细胞/球形紅細胞　spherocytes
球形红细胞的/球狀血球的　spherocytic
球形肌瘤/球形肌瘤　ball myoma
球形角膜/球形角膜　keratoglobus
球形晶状体/球狀晶狀體　spherophakia
球形乳房/球形乳房　spherical breast
球形视网膜脱离/球形視網膜脫離　globular detachment of retina
球形痰/球狀痰　globular sputum
球形体/球形體　spheroplast
球形细胞增多症/球狀血球症，球狀血球性貧血　spherocytosis
球形牙/球形牙　globodontia
球样细胞脑白质营养不良/球樣細胞腦白質營養不良　globoid cell leukodystrophy
球样细胞性脑白质营养不良/球樣細胞性腦白質營養不良症　globoid leukodystrophy
球样血管瘤/腎小球樣血管瘤　glomeruloid hemangioma
球柱镜片/球柱面鏡片　spherocylindrical lens
球柱[透]镜/球柱面透鏡　spherocylinder
球状带/球狀帶　zona glomerulosa
球状核/球狀核　globus nucleus, globus
球状瘤/球狀瘤　globular tumor
球状上颌囊肿/上頜鼻突狀囊腫　globulomaxillary cyst
球状石/球狀石　spherolith
球状突/胚胎球狀突　globular process
球状细胞/球狀細胞　spheroidal cell
球状小粒/球狀小粒　coccode
球狀血细胞性黄疸/球狀血球性黃疸　spherocytic jaundice
巯基化合物/巰基化合物　sulfhydryl compound
巯基试剂/巰基試劑　sulfhydryl reagent
巯基乙胺类/巰基乙胺類　mercaptoethylamines
巯基乙醇/巰基乙醇　mercaptoethanol
巯基乙酸锑钠/硫甘醇酸銻鈉　antimony sodium thioglycollate
巯基乙酰胺锑/硫甘醇醯胺銻　antimony thioglycollamide
巯[基]组氨酸/硫醇組織胺酸　thiolhistidine
巯乙酸盐类/巰乙醇酸鹽類　thioglycolates
齆/齆　rhinorrhea with clear discharge
区/區　area
区带电泳/區帶電泳　zone electrophoresis
区带离心法/區帶離心法　zonal centrifugation
区段乳房切除术/區段乳房切除術　segmental mastectomy
区基质/領域母質　territorial matrix
区间基质/領域間母質　interterritorial matrix
区域长度法/面積-長度方法　area-length method
区域定位图/區域定點陣圖　regional map

区域疗法/區域療法　zone therapy
区域麻醉/區域麻醉　regional anesthesia
区域性/局部的　regional
区域阻滞/區域阻斷麻醉　field block
驱虫斑鸠菊/驅蟲斑鳩菊　Vernonia anthelmintica
驱虫法/驅蟲法　expelling intestinal parasites method
驱虫攻下/驅蟲攻下　expelling intestinal parasites by purgation
驱虫药/驅蟲藥　insect repellent
驱动蛋白/驅動蛋白　kinesin
驱风药/驅風藥　carminative
驱蛔虫药/驅蛔蟲藥　ascaricide, lumbricide
驱蛔杀虫/驅蛔殺蟲　expelling and killing ascarid
驱虫剂/驅蟲劑　insectifuge
驱蛲虫药/驅蟯藥，殺蟯藥　oxyurifuge
驱气灌肠剂/驅氣灌腸劑　flatus enema
驱[蠕]虫药/驅[蠕]蟲藥　vermifuge
驱石剂/驅石藥　lithagogue
驱绦虫药/驅條蟲劑　taeniafuge
驱蚊剂/驅蚊劑　culicifuge
驱邪截疟/驅邪截瘧　expulsing pathogen for preventing malaria
驱血绷带/驅血繃帶　esmarch bandage
驱血法/驅血法　avascularization
驱血止血带/驅血止血帶　esmarch tourniquet
屈部湿疹/屈面濕疹　flexural eczema
屈侧银屑病/屈側銀屑病　flexural psoriasis
屈法/屈法　flexing manipulation
屈光/屈光　refraction
屈光不同/屈光不同　heterorefraction
屈光不正/不正视，非正视　ametropia
屈光不正性弱视/屈光不正性弱視　ametropic amblyopia
屈光不正眼/屈光不正眼　ametropic eye
屈光测量/眼折光调节力测定法　dioptometry
屈光测量法/眼折光力测定法　dioptoscopy
屈光参差/屈光不等　anisometropia
屈光参差性弱视/屈光參差性弱視　anisometropic amblyopia
屈光参差者/兩眼不等視者　anisometrope
屈光等同/兩眼折射力相等　isometropia
屈光计/屈光計　refractometer
屈光计检查/屈光計檢查　refractometry
屈光检查[法]/屈光檢查[法]　examination of refraction
屈光检查计/眼折光計，眼折光計　anaclasimeter
屈光检查器/屈光檢鏡　striascope
屈光力/屈光力　refractive power

屈光系统/折光系　dioptric system
屈光性屈光不正/屈光性屈光不正　refractive ametropia
屈光学/屈光學　dioptrics
屈光指数/屈光指數　refractive index
屈肌/屈肌　flexor muscle
屈肌强直/屈肌強直　flexor tetanus
屈肌支持带/屈肌支持帶　flexor retinaculum
屈肌总腱鞘/屈肌總腱鞘　common flexor sheath
屈髋伸膝试验/屈髖伸膝試驗　hip flexion and knee extension test
屈髋现象/髖屈曲現象　hip-flexion phenomenon
屈亮度/屈光度　diopter
屈面/屈面　flexion surface
屈[踇]短肌/屈[踇]短肌　Musculus flexor hallucis brevis
屈挠不能/屈撓不能，關節僵硬　acampsia
屈挠杆菌科感染/屈撓桿菌科感染　Flexibacteraceae infection
屈曲/向内弯　inflection
屈曲部网状着色异常/屈曲部網狀著色異常　reticular pigmented anomaly of flexure
屈曲骨折/彎曲性骨折　bending fracture
屈曲过度/屈曲過度　hyperflexion
屈曲挛缩/屈曲攣縮　flexion contracture
屈曲密螺旋体/軟螺旋體　Treponema refringen
屈曲指/屈曲指　camptodactylia
屈生酸/苯萘甲酸，草屈酸　chrysenic acid
屈斯特疝/Küster 氏疝　Küster hernia
屈腕试验/屈腕試驗　wrist bending test
屈昔多巴/屈昔多巴　droxidopa
屈膝背卧位/屈膝背臥位　dorsal recumbent position
屈戌关节/屈戌關節　hinge joint
屈展旋伸征/屈展旋伸徵象　fabere sign
祛风/祛風　dispelling wind-evil
祛风除湿/祛風除濕　dispelling wind and eliminating dampness
祛风化痰/祛風化痰　dispelling pathogenic wind and eliminating phlegm
祛风解肌/祛風解肌　dispelling pathogenic wind from muscles
祛风解痉/祛風解痙　dispelling pathogenic wind for resolving convulsion
祛风明目/祛風明目　dispelling pathogenic wind for improving eyesight
祛风明目法/祛風明目法　dispelling wind to brighten eye
祛风清热法/祛風清熱法　dispelling wind and

clearing heat
祛风燥湿/祛風燥濕 dispelling pathogenic wind and removing dampness
祛湿法/祛濕法 eliminating dampness method
祛湿剂/祛濕劑 desiccating formula
祛湿宣痹/祛濕宣痹 removing dampness and dredging channel blockade
祛暑解表/祛暑解表 dispelling summerheat to relieve exterior pattern
祛痰/祛痰 dispelling phlegm
祛痰法/祛痰法 expelling phlegm method
祛痰合剂/祛痰合劑 expectorant mixture
祛痰化浊/祛痰化濁 expelling phlegm and resolving turbidity
祛痰剂/祛痰劑 phlegm-expelling formula
祛痰宣痹/祛痰宣痹 expelling phlegm and dredging channel blockade
祛痰药/祛痰藥 expectorant
祛邪扶正/祛邪扶正 eliminating pathogen and strengthening vital qi
祛瘀/祛瘀 dispelling stasis
祛瘀排脓/祛瘀排膿 removing blood stasis and expelling pus
祛瘀生新/祛瘀生新 removing blood stasis for promoting tissue regeneration
躯干/軀幹 trunk, torso
躯干不全畸胎/軀體不全畸胎 perocormus
躯干迷走神经切断术/迷走神經幹切斷術 truncal vagotomy
躯干前曲症/軀幹彎曲症 campospasm
躯干湿疹/軀幹濕疹 eczema corporis
躯干下部痣/軀幹下部痣,游泳褲式母斑 bathing trunk nevus
躯干血管角化瘤/軀幹血管角化瘤 angiokeratoma corporis
躯裂畸胎/裂軀幹畸胎,裂體畸胎 schistocormus
躯裂[畸形]/裂軀幹畸形,裂體畸形 schistocormia
躯体变形障碍/軀體變形障礙 body dysmorphic disorder
躯体病/軀體病 somatopathy
躯体病幻想/軀體病幻想 somatophrenia
躯体病治疗/軀體治療 somatotherapy
躯体发育模式/軀體發育模式 body patterning
躯体肥厚/軀體肥厚 pachysomia
躯体感觉/軀體感覺 somatognosis
躯体感觉皮层/體感覺運動大腦皮質 somatic cortex
躯体感觉诱发电位/軀體感覺誘發電位 somatosensory evoked potential
躯体感觉障碍/軀體感覺障礙 somatosensory disorder
躯体感觉组元/身體感覺組元 somatic sensory component
躯体功能重建/軀體功能重建 physical function reconstruction
躯体机制/身體機構,軀體機構 somatic mechanism
躯体康复/軀體康復 physical rehabilitation
躯体裂/裂軀幹畸形,裂[椎]體畸形 somatoschisis
躯体论者/軀體論者 somatist
躯体X射线[照]片/軀體X光照片 somatogram
躯体神经功能综合征/體病性症候群 physiopathic syndrome
躯体神经纤维/軀體神經纖維 somatic nerve fiber
躯体死亡/全身死 somatic death
躯体特征/軀體特徵 somatic stigma
躯体痛/軀體痛,身體痛 somatalgia, somatic pain
躯体型障碍/軀體型障礙 somatoform disorder
躯体性精神病/軀體性精神病 somatopsychosis
躯体[性]神经功能病/軀體神經官能病 pathoneurosis
躯体[性]神经功能病的/體病性的 physiopathic
躯体依赖/軀體依賴 physical dependence
躯体诱导/軀體誘導 somatic induction
躯体运动组元/身體運動組元 somatic motor component
躯体症状化/軀體化 somatization
趋触性/趨觸性 thigmotaxis
趋电性/趨電性,向電性 electrotaxis
趋风性/趨風性 anemotropism
趋光性/趨光性,向光性,應光性 phototaxis
趋化的/趨化性的 chemotactic
趋化因子/趨化性因數 chemotactic factor
趋化因子受体/趨化因數受體 chemokine receptor
趋化因子抑制剂/趨化因數抑制劑 chemotactic factor inhibitor
趋化应答/趨化應答 chemotactic response
趋化作用/趨化性,向化性,向藥性 chemotaxis
趋交感神经细胞/趨交感神經細胞,親交感神經細胞 sympathicotropic cell
趋器官性/趨器官性 organotaxis
趋染色质性/趨核染質性 chromatotaxis
趋渗性/趨滲性 osmotaxis
趋势/趨勢,傾向 tendency
趋水性/趨水性 hydrotaxis
趋营养性/親營養性 trophotaxis
曲安奈德/曲安奈德 triamcinolone acetonide
曲安西龙/曲安西龍 triamcinolone

曲吡那敏/曲吡那敏　tripelennamine
曲鬓/曲鬢　qubin, GB7
曲部/[肾]盘曲部　pars convoluta
曲差/曲差　qucha, BL4
曲池/曲池　quchi, LI11
曲度远视/彎度[不足]性遠視　curvature hyperopia
曲氟尿苷/曲氟尿苷　trifluridine
曲骨/曲骨　qugu, RN2
曲剂/麴劑　fermented medicine
曲菌性角膜炎/麴菌素性角膜炎　aspergillus keratitis
曲率性近视/彎曲性近視,凸度性近視　curvature myopia
曲率性屈光不正/彎度不正視　curvature ametropia
曲率性散光/曲率性散光　curvature astigmatism
曲率性远视/曲度薄弱性遠視　curvature hypermetropia
曲马朵/曲馬朵　tramadol
曲霉核酸酶/麴黴核酸酶　aspergillus nuclease
曲霉菌病/麴菌病　aspergillosis
曲霉属/麴黴屬　*Aspergillus*
曲霉素/麴菌素,麴菌黑質　aspergillin
曲霉酸/麴黴酸　aspergillic acid
曲霉中毒/麴菌中毒　aspergillotoxicosis
曲霉肿/麴菌瘤　aspergilloma
曲美布汀/曲美布汀　trimebutine
曲美他嗪/曲美他嗪　trimetazidine
曲面断层X射线片/曲面斷層X線片　panoramic
曲帕拉醇/曲帕拉醇　triparanol
曲匹地尔/曲匹地爾　trapidil
曲普利啶/曲普利啶　triprolidine
曲普瑞林/曲普瑞林　triptorelin
曲泉/曲泉　ququan, LR8
曲酸/曲酸　kojic acid
曲他胺/三乙撑蜜胺　triethylenemelamine
曲托喹酚/曲托喹酚　tretoquinol
曲细精管索/細精索　seminiferous cord
曲线/曲線,彎　curve
曲线下面积/曲線下面積　area under curve
曲形釉质/卷曲性釉質　curled enamel
曲牙/下腭角　mandibular angle
曲垣/曲垣　quyuan, SI13
曲泽/曲澤　quze, PC3
曲张的/蜿蜒狀的　cirsoid
曲张静脉刀/静脈曲張刀　cirsotome
曲张静脉结扎术/静脈曲張結扎術　cirsodesis
曲张静脉切除术/曲張靜脈切除術　varicectomy
曲张静脉切开术/静脈曲張切開術　cirsotomy
曲张静脉炎/曲張靜脈炎　varicophlebitis
曲张静脉注射[疗]法/静脈曲張注射療法　cirsenchysis
曲张链丝菌素/曲張鏈絲菌素　streptovaricin
曲折/曲折　deflection
曲唑酮/曲唑酮　trazodone
瞿麦/瞿麥　lilac pink herb
蠼螋伤/蠼螋傷　anisolobis sting
取代化合物/取代化合物,置换化合物　substitution compound
取代基/取代基　substituent
取代基效应/取代基效應　substituent effect
取代记忆/取代記憶　replacement memory
6-APA6α-取代物/6-APA6α-取代物　6-APA6α-substituent
6-APA6β-取代物/6-APA6β-取代物　6-APA6β-substituent
7-ACA7α-取代物/7-ACA7α-取代物　7-ACA7α-substituent
7-ACA7β-取代物/7-ACA7β-取代物　7-ACA7β-substituent
7-ACA3-取代物修饰/7-ACA3-取代物修飾　7-ACA3-substituent modification
取皮机/切皮器,皮刀　dermatome
取皮术/取皮術　harvesting of skin grafts
取石钳/碎石鉗　lithotomy forceps
取嚏疗法/取嚏療法　sneezing therapy
取样/取樣　sampling
取样容积/取樣容積　sampling volume
龋/齲　caries
龋病学/齲蛀學　cariology
龋病易感性/齲病易感性　dental caries susceptibility
龋齿/齲齒,蛀牙　dental caries
龋齿活动性试验/齲齒活動性試驗　dental caries activity test
龋洞分离剂/齲洞隔離劑　cavity liner
龋发生/齲生成　cariogenesis
龋失补/齲失補　decay missing filling
龋失补牙/齲失補牙　decay missing filling tooth
龋失补牙面/齲失補牙面　decay missing filling surface
龋失补指数/齲失補指數　decay missing filling index
龋蚀性/齲蝕性　cariosity
龋质挖除/牙齒挖空　dental excavation
去饱和[作用]/去飽和作用　desaturation
去补体/補體移除　decomplementize
去除文身/去除文身　removing tattoo
去[大]脑紧张/除腦後緊張　acerebral tonus
去[大脑]皮质状态/去[大腦]皮質狀態　decortical

state
去大脑强直/除腦強硬　decerebrate rigidity
去大脑状态/去大腦狀態　decerebrate state
去蛋白[作用]/去蛋白作用　deproteinization
去毒簇溶血素/去毒類溶血素　hemolysoid
去毒生肌/去毒生肌　detoxication and promoting granulation
去恶清心汤/去惡清心湯　lochia relieving and heart clearing decoction, qu'e qingxin decoction
去分化/反分化，排除分化　dedifferentiation
去腐生肌/去腐生肌　eliminating necrotic tissues and promoting granulation
去腐生肌散/去腐生肌散　qufu shengji powder
去腐生肌药/去腐生肌藥　putridity removal and myogenic medicine
去腐消肿/去腐消腫　eliminating necrotic tissues and detumescence
去睾丸状态/去睪樣狀態　eunuchoid state
去梗阻后利尿/去梗阻後利尿　postobstructive diuresis
去冠器/去冠器　crown remover
去获能/除[獲]能　decapacitation
去甲二氢愈创木酸/去甲二氫愈創木酸　nordihydroguaiaretic acid
去甲环素/脱甲四環素　demecycline
去甲莨菪碱/正莨菪素　norhyoscyamine
去甲肾上腺素/正腎上腺素　noradrenaline, norepinephrine
去甲肾上腺素能神经元/去甲腎上腺素能神經元　noradre-nergic neuron
去甲替林/去甲替林　nortriptyline
去甲西泮/去甲西泮　nordazepam
去甲雄烷类/去甲雄烷類　norandrostanes
去甲孕酮类/去甲孕酮類　norprogesterones
去甲孕甾二烯类/去甲孕甾二烯類　norpregnadienes
去甲孕甾三烯类/去甲孕甾三烯類　norpregnatrienes
去甲孕甾烷类/去甲孕甾烷類　norpregnanes
去甲孕甾烯类/去甲孕甾烯類　norpregnenes
去甲甾类/去甲甾類　norsteroids
去离子水/去離子水　deionized water
去脑[法]/大腦截除法，除腦　decerebration
去脑皮质术/去腦皮質術　cerebral decortication
去皮/换膚　peeling
去皮质强直/去皮質強直　decorticate rigidity
去羟肌苷/去羥肌苷　didanosine
去羟米松/去氫氧迪皮質醇　desoximetasone
去氢表雄酮/還原雄性素　dehydroepiandrosterone
去氢胆固醇/脱氫膽固醇　desmosterol

去氢胆固醇类/去氫膽甾醇類　dehydrocholesterols
去氢胆酸/去氫膽酸　dehydrocholic acid
去氢抗坏血酸/去氫抗壞血酸　dehydroascorbic acid
去溶剂化/解溶作用　desolvation
去上皮/去上皮　de-epithelization
去上皮皮瓣/去上皮皮瓣　de-epithelized skin flap
去神经电位/去神經電位　denervation potential
去神经性肌萎缩/去神經性肌萎縮　denervated muscle atrophy
去神经性膀胱/去神經性膀胱，自主性膀胱　denervated bladder
去神经支配/失神經作用　denervation
去肾性高血压/去腎性高血壓　renoprival hypertension
去势细胞/閹割細胞　castration cell
去势治疗/閹割　castration
去适应[作用]/去適應作用，除去適應　deconditioning
去髓/除髓　emedullate
去铁胺/去鐵胺　deferoxamine
去铁草酰胺/鉗驖羥醯胺　desferrioxamine
去头分泌/斷頭分泌　decapitation secretion
去唾液酸糖蛋白受体/去唾液酸糖蛋白受體　asialoglycoprotein receptor
去唾液酸糖蛋白质类/去唾液酸糖蛋白質類　asialoglycoproteins
去味乙醇/除臭醇　deodorized alcohol
去污剂/清滌藥　detersive
去纤维蛋白法/脱纖維作用　defibrination
去纤维蛋白血/脱纖維素血液　defibrinated blood
去纤维蛋白综合征/去纖維蛋白症候群　defibrination syndrome
去血红蛋白/除去血紅素　dehemoglobinize
去氧孕烯/去氧孕烯　desogestrel
去乙酰毛花苷/去乙醯毛花苷　deslanoside
去油/去油　de-fatting
去脏术/去臟術　exenteration
去种特异性抗体/非特異性抗體　despeciated antibody
去种特异性血清/無種特異性血清　despeciated serum
圈套绷带/環套繃帶　loop bandage
圈套器/圈套器　snare
圈套烧灼术/圈套燒灼術　snare cautery
圈形卡环/圈形卡環　ring clasp
全氨基酸尿症/全胺基酸尿症　generalized aminoaciduria
全白内障/完全内障　total cataract

全鼻窦切除术/全鼻竇切除術　pansinusectomy
全鼻窦炎/全鼻竇炎　pansinusitis
全鼻再造术/全鼻再造術　total nose reconstruction
全鼻中隔/全中隔　panseptum
全臂长/全臂長　total arm length
全[部]感觉缺失/全部感覺缺失　total anesthesia
全部血细胞计数/全部血球計數　complete blood count
全草/全草　whole herb
全层角膜移植片/全層角膜移植片　full thickness corneal graft
全层角膜移植物/穿透性移植物　penetrating graft
全层皮移植片/全層移植物　full-thickness graft
全肠外营养/全營養注射劑　total parenteral nutrition, TPN
全程血尿/完全血尿　total hematuria
全垂体功能减退症/全腦下垂體機能不足　panhypopituitarism
全瓷冠/全瓷冠　all-ceramic crown
全蛋白/完整蛋白質　whole protein
全动脉炎/全動脈炎　panarteritis
全耳炎/全耳炎　panotitis
全反式维甲酸/全反維他命 A 酸　all-trans-retinoic acid
全肺静脉异位引流/全肺靜脈異位引流　total anomalous pulmonary venous drainage
全肺阻力/全部肺部血管抵抗力　total pulmonary resistance
全腹腔脏器移植/全腹腔臟器移植　whole abdominal multivisceral transplantation
全骨髓增生/骨髓全部增生　panmyelosis
全骨炎/全骨炎　general osteitis
全冠/完整牙冠　full crown
全颌种植体/全頜種植體　complete implant
全喉切开术/全喉切開術　complete laryngotomy
全厚瓣/全厚瓣　full thickness flap
全厚皮肤移植/全厚皮膚移植　full thickness skin transplantation
全厚皮片/全厚皮片　full thickness free skin graft
全畸形/全畸形　pantamorphia
全脊髓阻滞麻醉/全脊髓阻斷麻醉　total spinal block
全脊椎麻醉/全脊椎麻醉　total spinal anesthesia
全睑球粘连/全瞼粘連　pantankyloblepharon
全[浆分]泌腺/全泌腺　holocrine gland
全焦距透镜/全焦距透鏡　omnifocal lens
全结肠切除术/全結腸切除術　total colectomy
全结肠炎/全結腸炎　pancolitis

全景放射摄影术/全景放射攝影術　panoramic radiography
全局关系/全域關係　holotopy
全口义齿/全口假牙　complete denture
全口义齿修复学/全口義齒修復學　complete prosthodontics
全裂/全胚分裂　complete cleavage
全氯萘/全氯萘　perna
全氯萘病/全氯萘皮病，氯瘡病　perna disease
全麻分子学说/全麻分子學説　molecular theory of general anesthesia
全麻原理/全麻原理　mechanism of general anesthesia
全盲/全盲　total blindness
全酶/全酶　holoenzyme
全面康复/全面康復　comprehensive rehabilitation
全面质量管理/全面品質管制　total quality control, total quality management
全民健康保险/全民健康保險　universal coverage
全脑炎/全腦炎　panencephalitis
全能的/全能的　totipotential
全能干细胞/全能幹細胞　totipotent stem cell
全能造血干细胞/多潛能造血幹細胞　multipotential hematopoietic stem cell, multipotential hemopoietic stem cell
全凝集[反应]/全凝集　panagglutination
全[膀胱]壁纤维变性/全膀胱壁纖維變性　panmural fibrosis
全葡萄膜炎/全葡萄膜炎，全眼角膜炎　panuveitis
全[潜]能细胞/全[潛]能細胞　totipotent cell, totipotential cell
全染性/全染性　panchromia
全色盲/全色盲　achromatopsia
全色盲者/單色視者，完全色盲者　monochromat
全身白化病/全身白化病　total albinism
全身病性溃疡/全身病性潰瘍　constitutional ulcer
全身[播散]性的/全身的　generalized
全身脆弱性骨硬化/全身骨脆弱性硬化　osteopoikilosis
全身发作/全身發作　generalized seizure
全身肥胖症/全身肥胖病　adiposis universalis
全身辐射量计数/全身輻射量計數　whole-body counting
全身负荷/全身負荷　body burden
全身钙质沉着/全身鈣質沈著症　calcinosis universalis
全身感觉/全身感覺　general sense
全身感染/全身感染　general infection

全身关节炎/全身關節炎　hamarthritis
全身裹法/全身裹法　full pack
全身疾病/一般疾病　general disease
全身结核病/全身性結核　general tuberculosis
全身糠秕性秃发/全身糠秕性禿髮　alopecia pityroides universalis
全身麻痹症/全身麻痺　general paralysis
全身麻醉/全身麻醉法　general anesthesia
全身麻醉剂/全身麻醉劑　general anesthetic
全身麻醉药/全身麻醉藥,全身麻醉劑　general anesthetic
全身梅毒/全身性梅毒　constitutional syphilis
全身梅毒病/梅毒病,全身梅毒　syphilosis
全身弥漫性体血管角化瘤/全身彌漫性軀幹血管角化瘤　angiokeratoma corporis diffusum universale
全身性囊状骨炎/全身囊狀骨炎　osteitis cystica generalisata
全身偏侧萎缩/全身偏側萎縮　total hemiatrophy
全身强壮药/全身強壯藥　general tonic
全身适应综合征/全身適應症候群　general adaptation syndrome
全身体积描记术/全身體積描記術　whole body plethysmography
全身痛/全身痛　pantalgia
全身秃/全身禿　alopecia generalisata
全身脱毛/全身禿毛　alopecia universalis
全身萎缩/全身萎縮　general atrophy
全身兴奋剂/全身性興奮藥　general stimulant
全身性玻璃样变性/全身性玻璃樣體增生症　systemic hyalinosis
全身性痤疮/全身性痤瘡　acne generalis
全身性癫痫/全身性癲癇　generalized epilepsy
全身性淀粉样变[性病]/全身性澱粉樣變性病　systemic amyloidosis
全身性多中心性脂肪母细胞增生病/全身性多中心性脂肪母細胞增生症　systemic multicentric lipoblastosis
全身性非白血病性网状内皮组织增殖/全身性非白血病性網狀內皮病　systemic aleukemic reticuloendotheliosis
全身性感染/全身性感染　systemic infection
全身性红斑狼疮/全身性紅斑狼瘡　erythematosus
全身性疾病/系統病　systemic disease
全身性脊髓病/全身性脊髓病　systemic myelopathy
全身性进行性硬化病/全身性進行性硬化病　systemic progressive sclerosis
全身性牛痘/全身性牛痘　generalized vaccinia
全身性牛皮癣/全身牛皮癣　psoriasis universalis

全身性铍沉着病/全身性鈹沈著症　systemic berylliosis
全身性肉瘤病/全身性肉瘤病　general sarcomatosis
全身性水肿/全身水腫　anasarca
全身性幼稚型/全身幼稚型　universal infantilism
全身性脂肪营养不良/全身性脂質失養症　generalized lipodystrophy
全身营养/全身營養　general nutrition
全身照射/全身性照射法　whole-body irradiation
全身症状/全身症狀　constitutional symptom
全身脂肪营养不良/全身脂肪營養不良　total lipodystrophy
全身作用/全身作用　general action
全收缩期杂音/全收縮期雜音　holosystolic murmur
全体层摄影术/全體層照相術　pantomography
全听骨链[重建]赝复物/全聽骨鏈[重建]贗複物　total ossicular replacement prosthesis
全同胞/全同胞　fullsib
全头皮撕脱[伤]/全頭皮撕脱[傷]　total scalp avulsion injury
全秃/全秃　alopecia capitis totalis, alopecia totalis
全腿长/全腿長　total leg length
全胃肠外营养/全注射營養法　total parenteral nutrition
全无脑/全無腦畸形　pantanencephaly
全息摄影术/全方位照相術　holography
全T细胞试剂/泛T細胞試劑　pan T-cell reagent
全小肠移植/全小腸移植　whole small intestine transplantation
全蝎/全蠍　scorpion
全血/全血　whole blood
全血初细胞增生/母紅白血球血小板過多病　erythroleukothrombocythemia
全血管翳/全血管翳　total pannus
全血激活凝血时间/全血啟動凝血時間　activated blood clotting time
全血交换输血/全血交換輸血　whole blood exchange transfusion
全血凝固时间/全血凝固時間　whole blood coagulation time
全血细胞减少/全部血球減少　pancytopenia
全血细胞减少伴先天性缺陷/全血細胞減少合并先天性缺陷　pancytopenia with congenital defects
全血细胞溶解/全部血球溶解　pancytolysis
全颜面骨骨折/全顏面骨骨折　panfacial fracture
全眼球炎/全眼球炎　panophthalmitis
全胰十二指肠切除术/全胰十二指腸切除術　total pancreaticoduodenectomy

全胰腺移植/全胰腺移植 whole pancreas transplantation
全硬化/[完]全硬化 pansclerosis
全知/全知 omniscience
全肢断离者/無肢病例 basket case
全直肠结肠切除术/全部直腸及結腸切除術 panproctocolectomy
全质分泌/全漿分泌 holocrine
全质分泌腺/全質分泌腺 holocrine gland
全子宫卵巢切除术/全部子宮卵巢切除術 panhystero-oophorectomy
全子宫切除术/全部子宮切除術,子宮全切除術 panhysterectomy
全子宫输卵管卵巢切除术/全部子宮輸卵管卵巢切除術 panhysterosalpingo-oophorectomy
全子宫输卵管切除术/全部子宮輸卵管切除術 panhysterosalpingectomy
全自动双腔起搏/全自動雙腔起搏 fully automatic dual chamber pacing
全纵隔清扫术/全縱隔清掃術 en bloc mediastinal dissection
泉古菌门/泉古菌門 Crenarchaeota
拳/拳 fist
拳绷带/拳繃帶 closed fist bandage
拳击手骨折/拳擊手骨折 boxer fracture
拳击样舞蹈病/擊拳狀舞蹈病 hammering chorea
拳击员脑病/拳擊手腦病 punchdrunk
拳叩诊/拳叩診 fist percussion
拳参/拳參 bistort, bistort rhizome
蜷腿位置/蜷曲姿勢 coiled position
醛/醛 aldehyde
醛苷/醛苷 aldehyde glycoside
醛固酮/醛固酮 aldosterone
醛固酮合酶/醛固酮合酶 aldosterone synthase
醛固酮减少症/醛固酮缺乏 hypoaldosteronism
醛固酮拮抗药/醛固酮拮抗藥 aldosterone antagonists
醛固酮受体/醛固酮受體 aldosterone receptors
醛固酮腺瘤/醛固酮腺瘤 aldosterone-producing adenoma
醛固酮抑制药/醛固酮抑制劑 aldosterone inhibitor
醛固酮增多症/醛固醇過多症 hyperaldosteronism
醛还原酶/醛還原酶 aldehyde reductase
醛[基]赖氨酸/醛基賴胺酸 allysine
醛碱/醛基 aldin
醛连接酶/碳連酶,聚醛酶 carboligase
醛裂合酶类/醛裂合酶類 aldehyde-lyases
醛酶/醛酵素 aldehydase

醛歧化酶/醛變酶 aldehyde mutase
醛酸类/醛酸類 aldehydic acids
醛缩酶/醛縮酶 aldolase
醛糖/醛醣 aldose
醛糖二糖酸/醛醣二醣酸 aldobionic acid
醛糖苷/醛醣苷 aldoside
醛糖还原酶抑制药/醛醣還原酶抑制藥 aldose reductase inhibitor
醛糖酮糖异构酶类/醛醣酮醣異構酶類 aldose-ketose isomerases
醛酮转移酶类/醛酮轉移酶類 aldehyde-ketone transferases
醛脱氢酶/醛脱氫酶 aldehyde dehydrogenase
醛氧化还原酶类/醛氧化還原酶類 aldehyde oxidoreductases
醛氧化酶/醛氧化酶 aldehyde oxidase
醛甾酮/醛甾酮 aldosterone
醛甾酮过多症/腎上腺留鹽激素過多症 aldosteronism
醛甾酮过少症/醛甾酮過少症 aldosteronopenia
醛甾酮拮抗剂/醛固酮拮抗劑 aldosterone antagonist
醛甾酮类药/醛固酮類藥 aldosterones
醛甾酮瘤/留鹽激素瘤 aldosteronoma
醛甾酮尿/留鹽激素尿 aldosteronuria
醛甾酮生成/留鹽激素生成 aldosteronogenesis
醛甾酮抑制药/醛固酮抑制藥 aldosterone inhibitor
颧大肌/顴大肌,大顴肌 zygomaticus major, greater zygomatic muscle, zygomaticus major muscle
颧点/顴點,顴穴 zygion, jugale
颧疔/顴疔 furuncle on cheek, zygomatic ding
颧弓/顴弓 zygomatic arch, malar arch
颧弓韧带/顴弓韌帶 zygomatic ligament
颧弓位投照术/顴弓位投照術 roentgenography of zygomatic arch
颧骨/顴骨 zygomatic bone, cheek bone
颧骨点/方軛骨 jugale
颧骨额突/顴骨額突 frontal process of zygomatic bone
颧骨骨折/顴骨骨折 zygomatic fracture
颧骨眶隆起/顴骨眶隆起 orbital eminence of zygomatic bone
颧骨颞突/顴骨颞突 temporal process of zygomatic bone
颧骨缘结节/顴骨緣結節 marginal tubercle of zygomatic bone
颧颌点/顴頜點 zygomaxillare
颧红/顴紅 hectic cheek

颧肌/顴肌　zygomaticus
颧颊潮红/顴部潮紅　malar flush
颧疽/顴疽　zygomatic carbuncle
颧眶动脉/顴眶動脈　zygomaticoorbital artery
颧眶孔/顴眶孔　zygomaticoorbital foramen
颧髎/顴髎　quanliao, SI18
颧淋巴结/顴淋巴結　malar lymph node
颧面孔/顴面孔　zygomaticofacial foramen
颧面神经/顴面神經　zygomaticofacial nerve
颧面支/顴面支　zygomaticofacial branch
颧颞孔/顴顳孔　zygomaticotemporal foramen
颧颞神经/顴顳神經　zygomaticotemporal nerve
颧颞支/顴顳支　zygomaticotemporal branch
颧前孔/顴前孔　anterior zygomatic foramen
颧区/顴部　zygomatic region
颧上颌缝/顴頜縫　zygomaticomaxillary suture
颧神经/顴神經　zygomatic nerve, nerve zygomaticus
颧神经交通支/與顴神經交通支　communicating branch with zygomatic nerve
颧突/顴突　zygomatic process, malar process
颧突度/顴突度　zygomatic projection
颧小肌/顴小肌, 小顴肌　zygomaticus minor, lesser zygomatic muscle, zygomaticus minor muscle
颧痈/顴癰　zygomatic abscess
颧缘/顴緣　zygomatic margin
颧支/顴支　zygomatic branch
犬埃里希体/犬埃里希體　Ehrlichia canis
犬肠道孤病毒/犬腸道孤病毒　ECDO virus
犬齿肌/犬齒肌　canine muscle
犬传染性肝炎/犬傳染性肝炎　infectious canine hepatitis
犬的/犬的　canine
犬恶丝虫/犬心絲蟲　Dirofilaria immitis
犬吠样咳/犬吠樣欬嗽　dog cough
犬复孔绦虫/橢圓條蟲　Taenia elliptica
犬弓蛔虫感染/狗毒蛔蟲感染　toxocara canis infection
犬钩端螺旋体/犬疫螺旋體　Leptospira canicola
犬钩[口线]虫/犬鉤蟲　Ancylostoma caninum
犬嚼食欲/犬嚼食慾　canine appetite
犬疥疮/犬疥瘡　canine scabies
犬髋发育不良/犬髖發育不良　canine hip dysplasia
犬尿氨酸/犬尿素　kynurenine
犬尿胺/犬尿胺　kynuramine
犬尿喹啉酸/犬尿喹啉酸　kynurenic acid
犬乳头瘤病毒/犬乳頭狀瘤病毒　canine papilloma virus
犬属/犬屬　Canis
犬瘟热/犬瘟熱　canine distemper
犬瘟热病毒/犬瘟熱病毒　canine distemper virus
犬血巴尔通体/犬血巴通蟲　Haemobartonella canis
劝导交谈/勸導交談　persuasive communication
劝告/建議,忠告　advice
炔雌醇/乙炔基雌二醇　ethinyl estradiol
炔雌醚/炔雌醚　quinestrol
炔己蚁胺/炔己蟻胺　ethinamate
炔类/炔類　alkynes
炔诺酮/炔諾酮　norethindrone
炔孕酮/羥脱水孕酮　ethisterone
缺顶露脑畸胎/缺頂露腦畸胎　hyperencephalus
缺乏/缺乏,不足　deficiency, paucity
缺乏症/缺乏症　deficiency disease
缺乏症状/缺乏症狀　deficiency symptom
缺钙/鈣缺乏　acalcerosis
缺钙症/鈣缺乏病　acalcicosis
缺过氧化氢酶血症/缺過氧化氫酶血症　acatalasemia
缺口平移/缺口平移　nick translation
缺磷症/磷質缺乏病　aphosphorosis
缺氯性氮血[症]/低氯氮血症　chloropenic azotemia
缺盆/缺盆　quepen, ST12
缺盆疽/缺盆疽　quepen scrofula, scrofula in supraclavicular fossa
缺乳/缺乳　oligogalactia, agalactia, hypogalactia
缺乳·肝气郁结证/缺乳·肝氣鬱結證　oligogalactia with pattern of liver qi depression
缺乳·气血两虚证/缺乳·氣血兩虛證　oligogalactia with pattern of deficiency of both qi and blood
缺乳·痰浊阻滞证/缺乳·痰濁阻滯證　oligogalactia with pattern of blockade of phlegm-turbidity
缺失定位[法]/缺失定位[法]　deletion mapping
缺蚀菌落/咬痕狀菌落　bitten colony
缺水血[症]/血内缺乏水分　anhydremia
缺损/缺損　coloboma
缺损实验/缺點試驗　defect experiment
缺体生物/缺體生物　nullisomic
缺铁性贫血/缺鐵性貧血　iron deficiency anemia
缺铁性吞咽困难综合征/缺鐵性吞嚥困難症候群　sideropenic dysphagia syndrome
缺铁性咽下困难/缺鐵性消化不良及吞嚥困難　sideropenic dysphagia
缺隙保持器/間隙保持器　space maintainer
缺陷/缺損,不全　defect, deficiency
缺陷病毒/缺陷病毒　defective virus
缺血/缺血　ischemia
缺血后乳头肌断裂/缺血後乳頭肌斷裂

postischemic papillary muscle rupture
缺血后乳头肌功能不良/缺血後乳頭肌功能不良 postischemic papillary muscle dysfunction
缺血性肝炎/缺氧性肝炎 ischemic hepatitis
缺血性坏死/缺血性壞死 ischemic necrosis
缺血性肌挛缩/缺血性肌攣縮 ischemic contracture
缺血性结肠炎/缺血性結腸炎 ischemic colitis
缺血性溃疡/缺血性潰瘍 ischemic ulcer
缺血性挛缩/缺血性攣縮 ischemic contracture
缺血性麻痹/缺血性麻痺 ischemic palsy
缺血性脑血管疾病手术/缺血性腦血管疾病手術 operation for ischemic cerebrovascular diseases
缺血性神经病/缺血性神經病變 ischemic neuropathy
缺血性肾炎/缺血性腎炎 ischemic nephritis
缺血性视神经病变/缺血性視神經病變 ischemic optic neuropathy
缺血性水肿/缺血性水腫 ischemic edema
缺血性停搏/缺血性停搏 ischemic arrest
缺血性心脏病/缺血性心臟病 ischemic heart disease
缺血性腰痛/缺血性腰痛 ischemic lumbago
缺血预处理/缺血預處理 ischemic preconditioning
缺牙间隙/無牙隙,缺牙隙 edentulous space
缺盐综合征/缺鹽症候群 salt depletion syndrome
缺氧/缺氧 oxygen deficit
缺氧缺血性脑病/缺氧缺血性腦病 hypoxic ischemic encephalopathy
缺氧性脑病/缺氧性腦病變 hypoxic encephalopathy
缺氧性缺氧/缺氧性缺氧症 anoxic anoxia
缺氧性停搏/缺氧性停搏 anoxic arrest
缺氧指示剂/厭氧指示劑 anaerobic indicator
缺医地区/缺醫地區 medically underserved area
缺肢/缺肢,肢不全畸形 ectromelia
缺指畸形/缺指畸形 ectrodactylia
缺趾畸形/缺趾畸形 ectrodactylia
雀稗中毒/雀稗中毒 paspalism
雀斑/雀斑 ephelis, freckle
雀斑痣/雀斑痣 lentigo
雀斑状的/雀斑的 lentiginous
雀啄灸/雀啄灸 sparrow-pecking moxibustion
确定成分培养基/確定成分培養基,已知成分培養液 defined medium
确立细胞株/已建立之細胞族 established cell strain
群勃龙/群勃龍 trenbolone
群集/群集 swarm
群居性痢疾/收容所痢疾 asylum dysentery
群聚性眶周粉刺/群聚性眶周粉刺 grouped periorbital comedo
群落生态学/共同環境適應學,集體生態學 synecology
群凝集[反应]/群凝集[反應] group agglutination
群特异性抗原/群特異性抗原 group-specific antigen
群体传染/群眾傳染 herd infection
群体反应性抗体/群體反應性抗體 panel reaction antibody
群体家庭/群體家庭 group home
群体免疫/群眾免疫 herd immunity
群体免疫接种法/群體免疫接種法 mass immunization
群体药动学/群體藥動學 population pharmacokinetics
群体遗传学/群體遺傳學 population genetics

R

然谷/然谷　rangu, KI2
燃料热值/燃值　fuel value
燃烧/燃燒　burn
燃烧弹烧伤/燃燒彈燒傷　incendiary bomb burn
燃素/燃素　phlogiston
燃油/燃油　fuel oil
染发剂/染髮劑　hair dye
染工[膀胱]癌/染工[膀胱]癌　dye worker cancer
染料/染料　dye
染料积存/染料積存　dye pooling
染料激光器/染料雷射器　dye laser
染料流畅试验/染料流暢試驗　dye outflow test
染料木黄酮/染料木黄酮　genistein
染料排斥试验/染料排斥試驗　dye exclusion test
染料试验/染料試驗　dye test
染料稀释技术/染料稀釋技術　dye dilution technique
染料稀释曲线法/染料稀釋曲線法　dye dilution curve method
染料原液/染料原液　stock staining solution
染色/染色　staining
染色不足/弱染,染色過弱　understain
染色单体/染色單體　chromatid
染色过度/過度染色　overstain
染色剂/染色,染料　stain
染色检尿法/染色檢尿法　chromourinography
染色粒/染色粒　chromomere
染色输尿管镜检查/染色輸尿管鏡檢法　chromoureteroscopy
染色体/染色體　chromosome
X染色体/X染色體　X chromosome
Y染色体/Y染色體　Y chromosome
染色体臂/染色體臂　chromosome arm
染色体病/染色體病　chromosome disease
染色体不完整微核/染色體不完整微核　chromosome-defective micronuclei
染色体不稳定性/染色體不穩定性　chromosomal instability
染色体步移/染色體步移　chromosome walking
染色体重排/染色體重排　chromosome rearrangement
染色体脆性/染色體脆性　chromosome fragility

染色体脆性位点/染色體脆性位點　chromosome fragile site
染色体倒位/染色體倒位　chromosome inversion
染色体定位/染色體定位　chromosome positioning
染色体丢失/染色體丟失　chromosome loss
染色体断裂/染色體斷裂　chromosomal aberration, chromosome breakage
染色体多态性/染色體多態性　chromosomal polymorphism
染色体分离/染色體分離　chromosome segregation
染色体基因/染色體基因　chromogene
染色体畸变/染色體畸變　chromosome aberration
染色体交叉/染色體交叉　chromosomal chiasma
染色体结构/染色體結構　chromosome structure
染色体结合期/染色體接合期　synaptic phase
染色体介导耐药性/染色體介導耐藥性　chromosome-mediated resistance
染色体配对/染色體配對　chromosome pairing
染色体缺失/染色體缺失　chromosome deletion
[染色体]缺失综合征/缺失症候群　deletion syndrome
染色体21三体综合征/三染色體21症,唐氏症　trisomy 21 syndrome
染色体随体/附染色體　chromosomal satellite
染色体跳移/染色體跳移　chromosome jumping
染色体突变/染色體突變　chromosome mutation
染色体图/染色體圖　chromosome mapping
染色体图染/染色體圖染　chromosome painting
染色体外遗传/非染色體性遺傳　extrachromosomal inheritance
染色体文库/染色體文庫　chromosome library
染色体显带/染色體顯帶　chromosome banding
染色体显带技术/染色體顯帶技術　chromosome banding technique
染色体性别/染色體性別　chromosmal sex
染色体原位杂交/染色體原位雜交　in situ chromosomal hybridization
染色体障碍/染色體障礙　chromosome disorder
染色体组型分型/核型分析　karyotyping
染色微粒/染色體微粒,染色小粒　chromiole
染色胃液检查/胃液染色檢查法　gastric

chromoscopy
染色质/染色質 chromatin
染色质粒/嗜色粒,尼索氏小體 chromatic granule
染色质粒融合/核絲融合 mitapsis
染色质免疫沉淀法/染色質免疫沈澱法 chromatin immunoprecipitation
染色质溶解/核染質溶解 chromatolysis
染色质丝/核染質纖維 chromatic fiber
染色质碎裂/核染質破裂 chromatinorrhexis
染色质纹/紋染細胞 stichochrome
染色质屑/核染質小粒,核染質屑 chromatin dust
染色质移动/核染質移動 chromatocinesis
染深色的/著色過深的,濃染的 hyperchromatic
染苔/染苔 stained fur
染液/染液 staining solution
让德尔固定液/Gendre 氏固定液 Gendre fixing fluid
让苏尔病/Gensoul 氏病 Gensoul disease
饶舌癖/饒舌癖,贅語癖 verbomania
桡侧/橈側 radial
桡侧半肢畸形/橈側半肢畸形 radial hemimelia
桡侧返动脉/橈返動脈 radial recurrent artery
桡侧副动脉/橈側副動脈 radial collateral artery
桡侧副韧带/橈側副韌帶 radial collateral ligament
桡侧屈腕肌/橈側屈腕肌 flexor carpi ulnaris
桡侧伸腕肌腱周围炎/橈側伸腕肌腱周圍炎 perimyotenositis of extensor of radial aspect
桡侧腕长伸肌/橈側伸腕長肌 extensor carpi radialis longus
桡侧腕短伸肌/橈側伸腕短肌 extensor carpi radialis brevis
桡侧腕短伸肌囊/橈側伸腕短肌囊 bursa of extensor carpi radialis brevis
桡侧腕骨/橈側腕骨 radial carpal bone
桡侧腕屈肌/橈側屈腕肌 flexor carpi radialis
桡侧腕屈肌腱鞘/橈側屈腕肌腱鞘 tendinous sheath of flexor carpi radialis
桡侧腕伸肌腱鞘/橈側伸腕肌腱鞘 tendinous sheath of extensores carpi radialis
桡侧掌骨点/橈側掌骨點 metacarpale radiale
桡侧支动脉/橈側支動脈 collateral radial artery
桡尺骨间韧带/橈尺骨間韌帶 radioulnar interosseous ligament
桡尺骨切迹/橈尺骨切跡,橈骨乙狀窩 sigmoid cavity of radius
桡尺骨融合/橈尺骨融合 radioulnar synostosis
桡尺近侧关节/橈尺近側關節 proximal radioulnar joint, proximal radioulnar articulation
桡尺连结/橈尺韌帶聯合 radioulnar syndesmosis

桡尺上关节/橈尺上關節 superior cubitoradial articulation
桡尺下关节/橈尺下關節 inferior cubitoradial articulation
桡尺远侧关节/橈尺遠側關節 distal radioulnar joint, distal radioulnar articulation
桡尺远侧关节盘/橈尺遠側關節盤 discus articulatio radioulnaris distalis
桡动脉/橈動脈 radial artery
[桡动脉]腕掌支/[橈動脈]腕掌支 palmar carpal branch
桡骨/橈骨 radius, radial bone
桡骨背侧结节/橈骨背側結節 dorsal tubercle of radius
桡骨粗隆/橈骨粗隆 radial tuberosity
桡骨倒错反射/反橈骨反射 inverted radial reflex
桡骨点/橈側頭 radiale
桡骨干骨折/橈骨幹骨折 fracture of shaft of radius, radial shaft fracture
桡骨骨间缘/橈骨骨間緣 interosseous border of radius
桡骨骨折/橈骨骨折 radial fracture
桡骨关节凹/橈骨關節凹 articular fovea of radius
桡骨关节前韧带/橈腕關節前韌帶 anterior ligament of radiocarpal joint
桡骨冠状韧带/橈骨冠狀韌帶 coronary ligament of radius
桡骨后面/橈骨後面 posterior surface of radius
桡骨后缘/橈骨後緣 posterior border of radius
桡骨环状关节面/橈骨環狀關節面 articular circumference of radius
桡骨环状韧带/橈骨環狀韌帶 annular ligament of radius, annular ligament of digits of radius
桡骨茎突/橈骨莖突 styloid process of radius
桡骨茎突狭窄性腱鞘炎/橈骨莖突狹窄性腱鞘炎 de Quervain disease
桡骨颈/橈骨頸 neck of radius
桡骨前面/橈骨前面 anterior surface of radius
桡骨前缘/橈骨前緣 anterior border of radius
桡骨缺如/橈骨缺如,橈骨缺乏 absence of radius
桡骨体/橈骨體 shaft of radius
桡骨头/橈骨頭 head of radius
桡骨头半脱位/橈骨頭半脱位 radial head subluxation, subluxation of radial head
桡骨头骨折/橈[骨]頭骨折 fracture of head of radius, radius head fracture
桡骨外侧面/橈骨外側面 lateral surface of radius
桡骨弯曲/彎曲橈骨 radius curvus

桡骨窝/橈骨凹　radial depression
桡骨下1/3骨折合并下桡尺骨关节脱位/橈骨下1/3骨折合并下橈尺骨關節脫位　fracture of lower 1/3 of radius combined with dislocation of lower ulnaradius joint
桡骨小头半脱位/橈骨小頭半脱位　radial head subluxation
桡骨远端骨折/橈骨遠端骨折　distal fracture of radius
桡骨中下/橈骨中下　fracture of lower end of radius complicated with distal radioulnar dislocation
桡箕/橈箕　radial loop
桡静脉/橈静脈　radial vein
桡偏手/橈偏手　radial clubhand
桡浅神经/橈淺神經　superficial radial nerve
桡切迹/橈骨切跡　radial notch
桡深神经/橈深神經　deep radial nerve
桡神经/橈神經　radial nerve
桡神经病/橈神經病　radial neuropathy
桡神经沟/橈神經溝　groove for radial nerve, sulcus for radial nerve, radial groove
桡神经肌支/橈神經肌支　muscular branch of radial nerve
桡神经浅支/橈神經淺支　superficial branch of radial nerve
桡神经深支/橈神經深支　deep branch of radial nerve
桡神经指背神经/橈指指背神經　dorsal digital nerve of radial nerve
桡头/橈[側]頭　radial head
桡外静脉/橈外静脈　external radial vein
桡腕背侧韧带/橈腕背側韌帶　dorsal radiocarpal ligament
桡腕侧副韧带/橈腕側副韌帶　radial collateral ligament of carpus
桡腕关节/橈腕關節　radiocarpal joint, radiocarpal articulation
桡腕关节背侧韧带/橈腕關節背側韌帶　dorsal ligament of radiocarpal joint
桡腕韧带/橈腕韌帶　radiocarpal ligament
桡腕掌侧韧带/橈腕掌側韌帶　palmar radiocarpal ligament
桡窝/橈骨窩　radial fossa
桡指背神经/橈指背神經　radial dorsal digital nerve
桡足虫/橈足蟲　copepod
绕丹宁/繞丹寧　Rhodanine
绕道术后皮肤变化/繞道術後皮膚變化　skin change after by-pass operation
绕核性白内障/核周圍内障　perinuclear cataract
绕圈病/迴旋病　circling disease
绕转/繞轉,迴轉　revolution
惹迪韧带/Gerdy氏韌帶　Gerdy ligament
热按摩疗法/加熱按摩法　thermomassage
热保留/熱保留　heat retention
热闭/熱閉　heat blockade
热痹/熱痺　arthralgia caused by heat pathogen, heat bi
热变色效应/熱色效應　thermochromism effect
热病/熱病　pyreticosis
热病论/熱病論,發熱論　pyretography
热病性尿/熱病性尿　febrile urine
热病性荨麻疹/熱病性蕁麻疹　urticaria febrilis
热病学/熱病學　pyretology
热病饮食/熱病食物　fever diet
热病谵妄/熱病譫妄,熱性譫妄　febrile delirium
热潮红/熱潮紅　hot flash
热沉淀反应/熱沈澱法,煮沸沈澱　thermoprecipitation
热沉淀素试验/熱沈澱素試驗　thermoprecipitin test
热沉淀原/熱沈澱素原　thermoprecipitinogen
热炽津伤/熱熾津傷　injury of fluid due to exuberant heat
热穿通伤/熱穿通傷　heat perforating wound
热疮/熱瘡　heat sore, herpes simplex
热疮・肺胃热盛证/熱瘡・肺胃熱盛證　heat sore with pattern of heat exuberance in lung and stomach
热疮・风热外袭证/熱瘡・風熱外襲證　heat sore with pattern of external assault by wind-heat
热疮・阴虚内热证/熱瘡・陰虛内熱證　heat sore with pattern of yin deficiency and internal heat
热带/熱帶　hot band
热带崩蚀性溃疡/熱帶崩蝕性潰瘍　tropical phagedenic ulcer
热带病/熱帶病　tropical disease
热带臭虫/熱帶臭蟲　Cimex hemipterus
热带疮/熱帶瘡　tropical sore
热带痤疮/熱帶痤瘡　tropical acne
热带的/熱帶的　tropical
热带耳病/熱帶外耳道炎　tropical ear
热带腹股沟乳头[状]瘤/熱帶性腹股溝乳頭狀瘤　papilloma inguinale tropicum
热带腹泻/熱帶腹瀉　tropical diarrhea
热带棘皮瘤/熱帶棘皮瘤　acanthoma tropicum
热带假丝酵母/熱帶念珠菌　Candida tropicalis
热带痉挛性轻截瘫/熱帶痙攣性下身輕癱　tropical spastic paraparesis

热带溃疡/熱帶潰瘍　tropical ulcer
热带利什曼原虫/熱帶利什曼原蟲　Leishmania tropica
热带气候/熱帶氣候　tropical climate
热带嗜曙红细胞增多性哮喘/熱帶嗜伊紅血球增多性哮喘　tropical eosinophilic asthma
热带嗜酸粒细胞增多症/熱帶性嗜伊紅血球增多症　tropical eosinophilia
热带鼠恙虫/熱帶鼠恙蟲　tropical rat mite
热带无汗性衰弱/熱帶性汗閉性衰弱　tropical anhidrotic asthenia
热带象皮病/熱帶象皮病　elephantiasis tropica
热带性贲门痉挛/熱帶性賁門痙攣　tropical cardiospasm
热带性痤疮/熱帶性痤瘡　acne tropicalis
热带性肺嗜酸细胞浸润症/熱帶性肺嗜酸細胞浸潤症　tropical pulmonary eosinophilia
热带性汗闭/熱帶性汗閉　tropical anhidrosis
热带性健忘/熱帶性健忘　tropical amnesia
热带性口炎性腹泻/熱帶性口炎性腹瀉　tropical sprue
热带性脓性肌炎/熱帶性肌炎　bungpagga
热带性心肌内膜纤维化/熱帶性心肌内膜纖維化　tropical endomyocardial fibrosis
热带性咽下困难/熱帶咽難症　tropical dysphagia
热带医学/熱帶[病]醫學　tropical medicine
热带肿/熱帶腫病　tropical swelling
热点/熱覺點　hot spot
热电流/熱電流　thermocurrent
热电偶检测器/熱電偶檢測器　thermocouple detector
热电针/熱電針　thermo-electric needle
热毒/熱毒　heat-toxicity
热毒闭肺证/熱毒閉肺證　pattern of heat-toxicity blocking lung
热毒攻喉证/熱毒攻喉證　pattern of heat-toxicity invading throat
热毒攻舌证/熱毒攻舌證　pattern of heat-toxicity invading tongue
热毒内陷证/熱毒内陷證　pattern of interior invaded by heat-toxicity
热毒伤阴证/熱毒傷陰證　pattern of yin injured by heat-toxicity
热毒壅聚头面证/熱毒壅聚頭面證　pattern of heat-toxicity stagnated in head and face
热毒蕴结冲任/熱毒蘊結冲任　accumulation and binding of heat-poison in thoroughfare and conception channels

热遏/熱遏　blocked heat
热敷[法]/熱敷法　hot compress
热敷疗法/熱敷療法　hot compress therapy
热伏冲任/熱伏冲任　heat hiding in thoroughfare and conception channels, heat lodging in Chong and Conception Channels
热服/熱服　administered hot
热辐射/熱輻射　radiation of heat
热辐射烧伤/熱輻射燒傷　heat radiation burn
热辐射[线]/熱輻射線　caloradiance
热固性/熱成型　thermoset
热滚筒挤压伤/熱滾筒擠壓傷　hot roller crush injury
热滚筒烧伤/熱滾筒燒傷　hot roller burn
热裹法/熱濕布裹法　hot pack
热烘疗法/熱烘療法　baking after topical medication
热化学/熱化學　thermochemistry
热活检/熱活檢　hot biopsy
热激蛋白/熱休克蛋白　heat-shock protein
热激反应/熱休克反應　heat-shock response
热激红斑/温度性紅斑　erythema caloricum
热极生风/熱極生風　extreme heat causing wind
热觉过敏/熱覺過敏　hyperthermalgesia
热结/熱積聚　heat accumulation
热结旁流/熱結旁流　heat fecaloma with watery discharge
热结膀胱/熱結膀胱　heat accumulation of bladder
热解重量分析计/温度比重計　thermogravimeter
热厥/熱[昏]厥　heat syncope, syncope due to excessive heat
热卡摄取量/熱卡攝取量　calorie intake
热炕癌/熱炕癌，火籃癌　kangri cancer
热扩散/加熱擴散　thermodiffusion
热扩散时间/熱擴散時間　thermal diffusion time
热烙气管切开术/熱烙氣管切開術　thermotracheotomy
热烙手术/烙器手術　ignioperation
热烙术/熱烙術，熱灼法　thermocautery
热泪/熱淚　hot lacrimation
热离子发射/熱離子發射　thermionic emission
热离子学/熱離子學　thermionics
热离子整流器/熱離子整流器　thermionic rectifier
热力灭菌法/加熱滅菌法　thermal sterilization
热力学/熱力學　thermodynamics
热利诺综合征/Gélineau 氏症候群　Gélineau syndrome
热利耶病/Gerlier 氏病　Gerlier disease
热利耶综合征/Gerlier 氏症候群　Gerlier syndrome

热[量]/卡路里　caloric
热量器/熱量計器　caloriscope
热量商数/卡路里商,熱量係數　caloric quotient
热量摄取/熱量攝入　caloric intake
热量限制/熱量限制　caloric restriction
热疗法/熱療法　thermotherapy
热疗学/熱療學　thermatology
热淋/熱淋　heat stranguria, heat strangury
热淋·湿热下注证/熱淋·濕熱下注證　heat strangury with pattern of downward diffusion of damp-heat
热淋·阴虚湿热证/熱淋·陰虛濕熱證　heat strangury with pattern of yin deficiency and damp-heat
热硫化型硅橡胶/熱硫化型矽橡膠　heat-vulcanized silicone rubber
热秘/熱秘　heat constipation
热灭活法/無活性溫熱　thermoinactivation
热敏发光剂量测定法/熱發光劑量測定法　thermoluminescent dosimetry
热能分析器/熱能分析器　thermo-energy analyzer, TEA
热凝固疗法/熱凝固療法　thermal coagulation
热凝固术/加熱凝固法　thermocoagulation
热喷雾接口/熱噴霧接口　thermospray interface
热膨胀/熱脹　thermal expansion
热平衡/熱平衡　thermal balance
热迫大肠/熱迫大腸　heat invading large intestine
热气疗法/熱氣療法　thermaerotherapy
热气浴/熱氣浴　hot-air bath
热球蛋白/熱球蛋白　pyroglobulin
热球蛋白血[症]/熱沈澱球蛋白血症　pyroglobulinemia
热缺血时间/熱缺血時間　warm ischemia time
热扰心神证/熱擾心神證　pattern of heat disturbing heart-mind
热扰胸膈证/熱擾胸膈證　pattern of chest and diaphragm disturbed by heat
热入下焦证/熱入下焦證　pattern of heat invading lower jiao
热入心包/熱入心包　invasion of pericardium by heat
热入心包证/熱入心包證　pattern of invasion of the pericardium by heat
热入血分/熱入血分　heat invading blood phase
热入血室/熱入血室　heat invading blood chamber
热入血室证/熱入血室證　pattern of heat invading blood chamber
热伤肺络证/熱傷肺絡證　pattern of lung collaterals injured by heat
热伤神明/熱傷神明　heat affecting spirit, heat impairing the mind
热烧伤/灼傷,燒傷　thermal burn
热胜则肿/熱勝則腫　predominant heat causing swelling
热盛动风证/熱盛動風證　pattern of stirring wind due to intense heat
热盛动血证/熱盛動血證　pattern of stirring blood due to intense heat
热盛伤津证/熱盛傷津證　pattern of consumption of fluid due to intense heat
热衰竭/中暑衰竭　heat exhaustion
热水浴/熱[水]浴　hot bath
热丝线烧灼/熱絲線燒灼　hot-wire cautery
热塑性/熱塑[性]　thermoplastic
热损伤区[带]/熱損傷區[帶]　thermal injury zone
热痰证/熱痰證　heat-phlegm pattern
热探头凝固[术]/熱探頭凝固[術]　heater probe coagulation
热烫伤目/熱燙傷目　eye injured by overheat
热痛/熱痛　heat pain
热微量转移法/熱微量分離法　thermo micro-application separation, TAS
热稳定性/熱安定性　heat stability
热稀释法/熱稀釋法　thermodilution-method
热陷心包证/熱陷心包證　pattern of invasion of pericardium by heat
热哮/熱哮　heat wheezing
热邪/熱邪　heat pathogen
热性呼吸困难/熱性呼吸困難　thermal dyspnea
热性肌张力计/溫熱張力計,溫熱壓力計　thermotonometer
热性惊厥/熱性痙攣　febrile convulsion
热性视神经病变/熱性視神經病變　thermal optic neuropathy
热性痛觉/溫度痛覺,熱痛覺　thermalgesia
热性痛觉过敏/溫度痛覺過敏,熱痛覺過敏　thermohyperalgesia
热性痛觉缺失/熱性痛覺缺失　thermanalgesia
热性哮喘/熱性哮喘　heat asthma
热性荨麻疹/熱性蕁麻疹　heat urticaria
热性谵妄/熱性譫妄,熱病譫妄　pyretotyphosis
热压伤/熱壓傷　hot crush injury
热痒/熱癢　heat itching
热因热用/熱因熱用　treating false-heat pattern with heat methods
热应激障碍/熱應激障礙　heat stress disorders
热郁/熱鬱,熱滯　heat stagnation
热原/熱原　pyrogen

热原体属/熱原體屬　Thermoplasma
热熨法/熱熨法　hot compress
热瘴/熱瘴　pyrexic miasma
热者寒之/熱者寒之　treating heat pattern with cold methods
热阵/熱陣　heat array
热证/熱證　heat pattern
热致发光/熱致發光　thermoluminescence
热致死时间/熱滅菌時間　thermal death time
热肿/熱腫　heat swelling
热重量分析法/熱重法　thermogravimetry
热重于湿证/熱重於濕證　dampness-heat pattern with predominant heat
热灼术/熱灼術　heat cautery
人艾可病毒/人艾可病毒　Human Echovirus
人白细胞抗原/人白細胞抗原,組織配對抗原　human leukocyte antigen
人肠道病毒A型/人腸道病毒A型　human enterovirus A
人肠道孤[儿]病毒/人腸道孤病毒　enteric cytopathogenic human orphan virus
人肠滴虫/人腸滴蟲　Enteromonas hominis
人-宠物依恋/人-寵物依戀　human-pet bonding
人丹/人丹　rendan mini-pills
人单鞭滴虫/人體單鞭蟲　Cercomonas hominis
人胆酸/人膽酸　fellic acid
人等孢子球虫/人類同形孢子蟲　Isospora hominis
人痘接种术/人痘接種術,天花接種,引痘　variolation
人副流感病毒/人副流感病毒　human parainfluenza virus
人格/人格,人性　personality
人格病患并依赖诉讼/病態人格及依賴訴訟　personality disorder and recourse to litigation
人格发展/人格發展　personality development
人格分裂/人格分裂　split personality
人格解体/人格解體　depersonalization
人格论/人格學　personalistics
人格评价/人格評價　personality assessment
人格缺损性精神分裂症/人格缺損性思覺失調症　defect schizophrenia
人格试验/人格試驗　personality test
人格体质论/人格體質論　theory of personality and constitution
人格阴阳比例组成论/人格陰陽比例組成論　theory of personality composed by yin-yang proportion
人格障碍/人格障礙,性格障礙　character disorder, personality disorder

人工板/人工板　artificial plate
人工瓣膜机械性故障/人工瓣膜機械性故障　mechanical dysfunction of prosthetic valve
人工瓣膜机械性失效/人工瓣膜機械性失效　mechanical failure of prosthetic valve
人工瓣膜心内膜炎/人工瓣膜心內膜炎　prosthetic valve endocarditis
人工鼻/人工鼻,假鼻　artificial nose
人工齿/人工齒　artificial tooth
人工齿列/人工齒列　artificial dentition
人工的/人工的,人造的　artificial
人工低温/誘導性低體溫　induced hypothermia
人工冬眠/人工冬眠　artificial hibernation
人工耳/人工耳　artificial ear
人工肺/人工肺　artificial lung
人工肝/人工肝　artificial liver
人工感染/人工感染　artificial infection
人工肛门/人工肛門　artificial anus
人工骨/人工骨　artificial bone
人工固定式牙种植体/人工固定式牙植體　artificial fixtures dental implant
人工关节/人工關節　artificial joint
人工合成生物碱/人工贋鹼　artificial alkaloid
人工殆/人工咬合　artificial occlusion
人工喉/人工喉　artificial larynx
人工呼吸/人工呼吸　artificial respiration
人工呼吸器/人工呼吸器　artificial ventilator
人工获得性免疫/人工獲得性免疫　artificially acquired immunity
人工角膜/人工角膜　artificial cornea
人工角膜移植术/人工角膜移植術　artificial keratoplasty
人工晶[状]体/人工晶狀體　artificial lens
人工晶状体眼/人工晶狀體眼　pseudophakic eye
人工抗原/人工抗原　artificial antigen
人工泪液/人工淚液　artificial tears
人工流产/人工流産　artificial abortion
人工免疫/人工免疫性　artificial immunity
人工膜/人工膜　artificial membrane
人工耐毒法/人工耐毒法　mithridatism
人工尿道括约肌/人工尿道括約肌　artificial urinary sphincter
人工皮肤/人工皮膚　artificial skin
人工破膜术/人工破膜術　artificial rupture of membrane
人工气腹/人工氣腹　artificial pneumoperitoneum
人工气管置换术/人工氣管置換術　replacement of tracheal prosthesis

人工气候室/人工氣候室　phytotron
人工气胸/人工氣胸　artificial pneumothorax
人工器官/人工器官　artificial organ
人工前牙/人工前牙　artificial anterior teeth
人工热源照射法/人工發熱法　ignisation
人工乳突/人工乳突　artificial mastoid
人工神经网络/人工神經網路　artificial neural network
人工肾/人工腎臟　artificial kidney
人工生物器官/人工生物器官　bioartificial organ
人工授精/人工受精　artificial insemination, eutelegenesis
人工甜味剂/人工甘味劑　artificial sweetener
[人工]条件反射/條件反射　conditioned reflex
人工通气/人工通氣　artificial ventilation
人工瞳孔/人工瞳孔　artificial pupil
人工脱敏/人工減敏　artificial desensitization
人工唾液/人工涎　artificial saliva
人工喂养/人工餵養, 人工餵食, 人工哺養　artificial feeding
人工窝洞分类/人工窩洞分類法　artificial cavity classification
人工吸血管/人工吸血管　bdellepithecium
人工膝关节/人工膝關節　knee prosthesis
人工心脏/人工心臟　artificial heart
人工心脏瓣膜/人工心臟瓣膜　prosthetic heart valve
人工心脏起搏/人工心臟起搏　artificial cardiac pacing
人工心脏起搏器/人工心臟整律器　artificial pacemaker
人工心脏停搏/人工心臟停搏　induced heart arrest
人工选择/人爲淘汰, 人擇　artificial selection
人工血管/人工血管　artificial blood vessel
人工血管置换术/人工血管置換術　prosthetic vessel replacement
人工荨麻疹/人工蕁麻疹　urticaria factitia
人工牙根牙种植体/人工牙根牙植體　artificial tooth root dental implants
人工牙列/人工牙列　artificial articulation
人工眼/假眼　artificial eye
人工胰腺/人工胰腺　artificial pancreas
人工义齿/人工義齒　artificial denture
人工指甲/人工指甲　nail artificial
人工制品/人工製品　artifact
人工智能/人工智慧　artificial intelligence
人冠状病毒/人冠狀病毒　human coronavirus
人呼吸道合胞体病毒/人呼吸道合胞體病毒　human respiratory syncytial virus

[人]蛔虫/人蛔蟲　Ascaris lumbricoides
人机系统/人機系統　man-machine systems
人基因组/人基因組　human genome
人际关系/人際關係　interpersonal relations
人酵母菌/人酵母菌　blastocystis hominis
人结核/人結核　human tuberculosis
人科动物/人類　hominid
人口变革/人口變革, 人口變遷　demographic revolution
人口稠密地区/人口稠密地區　densely inhabited district
人口动力学/人口動力學　population dynamics
人口分布结构/人口分布結構　demographic structure
人口分析/人口分析　demographic analysis
人口静态统计法/人口普查統計法　census statistics method
人口控制/人口控制　population control
人口密度/人口密度　density of population
人口普查/人口普查, 人群調查　census of population
人口普查登记/人口普查登記　census-taking registration
人口普查统计区域/人口普查統計區域　census tract
人口群体/人口群體　population group
人口数据/人口數據　demographic data
人口特征/人口特徵　population characteristics
人口统计图/人口圖　demogram
人口统计学/人口統計學　demography
人口现象/人口現象　demographic behavior
人口学/人口學　larithmics
人口增长/人口增長　population growth
人口状况/人口狀況　demographic situation
人口自然增长/人口自然增長　natural increase of population
人口组成/人口組成　demographic composition
人[类]白细胞抗原/人[類]白細胞抗原　human leukocyte antigen
人类白细胞位点A/人類白血球基因位置A　human leukocyte locus A
人类活动/人類活動　human activities
人类活动学/人類動力學　anthropokinetics
人类基因组计划/人類基因組專案　human genome project
人类健康计划/人類健康計劃　healthy people programs
人类马蝇/人類馬蠅　human botfly
人类免疫缺陷病毒/人類免疫缺陷病毒　human immunodeficiency virus, HIV

人 643

人类免疫缺陷病毒感染/人類免疫不全病毒感染 HIV infection
人类疱疹病毒/人類皰疹病毒　human herpes virus
人类生物学/人類生物學,人及類人猿生物學 anthropobiology
人类实验/人類實驗　human experimentation
人类嗜T淋巴细胞病毒/人類嗜T淋巴細胞病毒 human T-lymphotropic virus
人类特性/人類特性　human characteristics
人类体型审定检查/人體檢查學　anthroposcopy
人类T细胞白血病-淋巴瘤病毒/人類T細胞白血病-淋巴瘤病毒　human T-cell leukemia-lymphoma virus
人类T细胞亲淋巴性病毒/人類T細胞親淋巴性病毒　human T-cell lymphoid virus
人类小病毒B19型/人類小病毒B19型　human parvovirus B19
人类学/人類學　anthropology
人类遗传学/人類遺傳學　human genetics
人卵泡刺激素/人卵泡刺激素　human follicle stimulating hormone
人名命名/人名命名　eponym
人名[命名]疾病/人名名詞病　eponymic disease
人疟/人瘧　human malaria
人蟠尾丝虫/人蟠尾絲蟲　blinding worm
人疱疹病毒3型/人類皰疹病毒第3型　human herpesvirus 3
人疱疹病毒6型/人類皰疹病毒第6型　human herpesvirus 6
人疱疹病毒7型/人類皰疹病毒第7型　human herpesvirus 7
人疱疹病毒8型/人類皰疹病毒第8型　human herpesvirus 8
人群监测/人群監測　population surveillance
人染色体/人染色體　human chromosomes
人绒毛膜促性腺素兴奋试验/絨毛膜促性腺素興奮試驗　human chorionic gonadotropin stimulation test
人乳/人乳　human milk
人乳光蛋白/蛋白石素,乳光素　opalisin
人乳头瘤病毒/人類乳頭瘤病毒,人類乳突病毒 human papillomavirus
人乳腺/人乳腺　human mammary gland
人身之神/人身之神　vitality of human
人参/人参　ginseng
人参健脾丸/人参健脾丸　renshen jianpi pill
人参养荣丸/人参養榮丸　renshen yangrong pill
人参叶/人参葉　ginseng leaf

人参再造丸/人参再造丸　renshen zaizao pill
人参皂苷类/人参皂貳類　ginsenosides
人生长激素/人類生長激素　human growth hormone
人事制之/人事制之　knowing patient's general condition in diagnosis
人寿保险/人壽保險　life insurance
人胎盘催乳激素/人胎盤催乳質　human placental lactogen
人体/人體　human body
人体病理学/人體病理學　human pathology
人体测量[法]/身體測量法　somatometry
人体测量器/人體測量器　anthropometer
人体测量术/人體測量法　anthropometry
人体测量学家/人體測量學家　anthropometrist
人体对称美/人體對稱美　symmetric beauty of body
人体工程/人體工程　human engineering
人体和谐美/人體和諧美　harmony beauty of body
人体黄金点/人體黄金點　golden point of body
人体黄金分割/人體黄金分割　golden section of body
人体黄金律/人體黄金律　golden rule of body
人体酵母/人體酵母菌　Saccharomyces hominis
人体节奏美/人體節奏美　rhythm beauty of body
人体解剖学/人體解剖學　human anatomy
人体均衡美/人體均衡美　balance beauty of body
人体轮廓线/人體輪廓線　body contour line
人体模型/人體模型　manikins
人体胚胎学/人體胚胎學,人體發生學　human embryology
人体曲线/人體曲線　body curve
人体线条/人體線條　body line
人体信息素类/人體資訊素類　human pheromones
人体形式美/人體形式美　formal beauty of body
人体运动电影照相机/活動攝影機　kinetoscope
人体整体美/人體整體美　ensemble beauty of body
[人]头虱/頭蝨　Pediculus humanus capitis
人为痤疮/人爲痤瘡　artificial acne
人为的/人爲的,人造的　factitious
人为构造/人工産物　artefact
人为甲状腺毒症/人爲甲狀腺毒症　factitia thyrotoxicosis
人为甲状腺功能亢进/人爲的甲狀腺機能亢進 factitous hyperthyrodidsm
人为皮肤病/人爲皮膚病　factitious skin disease
人为皮炎/人爲皮膚炎　dermatitis factitia
人为伤害/人爲傷害　factitial injury
人为水肿/人爲水腫　edema artefactum
人为脂膜炎/人爲脂膜炎　factitious panniculitis

人为紫癜/人爲紫癜　purpura factitia
人T细胞白血病病毒/人類T細胞白血病病毒　human T cell leukemia virus
人腺病毒/人腺病毒　human adenoviruse
人腺病毒感染/人腺病毒感染　human adenovirus infection
人型支原体/人黴漿菌　mycoplasma hominis
人血清黄疸/人血清黄疸　human serum jaundice
人血小板抗原/人血小板抗原　human platelet antigen
人咬伤/人咬傷　human bite
人迎/人迎　①site for taking carotid pulse ②renying ST9
人蚤/人蚤　Pulex irritans
人造的/人造的　factitia
人造腭/人造腭　artificial palate
人造腭帆/人造腭帆　artificial velum
人造沸石/人造沸石　permutite
人造沸石法/人造沸石法　permutit method
人造革/人造革　artificial leather
人造冠/人工牙冠　artificial crown
人造黑素/人造黑素, 類黑素　artificial melanin
人造黄油/人造黄油　margarine
人造黄油病/人造酪病　margarine disease
人造奶油/人造奶油, 凍化脂肪　oleotine
人造石/人造石　artificial stone
人造丝工人病/人造絲工人病　rayon-worker disease
人造移植骨/人造移植骨　artificial bone graft
人造樟脑/人造樟腦　artificial camphor
人中/人中　philtrum
人中疔/人中疔　furuncle on renzhong point, Renzhong ding
人中脊/人中脊　philtrum ridge
人种群/人種群　ethnic group
人种生物学/人種生物學　ethnobiology
人种心理学/人種心理學　ethnopsychology
人种学/人種學　ethnology
人字点/人字縫尖　lambda
人字缝合/人字縫合　lambdoidal suture
人字缝/人字縫　lambdoid suture
人字形绷带/人字形繃帶, 穗形繃帶　spica bandage
人字形韧带/人字形韌帶　lambdoid ligament
人字形石膏/人字形石膏　spica cast
人字形石膏绷带/人字形石膏繃帶　spica plaster bandaging
人字缘/人字緣　lambdoid border
人足前段/人足前段　human forefoot
壬苯醇醚/壬苯醇醚　nonoxynol
壬二酸/壬二酸　azelaic acid
壬酸/天竺葵酸　pelargonic acid
壬糖/壬糖　nonose
壬[烷]基/壬[烷]基　nonyl
仁斋直指方/仁齋直指方　Effective Recipes from Renzhai House
忍冬藤/忍冬藤　honeysuckle stem
刃厚皮片/刃厚皮片　razor graft
认同危机/自我認同危機　identity crisis
认音中枢/認音中樞　auditopsychic center
认知/認知　cognition
认知不协调/識別力不協調　cognitive dissonance
认知功能不全/認知功能不全　cognitive dysfunction
认知科学/認知科學　cognitive science
认知疗法/認知療法　cognitive therapy
认知心理学/認知心理學　cognitive psychology
认知行为治疗/認知行爲治療　cognitive behavioral therapy
认知性事件相关电位/認知性事件相關電位　cognitive event related potential
认知训练/認知訓練　cognitive training
认知障碍/認知意識障礙　gnostic disorder
任脉/任脈　conception channel, conception vessel
韧带/韌帶　ligament
韧带病/韌帶病　desmopathy
韧带成形术/韌帶成形術　syndesmoplasty
韧带缝术/韌帶縫合術　syndesmorrhaphy
韧带骨赘/韌帶骨贅　syndesmophyte
韧带固定术/韌帶固定術　syndesmopexy
韧带联合/韌帶聯合　syndesmosis
韧带论/韌帶論　syndesmography
韧带膜/韌帶膜　peridesmium
韧带膜炎/韌帶膜炎　peridesmitis
韧带内的/韌帶內的　intraligamentous
韧带破裂/韌帶破裂　desmorrhexis
韧带切除术/韌帶切除術　syndesmectomy
韧带切开术/韌帶切開法　desmotomy
韧带痛/韌帶痛　desmalgia
韧带位/韌帶位　ligamental position
韧带学/韌帶學　desmography
韧带炎/韌帶炎　desmitis
韧带异位/韌帶異位　syndesmectopia
韧带硬化/韌帶硬化　sclerodesmia
韧皮部/韌皮部　phloem
韧皮射线/韌皮射線　phloem ray
韧型纤维/韌型纖維　libriform fiber
妊娠/妊娠　pregnancy, gestation
妊娠斑/妊娠斑　cyasma
妊娠保持/妊娠保持　pregnancy maintenance

妊娠并发症/妊娠并發症　pregnancy complication
妊娠病/妊娠病　gestational disease
妊娠病脉/妊娠病脈　morbid pulse in pregnancy
妊娠常脉/妊娠常脈　regular pulse in pregnancy
妊娠初期/妊娠初期　the first pregnancy trimester
妊娠次数/妊娠次數　gravidity
妊娠大便不通/妊娠大便不通　gestational constipation
妊娠大便不通·脾肺气虚证/妊娠大便不通·脾肺氣虛證　gestational constipation with pattern of qi deficiency of spleen and lung
妊娠大便不通·胃肠气滞证/妊娠大便不通·胃腸氣滯證　gestational constipation with pattern of qi stagnating in stomach and intestine
妊娠大便不通·血虚津亏证/妊娠大便不通·血虛津虧證　gestational constipation with pattern of blood deficiency and fluid depletion
妊娠蛋白尿/妊娠蛋白尿　gestational proteinuria
妊娠蛋白质类/妊娠蛋白質類　pregnancy proteins
妊娠毒性/妊娠毒性　prenatal injury
妊娠恶阻/妊娠惡阻　hyperemesis gravidarum
妊娠恶阻·肝胃不和证/妊娠惡阻·肝胃不和證　hyperemesis gravidarum with pattern of disharmony between liver and stomach
妊娠恶阻·脾胃气虚证/妊娠惡阻·脾胃氣虛證　hyperemesis gravidarum with pattern of qi deficiency of spleen and stomach
妊娠恶阻·气阴两虚证/妊娠惡阻·氣陰兩虛證　hyperemesis gravidarum with pattern of deficiency of both qi and yin
妊娠恶阻·痰湿阻滞证/妊娠惡阻·痰濕阻滯證　hyperemesis gravidarum with pattern of stagnation and blockade of phlegm-damp
妊娠烦渴/妊娠煩渴　vexation and thirst during pregnancy
妊娠反应/妊娠反應　gestation reaction, pregnancy reaction
妊娠风疹/妊娠風疹　gestational rubella, rubella during pregnancy
妊娠腹痛/妊娠腹痛　abdominal pain during pregnancy
妊娠腹痛·气滞证/妊娠腹痛·氣滯證　abdominal pain during pregnancy with qi stagnation pattern
妊娠腹痛·虚寒证/妊娠腹痛·虛寒證　abdominal pain during pregnancy with deficiency-cold pattern
妊娠腹痛·血热证/妊娠腹痛·血熱證　abdominal pain during pregnancy with blood heat pattern
妊娠腹痛·血虚证/妊娠腹痛·血虛證　abdominal pain during pregnancy with blood deficiency pattern
妊娠腹痛·血瘀证/妊娠腹痛·血瘀證　abdominal pain during pregnancy with blood stasis pattern
妊娠肝内胆汁淤积症/妊娠肝内膽汁淤積症　intrahepatic cholestasis of pregnancy
妊娠高血压/妊娠高血壓　gestational hypertension
妊娠高血压综合征/妊娠高血壓症候群　pregnancy-induced hypertension syndrome
妊娠过程图/妊娠圖　pregnogram
妊娠黄体/妊娠黃體　corpus luteum of pregnancy
妊娠急性黄色肝萎缩/妊娠急性黃色肝萎縮　obstetric acute yellow liver atrophy
妊娠急性脂肪肝/妊娠急性脂肪肝　acute fatty liver of pregnancy
妊娠结局/妊娠結局　pregnancy outcome
妊娠禁忌[药]/妊娠禁忌　contraindications during pregnancy
妊娠惊悸/妊娠驚悸　gestational palpitation, palpitation during pregnancy
妊娠惊悸·心血虚证/妊娠驚悸·心血虛證　gestational palpitation with pattern of heart blood deficiency
妊娠惊悸·阴虚火旺证/妊娠驚悸·陰虛火旺證　gestational palpitation with pattern of exuberant fire due to yin deficiency
妊娠剧吐/妊娠性劇吐　hyperemesis gravidarum
妊娠率/妊娠率　pregnancy rate
妊娠脉/妊娠脈　pregnancy pulse
妊娠面斑/孕婦面貌　mask of pregnancy
妊娠末期/妊娠末期　the third pregnancy trimester
妊娠目病/妊娠目病　gestational eye disease
妊娠呕吐/妊娠嘔吐，孕吐　vomiting of pregnancy
妊娠疱疹/妊娠皰疹　gestational bleb, bleb during pregnancy
妊娠偏头痛/妊娠偏頭痛　migraine during pregnancy
妊娠贫血/妊娠貧血　anemia during pregnancy, gestational anemia
妊娠贫血·肝肾两虚证/妊娠貧血·肝腎兩虛證　gestational anemia with pattern of deficiency of both liver and kidney
妊娠贫血·气血两虚证/妊娠貧血·氣血兩虛證　gestational anemia with pattern of deficiency of both qi and blood
妊娠贫血·心脾两虚证/妊娠貧血·心脾兩虛證　gestational anemia with pattern of heart-spleen deficiency
妊娠期/妊娠期　gestation period
妊娠期大肠杆菌病/孕期大腸桿菌病　colibacillosis

gravidarum
妊娠期精神病/妊娠期精神病，懷孕期精神病 gestational psychosis
妊娠期类天疱疮/妊娠期類天皰瘡 pemphigoid gestationis
妊娠期肾炎/妊娠期腎炎 nephritis gravidarum
妊娠期肾盂炎/妊娠期腎盂炎 pyelitis gravidarum
妊娠丘疹性皮炎/妊娠丘疹性皮炎 papular dermatitis of pregnancy
妊娠肉芽肿/妊娠肉芽腫 granuloma gravidarum
妊娠乳痈/妊娠乳癰 mammary abscess in pregnancy
妊娠三月期/妊娠三月期 pregnancy trimesters
妊娠瘙痒性毛囊炎/妊娠期搔癢性毛囊炎 pruritic folliculitis of pregnancy
妊娠瘙痒性荨麻疹性丘疹及斑块/妊娠搔癢性蕁麻疹性丘疹及斑塊 pruritic urticarial papules and plaques of pregnancy
妊娠瘙痒[症]/妊娠搔癢[症] pruritus gravidarum
妊娠瘙痒症/妊娠搔癢症 gestational pruritus, pruritus during pregnancy
妊娠瘙痒症·风热证/妊娠搔癢症·風熱證 gestational pruritus with wind-heat pattern
妊娠瘙痒症·血虚证/妊娠搔癢症·血虛證 gestational pruritus with blood deficiency pattern
妊娠肾盂肾炎/妊娠腎盂腎炎 pyelonephritis of pregnancy
妊娠肾盂炎/妊娠腎盂炎 encyopyelitis
妊娠试验/妊娠試驗 pregnancy test
妊娠水肿/懷孕水腫 gestational edema
妊娠糖尿病/懷孕型糖尿病 gestational diabetes
妊娠特异性β1糖蛋白质类/妊娠特異性β1糖蛋白質類 pregnancy-specific beta 1-glycoproteins
妊娠晚期/妊娠晚期 late trimester of pregnancy
妊娠纹/妊娠紋，孕婦紋 striae gravidarum
妊娠舞蹈症/孕婦舞蹈病 chorea gravidarum
妊娠细胞/妊娠細胞 pregnancy cell
妊娠下肢抽筋/妊娠下肢抽筋 lower limbs spasm during pregnancy
妊娠下肢抽筋·肝血虚证/妊娠下肢抽筋·肝血虛證 lower limbs spasm during pregnancy with pattern of liver blood deficiency
妊娠下肢抽筋·感寒证/妊娠下肢抽筋·感寒證 lower limbs spasm during pregnancy with cold pattern
妊娠相关α2巨球蛋白类/妊娠相關α2巨球蛋白類 pregnancy-associated alpha 2-macroglobulins
妊娠相关血浆蛋白A/妊娠相關血漿蛋白A pregnancy-associated plasma protein-A
妊娠消渴/妊娠消渴 consumptive thirst during pregnancy
妊娠小便不通/妊娠小便不通 urine retention during pregnancy
妊娠小便不通·气虚证/妊娠小便不通·氣虛證 urine retention during pregnancy with qi deficiency pattern
妊娠小便不通·肾虚证/妊娠小便不通·腎虛證 urine retention during pregnancy with kidney deficiency pattern
妊娠泄泻/妊娠洩瀉 gestational diarrhea
妊娠泄泻·肝气犯脾证/妊娠洩瀉·肝氣犯脾證 gestational diarrhea with pattern of liver qi invading spleen
妊娠泄泻·脾肾阳虚证/妊娠洩瀉·脾腎陽虛證 gestational diarrhea with pattern of yang deficiency of spleen and kidney
妊娠泄泻·湿热[蕴结]证/妊娠洩瀉·濕熱[蘊結]證 gestational diarrhea with pattern of accumulation and binding of damp-heat
妊娠泄泻·食积证/妊娠洩瀉·食積證 gestational diarrhea with food retention pattern
妊娠性纤维软疣/妊娠性纖維軟疣 mollusca fibrosum gravidarum
妊娠眩晕/妊娠眩暈 dizziness during pregnancy
妊娠学/懷孕學 syllepsiology
妊娠血清/孕婦血清 pregnancy serum
妊娠痒疹/妊娠癢疹 prurigo gestationis
妊娠腰痛/妊娠腰痛 gestational lumbago
妊娠腰痛·风寒证/妊娠腰痛·風寒證 gestational lumbago with wind-cold pattern
妊娠腰痛·肾虚证/妊娠腰痛·腎虛證 gestational lumbago with kidney deficiency pattern
妊娠遗尿/妊娠遺尿 gestational enuresis
妊娠遗尿·脾肺气虚证/妊娠遺尿·脾肺氣虛證 gestational enuresis with pattern of qi deficiency of spleen and lung
妊娠遗尿·肾气虚证/妊娠遺尿·腎氣虛證 gestational enuresis with pattern of kidney qi deficiency
妊娠溢液/妊娠液漏 hydrorrhea gravidarum
妊娠龈瘤/妊娠齦瘤 pregnancy epulis
妊娠龈炎/妊娠齦炎 pregnancy gingivitis
妊娠诱发高血压/妊娠性高血壓 pregnancy-induced hypertension
妊娠脏躁/妊娠臟躁 hysteria during pregnancy
妊娠早期/妊娠早期 early trimester of pregnancy
妊娠谵语/妊娠譫語 delirium during pregnancy

妊娠诊法/妊娠診法　pregnancy diagnostics
妊娠中期/妊娠中期　mid trimester of pregnancy
妊娠中毒/妊娠中毒病　gestational toxicosis
妊娠滋养细胞肿瘤/妊娠滋養細胞腫瘤　gestational trophoblastic neoplasm
妊娠子烦/妊娠子煩　restlessness during pregnancy
妊娠子宫压迫肠梗阻/妊娠子宮壓迫性腸阻塞　ileus subparta
[妊娠]子痫/妊娠子癇　eclampsia gravidarum
妊娠紫癜/妊娠紫癜　gestational purpura, purpura during pregnancy
妊娠自体免疫性孕酮皮炎/孕婦自體免疫黃體激素皮膚炎　autoimmune progesterone dermatitis of pregnancy
日本法/日本法　Japanese method
日本蜡/日本蠟　Japan wax
日本脑炎/日本腦炎　Japanese encephalitis
日本脑炎病毒/日本腦炎病毒　Japanese encephalitis virus
日本脑炎疫苗/日本腦炎疫苗　Japanese encephalitis vaccine
[日本]七日热/日本七日熱　nanukayami disease
日本漆树/日本漆樹　Japanese lacquer tree
日本秋恙虫/日本秋恙蟲　tsutsugamushi
日本血凝病毒/日本血球凝集病毒　hemagglutinating virus of Japan
日本血吸虫/日本血吸蟲　schistosoma japonicum
日本血吸虫病/日本血吸蟲病　schistosomiasis japonicum
日晡潮热/日晡潮熱　afternoon tidal fever
日常生活活动/日常生活活動　activity of daily living
日常生活活动训练/日常生活活動訓練　training of activity of daily living
日常生活能力评定/日常生活能力評定　evaluation of activities of daily living
日发疟/日發瘧　quotidian malaria
日光关联性伤害/日光關聯性傷害　sun-related injury
日光空气疗法/日光空氣療法　helioaerotherapy
日光烙术/日光烙法　solar cautery
日光疗法/日光療法　heliotherapy
日光皮炎/日光皮炎　solar dermatitis
日光湿疹/日光性濕疹　solar eczema
日光性扁平苔藓/日光性扁平苔蘚　actinic lichen planus
日光性变性/日光性變性　actinic degeneration
日光性唇炎/日光唇炎,日曬性唇炎　solar cheilitis
日光性痤疮/日光性痤瘡　acne solaris
日光性粉刺/日光性粉刺　solar comedo
日光性粉刺性斑块/日光性粉刺性板塊　actinic comedonal plaque
日光性汗孔角化病/日光性汗孔角化症　actinic porokeratosis
日光性黑子/日光性小痣　solar lentigo
日光性角化病/光化性角化病　solar keratosis
日光性角化棘皮瘤/日光性角化棘皮瘤　actinic keratoacanthoma
日光性毛囊炎/日光性毛囊炎　actinic folliculitis
日光性皮炎/日光性皮膚炎　actinic dermatitis
日光性皮疹/日光性皮疹,手控除草機者皮膚炎　strimmer rash
日光性视网膜炎/日光性視網膜炎　solar retinitis
日光性苔藓/日光性苔蘚　lichen solaris
日光性弹力纤维病/日光性彈性纖維變性　solar elastosis
日光性弹性组织变性综合征/日光性彈性組織變性症候群　solar elastosis syndrome
日光性秃/日光性秃　actinic alopecia
日光性脱皮性唇炎/日光性脱皮性唇炎　cheilitis exfoliativa actinica
日光性网状细胞增生病/日光性網狀細胞增生病　actinoreticulosis
日光性荨麻疹/日光性蕁麻疹　light urticaria, solar urticaria
日光性痒疹/日光性癢疹　actinic prurigo
日光性紫癜/日光性紫癜　actinic purpura
日光性紫癜症/日光性紫癜症　purpura solaris
日光照射/日光照射　solar irradiation
日间护理中心/日間照護中心　day care center
日间磨牙症/日間磨牙症　diurnal bruxism
日间异常功能/日間異常功能　diurnal parafunction
日晒疮/日曬瘡　solar dermatitis
日晒疮·风燥血瘀证/日曬瘡·風燥血瘀證　solar dermatitis with pattern of wind-dryness and blood stasis
日晒疮·热毒外袭证/日曬瘡·熱毒外襲證　solar dermatitis with pattern of external assault by heat-toxin
日晒疮·湿热毒蕴证/日曬瘡·濕熱毒蘊證　solar dermatitis with pattern of dampness-heat toxin amassment
日晒红斑/日光性紅斑　erythema solare
日射病/日射病　sunstroke
日射光谱仪/日光射線分光測量儀　spectropyrheliometer
日射性脑炎/日射性腦炎,曝日腦炎　heliencephalitis

日食[性]盲/日蝕性盲　eclipse blindness
日蚀/日蝕　eclipse
日托医院/日托醫院　day hospital
日托幼儿园/日托幼稚園　child day care center
日月/日月　riyue, GB24
茸角/茸角　antler
荣格病/Jung氏病　Jung disease
荣枯老嫩/榮枯老嫩　lustrous-withered-tough-tender
荣舌/榮舌　lustrous tongue
绒促性素/絨促性素　chorionic gonadotrophin
绒毛/絨毛　villus
绒毛襞/絨毛皺襞　villous fold
绒毛管癌/絨毛管狀癌　villous duct cancer
绒毛间循环/絨毛間循環　intervillous circulation
绒毛结节状腱鞘炎/絨毛結節狀腱鞘炎　villonodular tenosynovitis
绒毛瘤/絨毛瘤　villoma
绒毛膜/絨毛膜　chorion
绒毛膜癌/絨毛膜癌　chorionic carcinoma
绒毛膜板/絨毛板　chorionic plate
绒毛膜采样/絨毛取樣　chorionic villus sampling
绒毛膜促性腺激素/絨毛膜促性腺激素　chorionic gonadotropin
绒[毛]膜的/絨毛膜的　chorionic
绒[毛]膜发生/絨毛膜生成　choriogenesis
绒[毛]膜瘤/絨毛膜瘤　chorioma
绒毛膜卵黄囊胎盘/絨毛卵黄囊胎盘　choriovitelline placenta
绒毛膜囊/絨毛囊　chorionic sac
绒[毛]膜内层/絨毛膜內層　endochorion
绒毛膜尿囊/絨毛膜尿囊　chorioallantois
绒毛膜尿囊胎盘/絨毛尿膜囊胎盘　chorioallantoic placenta
绒[毛]膜尿囊移植物/絨毛膜尿囊移植物　chorioallantoic graft
绒毛膜绒毛取样/絨毛膜絨毛取樣　chorionic villi sampling
绒毛膜外妊娠/絨毛膜腔外妊娠　exochorial pregnancy
绒[毛]膜血管瘤/絨毛膜血管瘤　chorangioma
绒[毛]膜血管内皮胎盘/絨毛膜血管内皮胎盘　hemoendothelial placenta
绒[毛]膜血管纤维瘤/絨毛膜血管纖維瘤　chorioangiofibroma
绒[毛]膜循环/絨毛膜循環　chorionic circulation
绒毛膜羊膜炎/絨毛羊膜炎　chorioamnionitis
绒[毛]膜增殖/絨毛膜增殖　chorioblastosis
绒毛尿囊膜/絨毛尿囊膜　chorioallantoic membrane

绒毛前胚/絨毛前期胚　previllous embryo
绒毛乳头状瘤/絨毛狀乳頭狀瘤　villous papilloma
绒毛胎盘/絨毛胎盘　villous placenta
绒毛吸取/絨毛吸取　villus aspiration
绒毛心/毛樣心,多毛心　hairy heart
绒毛性腱鞘炎/絨毛狀腱鞘炎　villous tenosynovitis
绒毛样的/絨毛的　villose
绒毛[与]结节性的/絨毛與結節的　villonodular
绒毛状癌/絨毛狀癌　carcinoma villosum
绒毛状滑膜炎/樹枝狀滑膜炎　dendritic synovitis
绒毛状腺瘤/絨毛腺瘤　villous adenoma
绒毛状心包炎/絨毛狀心包炎　pericarditis villosa
绒膜绒毛/絨毛膜絨毛　chorionic villus
绒膜性男性乳房增殖/絨毛膜性男性女乳症　choriogenic gynecomastia
绒球/絨球,小葉　flocculus
绒球脚/絨球腳　peduncle of flocculus
绒球小结叶/絨球小結葉　flocculonodular lobe
容积/容積　volume
容积计/容積計,容量計　volumenometer
容积控制通气/容積控制通氣　volume controlled ventilation
容积控制通气加叹气/容積控制通氣加嘆氣　volume controlled ventilation-sigh
容积摩尔渗透压浓度过低/低滲透性,滲透壓過低　hyposmolarity
容积渗摩尔浓度过多/滲透溶質度過高　hyperosmolarity
容积系数/容量係數　volume coefficient
容积性泻药/容積性緩瀉藥　osmotic laxative
容积转换型通气机/容積轉換型通氣機　volume-cycled ventilator
容量分布/容量分布　volume distribution
容量负荷过度/容積超過負荷　volume overload
容量依赖性高血压/容量依賴性高血壓　volume dependent hypertension
容貌/相貌面容　physiognomy
容貌耳长/容貌耳長　physiognomic ear length
容貌耳宽/容貌耳寬　physiognomic ear breadth
容貌缺陷/容貌缺陷　defect of physiognomy
容貌缺陷感/容貌缺陷感　defective sense of physiognomy
容痰管/痰[離心]管　sputum tube
溶癌素/溶癌[酵]素　carcinolysin
溶白细胞血清/溶白血球性血清　leukocytolytic serum
溶胞[作用]/溶胞[作用]　lysis
溶出度/溶離　dissolution

溶耵聍剂/溶耳垢劑　ceruminolytic
溶肝素/溶肝[細胞]素　hepatolysin
溶骨的/溶骨的,骨質溶解的　osteolytic
溶骨性癌/溶骨性癌　osteolytic cancer
溶化/溶化　solution, dissolve
溶化性[皮肤]结核/液化性結核病　tuberculosis colliquativa
溶剂/溶劑　solvent
溶剂萃取/溶劑抽取　solvent extraction
溶剂分解/溶化分解　solvolysis
溶剂蓝19/溶劑藍19　solvent blue 19
溶甲状腺素/溶甲狀腺素　thyrolysin
溶胶/溶膠,膠溶體　sol
溶解/溶解　dissolve
溶解度/溶解度　solubility
溶解激酶/溶纖維蛋白啟動酶　lysokinase
溶解纤维蛋白的/分解纖維蛋白的　fibrinolytic
溶解性病毒/細胞溶解病毒　lytic virus
溶解性坏死/溶解性壞死　lytic necrosis
溶解氧/溶解氧　dissolved oxygen
溶菌反应/溶菌反應　bacteriolytic reaction
溶菌剂/溶菌劑　bacteriolysant
溶菌介体/溶菌介體　bacteriolytic amboceptor
溶菌酶/溶菌酶,胞溶酶　lysozyme
溶菌素/溶菌素　bacteriolysin
溶菌血清/溶菌性血清　bacteriolytic serum
溶菌作用/細菌溶解,溶菌現象　bacteriolysis
溶蜡素/溶蠟素　cerolysin
溶淋巴组织血清/溶淋巴組織性血清　lymphatolytic serum
溶瘤病毒/溶瘤病毒　oncolytic virus
溶卵白素/溶卵白素,卵白溶素　ovolysin
溶螺旋体素/溶螺旋體素　spirochetolysin
溶媒/溶媒　menstruum
溶酶体/溶酶體　lysosome
溶酶体酶/溶酶體酶　lysosomal enzyme
溶酶体贮积症/胞溶體貯積症　lysosomal storage disease
溶内皮[细胞]血清/溶內皮細胞血清　endotheliolytic serum
溶皮素/溶皮素　dermolysin
溶脾素/脾溶素　splenolysin
溶葡萄球菌酶/溶葡萄菌素　lysostaphin
溶神经素/神經溶素　neurolysin
溶神经细胞素/神經細胞溶解素　neurocytolysin
溶石液灌注器/溶石藥注入器　litholyte
溶栓/血栓溶解　thrombolysis
溶素生成/溶素生成　lysinogenesis

溶素原/溶素生成抗原　lysinogen
溶髓鞘质素/溶髓鞘素　myelinolysin
溶细胞的/溶細胞的　cytolytic
溶细胞毒素/溶細胞毒素　synocytotoxin
溶纤维蛋白药/纖維蛋白分解白藥　fibrinolytic
溶心肌素/溶心肌素　cardiolysin
溶胸腺素/溶胸腺素　thymolysin
溶血/溶血,紅血球溶解　hemolysis
溶血产物/溶血産物　hemolysate
溶血单位/溶血單位　hemolytic unit
溶血磷脂/脱脂酸磷脂　lysophosphatide
溶血磷脂酶/溶血磷脂酶　lysophospholipase
溶血磷脂受体/溶血磷脂受體　lysophospholipid receptor
溶血磷脂素类/溶血磷脂素類　lysophospholipids
溶血磷脂酸受体/溶血磷脂酸受體　lysophosphatidic acid receptor
溶血磷脂酰胆碱类/溶血磷脂醯膽鹼類　lysophosphatidylcholines
溶血卵磷脂/脱脂酸卵磷脂　lysolecithin
溶血脑磷脂/脱脂酸腦磷脂　lysocephalin
溶血尿毒症综合征/溶血尿毒症症候群　hemolytic uremic syndrome
溶血蚀斑试验/溶血蝕斑試驗　hemolytic plaque assay
溶血试验/溶血試驗　hemolytic test
溶血栓药/溶血栓藥　thrombolytic
溶血素/溶血素,溶紅血球素　hemolysin
溶血素因子/溶血素因數　hemolysin factor
溶血小板性紫癜/溶血小板性紫癜　thrombocytolytic purpura
溶血性巴斯德菌/溶血性巴斯德拉菌　Pasteurella hemolytica
溶血性斑块技术/溶血性斑塊技術　hemolytic plaque technique
溶血性黄疸/溶血性黃疸　hemolytic jaundice
溶血性黄疸贫血病/溶血性黃疸貧血病　icteroanemia
溶血性介体/溶血介體　hemolytic amboceptor
β溶血性链球菌/乙型溶血性鏈球菌　beta-hemolytic streptococci
溶血性链球菌性坏疽/溶血性鏈球菌性壞疽　hemolytic streptococcal gangrene
溶血性尿毒综合征/溶血性尿毒症候群　hemolytic-uremic syndrome
溶血性疟/溶血性瘧　hemolytic malaria
溶血性贫血/溶血性貧血　hemolytic anemia
溶血性青光眼/溶血性青光眼　hemolytic glaucoma

溶血隐秘杆菌/溶血隱秘桿菌　Arcanobacterium hemolyticum
溶血指数/溶血指數　hemolytic index
溶血质/溶血質　hemolytic substance
溶血作用/溶血作用　hemolyzation
溶液/溶液　solution
溶液片剂/溶液錠劑　solution tablet
溶液型气雾剂/溶液型氣化噴霧劑　solution aerosol
溶源性/溶原性　lysogeny
溶源性菌株/溶原性菌株　lysogenic strain
溶质/溶質　solute
溶质性利尿/溶質性利尿　solute diuresis
溶锥虫[作用]/錐蟲溶解破壞　trypanolysis
溶组织内阿米巴/溶組織內阿米巴　Entamoeba histolytica
溶组织梭菌/溶組織梭狀芽孢桿菌　Clostridium histolyticum
熔点/熔點　melting point
熔距/熔距　melting range
熔融二氧化硅空心柱/熔融二氧化矽開口柱　fused-silica open tubular column, FSOTC
蝾螈毒碱/蝾螈素　salamanderin
融合/融合　fusion
融合癌基因蛋白质类/融合癌基因蛋白質類　fusion oncogene proteins
融合波群/融合波群　fusion complex
融合搏动/融合心跳　fusion beat
融合蛋白/融合蛋白質　fusion protein
融合痘/融合痘　variola confluens
融合基因/融合基因　fusion gene
融合肋/融合肋　fused rib
融合力/融合能力　fusion faculty
融合频率/融合頻率　fusion frequency
融合肾/并合腎　fused kidney
融合体/融合體　fusant
融合无形双焦点透镜/融合無形雙焦點透鏡　fused bifocal lens
融合线/融合線　fusion line
融合性脓疱病/融合性膿皰病　commissural impetigo
融合性天花/融合天花　confluent smallpox
融合性网状乳头状瘤病/融合性網狀乳突瘤病　confluent and reticulate papillomatosis
融合性荨麻疹/密集性蕁麻疹　urticaria conferta
融合牙/融齒　fused tooth
柔道慢跑者瘙痒病/柔道慢跑者搔癢病　judo jogger itch
柔肝息风/柔肝息風　softening liver for calming endogenous wind
柔和杂音/柔和雜音　soft murmur
柔红霉素/柔紅黴素　daunorubicin
柔痉/柔痙　hidrotic convulsion
柔韧性/柔韌性　pliability
柔软度/柔軟度　flexibility
柔弱葡萄孢/五月甲蟲黴菌　Botrytis tenella
柔弱足/衰弱足　weak foot
柔性/柔性　flexibility
揉擦剂/擦治藥　anatriptic
揉法/揉法　kneading manipulation
揉捻法/揉撚法　massaging and twisting manipulation
揉捏按摩法/揉捏按摩法　kneading massage
揉捏法/揉捏法,指捏法　kneading
鞣红/鞣紅　phlobaphene
鞣花鞣质/并没食子鞣質　ellagitannin
鞣花酸/土耳其鞣酸　ellagic acid
鞣皮法/皮革之硝化　tanning
鞣酸/鞣酸　tannic acid
鞣酸蛋白素/鞣酸蛋白素　tannate albumin
鞣酸甘油剂/鞣酸甘油劑　tannic acid glycerite
鞣酸奎宁/鞣酸奎寧　quinine tannate
鞣酸铝/鞣酸鋁　tannal
鞣酸酶/鞣酸酯酵素　tannase
鞣酸试验/鞣酸試驗　tannic acid test
鞣酸盐/鞣酸鹽　tannate
鞣酸胰岛素/鞣酸胰島素　tannate insulin
鞣质细胞/鞣質細胞　tannin cell
肉孢子虫/肉孢子蟲,肌芽孢蟲　sarcosporidium
肉孢子虫病/肌囊蟲病,肌芽孢蟲病　sarcocystosis
肉苁蓉/肉蓯蓉　desertliving cistanche
肉豆蔻/肉豆蔻　nutmeg
肉豆蔻肝/肉豆蔻肝　nutmeg liver
肉豆蔻脑/肉豆蔻腦　myristicol
肉豆蔻酸/肉豆蔻酸　myristic acid
肉豆蔻酸鲸蜡酯/肉豆蔻酸鯨蠟酯　cetyl myristate
肉豆蔻酸盐类/肉豆蔻酸鹽類　myristates
肉豆蔻萜/肉豆蔻油精　myristicene
肉豆蔻油/肉豆蔻油　nutmeg oil
肉毒毒素类/肉毒毒素類　botulinum toxins
肉毒杆菌/肉毒桿菌　Botulinus bacillus
肉毒杆菌毒素/肉毒桿菌毒素　botulinum toxin
肉[毒]碱缺乏病/肉[毒]鹼缺乏之病　carnitine deficiency
肉毒抗毒素/臘腸菌抗毒素　botulinum antitoxin
肉毒素/肉毒素　creotoxin
肉毒鱼类中毒/肉毒魚類中毒　ciguatera poisoning
肉毒质/肉毒質　creatoxicon

肉毒中毒/肉毒中毒　botulism
肉桂/肉桂　cassia bark, cassia, cinnamon
肉桂醇/桂醯基醇　cinnamyl alcohol
肉碱/副肉精,肉毒鹼　carnitine
肉碱 O-软脂酰转移酶/肉鹼 O-軟脂醯基轉移酶　carnitine O-palmitoyltransferase
肉碱酰基转移酶类/肉鹼醯基轉移酶類　carnitine acyltransferases
肉碱 O-乙酰基转移酶/肉鹼 O-乙醯基轉移酶　carnitine O-acetyltransferase
肉浸液/肉浸液　meat solution
肉浸质/肉浸質　zomidin
肉类加工业/肉類加工業　meat-packing industry
肉类饮食/肉類飲食　meat diet
肉瘤/肉瘤　flesh tumor, lipoma
肉瘤变/肉瘤變　sarcomatous change
肉瘤病/肉瘤病　sarcomatosis
肉瘤•肝郁痰凝证/肉瘤•肝鬱痰凝證　flesh tumor with pattern of liver depression and phlegm coagulation
肉瘤化肌瘤/肉瘤性肌瘤　myoma sarcomatodes
肉瘤•脾虚痰凝证/肉瘤•脾虛痰凝證　flesh tumor with pattern of spleen deficiency and phlegm coagulation
肉瘤生成/肉瘤生成　sarcomagenesis
肉瘤性癌/肉瘤性癌　carcinoma sarcomatodes
肉瘤性骨炎/肉瘤性骨炎　sarcomatous osteitis
肉瘤性甲状腺肿/肉瘤性甲狀腺腫　sarcomatous goiter
肉瘤性脑膜炎/肉瘤性腦膜炎　meningitis sarcomatosa
肉瘤性脂肪瘤/肉瘤性脂瘤　lipoma sarcomatodes
肉瘤样的/肉瘤狀的　sarcomatoid
肉瘤样反应/肉瘤樣反應　sarcoidal reaction
肉瘤样神经病/肉瘤樣神經病變　sarcoid neuropathy
肉轮/肉輪　flesh wheel
肉霉酸/肉黴酸　carolic acid
肉膜/肉層　panniculus carnosus
肉膜肌/肉膜肌　dartos muscle
肉膜状的/肉膜狀的　dartoic
肉膜状肌瘤/肉膜肌瘤　dartoic myoma
肉膜状平滑肌瘤/肉膜狀平滑肌瘤　dartoic leiomyoma
肉汤滤液结核菌素/肉羹濾液結核菌素　tuberculin bouillon filtrate
肉香质/肉香質　osmazome
肉行/肉行　muscle pestilence
肉芽形成/肉芽形成　granulation

肉芽性骨炎/肉芽性骨炎　osteitis granulosa
肉芽性腱鞘炎/肉芽性腱鞘炎　tenosynovitis granulosa
肉芽性尿道炎/肉芽性尿道炎　urethritis granulosa
肉芽性肾盂炎/肉芽性腎盂炎　pyelitis granulosa
肉芽性狭窄/肉芽組織性狹窄　granulation stenosis
肉芽增生性软下疳/菌樣下疳　fungating sore
肉芽肿/肉芽腫　granuloma
肉芽肿病/肉芽腫病　granulomatosis
肉芽肿疾病/肉芽腫疾病　granulomatous disease
肉芽肿荚膜杆菌/肉芽腫莢膜樣菌　Calymmatobacterium granulomatis
肉芽肿酵母/肉芽腫酵母菌,顆粒腫酵母菌　Saccharomyces granulomatosa
肉芽肿性/肉芽腫的　granulomatous
肉芽肿性唇炎/肉芽腫性唇炎　cheilitis granulomatosa
肉芽肿性喉炎/肉芽腫性喉炎　granulomatous laryngitis
肉芽肿性结肠炎/肉芽腫性結腸炎　granulomatous colitis
肉芽肿性酒渣鼻/肉芽腫性酒渣鼻　granulomatous rosacea
肉芽肿性淋巴瘤/肉芽腫性淋巴瘤　granulomatous lymphoma
肉芽肿性皮肤松弛症/肉芽腫性鬆弛狀皮膚　granulomatous slack skin
肉芽肿性前列腺炎/肉芽腫性前列腺炎　granulomatous prostatitis
肉芽肿性胃炎/肉芽腫性胃炎　granulomatous gastritis
肉芽肿性心肌炎/肉芽腫性心肌炎　granulomatous myocarditis
肉芽肿性牙龈瘤/肉芽腫性齦瘤　epulis granulomatosa
肉芽肿性炎/肉芽腫性炎　granulomatous inflammation
肉芽组织/肉芽組織　granulation tissue
肉眼/肉眼　naked eye
肉眼可见的/肉眼可見的　macroscopic
肉眼凝集反应/肉眼可見之凝集　macroscopic agglutination
肉眼损害/肉眼病變　gross lesion
肉样瘤病/班-伯二氏病,伯克氏肉樣瘤　Besnier-Boeck disease
肉样胎块/肉樣胎塊　fleshy mole
肉蝇/肉蠅　flesh fly
肉蝇属/肉蠅屬　*Sarcophaga*

肉瘿/肉瘿　flesh goiter, thyroid adenoma and cyst
肉瘿·气阴两虚证/肉瘿·氣陰兩虛證　flesh goiter with qi-yin deficiency pattern
肉瘿·气滞痰凝证/肉瘿·氣滯痰凝證　flesh goiter with pattern of qi stagnation and phlegm coagulation
肉硬/肉硬　stiff flesh
肉疣/肉疣　ecphyma
肉中毒/肉中毒　creatotoxism
肉柱/肉小梁　trabeculae carneae
肉足纲感染/肉足綱感染　Sarcodina infection
如丧神守/如喪神守　panic-striken
如意金黄散/如意金黃散　ruyi jinhuang powder
如银内障/如銀內障　silver cataract
铷-82/銣-82　rubidium-82
铷放射性同位素/銣放射性同位素　rubidium radioisotope
濡脉/濡脈　soft pulse
蠕虫/蠕蟲　helminth
蠕虫病/蠕蟲病　helminthic disease
蠕虫蛋白质类/蠕蟲蛋白質類　helminth proteins
蠕虫的/蠕蟲的　helminthic, verminous
蠕虫感染/蠕蟲感染　helminthic infection
蠕虫基因/蠕蟲基因　helminth gene
蠕虫寄生/蠕蟲寄生　helminthism
蠕虫抗体/蠕蟲抗體　helminth antibody
蠕虫抗原/蠕蟲抗原　helminth antigen
蠕虫瘤/蠕蟲瘤　helminthoma
蠕虫性动脉瘤/血寄生蟲性動脈瘤　verminous aneurysm
蠕虫性绞痛/蠕蟲性絞痛　verminous colic
蠕虫性脓肿/蠕蟲性膿腫　helminthic abscess
蠕虫性弹性瘤/蠕蟲性彈性瘤　helminthiasis elastica
蠕虫学/蠕蟲學　helminthology
蠕虫血红蛋白/蠕蟲血紅素　hemoerythrin
蠕虫样皮萎病/蠕蟲樣皮萎病　vermiculate atrophoderma
蠕虫状的/蠕蟲狀的　vermiform
蠕动/蠕動　peristaltic motion
蠕动迟缓/蠕動遲緩,蠕動減退　hypoperistalsis
蠕动过慢/蠕動徐緩　bradystalsis
蠕动过强/蠕動過強,蠕動過度　hyperperistalsis
蠕动停止/蠕動停止,無蠕動　aperistalsis
蠕动障碍/痛性蠕動,異常蠕動　dysperistalsis
蠕螨症/毛囊恙蟲病　demodectic acariasis
蠕行转移/蠕行轉移　caterpillaring transfer
蠕形螨病/恙蟲感染　demodicidosis
蠕形螨毛囊炎/蠕形蟲毛囊炎　demodex folliculitis
蠕形螨属/蠕形蟎屬　Demodex
乳/乳　milk
乳癌/乳[房]癌　mastocarcinoma
乳白型突变/乳白型突變　opal mutation
乳棒状杆菌/乳棒狀桿菌　corynebacterium lacticum
乳传播的/乳媒的　milk-borne
乳代用品/乳代用品　milk substitute
乳蛋白[质]/乳蛋白質　lactoprotein
乳蛋白质类/乳蛋白質類　milk proteins
乳冻/乳凍　matzoon
乳毒病/乳毒病　milk sickness
乳毒素/乳毒素　galactotoxin
乳多泡病毒/乳多泡病毒　papilloma-polyoma-simian vacuolating virus
乳蛾/乳蛾,扁桃腺炎　nippled moth, tonsillitis
乳蛾·肺肾阴虚证/乳蛾·肺腎陰虛證　tonsillitis with lung-kidney yin deficiency pattern
乳蛾·肺胃热盛证/乳蛾·肺胃熱盛證　tonsillitis with pattern of heat exuberance in lung and stomach
乳蛾·风热外袭证/乳蛾·風熱外襲證　tonsillitis with pattern of external assault by wind-heat
乳蛾·脾胃虚弱证/乳蛾·脾胃虛弱證　tonsillitis with spleen-stomach weakness pattern
乳蛾·痰瘀互结证/乳蛾·痰瘀互結證　tonsillitis with pattern of intermingled phlegm and stasis
乳儿剧吐/乳兒劇吐　hyperemesis lactentium
乳发/乳發　mammary cellulitis, suppurative mastitis
乳发·火毒炽盛证/乳發·火毒熾盛證　mammary cellulites with blazing fire-toxin pattern
乳发·正虚邪恋证/乳發·正虛邪戀證　mammary cellulites with pattern of healthy qi deficiency and lingering pathogen
乳房/乳房　breast, mamma
乳房瓣/乳房瓣　breast flap
乳房超声检查/乳房超聲檢查　mammary ultrasonography
乳房潮红/乳房潮紅　breast flush
乳房成形术/乳房成形術　mammoplasty
乳房初发育/青春期乳房開始發育　thelarche
乳房大小不等/左右乳房不等　anisomastia
乳房倒经/乳腺倒經　mastomenia
乳房动脉/乳房動脈　mammary artery
乳房肥大/乳腺肥大　hypermastia
乳房干板摄影术/胸部幹板放射線照相術　xeromammography
乳房固定术/乳房固定術　mastopexy
乳房过小/乳房過小　micromastia
乳房假体[纤维]包膜挛缩/乳房假體[纖維]包膜攣

缩　breast implant fibrous capsule contracture
乳房结核/乳房結核　tuberculosis of breast
乳房巨大性乳腺炎/腺肥大性乳腺炎　gargantuan mastitis
乳房瘘管/乳房瘻管　mammary fistula
乳房美容术/乳房美容術　breast cosmesis
乳房囊性增生/乳房囊性增生　cystic hyperplasia of the breast
乳房内侧支/乳房内側支　medial mammary branch
乳房内的/乳房内的　intramammary
乳房内动脉/乳房内動脈　internal mammary artery
乳房内脓肿/乳房内膿瘍　intramammary abscess
乳房旁淋巴结/乳房旁淋巴結　parammammary lymph node
乳房皮下切除术/乳房皮下切除術　subcutaneous mammectomy
乳房前的/乳房前的　premammary
乳房切除术/乳房切除術　mammectomy
乳房1/4切除术/乳房1/4切除術　quadrectomy of breast
乳房切除术后的/乳房切除術後　postmastectomy
乳房切除术后淋巴管肉瘤/乳房切除術後淋巴管肉瘤　postmastectomy lymphangiosarcoma
乳房切开术/乳房切開術　mastotomy
乳房切开引流术/乳房造口術，乳腺排膿法　mastostomy
乳房区/乳房部　mammary region
乳房全切除术/全部乳房切除術　total mastectomy
乳房热图描记[术]/温热乳腺記録術　thermomastography
乳房X射线摄影术/乳房X光攝影術　mammography
乳房X射线照片/乳房X光像　mammogram
乳房神经痛/乳房神經痛　mammary neuralgia
乳房湿疹/乳房濕疹　breast eczema
乳房缩小成形术/乳房縮小成形術　reductive mammoplasty
乳房疼痛/乳房疼痛　breast pain
乳房体/乳房體　body of breast
乳房痛/乳房痛　mammalgia
乳房外侧支/乳房外側支　lateral mammary branch
乳房外的/乳腺外的　extramammary
乳房外动脉/乳房外動脈　external mammary artery
乳房外佩吉特病/乳房外佩吉特病　extramammary Paget disease
乳房下垂/乳房下垂，乳房懸垂　mastoptosis
乳房下区/乳房下部　inframammary region
乳房悬韧带/乳房懸韌帶　suspensory ligament of breast
乳房芽/乳房芽　breast bud
乳房硬化/乳房硬化　zaranthan
乳房杂音/乳房雜音　mammary souffle
乳房再造术/乳房再造術　breast reconstruction
乳房增大/乳房增大　mastauxe
乳房增大成形术/增大乳房成形術　augmentation mammoplasty
乳房植入/乳房植入　breast implantation
乳房植入体/乳房植入體　breast prosthetic implant
乳房肿块切除术/乳房腫塊切除術　lumpectomy of breast
乳房组织增生/乳房組織增生　mammiplasia
乳疳/乳疳　mammary necrosis
乳膏/乳膏　cream
乳根/乳根　rugen, ST18
乳管扩张症/乳管擴張症　mammary duct ectasia
乳管炎/輸乳管炎　galactophoritis
乳光/乳光　opalescence
乳光蛋白/乳光蛋白　opalescin
乳果糖/乳果糖　lactulose
乳过氧化物酶/乳過氧化酶　lactoperoxidase
乳核/乳核　fibroadenoma of breast, mammary nodule
乳核·肝郁痰凝证/乳核·肝鬱痰凝證　mammary nodule with pattern of liver depression and phlegm coagulation
乳核·血瘀痰凝证/乳核·血瘀痰凝證　mammary nodule with pattern of blood stasis and phlegm coagulation
乳化/乳化　emulsification
乳化膏/乳化油膏　emulsifying ointment
乳化基质/乳化基劑　emulsifying base
乳化剂/乳化劑　emulsifier
乳化蜡/乳化臘　emulsifying wax
乳化器/乳化器　emulsator
乳环状试验/乳環狀試驗　milk ring test
乳积/乳積　infantile dyspepsia
乳剂/乳劑　emulsion
乳痂/乳痂　cradle cap
乳胶凝集试验/乳膠凝集試驗　latex agglutination test
乳胶体/乳膠體　emulsion colloid
乳疽/乳疽　mammary deep abscess
乳疽·肝郁胃热证/乳疽·肝鬱胃熱證　mammary deep abscess with pattern of liver depression and stomach heat
乳疽·气血两虚证/乳疽·氣血兩虛證　mammary

deep abscess with qi-blood deficiency pattern
乳疽•热毒炽盛证/乳疽•熱毒熾盛證 mammary deep abscess with blazing heat-toxin pattern
乳痨/乳癆 mammary tuberculosis, tuberculosis of breast
乳痨•气滞痰凝证/乳癆•氣滯痰凝證 mammary tuberculosis with pattern of qi stagnation and phlegm coagulation
乳痨•阴虚痰热证/乳癆•陰虛痰熱證 mammary tuberculosis with pattern of yin deficiency and phlegm-heat
乳痨•正虚邪恋证/乳癆•正虛邪戀證 mammary tuberculosis with pattern of healthy qi deficiency and lingering pathogen
乳酪螨/乳酪螨 cheese mite
乳酪样的/乾酪狀的 cheesy
乳类过敏反应/乳類過敏反應 milk hypersensitivity
乳疬/乳癧 gynecomastia, hypertrophy of breast
乳疬•肝气郁结证/乳癧•肝氣鬱結證 gynecomastia with liver qi stagnation pattern
乳疬•肾虚证/乳癧•腎虛證 gynecomastia with kidney deficiency pattern
乳链菌肽/乳鏈球菌素 nisin
乳疗法/牛奶療法 milk cure
乳磷酸盐/乳磷酸鹽 lactophosphate
乳瘘/乳瘻 milk fistula
乳漏/乳漏,乳房瘻管 mammary fistula
乳漏•阴虚痰热证/乳漏•陰虛痰熱證 mammary fistula with pattern of yin deficiency and phlegm-heat
乳漏•余毒未清证/乳漏•餘毒未清證 mammary fistula with uncleared remnant toxin pattern
乳漏•正虚毒恋证/乳漏•正虛毒戀證 mammary fistula with pattern of healthy qi deficiency and lingering toxin
乳媒介病/乳媒介病,乳傳播病 milk-borne disease
乳酶生/乳酶生 lactasin
乳糜/乳糜 chyle
乳糜池/乳糜池 chyle cistern
乳糜反流/乳糜反流 chylous reflux
乳糜管/乳糜管 chyliferous vessel
乳糜管扩张/乳糜管擴張 chylectasia
乳糜管瘤/乳糜管瘤 chylangioma
乳糜过多/乳糜過多 polychylia
乳糜淋巴水肿/乳糜性淋巴水腫 chylous lymphedema
乳糜囊肿/乳糜囊腫 chylous cyst
乳糜尿/乳糜尿 chylous urine, chyluria
乳糜气胸/乳糜氣胸 chylopneumothorax
乳糜生成的/乳糜生成的 chylopoietic
乳糜微粒/乳糜微粒 chylomicron
乳糜微粒血[症]/乳糜微粒血症 chylomicronemia
乳糜吸收/乳糜吸收 chylous absorption
乳糜小体/乳糜小體 chyle corpuscle
乳糜泻/乳糜瀉,粥狀瀉 celiac disease
乳糜泻综合征/乳糜瀉症候群 celiac syndrome
乳糜心包/乳糜性心包積液 chylopericardium
乳糜形成/乳糜生成,乳糜化作用 chylifaction
乳糜形成障碍/乳糜障礙,乳糜異常 dyschylia
乳糜[性]的/乳糜的 chylous
乳糜性腹膜炎/乳糜性腹膜炎 chyle peritonitis
乳糜性腹水/乳糜性腹水 chylous ascites
乳糜性水腹/乳糜腹 chyloperitoneum
乳糜性心包炎/乳糜性心包炎 chylopericarditis
乳糜性血尿/乳糜性血尿 chylous hematuria
乳糜胸/乳糜胸,胸腔水性乳糜 chylothorax
乳糜学/乳糜學 chylology
乳糜血[症]/乳糜血症 chylemia
乳糜样水囊肿/乳糜性水囊 chylous hydrocele
乳糜溢/乳糜漏,乳糜性洩 chylorrhea
乳糜正常/乳糜正常 euchylia
乳[内]脂/乳脂 milk fat
乳酿酶/乳澱粉酶 galactozymase
乳衄/乳衄 nipple bleeding, thelorrhagia
乳衄•肝郁火旺证/乳衄•肝鬱火旺證 nipple bleeding with pattern of liver depression and fire effulgence
乳衄•脾不统血证/乳衄•脾不統血證 nipple bleeding with pattern of spleen failing to control blood
乳癖/乳癖 breast lump, mammary hyperplasia
乳癖•冲任失调证/乳癖•沖任失調證 breast lump with pattern of thoroughfare-controlling vessels disharmony
乳癖•肝郁痰凝证/乳癖•肝鬱痰凝證 breast lump with pattern of liver depression and phlegm coagulation
乳癖消片/乳癖消片 rupixiao tablet
乳品酵母/乳内酵母菌 Saccharomyces galacticolus
乳品素食者/乳素食者 lactovegetarian
乳泣/乳泣 spontaneous lactation
乳清/乳清,乳漿 whey
乳清蛋白/乳清蛋白,乳白蛋白 lactalbumin
乳清疗法/乳清療法 whey cure
乳清酸/乳清酸 orotic acid
乳清酸核苷-5'-磷酸脱羧酶/乳清酸核苷-5'-磷酸

脱羧酶 orotidine-5'-phosphate decarboxylase
乳清酸磷酸核糖基转移酶/乳清酸磷酸核糖基轉移
　酶 orotate phosphoribosyltransferase
乳清酸尿/乳清酸尿 orotic aciduria
乳球蛋白/乳球蛋白 lactoglobulin
乳生成/乳生成 galactopoiesis
乳石/乳石 lacteal calculus
乳食疗法/乳食療法 lactotherapy
乳栓/乳栓 milk thrombus
乳酸/乳酸 lactic acid
乳[酸]杆菌科/乳酸桿菌科 Lactobacteriaceae
乳[酸]杆菌素/乳酸桿菌素 lactobacillin
乳酸鲸蜡酯/乳酸鯨蠟酯 cetyl lactate
乳酸林格液/乳酸林格液 Ringer lactate solution
乳酸钠/乳酸鈉 sodium lactate
乳酸钠林格/乳酸鈉林格 sodium lactate Ringer's
乳酸钠溶液/乳酸鈉液 sodium lactate solution
乳酸尿/乳酸尿症 lactaciduria
乳酸生成酶/乳酸酵素 lactic ferment
乳酸脱氢酶/乳酸脱氫酶 lactic dehydrogenase
乳酸脱氢酶活性病毒/乳酸脱氫酶活性病毒 lactate dehydrogenase-elevating virus
乳酸脱氢酶类/乳酸脱氫酶類 lactate dehydrogenases
乳酸性酸中毒/乳酸性酸中毒 lactic acidosis
乳酸血/乳酸血症 lactacidemia
乳酸亚铁/乳酸亞鐵 ferrous lactate
乳酸盐/乳酸鹽 lactate
乳酸盐林格溶液/乳酸鹽 Ringer 氏溶液 lactated Ringer solution
乳酸乙氧基苯胺/乳酸乙氧基苯胺 lactophenin
乳糖/乳糖 lactose
乳糖不耐受/不耐乳糖症 lactose intolerance
乳糖操纵子/乳糖操縱子 lac operon
乳糖合酶/乳糖合酶 lactose synthase
乳糖酶/乳糖酶 lactase
乳糖酶缺乏/乳糖酶缺乏 lactase deficiency
乳糖耐量试验/乳糖耐量試驗 lactose tolerance test
乳糖尿/乳糖尿症 lactosuria
乳糖试验/乳糖試驗 lactose test
乳糖酰基[神经]鞘氨醇类/乳酸醯基鞘氨醇類 lactosylceramides
乳糖因子类/乳糖因數類 lactose factors
乳铁蛋白/乳鐵蛋白 lactoferrin
乳头/乳頭 nipple, papilla
乳头被盖束/乳頭被蓋束 mammillotegmental tract
乳头层/乳頭層 papillary layer
乳头成形术/乳頭成形術 nipple plasty

乳头出血/乳頭出血 thelorrhagia
乳头点/乳頭點 thelion
乳头风/乳頭風 nipple wind, rhagadia mammae
乳头风·肝经湿热证/乳頭風·肝經濕熱證 nipple wind with pattern of dampness-heat in liver channel
乳头管/乳頭管 papillary duct
乳头肌/乳頭肌 papillary muscle
乳头肌断裂/乳頭肌斷裂 rupture of papillary muscle of heart
乳头肌功能不良/乳頭肌功能不良 dysfunction of papillary muscle
乳头肌劈开术/乳頭肌劈開術 splitting of papillary muscle
乳头间线/乳線 mammary line
乳头脚/乳頭腳 mamillary peduncle
乳头孔/乳頭孔 papillary foramen
乳头类圆线虫/乳頭狀擬圓蟲 strongyloides papillosus
乳瘤病毒/乳突瘤病毒 papilloma virus
乳头糜烂性腺瘤病/乳頭糜爛性腺瘤病 erosive adenomatosis of the nipple
乳头内陷/乳頭內陷 nipple retraction
乳头佩吉特病/乳頭 Paget 氏病 Paget disease of nipple
乳头膨起/乳頭豎起 thelerethism
乳头切除术/乳頭切除術 papillectomy
乳头切开刀/[十二指腸]乳頭切除刀 papillotome
乳头丘脑束/乳頭丘腦束 mamillothalamic tract
乳头区/乳頭部 mamillary region
乳头乳晕复合体/乳頭乳暈複合體 nipple-areola complex
乳头乳晕复合组织游离移植术/乳頭乳暈複合組織游離移植術 nipple-areola compound tissue free grafting
乳头乳晕再造术/乳頭乳暈再造術 nipple-areola reconstruction
乳头上部切开/乳頭上部切開 suprapapillary incision
乳头视网膜炎/视乳頭網膜炎 papilloretinitis
乳头体/乳頭體 mamillary body
乳头体脚/乳頭體腳 mamillary peduncle
乳头体内侧核/乳頭體內側核 medial mamillary nucleus
乳头体前核/乳頭體前核 premamillary nucleus
乳头体前静脉弓/乳頭體前靜脈弓 premamillary venous arch
乳头体丘脑的/乳頭體丘腦的 mammillothalamic
乳头体外侧核/乳頭體外側核 lateral mamillary

nucleus
乳头体中间核/乳頭體中間核　intermediate mamillary nucleus
乳头痛/乳頭痛　thelalgia
乳头突/乳頭突　papillary process
乳头下丛/乳突下網狀層　subpapillary plexus
乳头下毛细血管网/乳頭下皮膚毛細血管網　subpapillary network
乳头线/乳頭線　mamillary line
乳头腺瘤病/乳頭腺瘤病　adenomatosis of nipple
乳头小脓肿/乳突狀微小膿瘍　papillary microabscess
乳头炎/乳頭炎　acromastitis
乳头样肿瘤/乳頭樣腫瘤　papillary tumor
乳头移位/乳頭移位　nipple transposition
乳头溢液/乳頭溢液　nipple discharge
乳头增生性[鼻]窦炎/乳頭增生性鼻竇炎　papillary sinusitis
乳头状/乳頭狀　papillary
乳头状癌/乳頭狀癌　papilliferous carcinoma
乳头状汗管囊腺瘤/乳頭狀汗管囊腺瘤　syringocystadenoma papilliferum
乳头状汗腺腺瘤/乳頭狀汗腺腺瘤　hidradenoma papilliferum
乳头状汗腺腺性痣/乳頭狀汗腺腺性痣　nevus syringocystadenosus papilliferus
乳头状甲状腺癌/乳頭狀甲狀腺癌　papillary thyroid carcinoma
乳头状瘤/乳頭狀瘤　papilloma
乳头[状]瘤病/乳頭狀瘤病　papillomatosis
乳头[状]瘤病毒/乳頭瘤病毒　papillomavirus
乳头状瘤病毒感染/乳頭狀瘤病毒感染　papillomavirus infection
乳头[状]瘤的/乳頭狀瘤的　papillomatous
乳头[状]瘤性甲状腺肿/乳頭狀瘤性甲狀腺腫　papillomatous goiter
乳头状瘤样痣/乳頭狀瘤性痣　nevus papillomatosus
乳头状囊腺癌/乳頭狀囊腺癌　papillary cystadenocarcinoma
乳头状囊腺瘤/乳頭狀囊腺瘤　papillary cystic adenoma
乳头状体大脑脚束/乳頭狀體大腦腳束　mammillopeduncular tract
乳头状体盖膜束/乳頭狀體蓋膜束　mammillotegmental tract
乳头状体丘脑束/乳頭狀體丘腦束　mammillothalamic tract
乳头状涎腺瘤/乳頭狀涎腺瘤　sialadenoma papilliferum
乳头状腺癌/乳頭狀腺癌, 息肉狀腺癌　papillary adenocarcinoma
乳头状腺瘤/乳頭狀腺瘤　papilliform adenoma
乳头状腺囊瘤/乳頭狀腺囊瘤　papilloadenocystoma
乳头状小汗腺腺瘤/乳頭狀小汗腺瘤　papillary eccrine adenoma
乳头状小体/乳頭, 乳突　papillae
乳头状增生/乳頭狀增生　papillary hyperplasia
乳头状紫癜/乳頭狀紫癜病　purpura papillosa
乳突/乳突　mamillary process, mastoid process, mastoid
乳突壁/乳突壁　mastoid wall
乳突部/乳突部　mastoid part
乳突部耳炎/乳突性耳炎　otitis mastoidea
乳突成形术/乳突成形術　mastoidoplasty
乳突穿刺术/乳突穿刺術　mastoideocentesis
乳突导静脉/乳突導靜脈　mastoid emissary vein
乳突点/乳突點　mastoideale
乳突动脉/乳突動脈　mastoid artery
乳突窦/鼓竇, 鼓房　mastoid antrum
乳突窦入口/乳突竇入口　entrance to mastoid antrum
乳突多瘤空泡病毒/乳突多瘤空泡病毒　PAPOVA virus
乳突根治术/乳突根治術　radical mastoidectomy
乳突沟/乳突溝　mastoid groove
乳突骨/乳突骨　mastoid bone
乳突后入路/乳突後入路　retromastoid approach
乳突肌动脉/乳突肌動脈　myomastoid artery
乳突肌功能异常/乳突肌功能異常　papillary dysfunction
乳突积脓/乳突積膿　mastoid empyema
乳突尖/乳突穴　mastoidale
乳突角/乳突角　mastoid angle
乳突孔/乳突孔　mastoid foramen
乳突淋巴结/乳突淋巴結　mastoid lymph node
乳突瘤状增生/乳突瘤狀增生　papillomatous proliferation
乳突内[膜]炎/乳突腔炎　endomastoiditis
乳突内脓肿/乳突內膿瘍　intramastoid abscess
乳突旁突/乳突旁突　paramastoid process
乳突切除术/乳突竇切除術　mastoidectomy
乳突切迹/乳突切跡　mastoid notch
乳突上嵴/乳突上嵴　supramastoid crest
乳突痛/乳突痛　mastoidalgia
乳突凸/頂骨乳突角之頂部　entomion
乳突小房/乳突小房　mastoid cell

乳突小管/乳突小管 mastoid canaliculus
乳突囟/乳突囟 mastoid fontanelle
乳突炎/乳突炎 mastoiditis
乳突缘/乳突緣 mastoid border
乳突凿开术/乳突手術 mastoid operation
乳突支/乳突支 mastoid branch
乳突周炎/乳突外炎 extramastoiditis
乳突状汗管囊腺瘤/乳突狀汗管囊腺瘤 papillary syringocystadenoma
乳突状汗腺癌/乳突狀汗腺癌 papillary hidroma
乳突状或疣状病变/乳突狀或疣狀病變 papillary or verrucous lesions
乳突状瘤/乳突狀瘤 papillary cancer
乳微粒/乳微粒 lactoconium
乳酰胺/乳醯胺 lactamide
乳酰谷胱甘肽裂合酶/乳醯穀胱甘肽裂合酶 lactoylglutathione lyase
乳腺/乳腺 mammary gland
乳腺癌/乳腺癌 mammary cancer
乳腺癌切除术后淋巴管肉瘤/乳腺癌切除術後淋巴管肉瘤 postmastectomy lymphangiosarcoma
乳腺出血/乳腺出血 mastorrhagia
乳腺导管造影术/乳腺攝影 galactography
乳腺发育/乳腺發育 mammogenesis
乳腺发育不良/乳房發育不良 mammary dysplasia
乳腺管/乳腺管 ductus lactiferi
[乳腺]管内乳头状瘤/管內乳頭狀瘤 intracanalicular papilloma
乳腺过敏/乳房過敏 irritable breast
乳腺后脓肿/乳腺後膿腫 retromammary abscess
乳腺疾病/乳腺疾病 breast disease
乳腺脊/乳脊 mammary ridge
乳腺[结缔组织及上皮]增生症/乳腺增生病 cyclomastopathy
乳腺巨大纤维腺瘤/胸部巨纖維瘤 giant fibroadenoma of the breast
乳腺瘤/乳腺瘤 mastadenoma
乳腺囊肿/乳腺囊腫 breast cyst
乳腺脓肿/乳房膿腫 mammary abscess
乳腺佩吉特病/乳房佩吉特病 mammary Paget disease
乳腺痛/乳腺痛 mastalgia
乳腺外侧突/乳腺外側突 lateral process of mammary gland
乳腺外佩吉特病/乳房外佩吉特病 extramammary Paget disease
乳腺萎缩/乳腺萎縮 mammary gland atrophy
乳腺纤维囊性病/乳腺纖維囊性病 fibrocystic breast disease
乳腺腺病/乳腺腺病 adenosis of breast
乳腺小叶/乳腺小葉 lobule of mammary gland
乳腺炎/乳腺炎 mammitis
乳腺炎性癌/乳炎性癌 carcinoma mastitoides
乳腺叶/乳腺葉 lobe of mammary gland
乳腺硬癌/乳腺硬癌 mastoscirrhus
乳腺增生/乳腺增生 hyperplasia of mammary gland
乳腺褶/乳房皺襞 mammary fold
乳腺支/乳腺支 mammary branch
乳腺肿瘤/乳腺腫瘤 breast neoplasm
乳腺周炎/乳腺旁組織炎 paramastitis
乳腺自我检查/乳腺自我檢查 breast self-examination
乳香/乳香 frankincense
乳香试验/乳香試驗 mastic test
乳小管脓肿/乳小管膿腫 canalicular abscess
乳性鞘膜积液/積乳囊腫 galactocele
乳悬/乳懸 mastoptosis
乳血症/乳血症,血性乳汁,血乳 galactemia
乳牙/乳牙,乳齒,[短]暫齒 deciduous tooth
乳牙残余/乳牙殘餘 remnants of deciduous tooth
乳牙槽/乳牙齒槽 alveolus deciduus
乳牙列/初次生牙 primary dentition
乳牙早失/乳牙早失 premature shedding of deciduous tooth
乳牙滞留/乳牙滯留 retained deciduous tooth
乳岩/乳癌 breast cancer
乳岩·冲任失调证/乳癌·冲任失調證 breast cancer with pattern of thoroughfare-controlling vessels disharmony
乳岩·肝郁痰凝证/乳癌·肝鬱痰凝證 breast cancer with pattern of liver depression and phlegm coagulation
乳岩·脾胃虚弱证/乳癌·脾胃虛弱證 breast cancer with spleen-stomach weakness pattern
乳岩·气血两虚证/乳癌·氣血兩虛證 breast cancer with qi-blood deficiency pattern
乳岩·正虚毒炽证/乳癌·正虚毒熾證 breast cancer with pattern of healthy qi deficiency and blazing toxin
乳[液]比重计/乳液比重計 galactometer
乳液分泌抑制/乳液分泌抑制 galactischia
乳液生成/乳液形成 galactosis
乳液异常/乳液組成異常 galactacrasia
乳溢/乳液漏,溢乳 galactorrhea
乳营养法/乳液營養法 galactotrophy
乳痈/乳癰 acute mastitis

乳痈·气滞热壅证/乳癰·氣滯熱壅證 acute mastitis with pattern of qi stagnation and heat congestion
乳痈·热毒炽盛证/乳癰·熱毒熾盛證 acute mastitis with blazing heat-toxin pattern
乳痈·正虚毒恋证/乳癰·正虛毒戀證 acute mastitis with pattern of healthy qi deficiency and lingering toxin
乳油测定器/乳酪測定計 creamometer
乳晕/乳暈 areola of breast, areola of nipple
乳晕静脉丛/乳暈靜脈叢 plexus venosus areolaris
乳晕腺/乳暈腺 areolar gland
乳晕炎/乳暈炎 areolitis
乳晕缘切口/乳暈緣切口 periareolar incision
乳汁/乳汁 breast milk
乳汁管/乳汁管 laticiferous tube
乳汁减少/乳汁減少,泌乳不足 hypogalactia
乳汁囊肿/乳腺［囊］腫 milk cyst
乳汁失禁/乳汁失禁 incontinence of milk
乳汁自出/乳漏 galactorrhea
乳汁自出·肝经郁热证/乳汁自出·肝經鬱熱證 galactorrhea with pattern of heat stagnation in Liver Channel
乳汁自出·气虚证/乳汁自出·氣虛證 galactorrhea with qi deficiency pattern
乳脂计/乳脂計,乳油計 butyrometer
乳脂微粒/乳脂小體 milk corpuscle
乳脂小球/乳脂小球 milk globule
乳制品/乳製品 dairy product
乳制品业/乳製品業 dairying
乳中/乳中 ruzhong, ST17
乳中毒/乳中毒 galactotoxism
乳状剂/乳狀劑 emulsions
乳状尿/乳狀尿 milky urine
乳浊型气雾剂/乳劑型氣化噴霧劑 emulsion aerosol
入定/入定 enter the Ding
入静/入靜 entering tranquility
入口/入口 aditus
入口平面/入口平面 pelvic inlet plane
入口修形/入口修形 access preparation
入眠前状态/入眠前狀態 hypnagogic state
入魔/入魔 entrance of demons
入球微动脉/入球小動脈 afferent arteriole
入球小动脉/入球小動脈,輸入小動脈 afferent glomerular arteriole
入射角/入射角 angle of incidence
入射线/入射線 incident ray
入睡前幻觉/入睡前幻覺 hypnagogic hallucination
入学医学检查/入學健康檢查 entrance medical examination
入院/住院 admission
褥疮/褥瘡 bedsore, decubital ulcer, decubitus
褥疮·气血两虚证/褥瘡·氣血兩虛證 bedsore with qi-blood deficiency pattern
褥疮·气滞血瘀证/褥瘡·氣滯血瘀證 bedsore with pattern of qi stagnation and blood stasis
褥疮·蕴毒腐溃证/褥瘡·蘊毒腐潰證 bedsore with pattern of ulceration due to amassed toxin
褥式缝合/褥式縫合 mattress suture
褥式浆肌层缝合/霍爾斯氏縫合法 Halsted suture
软斑病细胞/軟斑病細胞 von Hansman cell
软布/軟膏布 mull
软垂疣/垂疣 acrochordon
软导管/彈性導管 flexible catheter
软钉胼/軟雞眼 heloma molle
软腭/軟腭 soft palate
软腭裂/軟腭裂 cleft soft palate
软腭-心-面综合征/Shprintzen氏症候群 Shprintzen syndrome
软腭阵挛/腭肌陣攣 palatal myoclonus
软法兰绒绷带/軟法蘭絨繃帶 domette bandage
软辐射/軟線放射 soft radiation
软膏/軟膏 ointment
软膏敷裹/軟膏敷裹 ointment dressing
软膏敷料/軟膏敷料 salve dressing
软膏管/軟膏管 ointment tube
软膏罐/軟膏罐 ointment jar
软膏基质/軟膏基質 ointment base
软膏剂/軟膏劑 ointment
软垢指数/軟垢指數 debris index
软骨/軟骨 cartilago
软骨癌/軟骨癌 chondrocarcinoma
软骨病/軟骨病 chondropathia
软骨病理学/軟骨病理學 chondropathology
软骨部/軟骨部 cartilaginous part
软骨成熟区/軟骨成熟區 zone of maturing cartilage
软骨成形术/軟骨造形術 chondroplasty
软骨成长不全/軟骨成長不全 achondrogenesis
软骨雏形/軟骨雛形 cartilage model
软骨刀/軟骨刀 chondrotome
软骨发育不良/軟骨發育不良,軟骨發育障礙 dyschondroplasia
软骨发育不全/軟骨發育不全,軟骨營養不良 chondrodysplasia, achondroplasia
软骨发育不全性侏儒/軟骨發育不全性侏儒 achondroplastic dwarf
软骨发育异常/軟骨發育異常 multiple congenital

enchondroma
软骨钙化区/軟骨鈣化區　zone of calcifying cartilage
软骨钙质沉着症/軟骨鈣質沈著病　chondrocalcinosis
软骨骼/軟骨骨骼　chondroskeleton
软骨骨化/軟骨[内]骨化　cartilaginous ossification
软骨骨瘤/軟骨骨瘤　chondrosteoma
软骨骨生成障碍/小肢型軟骨發育不良　dyschondrosteosis
软骨骺炎/軟骨骨骺炎　chondroepiphysitis
软骨化/軟骨化作用　cartilaginification
软骨坏死/軟骨壞死　chondronecrosis
软骨基质/軟骨基質　cartilage matrix
软骨疾病/軟骨疾病　cartilage disease
软骨间部/軟骨間部　intercartilaginous part
软骨间连结/軟骨間連結　interchondral joint
软骨间韧带/肋軟骨間韌帶　interchondral ligament
软骨胶/軟骨膠　chondrin
软骨胶球/軟骨膠球　chondrin ball
软骨胶素/軟骨膠糖　chondrosin
软骨节/軟骨節　chondromere
软骨结合/軟骨聯合　synchondrosis
软骨结合切除术/軟骨結合切除術　synchondrectomy
软骨结合切开术/軟骨結合切開術　synchondroseotomy
软骨连结/軟骨連結　cartilaginous joint
软骨瘤病/軟骨瘤病　chondromatosis
软骨颅/軟骨性顱　chondrocranium
软骨论/軟骨論　chondrography
软骨毛发发育不良/軟骨毛髮發育不全　cartilage-hair hypoplasia
软骨膜/軟骨膜　perichondrium
软骨膜骨/軟骨膜骨　perichondrial bone
软骨膜瘤/軟骨膜瘤　perichondroma
软骨膜[下]骨化/軟骨膜骨化　perichondral ossification
软骨膜炎/軟骨膜炎　perichondritis
软骨膜移植术/軟骨膜移植術　perichondrium grafting
软骨膜移植物/軟骨膜移植物　perichondrium graft
软骨囊/軟骨囊　cartilage capsule
软骨内成骨/軟骨內骨化　endochondral ossification
软骨内骨/軟骨內骨　intrachondrial bone
软骨内化骨/軟骨內化骨　endochondral bone
软骨内皮瘤/軟骨內皮瘤　chondroendothelioma
软骨黏蛋白/軟骨黏蛋白質　chondromucin
软骨黏液瘤/軟骨黏液瘤　chondromyxoma
软骨黏液肉瘤/軟骨黏液肉瘤　chondromyxosarcoma
软骨黏液样/軟骨黏液樣　chondromyxoid
软骨黏液样纤维瘤/軟骨黏液樣纖維瘤　chondromyxoid fibroma
软骨皮炎/軟骨皮膚炎　chondrodermatitis
软骨葡萄糖/軟骨葡萄糖　chondroglucose
软骨切除术/軟骨切除術　chondrectomy
软骨切开术/軟骨切開術　chondrotomy
软骨溶解/軟骨溶解,軟骨鬆解　chondrolysis
软骨肉瘤/軟骨肉瘤　chondrosarcoma
软骨肉瘤病/軟骨肉瘤病　chondrosarcomatosis
软骨软化/軟骨軟化　chondromalacia
软骨生成/軟骨生成　chondroplasia
软骨疏松/軟骨疏鬆　chondroporosis
软骨素/軟骨素　chondroitin
软骨素 ABC 裂合酶/軟骨素 ABC 裂合酶　chondroitin ABC lyase
软骨素裂合酶类/軟骨素裂合酶類　chondroitin lyases
软骨素硫酸酶类/軟骨素硫酸酶類　chondroitinsulfatases
软骨素硫酸盐类/軟骨素硫酸鹽類　chondroitin sulfates
软骨素-4-硫酸酯酶/軟骨素-4-硫酸酯酶　chondro-4-sulfatase
软骨[素]原/軟骨素原　chondrogen
软骨酸/軟骨酸　chondroitic acid
软骨痛/軟骨痛　chondralgia
软骨外丛/軟骨外叢　extrachondral plexus
软骨外胚层发育不良/軟骨外胚層發育不全　chondroectodermal dysplasia
软骨微粒/軟骨微粒,塵狀小體　chondroconia
软骨细胞/軟骨細胞　cartilage cell, chondrocyte
软骨[细胞]囊/軟骨細胞囊　cartilage cell capsule
软骨细胞柱/軟骨細胞柱　column of cartilage cell
软骨纤维瘤/軟骨纖維瘤　chondrofibroma
软骨陷窝/軟骨陷窩,軟骨基質　cartilage lacuna
软骨腺瘤/軟骨腺瘤　chondroadenoma
软骨小梁/軟骨小梁　cartilage trabecula
软骨屑移植术/軟骨屑移植術　diced cartilage grafting
软骨屑移植物/軟骨丁移植物　diced cartilage graft
软骨性部/軟骨[性]部　Pars cartilaginosa
软骨性外耳道/軟骨性外耳道　cartilaginous external acoustic meatus
软骨学/軟骨學　chondrology
软骨血管瘤/軟骨血管瘤　chondroangioma
软骨炎/軟骨炎　chondritis

软骨衍生生长因子/軟骨衍生生長因數 cartilage-derived growth factor
软骨样癌/軟骨性癌 chondroid cancer
软骨样汗管瘤/軟骨樣汗管瘤 chondroid syringoma
软骨样脂肪瘤/軟骨樣脂肪瘤 chondroid lipoma
软骨移植/軟骨移植 cartilage transplantation
软骨移植术/軟骨移植術 cartilage grafting
软骨移植物/軟骨移植物 cartilage graft
软骨营养不良/軟骨失養 chondrodystrophia
软骨营养不良性肌强直/軟骨營養不良性肌強直 chondrodystrophic myotonia
软骨疣/軟骨贅 chondrophyte
软骨增殖过多/軟骨增殖過度 hyperchondroplasia
软骨增殖区/軟骨增殖區 zone of proliferating cartilage
软骨脂瘤/軟骨脂肪瘤 chondrolipoma
软骨肿瘤/軟骨腫瘤 cartilaginous tumor
软骨周成骨/軟骨膜骨化, 脆膜骨化 perichondral ossification
软骨贮备区/軟骨貯備區 zone of reserve cartilage
软骨状的/軟骨狀的 chondroid
软骨组织/軟骨組織 cartilage tissue
软糊状的/糜爛的 pultaceous
软化/軟化 softening
软化斑/軟化斑 malacoplakia
软化囊肿/軟化囊腫 softening cyst
软化牙本质/軟化牙本質 soft dentin
软脊膜/軟脊膜 spinal pia mater
软脊膜齿状韧带/軟脊膜齒狀韌帶 denticulate ligament of spinal pia mater
软甲/軟爪甲 hapalonychia
软坚散结/軟堅散結 softening and resolving hard mass
软坚散结法/軟堅散結法 softening hardness and dispersing mass
软体动物毒液类/軟體動物毒液類 mollusk venoms
软胶囊剂/軟膠囊劑 soft capsule
软脚瘟/軟腳瘟 pestilence with flaccid leg
软疖/軟癤 soft furuncle
软离子化方法/軟離子化方法 soft ionization
软脉冲/軟脈衝 soft pulse
软毛青霉二酸酐/短毛酮酸 puberulonic acid
软毛青霉酸/短毛酸 puberulic acid
软膜/軟膜 pia mater, soft mask
软膜漏斗/軟膜漏斗 pial funnel
软膜神经胶[质]层/軟腦膜神經膠層 pia-glia
软木尘肺/軟木塵肺 suberosis
软木脂/軟木纖維質 suberin
软脑脊膜/軟腦脊膜 pia mater
软脑[脊]膜病/軟腦膜病 leptomeningopathy
软脑[脊]膜充血/軟腦膜充血 leptomeningeal hyperemia
软脑[脊]膜炎/軟腦膜炎 leptomeningitis
软脑膜/軟腦膜 cerebral pia mater
软肾病/髓樣腎病 pulpy kidney disease
软食/軟食 soft diet
软水/軟水 soft water
软体动物门/軟體動物門 Mollusca
软体动物似的/軟疣狀的 molluscoid
软下疳/軟下疳 chancroidal ulcer
软纤维瘤/軟纖維瘤 soft fibroma
软性角膜接触镜/軟性角膜接觸鏡 soft corneal contact lens
软性乳头状瘤/軟性乳頭狀瘤 papilloma molle
软药/軟藥 soft drug
软硬腭裂/軟硬腭裂 cleft soft and hard palate
软疣/軟疣 molluscum
软疣性痤疮/軟疣性痤瘡 acne molluscum
软疣性假瘤/軟疣性假瘤 molluscoid pseudotumour
软疣状痣/軟疣狀痣 nevus mollusciformis
软皂脂/甘油軟皂 mollin
软脂酸盐/棕櫚酸鹽 palmitate
软脂酸脂试验/軟脂試驗 palmin test
软质牙/軟化齒 malacotic teeth
软组织多形性透明性血管扩张性肿瘤/軟組織多形性透明化血管擴張性腫瘤 pleomorphic hyalinizing angioectatic tumor of soft part
软组织感染/軟組織感染 soft tissue infections
软组织骨化性纤维黏液瘤/軟組織骨化性纖維黏液瘤 ossifying fibromyxoid tumor of soft tissue
软组织假恶性骨瘤/軟組織假惡性骨瘤 pseudomalignant osseous tumor of soft tissue
软组织巨细胞成纤维细胞瘤/軟組織巨細胞纖維母細胞瘤 giant-cell fibroblastoma of soft tissue
软组织扩张器/軟組織擴張器 soft tissue expander
软组织扩张术/軟組織擴張術 soft tissue expansion
软组织嗜酸细胞肉芽肿/軟組織嗜伊紅球性肉芽腫 eosinophilic granuloma of the soft tissue
软组织损伤/軟組織損傷 soft tissue injuries
软组织提紧术/軟組織提緊術 soft tissue tightening
软组织腺泡状肉瘤/蜂窩狀肉瘤, 泡狀軟組織肉瘤 alveolar soft part sarcoma
软组织肿瘤/軟組織腫瘤 soft tissue neoplasms
朊病毒/朊病毒 prion
朊病毒病/朊病毒病 prion disease
朊间质/朊間質 proteose

蕤仁/蕤仁　hedge prinsepia nut
锐剥离/鋭器解剖　sharp dissection
锐疽/鋭疽　pilonidal disease
锐疽•气阴两虚证/鋭疽•氣陰兩虛證　pilonidal disease with qi-yin deficiency pattern
锐疽•湿热蕴结证/鋭疽•濕熱蘊結證　pilonidal disease with dampness-heat amassment pattern
锐疽•痰湿凝聚证/鋭疽•痰濕凝聚證　pilonidal disease with pattern of phlegm-dampness coagulation and aggregation
锐痛/鋭痛　sharp pain
锐缘支动脉/鋭緣支動脈　acute marginal artery
瑞德型豪猪状鱼鳞癣/瑞德型豪豬狀魚鱗癬　Rheydt type of ichthyosis hystrix
瑞列绦虫病/瑞列條蟲病　raillietiniasis
瑞莫必利/瑞莫必利　remoxipride
瑞士干酪样增生/瑞士乾酪樣增殖　Swiss-cheese hyperplasia
瑞斯西丁素/瑞斯托菌素　ristocetin
瑞特染色/賴特染色　Wright staining
瑞香苷/瑞白苷，瑞香素，白瑞香苷　daphnin
瑞香中毒/[白]瑞香中毒　daphnism
瑞竹堂经验方/瑞竹堂經驗方　Empirical Recipes from Auspicious Bamboo Hall
闰管/閏管　intercalated duct
闰盘/閏盤　intercalated disk
闰绍细胞/閏紹細胞　Renshaw cell
闰细胞/閏細胞　intercalary cell
润/潤　moistening
润肠药/潤腸藥　aperitive
润发油痤疮/髮油所致痤瘡　pomade acne
润肺化痰/潤肺化痰　moistening lung for removing phlegm
润肺止咳/潤肺止欬　moistening lung for arresting cough
润滑剂/潤滑劑　malactic
润滑性泻药/滑潤性瀉藥　emollient laxative
润湿性/潤濕性　wettability
润苔/潤苔　moist fur
润下/潤下　purgation by drugs of lubricant nature
润下剂/潤下劑　moistened cathartic formula
润燥/潤燥　moisturizing dryness-syndrome
润燥法/潤燥法　moistening dryness method
润燥化痰/潤燥化痰　moistening dryness for removing phlegm
润燥通便/潤燥通便　moistening dryness for relaxing bowels
润泽药/潤澤藥　lenitive
若虫/活動蛹　nymph
若丹明类/若丹明類　rhodamines
弱蛋白银/弱蛋白銀　Argyrol
弱化子/弱化子，致弱物　attenuator
弱脉/弱脈　weak pulse
弱染性/弱染性　amblychromasia
弱声助听器/微音助聽器　micracoustic
弱视/弱視　amblyopia
弱视•禀赋不足证/弱視•禀賦不足證　amblyopia with constitutional insufficiency pattern
弱视矫正法/弱視治療法　amblyopiatrics
弱视镜/弱視用鏡　amblyoscope
弱视•脾胃虚弱证/弱視•脾胃虚弱證　amblyopia with spleen-stomach weakness pattern
弱视性眼球震颤/弱視性眼球震顫　amblyopic nystagmus
弱视眼操练疗法/視力練習法　pleoptics
弱视者/弱視者　amblyope
弱性溃疡/弱性潰瘍　weak ulcer
弱银蛋白质/弱銀蛋白質　mild sliver protein
弱荧光/弱螢光　hypofluorescence

S

撒布/撒布　poudrage, sprinkle
撒布粉/撒布粉　epipastic
撒利汞茶碱液/撒利汞茶鹼液　salyrgan-theophylline solution
脎/脎　osazone
脎试验/脎試驗　osazone test
萨巴内耶夫-弗兰克手术/賽-弗二氏手術　Ssabanejew-Frank operation
萨布朗葡萄糖琼脂/薩布羅葡萄糖瓊脂　Sabourand glucose agar
萨尔迪诺-努范综合征/Saldino-Noonan 症候群　Saldino-Noonan syndrome
萨拉蒙综合征/Salamon 氏症候群　Salamon syndrome
萨拉细胞/Sala 氏細胞　Sala cell
萨卢斯征/薩盧斯徵　Salus sign
萨罗樟脑/水楊酸苯酯樟腦　salol camphor
萨满教/薩滿教　Shamanism
萨佩韧带/Sappey 氏韌帶　Sappey ligament
萨洒皂草配基/洋菝葜皂苷　sarsasapogenin
腮沟/腮溝　visceral groove
腮腺导管/腮腺導管　ductus parotideus
腮腺导管瘘/腮腺導管瘻　parotid duct fistula
腮腺的/腮腺的　parotidean
腮腺功能亢进/腮腺機能過旺　hyperparotidism
腮腺管/腮腺[導]管　parotid duct
腮腺管囊肿/腮腺管囊腫　parotid duct cyst
腮腺管乳头/腮腺管乳頭　papilla of parotid duct
腮腺后[间]隙综合征/腮腺後隙症候群　syndrome of retroparotid space
腮腺后静脉/腮腺後靜脈　posterior parotid vein
腮腺疾病/腮腺疾病　parotid diseases
腮腺/腮腺　parotid gland
腮腺筋膜/腮腺筋膜　parotid fascia
腮腺静脉/腮腺靜脈　parotid vein
腮腺淋巴结/腮腺淋巴結　parotid lymph node
腮腺囊肿/腮腺囊腫　parotid cyst
腮腺内丛/腮腺內叢　intraparotid plexus
腮腺脓肿/腮腺膿腫　parotid abscess
腮腺前静脉/面靜脈腮腺支　anterior parotid vein
腮腺浅部/腮腺淺部　superficial part of parotid gland
腮腺浅淋巴结/腮腺淺淋巴結　superficial parotid lymph node
腮腺切除术/腮腺切除術　parotidectomy
腮腺区/腮腺區　parotid region
腮腺深部/腮腺深部　deep part of parotid gland
腮腺深淋巴结/腮腺深淋巴結　deep parotid lymph node
腮腺神经/腮腺神經　parotid nerve
[腮腺]嗜酸粒细胞腺瘤/嗜酸顆粒細胞腺瘤　oxyphilic granular cell adenoma
腮腺涎/腮腺涎　parotid saliva
腮腺腺体瘘/腮腺腺體瘻　parotid gland fistula
腮腺炎/腮腺炎　parotitis
腮腺炎病毒/腮腺炎病毒　mumps virus
腮腺炎性睾丸炎/腮腺炎性睾丸炎　orchitis parotidea
腮腺炎疫苗/腮腺炎疫苗　mumps vaccine
腮腺咬肌区/腮腺嚼肌部　parotideomasseteric region
腮腺硬化/腮腺硬癌　parotidoscirrhus
腮腺支/腮腺支　parotid branch
腮腺肿瘤/腮腺腫瘤　parotid neoplasm
腮岩/腮巖,頰癌　rock-like cheek, carcinoma of cheek, cheek cancer
腮肿/痄腮　mumps
塞鼻法/塞鼻法　nasal plugging therapy
塞鼻疗法/塞鼻療法　nose-plugging therapy
塞茨变形呼吸/Seitz 氏變性呼吸　Seitz metamorphosing respiration
塞尔绷带/Sayre 氏繃帶　Sayre bandage
塞尔丁格技术/Seldinger 技術　Seldinger technique
塞尔夹板/Sayre 氏夾板　Sayre splint
塞尔托利细胞/Sertoli 氏細胞　Sertoli cell
塞尔托利细胞瘤/塞托利氏細胞瘤　Sertoli cell tumor
塞耳疗法/塞耳療法　ear-plugging therapy
塞克尔综合征/塞克爾症候群　Seckel syndrome
塞仑/塞蘭姆　thiram
塞利洛尔/塞利洛爾　celiprolol
塞流/塞流　blocking with haemostatic for arresting uterine hemorrhage
塞曼效应/濟曼氏效應　Zeeman effect

塞梅林韧带/Soemmering 氏韧带　Soemmering ligament
塞米施[角膜]溃疡/Saemisch 氏潰瘍　Saemisch ulcer
塞斯丹-雷蒙综合征/塞-雷二氏症候群　Cestan-Raymond syndrome
塞斯丹-舍奈茨综合征/塞-程二氏症候群　Cestan-Chenais syndrome
塞斯坦综合征/Cestan 氏症候群　Cestan syndrome
塞条/塞條　tent
塞托利细胞仅存综合征/塞托利細胞僅存症候群　Sertoli cell only syndrome
塞西亚病/Scythian 病　Scythian disease
塞药法/塞藥法　suppository method
塞扎里网状细胞增多综合征/史勒里氏網狀細胞增生症候群　Sézary reticulosis syndrome
塞扎里综合征/史勒里氏症候群　Sézary syndrome
噻苯哒唑/涕必靈　thiabendazole
噻吨类/噻噸類　thioxanthenes
噻二嗪类/噻二嗪類　thiadiazines
噻吩甲酰三氟丙酮/噻吩甲醯三氟丙酮　thenoyltrifluoroacetone
噻吩类/噻吩類　thiophenes
噻氯匹定/噻氯匹定　ticlopidine
噻吗洛尔/噻嗎洛爾　timolol
噻嘧啶/四氢基噻吩乙烯嘧啶　pyrantel
噻嘧啶酒石酸盐/噻嘧啶酒石酸鹽　pyrantel tartrate
噻嘧啶双羟萘酸盐/噻嘧啶雙羥萘酸鹽　pyrantel pamoate
噻嗪类/噻嗪類　thiazines
噻替派/硫替派　thiotepa
噻烯霉素类/噻烯黴素類　thienamycins
噻唑/噻唑　thiazole
噻唑烷二酮类/噻唑烷二酮類　thiazolidinediones
鳃的/鳃的　branchial
鳃窦/鳃竇　branchial sinus
鳃弓/鳃弧　branchial arch
鳃弓肌/鳃肌　branchial muscle
鳃[弓]下隆起/鳃下隆起　hypobranchial eminence
鳃沟/鳃溝　branchial groove
鳃管/鳃管　branchial duct
鳃后体/終鳃體, 後鳃體　ultimobranchial body
鳃节/鳃原節　branchiomere
鳃裂/鳃裂　branchial cleft
鳃裂癌/鳃裂癌　branchial carcinoma
鳃裂囊肿/鳃裂囊腫　branchial cyst
鳃裂原性囊肿/鳃裂原性囊腫　branchiogenetic cyst
鳃瘘/鳃瘻　branchial fistula
鳃膜/鳃膜　branchial membrane
鳃囊肿/鳃囊腫　branchial cyst
鳃器/鳃器　branchial apparatus
鳃原的/鳃裂原的　branchiogenous
赛比静脉/Sappey 氏静脉, 副脐静脉　vein of Sappey
赛得利兹粉/賽特鹽, 複方沸騰散　Seidlitz powder
赛德尔暗点/賽德爾暗點　Seidel scotoma
赛德黑尔姆溶液/Seyderhelm 氏溶液　Seyderhelm solution
赛庚啶/賽浦西他啶　cyproheptadine
赛克利嗪/賽克力嗪　cyclizine
赛拉嗪/賽拉嗪　xylazine
赛璐玢/賽璐芬, 透明紙　cellophane
赛璐珞线/假象牙線　celluloid thread
赛洛西宾/賽洛西賓　psilocybine
赛姆截肢术/賽姆截肢術　Syme amputation
赛跑者骨折/疾走者骨折　sprinter fracture
赛-舍综合征/Cestan-Chenais 二氏症候群　syndrome of Cestan-Chenais
赛特贝格病/賽特貝格病　Seitelberger disease
赛维兹光滑舌/Sandwith 氏光滑舌　Sandwith bald tongue
三胺/三胺　triamine
三胺五乙酸/三胺五乙酸　pentetic acid
三瓣的/有三瓣的　trivalve
三胞胎/三胞胎　trigemini
二倍频率/二倍頻率　tripler frequency
三倍体/三倍體　triploid
三倍性/三套染色體　triploidy
三苯甲基化合物/三苯甲基化合物　trityl compound
三苯甲烷/三苯甲烷　triphenylmethane
三苯乙烯/三苯乙烯　triphenylethylene
三壁骨下袋/三壁骨下袋　three-walled infrabony pocket
三臂[畸形]/三臂畸形　tribrachia
三臂卡环/三臂卡環　three-arm clasp
三边孔/三邊孔　trilateral foramen
三苄糖苷/乙基三苄基葡萄呋喃糖苷　tribenoside
三波长分光光度法/三波長分光光度法　three wavelength spectrophotometry
三波脉/三重搏脈　tricrotic pulse
三波脉波/三重搏波　tricrotic wave
三部九候/三部九候　three body parts and nine pulse taking sites
三才/三才　three life forces
三才整体论/三才整體論　theory of three life forces as unity
三才之道/三才之道　law of three life forces

三叉点/三叉點 triradius
三叉结节/三叉結節 trigeminal tubercle
三叉丘脑束/三叉丘腦束 trigeminothalamic tract
三叉丘系/三叉神經丘徑 trigeminal lemniscus
三叉取[膀胱]石钳/三叉取石器 trilabe
三叉神经/三叉神經 trigeminal nerve
三叉神经半月节甘油注射术/三叉神經半月節甘油注射術 glycerol injection of gasserian ganglion
三叉神经半月节射频热凝固术/三叉神經半月節射頻熱凝固術 radiofrequency thermocoagulation for gasserian ganglion
三叉神经的/三叉神經的 trifacial, trigeminal
三叉神经感觉根/三叉神經感覺根 sensory root of trigeminal nerve
三叉神经感觉根切断术/三叉神經感覺根切斷術 sensory rhizotomy of trigeminal nerve
三叉神经沟/三叉神經溝 trigeminal groove
三叉神经核/三叉神經核 trigeminal nucleus
三叉神经疾病/三叉神經疾病 trigeminal nerve disease
三叉神经脊束/三叉神經脊徑 spinal tract of trigeminal nerve
三叉神经脊束核/三叉神經脊徑核 spinal nucleus of trigeminal nerve
三叉神经脊髓核/三叉神經脊髓核 spino trigeminal nucleus
三叉神经节/三叉神經節 trigeminal ganglion
三叉神经节支/三叉神經節支 branch of trigeminal ganglion
三叉神经脑桥核/三叉神經腦橋核 pontine nucleus of trigeminal nerve
三叉神经腔/三叉神經腔 trigeminal cave
三叉神经丘脑的/三叉神經丘腦的 trigeminothalamic
三叉[神经]丘脑束/三叉神經丘腦徑 trigeminothalamic tract
三叉神经射频热凝固术/三叉神經射頻熱凝固術 radiofrequency thermocoagulation of trigeminal nerve
三叉神经失养性溃疡/三叉神經失養性潰瘍 trigeminal trophic ulceration
三叉神经痛/三叉[神經]痛 epileptiform neuralgia, trifacial neuralgia
三叉神经尾核/三叉神經尾核 trigeminal caudal nucleus
三叉神经性咳/三叉神經性欬嗽 trigeminal cough
三叉神经压迹/三叉神經壓痕,三叉神經切跡 trigeminal impression

三叉神经眼支撕脱术/三叉神經眼支撕脱術 avulsion of ophthalmic branch of trigeminal nerve
三叉神经营养综合征/三叉神經失養性潰瘍症候群 trigeminal trophic syndrome
三叉神经运动根/三叉神經運動根 motor root of trigeminal nerve
三叉神经运动核/三叉神經運動核 motor nucleus of trigeminal nerve
三叉神经支/三叉神經支 trigeminal branch
三叉神经中脑核/三叉神經中腦核 mesencephalic nucleus of trigeminal nerve
三叉神经中脑束/三叉神經中腦徑 mesencephalic tract of trigeminal nerve
三叉神经中央束/三叉神經中央束 central tract of trigeminal nerve
三叉形切口/三叉形切口 tripod incision
三叉形韧带/三叉形韌帶 ligament of Bigelow
三重复视/三重複視 triple vision
三重染料肥皂合剂/三染質肥皂合劑 triple dye-soap mixture
三重态/三重態 triplet state
三次肝移植/三次肝移植 tertiary liver transplantation
三醋精/三醋酸甘油 triacetin
三簇介体/三簇介體 triceptor
三氮烯/三氮烯 triazene
三等管等睾吸虫/三等管等睾吸蟲 isoparorchis trisimilitubis
三蒂皮瓣/三蒂皮瓣 tripedicle skin flap
三碘苯甲酸类/三碘苯甲酸類 triiodobenzoic acids
三碘化物/三碘化物 triiodide
三碘甲状腺氨酸/三碘甲狀腺胺酸 liothyronine
三碘甲状腺原氨酸/三碘甲狀腺原氨酸 triiodothyronine
三碘乙丙酸/三次乙二磺酸 triiodoethionic acid
三度房室传导阻滞/第三級房室傳導阻滯 the third-degree heart block
三度空间咬合器/三度空間咬合器 three dimensional articulator
三度烧伤/三度燒傷 the third-degree burn
三段排尿/三段排尿 triple voiding
三对基因杂种/三混種,三雜種 trihybrid
三对一胰岛素/三對一胰島素 three to one insulin
三耳畸胎/贅耳者 triotus
三发性甲状旁腺功能亢进症/三發性甲狀旁腺功能亢進症 tertiary hyperparathyroidism
三房心/三房心 cor triatriatum
三肺叶切除术/三肺葉切除術 trilobectomy

三分子水/三個水分子 trihydrol
三氟丙嗪/三氟丙嗪 triflupromazine
三氟哌丁苯/三氟哌丁苯 trifluperidol
三氟拉嗪/三氟拉嗪 trifluoperazine
三氟噻吨/氟哌噻顿 flupenthixol
三氟乙醇/三氟乙醇 trifluoroethanol
三氟乙酸/三氟乙酸 trifluoroacetic acid
三根叉受累/三根叉侵犯 trifurcation involvement
三根分叉部/三分叉 trifurcation
三光/三光 three lights, light of sun, moon and fire
三硅酸镁/三矽酸鎂 magnesium trisilicate
三核苷酸/三核苷酸 trinucleotide
三核苷酸重复/三核苷酸重複 trinucleotide repeat
三核苷酸重复扩增/三核苷酸重複擴增 trinucleotide repeat expansion
三踝骨折/三踝骨折 trimalleolar fracture
三环抗抑郁药/三環抗抑鬱藥 tricyclic antidepressive agent
三环类抗抑郁剂/三環抗憂鬱劑 tricyclic antidepressant
三黄膏/三黄膏 sanhuang plaster
三黄片/三黄片 sanhuang tablet
三级蛋白质结构/三級蛋白質結構 tertiary protein structure
三级功能性矫正装置/三級功能性矯正裝置 class III functional appliance
三级关系/三級關係 class III relationship
三级结构/三級結構，三級構造 tertiary structure
三级卵泡/三級卵泡 tertiary follicle
三级绒毛干/三級絨毛幹 tertiary stem villus
三级弹线牵引/三級彈線牽引 class III elastic
三级弯折/三級彎折 the third order bend
三级亚类/三級亞類 class III subdivision
三级异常咬合/三級異常咬合 class III malocclusion
三己糖神经酰胺类/三己糖基神經醯胺類 trihexosylceramides
三甲氨乙酸/三甲胺基乙酸 trimethylaminoacetic acid
三甲胺/三甲胺 trimethylamine
三甲复脉汤/三甲複脈湯 sanjia fumai decoction
三甲基硅烷化合物/三甲基矽烷化合物 trimethylsilyl compound
三甲基锡化合物/三甲基錫化合物 trimethyltin compound
三甲基乙酸/三甲基乙酸，特戊酸 pivalic acid
三甲卡因/三甲卡因 trimecaine
三甲利定/三甲利定 promedol
三甲曲沙/三甲曲沙 trimetrexate
三甲沙林/三甲沙林 trioxsalen
三甲双酮/三甲雙酮 trimethadione
三价的/三價[個體]的 trivalent
三尖瓣/三尖瓣 tricuspid valve
三尖瓣瓣环成形术/三尖瓣瓣環成形術 tricuspid annuloplasty
三尖瓣闭锁/三尖瓣閉鎖 tricuspid atresia
三尖瓣闭锁不全/三尖瓣閉鎖不全 tricuspid valve insufficiency
三尖瓣成形术/三尖瓣成形術 tricuspid valvoplasty
三尖瓣反流/三尖瓣反流 tricuspid regurgitation
三尖瓣关闭不全/三尖瓣閉鎖不全 tricuspid valve insufficiency
三尖瓣关闭不全卡尔庞捷修复术/三尖瓣關閉不全卡爾龐捷修復術 Carpentier repair of tricuspid incompetence
三尖瓣[区]杂音/三尖瓣雜音 tricuspid murmur
三尖瓣脱垂/三尖瓣脫垂 tricuspid valve prolapse
三尖瓣狭窄/三尖瓣狹窄 tricuspid stenosis
三尖的/三尖[瓣]的 tricuspid
三尖杉酯碱类/三尖杉酯鹼類 harringtonines
三间/三間 sanjian, LI3
三键/三鍵 triple bond
三焦/三焦 sanjiao, triple energy
三焦辨证/三焦辨證 pattern identification of sanjiao theory
三焦点镜片/三焦點透鏡 trifocal lens
三焦点眼镜/三焦點眼鏡 trifocal glass
三焦惊/三焦驚 convulsion due to triple-energizer disorders
三焦俞/三焦俞 sanjiaoshu, BL22
三角绷带/三角繃帶 triangular bandage
三角皱襞/三角皺襞 triangular fold
三角布绷带/三角布繃帶 cravat, cravat bandage
三角部/三角部 triangular part
三角带/三角帶 scarf bandage
三角沟/三角溝 triangular groove
三角骨/三角骨 triquetral bone
三角肌/三角肌 deltoid muscle, triangular muscle
三角肌粗隆/三角肌粗隆 deltoid tuberosity
三角肌动脉/三角肌動脈 deltoid artery
三角肌筋膜/三角肌筋膜 deltoid fascia
三角肌区/三角肌部 deltoid region
三角肌下的/三角肌下的 subdeltoid
三角肌下滑囊炎/肩峰下黏液囊炎 subdeltoid bursitis
三角肌下囊/三角肌下囊 subdeltoid bursa
三角肌胸肌三角/三角肌胸肌三角 delto-

ideopectoral triangle
三角肌支/三角肌支　deltoid branch
三角及管状毛/三角及管狀毛　pili trianguli et canaliculi
三角嵴/三角嵴　triangular ridge
三角毛/三角毛　pili trianguli
三角器/三角器　triple-angle
三角区脑膜瘤/三角區腦膜瘤　trigonal meningioma
三角韧带/三角韌帶　deltoid ligament
三角束/三角束　triangular tract
三角头畸胎/三角頭畸胎　trigocephalus
三角头[畸形]/三角頭畸形　trigonocephalia
三角窝/三角窩　triangular fossa
三角窝隆起/三角窩隆起　eminence of triangular fossa
三角纤维软骨复合体/三角纖維軟骨複合體　triangular fibrocartilage complex
三角[形]/三角[形]　triangle
三角形圈/三角形圈　delta loop
三角胸肌淋巴结/三角胸肌淋巴結　deltopectoral lymph node
三角针/三角針　triangular needle
三脚架种植体/三腳架種植體　tripod implant
三阶/三階　the third order
三精入卵/三精入卵　trispermy
三九胃泰/三九胃泰　sanjiu weitai capsules
三聚氰酸/三聚氰酸　tricyanic acid
三聚体/三聚體　trimer
三聚乙硫醛/三聚硫代乙醛　sulfoparaldehyde
三聚乙醛/三聚乙醛　Paraldehyde
三聚乙醛中毒/三聚乙醛中毒　paraldehydism
三棱/三棱　common buried rubber
三棱镜片/三棱鏡片　prismatic glasses lens
三棱镜视力计/棱鏡檢眼器　prismoptometer
三棱眼镜/棱晶眼鏡　prismatic spectacles
三棱针/三棱針　three-edged needle
三棱针疗法/三棱針療法　three-edged needle therapy
三里发/三里發　Zusanli cellulitis
三联律/三連律　trigeminy
三联脉/三聯脈　trigeminal pulse
三联免疫抑制治疗/三聯免疫抑制治療　triple immunosuppressive therapy
三联体/三聯體　triplet, triad
三联微管/三聯微管　triplomicrotubule
三磷酸腺苷酶/三磷酸腺苷酶　adenosine triphosphatase
三磷酸盐/三磷酸鹽　triphosphate
三菱形皮瓣/三菱形皮瓣　triple rhomboid skin flap

三硫化物/三硫化物　tersulfide
三卤甲烷/三鹵甲烷　trihalomethanes
三氯苯酚/三氯酚　trichlorophenol
三氯化碘/三氯化碘　iodine trichloride
三氯化砷/三氯化砷　arsenic chloride
三氯化锑/三氯化銻　butter of antimony
三氯化物/三氯化物　terchloride
三氯环氧丙烷/三氯環氧丙烷　trichloroepoxypropane
三氯磷酸酯/三氯磷酸酯　trichlorfon
三氯噻嗪/三氯甲基噻唑　trichlormethiazide
三氯三乙烯砷/三氯三乙烯砷　trichlorotrivinylarsine
三氯生/三氯生　triclosan
三氯叔丁醇/氯丁醇　chlorobutanol
三氯乙酸/三氯醋酸　trichloroacetic acid
三氯乙烷类/三氯乙烷類　trichloroethanes
三氯乙烯/三氯乙烯　trichloroethylene
三面畸胎/三面畸胎,三面連胎　triprosopus
三面接触镜/三面[接觸]鏡　three-mirror contact lens
三胚层的/三胚層的　tridermic
三胚层瘤/三胚瘤　tridermic tumor
三胚层胚盘/三胚層胚盤　trilaminar germ disc
三胚层形成/三胚層發生　tridermogenesis
三偏磷酸酯酶/三偏磷酸酯酶　trimetaphosphatase
三品/三品　three grades of drugs
三七/三七　sanqi
三七片/三七片　sanqi tablet
三七伤药片/三七傷藥片　sanqi shangyao tablet
三期梅毒/[第]三期梅毒　tertiary syphilis
三期切断术/第三期截斷術　tertiary amputation
三前臂[畸形]/三重前臂　triantebrachia
三[腔及其]内脏的/三腔臟腑的　trisplanchnic
三腔双囊管/三腔雙囊管　Sengstaken-Blakemore tube
三腔胃/三房胃　trifid stomach
三腔心/三腔心　trilocular heart
三羟化物/三氫氧化物　trihydrate
三羟基蒽醌/三羥蒽醌　anthragallol
三嗪类/三嗪類　triazines
三躯联胎/三軀連胎　somatotridymus
三[染色]体性/一套半染色體,三染色體　trisomia
三仁汤/三仁湯　sanren decoction
三日麻疹/三日麻疹　three-day measles
三日疟/三日[兩頭]瘧　quartan malaria
三日疟原虫/三日瘧原蟲,三日兩頭瘧蟲　Plasmodium malariae
三肉豆蔻甘油脂/三肉豆蔻甘油脂　myristic

triglyceride
三色[现象]/三原色性　trichroism
三色学说/三色學說　trichromatic theory
三射[染色]体/三射[染色]體　triradial chromosome
三圣散/三聖散　Three Sages powder
三室模型/三室模型　three-compartment model
三手[畸形]/三手畸形　tricheiria
三酸甘油脂脂肪酶/三酸甘油脂脂肪酶　triglycerides lipase
三羧酸类/三羧酸類　tricarboxylic acids
三羧酸循环/克列伯氏循環　Krebs cycle
三胎/三胎　triplets
三胎妊娠/三胎妊娠　triplet pregnancy
三肽/三肽　kyrin
三糖/三醣　trisaccharide
三糖酶/三醣酶　trisaccharidase
三体性/三染色體性　trisomy
三调/三調　three adjustments
三调合一/三調合一　three adjustments integrated into one
三萜/三萜　triterpene
三萜皂苷/三萜類皂苷　triterpenoid saponin
三萜皂苷元/三萜類皂苷元　triterpenoid sapogenin
三瞳[畸形]/三瞳畸形,三瞳症　triplokoria
三头肌/三頭肌　tricipital muscle
三头畸胎/三頭畸胎,三頭連胎　tricephalus
三头钳/三頭鉗　aderer
三烷锡化物/三烷錫化物　trialkyltin compound
三维超声心动描记术/三維超聲心動描記術　three-dimensional echocardiography
三维成像/三維成像　three-dimensional imaging
三维定量构效关系/三維定量構效關係　three-dimensional quantitative structure activity relationship, 3D-QSAR
三维结构/三維結構　three-dimensional structure
三维色谱图/三維層析圖　three-dimensional chromatogram
三物备急丸/三物備急丸　sanwu beiji pill
三烯甲雌醇核/三烯甲雌固醇　estratriene
三烯类/三烯類　trienes
三烯烃/烴三烯　alkatriene
三向辐射/三面放射,三向放射　triradiation
三相波/三相波　triphasic wave
三相的/三相的　triphasic
三相气雾剂/三相氣化噴霧劑　three-phase aerosol
三硝基苯磺酸/三硝基苯磺酸　trinitrobenzenesulfonic acid
三硝基苯甲硝胺/三硝基甲苯胺　tetryl
三硝基苯类/三硝基苯類　trinitrobenzenes
三硝基甲苯/三硝基甲苯　trinitrotoluene
三硝基甲苯中毒/三硝基甲苯中毒　trinitrotoluene poisoning
三硝基甲酚/三硝基甲酚　trinitrocresol
三硝酸甘油酯/硝酸甘油酯,三硝酸甘油基酯　nitroglycerin spirit
三硝酸甘油酯/三硝酸甘油　glyceryl trinitrate
三硝酸甘油酯中毒/三硝酸甘油酯中毒,硝基甘油中毒　glonoinism
三硝酸盐/三硝酸鹽　trinitrate
三辛酸甘油脂/三辛酸甘油脂　caprylic acid triglyceride
三溴化碘/三溴化碘　iodine tribromide
三溴化物/三溴化物　tribromide
三溴芦荟苷/三溴蘆薈苷　tribromaloin
三溴乙醇/三溴乙醇　tribromoethanol
三溴乙醇溶液/三溴乙醇溶液　tribromoethanol solution
三亚胺醌/三亞胺醌　triaziquone
三亚乙基磷酰胺/三亞乙基磷醯胺　triethylenephosphoramide
三阳并病/三陽并病　exogenous cold disease involving three yang channels
三阳合病/三陽合病　concurrent disease of three yang channels
三阳络/三陽絡　sanyangluo, SI8
三氧化二铋/三氧化物鉍　bismuth trioxide
三氧化二砷/三氧化二砷　arsenic trioxide
三氧化锑/三氧化二銻　antimony trioxide
三氧化物/三氧化物　trioxide
三叶皮瓣/三葉皮瓣　trilobed skin flap
三叶胎盘/三葉胎盤　placenta triloba
三叶形绷带/三葉形繃帶　trefoil bandage
三乙胺/三乙[醇]胺　triethylamine
三乙醇胺/三乙醇胺　triethanolamine
三乙四胺/三乙四胺　triethylenetetramine
三乙锡化合物/三乙錫化合物　triethyltin compound
三乙硝胺/三硝酸三乙醇胺酯　trolnitrate
三翼托架/三翼托架　triple bracket
三因/三因　three types of disease causes
三因极一病证方论/三因極一病證方論　Treatise on Diseases, Patterns and Prescriptions Related to Unification of the Three Etiologies
三因学说/三因學說　theory of three types of disease causes
三阴交/三陰交　sanyinjiao, SP6
三音律/三重節律　triple rhythm

三硬脂酸甘油脂/三硬脂酸甘油脂　stearic triglyceride
三油酸甘油脂/三油酸甘油酯　triolein
三郁/三鬱　three types of stagnation pattern
三元化合物/三級化合物　tertiary compound
三元素汞合金/三元素汞合金　ternary amalgam
三元酸/三酸基　triacid
三原子分子/三原子分子　triatomic molecule
三爪钳/三叉鉤　trielcon
三爪取弹钳/三爪取彈鉗　alphonsin
三肢切断术/三肢截斷術　triple amputation
三肢瘫/三肢癱瘓　triplegia
三指的/三指的　tridactyl
三趾的/三趾的　tridactyl
三酯[化合]物/三酯化合物　triester
三子养亲汤/三子養親湯　sanzi yangqin decoction
三足[畸形]/三足駢肢畸形　tripodia
三唑类/三唑類　triazoles
三唑仑/三唑侖　triazolam
伞襞/傘皺襞　fimbriated fold
伞兵骨折/傘兵骨折　paratrooper fracture
伞房花形的/傘房花的，傘形的　corymbose
伞房花形梅毒疹/傘狀花疹形梅毒疹　syphilid corymbiformis
伞房花序/傘房花序　corymb
伞形附着/陽傘狀附著　parasol insertion
伞形视网膜脱离/傘形視網膜脫離　umbrella detachment of retina
伞形酮/傘形酮　umbelliferone
伞状虹膜/陽傘狀虹膜　umbrella iris
伞状韧带/傘狀韌帶　laciniate ligament
散弹式处方/散彈式處方，雜湊處方　shotgun prescription
散光/散光　astigmatism
散光表/散光表　astigmatic chart
散光测量法/散光計檢法　astigmometry
散光带/散光帶　astigmatic band
散光计/散光計　astigmatometer
散光间距/散光間距　astigmatism interval
散光矫正镜/散光矯正鏡　hydroadiascope
散光镜/散光鏡　diverging meniscus
散光镜检查/散光鏡檢查　astigmatoscopy
散光镜片/亂視透鏡　astigmatic lens
散光描记器/散光描記器　astigmagraph
散光盘表/散光儀　astigmatic dial
散光轴/散光軸　astigmatism axis
散剂/散劑　powder
散焦光束/散焦光束　defocused beam
散脉/散脈　scattered pulse
散射辐射/分散放射　scattered radiation
散在重复序列/散在重複序列　interspersed repetitive sequences
散在神经元/散在神經元　sporadoneure
散阵/散陣　dissipating array
散装产品/散装産品　bulk products
散播型汗孔角化症/散播型汗孔角化症　porokeratosis disseminata
散布/散布　scatter
散发/散發　emission
散发病/散發病　sporadic disease
散发性斑疹伤寒/散發性斑疹傷寒　sporadic typhus
散发性呆小病/散發性呆小症　spontaneous cretinism
散发性高甘油三酯血症/散發性高甘油三酯血症　sporadic hypertriglyceridemia
散发性甲状腺肿/散發性甲狀腺腫　sporadic goiter
散发性弹力纤维分解皮肤萎缩/散發性彈力纖維分解皮萎病　atrophoderma elastolytica discreta
散发性跖汗孔角化病/散發性蹠汗孔角化病　porokeratosis plantaris discreta
散法/散法　dispersing manipulation
散寒除湿/散寒除濕　dispelling cold and removing dampness
散寒化饮/散寒化飲　dispelling cold and resolving fluid retention
散瞳剂性青光眼/散瞳劑性青光眼　mydriatic glaucoma
散瞳强直/散瞳性強硬　mydriatic rigidity
散瞳试验/散瞳試驗　mydriasis test
散瞳药/散瞳藥　mydriatics
桑白皮/桑白皮　cortex mori radicis, white mulberry root-bark
桑德病/Saunder 氏病　Saunder disease
桑德尔病/Sander 氏病　Sander disease
桑德尔灵敏度/桑德爾靈敏度　Sandell sensitivity
桑德曼-安德拉综合征/商得門-安得拉症候群，乏汗及牙齒缺損症　Sandmann-Andra syndrome
桑寄生/桑寄生，槲寄生　Viscum album, Chinese viscum herb
桑菊饮/桑菊飲　sangju drink
桑毛虫皮炎/桑毛蟲皮炎　euproctis similis dermatitis
桑拿浴/桑拿浴　sauna
桑螵蛸/桑螵蛸　mantis egg-case
桑螵蛸散/桑螵蛸散　sangpiaoxiao powder
桑普森囊肿/Sampson 氏囊腫　Sampson cyst
桑葚/桑葚　mulberry fruit

桑葚胚/桑葚胚　embryotic sphere
桑葚胚期/桑葚[體]期　morula stage
桑葚[胚]形成/桑葚體形成　morulation
桑葚形/桑葚形　morular shape
桑葚样细胞/桑葚狀細胞　morular cell
桑葚状磨牙/桑葚狀白齒　mulberry molar
桑葚状痣/桑葚狀痣　nevus morus
桑托里尼管/Santorini 氏管　duct of Santorini
桑托里尼肌/Santorini 氏肌肉　Santorini muscle
桑杏汤/桑杏湯　sangxing decoction
桑叶/桑葉　mulberry leaf
桑枝/桑枝　mulberry twig
嗓音外科学/嗓音外科學　phonosurgery
扫斑机/掃斑機　emaculation machine
扫掠注视/掃掠注視　saccadic fixation
扫描/掃描　scan
扫描电镜术/掃描電子顯微術　scanning electron microscopy
扫描电[子显微]镜/掃描電子顯微鏡　scanning electron microscope
扫描隧道显微镜检查/掃描隧道顯微鏡檢查　scanning tunneling microscopy
扫描探针显微镜检查/掃描探針顯微鏡檢查　scanning probe microscopy
扫描照相术/掃描造影術　scanography
扫视运动/掃視運動　saccadic movement
扫烟囱工人癌/掃煙囪工人癌　chimney sweeper cancer
瘙痒的/搔癢病的　pruritic
瘙痒症/搔癢病　pruritus
臊瘊/臊瘊　condyloma
臊瘊·肝经湿热证/臊瘊·肝經濕熱證　condyloma with pattern of dampness-heat in liver channel
臊瘊·脾虚湿困证/臊瘊·脾虛濕困證　condyloma with pattern of spleen deficiency and dampness retention
臊瘊·气滞血瘀证/臊瘊·氣滯血瘀證　condyloma with pattern of qi stagnation and blood stasis
色氨酸/色胺酸　tryptophan
1-色氨酸/1-色胺酸　1-tryptophan
色氨酸反应/色胺酸反應　tryptophan reaction
色氨酸合酶/色胺酸合酶　tryptophan synthase
色氨酸加氧酶/色胺酸加氧酶　tryptophan oxygenase
色氨酸 tRNA 连接酶/色胺酸 tRNA 連接酶　tryptophan-tRNA ligase
色氨酸酶/色胺酸酵素　tryptophanase
色氨酸尿/色胺酸尿症　tryptophanuria
色氨酸羟化酶/色胺酸羥化酶　tryptophan hydroxylase
色氨酸试验/色胺酸試驗　tryptophan test
色胺类/色胺類　tryptamines
色胺酸缺乏/色胺酸缺乏　tryptophan deficiency
色板/色板　shade guide
色蛋白/色[素]蛋白　chromoprotein
色调 B 度/乙種色調　tint B
色二孢霉菌毒病/色二孢黴菌中毒症　diplodiatoxicosis
色甘酸二钠/色甘酸二鈉　disodium cromoglycate
色甘酸钠/色甘酸鈉　sodium cromoglycate
色甘酸盐/色甘酸鹽　cromoglycate
色杆菌属/產色細菌屬　*Chromobacterium*
色光疗法/色光療法　color therapy
色汗症/色汗症　chromidrosis
色幻觉/心理色,想像色,意色　psychochrome
色幻视/色[彩]幻視　chromophose
色觉/色覺　color sense, color vision
色觉测量计/色覺測量計　chromatoskiameter
色觉检查/色覺檢查法　chromatoptometry
色觉检查[法]/色覺檢查[法]　examination of color sense
色觉检查器/色覺檢查計　chromoscope
色觉检查图/色覺檢查圖　color vision plate
色觉缺陷/色覺缺陷　color vision defect
色觉试验/色覺試驗　color perception test
色觉异常者/色覺不正常者　color deviant
色觉障碍/輕度色盲,部分色盲　dyschromatopsia
色觉正常/色視正常　euchromatopsy
色厥/色厥　sex syncope
色立体/有色三相體　color solid
色联觉/色幻覺,假色覺　psychochromesthesia
色脉合参/色脈合參　comprehensive consideration of both complexion and pulse manifestation
色满卡林/色滿卡林　cromakalim
色满类/色滿類　chromans
色盲/色盲　color blindness
色盲暗点/色盲暗點　color scotoma
色盲测验器/色盲測驗器　leukoscope
色盲检查镜/色盲檢查器　anomaloscope
色霉素类/色黴素類　chromomycins
色谱法/色譜法　chromatography
色谱工作站/層析工作站　chromatographic work station
色谱数据处理机/層析數據處理機　chromatographic data processor
色谱图/層析圖　chromatogram
色谱响应函数/層析回應函數　chromatographic

response function, CRF
色谱优化函数/層析最適化函數　chromatographic optimization function, COF
色情/淫蕩　salacity
色情精神病/色情精神病　erotic psychosis
色情狂/色情狂,花癲,色情性躁狂　eroticomania
色情狂者/色情狂者　erotomaniac
色弱/色弱　color weakness
色视野/色視野　color visual field
色视症/色幻覺,視色異常　chromatopsia
色素/色素　pigment
色素斑/色素斑　pigmented spot
色素播散综合征/色素播散症候群　pigment dispersion syndrome
色素不均/著色不等,染色不匀　anisochromasia
色素部/色素部　Pars pigmentosa
色素沉着/色素沈著　chromatosis, hyperpigmentation
色素沉着不足/色素過少,色素不足　hypopigmentation
色素沉着过多/色素沈著過度,著色過度　hyperpigmentation
色素沉着息肉综合征/色素沈著息肉症候群　Peutz-Jeghers syndrome
色素固定/色素固定　chromatopexis
色素过多/皮膚異色症　polychromia
色素过多症/色素增多　pleiochromia
色素减退/色素減退　hypopigmentation
色素[结缔]组织/色素結締組織　pigment connective tissue
色素颗粒/色素顆粒　pigment granule
色素内镜检查[术]/色素内鏡檢查[術]　dye endoscopy
色素尿/色素尿　chromaturia
色素缺乏/無色素症　achromia
色素缺乏斑/無色素斑　achromic patch
色素绒毛结节性滑膜炎/色素絨毛結節性滑膜炎　pigmented villonodular synovitis
色素溶解/色素破壞　pigmentolysis
色素溶素/色素溶素　pigmentolysin
色素上皮细胞/色素上皮細胞　pigment epithelial cell
色素舌/色素舌　pigmented tongue
色素生成/色素發生　pigmentogenesis
色素失禁/色素失禁　incontinence of pigment
色素失调/色素失調　pigmentary incontinence
色素失调症/色素失節病　incontinentia pigmenti
色素脱失/脱色　depigmentation
色素细胞/色素細胞　pigment cell

色素细胞瘤/色素母细胞瘤　chromatophoroma
色素细胞痣/色素細胞性母斑,色素細胞性痣　nevomelanocytic nevus
色素形成/色素生成,色素產生　chromogenesis
色素性扁平苔癣/色素性扁平苔癬　lichen planus pigmentosus
色素性多毛性表皮痣/色素性多毛性表皮痣　pigmented hairy epidermal naevus
色素性分界线/色素性分界線　pigmentary demarcation line
色素性汗腺顶端汗腺瘤/色素性汗腺頂端汗腺瘤　pigmented eccrine acrospiroma
色素性化妆品皮炎/色素性化妝品皮膚炎　pigmented cosmetic dermatitis
色素性基底细胞癌/色素性基底細胞癌　pigmented basal cell carcinoma
色素性基底细胞上皮瘤/色素性基底細胞上皮瘤　pigmented basal cell epithelioma
色素性疾病/色素性疾病　pigmentary disorder
色素性结石/色素性結石　pigmented stone
色素性口围红斑/色素性口圍紅斑　pigmented peribuccal erythema of Brocq
色素性毛囊囊肿/色素性毛囊囊腫　pigmented follicular cyst
色素性玫瑰疹/色素性玫瑰疹　roseola pigmentosa
色素性皮炎/色素性皮膚炎　pigmented dermatitis
色素性视网膜炎/視網膜色素變性　retinitis pigmentosa
色素性梭状细胞痣/色素性梭狀細胞痣　pigmented spindle cell nevus
色素性萎缩/色素性萎縮,著色性萎縮　pigmentary atrophy
色素性荨麻疹/著色性蕁麻疹　urticaria pigmentosa
色素性痒疹/色素性癢疹　prurigo pigmentosa
色素性真菌病/產色黴菌病　chromomycosis
色素性脂溢性角化症/色素性脂漏性角化症　pigmented seborrheic keratosis
色素性紫癜/色素性紫癜　pigmentary purpura
色素性紫癜性皮肤病/色素性紫癜性皮膚病　pigmentary purpuric dermatosis
色素性紫癜性皮疹/色素性紫癜性皮疹　pigmentary purpuric eruption
色素性紫癜性苔藓样皮肤病/色素性紫癜性苔蘚樣皮膚病　pigmented purpuric lichenoid dermatosis
色素性紫癜性苔藓样皮炎/苔癬樣紫斑色素性皮膚炎　pigmented purpuric lichenoid dermatitis
色素血管性斑痣性错构瘤病/色素血管性母斑症　phakomatosis pigmentovascularis

色素血栓/色素性血栓 pigmentary thrombus
色素异常症/色素沈著異常 dyschromatosis
色素质/漿染質,染色漿 chromatoplasm
色素痣/色素性斑痣 pigmented nevus
色酮/色酮 chromone
色原/色原質 chromogen
色原烷/色[原]烷 chromane
色泽/色澤 color and luster, sheeny complexion
色痣/色痣 pigmented mole
色紫/色紫 chrom violet
涩/澀 astringent
涩肠固脱剂/澀腸固脱劑 formula for astringing intestine and arresting proptosis
涩肠止泻/澀腸止瀉 relieving diarrhea with astringents
涩剂/澀劑 astringent formula
涩精止遗剂/澀精止遺劑 formula for astringing spermatorrhea
涩脉/澀脈 hesitant pulse
啬神养性/嗇神養性 banishing world desires to repose
铯放射性同位素/銫放射性同位素 cesium radioisotope
铯同位素/銫同位素 cesium isotope
塞因塞用/塞因塞用 treating obstructive pattern with tonifying methods
森林脑炎/森林腦炎 forest encephalitis
森林雅司病/美洲利什曼病 pian bois
森宁手术/森寧手術 Senning operation
森森伯纳综合征/Sensenbrenner 氏症候群 Sensenbrenner syndrome
森斯塔肯-布莱克穆尔管/森-布二氏管 Sengstaken-Blakemore tube
森西巴明/森西巴明 Sensibamine
僧帽水母属/僧帽水母屬 Physalia
僧帽状细胞/僧帽狀細胞 mitral cell
杀阿米巴药/殺阿米巴藥 amebacide
杀白细胞素/殺白血球素 leukocidin
杀孢子剂/殺芽孢藥 sporicide
杀病毒剂/殺病毒藥 viricide
杀成虫剂/殺成蟲劑 imagocide
杀虫剂/殺蟲劑 pesticide
杀虫剂皮炎/殺蟲劑所致皮膚炎 pesticide dermatitis
杀虫气雾剂/殺蟲氣化噴霧劑 insect aerosol
杀虫消疳/殺蟲消疳 destroying parasites for curing malnutrition
杀虫药/殺蟲藥 pesticide, insecticide
杀黑星菌素/殺黑星菌素 venturicidins

杀蛔虫药/殺蛔蟲藥 lumbricide
杀寄生虫剂/殺寄生蟲藥 parasiticides
杀假丝菌素/殺假絲菌素,殺念珠菌素 candicidin
杀结核菌素/殺結核菌素 tubercidin
杀结核菌药/殺結核菌藥 tuberculocide
杀疥螨药/殺疥蟲藥 scabicide
杀精子药/殺精子藥 spermaticide
杀菌剂/殺菌劑 bactericidal, agent bactericide, germicide
杀菌浓度/殺菌濃度 bactericidal concentration
杀菌素/殺菌素 bacteriocidin
杀菌温度/殺菌溫度 thermal death point
杀菌物质/殺菌物質 bactericidal substance
杀菌性抗生素/殺菌性抗生藥 bactericidal antibiotic
杀[昆]虫器/滅蟲器 disinsector
杀链球菌药/殺鏈球菌藥 streptococcicide
杀裂殖体药/殺裂殖體蟲藥 schizonticide
杀螺菌素/殺螺旋菌素 spirillicidin
杀螺菌药/殺螺旋菌劑 spirillicide
杀螺旋体药/殺螺旋體劑 spirocheticide
杀螨剂/殺蟎劑 acaricide
杀蛲虫剂/殺蟯藥 oxyuricide
杀疟原虫药/殺瘧原蟲劑 plasmodicide
杀配子[体]剂/殺配子藥,殺生殖體藥 gametocide
杀葡萄球菌剂/殺葡萄球菌劑 staphylocide
杀蠕虫药/殺蠕蟲藥 helminthicide
杀软体动物药/殺軟體動物藥 molluscacide
杀伤细胞/殺手細胞 killer cell
杀上皮[细胞]毒素/上皮细胞破壞毒素 epitheliotoxin
杀丝虫药/殺絲蟲藥 filaricide
杀绦虫药/殺條蟲藥 taeniacide
杀体表寄生虫剂/殺皮上寄生蟲藥,殺外寄生蟲藥 epizoicide
杀外寄生虫药/殺外寄生蟲藥 ectoparasiticide
杀微生物剂/殺微生物藥 microbicide
杀细胞药/殺細胞藥 cytocide
杀[细]菌的/殺菌的 bactericidal
杀[细]菌剂/殺菌藥 bactericide
杀纤毛虫毒素/殺纖毛蟲毒素 infusoriotoxin
杀线虫剂/殺線蟲藥 nematocide
杀血吸虫药/殺血吸蟲劑 schistosomacide
杀婴/殺嬰 infanticide
杀真菌剂/殺黴菌藥 fungicide
杀真菌药/抗黴菌藥,抑制黴菌感染藥 antifungal
杀枝曲菌素/殺黴菌素,殲分枝桿菌素 mycocidin
杀锥虫药/殺錐蟲藥 trypanocide
沙/沙 sand

沙癌/沙癌　psammocarcinoma
沙比桧中毒/薩界檜中毒　sabinism
沙丁胺醇/沙丁胺醇　albuterol
沙棘/沙棘　seabuckthorn fruit
沙解/沙解　subjee
沙可来新/溶肉瘤素　sarcolysin
沙奎那韦/沙喹納韋　saquinavir
沙拉新/沙拉新　saralasin
沙雷菌感染/沙雷菌感染　serratia infection
沙利度胺/沙利竇邁　thalidomide
沙利度胺事件/沙利度胺事件　thalidomide event
沙粒病毒科/沙粒病毒科　Arenaviridae
沙粒病毒科感染/沙粒病毒科感染　Arenaviridae infection
沙粒乳头状腺肌瘤/沙粒乳頭狀腺肌瘤　adenomyoma psammopapillare
沙粒腺瘤/沙粒腺瘤　adenoma psammosum
沙林/沙林,甲氟磷酸異丙酯　sarin
沙瘤/沙狀瘤　sand tumor
沙漏样杂音/沙漏狀雜音　hourglass murmur
沙滤试验/砂濾試驗　sand test
沙螨/恙蟲　chigger
沙门菌/沙門桿菌　Salmonella
沙门菌病/沙門菌病　salmonellosis
沙门菌感染/沙門菌感染　salmonella infection
沙门菌群/沙門菌群　salmonella group
沙门菌食物中毒/沙門菌食物中毒　salmonella food poisoning
沙门菌噬菌体/沙門菌噬菌體　salmonella phage
沙门氏菌菌苗/沙門氏菌菌苗　salmonella vaccine
沙漠疮/沙漠瘡　barcoo rot
沙漠气候/沙漠氣候　desert climate
沙漠热/沙漠熱　desert fever
沙平/沙平　sapin
沙肉瘤/沙質肉癌　psammosarcoma
沙赛尼亚克腋肌/Chassaignac 氏腋肌　Chassaignac axillary muscle
沙土浴/土浴　earth bath
沙乌尔管/沙烏爾氏管　Chaoul tube
沙乌尔[X 射线]疗法/沙烏爾氏治療　Chaoul therapy
沙眼/沙眼　trachoma
沙眼包涵体结膜炎/沙眼包涵體結膜炎　TRIC
沙眼腺/沙眼腺　trachoma gland
沙眼小体/砂眼小體,普-格二氏體　Prowazek-Greeff body
沙眼性角膜溃疡/沙眼性角膜潰瘍　trachomatous corneal ulcer
沙眼性血管翳/沙眼性血管翳　trachomatous pannus
沙眼衣原体/沙眼衣原體　chlamydia trachomatis
沙样瘤/沙樣瘤,沙狀瘤　psammoma
沙伊综合征/Scheie 氏症候群　Scheie syndrome
沙浴疗法/沙浴療法　ammotherapy
沙苑子/沙苑子　flatstem milkvetch seed
沙蚤/沙蚤　chigoe
沙状癌/沙狀癌　carcinoma psammosum
沙状小结节性腹膜炎/沙狀腹膜炎　peritonitis arenosa
纱布绷带/紗布繃帶　gauze bandage
砂晶/砂晶　sandy crystal
砂砾性的/沙質的　tophaceous
砂粒体/沙樣瘤小體　psammoma body
砂疗法/砂療法　sand therapy
砂囊/沙囊　gizzard
砂仁/砂仁　villous amomum fruit
砂烫/砂燙　heated with sand
砂纸片/砂紙片,砂紙盤　sand paper disc, sandpaper disk
砂纸条/砂紙磨帶　sand paper strip
砂纸状胆囊/沙紙狀膽囊　sandpaper gallbladder
痧证/痧證　sha disease
鲨胆固醇/鯊膽固醇　scymnol
鲨肝醇/鯊肝醇　batyl alcohol
鲨肝肌糖/犬鮫糖　scyllite
鲨革/鯊皮　shagreen
鲨革斑/鯊皮樣斑　shagreen patch
鲨肌醇/犬鮫醇,犬鮫酸　scyllitol
鲨样皮/鯊樣皮　shagreen skin
筛/篩[網]　sieve
筛斑/篩斑　maculae cribrosae
筛窦/篩竇　ethmoidal sinus
筛窦泪管炎/淚管鼻竇炎　dacryosinusitis
筛窦切除术/篩房切除術　ethmoidectomy
筛窦切开术/切入篩竇術　ethmoidotomy
筛窦炎/篩竇炎　ethmoidal sinusitis
筛沟/篩溝　ethmoidal sulcus
筛骨/篩骨　ethmoid bone, sieve bone
筛骨的/篩骨的　ethmoidal
筛骨蜂窠/篩骨蜂窠　bony ethmoidal cell
筛骨迷路/篩骨迷路　ethmoidal labyrinth
筛骨前动脉/篩前動脈　anterior ethmoidal artery
筛骨前神经/篩前神經　anterior ethmoidal nerve
筛骨筛板/篩骨的篩板　cribriform plate of ethmoid bone
筛骨筛漏斗/篩骨篩漏斗　ethmoidal infundibulum of ethmoid bone

筛骨外侧部/篩骨外側塊	ectethmoid bone
筛骨炎/篩骨炎	ethmoiditis
筛管/篩管	sieve tube
筛后动脉/篩後動脈	posterior ethmoidal artery
筛后孔/篩後孔,眶篩管	posterior ethmoidal foramen
筛后神经/篩後神經	posterior ethmoidal nerve
筛嵴/篩[骨]嵴	ethmoidal crest
筛筋膜/篩筋膜	cribriform fascia
筛静脉/篩靜脈	ethmoidal vein
筛孔/篩孔	cribriform foramina
筛孔样室间隔缺损/篩孔樣室間隔缺損	Swiss cheese ventricular septal defect
筛泪缝/篩淚縫	ethmoidolacrimal suture
筛漏斗/篩漏斗	ethmoidal infundibulum
筛泡/篩骨泡	ethmoidal bulla
筛前孔/篩前孔,眶顱管	anterior ethmoidal foramen
筛前神经鼻内支/篩前神經鼻内支	internal nasal branches of anterior ethmoidal nerve
筛前神经鼻外支/篩前神經鼻外支	external nasal branch of anterior ethmoidal nerve
筛前神经痛/篩前神經痛	anterior ethmoidal neuralgia
筛前神经综合征/篩前神經症候群	anterior ethmoid nerve syndrome
筛切迹/篩切跡	ethmoidal notch
筛区/篩區	cribriform area, area cribrosa
筛上颌缝/篩頜縫	ethmoidomaxillary suture
筛突/篩骨突	ethmoidal process
筛析/篩析	sieving
筛细胞/篩細胞	cribrose cell
筛小房/篩小房	ethmoidal cellules
筛形的/篩形的	ethmoid
筛形敷布/篩狀壓布	cribriform compress
筛形视野/篩狀視野,篩狀視界	cribriform field of vision
筛选/篩選	screening
筛选方法/篩選方法	screening technique
筛选模型/篩選模型	screening model
筛域/篩域	sieve area
筛[状]板/篩板	cribriform plate
筛状处女膜/篩狀處女膜	cribriform hymen
筛状的/篩狀的	cribriform, cribrose
筛状骨/篩狀骨	cribriform bone
筛状皮片/篩狀皮片	sieve skin graft
筛状移植片/篩狀移植物	sieve graft
晒干/曬乾	drying in sunshine
晒伤/曬傷	sunburn
晒伤反应/曬傷反應	sunburn reaction
山贝西溃疡/山貝西潰瘍	Zambesi ulcer
山伯格病/Schamberg 氏病	Schamberg disease
山慈姑指/鬱金香指	tulip finger
山慈菇/山慈菇	appendiculate cremastra pseudobulb, common pleione pseudobulb
山道年/山道年	santonin
山道年草/山道年草,土荆芥	wormseed
山道年试验/山道年試驗	santonin test
山道年酸/山道年酸	santoninic acid
山顶/山頂	culmen
山豆根/山豆根	Vietnamese sophora root and rhizome
山根/山根	nasal root
山梗烷醇酮/北美山梗菜素	lobeline
山环素/脱甲去氧四環素	sancycline
山金车/山金車	Arnica montana
山口隧道手术/山口隧道手術	Takeuchi tunnel operation
山榄烯/山欖烯	sapotalene
山梨醇/山梨醇	sorbitol
山梨醇溶液/清涼茶醇溶液	sorbitol solution
山梨聚糖/脱水山梨醇	sorbitan
山梨酸/山梨酸	sorbic acid
山梨糖/山梨糖	sorbose
山黧豆中毒/山黧豆素中毒	lathyrism
山黧豆中毒性骨病/山黧豆骨毒症	osteolathyrism
山莨菪碱/山莨菪鹼	anisodamine
山麦冬/山麥冬	liriope root tuber
山毛榉/山毛櫸	beech
山毛榉木馏油/山毛櫸木馏油	beechwood creosote
山柰/山柰	galanga resurrectionlily rhizome
山柰酚类/山柰酚類	kaempferols
山坡/坡	declive
山区绞痛/山區絞痛	hill colic
山羊关节炎脑炎病毒/山羊關節炎腦炎病毒	caprine arthritis-encephalitis virus
山羊天花/山羊天花	variola caprina
山羊样的/像羊的	caprillic
山药/山藥	common yam rhizome
山楂/山楂	hawthorn fruit
山茱萸/山茱萸	asiatic cornelian cherry fruit
珊瑚[的]/珊瑚	coral
珊瑚割伤/珊瑚割傷	coral cut
珊瑚溃疡/珊瑚潰瘍	coral ulcer
珊瑚皮炎/珊瑚皮膚炎	coral dermatitis
珊瑚状白内障/珊瑚狀内障	coralliform cataract
珊瑚状血栓/珊瑚狀血栓	coral thrombus

栅表细胞比/柵表細胞比　palisade ratio
闪避性溃疡/規避性潰瘍　elusive ulcer
闪变亮度计/閃光[光度]計　flicker meter
闪变亮度术/閃變光度測定法　flicker photometry
闪电击伤/閃電擊傷　lightning injury
闪电烧伤/閃電燒傷　lightning burn
闪电性神经[功能]病/閃電神經官能症　keraunoneurosis
闪电状偏头痛/閃電狀偏頭痛　fulgurating migraine
闪缎样视网膜/射線視網膜　shot-silk retina
闪缎样现象/閃緞樣現象　shot-silk phenomenon
闪罐/閃罐　quick cupping, successive flash cupping
闪光暗点/閃爍暗點　flittering scotoma
闪光标记/閃光標記　flash labeling
闪光的/閃光的　glistening
闪光幻视/閃光幻覺　spintherism
闪光融合/閃光融合　flicker fusion
闪光烧伤/閃焰灼傷　flash burn
闪光视觉诱发电位/閃光視覺誘發電位　flash visual evoked potential
闪光视网膜电图/閃光視網膜電圖　flash electroretinogram
闪光[信号装置]/閃光　flare
闪光性变性/閃光樣變性　glistening degeneration
闪火法/閃火法　fire twinkling method, flash-fire cupping
闪石石棉/閃石石棉　amphibole asbestos
闪烁光/閃爍　flicker
闪烁计数/閃爍計數　scintillation counting
闪烁计数计/閃爍計數器　scintillometer
闪烁镜/閃爍鏡　spinthariscope
闪烁扫描/閃爍掃描　scintiscan
闪烁扫描术/閃爍檢查　scintigraphy
闪烁扫描仪/閃爍掃描器　scintiscanner
闪烁摄影机/閃爍攝影機　scintillation gamma camera
闪烁视网膜电图/閃爍視網膜電圖　flicker electroretinogram
闪烁图/閃爍圖　scintigram
闪烁[照]片/閃爍照片　scintiphoto
闪蒸进样法/驟蒸進樣　flash evaporating injection
疝/疝　hernia
疝被盖/疝被蓋　hernial covering
疝病学/疝學　herniology
疝出/疝形成　herniation
疝穿刺术/疝穿刺術　herniopuncture
疝带/疝氣帶　truss
疝刀/疝刀　hernia knife
疝底/疝底　hernial fundus
疝复位/疝復位　hernia reduction
疝环/疝環　hernial ring
疝颈/疝頸　hernial neck
疝阑尾切除术/闌尾疝切除術　hernioappendectomy
疝囊/疝囊　hernia sac
疝内容物/疝內容物　hernial content
疝内修补术/赫尼亞內修補術　endoherniorrhaphy
疝气/疝[氣]　hernia
疝切开术/赫尼亞切開術　celotomy
疝水囊肿/赫尼亞囊積水　hernial hydrocele
疝性动脉瘤/脱出性動脈瘤　hernial aneurysm
疝修补术/疝修補術　herniorrhaphy
疝[修补]针/赫尼亞針　hernia needle
扇头蜱属/扇頭壁蝨屬　*Rhipicephalus*
扇形唇瓣/扇形唇瓣　fan lip flap
扇形磁场质谱仪/扇形磁場質譜儀　magnetic sector mass spectrometer
扇形虹膜切除术/弧三角虹膜切除術　sector iridectomy
扇形扫描/扇形掃描　sector scanning
扇形突变/扇形突變,角變　sector mutation
善悲/善悲　easily to be sorrowful
善饥症/劇飢症　limosis
善惊/善驚　easily to be frightened
善恐/善恐　easily to be terrified
善眠/善眠　lethargy
善怒/善怒　easily to be angry
善色/善色　benign complexion
善听者/善聽者　auditive
善忘/善忘　poor memory
善喜/善喜　easily to be overjoyed
膳食/膳食　diet
膳食调查/膳食調查　diet survey
膳食风尚/膳食風尚　diet fad
膳食服务/膳食服務　dietary service
膳食记录/膳食記錄　diet record
膳食疗法/膳食療法　diet therapy
膳食钠/膳食鈉　dietary sodium
膳食纤维/食物纖維　dietary fiber
膳食学/膳食學,飲食學　dietetics
鳝血疗法/鱔血療法　eel-blood therapy
伤病员分拣/傷兵之鑒別歸類法　triage
伤道/傷道　wound tract
伤道出口/傷道出口　exit of wound tract
伤道入口/傷道入口　entrance of wound tract
伤风/傷風　mild common cold
伤风鼻塞/傷風鼻塞　acute rhinitis, nasal

obstruction due to mild cold
伤风鼻塞·外感风寒证/傷風鼻塞·外感風寒證 nasal obstruction due to mild cold with pattern of external contraction of wind-cold
伤风鼻塞·外感风热证/傷風鼻塞·外感風熱證 nasal obstruction due to mild cold with pattern of external contraction of wind-heat
伤害/傷害 damage
伤害感受器/傷害受器 nociceptor
伤害性刺激/傷害性刺激 noxious stimulation
伤害性联合反应/傷害性聯合反應 nociassociation
伤害性疼痛/傷害性疼痛 nociceptive pain
伤害性影响/外傷影響 noci-influence
伤害性知觉/傷害識別 nociperception
伤寒/傷寒 ①typhoid ②exogenous cold disease, cold damage ③exogenous febrile disease
伤寒败血病/傷寒敗血病 typhoid septicemia
伤寒棒状杆菌/傷寒棒狀桿菌 Corynebacterium typhi
伤寒发癍/傷寒發癍 exogenous cold disease with ecchymoses
伤寒发狂/傷寒發狂 exogenous cold pattern with mania
伤寒肺炎/傷寒肺炎 typhopneumonia
伤寒副伤寒菌苗/傷寒副傷寒菌苗 typhoid-paratyphoid vaccine
伤寒[杆菌]性胃肠炎/傷寒菌性胃腸炎 gastroenteritis typhosa
伤寒菌毒症/傷寒菌毒症 typhobacillosis
伤寒菌苗/傷寒疫苗 antityphoid vaccine
伤寒菌素/傷寒菌素 typhoidin
伤寒菌素试验/傷寒菌素試驗，蓋-弗二氏試驗 typhoidin test
伤寒菌血症/傷寒菌血症 typhemia
伤寒劳复/傷寒勞復 recurrent exogenous cold disease caused by overstrain
伤寒肋病/傷寒肋病 typhoid rib
伤寒论/傷寒論 Treatise on Cold Pathogenic Diseases
伤寒明理论/傷寒明理論 Concise Exposition on Cold Pathogenic Diseases
伤寒热/傷寒病 typhoid fever
伤寒食复/傷寒食復 recurrent exogenous cold disease caused by improper diet
伤寒细胞/傷寒細胞 typhoid cell
伤寒小结/傷寒小結 typhoid nodule
伤寒性骨髓炎/傷寒性骨髓炎 typhoid osteomyelitis
伤寒性红斑/傷寒性紅斑 erythema typhosum
伤寒性脊柱[病]/傷寒脊柱病 typhoid spine
伤寒性甲状腺炎/傷寒性狀腺炎 eberthian strumitis
伤寒性脑膜炎/傷寒性腦膜炎 typhoid meningitis
伤寒性疟/傷寒性瘧 malaria typhoid
伤寒阳厥/傷寒陽厥 exogenous cold disease with yang syncope
伤寒阳盛格阴证/傷寒陽盛格陰證 exogenous cold disease with pattern of yin repelled by exuberant yang
伤寒样黄疸/傷寒狀黃疸 icterus typhoides
伤寒阴厥/傷寒陰厥 exogenous cold disease with yin cold limbs
伤寒阴盛格阳证/傷寒陰盛格陽證 exogenous cold disease with pattern of yang repelled by exuberant yin
伤寒阴阳毒/傷寒陰陽毒 exogenous cold disease with yin-yang poisoning
伤寒阴阳易/傷寒陰陽易 yin yang exchange of exogenous cold disease
伤寒杂病论/傷寒雜病論 Treatise on Cold Pathogenic and Miscellaneous Diseases
伤寒转闭/傷寒轉閉 conversion of exogenous cold disease to blockade
伤寒转痉/傷寒轉痙 conversion of exogenous cold disease to convulsion
伤寒转脱/傷寒轉脱 conversion of exogenous cold disease to collapse
伤寒状态/傷寒狀態 typhoid state
伤津/傷津 impairment of fluid
伤酒鼻衄/傷酒鼻衄 alcoholic epistaxis
伤酒恶寒/傷酒惡寒 alcoholism with aversion to cold
伤酒呕血/傷酒嘔血 alcoholic hematemesis
伤酒头痛/傷酒頭痛 alcoholic headache
伤口/創傷 wound
伤口感染/創傷感染 wound infection
伤口裂开/傷口裂開 wound dehiscence
伤口收缩/傷口收縮 wound contraction
伤口水肿/傷口水腫 wound edema
伤口愈合/傷口愈合 wound healing
伤湿止痛膏/傷濕止痛膏 shangshi zhitong plaster
伤食/傷食 food damage
伤暑/傷暑 mild summerheat stroke, sunstroke
商陆/商陸 pokeberry root
商陆有丝分裂原类/商陸有絲分裂原類 pokeweed mitogens
商陆中毒/商陸中毒 pokeberry root poisoning

商品中间体/商品中間體　merchant intermediate
商丘/商丘　shangqiu, SP5
商曲/商曲　shangqu, KI17
商阳/商陽　shangyang, LI1
上凹/上凹　superior fovea
上半[部]视网膜/視網膜上半部　upper retina
上半规管/上半規管　superior semicircular duct
上半月小叶/上半月小葉　superior semilunar lobule
上胞下垂/上胞下垂　drooping of upper eyelid, blepharoptosis, ptosis of eyelid
上胞下垂·禀赋不足证/上胞下垂·稟賦不足證　drooping of upper eyelid with constitutional insufficiency pattern
上胞下垂·风痰阻络证/上胞下垂·風痰阻絡證　drooping of upper eyelid with pattern of wind-phlegm obstructing collateral
上胞下垂·风中经络证/上胞下垂·風中經絡證　drooping of upper eyelid with pattern of wind striking channel and collateral
上胞下垂·脾气虚证/上胞下垂·脾氣虛證　drooping of upper eyelid with spleen qi deficiency pattern
上鼻道/上鼻道,鼻上道　superior nasal meatus, ethmoid fissure
上鼻甲/上鼻甲　superior nasal concha
上鼻甲骨/上鼻甲骨　superior nasal bone
上壁/上壁　superior wall
上臂长/上臂長　upper arm length
上鞭毛体/表鞭毛體,表鞭毛型　epimastigote
上表皮/上表皮　upper epidermis, epicuticle
上部/上部　superior part
上肠系膜动脉综合征/上腸繫膜動脈症候群　superior mesenteric artery syndrome
上冲/上銃　upper punch
上唇/上唇　upper lip
上唇鼻翼提肌/鼻唇舉肌　levator labii superioris alaeque nasi
上唇动脉/上唇動脈　superior labial artery
上唇方肌/上唇方肌　quadrate muscle of upper lip
上唇结节/上唇結節　tubercle of upper lip
上唇静脉/上唇靜脈　superior labial vein, vein of upper lip
上唇门齿肌/上唇門齒肌　musculi incisivi labii superioris
上唇提肌/上唇舉肌,提上唇肌　levator labii superioris, levator muscle of upper lip
上唇系带/上唇繫帶　frenulum of upper lip
上唇线/上唇線　upper lip line
上唇正中裂/上唇正中裂　median upper lip cleft

上唇支/上唇支　superior labial branch
上唇中点/上唇點　labrale superius
上的/上的　superior
上顶间骨/上頂間骨　suprainterparietal bone
上段/上段　superior segment
上段动脉/上段動脈　superior segmental artery
上段食管括约肌/上段食管括約肌　upper esophageal sphincter
上段下支气管/肺上葉下支氣管　bronchus segmentalis subsuperior
上段支气管/上段支氣管　superior segmental bronchus
上段[中胚层]肌/上胚節肌,體節背部肌　epimeric muscle
上腭痈/上腭癰　abscess of upper palate, upper palate abscess
上耳根/上耳根　shangergen
上腹/上腹　superior belly
上腹部/上腹部　epigastrium
上腹部搏动/上腹部搏動　epigastric pulsation
上腹部穿刺/上腹穿刺　epigastric puncture
上腹部寄生畸胎/上腹寄生胎,寄生性上腹連胎　epigastrius
上腹部痛/上腹部痛　epigastralgia
上腹部休克/上腹部休克　epigastric shock
上腹丛/上腹叢　epigastric plexus
上腹疝/上腹疝　epigastric hernia
上腹下丛/上腹下叢　superior hypogastric plexus
上腹[压痛]点/上腹壓痛點　epigastric spot
上橄榄核/上橄欖核　superior olivary nucleus
上橄榄体/上橄欖體　superior olive
上干/上幹　superior trunk
上根/上根　superior root
上宫之人/上宫之人　typical earth-phase person
上构件/上構件　upper member
上古天真论篇/上古天真論篇　Treatise on How to Keep Healthy
上鼓室/耳隱窩　attic
上鼓室切开术/上鼓室切開術　epitympanotomy
上鼓室炎/上鼓室炎　epitympanitis
上关/上關　shangguan, GB3
上关节面/上關節面　superior articular facet, superior articular surface
上关节突/上關節突　superior articular process
上寒下热证/上寒下熱證　pattern of upper cold and lower heat
上颌癌/上頜癌　maxillary cancer
上颌鼻嵴/上頜鼻嵴　maxilla nasal crest

上颌鼻突/上頜鼻突　maxilla nasal process
上颌侧位体层片/上頜側位體層片　lateral tomogram of maxillae
上颌的/上頜的　maxillary
上颌动脉/上頜動脈　maxillary artery
上颌动脉咽支/上頜動脈咽支　pharyngeal branch of maxillary artery
上颌窦/上頜竇　maxillary sinus, maxillary antrum
上颌窦冲洗/上頜竇沖洗　irrigation of maxillary sinus
上颌窦穿刺冲洗术/上頜竇穿刺沖洗術　puncture and irrigation of maxillary sinus
上颌窦根治术/上頜竇根治術　radical maxillary sinusotomy
上颌窦积脓/上頜竇積膿　empyema of antrum
上颌窦积液/上頜竇積水　antracele
上颌窦结石症/上頜竇結石症　maxillary antrolithiasis
[上颌]窦镜检查[法]/上頜竇鏡檢法，竇檢視法　antroscopy
[上颌]窦开窗术/上頜竇開窗術　antral window operation
上颌窦裂孔/上頜竇裂孔　maxillary hiatus
上颌窦黏膜下囊肿/上頜竇黏膜下囊腫　submucous cyst of maxillary sinus
上颌窦切开术/上頜竇切開術　maxillary sinusotomy
上颌窦痛/上頜竇痛　genyantralgia
[上颌]窦息肉/上頜竇息肉　antral polyp
上颌窦炎/上頜竇炎　genyantritis
上颌窦支/上頜竇支　maxillary sinus branch
上颌窦肿瘤/上頜竇腫瘤　maxillary sinus neoplasm
上颌额点/上頜額點　maxillofrontale
上颌腭沟/上頜腭溝　palatine groove of maxilla, sulci palatini maxillae
上颌发育不良/上頜發育不良　maxillary dysplasia
上颌缝/上頜縫　maxillary suture
上颌阜/上頜阜　maxillary rampart
上颌骨/上頜骨　maxillary bone, upper jaw bone
上颌骨部分切除术/上頜骨部分切除術　partial maxillectomy
上颌骨粗隆/上頜粗隆　maxillary tuberosity
上颌骨腭突/上頜骨腭突　palatine process of maxilla
上颌骨发育不全/上頜骨發育不全　maxillary deficiency
上颌骨骨髓炎/上頜骨骨髓炎　osteomyelitis of maxilla
上颌骨骨折/上頜骨骨折　maxilla fracture, maxillary fracture
上颌骨横骨折/上頜骨橫骨折　transverse maxillary fracture
上颌骨颊切迹/上頜骨頰切跡　maxillary buccal notch
上颌骨尖牙窝/上頜骨尖牙窩　canine fossa of maxilla
上颌骨间片段/上頜骨間片段　intermaxillary segment
上颌骨结构/上頜架構　architecture of maxilla
上颌骨眶下沟/上頜骨眶下溝　infraorbital groove of maxilla, sulcus infraorbitalis maxilla
上颌骨颞下面/上頜骨顳下面　infratemporal surface of maxilla
上颌骨前半切除术/上頜骨前半切除術　anterohemimaxillectomy
上颌骨切除术/上頜骨切除術　maxillectomy
上颌骨切开术/上頜骨切開術　maxillotomy
上颌骨切牙窝/上頜骨切牙窩　incisive fossa of maxilla
上颌骨全切除术/上頜骨全切除術　total maxillectomy
上颌骨手术性纤毛囊肿/上頜骨之手術性纖毛囊腫　surgical ciliated cyst of maxilla
上颌骨牙槽/上頜骨牙槽　dental alveoli of maxilla
上颌骨牙槽轭/上頜骨牙槽軛　juga alveolaria of maxilla
上颌骨牙槽弓/上頜骨牙槽弓　alveolar arch of maxilla
上颌骨牙槽骨/上頜骨牙槽骨　alveolar bone of maxilla
上颌骨牙槽间隔/上頜骨牙槽間隔　interalveolar septa of maxilla
上颌骨牙槽面/上頜齒槽面　alveolar surface of maxilla
上颌骨牙槽突/上頜[骨]齒槽突　alveolar process of maxilla, maxilla alveolar process
上颌骨牙根间隔/上頜骨牙根間隔　interradicular septa of maxilla
上颌骨炎/上頜骨炎　maxillitis
上颌管/上頜管　maxillary canal
上颌横断殆片/上頜橫斷殆片　occlusal film of maxillae
上颌横贯骨折/上頜橫貫骨折　transverse maxilla fracture
上颌后拉/上頜後拉　maxillary retraction
上颌后前体层片/上頜後前體層片　posterio-anterior tomogram of maxillae
上颌后缩/上頜後縮　maxillary retrusion

上颌积脓/上頜積膿　maxillary empyema
上颌畸形/上頜畸形　maxillary deformity
上颌疾病/上頜疾病　maxillary disease
上颌寄生胎/頜部寄生胎,寄生性頜部連胎　epignathus
上颌间缝/上頜間縫　intermaxillary suture
上颌间骨/上頜間骨　intermaxillary bone
上颌角/上頜角　maxillary angle
上颌结节/上頜結節　maxillary tuberosity, maxillary tubercle
上颌结节成形术/上頜結節成形術　maxillary tuberoplasty
上颌结节区/上頜結節區　maxilla tuberosity region
上颌结节注射法/上頜結節注射法　tuberosity injection
上颌截骨术/上頜截骨術　maxillary osteotomy
上颌静脉/上頜靜脈　maxillary vein
上颌空间重获/上頜空間重獲　maxillary space regaining
上颌扩张器/上頜擴張器　maxillary expansion appliance
上颌扩张[术]/上頜擴張術　maxillary expansion
上颌隆凸/上頜隆凸　maxillary protuberance
上颌面/上頜面　maxillary surface
上颌面部发育/上頜面部發育　maxillofacial development
上颌面部损伤/上頜面部損傷　maxillofacial injury
上颌面的/上頜與顏面的　maxillofacial
上颌面装置/上頜面裝置　maxillofacial appliance
上颌平面/上頜平面　maxillary plane
上颌前部截骨术/上頜前部截骨術　anterior maxillary osteotomy
上颌前孔/上頜前孔　anterior maxillary foramen
上颌前伸/上頜前突　maxillary protraction
上颌前突/上頜前突　anteroposterior maxillary excess
上颌前正中囊肿/正中前上頜囊腫　median anterior maxillary cyst
上颌筛骨嵴/上頜篩骨嵴　maxilla ethmoid crest
上颌舌弓/上頜舌弓　maxillary lingual arch
上颌神经/上頜神經　maxillary nerve, superior maxillary nerve
上颌神经丛/上頜神經叢　maxillary plexus
上颌神经脑膜支/上頜神經腦膜支　meningeal branch of maxillary nerve
上颌神经神经节支/上頜神經神經節支　ganglionic branch of maxillary nerve
上颌生长过度/上頜生長過度　maxillary excess

上颌收缩/上頜收縮　maxillary constriction
上颌体/上頜體　body of maxilla, upper jaw member
上颌突/上頜突　maxillary process
上颌外丛/上頜外叢　plexus maxillaris externus
上颌下的/上頜下的　inframaxillary
上颌牙/上頜齒　maxillary teeth
上颌牙槽长度/上頜牙槽長度　maxilloalveolar length
上颌牙槽弓/上頜牙槽弓　arcus alveolaris maxillae
上颌牙槽宽度/上頜牙槽寬度　maxilloalveolar breadth
上颌牙齿突出/上頜牙齒突出　maxillary dental protrusion
上颌牙错位/上頜齒異位　maxillary trusion
上颌牙的/上頜與齒的　maxillodental
上颌牙弓矫正线/上頜牙弓矯正線　maxillary archwire
上颌中切牙牙槽脊顶点/上頜中切牙牙槽脊頂點　superior prosthion
上颌肿瘤/上頜腫瘤　maxillary neoplasm
上颌锥状骨折/上頜錐狀骨折　pyramidal maxilla fracture
上横骨/胸骨柄即前胸骨　manubrium of sternum
上后锯肌/上後鋸肌　serratus posterior superior, superior posterior serratus muscle
上呼吸道感染/上呼吸道感染　upper respiratory tract infection
上滑膜/上滑膜　superior synovial membrane
上甲状旁腺/上甲狀旁腺　superior parathyroid gland
上睑/上瞼　upper eyelid
上睑板/上瞼板　superior tarsus
上睑板肌/上瞼板肌　superior tarsalis
上睑襞/上瞼襞　superior palpebral fold
上睑弓/上瞼弓　superior palpebral arch
上睑静脉/上瞼靜脈　superior palpebral vein
上睑提肌/上瞼舉肌,提上瞼肌　levator muscle of upper eyelid
上睑提肌缩短术/上瞼提肌縮短術　shortening operation of musculus levator palpebrae superioris
上交叉核/上交叉核　suprachiasmatic nucleus
上焦/上焦　upper jiao
上焦如雾/上焦如霧　upper jiao being organ of fogging
上焦湿热/上焦濕熱　dampness-heat in upper jiao
上焦湿热证/上焦濕熱證　pattern of dampness-heat in upper jiao
上角/上角　superior angle, superior cornu
上骱声/上骱聲　sound of relocation

上胫关节/上脛關節　superior tibial articulation
上巨虚/上巨虛　shangjuxu, ST37
上角之人/上角之人　typical wood-phase person
上髁/上髁　epicondyle
上髁骨折/上髁骨折　epicondylar fracture
上髁痛/[肱]上髁痛　epicondylalgia
上髁炎/[肱]上髁炎　epicondylitis
上肋凹/上肋凹　superior costal fossa
上肋横突韧带/上肋橫突韌帶　superior costotransverse ligament
上廉/上廉　shanglian, LI9
上髎/上髎　shangliao, BL31
上孖肌/上孖肌　gemellus superior
上门齿点/上門齒點　incision superius
上迷小管/上迷管　superior aberrant ductule
上泌涎核/上泌涎核　superior salivatory nucleus
上面/上面　superior surface, trochlear surface, facies superior
上内尖/上臼齒之内後齒冠隆　entocone
上内[向]隐斜视/上内轉隱斜眼　hyperesophoria
上尿路感染/上尿路感染　upper urinary tract infection
上颞线/上顳線　superior temporal line
上胚层/上胚層　epiblast
上皮/上皮　epithelium
上皮癌/上皮癌　epidermal cancer, epithelial cancer
上皮瘢痕/上皮瘢痕　epithelite
上皮包埋/上皮包涵物　epithelial inclusion
上皮岛/上皮島　epithelial island
上皮的/上皮的　epithelial
上皮发育不良/上皮變異　epithelial dysplasia
上皮附着/上皮附著　epithelial attachment
上皮隔/上皮橫膈　epithelial diaphragm
上皮根鞘/上皮根鞘　epithelial root sheath
上皮化/上皮化　epithelization
上皮-肌上皮癌/上皮肌上皮癌　epithelial-myoepithelial carcinoma
上皮-肌上皮小岛/上皮-肌上皮小島　epi-myoepithechial island
上皮基底膜/上皮基底膜　basement membrane epithelium
上皮脊/上皮脊　epithelial ridge
上皮瘤/上皮瘤　epithelial tumor, epithelioma
上皮瘤病/上皮瘤病　epitheliomatosis
上皮膜抗原/上皮膜抗原　epithelial membrane antigen
上皮内癌/上皮内癌　intraepithelial carcinoma
上皮内的/上皮内的　intraepithelial
上皮内囊肿/上皮内囊腫　intraepithelial cyst
上皮内陷/上皮套疊　epithelial invagination
上皮内腺/上皮内腺,上皮間腺　intraepithelial gland
上皮片移植/上皮片移植　epithelial sheet transplantation
上皮桥粒/上皮胞橋小體　desmosomes of epithelium
上皮清创术/上皮清創　epithelial debridement
上皮绒[毛]膜的/上皮絨毛膜的　epitheliochorial
上皮绒[毛]膜胎盘/上皮絨毛膜胎盤　epitheliochorial placenta
上皮溶解/上皮溶解,上皮崩解　epitheliolysis
上皮生长因子/上皮生長因數　epithelium growth factor
上皮剩余/上皮剩餘　epithelial rest
上皮栓/上皮栓　epithelial plug
上皮嗜中性粒细胞活化肽/上皮嗜中性球活化肽　epithelial neutrophil activating peptide
上皮脱屑/上皮剥落　epithalaxia
上皮网状细胞/上皮網狀細胞　epithelial reticular cell
上皮细胞/上皮細胞　epithelial cell
上皮细胞巢/上皮細胞巢　epithelial cell nest
上皮细胞管型/上皮細胞管型　epithelial cell cast
上皮细胞间张力原纤维/上皮細胞間張纖　intercellular tonofibrils of epithelium
上皮新月/上皮性新月體　epithelial crescent
上皮形成/上皮形成,上皮化　epithelialization
上皮性眼干燥症/眼球表面乾燥　xerophthalmia superficialis
上皮炎/上表皮炎　epitheliitis
上皮样的/上皮樣的　epithelioid
上皮样囊肿/上皮囊腫　epithelial cyst
上皮样平滑肌瘤/上皮平滑肌瘤　epithelioid leiomyoma
上皮样肉瘤/上皮樣肉瘤　epithelioid sarcoma
上皮样肉芽肿/上皮樣肉芽腫　epithelioid granuloma
上皮样细胞/上皮樣細胞　epithelioid cell
上皮样细胞肉芽肿/上皮樣細胞肉芽腫　epithelioid cell granuloma
上皮样细胞痣/上皮樣痣細胞母斑　epithelioid cell nevus
上皮样血管瘤/上皮樣血管瘤　epithelioid hemangioma
上皮样血管瘤病/上皮樣血管瘤病　epithelioid angiomatosis
上皮样血管内皮瘤/上皮樣血管内皮瘤　epithelioid hemangioendothelioma

上皮样血管肉瘤/上皮樣血管肉瘤 epithelioid angiosarcoma
上皮移植/上皮移植 epithelial transplantation
上皮原纤维/上皮原纖維 epitheliofibril
上皮珠/上皮珠 epithelial pearl
上皮组织/上皮組織 epithelial tissue
上偏盲/上偏盲 upper hemianopsia
上品/上品 top grade drug
上屏/上屏 shangping, TG1, upper tragus
上前臼齿第三尖/上前臼齒第三尖 tritocone
上前段/上前段 anterior superior segment
上前段动脉/上前段動脈 superior anterior segmental artery
上腔静脉/上腔靜脈 superior vena cava
上腔静脉梗阻/上腔靜脈梗阻 obstruction of superior vena cava
上腔静脉口/上腔靜脈口 orifice of superior vena cava
上腔静脉血栓性静脉炎/上腔靜脈血栓性靜脈炎 superior vena cava thrombophlebitis
上腔静脉综合征/上腔靜脈症候群 superior vena cava syndrome
上清丸/上清丸 shangqing pill
上清液/上清液 supernatant, supernatant fluid
上丘/上丘 superior colliculus
上丘白质层/上丘白質層 white matter layers of superior colliculus
上丘臂/上丘臂 brachium of superior colliculus
上丘带状层/上丘帶狀層 zonale layers of superior colliculus
上丘灰质层/上丘灰質層 gray matter layers of superior colliculus
上丘连合/上丘連合 commissure of superior colliculus
上丘脑/上丘腦 epithalamus
上丘丘系层/上丘丘系層 lemnisci layers of superior colliculus
上丘视层/上丘視層 optic layers of superior colliculus
上热下寒证/上熱下寒證 pattern of upper heat and lower cold
上筛斑/上篩斑 superior macula cribrosa
上商之人/上商之人 typical metal-phase person
上舌段/上舌段 superior lingular segment
上舌段支气管/肺舌葉上支氣管 superior lingular bronchus
上舌骨/舌骨上骨 epihyal bone
上舌支/舌上支 superior lingular branch

上射视野/超射视野,超射视界 overshot field of vision
上神经节/上神經節 superior ganglion
上升期/向上期 upstroke phase
上升支/上昇支 upstroke
上盛下虚/上盛下虛 upper excess and lower deficiency
上盛下虚证/上盛下虛證 pattern of upper excess and lower deficiency
上矢状窦/上矢狀竇 superior sagittal sinus
上矢状窦沟/上矢狀竇溝 sulcus for superior sagittal sinus, groove for superior longitudinal sinus
上市后监察/上市後監察,上市後監視 post marketing surveillance, PMS
上髓帆/上髓帆 superior medullary velum
上损及下/上損及下 deficiency transmitted from upper body to lower body
上体腔/上胚[體]腔 epicoeloma
上体性失调症/上體失調症 superior ataxia
上外侧面/上外側面 superolateral surface
上外[向]隐斜视/上外轉隱斜眼 hyperexophoria
上脘/上脘 shangwan, RN13
上尾骨韧带/上尾骨韌帶 superior coccygeal ligament
上位换气法/上位換氣法 upward ventilation
上位基因/上位基因 epistatic gene
上胃肠道/上胃腸道 upper gastrointestinal tract
上吻合静脉/上吻合靜脈 superior anastomotic vein
上下分消/上下分消 eliminating pathogens by phlegm elimination and purgation respectively
上下颌不等的/上下頜不等 anisognathous
上下颌不[相]称/上下頜不對稱 dysallilognathia
上下颌的/上下頜間 maxillomandibular
上下颌发育异常/上下頜異常 dysgnathia
上下颌发育障碍/上頜與下頜的發育障礙 maxillomandibular dysplasia
上下颌固定/上下頜固定 maxillomandibular fixation
上下颌固定术/上下頜固定術 mandibulomaxillary
上下颌关系/上下頜關係 jaw-to-jaw relationship
上下颌[颌间]固定/上下頜間固定 mandibulomaxillary fixation
上下颌间记录/上下頜與下頜記錄 maxillomandibular record
上下颌间咬合/上下頜間咬合 maxillomandibular bite
上下颌间隙/上下頜間隙 maxillomandibular space
上下颌正常/上下頜正常 eugnathia
上下颌支抗/上下頜錨定 maxillomandibular

anchorage
上下配穴法/上下配穴法 superior-inferior points association, superior-inferior points combination
上下性偏盲/上下性偏盲 altitudinal hemianopia
上项线/上項線 superior nuchal line
上消/上消 upper consumption
上消·肺热津伤证/上消·肺熱津傷證 upper consumption with pattern of fluid consumption due to lung heat
上消·燥热伤肺证/上消·燥熱傷肺證 upper consumption with pattern of dryness-heat injuring lung
上小脑脚/上小腦腳 superior cerebellar peduncle
上斜肌/眶上斜肌 superior obliquus
上斜肌腱鞘/上斜肌腱鞘 tendinous sheath of superior obliquus
上斜视/上斜眼 anotropia
上星/上星 shangxing, DU23
上行的/上行的 ascending
上行束/上行徑 ascending tract
上行穗形绷带/上行穗形繃帶 spica ascending bandage
上行性变性/上行性變性 ascending degeneration
上行性脊髓病/上行性脊髓病 ascending myelopathy
上行性脊髓灰质炎/上行性脊髓灰質炎 ascending poliomyelitis
上行性脊髓炎/上行性脊髓炎 ascending myelitis
上行性神经病/上行性神經病變 ascending neuropathy
上行性肾盂肾炎/上行性腎盂腎炎 ascending pyelonephritis
上行性肾盂炎/上行性腎盂炎 ascending pyelitis
上行咽喉神经丛/上行咽喉神經叢 ascending pharyngeal plexus
上胸骨/胸骨柄 episternum
上虚下实/上虛下實 upper deficiency and lower excess
上牙槽点/上牙槽點 supradentale
上牙槽后动脉/上齒槽後動脈 posterior superior alveolar artery
上牙槽后支/上牙槽後支 posterior superior alveolar branch
上牙槽前点/上牙槽前點 prosthion exoprothion
上牙槽前动脉/上齒槽前動脈 anterior superior alveolar artery
上牙槽前支/上牙槽前支 anterior superior alveolar branch
上牙槽神经/上牙槽神經 superior alveolar nerve
上牙槽突最侧点/上牙槽突最側點 ectomalare
上牙槽中支/上牙槽中支 middle superior alveolar branch
上牙槽最内点/上牙槽最內點 endomalare
上牙丛/上牙叢 superior dental plexus
上牙弓/上齒弓 upper dental arch
上牙龈支/上牙齦支 superior gingival branch
上牙支/上牙支 superior dental branch
上叶/上葉 superior lobe
上叶支/上葉支 superior lobar branch
上蚓部/上小腦蚓部 superior vermis
上隐斜/上隱斜 hyperphoria
上隐斜视/上隱斜眼,上轉斜眼 anophoria
上迎香/上迎香 shangyingxiang, EX-HN8
上游气道阻力/上游氣道阻力 upstream resistance
上釉/上釉 glazing
上羽之人/上羽之人 more wise and resourceful, typical water-phase person
上缘/上緣 superior border, superior margin
上运动神经元/上運動神經元 upper motor neuron
上肢/上肢 upper limb, upper extremity
上肢长/上肢長 upper extremity length
上肢带骨/上肢帶骨 shoulder girdle, bone of girdle of upper extremities
上肢带连结/上肢帶連結 joint of shoulder girdle
上肢带韧带/上肢帶韌帶 ligament of girdle of superior extremity
上肢骨/上肢骨 bone of upper limb
上肢骨骼/上肢骨骼 bone of upper extremity
上肢肌/上肢肌 muscle of upper limb
上肢肌节/上肢肌節 upper limb myotome
上肢浅静脉/上肢淺靜脈 superficial veins of upper limb
上肢深静脉/上肢深靜脈 deep vein of upper limb
上肢型脊髓痨/上肢型脊髓痨,脊髓上段痨 superior tabes
上直肌/上直肌 superior rectus
上徵之人/上徵之人 more irritable and quick, typical fire-phase person
上主静脉/上主靜脈 supracardinal vein
上纵隔/上縱隔 superior mediastinum
上纵肌/上縱肌 superior longitudinal muscle
上纵束/上縱束 superior longitudinal fasciculus
尚伯兰细菌滤器/夏伯蘭氏濾器 Chamberland filter
尚茨病/Schanz氏病 Schanz disease
尚茨截骨术/尚茨截骨術 Schanz osteotomy
尚茨综合征/Schanz氏症候群 Schanz syndrome
尚皮固定液/Champy氏固定液 Champy fixing fluid

尚特梅斯反应/夏特曼氏反應　Chantemesse reaction
尚药局/尚藥局　Bureau of the Administration of the Royal Medicinal Affairs
烧杯/燒杯　beaker
烧冲复合伤/燒沖複合傷　burnblast combined injury
烧放复合伤/燒放複合傷　burnradiation combined injury
烧焦[臭]味/焦氣,焦臭　empyreuma
烧伤/燒傷,灼傷　burn
烧伤瘢痕恶性变/燒傷瘢痕惡性變　malignant degeneration of burn scar
烧伤瘢痕挛缩/燒傷瘢痕攣縮　burned cicatricial contracture
烧伤并发症/燒傷并發症　complication of burn
烧伤病房/燒傷病房　burn unit
烧伤病人后送/燒傷病人後送　evacuation of burn patient
烧伤病人转送/燒傷病人轉送　transportation of burn patient
烧伤残余创面/燒傷殘餘創面　residual burn wound
烧伤处理/燒傷處理　burn care
烧伤创面/燒傷創面　burn wound
烧伤创面脓毒症/燒傷創面膿毒症　burn wound sepsis
烧伤创面愈合/燒傷創面愈合　burn wound healing
烧伤毒素/燒傷毒素　burn toxin
烧伤敷料/燒傷敷料　burn dressing
烧伤感染/燒傷感染　infection of burn
烧伤合并脊髓损伤/燒傷合并脊髓損傷　burn combined with spinal injury
烧伤合并中毒/燒傷合并中毒　burn combined with poisoning
烧伤后病毒感染/燒傷後病毒感染　postburn virus infection
烧伤后肺动脉楔压监测/燒傷後肺動脈楔壓監測　pulmonary artery wedge pressure monitoring following burns
烧伤后假性低钠血症/燒傷後假性低鈉血症　pseudohyponatremia following burn
烧伤后假性糖尿病/燒傷後假性糖尿病　pseudodiabetes of burn
烧伤后精神紊乱/燒傷後精神紊亂　postburn psychological disturbance
烧伤后脉搏血氧饱和度监测/燒傷後脈搏血氧飽和度監測　pulse oximetry monitoring following burns
烧伤后肾上腺出血/燒傷後腎上腺出血　postburn adrenal hemorrhage
烧伤后血比容监测/燒傷後血比容之監測　haematocrit monitoring following burns
烧伤•火毒内陷证/燒傷•火毒內陷證　burn with pattern of fire-toxin sinking inward
烧伤•火毒伤津证/燒傷•火毒傷津證　burn with pattern of fire-toxin injuring fluid
烧伤面积/燒傷面積　burn surface area
烧伤面积手掌估算法/燒傷面積手掌估算法　palm method for estimation of burn surface area
烧伤脑病/燒傷腦病　burn encephalopathy
烧伤•脾虚阴伤证/燒傷•脾虛陰傷證　burn with pattern of spleen deficiency and yin injury
烧伤•气血两虚证/燒傷•氣血兩虛證　burn with qi-blood deficiency pattern
烧伤深度/燒傷深度　depth of burn
烧伤性休克/燒傷性休克　burn shock
烧伤•阴伤阳脱证/燒傷•陰傷陽脫證　burn with pattern of yin injury and yang collapse
烧伤灾难/燒傷災難　burn disaster
烧伤指数/燒傷指數　burn index
烧伤中心/燒傷中心　burn center
烧蚀疗法/燒蝕療法　burning-eroding therapy
烧灼/燒灼　cauterize
烧灼术/燒灼術,烙術　cautery
芍药汤/芍藥湯　shaoyao decoction
杓关节面/杓關節面　arytenoid articular surface
杓会厌部/杓會厭部　aryepiglottic part
杓会厌肌/杓會厭肌　aryepiglottic muscle
杓间襞/杓間皺襞　interarytenoid fold
杓间切迹/杓間切跡　interarytenoid notch
杓斜肌/杓斜肌　oblique arytenoid
杓状的/杓狀　arytenoid
杓状会厌襞/杓狀會厭皺襞　aryepiglottic fold
杓状软骨/杓狀軟骨　arytenoid cartilage
杓状软骨底/杓狀軟骨底　base of arytenoid cartilage
杓状软骨关节面/杓狀軟骨關節面　articular surface of arytenoid cartilage
杓状软骨后面/杓狀軟骨後面　posterior surface of arytenoid cartilage
杓状软骨尖/杓狀軟骨尖　apex of arytenoid cartilage
杓状软骨内侧面/杓狀軟骨內側面　medial surface of arytenoid cartilage
杓状软骨前外侧面/杓狀軟骨前外側面　anterolateral surface of arytenoid cartilage
杓状软骨切除术/杓狀軟骨切除術　arytenoidectomy
少关节炎/少關節炎　pauciarthritis
少汗/少汗　hyphidrosis
少汗性外胚层发育不良/少汗性外胚層發育不全,無汗外胚層發育不全　hypohidrotic ectodermal

少汗症/汗過少,少汗　hypohidrosis
少黄卵/少黄卵　alecithal ovum
少见病/少見病　rare diseases
少节指/指骨缺少,缺指骨　hypophalangism
少节趾/趾骨缺少,缺趾骨　hypophalangism
少精子症/少精子症　oligospermatism, oligospermia
少尿/少尿　oliguria
少尿型肾[功能]衰竭/少尿型腎[功能]衰竭　oliguric renal failure
少树突神经胶质细胞/寡樹突神經膠質細胞　oligodendroglial cell
少睡习惯/厭睡　philagrypnia
少思/少思　lessening anxiety
少突胶质/少樹突神經膠細胞,寡樹突神經膠質細胞　oligodendroglia
少突胶质细胞/少突[神經]膠質細胞　oligodendrocyte
少突神经胶质/間膠質　oligodendroglia
少突神经胶质瘤/間膠質瘤　oligodendroglioma
少突神经胶质细胞/寡樹突膠質細胞,間膠質細胞　mesoglia cell, oligodendrocyte
少牙[畸形]/齒不足,齒過少　oligodontia
少欲/少欲　lessening desire
少渣饮食/低渣飲食　low residue diet
少指[畸形]/指不全　oligodactyly
少趾[畸形]/趾不全　oligodactyly
少冲/少沖　shaochong, HT9
少府/少府　shaofu, HT8
少腹/少腹　lateral lower abdomen
少腹急结/少腹急結　spasmodic pain in lower abdomen
少腹疽/少腹疽　carbuncle of lower abdomen, lower abdominal carbuncle
少腹痛/少腹痛　pain in lateral lower abdomen
少宫之人/少宮之人　atypical earth-phase person, more quick-witted
少海/少海　shaohai, HT3
少年胚胎性癌/少年胚胎性癌　juvenile embryonal carcinoma
少年期弹性组织增生/先天性彈性組織瘤　juvenile elastoma
少年型全身麻痹/幼年麻痺性癡呆　juvenile paresis
少商/少商　shaoshang, LU11
少商之人/少商之人　atypical metal-phase person, more serious
少小客忤/少小客忤　infantile convulsive seizure due to fright of seeing straigers

dysplasia

少阳病证/少陽病證　Shaoyang disease, Shaoyang pattern
少阳传阴/少陽傳陰　Shaoyang disease transmitting to interior
少阳坏病/少陽壞病　deteriorated case of Shaoyang disease
少阳之人/少陽之人　Shaoyang person
少阳中风/少陽中風　Shaoyang disease with wind affection
少阴便脓血证/少陰便膿血證　Shaoyin disease with purulent bloody stool pattern
少阴病证/少陰病證　Shaoyin disease, Shaoyin pattern
少阴寒化/少陰寒化　cold transformation of Shaoyin disease
少阴寒化证/少陰寒化證　Shaoyin disease with cold transformation pattern
少阴热化/少陰熱化　heat transformation of Shaoyin disease
少阴热化证/少陰熱化證　Shaoyin disease with heat transformation pattern
少阴热厥/少陰熱厥　Shaoyin disease with heat type cold limbs
少阴三急下证/少陰三急下證　Shaoyin disease with indications for three drastic catharsis
少阴伤寒/少陰傷寒　Shaoyin disease with cold damage
少阴下利证/少陰下利證　Shaoyin disease with diarrhea pattern
少阴咽痛证/少陰咽痛證　Shaoyin disease with sore throat pattern
少阴之人/少陰之人　Shaoyin person
少阴中风/少陰中風　Shaoyin disease with wind affection
少羽之人/少羽之人　atypical water-phase person, more introverted
少泽/少澤　shaoze, SI1
少徵之人/少徵之人　atypical fire-phase person, more suspicious
绍丁液/Schaudinn氏液　Schaudinn fluid
绍-赫饮食/Sauerbruch-Herrmannsdorfer二氏飲食　Sauerbruch-Herrmannsdorfer diet
绍曼综合征/Schaumann氏症候群　Schaumann syndrome
绍[舒]曼[小]体/Schaumann氏體　Schaumann body
绍塔-韦特海姆手术/史-章二氏手術　Schauta-Wertheim operation
绍兴本草/紹興本草　Shaoxing Bencao

哨笛音/哨笛音　sibilant rhonchi
哨点监测/哨點監測　sentinel surveillance
哨音/哨音　whistling murmur
舌/舌　①tongue, linguae ②she
舌白斑病/舌白斑病　leukoplakia lingualis
舌背/舌背　dorsum of tongue
舌背动脉/舌背動脈　dorsal artery of tongue
舌背静脉/舌背靜脈　dorsal lingual vein
舌背支/舌背支　dorsal lingual branch
舌扁桃体/舌扁桃體　lingual tonsil
舌扁桃体炎/舌扁桃腺炎　lingual tonsillitis
舌病/舌病　glossopathy
舌不知味/舌不知味　tasteless of tongue
舌侧倾斜/舌側傾斜　lingual inclination
舌侧托/舌面板　linguoplate
舌侧翼缘/舌凸緣　lingual flange
舌侧龈/舌面齦　lingual gingiva
舌侧支托/齒舌面托　lingual rest
舌颤/舌顫　trembling tongue
舌成形术/舌成形術　glossoplasty
舌疮/舌瘡　tongue sore
舌垂直肌/舌垂直肌　vertical muscle of tongue
舌唇的/舌與唇的　glossolabial
舌唇粘连术/舌唇粘連術　tongue-to-lip adhesion operation
舌刺/舌刺　tongue crib
舌底神经/舌底神經　sublingual nerve
舌底神经节/舌底神經結　sublingual ganglion
舌点/舌點　linguale
舌疔/舌疔　tongue pustule
舌动脉/舌動脈　lingual artery
舌动脉舌背支/舌動脈舌背支　dorsal lingual branch of lingual artery
舌动脉舌骨上支/舌動脈舌骨上支　suprahyoid branch of lingual artery
舌动描记器/舌動描記器　glossograph
舌短缩/舌短縮　shortened and contracted tongue
舌腭弓/舌腭弓　palatoglossal arch
舌腭肌/舌腭肌　glossopalatinus
舌缝术/舌縫合術　glossorrhaphy
舌干/舌乾　dry tongue
舌杆/舌側槓　lingual bar
舌根/舌根　tongue root, root of tongue
舌根前部/舌根前部　prebase
舌根腺/舌狀腺,舌根濾胞　lenticel
舌弓/舌弓　lingual arch
舌骨/舌骨　hyoid bone, lingual bone
舌骨板/舌骨板　hyoid bar

舌骨大角/舌骨大角　greater cornu of hyoid bone
舌骨动脉/舌骨動脈　hyoid artery
舌骨弓/舌骨弓,舌弧　hyoid arch
舌骨后囊/舌骨後囊　retrohyoid bursa
舌骨会厌韧带/舌骨會厭韌帶　hyoepiglottic ligament
舌骨肌/舌骨肌　muscle of hyoid bone
舌骨甲状韧带/舌骨甲狀韌帶　hyothyroid ligament
舌骨上的/舌骨上的　suprahyoid
舌骨上肌/舌骨上肌　suprahyoid muscle
舌骨上颈清扫术/舌骨上頸部切除　suprahyoid neck dissection
舌骨上囊肿/舌骨上囊腫　suprahyoid ranula
舌骨上韧带/舌骨上韌帶　epihyal ligament
舌骨上支/舌骨上支　suprahyoid branch
舌骨舌肌/舌骨舌肌　hyoglossus, hyoglossal muscle
舌骨舌肌底部/舌骨舌肌基部　hyobasioglossus
舌骨舌肌舌骨部/附在舌骨底部分的骨舌肌　basioglossus
舌骨体/舌骨體　body of hyoid bone
舌骨下肌/舌骨下肌　infrahyoid muscle
舌骨下淋巴结/舌骨下淋巴結　infrahyoid lymph node
舌骨下囊/舌骨下囊　infrahyoid bursa
舌骨下支/舌骨下支　infrahyoid branch
舌骨小角/舌骨小角　lesser cornu of hyoid bone
舌管/舌管　lingual duct
舌横肌/舌橫肌　transverse muscle of tongue, musculus transversus linguae
舌后坠/舌下垂　glossoptosis
舌回/舌迴　lingual gyrus
舌会厌韧带/舌會厭韌帶　glossoepiglottic ligament
舌会厌外侧襞/舌會厭外側皺襞　lateral glossoepiglottic fold
舌会厌正中襞/舌會厭中皺襞　median glossoepiglottic fold
舌肌/舌肌　muscle of tongue, lingualis
舌疾病/舌疾病　tongue disease
舌尖/舌尖　tongue apex, apex of tongue, proglossis
舌蹇[病]/舌謇[病]　stiff tongue disease
舌腱膜/舌腱膜　aponeurosis of tongue
舌角化病/舌角化病　keratosis linguae
舌结核/舌結核　tuberculosis of tongue
舌痉挛/舌痙攣　lingual spasm
舌静脉/舌靜脈　lingual vein
舌静脉曲张/舌靜脈擴張,舌痔　lingual hemorrhoid
舌卷/舌卷　curly tongue
舌菌/舌菌,舌癌　tongue cancer, tongue carcinoma
舌力计/舌力計　glossodynamometer

舌联桁/舌聯桁　hypobranchial eminence
舌裂/舌裂,裂舌,分歧舌　cleft tongue, fissured tongue
舌裂・肝肾阴虚证/舌裂・肝腎陰虛證　fissured tongue with liver-kidney yin deficiency pattern
舌裂[畸形]/舌裂畸形　schistoglossia
舌裂・胃阴不足证/舌裂・胃陰不足證　fissured tongue with stomach-yin deficiency pattern
舌裂・心火上炎证/舌裂・心火上炎證　fissured tongue with pattern of heart-fire flaring upward
舌裂・心脾两虚证/舌裂・心脾兩虛證　fissured tongue with heart-spleen deficiency pattern
舌淋巴结/舌淋巴結　lingual lymph node
舌滤泡/舌濾泡　lingual follicle, lingual follicles
舌麻/舌麻　numbness of tongue
舌盲孔/舌盲孔　foramen cecum of tongue, cecal foramen of tongue
舌面/舌面　lingual surface
舌面干/舌面幹　linguofacial trunk
舌面脊/齒冠之底脊　basal ridge
舌面隆凸/齒之舌面脊　cingulum
舌面[齲]洞/舌面齲齒腔洞　lingual cavity
舌面窝/舌側窩　lingual fossa
舌面隙/舌面隙,舌小凹　lingual pit
舌黏膜/舌黏膜　lingual mucous membrane
舌衄[病]/舌衄[病]　tongue bleeding
舌衄・心经积热证/舌衄・心經積熱證　tongue bleeding with pattern of accumulated heat in Heart Channel
舌衄・阴虚火旺证/舌衄・陰虛火旺證　tongue bleeding with pattern of exuberant fire due to yin deficiency
舌旁/舌旁　lateral side of tongue
舌偏侧肥大/半舌巨大　hemimacroglossia
舌前部外胚间叶层软骨黏液样瘤/舌前部外胚間葉層軟骨黏液樣瘤　ectomesenchymal chondromyxoid tumor of the anterior tongue
舌前腺/舌前腺　anterior lingual gland
舌钳/舌鉗　tongue forceps
舌强/舌強　stiff tongue
舌强语謇/舌強語謇　aphasia with stiff tongue
舌切除术/舌切除術　glossectomy
舌切开术/舌切開術　glossotomy
舌乳头/舌乳頭　lingual papilla, papilla of tongue, lingual papilla
舌乳头炎/舌乳頭炎　lingual papillitis
舌润/舌潤　moistened tongue
舌色/舌色　tongue color

舌涩/舌澀　aphasia with stiff tongue
[舌]上纵肌/[舌]上縱肌　superior longitudinal muscle
舌深动脉/舌深動脈　deep lingual artery
舌深静脉/舌深靜脈　deep lingual vein
舌神/舌神　tongue spirit
舌神经/舌神經　lingual nerve
舌神经鼓索交通支/舌神經鼓索交通支　communicating branch of lingual nerve with chorda tympani
舌神经神经节支/舌神經神經節支　ganglionic branch of lingual nerve
舌神经咽峡支/舌神經咽峽支　branch of lingual nerve to isthmus of fauces
舌生瘀斑/舌生瘀斑　ecchymosis on tongue
舌缩/舌縮　contracted tongue
舌苔/舌苔　fur, coated tongue
舌态/舌態　tongue condition
舌痰包/舌痰包　phlegmatic mass in tongue, sublingual gland cyst
舌体/舌體　body of tongue
舌痛[病]/舌痛[病]　glossodynia, tongue pain disease
舌退缩/舌退縮,舌收縮　glossocoma
舌歪/舌歪　wry tongue
舌痿/舌痿　flaccid tongue
舌舞蹈病/舞蹈病性舌　choreic tongue
舌习惯/舌習慣　tongue habit
舌系/舌系　sublingual vessel and ligament, tongue connector
舌系带/舌繫帶　frenulum of tongue, lingual frenum
舌系带短缩/舌繫帶短縮　ankyloglossia
舌系带过短/舌繫帶過短　ankyloglossum
舌系带切除术/舌粘連分離術　ankylotomy
舌下襞/舌下皺襞　sublingual fold
舌下的/舌下的　sublingual
舌下动脉/舌下動脈　sublingual artery
舌下阜/舌下肉阜　sublingual caruncle
舌下给药/舌下錠[劑]　sublingual administration
舌[下]颌裂/舌頜骨裂　hyomandibular cleft
舌下间隙/舌下間隙　sublingual space
舌下静脉/舌下靜脈　sublingual vein, ranine vein
舌下静脉曲张/舌下靜脈曲張　sublingual varices
舌下溃疡/舌下潰瘍　sublingual ulcer
舌下络脉/舌下絡脈　sublingual vessel
舌下面/舌下面　inferior surface of tongue
舌下囊肿/舌下囊腫　ranula, sublingual cyst
舌下囊肿修治术/舌下囊腫修治術　batrachoplasty

舌下黏膜/舌下黏膜　sublingual mucosa
舌下片剂/舌下片劑　sublingual tablet
舌下前置核/舌下前置核　nucleus prepositus hypoglossi
舌下神经/舌下神經　hypoglossal nerve, sublingual nerve
舌下神经伴行静脉/舌下神經并行靜脈　accompanying vein of hypoglossal nerve
舌下神经管/舌下神經管　hypoglossal canal
舌下神经管静脉丛/舌下神經管靜脈叢　venous plexus of hypoglossal canal
舌下神经核/舌下神經核　nucleus of hypoglossal nerve
舌下神经疾病/舌下神經疾病　hypoglossal nerve disease
舌下神经降支/舌下神經降支　descendens cervicis
舌下神经交通支/舌下神經交通支　communicating branch with hypoglossal nerve
舌下神经孔/舌下神經孔　hypoglossal foramen
舌下神经襻/舌下神經襻　loop of hypoglossal nerve
舌下神经三角/舌下神經三角　hypoglossal triangle
舌下神经舌支/舌下神經舌支　lingual branch of hypoglossal nerve
舌下神经性舌萎缩/舌下神經性舌萎縮　hypoglossal atrophy
舌下食物试验/舌下食物試驗　sublingual food test
舌下投药/舌下投藥　sublingual administration
舌下投药法/舌下用藥法　sublingual medication
舌下腺/舌下腺　sublingual gland
舌下腺凹/舌下腺凹　sublingual fossa
舌下腺大管/舌下腺大管　major sublingual duct
舌下腺导管/舌下腺導管　sublingual duct
舌下腺囊肿/舌下腺囊腫　sublingual gland cyst
舌下腺涎/舌下腺涎　sublingual saliva
舌下腺小管/舌下腺小管　minor sublingual duct
舌下腺炎/舌下腺炎　sublinguitis
舌下腺肿瘤/舌下腺腫瘤　sublingual gland neoplasm
舌下小神经/舌下小神經　lesser hypoglossal nerve
舌下炎/舌下炎　subglossitis
舌下周核/舌下周核　perihypoglossal nucleus
舌下纵肌/舌下縱肌　inferior longitudinal muscle of tongue
舌下[组织]炎/舌下組織炎　paraglossia
舌现象/舌現象　tongue phenomenon
舌腺/舌腺　lingual gland
舌腺涎/舌腺涎　lingual saliva
舌向错位/齒之舌側轉位　linguoversion
舌向𬌗[位]/齒舌側咬合　lingual occlusion
舌向移位/齒之舌側變位　linguoplacement
舌向阻生/舌向阻生　linguoangular impaction
舌象/舌象　tongue manifestation
舌象预后/舌象預後　glossomantia
舌形/舌形　tongue shape
舌形虫/舌形蟲　linguatulid
舌形虫病/舌形蟲病　pentastomiasis
舌咽部/舌咽部　glossopharyngeal part
舌咽的/舌[與]咽的　glossopharyngeal
舌咽肌/舌咽肌　glossopharyngeal muscle
舌咽神经/舌咽神經　glossopharyngeal nerve
舌咽神经扁桃体支/舌咽神經扁桃體支　tonsillar branch of glossopharyngeal nerve
舌咽神经鼓索交通支/舌咽神經鼓索交通支　communicating branch of glossopharyngeal nerve with chorda tympani
舌咽神经疾病/舌咽神經疾病　glossopharyngeal nerve disease
舌咽神经交通支/舌咽神經交通支　communicating branch with glossopharyngeal nerve
舌咽神经颈动脉窦支/舌咽神經頸動脈竇支　carotid sinus branch of glossopharyngeal nerve
舌咽神经上神经节/舌咽神經上神經節　superior ganglion of glossopharyngeal nerve
舌咽神经舌支/舌咽神經舌支　lingual branch of glossopharyngeal nerve
舌咽神经痛/舌咽神經痛　glossopharyngeal neuralgia
舌咽神经下神经节/舌咽神經下神經節　inferior ganglion of glossopharyngeal nerve
舌咽神经咽支/舌咽神經咽支　pharyngeal branch of glossopharyngeal nerve
舌咽杂音/咽下雜音　deglutition murmur
舌岩/舌巖　lingual carcinoma
舌岩·气阴两虚证/舌巖·氣陰兩虛證　lingual carcinoma with qi-yin deficiency pattern
舌岩·湿毒蕴结证/舌巖·濕毒蘊結證　lingual carcinoma with dampness-toxin amassment pattern
舌岩·心火炽盛证/舌巖·心火熾盛證　lingual carcinoma with blazing heart fire pattern
舌岩·阴虚火旺证/舌巖·陰虛火旺證　lingual carcinoma with pattern of yin deficiency and fire effulgence
舌炎/舌炎　glossitis
舌叶/舌葉　lingual folium
舌异位甲状腺/舌部甲狀腺　lingual thyroid
舌痈/舌癰　glossanthrax
舌釉沟/舌釉溝　lingual enamel groove
舌缘/舌緣　margin of tongue, lingual margin

舌诊/舌診　tongue inspection
舌正中沟/舌正中溝　median sulcus of tongue
舌支/舌支　lingular branch
[舌支]上部/[舌支]上部　superior part
舌质/舌質　tongue quality
舌中隔/舌中隔　septum of tongue
舌肿/舌腫[大]　swollen tongue, glossoncus
舌肿瘤/舌腫瘤　tongue neoplasms
舌周炎/舌周圍炎　periglossitis
舌灼痛/舌灼感覺　burning tongue
舌纵/舌縱　protracted tongue
蛇背疔/蛇背疔　snake-back ding
蛇串疮/蛇串瘡,帶狀皰疹　herpes zoster, snake-like sore
蛇串疮·肝经郁热证/蛇串瘡·肝經鬱熱證　snake-like sore with pattern of heat stagnation in liver channel
蛇串疮·脾虚湿困证/蛇串瘡·脾虛濕困證　snake-like sore with pattern of spleen deficiency and dampness retention
蛇串疮·气滞血瘀证/蛇串瘡·氣滯血瘀證　snake-like sore with pattern of qi stagnation and blood stasis
蛇床子/蛇床子　common cnidium fruit
蛇毒/蛇毒　snake venom
蛇毒疗法/蛇毒處理法　venomization
蛇毒溶血卵磷脂/卵磷脂蛇毒溶血素　lecithid
蛇毒性白细胞溶解/蛇毒性白血球崩解　venom leukocytolysis
蛇毒液类/蛇毒液類　snake venoms
蛇毒致炎酶/蝮蛇素酶　echidnase
蛇腹疔/蛇腹疔　snake-belly ding, snake-belly furuncle
蛇根混合碱/蛇根純浸膏　alseroxylon
蛇根碱/蛇根鹼　serpentine
蛇莓/蛇莓　Indian mock strawberry
蛇凝血素/蛇凝血素　hemocoagulin
蛇皮癣/蛇皮癬　ichthyosis
蛇皮癣·血虚风燥证/蛇皮癬·血虛風燥證　ichthyosis with pattern of wind-dryness due to blood deficiency
蛇皮癣·血瘀燥热证/蛇皮癬·血瘀燥熱證　ichthyosis with pattern of blood stasis and dryness-heat
蛇舌状虫病/蛇舌狀蟲病,洞頭蟲病　porocephaliasis
蛇头疔/蛇頭疔　snake-head ding, whitlow
蛇蜕/蛇蜕　snake slough
蛇纹石石棉/蛇紋石石棉　serpentine asbestos
蛇行状湿疹/蛇行狀濕疹　eczema serpinginosum
蛇眼疔/蛇眼疔　paronychia, snake-eye ding
蛇咬伤/蛇咬傷　snake bite
蛇咬中毒/蛇咬中毒　ophidism
舍脉从症/舍脈從症　precedence of symptoms over pulse manifestation
舍症从脉/舍症從脈　precedence of pulse manifestation over symptoms
设备污染/設備汙染　equipment contamination
社会保障/社會保障　social security
社会化医学/社會化醫學　socialized medicine
社会精神病学/社會精神病學　social psychiatry
社会康复/社會康復　social rehabilitation
社会适应/社會適應　social adjustment
社会[心理]卫生/社會衛生學　social hygiene
社会心理学/社會心理學　social psychology
社会行为药学/社會行爲藥學　social-behavioral pharmacy
社会药房/社區藥局　community pharmacy
社会医学/社會醫學　social medicine
社交恐怖症/社交恐怖症　social phobia
社区/社區　community
社区保健护理/社區保健護理　community health nursing
社区公共卫生体系/社區公共衛生體系　community public health system
社区护士/社區護理人員,分區護理人員　community nurse
社区获得性感染/社區獲得性感染　community-acquired infections
社区精神卫生/社區精神衛生　community mental health
社区精神卫生中心/社區精神衛生中心　community mental health center
社区卫生/社區衛生　community health
社区卫生保健信息系统/社區醫療信息系統　community health care information system
社区卫生辅助人员/社區衛生輔助人員　community health aid
社区卫生计划/社區衛生計劃　community health planning
社区卫生中心/社區衛生中心　community health center
社区牙周治疗需要指数/社區牙周治療需要指數　community periodontal index for treatment needs
社区医疗群/社區醫療群　family doctor integrated delivery system
社区医院/社區醫院　community hospital

社区组织/社區組織　community organization
舍利鲍姆溶液/Schallibaum 氏溶液　Schallibaum solution
舍莫瑞林/舍莫瑞林　sermorelin
舍曲林/舍曲林　sertraline
射工伤/射工傷　caterpillar sting
射精/射精　ejaculation
射精不良/射精不良　malemission
射精管/射精管　ejaculatory duct
射精过慢/射精徐緩　bradyspermatism
射毛[疗]法/射毛療法　pilojection
射频/放射頻率　radiofrequency
射频导管消融[术]/射頻導管消融[術]　radiofrequency catheter ablation
射频电疗法/射頻電療法　radiofrequency electrotherapy
射频起搏器/射頻起搏器　radiofrequency pacemaker
射频手术消融[术]/射頻手術消融[術]　radiofrequency surgical ablation
射气投置器/射氣發放器, 射氣治療器　emanator
射气治疗院/射氣療病院　emanatorium
射线/射線　ray
X 射线/X 射線　X-ray
γ 射线/γ 射線　gamma radiation
X 射线病/X 射線病, X 射線中毒　X-ray sickness
X 射线穿透力/X 射線的穿透力　hardness of X-ray
射线发生/放射線生成　actinogenesis
X 射线发生器/X 光产生器　X-ray generator
射线[发生]学/放射線學　actinogenics
X 射线光谱学/X 光光譜學　X-ray spectroscopy
射线间的/射線間的　interradial
X 射线胶片/X 光膠片　X-ray film
X 射线解剖学/X 射線解剖學　X-ray anatomy
X 射线宽束吸收测定法/X 光寬束吸收測定法　broad-beam absorption
射线疗法/放射線療學　actinotherapeutics
X 射线片夹/製作塗片 X 光射線　X-ray mount
X 射线束强度/X 光射線強度　intensity of an X-ray beam
射线透过性/射線透過性　radiability
X 射线显微分析/X 射線顯微分析　X-ray microanalysis
X 射线性脱发/X 射線性秃髮　X-ray alopecia
X 射线衍射图/X 射線繞射模式, X 射線繞射圖案　X-ray diffraction pattern
射线增敏剂/射線增敏劑　radiosensitizing agent
射线质/放射性物質, 放射原　actinogen
X 射线中毒/X 射線中毒　roentgen intoxication

X 射线装置的校正/X 光機校核　calibration of X-ray unit
射血分数/射血分數　ejection fraction
射血时间/射血時間　ejection time
射血时间指数/射血時間指數　ejection time index
射血时相指数/射出期指數　ejection phase index
摄法/攝法　pressing-kneading around inserted needle
摄领疮/攝領瘡　nape sore
摄取/攝取　uptake
摄生/攝生　regulating emotions and desires
摄生学/攝生學, 健康生活學　eubiotics
摄食过度/攝食過度　hyperphagia
摄食行为/攝食行爲　feeding behavior
摄食障碍/不正常食慾障礙　eating disorder
摄氏温度计/攝氏溫度計　Celsius thermometer
摄引作用/集菌作用　anachoresis
摄影测量法/攝影測量法　photogrammetry
摄影师湿疹/攝影師濕疹　photographers eczema
摄影术/照相術　photography
麝蓍草素/麝蓍草素　ivain
麝蓍油/麝蓍草餾油　ivaol
麝香/麝香　musk
麝香保心丸/麝香保心丸　shexiang baoxin pill
麝香草/麝香草　thymian
麝香草酚/麝香草酚, 麝香草腦　thymol
麝香草酚蓝/麝香草酚藍　coeruleum thymolis
麝香草酚浊度试验/麝香草酚濁度試驗　thymol turbidity test
麝香草脑/麝香草酚樟腦　thyme camphor
麝香草脑酞/麝香草腦酞　thymol phthalein
麝香祛痛气雾剂/麝香祛痛氣霧劑　shexiang qutong aerosol
麝香追风膏/麝香追風膏　shexiang zhuifeng plaster
申克孢子丝菌/Schenckii 氏孢子絲菌　Sporothrix schenckii
申脉/申脈　shenmai, B62, BL62
伸长反应/加長反應　lengthening reaction
伸长细胞/伸展細胞　tanycyte
伸肌/伸肌　extensor muscle
伸肌上支持带/伸肌上支持帶　superior extensor retinaculum
伸肌下支持带/伸肌下支持帶　inferior extensor retinaculum
伸肌支持带/伸肌支持帶　extensor retinaculum
伸筋草/伸筋草　common clubmoss herb
伸髋试验/伸髖試驗　hip extension test
伸面/伸面　extensor surface
伸屈法/伸屈法　stretching and flexing manipulation

伸入运动/伸入運動　emperipolesis
伸舌样白痴/克穆克氏白癡　Kalmuk idiocy
伸缩泡/伸縮泡　contractile vacuole
伸缩振动/伸縮振動　stretching vibration
伸腿臀位/伸腿臀位生產式　frank breech
伸展/伸展　unfolding
伸展过度/伸展過度　paratonia
伸展夹/伸展夾板　extension splint
伸指现象/指现象,格登氏现象　finger phenomenon
伸趾现象/足趾现象,巴賓斯基氏反射　toe phenomenon
身材矮小症/身材矮小症　short stature
身长/身長　body length
身高/身高　stature
身目俱黄/身目俱黃　yellow skin and eye
身热不扬/身熱不揚　hiding fever
身热夜甚/身熱夜甚　fever aggravated at night
身势学/身勢學　kinesics
身体部位/身體部位　body region
身体测量/身體測量　body size
身体成分/身體成分　body composition
身体的/身體的　physical
身体锻炼/身體鍛煉　exercise movement techniques
身体发育不全/身體發育不全　hyposomia
身体健全/身體健全　physical fitness
身体紧张型/軀體緊張　somatotonia
身体耐力/身體耐力　physical endurance
身体水分/身體水分　body water
身体体积描记法/身體體積描記器　body plethysmography
身体尪羸/身體尪羸　thin and weak body
身体吸引力/身體吸引力　physical attraction
身体依赖性/身體依賴性　physical dependence
身体自我/身體自我　body ego
身痛/身痛　pantalgia
身心放松技巧/身心放鬆技巧　mind-body and relaxation techniques
身心关系/身心關係　mind-body relation
身心合一/身心合一　body and mind integrated into one
身心失调/身心失調　somatopsychic disturbance
身心牙科学/身心牙醫學　psychosomatic dentistry
身心医学家/身心醫學醫師　psychosomaticist
身心有缺陷的人/肉體上、精神上或道德上有缺點者　defective
身痒/身癢　pruritus
身振摇/身振搖　body shaking
身之本/身之本　root of body

身重/身重　heavy body
身柱/身柱　shenzhu, DV12, GV12
参附汤/參附湯　shenfu decoction
参苓白术散/參苓白朮散　shenling baizhu powder
参苏饮/參蘇飲　shensu drink
砷/砷　arsenic
砷斑/砷斑　arsenic stain
砷毒性口炎/砷毒性口炎　arsenicalis stomatitis
砷毒性震颤/砷毒性震顫　arsenic tremor
砷分离/砷分離　arsenolysis
砷黑变病/砷劑黑變症　arsenical melanosis
砷化物/砷化物,砒化物　arsenide
砷剂/砷劑　arsenicals
砷剂癌/砷癌　arsenical carcinoma
砷剂促动作用/砷劑促動作用　arsenoactivation
砷角化病/砷中毒角化病　arsenical keratosis
砷疗法/砷療法　arsenization
砷硫酸试剂/砷硫酸試劑,羅森塔勒氏試劑　arsenic-sulfuric acid reagent
砷皮炎/砷劑皮膚炎　arsenical dermatitis
砷酸/砷酸　arsenic acid
砷酸胺/砷酸胺　arsenamide
砷酸钠/砷酸鈉,砒酸鈉　sodium arsenate
砷酸铅/砷酸鉛,砒酸鉛　lead arsenate
砷酸盐/砷酸鹽,砒酸鹽　arsenate
砷性皮肤溃疡/砷原性潰瘍　arsenic ulcer
砷盐/砷鹽　arsenic salt
砷原性黄疸/砷原性黃疸　arsenical jaundice
砷中毒/砷中毒　arsenic intoxication
砷中毒性神经病/砷原性神經病變　arsenic neuropathy
深底的/深底的　profundal
深瘰疽/深層瘰疽　deep felon
深部/深部　deep part
深部触诊法/深觸診　deep palpation
深部穿通痣/深入性母斑　deep penetrating nevus
深部感觉/深部感覺　bathesthesia
深部感觉迟钝/深覺遲鈍　bathyhypesthesia
深部感觉过敏/深[部感]覺過敏　bathyhyperesthesia
深部感觉缺失/深[部感]覺缺失　bathyanesthesia
深部狼疮/深部狼瘡　lupus profundus
深部梅毒瘤/深部樹膠樣腫　deep gummata
深部霉菌感染/深部黴菌感染　deep fungal infection
深部脑刺激法/深部腦刺激法　deep brain stimulation
深部脑电图/深部腦電圖　depth electroencephalogram
深部脑电图学/深部腦電圖學　depth

electroencephalography
深部真菌病/深部真菌病　deep mycosis
深层/[顱筋膜]深層　deep layer
深层反射/深層反射,深部反射　deep reflex
深层角膜炎/深層角膜炎,間質性角膜炎　deep keratitis
深[层]皮质/深[層]皮質　deep cortex
深[层]皮质单位/深[層]皮質單位　deep cortex unit
深[层]皮质复合体/深[層]皮質複合體　deep cortex complex
深层视网膜出血/深層視網膜出血　deep retinal hemorrhage
深层通气发酵/深層通氣發酵　submerged aerobic fermentation
深层掌侧动脉弓/深掌動脈弓　deep palmar arterial arch
深低温冷冻组织贮存/深低溫冷凍組織貯存　tissue storage by deep freezing
深度白痴/深度白癡,絕對白癡　absolute idiocy
深度[剂]量/深部劑量,深部組織受量　depth dose
深度烧伤/深度燒傷　deep burn
深度睡眠/深度睡眠　deep sleep
深度知觉/深覺　depth perception
深二度烧伤/深二度燒傷　deep the second degree burn
深分歧韧带/深分歧韌帶　deep bifurcated ligament
深覆盖/深覆蓋　deep overjet
深覆𬌗/深覆𬌗　deep overbite
深红酵母/紅色酵母菌　Saccharomyces rubrum
深呼吸/深呼吸　bathypnea
深筋膜/深筋膜　deep fascia
深静脉/深靜脈　deep vein
深静脉血栓形成/深層靜脈栓塞　deep vein thrombosis
深淋巴管/深淋巴管　deep lymphatic vessel
深淋巴结/深淋巴結　deep lymph node
深眠状态/類睡症　parasomnia
深染细胞/深色細胞　hyperchromatic cell
深色染色质/核深染質　hyperchromatin
深粟疹/深層粟粒疹　miliaria profunda
深头/深頭　deep head
深吸气性呼吸/深吸氣性呼吸　apneustic respiration
深在性红斑狼疮/深在性紅斑狼瘡　lupus erythematosus profundus
深支/深支　Ramus profundus
神/神　①vitality ②spirit ③mental activity ④spirit of pulse
神不守舍/神不守舍　instable mind

神藏/神藏　shencang, KI25
神道/神道　shendao, DU11
神灯照疗法/神燈照療法　lamp lighting up therapy
神封/神封　shenfeng, K23, KI23
神膏/神膏　spirit jelly, vitreum
神光/神光　spirit light
神光自见/神光自見　photopsia
神昏/神昏,意識喪失　unconsciousness
神机/神機　spiritual mechanism
神经/神經　nerve
神经安定药/神經安定藥　neuroleptic
神经氨酸类/神經氨酸類　neuraminic acids
神经氨酸酶/神經胺酸酶　neuraminidase
神经白细胞素/神經白細胞素　neuroleukin
神经板/神經板　neural plate
神经保护药/神經保護藥　neuroprotective agent
神经变[态反]应性/神經變應性　neuroallergy
神经变性/神經變性　nerve degeneration
神经变性疾病/神經變性疾病　neurodegenerative disease
神经病/神經病變　neuropathy
神经病的/神經病的　neuropathic
神经病电疗法/神經病電療法　neuroelectrotherapeutics
神经病毒/神經病毒　neurovirus
神经病患者/神經質者,神經病者　neuropath
神经病理学/神經病理學　neuropathology
神经病疗法/神經病療法　neuriatry
神经病体质/神經病體質　neuropathic constitution
神经病性关节病/神經病性關節病　neuropathic joint disease
神经病性关节炎/神經病性關節炎　neuropathic arthritis
神经病性肌萎缩/神經病性肌萎縮　neuropathic atrophy
神经病性水肿/神經病性水腫　neuropathic edema
神经病性秃发/神經病性秃髮　alopecia neurotica
神经病学/神經[病理]學　neurology
神经病学表现/神經病學表現　neurologic manifestation
神经病学检查/神經病學檢查　neurologic examination
神经病学诊断技术/神經病學診斷技術　neurological diagnostic technique
神经病诊断/神經病診斷法　neurodiagnosis
神经肠管/神經消化管　neurenteric canal
神经成形术/神經造形術,神經修補術　neuroplasty
神经冲动/神經興奮　nerve impulse

神经传导/神經傳導　neural conduction
神经传导速率/神經傳導速率　nerve conduction velocity
神经传导阻断/神經傳導阻滯　nerve blocking
神经[传]递质/神經傳導介質　neurotransmitter
神经垂体/神經垂體　neurohypophysis
神经垂体芽/神經垂體芽　neurohypophyseal bud
神经刺激器/神經刺激器　nerve stimulator
神经丛/神經叢　nerve plexus
神经丛麻醉/神經叢麻醉法　plexus anesthesia
神经丛损伤/神經叢損傷　injury of nerve plexus
神经丛炎/神經叢炎　plexitis
神经导航/神經導航　neuronavigation
神经递质/神經遞質　neurotransmitter
神经递质摄取抑制药/神經遞質攝取抑制藥　neurotransmitter uptake inhibitor
神经递质受体/神經遞質受體　neurotransmitter receptor
神经递质药/神經遞質藥　neurotransmitter agent
神经电/神經電流　neuroelectricity
神经电[流]描记术/神經電圖學　electroneurography
神经动脉硬化性绞痛/神經動脈硬化性絞痛　nerve angina
神经[毒]碱/神經鹼　neurine
神经毒理学/神經毒理學　neurotoxicology
神经毒力/神經毒性　neurovirulence
神经毒素/神經毒素　nerve toxin
神经断伤/神經斷傷,神經損斷　neurotmesis
神经发生/神經發生,神經生成　neurogenesis
神经发育学疗法/神經發育學療法　neurodevelopment therapy
神经放射摄影术/神經放射攝影術　neuroradiography
神经放射学/神經系放射學　neuroradiology
神经分布/神經分布　nerve supply
神经分泌/神經分泌　neurosecretion
神经分泌神经元/神經分泌神經元,神經分泌細胞　neurosecretory neuron
神经分泌系统/神經分泌系統　neurosecretory system
神经分泌细胞/神經分泌細胞　neurosecretory cell
神经分泌性消化不良/神經分泌性消化不良　neurosecretory dyspepsia
神经分析器/神經分析器　neural analyzer
神经分支节/節胚神經幹　hodoneuromere
神经分支新生/神經新支形成　neurocladism
神经缝合术/神經縫合術　neurorrhaphy
神经干/神經幹　nerve trunk

神经干细胞/神經幹細胞　neural stem cell
神经根/神經根　nerve root
神经根病/神經根病　radiculopathy
神经根神经病/脊神經根病變　radiculoneuropathy
神经根痛/神經根痛　root pain
[神经]根细胞/根細胞　root cell
神经根型颈椎病/神經根型頸椎病　cervical spondylotic radiculopathy
神经根炎/神經根炎　radiculitis
神经根综合征/脊神經根症候群　radicular syndrome
神经功能病/神經官能病,官能性神經病　neurotica
神经功能过旺/神經機能旺盛,神經興奮過度　neurosthenia
神经功能增强法/神經機能增強法　hyperneurotization
神经功能联系不能/神經機能聯繫失調　diaschisis
神经功能障碍/神經質　neurotic disorder
神经沟/神經溝　neural groove
神经沟未闭/神經溝不閉　asyntaxia dorsalis
神经固定/神經系定著　neurofixation
神经管/神經管　neural tube
神经管闭合不全/神經管閉合不全　dysrhaphia
神经管裂孔/神經管裂孔　neural hiatus
神经管腔/腦脊髓管　neurocoele
神经管缺陷/神經管缺陷　neural tube defect
神经管尾端遗迹/神經管尾端遺跡　coccygeal vestige
神经过敏症/神經過敏症　neuroticism
神经核/神經核　nucleus
神经核发育不全/中樞神經核發育不全　nuclear aplasia
神经黑变症/神經黑變症　neuromelanosis
神经化/神經化　neuralization
神经化学/神經化學　neurochemistry
神经回路/神經回路　neural circuit
[神经或胚胎]心房丛/[神經或胚胎之]心房叢　atrial plexus
神经肌电描记术/神經肌電描記術　electroneuromyography
神经肌肉表现/神經肌肉表現　neuromuscular manifestation
神经肌肉传递阻滞/神經肌肉傳導隔斷　neuromuscular block
神经肌肉刺激/神經肌肉刺激　neuromuscular stimulation
神经肌肉的/神經與肌的　neuromuscular
神经肌肉非去极化药/神經肌肉非去極藥　neuromuscular nondepolarizing agent
神经肌肉疾病/神經肌肉疾病　neuromuscular

disease
神经肌肉接头/神經肌肉接合點 neuromuscular junction
神经肌肉接头疾病/神經肌肉接頭疾病 neuromuscular junction disease
神经肌肉去极化药/神經肌肉去極化藥 neuromuscular depolarizing agent
神经肌肉收缩性/神經肌肉收縮性 neuromuscular contractility
神经肌肉药/神經肌肉藥 neuromuscular agent
神经肌肉张力过强/神經肌性張力過度 neuromuscular hypertension
神经肌肉障碍/神經肌肉障礙 neuromuscular disorder
神经肌肉阻断剂/神經肌肉阻斷劑 neuromuscular blocker
神经肌肉阻滞/神經肌肉阻滯,神經肌肉阻斷 neuromuscular blockade
神经肌肉阻滞药/神經肌肉阻滯藥 neuromuscular blocking agent
神经肌梭/神經肌梭 neuromuscular spindle
神经肌无力/神經肌無力 neuromyasthenia
神经肌细胞/神經肌細胞 neuromuscular cell
神经肌性动脉球/神經肌肉動脈小球 cutaneous glomus
神经肌炎/神經肌炎 neuromyositis
神经激素/神經激素 neurohormone
神经激肽 A/神經激肽 A neurokinin A
神经嵴/神經嵴 neural crest
神经脊髓炎/神經髓質炎 neuromyelitis
神经架桥法/神經架橋法 nerve bridging
神经腱鞘囊肿/神經腱鞘囊腫 ganglion cyst of nerve
神经腱梭/神經腱梭 neurotendinous spindle
神经降压肽/神經降壓肽 neurotensin
神经降压肽受体/神經降壓肽受體 neurotensin receptor
神经交叉吻合术/神經交叉吻合術 nerve cross anastomosis
神经胶质/神經膠質 neuroglia
神经胶质瘤/神經膠質瘤 glioma
神经胶质瘤病/神經膠質瘤病 gliomatosis
神经胶质肉瘤/肉瘤性神經膠瘤 glioma sarcomatosum
神经胶质细胞/神經膠質細胞 neuroglial cell, neuroglia cell
神经胶质细胞瘤/神經膠質細胞瘤 neurogliocytoma
神经胶质原纤维酸性蛋白质/神經膠質原纖維酸性蛋白質 glial fibrillary acidic protein
神经胶质增生/神經膠質增殖病 gliosis
神经角蛋白/神經角蛋白 neuroceratin
神经角质网/神經角質網 neurokeratin network
神经节/神經節 ganglion, nerve ganglion
［神经节］被囊细胞/［神經節］被囊細胞 capsular cell
神经节成神经细胞瘤/神經節神經母細胞瘤,神經節膠質母細胞瘤 ganglioneuroblastoma
神经节的/神經節的 ganglionic
神经节苷脂/神經節糖苷 ganglioside
神经节苷脂［贮积］病/神經節糖苷病 gangliosidosis
神经节瘤/神經節神經細胞瘤 ganglioneuroma
神经节切除术/神經節切除術 ganglionectomy
神经节神经胶质瘤/神經節性神經膠質瘤 ganglionic glioma
神经节细胞/神經節細胞 ganglionic cell, ganglion cell
神经节细胞缺乏［症］/無神經節症 aganglionosis
神经［节］细胞性神经瘤/神經節性神經瘤 ganglionar neuroma
神经节兴奋药/神經節興奮藥 ganglionic stimulant
神经节性涎/神經節性涎 ganglionic saliva
神经节炎/神經節炎 gangliitis
神经节支/神經節支 ganglionic branch
神经节周炎/神經節周圍炎 perigangliitis
神经节阻滞/神經節阻斷 ganglionic block
神经节阻滞药/神經節阻滯藥,神經節阻斷藥 ganglionic blocker
神经结构/神經結構 neuromechanism
神经解剖学/神經解剖學 neuroanatomy
神经精神病/神經性精神病 neuropsychopathy
神经精神病学/神經精神病學 neuropsychiatry
神经精神药理学/神經精神藥理學 neuropsychopharmacology
神经卡压综合征/神經卡壓症候群 nerve compression syndrome
神经科学/神經科學 neuroscience
神经壳质/神經甲殼素 neurochitin
神经孔/神經［管］孔 neuropore
神经控制［作用］/神經控制作用 neurarchy
神经叩击器/神經叩動器 neurokinet
神经淋巴瘤病/神經淋巴瘤病 neurolymphomatosis
神经磷脂酶缺乏/神經磷脂酶缺乏 sphingomyelinase deficiency
神经磷脂贮积病/神經磷脂貯積病 sphingomyelin storage disease
神经瘤/神經瘤 neuroma

神经瘤病/神經瘤病　neuromatosis
神经瘤样象皮病/神經瘤象皮病　pachydermatocele
神经螺旋体病/神經螺旋體病　neuroborreliosis
神经麻痹性角膜炎/神經痲痺性角膜炎　neuroparalytic keratitis
神经麻痹性水肿/神經痲痺性水腫　neuroparalytic edema
神经梅毒/神經梅毒　lues nervosa
神经梅毒复发/梅毒之神經再發症　neurorelapse
神经迷路炎/迷路神經纖炎　neurolabyrinthitis
神经免疫调节/神經免疫調節　neuroimmunomodulation
神经免疫学/神經免疫學　neuroimmunology
神经命名法/神經命名法　neuronymy
神经膜鞘/神經膜組織鞘　chitoneure
神经膜细胞/神經膜細胞　neurolemmal cell
神经末端/神經終端　teleneuron
神经末梢/神經末梢　nerve ending
神经母细胞瘤/神經母細胞瘤　neuroblastoma
神经脑脊髓病/神經腦脊髓病　neuroencephalomyelopathy
神经内的/神經内的　endoneural
神经内分泌癌/神經内分泌癌　neuroendocrine carcinoma
神经内分泌传导器/神經内分泌作用傳導物　neuroendocrine transducer
神经内分泌的/神經内分泌的　neuroendocrine
神经内分泌瘤/神經内分泌瘤　neuroendocrine tumor
神经内分泌学/神經内分泌學　neuroendocrinology
神经内镜/神經内窺鏡　neuroendoscope
神经内镜检查/神經内窺鏡檢查　neuroendoscopy
神经内麻醉/神經内麻醉　endoneural anesthesia
神经内麻醉法/神經内麻醉法　intraneural anesthesia
神经内膜/神經内膜,神經内衣　endoneurium
神经内膜炎/神經内衣炎　endoneuritis
神经旁的/神經旁的　paraneural
神经旁阻滞/神經旁阻斷麻醉　paraneural block
神经胚/神經[軸]胚　neurula
神经胚期/神經胚期　neurula period, neurula stage
神经胚形成/神經[軸]胚形成　neurulation
神经培养/神經培養　neural culture
神经皮肤黑色素痣序列征/神經皮膚黑色素痣序列徵　neurocutaneous melanosis sequence
神经皮肤综合征/神經皮膚症候群　neurocutaneous syndrome
神经破坏性阻滞/神經破壞性阻滯　neurolytic block
神经牵伸术/神經牽伸術　neurotony
神经鞘/神經鞘,神經膜　neurilemma
神经鞘瘤/神經鞘瘤,腦膜鞘瘤　neurinoma, sheath tumor
神经鞘膜/神經鞘膜　epilemma
神经鞘黏液瘤/神經鞘黏液瘤　neurothekeoma
神经鞘炎/神經外膜炎　adventitial neuritis
神经鞘脂贮积症/神經鞘脂病　sphingolipidosis
神经切除术/神經切除術　neurectomy
神经切断术/神經切斷術　neurotomy
神经切迹/神經切跡　nerve incisure
神经曲霉病/神經麴黴病　neuroaspergillosis
神经躯体性/神經軀體性　neurosomatic
神经融合术/神經湊合手術　nerve fusion
神经肉瘤/神經肉瘤　neurosarcoma
神经乳头/神經乳頭　neurothele
神经上皮/神經上皮　neuroepithelium
神经上皮瘤/神經上皮瘤　neuroepithelioma
神经上皮细胞/神經上皮細胞　neuroepithelial cell
神经上皮小体/神經上皮小體　neuroepithelial body
神经上皮肿瘤/神經上皮腫瘤　neuroepithelial tumor
神经烧伤/神經燒傷　burn of nerve
神经生理学/神經生理學　neurophysiology
神经生理学疗法/神經生理學療法　neurophysiological therapy
神经生物学/神經生物學　neurobiology
神经生长因子/神經生長因數　nerve growth factor
神经生长因子受体/神經生長因數受體　nerve growth factor receptor
神经适应/神經適應　nerve accommodation
神经受体/神經受器　neuroceptor
神经束/神經束　nerve tract
神经束[间]吻合术/神經束[間]吻合術　interfascicular nerve anastomosis
神经束膜/神經束膜　perineurium
神经束膜的/神經束膜的　perineurial
神经束膜瘤/神經束膜瘤　perineurioma
神经束膜内膜炎/神經内膜束膜炎　endoperineuritis
神经束膜炎/神經束膜炎　perineuritis
神经束上皮/神經束上皮　perineural epithelium
神经束切断术/纖維束切斷術　tractotomy
神经束移植/神經束移植　fascicular nerve transplantation
神经束移植物/神經束移植物　fascicular graft
神经衰弱/神經衰弱　nerve tire
神经衰弱性眩晕/神經衰弱性眩暈　neurasthenic vertigo
神经衰弱者/神經衰弱者　neurasthenic
神经衰弱综合征/神經衰弱症候群　neurasthenic syndrome

神经丝/神經絲　neurofilament
神经撕除术/神經撕除法　neuragmia
神经撕脱术/神經撕脱術　avulsion of nerve
神经松解术/神經鬆解術　neurolysis
神经髓鞘肿瘤/神經髓鞘腫瘤　nerve sheath tumor
神经损伤/神經損傷　injury of nerve
神经索/神經索　nerve funiculus
神经肽 Y/神經肽 Y　neuropeptide Y
神经肽类/神經肽類　neuropeptides
神经肽受体/神經肽受體　neuropeptide receptor
神经肽 Y 受体/神經肽 Y 受體　neuropeptide Y receptor
神经套管术/包神經術　tubulization
神经调节蛋白类/神經調節蛋白類　neuregulins
神经调质/神經調節物質　neuromodulator
神经通路/神經通路　neural pathway, nervous pathway
神经痛/神經痛　neuralgia
神经痛性肌萎缩/臂部神經炎　brachial neuritis
神经痛样的/神經痛樣的　neuralgiform
神经凸/神經凸　neurapophysis
神经突/神經突　neurite
神经外的/神經外的　extraneural
神经外科/神經外科　neurosurgery
神经外科手术/神經外科手術　neurosurgical procedure
神经外科医师/神經外科醫師　neurosurgeon
神经外膜/神經外膜,神經外衣　epineurium
神经外胚层的/神經外胚層的　neuroectodermal
神经外胚层发育不良/神經外胚層發育不全　neuroectodermal dysplasia
神经外胚层瘤/神經外胚瘤　neuroectodermal tumor
神经外伤/神經外傷　neurotrauma
神经网/神經網　nerve net
神经网络/神經網路　neural networks
神经微管/神經小管　neurotubule
神经微丝蛋白质类/神經微絲蛋白質類　neurofilament proteins
神经萎缩者/神經萎縮者　neuratrophic
神经吻合[术]/神經吻合[術]　neural anastomosis
神经系统/神經系[統]　nervous system
神经系统创伤/神經系統創傷　nervous system trauma
神经系统副肿瘤综合征/神經系統副腫瘤症候群　nervous system paraneoplastic syndrome
神经系统汞中毒/神經系統汞中毒　nervous system mercury poisoning
神经系统畸形/神經系統畸形　nervous system malformation
神经系统疾病/神經系統疾病　nervous system disease
神经系统酒精诱发性障碍/神經系統酒精誘發性障礙　nervous system alcohol-induced disorder
神经系[统]囊肿/神經系[統]囊腫　neural cyst
神经系统铅中毒/神經系統鉛中毒　nervous system lead poisoning
神经系统溶酶体贮积病/神經系統溶酶體貯積病　nervous system lysosomal storage disease
神经系统生理学/神經系統生理學　nervous system physiology
神经系统血吸虫病/神經系統血吸蟲病　neuroschistosomiasis
神经系统遗传变性障碍/神經系統遺傳變性障礙　nervous system heredodegenerative disorder
神经系统肿瘤/神經系統腫瘤　nervous system neoplasm
神经系统重金属中毒/神經系統重金屬中毒　nervous system heavy metal poisoning
神经系统状态/神經系現狀,神經系狀況　neurostatus
神经系统自身免疫疾病/神經系統自身免疫疾病　autoimmune diseases of the nervous system
神经细胞/神經細胞　nerve cell
神经细胞[胞]体/神經細胞體　neurosome
神经细胞固缩/神經細胞固縮　neuronal shrinkage
神经细胞瘤/神經細胞瘤　neurocytoma
神经细胞黏附分子类/神經細胞黏附分子類　neural cell adhesion molecules
神经细胞趋生物性/神經細胞趨生物性　neurobiotaxis
神经细胞[线状]排列/神經成分整列　neurotagma
神经细胞学/神經細胞學　neurocytology
神经细胞炎/神經細胞炎　celluloneuritis
神经细胞营养不良/神經細胞營養不良　neuroinidia
神经纤毛蛋白质类/神經纖毛蛋白質類　neuropilins
神经纤维/神經纖維　nerve fiber
神经纤维瘤/纖維神經瘤,神經纖維病　neurofibroma
神经纤维瘤病/神經纖維瘤病,多發性神經纖維瘤　neurofibromatoses, neurofibromatosis
神经纤维瘤性象皮病/神經纖維瘤性象皮病　elephantiasis neurofibromatosasis
神经纤维曲张/神經纖維曲張　neurovaricosis
神经纤维肉瘤/神經纖維肉瘤　neurofibrosarcoma
神经纤维束/神經纖維束　nerve fasciculus, nerve tract
神经纤维松解法/神經纖維梳裂法　combing

神经纤维素/神經纖維素 neurofibromin
神经纤维酸/神經纖維酸 fibril acid
神经纤维网/神經纖維網 feltwork
神经纤维脂肪瘤/神經之纖維脂肪瘤 fibrolipoma of nerve
神经酰胺类/神經醯胺類 ceramides
神经酰胺三己糖酶/神經醯胺三己糖酶 ceramide trihexosidase
神经效应器接点/神經效應器接點 neuroeffector junction
神经心理学/神經心理學 neuropsychology
神经心理学测验/神經心理學測驗 neuropsychological test
神经星形细胞瘤/神經星形細胞瘤 neuroastrocytoma
神经兴奋性过度/神經興奮性過強 hypertarachia
神经[兴奋性]运动/神經運動 nervimotion
神经行为学表现/神經行爲學表現 neurobehavioral manifestation
神经[型]囊尾蚴病/神經囊尾蚴蟲病 neurocysticercosis
神经性鼻炎/神經性鼻炎 rhinitis nervosa
神经性表皮脱落/神經性表皮脱落 neurotic excoriation
神经性步态障碍/神經性步態障礙 neurologic gait disorders
神经性肠梗阻/神經性腸梗阻 ileus of nervous origin
神经性大便失禁/神經性大便失禁 encopresis
神经性的/源自神經的,生成神經的 neurogenic
神经性耳鸣/神經性耳鳴 nervous tinnitus
神经性发热/神經性發熱 thermoneurosis
神经性放电/神經性放電 nervous discharge, neural discharge
神经性分泌作用/内分泌的神經作用 neurocrinia
神经性腹泻/神經性腹瀉 nervous diarrhea
神经性关节病/神經[性]關節病 neuroarthropathy
神经性呼吸/神經性呼吸 nervous respiration
神经性呼吸困难/呼吸困難精神官能症 dyspneoneurosis
神经性肌强直/神經性肌強直,肌痙攣 neuromyotonia
神经性叫喊/叫喊性神經病 neurophonia
神经性紧张/神經性緊張 neurogenic tonus
神经性痉挛/神經性痙攣 neurospasm
神经性纠发病/神經性糾髮病 plica neuropathica
神经性溃疡/神經性潰瘍 neurogenic ulcer
神经性聋/[聽]神經性聾症 nerve deafness
神经性麻痹/神經性麻痺 neuroparalysis
神经性能/神經特性,神經力 neurility
神经性尿崩症/神經性尿崩症 neurogenic diabetes insipidus
神经性呕吐/神經性嘔吐 nervous vomiting
神经性膀胱/神經性膀胱 nervous bladder
神经性皮炎/神經性皮炎 neurodermatitis
神经性贫血综合征/神經性貧血症候群 neuro-anemic syndrome
神经性气喘/神經性氣喘 nervous asthma
神经性乳头状瘤/神經性乳頭狀瘤 neuroticum papilloma
神经性贪食/神經性貪食 bulimia nervosa
神经性疼痛/神經性疼痛 neuropathic pain
神经性吞咽困难/神經性吞嚥困難 dysphagia nervosa
神经性萎缩/神經性肌萎縮 neural atrophy
神经性消化不良/神經性消化不良 nervous dyspepsia
神经性心绞痛/神經性心絞痛 angina nervosa
神经性休克/神經性休克 neurogenic shock
神经性循环衰弱/心臟神經衰弱,心臟神經官能病 cardiac neurasthenia
神经性厌食/神經性厭食症,精神性厭食症 anorexia nervosa
神经性阳痿/神經性陽痿 neurogenic impotence
神经性抑郁/神經性抑鬱 nervous depression
神经性营养不良/神經性營養不良 nervous dystrophy
神经性谵妄/神經性譫妄 delirium nervosum
神经性紫癜/神經性紫癜 purpura nervosa
神经学模型/神經學模型 neurological model
神经血管错构瘤/神經血管缺陷瘤 neurovascular hamartoma
神经血管的/神經血管的 neurovascular
神经血管蒂皮瓣/神經血管蒂皮瓣 neurovascular pedicle skin flap
神经血管束/神經血管束 neurovascular bundle
神经血管造影/神經血管造影 neuroangiography
神经循环衰弱症/神經系循環系無力,神經性循環無力 neurocirculatory asthenia
神经压碾/神經壓碾 nerve crush
神经炎/神經炎 neuritis
神经炎性肌萎缩/神經炎性肌萎縮 neuritic muscular atrophy
神经炎性皮肤萎缩/神經炎性皮萎病 atrophoderma neuriticum
神经炎性湿疹/神經炎性濕疹 eczema neuriticum

神经炎性秃发/神經炎性禿髮 alopecia neuritica
神经眼科学/神經眼科學 neuroophthalmology
神经眼血管瘤病/神經眼血管瘤病 neuroculo-angiomatosis
神经样的/神經樣的 neuroid
神经药理学/神經藥理學 neuropharmacology
神经胰岛复合体/經胰島複合體 neuroinsular complex
神经移入肌肉术/神經鬆解移地術 neurosarcokleisis
神经移位/神經移位 nerve transfer
神经移位术/神經移位術 nerve transposition
神经移植/神經移植 neural transplantation, nerve transplantation
神经移植术/神經再生,神經植入法 neurotization
神经移植物/神經移植物 nerve graft
神经遗传学/神經遺傳學 neurogenetics
神经抑制/神經抑制 neural inhibition
神经营养/神經營養 neurotrophy
神经营养不足/神經營養不足 neurotrophasthenia
神经营养的/神經營養的 neurotrophic
神经营养物质/神經營養物質 neurotrophic substance
神经营养性大疱性表皮松解症/神經營養性大皰性表皮鬆解症 epidermolysis bullosa neurotrophica
神经营养性关节炎/神經營養性關節炎 neurotrophic arthritis
神经营养性溃疡/神經[營養]性潰瘍 neurotrophic ulcer
神经营养性三叉神经综合征/神經營養性的三叉神經症候群 neurotrophic trigeminal syndrome
神经营养性萎缩/神經營養性萎縮 neurotrophic atrophy
神经营养因子/神經營養因數 neurotrophin
神经硬化症/神經硬化 neurosclerosis
神经[与]循环系统的/神經系與循環系的 neurocirculatory
神经语言学规划/神經語言學規劃 neurolinguistic programming
神经元/神經元,神經細胞 neuron
神经元变性/神經元變性 neuronal degeneration
神经元病/神經元病 neuronopathy
神经元发育不全/神經單位發育不全 neuronagenesis
神经元间接触/神經元間接觸 ephapse
神经[元]介质说/神經液學說 neurohumoralism
神经元可塑性/神經元可塑性 neuronal plasticity
神经元内血糖不足/神經缺糖症 oxyachrestia
[神经元]染质溶解/染色質溶解,核染質溶解,色素溶解 chromatolysis
神经元-神经胶质细胞黏附分子/神經元-神經膠質細胞黏附分子 neuron-glia cell adhesion molecule
神经元细胞黏附分子/神經元細胞黏附分子 neuronal cell adhesion molecule
神经元型/神經元型 neuron pattern
神经元炎/神經細胞炎,神經單位炎 neuronitis
神经元移植/神經元移植 neuron transplantation
神经元营养质/神經營養素 trophon
[神经元]中枢突/[神經元]中樞突 central process
[神经元]周围突/[神經元]周圍突 peripheral process
神经元周卫星细胞/神經元周衛星細胞 perineuronal satellite cell
神经原纤维/神經原纖維 neurofibril
神经原纤维缠结/神經原纖維纏結 neurofibrillary tangle
神经原纤维网/神經微纖維網 neurofibrillar network
神经原性感染/神經原性感染 neurogenic inflammation
神经原性关节病/神經原性關節病,神經病性關節病 neurogenic arthropathy
神经原性膀胱/神經發生性膀胱 neurogenic bladder
神经运动力/神經運動力 nervimotility
神经再生/神經再生 regeneration of nerve, nerve regeneration
神经张力性反应/神經性強直反應 neurotonic reaction
神经褶/神經褶 neural fold, medullary fold
神经症/神經症 neurosis
神经[症]性尿/神經性尿 nervous urine
神经症性障碍/神經症性障礙 neurotic disorder
神经脂瘤病/神經脂瘤病 neurolipomatosis
神经质/神經過敏 nervousness
神经质忧郁症/神經質憂鬱症 neurotic depressive disorder
神经痣/神經痣 neural nevus
神经中枢/神經中樞 nerve center
神经终器/神經終器 neuroterminal
神经[中]毒/神經[中]毒 neurotoxic
神经中毒性/神經[中]毒性 neurotoxicity
神经中毒症/神經中毒症 neurotoxia
神经中毒综合征/神經中毒症候群 neurotoxicity syndrome
神经周成纤维细胞瘤/神經周圍纖維組織母細胞瘤 perineural fibroblastoma
神经周浸润麻醉/神經旁浸潤麻醉法 paraneural infiltration

神经周淋巴隙/神經周圍淋巴道　perineural channel
神经周[围]的/神經周圍的　perineural
神经周围麻醉法/神經周圍麻醉法　perineural anesthesia
神经周围阻滞/神經周圍傳導阻滯　perineural block
神经轴分解/軸索崩解　axolysis
神经轴索静脉曲张/神經軸索曲張　filovaricosis
神经轴突营养不良/神經軸突營養不良　neuroaxonal dystrophy
神经追踪法/神經追蹤法　nerve tracing method
神经滋养管/神經血管　vasa nervorum
神经阻滞法/神經阻滯法　neural anesthesia
神经阻滞剂恶性综合征/安定藥惡性症候群　neuroleptic malignant syndrome
神经阻滞麻醉/神經阻滯麻醉法　nerve blocking anesthesia
神经组织/神經組織　nerve tissue, nervous tissue
神经组织蛋白质类/神經組織蛋白質類　nerve tissue proteins
神经组织耗损/神經組織耗損　neurophthisis
神经组织学/神經組織學　histoneurology
神经组织肿瘤/神經組織腫瘤　nerve tissue neoplasm
神经[作用]性激素/神經影響内分泌素　neurocrine
神愦/神憒　unconsciousness
神劳/神勞　mental exhaustion, over contemplation
神乱/神亂　delirium
神门/神門　shenmen
神秘主义/神秘主義　mysticism
神明/神明　mental activity
神农/神農　Shennong
神农本草经/神農本草經　Shennong's Classic of Materia Medica
神农本草经集注/神農本草經集注　Variorum of Shennong's Classic of Materia Medica
神疲/神疲　mental fatigue, spiritlessness
神曲/神曲　medicated leaven
神阙/神闕　shenque, RN8
神水/神水,水狀液　spirit water, aqueous humor, spiritual water
神水将枯/神水將枯　dry eye pattern, exhaustion of spirit water
神水将枯·肺阴虚证/神水將枯·肺陰虛證　exhaustion of spirit water with lung yin deficiency pattern
神水将枯·肝肾阴虚证/神水將枯·肝腎陰虛證　exhaustion of spirit water with liver-kidney yin deficiency pattern

神水将枯·气阴两虚证/神水將枯·氣陰兩虛證　exhaustion of spirit water with qi-yin deficiency pattern
神堂/神堂　shentang, BL44
神庭/神庭　shenting, DU24
神游[症]/神遊症　wandering impulsion
神志/神志　mentality
神志病/神志病　mental disease
神志不定/神志不定　disturbed mind
神志清醒的/清醒的　lucid
神志有辨/神志有辨　differentiation of mental activity and temperament
审视瑶函/審視瑤函　Precious Book of Ophthalmology
审症求因/審症求因　differentiation of symptoms and signs to identify etiology
肾/腎　kidney, renes
肾阿米巴病/腎阿米巴病　renal amebiasis
肾癌/腎癌　renal carcinoma, kidney cancer
肾癌·脾肾气虚证/腎癌·脾腎氣虛證　kidney cancer with pattern of qi deficiency of spleen and kidney
肾癌·湿热蕴毒证/腎癌·濕熱蘊毒證　kidney cancer with pattern of damp-heat and amassing poison
肾癌·阴虚内热证/腎癌·陰虛内熱證　kidney cancer with pattern of internal heat due to yin deficiency
肾癌·瘀血内阻证/腎癌·瘀血内阻證　kidney cancer with pattern of internal blockade of static blood
肾棒状杆菌/腎棒狀桿菌　Corynebacterium renale
肾包虫病/腎包蟲病　renal hydatid disease
肾包膜下测定/腎包膜下測定　subrenal capsule assay
肾被膜剥除术/腎被膜剝除術　nephrocapsulectomy
肾被膜切开术/腎被膜切開術　nephrocapsulotomy
肾病/腎病　nephrosis
肾病性水肿/腎病性水腫　nephrotic edema
肾病灶清除术/腎病灶清除術　renal cavernostomy
肾不纳气/腎不納氣　deficiency of kidney qi failing to control respiring qi
肾部分切除术/腎部分切除術　partial nephrectomy
肾藏精/腎藏精　kidney storing essence
肾藏志/腎藏志　kidney storing will
肾超声检查[术]/腎超聲檢查[術]　renal ultrasonography
肾充血/腎充血　nephremia
肾出血/腎出血　renal hemorrhage
肾出血性囊肿/腎出血性囊腫　hemorrhagic cyst of kidney
肾穿刺活检/腎穿刺活檢　renal needle biopsy

肾穿刺术/腎穿刺術　renipuncture
肾穿透伤/腎穿透傷　penetrating injury of kidney
肾丛/腎叢　renal plexus
肾挫伤/腎挫傷　contusion of kidney
肾错构瘤/腎錯構瘤　hamartoma of kidney
肾大盏/腎大盞　major renal calices
肾代偿性肥大/腎代償性肥大　renal compensatory hypertrophy
肾单位/腎[單]元　nephron
肾单位肾小球滤过率/腎單位腎小球濾過率　nephron glomerular filtration rate
肾蒂断裂/腎蒂斷裂　rupture of renal pedicle
肾蒂淋巴管剥脱术/腎蒂淋巴管剝脫術　stripping of renal lymphatic vessel
肾淀粉样变性/腎澱粉樣變性　amyloidosis of kidney
肾动静脉瘘/腎動靜脈瘻　renal arteriovenous fistula
肾动脉/腎動脈　renal artery
肾动脉梗阻/腎動脈梗阻　renal artery obstruction
肾动脉后支/腎動脈後支　posterior branch of renal artery
肾动脉后支后段动脉/腎動脈後支後段動脈　posterior segmental artery of posterior branch of renal artery
肾动脉疾病/腎動脈疾病　renal arterial disease
肾动脉瘤/腎動脈瘤　aneurysm of renal artery
肾动脉前支/腎動脈前支　anterior branch of renal artery
肾动脉前支上段动脉/腎動脈前支上段動脈　superior segmental artery of anterior branch of renal artery
肾动脉前支上前段动脉/腎動脈前支上前段動脈　superior anterior segmental artery of anterior branch of renal artery
肾动脉前支下段动脉/腎動脈前支下段動脈　inferior segmental artery of anterior branch of renal artery
肾动脉前支下前段动脉/腎動脈前支下前段動脈　inferior anterior segmental artery of anterior branch of renal artery
[肾动脉]输尿管支/[腎動脈]輸尿管支　ureteric branch of renal artery
肾动脉栓塞/腎動脈栓塞　thrombosis of renal artery
肾动脉栓塞术/腎動脈栓塞術　embolization of renal artery
肾动脉狭窄/腎動脈狹窄　renal artery stenosis
肾动脉纤维增生病/腎動脈纖維增生病　fibroplasia of renal artery
肾动脉血栓形成/腎動脈血栓形成　renal arterial thrombosis
肾动脉硬化梗塞疾病/腎動脈硬化梗塞疾病　atheroembolic renal disease
肾动脉硬化症/腎動脈硬化症　renal arteriosclerosis
肾动脉造影[术]/腎動脈造影[術]　renal arteriography
肾动脉粥样硬化症/腎動脈粥樣硬化症　renal arterial atherosclerosis
肾窦/腎竇　renal sinus
肾窦脂肪瘤样病/腎竇脂肪瘤樣病　renal sinus lipomatosis
肾毒物/腎毒物　nephrotoxicant
肾毒性/腎毒性　renal toxicity
肾毒性肾小球肾炎/腎毒性腎小球腎炎　nephrotoxic glomerulonephritis
肾毒性血清肾炎/腎毒性血清腎炎　nephrotoxic serum nephritis
肾段/腎段　renal segment
肾断层造影[术]/腎斷層造影術　nephrotomography
肾断层造影洗出法/腎斷層造影洗出法　washout method in nephrotomography
肾恶/腎惡　critical condition of kidney
肾恶性纤维组织细胞瘤/腎惡性纖維組織細胞瘤　malignant fibrous histiocytoma of kidney
肾恶燥/腎惡燥　kidney being averse to dryness
肾发生/腎發生　nephrogenesis
肾发育不良/腎發育不良　renal dysplasia
肾发育不全/腎發育不全　renal hypoplasia
肾肥大/腎肥大　renal hypertrophy
肾缝合术/腎縫合術　nephrorrhaphy
肾钙斑/腎鈣斑　Randall plaque
肾钙斑学说/腎鈣斑學說　theory of Randall plaque
肾钙化囊肿/腎鈣化囊腫　calcified cyst of kidney
肾钙质沉着症/腎鈣質沈著病　nephrocalcinosis
肾疳/腎疳　kidney gan disease
肾膈韧带/腎膈韌帶　diaphragmatic ligament of kidney
肾梗死/腎梗死　infarction of kidney
肾弓形动脉/腎弓形動脈　arcuate artery of kidney
肾弓形静脉/腎弓狀靜脈　arcuate vein of kidney
肾功能不全/腎功能不全　renal insufficiency
肾功能试验/腎功能試驗　kidney function test
肾[功能]衰竭/腎[功能]衰竭　kidney failure, renal failure
肾固定术/腎固定術　nephropexy
肾合膀胱/腎合膀胱　kidney being connected with bladder
肾后性急性肾[功能]衰竭/腎後性急性腎[功能]衰

竭　postrenal acute renal failure
肾化脓/腎化膿，腎膿腫　nephropyosis
肾毁蚀病/腎毀蝕病　nephrophagiasis
肾积水尿血/腎積水尿血　urohematonephrosis
肾积水血尿/腎積水血尿，水血腎，腎臟積血尿　hydrohematonephrosis
肾畸形/腎畸形　deformity of kidney
肾激肽系统/腎激肽系統　renal kallikrein system
肾及膀胱辨证/腎及膀胱辨證　pattern identification of kidney and bladder
肾疾病/腎疾病　kidney disease
肾假性瘤/腎假性瘤　pseudotumor of kidney
肾间腺/腎間腺　interrenal gland
肾绞痛/腎絞痛　renal colic
肾节/腎節　renal ganglion
肾结肠固定术/腎結腸固定術　nephrocolopexy
肾结肠下垂/腎結腸下垂　nephrocoloptosis
肾结核/腎結核　renal tuberculosis
肾结核对侧肾积水/腎結核對側腎積水　renal tuberculosis with contralateral hydronephrosis
肾结石/腎結石　nephrolithiasis
肾筋膜/腎筋膜　renal fascia
肾惊/腎驚　convulsion due to kidney disorder
肾精/腎精　kidney essence
肾精不足/腎精不足　insufficiency of kidney essence
肾精亏虚证/腎精虧虛證　pattern of deficiency of kidney essence
肾静脉/腎静脈　renal vein
肾静脉肾素/腎静脈腎素　renal vein renin
肾静脉栓塞/腎静脈栓塞　thrombosis of renal vein
肾静脉血栓形成/腎静脈血栓形成　renal venous thrombosis
肾静脉造影[术]/腎静脈造影[術]　renal venography
肾开窍于耳/腎開竅於耳　kidney opening at ear
肾颗粒细胞癌/腎顆粒細胞癌　granular cell carcinoma of kidney
肾溃疡/腎潰瘍　nephrelcosis
肾痨/腎痨　kidney consumption, renal tuberculosis
肾离体术/腎離體術　bench technique of kidney
肾粒状萎缩/腎粒狀萎縮　granular atrophy of kidney
肾良性肿瘤/腎良性腫瘤　benign renal tumor
肾裂伤/腎裂傷　laceration of kidney
肾淋巴瘤/腎淋巴瘤　renal lymphoma
肾淋巴母细胞瘤/腎淋巴母細胞瘤　renal lymphoblastoma
肾淋巴肉瘤/腎淋巴肉瘤　lymphosarcoma of kidney
肾瘤/腎瘤　nephroma
肾瘘/腎瘻　renal fistula
肾鹿角状结石/腎鹿角狀結石　staghorn stone of kidney
肾麻痹/腎麻痺　nephroparalysis
肾门/腎門　renal hilum
肾门上淋巴结切除术/腎門上淋巴結切除術　suprahilar lymphadenectomy
肾门脂肪瘤样病/腎門脂肪瘤樣病　lipomatosis of renal hilus
肾弥漫性脂瘤/腎彌漫性脂瘤　lipoma diffusum renis
肾面/腎面　renal surface
肾母细胞瘤基因/腎母細胞瘤基因　Wilms tumor gene
肾囊动脉/腎囊動脈　capsular artery
肾囊风/腎囊風，陰囊濕疹　scrotum eczema
肾囊风·湿热下注证/腎囊風·濕熱下注證　scrotum eczema with pattern of dampness-heat diffusing downward
肾囊静脉/腎囊静脈　capsular vein
肾囊性病/腎囊性病　renal cystic disease
肾囊肿/腎囊腫　renal cyst
肾囊肿形成/腎囊腫形成　nephrocystosis
肾内反流/腎內反流　intrarenal reflux
肾内肾积水/腎內腎積水　intrarenal hydronephrosis
肾酿酶/腎釀酶，腎酵素　nephrozymase
肾浓缩能力/腎濃縮能力　kidney concentrating ability
肾脓肿/腎膿腫　renal abscess
肾旁假囊肿/腎旁假囊腫　pararenal pseudocyst
肾旁囊肿/腎旁囊腫　paranephric cyst
肾旁脂体/腎旁脂體　pararenal adipose body of kidney
肾膀胱吻合术/腎膀胱吻合術　nephrocystanastomosis
肾膀胱炎/腎膀胱炎　nephrocystitis
肾泡/腎泡　renal vesicle
肾胚细胞瘤/腎胚細胞瘤　nephroblastoma
肾皮质/腎皮質　renal cortex, cortex renis
肾皮质坏死/腎皮質壞死　cortical necrosis of kidney
肾皮质脓肿/腎皮質膿腫　cortical abscess of kidney
肾皮质外层/腎皮質外層　cortex corticis
肾皮质腺瘤/腎皮質腺瘤　renal cortical adenoma
肾皮综合征/腎皮症候群　renocutaneous syndrome
肾脾固定术/腎脾固定術　nephrosplenopexy
肾平滑肌瘤/腎平滑肌瘤　leiomyoma of kidney
肾平滑肌肉瘤/腎平滑肌肉瘤　leiomyosarcoma of kidney
肾破裂/腎破裂　rupture of kidney
肾气/腎氣　kidney qi

肾气不固/腎氣不固　non-consolidation of kidney qi
肾气不固证/腎氣不固證　pattern of non-consolidation of kidney qi
肾气丸/腎氣丸　shenqi pills
肾气虚/腎氣虛　kidney qi deficiency
肾气虚证/腎氣虛證　pattern of kidney qi deficiency
肾前列腺素/腎前列腺素　renal prostaglandin
肾前性急性肾[功能]衰竭/腎前性急性腎[功能]衰竭　prerenal acute renal failure
肾前性尿毒症/腎前性尿毒症　prerenal uremia
肾前性无尿/腎前性無尿　prerenal anuria
[肾]浅皮质静脉/[腎]淺皮質靜脈　superficial cortical vein
肾切除术/腎切除術　nephrectomy
肾切开术/腎切開術　nephrotomy
肾缺如/腎缺如　renal agenesis, agenesis of kidney
肾热病/腎熱病　kidney heat disease
肾肉瘤/腎肉瘤　sarcoma of kidney
肾乳头/腎乳頭　renal papilla
肾乳头坏死/腎乳頭壞死　kidney papillary necrosis
肾乳头筛区/腎乳頭篩區　cribriform area of renal papilla
肾软化/腎軟化　nephromalacia
肾扫描/腎掃描　renal scan
肾善/腎善　favorable condition of kidney
肾上腺/腎上腺　suprarenal gland, adrenal gland
肾上腺病/腎上腺病　adrenalopathy
肾上腺丛/腎上腺叢　suprarenal plexus, adrenal plexus
肾上腺动脉/腎上腺動脈　suprarenal artery
肾上腺动脉造影[术]/腎上腺動脈造影[術]　adrenal arteriography
肾上腺毒素/腎上腺毒素　adrenotoxin
肾上腺非功能性皮质腺瘤/腎上腺非功能性皮質腺瘤　nonfunctional adrenocortical adenoma
肾上腺高血压/腎上腺高血壓　adrenal hypertension
肾上腺功能病/腎上腺功能病　adrenalism
肾上腺功能初现/腎上腺皮質功能初現　adrenarche
肾上腺功能减退/腎上腺功能減退　adrenal insufficiency
肾上腺功能亢进/腎上腺機能亢進　hyperadrenalism
肾上腺功能停滞/腎上腺功能停滯　adrenopause
肾上腺功能早现/腎上腺功能早現　premature adrenarche
肾上腺功能障碍/腎上腺機能障礙　dysadrenalism
肾上腺后面/腎上腺後面　posterior surface of adrenal gland
肾上腺疾病/腎上腺疾病　adrenal gland disease
肾上腺交感神经综合征/腎上腺交感神經症候群　adrenosympathetic syndrome
肾上腺结核/腎上腺結核　adrenal tuberculosis
肾上腺瘤/腎上腺瘤　suprarenoma
肾上腺门/腎上腺門　hilum of adrenal gland
肾上腺脑白质营养不良/腎上腺腦白質營養不良　adrenoleucodystrophy
肾上腺内侧缘/腎上腺內側緣　medial border of adrenal gland
肾上腺能阻滞/腎上腺能阻滯　adrenergic block
肾上腺皮质/腎上腺皮質　adrenal cortex
肾上腺皮质癌/腎上腺皮質癌　adrenocortical carcinoma
肾上腺皮质功能减退/腎上腺皮質功能減退　hypoadrenocorticism
肾上腺皮质功能减退症/腎上腺皮質功能減退症　adrenocortical insufficiency
肾上腺皮质功能亢进/腎上腺皮質功能亢進　hypercorticism
肾上腺皮质功能亢进性肥胖/腎上腺功能亢進性肥胖　hyperinterrenal obesity
肾上腺皮质功能试验/腎上腺皮質功能試驗　adrenal cortex function test
肾上腺皮质功能障碍/腎上腺皮質功能異常　dyscorticism
肾上腺皮质功能正常/腎上腺皮質功能正常　isoadrenocorticism
肾上腺皮质激素/腎上腺皮質素　adrenocortical hormone
肾上腺皮质激素类/腎上腺皮質激素類　adrenocortical hormones, adrenal cortex hormones
肾上腺皮质疾病/腎上腺皮質疾病　adrenal cortex disease
肾上腺皮质瘤/腎上腺皮質瘤　adrenocortical tumor
肾上腺皮质铁氧还原蛋白/腎上腺皮質鐵氧還原蛋白　adrenodoxin
肾上腺皮质系统/腎上腺皮質系統　interrenal system
肾上腺皮质腺瘤/腎上腺皮質腺瘤　adrenocortical adenoma
肾上腺皮质增生/腎上腺皮質增生　adrenal cortical hyperplasia
肾上腺皮质肿瘤/腎上腺皮質腫瘤　adrenal cortex neoplasms
肾上腺皮质综合征/腎上腺皮質症候群　adrenal cortical syndrome
肾上腺片移植/腎上腺片移植　adrenal slices transplantation

肾上腺前面/腎上腺前面 anterior surface of adrenal gland
肾上腺切除术/腎上腺切除術 adrenalectomy
肾上腺切除术综合征/腎上腺切除症候群 postadrenalectomy syndrome
肾上腺色素/腎上腺色素 adrenochrome
肾上腺上动脉/腎上腺上動脈 superior suprarenal artery
肾上腺肾面/腎上腺腎面 renal part of adrenal gland
肾上腺生殖综合征/腎上腺生殖症候群,腎上腺性生殖器症候群 adrenogenital syndrome
肾上腺剩余瘤/腎上腺剩餘瘤 adrenal rest tumor
α-肾上腺受体拮抗剂/α-腎上腺受體拮抗劑,甲型腎上腺受體拮抗劑 α-adrenergic antagonist
肾上腺素/腎上腺素 adrenalin
肾上腺素激动药/腎上腺素能激動藥 adrenergic agonist
肾上腺素能激动剂/腎上腺素能激動劑 adrenergic agonist
肾上腺素能α激动剂/腎上腺素能α激動劑 adrenergic α-agonist
肾上腺素能β激动剂/腎上腺素能β激動劑 adrenergic β-agonist
肾上腺素能拮抗剂/腎上腺素能拮抗劑 adrenergic antagonist
肾上腺素能α拮抗剂/腎上腺素能α拮抗劑 adrenergic α-antagonist
肾上腺素能摄取抑制剂/腎上腺素能攝取抑制劑 adrenergic uptake inhibitor
肾上腺素能神经/腎上腺素能神經 adrenergic nerve
肾上腺素能神经元/腎上腺素能神經元 adrenergic neuron
肾上腺素能神经元阻滞/腎上腺素能神經元阻滯 adrenergic-neuron-blocking
肾上腺素能神经支配/腎上腺素能神經支配 adrenergic innervation
肾上腺素能受体/腎上腺素能受體 adrenergic receptors
肾上腺素能β受体拮抗剂/腎上腺素能β受體拮抗劑 adrenergic β-antagonist
肾上腺素能药/腎上腺素能藥 adrenergic agent
肾上腺素尿/腎上腺素尿 adrenalinuria
肾上腺素溶液/腎上腺素溶液 epinephrine solution
肾上腺素生成/腎上腺素生成 adrenalinogenesis
肾上腺素受体/腎上腺素受體 adrenoceptor, adrenoreceptor
α-肾上腺素受体/α-腎上腺素受體,甲型腎上腺素受體 α adrenoreceptor
β-肾上腺素受体/β-腎上腺受體,乙型腎上腺受體 β adrenoreceptor
α-肾上腺素受体激动剂/α-腎上腺受體促效劑,甲型腎上腺受體促效劑 α-adrenoreceptor agonist
β-肾上腺素受体激动药/β-腎上腺接受器作用劑,乙型腎上腺接受器作用劑 β-adrenoreceptor agonist
肾上腺素受体拮抗药/腎上腺素能受體拮抗藥 adrenoreceptor antagonist
β-肾上腺素受体阻滞剂/β-腎上腺接受器阻滯劑,乙型腎上腺接受器阻滯劑 β-adrenoreceptor blocker
肾上腺素受体阻滞药/腎上腺素受體阻滯藥 adrenoreceptor blocker
肾上腺素血症/腎上腺素血症 adrenalinemia
肾上腺髓质/腎上腺髓質 adrenal medulla
肾上腺髓质三征/腎上腺髓質三徵 adrenomedullary triad
肾上腺髓质增生症/腎上腺髓質增生症 adrenal medulla hyperplasia
[肾上腺]胎性皮质/[腎上腺]胎性皮質 fetal cortex
肾上腺酮/腎上腺酮 adrenalone
肾上腺外副神经节瘤/腎上腺外副神經節瘤 extra-adrenal paraganglioma
肾上腺危象/腎上腺危象,愛迪生氏病危象 adrenal crisis
肾上腺下动脉/腎上腺下動脈 inferior suprarenal artery, inferior capsular artery
肾上腺腺瘤/腎上腺腺瘤 adrenal adenoma
肾上腺性白线/腎上腺性白線 white adrenal line
肾上腺性男性化/腎上腺性男性化 adrenal virilism
肾上腺性男性化综合征/腎上腺性男性化症候群 adrenal virilizing syndrome
肾上腺性组织/腎上腺性組織 adrenogenic tissue
肾上腺雄[甾]酮/腎上腺固酮 adrenosterone
肾上腺血管造影[术]/腎上腺血管造影[術] adrenal angiography
肾上腺压迹/腎上腺壓跡 suprarenal impression
肾上腺炎/腎上腺炎 adrenalitis
肾上腺氧化酶/腎上腺氧化酶 adrenoxidase
肾上腺样瘤/腎上腺樣瘤 hypernephroma
肾上腺移植/腎上腺移植 adrenal transplantation
肾上腺抑制药/腎上腺抑制劑 adrenostatic
[肾上腺]永久皮质/[腎上腺]永久皮質 permanent cortex
肾上腺中动脉/腎上腺中動脈 middle suprarenal artery
肾上腺中间质/腎上腺中間質 internal of suprarenal gland substance
肾上腺中央静脉/腎上腺中央靜脈 central vein of

adrenal gland, central vein of suprarenal gland
肾上腺肿大/腎上腺腫大　adrenomegaly
肾上腺肿瘤/腎上腺腫瘤　adrenal gland neoplasm
肾上腺综合征/腎上腺症候群　suprarenogenic syndrome
肾X射线造影术/腎臟X光攝影術　nephrography
［肾］深皮质静脉/［腎］深皮質靜脈　deep cortical vein
肾神经节/腎神經節　renal ganglia
肾神经鞘瘤/腎神經鞘瘤　schwannoma of kidney
肾失用性萎缩/腎失用性萎縮　disuse atrophy of kidney
肾石病/腎石病　lithonephria
肾石切除术/腎石切除術　lithonephrotomy
肾实质癌/腎實質癌　carcinoma of renal parenchyma
肾实质切开取石术/腎實質切開取石術　nephrolithotomy
肾嗜酸细胞瘤/腎嗜酸細胞瘤　renal oncocytoma
肾输尿管膀胱切除术/腎輸尿管膀胱切除術　nephroureterocystectomy
肾输尿管切除术/腎輸尿管切除術　nephroureterectomy
肾俞/腎俞　shenshu, BL23
肾俞漏/腎俞漏　shenshu fistula
肾俞虚痰/腎俞虛痰　spinal tuberculosis in shenshu
肾俞虚痰·肾阳虚证/腎俞虛痰·腎陽虛證　spinal tuberculosis in shenshu with kidney yang deficiency pattern
肾俞虚痰·肾阴虚证/腎俞虛痰·腎陰虛證　spinal tuberculosis in shenshu with kidney yin deficiency pattern
肾衰管型/腎衰管型　renal failure cast
肾衰指数/腎衰指數　renal failure index
肾水/腎水　edema due to dysfunction of kidney, kidney edema
肾水·膀胱停水证/腎水·膀胱停水證　kidney edema with pattern of water retention in bladder
肾水·气滞水停证/腎水·氣滯水停證　kidney edema with pattern of qi stagnation and water retention
肾水·肾阳虚证/腎水·腎陽虛證　kidney edema with pattern of kidney yang deficiency
肾水·下焦湿热证/腎水·下焦濕熱證　kidney edema with pattern of damp-heat in lower jiao
肾水·浊邪上逆证/腎水·濁邪上逆證　kidney edema with pattern of upward counterflowing of turbidity pathogen
肾素/腎［活］素　renin
肾素激活物/腎素激活物，腎素活化質　renin activator
肾素瘤/腎素瘤　reninoma
肾素-血管紧张素系统/腎素-血管緊張素系統　renin-angiotensin system
肾素依赖性高血压/腎素依賴性高血壓　renin-dependent hypertension
肾素抑制药/腎素抑制藥　renin inhibitor
肾髓质/腎髓質　renal medulla, kidney medulla
肾髓质管扩张/腎髓質管擴張　medullary ductal ectasia of kidney
肾髓质坏死/腎髓質壞死　medullary necrosis of kidney
肾髓质囊性病/腎髓質囊性病　medullary cystic disease of kidney
肾损伤/腎損傷　renal injury
肾探测图/腎膀胱探測圖　renocystogram
肾糖阈/腎糖閾，排糖閾　threshold sugar
肾替代疗法/腎替代療法　renal replacement therapy
肾痛/腎痛　nephralgia
肾透明细胞癌/腎透明細胞癌，腎亮細胞癌　clear cell carcinoma of kidney
肾透析/腎透析　renal dialysis
肾突出/腎膨出，腎赫尼亞　nephrocele
肾图/腎圖　nephrogram
肾托/腎托，腎墊　kidney pad
肾外尿毒症/腎外尿毒症　extrarenal uremia
肾外型肾盂/腎外型腎盂　extrarenal pelvis
肾外性氮血症/腎外性氮血症　extrarenal azotemia
肾网膜固定术/腎網膜固定術　nephro-omentopexy
肾为先天之本/腎爲先天之本　kidney being congenital origin
肾萎缩/腎萎縮　renal atrophy
肾痿/腎痿　kidney flaccidity
肾细胞癌/腎細胞癌　renal cell carcinoma
肾下垂/腎下垂　kidney ptosis, ptosis of kidney
肾纤维瘤/腎纖維瘤　renal fibroma
肾纤维样肉瘤/腎纖維樣肉瘤　renal fibroid sarcoma
肾纤维脂肪瘤样病/腎纖維脂肪瘤樣病　renal fibrolipomatosis
肾腺癌/腎腺癌　adenocarcinoma of kidney
肾腺瘤/腎腺瘤　renal adenoma
肾小管/腎小管　renal tubule
肾小管反流/腎小管反流　renal tubular backflow
肾小管破裂/腎小管破裂　tubulorrhexis
肾小管肾小球反馈机制/腎小管腎小球反饋機制　tubuloglomerular feedback mechanism
肾小管肾炎/腎小管腎炎　tubular nephritis
肾小管吸收/腎小管吸收　tubular resorption

肾小管性蛋白尿/腎小管性蛋白尿　tubular proteinuria
肾小管性低渗尿/腎小管性低滲尿　tubular hyposthenuria
肾小管性多尿/腎小管性多尿　tubular diuresis
肾小管性酸中毒/腎小管性酸中毒　renal tubular acidosis
肾小管最大排泄量/腎小管最大排洩量　maximal tubular excretory capacity
肾小囊/腎小囊　renal capsule
肾小囊腔/腎小囊腔　capsular space
肾小囊上皮/腎小囊上皮　capsular epithelium
肾小球/腎小球　glomerulus, renal glomerulus
肾小球被膜性肾炎/腎小球被膜性腎炎　glomerulocapsular nephritis
肾小球病/腎小球病　glomerulopathy
肾小球出球动脉/腎小球出球動脈,腎小球輸出動脈　efferent artery of glomerulus
肾小球出血/腎小球出血　glomerular hemorrhage
肾小球动脉/腎小球動脈　artery of glomerulus
肾小球基膜/腎小球基膜　glomerular basement membrane
肾小球滤过率/腎小球濾過率　glomerular filtration rate
肾小球滤过膜/腎小球濾過膜　glomerular filtration membrane
肾小球毛细血管/腎小球毛細血管,腎小球微血管　glomerular capillary
肾小球膜/腎小球膜　glomerular mesangium
肾小球囊/腎小球囊　glomerular capsule, Malpighian capsule
肾小球囊肿病/腎小球囊腫病　glomerulocystic disease
[肾小]球内系膜细胞/[腎小]球內繫膜細胞,内腎小球膜細胞　intraglomerular mesangial cell
[肾小]球旁复合体/近腎小球器,近腎絲球器　juxtaglomerular apparatus
肾小球旁器/近血管球細胞　juxtaglomerular apparatus
[肾小]球旁细胞/近腎小球細胞,腎近絲球細胞　juxtaglomerular cell
肾小球旁细胞肥大/近腎小球細胞肥大　juxtaglomerular cell hypertrophy
肾小球旁细胞增生症/近腎小球細胞增生　juxtaglomerular cell hyperplasia
肾小球旁增生并醛酯酮过多症/近腎小球增生并醛酯酮過多症　juxtaglomerular hyperplasia with hyperaldosteronism

肾小球清除率/腎小球清除率　glomerular clearance rate
肾小球入球小动脉/腎小球輸入小動脈　afferent artery of glomerulus
肾小球上皮/腎小球上皮　glomerular epithelium
肾小球上皮细胞病/腎小球上皮細胞疾病　glomerular epithelial cell disease
肾小球肾炎/腎小球腎炎　glomerular nephritis
肾小球肾炎患者/腎小球腎炎患者　brightic
肾小球通透性/腎小球通透性　glomerular permeability
[肾小]球外系膜细胞/[腎小]球外系膜細胞　extraglomerular mesangial cell
肾小球小管性肾炎/腎小球小管性腎炎　glomerulotubular nephritis
肾小球性蛋白尿/腎小球性蛋白尿　glomerular proteinuria
肾小球性血尿/腎小球性血尿　glomerular hematuria
肾小球血流动力学/腎小球血流動力學　glomerular hemodynamics
肾小球炎/腎小球炎,腎血管球炎,腎絲球炎　glomerulitis
肾小体/腎小體　renal corpuscle
肾小叶/腎小葉　renal lobule
肾小叶间动脉/腎小葉間動脈　interlobular artery of kidney
肾小叶间静脉/腎小葉間靜脈　interlobular veins of kidney
肾小盏/腎小盞,小腎盞　minor renal calice, infundibula of kidney
肾心痛/腎心痛　true heart pain with cold limbs caused by kidney disease
肾星状静脉/腎星狀靜脈　stellate veins of kidney
肾形胎盘/腎形胎盤　placenta reniformis
肾型斑疹伤寒/腎型斑疹傷寒,腎性斑疹傷寒　nephrotyphus
肾型伤寒/腎型傷寒,腎性傷寒　nephrotyphoid
肾性氨基酸尿/腎性氨基酸尿　renal aminoaciduria
肾性恶病质/腎性惡病質　urinary cachexia
肾性腹水/腎性腹水　ascites vulgatior
肾性高血压/腎性高血壓　renal hypertension
肾性佝偻病/腎性佝僂病　renal rickets
肾性骨软化症/腎性骨軟化症　renal osteomalacia
肾性骨营养障碍/腎性骨營養障礙　renal osteodystrophy
肾性骨硬化症/腎性骨硬化症　renal osteosclerosis
肾性呼吸困难/腎性呼吸困難　renal dyspnea
肾性尿崩症/腎性尿崩症　nephrogenic diabetes

insipidus
肾性气喘/腎性氣喘　renal asthma
肾性生长停滞综合征/腎性生長停滯症候群　renal growth failure syndrome
肾性水肿/腎性水腫　renal edema
肾性糖尿/腎性糖尿　renal glucosuria
肾性糖尿病/腎性糖尿病　renal diabetes
肾性血尿/腎性血尿　renal hematuria
肾性幼稚症/腎性幼稚症　renal infantilism
肾性侏儒综合征/腎性侏儒症候群　renal dwarfism syndrome
肾虚寒湿证/腎虛寒濕證　pattern of cold-dampness due to kidney deficiency
肾虚水泛/腎虛水泛　water diffusion due to kidney deficiency
肾虚髓亏证/腎虛髓虧證　pattern of marrow depletion due to kidney deficiency
肾旋转异常/腎旋轉異常　renal malrotation
肾血管重建术/腎血管重建術　renovascular reconstruction
肾血管疾病/腎血管疾病　renal vascular diseases
肾血管瘤/腎血管瘤　hemangioma of kidney
肾血管外皮细胞瘤/腎血管外皮細胞瘤　renal hemangiopericytoma
肾血管性高血压/腎血管性高血壓　renal vascular hypertension
肾血管硬化/腎血管硬化，血管性肾硬化病　nephroangiosclerosis
肾血管杂音/腎血管雜音　renovascular bruit
肾血管造影[术]/腎血管造影[術]　renal angiography
肾血浆流量/腎血漿流量　renal plasma flow
肾血流动力学/腎血流動力學　renal hemodynamics
肾血吸虫病/腎血吸蟲病　renal schistosomiasis
肾循环/腎循環　renal circulation
肾压迹/腎壓跡　renal impression
肾岩/腎巖　penis carcinoma
肾岩·火毒炽盛证/腎巖·火毒熾盛證　penis carcinoma with blazing fire-toxin pattern
肾岩·湿浊瘀结证/腎巖·濕濁瘀結證　penis carcinoma with pattern of intermingled dampness-turbidity and stasis
肾岩·阴虚火旺证/腎巖·陰虛火旺證　penis carcinoma with pattern of yin deficiency and fire effulgence
肾炎/腎[臟]炎　nephritis
肾炎性丹毒/腎炎性丹毒　nephroerysipelas
肾炎饮食/腎炎飲食　nephritic diet

肾炎综合征/腎炎症候群　nephritic syndrome
肾阳/腎陽　kidney yang
肾阳虚/腎陽虛　kidney yang deficiency
肾阳虚水泛证/腎陽虛水泛證　pattern of water diffusion due to kidney yang deficiency
肾阳虚证/腎陽虛證　pattern of kidney yang deficiency
肾叶/腎葉　renal lobe
肾叶间动脉/腎葉間動脈　interlobar artery of kidney
肾叶间静脉/腎葉間靜脈　interlobar veins of kidney
肾移植/腎移植　kidney transplantation
肾异位/腎異位　ectopia renis
肾异种组织肿瘤/腎異種組織腫瘤　heteroplastic tissue tumor of kidney
肾阴/腎陰　kidney yin
肾阴虚/腎陰虛　kidney yin deficiency
肾阴虚火旺证/腎陰虛火旺證　pattern of fire hyperactivity due to kidney yin deficiency
肾阴虚证/腎陰虛證　pattern of kidney yin deficiency
肾阴阳两虚证/腎陰陽兩虛證　pattern of kidney yin-yang deficiency
肾音描记图/腎音描記圖　phonorenogram
肾硬化症/腎硬化症　nephrosclerosis
肾痈/腎癰　renal carbuncle, kidney abscess
肾盂/腎盂　renal pelvis, kidney pelvis
肾盂癌/腎盂癌　carcinoma of renal pelvis
肾盂白斑病/腎盂白斑病　leukoplakia of renal pelvis
肾盂病/腎盂病　pyelopathy
肾盂测量法/腎盂測量法　pyelometry
肾盂成形术/腎盂成形術　nephropyeloplasty
肾盂充气照相术/腎盂充氣照相術　pneumokidney
肾盂回肠膀胱吻合术/腎盂迴腸膀胱吻合術　pelvioileoneocystostomy
肾盂积尿/腎盂積尿，尿肾病　uronephrosis
肾盂积脓/腎臟積膿，膿尿腎　uropyonephrosis
肾盂积水/腎盂積水，水肾，肾水腫　hydronephrosis
肾盂积血/腎盂積血，血肾　hematonephrosis
肾盂积血扩张/腎盂積血擴張，血性腎盂擴張　hemopyelectasis
肾盂间质反流/腎盂間質反流　pyelointerstitial backflow
肾盂检查法/腎盂檢視法　pelvoscopy
肾盂静脉反流/腎盂靜脈反流　pyelovenous backflow
肾盂静脉曲张/腎盂靜脈曲張　varix of pelvis
肾盂静脉炎/腎盂靜脈炎　pyelophlebitis
肾盂扩张/腎盂擴張　pyelectasis
肾盂淋巴反流/腎盂淋巴反流　pyelolymphatic backflow

肾盂鳞状细胞癌/腎盂鱗狀細胞癌 squamous cell carcinoma of renal pelvis
肾盂毛细血管扩张症/腎盂毛細血管擴張症 telangiectasis of renal pelvis
肾盂膀胱吻合术/腎盂膀胱造口吻合術 pyelocystostomosis
肾盂膀胱炎/腎盂膀胱炎 pyelocystitis
肾盂切开取石术/腎盂切開取石術 pyelolithotomy
肾盂切开术/腎盂切開術 pyelotomy
肾盂乳头状癌/腎盂乳頭狀癌 papillary carcinoma of renal pelvis
肾盂乳头状瘤/腎盂乳頭狀瘤 papilloma of renal pelvis
肾盂上皮细胞癌/腎盂上皮細胞癌 renal pelvis epithelioma
肾盂肾病/腎盂腎病 pyelonephrosis
肾盂肾炎/腎盂腎炎 pyelonephritis
肾盂肾盏扩张/腎盂腎盞擴張 pyelocaliectasis
肾盂输尿管成形术/腎盂輸尿管造形術 pyeloureteroplasty
肾盂输尿管扩张/腎盂輸尿管擴張 pyeloureterectasis
肾盂输尿管连接部狭窄/腎盂輸尿管連接部狹窄 stricture of pyeloureteric junction
肾盂输尿管松解术/腎盂輸尿管鬆解術 pelvioureterolysis
肾盂输尿管造影[术]/腎盂輸尿管造影術 pyeloureterography
肾盂腺癌/腎盂腺癌 pyeloadenocarcinoma
肾盂血管瘤/腎盂血管瘤 hemangioma of renal pelvis
肾盂压测定/腎盂壓測定 Whitaker test
肾盂炎/腎盂炎 pyelitis
肾盂移行细胞癌/腎盂移行細胞癌 transitional cell carcinoma of renal pelvis
肾盂源性囊肿/腎盂源性囊腫 pyelogenic cyst
肾盂造口术/腎盂造口術 pelviostomy
肾盂造瘘术/腎盂造瘺術，腎盂造口術 pyelostomy
肾盂造影术/腎盂造影術 pyelography
肾盂折术/腎盂折疊術 pyeloplication
肾盂肿瘤/腎盂腫瘤 tumor of renal pelvis
肾郁/腎鬱 stagnancy pattern of kidney qi
肾圆虫/腎圓蟲 Strongylus renalis
肾脏病学/腎病學 nephrology
肾脏冲击诊/腎臟衝擊診 kidney punch
肾脏毒理学/腎臟毒理學 nephrotoxicology
肾脏感染性疾病/腎臟感染性疾病 renal infectious diseases

肾脏皮质/腎臟皮質 cortical substance of kidney
肾脏相互平衡/腎臟相互平衡 renal counterbalance
肾脏用药/腎臟用藥 renal agents
肾造瘘术/腎造瘺術，腎造口術 nephrostomy
肾盏/腎盞 renal calice, kidney calice
肾盏积水/腎盞積水 hydrocalycosis
肾盏结核/腎盞結核 tuberculosis of calyx
肾盏静脉瘘/腎盞靜脈瘺 calyceal venous fistula
肾盏扩张/腎盞擴張 caliectasis
肾盏囊肿/腎盞囊腫 pyelogenic renal cyst
肾盏憩室/腎盞憩室 calyceal diverticulum
肾盏切除术/腎盞切除術 calicectomy
肾真菌病/腎真菌病 renal fungous disease
肾之府/腎之府 house of kidney
肾支/腎支 renal branches
肾脂肪瘤/腎脂肪瘤 lipoma of kidney
肾脂肪囊/腎脂肪囊 adeps renis
肾脂肪肉瘤/腎脂肪肉瘤 liposarcoma of kidney
肾直小管/腎直小管 Bellini fistula
肾指数/腎指數 renal index
肾志恐/腎志恐 kidney being associated with fear
肾肿瘤/腎腫瘤 kidney neoplasms
肾周吹气法/腎周圍灌氣法 perirenal insufflation
肾周积水/腎周積水 hydroperinephrosis
肾周囊肿/腎周囊腫 perinephric cyst
肾周脓肿/腎周膿腫 perinephric abscess
肾周血肿/腎周血腫 perirenal hematoma
肾周炎/腎周炎 perinephritis
肾轴性旋转/腎軸性旋轉 axial rotation of kidney
肾主封藏/腎主封藏 kidney governing storage
肾主骨/腎主骨 kidney dominating bone, kidney governing bone
肾主纳气/腎主納氣 kidney governing inspiration
肾主生殖/腎主生殖 kidney governing reproduction
肾主水液/腎主水液 kidney governing water metabolism
肾柱/腎柱 renal column
肾锥体/腎錐體 renal pyramid, pyramid of kidney
肾著/腎著 affection of kidney by cold-dampness, kidney disorder with cold painful waist
肾子/腎子 testicle and epididymis
肾子宫内膜异位症/腎子宫内膜異位症 endometriosis of kidney
肾紫癜/腎[型]紫癜 purpura of kidney, renal purpura
肾自截/腎自截 autonephrectomy
肾综合征出血热/腎綜合徵出血熱 hemorrhagic fever with renal syndrome

胂凡纳明/阿斯凡納明　arsphenamine
胂凡纳明钠/阿斯凡納明鈉　sodiarsphenamine
胂基水杨酸/胂基水楊酸　arsinosalicylic acid
胂硫醇/胂硫醇　arsthinol
胂酸/胂酸　arsonic acid
渗出/滲出　effusion
渗出物/滲出物,滲[出]液　exudate
渗出性出血/滲出性出血　exudative hemorrhage
渗出性多形红斑/滲出性多形性紅斑　erythema multiforme exudativum
渗出性关节炎/滲出性關節炎　exudative arthritis
渗出性滑膜炎/滲出性滑膜炎　synovitis effusionis
渗出性结核/滲出性結核　exudative tuberculosis
渗出性盘状苔藓样皮肤病/滲出性盤狀苔蘚樣皮膚病　exudative discoid and lichenoid dermatosis
渗出性肾炎/滲出性腎炎　exudative nephritis
渗出性视网膜脱离/滲出性視網膜脫離　exudative detachment of retina
渗出性心包炎/滲出性心包炎　effusive pericarditis
渗出性咽峡炎/滲出性咽峽炎　exudative angina
渗出性炎/滲出性炎　exudative inflammation
渗出液/滲出液　transudate
渗出液囊肿/滲出液囊腫　exudation cyst
渗漏/滲漏　leak
渗漏突变体/滲漏突變體　leaky mutant
渗漏突变株/滲漏突變株　leaky mutant
渗滤法/滲瀘法　percolation
渗脓/滲膿　pyecchysis
渗湿化痰/滲濕化痰　eliminating dampness and resolving phlegm
渗湿利水/滲濕利水　eliminating dampness and diuresis
渗透/滲透　permeation
渗透脆性/滲透脆性　osmotic fragility
渗透当量/滲透當量　osmotic equivalent
渗透疗法/滲透療法,高滲療法　osmotherapy
渗透麻醉法/滲透麻醉法　permeation anesthesia
渗透膜/滲透膜　osmotic membrane
渗透梯度/滲透梯度　osmotic gradient
渗透调节/滲透調節　osmoregulation
渗透性常数/滲透性常數　permeability constant
渗透性过高/滲透性過高　hyperpermeability
渗透性利尿/滲透性利尿　osmotic diuresis
渗透性利尿药/滲透性利尿藥　osmotic diuretics
渗透性休克/滲透性休克　osmotic shock
渗透压/滲透壓　osmotic pressure
渗透压浓度/滲透壓濃度　osmolar concentration
渗透[作用]/滲透[作用]　osmosis

渗压调节/滲壓調節,變滲透壓作用　poikilosmosis
渗压性利尿药/滲壓性利尿藥　osmotic diuretic
渗液性心包炎/滲液性心包炎　pericarditis with effusion
渗液性肿瘤/滲液性腫瘤　oozing tumor
葚孢菌素类/葚孢菌素類　sporidesmins
升/升　sheng
升部/昇部　ascending part
升动脉/昇動脈　ascending artery
升汞/昇汞,氯化汞,二氯化汞　mercuric chloride
升华/昇華　sublimation
升华硫/昇華硫,硫磺華　flowers of sulfur
升华樟脑/昇華樟腦,樟腦華　flowers of camphor
升降出入/昇降出入　ascending, descending, exiting and entering
升降浮沉/昇降浮沈　ascending and descending, floating and sinking
升结肠/昇結腸　ascending colon
升结肠系膜/昇結腸繫膜　ascending mesocolon, mesentery of ascending part of colon
升结肠周炎/昇結腸周圍炎　pericolitis dextra
升麻/升麻　largetrifoliolious bugbane rhizome
升麻葛根汤/升麻葛根湯　shengma gegen decoction
升线二波/昇線二波　anadicrotic wave
升线二波脉/昇線二波脈　anadicrotic pulse
升线三波脉/昇線三波脈　anatricrotic pulse
升线一波/昇線一波,昇線小隆波　anacrotic wave
升线一波脉/昇線一波脈,昇線小隆脈　anacrotic pulse
升压利尿药/昇壓利尿劑　hemopiesic diuretic
升支/昇支　ascending branch, ascending ramus
升支骨内植入体/昇支骨内植入體　ramus endosseous implant
升主动脉/昇主動脈　ascending aorta
生产/生產　manufacture
生成障碍/生成障礙　dyspoiesis
生存饮食/生存飲食　subsistence diet
生存者/生存者　existent
生地黄/生地黃　unprocessed rehmannia root
生发层/生髮層　stratum germinativum
生发剂/生髮劑　trichogen
生发细胞/生髮細胞　germinal cell
生发中心/生髮中心　germinal center
[生发中心]暗区/暗區　dark region
[生发中心]明区/亮區　light region
生骨节/生骨節　sclerotome
生后肾原基/生後腎原基　metanephrogenic blastema
生化变株/生化變株　biochemical mutant

生化毒理学/生化毒理學　biochemical toxicology
生化汤/生化湯　shenghua decoction
生化现象/生化現象　biochemical phenomena
生化药物/生化藥物　biochemical drug
生化药学/生化藥學　biochemical pharmacy
生化遗传学/生化遺傳學　biochemical genetics
生活变动事件/生活變動事件　life change event
生活方式/生活方式　life style
生活力缺乏性变性/生活力缺乏性變性　abiotrophic degeneration
生活力缺损/生活力缺損　abiatrophy
生活事件量表/生活事件量表　life event scale
生[活]体抵抗力/生體抵抗力　vital resistance
生活污水/生活汙水,民生汙水　domestic sewage
生活质量/生活品質　quality of life
生活周期/生命週期　life cycle
生机论/生機論　vitalism
生肌定痛/生肌定痛　promoting granulation and relieving pain
生肌节/生肌節　myotome
生肌收口/生肌收口　promoting granulation and wound healing
生肌收口药/生肌收口藥　myogenic and wound-healing medicine
生肌玉红膏/生肌玉紅膏　shengji yuhong plaster
生姜/生薑　fresh ginger
生角质区/生角質區　keratogenous zone
生精上皮/生精上皮　seminiferous epithelium, spermatogenic epithelium
生精上皮周期/生精上皮週期　cycle of seminiferous epithelium
生精细胞/生精細胞　spermatogenic cell
生精小管/生精小管,生精細管　seminiferous tubule
生理暗点/生理暗點　physiologic scotoma
生理功能测定/生理機能測定　physiometry
生理过程/生理過程　physiological processes
生理过程恒定/生理過程恆定　homeorrhesis
生理过敏性/生理性過敏　physiologic allergy
生理𬌗/生理𬌗　physiologic occlusion
生理化学/生理化學　physiochemistry
生理解毒剂/生理性解毒藥　physiological antidote
生理零度/生理零度　physiologic zero
生理盲点/生理盲點　physiological blind spot
生理盲点外露/生理盲點外露　baring of physiological blind spot
生理器官/生理器官　biorgan
生理生化特征/生理生化特徵　physiological and biochemical property
生理适应性/生理適應性　physiological adaption
生理无效腔/生理無效區,生理死腔　physiological dead space
生理无效腔占潮气量比值/生理無效腔占潮氣量比值　ratio of physiological dead space to tidal volume
生理吸收/生理吸收　physiological absorption
生理习惯/生理習慣　physiologic habit
生理性白细胞增多/生理性白血球增多　physiologic leukocytosis
生理性低丙种球蛋白血症/生理性丙型血球蛋白過少　physiologic hypogammaglobulinemia
生理性肥大/生理性肥大　physiologic hypertrophy
生理性钙化/生理性鈣化　physiologic calcification
生理性呼吸/生理性呼吸　physiologic respiration
生理性黄疸/生理性黃疸　physiologic jaundice
生理性记忆/生理性記憶　physiological memory
生理性拮抗/生理性拮抗　physiological antagonism
生理性配合禁忌/生理性配合禁忌　physiologic incompatibility
生理性贫血/生理性貧血　physiologic anemia
生理性鞣酸/生理性鞣酸　physiologic tannin
生理性缩复环/生理性縮複環　physiologic retraction ring
生理性萎缩/生理性萎縮　physiological atrophy
生理性新生血管化/生理性新生血管化　physiologic neovascularization
生理性眼球震颤/生理性眼球震顫,生理性眼震　physiological nystagmus
生理性眼震/生理性眼震,生理性眼球震顫　physiological nystagmus
生理学/生理學　physiology
生理学家/生理學家　physiologist
生理学监测/生理學監測　physiologic monitoring
生理学模式识别/生理學模式識別　physiological pattern recognition
生理学适应/生理學適應　physiological adaptation
生理盐溶液/生理鹽溶液　normal salt solution
生理盐水/生理鹽水　physiological sodium solution
生淋巴的/產生淋巴的　lymphogenous
生脉散/生脈散　shengmai powder
生脉注射液/生脈注射液　shengmai injections
生毛基/生毛基　germinal hair matrix
生命/生命　life
生命保障系统/生命保障系統　life support systems
生命点/生命點　vital point
生命价值/生命價值　value of life
生命三支柱/生命三要器　tripod of life

生命特征/生命徵象　vital sign
生命统计/生命統計　vital statistics
生命学/生命學　bionomy, biotics
生命支援疗法/生命支援療法　life support care
生命周期各时期/生命週期各時期　life cycle stages
生命自生/生命自生　biopoiesis
生皮肌节/生皮肌節　dermomyotome
生皮节/生皮節　dermatome
生氰作用/生氰作用,氰之生成　cyanogenesis
生热力/生熱力,產熱力　caloricity
生热学/生熱學,產生熱原理論　thermogenics
生乳热/生乳熱,產乳熱　galactopyra
生色化合物/生色化合物　chromogenic compounds
生色团/生色團　chromophore
生晒参/生曬參　dried fresh ginseng
生肾节/生腎節　nephromere, nephrotome
生肾索/生腎索　nephrogenic cord
生石灰/生石灰　quicklime
生食/生食　omophagia
生死检定法/生死檢定法,生死判驗法　bioscopy
生态毒理学/生態毒理學　ecotoxicology
生态体系/生態系[統]　ecological system, ecosystem
生态学/生態學　ecology
生态遗传学/生態遺傳學　ecogenetics
生痰/生痰　sputum crudum
生体毒素/生體毒素　biotoxin
生甜味基/生甜味基　gluciphore
生铁落饮/生鐵落飲　pig iron flakes drink, shengtieluo drink
生酮抗生酮比率/生酮抗生酮比率　ketogenic-antiketogenic ratio
生酮膳食/生酮飲食　ketogenic diet
生酮作用/酮體生成,酮產生　ketogenesis
生统遗传学/生化統計遺傳學　biometrical genetics
生物胺类/生物胺類　biogenic amines
生物胺受体/生物胺受體　biogenic amine receptor
生物半衰期/生物半衰期　biological half-life
生物瓣/生物瓣　bioprosthetic valve
生物标本库/生物標本庫　biological specimen bank
生物测定/生物測定　bioassay
生物传感技术/生物傳感技術　biosensing techniques
生物催化剂/生物催化劑,酵素　biocatalyst
生物大分子/生物大分子　biomacromolecule
生物等效性/生物等效性　bioequivalence
生物地理学/生物地理學　biogeography
生物电/生物電　bioelectricity
生物电能源/生物電能源　bioelectric energy sources
生物电位/生物電位　bioelectric potential

生物电子等排[体]/生物電子等排體　bioisostere
生物电子学/生物電子學　bioelectronics
生物蝶呤/生物喋呤　biopterin
生物毒/生物毒　biotoxin
生物毒理学/生物毒理學　biotoxicology
生物多样性/生物多樣性　biodiversity
生物发生律/生物發生律　biogenetic law
生物反应器/生物反應器　bioreactors
生物反应修饰剂/生物反應修飾劑　biological response modifier
生物分子/生物分子　biomolecule
生物分子核磁共振/生物分子核磁共振　biomolecular nuclear magnetic resonance
生物敷料/生物敷料　biologic dressing, biological dressing
生物个体/生物個體,生命體　bion
生物功能增强技术/生物功能增強技術　biomedical enhancement
生物合成/生物合成　biosynthesis
生物合成基因克隆/生物合成基因克隆　biosynthesis gene clone
生物合成途径/生物合成途徑　biosynthesis pathway, biosynthetic pathway
生物化学回馈/生物化學回饋　biochemical feedback
生物化学形态学/生化形態學　biochemorphology
生物化学性转移/生化學性轉移　biochemical metastasis
生物化学种族指数/生物化學種族指數　biochemical racial index
生物回馈/生物回饋　biofeedback
生物回馈疗法/生物回饋療法　biofeedback therapy
生物活性/生物活性　biological activity
生物活性物质/生物活性物質　bioactive substance
生物计/生物計　biometer
生物技术/生物技術法　biotechnology
生物假体/生物假體　bioprosthesis
生物检定/生物檢定　bioassay, biological identification
生物碱/生物鹼　alkaloid
生物碱测定法/生物鹼測定　alkalometry
生物碱类/生物鹼類　alkaloids
生物降解/生物降解,生物分解　biodegradation
生物胶体/生物膠體,生物膠質　biocolloid
生物节律/生物節律　biological rhythm
生物进化/生物進化　organic evolution
生物精神病学/生物精神病學　biological psychiatry
生物聚合物/生物聚合物,生體聚合物　biopolymer
生物可利用率/生體可利用率　bioavailability

生物克隆/生物克隆　organism cloning
生物恐怖/生物恐怖　bioterrorism
生物类黄酮/生物類黃酮　bioflavonoid
生物利用度/生物利用度　bioavailability, biological availability
生物量/生物量　biomass
生物疗法/生物療法　biological therapy
生物伦理问题/生物倫理問題　bioethical issues
生物伦理学/生物倫理學　bioethics
生物免疫抑制/生物免疫抑制　biological immunosuppression
生物膜/生物膜　biomembrane, biofilm
[生物膜]胞质片/[生物膜]胞質片　protoplasmic leaflet of biomembrane
[生物膜]外片/[生物膜]外片　extracellular leaflet of biomembrane
生物区系/生物區系,生物群　biota
生物染色剂/生物染色劑　biological dye, biological stain
生物渗透/生物滲透　biosmosis
生物衰老学/生物衰老學　catachronobiology
生物死亡/生物死亡　biological death
生物素/生物素　biotin
生物素标记探针/生物素標記探針　biotinylated probe
生物素酶/生物素酶　biotinidase
生物素酶缺乏/生物素酶缺乏　biotinidase deficiency
生物陶瓷/生物陶瓷　bioceramic
生物体 X 射线照相术/生物體 X 射線照相術　bioroentgenography
生物吞噬作用/生物吞噬作用　biophagism
生物卫星/生物衛星　biosatellite
生物无机化学/生物無機化學　bioinorganic chemistry
生物相容性/生物相容性　biocompatibility
生物相容性包被物质/生物相容性包被物質　biocompatible coated material
生物相容性材料/生物相容性材料　biocompatible material
生物效价测定/生物效價測定　estimation of biological potency
生物心理社会模式/生物心理社會模式　biopsychosocial model
生物[性]发光/生物發光　bioluminescence
生物[性]分解/生物分解,經生物崩解　biolysis
生物性溶血/生物性溶血　biologic hemolysis
生物性损伤/生物性損傷　biological injury
生物学保存/生物學保存　biological preservation

生物学变态/生物學變態　biological metamorphosis
生物学标记/生物學標記　biological markers
生物学价/生物學價,抗體生物價　biologic valence
生物学媒介/生物學媒介,生物性病媒　biological vector
生物学模型/生物學模型　biological models
生物学适应/生物學適應　biological adaptation
生物学特异性/生物學特異性,生物學專一性　biological specificity
生物学现象/生物學現象　biological phenomena
生物学诊断/生物學診斷　biological diagnosis
生物学肿瘤标记/生物學腫瘤標記　biological tumor markers
生物氧化/生物氧化　biological oxidation
生物药剂学/生物藥劑學　biopharmaceutics
生物医学/生物醫學　biomedicine
生物医学工程/生物醫學工程　biomedical engineering
生物医学技术/生物醫學技術　biomedical technology
生物医学技术评估/生物醫學技術評估　biomedical technology assessment
生物医学研究/生物醫學研究　biomedical research
生物因子/生物因子　biological factor
生物应答调节剂/生物應答調節劑　biological response modifier
生物有机化学/生物有機化學　bioorganic chemistry
生物元素/生物元素　bioelement
生物源单胺类/生物源單胺類　biogenic monoamines
生物源多胺类/生物源多胺類　biogenic polyamines
生物源性疾病/生物[源]性疾病,生物源病　bionosis
生物战/生物戰　biological warfare
生物指示剂/生物指示劑　biological indicator
生物制品/生物製品　biological product
生物致毒作用/生體中毒,生體致毒　biotoxication
生物钟/生物鐘　biological clock
生物钟紊乱/生物鐘紊亂　chronobiology disorder
生物转化/生物轉化　biotransformation
生物转运/生物轉運　biological transport
生心板/生心板　cardiogenic plate
生心区/生心區　cardiogenic area
生心中胚层/生心中胚層　cardiogenic mesoderm
生锈/生銹　rusting
生血管细胞团/生血管細胞團,血管生成性細胞叢　angiogenic cell cluster
生牙质纤维/生牙質纖維,牙質發生纖維,牙本質原纖維　dentinogenic fiber
生药/生藥　crude drug
生药拉丁名/生藥拉丁名　Latin name of crude drug

生药学/生藥學 pharmacognosy
生育不能/生育不能 impotentia generandi
生育酚/生育酚,維生素 E tocopherol
α-生育酚/α-生育酚 alpha-tocopherol
生育酚类/生育酚類 tocopherols
生育间隔/生育間隔 birth interval
生育力/生育力 fertility
生育三烯酚类/生育三烯酚類 tocotrienols
生育史/生育史 reproductive history
生育指数/生育指數 fertility index
生源/生源,生物體 biogen
生源合成/生源合成 biogenetic synthesis
生源说/生源説 biogenesis
生长/生長 growth
生长发育/生長發育 growth and development
生长激素/生長激素 growth hormone
生长激素类/生長激素類 growth hormones
生长激素瘤/生長激素瘤 somatotropinoma
生长激素缺乏性侏儒症/生長激素缺乏性侏儒症 growth hormone deficiency dwarfism
生长激素释放激素/生長激素釋放激素 growth hormone-releasing hormone
生长激素释放素试验/生長激素釋放素試驗 growth hormone-releasing hormone test
生长激素细胞/生長激素分泌細胞 somatotroph, STH cell
生长激素腺瘤/生長激素腺瘤 growth hormone adenoma
生长卵泡/生長卵泡 growing follicle
生长面/生長面 growth plate
生长谱/生長譜,[細菌]發育圖 auxanogram
生长期/生長期 trophophase
生长期秃/生長期秃 anagen alopecia
生长曲线/生長曲線,生長過程圖 auxodrome
生长调节素类/生長調節素類 somatomedins
生长调节素受体/生長調節素受體 somatomedin receptor
生长物质/生長物質 growth substance
生长型/生長型 vegetative form
生长抑素/生長抑素,生長激素釋放抑制因子 somatostatin
生长抑素瘤/體抑素瘤 somatostatinoma
生长抑素受体/生長抑素受體 somatostatin receptor
生长抑制物/生長抑制物 growth inhibitor
生长因子/生長因子,生長因數 growth factor
生长因子受体/生長因子受體 growth factor receptor
生长预测/生長預測 growth prediction

生长晕/生長暈,贅生物 outgrowth
生长障碍/生長障礙 vegetative disorder
生长锥/生長錐 growth cone
生之本/生之本 root of life
生汁兑入/生汁兑入 mix with fresh juice
生殖/生殖,繁殖 reproduction
生殖本能/生殖本能 genesic sense, reproductive sense
生殖道/生殖道 genital tract
生殖道绝育/生殖道絶育 reproductive sterilization
生殖毒理学/生殖毒理學 reproductive toxicology
生殖毒性/生殖毒性 preconception injuries
生殖股区/生殖腹股區域 genitocrural region
生殖工程/生殖工程 reproduction engineering
生殖沟/生殖溝 genital groove
生殖股神经/生殖股神經 genitofemoral nerve
生殖管/生殖管 genital duct
生殖会阴缝/生殖會陰縫 genitoperineal raphe
生殖技术/生殖技術 reproductive technique
生殖健康服务/生殖健康服務 reproductive health service
生殖结节/生殖結節 genital tubercle, cloacal tubercle
生殖控制药/生殖控制藥 reproductive control agents
生殖力障碍/生殖力障礙 dysgenesia
生殖裂/生殖裂 genital cleft
生殖隆起/生殖隆起 genital swelling
生殖泌尿道/泌尿生殖道 genitourinary tract
生殖免疫学/生殖免疫學 reproductive immunology
生殖尿道瘘/生殖尿道瘻 genitourinary fistula
生殖期精神病/生殖期精神病 generative psychosis
生殖器/生殖器 genitalia
生殖器成形术/生殖器成形術,生殖器整形術 genitoplasty
生殖器发育不良/生殖器發育不良 dysgenitalism
生殖器功能障碍/生殖器功能障礙 dysgenesis
生殖器官/生殖器官 genital organ
生殖器结核/生殖器結核 genital tuberculosis
生殖器密螺旋体/生殖器螺旋體 Treponema genitalis
生殖器疱疹/生殖器皰疹 herpes genitalis
生殖器支原体/生殖器支原體 Mycoplasma genitalium
生殖器肿大/生殖器腫大 genital swelling
生殖器状头畸胎/生殖器狀頭畸胎 aedoeocephalus
生殖权/生殖權 reproductive rights
生殖染色质/生殖染色質 sporetia

生殖上皮/生殖上皮 germinal epithelium
生殖索/生殖索,精索 genital cord
生殖突/生殖突 sexual swelling
生殖系统/生殖系統 reproductive system
生殖细胞/生殖細胞 genital cell, germ cell
生殖细胞瘤/生殖細胞瘤,胚細胞瘤 germinoma
生殖细胞索/性索 sex cords
生殖细胞系突变/生殖細胞系突變 germline mutation
生殖腺/生殖腺,性腺 gonad
生殖腺发生/生殖腺發生 gonadogenesis
生殖腺发育不全/性腺發育不良,生殖器發育不全 gonadal dysgenesis
生殖腺功能缺乏/生殖機能缺乏 agenitalism
生殖[腺]嵴/生殖嵴 gonadal ridge
生殖腺索/生殖腺索 gonadal cord
生殖小核/生殖小核 germline micronucleus
生殖小体/生殖小體 genital corpuscle
生殖行为/生殖行爲 reproductive behavior
生殖学/生殖學 genesiology
生殖医学/生殖醫學 reproductive medicine
生殖原肠系膜/生殖原腸繫膜 gonadial mesentery
生殖褶/生殖褶,生殖皺襞 genital fold
生殖支/生殖支 genital branch
生殖制止[法]/生殖制止,生殖阻遏 genesistasis
生殖周期/生殖週期 reproductive cycle
声襞/聲襞,聲帶 vocal fold
声波/聲波 sonic wave
声波谱图术/聲波譜圖術 sound spectrography
声波照相术/聲波照相術,音波攝影術 phonophotography
声创伤/聲創傷 acoustic trauma
声刺激/聲刺激 acoustic stimulation
声带/聲帶 vocal cord
声带固定术/聲帶固定術 cordopexy
声带肌/聲帶肌 vocal muscle
声带肌炎/聲帶肌炎,聲帶炎 myochorditis
声带接触性溃疡/聲帶接觸性潰瘍 contact ulcer of vocal cord
声带麻痹/聲帶麻痺 vocal cord paralysis
声带切除术/索帶切除術 cordectomy
声带突/聲帶突 vocal process
声带外移固定术/聲帶外移固定術 lateral cordopexy
声带息肉/聲帶息肉 polyp of vocal cord
声带小结/聲帶小節,聲帶結節 vocal nodule
声导抗/聲導抗 acoustic immitance
声定位/聲定位 sound localization

声反射松弛试验/聲反射鬆弛試驗 acoustic reflex relaxation test
声感受器/感音體,受音體 phonoreceptor
声门/聲門 glottis
声门测量术/聲門測量術 glottography
声门结核/聲門結核 tuberculosis of glottides
声门痉挛/聲門痙攣 glottic spasm
声门裂/聲門裂 fissure of glottis
声门裂测量计/聲門裂測量器 schistometer
声门区/聲[門]區 vocal area
声门上喉癌/聲門上喉癌 supraglottic carcinoma
声门上喉切除术/聲門上喉切除術 supraglottic laryngectomy
声门水肿/聲門水腫 glottic edema
声门图/聲門圖 glottogram
声门下喉癌/聲門下喉癌 subglottic carcinoma
声门下喉炎/聲門下喉炎 subglottic laryngitis
声门下腔/聲門下腔 infraglottic cavity
声门下水肿/喉下水腫 subglottic edema
声门下狭窄/聲門下狭窄 subglottic stenosis
声门型喉癌/聲門型喉癌 glottic carcinoma
声谱图/聲譜圖 sound spectrogram
声强度计/聲強度計 phonometer
声全息照相术/聲全息照相術,傳聲全方位照相術 acoustical holography
声韧带/聲韌帶 vocal ligament
声弱/聲[音低]弱 leptophonia
声弱症/聲弱症 microphonia
声色联觉/聲色聯覺,聞聲睹色 echophotony
声嗄/聲嗄,嘶啞 hoarseness
声嘶/聲嘶,聲嗄 light hoarseness, hoarseness, trachyphonia
声嘶失音按摩法/聲嘶失音按摩法 trachyphonia and aphonia massage
声探子/聲探子 drum probe
声图/聲圖 phonogram
声响过弱/聲響過弱,聲音過弱 hypophonesis
声学显微镜检查/聲學顯微鏡檢查 acoustic microscopy
声音/聲音 sound
声音变调/聲音變化,輕失音症 paraphonia
声音干扰/聲音干擾 interference of sound
声震损伤/聲震損傷 sound injury
声阻抗试验/聲阻抗試驗 acoustic impedance tests
圣多里尼环状括约肌/聖多里尼環狀括約肌 circular Santorini sphincter muscle
圣菲利波综合征/聖菲利波症候群 Sanfilippo syndrome

圣济经/聖濟經　Classic of Holy Benevolence
圣济总录/聖濟總錄　General Records of Holy Universal Relief
圣路易斯脑炎/聖路易斯腦炎　St. Louis encephalitis
圣路易斯脑炎病毒/聖路易斯腦炎病毒　St. Louis encephalitis virus
圣托里尼韧带/聖托里尼氏韌帶　Santorini ligament
剩余碱水解法/剩餘鹼水解法　residual basic hydrolysis method
剩余精核/剩餘精核,額外精核　merocyte
剩余尿/剩餘尿　residual urine
剩余亲和力/剩餘親合勢　residual affinity
剩余视野/剩餘視野　surplus field
尸阿托品/肉阿托品　ptomatropine
尸胺/屍毒　cadaverine
尸斑/屍斑　livor mortis
尸毒碱/屍毒鹼　pathomaine
尸毒性疣/剖屍結節　dissection tubercle
尸反应/屍反應　cadaveric reaction
尸碱血/屍鹼血　ptomainemia
尸碱中毒/屍鹼中毒　ptomainotoxism
尸僵/屍僵　postmortem rigidity, rigor mortis
尸厥/屍厥　cadaverous syncope
尸蜡/屍蠟　adipocere
尸冷/屍寒　algor mortis
尸体/屍體　cadaver
尸体保存/屍體保存,屍體塗油防腐法,制屍法　embalming
尸体测量器/屍體測定器　necrometer
尸体供者/屍體供者　cadaver donor
尸体解剖/屍體解剖　autopsy
尸体痉挛/屍體痙攣　cadaveric spasm
尸体面模/屍體面模　death mask
尸体皮/屍體皮　cadaver skin
尸体脾移植/屍體脾移植　cadaveric spleen transplantation
尸体剖检/屍體檢驗,驗屍　ptomatopsia
尸体肾移植/屍體腎移植　cadaveric renal transplantation
失弛缓症/失弛緩症,弛緩不能　achalasia
失蛋白性肠病/失蛋白性腸病　protein-losing enteropathy
失读[症]/失讀症　alexia
失活/失活　inactivation
失活牙/失活牙　devital tooth
失活中心/失活中心　inactivation center
失禁/失禁　incontinentia
失禁垫/失禁墊　incontinence pad
失精/失精　psychosomatic disease due to social stress
失精家/失精家　person suffering from seminal loss
失眠/失眠　wakefulness, insomnia
失眠患者/失眠患者　insomniac
失眠[症]/失眠[症]　insomnia
失母爱/失母愛　maternal deprivation
失母爱综合征/失母愛症候群　maternal deprivation syndrome
失热/失熱　loss of heat
失认症/失認症,認識不能,識別不能　agnosia
失荣/失榮　cervical carcinoma with cachexia, cervical malignancy with cachexia
失荣•气血两虚证/失榮•氣血兩虛證　cervical malignancy with cachexia with pattern of qi-blood deficiency
失荣•痰毒瘀结证/失榮•痰毒瘀結證　cervical malignancy with cachexia with phlegm-toxin-stasis intermingling pattern
失荣•痰气互结证/失榮•痰氣互結證　cervical malignancy with cachexia with pattern of intermingled phlegm and qi
失荣•瘀毒化热证/失榮•瘀毒化熱證　cervical malignancy with cachexia with pattern of stasis-toxin transforming into heat
失神/失神　loss of vitality
失神发作/失神發作　absence seizure
失神性癫痫/失神性癲癇　absence epilepsy
失声/失音　aphonia
失算[症]/失算[症],計算力缺失,計算不能　acalculia
失笑散/失笑散　shixiao powder
失效期/失效期　expiration date
失写性失语/失寫性失語　graphomotor aphasia
失写症/失寫症,書寫不能　agraphia
失血/失血　loss of blood
失盐性肾病/失鹽性腎病　salt-losing nephropathy
失盐性肾炎/失鹽性腎炎　salt-losing nephritis
失音/失音　loss of voice
失用性弱视/失用性弱視　disuse amblyopia
失用性萎缩/失用性萎縮　disuse atrophy
失用症/失用症　apraxia
失语韵[症]/語調缺失　aprosody
失语症/失語症　alogia
失语症学/失語症學　aphasiology
失乐感[症]/失樂感[症],旋律辨識障礙症　amusia
失张力发作/失張力發作,弛緩性癲癇發作　atonic seizure

失重模拟/失重模擬　weightlessness simulation
虱/蝨　lice
虱病/蝨病　pediculosis
虱草子碱/滅蝨草素　staphisagrine
虱疮/蝨瘡　louse sting
虱寄生/蝨寄生　lice infestations
虱螨/蝨蟎　straw mite
虱目/蝨目　Anoplura
虱属/蝨屬　Pediculus
虱蝇科/蝨蠅科　Hippoboscidae
虱状恙虫/蝨狀恙蟲　louse mite
狮弓蛔线虫/獅蛔蟲　Toxascaris leonina
狮面/獅面麻風　leontiasis
施蒂默病/施蒂默病　Stühmer disease
施莱希溶液/施萊希溶液　Schleich solution
施勒德综合征/施勒德症候群　Schroeder syndrome
施雷格线/施雷格線，齒廓線　Schreger line
施利希特试验/施利希特試驗　Schlichter test
施罗德病/施羅德病　Schroeder disease
施密特饮食/施密特飲食　Schmidt diet
施密特综合征/施密特症候群　Schmidt syndrome
施莫尔黄疸/夏莫爾氏黃疸　Schmorl jaundice
施莫尔结节/夏莫爾結節　Schmorl nodules
施莫尔体/夏莫爾體　Schmorl body
施虐狂/施虐狂　sadism
施虐受虐狂/施虐受虐狂　sadomasochism
施佩曲线/施佩曲線　curve of Spee
施皮格勒-芬特类肉瘤/施皮格勒-芬特類肉瘤　Spiegler-Fendt sarcoid
施皮格勒瘤/施皮格勒瘤　Spiegler tumor
施氏针/施氏針　Steinmann pin
施特恩贝格巨细胞/施特恩貝格巨細胞　Sternberg giant cell
施特劳斯针/施特勞斯針　Strauss needle
施特吕姆佩尔病/施特吕姆佩爾病　Strümpell disease
施特罗迈尔夹/施特羅邁爾夾板　Stromeyer splint
施滕德尔皿/施滕德爾皿　Stender dish
施图姆圆锥/施圖姆圓錐　Sturm conoid
施瓦巴赫试验/施瓦巴赫試驗　Schwabach test
施瓦茨曼现象/施瓦茲曼現象　Schwartzmann phenomenon
施万细胞/施萬細胞　Schwann cell
施万细胞瘤/施萬細胞瘤　Schwann cell tumor
施万增生/施萬增生　Schwann hyperplasia
施韦宁格尔-布齐型斑状萎缩/施韋寧格爾-布齊型斑塊萎縮　Schweninger-Buzzi type macular atrophy
施行巴[斯德]氏消毒/施行巴[斯德]氏消毒　pasteurize
施行灌肠/施行灌腸　clysterize
湿布包裹法/濕布包裹法　wet pack
湿疮/濕瘡，濕疹　eczema
湿疮·风热蕴肤证/濕瘡·風熱蘊膚證　eczema with pattern of wind-heat amassing in skin
湿疮·脾虚湿困证/濕瘡·脾虛濕困證　eczema with pattern of spleen deficiency and dampness retention
湿疮·湿热浸淫证/濕瘡·濕熱浸淫證　eczema with dampness-heat inundation pattern
湿疮·血虚风燥证/濕瘡·血虛風燥證　eczema with pattern of wind-dryness due to blood deficiency
湿单浴/濕單浴　sheet bath
湿痘/濕痘　wetpox
湿毒蕴结证/濕毒蘊結證　pattern of accumulated dampness-toxicity
湿度/濕度　humidity
湿度测定法/濕度測定法，測濕法　hygrometry
湿度计/濕度計　hygrometer
湿度记录器/濕度記錄器　hygrograph
湿肺/濕肺　wet lung
湿敷/濕敷　wet compress
湿敷疗法/濕敷療法　moisten compress therapy
湿敷料/濕敷料　moist dressing
湿化疗法/濕化療法　humidity therapy
湿化祛痰/濕化祛痰　humidification expectorant
湿剂/濕劑　moist formula
湿家/濕家　person suffering from dampness
湿脚气/濕腳氣　weak foot due to dampness, wet beriberi
湿啰音/濕啰音，水泡音　moist rale
湿疟/濕瘧，暑瘧，瘴瘧　damp malaria
湿热耳/濕熱耳　hot weather ear
湿热犯耳证/濕熱犯耳證　pattern of dampness-heat invading ear
湿热浸淫证/濕熱浸淫證　pattern of excessive dampness-heat
湿热痢/濕熱痢　damp-heat dysentery
湿热弥漫三焦证/濕熱彌漫三焦證　pattern of diffusive dampness-heat in sanjiao
湿热灭菌/濕熱滅菌　moist heat sterilization
湿热下注证/濕熱下注證　pattern of dampness-heat diffusing downward
湿热壅滞证/濕熱壅滯證　pattern of stagnant and jamming dampness-heat
湿热瘀阻证/濕熱瘀阻證　pattern of stagnant dampness-heat

湿热[蕴结]证/濕熱[蘊結]證　pattern of accumulated dampness-heat
湿热蕴脾/濕熱蘊脾　dampness-heat stagnating in spleen
湿热蕴脾证/濕熱蘊脾證　pattern of dampness-heat stagnating in spleen
湿热蒸舌证/濕熱蒸舌證　pattern of dampness-heat steaming tongue
湿热阻络证/濕熱阻絡證　pattern of dampness-heat blocking collaterals
湿润/濕潤　moist
湿润剂/濕潤劑　wetting agents
湿润性湿疹/濕潤性濕疹　weeping eczema
湿胜阳微/濕勝陽微　predominant dampness causing weak yang
湿胜[则]濡泻/濕勝[則]濡瀉　predominant dampness causing diarrhea
湿痰证/濕痰證　dampness-phlegm pattern
湿痛/濕痛　dampness pain
湿温[病]/濕温病　damp-warm disease
湿温伤寒/濕温傷寒　damp-warm disease with cold damage
湿温·湿遏卫气证/濕温·濕遏衛氣證　damp-warm disease with pattern of dampness inhibiting defense qi
湿温·湿困中焦证/濕温·濕困中焦證　damp-warm disease with pattern of dampness retaining in middle jiao
湿温·湿热弥漫三焦证/濕温·濕熱彌漫三焦證　damp-warm disease with pattern of damp-heat diffusing in sanjiao
湿温·湿热蕴毒证/濕温·濕熱蘊毒證　damp-warm disease with pattern of damp-heat and amassing poison
湿温·痰蔽心包证/濕温·痰蔽心包證　damp-warm disease with pattern of phlegm invading pericardium
湿温·邪阻膜原证/濕温·邪阻膜原證　damp-warm disease with pattern of pathogen blocking pleuro-diaphragmatic interspace
湿温·阳湿伤表证/濕温·陽濕傷表證　damp-warm disease with pattern of yang dampness injuring exterior
湿温·阴湿伤表证/濕温·陰濕傷表證　damp-warm disease with pattern of yin dampness injuring exterior
湿温·余邪未净证/濕温·餘邪未淨證　damp-warm disease with pattern of lingering remnant pathogen
湿吸杯/濕吸杯　wet cup
湿邪/濕邪　dampness pathogen
湿泻/濕瀉　damp diarrhea
湿性坏疽/濕性壞疽　moist gangrene
湿性坏死/濕性壞死　moist necrosis
湿性脚气病/濕性腳氣病　wet beriberi
湿性咳嗽/濕性欬嗽　moist cough
湿性黏滞/濕性黏滯　characteristic of dampness being sticky and stagnant
湿性趋下/濕性趨下　characteristic of dampness being descending
湿性哮喘/濕性氣喘　humid asthma
湿性重浊/濕性重濁　characteristic of dampness being heavy and turbid
湿痒/濕癢　dampness itching
湿疫/濕疫　damp pestilence
湿翳/濕翳　fungal keratitis, wet nebula
湿翳·热重于湿证/濕翳·熱重於濕證　wet nebula with pattern of heat predominating over dampness
湿翳·湿重于热证/濕翳·濕重於熱證　wet nebula with pattern of dampness predominating over heat
湿壅鼻窍证/濕壅鼻竅證　pattern of dampness invading nose
湿疣/濕疣　condylomata
湿疣病/濕疣病　condylomatosis
湿郁/濕鬱　damp stagnation, stagnation pattern of dampness
湿疹病/濕疹病　eczematosis
湿疹化/濕疹化　eczematization
湿疹失能指数/濕疹失能指數　eczema disability index
湿疹性表皮痣/濕疹性表皮痣　eczematous epidermal nevus
湿疹性多形性日光疹/濕疹性多形性日光疹　eczematous polymorphous light eruption
湿疹性睑缘炎/濕疹性瞼緣炎　eczematous blepharitis
湿疹性皮肤疾病/濕疹性皮膚疾病　eczematous skin diseases
湿疹性皮炎/濕疹性皮膚炎　eczematous dermatitis
湿疹样癌/濕疹樣癌　eczema carcinoma, eczematoid carcinoma
湿疹样脓疱病/濕疹狀膿皰病　impetigo eczematoides
湿疹样疹/濕疹樣疹,自激[性濕]疹　eczematid
湿疹样紫癜/濕疹樣紫癜,自激性濕疹樣紫癜　eczematid-like purpura
湿至干敷料/濕至乾敷料　wet-to-dry dressing
湿制颗粒/濕式顆粒　moist granulation, wet

granulation
湿中/濕中 damp parapoplexy
湿肿/濕腫 dampness swelling
湿重于热证/濕重於熱證 dampness-heat pattern with predominant dampness
湿装柱法/濕裝柱法,管柱濕裝法 wet packing method
湿阻/濕阻 damp obstruction
湿阻[病]/濕阻[病] damp obstruction disease
湿阻·脾虚湿困证/濕阻·脾虛濕困證 damp obstruction disease with pattern of damp retention due to spleen deficiency
湿阻气机/濕阻氣機 dampness hampering qi movement
湿阻·湿困脾胃证/濕阻·濕困脾胃證 damp obstruction disease with pattern of dampness retaining in spleen and stomach
湿阻·湿热中阻证/濕阻·濕熱中阻證 damp obstruction disease with pattern of obstruction of middle jiao by damp-heat
湿阻证/濕阻證 dampness retention pattern
蓍草/歐蓍草 yarrow
十八反/十八反 eighteen clashes, eighteen incompatible medicaments
十八[烷]醇/十八[烷]醇,硬脂酸醇 stearyl alcohol
十八烷基硅烷键合硅胶/十八烷基矽鍵結矽膠 octadecylsilane chemically bonded silica
十倍程/十倍程 decade
十滴水/十滴水 shidishui tincture
十二刺/十二刺 twelve techniques of needling
十二段锦/十二段錦 shi'erduanjin, twelve-sectioned exercise
十二经脉/十二經脈 twelve regular channels
十二[烷]醇/十二[烷]醇 dodecanol
十二烷基硫酸钠/十二烷基硫酸鈉 sodium dodecylsulfate, SDS
十二烷硫酸钠/十二烷硫酸鈉 sodium dodecyl sulfate
十二元环大环内酯类/十二元環巨環內酯類 12-membered ring macrolides
十二指肠/十二指腸 duodenum, shi'erzhichang, CO5
十二指肠闭锁/十二指腸閉鎖 duodenal atresia
十二指肠残端漏/十二指腸殘端漏 duodenal stump leakage
十二指肠大乳头/十二指腸大乳頭 major duodenal papilla
十二指肠胆囊造口吻合术/十二指腸膽囊造口吻合術 duodenocholecystostomy
十二指肠胆总管切开术/十二指腸輸膽管切開術 duodenocholedochotomy
十二指肠胆[总]管炎/十二指腸膽[總]管炎 duodenocholangitis
十二指肠动脉/十二指腸動脈 duodenal artery
十二指肠反流/十二指腸反流 duodenal regurgitation
十二指肠缝合术/十二指腸縫合術 duodenorrhaphy
十二指肠肝韧带/十二指腸肝韌帶 duodenohepatic ligament
十二指肠梗阻/十二指腸梗阻 duodenal obstruction
十二指肠钩虫/十二指腸鉤蟲 ancylostoma duodenale
十二指肠钩虫病/十二指腸鉤蟲病 ancylostomiasis duodenale
十二指肠冠/十二指腸冠,十二指腸帽 duodenal cap
十二指肠冠过大/十二指腸冠過大,大形十二指腸帽 megalobulbus
十二指肠后动脉/十二指腸後動脈 retroduodenal artery
十二指肠后隐窝/十二指腸後隱窩 retroduodenal recess
十二指肠回肠造口吻合术/十二指腸迴腸造口吻合術 duodenoileostomy
十二指肠疾病/十二指腸疾病 duodenal diseases
十二指肠假憩室/十二指腸假憩室 pseudodiverticulum of duodenum
十二指肠降部/十二指腸降部 descending part of duodenum
十二指肠镜/十二指腸鏡 duodenoscopes
十二指肠镜检查/十二指腸鏡檢查 duodenoscopy
十二指肠空肠襻不全旋转/十二指腸空腸襻不全旋轉 incomplete rotation of duodenojejunal loop
十二指肠空肠曲/十二指腸空腸曲 duodenojejunal flexure
十二指肠空肠窝疝/十二指腸空腸窩疝 duodenojejunal hernia
十二指肠空肠造口吻合术/十二指腸空腸造口吻合術 duodenojejunostomy
十二指肠溃疡/十二指腸潰瘍 duodenal ulcer
十二指肠瘘[管]/十二指腸瘻管 duodenal fistula
十二指肠内投药法/十二指腸內用藥法 transduodenal medication
十二指肠旁襞/十二指腸旁襞 paraduodenal fold
十二指肠旁疝/十二指腸旁疝 paraduodenal hernia
十二指肠旁隐窝/十二指腸旁隱窩 paraduodenal recess

十二指肠蹼/十二指腸蹼　duodenal web
十二指肠憩室/十二指腸憩室　duodenal diverticulum
十二指肠切除术/十二指腸切除術　duodenectomy
十二指肠切开术/十二指腸切開術　duodenotomy
十二指肠球/十二指腸球　duodenal bulb of duodenum
十二指肠乳头/十二指腸乳頭　major caruncle of Santorini
十二指肠上襞/十二指腸上襞　superior duodenal fold
十二指肠上部/十二指腸上部　superior part of duodenum
十二指肠上动脉/十二指腸上動脈　supraduodenal artery
十二指肠上曲/十二指腸上曲　superior duodenal flexure
十二指肠上隐窝/十二指腸上隱窩　superior duodenal recess, superior duodenal fossa
十二指肠X射线摄影/十二指腸X光攝影　duodenogram
十二指肠肾韧带/十二指腸腎韌帶　duodenorenal ligament
十二指肠升部/十二指腸昇部　ascending part of duodenum
十二指肠十二指肠吻合术/十二指腸與十二指腸吻合術　duodenoduodenostomy
十二指肠水平部/十二指腸水平部　horizontal part of duodenum
十二指肠松解术/十二指腸鬆解術，十二指腸剝離術　duodenolysis
十二指肠提肌/十二指腸提肌　muscle of Treitz
十二指肠胃反流/十二指腸胃返流　duodenogastric reflux
十二指肠系膜/十二指腸繫膜　mesoduodenum
十二指肠狭窄/十二指腸狹窄　duodenal stenosis
十二指肠下襞/十二指腸下襞　inferior duodenal fold
十二指肠下曲/十二指腸下曲　inferior duodenal flexure
十二指肠下隐窝/十二指腸下隱窩　inferior duodenal recess, inferior duodenal fossa
十二指肠腺/十二指腸腺　duodenal gland
十二指肠小肠造口吻合术/十二指腸小腸造口吻合術　duodenoenterostomy
十二指肠小乳头/十二指腸小乳頭　minor duodenal papilla
十二指肠悬肌/十二指腸提肌，提十二指腸肌　suspensory muscle of duodenum
十二指肠悬韧带/十二指腸懸韌帶，Treitz 氏韌帶　suspensory ligament of duodenum, ligament of Treitz
十二指肠压迹/十二指腸壓跡　duodenal impression
十二指肠炎/十二指腸炎　duodenitis
十二指肠幽门狭窄/十二指腸幽門狹窄　duodenopyloric constriction
十二指肠造口术/十二指腸造口術，十二指腸造瘻術　duodenostomy
十二指肠支/十二指腸支　duodenal branches
十二指肠制动器/十二指腸抑動器　duodenal brake
十二指肠肿瘤/十二指腸腫瘤　duodenal neoplasms
十二指肠周炎/十二指腸周圍炎　periduodenitis
十二指肠纵襞/十二指腸縱襞　longitudinal fold of duodenum
十灰散/十灰散　shihui powder
十剂/十劑　ten functional types of formularies
十九畏/十九畏　nineteen incompatibilities, nineteen medicaments of mutual restraint
十居里/十居里　decacurie
十六元环大环内酯类/十六元環巨環內酯類　16-membered ring macrolides
十氯酮/十氯酮　chlordecone
十七[烷]酸/十七[烷]酸，珠光脂酸　margaric acid
十七椎[穴]/十七椎[穴]　shiqizhui, EX-B8
十全大补丸/十全大補丸　shiquan dabu pills
十三鬼穴/十三鬼穴　thirteen empirical points for mental disorders
十三科/十三科　thirteen branches of medicine
十三碳二酸/十三碳二酸　brassilic acid
十四经/十四經　fourteen channels
十四经发挥/十四經發揮　Elucidation of Fourteen Channels
十四烷基硫酸钠/十四烷基硫酸鈉　sodium tetradecyl sulphate
十四烷硫酸钠/十四烷硫酸鈉　sodium tetradecyl sulfate
十四酰佛波乙酯/十四醯佛波乙酯　tetradecanoylphorbol acetate
十四元环大环内酯类/十四元環大環內酯類　14-membered ring macrolides
十烃铵化合物/十烴銨化合物　decamethonium compounds
十问/十問　ten questions
十香返生丸/十香返生丸　shixiang fansheng pills
十宣/十宣　shixuan, EX-UE11
十一碳烷/十一碳烷　undecane
十一碳烯酸/十一碳烯酸　undecylenic acid
十一碳烯酸类/十一碳烯酸類　undecylenic acids

十一烯酸锌/十一烯酸鋅　zinc undecylenate
十枣汤/十棗湯　shizao decoction
十字绷带/十字繃帶　crucial bandage
十字绷带法/十字繃帶法　crucial bandaging
十字隆起/十字隆起,十字凸　cruciform eminence
十字切开/十字形切開　crucial incision
十字韧带/十字韌帶　cruciform ligament
十字形吻合/十字形吻合　crucial anastomosis
石/[結]石　stone
石板/石板　slate
石板样贫血/石板樣貧血　slaty anemia
石菖蒲/石菖蒲　grassleaf sweetflag rhizome
石胆酸/石膽酸,膽酸結石　lithocholic acid
石蛾/石蛾　tonsil hypertrophy, chronic tonsillitis, stony moth
石膏/石膏　gypsum
石膏板绷带/石膏板繃帶　stucco-plaster bandage
石膏绷带法/石膏繃帶法　plaster bandaging
石膏沉着/石膏沈著　stycosis
石膏床/石膏床　plaster bed
石膏固定/石膏固定　plaster fixation
石膏管型综合征/石膏管型症候群　cast syndrome
石膏夹板/石膏夾板　plaster splint
石膏样发癣菌/石膏樣毛癬菌　Trichophyton gypseum
石骨症/石骨症　osteopetrosis
石关/石關　shiguan, KI18
石斛/石斛　dendrobium
石斛明目丸/石斛明目丸　shihu mingmu pill
石斛夜光丸/石斛夜光丸　shihu yeguang pill
石化耳/石化耳　petrified auricle
石化胎块/石[灰]化胎塊　stone mole
石灰变性/石灰變性　calcareous degeneration
石灰烧伤/石灰燒傷　lime burn
石灰质浸润/石灰浸潤　calcareous infiltration
石瘕/石瘕　stony uterine mass
石疖/石癤　stone furuncle, stony furuncle
石决明/石決明　abalone shell
石蜡/石蠟　paraffin
石蜡包埋/石蠟包埋　paraffin embedding
石蜡敷裹/石蠟敷料　paraffin dressing
石蜡敷糊/石蠟敷糊　pliable paraffin
石蜡[工]癌/石蠟癌　paraffin cancer
石蜡糊法/石蠟糊法　nujol mull method
石蜡疗法/石蠟療法　paraffin therapy
石蜡美容疗法/石蠟美容療法　cosmetic paraffin therapy
石蜡切片/石蠟切片　paraffin section

石蜡瘤/石蠟瘤,油性肉芽腫　oleogranuloma
石蜡软膏/石蠟軟膏　paraffin ointment
石蜡硬脂绷带/石蠟硬脂繃帶　paraffin and stearin bandage
石蜡灼伤/石蠟灼傷　paraffin burn
石淋/石淋　stony strangury, urolithic stranguria
石淋·肾气虚证/石淋·腎氣虛證　stony strangury with kidney qi deficiency pattern
石淋·肾阴虚证/石淋·腎陰虛證　stony strangury with kidney yin deficiency pattern
石淋·下焦湿热证/石淋·下焦濕熱證　stony strangury with pattern of dampness-heat in lower jiao
石淋·下焦瘀滞证/石淋·下焦瘀滯證　stony strangury with pattern of qi stagnation and blood stasis in lower jiao
石榴/石榴　granatum
石榴疽/石榴疽　olecranon carbuncle
石榴皮/石榴皮　pomegranate rind
石门/石門　shimen, RN5
石棉/石棉　asbestos
石棉沉着病/石棉沈著病,石棉入肺病　asbestosis
石棉带/石棉帶　asbestos ribbon
石棉小体/石棉小體　asbestos body
石棉业皮肤病/石棉業皮膚病　asbestos industry dermatosis
石棉疣/石棉疣　asbestos wart
石棉状变性/石棉狀變性　asbestos transformation
石棉状癣/石棉狀癬　asbestos-like tinea
石墨/石墨　graphite
石墨卡套/石墨卡套　graphite ferrule
石墨纤维变性/石墨纖維變性　graphite fibrosis
石墨悬液/石墨懸液　hydrokollag
石尿症/石尿[症]　lithuresis
石蕊/石蕊　lacmus
石蕊红素/石蕊紅素,石蕊紅質　erythrolein
石蕊牛乳试验/石蕊牛奶試驗　litmus milk test
石蕊乳/石蕊乳　litmus milk
石蕊[试]纸/石蕊試紙　litmus paper
石蕊素试纸/石蕊紅色試紙　azolitmin paper
石室秘录/石室秘錄　Medical Secrets Recorded in a Stone Room
石水/石水　stony edema
石蒜科生物碱类/石蒜科生物鹼類　amaryllidaceae alkaloids
石胎/石胎,胎兒石化　lithopedion
石胎盘/石胎盤,結石性胎盤　stone placenta
石炭酸/石炭酸　carbolic acid

石炭酸复红/石炭酸復紅　carbolfuchsin
石炭酸烧伤/石炭酸燒傷　phenol burn
石韦/石葦　shearer's pyrrosia leaf
石细胞/石細胞　stone cell
石样心/石樣心　stony heart
石药中毒/石藥中毒　stone drug poisoning
石叶属/石葉屬　Cladonia
石瘿/石癭　stony goiter, thyroid carcinoma
石瘿•痰毒瘀结证/石癭•痰毒瘀結證　stony goiter with phlegm-toxin-stasis intermingling pattern
石瘿•瘀热伤阴证/石癭•瘀熱傷陰證　stony goiter with pattern of stasis-heat injuring yin
石油/石油　petroleum
石油痤疮/石油痤瘡　petroleum acne
石油及其衍生物性皮肤病/石油及其衍生物所致皮膚病　petroleum and its derivative dermatosis
石油皮炎/石油皮炎　petroleum dermatitis
石鱼刺伤/石魚刺傷,海膽螫症　stonefish stings
时差反应/時差反應　jet lag
时辰毒性/時辰毒性　chronotoxicity
时辰药理学/時辰藥理學　chronopharmacology
时方/時方　nonclassical prescriptions
时复目痒/時復目癢　constant eye itching, seasonal eye itching
时复目痒•湿热夹风证/時復目癢•濕熱夾風證　seasonal eye itching with pattern of dampness-heat complicated by wind
时复目痒•外感风热证/時復目癢•外感風熱證　seasonal eye itching with pattern of external contraction of wind-heat
时复目痒•血虚生风证/時復目癢•血虛生風證　seasonal eye itching with pattern of blood deficiency generating wind
时复症/時復症　seasonal eye disease
时间常数/時間常數　time constant
时间对比敏感度/時間對比敏感度　temporal contrast sensitivity
时间感觉/時[間感]覺　time sense
时间觉障碍/時間覺障礙,時間意識紊亂　dischronation
时间疗法/時間療法　chronotherapy
时间谱带展宽/時間譜帶展寬　band broading in time
时间效应曲线/時間效應曲線　time effect curve
时间因素/時間因素　time factors
时间增益补偿/時間增益補償　time gain compensation
时间知觉/時間知覺　time perception
时间转换型通气机/時間轉換型通氣機　time-cycled ventilator
时空聚类分析/時空聚類分析　space-time clustering
时令病/時令病　seasonal disease
时期/[時]期　phase
时邪/時邪　seasonal pathogen
时行感冒/流行性感冒　influenza
时行感冒虚脱证/時行感冒虛脫證　influenza with collapse pattern
时行寒疫/時行寒疫　seasonal cold pestilence
时行伤寒/時行傷寒　epidemic exogenous cold disease
时疫/時疫　seasonal pestilence
时值测量[法]/時值測定法　chronaximetry
识别/識別　recognition
识神/識神　acquired mentality
实按灸/實按灸　paper or cloth-separated moxibustion, pressing moxibustion
实变/堅實變化,變實　consolidation
实喘/實喘　excessive dyspnea
实喘•风寒袭肺证/實喘•風寒襲肺證　excessive dyspnea with pattern of wind-cold invading lung
实喘•风热犯肺证/實喘•風熱犯肺證　excessive dyspnea with pattern of wind-heat invading lung
实喘•痰热壅肺证/實喘•痰熱壅肺證　excessive dyspnea with pattern of phlegm-heat congesting lung
实喘•痰湿蕴肺证/實喘•痰濕蘊肺證　excessive dyspnea with pattern of phlegm-damp amassing in lung
实喘•外寒内热证/實喘•外寒內熱證　excessive dyspnea with pattern of external cold and internal heat
实喘•外寒内饮证/實喘•外寒內飲證　excessive dyspnea with pattern of external cold and internal fluid
实喘•燥热伤肺证/實喘•燥熱傷肺證　excessive dyspnea with pattern of dryness-heat injuring lung
实寒证/實寒證　excessive cold pattern
实际安全量/實際安全[劑]量　virtual safety dose
实际碱过剩/實際鹼過剩　actual base excess
实际死亡率/實際死亡率　actual mortality
实际损伤/實際損傷　actual trauma
实际碳酸氢根/實際碳酸氫根　actual bicarbonate radical
实际碳酸氢盐/實際碳酸氫鹽　actual bicarbonate
实践/實習　practice
实脉/實脈　excess pulse

实秘/實秘　excessive constipation
实[囊]胚/實[體]囊胚,實胚　stereoblastula, parenchymula
实呕/實嘔　excessive vomiting
实呕·肝气犯胃证/實嘔·肝氣犯胃證　excessive vomiting with pattern of liver qi invading stomach
实呕·寒邪犯胃证/實嘔·寒邪犯胃證　excessive vomiting with pattern of cold pathogen invading stomach
实呕·食积证/實嘔·食積證　excessive vomiting with food retention pattern
实呕·暑湿证/實嘔·暑濕證　excessive vomiting with summerheat-damp pattern
实呕·痰饮停胃证/實嘔·痰飲停胃證　excessive vomiting with pattern of phlegm-fluid stagnated in stomach
实呕·外邪犯胃证/實嘔·外邪犯胃證　excessive vomiting with pattern of exogenous pathogen invading stomach
实呕·胃热证/實嘔·胃熱證　excessive vomiting with stomach heat pattern
实脾散/實脾散　shipi powder
实热证/實熱證　excessive heat pattern
实时频谱分析/即時頻譜分析　real time spectral analysis
实时软组织扩张术/即時軟組織擴張術　immediate soft tissue expansion
实时修复/即時修復　immediate repair
实时转移/實時轉移,即時轉移　immediate transfer
实体[感]觉/實體覺　stereognostic sense
实体瘤/實體瘤　solid tumor
实体听诊[法]/實體聽診法　stereoauscultation
实体显微镜/實體顯微鏡　stereo microscope
实邪/實邪　excessive pathogen
实性暗点/實性暗點,正性暗點　positive scotoma
实性畸胎瘤/實性畸胎瘤,固體畸胎瘤　solid teratoma
实性叩响/實[性]叩響　flat percussion resonance
实验/實驗　experiment
实验病/實驗病　experimental disease
实验病理学/實驗病理學　experimental pathology
实验动物/實驗動物　laboratory animals
实验动物科学/實驗動物科學　laboratory animal science
实验动物学/實驗動物學　experimental zoology
实验口腔医学/實驗口腔醫學　experimental stomatology
实验胚胎学/實驗胚胎學　experimental embryology

实验室/實驗室　laboratory
实验室感染/實驗室感染　laboratory infection
实验室管理规范/實驗室管理規範　good laboratory practice, GLP
实验室疾病/實驗室疾病　laboratory disease
实验室霉浆菌/實驗室黴漿菌　Mycoplasma laboratorium
实验室人员/實驗室人員　laboratory personnel
实验心理学/實驗心理學　experimental psychology
实验性白血病/實驗性白血病　experimental leukemia
实验性辐射损伤/實驗性輻射損傷　experimental radiation injury
实验性肝硬化/實驗性肝硬化　experimental liver cirrhosis
实验性肝肿瘤/實驗性肝腫瘤　experimental liver neoplasms
实验性高血压/實驗性高血壓　experimental hypertension
实验性关节炎/實驗性關節炎　experimental arthritis
实验性黑色素瘤/實驗性黑色素瘤　experimental melanoma
实验性肉瘤/實驗性肉瘤　experimental sarcoma
实验性乳房肿瘤/實驗性乳房腫瘤　experimental mammary neoplasm
实验性神经系统自身免疫性疾病/實驗性神經系統自身免疫性疾病　experimental nervous system autoimmune disease
实验性糖尿病/實驗性糖尿病　experimental diabetes mellitus
实验性植入物/實驗性植入物　experimental implant
实验性肿瘤/實驗性腫瘤　experimental neoplasm
实验医学/實驗醫學　experimental medicine
实验用化学品/實驗用化學品　laboratory chemicals
实验针灸学/實驗針灸學　subject of experimental acupuncture and moxibustion
实验治疗/實驗治療　experimental therapy
实音/[低]實音　flatness
实用人体运动学/實用人體運動學　applied kinesiology
实用性运动/實用性運動　practical exercise
实则阳明/實則陽明　excessive disease located in Yangming
实者泻其子/實者瀉其子　purging child viscera for treating excess of mother viscera
实者泻之/實者瀉之　treating excess pattern with purgative methods
实证研究/實證研究　empirical research

实质/實質,主質　parenchyma
实质内注射/實質內注射　parenchymatous injection
实质性出血/實質性出血　parenchymatous hemorrhage
实质性脊髓炎/實質性脊髓炎　parenchymatous myelitis
实质性甲状腺肿/實質性甲狀腺腫　parenchymatous goiter
实质性瘤/實質性瘤　parenchymatous tumor
实质性气肿/實質性氣腫　substantial emphysema
实质性乳腺炎/實質性乳腺炎　parenchymatous mastitis
实质性神经梅毒/實質性神經梅毒　parenchymatous neurosyphilis
实质性肾炎/實質性腎炎　parenchymatous nephritis
实质性水肿/實質性水腫　parenchymatous edema
实质性心肌炎/實質性心肌炎　parenchymatous myocarditis
实质炎/實質炎　parenchymatitis
实中夹虚/實中夾虛　excess complicated with deficiency
实肿/實腫　excess swelling
实足年龄/實足年齡　chronological age
拾物试验/拾物試驗　pick-up test
食虫椿象科昆虫/食蟲椿象科昆蟲　assassin bug
食床/食床　dental calculus
食道/食道　shidao, CO2, esophagus
食淀粉癖/嗜食澱粉　amylophagia
食窦/食竇　shidou, SP17
食粪癖/食糞癖　coprophagia
食复/食復　recurrence caused by dietary irregularity
食骨癖/食骨癖　osteophagia
食管/食管　esophagus
食管癌/食管癌,食道癌　esophageal cancer, esophagus cancer
食管瘢痕狭窄/食管瘢痕狹窄　cicatricial stricture of esophagus
食管贲门腺/食管賁門腺　esophageal cardiac gland
食管闭锁/食管閉鎖　esophageal atresia
食管襞折术/食管襞折術,食道折叠術,食道皺形成術　esophagoplication
食管病学/食管病學,食道學　esophagology
食管[长度]测量计/食管[長度]測量器,測食道長度器　esophagometer
食管肠吻合术/食管腸吻合術,食道腸吻合術　esophagoenterostomy
食管成形术/食管成形術,食道成形術,食道造形術　esophagoplasty
食管重复畸形/食管重複畸形　duplication of esophagus
食管穿孔/食管穿孔　esophageal perforation
食管丛/食管[神經]叢　esophageal plexus
食管刀/食道刀　esophagotome
食管导程/食管導程,食道導程　esophageal lead
食管动脉/食管動脈,食道動脈　esophageal artery
食管恶性黑[色]素瘤/食管惡性黑[色]素瘤　malignant melanoma of esophagus
食管腐蚀性灼伤/食管腐蝕性灼傷　corrosive burn of esophagus
食管腹部/食管腹部　abdominal part of esophagus
食管过短/食管過短,短食道畸形　brachyesophagus
食管喉头切除术/食管喉頭切除術,食道喉切除術　esophagolaryngectomy
食管后间隙/食管後間隙　retroesophageal space
食管环/食管環,食道環　esophageal ring
食管活动障碍/食管活動障礙　esophageal motility disorder
食管肌层切开术/食管肌層切開術,食道肌層切開術　esophagomyotomy
食管[肌]胃肌切开术/食管[肌]胃肌切開術,食道胃肌切開術　esophagogastromyotomy
食管疾病/食管疾病　esophageal diseases
食管结核/食管結核　tuberculosis of esophagus
食管颈部/食管頸部　cervical part of esophagus
食管痉挛/食道痙攣　esophageal spasm
食管静脉/食管靜脈　esophageal vein
食管静脉曲张/食管靜脈曲張　esophageal varice
食管静脉曲张内镜结扎[术]/食管靜脈曲張內鏡結扎[術]　endoscopic rubber banding for esophageal varice
食管静脉曲张硬化治疗[术]/食管靜脈曲張硬化治療[術]　sclerotherapy for esophageal varice
食管镜/食道鏡　esophagoscope
食管镜检查法/食道鏡檢查法　esophagoscopy
食管空肠胃吻合术/食道空腸胃吻合術　esophagojejunogastrostomosis
食管空肠吻合术/食管空腸吻合術　esophagojejunostomy
食管溃疡/食道潰瘍　esophageal ulcer
食管扩张/食道擴張[術]　esophagectasia
食管扩张器/食管擴張器　esophageal dilator
食管扩张探条/食管擴張探條　bougie for esophageal dilatation
食管裂孔/食管裂孔　esophageal hiatus, esophageal foramen
食管裂孔疝/食道裂孔疝　hiatal hernia

食管裂孔疝修补术/食管裂孔疝修補術　hiatal hernia repair
食管瘘/食道瘻　esophageal fistula
食管囊肿/食管囊腫　esophageal cyst
食管内听心器/食管内聽心器，體腔聽診器　endostethoscope
食管内压力测定/食管内壓力測定　intraesophageal manometry
食管黏膜撕裂症/食管黏膜撕裂症　Mallory-Weiss syndrome
食管黏膜息肉/食管黏膜息肉　polypus of esophageal mucosa
食管黏膜炎/食管黏膜炎，食道黏膜炎　endoesophagitis
食管旁疝/食管旁疝，食道旁疝　paraesophageal hernia
食管旁食管裂孔疝/食管旁食管裂孔疝　paraesophageal hiatus hernia
食管平滑肌瘤摘出术/食管平滑肌瘤摘出術　enucleation of esophageal leiomyoma
食管蹼/食道網狀組織　esophageal web
食管憩室/食管憩室　diverticulum of esophagus
食管憩室病/食管憩室病　esophageal diverticulosis
食管切除术/食管切除術　esophagectomy
食管切开术/食管切開術，食道切開術　esophagotomy
食管曲张静脉破裂/食管曲張静脈破裂　rupture of esophageal varices
食管软化[症]/食管軟化[症]，食道軟化　esophagomalacia
食管疝/食管疝　esophageal hernia
食管烧伤/食管燒傷　esophageal burn
食管神经丛/食道神經叢　esophageal plexus
食管神经性功能紊乱/食管神經性功能紊亂　neurogenic dysfunction of esophagus
食管失弛症/食管失弛症　esophageal achalasia
食管十二指肠吻合术/食道十二指腸吻合術　esophagoduodenostomy
食管食管吻合术/食管食管吻合術，食道食道吻合術　esophagoesophagostomy
食管受压性吞咽困难/食管受壓性吞嚥困難，食道受壓性吞嚥困難　dysphagia lusoria
食管酸灌注试验/食管酸灌注試驗　esophageal acid perfusion test
食管探条/食管探條，食道探條　esophageal bougie
食管探子/食管探子，食道探子　esophageal sound
食管痛/食管痛，食道痛　esophagalgia
食管胃底固定术/食管胃底固定術，食道胃底固定法　esophagofundopexy
食管胃底吻合术/食管胃底吻合術　esophagofundostomy
食管胃接合处/食管胃接合處　esophagogastric junction
食管胃镜检查/食管胃鏡檢查，食道胃鏡檢法　esophagogastroscopy
食管胃切除术/食管胃切除術，食道胃切除術　esophagogastrectomy
食管胃切除术与结肠间置术/食管胃切除術與結腸間置術　esophagogastrectomy with colon interposition
食管胃填塞/食管胃填塞，食道胃填塞　esophagogastric tamponade
食管胃吻合术/食管胃吻合術，食道胃吻合術　esophagogastrostomy
食管系膜/食管繫膜　mesoesophagus
食管狭窄/食管狭窄　esophageal stenosis
食管X线[照]片/食道X線[照]片，食道X光像　esophagogram
食管X线照相术/食道X線照相術，食道X光攝影術　esophagography
食管腺/食管腺，食道腺　esophageal gland
食管消化性溃疡/食管消化性潰瘍　peptic ulcer of esophagus
食管心动图/食管心動圖，食道心動波　esophageal cardiogram
食管性多涎症/食管性多涎症，食道唾液性症　esophagosalivary symptom
食管胸部/食管胸部　thoracic part of esophagus
食管[胸段]梗阻/食管[胸段]梗阻，食道哽塞　thoracic choke
食管压迹/食管壓跡　esophageal impression
食管言语/食管言語，食道言語　esophageal speech
食管炎/食管炎，食道炎　esophagitis
食管异位软骨/食管異位軟骨　ectopic cartilage of esophagus
食管异物/食管異物　foreign body in esophagus
食管运动功能失调/食管運動功能失調　esophageal motility dysfunction
食管造口术/食管造口術，食道造口術，食管造瘻術　esophagostomy
食管造瘘口/食管造瘻口，食道瘻孔　esophagostoma
食管支/食管支　esophageal branch
食管肿瘤/食管腫瘤　esophageal neoplasms
食管周炎/食道周圍炎　periesophagitis
食管自发性破裂/食管自發性破裂　spontaneous rupture of esophagus

食后痛/食後痛　postprandial pain
食积/食積　dyspepsia
食厥/食厥　crapulent syncope, syncope due to improper diet
食疗/食療,食治　dietotherapy
食疗本草/食療本草　Materia Medica for Dietotherapy
食毛癖/食毛癖,食髮癖　trichophagy
食糜/食糜　chyme
食糜生成/食糜生成,食糜形成,食糜化成　chymification
食糜泻/乳糜瀉,粥樣瀉　celiac flux
食糜溢/食糜溢,食糜漏　chymorrhea
食疟/食瘧　malaria due to improper diet
食品剥夺/食品剝奪　food deprivation
食品毒理学/食品毒理學　food toxicology
食品防腐剂/食品防腐劑　food preservatives
食品辐射/食品輻射　food irradiation
食品工艺学/食品工藝學　food technology
食品寄生虫学/食品寄生蟲學　food parasitology
食品检查/食品檢查　food inspection
食品立法/食品立法　food legislation
食品添加剂/食品添加劑　food additive
食品微生物学/食品微生物學　food microbiology
食品污染/食品汙染　food contamination
食品药物相互作用/食品藥物相互作用　food-drug interactions
食品着色剂/食品著色劑　food coloring agent
食谱制订/食譜制訂　menu planning
食人肉癖/食人肉［癖］,吃同類動物的肉　cannibalism
食肉动物/食肉動物　carnivore
食土癖者/食土癖者　geophagist
食团/食團,飯團　alimentary bolus
食物残渣/食物殘渣　food debris
食物存积性咽下困难/食物存積性嚥下困難,會厭窩性食物堆積吞嚥困難　vallecular dysphagia
食物毒/食物毒［素］　bromatotoxin
食物毒素/食物毒素　sitotoxin
食物毒性/食物毒性　dietotoxicity
食物感染/食物感染　food infection
食物过敏/食物過敏　food hypersensitivity
食物混黏液［作用］/食物混黏液［作用］,和涎,混涎　invisication
食物加工法/食物加工法　curing
食物进肠过速/食物進腸過速,食物進腸過度　tachyalimentation
食物链/食物鏈　food chain

食物螨/食物蟲　food mites
食物排除疗法/食物排出療法,檢測食物過敏飲食,去過敏原飲食　elimination diet
食物嵌塞/食物嵌塞　food impaction
食物缺乏病/食物缺乏病　food-deficiency disease
食物性毒血症/食物性毒血症,飲食性毒血症　alimentary toxemia
食物性酮尿/食物性酮尿　ketourine
食物性哮喘/食物性氣喘　food asthma
食物溢出道/食物溢出道　spillway of food
食物中毒/食物中毒,消化道中毒　food poisoning, alimentary intoxication
食性/食性　quality of food
食养/食養　health preserving with food
食医/食醫　dietetician
食医心鉴/食醫心鑒　Heart Mirror of Dietotherapy
食已则吐/食已則吐　vomiting right after eating
食㑊/食㑊　polyphagia with emaciation
食用疫苗/食用疫苗　edible vaccine
食用植物/食用植物　edible plant
食鱼蟹类中毒/食魚蟹類中毒　allergy after eating fish and crab, fish and crab poisoning
食郁/食鬱　food stagnation, stagnation pattern of food
食郁肉中毒/食鬱肉中毒　decayed flesh poisoning
食欲/食欲　appetite
食欲不振/食欲不振,食欲缺失　inappetence
食欲刺激药/食欲刺激藥　appetite stimulants
食欲调节/食欲調節　appetite regulation
食欲无常/食慾無常　capricious appetite
食欲液/食欲胃液　appetite juice
食欲抑制药/食欲抑制藥　appetite depressants
食欲障碍/食慾障礙　appetite disorder
食欲正常/食欲正常　eusitia
食欲中枢/食欲［平衡］中樞　appestat
食指/食指　index finger
食滞胃肠证/食滯胃腸證　pattern of retention of food in stomach
食中/食中　food stagnation parapoplexy
食诸肉中毒/食諸肉中毒　all toxic flesh poisoning
食浊阻滞聚证/食濁阻滯聚證　accumulation disease with pattern of food turbidity blockade
蚀斑技术/蝕斑技術　plaque technique
蚀斑形成细胞/蝕斑形成細胞,空斑形成細胞　plaque forming cell
蚀骨性脓肿/蝕骨性膿瘍　ossifluent abscess
蚀关节性脓肿/蝕關節性膿腫　arthrifluent abscess
蚀刻/［酸］蝕刻　etching

莳萝属/蒔蘿屬　Anethum
莳萝油/蒔蘿油　oil of dill
史必兹痣/史必兹痣,梭狀及上皮樣細胞痣　Spitz nevus
史登诺导管/史登諾導管　Steno duct
史国公药酒/史國公藥酒　shiguogong wine
史柯德氏敷料/史柯德氏敷料　Scott dressing
史密斯病/史密斯病　Smith disease
史密斯骨折/史密斯骨折　Smith fracture
史密斯抗原/史密斯抗原　Smith antigen
史密斯脱位/史密斯脫位　Smith dislocation
史密斯杂音/史密斯雜音　Eustace Smith murmur
矢气/矢氣,胃腸氣　flatus
矢状参考线/矢狀參考線,矢狀輔助線　sagittal reference line
矢状窦旁脑膜瘤/矢狀竇旁腦膜瘤,矢狀面腦膜瘤　parasagittal meningioma
矢状窦血栓形成/矢狀竇血栓形成　sagittal sinus thrombosis
矢状缝合/矢狀縫合　sagittal suture
矢状沟/矢狀溝　sagittal groove
矢状截骨术/矢狀截骨術　sagittal osteotomy
矢状面/矢狀面　sagittal plane
矢状劈开截骨术/矢狀劈開截骨術　sagittal split osteotomy
矢状束/矢狀束,矢狀徑　sagittal tract
矢状髓束/矢狀髓束,矢狀髓徑　sagittal medullary tract
矢状缘/矢狀緣　sagittal border
矢状轴/矢狀軸　sagittal axis
使君子/使君子　rangooncreeper fruit
使君子氨酸/使君子氨酸　quisqualic acid
始初反应/始初反應,起始作用　initial response
始基囊肿/始基囊腫　primordial cyst
士的宁/士的寧,番木鱉素,馬錢子素　strychnine
士的宁化/士的寧化,受番木鱉作用　strychnize
士的宁狂/士的寧狂,番木鱉癖　strychninomania
士的宁作用/士的寧作用,番木鱉作用　strychninization
士的宁中毒/士的寧中毒,番木鱉素中毒　strychninism
示波测量法/示波測量法,振動描記法　oscillometry
示波计/示波計,振動描記器　oscillometer
示波器/示波器　oscillograph
示波图/[電波像]示波圖,電波描記像　oscillogram
示波血压计/示波血壓計,振動血壓計　sphygmo-oscillometer
示差脉冲极谱法/示差脈衝極譜法　differential pulse polarography
示教检眼镜/示教檢眼鏡　demonstration ophthalmoscope
示意不能/示意不能,傳達不能　asemasia
示指/示指,食指　index finger
示指桡侧动脉/示指橈側動脈,食指橈側動脈　radial artery of index finger
示指伸肌/示指伸肌,伸食指肌　extensor indicis
示踪/示蹤,描記法,描記波　tracing
示踪元素/追蹤元素　tracer element
[世]代/世代　generation
世界针灸学会联合会/世界針灸學會聯合會　World Federation of Acupuncture-Moxibustion Societies
世医得效方/世醫得效方　Effective Formulae Handed Down for Generations
势能/勢能,位能　potential energy
试分娩/試分娩　trial of labor
试管/試管　test glass
试管培养/管中培養　tube culture
试管婴儿/試管嬰兒　test tube baby
试剂/試劑　reagent
试剂喷雾器/試劑噴霧器　reagent sprayer
试剂条/試劑條　reagent strips
试镜架/試[視]鏡架,試驗支架　trial frame
试镜箱/試[視]鏡箱,視力鏡盒　trial case
试视力字体/試視力字體,驗光圖型,配光字型　optotype
试胎/試胎　testing labor
试探穿刺/試探穿刺[法],試探穿刺術　exploratory puncture
试验/試驗　trial
试验集/試驗集,試驗組　test set
试验卡/試驗卡,視力卡　test card
试验前焦虑量表/試驗前焦慮量表　test anxiety scale
试[验溶]液/試液　test solution
试验膳食/試驗飲食　test diet
试验预期值/試驗預期值　predictive value of tests
视暗质/視暗質　scotopsin
视白质/視白質　leukopsin
视杯/視杯　optic cup, ocular cup
视辨距不良/視辨距不良　ocular dysmetria
视柄/視柄　optic stalk
视差/視差,移像感　parallax
视词中枢/視詞中樞,識字中樞　visual word center
视刺激器疗法/視刺激器療法　vision stimulator treatment
视错觉/視錯覺　optical illusions

视蛋白/視蛋白　opsin
视定若动/視定若動　static thing seen as motional
视动性眼震/視動性眼震,動景性眼球震顫　optokinetic nystagmus
视度/視度　oxyopter
视放射/視放射　optic radiation
视辐射/視輻射　optic radiation
视杆视锥层/視桿視錐層,桿狀錐狀細胞層　layer of rods and cones
视杆外段/視桿外段　rod outer segments
视杆细胞/視桿細胞　rod cell
视沟/視[叉]溝　optic groove, optic sulcus
视黄醇结合蛋白质类/視黄醇結合蛋白質類　retinol-binding proteins
视黄醛/視黄醛　retinaldehyde
视黄酸/視黄酸,維生素 A 酸　retinoic acid
视黄质/視黄質　visual yellow
视惑/視惑　disturbed vision, visual distortion
视[基]板/視基板,眼基板　ophthalmic placode, optic plate
视交叉/視[束]交叉,視神經交叉　optic chiasma
视交叉后静脉弓/視交叉後靜脈弓　retrochiasmatic venous arch
视交叉后隆起/視交叉後隆凸　postchiasmatic eminence
视交叉上核/視交叉上核　suprachiasmatic nucleus
视交叉支/視交叉支　chiasmatic branch
视交叉蛛网膜炎/視交叉蛛網膜炎　chiasmal arachnoiditis
视交叉综合征/視交叉症候群　chiasmatic syndrome
视角/視角　visual angle
视近性集合/視近性集合　proximal convergence
视觉/視覺　visual sense, vision
视觉差异/視覺差異　vision disparity
视觉电生理检查[法]/視覺電生理檢查[法]　examination of visual electrophysiology
视觉电生理学/視覺電生理學　visual electrophysiology
视觉分辨力/視覺分辨力　optic resolving power
视觉感受器/視覺感受器　visual receptor
视觉光学/視覺光學　visual optics
视觉记忆/視覺記憶　eye memory
视觉检查器/視覺檢查器　subjectoscope
视觉模拟评分法/視覺類比評分法　visual analogue scales
视觉模式识别/視覺模式識別　visual pattern recognition
视觉缺失/視覺缺失　optic anesthesia

视觉生理学/視覺生理學　visual physiology
视觉舒适/視覺舒適　euphoropsia
视觉先兆/視覺先兆　visual aura
视觉效率/視覺效率　visual efficiency
视觉心理区/視覺心理區　visuopsychic area
视觉性失语症/視覺性失語症　optic aphasia
视觉性失写症/視覺性失寫症　optic agraphia
视觉性眼球震颤/視原性眼球震顫　visual nystagmus
视觉学/視覺學　visionics
视觉眼电图/視覺眼電圖　visual electrooculogram
视觉异常/視覺異常　anomalopia
视觉诱发电位/視覺誘發電位　visual evoked potential
视觉障碍/視覺障礙　vision disorders
视空间觉失认[症]/視空間覺失認[症]　visual-spatial agnosia
视力/視力,視敏度　visual acuity
视力表/視力表　visual acuity chart
视力测定法/視力測驗法,驗光法　optometry
视力计/視力計　visuometer
视力检查[法]/視力檢查[法]　examination of visual acuity
视力减退/視力減退　visual deterioration
视力普查/視力普查　vision screening
视力试验/視力試驗　vision tests
视力损伤者/視力損傷者　visually impaired persons
视路/視路　visual pathway
视敏度/視敏度,視力　visual acuity
视脑/視腦,眼腦　ophthalmencephalon
视盘/視盤　optic disc
视盘陷凹/視盤陷凹,視神經乳頭陷凹　excavation of optic disc
视盘小疣/視盤小疣　optic disk drusen
视皮质/視皮質　visual cortex
视疲劳/視疲勞,眼力疲勞,眼無力　asthenopia, asth
视疲劳·肝气郁结证/視疲勞·肝氣鬱結證　asthenopia with liver qi stagnation pattern
视疲劳·肝肾两虚证/視疲勞·肝腎兩虛證　asthenopia with liver-kidney deficiency pattern
视疲劳·气血两虚证/視疲勞·氣血兩虛證　asthenopia with qi-blood deficiency pattern
视歧/視歧　diplopia, double vision
视器/視覺器官　visual organ, organ of vision
视前内侧核/視前内側核　medial preoptic nucleus
视前区/視前區,視前部　preoptic region, preoptic area
视前外侧核/視前外側核　lateral preoptic nucleus

视青质/視紫[藍]質　iodopsin
视区/視區　visual zone
视乳头/視乳頭　optic papilla
视乳头杯/視乳頭杯　cupped disk
视乳头水肿/視乳頭水腫　papilledema
视色质/視色質，视[網膜]色素　chromophane
视上垂体束/視上垂體束　supraopticohypophyseal tract
视上核/視上核　supraoptic nucleus
视上交叉/視上交叉　supraoptic decussation
视上连合/視上連合　supraoptic commissure
视上区/視上部　supraoptic region
视神经/視神經　optic nerve
视神经病变/視神經病變　optic neuropathy
视神经发育不全/視神經發育不全　aplasia of optic nerve
视神经管/視神經管　optic canal
视神经管减压术/視神經管減壓術　decompression of optic canal
视神经管内部/視神經管内部　intracanalicular part of optic nerve
视神经黑色素细胞瘤/視神經黑色素細胞瘤　melanocytoma of optic nerve
视神经疾病/視神經疾病　optic nerve disease
视神经脊髓炎/視神經脊髓炎　neuro-optic myelitis
视神经胶质瘤/眼神經膠質瘤　optic glioma
视神经睫状神经切除术/視神經睫狀神經切除術　opticociliary neurectomy
视神经孔/視神經孔　optic foramen
视神经孔鼻根间径/視神經孔鼻根間徑　opticonasion
视神经眶部/視神經眶部　orbital part of optic nerve
视神经颅内部/視神經顱内部　intracranial part of optic nerve
视神经脉络膜视网膜炎/視神經脈絡膜視網膜炎　neurochorioretinitis
视神经脉络膜炎/視神經脈絡膜炎　neurochoroiditis
视神经脑膜瘤/視神經腦膜瘤　meningioma of optic nerve
视神经内鞘/視神經内鞘　inner sheath of optic nerve
视神经盘/視神經盤，視神經乳頭　optic disc
视[神经]盘凹陷/視[神經]盤凹陷　excavation of optic disc
视[神经]盘病变/視[神經]盤病變　papillopathy
视[神经]盘缺损/視[神經]盤缺損　coloboma of optic disc
视[神经]盘视网膜病变/視[神經]盤視網膜病變　papilloretinopathy
视[神经]盘炎/視[神經]盤炎　papillitis
视[神经]盘直径/視[神經]盤直徑　disc diameter
视神经鞘膜瘤/視神經鞘膜瘤　optic nerve neurinoma
视神经乳头/視神經乳頭　papilla of optic nerve
视神经乳头水肿/視神經乳頭水腫　choked disc
视神经视网膜病/視神經視網膜病　neuroretinopathy
视神经视网膜炎/視神經視網膜炎　neuroretinitis
视神经撕脱/視神經撕脱　evulsion of optic nerve
视神经损伤/視神經損傷　optic nerve injuries
视神经外鞘/視神經外鞘　outer sheath of optic nerve
视神经萎缩/視神經萎縮　optic atrophy
视神经纤维层/視神經纖維層　layer of optic fibers
视神经血管环/視神經血管環　vascular circle of optic nerve
视神经炎/視神經炎　optic neuritis
视神经眼内部/視神經眼内部　intraocular part of optic nerve
视神经异位/視神經異位　heterotopy of optic nerve
视神经肿瘤/視神經腫瘤　optic nerve neoplasm
视神经周围炎/視神經周圍炎　optic perineuritis
视神经蛛网膜炎/視神經蛛網膜炎　opticoarachnoiditis
视束/視束，视徑[幹]　optic tract, ophthalmic tract
视束支/視束支　branches of optic tract
视听设备/視聽設備　audiovisual aids
视通路/視通路　visual pathway
视网膜/視網膜　retina
视网膜鼻侧上小动脉/視網膜鼻側上小動脈，視網膜上鼻小動脈　superior nasal arteriole of retina
视网膜鼻侧上小静脉/視網膜鼻側上小静脈　superior nasal venule of retina
视网膜鼻侧下小动脉/視網膜鼻側下小動脈，視網膜下鼻小動脈　inferior nasal arteriole of retina
视网膜鼻侧下小静脉/視網膜鼻側下小静脈　inferior nasal venule of retina
视网膜变性/視網膜變性　retinal degeneration
视网膜病变/視網膜病變　retinopathy
视网膜赤道部/視網膜赤道部，視網膜中間區　midperiphery
视网膜出血/視網膜出血　retinal hemorrhage
视网膜穿孔/視網膜穿孔　retinal perforation
视网膜电描记器/視網膜電描記器　electroretinograph
视网膜电描记术/視網膜電描記術　electroretinography
视网膜电图/視網膜電圖　electroretinogram
视网膜动脉/視網膜動脈　retinal artery

视网膜动脉闭塞/視網膜動脈閉塞 retinal artery occlusion
视网膜动脉搏动/視網膜動脈搏動 retinal arterial pulsation
视网膜动脉痉挛/視網膜動脈痙攣 retinal arteriospasm
视网膜动脉瘤/視網膜動脈瘤 retinal aneurysm
视网膜动脉压/視網膜動脈壓 retinal arterial pressure
视网膜动脉硬化/視網膜動脈硬化 retinal arteriosclerosis
视网膜对应点/視網膜對應點 corresponding retinal point
视网膜发绀/視網膜發紺 cyanosis retinae
视网膜发育不良/視網膜發育不良 retinal dysplasia
[视网膜]放射状胶质细胞/[視網膜]放射狀膠質細胞 radial neuroglia cell
视网膜感光迟钝/視網膜[感光]遲鈍 torpor retinae
视网膜格子样变性/視網膜格子樣變性 lattice degeneration of retina
视网膜光感减退/視網膜光感減退 aphotesthesia
视网膜虹膜部/視網膜虹膜部 pars iridica retinae
视网膜环状变性/視網膜環狀變性 circinate degeneration of retina
视网膜黄斑/視網膜黃斑 macula lutea retinae
视网膜疾病/視網膜疾病 retinal disease
视网膜检视镜/視網膜檢視鏡 stigmatometer
视网膜胶质瘤/視網膜神經膠質瘤 glioma retinae
[视网膜]节细胞层/[視網膜]節細胞層 layer of ganglion cell
视网膜结核/視網膜結核 tuberculosis of retina
视网膜睫状体部/視網膜睫狀體部 pars ciliaris retinae
视网膜静脉/視網膜靜脈 retinal vein
视网膜静脉闭塞/視網膜靜脈閉塞 retinal vein occlusion
视网膜静脉搏动/視網膜靜脈搏動 retinal venous pulsation
视网膜静脉分支阻塞/視網膜靜脈分支阻塞 branch retinal vein occlusion
视网膜静脉压/視網膜靜脈壓 retinal venous pressure
视网膜静脉炎/視網膜靜脈炎 retinal phlebitis
视网膜镜/視網膜鏡 retinoscopes
视网膜镜检查/視網膜鏡檢查 retinoscopy
视网膜巨动脉瘤/視網膜巨動脈瘤 retinal macroaneurysm
视网膜冷凝固定术/視網膜冷凝固定術 cryoretinopexy
视网膜裂孔/視網膜裂孔 retinal hole
视网膜绿色素/視網膜綠色素,視網膜綠質 chlorophane
视网膜脉络膜炎/視網膜脈絡[膜]炎 retinochoroiditis
视网膜盲部/視網膜盲部 pars blind retinae, pars caeca retinae
视网膜毛细管扩张/視網膜毛細管擴張 retinal telangiectasis
视网膜母细胞瘤/視網膜母細胞瘤 retinoblastoma
视网膜母细胞瘤蛋白质/視網膜母細胞瘤蛋白質 retinoblastoma protein
视网膜母细胞瘤基因/視網膜母細胞瘤基因 retinoblastoma gene
视网膜囊样变性/視網膜囊樣變性 cystoid degeneration of retina
视网膜内侧小动脉/視網膜內側小動脈 medial arteriole of retina
视网膜内侧小静脉/視網膜內側小靜脈 medial venule of retina
视网膜内层/視網膜內層 entoretina
[视网膜]内核层/内核層 inner nuclear layer
视网膜内间隙/視網膜內空隙 intraretinal space
[视网膜]内界膜/[視網膜]內限膜,内限界膜 inner limiting membrane
[视网膜]内网层/[視網膜]內網層 inner plexiform layer
视网膜颞侧上小动脉/視網膜顳側上小動脈,視網膜上顳小動脈 superior temporal arteriole of retina
视网膜颞侧上小静脉/視網膜顳側上小靜脈 superior temporal venule of retina
视网膜颞侧下小动脉/視網膜顳側下小動脈,視網膜下顳小動脈 inferior temporal arteriole of retina
视网膜颞侧下小静脉/視網膜顳側下小靜脈 inferior temporal venule of retina
视网膜胚瘤/視網膜胚瘤 dictyoma
视网膜劈裂症/視網膜劈裂症 retinoschisis
视网膜皮质/視網膜皮質 retinal cortex
视网膜平脱离/視網膜平脫離 flat detachment of retina
视网膜破裂/視網膜破裂 dialysis retinae
视网膜铺路石样变性/視網膜鋪路石樣變性 paving stone degeneration of retina
视网膜前出血/視網膜前出血 preretinal hemorrhage
视网膜前纤维增生/視網膜前纖維增生 preretinal fibrosis

视网膜切除术/視網膜切除術　retinectomy
视网膜切开术/視網膜切開術　retinotomy
视网膜缺损/視網膜缺損　coloboma of retina
视网膜缺血/視網膜缺血　retinal ischemia
视网膜色素层/視網膜色素層　pars pigmentosa retinae
视网膜色素类/視網膜色素類　retinal pigments
[视网膜]色素上皮层/[視網膜]色素上皮層　pigment epithelium layer
视网膜色素细胞/視網膜色素細胞　pigment cell of retina
视网膜神经部/視網膜神經部　pars nervosa retinae
视网膜神经节细胞/視網膜神經節細胞　retinal ganglion cell
视网膜视部/視網膜視部　pars optica retinae
[视网膜]双极细胞/雙極細胞　bipolar cell
视网膜水肿/視網膜水腫　retinal edema
视网膜痛/視網膜痛　neurodealgia
视网膜脱离/視網膜脫離,視網膜剥落　retina detachment, detachment of retina
视网膜脱离·肝肾阴虚证/視網膜脫離·肝腎陰虛證　retina detachment with liver-kidney yin deficiency pattern
视网膜脱离·脉络瘀阻证/視網膜脫離·脈絡瘀阻證　retina detachment with pattern of stasis and obstruction of vessel and collateral
视网膜脱离·脾虚湿困证/視網膜脫離·脾虛濕困證　retina detachment with pattern of spleen deficiency and dampness retention
[视网膜]外核层/外核層　outer nuclear layer
[视网膜]外界膜/外界膜　outer limiting membrane
视网膜外膜/視網膜外膜　epiretinal membrane
[视网膜]外网层/[視網膜]外網層　outer plexiform layer
[视网膜]网间细胞/[視網膜]網間細胞,網織層間細胞　interplexiform cell
视网膜微动脉瘤/視網膜微動脈瘤　retinal microaneurysm
视网膜萎缩/視網膜萎縮　neurodeatrophia
[视网膜]无长突细胞/[視網膜]無長突細胞,無軸突神經細胞　amacrine cell
视网膜下积液/視網膜下積液　subretinal fluid
视网膜下囊尾蚴病/視網膜下囊尾蚴病　subretinal cysticercosis
视网膜下丘脑纤维/視網膜下丘腦纖維　retinohypothalamic fiber
视网膜像/視[網膜]像　optogram
视网膜小疣/視網膜小疣　retinal drusen
视网膜新生血管化/視網膜新生血管化　retinal neovascularization
视网膜血管/視網膜血管　retinal vessel
视网膜血管病变/視網膜血管病變　retinal vasculopathy
视网膜血管阻塞/視網膜血管阻塞　ophthalmovascular choke
视网膜血管瘤病/視網膜血管瘤病　retinal angiomatosis
视网膜血管炎/視網膜血管炎　retinal vasculitis
视网膜血管纡曲/視網膜血管紆曲　tortuosity of retinal vessel
视网膜血压测量/視網膜血壓測量,視網膜動脈壓測量法　ophthalmodynamometry
视网膜血压计/視網膜血壓計　ophthalmodynamometer
视网膜循环时间/視網膜循環時間　retinal circulation time
视网膜炎/視網膜炎　retinitis
视网膜移位术/視網膜移位術,視網膜水腫切開術　hydrodictiotomy
视网膜照片/視網膜照片　retinograph
视网膜照相术/視網膜照像術　retinography
视网膜震荡/視網膜震蕩　commotio retinae
视网膜脂血症/視網膜脂血症　retinal lipemia
视网膜痣样色素沉着/視網膜痣樣色素沈著　nevoid pigmentation of retina
视网膜中层/視網膜中層　mesoretina
视网膜中央动脉/視網膜中央動脈,視網膜中心動脈　central artery of retina, central retinal artery
视网膜中央动脉阻塞/視網膜中央動脈阻塞　central retinal artery occlusion
视网膜中央静脉/視網膜中央靜脈　central vein of retina, central retinal vein
视网膜中央静脉阻塞/視網膜中央靜脈阻塞　central retinal vein occlusion
视网膜肿瘤/視網膜腫瘤　retinal neoplasm
视网膜锥体原生质/視網膜錐體原生質　conomyoidin
视网膜自发光感/視網膜自發光感,視網膜自生光　idioretinal light
视物变形症/視物變形症,變形視　metamorphopsia
视物[大小]不称症/視物[大小]不稱症　dysmetropsia
视物颠倒/視物顛倒　upside down vision
视物显大显小交替症/視物顯大顯小交替症,交替大小视症　micromegalopsia
视物显大症/巨大幻覺[妄想]　macropsia

视物显多症/視物顯多症　polyopsia
视物显小症/視物顯小症,小视症　micropsia
视物易色/視物易色　color confusion
视物易色•脾气虚证/視物易色•脾氣虛證　color confusion with spleen qi deficiency pattern
视物易色•肾精亏虚证/視物易色•腎精虧虛證　color confusion with kidney essence deficiency pattern
视物易形/視物易形　shape blindness, visual distortion
视细胞/視細胞　visual cell
视线/視線　line of sight
视线距/視線距　distance of visual line
视像不等/影像不等　aniseikonia
视像凑合/視像湊合　fusion of image
视形测定法/視形測定法　eidoptometry
视性失语症/視性失語症　visual aphasia
视性眼阵挛/視性眼陣攣　opsoclonus
视野/視野,範圍　visual field
视野岛/視野島　visual island
视野分析仪/視野分析儀　visual field analyser
视野计/視野計　perimeter
视野检查法/視野檢查法,視野測定法　perimetry
视野镜/視野鏡　cycloscope
视野缺损/視野缺損　defect of visual field
视野缩小/視野縮小　constriction of visual field
视叶/視葉　optic lobe
视衣/視衣　visual cloth
视隐窝/視隱窩　optic recess, chiasmatic recess
视瞻昏渺/視瞻昏渺　blurred vision, obscured vision
视瞻昏渺•肝气郁结证/視瞻昏渺•肝氣鬱結證　obscured vision with liver qi stagnation pattern
视瞻昏渺•肝肾阴虚证/視瞻昏渺•肝腎陰虛證　obscured vision with liver-kidney yin deficiency pattern
视瞻昏渺•气血两虚证/視瞻昏渺•氣血兩虛證　obscured vision with qi-blood deficiency pattern
视瞻昏渺•痰湿蕴结证/視瞻昏渺•痰濕蘊結證　obscured vision with phlegm-dampness amassment pattern
视瞻昏渺•瘀血阻络证/視瞻昏渺•瘀血阻絡證　obscured vision with pattern of static blood obstructing collateral
视瞻有色/視瞻有色　colored shade before eye
视瞻有色•肝气郁结证/視瞻有色•肝氣鬱結證　colored shade before eye with liver qi stagnation pattern
视瞻有色•肝肾两虚证/視瞻有色•肝腎兩虛證　colored shade before eye with liver-kidney deficiency pattern
视瞻有色•痰湿化热证/視瞻有色•痰濕化熱證　colored shade before eye with pattern of phlegm-dampness transforming into heat
视瞻有色•痰湿郁滞证/視瞻有色•痰濕鬱滯證　colored shade before eye with phlegm-dampness stagnation pattern
视瞻有色•阴虚火旺证/視瞻有色•陰虛火旺證　colored shade before eye with pattern of yin deficiency and fire effulgence
视正反斜/視正反斜　straight thing seen as oblique
视知觉/視知覺　visual perception
视直如曲/視直如曲　metamorphopsia, straight thing seen as crooked
视中枢/視[覺]中樞　optic center
视轴/視軸　optic axis, visual axis
视轴计/視軸計,視軸测定器　haploscope
视轴矫正法/視軸矯正術　orthoptics
视轴矫正器/視軸矯正器,矯眼器　orthoptoscope
视轴矫正医师/視軸矯正醫師,視軸矯正專家　orthoptist
视轴偏歪测量器/視軸偏歪測量器,視軸差度計　chiastometer
[视]锥细胞/[視]錐細胞　cone cell
视紫红质/視紫[紅]質　porphyropsin, rhodopsin
拭子/拭子　swab
柿蒂/柿蒂　persimmon calyx
是动病/是動病　disease caused by disorder of this channel
适当热量饮食/適當熱量飲食,正常熱量飲食　eucaloric diet
适当食物/適當食物　adequate diet
适当性红细胞增多症/適當性紅血球增多症　appropriate polycythemia
适量营养/適當營養　adequate nutrition
适形放射疗法/適形放射療法　conformal radiotherapy
适应比值/適應比值　accommodation ratio
适应不良行为/適應不良行爲　maladaptive behavior
适应计/適應計　adaptometer
适应卡尔曼滤波法/適應性卡爾曼濾波法　adaptive Kalman filtering method
适应酶/適應酶,適應酵素　adaptive enzyme
适应乳/適應乳　adapted milk
适应行为/適應行爲　adaptive behavior
适应性肥大/適應性肥大　adaptive hypertrophy
适应性活动/適應性活動　adaptive activity

适应性疾病/適應[疾]病 adaptation disease
适应[性]障碍/適應[性]障礙 adjustment disorder
适应障碍伴抑郁心境/適應障礙伴憂鬱心境,適應障礙症并發憂鬱情緒 adjustment disorder with depressed mood
适应证/適應證 indication
适[作用]/適應 adaptation
适于胎龄儿/適於胎齡兒 appropriate for gestational age infant
适者生存/適者生存 survival of the fittest
室/室 chamber, room
室壁动脉瘤/室壁動脈瘤 mural aneurysm
室壁激动时间/室壁激動時間 ventricular activation time
室壁运动/室壁運動 ventricular wall motion
室襞/室襞,褶 ventricular fold
室房传导/室房傳導 ventriculoatrial conduction
室管膜/室管膜 ependyma
室管膜病/室管膜病 ependopathy
室管膜层/室管層 ependymal layer
室管膜瘤/室管膜瘤 ependymoma
室管膜母细胞瘤/室管膜母細胞瘤,室管膜胚細胞瘤 ependymoblastoma
室管膜囊肿/室管膜囊腫 ependymal cyst
室管膜神经胶质瘤/室管膜神經膠質瘤 ependymal glioma
室管膜细胞/室管膜細胞 ependymal cell
室管膜下瘤/室管膜下瘤 subependymoma
室管膜下神经胶质瘤/室管膜下神經膠質瘤 subependymal glioma
室管膜炎/室管膜炎 ependymitis
室间隔/室間隔 interventricular septum
室间隔肌部/室間隔肌部 muscular part of interventricular septum
室间隔膜部/室間隔膜部 membranous part of interventricular septum
室间隔破裂/室間隔破裂 ventricular septal rupture
室间隔缺如/室間隔缺如 absence of the interventricular septum
室间隔缺损/室間隔缺損,心室中隔缺陷 ventricular septal defect, ventricular heart septal defect
室间隔缺损修补术/室間隔缺損修補術 repair of ventricular septal defect
室间隔支/室間隔支 branch of interventricular septum
室间沟/室間溝 interventricular groove
室间孔/室間孔 interventricular foramen
室内[传导]阻滞/室內傳導阻斷 intraventricular block
室内空气污染/室內空氣汙染 indoor air pollution
室内下水装置/室內下水裝置 house grainage
室襻/室襻 ventricular loop
室旁垂体束/室旁垂體束 paraventriculohypophyseal tract
室旁核/室旁核 paraventricular nucleus
室上嵴/室上嵴 supraventricular crest
室上性心动过速/室上性心動過速 supraventricular tachycardia
室温硫化型硅橡胶/室溫硫化型矽橡膠 room temperature vulcanized silicone rubber
室性搏动/心室搏動 ventricular beat
室性节律/室性節律 ventricular rhythm
室性快速性心律失常/室性快速性心律失常 ventricular tachyarrhythmia
室性流出道阻塞/室性流出道阻塞 ventricular outflow obstruction
室性期外收缩/室性期外收縮 ventricular extrasystole
室性[脱]逸搏[动]/心室逸搏 ventricular escape beat
室性心动过速/室性心動過速,心室性心搏快速 ventricular tachycardia
室性心律不齐/室性心率不齊,心室性不整脈 ventricular arrhythmia
室性早搏复合征/室性早搏複合徵 ventricular premature complex
室周器/室周器,心室周圍器官 circumventricular organs
室周纤维/室周纖維 periventricular fiber
铈放射性同位素/鈰放射性同位素 cerium radioisotope
铈同位素/鈰同位素 cerium isotope
舐食状杂音/舐食狀雜音 lapping murmur
释放综合征/釋放症候群 release syndrome
释义性妄想/釋義性妄想 delusion of interpretation
嗜癌性/嗜癌性,親癌性 carcinophilia
嗜表皮性/嗜表皮性,親表皮性 epidermotropism
嗜表皮性成淋巴细胞瘤/嗜表皮性成淋巴母細胞瘤,親表皮性淋巴母細胞瘤 epidermotropic lymphoblastoma
嗜表皮性网状细胞增多[症]/嗜表皮性網狀細胞增多[症],親表皮性網狀細胞增生症 epidermotropic reticulosis
嗜补体簇/嗜補體族,親補體族 complementophil group
嗜创伤癖/嗜創傷癖,好創傷癖 traumatophilia

嗜碘阿米巴囊肿/嗜碘阿米巴囊腫　iodamoeba cyst
嗜碘颗粒/嗜碘粒　iodophil granule
嗜碘性/嗜碘性　iodophilia
嗜动物性真菌/嗜動物性真菌　zoophilic fungus
[嗜锇]板层小体/[嗜鋨]板層體　osmiophilic lamellar body
嗜锇性/嗜鋨性　osmiophilia
嗜锇血小板/嗜鋨血小板　osmiophilic platelet
嗜二氧化碳噬细胞菌属/嗜二氧化碳噬纖細菌屬　Capnocytophaga
嗜肺军团菌感染/嗜肺軍團菌感染,退伍军人症桿菌感染　Legionella pneumophilia infection
嗜粪癖/嗜糞癖　coprophilia
嗜粪癖者/嗜糞癖者　coprophiliac
嗜钙性/嗜鈣性　calciphilia
嗜铬颗粒/嗜鉻顆粒　chromaffin granule
嗜铬粒蛋白类/嗜鉻粒蛋白類　chromogranin
嗜铬器官病/嗜鉻器官病,嗜鉻組織病　chromaffinopathy
嗜铬系统/嗜鉻系統　chromaffin system
嗜铬细胞/嗜鉻細胞　chromaffin cell
嗜铬细胞瘤/嗜鉻細胞瘤　chromaffin-cell tumor, phaeochromocytoma
嗜铬性/嗜鉻性　chromaffinity
嗜铬性副神经节/嗜鉻性副神經節　chromaffin paraganglia
嗜铬组织功能亢进/嗜鉻組織功能亢進,嗜鉻細胞機能過旺　hyperchromaffinism
嗜好与变应性接触性皮炎/嗜好與過敏性接觸性皮膚炎　hobbies and allergic contact dermatitis
嗜碱粒细胞/嗜鹼粒細胞　basophil
嗜碱粒细胞白血病/嗜鹼粒細胞白血病　basophilic cell leukemia
嗜碱粒细胞试验/嗜鹼[粒細胞]試驗　basophil test
嗜碱染色质/嗜鹼染色質,鹼基性核染質　basichromatin
嗜碱细胞/嗜鹼細胞　basophilic cell
嗜碱细胞腺瘤/嗜鹼細胞腺瘤　basophilic adenoma
嗜碱细胞性白血病/嗜鹼細胞性白血病,嗜鹼性血球白血病　basophilic leukemia
嗜碱性/嗜鹼性,嗜鹼現象　basophilia
嗜碱性白细胞/嗜鹼性白血球　basophilic leukocyte
嗜碱性白细胞减少/嗜鹼性白血球減少　basophilic leukopenia
嗜碱性白细胞增多/嗜鹼性白血球增多　basophilic leukocytosis
嗜碱性胞质副网素/嗜鹼性細胞副網質　basicytoparaplastin
嗜碱性变性/嗜鹼性變性　basic degeneration
嗜碱性成血红血细胞/嗜鹼性成紅血細胞,嗜鹼性母紅血球　basophilic erythroblast
嗜碱性副染色质/嗜鹼性副染色質,鹼基性副核染質,鹼基性核成形質　basiparachromatin, basicaryoplastin
嗜碱性副网素/嗜鹼性副網質,嗜鹼性副形成質　basiparaplastin
嗜碱性杆细胞/嗜鹼性桿細胞　basophilic band cell
嗜碱性杆状核粒细胞/嗜鹼性桿狀核粒細胞　basophilic granulocyte band form
嗜碱性粒/嗜鹼[性]粒　basophil granules
嗜碱性粒细胞/嗜鹼性粒細胞,嗜鹼性顆粒球　basophil, basophilic granulocyte
嗜碱性粒细胞脱颗粒试验/嗜鹼性粒細胞脫顆粒試驗　basophil degranulation test
嗜碱性染色微粒/嗜鹼性染色微粒,鹼基性染色小粒　basichromiole
嗜碱性退化/嗜鹼性退化　basophilic degeneration
嗜碱性晚幼粒细胞/嗜鹼性晚幼粒細胞,嗜鹼性後髓細胞　basophilic metamyelocyte
嗜碱性细胞/嗜鹼性細胞,嗜鹼白血球　basocyte
嗜碱性细胞减少[症]/嗜鹼性細胞減少　basocytopenia
嗜碱性细胞趋化因子/嗜鹼性細胞趨化因子　basophil chemotactic factor
嗜碱性细胞增多[症]/嗜鹼性細胞增多　basocytosis
嗜碱性早幼粒细胞/嗜鹼性早幼粒細胞　basophilic promyelocyte
嗜碱性中幼粒细胞/嗜鹼性中幼粒細胞　basophilic myelocyte
嗜碱异染性/鹼基性色素異染性　basometachromophil
嗜酒者/嗜酒者,酒徒　drunkard
嗜酒者互戒协会/嗜酒者互戒協會,隱名者戒酒俱樂部　alcoholics anonymous
嗜巨噬细胞抗体/嗜巨噬細胞抗體　macrophage cytophilic antibody
嗜冷生物/嗜冷生物　psychrophile
嗜龙胆紫物/嗜龍膽紫物　gentianophil
嗜猫癖/嗜貓癖　ailurophilia
嗜眠性脑炎/嗜眠性腦炎　lethargic encephalitis
嗜眠[症]/嗜眠症,病態的嗜眠　hypnosia
嗜派若宁性/嗜派若寧性　pyroninophilia
嗜派若宁性颗粒/嗜派若寧性顆粒　pyroninophilic granulations
嗜皮菌属/嗜皮菌屬　Dermatophilus
嗜品红粒/嗜品紅粒　fuchsinophil granules

嗜品红物/嗜品紅物　fuchsinophil
嗜品红性/嗜品紅性　fuchsinophilia
嗜热菌蛋白酶/嗜熱菌蛋白酶　Thermolysin
嗜热四膜虫/嗜熱四膜蟲　Tetrahymena thermophila
嗜色细胞/嗜色細胞,易染細胞　chromophil cell
嗜神经病毒/嗜神經病毒,親神經性病毒　neurotropic virus
嗜神经性/嗜神經性,親神經性　neurotropic
嗜兽癖/嗜獸癖　zoomania
嗜水气单胞菌/吸水性産氣單孢菌　Aeromonas hydrophila
嗜睡/嗜睡,嗜眠　lethargy, somnolence
嗜睡样昏迷/嗜睡樣昏迷　cataphora
嗜苏丹体/嗜蘇丹質　sudanophil
嗜酸副染色质/嗜酸副染色質,嗜酸副核網質　oxyparaplastin
嗜酸粒细胞白血病/嗜酸粒細胞白血病　eosinophilic cell leukemia
嗜酸粒细胞[过敏]趋化性因子/嗜酸粒細胞[過敏]趨化性因子,嗜伊紅球趨化因數　eosinophil chemotactic factor
嗜酸粒细胞减少/嗜伊粒細胞減少　eosinopenia
嗜酸粒细胞增多/嗜伊粒細胞增多　eosinophilia
嗜酸粒细胞增多肌痛综合征/嗜酸粒細胞增多肌痛症候群　eosinophilia-myalgia syndrome
嗜酸染色质/嗜酸染色質　lanthanin
嗜酸细胞过多/嗜酸細胞過多　hypereosinophilic
嗜酸细胞过多-肌痛综合征/嗜酸細胞過多-肌痛症候群　hypereosinophilia-myalgia syndrome
嗜酸细胞过氧化物酶/嗜酸細胞過氧化物酶　eosinophil peroxidase
嗜酸细胞活化趋化因子/嗜酸細胞活化趨化因子,伊紅趨素　eotaxin
嗜酸细胞颗粒蛋白质类/嗜酸細胞顆粒蛋白質類　eosinophil granule proteins
嗜酸细胞趋化因子/嗜酸細胞趨化因子　eosinophil chemotactic factor
嗜酸细胞肉芽肿/嗜酸細胞肉芽腫,嗜伊紅性肉芽腫　eosinophilic granuloma
嗜酸细胞腺瘤/嗜酸細胞腺瘤　eosinophil adenoma
嗜酸细胞性白血病/嗜酸細胞性白血病　eosinophilic leukemia
嗜酸细胞性肺/嗜酸細胞性肺　eosinophilic lung
嗜酸细胞性蜂窝[组]织炎/嗜酸細胞性蜂窩組織炎　eosinophilic cellulitis
嗜酸[细胞]性海绵样水肿/嗜酸[細胞]性海綿樣水腫　eosinophilic spongiosis
嗜酸[细胞]性筋膜炎/嗜酸[細胞]性筋膜炎　eosinophilic fasciitis
嗜酸[细胞]性溃疡/嗜伊紅球性潰瘍　eosinophilic ulcer
嗜酸[细胞]性脓疱性毛囊炎/嗜酸[細胞]性膿疱性毛囊炎　eosinophilic pustular folliculitis
嗜酸细胞性膀胱炎/嗜酸[細胞]性膀胱炎　eosinophilic cystitis
嗜酸[细胞]性舌溃疡/嗜酸[細胞]性舌潰瘍　eosinophilic ulcer of tongue
嗜酸细胞性胃肠炎/嗜酸[細胞]性胃腸炎　eosinophilic gastroenteritis
嗜酸细胞性胃炎/嗜酸細胞性胃炎　eosinophilic gastritis
嗜酸[细胞]性心内膜心肌病/嗜酸[細胞]性心内膜心肌病　eosinophilic endomyocardial disease
嗜酸[细胞]性血管炎/嗜酸[細胞]性血管炎　eosinophilic vasculitis
嗜酸[细胞]性血管中心性纤维化/嗜酸[細胞]性血管中心性纖維化　eosinophilic angiocentric fibrosis
嗜酸[细胞]性脂膜炎/嗜酸[細胞]性脂膜炎　eosinophilic panniculitis
嗜酸细胞阳离子蛋白质/嗜酸細胞陽離子蛋白質　eosinophil cationic protein
嗜酸细胞源神经毒素/嗜酸細胞源神經毒素　eosinophil-derived neurotoxin
嗜酸细胞增多-肌痛/嗜酸[細胞]增多-肌痛　eosinophilia-myalgia
嗜酸细胞增多性肝肥大综合征/嗜酸[細胞]增多性肝腫大症候群　eosinophilia-hepatomegaly syndrome
嗜酸细胞增多综合征/嗜酸細胞增多症候群　hypereosinophilic syndrome
嗜酸细胞增生性淋巴肉芽肿/嗜酸細胞增生性淋巴肉芽腫　eosinophilic lymphoid granuloma
嗜酸细胞主要碱性蛋白质/嗜酸細胞主要鹼性蛋白質　eosinophil major basic protein
嗜酸小体/嗜酸小體　eosinophilic body
嗜酸性/嗜酸性　acidophilia
嗜酸性白细胞增多症/嗜酸性白細胞增多症,嗜伊紅性白血球增多,嗜酸性白血球增多　eosinophilic leukocytosis
嗜酸性包涵体/嗜酸性包涵體,嗜伊紅性包涵體　eosinophilic inclusion body
嗜酸[性]胞质/嗜酸[性]胞質,嗜酸原漿,嗜酸細胞漿　oxyplasm
嗜酸性分叶核粒细胞/嗜酸性分葉核粒細胞　eosinophilic granulocyte segmented form
嗜酸性杆细胞/嗜酸性桿細胞　eosinophilic band cell

嗜酸性杆状核粒细胞/嗜酸性桿狀核粒細胞 eosinophilic granulocyte band form
嗜酸性坏死/嗜酸性壞死 acidophilic necrosis
嗜酸性胶原病/嗜酸性膠原病,嗜伊紅性膠原病 eosinophilic collagen disease
嗜酸性颗粒/嗜酸性顆粒 acidophilic granule
嗜酸性粒/嗜酸粒 acidophil granule
嗜酸性粒细胞/嗜酸性粒細胞,嗜酸性顆粒球,嗜伊紅血球 eosinophilic cell, eosinophilic granulocyte, eosinophil
嗜酸性粒细胞集落生成单位/嗜酸性粒細胞集落生成單位,單核細胞-巨噬細胞集落形成單位 colony forming unit eosinophil, CFU-EO
嗜酸性粒细胞减少/嗜酸性粒細胞減少 hypoeosinophilia
嗜酸性粒细胞性肺病/嗜酸性粒細胞性肺病 eosinophilic pneumonopathy
嗜酸性粒细胞增多/嗜酸性粒細胞增多 hypereosinophilia
嗜酸性脓肿/嗜酸性膿腫 eosinophilic abscess
嗜酸性晚幼粒细胞/嗜酸性晚幼粒細胞,嗜伊紅性後髓細胞 eosinophilic metamyelocyte
嗜酸[性]细胞/嗜酸細胞 acidophilic cell
嗜酸腺癌/嗜酸腺癌 oncocytic adenoma
嗜酸性腺瘤/嗜酸性腺瘤,嗜伊紅腺瘤 acidophilic adenoma, eosinophilic adenoma
嗜酸[性]小脓肿/嗜酸[性]小膿腫,嗜伊紅球性微膿瘍 eosinophilic microabscess
嗜酸性早幼粒细胞/嗜酸性早幼粒細胞,嗜伊紅性前髓細胞 eosinophilic promyelocyte
嗜酸[性]中幼粒细胞/嗜酸[性]中幼粒細胞,嗜伊紅性骨髓細胞 eosinophilic myelocyte
嗜酸性组织细胞增多症/嗜酸性組織細胞增多症,嗜伊紅球性組織細胞增生症 eosinophilic histiocytosis
嗜天青颗粒/嗜天青顆粒,嗜苯胺藍顆粒 azurophilic granule
嗜铁体/嗜鐵體,嗜鐵組織 siderophil
嗜同性抗体/嗜同性抗體,嗜同種抗體 isophil antibody
嗜卧/嗜臥 somnolence
嗜细胞群/嗜細胞群,親細胞族 cytophil group
嗜细胞[性]抗体/嗜細胞[性]抗體 cytophilic antibody
嗜溴剂癖/嗜溴劑癖,溴劑狂 bromomania
嗜血杆菌属/嗜血桿菌屬 Haemophilus
嗜血杆菌性脑膜炎/嗜血桿菌性腦膜炎 haemophilus meningitis
嗜血杆菌疫苗/嗜血桿菌疫苗,嗜血菌菌苗 Haemophilus caccine
嗜血红蛋白性/嗜血紅素 hemoglobinophilia
嗜血菌感染/嗜血菌感染 haemophilus infection
嗜血细胞性淋巴组织细胞增多症/嗜血細胞性淋巴組織細胞增多症 hemophagocytic lymphohistiocytosis
嗜血综合征/噬血症候群,吞噬血球症候群 hemophagocytic syndrome
嗜药癖/嗜藥癖,服藥癖 pharmacophilia
嗜夜癖/嗜[黑]夜癖 nyctophilia
嗜异/嗜異 paroxia
嗜异染细胞/嗜異染細胞 metachromatophil
嗜异性抗体/嗜異性抗體 heterophil antibody
嗜异性抗原/嗜異性抗原 heterophil antigen
嗜异性粒细胞/嗜異性粒細胞 heterophil granulocyte
嗜异性凝集试验/嗜異性凝集試驗 heterophil agglutination test
嗜银细胞瘤/嗜銀細胞瘤,親銀細胞瘤 argentaffinoma
嗜银细胞瘤综合征/嗜銀細胞瘤症候群,轉移性類癌瘤症候群 argentaffinoma syndrome
嗜银纤维/嗜銀纖維 argyrophilic fiber
嗜银性/嗜銀性 argyrophilic, argyrophilia
嗜欲/嗜欲 indulgence in sensual pleasure
嗜云癖/嗜雲癖,愛雲性精神病,雲翳嗜好 nephelopsychosis
[嗜]中性/嗜中性 neutrophilia
嗜中性白细胞/嗜中性白細胞,嗜中性白血球 neutrophil
嗜中性白细胞活化/嗜中性白細胞活化,嗜中性白細胞啟動 neutrophil activation
嗜中性白细胞增多/嗜中性白細胞增多,嗜中性白血球增多 neutrophilic leukocytosis
嗜中性白细胞增多症/嗜中性白血球增多症 neutrophilia
嗜中性带状细胞/嗜中性帶狀細胞 neutrophilic band cell
嗜中性皮肤炎/嗜中性皮膚炎 neutrophilic dermatitis
嗜中性细胞/[嗜]中性細胞,嗜中性白血球 neutrophil cell
嗜中性小汗腺炎/嗜中性小汗腺炎,嗜中性球汗腺炎 neutrophilic eccrine hidradenitis
嗜中性中幼粒细胞/嗜中性中幼粒細胞,嗜中性骨髓細胞 neutrophilic myelocyte
噬白细胞现象/噬白細胞現象,噬白血球作用

leukocytophagy
噬斑原位杂交/噬斑原位雜交 in situ plaque hybridization
噬尘细胞/噬塵細胞 coniophage
噬肝细胞/噬肝細胞 hepatophage
噬骨细胞/噬骨細胞,蝕骨細胞,破骨細胞 osteophage
噬黑素细胞/噬黑色素細胞 melanophage
噬红[细胞]细胞/噬紅[細胞]細胞,噬紅血球細胞 erythrophage
噬红细胞现象/噬紅細胞現象,噬紅血球現象 erythrophagia
噬红细胞作用/噬紅細胞作用,噬紅血球作用 erythrophagocytosis
噬肌细胞/噬肌細胞 myophage
噬菌体/噬菌體 bacteriophage
噬菌体溶解作用/噬菌體溶解,噬體崩解 phagelysis
噬菌体型/噬菌體型 lysotype
噬菌体学/噬菌體學 bacteriophagology
噬菌体展示/噬菌體顯示 phage display
噬菌调理素/噬菌調理素 bacteriorhodopsin
噬菌现象/噬菌[現象] bacteriophagia
噬色细胞/噬色細胞 chromophage
噬神经细胞/噬神經細胞 neuronophage
噬神经细胞作用/噬神經細胞作用 neuronophagy
噬髓鞘细胞/噬髓鞘細胞 axophage
噬铁细胞/噬鐵細胞 siderophage
噬细胞免疫/噬菌免疫 phagocytic immunity
噬细胞栓/噬細胞栓 phagocytic thrombus
噬血细胞/噬血細胞,噬紅血球細胞 hematophage
噬鱼腹蛇/噬魚腹蛇 moccasin
噬原虫细胞/噬原蟲細胞 protozoophage
噬脂细胞/噬脂細胞 lipophage
螫伤/螫傷 sting
螫伤反应/螫傷反應 stinging reaction
螫蝇属/螫蠅屬 *Stomoxys*
收呆至神汤/收呆至神湯 treasured decoction for relieving dementia
收割者肺/收割者肺,農夫肺 harvester lung
收肌/收肌 adductor muscle
收肌管/收肌管 adductor canal, subsartorial canal
收肌腱裂孔/收肌腱裂孔 adductor tendinous opening
收肌结节/收肌結節 adductor tubercle
收集透镜/收集透鏡 collective lens
收敛/收斂 convergence
收敛神气/收斂神氣 convergence of spirit and qi
收敛酸镉/收斂酸鎘 cadmium styphnate

收敛酸锌/收斂酸鋅 zinc styphnate
收敛性/收斂[性],收斂作用 astringency
收敛性苦味药/收斂性苦味劑,止血性苦味劑 styptic bitter
收敛药/收斂藥 astringent
收率/收率,産率 yield
收容入院/收容入院 institutionalization
收容入院青少年/收容入院青少年 institutionalized adolescent
收视返听/收視返聽 withdraw the sight and reverse hearing
收缩/收縮,攣縮 contraction
收缩板/收縮板 contractile disc
收缩波/收縮波 contraction wave
收缩储备力/收縮儲備力 contractile reserve
收缩蛋白质类/收縮蛋白質類 contractile proteins
收缩力/收縮力 contractility
收缩期储备/收縮期儲備,收縮性儲量 systolic reserve
收缩期高血压/收縮期高血壓 systolic hypertension
收缩期喀喇音/收縮期喀喇音 systolic click
收缩期脉搏曲线/收縮期脈波 sphygmosystole
收缩期末容积/收縮期末容積 endsystolic volume
收缩期末容积指数/收縮期末容積指數 endsystolic volume index
收缩期末压/收縮期末壓 endsystolic pressure
收缩期喷射喀喇音/收縮期噴射喀喇音 systolic ejection click
收缩期前奔马律/收縮期前奔馬律 presystolic gallop
收缩期前向活动/收縮期前向活動 systolic anterior motion
收缩期前杂音/收縮期前雜音 presystolic murmur
收缩期前震颤/收縮期前震顫 presystolic thrill
收缩期射血/收縮期射血 systolic discharge
收缩期心力衰竭/收縮期心力衰竭 systolic heart failure
收缩期压力梯度/心收縮壓力梯度 systolic gradient
收缩期杂音/收縮期雜音 systolic murmur
收缩期震颤/收縮期震顫 systolic thrill
收缩晚期杂音/收縮晚期雜音 late systolic murmur
收缩纤维细胞/收縮纖維細胞 contractile fiber cell
收缩压/收縮[期血]壓 systolic pressure
收缩压-时间指数/收縮壓-時間指數,收縮性壓力時間指數 systolic pressure-time index
收缩因子/收縮因子 contracting factor
收缩早期杂音/收縮早期雜音 early systolic murmur

收缩中期杂音/收縮中期雜音　midsystolic murmur
收缩状况/收縮狀況　contractile state
手/手　hand, manus
手背/手背　back of hand, dorsum of hand
手背腱膜/手背腱膜　aponeurosis dorsalis manus
手背筋膜/手背筋膜　dorsal fascia of hand
手背静脉丛/手背靜脈叢　dorsal venous plexus of hand
手背静脉网/手背靜脈網　dorsal venous rete of hand, rete venosum dorsale manus
手背皮下间隙/手背皮下間隙　dorsal subcutaneous space
手背热/手背熱　feverishness on dorsum of hand
手臂测力法/手臂測力法　arm ergometry
手臂骨骼/手臂骨骼　arm bones
手不全畸胎/手不全畸胎　perochirus
手部除皱术/手部除皺術　hand rhytidectomy
手部舟状骨/手部舟狀骨　scaphoid bone of hand
手颤/手顫　tremor of hand
手长宽度比/手長寬度比,手比值　hand ratio
手成形术/手成形術,手造形術　chiroplasty
手持视野计/手持視野計　hand held perimeter
手持压缩器/手持壓縮器,手用填壓器　hand condenser
手动增压泵/手動增壓泵　hand increasing pressure pump
手动铸压机/手[動]鑄壓機　hand casting presser
手恶性水肿/手惡性水腫　malignant edema of hand
手发背/手發背　cellulitis of hand dorsum, pyogenic carbuncle of back of hand
手发背•风热证/手發背•風熱證　cellulitis of hand dorsum with wind-heat pattern
手发背•火毒蕴结证/手發背•火毒蘊結證　cellulitis of hand dorsum with fire-toxin amassment pattern
手发背•气血两虚证/手發背•氣血兩虛證　cellulitis of hand dorsum with qi-blood deficiency pattern
手发背•湿热壅滞证/手發背•濕熱壅滯證　cellulitis of hand dorsum with pattern of dampness-heat congestion and stagnation
手法/手[推]法,操作法　manipulation
手法扩张术/用手擴張術　manual dilatation
手风琴状腹/手風琴狀腹　accordion abdomen
手骨/手骨　bone of hand, hand bone
手骨间背侧肌/手骨間背側肌　dorsal interosseous of hand
手骨筋膜鞘/手骨筋膜鞘　fascia sheath of hand bone
手关节/手關節　joints of hand
手关节病变/手關節病變　cheiroarthropathy
手关节炎/手關節炎　cheirarthritis
手汗/手汗　hand sweating
手[肌]痉挛/手痙攣,寫痙　cheirospasm
手畸形/手畸形　hand deformity
手肩综合征/手肩症候群　hand-shoulder syndrome
手厥阴心包经/手厥陰心包經　Jueyin Pericardium Channel of Hand, Jueyin Pericardium Meridian of Hand
手控呼吸器/手控呼吸器　manual respirator
手控通气/手控通氣　manual ventilation
手摸心会/手摸心會　differentiation by palpating the injured area
[手]内侧鞘/[手]內側鞘　medial compartment
手皮肤病/手皮膚病　hand dermatosis
手偏利/手偏利　handedness
手球员掌/手球員掌,手球戲掌傷　handball palm
手取胎盘术/手取胎盤術　manual removal of placenta
手拳不展/手拳不展　inextensible fist
手软/手軟　flaccidity of hand
手三里/手三里　shousanli, LI10
手三阳经/手三陽經　three yang channels of hand, three yang meridians of hand
手三阴经/手三陰經　three yin channels of hand, three yin meridians of hand
手烧伤/手燒傷　burn of hand
手少阳三焦经/手少陽三焦經　Shaoyang Sanjiao Channel of Hand, Shaoyang Sanjiao Meridian of Hand
手少阴心经/手少陰心經　Shaoyin Heart Channel of Hand, Shaoyin Heart Meridian of Hand
手湿疹/手濕疹　hand eczema
手势交流/手勢交流　manual communication
手[势]语/手語　cheirology
手术/手術　operation
手术并发症/手術并發症　operative complication
手术步骤/手術步驟　operating procedure
手术灯/手術燈　operating light
手术放大镜/手術放大鏡　operating loupe
手术后并发症/手術後并發症　postoperative complication
手术后出血/手術後出血　postoperative hemorrhage
手术后恶心呕吐/手術後噁心嘔吐　postoperative nausea and vomiting
手术后裂/手術後裂　postoperative cleft
手术后期间/手術後期間　postoperative period
手术后缺损/手术后缺損,手術性缺陷　operative defect

手术后疝/手術後疝　postoperative hernia
手术后梭状细胞结节/手術後梭狀細胞結節,創傷後梭狀細胞結節　postoperative spindle cell nodule
手术后疼痛/手術後疼痛　postoperative pain
手术后外科敷料/手術後外科敷料　postoperative surgical dressing
手术后心肌梗死/手術後心肌梗死　postoperative myocardial infarction
手术后医护/手術後醫護　postoperative care
手术恐惧症/手術恐懼症　ergasiophobia
手术疗法/手術療法　surgical therapy
手术期间/手術期間　intraoperative period
手术前护理/手術前護理　preoperative care
手术区/手術區　operating field
手术入路/手術入路　operative approach
手术失血/手術失血　surgical blood loss
手术示教室/手術示教室　operating theater
手术室/手術室,開刀房　operating room
手术室覆巾/手術室覆巾　operating room draping
手术室规则/手術室規則　operating room decorum
手术室护理/手術室護理　operating room nursing
手术室技术员/手術室技術員　operating room technician
手术室信息系统/手術室信息系統,手術室資訊系統　operating room information systems
手术台/手術檯　operation table
手术外固定/手術外固定,手術性外部固定　external surgical fixation
手术外套/手術外套,手術[套]衣　operating overall
手术显微镜/手術顯微鏡　operating microscope
手术形成结构/手術形成結構　surgically-created structure
手术性牙髓暴露/手術性牙髓曝露,手術露牙髓[術]　surgical pulp exposure
手术止血/手術止血　surgical hemostasis
手术中并发症/手術中并發症　intraoperative complication
手术中护理/手術中護理　intraoperative care
手术中监测/手術中監測　intraoperative monitoring
手术助理护士/手術助理護士,手術助理護理人員　scrub nurse
手损伤/手損傷　hand injury
手太阳小肠经/手太陽小腸經　Taiyang Small Intestine Channel of Hand, Taiyang Small Intestine Meridian of Hand
手太阴肺经/手太陰肺經　Taiyin Lung Channel of Hand, Taiyin Lung Meridian of Hand
手套/手套　glove
手套接触性皮炎/手套接觸性皮膚炎　glove dermatitis
手套区/手套區　glove area
手套式绷带/手套形繃帶　gauntlet bandage
手套式感觉缺失/手套式感覺缺失,手套狀感覺缺失　gauntlet anesthesia
手痛/手痛　cheiralgia
手推车/手推車　cart
[手]外侧鞘/[手]外側鞘　lateral compartment
手腕X光片/手腕X光片　hand-wrist radiograph
手五里/手五里　shouwuli, LI13
手小头间静脉/手小頭間靜脈　venae intercapitales manus
手性/手性　chirality
手性拆分/手性拆分　chiral separation
手性分子/手性分子　chiral molecule
手性固定相/手性固定相　chiral stationary phase, CSP
手性碳原子/手性碳原子　chiral carbon atom
手癣/手癬　tinea manuum
手阳明大肠经/手陽明大腸經　Yangming Large Intestine Channel of Hand, Yangming Large Intestine Meridian of Hand
手艺工痉挛/手工痙攣　handicraft spasm
手蚓状肌/手蚓狀肌　lumbrical muscle of hand
手硬/手硬　stiff hand
手用空气注射器/手用空氣注射器,手用空氣注射筒　hand air syringe
手用器械/手用器械　hand instrument
手浴/手浴　maniluvium
手运动觉/手運動覺　cheirocinesthesia
手掌/手掌　palm of hand, palm
手掌瘢痕挛缩/手掌瘢痕攣縮　scar contracture of palm
手掌部分萎缩/手掌部分萎縮　partial thenar atrophy
手掌侧静脉/手掌側靜脈　palmar metacarpal veins
手掌侧静脉网/手掌側靜脈網　palmar venous rete of hand
手掌多汗症/手掌多汗症　palmar hyperhidrosis
手掌黑癣/手掌黑癬　tinea nigra palmaris
手掌红斑/手掌紅斑　palmar erythema
手掌慢性肥厚性皮肤病/手掌慢性肥厚性皮膚病　chronic hypertrophic dermatosis of the palm
手掌脓疱病/手掌膿皰病　palmar pustulosis
手掌纹/手掌紋　palmar print
手指/[手]指　finger
手指背面/手指背面　dorsal surface of finger
手指骨/手指骨　ossa digitorum manus

手指间藏毛窦/手指間藏毛竇 interdigital pilonidal sinus
手指灵敏性/手指靈巧性 finger dexterity
手指挛急/手指攣急 spasm of finger
手指失认症/手指失認症,手指認識不能 finger agnosia
手指体积描记器/手指體積描記器 finger plethysmography
手指掌面/手指掌面 palmar surface of finger
手指支持/手指支持,指支托 finger rest
[手]中间鞘/[手]中間鞘 intermediate compartment
手舟骨/[手]舟骨 scaphoid bone
手镯/手鐲 bracelet
手镯试验/手鐲試驗 bracelet test
手足病医生/手足病醫生,手腳醫,足醫 chiropodist
手足搐搦/手足搐搦 tetany
手足搐搦静止期/破傷風靜止期 tetanode
手足疔疮/手足疔瘡 ding of hand and foot, deep-rooted sore of hand and foot, hard furuncle on hand and foot
手足疔疮·火毒蕴结证/手足疔瘡·火毒蘊結證 ding of hand and foot with fire-toxin amassment pattern
手足疔疮·热盛酿脓证/手足疔瘡·熱盛釀膿證 ding of hand and foot with pattern of suppuration due to heat exuberance
手足疔疮·湿热下注证/手足疔瘡·濕熱下注證 ding of hand and foot with pattern of dampness-heat diffusing downward
手足发绀/手足發紺 acrocyanosis
手足过长/手足過長,四肢過長 acrodolichomelia
手足汗出/手足汗出 sweating of hands and feet
手足胶原性斑块/手足膠原性斑塊 collagenous plaques of the hands and feet
手足厥逆/手足厥逆 deadly cold hand and foot
手足口病/手足口病,手足口症 hand-foot-mouth disease
手足逆胪/手足逆臚 cracked skin around nail
手足蠕动/手足蠕動 wriggling of limbs
手足痛/手足痛 cheiropodalgia
手足温度过低/手足溫度過低 acrohypothermy
手足心汗/手足心汗 sweating of palms and soles
手足心热/手足心熱 feverishness in palms and soles
手足徐动样痉挛/手足徐動樣痙攣 athetoid spasm
手足徐动症/手指徐動病 athetosis
手足医术/手足醫術 chiropody
守门员脱位/守門者脱位 gamekeeper dislocation
守气/守氣 maintaining needling sensation
首次通过心室显像术/首次通過心室顯像術 the first-pass ventriculography
首过代谢/首過代謝,首渡代謝 the first-pass metabolism
首过效应/首過效應,首渡效應 the first-pass effect
首剂效应/首劑效應 the first-dose response
首裂/首裂,初級裂 primary fissure
首如裹/首如裹 head with binding sensation
首乌藤/首烏藤 tuber fleeceflower stem
首乌丸/首烏丸 shouwu pills
首选药/首選藥 drug of the first choice
首要宿主/首要宿主 primary host
寿命/壽命 life span
寿命表/壽命表 life table
寿世保元/壽世保元 Longevity and Life Preservation
受盛化物/受盛化物 reservoir and transformation
受害尸体出血/受害屍體出血 cruentation
受检率/受檢率 examination rate
受精/受精 fertilization
受精龄/受精齡 fertilization age
受精卵/受精卵,受孕卵 fertilized ovum
受精卵胞质/受精卵胞質 cytuloplasm
受精卵核/受精卵核 maritonucleus
受精卵输卵管内移植/受精卵輸卵管內移植 zygote intrafallopian transfer
受精卵中心球/受精卵中心球,運動中心 kinetic center
受精膜/受精膜 fertilization membrane
受精[能]力/受精[能]力 fertility, fertilization ability
受精神分析者/受精神分析者 analysand
受精素/受精素 fertilizin
受精锥/受精錐 fertilization cone
受控环境/受控環境 controlled environment
受虐待儿童综合征/受虐待兒童症候群 battered child syndrome
受虐狂者/受虐狂者,受虐淫者 masochist
受虐癖/受虐癖,受虐淫,受虐色情 masochism
受[皮]区/受[皮]區 recipient site
受器控制钙离子通道/受器控制鈣離子管道 receptor-operated calcium channel
受氢体/受氫體 hydrogen acceptor
受体/受體 receptor
C3受体/C3受體 C3 receptor
受体储备/受體儲備 receptor reserve
受体蛋白质酪氨酸激酶类/受體蛋白質酪氨酸激酶類 receptor protein-tyrosine kinases
受体拮抗模型/受體拮抗模型 receptor-antagonist

model
受体聚集/受體聚集　receptor aggregation
受体调节/受體調節　receptor regulation
受体调控性通道/受體調控性通道　receptor operated channel
受体性萎缩/受體性萎縮　receptoric atrophy
受体学说/受體學說　receptor theory
β受体阻断剂/β受體阻斷劑　beta blocker
受调理[素作用]/受調理[素作用]　opsonize, opsonify
受位/受位　acceptor site
受氧体/受氧體　oxygen acceptor
受孕/受孕　conception
受孕期/受孕期　fertile period
受者预处理/受者預處理　recipient pretreatment
授精/授精　insemination
售后产品监测/售後產品監測　postmarketing product surveillance
兽性变性/獸性變質　theroid degeneration
兽医学/獸醫學　veterinary medicine
兽疫/獸疫　epizootic
兽疫传染/獸疫傳染,獸疫性感染,獸病性傳染　epizootic infection
兽疫性肝炎/獸疫性肝炎　epizootic hepatitis
兽疫性脑脊髓膜炎/獸疫性腦脊髓膜炎,動物流行性腦脊髓膜炎　epizootic cerebrospinal meningitis
兽疫性湿疹/獸疫性濕疹　eczema epizootica
瘦薄舌/瘦薄舌　thin tongue
瘦长体型/瘦長體型,瘦削體型,輕體型　leptosomatic habit
瘦长型者/瘦長體格者　leptosome
瘦果/瘦果　capsella
瘦弱/瘦弱　thinness
瘦素/瘦素　leptin
书写痉挛/書寫痙攣　writer spasm
书写困难/書寫困難,書寫障礙,失寫症　dysgraphia
书写区/書寫區　writing area
书写者麻痹/書寫者麻痺　scriveners palsy
枢椎/樞椎　axis
枢椎齿突/樞椎齒突　odontoid process of axis
叔醇/叔醇,三級醇　tertiary alcohol
叔丁基氢过氧化物/叔丁基氫過氧化物　tert-butyl hydroperoxide
叔丁基乙醇/叔丁基乙醇　tert-butyl alcohol
梳状肌/梳狀肌　musculi pectinati
舒巴坦/舒巴坦　sulbactam
舒必利/舒必利　sulpiride
舒-查现象/舒-查现象,Schultz-Charlton氏现象　Schultz-Charlton phenomenon
舒尔策束/舒爾策束,Schultze氏徑　Schultze tract
舒尔策胎盘/舒爾策胎盤,Schultze氏胎盤　Schultze placenta
舒尔策细胞/舒爾策細胞,嗅細胞　Schultze cell
舒尔茨-戴尔反应/舒爾茨-戴爾反應　Schultz-Dale reaction
舒尔茨束间束/舒爾茨束間束,垂點狀徑　comma tract of Schultze
舒尔茨综合征/舒爾茨症候群,Schultz氏症候群　Schultz syndrome
舒芬太尼/舒芬太尼　sufentanil
舒筋活络/舒筋活絡　relieving rigidity of muscles and activating collaterals
舒筋散结/舒筋散結　relieving rigidity of muscle and dissipate bind
舒筋止痛/舒筋止痛　relieving rigidity of muscle and relieving pain
舒林酸/舒林酸　sulindac
舒洛地尔/舒洛地爾　suloctidil
舒洛芬/舒洛芬　suprofen
舒马普坦/舒馬普坦　sumatriptan
舒适/舒適[化]　comfortization
舒张后杂音/舒張後雜音　postdiastolic murmur
舒张进针法/舒張進針法　skin stretching needle inserting
舒张末期压/舒張末期壓力　end-diastolic pressure
舒张末期压力容积关系/舒張末期壓力容積關係　end-diastolic pressure-volume relation
舒张期高血压/舒張期高血壓　diastolic hypertension
舒张期末容积/舒張期末容積　end-diastolic volume
舒张期末容积指数/舒張期末容積指數　end-diastolic volume index
舒张期末压/舒張期末壓　end-diastolic pressure
舒张期心力衰竭/舒張期心衰竭　diastolic heart failure
舒张期杂音/舒張期雜音　diastolic murmur
舒张期震颤/舒張期震顫　diastolic thrill
舒张前期杂音/舒張前[期]雜音　prediastolic murmur
T1舒张时间/T1舒張時間　T1 relaxation time
T2舒张时间/T2舒張時間　T2 relaxation time
舒张速率/舒張速率　relaxation rate
舒张压/舒張[期血]壓　diastolic pressure
舒张因子/舒張因子,舒張因數　relaxing factor
舒张早期奔马律/舒張早期奔馬率,不正常第三心音　protodiastolic gallop
舒张早期杂音/舒張早期雜音　early diastolic

murmur
舒张中期杂音/舒張中期雜音 mid-diastolic murmur
疏布绷带/疏布繃帶 open-wove bandage
疏风透疹/疏風透疹 dispelling wind to promote eruption
疏肝和胃/疏肝和胃 dispersing stagnated liver qi for regulating stomach
疏肝解郁/疏肝解鬱 dispersing stagnated liver qi for relieving qi stagnation
疏肝理气法/疏肝理氣法 dispersing liver and regulating qi
疏肝利胆/疏肝利膽 dispersing stagnated liver qi for promoting bile flow
疏经通脉反应/疏經通脈反應 meridians and collaterals clearing reaction
疏螺旋体感染/疏螺旋體感染 Borrelia infections
疏螺旋体属/疏螺旋體屬 *Borrelia*
疏溶剂作用/疏溶劑作用,壓[疏]溶媒作用 solvophobic interaction
疏散风邪/疏散風邪 dispelling wind pathogens
疏散外风剂/疏散外風劑 formula for dispersing external wind
疏水键/疏水鍵,壓水鍵 hydrophobic bond
疏水胶体/疏水膠質 hydrophobic colloid
疏水物质/疏水物質 hydrophobic substance
疏水性/疏水性 hydrophobicity
疏水作用/疏水作用,壓水作用 hydrophobic interaction
疏松部/疏鬆部 puffing
疏松骨折/疏鬆骨折 loose fracture
疏松结缔组织/疏鬆性結締組織 loose connective tissue
疏松性骨炎/疏鬆性骨炎,稀疏性骨炎 rarefying osteitis
疏五过论篇/疏五過論篇 Treatise on Patients' Social Status and Lifestyle
疏液胶体/疏液膠體,拒水膠體 lyophobic colloid
疏凿饮子/疏鑿飲子 shuzuo drink
输出层/輸出層 output layer
输出管/輸出管 efferent duct
输出量/排出量 output
输出淋巴管/輸出淋巴管 efferent lymphatic vessel
输出小管/輸出小管 efferent duct
输出小管圆锥/輸出小管圓錐 conus vasculosus
输接种血/輸接種血,接種血轉輸法 vaccinating transfusion
输精管/輸精管 deferent duct
输精管穿刺术/輸精管穿刺術 vasopuncture

输精管丛/輸精管叢 deferential plexus
输精管动脉/輸精管動脈 deferential artery
输精管缝合术/輸精管縫合術 vasorrhaphy
输精管附睾吻合术/輸精管附睾吻合術,附睾輸精管造口吻合術 epididymovasostomy
输精管附睾造影[术]/輸精管附睾造影[術],輸精管附睾放射線攝影術 vaso-epididymography
输精管睾丸吻合术/輸精管睾丸[造口]吻合術 vaso-orchidostomy
输精管壶腹/輸精管壺腹 ampulla of deferent duct, ampulla ductus deferentis
输精管畸形/輸精管畸形 deformity of vas deferens
输精管结核/輸精管結核 tuberculosis of vas deferens
输精管结扎术/輸精管結扎術 vasoligation
输精管精囊切除术/輸精管精囊切除術 vasovesiculectomy
输精管精囊炎/輸精管精囊炎 vasovesiculitis
输精管精囊造影[术]/輸精管精囊造影[術] vasoseminal vesiculography
输精管梅毒/輸精管梅毒 syphilis of vas deferens
输精管切除术/輸精管切除術 vasectomy
输精管切断术/輸精管切斷術 vasosection
输精管缺如/輸精管缺如 absence of vas deferens
输精管吻合术/輸精管[兩段造口]吻合術 vasovasostomy
输精管炎/輸精管炎 deferentitis
输精管造口术/輸精管造口術,輸精管造瘻術 vasostomy
输精管造影[术]/輸精管造影[術] vasography
输精管周炎/輸精管周[圍]炎 perideferentitis
输卵管/輸卵管 uterine tube, ovarian duct, Fallopian tube
输卵管闭锁/輸卵管閉鎖 atresia of uterine tube, atresia tubalis
输卵管襞/輸卵管[皺]襞 uterine tubal fold
输卵管部分切除造口术/輸卵管部分切除造口術 salpingostomatomy
输卵管成形术/輸卵管形成術 salpingoplasty
输卵管动脉/輸卵管動脈 fallopian artery
输卵管端/輸卵管端 superior extremity, tubal extremity
输卵管缝合术/輸卵管縫合術 salpingorrhaphy
输卵管腹膜/輸卵管腹膜,輸卵管外膜 perisalpinx
输卵管腹膜炎/輸卵管腹膜炎,輸卵管周圍炎 perisalpingitis
输卵管腹腔口/輸卵管腹腔口 abdominal orifice of uterine tube

输卵管固定术/輸卵管固定術　salpingopexy
输卵管壶腹/輸卵管壺腹　ampulla of uterine tube
输卵管肌层/輸卵管肌層,輸卵管肌組織　myosalpinx
输卵管肌[层]炎/輸卵管肌[層]炎,輸卵管肌組織炎　myosalpingitis
输卵管积脓/輸卵管積膿　pyosalpinx
输卵管积脓气/輸卵管積膿氣,輸卵管積氣膿,氣膿輸卵管　physopyosalpinx
输卵管积水/輸卵管積水　hydrosalpinx
输卵管积血/輸卵管積血　hematosalpinx
输卵管积液/輸卵管積液　sactosalpinx
输卵管疾病/輸卵管疾病　fallopian tube disease
输卵管间质部妊娠/輸卵管間質部妊娠　interstitial tubal pregnancy
输卵管绞痛/輸卵管絞痛　tubal colic
输卵管结核/輸卵管結核　tuberculosis of fallopian tube
输卵管结扎/輸卵管結扎　tubal ligation
输卵管静脉曲张/輸卵管靜脈曲張　tubo-ovarian varicocele
输卵管绝育/輸卵管絕育　tubal sterilization
输卵管开放试验/輸卵管開放試驗　fallopian tube patency test
输卵管扩张/輸卵管擴張　tubal dilatation
输卵管阔韧带妊娠/輸卵管闊韌帶妊娠　mesenteric pregnancy
输卵管淋病/輸卵管淋病　tubal gonorrhea
输卵管流产/輸卵管流產　tubal abortion
输卵管漏斗/輸卵管漏斗　infundibulum of uterine tube
输卵管卵巢囊肿/輸卵管卵巢囊腫　tubo-ovarian cyst
输卵管卵巢切除术/輸卵管卵巢切除術　salpingo-ovariectomy
输卵管卵巢疝/輸卵管卵巢疝,輸卵管卵巢赫尼亞　salpingo-oophorocele
输卵管卵巢炎/輸卵管卵巢炎　salpingo-oophoritis
输卵管卵巢周炎/輸卵管卵巢周[圍]炎　perisalpingo-ovaritis
输卵管内膜/輸卵管內膜　endosalpinx
输卵管内膜瘤/輸卵管內膜瘤　endosalpingoma
输卵管内膜炎/輸卵管內膜炎　endosalpingitis
输卵管内膜异位症/輸卵管內膜異位症　endosalpingiosis
输卵管扭转/輸卵管扭轉　tubatorsion
输卵管皮样囊肿/輸卵管皮樣囊腫　tubal dermoid
输卵管切除术/輸卵管切除術　salpingectomy
输卵管切开术/輸卵管切開術　salpingotomy
输卵管妊娠/輸卵管妊娠　tubal pregnancy, tubal gestation
输卵管妊娠破裂/輸卵管妊娠破裂　rupture of tubal pregnancy
输卵管伞/輸卵管傘　fimbria of uterine tube
输卵管伞突出/輸卵管傘突出,輸卵管傘脫垂　fimbriocele
输卵管疝/輸卵管疝,輸卵管赫尼亞[脫垂]　salpingocele
输卵管胎块/輸卵管胎塊　tubal mole
输卵管通气法/輸卵管通氣法　tubal insufflation
输卵管通气术/輸卵管通氣術　uterotubal insufflation
输卵管通液术/輸卵管通液術　hydrotubation
输卵管吻合术/輸卵管吻合術　anastomosis of tube
输卵管系膜/輸卵管繫膜　mesosalpinx
输卵管峡/輸卵管峽　isthmus of uterine tube, isthmus of fallopian tube
输卵管性不孕/輸卵管性不孕　tubal infertility
输卵管性痛经/輸卵管性痛經　tubal dysmenorrhea
输卵管性月经/輸卵管性月經　tubal menstruation
输卵管炎/輸卵管炎　salpingitis
输卵管移植术/輸卵管移植術　implantation of tube
输卵管造口术/輸卵管造口術　salpingostomy
输卵管造影术/輸卵管造影術,輸卵管X光攝影術　salpingography
输卵管粘连分离术/輸卵管粘連剝離術　salpingolysis
输卵管支/輸卵管支　tubal branch
输卵管直肠瘘/輸卵管直腸瘻　tuborectal fistula
输卵管肿瘤/輸卵管腫瘤　fallopian tube neoplasm
输卵管周炎/輸卵管周炎,輸卵管旁組織炎　parasalpingitis
输卵管子宫间妊娠/輸卵管子宮間妊娠,輸卵管子宮壁妊娠　interstitial pregnancy
输卵管子宫口/輸卵管子宮口　uterine orifice of uterine tube
输卵管阻塞/輸卵管阻塞,輸卵管閉塞　tubal occlusion
输尿管/輸尿管　ureter
输尿管癌/輸尿管癌　carcinoma of ureter
输尿管白斑病/輸尿管白斑病　leukoplakia of ureter
输尿管闭锁/輸尿管閉鎖　atresia of ureter
输尿管壁内部/輸尿管壁內部　intramural part of ureter
输尿管肠瘘/輸尿管腸瘻　ureteroenteric fistula
输尿管肠吻合术/輸尿管腸[造口]吻合術

ureteroenteroanastomosis
输尿管成形术/輸尿管成形術,輸尿管造形術 ureteroplasty
输尿管出血/輸尿管出血 ureterorrhagia
输尿管丛/輸尿管叢 ureteric plexus
输尿管电[流]图/輸尿管電圖 electroureterogram
输尿管发育不良/輸尿管發育不良 ureteral dysplasia
输尿管发育不全/輸尿管發育不全 ureteral hypoplasia
输尿管放线菌病/輸尿管放線菌病 actinomycosis of ureter
输尿管缝合术/輸尿管縫合術 ureterorrhaphy
输尿管腹部/輸尿管腹部 abdominal part of ureter
输尿管腹膜包裹术/輸尿管腹膜包裹術 ureteroperitonization
输尿管梗阻/輸尿管梗阻 ureteral obstruction
输尿管化脓/輸尿管化膿 ureteropyosis
输尿管回肠皮肤尿流改道[术]/輸尿管迴腸皮膚尿流改道[術] ureteroileal cutaneous diversion
输尿管回肠吻合术/輸尿管迴腸[造口]吻合術 ureteroileostomy
输尿管积尿/輸尿管積尿 uroureter
输尿管积脓/輸尿管積膿 pyoureter
输尿管积脓尿/輸尿管積膿尿 uropyoureter
输尿管积水/輸尿管積水 hydroureter
输尿管畸形/輸尿管畸形 deformity of ureter
输尿管疾病/輸尿管疾病 ureteral disease
输尿管间壁韧带/輸尿管間壁韌帶 interureteral ligament
输尿管间襞/輸尿管間襞 interureteric fold
输尿管绞痛/輸尿管絞痛 ureteral colic
输尿管结肠吻合术/輸尿管結腸吻合術 ureterocolic anastomosis
输尿管结核/輸尿管結核 tuberculosis of ureter
输尿管结石/輸尿管結石 ureter calculus
输尿管镜/輸尿管鏡 ureteroscope
输尿管镜检查/輸尿管鏡檢查,輸尿管内視鏡檢法 ureteroscopy
输尿管开口/輸尿管開口 orifice of ureter
输尿管开口异位/輸尿管開口異位 ectopic ureteral orifice
输尿管空肠皮肤尿流改道术/輸尿管空腸皮膚尿流改道術 ureterojejunal cutaneous diversion
输尿管口/輸尿管口 ureteric orifice
输尿管口镜检查/輸尿管口鏡檢查,輸尿管口膀胱鏡檢法 ureteral meatoscopy
输尿管口喷尿描记法/輸尿管口噴尿描記法,排尿節律描記法 urorhythmography
输尿管口切开术/輸尿管口切開術 ureteral meatotomy
输尿管口狭窄/輸尿管口狭窄 stricture of ureterovesical orifice
输尿管扩张/輸尿管擴張 dilatation of ureter
输尿管瘘/輸尿管瘻 ureteral fistula
输尿管梅毒/輸尿管梅毒 syphilis of ureter
输尿管黏液蓄积/輸尿管黏液蓄積,輸尿管積黏液 ureterophlegma
输尿管襻造瘘术/輸尿管襻造瘻術 loop ureterostomy
输尿管旁静脉/輸尿管旁静脈 paraureteric vein
输尿管膀胱成形术/輸尿管膀胱成形術 ureterovesicoplasty
输尿管膀胱镜/輸尿管膀胱鏡 ureterocystoscope
输尿管膀胱吻合术/輸尿管膀胱吻合術 ureteroneocystostomy
输尿管盆部/輸尿管盆部 pelvic part of ureter
输尿管皮肤尿流改道术/輸尿管皮膚尿流改道術 ureterocutaneous diversion
输尿管皮肤造口术/輸尿管皮膚造口[吻合]術 ureterocutaneostomy
输尿管皮肤造瘘术/輸尿管皮膚造瘻術 cutaneous ureterostomy
输尿管破裂/輸尿管破裂 ureterodialysis
输尿管-输尿管吻合术/輸尿管-輸尿管吻合術,經輸尿管之輸尿管造口術 transureteroureterostomy
输尿管憩室/輸尿管憩室 diverticulum of ureter
输尿管桥/輸尿管橋 ureteric bridge
输尿管切除术/輸尿管切除術 ureterectomy
输尿管切开取石术/輸尿管切開取石術,輸尿管石切除術 ureterolithotomy
输尿管切开术/輸尿管切開術 ureterotomy
输尿管缺如/輸尿管缺如 agenesis of ureter
输尿管乳头状癌/輸尿管乳頭狀癌 papillary carcinoma of ureter
输尿管乳头状瘤/輸尿管乳頭狀瘤 papilloma of ureter
输尿管疝/輸尿管疝,輸尿管赫尼亞 ureterocele
输尿管肾部分切除术/輸尿管腎部分切除術 ureteroheminephrectomy
输尿管肾镜/輸尿管腎[内視]鏡 ureterorenoscope
输尿管肾切除术/輸尿管腎切除術 ureteronephrectomy
输尿管肾盂成形术/輸尿管腎盂造形術 ureteropelvioplasty
输尿管肾盂连接处梗阻/輸尿管腎盂連接處梗阻

obstruction at ureteropelvic junction
输尿管肾盂连接处狭窄/輸尿管腎盂連接處狹窄 stricture of ureteropelvic junction
输尿管肾盂肾炎/輸尿管腎盂腎炎 ureteropyelonephritis
输尿管肾盂吻合术/輸尿管腎盂[新口]吻合術 ureteroneopyelostomy
输尿管肾盂炎/輸尿管腎盂炎 ureteropyelitis
输尿管肾盂造影[术]/輸尿管腎盂造影[術],輸尿管腎盂攝影術 ureteropyelography
输尿管石/輸尿管石 ureterolith
输尿管松解术/輸尿管鬆解術 ureterolysis
输尿管损伤/輸尿管損傷 ureteral injury
输尿管痛/輸尿管痛 ureteralgia
输尿管脱垂/輸尿管脱垂 prolapse of ureter
输尿管息肉/輸尿管息肉 polyp of ureter
输尿管狭窄/輸尿管狹窄 stricture of ureter
输尿管性痛经/輸尿管性痛經 ureteric dysmenorrhea
输尿管芽/輸尿管芽 ureteric bud
输尿管炎/輸尿管炎 ureteritis
输尿管移行细胞癌/輸尿管移行細胞癌 transitional cell carcinoma of ureter
输尿管移植[术]/輸尿管移植[術] transplantation of ureter
输尿管乙状结肠吻合术/輸尿管乙狀結腸[造口]吻合術 ureterosigmoidostomy
输尿管阴道瘘/輸尿管陰道瘻 ureterovaginal fistula
输尿管造口术/輸尿管造口術 ureterostomy
输尿管造影术/輸尿管造影術,輸尿管 X 光攝影法 ureterography
输尿管造影照片/輸尿管造影照片,輸尿管 X 光相片 ureterogram
输尿管支/輸尿管支 ureteric branches
输尿管直肠吻合术/輸尿管直腸吻合術 ureteroproctostomy
输尿管肿瘤/輸尿管腫瘤 tumor of ureter
输尿管周围纤维变性/輸尿管周圍纖維變性,輸尿管周圍纖維化 periureteric fibrosis
输尿管周围炎/輸尿管周圍炎 periureteritis
输尿管子宫内膜异位症/輸尿管子宮內膜異位症 endometriosis of ureter
输尿管阻塞/輸尿管阻塞 urteral obstruction
输乳窦/輸乳竇,排乳竇 lactiferous sinus
输乳管/輸乳管 lactiferous duct
输乳管窦/輸乳管竇 lactiferous sinus
输乳小管/輸乳小管 lactiferous tubule, canalicular duct

输入层/輸入層 input layer
输入疾病/輸入疾病,境外移入疾病 imported disease
输入静脉/輸入靜脈 afferent veins
输入淋巴管/傳入淋巴管 afferent lymphatic vessel
输入襻综合征/輸入襻症候群 afferent loop syndrome
输入性[肠]襻/輸入性[腸]襻 afferent loop
输色素细胞/噬色素細胞 pigmentophore
输[穴]/輸穴 shu-stream point
输血/輸血 transfuse
输血肝炎/輸血肝炎 transfusion hepatitis
输血后肝炎/輸血後肝炎 post-transfusion hepatitis
输血[后]肾炎/輸血腎炎 transfusion nephritis
输血浆法/輸血漿法,血漿轉輸法 plasma transfusion
输血器/輸血器,轉輸器 transfusion apparatus
输血清/輸血清 serum transfusion
输液泵/輸液泵 infusion pump
输液管/輸液管 tubing
输液剂/輸液劑 infusion solution
输注泵/輸注泵 infusion pump
蔬菜蛋白质类/蔬菜蛋白質類 vegetable proteins
蔬菜皮炎/蔬菜皮炎 dermatitis due to vegetable
蔬菜日光性皮炎/蔬菜日光性皮炎 vegetable-solar dermatitis
蔬食/蔬食,素食 vegetable diet
熟地黄/熟地黄 prepared rehmannia root
暑/暑 summerheat epilepsy
暑病/暑病 summerheat disease
暑喘/暑喘 summerheat dyspnea
暑毒失血/暑毒失血 blood loss due to summerheat poisoning
暑风/暑風 syncope from sunstroke
暑秽/暑穢 summerheat filth
暑疖/暑癤 summer boil, summer furuncle
暑痉/暑痙 summerheat convulsion
暑厥/暑厥 summerheat syncope
暑咳/暑欬 summerheat cough
暑渴/暑渴 summerheat thirst
暑痢/暑痢 summerheat dysentery
暑淋/暑淋 summerheat strangury
暑疟/暑瘧 summerheat malaria
暑气呕吐/暑氣嘔吐 summerheat vomiting
暑热动风证/暑熱動風證 pattern of stirring wind due to summerheat
暑[热]证/暑[熱]證 summerheat-heat pattern
暑痧/暑痧 summerheat sha disease

暑伤肺络证/暑傷肺絡證　pattern of lung collaterals injured by summerheat

暑伤津气证/暑傷津氣證　pattern of summerheat injuring fluid and qi

暑湿痹/暑濕痹　summerheat dampness with impediment

暑湿[病]/暑濕　summerheat dampness

暑湿喘逆/暑濕喘逆　summerheat dampness with panting

暑湿腹痛/暑濕腹痛　summerheat dampness with abdominal pain

暑湿流注/暑濕流注　deep multiple abscess due to summer dampness

暑湿流注·气阴两虚证/暑濕流注·氣陰兩虛證　deep multiple abscess due to summer dampness with qi-yin deficiency pattern

暑湿流注·暑湿交阻证/暑濕流注·暑濕交阻證　deep multiple abscess due to summerheat-dampness with pattern of summerheat-dampness collaborative obstruction

暑湿[内蕴]证/暑濕[内蘊]證　pattern of summerheat-dampness accumulated in interior

暑湿伤寒/暑濕傷寒　summerheat dampness with cold damage

暑湿·暑湿困阻中焦证/暑濕·暑濕困阻中焦證　summerheat dampness with pattern of summerheat-damp retaining in middle jiao

暑湿·暑湿弥漫三焦证/暑濕·暑濕彌漫三焦證　summerheat dampness with pattern of summerheat-damp diffusing in sanjiao

暑湿·暑湿伤气证/暑濕·暑濕傷氣證　summerheat dampness with pattern of summerheat-damp injuring qi

暑湿·暑湿在卫证/暑濕·暑濕在衛證　summerheat dampness with pattern of summerheat-damp in defensive phase

暑湿袭表证/暑濕襲表證　pattern of exterior attacked by summerheat-dampness

暑湿眩晕/暑濕眩暈　summerheat dampness with dizziness

暑湿·余热夹痰瘀证/暑濕·餘熱夾痰瘀證　summerheat dampness with pattern of lingering heat complicated with phlegm and static blood

暑痿/暑痿　summerheat flaccidity

暑温[病]/暑溫　summerheat warmth

暑温后遗症/暑溫後遺症　sequelae of summerheat warmth

暑温·津气欲脱证/暑溫·津氣欲脫證　summerheat warmth with pattern of verging depletion of qi and fluid

暑温·暑热动风证/暑溫·暑熱動風證　summerheat warmth with pattern of wind stirring by hot-summerheat

暑温·暑入心营证/暑溫·暑入心營證　summerheat warmth with pattern of summerheat invading heart nutrient phase

暑温·暑入血分证/暑溫·暑入血分證　summerheat warmth with pattern of summerheat invading blood phase

暑温·暑入阳明证/暑溫·暑入陽明證　summerheat warmth with pattern of summerheat invading Yangming

暑温·暑伤肺络证/暑溫·暑傷肺絡證　summerheat warmth with pattern of summerheat injuring lung collaterals

暑温·暑伤津气证/暑溫·暑傷津氣證　summerheat warmth with pattern of summerheat injuring fluid and qi

暑温·暑伤心肾证/暑溫·暑傷心腎證　summerheat warmth with pattern of summerheat injuring heart and kidney

暑邪/暑邪,暑熱邪氣　summerheat pathogen

暑泻/暑瀉　summerheat diarrhea

暑性升散/暑性昇散　characteristic of summerheat being ascending and dispersive

暑性炎热/暑性炎熱　characteristic of summerheat being scorching-hot

暑易夹湿/暑易夾濕　summerheat being likely to be mixed with dampness

暑易扰心/暑易擾心　summerheat being likely to disturb heart

暑瘵/暑瘵　summerheat phthisis

蜀黍毒碱/蜀黍毒鹼,玉蜀黍腐鹼　pellagrazein

蜀黍红疹颈圈/蜀黍紅疹頸圈　collarette

鼠/鼠　rat

鼠白血病病毒/鼠白血病病毒　murine leukemia virus

鼠类圆线虫/鼠類圓線蟲,鼠擬圓蟲　strongyloides ratti

鼠李糖/鼠李糖　rhamnose

鼠瘘/鼠瘻　tuberculous fistula

鼠脑脊髓炎病毒/鼠腦脊髓炎病毒　mouse encephalomyelitis virus

鼠乳/鼠乳　molluscum contagiosum, mouse nipple

鼠尾草/鼠尾草　Salvia officinalis

鼠尾草萃取物/鼠尾草萃取物　sage extract

鼠咬热/鼠咬熱 sodoku
鼠咬热螺旋菌/鼠咬熱螺旋菌 Spirillum minus
鼠疫/鼠疫 pestis, plague
鼠疫斑/鼠疫斑 plague spot
鼠疫杆菌感染/鼠疫桿菌感染 Yersinia infection
鼠疫菌苗/鼠疫疫苗 plague vaccine
鼠疫溃疡/鼠疫潰瘍 plague sore
薯蓣皂苷元/薯蕷皂苷[元] diosgenin
曙红Ⅰ蓝/曙紅Ⅰ藍 eosineⅠbluish
术后胆囊炎/術後膽囊炎 postoperative cholecystitis
术后瘘/術後瘻 postoperative fistula
术后脓胸/術後膿胸 postoperative empyema
术后胰腺炎/術後胰腺炎 postoperative pancreatitis
术前模型/術前模型 preoperative cast
术前栓塞术/術前栓塞術 preoperative embolization
术中胆管造影[术]/術中膽管造影[術] intraoperative cholangiography
术中内镜检查[术]/術中內鏡檢查[術] intraoperative endoscopy
术中软组织扩张术/術中軟組織擴張術 intraoperative soft tissue expansion
束/束 cord
束带畸形/束帶畸形 constriction band deformity
束带状感觉缺失/[束]帶狀感覺缺失 girdle anesthesia
束腹试验/束腹試驗,腰帶試驗 belt test
束骨/束骨 shugu, BL65
束间神经胶质/束間神經膠質 interfascicular neuroglia
束间束/束間束 interfascicular fasciculus
束旁核/束旁核 parafascicular nucleus
束支/束支 bundle branch
束支传导阻滞/束支傳導阻滯 bundle branch block
束中形成层/束中形成層 fascicular cambium
束状带/束狀帶 zona fasciculata
束状骨/束[狀]骨 bundle bone
束状回/束狀迴 fasciolar gyrus
束状角膜炎/束狀角膜炎 fascicular keratitis
树胶/樹膠 gum
树胶树脂/樹膠樹脂 gum resin
树胶样肿/樹膠樣腫 gumma
树胶肿/樹膠腫 gummy tumor
树胶肿样淋巴管炎/樹膠腫樣淋巴管炎,屠夫黴菌病 菌病 cladiosis
树-树突触/樹-樹突觸,樹突間突觸 dendrodendritic synapse
树-体突触/樹-體突觸,樹體神經元突觸 dendrosomatic synapse
树突/樹突 dendrite
树突棘/樹突棘 dendritic spine
树突细胞/樹突細胞 dendritic cell
树突运输/樹突運輸 dendritic transport
树蛙/樹蛙 tree frog
树枝状角膜炎/樹枝狀角膜炎 dendritic keratitis
树枝状溃疡/樹枝狀潰瘍 dendritic ulcer
树枝状赘疣/樹枝狀贅疣,樹枝狀贅生物 dendritic vegetation
树脂/樹脂 resin
树脂包埋/樹脂包埋 resin-embedding
树脂包埋技术/樹脂包埋技術 resin-embedding technique
树脂醇苷/樹脂醇苷 resinol glycoside
树脂道/樹脂道 resin canal
树脂黏固剂/樹脂黏固劑 resin cement
树-轴突触/樹-軸突觸,樹軸神經元突觸 dendroaxonic synapse
树状毛细血管扩张/樹狀毛細血管擴張,樹狀微血管 擴張 arborizing telangiectasia
竖棘肌/豎棘肌 erector muscle of spine
竖脊肌/豎脊肌 erector spinae
竖毛/豎毛 arrector pili
竖毛肌/豎毛肌 arrector pilli, arrector pili muscle, arrector pilli muscle
竖毛肌错构瘤/豎毛肌錯構瘤 arrector pili hamartoma
竖阴茎肌/豎陰莖肌 erector muscle of penis
腧府/腧府 shufu, KI27
腧募配穴法/腧募配穴法 back-shu points and front-mu points association, back-shu points and front-mu points combination
腧穴/腧穴 point
腧穴定位法/腧穴定位法 method of point location
腧穴特异性/腧穴特異性 specificity of point
腧穴学/腧穴學 subject of point
腧穴压痛/腧穴壓痛 tenderness of acupoints
腧穴注射疗法/腧穴注射療法 point-injection therapy
数量变异/數量變異 meristic variation
数量性状/數量性狀 quantitative trait
数量性状基因座位/數量性狀基因座位 quantitative trait loci
数量遗传学/數量遺傳學 quantitative genetics
数脉/[頻]數脈 rapid pulse, frequent pulse
数目畸变/數目畸變 numerical aberration
数值分类法/數值分類法 numerical taxonomy
数指/數指 counting fingers

数字冠状动脉造影术/數位冠狀動脈攝影術　digital coronary arteriography
数字减影血管造影术/数字減影血管造影術，數位減影血管造影術　digital subtraction angiography
数字解剖学/數字解剖學　digital anatomy
漱口/漱口　gargle
漱口剂/漱口劑，漱口藥　collutory
漱口水/漱口水　mouthwash
刷拭活检/刷拭活檢　brush biopsy
刷牙/刷牙　toothbrushing
刷样毛发/刷樣毛[髮]　brush-like hair
刷状细胞/刷狀細胞　brush cell
刷状缘/刷狀緣　brush border
刷[子]/刷子　brush
衰变/衰變　decay
衰减/衰減　attenuation
衰减全反射/衰減全反射　attenuated total reflectance, ATR
衰竭/衰竭，疲憊　exhaustion, failure
衰竭性精神病/衰竭性精神病　exhaustion psychosis
衰竭性阳痿/衰竭性陽痿，疲憊性陽痿　exhaustion impotence
衰竭性谵妄/衰竭性譫妄　exhaustion delirium
衰竭综合征/衰竭症候群　exhaustion syndrome
衰老/衰老　aging
衰老斑/衰老斑　senile plaque
衰老者/老耄者，年老昏憒者　dotard
衰弱/衰弱，無力　asthenia, weakness
衰弱性血栓/衰弱性血栓，虛弱性血栓　marantic thrombus, marantic thrombosis
衰退/衰退　decay
衰退期/衰老期，衰頹期　phase of decline
率谷/率谷　shuaigu, GB8
囟/囟　obex
栓剂/栓劑　suppository
栓剂基质/栓劑基劑　suppository base
栓塞/栓塞　embolism
栓塞后血栓形成/栓子性血栓形成　embolic thrombosis
栓塞形成/栓塞形成　embolization
栓塞性动脉瘤/栓塞性動脈瘤　embolic aneurysm
栓塞性梗死/栓子性梗死，栓子性梗塞　embolic infarction
栓塞性坏死/栓塞性壞死　embolic necrosis
栓塞性脓肿/栓塞性膿腫　embolic abscess
栓塞性肾炎/栓塞性腎炎　embolic nephritis
栓塞性痔/栓塞性痔　thrombosed hemorrhoid
栓状核/栓狀核　emboliform nucleus

栓子/栓子　embolus
栓子清除术/栓子切除術　embolectomy
双凹透镜/雙凹透鏡　concavoconcave lens
双白蛋白血[症]/雙白蛋白血症　bisalbuminemia
双瓣膜置换术/雙瓣膜置換術　double valve replacement
双孢子/雙孢子，雙芽孢　dispore
双胞胎/雙胞胎　twin
双胞胎细胞/雙胞胎細胞　twin cell
双苯甲亚胺/雙苯甲亞胺　bisbenzimide
双鼻/雙鼻[畸形]　birhinia
双鼻侧偏盲/雙鼻側偏盲　binasal hemianopsia
双臂卡环/雙臂卡環　two-arm clasp
双苄基异喹啉生物碱/雙苄基異喹啉生物鹼　bisbenzylisoquinoline alkaloid
双丙酮丙烯酰胺/雙丙酮丙烯醯胺　diacetone acrylamide
双RNA病毒科感染/雙RNA病毒科感染　birnaviridae infection
双波长一元线性回归法/雙波長[一元]線性回歸法　dual-wavelength linear regression method
双侧唇裂/雙側唇裂，雙側裂唇　bilateral cleft lip
双侧动脉导管/雙側動脈導管　bilateral ductus arteriosus
双侧腭裂/雙側腭裂　bilateral cleft palate
双侧肺炎/兩側肺炎，雙肺炎　double pneumonia
双侧两性畸形/雙側兩性畸形　bilateral gynandromorphism
双侧颞叶切除综合征/雙側顳葉切除症候群　Kluver-Bucy syndrome
双侧平衡/雙側平衡　bilateral equilibration
双侧擒拿法/雙側擒拿法　bilateral grasping massage for throat disease
双侧瘫痪/兩側癱瘓，對癱　diplegia
双侧脱位/兩處脫位　double dislocation
双侧像相同/雙側像相同，影像相等　iseiconia
双层绒型假体/雙層絨型假體　double velour prosthesis
双翅目/雙翅目　Diptera
双重睑术/雙重瞼術　double eyelid operation
双重结果/雙重結果　double effect
双重偏瘫/雙重偏癱　double hemiplegia
双重人格/雙重人格　dual personality
双重神经支配/雙重神經支配，二種神經支配　double innervation
双重生活/雙重生活　double life
双重听力试验/雙重聽力試驗　dichotic listening test
双重牙列/雙重牙列　double dentition

双重意识/雙重意識　double consciousness
双重杂合子/雙重雜合子,雙重雜合體　double heterozygote
双重诊断/雙重診斷　dual diagnosis
双重制约作用/雙重制約作用　double bind interaction
双出口/雙出口　double-outlet
双唇[症]/雙唇　double lip
双雌受精/雙雌受精　digyny
双醋酚丁/雙醋酚丁　oxyphenisatin acetate
双醋炔诺醇/雙醋炔諾醇　ethynodiol diacetate
双胆囊/雙膽囊　double gallbladder
双蛋白尿/雙蛋白尿　diploalbuminuria
双蒂皮瓣/雙蒂皮瓣　bipedicle skin flap
双碘甲状腺原氨酸类/雙碘甲狀腺原胺酸類　diiodothyronines
双碘喹啉/碘羥基喹啉　iodoquinol
双碘酪氨酸/二碘鉻胺[基]酸　diiodotyrosine
双丁酰环GMP/雙丁醯環GMP　dibutyryl cyclic GMP
双顶径/雙頂徑,頂骨間徑　biparietal diameter
双端固定桥/雙端固定橋　rigid fixed bridge
双对比灌肠/雙對比灌腸　double contrast enema
双耳交替冷热试验/雙耳交替冷熱試驗　alternate binaural bithermal caloric test
双耳交替响度平衡试验/雙耳交替響度平衡試驗　alternate binaural loudness balance test
双耳两分/雙耳兩分　dichotic
双耳同时冷热试验/雙耳同時冷熱試驗　simultaneous binaural bithermal caloric test
双二倍体/雙二倍體　amphidiploid
双二甲肼/雙二甲肼,四甲二肼　dicacodyl
双房性膀胱/雙房性膀胱　bilocular bladder
双肺叶切除术/雙肺葉切除術　pulmonary bilobectomy
双肺移植/雙肺移植　double lung transplantation
双酚A缩水甘油基异丁烯酸/雙酚A縮水甘油基異丁烯酸　bisphenol A-glycidyl methacrylate
双峰稽留热/雙峰稽留熱,雙重稽留熱　double continued fever
双呋脒腙/雙呋脒腙,硝呋文　nitrovin
双甘氨肽/雙甘胺肽,甘胺醯甘胺酸　glycylglycine
双胍类/雙胍類　biguanides
双关节肌/雙關節肌　two-joint muscle
双管结肠造口术/雙管結腸造口術　double barrel colostomy
双光束光学零位平衡系统/雙光束光學零位平衡系統　double beam optical-null system
双行睫/雙行睫,雙睫症　distichia
双核阿米巴腹泻/雙核阿米巴腹瀉　Dientamoeba diarrhea
双核阿米巴属/雙核阿米巴屬　*Dientamoeba*
双核苷酸重复/雙核苷酸重複　dinucleotide repeat
双核细胞/雙核細胞　tart cell
双核形成/雙核形成,雙核化　binucleation
双颌截骨术/雙頜截骨術　bimaxillary osteotomy
双颌前突/雙頜前突　bimaxillary protrusion
双踝骨折/雙踝骨折　bimalleolar fracture
双环呋喃/雙環呋喃,雙咪喃環　bifuran
双环维林/雙環維林　dicyclomine
双黄连口服液/雙黃連口服液　shuanghuanglian mixture
双黄酮/雙黃酮　biflavone
双黄酮类/雙黃酮類　biflavones
双回肠/雙迴腸,重複迴腸　duplex ileum
双箕斗/雙箕斗　double loop whorl
双极/雙極　twin pole
双极成神经细胞/雙極成神經細胞,雙極神經母細胞　bipolar neuroblast
双极导联/雙極導聯,雙極導程　bipolar lead
双极电凝器/雙極電凝器　bipolar electrocoagulator
双极电凝[术]/雙極電凝[術]　bipolar coagulation
双极电灼术/雙極電灼術　bipolar electric cautery
双极神经元/雙極神經元　bipolar neuron
双加氧酶类/雙加氧酶類　dioxygenases
双价抗体/雙價抗體　bivalent antibody
双价离子/雙價離子　doubly charged ion
双尖型/雙尖型　bicuspoid
双尖型白齿/雙尖樣白齒　bicuspoid molar
双尖牙/雙尖牙,小白齒　dens bicuspidatus
双尖牙空隙/雙尖牙空隙,小白齒空隙　bicuspid spaces
双尖牙托架/雙尖牙托架,小白齒用托架　bicuspid brackets
双键/雙鍵　double bond
双交联助听器/雙交聯助聽器　bilateral contralateral routing of signals aid
双焦点镜片/變焦[點]透鏡　bifocal lens
双焦点眼镜/雙焦點眼鏡　bifocal glasses
双角单颈子宫/雙角單頸子宮,單頸雙角子宮[畸形]　uterus bicornis unicollis
双角子宫/雙角子宮　uterus bicornis
双解磷/雙解磷　trimedoxime
双精入卵/雙精入卵　dispermy
双肼屈嗪/雙肼屈嗪　dihydralazine
双颈双头畸胎/雙頭雙頸畸胎　diauchenos

双镜头摄影机/雙鏡頭攝影機 bicamera
双髁状关节/雙髁狀關節 bicondylar joint
双孔钾通道/雙孔鉀通道 tandem-pore-domain potassium channels
双口畸胎/雙口畸胎 distomus
双口子宫/雙口子宫 uterus biforis
双脸畸胎/雙臉畸形 iniops
双链霉素/雙鏈黴素 streptoduocin
双量子转移实验/雙量子轉移實驗 double quantum transfer experiment
双磷酸甘油酸变位酶/雙磷酸甘油酸變位酶 bisphosphoglycerate mutase
双菱形皮瓣/雙菱形皮瓣 double rhomboid skin flap
双流子宫导管/雙流子宮導管,波士曼氏導管 bozeman catheter
双硫仑/雙硫侖,二硫龍 disulfiram
双硫仑样反应/雙硫侖樣反應,類二硫侖效應 disulfiram-like reaction
双硫腙/雙硫腙,二苯硫卡巴腙 dithizone
双卵孪生/二卵雙胞胎,異卵雙胞胎 dizygotic twins
双卵双胞儿/雙卵雙胎兒 binovular twins
双螺旋/雙螺旋 double helix
双螺旋模型/雙螺旋模型 double helix model
双氯非那胺/雙氯非那胺,二氯苯磺胺 dichlorphenamide
双氯酚/雙氯酚 dichlorophene
双氯西林/雙氯西林 dicloxacillin
双盲测验/雙盲測驗,雙盲試驗 double-blind test
双盲法/雙盲法 double-blind method
双毛[症]/雙毛症 districhiasis
双霉素/雙黴素 amphomycin
双嘧达莫/雙嘧達莫,二吡待摩 dipyridamole
双面畸胎/雙面畸胎 diprosopus
双面畸形/雙面畸形 diprosopus, diprosopy
双面夹角/雙面夾角 dihedral angle
双面联胎/雙面連胎,複面連胎 janiceps
双面荧光屏/雙面螢光屏 biplane fluoroscope
双[命]名法/雙命名法 binomial nomenclature
双目间接检眼镜/雙目間接檢眼鏡 binocular indirect ophthalmoscope
双目检眼镜/雙目檢眼鏡 binophthalmoscope
双能扫描投影放射摄影术/雙能掃描投影放射攝影術 dual-energy scanned projection radiography
双黏膜性瘘管/雙黏膜性瘻管 fistula bimucosa
双颞侧偏盲/雙顳側偏盲 bitemporal hemianopsia
双盘吸虫病/[雙盤]吸蟲病,瓜仁蟲病 distomiasis
双盘状胎盘/雙盤狀胎盤 bidiscoidal placenta
双膀胱/雙膀胱 duplicated bladder

双胚叶畸胎瘤/雙胚葉[畸胎]瘤 bidermoma
双片对比显微镜/[雙片]對比顯微鏡 comparascope
双歧杆菌属/雙歧桿菌屬 *Bifidobacterium*
双脐畸胎/雙臍畸胎,雙臍連胎 ensomphalus
双前臂畸形/雙前臂畸形 diantebrachia
双潜能/雙向潛能,雙重潛能 bipotentiality
双腔导管/雙腔導管,雙向導管 two-way catheter
双腔关节/雙腔關節,兩腔關節 bilocular joint
双腔脓肿/雙腔膿腫,兩室性膿腫 bicameral abscess
双腔吸虫病/雙腔吸蟲病 dicroceliasis
双腔右心室/雙腔右心室 double chamber of right ventricle
双腔支气管导管/雙腔支氣管導管 double lumen endobronchial tube
双腔子宫/雙腔子宫 uterus bilocularis
双[羟]香豆素/雙香豆素 dicoumarin
双桥基/雙橋基 double abutment
双亲/雙親 parents
双亲肾移植/雙親腎移植 parental renal transplantation
双亲向子女遗传传递/親代向子代的遺傳傳遞 parent-to-child transmission
双亲遗传/雙親遺傳,兩親性遺傳 amphigonous inheritance
双亲中值/雙親中值 midparent value
双青藤碱/雙青藤鹼 disinomenine
双氢胆固醇/雙氫膽固醇,二氫膽固醇 dihydrocholesterol
双氢睾酮/雙氫睾酮,二氫睾丸脂酮 dihydrotestosterone
双氢链霉素硫酸盐/雙氫鏈黴素硫酸鹽,硫酸二氫鏈黴素 dihydrostreptomycin sulfate
双氢吗啡/雙氫嗎啡,二氫嗎啡 dihydromorphine
双氢麦角胺/雙氫麥角胺 dihydroergotamine
双氢麦角考宁/雙氫麥角考寧,二氫麥角脂肪 dihydroergocornine
双氢麦角克碱/雙氫麥角克鹼,二氫麥角鹼 dihydroergocristine
双氢麦角隐亭/雙氫麥角隱亭,二氫麥角隱亭 dihydroergocryptine
双氢速甾醇/雙氫速甾醇,二氫速甾醇 dihydrotachysterol
双球面透镜/雙球面透鏡 bispherical lens
双曲钩端螺旋体/雙曲[鉤端]螺旋體 *Leptospira biflexa*
双曲线玻璃/雙曲線玻璃 hyperbolic glasses
双躯干畸胎/雙軀幹畸胎 disomus
双躯[畸形]/雙軀[畸形],雙體畸形 diplosomatia

双人疗法/雙人療法	couples therapy
双韧管状中柱/雙韌管狀中柱	amphiphloic siphonostele
双韧维管束/雙韌維管束	bicollateral vascular bundle
双乳头瓣/雙乳頭瓣	double papillae flap
双入口心室/雙入口心室	double inlet ventricle
双上颌横形骨折/雙上頜橫形骨折,Guerin氏骨折	Guerin fracture
双上腔静脉/雙上腔靜脈	double superior vena cava
双上身畸胎/雙上畸胎,前雙連胎	duplicitas anterior
双肾双输尿管畸形/雙腎雙輸尿管畸形	birenal and biureteral deformity
双生/雙生	twins
双生牙/雙生牙	geminated tooth
双生研究/雙生研究	twin study
双生子法/雙生子法	twin method
双生子卵性诊断/雙生子卵性診斷	zygosity diagnosis
双识别假说/雙識別假說	dual recognition hypothesis
双食管/雙食管,雙食道畸形	diesophagus
双手触诊/雙手觸診,兩手觸診法	bimanual palpation
双手进针法/雙手進針法	needle-inserting with both hands
双手叩诊/雙手叩法	bimanual percussion
双丝弓矫治器/雙絲弓矯治器	twin-wire appliance
双四氧嘧啶/雙四氧嘧啶	uroxin
双缩甲醇酰二水杨酸/雙縮甲醇醯二水楊酸,二甘醇醯二水楊酸	diglycoldisalicylic acid
双缩脲反应/雙[縮]脲反應,縮二脲反應	biuret reaction
双缩脲试验/雙[縮]脲試驗	biuret test
双缩脲试纸/雙縮脲試紙,雙脲紙	biuret paper
双胎/雙胎,雙生兒	co-twin, twins
双胎产妇/雙胎產婦	gemellipara
双胎疾病/雙胎疾病	diseases in twins
双胎妊娠/雙胎妊娠,雙孕	double gestation, twin pregnancy
双胎生成/雙胎生成	diembryony
双特异性抗体/雙特異性抗體	bispecific antibody
双头绷带卷/雙頭繃帶卷	double-ended roller
双头畸胎/雙頭畸胎	bicephalus
双头[畸形]/雙頭畸形	dicephaly
双臀腹胸联胎/雙臀[型]腹胸連胎	gastrothoracopagus dipygus
双臀畸胎/雙臀畸胎,雙骨盆畸形	dilecanus
双脱氧核苷类/雙脫氧核苷類,雙去氧核苷類	dideoxynucleosides
双脱氧腺苷/雙脫氧腺苷,雙去氧腺苷	dideoxyadenosine
双弯导管/雙彎導管	bicoudate catheter
双微体/雙微體	double minute
双下颌/雙下頜,雙頜畸形	augnathus
双[下]颌畸胎/雙下頜畸胎	dignathus
双下身畸胎/雙下身畸胎,後雙連胎	duplicitas posterior
双线/雙線	diplonema
双线期/雙線期	diplotene stage
双香豆素/雙[羥]香豆素	dicumarol
双香豆乙酯/雙香豆乙酯,雙香豆素酯	ethyl biscoumacetate
双向交叉抗药性/雙向交叉抗藥性	bidirectional cross resistance
双[向]扩散/雙擴散	double diffusion
双向扩散试验/雙向擴散試驗	double diffusion test
双向免疫电泳/雙向免疫電泳	two-dimensional immunoelectrophoresis
双向免疫扩散试验/雙向免疫擴散試驗	double immunodiffusion test
双向上腔静脉肺动脉吻合术/雙向上腔靜脈肺動脈吻合術	bidirection superior cavopulmonary anastomosis
双相情感障碍/雙相情感障礙	bipolar affective disorder
双相死亡率/雙相死亡率	two phase mortality
双相障碍/雙相障礙,雙極性障礙,躁鬱症	bipolar disorder
双硝苯脲二甲嘧啶醇/雙硝苯脲二甲嘧啶醇	nicarbazin
双小核草履虫/雙小核草履蟲	Paramecium aurelia
双心腔起搏器/雙心腔起搏器	dual chamber pacemaker
双心室肥厚/雙心室肥厚,兩心室肥厚	biventricular hypertrophy
双心体/雙心體,兩中心體	diplosome
双星[体]/雙星[體],兩星	amphiaster
双性现象/雙性現象,真性陰陽人	bisexuality
双雄受精/雙雄受精	diandry
双血卟啉醚/雙血卟啉醚,二血卟啉醚	dihematoporphyrin ether
双眼/兩眼	binoculus
双眼绷带/雙眼繃帶	binocular bandage
双眼绷带法/雙眼繃帶法	binocular bandaging
双眼单视/雙眼單視	binocular single vision

双眼单视界/雙眼單視界　horopter
双眼单视界曲线/雙眼單視界曲線　horopter curve
双眼单视镜/雙眼單視鏡,雙目鏡　binoscope
双眼等像/雙眼等像　iseikonia
双眼拮抗/雙眼拮抗　binocular rivalry
双眼屈光不等/雙眼屈光不等,兩眼屈光度不等　heterometropia
双眼视觉/雙眼視覺,兩眼視覺　binocular vision
双眼视像融合/雙眼視像融合,兩眼視像湊合　binocular fusion
双眼视野/雙眼視野　binocular visual field
双眼调节/雙眼調節　binocular accommodation
双眼注视/雙眼注視　binocular fixation
双羊膜囊双胎/雙羊膜囊雙胎　diamnionic twin pregnancy
双氧气/雙氧氣　oxozone
双叶皮瓣/雙葉皮瓣　bilobed skin flap
双叶胎盘/雙葉胎盤　bilobed placenta
双叶型人工瓣膜/雙葉型人工瓣膜,雙葉型機械瓣　bileaflet prosthetic valve
双叶阴囊/雙葉陰囊　bilobate scrotum
双叶状种植体/雙葉狀種植體　double blade implant
双因子杂合子/雙因子雜合子,雙異質接合子　diheterozygote
双阴道/雙陰道[畸形]　double vagina
双阴茎/雙陰莖[畸形]　double penis
双吲哚生物碱/雙吲哚生物鹼　bisindole alkaloid
双羽肌/雙羽肌　bipennate muscle
双圆柱透镜/雙圓柱透鏡,雙柱面透鏡　bicylindrical lens
双缘甲/雙緣甲　double-edge nails
双杂交系统技术/雙雜交系統技術　two-hybrid system technique
双折射/雙折射　birefringence
双折射物质/雙折射物質,雙折射粒　disdiaclast
双折射脂类/雙折射性脂類,雙折射性脂質　anisotropic lipoid
双指触诊/雙[指]觸診　double touch
双中心体/雙中心體,兩中心粒　diplosome
双轴关节/雙軸關節,兩軸關節　biaxial joint
双主动脉弓/雙主動脈弓　double aortic arch
双着丝粒染色体/雙著絲粒染色體,雙中節染色體　dicentric chromosome
双子宫[畸形]/雙子宫[畸形]　dimetria, double uterus
霜/霜　frost-like powder
霜剂/霜劑,乳膏　cream
爽身粉/爽身粉　dusting powder

水/水　water
水白疗/水白疗　palmar blister
水包油乳剂/水包油乳劑　oil-in-water emulsion
水不涵木/水不涵木　kidney failing to nourish liver, water failing to nourish wood
水槽征/水槽徵　flush-tank sign
水车状杂音/水車狀雜音　water-wheel murmur
水冲状脉/水冲狀脈　water-hammer pulse
水充盈法/水充盈法　water filling method
水传感染/水傳[感]染　water-borne infection
水传染病/水傳染病　water-borne disease
水当量/水當量　water equivalent
水道/水道　shuidao, ST28
水电解质平衡/水電解質平衡　water-electrolyte balance
水电解质失调/水電解質失調　water-electrolyte imbalance
水垫/水墊　water bed
水貂细胞病灶诱发病毒/水貂細胞病灶誘發病毒　mink cell focus-inducing virus
水痘/水痘　chickenpox, varicella
水痘病毒/水痘病毒　chickenpox virus
水痘带状疱疹病毒/水痘帶狀皰疹病毒　varicella-zoster virus
水痘带状疱疹脑炎/水痘帶狀皰疹腦炎　varicella zoster encephalitis
水痘接种/水痘接種　varicellation
水痘疱疹病毒/水痘皰疹病毒　herpesvirus varicella
水痘·热毒炽盛证/水痘·熱毒熾盛證　varicella with pattern of blazing heat-toxin
水痘·邪郁肺卫证/水痘·邪鬱肺衛證　varicella with pattern of pathogen stagnated in lung-defense phase
水痘性角膜炎/水痘性角膜炎　varicella keratitis
水痘疫苗/水痘疫苗　chickenpox vaccine
水毒/水毒　schistosome cercarial dermatitis
水飞/水飛　levigating, grinding in water
水飞蓟素/水飛薊素　silymarin
水分离/水分離　hydrodissection
水分/水分　shuifen, RN9
水分测定/水分測定　determination of water
水敷/水敷　water dressing
水沟/水溝　shuigou, DU26
水谷之海/水谷之海　reservoir of food and drink
水臌/水臌　water tympanites
水管周灰质/水管周灰質　periaqueductal gray
水寒射肺/水寒射肺　water-cold attacking lung
水合/水合　hydration
水合成[作用]/水合成作用　hydrosynthesis

水合氯醛/水合氯醛,水化氯醛　chloral hydrate
水合酶/水合酶　hydratase
水合氢离子/水合氫離子　hydrogen ion
水合萜二醇/水合萜二醇,水化松香腦　terpin hydrate
水合物/水合物　hydrate
水合作用/水合作用,水化作用　hydration
水红花子/水紅花子　prince's-feather fruit
水[化]合物/水化物　hydrate
水化酶/水化酶　hydrase
水剂青霉素/水劑青黴素　aqueous penicillin
水瘕/水瘕　watery abdominal mass
水煎/水煎　decoct with water
水检眼镜/水檢眼鏡,水層矯光器,水層檢眼器　orthoscope
水检眼镜检查/水檢眼鏡檢查,水層矯光術　orthoscopy
水胶模/水膠[壓]模　hydrocolloid impression
水胶体/水膠體　hydrocolloid
水胶体敷料/水膠體敷料　hydrocolloid bandage
水胶体印模材料/水膠體印模材料　hydrocolloid impression material
水结胸证/水結胸證　water chest binding pattern
水解/水解　hydrolysis, hydrolyzed
水解[产]物/水解産物　hydrolysate
水解蛋白注射液/水解蛋白注射液　protein hydrolysate injection
水解酶/水解酶,水解酵素　hydrolyzing enzyme
水解鞣质类/水解鞣質類　hydrolyzable tannins
水解物/水解物,水解基質　hydrolyte
水解作用/水解[作用]　hydrolysis
水浸法/水浸法　water immersion
水晶体皮质/水晶體皮質　cortex lentis
水净化/水淨化　water purification
水厥/水厥　water retention syncope
水克火/水克火　water restricting fire
水孔蛋白类/水孔蛋白類　aquaporins
水亏火旺/水虧火旺　blazing of fire due to yin deficiency
水蜡树花粉过敏咳/水臘樹花粉過敏欬,水臘樹欬嗽　privet cough
水疗法/水療法　hydrotherapy
水裂解酶/水裂解酶,去水酶　hydrolyase
水流操作法/水流操作法,水流技術　hydro-flow technique
水流冷却器/水流冷卻器　zero done
水轮/水輪　water wheel
水霉属/水[屬]黴,水生菌　Saprolegnia
水蜜丸/水蜜丸　water-honeyed pill
水母毒素/水母毒素,水母充血素　medusocongestin
水母发光蛋白/水母發光蛋白,水母螢光素　aequorin
水囊法/水囊法　water filled balloon method
水囊瘤/水囊瘤　hygroma
水囊性肌瘤/水囊性肌瘤　hydromyoma
水囊肿/水囊腫　hydrocyst
水囊肿切除术/水囊切除術　hydrocelectomy
水囊肿性睾丸肉样肿/水囊腫性睾丸肉樣腫,積水性陰囊肉腫　sarcohydrocele
水囊状淋巴管瘤/水囊狀淋巴管瘤,囊性水瘤　cystic hygroma
水脑/水腦　water brain
水泥烧伤/水泥燒傷,水泥蝕傷　cement burn
水泥湿疹/水泥濕疹　cement eczema
水逆/水逆　water regurgitation
水凝胶/水凝膠,水凝體　hydrogel
水牛背/水牛背　buffalo hump
水牛角/水牛角　buffalo horn
水牛颈/水牛頸　buffalo neck
水泡状变性/水囊狀變性　hydatidiform degeneration
水疱/水皰　blister, vesicle, phlycten
水疱病/水皰病　hydroa
水疱浆疗法/水皰漿療法　phlyctenotherapy
水疱试验/水皰試驗　blister test
水疱形成/水皰形成,水皰發生　vesiculation
水疱性红斑性狼疮/水皰性紅斑性狼瘡　burdock root extract
水疱性口炎印第安纳病毒/水皰性口炎印第安那病毒　vesicular stomatitis-Indiana virus
水疱性丘疹样糠疹/水皰性丘疹樣糠疹　papulovesicular pityriasis
水平板/水平板,水平層　horizontal plate
水平变形/水平變形　horizontal distortion
水平部/水平部　horizontal part
水平参考线/水平參考線,水平輔助線　horizontal reference line
水平测量器基座/水平測量器基座　horizontal surveyor base
水平重叠/水平重疊　horizontal overlap
水平传递/水平傳遞　horizontal transmission
水平对称/水平對稱　horizontal symmetry
水平复位瓣/水平復位瓣　horizontally repositioned flap
水平覆盖/水平覆蓋　overjet
水平骨折/水平骨折　horizontal fracture
水平衡/水平衡　water balance
水平滑动截骨术/水平滑動截骨術　horizontal sliding

osteotomy
水平基因转移/水平基因轉移　horizontal gene transfer
水平疾病传播/水平疾病傳播　horizontal disease transmission
水平角度/水平角度　horizontal angulation
水平截骨术/水平截骨術　horizontal osteotomy
水平裂/水平裂　horizontal fissure
水平面/水平面　horizontal plane
水平偏盲/水平偏盲　horizontal hemianopsia
水平上颌骨折/水平上頜骨折　horizontal maxilla fracture
水平细胞/水平細胞　horizontal cell
水平下颌关系/水平下頜關係　horizontal jaw relation
水平下颌移动/水平下頜移動　horizontal jaw movement
水平纤维/水平纖維　horizontal fiber
水平性眩晕/水平位眩暈　horizontal vertigo
水平性眼球震颤/水平性眼球震顫　horizontal nystagmus
水平性隐斜/水平性隱斜　horizontal phoria
水平牙根断裂/水平牙根斷裂　horizontal root fracture
水平轴/水平軸　horizontal axis
水平阻生/水平阻生　horizontal impaction
水气腹/水氣腹　hydraeroperitoneum
水气凌心/水氣凌心　water pathogen attacking heart
水气凌心证/水氣凌心證　pattern of water pathogen attacking heart
水气胸/水氣胸,肋膜腔積水充氣　hydropneumothorax
水芹烯/水芹烯　phellandrene
水泉/水泉　shuiquan, KI5
水溶胶/水溶膠,水懸膠體　hydrosol
水溶性基质/水溶性基質　water-soluble base
水溶性浸出物/水溶性浸出物　water-soluble extractive
水溶性维生素/水溶性維生素　water-soluble vitamin
水溶液/水溶液　aqua
水褥/水褥,水墊床　hydrostatic bed
水软化/水軟化　water softening
水疝/水疝　hydrocele
水生动植物/水生物動植物　aquatic
水生木/水生木　water generating wood
水湿内停证/水濕內停證　pattern of internal stagnation of fluid-dampness
水手皮肤/水手皮膚　sailor skin

水苏[四]糖/水蘇[四]糖,菜豆糖　stachyose
水突/水突　shuitu, ST10
水土不服/水土不服　non-acclimatization
水丸/水丸　watered pill
水微生物学/水微生物學　water microbiology
水污染/水汙染　water pollution
水污染物/水汙染物　water pollutants
水下按摩/水下按摩　underwater massage
水下爆炸性震伤/水下爆炸性震傷,水下衝擊　immersion blast
水下洗肠疗法/水下洗腸療法　underwater colonic irrigation
水下运动/水下運動　underwater exercise
水仙花疹/水仙花疹　lily rash
水相/水相　aqueous phase
水泻/水瀉　watery diarrhea
水泻剂/水瀉劑　hydragogue
水形人/水形人　water-phase person
水性霜/水性霜　aqueous cream
水性油脂/水性油脂　fluid greases
水选/水選　selection in water
水压/水壓　hydraulic pressure
水压扩张器/水壓擴張器　hydrostatic dilator
水压扩张术/水囊擴張術　hydrostatic dilatation
水压调节器/水壓調節器　hydrostat
水杨苷/水楊苷,水楊素　salicin
水杨醛/水楊醛　salicylaldehyde
水杨醛试验/水楊醛試驗　salicylaldehyde test
水杨酸/水楊酸　salicylic acid
水杨酸苯酯/水楊酸酯　phenol salicylate
水杨酸反应/水楊酸反應　salicylism reaction
水杨酸汞/水楊酸汞,柳酸汞　mercuric salicylate
水杨酸火棉胶/水楊酸火棉膠　salicylic acid collodion
水杨酸奎宁/水楊酸奎寧　quinine salicylate
水杨酸疗法/水楊酸療法　salicyltherapy
水杨酸棉/水楊酸棉　salicylated cotton
水杨酸钠/水楊酸鈉　sodium salicylate
水杨酸盐/水楊酸鹽　salicylate
水杨酸盐疗法/水楊酸劑療法　salicyl treatment
水杨酸盐血[症]/水楊酸血症　salicylemia
水杨酸中毒/水楊酸中毒　salicylism
水杨酸灼伤/水楊酸灼傷　acetylsalicylic acid chemical injuries
水杨酰胺/水楊酸胺　salicylamide
水杨酰苯胺类/水楊醯苯胺類　salicylanilides
水杨酰醋酸/水楊醯醋酸　salicyloacetic acid
水杨酰偶氮磺胺吡啶/水楊醯偶氮磺胺吡啶,水楊酸磺胺吡啶　salicylazosulfapyridine

水杨酰[替]苯胺/水楊醯[替]苯胺,水楊酸苯胺 salicylanilide
水样变性/水樣變性,水腫變性 hydropic degeneration
水样便/水樣便 watery stool
水样透明细胞/水樣透明細胞 wasserhelle cell
水俣病/水俣病 minamata disease
水源性瘙痒/水源性搔癢,水因性搔癢 aquagenic pruritus
水源性荨麻疹/水源性蕁麻疹,水因性蕁麻疹 aquagenic urticaria
水曰润下/水曰潤下 water characterized by moistening and descending
水运动/水運動 water movements
水蛭/水蛭 leech
水蛭病/水蛭病 hirudiniasis
水蛭素/水蛭素 hirudin
水蛭素疗法/水蛭素療法 hirudin therapy
水蛭吸血法/水蛭吸血法 leeching
水蛭咬伤/水蛭咬傷 leech bite
水中扩散/水内擴散 hydrodiffusion
水中运动疗法/水中運動療法 hydrokinesitherapy
水肿[病]/水腫[病] dropsy, edema
水肿形成/水腫形成 edematization
水肿性喉炎/水腫性喉炎 edematous laryngitis
水肿性肾病变/水腫性腎病變,浮腫性腎病 hydropic nephrosis
水肿性肾炎/水腫性腎炎 hydremic nephritis
水肿性荨麻疹/水腫性蕁麻疹 urticaria edematous
水中毒/水中毒 water intoxication
水煮/水煮 boil with water
水柱[式]肺活量计/水柱式肺[活]量計 hydrospirometer
水柱[式]脉搏描记器/水柱式脈博描記器,水媒脈波計 hydrosphygmograph
水恣泄/水恣洩 running watery diarrhea
水渍疮/水漬瘡 paddy-field dermatitis
水族馆肉芽肿/水族館肉芽腫,水族池肉芽腫 aquarium granuloma
睡梦性感觉过敏/睡夢性感覺過敏,夢寐性感覺過敏 oneiric hyperesthesia
睡梦状态/睡夢狀態 dreamy state
睡眠/睡眠 sleep, slumber
睡眠剥夺/睡眠剝奪 sleep deprivation
睡眠动作描记器/睡時運動描記器 hypnocinematograph
睡眠过度/睡眠過度,嗜眠 hypersomnia
睡眠呼吸暂停/睡眠呼吸暫停 sleep apnea
睡眠呼吸暂停综合征/睡眠呼吸暫停症候群 sleep apnea syndrome
睡眠-觉醒过渡障碍/睡眠-覺醒過渡障礙 sleep-wake transition disorder
睡眠觉醒障碍/睡眠覺醒障礙 sleep arousal disorder
睡眠困难/睡眠困難 dyscoimesis
睡眠麻痹/睡眠麻痺 sleep paralysis
睡眠期/睡眠期 sleep stage
睡眠疼痛/睡時痛 hypnalgia
睡眠学/睡眠學 hypnosophy
睡眠学习/睡眠學習 hypnopedia
睡眠异常/睡眠異常 parahypnosis
睡眠运动描记器/睡眠運動描記器,睡眠活動記錄器 somnocinematograph
睡眠障碍/睡眠障礙 sleep disorder, somnipathy
睡前期/睡前期,初眠,淺睡 predormitium
睡行症/睡行症 sleep walking
吮拇癖/吮拇癖,吸拇癖 sucking thumb
吮乳期动物/吮乳期動物 suckling animal
吮舌癖/吸舌[癖] sucking tongue
吮指[癖]/吸指癖 finger-sucking
顺铂/順鉑 cisplatin
顺产/順產,自然生產 spontaneous delivery
顺传/順傳 sequential transmission
顺磁性/順磁性 paramagnetism
顺磁性造影剂/順磁性造影劑 paramagnetic contrast medium
顺从性/依從性 compliance
顺错构象/順錯構象 synclinal conformation
顺叠构象/順疊構象 synperiplanar conformation
顺反异构/順反異構物 cis-trans isomerism
顺反异构酶类/順反異構酶類 cis-trans isomerases
顺反子/順反子 cistron
顺规性散光/順規性散光 astigmatism with rule
顺扭转/順扭轉,正扭轉 positive torsion
顺情从欲/順情從欲 desire satisfaction
顺情从欲疗法/順情從欲療法 desire satisfaction therapy
顺蠕动吻合[术]/順蠕動吻合[術],同蠕動向吻合術 isoperistaltic anastomosis
顺式/順式 cis
顺式构象/順式構象 cisoid conformation
顺势疗法/順勢療法 homeopathy, TCM homeopathy
顺势医疗处方集/順勢醫療處方集 homeopathic formularies
顺势医疗药典/順勢醫療藥典 homeopathic pharmacopoeias

顺势医疗者/順勢醫療者,顺势疗法派　homeopath
[顺]乌头酸酶/[順]烏頭酸酶　aconitase
顺向变性/順向變性　anterograde degeneration
顺向插入/順向插入　direct insertion
顺向轴突输送/順向軸突運輸　anterograde axonal transport
顺行记忆/順行記憶　anterograde memory
顺行肾盂造影[术]/順行腎盂造影[術]　antegrade pyelography
顺行栓塞/順行栓塞　direct embolism
顺行性传导阻滞/順行性傳導阻斷　antegrade block
顺行性心脏停搏液灌注/順行性心臟停搏液灌注　antegrade perfusion of cardioplegic solution
顺行性遗忘/順行性健忘　anterograde amnesia
顺序拔牙法/順序拔牙法　serial extraction
顺意疗法/順意療法　desire satisfaction therapy
顺应性/順應性　compliance
顺欲/順欲　desire satisfaction
顺证/順證　favorable pattern, pattern with good prognosis
顺志/順志　desire satisfaction
瞬膜/瞬膜　nictitating membrane
瞬目痉挛/瞬目痙攣　nictating spasm
瞬时空腔/瞬時空腔,暫態空腔　temporary cavity
说服疗法/説服療法　pithiatry
说理开导疗法/説理開導療法　reasoning therapy
说示不能/説示不能,示意不能　asemia
朔勒位/朔勒位,許勒位　Scholler position
朔伊尔曼病/朔伊爾曼病,舒爾曼病　Scheuermann disease
硕大利什曼原虫/碩大利什曼原蟲　Leishmania major
司法鉴定/司法鑒定　expert testimony
司法精神病学/司法精神病學　forensic psychiatry
司法精神病学鉴定/司法精神病學鑒定　forensic psychiatrics expertise
司可巴比妥/司可巴比妥　secobarbital
司立吉林/司立吉林　selegiline
司莫司汀/司莫司汀　semustine
司帕霉素/司帕黴素,稀疏黴素　sparsomycin
司他夫定/司他夫定　stavudine
司他霉素/司他黴素　distamycins
司坦唑醇/脂類促同化藥　stanozolol
司替罗磷/司替羅磷　tetrachlorvinphos
司天/司天　celestial manager qi
司外揣内/司外揣内　governing exterior to infer interior
丝/絲　filament, silk

Z丝/Z絲　Z filament
丝氨酸/絲胺酸　serine
丝氨酸蛋白酶/絲胺酸[蛋白]酶　serine proteinase
丝氨酸蛋白酶抑制剂/絲胺酸蛋白酶抑制劑　serine proteinase inhibitor
丝氨酸tRNA连接酶/絲胺酸tRNA連接酶　serine-tRNA ligase
丝氨酸内肽酶类/絲胺酸内肽酶類　serine endopeptidases
丝虫病/絲蟲病　filariasis
丝虫病肾病/絲蟲病腎病　filariasis nephropathy
丝虫病·湿热下注证/絲蟲病·濕熱下注證　filariasis with pattern of downward diffusion of damp-heat
丝虫属/絲蟲屬　Filaria
丝虫性睾丸炎/絲蟲性睾丸炎　filarial orchitis
丝虫性滑膜炎/絲蟲性滑膜炎　filarial synovitis
丝虫性脓肿/絲蟲病膿瘍　filarial abscess
丝虫性水囊肿/絲蟲性水囊腫　filarial hydrocele
丝虫性象皮病/[血]絲蟲性象皮病,真象皮病　filarial elephantiasis
丝虫周期性/絲蟲週期性,血絲蟲之週期發作性　filarial periodicity
丝绸样咿轧音/絲擦狀撚發音　silken crepitus
丝瓜络/絲瓜絡　luffa vegetable sponge
丝间质/絲間質　interfilar substance
丝胶/絲膠,絲蛋白　sericin
丝聚蛋白原/絲聚蛋白原　profilaggrin
丝连多形核白细胞/絲連多形核白細胞,有絲多形核白血球　filament polymorphonuclear
丝裂霉素/絲裂黴素　mitomycin
丝裂原/絲裂原　mitogen
丝裂原启动蛋白激酶类/絲裂原啟動蛋白激酶類　mitogen-activated protein kinases
丝球/絲球,絲團　skein
丝绒疝带/絲絨疝帶,絲團疝氣帶　yarn truss
丝素蛋白质类/絲素蛋白質類　fibroins
丝袜病/絲襪病　silk stocking disease
丝线/絲線　silk suture
丝线植入法/絲線植入法　silk implantation
丝心蛋白/絲[心]蛋白　fibroin
丝圆线虫/絲圓[線]蟲　Strongylus filaria
丝竹空/絲竹空　sizhukong, SJ23
丝状病毒科/絲狀病毒科　Filoviridae
丝状假足/絲狀假足　filopodium
丝状角膜炎/絲狀角膜炎　filamentary keratitis
丝状菌病/絲狀菌病　hyphomycosis
丝状乳头/絲狀乳頭,絲狀乳突　filiform papilla
丝状疣/絲狀疣　verruca filiformis

丝状真菌/絲狀真菌　filamentous fungus
丝足/絲[狀僞]足　filopodium
私立卫生设施/私立衛生設施　proprietary health facility
私立医院/私立醫院　private hospitals
私人开业/私人開業,私人醫業　private practice
私人开业护理/私人開業護理　private duty nursing
私生/私生　illegitimacy
私营医院/私營醫院　proprietary hospital
思/思　pensiveness, thought
思潮过敏/思潮過敏,思想過敏　hyperpsychosis
思考速度测验器/思想速度測驗器　noematachometer
思考速度描记器/思想速度描記器　noematachograph
思虑/思慮　thinking
思虑伤脾/思慮傷脾　worry impairing spleen
思梦/思夢　missing dream
思伤/思傷　impairment caused by anxiety
思伤脾/思傷脾　pensiveness impairing the spleen
思胜恐/思勝恐　reasoning to reducing fear
思为脾志/思爲脾志　spleen being associated with pensiveness
思维/思維　thinking
思维被夺/思維被奪　thought withdrawal
思维奔逸/思維奔逸　flight of thought
思维播散/思維播散　thought broadcasting
思维不连贯/思維不連貫,思想散漫,思想無緒　incoherence of thought
思维插入/思維插入　thought insertion
思维化声/思維化聲　audible thought
思维黏滞/思維黏滯　viscosity of thinking
思维贫乏/思維貧乏　poverty of thought
思维破裂/思維破裂　splitting of thought
思维松散/思維鬆散　looseness of thinking
思维云集/思維雲集　pressure of thought
思维障碍/思想障礙　thought disorder
思维中断/思維中斷　thought blocking
思想迟钝/思想遲鈍　hypopsychosis
思郁/思鬱　stagnation pattern caused by pensiveness
思则气结/思則氣結　pensiveness leading to qi knotting
思中/思中　stroke due to anxiety or over-thinking
斯宾塞-帕克疫苗/疫斯賓塞-帕克苗,史-帕二氏疫苗　Spencer-Parker vaccine
斯德奇综合征/斯德奇症候群,Sturge 氏症候群　Sturge syndrome
斯蒂尔病/斯蒂爾病　Still disease
斯蒂尔桥体/斯蒂爾橋體,史蒂爾氏橋體　Steele pontic
斯蒂尔-肖法综合征/斯蒂爾-肖法症候群,史-夏二氏症候群　Still-Chauffard syndrome
斯蒂尔牙面/斯蒂爾牙面　Steele facing
斯蒂尔杂音/斯蒂爾雜音,Steell 氏雜音　Steell murmur
斯蒂尔综合征/斯蒂爾症候群,Still 氏症候群　Still syndrome
斯蒂克勒综合征/斯蒂克勒症候群　Stickler syndrome
斯-哈综合征/斯-哈症候群,Stryker-Halbeisen 二氏症候群　Stryker-Halbeisen syndrome
斯基勒伦骨折/斯基勒倫骨折,Skillern 氏骨折　Skillern fracture
斯卡尔帕神经/斯卡爾帕神經,Scarpa 氏神經　Scarpa nerve
斯卡尔帕液/斯卡爾帕液,Scarpa 氏液　Scarpa fluid
斯卡托辛/斯卡托辛　skatosin
斯-卡-韦综合征/斯-卡-韋症候群,Sturge-Kalischer-Weber 三氏症候群　Sturge-Kalischer-Weber syndrome
斯科达叩响/斯科達叩響,Skodaic 氏叩響　Skodaic resonance
斯莱病/斯萊病,Sly 氏症候群　Sly syndrome
斯卢德神经痛/斯盧德神經痛,Sluder 氏神經痛　Sluder neuralgia
斯卢德综合征/斯盧德症候群,Sluder 氏症候群　Sluder syndrome
斯-莫综合征/斯-莫症候群,Stewart-Morel 二氏症候群　Stewart-Morel syndrome
斯内伦视力表/斯內倫視力表　Snellen chart
斯潘德克斯弹力纤维/斯潘得克斯彈力纖維　spandex
斯彭斯综合征/斯彭斯症候群,Spens 氏症候群　Spens syndrome
斯皮茨痣/斯皮茨痣　Spitz nevus
斯塔比肿/斯塔比肿　stabilarsan
斯塔尔氏耳I型/斯塔爾氏耳I型,Stahl 氏耳第一型　Stahl No.1 ear
斯塔尔氏耳II型/斯塔爾氏耳II型,Stahl 氏耳第二型　Stahl No.2 ear
斯塔林心脏法则/斯塔林心臟法則,Starling 氏定律　Starling law
斯塔斯-奥托法/斯塔斯-奧托法,史-歐二氏法　Stas-Otto method
斯坦纳分析法/斯坦納分析法　Steiner analysis
斯坦纳特病/斯坦納特病,Steinert 氏病　Steinert

斯坦因-利文撒尔综合征/斯坦因-利文撒爾症候群, 史-雷二氏症候群　Stein-Leventhal syndrome
斯特里特发育分期/斯特里特發育分期　Streeter developmental horizons
斯特罗恩病/斯特羅恩病, Strachan 氏病　Strachan disease
斯特诺管/斯特諾管, Steno 氏管, 腮腺管　duct of Steno
斯滕伯格病/斯滕伯格病, Sternberg 氏病　Sternberg disease
斯滕伯格-里德细胞/斯滕伯格-里德細胞, Sternberg-Reed 二氏細胞　Sternberg-Reed cell
斯滕特移植物/斯滕特移植物, Stent 氏移植物　Stent graft
斯廷博克单位/斯廷博克單位, 史提伯氏單位　Steenbock unit
斯图尔特-霍姆斯征/斯圖爾特-霍姆斯徵, 史-哈二氏徵象　Stewart-Holmes sign
斯图基反射/斯圖基反射, 史托吉反射　Stookey reflex
斯托克斯透镜/斯托克斯透鏡, Stokes 氏透鏡　Stokes lens
斯托克斯综合征/斯托克斯症候群, Stokes 氏症候群　Stokes syndrome
斯韦迪奥尔病/斯韋迪奧爾病, Swediaur 氏病　Swediaur disease
斯-亚病/斯-亞病, Stokes-Adams 二氏病　Stokes-Adams disease
斯-亚发作/斯-亞發作, Stokes-Adams 二氏發作　Stokes-Adams attack
斯-亚综合征/斯-亞症候群, Stokes-Adams 二氏症候群　Stokes-Adams syndrome
锶放射性同位素/鍶放射性同位素　strontium radioisotopes
锶同位素/鍶同位素　strontium isotopes
撕开/撕開　tear
撕裂/撕裂　laceration
撕裂伤/撕裂［創傷］　lacerated wound, laceration
撕裂音/軋軋聲　craquement
撕囊术/撕囊術　capsulorhexis
撕脱骨折/撕除性折斷　avulsion fracture
撕脱伤/撕脫傷　avulsion
嘶嘶声呼吸/嘶嘶聲呼吸　hissing respiration
死产/死產　stillbirth
死产率/死產率　mortinatality
死骨片/死骨片, 腐骨片　sequestrum
死骨切除术/死骨切除術　sequestrectomy
死后变化/死後變化　postmortem change
死后分娩/死後分娩　postmortem delivery
死后血凝块/死後血［凝］塊　postmortem clot
死后血栓/死後血栓　postmortem thrombus
死后诊断/死後診斷　paragnosis
死后自溶/死後自溶　postmortem autolysis
死精症/死精症　necrospermia
死前血块/死前血塊　antemortem clot
死前血栓/死前血栓　antemortem thrombus
死区/死區　dead tract
死胎/死胎, 胎兒死亡　fetal death
死亡/死［亡］　death
死亡本能/死亡本能　death instinct
死亡率/死亡率　mortality
死亡率图/死亡率圖　mortalogram
死亡热/死亡熱　death fever
死亡学/死亡學　thanatology
死亡证/死亡證　death certificates
死因/死因　cause of death
死因不明/死因不明, 不明死亡　dysoemia
死者/死者　dead
死指/死指　dead finger
四白/四白　sibai, ST2
四瓣 Z 成形术/四瓣 Z 成形術　four-flap Z-plasty
四倍体/四倍體, 四套染色體　tetraploid
四倍性/四倍性, 四套染色體　tetraploidy
四苯硼钠/四苯硼鈉　sodium tetraphenylborate
四苯硼酸钠/四苯硼酸鈉　sodium tetraphenylborate
四吡咯类/四吡咯類　tetrapyrroles
四臂畸胎/四臂畸形　tetrabrachius
四边孔/四邊孔　quadrilateral foramen
四鞭毛体/四鞭毛體　tetramastigote
四步触诊法/四步觸診法　four maneuvers of Leopold
四产妇/四產婦　quadripara
四簇介体/四簇介體　quadriceptor
四氮唑比色法/四氮唑比色法　tetrazoline colorimetry
四点测定/四點測定　four-point assay
四碘酚酞/四碘酚酞　phenoltetraiodophthalein
四碘酚酞钠/四碘［酚］酞鈉　tetiothalein sodium
四叠体/四疊體　corpora quadrigemina
四叠体静脉/四疊體靜脈　quadrigeminal vein
四叠体上臂/四疊體上臂　prebrachium
四叠体下臂/四疊體下臂　postbrachium
四渎/四瀆　sidu, SJ9
四耳畸胎/四耳畸胎　tetraotus
四分孢子/四分孢子　tetraspore

四分切/四分切法 quadrisection
四分体/四分體 tetrad
四缝/四縫 sifeng, EX-UE10
四氟乙烯均聚物/四氟乙烯均聚物 proplast
四个成串刺激/四個成串刺激 train of four stimulation
四管锁槽式带环/四管鎖槽式帶環,四溝托圈 four-channel bracket band
四海/四海 four seas
四环类抗生素/四環類抗生素 tetracycline antibiotics
四环类抗抑郁剂/四環類抗憂鬱藥 tetracyclic antidepressant
四环素/四環素 tetracycline
四环素抗药性/四環素抗藥性 tetracycline resistance
四环素色素牙/四環素色素牙 tetracycline pigmentation teeth
四级蛋白质结构/四級蛋白質結構 quaternary protein structure
四级结构/四級結構 quarternary structure
四极/四維,四桎 four limbs, four poles
四甲基/四甲基 tetramethyl
四甲基苯二胺/四甲基苯二胺 tetramethyl phenylenediamine
四甲基尿酸/四甲基尿酸 tetramethyluric acid
四[价]酸/四酸 tetracid
四尖牙/四尖齒 quadricuspid
四节律/四節律 quadruple rhythm
四君子汤/四君子湯 sijunzi decoction
四联律/四聯律 quadrigeminy
四联脉/四聯脈,四搏脈 quadrigeminal pulse
四联免疫抑制治疗/四聯免疫抑制治療 quadruple immunosuppressive therapy
四联症/四聯症 tetralogy
四氯酚酞/四氯酚酞,酚四氯酞 phenoltetrachlorophthalein
四氯酚酞试验/四氯酚酞試驗,酚四氯酞試驗 phenoltetrachlorophthalein test
四氯化碳/四氯化碳 carbon tetrachloride
四氯化碳性肾炎/四氯化碳性腎炎 carbon tetrachloride nephritis
四氯化碳中毒/四氯化碳中毒 carbon tetrachloride poisoning
四氯化物/四氯化物 tetrachloride
四氯乙烷/四氯乙烷 cellon
四氯乙烯/四氯乙烯 tetrachloroethylene
四满/四滿 siman, KI14
四咪唑/四咪唑 tetramisole

四妙勇安汤/四妙勇安湯 simiao yong'an decoction
四逆散/四逆散 sini powder
四逆汤/四逆湯 sini decoction
四气/四氣 four nature of drugs
四气调神大论篇/四氣調神大論篇 Treatise on the Managing of Emotions with the Qi of Four Seasons
四氢大麻酚/四氫大麻酚 tetrahydrocannabinol
四氢可的松/四氫可的松 tetrahydrocortisone
四氢萘类/四氫萘類 tetrahydronaphthalenes
四氢萘酮类/四氫萘酮類 tetralones
四氢尿苷/四氫尿苷 tetrahydrouridine
四氢皮质醇/四氫皮質醇 tetrahydrocortisol
四氢糖基二硫化硫胺素/四氫糖基二硫化硫胺素 thiamin tetrahydrofurfuryl disulfide
四氢叶酸/四氫葉酸 tetrahydrofolic acid
四氢叶酸脱氢酶/四氫葉酸脱氫酶 tetrahydrofolate dehydrogenase
四氢叶酸盐类/四氫葉酸鹽類 tetrahydrofolates
四氢异喹啉类/四氫異喹啉類 tetrahydroisoquinolines
四氢异喹啉生物碱/四氫異喹啉生物鹼 tetrahydroisoquinoline alkaloid
四氢罂粟林/四氫罂粟林 tetrahydropapaveroline
四乳[畸形]/四乳[畸形],畸形四乳房 tetramazia
四射染色体/四射染色體 quadriradial chromosome
四神聪/四神聰 sishencong, EX-HN1
四神丸/四神丸 sishen pill
四时调摄/四時調攝 health maintenance in four seasons
四手操作/四手操作 four-handed technique
四手畸胎/四手畸胎 tetrachirus
四胎/四胎 quadruplets
四胎妊娠/四胎妊娠 quadruplet pregnancy
四肽/四肽 tetrapeptide
四肽胃泌素/四肽胃泌素 tetragastrin
四糖/四醣 tetrasaccharide
四萜/四萜 tetraterpene
四头肌/四頭肌 quadriceps
四头肌试验/四頭肌試驗 quadriceps test
四腿畸胎/四腿畸胎 tetrascelus
四弯风/四彎風,特異反應性皮炎,異位性皮炎 atopic dermatitis of elbow and knee pits, four bends wind
四维超声心动描记术/四維超聲心動描記術 four-dimensional echocardiography
四物安神汤/四物安神湯 decoction of four ingredients for tranquilizing the mind, siwu anshen decoction

四物汤/四物湯　siwu decoction
四烯甲雌醇核/四烯甲雌醇核　estratetraene
四烯类/四烯類　tetraenes
四硝基甲烷/四硝基甲烷　tetranitromethane
四硝季戊醇/四硝季戊醇,四硝酸五蘇醇　niperyt
四星体/四星體　tetraster
四溴酚酞/四溴酚酞　tetrabromophenolphthalein
四溴酚酞钠/四溴[酚]酞鈉　tetrabromophthalein sodium
四溴荧光素/四溴螢光素　tetrabromofluorescein
四眼畸胎/四眼畸胎　tetranophthalmos
四眼双面畸胎/四眼雙面畸胎　diprosopus tetrophthalmos
四氧化锇/四氧化鋨　osmium tetroxide
四氧化物/四氧化物　tetroxide
四氧嘧啶/四氧嘧啶　alloxan
四氧嘧啶糖尿病/四氧嘧啶糖尿病　alloxan diabetes
四乙铵/四乙銨　tetraethylammonium
四乙铵化合物/四乙銨化合物　tetraethylammonium compounds
四乙基铅/四乙基鉛　tetraethyl lead
四乙酸盐/四乙酸鹽,四醋酸鹽　tetracetate
四异丙基焦磷酰胺/四異丙基焦磷醯胺　tetraisopropylpyrophosphamide
四原子分子/四原子分子　tetratomic molecule
四诊/四診　four diagnostic methods
四诊合参/四診合參　comprehensive analysis of data gained by four diagnostic methods
四肢/四肢　limbs, extremities
四肢不全/四肢不全　peromelia
四肢对称性色素沉着异常症/四肢對稱性色素沈著異常症　symmetrical dyschromatosis of the extremities
四肢发育不全[畸形]/四肢發育不全[畸形],肢骨發育不全畸形　ectromelia
四肢发育过度/四肢發育過度　acrometagenesis
四肢救助/四肢救助　limb salvage
四肢拘急/四肢拘急　spasm of limbs
四肢麻痹/四肢麻痺　quadriplegia
四肢麻痹站立支架/四肢麻痺站立支架,四肢麻痺支撐支架　quadriplegic standing frame
四肢强直/四肢強直　rigidity of limbs
四肢切断术/四肢切斷術,四肢截斷術　quadruple amputation
四肢轻瘫/四肢輕癱,四肢軟弱　tetraparesis
四肢瘫痪/四肢癱瘓　quardriplegia
四肢疼痛/四肢疼痛　limbs pain
四指叩诊/四指叩診,彈琴式叩法　piano percussion

四足动物/四足動物,四足獸　quadruped
四足畸胎/四足畸胎　tetrapus
四足行动/四腳行動,四腳爬行　tetrapodisis
四唑类/四唑類　tetrazoles
四唑鎓盐类/四唑鎓鹽類　tetrazolium salts
似曾相识症/似曾相識症　deja vu
似腹盘吸虫病/似腹盤吸蟲病,雙口吸蟲病　gastrodisciasis
似守非守/似守非守　seemingly kept on but not focusing
饲肥星形细胞/飼肥星形細胞,大圓形細胞形成的星形細胞　gemistocyte
饲管/飼管,給養管　feeding tube
饲鸟者肺病/飼鳥者肺病,過敏性肺泡炎　bird-breeder disease
忪悸/忪悸　severe palpitation
松柏醇试剂/松柏醇試劑　coniferyl alcohol reagent
松弛/鬆弛,弛緩　looseness, relaxation
松弛部/鬆弛部　flaccid part
松弛肌/鬆弛肌　laxator
松弛技术/鬆弛技術　relaxation techniques
松弛肩/鬆弛肩　loose shoulder
松弛素/鬆弛素　relaxin
松弛性/鬆弛性　lusitropic
松弛性睑外翻/鬆弛性瞼外翻,弛緩性瞼外翻　flaccid ectropion
松弛性皮肤张力线/鬆弛性皮膚張力線　relaxed skin tension lines
松弛性偏瘫/鬆弛性偏癱,肌張不全,低肌張　flaccid hemiplegia
松弛性瘫痪/鬆弛性癱瘓,弛緩性麻痺　flaccid paralysis
松达氯铵/松達氯銨　chlorisondamine
松动牙固定术/鬆動牙固定術　fixation of loosened tooth
松二糖/松二糖　turanose
松果体/松果體　pineal body, pineal gland
松果体病/松果體病　pinealopathy
松果体功能减退/松果體機能不足　hypopinealism
松果体功能亢进/松果體機能亢進　hyperpinealism
松果体功能缺失/松果體機能缺失　apinealism
松果体功能障碍/松果腺機能障礙　pinealism
松果体脚/松果體腳　peduncle of pineal body
松果体瘤/松果腺瘤　pinealoma
松果体切除术/松果體切除術,松果腺切除術　pinealectomy
松果体上隐窝/松果[體]上隱窩　suprapineal recess
松果体外侧静脉/松果體外側靜脈　lateral

epiphyseal vein
松果体细胞/松果體細胞,松果腺细胞　pinealocyte, pineal cell
松果体细胞瘤/松果體細胞瘤,松果腺[细胞]瘤　pinealocytoma
松果体隐窝/松果[體]隱窩　pineal recess
松果体肿瘤/松果體腫瘤　pineal gland tumor
松果体综合征/松果體症候群　epiphyseal syndrome, pineal syndrome
松果腺/松果腺　pineal gland
松果眼/松果眼　epiphyseal eye
松果隐窝/松果隱窩,松果體室,松果腺室　pineal ventricle
松花粉/松花粉　pine pollen
松节油/松節油　turpentine oil
松节油灌肠/松節油灌腸　turpentine enema
松节油萜/松節油萜　terebene
松节油中毒/松節油中毒　terebinthinism
松静阶段/鬆靜階段　relaxation and tranquility stage
松开主动脉钳夹/鬆開主動脈鉗夾　aortic declamping
松萝属/松蘿屬　Usnea
松毛虫皮炎/松毛蟲皮炎　dendrolimus dermatitis
松毛虫伤/松毛蟲傷　pine caterpillar sting
松皮癣/松皮癬　pine bark plaque, skin amyloidosis
松三糖/松三醣　melicitose
松石脂[肪]瘤/松石脂瘤　topholipoma
松香/松香　rosin
松香芹醇/松香芹醇　pinocarveol
松香酸/松香酸,樅酸　abietic acid
松香酸盐/松香酸鹽,樅酸鹽　abietate
松香烷二萜类/松香烷二萜類　abietane diterpenes
松质骨/鬆質骨,疏鬆骨,海綿質骨　cancellous bone, spongy bone, substantia spongiosa ossium
耸肩试验/聳肩試驗　trapezius muscle myosthenic test
苏氨酸/蘇胺酸　threonine
苏氨酸tRNA连接酶/蘇胺酸tRNA連接酶　threonine-tRNA ligase
苏氨酸脱水酶/蘇胺酸脫水酶　threonine dehydratase
苏打/蘇打　soda
苏打薄荷溶液/蘇打薄荷溶液　soda and mint solution
苏丹蓝CN/蘇丹藍CN　Sudan blue CN
苏丹绿4B/蘇丹綠4B　Sudan green 4B
苏格兰脑炎/蘇格蘭腦炎　Scotland encephalitis
苏合香/蘇合香　storax
苏合香丸/蘇合香丸　storax pill, suhexiang pills
苏-加综合征/蘇-加症候群,Sulzberger-Garbe二氏症候群　Sulzberger-Garbe syndrome
苏敬/蘇敬　Su Jing
苏拉明/蘇拉明,舒拉明　suramin
苏联东部地方性皮病/蘇聯東部地方性皮病,Sartian氏病　Sartian disease
苏木/蘇木　sappan wood
苏木红质氨/蘇木紅質氨　ammonia hemate
苏木精/蘇木精　hematoxylin
苏木精锶染剂/蘇木精鍶染料　hemastrontium, hematoxylin
苏木精-伊红染色/蘇木精-伊紅染色,H-E染色　hematoxylin-eosin staining, H-E staining
苏萨溶液/蘇薩溶液　susa solution
苏颂/蘇頌　Su Song
苏糖/蘇糖　threose
苏铁素/蘇鐵素　cycasin
苏型构型/蘇型構型　threo configuration
苏醒室/甦醒室　recovery room
苏醒药/甦醒藥,回醒劑　analeptic
苏云金芽孢杆菌/蘇雲金芽桿菌,蘇力菌　Bacillus thuringiensis
苏子降气汤/蘇子降氣湯　suzi jiangqi decoction
诉怨妄想狂/訴訟妄想[狂]　querulous paranoia
素髎/素髎　suliao, DU25
素食者/素食[主義]者　vegetarian
素食者膳食/素食者膳食　vegetarian diet
素问/素問　Plain Questions
素问玄机原病式/素問玄機原病式　Explanation to Mysterious Pathogenesis and Etiology Based on the Plain Questions
素心兰/素心蘭　chypre
素质/素質　diathesis
速度/速度　velocity
速度常数/速度常數　rate constant
速发型变态反应/即時性過敏,立即性過敏　immediate allergy
速发型超敏反应/立即型過敏　immediate hypersensitivity
速激肽类/速激肽類　tachykinins
速激肽受体/速激肽受體　tachykinin receptors
速率系数/速度係數　velocity coefficient
速食癖/速食癖,吞食快速　tachyphagia
速效救心丸/速效救心丸　suxiao jiuxin pills
速转实体镜/速轉實體鏡,速视器　tachistoscope
宿食/宿食　food retention
宿翳/宿翳　corneal scar, old nebula
宿主/宿主　host

宿主寄生虫关系/宿主寄生蟲關係 host-parasite relation
宿主抗移植物反应/宿主抗移植物反應 host versus graft reaction
粟疮/粟瘡 follicular conjunctivitis, millet sore
粟疮•脾虚湿困证/粟瘡•脾虛濕困證 millet sore with pattern of spleen deficiency and dampness retention
粟疮•湿热夹风证/粟瘡•濕熱夾風證 millet sore with pattern of dampness-heat complicated by wind
粟粒动脉瘤/粟粒動脈瘤 miliary aneurysm
粟粒坏死性痤疮/粟粒壞死性痤瘡 acne necrotica miliaris
粟粒性癌病/粟粒狀癌症 miliary carcinosis
粟粒性痤疮/粟粒性痤瘡 acne miliaria
粟粒性痘疮样痤疮/粟粒性痘瘡樣痤瘡 acne varioliformis miliaris
粟粒性结核/粟粒性結核 miliary tuberculosis
粟粒疹/粟粒疹 miliary eruption
粟粒疹后少汗症/粟粒疹後少汗症 postmiliarial hypohidrosis
粟粒疹热/粟粒疹熱 miliary fever
粟粒状天花/粟粒狀天花,粟粒狀痘瘡 variola miliaris
粟丘疹/粟丘疹 milium
塑化剂/塑化劑 plasticizer
塑胶工业/塑膠工業 plastics industry
塑料/塑膠 plastics
塑料安瓿/塑膠安瓿 plastic ampoule
塑料包埋/塑膠包埋 plastic embedding
塑料管微粒/塑膠管微粒 plastic tubing particle
塑料夹板/塑膠夾板 plastic splint
塑料喷护膜/塑膠噴護膜 vibesate
塑性凝胶/塑性凝膠,成形乳膠體 plastogel
酸/酸 sour, acid
酸白蛋白/酸白蛋白 acid albumin
酸败/酸敗 rancidity
酸不溶性灰分/酸不溶性灰分 acid-insoluble ash
酸潮/酸潮 acid tide
酸橙/酸橙 sour orange
酸定量器/酸定量器 acidimeter
酸度/酸度 acidity
酸反流/酸反流 acid reflux
酸酐/酸酐,脱水酸 anhydride
酸酐水解酶类/酸酐水解酶類 acid anhydride hydrolases
酸-枸橼酸-葡萄糖溶液/酸-枸橼酸-葡萄糖溶液,檸檬酸葡萄糖溶液 acid-citrate-dextrose solution
酸过多性呕吐/酸過多性嘔吐 hyperacid vomiting
酸化/酸化[作用],變酸 acidification
酸化磷酸氟化物/酸化磷酸氟化物 acidulated phosphate fluoride
酸化饮食/酸化飲食,酸灰性飲食 acid-ash diet
酸碱代谢/酸鹼代謝 acid-base metabolism
酸碱内环境稳定/酸鹼內環境穩定 acid-base homeostasis
酸碱平衡/酸鹼平衡 acid-base equilibrium, acid-base balance
酸碱平衡失调/酸鹼平衡失調 acid-base imbalance
酸碱伤目/酸鹼傷目 eye injured by acid and alkali
酸碱杂质测定器/酸鹼雜質測定器 ionoscope
酸觉/酸覺 acid sense
酸类/酸類 acids
酸绿/酸[性]綠 acid green
酸尿/酸[性]尿 aciduria
酸凝集/酸凝集 acid agglutination
酸缺乏/酸缺乏 anacidity
酸乳/酸乳 yogurt
酸乳产品/酸乳產品 cultured milk product
酸乳饮食/酸乳飲食 sour-milk diet
酸涩/酸澀 acerbity
酸烧伤/酸燒傷 acid burn
酸蚀处理/酸蝕處理 acid etching
酸痛/酸痛 aching pain, sour pain
酸细胞/酸細胞 acid cell
酸性氨基葡糖聚糖/酸性氨基葡糖聚糖,酸性糖胺聚糖 acid glycosaminoglycans
酸性氨基酸类/酸性氨基酸類 acidic amino acids
酸性氨基酸转运系统/酸性氨基酸轉運系統 acidic amino acid transport system
酸性单磷酸酯酶/酸性單磷酸酯酶 acid monophosphoesterase
酸性蛋白酶/酸性蛋白酶 acid protease
酸性地衣红-吉姆沙染色/酸性地衣紅-Giemsa染色 acid orcein-Giemsa stain
酸性碘铂酸盐溶液/酸性碘鉑酸鹽溶液 acidified iodoplatinate solution
酸性反应/酸性反應 acid reaction
酸性核蛋白/酸性核蛋白 acid nuclear protein
酸性酒石酸去甲肾上腺素/酸性酒石酸去甲肾上腺素,酸性酒石酸鹽正腎上腺素 levarterenol bitartrate
酸性酒石酸盐/酸性酒石酸鹽 acid tartrate
酸性磷酸酶/酸性磷酸[分解]酶 acid phosphatase
酸性磷酸酯酶/酸性磷酸酯酶 acid phosphoesterase
酸性硫酸盐/酸性硫酸鹽 acid sulfate

酸性麦芽糖酶缺乏/酸性麥芽糖酶缺乏 acid maltase deficiency
酸性钼酸盐试剂/酸性鉬酸鹽試劑 acid molybdate reagent
酸性黏多糖/酸性黏多醣 acidic mucopolysaccharide
酸性品红/酸性品紅,酸性複紅 acid fuchsin
酸性强直/酸性強直 acid rigidity
酸性[羟]高铁血红素/酸性[羥]高鐵血紅素,酸性正鐵血紅素 acid hematin
酸性染剂/酸性染劑,酸性色料 acid dye
酸性染料比色法/酸性染料比色法 acid-dye colorimetry
酸性神经酰胺酶/酸性神經醯胺酶 acid ceramidase
酸性碳酸盐/酸性碳酸鹽 acid carbonate
酸性糖苷神经鞘脂类/酸性糖苷神經鞘脂類 acidic glycosphingolipids
酸性外膜/酸性外膜,酸性包膜 acid mantle
酸性消化不良/酸性消化不良 acid dyspepsia, acid indigestion
酸性盐/酸性鹽 acid salt
酸性-α-乙酸萘酯酶/酸性-α-乙酸萘酯酶 acid-α-naphthyl acetate esterase
酸性正铁血红素测定法/酸性正鐵血紅素測定法,酸性血色質法 acid hematin method
酸性脂酶缺乏症/酸性脂酶缺乏症,酸性脂肪分解酶缺乏 acid lipase deficiency
酸性紫/酸性紫 acid violet
酸血[症]/酸血症 acidemia
酸枣仁/酸棗仁 spine date seed
酸枣仁汤/酸棗仁湯 suanzaoren decoction, wild jujube seed decoction
酸值/酸值,酸數 acid value
酸中和容量/酸中和容量,酸中和能力 acid-neutralizing capacity
酸中毒/酸毒,酸毒症 acid intoxication
蒜/蒜 Allium sativum
算术平均径/算術平均徑,平均直徑 average diameter
随访研究/隨訪研究 follow-up studies
随机对照试验/隨機對照試驗 randomized controlled trial
随机交配/隨機交配 random mating
随机扩增多态 DNA 技术/隨機擴增多態 DNA 技術 random amplified polymorphic DNA technique
随机筛选/隨機篩選 random screening
随机样本/隨機樣本 random sample
随机整合/隨機整合 random integration
随境转移/隨境轉移,分心性,注意散漫 distractibility
随体/隨體 satellite
随体联合/隨體聯合 satellite association
随意肌/隨意肌 voluntary muscle
随意肌松弛药/隨意肌鬆弛藥 voluntary muscle relaxant
随意型皮瓣/隨意型皮瓣 random pattern skin flap
随意运动/隨意運動 voluntary motion
髓/[骨]髓 pith, marrow
髓单核细胞/髓單核細胞 myelomonocytic
髓底壁/髓底壁,齒髓下壁 subpulpal wall
髓动脉/[脾]髓動脈 artery of the pulp
髓放线/髓放線,髓射線 medullary ray
髓沟/髓溝,背溝 medullary groove
髓冠/髓冠,牙冠髓 coronal pulp
髓管隔/髓管隔 neural septum
髓管网/髓管網 myelospongium
髓核/髓核,瓢核 nucleus pulposus
[髓]核溶解术/髓核溶解術 neucleolysis
髓核突出/髓核突出 hernia of the nucleus pulposus
髓坏死/髓壞死 pulp necrosis
髓浆状癌/髓漿狀癌,糜爛性癌 pultaceous carcinoma
髓角/髓角 pulp horn
髓节/髓節 myelomere
髓静脉/髓靜脈 pulp vein
髓亏证/髓虧證 pattern of marrow deficiency
髓磷脂变性/髓磷脂變性 myelinic degeneration
髓磷脂蛋白脂质蛋白质/髓磷脂蛋白脂質蛋白質 myelin proteolipid protein
髓磷脂蛋白质类/髓磷脂蛋白質類 myelin proteins
髓磷脂碱性蛋白质类/髓磷脂鹼性蛋白質類 myelin basic proteins
髓磷脂相关糖蛋白/髓磷脂相關糖蛋白 myelin-associated glycoprotein
髓母细胞瘤/髓母細胞瘤,神經管胚細胞瘤 medulloblastoma
髓内出血/[脊]髓内出血 intramedullary hemorrhage
髓内钉/髓內釘 intramedullary pin
髓内动静脉畸形/髓內動靜脈畸形 intramedullary arteriovenous malformation
髓内骨折固定术/髓內骨折固定術 intramedullary fracture fixation
髓内皮样囊肿/髓內皮樣囊腫,脊髓質內皮囊瘤 intramedullary dermoid
髓襻/髓襻 medullary loop
[髓襻]细段/細段 thin segment

髓旁肾单位/髓旁腎單位,近髓质肾元　juxtamedullary nephron
髓腔/髓腔　medullary cavity
髓鞘/髓鞘　myelin sheath
髓鞘发生/髓鞘發生,髓鞘質産生,髓鞘形成　myelogeny
髓鞘节/髓鞘節　medullary segment
髓鞘切迹/髓鞘切跡,施-蘭切跡　incisure of myelin
髓鞘染色/髓鞘染色　myelin staining
髓鞘染色法/髓鞘染色法　myelin staining method
髓鞘神经纤维/髓鞘神經纖維,有髓神經纖維　medullated nerve fiber
髓鞘生成区/髓鞘生成區,髓鞘形成區　myelinogenetic field
髓鞘脱失/髓鞘脱失　demyelinating
髓鞘形成/髓鞘形成　medullation, myelinization
髓鞘质病/髓鞘[白]質病,腦白質病　myelinopathy
髓鞘[质]分解/髓鞘質分解,髓鞘崩解　myelolysis
髓上皮瘤/髓上皮瘤,神經上皮瘤　medulloepithelioma
髓石/[齒]髓石　pulp stone
髓室/[齒]髓腔　pulp chamber
髓室底/髓室底　floor of pulp chamber
髓室顶/髓室頂　roof of pulp chamber
髓索/髓索　medullary cords
髓外造血/髓外造血,骨髓外造血作用　extramedullary hemopoiesis
髓[微]动脉/髓[微]動脈　pulp arteriole
髓萎缩/髓萎縮　pulp atrophy
髓系细胞/髓系細胞　myeloid cells
髓细胞瘤/[骨]髓細胞瘤　myelocytoma
髓细胞生成/髓細胞生成,骨髓形成,骨髓細胞製成　myelopoiesis
髓细胞生长酮酸/髓細胞生長酮酸　myelokentric acid
髓细胞性白血病/髓細胞性白血病,骨髓性白血病　myelocytic leukemia
髓[细胞]性多能干细胞/髓[細胞]性多能幹細胞　pluripotential myeloid-restricted stem cell
髓细胞性类白血病反应/髓細胞性類白血病反應,骨髓細胞性白血病樣反應　myelocytic leukemoid reaction
髓细胞血症/髓細胞血症　myelocythemia
髓纤维变性/髓纖維變性　pulp fibrosis
髓小球/髓小球,髓脂質小體　myelin globule
髓样白血病/髓樣白血病,骨髓細胞性白血病,骨髓性白血病　myeloid leukemia
髓样化生/髓樣化生,骨髓細胞化生　myeloid metaplasia
髓样瘤/髓樣瘤　encephaloid
髓之府/髓之府　fu-viscera of marrow
髓脂瘤/[脊]髓脂瘤　myelolipoma
髓质/髓質　medulla
髓质淋巴窦/髓[質淋巴]竇　medullary sinus
髓质瘤/髓質瘤　hylic tumor
髓质切除术/髓質切除術　medullectomy
髓周动静脉瘘/髓周動靜脈瘻　perimedullary arteriovenous fistula
髓周牙本质/髓周牙本質　circum pulpal dentin
髓状癌/髓狀癌　medullary carcinoma
髓椎体/髓椎體　neurocentrum
岁会/歲會　yearly weather
岁运/歲運　year evolutive phase
碎骨片/碎骨片　splinter
碎骨片清除术/碎骨片清除術,骨碎片切除術　esquillectomy
碎骨钳/碎骨鉗　osteophore
碎裂电位/碎裂電位　fragmented potential
碎裂声/碎裂聲　crackles
碎颅钳/碎顱器　cranioclast
碎颅术/碎顱術,顱骨摧碎術　cranioclasty
碎片/碎片,碎屑　chip, debris
碎片骨折/碎片骨折　chip fracture
碎片状坏死/碎片狀壞死,零碎性壞死　piecemeal necrosis
碎石[膀胱]镜/碎石鏡　lithotriptoscope
碎石器/碎石器　lithoclast
碎石清除术/碎石清除術,碎石洗出術　lithocenosis
碎石术/碎石術　lithotripsy
碎石洗出术/碎石洗出術,碎石清除術　litholapaxy
碎胎刀/碎胎刀,截胎刀,截胎器　embryotome
碎胎术/碎胎術,胎兒截開術,截胎術　embryotomy
碎语/碎語　word debris
隧道/隧道　burrow
隧道病/隧道病　tunnel disease
隧道伤/隧道傷　tunnel wound
隧道植皮术/隧道植皮術　tunnel skin grafting
孙络/孫絡　tertiary collaterals
孙囊/孫囊[腫]　granddaughter cyst
孙思邈/孫思邈　Sun Simiao
损害/損害,病灶　lesion, nuisance
损毁法/損毀法　lesion method
损容性皮肤病/損容性皮膚病　discosmetic dermatosis
损伤/損傷　impairment, injury
损伤电流/損傷電流　current of injury

损伤电位/損傷電位　injury potential
损伤后/損傷後　postinjury
损伤内证/損傷內證　inner disorder due to injury
DNA 损伤试验/DNA 損傷試驗　DNA injured test
损伤性背痛/損傷性背痛,外伤性背痛　backalgia
损伤严重度评分/損傷嚴重度評分　injury severity score
娑罗子/娑羅子　buck-eye seed
梭肌/梭肌　musculus fusiformis
梭菌感染/梭狀菌感染　clostridial infection
梭菌链球菌病/梭菌與鏈球菌病　fusostreptococcicosis
梭菌螺菌病/梭菌螺菌病,文生氏咽峡炎　fusospirillosis
梭菌螺菌感染/梭菌螺菌感染　fusospirillary infection
梭链孢酸/梭鏈孢酸　fusidic acid
梭内肌纤维/梭內肌纖維　intrafusal muscle fiber
梭形棒状杆菌/梭狀桿菌　Corynebacterium fusiforme
梭形杆菌感染/梭桿菌感染　Fusobacterium infection
梭形杆菌属/梭菌屬　*Fusobacterium*
梭形肌/梭形肌　fusiform muscle
梭形裂体吸虫/梭形裂體吸蟲　Schistosoma spindale
梭形切除[术]/梭形切除[術]　fusiform excision
梭形切口/梭形切口　fusiform incision
梭形细胞/梭狀細胞　fusiform cell, spindle cell
梭形细胞痣/梭形細胞痣　spindle cell nevus
梭形指/梭形指　spindle-shaped finger
梭状动脉瘤/梭狀動脈瘤　fusiform aneurysm
梭状回/梭狀迴　fusiform gyrus
梭状及上皮样细胞痣/梭狀及上皮樣細胞痣,史必兹痣　spindle and epithelioid cell nevus
梭状类[拟]杆菌/梭狀類[擬]桿菌,梭樣類桿菌　bacteroides fusiformis
梭状螺旋菌口炎/梭狀螺旋菌口炎,梭狀螺旋體性口炎　fusospirochetal stomatitis
梭状毛发/梭形毛髮　spindle hair
梭状胸/梭狀胸　fusiform thorax
梭状[芽孢]杆菌肽酶/梭狀芽孢桿菌肽酶　clostridiopeptidase
梭状芽孢杆菌性肾炎/梭狀芽孢桿菌性腎炎,梭菌性腎炎　clostridial nephritis
羧苄西林/羧苄西林　carbenicillin
羧化酶/羧化酵,羧基酵　carboxylase
羧化酶合酶缺乏/羧化酶合酶缺乏　holocarboxylase synthetase deficiency
羧基/羧基　carboxyl

羧基多肽酶/羧基多肽酶　carboxypolypeptidase
羧基裂解酶/羧基裂解酶　carboxy lyase
羧[基]肽酶/羧肽酶　carboxypeptidase
羧甲半胱氨酸/羧甲半胱氨酸　carbocysteine
羧甲[基]纤维素/羧甲基纖維素　carboxymethyl cellulose
羧酸/羧酸　carboxylic acid
羧酸酯酶/羧酸酯酶,脱糖酸酯酶　carboxylesterase
羧酸酯水解酶类/羧酸酯水解酶類　carboxylic ester hydrolases
羧肽酶 U/羧肽酶 U　carboxypeptidase U
羧肽酶类/羧肽酶類　carboxypeptidases
羧肽酶原/羧肽酶原,前羧勝肽酶　procarboxypeptidase
羧乙烯聚合物/羧乙烯聚合物　carboxyvinylpolymer
缩-2-氨基丙二酰脲酸/縮胺基丙二醯尿素酸　uramilic acid
缩氨基脲类/縮氨基脲類　semicarbazones
缩氨硫脲/縮氨硫脲　amithiozone
缩鼻术/縮鼻術　rhinomiosis
缩胆囊素拮抗药/縮膽囊素拮抗藥　cholecystokinin antagonist
缩胆囊素酶/縮膽囊素酶,激膽囊素分解酶　cholecystokinase
缩短反应/縮短反應　shortening reaction
缩二脲/雙脲　biuret
缩酚酸/縮酚[羧]酸,酚羧酸酯　depside
缩合反应/縮合反應　condensation reaction
缩合鞣质/縮合鞣質　condensed tannin
缩合物/縮合物　condensation substance, condensation compound
缩颌/縮頜　retrognathia
缩简言语/縮減語言,半截語言　clipped speech
缩脚痧/縮腳痧　spasmodic leg sha disease
缩聚物/縮聚物,濃縮聚合物　condensation polymer
缩硫醇/縮硫醇　mercaptol
缩脉管性菌毒素/縮脈管性菌毒素　anectasin
缩尿止遗/縮尿止遺　reducing urination for preventing enuresis
缩醛类/縮醛類　acetals
缩醛磷脂/縮醛磷脂　plasmalogen
缩肽类/縮肽類　depsipeptides
缩瞳剂性白内障/縮瞳劑性白內障　miotic cataract
缩瞳剂性青光眼/縮瞳劑性青光眼　miotic glaucoma
缩瞳药/縮瞳藥　miotics
缩微摄影/縮微攝影　microfilming
缩小甘露糖酸/縮小甘露糖酸　chitonic acid
缩小镜/縮小鏡　reducing lens

缩小妄想/縮小妄想　micromania
缩小妄想性谵妄/縮小妄想性譫妄,縮小妄想症譫妄　micromaniacal delirium
缩阴病/縮陰病　retracted genitals
缩阴·寒证/縮陰·寒證　genital retraction with cold pattern
缩阴·热证/縮陰·熱證　genital retraction with heat pattern
缩影 X 射线照相术/縮影 X 射線照相術,小片 X 射線攝影術　miniature roentgenography
缩余釉上皮/縮餘釉上皮　reduced enamel epithelium
缩窄/縮窄　coarctation
缩窄性心包炎/狹窄性心包炎　constrictive pericarditis
缩窄性心内膜炎/縮窄性心内膜炎　constrictive endocarditis
所不胜/所不勝　restraining
所生病/所生病　disease of viscera connecting with this channel
所胜/所勝　being restrained
索/索,帶　cord
索比容器/索比容器,Sorby 氏容器　Sorby cell
索丹绷带/索丹繃帶,Seutin 氏繃帶　Seutin bandage
索的/索的　funicular
索恩菌痢/索恩菌痢,桑納氏痢疾　Sonne dysentery
索尔特截骨术/索爾特截骨術　Salter osteotomy
索科芦荟苷/索科蘆薈苷　socaloin
索雷谱带/索雷譜帶,Soret 氏光譜帶　Soret band
索马里链霉菌/索馬利鏈黴菌　Streptomyces somaliensis
索曼/索曼,甲氟磷酸異己酯　soman
索莫吉单位/索莫吉單位　Somogyi unit
索旁软骨/索旁軟骨,索旁軟骨,副索軟骨　parachordal cartilage
索前板/前索板　prochordal plate
索瑞[光谱]带/索雷氏光譜帶　Soret band
索氏[脂肪]抽提器/索氏[脂肪]抽提器　Soxhlet extractor
索他洛尔/索他洛爾　sotalol
索烃类/索烴類　catenanes
索性脊髓[变性]病/索性脊髓變性病,脊髓索變性病　funicular myelosis
索状瘢痕/索狀瘢痕　cicatricial band
索状脊髓病/索狀脊髓病　funicular myelopathy
索状因子/索狀因數　cord factor
锁肛穿孔术/鎖肛穿孔術,人造肛門術,人工肛門術　proctotresia
锁肛痔/鎖肛痔　anorectal cancer, locked anus pile
锁肛痔·脾肾两虚证/鎖肛痔·脾腎兩虛證　anorectal cancer with spleen-kidney deficiency pattern
锁肛痔·气阴两虚证/鎖肛痔·氣陰兩虛證　anorectal cancer with qi-yin deficiency pattern
锁肛痔·气滞血瘀证/鎖肛痔·氣滯血瘀證　anorectal cancer with pattern of qi stagnation and blood stasis
锁肛痔·湿热蕴结证/鎖肛痔·濕熱蘊結證　anorectal cancer with dampness-heat amassment pattern
锁骨/鎖骨　①clavicle ②suogu, SF6
锁骨部/鎖骨部　clavicular part
锁骨骨折/鎖骨骨折　clavicular fracture, clavicle fracture
锁骨后上神经/鎖骨後上神經　posterior supraclavicular nerve
锁骨肩峰端/鎖骨肩峰端,鎖骨之外側端　external extremity of clavicle
锁骨颅骨发育不良/鎖骨顱骨發育不全　cleidocranial dysplasia
锁骨内上神经/鎖骨內上神經,前鎖骨上神經　anterior supraclavicular nerve
锁骨切断术/鎖骨切斷術　cleidotomy
锁骨切迹/鎖骨切跡　clavicular incisure of sternum
锁骨上部/鎖骨上部　supraclavicular part
锁骨上大窝/鎖骨上大窩　greater supraclavicular fossa
锁骨上肌/鎖骨上肌　supraclavicular muscle
锁骨上间隙/鎖骨上間隙　supraclavicular space
锁骨上淋巴结/鎖骨上淋巴結　supraclavicular lymph node
锁骨上内侧神经/鎖骨上內側神經　medial supraclavicular nerve
锁骨上神经/鎖骨上神經　supraclavicular nerve
锁骨上神经后支/鎖骨上神經後支　posterior supraclavicular nerve
锁骨上神经前支/鎖骨上神經前支　anterior supraclavicular nerve
锁骨上外侧神经/鎖骨上外側神經　lateral supraclavicular nerve
锁骨上小窝/鎖骨上小窩　lesser supraclavicular fossa
锁骨上中间神经/鎖骨上中間神經　intermediate supraclavicular nerve
锁骨十字形绷带/鎖骨十字繃帶　clavicular cross
锁骨体/鎖骨體　shaft of clavicle
锁骨痛风/鎖骨痛風　cleidagra
锁骨下部/鎖骨下部　ingrtaclavicular part
锁骨下动脉/鎖骨下動脈　subclavian artery
锁骨下动脉丛/鎖骨下[動脈]叢　subclavian plexus

锁骨下动脉沟/鎖骨下動脈溝　sulcus for subclavian artery
锁骨下动脉片主动脉成形术/鎖骨下動脈片主動脈成形術　subclavian arterial flap aortoplasty
锁骨下动脉窃血综合征/鎖骨下動脈阻塞症候群　subclavian steal syndrome
锁骨下动脉[血流]改道/鎖骨下動脈血流改道　subclavian steal
锁骨下干/鎖骨下幹　subclavian trunk
锁骨下肌/鎖骨下肌　musculus subclavius
锁骨下肌沟/鎖骨下肌溝　subclavian groove
锁骨下肌神经/鎖骨下肌神經　subclavian nerve
锁骨下静脉/鎖骨下靜脈　subclavian vein
锁骨下静脉沟/鎖骨下靜脈溝　sulcus for subclavian vein
锁骨下淋巴结/鎖骨下淋巴結　infraclavicular node
锁骨下襻/鎖骨下襻　subclavian subcalvia
锁骨下神经/鎖骨下神經　subclavian nerve
锁骨下脱位/鎖骨下脱位　subclavicular dislocation
锁骨下窝/鎖骨下窩　infraclavicular fossa
锁骨下杂音/鎖骨下雜音　subclavicular murmur
锁骨胸骨端/鎖骨胸骨端，鎖骨之内側端　internal extremity of clavicle
锁骨胸肌三角/鎖骨胸肌三角　clavipectoral triangle
锁骨压碎术/鎖骨壓碎術　cleidotripsy
锁骨折术/鎖骨折[斷]術　cleidorrhexis
锁骨征/鎖骨徵象　clavicular sign
锁骨支/鎖骨支　clavicular branch
锁骨中间上神经/鎖骨中間上神經　middle supraclavicular nerve
锁骨中线/鎖骨中線　midclavicular line
锁喉风/鎖喉風　lockjaw throat wind
锁喉痈/鎖喉癰　throat-locking cellulitis
锁喉痈·热伤胃阴证/鎖喉癰·熱傷胃陰證　throat-locking cellulitis with pattern of heat injuring stomach yin
锁喉痈·肉腐成脓证/鎖喉癰·肉腐成膿證　throat-locking cellulitis with pattern of decayed flesh becoming pus
锁喉痈·痰热蕴结证/鎖喉癰·痰熱蘊結證　throat-locking cellulitis with phlegm-heat amassment pattern
锁间韧带/鎖[骨]間韌帶　interclavicular ligament
锁口疔/鎖口疔　mouth-locking ding
锁链素/鎖鏈素　desmosine
锁链样扎法/鏈狀結扎　chain ligature
锁切迹/鎖骨切跡　clavicular notch
锁胸筋膜/鎖胸筋膜　clavipectoral fascia
锁阳/鎖陽　songaria cynomorium herb
锁阳固精丸/鎖陽固精丸　suoyang gujing pills
锁阴术/防止交媾術，陰部鋼閉法，鎖陰術　pharaonic circumcision

T

他精人工授精/他精人工授精　artificial insemination by donor, AID
他觉性耳鸣/他覺性耳鳴　objective tinnitus
他克林/他克林,四氢胺基吖啶　tacrine
他克莫司/他克莫司,他羅利姆　tacrolimus
他克莫司结合蛋白质类/他克莫司結合蛋白質類　tacrolimus binding proteins
他莫昔芬/他莫爾昔芬　tamoxifen
他人暗示/他人暗示　heterosuggestion
铊/鉈　thallium
铊放射性同位素/鉈放射性同位素　thallium radioisotopes
铊谷/鉈谷,硫化鉈谷　thalgrain
铊中毒/鉈中毒　thallitoxicosis
溻皮疮/溻皮瘡　dermatitis exfoliativa neonatorum
溻渍法/溻漬法　external medicinal liquid application
塔尔万病/塔爾萬病,Talfan 氏病　Talfan disease
塔夫内尔绷带/塔夫內爾繃帶,Tuffnell 氏繃帶　Tuffnell bandage
塔夫内尔饮食/塔夫內爾飲食,Tuffnell 氏飲食　Tuffnell diet
塔格糖/塔格糖　tagatose
塔红色染色/塔紅色染色　pagoda red
塔龙酸/塔龍酸　talonic acid
塔罗糖/塔羅糖,太洛糖　talose
塔皮亚综合征/塔皮亞症候群　Tapia syndrome
塔日酸/塔日酸　tariric acid
塔形肩/塔形肩　sugar-loaf shoulder
踏板运动试验/踏板運動試驗　treadmill exercise test
踏步试验/踏步試驗　stepping test
踏车运动试验/踏車運動試驗　bicycle exercise test
胎斑/胎斑　mongolian spot
胎部胚盘/胎部胚盤　embryonic blastoderm
胎产式/胎產式　fetal lie
胎产损伤/胎產損傷　infantile disease due to fetal injury
胎传/胎傳,胎兒感染　fetal infection
胎蛋白/胎蛋白　fetoprotein
胎动不安/胎動不安　threatened abortion
胎动不安·气血两虚证/胎動不安·氣血兩虛證　threatened abortion with pattern of deficiency of both qi and blood
胎动不安·肾虚证/胎動不安·腎虛證　threatened abortion with kidney deficiency pattern
胎动不安·外伤证/胎動不安·外傷證　threatened abortion with traumatic pattern
胎动不安·血热证/胎動不安·血熱證　threatened abortion with blood heat pattern
胎动不安·症瘕伤胎证/胎動不安·症瘕傷胎證　threatened abortion with pattern of abdominal mass injuring fetus
胎动感/胎動感,胎動初覺,胎初動期　quickening
胎毒/胎毒,胚胎毒性　fetal toxicity, fetal toxicosis
胎毒蕴热证/胎毒蘊熱證　pattern of accumulated heat due to fetal toxicity
胎［儿］/胎兒　fetus
胎儿氨基蝶呤效应/胎兒氨基喋呤效應　fetal aminopterin effect
胎儿苯妥英钠综合征/胎兒苯妥英鈉症候群　fetal dilantin syndrome
胎儿测量法/胎兒測量法　fetometry
胎儿测听[法]/胎兒測聽[法]　fetal audiometry
胎儿产前生活/[胎兒]產前生活　antenatal life
胎儿成熟度/胎兒成熟度　fetal maturity
胎儿蛋白质类/胎兒蛋白質類　fetal proteins
[胎儿]二次循环/二次循環　the second circulation
胎儿发育/胎兒發育　fetal development
胎儿反应停综合征/胎兒反應停症候群　fetal thalidomide syndrome
胎儿风疹综合征/胎兒風疹症候群　fetal rubella syndrome
胎儿附件/胎兒附件　appendages of the fetus
胎儿弓形体感染综合征/胎兒弓形體感染症候群　fetal toxoplasmosis syndrome
胎儿宫内窒息/胎兒宮內窒息　fetal asphyxia
胎儿呼吸/胎兒呼吸　fetal respiration
胎儿活动/胎[兒活]動　fetal movement
胎儿活力/胎兒活力　fetal viability
胎儿疾病/胎兒疾病　fetal disease
胎儿监测/胎兒監測　fetal monitoring
胎儿结核/胎兒結核　fetal tuberculosis

胎儿镜/胎兒[內視]鏡　fetoscope
胎儿镜检查/胎兒[內視]鏡檢查　fetoscopy
胎儿窘迫/胎兒窘迫　fetal distress
胎儿巨细胞病毒综合征/胎兒巨細胞病毒症候群　fetal cytomegalovirus syndrome
胎儿抗原/胎兒抗原　fetal antigen
胎儿梅毒/胎兒梅毒　syphilis fetalis
胎儿面娩出式/胎兒面娩出式　Schultz mechanism
胎儿母体输血/胎兒母輸血綜合徵　fetomaternal transfusion
胎儿皮脂/胎體皮脂,胎垢　vernix caseosa
胎儿期/胎兒期　fetal stage
胎儿[期]创伤无瘢痕愈合/胎兒[期]創傷無瘢痕愈合　fetal scarless wound healing
胎儿期疗法/胎兒期療法　fetal therapies
胎儿器官成熟度/胎兒器官成熟度　fetal organ maturity
胎儿缺碘效应/胎兒缺碘效應　fetal iodine deficiency effect
胎儿软骨营养不良/胎兒軟骨營養不良,胎兒軟骨失養　chondrodystrophia fetalis
胎儿肾/胎兒腎　fetal kidney
胎儿生长迟缓/胎兒生長遲緩　fetal growth retardation
胎儿水肿/胎兒水腫　hydrops fetalis
胎儿死亡率/胎兒死亡率　fetal mortality
胎儿-胎儿输血/雙胎輸血綜合徵　fetofetal transfusion
胎儿胎盘/胎兒胎盤　fetal placenta
胎儿体重/胎兒體重　fetal weight
胎儿外科/胎兒外科　fetal surgery
胎儿弯曲杆菌/胎兒彎曲桿菌　Campylobacter fetus
胎儿吸收/胎兒吸收　fetal resorption
胎儿下降感/胎兒下降感,腹輕感　lightening
胎儿向母体出血/胎兒-母體出血　fetomaternal hemorrhage
胎儿心率/胎兒心率　fetal heart rate
胎儿心音描记/胎兒心音描記　fetal phonocardiography
胎儿心脏/胎兒心臟　fetal heart
胎[儿]性心内膜炎/胎兒心內膜炎　fetal endocarditis
胎儿休克/胎兒休克　fetal shock
胎儿学/胚兒學,胚胎學　fetology
胎儿血红蛋白/胎兒血紅蛋白,胎兒血紅素　fetal hemoglobin
胎儿血液循环/胎兒[血液]循環　fetal circulation
胎儿研究/胎兒研究　fetal research
胎儿羊膜索/胎兒羊膜索　fetoamniotic band

胎儿移位/胎兒變位　fetal displacement
胎儿乙内酰脲综合征/胎兒乙內醯脲症候群,胎兒酒精症候群　fetal hydantoin syndrome
胎儿营养/胎兒營養　cyotrophy
胎儿营养失调/胎兒營養失調　fetal nutrition disorder
胎儿幼红细胞增多症/胎兒幼紅細胞增多症　fetal erythroblastosis
胎儿杂音/胎兒雜音　fetal souffle
胎儿X射线照相术/胎兒X射線照相術,胎兒造影術　fetography
[胎儿之]髋臼骨/[胎兒之]髖臼骨　os acetabuli
胎方位/胎方位　fetal position
胎肥/胎肥　neonatal adiposis
胎粪/胎糞　meconium
胎粪绞痛/胎糞絞痛　meconial colic
胎粪吸入综合征/胎糞吸入症候群　meconium aspiration syndrome
胎粪性便秘/胎糞性便秘　meconium constipation
胎粪性肠梗阻/胎糞性腸梗阻,胎糞腸塞　meconium ileus
胎粪性腹膜炎/胎糞性腹膜炎　meconium peritonitis
胎粪溢/胎糞瀉　meconiorrhea
胎风赤烂/胎風赤爛　infantile marginal blepharitis
胎缝性淋巴管瘤/胎裂性淋巴管瘤　fissural lymphangioma
胎肛膜/胎肛膜　meconic membrane
胎寒/胎寒　neonatal cold
胎患内障/胎患內障　congenital cataract
胎患内障·胎毒上攻证/胎患內障·胎毒上攻證　congenital cataract with pattern of fetal toxin attacking upward
胎患内障·先天不足证/胎患內障·先天不足證　congenital cataract with congenital insufficiency pattern
胎黄/胎黃　fetal jaundice, neonatal jaundice
胎黄动风证/胎黃動風證　fetal jaundice with pattern of wind stirring
胎黄·寒湿凝滞证/胎黃·寒濕凝滯證　fetal jaundice with pattern of stagnation and congelation of cold-damp
胎黄·湿热郁蒸证/胎黃·濕熱鬱蒸證　fetal jaundice with pattern of stagnation and steaming of damp-heat
胎黄虚脱证/胎黃虛脫證　fetal jaundice with collapse pattern
胎黄·瘀积发黄证/胎黃·瘀積發黃證　fetal jaundice with pattern of blood stasis and amassment

胎记/胎記　birthmark
胎浆膜/胎[儿的]漿膜　serolemma
胎教/胎教　fetal education
胎癥疮/胎癥瘡　infantile eczema
胎癥疮·脾虚湿困证/胎癥瘡·脾虛濕困證　infantile eczema with pattern of spleen deficiency and dampness retention
胎癥疮·胎火湿热证/胎癥瘡·胎火濕熱證　infantile eczema with pattern of fetal fire and dampness-heat
胎龄评估/胎齡評估　assessment of gestational age
胎瘤/胎瘤　neonatal fetal mass
胎漏/胎漏　threatened abortion, vaginal bleeding during pregnancy
胎漏·跌扑损伤证/胎漏·跌撲損傷證　vaginal bleeding during pregnancy with pattern of injury due to falling
胎漏·气血两虚证/胎漏·氣血兩虛證　vaginal bleeding during pregnancy with pattern of deficiency of both qi and blood
胎漏·肾虚证/胎漏·腎虛證　vaginal bleeding during pregnancy with kidney deficiency pattern
胎漏·虚寒证/胎漏·虛寒證　vaginal bleeding during pregnancy with deficiency-cold pattern
胎漏·虚热证/胎漏·虛熱證　vaginal bleeding during pregnancy with deficiency-heat pattern
胎漏·血热证/胎漏·血熱證　vaginal bleeding during pregnancy with blood heat pattern
胎漏·瘀血证/胎漏·瘀血證　vaginal bleeding during pregnancy with static blood pattern
胎毛/胎毛　lanugo hair
胎膜/胎膜　fetal membrane
胎膜破裂/胎膜破裂　rupture of membranes
胎膜石化/胎膜石化　lithokelyphos
胎膜胎儿石化/胎兒胎膜石化　lithokelyphopedion
胎膜先破/胎膜先破　early rupture of membrane
胎膜早破/胎膜早破　premature rupture fetal membrane
胎内[成]胎/胎内[成]胎　intrafetation
胎内寄生胎/胎内[畸]胎　endocymic monster
胎内胎[畸形]/胎内胎,套叠胎　fetal inclusion
胎盘/胎盤　placenta
胎盘边缘血窦破裂/胎盤邊緣血竇破裂　rupture of placental marginal sinus
胎盘病/胎盤病　placentopathy
胎盘剥离/胎盤剝離　placental separation
胎盘部位滋养层瘤/胎盤部位滋養層瘤　placental site trophoblastic tumor

胎盘促性腺激素/胎盤促性腺激素,胎盤生殖素　cyonin
胎盘催乳激素/胎盤催乳激素　placental lactogen
胎盘催乳素/胎盤泌乳素　galactagogin
胎盘发生/胎盤發生　placentogenesis
胎盘分离/胎盤分離　separation of placenta
胎盘隔/胎盤隔　placental septum
胎盘梗死/胎盤梗死　placental infarction
胎盘功能不全/胎盤官能不全　placental insufficiency
胎盘功能试验/胎盤功能試驗　placental function tests
胎盘呼吸/胎盤呼吸　placenta respiration
胎盘激素类/胎盤激素類　placental hormones
胎盘疾病/胎盤疾病　placenta diseases
胎盘碱性磷酸酶/胎盤鹼性磷酸酶　placental alkaline phosphatase
胎盘结核/胎盤結核　placental tuberculosis
胎盘瘤/胎盤瘤　placentoma
胎盘娩出/胎盤娩出　placental expulsion
胎盘母体部/胎盤母體部,母體胎盤　maternal placenta
胎盘排出/胎盤排出　expulsion of placenta
胎盘屏障/胎盤屏障　placental barrier
胎盘嵌顿/胎盤嵌頓,箝閉胎盤　incarcerated placenta, placental incarceration
胎盘绒毛炎/胎盤絨毛炎　villositis
胎盘溶素/胎盤溶素　placentolysin
胎盘输血/胎盤輸血　placental transfusion
胎盘水肿/胎盤水腫　placental edema
胎盘胎儿部/胎盤胎兒部,胎兒胎盤　fetal placenta, pars fetalis placentae
胎盘提取物/胎盤提取物　placental extracts
胎盘停滞/胎盤停滯　retention of placenta
胎盘形成/胎盤形成,胎盤生成　placentation
胎盘形成期出血/胎盤形成期出血　placentation bleeding
胎盘学/胎盤學　placentology
胎盘学家/胎盤學家　placentologist
胎盘[血]窦/胎盤竇　placental sinus
胎盘血栓形成/胎盤血栓形成　placental thrombosis
胎盘血液循环/胎盤[血液]循環　placental circulation
胎盘炎/胎盤炎　placentitis
胎盘杂音/胎盤雜音　placental murmur
胎盘早剥/胎盤早剝,胎盤早期剝離,胎盤剝落過早　abruptio placentae, abruption placenta
胎盘[早期]脱离/胎盤[早期]脫離,胎盤脫落　ablatio placentae

胎盘造影术/胎盤造影術,胎盤 X 光攝影術　placentography
胎盘[造影]照片/胎盤[造影]照片,胎盤顯影照片　placentogram
胎盘粘连/胎盤粘連　placental adherence
胎盘滞留/胎盤滯留　placental retention
胎盘子宫部/胎盤子宮部,胎盤母體部　pars uterina placentae
胎怯/胎怯　fetal debility
胎怯・脾肾气虚证/胎怯・脾腎氣虛證　fetal debility with pattern of qi deficiency of spleen and kidney
胎怯・肾精薄弱证/胎怯・腎精薄弱證　fetal debility with pattern of feeble kidney essence
胎球蛋白/胎球蛋白　fetuin
胎热/胎熱　neonatal fever
胎生/胎生　viviparity
胎生青记/胎生青記,胎痣　birthmark
胎生牙/胎生牙,胎生齒　natal tooth
胎势/胎勢　fetal attitude
胎水过少/胎水過少　oligohydramnios
胎死不下/胎死不下　missed abortion or retention of dead fetus, retention of dead fetus
胎死不下・气血两虚证/胎死不下・氣血兩虛證　missed abortion or retention of dead fetus with pattern of deficiency of both qi and blood
胎死不下・气滞血瘀证/胎死不下・氣滯血瘀證　missed abortion or retention of dead fetus with pattern of qi stagnation and blood stasis
胎体营养物/胚胎營養質　embryotroph
胎头变形/胎頭變形　moulding of head
胎头拨露/胎頭撥露　head visible on vulval gapping
胎头刀/胎頭刀　cephalotome
胎头倒转术/胎頭轉向術,頭式轉向術　cephalic version
胎头浮/胎頭浮,浮動胎頭　floating head
胎头过度仰伸/胎頭過度仰伸　hyperextension of fetal head
[胎]头后出/胎頭後出　aftercoming head
胎头入盆/胎頭入盆　engagement of head
胎头水肿/胎頭水腫,先鋒頭　caput succedaneum
胎头吸引术/胎頭吸引術　vacuum extraction
胎头血肿/胎頭血腫　hematocephalus
胎头着冠/胎頭著冠　crowning of head
胎臀倒转术/胎臀倒轉術,盆式轉向術　pelvic version
胎臀牵引术/胎臀牽引術　extraction of breech
胎萎不长/胎萎不長　retarded growth of fetus
胎萎不长・脾肾阳虚证/胎萎不長・脾腎陽虛證　retarded growth of fetus with pattern of yang deficiency of spleen and kidney
胎萎不长・气血两虚证/胎萎不長・氣血兩虛證　retarded growth of fetus with pattern of deficiency of both qi and blood
胎萎不长・阴虚血热证/胎萎不長・陰虛血熱證　retarded growth of fetus with pattern of blood heat due to yin deficiency
胎位倒转术/胎位倒轉術　fetal version
胎先露/胎先露　fetal presentation
胎心分娩力描记法/胎心分娩力描記法,胎兒心率數計法　cardiotocography
胎心率监测/胎心率監測　fetal heart rate monitoring
胎心[音]节律/胎心[音]節律　fetal rhythm
胎形/胎形　fetal morphology
胎性腺瘤/胎性腺瘤　fetal adenoma
胎血/胎血　fetal blood
胎样心音/胎樣心音,胎音調　embryocardia
胎衣/胎衣,胎盤　embryonic envelope, placenta
胎元/胎元　fetal primordial qi
胎脂/胎脂,胎[兒]皮脂　vernix caseosa
胎中胎/胎內胎　fetus in fetu
胎足倒转术/胎足倒轉術,胎足轉向術,足式轉向術　podalic version
台秤/檯秤　platform balance
台[罗德]氏液/Tyrode 氏溶液　Tyrode solution
台盼罗散/臺盼羅散,鹵副複紅　tryparosan
苔黑酚试验/苔黑酚試驗,二羥基甲苯試驗　orcinol test
苔色/苔色　fur color
苔属/苔屬　Carex plant
苔藓/苔蘚　moss
苔藓化/苔蘚化　lichenification
苔藓细胞/苔蘚細胞,苔狀細胞　mossy cell
苔藓纤维/苔蘚纖維　mossy fiber
苔藓样变/苔蘚樣變　lichenification
苔藓样副银屑病/苔蘚樣副銀屑病　lichenoid parapsoriasis
苔藓样角化病/苔蘚樣角化病　lichenoid keratosis
苔藓样糠疹/苔癬狀糠疹　pityriasis lichenoides
苔藓样类银屑病/苔蘚樣類銀屑病,苔蘚狀類乾癬　parapsoriasis lichenoides
苔藓样条纹状汗孔角化症/苔蘚樣條紋狀汗孔角化症　porokeratosis striata lichenoides
苔藓样疹/苔蘚樣疹　lichenoid eruption
苔藓状湿疹/苔蘚狀濕疹　eczema lichenoid
苔藓状痣/苔蘚狀痣　nevus lichenoides
苔质/苔質　fur character

苔状足疣/苔狀足疣　mossy foot
太白/太白　taibai, SP3
太冲/太冲　taichong, LR3
太极拳/太極拳　Taiji quan
太空运动病/太空運動病　space motion sickness
太平惠民和剂局方/太平惠民和劑局方　Prescriptions of the Bureau of Taiping People's Welfare Pharmacy
太平圣惠方/太平聖惠方　Taiping Holy Prescriptions for Universal Relief
太藤病/太藤病,嗜酸球性膿疱性毛囊炎　Ofuji disease
太田痣/太田痣　nevus of Ota
太息/太息　sighing
太溪/太溪　taixi, KI3
太阳病误治证/太陽病誤治證　Taiyang disease due to improper treatment
太阳病证/太陽病[證]　Taiyang disease, Taiyang pattern
太阳坏病/太陽壞病　deteriorated case of Taiyang disease
太阳痞证/太陽痞證　Taiyang disease with abdominal distension
太阳伤寒证/太陽傷寒證　Taiyang disease with cold damage pattern
太阳少阳并病/太陽少陽并病　Taiyang disease involving Shaoyang Channel
太阳少阳合病/太陽少陽合病　concurrent disease of Taiyang and Shaoyang Channels
太阳神经丛麻痹/太陽神經叢麻痺　abepithymia
太阳蓄血/太陽蓄血　Taiyang disease of blood retention
太阳蓄血证/太陽蓄血證　Taiyang disease with stagnated blood pattern
太阳[穴]/太陽[穴]　taiyang, EX-HN5
太阳眼镜/太陽眼鏡　sun glasses
太阳阳明并病/太陽陽明并病　Taiyang disease involving Yangming Channel
太阳阳明合病/太陽陽明合病　concurrent disease of Taiyang and Yangming Channels
太阳之人/太陽之人　Taiyang person
太阳中风证/太陽中風證　pattern of affection of Taiyang by wind, Taiyang disease with wind affection
太医/太醫　palace physician
太医局/太醫局　Imperial Medical Service
太医署/太醫署　Imperial Medical Academy
太医院/太醫院　Imperial Academy of Medicine
太乙/太乙　taiyi, ST23
太乙神针/太乙神針　taiyi miraculous moxa roll
太阴病证/太陰病證　Taiyin disease, Taiyin pattern
太阴发黄/太陰發黃　Taiyin disease with jaundice
太阴寒湿/太陰寒濕　Taiyin cold-dampness
太阴伤寒/太陰傷寒　Taiyin disease with cold damage
太阴虚寒/太陰虛寒　Taiyin deficiency-cold
太阴之人/太陰之人　Taiyin person
太阴中风/太陰中風　Taiyin disease with wind affection
太渊/太淵　taiyuan, LU9
太子参/太子參　heterophylly falsestarwort root
肽/肽　peptide
肽分泌细胞/肽分泌細胞　peptide-secretory cell
肽合酶类/肽合酶類　peptide synthases
肽核酸类/肽核酸類　peptide nucleic acids
肽基二肽酶A/肽基二肽酶A　peptidyl-dipeptidase A
肽基脯氨酰异构酶/肽基脯氨醯異構酶　peptidylprolyl isomerase
肽基转移酶类/肽基轉移酶類　peptidyl transferases
肽键/肽鍵　peptide bond
肽聚糖/肽聚糖　peptidoglycan
肽聚糖糖基转移酶/肽聚糖糖基轉移酶　peptidoglycan glycosyltransferase
肽库/肽庫　peptide library
肽类激素/肽類激素　peptide hormones
肽类抗生素/肽類抗生素　peptide antibiotic
肽链/肽鏈　peptide chain
肽链端解酶/肽鏈端解酶　exopeptidase
肽链内切酶/肽鏈内切酶,勝肽內酵素,勝肽內酶　endopeptidase
肽酶/肽酶,勝酵素　peptase
肽纳米管/肽納米管　peptide nanotube
肽能神经元/肽能神經元　peptidergic neuron
肽谱/肽譜　peptide mapping
肽起始因子类/肽起始因數類　peptide initiation factors
肽生物合成/肽生物合成　peptide biosynthesis
肽受体/肽受體　peptide receptors
肽水解酶类/肽水解酶類　peptide hydrolases
肽碎片/肽碎片　peptide fragment
肽糖脂/肽糖脂　peptidoglycolipid
肽延伸因子/肽延伸因數　peptide elongation factors
肽终止因子/肽終止因數　peptide termination factors
钛/鈦　titanium
β钛矫正线/β鈦矯正線,貝他鈦絲弓　beta-titanium

archwire
钛角之人/鈦角之人 atypical wood-phase person, more enterprising
钛镍丝/鈦鎳絲 titanium-nickel wire
钛商之人/鈦商之人 atypical metal-phase person, more self-disciplined
钛试剂/試鈦靈 tiron
钛酸钴/鈦酸鈷 cobalt titanium oxide
钛云母/鈦雲母 odenite
泰勒病/泰勒病,Theiler 氏病 Theiler disease
泰勒夹/泰勒夾,Taylor 氏夾板 Taylor splint
泰勒饮食/泰勒飲食,Taylor 氏飲食 Taylor diet
泰累尔梨浆虫病/泰累爾梨漿蟲病,泰勒蟲病 theileriasis
泰洛星/泰洛星,泰樂菌素 tylosin
泰-萨克斯病/泰-薩克斯病,塔-賽二氏病,黑矇性家族性癡愚 Tay-Sachs disease
泰森病/Thaysen 氏病 Thaysen disease
泰山压顶/泰山壓頂 Mount-Tai pressing atop
泰氏脉络膜炎[病]/泰氏脈絡膜炎[病],Tay 氏病 Tay disease
酞氨西林/酞胺西林,氨苄青黴素羥基酞酯 talampicillin
酞嗪类/酞嗪類 phthalazines
酞酸二甲酯/酞酸二甲酯 dimethyl phthalate
贪食癖/貪食癖 phagomania
贪食症/貪食症,食欲過盛,善飢 bulimia
瘫痪[病]/癱瘓[病],麻痺 paralysis
瘫痪发作/癱瘓發作 paralytic stroke
瘫痪型狂犬病/癱瘓型狂犬病 paralytic hydrophobia
弹拨法/彈撥法 poking channels manipulation
弹法/彈法 needle-handle flicking
弹簧固定桥/彈簧固定橋 spring fixed bridge
弹簧天平/彈簧天平 spring balance
弹筋法/彈筋法 sinew-flicking manipulation
弹力波传导试验/彈力波傳導試驗 elastic wave propagation tests
弹力长袜/彈性襪 elastic stocking
弹力牵引/彈性牽引 elastic traction
弹力牵引夹板/彈力牽引夾板 elastic traction splint
弹力素病/彈力素病 elastin disease
弹力纤维/彈力纖維 elastic fiber
弹力纤维变性/彈力纖維變性 elastotic degeneration
弹力纤维瘤/彈性[蛋白]纖維瘤 elastofibroma
弹力纤维营养不良/彈力纖維營養不良 elastic dystrophy
弹力纤维脂肪瘤/彈力纖維脂肪瘤 elastofibrolipoma
弹力性皮肤/彈性性皮膚,彈性皮 elastic skin
弹力衣/彈力衣 pressure garment
弹力痣/彈力痣 elastic nevus
弹力组织小纤维蛋白/彈力組織小纖維蛋白 elastic tissue fibrillar protein
弹力组织痣/彈力組織痣 elastic tissue nevus
弹跳指/彈簧指 spring finger
弹响髋/彈響髖,髖關節彈響 snapping hip
弹响试验/彈響試驗 snapping test
弹响指/彈響指 snapping finger
弹性绷带/彈性繃帶,橡膠繃帶 elastic bandage
弹性测定法/彈性測定法 elastometry
弹性层/彈性層 elastica
弹性蛋白酶/彈性蛋白酶 elastase
弹性蛋白原/彈性蛋白原 tropoelastin
弹性动脉/彈性動脈 elastic artery
弹性火棉胶/彈性火棉膠 collodion elastique
弹性假黄瘤/彈性[纖維]假黄瘤 pseudoxanthoma elasticum
弹性[结缔]组织/彈性結締組織 elastic connective tissue
弹性结扎线/彈性結紮線 elastic ligature
弹性聚硅酮类/彈性聚矽酮類 silicone elastomers
弹性凝胶/彈性凝膠,彈性乳膠 elastogel
弹性皮肤/彈性皮膚 cutis elastica
弹性软骨/彈性軟骨 elastic cartilage
弹性体/彈性體 elastomers
弹性纤维/彈性纖維 elasticum, elastic fiber
弹性纤维层/彈性纖維層 elastic fibrous layer
弹性样物质/彈性樣[物]質,彈力質 elastoid
弹性样组织变性/彈力樣[組織]變性 elastoid degeneration
弹性衣/彈性衣 pressure garments
弹性圆锥/彈性圓錐 elastic conus
弹性组织/彈性組織,彈力組織 elastic tissue
弹性组织变性/彈性組織變性 elastosis
弹性组织离解/彈性組織離解,彈性質溶解 elastolysis
弹性[组织]瘤/彈性組織瘤 elastoma
弹性[组织]黏蛋白/彈性組織黏蛋白 elastomucin
弹性组织[缺乏]病/彈性組織缺乏 elastopathy
弹性组织[纤维]破裂/彈性組織[纖維]破裂,彈性組織内的彈性纖維破裂 elastorrhexis
弹跃性瞳孔/彈躍性瞳孔,跳躍狀瞳孔 bounding pupil
痰/痰 sputum, phlegm
痰毒/痰毒 phlegmatic toxin
痰毒·风热痰火证/痰毒·風熱痰火證 phlegmatic toxin with pattern of wind-heat and phlegm-fire

痰毒·肝郁痰火证/痰毒·肝鬱痰火證　phlegmatic toxin with pattern of liver depression and phlegm-fire

痰毒·热盛酿脓证/痰毒·熱盛釀膿證　phlegmatic toxin with pattern of suppuration due to heat exuberance

痰毒·湿热蕴结证/痰毒·濕熱蘊結證　phlegmatic toxin with dampness-heat amassment pattern

痰毒·余毒凝滞证/痰毒·餘毒凝滯證　phlegmatic toxin with pattern of remnant toxin coagulation and stagnation

痰火闭窍证/痰火閉竅證　pattern of phlegm-fire blocking orifices, pattern of the heart fogged by phlegm-fire

痰火扰神/痰火擾神　phlegm-fire disturbing mind

痰火扰神证/痰火擾神證　pattern of phlegm-fire disturbing mind

痰火扰心/痰火擾心　phlegm-fire disturbing heart

痰火扰心证/痰火擾心證　pattern of phlegm-fire disturbing heart

痰厥/痰厥　phlegm syncope

痰菌检查率/痰菌檢查率　sputum examination rate

痰菌阴转率/痰菌陰轉率　sputum negative conversion rate

痰蒙清窍证/痰蒙清竅證　pattern of phlegm covering clear orifices

痰蒙心窍/痰蒙心竅　phlegm covering heart orifices

痰蒙心窍证/痰蒙心竅證　pattern of phlegm covering heart orifices

痰凝胞宫证/痰凝胞宮證　pattern of coagulated phlegm in uterus, pattern of coagulated phlegm in womb

痰疟/痰瘧　phlegm malaria

痰气互结证/痰氣互結證　pattern of intermingled phlegm and qi, pattern of phlegm and qi blockage

痰热动风证/痰熱動風證　pattern of stirring wind due to phlegm-heat

痰热犯鼻证/痰熱犯鼻證　pattern of phlegm-heat invading nose

痰热结胸证/痰熱結胸證　pattern of phlegm-heat accumulated in chest

痰热内闭证/痰熱內閉證　pattern of phlegm-heat blocking internally

痰热内扰证/痰熱內擾證　pattern of phlegm-heat attacking internally

痰热壅肺证/痰熱壅肺證　pattern of phlegm-heat obstructing lung

痰湿泛耳证/痰濕泛耳證　pattern of phlegm-dampness invading ear

痰湿阻络证/痰濕阻絡證　pattern of phlegm-dampness blocking collaterals

痰食互结证/痰食互結證　pattern of food intermingled with phlegm

痰痛/痰痛　phlegm pain

痰哮/痰哮　phlegm wheezing

痰饮[病]/痰飲[病]　phlegm-fluid retention

痰饮·脾阳虚证/痰飲·脾陽虛證　phlegm-fluid retention with pattern of spleen yang deficiency

痰饮·饮留胃肠证/痰飲·飲留胃腸證　phlegm-fluid retention with pattern of fluid retention in stomach and intestines

痰饮·饮邪化热证/痰飲·飲邪化熱證　phlegm-fluid retention with pattern of pathogenic fluid transforming into heat

痰瘀互结证/痰瘀互結證　pattern of intermingled phlegm and blood stasis

痰瘀生风/痰瘀生風　phlegm stasis causing wind

痰瘀阻肺证/痰瘀阻肺證　pattern of phlegm and blood stasis obstructing lung

痰郁/痰鬱　phlegm stagnation, stagnation pattern of phlegm

痰证/痰證　phlegm pattern

痰肿/痰腫　phlegm swelling

痰浊上蒙证/痰濁上蒙證　pattern of turbid phlegm covering upper orifices

痰浊阻肺/痰濁阻肺　turbid phlegm obstructing lung

痰浊阻肺证/痰濁阻肺證　pattern of turbid phlegm obstructing lung

痰阻心脉证/痰阻心脈證　pattern of phlegm blocking heart vessel

檀香/檀香　sandalwood

檀香木/檀香木　sandalwood

坦纳林/坦納林　tannalin

毯/[腦]毯　tapetum

毯层视网膜变性/斑層視網膜變性　tapetoretinal degeneration

毯状细胞/毯狀細胞　tapetal cell, tapetum cell

叹气/嘆氣　sigh

叹气[息]样呼吸/嘆氣[息]樣呼吸，唷嘆狀呼吸　sighing respiration

叹息式呼吸困难/嘆息性呼吸困難　sighing dyspnea

炭化/炭化　char

炭疽/炭疽　anthrax

炭疽菌苗/炭疽菌苗　anthrax vaccine

炭疽菌黏液素/炭疽菌黏液素，炭疽預防素　anthracomucin

炭疽菌素/炭疽菌素　anthracin
炭疽芽孢杆菌/炭疽[孢芽]桿菌　Bacillus anthracis
炭粒凝集试验/炭粒凝集試驗　charcoal agglutination test
炭疗法/炭末療法　anthracotherapy
炭末沉着[病]/炭末沈著病,炭末入肺病　anthracosis
探查电极/探查電極,檢查電極　exploring electrode
探查针/探查針　exploring needle
探宫腔术/探宮腔術　sounding of uterine cavity
探究行为/探究行爲　exploratory behavior
探视病人者/探視病人者　visitors to patients
探条扩张[术]/探條擴張[術]　bougienage
探吐法/探吐法　inducing vomiting method
探针/探針　probe
探针式注射器/探針式注射器　probe syringe
碳/碳　carbon
碳氮连接酶类/碳氮連接酶類　carbon-nitrogen ligases
碳氮裂合酶类/碳氮裂合酶類　carbon-nitrogen lyases
碳二亚胺/碳二醯胺　carbodiimide
碳放射性同位素/碳放射性同位素　carbon radioisotopes
碳管/碳管　carbon tube
碳黑/碳黑　carbon black
碳化/碳化　carbonize
碳化二亚胺类/碳化二亞胺類　carbodiimides
碳化钨钴/碳化鎢鑽　carbide bur
碳化物/碳化物　carbide
碳化[作用]/碳化[作用]　carbonization
碳环酸类/碳環酸類　carbocyclic acids
碳链[裂解]酶/碳鏈[裂解]酶,解連碳酵素,解重碳酵素　desmolase
碳硫连接酶类/碳硫連接酶類　carbon-sulfur ligases
碳硫裂合酶类/碳硫裂合酶類　carbon-sulfur lyases
碳霉素/碳黴素,嘉賓黴素　carbomycin
碳末石末沉着病/碳末石末沈著病,碳末矽末沈著病　anthracosilicosis
碳纳米管/碳納米管　carbon nanotubes
碳青霉烯类/碳青黴烯類　carbapenems
碳氢化合物皮炎/碳氫化合物皮炎　dermatitis due to hydrocarbon
碳氢化合物中毒/碳氫化合物中毒　hydrocarbarism
碳染料/碳染料　carbon stain
碳水化合物/碳水化合物　carbohydrate
碳水化合物差向异构酶类/碳水化合物差向異構酶類　carbohydrate epimerases
碳水化[合]物代谢/碳水化[合]物代謝　carbohydrate metabolism
碳水化合物构象/碳水化合物構象　carbohydrate conformation
碳水化合物缺乏糖蛋白综合征/碳水化合物缺乏糖蛋白症候群　carbohydrate-deficient glycoprotein syndrome
碳水化合物脱氢酶类/碳水化合物脫氫酶類　carbohydrate dehydrogenases
碳水化合物序列/碳水化合物序列　carbohydrate sequence
碳水化物部分/碳水化合物部分,糖部分　carbohydrate moiety
碳酸/碳酸　carbonic acid
碳酸铵/碳酸銨　ammonium carbonate
碳酸钙/碳酸鈣　calcium carbonate
碳酸酐酶/碳酸酐酶　carbon anhydrase
碳酸酐酶抑制剂/碳酸酐酶抑制劑　carbonic anhydrase inhibitors
碳酸酐酶抑制药/碳酸酐酶抑制藥　carbonic anhydrase inhibitor
碳酸锂/碳酸鋰　lithium carbonate
碳酸木馏油/碳酸木餾油　creosote carbonate
碳酸钠/碳酸鈉　sodium carbonate
碳酸尿[症]/碳酸尿　carbonuria
碳酸氢钾/碳酸氫鉀　potassium bicarbonate
碳酸氢钠/碳酸氫鈉　sodium bicarbonate
碳酸氢盐/碳酸氫鹽,重碳酸鹽　dicarbonate
碳酸氢盐缓冲液/碳酸氫鹽緩衝液,重碳酸鹽緩衝系統　bicarbonate buffer
碳酸缺乏性碱中毒/碳酸缺乏性鹼中毒　acapnial alkalosis
碳酸水淋浴器/碳酸水冲浴器　ombrophore
碳酸血红蛋白/碳酸血紅蛋白,碳醯胺基血紅素　carbhemoglobin
碳酸亚铁/碳酸亞鐵　ferrous carbonate
碳酸盐/碳酸鹽　carbonate
碳酸盐饮料/碳酸鹽飲料　carbonated beverage
碳碳连接酶类/碳碳連接酶類　carbon-carbon ligases
碳碳裂合酶类/碳碳裂合酶類　carbon-carbon lyases
碳碳双键异构酶类/碳碳雙鍵異構酶類　carbon-carbon double bond isomerases
碳同位素/碳同位素　carbon isotope
碳头孢烯类/碳頭孢烯類　carbacephems
碳酰胆碱/碳醯膽鹼　carbachol
碳酰氰化物对三氟甲氧苯基腙/碳醯氰化物對三氟甲氧苯基腙　carbonyl cyanide p-trifluoromethoxyphenyl hydrazone

碳酰氰化物间-氯苯基腙/碳醯氰化物間-氯苯基腙　carbonyl cyanide m-chlorophenyl hydrazone
碳锌电池/碳鋅電池　zinc-carbon cell
碳循环/碳循環　carbon cycle
碳氧肌红蛋白/碳氧肌紅蛋白,一氧化碳肌血球素　carboxymyoglobin
碳氧连接酶类/碳氧連接酶類　carbon-oxygen ligases
碳氧裂合酶类/碳氧裂合酶類　carbon-oxygen lyases
碳氧血红蛋白/碳氧血紅蛋白,一氧化碳血紅素　carboxyhemoglobin
碳种植体/碳種植體　carbon implant
汤剂/湯劑　decoction
汤姆森彩绒试验/湯姆森彩絨試驗　Thomson wool skeins test
汤姆森综合征/湯姆森症候群,Thomson 氏症候群,白内障-微血管擴張-色素沈著症候群　Thomson syndrome
汤头歌诀/湯頭歌訣　Recipes in Rhymes
汤液本草/湯液本草　Materia Medica for Decoctions
汤液醪醴论篇/湯液醪醴論篇　Treatise on Medicinal Decoctions
羰花青/羰花青　carbocyanine
唐南平衡/唐南平衡,多南平衡　Donnan equilibrium
唐慎微/唐慎微　Tang Shenwei
唐氏综合征/唐氏症候群　Down syndrome
唐斯分析法/唐斯分析法　Downs analysis
糖/糖　sugar
糖胺聚糖/[葡萄]糖胺聚糖　glycosaminoglycan
糖醇类/糖醇類　sugar alcohols
糖醇脱氢酶类/糖醇脫氫酶類　sugar alcohol dehydrogenases
糖蛋白/糖蛋白　glycoprotein
糖蛋白分泌细胞/糖蛋白分泌細胞　glycoprotein-secretory cell
糖氮比率/糖氮比值　dextrose-nitrogen ratio
糖锭[剂]/糖錠,錠劑　troche
糖负荷/糖負荷　glucose load
糖苷/糖苷　glycoside
糖苷神经鞘脂类/糖苷神經鞘脂類　glycosphingolipids
糖苷水解酶类/糖苷水解酶類　glycoside hydrolases
糖果/糖果　candy
糖化[作用]/糖化[作用]　saccharification, saccharify
糖混合物/糖混合物　sugar mixture
糖基化/糖基化　glycosylation
糖基化血红蛋白 A/糖基化血紅蛋白 A　Glycosylated Hemoglobin A
糖基磷脂酰肌醇类/糖基磷脂醯肌醇類　glycosylphosphatidylinositols
糖基神经酰胺酶/糖基神經醯胺酶　glycosylceramidase
糖基转移酶类/糖基轉移酶類　glycosyltransferases
糖浆剂/糖漿[劑]　syrup
糖酵解/糖酵解　glycolysis
糖酵解酶/糖酵解酶,肝糖分解酶,糖類分解酶　glycolytic enzyme
糖精/糖精　gluside
糖精钠/糖精鈉　saccharin sodium
糖类/糖類　carbohydrate, saccharide
糖量计/糖量計,測糖器　saccharimeter
糖磷酸盐类/糖磷酸鹽類　sugar phosphates
糖磷脂/糖磷脂　glycophospholipids
糖硫羰酸/糖硫羰酸　glucothionic acid
糖酶/糖酶,碳水化物酵素　carbohydrase
糖蜜/糖蜜　molasses
糖耐量减低/糖耐量減低　impaired glucose tolerance
糖耐受性/糖耐受性　sugar tolerance
糖尿/糖尿　glucosuria
糖尿病/糖尿病　diabetes
糖尿病白内障/糖尿病性白內障　diabetic cataract
糖尿病并发症/糖尿病并發症　diabetes complications
糖尿病单一神经病变/糖尿病單一神經病變　diabetic mononeuropathy
糖尿病多发神经病变/糖尿病多發神經病變　diabetic polyneuropathy
糖尿病高渗性昏迷/糖尿病高滲性昏迷　diabetic hyperosmolar coma
糖尿病高脂血症/糖尿病高脂血症　diabetic hyperlipemia
糖尿病患者/糖尿病患者　diabetic
糖尿病患者妊娠/糖尿病患者妊娠　pregnancy in diabetics
糖尿病黄瘤/糖尿病黃瘤　diabetic xanthoma
糖尿病昏迷/糖尿病[性]昏迷　diabetic coma
糖尿病肌萎缩/糖尿病肌萎縮　diabetic amyotrophy
糖尿病皮肤病变/糖尿病皮膚病變,糖尿病皮膚症　diabetic dermopathy
糖尿病膳食/糖尿病膳食,糖尿病飲食　diabetic diet
糖尿病神经病变/糖尿病性神經病變　diabetic neuropathy
糖尿病肾病/糖尿病腎病　diabetic nephropathy
糖尿病肾乳头坏死/糖尿病腎乳頭壞死　diabetic renal papillary necrosis
糖尿病视网膜病变/糖尿病視網膜病變,糖尿病性視網膜病　diabetic retinopathy

糖尿病视网膜病变·肝肾两虚证/糖尿病視網膜病變·肝腎兩虛證　diabetic retinopathy with liver-kidney deficiency pattern
糖尿病视网膜病变·气阴两虚证/糖尿病視網膜病變·氣陰兩虛證　diabetic retinopathy with qi-yin deficiency pattern
糖尿病视网膜病变·阴阳两虚证/糖尿病視網膜病變·陰陽兩虛證　diabetic retinopathy with yin-yang deficiency pattern
糖尿病手指粗隆/糖尿病之手指粗隆　finger pebbles in diabetes mellitus
糖尿病酮症酸中毒/糖尿病酮症酸中毒　diabetic ketoacidosis
糖尿病微动脉瘤/糖尿病微動脈瘤　diabetic microaneurysm
糖尿病心肌病/糖尿病心肌病　diabetic cardiomyopathy
糖尿病心脏病/糖尿病心臟病　diabetic cardiopathy
糖尿病性大疱病/糖尿病性大皰病,糖尿病性水皰症　bullosis diabeticorum
糖尿病性耳疾/糖尿病性耳疾　diabetic ear
糖尿病性肺结核/糖尿病性肺結核,糖尿病癆　diabetic phthisis
糖尿病性红斑/糖尿病性紅斑,糖尿病性紅變症　diabetic rubeosis
糖尿病[性]坏疽/糖尿病性壞疽　diabetic gangrene
糖尿病性溃疡/糖尿病性潰瘍　diabetic ulcer
糖尿病性瘙痒症/糖尿病性搔癢症　diabetic pruritus
糖尿病性肾小球肾炎/糖尿病性腎小球腎炎　diabetic glomerulonephritis
糖尿病性湿疹/糖尿病性濕疹　eczema diabeticorum
糖尿病性酸中毒/糖尿病性酸中毒,糖尿病酸血症　diabetic acidosis
糖尿病性颜面发红/糖尿病性顏面發紅　rubeosis faciei diabetica
糖尿病性阳痿/糖尿病性陽痿　diabetic impotence
糖尿病性硬肿病/糖尿病性硬腫病　scleredema of diabetes mellitus
糖尿病性脂性渐进性坏死/糖尿病性脂性漸進性壞死,糖尿病性類脂質漸進性壞死　necrobiosis lipoidica diabeticorum
糖尿病血管病变/糖尿病血管病變　diabetic angiopathies
糖尿病增殖性视网膜病/糖尿病增殖性視網膜病　diabetic proliferative retinopathy
糖尿病疹/糖尿病疹　diabetid
糖尿病脂性渐进性坏死/糖尿病脂性漸進性壞死　diabetic lipoidic necrobiosis
糖尿病周围血管病/糖尿病周圍血管病　diabetic peripheral angiopathy
糖尿病足/糖尿病足　diabetes mellitus foot
糖尿定量器/糖尿病尿糖計　picrosaccharometer
糖皮质激素类/糖皮質激素類　glucocorticoids
糖皮质激素受体/糖皮質激素受體　glucocorticoid receptors
糖皮质类固醇可抑制性醛固酮症/糖皮質類固醇可抑制性醛固酮症　glucocorticoid suppressible aldosteronism
糖醛酸/糖醛酸　uronic acid
糖[肾上腺]皮质激素/糖[腎上腺]皮質激素,腎上腺促糖皮質激素　glucocorticoid
糖酸类/糖酸類　sugar acids
糖肽/糖肽　glycopeptide
糖肽类/糖肽類　glycopeptides
糖肽类抗生素/糖肽類抗生素　glycopeptide antibiotics
糖涎/糖涎　melitoptyalism
糖消化不良/糖消化不良　sugar indigestion
糖[新陈]代谢/糖新陳代謝　saccharometabolism
糖血症/糖血症　glucohemia
糖衣片剂/糖衣片劑,糖衣錠[劑]　sugar coated tablet
糖原/糖原　glycogen
糖原变性/糖原變性,肝糖變性　glycogenic degeneration
糖原分解不足/糖原質分解不足　hypoglycogenolysis
糖原分解过度/糖原分解過度　hyperglycogenolysis
糖原分解神经/糖原分解神經,肝糖分解神經　glycogenolytic nerve
糖原合成酶/糖原合成酶　glycogen synthase
糖原合成酶激酶类/糖原合成酶激酶類　glycogen synthase kinases
糖原合酶D磷酸酶/糖原合酶D磷酸酶　glycogen-synthase-D phosphatase
糖原颗粒/糖原顆粒,肝糖顆粒　glycogen granule
糖原磷酸化酶/糖原磷酸化酶　glycogen phosphorylase
糖原缺乏/糖原缺乏,肝糖儲藏不能,肝細胞無儲藏澱粉能力　azoamyly
糖原脱支酶系统/糖原脱支酶系統　glycogen debranching enzyme system
糖原性肾病/糖原性腎病,肝糖性腎病變　glycogen nephrosis
糖原异生[作用]/糖原異生[作用],糖類合成　neoglycogenesis
糖原贮积病/糖原貯積病,肝糖儲藏疾病　glycogen

storage diseases
糖原贮积病Ⅲ型/糖原貯積病Ⅲ型,糖原貯積病第三型　limit dextrinosis
糖原贮积症/糖原貯積症,肝糖貯積病　glycogen storage disease
糖原贮积症Ⅰ型/糖原貯積症Ⅰ型,肝糖貯積病第一型　glycogen storage disease type Ⅰ
糖原贮积症Ⅲ型/糖原貯積症Ⅲ型,肝糖貯積病第三型　glycogen storage disease type Ⅲ
糖原贮积症Ⅳ型/糖原貯積症Ⅳ型,肝糖貯積病第四型　glycogen storage disease type Ⅳ
糖杂体/糖雜體　heteroside
糖甾类/糖甾類　glucosteroids
糖甾类拮抗药/糖固醇拮抗藥　glucosteroid antagonists
糖脂/糖脂　glycolipid
糖脂类/糖脂類　glycolipids
糖脂贮积病/糖脂貯積病　glycolipidosis
烫/燙　scalding
烫伤/燙傷　scald
烫[制]/燙[制]　scalding
绦虫/條蟲　cestode, tapeworm
绦虫病/條蟲病　taeniasis
绦虫病·虫积肠道证/條蟲病·蟲積腸道證　taeniasis with pattern of accumulation of worms in intestine
绦虫病·脾胃气虚证/條蟲病·脾胃氣虛證　taeniasis with pattern of qi deficiency of spleen and stomach
绦虫毒素/條蟲毒素　teniotoxin
绦虫感染/條蟲感染　tapeworm infections
绦虫学/條蟲學　cestodology
逃逸反应/逃逸反應　escape reaction
桃花癍/桃花癍　peach flower macula
桃金娘/桃金娘　myrtle
桃仁/桃仁　peach seed
陶-宾病/陶-賓病,Taussig-Bing 二氏病　Taussig-Bing disease
陶瓷金属黏固剂/陶瓷金屬黏固劑　cermet cements
陶瓷滤器/陶瓷濾器　ceramic filter
陶瓷修复/陶瓷修復　ceramic restoration
陶道/陶道　taodao, DU13
陶工硅肺病/陶工硅肺病,陶工矽肺症　potters silicosis
陶工哮喘/陶工哮喘　potters asthma
陶罐/陶罐　pottery cup
陶弘景/陶弘景　Tao Hongjing
陶西格-宾综合征/陶西格-賓症候群,陶-賓二氏症候群　Taussig-Bing syndrome
陶针疗法/陶針療法　pottery needle therapy
淘汰药品/淘汰藥物　obsolete drugs
套层/套[膜]層,外套層　mantle layer
套沟/套溝　mantle groove
套管插入术/套管插入法　cannulation
套管冷冻[探]头/套管冷凍[探]頭　trocar cryoprobe
套膜沟/套[膜]溝　pallial groove
套入法尿道成形术/套入法尿道成形術　badenoch urethroplasty
套针/套針　trocar
套装论/套裝論,生成論,先成論　encasement theory
套状移植物/套狀移植物　gauntlet graft
特登绷带/特登繃帶,Theden 氏繃帶　Theden bandage
特定穴/特定穴　specific point
特发性/特發性,自發的,原發的　idiopathic
特发性瘢痕疙瘩/特發性瘢痕疙瘩　idiopathic keloid
特发性逼尿肌协同失调/特發性逼尿肌協同失調　idiopathic detrusor dyssynergia
特发性不育症/特發性不育症　idiopathic infertility
特发性低血色素性贫血/特發性低血色素性貧血,特發性低色性貧血　idiopathic hypochromemia
特发性滴状色素减少症/特發性滴狀色素減少症,特發性斑點樣黑色素減少病　idiopathic guttate hypomelanosis
特发性癫痫/特發性癲癇　idiopathic epilepsy
特发性肥大/特發性肥大　idiopathic hypertrophy
特发性肥厚性主动脉瓣下狭窄/自發性肥厚性主動脈下部狹窄　idiopathic hypertrophic subaortic stenosis
特发性肺动脉干扩张/特發性肺動脈幹擴張　idiopathic dilatation of pulmonary trunk
特发性肺动脉扩张/特發性肺動脈擴張　idiopathic pulmonary arterial dilation
特发性肺含铁血黄素沉着症/特發性肺含鐵血黃素沈著症　idiopathic pulmonary hemosiderosis
特发性肺间质纤维化/特發性肺間質纖維化　idiopathic pulmonary interstitial fibrosis
特发性腹膜后纤维化/特發性腹膜後纖維化　idiopathic retroperitoneal fibrosis
特发性高血压/特發性高血壓　idiopathic hypertension
特发性骨脆弱/特發性骨脆弱,不明性骨脆弱　osteopsathyrosis idiopathic
特发性肌痉挛/特發性肌痙攣　idiopathic muscular spasm
特发性肌萎缩/原發性肌萎縮　idiopathic muscular atrophy
特发性疾病/特發[性疾]病　idiopathic disease

特发性局灶性肾小球肾炎/特發性局灶性腎小球腎炎　idiopathic focal glomerulonephritis
特发性扩张/特發性擴張　idiopathic dilatation
特发性弥漫性溃疡/特發性彌漫性潰瘍　idiopathic diffuse ulcer
特发性尿钙增多症/特發性尿鈣增多症　idiopathic hypercalcinuria
特发性皮肤萎缩/特發性皮膚萎縮　atrophia cutis idiopathica
特发性鞘膜积液/特發性鞘膜積液　idiopathic hydrocele
特发性热/特發性熱　essential fever
特发性嗜睡症/特發性嗜睡症　idiopathic hypersomnolence
特发性水肿/自發性水腫　idiopathic edema
特发性哮喘/特發性哮喘　true asthma
特发性心动过速/自發性心動快速　essential tachycardia
特发性心肌病/特發性心肌病　idiopathic cardiomyopathy
特发性心室搏动/特發性心室搏動　idioventricular beat
特发性性早熟症/特發性性早熟症　idiopathic sexual precocity
特发性眩晕/特發性眩暈,自發性眩暈　essential vertigo
特发性血尿/特發性血尿,自發性血尿　essential hematuria
特发性血小板减少症/特發性血小板減少症,原發性血小板減少症　essential thrombocytopenia
特发性阴囊坏疽/特發性陰囊壞疽　Fournier gangrene of scrotum
特发性震颤/特發性震顫　essential tremor
特发性中性白细胞减少/特發性中性白細胞減少,自發性嗜中性白血球減少病　idiopathic neutropenia
特发性纵隔炎/特發性縱隔炎　idiopathic mediastinitis
特非那定/特非那定　terfenadine
特氟隆/鐵弗龍　teflon
特拉唑嗪/特拉唑嗪　terazosin
特赖茨疝/特賴茨疝,Treitz 氏疝　Treitz hernia
特兰塔斯小点/特蘭塔斯小點,泰特斯氏小斑　Trantas dots
特劳贝征/特勞貝徵,Traube 氏徵象　Traube sign
特雷弗病/特雷弗病,Trevor 氏病　Trevor disease
特里综合征/特里症候群,Terry 氏症候群　Terry syndrome
特立帕肽/特立帕肽　teriparatide

特鲁朗静脉/特魯朗靜脈,Trolard 氏静脉　Trolard vein
特鲁索病/特魯索病,Trousseau 氏病　Trousseau disease
特鲁索综合征/特魯索症候群,Trousseau 氏症候群　Trousseau syndrome
特伦德伦堡塞子/特倫德倫堡塞子,Trendelenburg 氏塞子　Trendelenburg tampon
特伦德伦堡试验/特倫德倫堡試驗　Trendelenburg test
特伦德伦伯格套管/特倫德倫伯格套管,特倫伯氏插管　Trendelenburg cannula
特纳牙/特納齒　Turner tooth
特纳综合征/特納症候群　Turner syndrome
特普他林/特普他林　terbutaline
特殊儿童/特殊兒童　exceptional child
特殊分化黏膜/特殊分化黏膜　specialized mucosa
特殊感觉/特殊感覺　special sense
特殊教育/特殊教育　special education
特殊颗粒/特殊顆粒　specific granule
特殊内脏感觉/特殊內臟感覺　special visceral sense
特殊内脏运动/特殊內臟運動　special visceral motor
特殊躯体感觉/特殊軀體感覺　special somatic sense
特殊抑制剂/特殊抑制劑　specific inhibitor
特殊意义妄想/特殊意義妄想　delusion of special significance
特威德二角/特威德二角　Tweed triangle
特效药/特效藥　specific medicine
特性黏度/特性黏度,固有黏度　intrinsic viscosity
特许专卖药/特許專賣藥　proprietary medicine
特异病/特異病,特殊病　specific disease
特异病征性/特異病徵性　pathognomonic
特异刺激/特異刺激　specific stimulation
特异蛋白质/特異[性]蛋白質　specific protein
特异反应/特異反應,專一性反應　specific reaction
特异反应比速/特異反應速度,特異反應速率,專一性反應速率　specific reaction rate
特异突触/特異突觸　specific synapses
特异性/特異性,專一性　specificity
特异性免疫/特異性免疫　specific immunity
特异性尿道炎/特異性尿道炎　specific urethritis
特异性热病谵妄/特異性熱症譫妄　specific febrile delirium
特异性血清/特異性血清,特殊血清　specific serum
特异质/特異[體]質　idiosyncrasy
特应病/特異病,異位病　atopy disease
特应性/特[異反]應性　atopy
特应性鼻炎/特應性鼻炎,異位性鼻炎　atopic

rhinitis
特应性变态反应/特應性變態反應　atopic allergy
特应性反应/特應性反應,異位性反應　atopic reaction
特应性疾病/特應性疾病,異位性疾病　atopic disease
特应性皮炎/特應性皮炎,異位性皮膚炎　atopic dermatitis
特应性皮炎样疹/特應性皮炎樣疹,異位性皮膚炎樣疹　atopic dermatitis like eruption
特应性湿疹/特應性濕疹,異位性皮膚炎　atopic eczema
特应性素质/特應性素質,異位性體質　atopic diathesis
特应性荨麻疹/特應性蕁麻疹,異位性蕁麻疹　atopic urticaria
特约医疗/特約醫療　contract practice
特征/特徵　feature
特征射线/特性射線　characteristic ray
特征X射线/標識X射線　characteristic X-radiation
特征向量投影/特徵向量投影　eigenvector projection
特征选择/特徵選擇　feature selection
特制色条/特製色條　custom shade tab
特质/特質,特性　trait
疼痛/疼痛　pain
疼痛测定/疼痛測定　pain measurement
疼痛测量法/疼痛測量法,疼痛計量　dolorimetry
疼痛反应/疼痛反應　pain reaction
疼痛感受器/疼痛感受器　nociceptors
疼痛弧试验/疼痛弧試驗　painful arc test
疼痛缓解/疼痛緩解　pain relief
疼痛恐惧症/疼痛恐懼症　algophobia
疼痛门诊/疼痛門診　pain clinic
疼痛受体/痛覺受體　pain receptor
疼痛性蓝肿/疼痛性藍腫,有痛性青股腫　phlegmasia cerulea dolens
疼痛性青肿综合征/疼痛性青腫症候群,痛性淤青症候群　painful bruising syndrome
疼痛诊所/疼痛診所　pain clinics
滕雷恩氏征象/滕霍恩氏徵象　ten Horn's sign
滕喜隆/滕喜隆,依酚氯銨　edrophonium
藤黄/藤黄　gamboge
藤黄酸/藤黄酸　gambogic acid
剔甲癖/剔甲癖,爪甲摘取狂　onychotillomania
梯度/梯度　gradient
梯度-回音影像序列/梯度-回音影像序列　gradient-echo imaging sequence
梯度离心/梯度離心　gradient centrifugation
梯度平板法/梯度平板法　gradient plating
梯度洗脱/梯度洗脱,梯度沖洗　gradient elution
梯级征/梯級徵,登級徵象　stairs sign
梯密度离心法/梯密度離心法　density gradient centrifugation
梯形夹板/梯形夾　ladder splint
梯形钳/梯形鉗　youngloop bending pliers
梯[形]头/梯[形]頭,階突頭　bathrocephaly
锑化物/銻二元化合物　antimonid
锑皮炎/銻皮膚炎　antimony dermatitis
锑酸/銻酸　antimonic acid
锑氧基/銻氧基　antimonyl
踢伤/踢傷　kicking injury
提按端挤/提按端擠　holding-lifting-squeezing-pressing manipulation
提插/提插　lifting and thrusting of needle
提插补泻/提插補瀉　lifting-thrusting reinforcing-reducing method
提法/提法　lifting manipulation
提肌/提肌,舉肌　levator
提肌圆枕/提肌圓枕　torus levatorius, torus of levator
提捏进针法/提捏進針法　skin-pinching up needle inserting
提脓拔毒/提膿拔毒　eliminating pus and toxicity
提脓去腐/提膿去腐　eliminating pus and necrotic tissues
提脓去腐药/提膿去腐藥　pus-discharging and putridity removing medicine
提前发作/提前發作　subintrance
提前医护计划/提前醫護計劃　advance care planning
提琴状胎盘/提琴狀胎盤　panduriform placenta
提取/提取,抽提,萃取　extraction, extract
提取容量法/提取容量法,抽提滴定法　extraction titration
提取物/提取物,抽提物　extract
提取重量法/提取重量法,抽取重量法　extraction gravimetry
提塞留斯电泳仪/提塞留斯電泳儀,泰塞利氏電泳儀器,提塞利氏電泳儀　Tiselius apparatus
提上睑肌折叠术/提上瞼肌折疊術　pleating of levator palpebrae superioris
提醒者系统/提醒者系統　reminder systems
提早发作/提早發作,早發　prolepsis
提踵试验/提踵試驗　Ely test
啼鸣呼吸/啼鳴呼吸,啼狀呼吸音　crowing respiration
蹄骨/蹄骨　coffin bone

体/體 body
体被/體被，全體皮膚 common integument
体[壁]感受器/體[壁]感受器，軀體受器 somatoceptor
体壁肌节/體壁肌節 body wall myotome
体壁瘘/體壁瘺 parietal fistula
体壁羊膜/體壁羊膜 pleuramnion
体壁中胚层/體壁中胚層 somatic mesoderm
体表标测/體表標測 surface mapping
体表电位图/體表電位圖，體表電點陣圖 body surface potential mapping
体表高频振荡/體表高頻振盪 high frequency oscillation of body surface
体表寄生虫病/體表寄生蟲病，皮上寄生蟲病 epizoonosis
体表降温/體表降溫 surface cooling
体表解剖标志定位法/體表解剖標志定位法 method of anatomical landmark
体表面积/體表面積 body surface area
体表温度测量器/體表溫度測量器 thermointegrator
体层[X射线]照片/斷層照片，體層照片 stratigram
体层摄影术/體層攝影術，斷層X射線檢法 tomography
体察/體察 experience and observe
体臭恐惧/體臭恐懼 bromidrosiphobia
体蒂/體柄，體蒂 body stalk
体动X射线体层照相术/體動X射線體層照相術，自體移動X光照相術 autotomography
体干神经系统/體幹神經系統，軀壁神經系統，軀體神經系統 somatic nervous system
体格检查/體格檢查，身體檢查 physical examination
体格指数/體格指數 body build index
体积测定法/體積測定法 stereometry
体积计/體積計 stereometer
体积描记器/體積[變化]描記器 plethysmograph
体积描记术/體積描記法 plethysmography
体积描记图/體積描記像 plethysmogram
体积膨胀/體積膨脹 cubical expansion
体节/體節 somite, metamere
体节胚/體節[期]胚 somite embryo
体节前胚胎/體節前胚胎，前原節期 presomite
体静脉/體[循環]靜脈 systemic vein
体力测量法/肌力測定法，體力測定法 sthenometry
体力过盛/體力過盛 hypersthenia
体疗美容/體療美容 physical therapeutic cosmetics
体裂[下肢缺损]畸形/體裂[畸形] schistosomia
体毛/體毛 hairs, body hair
体内/[身]體内 in vivo

体内蛋白质[分散]稳定/體内蛋白質分散穩定 prostaxia
体内分泌物/體内分泌物 bodily secretions
体内活体染色/體内活體染色 intravital staining, vital staining
体内寄生虫/體内寄生蟲 endoparasites
体内人工心脏/體内人工心臟 intracorporeal heart
体内试验/體内試驗 in vivo test
体内受精/體内受精 in vivo fertilization, internal fertilization
体内外控制/體内外控制 internal-external control
体能测定/體能測定 fitness test
体佩助听器/體佩助聽器 body-worn hearing aid
体腔/體腔 body cavity
体腔动物/體腔動物 coelomate
体腔管/體腔管 coelomic duct
体腔肌/體腔肌，體壁肌 coelomyarian
体腔寄生物/體腔寄生物 celozoic parasite
体腔流电疗法/體腔流電療法，器官内部感應電化療法 intragalvanization
体腔膜/體腔膜 celarium
体腔内无线电探测器/體腔内無線電測壓器 endoradiosonde
体腔X射线管/體腔X射線管，體腔X光球管 endodiascope
体腔X射线检查/體腔X射線檢查，體腔X光檢查 endodiascopy
体染色[神经]细胞/體染色細胞 somatochrome
体神经/體神經 somatic nerve
体虱/體蝨 body lice
体虱病/體蝨病 pediculosis corporis
体视学/體視學，立體測量學 stereology
体-树突触/體-樹[神經元]突觸 somato-dendritic synapse
体-体突触/體-體[神經元]突觸 somato-somatic synapse
体外/體外，試管内 in vitro
体外超滤作用/體外超濾作用 extracorporeal ultrafiltration
体外冲击波碎石术/體外衝擊波碎石術，體外震波碎石術 extracorporeal shock wave lithotripsy
体外动静脉短路/體外動靜脈短路 external arteriovenous shunt
体外发生/體外發生 ectogenesis
体外肝灌注/體外肝灌注 extracorporeal liver perfusion
体外光化学治疗/體外光化療法 extracorporeal photochemotherapy

体外活体染色/體外活體染色 supravital staining
体外寄生虫/體外寄生蟲 ectoparasites
体外寄生虫感染/體外寄生蟲感染 ectoparasitic infestation
体外抗原/外抗原體 ectoantigen
体外膜氧合作用/體外膜氧合作用 extracorporeal membrane oxygenation
体外起搏器/體外起搏器 external pacemaker
体外试验/體外試驗 in vitro test
体外受精/體外受精 in vitro fertilization, fertilization in vitro
体外心/體外心,心異位 ectopia cordis
体外性脓毒症/體外性膿毒症,外[因性]敗血病 exosepsis
体外循环/體外循環 extracorporeal circulation
体外氧合作用/體外氧合作用 extracorporeal oxygenation
体位/體位 posture
体位保持/體位保持 positioning
体位性蛋白尿/體位性蛋白尿 postural proteinuria
体位性缺血/體位性缺血 postural ischemia
体位性眩晕/體位性眩暈,姿勢性眩暈 positional vertigo
体位性震颤/體位性震顫,姿勢性震顫 postural tremor
体位引流/體位引流,順位洩液法,雙更體位洩液法 postural drainage
体温/體溫 body temperature
体温变化/體溫變化 body temperature changes
体温反常/體溫反常 thermic inversion
体温计/體溫計,臨床溫度計 clinical thermometer
体温[全日]恒定/體溫均一,全日體溫不變 monothermia
体温调节/體溫調節 body temperature regulation
体细胞/體細胞 somatic cell
体细胞互换/體細胞互換 somatic crossing over
体细胞基因治疗/體細胞基因治療 somatic cell gene therapy
体细胞抗原/體[細胞]抗原 somatic antigen
体细胞染色体配对/體細胞染色體配對 somatic pairing
体细胞突变/體[細胞]突變 somatic mutation
体细胞突变学说/體細胞突變學說 somatic mutation theory
体细胞遗传学/體細胞遺傳學 somatic cell genetics
体细胞杂种/體細胞雜種 somatic cell hybrid
体象/體像 body image
体象变形/體像變形 body image distortion
体象蔑视/體像蔑視 body image disparagement
体象手术/體像手術 body image surgery
体象障碍/體像障礙 body image disturbance
体象治疗/體像治療 body image treatment
体形变异/體形變異 allometron
体形塑造/體形塑造 body contouring
体型/體型 somatotypes
体型决定[法]/體型決定法 somatotyping
体型指数/體型指數 habitus index
体癣/體癬 tinea corporis
体循环/體循環,大循環,全身循環 greater circulation, general circulation, systemic circulation
体液/體液 body fluid
体液白蛋白/體液白蛋白 circulating albumin
体液不调/體液不調,惡液質 dyscrasia
体液分布/體液分布 body fluid compartments
体液检验学/體液檢驗學 ecsomatics
体液抗体/體液抗體 humoral antibody
体液免疫/體液免疫 humoral immunity
体液学说/體液學說 humoralism
体液循环停止/體液循環停止 acyclia
体液转移/體液轉移 fluid shift
体育/體育 physical education
体育运动/體育運動 sports
体征/體徵,身體徵象 physical sign
体质/體質 somatoplasm, body constitution, constitution
体质病/體質病,全身病 constitutional disease
体质心理学/體質心理學 constitutional psychology
体质型异常/體質異常 ectypia
体质性肝功能不良/體質性肝機能不良 constitutional hepatic dysfunction
体质性黄疸/體質性黃疸 constitutional jaundice
体质性痒疹/體質性癢疹 prurigo diathesique
体质性抑郁/體質性抑鬱 constitutional depression
体质医学/體質醫學 constitutional medicine
体中心温度/體中心溫度 body core temperature
体重/體重,身體重量 body weight
体重比率/體重比率 body-weight ratio
体重变化/體重變化 body weight changes
体重减轻/體重減輕 weight loss
体重身长指数/體重身長指數 baric index
体重增长/體重增長 weight gain
体重指数/人體品質指數 body mass index
体-轴突触/體-軸[神經元]突觸 somato-axonic synapse
剃刀/剃[毛]刀 razor
剃须后洗液/剃鬚後洗液,鬍後乳液 aftershave

lotion
替补骨/替補骨,软骨性骨 substitution bone
替代疗法/替代療法,另類療法 alternative therapy
替代品/替代品,替代藥 succedaneum
替代性肥大/替代性肥大 vicarious hypertrophy
替代性明希豪森综合征/替代性明希豪森症候群,替代性米肖森症候群 Münchhausen syndrome by proxy
替代性气肿/替代性氣腫 vicarious emphysema
替代性纤维变性/替代性纖維變性,替代性纖維化 replacement fibrosis
替代性增生/替代性增生 replacement hyperplasia
替代医学/替代醫學,另類醫療 alternative medicine
替卡西林/替凱西林 ticarcillin
替考拉宁/替考拉寧 teicoplanin
替来他明/替來他明 tiletamine
替利定/替利定 tilidine
替洛隆/替洛隆 tilorone
替马西泮/替馬西泮 temazepam
替美福司/替美福司 temefos
替尼泊苷/替尼泊甙 teniposide
替尼酸/替尼酸 ticrynafen
替普罗肽/替普羅肽 teprotide
替身母亲/替身母親 surrogate mother
替身综合征/替身症候群 capgras syndrome
替沃噻吨/替沃噻噸 thiothixene
替硝唑/替硝唑,他咪唑 tinidazole
嚏/嚏 sneeze
天才儿童/天才兒童 gifted child
天池/天池 tianchi, PC1
天冲/天沖 tianchong, GB9
天窗/天窗 tianchuang, SI16
天地之神/天地之神 vitality of nature
天鼎/天鼎 tianding, LI17
天冬/天冬 cochinchinese asparagus root
天冬氨酸/天門冬酸 aspartic acid
天冬氨酸氨基转移酶类/天門冬胺酸胺基轉移酶類,天門冬胺酸轉胺酶類 aspartate aminotransferases
天冬氨酸半醛脱氢酶/天門冬胺酸半醛脱氫酶 aspartate-semialdehyde dehydrogenase
天冬氨酸激酶/天門冬胺酸激酶 aspartate kinase
天冬氨酸激酶高丝氨酸脱氢酶/天門冬胺酸激酶高絲胺酸脱氫酶 aspartokinase homoserine dehydrogenase
天冬氨酸 tRNA 连接酶/天門冬胺酸 tRNA 連接酶 aspartate-tRNA ligase
天冬氨酸裂氨酶/天門冬胺酸裂胺酶 aspartate ammonia lyase

天冬氨酸酶/天門冬胺酸酶 aspartase
天冬氨酸内肽酶类/天門冬胺酸内肽酶類 aspartic endopeptidases
天冬氨酸脱氢酶/天門冬胺酸脱氫酶 aspartic dehydrogenase
天冬氨酸盐/天門冬胺酸鹽 aspartate
天冬氨酸转氨甲酰酶/天門冬胺酸轉胺甲醯酶 aspartate carbamoyltransferase
天冬氨酰基葡萄糖尿/天門冬葡萄糖胺尿 aspartyl glycosaminuria
天冬氨酰葡糖脱氨基酶/天門冬胺醯葡糖脱氨基酶 aspartylglucosylaminase
天冬氨酰糖基胺/天門冬胺醯糖胺 aspartylglycosylamine
天冬胱甘肽/天門冬酸胱甘肽 asparthione
天冬酰胺/天門冬醯胺,天[門]冬素 asparagine
天冬酰胺连接酶/天門冬醯胺連接酶 aspartate-ammonia ligase
天冬酰胺酶/天門冬醯胺酶 asparaginase
天符/天符 coincidence of heavenly qi
天府/天府 tianfu, LU3
天花/天花,痘瘡 smallpox, variola
天花病毒/天花病毒 smallpox virus
天花粉/天花粉 snakegourd root
天花粉蛋白/天花粉蛋白,天花粉素 trichosanthin
天花红斑/天花紅斑,天花紅疹 alices
天花接种/天花接種,人痘接種 variolation
天花性睾丸炎/天花性睾丸炎,痘瘡性睾丸炎 orchitis variolosa
天花性脓疱病/天花性膿皰病 impetigo varioiosa
天花性紫癜/天花性紫癜,痘瘡紫癜病 purpura variolosa
天花疫苗/天花疫苗,牛痘苗 smallpox vaccine
天宦/天宦 congenital eunuch
天井/天井 tianjing, SJ10
天葵子/天葵子 muskrootlike semiaquilegia root
天蓝色/天藍色,深藍 coeruleus
天髎/天髎 tianliao, SJ15
天癸/天癸 sex promoter, tiangui
天麻/天麻 tall gastrodia tuber
天麻钩藤饮/天麻鉤藤飲 tianma gouteng drink
天麻丸/天麻丸 tianma pills
天南星/天南星 jackinthepulpit tuber
天疱疮/天皰瘡 pemphigus, pemphigus and pemphigoid
天疱疮抗原/天皰瘡抗原 pemphigus antigen
天疱疮·脾虚湿困证/天皰瘡·脾虛濕困證 pemphigus and pemphigoid with pattern of spleen

deficiency and dampness retention
天疱疮·气阴两虚证/天皰瘡·氣陰兩虛證　pemphigus and pemphigoid with qi-yin deficiency pattern
天疱疮·热毒炽盛证/天皰瘡·熱毒熾盛證　pemphigus and pemphigoid with blazing heat-toxin pattern
天疱疮·心火脾湿证/天皰瘡·心火脾濕證　pemphigus and pemphigoid with pattern of heart fire and spleen dampness
天疱疮样天花/天皰瘡狀痘瘡　variola pemphigosa
天气/天氣　celestial qi
天青蛋白/天青蛋白　azurin
天青染料/天青染料　azure stains
天泉/天泉　tianquan, PC2
天然白蛋白/天然白蛋白，天然蛋白素　native albumin
天然产物/天然産物　natural product
天然齿/天然齒　natural tooth
天然蛋白/天然蛋白[質]　native protein
天然抗体/天然抗體　natural antibody
天然蜡/天然蠟　natural waxes
天然免疫/天然免疫，自然免疫　natural immunity
天然免疫性/天然免疫性　autarcesis
天然免疫学/天然免疫學，天然免疫論　autarcesiology
天然耐受[性]/天然耐受[性]　natural tolerance
天然耐药/天然耐藥　natural drugresistance
天然培养基/天然培養基　natural medium
天然杀伤细胞/天然殺傷細胞　natural killer cell
天然树脂/天然樹脂　natural resin
天然调湿因子/天然調濕因數　natural moisturizing factor
天然牙列/天然牙列，天然齒列　natural dentition
天然药物/天然藥物　natural crude drug, natural medicine
天人合一/天人合一　heaven and men integrated into one, unity of heaven and humanity
天人相应/天人相應　correspondence between human body and natural environment, correspondence between man and universe
天容/天容　tianrong, SI17
天枢/天樞　tianshu, ST25
天台乌药散/天台烏藥散　tiantai wuyao powder
天突/天突　tiantu, RN22
天王补心丹/天王補心丹　tianwang buxin mini-pills
天溪/天溪　tianxi, SP18
天仙藤/天仙藤　dutchmanspipe vine
天仙子/天仙子　henbane seed
天行赤眼/天行赤眼　epidemic conjunctivitis, epidemic red eye
天行赤眼暴翳/天行赤眼暴翳　epidemic keratoconjunctivitis, epidemic red eye with acute nebula
天行赤眼暴翳·肺热壅盛证/天行赤眼暴翳·肺熱壅盛證　epidemic red eye with acute nebula with pattern of lung-heat congestion and excessiveness
天行赤眼暴翳·肝火偏盛证/天行赤眼暴翳·肝火偏盛證　epidemic red eye with acute nebula with pattern of liver fire excessiveness
天行赤眼暴翳·余毒未清证/天行赤眼暴翳·餘毒未清證　epidemic red eye with acute nebula with uncleared remnant toxin pattern
天行赤眼·初感疠气证/天行赤眼·初感癘氣證　epidemic red eye with pattern of new contraction of epidemic qi
天行赤眼·热毒炽盛证/天行赤眼·熱毒熾盛證　epidemic red eye with blazing heat-toxin pattern
天行赤眼·疫热伤络证/天行赤眼·疫熱傷絡證　epidemic red eye with pattern of epidemic heat injuring collateral
天牖/天牖　tianyou, SJ16
天灾性精神病/天災性精神病　catastrophe psychosis
天竺葵/天竺葵　geranium
天竺鼠最大化试验/天竺鼠最大化試驗　guinea-pig maximization test
天柱/天柱　tianzhu, BL10
天柱疽/天柱疽　Dazhui carbuncle
天宗/天宗　tianzong, SI11
添加/添加　addition
添加辅食/添加輔食　adding food supplements
添加剂/添加劑，添加物　additive
添加性生长/添加性生長　accretionary growth
田径运动/田徑運動　track and field
田鼠体畸胎/田鼠體畸胎　aspalasoma
恬惔虚无/恬惔虛無　tranquilize the mind and stay empty
甜菜/甜菜　beet
甜菜苷/甜菜苷，甜菜紅素　betanin
甜菜根糖/甜菜根糖　teutlose
甜菜碱/甜菜素　betaine
甜橙/甜橙　Citrus sinensis
甜味剂/甜味劑　sweeting agent
填充式胸廓成形术/填充式胸廓成形術　plombage thoracoplasty
填空性水肿/補空性水腫　edema ex vacuo

填料/填料,充填物　packing material
填塞/填塞,填閉　obturation
填塞法/填塞法　plugging
填塞管/堵塞管　tampon tube
填塞器/填塞器　packer
填质性远视/填質性遠視,折射率性遠視　index hyperopia
挑刺法/挑刺法　pricking blood therapy
挑选/挑選　sorting
挑治疗法/挑治療法　pricking method
条[棒]/條[棒],棒,槓　bar
条剂/條劑　stripe formula
条件/狀況　condition
条件刺激物/條件刺激物　conditioned stimulus
条件反射/條件反射　conditioned reflex
条件反射测听[法]/條件反射測聽[法]　conditioned reflex audiometry
条件概率/條件概率　conditional probability
条件激发病/條件激發病　conditional disease
条件溶血试验/條件溶血試驗　conditioned hemolysis test
条件性培养基/條件性培養基　conditioned culture media
条口/條口　tiaokou, ST38
条索状卵巢/條索狀卵巢　streak ovary
条纹/條紋　striation
条纹状骨肥厚/條紋狀骨肥厚　flowing hyperostosis
条纹状汗孔角化病/條紋狀汗孔角化病　striate porokeratosis
条纹状苔癣/[條]紋狀苔蘚　lichen striatus
条形斑点杂交/條形斑點雜交　slot blot hybridization
条蕈毒素/條蕈毒素,白蕈毒素　amanita toxin
条皂/塊狀皂　bar soap
条状角膜炎/條[紋]狀角膜炎　alphabet keratitis
条状鳞癣/線狀[魚]鱗癬　linear ichthyosis
条状皮肤角化病/條狀皮膚角化病,紋狀皮膚角皮症　striate keratoderma
调拌/調拌　spatulation
调变/調變　modulation
调补冲任/調補衝任　strengthening thoroughfare and conception channels
调和肝脾/調和肝脾　harmonizing liver and spleen
调和气血/調和氣血　harmonizing qi and blood
调和药/調和藥　harmonizing drug
调和营卫/調和營衛　harmonizing yingfen and weifen
调𬌗/調𬌗,咬合修正　occlusal adjustment
调剂/調劑,調合,配方　dispense, compounding
调节/調節　accommodation
调节反射/調節反射　accommodation reflex
调节幅度/調節幅度　amplitude of accommodation
调节过度/過度調節　excessive accommodation
调节基因/調節基因　regulatory gene, regulator gene
调节计/調節計　accommodatometer
调节近点/調節近點　near point of accommodation
调节痉挛/調節痙攣,調適痙攣　spasm of accommodation
调节麻痹/調節麻痺　paralysis of accommodation
调节受抑/調節受抑　cyclodamia
调节衰退/調節衰退　accommodative failure
调节性光幻视/調節性光幻視　accommodation phosphene
调节性集合/調節性集合　accommodative convergence
调节性视疲劳/調節性視疲勞,調節性眼力疲勞　accommodative asthenopia
调节性斜视/調節性斜視　accommodative squint
调节性旋转隐斜视/調節性旋轉隱斜視,調節性轉動斜視　accommodative cyclophoria
调节远点/調節遠點　far point of accommodation
调节子/調節子　regulon
调经/調經　regulating menstruation
调经论篇/調經論篇　Discussion on Regulating the Meridians
调聚物/調聚物　telomer
调理肠胃/調理腸胃　coordinating intestines and stomach
调理冲任/調理衝任　coordinating Chong and Conception Vessels
调理免疫/調理免疫,調理素免疫性　opsonic immunity
调理情欲/調理情欲　regulating emotions and desires
调理素/調理素　opsonin
调理素定量法/調理素定量法　opsonometry
调理素疗法/調理素療法　opsonotherapy
调理素学/調理素學　opsonology
调理素原/調理素原,調理素抗原質　opsonogen
调理素专家/調理素專家　opsonist
调理性粘连/調理性粘連　opsonic adherence
调理阴阳/調理陰陽　coordinating yin and yang
调理指数/調理素指數,調理係數　opsonic index
调情于中适/調情於中適　regulating emotions to a proper state
调摄心身/調攝心身　psychosomatic adjustment
调身/調身　adjustment of body
调身养神/調身養神　doing exercise to repose
调味剂/調味劑　flavoring agents

调味品/調味品　condiments
调息/調息　adjustment of breath
调心/調心　adjustment of mind
调整/調整　adjustment
调整溶液/調整溶液　adjusted solution
调整型发育/調整型發育　regulatory development
调知于中适/調知於中適　regulating cognition to a proper state
J-调制法/J-調制法　J-modulation method
调制中频电疗法/調製中頻電療法　modulated medium frequency electrotherapy
调质/調質　modulator
跳弹伤/跳彈傷　ricocheted bullet wound
跳行转移/跳行轉移　waltzing transfer
跳痛/跳痛　starting pain
跳跃进化/跳躍演化　saltatory evolution
跳跃纤维/跳躍纖維　transilient fiber
跳跃性病变/跳躍性病變　skip lesion
跳跃性舞蹈病/跳躍性舞蹈病　dancing chorea
跳跃性血栓形成/跳躍性血栓形成　jumping thrombosis
跳跃运动/跳躍運動　jumping exercise
跳蚤/跳蚤　flea
跳蚤叮咬/跳蚤叮咬　flea bite
贴标签/貼標籤　labeling
贴棉法/貼棉法　burning cotton method, cotton fire cupping
贴片/貼片　paster
萜/萜　terpene
萜类/萜類　terpenoid
萜类生物碱/萜類生物鹼　terpenoid alkaloid
萜品醇/萜品醇, 松脂醇, 松香醇　terpineol
萜中毒/萜中毒　terpenism
铁螯合剂/鐵螯合劑　iron chelating agent
铁卟啉蛋白/鐵卟啉蛋白　iron porphyrin protein
铁超负荷/鐵超負荷　iron overload
铁尘肺/鐵塵肺, 鐵屑沈著病　pneumoconiosis siderotica
铁沉着肝/鐵[沉著]肝　iron liver
铁代谢障碍/鐵代謝障礙　iron metabolism disorders
铁蛋白/鐵蛋白　ferritin
铁笛丸/鐵笛丸　tiedi pill
铁放射性同位素/鐵放射性同位素　iron radioisotope
铁粉/鐵粉　iron powder
铁化合物/鐵化合物　iron compounds
铁剂疗法/鐵[劑]療法　ferrotherapy
铁结合蛋白质类/鐵結合蛋白質類　iron-binding proteins

铁粒幼细胞性贫血/鐵粒幼細胞性貧血　sideroblastic anemia
铁硫蛋白/鐵硫蛋白　iron-sulfur protein
铁硫蛋白质类/鐵硫蛋白質類　iron-sulfur proteins
铁尿病/鐵尿病　siderinuria
铁氰化物/鐵氰化物　ferricyanides
铁缺乏[症]/鐵缺乏　asiderosis
铁色皮[症]/鐵色[皮]病, 皮膚鐵色病　sideroderma
铁杉/鐵杉　hemlock
铁石棉/鐵石棉　amosite asbestos
铁苏木精染剂/鐵蘇木精染劑, 鐵蘇木素　iron hematoxylin
铁调节蛋白质类/鐵調節蛋白質類　iron-regulatory proteins
铁同位素/鐵同位素　iron isotopes
铁线虫病/鐵線蟲病　gordiasis
铁线莲属/鐵線蓮屬　*Clematis*
铁屑检查听音器/鐵屑檢查聽音器　siderophone
铁锈色[样]痰/鐵銹色[樣]痰, 銹色痰　rusty sputum
铁絮状反应/鐵絮狀反應, 鐵抗原絮凝作用　ferroflocculation
铁血黄素沉着病/鐵血黃素沉著病, 含鐵血紅素沈積症　haemosiderosis
铁盐/鐵鹽　iron salt
铁氧化还原蛋白/鐵氧化還原蛋白, 光化鐵蛋白　ferredoxin
铁右旋糖酐复合物/鐵右旋糖酐複合物　iron-dextran complex
铁载体/鐵載體　siderophores
铁质沉着性脾肉芽肿病/鐵質沈著性脾肉芽腫病　splenogranulomatosis siderotica
铁[质]缺乏/鐵質缺乏　sideropenia
呫吨类/呫噸類　xanthenes
听齿/聽齒　auditory teeth of Huschke
听辐射/聽輻射　acoustic radiation, auditory radiation
听宫/聽宮　tinggong, SI19
听骨肌/聽骨肌　muscle of auditory ossicles
听骨链成形术/聽小骨成形術　ossiculoplasty
听骨韧带/聽骨韌帶　ligament of auditory ossicles
听幻觉/聽幻覺, 幻聽　pseudacousis
听会/聽會　tinghui, GB2
听[基]板/耳基板　otic placode
听崤/聽崤　acoustic crest
听结节/聽結節　acoustic tubercle
听觉/聽覺　sense of hearing
听觉不良/聽覺不良　dysacousia
听觉迟钝/聽覺遲鈍, 弱聽　amblyacousia
听觉反射/聽覺反射　acoustic reflex

听觉过敏/聽覺過敏　hyperacusis
听觉减退/聽覺減退,聽覺遲鈍　acoustic hypoesthesia
听觉皮质/聽[覺]皮質　auditory cortex
听觉疲劳/聽覺疲勞　auditory fatigue
听觉区域/聽覺區域,聽區　auditory area
听觉丧失/聽覺喪失,失聰,聾　hearing loss
听觉失认[症]/聽覺缺失症　auditory agnosia
听觉通路/聽覺通路　auditory pathway
听觉先兆/聽覺性先兆　auditory aura
听觉性健忘[症]/聽覺性健忘[症],音記憶不能　acousmatamnesia
听觉性失语[症]/聽覺性失語[症],聽性失語症　acoustic aphasia, auditory aphasia
听[觉性书]写不能/聽寫不能　acoustic agraphia
听觉诱发电位/聽覺誘發電位　auditory evoked potential
听觉语音/聽覺語音,語響　vocal resonance
听觉障碍/聽覺障礙　auditory perceptual disorder
听觉中枢/聽覺中樞　auditory center, acoustic center
听叩诊/聽叩診　auscultatory percussion
听力/聽[覺]　hearing
听力测验法/聽力測驗法　acoumetry
听力级/聽力級,聽力程度　hearing level
听力检查/聽力檢查　hearing test
听力受损者/聽力受損者　hearing impaired person
听力图/聽力圖,聽力記錄單　audiogram
听力学/聽力學　audiology
听力障碍/聽力障礙　hearing disorder
听力障碍康复/聽力障礙康復　rehabilitation of hearing impaired
听脉血压计/聽脈血壓計,聽力測壓器　sphygmometroscope
听毛/聽毛　auditory hairs
听毛细胞/聽毛細胞　acoustic hair cell
听泡/耳囊　otic vesicle
听泡壁/聽胞壁　periotic wall
听器/聽器　acoustic apparatus
听球/聽球　auditory bulb
听神经/聽神經　auditory nerve
听神经核/聽神經核　auditory nucleus
听神经瘤/聽神經瘤　acoustic nerve tumor
听神经[神经]鞘瘤/聽神經鞘瘤　acoustic schwannoma
听神经纤维瘤/聽神經纖維瘤　acoustic neurofibromatosis
听神经中央束/聽神經中央束　central tract of auditory nerve
听声音/聽聲音　listening
听石探杆/聽石探桿,檢石聲器　lithophone
听视触觉刺激/聽視觸覺刺激　audio-visual-tactile stimulation
听束/聽束　auditory tract
听窝/聽窩,聽碟　auditory saucer
听细胞/聽細胞　auditory cell
听弦/聽弦　auditory string
听小骨/聽小骨　auditory ossicles, phonophore
听小骨关节/聽小骨關節　joints of auditory ossicles, articulations of auditory ossicles
听小骨肌/聽小骨肌　muscles of auditory ossicles
听小骨假体/聽小骨假體　ossicular prosthesis
听小骨切除术/聽小骨切除術　ossiculectomy
听小骨切开术/聽小骨切開術　ossiculotomy
听小骨韧带/聽小骨韌帶　ligaments of auditory ossicles
听小骨置换/聽小骨置換　ossicular replacement
听[性]脑干反应/聽[性]腦幹反應　auditory brainstem response
听性强直/聽性強直　acoustic tetanus
听野/聽野,聽[覺]界　auditory field
听音不能/聽音不能　asonia
听音叩诊/聽音叩診　auditory percussion
听音转眼反射/聽音轉眼反射　audito-oculogyric reflex
听语遗忘/聽語遺忘,聽覺性健忘　auditory amnesia
听域下频率/聽閾下頻率　subsonic frequency
听阈/聽閾　auditory threshold
听阈级/聽閾級　hearing threshold level
听诊/聽診[法]　auscultation
听诊录音机/聽診錄音機,聽診答錄機　phonostethograph
听诊器/聽診器　stethoscopes
听诊器检查/聽診器檢法　stethoscopy
听诊三角/聽診三角　triangle of auscultation
听诊无音间隙/聽診[無音間]隙,無音隙　auscultatory gap
听诊音过强/聽診音過強,聲音過強　hyperechema
烃类/烴類　hydrocarbons
烃类基质/烴類基劑　hydrocarbon base
烃液/烴液　hydrocarbonous fluid
烃油/烴油,白色油狀烴　hydrocarbon oil
廷德尔光/廷德爾光,泰德爾氏光　Tyndall light
廷孔/廷孔　vaginal orifice
停经/停經　suppressed menstruation
停经后前额纤维化秃发/停經後前額纖維化禿髮　postmenopause frontal fibrosing alopecia

停药综合征/停藥症候群　withdrawal syndrome
停饮/停飲　stagnant fluid retention
停止/停止　stop
停滞的/停滯的,静止的　stationary
葶苈子/葶藶子　tansymustard seed, pepperweed seed
挺舌/挺舌　tongue thrust
艇角/艇角　tingjiao, angle of superior concha, CO8
艇中/艇中　tingzhong, center of superior concha
通鼻/通鼻　relieving stuffy nose, unblocking stuffy nose
通草/通草　ricepaperplant pith
通畅引流法/通暢引流法　free drainage
通道/通道,管道,路　channel, passage
通道区/通道區　confined space
通道细胞/通道細胞　passage cell
通电期间强直/通電期間強直,持久強直,連續強直　duration tetany
通耳/通耳　improving hearing, unblocking stuffy ear
通腑排脓/通腑排膿　catharsis and expelling pus
通关散/通關散　tongguan powder
通贯型/通貫型　simple crease
通剂/通劑　obstruction-removing formula
通经/通經　promoting menstruation
通经药/通經藥,調經藥　emmenagogue
通睛/通睛　concomitant esotropia, crosseye
通睛·禀赋不足证/通睛·禀賦不足證　crosseye with constitutional insufficiency pattern
通睛·经络挛滞证/通睛·經絡攣滯證　crosseye with pattern of channel-collateral spasm and stagnation
通里/通里　tongli, HT5
通络下乳/通絡下乳　dredging collateral for promoting lactation
通气不足/換氣不足　hypoventilation
通气分布不均/通氣分布不均　maldistribution of ventilation
通气-灌注肺扫描/換氣-灌注肺掃描　ventilation-perfusion lung scanning
通气机/通氣機,通氣器,換氣筒　ventilator
通气机撤除法/通氣機撤除法　ventilator weaning
通气量/通氣量　air flow
通气试验/通氣試驗　ventilation test
通气与血流灌注比值/通氣與血流灌注比值　ventilation/perfusion ratio
通气与血流灌注比值失调/通氣與血流灌注比值失調　ventilation/perfusion mismatching
通窍/通竅　unblocking stuffy orifice
通乳/通乳　lactogenesis

通乳消痈/通乳消癰　promoting lactation for resolving carbuncle
通天/通天　tongtian, BL7
通透酶/通透酶　permease
通透性/通透性　permeability
通透性增高因子/通透性增高因子　permeability increasing factor
通泄/通洩　eliminating heat-evil by purgation
通宣理肺丸/通宣理肺丸　tongxuan lifei pills
通因通用/通因通用　treating incontinent pattern with dredging methods
通用电光[窥]镜/通用電光[窺]鏡,全能電檢器　panelectroscope
通用刮治器/通用刮治器　universal curette
通用过程术语学/通用過程術語學　current procedural terminology
通用解毒药/通用解毒藥　universal antidote
通用名药物/通用名藥物　generic drug
通用[液体]比重计/通用[液體]比重計,全能比重計　panhydrometer
通用医疗保健服务编码系统/通用醫療保健服務編碼系統　healthcare common procedure coding system
同胞/同胞　sibling
同胞关系/同胞關係　sibling relation
同胞配对法/同胞配對法　sibpair method
同胞肾移植/同胞腎移植　sibling renal transplantation
同辈效应/同輩效應,世代效應　cohort effect
同病相怜症/同病相憐症　alteregoism
同病血清/同[種]病血清　isoserum
同病异治/同病異治　treating same disease with different methods
同步搏动/同步搏動　synchronous pulsation
同步化/同步化　synchronization
同步加速器/同步加速器　synchrotron
同步间歇强制通气/同步間歇強制通氣　synchronous intermittent mandatory ventilation
同步起搏/同步起搏,同步調整　synchronous pacing
同步起搏器/[心臟]同步起搏器　synchronous pacemaker
同步心室辅助/同步心室輔助　synchronized ventricular assistance
同侧偏利/同側偏利　dominant laterality
同侧偏盲/同側偏盲　homonymous hemianopsia
同侧细胞/同側細胞　tautomeral cell
同侧性复视/同側[性]複視　direct diplopia
同侪集群/同儕集群　peer group

同等[辐射]量/同等輻射量　isodose
同等位基因/同等位基因　isoallele
同端吸盘虫病/同端吸盤蟲病,副雙口吸蟲病　paramphistomiasis
同多糖/同多醣　homopolysaccharide
同分异构[体]/同分異構[物]　isomer
同功酶/同功酶　isozyme
同功能物质/同功能物質　isotelic substance
同功凝固酶/同功凝固酶　isocoagulase
同核体/同核體　homokaryon
同化激素类/同化激素類　anabolic hormones
同化剂/同化劑　anabolic agents
同基因骨髓移植/同基因骨髓移植　isogeneic bone marrow transplantation
同基因移植/同基因移植　syngeneic transplantation
同基因移植物/同基因移植物　syngeneic graft
同晶型/同晶型　isomorphism
同聚物/同聚物　homopolymer
同类系/同類系　congenic strain
同龄人/同齡人　age cohort
同名经配穴法/同名經配穴法　combination of points of namesake channels, combination of points of namesake meridians
同盘吸虫属/同盤吸蟲屬　*Paramphistomum*
同配生殖/同配生殖　homogamy
同期复孕/同期複孕　superfecundation
同期胰肾联合移植/同期胰腎聯合移植　simultaneous pancreas and renal transplantation
同期遗传/同期遺傳　homochronous inheritance
同三晶形/同三晶形　isotrimorphism
同身寸/同身寸　body cun, proportional unit of body
同渗容摩/同滲容摩　osmolarity
同时的/同時的,并行的　concurrent
同时感染/同時感染　coinfection
同时视/同時視　simultaneous perception
同时新生/同時新生　synkainogenesis
同时兴奋/同時興奮　coexcitation
同视机/同視器,合視器　synoptophore
同属移植/同屬移植　isoplastic transplantation
同属移植片/同屬移植片　isoplastic graft
同素异形胶体/同素異形膠體　allocolloid
同素异形体/同素異形體　allotrope
同位素/同位素　isotope
同位素标记/同位素標記　isotope labeling
同位素二重稀释法/同位素二重稀釋法　double isotope dilution method
同位素分离器/同位素[電磁]分離器　isotron
同位素示踪/同位素示蹤,同位素標蹤　isotopic tracing
同位素效应/同位素效應　isotope effect
同位素学/同位素學　isotopology
同位痛/同位痛　homotopic pain
同位移植/同位移植　homotopic transplantation
同窝/同窩　brood
同系[化合]物/同系[化合]物　homologen
同系移植物/同系移植物,同種形成移植物　isogeneic graft
同线性/同線性　synteny
同向重复[序列]/同向重複[序列]　direct repeat
同向偏斜/同向偏斜,共軛偏向,共同偏向　conjugate deviation
同向性病毒/同向性病毒　ecotropic virus
同效维生素/同效維生素,擬維生素　vitamer
同心板/同心板　concentric lamella
同心的/同心的　concentric
同心发癣菌/同心髮癬菌,疊瓦毛癬菌　Trichophyton concentricum
同心曲霉/同心麴黴　Aspergillus concentricus
同心性萎缩/同心性萎縮　concentric atrophy
同心性血管周围肌瘤/同心性血管周圍肌瘤　concentric perivascular myoma
同心性[子宫]纤维瘤/同心性纖維瘤　concentric fibroma
同形孢子/同形孢子　homospore
同形反应/同形反應　isomorphic response
同形结合/同形接合,同式結合　isogame
同形配子/同形配[偶]子,同式配子　isogamete, homogamete
同形配子产生/同形配子產生　isogamety
同形现象/同形現象　isomorphic phenomenon
同形小配子/同形小配子,同式小配偶子　isomicrogamete
同形新生/同形新生,同形產生　homomorphosis
同形杂种/同形雜種　isophan
同型/同型,同範　homotype
同型变异/同型變異　isotypic variation
同型胱氨酸尿性白内障/同型胱胺酸尿性白內障　homocystinuria cataract
同型种/同型種　phenon
同性恋/同性戀[愛],同性性欲　homosexuality
同性恋者/同性戀者　homosexual
同性性早熟/同性性早熟　isosexual precocious puberty
同血统移植法/同源移植法　syngenesioplastic transplantation
同血统移植术/同血统移植法,同源移植法

syngenesiotransplantation
同源病/同源病　congenerous disease
同源重组/同源重組　homologous recombination
同源动物/同源動物　congenic animal
同源多倍体/同源多倍體,自體多套染色體　autopolyploid
同源多倍性/同源多倍性,自體多套染色體性　autopolyploidy
同源二倍体/同源二倍體,自體雙套染色體　autodiploid
同源二倍性/同源二倍性,自體雙套染色體狀態　autodiploidy
同源节律/同源節律,原地節律　homogenetic rhythm
同源框/同源框　homoeobox
同源框基因/同源框基因　homoeobox gene
同源框顺序/同源框順序　homoeobox sequence
同源疗法/同源療法,同種病質療法　isopathy
同源片段/同源片段　homologous fragment
同源区/同源區　homology region
同源染色体/同源染色體　homologous chromosome
同源体/同源體　autoploid
同源物/同源物　congener
同源细胞群/同源細胞群　isogenous group
同源性/同源性　homology
同源性抗原/同源性抗原,同種抗原　homologous antigen
同源性皮炎/同源性皮[膚]炎　clonal dermatitis
同源血管床/同源血管床　cognate vascular bed
同源异形/同源異形　homoeosis
同源异形突变体/同源異形突變體　homoeotic mutant
同源[异型]框/同源[異型]框,同源盒　homeobox
同支吻合术/同支吻合術　homocladic anastomosis
同质刺激/同種刺激　isostimulation
同质性疾病/同質性疾病　homologous disease
同质异晶体/同質異晶體　paramorph
同质异晶[现象]/同質異晶　paramorphism
同质异形[现象]/同質異形[現象]　dysmorphism
同种白细胞凝集素/同種白細胞凝集素　isoleucoagglutinin
同种刺激法/同種刺激法　homostimulation
同种刺激剂/同種刺激劑　homostimulant
同种毒素/同種毒素,同族毒素　homoiotoxin
同种肺氧合/同種肺氧合　homologous lung oxygenation
同种骨成形术/同種骨成形術,同質骨造形術　homeo-osteoplasty
同种过敏反应/同種過敏反應,同種過敏性　homologous anaphylaxis
同种精子毒素/同種精子毒素　isospermotoxin
同种抗体/同種抗體　isoantibodies
同种抗原/同種抗體原　isoantigen
同种免疫/同種[異體]免疫　alloimmunity
同种凝集素/同種凝集素　isoagglutinin
同种气管置换术/同種氣管置換術　tracheal homograft replacement
同种溶解/同種[組織]溶解　homolysis
同种溶素/同種溶素　homolysin
同种溶细胞素/同種溶細胞素　isocytolysine
同种肾毒素/同種腎毒素　isonephrotoxin
同种生物/同種生物　conspecific
同种物/同種物　isoplassont
同种细胞毒素/同種細胞毒素　isocytotoxin
同种心脏瓣膜/同種心臟瓣膜　homologous cardiac valve
同种型/同型　isotype
同种血清/同種血清　homologous serum
同[种]血清型/同種血清型　homologous serotype
同种血清性肝炎/同種血清性肝炎　homologous serum hepatitis
同种血清性黄疸/同種血清性黄疸　homologous serum jaundice
同种牙移植术/同種牙移植術　homotransplantation of tooth
同种移植/同種移植　homologous transplantation, homoplastic transplantation
同种移植物/同種移植物　homeograft
同种移植物反应/同種移植物反應　homograft reaction
同种异基因/同種異基因　allogene
同种异基因效应/同種異基因效應　allogenic effect
同种异基因抑制作用/同種異基因抑制作用,同種抑制　allogenic inhibition
同种异体抗原/同種異體抗原　allotypic antigen
同种异体皮肤移植/同種異體皮膚移植　allogenic skin graft
同种异体移植物/同種異體移植物　allogenic graft
同种异体移植物反应/同種[異體]移植物反應　allograft reaction
同种异体组织不相容性/同種異體組織不相容性　allohistoincompatibility
同种异体组织相容性/同種異體組織相容性　allohistocompatibility
同种异型/同種異型　allotype
同种异型标记/同種異體標記　allotypic marker
同种异型决定簇/同種異型決定簇　allotypic

determinant
同种异型位/同種異型位,異位點 allotope
同种组织移植/同種組織移植 allogenic transplantation
同轴针电极/同軸針電極 coaxial needle electrode
桐油中毒/桐油中毒 tung oil poisoning
铜/銅 copper
铜毒性绞痛/銅毒性絞痛,銅工絞痛 copper colic
铜放射性同位素/銅放射性同位素 copper radioisotope
铜肥皂试验/銅肥皂試驗 copper soap test
铜宫内避孕器/銅宮內避孕器 copper intrauterine device
铜汞合金/銅汞合金 copper amalgam
铜绿假单胞菌/銅綠假單胞菌,綠膿桿菌 Pseudomonas aeruginosa
铜酶/銅酶 copper enzyme
铜黏固剂/銅黏固粉 copper cement
铜刨花/銅刨花 copper turning
铜圈/銅圈 copper band
铜丝动脉/銅絲動脈 copper-wire artery
铜锈/銅銹 aerugo
铜血症/銅血症 cupremia
铜针疗法/銅針療法 copper needle therapy
铜蒸气激光器/銅蒸氣激光器,銅蒸氣雷射 copper vapor laser
铜中毒/銅中毒 copper poisoning
童声/童聲 puberphonia
童样痴呆/童樣癡呆 puerilism
酮/酮 ketone
酮病/酮病 ketosis
酮醇/酮醇 ketone alcohol
酮胆固醇类/酮膽固醇類,酮膽甾醇類 ketocholesterols
酮胆烷酸/酮烷膽酸 ketocholanic acid
酮丁糖/酮丁糖 ketotetrose
酮咯酸/酮咯酸 ketorolac
酮咯酸氨丁三醇/酮咯酸氨丁三醇 ketorolac tromethamine
酮过多/酮過多 hyperketosis
酮基化[作用]/酮基化[作用],酮化 ketonization
酮康唑/酮康唑 ketoconazole
酮类/酮類 ketones
酮洛芬/酮洛芬 ketoprofen
酮内酯类抗生素/酮內酯類抗生素 ketolides
酮尿[症]/酮尿 ketonuria
酮醛/酮醛 keto-aldehyde
酮色林/酮色林 ketanserin

酮四氢菲/酮四氫菲 keto-tetrahydrophenanthrene
酮酸/酮酸 keto acid
酮酸疗法/酮酸療法 keto acid therapy
酮酸裂解酶/酮酸裂解酶,酮酸溶解酶 keto acid-lyase
酮酸中毒/酮酸中毒 ketoacidosis
酮糖/酮醣 ketose
酮糖尿/酮醣尿 ketosuria
酮体类/酮體類 ketone bodies
酮体生成/酮生成 ketoplasia
酮替芬/酮替芬 ketotifen
酮肟/酮肟 ketoxime
酮戊二酸类/酮戊二酸類 ketoglutaric acids
酮戊二酸脱氢酶复合物/酮戊二酸脫氫酶複合物 ketoglutarate dehydrogenase complex
酮血[症]/酮血症 ketonemia
酮亚胺/酮亞胺 ketimine
酮氧化还原酶类/酮氧化還原酶類 ketone oxidoreductases
酮硬脂酸/酮硬脂酸 ketostearic acid
酮甾类/酮甾類 ketosteroid
瞳间线/瞳間線 interpupillary line
瞳孔/瞳孔 pupil
瞳孔闭锁/瞳孔閉鎖 seclusion of pupil
瞳孔变形/瞳孔變形,瞳孔異常 discoria
瞳孔测量[法]/瞳孔測量法 pupillometry
瞳孔齿轮样运动/瞳孔齒輪樣運動 cogwheel movement of pupil
瞳孔大小不等/瞳孔大小不等 anisocoria
瞳孔等大/瞳孔等大,等徑瞳孔 isocoria
瞳孔对光反应/瞳孔對光反應 reaction of pupil to light
瞳孔反射/瞳孔反射 pupillary reflex
瞳孔反应迟钝/瞳孔反應遲鈍 asthenocoria
瞳孔反应消失/瞳孔反應消失 pupillatonia
瞳孔畸形/瞳孔畸形 deformed pupil
瞳孔计/瞳孔計 pupillometer
瞳孔检影法/瞳孔檢影法,視網膜鏡檢法 coroscopy
瞳孔紧张症/瞳孔緊張症,瞳孔強直性反應 pupillotonia
瞳孔镜/瞳孔鏡 pupilloscope
瞳孔距离/瞳間距,眼間距 interpupillary distance
瞳孔距离测量尺/瞳孔距離測量尺 interpupillary distance rule
瞳孔距离计/瞳孔距離計 interpupillary gauge
瞳孔开大/瞳孔擴大,瞳孔散大 platycoria
瞳孔开大肌/瞳孔開大肌 dilator pupillae, dilator muscle of pupil, dilator pupillae muscle

瞳孔扩大/瞳孔擴大　dilatation of pupil
瞳孔扩大肌/瞳孔擴大肌　pupil dilatator muscle
瞳孔括约肌/瞳孔括約肌　sphincter pupillae
瞳孔描记器/瞳孔描記器,瞳孔記錄儀　pupillograph
瞳孔膜/瞳孔膜　pupillary membrane
瞳孔膜闭/瞳孔膜閉,瞳孔遮閉,瞳孔閉合　occlusion of pupil
瞳孔膜存留/瞳孔膜存留,永存性瞳孔膜　persistent pupillary membrane
瞳孔旁移术/瞳孔旁移術,瞳孔遷移術,遷瞳術　coroparelcysis
瞳孔散大/瞳孔散大　mydriasis
瞳孔散缩图/瞳孔[散縮]圖　pupillogram
瞳孔失调/瞳孔失調　pupil disorder
瞳孔缩小/瞳孔縮小　miosis
瞳孔狭小/瞳孔狹小　stenocoriasis
瞳孔狭窄/瞳孔狹窄　corestenoma
瞳孔形成/瞳孔形成,假瞳術　coremorphosis
瞳孔药效试验/瞳孔藥效試驗　pupillary pharmacodynamic test
瞳孔异位/瞳孔異位　ectopia pupillae
瞳孔缘/瞳孔緣　pupillary margin
瞳孔阻滞/瞳孔阻滯　pupillary block
瞳神/瞳神,瞳孔　pupil
瞳神病/瞳神病　pupil disease
瞳神干缺/瞳神乾缺　dry defective pupil, pupillary metamorphosis
瞳神干缺·肝胆实热证/瞳神乾缺·肝膽實熱證　dry defective pupil with pattern of liver-gallbladder excessive heat
瞳神干缺·肝肾阴虚证/瞳神乾缺·肝腎陰虛證　dry defective pupil with liver-kidney yin deficiency pattern
瞳神干缺·脾肾阳虚证/瞳神乾缺·脾腎陽虛證　dry defective pupil with spleen-kidney yang deficiency pattern
瞳神紧小/瞳神緊小　contracted pupil, iridocyclitis, papillary seclusion
瞳神紧小·风湿夹热证/瞳神緊小·風濕夾熱證　contracted pupil with pattern of wind-dampness complicated by heat
瞳神紧小·肝胆实热证/瞳神緊小·肝膽實熱證　contracted pupil with pattern of liver-gallbladder excessive heat
瞳神紧小·肝经风热证/瞳神緊小·肝經風熱證　contracted pupil with pattern of wind-heat in liver channel
瞳神紧小·阴虚火旺证/瞳神緊小·陰虛火旺證　contracted pupil with pattern of yin deficiency and fire effulgence
瞳神散大/瞳神散大　enlarged pupil, mydriasis
瞳神欹侧/瞳神欹側　pupil deformation and dislocation, pupillary metamorphosis due to anterior synechia
瞳子髎/瞳子髎　tongziliao, GB1
统计质量控制/統計質量控制,統計品管　statistical quality control, SQC
统计资料说明/統計資料說明　statistical data interpretation
统一医学语言系统/統一醫學語言系統　unified medical language system
桶柄状骨折/桶柄狀骨折　bucket-handle fracture
桶状胸/桶狀胸　barrel-shaped thorax
筒箭毒碱/筒箭毒鹼　tubocurarine
筒线虫病/筒線蟲病　gongylonemiasis
筒状乳房/筒狀乳房　cylindrical breast
痛/痛　pain
痛痹/痛痺　painful bi, arthralgia aggravated by cold, arthralgia caused by cold pathogen
痛风/痛風　gout
痛风·肝肾阴虚证/痛風·肝腎陰虛證　gout with pattern of liver-kidney yin deficiency
痛风虹膜炎/尿酸性虹膜炎,痛風性虹膜炎　uratic iritis
痛风尿/痛風[性]尿　gouty urine
痛风肾病/痛風腎病　gouty nephropathy
痛风·湿热[蕴结]证/痛風·濕熱[蘊結]證　gout with pattern of accumulation and binding of damp-heat
痛风石/痛風石　gouty tophi
痛风石痛风/痛風石痛風　tophaceous gout
痛风·痰浊阻滞证/痛風·痰濁阻滯證　gout with pattern of blockade of phlegm-turbidity
痛风体质/痛風體質　gouty diathesis
痛风性关节炎/痛風性關節炎　gouty arthritis
痛风性溃疡/痛風[性]潰瘍　gouty ulcer
痛风性尿道炎/痛風性尿道炎　gouty urethritis
痛风性舌痛/痛風性舌痛　glottagra
痛风饮食/痛風飲食　gout diet
痛风·瘀热阻滞证/痛風·瘀熱阻滯證　gout with pattern of blockade of static blood and heat
痛经/痛經　dysmenorrhea, painful menstruation
痛经·肝肾两虚证/痛經·肝腎兩虛證　dysmenorrhea with pattern of deficiency of both liver and kidney
痛经·寒湿凝滞证/痛經·寒濕凝滯證　dysmenorrhea with pattern of stagnation and congelation of cold-damp

痛经·气血两虚证/痛經·氣血兩虛證 dysmenorrhea with pattern of deficiency of both qi and blood
痛经·气滞血瘀证/痛經·氣滯血瘀證 dysmenorrhea with pattern of qi stagnation and blood stasis
痛经·湿热瘀阻证/痛經·濕熱瘀阻證 dysmenorrhea with pattern of blockade of damp-heat and static blood
痛经·阳虚内寒证/痛經·陽虛內寒證 dysmenorrhea with pattern of yang deficiency and internal cold
痛觉/痛覺 sense of pain
痛觉测验法/痛覺測量法 algometry
痛觉过敏/痛覺過敏 hyperalgesia
痛觉计/痛覺計 algesimeter
痛觉减退/痛覺減退 hypalgesia
痛觉缺失/痛覺缺失,無痛 analgia
痛觉神经/痛覺神經 pain nerve
痛觉时间计/痛覺時間計 algesichronometer
痛痛病/痛痛病 itai-itai disease
痛无定处/痛無定處 migratory pain
痛泻要方/痛瀉要方 tongxieyao formula
痛性非化脓性肋软骨肿胀/痛性非化膿性肋軟骨腫脹 painful nonsuppurative swelling of costal cartilage
痛性感觉缺失/痛性感覺缺失,痛性麻木 anesthesia dolorosa
痛性痉挛/痛性痙攣 cramp
痛性排尿/痛性排尿,排尿疼痛 alginuresis
痛性牵连感觉/痛性牽連感覺 synesthesialgia
痛性眼肌麻痹综合征/痛性眼肌麻痺症候群 Tolosa-Hunt syndrome
痛性营养障碍/痛性營養障礙,痛性失養症 algodystrophy
痛性脂肪病/痛性脂肪病,痛性肥胖病 adiposis dolorosa
痛性脂肪突出/痛性脂肪突出 painful fat herniation
痛压测验法/痛壓測驗法,痛壓度計 palpatometry
痛有定处/痛有定處 fixed pain
痛阈/痛閾 pain threshold
痛足综合征/痛足症候群,足痛症候群 feet painful syndrome
偷窃恐怖/偷竊恐怖,竊盜恐懼症 cleptophobia
偷窃狂/竊[盜]癖,竊癖者 kleptomania
头/頭[部] head, caput
头半棘肌/頭半棘肌 semispinalis capitis, musculus semispinalis capitis
头孢氨苄/頭孢氨苄 cefalexin, cephalexin
头孢呋辛/頭孢呋辛 cefuroxime
头孢哌酮/頭孢哌酮 cefoperazone

头孢磺啶/頭孢磺啶 cefsulodin
头孢甲肟/頭孢甲肟 cefmenoxime
头孢菌病/頭孢菌病 cephalosporiosis
头孢菌属/頭胞菌屬 Cephalosporium
头孢菌素抗药性/頭孢菌素抗藥性 cephalosporin resistance
头孢菌素类/頭孢菌素類 cephalosporins
头孢菌素酶/頭孢菌素酶,頭孢菌素酵素 cephalosporinase
头孢克洛/頭孢克洛 cefaclor
头孢克肟/頭孢克肟 cefixime
头孢拉啶/頭孢拉啶 cephradine
头孢来星/頭孢來星,先鋒黴素Ⅲ,頭孢菌格來新 cephaloglycin
头孢霉属/頭孢黴屬 Cephalosporium
头孢美唑/頭孢美唑 cefmetazole
头孢孟多/頭孢孟多 cefamandole
头孢尼西/頭孢尼西 cefonicid
头孢匹林/頭孢匹林 cephapirin
头孢羟氨苄/頭孢羥氨苄 cefadroxil
头孢曲嗪/頭孢曲嗪 cefatrizine
头孢曲松/頭孢曲鬆 ceftriaxone
头孢噻啶/頭孢噻啶,先鋒黴素Ⅱ,頭孢子菌利定 cephaloridine
头孢噻吩/頭孢噻吩,先鋒黴素Ⅰ,頭孢菌新素 cephalothin
头孢噻肟/頭孢噻肟 cefotaxime
头孢他啶/頭孢他啶 ceftazidime
头孢体/頭孢體,頭孢蟲 cephalont
头孢替安/頭孢替安 cefotiam
头孢替坦/頭孢替坦 cefotetan
头孢西丁/頭孢西丁,孢菌素 cefoxitin
头孢乙腈/頭孢乙腈 cephacetrile
头孢唑林/頭孢唑林 cefazolin
头孢唑肟/頭孢唑肟 ceftizoxime
头臂动脉/頭臂動脈,頭肱動脈 brachiocephalic artery
头臂干/頭臂幹 brachiocephalic trunk
头臂静脉/頭臂靜脈 brachiocephalic vein
头臂缺血/頭臂[局部]缺血 brachiocephalic ischemia
头不全畸胎/頭不全畸胎 paracephalus
头不全无上肢畸胎/頭不全無上肢畸胎,無頭臂有肩畸胎 omacephalus
头不全胸部寄生胎/頭不全胸部寄生胎,頭不全之胸連畸胎 thoracoparacephalus
头部/頭[部] head
头部绷带法/頭部繃帶法 head bandaging
头[部]病/頭[部]病 cephalopathy

头部倒经/頭部倒經 cephalomenia
头部防护装置/頭部防護裝置 head protective devices
头部过短[症]/頭部過短症 hyperbrachycephaly
头部寄生胎/頭部寄生胎 cephalopagus parasiticus
头部寄生肢畸胎/頭部寄生肢畸胎,頭肢畸胎 cephalomelus
头部联胎/頭部連胎 cephalodymus
头部联胎畸形/頭部連胎畸形 cephalodymia
头部毛囊周围炎/頭部毛囊周圍炎 perifolliculitis capitis
头部内伤/頭部內傷 internal injury of head
头部脓肿性穿掘性毛囊周围炎/膿皰成癥性頭部毛囊周圍炎 perifolliculitis capitis abscedens et suffodiens
头部破伤风/頭部破傷風 cephalic tetanus
头部完整的[畸胎]/頭部完整的,全頭的 holocephalic
头部形成/頭部形成 cephalogenesis
头部优势发育/頭部器官優勢發育 cephalization
头部运动/頭部運動 head movements
头测量器/頭測量器,測顱器 cephalometer
头长肌/頭長肌 longus scapitis
头带/頭帶 head band
头低脚高位/頭低腳高位,德臺堡氏臥位 Trendelenburg position
头低位/頭低位 head-down tilt
头顶寄生畸胎/頭頂寄生畸胎,髮部不全寄生胎 epicomus
头耳指数/耳頂指數 auriculovertical index
头发育不全畸胎/頭發育不全畸胎,篩形頭畸胎 ethmocephalus
头发/[頭]髮 hair of head
头发断裂面/頭髮斷裂面 split ends
头发移植物/頭髮移植物 hair graft
头风/頭風 intermittent headache
头风·肝肾阴虚证/頭風·肝腎陰虛證 intermittent headache with pattern of liver-kidney yin deficiency
头风·肝阳上亢证/頭風·肝陽上亢證 intermittent headache with pattern of liver yang hyperactivity
头风·气血两虚证/頭風·氣血兩虛證 intermittent headache with pattern of deficiency of both qi and blood
头风·痰浊上扰证/頭風·痰濁上擾證 intermittent headache with pattern of upward disturbance of phlegm-turbidity
头风·瘀阻脑络证/頭風·瘀阻腦絡證 intermittent headache with pattern of static blood blocking brain collateral
头高背卧位/頭高背臥位,背臥舉高位 dorsal elevated position
头沟/頭溝 cephalic groove
头固定器/頭固定器,頭支援器 cephalostat
头汗/頭汗 head sweating
头颌不全长嘴畸胎/頭頜不全長嘴畸胎,長鼻嘴并腦畸胎 stomencephalus
头后大直肌/頭後大直肌,大頭後直肌 rectus capitis posterior major
头后点/頭後點 opisthocranion
头后小直肌/小頭後直肌 rectus capitis posterior minor
头昏/眩暈 vertigo
头肌/頭肌 muscles of head
头棘肌/頭棘肌 spinalis capitis
头夹肌/頭夾肌 splenius capitis, musculus splenius capitis
头绞痛/頭絞痛 angina capitis
头巾状瘤/頭巾狀瘤 turban tumor
头颈部肿瘤/頭頸部腫瘤 head and neck neoplasms
头静脉/頭靜脈 cephalic vein
头联双胎/頭聯[雙]胎 cephalopagus, craniopagus
头裂畸胎/頭裂畸胎,裂頭[畸胎] schistocephalus
头裂[畸形]/頭裂畸形 schizocephalia
头临泣/頭臨泣 toulinqi, GB15
头颅穿刺术/頭顱穿刺術 cephalocentesis
头颅骨/頭顱[骨] skull
头颅透光试验/頭顱透光試驗 transillumination of skull
头[颅]血肿/頭血腫,頭血瘤 cephalohematoma
头帽/頭網 headgear
头帽期/頭帽期 cap phase
头霉素类/頭黴素類 cephamycins
头盆不称/頭盆不稱,胎頭與骨盆不相稱 cephalopelvic disproportion
头皮/頭皮,頭蓋 scalp
头皮白痂病/頭皮白痂病,頭皮白痂癬 witkop
头皮层间蜂窝[组]织炎/頭皮切割性蜂窩組織炎 dissecting cellulitis of scalp
头皮挫伤/頭皮挫傷 scalp contusion
头皮单纯糠疹/頭皮單純糠疹 pityriasis simplex capitis
头皮发育不全/頭皮發育不全 hypoplasia of scalp
头皮夹/頭皮夾 scalp clip
头皮糠疹/頭皮糠疹 pityriasis capitis
头皮裂伤/頭皮裂傷 scalp laceration
头皮麻木/頭皮麻木 numbness of scalp

头皮毛发瘤/頭皮毛髮瘤 pilar tumor of scalp
头皮糜烂性脓疱性皮肤病/頭皮糜爛性膿皰性皮膚病 erosive pustular dermatosis of scalp
头皮皮肤病/頭皮皮膚病 scalp dermatosis
头皮切口/頭皮切口 incision of scalp
头皮瘙痒[症]/頭皮搔癢[症] pruritus capitis
头皮湿疹/頭皮濕疹 eczema capitis
头皮撕脱/頭皮撕脱 scalp avulsion injury
头皮撕脱伤/頭皮撕脱傷 scalp avulsion
头皮缩减术/頭皮減縮手術 scalp reduction surgery
头皮痛/頭皮痛 scalp pain
头皮下气瘤/頭皮下氣瘤 extracranial pneumatocele
头皮屑/頭皮[病態脱]屑 dandruff
头皮血肿/頭皮血腫 scalp hematoma
头皮血肿抽吸术/頭皮血腫抽吸術 aspiration of hematoma of scalp
头皮针疗法/頭[皮]針療法 scalp acupuncture therapy
头气肿/頭[部]氣腫 physocephaly
头前直肌/頭前直肌 rectus capitis anterior
头窍阴/頭竅陰 touqiaoyin, GB11
头曲/頭曲 cephalic flexure
头上斜肌/頭上斜肌 obliquus capitis superior
头神经节丛/頸神經叢 cephalic ganglionated plexus
头虱病/頭蝨病 pediculosis capitis
头水囊肿/頭水囊腫 cephalhydrocele
头水肿/頭水腫 edema capitis
头索/頭索 cephalochord
头听诊器/頭聽診器 head stethoscope
头痛[病]/頭痛[病] cephalalgia, headache
头痛·风寒证/頭痛·風寒證 headache with wind-cold pattern
头痛·风热证/頭痛·風熱證 headache with wind-heat pattern
头痛·风湿证/頭痛·風濕證 headache with wind-damp pattern
头痛·肝风内动证/頭痛·肝風内動證 headache with pattern of internal stirring of liver wind
头痛·肝阳上亢证/頭痛·肝陽上亢證 headache with pattern of liver yang hyperactivity
头痛·气虚证/頭痛·氣虛證 headache with qi deficiency pattern
头痛·肾精亏虚证/頭痛·腎精虧虛證 headache with pattern of kidney essence insufficiency
头痛·食积证/頭痛·食積證 headache with food retention pattern
头痛·痰厥证/頭痛·痰厥證 headache with pattern of phlegm syncope
头痛·痰浊上扰清窍证/頭痛·痰濁上擾清竅證 headache with pattern of phlegm-turbidity disturbing clear orifices
头痛·血虚证/頭痛·血虛證 headache with blood deficiency pattern
头痛·瘀血闭阻证/頭痛·瘀血閉阻證 headache with pattern of blockade of static blood
头痛症/頭痛症 headache disorders
头突/頭突 head process
头外侧直肌/頭外側直肌 rectus capitis lateralis
头围/頭圍 head circumference
头围增长过速/頭圍增長過速 over growth of skull
头维/頭維 touwei, ST8
头尾轴/頭尾軸 cephalocaudal axis
头位产/頭位產, 露頭生產 head birth
头下骨折/頭下骨折 subcapital fracture
头下斜肌/頭下斜肌 obliquus capitis inferior
头先露/頭產式 head presentation
头项强痛/頭項強痛 rigidity of nape and headache
头项软/頭項軟 flaccidity of neck
头型/頭型 head type
头胸/頭胸 cephalothorax
头胸腹联胎/頭胸腹聯胎 cephalothoracoventropagus
头胸联胎/頭胸聯胎 cephalothoracopagus
头悬吊/頭懸吊, 頭部懸吊法 cephalic suspension
头癣/[禿]髮癬 tinea capitis
头血囊肿/頭血囊[腫] cephalhematocele
头眼反射/頭眼反射, 動眼運動反射 oculocephalogyric reflex
头摇/頭搖 head tremor
头影测量学/頭[影]測量學, 測顱學 cephalometrics
头影描绘图/頭影描繪圖, 測顱描記法 cephalometric tracing
头晕[病]/頭暈, 頭風 dizziness
头胀/頭脹 fullness in head
头褶/頭褶 cephalic fold, head fold
头震颤/頭震顫 tremor capitis
头正中静脉/頭正中静脈 median cephalic vein
头中鸣响/頭中鳴響 ringing in the head
头重/頭重 heavy sensation of head
头状骨/頭狀骨 capitate bone
头最长肌/頭最長肌 longissimus capitis
投射/投射 projection
投射技术/投射技術 projective technique
投射镜/投射器 projectoscope
投射神经/投射神經 projection nerve
投射神经元/投射神經元, 投射神經單位 projection neuron

投射束/投射徑　projection tract
投射物/投射物　missile projectile
投射纤维/投射纖維　projection fiber
投药途径/投藥途徑　drug administration route
投影[放大]器/投影器　balopticon
投影描绘器/投影描繪器　camera lucida
投影视野计/投影視野計　projection perimeter
投掷症/投擲症　ballism
骰骨/骰骨　cuboid bone
骰骨粗隆/骰骨粗隆　tuberosity of cuboid bone
骰关节面/骰[骨]關節面　cuboid articular surface
骰舟背侧韧带/骰舟背側韌帶,背側骰舟韌帶　dorsal cuboideonavicular ligament
骰舟韧带/骰舟韌帶　cubonavicular ligament
骰舟足底韧带/骰舟蹠側韌帶,足底骰舟韌帶　plantar cuboideonavicular ligament
透壁性心肌梗死/透壁性心肌梗死　transmural myocardial infarction
透关射甲/透關射甲　going through passes to reach nails, venule going through all passes to reach nail
透光法/透光法　light transmittance method
透见荧光/透見螢光　transmitted fluorescence
透镜/透鏡　lenses
透明/透明　clearing
透明变性梭状细胞瘤/透明變性梭狀細胞瘤　hyalinizing spindle cell tumor
透明层/透明層　stratum lucidum
透明带/透明帶　zona pellucida
透明带反应/透明層反應　zona reaction
透明蛋白/透明蛋白,透明質　hyalin
透明蛋白尿/透明蛋白尿,透明質尿　hyalinuria
透明蛋白原/玻明蛋白原,透明質原　hyalogen
透明度计/透明度計　diaphanometer
透明肺/透明肺　hyperlucent lung
透明隔/透明隔　septum pellucidum
透明隔板/透明隔板　lamina of septum pellucidum
透明隔后静脉/透明隔後靜脈　posterior vein of septum pellucidum
透明隔静脉/透明隔靜脈　septum pellucidum vein, vein of septum pellucidum
透明隔开窗术/透明隔開窗術　fenestration of septum pellucidum
透明隔前静脉/透明隔前靜脈　anterior vein of septum pellucidum
透明隔腔/透明隔腔　cavity of septum pellucidum
透明隔-视神经发育不良/透明隔-視神經發育不良　septo-optic dysplasia
透明管型/透明管型,透明圓柱　hyaline cast

透明化/透明化　hyalinizing
透明胶带/透明膠帶　scotch tape
透明角质颗粒/透明角質顆粒　keratohyalin granule
透明毛圆线虫/玻璃毛圓線蟲,玻璃毛狀圓蟲　Trichostrongylus vitrinus
透明毛质颗粒/透明毛質顆粒　trichohyalin granule
透明膜病/透明膜病　hyaline membrane disease
透明软骨/透明軟骨　hyaline cartilage
[透明]软骨结合/軟骨結合　Synchondrosis(拉)
透明丝孢霉病/透明絲孢黴病　hyalohyphomycosis
透明梭状细胞瘤合并巨大玫瑰结/透明梭狀細胞瘤合併巨大玫瑰結　hyalinizing spindle cell tumor with giant rosettes
透明细胞/透明細胞　clear cell
透明[细胞]癌/透明[細胞]癌,玻質狀癌　hyaline carcinoma
透明细胞汗管瘤/透明細胞汗管瘤　clear cell syringoma
透明细胞汗腺瘤/透明細胞汗腺瘤　clear cell hidradenoma
透明细胞汗腺腺瘤/透明細胞汗腺腺瘤　clear cell hidroadenoma
透明细胞肌上皮瘤/透明細胞肌上皮瘤　clear cell myoepithelioma
透明细胞棘皮瘤/透明細胞棘皮瘤　clear cell acanthoma
透明细胞肉瘤/透明細胞肉瘤　clear cell sarcoma
透明细胞腺癌/透明細胞腺癌　clear cell adenocarcinoma
透明性浆膜炎/透明性漿膜炎　hyaloserositis
透明性角膜溃疡/透明性角膜潰瘍　transparent ulcer of cornea
透明血栓/透明血栓,玻質狀血栓　hyaline thrombus
透明牙本质/透明牙[本]質　transparent dentin
透明质/透明質,透明漿　hyaloplasm
透明质酸/透明質酸　hyaluronic acid
透明质酸酶/透明質酸酶,玻尿酸酵素　hyaluronidase
透明质酸钠/玻糖醛酸鈉　sodium hyaluronate
透明质酸葡糖胺酶/透明質酸葡糖胺酶　hyaluronoglucosaminidase
透明质酸盐/透明質酸鹽,玻尿酸鹽　hyalurate
透明质酸酯/透明質酸酯,玻尿酸酯　hyalurate
透明质酸酯裂解酶/透明質酸酯溶解酶　hyaluronate lyase
透脓散/透膿散　tounong powder
透脓生肌/透膿生肌　promoting pus drainage and granulation

透皮治疗系统/經皮治療系統　transdermal therapeutic system
透热法/內热法　endothermy
透热疗法/透熱［療法］　diathermy
透热 X 射线疗法/透熱 X 射線療法　thermoradiotherapy
透热转气/透熱轉氣　clearing heat of yingfen to qifen
透射电镜/透射電鏡,透過電子顯微鏡　transmission electron microscope
透射电镜术/透射電鏡術,掃描透射電子顯微術　transmission electron microscopy
透射学/透射學　penetrology
透视镜/透視鏡,檢影屏,螢光屏　photoscope
透析/透析　dialysis
透析不平衡综合征/透析不平衡症候群　dialysis dysequilibrium syndrome
透析分流/透析分流　dialysis shunt
透析率/透析［進行速］率　dialysance
透析器/透析器　dialyzer, dialyser
透析失衡综合征/透析失衡症候群　dialysis disequilibrium syndrome
透析性骨病/透析性骨病　dialytic osteopathy
透析性联体生活/透析性連體生活　dialytic parabiosis
透析液/透析液　dialyzate, dialysate
透照灯/透照燈,透照鏡　diaphane
透照法/透照法　transillumination
透照摄影术/透照攝影術　diaphanography
凸出切平面/凸出切平面　convex incisal plane
凸颌/凸頜　prognathism
凸颏/凸頦　galoche chin
凸眼-大舌-巨人症综合征/凸眼-大舌-巨人症症候群　exophthalmos-macroglossia-gigantism syndrome
凸柱镜片/凸柱鏡片　convex cylindrical lens
秃发/禿髮　baldness
秃发恐惧症/禿髮恐懼症,懼禿症　peladophobia
突变/突變　mutation
突变蛋白质/突變蛋白［質］　mutein
突变基因/突變基因　mutant gene
突变瘤/突變瘤　progonoma
突变率/突變率　mutation rate
突变论/突變［理］論　catastrophe theory
突变频率/突變頻率　mutant frequency
突变生物合成/突變生物合成　mutabiosynthesis
突变体/突變體,突變株,變異株　mutant
突变子/突變子　muton
突出/突出,凸出,前垂　proptosis, protrusion
突触/突觸　synapse
突触传递/突觸傳遞　synaptic transmission
突触传递物质/突觸傳導物質　ad substance
突触带/突觸帶　synaptic ribbon
突触蛋白类/突觸蛋白類　synapsins
突触后部/突觸後部　postsynaptic element, postsynaptic portion
突触后成分/突觸後成分　postsynaptic element
突触后膜/突觸後膜　postsynaptic membrane
突触后染色质纽/突觸後染色質紐　auxospireme
突触间隙/突觸間隙　synaptic cleft, synaptic space
突触结/突觸結　synaptic bouton
突触膜/突觸膜　synaptic membrane
突触囊泡/突觸囊泡,突觸小泡　synaptic vesicle
突触囊泡蛋白/突觸囊泡蛋白　synaptophysin
突触前部/突觸前部　presynaptic element
突触前成分/突觸前成分　presynaptic element
突触前膜/突觸前膜　presynaptic membrane
突触前末梢/突觸前末梢　presynaptic terminal
突触前受体/突觸前受體　presynaptic receptor
突触体/突觸體　synaptosome
突触［小］泡/突觸小泡,突觸囊泡　synaptic vesicle
突触［小］球/突觸［小］球　synaptic glomerulus
突触小体/突觸小體　synaptic knob
突触学/突觸學　synaptology
突触学说/突觸學說　synaptic theory
突发性聋/突發性聾　sudden deafness
突发性听觉丧失/突發性聽覺喪失　sudden hearing loss
突破性出血/突破性出血　breakthrough bleeding
突起睛高/突起睛高　acute inflammation of orbit with protrusion of eyeball, sudden eyeball protrusion
突起睛高·风火热毒证/突起睛高·風火熱毒證　sudden eyeball protrusion with pattern of wind-fire-heat toxin
突起睛高·火毒内陷证/突起睛高·火毒內陷證　sudden eyeball protrusion with pattern of fire-toxin sinking inward
突然变异/突然變異　halmatogenesis
突然进化/突然進化,意外性進化　emergent evolution
突眼比较计/凸眼比較計,眼球凸度計　orthometer
突眼计/凸眼計,眼球凸出度量計　proptometer
突眼性甲状腺肿/凸眼性甲狀腺腫　exophthalmic goiter
突眼性甲状腺肿心动过速/凸眼甲狀腺腫性心搏快速　tachycardia strumosa exophthalmica

突眼性眼肌麻痹/凸眼性眼肌癱瘓　exophthalmic ophthalmoplegia
图表死亡率/圖表死亡率　tabular mortality
图顿巨细胞/圖頓巨細胞　Touton giant cell
图距/圖距　map distance
图距单位/圖距單位　map unit
图雷恩多发性角化病/圖雷恩多發性角化症，Touraine 氏多發性角化症　polykeratosis of Touraine
图雷纳多发角化病/圖賴納多發角化病　Touraine polykeratosis
图书缩影胶片/圖書縮影膠片，圖書影片　bibliofilm
图像分析/圖像分析　image analysis
图像分析系统/圖像分析系統　image analysis system
图像分析仪/圖像分析儀　image analyzer
图像视觉诱发电位/圖像視覺誘發電位　pattern visual evoked potential
图像视网膜电图/圖像視網膜電圖　pattern electroretinogram
图像细胞测定/圖像細胞測定　image cytometry
图像增强/圖像增強　image enhancement
图形/圖　figure
图轴描记器/圖軸描記器　axograph
图状银屑病/圖狀銀屑病，圖形牛皮癬　psoriasis figurata
徒手肌力测定/徒手肌力測定　manual muscle test
徒手取皮/徒手取皮　free-hand excision of skin graft
徒手体操/徒手體操　free-hand exercise
涂布培养/塗布培養　spread plate cultivation
涂擦法/塗擦法　illinition
涂擦剂/塗擦藥　inunctum
涂氟/塗氟　fluoridize
涂抹/塗抹，塗布　daub, painting, smearing
涂片/塗片，抹片　smear
涂片层/塗片層　smear layer
涂碳种植体/塗碳種植體　carbon coated implant
涂眼药膏法/塗眼藥膏法　application of eye ointment
涂药膏/塗藥膏　anoint, unction
涂药器/塗藥器　medicator
屠夫疣/屠夫疣　butcher wart
屠宰场湿疹/屠宰場濕疹　slaughter house eczema
土贝母/土貝母　paniculate bolbostemma
土炒/土炒　fried with earth
土耳其斯坦溃疡/土耳其斯坦潰瘍　Turkestan ulcer
土风疮/土風瘡　local wind sore, urticaria populosa
土风疮·风热犯表证/土風瘡·風熱犯表證　urticaria papulosa with pattern of wind-heat assailing exterior
土风疮·胃肠湿热证/土風瘡·胃腸濕熱證　urticaria papulosa with pattern of dampness-heat in stomach and intestine
土茯苓/土茯苓　glabrous greenbrier rhizome
土金属磷酸盐/土金屬磷酸鹽　earthy phosphate
土荆芥/土荆芥　Chenopodium ambrosioides
土荆皮/土荆皮　golden larch bark
土克水/土克水　earth restricting water
土拉菌病/土拉菌病，土拉倫斯病　tularemia
土拉菌素/土拉菌素　tularine
土拉热杆菌性结膜炎/土拉熱桿菌性結膜炎，土勒菌結膜炎　squirrel plague conjunctivitis
土霉素/土黴素　oxytetracycline
土木香/土木香　inula root
土牛膝/土牛膝　native achyranthes root
土曲霉/土麴菌　Aspergillus terreus
土壤传染/土壤傳染　soil infection
土壤杆菌属/土壤桿菌屬，農桿菌屬　*Agrobacterium*
土壤微生物/土壤微生物　soil microorganism
土壤污染物/土壤汙染物　soil pollutant
土生金/土生金　earth generating metal
土形人/土形人　earth-phase person
土样舌/土狀舌苔　earthy tongue
土爰稼穑/土爰稼穡　earth characterized by sowing and reaping
吐虫/吐蟲　helminthemesis
吐法/吐法　emesis method
吐粪/吐糞　stercoraceous vomiting
吐根/吐根　ipecac
吐根酸/吐根酸　ipecacuanhic acid
吐蛔/吐蛔　vomiting ascaris
吐酒石疗法/吐酒石療法　tartarization
吐舌/吐舌　protruding tongue, wagging tongue
吐舌习惯/吐舌習慣　tongue thrusting
吐瘦/吐瘦，嘔吐性萎縮　emetatrophia
吐酸/吐酸，胃酸逆流　acid regurgitation
吐酸·寒证/吐酸·寒證　acid regurgitation with cold pattern
吐酸·热证/吐酸·熱證　acid regurgitation with heat pattern
吐痰/吐痰，噴液　spitting
吐泻药/吐瀉藥　emetocathartic
吐血/吐血　hematemesis
吐血·暴食伤胃证/吐血·暴食傷胃證　hematemesis with pattern of crapulence injuring stomach
吐血[病]/吐血[病]，嘔血　hematemesis
吐血·肝火犯胃证/吐血·肝火犯胃證　hematemesis

with pattern of liver fire invading stomach
吐血·肝胃阴虚证/吐血·肝胃陰虛證　hematemesis with pattern of yin deficiency of liver and stomach
吐血·脾不统血证/吐血·脾不統血證　hematemesis with pattern of failure of spleen to control blood
吐血·胃火炽盛证/吐血·胃火熾盛證　hematemesis with pattern of blazing stomach fire
吐血涎症/吐血涎症　hemosialemesis
吐血·瘀阻胃络证/吐血·瘀阻胃絡證　hematemesis with pattern of static blood blocking stomach collateral
钍化合物/釷化合物　thorium compounds
钍射气/釷射氣　thorium emanation
钍照片/釷照片,釷相片,釷照相　thoriagram
兔耳测试/兔耳測試　rabbit-ear test
兔肤蝇/兔蠅　rabbit botfly
兔化法/兔化法,兔體通過減毒法　lapinization
兔口腔乳头[状]瘤/兔口腔乳頭狀瘤　rabbit oral papilloma
兔[密]螺旋体/兔螺旋體　Treponema cuniculi
兔缺/兔缺　harelip
兔乳头[状]瘤/兔乳頭狀瘤　rabbit papilloma
菟丝子/菟絲子　dodder seed
团块结核疹/團塊結核疹,密聚性結核　tuberculosis conglomerata
团块肾/團塊腎,塊狀腎　lump kidney
团块细胞/團塊細胞　clump cell
团体[性]痢疾/集體[性]痢疾　institutional dysentery
团状结核疹/團狀結核疹　tuberculosis conclamata
推扳疗法/推扳療法　pushing and pulling manipulation
推迟性排泄性尿路造影[术]/推遲性排洩性尿路造影[術],延緩性排洩性尿路造影[術]　delayed excretory urography
推出/推出,壓出　detrusion
推动力缺乏/推出力缺乏,欠缺動機　poor motivation
推法/推法　pushing manipulation
推脊/推脊　spinal pushing
推进皮瓣/推進皮瓣,前徙瓣　advancement flap, advancement skin flap
推拿/推拿,按摩　massage
推拿疗病派/推拿療病派,推拿療病法　naprapathy
推拿疗病者/推拿療病者　naprapath
推片力/推錠力　ejection force
推切剥离/推切剝離　cleavage dissection
推寻/推尋　pulse searching
癞疝/癞疝　serious indirect hernia

腿/腿　leg
腿部高血压性溃疡/腿部高血壓性潰瘍　hypertensive ulceration of leg
腿侧弯/腿側彎,腿旁彎　cnemoscoliosis
腿长不等/腿長不等　leg length inequality
腿溃疡/腿潰瘍　leg ulcer
腿皮肤病/腿皮膚病　leg dermatosis
腿损伤/腿損傷　leg injuries
腿痛/腿痛　skelalgia
腿无力/腿無力　skelasthenia
腿象皮肿/腿象皮病　elephantiasis of leg
腿型/腿型　leg type
腿征/腿徵[象]　leg sign
腿足肿胀/腿足腫脹,足腫大　tama
退变性精神病/退變性精神病　degenerative psychosis
退变性麻痹/退變性麻痺　degenerative paralysis
退化/退化　catagenesis
退化肌/退化肌　vestigial muscle
退化型/退化型,衰退型,衰殘型　degeneration form, involution form
退热[疗]法/退熱[療]法　antipyresis
退热[期]/熱退期　defervescence
退热药/退熱藥　defervescent
退色痣/褪色痣,色素脱失性母斑　nevus depigmentosus
退伍军人医院/退伍軍人醫院　veterans hospital
退行/變性,變質,退化　degeneration
退行关节病/退行性關節病,退化性關節病　degenerative joint disease
退行关节炎/退行性關節炎,退化性關節炎　degenerative arthritis
退行神经痛/退行性神經痛,退化性神經痛　degenerative neuralgia
退行生长/退行生長,逆生長　degrowth
退行性癌/退行性癌,逆行性癌　retrograde cancer
退行性非典型组织细胞增生症/退行性非典型組織細胞增生症　regressive atypical histiocytosis
退行性改变/退化性變化　degenerative change
退行性睑外翻/退行性瞼外翻　degenerative ectropion
退行性近视/退行性近視　degenerative myopia
退行性肾炎/變性腎炎　degenerative nephritis
退行性萎缩/退化性萎縮　degenerative atrophy, reversionary atrophy
退行性转移/退行性轉移　retrograde metastasis
退翳明目/退翳明目　removing nebula for improving eyesight

退翳明目法/退翳明目法　removing nebula to brighten eye
蜕变中间物质/蜕變中間產物,射線暫產物　metabolon
蜕膜/蜕膜　decidua
蜕膜病/蜕膜病,蜕膜組織異位症　deciduosis
蜕膜反应/蜕膜反應,蜕化作用　decidua reaction
蜕膜管型/蜕膜管型　decidual cast
蜕膜化/蜕膜化　decidualization
蜕膜瘤/蜕膜瘤　deciduoma
蜕膜脐/蜕膜臍　decidual umbilicus
蜕膜胎盘/蜕膜胎盤,脱落胎盤　deciduate placenta
蜕膜脱落/蜕落　deciduation
蜕膜细胞/蜕膜細胞　decidual cell
蜕膜性子宫内膜炎/蜕膜性子宫內膜炎　decidual endometritis
蜕膜炎/蜕膜炎　deciduitis
蜕皮/蜕皮　molting
蜕皮后期/蜕皮後期　postecdysis
蜕皮激素/蜕皮激素　ecdysone
蜕皮前期/蜕皮前期　proecdysis
蜕皮甾体/蜕皮甾體　ecdysteroid
蜕皮甾酮/蜕皮甾酮　ecdysterone
褪黑激素/褪黑激素,抗黑變激素　melatonin
褪黑激素受体/褪黑激素受體　melatonin receptor
褪色/褪色　color fading
吞服/吞服　deglutition, swallow
吞脓/吞膿　pyophagia
吞气症/吞氣症　aerophagy
吞砷癖/吞砷癖　arsenophagy
吞食梗塞/吞食梗塞　blockage in deglutition
吞噬/吞噬　phagocytize
吞噬溶酶体/吞噬溶酶體　phagolysosome
吞噬[神经]胶质作用/吞噬[神經]膠質作用,神經膠細胞吞噬作用　gliophagia
吞噬体/吞噬體　phagosome
吞噬细胞/吞噬細胞　phagocyte
吞噬细胞疾病/吞噬細胞疾病　phagocytic cell disorder
吞噬细胞溶解/吞噬細胞崩解　phagolysis
吞噬细胞杀菌功能不良/吞噬細胞殺菌功能不良　phagocyte bactericidal dysfunction
吞噬细胞素/吞噬細胞素　phagocytin
吞噬性小神经胶质细胞/吞噬性小神經膠質細胞　phagocytic microglia
吞噬血细胞作用/吞噬血細胞作用,噬血球作用　hemocytophagia
吞噬指数/吞噬[細胞]指數,噬細胞指數　phagocytic index
吞噬作用/吞噬作用　phagocytosis
吞涎症/吞涎症　sialophagia
吞线试验/吞線試驗　string test
吞血细胞噬细胞/吞血細胞噬細胞,吞紅血球之噬細胞　globuliferous phagocyte
吞[血液]色素噬细胞/吞[血液]色素噬細胞,含黑色素之吞噬細胞　melaniferous phagocyte
吞咽/吞嚥　swallowing
吞咽不能/吞嚥不能　aglutition
吞咽反射/吞嚥反射　swallowing reflex
吞咽困难/吞嚥困難,嚥物困難,嚥下困難　dysphagia
吞咽痛/[吞]嚥痛　odynophagia
吞咽障碍/吞嚥障礙　deglutition disorder
豚草皮炎/豚草皮炎　ragweed dermatitis
豚鼠阴囊肿胀反应/豚鼠陰囊腫脹反應　Neill-Mooser reaction
豚脂/豚脂　adeps
豚脂状蛋白/豚脂狀蛋白　lardacein
臀/臀　①buttock ②tun, AH7
臀部/臀部　rump
臀部寄生胎/臀部寄生胎,寄生性臀部連胎　pygopagus parasiticus
臀部联胎畸形/臀部連胎畸形　pygopagy
臀部联体儿/臀部連胎　pygopagus
臀部美容术/臀部美容術　aesthetic buttock surgery
臀大肌/臀大肌　gluteus maximus
臀大肌转子囊/臀大肌轉子囊　trochanteric bursa of gluteus maximus
臀大肌坐骨囊/臀大肌坐骨囊　sciatic bursa of gluteus maximus
臀沟/臀溝　gluteal sulcus
臀股皱褶/臀股皺褶　gluteofemoral crease
臀红/臀紅　red buttock
臀后线/臀後線　posterior gluteal line
臀厚/臀厚　hip thickness
臀肌粗隆/臀肌粗隆　gluteal tuberosity
臀肌间囊/臀肌間囊　intermuscular bursae of glutei
臀肌腱膜/臀肌腱膜　gluteal aponeurosis
臀肌筋膜炎/臀肌筋膜炎　gluteus myofascitis
臀肌挛缩/臀肌攣縮　gluteus contracture
臀肌移植术/臀肌移植術　gluteus transplantation
臀筋膜/臀肌膜　gluteal fascia
臀联双胎/臀聯雙胎,臀部聯胎　pygopagus
臀裂/臀裂　clunial cleft
臀淋巴结/臀淋巴結　gluteal lymph node
臀面/臀面　gluteal surface

臀内侧皮神经/臀内側皮神經,臀上皮神經　middle clunial nerve
臀前线/臀前線　anterior gluteal line
臀疝/臀疝　gluteal hernia
臀上动脉/臀上動脈　superior gluteal artery
臀上动脉浅支/臀上動脈淺支　superficial branch of superior gluteal artery
臀上动脉深支/臀上動脈深支　deep branch of superior gluteal artery
臀上动脉深支上支/臀上動脈深支上支　superior branch of deep branch of superior gluteal artery
臀上动脉深支下支/臀上動脈深支下支　inferior branch of deep branch of superior gluteal artery
臀上静脉/臀上靜脈　superior gluteal vein
臀上淋巴结/臀上淋巴結　superior gluteal lymph node
臀上皮神经/臀上皮神經　superior clunial cutaneous nerve
臀上神经/上臀神經　superior gluteal nerve
臀痛/臀部痛　pygalgia
臀围/臀圍　hip circumference
臀位分娩/臀位分娩,臀式產　breech delivery
臀位助产/臀位助產　assisted breech delivery
臀下侧皮神经/臀下側皮神經　inferior cluneal nerve
臀下动脉/臀下動脈　inferior gluteal artery
臀下静脉/臀下靜脈　inferior gluteal vein
臀下淋巴结/臀下淋巴結　inferior gluteal lymph node
臀下皮神经/臀下皮神經　inferior clunial nerve
臀下神经/臀下神經　inferior gluteal nerve
臀下线/臀下線　inferior gluteal line
臀先露/臀先露[產式],臀產式,臀位生產式　breech presentation
臀小肌/臀小肌　gluteus minimus, musculus gluteus minimus
臀小肌转子囊/臀小肌轉子囊　trochanteric bursa of gluteus minimus
臀痈/臀癰　gluteal cellulitis, pyogenic carbuncle of buttock
臀痈·气血两虚证/臀癰·氣血兩虛證　gluteal cellulitis with qi-blood deficiency pattern
臀痈·湿火蕴结证/臀癰·濕火蘊結證　gluteal cellulitis with dampness-fire amassment pattern
臀痈·湿痰凝结证/臀癰·濕痰凝結證　gluteal cellulitis with pattern of dampness-phlegm coagulating and intermingling
臀脂过多/臀脂過多,女臀過肥　steatopygia
臀中侧皮神经/臀中側皮神經　middle cluneal nerve

臀中肌/臀中肌　gluteus medius
臀中肌转子囊/臀中肌轉子囊　trochanteric bursa of gluteus medius
臀中皮神经/臀中皮神經　middle clunial nerve
臀中神经/臀中神經　middle gluteal nerve
托比-艾尔试验/特-埃二氏試驗　Tobey-Ayer test
托吡卡胺/托吡卡胺　tropicamide
托泊替坎/托泊替坎　topotecan
托布津/托布津　thiophanate
托槽/托槽,支持器,撐架　bracket
托槽黏着定位器/托槽黏著定位器　bracket positioning gauge
托达罗腱/托達羅腱　Todaro tendon
[托]带/[托]帶,束帶　girdle
托德麻痹/托德麻痺,Todd 氏麻痺　Todd palsy
托德瘫痪/托德癱瘓　Todd paralysis
托德体/托德體　Todd bodies
托酚酮/托酚酮　tropolone
托管/託管　trust
托管人/託管人　trustees
托颌法/托頜法　jaw thrust
托架/托架　brackets
托兰/托蘭,托朗　troland
托雷克手术/托雷克手術　Torek operation
托里排脓/托裏排膿　expelling pathogens by strengthening vital qi and expelling pus
托利契利真空/托利契利真空　Torricellian vacuum
托洛氯铵/托洛氯銨　tolonium chloride
托洛萨-亨特综合征/痛性眼肌麻痺症候群　Tolosa-Hunt syndrome
托马-蔡斯计数池/托馬-蔡司計數池,Thoma-Zeiss 二氏計數池　Thoma-Zeiss counting cell
托马塞利综合征/托馬塞利症候群,Tommaselli 氏症候群　Tommaselli syndrome
托马斯后夹/托馬斯後夾,Thomas 氏後夾板　Thomas posterior splint
托马斯夹板/托馬斯夾板　Thomas splint
托马斯征/托馬斯徵　Thomas sign
托马液/托馬液,Thoma 氏液　Thoma fluid
托美丁/托美丁　tolmetin
托姆森现象/托姆森現象　Thomsen phenomenon
托姆斯颗粒层/托姆斯顆粒層　Tomes granular layer
托萘酯/托萘酯,甲基甲苯基硫代甲胺酸　tolnaftate
托哌酮/托哌酮　tolperisone
[托]盘/盤　tray
托盘疔/托盤疔　midpalmar space infection, palmar ding
托屈嗪/托屈嗪　todralazine

托瑞米芬/托瑞米芬　toremifene
托腮痈/托腮癰　cheek abscess
托烷类/托烷類　tropanes
托牙平衡/托牙平衡　denture balance
托牙性溃疡/托牙性潰瘍,托牙瘡　denture sore
托牙翼缘/托牙翼緣,全口假牙凸緣　denture flange
拖出术/拖出術　pullthrough operation
拖线引流/拖線引流　thread pulling drainage
拖曳足/拖曳足　shuffle foot
脱氨[基]/脱胺[基作用]　deamination, deaminize
脱氨基精氨酸血管升压素/脱胺基精胺酸血管昇壓素　deamino arginine vasopressin
脱氨[基]酶/脱醯胺酶　deamidizing enzyme
脱氨酶类/解氨酶類　ammonia-lyases
脱垂/脱垂,脱出　prolapse
脱醇[作用]/脱醇[作用],去醇作用,除醇　dealcoholization
脱氮/脱氮,除氮作用　denitrification
脱碘作用/脱碘　deiodination
脱发/脱髮,秃[髮]　alopecia
脱发酵母/髮部酵母　Saccharomyces capillitii
脱发性痤疮/脱髮性痤瘡,秃性痤瘡　acne decalvans
脱辅蛋白质/脱輔蛋白質,去輔基蛋白質　apoprotein
脱辅蛋白质类/脱輔蛋白質類　apoproteins
脱辅[基]蛋白质/缺輔基蛋白質　apoprotein
脱辅酶类/脱輔酶類　apoenzymes
脱钙/脱鈣,脱石灰　decalcify
脱钙骨/脱鈣骨　decalcified bone
脱钙骨基质/脱鈣骨基質　decalcified bone matrix
脱钙技术/脱鈣技術　decalcification technique
脱钙性骨炎/脱鈣性骨炎　decalcifying osteitis
脱钙液/脱鈣液　decalcifying fluid
脱肛/脱肛,肛門脱出　anal prolapse, rectal prolapse, prolapsed anus
脱肛·脾虚气陷证/脱肛·脾虛氣陷證　rectal prolapse with pattern of spleen deficiency and qi sinking
脱肛·肾气不固证/脱肛·腎氣不固證　rectal prolapse with pattern of unconsolidation due to kidney qi deficiency
脱肛·湿热下注证/脱肛·濕熱下注證　rectal prolapse with pattern of dampness-heat diffusing downward
脱肛·血热肠燥证/脱肛·血熱腸燥證　rectal prolapse with pattern of blood heat and intestine dryness
脱汗/脱汗　sweating of dying
脱甲/脱甲　defluvium unguium
脱甲病/脱甲病,無[爪]甲　onychomadesis
脱甲基[作用]/脱甲基[作用],去甲烷作用,去甲基作用　demethylation

脱甲症/脱甲症　alopecia unguium
脱肩/脱肩　knocked-down shoulder
脱缰/脱繮　runaway
脱焦痂/脱焦痂　separation of eschar
脱节性肾小管性酸中毒/脱節性腎小管性酸中毒　dislocation renal tubular acidosis
脱臼骨折/脱臼骨折　dislocation fracture
脱疽/脱疽　gangrene, gangrene of digit
脱疽·寒湿阻络证/脱疽·寒濕阻絡證　gangrene with pattern of cold-dampness obstructing collateral
脱疽·气血两虚证/脱疽·氣血兩虛證　gangrene with qi-blood deficiency pattern
脱疽·热毒伤阴证/脱疽·熱毒傷陰證　gangrene with pattern of heat-toxin injuring yin
脱疽·湿热毒盛证/脱疽·濕熱毒盛證　gangrene with pattern of dampness-heat toxin excessiveness
脱疽·血脉瘀阻证/脱疽·血脈瘀阻證　gangrene with pattern of blood vessels stasis and obstruction
脱离/脱離　ablatio
脱磷酸[作用]/脱磷酸[作用],除磷酸化作用　dephosphorylation
脱硫弧菌科感染/脱硫弧菌科感染　desulfovibrionaceae infections
脱硫酶/脱硫酶　desulfurase
脱硫生物素/去硫生物素　desthiobiotin
脱漏搏动/脱漏搏動,搏動脱漏　dropped beat
脱氯[作用]/脱氯[法]　dechloridation
脱落/脱落　defluvium
脱落法细胞学检查[术]/脱落法細胞學檢查[術]　exfoliative cytologic examination
脱落酸类/脱落酸類　abscisic acid
脱落性骨炎/脱落性骨炎　exfoliative osteitis
脱麻醉药/脱麻醉藥,失麻醉藥　denarcotize
脱毛/脱毛　depilation
脱毛[发]剂/脱毛[髮]劑,除髮藥　depilatory
脱毛剂量/脱毛劑量　epilating dose
脱毛术/脱毛術,拔毛,除毛法　epilation
脱镁叶绿素/脱鎂葉綠素　pheophytin
脱免疫/脱免疫,使無免疫性,使喪失免疫性　disimmunize
脱敏/脱敏　desensitization
脱敏剂/脱敏劑,去敏[感]藥　desensitizer
脱敏疗法/脱敏療法　desensitization therapy
脱敏性免疫/脱敏性免疫　iathergy
脱囊/脱囊,出囊,自囊逸出　excystation, scrotal necrosis
脱囊·肝肾阴虚证/脱囊·肝腎陰虛證　scrotal necrosis with liver-kidney yin deficiency pattern

脱囊·湿热下注证/脱囊·濕熱下注證 scrotal necrosis with pattern of dampness-heat diffusing downward
脱皮/脱皮 desquamating
脱嘌呤核酸/脱嘌呤核酸 apurinic acid
脱气/脱氣 degassing
脱气水/脱氣水 deaerated water
脱氢胆固醇/脱氫膽固醇,去氫膽固醇 dehydrocholesterol
脱氢胆酸排出增多/脱氫膽酸排出增多,去氫膽酸過多 dehydrocholaneresis
脱氢胆酸盐/脱氫膽酸鹽,去氫膽酸鹽 dehydrocholate
脱氢睾酮环戊烯醚/脱氫睾酮環戊烯醚 quinbolone
脱氢硫胺试验/脱氫硫胺試驗,硫色素試驗 thiochrome test
脱氢酶/脱氫酶,脱氫酵素,去氫酵素 dehydrogenase
脱氢肽酶/脱氫肽酶,去氫勝肽酵素 dehydropeptidase
脱氢雄酮/脱氫脂酮,去氫男性脂酮 dehydroandrosterone
脱氢紫堇碱/脱氫紫堇鹼,去氫延胡索素 dehydrocorydaline
脱巯基酶/脱氫基酶,脱硫化氫酶 desulfhydrase
脱色剂/脱色劑 bleaching agent
脱[神经]髓鞘/脱髓鞘 demyelinate
脱胨结核菌素/脱胨結核菌素,脱蛋白結核菌素 albumose-free tuberculin
脱水/脱水 dehydration
脱水毒蕈碱/脱水毒蕈鹼 anhydromuscarine
脱水剂/脱水劑 dehydrant
脱水酶/脱水酵素 dehydratase
脱水器/除水器 dehydrator
脱水热/脱水熱 dehydration fever
脱水托品/脱水托品,失水特羅品 tropidine
脱水蔗糖/脱水蔗糖,聚蔗糖 saccharosan
脱髓鞘疾病/脱髓鞘疾病 demyelinating diseases
脱髓鞘性脑病/脱髓鞘性腦病 demyelinating encephalopathy
脱髓鞘[作用]/脱髓鞘[作用] demyelination
脱羧/脱羧[基作用] decarboxylation
脱羧酶/脱羧基酵素 decarboxylase
脱羧酶抑制药/脱羧酶抑制藥 decarboxylase inhibitor
脱烷基化/脱烷基化 dealkylation
脱位/脱位 dislocation
脱位复位术/脱位回復術 reduction of dislocation
脱位·肝肾亏虚证/脱位·肝腎虧虛證 dislocation with liver-kidney deficiency pattern
脱位·气血两虚证/脱位·氣血兩虛證 dislocation with qi-blood deficiency pattern
脱位·血瘀气滞证/脱位·血瘀氣滯證 dislocation with pattern of blood stasis and qi stagnation
脱酰胺[作用]/脱醯胺作用 deamidation
脱酰[基]酶/脱醯基酶 deacylase
脱屑/脱屑 desquamation
脱屑性耳炎/脱屑性耳炎 otitis desquamativa
脱屑性肺炎/脱屑性肺炎,落屑性肺炎 desquamative pneumonia
脱屑性红皮病/脱屑性紅皮症,脱皮性紅皮症 erythroderma desquamativum
脱屑性肾炎/脱屑性腎炎,落屑性腎炎 desquamative nephritis
脱形/脱形 extreme emaciation
脱牙/脱牙,落齒,牙齒脱落 dedentition
脱阳/脱陽 collapse of yang qi
脱氧/去氧,除氧 deoxidize
脱氧胞苷/去氧胞苷 deoxycytidine
脱氧胞苷核苷酸类/去氧胞苷核苷酸類 deoxycytidine nucleotides
脱氧胞苷激酶/去氧胞苷激酶 deoxycytidine kinase
脱氧胞苷-磷酸/去氧胞苷-磷酸 deoxycytidine monophosphate
脱氧胞苷酸/去氧胞苷酸 deoxycytidylic acid
脱氧胆酸/去氧膽酸 deoxycholic acid
脱氧胆酸排出增多/去氧膽酸排出增多 deoxycholaneresis
脱氧合[作用]/去氧法,除氧作用 deoxygenation
脱氧核苷/去氧核苷 deoxynucleoside
脱氧核糖/去氧核糖 deoxyribose
脱氧核糖核蛋白/去氧核糖核蛋白 deoxyribonucleoprotein
脱氧核糖核苷/去氧核糖核苷 deoxyribonucleoside
脱氧核糖核苷酸/去氧核糖核苷酸 deoxyribonucleotide
脱氧核糖核酸/去氧核糖核酸 deoxyribonucleic acid
脱氧核糖核酸聚合酶/去氧核糖核酸聚合酶 DNA polymerase
脱氧核糖核酸连接酶/去氧核糖核酸連接酶 DNA ligase
脱氧核糖核酸酶/去氧核糖核酸酶 deoxyribonuclease
脱氧核糖核酸钠/去氧核糖核酸鈉 sodium deoxyribonucleic acid
脱氧核糖核酸外切酶类/去氧核糖核酸外切酶類 exodeoxyribonucleases

脱氧核糖嘧啶光裂合酶/去氧核糖嘧啶光裂解酶 deoxyribodipyrimidine photolyase
脱氧麻黄碱/去氧麻黄素 desoxyephedrine
脱氧吗啡/去氧嗎啡,還原嗎啡 desoxymorphine
脱氧鸟苷/去氧鳥苷 deoxyguanosine
脱氧鸟苷酸/去氧鳥嘌呤核苷酸 deoxyguanylic acid
脱氧鸟嘌呤核苷酸类/去氧鳥嘌呤核苷酸類 deoxyguanine nucleotides
脱氧尿苷/去氧尿嘧啶核苷 deoxyuridine
脱氧尿苷核苷酸类/去氧尿苷核苷酸類 deoxyuracil nucleotides
脱氧皮质酮/去氧皮質脂酮 desoxycorticosterone
脱氧皮质[甾]酮/去氧腎上腺皮質脂酮 cortexone
脱氧葡萄糖/去氧葡萄糖 deoxyglucose
脱氧葡萄糖法/脱氧葡萄糖法 deoxyglucose method
脱氧肾上腺素/去氧腎上腺素 deoxyepinephrine
脱氧糖/去氧糖 desoxy-sugar
脱氧糖类/去氧糖類 deoxy-sugars
脱氧腺苷类/去氧腺苷類 deoxyadenosines
脱氧腺苷酸/去氧單磷酸腺苷 deoxyadenylic acid
脱氧腺嘌呤核苷酸类/去氧腺嘌呤核苷酸類 deoxyadenine nucleotides
脱氧[作用]/去氧,除氧作用 deoxidation
脱叶菌素类/脱葉[菌]素類 exfoliatins
脱衣癖/脱衣癖 ecdysiasm
脱乙酰头孢菌素 C/脱乙醯頭孢菌素 C deacetyl cephalosporin C, DCPC
脱阴/脱陰 collapse of yin qi
脱瘾现象/脱癮現象 abstinence phenomenon
脱瘾综合征/脱癮症候群 abstinence syndrome
脱营/脱營 psychosomatic disease due to emotional stress
脱油酸卵磷脂/脱油酸卵磷脂 desoleolecithin
脱羽恙虫/脱羽恙蟲 depluming mite
脱证/[氣]脱證 collapse pattern, desertion disease
脱支/脱支,去分支 debranching
脱支链糖原贮积病/脱支鏈糖原積貯病 debrancher glycogen storage disease
脱支酶缺乏/脱支酶缺乏,去分支酶缺乏 debranching enzyme deficiency
脱脂乳/脱脂乳,去油乳 skimmed milk
脱植基叶绿素类/脱植基葉綠素類 chlorophyllides
脱痔/脱痔 prolapsed hemorrhoid
驼背/駝背 bent back
驼背矫正器/駝背矯正器,駝背帶 kyphotone
驼鼻/駝鼻 hump nose
驼峰/駝峰 rider peak
驼峰样电子致密沉积物/駝峰樣電子致密沈積物 humplike electron dense deposits
妥布霉素/妥布拉黴素 tobramycin
妥卡尼/妥卡尼 tocainide
妥拉磺脲/妥拉磺脲 tolazamide
妥拉唑林/托拉佐林,苄咪唑啉 tolazoline
椭圆凹/橢圓凹,長方凹 oblong fovea
椭圆关节/橢圓[動]關節 ellipsoidal joint
椭圆酵母/橢圓酵母,橢圓形酵母菌 Saccharomyces ellipsoideus
椭圆囊/橢圓囊 utricle
椭圆囊斑/橢圓囊斑,前列腺囊斑,橢囊斑 macula utriculi
椭圆囊壶腹神经/橢圓囊壺腹神經 utriculoampullary nerve
椭圆囊球囊管/橢圓囊球囊管 ductus utriculosaccularis
椭圆囊神经/橢圓囊神經 utricular nerve
椭圆囊炎/橢圓囊炎 utriculitis
椭圆囊隐窝/橢圓囊隱窩 elliptical recess
椭圆偏振/橢圓偏振,橢圓偏極[化] elliptical polarization
椭圆球囊管/橢圓球囊管 utriculosaccular duct
椭圆体/橢圓體 ellipsoid
椭圆形红细胞/橢圓紅血球 elliptocyte
椭圆形红细胞性贫血/橢圓形紅血球性貧血,駝狀貧血 cameloid anemia
椭圆形红细胞增多症/橢圓形紅血球增多症,橢圓紅血球症 elliptocytosis
拓奎反应/拓奎反應,绿奎宁反應 Thalleoquin reaction
拓扑指数/拓撲指數 topological index
唾腺电[流]图/唾液腺電圖 electrosalivogram
唾血/唾血 spitting blood
唾液/唾液 saliva
唾液薄膜/唾液薄膜 salivary pellicle
唾液蛋白质类/唾液蛋白質類 salivary proteins
唾液[分泌]过少/唾液分泌過少,缺涎 hyposialosis
唾液[分泌]减少/唾液分泌減少,涎分泌過少 oligoptyalism
唾液管/唾腺管 salivary duct
唾液缺乏性消化不良/唾液[缺乏]性消化不良 salivary dyspepsia
唾液酸/唾液酸,涎酸 sialic acid
唾液酸贮积病/唾液酸貯積病 sialic acid storage disease
唾液酸转移酶类/唾液酸轉移酶類 sialyltransferases
唾液糖蛋白类/唾液糖蛋白類 sialoglycoproteins

唾液腺/唾液腺 salivary gland
唾液腺病毒/唾液腺病毒,涎腺病毒 salivary gland virus
唾液腺绞痛/唾[液]腺絞痛 salivary colic
唾液腺囊肿/唾液腺囊腫 cyst of salivary gland
唾液消化/唾液消化,涎消化 salivary digestion
唾液学/唾液學,涎學 sialology
唾液药物浓度/唾液藥物濃度 saliva drug level
唾液溢流/唾液溢流 overflow of saliva
唾液诊断学/涎液診斷學 sialosemeiology
唾液支原体/唾液支原菌,涎黴漿菌 Mycoplasma salivarium

W

挖蛤者痒/挖蛤者癢病　clam digger itch
挖治器/挖[出]器　excavator
蛙粪霉菌病/蛙糞黴病　basidiobolomycosis
蛙粪霉属/蛙糞黴屬　*Basidiobolus*
蛙面/蛙面,蛙臉,蛙狀面容　frog face
蛙皮缩胆囊肽/蛙皮縮膽囊肽　cerulein
娃儿藤碱/娃兒藤鹼,鷗蔓鹼　tylophorine
瓦尔萨尔瓦窦/瓦爾薩爾瓦竇,Valsalva 氏竇　sinus of Valsalva
瓦格纳试剂/瓦格納試劑,碘化鉀碘試劑　Wagner's reagent
瓦格斯塔夫骨折/瓦格斯塔夫骨折,Wagstaffe 氏骨折　Wagstaffe fracture
瓦工麻痹/瓦工麻痺　hod-carrier palsy
瓦拉明/瓦拉明,水化戊烯草脂　valamin
瓦楞子/瓦楞子,半開魁蛤　clam shell
瓦利病/瓦利病,Vallee 氏病　Vallee disease
瓦利-里特尔定律/瓦利里特爾定律,瓦-利二氏定律　Valli-Ritter law
瓦伦贝格综合征/瓦倫貝格症候群,Wallenberg 氏症候群　Wallenberg syndrome
瓦伦丁夹板/瓦倫丁夾板,Valentine 氏夾板　Valentine splint
瓦[萨尔]氏疟原虫/瓦[薩爾]氏瘧原蟲,松鼠瘧蟲　Plasmodium vassali
瓦生氏腹盘吸虫/瓦生氏腹盤吸蟲　Amphistoma watsoni
瓦[生]氏瓦生吸虫/瓦[生]氏瓦生吸蟲,華生尼氏雙口吸蟲　Watsonius watsoni
瓦氏巨球蛋白血症肾病/瓦氏巨球蛋白血症腎病　renal disease in Waldenstroms macroglobulinemia
瓦斯爆炸伤/瓦斯爆炸傷　gas explosion burn
瓦松毒素/瓦松毒素　cotyledontoxin
瓦滕贝格病/瓦藤貝格病,Wartenberg 氏病　Wartenberg disease
瓦因加滕综合征/瓦因加藤症候群,Weingarten 氏症候群　Weingarten syndrome
袜套牵引/襪套牽引　stocking traction
歪鼻/歪鼻　wry nose
歪口/歪口　distorted mouth
外板/外板　outer plate, external lamina

外半规管侧凸/半規管外側凸　prominence of lateral semicircular canal
外包缝合法/外包縫合法　outpocketing
外孢子膜/外孢子膜,外芽孢膜　exosporium
外[胞]浆溶解/外胞漿崩解　ectolysis
外鼻/外鼻　external nose, waibi
外壁绒型假体/外壁絨型假體　external velour prosthesis
外臂肌间韧带/外臂肌間韌帶　external intermuscular ligament of arm
外表检视法/外表檢視法,外診法　ectoscopy
外部感觉/外界感覺　external sensation
外侧/外側　lateral
外侧半月板/外側半月板　lateral meniscus
外侧背核/外側背核　lateral dorsal nucleus
外侧鼻突/外側鼻突　lateral nasal process, lateral nasal prominence
外侧壁/外側壁　lateral wall
外侧部/外側部　lateral part
外侧苍白球/外側蒼白球　lateral globus pallidus
外侧唇/外側唇　lateral lip
外侧底段/外側底段　lateral basal segment
外侧底段支气管/外側底段支氣管　lateral basal segmental bronchus
外侧底支/外側底支　lateral basal branch
外侧段/外側段　lateral segment
外侧段动脉/外側段動脈　lateral segmental artery
外侧段支气管/外側段支氣管　lateral segmental bronchus
外侧腭突/外側腭突　lateral palatine process
外侧根/外側根　lateral root
外侧弓状韧带/外側弓狀韌帶　lateral arcuate ligament
外侧沟/外側溝　lateral sulcus
外侧沟后支/外側溝後支　posterior ramus of lateral sulcus
外侧沟前支/外側溝前支　anterior ramus of lateral sulcus
外侧沟升支/外側溝昇支　ascending ramus of lateral sulcus
外侧固有束/外側固有束　lateral fasciculus proprius

外侧腘绳肌腱/膕外側腱　outer hamstring
外侧核群/外側核群　lateral nuclear group
外侧后核/外側後核　lateral posterior nucleus
外侧混合束/外側混合徑　mixed lateral tract
外侧甲状软骨舌骨韧带/外側甲狀軟骨舌骨韌帶　ligamentum thyrohyoideum laterale
外侧角/外側角　lateral angle
外侧脚/外側腳　lateral crus
外侧结节/外側結節　lateral tubercle
外侧颈窦/外側頸竇　lateral cervical sinus
外侧髁/外[侧]髁　lateral condyle
外侧髁上嵴/外側髁上嵴　lateral supracondylar ridge
外侧髁上线/外側髁上線　lateral supracondylar line
外侧淋巴结/外側淋巴結　lateral lymph node
外侧面/外側面　lateral surface, facies lateralis
外侧皮支/外側皮支　lateral cutaneous branch
外侧前庭神经核/外側前庭神經核　lateral vestibular nucleus
外侧丘脑核/外側丘腦核　lateral thalamic nucleus
外侧丘系/外側丘系　lateral lemniscus
外侧丘系核/外側丘系核　nucleus of lateral lemniscus
外侧丘系束/外側丘系束　lateral fillet tract
外侧韧带/外側韌帶　lateral ligament
外侧软骨板/外側軟骨板　lateral cartilaginous lamina
外侧伞状韧带/外側傘狀韌帶　external laciniate ligament
外侧舌膨大/外側舌膨大　lateral tongue swelling
外侧束/外側束　lateral cord
外侧髓板/外側髓板　lateral medullary lamina
外侧索/外側索　lateral funiculus
外侧头/外側頭　lateral head
外侧突/外側突　lateral process
外侧网状核/外側網狀核　lateral reticular nucleus
外侧膝状体/外側膝狀體　lateral geniculate body
外侧膝状体核/外側膝狀體核　lateral geniculate nucleus
外侧膝状体支/外側膝狀體支　branch of lateral geniculate body
外侧陷窝/外側陷窩　lateral lacunae
外侧腺支/外側腺支　lateral glandular branch
外侧楔骨/外側楔骨　lateral cuneiform bone, external cuneiform bone
外侧嗅回/外側嗅迴　lateral olfactory gyrus
外侧嗅纹/外側嗅紋　lateral olfactory stria
外侧隐窝/外側隱窩　lateral recess
外侧缘/外側緣　lateral border
外侧缘静脉/外側緣靜脈　lateral marginal vein
外侧支/外側支　lateral branch
外侧直径/外側直徑　direct lateral tract
外侧直静脉/外側直靜脈　lateral direct veins
外侧肘后肌/外側肘後肌　lateral anconeus muscle
外侧纵纹/外側縱紋　lateral longitudinal stria
外层瘤/外層瘤,裹膜瘤　rind tumor
外层渗出性视网膜病变/外層滲出性視網膜病變　external exudative retinopathy
外层心包炎/外層心包炎　external pericarditis
外出血/外出血　external hemorrhage
外唇/外唇　outer lip
外倒转术/外倒轉術,腹式轉向術　abdominal version
外[电]阻/外電阻　external resistance
外动脉瘤/[體腔]外動脈瘤　external aneurysm
外毒素/外毒素　exotoxin
外耳/外耳　①external ear, concha ②wai'er, TG1u
外耳道/外耳道　external acoustic meatus
外耳道闭锁/外耳道閉鎖　atresia of external acoustic meatus, atresia of external auditory canal
外耳道骨性部/外耳道骨性部　bony part of external acoustic meatus
外耳道疖/外耳道癤,癤性耳炎　furuncular otitis
外耳道软骨/外耳道軟骨　cartilage of external acoustic meatus
外耳道软骨部/外耳道軟骨部　cartilaginous part of external acoustic meatus
外耳道软骨切迹/外耳道軟骨切跡　notches in cartilage of external acoustic meatus
外耳道神经/外耳道神經　nerve to external acoustic meatus
外耳道栓/外耳道栓　meatal plug
外耳道峡/外耳道峽　isthmus of external acoustic meatus
外耳道狭窄/外耳道狹窄　stricture of external auditory canal
外耳道异物/外耳道異物　foreign body entering ear
外耳道再造术/外耳道再造術　reconstruction of external auditory canal
外耳耳廓韧带/外耳耳廓韌帶　ligament of auricle of external ear
外耳畸形/外耳畸形　deformity of external ear
外耳门/外耳門　external acoustic pore
外耳门上缘点/外耳門上緣點　porion
外耳炎/外耳炎　otitis external
外翻/外翻　eversion
外翻肌/外翻肌　evertor
外翻畸形足/外翻畸形足　valgus club foot
外翻足/外翻足　valgus

外分泌/外分泌　external secretion
外分泌部胰腺/外分泌部胰腺　exocrine pancreas
外分泌汗腺/外分泌汗腺　eccrine gland
外分泌物/外分泌物　eccrine
外分泌腺/外分泌腺　exocrine glands
外分泌[性]/外分泌性　exocrinosity
外分泌学/外分泌學　exocrinology
外分泌肢端汗腺瘤/外分泌肢端汗腺瘤　eccrine acrospiroma
外风证/外風證　exogenous wind pattern
外敷法/外敷法　topical application
外附肌/外部肌　extrinsic muscle
外腹股沟韧带/外腹股溝韌帶　external inguinal ligament
外感/外感[病證]　exogenous disease
外感高热/外感高熱　exogenous high fever
外感咳嗽/外感欬嗽　exogenous cough
外感咳嗽·风热证/外感欬嗽·風熱證　exogenous cough with wind-heat pattern
外感咳嗽·风燥证/外感欬嗽·風燥證　exogenous cough with wind-dryness pattern
外感咳嗽·火热证/外感欬嗽·火熱證　exogenous cough with fire-heat pattern
外感咳嗽·凉燥证/外感欬嗽·涼燥證　exogenous cough with cool-dryness pattern
外感咳嗽·暑湿证/外感欬嗽·暑濕證　exogenous cough with summerheat-damp pattern
外感咳嗽·外寒内热证/外感欬嗽·外寒內熱證　exogenous cough with pattern of external cold and internal heat
外感咳嗽·温燥证/外感欬嗽·溫燥證　exogenous cough with warm-dryness pattern
外感热病/外感熱病,傷寒,外感溫病　exogenous febrile disease, heat disease
外感受器/外感[受]器,外界接受器　exteroceptor
外感受神经系统/外感神經系統　exteroceptive nervous system
外感头痛/外感頭痛　exogenous headache
外感泄泻/外感洩瀉　exogenous diarrhea
外感眩晕/外感眩暈　exogenous vertigo
外巩膜沟/外鞏膜溝　external scleral sulcus
外共生生物/外共生生物　ectosymbiont
外购服务/外購服務　outsourced services
外骨半规管/外[骨]半規管　lateral semicircular canal
外骨壶腹/外骨壺腹　lateral bony ampulla
外固定/外固定　external fixation
外固定器/外固定器　external fixator

外固定器疗法/外固定器療法　external fixator treatment
外关/外關　waiguan, SJ5
外观容量分布/外觀容量分布　apparent volume distribution
外国医学研究生/外國醫學研究生　foreign medical graduate
外果皮/外果皮　exocarp
外呼吸/外呼吸　external respiration
外壶腹神经/外壺腹神經　lateral ampullary nerve
外踝/外踝　lateral malleolus, external malleolus
外踝点/外踝點　lateral malleolus point, malleolus fibula point
外踝骨折/外踝骨折　fracture of external malleolus
外踝关节面/外踝關節面　articular facet of lateral malleolus
外踝尖[穴]/外踝尖[穴]　waihuaijian, EX-LE9
外踝面/外踝面　lateral malleolar facet
外踝皮下囊/外踝皮下囊　subcutaneous bursa of lateral malleolus
外踝前动脉/外踝前動脈,前外踝動脈　lateral anterior malleolar artery
外踝网/外踝網　lateral malleolar rete
外踝窝/外踝窝　lateral malleolar fossa
外踝支/外踝支　lateral malleolar branch
外环骨板/外環骨板,骨外板　outer circumferential lamella
外喙锁韧带/外喙鎖韌帶　external coracoclavicular ligament
外积[生长]学说/外積[生長]學說,累積說　apposition theory
外基因子/外基因子　exogenote
外激素/外激素　ectohormone
外寄生物/外寄生物　ectoparasite
外加生长/外加生長　appositional growth
外监护/外監護　external electronic monitoring
外睑腺炎/外瞼腺炎　external hordeolum
外界定向力障碍/外界定向力障礙　allopsychic disorientation
外胫夹/外脛夾,脛骨夾板　shin splint
外科保持法/外科保持法　surgical retention
外科病理学/外科病理學　surgical pathology
外科补益法/外科補益法　tonifying method
外科床/外科床　surgical bed
外科动静脉转流术/外科動靜脈轉流術　surgical arteriovenous shunt
外科动脉瘤/外科動脈瘤　surgical aneurysm
外科缝合器/外科縫合器　surgical stapler

外科缝合器缝合/外科縫合器縫合　surgical stapling
外科汞溴红溶液/外科汞溴紅溶液,外科用紅溴汞溶液　surgical merbromin solution
外科骨印模/外科骨印模,手術性骨印模　surgical bone impression
外科和营法/外科和營法　nutrient-blood-harmonizing method
外科疾病/外科疾病　surgical disease
外科减压术/外科減壓術　surgical decompression
外科结/外科結　surgical knot
外科结核/外科結核　surgical tuberculosis
外科解表法/外科解表法　exterior-relieving method
外科解剖学/外科解剖學　surgical anatomy
外科精要/外科精要　Essence of External Diseases
外科颈/外科頸　surgical neck
外科口腔正畸学/外科口腔正畸學　surgical orthodontics
外科理湿法/外科理濕法　dampness-removing method
外科疗法/外科療法　surgical treatment
外科麻醉/外科[手術]麻醉　surgical anesthesia
外科门腔分流术/外科門腔分流術　surgical portacaval shunt
外科门体分流术/外科門體分流術　surgical portasystemic shunt
外科门诊中心/外科門診中心　surgicenter
外科皮瓣/外科皮瓣　surgical flap
外科脾肾分流术/外科脾腎分流術　surgical splenorenal shunt
外科器械/外科器械　surgical instruments
外科器械学/外科器械學,外科用具學　acidology
外科清热法/外科清熱法　heat-clearing method
外科祛痰法/外科祛痰法　expelling-phlegm method
外科纱布/外科紗布　surgical sponge
外科伤口感染/外科傷口感染　surgical wound infection
外科设备/外科設備　surgical equipment
外科石膏/外科石膏　surgical cast
外科手术/外科手術　operative surgical procedure
外科手术保险/外科手術保險　surgical insurance
外科手术学/外科手術學　operative surgery
外科手套/外科手套　surgical gloves
外科调胃法/外科調胃法　stomach-harmonizing method
外科通里法/外科通裡法　interior-dredging method
外科网/外科網　surgical mesh
外科温通法/外科溫通法　warm-dredging method
外科吻合术/外科吻合術　surgical anastomosis

外科行气法/外科行氣法　qi-activating method
外科性腹部/外科性腹部　surgical abdomen
外科性气肿/外科性氣腫　surgical emphysema
外科休克/外科休克　surgical shock
外科学/外科[學]　surgery
外科学肛管/外科學肛管　surgical anal canal
外科学诊断技术/外科學診斷技術　surgical diagnostic technique
外科医师/外科醫師　surgeon
外科用高频电流/外科[用高頻]電流　surgical current
外科用氯化苏打溶液/外科用氯化蘇打溶液　surgical solution of chlorinated soda
外科针/外科針　surgeon needle
外科正宗/外科正宗　Orthodox Manual of External Diseases
外科证治全生集/外科[證治]全生集　Life-saving Manual of Diagnosis and Treatment of External Diseases
外科专业/外科專業　surgical specialty
外[颗]粒层/外[顆]粒層　external granular layer
外[颗]粒层纹/外[顆]粒層紋　stria of external granular layer
外髁/外髁　external condyle
外壳蛋白质复合物/外殼蛋白質複合物　coat protein complex
外括约肌成形术/外括約肌成形術　external sphincteroplasty
外[来]暗示/外來暗示　ectosuggestion
外来物/外來物　exotic
外劳宫/外勞宮　wailaogong, EX-UE8
外力作用/外力作用　exogenic action
外臁疮/外臁瘡　lateral shank ulcer
外淋巴/外淋巴　perilymph
外淋巴管/外淋巴管　perilymphatic duct
外淋巴瘘/外淋巴瘻　perilymphatic fistula
外淋巴漏/外淋巴漏　perilymphorrhea
外淋巴隙/外淋巴隙　perilymphatic space
外淋巴液/外淋巴液　perilymph fluid
外陵/外陵　wailing, ST26
外瘘/外瘺管　external fistula
外螺旋沟/外螺旋溝　external spiral sulcus
外盲瘘/外盲瘻管　external blind fistula
外[毛]根鞘/外根鞘　external root sheath, outer root sheath
外毛细胞/外毛細胞　outer hair cell
外貌吸引力/外貌吸引力　appearance attraction
外泌汗腺/外泌汗腺　eccrine sweat gland

外面/外面　external surface
外膜/外膜　adventitia
外膜壶腹/外膜壺腹　lateral membranous ampulla
外膜细胞/外膜細胞　adventitial cell
外膜真皮巨大纤维黏液样瘤/外膜真皮之巨大纖維黏液樣瘤　giant fibromyxoid tumor of the adventitial dermis
外囊/外囊　external capsule
外囊出血/外囊出血　external capsule hemorrhage
外脑[脊]膜/外腦[脊]膜,腦外膜　exomeninx
外尿流改道术/外尿流改道術　external urinary diversion
外胚层/外胚層　ectoderm
外胚层病/外胚層病　ectodermosis
外胚层发育不良症/外胚層發育不良症,外胚層器官發育不良,外胚層發育異常　ectodermal dysplasia
外胚层沟/外胚層溝　ectodermal groove
外胚层肌/外胚層肌　ectodermal muscle
外胚层间质瘤/外胚層間質瘤　ectomesenchymoma
外胚层缺损/外胚層缺損　ectodermal defect
外胚层体型者/外胚層體型者　ectomorph
外胚层泄殖腔/外胚層洩殖腔　ectodermal cloaca
外胚层性神经梅毒/外胚層性神經梅毒　ectodermogenic neurosyphilis
外[胚层原]中胚层/外中胚層　ectomesoblast
外胚乳/外胚乳　perisperm
外皮深层/皮膚深層　enderon
外皮形成/外皮形成,表皮形成　cuticularization
外嵌植皮术/外嵌植皮術　onlay skin grafting
外切核酸酶/外切核酸酶　exonuclease
外切核酸酶类/外切核酸酶類　exonucleases
外切核糖核酸酶类/外切核糖核酸酶類　exoribonucleases
外倾/外傾　extraversion
外倾[性格]者/外傾[性格]者,精神外向者　extravert
外丘/外丘　waiqiu, GB36
外韧维管束/外韌維管束,并立型維管束　collateral vascular bundle
外疝/外疝　external hernia
外伤/外傷　external injury
外伤后应激障碍/創傷後精神壓力障礙　post-traumatic stress disorder
外伤后谵妄/外傷後譫妄　delirium post-traumaticum
外伤性白内障/外傷性白內障　traumatic cataract
外伤性变性/外傷性變性　traumatic degeneration
外伤性表皮囊肿/外傷性表皮囊腫　traumatic epidermal cyst
外伤性表皮样囊肿/外傷性表皮樣囊腫　traumatic epidermoid cyst
外伤性肺气肿/創傷性肺氣腫　traumatic emphysema
外伤性感觉缺失/外傷性感覺缺失　traumatic anesthesia
外伤性脊髓病/外傷性脊髓病　traumatic myelopathy
外伤性脊髓空洞症/創傷性脊髓空洞症　traumatic syringomyelia
外伤性脊髓炎/外傷性脊髓炎　traumatic myelitis
外伤性角膜炎/外傷性角膜炎　traumatic keratitis
外伤性截瘫/外傷性截癱　traumatic paraplegia
外伤性溃疡/外傷性潰瘍　traumatic ulcer
外伤性囊肿/創傷性囊腫　traumatic cyst
外伤性脑膜炎/外傷性腦膜炎　traumatic meningitis
外伤性尿道瘘/外傷性尿道瘺　traumatic urethral fistula
外伤性青光眼/外傷性青光眼　traumatic glaucoma
外伤性脱位/外傷性脫位　traumatic dislocation, unifacet dislocation
外伤性心包炎/創傷性心包炎　traumatic pericarditis
外伤性血栓/創傷性血栓　traumatic thrombus
外伤性血栓形成/外傷性血栓形成　traumatic thrombosis
外伤性胰腺炎/外傷性胰腺炎　traumatic pancreatitis
外伤性癔症/外傷性癔病　traumatic hysteria
外伤性脂肪坏死/外傷性脂肪壞死　traumatic fat necrosis
外伤性直肠炎/外傷性直腸炎　traumatic proctitis
外上段静脉/外上段靜脈　lateral superior segment vein
外上髁/外上髁　lateral epicondyle
外[神经]胶质/外膠質　ectoglia
外肾小球/外腎小球　external glomerulus
外渗/外滲　extravasation
外生骨疣/外生骨疣　exostoses
外生骨疣切除术/外生骨疣切除術　exostosectomy
外生软骨瘤/外生軟骨瘤　ecchondroma
外生[性]骨疣/外生骨贅　exostosis
外生性生长/外生性生長　exophytic growth
外生殖器/外生殖器　①external genital organ ②waishengzhiqi, HX4
外生殖器带状疱疹/外生殖器帶狀皰疹　herpes zoster of external genitalia
外生殖器毒物性皮炎/外生殖器毒物性皮炎　dermatitis venenata of external genitalia
外生殖器汗腺腺瘤/外生殖器汗腺腺瘤　syringoma of external genitalia

外生殖器红癣/外生殖器紅癬　erythrasma of external genitalia
外生殖器淋菌性脓疮/外生殖器淋菌性膿瘡　extragenital gonococcal ecthyma
外生殖器梅毒/外生殖器梅毒　extragenital syphilis
外生殖器疱疹样皮炎/外生殖器皰疹樣皮炎　dermatitis herpetiformis of external genitalia
外生殖器萎缩/外生殖器萎縮　atrophy of external genitalia
外生殖器血管角化瘤/外生殖器血管角化瘤　angiokeratoma of external genitalia
外生殖器血管神经性水肿/外生殖器血管神經性水腫　angioneurotic edema of external genitalia
外髓板/外髓板　external medullary lamina
外隧道/外隧道　outer tunnel
外胎盘/外胎盤,胎盘外部　ectoplacenta
外胎盘锥/外胎盤[圓]錐　ectoplacental cone
外台秘要方/外臺秘要方　Arcane Essentials from the Imperial Library
外肽酶/外肽酶　exopeptidase
外弹性膜/外彈性膜　external elastic lamina, external elastic membrane
外套层瘤/外套層瘤,包膜瘤　mantleoma
外推系数/外插係數　extrapolation coefficient
外围巨细胞修复性肉芽肿/外圍巨細胞修復性肉芽腫　peripheral giant-cell reparative granuloma
外吸渗/外吸滲,外逸　exsorption
外吸收/外吸收　external absorption
外下段静脉/外下段靜脈　lateral inferior segment vein
外下隐斜视/外下隱斜視　exocataphoria
外纤毛细胞/外纖毛細胞　external ciliated cell
外显率/外顯率,遗传特质表现频率　penetrance
外显子/外顯子　exon
外消旋[变]体/外消旋體　racemic modification
外消旋[化合]物/外消旋[化合]物　racemic compound, racemate
外消旋混合物/外消旋混合物　racemic mixture
外斜视/外斜視,散開性斜視　exotropia
外星性皮炎/外星性皮炎　extraterrestrial dermatitis
外形高点/外形高點,外形界線之高度　height of contour
外形性别/外形性別,形態性別　morphological sex
外形修整/外形修復　contouring
外旋转/外旋轉　external rotation
外旋转斜视/外[旋轉]斜視　excyclotropia
外旋转隐斜/外旋轉隱斜,外隱斜視　excyclophoria
外眼电图/外眼電圖　extraoculogram

外眼检查[法]/外眼檢查[法]　examination of external eye
外移行/外移行　external transmigration
外遗传致癌物/外遺傳致癌物　epigenetic carcinogens
外因/外因　external cause
外因病/外因病　exopathy
外因性动脉瘤/外因性動脈瘤　exogenous aneurysm
外因性感染/外因性感染　exogenous infection
外因性疾病/外因性疾病　enthetic disease
外因性凝血/外因性凝血　extrinsic coagulation
外因性中毒/外因性中毒　exogenic toxicosis
外阴病/外陰病,女陰病　vulvopathy
外阴道肛门[畸形]/外陰道肛門[畸形],女陰陰道肛　vulvar anus, vulvovaginal anus
外阴缝术/外陰縫術,女陰縫合術　episiorrhaphy
外阴根治术/外陰根治術　radical vulvectomy
外阴会阴缝术/外陰會陰縫術,女陰會陰縫合術　episioperineorrhaphy
外阴疾病/外陰疾病　vulvar disease
外阴结核/外陰結核　vulval tuberculosis
外阴溃疡/外陰潰瘍,陰疳,陰部壞疽　cancrum pudendi
外阴裂/外陰裂,外陰部裂隙　fissura pudendi
外阴佩吉特病/外陰佩吉特病,女陰 Paget 氏病　Paget disease of vulva
外阴切除术/外陰切除術,女陰切除術　vulvectomy
外阴瘙痒症/外陰搔癢症,女陰搔癢　pruritus vulvae
外阴臊疣/外陰臊疣　condyloma of vulva
外阴性阴道痉挛/外陰性陰道痙攣　vulvar vaginismus
外阴血管角化瘤/外陰血管角化瘤,女陰血管角化瘤　angiokeratoma of vulva
外阴血囊肿/外陰血囊腫,陰部血囊　pudendal hematocele
外阴熏洗/外陰熏洗　vulval steaming and douche
外阴阴道炎/外陰陰道炎,女陰陰道炎　vulvovaginitis
外阴营养不良/外陰營養不良　vulvar dystrophy
外阴肿瘤/外陰腫瘤　vulvar neoplasms
外隐静脉/外隱靜脈　external saphenous vein
外隐斜/外隱斜,外轉隱斜眼　exophoria
外用/外用　external application
外用氟化物/外用氟化物　topical fluoride
外用酒精/外用酒精　rubbing alcohol
外用药/外用藥　externally applied agent
外用液体药剂/外用液體藥劑,外用液體製劑　liquid preparation for external use
外釉上皮/外釉上皮　outer enamel epithelium,

external enamel epithelium
外原肠胚/外原腸胚　exogastrula
外原肠胚形成/外原腸胚形成　exogastrulation
外源代谢/外源代謝,外生性代谢　exogenous metabolism
外源基因/外源基因　exogenous gene
外源凝集素/外源凝集素　lectin
外源物/外源物　xenobiotics
外源性变应性肺泡炎/外源性變應性肺泡炎,外因性過敏肺泡炎　extrinsic allergic alveolitis
外源性高胆固醇血症/外源性高膽固醇血症　exogenous hypercholesterolemia
外源性高甘油三酯血症/外源性高甘油三脂血症,外源性高三酸甘油脂血症　exogenous hypertriglyceridemia
外源性类脂性肺炎/外源性類脂性肺炎　exogenous lipoid pneumonia
外源性染色/外源性染色　extrinsic staining
外源性哮喘/外因性氣喘　extrinsic asthma
外源性中毒/外源性中毒　heterointoxication
外源性重感染/外源性重感染　exogenous superinfection
外在神经支配/外在神經支配　extrinsic innervation
外燥证/外燥證　exogenous dryness pattern
外展/外展　abduction
外展过度/過度外展　hyperabduction
外展肌/外展肌　abductor
外展夹板/外展夾板　abduction splint
外展拇长肌/外展拇長肌　musculus abductor pollicis longus
外展[踇]肌/外展[踇]肌　abductor hallucis
外展神经/外展神經　abducent nerve
外障/外障　external ophthalmopathy
外枕骨/外枕骨　exoccipital bone
外证/外證　exterior pattern
外支/外支　external branch
外直肌/外直肌　lateral rectus
外直肌腱膜/外直肌腱膜　lacertus of lateral rectus
外指细胞/外指細胞,戴特斯细胞　outer phalangeal cell
外治法/外治法　external therapy, external treatment
外致密纤维/外致密纖維　outer coarse fiber, outer dense fiber
外痔/外痔　external hemorrhoid
外痔·脾虚气陷证/外痔·脾虛氣陷證　external hemorrhoid with pattern of spleen deficiency and qi sinking
外痔·气滞血瘀证/外痔·氣滯血瘀證　external hemorrhoid with pattern of qi stagnation and blood stasis
外痔·湿热下注证/外痔·濕熱下注證　external hemorrhoid with pattern of dampness-heat diffusing downward
外置移植物/外置移植物　onlay graft
外周导管插入术/外周導管插入術　peripheral catheterization
外周感受器/外周感受器,末梢感受器　peripheroceptor
外周耐受/外周耐受　peripheral tolerance
外周神经刺激/外周神經刺激　peripheral nerve stimulation
外周神经胶质瘤/末梢神經膠質瘤　peripheral glioma
外周性光幻视/末梢性光幻視　peripherophose
外周性痛/外周性痛,離心性疼痛　excentric pain
外周性脱羧酶抑制药/外周性脱羧酶抑制藥,末梢脱羧酶抑制劑　peripheral decarboxylase inhibitor
外周性影幻视/末梢性影幻視,周圍影幻視　peripheraphose
外周血干细胞移植/外周血幹細胞移植　peripheral blood stem cell transplantation
外周血管疾病/外周血管疾病　peripheral vascular disease
外周血管扩张药/周邊血管擴張藥　peripheral vasodilator
外周血管阻力/周邊血管抵抗力　peripheral vascular resistance
外柱细胞/外柱細胞　outer pillar cell
外转胎位术/外轉胎位術,外倒轉術　external version
外椎骨静脉丛/外椎骨静脈叢　external vertebral plexus
外锥体[细胞]层/外錐體[細胞]層　external pyramidal layer
外[子]宫颈/外子宫頸　exocervix
外眦/外眥　lateral angle of eye
外眦间距/外眥間距　outer canthic diameter
弯/彎　bend
弯刀综合征/彎刀症候群　scimitar syndrome
弯骨矫形术/彎骨矯形術,彎骨矯直術　osteotomoclasia
弯节锥蝽/彎節錐蝽　Panstrongylus geniculatus
弯曲/彎曲　flexure
弯曲部位网状色素异常/彎曲部位網狀色素異常　reticulate pigmented anomaly of flexure

弯曲杆菌感染/彎曲桿菌感染　Campylobacter infection
弯曲杆菌属/彎曲桿菌屬　*Campylobacter*
弯曲菌病/彎曲桿菌病　campylobacteriosis
弯曲菌肠炎/彎麴菌腸炎　Campylobacter enteritis
弯曲牙/彎曲牙　dilaceration of tooth
弯曲振动/彎曲振動　bending vibration
弯曲足/彎曲足　crooked foot
弯手机/彎機頭　contra-angle handpiece
弯形切口/彎形切口,曲棍球棒形切開術　hockey stick incision
弯腰扶椅位/彎腰扶椅位　bending with chair supporting position
弯月形镜片/彎月形鏡片,凸凹透鏡　meniscus lens
弯针/彎針　curved needle, bending of needle
弯指/彎指,手指彎曲變形　dactylogryposis
蜿蜒状动脉瘤/蜿蜒狀動脈瘤　diffuse arterial ectasia
豌豆骨/豌豆骨　pisiform bone
豌豆骨关节/豌豆骨關節　joint of pisiform bone
豌豆关节/豌豆關節　articulation of pisiform bone
豌豆球蛋白/豌豆球蛋白,蠶豆蛋白　vicilin
豌豆汤样粪/豌豆湯樣糞,碗豆羹狀糞　pea soup stool
丸[剂]/丸[劑]　pill
丸块/丸塊　massa
丸药/丸藥,小丸　pellet
完带汤/完帶湯　wandai decoction
完谷不化/完穀不化　diarrhea with undigested food
完骨/完骨,乳突　①mastoideum, mastoid process ②wangu, GB12 point
完全变性反应/完全變性反應　reaction of total degeneration
完全并指/完全并指　complete syndactyly
完全并趾/完全并趾　complete syndactyly
完全蛋白质/完全蛋白質　complete protein
完全对称性双畸胎/完全對稱性雙畸胎,對稱雙畸胎　cenadelphus
完全发育期/完全發育期　metaplasis
完全房室阻断/完全房室阻斷　complete block
完全骨折/完全骨折　complete fracture
完全虹膜麻痹/完全虹膜麻痺　complete iridoplegia
完全激动药/完全激動藥　full agonist
完全拮抗药/完全拮抗藥　full antagonist
完全抗体/完全抗體　complete antibody
完全抗原/完全抗原　complete antigen
完全流产/完全流産　complete abortion
完全卵裂/完全卵裂　complete cleavage, holoblastic cleavage
完全培养基/完全培養基　complete medium, CM
完全偏盲/完全偏盲,絕對偏盲　absolute hemianopia
完全前置胎盘/完全前置胎盤　placenta praevia totalis
完全疝/完全疝　complete hernia
完全失神经支配/完全失神經支配　total denervation
完全脱位/完全脱位　complete dislocation
完全型大动脉转位/完全型大動脈轉位　complete transposition of great artery
完全性房室传导阻滞/完全性房室傳導阻滯,心臟傳導完全阻斷　complete heart block
完全性房室通道/完全性房室通道　complete atrioventricular canal
完全性瘘/完全性瘘,全瘘管　complete fistula
完全性[脑]卒中/完全性[腦]卒中　complete stroke
完全性前置胎盘/完全性前置胎盤　total placenta praevia
完全性失语[症]/完全性失語[症]　total aphasia, global aphasia
完全性遗忘/完全性遺忘　global amnesia
完全再生/完全再生　holomorphosis
完善行为/完善行爲　consummatory behavior
完整活组织检查/完整活組織檢查,全切除活組織檢查法　total biopsy
顽固性溃疡/頑[固]性潰瘍　intractable ulcer
顽固性疼痛/頑固性疼痛　intractable pain
顽固性荨麻疹/頑固性蕁麻疹,久存性蕁麻疹　urticaria perstans
顽固性银屑病/頑固性銀屑病,頑固性乾癬　psoriasis inverterata
顽抗者/頑抗者　recalcitrant
顽湿聚结/頑濕聚結,結節性癢疹　accumulation of stubborn dampness, prurigo nodularis
顽湿聚结·湿热风毒证/頑濕聚結·濕熱風毒證　accumulation of stubborn dampness with pattern of dampness-heat and wind-toxin
顽湿聚结·血瘀风燥证/頑濕聚結·血瘀風燥證　accumulation of stubborn dampness with pattern of blood stasis and wind-dryness
顽童面容/頑童面容　elfin face
烷撑二醇/烷二醇　alkylene glycol
烷化雌激素甾类/烷化雌激素甾類　alkylated estrogenic steroids
烷化剂/烷化劑　alkylating agent
烷化作用/烷化作用,烴基化作用　alkylation
烷基/烴基　alkyl
烷基胺/烷基胺,烴胺　alkylamine
烷基汞化合物/烷基汞化合物　alkylmercury

compound
烷基化/烷基化　alkylate
烷基化抗肿瘤药/烷基化抗腫瘤藥　alkylating antineoplastic agent
烷基三甲基季铵类化合物/烷基三甲基銨類化合物　alkyl trimethyl ammonium compound
烷属化合物/石蠟化合物　paraffin compound
2-烷-N-羧甲-N-羟乙咪唑啉甜菜碱/2-烷-N-羧甲-N-羥乙咪唑啉甜菜鹼　2-alkyl-N-carboxymethyl-N-hydroxyethyl imidazolinium betaine
烷烃1-单氧酶/烷烴1-單氧酶　alkane 1-monooxygenase
烷烃类/烷烴類　alkanes
烷氧基测定/烷氧基測定　alkoxy determination
挽救疗法/挽救療法　salvage therapy
晚电位/晚電位　late potential
晚发性精神分裂症/晚發性精神分裂症　late schizophrenia
晚感受器电位/晚感受器電位　late receptor potential
晚期/後期　advanced stage
晚期产后出血/晚期產後出血　late postpartum hemorrhage, late stage of postpartum hemorrhage
晚期减速/晚期減速　late deceleration
晚期流产/後期流產　late abortion
晚期梅毒/晚期梅毒　lues tarda
晚期尿毒症/晚期尿毒症　late stage uremia
晚期胎死/晚期死胎　late fetal death
晚期血吸虫病/晚期血吸蟲病　advanced stage of schistosomiasis
晚期婴儿型家族性黑矇性痴呆/晚期嬰兒型家族性黑矇性癡呆,比-傑二氏病　Bielschowsky-Jansky disease
晚幼红细胞/晚幼紅細胞,變型母紅血球　metarubricyte
晚幼粒细胞/晚幼粒細胞,後髓細胞　metamyelocyte
脘腹积证/脘腹積證　amassment disease of epigastrium and abdomen
脘腹痛/脘腹痛　epigastric pain
万病回春/萬病回春　Curative Measures for All Diseases
万古霉素/萬古黴素　vancomycin
万古霉素抗药性/萬古黴素抗藥性　vancomycin resistance
万密斋医学全书/萬密齋醫學全書　Wan Mizhai's Complete Medical Book
万氏牛黄清心丸/萬氏牛黃清心丸　wanshi niuhuang qingxin pills
万应锭/萬應錠　wanying troches

万应药/萬應藥　polychrest
腕/腕　wrist, wan, SF2
腕背侧韧带/腕背側韌帶　dorsal carpal ligament
腕背侧网/腕背側網,背側腕弓　posterior carpal arch
腕背后侧环状韧带/腕背後側環狀韌帶　dorsal posterior annular ligament of wrist
腕背网/腕背網　dorsal carpal rete
腕背支/腕背支　dorsal carpal branch
腕部瘢痕挛缩/腕部瘢痕攣縮　scar contracture of wrist
腕尺侧副韧带/腕尺側副韌帶　ulnar carpal collateral ligament
腕尺侧管/腕尺側管　ulnar carpal canal
腕尺外侧韧带/腕尺外側韌帶　ulnar lateral ligament of carpus
腕带蛇舌状虫/腕帶狀洞頭蟲　Armillifer armillatus
腕辐状韧带/腕輻狀韌帶　radiate carpal ligament
腕骨/腕骨　①carpal bone, carpale, carpus ②wangu, SI4
腕骨沟/腕溝　carpal groove, sulcus of wrist
腕骨骨折/腕骨骨折　wrist fracture
腕骨间背侧韧带/腕骨間背側韌帶　dorsal intercarpal ligament
腕骨间骨间韧带/腕骨間骨間韌帶　interosseous intercarpal ligament
腕骨间关节/腕骨間關節　intercarpal joint, intercarpal articulation
腕骨间掌侧韧带/腕骨間掌側韌帶　palmar intercarpal ligament
腕骨切除术/腕切除術　carpectomy
腕关节/腕關節　carpal articulation
腕关节面/腕關節面　carpal articular surface
腕关节扭伤/腕關節扭傷　sprain of wrist joint
腕关节深总韧带/腕關節深總韌帶　deep common ligament of wrist joint
腕关节炎/腕關節炎　carpal arthritis
腕管/腕管　carpal canal, flexor canal
腕管综合征/腕管症候群　carpal tunnel syndrome
腕管综合征·风寒湿阻证/腕管症候群·風寒濕阻證　carpal tunnel syndrome with wind-cold-dampness obstruction pattern
腕管综合征·血瘀气滞证/腕管症候群·血瘀氣滯證　carpal tunnel syndrome with pattern of blood stasis and qi stagnation
腕后区/腕後部　posterior region of wrist
腕疽/腕疽　tuberculous arthritis of wrist
腕内侧韧带/腕內側韌帶　medial ligament of wrist
腕前区/腕前部　anterior region of wrist

腕桡侧副韧带/腕橈側副韌帶　radial carpal collateral ligament
腕桡侧管/腕橈側管　radial carpal canal
腕桡外侧韧带/腕橈外側韌帶　radial lateral ligament of carpus
腕三角关节盘/腕三角關節盤　triangular disc of wrist
腕三角软骨挤压试验/腕三角軟骨擠壓試驗　crushing test of wrist triangular cartilage
腕三角纤维软骨损伤/腕三角纖維軟骨損傷　injury of triquetral fibrocartilage
腕伸肌紧张试验/腕伸肌緊張試驗　Mills sign
腕损伤/腕損傷　wrist injury
腕下垂/腕下垂，垂腕　wristdrop
腕楔状骨/腕楔狀骨　cuneiform bone of carpus
腕痈/腕癰　wrist abscess
腕掌背侧韧带/腕掌骨背側韌帶　dorsal carpometacarpal ligament
腕掌侧网/前腕弓　anterior carpal arch
腕掌骨间韧带/腕掌骨間韌帶　interosseous carpometacarpal ligament
腕掌关节/腕掌關節　carpometacarpal joint, carpometacarpal articulation
腕掌拇指关节/腕掌拇指關節　the first carpometacarpal articulation
腕掌前韧带/腕掌前韌帶　anterior carpometacarpal ligament
腕掌掌侧韧带/腕掌骨掌側韌帶　palmar carpometacarpal ligament
腕掌支/腕掌支　palmar carpal branch
腕中关节/腕中關節　mediocarpal joint
腕中心骨/腕中心骨　carpal central bone
腕舟骨折/腕舟[狀]骨骨折　fracture of scaphoid bone of wrist
腕足痉挛/腕足痙攣　carpopedal spasm
尪痹/尪痹　aggravated bi
尪痹颗粒/尪痹顆粒　wangbi granule
亡阳/亡陽，脱陽　yang depletion
亡阳证/亡陽證　yang depletion pattern
亡阴/亡陰，脱陰　yin depletion
亡阴证/亡陰證　yin depletion pattern
王不留行/王不留行　cowherb seed
王清任/王清任　Wang Qingren
王叔和/王叔和　Wang Shuhe
网/網　rete
网板/網板　reticular lamina
网格蛋白/網格蛋白　clathrin
网格蛋白包被小泡/網格蛋白包被小泡　clathrin-coated vesicle
网格蛋白轻链/網格蛋白輕鏈　clathrin light chain
网格蛋白重链/網格蛋白重鏈　clathrin heavy chain
网膜/網膜　omentum
网膜肠疝/網膜腸疝，網膜腸赫尼亞　epiploenterocele
网膜成形术/網膜成形術　epiploplasty
网膜带/網膜帶　omental band
网膜缝合术/網膜縫合術　epiplorrhaphy
网膜梗死/網膜梗死　omental infarction
网膜股疝/網膜股疝，網膜股赫尼亞　epiplomerocele
网膜固定术/網膜固定術　epiplopexy
网膜结节/網膜結節　omental tuberosity
网膜孔/網膜孔　omental foramen
网膜孔淋巴结/網膜孔淋巴結　lymph node of omental foramen
网膜门静脉造影术/網膜門靜脈造影術　omentoportography
网膜囊/網膜囊　omental bursa
网膜囊前庭/網膜囊前庭　vestibule of omental bursa
网膜囊上隐窝/網膜囊上隱窩　superior omental recess
网膜囊下隐窝/網膜囊下隱窩　inferior omental recess
网膜囊肿/網膜囊腫　omental cyst
网膜内疝/網膜內疝　hernia intraepiploica
网膜扭转/網膜扭轉　omental torsion
网膜脓肿/網膜膿腫　epiploic abscess
网膜脾固定术/網膜脾固定術　omentosplenopexy
网膜脐疝/網膜臍疝，網膜臍赫尼亞　epiplomphalocele
网膜切除术/網膜切除術　epiploectomy
网膜切开术/網膜切開術　omentotomy
网膜肉芽脐疝/網膜肉芽臍疝，網膜內贅性臍疝氣，網膜肉贅性臍赫尼亞　epiplosarcomphalocele
网膜疝/網膜疝，網膜赫尼亞　epiplocele
网膜突出/網膜突逸　omental hernia
网膜系膜/網膜繫膜　meso-omentum
网膜炎/[大]網膜炎　epiploitis
网膜移植/網膜移植　omentum transplantation
网膜移植物/網膜移植物　omental graft
网膜阴囊疝/網膜陰囊疝，網膜陰囊赫尼亞　epiploscheocele
网膜支/網膜支　epiploic branch, omental branch
网球肩病/網球肩病　tennis shoulder
网球腕/網球腕，網球員腕病　tennis wrist
网球肘/網球肘，網球員肘病，橈肱骨黏液囊炎　tennis elbow
网染细胞/網染細胞　arkyochrome

网尾线虫感染/網尾線蟲感染　Dictyocaulus infection
网纹染细胞/網紋染細胞　arkyostichochrome
网纹细胞/網紋細胞　reticulated cell
网硬蛋白/網硬蛋白,網硬素　reticulin
网织红细胞/網狀紅血球,網狀細胞　reticulocyte
网质/網質　polioplasm
网状变性/網狀變性　reticular degeneration
网状部/網狀部　reticular part
网状层/網狀層　reticular layer
网状带/網狀帶　zona reticularis
网状红斑性黏蛋白沉积症/網狀紅斑性黏蛋白沈積症　reticular erythematous mucinosis
网状红斑萎缩性毛囊炎/網狀紅斑[萎縮]性毛囊炎　folliculitis ulerythematosa reticulata
网状红细胞/網狀紅細胞,網狀紅血球　reticulocyte
网状基质/網狀質　pseudostructure
网状激活系统/網狀激活系統,網狀活化系統　reticular activating system
网状脊髓束/網狀脊髓徑　reticulospinal tract
网状结构/網狀結構　reticular formation
网状类银屑病/網狀類銀屑病　parapsoriasis retiformis
网状内皮系统/網狀內皮系統　reticuloendothelial system, RES
网状内皮细胞/網狀內皮細胞　reticuloendothelial cell
网状内皮组织/網狀內皮組織　reticuloendothelium
网状内皮组织增殖/網狀內皮組織增殖　reticuloendotheliosis
网状内皮组织增殖病毒/網狀內皮組織增殖病毒　reticuloendotheliosis virus
网状黏质/網狀黏質　magma reticulare
网状皮肤萎缩/網狀皮膚萎縮,網狀皮萎病　atrophoderma reticulatum
网状皮片/網狀皮片　mesh free skin graft
网状皮片取皮机/網狀皮片取皮機　mesh graft dermatome
网状青斑/網狀青斑　livedo reticularis
网状色素性疾患/網狀色素性疾病　reticular pigment disorder
网状细胞/網狀細胞　reticular cell
网状细胞计数/網狀細胞計數　reticulocyte count
网状细胞肉瘤/網狀細胞肉瘤　clasmocytoma
网状细胞增多[症]/網狀細胞增多症　reticulosis
网状纤维/網狀纖維　reticulum fiber, reticular fiber
网状纤维染色/網狀纖維染色　reticulin fiber staining
网状小脑纤维/網狀小腦纖維　reticulocerebellar fiber
网状肢端色素沉着症/網狀肢端色素沈著症　acropigmentation of reticularis
网状植皮术/網狀植皮術　mesh grafting
网状中柱/網狀中柱　dictyostele
网状组织/網狀組織　reticulum
网状组织细胞瘤/網狀組織細胞瘤　reticulohistiocytoma
网状组织细胞肉芽肿/網狀組織細胞肉芽腫　reticulohistiocytic granuloma
网状组织细胞增生症/網狀組織細胞增生症　reticulohistiocytosis
往返性杂音/往返性雜音　to and fro murmur
往复隔膜泵/往復隔膜泵　reciprocating diaphragm pump
往复式装置/往復式裝置　to and fro system
妄想/妄想　delusion
妄想痴呆患者/妄想癡呆[患]者　paraphrenic
妄想狂者/妄想狂者　paranoiac
妄想心境/妄想心境　delusional mood
妄想性知觉/妄想性知覺　delusional perception
妄言/妄言　delirious speech
妄语/妄語　delirious speech
忘忧散/忘憂散　powder for infertile men
望鼻前庭/望鼻前庭　inspection of nasal vestibule
望鼻腔/望鼻腔　inspection of nasal cavity
望鼻涕/望鼻涕　inspection of snivel
望鼻血/望鼻血　inspection of nose bleeding
望鼻咽部/望鼻咽部　inspection of nasopharynx
望带下/望帶下　inspection of vaginal discharge
望恶露/望惡露　inspection of lochia
望耳郭/望耳郭　inspection of auricle
望耳孔/望耳孔　inspection of external acoustic meatus
望耳膜/望耳膜　inspection of tympanic membrane
望耳周/望耳周　inspection of periotic skin
望颌面/望頜面　inspection of maxillo-facial region
望喉腔/望喉腔　inspection of laryngeal cavity
望喉外部/望喉外部　inspection of external larynx
望喉咽部/望喉咽部　inspection of laryngopharynx
望经血/望經血　inspection of menstrual blood
望口唇/望口唇　inspection of lip
望口腔黏膜/望口腔黏膜　inspection of oral mucosa
望口咽部/望口咽部　inspection of oropharynx
望络脉/望絡脈　inspection of collateral
望面色/望面色　inspection of complexion
望目/望目　inspection of eyes
望排出物/望排出物　inspection of excreta
望皮肤/望皮膚　inspection of skin, observation of

skin
望人中/望人中 inspection of philtrum
望乳房/望乳房 inspection of breast
望乳汁/望乳汁 inspection of breast milk
望色/望色 inspection of color
望舌体/望舌體 inspection of tongue body
望神/望神 inspection of spirit, inspection of vitality
望态/望態 inspection of gesture and behavior
望外鼻/望外鼻 inspection of external nose
望五官/望五官 inspection of five apertures
望形/望形 inspection of body statue
望形态/望形態 inspection of body statue and movements
望牙齿/望牙齒 inspection of tooth
望眼神/望眼神 inspection of eye expression, inspection of eye spirit
望阴道/望陰道 inspection of vagina
望阴户/望陰戶 inspection of vulva
望龈肉/望齦肉 inspection of gum
望远镜试验/望遠鏡試驗 telescope test
望诊/望診 inspection
危害/危害 hazard
危害废弃物/危害廢棄物 hazardous waste
危害减少/危害減少 harm reduction
危害物质/危害物質 hazardous substance
危害性/危害性 hazardness
危机干预/危機干預 crisis intervention
危急性出血/危急性出血 critical hemorrhage
危险处理/危險處理 risk management
危险行为/危險行爲 dangerous behavior
危险行为因素监测系统/危險行爲因素監測系統 behavioral risk factor surveillance system
危险性评估/危險性評估 risk assessment
危险因素/危險因素 risk factors
危象/危象,危症 crisis
危重病/危重病 critical illness
危重病人医疗/危重病人醫療 critical care
危重症医学/危重症醫學 critical care medicine
威策尔胃造口术/威策爾胃造口術 Witzel gastrostomy
威尔金森三角/威爾金森三角,維金森三角 Wilkinson triangle
威尔尼克综合征/威爾尼克症候群,Wernicke 氏症候群 Wernicke syndrome
威尔逊肌/威爾遜肌,Wilson 氏肌 Wilson muscle
威尔逊综合征/威爾遜症候群,Wilson 氏症候群 Wilson syndrome
威尔逊阻断/威爾遜阻斷,Wilson 氏阻斷 Wilson block
威克姆纹/威克姆紋 Wickham striae
威利斯垂直距离测量尺/威利斯垂直距離測量尺 Willis bite gauge
威利斯神经/威利斯神經,Willis 氏神經,副神經 nerve of Willis
威利斯误听/威利斯誤聽 Willis paracusia
威廉斯综合征/威廉斯症候群 Williams syndrome
威灵仙/威靈仙 Chinese clematis root
威姆斯赫斯特起电机/威姆斯赫斯特起電機,維斯特氏起電機 Wimshurst machine
威塞利韧带/威塞利韌帶,Vesalius 氏韌帶,腹股溝韌帶 Vesalius ligament
威沙特试验/威沙特試驗,威夏特氏試驗 Wishart test
微/微 micro
微孢子/微孢子 microsporidia
微孢子虫病/微孢子蟲病 microsporidiosis
微胞粒间液/微胞粒間液 intermicellar fluid
微波/微波 microwave
微波疗法/微波療法 microwave therapy
微波灭菌/微波滅菌 microwave sterilization
微波凝固[术]/微波凝固[術] microwave coagulation
微波烧伤/微波燒傷 microwave burn
微波消融[术]/微波消融[術] microwave ablation
微波性白内障/微波性白內障 microwave cataract
微测压计/微測壓計 microtonometer
微差体积描记法/微差體積描記法,微量體積改變描記法 microplethysmography
微创性外科手术/微創性外科手術 minimally invasive surgical procedure
微单位/微單位 microunit
微滴反应/減滴質反應,小滴反應 miostagmin reaction
微滴核/微滴核 droplet nucleus
微电极/微電極 microelectrode
微动关节/微動關節 amphiarthrosis
微动脉瘤/微動脈瘤 microaneurysm
微动物区系/微動物區系 microfauna
微分干涉相差显微镜/鑒別性干擾-相差顯微鏡 differential interference-contrast microscope
微粉化/微粉化 micronise
微粉磨/微粉磨 micronizer
微伏[特]/微伏特 microvolt
微观不均一性/微觀不均一性,微異質性 microheterogeneity
微管/微管 microtubule

微管蛋白/微管蛋白　tubulin
微管蛋白质类/微管蛋白質類　microtubule proteins
微管相关蛋白质类/微管相關蛋白質類　microtubule-associated proteins
微管学说/微管學說　microtubule theory
微管组织中心/微管組織中心　microtubule-organizing center
微过滤/微過濾　microfiltration
微核/微核,小核　micronucleus
微核试验/微核試驗　micronucleus test
微胶粒/微膠粒　micelle
微晶皮肤磨削术/微晶皮膚磨削術　dermabrasion by microcrystal
微晶[体]/微晶體　microcrystal
微晶纤维素/微晶纖維素　microcrystalline cellulose
微晶学说/微晶學說　microcrystal theory
微精氨基琥珀酸尿/微精胺基琥珀酸尿　microargininosuccinic aciduria
微静脉血管瘤/微[細]靜脈血管瘤　microvenular hemangioma
微居里/微居里　microcurie
微居里小时/微居里小時　microcurie-hour
微克/微克　microgram
微孔过滤/微孔過濾　microfiltration
微孔过滤器/微孔過濾器　micropore filter
微孔滤器/微孔濾器　micropore filter
微孔膜/微孔膜　microporous membrane
微粒/微粒　particle, particulate
微粒辐射/微粒輻射　corpuscular radiation
微粒化/使變小　micronize
微粒监测/微粒監測　particulate matter monitoring
微粒皮片/微粒皮片　microne free skin graft
微粒体/微粒體　microsome
微粒直径测定法/微粒直徑測定法,纖維徑測量法　eriometry
微粒直径测定器/微粒直徑測定器,纖維徑測定器　eriometer
微粒植皮术/微粒植皮術　granular skin grafting
微梁网/微梁網　microtrabecular lattice, microtrabecular network
微量比色计/微量比色計　microcolorimeter
微量测定[法]/微量檢定法　microdetermination
微量沉淀[反应]/微量沈澱反應　microprecipitation
微量沉淀试验/微量沈澱試驗　microprecipitation test
微量分析/微量分析[法],精微分析法　microanalysis
微量灌肠/微量灌腸　microclyster
微量呼吸计/微量呼吸計　microrespirometer
微量灰化法/微量灰化法,微量燒灰測定法　microincineration
微量冷热试验/微量冷熱試驗　minimal caloric test
微量淋巴细胞毒性试验/微量淋巴細胞毒性試驗　microlymphocytotoxicity test
微量黏度计/微量黏度計　microviscosimeter
微量天平/微量天秤,精微天秤　microbalance
微量调节注射器/微量調整注射器　microsyringe
微量血气计/微量血氣[測量]計　microaerotonometer
微量血细胞比容/微量血細胞比容,微量血球容積測定法　microhematocrit
微量[液体]测压计/微量[液體]測壓計,微小測壓計,流體壓力計　micromanometer
微量营养素/微量營養素,微量滋養質　nutrilite
微量营养系/微量營養系　micronutrients
微量元素/微量元素　trace element
微量注射/微量注射　microinjections
微量注射器/微量注射器　microsyringe, microinjector
微流体分析技术/微流體分析技術　microfluidic analytical technique
微滤泡性甲状腺肿/微濾泡性甲狀腺腫　microfollicular goiter
微伦琴/微倫琴,微量X光線單位　microroentgen
微脉/微脈　faint pulse
微脉管系统/微脈管系統　microvasculature
微囊化/微囊化　microencapsulation
微囊剂/微囊劑　microcapsule
微囊片/微囊錠[劑]　microencapsule tablet
微囊肿性附件癌/微囊腫性附件癌,微囊腫性附屬器癌　microcystic adnexal carcinoma
微囊注射液/微囊注射液　microencapsule injection
微脓肿/微膿腫　microabscess
微泡式氧合器/微泡式氧合器　microbubble oxygenator
微气泡/微氣泡　microbubbles
微嵌合体/微嵌合體　microchimera
微球/微球　microsphere
β2-微球蛋白/β2-微球蛋白,乙二型微球蛋白　bata2-microglobulin
微球菌核酸酶/微球菌核酸酶　micrococcal nuclease
微球体/微球體　microspheres
微热/微熱,輕熱　eupyrexia, mild fever
微绒毛/微絨毛　microvillus
微容量计数法/微容量計數法,微容量測定　microvolumetry
微弱呼吸/微弱呼吸　feeble respiration

微升/微立,微公升　microliter
微升毛细管/微升毛細管　microcap
微生态系/微[小]生態系,微小環境適應系　microecosystem
微生物/微生物　microbe
微生物测定[法]/微生物鑒定,微生物檢定　microbioassay
微生物光感受器/微生物光感受器　microbial photoreceptor
微生物集落计数/微生物集落計數　microbial colony count
微生物胶原酶/微生物膠原酶　microbial collagenase
微生物抗药性/微生物抗藥性　microbial drug resistance
微生物敏感性试验/微生物敏感性試驗　microbial sensitivity test
微生物区系/微生物區系　microflora
微生物视紫质/微生物視紫質　microbial rhodopsin
微生物效价测定/微生物效價測定　microbiological assay
微生物性湿疹/微生物性濕疹　microbial eczema
微生物学技术/微生物學技術　microbiological technique
微生物学家/微生物學家　microbiologist
微生物学现象/微生物學現象　microbiologic phenomena
微生物约物/微生物藥物　microbial medicine
微生物药学/微生物藥學　microbial pharmacy
微时计/微時計　chronograph
微栓子/微栓子　microemboli
微丝/微絲　microfilament
微丝蛋白质类/微絲蛋白質類　microfilament proteins
微丝蚴血/幼絲蟲血症　microfilaremia
微体/微體　microbody
微体[新陈]代谢/微體新陳代謝　micrometabolism
微透析/微透析　microdialysis
微团/微團,膠粒　micelle
微瓦[特]/微瓦特　microwatt
微丸/微丸　mini-pill
微卫星重复/微衛星重複　microsatellite repeat
微温浴/微溫浴　tepid bath
微细胞/微細胞　microcell
微细血管血管瘤/微細血管血管瘤　microcapillary hemangioma
微纤维/微纖維　microfibril
微纤维蛋白质/微纖維蛋白質　fibrillar protein
微腺瘤/微[小]腺瘤　microadenoma

微小病变/微小病變,微小改變疾病　minimal change disease, nil disease
微小病变型肾病/微小病變型腎病　minimal change nephrosis
微小 RNA 病毒/小核糖核酸病毒　picornavirus
微小环境/微小環境　microenvironment
微小剂量/微[小]劑]量　microdosage
微小膜壳绦虫/微小膜殼條蟲,短小包膜蟲,短小條蟲　Hymenolepis nana
微小内蜒阿米巴/短小内[蜒]阿米巴　Endolimax nana
微笑分析/微笑分析　smile analysis
微笑构成/微笑構成　components of smile
微笑美学/微笑美學　smile aesthetics
微笑线/微笑線　smile lines
微斜视/微斜視　microtropia
微芯片电泳/微芯片電泳,微晶片電泳　microchip electrophoresis
微型计算机/微型計算機,微型電腦　microcomputer
微血管/微血管,毛细血管　micrangium
微血管病/微血管病,毛細血管病　microangiopathy
微血管病性溶血性贫血/微血管病性溶血性貧血　microangiopathic hemolytic anemia
微血管吻合[术]/微血管吻合[術]　microvascular anastomosis
微血管性心绞痛/微血管性心絞痛　microvascular angina
微血栓/微血栓　microthrombus
微循环/微循環　microcirculation
微音留声器/微音揚聲器　microphonograph
微原纤维/微原纖維　microfibril
微阵列分析/微陣列分析　microarray analysis
微[植]皮刀/微植皮刀　microdermatome
微注射/微注射　microinjection
煨[制]/煨,焙烤　roasting, roasting in ashes
韦伯试验/韋伯試驗　Weber test
韦伯膝总韧带/[韋伯]膝總韌帶,Weber 氏總韌帶　common ligament of Weber
韦伯综合征/韋伯症候群,Weber 氏症候群　syndrome of Weber
韦德尼希-霍夫曼麻痹/韋德尼希-霍夫曼麻痺,Werdnig-Hoffmann 二氏麻痺　Werdnig-Hoffmann paralysis
韦-迪病/韋-迪病,Weber-Dimitri 二氏病　Weber-Dimitri disease
韦-杜综合征/韋-杜症候群,Weber-Dubler 二氏症候群　Weber-Dubler syndrome
韦尔病/韋爾病,Weil 氏病,螺旋體性黃疸　Weil

disease
韦尔波疝/韋爾波疝,Velpeau 氏疝　Velpeau hernia
韦尔加泪沟/韋爾加淚溝,Verga 氏淚溝　Verga lacrimal groove
韦尔姆斯瘤/韋爾姆斯瘤,Wilms 氏瘤　Wilms tumor
韦尔内综合征/韋爾內症候群,Vernet 氏症候群　Vernet syndrome
韦尔斯综合征/威爾斯症候群　Wells syndrome
韦格纳肉芽肿病/韋格納肉芽腫病　Wegner granulomatosis
韦金斯基现象/韋金斯基現象　Wedensky phenomenon
韦金斯基效应/韋金斯基效應　Wedensky effect
韦金斯基易化作用/韋金斯基易化作用　Wedensky facilitation
韦兰德溃疡/韋蘭德潰瘍,Welander 氏潰瘍　Welander ulcer
韦尼克病/韋尼克病　Wernicke disease
韦尼克脑病/韋尼克腦病,Wernicke 氏腦病　Wernicke encephalopathy
韦尼克区/韋尼克區　Wernicke area
韦尼克综合征/韋尼克症候群　Wernicke syndrome
韦氏比重秤法/韋氏比重稱法,流體靜力比重稱法　hydrostatic method
韦氏成人智力量表/韋氏成人智力量表　Wechsler adult intelligence scale
韦氏儿童智力量表/韋氏兒童智力量表　Wechsler intelligence scale for children
韦氏肉芽肿病/韋氏肉芽腫病　Wegener granulomatosis
韦氏智力量表/韋氏智力量表　Wechsler scale
韦斯特法尔比重天平/韋斯特法爾比重天平,Westphal 氏比重天平　Westphal balance
韦斯特法尔病/韋斯特法爾病,Westphal 氏病　Westphal disease
韦特岛病/韋特島病　Islet of Wight disease
韦特海姆夹/韋特海姆夾,Wertheim 氏夾　Wertheim splint
违法流产/違法流產　criminal abortion
违拗症/違拗症　negativism
围刺法/圍刺法　encircling needling
围绝经期/圍絕經期　perimenopause
围绝经期妇女/圍絕經期婦女　perimenopausal woman
围模蜡/塑模蠟　boxing wax
围裙湿疹/圍裙狀濕疹　apron eczema
围裙状黏膜瓣/圍裙狀黏膜瓣　apron mucosal flap
围生期/圍生期,圍產期　perinatal stage

围生期死亡率/圍生期死亡率,圍產期死亡率　perinatal mortality
围生期心脏病/圍生期心臟病　perinatal heart disease
围生期药理学/圍生期藥理學,圍產期藥理學　perinatal pharmacology
围生期医护/圍生期醫護　perinatal care
围生医学/圍生醫學,嬰兒出生前後學　perinatology
围手术期护理/圍手術期護理　perioperative nursing
围手术期医护/圍手術期醫護　perioperative care
围心腔/圍心腔　pricardial coelom
维持蛋白/維持蛋白質　maintenance protein
维持剂量/維持劑量　maintenance dose
维持气道通畅/維持氣道通暢　airway maintenance
维持性透析/維持性透析　maintenance dialysis
维道/維道　weidao, GB28
维多利亚橙黄/維多利亞橙黃　Victoria orange
维多利亚绿/維多利亞綠　Victoria green
维厄桑斯静脉/維厄桑斯靜脈,Vieussens 氏靜脈,心前靜脈　veins of Vieussens
维尔德穆特耳/維爾德穆特耳,Wildermuth 氏耳　Wildermuth ear
维尔纳综合征/維爾納症候群　Werner syndrome
维尔皮安萎缩/維爾皮安萎縮,Vulpian 氏萎縮　Vulpian atrophy
维尔松管/維爾松管,Wirsung 氏管,胰管　duct of Wirsung
维管束/維管束　vascular bundle
维吉霉素/維吉黴素　virginiamycin
维甲类 X 受体/維甲類 X 受體　retinoid X receptor
维甲酸/維甲酸,維生素 A 酸　tretinoin
维甲酸受体/維甲酸受體　retinoic acid receptor
维卡特试针/維卡特試針,Vicat 氏針　Vicat needle
维克海默液/維克海默液,Wickersheimer 氏液　Wickersheimer fluid
n 维空间/n 維空間　n-dimensional space
维库溴铵/維庫溴銨　vecuronium
维拉[肠]瘘/維拉[腸]瘻,Vella 氏瘻　Vella fistula
维拉雷综合征/維拉雷症候群,Villaret 氏症候群　Villaret syndrome
维拉帕米/維拉帕米　verapamil
维洛沙秦/維洛沙秦　viloxazine
维尼亚尔细胞/維尼亞爾細胞,Vignal 氏細胞　Vignal cell
维萨里骨/維薩里骨,種子[狀]骨　vesalianum
维萨里静脉/維薩里靜脈,導靜脈　vesalian vein
维生素/維生素　vitamin
维生素 A/維生素 A　vitamin A

维生素 B_1/维生素 B_1,硫胺素　thiamine
维生素 B_2/维生素 B_2　vitamin B_2
维生素 B_6/维生素 B_6　vitamin B_6
维生素 B_{12}/维他命 B_{12}　cyanocobalamin
维生素 C/维生素 C,抗坏血酸　vitamin C
维生素 D/维生素 D　vitamin D
维生素 D_2/维生素 D_2　vitamin D_2
维生素 E/维生素 E　vitamin E
维生素 K/维生素 K　vitamin K
维生素 K_1/维生素 K_1　vitamin K_1
维生素 U/维生素 U　vitamin U
维生素 D_3 胆酯醇/维生素 D_3 膽酯醇　vitamin D_3-cholecalciferol
维生素 D 反应元件/维生素 D 反應元件　vitamin D response element
维生素分析器/维生素分析器　vitameter
维生素过多症/维生素過多症　supervitaminosis
维生素 A 过多症/维生素 A 過多症　hypervitaminosis A
维生素 D 过多症/维生素 D 過多症　hypervitaminosis D
维生素拮抗物/維生素拮抗物,維生素對抗劑　vitagonist
维生素 D 结合蛋白质/维生素 D 結合蛋白質　vitamin D-binding protein
维生素类/维生素類　vitamins
维生素缺乏/维生素缺乏　vitamin deficiency
维生素 A 缺乏/維生素 A 缺乏　vitamin A deficiency
维生素 B 缺乏/維生素 B 缺乏　vitamin B deficiency
维生素 B_6 缺乏/維生素 B_6 缺乏　vitamin B_6 deficiency
维生素 B_{12} 缺乏/維生素 B_{12} 缺乏　vitamin B_{12} deficiency
维生素 D 缺乏/維生素 D 缺乏　vitamin D deficiency
维生素 E 缺乏/維生素 E 缺乏　vitamin E deficiency
维生素 K 缺乏/維生素 K 缺乏　vitamin K deficiency
维生素 C 缺乏病/维生素 C 缺乏病　vitamin C deficiency
维生素 A 缺乏检眼器/維生素 A 缺乏檢眼器,維生素檢鏡　vitaminoscope
维生素缺乏性营养障碍/維生素缺乏性營養障礙　vitanition
维生素缺乏症/維生素缺乏症　avitaminosis
维生素 A 缺乏症/維生素 A 缺乏症　hypovitaminosis A
维生素 B_1 缺乏症/維生素 B_1 缺乏症　thiamine-deficiency
维生素 D_2 溶液/維生素 D_2 溶液,導鈣素溶液　calciferol solution
维生素 A 酸/维生素 A 酸　vitamin A acid
维生素 A 酸类/维生素 A 酸類　retinoids
维生素学/維生素學,維生素論　vitaminology
维生素 D 依赖性钙结合蛋白/維生素 D 依賴性鈣結合蛋白　vitamin D-dependent calcium-binding protein
维生素 D 依赖性佝偻病Ⅰ型/維生素 D 依賴性佝僂病Ⅰ型　vitamin D-dependent rickets typeⅠ
维生素 A 油/维生素 A 油　vitamin A-oil
维生素油剂/維生素油液　oleovitamin
维氏分析法/威氏分析法　Wits analysis
维提阿丁/維提阿丁　vitiatin
维希曼哮喘/維希曼哮喘,Wichmann 氏氣喘　Wichmann asthma
伪超常传导/偽超常傳導　pseudosupernormal conduction
伪递质/偽遞質　false transmitter
伪聋/偽聾　simulated deafness
伪盲/偽盲　simulated blindness
伪膜性小肠结肠炎/偽膜性小腸結腸炎,假膜性腸炎　pseudomembranous enterocolitis
伪品/偽品　counterfeit drug
伪阴性/偽陰性　false negativity
伪足/偽足,假足　pseudopodia
苇茎汤/葦莖湯　weijing decoction
尾/尾　cauda
尾孢霉病/尾孢黴菌病　cercosporamycosis
尾背侧锯肌/尾背側鋸肌　musculus serratus dorsalis caudalis
尾部发育不良/尾部發育不良　caudal dysplasia
尾[部]肌节/尾[部]肌節　caudal myotome
尾草履虫/尾草履蟲　Paramecium caudatum
尾侧/尾側　caudal
尾侧韧带/尾韌帶　caudal ligament
尾肠/尾腸　tailgut
尾丛/尾骨叢　coccygeal plexus, plexus coccygeus
尾段/尾段　coccygeal segments
尾骨/尾骨　coccyx, coccygeal bone
尾骨骨折/尾骨骨折,尾椎骨折　coccygeal fracture, coccyx fracture
尾骨肌/尾骨肌　coccygeus
尾骨角/尾骨角　cornu of coccyx, coccygeal horn
尾骨切除术/尾骨切除術　coccygectomy
尾骨切开术/尾骨切開術　coccygotomy
尾骨神经/尾骨神經　nervus coccygeus
尾骨痛/尾骨痛　coccydynia
尾骨血管球/尾骨血管叢　coccygeal vascular plexus

尾骨[血管]体/尾骨體　coccygeal body
尾骨诸肌/尾骨諸肌　coccygeal muscle
尾管/尾管　caudal tube
尾核横静脉/尾核橫靜脈　transverse caudate vein
尾核纵静脉/尾核縱靜脈　longitudinal caudate vein
尾瘘/尾瘻,尾骨瘻管　coccygeal fistula
尾间发/尾間發　coccygeal abscess
尾间骨/尾間骨　coccyx
尾间痛/尾間痛　coccygeal pain
[尾]末段/尾部,精尾　end piece
尾皮支持带/尾皮支持帶　caudal retaining band
尾神经/尾神經　coccygeal nerve
尾神经后支/尾神經後支　posterior branch of coccygeal nerve
尾神经前支/尾神經前支　anterior branch of coccygeal nerve
尾痛症/尾痛症,尾骨痛　coccygodynia
尾纤虫/尾纖蟲　Uronema caudatum
尾小凹/尾小凹　coccygeal foveola
尾蚴膜反应/尾蚴膜反應　cercarien hullen reaction
尾蚴性皮炎/尾蚴性皮膚炎　cercarial dermatitis
尾褶/尾褶　tail fold
尾状核/尾狀核　caudate nucleus
尾状核静脉/尾狀核靜脈　veins of caudate nucleus
尾状核体/尾狀核體　body of caudate nucleus
尾状核头/尾狀核頭　head of caudate nucleus
尾状核尾/尾狀核尾　tail of caudate nucleus
尾状核尾支/尾狀核尾支　branches of tail of caudate nucleus
尾状突/尾狀突　caudate process
尾状叶/尾狀葉　caudate lobe
尾状叶动脉/尾狀葉動脈　artery of caudate lobe
尾状叶右管/尾[狀]葉右管　right duct of caudate lobe
尾状叶支/尾狀葉支　caudate branch
尾状叶支后支/尾狀葉支後支　posterior branch of caudate branch
尾状叶支前支/尾狀葉支前支　anterior branch of caudate branch
尾状叶左管/尾[狀]葉左管　left duct of caudate lobe
尾椎/尾椎　coccygeal vertebra
纬线裂/緯線裂,緯面分裂　latitudinal cleavage
委陵菜/委陵菜　Chinese cinquefoil
委内瑞拉螺旋体/委内瑞拉[回歸熱]螺旋體　Borrelia venezuelensis
委内瑞拉马脑脊髓炎/委内瑞拉馬腦脊髓炎　Venezuelan equine encephalomyelitis
委内瑞拉马脑炎/委内瑞拉馬腦炎　Venezuelan equine encephalitis
委阳/委陽　weiyang, BL39
委中/委中　weizhong, BL40
委中毒/委中毒　Weizhong abscess, acute pyogenic infection of popliteal fossa, acute pyogenic popliteal lymphadenitis
委中毒•气血两虚证/委中毒•氣血兩虛證　Weizhong abscess with qi-blood deficiency pattern
委中毒•气滞血瘀证/委中毒•氣滯血瘀證　Weizhong abscess with pattern of qi stagnation and blood stasis
委中毒•湿热蕴结证/委中毒•濕熱蘊結證　Weizhong abscess with dampness-heat amassment pattern
萎黄病/萎黄病　chlorosis, green sickness
萎黄病[性]肾炎/萎黄病與蛋白尿症　chlorobrightism
萎缩/萎縮　atrophia, atrophy
萎缩纹/萎縮紋　striae atrophica
萎缩纤维化/萎縮纖維化,纖維變性及萎縮　fibroatrophy
萎缩性/萎縮性　atrophic
萎缩性癌/萎縮性癌　carcinoma atrophicans
萎缩性白斑症/萎縮性白斑病　atrophic leukoplakia
萎缩性白色斑点/萎縮性白色斑點　atrophic white spot
萎缩性瘢痕/萎縮性瘢痕　atrophic scar
萎缩性鼻窦炎/萎縮性鼻竇炎　atrophic sinusitis
萎缩性鼻炎/萎縮性鼻炎　atrophic rhinitis
萎缩性扁平苔藓/萎縮性扁平苔蘚　atrophic lichen planus
萎缩性痤疮/萎縮性痤瘡　acne atrophica
萎缩性大疱性表皮松解/萎縮性水皰性表皮鬆解症　epidermolysis bullosa atrophicans
萎缩性多软骨炎/萎縮性多軟骨炎　atrophic polychondritis
萎缩性[肺]气肿/萎縮性[肺]氣腫,小肺性氣腫　atrophic emphysema, small-lunged emphysema
萎缩性骨折/萎縮性骨折　atrophic fracture
萎缩性关节炎/萎縮性關節炎　atrophic arthritis
萎缩性喉炎/萎縮性喉炎　atrophic laryngitis
萎缩性肌疾病/萎縮性肌疾病　atrophic muscular disorder
萎缩性肌强直/萎縮性肌強直病,營養不良肌強直病　myotonia atrophica
萎缩性脊髓空洞症/萎縮性脊髓空洞症　syringomyelia atrophica
萎缩性结缔组织病性脂膜炎/萎縮性結締組織病性

脂层炎　atrophic connective tissue disease panniculitis
萎缩性狼疮/萎縮性狼瘡　lupus atrophicans
萎缩性毛发角化病/萎縮性毛髮角化病,萎縮毛角化病　keratosis pilaris atrophicans
萎缩性皮炎/萎縮性皮膚炎　dermatitis atrophicans
萎缩性舌炎/萎縮性舌炎　atrophic glossitis
萎缩性脱发/萎縮性脱髮,萎縮性禿髮　alopecia atrophicans
萎缩性胃炎/萎縮性胃炎　atrophic gastritis
萎缩性咽炎/萎縮性咽炎　atrophic pharyngitis
萎缩性眼睑下垂/萎縮性眼瞼下垂　ptosis atrophica
萎缩性硬斑病/萎縮性硬斑病　morphea atrophica
萎陷肺啰音/萎陷肺啰音,陷落部水泡音　collapse rale
萎陷疗法/萎陷療法,陷落療法,壓縮療法　collapse therapy
萎锈灵/萎銹靈　carboxin
萎叶/萎葉　betel
萎叶性颊癌/萎葉性頰癌,檳榔癌　buyo cheek cancer
猥亵儿童/猥褻兒童　sexual child abuse
痿病/痿病　flaccidity disease
痿病·肺热津伤证/痿病·肺熱津傷證　flaccidity disease with pattern of fluid consumption due to lung heat
痿病·肝肾两虚证/痿病·肝腎兩虛證　flaccidity disease with pattern of deficiency of both liver and kidney
痿病·脾胃气虚证/痿病·脾胃氣虛證　flaccidity disease with pattern of qi deficiency of spleen and stomach
痿病·湿热浸淫证/痿病·濕熱浸淫證　flaccidity disease with pattern of inundated damp-heat
痿病·瘀血阻络证/痿病·瘀血阻絡證　flaccidity disease with pattern of static blood blocking collaterals
鲔精蛋白/鮪精蛋白　thynnin
卫分/衛分　defense tier, weifen
卫分证/衛分證　weifen pattern
卫气/衛氣　defensive qi
卫气同病/衛氣同病　disease involving both defensive and qi phases
卫气同病证/衛氣同病證　pattern of disease involving both defensive and qi phases
卫气虚/衛氣虛　deficiency of defensive qi
卫气营血辨证/衛氣營血辨證　nutrient and blood phases, pattern identification of defensive
卫生/衛生　health
卫生保健调查/衛生保健調查　health care survey
卫生保健费用/衛生保健費用　health care cost
卫生保健辅助人员/衛生保健輔助人員　allied health personnel
卫生保健改革/衛生保健改革　health care reform
卫生保健公平提供/衛生保健公平提供　health care rationing
卫生保健联合体/衛生保健聯合體　health care coalition
卫生保健评价机制/衛生保健評價機制　health care evaluation mechanism
卫生保健提供/衛生保健提供　delivery of health care
卫生保健同行评议/衛生保健同行評議　health care peer review
卫生保健质量/衛生保健品質　quality of health care
卫生保健质量保证/衛生保健品質保證　health care quality assurance
卫生保健质量指标/衛生保健品質指標　health care quality indicator
卫生保健组织鉴定联合委员会/衛生保健組織鑒定聯合委員會　joint commission on accreditation of health care organizations
卫生处理/衛生處理,清潔衛生法　sanitization
卫生动力学/衛生動力學　health transition
卫生服务/衛生服務　health services
卫生服务管理/衛生服務管理　health services administration
卫生服务滥用/衛生服務濫用　health services misuse
卫生服务使用研究/衛生服務使用研究　marketing of health service
卫生服务需求/衛生服務需求　health services need and demand
卫生服务研究/衛生服務研究　health services research
卫生服务易得程度/衛生服務易得程度　health services accessibility
卫生工程/衛生工程　sanitary engineering
卫生工作重点/衛生工作重點　health priority
卫生化/衛生化　hygienization
卫生计划方针/衛生計劃方針　health planning guideline
卫生计划技术援助/衛生計劃技術援助　health planning technical assistance
卫生计划实施/衛生計劃實施　health plan implementation
卫生计划委员会/衛生計劃委員會　health planning

council
卫生计划资助/衛生計劃資助　health planning support
卫生计划组织/衛生計劃組織　health planning organization
卫生经费支出/衛生經費支出　health expenditure
卫生排水系统/衛生排水系統　sanitary drainage
卫生桥/衛生橋　sanitary bridge
卫生桥体/衛生橋體　sanitary pontic
卫生人力/衛生人力　health manpower
卫生人员/衛生人員　health personnel
卫生设施/衛生設施　health facility
卫生设施搬迁/衛生設施搬遷　health facility moving
卫生设施负责人员/衛生設施負責人員　health facility administrator
卫生设施管理人员/衛生設施管理人員　hospitalist
卫生设施规模/衛生設施規模　health facility size
卫生设施合并/衛生設施合并　health facility merger
卫生设施环境/衛生設施環境　health facility environment
卫生设施计划/衛生設施計劃　health facility planning
卫生食品/衛生食品　health food
卫生物理学/衛生物理學　health physics
卫生系统机构/衛生系統機構　health systems agency
卫生系统计划/衛生系統計劃　health systems plan
卫生学/衛生學　hygiene
卫生学家/衛生學家　hygienist
卫生有关职业/衛生有關職業　allied health occupation
卫生展览会/衛生展覽會　health fair
卫生战略/衛生策略　health strategy
卫生政策/衛生政策　health policy
卫生职业/衛生職業　health occupation
卫生职业院校/衛生職業院校　health occupation school
卫生专业/健康專業　health profession
卫生专业学生/衛生專業學生　health occupation student
卫生资源/衛生資源　health resource
卫氏并殖吸虫/肺并殖器吸蟲,肺蛭　Paragonimus westermani
卫氏并殖吸虫病/衛氏并殖吸蟲病　paragonimiasis westermani
卫星病毒/衛星病毒　satellite virus
卫星细胞/衛星細胞　satellite cell
卫星现象/陪星狀態,衛星狀態　satellitosis
卫星医院/衛星醫院　satellite hospital
卫星状疤痕/衛星狀疤痕　stellate scar
卫阳被遏/衛陽被遏　defensive yang being obstructed
卫营同病/衛營同病　disease involving both defensive and qi phases
未参加医疗保险者/未參加醫療保險者　medically uninsured
未产妇/未產婦　nullipara
未成年人/未成年人　minor
未成熟白细胞/未成熟白血球　neocyte
未成熟白细胞血症/未成熟白血球症　neocytosis
未成熟畸胎瘤/未成熟畸胎瘤　immature teratoma
未成熟型/未成熟型　juvenile form
未定带/未定帶　zona incerta
未定尖尾线虫/未定尖尾線蟲　Oxyuris incognita
未定类麻风/未定類麻風,未定型麻風　indeterminate leprosy
未定类树突状细胞/未定類樹突狀細胞,未定型樹狀細胞　indeterminate dendritic cell
未定型细胞瘤/未定型細胞瘤　indeterminate cell tumor
未分化癌/未分化癌　undifferentiated carcinoma
未分化的/未分化的　undifferentiated
未分化甲状腺癌/未分化甲狀腺癌　undifferentiated thyroid carcinoma
未分化间充质细胞/未分化間充質細胞,未分化間葉細胞　undifferentiated mesenchymal cell
未分化淋巴瘤/未分化性淋巴瘤　undifferentiated lymphoma
未分化[胚]组织/未分化的胚胎組織　indifferent tissue
未分化生殖器/未分化生殖器　indifferent genitalia
未分化细胞/未分化細胞　anaplastic cell, undifferentiated cell
未分化细胞性白血病/未分化細胞白血病　undifferentiated cell leukemia
未分化性腺/未分化性腺　indifferent gonad
未分类病毒/未分類病毒　unclassified viruse
未复位的脱位/未復[位]的脫位　unreduced dislocation
未接触抗原者/未接觸抗原者　antigenic virgin
未经产/未經產　nulliparity
未萌出牙/未萌出牙,未出齒　unerupted tooth
未[能]旋转/未[能]轉動,轉動缺失　nonrotation
未破卵泡黄素化综合征/未破卵泡黃素化症候群　luteinized unruptured follicle syndrome
未消化粪/未消化糞　undigested stool
未孕妇/未孕婦　nulligravida

未知原发灶肿瘤/未知原發灶腫瘤　unknown primary neoplasm
未足月妊娠/未足月妊娠,不完全妊娠　incomplete pregnancy
位变异构体/位變異構體,同質異性物　metamer
位点/位點,位置,地位　site
位觉/位覺,姿勢感覺　sense of position
位觉砂/位覺砂　statoconia
位觉砂膜/位覺砂膜,耳砂膜,耳石膜,位砂膜　statoconic membrane
位置[感]觉/部位感覺　topesthesia
位置失认[症]/位置失認[症]　atopognosia
位置效应/位置效應　position effect
位置信息/位置信息,位置訊息　positional information
位置性眼震/位置性眼震,位置性眼球震顫　positional nystagmus
位置异构/位置[同質]異構　position isomerism
位阻/位阻,立體障礙　steric hindrance
味/味[覺]　taste
味幻觉/味幻覺,味錯覺,錯味　pseudogeusia
味觉/味覺　gustatory sense
味觉迟钝/味覺遲鈍,鈍味　amblygeustia
味觉倒错/味覺顛倒,味覺異常　parageusia
味觉过敏/味覺過敏　hypergeusesthesia
味觉减退/味覺減退,味覺遲鈍　hypogeusia
味觉缺失/味覺缺失　gustatory anesthesia
味觉丧失/味覺喪失　ageusia
味觉神经/味覺神經　nerve of taste
味觉细胞/味覺細胞　gustatory cell
味觉性出汗/味覺性出汗　gustatory sweating
味觉性出汗综合征/味覺性出汗症候群　gustatory sweating syndrome
味觉性多汗症/味覺性多汗症　gustatory hyperhidrosis
味觉性失语/味覺失語症　ageusic aphasia
味觉阈/味覺閾　taste threshold
味觉障碍/味覺障礙　taste disorder
味孔/味孔　gustatory pore, taste pore
味蕾/味蕾　taste bud
[味蕾]基细胞/基細胞　basal cell
味盲/味盲[症],味失辨症,味覺消失　taste blindness
味器/味[覺]器,味官　gustatory organ
味细胞/味[蕾]細胞　taste cell
味腺/味腺　taste gland
畏光/畏光　photophobia
畏寒/畏寒　fear of cold

畏食/畏食[症],進食恐懼症　sitophobia
胃/胃　①stomach ②stomach qi of pulse ③wei, CO4
胃癌/胃癌　gastric cancer, stomach cancer
胃癌·肝胃不和证/胃癌·肝胃不和證　stomach cancer with pattern of disharmony between liver and stomach
胃癌·脾胃虚寒证/胃癌·脾胃虛寒證　stomach cancer with pattern of deficiency-cold of spleen and stomach
胃癌·痰湿瘀结证/胃癌·痰濕瘀結證　stomach cancer with pattern of stagnation and congelation of phlegm-damp
胃癌·胃热伤阴证/胃癌·胃熱傷陰證　stomach cancer with pattern of stomach heat injuring yin
胃癌·瘀毒内结证/胃癌·瘀毒內結證　stomach cancer with pattern of internal binding of static blood and poison
胃半切除术/胃半切除術,半胃切除術　hemigastrectomy
胃背系膜/胃背繫膜,背側胃繫膜　dorsal mesogastrium
胃贲门部/胃賁門[部]　cardiac stomach
胃泵/胃泵,胃唧筒　stomach pump
胃壁肌层/胃壁肌層　muscular layer of stomach wall
胃壁[X射线]照相术/胃壁[X射線]照相術,胃壁X光照相術　gastric parietography
胃壁细胞/胃壁細胞　gastric parietal cell
胃病/胃病　gastropathy
胃病性手足搐搦/胃病性手足搐搦,胃病性肢搦病　gastric tetany
胃病性哮喘/胃病性氣喘　gastric asthma
胃病性眩晕/胃[病]性眩暈　gastric vertigo, stomachal vertigo
胃病学/胃[病]學　gastrology
胃病学家/胃病學家　gastrologist
胃不和/胃不和　discomfort in stomach
胃部分切除术/部分胃切除術　partial gastrectomy
胃残端/胃殘端　gastric stump
胃仓/胃倉　weicang, BL50
胃肠病学/胃腸[病]學　gastroenterology
胃肠病学家/胃腸病學家　gastroenterologist
胃肠病用药/胃腸病用藥　gastrointestinal agent
胃肠插管法/胃腸插管法　gastrointestinal intubation
胃肠成形术/胃腸成形術　gastroenteroplasty
胃肠出血/胃腸出血　gastrointestinal bleeding
胃肠道/胃腸道　gastrointestinal tract
胃肠道间质肿瘤/胃腸道間質腫瘤　gastrointestinal

stromal tumor
胃肠道抗感染药/胃腸道抗感染藥　gastrointestinal anti-infective
胃肠道毛细血管/胃腸道毛細血管,胃腸道微血管　gastrointestinal capillary
胃肠道内窥镜检查/胃腸道內窺鏡檢查　gastrointestinal endoscopy
胃肠电吻合术/電胃腸吻合術　electrogastroenterostomy
胃肠活动/胃腸活動　gastrointestinal motility
胃肠激素类/胃腸激素類　gastrointestinal hormones
胃肠激素受体/胃腸激素受體　gastrointestinal hormone receptor
胃肠疾病/胃腸病　gastrointestinal disease
胃肠结核/胃腸結核　gastrointestinal tuberculosis
胃肠瘘/胃腸瘻[管]　gastrointestinal fistula
胃肠内窥镜/胃腸內窺鏡　gastrointestinal endoscope
胃肠内容物/胃腸內容物　gastrointestinal content
胃肠切开术/胃腸切開術　gastroenterotomy
胃[肠]石/胃腸[石],糞石,腸胃結石　bezoar
胃肠通过试验/胃腸通過試驗　gastrointestinal transit
胃肠痛/胃腸[神經]痛　gastroenteralgia
胃肠外输注/胃腸外輸注　parenteral infusion
胃肠外消化/胃腸外消化,非經腸的消化,消化道外消化　parenteral digestion
胃肠外营养/胃腸外營養　parenteral nutrition
胃肠下垂/胃腸下垂　gastroenteroptosis
胃肠消化/胃腸道消化　gastrointestinal digestion
胃肠消化不良/胃腸性消化不良　gastrointestinal dyspepsia
胃肠型紫癜/胃腸型紫癜[症]　purpura gastrointestinalis
胃肠炎/胃腸炎　gastroenteritis
胃肠液/胃腸液　gastrointestinal fluid
胃肠胰内分泌系统/胃腸胰內分泌系統　gastro-entero-pancreatic endocrine system
胃肠造口吻合术/胃腸造口吻合術　gastroenterostomy
胃肠肿瘤/胃腸腫瘤　gastrointestinal neoplasm
胃成形术/胃成形術,胃造形術　gastroplasty
胃充气造影术/胃充氣造影術,胃充氣X光攝影法　pneumogastrography
胃虫/胃蟲　stomach worm
胃重复[畸形]/胃重複[畸形]　reduplication of stomach
胃出口梗阻/胃出口梗阻　gastric outlet obstruction
胃出血/胃出血　gastric hemorrhage
胃次全切除术/胃次全切除術,大部分胃切除術　subtotal gastrectomy
胃丛/胃叢　gastric plexus, plexus gastrici
胃促胰酶/胃促胰酶　chymase
胃大弯/胃大彎　greater curvature of stomach
胃蛋白酶/胃蛋白酶,胃液素,消化素　pepsin
胃蛋白酶A/胃蛋白酶A　pepsin A
胃蛋白酶处理/胃蛋白酶處理,加胃液素,以胃液處理　pepsinate
胃蛋白酶分泌/胃蛋白酶分泌,胃液素分泌　pepsinia
胃蛋白酶过多/胃蛋白酶過多　hyperpepsinia
胃蛋白酶过少/胃蛋白酶過少　hypopepsinia
胃蛋白酶尿/胃蛋白酶尿,胃泌素尿　pepsinuria
胃蛋白酶缺乏/胃蛋白酶缺失　anapepsia
胃蛋白酶盐剂/胃蛋白酶鹽劑,消化鹽　peptic salt
胃蛋白酶原/胃蛋白酶原,胃泌素原,消化素原　pepsinogen
胃蛋白酶原A/胃蛋白酶原A　pepsinogen A
胃蛋白酶原C/胃蛋白酶原C　pepsinogen C
胃刀/胃刀　gastrotome
胃底/胃底　fundus of stomach, gastric fundus
胃底切除术/胃底切除術　fundusectomy
[胃]底腺/胃底腺　fundic gland
胃底折叠术/胃底折疊術　fundoplication
胃动电流描记法/胃動電流描記法,胃電圖測定　electrogastrography
胃动电流描记器/胃動電流描記器,胃電描記器　electrogastrograph
胃动电流图/胃電圖　electrogastrogram
胃动描记器/胃動描記器　gastrograph
胃窦十二指肠[溃疡]切除术/胃竇及十二指腸切除術　antroduodenectomy
胃窦血管扩张/胃竇血管擴張　gastric antral vascular ectasia
胃毒素/胃毒素　gastrotoxin
胃毒血清/胃毒[性]血清　gastrotoxic serum
胃短动脉/胃短動脈　short gastric artery
胃短静脉/胃短靜脈　short gastric vein
胃分解蛋白酶/胃分解蛋白酶　gastricsin
胃蜂窝[组]织炎/胃蜂窩[組]織炎　linitis
胃缝术/胃縫[合]術　gastrorrhaphy
胃腹膜炎/胃腹膜炎　gastroperitonitis
胃腹系膜/胃腹繫膜,腹側胃繫膜　ventral mesogastrium
胃肝韧带/胃肝韌帶　gastrohepatic ligament
胃肝炎/胃肝炎　gastrohepatitis
胃膈韧带/胃膈韌帶　gastrophrenic ligament
胃垢/胃垢　sordes gastricae

胃固定术/胃固定術　gastropexy
胃冠状神经丛/胃冠狀神經叢　gastric coronary plexus
胃管/胃管　gastric canal
胃管饲法/胃管飼法,胃道灌食法　gastrogavage
胃过敏/胃過敏　irritability of the stomach
胃寒/胃寒　stomach cold
胃后壁/胃後壁　posterior wall of stomach, paries posterior gastricus
胃后表面/胃後面　posterior surface of stomach
胃后丛/胃後叢　plexus gastricus posterior
胃后动脉/胃後動脈　posterior gastric artery
胃后静脉/後胃靜脈　posterior gastric vein
胃后支/胃後支　posterior gastric branch
胃缓/胃緩　down-bearing stomachache
胃缓·脾虚气陷证/胃緩·脾虚氣陷證　down-bearing stomachache with pattern of qi collapse and spleen deficiency
胃缓·胃阴虚证/胃緩·胃陰虚證　down-bearing stomachache with pattern of stomach yin deficiency
胃回肠吻合术/胃迴腸吻合術　gastroileostomy
胃回肠炎/胃迴腸炎　gastroileitis
胃火炽盛/胃火熾盛　exuberance of stomach fire
胃火炽盛证/胃火熾盛證　pattern of exuberance of stomach fire
胃火燔龈证/胃火燔齦證　pattern of stomach fire flaring gum
胃肌轻瘫/胃[肌]輕癱　gastroparesis
胃肌无力/胃肌無力　myasthenia gastrica
胃积气/胃内積氣　aerogastria
胃积食绞痛/胃積食絞痛　saburral colic
胃疾病/胃疾病　stomach disease
胃家实/胃家實　excessive heat in stomach and intestine, excess of stomach and intestine
胃降温法/胃降溫法,胃低温　gastric hypothermia
胃角切迹/胃[角]切跡　gastric notch
胃绞痛/胃絞痛　gastric colic
胃结肠干/胃結腸幹　gastrocolic trunk
胃结肠瘘/胃結腸瘻　gastrocolic fistula
胃结肠切开术/胃結腸切開術　gastrocolotomy
胃结肠韧带/胃結腸韌帶　gastrocolic ligament
胃结肠吻合术/胃結腸[造口]吻合術　gastrocolostomy
胃结肠炎/胃結腸炎　gastrocolitis
胃结核/胃結核　tuberculosis of stomach
胃津/胃津　stomach fluid
胃近端迷走神经切断术/胃近端迷走神經切斷術　proximal gastric vagotomy

胃惊/胃驚　convulsion due to stomach disorder
胃痉挛/胃痙攣　gastrospasm
胃镜/胃鏡　gastroscope
胃镜检查/胃鏡檢查　gastroscopy
胃空肠结肠瘘/胃空腸結腸瘻　gastrojejunocolic fistula
胃空肠食管吻合术/胃空腸食道吻合術　gastrojejunoesophagostomy
胃空肠吻合术/胃空腸吻合術　gastrojejunostomy
胃空肠性便秘/胃空腸性便秘　gastrojejunal constipation
胃空痛/胃空痛　gastralgokenosis
胃溃疡/胃潰瘍　gastric ulcer
胃扩张/胃擴張　dilatation of stomach
胃淋巴结/胃淋巴結　gastric lymph node
胃瘘/胃瘻　gastric fistula
胃瘘管饲法/胃瘻管飼法,胃瘘灌食法　gastrostogavage
胃瘘注洗法/胃瘻注洗法,胃瘘洗胃法　gastrostolavage
胃螺旋体病/胃螺旋體病　gastric spirochetosis
胃麻痹/胃麻痺　gastroparalysis
胃毛细血管/胃毛細血管,胃微血管　gastric capillary
胃酶解血管紧张肽/胃酶解血管緊張肽,胃蛋白酶解高血壓肽　pepsitensin
胃酶细胞/胃液細胞　peptic cell
胃酶抑素类/胃酶抑素類　pepstatins
胃霉菌病/胃黴菌病　gastromycosis
胃泌素/胃泌[激]素　gastrin
胃泌素类/胃泌素類　gastrins
胃泌素瘤/胃泌素瘤　gastrinoma
胃泌素释放肽/胃泌素釋放肽　gastrin-releasing peptide
胃泌酸调节素/胃泌酸調節素　oxyntomodulin
胃泌酸细胞/胃泌酸細胞　gastric oxyntic cell
胃面/胃面　gastric surface
胃纳呆滞/胃納呆滯,厭食症　anorexia
胃内残渣/胃内殘渣　gastric residuum
胃内积血清/胃内積血清　serogastria
胃内压测量器/胃内壓測量器,胃壓力計　gastrotonometer
胃内照相机/胃内照相機　gastrocamera
胃内照相术/胃内照相法　gastrophotography
胃黏蛋白/胃黏蛋白　gastric mucin
胃黏膜/胃黏膜　gastric mucosa
胃黏膜脱垂/胃黏膜脱垂　prolapse of gastric mucosa
胃黏膜炎/胃黏膜炎　endogastritis
胃黏液多糖/胃[黏液]多醣　gastric polysaccharide

胃黏液溢/胃黏液溢,胃黏液過量分泌,胃黏液漏　gastromyxorrhea
胃扭转/胃扭轉　gastric volvulus
胃排空/胃排空　gastric emptying
胃旁路术/胃旁路術　gastric bypass
胃膨出/胃膨出,胃脱疝　gastrocele
胃皮/胃皮　gastrodermis
胃皮肤综合征/胃皮[膚]症候群　gastrocutaneous syndrome
胃脾韧带/胃脾韌帶　gastrosplenic ligament
胃破裂/胃破裂　stomach rupture
胃气/胃氣　stomach qi
胃气不降/胃氣不降　failure of stomach qi to descend
胃气囊装置/胃氣囊裝置　gastric balloon
胃气上逆/胃氣上逆　adverse rising of stomach qi
胃气上逆证/胃氣上逆證　pattern of adverse rising of stomach qi
胃气虚/胃氣虛　deficiency of stomach qi
胃气虚证/胃氣虛證　pattern of deficiency of stomach qi
胃气胀/胃氣脹　bloating
胃憩室/胃憩室　gastric diverticulum
胃憩室病/胃憩室病　stomach diverticulosis
胃前壁/胃前壁　anterior wall of stomach
胃前丛/胃前叢　plexus gastricus anterior
胃前支/胃前支　anterior gastric branch
胃切除后综合征/胃切除後症候群　postgastrectomy syndrome
胃切除术/胃切除術　gastrectomy
胃切开术/胃切開術　gastrotomy
胃倾倒症/胃傾倒症,傾倒胃　dumping stomach
胃穹窿/胃穹窿　fornix of stomach
胃区/胃區　gastric area
胃全切除术/胃全切除術,全胃切除術　total gastrectomy
胃热/胃熱　stomach heat
胃热消谷/胃熱消穀　stomach heat accelerating digestion
胃蠕虫病/胃蠕蟲病　stomach worm disease
胃软化/胃軟化　gastromalacia
胃上丛/胃上叢　plexus gastricus superior
胃神根/胃神根　spirit and root of pulse
胃神经/胃神經　gastric nerve
胃神经根炎/胃神經根炎　gastroradiculitis
胃渗血/胃滲血　gastrostaxis
胃十二指肠丛/胃十二指腸叢　plexus gastroduodenalis
胃十二指肠动脉/胃十二指腸動脈　gastroduodenal artery
胃十二指肠镜检查/胃十二指腸鏡檢法　gastroduodenoscopy
胃十二指肠瘘/胃十二指腸瘻　gastroduodenal fistula
胃十二指肠切除术/胃十二指腸切除術　gastroduodenectomy
胃十二指肠吻合术/胃十二指腸吻合術　gastroduodenostomy
胃十二指肠炎/胃十二指腸炎　gastroduodenitis
胃石/胃石　gastrolith
胃石病/胃石病　gastrolithiasis
胃食管反流/胃食管反流,胃食道回流　gastroesophageal reflux
胃食管疝/胃食道疝　gastroesophageal hernia
胃食管吻合术/胃食道[造口]吻合術　gastroesophagostomy
胃食管炎/胃食道炎　gastroesophagitis
胃食管癔球/胃食管癔球　gastroesophageal globus hystericus
胃俞/胃俞　weishu, BL21
胃刷/胃刷　stomach brush
胃松解术/胃鬆解術　gastrolysis
胃苏颗粒/胃蘇顆粒　weisu granule
胃酸/胃酸　gastric acid
胃酸过多[症]/胃酸過多　hyperchlorhydria
胃酸过少[症]/胃酸過少　hypochlorhydria
胃酸缺乏/胃酸缺乏,胃内鹽酸缺乏　achlorhydria
胃酸缺乏性胃炎/胃酸缺乏性胃炎　achlorhydric gastritis
胃酸缺乏性消化不良/胃酸缺乏性消化不良,無酸性消化不良　anacidic dyspepsia
胃体/胃體　body of stomach
胃通过时间/胃通過時間,胃程時間　gastric transit time
胃痛[病]/胃痛[病]　gastralgia, stomachache, stomach pain
胃痛·肝气犯胃证/胃痛·肝氣犯胃證　stomachache with pattern of liver qi invading stomach
胃痛·肝胃郁热证/胃痛·肝胃鬱熱證　stomachache with pattern of heat stagnation in liver and stomach
胃痛·寒邪犯胃证/胃痛·寒邪犯胃證　stomachache with pattern of cold pathogen invading stomach
胃痛·脾胃虚寒证/胃痛·脾胃虛寒證　stomachache with pattern of deficiency-cold of spleen and stomach
胃痛·脾胃阴虚证/胃痛·脾胃陰虛證　stomachache with pattern of yin deficiency of spleen and stomach

胃痛·湿热中阻证/胃痛·濕熱中阻證 stomachache with pattern of damp-heat blocking middle jiao
胃痛·食积证/胃痛·食積證 stomachache with food retention pattern
胃痛·痰湿内积证/胃痛·痰濕內積證 stomachache with pattern of internal amassment of phlegm-damp
胃痛·胃火炽盛证/胃痛·胃火熾盛證 stomachache with pattern of blazing stomach fire
胃痛·瘀阻胃络证/胃痛·瘀阻胃絡證 stomachache with pattern of static blood blocking stomach collateral
胃透照灯/胃透照燈 gastrodiaphane
胃透照镜检查/胃透照鏡檢查,胃照鏡檢法 gastrodiaphanoscopy
胃外瘘/胃外瘺 gastrocutaneous fistula
胃外膜炎/胃外膜炎,胃腹膜炎 exogastritis
胃脘下俞/胃脘下俞 weiwanxiashu, EX-B3
胃网膜丛/胃網膜叢 gastroepiploic plexus
胃网膜动脉/胃網膜動脈 gastroepiploic artery
胃网膜静脉/胃網膜静脈 gastroepiploic vein
胃网膜右动脉/胃網膜右動脈 right gastroepiploic artery
胃网膜右动脉网膜支/胃網膜右動脈網膜支 epiploic branch of right gastroepiploic artery
胃网膜右动脉胃支/胃網膜右動脈胃支 gastric branch of right gastroepiploic artery
胃网膜右静脉/胃網膜右静脈 right gastroepiploic vein, right gastroomental vein
胃网膜右淋巴结/胃網膜右淋巴結 right gastroomental lymph node
胃网膜左动脉/胃網膜左動脈 left gastroepiploic artery
胃网膜左动脉网膜支/胃網膜左動脈網膜支 epiploic branch of left gastroepiploic artery, omental branch of left gastroepiploic artery
胃网膜左动脉胃支/胃網膜左動脈胃支 gastric branch of left gastroepiploic artery
胃网膜左静脉/胃網膜左静脈 left gastroomental vein, left gastroepiploic vein
胃网膜左淋巴结/胃網膜左淋巴結 left gastroomental lymph node
胃吻合术/胃吻合術 gastroanastomosis
胃窝/胃窩 pit of stomach
胃息肉病/胃息肉病 polyposis gastrica
胃喜润恶燥/胃喜潤惡燥 stomach liking moistness and disliking dryness
胃系膜/胃繫膜 mesogaster
胃狭窄/胃狹窄 gastrostenosis
胃下垂/胃下垂 gastroptosis
胃下丛/胃下叢 plexus gastricus inferior
胃纤维镜/胃纖維鏡 gastrofiberscope
胃腺/胃腺 gastric gland
胃腺癌/胃腺癌 gastric adenocarcinoma
胃腺炎/胃腺炎 gastradenitis
胃消化/胃消化 gastric digestion
胃消化不良/胃消化不良 gastric indigestion
胃消化毒素/胃消化毒素 peptinotoxin
胃小凹/胃小凹 gastric pit, gastric foveola
胃小肠结肠吻合术/胃小腸結腸吻合術 gastroenterocolostomy
胃小肠结肠炎/胃小腸結腸炎 gastroenterocolitis
胃小弯/胃小彎 lesser curvature of stomach
胃小窝/胃小窩 alveolus of stomach
胃心痛/胃心痛 true heart pain with cold limbs caused by stomach disease
胃心综合征/胃心症候群 gastrocardiac syndrome
胃性咳嗽/胃性欬嗽 stomach cough
胃压迹/胃壓跡 gastric impression
胃炎/胃炎 gastritis
胃炎性黑矇/胃炎性黑矇,口臭性黑矇 saburral amaurosis
胃阳/胃陽 stomach yang
胃液/胃液 gastric juice
胃液[分泌]过多/胃液分泌過多 hyperchylia
胃液[分泌]过少/胃液分泌過少 hypochylia
胃液分析/胃液分析 gastric analysis
胃液缺乏/胃液缺乏症 achylia gastrica
胃液缺乏性贫血/消化液缺乏性貧血 achylic anemia
胃液酸度测定/胃液酸度測定 gastric acidity determination
胃液[游离]盐酸正常/胃液[游離]鹽酸正常,胃内鹽酸度正常 euchlorhydria
胃胰襞/胃胰皺襞 gastropancreatic fold
胃胰[腺]炎/胃胰炎 gastropancreatitis
胃阴/胃陰 stomach yin
胃阴虚/胃陰虛 deficiency of stomach yin
胃阴虚证/胃陰虛證 pattern of deficiency of stomach yin
胃蝇科/胃蠅科 Gasterophilidae
胃幽门端扩大/胃幽門端擴大 prognathion dilatation
胃右动脉/胃右動脈 right gastric artery
胃右静脉/胃右静脈 right gastric vein
胃右淋巴结/胃右淋巴結 right gastric lymph node
胃造口术/胃造口術 gastrostomy
胃燥津伤证/胃燥津傷證 pattern of fluid injury due to stomach dryness

胃胀／胃脹　stomach distension
胃折术／胃折[疊]術　gastroplication
胃支／胃支　gastric branch
胃肿瘤／胃腫瘤　stomach neoplasm
胃周期／胃週期　gastric cycle
胃[皱]襞／胃皺襞　gastric fold
胃潴留／胃瀦留　gastric retention
胃主受纳／胃主受納　stomach receiving food and drink
胃主细胞／胃主細胞　gastric chief cell
胃灼热／胃[心]灼熱，心口灼熱　heartburn
胃左动脉／胃左動脈　left gastric artery, left coronary artery of stomach
胃左动脉食管支／胃左動脈食管支　esophageal branch of left gastric artery
胃左静脉／胃左靜脈　left gastric vein
胃左淋巴结／胃左淋巴結　left gastric lymph node
胃左下动脉／胃左下動脈　left inferior gastric artery
喂饲方法／餵飼方法　feeding method
喂养／餵養　feeding
蔚蓝色内障／蔚藍色內障，藍內障　blue cataract
魏贝尔-帕拉德体／魏貝爾-帕拉德體，韋伯爾-帕烈得體　Weibel-Palade body
魏尔·米切尔疗法／魏爾·米切爾療法，韋米·契爾氏療法　Weir Mitchell treatment
魏尔征象／魏爾徵象，威利氏徵象　Weill sign
魏特布雷希特韧带／魏特布雷希特韌帶，Weitbrecht 氏韌帶　Weitbrecht ligament
魏因加特纳病／魏因加特納病，Weingartner 氏病　Weingartner disease
温／溫　warm
温病／溫病　warm disease
温病劳复／溫病勞復　recurrent warm disease caused by overstrain
温病食复／溫病食復　recurrent warm disease caused by improper diet
温病条辨／溫病條辨　Detailed Analysis of Epidemic Warm Diseases
温病学／溫病學　science of epidemic febrile disease of traditional Chinese medicine
温病学派／溫病學派　school of warm disease
温病阴阳易／溫病陰陽易　yin yang exchange of warm disease
温补脾胃／溫補脾胃　warmly invigorating spleen and stomach
温补脾阳／溫補脾陽　warmly invigorating spleen yang
温补肾阳／溫補腎陽　warmly invigorating kidney yang
温补心肺／溫補心肺　warmly invigorating heart and lung
温补心阳／溫補心陽　warmly invigorating heart yang, warm tonifying heart yang
温差电制冷／溫差電製冷　freezing by thermoelectric action
温刺激物／溫熱刺激　thermal stimulus
温胆汤／溫膽湯　decoction for clearing away gallbladder heat, wendan decoction
温毒[病]／溫毒[病]　warm-toxin disease
温毒发瘢／溫毒發瘢　warm-toxin disease with ecchymoses
温度／溫度　temperature
温度测量法／溫度測量法，測計溫法　thermometry
温度差别触诊法／溫度差別觸診法，溫度差別按診法　thermopalpation
温度[感]觉／溫度覺，冷熱覺　thermesthesia
温度[感]觉测量器／溫度[感]覺測量器，溫度覺計　thermesthesiometer
温度[感]觉迟钝／溫度覺遲鈍　thermhypesthesia
温度感觉缺失／溫度感覺缺失，溫覺缺失　thermal anesthesia
温度感受器／溫度感受器　thermoreceptor
温度感受体／感熱體，熱接受體　thermoreceptor
温度计／溫度計　thermometers
温度记录法／溫度記錄法　thermography
温度记录器／溫度記錄器　thermograph
温度觉／溫度覺　thermic sense
温度觉过敏／溫度覺過敏　thermohyperesthesia
温度觉缺失／溫度覺缺失　thermanesthesia
温度调节／溫度調節，節溫　thermoregulation
温度性收缩／溫度性收縮，變溫性收縮　thermosystaltism
温度性水肿／溫熱性水腫　thermal edema
温法／溫法　warming method
温肺散寒／溫肺散寒　warming lung for dispelling cold
温服／溫服　administered warm
温和灸／溫和灸　mild-warm moxibustion
温和噬菌体／溫性噬菌病毒　temperate phage
温化寒痰／溫化寒痰　warmly resolving cold-phlegm
温化水湿剂／溫化水濕劑　formula for warmly resolving watery dampness
温经／溫經　warming womb and channel
温经活血／溫經活血　warming channel and activating blood circulation
温经散寒／溫經散寒　warming channel for dispelling

温经散寒剂/溫經散寒劑 formula for warming channel for dispersing cold
温经汤/溫經湯 wenjing decoction
温经止血/溫經止血 warming channel for arresting bleeding
温灸器灸/溫灸器灸 moxibustion with moxibustioner
温觉/溫覺 warmth sensation
温开剂/溫開劑 warm formula for resuscitation
温克巴赫病/溫克巴赫病,Wenckebach 氏病 Wenckebach disease
温克尔病/溫克爾病,Winckel 氏病 Winckel disease
温克勒病/溫克勒病,Winkler 氏病 Winkler disease
温克曼病/溫克曼病,Winkelman 氏病 Winkelman disease
温里法/溫里法 warming interior method
温里剂/溫里劑 warming interior formula
温溜/溫溜 wenliu, LI7
温疟/溫瘧 warm malaria
温脾汤/溫脾湯 wenpi decoction
温清并用/溫清并用 using warming and heat-clearing simultaneously
温泉/溫泉 spa
温泉黄粉/溫泉黃粉,礦泉硫 sulfuraria
温泉泥疗法/溫泉泥療法 fangotherapy
温热[病]/溫熱病 warm-heat disease
温热性眼球震颤/溫熱性眼球震顫 caloric nystagmus
温热遗症/溫熱遺症 sequelae of warm-heat disease
温热遗症·不便/溫熱遺症·不便 constipation as a sequela of warm-heat disease
温热遗症·不寐/溫熱遺症·不寐 insomnia as a sequela of warm-heat disease
温热遗症·不食/溫熱遺症·不食 anorexia as a sequela of warm-heat disease
温热遗症·额热/溫熱遺症·額熱 hot forehead as a sequela of warm-heat disease
温热遗症·耳聋/溫熱遺症·耳聾 deafness as a sequela of warm-heat disease
温热遗症·发疮/溫熱遺症·發瘡 ulceration as a sequela of warm-heat disease
温热遗症·发痿/溫熱遺症·發痿 flaccidity as a sequela of warm-heat disease
温热遗症·发颐/溫熱遺症·發頤 swollen cheek as a sequela of warm-heat disease
温热遗症·发蒸/溫熱遺症·發蒸 steaming heat as a sequela of warm-heat disease
温热遗症·发肿/溫熱遺症·發腫 edema as a sequela of warm-heat disease
温热遗症·腹热/溫熱遺症·腹熱 abdominal heat as a sequela of warm-heat disease
温热遗症·昏沉/溫熱遺症·昏沉 lethargy as a sequela of warm-heat disease
温热遗症·肌肤甲错/溫熱遺症·肌膚甲錯 chapped skin as a sequela of warm-heat disease
温热遗症·惊悸/溫熱遺症·驚悸 palpitation as a sequela of warm-heat disease
温热遗症·咳嗽/溫熱遺症·欬嗽 cough as a sequela of warm-heat disease
温热遗症·妄言/溫熱遺症·妄言 delirium as a sequela of warm-heat disease
温热遗症·喜唾/溫熱遺症·喜唾 frequent spitting as a sequela of warm-heat disease
温热遗症·下血/溫熱遺症·下血 bloody stool/hematuria as sequelae of warm-heat disease
温热遗症·遗精/溫熱遺症·遺精 seminal emission as a sequela of warm-heat disease
温热遗症·语謇/溫熱遺症·語謇 sluggish speech as a sequela of warm-heat disease
温热遗症·怔忡/溫熱遺症·怔忡 severe palpitation as a sequela of warm-heat disease
温热遗症·自汗盗汗/溫熱遺症·自汗盜汗 spontaneous and night sweating as sequelae of warm-heat disease
温肾/溫腎 warming the kidney
温肾散寒/溫腎散寒 warming kidney for dispelling cold
温室效应/溫室效應 greenhouse effect
温水浴/溫水浴,微温浴 lukewarm bath
温斯洛韧带/溫斯洛韌帶,Winslow 氏韌帶 Winslow ligament
温特博特姆征/溫特博特姆徵 Winterbottom sign
温通小肠/溫通小腸 warmly dredging small intestine
温胃散寒/溫胃散寒 warming stomach for dispelling cold
温下剂/溫下劑 warm cathartic formula
温型抗体/溫型抗體 warm antibody
温[型]凝集素/溫熱凝集素 warm agglutinin
温血/溫血 warming blood
温血凝素/溫血球凝集素 warm hemagglutinin
温阳/溫陽 warming yang
温阳化饮/溫陽化飲 warming yang for resolving fluid retention
温阳利水/溫陽利水 warming yang for diuresis

| 温阳散寒/溫陽散寒 warming yang for dispelling cold
| 温阳通便/溫陽通便 warming yang for relaxing bowels
| 温阳行气/溫陽行氣 warming yang for activating qi-flowing
| 温阳益气/溫陽益氣 warming yang and benefiting qi
| 温疫论/溫疫論 On Plague Diseases
| 温浴/溫[水]浴 warm bath
| 温脏安蛔/溫臟安蛔 calming intestinal ascarid by warming method
| 温燥/溫燥 warm dryness
| 温燥化痰剂/溫燥化痰劑 formula for resolving phlegm with warm drugs
| 温燥证/溫燥證 warm-dryness pattern
| 温针灸/溫針灸 needle warming through moxibustion, warming needle moxibustion
| 温中散寒/溫中散寒 warming spleen and stomach for dispelling cold
| 温中散寒剂/溫中散寒劑 formula for warming interior for dispersing cold
| 瘟病毒感染/瘟病毒感染 Pestivirus infections
| 瘟毒/瘟毒 pestilent toxicity
| 瘟毒下注证/瘟毒下注證 pattern of pestilential toxicity invading downward
| 瘟热/瘟熱 distemper
| 瘟疫/瘟疫 epidemic infectious disease, pestilence
| 文唇/文唇 tattooing lip
| 文唇线/文唇線 tattooing lip line
| 文化交叉比较/文化交叉比較 cross-cultural comparison
| 文火/文火 mild fire
| 文眉/文眉 tattooing eyebrow
| 文丘里流量计/文丘里流量計 venturimeter
| 文森特螺旋体/文森特螺旋體,Vincenti 氏螺旋體 Treponema Vincenti
| 文身/文身[法],黥墨法 tattooing
| 文身肉芽肿/文身肉芽腫 tattoo granuloma
| 文氏曲霉/文氏麴黴,Wentii 氏麴黴菌 Aspergillus Wentii
| 文氏型房室传导阻滞/文氏型房室傳導阻滯 Wenckebach atrioventricular block
| 文学中医学/文學中醫學 medicine in literature
| 文眼线/文眼線 tattooing lid margin
| 文娱疗法/文娛療法 recreational therapy
| 文字视觉/字视力 word vision
| 纹/紋 striae
| 纹静脉/紋靜脈 striate vein

纹孔/紋孔 pit
纹理/紋理 striation
纹色/紋色 color of venule
纹状染色细胞/紋狀染色細胞 stichochrome cell
纹状视网膜炎/紋狀視網膜炎 striate retinitis
纹状体/紋狀體 corpus striatum, striatum
纹状体电[流]图/紋狀體電圖 electrostriatogram
纹状体黑质变性/紋狀黑體變性 striatonigral degeneration
纹状体黑质束/紋狀體黑質束,紋狀體黑質徑 strionigral tract
纹状体静脉/紋狀體靜脈 striate vein
纹状体内侧动脉/紋狀體內側動脈 medial striate artery
纹状体皮质综合征/紋狀體皮質症候群 striocortical syndrome
纹状体外侧动脉/紋狀體外側動脈 lateral striate artery
纹状体小脑性震颤/紋狀體小腦性震顫 striocerebellar tremor
纹状缘/紋狀緣 striated border
闻带下/聞帶下 smelling vaginal discharge
闻恶露/聞惡露 smelling lochia
闻月经/聞月經 smelling menstrual blood
闻诊/聞診 listening and smelling
蚊虫叮咬伤/蚊蟲叮咬傷 insect sting
蚊虫叮咬伤·热毒蕴结证/蚊蟲叮咬傷·熱毒蘊結證 insect sting with heat-toxin amassment pattern
蚊叮伤/蚊叮傷 mosquito sting
蚊叮咬/蚊叮咬 mosquito bite
蚊科/蚊科 Culicidae
蚊式止血钳/小止血鉗 mosquito forceps
蚊体内生环/蚊內週期 mosquito cycle
蚊子/蚊 mosquito
吻/吻 labial commissure
吻合管/吻合管 anastomotic vessel
吻合口/吻合口 anastomotic stoma
吻合口溃疡/吻合口潰瘍 stoma ulcer
吻合[术]/吻合[術] anastomosis
吻合性静脉曲张/吻合性靜脈曲張 anastomotic varix
稳定臂/穩定臂 stabilizing arm
稳定度测定器/穩定度測定器 stabilograph
稳定骨折/穩定骨折 stable fracture
稳定剂/安定劑 stabilizer
稳定胶体/穩定膠質 stable colloid
稳定同位素/穩定同位素,安定同位素 stable isotope

稳定型心绞痛/穩定型心絞痛　stable angina pectoris
稳定性/安定性　stability
稳定性加速实验/安定性加速試驗　accelerated stability test
稳定性膀胱/穩定性膀胱　stable bladder
稳定性试验/安定性試驗　stability study
稳定性萎缩瘢痕/穩定性萎縮瘢痕　stable atrophic scar
稳定状态/穩定狀態　steady state
稳定作用/安定作用　stabilization
稳态血药浓度/穩態血藥濃度　steady plasma-drug concentration
稳态血药浓度峰值/穩態血中濃度最高值　maximum value of steady plasma-drug concentration
稳态血药浓度谷值/穩態血藥濃度谷值　minimum value of steady plasma-drug concentration
问鼻塞/問鼻塞　inquiry of nasal obstruction
问鼻涕/問鼻涕　inquiry of snivel
问鼻痛/問鼻痛　inquiry of nasal pain
问齿舌衄/問齒舌衄　inquiry of gum and tongue bleeding
问初潮/問初潮　inquiring about menarche
问带下/問帶下　inquiring about vaginal discharge
问耳聋/問耳聾　inquiry of deafness
问耳鸣/問耳鳴　inquiry of tinnitus
问耳痛/問耳痛　inquiry of earache
问发音/問發音　inquiry of phonation
问汗/問汗　inquiry about sweating
问呼吸/問呼吸　inquiry of breath
问咳嗽痰涎/問欬嗽痰涎　inquiry of cough and sputum
问口干/問口乾　inquiry of dry mouth
问口腔内疼痛/問口腔內疼痛　inquiry of oral pain
问口味/問口味　inquiry of oral taste
问乳汁/問乳汁　inquiring about breast milk
问吞咽/問吞嚥　inquiry of deglutition
问嗅觉/問嗅覺　inquiry of olfactory sensation
问眩晕/問眩暈　inquiry of vertigo
问咽喉疼痛/問咽喉疼痛　inquiry of sore throat
问咽喉异物感/問咽喉異物感　inquiry of sensation of foreign body in throat
问月经/問月經　inquiring about menstruation
问孕候/問孕候　inquiring about pregnant symptoms
问诊/問診　asking, inquiry
问周期/問週期　inquiring about menstrual cycle
翁雷手术/歐布雷氏手術　Ombredanne operation
翁纳-帕彭海姆染剂/烏-帕二氏染劑　Unna-Pappenheim stain
鎓类化合物/鎓類化合物　onium compounds
涡虫/渦蟲　planarian
涡静脉/渦靜脈　vorticose vein, venae vorticosae, vortex vein
涡流型微孔氧合器/渦流型微孔氧合器　vortex microporous oxygenator
涡纹状神经纤维瘤/渦紋狀神經纖維瘤　storiform neurofibroma
涡旋/渦　vortex
涡状细胞/渦狀細胞　vortex cell
窝洞/窩洞,腔窩　cavity
窝洞涂剂/窩洞[塗]劑,洞護塗劑,洞襯劑　cavity varnish
窝洞预备/窩洞預備,洞製備法　cavity preparation
窝沟封闭剂/窩溝封閉劑　pit and fissure sealant
窝沟龋/窩溝齲　pit and fissure caries
窝后结节/窩後結節　postglenoid tubercle
窝后孔/窩後孔,臼後孔　postglenoid foramen
窝状角质松解症/窩狀角質鬆解症,凹性角質層分離　pitted keratolysis
蜗背侧核/蝸背側核　dorsal cochlear nucleus
蜗窗/蝸窗　fenestra cochleae
蜗窗嵴/蝸窗嵴　crest of fenestra cochleae
蜗窗小窝/蝸窗小窩,蝸窗小凹　fossula of fenestra cochleae
蜗底/蝸底　base of cochlea
蜗顶/蝸頂　cupula of cochlea
蜗腹侧核/蝸腹側核　ventral cochlear nucleus
蜗管/[耳]蝸管　cochlear duct
蜗管顶盲端/蝸管頂盲端　cupular cecum of cochlear duct
蜗管鼓壁/蝸管鼓壁　tympanic wall of cochlear duct
蜗管静脉/蝸管靜脈　vein of canaliculus of cochlea
蜗管前庭壁/蝸管前庭壁,前庭膜　vestibular wall of cochlear duct
蜗管前庭盲端/蝸管前庭盲端　vestibular cecum of cochlear duct
蜗管腔/蝸管腔　auditory duct
蜗管外壁/蝸管外壁　external wall of cochlear duct
蜗管隐窝/[耳]蝸隱窩　cochlear recess
蜗后性聋/蝸後性聾　retrocochlear deafness
蜗孔/蝸孔　helicotrema
蜗螺旋管/蝸螺旋管　cochlear spiral canal
蜗迷路/[耳]蝸迷路　cochlear labyrinth
蜗内电位/蝸內電位　endocochlear potential
蜗牛甾醇/蝸牛甾醇,蝸脂醇　helisterine
蜗区/蝸區　cochlear area

蜗神经/[耳]蜗神經　cochlear nerve
[蜗神经]交通支/[蝸神經]交通支　communicating branch of vestibular nerve with cochlear nerve
蜗神经节/[耳]蝸神經節　cochlear ganglion
蜗水管/蝸水管,蝸小管　aqueduct of cochlea, cochlear aqueduct
蜗水管静脉/蝸水管靜脈　vein of cochlear aqueduct
蜗水管内口/蝸水管內口　internal aperture of cochlear aqueduct
蜗水管外口/蝸小管外口　external aperture of aqueduct of cochlea
蜗支/蝸支　cochlear branch
蜗轴/蝸軸　modiolus
蜗轴板/蝸軸板　lamina of modiolus cochleae
蜗轴底/蝸軸底　base of modiolus of cochlea
蜗轴螺旋管/蝸軸螺旋管　spiral canal of modiolus
蜗轴螺旋静脉/蝸軸螺旋靜脈　spiral vein of modiolus, vena spiralis modioli
蜗轴纵管/蝸軸縱管　longitudinal canals of modiolus cochleae
蜗状关节/蝸狀關節　screw articulation
肟类/肟類　oximes
沃尔夫定律/沃爾夫定律　Wolff law
沃尔夫管/沃爾夫氏導管,小肾管　Wolffian duct
沃尔夫管囊肿/沃爾夫氏囊腫　Wolffian cyst
沃尔夫-帕金森-怀特综合征/沃爾夫-帕金森-懷特症候群,維-帕-懷三氏症候群　Wolff-Parkinson-White syndrome
沃尔夫移植物/沃爾夫氏移植物　Wolff graft
沃尔曼病/沃爾曼病,Wolman氏病　Wolman disease
沃-弗综合征/華-弗二氏症候群　Waterhouse-Friderichsen syndrome
沃克病/沃克病,Kwok氏病　Kwok disease
沃勒变性/沃勒變性,華-勒二氏變性　Wallerian degeneration
沃罗诺夫环/沃羅諾夫環,沃諾爾環　Woronoff ring
沃-罗综合征/沃-羅症候群,Ward-Romano氏症候群　Ward-Romano syndrome
沃森-克里克螺旋结构形/沃森-克里克螺旋結構形,華-克二氏雙螺旋　Watson-Crick helix
沃森-施瓦茨试验/華史氏試驗　Watson-Schwartz test
沃特斯顿手术/沃特斯頓手術　Waterston operation
卧病在家者/臥病在家者　homebound person
卧床疗养/臥床療法　clinotherapy
卧床休息/臥床休息　bed rest
卧倒性心动过缓/臥倒性心搏徐緩　clinostatic bradycardia

卧位/臥位　clinostatism
握笔状手/握筆狀手,書寫狀手　writing hand
握柄磨光器/握柄磨光器,擦牙木簽把持器　porte-polisher
握力/握力　hand strength
握力负荷试验/握力負荷試驗　handgrip stress test
握拳尺偏试验/握拳尺偏試驗　Finkelsein sign
乌丹电流/烏丹電流,奧丁電流　Oudin current
乌丹共振器/烏丹共振器,奧丁氏共振器　Oudin resonator
乌得鲁胶/烏得魯膠,東印度醫用橡樹　udruj
乌风内障/烏風內障　dark wind glaucoma
乌风内障·肝胆实热证/烏風內障·肝膽實熱證　dark wind glaucoma with pattern of liver-gallbladder excessive heat
乌风内障·血瘀气滞证/烏風內障·血瘀氣滯證　dark wind glaucoma with pattern of blood stasis and qi stagnation
乌风内障·阴虚火旺证/烏風內障·陰虛火旺證　dark wind glaucoma with pattern of yin deficiency and fire effulgence
乌干达S病毒/烏干達S型病毒　Uganda S virus
乌鸡白凤丸/烏雞白鳳丸　wuji baifeng pills
乌拉坦/烏拉坦　urethane
乌洛托品/烏洛托品,六次甲基四胺,六甲烯四胺　methenamine
乌梅/烏梅　smoked plum
乌梅丸/烏梅丸　wumei pills
乌瑞替派/烏瑞替派　uredepa
乌痧/烏痧　sha disease with blackish complexion
乌梢蛇/烏梢蛇　black-tail snake
乌头/烏頭　aconite
乌头碱/烏頭素　aconitine
乌头类中毒/烏頭類中毒　aconite poisoning
乌头酸/烏頭酸　aconitic acid
乌头酸水合酶/烏頭酸水合酶　aconitate hydratase
乌头原碱/烏頭原鹼,阿可寧　aconine
乌药/烏藥　combined spicebush root
乌扎拉根/烏扎拉根,烏柴拉　uzara
污斑细胞/汙斑細胞　smudge cell
污秽恐怖者/汙穢恐怖者,不潔恐懼症者　mysophobiac
污泥梭状芽孢杆菌/汙泥梭狀芽孢桿菌,Sordellii氏梭狀芽孢桿菌　Clostridium sordellii
污泥消化法/汙泥消化法,汙泥生化法消化　sludge digestion
污染伤口/汙染傷口　contaminated wound
污染物/汙染物　contaminant

污水/汙水　sewage
污水处理法/汙水處理法,下水汙物處置法,糞汙處理法　sewage treatment
污水生物/汙水生物　saprobe
污物/汙物　filth
巫术/巫術　witchcraft
巫术综合征/巫術症候群,人工性接觸性蕁麻疹　witchcraft syndrome
钨铬钴合金/鎢鈷鉻合金　stellite
钨化合物/鎢化合物　tungsten compound
钨酸/鎢酸　tungstic acid
钨酸盐/鎢酸鹽　tungstate
屋翳/屋翳　wuyi, S15, ST15
无瘢痕皮肤磨削术/無瘢痕皮膚磨削術　scar-free skin resurfacing
无半乳糖尿/無半乳糖尿　agalactosuria
无包皮[畸形]/無包皮畸形,先天無包皮　aposthia
无被囊神经小球/無被囊神經小球　nonencapsulated nerve glomerulus
无鼻[畸形]/無鼻畸形　arhinia
无臂畸胎/無臂畸胎　abrachius
无鞭毛体/無鞭毛體,無鞭毛型　amastigote
无标记细胞/無標記細胞　null cell
无病例临床讲解/無病例臨床講解　dry clinic
无病生存/無病生存　disease-free survival
无长突神经元/無長突神經元,無軸突神經細胞　amacrine neuron
无长突细胞/無長突細胞　amacrine cell
无衬垫夹/無襯墊夾　unpadded splint
无抽搐性电休克治疗/無抽搐性電休克治療　nonconvulsive ECT
无臭/無臭　odorless
无创[伤]缝针/無創[傷]縫針　atraumatic suture needle
无创[伤]技术/無創[傷]技術　atraumatic technique
无创脱位/無創脫位,單純脫位　closed dislocation
无创性方法/無創性方法　noninvasive method
无唇[畸形]/無唇畸形　acheilia
无胆色素粪/無膽色素糞　acholic stool
无胆色素尿/無膽色[素]尿,無膽尿　acholuria
无胆色素尿性黄疸/無膽尿性黃疸　acholuric jaundice
无胆汁[症]/無膽汁[症],膽汁缺乏　acholia
无蛋白免疫原/無蛋白免疫原　isopatin
无蛋白溶液/無蛋白溶液　protein-free solution
无骶[畸形]/無骶畸形,骶骨缺失　asacria
无蒂囊肿/無蒂囊腫,無柄囊腫　sessile cyst
无顶冠状静脉窦综合征/無頂冠狀靜脈竇症候群　unroofed coronary sinus syndrome
无定形病/無定形病[症]　amorpha
[无定形]基质/[無定形]基質　amorphous ground substance
无定形畸胎/無體形怪胎　amorphus
无定形胎/無定形胎　fetus amorphus
无定形胰岛素/無定形胰島素　amorphous insulin
无动性躁狂/無動性躁狂,運動不能性躁狂　akinetic mania
无痘天花/無痘天花　variola sine eruptione
无毒性效应剂量/無[毒性]效應劑量　non-observed effect dose, NOED
无毒血清沉淀/無毒血清沈澱　petit serum
无恶露/無惡露,缺乏惡露　alochia
无耳/無耳　anotia
无耳垂耳/無耳垂耳,Cagot 氏耳　Cagot ear
无耳垂畸形/無耳垂畸形,Aztec 耳,無耳垂耳　Aztec ear
无耳海豹类/無耳海豹類　earless seals
无耳畸胎/無耳畸胎　anotus
无耳畸形/無耳畸形　anotia
无二氧化碳水/無二氧化碳水　carbon dioxide-free water
无反射性膀胱/無反射性膀胱　nonreflex bladder
无反应性/無反應性,無力,應變性缺失　anergy
无反应性结核病/無反應性結核病　nonreactive tuberculosis
无肺[畸形]/無肺畸形　apneumia
无缝带环/無縫帶環　seamless band
无缝冠压模机/無縫冠壓模機　swager for seamless shell
无缝壳冠/無縫殼冠　seamless shell crown
无麸质饮食/無麩質飲食　gluten-free diet
无复吸入活瓣/無複吸入活瓣　nonrebreathing valve
无复吸入装置/無複吸入裝置　nonrebreathing system
无肝期/無肝期　anhepatic phase
无感觉失水/無感覺失水　insensible water loss
无睾畸形/無睾丸畸形　anorchidism
无睾者/無睾者　anorchid
无睾症/無睾症　anorchia
无根苔/無根苔　rootless fur
无功能肾上腺瘤/無功能腎上腺瘤　non-functional adrenal tumor
无功能性𬌗/無功能性𬌗,齒功能喪失性咬合　non-functional occlusion
无功能肿瘤/無功能腫瘤,無機能性腫瘤　non-functional tumor

无光感／無光感　no light perception
无汗／無汗　anhidrosis
无汗性外胚层发育不良／無汗外胚層發育不全　anhidrotic ectodermal dysplasia
无汗症／無汗症　anidrosis
无核胞浆膨胀／無核胞漿膨脹,擴張之無核胞漿　chasmatoplasson
无核红细胞／無核紅細胞　erythroplastid
无核裂卵／無核［裂］卵,單卵　monerula
无核细胞／無核細胞　cytode
无核原虫类／無核原蟲類,單蟲類　monera
无颌［畸形］／無頜［畸形］　agnathia
无颌类／無頜類　agnathans
无黑色素黑色素瘤／無黑色素黑色素瘤,無色素性黑色瘤　amelanotic melanoma
无黑色素小痣性恶性黑色素瘤／無黑色素小痣性惡性黑色素瘤　amelanotic lentigo maligna melanoma
无横纹肌／無橫紋肌　nonstriated muscle
无虹膜／無虹膜　aniridia
无后颅［畸形］／無後顱［畸形］,無後頭顱畸形　notancephalia
无呼吸音／無呼吸音　suppressed respiration
无花果蛋白酶／無花果蛋白酶　ficin
无环酸类／無環酸類　acyclic acids
无环烃类／無環烴類　acyclic hydrocarbons
无黄疸型病毒性肝炎／無黃疸型病毒性肝炎　anicteric virus hepatitis
无机化学品／無機化學品　inorganic chemical
无机碱皮肤损伤／無機鹼皮膚損傷　inorganic alkaline cutaneous trauma
无机焦磷酸酶／無機焦磷酸酶　inorganic pyrophosphatase
无机硫酸盐／無機硫酸鹽,預成性硫酸鹽,礦物性硫酸鹽　preformed sulfates
无机酸皮肤损伤／無機酸皮膚損傷　inorganic acid cutaneous trauma
无机碳化合物／無機碳化合物　inorganic carbon compounds
无机物／無機物　mineral
无畸变极化转移增益法／無畸變極化轉移增益法　distortionless enhancement by polarization transfer, DEPT
无畸透镜／無畸透鏡,正视透镜　orthoscopic lens
无极成神经细胞／無極神經母細胞　apolar neuroblast
无极分子／無極分子,非极性分子　nonpolar molecule
无极细胞／無極細胞　apolar cell
无脊髓畸胎／無脊髓畸胎　amyelus
无脊髓［畸形］／無脊髓畸形　amyelia
无脊椎动物／無脊椎動物,無脊類動物　invertebrate
无脊椎动物光感受器／無脊椎動物光感受器　invertebrate photoreceptor
无脊椎动物激素类／無脊椎動物激素類　invertebrate hormones
无脊椎动物神经节／無脊椎動物神經節　invertebrate ganglia
无脊椎动物肽受体／無脊椎動物肽受體　invertebrate peptide receptor
无脊［椎动物］血红蛋白／無脊［椎動物］血紅蛋白,凝血紅素　erythrocruorin
无尖牙／無尖牙　cuspless tooth
无睑［畸形］／無瞼［畸形］　ablepharon
无焦痂单层皮肤磨削术／無焦痂單層皮膚磨削術　single layer eschar-free skin resurfacing
无焦痂分层皮肤磨削术／無焦痂分層皮膚磨削術　layer by layer eschar-free skin resurfacing
无结石性胆囊炎／無結石性膽囊炎　acalculous cholecystitis
无茎真菌病／無莖黴菌病　acaulinosis
无晶状体／無晶狀體　aphakia
无精／無精　aspermatism
无精子发生／無精子發生,精子無法生成,精子形成不能　aspermatogenesis
无颈子宫／無頸子宮［畸形］　uterus acollis
无菌／無菌　asepsis
无菌操作／無菌操作　aseptic processing
无菌操作室／無菌操作室　aseptic processing room
无菌敷料／無菌敷料　aseptic dressing
无菌结晶／無菌結晶　aseptic crystallization
无菌区／無菌區　aseptic area
无菌溶液／無菌溶液　sterile solution
无菌伤口／無菌傷口,無菌創傷　aseptic wound
无菌生物／無菌生物　germ-free life
无菌室／無菌室　sterile room
无菌术／無菌術　asepsis
无菌脱脂纱布／滅菌脫脂紗布,滅菌吸水紗布　sterile absorbent gauze
无菌外科学说／無菌外科學說　asepticism
无菌性腹膜炎／無菌性腹膜炎　aseptic peritonitis
无菌性梗死／無菌性梗死　aseptic infarct
无菌性坏死／無菌性壞死　aseptic necrosis
无菌性脑膜炎／無菌性腦膜炎　aseptic meningitis, sterile meningitis
无菌性炎症／無菌性炎症　aseptic inflammation
无菌制品／無菌製品　sterile product
无菌状态／無菌狀態　aseptic condition

无颗粒性/無顆粒性　agranular
无口/無口[畸形]　astomia
无口鼻独眼并耳畸胎/無口鼻獨眼[并耳]畸胎,光面畸胎　opocephalus
无口鼻眼畸胎/無口鼻眼畸胎,無眼、口、鼻之畸胎　triencephalus
无口畸胎/無口畸胎　astomus
无口[畸形]/無口畸形　astomia
无肋/無肋畸形　apleuria
无泪/淚缺乏　alacrimia
无力/無力,弛緩　atony
无力性腹泻/無力性腹瀉　atonic diarrhea
无力性溃疡/無力性潰瘍　atonic ulcer
无力性木僵/無力性木僵　anergic stupor
无力性痛风/無力性痛風　asthenic gout
无力性胸/無力性胸　asthenic thorax
无粒白细胞/無顆粒白血球　agranulocyte, nongranular leukocyte
无颅盖/無顱蓋,無顱畸形　acrania
无颅畸胎/無顱畸胎　acranius
无颅[畸形]/無顱畸形　acrania
无卵性月经/無卵性行經　anovulational menstruation
无脉病/無脈病　pulseless disease
无脉络膜/無脈絡膜[畸形],脈絡膜缺失　choroideremia
无毛的/無毛的　glabrous
无毛丘疹/無毛丘疹　atrichia with papular eruption
无酶症/無酵症,酵素缺乏症　anenzymia
无面畸胎/無面畸胎　aprosopus
无面[畸形]/無面畸形　aprosopia
无名动脉/無名動脈　innominate artery
无名静脉/無名静脈　innominate vein
无名孔/無名孔　innominate foramen
无名小管/無名小管　innominate canaliculus
无名质/無名質　substantia innominata
无名肿毒/無名腫毒　acute subcutaneous pyogenic infection, unknown swelling toxin
无明显有害效应剂量/無明顯有害效應劑量　no-observed-adverse-effect level
无脑回[畸形]/無腦迴畸型　agyria
无脑畸胎/無腦畸胎　anencephalus
无脑畸形/無腦[畸形]　anencephaly
无脑脊髓畸胎/無腦脊髓畸胎　amyelencephalus
无脑脊髓[畸形]/無腦脊髓畸形　amyelencephalia
无脑有颈畸形/[無頭]無腦有頸畸形　deranencephalia
无能力/無能力,官能不足　incapacity
无能力者/無能力者　incompetent
无念/無念　without idea
无尿症/無尿[症]　anuria
无排卵/排卵停止　anovulation
无排卵性不孕/無排卵性不孕　anovulatory infertility
无排卵性功能失调性子宫出血/無排卵性功能失調性子宫出血　anovulatory dysfunctional uterine bleeding
无排卵性月经/無排卵性月經　anovulatory menstruation
无排卵周期/無排卵週期　anovulatory cycle
无膀胱[畸形]/無膀胱畸形　acystia
无皮[畸形]/無皮畸形　adermia
无脾/無脾　asplenia
无脾畸形/無脾畸形　alienia
无脾综合征/無脾症候群　asplenia syndrome
无嘌呤膳食/無嘌呤飲食　purine-free diet
无脐综合征/無臍症候群　absent navel syndrome
无气流期/無氣流期　period of zero flow
无球面像差焦点/無球面像差焦點,消球差焦點　aplanatic focus
无躯干畸胎/無軀幹畸形　asoma
无热/無熱的　afebrile
无热流产/無熱性流産　afebrile abortion
无热谵妄/無熱譫妄　afebrile delirium
无乳房/無乳房　amastia
无乳腺[畸形]/無乳腺畸形,無乳房畸形　amazia
无乳支原体/無乳支原體　Mycoplasma agalactiae
无色淀粉样蛋白/無色澱粉樣質　achrooamyloid
无色杆菌科/無色桿菌科　Achromobacteriaceae
无色糊精/白色糊精　leukodextrin
无色花色苷/白花色素苷　leucoanthocyanin
无色花色素/白花色素　leucoanthocyanidin
无色尿/無色尿　achromaturia
无色素痣/無色素母斑　achromic naevus
无色肽/無色肽　acropeptide
无色网/無色網,非染質網　achromatic net
无上体畸胎/[無頭]無上體畸胎　peracephalus
无舌[畸形]/無舌[畸形],先天性無舌畸形　aglossia
无舌锁口[畸形]/無舌鎖口[畸形],無舌無口畸形　aglossostomia
无舌无指综合征/無舌無指症候群,先天性無舌及無指畸形症候群　aglossia-adactylia syndrome
无舌无趾综合征/無舌無趾症候群,先天性無舌及無趾畸形症候群　aglossia-adactylia syndrome
无伸展性/無伸展性　inextensibility
无肾[畸形]/無腎[畸形],腎發育不全　anephrogenesis
无肾小球肾/無腎小球腎　aglomerular kidney

无生殖器畸胎／無生殖器畸胎　agenosomus
无生殖腺者／無生殖腺者　agonad
无生殖腺[状态]／無生殖腺[狀態]，無性腺症　agonadism
无声唇语／無聲唇語，腦語　endophasia
无声嗫语／無聲囁語，暗语，嘔語　mussitation
无时冷泪／無時冷淚　constant cold tear, constant epiphora
无收缩／無收縮　asystole
无手[畸形]／無手畸形　acheiria
无手足[畸形]／無手足[畸形]，無手無足畸形　acheiropodia
无水酒精／無水酒精，純酒精，純醇　absolute alcohol
无水羊毛脂／無水羊毛脂　anhydrous lanolin
无水乙醇／無水乙醇　absolute ethanol
无丝分裂／無絲分裂　amitosis
无丝嗜中性白细胞／無絲嗜中性白血球　nonfilamented neutrophil
无酸／無酸[性]，缺酸　inacidity
无髓鞘神经纤维／無髓鞘神經纖維　nonmedullated nerve fiber
无髓牙／無髓齒　pulpless tooth
无胎盘类／無胎盤類　implacentalia
无碳复写纸／無碳複寫紙　carbonless copy paper
无特异性病原体有机物／無特異性病原體有機物　specific pathogen-free organism
无体形畸胚／無體形畸胚　embryonic anideus
无体形臀部寄生胎／無體型臀部寄生胎，臀部無定形連胎　pygoamorphus
无体植物／無體植物　asomatophyte
无瞳孔[畸形]／無瞳孔[畸形]　acorea
无痛性黄疸／無痛性黃疸　painless jaundice
无痛性溃疡／無痛潰瘍　indolent ulcer
无痛性心绞痛／無痛性心絞痛　angina pectoris sine dolore
无头畸胎／無頭畸胎　acephalus
无头疽／無頭疽　headless abscess, deep carbuncle, suppurative osteomyelitis and arthritis
无头囊／無頭囊，無頭孢蟲　acephalocyst
无头无臂[畸形]／無頭無臂畸形　acephalobrachia
无头无脊柱[畸形]／無頭無脊柱畸形　acephalorhachia
无头无口[畸形]／無頭無口畸形　acephalostomia
无头无手[畸形]／無頭無手畸形　acephalochiria
无头无心[畸形]／無頭無心畸形　acephalocardia
无头无胸[畸形]／無頭無胸畸形　acephalothoracia
无头无足[畸形]／無頭無足畸形　acephalopodia
无头胸上腹[畸形]／無頭胸上腹[畸形]，無頭無腹畸形　acephalogastria
无蜕膜类[动物]／無蛻膜類動物　indecidua
无蜕膜胎盘／無蛻膜胎盤　indeciduate placenta
无尾觉器线虫／無尾覺器線蟲　aphasmid
无胃[畸形]／無胃畸形　agastria
无细胞层／無細胞層　cell-free zone
无细胞系统／無細胞系統　cell-free system
无细胞牙骨质／無細胞牙骨質　acellular cementum
无细胞疫苗／無細胞疫苗　acellular vaccine
无下颌并耳畸胎／無下頜并耳畸胎　otocephalus
无[下]颌畸胎／無下頜畸胎　agnathus
无下颌头面畸形／下頜頭面畸形，無下頜頭[畸形]　agnathocephalia
无先兆偏头痛／無兆性偏頭痛　migraine without aura
无限外韧维管束／無限外韌維管束，無限并立型維管束　unclosed collateral bundle
无小脑[畸形]／無小腦畸形　notanencephalia
无效等位基因／無效等位基因　amorphic gene
无效腔／無效腔，死腔　dead space
无心畸形／無心畸形　acardia
无心寄生胎畸胎／全無心畸胎　holoacardius
无行为能力／無行為能力　incapability
无性繁殖／無性繁殖　vegetative propagation
无性生殖／無性生殖　asexual reproduction
无性生殖体／無性生殖體　agamete
无性生殖周期／無性生殖週期　asexual cycle
无性世代／無性世代　asexual generation
无性细胞瘤／無性細胞瘤　dysgerminoma
无胸骨[畸形]／無胸骨畸形　asternia
无胸腺／無胸腺，胸腺機能缺失　athymism, athymismus
无胸腺小鼠／無胸腺小鼠　athymic mice
无嗅脑[畸形]／無嗅腦畸形　arhinencephalia
无血管移植物／無血管移植物　avascular graft
无血清培养基／無血清培養基　serum-free medium
无牙／無齒[畸形]　anodontia
无牙颌／無牙頜　edentulous jaw
无牙[颌]印模托盘／無牙[頜]印模托盤　edentulous impression tray
无牙患者治疗学／無牙患者治療學　edentics
无牙口腔／無牙口腔　edentate mouth
无牙区带蒂移植瓣／無牙區帶蒂移植瓣　edentulous-area grafts flap
无盐饮食／無鹽飲食，無鹽食物，除鹽食物　salt-free diet
无盐掌宁／無鹽掌寧，南美仙人掌素　anhalonine
无眼[畸形]／無眼[畸形]　anophthalmia

无眼畸胎/無眼畸形　anophthalmus
无羊膜动物/無羊膜動物　anamniote
无氧阈/無氧閾　anaerobic threshold
无义密码子/無義密碼子　nonsense codon
无义突变/無義突變　nonsense mutation
无阴道/無陰道［畸形］　absence of vagina
无应激试验/無應激試驗　non-stress test
无运动/無運動，無動力　akinesis
无责任能力/無責任能力　irresponsibility
无障碍通行/無障礙通行　barrier free accessibility
无针［高压］喷射注射器/無針［高壓］噴射注射器，皮膚無針噴注器　dermojet
无疹性带状疱疹/無疹性帶狀皰疹　zoster sine herpete
无症状病/無症狀病　silent disease
无症状［性］感染/無症狀性感染　subclinical infection
无症状性细菌尿/無症狀性細菌尿　asymptomatic bacteriuria
无症状性［心肌］缺血/無症狀性缺血　silent ischemia
无肢［畸形］/無肢畸形　amelia
无β脂蛋白血症/無β-脂蛋白血症，血清β-脂蛋白缺乏症　abetalipoproteinemia
无脂饮食/無脂食物　fat-free diet
无指畸形/無指畸形　aphalangia
无趾畸形/無趾畸形　aphalangia
无重力状态/無重力狀態　gravity free state
无着丝粒断片/無著絲粒斷片　acentric fragment
无子宫［畸形］/無子宮畸形　ametria, absence of uterus
无足［畸形］/無足畸形　apodia, apus
无左右定向力/無左右定向力　right-left disorientation
吴策线虫病/吳策線蟲病，伍克勒氏絲蟲病　Wuchereriasis
吴普本草/吳普本草　Wu Pu Bencao
吴瑭/吳瑭　Wu Tang
吴有性/吳有性　Wu Youxing
吴茱萸/吳茱萸　medicinal evodia fruit
吴茱萸次碱/吳茱萸次鹼　rutaecarpine
吴茱萸汤/吳茱萸湯　wuzhuyu decoction
蜈蚣/蜈蚣，百足蟲　centipede
蜈蚣毒［液］/蜈蚣毒　centipede venom
蜈蚣蜇伤/蜈蚣螫傷　centipede sting
蜈蚣中毒/蜈蚣中毒　centipede poisoning
五瓣成形术/五瓣成形術　five-flap plasty
五倍体/五倍體　pentaploid
五倍子/五倍子　Chinese gall

五迟/五遲　five kinds of retardations, five retardations
五迟・肝肾两虚证/五遲・肝腎兩虛證　five retardations with pattern of deficiency of both liver and kidney
五迟・痰瘀阻滞证/五遲・痰瘀阻滯證　five retardations with pattern of blockade of phlegm and static blood
五迟・心脾两虚证/五遲・心脾兩虛證　five retardations with pattern of heart-spleen deficiency
五重峰/五重峰　quintet
五处/五處　wuchu, BL5
五刺/五刺　five techniques of needling
五疸/五疸　five jaundices
五夺/五奪　five exhaustions
五方/五方　five orientations
五风内障/五風內障　five wind glaucoma
五氟利多/五氟利多　penfluridol
五福化毒丸/五福化毒丸　wufu huadu pills
五官/五官　five sense apertures
五华/五華　five lustre
五积散/五積散　wuji powder
五加皮/五加皮　cortex acanthopanacis radicis, acanthopanax root bark
五尖牙/五尖牙　quinquecuspid
五劳/五勞　five consumptions, five types of strain
五联症/五聯症，五合要素，五合症候　pentalogy
五灵脂/五靈脂　flying squirrel's droppings
五苓散/五苓散　wuling powder
五氯苯酚/五氯酚　Pentachlorophenol
五轮/五輪　five wheels
五轮八廓/五輪八廓　five wheels and eight regions
五轮辨证法/五輪辨證法　five-wheel pattern differentiation
五轮学说/五輪學說　five-wheel theory
五磨饮子/五磨飲子　five milled ingredients decoction
五年生存率/五年存活率　five-year survival rate
五年死亡率/五年死亡率　five-year mortality rate
五皮饮/五皮飲　wupi drink
五禽戏/五禽戲　five mimic-animal exercise, wuqinxi
五仁润肠丸/五仁潤腸丸　wuren runchang pills
五仁丸/五仁丸　wuren pills
五日热巴尔通体/五日熱巴爾通體　Bartonella quintana
五软/五軟　five infantile flaccidity, five kinds of flaccidity
五色/五色　five colors

五色带/五色帶　multicolored vaginal discharge
五色带[病]/五色帶[病]　parti-colored vaginal discharge
五色带·湿热下注证/五色帶·濕熱下注證　parti-colored vaginal discharge with pattern of downward diffusion of damp-heat
五色带·五脏虚损证/五色帶·五臟虛損證　parti-colored vaginal discharge with pattern of deficiency of five zang-viscera
五色主病/五色主病　diagnostic significance of five colors
五善/五善　five favorable conditions
五神/五神　five emotions, five mental activities
五神脏/五神臟　five organs related to mental activities
五声/五聲　five sounds
五十动/五十動　fifty beats
五十二病方/五十二病方　Prescriptions for Fifty-two Diseases, 52 Bing Fang
五石散/五石散　five minerals powder
五时/五時　five seasons
五枢/五樞　wushu, GB27
五输配穴法/五輸配穴法　five-shu points association, five-shu points combination
五输穴/五輸穴　five-shu point
五态人/五態人　five types of constitution
五态人格测验/五態人格測驗　five types of personality test
五肽/五肽，戊勝　pentapeptide
五肽胃泌素/五肽胃泌素　pentagastrin
五糖/五[碳]糖　pentosaccharide
五体/五體　five body constituents
五痿/五痿　five flaccidity
五味/五味　five flavors
五味偏嗜/五味偏嗜　flavor predilection
五味消毒饮/五味消毒飲　wuwei xiaodu drink
五味子/五味子　Chinese magnoliavine fruit
五烯甲雌醇核/五烯甲雌醇核　estrapentaene
五烯类/五烯類　pentaenes
五邪/五邪　five pathogens
五心烦热/五心煩熱　feverish sensation in the chest, dysphoria with feverish sensation in chest, palms and soles
五行/五行　five phases
五行人/五行人　persons with characteristics of the five phases
五行相乘/五行相乘　over-restriction of five phases
五行相克/五行相克　mutual restriction of five phases
五行相生/五行相生　mutual generation of five phases
五行相侮/五行相侮　counter-restriction of five phases
五行学说/五行學説　five phases theory, five-phase theory
五溴化碘/五溴化碘　iodine pentabromide
五氧化二碘/五氧化二碘　iodine pentoxide
五氧化二锑/五氧化二銻　antimony pentoxide
五氧化物/五氧化物　pentoxide
五液/五液　five humors
五音/五音　five tones
五音疗法/五音療法　five-sound therapy
五硬/五硬　five kinds of stiffness, five stiffness
五元素汞合金/五元素汞合金　quinary amalgam
五运/五運　five evolutive phases
五脏/五臟　five zang viscera
五脏痹/五臟痺　five zang-viscera bi
五脏别论篇/五臟別論篇　Treatise on the Five Zang Organs
五脏疳/五臟疳　gan disease of five zang-viscera
五脏咳/五臟欬　five zang-viscera cough
五脏情志论/五臟情志論　theory of zang-fu organs and emotions
五脏郁证/五臟鬱證　stagnation pattern of the five zang organs
五志/五志　five emotions
五志过极/五志過極　extreme frustration of five emotions
五志化火/五志化火　five emotions transforming into fire
五子衍宗丸/五子衍宗丸　wuzi yanzong pills
午后潮热/午後潮熱　tidal fever in the afternoon
午时茶颗粒/午時茶顆粒　wushicha granules
伍德布里奇疗法/伍德布里奇療法，伍布里氏療法　Woodbridge treatment
伍德光/伍德光，Wood 氏燈　Wood light
伍尔皮安试验/伍爾皮安試驗，華爾安氏試驗　Vulpian test
武火/武火　strong fire
武靴叶属/武靴葉屬　Gymnema
武装巨噬细胞/武裝巨噬細胞　armed macrophage
舞蹈病持续状态/舞蹈病持續狀態　status choreicus
舞蹈病样综合征/舞蹈病症候群　chorea syndrome
舞蹈狂/舞蹈病　choromania
舞蹈疗法/舞蹈療法　dance therapy
舞蹈徐动症/舞蹈手足痙病　choreoathetosis

舞蹈者足/舞蹈者足 dancer foot
舞蹈症性障碍/舞蹈症性障礙 choreatic disorders
戊巴比妥/戊基巴比妥 pentobarbital
戊醇/戊醇 amyl alcohol
戊醇类/戊醇類 pentanols
戊醇生成发酵/戊醇生成發酵,戊基發酵 amylic fermentation
戊醇中毒/戊醇中毒 amylism
戊二醛/戊二醛 glutaral
戊二酸盐类/戊二酸鹽類 glutarates
α-戊桂皮醛/α-戊桂皮醛 α-amyl cinnamic aldehyde
戊基/戊[烷]基 amyl
戊基氯/戊基氯,氯化戊基 amyl chloride
戊基止痛胶体/戊基止痛膠體 amyl anodyne colloid
戊聚糖/戊聚糖 pentosan
戊醛/戊酸醛 valeric aldehyde
戊醛糖/戊醛醣 aldopentose
戊沙溴铵/戊沙溴銨,甲苯基戊酸二乙胺乙酯 valethamate
戊双脒/戊雙脒,雙對脒基苯氧基戊烷 pentamidine
戊四硝酯/戊四硝酯,四硝基五紅藓醇 pentaerythritol tetranitrate
戊四烟酯/戊四煙酯 niceritrol
戊四唑/戊四唑 pentylenetetrazole
戊酸/戊酸,纈草酸 valerianic acid
戊酸雌二醇/戊酸雌二醇 estradiol valerate
戊酸类/戊酸類 pentanoic acids
戊酸盐类/戊酸鹽類 valerates
戊糖/戊糖 pentose
戊糖苷/戊糖苷 pentoside
戊糖苷酶/戊糖酵素 pentosidase
戊糖核酸/戊糖核酸 pentosenucleic acid
戊糖基/戊糖基 pentosyl
戊糖基转移酶类/戊糖基轉移酶類 pentosyl transferases
戊糖类/戊糖類 pentoses
戊糖磷酸类/戊糖磷酸類 pentose phosphates
戊糖磷酸途径/磷酸戊糖路徑 pentose phosphate pathway
戊糖尿/戊糖尿 pentosuria
戊糖旁路/戊糖分路 pentose shunt
戊糖脎/戊糖脎 pentosazon
戊糖血[症]/戊糖血[症] pentosemia
戊酮类/戊酮類 pentanones
戊烷/戊烷 pentane
戊烯/戊烯 amylene
戊烯麻醉/戊烯麻醉 amylene anesthesia
戊型病毒性肝炎/戊型病毒性肝炎 viral hepatitis type E
戊型肝炎/戊型肝炎 hepatitis E
戊型肝炎病毒/戊型肝炎病毒 hepatitis E virus
芴类/芴類 fluorenes
物镜/接物鏡 objective lens
物理变应性/物理性過敏 physical allergy
物理刺激/物理刺激 physical stimulation
物理化学/物理化學 physical chemistry
物理疗法/物理療法 physical therapy
物理美容学/物理美容學 physical cosmetology
物理染色体图/物理染色體圖 physical chromosome mapping
物理[性损]伤/物理[性损]傷 physical injury
物理性荨麻疹/物理性蕁麻疹 physical urticaria
物理性质/物理性質 physical property
物理学配伍禁忌/物理學配伍禁忌,物理性配伍禁忌 physical incompatibility
物理药学/物理藥學 physical pharmacy
物理医学/物理醫學,理療學 physical medicine
物理医学家/物理[派]醫學家 iatrophysicist
物理医学与康复[学]/物理醫學與康復[學] physical medicine and rehabilitation
物理影响妄想/物理影響妄想 delusion of physical influence
物理应力/物理應力 mechanical stress
物理诱变剂/物理誘變劑 physical mutagen
物理预防/物理預防 physical prophylaxis
物理原[因]病/物理原[因]病 physinosis
物理诊断/物理診斷 physical diagnosis
物理治疗/物理治療 physiotherapy
物理治疗学/物理治療[醫]學 physiatry
物盲/物[體]盲,物體失辨症 object blindness
物损真睛/物損真睛 ocular penetration, traumatic injury of lens
物体巨大感/物體巨大感,大認知 macrostereognosia
物体旋转性眩晕/物體旋轉性眩暈,物景[轉動性]眩暈 objective vertigo
物我两忘/物我兩忘 both material and oneself been forgotten
物质/物質 substance
H物质/H物質 H substance
P物质/P物質 substance P
α物质/α物質,甲型質 alpha substance
β物质/β物質,乙型質 beta substance
物质代谢/物質代謝 substance metabolism
物质戒断综合征/物質戒斷症候群 substance withdrawal syndrome
物质滥用检测/物質濫用檢測 substance abuse

detection
物质滥用治疗中心/物質濫用治療中心　substance abuse treatment center
物质缺失性综合征/物質缺失性症候群　depletion syndrome
物质相关性障碍/物質相關性障礙　substance-related disorder
物质诱发性精神病/物質誘發性精神病　substance-induced psychosis
误差/誤差,錯誤　error
误差修正反馈法/誤差修正反饋法　error correct feed-back method
误听/誤聽　paracusia
误吸/誤吸　aspiration

误义突变/誤義突變　missense mutation
误诊/誤診　diagnostic error
误治/誤治　wrong treatment
恶风/惡風　aversion to wind
恶寒/惡寒　aversion to cold
恶寒发热/惡寒發熱　aversion to cold with fever
恶寒战栗/惡寒顫慄　shaking chill
恶热/惡熱　aversion to heat
雾化疗法/霧化療法　nebulization therapy
雾化器/霧化器,噴霧器　nebulizer
雾视法/霧視法　fogging method
雾视[症]/霧視[症],幻影症　scieropia
寤寐/寤寐　waking and sleeping
寤梦/寤夢　dream of daytime activity

X

西班牙绞带/西班牙絞帶　Spanish windlass
西班牙流行性感冒/西班牙流行性感冒　Spanish influenza
西班牙式止血带/西班牙式止血帶　Spanish tourniquet
西班牙蝇/西班牙蒼蠅　Spanish fly
西吡氯铵/西吡氯銨　cetylpyridinium
西伯鼻孢子虫/西伯鼻孢子蟲，Seeberi 氏鼻芽孢菌　Rhinosporidium seeberi
西布森沟/西布森溝，Sibson 氏溝　Sibson groove
西布森腱膜/西布森腱膜，Sibson 氏腱膜　Sibson aponeurosis
西登哈姆咳/西登哈姆欬，Sydenham 氏欬嗽　Sydenham cough
西登哈姆舞蹈病/西登哈姆舞蹈病，Sydenham 氏舞蹈症　Sydenham chorea
西方马脑脊髓炎/西方馬腦脊髓炎　western equine encephalomyelitis
西方马脑炎/西方馬腦炎　western equine encephalitis
西方马脑炎病毒/西方馬腦炎病毒　western equine encephalitis virus
西方型马脑脊髓炎病毒/西方型馬腦脊髓炎病毒，西部馬腦脊髓炎病毒　WEE virus
西格玛反应/西格瑪反應，梅毒凝絮反應　sigma reaction
西瓜属/西瓜屬　Citrullus
西瓜霜润喉片/西瓜霜潤喉片　xiguashuang runhou tablets
西瓜子素/西瓜子素，垂瓜黃質，甜瓜黃苷　cucurbocitrin
西-哈细胞/西-哈細胞，鐮狀細胞　Siemens-Halske cell
西河柳/西河柳　Chinese tamarisk twig
西红花/西紅花　saffron
西红柿/番茄　tomato
西黄蓍胶浆/西黃蓍膠漿　tragacanth mucilage
西卡尔综合征/西卡爾症候群，Sicard 氏症候群　Sicard syndrome
西-柯综合征/西-柯症候群，Silvestrini-Corda 二氏症候群　Silvestrini-Corda syndrome
西拉普利/西拉普利　cilazapril
西里[肠]瘘/西里[腸]瘻，Thiry 氏腸瘻　Thiry fistula
西里-韦拉肠瘘/西里-韋拉腸瘻，Thiry-Vella 二氏瘻　Thiry-Vella fistula
西罗霉素/西羅黴素　cirolemycin
西罗莫司/西羅莫司　sirolimus
西玛嗪/西馬嗪　Simazine
西门利克森林病毒/西門利克森林病毒，森立奇森林病毒　Semliki forest virus
西门子综合征/西門子症候群，Siemens 氏症候群　Siemens syndrome
西蒙病灶/西蒙病灶　Simon foci
西蒙综合征/西蒙症候群，Simon 氏症候群　Simon syndrome
西咪替丁/西咪替丁　cimetidine
西米拉状粪/西米拉狀糞　sago-grain stool
西米脾/西米脾　sago spleen
西莫纳尔特系带/西莫納爾特繫帶，Simonart 氏帶　Simonart band
西姆布病毒/西姆布病毒，Simbu 病毒　Simbu virus
西尼罗病毒/西尼羅河病毒　West Nile virus
西尼罗热/西尼祿熱　West Nile fever
西诺沙星/西諾沙星　cinoxacin
西诺沙酯/西諾沙酯，辛諾賽　cinoxate
西皮饮食/西皮飲食，消化性潰瘍飲食　sippy diet
西曲溴铵化合物/西曲溴銨化合物，西曲銨化合物　cetrimonium compounds
西沙必利/西沙必利　cisapride
西索米星/西索米星，紫蘇黴素　sisomicin
西酞普兰/西酞普蘭　citalopram
西替利嗪/西替利嗪　cetirizine
西瓦特皮肤异色病/西瓦特皮膚異色病　Civatte poikiloderma
西瓦特体/西瓦特體，Civatte 氏小體　Civatte body
西洋参/西洋参　American ginseng
西印度苦香皮/西印度苦香皮　cortex cascarillae
西印度糖蜜/西印度糖蜜　West India molasses
西藏传统医学/西藏傳統醫學　Tibetan traditional medicine
西佐喃/西左非蘭　Sizofiran

吸虫/吸蟲　fluke
吸虫病/吸蟲病　trematodiasis
吸虫感染/吸蟲感染　trematode infection
吸大麻烟/吸大麻煙　marijuana smoking
吸附/吸附　adsorption
吸附剂/吸附劑　adsorbent
吸附解毒/吸附解毒　sorption detoxification
吸附类毒素/吸附性類毒素　adsorbed toxoid
吸附物/吸附物　adsorbate
吸附洗脱试验/吸附洗脱試驗　adsorption elution test
吸管虫/吸管蟲　suctorian
吸光度/吸光度　absorbance
吸光度比值/吸光度比值　absorbance ratio
吸光系数/吸光係數,比吸光度　specific absorbance
吸颊[症]/吸頰　sucking cheek
吸量管/吸量管　pipet
吸留气体/吸留氣體,封闭氣體　occluded gas
吸气测量计/吸氣[測量]計　inspirometer
吸气活瓣/吸氣活瓣　inspiratory valve
吸气肌痉挛/吸氣肌痙攣　inspiratory spasm
吸气困难/吸氣困難　inspiratory dyspnea
吸气量/吸氣量　inspiratory capacity
吸气末暂停/吸氣末暫停　endinspiratory pause
吸气末正压/吸氣末正壓　endinspiratory positive pressure
吸气驱动压/吸氣驅動壓　inspiratory driving pressure
吸气性创伤/吸氣性創傷　sucking wound
吸乳器/吸乳器,吸乳唧筒,抽乳筒　breast pump
吸入/吸入　inhalation
吸入暴露/吸入暴露　inhalation exposure
吸入储备仓/吸入儲備倉　inhalation spacer
吸入毒理学/吸入毒理學　inhalation toxicology
吸入法/吹入[法],吹氣法　insufflation
吸入麻醉/吸入麻醉　respiration anesthesia
吸入麻醉药/吸入麻醉藥,吸入性麻醉劑　inhalation anesthetic
吸入气/吸入氣　inspired gas
吸入气雾剂/吸入氣霧劑,吸入型氣化噴霧劑　inhalation aerosol
吸[入]器/吸[入]器　inspirator, inhaler
吸入投药/吸入投藥　inhalation administration
吸入物/吸入物　inhalant
吸入性肺炎/吸入性肺炎　aspiration pneumonia
吸入性结核/吸入性結核　aerogenic tuberculosis
吸入性烧伤/吸入性燒傷　inhalation burn
吸入性损伤/吸入性損傷　inhalation injury
吸入氧比例/吸入氧比例　fraction of inspiratory oxygen
吸湿性膨胀/吸濕性擴張　hygroscopic expansion
吸收不良/吸收不良　malabsorption
吸收不良综合征/吸收不良性症候群　malabsorption syndrome
吸收促进剂/吸收增進劑　absorption enhancer
吸收法/吸收法　absorption method
吸收分数/吸收分數,吸收分率　absorption fraction
吸收[光]带/吸收帶,吸光帶　absorption band
吸收[光]谱/吸收光譜　absorption spectrum
吸收基质/吸收基劑　absorption base
吸收剂/吸收劑　absorbent, absorber
吸收抗原/吸收抗原　absorben
吸收力/吸收力,吸光率　absorbency
吸收量/吸收量　absorbed dose
吸收[谱]线/吸收線　absorption line
吸收器/吸收器　absorption apparatus
吸收腔隙/吸收腔隙,霍希普氏腔隙　absorption lacuna
吸收体/吸收體,吸收器,吸收劑　absorber
吸收透镜/吸收透鏡　absorption lens
吸收系数/吸收係數　coefficient of absorption
吸收细胞/吸收細胞　absorptive cell
吸收陷窝/吸收腔隙　absorption lacuna
吸收性黄疸/吸收性黄疸　absorption jaundice
吸收性基质/吸收性基質　absorption base
吸收性明胶海绵/吸收性明膠海綿　absorbable gelatin sponge
吸收[作用]/吸收　absorption
吸水明胶片/吸水明膠片,吸收性膠膜　absorbable gelatin film
吸水性气哽/吸水性氣哽,水哽塞,吸水性窒息　water choke
吸吮反射/吮吸反射　sucking reflex
吸吮水疱/吮吮水皰　sucking blister
吸吮线虫病/吮吮絲蟲病,瞼絲蟲病　thelaziasis
吸吮行为/吸吮行爲　sucking behavior
吸涎器/吸涎器,排涎器　saliva ejector
吸血/吸血　sucking blood
吸血蝙蝠/吸血蝙蝠　vampire
吸血昆虫/吸血[昆]蟲　hematophagous bug
吸血器/吸血器,放血計量器　bdellometer
吸烟/吸煙　smoking
吸烟癌/吸煙癌,煙徒癌　smoker cancer
吸烟斑/吸煙斑　smoking patch
吸烟戒断/吸煙戒斷　tobacco use cessation
吸烟性黑斑[症]/吸煙性黑斑[症]　smoker's

melanoplakia
吸烟者/吸煙者 smoker
吸烟者呼吸综合征/吸煙者呼吸症候群 smoker respirtory syndrome
吸烟者角化病/吸煙者角化症 smoker keratosis
吸烟者面容/吸煙者面容 smoker face
吸烟者气喘/吸煙者氣喘 smoker asthma
吸烟者消化不良/嗜煙者消化不良 smoker dyspepsia
吸烟者眩晕/嗜煙者眩暈,煙徒眩暈 smoker vertigo
吸叶/吸葉 bothridium
吸液针/吸液針,吸引針 aspirating needle
吸引/吸引 attraction
吸引导液法/吸引導流法 aspiration drainage
吸引管/吸引管 suction catheter
吸引活检[术]/吸引活檢[術] suction biopsy
吸着剂/吸著劑 sorbent
吸足/吸[吮]足 sucker foot
希阿利-阿诺尔德综合征/希阿利-阿諾爾德症候群,契-亞二氏症候群 Chiari-Arnold syndrome
希阿利综合征/希阿利症候群,Chiari氏症候群 Chiari syndrome
希波克绷带/希波克繃帶,Hippocrates氏繃帶 Hippocrates bandage
希波克拉底誓言/希波克拉底誓言,希氏誓言 Hippocratic Oath
希波克拉底医派者/希波克拉底醫派者,希派治療體系信奉者 Hippocratist
希波克拉底振荡音/希波克拉底振盪音,希波拉氏振盪聲 Hippocratic sound
希-德综合征/希-德症候群,Shy-Drager症候群 Shy-Drager syndrome
希恩手术/希恩手術,契恩氏手術 Chiene operation
希恩-西蒙病/希恩-西蒙病,Sheehan-Simmond氏病 Sheehan-Simmond disease
希恩综合征/希恩症候群 Sheehan syndrome
希尔施普龙病/希爾施普龍病 Hirschsprung disease
希尔食管裂孔疝修补术/希爾食管裂孔疝修補術 Hill hiatal hernia repair
希尔维氏窝/希爾維氏窩,西維爾氏窩,大腦側窩 Sylvian fossa
希夫碱类/希夫鹼類 Schiff bases
希-弗综合征/希-弗症候群,Chiari-Frommel二氏症候群 Chiari-Frommel syndrome
希林试验/希林[氏]試驗 Schilling test
希帕胺/希帕胺 Xipamide
希齐希试验/希齊希試驗,希茲格氏試驗 Hitzig test
希氏多孔针刺结核菌素试验/希氏多孔針刺結核菌素試驗 Heaf multiple puncture tuberculin test
希氏束/希[斯]氏束,房室束 bundle of His
希氏束电图/希氏束電圖,心臟希氏束電描記圖 His bundle electrogram
希氏束电位分裂/希氏束電位分裂 split of His potential
希斯管/希氏管,His氏管 duct of His
希斯荚膜染色法/希斯荚膜染色 Hiss capsule stain
希托夫管/希托夫管,希多氏管,柯魯克氏管 Hittorf tube
昔奈福林/昔奈福林,昔內弗林 Synephrine
析因分析/析因分析,因子分析 factor analysis
析因实验/析因實驗 factorial experiment
息贲/息賁 lung amassment
息风定痫/息風定癇 arresting epilepsy by calming endogenous wind
息风解痉/息風解痙 relieving spasm by calming endogenous wind
息肉/息肉 polyp
息肉病/息肉病 polyposis
息肉刀/息肉刀 polypotome
息肉分块切除[术]/息肉分塊切除[術] piecemeal polypectomy
息肉夹碎器/息肉壓碎器 polypotrite
息肉切除[术]/息肉切除[術],息肉割除術 polypectomy
息肉手法摘除术/息肉手法摘除術 digital polypectomy
息肉性结肠炎/息肉性結腸炎 polypous colitis
息肉性胃炎/息肉性胃炎 polypous gastritis
息肉性心内膜炎/息肉性心內膜炎 polypous endocarditis
息肉样鼻炎/息肉狀鼻炎 polypoid rhinitis
息肉样黑变症/息肉樣黑變症 polypoid melanosis
息肉样畸胎瘤/息肉狀畸胎瘤 polypoid teratoma
息肉样瘤/息肉狀瘤 polypoid tumor
息肉样腺癌/息肉狀腺癌 polypoid adenocarcinoma
息肉样增生/息肉狀增生 polypoid hyperplasia
息肉痔/息肉痔,直腸息肉 rectal polyp
息肉痔·大肠湿热证/息肉痔·大腸濕熱證 rectal polyp with pattern of dampness-heat in large intestine
息肉痔·风伤肠络证/息肉痔·風傷腸絡證 rectal polyp with pattern of wind injuring intestine collaterals
息肉痔·脾气虚证/息肉痔·脾氣虛證 rectal polyp with spleen qi deficiency pattern
息肉痔·气滞血瘀证/息肉痔·氣滯血瘀證 rectal

polyp with pattern of qi stagnation and blood stasis
息肉状腺瘤/息肉狀腺瘤　polypoid adenoma
息肉状腺瘤病/息肉狀癌病　polypoidosis
息止位垂直关系/息止位垂直關係　vertical relation of rest position
硒/硒　selenium
硒代胱氨酸/硒代胱氨酸　selenocysteine
硒代甲硫氨酸/硒代甲硫胺酸,硒蛋胺酸　selenomethionine
硒放射性同位素/硒放射性同位素　selenium radioisotope
硒胱氨酸/硒胱胺酸　selenium cystine
硒化合物/硒化合物　selenium compound
硒化氢/硒化氫　hydrogen selenide
硒化物/硒化物　selenide
硒酸盐/硒酸鹽　selenate
硒中毒/硒中毒　selenosis
悉尼酮类/悉尼酮類,斯德酮類　sydnones
悉尼线/悉尼線　Sidney line
烯丙胺/烯丙胺,丙烯胺　allylamine
烯丙雌醇/烯丙雌醇　allylestrenol
烯丙甘氨酸/烯丙甘胺酸,丙烯基甘胺酸　allylglycine
烯丙化合物/烯丙化合物　allyl compound
烯丙基异丙乙酰胺/烯丙基異丙乙醯胺　allylisopropylacetamide
烯丙吗啡/烯丙嗎啡　nalorphine
烯醇/烯醇　enol
烯醇化/烯醇化　enolization
烯醇型/烯醇型,烯醇式　enol form
烯烃类/烯烴類　alkenes
烯酰 CoA 水合酶/烯醯 CoA 水合酶　enoyl-CoA hydratase
烯脂酸/烯脂酸,烯屬酸　olefinic acid
稀氨溶液/稀氨溶液　diluted ammonia solution
稀次醋酸铅溶液/稀[釋]次醋酸鉛溶液　diluted lead subacetate solution
稀次氯酸钠溶液/稀[釋]次氯酸鈉溶液　diluted sodium hypochlorite solution
稀发月经过多/稀法月經過多,月經來潮次數少而量多　oligohypermenorrhea
稀发月经过少/稀法月經過少,月經來潮次數少而量亦少　oligohypomenorrhea
稀毛症/稀毛症　hypotrichosis
稀氢氧化铵溶液/稀氫氧化氨溶液　diluted ammonium hydroxide solution
稀释/稀釋　dilution
稀释达金溶液/稀釋達金溶液,改良 Dakin 氏溶液　modified Dakin solution
稀释法/稀釋法　dilution method
稀释剂/稀釋劑,稀釋藥　diluent agent, diluent
稀释染液/稀釋染液　diluted staining solution
稀释性祛痰药/稀釋性祛痰藥　diluent expectorant
稀疏性狼疮/稀疏性狼瘡　lupus discretus
稀土金属元素混合物/稀土金屬元素混合物　lucium
稀土元素/稀土元素　rare earth element
稀血性腹水/稀血性腹水,水血症性腹水　hydremic ascites
稀血性红细胞减少/稀血性紅細胞減少,多漿性紅血球減少　hydro-oligocythemia
稀血性水肿/稀血性水腫　hydremic edema
稀有放线菌/稀有放線菌　rare actinomycete
犀角地黄汤/犀角地黃湯　xijiao dihuang decoction
锡多磷酸盐类/錫多磷酸鹽類　tin polyphosphate
锡放射性同位素/錫放射性同位素　tin radioisotope
锡氟化物/錫氟化物　tin fluoride
锡化合物/錫化合物　tin compound
锡克试验/錫克試驗,席克氏試驗　Schick test
锡兰病/錫蘭病　Ceylon sickness
锡酸/錫酸　stannic acid
锡酸盐/錫酸鹽　stannate
溪谷热/溪谷熱,山谷熱,球黴菌病　valley fever
豨莶草/豨薟草　siegesbeckia herb
蜥蜴咬伤/蜥蜴咬傷　lizard bite
膝/膝　knee, xi, AH4
膝闭锁/膝閉鎖　locked knee
膝反屈/膝反屈　genu recurvatum
膝反射/膝反射　knee jerk reflex
膝反张/膝反張　knee recurvatum
膝盖以上/膝以上　above knee
膝高低征/膝高低徵　Allis' sign
膝弓状韧带/膝弓狀韌帶　arcuate ligament of knee
膝骨关节炎/膝骨關節炎　knee osteoarthritis
膝关/膝關　xiguan, LR7
膝关节/膝關節　knee joint, articulation of knee
膝关节半月板损伤/膝關節半月板損傷　injury of meniscus of knee joint, meniscus injury of knee
膝关节创伤性滑膜炎/膝關節損傷性滑膜炎　traumatic synovitis of knee joint
膝关节过伸试验/膝關節過伸試驗　hyperextension test of knee joint
膝关节肌/膝關節肌　articularis genus
膝关节夹/膝關節夾,湯馬斯氏膝夾　knee splint
膝关节交叉韧带损伤/膝關節交叉韌帶損傷　injury of cruciate ligament of knee joint
膝关节交锁/膝關節交鎖　locking of knee

膝关节内侧半月板/膝關節內側半月板　medial meniscus of knee joint
膝关节内外侧副韧带损伤/膝關節內外側副韌帶損傷　injury of medial and lateral ligaments of knee joint
膝关节水肿/膝關節水腫,膝關節積水　water on the knee
膝关节弹跳征/膝關節彈跳徵　bounce sign of knee joint
膝关节脱位/膝關節脫位　dislocation of knee joint, knee dislocation
膝关节网/膝關節網　genicular articular rete
膝关节粘连松解器/膝關節粘連鬆解器,碎膝器　genuclast
膝冠状韧带/膝冠狀韌帶　coronary ligament of knee
膝横韧带/膝橫韌帶　transverse ligament of knee
膝后交叉韧带/膝後交叉韌帶,後膝十字韌帶　posterior cruciate ligament of knee
膝后区/膝後部　posterior region of knee
膝后韧带/膝後韌帶　posterior ligament of knee
膝降动脉/膝降動脈　descending genicular artery
膝交叉韧带/膝交叉韌帶,膝十字韌帶　cruciate ligament of knee, cruciate ligaments of knee
膝静脉/膝靜脈　genicular vein, genicular veins
膝内/膝內　xinei, EX-LE3
膝内侧副韧带/膝內側副韌帶　knee medial collateral ligament
膝内侧韧带/膝內側韌帶　medial ligament of knee
膝内翻/膝內翻,弓形腿　genu varum
膝前交叉韧带/膝前交叉韌帶,膝前十字韌帶　anterior cruciate ligament of knee
膝前囊/膝前囊　genual bursa
膝前区/膝前部　anterior region of knee
膝屈曲畸形/膝屈曲畸形　flexion deformity of knee
膝上截肢/膝上截肢　above knee amputation
膝上内侧动脉/膝上內側動脈　medial superior genicular artery
膝上外侧动脉/膝上外側動脈　lateral superior genicular artery
膝损伤/膝損傷　knee injury
膝脱位/膝脫位　knee dislocation
膝外翻/膝外翻,叉形腿　genu valgum
膝弯痈/膝彎癰　poples abscess
膝下内侧动脉/膝下內側動脈　medial inferior genicular artery
膝下内动脉/膝下內動脈　medial inferior genicular artery
膝下外侧动脉/膝下外側動脈　lateral inferior genicular artery
膝胸[卧]位/膝胸[臥]位　knee-chest position
膝眼/膝眼　xiyan, EX-LE5
膝阳关/膝陽關　xiyangguan, GB33
膝翼状韧带/膝翼狀韌帶　alar ligaments of knee
膝痈/膝癰　knee abscess
膝脂体/膝脂體　patellar fat pad
膝中动脉/膝中動脈　middle genicular artery
膝肿痛/膝腫痛　swelling and pain in knee
膝状节神经痛/膝狀神經節痛　geniculate neuralgia
膝状神经节/膝狀神經節　geniculate ganglion
膝状神经节性耳痛/膝狀神經節性耳痛　geniculate otalgia
膝状体/膝狀體　geniculate bodies
膝状体静脉/膝狀體靜脈　vein of the geniculate body
膝总韧带/膝總韌帶　common ligament of knee
习服/習服　acclimatization
习惯病/習慣病　habit disease
习惯性/習慣性　habituation
习惯性抽搐/習慣性抽搐　habit tics
习惯性疾患/習慣性疾患,沓慣不正常障礙　habit disorder
习惯性脊柱侧凸/習慣性脊柱側凸,習慣性脊柱側彎　habit scoliosis
习惯性痉挛/習慣性痙攣　habit spasm
习惯性流产/習慣性流產　habitual abortion
习惯性逆转/習慣性逆轉　habit reversal
习惯性脱位/習慣性脫位　habitual dislocation, recurrent dislocation
习以平惊/習以平驚　calming the frightened
席尔德病/席爾德病,希爾德病　Schilder disease
席尔默试验/席爾默試驗,Schirmer氏試驗　Schirmer test
席夫碱/席夫鹼,希夫鹼　Schiff base
席夫试验/席夫試驗,希夫氏試驗　Schiff test
席林白血病/席林白血病,Schilling氏白血病　Schilling leukemia
席纹状/席紋狀,漩渦狀　storiform
洗鼻法/洗鼻法　method of nasal douche
洗涤法/洗滌法　rinsing and compressing method
洗涤剂/洗滌劑,清潔劑　detergent
洗涤盆/洗滌盆　sink
洗耳海绵/耳用海綿　ear sponge
洗耳疗法/洗耳療法　ear-washing therapy
洗发精/洗髮精　shampoos
洗剂/洗劑,乳液　lotion
洗眉[术]/洗眉[術]　washing eyebrow

洗漂/洗漂　washing and blanching, washing and rinsing
洗润/洗潤　rinsing moistening
洗手/洗手　handwashing
洗脱/洗脱　elution
洗脱剂/洗脱劑　eluant
洗脱物/沖洗液　eluate
洗胃/洗胃　gastric lavage
洗心汤/洗心湯　dementia relieving decoction
洗眼杯/洗眼杯　eyebath
洗眼法/洗眼法　douche therapy for eye
洗眼壶/洗眼壺　undine
洗眼剂/洗眼藥　eye wash
洗眼受水器/洗眼受水器　eye bath basin
洗衣板状头盖/洗衣板狀頭蓋　washboard scalp
洗衣妇手/洗衣婦手　washerwoman hand
洗衣工痒病/洗衣工癢病,洗衣癬　dhobie itch
洗冤录/洗冤錄　Records for Washing Away of Wrong Cases
洗制硫/洗制硫　washed sulfur
徙前术/前進縫合術　prorrhaphy
喜悲/喜悲　easily to be sorrowful
喜惊/喜驚　easily to be frightened
喜梦/喜夢　dreamfulness, joyful dream
喜怒/喜怒　easily to be angry
喜怒不节/喜怒不節　incalculable moods
喜怒伤气/喜怒傷氣　excessive joy and anger impairing qi
喜伤心/喜傷心　overjoy impairing heart
喜胜悲/喜勝悲　amusing to eliminate sadness
喜食异物/喜食異物　addiction to eating foreign bodies
喜树碱/喜樹鹼　camptothecin
喜忘/喜忘　poor memory
喜为心志/喜爲心志　heart being associated with joy
喜笑不休/喜笑不休　compulsive laughter
喜则气缓/喜則氣緩　excessive joy leading to qi loose, overjoy leading to sluggishness of heart qi
喜中/喜中　strok due to severe sudden joy
戏剧样人格障碍/戲劇樣人格障礙　histrionic personality disorder
系带/繫帶　fraenum
系带切断术/繫帶切除術　frenectomy
系带切开术/繫帶切開術,繫帶切斷術　frenotomy
系固斑块/繫固斑塊　anchoring plaque
系固细纤维/繫固細纖維　anchoring filament
系固小纤维/繫固小纖維　anchoring fibril
系列学习/系列學習　serial learning
系膜毛细血管性肾小球肾炎/繫膜毛細血管性腎小球腎炎　mesangial capillary glomerulonephritis
系膜小肠/繫膜小腸　jejunoileal intestine
系膜性 IgA/IgG 肾盂肾炎/繫膜性 IgA/IgG 腎盂腎炎,間質細胞 IgA/IgG 腎盂腎炎　mesangial IgA disease/IgG disease
系膜缘/繫膜緣　mesenteric border
系膜增生性肾小球肾炎/繫膜增生性腎小球腎炎　mesangial proliferative glomerulonephritis
系谱/系譜　pedigree
系数/係數　coefficient
系数倍率法/係數倍率法　K-ratio method, signal multiplier method
系锁槽式带环/繫鎖槽式帶環,可縛托帶環　tie bracket band
系统/系統　system
系统解剖学/系統解剖學　descriptive anatomy, systematic anatomy
系统矩阵组合法/系統矩陣組合法　system matrix combination method
系统模型/系統模型　system model
系统生物学/系統生物學　systems biology
系统适用性/系統適合性　system suitability
系统性变性/系統[性]變性　system degeneration
系统性肥大细胞增生症/系統性肥大細胞增生症　systemic mastocytosis
系统性红斑狼疮/全身性紅斑性狼瘡　systemic lupus erythematosus
系统性红斑狼疮听力损失/系統性紅斑性狼瘡聽力喪失　hearing loss in SLE
系统性脊髓炎/系統性脊髓炎　systematic myelitis
系统性弹力纤维断裂/系統性彈力纖維斷裂　systematized elastorrhexis
系统性血管炎/系統性血管炎　systemic vasculitis
系统性炎症反应综合征/系統性炎症反應綜合徵　systemic inflammatory response syndrome
系统性硬化病/系統性硬化病,全身性硬化　systemic sclerosis
系统性硬皮病/系統性硬皮病,全身性硬皮病　systemic scleroderma
系统综合/系統綜合　systems integration
细胞/細胞　cell
A 细胞/A 細胞　A cell
P 细胞/P 細胞　P cell
α 细胞/α 細胞　α cell
β 细胞/β 細胞　β cell
γ 细胞/γ 細胞,伽馬細胞　γ cell
δ 细胞/δ 細胞　δ cell

细胞板/細胞板　cell plate
细胞包涵体/細胞包涵體　cell inclusion
细胞包涵物/細胞内包涵物　cell inclusion
细胞保护/細胞保護　cytoprotection
细胞壁/細胞壁　cell wall
细胞壁支架/細胞壁支架　cell wall skeleton
细胞变异/細胞變異　cytometaplasia
细胞表面标记/細胞表面標志　cell surface marker
细胞表面生物学/外膜生物學　ectobiology
细胞表面受体/細胞表面受體　cell surface receptor
细胞表面突出/細胞表面突出　cell surface extension
I细胞病/I細胞[疾]病　I cell disease
细胞病变发生/細胞病變發生　cytopathogenesis
细胞病理学/細胞病理學　cytopathology
细胞不溶质/細胞不溶質,细胞内不溶物　ellipsin
细胞巢/細胞巢　cell nest
细胞存活/細胞存活　cell survival
细胞大小/細胞大小　cell size
细胞单采法/細胞單採法,血细胞去除術　cytapheresis
细胞等大/細胞等大　isocytosis
细胞低氧/細胞低氧　cell hypoxia
细胞低氧射线增敏药/細胞低氧射[線]增敏藥　hypoxic cell radiosensitizer
细胞凋亡/細胞凋亡　apoptosis
细胞凋亡易感蛋白/細胞凋亡易感蛋白　cellular apoptosis susceptibility protein
细胞动力传导/細胞動力傳導　cellular mechanotransduction
细胞毒试验/細胞毒試驗　cytotoxicity test
细胞毒素/細胞毒素　cytotoxin
细胞毒素过敏症/細胞毒素過敏症,细胞毒性過敏反應　cytotoxic anaphylaxis
细胞毒素中毒/細胞毒素中毒　cytotoxicosis
细胞毒性/細胞毒性　cytotoxicity
细胞毒[性]抗体/細胞毒[性]抗體　cytotoxic antibody
细胞毒性T[淋巴]细胞/細胞毒性T[淋巴]細胞　cytotoxic T cell, Tc cell
细胞发生/細胞發生,细胞生成　cytogenesis
细胞肥大包涵体综合征/細胞肥大包涵體症候群　cytomegalic inclusion syndrome
细胞分化/細胞分化　cell differentiation
细胞分级分离/細胞分級分離　cell fractionation
细胞分离/細胞分離　cell separation
细胞分裂/細胞分裂　cell division
细胞分裂前期/細胞分裂前期,核分裂之前期　prophase
细胞分裂素/細胞分裂素,细胞激肽　cytokinin
细胞分裂完全抑制/有絲分裂完全抑制,有絲分裂中止　stathmokinesis
细胞分析器/細胞分析機　cytoanalyzer
细胞骨架/細胞骨架,细胞支架　cytoskeleton
细胞骨架丝/細胞骨架絲　cytoskeletal filament
细胞骨架学说/細胞骨架學説　cytoskeleton theory
细胞光度测定法/細胞光度測定法　cytophotometry
细胞光度计/細胞光度計　cytophotometer
细胞过多/細胞過多　hypercellularity
细胞核/細胞核　cell nucleus, nucleus
细胞核测量法/細胞核測驗法　karyometry
细胞核分裂/細胞核分裂　cell nucleus division
细胞核结构/細胞核結構　cell nucleus structure
细胞核内[生长]环/核内週期　intranuclear cycle
细胞核仁/細胞核仁　cell nucleolus
细胞核试验/細胞核[子]試驗　nuclear test
细胞核细胞质转运蛋白质类/細胞核細胞質轉運蛋白質類　nucleocytoplasmic transport proteins
细胞核主动转运/細胞核主動轉運　cell nucleus active transport
T细胞红皮病/T細胞紅皮症　T cell erythroderma
细胞呼吸/細胞呼吸　cell respiration
细胞互应性/細胞互應性,细胞相應作用　cytobiotaxis
细胞化学/細胞化學　cytochemistry
细胞化学作用/細胞化學作用　cytochemism
细胞坏死/細胞壞死　cytonecrosis
细胞坏死毒素/細胞壞死毒素　necrocytotoxin
细胞黄/細胞黄,核黄素磷酸脂　cytoflav
细胞回收器/細胞回收器　cell saver
细胞活素/細胞活素,细胞因子　cytokine
细胞基质连接部/細胞基質連接部　cell-matrix junctions
细胞激素/細胞激素,细胞内泌素　cytohormone
细胞激肽类/細胞激肽類　cytokinins
细胞极性/細胞極性　cell polarity
细胞集合/細胞集合　cell aggregation
细胞计数/細胞計數　cell count
细胞间丛/細胞間叢　intercellular plexus
细胞间分泌小管/細胞間分泌小管　intercellular secretory canaliculus
细胞间甲型球蛋白皮肤病/細胞間甲型球蛋白皮膚病　intercellular IgA dermatosis
细胞间胶质/細胞接合質　intercellular cement
细胞间接合部/細胞間接合部　intercellular junction
细胞间黏接物质/細胞間黏接物質,细胞間結合質　intercellular cement substance

细胞间黏着分子/細胞間黏著分子　intercellular adhesion molecule
细胞间桥/[細]胞間橋　intercellular bridge
细胞间隙/[細]胞間隙　intercellular space
细胞间质/細胞間質　intercellular substance
细胞交流/細胞交流　cell communication
细胞接触抑制/細胞接觸抑制　cell contact inhibition
细胞接触诱导/細胞接觸誘導　cell contact guidance
细胞结构/細胞結構　cellular structure
细胞结合[性]抗体/細胞結合[性]抗體　cell bound antibody
细胞介导的淋巴细胞毒性/細胞介導的淋巴細胞毒性　cell-mediated lymphocytotoxicity
细胞介导免疫/細胞[介導]免疫,細胞媒介免疫　cell-mediated immunity
细胞浸润/細胞浸潤　cellular infiltration
细胞抗原/細胞抗原　cell antigen
细胞抗争/細胞抗争　cytomachia
细胞颗粒/細胞顆粒　cell granulation
细胞克隆/細胞克隆　cell clone
细胞连接/細胞連接,細胞接合　cell junction
细胞疗法/細胞療法　cytotherapy
T细胞淋巴瘤/T細胞淋巴瘤　T cell lymphoma
细胞瘤/細胞瘤　cytoma
细胞免疫/細胞免疫　cell immunity
细胞膜/細胞膜　cell membrane
细胞膜结构/細胞膜結構　cell membrane structure
细胞膜水解酶/細胞膜水解酶,胞體水解酵素,胞質水解劑　cytohydrolist
细胞膜通透性/細胞膜通透性　cell-membrane permeability
细胞膜有被小窝/細胞膜有被小窩　cell-membrane coated pit
[细]胞内的/細胞内的　intracellular
细胞内分泌小管/細胞内分泌小管　intracellular secretory canaliculus
细胞内分生孢子/細胞内分生孢子,内生孢子,内芽孢　endogonidium
细胞内含物/細胞内含物,細胞内包涵物,細胞内異物　endocyte
细胞内涵物/細胞内涵物,胞涵物　cell inclusion
细胞内间隙/細胞内間隙　intracellular space
细胞内酶/細胞内酶,細胞内酵素　intracellular enzyme
细胞内膜/細胞内膜　intracellular membrane
细胞内液/細胞内液　intracellular fluid
细胞黏附/細胞黏附,細胞接著　cell adhesion
细胞黏附分子/細胞黏附分子　cell adhesion molecule
细胞黏着/細胞黏著　cell adhesion
细胞黏着素受体/細胞黏著素受體　cytoadhesin receptor
细胞尿[症]/細胞尿[症]　cyturia
细胞排斥/細胞[性]排斥　cellular rejection
细胞培养/細胞培養　cell culture
细胞培养技术/細胞培養技術　cell culture technique
细胞破碎/細胞破碎　cytoclasis
细胞谱系/細胞[譜]系　cell lineage
细胞器/細胞器　cell organelle
细胞迁移/細胞遷移,細胞移動　cell migration
细胞迁移素/細胞遷移素,溢出類脂質　ergusia
细胞球形体/細胞球形體　cellular spheroid
细胞区室化/細胞區室化　cell compartmentation
细胞趋化素/細胞趨化素　cytotaxin
细胞趋化素原/細胞趨化素原　cytotaxigen
细胞趋向性/細胞趨向性,趨細胞性,親細胞性　cytotaxis
细胞群/細胞塊　cell mass
细胞韧性/細胞韌性　cellular tenacity
细胞溶胶/細胞溶質,細胞液　cytosol
细胞溶解/細胞溶解　cytolysis
细胞溶解液/細胞溶解液　cytolysate
细胞溶酶体/細胞溶酶體　cytolysosome
细胞溶素/溶細胞素,溶細胞素　cytolysin
细胞融合/細胞融合　cell fusion
细胞色素/細胞色素　cytochrome
细胞色素类/細胞色素類　cytochromes
细胞杀害[作用]/細胞殺害作用　cytoctony
细胞生理学/細胞生理學　cell physiology
细胞生物学/細胞生物學　cell biology
细胞生长过程/細胞生長過程　cell growth processes
细胞生长素/細胞生長素　archusia
细胞生长抑制剂/細胞[生長]抑制劑　cytostatic
细胞识别/細胞識別　cell recognition
细胞受体/細胞受體　cell receptor
细胞输注/細胞輸注　cell infusion
细胞衰老/細胞衰老　cell aging
细胞栓塞/細胞栓塞　cellular embolism
细胞栓子/細胞栓子　cell embolus
细胞死亡/細胞死亡　cell death
细胞松弛素/細胞鬆弛素,細胞弛緩素　cytochalasin
细胞损伤/細胞損傷　cell injury
细胞损伤毒素/細胞損傷毒素,細胞毒[素]　cytost
细胞提取物/細胞提取物　cell extract
[细]胞体/細胞體　cell body
细胞通过时间/細胞通過時間　cell transit time

细胞通讯/細胞通訊,胞間聯繫　intercellular communication
细胞透过液/細胞穿透液　transcellular fluid
细胞突/細胞突　cell process
细胞吞噬指数/細胞吞噬指數,噬細胞指數　cytophagic index
细胞吞噬作用/細胞吞噬作用,噬胞體作用　cytophagocytosis
细胞脱颗粒/細胞脱顆粒　cell degranulation
细胞外胆固醇沉着病/細胞外膽固醇沈著病　extracellular cholesterosis
细胞外基质/細胞外基質　extracellular matrix
细胞外基质蛋白质类/細胞外基質蛋白質類　extracellular matrix proteins
细胞外隙/細胞外隙　extracellular space
细胞外信号调节 MAP 激酶类/細胞外信號調節 MAP 激酶類　extracellular signal-regulated MAP kinases
细胞外液/細胞外液　extracellular fluid
细胞网/胞質綱　cytoreticulum
细胞物理学/細胞物理學　cytophysics
细胞吸管/細胞吸管　cytopipette
细胞系/細胞系　cell line
细胞形态学/細胞形態學　cytomorphology
细胞形状/細胞形狀　cell shape
细胞性蓝痣/細胞性藍痣　cellular blue nevus
细胞性生殖/細胞性生殖　cytogenic reproduction
细胞性血管纤维瘤/細胞性血管纖維瘤　cellular angiofibroma
细胞[性]肿瘤/細胞性腫瘤　cellular tumor
细胞悬液/細胞懸液　cell suspension
细胞学/細胞學　cytology
细胞学技术/細胞學技術　cytological technique
细胞学说/細胞學說　cell doctrine
细胞牙骨质/細胞牙骨質,細胞齒堊質　cellular cementum
细胞样小体/細胞樣小體,細胞狀體　cytoid bodies
细胞液/細胞液　cell sap
细胞衣/細胞衣,細胞外被　cell coat
细胞移植/細胞移植　cell transplantation
细胞遗传学/細胞遺傳學　cytogenetics
细胞遗传学分析/細胞遺傳學分析　cytogenetic analysis
细胞遗传学家/細胞遺傳學家　cytogeneticist
细胞因子/細胞激素　cytokine
细胞因子受体/細胞因數受體　cytokine receptor
细胞游走抑制/細胞遊走抑制　cell migration inhibition
细胞原位杂交/細胞原位雜交　in situ cytohybridization
细胞运动/細胞運動　cell movement
细胞杂交/細胞雜交　cell hybridization
细胞增大/細胞增大　cell enlargement
细胞增大性生长/細胞增大性生長　auxetic growth
细胞增多性生长/細胞增多性生長　multiplicative growth
细胞增殖/細胞增殖　cell proliferation
细胞[增殖]抑制药/細胞[增殖]抑制藥　cytostatic
细胞真菌病/細胞黴菌病　cytomycosis
细胞诊断/細胞診斷[法]　cytodiagnosis
细胞支架/細胞支架,細胞骨架　cytoskeletal
细胞支架蛋白质类/細胞支架蛋白質類　cytoskeletal proteins
细胞质/細胞質,胞體漿　cytoplasm
细胞质基因/細胞質基因,胞體漿基因,胞體漿遺傳因數　plasmagene
细胞质基因组/細胞質基因組,胞質基因　cytoplasmic genome
细胞质颗粒/細胞質顆粒,細胞漿粒　cytoplasmic granule
细胞质内精子注射/細胞質内精子注射　intracytoplasmic sperm injection
细胞质桥/細胞質橋　cytoplasmic bridge
细胞质天冬氨酸氨基转移酶/細胞質天冬胺酸胺基轉移酶　cytoplasmic aspartate aminotransferase
细胞质遗传/胸漿性遺傳　cytoplasmic inheritance
细胞痣/細胞痣,細胞母斑　cellular nevus
细胞中纬线/細胞中緯線　equator of cell
细胞肿胀/細胞腫脹　cellular swelling
细胞[中]毒类药/細胞[中]毒類藥,細胞毒性藥　cytotoxic drug
细胞周期/細胞週期　cell cycle
细胞周期蛋白类/細胞週期蛋白類　cyclins
细胞周期蛋白质类/細胞週期蛋白質類　cell cycle proteins
细胞周期蛋白质依赖激酶类/細胞週期蛋白質依賴激酶類　cyclin-dependent kinases
细胞周围细胞/細胞周圍細胞　pericellular cell
细胞株/細胞株　cell strain
细胞滋养层/細胞滋養層　cytotrophoblast
细胞滋养层壳/細胞滋養層殼,滋養發生層　cytotrophoblastic shell
细胞滋养层细胞柱/細胞滋養層細胞柱　cytotrophoblastic cell column
细胞组合/細胞組合　cellular association
细胞[组织]发生/細胞[組織]發生,細胞組織構造之

發生　cytohistogenesis
细胞[组织]溶解/[細胞]組織溶解　cathepsis
细病毒组/細病毒組,纖細病毒　tenuivirus
细长小刀/細長[小]刀,小刀　bistoury
细长指/細長指　leptodactyly
细长趾/細長趾　leptodactyly
细滴虫/細滴蟲,細鞭體,細鞭蟲　leptomonad
细沟/細溝　rill channel
细肌丝/細肌絲　thin myofilament
细精管/細精管　seminiferous tubule
细交链孢菌酮酸/細交鏈孢菌酮酸,替奴佐酸　tenuazonic acid
细菌/細菌　bacterium
细菌孢子/細菌孢子　bacterial spore
细菌胞浆素/細菌胞漿素,菌漿素　bacterioplasmin
细菌变异/細菌變異　bacterial dissociation
细菌病/細菌病　bacteriosis
细菌病毒/細菌[性]病毒　bacterial virus
细菌病因学/細菌病因學　bacterial etiology
细菌沉淀素/細菌沈澱素　bacterioprecipitin
细菌重组/細菌重組　bacterial recombination
细菌蛋白质/細菌蛋白質　bacterioprotein
细菌蛋白质类/細菌蛋白質類　bacterial proteins
细菌毒素/細菌毒素　bacteriotoxin
细菌毒素类/細菌毒素類　bacterial toxins
细菌毒性子宫内膜炎/菌毒[性]子宫内膜炎　bacteriotoxic endometritis
细菌毒血症/細菌毒血症　bacteriotoxemia
细菌多糖类/細菌多醣類　bacterial polysaccharides
[细菌]发育培养检查法/[細菌]發育培養檢查法,[細菌]發育檢查法　auxanography
细菌分型技术/細菌分型技術　bacterial typing technique
细菌感染/細菌感染　bacterial infection
细菌过度繁殖综合征/細菌過度繁殖症候群,細菌過度生長症候群　bacterial overgrowth syndrome
细菌回复突变试验/細菌回復突變試驗,安氏試驗　Ames test
细菌基因/細菌基因　bacterial gene
细菌基因表达调控/細菌基因表達調控　bacterial gene expression regulation
细菌基因组/細菌基因組　bacterial genome
细菌激酶/細菌性激酶　bacterial kinase
细菌荚膜/細菌莢膜　bacterial capsule
细菌菌苗/細菌菌苗　bacterial vaccine
细菌抗体/細菌抗體　bacterial antibody
细菌抗药性/細菌抗藥性　bacterial drug resistance
细菌抗原/細菌抗原　bacterial antigen

细菌疗法/細菌療法　bacillotherapy
细菌酶/細菌酶,細菌酵素　bacterial enzyme
细菌内毒素/細菌内毒素　bacterial endotoxin
细菌黏附/細菌黏附　bacterial adhesion
细菌黏着素/細菌黏著素　bacterial adhesin
细菌尿/菌尿症　bacteriuria
细菌脲酶/胺酵素　urasin
细菌凝块/細菌凝塊　clump
细菌凝血素/細菌凝血素　bacteriohemagglutinin
细菌[培养]滤液/細菌濾液　antivirus
细菌染色体/細菌染色體　bacterial chromosome
细菌溶血素/細菌溶血素　bacteriohemolysin
细菌生理学/細菌生理學　bacterial physiology
细菌噬菌体/細菌噬菌體　bacteriophage
细菌栓塞/細菌栓塞　bacterial embolism
细菌栓子/細菌栓子　bacterial embolus
细菌素/細菌素　bacteriocin
细菌素质粒/細菌素質粒　bacteriocin plasmid
细菌调理素/細菌調理素　bacterio-opsonin
细菌外膜蛋白质类/細菌外膜蛋白質類　bacterial outer membrane proteins
细菌纤毛/細菌纖毛　bacterial fimbriae
细菌[显微]镜检查/細菌顯微鏡檢查,細菌顯微鏡檢法　bacterioscopy
细菌性变态反应/細菌性變態反應,細菌變應性,細菌性過敏　bacterial allergy
细菌性变性/細菌性變性　bacillary degeneration
细菌性肠菌病/細菌性腸菌病,腸細菌病　enteromycosis bacteriacea
细菌性动脉瘤/細菌性動脈瘤,菌病性動脈瘤　bacterial aneurysm
细菌性肺炎/細菌性肺炎　bacterial pneumonia
细菌性腹泻/細菌性腹瀉　bacterial diarrhea
细菌性肝脓肿/細菌性肝膿腫　bacterial liver abscess
细菌性假霉菌病/細菌性假黴菌病　bacterial pseudomycosis
细菌性间质性肾炎/細菌性間質性腎炎　bacterial interstitial nephritis
细菌性角膜炎/細菌性角膜炎　bacterial keratitis
细菌性结膜炎/細菌性結膜炎　bacterial conjunctivitis
细菌性瘤/細菌性瘤,菌瘤　bacteriophytoma
细菌性毛囊炎/細菌性毛囊炎　bacterial folliculitis
细菌性脑膜炎/細菌性腦膜炎　bacterial meningitis
细菌性尿道炎/細菌性尿道炎　bacterial urethritis
细菌性膀胱炎/細菌性膀胱炎　bacterial cystitis
细菌性皮肤疾病/細菌性皮膚疾病　bacterial skin diseases

细菌性葡萄膜炎/細菌性葡萄膜炎　bacterial uveitis
细菌性前列腺炎/細菌性前列腺炎　bacterial prostatitis
细菌性热原质/細菌性熱原質,細菌發熱質,内毒素　bacterial pyrogen
细菌性肾炎/細菌性腎炎　bacterial nephritis
细菌性肾盂肾炎/細菌性腎盂腎炎　bacterial pyelonephritis
细菌性食物中毒/細菌性食物中毒　bacterial food poisoning
细菌性哮喘/細菌性氣喘　bacterial asthma
细菌性心包炎/細菌性心包炎　bacterial pericarditis
细菌性心肌炎/細菌性心肌炎　bacterial myocarditis
细菌性心内膜炎/細菌性心內膜炎　bacterial endocarditis
细菌性性传播疾病/細菌性性傳播疾病　bacterial sexually transmitted disease
细菌性牙髓炎/細菌性牙髓炎　anachoretic pulpitis
细菌性眼感染/細菌性眼感染　bacterial eye infection
细菌性阴道病/細菌性陰道病　bacterial vaginosis
细菌性赘生物/細菌性贅生物　bacterial vegetation
细菌性紫癜/細菌性紫癜　bacterial purpura
细菌学/細菌學　bacteriology
细菌学技术/細菌學技術　bacteriological technique
细菌学失败率/細菌學失敗率　bacteriological failure rate
细菌叶绿素/細菌葉綠素　bacteriochlorophyll
细菌叶绿素 A/細菌葉綠素 A　bacteriochlorophyll A
细菌胰蛋白酶/細菌胰蛋白酶　bacteriotrypsin
细菌移位/細菌移位　bacterial translocation
细菌荧光素酶类/細菌螢光素酶類　bacterial luciferases
细菌载色体/細菌載色體　bacterial chromatophore
细菌疹/細菌疹　bacterial exanthem
细菌指数/細菌指數　bacterial index
细菌质/細菌質　bacterial substance
细菌转化/細菌轉化,細菌變型　bacterial transformation
细菌转铁蛋白受体复合物/細菌轉鐵蛋白受體複合物　bacterial transferrin receptor complex
细粒棘球绦虫/細粒棘球絛蟲　Echinococcus granulosus
细粒棘球蚴病/細粒棘球蚴病　echinococcosis granulosa
细粒状呼吸音/顆粒呼吸音　granular respiration
细淋巴管病/細淋巴管病　microadenopathy
细螺旋体/細螺旋體　treponema gracile
细脉/細脈　pulsus parvus, thready pulse
细捻发音/細捻發音,爆裂狀水泡音　crackling rale
细弱密螺旋体/細弱[密]螺旋體　treponema pertenue
细湿啰音/細濕啰音　fine rale
细食/細[質飲]食,無刺激性飲食　smooth diet
细丝弓矫治器/細絲弓矯治器　light-wire appliance
细丝钳/細絲鉗　light-wire plier
细探子描记器/細探子描記器,探針描記器　stylus tracer
细[微]小病毒/細[微]小病毒,微小病毒　parvovirus
细线期/細線期　leptotene stage
细线前期/細線前期　proleptotene stage
细小病毒/細小病毒　picodnavirus
细小病毒科感染/細小病毒科感染　Parvoviridae infection
细小 RNA 病毒科感染/細小 RNA 病毒科感染　picornaviridae infection
细小主动脉根/細小主動脈根　small aortic root
细辛/細辛　manchurian wildginger
细辛脑/細辛腦　asaron
细叶土木香苦素/細葉土木香苦素　tenulin
细针抽吸活组织检查/細針抽吸活組織檢查,細針抽吸活檢　fine-needle aspiration biopsy
细针活组织检查/細針活組織檢查　fine-needle biopsy
细支气管/細支氣管　bronchiole
细支气管肺泡癌/細支氣管肺泡癌　bronchioloalveolar carcinoma
细支气管肺泡腺癌/細支氣管肺泡腺癌　bronchioloalveolar adenocarcinoma
细支气管扩大/細支氣管擴大,細支氣管腫大　bronchiocele
细支气管扩张/細支氣管擴張　bronchiolectasis
细支气管炎/細支氣管炎　bronchiolitis
细支气管周炎/細支氣管周[圍]炎　peribronchiolitis
郄门/郄門　ximen, PC4
郄穴/郄穴　xi-cleft point
隙裂骨折/隙裂骨折　fissured fracture
虾螯状畸形/蝦螯狀畸形,龍蝦爪畸形　lobster claw deformity
虾红素/蝦紅素,甲殼紅質　astacene
虾尾状导管/蝦尾狀導管,龍蝦尾導管　lobster tail catheter
虾爪状畸形/蝦爪狀畸形,手腳蝦爪畸型　lobster claw deformity
侠白/俠白　xiabai, LU4
侠溪/俠溪　xiaxi, GB43
侠瘿瘤/俠瘿瘤　parathyroid gland accentuation

峡/峽　isthmus
峡部切除术/峽[部]切除術　isthmectomy
狭鼻类/狹鼻類　catarrhina
狭长头/狹長頭,細頭畸形　leptocephaly
狭长头者/狹長頭者,細頭者,細頭畸胎　leptocephalus
狭束吸收/狹束吸收　narrow-beam absorption
狭缩蛇舌状虫/收縮洞頭蟲　Porocephalus constrictus
狭窄/狹窄　stenosis, stricture
狭窄后扩张术/狹窄後擴張術　post-stenotic dilatation
狭窄切开刀/狹窄切開刀　stricturotome
狭窄切开术/狹窄切開術　stricturotomy
狭窄性腱鞘炎/狹窄性腱[鞘]炎　stenosing tendinitis, stenosing tenosynovitis, tenosynovitis stenosans
狭窄性吞咽困难/狹窄性吞嚥困難　dysphagia constricta
狭窄性杂音/狹窄性雜音　stenosal murmur
下凹/下凹　inferior fovea
下半[部]视网膜/下半[部]視網膜,視網膜下半部　lower retina
下半部头痛/下半部頭痛　lower-half headache
下半月小叶/下半月小葉　inferior semilunar lobule
下鼻道/下鼻道,鼻下道　inferior nasal meatus
下鼻甲/下鼻甲　inferior nasal concha
下鼻甲骨/下鼻甲骨　inferior turbinate bone
下壁/下壁　inferior wall
下表皮/下表皮　lower epidermis
下部/下部　inferior part
下部结构/下部結構　infrastructure
下部肾单位/下部腎單位,腎單位下部　lower nephron
下侧腹露脏下肢不全畸胎/下側腹露臟下肢不全畸胎,凸臟下肢不全畸形,殘疾體形畸形　cyllosoma
下层清液/下層清液,沈澱液　subnatant
下超殆/下超殆,突下頜咬合　underhung bite
下齿丛/下齒叢　plexus dentalis inferior
下冲/下銃　lower punch
下垂/下垂,脱出　ptosis
下垂心/下垂心,懸垂心　hanging heart
下垂足/下垂足,懸擺足,垂足　dangle foot
下垂足夹/下垂足夾　drop foot splint
下唇/下唇　lower lip
下唇动脉/下唇動脈　inferior labial artery
下唇方肌/下唇方肌　quadrate muscle of lower lip
下唇静脉/下唇靜脈　inferior labial vein

下唇系带/下唇繫帶　frenulum of lower lip
下唇线/下唇線　lower lip line
下唇正中裂/下唇正中裂　median lower lip cleft
下唇中点/下唇[中]點　labrale inferius
下次尖/[下頜臼齒之]下次尖　hypoconid
下次小尖/下次小尖,下頜臼齒之下末尖　hypoconulid
下端/下端　inferior extremity
下段/下段　inferior segment
下段动脉/下段動脈　inferior segmental artery
下段肌/下段肌,下胚節肌,體節腹外側肌　hypomeric muscle
下段食管括约肌/下段食管括約肌　lower esophageal sphincter
下颌突/下頜突　mandibular prominence
下耳根/下耳根　xiaergen, lower ear root, R3
下法/下法　purgative method
下腹/下腹　inferior belly, hypogastrium
下腹部/下腹部　hypogastrium
下腹丛/下腹叢　plexus hypogastricus
下腹动脉闭锁/下腹動脈閉鎖　obliterated hypogastric artery
下腹静脉/腹下靜脈　hypogastric vein
下腹联胎/下腹連胎　hypogastropagus
下腹裂[畸形]/下腹裂畸形　hypogastroschisis
下腹切开术/骨盆切開術　etrotomy
下腹上丛/下腹上叢　plexus hypogastricus superior
下腹下丛/下腹下叢　inferior hypogastric plexus, plexus hypogastricus inferior
下疳样脓皮病/下疳狀膿皮病　chancriform pyoderma
下疳状综合征/下疳狀症候群　chancriform syndrome
下橄榄核/下橄欖核　inferior olivary nucleus
下橄榄核门/下橄欖核門　hilum of inferior olive
下橄榄体/下橄欖體　inferior olive
下干/下幹　inferior trunk
下根/下根　inferior root
下关/下關　xiaguan, ST7
下关节间隙/下關節間隙　JS inferior
下关节面/下關節面　inferior articular facet, inferior articular surface
下关节突/下關節突　inferior articular process
下合穴/下合穴　lower-he-sea point
下颌闭合弧/下頜閉合弧　arcs of mandibular closure
下颌不对称/下頜不對稱　mandibular asymmetry
下颌重置装置/下頜重置裝置　mandibular repositioning appliance

下颌底/下頜底　base of mandible
下颌底座/下頜底座　mandibular base
下颌动脉/下頜動脈　mandibular artery
下颌发育不足/下頜發育不足　mandibular deficiency
下颌发育过度/下頜發育過剩　mandibular excess
下颌反常运动/下頜脫軌運動　perverted mandibular movement
[下]颌反射/下頜反射　mandibular reflex
下颌根尖下截骨术/下頜根尖下截骨術　mandibular subapical osteotomy
下颌弓/下頜弧　mandibular arch
下颌骨/下頜骨　mandible
下颌骨侧位投照术/下頜骨側位投照術　lateral position roentgenography of mandible
下颌骨齿槽突/下頜骨齒槽突　mandible alveolar process
下颌骨重建术/下頜骨重建術　mandibular reconstruction
下颌骨发育不良/下頜發育不良　mandibular hypoplasia
下颌骨发育不全/下頜顏面成骨不全　mandibulofacial dysostosis
下颌骨骨折/下頜骨骨折　mandible fracture
下颌骨冠突/下頜骨冠突　coronoid process of mandible
下颌骨颌下小窝/下頜骨頜下小窩　fovea submaxillaris mandibulae
下颌骨后前位投照术/下頜骨後前位投照術　posterio-anterior position of mandibular roentgenography
下颌骨滑动运动/下頜骨滑行運動　gliding movements of mandible
下颌骨化中心/下頜骨化中心　dentary center
下颌骨角/下頜骨角　angle of mandible
下颌骨截骨术/下頜截骨術　mandibular osteotomy
下颌骨颈部/下頜骨頸部　neck of the mandible
下颌骨颏部口腔内显露法/下頜骨頦部口腔内顯露法　degloving
下颌骨髁突/下頜髁　condyle of mandible
下颌骨髁状突/下頜骨髁狀突　mandibular condyle
下颌骨面骨成骨异常/下頜骨顏面骨成骨異常　dysostosis mandibulo-facialis
下颌骨切除术/下頜骨切除術　mandibulectomy
下颌骨舌下小窝/下頜骨舌下小窩　fovea sublingualis mandibulae
下颌骨下缘/下頜骨下緣　inferior border of mandible
下颌骨斜线/下頜骨斜線　oblique line of mandible

下颌骨牙槽/下頜骨牙槽　dental alveoli of mandible
下颌骨牙槽部/下頜骨牙槽部　alveolar part of mandible
下颌骨牙槽轭/下頜骨牙槽軛　alveolar yoke of mandible
下颌骨牙槽弓/下頜骨牙槽弓　alveolar arch of mandible
下颌骨牙槽骨/下頜骨牙槽骨　alveolar bone of mandible
下颌骨牙槽间隔/下頜骨牙槽間隔　interalveolar septa of mandible
下颌骨牙根间隔/下頜骨牙根間隔　interradicular septa of mandible
下颌骨颜面发育不全/下頜面骨發育不全　mandibulofacial dysostosis
下颌骨眼面畸形/下頜骨眼面畸形　mandibulo-oculofacial dyscephaly
下颌骨翼状小窝/下頜骨翼狀小窩　pterygoid fossa of inferior maxillary bone
下颌骨折/下頜骨折　mandibular fracture
下颌关节/下頜關節　mandibular joint
下颌关节盘/下頜關節盤　mandibular disc
下颌关节神经痛/下頜關節神經痛　mandibular joint neuralgia
下颌关节突交切点/下頜關節突交切點　articulare
下颌[关节]脱位/下頜關節脱位　mandibular dislocation
下颌关节外韧带/下頜關節外韌帶　external ligament of mandibular articulation
下颌关节炎/下頜關節炎　mandibular arthritis
下颌冠状突/下頜冠狀突，喙突　corone
下颌管/下頜管　mandibular canal
下颌过小/下頜過小　micromandibulare
下颌横断殆片/下頜横斷殆片　occlusal film of mandible
下颌后静脉/下頜後静脈　retromandibular vein
下颌后缩/下頜後收　mandibular retraction
下颌后移/下頜後移　mandibular setback
下颌滑动/下頜滑動　mandibular glide
下颌滑行运动/下頜滑行運動　mandibular glide movement
下颌回缩征/下頜回縮，頜退縮徵象　chin-retraction sign
下颌肌整形术/下頜肌整形術　mandibular myoplasty
下颌基底覆盖/下頜基底覆蓋　mandibular basal coverage
下颌疾病/下頜疾病　mandibular disease

下颌嵴/下頜牙嵴　mandibular ridge
下颌寄生畸胎/下頜寄生畸胎,肌連下頜畸胎　myognathus
下颌寄生胎/下頜寄生胎　hypognathus
下颌假体/下頜假體　mandibular prosthesis
下颌假体植入/下頜假體植入　mandibular prosthesis implantation
下颌间缝/下頜骨間縫　intermandibular suture
下颌角/下頜角　angle of mandible, gonial angle, mandibular angle
下颌角点/下頜角點　gonion
下颌角骨折/下頜角骨折　mandible angle fracture
下颌角前凹/下頜角前凹　pregonium
下颌颈/下頜頸　neck of mandible
下颌颈部嵴/下頜頸部嵴　mandibular neck crest
下颌咀嚼运动/下頜骨咀嚼運動　masticatory mandibular movement
下颌髁骨折/下頜髁骨折　mandible condyle fracture
下颌髁突切除术/下頜髁突切除術　mandibular condylectomy
下颌髁状突/下頜髁狀突　capitulum mandibulae
下颌孔/下頜孔　mandibular foramen, foramen inferior dental
下颌联合/下頜聯合　mandibular symphysis, mentalis symphysis
下颌联合部骨折/下頜聯合部骨折　mandible symphysis fracture
下颌联合点/下頜聯合點,連合穴　symphysion
下颌裂/下頜裂　mandibular cleft
下颌淋巴结/下頜淋巴結　mandibular lymph node, mandibular lymph nodes
下颌隆凸/下頜[骨]隆凸　torus mandibularis
下颌面骨发育不良/下頜面骨發育不良　mandibular facial dysostosis
下颌模型/下頜模型　mandibular cast
下颌囊肿/下頜囊腫　mandibular cyst
下颌内板骨化中心/下頜内板骨化中心,頰肌骨化中心　splenial center
下颌平衡/下頜平衡　mandibular equilibration
下颌平面/下頜平面　mandibular plane
下颌前伸/下頜前伸　mandibular protraction
下颌前突/下頜骨凸頜畸形　mandibular prognathism
下颌切迹/下頜切跡　mandibular notch
下颌韧带/下頜韌帶　mandibular ligament
下颌软骨结合/下頜軟骨結合　mandibular synchondrosis
下颌舌骨动脉/下頜舌骨動脈　mylohyoid artery
下颌舌骨缝/下頜舌骨縫　mylohyoid raphe
下颌舌骨沟/下頜舌骨溝　mylohyoid groove, mylohyoid sulcus of mandible
下颌舌骨肌/下頜舌骨肌　mylohyoid
下颌舌骨肌神经/下頜舌骨肌神經　mylohyoid nerve
下颌舌骨肌线/下頜舌骨線　mylohyoid line
下颌舌骨肌支/下頜舌骨肌支　mylohyoid branch
下颌舌骨区/下頜舌骨區　mylohyoid region
下颌舌骨线/下頜舌骨線　mylohyoid line
下颌舌骨帐幕/下頜舌骨帳幕　mylohyoid curtain
下颌舌肌/下頜舌肌　myloglossus
下颌舌面板/下頜舌面板　mandibular linguoplate
下颌神经/下頜神經　mandibular nerve, submaxillary nerve
[下颌神经]脑膜支/[下頜神經]腦膜支　meningeal branch of mandibular nerve
下颌神经阻滞麻醉/下頜神經阻滯麻醉　mandibular block anesthesia
下颌升支侧位体层片/下頜昇支側位體層片　lateral tomogram of ramus
下颌升支内侧隆突阻滞麻醉/下頜昇支内側隆突阻滯麻醉　block anesthesia at internal ramus prominence
下颌升支切线位投照术/下頜昇支切線位投照術　tangential position roentgenography of mandibular ramus
下颌手法操作/下頜手法操作　mandibular manipulation
下颌损伤/下頜損傷　mandibular injury
下颌体/下頜體　body of mandible, lower jaw member
下颌体位/下頜體位　posture of mandible
下颌头/下頜頭　head of mandible
下颌头套/下頜頭套　headgear mandibular
下颌突/下頜[骨]突　mandibular process
下颌退缩/下頜退縮　mandibular retrognathism
下颌脱臼/下頜脱臼　jaw dislocation
下颌位/下頜位　mandibular position
下颌窝/下頜窝,下頜凹　mandibular fossa
下颌窝关节盂韧带/下頜窝關節盂韌帶　glenoid ligament of mandibular fossa
下颌息止位/下頜息止位　rest position of mandible
下颌徙前术/下頜徙前術　mandibular advancement
下颌下间隙/下頜下間隙　submandibular space
下颌下淋巴结/下頜下淋巴結　submandibular lymph node
下颌下三角/下頜下三角　submandibular triangle
下颌下神经节/下頜下神經節　submandibular ganglion

下颌下神经节副交感根/下頜下神經節副交感根 parasympathetic root of submandibular ganglion

下颌下神经节感觉根/下頜下神經節感覺根 sensory root of submandibular ganglion

下颌下神经节交感根/下頜下神經節交感根 sympathetic root of submandibular ganglion

下颌下腺/下頜下腺 submandibular gland

下颌下腺凹/[下]頜下腺凹 submandibular fossa, submandibular fovea

下颌下腺管/[下]頜下腺管 submandibular duct

下颌腺/下頜腺 mandibular gland

下颌小舌/下頜小舌 mandibular lingula

下颌小头/下頜骨髁狀突頭 head of condyloid process of mandible

下颌斜角/下頜斜角 cant of the mandible

下颌U型钉骨板/下頜U型釘骨板 mandibular staple bone plate

下颌牙/下頜齒 mandibular tooth

下颌牙槽座点/下頜牙槽座點,高頦點 point B

下颌[牙床]丰厚度/下頜[牙床]豐厚度 mandibular fullness

下颌牙弓矫正线/下頜牙弓矯正線 mandibular archwire

下颌咽部/下頜咽部 mylopharyngeal part

下颌咽肌/下頜咽肌 mylopharyngeal muscle

下颌义齿/下頜義齒 mandibular denture

下颌印模/下頜印模 lower impression, mandibular impression

下颌圆枕/下頜圓枕 mandibular torus

下颌缘/下頜緣 mandibular border

下颌缘支/下頜緣支 marginal mandibular branch

下颌运动/下頜運動 movements of mandible

下颌运动复制器/下頜運動複製器 gnathic replicator

下颌运动描记仪/下頜運動描記儀 mandibular kinesiograph

下颌运动自如/下頜運動自如 unlocking of mandible

下颌正中关系/下頜正中關係 mandibular centric relation

下颌正中囊肿/下頜正中囊腫 median mandibular cyst

下颌支/下頜支 ramus of mandible, mandibular ramus

下颌支截骨术/下頜支截骨術 osteotomy of ramus

下颌支支架种植体/下頜支支架種植體 ramus frame implant

下颌中点/下頜正中點 median mandibular point

下颌中切牙切缘点/下頜中切牙切緣點 incision inferius

下颌中切牙牙槽嵴顶点/下頜中切牙牙槽嵴頂點 infradentale

下颌肿瘤/下頜腫瘤 mandibular neoplasm

下颌轴/下頜軸 mandibular axis

下颌注射/下頜注射 mandibular injection

下后的/下後方 inferoposterior

下后尖/下後尖,下白齒內前尖 metaconid

下后锯肌/下後鋸肌 serratus posterior inferior

下滑膜/下滑膜 inferior synovial membrane

下级无头畸胎/下級無頭畸胎,脊髓無頭畸胎 myelacephalus

下甲状旁腺/下甲狀旁腺 inferior parathyroid gland

下睑/下瞼 lower eyelid

下睑板/下瞼板 inferior tarsus

下睑板肌/下瞼板肌 inferior tarsalis, inferior tarsal muscle

下睑袋/下瞼袋 baggy deformity of lower eyelid

下睑袋修复术/下瞼袋修復術 prosthesis of baggy deformity

下睑弓/下瞼弓 inferior palpebral arch

下睑紧缩术/下瞼緊縮術 lower eyelid tightening

下睑静脉/下瞼靜脈 inferior palpebral vein, vein of lower eyelid

下睑支/下瞼支 inferior palpebral branches

下降/降下,下垂 descent

下焦/下焦 lower jiao

下焦如渎/下焦如瀆 lower jiao being organ of draining

下焦湿热/下焦濕熱 dampness-heat in lower jiao

下焦湿热证/下焦濕熱證 pattern of dampness-heat in lower jiao

下角/下角 inferior horn

下胫关节/下脛關節,脛骨關節 tibial articulation

下巨虚/下巨虛 xiajuxu, ST39

下来/下來 alighting

下肋凹/下肋凹,肋下凹 inferior costal fovea, costal pit

下廉/下廉 xialian, LI8

下髎/下髎 xialiao, BL34

下孖肌/下孖肌 gemellus inferior

下迷小管/下迷管 inferior aberrant ductules

下泌涎核/下泌涎核 inferior salivatory nucleus

下面/下面 inferior surface, facies inferior

下磨牙后部/下磨牙後部,下白齒後尖 talonid

下内尖/下內尖,下白齒之內後齒冠隆 entoconid

下内[向]隐斜视/下內[向]隱斜視,下內轉隱斜眼

hypoesophoria
下尿路感染/下尿路感染　lower urinary tract infection
下颞线/下顳線　inferior temporal line
下胚层/下胚層　hypoblast
下胚叶/下胚葉　hypenchyme
下胚轴/下胚軸　hypocotyl
下皮/下皮　hypodermis
下皮纤维/下皮纖維　hypodermal fiber
下偏盲/下偏盲　lower hemianopsia
下品/下品　low grade drug
下屏/下屏　lower tragus, xiaping, TG2
下前第三尖/下前[白齒]第三尖　tritoconid
下前段/下前段　anterior inferior segment
下前段动脉/下前段動脈　inferior anterior segmental artery
下腔静脉/下腔靜脈　inferior vena cava
下腔静脉瓣/下腔靜脈瓣,歐氏瓣　valve of inferior vena cava, Eustachian valve
下腔静脉口/下腔靜脈口　orifice of inferior vena cava
下丘/下丘　inferior colliculus
下丘臂/下丘臂　brachium of inferior colliculus
下丘核/下丘核　nucleus of inferior colliculus
下丘连合/下丘連合　commissure of inferior colliculus
下丘脑/下丘腦,丘腦下部　hypothalamus
下丘脑背内侧核/下丘腦背內側核　dorsomedial hypothalamic nucleus
下丘脑垂体束/下丘腦垂體束　hypothalamohypophyseal tract
下丘脑-垂体系统/下丘腦-垂體系統　hypothalamo-hypophyseal system
下丘脑腹内侧核/下丘腦腹內側核　ventromedial hypothalamic nucleus
下丘脑弓状核/下丘腦弓狀核　arcuate nucleus of hypothalamus
下丘脑沟/下丘腦溝,丘腦下部溝　hypothalamic sulcus
下丘脑核支/丘腦下部核支　branch of hypothalamic nucleus
下丘脑后核/下丘腦後核　posterior hypothalamic nucleus
下丘脑后区/下丘腦後區　posterior hypothalamic nucleus
下丘脑激素类/下丘腦激素類　hypothalamic hormones
下丘脑疾病/下丘腦疾病　hypothalamic disease

下丘脑脊髓纤维/下丘腦脊髓纖維　hypothalamospinal fiber
下丘脑皮质纤维/下丘腦皮質纖維　hypothalamocortical fiber
下丘脑前核/下丘腦前核,丘腦下部前核　anterior hypothalamic nucleus
下丘脑前区/下丘腦前部　anterior hypothalamic region
下丘脑切开术/丘腦切開術,丘腦下部切開術　hypothalamotomy
下丘脑乳头状体/[下丘腦]乳頭狀體,丘腦下部乳頭狀結節　mamillary tubercle of hypothalamus
下丘脑室旁核/下丘腦室旁核　paraventricular hypothalamic nucleus
下丘脑外侧核/下丘腦外側核,外側下丘腦核　lateral hypothalamic nucleus
下丘脑外侧区/下丘腦外側區,下丘腦外側部　lateral hypothalamic region
下丘脑性闭经/下丘腦性閉經,下丘腦性停經　hypothalamic amenorrhea
下丘脑性甲状腺功能减退症/下丘腦性甲狀腺功能減退症　hypothalamic hypothyroidism
下丘脑性甲状腺功能亢进症/下丘腦性甲狀腺功能亢進症　hypothalamic hyperthyroidism
下丘脑支/下丘腦支　hypothalamic branch
下丘脑肿瘤/下丘腦腫瘤　hypothalamic neoplasm
下丘脑综合征/下丘腦症候群　hypothalamic syndrome
下乳/下乳　promoting lactation
下筛斑/下篩斑　inferior macula cribrosa
下舌段/下舌段　inferior lingular segment
下舌段支气管/下舌段支氣管,肺舌葉下支氣管　inferior lingular bronchus
下舌支/舌下支　inferior lingular branch
下身负压/下身負壓　lower body negative pressure
下身感觉缺失/下身感覺缺失　para-anesthesia
下神经节/下神經節　inferior ganglion
下肾单位肾病/下腎單位腎病,腎單位下部腎病　lower nephron nephrosis
下矢状窦/下矢狀竇　inferior sagittal sinus, inferior sagittal sinuses
下视丘疾病/下視丘疾病　hypothalamic disease
下髓帆/下髓帆　inferior medullary velum
下损及上/下損及上　deficiency transmitted from lower body to upper body
下胎/下胎　induced abortion
下体腔/下體腔　hypocoelom
下托/下托,下腳　subiculum

下托复合体/下托複合體　subicular complex
下外侧方/下外側方　inferolateral
下外侧面/下外側面　inferolateral surface
下外[向]隐斜视/下外[向]隱斜視,下外轉隱斜眼　hypoexophoria
下脘/下脘　xiawan, RN10
下位换气法/下位換氣法　downward ventilation
下胃肠道/下胃腸道　lower gastrointestinal tract
下吻合静脉/下吻合靜脈　inferior anastomotic vein
下项线/下項線　inferior nuchal line
下消/下消　lower consumption
下消·津伤燥热证/下消·津傷燥熱證　lower consumption with pattern of dryness-heat injuring fluid
下消·气阴两虚证/下消·氣陰兩虛證　lower consumption with pattern of deficiency of both qi and yin
下消·肾阴虚证/下消·腎陰虛證　lower consumption with pattern of kidney yin deficiency
下消·阴阳两虚证/下消·陰陽兩虛證　lower consumption with pattern of deficiency of both yin and yang
下消·瘀血闭阻证/下消·瘀血閉阻證　lower consumption with pattern of blockade of static blood
下小脑脚/下小腦腳　inferior cerebellar peduncle
下斜肌/[眶]下斜肌　inferior obliquus
下斜曲线/下斜曲線　recline pressure curve
下斜韧带/下斜韌帶　inferior oblique ligament
下斜视/下斜視　hypotropia
下行垂点状束/下行垂點狀束,下行逗點狀徑　descending comma tract
下行前侧束/下行前側束,下行前側徑　anterolateral descending tract
下行束/下行束,下行徑　descending tract
下行穗形绷带/下行穗形繃帶　spica descending bandage
下行性变性/下行[性]變性　descending degeneration
下行性脊髓病/下行性脊髓病　descending myelopathy
下行性脊髓炎/下行性脊髓炎　descending myelitis
下行性神经病/下行性神經病變　descending neuropathy
下牙槽点/下牙槽點　infradentale
下牙槽动脉/下齒槽動脈　inferior alveolar artery, inferior dental artery
下牙槽前点/下牙槽前點　infradentale anterius
下牙槽神经/下齒槽神經　inferior alveolar nerve, inferior dental nerve
下牙丛/下牙叢,下齒叢　inferior dental plexus
下牙错位/下牙錯位,下頜齒異位　mandibular trusion
下牙弓/下齒弓　lower dental arch
下牙龈支/下牙齦支　inferior gingival branch
下牙支/下牙支　inferior dental branch
下咽/下咽[腔],咽下部　hypopharynx
下咽镜检查/下咽鏡檢查,咽下部鏡檢查　hypopharyngoscopy
下咽[窥]镜/下咽[窺]鏡,下咽腔鏡,咽下部鏡　hypopharyngoscope
下咽肿瘤/下咽腫瘤　hypopharyngeal neoplasm
下眼睑皱襞/下眼瞼皺襞　inferior palpebral fold
下叶/下葉　inferior lobe
下叶上支/下葉上支　superior branch of inferior lobe
下叶支/下葉支　inferior lobar branch
下意识/下意識,隐意,潜意識　subconsciousness
下蚓部/下[小腦]蚓部　inferior vermis
下蚓静脉/下蚓靜脈　inferior vein of vermis, inferior vermian vein
下隐斜视/下[轉]隱斜視　hypophoria
下游气道阻力/下游氣道阻力　downstream resistance
下原尖/下原尖　protoconid
下缘/下緣　inferior border, inferior margin
下运动神经元/下運動神經元　lower motor neuron
下支/下支　inferior branch
下肢/下肢　lower limb, lower extremity
下肢不等长/下肢不等長　leg length discrepancy
下肢不宁综合征/下肢不寧症候群　restless leg syndrome
下肢不全畸胎/下肢不全畸胎　peropus
下肢长/下肢長　lower extremity length
下肢带骨/下肢帶骨　pelvic girdle
下肢带连结/下肢帶連結　joint of pelvic girdle
下肢带韧带/下肢帶韌帶　ligament of girdle of inferior extremity
下肢骨/下肢骨　bone of lower limb
下肢肌/下肢肌　muscle of lower limb
下肢肌节/下肢肌節　lower limb myotome
下肢浅静脉/下肢淺靜脈　superficial vein of lower limb
下肢深静脉/下肢深靜脈　deep vein of lower limb
下肢痛/下肢痛　melosalgia
下直肌/下直肌　inferior rectus
下志室/下志室　xiazhishi, EX-B5
下主静脉/下主靜脈　subcardinal vein
下纵隔/下縱隔　inferior mediastinum

下纵肌/下縱肌　inferior longitudinal muscle
下纵束/下縱束　inferior longitudinal fasciculus
夏疮/夏瘡　summer sore
夏尔科综合征/夏爾科症候群,Charcot 氏症候群　Charcot syndrome
夏季唇炎/夏令唇炎　summer cheilitis
夏季痤疮/夏季痤瘡　acne aestivalis
夏季热/夏季熱,疰夏　summer fever
夏季热·上盛下虚证/夏季熱·上盛下虛證　summer fever with pattern of upper excess and lower deficiency
夏季热·暑伤肺胃证/夏季熱·暑傷肺胃證　summer fever with summerheat injuring lung and stomach
夏季瘙痒[症]/夏季搔癢[症]　pruritus aestivalis
夏季水疱/夏季水皰　hydroa aestivale
夏季哮喘/夏季哮喘　summer asthma
夏季疹/夏季疹　summer eruption
夏科动脉/夏科動脈,Charcot 氏動脈　Charcot artery
夏科动脉瘤/夏科動脈瘤,Charcot 氏動脈瘤　Charcot aneurysm
夏科关节/夏科關節,Charcot 氏關節　Charcot joint
夏科关节病/夏科關節病,Charcot 氏關節病　Charcot arthropathy
夏科关节炎/夏科關節炎,Charcot 氏關節炎　Charcot arthritis
夏科-马里-图斯病/夏科-馬里-圖斯病,夏-馬-托三氏病　Charcot-Marie-Tooth disease
夏科-诺伊曼晶体/夏科-紐二氏結晶,夏-紐二氏結晶　Charcot-Neumann crystals
夏科痛/夏科痛,Charcot 氏疼痛　Charcot pain
夏科足/夏科足,Charcot 氏足　Charcot foot
夏枯草/夏枯草　common selfheal fruit-spike
夏令/夏令　summer
夏令瘙痒/夏令搔癢　summer itch
夏令痒疹/夏季癢疹　prurigo aestivale
夏秋疟/夏秋瘧　aestivo-autumnal malaria
夏斯特病/夏斯特病,Chester 氏病　Chester disease
夏天无/夏天無　decumbent corydalis rhizome
夏-魏-巴综合征/夏-魏-巴症候群,Charcot-Weiss-Barker 三氏症候群　Charcot-Weiss-Barker syndrome
夏至草/歐夏至草,苦薄荷　horehound
仙方活命饮/仙方活命飲　xianfang huoming drink
仙鹤草/仙鶴草　hairyvein agrimonia herb
仙客来苷/仙客來苷,歐紫羅蘭素　cyclamin
仙茅/仙茅　common curculigo rhizome
仙人球中毒/仙人球中毒,南美仙人掌中毒　mescalism
仙人梳碱/仙人梳鹼,仙人掌毒贋鹼　pectenine
仙人掌/仙人掌　cactus
仙人掌皮炎/仙人掌皮膚炎　sabra dermatitis
仙人掌肉芽肿/仙人掌肉芽腫　cactus granuloma
仙台病毒/仙臺病毒　Sendai virus
先成论/先成論　preformation theory
先导化合物/先導化合物　lead compound
先导[化合]物优化/先導[化合]物優化,先道物最適化　lead optimization
先导链/先導鏈　leading strand
先发性精神病/提前性精神病　anticipatory insanity
先煎/先煎　decocted earlier
先露异常/先露異常,產位異常　malpresentation
先男后女两性畸形/先男後女兩性畸形　protandrous hermaphroditism
先女后男两性畸形/先女後男兩性畸形　protogynous hermaphroditism
先期辅导/先期輔導,預期性導引　anticipatory guidance
先驱麻醉/先驅麻醉,初期麻醉　prenarcosis
先天变异/先天[性]變異　inborn variation
先天病/先天病　congenital disease
先天肥大性幽门狭窄/先天肥大性幽門狹窄,先天性肥厚性幽門狹窄　congenital hypertrophic pyloric stenosis
先天肥胖性巨体/先天肥胖性巨體,先天性脂肪性巨體　macrosomatia adiposa congenita
先天骨折/先天[性]骨折　congenital fracture
先天混合性黏液瘤/先天[性]混合性黏液瘤　congenital mixed myxoma
先天畸形/先天[性]畸形　congenital malformation
先天鳞癣/先天[性魚]鱗癬,先天性角化病　ichthyosis congenita
先天免疫/先天免疫,自然免疫性　innate immunity
先天缺失/先天[性]缺失　congenital absence
先天缺损/先天缺損　ectrogeny
先天溶血性黄疸/先天溶血性黃疸　congenital hemolytic jaundice
先天三角形秃发/先天三角形禿髮　alopecia triangularis congenitalis
先天疝/先天[性]疝　congenital hernia
先天秃发/先天禿髮　congenital alopecia
先天脱位/先天[性]脱位　congenital dislocation
先天无神经节性巨结肠/先天無神經節性巨大結腸,先天性無神經節細胞巨大結腸症,赫氏病　congenital aganglionic megacolon
先天性/先天性　congenital
先天性氨基酸代谢障碍/先天性胺基酸代謝障礙

先天性氨基酸代谢障碍/先天性胺基酸代謝障礙 inborn error of amino acid metabolism
先天性氨基酸转运障碍/先天性胺基酸轉運障礙 inborn amino acid transport disorder
先天性白痴/先天性白癡 genetous idiocy
先天性白内障/先天性白内障 congenital cataract
先天性白血病/先天性白血病 congenital leukemia
先天性扳机拇指/先天性扳機拇指 congenital trigger thumb
先天性丙酮酸代谢障碍/先天性丙酮酸代謝障礙 inborn error of pyruvate metabolism
先天性并指/先天性并指 congenital syndactyly
先天性重唇/先天性重唇 congenital double lip
先天性喘鸣/先天性喘鳴 congenital stridor
先天性垂直距骨/先天性垂直距骨 congenital vertical talus
先天性唇窦道/先天性唇竇道 congenital lip sinus
先天性毳毛性多毛症/先天性毳毛性多毛症 congenital hypertrichosis lanuginosa
先天性大脑性麻痹/先天性大腦性麻痺,先天腦性麻痺 congenital cerebral palsy
先天性代谢缺陷/先天性代謝缺陷 inborn error of metabolism
先天性单指/先天性單指 monodactyly
先天性胆总管扩张/先天性膽總管擴張 congenital choledochus dilatation
先天性胆总管囊肿/先天性膽總管囊腫 congenital choledochus cyst
先天性镫骨固定/先天性鐙骨固定 congenital fixation of stapes
先天性动静脉交通/先天性動靜脈交通 congenital arteriovenous communication
先天性动静脉瘘/先天性動靜脈瘻[管] congenital arteriovenous fistula
先天性短颈综合征/先天性短頸症候群 Klippel-Feil syndrome
先天性短食管/先天性短食管 congenital short esophagus
先天性多发性关节松弛/多發性先天性關節異常鬆弛 arthrochalasis multiplex congenita
先天性耳凹/先天性耳凹 congenital auricular pit
先天性耳郭囊肿/先天性耳郭囊腫 congenital auricular cyst
先天性耳前瘘/先天性耳前瘻[管] congenital fistula auris
先天性耳裂隙/先天性耳裂[隙] fissura auris congenita
先天性耳聋/先天性耳聾 congenital deafness
先天性耳瘘/先天性耳瘻 congenital auricular fistula
先天性耳前窦道/先天性耳前竇道 congenital preauricular sinus
先天性耳前瘘管/先天性耳前瘻管,先天性耳廓前瘻 congenital preauricular fistula
先天性耳前囊肿/先天性耳前囊腫 congenital preauricular cyst
先天性非球形红细胞溶血性贫血/先天性非球形紅細胞溶血性貧血 congenital non-spherocytic hemolytic anemia
先天性肥大性幽门狭窄/先天性肥大性幽門狹窄 congenital hypertrophic pyloric stenosis
先天性肺动静脉瘘/先天性肺動靜脈瘻[管] congenital pulmonary arteriovenous fistula
先天性肺静脉狭窄/先天性肺靜脈狹窄 congenital pulmonary vein stenosis
先天性肺囊肿/先天性肺囊腫 congenital pulmonary cyst
先天性肺泡发育不全/先天性肺泡發育不全 congenital alveolar dysplasia
先天性肺叶性肺气肿/先天性肺葉性肺氣腫 congenital lobar emphysema
先天性风疹综合征/先天性風疹症候群 congenital rubella syndrome
先天性腹股沟疝/先天性腹股溝疝 congenital inguinal hernia
先天性肝囊肿/先天性肝囊腫 congenital cyst of liver
先天性肝内胆管扩张/先天性肝内膽管擴張 congenital intrahepatic duct dilatation
先天性肝纤维化/先天性肝纖維化,先天性肝纖維變性 congenital hepatic fibrosis
先天性肝性卟啉症/先天性肝性卟啉病,先天性肝紫質病 congenital hepatic porphyria
先天性肝硬化/先天性肝硬化 congenital cirrhosis
先天性肛门闭锁/先天性肛門閉鎖 congenital anal atresia
先天性肛门瘘管/先天性肛門瘻管 congenital anal fistula
先天性肛门狭窄/先天性肛門狹窄 congenital anal stenosis
先天性肛门直肠畸形/先天性肛門直腸畸形 congenital anorectal malformation
先天性高氨血症/先天性高氨血症 congenital hyperammonemia
先天性睾丸发育不全/先天性睾丸發育不全,克蘭費爾特氏症候群 Klinefelter syndrome
先天性膈疝/先天性膈疝 congenital diaphragmatic hernia

先天性弓形虫病/先天性弓形蟲病　congenital toxoplasmosis
先天性钴胺传递蛋白Ⅱ缺乏/先天性鈷胺傳遞蛋白Ⅱ缺乏　congenital transcobalamin Ⅱ deficiency
先天性关节挛缩/先天性關節攣縮　congenital arthrogryposis
先天性果糖代谢障碍/先天性果糖代謝障礙　inborn error of fructose metabolism
先天性黑矇/先天性黑矇　congenital amaurosis
先天性黑素细胞痣/先天性黑色素細胞痣　congenital melanocytic nevus
先天性红细胞生成性卟啉/先天性紅細胞生成性卟啉,先天性紅血球生成性紫質症　congenital erythropoietic porphyria
先天性红细胞生成性卟啉病/先天性紅細胞生成性卟啉病,Gunther氏病　Gunther disease
先天性喉喘鸣/先天性喉喘鳴　congenital laryngeal stridor
先天性喉痉挛/先天性喉痙攣　congenital laryngeal spasm
先天性厚甲综合征/先天性厚甲症候群　pachyonychia congenita syndrome
先天性环/先天性環　congenital ring
先天性环状缩窄/先天性環狀縮窄　congenital ring constriction
先天性黄疸/先天性黄疸　congenital jaundice
先天性肌发育不全/先天性肌發育不全　amyoplasia congenita
先天性肌强直/先天性肌強直　congenital myotonia
先天性肌无力综合征/先天性肌無力症候群　congenital myasthenic syndromes
先天性肌张力缺失/先天性肌張力缺失　congenital amyotonia
先天性畸胎瘤/先天性畸胎瘤　congenital teratoma
先天[性]畸形/先天[性]畸形　congenital malformation
先天性疾病/先天性疾病　congenital disease
先天性脊柱侧凸/先天性脊柱側凸,先天性脊柱側彎　congenital scoliosis
先天性家族性非溶血性黄疸/先天性家族性非溶血性黄疸　congenital familial nonhemolytic jaundice
先天性甲肥厚/先天性[指]甲肥厚,先天性[趾]甲肥厚　pachyonychia congenita
先天性甲状腺功能减退症/先天性甲狀腺功能減退症　congenital hypothyroidism
先天性甲状腺肿/先天性甲狀腺腫　congenital goiter
先天性睑内翻/先天性瞼內翻　congenital entropion
先天性颈裂[畸形]/[先天性]頸裂畸形,先天性頸部裂隙　tracheloschisis
先天性交替性甲营养不良/先天性交替性甲營養不良　congenital alternate nail dystrophy
先天性角化不良/先天性角化不良　congenital dyskeratosis
先天性角膜混浊/先天性角膜混濁　congenital corneal opacity
先天性结肠扩张/先天巨結腸擴張　congenital dilatation of colon
先天性金属代谢缺陷/先天性金屬代謝缺陷　inborn errors metal metabolism
先天性筋膜营养不良/先天性筋膜營養不良,先天性筋膜失養　congenital fascial dystrophy
先天性进行性脂质营养不良/先天進行性脂質營養不良,先天進行性脂質失養症　congenital progressive lipodystrophy
先天性胫骨假关节/先天性脛骨假關節　congenital pseudoarthrosis of tibia, congenital tibia pseudoarthrosis
先天性巨结肠/先天性巨結腸　congenital megacolon
先天性巨肾盏/先天性巨腎盞　congenital megacalycosis
先天性巨输尿管/先天性巨輸尿管　congenital megaloureter
先天性巨形色素痣/先天性巨形色素痣　congenital giant pigmented nevus
先天性髋骨发育不全/先天性髖骨發育不全　congenital dysplasia of the hip
先天性髋关节脱臼/先天性髖關節脱臼　congenital dislocation of hip
先天性髋关节脱位/先天性髖關節脱位　congenital dislocation of hip joint, congenital hip dislocation
先天性髋内翻/先天性髖內翻　congenital coax vara
先天性髋脱位/先天性髖脱位　congenital dislocation of hip
先天性泪囊瘘/先天性淚囊瘻　congenital lacrimal sac fistula
先天性类白血病反应/先天性類白血病反應　congenital leukemoid reaction
先天性两侧手足徐动症/[先天性]兩側手足徐動症　double athetosis
先天性淋巴水肿/先天性淋巴水腫　congenital lymphedema
先天性鳞癣样红皮病/先天性鱗癬樣紅皮症,先天性魚鱗癬狀紅皮症　congenital ichthyosiform erythroderma
先天性卵巢发育不全/先天性卵巢發育不全,透纳[氏]症　Turner syndrome

先天性马蹄内翻足/先天性馬蹄内翻足　congenital equinovarus, congenital talipes equinovarus

先天性盲/先天性盲　congenital blindness

先天性毛痣/先天性毛痣　congenital hairy nevus

先天性梅毒/先天[性]梅毒　congenital syphilis

先天性弥漫性皮色斑驳/先天性彌漫性皮色斑駁　congenital diffuse mottling of the skin

先天性脑动脉瘤/先天性腦動脈瘤　congenital cerebral aneurysm

先天性脑积水/先天性腦積水,先天性水腦,慢性水腦　congenital hydrocephalus

先天性内在因子缺乏/先天性内在因子缺乏,先天性内生性因數缺乏　congenital intrinsic factor deficiency

先天性黏液水肿/先天性黏液水腫　congenital myxedema

先天性膀胱颈肥大/先天性膀胱頸肥大　congenital hypertrophy of the bladder neck

先天性膀胱颈挛缩/先天性膀胱頸攣縮　congenital contracture of bladder neck

先天性皮肤发育不全/先天性皮膚成形不全　aplasia cutis congenita

先天性皮肤黑色素细胞增生症/先天性皮膚黑色素細胞增生症　congenital dermal melanocytosis

先天性皮肤缺乏/先天性皮膚缺乏　congenital absence of the skin

先天性皮肤萎缩/先天性皮膚萎縮　atrophia cutis congenita

先天性皮肤异色病/先天性多形皮膚萎縮症　poikiloderma congenitale

先天性皮肤异色症/先天性皮膚異色症　congenital poikiloderma

先天性皮脂腺增生/先天性皮脂腺增生　congenital sebaceous gland hyperplasia

先天性嘌呤嘧啶代谢缺陷/先天性嘌呤嘧啶代謝缺陷　inborn errors of purine-pyrimidine metabolism

先天性脐疝/先天性臍疝[氣],先天性臍赫尼亞　congenital umbilical hernia

先天性气管食管瘘/先天性氣管食管瘻　congenital tracheoesophageal fistula

先天性鞘膜积液/先天性鞘膜積液,先天性水囊　congenital hydrocele

先天性青光眼/先天性青光眼,牛眼症　congenital glaucoma

先天性全身静脉扩张/先天性全身靜脈擴張,先天性廣泛性靜脈擴張症　congenital generalized phlebectasia

先天性全身性肌发育不良/先天性全身性肌發育不良　musculorum generalisata congenitale hypoplasia

先天性全身性水肿/先天性全身性水腫　congenital generalized dropsy

先天性全身性纤维瘤病/先天性廣泛性纖維瘤病　congenital generalized fibromatosis

先天性全身性脂质营养不良/先天性全身性脂質營養不良,先天性廣泛性脂肪失養　congenital generalized lipodystrophy

先天性缺掌骨[畸形]/先天性缺掌骨[畸形],先天性掌骨缺損症　ectrometacarpia

先天性缺肢/先天性缺肢,先天性無肢畸形　lipomeria

先天性缺跖骨[畸形]/先天性缺蹠骨[畸形],先天性蹠骨缺損症　ectrometatarsia

先天性缺指骨[畸形]/先天性缺指骨[畸形],先天性指骨不全症　ectrophalangia

先天性缺趾骨[畸形]/先天性缺趾骨[畸形],先天性趾骨不全症　ectrophalangia

先天性桡尺骨融合/先天性橈尺骨融合　congenital radioulnar synostosis

先天性乳房及乳头缺乏/先天性乳房及乳頭缺乏　congenital absence of the breasts and nipples

先天性乳糖酶缺乏/先天性乳糖酶缺乏　congenital lactase deficiency

先天性弱视/先天性弱視　congenital amblyopia

先天性上腹壁疝/先天性上腹壁疝　congenital epigastric hernia

先天性上睑下垂/先天性上瞼下垂　congenital ptosis

先天性上肢畸形/先天性上肢畸形　congenital upper extremity deformity

先天性肾病综合征/先天性腎病症候群　congenital nephrotic syndrome

先天性肾囊性[疾]病/先天性腎囊性[疾]病　congenital renal cystic disease

先天性肾上腺皮质增生[症]/先天性腎上腺皮質增生症　congenital adrenal cortical hyperplasia

先天性肾上腺增生/先天性腎上腺增生　congenital adrenal hyperplasia

先天性肾小管输尿障碍/先天性腎小管輸尿障礙　inborn errors of renal tubular transport

先天性肾性失盐综合征/先天性腎性失鹽症候群　congenital renal saltlosing syndrome

先天性肾炎/先天性腎炎　congenital nephritis

先天性肾脏及视网膜发育不良/遺傳性腎臟及視網膜發育不全　hereditary renal-retinal dysplasia

先天性食管闭锁/先天性食管閉鎖　congenital esophageal atresia

先天性食管裂孔疝/先天性食管裂孔疝　congenital

先天性食管裂孔疝/先天性食管裂孔疝 congenital esophageal hiatal hernia
先天性食管狭窄/先天性食管狭窄 congenital stenosis of esophagus
先天性视网膜剥离/先天性視網膜剝離 congenital detachment of retina
先天性室间隔瘤/先天性室間隔瘤 congenital aneurysm of ventricular septum
先天性手畸形/先天性手畸形 congenital hand deformities
先天性竖毛肌错构瘤/先天性豎毛肌錯構瘤 congenital arrector pili hamartoma
先天性双侧面瘫综合征/先天性雙側面癱症候群 congenital facial diplegia syndrome
先天性水痘综合征/先天性水痘症候群 congenital varicella syndrome
先天性水俣病/先天性水俣病 congenital minamata disease
先天性髓过氧化物酶缺乏症/先天性髓過氧化物酶缺乏症,先天性髓過氧化酶缺乏 congenital myeloperoxidase deficiency
先天性碳水化合物代谢障碍/先天性碳水化合物代謝障礙 inborn error of carbohydrate metabolism
先天性特发性心肌肥厚/先天性特發性心肌肥厚 congenital idiopathic hypertrophy of heart
先天性瞳孔异位/先天性瞳孔異位 ectopia pupillae congenita
先天性痛觉缺失/先天性痛覺缺失 congenital pain insensitivity
先天性秃发/先天性秃髪 alopecia congenitalis
先天性外胚层缺损/先天性外胚層缺損 congenital ectodermal defect
先天性胃扭转/先天性胃扭轉 congenital gastric volvulus
先天性无耳/先天性無耳 congenital anotia
先天性无发/先天性無髮,先天毛髮缺乏,先天秃 congenital alopecia
先天性无泪症/先天性無淚症 alacrimia congenita
先天性无毛症/先天性無毛症 atrichia congenita
先天性无神经节症/先天性無神經節症 congenital aganglionosis
先天性无痛症/先天性無痛症 congenital absence of pain
先天性无阴道/先天性無陰道 congenital absence of vagina
先天性无指/先天性無指,無指畸形 adactyly
先天性无趾/先天性無趾,無趾畸形 adactyly
先天性吸收不良/先天性吸收不良 congenital malabsorption
先天性稀毛症/先天性稀毛症 congenital hypotrichosis
先天性下唇瘘管/先天性下唇瘺管 congenital fistulas of lower lip
先天性下肢畸形/先天性下肢畸形 congenital lower extremity deformities
先天性涎腺缺失/先天性涎腺缺失 congenital absence of salivary gland
先天性限界性多毛症/先天性限界性多毛症 congenital circumscribed hypertrichosis
先天性小口或无口/先天性小口或無口,口萎縮 lipostomy
先天性斜颈/先天性斜頸 congenital torticollis
先天性心包缺损/先天性心包缺陷,先天性心包膜缺陷 congenital pericardial defect
先天性心脏病/先天性心臟病 congenital heart disease
先天性心脏横纹肌瘤/先天性心臟橫紋肌瘤 congenital rhabdomyoma of heart
先天性心脏缺损/先天性心臟缺損 congenital heart defect
先天性胸骨后膈疝/先天性胸骨後膈疝 Morgagni hernia
先天性血管瘤/先天性血管瘤 congenital hemangioma
先天性牙龈瘤/先天性牙齦瘤 congenital epulis
先天性颜面外胚层发育异常/先天性顔面外胚層發育異常 congenital ectodermal dysplasia of the face
先天性眼震/先天性眼震,先天性眼球震颤 congenital nystagmus
先天性遗传性疾病/先天性遺傳性疾病 inborn genetic disease
先天性异位输尿管/先天性異位輸尿管 congenital ectopic ureter
先天性阴道闭锁/先天性陰道閉鎖 congenital atresia of vagina
先天性阴茎弯曲/先天性陰莖彎曲 congenital curvature of penis
先天性营养性水肿/先天性營養性水腫 congenital trophedema
先天性甾类代谢障碍/先天性甾類代謝障礙 inborn errors of steroid metabolism
先天性再生不良性贫血/先天性發育不全性貧血 congenital hypoplastic anemia
先天性再生障碍性贫血/先天性再生障礙性貧血 congenital aplastic anemia
先天性造红细胞性紫质症/先天性造紅血球性紫質症 congenital erythropoietic porphyria

先天性肢端过小综合征/先天性肢端過小症候群 congenital acromicria syndrome
先天性肢畸形/先天性肢畸形 congenital limb deformity
先天性脂质代谢缺陷/先天性脂質代謝缺陷 inborn error of lipid metabolism
先天性直肠闭锁/先天性直腸閉鎖 congenital rectal atresia
先天性直肠狭窄/先天性直腸狹窄 congenital stenosis of rectum
先天性指关节融合/先天性指關節融合 congenital symphalangia
先天性趾关节融合/先天性趾關節融合 congenital symphalangia
先天性痣细胞痣/先天性痣細胞痣 congenital nevocytic nevus
先天性肿瘤/先天性腫瘤 congenital tumor
先天性紫绀/先天性發紺 congenital cyanosis
先天性足畸形/先天性足畸形 congenital foot deformity
先天性足外翻畸形/先天性足外翻畸形 congenital convex club foot
先天之精/先天之精 congenital essence
先天痣/先天痣 nevus maternus
先占免疫/先占免疫,占先性免疫力 preemptive immunity
先兆/先兆 aura
先兆痉挛/先兆痙攣 protospasm
先兆临产/先兆臨産 threatened labor
先兆流产/先兆流産,危迫性流産 threatened abortion
先兆乳腺病/先兆乳腺病,前驅性乳房 proemial breast
先兆症状/先兆症狀,預兆症狀 signal symptom
先兆子痫/初期子癇,子癇先兆 preeclampsia
先兆子痫·脾虚肝旺证/先兆子癇·脾虛肝旺證 preeclampsia with pattern of spleen deficiency and liver hyperactivity
先兆子痫·阴虚动风证/先兆子癇·陰虛動風證 preeclampsia with pattern of wind stirring due to yin deficiency
先证者/先證者,淵源者 proband
纤连蛋白类/纖連蛋白類 fibronectins
纤毛/纖毛 cilia, cilium
纤毛虫/纖毛蟲 ciliophoran
纤毛[虫]纲/纖毛綱 Ciliata
纤毛虫[性]痢疾/纖毛蟲痢疾 ciliary dysentery
纤毛菌病/纖毛菌病 leptothricosis

纤毛抗原/纖毛抗原 fibrial antigen
纤毛囊肿/纖毛囊腫 ciliated cyst
纤毛起搏点/纖毛[細胞]起搏點 cilium pacemaker
纤毛上皮/纖毛上皮,細毛上皮 ciliated epithelium
纤毛上皮毒素/细毛上皮毒素 trichotoxin
纤毛上皮囊肿/纖毛上皮囊腫 ciliated epithelial cyst
纤毛细胞/纖毛細胞 ciliated cell
纤毛亚门感染/纖毛亞門感染 Ciliophora infection
纤毛运动/纖毛運動 ciliary motion
纤毛运动障碍/纖毛運動障礙 ciliary motility disorders
纤溶酶/胞漿素 plasmin
纤溶酶原/纖溶酶原,血纖蛋白溶解酶原 plasminogen
纤溶酶原激活物/纖溶酶原啟動劑 plasminogen activator
纤溶酶原激活物抑制物/纖溶酶原啟動物抑制物 plasminogen activator inhibitor
纤溶酶原灭活剂/纖溶酶原滅活劑 plasminogen inactivator
纤丝病毒科感染/纖絲病毒科感染 Filoviridae infection
纤维癌/纖維癌 carcinoma fibrosum
纤维斑块/纖維斑塊 fibrous plaque
纤维闭塞性细支气管炎/纖維閉塞性細支氣管炎,阻塞性纖維性細支氣管炎 bronchiolitis fibrosa obliterans
纤维层/纖維層 fibrous layer
纤维颤动性肌阵挛/纖維顫動性肌陣攣,肌微纖維顫動 fibrillary myoclonia
纤维成淋巴管细胞瘤/纖維成淋巴管細胞瘤,纖維淋巴血管母細胞瘤 fibrolymphoangioblastoma
纤维成形性反应/纖維形成性反應 desmoplastic reaction
纤维蛋白/纖維蛋白,纖維素 fibrin
纤维蛋白海绵/纖維蛋白海綿,纖維素海綿 fibrin sponge
纤维蛋白激酶/纖維蛋白激酶,組織激酶 tissue kinase
纤维蛋白裂解产物/纖維蛋白裂解產物 fibrin split product
纤维蛋白尿/纖維蛋白尿,纖維素尿 fibrinuria
纤维蛋白泡沫/纖維蛋白泡沫 fibrin foam
纤维蛋白溶解/纖維蛋白溶解,纖維蛋白分解 fibrinolysis
纤维蛋白溶解性紫癜/纖維蛋白溶解性紫癜,溶纖維素性紫癜病 fibrinolytic purpura
纤维蛋白溶解药/纖維蛋白溶解藥 fibrinolytic

agents
纤维蛋白溶解抑制剂/纖維蛋白溶解抑制劑 fibrinolysis inhibitor
纤维蛋白溶解综合征/纖維蛋白溶解症候群 fibrinolysis syndrome
纤维蛋白溶酶原/纖維蛋白溶酶原,胞漿素原 plasminogen
纤维蛋白肽A/纖維蛋白肽A fibrinopeptide A
纤维蛋白肽B/纖維蛋白肽B fibrinopeptide B
纤维蛋白套/纖維蛋白套 fibrin sleeve
纤维蛋白纤维蛋白原降解物/纖維蛋白纖維蛋白原降解物 fibrin fibrinogen degradation product
纤维蛋白形成/纖維蛋白形成,纖維素生成,纖維蛋白生成 fibrinogenesis
纤维蛋白形成后纤维变性/纖維蛋白形成後纖維變性 postfibrinous fibrosis
纤维蛋白性鼻炎/纖維[蛋白]性鼻炎 fibrinous rhinitis
纤维蛋白性肺炎/纖維蛋白性肺炎,纖維素性肺炎 fibrinous pneumonia
纤维蛋白性滑膜炎/纖維蛋白性滑膜炎 fibrinous synovitis
纤维蛋白性胃炎/纖維蛋白性胃炎 fibrinous gastritis
纤维蛋白性血栓/纖維蛋白性血栓 fibrinous thrombus
纤维蛋白性咽峡炎/纖維蛋白性咽峽炎 fibrinous angina
纤维蛋白性炎/纖維蛋白性炎,纖維素性炎症 fibrinous inflammation
纤维蛋白性粘连/纖維蛋白性粘連 fibrinous adhesion
纤维蛋白性支气管炎/纖維蛋白性支氣管炎 fibrinous bronchitis
纤维蛋白样变性/纖維蛋白樣變性 fibrinoid degeneration
纤维蛋白样坏死/纖維蛋白樣壞死 fibrinoid necrosis
纤维蛋白原/纖維蛋白原,纖維素原 fibrinogen
纤维蛋白原缺乏血症/纖維蛋白原缺乏血症,血纖維蛋白原缺乏症 afibrinogenemia
纤维蛋白原溶解/纖維蛋白原溶解,纖維蛋白原分解 fibrinogenolysis
纤维蛋白原试验/纖維蛋白原試驗,纖維素原試驗 fibrinogen test
纤维蛋白原受体/纖維蛋白原受體 fibrinogen receptor
纤维蛋白原血症/纖維蛋白原血症,纖維蛋白原過多 fibrinogenemia

纤维蛋白组织黏着剂/纖維蛋白組織黏著劑 fibrin tissue adhesive
纤维二糖/纖維[二]糖,纖維雙糖 cellobiose
纤维二糖酶/纖維[二]糖酶 cellase
纤维发生/纖維發生,纖維生成,纖維形成 fibrogenesis
纤维管胞/纖維狀假導管胞 fiber tracheid
纤维[光导]支气管镜检查[术]/纖維[光導]支氣管鏡檢查[術] fiberoptic bronchoscopy
纤维光学/纖維光學 fiber optics
纤维化/纖維化,纖維變性,纖維組織生成 fibrosis
纤维化肺/纖維化肺,肺纖維變性 fibroid lung
纤维化肉瘤/纖維化肉瘤 sclerosarcoma
纤维环/纖維環 annulus fibrosus
纤维黄瘤/纖維黄瘤,纖維性黄色瘤 fibroxanthoma
纤维肌瘤/纖維肌瘤 fibromyoma
纤维肌瘤切除术/纖維肌瘤切除術 fibromyomectomy
纤维肌肉肥大/纖維肌肉肥大 fibromuscular hypertrophy
纤维肌肉增生/纖維肌肉增生 fibromuscular hyperplasia
纤维肌痛/纖維肌痛 fibromyalgia
纤维肌型主动脉瓣下狭窄/纖維肌型主動脈瓣下狹窄 fibromuscular subvalvular aortic stenosis
纤维肌性发育不良/纖維肌性發育不全 fibromuscular dysplasia
纤维肌炎/纖維肌炎 fibromyositis
纤维己糖/纖維己糖 cellohexose
纤维胶原类/纖維膠原類 fibrillar collagens
纤维胶质/纖維[組織]膠質 fibroglia
纤维胶质瘤/纖維膠質瘤 fibroglioma
纤维胶质原纤维/纖維膠質微纖維 fibroglia fibril
纤维角化瘤/纖維角化瘤 fibrokeratoma
纤维镜/纖維鏡 fiberscope
纤维篮/纖維籃 fiber basket
纤维肋/纖維肋 circumferential rib, fibrous rib, semicircular rib
纤维连接/纖維連結,纖維關節 fibrous joint
纤维连接蛋白/纖維連接蛋白,纖維結合素 fibronectin
纤维瘤/纖維瘤 fibroma
纤维瘤病/纖維瘤病,纖維瘤生成 fibromatosis
纤维瘤切除术/纖維瘤切除術 fibromectomy
纤维毛囊瘤/纖維毛囊瘤 fibrofolliculoma
纤维膜/纖維膜 fibrous membrane
纤维膜型主动脉瓣下狭窄/纖維膜型主動脈瓣下狹窄 fibromembranous subvalvular aortic stenosis

纤维膜炎/纖維膜炎　inohymenitis
纤维囊/纖維囊　fibrous capsule
纤维囊瘤/纖維囊瘤　fibrocystoma
纤维囊性病/纖維囊性病　fibrocystic disease
纤维囊性骨炎/纖維囊性骨炎,囊狀纖維性骨炎　osteitis fibrosa cystica
纤维内镜/纖維内鏡　fiberendoscope
纤维黏液瘤/纖維黏液瘤　myxoma fibrosum
纤维黏液肉瘤/纖維黏液肉瘤　fibromyxosarcoma
纤维黏液样肉瘤/纖維黏液樣肉瘤　fibromyxoid sarcoma
纤维鞘/纖維鞘　circumferential fiber, fibrous sheath
纤维鞘环状部/纖維鞘環狀部　annular part of fibrous sheath
纤维鞘交叉部/纖維鞘交叉部　cruciform part of fibrous sheath
纤维溶解性出血/纖維溶解性出血　fibrinolytic hemorrhage
纤维肉瘤/纖維肉瘤　fibrosarcoma
纤维肉芽肿性胃炎/纖維性肉芽腫性胃炎　gastritis granulomatosa fibroplastica
纤维乳头瘤/纖維乳頭[狀]瘤　fibropapilloma
纤维软骨/纖維軟骨　fibrocartilage
纤维软骨环/纖維軟骨環　fibrocartilaginous ring
纤维软骨瘤/纖維軟骨瘤　fibrochondroma
纤维软骨炎/纖維軟骨炎　fibrochondritis
纤维三糖/纖維三醣,纖維丙醣　cellotriose
纤维上皮瘤/纖維上皮瘤　fibroepithelioma
纤维上皮乳头状瘤/纖維性上皮乳頭狀瘤　fibroepithelial papilloma
纤维上皮肿瘤/纖維上皮腫瘤　fibroepithelial neoplasm
纤维石/纖維石　inolith
纤维束/纖維束　fiber tract
纤维四糖/纖維四醣,纖維丁醣　cellotetrose
纤维素/纖維素　cellulose
纤维素酶/纖維素酶,木纖維質酵素　cellulase
纤维髓样癌/纖維髓狀癌　carcinoma fibromedullare
纤维弹性组织增生/纖維彈性組織增生,纖維組織與彈力組織增殖　fibroelastosis
纤维息肉/纖維息肉　fibropolypus
纤维细胞/纖維細胞　fiber cell
纤维腺病/纖維腺病,纖維腺腫大　fibroadenosis
纤维腺瘤/纖維腺瘤　fibroadenoma
纤维相关胶原类/纖維相關膠原類　fibril-associated collagens
纤维心包/纖維心包,心包纖維層　fibrous pericardium
纤维形成性素质/纖維形成性素質,成纖維性體質　fibroplastic diathesis
纤维性肺炎/纖維性肺炎　fibrous pneumonia
纤维性肌炎/纖維變性肌炎　fibromyitis
纤维性甲状腺炎/纖維性甲狀腺炎　fibrous thyroiditis
纤维性甲状腺肿/纖維性甲狀腺腫　fibrous goiter
纤维性假晶状体[症]/纖維性假晶狀體病　pseudophakia fibrosa
纤维性结核/纖維性結核[病],纖維樣癆病　fibrotuberculosis
纤维性颞下颌关节强直/纖維性顳下頜關節強直　fibrous ankylosis of TMJ
纤维性丘疹/纖維性丘疹　fibrous papule
纤维性[神经]胶质/纖維性[神經]膠質,原纖維膠質　fibrillary glia
纤维性腺块/纖維性腺塊　adenoma fibrosum
纤维性心包炎/纖維性心包炎　fibrinous pericarditis
纤维性心肌炎/纖維性心肌炎　fibrous myocarditis
纤维性心内膜炎/纖維性心内膜炎　endocarditis fibrosa
纤维性星形胶质细胞/纖維性星形膠質細胞,纖維性星狀細胞　fibrous astrocyte
纤维性星形细胞瘤/纖維性星[形]細胞瘤　pilocytic astrocytoma
纤维性牙龈瘤/纖維性牙齦瘤,纖維腫樣齦瘤　epulis fibromatosa
纤维性炎性增生/纖維[性]炎性增生　fibrous inflammatory hyperplasia
纤维性异常增殖症/纖維性異常增殖症,增生性纖維化　proliferative fibrosis
纤维性粘连/纖維性粘連　fibrous adhesion
纤维性肿瘤/纖維性腫瘤　fibrous lump
纤维性组织细胞瘤/纖維性組織細胞瘤　fibrous histiocytoma
纤维胸/纖維胸　fibrothorax
纤维血管瘤/纖維血管瘤　fibroangioma
纤维硬化/纖維硬化　fibrosclerosis
纤维脂瘤/纖維脂瘤　lipoma fibrosum
纤维质消化检查/纖維質消化檢查,纖維檢診法　fibrinoscopy
纤维状断裂/纖維狀斷裂　fibrous fracture
纤维状肌病/纖維狀肌病,桿狀體肌病　nemaline myopathies
纤维组织发育不良/纖維組織發育不良,纖維性發育不良　fibrous dysplasia
纤维组织形成/纖維組織形成　fibrose
纤维组织炎/纖維組織炎　fibrositis

纤维组织硬化/纖維組織硬化　inosclerosis
纤维组织肿瘤/纖維組織腫瘤　fibrous tissue neoplasm
氙放射性同位素/氙放射性同位素　xenon radioisotope
氙同位素/氙同位素　xenon isotope
掀起型骨折/掀起型骨折,隆起骨折　elevated fracture
酰胺/醯胺　amide
酰胺氮/醯胺氮質,胺基氮質　amide nitrogen
酰胺合酶类/醯胺合酶類　amide synthases
酰胺黑/醯胺黑　amido black
酰胺类/醯胺類　amides
酰胺磷酸核糖基转移酶/醯胺磷酸核糖基轉移酶　amidophosphoribosyltransferase
酰胺酶/醯胺酶　amidase
酰胺水解酶类/醯胺[基]水解酶類　amidohydrolases
酰胺转移酶/醯胺轉移酶　amidotransferase
酰毒毛花苷元/醯毒毛花苷元,乙醯毒毛旋花子苷配質　acetylstrophanthidin
酰化[作用]/醯化[作用],醯基化,加醯基作用　acidylation
酰[基]/醯基　acyl
酰基变位酶/醯基變位酶　acylmutase
酰基辅酶A/醯基輔酶A　acyl coenzyme A
酰基磷酸酯酶/醯基磷酸酯酶,醯基磷酸鹽水解酵素　acylphosphatase
酰基[神经]鞘氨醇/醯基鞘胺醇　ceramide
酰基[神经]鞘氨醇酶/醯基鞘胺醇酶　ceramidase
酰基CoA脱氢酶/醯基CoA脱氫酶,醯基輔酶A脱氫酶　acyl-CoA dehydrogenase
酰基CoA氧化酶/醯基CoA氧化酶　acyl-CoA oxidase
酰基载体蛋白质/醯基載體蛋白質　acyl carrier protein
酰基[转移]酶/醯基[轉移]酶,醯酶　acylase
酰基转移酶类/醯基轉移酶類　acyltransferases
酰脲/醯脲　ureide
酰替苯胺类/醯[替]苯胺類　anilides
酰亚胺/醯亞胺　imide
酰亚胺酯类/醯亞胺酯類　imidoesters
鲜地黄/鮮地黄　fresh rehmannia root
鲜红舌/深紅舌　cardinal tongue
鲜药/鮮藥　fresh crude drug, fresh medicine
鲜竹沥/鮮竹瀝　fresh bamboo sap
弦脉/弦脈　wiry pulse, stringy pulse
弦[线]电流计/弦線電流計,絲電流計　thread galvanometer
涎淀粉酶原/涎澱粉酶原,涎液素原,涎酵素原　ptyalinogen
涎反应/涎[液]反應　ptyaloreaction
涎管/涎管　sialodochium
涎管成形术/涎管成形術,涎腺管造形術　sialodochoplasty
涎管扩张/涎管擴張[術]　ptyalectasis
涎管X射线[造影]片/涎管X射線[造影]片,涎腺管X光像　sialogram
涎管[X射线]造影术/涎管[X射線]造影術,涎管X光照相術　ptyalography
涎管狭窄/涎管狭窄　sialostenosis
涎管炎/涎管炎　sialodochitis
涎瘤/涎瘤　sialoma
涎瘘/涎瘻　salivary fistula
涎石/涎石　sialolith, salivary stone
涎石病/涎石病　sialolithiasis
涎石摘除术/涎石摘除術,涎石切除術　sialolithotomy
涎石症/涎石症　salivary calculi
涎酸贮积症/涎酸貯積症,涎液腺病　sialidosis
涎细胞/涎細胞,唾腺細胞　salivary cell
涎腺/涎腺,唾液腺　salivary gland
涎腺导管/涎腺導管　salivary duct
涎腺导管癌/涎腺導管癌　salivary duct carcinoma
涎腺导管闭锁/涎腺導管閉鎖　salivary gland duct atresia
涎腺导管结石/涎腺導管結石　salivary duct calculi
涎腺导管扩张/涎腺導管擴張　dilation of salivary gland duct
涎腺分泌抑制/涎液分泌抑制　sialoschesis
涎腺化生/涎腺化生　sialometaplasia
涎腺结石/涎腺結石　salivary gland calculi
涎腺瘘/涎腺瘻　salivary gland fistula
涎腺囊肿/涎囊腫　sialocele
涎腺切除术/涎腺切除術　sialoadenectomy
涎腺切开引流术/涎腺切開引流術　sialoadenotomy
涎腺融合/涎腺融合　fusion of salivary gland
涎腺下颌骨舌侧陷入/涎腺下頜骨舌側陷入　lingual mandibular salivary gland depression
涎腺涎管[X射线]造影术/涎腺涎管[X射線]造影術,涎腺攝影術　sialadenography
涎腺炎/涎腺炎　sialadenitis
涎腺造影术/涎腺造影術,涎管X射線攝影術　sialography
涎腺增生/涎腺增生　hyperplasia of salivary gland
涎腺肿大[症]/涎腺腫大[症],涎液流出　sialosis
涎腺肿瘤/涎腺腫瘤　salivary gland neoplasm

涎液疾病/涎液疾病　salivary gland disease
涎[液]抑胃素/涎液抑胃素　sialogastrone
衔接蛋白复合物/銜接蛋白複合物　adaptor protein complex
衔接蛋白复合物亚单位/銜接蛋白複合物亞單位　adaptor protein complex subunit
衔接联会/銜接聯會,[染色體的]對端接合　telosynapsis
衔接性精神病/連續性精神病,續發性精神病　consecutive insanity
衔接易位/銜接易位　tandem translocation
痫病/癇病　epilepsy
痫病·发作期/癇病·發作期　attacking stage of epilepsy, seizure
痫病·风痰闭窍证/癇病·風痰閉竅證　epilepsy with syndrome of wind-phlegm blocking orifices
痫病·肝火痰热证/癇病·肝火痰熱證　epilepsy with syndrome of liver-fire and phlegm-heat
痫病·肝肾阴虚证/癇病·肝腎陰虛證　epilepsy with syndrome of yin deficiency of liver and kidney
痫病·脾虚湿困证/癇病·脾虛濕困證　epilepsy with syndrome of damp retention due to spleen deficiency
痫病·痰火扰神证/癇病·痰火擾神證　epilepsy with syndrome of phlegm-fire disturbing spirit
痫病·心脾两虚证/癇病·心脾兩虛證　epilepsy with syndrome of deficiency of both heart and spleen
痫病·心肾两虚证/癇病·心腎兩虛證　epilepsy with syndrome of deficiency of heart and kidney
痫病·休止期/癇病·休止期　quiescent stage of epilepsy
痫病·血虚动风证/癇病·血虛動風證　epilepsy with syndrome of wind stirring due to blood deficiency
痫病·瘀阻脑络证/癇病·瘀阻腦絡證　epilepsy with syndrome of static blood blocking brain collateral
嫌色细胞/嫌色細胞,難染細胞　chromophobe cell
嫌色性腺瘤/嫌色性腺瘤,拒染色細胞腺瘤　chromophobe adenoma
显汗/顯汗　sensible perspiration
显花植物甾醇/顯花植物甾醇,顯脂醇　phanerosterol
显热/顯熱,可感熱　sensible heat
显示液/顯示[溶]液　disclosing solution
显示杂合子/顯示雜合子　manifesting heterozygote
显微操作/顯微操作,微小操作法　micromanipulation
显微操作器/顯微操作器,微小操作器　micromanipulator
显微操作术/顯微鏡技術,顯微鏡操作　micrergy

显微操作针/顯微操作針,微針　microneedle
显微电影摄术/顯微電影攝影術　microcinematography
显微电影照相术/顯微電影照相術,顯微鏡標本活動影片制法　microkinematography
显微多血管炎/顯微多血管炎　microscopic polyangiitis
显微放射照片/顯微放射照片,X光顯微攝影照相像　microradiogram
显微放射照相术/顯微放射照相術,X光顯微攝影術　microradiography
显微放射自显影/顯微[放射]自顯影　microautoradiograph
显微放射自显影术/顯微放射自顯影術　microautoradiography
显微分光光度计/顯微分光光度計　microspectrophotometer
显微分光镜/顯微分光鏡　microspectroscope
显微分光亮度法/顯微分光光度法　microspectrophotometry
显微缝合/顯微縫合　micro suture
显微光密度计/顯微光密度計　microdensitometer
显微活体解剖/顯微活體解剖　microvivisection
显微技术/顯微技術　microtechnic
显微鉴定/顯微鑒定,顯微鑒別　microscopical identification
显微解剖/顯微解剖,顯微鏡剖檢法　microdissection
显微解剖学/顯微解剖學,組織學　microscopic anatomy
显微镜/顯微鏡　microscope
显微镜检查/顯微鏡檢查　microscopy
显微镜凝集反应/顯微鏡凝集反應,顯微凝集　microscopic agglutination
显微镜视野/顯微鏡視野　field of a microscope
显微镜[载物]台/顯微鏡[載物]台　microstat
显微美容外科/顯微美容外科　aesthetic microsurgery
显微描绘器/顯微描繪器　camera lucida
显微切片/顯微切片,顯微解剖術　microsection
显微摄影术/顯微攝影術,顯微照相術　photomicrography, microphotography
显微神经外科[学]/顯微神經外科[學],顯微鏡下神經外科　microneurosurgery
显微[神经]血管减压术/顯微[神經]血管減壓術　microsurgical neurovascular decompression
显微投影/顯微投影　microprojection
显微投影器/顯微投影器　microprojector
显微外科技术/顯微外科技術　microsurgical

technique
显微外科手术/顯微外科[手術] microsurgery
显微血管外科/顯微血管外科 microvascular surgery
显微照片/顯微照片 microphotograph
显微照相/顯微照相 photomicrograph
显微照相器/照相顯微鏡 photomicroscope
显微折射计/顯微折射計 microrefractometer
显微组织学/顯微鏡組織學 microhistology
显小性幻觉/顯小症幻覺 microptic hallucination
显形的/顯形的 delomorphic
显形细胞/顯形細胞 delomorphous cell
显性补体/顯性補體,主補體 dominant complement
显性的/顯性 dominant
显性负效应/顯性負效應 dominant negative effect
显性感染/顯性感染 apparent infection
显性基因/顯性基因 dominant gene
显性频率/顯性頻率 dominant frequency
显性受体/顯性受體,優勢受體,主受體 dominant receptor
显性性状/顯性[性狀] dominant character
显性遗传/顯性遺傳,優性遺傳 dominant inheritance
显性遗传先天性鱼鳞病样红皮病/顯性遺傳先天性魚鱗病樣紅皮病,顯性遺傳先天性魚鱗癬樣紅皮症 dominant congenital ichthyosiform erythroderma
显性遗传寻常鱼鳞病/顯性遺傳尋常魚鱗癬 dominant ichthyosis vulgaris
显性营养不良型大疱性表皮松解[症]/顯性營養不良型大皰性表皮鬆解[症] epidermolysis bullosa dystrophic dominant, dominant dystrophic epidermolysis bullosa
显性远视/顯性遠視 manifest hypermetropia
显性致死试验/顯性致死試驗 dominant lethal test
苋紫溶液/莧紫[素]溶液 amaranth solution
现场抢救/現場搶救 salvage at scene
现代生物学/現代生物學,新生物學 neontology
现代药/現代[新]藥 modern drug
现实感丧失/現實感喪失,現實解體 derealization
现实治疗/現實治療 reality therapy
现象/現象 phenomenon
限定责任能力/限定責任能力 delimited responsibility
限度检查/限度檢查 limit test
限界性角膜切开术/限界性角膜切開術 delimiting keratotomy
限钠膳食/限鈉膳食 sodium-restricted diet
限速步骤/限速步驟,速率决定步驟 rate-limiting step
限性基因/限性基因 sex-limited gene
限性遗传/限性遺傳 sex-limited inheritance
限制/限制 restrict, restriction
限制蛋白质膳食/限制蛋白質膳食 protein-restricted diet
限制酶/限制酶 restriction enzyme
限制性疾病/限制性疾病,局限性疾病 restrictive disease
限制[性内切核酸]酶/限制[性内切核酸]酶 restriction endonuclease
限制性内切酶图谱法/限制性内切酶圖譜法 restriction mapping
限制性片段长度多态性/限制性片段長度多態性 restriction fragment length polymorphism
限制性通气障碍/限制性通氣障礙 restrictive ventilatory disorder
限制性心肌病/限制性心肌病 restrictive cardiomyopathy
限制脂肪膳食/限制脂肪膳食 fat-restricted diet
线/線 line
M线/M線 M line
Z线/Z線 Z line
线虫/線蟲 nemathelminth
线虫病/線蟲[寄生]病 nematodiasis
线虫传多面体病毒/線蟲傳多面體病毒,蠕傳多角體病毒組 Nepovirus
线虫感染/線蟲感染 threadworm infection
线虫学/線蟲學 nematology
线瘊/線瘊 verruca filiformis
线剂/線劑 thread formula
线角/線角 line angle
线粒体/線粒體 mitochondrion
线粒体粗肿/線粒體粗腫,線粒體腫厚 pachynesis
线粒体蛋白质类/線粒體蛋白質類 mitochondrial proteins
线粒体肌病/線粒體肌病 mitochondrial myopathy
线粒体基因/線粒體基因 mitochondrial gene
线粒体疾病/線粒體疾病 mitochondrial disease
线粒体嵴/線粒體嵴 mitochondrial crista
线粒体膜转运蛋白质类/線粒體膜轉運蛋白質類 mitochondrial membrane transport proteins
线粒体脑肌病/線粒體腦肌病 mitochondrial encephalomyopathy
线粒体鞘/粒線體鞘 mitochondrial sheath
线粒体天冬氨酸氨基转移酶/線粒體天冬氨酸氨基轉移酶 mitochondrial aspartate aminotransferase
线粒体系/線粒體系,原漿小體,粒線體 chondriome

线粒体遗传/粒線體遺傳 mitochondrial inheritance
线粒体质子转运 ATP 酶/線粒體質子轉運 ATP 酶 mitochondrial proton-translocating ATPase
线粒体肿胀/線粒體腫脹 mitochondrial swelling
线切术/線切術,絲帶切斷法 seriscission
线圈损害/線圈損害,線環狀損害 wire-loop lesion
线形病毒组/線形病毒組 closterovirus
线形骨折/線狀骨折 linear fracture
线形探条/線形探條,細探條,細探子 filiform
线性动力学/線性動力學 linear kinetics
线性规划法/線性規劃法,線性程控法 linear programming method
线性模型/線性模型 linear model
线性扫描/線性掃描 linear scanning
线性萎缩/線性萎縮 linear atrophy
线性学习机/線性學習機 linear learning machine
线性自由能/線性自由能 linear free energy
线压法/線壓法,血管之絲壓法 filopressure
线状瘢痕/線狀瘢痕 linear scar
线状扁平苔癣/線狀扁平苔癣 lichen planus linearis
线状刀/線狀刀 linear knife
线状颅骨切除术/線狀顱骨切除術 linear craniectomy
线状 IgA 皮肤病/線狀 IgA 皮膚病 linear IgA dermatosis
线状皮脂腺痣综合征/線狀皮脂腺痣症候群 linear sebaceous nevus syndrome
线状乳头状瘤/線狀乳頭狀瘤 papilloma lineare
线状湿疹/線狀濕疹 linear eczema
线状体肌病/線狀體肌病 nemaline myopathy
线状硬皮病/線狀硬皮病 linear scleroderma
陷凹区/陷凹區 bay region
陷谷/陷谷 xiangu, ST43
陷窝/陷窩 lacunae
陷窝韧带/陷窩韌帶 lacunar ligament
陷窝韧带股疝/陷窩韌帶[股]疝 laugier hernia
陷窝性扁桃体炎/陷窩性扁桃體炎,乾酪狀扁桃腺炎 caseous tonsillitis
陷窝性咽峡炎/陷窩性咽峡炎 lacunar angina
腺/腺 gland
腺癌/腺癌 adenocarcinoma
腺被囊/腺被囊,腺外衣,腺被膜 glandilemma
腺病/腺病 adenopathy
腺病毒/腺病毒 adenovirus
腺病毒科感染/腺病毒科感染 adenoviridae infection
腺病毒早期蛋白质类/腺病毒早期蛋白質類 adenovirus early proteins
腺病性鼻炎/腺病性鼻炎 scrofulous rhinitis
腺病质性睑炎/腺病質性瞼炎 blepharitis scrofulosa
腺垂体/腺垂體 adenohypophysis
腺垂体[前叶]/垂體前葉 adenohypophysis
腺垂体切除术/垂體前葉切除[術] adenohypophysectomy
腺蜂窝[组]织炎/腺蜂窩組織炎 adenocellulitis
腺苷/腺苷[酸] adenosine
腺苷二磷酸/腺苷二磷酸 adenosine diphosphate
腺苷二磷酸核糖/腺苷二磷酸核糖 adenosine diphosphate ribose
腺苷二磷酸葡萄糖/腺苷二磷酸葡萄糖 adenosine diphosphate glucose
腺苷二磷酸糖类/腺苷二磷酸糖類 adenosine diphosphate sugars
腺苷高半胱氨酸酶/腺苷高半胱氨酸酶 adenosylhomocysteinase
腺苷激酶/腺苷激酶 adenosine kinase
腺苷甲硫氨酸脱羧酶/腺苷甲硫氨酸脱羧酶 adenosylmethionine decarboxylase
腺苷磷硫酸/腺苷磷硫酸 adenosine phosphosulfate
腺苷-磷酸/腺苷-磷酸,單磷酸腺苷 adenosine monophosphate
腺苷酶/腺苷酸酵素 adenosinase
腺苷三磷酸/腺苷三磷酸 adenosine triphosphate
腺苷三磷酸酶/腺苷三磷酸酶 adenosine triphosphatase
腺苷三磷酸双磷酸酶/腺苷三磷酸雙磷酸酶 apyrase
腺苷酸环化酶/腺苷酸環化酶 adenylate cyclase
腺苷酸环化酶毒素/腺苷酸環化酶毒素 adenylate cyclase toxin
腺苷酸[基]琥珀酸/腺苷酸[基]琥珀酸,腺苷基琥珀酸盐 adenylosuccinate
腺苷酸基琥珀酸合酶/腺苷酸基琥珀酸合酶,腺苷基琥珀酸合成酶 adenylosuccinate synthase
腺苷酸基琥珀酸[裂解]酶/腺苷酸基琥珀酸[裂解]酶 adenylosuccinase, adenylosuccinate lyase
腺苷酸激酶/腺苷酸激酶 adenylate kinase
腺苷酸脱氨酶/腺嘌呤酸脱胺基酵素 adenylic acid deaminase
腺苷脱氨酶/腺苷酸脱胺基酵素,腺苷[酸]脱胺酶 adenosine deaminase
腺苷酰亚氨二磷酸/腺苷醯亞氨二磷酸 adenylyl imidodiphosphate
腺功能减退/腺功能減退,腺機能不足 hypoadenia
腺功能衰弱/腺功能衰退,腺無力,腺機能減弱 adenasthenia
腺管征/腺管徵,管徵象 duct sign

腺肌瘤/腺肌瘤　adenomyoma
腺肌瘤病/腺肌瘤病　adenomyomatosis
腺肌肉瘤/腺肌肉瘤　adenomyosarcoma
腺肌上皮瘤/腺肌上皮瘤　adenomyoepithelioma
腺肌纤维瘤/腺肌纖維瘤　adenomyofibroma
腺棘皮瘤/腺棘皮瘤　adenoacanthoma
腺节/腺節　adenomere
腺联病毒/腺聯病毒,腺病毒相關病毒　adeno-associated virus
腺淋巴瘤/腺淋巴瘤,淋巴腺瘤　adenolymphoma
腺鳞/腺鱗　glandular scale
腺鳞状癌/腺鱗狀癌　adenosquamous carcinoma
腺瘤/腺瘤　adenoma
腺瘤病/腺瘤病　adenomatosis
腺瘤性癌/腺瘤性癌　carcinoma adenomatosum
腺瘤性甲状腺肿/腺瘤狀甲狀腺腫　adenomatous goiter
腺瘤性息肉/腺瘤性息肉　adenomatous polyp
腺瘤样瘤/腺瘤樣瘤　adenomatoid tumor
腺瘤样皮脂腺增生/腺瘤樣皮脂腺增生　adenomatous sebaceous hyperplasia
腺瘤状鼻窦炎/腺瘤狀鼻竇炎　adenomatous sinusitis
腺瘤状结肠息肉蛋白/腺瘤狀結腸息肉蛋白　adenomatous polyposis coli protein
腺毛/腺毛　glandular hair
腺囊瘤/腺囊瘤,腺囊腫　adenocyst
腺囊性病/腺囊性病　adenocystic disease
腺囊肿/腺囊腫　adenocele
腺囊肿性卵巢/腺囊腫性卵巢　adenocystic ovary
腺囊状黏液癌/腺囊狀黏液癌　adenocystic mucinous carcinoma
腺内淋巴结/腺内淋巴結　intraglandular lymph node
腺泡/腺泡　alveolus of a gland, acinus, alveolus
腺泡癌/腺泡癌　acinous cancer, acinous carcinoma
腺泡细胞癌/腺泡細胞癌　acinar cell carcinoma
腺泡细胞瘤/腺泡細胞瘤　acinic cell tumor
腺泡型横纹肌肉瘤/腺泡型橫紋肌肉瘤,齒槽橫紋肌肉瘤　alveolar rhabdomyosarcoma
腺泡炎/腺泡炎　acinitis
腺泡样腺癌/腺泡狀腺癌　acinar adenocarcinoma
腺嘌呤/腺嘌呤　adenine
腺嘌呤次黄嘌呤/腺嘌呤次黄嘌呤,亞黄腺嘌呤　adenine hypoxanthine
腺[嘌呤核]苷酸/腺[嘌呤核]苷酸　adenylate
腺嘌呤核苷酸类/腺嘌呤核苷酸類　adenine nucleotides
腺嘌呤核苷酸转运体/腺嘌呤核苷酸轉運體　adenine nucleotide translocator

腺[嘌呤核]苷酰基/腺[嘌呤核]苷醯基　adenylyl
腺嘌呤[基]/腺嘌呤基,腺苷基　adenyl
腺嘌呤基环化酶/腺嘌呤基環化酶　adenylcyclase
腺嘌呤磷酸核糖基转移酶/腺嘌呤磷酸核糖基轉移酶　adenine phosphoribosyltransferase
腺嘌呤三磷酸酶/腺嘌呤三磷酸酶　adenine triphosphatase
腺嘌呤[脱氨]酶/腺嘌呤酶　adenase
腺嘌呤胸腺嘧啶富集序列/腺嘌呤胸腺嘧啶富集序列　AT rich sequence
腺平滑肌纤维瘤/腺平滑肌纖維瘤　adenoleiomyofibroma
腺切除术/腺切除術　adenectomy
腺热/[淋巴]腺热　glandular fever
腺肉瘤/腺肉瘤　adenosarcoma
腺软骨瘤/腺軟骨瘤　adenochondroma
腺软化/腺軟化　adenomalacia
腺上皮/腺上皮　glandular epithelium
腺上皮瘤/腺上皮瘤　adenoepithelioma
腺X射线照相术/腺X射線照相術　adenography
腺实质/腺實質　glandular substance of prostate
腺体/腺體　gland
腺痛/腺痛　adenalgia
腺系统/腺系　glandular system
腺细胞/腺細胞,分泌細胞　glandular cell
腺纤维化/腺纖維化,腺之纖維變性　fibroadenia
腺纤维瘤/腺纖維瘤　adenofibroma
腺小叶/腺小葉　glandular lobule
腺性成釉细胞瘤/腺性成釉細胞瘤,腺釉質母細胞瘤　adenoameloblastoma
腺性唇炎/腺性唇炎　cheilitis glandularis
腺性尿道炎/腺性尿道炎　urethritis glandularis
腺性脓疱病/腺[腫]性膿疱病　impetigo adenosa
腺性膀胱炎/腺性膀胱炎　glandular cystitis
腺性肾盂炎/腺性腎盂炎　pyelitis glandularis
腺学/腺學　adenology
腺炎/[淋巴]腺炎　adenitis
腺样癌/腺樣癌,類腺癌　adenoid cancer, adenoid carcinoma
腺样痤疮/腺樣痤瘡　adenoid acne
腺样瘤/腺樣瘤,類腺瘤　adenoid tumor
腺样囊性癌/腺樣囊性癌　adenoid cystic carcinoma
腺样上皮癌/腺樣上皮癌　carcinoma epitheliale adenoides
腺样体/腺樣體　adenoid body
腺样体切除术/腺樣增殖切除術　adenoidectomy
腺样增殖体/腺樣增殖體　adenoid vegetation
腺样组织/腺樣組織　adenoid tissue

腺异位/腺異位　adenectopia
腺硬化/腺硬化　adenosclerosis
腺增大/腺增大　hyperadenosis
腺支/腺支　glandular branch
腺脂瘤/腺脂瘤　adenolipoma
腺脂瘤病/腺脂瘤病　adenolipomatosis
腺周炎/腺周圍炎　periadenitis
腺组织异常/腺組織異常　heteradenia
乡村医院/鄉村醫院　rural hospital
相对暗点/相對暗點　relative scotoma
相对骨导/相對骨導　relative bone conduction
相对缓脉/相對緩脈　relative infrequent pulse
相对集合/相對集合　relative convergence
相对价值表/相對價值表　relative value scale
相对密度/相對密度　relative density
相对面溃疡/相對面潰瘍　kissing ulcer
相对黏度/相對黏度　relative viscosity
相对强度/相對強度　relative intensity
相对生物利用度/相對生物利用度,相對生體可用率　relative bioavailability
相对生物学效应/相對生物[學]效率　relative biological effectiveness
相对湿度/相對濕度　relative humidity
相对视野/相對視野　relative visual field
相对调节/相對調節　relative accommodation
相对性白细胞增多症/相對性白血球增多症　relative leukocytosis
相对性红细胞增多症/相對性紅血球過多症　relative polycythemia
相恶/相惡　mutual inhibition
相反/相反,拮抗,反常　clashing, antagonism, inverse
相反贯注/相反貫注,對抗精神貫注,反感　counterinvestment
相关分化/相關分化　correlative differentiation
相关系数/相關係數　correlation coefficient
相关性检验/相關性檢驗　correlation test
相互凝集反应/相互凝集反應,交互凝集　interagglutination
相互适应/相互適應　coadaptation
相互易位/相互易位　reciprocal translocation
相互诱导/相互誘導,交互抑制　reciprocal induction
相继服药法/相繼服藥法　coup sur coup
相加/相加　addition
相加作用/等加效果　additive effect
相间分离/相間分離　alternate segregation
相兼脉/相兼脈　concurrent pulse
相克/相克　restriction

相控阵/相控陣　phased array
相邻分离/相鄰分離　adjacent segregation
相邻基因综合征/相鄰基因症候群,鄰近基因症候群　contiguous gene syndrome
相嵌连接/相嵌連接　interdigitating junction
相容性/相容性　compatibility
相溶解度分析/相溶解度分析　phase solubility analysis
相杀/相殺　counteract the toxicity of another drug, counteract toxicity of another drug
相生/相生　generation
相使/相使　mutual enhancement
相思豆毒蛋白/相思豆毒蛋白,相思豆毒素　abrin
相思豆中毒/相思豆中毒　abrism
相思豆[中毒性]眼炎/相思豆[中毒]性眼炎,相思豆眼炎　jequirity ophthalmia
相似性/相似性　similarity
相特征常数/相特徵常數,相專一性常數　phase specific constant
相畏/相畏　incompatibility
相须/相須　mutual promotion
香草基扁桃酸/香草基杏仁酸　vanillyl mandelic acid
香草醛/香草醛,香草精　vanillin
香草酸/香草酸　vanillic acid
香草酸二乙酰胺/香草酸二乙醯胺　ethamivan
香菖/香菖,白鳶尾　orris
香豆雌酚/香豆雌酚　coumestrol
香豆素/香豆素　coumarin
香豆素苷/香豆素苷,香豆素配糖體　coumarin glycoside
香豆酸类/香豆酸類　coumaric acids
香蜂草抽提液/香蜂草抽提液　balm mint extract
香附/香附　nutgrass galingale rhizome
香菇多糖/香菇多醣　lentinan
香加皮/香加皮　Chinese silkvine root-bark
香连片/香連片　xianglian tablets
香连丸/香連丸　xianglian pills
香料/香料　spice
香料酒精/香料酒精,香料醑　perfumed spirit
香料皮炎/香料皮炎,香料性皮膚炎　perfume dermatitis
香料调味品/香料調味品　spices
香茅/香茅,雄刈萱　citronella
香茅醇/香茅醇　citronellol
香茅醛/香茅醛　citronellal
香柠檬油/香檸檬油,佛手柑油　Bergamot oil
香薷/香薷　Chinese mosla
香薷散/香薷散　xiangru powder

香砂六君丸/香砂六君丸　xiangsha liujun pills
香砂养胃丸/香砂養胃丸　xiangsha yangwei pills
香砂枳术丸/香砂枳尢丸　xiangsha zhizhu pills
香石竹潜病毒组/香石竹潛病毒組,石竹隱潛病毒組　Carlavirus
香树脂/香樹脂,香膠,香膏　balsam
香苏散/香蘇散　xiangsu powder
香药/[芳]香藥　aromatic drug
香橼/香櫞　citron fruit
香脂/香脂　balsam
香脂酸/香脂酸　balsamic acid
箱式呼吸器/箱式呼吸器,小室狀呼吸器　cabinet respirator
箱式夹/箱式夾[板]　box splint
镶嵌发育/鑲嵌發育　mosaic development
镶嵌工业/鑲嵌工業　plating industry
镶嵌骨/鑲嵌骨　mosaic bone
镶嵌细胞/鑲嵌細胞　mosaic cell
镶嵌现象/鑲工態　mosaicism
镶嵌型发育/鑲嵌型發育,鑲嵌式發育　mosaic development
镶嵌杂种/鑲嵌雜種,嵌合型雜種　mosaic hybrid
镶嵌状疣/鑲嵌狀疣,鑲工疣　mosaic wart
响度不适级/響度不適級　loudness discomfort level
响度感觉/響度感覺　loudness perception
响度重振/響度重振　loudness recruitment
响肩/響肩　noisy shoulder
响尾蛇胺/響尾蛇胺　crotamine
响尾蛇毒素/響尾蛇毒素,響尾蛇神經毒　crotoxin
响尾蛇毒液类/響尾蛇毒液類　crotalid venoms
响尾蛇素/響尾蛇素,響尾蛇毒蛋白　crotalin
响尾蛇咬伤/響尾蛇咬傷　pit viper bite
响应面/響應面,回應面　response surface
响应时间/響應時間,回應時間　response time
向背中线/向背中線　dorsimesad
向尺侧/向尺骨　ulnad
向唇/向唇　labially
向电性/向電性,趨電性　galvanotropism
向顶孔间点/向頂孔間點,向頂穴,向頂圖　obeliad
向额[面]/向額　frontad
向腹背/向腹背　ventrodorsad
向钙性/向鈣性,趨鈣性　calciotropism
向光性/向光性　phototropism
向红团/向紅團　bathochrome
向基底/向底面　basad
向胫侧/向胫面　tibiad
向口/向口　orad
向量导联/向量導聯　vector lead
向量图/向量圖　vector diagram
向量眼电图/向量眼電圖　vector electrooculogram
向流性/向流性　rheotaxis
向颅/向[頭]顱　craniad
向眉间/向眉間　glabellad
向末端/向末端,向終端　terminad
[向内]突入/向内突入　intrusion
向内脏/向[内]臟,向臟腑　viscerad
向皮肤/向皮膚　dermad
向气性/向氣性,趨氣性　aerotropism
向前奔跑性先兆/[向前]奔跑性先兆　aura procursiva
向前脱位/向前脱位　forward dislocation
向群性/向群性,對社會及公共關係有興趣　koinotropy
向伤性/向傷性,趨傷性　traumatropism
向上调节/向上調節　up regulation
向上脱位/向上脱位　upward dislocation
向舌/向舌　lingually
向神经/向神經[軸]　neurad
向水性/向水性,趨水性　hydrotropism
向体躯后面/向體軀後面,向身體後面　posteriad
向头侧/向頭[側]　cephalad
向尾[侧]/向尾[側],向尾端　caudad
向温性/向温性,趨温性　thermotropism
向下调节/向下調節　down regulation
向下移位/[向]下移位　infraplacement
向心收缩/向心收縮　concentric contraction
向心性肥大/同心性肥大　concentric hypertrophy
向心性肥胖/向心性肥胖　central obesity
向性/[趨]向性　tropism
向胸骨/向胸骨　sternad
向压性/向壓性,趨壓性　barotaxis
向龈/向[牙]齦　gingivally
向右[侧]/向右　dextrad
向远侧/向遠側　distad
向枕外隆凸尖/向枕外隆凸尖,向枕穴　iniad
向重力性/向重力性　gravitropism
项背肌筋膜炎/項背肌筋膜炎　dorsonuchal myofascitis
项背筋膜炎/項背筋膜炎　fasciitis of nape muscle
项背拘急/項背拘急　spasm of nape and back
项部瘢痕疙瘩性痤疮/項部斑痕疙瘩性痤瘡,頸部蟹足腫性痤瘡　acne keloidalis nuchae
项横肌/項橫肌,頸橫肌　musculus transversus nuchae
项红斑/頸[部]紅斑　erythema nuchae
项筋膜/項筋膜　nuchal fascia

项平面/項平面　nuchal plane
项强/項強　stiff neck
项韧带/項韌帶,頸韌帶　ligamentum nuchae
G0 相/G0 相　G0 phase
G1 相/G1 相　G1 phase
G2 相/G2 相　G2 phase
相变/相變　phase transition
相变制冷/相變製冷　freezing by change of state
相差显微镜/[位]相差顯微鏡　phase microscope, phase contrast microscope
相差显微镜检查/相差顯微鏡檢查　phase-contrast microscopy
相度/相度　examination
相火/相火　ministerial fire
相火妄动/相火妄動　hyperactivity of ministerial fire
相火妄动证/相火妄動證　pattern of hyperactivity of ministerial fire, pattern of ministerial fire hyperactivity
相面术/相[面]法　metoposcopy
相转移催化/相轉移催化　phase transfer catalysis
象鼻虫类/象鼻蟲類　weevils
象鼻术/象鼻術　elephant trunk technique
象差计/象差計　aberrometer
象皮病样热/象皮病樣熱　elephantoid fever
象皮肿/象皮病　elephantiasis
象皮肿病变组织切除植皮术/象皮腫病變組織切除植皮術　elephantiasic tissue excision and skin grafting
象皮肿大网膜瓣转移引流术/象皮腫大網膜瓣轉移引流術　omental flap transferring for elephantiasis
象皮肿去表皮皮瓣埋入术/象皮腫去表皮皮瓣埋入術　Thompson buried dermis flap operation for elephantiasis
象人/象人　elephant man
象限盲/象限盲　quadrantanopsia
象限性头痛/象限[性]頭痛　quadrantal cephalalgia
象形性失语症/象形性失語症,圖案性失語症　pictorial aphasia
象牙质样外生骨疣/象牙質[樣]外生骨疣　ivory exostosis
象征性思维/象徵性思維　symbolic thinking
像/像　like
橡胶/橡膠　rubber
橡胶工/橡膠工　rubber worker
橡胶皮炎/橡膠皮炎　rubber dermatitis
橡皮绷带/橡皮繃帶　India-rubber bandage
橡皮管止血带/橡皮[管]止血帶　rubber tourniquet
橡皮圈/橡皮圈,橡皮氣褥　rubber cushion
橡皮塞/橡皮塞　rubber closure, rubber stopper
橡皮性口疮/橡皮性口[腔]瘡　rubber sore mouth
橡皮障/橡皮障　rubber dam
橡皮障打孔器/橡皮障打孔器,橡皮障鑽孔器　rubber dam punch
橡皮障夹/橡皮障夾　rubber dam clamp
橡皮障夹钳/橡皮障夾鉗　rubber dam clamp forceps
橡皮障架/橡皮障架　rubber dam frame
橡皮纸/橡皮紙　protectin
肖尔茨病/夏爾茲氏病　Scholz disease
肖法尔-斯蒂尔综合征/肖法爾-斯蒂爾症候群,Chauffard-Still 二氏症候群　Chauffard-Still syndrome
肖法尔综合征/肖法爾症候群,Chauffard 氏症候群　Chauffard syndrome
肖格伦综合征/肖格倫症候群,舍葛蘭症候群　Sjogren syndrome
肖帕尔关节/肖帕爾關節,Chopart 氏關節　Chopart articulation
肖普乳头状瘤/肖普乳頭狀瘤,索普氏乳頭狀瘤　Shope papilloma
肖普纤维瘤病毒/肖普纖維瘤病毒,Shope 氏纖維瘤病毒　Shope fibroma virus
逍遥散/逍遥散　ease powder, xiaoyao powder
逍遥型/逍遥型　ambulatory type
消除/排除　elimination
消除速率常数/排除速率常數　climination rate constant
消[导]法/消[導]法　promoting removing digestion method
消毒/消毒　disinfection
消毒剂/消毒劑　disinfectant
消毒药/消毒藥　disinfectant
消法/消法　resolving method
消费品安全/消費品安全　consumer product safety
消费者辩护/消費者辯護　consumer advocacy
消风散/消風散　xiaofeng powder
消谷善饥/消穀善飢　rapid digestion of food and polyorexia
消耗/消耗,空竭　consumption, depletion
消耗病/消耗病　wasting disease
消耗试验/消耗試驗　consumption test
消耗性凝血病变/消耗性凝血病變　comsumption coagulopathy
消耗性心内膜炎/消耗性心內膜炎　marantic endocarditis
消耗综合征/消耗症候群　wasting syndrome
消化/消化　digestion

消化不良/消化不良,不消化 dyspepsia, indigestion
消化不良性腹泻/消化不良性腹瀉 lienteric diarrhea
消化不良性绞痛/消化不良性心絞痛 angina dyspeptica
消化不良性尿/消化不良性尿 dyspeptic urine
消化不良性哮喘/消化不良性哮喘 asthma dyspeptica
消化池/腐化池 digestion tank
消化道/消化道 alimentary tract
消化道感染/消化道感染 alimentary infection
消化管/消化管 alimentary duct
消化酶/消化酶 digestive enzyme
消化内镜[学]/消化內鏡[學] digestive endoscopy
消化器/消化器 digestive apparatus
消化生理学/消化生理學 digestive physiology
消化系统/消化系統 alimentary system, digestive apparatus, digestive system
消化系统畸形/消化系統畸形 digestive system abnormality
消化系统疾病/消化系統疾病 digestive system diseases
消化系统结核/消化系統結核 tuberculosis of digestive system
消化系统瘘/消化系統瘻 digestive system fistula
消化系统内窥镜检查/消化系統內窺鏡檢查 digestive system endoscopy
消化系统外科手术/消化系統外科手術 digestive system surgical procedure
消化系统诊断技术/消化系統診斷技術 digestive system diagnostic technique
消化系统肿瘤/消化系統腫瘤 digestive system neoplasms
消化腺/消化腺 alimentary gland, digestive gland
消化性白细胞增多/消化性白血球增多 digestive leukocytosis
消化性溃疡/消化性潰瘍 peptic ulcer
消化性溃疡出血/消化性潰瘍出血 peptic ulcer hemorrhage
消化性溃疡穿孔/消化性潰瘍穿孔 peptic ulcer perforation
消化性食管炎/消化性食管炎 peptic esophagitis
消化药/消化藥 digestive
消化液缺乏/消化液缺乏,乳糜缺乏 achyiosia
消咳喘糖浆/消欬喘糖漿 xiaokechuan syrup, xiaokechuan tangjiang
消渴/消渴 wasting-thirst, consumptive thirst
消渴肺病/消渴肺病 consumptive thirst involving lung
消渴肝病/消渴肝病 consumptive thirst involving liver
消渴脉痹/消渴脈痺 consumptive thirst with pattern of vessel painful impediment
消渴脑病/消渴腦病 consumptive thirst involving brain
消渴肾病/消渴腎病 consumptive thirst involving kidney
消渴心病/消渴心病 consumptive thirst involving heart
消泺/消濼 xiaoluo, SJ12
消泡剂/消泡劑,抗發泡劑 antifoaming agent, defoaming agent
消泡室/消泡室 defoaming compartment
消痞化积/消痞化積 relieving oppression and masses, relieving and eliminating mass
消球差透镜/消球差透鏡 aplanatic lens
消球[面]差/消球差 aplanatism
消融/消融 ablation
消融疗法/消融療法,摘除治療 ablation therapy
消散剂/消散劑 discussive
消散性骨病/消散性骨病,骨骼消失病 disappearing bone disease
消散药/消散藥 dispersing medicine
消色差透镜/消色差透鏡 achromatic lens
消色差物镜/消色差[接]物鏡 achromatic objective
消食化滞/消食化滯 resolving food stagnation, relieving dyspepsia
消食剂/消食劑 digestive formula
消瘦/消瘦 emaciation
消瘦性水肿/消瘦性水腫 marantic edema
消栓通络片/消栓通絡片 xiaoshuan tongluo tablets
消栓再造丸/消栓再造丸 xiaoshuan zaizao pills
消水肿药/消水腫藥,治水腫劑 anti-edemic, antiedemic
消退/消退 subside
消退试验/消退試驗 extinction test
消旋蛋白质/消旋蛋白質 racemlzed protein
消旋化/消旋化 racemization
消旋酶/消旋酶 racemase
消旋型/消旋型 recemic form
消旋[作用]/外消旋 racemization
消炎药/消炎藥,消炎劑 anti-inflammatory drug, antiinflammatory agent
消炎镇痛药/消炎鎮痛藥 anti-inflammatory analgesic
消痈散疖/消癰散癤 resolving carbuncle and expulsing boil

消痔灵/消痔靈　xiaozhiling injection
消肿生肌/消腫生肌　detumescence and promoting granulation
消肿药/消腫劑　antioncotic
硝氨丙吖啶/硝氨丙吖啶　nitracrine
硝苯地平/硝苯地平　nifedipine
硝碘酚腈/硝碘酚腈　nitroxinil
硝呋太尔/硝呋太爾　nifuratel
硝呋莫司/硝呋莫司　nifurtimox
硝化[作用]/硝化,硝基代入　nitration
硝[基]胺/硝胺　nitramine
硝基苯/硝基苯　nitrobenzene
硝基苯半乳糖苷类/硝基苯半乳糖苷類　nitrophenylgalactosides
硝基[苯]酚/硝基酚　nitrophenol
硝基苯甲醚/硝基甲苯醚　nitro-anisol
硝基苯甲酸盐/硝基苯甲酸鹽,硝基苯類　nitrobenzoate
硝基酚类/硝基酚類　nitrophenols
硝基呋喃类/硝基呋喃類　nitrofurans
硝基呋喃类药/硝基呋喃類藥　nitrofurans
硝基化合物/硝基化合物　nitro compound
硝基还原酶类/硝基還原酶類　nitroreductases
硝基甲烷/硝基甲烷　nitromethane
硝基精氨酸/硝基精氨酸　nitroarginine
硝基喹啉类/硝基喹啉類　nitroquinolines
硝基链烷类/硝基鏈烷類　nitroparaffins
硝基咪唑类/硝基咪唑類　nitroimidazoles
硝基羟基碘苯乙酸酯/硝基羥基碘苯乙酸酯　nitrohydroxyiodophenylacetate
硝基氢氰酸盐试验/硝基氫氰酸鹽試驗,硝基普鲁士酸鹽試驗　nitroprusside test
硝甲酚汞/硝甲酚汞,硝基汞甲酚　nitromersol
硝米芬/硝米芬　nitromifene
硝普盐/硝普鹽　nitroprusside
硝酸/硝酸　nitric acid
硝酸苯汞/硝酸苯汞　phenylmercuric nitrate
硝酸甘油/硝基甘油,三硝酸甘油酯　nitroglycerin
硝酸类/硝酸類,亞硝酸和硝酸之總稱　nitrose
硝酸硫酸镁试验/硝酸硫酸鎂試驗　nitric acid-magnesium sulfate test
硝酸毛果芸香碱/硝酸毛果芸香鹼　pilocarpine nitrate
硝酸钠/硝酸鈉　sodium nitrate
硝酸铅/硝酸鉛　lead nitrate
硝酸烧伤/硝酸燒傷　nitric acid burn
硝酸盐还原酶类/硝酸鹽還原酶類　nitrate reductases
硝酸盐类/硝酸鹽類　nitrates
硝酸盐酶/硝酸鹽酶,硝酸鹽酵素　nitratase
硝酸异山梨酯/硝酸異山梨醇,異山梨醇硝醇脂　isosorbide dinitrate
硝酸银/硝酸銀　argent nitrate
硝酸铀酰/硝酸鈾醯基　uranyl nitrate
硝西泮/硝西泮　nitrazepam
硝酰基/硝醯基　nitroxyl
硝盐酸/硝鹽酸　nitrohydrochloric acid
小凹/小凹　foveolae
小凹形成/小凹形成,輕凹形成　delling
小白蛋白/小白蛋白　parvalbumins
小斑点/小斑點　speckle
小斑块副银屑病/小斑塊副銀屑病　small plaque parapsoriasis
小板块状类牛皮癣/小板塊狀類乾癬　parapsoriasis en petites plaque
小孢子/小芽孢　microspore
小孢子病/小孢子病　nosema disease
小孢子虫/小孢子蟲　microsporidian
小孢子菌病/小孢子菌病,小芽孢癬菌病　microsporosis
小孢子菌疹/小孢子菌疹,小芽孢菌病疹　microsporid
小鼻/小鼻畸形,鼻小畸形　microrhinia
小便不利/小便不利　dysuria
小便不通/小便不通　urinary stoppage
小便黄赤/小便黄赤　deep-colored urine
小便浑浊/小便渾濁　turbid urine
小便夹精/小便夾精　semen in urine
小便频数/排尿频繁　frequent micturition
小便清长/小便清長　clear urine in large amounts
小便涩痛/小便澀痛　difficulty and pain in micturition
小便失禁/小便失禁,尿失禁　aconuresis, incontinence of urine
小 RNA 病毒/小 RNA 病毒　picornavirus
小 RNA 病毒病/小 RNA 病毒病,小核糖核酸病毒病　picornavirus disease
小檗碱/小檗素　berberine
小檗因生物碱类/小檗因生物鹼類　berberine alkaloids
小柴胡汤/小柴胡湯　xiaochaihu decoction
小产/小產　late abortion, miscarriage
小肠/小腸　small intestine, xiaochang, CO6
小肠胆囊吻合术/小腸膽囊[造口]吻合術　enterocholecystostomy
小肠恶性淋巴瘤/小腸惡性淋巴瘤　small intestinal

malignant lymphoma
小肠梗阻/小腸梗阻　small intestine obstruction
小肠肌层/小腸肌層　muscular layer of small intestine
小肠结肠瘘/小腸結腸瘻管　enterocolic fistula
小肠结肠切除术/小腸大腸切除術　enterocolectomy
小肠结肠吻合术/小腸結腸吻合術　enterocolostomy
小肠结肠炎/小腸結腸炎，大小腸炎　enterocolitis
小肠惊/小腸驚　convulsion due to small intestine disorders
小肠镜检查[术]/小腸鏡檢查[術]　small intestinal endoscopy
小肠溃疡/小腸潰瘍　small intestinal ulcer
小肠瘘/小腸瘻　small bowel fistula
小肠密螺旋体/小腸密螺旋體，腸螺旋體　Treponema intestinale
小肠排列术/小腸排列術　plication of small intestine
小肠襻/小腸襻　pontoon
小肠容积描记术/小腸容積描記術　intestinal plethysmography
小肠实热/小腸實熱　excessive heat of small intestine
小肠实热证/小腸實熱證　pattern of excessive heat of small intestine
小肠俞/小腸俞　xiaochangshu, BL27
小肠系膜/小[腸]繫膜　mesenteriolum
小肠虚寒/小腸虚寒　deficiency-cold of small intestine
小肠移植/小腸移植　small intestine transplantation
小肠阴道裂/小腸陰道裂[隙]　fissura enterovaginalis
小肠淤滞综合征/小腸淤滯症候群　small intestinal stasis syndrome
小成红血细胞/小胚紅血球，小母紅血球　microblast
小齿畸形/小齒畸形　microdontism
小齿密螺旋体/小齒螺旋體　Treponema microdentium
小唇/小唇[畸形]　microcheilia
小带间隙/小帶間隙，懸器隙　zonular space
小带纤维/小帶纖維　zonular fiber
小袋虫病/小袋蟲病　balantidiasis
小袋虫性结肠炎/毛囊蟲性結腸炎　balantidial colitis
小袋虫[性]痢疾/小袋蟲[性]痢疾，毛囊蟲痢疾　balantidial dysentery
小滴/小滴，飛沫　droplet
小滴反应/小滴反應，減滴質反應　small-drop reaction
小地区分析/小地區分析　small-area analysis

小动静脉吻合/小動靜脈吻合　arteriolovenular anastomosis
小动脉/小動脈　arteriole, small artery
小动脉肝脏发育不良/小動脈肝臟發育不良　arteriohepatic dysplasia
小动脉坏死/小動脈壞死　arteriolonecrosis
小动[脉]静脉桥/小動[脈]靜脈橋，毛細動靜脈橋　arteriolovenular bridge
小动脉心腔小管/小動脈心腔小管，動脈腔小管　arterioluminal vessel
小动脉性坏死/小動脈性壞死　arteriolar necrosis
小动脉性肾硬化症/小動脈性腎硬化[症]　arteriolar nephrosclerosis
小动脉血窦小管/小動脈血竇小管，動脈竇脈隙小管　arteriosinusoidal vessel
小动脉炎/小動脈炎　arteriolitis
小动脉硬化/小動脈硬化　arteriolosclerosis
小多角骨/小多角骨　trapezoid bone, lesser trapezium
小腭动脉/小腭動脈　minor palatine artery
小腭管/小腭管　lesser palatine canal
小腭孔/小腭孔　foramen lesser palatine
小儿暴惊/小兒暴驚　sudden child frightened
小儿便秘/小兒便秘　infantile constipation
小儿痴呆/小兒癡呆　infantile dementia
小儿癫/小兒癲，胎病[風痰]　infantile epilepsy
小儿癫·发作期/小兒癲·發作期　seizure stage of infantile epilepsy
小儿癫·肝肾两虚证/小兒癲·肝腎兩虛證　infantile epilepsy with pattern of deficiency of both liver and kidney
小儿癫·脾肾气虚证/小兒癲·脾腎氣虛證　infantile epilepsy with pattern of qi deficiency of spleen and kidney
小儿癫·脾虚湿困证/小兒癲·脾虛濕困證　infantile epilepsy with pattern of damp retention due to spleen deficiency
小儿癫·心脾两虚证/小兒癲·心脾兩虛證　infantile epilepsy with pattern of heart-spleen deficiency
小儿癫·休止期/小兒癲·休止期　quiescent stage of infantile epilepsy
小儿肺炎/小兒肺炎　infantile pneumonia
小儿风/小兒風　infantile wind epilepsy
小儿腹痛[病]/小兒腹痛[病]　infantile abdominal pain, abdominal pain in children
小儿腹痛·腹部中寒证/小兒腹痛·腹部中寒證　infantile abdominal pain with pattern of cold attacking abdomen

小儿腹痛·脾胃虚寒证/小兒腹痛·脾胃虛寒證 infantile abdominal pain with pattern of deficiency-cold of spleen and stomach

小儿腹痛·气滞血瘀证/小兒腹痛·氣滯血瘀證 infantile abdominal pain with pattern of qi stagnation and blood stasis

小儿腹痛·乳食积滞证/小兒腹痛·乳食積滯證 infantile abdominal pain with pattern of milk and food stagnation

小儿腹痛·胃肠积热证/小兒腹痛·胃腸積熱證 infantile abdominal palm with pattern of accumulated heat in stomach and intestine

小儿肝炎颗粒/小兒肝炎顆粒 xiao'er ganyan granules

小儿肝移植/小兒肝移植 pediatric liver transplantation

小儿感冒/小兒感冒 infantile common cold

小儿感冒·风寒束表证/小兒感冒·風寒束表證 infantile common cold with pattern of wind-cold tightening exterior

小儿感冒·风热袭表证/小兒感冒·風熱襲表證 infantile common cold with pattern of wind-heat invading exterior

小儿感冒·夹惊/小兒感冒·夾驚 infantile common cold complicated with fright

小儿感冒·夹痰/小兒感冒·夾痰 infantile common cold complicated with phlegm

小儿感冒·夹滞/小兒感冒·夾滯 infantile common cold complicated with dyspepsia

小儿感冒颗粒/小兒感冒顆粒 xiao'er ganmao granules

小儿感冒·暑湿袭表证/小兒感冒·暑濕襲表證 infantile common cold with pattern of summerheat-damp invading exterior

小儿钩虫病/小兒鉤蟲病 infantile ancylostomiasis

小儿汗证/小兒汗證 sweating disease in children

小儿回春丹/小兒回春丹 xiao'er huichun mini-pills

小儿蛔虫病/小兒蛔蟲病 infantile ascariasis

小儿蛔虫病·虫积肠道证/小兒蛔蟲病·蟲積腸道證 infantile ascariasis with pattern of accumulation of worms in intestine

小儿蛔虫病·脾胃气虚证/小兒蛔蟲病·脾胃氣虛證 infantile ascariasis with pattern of qi deficiency of spleen and stomach

小儿姜片虫病/小兒薑片蟲病 infantile fasciolopsiasis

小儿结核/幼兒型結核病 childhood tuberculosis

小儿惊/小兒驚 infantile frightened epilepsy

小儿厥证/小兒厥證 infantile syncope, infantile syncope pattern

小儿厥证·寒厥/小兒厥證·寒厥 infantile cold syncope

小儿厥证·气厥/小兒厥證·氣厥 infantile qi syncope

小儿厥证·热厥/小兒厥證·熱厥 infantile heat syncope

小儿厥证·食厥/小兒厥證·食厥 infantile crapulent syncope

小儿厥证·痰厥/小兒厥證·痰厥 infantile phlegm syncope

小儿厥证·血厥/小兒厥證·血厥 infantile blood syncope

小儿康复/小兒康復 habilitation

小儿咳嗽[病]/小兒欬嗽 infantile cough

小儿咳嗽·肺气虚证/小兒欬嗽·肺氣虛證 infantile cough with pattern of lung qi deficiency

小儿咳嗽·肺阴虚证/小兒欬嗽·肺陰虛證 infantile cough with pattern of lung yin deficiency

小儿咳嗽·风寒袭肺证/小兒欬嗽·風寒襲肺證 infantile cough with pattern of wind-cold invading lung

小儿咳嗽·风热犯肺证/小兒欬嗽·風熱犯肺證 infantile cough with pattern of wind-heat invading lung

小儿咳嗽·痰热壅肺证/小兒欬嗽·痰熱壅肺證 infantile cough with pattern of phlegm-heat congesting lung

小儿咳嗽·痰湿蕴肺证/小兒欬嗽·痰濕蘊肺證 infantile cough with pattern of phlegm-damp amassing in lung

小儿客忤/小兒客忤 infantile convulsive seizure due to fright of seeing straigers

小儿口疮/小兒口瘡 infantile oral ulcer, oral aphthae in children

小儿口疮·气血两虚证/小兒口瘡·氣血兩虛證 infantile oral ulcer with pattern of deficiency of both qi and blood

小儿口疮·心火上炎证/小兒口瘡·心火上炎證 infantile oral ulcer with pattern of heart-fire flaring upward

小儿口疮·心脾积热证/小兒口瘡·心脾積熱證 infantile oral ulcer with pattern of accumulated heat in heart and spleen

小儿口疮·虚火上浮证/小兒口瘡·虛火上浮證 infantile oral ulcer with upward floating of deficient fire

小儿烂喉丹痧/小兒爛喉丹痧 infantile scarlet fever

小儿烂喉丹痧•气营两燔证/小兒爛喉丹痧•氣營兩燔證　infantile scarlet fever with pattern of blazing heat in both qi and nutrient phases

小儿烂喉丹痧•邪侵肺卫证/小兒爛喉丹痧•邪侵肺衛證　infantile scarlet fever with pattern of pathogen invading lung-defense phase

小儿烂喉丹痧•邪退阴伤证/小兒爛喉丹痧•邪退陰傷證　infantile scarlet fever with pattern of yin injury after pathogen subsidence

小儿痢疾/小兒痢疾　infantile dysentery

小儿淋证/小兒淋證　infantile stranguria

小儿淋证•膀胱湿热证/小兒淋證•膀胱濕熱證　infantile stranguria with pattern of damp-heat in bladder

小儿淋证•脾肾气虚证/小兒淋證•脾腎氣虛證　infantile stranguria with pattern of qi deficiency of spleen and kidney

小儿麻痹症/小兒麻痺症　infantile paralysis, poliomyelitis

小儿麻痹症•肝肾两虚证/小兒麻痺症•肝腎兩虛證　infantile paralysis with pattern of deficiency of both liver and kidney

小儿麻痹症•气虚血瘀证/小兒麻痺症•氣虛血瘀證　infantile paralysis with pattern of qi deficiency and blood stasis

小儿麻痹症•邪郁肺胃证/小兒麻痺症•邪鬱肺胃證　infantile paralysis with pattern of pathogen stagnated in lung and stomach

小儿麻痹症•邪注经络证/小兒麻痺症•邪注經絡證　infantile paralysis with pattern of pathogen diffusing into channel-collaterals

小儿囊虫病/小兒囊蟲病　infantile cysticercosis

小儿蛲虫病/小兒蟯蟲病　infantile oxyuriasis

小儿内镜检查[术]/小兒內鏡檢查[術]　pediatric endoscopy

小儿内伤咳嗽/小兒內傷欬嗽　infantile endogenous cough

小儿黏液水肿/小兒黏液水腫　childhood myxedema

小儿尿频/小兒尿頻　infantile frequent urination

小儿尿频•脾肾气虚证/小兒尿頻•脾腎氣虛證　infantile frequent urination with pattern of qi deficiency of spleen and kidney

小儿尿频•阴虚内热证/小兒尿頻•陰虛內熱證　infantile frequent urination with internal heat due to yin deficiency

小儿尿浊/小兒尿濁　infantile urinary turbidity

小儿疟疾/小兒瘧疾　infantile malaria

小儿呕吐/小兒嘔吐　infantile vomiting

小儿呕吐•肝气犯胃证/小兒嘔吐•肝氣犯胃證　infantile vomiting with pattern of liver qi invading stomach

小儿呕吐•脾胃虚寒证/小兒嘔吐•脾胃虛寒證　infantile vomiting with pattern of deficiency-cold of spleen and stomach

小儿呕吐•乳食积滞证/小兒嘔吐•乳食積滯證　infantile vomiting with pattern of milk and food stagnation

小儿呕吐•外邪犯胃证/小兒嘔吐•外邪犯胃證　infantile vomiting with pattern of exogenous pathogen invading stomach

小儿呕吐•胃热气逆证/小兒嘔吐•胃熱氣逆證　infantile vomiting with pattern of stomach heat and qi counter-flowing

小儿脐风/小兒臍風　neonatal tetanus

小儿乳蛾/小兒乳蛾　infantile nippled moth, infantile tonsillitis

小儿乳蛾•肺胃阴虚证/小兒乳蛾•肺胃陰虛證　infantile tonsillitis with pattern of yin deficiency of lung and stomach

小儿乳蛾•风热搏结证/小兒乳蛾•風熱搏結證　infantile tonsillitis with pattern of intermingling of wind-heat

小儿乳蛾•热毒炽盛证/小兒乳蛾•熱毒熾盛證　infantile tonsillitis with blazing heat-toxin

小儿神经外科[学]/小兒神經外科[學]　pediatric neurosurgery

小儿肾移植/小兒腎移植　pediatric renal transplantation

小儿时行感冒/小兒時行感冒　infantile influenza

小儿暑温/小兒暑溫　infantile summerheat warm disease, infantile warm disease in summer

小儿暑温•风邪留络证/小兒暑溫•風邪留絡證　infantile summerheat warm disease with pattern of wind pathogen stagnating in collaterals

小儿暑温•肝风内动证/小兒暑溫•肝風內動證　infantile summerheat warm disease with pattern of internal stirring of liver wind

小儿暑温•内闭外脱证/小兒暑溫•內閉外脫證　infantile summerheat warm disease with pattern of internal blockade and external collapse

小儿暑温•气虚血瘀证/小兒暑溫•氣虛血瘀證　infantile summerheat warm disease with pattern of qi deficiency and blood stasis

小儿暑温•气营两燔证/小兒暑溫•氣營兩燔證　infantile summerheat warm disease with pattern of blazing heat in both qi and nutrient phases

小儿暑温·热入营血证/小兒暑溫·熱入營血證 infantile summerheat warm disease with pattern of heat invading nutrient and blood phases

小儿暑温·痰火内扰证/小兒暑溫·痰火内擾證 infantile summerheat warm disease with pattern of internal disturbance of phlegm-fire

小儿暑温·痰蒙清窍证/小兒暑溫·痰蒙清竅證 infantile summerheat warm disease with pattern of phlegm clouding clear orifices

小儿暑温·卫气同病证/小兒暑溫·衛氣同病證 infantile summerheat warm disease with pattern of involving both defense and qi phases

小儿暑温·阴虚内热证/小兒暑溫·陰虛内熱證 infantile summerheat warm disease with pattern of internal heat due to yin deficiency

小儿暑温·营卫不和证/小兒暑溫·營衛不和證 infantile summerheat warm disease with pattern of disharmony between nutrient and defense phases

小儿水肿·变证/小兒水腫·變證 deteriorated case of infantile edema

小儿水肿[病]/小兒腫病,小兒浮腫 infantile edema

小儿水肿·常证/小兒水腫·常證 regular cases of infantile edema

小儿水肿·肺脾气虚证/小兒水腫·肺脾氣虛證 infantile edema with pattern of qi deficiency of lung and spleen

小儿水肿·风水相搏证/小兒水腫·風水相搏證 infantile edema with pattern of intermingling of wind and water

小儿水肿·脾肾阳虚证/小兒水腫·脾腎陽虛證 infantile edema with pattern of yang deficiency of spleen and kidney

小儿水肿·脾虚湿困证/小兒水腫·脾虛濕困證 infantile edema with pattern of damp retention due to spleen deficiency

小儿水肿·湿热内侵证/小兒水腫·濕熱内侵證 infantile edema with pattern of internal invasion of damp-heat

小儿水肿·水毒内闭证/小兒水腫·水毒内閉證 infantile edema with pattern of internal blockade of water-poison

小儿水肿·水气凌心证/小兒水腫·水氣淩心證 infantile edema with pattern of water qi invading heart

小儿水肿·邪陷心肝证/小兒水腫·邪陷心肝證 infantile edema with pattern of pathogen invading heart and liver

小儿丝虫病/小兒絲蟲病 infantile filariasis

小儿痰/小兒痰 infantile phlegm epilepsy

小儿绦虫病/小兒條蟲病 infantile taeniasis

小儿推拿/小兒推拿 infantile massage

小儿脱肛/小兒脱肛 infantile proctoptosis, infantile rectocele

小儿脱证/小兒脱證 infantile collapse, infantile desertion pattern

小儿脱证·阳气暴脱证/小兒脱證·陽氣暴脱證 infantile collapse with pattern of sudden collapse of yang qi

小儿脱证·阴虚液脱证/小兒脱證·陰虛液脱證 infantile collapse with pattern of fluid depletion and yin deficiency

小儿脱证·阴阳两脱证/小兒脱證·陰陽兩脱證 infantile collapse with pattern of collapse of both yin and yang

小儿外感咳嗽/小兒外感欬嗽 infantile exogenous cough

小儿外科/小兒外科 pediatric surgery

小儿痿病/小兒痿病 infantile flaccidity

小儿痫病/胎病[風痰] infantile epilepsy

小儿小肠移植/小兒小腸移植 pediatric small intestine transplantation

小儿哮喘/小兒哮喘 infantile asthma

小儿哮喘·发作期/小兒哮喘·發作期 attacking stage of infantile asthma

小儿哮喘·肺脾气虚证/小兒哮喘·肺脾氣虛證 infantile asthma with pattern of qi deficiency of lung and spleen

小儿哮喘·缓解期/小兒哮喘·緩解期 remitting stage of infantile asthma

小儿哮喘·脾气虚证/小兒哮喘·脾氣虛證 infantile asthma with pattern of spleen qi deficiency

小儿哮喘·肾虚不纳证/小兒哮喘·腎虛不納證 infantile asthma with pattern of failure to receive qi due to kidney deficiency

小儿哮喘·外寒内热证/小兒哮喘·外寒内熱證 infantile asthma with pattern of external cold and internal heat

小儿哮喘·虚实夹杂证/小兒哮喘·虛實夾雜證 infantile asthma with pattern of intermingling of deficiency and excess

小儿泄泻·变证/小兒洩瀉·變證 deteriorated case of infantile diarrhea

小儿泄泻·常证/小兒洩瀉·常證 regular case of infantile diarrhea

小儿泄泻·风寒证/小兒洩瀉·風寒證 infantile diarrhea with wind-cold pattern

小儿泄泻·脾肾阳虚证/小兒洩瀉·脾腎陽虛證 infantile diarrhea with pattern of yang deficiency of spleen and kidney

小儿泄泻·脾虚证/小兒洩瀉·脾虛證 infantile diarrhea with spleen deficiency pattern

小儿泄泻·气阴两虚证/小兒洩瀉·氣陰兩虛證 infantile diarrhea with pattern of deficiency of both qi and yin

小儿泄泻·伤食证/小兒洩瀉·傷食證 infantile diarrhea with pattern of improper diet

小儿泄泻·湿热[蕴结]证/小兒洩瀉·濕熱[蘊結]證 infantile diarrhea with pattern of accumulation and binding of damp-heat

小儿泄泻·阴竭阳脱证/小兒洩瀉·陰竭陽脱證 infantile diarrhea with pattern of yin depletion and yang collapse

小儿心悸[病]/小兒心悸[病] infantile palpitation

小儿心悸·水气凌心证/小兒心悸·水氣凌心證 infantile palpitation with pattern of water qi invading heart

小儿心悸·心脾两虚证/小兒心悸·心脾兩虛證 infantile palpitation with pattern of heart-spleen deficiency

小儿心悸·心虚胆怯证/小兒心悸·心虛膽怯證 infantile palpitation with pattern of heart deficiency and timidity

小儿心悸·心血瘀阻证/小兒心悸·心血瘀阻證 infantile palpitation with pattern of blockade due to heart blood stasis

小儿心悸·心阳虚证/小兒心悸·心陽虛證 infantile palpitation with pattern of heart yang deficiency

小儿心悸·阴虚火旺证/小兒心悸·陰虛火旺證 infantile palpitation with pattern of exuberant fire due to yin deficiency

小儿虚证感冒/小兒虛證感冒 deficient type infantile common cold

小儿血吸虫病/小兒血吸蟲病 infantile schistosomiasis, infantile schitosomiasis

小儿厌食/小兒厭食 infantile anorexia

小儿厌食·脾胃气虚证/小兒厭食·脾胃氣虛證 infantile anorexia with pattern of qi deficiency of spleen and stomach

小儿厌食·脾胃阴虚证/小兒厭食·脾胃陰虛證 infantile anorexia with pattern of yin deficiency of spleen and stomach

小儿阳水/小兒陽水 infantile yang edema

小儿样呼吸音/小兒樣呼吸音 puerile respiration

小儿药证直诀/小兒藥證直訣 Key to Therapeutics of Children's Diseases

小儿遗尿/小兒遺尿 infantile enuresis

小儿遗尿·肺脾气虚证/小兒遺尿·肺脾氣虛證 infantile enuresis with pattern of qi deficiency of lung and spleen

小儿遗尿·肝经湿热证/小兒遺尿·肝經濕熱證 infantile enuresis with pattern of damp-heat in liver channel

小儿遗尿·肾气不固证/小兒遺尿·腎氣不固證 infantile enuresis with pattern of unconsolidated kidney qi

小儿遗尿·心肾不交证/小兒遺尿·心腎不交證 infantile enuresis with pattern of incoordination between heart and kidney

小儿疫毒痢/小兒疫毒痢 infantile fulminant dysentery

小儿疫毒痢·内闭外脱证/小兒疫毒痢·內閉外脱證 infantile fulminant dysentery with pattern of internal blockade and external collapse

小儿疫毒痢·疫毒内闭证/小兒疫毒痢·疫毒內閉證 infantile fulminant dysentery with pattern of internal blockade of pestilent toxin

小儿阴水/小兒陰水 infantile yin edema

小儿瘀血/小兒瘀血 static blood epilepsy

小儿指纹/小兒指紋 infantile hand venule, infantile venule of index finger

小儿至宝丸/小兒至寶丸 xiao'er zhibao pills

小儿疰夏/小兒疰夏 summer non-acclimation in children, summer non-acclimatization in infant

小儿疰夏·脾胃气虚证/小兒疰夏·脾胃氣虛證 summer non-acclimatization in infant with pattern of qi deficiency of spleen and stomach

小儿疰夏·湿困脾胃证/小兒疰夏·濕困脾胃證 summer non-acclimatization in infant with pattern of dampness retaining in spleen and stomach

小儿紫癜/小兒紫癜 infantile purpura

小儿紫癜·风热扰络证/小兒紫癜·風熱擾絡證 infantile purpura with pattern of wind-heat disturbing collaterals

小儿紫癜·脾肾阳虚证/小兒紫癜·脾腎陽虛證 infantile purpura with pattern of yang deficiency of spleen and kidney

小儿紫癜·气不摄血证/小兒紫癜·氣不攝血證 infantile purpura with pattern of failure of qi to keep blood

小儿紫癜·气滞血瘀证/小兒紫癜·氣滯血瘀證 infantile purpura with pattern of qi stagnation and blood stasis

小儿紫癜•血热伤络证/小兒紫癜•血熱傷絡證　infantile purpura with pattern of blood-heat injuring collaterals
小儿紫癜•阴虚火旺证/小兒紫癜•陰虛火旺證　infantile purpura with pattern of exuberant fire due to yin deficiency
小耳/小耳　microtia
小耳畸形/小耳[畸形],耳過小,耳郭發育不全　microtia
小发作/[癲癇]小發作　petit mal
小发作持续状态/小發作持續狀態,癲癇小發作狀態　petit mal status
小反刍动物瘟疫病毒/小反芻動物瘟疫病毒　Pestes-des-petits-ruminants virus
小泛素相关修饰蛋白质类/小泛素相關修飾蛋白質類　small ubiquitin-related modifier proteins
小方/小方　minor prescription
小方脉/小方脈　medical department for children
小房/小房　areola
小[分]裂球/小分裂球　micromere
小粉孢子/小粉狀孢子　microaleuriospore
小腹痛/小腹痛,少腹痛　lower abdominal pain
小肝/小肝,肝小畸形　microhepatia
小睾丸/小睾丸[畸形]　micro-orchidia
小根/小根,支根　rootlet
小谷/小谷　valley
小骨/小骨　ossicle
小骨空/小骨空　xiaogukong, EX-UE6
小骨盆/小骨盆　lesser pelvis
小冠椰子蜡/小冠椰子蠟　ouricury wax
小管/小管　canaliculi, tubule
小管间牙本质/小管間牙本質　intertubular dentin
小管间质肾小管间质/腎小管間質,腎小管與組織間隙　tubulointerstitial
小管间质性肾病/小管間質性腎病　tubulointerstitial nephropathy
小管内纤维瘤/小管内纖維瘤　intracanalicular fibroma
小管期/小管期,微管期　canalicular period
小管性肾炎/小管性腎炎　tubular nephritis
小管周牙本质/小管周齒質　peritubular dentin
小管转运/小管轉運　tubular transport
小海/小海　xiaohai, SI8
小汗腺癌/小汗腺癌　eccrine carcinoma
小汗腺汗管囊腺瘤/[小]汗腺汗管囊腺瘤　eccrine syringocystadenoma
小汗腺汗管纤维腺瘤/[小]汗腺汗管纖維腺瘤,汗腺汗管纖維腺瘤　eccrine syringofibroadenoma

小汗腺汗孔癌/[小]汗腺汗孔癌　eccrine porocarcinoma
小汗腺汗孔瘤/小汗腺汗孔瘤　eccrine poroma
小汗腺囊瘤/小汗腺囊瘤　eccrine hidrocystoma
小汗腺囊腺瘤/小汗腺囊腺瘤　eccrine cystadenoma
小汗腺上皮瘤/小汗腺上皮瘤　eccrine epithelioma
小汗腺腺瘤/小汗腺腺瘤　eccrine hidroadenoma
小汗腺血管瘤性错构瘤/小汗腺血管瘤性錯構瘤　eccrine angiomatous hamartoma
小汗腺血管瘤痣/小汗腺血管瘤痣　eccrine angiomatous nevus
小汗腺痣/小汗腺痣　eccrine nevus
小核核糖核蛋白类/小核核糖核蛋白類　small nuclear ribonucleoproteins
小核仁核糖核蛋白类/小核仁核糖核蛋白類　small nucleolar ribonucleoproteins
小颌/小頜[畸形]　micrognathia
小颌弓间距离/小頜弓間距離　small interarch distance
小颌畸形/小頜畸形　micrognathism
小红细胞/小紅血球　microcyte
小红细胞性贫血/小紅血球性貧血　microcytic anemia
小红细胞症/小紅細胞症,小紅血球增多症　microcytosis
小户嫁痛/小户嫁痛　vaginal pain during the first coitus
小花芫硷/小花煙鹼　micranthine
小环/小環　circellus
小环结扎术/孔眼栓結術　eyelet wiring
小茴香/小茴香　fennel
小活络丹/小活絡丹　xiaohuoluo mini-pills
小棘苔癣/棘狀苔蘚　lichen spinulosus
小集落支原体/小集落支原體,小菌落黴漿菌　tiny mycoplasma
小脊髓/小脊髓[畸形]　micromyelia
小剂量激光疗法/小劑量激光療法,小劑量雷射療法　low-level laser therapy
小蓟/小薊　field thistle herb
小蓟饮子/小薊飲子　xiaoji drink
小建中汤/小建中湯　xiaojianzhong decoction
小胶质/小神經膠質[細胞]　microglia
小角/小角　lesser cornu, lesser horn
小角结节/小角結節,史托里氏軟骨隆凸　corniculate tubercle, eminence of cartilage of Santorini
小角膜/小角膜畸形　microcornea
小角软骨/小角狀軟骨　corniculate cartilage
小角舌肌/小角舌肌　chondroglossus

小角咽部/小角咽部　chondropharyngeal part
小角样结节/小角樣結節,小角狀結節　corniculate tubercle
小结/小結　nodule
小结肠/小結腸[畸形]　microcolon
小结间区/小結間區　internodule zone
小结节/小結節　lesser tubercle
小结节嵴/小結節嵴　crest of lesser tubercle
小结帽/小結帽　nodule cap
小结石病/小結石病,細石病　microlithiasis
小结树突细胞/[小]結樹突細胞,濾泡樹突細胞,毛囊樹突狀細胞　follicular dendritic cell
小结相关上皮细胞/小結相關上皮細胞　follicular associated cell
小结胸证/小結胸證　minor chest binding pattern
小金丹/小金丹　xiaojin mini-pills
小金丸/小金丸　xiaojin pills
小晶状体/小晶狀體[畸形]　microphakia
小精灵面容综合征/小精靈面容症候群,精靈臉症候群,小鬼臉症候群　elfin facies syndrome
小颈子宫/小頸子宮[畸形]　uterus parvicollis
小静脉/小靜脈　small vein, venule
小静脉孔/小靜脈孔,席比辛氏孔　thebesian foramen
小静脉炎/小靜脈炎　venulitis
小颏/小頦畸形　microgenia
小颗粒细胞/小顆粒細胞　small granule cell
小孔镜/小孔鏡,裂隙眼鏡　stenopeic spectacles
小口/小口[畸形]　microstomia, small mouth
小块/小塊[金屬]　nugget
小连接体/小連接體,次要接部　minor connector
小梁/小梁,小柱　trabecula
小梁变性/[支氣管]小梁狀變性　trabecular degeneration
小梁成形术/小梁成形術　trabeculoplasty
小梁穿刺术/小梁穿刺術　trabeculopuncture
小梁动脉/小梁動脈　trabecular artery
小梁骨/小梁骨　trabecular bone
小梁间隙/小梁間隙　intertrabecular space, trabecular space
小梁结构/小梁結構　trabecularism
小梁静脉/小梁靜脈　trabecular vein
小梁切除术/小梁切除術,小梁切開術　trabeculectomy
小梁切开刀/小梁切開刀　trabeculotome
小梁切开术/小梁切開術　trabeculotomy
小梁网/小梁網　trabecular reticulum, trabecular meshwork
小梁形成/小梁形成　trabeculation

小梁硬化/小梁硬化　trabecular sclerosis
小梁周围淋巴窦/小梁周圍淋巴竇　peritrabecular sinus
小[量]输血/小[量]輸血,微量輸血法　microtransfusion
小淋巴细胞/小淋巴細胞,小淋巴球　small lymphocyte
小淋巴细胞淋巴瘤/小淋巴細胞淋巴瘤　small lymphocytic lymphoma
小淋巴样细胞/微小淋巴球樣細胞　microlymphoidocyte
小菱形肌/小菱形肌　rhomboideus minor, lesser rhomboid muscle
小麦过敏/小麥過敏　wheat hypersensitivity
小麦胚/小麥胚　wheat germ
小麦糖/小麥糖　triticin
小满月/小滿月　a month after delivery
小棉球/小棉球　cotton pellet
小棉球试验/小棉球試驗　cotton pellet test
小面者/小面者,小面畸形　microprosopus
小墨蜱属/黑色蟲　Melanolestes
小母鸡病/小母雞病,小母雞腎盂腎炎　pullet disease
小囊/小囊　microcyst
小脑/小腦　cerebellum
小脑板/小腦板　cerebellar plate
小脑半球/小腦半球　cerebellar hemisphere
小脑背侧裂/小腦背側裂　fissura dorsolateralis cerebelli
小脑被盖束/小腦被蓋束　cerebellotegmental tract
小脑扁桃体/小腦扁桃體　tonsil of cerebellum
小脑扁桃体疝/小腦扁桃體疝　tonsillar hernia
小脑扁桃体支/小腦扁桃體支　cerebellar tonsillar branch
小脑变性/小腦變性　cerebellar degeneration
小脑病步态/小腦病步態　cerebellar gait
小脑病性强直/小腦病性強直,小腦性僵直　cerebellar rigidity
小脑出血/小腦出血　cerebellar hemorrhage
小脑第一裂隙/小腦第一裂隙,小腦主裂隙　fissura prima cerebelli
小脑共济失调/小腦共濟失調,小腦性[運動]失調症　cerebellar ataxia
小脑谷/小腦谷,小腦溪　cerebellar vallecula
小脑核/小腦核　cerebellar nucleus
小脑红核脊髓束/小腦紅核脊髓束,小腦紅核脊徑　cerebellorubrospinal tract
小脑后切迹/小腦後切跡　posterior cerebellar notch,

marsupial notch
小脑后上静脉/小腦後上靜脉　posterior superior cerebellar vein
小脑后外侧裂隙/小腦後外側裂　fissura posterolateralis cerebelli
小脑后下静脉/小腦後下靜脉　posterior inferior cerebellar vein
小脑后叶/小腦後葉　posterior lobe of cerebellum
小脑回/小腦迴,腦迴過小畸形　microgyrus
小脑活树/小腦活樹　arbor vitae, arbor vitae cerebelli
小脑疾病/小腦疾病　cerebellar disease
小脑脊束/小腦脊束　tract fasciculus cerebello-spinalis
小脑脊髓束/小腦脊髓束,小腦脊徑　cerebellospinal tract
小脑脚/小腦腳　cerebellar stalk
小脑静脉/小腦靜脉　cerebellar vein
小脑镰/小腦鐮　cerebellar falx, falx cerebelli
小脑裂/小腦裂　cerebellar fissure
小脑裂隙/小腦裂隙　fissura cerebelli
小脑幕/小腦幕　tentorium of cerebellum
小脑幕底支/小腦幕底支　tentorial basal branch
小脑幕脑膜瘤/小腦幕腦膜瘤,幕上腦膜瘤　tentorial meningioma
小脑幕切迹/小腦幕切跡　incisure of tentorium of cerebellum
小脑幕缘支/小腦幕緣支　tentorial marginal branch
小脑幕支/小腦幕支　tentorial branch
小脑脑桥角/小腦腦橋角　cerebellopontine angle
小脑脑桥角脑膜瘤/小腦腦橋角腦膜瘤　meningioma of cerebellopontine angle
小脑脑桥角综合征/小腦腦橋角症候群　syndrome of cerebellopontine angle
小脑皮质/小腦皮質　cerebellar cortex, cortex cerebelli
小脑皮质分子层/小腦皮質分子層　molecular layer of cerebellar cortex
小脑皮质颗粒层/小腦皮質顆粒層　granular layer of cerebellar cortex
小脑皮质梨形细胞层/小腦皮質梨形細胞層　piriform cell layer of cerebellar cortex
小脑前切迹/小腦前切跡　anterior cerebellar notch
小脑前上静脉/小腦前上靜脉　anterior superior cerebellar vein
小脑前庭束/小腦前庭束　cerebellovestibular tract
小脑前下静脉/小腦前下靜脉　anterior inferior cerebellar vein

小脑前叶/小腦前葉　anterior lobe of cerebellum
小脑切除[法]/小腦切除　decerebellation
小脑丘脑束/小腦丘脑束,小腦視丘徑　cerebellothalamic tract
小脑上动脉/小腦上動脉　superior cerebellar artery
小脑上脚/小腦上腳　superior cerebellar peduncle
小脑上脚交叉/小腦上腳交叉　decussation of superior cerebellar peduncle
小脑上静脉/小腦上靜脉　superior cerebellar vein
小脑神经胶质增生/小腦神經膠質增生　cerebellar gliosis
小脑树状白质/小腦樹狀白質　arborescent white substance of cerebellum
小脑水平裂/小腦水平裂　fissura horizontalis cerebelli
小脑髓质/小腦髓質　cerebellar medulla
小脑体/小腦體　corpus of cerebellum
小脑突出/小腦膨出　parencephalocele
小脑窝/小腦窩　cerebellar fossa
小脑下后动脉/小腦下後動脉　posterior inferior cerebellar artery
小脑下脚/小腦下腳　inferior cerebellar peduncle
小脑下静脉/小腦下靜脉　inferior cerebellar vein
小脑下前动脉/小腦下前動脉　anterior inferior cerebellar artery
小脑小球/小腦小球　cerebellar glomerulus
小脑小山/小腦小山　monticulus cerebelli
小脑小叶/小腦小葉　subfolium
小脑性构音障碍/小腦性構音障礙,小腦性口吃　cerebellar dysarthria
小脑性麻痹/小腦性麻痺　cerebellar palsy
小脑压迫圆锥/小腦壓迫圓錐,小腦受壓錐體　cerebellar pressure cone
小脑延髓池/小腦延髓池　cisterna magna
小脑延髓池穿刺/小腦延髓池穿刺[術]　cisternal puncture
小脑炎/小腦炎　cerebellitis
小脑叶片/小腦葉片　cerebellar folia
小脑蚓[部]/小腦蚓部,蠕蟲　vermis, cerebellar vermis
小脑中脚/小腦中腳　middle cerebellar peduncle
小脑中央前静脉/小腦中央前靜脉　precentral cerebellar vein
小脑肿瘤/小腦腫瘤　cerebellar neoplasm
小脑综合征/小腦症候群　cerebellar syndrome
小脑纵隔/小腦縱隔　mediastinum cerebelli
小牛胸腺核糖核酸酶/小牛胸腺核糖核酸酶　calf thymus ribonuclease

小牛血清/小牛血清　calf serum
小脓疱疹/小膿皰疹　impetigo incognito
小疱性湿疹/小皰性濕疹,小水泡性濕疹　eczema vesiculosum
小疱性紫癜病/小皰性紫癜病　purpura vesiculosa
小皮板/小皮板,角皮層　cuticular plate
小平面/小平面　facet
小气候/小氣候　microclimate
小腔形成/小腔形成　loculation
小强荧光细胞/小強螢光細胞　SIF cell, small intensely fluorescent cell
小青龙汤/小青龍湯　xiaoqinglong decoction
小丘/[小]丘,小阜　nodule
小丘疹样荨麻疹/小丘疹樣蕁麻疹　micropapular urticaria
小球间牙本质/小球間牙本質,球間隙牙本質,小球間齒質　interglobular dentin
小球[体]/小球　spherule
小球状石/小球狀石　microspherolith
小躯干/小軀幹[畸形]　nanocormia
小染色体/小染色體　small chromosome
小乳头/小乳頭,乳頭過小　microthelia
小上颌畸形/小上頜畸形　micromaxillary deformity
小舌/小舌[畸形]　microglossia
小神经胶质细胞/小神經膠質細胞,微膠質細胞　microglial cell
小神经胶质细胞瘤/小神經膠質細胞瘤,微神經膠質細胞瘤　microglioma
小拭子/小拭子,小墊布　pledget
小室/小室,私室　cabinet
小嗜酸细胞/小嗜酸細胞　microxycyte
小噬细胞/小噬細胞　microphage
小收肌/小收肌,内收小肌　adductor minimus
小手/小手[畸形]　microcheiria
小手术/小手術　minor surgery
小鼠保护试验/小鼠保護試驗　mouse protection test
小束/小束　fasciculus
小[水]疱/小水皰　phlyctenule
小水疱病/小水皰病　phlyctenulosis
小体/小體　corpuscle
小瞳孔/小瞳孔[畸形]　microcoria
小头/小頭[畸形]　microcephaly, capitulum
小头[畸形]/小頭症　nanocephaly
小头间静脉/小頭間靜脈　venae intercapitales
小头韧带/小頭韌帶　capitular ligament
小头者/小頭者,頭小畸胎　microcephalus
小腿长/小腿長　shank length
小腿骨间膜/小腿骨間膜　crural interosseous membrane
小腿骨间神经/小腿骨間神經　interosseous nerve of leg
小腿过短/小腿過短,小脛骨畸形　microcnemia
小腿红绀病/小腿紅紺病,絲襪病　erythrocyanosis crurum
小腿后骨筋膜鞘/小腿後骨筋膜鞘　posterior osseofascial compartments of leg
小腿后肌间隔/小腿後肌間隔　posterior crural intermuscular septum
小腿后区/小腿後部　posterior crural region
小腿筋膜/小腿筋膜　crural fascia, crural aponeurosis
小腿美容术/小腿美容術　aesthetic shank surgery
小腿内侧皮支/小腿内側皮支　medial crural cutaneous branch
小腿前骨筋膜鞘/小腿前骨筋膜鞘　anterior osseofascial compartment of leg
小腿前肌间隔/小腿前肌間隔　anterior crural intermuscular septum
小腿前区/小腿前區,小腿前部　anterior crural region
小腿三头肌/小腿三頭肌　triceps surae
小腿十字韧带/小腿十字韌帶　cruciate ligament of leg
小腿痛/小腿痛　scelalgia
小腿外侧骨筋膜鞘/小腿外側骨筋膜鞘　lateral osseofascial compartment of leg
小腿外侧区/小腿外側區,小腿外側部　lateral crural region
小腿足长指数/小腿足長指數,下腿及腳指數　lower leg-foot index
小唾液腺/小唾液腺　minor salivary gland
小外科手术/小外科手術　minor surgical procedure
小网膜/小網膜　lesser omentum
小网膜孔疝/小網膜孔疝　hernia of foramen of Winslow
小卫星DNA/小衛星DNA　minisatellite DNA
小卫星重复/小衛星重複　minisatellite repeat
小窝/小窩,細胞質膜微囊　alveoli, caveolae
小窝蛋白/小窩蛋白,細胞質膜微囊蛋白　caveolin
小无裂细胞淋巴瘤/小無裂細胞淋巴瘤　small noncleaved-cell lymphoma
小细胞癌/小細胞癌　small cell carcinoma
小细胞部/小細胞部　parvocellular part
小细胞淋巴瘤/小細胞淋巴瘤　small-cell lymphoma
小细胞溶酶/小細胞溶酶,小細胞溶解酵素　microcytase

小细胞肉瘤/小細胞肉瘤　small cell sarcoma
小细胞网状核/小細胞網狀核　parvocellular reticular nucleus
小细胞质核糖核蛋白类/小細胞質核糖核蛋白類　small cytoplasmic ribonucleoproteins
小下颌畸形/小下頜畸形　micromandibular deformity
小涎腺/小涎腺　minor salivary gland
[小]腺/[小]腺　glandula
小斜角肌/小斜角肌　scalenus minimus, musculus scalenus minimus
小型分生孢子/小型分生孢子,小型頂端芽孢　microconidium
小型银汞合金输送器/小型銀汞合金輸送器　miniature amalgam carrier
小型有丝分裂/小型有絲分裂,小有絲分裂　elassosis
小续命汤/小續命湯　xiaoxuming decoction
小血管炎/小血管炎,多發性血管炎　polyangitis
小血管注射/小血管注射器,微細注射　fine injection
小血栓形成/小血栓形成,微血栓症　microthrombosis
小血小板/小血小板　microplastocyte
小循环/小循環,肺循環　lesser circulation
小牙/小牙,小齒,小牙畸症　microdontia
小眼/小眼[畸形]　microphthalmia
小眼虫/小眼蟲　Euglena gracilis
小叶/小葉　lobule
小叶间胆管/小葉間膽管　interlobular bile duct, ductuli interlobulares
小叶间导管/小葉間[導]管　interlobular duct
小叶间动脉/[小]葉間動脈　interlobular artery
小叶间隔/小葉中隔　interlobular septum
小叶间静脉/小葉間靜脈　interlobular vein
小叶间气肿/小葉間氣腫　interlobular emphysema
小叶间小管/小葉間小管　interlobular ductuli
小叶内导管/小葉內[導]管　intralobular duct
小叶内静脉/小葉內靜脈　intralobular vein
小叶下静脉/小葉下靜脈　sublobular vein
小叶性肺不张/小葉性肺不張　lobular atelectasis
小叶性肾小球肾炎/小葉性腎絲球腎炎　lobular glomerulonephritis
小叶支气管/小葉支氣管　bronchus segmentales
小叶中心性胰腺炎/小葉中心性胰腺炎,中央葉胰炎　centrilobar pancreatitis
小叶周围性胰炎/[小]葉周圍性胰炎　perilobar pancreatitis
小叶状癌/小葉狀癌　lobular carcinoma

小翼/小翼　lesser wing
小阴唇/小陰唇　lesser lip of pudendum
小阴唇切除术/陰唇切除術　nymphectomy
小阴唇炎/小陰唇炎　nymphitis
小阴唇粘连/小陰唇粘連　adhesion of labia minora
小阴唇肿/小陰唇腫大　nymphoncus
小阴茎/小陰莖[畸形],陰莖過小　micropenis
小隐静脉/小隱靜脈　small saphenous vein
小蝇属/小蠅屬　Siphunculina
小幼红细胞/小幼紅細胞,微小正紅母血球　micronormoblast
小于胎龄婴儿/小於胎齡嬰兒　small for gestational age infant
小鱼际/小魚際,對魚際肌　hypothenar, hypothenar eminence
小鱼际筋膜/小魚際筋膜　hypothenar fascia
小圆肌/小圓肌　teres minor, musculus teres minor
小圆线虫/小圓線蟲　Strongylus micrurus
小折返/小折返　microreentry
小指/小指　little finger, auricular finger
小指背静脉/小指背靜脈　salvatella vein
小指短屈肌/小指短屈肌,屈小指短肌　flexor digiti minimi brevis, musculus flexor digiti minimi brevis manus
小指对掌肌/小指對掌肌　opponens digiti minimi
小指伸肌/伸小指肌　extensor digiti minimi, extensor muscle of little finger
小指伸肌腱鞘/伸小指肌腱鞘　tendinous sheath of extensor digiti minimi
小指弯曲/小指彎曲　streptomicrodactyly
小指展肌/小指展肌,外展小指肌　abductor digiti minimi, abductor muscle of little finger
小趾/小趾　little toe
小趾短屈肌/小趾短[屈]肌,屈小趾短肌　flexor digiti minimi brevis, musculus flexor digit minimi brevis pedis
小趾对跖肌/小趾對蹠肌　opponens digiti minimi of foot
小趾展肌/小趾展肌,外展小趾肌　abductor digiti minimi
小蛛立克次体/小蛛立克次體　Rickettsia akari
小烛树蜡/小燭樹蠟,大戟蠟　candelilla wax
小柱/小柱　columella
小柱性细胞癌/小柱性細胞癌　trabecular cell carcinoma
小转子/小轉子,小粗隆　lesser trochanter
小眦漏/小眥漏　external canthus leaking eye
小足者/小足者,足小畸胎,足小者　micropus

小组护理/小组護理　team nursing
小嘴[畸形]/小口畸形　hypostomia
哮病/哮病,喘鸣,氣喘　asthma, wheezing
哮病·不发作期/哮病·不發作期　intermittent stage of wheezing
哮病·发作期/哮病·發作期　attacking stage of wheezing
哮病·肺肾气虚证/哮病·肺腎氣虛證　wheezing with pattern of qi deficiency of lung and kidney
哮病·脾肺气虚证/哮病·脾肺氣虛證　wheezing with pattern of qi deficiency of spleen and lung
哮喘/哮喘,氣喘　asthma
哮喘持续状态/哮喘持續狀態　status asthmaticus
哮喘发作/哮喘發作,氣喘發作　asthmatic attack
哮喘-湿疹综合征/哮喘-濕疹綜合徵,氣喘-濕疹綜合徵　asthma-eczema complex
哮喘性肺嗜酸细胞浸润症/哮喘性肺嗜酸細胞浸潤症,氣喘性肺嗜酸細胞浸潤症　asthmatic pulmonary eosinophilia
哮喘样喘鸣/哮喘性哮鳴,氣喘性哮鳴　asthmatoid wheeze
哮吼/哮吼,嘶吼　croup
哮吼性咽喉痛/哮吼性咽喉痛,哮吼式喉痛　croupous sore throat
哮吼相关病毒/哮吼相關病毒　croup-associated virus CA
哮鸣/哮鳴,喘鳴　wheeze, wheezing
笑病/笑病　laughing sickness
笑不休/笑不休　compulsive laughter
笑肌/笑肌　musculus risorius
笑气和氧麻醉/笑氣和氧麻醉　gas and oxygen anesthesia
笑靥/[笑]靨　dimple
笑靥成形术/笑靨成形術　dimple formation
效价/效價　titer
效率/效率　efficiency
效能/療效,有效性　efficacy
效应/效應　effect
效应[淋巴]细胞/效應[淋巴]細胞　effector lymphocyte
效应 T 淋巴细胞/效應 T 淋巴球　effector T lymphocyte
效应器/效應器　effector
效应物/效應物　effector
效应物部位/效應物部位　effector site
效应细胞/效應細胞,作用細胞　effector cell
效应 T 细胞/效應 T 細胞　effector T cell
效应修正因子/效應修正因子,效應修正因數　effect modifier
楔/楔　wedge
楔骨/楔骨　cuneiform bone
楔间背侧韧带/楔間背側韌帶,背側楔間韌帶　dorsal intercuneiform ligament
楔间骨间韧带/楔間骨間韌帶　interosseous intercuneiform ligament
楔间关节/楔間關節　intercuneiform joint
楔间足底韧带/楔間足底韌帶,楔間蹠側韌帶,蹠側楔間韌帶　plantar intercuneiform ligament
楔前动脉/楔前動脈　precuneal artery
楔前叶/楔前葉,前楔葉　precuneus
楔束/楔[狀]束,Burdach 氏束　fasciculus cuneatus, tract of Burdach
楔束核/楔束核　cuneate nucleus
楔束结节/楔束結節　cuneate tubercle
楔骰背侧韧带/楔骰背側韌帶,背側楔骰韌帶　dorsal cuneocuboid ligament
楔骰骨间韧带/楔骰骨間韌帶,骨間楔骰韌帶　interosseous cuneocuboid ligament, cuneocuboid interosseous ligament
楔骰关节/楔骰關節　cuneocuboid joint
楔骰足底韧带/楔骰足底韌帶,楔骰蹠側韌帶,足底楔骰韌帶　plantar cuneocuboid ligament
楔小脑纤维/楔小腦纖維　cuneocerebellar fiber
楔形短头[畸形]/楔型短頭畸形　brachysphenocephaly
楔形核/楔形核　cuneiform nucleus
楔形切除[术]/楔形切除[術]　wedge excision
楔形切骨术/楔形切骨術,楔狀截骨術　cuneiform osteotomy
楔形头[畸形]/楔狀頭畸胎　sphenocephaly
楔形下核/楔形下核　subcuneiform nucleus
楔叶/楔[狀]葉　cuneus
楔跖骨间韧带/楔蹠骨間韌帶　interosseous cuneometatarsal ligament
楔舟背侧韧带/楔舟背側韌帶,背側楔舟韌帶　dorsal cuneonavicular ligament
楔舟关节/楔舟關節　cuneonavicular joint, cuneonavicular articulation
楔舟足底韧带/楔舟足底韌帶,楔舟蹠側韌帶,足底楔舟韌帶　plantar cuneonavicular ligament
楔状结节/楔狀結節　cuneiform tubercle
楔状缺损/楔狀缺損　wedge-shaped defect
楔状软骨/楔狀軟骨　cuneiform cartilage
楔状隙/楔狀隙　embrasure
歇止脉/歇止脈　stopped pulse
蝎/蠍　scorpion

蝎毒[液]/蠍毒　scorpion venom
蝎蜇伤/蠍螫傷　scorpion sting
蝎蜇中毒/蠍螫中毒,中蠍毒　scorpionism
协调/協調性　coordination
协调性联带运动/協調性聯帶運動　coordination synkinesia
协调性异种移植/協調性異種移植　concordant xenotransplantation
协调运动/協調運動　coordination exercise
协调状态/相關狀態　correlated state
协同/協同,增效作用　synergism, synergia
协同不能/協同不能　asynergy
协同沉淀[反应]/聯合沈澱,共同沈澱　coprecipitation
协同动作不能/協同動作不能　asynergia
协同[动作]不足/協同動作不足,共濟力不足　hyposynergia
协同动作障碍/協同動作障礙,共濟不能,失調症　dyssynergia
协同感觉缺失/協同感覺缺失　synergistic anesthesia
协同肌/協同肌　congenerous muscle
协同凝集[反应]/協同凝集　coagglutination
协同收缩/協同收縮,同濟收縮　cocontraction
协同性坏疽/協同性壞疽　synergistic gangrene
协同运动/協同運動　synergy movement
协同转运子/協同轉運子　symporter
协助细胞/協助者細胞　helper cell
协助自杀/協助自殺　assisted suicide
邪闭/邪閉　pathogen block
邪伏膜原证/邪伏膜原證　pattern of pathogen hidden in interpleuro-diaphramatic space
邪气/邪氣　pathogenic qi
邪气盛/邪氣盛　excess of pathogenic qi
邪郁少阳/邪鬱少陽　stagnant pathogen of Shaoyang
邪正盛衰/邪正盛衰　rising and falling of vital qi and pathogen
胁腹痛/脅腹痛　flank pain
胁疽/脅疽　chest and hypochondrium tuberculosis
胁肋/脅肋　lateral thorax
胁痛/脅痛　hypochondriac pain
胁痛[病]/脅痛[病],季肋痛　hypochondriac pain
胁痛·胆腑郁热证/脅痛·膽腑鬱熱證　hypochondriac pain with pattern of heat stagnation in gallbladder
胁痛·肝火胁痛证/脅痛·肝火脅痛證　hypochondriac pain with liver fire pattern
胁痛·肝经湿热证/脅痛·肝經濕熱證　hypochondriac pain with pattern of damp-heat in liver channel
胁痛·肝气郁结证/脅痛·肝氣鬱結證　hypochondriac pain with pattern of liver qi depression
胁痛·肝虚证/脅痛·肝虛證　hypochondriac pain with liver deficiency pattern
胁痛·肝阴虚证/脅痛·肝陰虛證　hypochondriac pain with pattern of liver yin deficiency
胁痛·瘀血阻络证/脅痛·瘀血阻絡證　hypochondriac pain with pattern of static blood blocking collaterals
胁痈/脅癰　hypochondrium abscess
偕耦/偕耦　geminal coupling
斜绷带/斜繃帶　oblique bandage
斜边骨折/斜邊骨折　pond fracture
斜部/斜部　oblique part
斜产位/斜產位,斜產式　oblique presentation
斜刺/斜刺　oblique insertion of needle
斜方骨/斜方骨　os trapezium
斜方肌/斜方肌　trapezius, musculus trapezius
斜方肌腱下囊/斜方肌腱下囊　subtendinous bursa of trapezius
斜方韧带/斜方韌帶　trapezoid ligament
斜方体/斜方體　trapezoid body
斜方体核/斜方體核　trapezoid nucleus
斜方线/斜方線,菱形線　trapezoid line
斜方形/斜方形,斜方骨　trapezium
斜飞脉/斜飛脈　oblique flying pulse
斜副腕韧带/斜副腕韌帶　oblique accessory carpal ligament
斜脊/斜脊　oblique ridge
斜角带/斜角帶　diagonal band
斜角肌/斜角肌　scalenus muscle
斜角肌淋巴结/斜角肌淋巴結　scalene lymph node
斜角肌切除术/斜角肌切除術　scalenectomy
斜角肌切开术/斜角肌切開術,斜角肌切断術　scalenotomy
斜角肌综合征/斜角肌症候群　scalenus syndrome
斜颈/斜頸,歪頸　torticollis, wryneck
斜径/斜徑　oblique diameter
斜裂/斜裂　oblique fissure
斜裂隙/斜裂隙　fissura obliqua
斜面导板/斜面導板　inclined bite plate
斜面培养/斜面培養　slant cultivation
斜坡/斜坡　clivus
斜坡前中点/斜坡前中點,坡穴　clition
斜坡支/斜坡支　clival branch
斜韧带/斜韌帶　oblique ligament
斜疝/斜疝　oblique hernia
斜视/斜視,斜眼　strabismus
斜视刀/斜視刀　strabotome
斜视[度]测量法/斜視度測量法　strabometry

斜视钩/斜眼鉤　squint hook
斜视计/斜視計　strabismometer
斜视剪/斜視剪　strabismus scissors
斜视角/斜視角　angle of strabismus
斜视镜检查/斜視鏡檢查　heteroscopy
斜视内镜/斜視內鏡　oblique viewing endoscope
斜视镊/斜視鑷　strabismus forceps
斜视偏向/斜視偏向　strabismic deviation
斜视性弱视/斜視性弱視　strabismic amblyopia
斜视学/斜視[研究]學　strabismology
斜视眼/斜視眼　squinting eye
斜视眼针/斜視眼針　strabismus needle
斜视[治疗]手术/斜視手術　strabotomy
斜索/斜索　oblique cord
斜瞳孔/[歪]斜瞳孔　skew pupil
斜头/斜頭　oblique head
斜骰舟韧带/斜骰舟韌帶　oblique cuboideonavicular ligament
斜纹孔/斜紋孔　oblique pit
斜卧呼吸/斜臥呼吸,平臥呼吸　platypnea
斜卧菌素/斜臥菌素　decumbin
斜纤维/斜纖維　oblique fiber
斜线/斜線　oblique line
斜行截骨术/斜行截骨術　oblique osteotomy
斜形骨折/斜[形]骨折　oblique fracture
斜形头/斜形頭,斜頭畸形　plagiocephaly
斜掌侧腕掌韧带/斜掌側腕掌韌帶　oblique palmar carpometacarpal ligament
斜轴散光/斜性散光　oblique astigmatism
斜轴牙/斜軸牙　axisversion
斜蛛属/斜蛛屬,棕蜘蛛　*Loxosceles*
谐音癖/諧音癖　assonance
谐音联想/聲音聯想,音響聯想　clang association
携带者/攜帶者,帶菌者,帶原者　carrier
鞋匠痉挛/鞋匠痙攣　shoemaker spasm
鞋匠胸/鞋匠胸　cobbler chest
鞋皮肤炎/鞋皮膚炎　shoes dermatitis
鞋皮炎/鞋皮炎　shoe dermatitis
缬氨霉素/纈胺黴素　valinomycin
缬氨酸/纈胺酸　valine
缬氨酸 tRNA 连接酶/纈氨酸 tRNA 連接酶　valine-tRNA ligase
缬氨酸血/纈胺酸血　valinemia
泄剂/洩劑　purgative formula
泄精/洩精　seminal emission
泄泻[病]/洩瀉　diarrhea
泄泻·肝气郁结证/洩瀉·肝氣鬱結證　diarrhea with pattern of liver qi depression

泄泻·寒湿证/洩瀉·寒濕證　diarrhea with cold-damp pattern
泄泻·伤酒证/洩瀉·傷酒證　diarrhea with alcoholism pattern
泄泻·伤食证/洩瀉·傷食證　diarrhea with pattern of improper diet
泄泻·湿热[蕴结]证/洩瀉·濕熱[蘊結]證　diarrhea with pattern of accumulation and binding of damp-heat
泄泻·暑湿证/洩瀉·暑濕證　diarrhea with summerheat-damp pattern
泄泻·痰积证/洩瀉·痰積證　diarrhea with pattern of phlegm accumulation
泄殖道/洩殖道　urodeum
泄殖腔/洩殖腔　cloaca
泄殖腔存留/洩殖腔存留　persistent cloaca
泄殖腔管/洩殖腔管　cloacal duct
泄殖腔畸形/洩殖腔畸形　cloacal deformity
泄殖腔膜/洩殖腔膜　cloacal membrane
泻白散/瀉白散　xiebai powder
泻肺逐饮/瀉肺逐飲　eliminating pathogens from lung for expelling fluid retention
泻根属/瀉根屬,歐薯蕷屬　*Bryonia*
泻火解毒法/瀉火解毒法　purging fire and detoxifying
泻剂/瀉劑,腸刺激藥,瀉藥　intestinal stimulant
泻鼠李/瀉鼠李,洋鼠李　buckthorn berry
泻酸/[洩]瀉酸,瀉藥　cathartic acid
泻下不爽/瀉下不爽　non-smooth diarrhea
泻下剂/瀉下劑　formula for purgation
泻下逐水/瀉下逐水　expelling water retention with drastic purgative
泻药/瀉藥　cathartic, purgative, Cathartics
泻药性结肠/瀉藥性結腸　cathartic colon
谢-奥二氏病/謝-奥二氏病　Schlatter-Osgood disease
谢德胸廓成形术/謝德胸廓成形術　Schede thoracoplasty
谢尔曼-布尔坎单位/謝爾曼-布爾坎單位,謝-布二氏單位　Sherman-Bourquin unit
谢尔曼单位/謝爾曼單位,謝孟氏單位　Sherman unit
薤白/薤白　longstamen onion bulb
蟹睛/蟹睛　corneal perforation and iridoptosis, crab-eye
蟹睛·肝胆实热证/蟹睛·肝膽實熱證　crab-eye with pattern of liver-gallbladder excessive heat
蟹睛·阴虚火旺证/蟹睛·陰虛火旺證　crab-eye with

pattern of yin deficiency and fire effulgence
蟹足肿/蟹足腫 crab feet swelling, keloid
蟹足肿·瘀血阻络证/蟹足腫·瘀血阻絡證 crab feet swelling with pattern of static blood obstructing collateral
心/心[臟] heart, xin, CO15
心瓣刀/心瓣刀 cardiovalvulotome
心瓣膜/心瓣膜 cardiac valve
心瓣膜成形术/心瓣膜成形術, 心瓣膜整形術 cardiac valvuloplasty
[心]瓣膜动脉瘤/[心]瓣膜動脈瘤, 心瓣瘤 valvular aneurysm
心瓣炎/心瓣[膜]炎 cardiovalvulitis
心包/心包, 心囊 pericardium
心包壁层/心包壁層 parietal layer of pericardium, parietal pericardium
心包穿刺术/心包[放液]穿刺術 pericardiocentesis
心包缝术/心包縫[合]術 pericardiorrhaphy
心包膈动脉/心包膈動脈 pericardiacophrenic artery
心包膈静脉/心包膈靜脈 pericardiacophrenic vein
心包横窦/心包橫竇 transverse sinus of pericardium
心包后动脉/心包後動脈 posterior pericardiac artery
心包积脓/心包積膿, 心包蓄膿, 膿心包 empyema of pericardium, pyopericardium
心包积气/心包積氣 pneumopericardium
心包积水/心包積水 hydrocardia
心包积血/心包積血 hemopericardium
心包积液/心包積液, 心包滲液 hydropericardium, pericardial effusion
心包浆膜层/心包漿膜層, 漿液性心包 serous pericardium
心包静脉/心包靜脈 pericardial vein, pericardiac vein
心包镜检查/心包鏡檢查 pericardioscopy
心包叩击音/心包叩擊音, 心包膜敲擊聲 pericardial knock
心包络/心包[絡] pericardium
心包络病/心包絡病 pericardium disease
心包摩擦音/心包摩擦音 pericardial friction rub
心包囊肿/心包囊腫 pericardial cyst
心包憩室/心包憩室 pericardial diverticulum
心包前淋巴结/心包前淋巴結 prepericardial lymph node
心包腔/心包腔 pericardial cavity
心包腔内脾组织植入/心包腔內脾組織植入 pericardial splenosis
心包腔粘连/心[包腔]粘連, 心包黏塞 concretio cordis

心包切除术/心包切除術 pericardectomy
心包切开后综合征/心包[膜]切開後症候群 post-pericardiotomy syndrome
心包切开术/心包切開術 pericardiotomy
心包绒毛/心包絨毛 pericardial villus
心包松解术/心包鬆解術 pericardiolysis
心包填塞/心包填塞 pericardial tamponade
心包外侧及内侧炎/心包外側及內側炎 pericarditis externa et interna
心包外侧淋巴结/心包外側淋巴結 lateral pericardial lymph node
心包外全肺切除术/心包外全肺切除術 extrapericardial pneumonectomy
心包纤维层/心包纖維層, 纖維性心包 fibrous pericardium
心包斜窦/心包斜竇 oblique sinus of pericardium
心包心肌炎/心包心肌炎 perimyocarditis
心包胸膜/心包胸膜 pericardiac pleura
心包胸膜管/心包胸膜管 pericardiopleural canal
心包炎/心包炎 pericarditis
心包炎性假肝硬变/心包炎性假[肝]硬變 pericarditic pseudocirrhosis
心包液/心包液 liquor pericardii
心包杂音/心包雜音 pericardial murmur
心包脏层/心包臟層 visceral layer of pericardium, cardiac pericardium
心包造口[技]术/心包造口[技]術 pericardial window technique, pericardiostomy
心包粘连术/心包粘連術 pericardiosymphysis
心包震颤/心包膜震顫 pericardial fremitus
心包支/心包支 pericardial branch
心包肿瘤/心包腫瘤 pericardial tumor
心包周炎/心包周[膜]炎 peripericarditis
心包纵隔炎/心包縱隔炎 pericardiomediastinitis
心背系膜/心背繫膜, 背心繫膜 dorsal mesocardium
心痹/心痹 heart bi
心表面降温/心表面降溫 epicardial cooling
心病毒感染/心病毒感染 Cardiovirus infection
心病还需心药医/心病還需心藥醫 Worry is only cured by heartening news.
心[病]性咯血/心[病]性欬血, 心臟病性欬血 cardiac hemoptysis
心病性哮喘/心病性哮喘, 謝-史二氏氣喘, 心[因]性氣喘 cardiasthma, Cheyne-Stokes asthma
心搏[动]/心搏動, 心跳動 heart beat
心搏动脉间期/心[搏]動脈期間 cardioarterial interval
心搏快慢交替/心搏快慢交替, 緩急脈搏

bradytachycardia
心搏停止/心搏停止　asystolia
心搏骤停/心搏驟停　sudden cardiac arrest
心藏神/心藏神　heart storing spirit
心冲击描记器/心衝擊描記器,心臟射出容量描记器　ballistocardiograph
心冲击[描记]图/心衝擊[描記]圖,心臟排血容量描記圖,心臟射出容量描記圖　ballistocardiogram
心传导系/心傳導系　conduction system of heart
心传导系统/心搏調整結構　cardionector
心磁波描记器/心磁波描記器　magnetocardiograph
心丛/心叢　cardiac plexus
心大静脉/心大靜脈　great cardiac vein
心导管/心導管　cardiac catheter
心导管检查/心導管檢查,心臟導管插入術　cardiac catheterization
心底/心[臟基]底　cardiac base, base of heart
[心电传导]梯形图/梯形圖　ladder diagram
心电动力描记术/心電動力描記術,運動心電圖描記術　ergocardiography
心电动力图/心電動力圖,運動心電圖　ergocardiogram
心电描记器/心電描記器,心動電流描記器,心動電流機　electrocardiograph
心电描记术/心電描記術,心動電流描記法,心電圖測定　electrocardiography
心电图/心電圖,心動電流像,電心圖　electrocardiogram, ECG
心电图运动试验/心電圖運動試驗　ECG exercise test
心电向量描记术/心電[向]量描記術,向量心電描記術　vector cardiography
心电向量图/心電向量[描記]圖,向量心電圖　vector cardiogram
心电阻描记法/心電阻描記法,阻抗心動圖描記法　rheocardiography
心电阻图/心電阻圖,阻抗心動圖,心阻抗圖　rheocardiogram
心动冲击描记术/心動衝擊描記術,心臟射出容量描記法　ballistocardiography
心动过缓/心動過緩,心搏徐緩,緩慢性不整脈　bradyarrhythmia, bradycardia
心动过缓-过速综合征/心動過緩-過速症候群,慢快症候群　bradytachy arrhythmia syndrome
心动过缓-心动过速综合征/心動過緩-心動過速症候群,頻緩脈症候群　bradycardia-tachycardia syndrome
心动过速/心搏過速,心搏快速,心搏頻率過速　tachycardia
心动脉搏描记器/心動脈搏描記器　cardiosphygmograph
心动脉搏图/心動脈搏圖,心動脈搏描記波　cardiosphygmogram
心动脉瘤/心[臟]動脈瘤　cardiac aneurysm
心动脉球/心動脈球　bulbus arteriosus cordis
心动描记术/心動描記術,心動描記法　cardiography
心动调节结构假说/心搏調整結構假説　cardionector hypothesis
心动图/[胸前]心動圖　kinetocardiogram
心动心音脉搏描记器/心動心音脈搏描記器,心動脈搏計　sphygmocardioscope
心动压力图/心臟壓力描記波　piezocardiogram
心动抑制剂/心動抑制劑　cardioinhibitor
心动周期/心動週期　cardiac cycle
心动周期选择性显影机/心動週期選擇性顯影機　cardiocairograph
心段支气管/心段支氣管,心葉支氣管　cardiac bronchus
心恶/心惡　critical condition of heart
心恶热/心惡熱　heart being averse to heat
心耳/心耳　auricle of heart, atrial appendage
心耳凹/心耳凹　auricular depression
心烦/心煩　vexation
心房/心房　cardiac atrium, atrium
心房搏动/心房搏動　atrial beat
心房颤动/心房顫動,心房震顫　atrial fibrillation
心房触发型起搏/心房觸發型起搏　atrial triggered pacing
心房促钠排泄肽/心房促鈉排瀉肽,心房利尿鈉勝肽　atrial natriuretic peptide
心房反射/心房反射　atrial reflex
心房肥大/心房肥大　atrial hypertrophy
心房分离/心房分離,兩心房電傳導獨立　atrial dissociation
心房梗死/心房梗死,心房梗塞　atrial infarction
心房功能/心房功能　atrial function
心房过早除极/心房過早除極,心房早期去極化　atrial premature depolarization
心房肌球蛋白/心房肌球蛋白　atrial myosin
心房肌细胞/心房肌細胞　atrial myocardial cell
[心]房间隔/心房中隔　atrial septum
心房间沟/心房間沟　interatrial groove
心房利钠激素/心房利鈉激素　atrial natriuretic hormone
心房内传导阻滞/心房内傳導阻滯　intra-atrial block
心房内折返/心房内折返,心房内回路　intra-atrial

reentry
心房黏液瘤/心房黏液瘤　atrial myxoma
心房扑动/心房撲動　atrial flutter
心房期外收缩/心房早期收縮　atrial premature contraction
心房期外收缩综合征/心房期外收縮綜合徵,心房早期收縮複徵　atrial premature complex
心房[起搏]电极/心房[起搏]電極　atrial lead
心房特殊颗粒/心房特殊顆粒　specific atrial granule
心房停搏/心房停搏,心房停止　auricular arrest
心房同步心室起搏/心房同步心室起搏　atrial synchronous ventricular pacing
心房同步心室抑制型起搏/心房同步心室抑制型起搏　atrial synchronous ventricular inhibited pacing
心房吻合支/心房吻合支　atrial anastomotic branch
心房希氏束/心房希氏束[徑]　atriohisian tract
心房纤维性颤动/心房纖維[性]顫動　auricular fibrillation
心房心室连接不协调/心房心室連接不協調　atrioventricular discordant connection
心房性传导阻滞/心房性傳導阻滯,心房性傳導阻斷　auricular block
心房性心动过速/心房性心動過速,心房性心搏快速　auricular tachycardia
心房压/心房壓　atrial pressure
心房异步起搏/心房異步起搏,心房非同步起搏　atrial asynchronous pacing
心房异构/心房異構　atrial isomerism
心房抑制型起搏/心房抑制型起搏　atrial inhibited pacing
心房引流/心房引流　atrial drainage
心房早搏复合征/心房早搏複合徵　atrial premature complex
心房支/心房支　Rami atriales
心房中间支/心房中間支　intermediate branch of atrium
心房转位术/心房轉位術　atrial switch procedure
心肥大/心肥大,巨心　megacardia
心肺标本/心肺標本　heart-lung preparation
心肺分流术/心肺分流[術]　cardiopulmonary bypass
心肺复苏术/心肺復甦術　cardiopulmonary resuscitation
心肺机/心肺機　heartlung machine
心肺联合移植/心肺聯合移植　combined heart and lung transplantation
心肺面/心肺面　pulmonary surface of heart
心肺耐力/心肺耐力　cardiorespiratory capacity
心肺脑复苏/心肺腦復甦　cardiopulmonarycerebral resuscitation
心肺气虚/心肺氣虛　qi deficiency of heart and lung
心肺气虚证/心肺氣虛證　pattern of qi deficiency of heart and lung
心肺叶固定术/心肺固定術　cardiopneumonopexy
心肺移植/心肺移植　heart-lung transplantation
心肺运动描记器/心肺運動描記器　cardiopneumograph
心肺杂音/心肺雜音　cardiopulmonary murmur
心风/心風　heart disease caused by wind
心肝火旺/心肝火旺　exuberant fire of heart and liver
心肝火旺证/心肝火旺證　pattern of exuberant fire of heart and liver
心肝角/心肝角　cardiohepatic angle
心肝血虚/心肝血虛　heart-liver blood deficiency
心肝肿大/心肝腫大　cardiohepatomegaly
心疳/心疳　heart gan disease
心膈面/心膈面　diaphragmatic surface of heart
心功能不全/心機能不全　cardiac insufficiency
心冠后丛/心冠後叢　plexus coronarius cordis posterior
心冠前丛/心冠前叢　anterior coronary plexus of heart
心管/心管　cardiac tube
心过小/心過小,小心[畸形]　microcardia
心合小肠/心合小腸　heart being connected with small intestine
心坏死/心[臟]壞死　cardionecrosis
心慌/心慌,心悸　palpitation
心火炽盛证/心火熾盛證　blazing heart fire pattern
心火亢盛/心火亢盛　hyperactivity of heart fire
心火上炎/心火上炎　heart-fire flaring upward
心火上炎证/心火上炎證　pattern of heart-fire flaring upward
心肌/心肌　myocardium, cardiac muscle
心肌保护/心肌保護　myocardial preservation
心肌病/心肌病　cardiomyopathy
心肌成形术/心肌成形術　cardiomyoplasty
心肌挫伤/心肌挫傷　myocardial contusion
心肌冬眠/心肌冬眠　myocardial hibernation
心肌窦状隙/心肌[内]竇狀隙　myocardial sinusoid
心肌断裂/心肌斷裂　fragmentation of myocardium
心肌顿抑/心肌功能喪失　myocardial stunning
心肌缝合术/心肌縫合術　myocardiorrhaphy
心肌梗死/心肌梗死　myocardial infarction
心肌梗死后综合征/心肌梗死後症候群,心肌梗塞後症候群　postmyocardial infarction syndrome

心肌梗死块切除术/心肌梗死塊切除術　myocardial infarctectomy

心肌梗死形成/心梗塞形成　cardiac infarction

心肌工作能力/心肌工作能力　myocardial performance

心肌功能不全/心肌功能不全,心肌官能不全　myocardial insufficiency

心肌固定术/心肌固定術　cardiomyopexy

心肌灌注影像/心肌灌注影像　myocardial perfusion imaging

心肌肌球蛋白/心肌肌球蛋白　cardiac myosin

心肌疾病/心肌疾病　cardiomyopathy

心肌膜/心肌[膜],心肌层　myocardium

心肌[起搏]电极/心肌[起搏]電極　myocardial lead

心肌缺血/心肌[局部]缺血　myocardial ischemia

心肌缺血预处理/心肌缺血預處理　myocardial ischemic preconditioning

心肌收缩/心肌收縮　myocardial contraction

心肌收缩药/心肌收縮藥　cardiac inotropic drug

心肌衰竭/心肌衰竭　myocardial failure

心肌撕裂/心肌撕裂　myocardial laceration

心肌外膜网/心肌外膜網　myoepicardial reticulum

心肌外套层/心肌外套層　myoepicardial mentle

心肌细胞/心[臟]肌細胞　cardiac myocyte, myocardial cell, cardiac muscle cell

心肌纤维/心肌纖維　cardiac muscle fiber

心肌效率/心肌效率　myocardial efficiency

心肌心包炎/心肌心包炎　myopericarditis

心肌[心]内膜炎/心肌[心]內膜炎,心内膜肌炎　endomyocarditis

心肌心外包膜/心肌心外包膜　myoepicardial mantle

心肌性心动过缓/心肌性心動過緩,心肌性心搏徐緩　cardiomuscular bradycardia

心肌血管重建术/心肌血管重建術　myocardial revascularization

心肌炎/心肌炎　myocarditis

心肌炎病毒/心肌炎病毒　myocarditis virus

心肌抑郁/心肌抑鬱　myocardial depression

心肌抑制因子/心肌抑制因子,心肌抑制因數　myocardial depressant factor

心肌运动描记器/心肌運動描記器　myocardiograph

心肌运动[描记]图/心肌[運動描記]波　myocardiogram

心肌再灌注/心肌再灌注　myocardial reperfusion

心肌再灌注损伤/心肌再灌注損傷　myocardial reperfusion injury

心肌脂肪变性/心肌脂肪變性　cardiomyolipsis

心肌组织细胞/心組織細胞　cardiac histiocyte

心及小肠辨证/心及小腸辨證　pattern identification of heart and small intestine

心悸[病]/心悸,驚跳病　palmus, palpitation

心悸·肝肾阴虚证/心悸·肝腎陰虛證　palpitation with pattern of yin liver-kidney yin deficiency

心悸·脾肾阳虚证/心悸·脾腎陽虛證　palpitation with pattern of yang deficiency of spleen and kidney

心悸·水气凌心证/心悸·水氣凌心證　palpitation with pattern of water qi invading heart

心悸·痰火扰神证/心悸·痰火擾神證　palpitation with pattern of phlegm-fire disturbing spirit

心悸·痰浊阻滞证/心悸·痰濁阻滯證　palpitation with pattern of blockade of phlegm-turbidity

心悸·邪毒犯心证/心悸·邪毒犯心證　palpitation with pattern of pathogenic poison invading heart

心悸·心脾两虚证/心悸·心脾兩虛證　palpitation with pattern of heart-spleen deficiency

心悸·心气虚证/心悸·心氣虛證　palpitation with pattern of heart qi deficiency

心悸·心虚胆怯证/心悸·心虛膽怯證　palpitation with pattern of heart deficiency and timidity

心悸·心阳不振证/心悸·心陽不振證　palpitation with pattern of debilitated heart yang

心悸·血脉瘀阻证/心悸·血脈瘀阻證　palpitation with pattern of static blood blocking blood vessels

心悸·阴虚火旺证/心悸·陰虛火旺證　palpitation with pattern of exuberant fire due to yin deficiency

心悸·阴血不足证/心悸·陰血不足證　palpitation with pattern of yin blood insufficiency

心尖/心尖　cardiac apex

心尖搏动/心尖搏動　apex beat

心尖冲动/心尖衝動　apical impulse

心尖切迹/心尖切跡　cardiac apical incisure

心尖收缩期杂音/心尖收縮期雜音　apical systolic murmur

心尖舒张期杂音/心尖舒張期雜音　apical diastolic murmur

心尖四腔观/心尖四腔觀　apical four chamber view

心尖心动描记法/心尖搏動描記法　apexcardiography

心尖心动图/心尖跳動圖　apexcardiogram

心尖心肌梗死/心尖心肌梗死　apical myocardial infarction

心尖杂音/心尖雜音　apex murmur, apical murmur

心间隔/心間隔,心中隔　cardiac septum, heart septum

心间隔缺损/心間隔缺損　heart septal defect

心减压神经/心減壓神經　cardiac depressor nerve

心胶质/心膠質,心凍膠　cardiac jelly
心绞痛/心絞痛　angina cordis
心绞痛恐惧症/心絞痛恐懼症　anginophobia
心绞痛晕厥/心絞痛暈厥　syncope anginosa
心绞痛综合征/心絞痛症候群　anginal syndrome
心结缔织炎/心結締組織炎　ethmocarditis
心结节病/心結節病,心臟肉瘤病　cardiac sarcoidosis
心惊/心驚　convulsion due to heart disorder
心静脉/心靜脈　cardiac vein
心厥/心厥　heart syncope
心开窍于舌/心開竅於舌　heart opening at tongue
心理测定学/心理測定學　psychometrics
心理测验学家/心理測驗學家,心理測驗師　psychometrician
心理[测验]诊断术/心理[測驗]診斷術,心理診斷　psychodiagnosis
心理反应描记器/心理反應描記儀　psychergograph
心理规律学/心理規律學,心理律則學　psychonomy
心理过程/心理過程　mental process
心理活动测时法/心理活動測時法,心理活動速度测定法　psychodometry
心理活动测时器/心理活動測時器,心理活動速度計　psychodometer
心理机理/心理機理　mental mechanism
心理剧/心理劇,心理表演療法　psychodrama
心理疗法/心理療法　psychotherapy
心理流电皮反应/心理流電皮反應　psychogalvanic skin response
心理评定/心理評定　psychological evaluation
心理社会剥夺/心理社會剥奪,心理及社會意識低下　psychosocial deprivation
心理社会因素/心理社會因素　psychosocial factor
心理生理性障碍/心理生理性障礙　psychophysiologic disorder
心理生理学/精神生理學　psychophysiology
心理数学/心理數學　psychomathematics
心理性别/心理性別　psychological sex
心理性性功能障碍/心理性性功能障礙　psychological sexual dysfunction
心理学/心理學　psychology
心理学不应期/心理學不應期　psychological refractory period
心理学回馈/心理學回饋　psychological feedback
心理学技术/心理學技術　psychological technique
心理学家/心理學家　psychologist
心理学交谈/心理學交談　psychological interview
心理学模型/心理學模型　psychological model
心理学试验/心理學試驗　psychological test
心理学适应/心理性適應　psychological adaptation
心理学脱敏作用/心理學脱敏作用　psychologic desensitization
心理学应激/心理學應激　psychological stress
心理语言学/心理語言學　psycholinguistics
心理战/心理戰　psychological warfare
心理治疗过程/心理治療過程　psychotherapeutic process
心理咨询/心理諮詢　psychological counselling
心力不足/心力不足　hypodynamia cordis
心力贯注/精神貫注　cathexis
心力衰竭/心力衰竭,心臟衰竭　cardiac failure
心力衰竭性肺/心力衰竭性肺,心病性肺臟　cardiac lung
心裂[畸形]/心裂[畸形],雙心　diplocardia
心磷脂/心磷脂　cardiolipin
心灵感应/心靈感應,兩心感通,傳心術　telepathy
心律/心[節]律　cardiac rhythm
心律不齐/心律不齊,心律不整　arrhythmia cordis
心律失常/心率失常,無節律,節律不齊,心律不整　arrhythmia
心律失常性右心室发育不良/心律失常性右心室發育不良　arrhythmogenic right ventricular dysplasia
心率/心率　cardiac rate
心率计/心率計,心動數計　cardiotachometer
心率计录法/心率記錄法,心動數計法　cardiotachometry
心率心搏节律/心率心搏節律,心動節律　rhythm of heart
心乱/心亂　disturbing thought
心脉痹阻证/心脈痹阻證　pattern of blockade of heart vessel
心脉搏胸[运]动描记器/心脈搏胸[運]動描記器,全部搏動描記器　pansphygmograph
心脉通片/心脈通片　xinmaitong tablet
心-面-皮肤综合征/心-[顔]面-皮膚症候群　cardiofaciocutaneous syndrome
心钠素/心鈉素　atrial natriuretic factor
心钠素受体/心鈉素受體　atrial natriuretic factor receptor
心内膜/心內膜　endocardium
心内膜标测/心內膜標測　endocardial mapping
心内膜垫/心內膜墊　endocardial cushion
心内膜垫缺损/心內膜墊缺損　endocardial cushion defect
心内膜[起搏]电极/心內膜[起搏]電極　endocardial lead
心内膜切除术/心內膜切除術　endocardiectomy

心内膜弹力纤维增生症/心內膜纖維彈性組織增生症 endocardial fibroelastosis
心内膜下层/心內膜下層 subendocardial layer
心内膜下缺血/心內膜下[局部]缺血 subendocardial ischemia
心内膜下心肌梗死/心內膜下心肌梗死 subendocardial myocardial infarction
心内膜下支/心內膜下支 subendocardial branch
心内膜心包炎/心內膜心包炎 endopericarditis
心内膜心肌病/心內膜心肌病 endomyocardial disease
心内膜心肌活检[术]/心內膜心肌活檢[術] endomyocardial biopsy
心内膜心肌纤维化症/心內膜[心肌]纖維化症,心肌內膜心臟纖維化,心內膜纖維變性 endomyocardial fibrosis
心内膜炎/心內膜炎 endocarditis
心内膜硬化/心內膜硬化 endocardial sclerosis
心内膜杂音/心內雜音 endocardial murmur
心内血回收/心內血回收 cardiotomy blood return
心内血回收管路/心內血回收管路 cardiotomy return line
心内血回收滤器/心內血回收濾器 cardiotomy filter
心内血回收贮血器/心內血回收貯血器 cardiotomy reservoir
心内血栓形成/心血栓形成 cardiac thrombosis
心内注射/心內注射 intracardiac injection
心排血量/心排血量,心搏出量,心輸出量 cardiac output
心排血指数/心[臟]排血指數 cardiac index
心脾固定术/心脾固定術 cardiosplenopexy
心脾两虚/心脾兩虛 heart-spleen deficiency
心脾两虚证/心脾兩虛證 pattern of heart-spleen deficiency
心平气和/心平氣和,心神安寧 ataraxia
心气/心氣 heart qi
心气不定/心氣不定 instability of heart qi
心气不固/心氣不固 insecurity of heart qi
心气不宁/心氣不寧 restlessness of heart qi
心气不收/心氣不收 insecurity of heart qi
心气热/心氣熱 heart qi heat
心气实/心氣實 heart qi excess
心气虚/心氣虛 heart qi deficiency
心气虚血瘀证/心氣虛血瘀證 pattern of heart qi deficiency and blood stasis
心气虚证/心氣虛證 pattern of heart qi deficiency
心气血两虚证/心氣血兩虛證 pattern of heart qi-blood deficiency
心气阴两虚证/心氣陰兩虛證 pattern of heart qi-yin deficiency
心前丛/心前叢 anterior cardiac plexus
心前间隙积气/心前[間隙]積氣,心口積氣 pneumoprecordium
心前静脉/心前靜脈 anterior cardiac vein
心前区导联/心前區導聯,胸前導程,心前導程 precordial lead
心前区重击/心前重擊 precordial thump
[心]前室间沟/前室間溝 anterior interventricular groove
心浅丛/心淺叢 superficial cardiac plexus
心[腔]积气/心[腔積]氣 pneumatocardia
心腔内息肉/心臟息肉 cardiac polyp
心腔内异物/心腔内異物 foreign body in cardiac chamber
心腔狭窄/心腔狹窄 cardiac stenosis
心窍/心竅 tongue, window of the heart
心切迹/心切跡 cardiac notch
心情易变/心境易變 poikilothymia
心球/心球 bulbus cordis
心热/心熱 heart heat
心热病/心熱病 heart heat disease
心热证/心熱證 pattern of heart heat
心疝/心疝 hernia cordis
心善/心善 favorable condition of heart
心身疾病/心身疾病,身心症 psychosomatic disease
心身健康调查表/心身健康調查表 psychosomatic inventory
心身医学/心身醫學 psychosomatic medicine
心身障碍/心身障礙,精神身體障礙 psychosomatic disorder
心深丛/心深叢 deep cardiac plexus
心神/心神 heart mental activity
心神感知论/心神感知論 theory of heart governing mental activity
心神经节/心神經節 cardiac ganglion
心神经痛/心神經痛 cardiac neuralgia
心神内闭/心神内閉 pathogens shut in the heart
心肾不交/心腎不交 disharmony between heart and kidney, failure of the normal physiological coordination between the heart and kidney, non-interaction between the heart and kidney
心肾不交证/心腎不交證 pattern of disharmony between heart and kidney, pattern of failure of the normal physiological coordination between the heart and kidney
心肾相交/心腎相交 coordination between heart and

kidney, intercourse between heart and kidney
心肾阳虚证/心腎陽虛證 pattern of yang deficiency of heart and kidney
心肾阴虚证/心腎陰虛證 pattern of yin deficiency of heart and kidney
心实/心實 heart excess
心实证/心實證 pattern of excessive heart pathogens
心室/心室 cardiac ventricle
心室按需型起搏器/心室按需型起搏器 ventricular demand pacemaker
心室凹/心室[性]凹 ventricular depression
心室壁瘤/心室壁瘤,心室囊狀瘤 ventricular aneurysm
心室颤动/心室[纖維]顫動 ventricular fibrillation
心室充盈/心室充盈 ventricular filling
心室重复反应/心室重複反應 repetitive ventricular response
心室重构/心室重構 ventricular remodeling
心室触发型起搏/心室觸發型起搏 ventricular triggered pacing
心室发育不良/心室發育不良 ventricle dysplasia
心室肥大/心室肥大 ventricular hypertrophy
心室辅助装置/心室輔助裝置 ventricular assist device
心室复合体/心室複合體 ventricular complex
心室功能/心室功能 ventricular function
心室功能障碍/心室功能障礙 ventricular dysfunction
心室沟/心室溝 ventricular groove
心室过早去极化/心室早期去極化 premature ventricular depolarization
心室肌切开术/心室肌切開術 ventriculomyotomy
心室肌球蛋白/心室肌球蛋白 ventricular myosin
[心]室间隔/心室中隔 ventricular septum
心室间隔穿孔/心室間隔穿孔 perforation of ventricular septum
心室间隔缺陷/心室間隔缺陷 ventricular septal defect
心室间沟/心室間溝 interventricular groove
心室间前动脉/心室間前動脈,前室間動脈 anterior interventricular artery
心室减压术/心室減壓術 ventricular decompression
心室阶差/心室階差 ventricular gradient
心室静脉/心室靜脈 ventricular vein
心室劳损/心室勞損 ventricular strain
心室流出道/心室流出道 ventricular outflow tract
心室流入道/心室流入道 ventricular inflowing tract
心室坪/心室坪,脈波線之心室性高丘,心室岡 ventricular plateau
心室扑动/心室撲動 ventricular flutter
心室期前复合波/心室期前複合波,心室早期收縮 premature ventricular complex
心室[起搏]电极/心室[起搏]電極 ventricular lead
心室切开术/心室切開術 ventriculotomy
心室热绝缘/心室熱絕緣 ventricular heat insulation
心室神经节/心室神經節 ventricular ganglia
心室收缩/心室收縮 ventricular systole
心室收缩末期容积/心室收縮末期容積 end-systolic volume
[心室]舒张末期容量/心室舒張末期容積 end-diastolic volume
心室同步型起搏器/心室同步型起搏器 ventricular synchronized pacemaker
心室脱逸/心室脫逸 ventricular escape
心室性早期收缩/心室性早期收縮 ventricular premature beat
心室压/心室壓 ventricular pressure
心室异步起搏/心室異步起搏,心室非同步起搏 ventricular asynchronous pacing
心室抑制型起搏/心室抑制型起搏 ventricular inhibited pacing
心室优势/心室優勢,心室偏重 ventricular preponderance
心室早期复合波/心室早期複合波 ventricular premature complex
心室早期收缩/心室早期收縮 premature ventricular beat
心室造影照片/心室造影照片,心室 X 光像 ventriculogram
心室自动收缩/心室自動收縮 automatic ventricular contraction
心室自主心律/心室自主性節律 idioventricular rhythm
心收缩正常/心收縮正常 eusystole
心舒期/心舒[張]期 diastole
[心]舒期延长/[心]舒期延長,心舒張期延長 bradydiastole
心舒张后期/心舒張後期 diastasis cordis
心输出量/心輸出量,搏量 kinemia
心输出量过多/心輸出量過多,心搏量過多 hyperkinemia
心俞/心俞 xinshu, BL15
心衰细胞/心衰細胞 heart failure cell
心水/心水 heart edema
心忪/心忪 severe palpitation
心缩期/收縮期 systole

心跳呼吸停止/心肺停止　cardiopulmonary arrest
心痛/心[臟]痛　cardiodynia, heart pain
心痛·寒凝心脉证/心痛·寒凝心脈證　heart pain with pattern of yang deficiency and cold congelation
心痛·火邪热结证/心痛·火邪熱結證　heart pain with pattern of binding of heat and fire pathogen
心痛·气阴两虚证/心痛·氣陰兩虛證　heart pain with pattern of deficiency of both qi and yin
心痛·气滞心胸证/心痛·氣滯心胸證　heart pain with pattern of qi stagnating in chest
心痛·痰浊闭阻证/心痛·痰濁閉阻證　heart pain with pattern of blockade of phlegm-turbidity
心痛·心气虚证/心痛·心氣虛證　heart pain with pattern of heart qi deficiency
心痛·心阳虚证/心痛·心陽虛證　heart pain with pattern of heart yang deficiency
心痛·心阴虚证/心痛·心陰虛證　heart pain with pattern of heart yin deficiency
心痛·瘀血闭阻证/心痛·瘀血閉阻證　heart pain with pattern of blockade of static blood
心突出/心突出,心臟赫尼亞　cardiocele
心外膜/心外膜　epicardium
心外膜标测/心外膜標測　epicardial mapping
心外膜[起搏]电极/心外膜[起搏]電極　epicardial lead
心外膜切除术/心外膜切除術　epicardiectomy
心外膜松解术/心外膜鬆解術　epicardiolysis
心外杂音/心外雜音　exocardial murmur
心网膜固定术/心[臟]網膜固定術　cardio-omentopexy
心危象/心危象　cardiac crisis
心痿/心痿　heart flaccidity
心胃火燔/心胃火燔　exuberant fire of heart and stomach
心胃痛/心胃痛　heart and stomach pain
心涡/心渦　vortex of heart
心窝/心窩,前心凹　precordial depression
心无所依/心無所依　failure of disturbed mind to calm down
心系膜/心繫膜　mesocardium
心下悸/心下悸　epigastric throb
心下囊/心下[黏液]囊　infracardiac bursa
心下痞/心下痞　epigastric oppression
心下支结/心下支結　feeling obstructed in epigastrium
心纤维三角/心纖維三角　fibrous trigone of heart
心小静脉/心小靜脈　small cardiac vein
心小静脉血流/心小靜脈血流　thebesian flow

心心包固定术/心[臟]心包固定術　cardiopericardiopexy
心心包炎/心心包炎　cardiopericarditis
心兴奋剂/心興奮藥　cardiac stimulant
心兴奋药/心興奮藥,強心劑　cardiant
心性肝硬变/心性肝硬變,心臟性肝硬化　cardiocirrhosis
心胸横径指数/心胸橫徑指數　cardiothoracic index
心胸肋面/心胸肋面,心臟胸骨與肋骨面　sternocostal surface of heart
心虚/心虛　heart deficiency
心虚胆怯/心虛膽怯　timidity due to heart qi deficiency
心虚胆怯证/心虛膽怯證　pattern of timidity due to heart qi deficiency
心血/心血　heart blood
心血管病/心[臟]血管病　angiocardiopathy
心血管分流/心血管分流　cardiovascular shunt
心血管畸形/心血管畸形　cardiovascular abnormality
心血管疾病/心血管疾病　cardiovascular disease
心血管结核/心血管結核　cardiovascular tuberculosis
心血管梅毒/心血管梅毒,心臟血管性梅毒　cardiovascular syphilis
心血管模型/心血管模型　cardiovascular model
心血管去适应性/心血管去適應性　cardiovascular deconditioning
心血管妊娠并发症/心血管妊娠并發症　cardiovascular pregnancy complication
心血管神经衰弱/心血管神經衰弱　phrenocardia
心血管生理过程/心血管生理過程　cardiovascular physiologic process
心血管生理现象/心血管生理現象　cardiovascular physiologic phenomena
心血管生理学/心血管生理學　cardiovascular physiology
心血管外科手术/心血管外科手術　cardiovascular surgical procedure
心血管系统/心血管系統　cardiovascular system
心血管系统毒理学/心血管系統毒理學　cardiovascular toxicology
心血管性眩晕/心[臟]血管性眩暈　cardiovascular vertigo
心血管学/心[臟]血管學　cardioangiology
心血管药/心血管[系]藥　cardiovascular drug
心血管药物/心血管藥物　cardiovascular agent
心血管荧光电影照相术/心血管螢光電影照相術,心血管活動攝影術　cineangiocardiography
心血管造影术/心血管造影術,心血管X光顯影術

angiocardiography
心血管造影照片/心血管造影照片,心血管 X 光顯影片　angiocardiogram
心血管诊断技术/心血管診斷技術　cardiovascular diagnostic technique
心血失养/心血失養　failure of heart blood to nourish, malnutrition of heart blood
心血虚/心血虛　heart blood deficiency
心血虚证/心血虛證　pattern of heart blood deficiency
心血瘀阻/心血瘀阻　stagnant blockade of heart blood
心压迹/心壓跡　cardiac impression
心阳/心陽　heart yang
心阳暴脱证/心陽暴脫證　pattern of sudden collapse of heart yang
心阳不振/心陽不振　devitalization of heart yang
心阳虚/心陽虛　heart yang deficiency
心阳虚血瘀证/心陽虛血瘀證　pattern of heart yang deficiency and blood stasis
心阳虚证/心陽虛證　pattern of heart yang deficiency
心抑制药/心[臟]抑制藥　cardiac depressant
心[因]性呼吸困难/心因性呼吸困難　cardiac dyspnea
心因性痛经/心因性痛經,精神性痛經　psychogenic dysmenorrhea
心因性头痛/心因性頭痛　psychogenic headache
心阴/心陰　heart yin
心阴不足/心陰不足　insufficiency of heart yin
心阴虚/心陰虛　heart yin deficiency
心阴虚证/心陰虛證　pattern of heart yin deficiency
心阴阳两虚证/心陰陽兩虛證　pattern of heart yin-yang deficiency
心音/心音　the heart sound
心音导管检查法/心音導管檢查法,音導管檢查法　phonocatheterization
心音鉴定器/心音鑒定器,心音計　systolometer
心音描记器/心音描記器　phonocardiograph
心音描记术/心音描記術　phonocardiography
心音图/心音圖,心音[描记]像　phonocardiogram
心营过耗/心營過耗　over consumption of heart nutrient
心影/心[陰]影　heart shadow
心硬化/心硬化　cardiosclerosis
心右冠丛/心右冠叢　right coronary plexus of heart
心右缘/心右緣　right border of heart
心郁/心鬱　stagnation pattern of heart qi
心源性肝硬化/心源性肝硬化　cardiac cirrhosis

心源性水肿/心源性水腫,心因性水腫　cardiac dropsy
心源性哮喘/心源性哮喘,心[因]性氣喘,心病性哮喘　cardiac asthma, Cheyne-Stoke asthma
心源性哮喘综合征/心源性哮喘症候群,心病性哮喘症候群　cardiac asthma syndrome
心源性休克/心源性休克,心因性休克,心臟性休克　cardiogenic shock
心源性眩晕/心源性眩暈,心因性眩暈　cardiac vertigo
心[脏]/心[臟]　heart
心脏按摩/心臟按摩　cardiac massage
心脏按压/心臟按壓　cardiac compression
心脏瓣膜/心臟瓣膜　heart valve
心脏瓣膜疾病/心臟瓣膜疾病　heart valve disease
心脏瓣膜假体植入/心臟瓣膜假體植入　heart valve prosthesis implantation
心[脏]瓣膜破裂/心[臟]瓣膜破裂　cardiac valve rupture
心脏瓣膜脱垂/心臟瓣膜脫垂　heart valve prolapse
心[脏]瓣膜置换术/心[臟]瓣膜置換術　cardiac valve replacement
心脏病/心臟病　cardiac disease
心脏病患者/心臟病患者　cardiopath
心脏病恐惧症/心臟病恐懼症,心病恐怖　cardiophobia
心脏病疗法/心臟病療法　cardiotherapy
心脏病学/心臟病學　cardiology
心脏病医疗设施/心臟病醫療設施　cardiac care facility
心脏病饮食/心臟病飲食　cardiac diet
心脏超声造影[术]/心臟超聲造影[術]　contrast echocardiography
心脏成肌细胞/心臟成肌細胞　cardiac myoblast
心脏冲动/心臟衝動,心搏動　cardiac impulse
心脏除颤/心臟除顫,去心房纖維顫動,去心室纖維顫動　defibrillation
心脏储备力/心臟儲備力,心餘力　cardiac reserve
心脏穿刺术/心臟穿刺術　cardiocentesis
心脏传导系统/心臟傳導系統　heart conduction system
心脏传导阻滞/心臟傳導阻滯　heart block
心脏导管插入术/心臟導管插入術　heart catheterization
心脏电机械分离/心臟電機械分離　cardiac electromechanical dissociation
心脏电生理学技术/心臟電生理學技術　cardiac electrophysiologic technique

心脏动力学/心臟動力學　cardiodynamics
心脏发生/心臟發育,心臟發生　cardiogenesis
心脏房室沟/心臟房室溝　atrioventricular groove
心脏肥大/心臟肥大　hypertrophy of heart
心脏辅助装置/心臟輔助裝置　heart-assist device
心脏复律/心律轉變法,復律法　cardioversion
心脏功能/心臟功能　cardiac function
心脏功能试验/心臟功能試驗　heart function test
心脏黑变/心臟黑[病]變　cardiomelanosis
心脏呼吸[的]/心臟[與]呼吸的　cardiorespiratory
心脏激素/心臟激素,心內泌素　cardiac hormone
心脏疾病/心臟疾病　heart disease
心脏甲状腺中毒病/心臟甲狀腺中毒病　cardiothyrotoxicosis
心脏交替/心臟交替,心臟脈搏強弱交替現象　alternans of the heart
心脏窘迫不适/心臟窘迫不適　cardiac distress
心脏扩大/心臟擴大　cardiac dilatation
心脏扩张/心[臟]擴張　dilatation of heart
心脏黏液瘤/心臟黏液瘤　cardiac myxoma
心脏破裂/心臟破裂　cardiorrhexis
心脏起搏/心臟起搏[法]　cardiac pacing
心脏切开术后心包炎/心臟切開術後心包炎　postcardiotomy pericarditis
心脏切开术后综合征/心臟切開術後症候群　postcardiotomy syndrome
心脏容量/心臟容量,心容積　cardiac volume
心脏乳头状弹力纤维瘤/心臟乳頭狀彈力纖維瘤　papillary fibroelastoma of heart
心脏神经/心臟神經,內臟神經　cardiac nerve, splanchnic nerve
心脏室壁瘤/心臟室壁瘤　heart aneurysm
心脏收缩期卡嗒音/心臟收縮期卡嗒音　systolic clicking sound
心脏收缩中期喀喇音/心臟收縮中期喀喇音　mid-systolic click
心脏手术/心臟手術　heart surgery
心脏损伤/心臟損傷　heart injury
心脏听诊/心臟聽診　heart auscultation
心脏停搏/心臟停搏　heart arrest
心脏停搏[法]/心臟麻痺　cardioplegia
心脏停搏液/心臟停搏液　cardioplegic solution
心脏外科手术/心臟外科手術　cardiac surgical procedure
心脏外形/心臟外形　cardiac outline
心脏萎缩/心臟萎縮　cardiac atrophy
心脏细菌感染/心臟細菌感染　cardiobacterium infection
心脏下垂/心臟下垂　cardioptosis
心脏纤维支架/心臟纖維支架　fibrous skeleton of heart
心脏线粒体/心臟線粒體　heart mitochondria
心脏性猝死/心臟性猝死　sudden cardiac death
心脏胸骨肋骨面/心臟胸骨肋骨面　sternocostal surface of heart
心脏旋转不良/心臟旋轉不良　malrotation of heart
心[脏]炎/心[臟]炎　carditis
心脏移植/心臟移植　heart transplantation
心脏异位/心[臟]異位,異位心　ectopia cordis
心脏右面/心[臟]右面　right surface of heart
心脏运动描记术/胸前心動描記術　kinetocardiography
心脏杂音/心[臟]雜音　cardiac murmur
心脏支持泵/心臟支持泵,心臟支持幫浦　cardiopulmonary support pump
心脏肿瘤/心臟腫瘤　cardiac tumor
心脏左冠状动脉/心臟左冠狀動脈　left coronary artery of heart
心脏做功指数/心臟做功指數　cardiac work index
心振动[描记]图/心振動[描記]圖,心音振動描記圖　vibrocardiogram
心振动心音描记器/心振動心音描記器,心音振動描記器　vibrophonocardiograph
心震描记法/心震描記法,心臟振動描記法　seismocardiography
心震图/心震圖,心臟振動描記　seismocardiogram
心志喜/心志喜　heart being associated with joy
心智/心智　mind
心智不全/心智不全　mental defective
心中懊恢/心中懊憹,胃灼熱　heartburn
心中懊恼/心中懊惱　vexation
心中憺憺大动/心中憺憺大動　empty sensation in heart, violent palpitation
心中静脉/心中靜脈　middle cardiac vein
心中神经/心中神經,中側心神經　middle cardiac nerve
心主神明/心主神明　heart governing mental activity
心主神明论/心主神明論　theory of heart governing mental activity
心主血脉/心主血脈　heart governing blood and vessels
心浊音区测定法/心[臟]濁音區測定法　cardiotopometry
心最小静脉/心最小靜脈　smallest cardiac vein
心最小静脉孔/[心最]小靜脈孔　foramina venarum minimarum

心最小静脉循环/心最小静脈循環,提比西恩氏循環 Thebesian circulation
芯片分析技术/芯片分析技術,晶片分析技術 microchip analytical procedure
辛/辛 pungent
辛胺醇/辛胺醇 heptaminol
辛醇类/辛醇類 octanols
辛德比斯病毒/辛德比斯病毒,Sindbis 病毒 Sindbis virus
辛德毕斯病/辛德畢斯病 Sindbis disease
辛二酸/辛二酸,軟木酸 suberic acid
辛伐他汀/斯伐他汀 simvastatin
辛寒生津/辛寒生津,辛寒解表 promoting the production of body fluid with drugs of pungent taste and cold nature
辛卡利特/辛卡利特 sincalide
辛可卡因/辛可卡因 cinchocaine
辛辣食物/辛辣食物 spicy food
辛凉解表/辛涼解表 resolving exterior pattern with pungent and cool natured drugs, dispelling the evil in the superficies with drugs of pungent taste and cool nature
辛凉解表剂/辛涼解表劑 formula for relieving exterior pattern with pungent and cool natured drugs
辛凉清热/辛涼清熱 clearing heat with pungent and cool-natured drugs
辛那色林/辛那色林 Cinanserin
辛普森夹/辛普森夾,Simpson 氏夾板 Simpson splint
辛酸/辛酸 caprylic acid
辛酸鲸蜡酯/辛酸鯨蠟酯 cetyl caprilate
辛酸钠/辛酸鈉 sodium caprylate
辛酸盐/辛酸鹽 caprylate
辛糖/辛糖 octose
辛脱克桂皮/辛托克桂皮,東印度類桂皮 sintoc
辛烷类/辛烷類 octanes
辛温解表/辛溫解表 relieving exterior pattern with pungent and warm natured drugs, dispelling the evil in the superficies with drugs of pungent taste and warm nature
辛温解表剂/辛溫解表劑 formula for relieving exterior pattern with pungent and warm natured drugs
辛温开窍/辛溫開竅 resuscitation with pungent and warm natured drugs
辛夷/辛夷 biond magnolia flower-bud
欣顿试验/欣頓試驗,希頓氏試驗 Hinton test
欣快/欣快 euphoria
欣快剂/欣快藥 euphoriant
锌/鋅 zinc
锌放射性同位素/鋅放射性同位素 zinc radioisotope
锌化合物/鋅化合物 zinc compound
锌绞痛/鋅絞痛 zinc colic
锌明胶/鋅明膠 zinc gelatin
锌缺乏综合征/鋅缺乏症候群 zinc deficiency syndrome
锌同位素/鋅同位素 zinc isotope
锌铜电池/鋅銅電池 zinc-copper cell
锌皂/鋅皂 zinc soap
锌指/鋅指 zinc finger
锌指蛋白/鋅指蛋白 zinc finger protein
锌中毒性寒战/鋅中毒性寒戰,鋅匠熱,金屬蒸煙熱 spelter chill
新产后/新產後 new postpartum
新城疫/新城雞瘟 Newcastle disease
新城疫病毒/新城雞瘟病病毒 Newcastle disease virus
新出现传染病/新出現傳染病 emerging communicable disease
新达尔文主义/新達爾文主義 neodarwinism
新大陆沙粒病毒/新大陸沙粒病毒 New World Arenavirus
新蝶呤/新喋呤 neopterin
新杆状线虫/新桿狀線蟲 caenorhabditis
新感/新感 new affection
新感春温/新感春溫 newly contracted spring warmth
新感温病/新感溫病 newly contracted warm disease
新骨折/新骨折 fresh fracture
新黄酮类/新黃酮類 neoflavonoids
新吉密春/新吉密春 neogermitrine
新几内亚震颤病/新幾內亞震顫病,庫魯病 kuru
新加坡耳/新加坡耳,耳黴菌病 Singapore ear
新结核菌素/新結核菌素 new tuberculin
新九分法/新九分法 modified rule of nine
新抗原/新抗原 neoantigen
新苦楝素/新苦楝素 neoquassin
新郎病/新郎病 bridegrooms disease
新立克次体属/新立克次體屬,里氏新立克次體屬 *Neorickettsia*
新霉素/新黴素 neomycin
新霉素 B/新黴素 B framycetin
新木脂体/新木脂素 neolignan
新脑/新腦 neencephalon
新皮层/新外表 neopallium

新皮质/新[脑]皮质　neocortex, neopallium
[新皮质]多形[细胞]层/[新皮質]多形[細胞]層　polymorphic layer of neocortex
新皮质分子层/新皮質分子層　molecular layer of neocortex
新皮质内颗粒层/新皮質內顆粒層　internal granular layer of neocortex
新皮质内锥体[细胞]层/新皮質內錐體[細胞]層　internal pyramidal layer of neocortex
新皮质外颗粒层/新皮質外顆粒層　external granular layer of neocortex
新皮质外锥体[细胞]层/新皮質外錐體[細胞]層　external pyramidal layer of neocortex
新品红/新複紅　isorubin
新清宁片/新清寧片　xinqingning tablets
新丘脑/新丘腦,丘腦新成部　neothalamus
新生/新生　neogenesis
新生动物/新生動物　newborn animals
新生儿/新生兒　neonatus
新生儿白化病/新生兒白化病　neonatal albinism
新生儿败血症/新生兒敗血症　septicemia of the newborn
新生儿暴发性紫癜/新生兒猛爆性紫瘢病　neonatal purpura fulminans
新生儿剥落性皮炎/新生兒剥落性皮膚炎　dermatitis exfoliativa neonatorum
新生儿剥脱性皮炎/新生兒剝脫性皮炎　exfoliative dermatitis of the newborn
新生儿层状脱屑/新生兒層狀[魚鱗癬]脫屑　lamellar desquamation of the newborn
新生儿肠病性肢端皮炎/新生兒腸病性肢端皮膚炎　neonatal acrodermatitis enteropathica
新生儿出血性疾病/新生兒出血性疾病　haemorrhagic disease of the newborn
新生儿痤疮/新生兒痤瘡　acne neonatorum
新生儿大脑白质退化症/新生兒大腦白質退化症　neonatal adrenoleukodystrophy
新生儿单纯疱疹/新生兒單純疱疹　neonatal herpes simplex
新生儿低血钙/新生兒低血鈣　hypocalcemia of newborn
新生儿低血糖/新生兒低血糖　hypoglycemia of newborn
新生儿肺出血/新生兒肺出血　pulmonary hemorrhage of the newborn
新生儿肺透明膜病/新生兒肺透明膜病　hyaline membrane disease of the newborn
新生儿肺炎/新生兒肺炎　neonatal pneumonia
新生儿肺炎病毒/新生兒肺炎病毒　newborn pneumonitis virus
新生儿肺炎·肺热血瘀证/新生兒肺炎·肺熱血瘀證　neonatal pneumonia with pattern of lung heat and blood stasis
新生儿肺炎·风寒袭肺证/新生兒肺炎·風寒襲肺證　neonatal pneumonia with pattern of wind-cold invading lung
新生儿肺炎·风热犯肺证/新生兒肺炎·風熱犯肺證　neonatal pneumonia with pattern of wind-heat invading lung
新生儿肝炎综合征/新生兒肝炎症候群　neonatal hepatitis syndrome
新生儿高胆红素血症/新生兒高膽色素血症　neonatal hyperbilirubinemia
新生儿红斑/新生兒紅斑　erythema neonatorum
新生儿红斑狼疮/新生兒紅斑狼瘡　neonatal lupus erythematosus
新生儿红细胞增多症/新生兒紅細胞增多症　polycythemia of the newborn
新生儿呼吸窘迫综合征/新生兒呼吸窘迫症候群　newborn respiratory distress syndrome
新生儿呼吸暂停/新生兒呼吸暫停　apnea of the newborn
新生儿护理/新生兒護理　neonatal nursing
新生儿坏死性小肠结肠炎/新生兒壞死性小腸結腸炎　necrotizing enterocolitis of the newborn
新生儿黄疸/新生兒黃疸　icterus neonatorum
新生儿肌无力/新生兒肌無力　neonatal myasthenia
新生儿甲状腺功能亢进症/新生兒甲狀腺功能亢進症　neonatal hyperthyroidism
新生儿假月经/新生兒假月經　pseudomenstruation of the newborn
新生儿惊撅/新生兒驚撅　convulsion of the newborn
新生儿咖啡牛奶斑/新生兒咖啡牛奶斑　neonatal cafe au lait spot
新生儿卡介苗接种率/新生兒卡介苗接種率　newborn BCG vaccination rate
新生儿泪囊炎/新生兒淚囊炎　neonatal dacryocystitis
新生儿颅内出血/新生兒顱內出血　intracranial hemorrhage of the newborn
新生儿脑炎/新生兒腦炎　encephalitis neonatorum
新生儿尿布皮炎/新生兒尿布皮膚炎　neonatal diaper dermatitis
新生儿脓疱病/新生兒膿疱病　impetigo neonatorum
新生儿皮肤附属器息肉/新生兒皮膚附屬器息肉　adnexal polyp of neonatal skin

新生儿皮下坏疽/新生兒皮下壞疽 neonatal subcutaneous gangrene
新生儿皮下脂肪坏死/新生兒皮下脂肪壞死症 adiponecrosis subcutanea neonatorum
新生儿贫血/新生兒貧血 neonatal anemia
新生儿破伤风/新生兒破傷風,臍風 tetanus neonatorum
新生儿期/新生兒期 neonatal stage
新生儿缺氧/新生兒缺氧症 anoxia neonatorum
新生儿溶血病/新生兒溶血病 haemolytic disease of the newborn, hemolytic disease of newborn
新生儿溶血性贫血/新生兒溶血性貧血 hemolytic anemia of newborn
新生儿乳房增大/新生兒乳房增大 enlargement of breast in the newborn
新生儿乳腺炎/新生兒乳腺炎 mastitis neonatorum
新生儿腮腺炎/新生兒腮腺炎 parotitis neonatorum
新生儿筛查/新生兒篩查 neonatal screening
新生儿生理性脱皮/新生兒生理性脱皮 physiological scaling of the newborn
新生儿湿肺/新生兒濕肺 wet lung of the newborn
新生儿水疱性表皮松解症/新生兒水皰性表皮鬆解症 neonatal epidermolysis bullosa
新生儿水肿/新生兒水腫 edema neonatorum
新生儿胎记/新生兒胎記 neonatal birthmark
新生儿糖尿病/新生兒糖尿病 neonatal diabetes mellitus
新生儿特发性呼吸窘迫/新生兒特發性呼吸窘迫,新生兒自發性呼吸困難 idiopathic respiratory distress of the newborn
新生儿天疱疮/新生兒天皰瘡 pemphigus neonatorum
新生儿脱瘾综合征/新生兒脱癮症候群,新生兒禁戒症候群 neonatal abstinence syndrome
新生儿吸入综合征/新生兒吸入症候群 aspiration syndrome of the newborn
新生儿先天性毛细血管扩张性大理石样皮肤/新生兒先天性微血管擴張性大理石狀皮斑 neonatal cutis marmorata telangiectatica congenita
新生儿先天性皮肤成形不全/新生兒先天性皮膚成形不全 neonatal aplasia cutis congenita
新生儿行为评分/新生兒行爲評分 neonatal behavioral assessment scale
新生儿学/新生兒學 neonatology
新生儿学家/新生兒學家 neonatologist
新生儿咽血综合征/新生兒嚥血症候群 swallowed blood syndrome of the newborn
新生儿眼炎/新生兒眼炎,新生兒眼膿溢 ophthalmia neonatorum
新生儿异位性皮炎/新生兒異位性皮膚炎 neonatal atopic dermatitis
新生儿硬化病/新生兒硬化病 sclerema neonatorum
新生儿硬脑膜下出血/新生兒硬腦膜下出血 neonatal subdural hemorrhage
新生儿硬皮病/新生兒硬皮病 scleroderma neonatorum
新生儿硬皮症/新生兒硬皮症 sclerema neonatorum
新生儿硬肿病/新生兒硬腫病 scleredema neonatorum
新生儿硬肿病·寒凝血瘀证/新生兒硬腫病·寒凝血瘀證 scleredema neonatorum of cold congelation and blood stasis
新生儿硬肿病·阳气虚衰证/新生兒硬腫病·陽氣虚衰證 scleredema neonatorum of yang qi exhaustion
新生儿暂时性脓疱病/暫時性新生兒膿皰症 transient neonatal pustulosis
新生儿暂时性脓疱性黑变病/新生兒暫時性膿皰性黑變病 transient neonatal pustular melanosis
新生儿暂时性萎缩性红斑/新生兒暫時性萎縮性紅斑 erythema atrophicans transient neonatorum
新生儿枕部脱发/新生兒枕部秃髮 neonatal occipital alopecia
新生儿窒息/新生兒窒息 asphyxia neonatorum
新生儿中毒性红斑/新生兒毒性紅斑 erythema toxicum neonatorum
新生儿重黄疸/新生兒重症黄疸 icterus gravis neonatorum
新生儿重症肌无力/新生兒重症肌無力 neonatal myasthenia gravis
新生儿重症监护/新生兒重症監護 neonatal intensive care
新生儿重症监护病房/新生兒重症監護病房 neonatal intensive care units
新生儿重症监护治疗病房/新生兒重症監護治療病房 neonatal intensive care unit
新生儿紫癜/新生兒紫癜病 purpura of newborn, purpura neonatorum
新生霉素/新生黴素 Novobiocin
新生期耐受[性]/新生期耐受[性] neonatal tolerance
新生物/新生物,贅生物 neoplasm
新生线/新生線 neonatal line
新生血管性青光眼/新生血管性青光眼 neovascular glaucoma
新生易位/新生易位 de novo translocation

新生婴儿/新生嬰兒　newborn infant
新生运动单位动作电位/新生運動單位動作電位　nascent motor unit action potential
新斯的明/新斯的明,新斯弟格明　Neostigmine
新钍/新釷　mesothorium
新脱位/新[鲜]脱位　recent dislocation
新纹状体/新紋狀體　neostriatum
新希波克拉提斯派医学/新希波克拉提斯派醫學　neo hippocratic medicine
新鲜骨折/新[鲜]骨折　fresh fracture
新鲜气流/新鮮氣流　fresh gas flow
新小脑/新小腦　neocerebellum
新小脑发育不全/新小腦發育不全　neocerebellar agenesis
新形体形成/新[形體]形成　neomorphism
新修本草/新修本草　Newly Revised Materia Medica
新药/新藥　new drugs
新药申请/新藥申請　new drug application
新翳/新翳　new nebula
新语/新語[症],新句　neologism
新月/新月,半月　demilune
新月体/新月形　crescent
新月体肾小球肾炎/新月形腎絲球腎炎　crescentic glomerulonephritis
新月细胞/新月形細胞　crescent cell
新针灸学/新針灸學　new acupuncture and moxibustion
囟会/囟會　xinhui, DU22
囟[门]/囟[門]　fontanel, fontanelle
囟门不合/囟門不合　failure of closure of fontanel
囟门高突/囟門高突　bulging fontanel, bulging fontanel in infant
囟门紧张/囟門緊張　tense fontanel
囟门宽大/囟門寬大　widened fontanel
囟门下陷/囟門下陷　sunken fontanel, sunken fontanel in infant
囟门早闭/囟門早閉　premature closure of fontanel
信号处理/信號處理,訊號處理　signal processing
信号传导/信號傳導　signal transduction
信号检测/信號檢測　signal detection
信号平均值/信號平均[化]　signal averaging
信号识别颗粒/信號識別顆粒　signal recognition particle
信号转导衔接蛋白质类/信號轉導銜接蛋白質類　signal transducing adaptor proteins
信使RNA/信使RNA,資訊核糖核酸　messenger RNA
信息交流媒体/信息交流媒體,資訊交流媒體　communication media
信息交流障碍/信息交流障礙,資訊交流障礙　communication barrier
信息素类/信息素類,資訊素類　pheromone
信息素受体/信息素受體,資訊素受體　pheromone receptor
信仰疗法/信仰療法,信心療法　faith healing
兴奋/興奮　stimulation
兴奋波/興奮波　excitation wave
兴奋反射性神经/刺激反射性神經　excitoreflex nerve
兴奋分泌性神经/刺激分泌性神經　excitosecretory nerve
兴奋过度/興奮過度　hypererethism
兴奋剂/興奮劑,促效劑,作用劑　agonist, stimulant
兴奋扩散/興奮擴散,興奮照射　irradiation of excitation
兴奋留迹/興奮留跡　engraphia
兴奋收缩耦联/興奮收縮耦聯,興奮收縮配合　excitation-contraction coupling
兴奋物质/興奮物質　excitatory substance
兴奋性氨基酸激动剂/興奮性氨基酸激動劑　excitatory amino acid agonist
兴奋性氨基酸拮抗剂/興奮性氨基酸拮抗劑　excitatory amino acid antagonist
兴奋性氨基酸类/興奮性氨基酸類　excitatory amino acids
兴奋性氨基酸药/興奮性氨基酸藥　excitatory amino acid agent
兴奋[性]缺失/興奮缺失,興奮性不足　anerethisia
兴奋性突触/興奮性突觸　excitatory synapse
兴奋性突触后电位/興奮性突觸後電位　excitatory postsynaptic potential
兴奋性休克/興奮性休克　erethismic shock
兴奋状态/激動狀態　affective state
兴奋[作用]/興奮[作用],刺激作用　stimulation
星点/星點　asterion
星球腔/星球腔　astrocoele
星群视野计/星群視野計　multiple stars perimeter
星图/星圖　star graph
星网层/星網層,星狀網　stellate reticulum
星细胞/星細胞　star cell
星形孢菌素/星形孢菌素　staurosporin
星形玻璃体炎/星狀玻璃體炎　asteroid hyalitis
星形骨折/星狀骨折　stellate fracture
星形胶质细胞/星形膠質細胞　astrocyte
星形母细胞瘤/星[形]母細胞瘤　astroblastoma
星形上皮网状细胞/星形上皮網狀細胞　stellate

epithelial reticular cell
星形神经胶质/星形神經膠質 astroglia
星形网/星狀網 stellate reticulum
星形细胞/星形細胞,星狀細胞 stellate cell, astrocyte
星形细胞瘤/星形細胞瘤,星狀神經膠質瘤 astrocytic glioma
星形细胞突破折/星形細胞突破折,星細胞突碎裂 clasmatodendrosis
星形细胞增生/星形細胞增生,星形细胞增多症 astrocytosis
星翳/星翳 star nebula
星状包涵体/星狀包涵體 asteroid inclusion body
星状绷带/星狀繃帶 stellate bandage
星状病毒科感染/星狀病毒科感染 Astroviridae infection
星状静脉/星狀靜脈 stellate vein
星状磷酸盐/星狀磷酸鹽 stellar phosphate
星状毛/星狀毛 stellate hair
星状韧带/星狀韌帶 stellate ligament
星状神经节/星狀神經節 stellate ganglion
星状神经节切除术/星狀神經節切除術 stellate ganglionectomy
星状神经节阻断/星狀神經節阻斷 stellate block
星状神经节阻滞术/星狀神經節阻滯術 stellate ganglion block
星状细胞合体/星狀細胞合體 gliarase
星状小静脉/星狀小靜脈 stellate venule
星状小体/星狀體 asteroid body
猩红/猩紅 scarlet
猩红热/猩紅熱 scarlatina
猩红热滑膜炎/猩紅熱滑膜炎 scarlatinal synovitis
猩红热肾炎/猩紅熱腎炎 scarlatinal nephritis
猩红热心肌炎/猩紅熱心肌炎 scarlatinal myocarditis
猩红热性关节炎/猩紅熱性關節炎 scarlatinal arthritis
猩红热性咽峡炎/猩紅熱咽峽炎 angina scarlatinosa
猩红热样风疹/猩紅熱樣風疹 rubeola scarlatina
猩红热样红斑/猩紅熱樣紅斑 scarlatiniform erythema
猩红色/猩紅色 scarlet
猩猩科/猩猩科 Pongidae
行痹/行痹,風痹 migratory bi, arthralgia caused by wind pathogen, migratory arthralgia
行迟/行遲 retardation in walking
行动/行動 action
行动障碍/移動障礙 motility disorder

行间/行間 xingjian, LR2
行经/行經 menstruating
行经畸胎/行經性畸胎 emmenic monster
行军骨折/行軍骨折 march fracture
行军性血红蛋白尿症/行軍性血紅蛋白尿症,行軍性血紅素尿 march hemoglobinuria
行军足/行軍足 march foot
行气剂/行氣劑 formula for activating qi flowing
行气降逆/行氣降逆 activating qi for lowering adverse qi
行为/行爲 act
行为不良/犯罪行爲 delinquency
行为毒理学/行爲毒理學 behavioral toxicology
行为精神病学/行爲精神病學 orthopsychiatry
行为纠正疗法/行爲糾正療法 implosive therapy
行为科学/行爲科學 behavioral science
行为疗法/行爲療法 behavior therapy
行为模式/行爲模式,行爲範型 behavior pattern
行为失检/行爲失檢,動作失宜,舉動失當 misaction
行为听力图/行爲聽力圖 behavioral audiogram
行为学家/行爲學家 ethologist
行为研究/行爲研究 behavioral research
行为医学/行爲醫學 behavioral medicine
行为遗传学/行爲遺傳學 behavioral genetics
行为异常/行爲異常 dystropy
行为障碍/行爲障礙 behavior disorder
行为症状/行爲症狀 behavioral symptom
行为支配/行爲支配 behavior control
行针/行針 manipulating needle
行针手法/行針手法 needling manipulation
行走前运动/行走前運動,早期行動 prelocomotion
T形绷带/T形繃帶,T形環帶 T-band matrix
形成/形成 formation
形成层/形成層 cambium
形成性硬结/成形性硬結 plastic induration
J形钩/J形鉤 J hook
T形夹/T形夾 T splint
形觉/形覺,立體覺 form sense
形觉剥夺性弱视/形覺剝奪性弱視 form deprivation amblyopia
形觉检查[法]/形覺檢查[法] examination of form sense
形神合一/形神合一 unity of physique and spirit
形式/形式 form
形视野/形視野 form visual field
形态/形態 appearance
形态测定法/形態測定法 morphometry

形态成分/形態成分,形態要素　morphological element
形态发生/形態發生　morphogenesis
形态发生场/形態發生場,形態演發場　morphogenetic field
形态发生梯度/形態發生梯度,形態演發梯度　morphogenetic gradient
形态分化/形態分化　morphodifferentiation
形态渐失/形態漸失　apeidosis
形态生成区/形態生成區　morphogenetic field
形态生长型/形態生長型　morphogenetic pattern
形态特征/形態特徵　morphological characteristic
形态物理学/形態物理學　morphophysics
形态相似/形態相似　plesiomorphism
形态心理学/形態心理學　morphopsychology
形态学/形態學　morphology
形态再造/形態再造　morphologic reconstruction
形态正常/形態正常　eumorphism
形体感觉/形體感覺　symbolia
J形头套/J形頭套　J hook headgear
形象后效应/形象後效應　figural aftereffect
"X"形血管吻合/"X"形血管吻合　X shape vascular anastomosis
形与神俱/形與神俱　psychosomatic harmony
形状/形狀　form, shape
形状板/形狀板,測智模型板　formboard
形状知觉/形狀知覺　form perception
C型病毒/C型病毒　C type virus
M型超声心动描记术/M型超聲心動描記術,M型心臟超音波圖　M-mode echocardiography
A型超声心动图/A型超聲心動圖,A型心臟超音波圖　A-mode echocardiography
U型腭主连接体/U型腭主連接體　U-shaped palatal major connector
Ⅰ型肺泡细胞/Ⅰ型肺泡細胞　type Ⅰ alveolar cell
Ⅱ型肺泡细胞/Ⅱ型肺泡細胞　type Ⅱ alveolar cell
C型截骨术/C型截骨術　C osteotomy
A型精原细胞/A型精原細胞　type A spermatogonium
B型精原细胞/B型精原細胞　type B spermatogonium
C型卡环/C型卡環　C clasp
α-2型抗胞浆素/甲2型抗胞漿素　α 2 antiplasmin
型片/型片　matrix band
α-1型球蛋白/α-1型球蛋白,阿爾法第一型球蛋白　α 1 globulin
α-2型球蛋白/α-2型球蛋白,阿爾法第二型球蛋白　α 2 globulin

B型心脏超音波图/B型心臟超音波圖　B-mode echocardiography
A型行为/A型行爲　type A behavior
B型行为/B型行爲　type B behavior
α-1型岩藻糖苷酶/α-1型岩藻糖苷酶,阿爾法第一型岩藻糖苷酶　α 1 fucosidase
C型植体/C型植體　C implant
X型组织细胞增多症/X型組織細胞增多症　X histiocytosis
Y型组织细胞增多症/Y型組織細胞增多症,疣狀黃瘤　Y histiocytosis
醒后抑郁[症]/醒後抑鬱　postdormital depression
醒梦状态/醒夢狀態,夢醒症,夢狀幻覺　oneirism
醒睡周期/醒睡週期　sleep-wake cycle
杏/杏　armeniaca
杏核颗粒/杏核顆粒　apricot core grain
杏仁/杏仁　apricot kernel
杏仁粉/[甜]杏仁粉　almond seed kernel powder
杏仁复合体/杏仁複合體　amygdaloid complex
杏仁腹侧通路/杏仁腹側通路　ventral amygdaloid pathway
杏仁核/杏仁核　amygdala
杏仁裂/杏仁裂,扁桃狀裂隙　amygdaline fissure
杏仁前区/杏仁前區　anterior amygdaloid area
杏仁酸/杏仁酸　amygdalic acid
杏仁酸安替比林/杏仁酸安替比林　antipyrine mandelate
杏仁酸铵/杏仁酸銨　ammonium mandelate
杏仁酸乌洛托品/杏仁酸烏洛托品,杏仁酸六甲烯四胺　methenamine mandelate
杏仁体/杏仁體　amygdaloid body
杏仁体支/杏仁體支　branch of amygdaloid body
杏仁酰对乙氧苯胺/杏仁酸醯對乙氧基苯胺　amygdalophenin
杏仁油/[甜]杏仁油　almond-oil, apricot kernel oil
杏仁油提液/杏仁油提液　apricot kernel extract
杏仁止咳糖浆/杏仁止欬糖漿　xingren zhike syrup
杏仁中毒/杏仁中毒　poisoning of bitter apricot seed
杏苏散/杏蘇散　xingsu powder
幸存患者/倖存患者　survivor
性/性　sex
性爱学/性[愛]學　erotology
性伴侣/性伴侶　sexual partner
性鞭毛/性鞭毛　sex pili
性变态/性變態,性欲不正常　paraphilia
性别/性別　sex, sexuality
性别比率/性別比率　sex ratio
性别分布/性別分布　sex distribution

性别分化/性[别]分化　sex differentiation
性别改变术/性別改變術　sex change operation
性别决定/性別決定　sex determination
性别控制/性別控制　sex control
性别特性/性別特性　gender identity
性别因素/性別因素　sex factor
性别预选/性別預選　sex preselection
性病/性病　venereal disease
[性病]黏液溢出/[性病]黏液溢出,膿漏　blennorrhagia
性病尿道炎/性病尿道炎,花柳性尿道炎　urethritis venerea
性病湿疣/性病濕疣,尖形疣　pointed wart, venereal wart
性病性淋巴肉芽肿/性病性淋巴肉芽腫　climatic bubo
性病性淋巴肉芽肿病毒/性病性淋巴肉芽腫病毒　lymphogranuloma venereum virus
性病[性]梅毒/性病性梅毒　venereal syphilis
性病性尿道炎/性病性尿道炎　venereal urethritis
性病性肉芽肿/性病性肉芽腫,花柳性肉芽腫　granuloma venereum
性病性乳头状瘤/花柳性乳頭狀瘤　papilloma venereum
性病性软下疳/性病性軟下疳　venereal sore
性病学/性病學,花柳病學,花柳科學　venereology
性病学家/性病學家,花柳病醫師,花柳病專家　venereologist
性病样溃疡/性病狀潰瘍　veneroid ulcer
性成熟/性成熟　sexual maturation
性传播/性傳播,性行爲傳染　sexually transmitted
性传播疾病/性傳播疾病　sexually transmitted diseases
性导/性導　sexduction
性发育/性發育　sexual development
性犯罪/性犯罪　sex offense
性分化/性分化　sex differentiation
性分化异常/性分化異常　disorder of sex differentiation
性分化障碍/性分化障礙　sex differentiation disorder
性复[合]体/性複合體　sex complex
性感觉异常/性感覺異常　paresthesia sexualis
性感缺乏/性感缺失　sexual anesthesia
性格/性格　character
性格分析/性格分析　character analysis
性功能/性功能　sexual function
性活动/性活動　sexual activity
性激素/性激素　sex hormone

性激素接合球蛋白/性荷爾蒙接連球蛋白　sex-hormone-binding globulin
性激素类/性激素類　sex hormones
性交/性交,交合　coitus
性交不能症/性交不能,交合不能　apareunia
性交的/性交的　venereal
性交后避孕/性交後避孕　postcoital contraception
性交后避孕药/性交後避孕藥　postcoital contraceptive
性交后出血/性交後出血　postcoital bleeding
性交后试验/性交後試驗　postcoital test
性交后休克/性交後休克　sexual shock
性交恐惧症/性交恐懼症,交媾恐懼症,懼交配症　coitophobia, genophobia
性交困难/性交困難　dyspareunia
性交龄/性交齡　coital age
性交性气喘/性[交性]氣喘　sexual asthma
性交疹病毒/性交疹病毒,媾疹病毒　coital exanthema virus
性交中断/性交中斷　coitus interruptus
性教育/性教育　sex education
性快感/性快感,性高潮　orgasm
性快感缺失/性快感缺失,性高潮缺失　anorgasmy
性冷/性冷　asexuality
性连锁遗传/性連[鎖]遺傳　X-linked inheritance
性联鱼鳞病/性聯魚鱗病　sex-linked ichthyosis
性母细胞/性母細胞,發育[母]細胞　auxocyte
性器期/性器期,生殖器時期　genital stage
性嵌合体/性嵌合體,雌雄嵌合體　sexual mosaic
性倾向紊乱/性傾向紊亂　sexual orientation disturbance
性情/性情　temperament
性情有辨/性情有辨　differentiation of temperament
性区/性區,生殖區　genital area
性染色体/性染色體　sex chromosome
性染色体畸变/性染色體畸變　sex chromosome aberration
性染色体障碍/性染色體障礙　sex chromosome disorder
性染色质/性染色質　sex chromatin
性骚扰/性騷擾　sexual harassment
性生活/性生活　sexual life
性手册/性手冊　sex manual
性索间质细胞瘤/性索間質細胞瘤　sex cord-mesenchymal tumor
性索-性腺间质瘤/性索-性腺間質瘤　sex cord-gonadal stromal tumor
性卫生/性衛生　sex hygiene

性味/性味　nature and flavor
性细胞/性細胞,生殖细胞　sexual cell
性腺/性腺　gonad
性腺发育不全/性腺發育不全　germinal aplasia
性腺功能减退性肥胖/性腺功能減退性肥胖,生殖腺官能不足性肥胖　hypogonad obesity
性腺功能减退症/性腺功能減退症,性腺機能不足　hypogonadism
性腺功能亢进/生殖腺機能亢進　hypergonadism
性腺基质细胞瘤/性腺基質細胞瘤　gonadal stromal tumor
性腺激素/性腺激素　gonadal hormone
性腺激素释放荷尔蒙/性腺激素釋放荷爾蒙　gonadotrophin releasing hormone
性腺静脉造影[术]/性腺靜脈造影[術]　gonadovenography
性腺胚细胞瘤/性腺母細胞瘤　gonadoblastoma
性腺缺如/性腺缺如　gonadal agenesis
性腺性别/性腺性別　gonadal sex
性腺性逆转/性腺性逆轉　gonadal sex reversal
性腺甾类激素/性腺甾類激素　gonadal steroid hormones
性腺障碍/性腺障礙　gonadal disorder
性腺组织肿瘤/性腺組織腫瘤　gonadal tissue neoplasm
性心理发育/性心理發育,性心理發展　psychosexual development
性行为/性行爲　sexual behavior
性选择/性選擇　sexual selection
性学/性學　sexology
性因素/性因素　sex factor
性幼稚症/性幼稚病　sexual infantilism
性诱引剂/性誘引劑　sex attractant
性欲/性欲　libido
性欲倒错/性欲倒错　paraphilias
性欲倒错者/性慾倒錯者,性欲不正常者　paraphiliac
性欲发生/性慾發生　erotogenesis
性欲发生区/性慾發生區,動情區　erogenous zone
性欲感觉/性慾感覺　sexual sense
性欲减退/性感減退,性感缺乏　hyposexuality
性欲节制/性欲節制　sexual abstinence
性欲亢进/性慾亢進,性欲過度　hypersexuality
性欲恐惧症/性慾恐懼症,戀愛恐懼症,性交恐懼症　erotophobia
性欲缺乏/性欲缺乏　asexuality
性欲缺失/性慾缺乏,性感缺乏　anaphrodisia
性欲无度/性慾無度,性慾未節制　sexual incontinence

性欲性精神变态者/性欲性精神變態者　sexual psychopath
性欲异常/性慾異常,性表現異常　sexopathy
性欲异常者/性慾異常者,變態性欲者,色情變態者　erotopath
性早熟/性早熟　sexual precosity, sexual prematurity
性早熟·肝郁化火证/性早熟·肝鬱化火證　sexual prematurity with pattern of liver depression transforming into fire
性早熟·阴虚火旺证/性早熟·陰虛火旺證　sexual prematurity with pattern of exuberant fire due to yin deficiency
性征/性徵　sex characteristics
性周期/性週期　sexual cycle
性转变综合征/性轉變症候群　sex reversal syndrome
性状/性狀　characteristics
性咨询/性諮詢　sex counseling
凶恶的/凶惡的　flagitious
兄弟情结/兄弟情結,凱因氏情結　Cain complex
芎归养荣汤/芎歸養榮湯　beautifying decoction with ligusticum and angelica
芎菊上清丸/芎菊上清丸　xiongju shangqing pills
汹涌发酵/洶湧發酵,狂暴性發酵　stormy fermentation
胸/胸[廓],胸腔　①thorax ②xiong, AH10
胸半棘肌/胸半棘肌　semispinalis thoracis, musculus semispinalis thoracis
胸背动脉/胸背動脈　thoracodorsal artery
胸背静脉/胸背靜脉　thoracodorsal vein
胸背区/胸背區　thoracodorsal region
胸背神经/胸背神經　thoracodorsal nerve
胸痹/胸痺　chest bi, chest painful impediment
胸壁/胸壁　thoracic wall, chest wall
胸壁反常运动/胸壁反常運動　paradoxical movement of chest wall
胸壁高频振荡/胸壁高頻振盪　high frequency oscillation of chest wall
胸壁畸形/胸壁畸形　chest wall deformity
胸壁瘘/胸[壁]瘻　thoracic fistula
胸壁浅表血栓性静脉炎/胸壁淺表血栓性靜脈炎　Mondor disease
胸壁浅静脉/胸壁淺靜脈　thoracic superficial vein
胸壁缺损重建术/胸壁缺損重建術　reconstruction of defect of chest wall
胸壁嗜酸[性]细胞肉芽肿/胸壁嗜酸[性]細胞肉芽腫　eosinophilic granuloma of chest wall
胸壁顺应性/胸壁順應性　chest wall compliance

胸壁心异位/胸壁心異位　ectopia cordis pectoralis
胸壁震荡通气/胸壁震蕩通氣　chest wall oscillation
胸部/胸部　thoracic part, chest
胸部动脉/胸部動脈　thoracic arteries
胸部多肢畸胎/胸部多肢畸胎　pleuromelus
胸部放射摄影术/胸部放射攝影術　thoracic radiography
胸部横突间肌/胸部橫突間肌　intertransverse muscle of thorax
胸部积脓/膿性胸膜炎　thoracic empyema
胸部疾病/胸部疾病　thoracic disease
胸部寄生胎/胸部寄生胎　thoracopagus parasiticus, thoracoparasitus
胸部联胎/胸部連胎　synthorax
胸部内伤/胸[部]内傷　internal injury of chest
胸部平面图/胸部平面圖　planithorax
胸部切口/胸部切口　thoracic incision
胸部X射线普查/胸部X線普查　mass chest X-ray
胸部损伤/胸部損傷　thoracic injury
胸部弯曲/胸部彎曲　thoracic curve
胸部语颤/胸部語顫,胸部震顫　pectoral fremitus
胸部肿瘤/胸部腫瘤　thoracic neoplasm
胸侧联胎/胸側連胎　hemipagus
胸长动脉/胸長動脈　long thoracic artery
胸长静脉/胸長靜脈　long thoracic vein
胸长神经/胸長神經　long thoracic nerve
胸大肌/胸大肌　pectoralis major, greater pectoral muscle
胸大肌腹部/胸大肌腹部　abdominal part of pectoralis major
胸大肌缺如/胸大肌缺如　absence of pectoralis major
胸大肌锁骨部/胸大肌鎖骨部　clavicular part of pectoralis major
胸大肌胸肋部/胸大肌胸肋部　sternocostal part of pectoralis major
胸带/胸帶　chest bandage
胸导管/胸導管　thoracic duct
胸导管腹部/胸導管腹部　abdominal part of thoracic duct
胸导管弓/胸導管弓　arch of thoracic duct
胸导管结扎术/胸導管結紮術　ligation of thoracic duct
胸导管颈部/胸導管頸部　cervical part of thoracic duct
胸导管胸部/胸導管胸部　thoracic part of thoracic duct

胸导管引流/胸導管引流　thoracic duct drainage
胸导联/胸導聯,胸前導程　chest lead
胸动脉/胸動脈　thoracic artery
胸动描记器/胸[廓運]動描記器　cyrtograph
胸段(1-12)/胸段(1-12)　thoracic segment (T)(1-12)
胸肺支/胸肺支　thoracic pulmonary branch
胸腹壁静脉/胸腹壁靜脈　thoracoepigastric vein
胸腹隔膜/胸腹[隔]膜　pleuroperitoneal membrane
胸腹联合切口/胸腹聯合切口　thoracoabdominal incision
胸腹联双胎/胸腹聯雙胎　thoracoventropagus
胸腹联胎/胸腹連胎　thoracogastrodidymus
胸腹裂/胸腹裂　thoracogastroschisis
胸腹裂[畸形]/胸腹裂[畸形],裂胸腹[畸形]　thoracoceloschisis
胸腹裂孔/胸腹裂孔,膈裂　pleuroperitoneal foramen
胸腹膜管/胸腹膜管　pleuroperitoneal canal
胸腹膜黄变病/[胎兒]胸腹膜黄化病變　cirrhonosus
胸腹膜孔/胸腹膜孔　pleuroperitoneal opening
胸腹膜裂孔疝/胸腹膜裂孔疝　pleuroperitoneal hiatal hernia
胸腹切开术/胸腹切開術,胸腹剖開術　thoracolaparotomy
胸苷/胸[腺核]苷　thymidine
胸苷激酶/胸苷激酶　thymidine kinase
胸苷-磷酸/胸苷-磷酸　thymidine monophosphate
胸苷磷酸化酶/胸苷磷酸化酶　thymidine phosphorylase
胸苷酸合酶/胸苷酸合成酶　thymidylate synthase
胸骨/胸骨　sternum
胸骨板/胸骨板,[胚胎]胸骨脊　sternal bar
胸骨部/胸骨部　sternal part
胸骨穿刺/胸骨穿刺術　sternal puncture
胸骨穿孔术/胸骨穿孔術　sternotrypesis
胸骨端/胸骨端　sternal end
胸骨翻转术/胸骨翻轉術　sternoturnover operation
胸骨沟/胸骨溝　sternal groove
胸骨骨折/胸骨骨折　sternal fracture
胸骨关节/胸骨關節　sternal articulation
胸骨关节面/胸骨關節面　sternal articular facet
胸骨后动脉/胸骨後動脈　posterior sternal artery
胸骨后甲状腺/胸骨後甲狀腺　retrosternal thyroid
胸骨后甲状腺肿/胸骨後甲狀腺腫　substernal goiter
胸骨后间隙/胸骨後間隙　retrosternal space
胸骨后疝/胸骨後疝　retrosternal hernia
胸骨肌/胸骨肌　sternalis, musculus sternalis
胸骨甲状肌/胸骨甲狀肌　sternothyroid

胸骨剑突/胸骨劍突　xiphoid cartilage
胸骨剑突联胎/胸骨劍突連胎　sternoxiphopagus
胸骨角/胸骨角　sternal angle
胸骨角度测量器/胸骨角度測量器　sternogoniometer
胸骨节/胸骨節　sternebra
胸骨结合/胸骨結合　sternal synchondrosis
胸骨联胎/胸骨連胎　sternodymus
胸骨联胎畸形/胸骨連胎畸形　sternodymia
胸骨裂/胸骨裂[隙]　cleft sternum
胸骨膜/胸骨膜　sternal membrane
胸骨旁淋巴结/胸骨旁淋巴結　parasternal lymph node
胸骨旁线/胸骨旁線　parasternal line
胸骨平面/胸骨平面　planum sternale
胸骨切开术/胸骨切開術　sternotomy
胸骨区/胸骨區　sternal region
胸骨软骨结合/胸骨軟骨結合　sternal synchondrosis
胸骨上搏动/胸骨上搏動　suprasternal pulsation
胸骨上骨/胸骨上骨　suprasternal bone
胸骨上间隙/胸骨上間隙　suprasternal space
胸骨舌骨肌/胸[骨]舌骨肌　sternohyoid muscle
胸骨[髓]活组织检查/胸骨[髓]活組織檢查, 胸骨活組織檢查法　sternal biopsy
胸骨体/胸骨體　body of sternum, gladiolus
胸骨痛/胸骨痛　sternodynia
胸骨下角/胸骨下角　infrasternal angle
胸骨线/胸骨線　sternal line
胸骨心包韧带/胸骨心包韌帶　sternopericardial ligament
胸骨支/胸[骨]支　sternal branch
胸管/胸管　chest tube
胸汗/胸汗　chest sweating
胸核/胸核　thoracic nucleus
胸横肌/胸橫肌　transversus thoracis
胸横突间肌/胸橫突間肌　intertransversarii thoracis, musculi intertransversarii thoracis
胸厚/胸厚　chest thickness
胸回旋肌/胸迴旋肌　rotatores thoracis, musculus rotatores thoracis
胸肌/胸肌　muscle of thorax, pectoralis
胸肌间淋巴结/胸肌間淋巴結　interpectoral lymph node
胸肌筋膜/胸肌筋膜　pectoral fascia
胸肌痉挛/胸肌痙攣　stethospasm
胸肌静脉/胸肌靜脈　pectoral vein
胸肌淋巴结/胸肌淋巴結　pectoral lymph node
胸肌麻痹/胸肌麻痺　stethoparalysis
胸肌区/胸肌區, 胸肌部　pectoral region
胸肌填塞法/胸肌填塞法　myotamponade
胸肌痛/胸肌痛　thoracomyodynia
胸畸形/胸[廓]畸形　thoracocyllosis
胸棘肌/胸棘肌　spinalis thoracis
胸棘间肌/胸部棘間肌　interspinale thoracis
胸甲式呼吸器/胸甲狀呼吸器　cuirass respirator
胸甲状腺肿/胸甲狀腺腫　thoracic goiter
胸肩峰动脉/胸肩峰動脈　thoracoacromial artery
[胸肩峰动脉]肩峰支/[胸肩峰動脈]肩峰支　acromial branch
[胸肩峰动脉]胸肌支/[胸肩峰動脈]胸肌支　pectoral branch
胸肩峰静脉/胸肩峰靜脈　thoracoacromial vein
胸交感神经切除术/胸交感神經切除術　thoracic sympathectomy
胸廓/胸廓　thoracic cage
胸廓部分切除术/胸廓[部分]切除術　thoracectomy
胸廓测量法/胸廓測量法, 測胸圍法　thoracometry
胸廓成形术/胸廓成形術, 胸廓造型術, 胸部缺陷修補術　thoracoplasty
胸廓出口综合征/胸廓出口症候群　thoracic outlet syndrome, syndrome of chest outlet
胸廓骨/胸廓骨　thoracic bone
胸廓筋膜/胸廓筋膜　thoracic fascia
胸廓扩张不能性呼吸困难/胸廓不擴張性呼吸困難　nonexpansional dyspnea
胸廓连结/胸廓連結　thoracic joint
胸廓内动脉/胸廓內動脈　internal thoracic artery
胸廓内动脉冠状动脉旁路移植术/胸廓內動脈冠狀動脈旁路移植術　internal mammary artery coronary artery bypass grafting
胸廓内动脉-冠状动脉吻合术/胸廓內動脈-冠狀動脈吻合術　internal mammary-coronary artery anastomosis
[胸廓内动脉]肋间前支/[胸廓內動脈]肋間前支　anterior intercostal branch
[胸廓内动脉]气管支/[胸廓內動脈]氣管支　tracheal branch
[胸廓内动脉]乳房内侧支/[胸廓內動脈]乳房內側支　medial mammary branch
[胸廓内动脉]胸骨支/[胸廓內動脈]胸骨支　sternal branch
[胸廓内动脉]胸腺支/[胸廓內動脈]胸腺支　thymic branch
[胸廓内动脉]纵隔支/[胸廓內動脈]縱隔支　mediastinal branch
胸廓内静脉/胸廓內靜脈　internal thoracic vein

胸廓切开术/胸廓切開術　thoracotomy
胸廓曲度计/胸[廓]曲度計　stethogoniometer
胸廓曲度描记器/胸廓曲度描記器　stethocyrtograph
胸廓上口/胸廓上口　inlet of thorax, superior aperture of thorax
胸廓狭窄/胸廓狹窄,胸部狭小　thoracostenosis
胸廓下口/胸廓下口　inferior aperture of thorax, outlet of thorax
胸廓造口术/胸廓造口術　thoracostomy
胸廓粘连松解术/胸廓粘連鬆解術,胸壁鬆解術,胸廓切離術　thoracolysis
胸廓支气管切开术/胸式支氣管切開術　thoracobronchotomy
胸廓指数/胸廓指數,胸径指数　thoracic index
胸肋/胸肋　sternal rib
胸肋部/胸肋部　sternocostal part
胸肋辐状韧带/胸肋輻狀韌帶　radiate sternocostal ligament
胸肋关节/胸肋關節　sternocostal joint, costosternal articulation
胸肋关节间韧带/胸肋關節間韌帶　ligamentum sternocostal interarticulare
胸肋关节内韧带/胸肋關節內韌帶　intraarticular sternocostal ligament
胸肋裂孔/胸肋裂孔　sternocostal hiatus
胸肋面/胸肋面　sternocostal surface
胸肋软骨关节/胸肋軟骨關節　chondrosternal articulation
胸肋三角/胸肋三角　sternocostal triangle
胸肋锁骨骨肥厚/胸肋鎖骨骨肥厚　sternocostoclavicular hyperostosis
胸肋锁骨间骨炎/胸肋鎖骨間骨炎　intersternocostoclavicular osteitis
胸联双胎/胸部聯胎　thoracopagus
胸闷/胸悶　oppression in chest
胸膜/胸膜　pleura
胸膜壁层/胸膜壁層　pleura costalis
胸膜壁层炎/胸膜壁層炎　corticopleuritis
胸膜剥除术/胸膜剝除術　pleural decortication
胸膜[部分]切除术/胸膜切除術　pleurectomy
胸膜残腔/胸膜殘腔　pleural residual space
胸膜胆囊炎/胸膜膽囊炎　pleurocholecystitis
胸膜顶/胸膜頂　cupula of pleura
胸膜反折处/胸膜反折處　reflection of pleura
胸膜肺区/胸膜肺區　pleuropulmonal region
胸膜肺松解术/胸膜肺鬆解術　pleuropneumonolysis
胸膜肺瘘/肋膜肺瘻　pleuropulmonary fistula
胸膜肺炎/胸膜[炎兼]肺炎　pleuropneumonia
胸膜腹膜管/肋膜腹膜管　pleuroperitoneal duct
胸膜肝炎/胸膜肝炎　pleurohepatitis
胸膜固定术/胸膜固定術　pleurodesis
胸膜疾病/胸膜疾病　pleural disease
胸膜间皮瘤/胸膜間皮瘤　mesothelioma of pleura
胸膜结核/胸膜結核　pleural tuberculosis
胸膜摩擦音/胸膜摩擦音　pleuritic rub
胸膜内肺松解术/胸膜内肺鬆解術　intrapleural pneumonolysis
胸膜内注射/胸腔内注射　intrapleural injection
胸膜捻发音/胸膜撚發音　pleural crackle
胸膜腔/胸膜腔　pleural cavity
胸膜腔灌洗/胸膜腔灌洗　pleural lavage
胸膜腔灌洗术/胸膜腔灌洗術,胸膜與腔内注射灌注法　pleuroclysis
胸膜腔降温/胸膜腔降温　pleural cooling
胸膜腔镜检查/胸膜檢視法　pleuroscopy
胸膜腔X射线照相术/胸膜腔X射線照相術,胸膜X光檢查法　pleurography
胸膜腔渗液/胸膜腔滲液　pleurorrhea
胸膜腔引流术/胸膜腔引流術　drainage of pleural cavity
胸膜切开术/胸膜切開術　pleurotomy
胸膜切缘/胸膜切緣　cut edge of pleura
胸膜全肺切除术/胸膜全肺切除術　pleuropneumonectomy
胸膜撒粉法/胸膜撒粉法　pleural poudrage
胸膜上膜/胸膜上膜　suprapleural membrane
胸膜石/胸膜石　pleurolith
胸膜食管肌/胸膜食管肌　pleuroesophageal muscle
胸膜松解术/胸膜鬆解術,肺鬆解術　pleurolysis
胸膜痛/胸膜痛　pleuritic pain
胸膜外肺松解术/胸膜外肺鬆解術　extrapleural pneumonolysis
胸膜外气胸/肋膜外氣胸　extrapleural pneumothorax
胸膜外纤维层剥除术/胸膜外纖維層剝除術,肋膜增厚剥脱術　decortication of lung
胸膜下肺小疱/胸膜下肺小皰　subpleural bleb
胸膜下疱/胸膜下皰　pleural bleb
胸膜心包剥除术/胸膜心包剝除術　pleuropericardial decortication
胸膜心包膜管/肋膜心包膜管　pleuropericardial duct
胸膜心包炎/胸膜[炎兼]心包炎　pleuropericarditis
胸膜心包杂音/胸膜包性雜音　pleuropericardial murmur
胸膜型伤寒/胸膜型傷寒　pleurotyphoid
胸膜性咳嗽/胸膜性欬嗽　pleuritic cough

胸膜胸壁固定术/胸膜壁層固定術 pleuroparietopexy
胸膜休克/胸膜[性]休克 pleural shock
胸膜炎/胸膜炎 pleurisy
胸膜隐窝/胸膜隱窩 pleural recess
胸膜脏层/胸膜臟層 pleural pulmonalis
胸膜增厚/胸膜肥厚 pleural thickening
胸膜粘连/胸膜粘連 pleural adhesion
胸膜震颤/胸膜震顫 pleural fremitus
胸膜支气管炎/胸膜支氣管炎 pleurobronchitis
胸膜肿瘤/胸膜腫瘤 pleural neoplasm
胸膜周炎/胸膜周[圍]炎 peripleuritis
胸内侧神经/胸内側神經 medial pectoral nerve
胸内回声/胸内回響 echophony
胸内甲状腺/胸[廓]内甲狀腺 intrathoracic thyroid
胸内筋膜/胸内筋膜 endothoracic fascia
胸内肾/胸内腎 thoracic kidney
胸内脏神经节/胸内臟神經節 thoracic splanchnic ganglion
胸髂肋肌/胸髂肋肌 iliocostalis thoracis
胸前位心/胸前位心 pectoral heart
胸腔/胸腔 thoracic cavity
胸腔穿刺术/胸膜穿刺術 pleuracentesis
胸腔积脓/胸腔積膿 pleural empyema
胸腔积液/胸腔積液,胸膜滲液,肋膜腔積水 hydrothorax, pleural effusion
胸腔镜/胸腔鏡 thoracoscope
胸腔镜肺活体组织检查/胸腔鏡肺活體組織檢查,胸腔鏡肺活檢 thoracoscopic lung biopsy
胸腔镜检查/胸腔鏡檢法 thoracoscopy
胸曲/胸曲 thoracic curvature
胸上动脉/胸上動脈 superior thoracic artery
胸[X射线]透视机/胸[X射線]透視機,胸部X光透視機 stethendoscope
胸神经/胸神經 thoracic nerve
胸神经后支/胸神經後支 posterior branch of thoracic nerve
胸神经后支内侧支/胸神經後支内側支 medial branch of posterior branch of thoracic nerve
胸神经后支外侧支/胸神經後支外側支 lateral branch of posterior branch of thoracic nerve
胸神经节/胸神經節 thoracic ganglion
胸神经前支/胸神經前支 anterior branch of thoracic nerve
胸式呼吸/胸式呼吸 thoracic respiration
胸水/肋膜腔積水 hydrothorax
胸锁骨炎/胸鎖骨炎 sternoclavicular osteitis
胸锁关节/胸鎖關節 sternoclavicular joint, sternoclavicular articulation
胸锁关节间软骨/[胸骨與]胸鎖關節間軟骨 omosternum
胸锁关节盘/胸鎖關節盤 sternoclavicular disc
胸锁关节脱位/胸鎖關節脱位,胸骨鎖骨關節脱臼 sternoclavicular dislocation
胸锁后韧带/胸鎖後韌帶 posterior sternoclavicular ligament
胸锁前韧带/胸鎖前韌帶 anterior sternoclavicular ligament
胸锁乳突肌/胸鎖乳突肌 sternocleidomastoid
胸锁乳突肌静脉/胸鎖乳突肌静脈 sternocleidomastoid vein
胸锁乳突肌区/胸鎖乳突肌部 sternocleidomastoid region
胸锁乳突肌血肿/胸鎖乳突肌血腫 sternocleidomastoid hematoma
胸锁乳突肌支/胸鎖乳突肌支 sternocleidomastoid branch
胸锁乳突静脉/胸鎖乳突静脈 sternocleidomastoid vein
胸痛/胸痛 chest pain
胸外侧动脉/胸外側動脈 lateral thoracic artery
胸外侧静脉/胸外側静脈 lateral thoracic vein, vena thoracica lateralis
胸外侧神经/胸外側神經 lateral pectoral nerve
胸外科手术/胸外科手術 thoracic surgical procedure
胸外科学/胸外科學 thoracic surgery
胸外啰音/胸外啰音,胸外性水泡音 extrathoracic rale
胸弯曲/胸[廓]彎曲 thoracocyrtosis
胸危象/胸危象 thoracic crisis
胸围/胸圍 chest circumference
胸狭窄/胸[廓]狭窄 stenothorax
胸下点/胸下點 substernale
胸腺/胸腺 thymus
胸腺癌/胸腺癌 thymic carcinoma
胸腺白血病抗原/胸腺白血病抗原 thymus leukemia antigen
胸腺毒血清/胸腺毒性血清 thymotoxic serum
胸腺发育不全/胸腺發育不全 thymic dysplasia
胸腺肥大/胸腺肥大 hypertrophy of thymus
[胸腺]抚育细胞/[胸腺]撫育細胞,培細胞,營養細胞 nurse cell
胸腺功能减退/胸腺功能減退,胸腺機能不足 hypothymism
胸腺功能障碍/胸腺機能障礙 cacothymia
胸腺功能正常/胸腺功能正常,胸腺活動力正常

euthymism
胸腺核苷酸/胸腺[核苷]酸　thymic acid
胸腺激素/胸腺激素　nucleosin
胸腺激素类/胸腺激素類　thymus hormones
胸腺甲状旁腺发育不全/胸腺甲狀旁腺發育不全　thymiparathyroid aplasia
胸腺静脉/胸腺靜脈　thymic vein
胸腺溃疡/胸腺潰瘍　thymelcosis
胸腺瘤/胸腺瘤　thymoma
胸腺嘧啶/胸腺嘧啶　thymine
胸腺嘧啶核苷酸类/胸腺嘧啶核苷酸類　thymine nucleotides
胸腺嘧啶DNA糖基化酶/胸腺嘧啶DNA糖基化酶　thymine DNA glycosylase
胸[腺嘧啶脱氧核]苷酸/胸[腺嘧啶脱氧核]苷酸,胸腺[嘧啶]核苷酸　thymidylic acid
胸腺嘧啶原酸/胸腺嘧啶原酸　thyminic acid
胸腺囊肿/胸腺囊腫　thymic cyst
胸腺喷丁/胸腺喷丁　thymopentin
胸腺皮质/胸腺皮質　cortex of thymus, thymic cortex
胸腺切除术/胸腺切除術　thymectomy
胸腺上皮细胞/胸腺上皮細胞　thymic epithelial cell
胸腺生成素类/胸腺生成素類　thymopoietins
胸腺生长激素/胸腺生長激素,胸腺發育素　thymocrescin
胸腺素/胸腺[激]素　thymosin
胸腺髓质/胸腺髓質　thymic medulla
胸腺髓质增生/胸腺髓質增生　thymic medullary hyperplasia
胸腺提取物/胸腺提取物　thymus extract
胸腺体液因子/胸腺體液因子　thymic humoral factor
胸腺体质/胸腺體質　status thymicus
胸腺外固定术/胸腺外固定術　exothymopexy
胸腺细胞/胸腺細胞　thymocyte cell, thymocyte
胸腺细胞移植/胸腺細胞移植　thymocyte cell transplantation
胸腺小体/胸腺小體　thymic corpuscle
胸腺小叶/胸腺小葉　thymic lobule
胸腺性白血病/胸腺性白血病　thymic leukemia
胸腺性气喘/胸腺性氣喘　thymic asthma
胸腺驯育/胸腺馴育　thymic education
胸腺咽管/胸腺咽管　thymopharyngeal duct
胸腺炎/胸腺炎　thymitis
胸腺衍生细胞/胸腺衍生細胞　thymus derived cell
胸腺依赖淋巴细胞/胸腺依賴淋巴細胞,胸腺依存性淋巴球　T cell, T lymphocyte, thymus dependent lymphocyte
胸腺依赖区/胸腺依賴區　thymus dependent area, thymus dependent region
胸腺依赖性抗原/胸腺依賴性抗原　thymus dependent antigen
胸腺依赖性缺乏/胸腺依賴性缺乏　thymus dependent deficiency
胸腺移植/胸腺移植　thymus transplantation
胸腺遗留/胸腺遺留,殘餘胸腺　thymokesis
胸腺原基/胸腺原基　primordium of thymus
胸腺增生/胸腺增生　thymus hyperplasia
胸腺支/胸腺支　thymic branch
胸腺组织转移/胸腺組織轉移,胸腺性遷徙　thymometastasis
胸乡/胸鄉　xiongxiang, SP19
胸小肌/胸小肌　pectoralis minor, musculus pectoralis minor
胸小肌发育不良/胸小肌發育不良　dysplasia of pectoralis minor
胸小肌缺如/胸小肌缺如　absence of pectoralis minor
胸胁苦满/胸脅苦滿　fullness and discomfort in chest and hypochondrium
胸心包隔膜/胸心包隔膜,胸膜圍心膜　pleuropericardial membrane
胸心神经/胸心神經　thoracic cardiac nerve
胸心血管外科学/胸心血管外科學　thoracic and cardiovascular surgery
胸心支/胸心支　thoracic cardiac branch
胸腰筋膜/胸腰筋膜　thoracolumbar fascia
胸腰椎椎体骨折/胸腰椎椎體骨折　thoracolumbar fracture
胸语音/胸語音　pectoriloquy
胸中点/胸中點　mesosternale
胸主动脉/胸主動脈　thoracic aorta
胸主动脉丛/胸主動脈叢　thoracic aortic plexus
胸主动脉瘤/胸主動脈瘤　thoracic aortic aneurysm
胸主动脉神经/胸主動脈神經　thoracic aortic nerve
[胸主动脉]纵隔支/[胸主動脈]縱隔支　mediastinal branch
胸椎/胸椎[骨]　①thoracic vertebra, whettle bones ②xiongzhui, AH11
胸椎骨折/胸椎骨折　fracture of thoracic vertebrae
胸椎小关节错缝/胸椎小關節錯縫　dislocation of small joint of thoracic vertebrae
胸椎小关节紊乱症/胸椎小關節紊亂症　thoracal facetjoint disturbance
胸纵静脉/胸縱靜脈　longitudinal thoracic vein

胸最长肌/胸最長肌　longissimus thoracis
胸最上动脉/胸最上動脈　highest thoracic artery
雄二烯类/雄二烯類　androstadienes
雄核发育/雄核發育　androgenesis
雄核卵块发育/雄核卵塊發育,男核卵發育　andromerogony
雄核生殖体/雄核生殖體　arrhenokaryon
雄黄/雄黄　realgar
雄黄中毒/雄黄中毒　realgar poisoning
雄激素/雄性素,男性激素　androgen
雄激素不敏感综合征/雄激素不敏感症候群,雄性激素失敏症候群　androgen insensitivity syndrome
雄激素分泌过少/雄性素分泌不足,睾丸間質細胞機能不足　hypoleydigism
雄激素化/雄激素化,女子男性化　androgenization
雄激素拮抗药/雄激素拮抗藥　androgen antagonist
雄激素结合蛋白质/雄激素結合蛋白質　androgen-binding protein
雄激素类/雄激素類　androgens
雄激素受体/雄激素受體　androgen receptor
雄激素性秃发/雄激素性秃髮　androgenetic alopecia
雄激素依赖性多毛症/雄激素依賴性多毛症　androgen-dependent hirsutism
雄激素依赖综合征/雄激素依賴症候群　androgen-dependent syndrome
雄激素增多症/雄性素過多症　hyperandrogenism
雄烯二酮/雄烯二酮　androstenedione
雄性不育/雄性不育　male infertility
雄[性交]配素/雄配子内泌素　androgamone
雄[性]配子/雄[性]配子　male gamete
雄性生殖器/雄性生殖器　male genitalia
雄性生殖器疾病/雄性生殖器疾病　male genital disease
雄性生殖器肿瘤/雄性生殖器腫瘤　male genital neoplasm
雄[性]原核/雄性原核　male pronucleus
雄甾酮/雄甾酮,雄[性]脂酮　androsterone
雄[甾]烷/雄[甾]烷,雄脂烷　androstane
雄[甾]烷醇类/雄[甾]烷醇類　androstanols
雄[甾]烷醇酮/雄[甾]烷醇酮　androstanolone
雄[甾]烷二醇/雄[甾]烷二醇　androstanediol
雄[甾]烷二酮/雄[甾]烷二酮　androstanedione
雄[甾]烷类/雄甾烷類　androstanes
雄[甾]烯/雄[性]烯　androstene
雄甾烯醇类/雄甾烯醇類　androstenols
雄[甾]烯二醇/雄烯二醇　Androstenediol
雄甾烯类/雄甾烯類　androstenes
熊果/熊果　bear berry
熊果苷/熊果苷,熊果葉素　arbutin
熊果酸/熊果酸　ursolic acid
熊去氧胆酸/熊去氧膽酸　ursodeoxycholic acid
休克/休克　shock
休克肺/休克肺　shock lung
休克抗原/休克抗原　shock antigen
休克器官/休克器官　shock organ
休克型肺炎/休克型肺炎　pneumonia with shock
休眠细胞/睡眠細胞　sleeping cell
休纳曼病/休納曼病,Hünermann 氏病　Hünermann disease
休斯手术/休斯手術　Hughes operation
休息/休息　rest
休息痢/休息痢　intermittent dysentery, recurrent dysentery
休息痢·发作期/休息痢·發作期　attacking stage of intermittent dysentery
休息痢·寒热错杂证/休息痢·寒熱錯雜證　intermittent dysentery with pattern of intermingled heat and cold
休息痢·缓解期/休息痢·緩解期　remittent stage of intermittent dysentery
休息痢·脾气虚证/休息痢·脾氣虛證　intermittent dysentery with pattern of spleen qi deficiency
休息痢·脾阳虚证/休息痢·脾陽虛證　intermittent dysentery with pattern of exhaustion of spleen yang
休息痢·瘀血内阻证/休息痢·瘀血內阻證　intermittent dysentery with pattern of internal blockade of static blood
休止角/休止角,安息角　angle of repose
休止期/休止期　ambiguous phase
休止期秃发/休止期秃髮　telogen alopecia
休止细胞/休止細胞,静息細胞,静止細胞　resting cell
休止性长出/休止性長出　arrested eruption
休止游走细胞/静止遊走細胞　resting wandering cell
修复/修復　repair
修复前口腔外科手术/修復前口腔外科手術　preprosthetic oral surgical procedure
修复前外科学/修復前外科學　preprosthetic surgery
修复外科手术/修復外科手術　reconstructive surgical procedure
修复性牙本质/修復性牙本質　reparative dentin
修复学家/修復學家,補缺學專家,補綴學專家　prosthetist
修面痉挛/修面痙攣,剃髮痙攣,剃鬚痙攣　keirospasm
修切标本/修切標本　excarnation

修事/修事 processing
修饰/修飾 modification
修饰基因/修飾基因,變更基因 modifying gene
修饰酶/修飾酶 modification enzyme
修整器/修整器 trimmer
羞愧疗法/羞愧療法 shame-induced therapy
袖形切断术/袖形切斷術,袖形截斷術 coat-sleeve amputation
袖珍面罩/袖珍面罩 pocket mask
袖珍膀胱内压测量器/袖珍膀胱内壓測量器,微小膀胱[容量]壓力計 microcystometer
袖状移植物/袖狀移植物 sleeve graft
嗅成神经细胞瘤/嗅神經母細胞瘤 olfactory neuroblastoma
嗅沟/嗅溝 olfactory sulcus
嗅沟脑膜瘤/嗅溝腦膜瘤 olfactory groove meningioma
嗅回静脉/嗅迴静脈 vein of olfactory gyrus
嗅结节/嗅結節 olfactory tubercle
嗅静脉/嗅静脈 olfactory vein
嗅距单位/嗅距單位,嗅閾,嗅覺單位 olfactie
嗅觉/嗅覺 sense of smell
嗅觉测量[法]/嗅覺測量[法],嗅覺檢法 olfactometry
嗅觉成感觉神经细胞瘤/嗅覺成感覺神經細胞瘤 olfactory esthesioneuroblastoma
嗅觉倒错/嗅覺倒錯,嗅覺障礙 parosmia
嗅觉过敏/嗅覺過敏,嗅覺過強 hyperosmia
嗅觉计/嗅覺計 olfactometer
嗅觉减退/嗅覺減退 hyposmia
嗅觉缺失/嗅覺缺失 olfactory anesthesia
嗅、生殖器发育不全/嗅、生殖器發育不全 olfactory genital dysplasia
嗅觉受体神经元/嗅覺受體神經元 olfactory receptor neuron
嗅觉性多汗症/嗅覺性多汗症 olfactory hyperhidrosis
嗅觉性失语/嗅覺失語症 anosmic aphasia
嗅觉学/嗅[覺]學 osmology
嗅觉异常/嗅覺異常 heterosmia, abnormal olfaction
嗅觉障碍/嗅覺障礙 olfaction disorder
嗅觉障碍学/嗅覺障礙論 osmonosology
嗅毛/嗅毛 olfactory hair
嗅敏度单位/嗅敏度單位,嗅覺敏銳度 olfactus
嗅脑/嗅腦 olfactory brain
嗅脑沟/嗅[腦]溝 rhinal sulcus
嗅黏膜/嗅黏膜 olfactory mucosa
嗅泡/嗅泡,嗅囊 olfactory vesicle

嗅皮层/嗅[覺]皮質 olfactory cortex
嗅谱图/嗅譜圖 olfactory spectrogram
嗅器/嗅器,嗅官 olfactory organ
嗅球/嗅球 olfactory bulb
嗅区/嗅區,嗅部 olfactory region
嗅区被盖束/嗅區被蓋束 olfactotegmental tract
嗅三角/嗅三角 olfactory trigone
嗅上皮/嗅[覺]上皮 olfactory epithelium
嗅神经/嗅[覺]神經 olfactory nerve
嗅神经疾病/嗅神經疾病 olfactory nerve disease
嗅神经孔/嗅神經孔 olfactory foramen
嗅试验/嗅試驗 olfactory test
嗅束/嗅束,嗅徑 olfactory tract
嗅丝/嗅絲 fila olfactoria
嗅通路/嗅通路 olfactory pathway
嗅妄想/嗅妄想 olfactory delusion
嗅窝/嗅窩 olfactory pit
嗅细胞/嗅細胞 olfactory cell
嗅[纤]毛/嗅[纖]毛 olfactory cilium
嗅腺/嗅腺 olfactory gland
嗅叶沟/嗅葉溝 olfactory groove
嗅[叶]脚/嗅腳 olfactory peduncle
溴百里酚蓝/溴百里酚藍 bromthymol blue
溴苯/溴[化]苯 bromobenzene
溴苯类/溴[化]苯類 bromobenzenes
溴苯磷/溴苯磷 leptophos
溴苯那敏/抗組織胺劑 brompheniramine
溴苯酸盐类/溴苯酸鹽類 bromobenzoates
溴吡斯的明/溴吡斯的明 pyridostigmine bromide
溴苄铵甲苯磺酸盐/溴苄銨托西酸鹽 bretylium tosylate
溴苄胺化合物/溴苄胺化合物 bretylium compound
溴痤疮/溴痤瘡 bromide acne
溴[代苯]酚/溴酚 bromphenol
溴代琥珀酰亚胺/溴琥珀醯亞胺 bromosuccinimide
N-溴代邻苯二甲酰亚胺滴定法/N-溴代苯二甲醯亞胺滴定法 N-bromophthalimide titration
溴代烃/溴代烴,溴化乙烷 hydrobromic ether
溴碘中毒/溴碘中毒 bromoiodism
N-溴丁二酰亚胺滴定法/N-溴丁二醯亞胺滴定法 N-bromosuccinimide titration
溴放射性同位素/溴放射性同位素 bromine radioisotope
溴酚蓝/溴酚藍 coeruleum bromophenolis
溴化苄/溴化苄,溴化苯甲基 benzyl bromide
溴化碘/溴化碘 iodine bromide
溴化度米芬/溴化度米芬,溴化多米芬 domiphen bromide

溴化合物/溴化合物　bromine compound
溴化鲸蜡三甲铵/溴化鯨蠟三甲銨　cetyl trimethyl ammonium bromide
溴化锂/溴化鋰　lithium bromide
溴化硫胺/溴化硫胺[素]　thiamin bromide
溴化氰/溴化氰　cyanogen bromide
溴化氰试剂/溴化氰試劑　cyanogen bromide reagent
溴化十六烷基三甲铵/溴化十六烷基三甲銨　cetrimide
溴化十烃季铵/溴化十烃季銨,溴化十甲烯銨　decamethonium bromide
溴化烃类/溴化烴類　brominated hydrocarbons
溴化物/溴化物　bromide
溴化新斯的明/溴化新斯的明,溴化新斯弟格明　neostigmine bromide
溴化乙锭/溴化乙錠　ethidium bromide
溴化甾类/溴化甾類　brominated steroids
溴环葡萄糖吡咯/溴化吡咯糖　glycopyrronium bromide
溴己新/溴己新　bromhexine
溴甲酚蓝/溴甲酚藍　coeruleum bromocresolis
溴甲酚绿/溴甲酚綠　bromcresol green
溴甲酚紫/溴甲酚紫　bromcresol purple
溴甲基后马托品/溴甲基後馬托品　homatropine methylbromide
溴金酸/溴金酸　bromauric acid
溴克立辛/溴克利辛　brocresine
溴尿苷/溴尿苷　broxuridine
溴尿嘧啶/溴尿嘧啶　bromouracil
溴哌喷酯/溴哌噴酯,溴化哌苯偶酯　pipenzolate bromide
溴麝香草酚蓝/溴麝香草酚藍　bromothymol blue
溴水杨醇/溴水楊醇　bromosaligenin
溴酸/溴酸　bromic acid
溴酸钠/溴酸鈉　sodium bromate
溴酸盐滴定法/溴酸鹽滴定法　bromate titration
溴酸盐类/溴酸鹽類　bromates
溴脱氧胞苷/溴脱氧胞苷,溴去氧胞苷　bromodeoxycytidine
溴脱氧尿苷/溴脱氧尿苷,溴去氧尿苷　bromodeoxyuridine
溴西泮/溴西泮　bromazepam
溴异戊酰脲/溴異戊[醯]脲　bromisovalum
溴隐亭/溴隱亭　bromocriptine
溴疹/溴疹　bromoderma
须/鬚　barba
须部假性毛囊炎/鬚部假性毛囊炎　pseudofolliculitis barbae
须部湿疹/鬚部濕疹　eczema barbae
须疮/鬚瘡　acne mentagra
须疮样瘢痕性红斑/鬚瘡樣疤痕性紅斑　ulerythema sycosiforme
须疮样痤疮/鬚瘡狀痤瘡　acne sycosiformis
须疮样湿疹/鬚瘡狀濕疹　eczema sycomatosum
须发癣菌/鬚毛癬菌　trichophyton mentagrophytes
须发早白/鬚髮早白　premature graying hair
须[根]/鬚[根]　fibrous root, rootlet
须毛/鬚毛　vibrissae
须毛假性毛囊炎/鬚毛假性毛囊炎　pseudofolliculitis vibrissae
须眉性男性化/眉鬚型男性化　prosopopilary virilism
须曲霉/鬚麴黴,鬚麴菌　Aspergillus barbae
须癣/鬚癬　tinea barbae
虚/虚,缺乏,不足　deficiency
虚喘/虚喘　deficient dyspnea, dyspnea of deficiency type
虚喘·脾肺气虚证/虚喘·脾肺氣虛證　deficient dyspnea with pattern of qi deficiency of both spleen and lung
虚喘·肾阳衰微证/虚喘·腎陽衰微證　deficient dyspnea with pattern of kidney yang exhaustion
虚喘·肾阴虚证/虚喘·腎陰虛證　deficient dyspnea with pattern of kidney yin deficiency
虚烦/虚煩　vexing chest heat in a deficiency condition
虚烦不得眠/虚煩不得眠　insomnia due to vexation
虚烦不得卧/虚煩不得臥　insomnia due to vexation
虚寒痢/虚寒痢　deficiency-cold dysentery
虚幻性动脉瘤/虚幻性[腹主]動脈瘤　phantom aneurysm
虚黄/虚黃　deficient jaundice
虚火上炎/虚火上炎　flaring up of deficient fire
虚火上炎证/虚火上炎證　pattern of flaring up of deficient fire
虚火灼龈证/虚火灼齦證　pattern of deficient fire flaring gum
虚焦点/虚焦點　virtual focus
虚劳/虚勞　consumptive disease
虚劳[病]/勞病,消耗性疾病　consumptive disease
虚劳·肺气虚证/虚勞·肺氣虛證　consumptive disease with pattern of lung qi deficiency
虚劳·肺肾气虚证/虚勞·肺腎氣虛證　consumptive disease with pattern of qi deficiency of lung and kidney
虚劳·肺阴虚证/虚勞·肺陰虛證　consumptive disease with pattern of lung yin deficiency

虚劳·肝肾阴虚证/虛勞·肝腎陰虛證 consumptive disease with pattern of liver-kidney yin deficiency
虚劳·肝血虚证/虛勞·肝血虛證 consumptive disease with pattern of liver blood deficiency
虚劳·肝阴虚证/虛勞·肝陰虛證 consumptive disease with pattern of liver yin deficiency
虚劳·脾气虚证/虛勞·脾氣虛證 consumptive disease with pattern of spleen qi deficiency
虚劳·脾肾阳虚证/虛勞·脾腎陽虛證 consumptive disease with pattern of yang deficiency of spleen and kidney
虚劳·脾胃阴虚证/虛勞·脾胃陰虛證 consumptive disease with pattern of yin deficiency of spleen and stomach
虚劳·脾血虚证/虛勞·脾血虛證 consumptive disease with pattern of spleen blood deficiency
虚劳·脾阳虚证/虛勞·脾陽虛證 consumptive disease with pattern of spleen yang deficiency
虚劳·气阴两虚证/虛勞·氣陰兩虛證 consumptive disease with pattern of deficiency of both qi and yin
虚劳·肾精亏虚证/虛勞·腎精虧虛證 consumptive disease with pattern of kidney essence insufficiency
虚劳·肾气虚证/虛勞·腎氣虛證 consumptive disease with pattern of kidney qi deficiency
虚劳·肾阳虚证/虛勞·腎陽虛證 consumptive disease with pattern of kidney yang deficiency
虚劳·肾阴虚证/虛勞·腎陰虛證 consumptive disease with pattern of kidney yin deficiency
虚劳·肾阴阳两虚证/虛勞·腎陰陽兩虛證 consumptive disease with pattern of deficiency of both kidney yin and kidney yang
虚劳·心脾两虚证/虛勞·心脾兩虛證 consumptive disease with pattern of heart-spleen deficiency
虚劳·心气虚证/虛勞·心氣虛證 consumptive disease with pattern of heart qi deficiency
虚劳·心肾阳虚证/虛勞·心腎陽虛證 consumptive disease with pattern of yang deficiency of both heart and kidney
虚劳·心血虚证/虛勞·心血虛證 consumptive disease with pattern of heart blood deficiency
虚劳·心阳虚证/虛勞·心陽虛證 consumptive disease with pattern of heart yang deficiency
虚劳·心阴虚证/虛勞·心陰虛證 consumptive disease with pattern of heart yin deficiency
虚里疼痛/虛里疼痛 pain at xuli
虚脉/虛脈 feeble pulse
虚秘/虛秘 deficient constipation
虚疟/虛瘧 deficient malaria
虚呕/虛嘔 deficient vomiting
虚呕·脾胃气虚证/虛嘔·脾胃氣虛證 deficient vomiting with pattern of qi deficiency of spleen and stomach
虚呕·脾胃虚寒证/虛嘔·脾胃虛寒證 deficient vomiting with pattern of deficiency-cold of spleen and stomach
虚呕·脾胃阳虚证/虛嘔·脾胃陽虛證 deficient vomiting with pattern of yang deficiency of spleen and stomach
虚呕·胃阴虚证/虛嘔·胃陰虛證 deficient vomiting with pattern of stomach yin deficiency
虚弱老人/虛弱老人 frail elderly
虚实辨证/虛實辨證 pattern identification of excess and deficiency
虚实夹杂/虛實夾雜 intermingled deficiency and excess
虚实夹杂证/虛實夾雜證 pattern of intermingled deficiency and excess
虚实真假/虛實真假 true-false of excess-deficiency
虚体感冒/虛體感冒 common cold in debilitated constitution
虚脱/虛脫 collapse
虚脱性斑疹伤寒/虛脫性斑疹傷寒 collapsing typhus
虚脱谵妄/虛脫譫妄 collapse delirium
虚无妄想/虛無妄想 nihilistic delusion
虚陷/虛陷 deficiency inward collapse
虚邪/虛邪 deficient pathogen
虚性暗点/虛性暗點,負性暗點 negative scotoma
虚阳上浮/虛陽上浮 deficient yang with upper manifestation
虚则太阴/虛則太陰 deficient disease located in Taiyin
虚者补其母/虛者補其母 reinforcing mother viscera for treating deficiency of child viscera
虚者补之/虛者補之 treating deficiency pattern with tonifying methods
虚中/虛中 deficient parapoplexy
虚中夹实/虛中夾實 deficiency complicated with excess
虚肿/虛腫 deficiency swelling
需求估价/需求估價 needs assessment
需氧呼吸/需氧呼吸 aerobic respiration
需氧菌呼吸酶/需氧菌呼吸酶,供氣酶 aerase
需氧量/需氧量 oxygen requirement
需氧生活/需氧生活 aerobiosis
需氧脱氢酶/需氧脫氫酶 aerobic dehydrogenase

需要证明/需要證明　certificate of need
徐长卿/徐長卿　paniculate swallowwort root
徐发/徐發,起病隐袭　insidious onset
徐疾补泻/徐疾補瀉　slow-rapid reinforcing-reducing method
徐灵胎医学全书/徐靈胎醫學全書　Xu Lingtai's Complete Medical Book
许克韧带/許克韌帶,Hueck 氏韧带　Hueck ligament
许勒尔综合征/許勒爾症候群,Schüller 氏症候群　Schüller syndrome
许佩尔病/許佩爾病,Hueppe 氏病　Hueppe disease
许特尔细胞癌/許特爾細胞癌,Hürthle 氏細胞癌　Hürthle cell carcinoma
许特尔细胞腺瘤/許特爾細胞腺瘤,Hürthle 氏細胞腺瘤　Hürthle cell adenoma
许瓦茨曼反应/許瓦茨曼反應　Schwartzman reaction
醑剂/醑劑　spiritus
旭日型静脉曲张/旭日型靜脈曲張　sunburst varicosity
序贯式主动脉冠状动脉搭桥术/序貫式主動脈冠狀動脈搭橋術　sequential aortocoronary bypass grafting
序贯试验/序貫試驗　sequential trial
序贯透析/序貫透析　sequential dialysis
序列/序列　sequence
序列比对/序列比對　sequence alignment
序列标记位点/序列標記位[元]點　sequence tagged site
序列分析/序列分析　sequence analysis
序列分析仪/序列[分析]儀,定序儀　sequenator, sequencer
序列缺失/序列缺失　sequence deletion
序列特异的寡核苷酸探针/序列特異的寡核苷酸探針　sequence specific oligonucleotide probe
序列同源性/序列同源性　sequence homology
序列征/序列徵,複徵,症候群　sequence
叙利亚溃疡/敘利亞潰瘍　Syrian ulcer
叙翁神经/敘翁神經,Cyon 氏神經　Cyon nerve
续存性动脉干/續存性動脈幹　persistent truncus arteriosus
续存性甲状舌管/續存性甲狀舌管,永存性甲狀腺舌管　persistent thyroglossal duct
续断/續斷　himalayan teasel root
续发性精神病态/續發性精神病態,病中疑懼症　epinosis
续筋接骨/續筋接骨　reunion of fractured tendons and bones
续名医类案/續名醫類案　A Supplement to Classified Case Records of Distinguished Physicians, Supplement to Classified Case Records of Celebrated Physicians
絮凝/凝絮[現象]　flocculation
絮凝试验/絮凝試驗　flocculation test
絮片状变性/絮片狀變性,葉狀變性　floccular degeneration
絮状反应/絮狀反應,凝絮反應　flocculation reaction
絮状麦皮癣菌/絮狀表皮癬菌　Epidermophyton floccosum
蓄积/蓄積　accumulation
蓄积毒性/蓄積毒性　cumulative toxicity
蓄气性腹膜炎/蓄氣性腹膜炎　gas peritonitis
蓄水证/蓄水證　stagnated fluid pattern
蓄血证/蓄血證　stagnated blood pattern
宣肺化痰/宣肺化痰　ventilating lung qi for dissipating phlegm
宣肺降逆/宣肺降逆　ventilating lung qi for lowering adverse qi
宣肺利水/宣肺利水　ventilating lung qi for diuresis
宣肺通气/宣肺通氣　ventilating lung qi
宣剂/宣劑　diffusing formula
宣明论方/宣明論方　Clear Synopsis on Recipes
宣明五气篇/宣明五氣篇　On Five Qi
喧嚷谵妄/喧嚷譫妄　noisy delirium
喧噪呼吸/喧噪呼吸　noisy respiration
玄府/汗[腺]孔　sweat pore
玄妙散/玄妙散　mysterious powder with figwort
玄明粉/玄明粉　sodium sulfate powder
玄参/玄參　figwort root
悬垂腹/懸垂腹　pendulous abdomen
悬垂肾/懸垂腎　nephrospasis
悬滴培养[物]/懸滴培養　hanging-drop culture
悬吊绷带/懸吊繃帶　suspensory bandage
悬吊绷带法/懸吊繃帶法　suspensory bandaging
悬吊夹板/懸吊夾板　suspension splint
悬浮时间/混懸時間　suspension time
悬浮[液]/懸浮[液],混懸劑　suspension
悬挂干湿球湿度计/懸擺式空氣濕度計　sling psychrometer
悬块培养[物]/懸塊培養,懸基培養　hanging-block culture
悬厘/懸厘　xuanli, GB6
悬颅/懸顱　xuanlu, GB5
悬起灸/懸起灸　over skin moxibustion, suspension moxibustion
悬韧带/懸韌帶　suspensory ligament
悬枢/懸樞　xuanshu, DU5

悬锁卡环/懸鎖卡環　swing lock clasp
悬突/懸突,外突,突出物　overhang
悬液/懸液　suspension
悬饮/懸飲　suspending fluid, suspending fluid retention
悬饮·肺络不畅证/懸飲·肺絡不暢證　suspending fluid retention with pattern of impediments of lung collaterals
悬饮·阴虚内热证/懸飲·陰虛內熱證　suspending fluid retention with pattern of internal heat due to yin deficiency
悬饮·饮停胸胁证/懸飲·飲停胸脅證　suspending fluid retention with pattern of fluid retaining in chest and hypochondrium
悬痈/懸癰　Huiyin abscess
悬雍垂/懸雍垂　uvula
悬雍垂部分切除术/懸雍部分切除術　cionotomy
悬雍垂刀/懸雍垂刀　kiotome
悬雍垂缝术/懸雍縫合術,裂腭縫合術　staphylorrhaphy
悬雍垂过长/懸雍垂過長,懸雍垂下垂　cionoptosis
悬雍垂肌/懸雍垂肌　uvularis
悬雍垂裂/懸雍垂裂,兩歧懸雍垂　bifid uvula
悬雍垂钳/懸雍垂鉗　staphylagra
悬雍垂切除术/懸雍垂切除術　staphylectomy
悬雍垂[软腭]成形术/懸雍垂成形術　staphyloplasty
悬雍垂[软腭]裂/懸雍垂裂　staphyloschisis
悬雍垂水肿/懸雍垂水腫　staphyledema
悬雍垂松弛/懸雍垂鬆弛　staphylodialysis
悬雍垂下垂/懸雍垂下垂　staphyloptosis, uvular ptosis
悬雍垂血肿/懸雍垂血腫　staphylhematoma
悬雍垂咽峡炎/懸雍垂咽峽咽,葡萄球菌咽炎　staphyloangina
悬雍垂延长/懸雍垂延長　himantosis
悬雍垂炎/雍懸垂炎　cionitis
悬钟/懸鐘　xuanzhong, GB39
悬珠痔/懸珠痔　fibropapilloma of anus, suspending bead pile
悬珠痔·气滞血瘀证/懸珠痔·氣滯血瘀證　fibropapilloma of anus with pattern of qi stagnation and blood stasis
悬珠痔·湿热下注证/懸珠痔·濕熱下注證　fibropapilloma of anus with pattern of dampness-heat diffusing downward
旋动脉/[迴]旋動脈　circumflex artery
旋耳疮/旋耳瘡,耳濕疹　ear eczema, eczema of ear
旋耳疮·风热湿邪证/旋耳瘡·風熱濕邪證　ear eczema with wind-heat-dampness pattern
旋耳疮·血虚风燥证/旋耳瘡·血虛風燥證　ear eczema with pattern of wind-dryness due to blood deficiency
旋腓骨支/旋腓骨支　circumflex fibular branch
旋覆代赭石汤/旋覆代赭石湯　xuanfu daizheshi decoction
旋覆花/旋覆花　inula flower
旋肱后动脉/旋肱後動脈　posterior humeral circumflex artery
旋肱后静脉/旋肱後静脈　posterior humeral circumflex vein
旋肱前动脉/旋肱前動脈　anterior humeral circumflex artery
旋肱前静脉/旋肱前静脈　anterior humeral circumflex vein
旋股内侧动脉/旋股内側動脈,股動脈内側迴旋支　medial femoral circumflex artery
旋股内侧动脉横支/旋股内側動脈横支　transverse branch of medial femoral circumflex artery
旋股内侧动脉髋臼支/旋股内側動脈髋臼支　acetabular branch of medial femoral circumflex artery
旋股内侧动脉浅支/旋股内側動脈淺支　superficial branch of medial femoral circumflex artery
旋股内侧动脉深支/旋股内側動脈深支　deep branch of medial femoral circumflex artery
旋股内侧动脉升支/旋股内側動脈昇支　ascending branch of medial femoral circumflex artery
旋股内侧静脉/旋股内側静脈　medial femoral circumflex vein
旋股内侧深动脉/旋股内側深動脈　internal deep circumflex artery
旋股外侧动脉/旋股外側動脈　lateral femoral circumflex artery
旋股外侧动脉横支/旋股外側動脈横支　transverse branch of lateral femoral circumflex artery
旋股外侧动脉降支/旋股外側動脈降支　descending branch of lateral femoral circumflex artery
旋股外侧动脉升支/旋股外側動脈昇支　ascending branch of lateral femoral circumflex artery
旋股外侧静脉/旋股外側静脈　lateral femoral circumflex vein, lateral circumflex femoral vein
旋光度/旋光度　optical rotation
旋光计/旋光計　polarimeter
旋光镜检查/偏光鏡檢查　polariscopic examination
旋光率/旋光率,比旋率　specific rotation
旋光尿糖计/測尿糖旋光鏡　diabetometer

旋光色觉镜/旋光色覺鏡　ophthalmoleukoscope
旋光色散/旋光色散,旋光分散　optical rotatory dispersion
旋光异构/旋光異構,光學[同質]異構　optical isomerism
旋后/旋後　supination
旋后肌/旋後肌　supinator
旋后肌嵴/旋後肌嵴　supinator crest
旋后肌综合征/旋後肌綜合徵　supinator pattern
旋肩胛动脉/旋肩胛動脈　circumflex scapular artery, circumflex artery of scapula
旋肩胛静脉/旋肩胛靜脈　circumflex scapular vein
旋螺风/旋螺風　balanoposthitis
旋毛虫/旋毛蟲　trichinella spiralis
旋毛虫病/旋毛蟲病　flesh-worm disease
旋毛虫栓塞/旋毛蟲栓塞　trichinous embolism
旋毛虫性肌炎/旋毛蟲性肌炎　trichinous myositis
旋盘尾丝虫/旋盤尾絲蟲,蟠尾絲蟲　Onchocerca volvulus
旋髂浅动脉/旋髂淺動脈　superficial iliac circumflex artery
旋髂浅静脉/旋髂淺靜脈　superficial iliac circumflex vein, superficial circumflex iliac vein
旋髂深动脉/旋髂深動脈　deep iliac circumflex artery
旋髂深动脉升支/旋髂深動脈昇支　ascending branch of deep iliac circumflex artery
旋髂深静脉/旋髂深靜脈　deep iliac circumflex vein, deep circumflex iliac vein
旋前/旋前　pronation
旋前方肌/旋前方肌　pronator quadratus, musculus pronator quadratus
旋前肌粗隆/旋前肌粗隆　pronator tuberosity
旋前屈肌/旋前屈肌　pronatoflexor
旋前圆肌/旋前圓肌　pronator teres, musculus pronator teres
旋前圆肌尺骨头/旋前圓肌尺骨頭　ulnar head of pronator teres
旋前圆肌肱骨头/旋前圓肌肱骨頭　humeral head of pronator teres
旋前圆肌综合征/旋前圓肌綜合徵　pronator pattern
旋前征/旋前徵[象]　pronation sign
旋锐形线虫/旋銳形線蟲,螺旋絲狀蟲　Acuaria spiralis
旋神经/旋神經　circumflex nerve
旋头痉挛/旋頭痙攣　rotatory spasm
旋尾目感染/旋尾目感染　Spirurida infections
旋斜计/旋斜計,眼肌偏轉力計　clinometer
旋眼痉挛/旋眼痙攣　oculogyric spasm
旋凿状齿/旋鑿狀齒　screw-driver teeth
旋支/旋支　circumflex branch
旋转棒性能试验/旋轉棒性能試驗　rotarod performance test
旋转不良/旋轉不良,旋轉失常,旋轉不當　malrotation
旋转磁场疗法/旋轉磁場療法　rotated magnetic field therapy
旋转法/旋轉法　rotating manipulation
旋转复位法/旋轉復位法　rotative restoration
旋转管/旋轉管　roll tube
旋转-回音序列/旋轉-回音序列　spin-echo sequence
旋转计/旋轉計　tropometer
旋转黏度计/旋轉[式]黏度計　rotating cylinder viscometer
旋转皮瓣/旋轉皮瓣　rotated skin flap
旋转屈伸/旋轉屈伸　rotation and flexion-extension
旋转试验/旋轉試驗　rotation test
旋转斜视/旋轉斜視　cyclotropia
旋转性头震颤/旋轉性頭震顫　head nystagmus
旋转性眩晕/旋轉性眩暈　rotary vertigo
旋转性眼球震颤/旋轉性眼球震顫　rotatory nystagmus
旋转压片机/旋轉壓片機,旋轉式壓錠機　rotary tablet machine
旋转异构体/旋轉異構體　rotamer
旋转隐斜/轉動斜眼,周轉隱斜視　cyclophoria
旋转隐斜视计/旋轉隱斜視計,轉動斜視計　cyclophorometer
旋锥蝇属/螺旋蠅屬　*Cochliomyia*
漩涡浴/漩[渦]浴　whirlpool bath
璇玑/璇璣　xuanji, RN21
选色/選色　shade selection
选用药/選用藥,首選藥物　drug of choice
选择/選擇　selection
选择毒性/選擇[性]毒性　selective toxicity
选择婚配/選擇婚配,選擇性交配　assortative mating
选择偏倚/選擇偏倚　selection bias
选择去偶/選擇[性]去偶　selective decoupling
选择松弛/選擇鬆弛　relaxation of selection
选择素类/選擇素類　selectins
选择系数/選擇係數　selection coefficient
选择行为/選擇行為　choice behavior
选择性/選擇性　selectivity
选择性雌激素受体调节剂/選擇性雌激素受體調節劑　selective estrogen receptor modulator
选择性蛋白尿/選擇性蛋白尿　selective proteinuria

选择性脊神经后根切断术/選擇性脊神經後根切斷術　selective posterior rhizotomy
选择性剪接/選擇性剪接　alternative splicing
选择性颈部廓清[术]/選擇性頸部淋巴擴清術　elective neck dissection
选择性迷走神经切断术/選擇性迷走神經切斷術　selective vagotomy
选择性免疫球蛋白缺陷/選擇性免疫球蛋白缺陷　selective immunoglobulin deficiency
选择性培养基/選擇性培養基　selective medium
选择性亲和力/選擇性親和力　elective affinity
选择性 IgA 缺陷/選擇性 IgA 缺陷,選擇性免疫球蛋白 A 缺乏　selective IgA deficiency
选择性 IgM 缺陷/選擇性 IgM 缺陷,選擇性免疫球蛋白 M 缺乏　selective IgM deficiency
选择性 X 射线摄影术/選擇性 X 射線攝影術　selective roentgenography
选择性肾动脉造影[术]/選擇性腎動脈造影[術]　selective renal arteriography
选择性外科手术/選擇性外科手術　elective surgical procedures
选择[性]吸收/選擇性吸收　selective absorption
选择性心血管造影[术]/選擇性心血管造影[術]　selective angiocardiography
选择性紫外线 B 光治疗/選擇性紫外線 B 光治療　selective ultraviolet B phototherapy
选择学说/選擇學說　selective theory
选择压力/選擇壓力　selection pressure
选择优势/選擇優勢　selection advantage
癣/癣　ringworm, tinea
癣菌性脱发/癣菌性禿髮　trichophytic alopecia
癣湿药水/癣濕藥水　xuanshi solution
眩晕[病]/眩暈　vertigo
眩晕持续状态/暈眩持續狀態　status vertiginous
眩晕·肝火上炎证/眩暈·肝火上炎證　endogenous vertigo with pattern of flaring up of liver fire
眩晕·肝阳上亢证/眩暈·肝陽上亢證　endogenous vertigo with pattern of liver yang hyperactivity
眩晕·痰湿阻滞证/眩暈·痰濕阻滯證　vertigo with pattern of stagnation and blockade of phlegm-damp
眩晕·痰浊上扰证/眩暈·痰濁上擾證　endogenous vertigo with pattern of upward disturbance of phlegm-turbidity
眩晕·外感风寒证/眩暈·外感風寒證　vertigo with pattern of exogenous wind-cold
眩晕·外感暑湿证/眩暈·外感暑濕證　vertigo with pattern of exogenous summerheat-damp
眩晕·外感燥火证/眩暈·外感燥火證　vertigo with pattern of exogenous dryness-fire
眩晕·瘀血阻窍证/眩暈·瘀血阻竅證　endogenous vertigo with pattern of static blood blocking orifices
削除疗法/削除療法　shaving therapy
削痂术/削痂術　eschar shaving
靴状心/靴狀心　coeur en sabot
学科间信息交流/學科間資訊交流　interdisciplinary communication
学龄儿童/學齡兒童　school child
学龄期/學齡期　school stage
学龄前儿童/學齡前兒童　preschool child
学龄前期/學齡前期　preschool stage
学生保健服务/學生保健服務　student health service
学生近视/學生近視,學齡兒童近視　school myopia
学习过度/學習過度　overlearning
学习无助状态/學習無助狀態　learned helplessness
学习障碍/學習障礙　learning disorder
学语后聋/學語後聾,學話後聾　postlingual deafness
学语前聋/學語前聾,學話前聾　prelingual deafness
雪白曲霉/雪白黴菌　Aspergillus niveus
雪崩学说/雪崩[狀神經興奮漸強]學說　avalanche theory
雪崩状传导/雪崩狀傳導　avalanche conduction
雪貂瘟热病毒/雪貂瘟熱病毒　ferret distemper virus
雪花状内障/雪花狀內障,雲片狀內障,暴風雪狀內障　snowflake cataract
雪茄状小体/雪茄狀小體　cigar body
雪镜/雪鏡　snow glasses
雪口/雪口　oral candidiasis, thrush
雪盲/雪盲　snow blindness
雪泥疗法/雪泥療法,雪水療法　slush treatment
雪球树皮/雪球樹皮　cramp bark
雪上一支蒿中毒/雪上一支蒿中毒　Aconitum kongboense poisoning
鳕肝尸胺/鳕肝屍胺,肝油酸毒　morrhuin
鳕[鱼]/鳕[魚],鳕鱉　morrhua
鳕鱼肝油/鳕[魚]肝油　cod liver oil
鳕组蛋白/鳕組蛋白,鳕精組織蛋白　gaduhiston
血/血　blood
血白蛋白/血清白蛋白　blood albumin
血白蛋白过多/血白蛋白過多,高白蛋白血症　hyperalbuminemia
血白蛋白减少/血白蛋白減少,低蛋白血症　hypalbuminemia
血孢子虫/血孢子蟲　haemosporidium
血泵/血泵　blood pump
血比热/血比熱　specific heat of blood
血比重计/血比重計　hemabarometer

血吡咯/血吡咯　hemopyrrol
血鞭毛虫/血鞭毛蟲　hemoflagellate
血便/血便,血糞　bloody stool
血冰点降低测定法/血冰點降低測定法,血液冰點測定法　hemocryoscopy
血病及气/血病及氣　blood disease involving qi
血卟啉光辐射疗法/血卟啉光輻射療法,血卟啉光照療法　hematoporphyrin photoradiation
血卟啉类/血卟啉類　hematoporphyrins
血卟啉尿/血卟啉尿,血紫質尿　hematoporphyrinuria
血卟啉衍生物/血卟啉衍生物　hematoporphyrin derivative
血补体/血補體,血防禦素　hemalexin
血尘/血塵　dust corpuscle
血沉/血沈　blood sedimentation
血沉淀素/血沈澱素　hemoprecipitin
血沉指数/血沈指數,沉降指數　sedimentation index
血沉棕黄层/血沈棕黃層,血塊黃層　buffy coat
血成分测定法/血[液]成分測定法　hematometry
血传病原体/血傳病原體　blood-borne pathogen
血胆固醇试验/血膽固醇試驗　blood cholesterol test
血胆固醇正常/血膽固醇量正常　normocholesterolemia
血胆碱酯酶缺乏/血中膽素酯酶缺乏　esterapenia
血胆素尿/血膽素尿,血膽紅素尿症　hemobilinuria
血蛋白电泳/血蛋白電泳　blood protein electrophoresis
血蛋白疾病/血蛋白疾病　blood protein disorder
血蛋白正常/血蛋白正常　normoproteinemia
血蛋白质类/血蛋白質類　blood proteins
血岛/血島　blood island
血窦/血竇[狀隙]　blood sinusoid
血窦循环/血竇循環,竇狀隙循環　sinusoidal circulation
血发酵/血[液]發酵　hematozymosis
血房水屏障/血房水屏障,血房液障壁　blood-aqueous barrier
血分/血分　blood tier, xuefen
血分光镜/血[液]分光鏡　hematoscope
血分光镜检查/血[液]分光鏡檢查　hematoscopy
血分热毒/血分熱毒　heat-toxicity in xuefen
血分瘀热/血分瘀熱　stagnated heat in xuefen
血分证/血分證　xuefen pattern
血风疮/血風瘡　general papular eczema
血府逐瘀汤/血府逐瘀湯　decoction for removing blood stasis in the chest, xuefu zhuyu decoction
血钙正常/血鈣正常　normocalcemia
血钙指数/血鈣指數　calcium index

血干燥物质测定法/血[液]乾燥成分測定法　hygremometry
血-肝源性黄疸/血-肝源性黃疸　hemato-hepatogenous jaundice
血睾屏障/血睾屏障　blood-testis barrier
血根草/血根[草],血根樹　bloodroot
血供/血供,血液供給　blood supply
血管/血管　blood vessel
血管暗点/血管暗點,血管性盲點　angioscotoma
血管暗点测量法/血管暗點測量法,血管性盲點測記法　angioscotometry
[血管]闭塞性疾病/[血管]閉塞性疾病,動脈阻塞疾病　occlusive disease
血管[闭塞性]综合征/血管[閉塞性]症候群,血管性症候群　vascular syndrome
血管[壁]坏死/血管壞死　angionecrosis
血管病/血管病　angiopathy
血管病变/血管病變　vasculopathy
血管病变性眩晕/血管病性眩暈　angiopathic vertigo
血管病理学/血管病理學　angiopathology
血管病性神经病/血管病性神經病　angiopathic neuropathy
血管成肌纤维细胞瘤/血管肌纖維母細胞瘤　angiomyofibroblastoma
血管成肌纤维细胞瘤样瘤/血管肌纖維母細胞瘤樣瘤　angiomyofibroblastoma-like tumor
血管成形术/血管成形術,血管造形術　angioplasty
血管床/血管床　vascular bed
血管丛/血管叢　vascular plexus
血管脆弱/血管脆弱　angiopsathyrosis
血管毒/血管毒　vascular poison
血管对合器/血管對合器　vessel approximator
血管发生/血管發生,血管生成　angiogenesis
血管发育不良/血管發育不良　angiodysplasia
血管反射/血管反射　vasoreflex
血管分叉口栓子/血管分叉栓子,騎馬狀栓子　saddle embolus
血管缝合/血管縫合　vascular suture
血管缝合术/血管縫合術　angiorrhaphy
血管感觉神经/血管感覺神經　vasosensory nerve
血管梗塞性肾切除/血管梗塞性腎切除　angioinfarction nephrectomy
血管构造/血管構造,血管構築　angioarchitecture
血管骨肥大综合征/血管骨肥大症候群　angio-osteohypertrophy syndrome
血管环/血管環,脈管環　vascular ring
血管活性肠多肽瘤/血管活性腸多肽瘤,胰腺瘤　vipoma

血管活性肠肽/血管活性腸肽　vasoactive intestinal peptide
血管活性肠肽受体/血管活性腸肽受體　vasoactive intestinal peptide receptor
血管[肌]层/血管[肌]層　vascular layer
血管[肌层]透明变性/血管肌層透明變性　angiohyalinosis
血管肌瘤/血管肌瘤　angiomyoma
血管肌肉瘤/血管肌肉瘤　angiomyosarcoma
血管肌脂瘤/血管肌脂瘤　angiomyolipoma
血管极/血管極　vascular pole
血管疾病/血管疾病　vascular disease
血管加压药/血管加壓藥　vasopressor
血管假体植入/血管假體植入　blood vessel prosthesis implantation
血管减压/血管減壓，抑制血管阻力，使血壓下降　vasodepression
血管减压药/血管減壓藥　vasodepressor
血管角质瘤/血管角質瘤　angiokeratoma
血管节/血管節　angiotome
血管紧张/血管緊張　angiotonia
血管紧张失调/血管緊張失調，血管緊張度不等狀態　angioataxia
血管紧张素/血管張力素　angiotensin
血管紧张素类/血管緊張素類　angiotensins
血管紧张素酶/血管緊張素酶，昇壓素酶　hypertensinase
血管紧张素受体/血管緊張素受體　angiotensin receptor
血管紧张素受体拮抗药/血管緊張素受體拮抗藥　angiotensin receptor antagonist
血管紧张素酰胺/血管緊張素醯胺　angiotensin amide
血管紧张素原/血管緊縮素原　angiotensinogen
血管紧张素转化酶抑制药/血管緊張素轉化酶抑制藥　angiotensin converting enzyme inhibitor
血管紧张素转换酶/血管張力素轉換酶　angiotensin-converting enzyme
血管紧张素转换酶抑制药/血管緊張素轉換酶抑制藥　angiotensin-converting enzyme inhibitor
血管痉挛/血管痙攣　vasospasm
血管痉挛病/血管痙攣性病　angiospasmodic disease
血管痉挛性感觉缺失/血管痙攣性感覺缺失　angiospastic anesthesia
血管痉挛性中心视网膜炎/血管痙攣性中心視網膜炎，中央血管痙攣性視網膜炎　central angiospastic retinitis
血管镜检查/血管鏡檢查　angioscopy

血管口径张力计/血管運動描記器，血管張力計　angiometer
血管溃疡/血管潰瘍　angionoma
血管扩张/血管擴張　angiectases
血管扩张剂/血管擴張劑　vasodilator
血管扩张器/血管擴張器　vessel dilator
血管扩张性癌/血管擴張性癌　telangiectatic cancer
血管扩张性肌瘤/血管擴張性肌瘤，毛細血管擴張性肌瘤　myoma telangiectodes
血管扩张性黏液瘤/血管擴張性黏液瘤　telangiectatic myxoma
血管扩张性息肉/血管擴張性息肉　polypus telangiectodes
血管扩张药/血管擴張藥　vasodilator
血管扩张痣/血管擴張痣　nevus angiectodes
血管淋巴管瘤/血管淋巴管瘤　angiolymphangioma
血管淋巴样增生伴毛囊性黏蛋白病/血管淋巴球增生伴毛囊性黏液素病　angiolymphoid hyperplasia with follicular mucinosis
血管淋巴样增生伴嗜酸细胞增多/血管淋巴球增生伴嗜伊紅球增多　angiolymphoid hyperplasia with eosinophilia
血管淋巴样增生伴嗜酸性粒细胞增多/血管淋巴樣增生伴嗜酸性球細胞增多　angiolymphoid hyperplasia with eosinophila
血管瘤/血管瘤　hemangioma
血管瘤病/血管瘤病　hemangiomatosis
血管瘤出血/血管瘤出血　hemangioma with hemorrhage
血管瘤性息肉/血管瘤狀息肉　polypus angiomatodes
血管瘤样纤维性组织细胞瘤/血管瘤樣纖維性組織細胞瘤　angiomatoid fibrous histiocytoma
血管瘤状痣/血管瘤狀痣　nevus angiomatodes
血管瘘/血管瘻　vascular fistula
血管漏斗/血管漏斗　vascular funnel
血管麻痹/血管麻痺　angioparalysis
血管迷走[神经]反射/血管迷走[神經]反射　vasovagal reflex
血管迷走[神经]性发作/血管迷走神經性發作　vasovagal attack
血管迷走神经性晕厥/血管迷走神經性暈厥　vasovagal syncope
血管迷走神经综合征/血管迷走神經症候群　vasovagal syndrome
血管免疫母细胞淋巴结病/血管免疫母細胞性淋巴腺病　angioimmunoblastic lymphadenopathy
血管免疫母细胞性淋巴结病伴异常蛋白血症/血管免疫母細胞性淋巴腺病變伴異常蛋白血症

angioimmunoblastic lymphadenopathy with dysproteinemia
血管膜部/血管膜部,葡萄腹部 uveal part
血管内低强度激光照射疗法/血管内低强度雷射照射療法 intravascular low level laser irradiation therapy
血管内化脓性肉芽肿/血管內化膿性肉芽腫 intravascular pyogenic granuloma
血管内激光照射疗法/血管內雷射照射療法 intravascular laser irradiation therapy
血管内筋膜炎/血管內肌膜炎 intravascular fasciitis
血管内膜炎/血管內膜炎 endovasculitis
血管内凝集/血管內凝集 intravascular agglutination
血管内凝结/血管內凝結 intravascular agglutinative
血管内皮/血管內皮 vascular endothelium
血管内皮瘤/血管內皮瘤 angioendothelioma
血管内皮瘤病/血管內皮[細胞]瘤病 angioendotheliomatosis
血管内皮生长因子/血管內皮生長因子 vascular endothelial growth factor
血管内乳头状内皮增生/血管內乳突狀內皮增生 intravascular papillary endothelial hyperplasia
血管内乳头状血管内皮瘤/血管內乳突狀血管內皮瘤 endovascular papillary angioendothelioma
血管内血凝固/血管內血凝固,血管內凝血 intravascular clotting
血管内氧合/血管內氧合 intravascular oxygenation
血管内造血/血管內造血 intravascular hematopoiesis, intravascular hemopoiesis
血管内支架/血管內支架 endovascular stent
血管内治疗/血管內治療 endovascular treatment
血管黏液瘤/血管黏液瘤 angiomyxoma
血管旁路移植术/血管旁路移植術 blood vessel by-pass grafting
血管胚层/血管胚層,血管母細胞,成血管細胞 angioderm
血管平滑肌瘤/血管[平滑]肌瘤 angioleiomyoma
血管破坏/血管破壞 angiolysis
血管前间隙/血管前間隙 prevascular space
血管前置/血管前置 vasa previa
血管腔内扩张术/血管腔內擴張術 intraluminal dilatation
血管腔隙/血管腔隙 lacuna vasorum, vascular compartment
血管强壮药/血管強壯藥,強血管藥 vascular tonic
血管切除术/血管切除術 angiectomy
血管切开术/血管切開術 angiotomy
血管轻瘫/血管輕癱 vasoparesis
血管球/血管球 glomus
血管球肌瘤/脈絡球血管肌瘤 glomangiomyoma
血管球瘤/血管球瘤,脈絡球血管瘤 glomangioma
血管球体/血管球體 glomus body
血管容量/血管容量 vascular capacitance
血管肉瘤/血管肉瘤 angiosarcoma
血管软骨瘤/血管軟骨瘤 angiochondroma
血管上[肌]层/血管上[肌]層 supravascular layer
血管烧伤/血管燒傷 burn of blood vessel
血管神经/血管神經 vascular nerve
血管神经病/血管神經病[變] angioneuropathy
血管神经病体质/血管神經性體質 vasoneurotic constitution
血管神经肌瘤/血管神經肌瘤 angioneuromyoma
血管神经胶质瘤/血管神經膠瘤 angioglioma
血管神经胶质瘤病/血管神經膠瘤病 angiogliomatosis
血管神经切除术/血管神經切除術 angioneurectomy
血管神经切断术/血管神經切開術 angioneurotomy
血管神经痛/血管神經痛 angioneuralgia
血管神经性血尿/血管神經性血尿 angioneurotic hematuria
血管神经性紫癜/血管神經性紫癜,血管神經病性紫癜病 purpura angioneurotica
血管升压素受体/血管昇壓素受體 vasopressin receptor
血管生成/血管生成 angiogenesis
血管生成蛋白质类/血管生成蛋白質類 angiogenic proteins
血管生成素/血管生成素 angiopoietin
血管生成调节剂/血管生成調節劑 angiogenesis modulating agent
血管生成抑制剂/血管生成抑制劑 angiogenesis inhibitor
血管生成诱导剂/血管生成誘導劑 angiogenesis inducing agent
血管石样变性/血管石樣變性,血管結石性變性 angiolithic degeneration
血管收缩/血管收縮,血管緊縮,血管縮小 vasoconstriction
血管收缩神经/血管收縮神經,血管緊縮神經 vasoconstrictor nerve
血管收缩性止血剂/血管性止血劑 vascular styptic
血管收缩药/血管收縮藥 vasoconstrictor, vasoconstrictor agent
血管舒缓素/血管舒緩素,微血管增滲素 kallikrein
血管舒缓素-激肽系统/血管舒緩素-激肽系統 kallikrein-kinin system

血管舒缩/血管舒縮,血管活動,血管運動 angiokinesis
血管舒缩力/血管舒縮力,血管運動力 vasomotoricity
血管舒缩神经/血管運動神經 vasomotor nerve
血管舒缩失调/血管運動性失調[症] vasomotor ataxia
血管舒缩系统/血管舒縮系統 vasomotor system
血管舒缩性鼻炎/血管運動性鼻炎 vasomotor rhinitis
血管舒缩性心绞痛/血管舒縮性心絞痛,血管收縮性心絞痛 vasomotor angina
血管舒缩性肿胀/血管舒縮[性]腫脹 vasomotor tumentia
血管舒缩药/血管舒縮藥 vasomotor
血管舒张/血管舒張,血管擴張 vasodilation
血管舒张神经/血管舒張神經 vasodilator nerve
血管舒张药/血管舒張藥 vasodilator agent
血管松弛药/血管鬆弛藥 vessel relaxant
血管痛/血管痛 angialgia
血管透热凝固术/血管透熱凝固法 angiodiathermy
血管外肺水/血管外肺水 extravascular lung water
血管外科手术/血管外科手術 vascular surgical procedure
[血管]外膜/[血管]外膜 adventitia, tunica adventitia
血管外皮细胞瘤/血管外皮細胞瘤,血管周皮細胞瘤 haemangiopericytoma
血管外血块/血管外血塊 external clot
血管外液/血管外液 extravascular fluid
血管外造血/血管外造血 extravascular hematopoiesis, extravascular hemopoiesis
血管网/血管網,血管叢,脈管網 vasoganglion
血管网状内皮瘤/血管網狀內皮瘤 angioreticuloendothelioma
血管网状内皮细胞瘤/血管網狀內皮細胞瘤 angioreticuloma
血管萎缩性皮肤异色病/血管萎縮性皮膚異色病 poikiloderma vasculare atrophicans
血管未闭/血管未閉 vascular patency
血管纹/血管紋 stria vascularis
血管无力/血管無力,血管無緊張 angiasthenia
血管系膜/血管繫膜 mesangium
血管系统/血管系[統] blood-vascular system
血管细胞黏附分子/血管細胞黏附分子 vascular cell adhesion molecule
血管狭窄/血管狹窄 angiostenosis
血管纤维瘤/血管纖維瘤 angiofibroma
血管纤维脂肪瘤/血管纖維脂肪瘤 angiofibrolipoma
血管显露/血管顯露 exposed vessel
血管显微镜检查/血管顯微鏡檢查 microscopic angioscopy
血管象皮病/血管象皮病 angioelephantiasis
血管心脏炎/血管心臟炎,心臟血管炎 angiocarditis
血管性成釉细胞瘤/血管性成釉細胞瘤,釉質母細胞血管瘤 ameloblastic hemangioma
血管性痴呆/血管性癡呆 vascular dementia
血管性骨炎/血管性骨炎 vascular osteitis
血管性坏疽/血管性壞疽 vascular gangrene
血管性扩张性肥大/血管性擴張性肥大 hemangiectatic hypertrophy
血管性联体生活/血管性連體生活 vascular parabiosis
血管性黏液瘤/血管性黏液瘤 vascular myxoma
血管性皮肤疾病/血管性皮膚疾病 vascular skin disease
血管性水肿/血管性水腫 angio-oedema
血管性痛经/血管性痛經 vascular dysmenorrhea
血管性头痛/血管性頭痛 vascular headache
血管[性]萎缩性皮肤异色病/血管[性]萎縮性皮膚異色病,血管性多形皮膚萎縮症 poikiloderma atrophicans vasculare
血管性血友病/血管性血友病 von Willebrand disease
血管性牙质/血管性牙質,血管齒質 vasodentin
血管性阳痿/血管性陽痿 vasculogenic impotence
血管性脂肪瘤/血管性脂肪瘤 vascular lipoma
血管性中心性成肌纤维细胞瘤/血管性中心性肌纖維母細胞瘤 angiocentric myofibroblastic tumor
血管性紫癜/血管性紫癜病 vascular purpura
血管悬吊/血管懸吊 vascular sling
血管血栓形成/血管血栓形成 vascular thrombosis
血管压迫法/血管壓迫法,壓迫止血法 angiopressure
血管压轧钳/血管壓軋鉗,血管壓迫器 angioclast
血管压轧术/血管壓軋術,壓碎血管止血法 angiotripsy
血管炎[病]/血管炎[病] vasculitides
血管样纹/血管樣紋,血管樣條紋症 angioid streak
血管移植/血管移植 blood vessel transplantation
血管移植术/血管移植術 blood vessel grafting
血管移植物/血管移植物 blood vessel graft
血管移植物闭塞/血管移植物閉塞 vascular graft occlusion
血管异位/血管異位,血管錯位 angiectopia
血管抑制蛋白质类/血管抑制蛋白質類 angiostatic

proteins
血管抑制素类/血管抑制素類　angiostatins
血管抑制型晕厥/血管抑制性暈厥　vasodepressor syncope
血管抑制药/血管抑制藥　vasoinhibitor
血管翳/角膜翳　pannus
血管荧光摄影机/血管活動攝影機　cineangiograph
血管荧光摄影术/血管活動攝影術　cineangiography
血管硬化/血管硬化　angiosclerosis
血管硬化性坏疽/血管硬化性壞疽　angiosclerotic gangrene
血管硬化性肌无力/血管硬化性肌無力　angiosclerotic myasthenia
血管原性休克/血管性休克　vasogenic shock
血管圆线虫病/血管圓線蟲病　angiostrongyliasis
血管运动性肾病/血管運動性腎病　vasomotor nephropathy
血管运动性中耳炎/血管運動性中耳炎　otitis media vasomotorica
血管杂音/血管雜音　vascular murmur
血管造口术/血管造口術　angiostomy
血管造影导管/血管造影導管　angiographic catheter
血管造影术/血管造影術,血管 X 光顯影術　angiography
血管造影照片/血管造影照片,血管 X 光顯影圖　angiogram
血管增大/血管增大　angiomegaly
血管增生/血管增生　angioplasia
血管振荡床/血管振盪床　vasoscillator bed
血管［正常］充盈/血管［正常］充盈,血管飽滿,血管充實　turgor vitalis
血管脂肪平滑肌瘤/血管脂肪平滑肌瘤　angiolipoleiomyoma
血管脂瘤/血管脂［肪］瘤　angiolipoma
血管止血障碍/血管止血障礙　vascular hemostatic disorder
血管痣/血管痣　vascular nevus
血管中膜/動脈中膜　tunica media
血管中心性免疫增生性病变/血管中心性免疫增生性病變,血管中心性免疫增生性病灶　angiocentric immunoproliferative lesion
血管肿瘤/血管腫瘤　vascular neoplasm
血管周瘤/血管周［圍］瘤　periangioma
血管周围浸润/血管周圍浸潤　perivascular infiltration
血管周围细胞/血管周圍細胞　perivascular cell
血管周围纤维瘤/血管周圍纖維瘤　perivascular fibroma
血管周围纤维囊/血管周圍纖維囊　perivascular fibrous capsule
血管周隙/血管周隙　perivascular space
血管周性甲状腺肿/血管周圍性甲狀腺腫　perivascular goiter
血管周炎/血管周［圍］炎　periangiitis
血管周足/血管周足　perivascular foot
血管注射/血管［内］注射　intravascular injection
血管滋养管/血管滋養管　vasa vasorum
血管阻力/血管阻力,血管抵抗力　vascular resistance
血管阻塞危象/血管阻塞危象　vasoocclusive crisis
血管组织肿瘤/血管組織腫瘤　vascular tissue neoplasm
血管样条纹/血管樣條紋,血管狀痕　angioid streak
血灌瞳神/血灌瞳神　hyphema and vitreous hemorrhage
血灌瞳神·肝胆实热证/血灌瞳神·肝膽實熱證　hyphema and vitreous hemorrhage with pattern of liver-gallbladder excessive heat
血灌瞳神·虚火伤络证/血灌瞳神·虛火傷絡證　hyphema and vitreous hemorrhage with pattern of deficiency-fire injuring collateral
血灌瞳神·血热妄行证/血灌瞳神·血熱妄行證　hyphema and vitreous hemorrhage with pattern of bleeding due to blood heat
血灌瞳神·瘀血内阻证/血灌瞳神·瘀血內阻證　hyphema and vitreous hemorrhage with pattern of internal obstruction of static blood
血海/血海　xuehai, blood sea, SP10
血寒/血寒　cold in blood
血寒证/血寒證　pattern of cold in blood
血汗/血汗　bloody sweating
血汗·肝胃火炽证/血汗·肝胃火熾證　bloody sweating with pattern of blazing fire of liver and stomach
血汗·气血两虚证/血汗·氣血兩虛證　bloody sweating with pattern of deficiency of both qi and blood
血汗·阴虚火旺证/血汗·陰虛火旺證　bloody sweating with pattern of exuberant fire due to yin deficiency
血汗［症］/血汗［症］　bloody sweat
血褐质/血褐質,血暗棕質　hemaphein
血褐质尿症/血褐質尿症　hemapheism
血褐质性黄疸/血褐［質］性黄疸　hemapheic jaundice
血红蛋白/血紅蛋白,血紅素　hemoglobin
血红蛋白变体/血紅蛋白變體,異常血紅蛋白

hemoglobin variant
血红蛋白病/血紅蛋白病　hemoglobinopathies
血红蛋白测定法/血紅蛋白測定法,血紅素檢查法　hemoglobinometry
血红蛋白胆汁/血紅蛋白膽汁,膽汁内含血紅素,血紅素膽症　hemoglobinocholia
血红蛋白分光光度计/血紅蛋白分光光度計,血液分光光度計　hematospectrophotometer
血红蛋白分解/血紅蛋白分解,血紅素分解　hemoglobinolysis
血红蛋白管型/血紅蛋白管型,血紅素圓柱　hemoglobin cast
血红蛋白光度测定计/血紅蛋白光度測定計,血紅素光度測定計　hemophotometer
血红蛋白过少/血紅蛋白過少,血紅素不足　oligochromemia
血红蛋白计/血紅蛋白計,血紅素計,血質計　hematinometer
血红蛋白浸渗/血紅蛋白浸滲,血紅素吸收　hemoglobin imbibition
血红蛋白类/血紅蛋白類　hemoglobins
血红蛋白林格溶液/血紅蛋白林格溶液,血紅素 Ringer 氏溶液　hemoglobin Ringer solution
血红蛋白尿/血紅蛋白尿,血紅素尿　hemoglobinuria
血红蛋白血色原/血紅蛋白血色原,變性血紅素　hemoglobin hemochromogen
血红蛋白血[症]/血紅素血症　hematospherinemia
血红蛋白溢/血紅蛋白溢,血紅素漏　hemoglobinorrhea
血红扇头蜱/血紅扇頭蜱,血色扇頭壁蝨　Rhipicephalus sanguineus
血红素/血紅素,血質　haem
血红素蛋白/血紅素蛋白[質]　hemoprotein
血红素合成酶缺乏/[原]血紅素合成酶缺乏　heme synthetase deficiency
血红素氧化酶/血紅素氧化酶　heme oxygenase
血红旋尾线虫/血紅旋尾線蟲　Spirocerca sanguinolenta
血[红]异刺皮螨/血異刺皮蟎　Allodermanyssus sanguineus
血糊精/血糊精　dystrophodextrin
血迹/血跡　blood stain
血钾正常/血鉀正常,正常血鉀　normokalemia
血碱度计/血鹼度計　hemoalkalimeter
血箭/血箭　hematohidrosis
血浆/血漿　blood plasma
血浆白蛋白/血漿白蛋白　plasma albumin
血浆半衰期/血漿半衰期　plasma half-life
血浆病/血漿病　hematoplasmopathy
血浆除去法/血漿除去法,去血漿法　plasma depletion
血浆促凝血先质缺乏/血漿促凝血先質缺乏,前血漿凝血活素缺乏　plasma thromboplastic antecedent deficiency
血浆代用品/血漿代用品　plasma substitute
血浆蛋白及链球菌激酶活化聚合体/血漿蛋白及鏈球菌激酶活化聚合體　plasminogen streptokinase activator complex
血浆蛋白原活化因子抑制物第一型/血漿蛋白原活化因子抑制物第一型　plasminogen activator inhibitor type 1
血浆蛋白质/血漿蛋白質　plasma protein
血浆蛋白组分/血漿蛋白組分　plasma protein fraction
血浆过多/血漿過多　polyplasmia
血浆激肽释放酶/血漿激肽釋放酶,血漿微血管增滲酶　plasma kallikrein
血浆减少/血漿減少　mioplasmia
血浆胶质渗透压/血漿膠質滲透壓　plasma colloid osmotic pressure
血浆扩容剂/血漿擴容劑,血漿膨脹劑　plasma expander
血浆疗法/血漿療法　plasmatherapy
血浆凝血激酶因子 D/血漿凝血激酶因子 D,血漿凝血質 D 因子　plasma thromboplastin factor D
血浆凝血质 B 因子/血漿凝血質 B 因子,血漿凝血質 B 因子　plasma thromboplastin factor B
血浆撇清现象/血漿撇清現象　skimming plasma
血浆清除率/血漿清除率　plasma clearance
血浆去除术/血漿去除術,血漿除去術,去血漿法　plasmapheresis
血浆容量/血漿容量　plasma volume
血浆肾素活性/血漿腎素活性　plasma renin activity
血浆水解物/血漿水解物　hydrolysate plasma
血浆糖分过多/血漿糖分過多　hyperglycoplasmia
血浆铜蓝蛋白/血漿銅藍蛋白　ceruloplasmin
血浆性出血/血漿性出血　plasma hemorrhage
血浆药物浓度/血漿中藥物濃度　plasma drug level
血浆增容剂/血漿增容劑　plasma extender
血浆置换/血漿置換,血漿交換　plasma exchange
血结/血結　hemonode
血结胸证/血結胸證　chest binding pattern with static blood
血竭/血竭　draconis resin
血竭散/血竭散　Dragon's blood powder
血晶/血晶　blood crystal

血精/血精　hematospermia
血厥/血厥,鬱厥　blood syncope, syncope due to lack of blood, syncope due to excessive bleeding
血厥·实证/血厥·實證　blood syncope with excess pattern
血厥·虚证/血厥·虛證　blood syncope with deficiency pattern
血库/血庫　blood bank
血块/血塊　clot
血块凝缩/血塊凝縮　clot retraction
血蓝蛋白/血藍蛋白,血藍質　Hemocyanin
血泪溢/血淚溢[出],血淚　dacryohemorrhea
血泪症/血淚症,色淚症　chromodacryorrhea
血类辨别法/血類辨別法,血液鑒別法,血液種屬辨別法　hematalloscopy
血量/血[容]量　blood volume
血量测定/血量測定　blood volume determination
血量减少/血[量過]少　oligohemia
血量正常/血量正常　normovolemia
血离子浓度变异/血液離子濃度變異,血液離子濃度變動　poikilionia
血淋/血淋　hematuric strangury, stranguria due to hematuria
血淋巴/血淋巴　hemolymph
血淋巴结/血淋巴結　hemal node, hemolymph node
血淋巴细胞毒素/血球淋巴細胞毒素　hemolymphocytotoxin
血流/血流　blood stream
血流导向气囊导管/血流導向氣囊導管　balloon tipped flow-directed catheter
血流动力学/血液動力學　hemodynamics
血流量/血流量　blood flow
血流量计/血流量計　blood flowmeter
血流速度/血流速度　blood flow velocity
血流速度计/血流速度計　tachometer
血流速度描记法/血流速度描記法　tachography
血流速度描记器/血液速度描記器　dromograph
血流速度描记图/血流速度描記圖,血流速度描記像　tachogram
血流速度照相器/血流速度照相器,照相血流速度計　photohematachometer
血流速率/血流速率　rate of blood flow
血瘤/血瘤　blood tumor, angioma
血瘤·肝经火旺证/血瘤·肝經火旺證　blood tumor with pattern of effulgent fire in liver channel
血瘤·脾失统摄证/血瘤·脾失統攝證　blood tumor with pattern of spleen failing to control and manage
血瘤·肾伏郁火证/血瘤·腎伏鬱火證　blood tumor with pattern of stagnated fire hidden in kidney
血瘤·心火妄动证/血瘤·心火妄動證　blood tumor with pattern of frenetic stirring of heart fire
血卵磷脂过多/血卵磷脂過多　hyperlecithinemia
血绿蛋白/血綠蛋白　chlorocruorin
血绿透明蛋白原/血綠透明蛋白原,螺旋透明蛋白原　spirographin
血滤泡素过多/血濾泡素過多,高濾泡素血症　hyperfolliculinemia
血轮/血輪　blood wheel
血矛线虫病/血矛線蟲病　haemonchosis
血膜/血膜　blood film
血膜式氧合器/血膜式氧合器　film oxygenator
血沫痧/血沫痧　bloody froth sha disease
血囊肿/血囊腫　blood cyst
血-脑脊液屏障/血-腦脊液屏障　blood-CSF barrier, BCB
血脑屏障/血腦屏障,血腦障壁,血腦障礙　blood-brain barrier
血[内]淋巴细胞减少/血[内]淋巴細胞減少,血内淋巴球過少　hypolymphemia
血[内]尿素过少/血内尿素過少　hypouremia
血[内]尿酸正常/血[内]尿酸正常,正常尿酸血　normouricemia
血内凝血激酶过少综合征/血内凝血激酶過少症候群　hypothromboplastinemic syndrome
血[内]凝血酶过少/血[内]凝血酶過少,低凝血激酶血症　hypothromboplastinemia
血[内]球蛋白异常/血[内]球蛋白異常,血中球蛋白異常　dysglobulinemia
血[内]铁过少/血鐵過少　hypoferremia
血尿/血尿　haematuria
血尿素氮/血[液]尿素氮　blood urea nitrogen
血尿素廓清试验/血尿素廓清試驗,血尿素清除力試驗　blood-urea clearance test
血尿素清除率/血尿素清除率,血尿素廓清力　blood-urea clearance
血尿性淋病/血尿性淋病　haemorrhagic gonorrhea
血凝固不全/血[液]凝固不全　athrombia
血凝集/血凝集,血球凝集作用　hemagglutination
血凝集试验/血凝集試驗　hemagglutination test
血凝集抑制试验/血凝集抑制試驗　hemagglutination inhibition test
血凝试验/血凝試驗　hemagglutination test
血凝素类/血凝素類　hemagglutinins
血凝抑制反应/血凝抑制反應,血球凝集抑制反應　hemagglutination-inhibition reaction
血凝抑制试验/血凝抑制試驗　hemagglutination

inhibition test
血浓缩/血濃縮　hemoconcentration
血脓肿/血[性]膿腫　hematapostema
血疱/血皰　bloody bulla, blood blister
血脐疝/血臍疝,血性臍膨出　hematomphalocele
血气/血氣,血液氣體　blood gas
血气分析/血氣分析　blood gas analysis
血气界面/血氣界面　blood gas interface
血气屏障/血氣屏障　blood-air barrier
血气心包/血氣心包,心包積血氣　hemopneumopericardium
血气形志篇/血氣形志篇　Qi Disorders, Treatise on Blood
血气胸/血氣胸　hemopneumothorax
血清/血清　serum
血清白蛋白/血清白蛋白,血清蛋白素　serum albumin
血清白蛋白尿/血清[白]蛋白尿　seroalbuminuria
血清白蛋白缺乏症/血内白蛋白缺乏症,血清白蛋白缺少症　analbuminemia
血清病/血清病　serum sickness
血清病性荨麻疹/血清病性蕁麻疹　serum sickness urticaria
血清不应性/血清不應性,血清抵抗性　seroresistance
血清蛋白质/血清蛋白質　serum protein
血清淀粉样P成分/血清澱粉樣P成分　serum amyloid P-component
血清淀粉样蛋白A/血清澱粉樣蛋白A　serum amyloid A
血清毒素/血清毒素　serotoxin
血清反应/血清反應　orrhoreaction
血清反应因子/血清反應因子　serum response factor
血清反应组件/血清反應組件,血清反應元件　serum response element
血清分离法/血清分離　serapheresis
血清分型/血清分型　serotyping
血清过敏反应/血清過敏[性]反應　seroanaphylactic reaction
血清过敏性/血清過敏性　sero-anaphylaxis
血清过敏症/血清過敏[症]　serum anaphylaxis
血清黄色素/血清黄色素　xanthorubin
血清黄素/血[清]黄素　hemolutein
血清黄体素/血清黄體素　serum lutein
血清菌苗免疫法/血液疫苗免疫法,血液疫苗接種法　serovaccination
血清类黏蛋白/血清類黏蛋白　orosomucoid

血清疗法/血清療法　serum therapy
血清流行病学/血清流行病學　seroepidemiology
血清流行病学研究/血清流行病學研究　seroepidemiologic study
血清酶/血清酶,血清酵素　seroenzyme
血清免疫/血清免疫　seroimmunity
血清黏液/血清黏液　seromucus
血清凝集镜检查/血清凝集鏡檢查　seroscopy
血清培养物/血清培養物　seroculture
血清前列腺酸性磷酸酶/血清前列腺酸性磷酸酶　prostatic fraction of serum acid phosphatase
血清球蛋白/血清球蛋白　seroglobulin
血清球蛋白类/血清球蛋白類　serum globulins
血清溶素/血清溶素　serolysin
血清色素/血清色素,血清色質　serochrome
血清杀菌试验/血清殺菌試驗　serum bactericidal test
血清渗出/血清滲出　exoserosis
血清生成/血清生成　serogenesis
血清生理学/血清生理學　serophysiology
血清试验/血清試驗　serum test
血清水/血清水　serum water
血清素/血清素　serotonin
血清素激动药/血清素激動藥　serotonin agonist
血清素拮抗药/血清素拮抗藥　serotonin antagonist
血清素类药/血清素類藥　serotonin agent
血清素摄取抑制药/血清素攝取抑制藥　serotonin uptake inhibitor
血清素受体/血清素受體　serotonin receptor
血清素综合征/血清素症候群　serotonin syndrome
血清糖蛋白/血清糖蛋白　seroglycoid
血清显红反应/血清顯紅反應　epiphanin reaction
血清效价回升/血清效價回昇　serorelapse
血清[型]肝炎/血清性肝炎　serum hepatitis
血清性肾炎/血清性腎炎　serum sickness nephritis
血清休克/血清休克　serum shock
血清学/血清學　serology
血清学决定簇/血清學決定簇　serological determinant
血清学试验/血清學試驗　serologic test
血清荨麻疹/血清蕁麻疹　serum urticaria
血清药物浓度/血清藥物濃度　serum drug level
血清抑制剂/血清抑制劑　serum inhibitor
血清阴性/血清[檢查]陰性　seronegativity
血清阴性脊柱关节病/血清陰性脊柱關節病　seronegative spondyloanthropathy
血清预防/血清預防法　seroprophylaxis
血清预后/血清預後　seroprognosis

血清诊断/血清診斷法　serodiagnosis
血清疹/血清疹　serum eruption
血清脂酶/血清脂酶,血清脂肪酵素　serolipase
血清中和试验/血清中和試驗　serum neutralization test
血清肿/血清腫　seroma
血清中毒/血清中毒　serum intoxication
血清转化[现象]/血清轉化　seroconversion
血热/血熱　heat in blood
血热肠燥证/血熱腸燥證　pattern of intestine dryness due to blood heat
血热动风证/血熱動風證　pattern of stirring wind due to blood heat
血绒毛膜胎盘/血[性]絨毛膜胎盤　hemochorial placenta
血容积测量法/血容積測量法,血液容積測定法　hematoncometry
血容量不足/血容量不足,循環血量減少　hypovolemia
血容量测定法/血容量測定法　hemovolumetry
血容量过多/血[容]量過多,多血症　hypervolemia
血容量扩充药/血容量擴充藥　plasma volume expander
血乳酸过多症/血乳酸過多[症]　hyperlactacidemia
血色病/血色病,血色素沈積症　haemochromatosis
血色蛋白/血色蛋白[質]　hemochromoprotein
血色过浓/血色過濃　hemachrosis
血色囊肿/血色囊腫　sanguineous cyst
血色素/血色素　hemachrome
血色素沉着症/血色素沈著病　hemochromatosis
血色原/血色原　hemochromogen
血色正常-大红细胞性贫血/正常血色-大紅細胞性貧血,大紅血球正常血色性貧血　macrocytic-normochromic anemia
血色指数过低/血色指數過低　hypochromemia
血色指数过高/血色素指數過高　hyperchromemia
血色质增多/血色質增多　polychromemia
血疝/血疝　hernia due to blood stasis
血神经屏障/血神經屏障　blood-nerve barrier
血-生精小管屏障/血-生精小管屏障　blood-seminiferous tubule barrier
血生型/棲血的　sanguicolous
血-视网膜屏障/血-視網膜屏障　blood-retina barrier
血栓/血栓　thrombus
血栓闭塞性动脉炎/血栓閉塞性動脈炎　thromboarteritis obliterans
血栓玻璃样变性/血栓玻璃[質]樣變性　hematohyaloid degeneration

血栓动脉内膜切除术/血栓動脈内膜切除術,血栓性動脈切除術　thromboendarterectomy
血栓噁烷-A合酶/血栓[噁]烷-A合酶　thromboxane-A synthase
血栓噁烷类/血栓[噁]烷類　thromboxanes
血栓噁烷受体/血栓[噁]烷受體　thromboxane receptor
血栓静脉炎性脾大/血栓静脈炎性脾大,血栓性静脈炎性脾臟巨大症　thrombophlebitic splenomegaly
血栓切除术/血栓切除術　thrombectomy
血栓溶解疗法/血栓溶解療法　thrombolytic therapy
血栓收缩蛋白/血栓收缩蛋白,栓塞縮回素　thrombosthenin
血栓栓塞/血栓栓塞　thromboembolism
血栓栓塞性综合征/血栓栓塞性症候群　thromboembolic syndrome
血栓素/血栓素　thromboxane
血栓弹力描记术/血栓彈性描記法　thrombelastography
血栓调节蛋白/血栓調節蛋白　thrombomodulin
血栓形成/血栓形成　thrombosis
血栓形成倾向/栓塞質　thrombophilia
血栓形成物质/血栓形成質　thromboplastic substance
血栓[性]动脉炎/血栓動脈炎　thromboarteritis
血栓性梗塞/血栓性梗塞　thrombotic infarct
血栓性坏疽/血栓性壞疽　thrombotic gangrene
血栓性静脉炎/血栓性静脈炎　thrombophlebitis
血栓性静脉炎后综合征/血栓静脈炎後症候群　postthrombophlebitic syndrome
血栓[性]淋巴管炎/血栓性淋巴管炎　thrombolymphangitis
血栓性脉管炎/血栓性脈管炎,血栓性血管炎　thromboangiitis
血栓性外痔/血栓性外痔　thrombosed external hemorrhoid
血栓[性]心内膜炎/血栓性心内膜炎　thromboendocarditis
血栓性血小板减少性肾损害/血栓性血小板减少性腎損害　renal damage in thrombotic thrombocytopenia
血栓性血小板减少性紫癜/血栓形成性血小板减少性紫癜病　thrombotic thrombocytopenic purpura
血栓[性]硬膜窦炎/血栓性硬膜竇炎　thrombosinusitis
血栓性淤滞/血栓性淤滯,栓塞性淤滯　thrombostasis
血酸过少/血酸過少,低酸血症,血酸減少

hypacidemia
血随气逆/血隨氣逆　bleeding due to qi reversed flow
血痰/血痰　sputum cruentum
血碳酸过多性酸中毒/血碳酸過多性酸中毒,高血碳酸性酸血症　hypercapnic acidosis
血碳酸正常/血碳酸正常　eucapnia
血糖/血糖　blood glucose
血糖苷脂/血糖苷脂　hematoside
血糖量正常/血糖量正常　normoglycemia
血糖缺乏/血糖缺乏　aglycemia
血糖异常/血糖異常　pathoglycemia
血糖正常/血糖正常　euglycemia
血糖指数/血糖指數　glycemic index
血糖自我监测/血糖自我監測　blood glucose self-monitoring
血体/血體　corpus hemorrhagicum
血铁黄素/血鐵黃素,含鐵血紅素　haemosiderin
血统/血統　blood line
血透明质/血透明質,血玻璃樣質　hematohyaloid
血脱/血脱　blood collapse, blood depletion
血脱证/血脱證　pattern of blood depletion
[血]外渗性囊肿/外滲性囊腫　extravasation cyst
血为气母/血爲氣母　blood being mother of qi
血吸虫病/血吸蟲病　bilharziasis, schistosomiasis
血吸虫瘤/[住]血吸蟲瘤　bilharzioma
血吸虫皮炎/血吸蟲皮炎,血吸蟲性皮膚炎　schistosome dermatitis
血吸虫肉芽肿/血吸蟲[性]肉芽腫　schistosomal granuloma
血吸虫色素/血吸蟲色素　schistosomal pigment
血吸虫属/血吸蟲屬　Bilharzia
血吸虫尾蚴皮炎/血吸蟲尾蚴皮炎　schistosome cercarial dermatitis
血吸虫[性]痢疾/住血吸蟲痢疾　bilharzial dysentery
血细胞/血細胞,血球　blood cell
血细胞比容/血細胞比容　hematocrit
血细胞发生/血細胞發生,造血[作用]　hematopoiesis, hemopoiesis, hemocytopoiesis
血细胞过多/血細胞過多　hypercytosis
血细胞计数/血細胞計數　blood cell count
血细胞计数法/血細胞計數法,血球計數法　hematimetry
血细胞计数器/[血]細胞計數器　cytometer
血细胞减少/血細胞減少,血球過少　hypocytosis
[血]细胞内变性/[血]細胞內變性,血球內變性　endoglobular degeneration
血细胞尿/血細胞尿,血球尿　hematocyturia

血细胞染色过深/血細胞染色過深,血球著色過深　hypercytochromia
血细胞溶解/血細胞溶解,血球溶解　cythemolysis
血细胞渗出/血細胞滲出,血球滲出,血球游出　diapedesis
血细胞生成/血細胞生成,血液生成,造血　hematopoiesis
血细胞糖分过少/血細胞糖分過少,細胞葡萄糖不足,血球葡萄糖含量不足　cytoglycopenia
血细胞团集器/血細胞團集器,血球團集器　cytoglomerator
血细胞吸附/血細胞吸附,血球吸著現象　hemadsorption
血细胞吸附病毒1型/血細胞吸附病毒1型,附血型病毒/第一型[HA1]病毒　hemadsorption virus/type 1 HA1 virus
血细胞吸附病毒2型/血細胞吸附病毒2型,附血型病毒/第二型[HA2]病毒　hemadsorption virus/type 2 HA2 virus
血细胞吸附抑制试验/血細胞吸附抑制試驗　hemadsorption inhibition test
血细胞学/血細胞學,血球學　hemocytology
血细胞压积/血細胞壓積,沈澱血球容量　packed-cell volume
血细胞压碎/血細胞壓碎,血球壓碎　hemocytotripsis
血细胞增多/血細胞增多,血球增多　hematocytosis
血细胞照片/血細胞照片,血球攝影像,血球相片　hemaphotograph
血细胞正常/血細胞正常,血球正常[狀態]　normocytosis
血[细菌]培养/血[液]細菌培養,血培養　hemoculture
血纤蛋白溶解/[血]纖維蛋白溶解　fibrinolysis
血纤蛋白溶解系统/[血]纖維蛋白溶解系統　fibrinolytic system
血纤[维蛋白溶酶原]激活酶/[血]纖維蛋白活化酵素　fibrinokinase
血纤维蛋白肽/[血]纖維蛋白勝肽　fibrinopeptide
血纤维蛋白原过少/[血]纖維蛋白原過少　hypofibrinogenemia
血象/血象,血[球]相　blood picture
血小板/血小板　blood platelet, thrombocyte
血小板病/血小板病　thrombocytopathy
血小板不减性紫癜/血小板不減性紫瘢　non-thrombocytopenic purpura
血小板功能不全/血小板功能不足　thrombasthenia
血小板功能不全性紫癜/血小板功能不足性紫癜病　thrombasthenic purpura

血小板功能试验/血小板功能試驗 platelet function test
血小板功能调节药/血小板功能調節藥 platelet function regulator
血小板活化/血小板活化 platelet activation
血小板活化因子/血小板活化因子 platelet activating factor
血小板疾病/血小板疾病 blood platelet disorder
血小板计数/血小板計數 platelet count
血小板减少伴桡骨缺损综合征/血小板減少伴橈骨缺損症候群 thrombocytopenia-absent radii syndrome
血小板减少性血管瘤综合征/血小板減少性血管瘤症候群 thrombopenia-haemangioma syndrome
血小板减少性紫癜/血小板減少性紫癜 thrombocytopenic purpura, thrombopenic purpura
血小板减少[症]/血小板減少症 thrombopeny
血小板间接计数/血小板間接計數 indirect platelet count
血小板聚集/血小板聚集 platelet aggregation
血小板聚集抑制剂/血小板聚集抑制劑 platelet aggregation inhibitor
[血小板]颗粒区/[血小板]顆粒區,顆粒狀區 granulomere
血小板膜糖蛋白类/血小板膜糖蛋白類 platelet membrane glycoproteins
血小板[内皮细胞]黏附分子/血小板[内皮細胞]黏著分子 platelet adhesion molecule
血小板黏附/血小板黏附,血小板粘連 platelet adhesiveness
血小板凝集素/血小板凝集素 platelet agglutinin
血小板凝集因子/血小板凝集因子 platelet aggregation factor
β-血小板球蛋白/乙型-凝血球蛋白 beta-thromboglobulin
血小板去除法/血小板去除法,小板破壞 plateletpheresis
血小板溶解/血小板破壞 thrombocytolysis
血小板溶素/血小板溶素 plakins
血小板生成/血小板生成 thrombopoiesis
血小板生成型巨核细胞/血小板生成型巨核細胞 platelet-producing megakaryocyte
血小板输注/血小板輸注 platelet transfusion
[血小板]透明区/血小板透明區,血小板透明部 hyalomere
血小板消耗性出血障碍/血小板消耗性出血障礙 consumptive thrombohemorrhagic disorder
血小板[性]血栓形成/血小板[性]血栓形成,血小板性栓塞 plate thrombosis
血小板血栓/血小板血栓 platelet thrombus
血小板衍生生长因子/血小板衍生生長因子 platelet-derived growth factor
血小板因子/血小板因子 platelet factor
血小板源生长因子受体/血小板源生長因子受體 platelet-derived growth factor receptor
血小板源生长因子α受体/血小板源生長因子α受體 platelet-derived growth factor alpha receptor
血小板源性生长因子/血小板源性生長因子 platelet-derived growth factor
血小板增多/血小板增多[症] thrombocytosis
血小板直接计数/血小板直接計數 direct platelet count
血小板贮池缺如/血小板貯池缺如 platelet storage pool deficiency
血型/血型 blood type
血型不合/血型不合,血型不相合性 blood group incompatibility
血型分类/血型分類,血液分型法 typing of blood
血型抗原/血型抗原 blood group antigen
血型糖蛋白/血型糖蛋白 glycophorin
血型物质/血型物質 blood group substance
血性穿刺/血性穿刺,血性穿放 bloody tap
血性恶露/血性惡露,漿性產後排出物 lochia sanguinolenta
血性腹水/血性腹水 sanguineous ascites
血性精液/血性精液 hemospermia
血性精液囊肿/血性精液囊腫 hematospermatocele
血性乳糜尿/血[性]乳糜尿 hematochyluria
血性渗出[液]/血性滲漏液 blood effusion
血性渗液/血性滲液 bloody effusion
血性胎块/血性胎塊 blood mole
血胸/血胸,胸腔積血 hemothorax
血-胸腺屏障/血-胸腺屏障 blood-thymus barrier
血虚/血虛 blood deficiency
血虚肠燥证/血虛腸燥證 pattern of intestine dryness due to blood deficiency
血虚动风证/血虛動風證 pattern of stirring wind due to blood deficiency
血虚风燥证/血虛風燥證 pattern of wind and dryness due to blood deficiency
血虚寒凝证/血虛寒凝證 pattern of coagulation cold due to blood deficiency
血虚津亏证/血虛津虧證 pattern of blood deficiency and depleted fluid
血虚生风/血虛生風 blood deficiency causing wind
血虚证/血虛證 pattern of blood deficiency

血虚作痒/血虛作癢　itching due to blood deficiency
血循环加速合并高血压/血循環加速合并高血壓　hypersphyxia
血压/血壓　blood pressure
血压测定/血壓測定　blood pressure determination
血压测定法/血壓測量法　hemodynamometry
血压计/血壓計　sphygmomanometer
血压监测仪/血壓監測儀　blood pressure monitor
血压描记器/脈壓描記器　sphygmometrograph
血压血液黏度测量法/血壓血液黏度測量法　sphygmoviscosimetry
血压异常/血壓異常　dysarteriotony
血盐过多/血鹽過多[症]　hyperalonemia
血氧测定法/血氧測定法,血氧定量法　oximetry
血氧测定器/血氧測定器,血氧描記器　oxyhemograph
血氧合[作用]指数/血氧合[作用]指數,血液氧合指数　hematopneic index
血氧计/血氧計　oximeter
血氧谱/血氧譜,血氧描計圖　oxyhemogram
血样癌/血樣癌　hematoid carcinoma
血样采集/血樣採集　blood specimen collection
血药浓度/血藥濃度　blood drug level
血[液]/血[液]　blood
血液保存/血液保存　blood preservation
血液变性/血液變性　blood denaturation
血液病/血液病　hematologic disease
血液病理学/血液病理學　hematopathology
血液不足/血液不足,血液减少　hematopenia
血液成分除去法/血液成分除去法　blood component removal
血液成分输血/血液成分輸血　blood component transfusion
血液代用品/血液代用品　blood substitute
血液淀粉酶/血[液]澱粉酶　hemodiastase
血液动力学过程/血液動力學過程　hemodynamic process
血液动力学现象/血液動力學現象　hemodynamic phenomena
血液毒理学/血液毒理學　hematotoxicology
血液废物潴留/血内廢物鬱滯　triphthemia
血液分析/血液分析　hemanalysis
血液复温/血液復溫　blood rewarming
血液灌注/血液灌注[法]　hemoperfusion
血液化学分析/血液化學分析　blood chemical analysis
血液结合素/血液結合素,血基質結合糖蛋白　hemopexin
血[液]浸润/血液浸潤　sanguineous infiltration
血液净化/血液淨化　blood purification
血液疗法/血[液]療法　hematherapy
血液流变学/血液流變學　hemorheology
血液滤过/血液濾過[術]　hemofiltration
血液黏度/血液黏度　blood viscosity
血液黏液瘤伴上皮成分/血液黏液瘤伴上皮成分　angiomyxoma with epithelial component
血液凝固/血液凝固　blood coagulation
血液凝固试验/血液凝固試驗　blood coagulation test
血液凝固因子/血液凝固因子　blood coagulation factor
血液凝固因子抑制剂/血液凝固因子抑制劑　blood coagulation factor inhibitor
血液凝固障碍/血液凝固障礙　blood coagulation disorder
血液浓缩/血液濃縮,血液濃厚　pachyhemia
血液浓缩器/血液濃縮器　hemoconcentrator
血液妊娠并发症/血液妊娠并發症　hematologic pregnancy complication
血液杀菌作用/血液殺菌作用　blood bactericidal activity
血液渗出/血液滲出　hematopedesis
血液渗性/血液滲[透]性　hemotonia
血液生理过程/血液生理過程　blood physiologic process
血液生理现象/血液生理現象　blood physiologic phenomena
血液生理学/血液生理學　blood physiology
血液透析/血液透析[術]　haemodialysis
血液透析滤过/血液透析濾過,血液透析過濾　hemodiafiltration
血液透析器/血液透析器,血液析離器　hemodialyzer
血液透析液/血液透析液　hemodialysis solution
血液湍流/血液湍流　turbulent blood flow
血液微聚集体/血液微聚集體　blood microaggregate
血液稀释/血液稀釋　hemodilution
血液心脏停搏[法]/血液心臟停搏[法]　blood cardioplegia
血液心脏停搏液/血液心臟停搏液　blood cardioplegic solution
血液新陈代谢/血液新陳代謝　hemetaboly
血液学/血液學　hematology
血液学家/血液學[專]家　hematologist
血液学试验/血液學試驗　hematologic test
血液学药物/血液學藥物　hematologic agent
血液循环/血液循環　blood circulation
血液循环时间/血液循環時間　blood circulation time

血液循环停止/血液循環停止　adiemorrhysis
血液有形成分/血液有形成分　blood formed element
血液郁滞性血栓/血液鬱滯性血栓　hematostatic thrombus
血液预充/血液預充　blood priming
血液再组成/血液再組成　blood reconstitution
血液制品/血液製劑　blood product
血液中血红蛋白饱和度/血液中血紅蛋白飽和度　saturation of hemoglobin in the blood phase
血液肿瘤/血液腫瘤　hematologic neoplasm
血液紫外线照射充氧疗法/血液紫外線照射充氧療法　ultraviolet blood irradiation and oxygenation
血液自凝性/血液自凝性,血内纖維素增多　inopexia
血翳包睛/血翳包睛　heavy drooping pannus, pannus, vascular nebula
血营养障碍/血營養障礙,血液營養不良　hematodystrophy
血影蛋白/血影蛋白　spectrin
血影细胞/血影細胞,幻影細胞,幽靈細胞　ghost cell
血影细胞性青光眼/血影細胞性青光眼　ghost cell glaucoma
血疣/血疣　blood wart
血友病/血友病　bleeder's disease
血友病B/血友病B,乙型血友病　hemophilia B
血友病[患]者/血友病[患]者　hemophiliac
血友病基因携带者/血友病基因攜帶者　hemophilia carrier
血友病性出血/血友病性出血　hemophilic hemorrhage
血友病性关节炎/血友病性關節炎　hemophilic arthritis
血瘀/血瘀　blood stasis
血瘀耳窍证/血瘀耳竅證　pattern of blood stasis in ear
血瘀气滞证/血瘀氣滯證　pattern of blood stasis and stagnant qi
血瘀舌下证/血瘀舌下證　pattern of sublingual blood stasis
血瘀证/血瘀證　pattern of blood stasis
血余炭/血餘炭　carbonized hair
血郁/血鬱　blood stagnation, stagnation pattern of blood
血原虫/血原蟲　hematozoon
血原性骨炎/血原性骨炎　hematogenous osteitis
血原性黄疸/血原性黃疸　hematogenous jaundice
血原性结核病/血原性結核病　hematogenous tuberculosis
血原性肾盂肾炎/血原性腎盂腎炎　hematogenous pyelonephritis
血原性肾盂炎/血原性腎盂炎　hematogenous pyelitis
血原性铁质沉着/血原性鐵質沈著　hematogenous siderosis
血原性休克/血原性休克　hematogenic shock
血缘关系/血緣[關係],血族關係　sibship
血运重建/血運重建　revascularization
血燥生风/血燥生風　blood dryness causing wind
血证/血證,血狀病,血液病　blood disease, blood pattern
血症论/血症論　On Blood Patterns
血之府/血之府　house of blood
血β脂蛋白异常/血β脂蛋白異常,血乙型脂蛋白異常　dysbetalipoproteinemia
血脂粒/血脂粒,脂肪微粒　lipomicron
血脂异常/血脂異常　dyslipidemia
血肿/血腫　haematoma
血肿性胎块/血腫性胎塊　hematomole
血中毒/血中毒　hematotoxicosis
血主濡之/血主濡之　blood being responsible for nurturing body
熏法/熏法　fumigation
熏剂/熏劑　fumigant
熏洗疗法/熏洗療法　fumigation and washing therapy
熏烟消毒法/薰煙消毒法　fumigation
熏眼法/熏眼法　fumigating therapy for eye
熏衣草属/熏衣草屬　Lavandula
熏蒸疗法/薰蒸療法　fumigation and steaming therapy
寻常痤疮/單純痤瘡　common acne
寻常狼疮/尋常狼瘡　tuberculosis luposa
寻常臁疮/尋常臁瘡　ecthyma vulgaris
寻常鳞癣/尋常鱗癬,普通鱗癬　ichthyosis vulgaris
寻常脓疱病/尋常膿疱病　impetigo vulgaris
寻常秃发/尋常禿髮　common baldness
寻常型天疱疮/尋常[型]天疱瘡　pemphigus vulgaris
寻常性龟头包皮炎/尋常性龜頭包皮炎　balanoposthitis vulgaris
寻常性天疱疮抗原/尋常性天疱瘡抗原　pemphigus vulgaris antigen
寻常性须疮/尋常[性]鬚瘡　sycosis vulgaris
寻常性银屑病/尋常性銀屑病,牛皮癬　psoriasis vulgaris
寻常疣/尋常疣　common wart, verruca vulgaris
寻常圆线虫/尋常圓線蟲　Strongylus vulgaris
寻开口/尋開口　gaining access

巡回护士/巡迴護士 circulating nurse
荨麻疹/蕁麻疹 urticaria
荨麻疹的/蕁麻疹的 urticarial
荨麻疹性热/蕁麻疹性發燒 urticarial fever
荨麻疹性血管炎/蕁麻疹性血管炎 urticarial vasculitis
荨麻疹样丹毒/鑽石形疹 diamonds
荨麻疹样紫癜/藍麻疹狀紫癜病 purpura urticans
荨麻疹状痤疮/蕁麻疹樣痤瘡 acne urticata
循法/循法 mild pressing along channel course, mild pressing along meridian course
循规性散光/循規性散光,循例散光 astigmatism with the rule
循环/循環 circulation
循环率/循環率,血行率 circulation rate
循环生理学/循環生理學 physiology circulation
循环时间/循環時間 circulation time
循环衰竭/循環衰竭 circulatory failure
循环停止/循環停止 circulatory arrest
循环系统/循環系統 circulatory system
循环型精神病/循環[型]精神病,更替性精神病 circular insanity
循环型情感障碍/循環型情感障礙 cyclothymic disorder
循环型人格障碍/循環型人格障礙 cyclothymic personality disorder
循环性精神病/循環[性]精神病 folie circulaire
循环性缺氧/循環性缺氧 circulatory hypoxemia
循环性虚脱/循環性虛脫 circulatory collapse
循环胸腺因子/循環胸腺因子 circulating thymic factor
循环血量/循環血量,循環容量 circulation volume

循环训练[法]/循環訓練[法] circuit training
循环障碍/循環障礙,血行障礙 disturbance of circulation
循环障碍性缺氧/循環障礙性缺氧,血流阻滞性缺氧症 stagnant anoxia
循环支持装置/循環支持裝置 circulatory support device
循经传/循經傳 sequential transmission along channel
循经感传/循經感傳 propagated sensation along channel
循衣摸床/循衣摸床 carphology, floccillation
循证医学/循證醫學 evidence-based medicine
鲟毒/鱘毒[素] acipenserin
训练方案/訓練方案 training program
训练集/訓練集,訓練組 training set
驯化 T[淋巴]细胞/馴化 T[淋巴]細胞 educated T lymphocyte
蕈毒碱中毒/蕈毒鹼中毒,蠅菌素中毒 muscarinism
蕈形体/蕈形體 mushroom body
蕈形香菇/蕈形香菇 shiitake mushroom
蕈样肉芽肿/蕈樣肉芽腫 granuloma fungoides
蕈样下疳/蕈狀下疳 fungating chancre
蕈样真菌病/蕈樣黴菌病,蕈樣肉芽腫 mycosis fungoides
蕈中毒/蕈中毒 mushroom poisoning
蕈状癌/蕈狀癌 fungous cancer
蕈状溃疡/蕈狀潰瘍 fungating ulcer
蕈状乳头/蕈狀乳頭 fungiform papilla
蕈状膝关节炎/蕈狀膝關節炎 fungous gonitis
蕈状赘肉/蕈狀贅肉 fungosity

Y

丫痛/丫癃 abscess between fingers
压凹性水肿/壓凹性水腫 pitting edema
压扁胎/壓扁胎[兒] fetus compressus
压出/壓出 detrusion
压疮/壓瘡,褥瘡 bed sore, pressure sore, decubitus
压疮性坏死/褥瘡性壞死 decubital necrosis
压电效应/壓電效應 piezoelectric effect
压动性瘢痕/壓動性瘢痕,壓力性瘢痕 manometric cicatrix
压灌法/壓灌法,加壓充填法 pressure filling
压痕测验/壓痕測驗 indentation test
压觉/壓[迫感]覺 piesesthesia
压觉电测计/壓覺電測器 baroelectroesthesiometer
压觉感受器/壓覺感受器,壓力受體 pressure receptor
压力/壓[力] pressure
压力安全阀/壓力安全閥 popoff valve
压力绷带/壓迫繃帶 pressure bandage
压力波/壓力波 pressure wave
压力测量器/壓力測量器,壓力計 pressometer
压力超声心动描记术/壓力超聲心動描記術 stress echocardiography
压力辅助通气/壓力輔助通氣 pressure assisted ventilation
压力负荷过度/壓力負荷過度,壓力過荷 pressure overload
压力感/壓力感,壓覺 pressure sense
压力感受器/壓力感受器,壓力接受器 baroreceptor
压力感受器反射/壓力感受器反射 baroreflex
压力感受神经/壓力感受神經 pressoreceptor nerve
压力换能器/壓力換能器 pressure transducer
压力计/壓覺計 piesimeter
压力阶差/壓力階差,壓力梯度 pressure gradient
压力控制通气/壓力控制通氣 pressure controlled ventilation
压力麻醉/壓力麻醉,高壓麻醉法 high pressure anesthesia
压力时间指数/壓力時間指數 pressure-time index
压力试验/壓力試驗 stress testing
压力-体积关系/壓力體積關係 pressure-volume relation

压力性尿失禁/壓力性尿失禁,壓抑性失禁 stress incontinence
压力性尿失禁悬吊术/壓力性尿失禁懸吊術 sling procedure for stress incontinence
压力性气胸/壓力[性]氣胸 pressure pneumothorax
压力支持/壓力支持 pressure support
压力转换型通气机/壓力轉換型通氣機 pressure-cycled ventilator
压模器/壓模器,齒科塑形器 swager
压片法/壓片法,壓錠法 halide disk method, pellet method, wafer method
压片机/壓錠機 tablet machine
压迫绷带法/壓迫繃帶法 pressure bandaging
压迫疗法/壓迫療法 compression treatment
压迫性发绀/壓迫性發紺 compression cyanosis
压迫性坏死/壓迫性壞死 pressure necrosis
压迫性脊髓炎/壓迫性脊髓炎 compression myelitis
压迫性咳/壓迫性欬[嗽] compression cough
压迫性溃疡/壓迫性潰瘍 oppressive ulcer
压迫性麻痹/壓迫性麻痺 pressure palsy
压迫性神经炎/壓迫性神經炎 pressure neuritis
压迫性脱发/壓迫性脫髮,壓力性禿髮 pressure alopecia
压迫性萎缩/壓迫性萎縮 compression atrophy
压迫性血栓形成/壓迫性血栓形成 compression thrombosis
压迫性荨麻疹/壓力性蕁麻疹 pressure urticaria
压迫性[循环]停滞/壓迫性停滯 pressure stasis
压迫[阻滞]麻醉/壓迫麻醉 compression anesthesia
压热器法/壓熱器法,熱壓消毒法 autoclave method
压伤/壓傷 compression injury
压舌板/壓舌板,壓舌器 tongue depressor
压缩骨折/壓縮骨折,壓迫性骨折 compression fracture
压缩气病/壓縮氣病 compressed-air sickness
压缩气疗法/壓縮氣療法 aeropiesotherapy
压缩热气按摩法/[壓縮]熱氣按摩法 pneumothermomassage
压缩室效应/壓縮室效應 compression chamber effect
压缩性肺容积丧失/壓縮性肺容積喪失 compressed

lung volume loss
压缩性骨折/壓縮性骨折 compression fracture
压缩性颅骨骨折/壓縮性顱骨骨折 depressed skull fracture
压痛/壓痛,觸痛 tenderness
压痛测定法/壓痛測定法,壓痛檢法 algeoscopy
压陷眼压计/壓陷眼壓計 impression tonometer
压抑/壓抑,阻遏,阻抑 repression
压抑疗法/壓抑療法 penalization
压抑致敏/壓抑致敏 repression-sensitization
压印/壓印,皮印,皮痕 autogram
压应力/壓應力 compressive stress
压榨机/壓榨機,壓榨器 presser
压制片/壓制片,壓制錠 compressed tablet
押手/押手 pressing hand
鸦胆子/鴉膽子 java brucea fruit
鸦片粉/鴉片粉,粉狀鴉片 powdered opium
鸦片戒断竖毛现象/鴉片戒斷[症候群之]竖毛现象 piloerection in opiate abstinence syndrome
鸦片乳酸/鴉片乳酸 thebolactic acid
鸦片瘾/鴉片癖 opiomania
鸦片瘾者/鴉片癖者 opiomaniac
鸦片制剂/鴉片[製]劑 opiate
鸦片紫碱/鴉片[紫]鹼 porphyroxine
鸭步[态]/鴨步[態],摇摆步态 waddling gait
鸭肝炎病毒/鴨肝炎病毒 duck hepatitis virus
鸭密螺旋体/鴨螺旋體 Treponema anatum
鸭胚疫苗/鴨胚疫苗 duck embryo vaccine
鸭脾坏死病毒/鴨脾壞死病毒 Trager duck spleen necrosis virus
鸭气管吸虫/鴨氣管[食道]吸蟲 Tracheophilus cymbius
鸭跖草/鴨蹠草 dayflower herb
鸭嘴阀/鴨嘴閥 duckbill valve
鸭嘴花属/鴨嘴花屬 Adhatoda
牙/牙,齒 ①teeth, odonto ②ya, LO1
[牙]白垢/[牙齒]白垢 materia alba
牙板/牙板,齒板 dental lamina
牙包埋/齒包埋 dental inclusion
牙被动萌出/牙被動萌出 passive tooth eruption
牙本质/牙本質,齒質 dentine, ebur dentis, dentin
牙[本]质壁/牙本質壁 dentin wall
牙[本]质变红/牙本質變紅 dentin blush
牙[本]质挫平/牙本質挫平 dentin filing
牙[本]质发生/牙[本]質發生,牙質形成 dentinogenesis
牙本质发生不全/牙[本]質發生不全,牙[本]質生長不全 dentinogenesis imperfect

牙[本]质发育不全/牙本質發育不全 dentinal dysplasia
牙[本]质发育异常/牙本質發育異常 dentin dysplasia
牙[本]质钙化不全[症]/牙本質鈣化不全[症] dentin hypocalcification
牙[本]质管/牙本質管 dentinal canal
牙[本]质过敏/牙本質過敏 dentin hypersensitivity
牙本质基质/牙本質基質,齒質基質 dentin matrix, dentinal matrix
牙[本]质痂/牙本質痂 dentin callus
牙[本]质可溶性/牙本質可溶性 dentin solubility
牙[本]质瘤/牙質瘤 dentinoma
牙[本]质敏感[症]/牙本質敏感 hyperesthesia of dentin
牙[本]质内死区/牙[本]質内死區,牙本質内死道 dead tract in dentin
牙[本]质黏结剂/牙本質黏結劑 dentin-bonding agent
牙[本]质屏障/牙本質屏障 dentin barrier
牙[本]质桥/牙本質橋 dentinal bridge
牙本质鞘/牙本質鞘,齒質鞘 dentinal sheath
牙本质生长线/牙本質生長線,齒質生長線 incremental line
牙[本]质碎片/牙本質碎片 dentin chips
牙[本]质碎屑/牙本質碎屑 dentinal debris
牙[本]质通透性/牙本質通透性 dentin permeability
牙[本]质瓦叠线/牙本質瓦疊線 imbrication line of dentin
牙[本]质微屑/牙本質微屑 dentin dust
牙[本]质纤维/牙本質纖維 dentinal fiber
牙[本]质象牙化/牙[本]質象牙化,牙本質變性 eburnation of dentin
牙本质小管/牙本質小管,齒質小管 dentinal tubule
牙[本]质牙骨质界/牙本質牙骨質界,牙質釉質界,齒質齒堊質界 dentinocemental junction
牙[本]质-牙髓/牙本質-牙髓 dentin-pulp
牙[本]质牙髓复合体/牙本質牙髓複合體 dentinopulpal complex
牙[本]质液/牙本質液 dentinal liquor
牙[本]质釉面横纹/牙本質釉面橫紋,牙本質橫紋 dentinal perikymata
牙[本]质釉质交界/牙本質牙釉質交界 dentinoenamel junction
牙[本]质釉质界/牙[本]質釉質界,釉質齒質結合 amelodentinal junction
牙[本]质釉质连合/牙[本]質釉質連合,牙本質牙釉質交界 dentinoenamel junction

牙[本]质釉质膜/牙本質釉質膜　dentino-enamel membrane
牙[本]质增生线/牙本質增生線　incremental line of dentin
牙比色系统/牙比色系統　tooth shade system
牙变色/牙變色　tooth discoloration
牙表膜/牙表膜　dental pellicle
牙病/牙病　odontopathy
牙病学/齒病論　pathodontia
牙病灶感染/牙病灶感染　dental focal infection
牙病治疗学/牙科治療學　dental therapeutics
牙材料销售商/牙材銷售商　dental dealer
牙槽/牙槽,齒槽　dental alveoli, alveolus dentis
牙槽部/齒槽部　alveolar part
牙槽成形术/牙槽成形術,齒槽突整形術　alveoloplasty
牙槽出血/牙槽出血,齒槽出血　alveolar hemorrhage
牙槽唇沟/牙槽唇溝,齒槽唇溝　alveololabial groove
牙槽动脉/牙槽動脈,齒槽動脈　alveolar artery
牙槽轭/牙槽軛,齒槽隆凸　juga alveolaria
牙槽弓/牙槽弓,齒槽弓　alveolar arch
牙槽骨/牙槽骨,齒槽骨　alveolar bone
牙槽骨切除术/牙槽骨切除術,齒槽切除術　alveolectomy
牙槽骨髓炎/牙槽骨髓炎,齒槽骨髓炎　alveolar osteomyelitis
牙槽骨质丢失/牙槽骨質丟失,齒槽骨質丟失　alveolar bone loss
牙槽管/牙槽管,齒槽管　alveolar canal
牙槽后动脉/牙槽後動脈　posterior superior dental artery
牙槽基骨/牙槽基骨　alveolar basal bone
牙槽嵴/牙槽嵴　alveolar ridge
牙槽嵴顶/牙槽嵴頂　alveolar ridge crest
牙槽嵴纤维/牙槽嵴纖維,齒槽嵴纖維　alveolar crest fiber
牙槽嵴形态学/牙槽嵴形態學　alveolar ridge morphology
牙槽嵴延展术/牙槽嵴延展術　alveolar ridge extension
牙槽嵴增高术/牙槽嵴增高術　alveolar ridge augmentation
牙槽间隔/牙槽間隔,齒槽間隔　interalveolar septa
牙槽孔/牙槽孔,齒槽孔　alveolar foramen
牙槽裂/牙槽裂　alveolar cleft
牙槽瘘/牙槽瘘,齒槽瘘管　alveolar fistula
牙槽黏膜/牙槽黏膜　alveolar mucosa
牙槽脓溢/牙槽膿溢,牙骨質損害　alveolysis
牙槽脓肿/牙槽膿腫,齒槽膿腫　alveolar abscess
牙槽前动脉/牙槽前動脈　anterior dental artery
牙槽切开术/牙槽切開術,齒槽切開術　alveolotomy
牙槽舌沟/牙槽舌溝,齒槽舌溝　alveololingual groove
牙槽神经/牙槽神經　superior alveolar nerve
牙槽痛/牙槽痛,[手術後]齒醴窩痛　alveolalgia
牙槽突/牙槽突,齒槽突　alveolar process
牙槽突部分切除术/牙槽突部分切除術,齒槽突部分切除術　alveolomerotomy
牙槽突点/牙槽突點　alveolon
牙槽萎缩/牙槽萎縮,齒槽萎縮　alveolar atrophy
牙槽窝/牙槽窩　tooth socket
牙槽炎/牙槽炎,齒槽炎　odontobothritis
牙槽龈/牙槽齦,齒槽齦　alveolar gingiva
牙槽龈纤维/牙槽齦纖維　alveologingival fiber
牙槽粘连/齒槽[骨]粘連　tooth ankylosis
牙槽正中囊肿/牙槽正中囊腫　median alveolar cyst
牙槽中点/牙槽中點,齒槽穴　alveolar point
牙测量器/牙測量器,齒尺　dentimeter
牙测量学/牙測量學　odontometry
牙长轴/牙長軸　long axis of tooth
牙沉积物/牙沈積物　dental deposit
牙成釉细胞瘤/牙成釉細胞瘤,牙釉質母細胞瘤　odontoameloblastoma
牙齿暴露量/牙齒暴露量　tooth display
牙齿大小/牙齒大小　tooth size
牙齿浮动/牙齒浮動　luxated teeth
牙齿光泽/牙齒光澤　tooth gloss
牙齿焦黑/牙齒焦黑　blackening of teeth
牙齿近中移动/牙齒近中移動　mesial movement of teeth
牙齿可见度/牙齒可見度　tooth visibility
牙齿萌出/牙齒萌出　eruption of teeth
牙齿磨损/齒質摩損　abrasio dentium
牙齿松动度/牙齒鬆動度　tooth mobility
牙齿松动度增加/增加的牙齒搖動性　increased tooth mobility
牙齿酸弱/牙齒酸弱　weak teeth with aching
牙[齿]髓石/牙[齒]髓石　denticle
牙齿形态学/牙齒形態學　dental morphology
牙齿修复剂/牙齒修復劑　dental restoration agent
牙齿移植/牙齒移植　tooth transplantation
牙齿拥挤/牙齒擁擠　crowded teeth
牙唇面/牙唇面　labial surface of tooth
牙瓷料/牙瓷料　dental porcelain
牙垫/牙墊,咬塊　bite block
牙钉/牙釘　dental pins

牙洞衬料/牙洞襯料　dental cavity lining
牙腭面/牙腭面　palatal surface of tooth
牙发生/牙發生　odontogenesis
牙发育/牙發育　development of tooth
牙发育不全/牙發育不全,齒發育不全　dental aplasia
牙氟中毒/牙[齒]氟中毒,牙齒氟斑點　dental fluorosis
牙符记法/牙符記法,牙型描記法　dentography
牙腐蚀/牙腐蝕　tooth erosion
牙钙化/牙鈣化　tooth calcification
牙疳/牙疳　gum gan disease, ulcerative gingivitis
牙膏/牙膏　toothpaste
牙根/牙根,齒根　root of tooth
牙根拔除术/牙根拔除術　extraction of dental root
[牙]根端囊肿/牙根[端]囊腫　radiculodental cyst
[牙]根覆盖/牙根覆蓋　root coverage
牙根管/牙根管,齒根管　pulp canal, root canal
牙根尖/牙根尖,齒根尖　apex of root of tooth, tooth apex
牙根尖孔/牙根尖孔,齒根尖孔　apical foramen, apical foramen of tooth
牙根间隔/牙根間隔,齒根間隔　interradicular septa
[牙]根面平整术/[牙]根面平整術,牙根平滑術　root planing
牙根钳/牙根鉗　rhizagra
牙根龋/牙根齲　root caries
牙根融合/牙根融合　fusion of root
牙根髓/牙根髓,齒根髓　radicular pulp
牙根挺/牙根梃[子]　root elevator
牙根吸收/牙根吸收　root resorption
牙根周刮除术/牙根周[圍]刮除術　periapical curettage
牙根周溃坏/牙根周潰壞,齒根旁組織敗壞　pararhizoclasia
牙弓/牙弓,齒[列]弓　dental arch
牙弓粗线/牙弓粗線　heavy arch wire
牙弓间隙/牙弓間隙　interarch space
牙弓间协调/牙弓間協調　interarch compatibility
牙弓宽度/牙弓寬度　arch width
牙弓扩展/牙弓擴張　arch expansion
牙弓扩张/牙弓擴張,腭弓擴大　expansion of the arch
牙弓收缩/牙弓收縮　dental arch contraction
牙弓特质/牙弓特質　arch trait
牙弓位置/牙弓位置　arch position
牙弓形状/牙弓形狀　arch-form
牙弓之间牙齿大小不调/牙弓之間牙齒大小不調　interarch tooth size discrepancy
牙沟/牙溝　dental groove
牙沟液/牙溝液,牙齦縫液　gingival crevicular fluid
牙垢/牙垢　dental debris
牙垢症/牙垢症,牙結石症　odontolithiasis
牙骨膜纤维/牙骨膜纖維　dentoperiosteal fiber
牙骨质/牙骨質　cementum
牙骨质层板/牙骨質層板　cementum lamina
牙骨质发育不全[症]/牙骨質發育不全[症]　cemental hypoplasia
牙骨质化纤维瘤/牙骨質化纖維瘤,齒堊質纖維瘤　cementifying fibroma
牙骨质棘/牙骨質棘　cemental spike
牙骨质瘤/牙骨質瘤　cementoma
牙骨质破坏/牙骨質破壞　cementoclasia
牙骨质器/牙堊質器　cement organ
牙骨质生成/牙骨質生成,齒骨質形成　cementification
牙骨质撕裂/牙骨質撕裂　cemental tear
牙骨质细胞/牙骨質細胞　cementocyte
牙骨质陷窝/牙骨質陷窩　cementum lacunae
牙骨质小皮/牙骨質小皮　cemental cuticle
牙骨质小体/牙骨質小體　cementicle
牙骨质形成/牙骨質形成　cementogenesis
牙骨质炎/牙骨質炎　cementitis
牙骨质增生/牙骨質增生,齒骨質增殖,堊質增生　cementum hyperplasia, hypercementosis
牙固位装置/牙固位裝置,牙弓契合板　dental clutch
牙固有组织/牙固有組織,牙齒組織　propriodentium
牙刮器/牙刮[器]　odontoglyph
牙关节炎/牙關節炎　dental arthritis
牙关紧闭/牙關緊閉　trismus, lockjaw
牙冠/牙冠,齒冠　crown of tooth, dental crown
牙冠错位/牙冠錯位,齒冠異位　coronal trusion
牙冠覆盖体/牙冠覆蓋體　dental veneer
牙冠囊肿/牙冠囊腫　coronodental cyst
牙冠腔/髓室　pulp chamber
牙冠伸长术/牙冠伸長術　crown lengthening
牙冠髓/齒冠髓　coronal pulp
牙冠型盒/牙冠型盒,牙冠製模盤　crown flask
牙冠折断/牙冠折斷,牙冠骨折　crown fracture
牙𬌗/牙𬌗　dental occlusion
牙𬌗架/牙𬌗架　dental articulator
牙痕舌/牙痕舌　crenated tongue
牙横嵴/牙橫嵴　transverse crest of tooth, transverse ridge of tooth
牙基嵴/牙基嵴　basal of tooth ridge
牙畸形/牙畸形　tooth abnormality

牙及牙槽外科学/牙及牙槽外科學　dental and alveolar surgery
牙疾病/牙疾病　tooth disease
牙疾病预防/牙疾病預防,牙科預防法　dental prophylaxis
牙夹板/齒夾板　dental splint
牙颊面/牙頰面　buccal surface of tooth
牙尖/牙尖,齒峰,齒尖　cuspis of tooth, dental cusp
牙尖干扰/牙尖干擾　cuspal interference
[牙]尖高[度]/牙尖高度　cusp height
牙尖间殆/牙尖間殆,牙尖嵌合　interdigitation
牙尖交错殆/牙尖交錯殆　intercuspal occlusion
牙尖交错位/牙尖交錯位　intercuspal position
[牙]尖角/牙尖角　cusp angle
[牙]尖-平面角/牙尖-平面角　cusp-plane angle
牙尖吻合/牙尖咬合,齒尖咬合　intercuspation
[牙]尖窝关系/尖窩關係　cusp-fossa relation
牙尖斜度/牙尖斜度　inclination of cusp
牙间按摩器/牙間按摩器　interdental stimulator
牙间沟/牙間溝　interdental groove
牙间隙/牙間隙,齒間隙　interdental space
牙间隙牙刷/牙間隙牙刷　interproximal brush
牙间龈/牙間齦,齒間齦　septal gingiva
牙健康调查/牙健康調查　dental health survey
牙胶尖/牙膠尖　gutta percha point
牙胶锥/牙膠錐　gutta percha cone
牙接触区/牙接觸區　contingent area of tooth
牙结节/牙結節,齒結節　tubercle of tooth
牙近中面/牙近中面　mesial surface of tooth
牙颈[部]/牙頸[部],齒頸　dental cervix, neck of tooth
牙颈部龋/牙頸部齲　cervical caries
牙颈线/牙[齒]頸線　cervical line
牙颈釉质嵴/牙頸釉質嵴　cervico-enamel ridge
牙菌斑/牙菌斑,齒[菌]斑　dental plaque
牙菌斑指数/牙菌斑指數　dental plaque index
牙科包埋材料/牙科包埋材料　dental investment
牙科保健服务/牙科保健服務　dental health service
牙科保健员/牙科保健員,牙醫助理　dental hygienist
牙科保险/牙科保險　dental insurance
牙科报刊写作/牙科報刊寫作　dental journalism
牙科材料/牙科材料　dental material
牙科操作/牙科治療　dental procedure
牙科处方集/牙科處方集　dental formulary
牙科词典/牙科詞典　dental dictionary
牙科催眠术/牙科催眠術　dental hypnosis
牙[科]法医学/牙[科]法醫學　dental jurisprudence
牙科放射摄影术/牙科放射攝影術　dental radiography
牙科废弃物/牙科廢棄物　dental waste
牙科费用/牙科費用　dental fee
牙科辅助人员/牙科輔助人員　dental auxiliary
牙科高速技术/牙科高速技術　dental high-speed technique
牙科高速设备/牙科高速設備　dental high-speed equipment
牙科工艺学/牙科工藝學　dental technology
牙科工作人员/牙科工作人員　dental staff
牙科汞合金/牙科汞合金　dental amalgam
牙科刮治术/牙科刮治術　dental scaling
牙科焊接/牙科焊接　dental soldering
牙科合金/牙科合金　dental alloy
牙科记录/牙科記錄　dental record
牙科技师/牙科技師　dental technician
牙科健康教育/牙科健康教育　dental health education
牙科教育/牙科教育　dental education
牙科经济学/牙科經濟學　dental economics
牙科卡环/牙科卡環　dental clasp
牙科开业医生/牙科開業醫生　dental general practice
牙科烤瓷学/牙科烤瓷學,假齒烤瓷學　ceramodontics
牙科立法/牙科立法　dental legislation
牙科联合开业/牙科聯合開業　dental group practice
牙科联合开业诊疗/牙科聯合開業診療　dental partnership practice
牙科伦理学/牙科倫理學　dental ethics
牙科麻醉/牙科麻醉　dental anesthesia
牙科美学/牙科美學　dental esthetics
牙科模型观测器/牙科模型觀測器　dental cast surveyor
牙科黏固剂/牙科黏固劑　dental cement
牙科盘/牙科盤　dental disk
牙科器械/牙科器械　dental instrument
牙科去黏固术/牙科去黏固術　dental debonding
牙科人造石/牙科人造石,齒髓石　dental stone
牙科设备/牙科設備　dental equipment
牙科设施/牙科設施　dental facility
牙科摄影术/牙科攝影術　dental photography
牙科生理学/牙科生理學　dental physiology
牙科石膏/牙科石膏,牙科硬膏劑　dental plaster
牙科实验室/牙科實驗室　dental laboratory
牙科探针/牙科探針　dental explorer
牙科调拌刀/牙科調拌刀　dental spatula
牙科围模材料/牙科圍模材料　dental casting

investment
牙科卫生人员/牙科衛生人員 dental hygienist
牙科消毒剂/牙科消毒劑 dental disinfectant
牙科信息学/牙科信息學,牙科資訊學 dental informatics
牙科许可证/牙科許可證 dental licensure
牙科学/牙科[學] dentistry
牙科学会/牙科學會 dental society
牙科学名词/牙科命名法 odontonomy
牙科学生/牙科學生 dental student
牙科学史/牙科學史 history of dentistry
牙科医疗/牙科醫療 dental care
牙科印模材料/牙科印模材料 dental impression material
牙科印模技术/牙科印模技術 dental impression technique
牙科凿子/牙科鑿子 dental chisel
牙科哲学/牙科哲學 dental philosophy
牙科诊疗工作管理/牙科診療工作管理 dental practice management
牙科诊室/牙科診室 dental office
牙科诊所/牙科診所 dental clinics
牙科治疗焦虑/牙科治療焦慮 dental anxiety
牙科[治疗]学/牙科學 odontiatria
牙科助理/牙科助理 dental assistant
牙科助手椅旁凳/牙科助手椅旁凳 dental assisting chair side stool
牙科注射器/牙科注射器,牙齒唧筒 dental syringe
牙科铸造技术/牙科鑄造技術 dental casting technique
牙科专业/牙科專業 dental specialty
牙科综合治疗台/牙科綜合治療檯 dental unit
牙空气喷磨机/牙空氣噴磨機 dental air abrasion
牙块/牙塊 teeth block
牙蕾/牙蕾 tooth bud
牙列/牙列 dentition
牙列不正/牙列不正,牙列不整 odontoloxia
牙裂/牙裂 dental fissure
牙裂综合征/牙裂症候群 cracked tooth syndrome
牙邻接面/牙鄰接面 approximal surface of tooth
牙瘤/牙[質]瘤 odontoma
牙瘘管/牙瘺管,齒[槽]瘺 dental fistula
牙萌出/牙萌出,出齒,生齒 tooth eruption
[牙]面/假牙面 facing
牙面描记器/牙面描記器,齒面描記器 odontograph
牙面描记图/牙面描記圖,齒面描記像 odontogram
牙面外观/牙面外觀 dentofacial appearance
牙模型/牙模型,口齒模型 dental cast

牙磨擦音/牙摩擦音 stridor dentium
牙磨耗/牙磨耗 tooth attrition
牙磨损/牙磨損 tooth abrasion
牙囊/牙囊,齒囊 dental sac
牙囊肿/牙囊腫,齒囊腫 dental cyst
牙内钉/牙内釘 endodontic pin
牙内吸收/牙内吸收 internal resorption of tooth
牙内陷/牙内陷 dens invaginatus
牙黏龈盖切除术/牙黏膜蓋切除術 operculectomy
牙脓肿/牙膿腫 dental abscess
[牙]排列/牙排列 alignment
牙排列不齐/牙排列不齊 irregular tooth alignment
牙旁囊肿/牙旁囊腫,牙周囊腫 paradental cyst
牙抛光/牙拋光 dental polishing
牙胚/牙胚,齒胚 tooth germ, dental germ
牙片/牙[科照]片 dental film
牙漂白/牙漂白 teeth bleaching
牙前庭面/牙前庭面 vestibular surface of tooth
牙腔/牙腔 dental cavity
牙桥基/牙橋基 dental abutment
牙切除术/牙齒切除術 odontectomy
牙切开术/牙切開術 odontotomy
牙切缘/牙切緣 incisal margin of tooth
牙侵蚀症/牙侵蝕症,齒質腐損 dental erosion
牙缺失/牙缺失 tooth loss
牙融合/融合牙 tooth fusion
牙乳头/牙乳頭,齒乳頭 papilla of tooth, dental papilla
牙三角嵴/牙三角嵴 triangular crest of tooth, triangular ridge of tooth
牙色/牙色 tooth color
牙舌面/牙舌面 lingual surface of tooth
牙 X 射线[照]片/牙 X 射線[照]片,齒 X 光像 odontoradiograph
牙神经痛/牙神經痛 dental neuralgia
牙渗透性/牙通透性 tooth permeability
牙生长不全/牙生長不全,牙質形成不全 odontogenesis imperfecta
牙失矿质/牙失礦質 tooth demineralization
牙石/牙石,齒石 dental calculus
牙石指数/牙石指數 calculus index
牙蚀/牙蝕 dental etching
牙始基/牙始基 primordia of tooth
牙式/牙式,齒列,齒式 dental formula
牙[视]错觉/牙[視]錯覺 dental illusion
牙[数]过多/牙[數]過多,齒過多 hyperdontia
牙撕脱/牙撕脱 tooth avulsion
牙松[动]/牙鬆,牙[齒]鬆動 odontoseisis

牙酸蚀/牙酸蝕　dental acid etching
牙髓/牙髓,齒髓　dental pulp
牙髓暴露/牙髓暴露　dental pulp exposure
[牙]髓变性/牙髓變性　pulp degeneration
牙髓病学/牙髓病學,根管治疗学　endodontics
牙髓病学家/牙髓病學家,根管治疗专家　endodontist
[牙]髓充血/牙髓充血　pulp hyperemia
[牙]髓肥大/牙髓肥大　pulp hypertrophy
牙髓覆盖术/牙髓覆蓋術　dental pulp capping
牙髓钙化/牙髓鈣化　dental pulp calcification
[牙]髓化生/牙髓化生　pulp metaplasia
[牙]髓坏疽/牙髓壞疽　pulp gangrene
牙髓坏死/牙髓壞死　dental pulp necrosis
牙髓活力测验器/牙髓活力測驗器　vitalometer of dental pulp
[牙]髓活力电测验器/牙髓活力電測驗器　electric vitalometer
牙髓疾病/牙髓疾病　dental pulp disease
[牙]髓渐进性坏死/牙髓漸進性壞死　pulp necrobiosis
[牙]髓脓肿/牙髓膿腫　pulp abscess
牙髓腔/牙髓腔　dental pulp cavity
[牙]髓切断术/[牙]髓切斷術,牙髓切開術　pulpotomy
[牙]髓疝/牙髓疝　hernia of pulp
牙髓失活/牙髓失活　devitalization of dental pulp
[牙]髓失活剂/[牙]髓失活劑,失活劑　pulp devitalizer
牙髓失活术/牙髓失活術　dental pulp devitalization
牙髓试验/牙髓試驗　dental pulp test
[牙]髓塑化剂/牙髓塑化劑　pulp resinifying agent
[牙]髓塑化治疗/牙髓塑化治療　pulp resinifying therapy
牙髓探针/牙髓探針　endodontic explorer
[牙]髓痛/牙髓痛　pulpalgia
[牙]髓网状萎缩/牙髓網狀萎縮　pulp reticular atrophy
[牙]髓息肉/牙髓息肉　pulp polyp
[牙]髓纤维性变/牙髓纖維性變　fibrous degeneration of pulp
牙髓牙[本]质复合体/牙髓牙本質複合體　pulpodentinal complex
牙髓牙周联合病变/牙髓牙周聯合病變　periodontic endodontic lesion
牙髓炎/牙髓炎　pulpitis
牙髓摘除[术]/牙髓摘除[術]　pulp extirpation
牙损伤/牙損傷　tooth injury

牙索/牙索,齒索　dental cord
牙体比较解剖学/牙體比較解剖學,比较牙科解剖學,比較牙體形態學　comparative dental anatomy
牙体发育异常/牙體發育異常,牙齒發育不良,牙齒發育障礙　odontodysplasia
牙体解剖学/牙科解剖學　dental anatomy
牙体外科学/牙科手術學　operative dentistry
牙体植入学/牙科植入學　implantodontics
牙挺/牙挺　dental elevator
牙痛/牙痛　dentalgia, toothache
牙痛·风寒证/牙痛·風寒證　toothache with wind-cold pattern
牙痛·风热证/牙痛·風熱證　toothache with wind-heat pattern
牙痛·胃火证/牙痛·胃火證　toothache with stomach fire pattern
牙痛·虚火证/牙痛·虛火證　toothache with deficiency-fire pattern
牙脱落/牙脱落　tooth exfoliation
牙窝洞制备/牙窩洞製備　dental cavity preparation
牙吸收/牙吸收　tooth resorption
牙吸收器/牙吸收器,齒吸收器　absorbent organ
牙下沉/牙下沈,淹没齒,粘連齒　submerged tooth
牙线/牙線　dental floss
牙线夹/牙線夾　dental floss holder
牙小管/牙小管　canaliculus dentalis
牙泄漏/牙洩漏　dental leakage
牙型/牙型　dental pattern
牙修复磨损/牙修復磨損　dental restoration wear
牙修复失效/牙修復失效　dental restoration failure
牙修复体/牙修復體,補齒器　dental prosthesis
牙修复体固位/牙修復體固位　dental prosthesis retention
牙修复体设计/牙修復體設計　dental prosthesis design
牙修复体修补/牙修復體修補　dental prosthesis repair
牙宣/牙宣　gingival atrophy, periodontal disease
牙宣·气血两虚证/牙宣·氣血兩虛證　periodontal disease with qi-blood deficiency pattern
牙宣·肾阴虚证/牙宣·腎陰虛證　periodontal disease with kidney yin deficiency pattern
牙宣·胃火炽盛证/牙宣·胃火熾盛證　periodontal disease with blazing stomach fire pattern
牙牙比例/牙牙比例　tooth-to-tooth proportion
牙牙槽骨粘连/牙牙槽骨粘連　dental ankylosis
牙岩/牙巖,齒齦癌　rock-like gum, carcinoma of gum, gum cancer

牙咬痈/牙咬癰　acute wisdom tooth pericoronitis
牙咬痈·风热上扰证/牙咬癰·風熱上擾證　acute wisdom tooth pericoronitis with pattern of wind-heat disturbing upward
牙咬痈·肝胆火盛证/牙咬癰·肝膽火盛證　acute wisdom tooth pericoronitis with pattern of liver-gallbladder fire excessiveness
牙医病人关系/牙醫病人關係　dentist-patient relation
牙医车床/牙醫車床　dental lathe
牙医师/牙醫師　dentist
牙医诊疗模式/牙醫診療模式　dentist's practice pattern
牙移动/牙移動　tooth movement
牙移位/牙移位　tooth migration
牙因概念/牙因概念　dentogenic concept
牙龈/牙齦,齒齦　gingiva, gum
牙龈按摩/牙齦按摩,齦按摩法　gingival massage
牙龈成形术/牙齦成形術,牙齦修補術　gingivoplasty
牙龈出血/牙齦出血　gingival hemorrhage
牙龈袋/[牙]齦袋　gingival pocket
牙龈刀/牙齦刀　gingivectomy knife
牙龈点彩/牙齦點彩,齦彩斑　gingival stippling
牙龈肥大/牙齦肥大　gingival hypertrophy
牙龈疾病/牙齦疾病　gingival disease
牙龈溃烂/牙齦潰爛　ulcer of gum
牙龈裂/牙齦裂　gingival cleft
牙龈囊肿/牙齦囊腫　gingival cyst
牙龈脓肿/[牙]齦膿腫　gum boil
牙龈切除术/[牙]齦切除術　gingivectomy
牙龈乳头/牙齦乳頭,齒齦乳頭　gingival papilla
牙龈上皮/[牙]齦上皮　gingival epithelium
牙龈生长过度/牙齦生長過度　gingival overgrowth
牙龈退缩/齒齦退縮　gingival recession
牙龈萎缩/牙齦萎縮　gingival atrophy
牙龈下刮治术/牙齦下刮治術,牙齦下刮除術　subgingival curettage
牙龈纤维瘤病/牙齦纖維瘤病　gingival fibromatosis
牙龈形态学/牙齦形態學　gingival morphology
牙龈炎/[牙]齦炎　gingivitis
牙龈缘/牙齦緣　gingival margin
牙龈增生/牙齦增生　gingival hyperplasia
牙龈支/牙齦支　gingival branch
牙龈肿瘤/牙齦腫瘤　gingival neoplasm
牙龈肿痛/牙齦腫痛　swelling and aching of gum
牙龈座/牙齦座　gum block
牙隐裂/牙隱裂　cracked tooth
牙印检查/牙印檢查,牙痕鑒定術　odontoscopy
牙印模/牙印模,齒壓跡　dental impression
牙应力分析/牙應力分析　dental stress analysis
牙痈/牙癰　gum abscess, periapical periodontitis
牙用带环/牙用帶環　dentate band
牙[有机或蛋白]基质/牙基質　dentoidin
牙釉质/牙釉質　enamel
牙釉质蛋白质类/牙釉質蛋白質類　dental enamel proteins
牙釉质发育不全/牙釉質發育不全　dental enamel hypoplasia
牙釉质可溶性/牙釉質可溶性　dental enamel solubility
牙釉质裂纹/牙釉質裂紋,釉質裂隙　enamel fissure
牙釉质密固/牙鈾質密固　eburnitis
牙釉质通透性/牙釉質通透性　dental enamel permeability
牙预科教育/牙預科教育　predental education
牙缘嵴/牙緣嵴　marginal crest of tooth, marginal ridge of tooth
牙源性钙化上皮瘤/牙源性鈣化上皮瘤,鈣化性上皮成齒瘤　calcifying epithelial odontogenic tumor
牙[源]性感染/牙[源]性感染,齒源性感染　odontogenic infection
牙源性角化囊肿/牙源性角化囊腫　odontogenic keratocyst
牙源性溃疡/牙源性潰瘍,齒性潰瘍　dental ulcer
牙源性囊肿/牙源[性]囊腫　odontogenic cyst
牙源性黏液瘤/牙源性黏液瘤,齒發性黏液瘤　odontogenic myxoma
牙源性上皮性肿瘤/牙源性上皮性腫瘤　epithelial odontogenic tumor
牙源性透明细胞瘤/牙源性透明細胞瘤　clear cell odontogenic tumor
牙源性纤维瘤/牙源性纖維瘤,齒源性纖維瘤　odontogenic fibroma
牙源性纤维肉瘤/牙源性纖維肉瘤　odontogenic fibrosarcoma
牙源性腺瘤样瘤/牙源性腺瘤樣瘤　adenomatoid odontogenic tumor
牙源性肿瘤/牙源性腫瘤,齒源性腫瘤　odontogenic tumor
牙远中面/牙遠中面　distal surface of tooth
牙再矿化/牙再礦化　tooth remineralization
牙再植术/牙再植術　tooth replantation
牙粘合/牙粘合　dental bonding
牙折断/牙折斷　tooth fracture
牙折裂/牙折裂,牙破折　odontoclasis
牙支/齒支　dental branch

牙支持/牙支持　tooth support
牙支持式/牙支持式　tooth-borne type
牙指数/牙指數，齒指數　dental index
牙制备/牙製備　tooth preparation
牙质/牙質　dentine of tooth
牙质骨质瘤/牙質骨[質]瘤　dentinosteoid
牙质管系统/牙質管系統，齒質系　dentinal system
牙质溶解/牙質溶解，牙質崩解　odontolysis
牙质痛/牙質痛　dentinalgia
牙质小管/牙質小管　dentinal tubule
牙质小管鞘/牙齒質小管鞘，齒質[小管]鞘　dentinal sheath
牙质小管炎/牙質[小管]炎　dentinitis
牙质形成/牙質形成　dentinification
牙质硬化/牙[本]質硬化　dentinal sclerosis
牙质釉质膜/牙質釉質膜，牙本質牙釉質膜　dentinoenamel membrane
牙质原/牙質原，牙母質　odontogen
牙中线/牙中線　tooth midline
牙中牙/牙中線，齒中齒　dens in dente
牙种植/牙種植　dental implantation
牙种植术/牙種植術　implantation of tooth
牙种植体/牙種植體　dental implant
牙周变性/齒骨膜病　periodontosis
牙周病学/牙周病學　periodontics
牙周病学家/牙周病專家　periodontist
牙周病指数/牙周病指數　periodontal disease index
牙周创伤/牙周創傷　periodontal traumatism
牙周锉/牙周銼　periodontal file
牙周袋/牙周袋，齒[周]袋　periodontal pocket
牙周袋标记镊/牙周袋標記鑷　pocket marking plier
牙周袋探针/牙周探針　pocket probe
牙周翻瓣术/牙周翻瓣術　periodontal flap surgery
牙周敷料/牙周敷料　periodontal dressing
牙周附着丢失/牙周附著丟失　periodontal attachment loss
牙周刮出物/牙周刮出物，牙根膜刮除物　apoxemena
牙周[疾]病/牙周疾病　periodontal disease
牙周计/牙周計　dental perimeter
牙周记录表/牙周記錄表　periodontal chart
牙周夹/牙周夾　periodontal splint
牙周溃坏/牙周潰壞，齒根膜崩解，牙周膜崩解　periodontoclasia
牙周麻醉/牙周麻醉　peridental anesthesia
牙周美学/牙周美學　periodontal aesthetics
牙周膜/牙周膜，齒周膜　periodontal membrane, periodontium
牙周膜浸润麻醉/牙周膜浸潤麻醉　periodontal infiltration anesthesia
牙周膜纤维变性/牙周膜纖維變性，牙周膜纖維化　pericemental fibrosis
牙周膜炎/牙周膜炎，齒骨膜炎，齒周膜炎　pericementitis
牙周囊肿/牙周囊腫　periodontal cyst
牙周脓溢/牙周膿溢，周圍化膿　peripyema
牙周脓肿/牙周膿腫，齒周膜膿腫　periodontal abscess
牙周塞治剂/牙周塞治劑　periodontal pack
牙周塞治术/牙周塞治術　periodontal packing
牙周上皮剩余/牙周上皮剩餘　periodontal epithelial rest
牙周萎缩/牙周萎縮　periodontal atrophy
牙周纤维/牙周纖維，齒周韌帶　desmodontium
牙周协同破坏区/牙周協同破壞區　zone of co-destruction
牙周新附着/牙周新附著　new-attachment of periodontium
牙周修复体/牙周修復體　periodontal prosthesis
牙周牙髓联合治疗/牙周牙髓聯合治療　combined periodonto-endodontic therapy
牙周炎/牙周炎，齒骨膜炎　periodontitis
牙周引导组织再生/牙周引導組織再生　periodontal guided tissue regeneration
牙周再附着/牙周再附著　re-attachment of periodontium
牙周支/齒周支　peridental branch
牙周指数/牙周指數　periodontal index
牙周组织/牙周組織，齒骨膜，齒根膜　periodontium
牙周组织激惹区/牙周組織激惹區　irritation zone of periodontium
牙助听器/牙助聽器，聾者聽牙聲器　dentaphone
牙自动萌出/牙自動萌出　active tooth eruption
牙阻生/牙阻生，牙齒嵌塞　dental impaction
牙组成部分/牙組成部分　tooth component
牙钻/牙鑽　bur
芽孢杆菌科感染/芽孢桿菌科感染　Bacillaceae infection
芽孢杆菌噬菌体/芽孢桿菌噬菌體　Bacillus phage
芽囊原虫感染/芽囊原蟲感染　Blastocystis infection
芽生孢子/芽生孢子　blastospore
芽生菌病/芽生[黴]菌病，酵母菌病　blastomycosis
芽生菌病样脓皮病/芽生黴菌病樣膿皮症　blastomycosis-like pyoderma
芽生菌属产色真菌病/芽生菌屬產色黴菌病　Phialophora chromoblastomycosis

芽生菌素/芽生黴素　blastomycin
芽生菌性皮炎/芽生黴菌性皮炎,芽生黴菌性皮膚炎　blastomycetic dermatitis
芽生菌性指间糜烂/芽生[黴]菌性指間糜爛　erosio interdigitalis blastomycetica
芽生菌性趾间糜烂/芽生[黴]菌性趾間糜爛　erosio interdigitalis blastomycetica
芽生霉菌属/芽生黴菌屬　Blastomyces
芽[体]/芽　bud
芽枝酵母病/芽枝酵母病,球芽枝黴菌病　blastodendriosis
芽殖裂头蚴/增生性幼條蟲　Sparganum proliferum
芽殖裂头蚴病/芽殖裂頭蚴病　sparganosis proliferum
蚜虫/蚜蟲　aphid
哑铃形晶体/啞鈴形結晶　dumbbell crystal
哑铃形脓肿/啞鈴型膿腫,領扣狀膿腫　collar-button abscess
哑铃状瘤/啞鈴狀瘤　dumbbell tumor
哑门/啞門　yamen, DU15
哑疟/啞瘧　dumb ague
哑人/啞人,啞者　mute
哑瘴喉风/啞瘴喉風　lockjaw-aphasia throat wind
哑[症]/啞症　dumbness
雅达松-佩利扎里皮肤松弛症/雅達松-佩利扎里皮膚鬆弛症,Jadassohn-Pellizari氏皮膚鬆弛症　Jadassohn-Pellizari anetoderma
雅达松皮肤松弛/雅達松皮膚鬆弛,Jadassohn氏皮膚鬆弛症　anetoderma of Jadassohn
雅各贝乌斯手术/雅各貝烏斯手術,賈科貝氏手術　Jacobaeus operation
雅各布-克罗伊茨费尔特病/雅各布-克羅伊茨費爾特病,賈-柯二氏病　Jakob-Creutzfeldt disease
雅各布森丛/雅各布森叢,Jacobson氏叢　Jacobson plexus
雅各布森神经/雅各布神經,Jacobson氏神經　Jacobson nerve
雅凯病/雅凱病,Jacquet氏病　Jacquet disease
雅克特综合征/雅各特症候群,Jacquet氏症候群　Jacquet syndrome
雅里施-赫克斯海默反应/雅里施-赫克斯海默反應,Jarisch-Herxheimer氏反應　Jarisch-Herxheimer reaction
雅司病/雅司病　framboesia
雅司瘤/雅司瘤　framboesioma
雅司疹/雅司[病]疹　yaw
雅韦勒液/雅韋勒液,Javelle氏溶液,次氯酸鉀溶液　Javelle solution

亚氨基/亞胺基,二價胺基　imidogen
亚氨基酸/亞胺基酸　imino acid
亚胺/亞胺　imine
亚胺[代]甲基/亞胺甲基　formimino
亚胺甲基谷氨酸/亞胺甲穀胺酸　formiminoglutamic acid
亚胺硫磷/亞胺硫磷　phosmet
亚胺培南/亞胺培南　imipenem
亚白血病性白血病/亞白血病性白血病,白血球缺乏性白血病　subleukemic leukemia
亚单位疫苗/亞單位疫苗　subunit vaccine
亚单元/亞單位,次級單位　subunit
亚碲酸盐/亞碲酸鹽　tellurite
亚碘酰基苯甲酸/亞碘醯苯甲酸　iodosobenzoic acid
亚丁溃疡/亞丁潰瘍,Aden氏潰瘍　Aden ulcer
亚二倍体/亞二倍體　hypodiploid
亚砜类/亞碸類　sulfoxides
亚核/亞核,次核　subnucleus
亚红斑量/亞紅斑量　suberythema dose
亚磺酸/亞磺酸　sulfinic acid
亚急性病/亞急性病　subacute disease
亚急性毒性/亞急性毒性　subacute toxicity
亚急性肝炎/亞急性肝炎　subacute hepatitis
亚急性坏死性脊髓炎/亞急性壞死性脊髓炎　subacute necrotic myelitis
亚急性坏死性脑病/亞急性壞死性腦病　subacute necrotizing encephalopathy
亚急性脊髓炎/亞急性脊髓炎　subacute myelitis
亚急性甲状腺炎/亞急性甲狀腺炎　subacute thyroiditis
亚急性结节性游走性脂膜炎/亞急性結節性遊走性脂膜炎　subacute nodular migratory panniculitis
亚急性结节移形性脂层炎/亞急性結節移形性脂層炎　subacute nodular migrating panniculitis
亚急性阑尾炎/亞急性闌尾炎　subacute appendicitis
亚急性联合硬化/亞急性聯合硬化　subacute combined sclerosis
亚急性皮肤红斑狼疮/亞急性皮膚紅斑狼瘡　subacute cutaneous lupus erythematosus
亚急性期医疗护理/亞急性期醫療護理　subacute care
亚急性肾炎/亞急性腎炎　subacute nephritis
亚急性湿疹/亞急性濕疹　subacute eczema
亚急性细菌性心内膜炎/亞急性細菌性心內膜炎　subacute bacterial endocarditis
亚急性血行播散型肺结核/亞急性血行播散型肺結核　subacute hematogenous pulmonary tuberculosis
亚急性炎/亞急性炎症　subacute inflammation

亚急性硬化性全脑炎/亞急性硬化性全腦炎 subacute sclerosing panencephalitis
亚急性重型肝炎/亞急性重型肝炎 subacute severe hepatitis
亚甲基单位/亞甲基單位,[二]次甲基單位 methylene unit, MU
亚甲基四氢叶酸还原酶/亞甲基四氫葉酸還原酶 methylenetetrahydrofolate reductase
亚甲基四氢叶酸脱氢酶/亞甲基四氫葉酸脱氫酶 methylenetetrahydrofolate dehydrogenase
亚甲蓝/亞甲藍 methylene blue
亚甲蓝试验/亞甲藍試驗,次甲基藍試驗 methylene blue test
亚精胺/亞精胺,精胺素 spermidine
亚类/亞類 subset
亚历山大/亞歷山大,Alexander 氏 Alexander
亚历山大病/亞歷山大病,Alexander 氏病 Alexander disease
亚历山大皮肤松弛症/亞歷山大皮膚鬆弛症 anetoderma of Alexander
亚临床型糖尿病/亞臨床型糖尿病,假性糖尿病 pseudodiabete
亚磷酸/亞磷酸 phosphorous acid
亚磷酸盐/亞磷酸鹽 phosphite
亚硫酸/亞硫酸 sulfurous acid
亚硫酸氢钠/亞硫酸氫鈉,酸性亞硫酸鈉 sodium bisulfite
亚硫酸氢盐/亞硫酸氫鹽,酸性亞硫酸鹽 bisulfite
亚硫酸盐/亞硫酸鹽 sulphites
亚硫酰/亞硫氧基 thionyl
亚硫酰基/亞磺醯基 sulfinyl
亚氯酸/亞氯酸 chlorous acid
亚氯酸盐/亞氯酸鹽 chlorite
亚麻/亞麻 flax
亚麻苦苷/亞麻苦苷 linamarin
亚麻酸类/亞麻酸類 linolenic acids
亚麻油脂/亞麻脂 linolein
亚麻子/亞麻子 flaxseed
亚麻[子]油/亞麻[仁]油 linseed oil, flaxseed oil
亚慢性病/亞慢性病 subchronic disease
亚梅毒/亞梅毒 parasyphillis
亚锰酸/亞錳酸 manganous acid
亚捻发音/亞撚發音 subcrepitation
亚诺德深分歧韧带/亞諾德深分歧韌帶,Arnold 氏深分歧韌帶 deep bifurcate ligament of Arnold
亚群/亞群 subpopulation
亚砷酸/亞砷酸,亞砒酸 arsenous acid
亚砷酸钾/亞砷酸鉀,亞砒酸鉀 postassium arsenite
亚砷酸钾溶液/亞砷酸鉀溶液 potassium arsenite solution
亚砷酸溶液/亞砷酸溶液 arsenious acid solution
亚砷酸牙髓失活剂/亞砷酸牙髓失活劑 arsenious acid pulp devitalizer
亚砷酸盐/亞砷酸鹽,亞砒酸鹽 arsenite
亚速起搏/亞速起搏 underdrive pacing
亚铁螯合酶/亞鐵螯合酶 ferrochelatase
亚铁化合物/亞鐵化合物,低鐵化合物 ferrous compound
亚铁氰化物/亞鐵氰化物 ferrocyanide
亚铁氰酸/亞鐵氰酸 ferrocyanic acid
亚稳[状]态/亞穩[狀]態,非完全安定狀態 metastable state
亚硒酸/亞硒酸 selenious acid
亚硒酸钠/亞硒酸鈉 sodium selenite
亚细胞病理学/亞細胞病理學 subcellular pathology
亚细胞部分/亞細胞部分 subcellular fraction
亚线粒体颗粒/亞線粒體顆粒 submitochondrial particle
亚硝胺/亞硝[基]胺 nitrosamine
亚硝化[作用]/亞硝酸化 nitrosification
亚硝基胍/亞硝基胍 nitrosoguanidine, NTG
亚硝基胍类/亞硝基胍類 nitrosoguanidines
亚硝基化合物/亞硝基化合物 nitroso compound
亚硝基甲基乌拉坦/亞硝基甲基烏拉坦 nitroso methylurethane
亚硝基脲化合物/亞硝基脲化合物 nitrosourea compound
亚硝基取代[作用]/亞硝基取代[作用],亞硝基置換 nitrososubstitution
亚硝基铁氰酸/亞硝基鐵氰酸 nitroferrocyanic acid
亚硝基吲哚/亞硝基吲哚 nitroso-indol
亚硝酸/亞硝酸 nitrous acid
亚硝酸钠/亞硝酸鈉 sodium nitrite
亚硝酸盐还原酶类/亞硝酸鹽還原酶類 nitrite reductases
亚硝酸盐类/亞硝酸鹽類 nitrites
亚硝酸盐尿/亞硝酸鹽尿 nitrituria
亚硝酸盐尿平衡/亞硝酸鹽尿平衡 nitrituria balance
亚硝酸盐样反应/亞硝酸鹽樣反應 nitritoid reaction
亚硝酸盐样危象/亞硝酸鹽樣危象 nitritoid crisis
亚硝酸盐样休克/亞硝酸鹽樣休克 nitritoid shock
亚硝酸盐样综合征/亞硝酸鹽樣症候群 nitritoid syndrome
亚硝酸乙酯/亞硝酸乙酯 ethyl nitrite
亚硝酸乙酯醑/亞硝酸乙基醑 ethyl nitrite spirit
亚硝酸异戊酯/亞硝酸[異]戊酯 amyl nitrite

亚硝酰基/亞硝醯基　nitrosyl
亚血友病/亞血友病,次血友病　deuterohemophilia
亚叶酸/亞葉酸　leucovorin
亚乙烯腺苷三磷酸/亞乙烯腺苷三磷酸　ethenoadenosine triphosphate
亚油酸/亞[麻]油酸　linoleic acid
亚油酸乙酯/亞[麻]油酸乙酯　ethyl linoleate
亚致死基因/亞致死基因　sublethal gene
亚种/亞種　subspecies
亚洲霍乱/亞洲[型]霍亂,亞細亞霍亂　Asiatic cholera
氩/氩　argon
氩激光器/氩雷射器　argon laser
氩离子激光疗法/氩離子雷射療法　argon ion laser therapy
咽/咽　pharynx
咽白喉/咽[門]白喉　faucial diphtheria
咽瘢痕性狭窄/咽瘢痕性狹窄　cicatricial stricture of pharynx
咽瓣/咽[壁]瓣　pharyngeal flap
咽鼻炎/咽鼻[部]炎　pharyngorhinitis
咽扁桃体/咽扁桃體　pharyngeal tonsil
咽扁桃体炎/咽扁桃體炎,腺樣增殖體咽炎　adenopharyngitis
咽扁桃腺/咽扁桃腺,第三扁桃腺　pharyngeal tonsil, the third tonsil
咽病/咽病　pharyngopathy
咽病疗法/咽病療法　pharyngotherapy
咽部吹药法/咽部吹藥法　method of throat insufflation
咽部感觉缺失/咽部感覺缺失　pharyngeal anesthesia
咽[部]角化病/咽角化病　keratosis pharyngea
咽部造口/咽部造口　pharyngostoma
咽侧切开术/咽側切開術　lateral pharyngotomy
咽侧体/咽側體　corpora allata
咽成形术/咽成形術　pharyngoplasty
咽出血/咽出血　pharyngorrhagia
咽垂体/咽[部腦下]垂體　pharyngeal hypophysis
咽丛/咽叢　pharyngeal plexus
咽刀/咽刀　pharyngotome
咽导管/咽門導管　faucial catheter
咽[腭]帆功能不全/咽[腭]帆功能不全,咽與腭功能不全　velopharyngeal insufficiency
咽腭弓/腭咽弓　palatopharyngeal arch
咽腭肌/咽腭肌　musculus palatopharyngeus
咽缝/咽縫　raphe of pharynx
咽干/咽乾　dry throat
咽干燥/咽乾燥　pharyngoxerosis

咽沟/咽溝　pharyngeal groove
咽鼓管/咽鼓管　auditory tube
咽鼓管半管/咽鼓管半管　semicanal for auditory tube
咽鼓管扁桃体/咽鼓管扁桃體,耳咽管扁桃腺　tubal tonsil, eustachian tonsil
咽鼓管插管法/咽鼓管插管法,耳咽管導管插入法　salpingocatheterism
咽鼓管成形术/咽鼓管成形術　eustachian tuboplasty
咽鼓管吹张术/咽鼓管吹張術　eustachian tube insufflation
咽鼓管导管/耳咽管導管,歐氏管導管　eustachian catheter
咽鼓管导管吹张术/咽鼓管導管吹張術　eustachian catheterization
咽鼓管点/咽鼓管點　salpingion
咽鼓管电图/咽鼓管電圖　electrotubogram
咽鼓管腭襞/咽鼓管腭[皺]襞,耳咽管腭皺襞　nasopharyngeal fold
咽鼓管沟/咽鼓管溝　sulcus for auditory tube
咽鼓管骨部/咽鼓管骨部　bony part of auditory tube
咽鼓管鼓室口/咽鼓管鼓室口　tympanic opening of auditory tube
咽鼓管鼓室隐窝/咽鼓管鼓室隱窩,耳咽管鼓室隱窩　tubotympanic recess
咽鼓管镜检查/耳咽管鏡檢查法　salpingoscopy
咽鼓管气房/咽鼓管氣房,咽鼓管含氣小房　tubal air cell
咽鼓管软骨/咽鼓管軟骨　cartilage of auditory tube
咽鼓管软骨部/咽鼓管軟骨部　cartilaginous part of auditory tube
咽鼓管声测[法]/咽鼓管聲測[法]　sonotubometry
咽鼓管峡/咽鼓管峽　isthmus of auditory tube
咽鼓管狭窄/咽鼓管狹窄　eustachian tube stenosis
咽鼓管咽襞/咽鼓管咽[皺]襞　salpingopharyngeal fold
咽鼓管咽肌/咽鼓管咽肌　salpingopharyngeus, salpingopharyngeal muscle
咽鼓管咽口/咽鼓管咽口　pharyngeal opening of auditory tube
咽鼓管炎/咽鼓管炎,耳咽道炎,歐氏管炎　eustachian salpingitis
咽鼓管溢/咽鼓管溢,耳咽管漏　tuborrhea
咽鼓管圆枕/咽鼓管圓枕　torus tubarius
咽鼓管自行吹张法/咽鼓管自行吹張法　self-inflation of eustachian tube, valsalva maneuver
咽鼓管阻力测量[法]/咽鼓管阻力測量[法]　tuboresistometry

咽鼓管阻力计/咽鼓管阻力計　tuboresistometer
咽鼓管阻塞/咽鼓管阻塞,耳道阻塞　tubal block
咽鼓室管沟/咽鼓室管溝,耳咽管沟　pharyngotympanic groove
咽鼓室性头痛/咽鼓室性頭痛,里格氏病　pharyngotympanic cephalalgia
咽喉/咽喉　throat, yanhou, pharynx larynx, TG3
咽喉病/咽喉[疾]病　throat disease
咽喉病刺烙法/咽喉病刺烙法　puncture cauterization method for throat disease
咽喉病刺破排脓法/咽喉病刺破排膿法　expelling pus by puncturing for throat disease
咽喉病导引法/咽喉病導引法　daoyin for throat disease
咽喉病敷贴法/咽喉病敷貼法　application method for throat disease
咽喉病烙治法/咽喉病烙治法　cauterization method for throat disease
咽喉部切诊/咽喉部切診　palpation of throat
咽喉部闻诊/咽喉部聞診　auscultation and olfaction of larynx and pharynx
咽喉梗塞不利/咽喉梗塞不利　sticking sensation in throat
咽喉菌/咽喉菌　throat cancer
咽喉菌·火毒蕴结证/咽喉菌·火毒蘊結證　throat cancer with fire-toxin amassment pattern
咽喉菌·气血凝结证/咽喉菌·氣血凝結證　throat cancer with pattern of qi-blood coagulating and intermingling
咽喉菌·痰浊凝聚证/咽喉菌·痰濁凝聚證　throat cancer with pattern of phlegm-turbidity coagulation and aggregation
咽喉科/咽喉科　department of pharynx and larynx
咽喉口腔病雾化吸入法/咽喉口腔病霧化吸入法　spray inhalation for oral and throat disease
咽喉口腔病蒸气吸入法/咽喉口腔病蒸氣吸入法　vapor inhalation for oral and throat disease
咽喉瘤/咽喉瘤　throat tumor
咽喉瘤·气滞血瘀证/咽喉瘤·氣滯血瘀證　throat tumor with pattern of qi stagnation and blood stasis
咽喉瘤·痰浊凝聚证/咽喉瘤·痰濁凝聚證　throat tumor with pattern of phlegm-turbidity coagulation and aggregation
咽喉食管全切除术/咽喉食管全切除術　total pharyngolaryngoesophagectomy
咽喉损伤/咽喉損傷　throat injury
咽喉损伤·热毒壅盛证/咽喉損傷·熱毒壅盛證　throat injury with pattern of heat-toxin congestion and excessiveness
咽喉损伤·血瘀咽喉证/咽喉損傷·血瘀咽喉證　throat injury with pattern of blood stasis in throat
咽喉疼痛按摩法/咽喉疼痛按摩法　massage for sore throat
咽喉性咳/咽[喉]性欬　throat cough
咽喉炎/咽喉炎　pharyngolaryngitis
咽喉支/咽喉支　laryngopharyngeal branch
咽喉肿痛/咽喉腫痛　inflamed and sore throat, swelling and pain in throat
咽后壁瓣/咽後壁瓣　postpharyngeal flap
咽后间隙/咽後間隙　retropharyngeal space
咽后淋巴结/咽後淋巴結　retropharyngeal lymph node
咽后脓肿/咽後膿腫　hippocratic angina
咽呼吸/咽呼吸　pharyngeal respiration
咽会厌襞/咽會厭[皺]襞　pharyngoepiglottic fold
咽肌/咽肌　muscle of pharynx, muscle of deglutition
咽肌层/咽肌層　muscular layer of pharynx
咽肌炎/咽肌炎　juxtangina
咽疾病/咽疾病　pharyngeal disease
咽角化症/咽角化症　pharyngeal keratosis
咽结核/咽結核　tuberculosis of pharynx
咽结节/咽結節　pharyngeal tubercle
咽结膜热/咽結膜熱,咽結合膜炎　pharyngoconjunctival fever
咽结膜热病毒/咽結膜熱病毒　pharyngoconjunctival fever virus
咽结膜炎/咽結膜炎　pharyngoconjunctivitis
咽痉挛/咽痙攣　pharyngospasm
咽静脉/咽靜脈　pharyngeal vein
咽静脉丛/咽靜脈叢　pharyngeal venous plexus
咽镜检查/咽鏡檢查　pharyngoscopy
咽菌/咽菌　carcinoma of pharynx
咽科学/咽科學,咽病學　pharyngology
咽裂/咽裂[隙]　pharyngeal cleft
咽瘘/咽瘻　pharyngeal fistula
咽颅底筋膜/咽顱底筋膜　pharyngobasilar fascia
咽路/咽路　esophagus
咽麻痹/咽麻痺　pharyngoparalysis
咽盲孔/咽盲孔　cecal foramen of pharynx
咽门/咽門　fauces
咽囊/咽囊　pharyngeal bursa, pharyngeal pouch
咽囊炎/咽囊炎　pharyngeal bursitis
咽内切开术/咽內切開術　internal pharyngotomy
咽黏液溢/咽黏液溢[流],咽漏　pharyngorrhea
咽旁间隙/咽旁間隙　parapharyngeal space
咽旁脓肿/咽旁膿腫　parapharyngeal abscess

咽憩室/咽憩室　pharyngeal diverticulum
咽腔/咽腔　cavity of pharynx
咽腔过大/咽腔過大　pharyngomegaly
咽切除术/咽切除術　pharyngectomy
咽切开术/咽切開術　pharyngotomy
咽穹窿/咽穹窿　vault of pharynx
咽腮管/咽腮管　pharyngobranchial duct
咽上骨/咽上骨　suprapharyngeal bone
咽上缩肌/咽上縮肌,上咽縮肌　superior constrictor of pharynx
咽上缩肌颊咽部/咽上縮肌頰咽部　buccopharyngeal part of superior constrictor of pharynx
咽上缩肌舌咽部/咽上縮肌舌咽部　glossopharyngeal part of superior constrictor of pharynx, pars glossopharyngea musculi constrictoris pharyngis superioris
咽上缩肌下颌咽部/咽上縮肌下頜咽部　mylopharyngeal part of superior constrictor of pharynx
咽上缩肌翼咽部/咽上縮肌翼咽部　pterygopharyngeal part of superior constrictor of pharynx, pars pterygopharyngea musculi constrictoris pharyngis superioris
咽舌肌/咽舌肌　pharyngoglossus
咽神经症/咽神經症　neurosis of pharynx
咽升动脉/咽昇動脈　ascending pharyngeal artery
咽石/咽石　pharyngolith
咽食管憩室/咽食管憩室　pharyngoesophageal diverticulum
咽痛/咽痛　pharyngalgia, sore throat
咽突出/咽凸出,咽赫尼亞　pharyngocele
咽外侧间隙/咽外側間隙　lateropharyngeal space
咽外切开术/咽外切開術　external pharyngotomy
咽峡/咽峽　isthmus of fauces, isthmus faucium
咽峡痉挛/咽峽痙攣　isthmospasm
咽峡炎/咽峽炎　angina
咽峡炎酵母/咽峽炎酵母[菌]　Saccharomyces anginae
咽峡支/咽峽支　branches to isthmus of fauces
咽狭窄/咽狹窄　pharyngostenosis
咽下部憩室/咽部下憩室　hypopharyngeal diverticulum
咽下缩肌/咽下縮肌,下咽縮肌　inferior constrictor of pharynx, inferior constrictor muscle of pharynx
咽下缩肌环咽部/咽下縮肌環咽部　cricopharyngeal part of inferior constrictor of pharynx, pars cricopharyngea musculi constrictoris pharyngis inferioris
咽下缩肌甲咽部/咽下縮肌甲咽部　thyropharyngeal part of inferior constrictor of pharynx, pars thyropharyngea musculi constrictoris pharyngis inferioris
咽型伤寒/咽型傷寒　pharyngotyphoid
咽咽鼓管炎/咽耳咽管炎　pharyngosalpingitis
咽炎/咽炎　pharyngitis
咽炎疹/咽喉疹　pharyngitid
咽隐窝/咽隱窩　pharyngeal recess
咽硬结/咽硬結,咽硬斑　pharyngoscleroma
咽造口术/咽[部]造口術　pharyngostomy
咽真菌病/咽真菌病　pharyngomycosis
咽疹/咽疹,咽紅斑　pharyngeal rash
咽支/咽支　pharyngeal branch
咽中缩肌/咽中縮肌,內咽縮肌　middle constrictor of pharynx, middle constrictor muscle of pharynx
咽中缩肌大角咽部/咽中縮肌大角咽部　ceratopharyngeal part of middle constrictor of pharynx
咽中缩肌小角咽部/咽中縮肌小角咽部　chondropharyngeal part of middle constrictor of pharynx
咽肿/咽腫　throat swelling
咽肿瘤/咽腫瘤　pharyngeal neoplasm
咽周间隙/咽周間隙　peripharyngeal space
咽阻塞/咽阻塞　pharyngemphraxis
胭脂虫蜡/胭脂蟲蠟,胭脂蟲素　coccerin
胭脂红/胭脂[蟲]紅　cochineal
胭脂红溶液/胭脂紅溶液　cochineal solution
胭脂红酸/胭脂紅酸,洋紅酸　carminic acid
烟/煙　fume
烟斑/煙斑　smoker's patch
烟草/煙草,煙葉　tobacco
烟草毒性心/煙毒心,煙毒性心臟　tobacco heart
烟草花叶病毒/煙草花葉[病]病毒　tobacco mosaic virus
烟草花叶病毒组/煙草花葉病毒組　tobamovirus
烟草花叶卫星病毒/煙草花葉衛星病毒　tobacco mosaic satellite virus
烟草坏死卫星病毒/煙草壞死衛星病毒　tobacco necrosis satellite virus
烟草性口炎/煙草性口炎,尼古丁口炎　stomatitis nicotina
烟草烟污染/煙草煙汙染　tobacco smoke pollution
烟草中毒/煙草中毒　tobacco poisoning
烟草中毒性弱视/煙草中毒性弱視　tobacco amblyopia
烟囱清扫工癌/煙囪清掃工癌,煙囪掃除者癌

chimney-sweeper cancer
烟斗颌/煙斗頜　pipe jaw
烟管癌/煙斗癌　claypipe cancer
烟管状便/煙管狀便,煙管軸狀糞　pipe-stem stool
烟灰/［煤］煙灰　soot
烟碱激动剂/煙鹼激動劑　nicotinic agonist
烟碱拮抗剂/煙鹼拮抗劑　nicotinic antagonist
烟碱受体/煙鹼受體　nicotinic receptor
烟碱酸/煙鹼酸　nicotine acid
烟碱酸苄酯/煙鹼酸苄酯　benzyl nicotinate
烟碱性口炎/煙鹼性口炎　nicotinic stomatitis
烟碱中毒/煙鹼中毒,煙草素中毒　nicotinism
烟肼酰胺/煙肼醯胺,尼亞拉胺　Nialamide
烟卷式引流/卷煙式洩管　cigarette drain
烟曲菌/煙麴菌,薰煙色麴菌　Aspergillus fumigatus
烟曲霉酸/煙麴黴酸　helvolic acid
烟色尿/煙色尿　smoky urine
烟酸类/煙酸類　nicotinic acids
烟酸缺乏病/煙［草］酸缺乏病　aniacinosis
烟酸试验/煙酸試驗　niacin test
烟雾化［作用］/煙霧化［作用］,使霧狀化　aerosolization
烟雾吸入损伤/煙霧吸入損傷　smoke inhalation injury
烟酰胺/煙［鹼］醯胺　niacinamide
烟酰胺单核苷酸/煙醯胺單核苷酸,煙草醯胺單核苷酸　nicotinamide mononucleotide
烟酰胺核苷酸腺嘌呤转移酶/煙醯胺核苷酸腺嘌呤轉移酶　nicotinamide-nucleotide adenylyltransferase
烟酰胺酶/煙醯胺酶　nicotinamidase
烟酰胺缺乏病/煙草醯胺缺乏病　aniacinamidosis
烟酰胺血［症］/煙醯胺血［症］,煙草醯胺血症　nicotinamidemia
［烟］熏剂/［煙］熏劑　smoke fumigant
阉割焦虑/閹割焦慮,去勢恐懼　castration anxiety
阉割情结/閹割情結,閹割後心理簇　castration complex
淹没辐射/湮滅放射　annihilation radiation
延迟毒性/延遲毒性　delayed toxicity
延迟缝合/延遲縫合　delayed suture
延迟后除极/延遲後除極　delayed afterdepolarization
延迟青春期/延遲青春期　delayed puberty
延迟神经毒性/延遲神經毒性　delayed neurotoxicity
延迟性脾破裂/延遲性脾破裂　delayed rupture of spleen
延迟修复/延遲修復　delayed repair
延迟愈合/延遲愈合　delayed union
延迟转移/延遲轉移　delayed transfer

延胡索/延胡索　Rhizoma Corydalis（拉）
延胡索酸氢化酶/延胡索酸氫化酶　fumaric hydrogenase
延胡索酸水合酶/延胡索酸水合酶　fumarate hydratase
延胡索酸盐/延胡索酸鹽,丁烯二酸鹽　fumarate
延胡索酸盐类/延胡索酸鹽類　fumarates
延命术/延命術,延命［法］　apothanasia
延期植皮术/延期植皮術　delayed skin grafting
延伸卡环/延伸卡環　extension clasp
延髓/延髓　medulla oblongata, oblongata
延髓出血/延髓出血　medulla oblongata hemorrhage
延髓弓状核/延髓弓狀核　arcuate nucleus of medulla oblongata
延髓孤束/延髓孤束,延髓孤立徑　solitary tract of medulla oblongata
延髓后正中静脉/延髓後正中靜脈　posteromedian medullary vein
延髓脊髓灰质炎/延腦［性］脊髓灰質炎　bulbar poliomyelitis
延髓静脉/延髓靜脈　veins of medulla oblongata
延髓空洞症/延髓空洞病　syringobulbia
延髓连合核/延髓連合核　commissural nucleus of medulla oblongata
延髓麻痹/延髓麻痺,延髓性癱瘓　bulbar palsy
延髓麻醉/脊隨麻醉　medullary anesthesia
延髓盲孔/延髓盲孔　cecal foramen of medulla oblongata
延髓脑桥沟/延髓腦轎溝　bulbopontine sulcus
延髓内侧支/延髓內側支　medial oblongatal branch
延髓前交叉综合征/延髓前交叉症候群　anterior cross bulbar syndrome
延髓前外侧沟/延髓前外側溝　anterolateral sulcus of medulla oblongata, anterolateral groove of medulla
延髓前外侧静脉/延髓前外側靜脈　anterolateral medullary vein
延髓前正中静脉/延髓前正中靜脈　anteromedian medullary vein
延髓前正中裂/延髓前正中裂［隙］　anterior median fissure of medulla oblongata
延髓上横静脉/延髓上橫靜脈　superior transverse medullary vein
延髓束/延髓束　bulbar tract
延髓外侧静脉/延髓外側靜脈　lateral medullary vein
延髓外侧支/延髓外側支　lateral oblongatal branch
延髓外侧综合征/延髓外側症候群　lateral medullary syndrome

延髓网状脊髓束/延髓網狀脊髓徑 bulboreticulospinal tract
延髓下横静脉/延髓下橫靜脈 inferior transverse medullary vein
延髓性感觉缺失/延髓性感覺缺失 bulbar anesthesia
延髓性共济失调/延髓性運動失調 bulbar ataxia
延髓性麻痹/延髓性麻痺 bulbar paralysis
延髓中缝/延髓中縫 raphe of medulla oblongata
延髓中横静脉/延髓中橫靜脈 middle transverse medullary vein
延髓蛛网膜下腔/延髓的蛛網膜下腔 subarachnoid cavity of medulla oblongata
延髓综合征/延髓症候群 bulbar syndrome
延续生命支持/延續生命支持,延續生命支援 prolonged life support
延续睡眠法/持久睡眠法 prolonged sleep
严格评价/嚴格評讀 critical appraisal skill
严重急性呼吸综合征/嚴重急性呼吸症候群 severe acute respiratory syndrome
言语/言語 speech
言语病理学/言語病理學 lalopathology
言语病学/言語病學 laliatry
言语不利/言語不利 inarticulateness
言语不清/言語不清,言語艱難 barylalia
言语参数测量/言語參數測量 speech production measurement
言语测听法/言語測聽法 speech audiometry
言语重复/言語重複[症],憂語症 palilalia
言语错乱/言語錯亂 paraphasia
言语发音试验/言語發音試驗 speech articulation test
言语干扰级/言語干擾級 speech interference level
言语功能测试/言語功能測試 speech function test
言语共济失调/言語[共濟]失調 ataxiophemia
言语过慢/言語過慢,言語徐緩 bradyarthria
言语急促/言語急促,促語症 oxylalia
言语检察阈/言語檢察閾 speech detection threshold
言语接受阈/言語接受閾 speech reception threshold
言语接受阈试验/言語接受閾試驗 speech reception threshold test
言语困难/出語困難,構音困難 dyslalia
言语理解/言語理解 lalognosis
言语理解困难/解語不能 logasthenia
言语理解力/言語理解力 speech intelligibility
言语疗法/言語療法 speech therapy
言语凌乱/言語凌亂 gibberish
言语器官麻痹/言語器官麻痺,言語肌性麻痺 laloplegia
言语腔韵失调/[言語]韻調失調,言語失韻 hypoprosody
言语涩滞/言語澀滯 angophrasia
言语声律障碍/言語[聲律]障礙 dysprosody
言语声学/言語聲學 speech acoustics
言语识别测验/言語識別測驗 speech discrimination test
言语识别率/言語識別率 speech discrimination score
言语[思维]连贯不能/言語[思維]連貫不能,思想連貫不能 asyndesis
言语行为/言語行爲 verbal behavior
言语性强化/言語性強化 verbal reinforcement
言语学习/言語學習 verbal learning
言语训练/言語訓練 speech training
言语异常/言語異常 heterophthongia
言语语言病理学/言語語言病理學 speech-language pathology
言语杂乱/言語雜亂 schizophasia
言语障碍/言語障礙 speech disorder
言语知觉/言語知覺 speech perception
言语重浊/言語重濁 pyknophrasia
岩/巖 cancer, carcinoma
岩部/岩部,錐體 petrosal part, petrous part
岩部后面/岩部後面 posterior surface of petrous part
岩部后缘/岩部後緣 posterior border of petrous part
岩部尖/岩部尖,錐體尖 apex of petrous part
岩部静脉/岩部靜脈 vena petrosa
岩部前面/岩部前面 anterior surface of petrous part
岩部前缘/岩部前緣 anterior border of petrous part
岩部上缘/岩部上緣 superior border of petrous part
岩部下面/岩部下面 inferior surface of petrous part
岩大浅神经沟/岩大淺神經溝 groove of great superficial petrosal nerve
岩大神经/岩大神經 greater petrosal nerve
岩大神经沟/岩大神經溝 sulcus for greater petrosal nerve
岩大神经管裂孔/岩大神經管裂孔 hiatus of canal for greater petrosal nerve
岩蝶韧带/岩蝶韌帶 petrosphenoid ligament
岩骨斜坡脑膜瘤/岩骨斜坡腦膜瘤 petroclival meningioma
岩鼓裂/岩鼓裂,格拉塞氏裂 petrotympanic fissure, glaserian fissure
岩尖切除术/岩[根]尖切除術 apicectomy
岩静脉/岩靜脈 petrosal vein

岩孔/岩孔，無名小管　innominate canaliculus
岩鳞裂/岩鱗裂,岩鱗間裂隙　petrosquamous fissure, fissura petrosquamosa
岩棉/岩棉　rockwool
岩上窦/岩上竇　superior petrosal sinus
岩上窦沟/岩上竇溝　groove for the superior sagittal sinus
岩深神经/岩深神經　deep petrosal nerve
岩石草/岩蘭草　vetiver
岩下窦/岩下竇　inferior petrosal sinus
岩下窦沟/岩下竇溝　sulcus for inferior petrosal sinus
岩下窦取样/岩下竇取樣　petrosal sinus sampling
岩小浅神经沟/岩小淺神經溝　groove of small superficial petrosal nerve
岩小神经/岩小神經　lesser petrosal nerve
岩小神经沟/岩小神經管　sulcus for lesser petrosal nerve
岩小神经管裂孔/岩小神經管裂孔　hiatus of canal for lesser petrosal nerve
岩小窝/岩小窩,岩小凹　petrosal fossula
岩性溃疡/岩性潰瘍,巖性潰瘍　cancerous ulcer
岩咽肌/岩咽肌　petropharyngeus
岩藻聚糖/岩藻聚糖　fucosan
岩藻糖/岩藻糖　fucose
岩藻糖苷/岩藻糖苷　fucoside
岩藻糖苷酶/岩藻糖苷酶　fucosidase
岩藻糖苷贮积症/岩藻糖苷貯積病　fucosidosis
岩藻糖基半乳糖 α-N-乙酰氨基半乳糖转移酶/岩藻糖基半乳糖 α-N-乙醯胺基半乳糖轉移酶　fucosyl galactose alpha-N-acetylgalactosaminyltransferase
岩藻糖基转移酶类/岩藻糖基轉移酶類　fucosyltransferases
岩枕骨结合关节/岩枕骨[结合]關節　petrooccipital articulation
岩枕间裂隙/岩枕間裂隙　fissura petrooccipitalis
岩枕结合/岩枕[軟骨]结合　petrooccipital synchondrosis
岩枕裂/岩枕裂　petrooccipital fissure
岩支/岩支　petrosus branch
岩中浅神经/岩中淺神經　superficial middle petrosal nerve
岩锥切除术/岩部切除術　petrosectomy
岩锥炎/岩[锥]炎,岩顳骨部炎　petrositis
炎性白细胞增多/炎性白血球增多　inflammatory leukocytosis
炎性肠病/炎性腸病,炎症性腸道病　inflammatory bowel disease
炎性充血/炎性充血　inflammatory hyperemia
炎性肥大/炎性肥大　inflammatory hypertrophy
炎性根旁囊肿/炎性根旁囊腫　inflammatory collateral cyst
炎性脊柱侧凸/炎性脊柱側凸,發炎性脊柱側彎　inflammatory scoliosis
炎性假瘤/炎性假瘤　inflammatory pseudotumor
炎性绞痛/炎性絞痛　inflammatory colic
炎性巨噬细胞/炎性巨噬細胞　inflammatory macrophages
炎性溃疡/炎性潰瘍　inflamed ulcer
炎性类酶/炎性類酶　phlogisticozymoid
炎性淋巴/炎性淋巴　inflammatory lymph
炎性黏液透明瘤/炎性黏液透明瘤,發炎性黏液透明性瘤　inflammatory myxohyaline tumor
炎性水肿/炎性水腫　inflammatory edema
炎性痛经/炎性痛經　inflammatory dysmenorrhea
炎性吞咽困难/[發]炎性吞嚥困難　dysphagia inflammatoria
炎性萎缩/炎性萎縮　inflammatory atrophy
炎性息肉/[發]炎性息肉　inflammatory polyp
炎性纤维增生/炎性纖維增生　inflammatory fibrous hyperplasia
炎性线状疣状表皮痣/炎性線狀疣狀表皮痣　inflammatory linear verrucous epidermal nevus
炎性消化不良/炎性消化不良　inflammatory dyspepsia
炎性椎管积水/炎性脊髓積水　hydrorachitis
炎症/炎症　phlegmasia
炎症后白斑病/炎症後白皮症,發炎後白皮症　postinflammatory leukoderma
炎症后过度黑变病/炎症後過度黑變病,發炎後黑色素過度沈著症　postinflammatory hypermelanosis
炎症后黑变病/炎症後黑變病,發炎後黑色素沈著症　postinflammatory melanosis
炎症后弹性组织溶解及皮肤松垂/發炎後彈性纖維溶解及皮膚鬆垂[症]　postinflammatory elastolysis and cutis laxa
炎症介导素类/炎症介導素類　inflammation mediators
炎症趋化因子类/炎症趨化因子類　chemokines
炎症细胞/炎症細胞　inflammatory cell
沿光照部位分布的/沿光照部分分布的　photodistributed
沿神经蔓延/神經路徑傳播　neuroprobasia
沿爪疗/沿爪疔　ding along nail edge
研究用诊断标准/研究用診斷標準　research

diagnostic criterion
研究中新药/研究中藥品　investigational drug
研磨/研磨　grind, triturate
研磨工哮喘/研磨工哮喘　grinder asthma
研磨器/研製器　triturator
盐/鹽　salt
盐分级分离/鹽分級分離　salt fractionation
盐化/鹽化,變化爲鹽　salify
盐类/鹽類　salts
盐类泻药/鹽類瀉藥　saline cathartic
盐卤中毒/鹽鹵中毒　bittern poisoning
盐皮质激素类/鹽皮質激素類　mineralocorticoids
盐皮质激素受体/鹽皮質激素受體　mineralocorticoid receptor
盐桥/鹽橋　salt bridge
盐溶/鹽溶　salting in
盐溶液/鹽溶液　salt solution
盐水浮集法/鹽水浮集法,鹽水漂浮法　brine flotation method
盐水输注/鹽水輸注　saline infusion
盐水浴/鹽水浴　brine bath
盐酸/鹽酸　hydrochloric acid
盐酸吖啶黄/鹽酸吖啶黃[素]　acriflavine hydrochloride
盐酸阿朴吗啡/鹽酸阿朴嗎啡　apomorphine hydrochloride
盐酸氨基吖啶/鹽酸氨基吖啶　aminacrine hydrochloride
盐酸半胱氨酸/鹽酸半胱胺酸,鹽酸硫胱胺酸　cysteine hydrochloride
盐酸苯海拉明/鹽酸苯海拉明　benzhydramine hydrochloride
盐酸苯海索/鹽酸苯海索　benzhexol hydrochloride
盐酸吡哆醇/鹽酸吡哆醇　pyridoxine hydrochloride
盐酸丙卡巴肼/鹽酸丙卡巴肼,鹽酸甲苄肼　procarbazine hydrochloride
盐酸达克罗宁/鹽酸達克羅寧　dyclonine hydrochloride
盐酸狄布卡因/鹽酸狄布卡因,鹽酸奴白卡因　dibucaine hydrochloride
盐酸丁卡因/鹽酸丁卡因　tetracaine hydrochloride
盐酸二甲异喹/鹽酸二甲異喹　dimethisoquin hydrochloride
盐酸二氢吗啡酮/鹽酸二氫嗎啡酮　hydromorphone hydrochloride
盐酸二乙酰吗啡/鹽酸二乙醯嗎啡,鹽酸海洛因　diacetylmorphine hydrochloride
盐酸海克卡因/鹽酸海克卡因,鹽酸己基卡因　hexylcaine hydrochloride
盐酸甲基育亨烷/鹽酸甲基育亨烷,甲基育亨烷鹽酸鹽　mimbane hydrochloride
盐酸精氨酸/鹽酸精胺酸　arginine hydrochloride
盐酸卡马风/鹽酸卡馬風,抗阿米巴原蟲藥　bialamicol hydrochloride
盐酸奎宁/鹽酸奎寧　quinine hydrochloride
盐酸硫胺素/鹽酸硫胺素　thiamin hydrochloride
盐酸氯苯丁嗪/鹽酸氯苯丁嗪　buclizine hydrochloride
盐酸氯环嗪/鹽酸氯環嗪　chlorcyclizine hydrochloride
盐酸氯普鲁卡因/鹽酸氯普魯卡因　chloroprocaine hydrochloride
盐酸麻黄碱/鹽酸麻黃素　ephedrine hydrochloride
盐酸毛果芸香碱/鹽酸毛果芸香鹼　pilocarpine hydrochloride
盐酸纳洛酮/鹽酸納洛酮　naloxone hydrochloride
盐酸萘甲唑啉溶液/鹽酸萘甲唑啉溶液　naphazoline hydrochloride solution
盐酸萘唑啉/鹽酸萘唑啉　naphazoline hydrochloride
盐酸普鲁卡因酰胺/鹽酸普魯卡因[醯]胺　procainamide hydrochloride
盐酸去甲麻黄碱/鹽酸去甲麻黃鹼　phenylpropanolamine hydrochloride
盐酸烧伤/鹽酸燒傷　hydrochloric acid burn
盐酸肾上腺素/鹽酸腎上腺素　adrenalin hydrochloride
盐酸双环胺/鹽酸雙環胺　dicyclomine hydrochloride
盐酸四环素/鹽酸四環素　tetracycline hydrochloride
盐酸脱氢肾上腺素溶液/鹽酸去氫腎上腺素溶液　phenylephrine hydrochloride solution
盐酸脱氧麻黄碱/鹽酸脱氧麻黃鹼,鹽酸去氧麻黃鹼　methamphetamine hydrochloride
盐酸烷基二胺乙基甘氨酸溶液/鹽酸烷基二胺乙基甘胺酸溶液　alkyldiaminoethylglycine hydrochloride solution
盐酸西尼二胺/鹽酸西尼二胺,鹽酸噻吩甲二胺　thenyldiamine hydrochloride
盐酸消旋麻黄素溶液/消旋鹽酸麻黃素溶液　racephedrine hydrochloride solution
盐酸乙基吗啡/鹽酸乙基嗎啡　ethylmorphine hydrochloride
盐酸异丙肾上腺素/鹽酸異丙基腎上腺素　isoproterenol hydrochloride
盐酸罂粟碱/鹽酸罌粟鹼　papaverine hydrochloride
盐酸优加托品/鹽酸優加托品,鹽酸優卡阿托品　eucatropine hydrochloride

盐酸组氨酸/鹽酸組[織]胺酸　histidine monohydrochloride
盐析/鹽析　salting out
盐细菌视紫红质/鹽細菌視紫紅質　halorhodopsin
盐腺/鹽腺　salt gland
盐液比重计/鹽液濃度計　salimeter
盐液密度计/鹽液密度計,鹽量計　salinometer
盐蒸/鹽蒸　steaming with salt-water
盐制/鹽制　processing with salt-water
盐炙/鹽炙　stir-frying with salt-water
[颜]面/顏面　facial surface
颜面疔疮/顏面疔瘡　facial ding, facial deep-rooted sore, facial hard furuncle
颜面疔疮·火毒炽盛证/顏面疔瘡·火毒熾盛證　facial ding with blazing fire-toxin pattern
颜面疔疮·热毒蕴结证/顏面疔瘡·熱毒蘊結證　facial ding with heat-toxin amassment pattern
颜面浮肿/顏面浮腫　facial edema
[颜]面感觉缺失/顏面感覺缺失　facial anesthsia
[颜]面角/顏面角　facial angle
[颜]面肉芽肿/顏面肉芽腫　granuloma faciale
[颜]面外面肉芽肿/顏面外顏面肉芽腫　extrafacial granuloma faciale
颜面增生/顏面增生　facial hyperplasia
颜色/色　color
颜色匹配/顏色匹配比色　color matching
衍射/衍射,繞射　diffraction
衍射光谱/衍射光譜,繞射光譜　diffraction spectrum
衍射光栅/衍射光柵,繞射光柵　diffraction grating
衍生蛋白/衍生蛋白,衍化蛋白質　derived protein
衍生化反应小管/衍生化反應小管,衍生反應小瓶　derivatizing reaction vial
衍生染色体/衍生染色體　derivative chromosome
衍生物/衍生物　derivative
衍生性循环/衍生性循環　derivative circulation
眼/眼　①eye, oculi ②yan, LO5
眼白化病/眼白化病　ocular albinism
眼胞疔/眼胞疔　ding of eyelid
眼胞瘀痛/眼胞瘀痛　blood stasis and pain of eyelid, stasis and pain due to eyelid contusion
眼保健按摩/眼保健按摩　health massage for eyes
眼保健操/眼保健操　eye-care massage
眼绷带/眼繃帶　eye bandage
眼壁硬度/眼壁硬度　ocular rigidity
眼壁硬度系数/眼壁硬度係數　coefficient of ocular rigidity
眼病/眼病,眼的病症　ocular disease
眼病理学/眼病理學　pathology of eye

眼病性脊柱侧凸/眼病性脊柱側凸　ocular scoliosis
眼病性眩晕/眼[病]性眩暈　ocular vertigo
眼玻璃体膜下出血/眼玻璃體[膜]下出血　subhyaloid hemorrhage
眼部注射法/眼部注射法　ocular injection
眼铲/眼鏟　eye spud
眼颤动/眼顫動　ophthalmodonesis
眼成形术/眼成形術,眼造形術,眼修補術　ophthalmoplasty
眼齿指发育不良/眼齒指發育不全　oculodentodigital dysplasia
眼出血/眼出血　eye hemorrhage
眼挫伤/眼挫傷　ocular contusion
眼带/眼帶　ocular band
眼带状疱疹/眼帶狀皰疹　ophthalmic zoster
眼丹/眼丹　erysipelas of eyelid, eyelid cellulitis
眼丹·风毒束睑证/眼丹·風毒束瞼證　eyelid cellulitis with pattern of wind-toxin fettering eyelid
眼丹·热毒壅盛证/眼丹·熱毒壅盛證　eyelid cellulitis with pattern of heat-toxin congestion and excessiveness
眼丹·正虚邪恋证/眼丹·正虛邪戀證　eyelid cellulitis with pattern of healthy qi deficiency and lingering pathogen
眼单位/眼單位　eye unit
眼胆固醇沉着症/眼膽固醇沈著症　cholesterolosis bulbi
眼蛋白质类/眼蛋白質類　eye proteins
眼底/眼底　fundus oculi
眼底反射/眼底反射　fundus reflex
眼底反射试验/眼底反射試驗,視網膜拾影法　fundus reflex test
眼底黄斑/眼底黃斑,眼底黃色斑點症　fundus flavimaculatus
眼底检查[法]/眼底檢查[法]　examination of ocular fundus
眼底镜/眼底鏡　funduscope
眼底镜检查/眼底鏡檢查　funduscopy
眼底显微镜检查/眼底顯微鏡檢查　fundus microscopy
眼底照相机/眼底照相機　fundus camera
眼底照相[术]/眼底照相[術]　fundus photography
眼蒂/眼蒂,視莖　optic stalk
眼点/眼點　eyespot
眼电描记术/眼電描記術　electro-oculography
眼电图/眼電圖　electro-oculogram
眼垫/眼墊　eye pad
眼动测位镜/眼動測位鏡,并行視線計　isoscope

眼动电图/眼動電圖,眼电[流]图 electro-oculogram
眼动电图描记法/眼動電圖描記法,眼電流描記法 electro-oculography
眼动脉/眼動脈 ophthalmic artery
眼动脉压/眼動脈壓 ophthalmic arterial pressure
眼动脉造影[术]/眼動脈造影[術] ocular angiography
眼动危象/眼動危象 oculogyric crisis
眼动眼电图/眼動眼電圖 eye movement electro-oculogram
眼毒理学/眼毒理學 ophthotoxicology
眼毒素/眼毒素 ophthalmotoxin
眼耳发育异常/眼耳發育不全 oculoauricular dysplasia
眼-耳-脊椎发育不良/眼耳脊椎發育不良 oculo-auriculo-vertebral dysplasia
眼耳平面/眼耳平面 eye-ear plane
眼反应/眼反應 oculoreaction
眼防护装置/眼防護裝置 eye protective device
眼房/眼[前]房 aqueous chamber
眼房水/眼[前]房水 aqueous humor
眼副器/眼副器 accessory organs of eye
眼干燥症/眼乾燥症,眼乾燥病,乾眼症 ophthalmoxerosis
眼疳/眼疳 eye gan disease
眼感染/眼感染 eye infection
眼跟踪试验/眼跟蹤試驗 eye tracking test
眼弓形虫病/眼弓形蟲病 ocular toxoplasmosis
眼黑变病/眼黑變病 ophthalmomelanosis
眼会聚/眼會聚 ocular convergence
眼肌/眼肌 muscle of eye, ocular muscle
眼肌病/眼肌病 ocular myopathy
眼肌操练器/眼肌運動器 phorotone
眼肌筋膜/眼肌筋膜,肌膜 muscular fascia
眼肌静脉/眼肌靜脈 vein of ocular muscle
眼肌力计/眼肌力計 optomyometer
眼肌麻痹/眼肌麻痺,眼肌癱瘓 ophthalmoplegia
眼肌麻痹性[周期性]偏头痛/眼肌麻痺性偏頭痛 ophthalmoplegic migraine
眼肌模型/眼動模型 ophthalmotrope
眼肌切开术/眼肌切開術 ophthalmomyotomy
眼肌失调矫正器/眼肌失調矯正器 metronoscope
眼肌衰弱性直视/眼肌衰弱性直視,眼肌全部微弱 asthenic orthophoria
眼肌运动矫正器/眼肌矯正器 myoculator
眼肌折叠术/眼肌折疊術 cinching
眼畸形/眼畸形 eye abnormality
眼疾病/眼疾病 eye disease

眼睑/眼瞼,眼皮,眼簾 eyelid
眼睑成形术/眼瞼成形術,瞼整形術 blepharoplasty
眼睑痤疮/眼瞼痤瘡 acne ciliaris
眼睑丹毒/眼瞼丹毒 erysipelas palpebrae
眼睑垫板/眼瞼墊板 eyelid plate
眼睑淀粉样变性/眼瞼澱粉樣變性 amyloid degeneration of eyelid
眼睑分裂痣/眼瞼分裂痣 divided nevus of eyelid
眼睑浮肿/眼瞼浮腫 eyelid edema, eyelid swelling
眼睑功能不全/眼瞼功能不全 insufficiency of the eyelid
眼睑黄斑瘤/眼瞼黄斑瘤 xanthelasma palpebrarum
眼睑黄色瘤/眼瞼黄色瘤,瞼黄瘤 xanthoma palpebrarum
眼睑基底细胞癌/眼瞼基底細胞癌 basal cell carcinoma of eyelid
眼睑疾病/眼瞼疾病 eyelid disease
眼睑浆细胞瘤/眼瞼漿細胞瘤 plasmocytoma of eyelid
眼睑疖/眼瞼癤 furuncle of eyelid
眼睑痉挛/[眼]瞼痙攣 blepharospasm
眼睑拉钩/眼瞼拉鉤,瞼牽開器 eyelid retractor
眼睑鳞状细胞癌/眼瞼鱗狀細胞癌 squamous cell carcinoma of eyelid
眼睑脓肿/眼瞼膿腫 palpebral abscess
眼睑皮肤松弛症/眼瞼皮膚鬆弛症,瞼皮鬆垂 blepharochalasis
眼睑皮下瘀血/眼瞼皮下瘀血 ecchymosis of eyelid
眼睑皮样囊肿/眼瞼皮樣囊腫 dermoid cyst of eyelid
眼睑皮脂囊肿/眼瞼皮脂囊腫 steatoma of eyelid
眼睑气肿/眼瞼氣腫 blepharoemphysema
眼睑缺损/眼瞼缺損,瞼裂開,瞼殘缺 blepharocoloboma
眼睑热病性疱疹/眼瞼熱病性皰疹 herpes febrilis palpebrae
眼睑乳头状瘤/眼瞼乳頭狀瘤 papilloma of eyelid
眼睑色素痣/眼瞼色素痣 pigmented nevus of eyelid
眼睑湿疹/眼瞼濕疹 eczema palpebrae
眼睑水肿/眼瞼水腫,瞼浮腫 blepharoedema
眼睑条件反射/眼瞼條件反射 eyelid conditioning
眼睑外翻/眼瞼外翻 ectropion
眼睑下垂/[眼]瞼下垂 blepharoptosis, ptosis
眼睑腺瘤/[眼]瞼腺瘤 blepharoadenoma
眼睑血管瘤/眼瞼血管瘤 hemangioma of eyelid
眼睑炎/[眼]瞼炎 blepharitis
眼睑缘表皮内上皮癌/眼瞼緣表皮内上皮癌 intraepidermal carcinoma of the eyelid margin

眼睑再造术/眼瞼再造術　reconstruction of eyelid
眼睑肿瘤/眼瞼腫瘤　eyelid neoplasm
眼腱炎/眼腱炎　ophthalmodesmitis
眼角/眼角　canthi
眼-脚综合征/眼-腳症候群　eye-foot syndrome
眼结核/眼結核　ocular tuberculosis
眼结膜内层/眼結膜內層　adnata
眼介质屈光计/眼介質屈光計,介質折射誤差儀　mediaometer
眼静脉切开术/眼靜脈切開術,眼瀉血法　ophthalmophlebotomy
眼镜/眼鏡　eyeglasses
眼镜处方/眼鏡處方　prescription of spectacles
眼镜架/眼鏡架　spectacle frame
眼镜蛇/眼鏡蛇　cobra
眼镜蛇毒溶血素/眼鏡蛇溶血素　cobralysin
眼镜蛇毒液类/眼鏡蛇毒液類　cobra venoms
眼镜蛇毒中毒/眼鏡蛇毒中毒　cobraism
眼镜蛇科毒液类/眼鏡蛇科毒液類　elapid venoms
眼镜蛇溶血毒素/眼鏡蛇溶血毒素　cobra hemotoxin
眼镜蛇神经毒素类/眼鏡蛇神經毒素類　cobra neurotoxins
眼镜师/眼鏡師,眼鏡家　optician
眼剧痛/眼劇痛　ophthalmagra
眼距测量器/眼距測量器,兩眼距離計,眼距計　vuerometer
眼距过宽/眼距過寬,兩眼距離過遠　ocular hypertelorism
眼距过窄/眼距過窄,兩眼距離過近　ocular hypotelorism
眼科/眼科　department of ophthalmology
眼科光学/眼鏡光學　opticianry
眼科器械/眼科器械　ophthalmological instrument
眼科手术学/眼科手術學　ophthalmic surgery
眼科学/眼科學　ophthalmology
眼科医师助理/眼科醫師助理　ophthalmic assistant
眼科照相[术]/眼科照相[術]　ophthalmic photography
眼科诊断技术/眼科診斷技術　ophthalmological diagnostic techniques
眼科治疗学/眼病治療學　ophthalmiatrics
眼科注射器/眼科注射器　ophthalmosyringe
眼库/眼庫　eye bank
眼眶/眼眶　orbital cavity
眼眶动脉瘤/眼眶動脈瘤　orbital aneurysm
眼眶蜂窝[组]织炎/眼眶蜂窩纖炎,眶蜂窩組織炎　orbital cellulitis
眼眶骨/眼眶骨　orbital bone
眼眶肌/眼眶肌　musculus orbitalis
眼眶结核/眼眶結核　orbital tuberculosis
[眼]眶脓肿/眶膿腫　orbital abscess
眼眶上神经/眼眶上神經　supraorbital nerve
眼眶植入物/眼眶植入物　orbital implant
眼淋病/眼淋病　ophthalmic gonorrhea
眼瘤/眼瘤　eye tumor
眼轮匝肌/眼輪匝肌　orbicularis oculi, musculus orbicularis oculi
眼轮匝肌反应/[眼]輪匝肌反應　orbicularis reaction
眼轮匝肌睑部/眼輪匝肌瞼部,眼輪肌眼瞼部　palpebral part of orbicularis oculi, pars palpebralis musculi orbicularis oculi
眼轮匝肌睫部/眼輪匝肌睫部,里奧郎肌　Riolan muscle
眼轮匝肌紧缩术/眼輪匝肌緊縮術　tightening operation of orbicularis
眼轮匝肌眶部/眼輪匝肌眶部　orbital part of orbicularis oculi
眼轮匝肌泪部/眼輪匝肌淚部　lacrimal part of orbicularis oculi
眼轮匝肌泪嵴部/眼輪匝肌淚嵴部,眼輪肌淚部　pars lacrimalis musculi orbicularis oculi
眼轮匝肌切除术/瞼括約肌切除術　blepharosphincterectomy
眼轮匝肌现象/輪匝肌現象　orbicularis phenomenon
眼轮匝肌悬吊术/眼輪匝肌懸吊術　suspension operation of orbicularis
眼轮匝肌征/眼輪匝肌徵[象]　orbicularis sign
眼囊/眼[軟骨]囊,視軟骨囊　optic capsule
眼囊尾蚴病/眼囊尾蚴病　ocular cysticercosis
眼脑膜静脉/眼腦膜靜脈　ophthalmomeningeal vein
眼脑肾综合征/眼腦腎症候群　oculocerebrorenal syndrome
眼内部/眼內部　intraocular part
眼内出血/眼內出血　intraocular hemorrhage
眼内灌注液/眼內灌注液　intraocular irrigating solution
眼内光凝术/眼內光凝術　endophotocoagulation
眼内黑色瘤/眼內黑色素瘤　intraocular melanoma
眼内肌/眼內肌　intraocular muscle
眼内激光/眼內激光,眼內雷射　endolaser
眼内角点/眼內角點　endocanthion
眼内晶体植入/眼內晶體植入　intraocular lens implantation
眼内媒质镜/眼內媒質鏡,眼内視鏡　entoptoscope
眼内媒质镜检查/眼內媒質鏡檢查,眼内視鏡檢法　entoptoscopy

眼内[容]炎/眼球内炎　entophthalmia
眼内容摘除术/眼内容摘除術　evisceration of eyeball
眼内渗液/眼内滲液　ophthalmosynchysis
眼内显微剪/眼内顯微剪　intraocular microscissor
眼内显微镊/眼内顯微鑷　intraocular microforceps
[眼]内旋/[眼]内旋　adtorsion
眼[内]压/眼[内]壓,眼球内壓力　intraocular pressure
眼内炎/眼内[部]炎　endophthalmitis
眼内液/眼球内液　intraocular fluid
眼内异物/眼内異物　intraocular foreign body
眼内异物摘出术/眼内異物摘出術　extraction of intraocular foreign body
眼内直肌功能不全/眼内肌功能不全　insufficiency of the interni
眼内注射/眼[球]内注射　intraocular injection
眼-黏膜综合征/眼黏膜症候群　ocular-mucous membrane syndrome
眼盘尾丝虫病/眼盤尾絲蟲病　ocular onchocerciasis
眼旁肿瘤/眼旁瘤　parophthalmoncus
眼泡/眼胞　ocular vesicle
眼皮肤白化病/眼皮膚白化病　oculocutaneous albinism
眼皮肤黑素细胞增多症/眼皮膚黑素細胞增多症,眼部皮膚黑色素細胞增生症　oculodermal melanocytosis
眼皮肤痣/眼皮膚痣,眼皮膚母斑　oculocutaneous nevus
眼疲劳/眼疲勞　eyestrain
眼疲劳患者/眼疲勞患者,眼力疲勞者　asthenope
眼偏视/眼偏視,不直視,歪視　anorthopia
眼扑动/眼撲動　ocular flutter
眼前半段/眼前半段　anterior eye segment
眼前房/眼前房　camera anterior bulbi
眼前房窦/眼前房竇　sinus of anterior chamber
眼前房积脓/前[前]房積膿　hypopyon
眼球/眼球　eyeball
眼球赤道/眼球赤道　equator of eyeball
眼球穿孔伤/眼球穿孔傷　perforating injury of eyeball
眼球挫伤/眼球挫傷　contusion of eyeball
眼球发绀/眼球發紺　cyanosis bulbi
眼球浮动/眼球浮動　ocular bobbing
眼球固定法/眼球固定法,眼支持法　ophthalmostasis
眼球固定器/眼球固定器,支眼器　ophthalmostat
[眼]球后出血/球後出血　retrobulbar hemorrhage
眼球肌/眼球肌　musculi bulbi

眼球结膜/眼球結膜　conjunctiva of eyeball
眼球筋膜鞘/眼球筋膜鞘　sheath of eyeball
眼球筋膜炎/眼球筋膜炎　ocular tenonitis
眼球痨/眼球痨　phthisis bulbi
眼球模型/眼球模型　eyeball phantom
眼球囊/眼球囊　ocular capsule
眼球内膜/眼球内膜　internal tunic of eyeball
眼球内容摘除术/眼球内容摘除術　eye evisceration
眼球内陷/眼球内陷　endophthalmos
眼球内轴/眼球内軸　internal axis of eyeball
眼球内注射/眼球内注射　intraocular injection
眼球破裂/眼球破裂　eyeball rupture
眼球鞘/眼球鞘　sheath of eyeball
眼球切开术/眼球切開術　ophthalmotomy
眼球容量/眼球容量　ocular volume
眼球软化/眼球軟化　ophthalmomalacia
眼球上癌/眼球上癌　epibulbar carcinoma
眼球撕脱/眼球撕脱　evulsion of bulb
眼球铁质沉着/眼球鐵質沈著　siderosis bulbi
眼球突出/眼球突出,眼球凸出,凸眼　ophthalmocele
眼球突出测量法/眼球突出測量法,眼球凸出測量法　exophthalmometry
眼球突出计/眼球突出計,眼球凸出度測量計　exophthalmometer
眼球脱位/眼球脱位　luxation of eyeball
眼球外轴/眼球外軸　external axis of eyeball
眼球萎缩/眼球萎縮　atrophy of eyeball
眼球下转/眼球下轉　subduction
眼球纤维膜/眼球纖維膜　fibrous tunic of eyeball
眼球斜视痉挛综合征/眼球斜視痙攣症候群　opsoclonus-myoclonus syndrome
眼球悬韧带/眼球懸韌帶　suspensory ligament of eyeball
眼球旋转/眼球旋轉　cycloduction
眼球血管膜/眼球血管膜　vascular tunic of eyeball
眼球压迫器/眼球壓迫器　bulbar compressor
眼球压迫试验/眼球壓迫試驗　bulbar compression test
眼球异位/眼球異位　ectopia bulbi
眼球运动/眼球運動　eye movement
眼球运动障碍/眼球運動障礙　ocular motility disorder
眼球运动照相机/眼动攝影器　ophthalmograph
眼球摘除匙/眼球摘除匙　enucleation spoon
眼球摘除剪/眼球摘除剪　enucleation scissor
眼球摘除术/眼球摘除術,眼球剜出術　enucleation of eyeball
眼球震颤/眼球震顫　nystagmus

眼球震颤肌阵挛症/眼球震顫肌陣攣症,眼球震顫與肌痙攣 nystagmus-myoclonus
眼球震颤描记器/眼球震顫描記器 nystagmograph
眼球震颤样跳动/眼球震顫樣跳動 nystagmoid jerking
眼球正位/眼球正位 mesoropter
眼区/眼區 eye area
眼屈光/眼内折射 ocular refraction
眼屈光测量法/眼屈光測量法,眼折射力檢法 ophthalmometry
眼屈光学/眼屈光學 dioptrics of eye
眼缺血综合征/眼缺血症候群 ocular ischemia syndrome
眼扫视/眼掃視 saccades
眼色素/眼色素 ommochrome
眼色素层巩膜炎/葡萄膜鞏膜炎 uveoscleritis
眼色素层黑素瘤/眼色素層黑素瘤,葡萄膜黑色瘤 uveal melanoma
眼色素层脑膜炎/眼色素層腦膜炎 uveomeningitis
眼色素层腮腺热/眼色素層腮腺熱,葡萄膜腮腺炎 uveoparotid fever
眼色素层腮腺炎性多神经炎/眼色素層腮腺炎性多神經炎,葡萄膜腮腺炎性多神經炎 uveoparotitic polyneuritis
眼色素上皮/眼色素上皮 pigment epithelium of eye
眼上静脉/眼上静脈 superior ophthalmic vein
眼烧伤/眼燒傷 burn of eye
眼神经/眼神經 ophthalmic nerve
眼神经节复合体/眼神經節複合體 ophthalmoganglionar complex
眼神经血管瘤/眼神經血管瘤 ocular neuroangiomatosis
眼神经炎/眼神經炎 ophthalmoneuritis
眼渗血/眼滲血 ophthalmorrhea
眼生理过程/眼生理過程 ocular physiologic process
眼生理现象/眼生理現象 ocular physiologic phenomena
眼生理学/眼生理學 ocular physiology
眼适应/眼適應 ocular adaptation
眼水肿/眼水腫 edema oculi
眼撕裂伤/眼撕裂傷 laceration of eye
眼损伤/眼損傷 eye injury
眼天疱疮/眼[部]天疱瘡 ocular pemphigus
眼调节/眼調節 ocular accommodation
眼调节计/眼調節計,測點儀 punctumeter
眼铁质沉着症/眼鐵質沈著症 ocular siderosis
眼铜质沉着症/眼銅屑沈著病 ocular chalcosis
眼痛/眼痛 ophthalmalgia

眼透照镜/眼透照器,眼澈照器 ophthalmodiaphanoscope
眼透照器/眼透照器 ocular transilluminator
眼外肌/眼外肌 extraocular muscle
眼外肌后徙术/眼外肌後徙術 recession of extraocular muscle
眼外肌麻痹/眼外肌麻痺 ophthalmoplegia externa
眼外肌前徙术/眼外肌前徙術 advancement of extraocular muscle
眼外肌缩短术/眼外肌縮短術 resection of extraocular muscle
眼外肌纤维化/眼外肌纖維化 fibrosis of extraocular muscle
眼外肌折叠术/眼外肌折疊術 pleating of extraocular muscle
眼外角点/眼外角點 ectocanthion
眼外科手术/眼外科手術 ophthalmologic surgical procedure
眼外伤/眼外傷 ocular injury
眼外直肌/眼外直肌 extrarectus
眼外直肌功能不全/眼外直肌功能不全,眼外肌功能不足 insufficiency of the externi
眼外转/眼外轉,眼外傾 abtorsion
眼萎缩/眼萎縮 ophthalmatrophia
眼温度计/眼溫度計 ophthalmothermometer
眼窝/眼窩 eye socket
眼窝狭窄/眼窩狹窄 stenotic eye socket
眼窝再造/眼窩再造 reconstruction of eye socket
眼窝再造术/眼窩再造術 reconstruction of contracted socket
眼下颌颅面骨畸形/眼下頜顱面骨畸形 oculomandibulodyscephaly
眼下静脉/眼下静脈 inferior ophthalmic vein
眼下斜肌/眼下斜肌 inferior oblique muscle of eyeball
眼显微手术/眼顯微手術 ophthalmic microsurgery
眼像不平衡透镜/影像不平衡透鏡,影像不等透鏡 aniseikonic lens
眼心反射/眼心反射 oculocardiac reflex
眼性偏头痛/眼性偏頭痛 ophthalmic migraine
眼性眼球震颤/眼[病]性眼球震顫 ocular nystagmus
眼癣/眼癬 eyelid eczema, eyelid lichen
[眼]血管膜/眼血管膜 vascular tunic
眼血流图/眼血流圖 rheoophthalmogram
眼压/眼[球内]壓 intraocular tension, intraocular pressure
眼压过高/眼壓過高 ocular hypertension

眼压计／眼壓計　tonometer
眼压计标准化／眼壓計標準化　standardization of tonometer
眼压检查法／眼壓檢查法　tonometry
眼咽肌营养不良／眼咽肌營養不良　oculopharyngeal muscular dystrophy
眼咽营养不良／眼咽營養不良，外眼肌咽肌失養　oculopharyngeal dystrophy
眼炎／眼炎　ophthalmia
眼炎患者／眼炎患者　ophthalmiac
眼[羊狂蝇]蛆病／眼[羊狂蠅]蛆病，眼内蝇蛆病　ophthalmomyiasis
眼药水／眼藥水　eye drop
眼异物／眼異物　eye foreign body
眼影像计／眼影像計　ophthalmoeikonometer
眼硬癌／眼硬癌　scirrhophthalmia
眼用锭剂／眼用錠劑　eye lozenge
眼用膏剂／眼用膏劑　eye ointment
眼用膜剂／眼用膜劑　eye pellicle
眼用软膏／眼用軟膏　ophthalmic ointment
眼用散剂／眼用散劑　eye powder
眼用水剂／眼用水劑　eye drop and lotion
眼用硝酸银溶液／眼用硝酸銀溶液　sliver nitrate ophthalmic solution
眼用制剂／眼用製劑　ophthalmic preparation
眼优势／視優勢　ocular dominance
眼浴／眼浴　ophthalmic bath
眼罩／眼罩　eye shield
眼真菌病／眼黴菌病　ophthalmomycosis
眼震电流描记术／眼震電流描記術，眼震顫電流描記法　electronystagmography
眼震电流描记图／眼震電[流描記]圖　electronystagmogram
眼肿瘤／眼腫瘤　eye neoplasm
眼周[组织]炎／眼周[組織]炎，眼旁[結締組織]炎　parophthalmia
眼轴／眼軸　axis of eyeball
眼珠／眼珠　eyeball
眼注视／眼注視　ocular fixation
眼转动计／眼轉動計，眼動測定器　ophthalmotropometer
眼眦部瘢痕畸形／眼眥部瘢痕畸形　scar deformity of canthus
眼组织胞浆菌病／眼組織胞漿菌病　ocular histoplasmosis
厌臭症／厭臭症，異臭厭惡症　osmodysphoria
厌锇血小板／厭鋨血小板　osmiophobic platelet
厌恶法／厭惡法　disgusting therapy

厌恶疗法／厭惡療法　aversive therapy
厌恶行为／厭惡行爲　aversive behavior
厌烦／厭煩　boredom
厌食[病]／厭食[病]，厭食症，食欲喪失　anorexia
厌食-恶病质综合征／厭食-惡病質症候群，厭食性惡病質症候群　anorexia-cachexia syndrome
厌食症／厭食[症]，拒食　fastidium
厌糖[现象]／厭糖現象　saccharocoria
厌氧蛋白分解酶／厭氧蛋白分解酶，嫌氧蛋白分解酵素　anaerobiase
厌氧菌／厭氧菌　anaerobe
厌氧菌性蜂窝[组]织炎／厭氧菌性蜂窩織炎，厭氧性蜂窩組織炎　anaerobic cellulitis
厌氧酶／厭氣酶，厭氣酵素　anaerase
厌氧生活／厭氧生活　anaerobiosis
厌氧性肌炎／厭氧性肌炎　anaerobic myositis
厌饮／厭飲　antiposia
咽气声／咽氣聲　inructation
咽气涎癖／咽氣涎癖，吞氣咽涎症　aerosialophagy
验电器／驗電器　electroscope
验恶露／驗惡露　observing lochia
验方／驗方　experiential effective recipe
验方新编／驗方新編　New Compilation of Effective Recipes
验光师／驗光師，視力測量師　optist
验光透镜／驗光透鏡　test lens
验尸／驗屍　postmortem
验湿器／驗濕器，空氣濕度計，測濕器　hygroscope
验温器／驗溫器，檢溫器　thermoscope
焰状细胞／焰狀細胞　flame cell
燕麦／燕麥　oat
燕麦蛋白／燕麥蛋白　avenin
燕麦片／燕麥片，燕麥粉　farina avena
燕麦形细胞／燕麥形細胞，燕麥狀細胞　oat-shaped cell
燕麦性肠结石／燕麥性腸[結]石　avenolith
燕窝／燕窩　cubilose
燕子臭虫／燕子臭蟲　swallow bug
羊鼻蝇／羊鼻蠅　sheep nostril fly
羊传染性口疮病毒／羊傳染性口瘡病毒　orf virus
羊痘／羊痘　goatpox
羊痘病毒／羊痘病毒　sheep-pox virus
羊痘接种／羊痘接種法　clavelization
羊肺腺瘤病／羊肺腺瘤病　ovine pulmonary adenomatosis
羊肺炎支原体／羊肺炎支原體　mycoplasma ovipneumoniae
羊粪样便／羊糞樣便　sheep-dung stool

羊胡疮/羊鬍瘡　sycosis
羊接触传染性脓疱病毒/羊接觸傳染性膿皰病毒　contagious ecthyma virus of sheep
羊筋痧/羊筋痧　sheep-tendon-like sha disease
羊毛粗脂/羊毛粗脂　suint
羊毛黄/羊毛黄　lanaurin
羊毛痧/羊毛痧　wool-like sha disease
羊毛甾醇/羊毛甾醇　lanosterol
羊毛甾烷/羊毛甾烷, 羊毛类固醇烷　lanostane
羊毛脂/羊毛脂　lanolin
羊毛脂甾醇/羊毛脂固醇　agnosterol
羊毛状发/羊毛狀髮　woolly hair
羊膜/羊膜　amnion
羊膜穿刺术/羊膜切開術　amniotomy
羊膜穿破器/羊膜穿破器, 羊膜刀　amniotome
羊膜带综合征/羊膜帶症候群　amniotic band syndrome
羊膜的/羊膜的　amniotic
羊膜动物类/羊膜動物類　amniota
羊膜缝/羊膜縫　amniotic raphe
羊膜管/羊膜管　amniotic duct
羊膜镜/羊膜鏡　amnioscope
羊膜镜检查/羊膜鏡檢法　amnioscopy
羊膜囊/羊膜囊　amniotic sac
羊膜破裂/羊膜破裂　amniorrhexis
羊膜脐/羊膜臍　amniotic umbilicus
羊膜腔/羊膜腔　amniotic cavity
羊膜腔穿刺术/羊膜穿刺術　amniocentesis
羊膜腔造影术/羊膜腔造影術, 羊膜腔顯影術　amniography
羊膜绒毛/羊膜絨毛　amniotic villus
羊膜索/羊膜帶　amniotic band
羊膜形成/羊膜形成　amniogenesis
羊膜炎/羊膜炎　amnionitis
羊膜早破畸形谱/羊膜早破畸形譜　early amnion rupture spectrum
羊膜粘连/羊膜粘連　amniotic adhesion
羊膜褶/羊膜褶　amniotic fold
羊皮纸/羊皮紙　parchment
羊皮纸样皮肤/羊皮紙狀皮膚, 皮膚萎縮　parchment skin
羊皮纸样右心室/羊皮紙樣右心室　parchment right ventricle
羊皮纸纸浆/羊皮紙紙漿　parchment pulp
羊瘙痒症/羊搔癢症　scrapie
羊水/羊水, 羊膜液　amniotic fluid
羊水过多/羊水過多　polyhydramnios
羊水过少/羊水過少　oligohydramnios
羊水积气/羊水積氣, 羊膜水積氣症　pneumoamnios
羊水栓塞/羊水栓塞　amnionic fluid embolism
羊水吸入综合征/羊水吸入症候群　amnionic fluid aspiration syndrome
羊水细胞/羊水細胞　amniocyte
羊水细胞培养/羊水細胞培養　amniotic cell culture
羊水溢/羊水漏　amniorrhea
羊绦虫/羊條蟲　Taenia ovis
羊跳跃病/羊跳躍病　louping ill
羊跳跃病病毒/羊跳躍病病毒, 羊蹠毒病病毒　louping ill virus
羊鸣音/羊鳴音, 羊[音語]聲　tragophonia
羊蝇蛆/羊蠅蛆, 羊蛆病　sheep maggot
羊脂/羊脂　adeps ovillus
阳/陽　yang
阳白/陽白　yangbai, GB14
阳病入阴/陽病入陰　yang disease involving yin
阳池/陽池　yangchi, SJ4
阳毒/陽毒　yang poisoning
阳毒发狂/陽毒發狂　yang toxicosis with mania
阳辅/陽輔　yangfu, GB38
阳纲/陽綱　yanggang, BL48
阳谷/陽谷　yanggu, SI5
阳和汤/陽和湯　yanghe decoction
阳化气/陽化氣　yang transforming qi
阳黄/陽黄　yang jaundice
阳黄·胆腑郁热证/陽黄·膽腑鬱熱證　yang jaundice with pattern of heat stagnation in gallbladder
阳黄·肝胆湿热证/陽黄·肝膽濕熱證　yang jaundice with pattern of damp-heat in liver and gallbladder
阳黄·热重于湿证/陽黄·熱重於濕證　yang jaundice with pattern of heat predominating over dampness
阳黄·湿困脾胃证/陽黄·濕困脾胃證　yang jaundice with pattern of dampness retaining in spleen and stomach
阳黄·湿热兼表证/陽黄·濕熱兼表證　yang jaundice with superficial pattern and damp-heat
阳黄·湿重于热证/陽黄·濕重於熱證　yang jaundice with pattern of dampness predominating over heat
阳极传导阻滞/陽極傳導阻滯　anodal block
阳极[电]紧张/陽極緊張　anelectrotonus
阳极电紧张状态/陽極[電]緊張狀態　anelectrotonic state
阳极断电强直/陽極斷電強直　anodal opening tetanus
阳极断电收缩/陽極斷電收縮　anodal opening contraction
阳极断电阵挛/陽極斷電陣攣, 陽極停電性陣攣

anodal opening clonus
阳极似阴/陽極似陰 extreme yang with yin manifestation
阳极通电强直/陽極通電強直,陽極關閉性強直 anodal closure tetanus
阳极通电收缩/陽極通電收縮 anodal closure contraction
阳极通电阵挛/陽極通電性陣攣 anodal closure clonus
阳交/陽交 yangjiao, GB35
阳狂/陽狂 yang manic psychosis
阳离子/陽離子 cation, positive ion
阳离子氨基酸转运蛋白/陽離子胺基酸轉運蛋白 cationic amino acid transporter
阳离子发生物/陽離子發生物,陽離子原 cationogen
阳离子交换膜/陽離子交換膜 cation exchange membrane
阳离子交换树脂/陽離子交換樹脂 cation exchange resin
阳离子交换树脂类/陽離子交換樹脂類 cation exchange resins
阳离子转运蛋白质类/陽離子轉運蛋白質類 cation transport proteins
阳陵泉/陽陵泉 yanglingquan, GB34
阳明病证/陽明病[證] Yangming disease, Yangming pattern
阳明发黄/陽明發黃 Yangming disease with jaundice
阳明腑实/陽明腑實 Yangming fuviscera excess
阳明腑证/陽明腑證 pattern of fuviscera of Yangming, Yangming fu-viscus pattern
阳明经证/陽明經證 Yangming Channel pattern
阳明伤寒/陽明傷寒 Yangming disease with cold affection
阳明虚寒/陽明虛寒 Yangming deficiency-cold
阳明蓄血证/陽明蓄血證 Yangming disease with stagnated blood pattern
阳明燥热/陽明燥熱 Yangming dryness-heat
阳明中风/陽明中風 Yangming disease with wind affection
阳明中寒/陽明中寒 Yangming disease with direct cold attack
阳气/陽氣 yang qi
阳气暴脱证/陽氣暴脱證 pattern of sudden yang collapse
阳强/陰縱 persistent erection of penis
阳跷脉/陽蹻脈 Yang Heel Channel, Yang Heel Vessel
阳神/陽神 soul
阳盛/陽盛 yang excessiveness
阳水/陽水 yang edema
阳水·风水相搏证/陽水·風水相搏證 yang edema with pattern of intermingling of wind and water
阳水·湿热[蕴结]证/陽水·濕熱[蕴結]證 yang edema with pattern of accumulation and binding of damp-heat
阳水·水湿浸渍证/陽水·水濕浸漬證 yang edema with pattern of retention and diffusion of water-damp
阳损及阴/陽損及陰 yang deficiency involving yin
阳损及阴证/陽損及陰證 pattern of yang deficiency involving yin
阳亡阴竭证/陽亡陰竭證 pattern of depletion of yang involving yin
阳微结/陽微結 binding with yang debility
阳维脉/陽維脈 Yang Link Channel, Yang Link Vessel
阳痿[病]/陽痿,性無能 impotence
阳痿·肝气郁结证/陽痿·肝氣鬱結證 impotence with pattern of liver qi depression
阳痿·惊恐伤肾证/陽痿·驚恐傷腎證 impotence with pattern of scare impairing kidney
阳痿·命门火衰证/陽痿·命門火衰證 impotence with pattern of declination of vital gate fire
阳痿·湿热下注证/陽痿·濕熱下注證 impotence with pattern of downward diffusion of damp-heat
阳痿·心脾两虚证/陽痿·心脾兩虛證 impotence with pattern of heart-spleen deficiency
阳溪/陽溪 yangxi, LI5
阳邪/陽邪 yang pathogen
阳性/陽性 positive
阳性趋电性/正電向性,陽電向性 positive electrotropism
阳性掌骨征/陽性掌骨徵 positive metacarpal sign
阳性转录延伸因子B/陽性轉錄延伸因子B positive transcriptional elongation factor B
阳虚/陽虛 yang deficiency
阳虚痹/陽虛痹 arthralgia due to yang deficiency, yang deficiency bi
阳虚寒凝证/陽虛寒凝證 pattern of yang deficiency and coagulated cold
阳虚气滞证/陽虛氣滯證 pattern of yang deficiency and qi stagnation
阳虚生寒/陽虛生寒 cold manifestation due to yang deficiency
阳虚水泛证/陽虛水泛證 pattern of water

overflowing due to yang deficiency
阳虚痰凝证/陽虛痰凝證 pattern of yang deficiency and coagulated phlegm
阳虚外感证/陽虛外感證 pattern of exogenous disease due to yang deficiency
阳虚血瘀证/陽虛血瘀證 pattern of yang deficiency and blood stasis
阳虚证/陽虛證 yang deficiency pattern
阳易/陽易 yang exchange
阳燥/陽燥 dryness due to excess of yang
阳证/陽證 yang pattern
杨继洲/楊繼洲 Yang Jizhou
杨梅疮/楊梅瘡 red bayberry sore, syphilitic skin lesion
杨梅结毒/楊梅結毒 syphilis of pharynx
杨梅舌/楊梅舌 myrica tongue
杨梅瘟/楊梅瘟 red bayberry-like pestilence
杨氏综合征/楊氏症候群,Young 氏症候群 Young syndrome
佯病/佯病 pathomimicry
疡科心得集/瘍科心得集 Experience Gained in Treating External Diseases
疡医/瘍醫 royal surgeon
洋地黄/洋地黄,毛地黄 digitalis
洋地黄酊/洋地黄酊,毛地黄酊 digitalis tincture
洋地黄毒苷/洋地黄毒苷,毛地黄毒質,毛地黄毒素 digitoxin
洋地黄毒苷配基/洋地黄毒苷配基,毛地黄毒苷配基 digitoxigenin
洋地黄粉/洋地黄粉,毛地黄粉 powdered digitalis
洋地黄糖苷类/洋地黄糖甙類 digitalis glycosides
洋地黄皂苷/洋地黄皂苷,毛地黄皂苷 digitonin
洋甘菊花粉/洋甘菊花粉 chamomile powder
洋甘菊油/[洋]甘菊油 chamomile oil
洋红舌/洋紅舌,複紅色舌 magenta tongue
洋茴香碱/洋茴香鹼 anisine
洋茴香醑/洋茴香醑 anise spirit
洋蕺菜根/洋蕺菜[根] mansa
洋蓟酶/洋薊酶,紅藍花凝乳酵素 cynarase
洋金花/洋金花 datura flower
洋蓍草/[洋]蓍草 milfoil
烊化/烊化 melt
仰伸/仰伸 extention
仰卧挺腹试验/仰臥挺腹試驗 supinating and throwing out belly test
仰卧位/仰臥位,背臥位 supine position
仰趾弓形足/仰趾弓形足,仰趾空凹足 calcaneocavus

仰趾内翻足/仰趾内翻足 talipes calcaneovarus
仰趾外翻足/仰趾外翻足 talipes calcaneovalgus
仰趾足/仰趾足 talipes calcaneus
养肝/養肝 nourishing the liver
养老/養老 yanglao, SI6
养鸟者肺/養鳥者肺 bird fancier's lung
养神/養神 reposing
养神汤/養神湯 mind nourishing decoction
养生/養生 health maintenance
养胎/養胎 nurturing fetus
养胃/養胃 nourishing the stomach
养胃舒胶囊/養胃舒膠囊 yangweishu capsule
养心安神/養心安神 nourishing the heart and calming the mind
养心汤/養心湯 heart nourishing decoction
养性/養性 disciplining one's temperaments
养性延命录/養性延命錄 Recordings of the Healing Art and Health Preservation
养血安神/養血安神 nourishing blood and calming mind
养血安神丸/養血安神丸 decoction for nourishing blood and calming mind, yangxue anshen pills
养血明目/養血明目 nourishing blood for improving eyesight
养血清心汤/養血清心湯 decoction for nourishing blood and clearing heat from the heart
养血生肌/養血生肌 nourishing blood and promoting granulation
养血胜风汤/養血勝風湯 decoction for nourishing blood and expelling wind
养血调经/養血調經 nourishing blood for regulating menstruation
养血息风/養血息風 nourishing blood for calming endogenous wind
养阴/養陰 nourishing yin
养阴清肺汤/養陰清肺湯 yangyin qingfei decoction
养阴生肌/養陰生肌 nourishing yin and promoting granulation
养殖/養殖 breed
氧/氧 oxygen
氧虫荧光素/氧蟲螢光素 oxyluciferin
氧蛋白酸/氧蛋白酸 oxyproteic acid
氧氮杂草类/氧氮雜草類 oxazepines
氧碘化物/氧碘化物 oxyiodide
氧放射性同位素/氧放射性同位素 oxygen radioisotope
氧分压/氧分壓 partial pressure of oxygen
氧氟沙星/氧氟沙星 ofloxacin

氧含量/氧含量　oxygen content
氧耗量/氧耗量，耗氧量　oxygen consumption
氧合肌红蛋白/氧和肌紅蛋白，氧化肌球素，氧化肌血球素　oxymyoglobin
氧合酶类/氧合酶類　oxygenases
氧合器/氧合器　oxygenator
氧合血红蛋白/氧合血紅蛋白　oxyhemoglobin
氧合作用/氧合作用，氧化　oxygenation
氧化不足性碳酸尿[症]/氧化不足碳酸尿　dysoxidative carbonuria
氧化蛋白酸/氧化蛋白酸　alloxyproteic acid
氧化氮类/氧化氮類　nitrogen oxides
氧化氘/重水　deuterium oxide
氧化毒素/氧化毒素　oxytoxin
氧化蒽酚/氧化蒽酚　oxanthranol
氧化钙/氧化鈣　calcium oxide
氧化过度/氧化過度　hyperoxidation
氧化焊媒/氧化焊劑　oxidizing flux
氧化合物/氧化合物　oxygen compound
氧化还原酶/氧化還原酶，氧化還原酵素　oxidoreductase, redox enzyme
氧化还原指示剂/氧化還原指示[劑]　redox indicator
氧化还原[作用]/氧化還原[作用]　redox
氧化肌细胞色素/氧化肌血黑質　oxymyohematin
氧化剂/氧化劑　oxidant
氧化结核菌素/氧化結核菌素　oxytuberculin
氧化锂/氧化鋰　lithia
氧化力不足/氧化力不足　asthenoxia
氧化磷酸化/氧化磷酸化　oxidative phosphorylation
氧化磷酸化偶联因子/氧化磷酸化偶聯因子　oxidative phosphorylation coupling factor
氧化铝/氧化鋁　alumina, aluminum oxide
氧化铝种植体/氧化鋁種植體　aluminum oxide implant
氧化铝柱色谱法/氧化鋁柱層析法　alumina column chromatography
氧化酶/氧化酶　oxidation enzyme
氧化镁/氧化鎂　magnesium oxide
氧化偶氮苯/氧[化]偶氮苯　azoxybenzene
氧化偶氮化合物/氧[化]偶氮化合物　azoxy compound
氧化偶氮甲烷/氧化偶氮甲烷　azoxymethane
氧化树脂/氧化樹脂　resene
氧化锶/氧化鍶　strontia
氧化苏木精/氧化蘇木精，蘇木紅[質]　hematein
氧化苏木精化合物/氧化蘇木精化合物　hemate
氧化物/氧化物　oxide
氧化纤维素/氧化纖維素，氧化木纖維質　oxidized cellulose
氧化锌/氧化鋅　zinc oxide
氧化锌碘仿糊/氧化鋅碘仿糊　zipp paste
氧化锌丁香油酚/氧化鋅丁香油酚　zinc-oxide-eugenol
氧化锌丁香油酚粘固剂/氧化鋅丁香油酚黏固劑　zinc-oxide-eugenol cement
氧化锌丁香油酚印模糊剂/氧化鋅丁香油酚印模糊劑　zinc-oxide-eugenol impression paste
氧化性应激/氧化性應激　oxidative stress
氧化血色素/氧化血色素，氧合血紅素　oxygenated hemoglobin
氧化亚氮/氧化亞氮，一氧化二氮，笑氣　nitrous oxide
氧化亚氮麻醉/氧化亞氮麻醉，笑氣麻醉　nitrous oxide anesthesia
氧化孕烯/氧化孕烯，酮孕烯　ketopregnene
氧化震颤素/氧化震顫素　oxotremorine
氧化状态/氧化狀態　oxidation state
氧离曲线/氧離曲線　oxygen dissociation curve
氧量计面具/氧量計面具，氧氣罩　meter mask
氧疗/氧療，氧氣療法　oxygen therapy
氧硫杂环己二烯/氧硫雜環己二烯　oxathiin
氧弥散系数/氧彌散係數　oxygen diffusion coefficient
氧醚疗法/氧醚[吸入]療法　oxyetherotherapy
氧幕/氧幕　oxygen tent
氧嘌呤/氧嘌呤　puron
氧瓶燃烧法/氧瓶燃燒法　oxygen flask combustion
氧气脊髓造影术/氧脊髓X光攝影術　oxygen myelography
氧嗪酸/氧嗪酸　oxonic acid
氧青霉烷类/氧青黴烷類　oxapenams
氧氰化汞/氧氰化汞　mercuric oxycyanide
氧容量/氧容量　oxygen capacity
氧山道年/氧[基]山道年　oxysantonin
氧输送/氧輸送　oxygen delivery
氧-酸裂合酶类/氧-酸裂合酶類　oxo-acid-lyases
氧同位素/氧同位素　oxygen isotope
氧头孢烯类/氧頭孢烯類　oxacephems
氧吸入疗法/氧吸入療法　oxygen inhalation therapy
氧吸收/氧吸收　oxygen absorption
氧烯洛尔/氧烯洛爾　oxprenolol
氧消耗率/氧消耗率，耗氧率　oxygen consumption rate
氧雄龙/氧雄龍　oxandrolone
氧血卟啉/氧血卟啉，氧合血紫質

oxyhematoporphyrin
氧乙烷/氧乙烷　ethyl oxide
氧杂蒽/氧雜蒽,黄嘌呤素　xanthene
氧杂蒽酮/氧雜蒽酮,黄嘌呤酮,山嗊　xanthone
氧张力/氧張力　oxygen tension
氧中毒/氧中毒　oxygen intoxication
氧自由基/氧自由基　oxygen derived free radical
痒/癢　itching
痒病/癢病　itch disease
痒觉/癢覺　itching sensation
痒螨病/癢蟎病,痂恙蟲病　psoroptic acariasis
痒螨属/癢蟎屬,慪蟎屬　Psoroptes
痒性紫癜/癢性紫癜,搔癢性紫癜病　itching purpura
痒疹/癢疹　prurigo
痒疹型大疱表皮松解症/癢疹性水皰性表皮鬆解症　epidermolysis bullosa pruriginosa
样本大小/樣本大小　sample size
恙虫病/恙蟲病　tsutsugamushi disease
恙虫属/恙蟲屬　Acarus
恙螨/恙蟎　chigger
恙螨病/恙蟎病,潜蚤病　chigger disease
恙螨叮咬/恙蟎叮咬　chigger bite
夭疽/夭疽　carbuncle of mastoid
腰/腰　waist
腰背部肌筋膜炎/腰背部肌筋膜炎　lumbodorsal myofascitis
腰背筋膜/腰背筋膜　lumbodorsal fascia
腰背偻俯/腰背僂俯　kyphosis
腰部/腰部　lumbar part, lumbar region
腰[部]肌节/腰[部]肌節　lumbar myotome
腰部脊髓/腰[部]脊髓　lumbar spinal cord
腰部结肠切开术/腰[部]結腸切開術,經腰結腸切開術　lumbocolotomy
腰部结肠造口术/腰[部]結腸造口術,經腰結腸造口術　lumbocolostomy
腰部阑尾炎/腰部闌尾炎　lumbar appendicitis
腰部联胎/腰部聯胎　psodymus
腰部切开术/腰[部]切開術　osphyotomy
腰部弯曲/腰部彎曲　lumbar curve
腰部斜扳法/腰部斜扳法　lumbar oblique thrust
腰部脊髓腔-腹腔分流术/腰部脊髓腔-腹腔分流術,腰與腹膜分流　lumboperitoneal shunt
腰丛/腰叢　lumbar plexus
腰大肌/腰大肌　psoas major, greater psoas muscle
腰[大]肌炎/腰大肌炎　psoitis
腰大肌征/腰大肌徵　psoas sign
腰带痈/腰帶癰　abscess around waist
腰骶部/腰骶部　lumbosacral region

腰骶丛/腰薦叢　lumbosacral plexus
腰骶干/腰薦幹　lumbosacral trunk
腰骶连结/腰薦關節　lumbosacral joint
腰骶膨大/腰薦膨大　lumbosacral enlargement
腰骶椎/腰骶椎　yaodizhui, AH9, lumbosacral vertebrae
腰点/腰點　lumbale
腰动脉/腰動脈　lumbar artery
腰动脉背侧支/腰動脈背側支　dorsal branch of lumbar artery
腰动脉脊支/腰動脈脊支　spinal branch of lumbar artery
腰段(1-5)/腰段(1-5)　lumbar segments (L)(1-5)
腰方肌/腰方肌　quadratus lumborum
腰腹股沟神经/腰腹股溝神經　lumboinguinal nerve
腰骨/腰骨　lumbar bone
腰果/腰果　cashew nut
腰果壳油皮炎/腰果殼油皮[膚]炎　cashew nutshell oil dermatitis
腰果树/腰果樹　cashew
腰横突间内侧肌/腰部横突間内側肌　intertransversarii mediales lumborum
腰横突间外侧肌/腰部横突間外側肌　intertransversarii laterales lumborum
腰厚/腰厚　waist thickness
腰回旋肌/腰迴旋肌　rotatores lumborum
腰肌/腰肌　psoas muscle
腰肌劳损/腰肌勞損　lumbar muscle strain
腰肌劳损·肝肾亏虚证/腰肌勞損·肝腎虧虛證　lumbar muscle strain with liver-kidney deficiency pattern
腰肌劳损·寒湿证/腰肌勞損·寒濕證　lumbar muscle strain with cold-dampness pattern
腰肌劳损·湿热证/腰肌勞損·濕熱證　lumbar muscle strain with dampness-heat pattern
腰肌劳损·瘀血证/腰肌勞損·瘀血證　lumbar muscle strain with static blood pattern
腰肌脓肿/腰肌膿腫　psoas abscess
腰棘间肌/腰[部]棘間肌　interspinale lumborum
腰交感神经[节]切除术/腰交感神經切除術　lumbar sympathectomy
腰静脉/腰静脈　lumbar vein
腰肋/腰肋　lumbar rib
腰肋弓/腰肋弓　arcus lumbocostalis
腰肋韧带/腰肋韌帶　lumbocostal ligament
腰肋三角/腰肋三角　lumbocostal triangle
腰冷/腰冷　coldness in waist
腰淋巴结/腰淋巴結　lumbar lymph node

腰内脏神经/腰內臟神經　lumbar splanchnic nerve
腰奇/腰奇　yaoqi, EX-B9
腰髂肋肌/腰髂肋肌　iliocostalis lumborum
腰曲/腰曲　lumbar curvature
腰三角/腰三角　lumbar triangle
腰疝/腰疝　lumbar hernia
腰上三角/腰上三角　superior lumbar triangle
腰神经/腰神經　lumbar nerve
腰神经后支/腰神經後支　posterior branch of lumbar nerve
腰神经节/腰神經節　lumbar ganglion
腰神经内侧支/腰神經內側支　medial branch of lumbar nerve
腰神经前支/腰神經前支　anterior branch of lumbar nerve
腰神经外侧支/腰神經外側支　lateral branch of lumbar nerve
腰升静脉/腰昇靜脈　ascending lumbar vein
腰俞/腰俞　yaoshu, DU2
腰酸/腰酸　soreness of loins
腰髓炎/腰髓炎　osphyomyelitis
腰痛[病]/腰痛[病]　low back pain, lumbago
腰痛点/腰痛點　yaotongdian, EX-UE7
腰痛·风寒证/腰痛·風寒證　lumbago with wind-cold pattern
腰痛·风热证/腰痛·風熱證　lumbago with wind-heat pattern
腰痛·风湿证/腰痛·風濕證　lumbago with wind-damp pattern
腰痛·肝气郁结证/腰痛·肝氣鬱結證　lumbago with pattern of liver qi depression
腰痛·寒湿证/腰痛·寒濕證　lumbago with cold-damp pattern
腰痛·脾湿证/腰痛·脾濕證　lumbago with spleen damp pattern
腰痛·肾虚证/腰痛·腎虛證　lumbago with kidney deficiency pattern
腰痛·湿热[蕴结]证/腰痛·濕熱[蘊結]證　lumbago with pattern of accumulation and binding of damp-heat
腰痛·湿痰证/腰痛·濕痰證　lumbago with damp-phlegm pattern
腰痛·瘀血证/腰痛·瘀血證　lumbago with static blood pattern
腰腿痛/腰腿痛　pain in lower extremities and waist
腰臀比/腰臀比　waist-hip ratio
腰臀部筋膜炎/腰臀部筋膜炎　fasciitis of waist and gluteal region

腰围/腰圍　waist circumference
腰膝酸软/腰膝酸軟　soreness and weakness of waist and knees
腰下连胎/骨盆連胎　lecanopagus
腰下三角/腰下三角　inferior lumbar triangle
腰小肌/腰小肌　psoas minor, musculus psoas minor
腰眼/腰眼　yaoyan, EX-B7
腰阳关/腰陽關　yaoyangguan, DU3
腰宜/腰宜　yaoyi, EX-B6
腰硬/腰硬　stiff loin
腰支/腰支　lumbar branch
腰重/腰重　heaviness in waist
腰椎/腰椎　lumbar vertebra
腰椎穿刺/腰椎穿刺[術]　lumbar puncture
腰椎穿刺后头痛/腰椎穿刺後頭痛　lumbar puncture headache
腰椎穿刺针/腰椎穿刺針　lumbar puncture needle
腰椎骶化/腰椎骶化　lumbar sacralization
腰椎副突/腰椎副突　accessory process of lumbar vertebra
腰椎骨折/腰椎骨折　fracture of lumbar vertebra
腰椎管狭窄症·风寒闭阻证/腰椎管狹窄症·風寒閉阻證　lumbar spinal canal stenosis with wind-cold blockage pattern
腰椎管狭窄症·气虚血瘀证/腰椎管狹窄症·氣虛血瘀證　lumbar spinal canal stenosis with pattern of qi deficiency and blood stasis
腰椎管狭窄症·肾气亏虚证/腰椎管狹窄症·腎氣虧虛證　lumbar spinal canal stenosis with kidney-qi deficiency pattern
腰椎后关节紊乱症/腰椎後關節紊亂症　disturbance of postlumbar joint
腰椎滑脱症/腰椎滑脫症　lumbar spondylolisthesis
腰椎滑脱症·风寒湿阻证/腰椎滑脫症·風寒濕阻證　lumbar spondylolisthesis with wind-cold-dampness obstruction pattern
腰椎滑脱症·肝肾亏虚证/腰椎滑脫症·肝腎虧虛證　lumbar spondylolisthesis with liver-kidney deficiency pattern
腰椎滑脱症·血瘀气滞证/腰椎滑脫症·血瘀氣滯證　lumbar spondylolisthesis with pattern of blood stasis and qi stagnation
腰椎化/腰椎化　lumbarization
腰椎间盘突出[症]/腰椎間盤突出[症]　prolapse of lumbar intervertebral disc, lumbar intervertebral disc prolapse
腰椎间盘突出症·风寒湿阻证/腰椎間盤突出症·風寒濕阻證　lumbar intervertebral disc prolapse with

wind-cold-dampness obstruction pattern
腰椎间盘突出症•肝肾亏虚证/腰椎間盤突出症•肝腎虧虛證　lumbar intervertebral disc prolapse with liver-kidney deficiency pattern
腰椎间盘突出症•湿热闭阻证/腰椎間盤突出症•濕熱閉阻證　lumbar intervertebral disc prolapse with dampness-heat blockage pattern
腰椎间盘突出症•血瘀气滞证/腰椎間盤突出症•血瘀氣滯證　lumbar intervertebral disc prolapse with pattern of blood stasis and qi stagnation
腰椎麻醉/腰髓麻醉法　lumbar anesthesia
腰椎乳突/腰椎乳突　mamillary process of lumbar vertebra
腰椎椎管狭窄症/腰椎椎管狹窄症　lumbar spinal canal stenosis, straitness of lumbar vertebra
腰最下动脉/腰最下動脈　lowest lumbar artery
腰坐骨综合征/腰[骼]坐骨症候群　lumbosciatic syndrome
摇摆触碰/搖擺觸碰　sway-and-feel manipulation
摇床/搖床　swing bed
摇动床/搖擺床　rocking bed
摇动法/搖動法,震動法,搖動振盪　shaking
摇动切片机/搖動切片機,搖擺式切片機　rocking microtome
摇法/搖法　needle-handle shaking, rotating and shaking manipulation
摇晃婴儿综合征/搖晃嬰兒症候群　shaken baby syndrome
摇混液/搖混[乳]液　shake lotion
摇篮测听图/搖籃測聽圖　cribogram
摇溶性/搖溶性,變凝性　thixotropism
摇尾幼虫皮炎/搖尾幼蟲皮膚炎　el Caribe dermatitis
摇蚊科/搖蚊科　Chironomidae
摇椅底足/搖椅[底]足　rocker bottom foot
遥测计/遙測計　telemeter
遥测术/遙測術,遠距測量法　telemetry
遥测温度计/遙測溫度計,遠距溫度計　telethermometer
遥测心电图/遙測心電圖,遠距心電圖記錄　telecardiogram
咬/咬　biting
咬唇症/咬唇症　lip biting
咬合/咬合　articulation
咬合错位/咬合錯位　crossbite
咬合间隙/咬合間隙,咬合距隙　interocclusal clearance
咬合力/咬合力　bite force

咬合力计/咬合力計,頜力計　gnathodynamometer
咬合试纸/咬合試紙　articulating paper
咬肌/咬肌,嚼肌　masseter
咬肌粗隆/咬肌粗隆,嚼肌粗隆　masseteric tuberosity
咬肌动脉/咬肌動脈,嚼肌動脈　masseteric artery
咬肌筋膜/咬肌筋膜,嚼肌筋膜　masseteric fascia
咬肌静脉/咬肌靜脈,嚼肌靜脈　masseteric vein
咬肌皮肤韧带/咬肌皮膚韌帶　masseteric cutaneous ligament
咬肌浅部/咬肌淺部,嚼肌淺部　superficial part of masseter
咬肌深部/咬肌深部,嚼肌深部　deep part of masseter
咬肌神经/咬肌神經,嚼肌神經　masseteric nerve
咬颊症/咬頰症　cheek biting
咬甲癖/咬甲癖　nail biting
咬甲癖者/咬甲癖者　onychophagist
咬紧牙/咬緊牙　tooth clinching
咬伤/咬傷　bite
咬应力/咬應力　bite stress
咬指甲癖/咬指甲癖　nail biting
药材/藥物　crude drug, crude medicine
药材生产/藥材生產　production of medicinal materials
药代动力学/藥物動力學　pharmacokinetics
药典/藥典　pharmacopeia
药动团/藥動團　kinetophore
药动学拮抗/藥動學拮抗　pharmacokinetic antagonism
药兜疗法/藥兜療法　medicinal bag therapy
药毒疹/藥毒疹,藥物皮膚炎　dermatitis medicamentosa, medicinal poison rash
药毒疹•气阴两虚证/藥毒疹•氣陰兩虛證　drug eruption with qi-yin deficiency pattern
药毒疹•热毒入营证/藥毒疹•熱毒入營證　drug eruption with pattern of heat-toxin entering nutrient phase
药毒疹•湿毒蕴结证/藥毒疹•濕毒蘊結證　drug eruption with dampness-toxin amassment pattern
药对/藥對　couplet medicines
药方书/藥方書　dispensatories
药房/藥房　drug store, pharmacy
药房工作规范/藥房工作規範,藥局優良執業作業規範　Good Pharmacy Practice, GPP
药费支出/藥費支出　drug cost
药膏疗法/藥膏療法　ointment therapy
药罐[法]/藥罐[法]　medicated cupping

药行/藥行　trade association of drugs
药剂/［藥］剂　agent
药剂师/藥劑師　pharmacists
药剂师工作保险/藥劑師工作保險　pharmaceutical services insurance
药剂师助手/藥劑師助手　pharmacists' aides
药剂天平/藥劑天平，配藥天平，調劑天平　prescription balance
药剂学/藥劑學，製藥學　pharmaceutics
药酒/藥酒　medicinal wine
药理活性物质/藥理活性物質　pharmacological active substance
药理学/藥理學　pharmacology
药理学家/藥理學家　pharmacologist
药理学配伍禁忌/藥理性配伍禁忌　pharmacological incompatibility
药理作用/藥理作用　pharmacologic action
药品/藥品　drug
药品法/藥品法　Medicine Act
药品供应规范/優良藥品供應規範　Good Supplying Practice, GSP
药品监督员/藥品監督員　pharmaceutical inspector
药品说明书/藥品說明書，藥品仿單　package insert
药品调剂规范/藥品調劑規範，藥品優良調劑作業規範　Good Dispensing Practice, GDP
药品虚假需要/藥品虛假需要，藥品的偽性需求　false demands on drugs
药品质量控制/藥品質量控制，藥品品管　drug quality control
药品注册商标/藥品註冊商標　registered trade mark of drugs
药筛/藥篩　medicinal sieve
药师/藥師　pharmacist
药史/藥［物］史　drug history
药市/藥市　drug market
药事管理/藥事管理，藥劑學管理　pharmacy administration
药蜀葵/［藥］蜀葵　marshmallow
药蜀葵［根］/藥蜀葵［之］根，藥蜀葵　althea
药薯/藥薯　Ipomea
药栓疗法/藥栓療法　medicinal suppository therapy
药筒拔法/藥筒拔法　medicated cup drainage
药王/藥王　king of medicine, yao wang
药物/藥物　drug
药物包装/藥物包裝　drug packaging
药物变态反应/藥物變態反應，藥物過敏反應　drug allergy
药物标签/藥物標簽　drug labeling

药物不良反应/藥物不良反應　adverse drug reaction, ADR
药物不良相互作用/藥物不良交互作用　adverse drug interaction
药物采购/藥物採購　drug purchase
药物残留物/藥物殘留物　drug residue
药物测量学/藥物測量學　pharmacometrics
药物成瘾性/藥物成癮性　drug addiction
药物处方/藥物處方　drug prescription
药物处置/藥物［之體內］處置　disposition of drug
药物传递系统/藥物傳遞系統，藥物遞送系統　drug delivery system
药物代谢/藥物代謝　metabolism of drug, drug metabolism
药物代谢动力学/藥物代謝動力學，藥動學　pharmacokinetics
药物代谢解毒/藥物代謝解毒　drug metabolic detoxication
药物代谢酶/藥物代謝酶　drug metabolism enzyme
药物-蛋白结合置换/藥物-蛋白結合置換　drug-protein binding displacement
药物滴注/藥物滴注　drug instillation
药物动力学相互作用/藥物動力學相互作用，藥動性交互作用　pharmacokinetic interaction
药物毒理学/藥物毒理學　drug toxicology
药物毒性/藥物毒性　drug toxicity
药物法学/藥物法學　pharmaceutical jurisprudence
药物反应/藥物反應　drug reaction
药物防腐剂/藥物防腐劑　pharmaceutical preservative
药物放射学/藥物放射學　pharmacoradiography
药物费用/藥物費用　pharmaceutical fee
药物分布/藥物分布　distribution of drug
药物分析/藥物分析　pharmaceutical analysis
药物附加剂/藥物附加劑　pharmaceutic aid
药物副反应报告系统/藥物副反應報告系統　adverse drug reaction reporting system
药物过敏/藥物過敏　drug hypersensitivity
药物过敏反应/藥物［爭性］過敏反應　drug anaphylaxis
药物化学/藥物化學　medicinal chemistry, pharmaceutical chemistry
药物记载学/藥物記載學　pharmacography
药物剂量效应关系/藥物劑量效應關係　drug dose-response relationship
药物剂量学/［藥物］剂量學　dosimetric medicine
药物剂型/藥物劑型　pharmaceutical dosage form
药物监测/藥物監測　drug monitoring

药物拮抗作用/藥物拮抗作用　drug antagonism
药物经济学/藥物經濟學　pharmacoeconomics, PE
药物警戒/藥物警戒　pharmacovigilance
药物灸/藥物灸　medicinal blister-causing moxibustion, medicinal moxibustion
药物抗性/化學抵抗力, 化學抗性　chemoresistance
药物滥用/藥物濫用　drug abuse
药物立法/藥物立法　drug legislation
药物利用/藥物利用　drug utilization
药物利用评价/藥物使用評估　drug utilization review, DUR
药物利用评审/藥物利用評審　drug utilization review
药物利用指数/藥物利用指數　drug utilization index
药物疗法/藥物療法　medication therapy, drug therapy
药物流行病学/藥物流行病學　pharmacoepidemiology
药物脉冲疗法/藥物脈衝療法　drug pulse therapy
药物美容/藥物美容　drug cosmetics
药物目录/藥物目錄　drug catalog
药物耐受性/藥物耐受性, 耐藥性　drug tolerance
药物浓度/藥物濃度　drug concentration, drug level
药物排泄/藥物排洩　excretion of drug
药物配伍/藥物配伍[性]　compatibility of drug
药物配伍禁忌/藥物配伍禁忌　drug incompatibility
药物批准/藥物批準　drug approval
药物皮炎/藥物皮[膚]炎　dermatitis medicamentosa
药物癖/藥物癖, 服藥癖, 給藥狂　pharmacomania
药物评价/藥物評價　drug evaluation
药物前体/藥物前體　prodrug
药物潜伏化/藥物潛伏化　drug latentiation
药物筛选/藥物篩選　drug screening
药物设计/藥物設計　drug design
药物生理作用/藥物生理作用　physiological effect of drug
药物市场学/藥物市場學　pharmaceutical marketing
药物释放系统/藥物釋放系統　drug delivery system
药物受体/藥物受體　drug receptor
药物体内过程/藥物[的]體內過程　fate of drug
药物调剂/藥物調劑　drug compounding
药物稳定性/藥物穩定性　drug stability
药物污染/藥物汙染　drug contamination
药物吸收/[藥物]吸收　absorption of drug
药物习惯性/藥物習慣性　drug habituation
药物相互作用/藥物相互作用　drug-drug interaction
药物协同作用/藥物協同作用　drug synergism
药物信息/藥物資訊　drug information

药物信息机构/藥物資訊機構　drug information service
药物性白内障/藥物性白內障　drug-induced cataract
药物性鼻炎/藥物性鼻炎　medicamentous rhinitis
药物性痤疮/藥[物性]痤瘡　acne medicamentosa, drug acne
药物性肺病/藥物性肺病　drug-induced pulmonary disease
药物性畸形/藥物性畸形　drug-induced abnormalities
药物性假性淋巴瘤/藥物性假性淋巴瘤　drug-induced pseudolymphoma
药物性间质性肾炎/藥物性間質性腎炎　drug-induced interstitial nephritis
药物性精神病/藥物性精神病　drug psychosis
药物性静坐不能/藥物性靜坐不能　drug-induced akathisia
药物性狼疮/藥物性狼瘡, 藥物引起之狼瘡　drug-induced lupus
药物性皮肤栓塞/藥物性皮膚栓塞　embolia cutis medicamentosa
药物性强直/藥物性強直, 藥物性痙攣　drug tetanus
药物性脱发/藥物性脫髮, 藥物性禿髮　alopecia medicamentosa
药物性荨麻疹/藥物[性]蕁麻疹　urticaria medicamentosa
药物性运动障碍/藥物性運動障礙　drug-induced dyskinesia
药物性紫癜/藥物性紫癜[病]　drug purpura
药物学/藥物學　materia medica
药物依赖/藥癮　drug dependence
药物依赖性/藥物依賴性　drug dependence
药[物]瘾/藥癮　drug habit
药物浴/藥物浴, 加藥浴　medicated bath
药物载体/藥物載體　drug carrier
药物诊断/藥物診斷[法]　pharmacodiagnosis
药物植入物/藥物植入物　drug implant
药物制剂/藥物製劑　pharmaceutical preparation
药物治疗学/藥物治療學　pharmacotherapeutics
药物致病机理/藥物致病機理, 藥物性發病　drug pathogenesis
药物中毒/藥物中毒　drug poisoning
药物贮藏/藥物貯藏　drug storage
药物转化/藥物轉化　transformation of drug
药物转运/藥物轉運　transport of drug
药物佐剂/藥物佐劑　pharmaceutic adjuvant
药西瓜/藥西瓜　bitter cucumber
药西瓜苷/藥西瓜苷, 藥西瓜素　colocynthin

药西瓜中毒/藥西瓜中毒　colocynthidism
药线疗法/藥線療法　medicated thread therapy
药线引流/藥線引流　medicated thread drainage
药箱/藥箱　medicine chest
药效[基]团/藥效原子　pharmacophore
药效学/藥效學,藥力學　pharmacodynamics
药效学相互作用/藥效學相互作用,藥效性交互作用　pharmacodynamic interaction
药性赋/藥性賦　Yaoxing Fu
药学/藥學　pharmacy
药学词典/藥學詞典　pharmaceutic dictionary
药学服务/藥學服務　pharmaceutical service
药学教育/藥學教育　pharmacy education
药学经济学/藥學經濟學　pharmaceutical economics
药学立法/藥學立法　pharmacy legislation
药学伦理学/藥學倫理學　pharmacy ethics
药学史/藥學史　pharmaceutical history
药学许可证/藥學許可證　pharmacy licensure
药学学会/藥學學會　pharmaceutical society
药学学生/藥學學生　pharmacy student
药学院校/藥學院校　pharmacy school
药养/藥養　health preserving with drug
药引/藥引　medicinal usher
药瘾/藥癮,嗜藥成癖　drug addiction
药用辅料/藥用輔料　pharmaceutic adjuvant
药用衡量/藥用衡量,藥衡　apothecaries weight
药用气体/藥用氣體　medicinal gas
药用溶液/藥用溶液　pharmaceutical solution
药用植物/藥用植物　medicinal plant
药用植物学/藥用植物學　pharmaceutical botany, medicinal botany
药用植物资源/藥用植物資源　resource of medicinal plant
药用制剂/藥用製劑　pharmaceutical preparation
药浴疗法/藥浴療法　medicinal bath therapy
药园/藥園　medicinal garden
药源性疾病/藥源性疾病　drug-induced disease
药熨疗法/藥熨療法　hot medicinal compress therapy
药枕疗法/藥枕療法　medicinal pillow therapy
药疹/藥疹　medicinal eruption
要素饮食/要素飲食　elemental diet
钥孔状瞳孔/鑰孔狀瞳孔　keyhole pupil
耶尔森菌感染/耶爾森菌感染　Yersinia infection
耶尔森菌假结核感染/耶爾森菌假結核感染　Yersinia pseudotuberculosis infection
耶格近视力表/耶格近視力表　Jaeger chart
耶基思-布里奇测验/耶斯基-布里奇測驗,耶-伯二氏試驗　Yerkes-Bridges test
耶斯纳淋巴细胞浸润/耶斯納淋巴細胞浸潤　Jessner lymphocytic infiltration
椰子/椰子　coconut
椰子核皮炎/椰子核皮炎　copra dermatitis
椰子螨皮炎/椰子螨皮炎,椰子肉癢病　copra itch
椰子油二甲甘氨酸/椰子油二甲甘胺酸　cocodimethyl glycine
椰子油烷基甜菜碱/椰子油烷基甜菜鹼　cocobetaine
椰子油烷基氧化二甲/椰子油烷基氧化二甲胺　cocodimethyl amine oxide
椰子油脂酸/椰子油脂酸　coconut fatty acid
椰子油脂酸单乙醇酰胺/椰子油脂酸單乙醇醯胺　coconut fatty acid monoethanolamide
椰子油脂酸二乙醇酰胺/椰子油脂酸二乙醇醯胺　coconut fatty acid diethanolamide
椰子油脂酸三甘油酯/椰子油脂酸三甘油酯　coconut fatty acid triglyceride
椰子油脂酸水解胶原蛋白/椰子油脂酸水解膠原蛋白　coco-hydrolyzed collagen
噎膈[病]/噎膈,吞嚥困難　dysphagia
噎膈·津亏热结证/噎膈·津虧熱結證　dysphagia with pattern of fluid insufficiency and heat binding
噎膈·气虚阳微证/噎膈·氣虛陽微證　dysphagia with pattern of qi deficiency and yang debility
噎膈·痰气阻膈证/噎膈·痰氣阻膈證　dysphagia with pattern of phlegm-qi blocking diaphragm
噎膈·痰瘀互结证/噎膈·痰瘀互結證　dysphagia with pattern of intermingling of phlegm and static blood
噎膈·瘀血闭阻证/噎膈·瘀血閉阻證　dysphagia with pattern of blockade of static blood
野百合碱/野百合鹼,農吉利鹼　monocrotaline
野病毒/野生病毒　wild virus
野葛酸/野葛[揮發性]酸　toxicodendric acid
野菊花/野菊花　wild chrysanthemum flower
野山参/野山參　wild ginseng
野生动物/野生動物　wild animal
野生型/野生型　wild type
野屎风/野屎風　hookworm dermatitis
野桐属/野桐屬　*Mallotus*
野樱桃/野櫻桃　choke cherry
野战外科学/野戰外科學　field surgery
野战止血带/戰地止血帶　field tourniquet
叶/葉　leaf, lobe
叶吡咯/葉吡咯　phyllopyrrole
叶卟啉/葉卟啉　phylloporphyrin
叶赤素/葉紅質　phylloerythrin
叶桂/葉桂　Ye Gui

叶红素/葉紅素,葉紅質　erythrophyll
叶黄素/葉黃素,黃體素,黃色素　lutein
叶间导管/腺葉間管　interlobar duct
叶间静脉/葉間靜脈　interlobar vein
叶间裂/葉間裂[隙]　fissura interlobaris
叶间面/葉間面　interlobar surface
叶间胸膜炎/葉間胸膜炎　interlobitis
叶绿醇/植物醇　phytol
叶绿素/葉綠素,葉綠質　chlorophyll
叶绿素蛋白/葉綠[素]蛋白　phyllochlorin
叶绿素酶/葉綠素酶,葉綠素酵素　chlorophylase
叶绿酸/葉綠酸　chlorophyllin
叶绿体/葉綠體　chloroplast
叶绿体质子移位 ATP 酶/葉綠體質子移位 ATP 酶　chloroplast proton-translocating ATPases
叶脉/葉脈　vein
叶内部/葉內部　intralobar part
叶内型肺隔离症/葉內型肺隔離症　intralobar pulmonary sequestration
叶片引导器/葉片引導器　blade guide
叶切除术/葉切除術　lobectomy
叶切断术/葉切斷術,腦葉切開術　lobotomy
叶肉/葉肉　mesophyll
叶酸/葉酸　folic acid
叶酸拮抗剂/葉酸拮抗劑　folic acid antagonist
叶酸钠/葉酸鈉　sodium folate
叶酸缺乏/葉酸缺乏　folic acid deficiency
叶酸盐/葉酸鹽　folate
叶外型肺隔离症/葉外型肺隔離症　extralobar pulmonary sequestration
叶下部/葉下部　infralobar part
叶性肺气肿/葉性肺氣腫　lobar emphysema
叶炎/葉炎　lobitis
叶支气管/葉支氣管　lobar bronchus
叶状/葉狀,葉形　lobation
叶状骨内植体/葉狀骨內植入體,刃形骨內植體　blade endosseous implant
叶状骨内植入体导缘/葉狀骨內植入體導緣,刃形骨內植體之導緣　leading edge of blade endosseous implant
叶状骨内植入体肩部/葉狀骨內植入體肩部,刃形骨內植體之肩臺　shoulder of blade endosseous implant
叶状假足/葉狀假足　lobopodium
叶状瘤/葉狀瘤　phyllodes tumor
叶状乳头/葉狀乳頭　foliate papilla
叶状乳头炎/葉狀乳頭炎　foliate papillitis
叶状胎盘/葉狀胎盤,分葉胎盤　lobed placenta

叶状植物/葉狀[體]植物　thallophyte
叶状种植体/葉狀種植體　blade implantation
夜蛋白尿[症]/夜蛋白尿　noctalbuminuria
夜发性眩晕/夜間[性]眩暈　nocturnal vertigo
夜间呼吸困难/夜間呼吸困難　nocturnal dyspnea
夜间护理/夜間護理　night care
夜间麻痹/夜間肢體麻痺　night palsy
夜间失声/夜間失音　nyctaphonia
夜间痛/夜間痛　night pain
夜间性肌阵挛综合征/夜間性肌陣攣症候群　nocturnal myoclonus syndrome
夜间性突发性张力障碍/夜間性突發性張力障礙　nocturnal paroxysmal dystonia
夜间遗尿症/夜間遺尿　nocturnal enuresis
夜间阴茎勃起试验/夜間陰莖勃起試驗　nocturnal penile tumescence test
夜间阵发性呼吸困难/夜間陣發性呼吸困難　nocturnal paroxysmal dyspnea
夜近视/夜近視　night myopia
夜惊/夜驚　night terror
夜盲/夜盲症　night blindness
夜盲计/夜盲計　nyctometer
夜盲者/夜盲者　nyctalope
夜明砂/夜明砂　bat's droppings
夜磨牙症/夜磨牙症　sleep bruxism
夜尿多/夜尿多　frequent urination at night
夜尿症/夜[頻]尿症　nocturia
夜疟/夜瘧　nocturnal malaria
夜热早凉/夜熱早涼　night fever abating at dawn
夜啼/夜啼　night crying of baby, night crying, nocturnal crying
夜啼·惊恐伤神证/夜啼·驚恐傷神證　nocturnal crying with pattern of fright injuring spirit
夜啼·脾虚中寒证/夜啼·脾虛中寒證　nocturnal crying with pattern of spleen deficiency and cold attack
夜啼·心经积热证/夜啼·心經積熱證　nocturnal crying with pattern of accumulated heat in the heart meridian
夜痛/夜痛,睡痛　nyctalgia
夜现丝虫/夜現[幼]絲蟲　filaria nocturna
夜用护板/夜用護板　night guard
射干/射干　blackberry lily rhizome
液/液　liquor, turbid fluid
液氮疗法/液氮療法　liquid nitrogen treatment
液电碎石术/液電碎石術　electrohydraulic lithotripsy
液化/液化,溶化　liquefaction
液化内障/液性內障　fluid cataract

液化性坏死/液化性壞死　colliquative necrosis
液化性皮肤结核病/液化性皮膚結核病,溶解性皮結核　tuberculosis cutis colliquativa
液化性软化/液化性軟化　colliquative softening
液化性脂膜炎/液化性脂膜炎　liquefying panniculitis
液化智力/液化智力　fluid intelligence
液晶/液晶　liquid crystal
液流描记器/液流描記器,液體流壓描記器　hydrophorograph
液门/液門　yemen, SJ2
液面监测器/液面監測器　level sensor
液[平]面/液面　fluid level
液态/液態　liquid state
液态硅橡胶/液態矽橡膠　fluid silicone rubber
液态空气/液態空氣　air liquid
液态石蜡/液態石臘　paraffin liquid
液体/液體　fluid
液体比色法/液體比色法,色調檢法,色調計用法　tintometry
液体比重测定法/液體比重測定法　areometry
液体比重计/液體比重計　areometer
液体彩色浊度计/液性測定儀　skopometer
液体丢失/液體丟失　fluid loss
液体废弃物处理/液體廢棄物處理　fluid waste disposal
液体基质/液體母質,液性母質,母組織液　fluid matrix
液体卡介苗/液體卡介苗　fresh liquid BCG vaccine
液体类毒素/流體類毒素　fluid toxoid
液体离子蒸发/液體離子蒸發　liquid ion evaporation, LIE
液体排出/液體排出　discharge of fluid
液体平衡/液體平衡　fluid balance
液体闪烁计数/液體閃爍計數　liquid scintillation counting
液体通气/液體通氣　liquid ventilation
液体蓄积/液體蓄積　fluid accumulation
液体药剂/液體製劑　liquid preparation
液体转移/液體轉移　fluid shift
液脱/液脱　fluid depletion, turbid fluid depletion
液脱证/液脱證　pattern of turbid fluid depletion
液相色谱法/液相色譜法,液相層析法　liquid chromatography
液相色谱-质谱联用仪/液相色譜-質譜聯用儀,液相層析質譜儀　liquid chromatograph/mass spectrometer, LC/MS
液溢/液溢,液漏　hydrorrhea
液汁疗法/液汁療法　opotherapy

液质瘤/液質瘤　fluid tumor
液状便/液狀糞　liquid stool
液状排出物/液狀排出物　fluid discharge
液状葡萄糖/液狀葡萄糖,葡萄糖液　liquid glucose
液状石蜡/液體石蠟,流動石蠟　liquid paraffin
液状石蜡瘤/液狀石蠟瘤,軟石蠟瘤　petrolatoma
腋/腋[部]　axilla
腋臭/腋臭　tragomaschalia
腋丛/腋[淋巴]叢　plexus axillaris
腋动脉/腋動脈　axillary artery
腋动脉瘤/腋動脈瘤　axillary aneurysm
腋汗/腋汗　armpit sweating
腋后线/腋後線　posterior axillary line
腋肩肘吊带/腋肩肘吊帶　A-S-E bandage
腋筋膜/腋筋膜　axillary fascia
腋静脉/腋靜脈　axillary vein, vena axillaris
腋淋巴管丛/腋淋巴管叢　axillary lymphatic plexus
腋淋巴结/腋淋巴結　axillary lymph node
腋挛缩/腋攣縮　axillary contracture
腋毛/腋毛　axillary hair
腋毛菌病/腋毛菌病　trichomycosis axillaris
腋毛移植[术]/腋毛移植[術]　axillary hair grafting
腋前线/腋前線　anterior axillary line
腋鞘/腋鞘　axillary sheath
腋区/腋部　axillary region
腋神经/腋神經　axillary nerve
腋神经肌支/腋神經肌支　muscular branch of axillary nerve
腋窝/腋窝　axillary fossa, armpit
腋窝后点/腋窝後點　posterior armpit point
腋窝瘤/腋部瘤　maschaloncus
腋窝脓肿/腋部膿腫　axillary abscess
腋窝前点/腋窝前點　anterior armpit point
腋窝悬韧带/腋窝懸韌帶　suspensory ligament of axilla
腋腺炎/腋腺炎　maschaladenitis
腋痈/腋癰　acute pyogenic axillary lymphadenitis, axillary abscess
腋痈·风温阻络证/腋癰·風溫阻絡證　axillary abscess with pattern of wind-warm obstructing collaterals
腋痈·肝郁痰火证/腋癰·肝鬱痰火證　axillary abscess with pattern of liver depression and phlegm-fire
腋痈·热毒壅滞证/腋癰·熱毒壅滯證　axillary abscess with pattern of heat-toxin congestion and stagnation
腋中线/腋中線　midaxillary line

一氨基酸/一胺基酸,單胺基酸　monamino acid
一般鉴别试验/一般鑒別試驗　general identification test
一般内脏感觉/一般內臟感覺　general visceral sense
一般内脏运动/一般內臟運動　general visceral motor
一般曲线/一般曲線　general curve
一般躯体感觉/一般軀體感覺　general somatic sense
一般躯体运动/一般體壁運動　general somatic motor
一般作用/一般作用　general effect
一匙量/一匙[量]　spoonful
一次性注射器/一次性注射器,拋棄式注射器　disposable syringe
一度空间咬合器/一度空間咬合器　one-dimensional articulator
一度烧伤/一度燒傷　the first degree burn
一儿性不育/一兒性不育,單兒性不孕　one-child sterility
一夫一妻制/一夫一妻制　monogamy
一个基因一个酶假说/一個基因一個酶假說,基因酶假說　one gene-one enzyme hypothesis
一贯煎/一貫煎　yiguan decoction
一过性波/一過性波　transient wave
一过性高血压/一次性高血壓,暫時性高血壓　transient hypertension
一过性黑矇/一次性黑矇,暫時性黑矇　amaurosis fugax
一过性盲/一過性盲　transitional blindness
一过性谵妄/一次性譫妄,暫時性譫妄　transitory delirium
一级动力学/一級動力學　the first order kinetics
一级苷/一級苷　primary glycoside
一级结构/一級結構,初生構造　primary structure
一级堂表亲/一級堂表親　the first cousin
一级弯折/一級彎折　the first order bend
一级异常𬌗/一級異常𬌗,一级異常咬合　class I malocclusion
一氯化物/一氯化物,單氯化物　monochloride
一期缝合/一期縫合,早期縫合　primary suture
一期截肢术/一期截肢術,第一期截斷術　primary amputation
一期梅毒/一期梅毒,初期梅毒　primary syphilis
一期小肠移植/一期小腸移植　one stage small intestine transplantation
一期修复/一期修復　one stage repair
一期延迟缝合/一期延遲縫合,早期延遲縫合　primary delayed suture
一期愈合/一期愈合　primary healing
一日量/一日[劑]量,一晝夜量　daily dose
一日尿量测定法/[一日]尿量測定法　uronoleometry
一日药剂/一日藥劑,晝夜丸,一晝夜片　diurnule
一室模型/一室模型　one-compartment model
一碳环/一碳環,環碳圜　carbocyclic ring
一体型根柱牙冠/一體型根柱牙冠　one-piece post crown
一酰胺/一醯胺,單醯胺　monamide
一溴樟脑/一溴樟腦　monobromated camphor
一氧化氮/[一]氧化氮　nitric oxide
一氧化碳/一氧化碳　carbon monoxide
一氧化碳中毒/一氧化碳中毒　carbon monoxide poisoning
一氧化物/一氧化物　monoxide
一氧化物酶/一氧化物酶,單氧合酶　monoxygenase
一元醇/一元醇,單羥醇　monohydric alcohol
一元酸/一元酸,單鹽基性酸,單元酸　monobasic acid
一致性/一致性　concordance
伊波加因/伊波加因,伊柏格鹼　ibogaine
伊达比星/伊達比星　idarubicin
伊短菌素/伊短菌素　edeine
伊顿因子/伊頓因子,肺炎黴漿菌　Eaton agent
伊尔斯病/伊爾斯病,埃爾斯氏病　Eales disease
伊格尔试验/伊格爾試驗,埃格氏試驗　Eagle test
伊红/伊紅　eosin
伊拉地平/伊拉地平　isradipine
伊兰花/伊蘭花　ylang-ylang
伊利诺斯病毒/伊利諾斯病毒,Illinois病毒　Illinois virus
伊洛前列素/伊洛前列素　Iloprost
伊普吲哚/伊普吲哚　iprindole
伊曲康唑/伊曲康唑　itraconazole
伊塔尔-肖勒瓦征/伊塔爾-肖勒瓦徵,伊-古二氏徵象　Itard-Cholewa sign
伊藤-伦谢纳试验/伊藤-倫謝納試驗,伊-林二氏試驗　Ito-Reenstierna test
伊韦马克综合征/伊韋馬克症候群,Ivemark症候群　Ivemark syndrome
伊维菌素/伊維菌素　ivermectin
伊文思公式/伊文思公式　Evans formula
伊文思蓝/伊文思藍,伊文斯[氏]藍　Evans Blue
伊蚊属/伊蚊屬,黑斑蚊屬　Aedes
衣阿华支原体/衣阿華支原體　mycoplasma iowae
衣蠹蛋白酶/衣蠹蛋白酶　clothes-moth proteinase
衣壳蛋白质类/衣殼蛋白質類　capsid proteins

衣霉素/衣黴素 tunicamycin
衣物性紫癜/衣物性紫癜 clothing purpura
衣原体/衣原體,披衣菌體 mantle bacterium
衣原体病/衣原體病,披衣菌病 chlamydiosis
衣原体肺炎/衣原體肺炎 chlamydia pneumonia
衣原体感染/衣原體感染,披衣菌感染 chlamydial infection
衣原体科感染/衣原體科感染 Chlamydiaceae infection
衣原体属/衣原體屬 Bedsonia
衣原体性结膜炎/衣原體性結膜炎 chlamydial conjunctivitis
衣原体性尿道炎/衣原體性尿道炎 chlamydial urethritis
衣原体血症/衣原體血症 chlamydemia
医案/醫案,病歷卡,病史檔案 medical record
医道/醫道 healing art
医方集解/醫方集解 Collected Exegesis of Recipes
医贯/醫貫 Key Link of Medicine
医护疗养所/醫護療養所 nursing home
医患沟通/醫病溝通 doctor-patient communication
医患关系/醫患關係,醫病關係 doctor-patient relationship
医患合作/醫患合作 doctor and patient cooperation
医患互动/醫病互動 doctor-patient interaction
医经/醫經 medical classic
医疗悲观主义/醫療悲觀主義 therapeutic pessimism
医疗补助/醫療補助 medical assistance
医疗差错/醫療差錯 medical error
医疗处理/醫療處理 medical care
医疗储蓄存款账户/醫療儲蓄存款賬戶 medical savings account
医疗法/醫療法 medical care act
医疗费用/醫療費用 medical fee
医疗费用无力承担/醫療費用無力承擔 medical indigency
医疗分类/醫療分類 medical care triage
医疗服务限制/醫療服務限制 gatekeeping
医疗护理提供者/醫療護理提供者 caregiver
医疗器械/醫療器材 medical device
医疗事故/醫療事故,醫學處置失當 malpractice, medical malpractice
医疗谈话/醫療面談 medical interview
医疗体操/醫療體操 medical gymnastics
医疗委员会/醫學委員會 medical board
医疗性行走/醫療性行走 therapeutic walking
医疗艺术/醫療藝術 medical treatment art

医疗职业/醫業,醫界 medical profession
医林改错/醫林改錯 Corrections of Errors in Medical Works, Correction of Errors in Medical Classics
医门法律/醫門法律 The Rules and Laws of Medicine
医生/醫生 doctor, physician
医生病人关系/醫生病人關係 physician-patient relation
医生护士关系/醫生護士關係 physician-nurse relation
医生拒绝医治/醫生拒絕醫治 refusal to treat
医生自我转诊/醫生自我轉診 physician self-referral
医圣/醫聖 medical sage
医心赤诚/醫心赤誠 treating patient with absolute sincerity
医学/醫學 medicine
医学纲目/醫學綱目 Compendium of Medicine
医学教育/醫學教育 medical education
医[学]昆虫学/醫[學]昆蟲學,醫用昆蟲學 medical entomology
医学伦理学/醫學倫理學 medical ethics
医学心悟/醫學心悟 medicine comprehended
医学信息学/醫學信息學,醫學資訊 medical informatics
医学院/醫學院 medical college
医医病书/醫醫病書 corrections of errors for doctors
医用胚胎学/醫用胚胎學 medical embryology
医源病/醫源病 iatrogenic disease
医源性多毛症/醫源性多毛症 iatrogenic hirsutism
医源性甲状腺功能亢进/醫源性甲狀腺機能亢進 iatrogenic hyperthyroidism
医源性精神障碍/醫源性精神障礙 iatrogenic mental disorder
医源性青光眼/醫源性青光眼 iatrogenic glaucoma
医源性阳痿/醫源性陽痿 iatrogenic impotence
医院工作者/醫院工作者 hospital worker
医院药房/醫院藥局 hospital pharmacy
医院药学/醫院藥學 hospital pharmacy
医宗金鉴/醫宗金鑒 Golden Mirror of Medicine
依地酸/依地酸 edetic acid
依地酸[二]钠/依地酸二鈉 disodium edetate
依地酸钙[二]钠/依地酸鈣[二]鈉,二鈉依地酸鈣 calcium disodium edetate
依地酸盐/依地酸鹽 edetate
依氟鸟氨酸/依氟鳥胺酸 eflornithine
依附/依附,黏著,黏附 adherence
依附寄生/依附寄生 micropredation

依附寄生物/依附寄生者　micropredator
依可碘酯/依可碘酯　echothiophate iodide
依赖/依赖　dependent
依赖病毒/依赖病毒　dependovirus
依赖性分化/依赖性分化,被动分化,隨應分化　dependent differentiation
依赖性人格障碍/依賴性人格障礙　dependent personality disorder
依米丁/依米丁,吐根素,吐根鹼　emetine
依那普利/依那普利,伊那拉普利　enalapril
依那普利拉/依那普利拉　enalaprilat
依诺肝素/依諾肝素　enoxaparin
依诺沙星/依諾沙星　enoxacin
依诺昔酮/依諾昔酮　enoximone
依匹唑/依匹唑　epirizole
依前列醇/依前列醇　epoprostenol
依前列醇受体/依前列醇受體　epoprostenol receptor
依沙吖啶/依沙吖啶,黄藥水　rivanol
依索庚嗪/依索庚嗪　ethoheptazine
依索唑胺/依索唑胺　ethoxzolamide
依他尼酸/依他尼酸,埃酒克林酸　ethacrynic acid
依他酸/依他酸　egtazic acid
依他硝唑/依他硝唑　etanidazole
依他唑酯/依他唑酯　etazolate
依替福林/依替福林　etilefrine
依替卡因/依替卡因　etidocaine
依托泊苷/依托泊苷　etoposide
依托度酸/依托度酸　etodolac
依托格鲁/依托格魯,三甘醇二縮水甘油醚　ethoglucid
依托红霉素/依托紅黴素,無味紅黴素　erythromycin estolate
依托咪酯/依托咪酯　etomidate
咿轧音腱鞘炎/咿軋音腱鞘炎,碎裂音性腱鞘炎　tenosynovitis crepitans
铱/銥　iridium
铱放射性同位素/銥放射性同位素　iridium radioisotopes
噫气/噫氣　belching
譩譆/譩譆　yixi, BL45
仪式行为/儀式行爲　ritualistic behavior
饴糖/飴糖,禾穀糖　cerealose
怡悦畅怀疗法/怡悦暢懷療法　cheerful mood therapy
怡悦开怀/怡悦開懷　having cheerful mood
胰/胰,胰腺,胰臟　pancreas
胰癌/胰癌　pancreas cancer
胰癌·肝胆湿热证/胰癌·肝膽濕熱證　pancreas cancer with pattern of damp-heat in liver and gallbladder
胰癌·气血两虚证/胰癌·氣血兩虛證　pancreas cancer with pattern of deficiency of both qi and blood
胰癌·气血瘀滞证/胰癌·氣血瘀滯證　pancreas cancer with pattern of qi stagnation and blood stasis
胰癌·湿浊阻遏证/胰癌·濕濁阻遏證　pancreas cancer with pattern of damp-turbidity blockade
胰背动脉/胰背動脈　dorsal pancreatic artery
胰病/胰病　pancreatopathy
胰病皮肤征/胰臟疾病的皮膚特徵　skin manifestations of pancreatic disease
胰病性便/胰病性糞　pancreatic stool
胰丛/胰叢　pancreatic plexus
胰大动脉/胰大動脈　great pancreatic artery
胰瘅/胰瘅　pancreatic fever
胰胆/胰膽　yidan, CO11, pancreas and gallbladder
胰胆管/胰膽管　pancreatobiliary duct
胰[蛋白]胨/胰[化]腖,胰[化]蛋白腖　tryptone
胰蛋白酶/胰蛋白酶,胰蛋白酵素　trypsin
胰蛋白酶[分泌]障碍/胰蛋白酶[分泌]障礙,胰蛋白酵素不足　dystrypsia
胰蛋白酶化/胰蛋白酶化　trypsinize
胰蛋白酶抑制剂/胰蛋白酶抑制劑　trypsin inhibitor
胰蛋白酶原/胰蛋白酶原　trypsinogen
胰岛/胰島　pancreatic islet
胰岛分离/胰島分離　islet isolation
胰岛功能亢进性肥胖/胰島功能亢進性肥胖,胰島官能過旺性肥胖　hyperinsulinar obesity
胰岛假说/胰島假說　insular hypothesis
胰岛瘤/胰島瘤　insulinoma
胰岛母细胞增生症/胰島母細胞增生症　nesidioblastosis
胰岛培养/胰島培養　islet culture
胰岛切除术/胰島切除術　nesidiectomy
胰岛素/胰島素　insipi
胰岛素分泌过少/胰島素[分泌]過少　hypoinsulinism
胰岛素昏迷/胰島素昏迷　insulin coma
胰岛素拮抗药/胰島素拮抗藥　insulin antagonists
胰岛素抗体/胰島素抗體　insulin antibody
胰岛素抗药性/胰島素抗藥性,抗胰島素性　insulin resistance
胰岛素酶/胰島素酶　insulinase
胰岛素受体/胰島素受體　insulin receptor
胰岛素受体激酶/胰島素受體激酶　insulin receptor kinase

胰岛素输注系统/胰島素輸注系統　insulin infusion system
胰岛素性脂肪萎缩/胰島素性脂質營養不良　insulinlipodystrophy
胰岛素休克治疗/胰島素休克治療　insulin shock therapy
胰岛素血[症]/胰島素血症　insulinemia
胰岛素样生长因子/胰島素樣生長因子　insulin-like growth factor
胰岛素样生长因子结合蛋白质类/胰島素樣生長因子結合蛋白質類　insulin-like growth factor binding proteins
胰岛素依赖型糖尿病/胰島素依賴型糖尿病　insulin-dependent diabetes mellitus
胰岛素与精蛋白锌胰岛素3∶1混合剂/胰島素精蛋白鋅胰島素3∶1混合劑　three-to-one insulin
胰岛素原/前胰島素　proinsulin
胰岛素注射液/胰島素注射液　insulin injection
胰岛细胞/胰島細胞　islet cell
[胰岛]PP细胞/PP細胞　PP cell
胰岛细胞癌/胰島細胞癌　islet cell carcinoma
胰岛细胞瘤/胰島細胞瘤　islet cell tumor
胰岛细胞腺瘤/胰島細胞腺瘤　islet cell adenoma
胰岛细胞移植/胰島細胞移植　islet cell transplantation
胰岛细胞增生/胰島細胞增生　islet cell hyperplasia
胰岛[腺]瘤/胰島腺瘤, 藍氏細胞腺瘤　Langerhansian adenoma
胰岛-腺泡门脉系统/胰島-腺泡門脈系統　islet-acinus portal system
胰岛炎/胰島炎　insulitis
胰岛移植/胰島移植　islet transplantation
胰淀粉酶/胰澱粉酶　pancreatic amylase
胰胨分解/胰化蛋白腖分解　tryptolysis
胰多肽/胰多肽　pancreatic polypeptide
胰反应/胰反應　pancreatic reaction
胰副管/胰副管　ductus pancreaticus accessorius
胰肝综合征/胰肝症候群　pancreaticohepatic syndrome
胰高血糖素/胰高血糖素, 昇糖素　glucagon
胰高血糖素瘤/胰高血糖素瘤, 昇糖素瘤　glucagonoma
胰高血糖素瘤综合征/胰高[血]糖素瘤症候群, 壞死溶解性移性紅斑　glucagonoma syndrome
胰高血糖素受体/胰高血糖素受體　glucagon receptor
胰功能不全/胰機能不全　pancreatic insufficiency
胰钩突/胰鉤突　uncinate process of pancreas
胰管/胰管　pancreatic duct, ductus pancreaticus
胰管结扎式胰腺移植/胰管結扎式胰腺移植　duct ligation pancreas transplantation
胰管检查[术]/胰管檢查[術]　pancreatoscopy
胰管空肠吻合术/胰和空腸吻合術　pancreaticojejunostomy
胰管括约肌/胰管括約肌　sphincter of pancreatic duct
胰管十二指肠吻合术/胰管十二指腸[造口]吻合術　pancreaticoduodenostomy
胰管填塞式胰腺移植/胰管填塞式胰腺移植　duct obstruction pancreas transplantation
胰管未汇合/胰管未匯合　nonfusion of pancreatic duct
胰管胃吻合术/胰管胃[造口]吻合術　pancreaticogastrostomy
胰管小肠吻合术/胰管小腸吻合術, 胰管腸造口吻合術　pancreaticoenterostomy
胰管[潴留]囊肿/胰管囊腫　pancreatic ranula
胰管阻塞/胰管阻塞　pancreatemphraxis
胰后面/胰後面　posterior surface of pancreas
胰积水/胰積水　hydropancreatosis
胰激肽/胰激肽, 卡里定　kallidin
胰激肽原/胰激肽原　kallidinogen
胰结核/胰結核　tuberculosis of pancreas
胰颈/胰頸　neck of pancreas
胰静脉/胰靜脈　pancreatic vein
胰淋巴结/胰淋巴結　pancreatic lymph node
胰瘤/胰瘤　pancreatoncus
胰酶/胰酶, 胰消化素, 胰酵素　pancreatin
胰酶灌肠剂/胰酶灌腸劑　pancreatic enema
胰酶盐剂/胰镁鹽劑, 胰鹽, 消化鹽　pancreatic salt
胰脾韧带/胰脾韌帶　pancreaticosplenic ligament
胰前动脉/胰前動脈　prepancreatic artery
胰前面/胰前面　anterior surface of pancreas
胰前缘/胰前緣　anterior border of pancreas
胰切迹/胰[腺]切跡　notch of pancreas
胰切开取石术/胰切開取石術, 胰石切除術　pancreolithotomy
胰切开术/胰切開術　pancreatomy
胰上淋巴结/胰上淋巴結　superior pancreatic lymph node
胰上缘/胰上緣　superior border of pancreas
胰肾联合移植/胰腎聯合移植　combined pancreas and renal transplantation
胰升糖素试验/胰昇糖素試驗　glucagon test
胰十二指肠静脉/胰十二指腸靜脈　pancreaticoduodenal vein

胰十二指肠淋巴结/胰十二指腸淋巴結　pancreaticoduodenal lymph node
胰十二指肠切除术/胰十二指腸切除術　pancreaticoduodenectomy
胰十二指肠上后动脉/胰十二指腸上後動脈　posterior superior pancreaticoduodenal artery
胰十二指肠上后动脉十二指肠支/胰十二指腸上後動脈十二指腸支　duodenal branch of posterior superior pancreaticoduodenal artery
胰十二指肠上后动脉胰支/胰十二指腸上後動脈胰支　pancreatic branch of posterior superior pancreaticoduodenal artery
胰十二指肠上后静脉/胰十二指腸上後靜脈　superior posterior pancreaticoduodenal vein
胰十二指肠上淋巴结/胰十二指腸上淋巴結　superior pancreaticoduodenal lymph node
胰十二指肠上前动脉/胰十二指腸上前動脈　anterior superior pancreaticoduodenal artery
胰十二指肠上前动脉十二指肠支/胰十二指腸上前動脈十二指腸支　duodenal branch of anterior superior pancreaticoduodenal artery
胰十二指肠上前动脉胰支/胰十二指腸上前動脈胰支　pancreatic branch of anterior superior pancreaticoduodenal artery
胰十二指肠上前静脉/胰十二指腸上前靜脈　superior anterior pancreaticoduodenal vein
胰十二指肠下动脉/胰十二指腸下動脈　inferior pancreaticoduodenal artery
胰十二指肠下动脉后支/胰十二指腸下動脈後支　posterior branch of inferior pancreaticoduodenal artery
胰十二指肠下动脉前支/胰十二指腸下動脈前支　anterior branch of inferior pancreaticoduodenal artery
胰十二指肠下后静脉/胰十二指腸下後靜脈　inferior posterior pancreaticoduodenal vein
胰十二指肠下淋巴结/胰十二指腸下淋巴結　inferior pancreaticoduodenal lymph node
胰十二指肠下前静脉/胰十二指腸下前靜脈　inferior anterior pancreaticoduodenal vein
胰十二指肠移植/胰十二指腸移植　pancreas-duodenal transplantation
胰石/胰[结]石　pancreatolith
胰石病/胰[結]石病　pancreatolithiasis
胰石切除术/胰[結]石切除術　pancreatolithectomy
胰弹性蛋白酶/胰彈性蛋白酶　pancreatic elastase
胰体/胰[腺]體　body of pancreas
胰痛/胰痛　pancrealgia
胰头/胰[腺]頭　head of pancreas
胰尾/胰[腺]尾　tail of pancreas
胰尾动脉/胰尾動脈　caudal pancreatic artery
胰下动脉/胰下動脈　inferior pancreatic artery
胰下淋巴结/胰下淋巴結　inferior pancreatic lymph node
胰下面/胰下面　inferior surface of pancreas
胰下缘/胰下緣　inferior border of pancreas
胰腺/胰[腺]　pancreas
胰腺癌/胰腺癌　pancreatic carcinoma
胰腺创伤/胰腺創傷　pancreatic trauma
胰腺分裂/胰腺分裂,分裂胰　pancreas divisum
胰腺蜂窝[组]织炎/胰[腺]蜂窩織炎,胰臟蜂窩組織炎　pancreatic phlegmon
胰腺钙化/胰腺鈣化　calcification of pancreas
胰腺功能减退/胰腺功能減退,胰臟機能不足　hypopancreatism
胰腺功能试验/胰腺功能試驗　pancreatic function test
胰腺功能异常/胰腺功能異常,胰臟機能異常　heteropancreatism
胰腺功能障碍/胰腺功能障礙,胰機能障礙　dyspancreatism
胰腺功能正常/胰腺功能正常,胰機能正常　eupancreatism
胰腺管/胰腺管　pancreatic duct
胰腺管癌/胰腺管癌　pancreatic ductal carcinoma
胰腺核糖核酸酶/胰腺核糖核苷酸,胰植物核酸酵素　pancreatic ribonuclease
胰腺激素类/胰腺激素　pancreatic hormone
胰腺激素受体/胰腺激素受體　pancreatic hormone receptor
胰腺疾病/胰腺疾病　pancreatic disease
胰腺假囊肿/胰[腺]假囊腫　pancreatic pseudocyst
胰腺瘘/胰腺瘺　pancreatic fistula
胰腺囊肿/胰[腺]囊腫　pancreatic cyst
胰腺脓肿/胰腺膿腫　abscess of pancreas
胰腺切除术/胰[腺]切除術　pancreatectomy
胰腺提取物/胰腺提取物　pancreatic extract
胰腺外分泌功能不全/胰腺外分泌功能不全　exocrine pancreatic insufficiency
胰腺外瘘/胰腺外瘺　external fistula of pancreas
胰腺性糖尿病/胰[腺]性糖尿病　pancreatic diabetes
胰腺炎/胰腺炎,胰臟炎　pancreatitis
胰腺移植/胰腺移植　pancreas transplantation
胰腺异位/胰腺異位　heterotopic pancreas
胰腺肿瘤/胰腺腫瘤　pancreatic neoplasm
胰腺周围脓肿/胰腺周圍膿腫　peripancreatic abscess

胰芽/胰芽　pancreatic bud
胰液/胰液　pancreatic juice
胰液[分泌]过多/胰液分泌過多,胰腺機能亢進　hyperpancreorrhea
胰液分泌过少/胰臟分泌過少　hypopancreorrhea
胰液回流/胰液回流　pancreatic reflux
胰痈/胰癰　pancreatic abscess
胰源性腹水/胰源性腹水　pancreatic ascites
胰造影术/胰攝影術　pancreatography
胰胀/胰脹　pancreatic distension
胰支/胰[腺]支　pancreatic branch
胰脂肪坏死/胰脂質壞死　pancreatic fat necrosis
胰脂[肪]酶/胰脂酶　pancrelipase
胰脂酶抑制药/胰脂酶抑制藥　pancreatic lipase inhibitor
胰脂酶原/胰脂酶原,胰脂酵素原　steapsinogen
胰制剂疗法/胰製劑療法,胰劑調法　pancreotherapy
胰周炎/胰周[圍]炎　peripancreatitis
胰组织破坏/胰組織破壞,胰崩解　pancreatolysis
移动接口电泳/移動接口電泳,移動區帶電泳　moving boundary electrophoresis
移动性痉挛/[移]動性痙攣　mobile spasm
移动性盲肠/移動性盲腸　mobile caecum
移动性起搏点/移動性起搏點,遊走性整律　wandering pacemaker
移动性水肿/移動性水腫,走動性水腫　ambulant edema
移动性浊音/移動性濁音　shifting dullness
移动抑制因子/移動抑制因子　migration inhibitory factor
移精变气论篇/移精變氣論篇　Treatise on Transformation of Essence and Qi
移码突变/移碼突變　frameshift mutation
移情/移情,同理心　empathy, transference
移酸滴管/移酸滴管,酸劑滴管,滴酸器　portacid
移位/移位　displacement
移位髌[骨]/移位髕[骨],滑脫髕　slipping patella
移行肌电复合波/移行肌電複合波　migrating myoelectric complex
移行期/移行期　migratory stage
移行上皮/移行上皮,過渡上皮　transitional epithelium
移行细胞/移行細胞　transitional cell
移行细胞癌/移行細胞癌　transitional cell carcinoma
移行性环状红斑角皮症/移行性環狀紅斑角皮症　erythrokeratoderma annularis migrans
移行性结节性红斑/移行性結節性紅斑　erythema nodosum migrans
移行性区域性剥落/移行性區域性剝落　exfoliatio areata migrans
移行性掌跖角化病/移行性掌蹠角化病　keratosis palmoplantaris migrans
移植/移植　transplant
移植后淋巴增生性疾病/移植後淋巴增生性疾病　post-transplant lymphoproliferative disease
移植瘤/移植瘤　transplanted tumor
移植免疫/移植免疫　transplantation immunity
移植免疫学/移植免疫學　transplantation immunology
移植命名学/移植命名學　transplantation terminology
移植耐受/移植耐受　transplantation tolerance
移植片/移植片　graft
移植嵌合体/移植嵌合體　transplantation chimera
移植肾病/移植腎病　transplant nephropathy
移植肾功能延迟/移植腎功能延遲　delayed renal graft function
移植肾活组织检查/移植腎活組織檢查,移植腎活檢　renal graft biopsy
移植肾原病复发/移植腎原病復發　recurrence of original disease in transplanted kidney
移植术/移植術　grafting
移植物/移植物　transplant
移植物存活/移植物存活　graft survival
移植物抗白血病反应/移植物白血病反應　graft versus leukemia effect
移植物抗宿主病/移植物抗宿主病　graft-versus-host disease
移植物抗宿主反应/移植物抗宿主反應　graft-versus-host reaction
移植物免疫耐受增强法/移植物免疫耐受增強法　immunologic graft enhancement
移植物排斥/移植物排斥　graft rejection
移植物宿主相互排斥病/移植物宿主相互排斥病　mutual graft versus host disease
移植物照射/移植物照射　graft irradiation
移植心脏复跳/移植心臟復跳　graft cardiac rebeating
移植性转移/移植性轉移　transplantation metastasis
移植胰假性囊肿/移植胰假性囊腫　graft pancreatic pseudocyst
移植胰胰瘘/移植胰胰瘻　graft pancreatic fistula
移植胰胰腺炎/移植胰胰腺炎　graft pancreatitis
移植预处理/移植預處理　transplantation conditioning
移中心眼镜/移中心眼鏡,偏心眼鏡　decentered

spectacles
移转/移轉,规避　aversion
遗传/遺傳　inheritance
遗传背景/遺傳背景　genetic background
遗传变异/遺傳變異　genetic variation
遗传标记/遺傳標記,先天性標志　genetic marker
遗传病/遺傳病　heredopathia
遗传不分离/遺傳不分離　genetic nondisjunction
遗传重组/遺傳重組　genetic recombination
遗传出血性毛细血管扩张/遺傳出血性毛細血管擴張,奥-韋-朗三氏病　Osler-Weber-Rendu disease
遗传毒理学/遺傳毒理學　genetic toxicology
遗传毒性致癌物/遺傳毒性致癌物　genotoxic carcinogen
遗传度/遺傳度,遺傳力,可遺傳性　heritability
遗传多态现象/遺傳多態現象　genetic polymorphism
遗传范本/遺傳範本　genetic template
遗传方式/遺傳方式　inheritance pattern
遗传负荷/遺傳負荷　genetic load
遗传复合体/遺傳複合體　genetic compound
遗传工程/遺傳工程　genetic engineering
遗传互补测验/遺傳互補測驗　genetic complementation test
遗传疾病/遺傳疾病　genetic disease
遗传疾患/遺傳疾患　genetic disorder, inherited disorder
遗传交叉/遺傳交叉　genetic cross
遗传交换/遺傳交換　genetic crossing over
遗传接合/遺傳接合　genetic conjugation
遗传结构/遺傳結構　genetic structure
遗传距离/遺傳距離　genetic distance
遗传决定论/遺傳決定論　genetic determinism
遗传流行病学/遺傳流行病學　genetic epidemiology
遗传梅毒/遺傳梅毒　hereditary syphilis
遗传密码/遺傳密碼　genetic code
遗传漂变/遺傳漂變,基因漸進性改變　genetic drift
遗传筛查/遺傳篩查　genetic screening
遗传上位性/遺傳上位性　genetic epistasis
遗传数量性状/遺傳數量性狀　heritable quantitative trait
遗传死亡/遺傳[性]死亡　genetic death
遗传素质/遺傳素質,遺傳誘因　heredodiathesis
遗传体质性疾病/遺傳體質性疾病,遺傳性體質病　heredoconstitutional disease
遗传现象/遺傳現象　genetic phenomena
遗传限度/遺傳限度,先天的限制　genetic limitation
遗传信息/遺傳資訊　genetic information
遗传性变态反应/遺傳性過敏　hereditary allergy

遗传性表皮多囊病/遺傳性表皮多囊症,遺傳性表皮多囊疾病　hereditary epidermal polycystic disease
遗传性别/遺傳性別,基因性別　genetic sex
遗传性不耐果糖[症]/遺傳性不耐果糖症　hereditary fructose intolerance
遗传性残毁性角化病/遺傳性殘毀性角化病　keratoma hereditaria mutilans
遗传性出血性毛细血管扩张/遺傳性出血性毛細血管擴張,遺傳性出血性小血管擴張　hereditary hemorrhagic telangiectasis
遗传性出血性紫癜/遺傳性出血性紫癜[病]　hereditary purpura hemorrhagica
遗传性大疱性表皮松解/遺傳性大皰性表皮鬆解,遺傳性水皰性表皮鬆解症　epidermolysis bullosa hereditaria
遗传性代谢缺陷/遺傳性代謝缺陷　inborn error of metabolism
遗传性对称性色素异常症/遺傳性對稱性色素異常症　hereditary symmetrical dyschromatosis
遗传性多发良性囊样上皮瘤/遺傳性多發良性囊樣上皮瘤　hereditary multiple benign cystic epithelioma
遗传性非息肉性结直肠肿瘤/遺傳性非息肉性結直腸腫瘤　hereditary nonpolyposis colorectal neoplasm
遗传性粪卟啉病/遺傳性糞卟啉病　hereditary coproporphyria
遗传性高胆红素血症/遺傳性高膽紅素血症　hereditary hyperbilirubinemia
遗传性共济失调/遺傳性共濟失調,遺傳性失調症　hereditary ataxia
遗传性黄斑变性/遺傳性黃斑變性　hereditary macular digeneration
遗传性黄嘌呤尿症/遺傳性黃嘌呤尿症　hereditary xanthinuria
遗传性疾病/遺傳性疾病　genetic disease
遗传性疾患/遺傳性疾患,遺傳性障礙　hereditary disorder
遗传性角膜营养不良/遺傳性角膜營養不良　hereditary corneal dystrophy
遗传性进行性黏蛋白组织细胞增生症/遺傳性進行性黏蛋白組織細胞增生症,遺傳性進行性黏液性組織球增生症　hereditary progressive mucinous histiocytosis
遗传性痉挛脊髓麻痹/遺傳性痙攣脊髓麻痺　hereditary spastic spinal paralysis
遗传性痉挛性截瘫/遺傳[性]痙攣性截癱　hereditary spastic paraplegia

遗传性局限性瘙痒症/遺傳性局限性搔癢症 hereditary localized pruritus
遗传性良性上皮内角化不良/遺傳性良性上皮內角化不良, Witkop-von Sallmann 二氏病 hereditary intraepithelial dyskeratosis, Witkop-von Sallmann disease
遗传性淋巴水肿/遺傳性淋巴水腫 hereditary lymphedema
遗传性慢性进行性肾炎/遺傳性慢性進行性腎炎 hereditary progressive chronic nephritis
遗传性免疫性肾炎/遺傳性免疫性腎炎 hereditary immunonephritis
遗传性黏膜上皮发育不良/遺傳性黏膜上皮發育不良 hereditary mucoepithelial dysplasia
遗传性皮肤病/遺傳性皮膚病 genodermatosis
遗传性皮肤病学/遺傳性皮膚病學 genodermatology
遗传性皮肤疾病/遺傳性皮膚疾病 genetic skin disease
遗传性葡萄糖醛酰基转移酶缺乏症/遺傳性葡萄糖醛醯基轉移酶缺乏症 hereditary deficiency of glucuronyl transferase
遗传性青少年性角膜上皮营养不良/遺傳性青少年性角膜上皮營養不良 hereditary juvenile epithelial dystrophy of cornea
遗传性球形红细胞增多症/遺傳性球形紅細胞增多症,遺傳性球狀紅血球症 hereditary spherocytosis
遗传性乳光牙本质/遺傳性乳[光]牙本質 hereditary opalescent dentin
遗传性乳清酸尿症/遺傳性乳[清]酸尿病 hereditary orotic aciduria
遗传性肾小球肾炎/遺傳性腎小球腎炎 hereditary glomerulonephritis
遗传性肾炎/遺傳性腎炎 hereditary nephritis
遗传性视神经萎缩/遺傳性視神經萎縮 hereditary optic atrophy
遗传性视神经炎/遺傳性視神經炎 hereditary optic neuritis
遗传性脱发/遺傳性脫髮,遺傳性禿髮 hereditary alopecia
遗传性椭圆形红细胞增多症/遺傳性橢圓形紅細胞增多症 hereditary elliptocytosis
遗传性外胚层发育不良/遺傳性外胚層發育不全 hereditary ectodermal dysplasia
遗传性小脑共济失调/遺傳性小腦共濟失調,遺傳性小腦性失調症 hereditary cerebellar ataxia
遗传性血管性水肿/遺傳性血管性水腫 hereditary angioedema
遗传性血尿/遺傳性血尿 hereditary hematuria
遗传性血小板功能不全/遺傳性血小板機能不全,遺傳性出血性紫癜病 hereditary thrombasthenia
遗传性血小板机能不全/遺傳性血小板機能不全,遺傳性出血性紫癜病 hereditary thrombasthenia
遗传性血液凝集障碍/遺傳性血液凝集障礙 inherited blood coagulation disorder
遗传性眼疾病/遺傳性眼疾病 hereditary eye disease
遗传性易位/遺傳性易位 inherited translocation
遗传性营养失调病/遺傳性營養失調病,遺傳性營養病 genetotrophic disease
遗传性硬化性皮肤异色症/遺傳性硬化性皮膚異色症 hereditary sclerosing poikiloderma
遗传性釉质发育异常[症]/遺傳性釉質發育異常[症] hereditary enamel dysplasia
遗传性釉质生长不全/遺傳性釉質生長不全,遺傳性齒釉質發育不全 hereditary enamel hypoplasia
遗传性掌红斑/遺傳性[手]掌紅斑 erythema palmare hereditarium
遗传性掌跖角化病/遺傳性掌蹠角化病 hereditary palmoplantar keratoderma
遗传性掌跖角皮症/遺傳性掌蹠角皮症 palmoplantar keratodermia hereditarium
遗传性正铁血红蛋白血性发绀/遺傳性正鐵血紅蛋白血性發紺,遺傳變性血紅素發紺 hereditary methemoglobinemic cyanosis
遗传性肢端皮肤异色萎缩症/遺傳性肢端皮膚異色萎縮症 hereditary acropoikiloderma
遗传性中枢神经系统脱髓鞘疾病/遺傳性中樞神經系統脫髓鞘疾病 hereditary central nervous system demyelinating disease
遗传性肿瘤综合征/遺傳性腫瘤症候群 hereditary neoplastic syndrome
遗传性紫癜/遺傳性紫癜 hereditary purpura
遗传学/遺傳學 genetics
遗传学服务/遺傳學服務 genetic service
遗传学过程/遺傳學過程 genetic process
遗传学技术/遺傳學技術 genetic technique
遗传学家/遺傳學家 geneticist
遗传学模型/遺傳學模型 genetic model
遗传学数据库/遺傳學資料庫 genetic database
遗传学研究/遺傳學研究 genetic research
遗传药理学/遺傳藥理學 pharmacogenetics
遗传药理学不良反应/遺傳藥理學[型藥物]不良反應 pharmacogenetical adverse drug reaction
遗传异质性/遺傳異質性 genetic heterogeneity
遗传抑制/遺傳抑制 genetic suppression
遗传易患性/遺傳易患性 hereditary susceptibility
遗传易位/遺傳易位 genetic translocation

遗传隐私/遺傳隱私　genetic privacy
遗传印记/遺傳印記　genetic imprinting
遗传杂交/遺傳雜交　genetic hybridization
遗传载体/遺傳載體　genetic vector
遗传早现/遺傳早現　genetic anticipation
遗传增强/遺傳增強　genetic enhancement
遗传致死/遺傳致死　genetic lethal
遗传转导/遺傳轉導　genetic transduction
遗传转化/遺傳轉化　genetic transformation
遗传转录/遺傳轉錄　genetic transcription
遗传咨询/遺傳諮詢　genetic counseling
遗腹受孕/遺腹受孕　posthumous conception
遗后听觉/遺後聽覺　auditory after-sensation
遗精[病]/遺精[病]　seminal emission, spermatorrhea, nocturnal emission
遗精·肝火偏盛证/遺精·肝火偏盛證　spermatorrhea with pattern of liver fire exuberance
遗精·君相火旺证/遺精·君相火旺證　spermatorrhea with pattern of blazing monarchic and ministerial fire
遗精·劳伤心脾证/遺精·勞傷心脾證　spermatorrhea with pattern of overstrain injuring heart and spleen
遗精·肾气不固证/遺精·腎氣不固證　spermatorrhea with pattern of unconsolidated kidney qi
遗精·肾阳衰微证/遺精·腎陽衰微證　spermatorrhea with pattern of kidney yang exhaustion
遗精·肾阴虚证/遺精·腎陰虛證　spermatorrhea with pattern of kidney yin deficiency
遗精·湿热下注证/遺精·濕熱下注證　spermatorrhea with pattern of downward diffusion of damp-heat
遗精·痰火内蕴证/遺精·痰火內蘊證　spermatorrhea with pattern of internal retention of phlegm-fire
遗精·心肾不交证/遺精·心腎不交證　spermatorrhea with pattern of incoordination between heart and kidney
遗精·阴虚火旺证/遺精·陰虛火旺證　spermatorrhea with pattern of exuberant fire due to yin deficiency
遗觉像/遺覺像　eidetic imagery
遗留性皮样囊瘤/遺傳性皮樣囊瘤,隔離性皮囊瘤　sequestration dermoid
遗漏心搏/遺漏心搏,脫漏脈動　missed beat
遗尿[病]/遺尿　enuresis
遗尿·肺脾气虚证/遺尿·肺脾氣虛證　enuresis with pattern of qi deficiency of lung and spleen
遗尿·肾督不足证/遺尿·腎督不足證　enuresis with pattern of insufficiency of kidney and governor vessel
遗尿·湿热下注证/遺尿·濕熱下注證　enuresis with pattern of downward diffusion of damp-heat
遗尿·下焦虚冷证/遺尿·下焦虛冷證　enuresis with pattern of deficiency-cold in lower jiao
遗尿·下焦蓄血证/遺尿·下焦蓄血證　enuresis with pattern of blood amassment in lower jiao
遗尿·心肾阴虚证/遺尿·心腎陰虛證　enuresis with pattern of yin deficiency in heart and kidney
遗忘/遺忘,記憶缺失,健忘　amnesia
遗忘性表情不能/遺忘性表情不能,遺忘性表情缺失　amnesic amimia
遗忘性色盲/遺忘性色盲　amnesic color blindness
遗忘性失用/遺忘性失用,健忘性失用症　amnestic apraxia
遗忘性失语/遺忘性失語,記憶障礙性失語症,健忘失語症　amnemonic aphasia, amnesic aphasia
遗忘性失语症/遺忘性失語症,言語健忘,健忘性失語症　verbal amnesia
遗忘因子法/遺忘因子法　forgetting factor method
遗忘止痛[法]/遺忘止痛[法],忘痛法　amnalgesia
遗忘综合征/遺忘症候群,健忘症候群　amnestic syndrome
遗嘱/遺囑　will
疑病患者/疑病患者　hypochondriac
疑病性神经症/疑病性神經症　hypochondrical neurosis
疑病症/疑病[症],臆想病　hypochondriasis
疑层/疑層　ambiguous layer
疑核/疑核　nucleus ambiguus
疑核脊髓丘脑麻痹/疑核脊髓丘腦麻痹　ambiguospinothalamic paralysis
疑核综合征/疑核症候群　syndrome of nucleus ambiguus
乙胺/乙胺　ethylamine
乙胺雌酚/乙胺雌酚　ethamoxytriphetol
乙胺丁醇/乙胺丁醇　ethambutol
乙胺类/乙胺類　ethylamine
乙胺嘧啶/乙胺嘧啶,吡拉美胺　pyrimethamine
乙胺嗪/乙胺嗪　diethylcarbamazine
乙拌磷/乙拌磷　disulfoton
乙叉二氯/乙叉二氯,氯化亞乙基　ethidene chloride
乙橙/乙基橙　ethyl orange
乙醇/乙醇　ethyl alcohol
乙醇胺/乙醇胺,胺基乙醇　ethanolamine
乙醇胺氨裂合酶/乙醇胺氨裂合酶　ethanolamine ammonia-lyase
乙醇胺磷酸转移酶/乙醇胺磷酸轉移酶　ethanolamine phosphotransferase
乙醇酸盐类/乙醇酸鹽類　glycolates

乙醇盐/乙醇鹽,乙醇化物　ethylate
乙雌烯醇/乙烯雌醇　ethylestrenol
乙蔗酚/乙蔗酚　diethylstilbestrol
乙碘油/乙碘油　ethiodized oil
乙二胺/乙二胺　ethylenediamine
乙二胺类/乙二胺類　ethylenediamines
乙二胺溶液/乙二胺溶液　ethylenediamine solution
乙二胺四乙酸/乙二胺四乙酸　ethylenediaminetetraacetic acid, EDTA
乙二胺四乙酸试验/乙二胺四乙酸試驗　EDTA infusion test
乙二醇/乙二醇　ethylene glycol
乙二醇丁醚/乙二醇丁醚　ethylene glycol monobutyl ether
乙二醇甲醚/乙二醇甲醚　ethylene glycol monomethyl ether
乙二醇乙醚/乙二醇乙醚　ethylene glycol monoethyl ether
乙二醛/乙二醛　biformyl
乙肝宁颗粒/乙肝寧顆粒　yiganning granule
乙酐/乙酐　acetic anhydride
乙琥胺/乙琥胺　ethosuximide
乙基/乙[烷]基　ethyl
乙基巴豆酰脲/乙基巴豆醯脲　ectylurea
乙基苯/乙[基]苯　ethyl benzene
乙基苯妥英/乙[基]苯妥英　ethotoin
乙基丙烯酸盐聚合物/乙基丙烯酸鹽共聚物　ethyl acrylate copolymer
乙基二甲基氨基丙碳化二亚胺/乙基二甲基胺基丙碳化二亞胺　ethyl dimethylaminopropyl carbodiimide
乙基汞化合物/乙基汞化合物　ethyl mercury compound
乙基化/乙基化[作用]　ethylation
乙基己二醇/乙基己二醇　ethohexadiol
乙基麻黄碱/乙基麻黃鹼　etafedrine
乙基马来酰亚胺/乙基馬來醯亞胺　ethylmaleimide
乙基吗啡/乙基嗎啡　ethylmorphine
乙基吗啡-N-脱甲基酶/乙基嗎啡-N-脫甲基酶　ethylmorphine N-demethylase
10-乙基-10-去氮-氨基蝶呤/10-乙基-10-去氮-胺基喋呤　10-ethyl-10-deaza-aminopterin
乙基纤维素/乙基纖維素　ethylcellulose
乙基香草醛/乙[基]香草醛　ethyl vanillin
乙基亚硝脲/乙基亞硝脲　ethylnitrosourea
乙基异丙肾上腺素/乙基異丙腎上腺素,去甲腎上腺素　isoetharine
乙腈类/乙腈類　acetonitriles

乙硫氨酸/乙硫胺[基酪]酸　ethionine
乙硫醇/乙硫醇　ethyl mercaptan
乙硫醇酸钙/乙硫醇酸鈣　calcium thioglycollate
乙硫异烟胺/乙硫異煙胺　ethionamide
乙氯维诺/乙氯維諾,氯乙基戊烯炔醇　ethchlorvynol
乙醚/乙醚　ether
乙醚滴定器/醚量計,醚滴數計　etherometer
乙醚麻醉/乙醚麻醉　ether anesthesia
乙醚喷雾/乙醚噴霧　ether spray
乙醚征/乙醚徵[象]　ether sign
乙脒/乙脒,醋脒　acetamidine
乙内酰苯硫脲/乙内醯苯硫脲,苯硫乙内醯脲　phenylthiohydantoin
乙内酰脲/乙内醯脲　hydantoin
乙内酰脲盐/乙内醯脲鹽　hydantoinate
乙醛/乙醛　ethanal
乙醛酸循环体类/乙醛酸循環體類　glyoxysomes
乙醛酸盐类/乙醛酸鹽類　glyoxylates
乙醛糖/己醛醣　aldohexose
乙醛脱氢酶/乙醛脫氫酶,乙醛脫氫酵素　acetaldehyde dehydrogenase
乙醛[氧化]酶/乙醛[氧化]酶,乙醛酵素,醋醛酶　acetaldehydase
乙炔/乙炔,電石氣　acetylene
乙炔雌二醇/乙炔雌二醇　ethinyl estradiol
乙炔基/乙炔基　acetenyl
乙炔基睾酮/乙炔睾脂酮　ethinyl testosterone
乙酸-丙二酸途径/乙酸-丙二酸途徑　acetate-malonate pathway
乙酸钙/乙酸鈣　calcium acetate
乙酸甘油酯/醋酸甘油　acetin
乙酸[和]亚铁氰化钾试验/醋酸及亞鐵氰化鉀試驗　acetic acid and potassium ferrocyanide test
乙酸环丙孕酮/乙酸環丙孕酮,醋酸環孕酮　cyproterone acetate
乙酸激酶/乙酸激酶,乙醯酶　acetokinase
乙酸-甲瓦龙酸途径/乙酸-甲瓦龍酸途徑　acetate-mevalonate pathway
乙酸钾/乙酸鉀,醋酸鉀　potassium acetate
乙酸钠/乙酸鈉,醋酸鈉　sodium acetate
乙酸 dl-α-生育酚/乙酸 dl-α-生育酚　dl-α-tocopherol
乙酸试验/乙酸試驗,醋酸試驗　acetic acid test
乙酸锌/乙酸鋅,醋酸鋅　zinc acetate
乙酸盐类/乙酸鹽類　acetates
乙酸乙烯酯共聚物乳液/乙酸乙烯酯共聚物乳液　vinyl acetate copolymer emulsion

乙酸乙酯/醋酸乙酯　ethyl acetate
乙酸铀试法/乙酸鈾試法,醋酸鈾法　uranium acetate method
乙酮醇/乙酮醇　ketol
乙烷/乙烷　ethane
乙烯/乙烯　ethylene
乙烯化合物/乙烯化合物　vinyl compound
乙烯聚合体/乙烯聚合體,聚乙烯　polyvinyl
乙烯类/乙烯類　ethylenes
乙烯类聚合物/乙烯類聚合物　polyvinyls
乙烯硫脲/乙烯硫脲　ethylene thiourea
乙烯麻醉/乙烯麻醉　ethylene anesthesia
乙烯树脂/乙烯樹脂　vinyl resin
乙烯亚胺反应/乙烯亞胺反應　ethylene imine reaction
乙酰氨苯磺胺/乙醯氨苯磺胺　acetylsulfanilamide
乙酰氨基苯甲酸/乙醯胺基苯甲酸　acetylaminobenzoic acid
乙酰氨基酚/乙醯胺基酚　acetyl aminophenol
乙酰氨基葡糖苷酶/乙醯胺基葡糖苷酶　acetylglucosaminidase
乙酰胺/乙醯胺,醋醯胺　acetamide
乙酰百里香酚/乙醯百里香酚,乙醯麝香草酚　acetylthymol
乙酰半胱氨酸/乙醯半胱胺酸　acetylcysteine
N-乙酰半胱氨酸/N-乙醯半胱胺酸　N-acetylcysteine
N-乙酰-L-半胱氨酸/N-乙醯-L-半胱胺酸　N-acetyl-L-cysteine
乙酰半乳糖胺/乙醯半乳糖胺　acetylgalactosamine
乙酰胞壁酰-丙氨酰-异谷酰胺/乙醯胞壁醯-丙氨醯-異穀醯胺　acetylmuramyl-alanyl-isoglutamine
乙酰苯/乙醯苯　acetyl benzene
乙酰苯胺/乙醯苯胺　acetanilide
乙酰苯胺类/乙醯苯胺類　acetanilides
乙酰苯甲酰乌头原碱/乙醯苯甲醯烏頭原鹼　acetyl benzaconine
乙酰苯肼/乙醯苯肼　acetylphenylhydrazine
乙酰蓖麻油酸甘油酯/乙醯蓖麻油酸甘油酯　acetyl glyceryl ricinoleate
乙酰丙嗪/乙醯丙嗪　acepromazine
乙酰丙酸/乙醯丙酸　levulinic acid
乙酰胆碱/乙醯膽鹼　acetylcholine
乙酰胆碱心脏停搏/乙醯膽鹼心臟停搏　acetylcholine cardiac arrest
乙酰胆碱酯酶/乙醯膽鹼酯酶　acetylcholinesterase
乙酰胆碱酯酶抑制药/乙醯膽鹼酯酶抑制藥　acetylcholinesterase inhibitor

乙酰丁香酚/乙醯丁香酚　aceteugenol
乙酰辅酶 A/乙醯輔酶 A　acetylcoenzyme A
乙酰汞辛酚/乙醯汞辛酚　acetomeroctol
乙酰化羊毛脂醇/乙醯化羊毛脂醇　acetylated lanolin alcohol
乙酰化羊毛脂醇聚氧乙烯/乙醯化羊毛脂醇聚氧乙烯　acetylated polyoxyethylene lanolin alcohol
乙酰化作用/乙醯化[作用]　acetylization
乙酰磺胺胍/乙醯磺胺胍　acetylsulfaguanidine
乙酰磺胺嘧啶/乙醯磺胺嘧啶　acetylsulfadiazine
乙酰磺胺噻唑/乙醯磺胺噻唑　acetylsulfathiazole
乙酰磺胺异χ唑/乙醯磺胺異χ唑　acetyl sulfisioxazole
乙酰[基]/乙醯基　acetyl
乙酰基转移酶/乙醯[基轉移]酶　acetylase, acetyltransferase
乙酰基转移酶类/乙醯基轉移酶類　acetyltransferases
乙酰甲醇/乙醯甲醇　acetyl carbinol
乙酰甲胆碱/乙醯甲膽鹼,乙醯甲基膽素　methacholine
乙酰-β-甲基胆碱/乙醯-β-甲基膽素　acetyl-beta-methylcholine
乙酰甲基甲醇/甲基乙醯原醇　acetylmethyl carbinol
乙酰甲硫氨酸尿囊素/乙醯甲硫胺酸尿囊素　allantoin acetyl methionine
乙酰解[作用]/乙醯解[作用],乙醯分解作用　acetolysis
乙酰卡尼/乙醯卡尼　acecainide
乙酰 CoA 连接酶/乙醯 CoA 連接酶　acetate-CoA ligase
乙酰磷酸酶/乙醯磷酸酶,乙醯磷酸酯解酶　acetylphosphatase
乙酰磷酸盐/乙醯磷酸鹽　acetylphosphate
乙酰硫胆碱/乙醯硫膽鹼　acetylthiocholine
乙酰氯/乙醯氯,氯化乙醯基　acetyl chloride
乙酰毛地黄毒素/乙醯毛地黃毒素　acetyldigitoxin
乙酰没食子酚/乙醯没食子酚　acetpyrogall
乙酰柠檬酸三丁酯/乙醯檸檬酸三丁酯　acetyl tributyl citrate
乙酰葡萄糖胺/乙醯葡萄糖胺,乙醯胺基葡萄糖　acetylglucosamine
乙酰鞣酸/乙醯鞣酸　acetyltannin
乙酰肉毒碱/乙醯肉[毒]鹼　acetylcarnitine
乙酰乳酸合酶/乙醯乳酸合酶　acetolactate synthase
乙酰胂胺/乙醯胂胺,醋[阿]胂　acetphenarsine
乙酰 CoA 水解酶/乙醯 CoA 水解酶　acetyl-CoA hydrolase

乙酰水杨酸/乙醯水楊酸　acetylsalicylic acid
乙酰水杨酸苯酯/乙醯水楊酸苯酯　acetyl salol
乙酰 CoA 羧化酶/乙醯輔酶 A 羧化酶　acetyl-CoA carboxylase
乙酰纤维素粉/乙醯纖維素粉　acetyl cellulose powder
乙酰血清素 N-甲基转移酶/乙醯血清素 N-甲基轉移酶　acetylserotonin N-methyltransferase
乙酰羊毛脂/乙醯羊毛脂,乙醯化羊毛脂　acetylated lanolin
乙酰洋地黄毒苷类/乙醯洋地黃毒甙類　acetyldigitoxins
乙酰氧乙苯胺/乙醯氧乙苯胺　acetophenetidin
乙酰氧乙酰氨基芴/乙醯氧乙醯胺基芴　acetoxyacetylaminofluorene
乙酰乙酸/乙醯乙酸,酮醋酸　acetoacetic acid
乙酰乙酸尿/乙醯乙酸尿,酮醋酸尿　acetoacetic aciduria
乙酰乙酸血/乙醯乙酸血,酮醋酸血症　diacetemia
乙酰乙酸盐/乙醯乙酸鹽,酮醋酸鹽　diacetate
乙酰乙酸盐类/乙醯乙酸鹽類　acetoacetates
乙酰酯酶/乙醯酯酶　acetylesterase
乙酰唑胺/乙醯唑胺,醋唑磺胺　acetazolamide
乙型[病毒性]肝炎/乙型[病毒性]肝炎　viral hepatitis type B
乙型副伤寒菌性胃肠炎/乙型副傷寒菌性胃腸炎　gastroenteritis paratyphosa B
乙型肝炎表面抗原/乙型肝炎表面抗原　hepatitis B surface antigen
乙型肝炎病毒/乙型肝炎病毒　hepatitis B virus
乙型肝炎核心抗原/乙型肝炎核心抗原　hepatitis B core antigen
乙型肝炎抗体/乙型肝炎抗體　hepatitis B antibody
乙型肝炎抗原/乙型肝炎抗原　hepatitis B antigen
乙型肝炎 e 抗原/乙型肝炎 e 抗原　hepatitis B e-antigen
乙型肝炎免疫球蛋白/乙型肝炎免疫球蛋白,B 型肝炎免疫球蛋白　hepatitis B immunoglobulin
乙型肝炎相关性肾小球肾炎/乙型肝炎相關性腎小球腎炎　hepatitis B associated glomerulonephritis
乙型肝炎疫苗/乙型肝炎疫苗　hepatitis B vaccine
乙型上行性脊髓炎病毒/乙型上行性脊髓炎病毒　ascending myelitis B virus
乙型水解酶缺乏/乙型水解酶缺乏　β-hydroxylase deficiency
乙氧二羟丁酮/乙氧二羥丁酮　kethoxal
乙氧汞林/乙氧汞林　merethoxylline
乙氧基苯酸/乙氧基苯酸　ethoxybenzoic acid
乙氧喹/乙氧喹　ethoxyquin
乙状窦/乙狀竇　sigmoid sinus
乙状窦沟/乙狀竇溝　sigmoid sulcus, sulcus for sigmoid sinus
乙状窦后入路/乙狀竇後入路　retrosigmoid approach
乙状窦前入路/乙狀竇前入路　presigmoid approach
乙状结肠/乙狀結腸　sigmoid colon, sigmoid
乙状结肠动脉/乙狀結腸動脈　sigmoid artery
乙状结肠固定术/乙狀結腸固定術　romanopexy
乙状结肠疾病/乙狀結腸疾病　sigmoid disease
乙状结肠间疝/乙狀結腸間疝　intersigmoid hernia
乙状结肠间隐窝/乙狀結腸間隱窩　intersigmoid recess
乙状结肠结核/乙狀結腸結核　tuberculosis of sigmoid colon
乙状结肠静脉/乙狀結腸靜脈　sigmoid vein
乙状结肠镜/乙狀結腸鏡　sigmoidoscope
乙状结肠镜检查/乙狀結腸鏡檢查　sigmoidoscopy
乙状结肠淋巴结/乙狀結腸淋巴結　sigmoid lymph node
乙状结肠膀胱/乙狀結腸膀胱　sigmoid conduit
乙状结肠膀胱扩大术/乙狀結腸膀胱擴大術　sigmoid augmentation cystoplasty
乙状结肠切除术/乙狀結腸切除術　sigmoidectomy
乙状结肠切开术/乙狀結腸切開術　sigmoidotomy
乙状结肠系膜/乙狀結腸繫膜　sigmoid mesocolon, mesentery of sigmoid colon
乙状结肠系膜固定术/乙狀結腸繫膜固定術　mesosigmoidopexy
乙状结肠系膜炎/乙狀結腸繫膜炎　mesosigmoiditis
乙状结肠炎/乙狀結腸炎　sigmoiditis
乙状结肠乙状结肠吻合术/乙狀結腸乙狀結腸吻合術,乙狀結腸間造口術　sigmoidosigmoidostomy
乙状结肠造口术/乙狀結腸造口術　sigmoidostomy
乙状结肠直肠造口术/乙狀結腸直腸吻合術　sigmoidoproctostomy
乙状结肠肿瘤/乙狀結腸腫瘤　sigmoid neoplasm
乙状结肠周炎/乙狀結腸周圍炎　perisigmoiditis
已溶血/已溶血,洩色血　laky blood
已修正主模型/已修正主模型　altered master cast
以病治病法/以病治病法　nosotherapy
以偏纠偏/以偏糾偏　emotional therapy corresponding with five elements
以情胜情/以情勝情　emotionally checking therapy
以情胜情疗法/以情勝情療法　emotionally checking therapy
以色列放线菌/以色列放線菌　Actinomyces israelii

以诈治诈/以詐治詐　treating feigned illness with a feigned method
钇放射性同位素/釔放射性同位素　yttrium radioisotope
钇铝石榴子石激光疗法/釔鋁石榴子石雷射療法　yttrium aluminum garnet laser therapy
钇同位素/釔同位素　yttrium isotope
蚁毒液类/蟻毒液類　ant venoms
蚁咬[皮]病/蟻咬[皮]症,蟻中毒　formiciasis
蚁蜇伤/蟻螫傷　ant sting
蚁走感/蟻走感,蟻行感　formication
蚁走感征/蟻走感徵象,泰諾氏徵象　formication sign
椅式/椅型　chair form
酏剂/酏劑　elixir
义齿/義齒,假牙　denture, trial denture
义齿边缘/義齒邊緣　denture border
义齿衬底/義齒襯底,托牙墊底術　denture rebasing
义齿衬垫材料/義齒襯墊材料　denture liner
义齿承托区/義齒承托區,假牙支撐區　denture-bearing area
义齿固位/義齒固位,假牙位置保留　denture retention
义齿基托/義齒基托　denture base
义齿基托美学/義齒基托美學　denture base aesthetics
义齿技师/義齒技師　denturist
义齿精密附着体/義齒精密附著體　denture precision attachment
义齿美学/義齒美學　denture aesthetics
义齿黏附剂/義齒黏附劑,假牙黏著物　denture adhesive
义齿清洁剂/義齒清潔劑　denture cleanser
义齿热处理/義齒熱處理　processing of denture
义齿设计/義齒設計　denture design
义齿识别标志/義齒識別標志　denture identification marking
义齿填塞/義齒填塞　denture packing
义齿吸附作用/義齒吸附作用　denture adsorption
义齿型盒/義齒型盒,牙托鑄型盒　denture flask
义齿性口腔痛/義齒性口腔痛,托牙口瘡　denture sore mouth
义齿性口炎/義齒性口炎,全口假牙性口角炎　denture stomatitis
义齿性增生/義齒性增生,齒列肥大　denture hypertrophy
义齿修补/義齒修補　denture repair
义齿修复术/義齒修復術,補綴術,贋複術　prosthodontics
义颌/義頜　surgical prosthesis
义眼/義眼,假眼　ocular prosthesis
艺术解剖学/藝術解剖學　artistic anatomy
艺术疗法/藝術療法　art therapy
艺术中医学/藝術中醫學　medicine in art
异倍体/異倍體　heteroploid
异倍性/異倍性,染色體異數性　heteroploidy
异丙巴比妥/異丙巴比妥　probarbital
异丙醇/異丙醇　isopropanol
异丙醇-氮-对苯次酚基二铵/異丙醇-氮-對苯次酚基二銨　isopropyl-n-phenyl-p-phenylenediamine
异丙氟磷/[異]丙氟磷　diisopropyl fluorophosphate
异丙氟磷溶液/異丙氟磷溶液,氟磷酸二異丙脂溶液　diisopropyl fluorophosphate solution
异丙基/異丙基　isopropyl
异丙基肾上腺素/異丙基腎上腺素　isoproterenol
异丙硫半乳糖苷/異丙硫半乳糖苷　isopropyl thiogalactoside
异丙嗪/異丙嗪　promethazine
异丙肾上腺素/異丙[去甲]腎上腺素　isoprenaline
异丙托铵/異丙托銨　ipratropium
异丙硝唑/異丙硝唑　ipronidazole
异丙烟肼/異丙煙肼,異煙鹼異丙醯膽　iproniazid
异病同治/異病同治　treating different diseases with the same method
异步起搏器/異步起搏器,心臟非同步起搏器　asynchronous pacemaker
异步型房室顺序起搏/異步型房室順序起搏,非同步型房室順序起搏　asynchronous atrioventricular sequential pacing
异侧感觉/異側感覺　allochiria
异侧两性畸形/異側兩性畸形,半身半陰陽,中分性半陰陽　dimidiate hermaphroditism
异侧偏盲/異側偏盲　heteronymous hemianopsia
异侧细胞/異側細胞,異質細胞　heteromeral cell
异常/異常　abnormal, abnormality, anomaly
异常𬌗/異常𬌗,咬合異常　abnormal occlusion
异常丙种球蛋白血症/異常丙種球蛋白血症,血中伽馬球蛋白異常　dysgammaglobulinemia
异常搏动/異常搏動,異常脈動　anomalous beat
异常蛋白血症紫癜/異常蛋白血症紫癜　purpura dysproteinemia
异常毒性/異常毒性　undue toxicity
异常反射/異常反射　abnormal reflex
异常复合波/異常複合波,反常複合波　anomalous complex
异常构造/異常構造　anomalous structure

异常汉森酵母/異常漢遜酵母　Hansenula anomala
异常红细胞/異常紅細胞　abnormal erythrocyte
异常欢乐/異常歡樂,快樂狂　hedonia
异常寄生物/異常寄生物　xenoparasite
异常危象/異常危象,異常劇變期　heterocrisis
异常纤维蛋白原类/異常纖維蛋白原類　abnormal fibrinogen
异常纤维蛋白原血症/異常纖維蛋白原血症,血纖維蛋白原異常　dysfibrinogenemia
异常血红蛋白病/異常血紅蛋白病　abnormal hemoglobinopathy
异常血红蛋白类/異常血紅蛋白類　abnormal hemoglobins
异常牙尖间殆/異常牙尖間殆,上下齒咬合不良　malinterdigitation
异常荧光/異常螢光　abnormal fluorescence
异臭/異臭　foreign odor
异处感觉/異處感[受觸]覺　allochesthesia
异处性畸胎瘤/異處性畸胎瘤　heterochthonous teratoma
异刺皮螨属/異刺皮蟎屬　Allodermanyssus
异翠雀碱/異翠雀鹼,飛燕草素同質異構物　delphisine
异等位基因/異等位基因　heteroallele
异狄氏剂/異狄氏劑　endrin
异淀粉酶/異澱粉酶　isoamylase
异丁醇/異丁醇　isobutanol
异丁芬酸/異丁芬酸,對異丁苯基醋酸　ibufenac
异丁嗪/異丁嗪　trimeprazine
异丁酸/異丁酸,異酪酸　isobutyric acid
异东莨菪醇/異東莨菪醇　oscine
异噁唑类/異噁唑類　isoxazoles
异酚处理法/異酚使用法　isophenolization
异氟磷/異氟磷,氟磷酸異丙酯　isoflurophate
异氟醚/異氟醚,異氟甲氧氟烷　isoflurane
异构化/異構化　isomerization
异构酶类/異構酶類　isomerases
异构现象/異構現象,同質異構,同質異性　isomerism
异固缩/異固縮　heteropyknosis
异国语言涩滞/異國語言澀滯,外語發音困難　barbaralalia
异核黄素/異[構]核黃素,異乳黃素　isoriboflavin
异核体/異核體　heterokaryon
异化能量消耗/異化能量消耗　catabolergy
异化[作用]/異化[作用]　disassimilation
异环磷酰胺/異環磷醯胺　ifosfamide
异黄酮/異黃酮　isoflavone

异黄酮类/異黃酮類　isoflavones
异黄烷酮/異黃烷酮　isoflavanone
异肌酸酐/異肌[胺]酸酐　isocreatinine
异基因骨髓移植/異基因骨髓移植　allogeneic bone marrow transplantation
异己酮/異己酮　hexone
异尖线虫病/異尖線蟲病　anisakiasis
异经取穴/異經取穴　point selection on related channels, point selection on related meridians
异腈化苯/異腈化苯　phenyl isocyanide
异卡波肼/異卡波肼　isocarboxazid
异康唑/異康唑　isoconazole
异抗坏血酸/異抗壞血酸　erythorbic acid
异克舒令/異克舒林　isoxsuprine
异喹胍/異喹胍　debrisoquin
异喹啉类/異喹啉類　isoquinolines
异喹啉生物碱/異喹啉生物鹼　isoquinoline alkaloid
异亮氨酸/異亮胺酸,異白胺酸　isoleucine
异亮氨酸 tRNA 连接酶/異亮氨酸 tRNA 連接酶　isoleucine-tRNA ligase
异硫氰酸/異硫氰酸　isosulfocyanic acid
异硫氰酸丁酯/異硫氰酸丁酯　butyl isothiocyanate
异硫氰酸盐/異硫氰酸鹽　isothiocyanate
异硫氰酸荧光素/異硫氰酸螢光素　fluorescein isothiocyanate, FITC
异马烯雌[甾]酮/異馬烯雌酮　hippulin
异麦芽糖/異麥芽糖　isomaltose
异柠檬酸/異檸檬酸　isocitric acid
异柠檬酸裂合酶/異檸檬酸裂合酶　isocitrate lyase
异柠檬酸脱氢酶/異檸檬酸脫氫酶　isocitrate dehydrogenase
异柠檬酸盐类/異檸檬酸鹽類　isocitrates
异配生殖/異配生殖,異形配子結合　anisogamy
异期复孕/異期複孕,重複受孕　superfetation
异前列腺素/異前列腺素　isoprostanes
异氰化乙酰/異氰化乙醯,乙醯異腈　acetyl isocyanide
异氰酸盐类/異氰酸鹽類　isocyanates
异氰酸荧光素/異氰酸螢光素　fluorescein isocyanate
异炔诺酮/異炔諾酮,烴炔諾酮　norethynodrel
异染[颗]粒/異染[顆]粒,異染小粒　metachromatic granule
异染色体/異染色體　heterochromosome
异染色质/異染色質　heterochromatin
异染性/異染性,變色反應性　metachromasia
异染性脑白质病/異染性腦白質病　metachromatic leukoencephalopathy
异染性脑白质营养不良/異染性腦白質營養不良症

metachromatic leukodystrophy
异乳糖/異乳糖　allolactose
异色[性]/異色　heterochromia
异色性虹膜睫状体炎/異色虹膜睫狀體炎　heterochromic iridocyclitis
异色性皮肌炎/異色性皮肌炎,皮膚異色病　poikilodermatomyositis
异色异构[现象]/同質異色異構物　chromoisomerism
异山梨酯/異山梨酯　isosorbide
异肾上腺素/甲基去甲腎上腺素　nordefrin
异生物质/異生物質　xenobiotics
异时性节律/異時性節律　metachronous rhythm
异食癖/異食癖,嗜異癖　pica
异嗜白细胞/異嗜白細胞　heterophil
异丝氨酸/異構絲胺基酸　isoserine
异锁链赖氨素/異鎖鏈賴胺素　isodesmosine
异糖质酸/異葡萄酸　isosaccharic acid
异体骨成形术/異種骨成形術,異種骨移植術　hetero-osteoplasty
异体接种/異種疫苗接種　heteroinoculation
异体皮肤的/異體皮膚的　heterodermic
异体皮移植片/異體皮移植物　heterodermic graft
异体受精/交互受精　cross fertilization
异体血清疗法/異體血清療法　heteroserotherapy
异体移植[术]/異體移植[法]　heteroplastic transplantation, allotransplantation
异体移植物/異體移植物　heterologous graft
异体移植细胞毒性/異體移植細胞毒性　allograft cytotoxity
异天冬氨酸/異天冬胺酸　isoaspartic acid
异头物/異頭物　anomer
异[吞]噬体/異噬體,異體吞噬泡　heterophagosome
异维 A 酸/異維 A 酸　isotretinoin
异尾类/異尾類　anomura
异位/異位　dystopia
异位搏动/異位搏動,額外搏動,異位脈動　ectopic beat
异位促性腺素综合征/異位促性腺素症候群　ectopic gonadotropin syndrome
异位的/異位的　atopic, ectopic
异位房性心动过速/異位房性心動過速　ectopic atrial tachycardia
异位肺叶/異位肺葉　ectopic lung lobe
异位肝移植/異位肝移植　heterotopic liver transplantation
异位感觉/異處感覺　allesthesia
异位肛门/異位肛門　preternatural anus

异位睾丸/異位睾丸　ectopic testis
异位骨/異位骨　heterotopic bone
异位回肠阴道肛门/異位迴腸陰道肛門　preternatural ileovaginal anus
异位基底细胞癌/異位基底細胞癌　aberrant basal cell carcinoma
异位激素类/異位激素類　ectopic hormones
异位激素综合征/異位激素症候群　ectopic hormone syndrome
异位甲/異位甲　ectopic nail
异位甲状旁腺/異位甲狀旁腺,異位副甲狀腺　ectopic parathyroid gland
异位甲状旁腺功能亢进症/異位甲狀旁腺功能亢進症　ectopic hyperparathyroidism
异位甲状腺/異位甲狀腺　ectopic thyroid gland, aberrant thyroid
异位甲状腺组织/異位甲狀腺組織　eccyesis thyroid tissue
异位交界性心动过速/異位交界性心動過速　ectopic junctional tachycardia
异位节律/異位節律　ectopic rhythm
异位泌乳/異位泌乳　galactometastasis
异位膜/異位膜　adventitious membrane
异位排尿/異地洩尿症　planuria
异位皮脂腺/異位皮脂腺　ectopic sebaceous gland
异位起搏点/異位起搏點　ectopic pacemaker
异位妊娠/異位妊娠,[子]宫外孕　ectopic pregnancy, eccyesis
异位妊娠·包块型/異位妊娠·包塊型　ectopic pregnancy with mass formation
异位妊娠·不稳定型/異位妊娠·不穩定型　unstable ectopic pregnancy
异位妊娠·未破损期/異位妊娠·未破損期　non-rupture stage of ectopic pregnancy
异位妊娠·休克型/異位妊娠·休克型　ectopic pregnancy with shock
异位妊娠·已破损期/異位妊娠·已破損期　rupture stage of ectopic pregnancy
异位肾/異位腎　ectopic kidney
异位输尿管/輸尿管異位　ectopic ureter
异位胎切除术/異位妊娠切開術,子宮外妊娠切開術　ectopotomy
异位痛/異位痛　heterotopic pain
异位痛经/補償性痛經,異位性痛經　vicarious dysmenorrhea
异位涎腺/異位涎腺　heterotopic salivary gland
异位小肠移植/異位小肠移植　heterotopic small intestine transplantation

异位心/異位心　ectocardia
异位心脏移植/異位心臟移植　heterotopic cardiac transplantation
异位性骨化/異位骨化　heterotopic ossification
异位性骨髓组织生成/異位性骨髓組織生成　ectopic myelopoiesis
异位性黑变病/異位性黑變症　ectopic melanosis
异位性蒙古斑/異位性蒙古斑　aberrant Mongolian spot
异位性痛风/異位性痛風　retrocedent gout
异位性心动过速/異位性心搏快速　ectopic tachycardia
异位牙/異位齒,錯位齒　malposed tooth
异位牙萌出/異位牙萌出　ectopic tooth eruption
异位胰腺移植/異位胰腺移植　heterotopic pancreas transplantation
异位胰组织/異位性胰組織　heterotopic pancreatic tissue
异位移植/異位移植法　heterotopic transplantation
异位移植物/異位移植物　heterotopic graft
异位阴道肛门/異位陰道肛門　preternatural vaginal anus
异位植入/異位植入　ectopic implantation
异位 ACTH 综合征/異位 ACTH 症候群　ectopic ACTH syndrome
异位 ADH 综合征/異位 ADH 症候群　ectopic ADH syndrome
异温[现象]/異溫現象,體溫調變　heterothermy
异戊胺/異戊胺　isoamylamine
异戊巴比妥/異戊巴比妥　amobarbital
异戊醇/異戊醇　isoamyl alcohol
异戊二烯/異戊二烯　isoprene
异戊酸/異戊酸,異纈草酸　isovaleric acid
异戊酸血[症]/異戊酸血症　isovaleric acidemia
异戊烯腺苷/異戊烯腺苷　isopentenyl adenosine
异物/異物　foreign body
异物反应/異物反應　foreign body reaction
异物感/異物感　foreign body sensation
异物梗喉/異物梗喉　laryngeal foreign body
异物巨细胞/異物巨細胞　foreign body giant cell
异物肉芽肿/異物肉芽腫　foreign body granuloma
异物入耳/耳内異物　foreign body in ear
异物入目/異物入目　foreign body entering eye, foreign body in eye
异物入目·睛伤邪侵证/異物入目·睛傷邪侵證　foreign body entering eye with pattern of eye trauma with pathogen invasion
异物入目·睛伤邪盛证/異物入目·睛傷邪盛證　foreign body entering eye with pattern of eye trauma with pathogen excessiveness
异物性阑尾炎/異物性闌尾炎　foreign body appendicitis
异物性铁质沉着/異物性鐵質沈著　xenogenous siderosis
异物性眼炎/異物性眼炎　xenophthalmia
异物游走/異物遊走　foreign body migration
异物针/異物針　foreign body needle
异物周炎/異物周炎　perialienitis
异纤维二糖/異木纖維糖　isocellobiose
异向性病毒/異向性病毒　xenotropic virus
异形孢子/異形孢子　heterospore
异形成红细胞/異形母紅血球　poikiloblast
异形发育/異形發育,發育錯誤　heterometaplasia
异形骨/異形骨　os irregulare
异形红细胞/異形紅血球　poikilocyte
异形红细胞症/異形紅血球症　poikilocythemia
异形配子/異形配子　anisogamete
异形吸虫病/異形吸蟲病　heterophyiasis
异形吸虫属/異形吸蟲屬　*Heterophyes*
异形血小板/異形血小板　poikiloplastocyte
异形异形吸虫/異形異形吸蟲　Heterophyes heterophyes
异型/異型種　xenotype
异型溶酶体/異溶酶體　heterolysosome
异型细胞形成/異形細胞形成　poikilocarynosis
异性恋/異體性欲　heterosexuality
异性性早熟/異性性早熟　heterosexual precocious puberty
异性装扮癖/異性衣装癖　eonism
异雄甾酮/異構雄酮　isoandrosterone
异烟肼/異煙肼　isoniazid
异烟肼神经[炎]病变/異煙酸神經病變　isoniazid neuropathy
异烟酸/異煙鹼酸　isonicotinic acid
异养生物/異養生物,非自養生物　heterotroph
异硬脂酸铝/異硬脂酸鋁　aluminium isostearate
异硬脂酸鲨鱼肝油酯/異硬脂酸鯊魚肝油酯　batyl isostearate
异源倍体/異源倍體　alloploid
异源倍性/異源倍性　alloploidy
异源多倍体/異源多倍體　allopolyploid
异源多倍性/異源多倍性　allopolyploidy
异源二倍体/有兩組異種染色體　allodiploid
异源二倍性/有兩組異種染色體的狀態　allodiploidy
异源三聚体 GTP 结合蛋白质类/異源三聚體 GTP 結合蛋白質類　heterotrimeric GTP-binding

proteins
异源双链分析/異源雙鏈分析　heteroduplex analysis
异源四倍体/異質四倍體　allotetraploid
异源体/異質漿粒群，異質移植物　alloplast
异支吻合术/異支吻合術　heterocladic anastomosis
异质肠石/異質腸石　heterolith
异质角膜成形术/人工角膜修補術　allokeratoplasty
异质节律/異地節律　heterogenetic rhythm
异质同晶异构/異質同晶之化合物　allodesmism
异质性抗原/異質性抗原　heterogenic antigen
异质[原]性/異質性，不均匀性，多相性　heterogeneity
异种补体/異種補體　heterocomplement
异种材料心脏瓣膜/異種材料心臟瓣膜　xenograft heart valve
异种刺激/異種刺激，異質刺激法，異種抗原刺激法　heterologous stimulus
异种蛋白/異性蛋白　foreign protein
异种的/異質的，異源的　heterogenetic, heterologous
异种动物/異種動物　outbred strains animal
异种肺氧合/異種肺氧合　heterologous lung oxygenation
异种过敏反应/異種過敏性　heterologous anaphylaxis
异种菌苗疗法/異種疫苗療法　heterovaccine therapy
异种抗体/異種抗體　heteroantibody
异种抗原/異種抗原　heteroantigen
异种免疫/異種免疫　heteroimmunity
异种免疫质/異種免疫質　heteroimmune substance
异种凝集反应/異種凝集　heteroagglutination
异种凝集素/異種凝集素　heteroagglutinin
异种皮肤移植/異體皮成形術，異體補皮術，異體皮膚修補術　dermatoheteroplasty
异种气管置换术/異種氣管置換術　tracheal heterograft replacement
异种溶解/異種溶解　heterolysis
异种溶素/異種溶素　heterolysin
异种溶血素/異種溶血素　heterohemolysin
异种特异性/異種特異性　heterospecific
异种细胞毒素/異種細胞毒素　heterocytotoxin
异种细胞溶素/異種溶細胞素　heterocytolysin
异种心脏瓣膜/異種心臟瓣膜　heterologous cardiac valve
异种血清/異種血清　heterologous serum
异种牙移植术/異種牙移植術　allogenic tooth transplantation
异种胰蛋白酶/殊胰蛋白酶　heterotrypsin
异种移植/異種形成移植物　xenoplastic graft
异种移植的/異種移植的　heteroplastic
异种移植模型抗肿瘤试验/異種移植模型抗腫瘤試驗　xenograft model antitumor assay
异种移植物/異種移植物　heteroplastic graft
异种疫苗/異種疫苗　heterologous vaccine
异种组织/異種組織　heteroplasm
异株/異株　heterologous strain
抑癌基因/抑癌基因　antioncogene
抑菌剂/抑菌劑　bacteriostatic agent
抑菌圈/抑菌圈　inhibition zone
抑菌性抗生素/抑菌性抗生藥　bacteriostatic antibiotic
抑情顺理疗法/抑情順理療法　emotion and cognition regulating therapy
抑球虫剂/抑球蟲劑　coccidiostatic
抑素/抑素　chalone
抑肽酶/抗蛋白酶酞　aprotinin
抑郁/抑鬱　depression of spirit
抑郁性/抑鬱的　depressive
抑郁性幻觉/抑鬱性幻覺　depressive hallucination
抑郁性木僵[症]/抑鬱性木僵　depressive stupor
抑郁性神经病/抑鬱性精神病　depressive psychosis
抑郁性神经症/憂鬱性精神官能症　depressive neurosis
抑郁性妄想/抑鬱妄想　depressive delusion
抑郁性谵妄/抑鬱性譫妄　delirium depressivum
抑郁状态/抑鬱狀態　depressive state
抑郁自评量表/抑鬱自評量表　self-rating depressive scale
抑郁综合征/憂鬱症候群　depressive syndrome
抑制/抑制　depression, inhibition, suppression
抑制肠蠕动药/便秘劑　costive
抑制带/阻礙區　inhibition zone
抑制蛋白/抑制蛋白　arrestin
抑制放射变应原吸附试验/抑制放射性過敏原吸附試驗　radioallergosorbent test inhibition, RAST inhibition
抑制基因/抑制基因　suppressor gene
抑制剂/抑制劑　inhibitor
抑制扩散/抑制照射　irradiation of inhibition
抑制倾向者/抑制傾向者　inhibitrope
抑制韧带/抑制韌帶　check ligament
抑制神经/抑制神經　inhibitory nerve
抑制素/抑制素　inhibin
抑制物缺乏学说/抑制物缺乏學說　theory of insufficient inhibitor
抑制细胞/抑制細胞　suppressor cell
抑制细胞活性/抑制細胞活性　cytostatic activity

抑制型起搏/抑制型起搏　inhibited pacing
抑制性T[淋巴]细胞/抑制性T[淋巴]細胞　suppressor T cell
抑制性突触/抑制性突觸　inhibitory synapse
抑制药/抑制藥　depressant
抑制真菌剂/黴菌抑制劑　fungistat
抑制中枢/抑制中樞　inhibitory center
抑制状态/抑制狀態　inhibitory state
呓语性失语/亂語性失語症　gibberish aphasia
呓语性书写不能/囈語性書寫不能　jargon agraphia
呓语性谵妄/囈語性譫妄　lingual delirium
易饱症/易飽症,飽感過早　hypercoria
易感人群/易感人群,易感者　susceptible
易感性/易感性　munity
易寒易热/易寒易熱　vulnerable to manifestation of heat and cold
易化技术/易化技術　facilitation technique
易化扩散/促進性擴散　facilitate diffusion
易化转运/促進性輸送　facilitory transport
易患基因/易患基因　susceptibility gene
易患性/易患性　liability
易黄汤/易黄湯　yihuang decoction
易激惹/興奮增盛,過敏　irritability
易筋经/易筋經　Changing Tendon Exercise, Muscle-Tendon Strengthening Exercise
易惊醒/易驚醒　troubled sleep
易扪主动脉/觸知性主動脈　palpable aorta
易疲[劳]性/易疲性　fatigability
易燃物/易燃物　inflammable
易染质/易染質　chromophil substance
易溶胶质/易溶膠質　lyotropic colloid
易伤人群/易傷人群　vulnerable population
易碳化物/易碳化物質　readily carbonizable substance
易位/易位　translocation
易位温度计/移動性溫度計　metastatic thermometer
易消化膳食/輕淡食物　light diet
易性转化癖/變性欲癖　transsexualism
易性装扮癖/喜好穿奇装異服之變態　transvestism
易虚易实/易虛易實　vulnerable to manifestation of deficiency and excess
易氧化物/易氧化物質　readily oxidizable substance
易装癖/易裝癖,衣裝倒錯症,異性裝扮　cross dressing
疫病/疫病　pestilential disease
疫疔/疫疔　cutaneous anthrax
疫疔·疫毒蕴结证/疫疔·疫毒蘊結證　cutaneous anthrax with pestilent toxin amassment pattern
疫毒痢/疫[毒]痢,奇恆痢　fulminant dysentery
疫毒内闭证/疫毒內閉證　pattern of blockage of the interior by pestilential toxin, pattern of epidemic toxin blocked internally
疫毒侵袭证/疫毒侵襲證　pattern of epidemic toxin invasion
疫喉/疫喉　pestilent throat
疫痉/疫痙　pestilence with convulsion
疫厥/疫厥　pestilence with syncope
疫痢/疫痢　ekiri
疫苗/疫苗　vaccine
疫苗接种后脑脊髓炎/疫苗接種後腦脊髓炎　postvaccinal encephalomyelitis
疫源探查者/菌媒學家　phorologist
疫疹/疫疹　pestilence with petechiae
疫疹·风热伤络证/疫疹·風熱傷絡證　pestilence with petechiae with pattern of wind-heat injuring collaterals
疫疹·气营两燔证/疫疹·氣營兩燔證　pestilence with petechiae with pattern of blazing heat in both qi and nutrient phases
疫疹·热迫营血证/疫疹·熱迫營血證　pestilence with petechiae with pattern of toxin entering nutrient and blood phases
疫疹·卫气同病证/疫疹·衛氣同病證　pestilence with petechiae with pattern of involving both defense and qi phases
疫疹·邪犯肝心证/疫疹·邪犯肝心證　pestilence with petechiae with pattern of pathogen invading liver and heart
疫疹·邪阻膜原证/疫疹·邪阻膜原證　pestilence with petechiae with pattern of pathogen blocking pleuro-diaphragmatic interspace
疫疹·血热妄行证/疫疹·血熱妄行證　pestilence with petechiae with pattern of bleeding due to blood heat
疫疹·余邪未净证/疫疹·餘邪未淨證　pestilence with petechiae with pattern of lingering remnant pathogen
疫疹·正气暴脱证/疫疹·正氣暴脫證　pestilence with petechiae with pattern of sudden collapse of vital qi
益火消阴/益火消陰　boosting source of fire for eliminating abundance of yin
益母草/益母草　motherwort herb
益母草膏/益母草膏　yimucao paste
益气/益氣　benefiting qi, benefiting vital energy
益气安神/益氣安神　benefiting qi and tranquilizing

the mind, benefiting qi for tranquillization
益气固表/益氣固表　invigorating qi for consolidating exterior
益气活血/益氣活血　benefiting qi for activating blood circulation
益气解表/益氣解表　benefiting qi for relieving exterior pattern
益气摄精/益氣攝精　benefiting qi for consolidating semen
益气生肌/益氣生肌　benefiting qi for promoting granulation
益气生津/益氣生津　benefiting qi for promoting production of fluid, benefiting vital energy and promoting the production of body fluid
益气生血/益氣生血　benefiting qi for promoting production of blood
益气养血法/益氣養血法　replenishing qi and nourishing blood
益气滋阴/益氣滋陰　benefiting qi and nourishing yin
益胃/益胃　benefiting the stomach
益胃汤/益胃湯　yiwei decoction
益元散/益元散　yiyuan powder
益智药/益智藥　nootropic
逸搏/逃脱脈動　escape beat
逸搏心律/逸脱節律　escape rhythm
意/意　idea, intention
意大利式鼻成形术/義大利式補鼻術　Italian rhinoplasty
意大利式手术/義大利手術　Italian operation
意联/意聯　punning
意疗/意療　byname for psychological therapy
意念/意念　awareness
意念性动作的/意想性運動的　ideokinetic
意念性疼痛/想像痛　ideogenous pain
意舍/意舍　yishe, BL49
意识/意識　consciousness
意识错乱/精神混亂　confusion
意识混浊/意識混濁　clouding of consciousness
意识丧失/神志喪失, 人事不省, 無知覺　unconsciousness
意识域/意識界　field of consciousness
意识运动性失用症/意想運動性失用症　ideomotor apraxia
意识障碍/意識障礙　consciousness disorder
意守/意守　keep the mind on
意外出血/意外出血　accidental hemorrhage
意外的/意外的　accidentally
意外跌倒/意外跌倒　accidental fall
意外流产/意外流産　accidental abortion
意外妊娠/意外妊娠　unplanned pregnancy
意外事故/意外事故　accident
意外事故保险/意外傷害保險　accident insurance
意外性痘/意外痘　accidental vaccinia
意外性纹身/意外性紋身　accidental tattoo
意想性的/意想的　ideogenous
意想性运动的/精神性運動的　ideomotor
意向倒错/意志顛倒　parabulia
意向性痉挛/意向性痙攣　intention spasm
意向性震颤/意向性震顫　intentional tremor
意志/意志　will, volition
意志过强/意志過強, 意志高強　hyperbulia
意志缺失/意志缺失　aboulia
意志缺失狂/意志缺失狂　aboulomania
溢出/溢出, 溢流　overflow
溢出物/溢出物　effluvium
溢出性蛋白尿/溢出性蛋白尿　overflow proteinuria
溢出性糖尿病/溢出性糖尿病　overflow diabetes
溢饮/溢飲　anasarcous fluid retention
薏苡仁/薏苡仁　coix seed
薏苡属/薏苡屬　*Coix*
翳/翳　lens opacity
翳风/翳風　yifeng, SJ17
翳明/翳明　yiming, EX-HN14
翼/翼　ala
翼凹/翼狀凹　pterygoid depression
翼板/翼板　alar plate
翼部/翼部　alar part, dilatator naris
翼点/翼點, 翼穴　pterion
翼点入路/翼點入路　pterion approach
翼蝶骨/蝶翼骨　alisphenoid bone
翼腭沟/翼腭溝　pterygopalatal groove
翼腭管注射法/翼腭管注射法　pterygopalatine canal injection
翼腭裂/翼腭間裂隙　fissura pterygopalatina
翼腭神经节/翼腭神經節　pterygopalatine ganglion
翼腭神经节副交感根/翼腭神經節副交感根　parasympathetic root of pterygopalatine ganglion
翼腭神经节感觉根/翼腭神經節感覺根　sensory root of pterygopalatine ganglion
翼腭神经节交感根/翼腭神經節交感根　sympathetic root of pterygopalatine ganglion
翼腭神经节眶支/翼腭神經節眶支　orbital branch of pterygopalatine ganglion
翼腭窝/翼腭凹　pterygopalatine fossa
翼腭窝综合征/翼腭窩症候群　pterygopalatine fossa syndrome

翼方软骨/翼方軟骨　pterygoquadrate cartilage
翼钩/翼突鉤　pterygoid hamulus
翼钩沟/翼鉤溝　sulcus of pterygoid hamulus
翼骨/翼骨　pterygoid bone
翼管/翼管　pterygoid canal
翼管动脉/翼管動脈,威迪恩氏動脈　artery of pterygoid canal
翼管静脉/翼管靜脈　vein of pterygoid canal
翼管神经/翼管神經　nerve of pterygoid canal
翼管神经丛/翼管神經叢,威迪恩氏叢　Vidian plexus
翼管神经切除术/翼管神經切除術　Vidian neurectomy
翼管神经痛/翼管神經痛　Vidian neuralgia
翼管支/翼管支　branch of pterygoid canal
翼肌凹/翼肌凹　pterygoid fovea
翼肌粗隆/翼肌粗隆　pterygoid tuberosity
翼肌支/翼支　pterygoid branch
翼棘肌/翼棘肌　pterygospinous muscle
翼棘韧带/翼棘韌帶　pterygospinous ligament
翼棘突/翼棘突　pterygospinous process
翼静脉丛/翼靜脈叢　pterygoid venous plexus
翼内肌/翼内[側]肌　medial pterygoid muscle
翼内肌神经/翼内肌神經　medial pterygoid nerve
翼内肌神经交通支/翼内肌神經交通支　communicating branch with medial pterygoid nerve
翼内神经/翼内神經　internal pterygoid nerve
翼切迹/翼切跡　pterygoid fissure, pterygoid notch, fissura pterygoidea
翼上骨/翼上骨　epipteric bone
翼上颌间裂隙/翼上頜間裂隙　fissura pterygomaxillaris
翼上颌裂/翼上頜裂　pterygomaxillary fissure
翼上颌韧带/翼上頜韌帶　pterygomaxillary ligament
翼上颌延伸种植体/翼上頜延伸種植體　maxillary pterygoid extension implant
翼神经/翼神經　pterygopalatine nerve
翼突/翼突　pterygoid process
翼突钩/翼突鉤　pterygoid hamulus
翼突钩沟/翼鉤溝　hamular groove
翼突脑膜动脉/翼突腦膜動脈　pterygomeningeal artery
翼突内侧板/翼突内側板　medial pterygoid plate
翼突外侧板/翼突外側板　lateral pterygoid plate
翼突下颌缝/翼突下頜縫　pterygomandibular raphe
翼外侧肌/翼外側肌　musculus pterygoideus lateralis
翼外肌/翼外肌　lateral pterygoid
翼外肌神经/翼外肌神經　lateral pterygoid nerve
翼窝/翼突窩　pterygoid fossa
翼下颌间隙/翼下頜間隙　pterygomandibular space
翼下颌韧带/翼下頜韌帶　pterygomandibular ligament
翼下颌注射法/翼下頜注射法　pterygomandibular injection
翼咽部/翼咽部　pterygopharyngeal part
翼咽肌/翼咽肌　pterygopharyngeal muscle
翼缘区/翼緣區　flange area
翼状板翼腭沟/翼狀板翼腭溝　pterygopalatine groove of pterygoid plate
翼状襞/翼狀[皺]襞　alar fold
翼状层/翼狀層　pterygoid lamina
翼状导管/附翼導管　winged catheter
翼状的/翼狀的　pterygoid
翼状肌/翼狀肌　pterygoid muscle
翼状肩胛[骨]/翼狀肩胛　alar scapula
翼状胬肉/翼狀胬肉　pterygium
翼状胬肉切除术/翼狀胬肉切除術　excision of pterygium
翼状胬肉转位术/翼狀胬肉轉位術　pterygium transplantation
翼状韧带/翼狀韌帶　alar ligament
翼状细胞/翼狀細胞　wing cell
癔病的/癔病的　hysterical
癔病患者/癔病患者　hysteric
癔病脊髓痨/癔病脊髓痨　hysterotabetism
癔病尿/癔病尿　hysterical urine
癔病性半侧舌唇痉挛/癔病性舌唇單側痙攣　hysterical glossolabial hemispasm
癔病性感觉缺失/癔病性感覺缺失　hysterical anesthesia
癔病性共济失调/癔病性運動失調　hysteric ataxia
癔病性关节痛/癔病性關節痛　hysterical arthralgia
癔病性肌痛/癔病性肌痛　hysterical myodynia
癔病性缄默症/癔病性緘默症　hysterical mutism
癔病性痉挛/癔病性痙攣　hysteric spasm
癔病性盲/癔病性盲　hysterical blindness
癔病性乳房/癔病性乳房　hysterical breast
癔病性[食管]狭窄/癔病性食管狹窄　hysterical stricture
癔病性视力障碍/癔病性視力障礙　hysteropia
癔病性视力障碍者/癔病性視力障礙患者　hysterope
癔病性水肿/癔病性水腫　hysterical edema
癔病性狭窄/癔病性狹窄　hysterical stenosis
癔病性心绞痛/癔病性心絞痛　hysteric angina
癔病谵妄/癔病譫妄　delirium hystericum
癔球性吞咽困难/癔球性吞嚥困難　dysphagia

globosa
癔症/癔病　hysteria
癔[症]球/臆球症　globus hystericus
癔症性瘫痪/歇斯底里性麻痹　hysterical paralysis
癔症性眩晕/癔病性眩暈　hysterical vertigo
癔症性遗忘/癔症性遺忘　hysterical amnesia
因地制宜/因地制宜　treatment in accordance with local conditions
因人制宜/因人制宜　treatment in accordance with patient's individuality
因时制宜/因時制宜　treatment in accordance with seasonal conditions
因虚致实/因虛致實　excess resulted from deficiency
因阵/因陣　adaptation array
因子/因子　factor
因子Ⅴ缺乏[症]/因子Ⅴ缺乏[症]　factor Ⅴ deficiency
因子Ⅶ缺乏[症]/因子Ⅶ缺乏[症]　factor Ⅶ deficiency
因子Ⅹ缺乏[症]/因子Ⅹ缺乏[症]　factor Ⅹ deficiency
因子Ⅺ缺乏[症]/因子Ⅺ缺乏[症]　factor Ⅺ deficiency
因子Ⅻ缺乏[症]/因子Ⅻ缺乏[症]　factor Ⅻ deficiency
因子ⅩⅢ缺乏[症]/因子ⅩⅢ缺乏[症]　factor ⅩⅢ deficiency
阴/陰　yin
阴包/陰包　yinbao, LR9
阴病出阳/陰病出陽　yin disease involving yang
阴部的/陰部的　pudendal
阴部管/陰部管　pudendal canal
阴部溃疡/陰部潰瘍　pudendal ulcer
阴部内动脉/陰部內動脈　internal pudendal artery
阴部内静脉/陰部內靜脈　internal pudendal vein
阴部热疮/陰部熱瘡　genitalia herpes
阴部热疮·肝经湿热证/陰部熱瘡·肝經濕熱證　genitalia herpes with pattern of dampness-heat in liver channel
阴部热疮·正虚邪恋证/陰部熱瘡·正虛邪戀證　genitalia herpes with pattern of healthy qi deficiency and lingering pathogen
阴部疝/陰部疝　pudendal hernia
阴部神经/陰部神經　pudendal nerve
阴部痛/陰部痛　pudendagra
阴部外动脉/陰部外動脈　external pudendal artery
阴部外动脉阴唇前支/[陰部外動脈]陰唇前支　anterior labial branch of external pudendal artery
阴部外动脉阴囊前支/[陰部外動脈]陰囊前支　anterior scrotal branch of external pudendal artery
阴部外静脉/陰部外靜脈　external pudendal vein
阴疮/陰瘡　sore of vulvae, vulval sore
阴疮·寒湿证/陰瘡·寒濕證　vulval sore with cold-damp pattern
阴疮·气虚夹热证/陰瘡·氣虛夾熱證　vulval sore with pattern of qi deficiency complicated with heat
阴疮·热毒证/陰瘡·熱毒證　vulval sore with heat-toxin pattern
阴吹/陰吹　flatus vaginalis
阴吹·气虚证/陰吹·氣虛證　flatus vaginalis with qi deficiency pattern
阴吹·气郁证/陰吹·氣鬱證　flatus vaginalis with qi depression pattern
阴吹·痰湿证/陰吹·痰濕證　flatus vaginalis with phlegm-damp pattern
阴吹·胃燥证/陰吹·胃燥證　flatus vaginalis with stomach dryness pattern
阴唇后动脉/陰唇後動脈　posterior labial artery
阴唇后静脉/陰唇後靜脈　posterior labial vein
阴唇后疝/陰唇後疝　posterior labial hernia
阴唇后神经/陰唇後神經　posterior labial nerve
阴唇后支/陰唇後支　posterior labial branch
阴唇间沟/大小陰唇溝　nympholabial furrow
阴唇美容术/陰唇美容術　aesthetic labia surgery
阴唇前动脉/陰户唇前動脈　anterior labial artery of vulva
阴唇前静脉/陰唇前靜脈　anterior labial vein
阴唇前连合/大陰唇前連合　anterior commissure of labia
阴唇前神经/陰唇前神經　anterior labial nerve
阴唇前庭炎/陰唇前庭炎　vestibulitis vulvai
阴唇前支/陰唇前支　anterior labial branch
阴唇韧带/陰唇韌帶　labial ligament
阴唇疝/陰唇疝　labial hernia
阴唇突/陰唇隆起　labial swelling
阴唇系带/陰唇繫帶　frenulum of pudendal labia
阴唇阴囊隆起/陰唇陰囊隆起　labioscrotal swelling
阴唇阴囊突/陰唇陰囊隆起　labioscrotal swelling
阴道/陰道　vagina
阴道板/陰道板　vaginal plate
阴道闭合术/陰道閉合術　colpocleisis
阴道闭锁/陰道閉鎖　atresia of vagina, vaginal atresia, atresia vaginae
阴道壁修补术/陰道壁修補術　repair of vaginal wall
阴道病/陰道病　vaginopathy
阴道测量器/陰道測量器　vaginometer

阴道插物保持器/陰道塞藥器　colpostat
阴道成形术/陰道造形術,陰道整形術　colpoplasty
阴道冲洗/陰道沖洗　vaginal douching, vaginal douche
阴道出血/陰道出血　colporrhagia
阴道的/陰道的　vaginal
阴道电热器/陰道電熱器　colpotherm
阴道动脉/陰道動脈　vaginal artery
阴道缝合术/陰道縫合術　colporrhaphy
阴道干燥/陰道乾燥　colpoxerosis
阴道肛门畸形/陰道肛門　vaginal anus
阴道隔/陰道隔　vaginal septum
阴道隔切开术/陰道隔切開術　incision of vaginal septum
阴道固定术/陰道固定術　colpopexy
阴道后壁/陰道後壁　posterior wall of vagina
阴道后壁膨出/道格拉斯疝突,陰道後壁疝突症　douglascele
阴道后疝/陰道後疝　posterior vaginal hernia
阴道会阴成形术/陰道會陰造形術　colpoperineoplasty
阴道会阴缝合术/陰道會陰縫合術　colpoperineorrhaphy
阴道会阴切开术/陰道會陰切開術　vaginiperineotomy
阴道肌层炎/陰道肌層炎　myocolpitis
阴道积恶露/陰道惡露不下　lochiocolpos
阴道积脓/陰道積膿　pyocolpos
阴道积气/陰道積氣　aerocolpos
阴道积血/陰道積血,陰道經血積留　hematocolpos
阴道疾病/陰道疾病　vaginal disease
阴道结肠瘘/陰道結腸瘻　vagino-colic fistula
阴道紧缩术/陰道緊縮術　vaginal tightening surgery
阴道痉挛/陰道痙攣　vaginismus
阴道静脉丛/陰道靜脈叢　vaginal venous plexus
阴道镜/陰道鏡　colposcope
阴道镜检查/陰道鏡檢法　colposcopy
阴道口/陰道口　vaginal orifice
阴道口扩大术/陰道口擴大術　perineoplasty of vaginal outlet
阴道扩张/陰道擴張,陰道膨脹　colpectasia
阴道扩张术/陰道擴張術　colpeurysis
阴道瘘/陰道瘻　vaginal fistula
阴道瘘子宫颈缝术/子宮頸瘻縫合術　trachelosyringorrhaphy
阴道毛滴虫/陰道滴蟲　Trichomonas vaginalis
阴道毛滴虫病/陰道滴蟲病　trichomoniasis
阴道霉菌病/陰道黴菌病　vaginomycosis
阴道模具/陰道模具　vaginal stent
阴道纳药/陰道納藥　encolpism
阴道内儿哭/陰道內兒啼　vagitus vaginalis
阴道内膀胱膨出/陰道膀胱赫尼亞　colpocystocele
阴道内培养/陰道內培養　intravaginal culture, IVC
阴道内投药/陰道內投藥　intravaginal administration
阴道黏膜增生/陰道黏膜增殖　colpohyperplasia
阴道黏液蓄积/黏液性陰道　mucocolpos
阴道尿道隆嵴/陰道尿道隆凸　urethral carina of vagina
阴道脓囊肿/陰道膿囊腫　pyocolpocele
阴道排出物/陰道排出物　vaginal discharge
阴道旁淋巴结/陰道旁淋巴結　paravaginal lymph node
阴道膀胱壁切开输尿管露出术/陰道膀胱式輸尿管露出術　colpocystoureterocystotomy
阴道膀胱成形术/陰道膀胱壁造形術　colpocystoplasty
阴道膀胱切开术/陰道式膀胱切開術　colpocystotomy
阴道膀胱输尿管切开术/陰道膀胱輸尿管切開術,陰道膀胱式輸尿管露出術　colpoureterocystotomy
阴道膀胱炎/陰道膀胱炎　colpocystitis
阴道皮瓣移植形成术/陰道皮瓣移植形成術　construction of vagina by skin flap grafting
阴道皮片移植形成术/陰道皮片移植形成術　construction of vagina by inlay split-thickness skin grafting
阴道破裂/陰道破裂,陰道裂傷　colporrhexis
阴道气响/陰道洩氣　flatus vaginalis
阴道前壁/陰道前壁　anterior wall of vagina
阴道前庭/陰道前庭,女陰前庭　vaginal vestibule, vestibule of vulva
阴道前庭肛门/異位前庭肛門　preternatural vestibular anus
阴道前庭窝/陰道前庭窩　vestibular fossa of vagina
阴道腔/陰道腔　vaginal canal
阴道切除术/陰道切除術　colpectomy
阴道切开术/陰道切開術　colpotomy
阴道穹侧部/陰道穹側部　lateral part of vaginal fornix
阴道穹后部/陰道穹後部　posterior part of vaginal fornix
阴道穹隆/陰道穹窿　fornix of vagina
阴道穹前部/陰道穹前部　anterior part of vaginal fornix
阴道缺如/陰道缺如　absence of vagina
阴道塞/交合後塞子　copulation plug

阴道塞[子]/陰道塞子　vaginal tampon
阴道疝/陰道疝　vaginal hernia
阴道X射线[照]片/陰道X光片　vaginogram
阴道X射线照相术/陰道[X光]攝影術　vaginography
阴道神经/陰道神經　vaginal nerve
阴道式腹腔穿刺术/陰道腹腔穿刺術　colpoceliocentesis
阴道式卵巢切除术/陰道式卵巢切除式　vaginal ovariotomy
阴道式剖腹术/陰道式剖腹術　colpoceliotomy
阴道[式]子宫肌瘤切除术/陰道式子宮肌瘤切除術　colpomyomectomy
阴道式子宫切除术/陰道式子宮切除術　vaginal hysterectomy
阴道输尿管切开术/陰道式輪尿管切開術　colpoureterotomy
阴道栓剂/陰道栓劑　vaginal suppository
阴道松弛/陰道鬆弛　vaginal relaxation
阴道痛/陰道痛　colpalgia
阴道投药法/陰道內給藥　encolpism
阴道涂片/陰道塗片　vaginal smear
阴道涂片检查/陰道塗片檢查　vaginal smear examination
阴道细胞涂片谱/陰道細胞塗片圖譜　colpocytogram
阴道细胞学/陰道細胞學　colpocytology
阴道狭窄/陰道狹窄　stenosis of vagina
阴道狭窄切开术/陰道狹窄切開術　colpostenotomy
阴道下垂/陰道下垂,陰道脫垂　colpoptosis
阴道显微镜/陰道顯微鏡　colpomicroscope
阴道显微镜检查/陰道顯微鏡檢法　colpomicroscopy
阴道小肠膨出/陰道小腸膨出　vaginal enterocele
阴道形成术/陰道形成術　construction of vagina
阴道性痛经/陰道性痛經　vaginal dysmenorrhea
阴道血囊肿/陰道血囊腫　vaginal hematocele
阴道炎/陰道炎　vaginitis
阴道阴唇的/陰道與陰唇的　vaginolabial
阴道阴唇疝/陰道陰唇疝　vaginolabial hernia
阴道引流/陰道引流　vaginal drainage
阴道再造术/陰道再造術　reconstruction of vagina
阴道褶/陰道褶,陰逆襞積　rugae of vagina
阴道支/陰道支　vaginal branch
阴道直肠固定术/陰道式直腸固定術　colporectopexy
阴道指诊/陰道觸診　vaginal touch
阴道肿瘤/陰道腫瘤　vaginal neoplasm
阴道周组织/陰道旁組織　paracolpium
阴道周[组织]炎/陰道旁組織炎　paracolpitis

阴道皱襞柱/陰道皺襞柱　columns of rugae of vagina
阴道注射/陰道注射　vaginal injection
阴道子宫积血/陰道子宮積血　hematocolpometra
阴蒂/陰蒂,陰核　clitoris
阴蒂包皮/陰蒂包皮　prepuce of clitoris
阴蒂背动脉/陰蒂背動脈　dorsal artery of clitoris
阴蒂背静脉/陰蒂背静脈　dorsal vein of clitoris
阴蒂背浅静脉/陰蒂背淺静脈　superficial dorsal vein of clitoris
阴蒂背深静脉/陰蒂背深静脈　deep dorsal vein of clitoris
阴蒂背神经/陰蒂背神經　dorsal nerve of clitoris
阴蒂海绵丛/陰蒂海綿竇[神經]叢　cavernous plexus of clitoris
阴蒂海绵体/陰蒂海綿體　cavernous body of clitoris
阴蒂海绵体神经/陰蒂海綿體神經　cavernous nerve of clitoris
阴蒂脚/陰蒂腳　crus of clitoris
阴蒂筋膜/陰蒂筋膜　fascia of clitoris
阴蒂切除术/陰蒂切除術　clitoridectomy
阴蒂切开术/陰蒂切開術,婦人環割術　clitoridotomy
阴蒂深动脉/陰蒂深動脈　deep artery of clitoris
阴蒂深静脉/陰蒂深静脈　deep vein of clitoris
阴蒂体/陰蒂體　body of clitoris
阴蒂头/陰蒂頭　glans of clitoris
阴蒂危象/陰蒂危象　clitoris crisis
阴蒂系带/陰蒂繫帶　frenulum of clitoris
阴蒂悬韧带/陰蒂懸韌帶　suspensory ligament of clitoris
阴蒂炎/陰蒂炎　clitoriditis
阴都/陰都　yindu, KI19
阴毒/陰毒　yin poisoning
阴毒伤寒/陰毒傷寒　exogenous cold disease with yin toxicosis
阴阜/陰阜　mons pubis
阴干/陰乾　drying in shade, drying in the shade
阴沟肠道菌素/陰溝腸道菌素　Cloacin
阴沟气/陰溝氣　sewer gas
阴垢/陰垢　smegma
阴谷/陰谷　yingu, KI10
阴汗/陰汗　perineal sweating
阴户/陰戶,女陰　vaginal door, vulva
阴户囊肿/陰戶囊腫　vaginal cyst
阴黄/陰黃　yin jaundice
阴黄·肝脾不调证/陰黃·肝脾不調證　yin jaundice with pattern of disharmony between liver and spleen
阴黄·寒湿证/陰黃·寒濕證　yin jaundice with cold-

damp pattern

阴黄·脾虚湿困证/陰黄·脾虛濕困證　yin jaundice with pattern of damp retention due to spleen deficiency

阴黄·湿热[蕴结]证/陰黄·濕熱[蘊結]證　yin jaundice with pattern of accumulation and binding of damp-heat

阴黄·血瘀肝郁证/陰黄·血瘀肝鬱證　yin jaundice with pattern of blood stasis and liver depression

阴黄·阳虚寒凝证/陰黄·陽虛寒凝證　yin jaundice with pattern of yang deficiency and cold congelation

阴极/陰極　cathode

阴极电解法/陰極電解法　katholysis

阴极电解质/陰極電解物　catholyte

阴极电紧张/陰極電緊張　catelectrotonus

阴极电紧张状态/陰極緊張狀態　catelectrotonic state

阴极断电强直/陰極開放性強直　cathodal opening tetanus

阴极断电收缩/陰極斷電收縮,陰極開放性收縮　cathodal opening contraction

阴极断电阵挛/陰極停電性陣攣,陰極開放性痙攣　cathodal opening clonus

阴极[射]线管/陰極射線管　cathode-ray tube

阴极似阳/陰極似陽　extreme yin with yang manifestation

阴极通电强直/陰極封閉性強直,陰極關閉性強直　cathodal closure tetanus

阴极通电收缩/陰極封閉性收縮　cathodal closure contraction

阴极通电阵挛/陰極通電性陣攣,陰極封閉性痙攣　cathodal closure clonus

阴交/陰交　yinjiao, RN7

阴结/陰結　yin binding

阴竭阳脱/陰竭陽脱　depletion of yin causing yang collapse

阴竭阳脱证/陰竭陽脱證　pattern of depletion of yin causing yang collapse

阴茎/陰莖　penis, phallus

阴茎阿米巴病/陰莖阿米巴病　amoebiasis of penis

阴茎癌/陰莖癌　carcinoma of penis

阴茎癌前期病变/陰莖癌前期病變　precancerous lesion of penis

阴茎白斑病/陰莖白斑病　leukoplakia penis

阴茎包涵囊肿/陰莖包涵囊腫　inclusion cyst of penis

阴茎包皮/陰莖包皮　prepuce of penis

阴茎背/陰莖背　dorsum of penis

阴茎背动脉/陰莖背動脈　dorsal artery of penis

阴茎背静脉/陰莖背靜脈　dorsal vein of penis

阴茎背浅静脉/陰莖背淺靜脈　superficial dorsal vein of penis

阴茎背深静脉/陰莖背深靜脈　deep dorsal vein of penis

阴茎背神经/陰莖背神經　dorsal nerve of penis

阴茎勃起/陰莖勃起　erection of penis

阴茎成形术/陰莖造形術　phalloplasty

阴茎出血/陰莖出血　phallorrhagia

阴茎挫伤/陰莖挫傷　contusion of penis

阴茎的/陰莖的　penile

阴茎动脉/陰莖動脈　artery of penis

阴茎动脉瘤/陰莖動脈瘤　phallaneurysm

阴茎发育不全/陰莖發育不全　agenesis of penis

阴茎放线菌病/陰莖放線菌病　actinomycosis of penis

阴茎缝/陰莖縫　raphe of penis

阴茎根/陰莖根　root of penis

阴茎骨/陰莖骨　penis bone

阴茎骨化/陰莖骨化　ossification of penis

阴茎海绵丛/陰莖海綿叢　plexus cavernosus penis

阴茎海绵体/陰莖海綿體　cavernous body of penis

阴茎海绵体白膜/陰莖海綿體白膜　albuginea of penis cavernous body

阴茎海绵体丛/陰莖海綿[神經]叢　cavernous plexus of penis

阴茎海绵体静脉/陰莖海綿體靜脈　venae cavernosae penis

阴茎海绵体腔/陰莖海綿體腔　caverns of penis cavernous body

阴茎海绵体神经/陰莖海綿體神經　cavernous nerves of penis

阴茎海绵体小梁/陰莖海綿體小梁　trabecula of penis cavernous body

阴茎海绵体炎/陰莖海綿體炎　spongiositis

阴茎海绵体硬节症/陰莖海綿體硬節症　plastic induration of the penis

阴茎海绵体造影[术]/陰莖海綿體造影[術]　cavernosography

阴茎黑色素瘤/陰莖黑色素瘤　melanoma of penis

阴茎坏死/陰莖壞死　gangrene of penis

阴茎环状硬节性淋巴管炎/陰莖環狀硬節性淋巴管炎　circular indurated lymphangitis of penis

阴茎基底细胞癌/陰莖基底細胞癌　basal cell carcinoma of penis

阴茎畸形/陰莖畸形　deformity of penis

阴茎疾病/陰莖疾病　penile disease

阴茎假瘤/陰莖假瘤　penile pseudotumor
阴茎假体/陰莖假體　penile prosthesis
阴茎假体植入/陰莖假體植入　penile implantation
阴茎绞窄/陰莖絞窄　strangulation of penis
阴茎脚/陰莖腳　crus of penis
阴茎结核/陰莖結核　tuberculosis of penis
阴茎结核疹/陰莖結核疹　penile tuberculide
阴茎结节/陰莖結節　penile nodule
阴茎截断[术]/陰莖截斷[術]　amputation of penis
阴茎近端型尿道下裂/陰莖近端型尿道下裂　proximal shaft hypospadias
阴茎颈/陰莖頸　neck of penis
阴茎裂/裂陰莖　penischisis
阴茎淋巴网状组织恶性病/陰莖淋巴網狀組織惡性病　lymphoreticular malignancy of penis
阴茎鳞状细胞癌/陰莖鱗狀細胞癌　squamous cell carcinoma of penis
阴茎鳞状细胞原位癌/陰莖鱗狀細胞原位癌　squamous cell carcinoma of penis in situ
阴茎瘘/陰莖瘻　penil fistula
阴茎螺旋动脉/陰莖螺旋動脈　helicine artery of penis
阴茎梅毒/陰莖梅毒　syphilis of penis
阴茎美容术/陰莖美容術　aesthetic penis surgery
阴茎囊肿/陰莖囊腫　cyst of penis
阴茎黏液样囊肿/陰莖黏液樣囊腫　penile mucoid cyst
阴茎尿道/陰莖尿道　penile urethra
阴茎尿道下裂/陰莖尿道下裂　penile hypospadia
阴茎扭转/陰莖扭轉　distortion of penis
阴茎皮肤撕脱伤/陰莖皮膚撕脱傷　avulsion of penis
阴茎皮样囊肿/陰莖皮樣囊腫　dermoid cyst of penis
阴茎皮脂腺囊肿/陰莖皮脂腺囊腫　sebaceous cyst of penis
阴茎前阴囊/陰莖前陰囊　prepenile scrotum
阴茎钳/陰莖壓迫鉗　jugum penis
阴茎浅筋膜/陰莖淺筋膜　superficial fascia of penis
阴茎切除术/陰莖切除術　peotomy
阴茎切开术/陰莖切開術　phallotomy
阴茎球/陰莖球　bulb of penis
阴茎球动脉/陰莖球動脈　artery of bulb of penis
阴茎球体静脉/陰莖球體靜脈　vein of bulb of penis
阴茎缺失/陰莖缺失　absence of penis
阴茎人工结节/陰莖人工結節　artificial penile nodule
阴茎上曲/陰莖上彎　phallanastrophe
阴茎深动脉/陰莖深動脈　deep artery of penis
阴茎深筋膜/陰莖深筋膜　deep fascia of penis
阴茎深静脉/陰莖深靜脈　deep vein of penis
阴茎损伤/陰莖損傷　injury of penis
阴茎痰核/陰莖痰核　Peyronie's disease, phlegmatic tubercle of penis
阴茎痰核·痰浊凝聚证/陰莖痰核·痰濁凝聚證　phlegmatic tubercle of penis with pattern of phlegm-turbidity coagulation and aggregation
阴茎痰核·阴虚痰热证/陰莖痰核·陰虛痰熱證　phlegmatic tubercle of penis with pattern of yin deficiency and phlegm-heat
阴茎体/陰莖體　body of penis, shaft of penis
阴茎痛/陰莖痛　phallalgia
阴茎头/陰莖頭,龜頭　glans
阴茎头白斑病/陰莖頭白斑病　leukoplakia of glans penis
阴茎头冠/陰莖頭冠　corona of glans of penis
阴茎头型尿道上裂/陰莖尿道上裂　balanic epispadias
阴茎头型尿道下裂/龜頭部尿道下裂　balanic hypospadias
阴茎头炎/陰莖頭炎,龜頭炎　balanitis
阴茎头炎及阴茎头包皮炎/陰莖頭炎及陰莖頭包皮炎　balanitis and balanoposthitis
阴茎头中隔/陰莖頭隔　septum of glans
阴茎脱位/陰莖脱位　dislocation of penis
阴茎外侧沟/陰莖外側溝　lateral phallic groove
阴茎弯曲/陰莖彎曲　phallocampsis
阴茎系韧带/陰莖繫韌帶　fundiform ligament of penis
阴茎下弯/陰莖下彎　chordee of penis
阴茎纤维瘤病/陰莖纖維瘤病　penile fibromatosis
阴茎纤维性海绵体炎/陰莖纖維性海綿體炎　fibrous cavernositis of penis
阴茎型尿道上裂/陰莖尿道上裂　penile epispadias
阴茎型尿道下裂/陰莖[部]尿道下裂　penile hypospadias
阴茎悬韧带/陰莖懸韌帶　suspensory ligament of penis
阴茎血管瘤/陰莖血管瘤　penile angioma
阴茎血肿/陰莖血腫　hematoma of penis
阴茎延长术/陰莖延長術　lengthening of penis
阴茎炎/陰莖炎　penitis
阴茎液溢/陰莖漏　phallorrhea
阴茎异常勃起/陰莖異常勃起　priapism
阴茎阴囊的/陰莖陰囊的　penoscrotal
阴茎阴囊尿道下裂/陰莖陰囊尿道下裂　penoscrotal hypospadia
阴茎阴囊皮肤撕脱[伤]/陰莖陰囊皮膚撕脱[傷]　avulsion of penile and scrotal skin

阴茎阴囊象皮肿/陰莖陰囊象皮腫 elephantiasis of penis and scrotum
阴茎阴囊型尿道下裂/陰莖陰囊部尿道下裂 penoscrotal hypospadias
阴茎阴囊绉襞/陰莖陰囊皺襞 penoscrotal fold
阴茎硬化性淋巴管炎/陰莖硬化性淋巴管炎 sclerosing lymphangitis of the penis
阴茎硬结/陰莖硬結 penile induration
阴茎原位癌/陰莖原位癌 penile intraepithelial neoplasia
阴茎远端型尿道下裂/陰莖遠端型尿道下裂 distal shaft hypospadias
阴茎再造[术]/陰莖再造[術] reconstruction of penis
阴茎折断/陰莖折斷 fracture of penis
阴茎中隔/陰莖隔 septum of penis
阴茎肿瘤/陰莖腫瘤 penile neoplasm
阴茎转位/陰莖轉位 translocation of penis
阴静阳躁/陰靜陽躁 steady yin and vexed yang
阴厥/陰厥 yin cold limbs
阴狂/陰狂 yin manic psychosis
阴冷/陰冷 sense of coldness extending into external genitals, vulval coldness
阴冷·风寒束表证/陰冷·風寒束表證 vulval coldness with pattern of wind-cold tightening exterior
阴冷·肾阳衰微证/陰冷·腎陽衰微證 vulval coldness with pattern of kidney yang exhaustion
阴离子电泳/陰離子電泳,陽極電透法 anaphoresis
阴离子交换膜/陰離子交換膜 anion exchange membrane
阴离子交换树脂/陰離子交換樹脂 anion exchange resin
阴离子交换树脂类/陰離子交換樹脂類 anion exchange resins
阴离子移变[现象]/陰離子趨性 anionotropy
阴离子转运蛋白质类/陰離子轉運蛋白質類 anion transport proteins
阴廉/陰廉 yinlian, LR11
阴陵泉/陰陵泉 yinlingquan, SP9
阴毛/陰毛 pubic hair
阴毛初生/陰毛初生 pubarche
阴毛美容术/陰毛美容術 aesthetic pubes surgery
阴毛移植[术]/陰毛移植[術] pubic hair grafting
阴门/陰道口 vaginal orifice
阴门帘/女陰唇過長 velamen vulvae
阴囊/陰囊 scrotum
阴囊癌/陰囊癌 carcinoma scroti

阴囊壁结核/陰囊壁結核 tuberculosis of scrotal wall
阴囊苍白细胞棘皮瘤/陰囊蒼白細胞棘皮瘤 pale cell acanthoma of the scrotum
阴囊成形术/陰囊造形術,陰囊修補術 oscheoplasty
阴囊挫伤/陰囊挫傷 contusion of scrotum
阴囊的/陰囊的 scrotal
阴囊对裂/陰囊對裂 bifid scrotum
阴囊多发性尿瘘/陰囊多發性尿瘺 watering-can scrotum
阴囊发育不全/陰囊發育不全 hypoplasia of scrotum
阴囊放线菌病/陰囊放線菌病 actinomycosis of scrotum
阴囊缝/陰囊縫 raphe of scrotum
阴囊钙化性皮脂腺囊肿/陰囊鈣化性皮脂腺囊腫 calcified sebaceous cyst of scrotum
阴囊钙质沉着症/陰囊鈣質沈著症 calcinosis of scrotum
阴囊后动脉/陰囊後動脈 posterior scrotal artery
阴囊后静脉/陰囊後靜脈 posterior scrotal vein
阴囊后神经/陰囊後神經 posterior scrotal nerve
阴囊后阴茎/陰囊後陰莖 retroscrotal penis
阴囊后支/陰囊後支 posterior scrotal branch
阴囊坏疽/陰囊壞疽 gangrene of scrotum
阴囊积尿/陰囊積尿 urocele
阴囊积血/陰囊積血 hematoscheocele
阴囊畸形/陰囊畸形 deformity of scrotum
阴囊角化囊肿/陰囊角化囊腫 keratinous cyst of scrotum
阴囊结核/陰囊結核 tuberculosis of scrotum
阴囊结石/陰囊結石 calculus of scrotum
阴囊淋巴管扩张/陰囊淋巴管擴張 lymph scrotum
阴囊瘤/陰囊瘤 oscheoma
阴囊隆起/陰囊隆起 scrotal swelling
阴囊瘘/陰囊瘺 scrotal fistula
阴囊念珠菌病/陰囊念珠菌病 candidiasis scrotalis
阴囊脓肿/陰囊膿腫 abscess of scrotum
阴囊皮肤梅毒/陰囊皮膚梅毒 syphilis of scrotal skin
阴囊皮脂腺囊肿/陰囊皮脂腺囊腫 sebaceous cyst of scrotum
阴囊前动脉/陰囊前動脈 anterior scrotal artery
阴囊前静脉/陰囊前靜脈 anterior scrotal vein
阴囊前神经/陰囊前神經 anterior scrotal nerve
阴囊前支/陰囊前支 anterior scrotal branch
阴囊[鞘膜]水囊肿/積水性陰囊赫尼亞,陰囊積水赫尼亞 oscheohydrocele
阴囊切除术/陰囊切除術 scrotectomy

阴囊缺如/陰囊缺如　agenesis of scrotum
阴囊肉膜/陰囊肉膜　dartos muscle of scrotum
阴囊瘙痒[症]/陰囊搔癢[症]　pruritus scroti
阴囊疝/陰囊疝　scrotal hernia
阴囊舌/陰囊舌　scrotal tongue
阴囊石/陰囊[皮脂腺結]石　oscheolith
阴囊水囊肿/陰囊水囊,陰囊積水　scrotal hydrocele
阴囊丝虫病/陰囊絲蟲病　filariasis of scrotum
阴囊损伤/陰囊損傷　injury of scrotum
阴囊特发性钙化/陰囊特發性鈣化　idiopathic calcinosis if scrotum
阴囊象皮病/陰囊象皮病　elephantiasis scroti
阴囊血管角化瘤/陰囊血管角化瘤　angiokeratoma scroti
阴囊血管瘤/陰囊血管瘤　hemangioma of scrotum
阴囊血肿/陰囊血腫　hematoma of scrotum
阴囊炎/陰囊炎　oscheitis
阴囊异位/陰囊異位　ectopia of scrotum
阴囊阴茎粘连/陰囊陰莖粘連　synoscheos
阴囊脂肪瘤/陰囊脂肪瘤　lipoma of scrotum
阴囊脂肿/陰囊脂腫　steatocele
阴囊中隔/陰囊隔　septum of scrotum
阴囊肿瘤/陰囊腫瘤　tumor of scrotum
阴囊转位/陰囊轉位　translocation of scrotum
阴平阳秘/陰平陽秘　relative equilibrium of yin-yang
阴气/陰氣　yin qi
阴跷脉/陰蹻脈　Yin Heel Channel, Yin Heel Vessel
阴痧/陰痧　yin sha disease
阴神/陰神　corporeal soul
阴盛/陰盛　yin excessiveness
阴盛阳衰证/陰盛陽衰證　pattern of yang deficiency due to yin excess
阴虱/陰蝨　phthirus pubis
阴虱病/陰蝨病　pediculosis pubis
阴市/陰市　yinshi, ST33
阴水/陰水　yin edema
阴水·脾虚湿困证/陰水·脾虛濕困證　yin edema with pattern of damp retention due to spleen deficiency
阴水·阳虚水泛证/陰水·陽虛水泛證　yin edema with pattern of water overflowing due to yang deficiency
阴水·瘀水互结证/陰水·瘀水互結證　yin edema with pattern of binding of static blood and water
阴缩/陰縮,縮陰　koro
阴损及阳/陰損及陽　yin deficiency involving yang
阴损及阳证/陰損及陽證　pattern of yin deficiency involving yang
阴挺/陰挺　uterine or vaginal prolapse, uterine prolapse
阴挺·脾虚气陷证/陰挺·脾虛氣陷證　uterine or vaginal prolapse with pattern of spleen deficiency and qi collapse
阴挺·肾气不固证/陰挺·腎氣不固證　uterine or vaginal prolapse with pattern of unconsolidated kidney qi
阴挺·湿热下注证/陰挺·濕熱下注證　uterine or vaginal prolapse with pattern of downward diffusion of damp-heat
阴痛/陰痛　vaginal pain
阴痛·肝气郁结证/陰痛·肝氣鬱結證　vaginal pain with pattern of liver qi depression
阴痛·肝肾两虚证/陰痛·肝腎兩虛證　vaginal pain with pattern of deficiency of both liver and kidney
阴痛·寒滞肝脉证/陰痛·寒滯肝脈證　vaginal pain with pattern of cold stagnation in liver channel
阴维脉/陰維脈　yin link channel, yin link vessel
阴郄/陰郄　yinxi, HT6
阴邪/陰邪　yin pathogen
阴性的/陰性的,負的　negative
阴性趋电性/負電向性,陰電向性　negative electrotropism
阴性预告值/陰性預測值　negative predictive value
阴虚/陰虛　yin deficiency
阴虚痹/陰虛痹　arthralgia due to yin deficiency, yin deficiency bi
阴虚肠燥证/陰虛腸燥證　pattern of intestine dryness due to yin deficiency
阴虚齿燥证/陰虛齒燥證　pattern of teeth dryness due to yin deficiency
阴虚动风证/陰虛動風證　pattern of stirring wind due to yin deficiency
阴虚动血证/陰虛動血證　pattern of stirring blood due to yin deficiency
阴虚发热/陰虛發熱　fever due to yin deficiency
阴虚肺燥证/陰虛肺燥證　pattern of lung dryness due to yin deficiency
阴虚风动/陰虛風動　stirring wind due to yin deficiency
阴虚火旺/陰虛火旺　exuberant fire due to yin deficiency
阴虚火旺证/陰虛火旺證　pattern of exuberant fire due to yin deficiency
阴虚津亏证/陰虛津虧證　pattern of yin deficiency and depletion of fluid
阴虚痢/陰虛痢　yin deficiency dysentery

阴虚内热证/陰虛內熱證 pattern of endogenous heat due to yin deficiency
阴虚湿热证/陰虛濕熱證 pattern of yin deficiency and dampness-heat
阴虚外感证/陰虛外感證 pattern of exogenous disease due to yin deficiency
阴虚血热证/陰虛血熱證 pattern of yin deficiency and blood heat
阴虚血瘀证/陰虛血瘀證 pattern of yin deficiency and blood stasis
阴虚血燥证/陰虛血燥證 pattern of yin deficiency and blood dryness
阴虚咽喉失濡证/陰虛咽喉失濡證 pattern of loss of moistening of throat due to yin deficiency
阴虚阳亢/陰虛陽亢 hyperactivity of yang due to yin deficiency
阴虚阳亢证/陰虛陽亢證 pattern of hyperactivity of yang due to yin deficiency
阴虚证/陰虛證 yin deficiency pattern
阴癣/陰癬 tinea inguinalis
阴阳/陰陽 yin-yang
阴阳辨证/陰陽辨證 pattern identification of yin-yang
阴阳并补剂/陰陽并補劑 formula for benefiting both yin and yang
阴阳对立/陰陽對立 opposition of yin-yang
阴阳二十五人/陰陽二十五人 25 types of constitution beased on yin and yang, Yin-yang 25 Constitational Types
阴阳格拒/陰陽格拒 expulsion of yin-yang
阴阳和平之人/陰陽和平之人 person of harmonious yin-yang
阴阳互根/陰陽互根 mutual rooting of yin-yang
阴阳离决/陰陽離決 divorce of yin-yang
阴阳离子平衡/陰陽離子平衡 anion-cation balance
阴阳两虚/陰陽兩虛 deficiency of both yin and yang
阴阳两虚证/陰陽兩虛證 pattern of deficiency of both yin and yang
阴阳偏盛/陰陽偏盛 excess of either yin or yang
阴阳偏衰/陰陽偏衰 deficiency of either yin or yang
阴阳失调/陰陽失調 yin-yang disharmony
阴阳睡梦论/陰陽睡夢論 doctrine of sleep and dream guided by yin-yang theory
阴阳消长/陰陽消長 waxing and waning of yin-yang
阴阳心身发展学说/陰陽心身發展學說 theory of psychosomatic development based on yin-yang
阴阳学说/陰陽學說 yin-yang theory
阴阳易/陰陽易 yin yang exchange

阴阳应象大论篇/陰陽應象大論篇 Treatise on the Cause of Diseases from Yin & Yang Imbalances
阴阳转化/陰陽轉化 mutual convertibility of yin-yang
阴阳自和/陰陽自和 natural harmony of yin-yang
阴痒[病]/陰癢[病] pruritus vulvae
阴痒·肝经湿热证/陰癢·肝經濕熱證 pruritus vulvae with pattern of damp-heat in liver channel
阴痒·阴虚血燥证/陰癢·陰虛血燥證 pruritus vulvae with pattern of yin deficiency and blood dryness
阴易/陰易 yin exchange
阴燥/陰燥 vulvae dryness, vulval dryness
阴燥·肝肾阴虚证/陰燥·肝腎陰虛證 vulval dryness with pattern of liver-kidney yin deficiency
阴燥·脾肾阳虚证/陰燥·脾腎陽虛證 vulval dryness with pattern of yang deficiency of spleen and kidney
阴燥·血虚化燥证/陰燥·血虛化燥證 vulval dryness with pattern of blood deficiency transforming into dryness
阴躁/陰躁 restlessness due to excess of yin
阴证/陰證 yin pattern
阴肿/陰腫 vulval swelling
阴肿·肝经湿热证/陰腫·肝經濕熱證 vulval swelling with pattern of damp-heat in liver channel
阴肿·寒湿证/陰腫·寒濕證 vulval swelling with cold damp pattern
阴肿·气陷证/陰腫·氣陷證 vulval swelling with pattern of qi collapse
阴肿·气滞水停证/陰腫·氣滯水停證 vulval swelling with pattern of qi and water stagnation
阴肿·外伤证/陰腫·外傷證 vulval swelling with traumatic pattern
茵陈/茵陳 virgate wormwood herb
茵陈蒿汤/茵陳蒿湯 yinchenhao decoction
茵陈五苓散/茵陳五苓散 yinchen wuling powder
音波按摩法/顫音按摩法 phonomassage
音波空气按摩法/音氣按摩法 phonopneumomassage
音叉/音叉 tuning fork
音叉听诊法/音叉聽診法 phonoauscultation
音叉振动自感测验法/自聲測量法 autophonometry
音调变异/音調變異 xenophonia
音调辨别/音調辨別 pitch discrimination
音[调]感[觉]/音覺 tone sense
音调知觉/音調知覺 pitch perception
音定向不能/音定向暗點 aural scotoma
音符/符號,音 note

音符失写症/音符失寫症　musical agraphia
音节盲/音節失辨症　syllabic blindness
音联觉/音幻覺,幻音　phonism
音频电疗[法]/音頻電療法　audiofrequency electrotherapy
音色不良/發音不良　dystimbria
音衰变试验/音衰變試驗　tone decay test
音素/音素　phoneme
音讯电疗法/音訊電療法　audiofrequency current therapy
音域/音域　vocal range
音乐电疗法/音樂電療法　musical electrotherapy
音乐疗法/音樂療法　music therapy, musicotherapy
音乐性杂音/樂音性雜音　musical murmur
音乐镇痛/音樂止痛　audioanalgesia
音振动描记器/音振動顯形器　tonophant
殷门/殷門　yinmen, BL37
铟-111/銦-111　indium-111
铟放射性同位素/銦放射性同位素　indium radioisotope
银/銀　silver
银叉样变形/銀叉狀變形　silver-fork deformity
银叉状骨折/銀叉狀骨折　silver-fork fracture
银柴胡/銀柴胡　star-wort root
银肠线/銀制腸線　silverized catgut
银蛋白质/銀蛋白質　sliver protein
银蛋白质类/銀蛋白質類　silver proteins
银电极/銀電極　silver electrode
银汞沉着症/銀汞沈著症　amalgam pigmentation
银汞合金/銀汞合金　silver amalgam
银化合物/銀化合物　silver compound
银莲花属/白頭翁屬　Anemone
银翘散/銀翹散　yinqiao powder
银染色[法]/銀染[色法]　silver staining
银十字/銀色十字　silver cross
银网植入法/銀絲網植入法　filigree implantation
银屑病/牛皮癬　psoriasis
银屑病失能指数/乾癬失能指數　psoriasis disability index
银屑病样皮炎/乾癬樣皮膚炎　psoriasiform dermatitis
银屑病型红皮症/乾癬性紅皮症　erythroderma psoriatica
银杏/銀杏　Ginkgo biloba
银杏苦内酯类/銀杏苦內酯類　ginkgolides
银杏内酯类/銀杏内酯類　bilobalides
银杏叶/銀杏葉　ginkgo leaf
银血[病]/銀血病　argyremia
银易染性/嗜銀現象　argyrophilia
银质沉着病/銀質沈著病　argyria
淫邪发梦/淫邪發夢　Treatise on Dreams and Treatment
淫羊藿/淫羊藿　epimedium herb
龈/[牙]齦　gum
龈癌/齦癌　ulocarcinoma
龈按摩/牙齦滋養法　ulotripsis
龈瓣/齦片　gingival flap
龈变性/牙齦變性　gingivosis
龈出血/齒齦出血　oulorrhagia
龈刀/齦刀　gingival lancet
龈点/齦點　prosthion
龈沟/齦溝　gingival groove, gingival sulcus
龈沟液测量仪/齦溝液測量儀　periotron
龈沟液取样纸条/齦溝液取樣紙條　perio paper
龈谷/齦谷　gingival col
龈裹牙/牙蓋　odontoclamis
龈交/齦交　yinjiao, DU28
龈口炎/齦口炎　gingivostomatitis
龈溃疡/齦潰瘍　ulocace
龈流血指数/齦流血指數　index of gingival bleeding
龈瘤/齦瘤,齒旁瘤　epulis
龈平面/齦平面　gingival plane
龈曲线/齒齦彎曲　gingival curvature
龈乳头/齦乳頭　gingival papilla
龈乳头炎/乳突狀齦炎　papillary gingivitis
龈上牙石/齦上積石　supragingival calculus
龈舌炎/齦舌炎　gingivoglossitis
龈痛/齦痛　gingivalgia
龈下刮治器/齦下刮治器　subgingival curette
龈下外形/齦下外形　subgingival contour
龈下牙石/齦下石　subgingival calculus
龈纤维瘤/齦纖維瘤　epulofibroma
龈纤维瘤病多毛综合征/齦纖維瘤病多毛症候群　fibromatosis gingivae hypertrichosis syndrome
龈线/齦線　gingival line
龈象皮病/巨大齦　macrogingivae
龈牙单位/齦牙單位　dentogingival unit
龈牙结合部/齦牙結合部　dentogingival junction
龈牙纤维/齦牙纖維　dentogingival fiber
龈炎指数/齦炎指數　index of gingivitis
龈缘/齦緣　gingival margin
龈缘高点/齦緣高點　gingival zenith
龈缘高度/齦緣高度　gingival height
龈缘突/齦緣突　gingival convexity
龈中隔/齦隔　gingival septum
引产/引產,人工分娩　induced labor

引产术/引產術　induction of labor
引出/引出　elicit
引带的/引帶的　gubernacular
引导/導引,導子　guidance, guide
引导杆/引導桿　guiding rod
引导骨再生/引導骨再生　guided bone regeneration
引导机理/引導機轉　guidance mechanism
引导组织再生术/引導組織再生術　guided tissue regeneration
引发剂/引發劑　initiator
引发阶段/引發階段　initiating stage
引发体/引發體　primosome
引火归原/引火歸原　conducting fire back to its origin
引经/引經　channel affinity, channel ushering
引经药/引經藥　channel ushering drug
引力/引力　gravitation
引流法/引流法　drainage method
引流管/引流管　drain
引流疗法/引流療法　drainage therapy
引流术/引流　drainage
引起痤疮的/引起痤瘡的　acnegenic
引起免疫的/導致免疫的　immunifacient
引起湿疹的/濕疹原的　eczematogenic
引物/引子　primer
引物延伸/引物延伸　primer extension
引向腹侧/向腹引動,腹引　ventriduct
引牙萌发管/引牙萌發管,引齒管　gubernacular canal
引种后牛痘/引痘性牛痘　variolovaccinia
吲达帕胺/吲達帕胺　indapamide
吲哚丙酸/吲哚丙酸　indopropionic acid
吲哚酚/靛基酚　indophenol
吲哚酚尿/氧靛基質尿　indoxyluria
吲哚酚血/氧靛基質血　indoxylemia
吲哚苷/吲哚苷,吲哚配糖體　indole glycoside
吲哚菁绿/靛氰藍綠　indocyanine green
吲哚克索/雙甲氧苯基吲哚　indoxole
吲哚拉明/吲哚納明,吲哚乙基,啶基苯醯胺　indoramin
吲哚类/吲哚類　indoles
吲哚里西啶生物碱/吲哚聯啶生物鹼　indolizidine alkaloid
吲哚-3-磷酸甘油酯合酶/吲哚-3-磷酸甘油酯合酶　indole-3-glycerol-phosphate synthase
吲哚洛尔/吲哚洛爾　pindolol
吲哚洛芬/吲哚洛芬　indoprofen
吲哚美辛/吲哚美辛　indometacin

吲哚尿/靛基質尿　indoluria
吲哚生物碱/吲哚生物鹼　indole alkaloid
吲哚生物碱类/吲哚生物鹼類　indole alkaloids
吲哚乙酸类/吲哚乙酸類　indoleacetic acids
吲哚乙酸尿/靛基醋酸尿　indolaceturia
吲嗪/吲嗪　indolizine
吲唑类/吲唑類　indazoles
饮/飲　drink, fluid retention
饮海水/掇入海水　mariposia
饮酒/飲酒　alcohol drinking
饮酒恐怖/飲酒恐懼症　dipsophobia
饮料/飲料　beverage
饮留胃肠证/飲留胃腸證　pattern of fluid retained in stomach and intestines
饮尿/飲尿　uriposia
饮片/飲片　prepared drug in pieces
饮膳正要/飲膳正要　Principles of Correct Diet
饮食禁忌/飲食禁忌　dietetic contraindication
饮食疗法/食物療法　bromatherapy
饮食美容/飲食美容　diet cosmetics
饮食所伤/飲食所傷　injury due to diet
饮食调理/飲食調理　dietetic regulation
饮食习惯/飲食習慣　food habit
饮食性高三酸甘油酯血症/飲食性高三酸甘油酯血症　alimentary hypertriglyceridemia
饮水/飲水　drinking
饮水淡化法/飲水淡化法　potification
饮水困难/飲水困難　dysdipsia
饮水试验/飲水試驗　water drinking test
饮水行为/飲水行爲　drinking behavior
饮水则呛/飲水則嗆　choke when drinking
饮停胸胁证/飲停胸脅證　pattern of fluid retained in chest and hypochondrium
饮液细胞/吸飲細胞,吸液細胞　pinocyte
饮液作用/漿液吞噬作用　hydrophagocytosis
饮溢四肢证/飲溢四肢證　pattern of fluid retention overflowing in limbs
饮用水/飲用水,可飲水　potable water
饮证/飲證　fluid retention pattern
蚓部小结/蚓部小結　nodule of vermis
蚓垂/蚓垂,小腦懸雍垂　uvula of vermis
蚓结节/蚓結節　tuber of vermis
蚓上静脉/蚓上靜脈　superior vein of vermis, superior vermian vein
蚓下静脉/蚓下靜脈　inferior vein of vermis, inferior vermian vein
蚓叶/蚓葉　folium of vermis
蚓狀肌/蚓狀肌　lumbrical

蚓锥体/蚓[部]錐體　pyramid of vermis, pyramid of cerebellum
隐白/隱白　yinbai, SP1
隐白血病/隱白血病　cryptoleukemia
隐孢子虫/隱孢子蟲　cryptosporidium
隐孢子虫病/隱孢子蟲病　cryptosporidiosis
隐蔽的/隱蔽的,隱藏的　masked
隐蔽决定簇/隱藏決定體　hidden determinant
隐蔽抗原/隱蔽抗原　hidden antigen
隐蔽切口/隱蔽切口　hidden incision
隐蔽细胞/隱蔽細胞　veiled cell
隐藏的/隱藏的,隱匿的　occult
隐翅虫/隱翅蟲　staphylinid
隐翅虫皮炎/隱翅蟲皮炎　paederus dermatitis
隐滴虫/隱滴蟲　cryptomonad
隐耳/隱耳畸形　cryptotia
隐发性的/隱原性　cryptogenic
隐肛/隱肛　covered anus
隐睾/隱睾　undescended testis
隐睾固定术/隱睾固定術　cryptorchidopexy
隐睾切除术/隱睾切除術　cryptorchidectomy
隐睾移植术/睾丸移植腹腔内法　orchidocelioplasty
隐沟/隱溝　subsulcus
隐含层/隱含層　hidden layer
隐花青/隱花青　koha
隐花植物/隱花植物　cryptogam
隐静脉/隱靜脈　saphenous vein
隐静脉的/隱靜脈的　saphenous
隐静脉腹膜造口[引流]术/隱靜脈腹膜造口吻合術　venoperitoneostomy
隐静脉孔/隱靜脈孔　saphenous opening
隐静脉裂孔/隱靜脈裂孔,卵圓窩　saphenous hiatus
隐静脉切除术/隱靜脈切除術　saphenectomy
隐静脉曲张/隱靜脈曲張　saphenous varix
隐静脉移植物/隱靜脈移植物　saphenous vein graft
隐匿出血/隱藏性出血　occult hemorrhage
隐匿型肾小球肾炎/隱匿型腎小球腎炎　latent glomerulonephritis
隐匿性出血/隱匿性出血　concealed hemorrhage
隐匿性传导/隱匿性傳導　concealed conduction
隐匿性附加径路/隱匿性附加徑路　concealed accessory pathway
隐匿性甲状腺功能亢进/無症狀的甲狀腺機能亢進　masked hyperthyroidism
隐匿性溃疡/隱蔽性潰瘍　concealed ulcer
隐匿性阑尾炎/隱蔽性闌尾炎　masked appendicitis
隐匿性疟/隱蔽性瘧　larvate malaria
隐匿性疝/隱性疝　concealed hernia
隐匿性糖尿病/掩蔽性糖尿病　masked diabetes
隐匿性痛风/無症狀痛風　masked gout
隐匿性抑郁[症]/隱匿性抑鬱[症]　masked depression
隐匿阴茎/隱匿陰莖　concealed penis
隐尿酸/隱尿酸　cryptophanic acid
隐氢图/隱氫圖　hydrogen-suppressed graph
隐球菌病/隱球菌病　cryptococcosis
隐球菌属/隱球菌　*Cryptococcus*
隐球菌性脑膜炎/囊球菌性腦膜炎　cryptococcal meningitis
隐神经/隱神經　saphenous nerve
隐私空间/隱私空間　personal space
隐私权/隱私權　privacy
隐痛/鈍痛　dull pain
隐头畸胎/隱頭畸胎,匿頭畸胎　cryptocephalus
隐窝/隱窩　recess
隐窝结石/隱窩結石　cryptolith
隐窝切除术/隱窩切除術　cryptectomy
隐窝细胞/隱窩細胞　pit cell
隐窝炎/隱窩炎　cryptitis
隐斜/斜眼,視軸偏向　phoria
隐斜测量[法]/斜眼測驗法　phorometry
隐斜测量计/斜眼測驗器　phorometer
隐斜视/隱斜視　heterophoria
隐斜视矫正镜/斜眼矯正鏡　phoriascope
隐斜性视疲劳/隱斜性視疲勞　heterophoric asthenopia
隐斜[眼]计/隱斜眼測驗器　convergiometer
隐斜眼痛/隱斜眼痛　heterophoralgia
隐形细胞/隱形細胞　adelomorphous cell
隐性/隱性　recessive
隐性病毒/隱性病毒　masked virus
隐性癫痫/隱性癲癇　larval epilepsy
隐性动脉瘤/隱性動脈瘤　silent aneurysm
隐性感染/不顯感染,無症狀性感染　inapparent infection
隐性黄疸/隱發性黃疸　occult jaundice
隐性积脓/隱蓄膿　cryptoempyema
隐性基因/隱性基因　recessive gene
隐性脊柱裂/隱性脊柱裂　spina bifida occulta
隐性颅裂/隱性顱裂　craniobifida occulta
隐性乳突炎/隱性乳突炎　latent mastoiditis
隐性肾病/隱性腎病　larval nephrosis
隐性酸中毒/隱性酸中毒　camouflaged acidosis
隐性先天鱼鳞癣样红皮症/隱性先天魚鱗癬樣紅皮症　recessive congenital ichthyosis erythroderma
隐性眼球震颤/隱性眼球震顫　latent nystagmus

隐性营养不良型大疱性表皮松解[症]/隱性營養不良型大皰性表皮鬆解[症]　epidermolysis bullosa dystrophic recessive
隐性营养不良性大疱性表皮松解/隱性全身營養不良性大皰性表皮裂解症　recessive dystrophic epidermolysis bullosa
隐性远视/隱性遠視　latent hypermetropia
隐性月经/隱[行月]經　cryptomenorrhea
隐性中耳炎/隱性中耳炎　latent otitis media
隐眼[畸形]/隱眼畸形　cryptophthalmus, cryptophthalmia
隐眼[畸形]综合征/隱頭畸胎症候群　cryptophthalmos syndrome
隐缘/隱緣　hidden margin
隐源性感染/隱原性傳染　cryptogenic infection
隐源性脓毒症/隱發性膿血症　cryptogenic pyemia
隐源性破伤风/隱發性破傷風　cryptogenic tetanus
隐源性肝硬化/隱源性肝硬化　cryptogenic cirrhosis
隐支/隱支　saphenous branch
瘾疹/癮疹,蕁麻疹,風疹塊　hidden rash, urticaria
瘾疹·风寒束表证/癮疹·風寒束表證　hidden rash with pattern of wind-cold fettering exterior
瘾疹·风热袭表证/癮疹·風熱襲表證　hidden rash with pattern of wind-heat assaulting exterior
瘾疹·气血两虚证/癮疹·氣血兩虛證　hidden rash with qi-blood deficiency pattern
瘾疹·气滞血瘀证/癮疹·氣滯血瘀證　hidden rash with pattern of qi stagnation and blood stasis
瘾疹·卫表不固证/癮疹·衛表不固證　hidden rash with pattern of unconsolidation of defensive exterior
瘾疹·胃肠湿热证/癮疹·胃腸濕熱證　hidden rash with pattern of dampness-heat in stomach and intestine
印度八角枫/印度八角楓　Alangium lamarckii
印度斑疹伤寒/印度之一種斑疹傷寒　Kumaon fever
印度红木/苦樹皮　Soymida febrifuga
印度回归热螺旋体/印度回歸熱螺旋體,卡德氏螺旋體　Borrelia carteri
印度胶/印度膠,加利膠　ghatti gum
印度解热合剂/印度退熱劑　sudarshan shurna
印度乳胶/印度樹膠　panchontee
印度式鼻成形术/印度式補鼻術　Indian rhinoplasty
印防己毒素/印度防己毒素　picrotoxin
印防己毒素中毒/印度防己毒中毒　picrotoxinism
印防己苷/印度防己素　anamirtin
印迹/印象　blotting
DNA 印迹/DNA 印跡　Southern blot
RNA 印迹/RNA 印跡　Northern blot
印加骨/印加骨　Inca bone
印戒细胞/戒環細胞　signet ring cell
印戒细胞癌/印環細胞癌　signet ring cell carcinoma
印模/印模　impression
印模材料/印模材料　impression material
印模膏/印模膏　modelling compound
印模糊剂/印模糊劑　impression paste
印模面/印模面　impression surface
印模区/印模區　impression area
印模石膏/印模石膏　complaster
印模托盘/印模盤　impression tray
印片法细胞学检查[术]/印片法細胞學檢查[術]　imprint cytologic examination
印刷工麻痹/印刷工麻痺　printer palsy
印刷工气[哮]喘/印刷工氣喘　printer asthma
印堂/印堂　yintang, EX-HN3
茚地那韦/英地那韋　indinavir
茚类/茚類　indenes
茚满类/茚滿類　indans
茚三酮/茚三酮　ninhydrin
茚三酮试剂/茚三酮試劑　ninhydrin reagent
英尺烛光/英尺燭光　foot-candle
英国黑汗热/英國黑汗熱　anglicus sudor
英国式鼻成形术/英式補鼻術　English rhinoplasty
英普咪定/英普咪定　impromidine
婴儿/嬰兒　infant
婴儿安全出生/活[胎生]産　live birth
婴儿保温箱/嬰兒保溫箱　infant incubator
婴儿鼻塞/嬰兒鼻塞　snuffle
婴儿痴呆/嬰兒癡呆　infantile dementia
婴儿猝死/嬰兒猝死　sudden infant death
婴儿猝死综合征/嬰兒猝死症候群　sudden infant death syndrome
婴儿发育表/嬰兒發育表　baby grid
婴儿肥大性胃部狭窄/嬰兒肥大性胃部狹窄　infantile hypertrophic gastric stenosis
婴儿粉/嬰兒撲粉,嬰兒爽身粉　baby powder
婴儿福利/嬰兒福利　infant welfare
婴儿腹部远心性脂肪营养不良/嬰兒腹部遠心性脂肪營養不良　lipodystrophia centrifugalis abdominalis infantilis
婴儿腹泻/嬰兒腹瀉　infantile diarrhea
婴儿腹泻病/嬰兒腹瀉疾病　infantile celiac disease
婴儿肝/嬰兒肝　infantile liver
婴儿孤独症/嬰兒孤獨癖　infantile autism
婴儿骨皮质增生症/嬰兒骨外組織肥厚症　infantile cortical hyperostosis
婴儿骨外层肥厚/增殖性骨外骨贅　hyperplastic

婴儿骨膜增生/嬰兒骨膜增生 infantile periostosis
婴儿固缩细胞增多症/嬰兒固縮細胞增多症 infantile pyknocytosis
婴儿黑变性神经外胚层瘤/嬰兒黑變性神經外胚層瘤 melanotic neuroectodermal tumor of infancy
婴儿护理/嬰兒護理 infant care
婴儿滑石粉/嬰兒滑石粉 baby talcum powder
婴儿坏疽性皮炎/嬰兒壞疽性皮膚炎 dermatitis gangrenosa infantum
婴儿环状红斑/嬰兒環狀紅斑 annular erythema of infancy
婴儿肌纤维瘤病/嬰兒肌纖維瘤病 infantile myofibromatosis
婴儿痉挛/嬰兒痙攣 infantile spasm
婴儿颗粒细胞龈瘤/嬰兒之顆粒細胞齦瘤 granular cell epulis of infancy
婴儿雷夫叙姆病/嬰兒雷弗蘇姆病 infantile refsum disease
婴儿利什曼原虫/嬰兒利什曼體 Leishmania infantum
婴儿脑炎/嬰兒腦炎 infantile encephalitis
婴儿黏液水肿/嬰兒黏液水腫 infantile myxedema
婴儿尿布/嬰兒尿布 infant diaper
婴儿配方/嬰兒配方 infant formula
婴儿皮肤急性出血性水肿/嬰兒皮膚急性出血性水腫 infantile acute hemorrhagic edema of the skin
婴儿皮肤黏蛋白沉积病/嬰兒皮膚黏液素病 cutaneous mucinosis of infancy
婴儿期/嬰兒期 infancy, babyhood
婴儿[期]的/嬰兒的 infantile
婴儿期神经轴突营养不良/嬰兒神經軸突退化 infantile neuroaxonal dystrophy
婴儿期纤维性错构瘤/嬰兒纖維性錯構瘤 fibrous hamartoma of infancy
婴儿期肢端脓疱病/嬰兒肢端膿皰症 acropustulosis of infancy
婴儿鞘膜积液/嬰兒鞘膜水囊腫 infantile hydrocele
婴儿色素性神经外胚层肿瘤/嬰兒色素性神經外胚層腫瘤 pigmented neuroectodermal tumor of infancy
婴儿疝/幼兒疝 infantile hernia
婴儿设备/嬰兒設備 infant equipment
婴儿肾/嬰兒腎 infantile kidney
婴儿生后休止期脱发/嬰兒出生後休止期落髮 postnatal telogen effluvium of infant
婴儿食品/嬰兒食品 infant food
婴儿室/嬰兒室 nursery
婴儿死亡率/嬰兒死亡率 infant mortality

婴儿松弛综合征/嬰兒鬆弛症候群 floppy infant syndrome hypotonia
婴儿苔藓/出牙疹 strophulus
婴儿臀部肉芽肿/嬰兒臀部肉芽腫 granuloma gluteale infantum
婴儿萎缩/幼兒萎縮症 infantile atrophy
婴儿喂养/嬰兒餵養 feeding baby
婴儿吸吮用假乳头/嬰兒吸吮用假乳頭 pacifier
婴儿行为/嬰兒行爲 infant behavior
婴儿型疝/幼兒疝[氣] infantile hernia
婴儿颜面头部急性湿疹/嬰兒顏面頭部急性濕疹 eczema infantum acutum faciei et capitis
婴儿样骨盆/幼兒型骨盆 infantile pelvis
婴儿样语/言語模糊不清,如嬰兒似的聲音 lallation
婴儿医院/嬰兒醫院 infantorium
婴儿营养障碍/嬰兒營養障礙 infant nutrition disorder
婴儿指/嬰兒指 infantile digital
婴儿指纤维瘤/嬰兒指纖維瘤 infantile digital fibroma
婴儿趾/嬰兒趾 infantile digital
婴儿趾纤维瘤/嬰兒趾纖維瘤 infantile digital fibroma
婴幼儿期/嬰兒期及孩童期 infancy and childhood
婴幼儿型青光眼/嬰兒期青光眼 infantile glaucoma
罂粟/罌粟 poppy
罂粟碱/罌粟鹼,罌粟素 papaverine
罂粟壳/罌粟殼 poppy capsule
罂粟子/罌粟子 mawseed
樱桃/櫻桃 cherry
樱桃苷/野櫻素 prunin
樱桃红斑/櫻桃紅點 cherry-red spot
樱桃糖浆/櫻桃糖漿 cherry syrup
樱桃状血管瘤/櫻桃狀血管瘤 cherry angioma
鹦鹉病毒/鸚鵡病毒 parrot virus
鹦鹉颌/鸚鵡頜 parrot jaw
鹦鹉热/鸚鵡熱 psittacosis
鹦鹉热衣原体/鸚鵡熱衣原體 Chlamydia psittaci
膺窗/膺窗 yingchuang, ST16
鹰鼻/鷹鼻 hooknose
鹰钩鼻/鷹鉤鼻 aquiline nose
鹰爪带/鷹爪帶 accipiter
鹰爪手/鷹爪手 claw hand
鹰嘴/鷹嘴[突] olecranon
鹰嘴的/鷹嘴的 olecranal
鹰嘴腱内囊/鷹嘴腱內囊 intratendinous bursa of olecranon
鹰嘴皮下囊/鷹嘴皮下囊 subcutaneous bursa of

olecranon
鹰嘴窝/鷹嘴窩　olecranon fossa
迎风冷泪/迎風冷淚　cold tear induced by wind, epiphora induced by wind
迎香/迎香　yingxiang, LI20
迎香穴按摩/迎香穴按摩　massage of Yingxiang point
荥[穴]/滎穴　ying-spring point
荧光/螢光　fluorescence
荧光胺/螢光胺　fluorescamine
荧光测量[法]/螢光測定法　fluorometry
荧光蛋白/二氫化螢光素　fluorescin
荧光分析法/螢光光度測定法　fluorimetry
荧光辐射/螢光輻射　fluorescent radiation
荧光共振能量转移/螢光共振能量轉移　fluorescence resonance energy transfer
荧光光度测定法/螢光光度測定法　fluorophotometry
荧光光谱法/螢光光譜法　fluorescence spectrometry
荧光剂/螢光劑　fluorescent agent
荧光抗体技术/螢光抗體技術　fluorescent antibody technique
荧光喹诺酮类/螢光喹諾酮類　fluoroquinolones
荧光密螺旋体抗体吸收试验/螢光密螺旋體抗體吸收試驗　fluorescent treponemal antibody-absorption test
荧光免疫分析/螢光免疫分析　fluorescence immunoassay, FIA
荧光偏振/螢光偏振　fluorescence polarization
荧光偏振免疫分析/螢光偏極免疫分析　fluorescence polarization immuno assay, FPIA
荧光漂白恢复技术/螢光漂白恢復技術　fluorescence recovery after photobleaching
荧光染料/螢光染料　fluorescent dye
荧光染色[法]/螢光染色[法]　fluorescent staining method, fluorescence staining
荧光X射线摄影术/螢光攝影術　photofluorography
荧光X射线[照]片/螢光攝影　photofluorogram
荧光X射线照相机/螢光X射線照相機　photofluoroscope
荧光X射线照相术/螢光X射線照相術　fluorography
荧光渗漏/螢光滲漏　fluorescence leakage
荧光素/螢光素　fluorescein
荧光素标记法/螢光素標記法　fluorescein labeling method
荧光素标记抗体/螢光素標記抗體　fluorescein labelled antibody

荧光素充盈/螢光素充盈　fluorescein filling
荧光素酶类/螢光素酶類　luciferases
荧光素钠/螢光素鈉，螢紅素鈉　uranin
荧光素尿/螢光素尿　fluoresceinuria
荧光素试验/螢光素試驗　fluorescein test
荧光素血管造影术/螢光素血管造影術　fluorescein angiography
荧光素-5-异硫氰酸盐/螢光素-5-異硫氰酸鹽　fluorescein-5-isothiocyanate
荧光透视检查/螢光透視檢查　fluoroscopy
荧光细胞/螢光細胞　fluorocyte
荧光显微镜/螢光顯微鏡　fluorescence microscope
荧光显微镜检查/螢光顯微鏡檢查　fluorescence microscopy
荧光原位杂交/螢光原位雜交　fluorescence in situ hybridization
荧光遮蔽/螢光遮蔽　blocked fluorescence
荧光组织化学/螢光組織化學　fluorescence histochemistry
荧光组织化学法/螢光組織化學法　fluorescence histochemical method
荧烷/螢光素母體　fluorane
萤火虫类/螢火蟲類　fireflies
萤火虫荧光素/螢火蟲螢光素　firefly luciferin
萤火虫荧光素酶类/螢火蟲螢光素酶類　firefly luciferases
萤石物镜/螢石接物鏡　fluorite objective
营分/營分　nutrient tier, yingfen
营分证/營分證　yingfen pattern
营气/營氣　nutrient qi
营卫不和/營衛不和　disharmony between nutrient qi and defensive qi
营血/營血　nutrient-blood
营养保健品/營養保健品　dietary supplement
营养补剂/營養補充劑　nutritional supplement
营养不良/營養不良　dystrophia
营养不良的/營養不良的　dystrophic
营养不良水肿/飢餓水腫　hunger edema
营养不良性闭经/營養不良性閉經　malnutritional amenorrhea
营养不良性大疱性表皮松解症/失養性水皰性表皮鬆解症　dystrophic epidermolysis bullosa
营养不良性钙化/營養不良性鈣化　dystrophic calcification
营养不良性肌强直/肌强直性營養不良　myotonic dystrophy
营养不良性肌强直病/失養性肌强直　myotonia dystrophica

营养不良性溃疡/營養[不良]性潰瘍　trophic ulcer
营养不良性皮肤钙沉着症/失養性皮膚鈣沈著病　dystrophic calcinosis cutis
营养不良性水肿/營養不良性水腫　alimentary edema
营养不良性水肿综合征/營養不良性水腫症候群　nutritional edema syndrome
营养不良性萎缩/營養不良性萎縮　malnutrition atrophy
营养不良性消瘦/營養不良性消瘦　nutritional marasmus
营养不足/營養不足　subnutrition
营养的/營養的　nutritional
营养调查/營養調查　nutrition survey
营养动力学/營養動力學　trophodynamics
营养功能/營養性，營養力　trophicity
营养灌肠剂/營養灌腸劑　nutrient enema
营养过度/過度營養法　hyperalimentation
营养过度病/營養過度病　hyperalimentosis
营养过剩/營養過剩　overnutrition
营养佳良/營養良好　eutrophia
营养价值/營養[價]值　nutritive value
营养孔/營養孔　nutrient foramen
营养疗法/營養療法　nutrition therapy
营养卵黄/營養[卵]黄　tropholecithus
营养培养基/營養培養基　nutrient medium
营养评价/營養評價　nutrition assessment
营养缺乏/營養缺乏,营养不良　denutrition
营养缺乏疾患/營養缺乏疾患　nutritional-deficiency disorder
营养[缺乏]性贫血/缺乏性貧血　deficiency anemia
营养缺乏性湿疹/營養缺乏性濕疹　nutritional-deficiency eczema
营养缺失/營養缺失　defective nutrition
营养缺陷型/營養缺陷型　auxotroph
营养膳食/滋養飲食　nourishing diet
营养神经/營養神經　trophic nerve
营养神经[病]性萎缩/營養神經病性萎縮　trophoneurotic atrophy
营养神经[功能]病/營養神經機能病,神經性營養病　trophoneurosis
营养神经[功能]病的/營養性神經機能病的　trophoneurotic
营养[神经]性坏疽/營養神經性壞疽　trophic gangrene
营养神经性溃疡/營養神經病性潰瘍　trophoneurotic ulcer
营养神经性麻风/營養神經性麻風　trophoneurotic leprosy
营养[素]缺乏病/營養素缺乏病　deprivation disease
营养特需型/營養特需型　idiotroph
营养物[质]/營養素,滋養的　nutrient
营养[性]病/營養障礙病　trophonosis
营养性男性乳房增殖/營養性男性乳房增殖　nutritional gynecomastia
营养性贫血/營養性貧血　nutritional anemia
营养性神经病/營養性神經病變　nutritional neuropathy
营养性水肿/營養性水腫病,下肢硬腫病　trophedema
营养性损害/營養性損害　trophic lesion
营养性肢痛症/營養性肢痛症　acrotrophodynia
营养需要/營養需要　nutritional requirement
营养学/營養學　alimentology
营养学家/營養管理人,飲食管理人　nutritionist
营养血管/營養血管　nutrient vessel
营养异常/營養異常　anomalotrophy
营养异常性巨大发育/巨體發育異常　macrodystrophia
营养障碍/營養障礙　nutrition disorder, trophic disturbance
营养障碍难产综合征/營養障礙難產症候群　dystrophia-dystocia syndrome
营养障碍性肝炎/營養障礙性肝炎　trophopathic hepatitis
营养政策/營養政策　nutrition policy
营养支持/營養支持　nutritional support
营养状况/營養狀況　nutritional status
营养作用过慢/營養作用徐緩　bradytrophia
营阴损伤/營陰損傷　nutrient qi and yin fluid being damaged
蝇类/蠅類　flies
蝇蛆病/[蠅]蛆病　myiasis
蝇蕈醇/蠅蕈醇　muscimol
蝇蕈毒素/瓢蕈毒素　amanitotoxin
影幻视/影幻視,眼前暗影　aphose
影响妄想/易受外界影響而生幻想　delusion of influence
影像/影像　image
影像计/影像檢查計　eikonometer
影像密度测定法/影像密度測量法　videodensitometry
影像清晰区/鑒定明確區　area of critical definition
影印平板培养/複製平板培養　replica plating
瘿/甲狀腺腫　goiter
瘿劳/瘿勞　goiter exhaustion, hypothyrea

瘿气/瘿氣 goiter qi, hyperthyreosis
瘿气·肝郁火旺证/瘿氣·肝鬱火旺證 goiter qi with pattern of liver depression and fire effulgence
瘿气·心脾气虚证/瘿氣·心脾氣虛證 goiter qi with heart-spleen qi deficiency pattern
瘿气·阴虚阳亢证/瘿氣·陰虛陽亢證 goiter qi with pattern of yin deficiency and yang hyperactivity
瘿痈/瘿癰 thyroiditis
瘿痈·风热痰凝证/瘿癰·風熱痰凝證 thyroiditis with pattern of wind-heat and phlegm coagulation
瘿痈·气滞痰凝证/瘿癰·氣滯痰凝證 thyroiditis with pattern of qi stagnation and phlegm coagulation
应对策略/因應策略 coping strategy
应激反应/壓力反應 stress reaction
应激性不良/興奮不良,感受性不良 dyserethesia
应激性高脂血症/應激性高脂血症 stress hyperlipidemia
应激性红细胞增多/壓力紅血球增多症 stress polycythemia
应激性溃疡/應激性潰瘍 stress ulcer
应激性糖尿病/應激性糖尿病 stress diabetes
应激源/壓力源 stressor
应激障碍/精神壓力障礙 stress disorder
应急剂量/緊急劑量 emergency dose
应力/應力,壓迫 stress, stress force
应力副承托区/應力副承托區 secondary stress-bearing area
应力骨折/應力[性]骨折 stress fracture
应力缓冲器/壓力減除器 stress breaker
应力缓冲式桥/應力緩衝式橋 broken stress bridge
应力性骨折/應力性骨折 stress fracture
应力主承托区/應力主承托區 primary stress-bearing area
应用解剖学/應用解剖學 applied anatomy
应用免疫学/應用免疫學 applied immunology
应用心理学/應用心理學 applied psychology
应指/應指 palpable fluctuation
硬癌/硬癌 carcinoma durum
硬癌的/硬癌的 scirrhous
硬斑病/硬斑病 morphea
硬斑病样基底细胞上皮瘤/硬斑病樣基底細胞上皮瘤 morphea-like basal cell epithelioma
硬蛋白/硬蛋白 scleroprotein
硬度/硬度 hardness
硬度计/硬度計 sclerometer
硬度试验/硬度試驗 hardness test
硬腭/硬腭 hard palate

硬腭裂/硬腭裂 cleft hard palate
硬膏布/硬膏布 plaster mull
硬膏[剂]/硬膏劑,膏藥 plaster
硬膏脱毛[发]法/膏藥除髮 dropacism
硬骨板/硬骨板 lamina dura
硬后镀金/硬後鍍金 aftergilding
硬化/硬化 cirrhosis, sclerosis
硬化变性/硬化性變性 sclerotic degeneration
硬化病/硬化病 scleredema
硬化骨骼/硬化骨骼 scleroskeleton
硬化剂/硬化劑 sclerosing agent
硬化[剂]溶液/硬化溶液 sclerosing solution
硬化剂注入疗法/硬化劑注入療法 sclerosing agent injection therapy
硬化疗法/硬化療法 sclerotherapy
硬化萎缩的/硬化萎縮的 scleroatrophic
硬化萎缩苔藓/硬化萎縮性苔蘚 lichen sclerosus et atrophicus
硬化型乳突炎/硬化性乳突炎 sclerosing mastoiditis
硬化性胆管炎/硬化性膽管炎 sclerosing cholangitis
硬化性的/硬化的 sclerotic
硬化性耳炎/硬化性耳炎 otitis sclerotica
硬化性非化脓骨髓炎/硬化性非化膿骨髓炎 sclerosing nonsuppurative osteomyelitis
硬化性骨髓炎/硬化[性]骨髓炎 sclerosing osteomyelitis
硬化性骨炎/硬化性骨炎 sclerosing osteitis
硬化性汗腺导管癌/硬化性汗管癌 sclerosing sweat duct carcinoma
硬化性脊髓炎/硬化性脊髓炎 sclerosing myelitis
硬化性角膜炎/硬化性角膜炎 sclerosing keratitis
硬化性狼疮/硬化性狼瘡 lupus sclerosus
硬化性淋巴管炎/硬化性淋巴管炎 sclerosing lymphangitis
硬化性卵巢炎/硬化性卵巢炎 sclero-oophoritis
硬化性黏液水肿/硬化性黏液水腫 scleromyxedema
硬化性皮肤结核/硬結性皮結核 tuberculosis cutis indurativa
硬化性上皮错构瘤/硬化性表皮錯構瘤 sclerosing epithelial hamartoma
硬化性湿疹/硬化性濕疹 eczema sclerosum
硬化性腺炎/硬性腺炎 scleradenitis
硬化性血管瘤/硬化血管瘤 sclerosing hemangioma
硬化性脂肪肉芽肿/硬化性脂肪肉芽腫 sclerosing lipogranuloma
硬化性中耳炎/硬化性中耳炎 otitis media sclerotica
硬化性注射/硬化性注射法 sclerosing injection
硬鸡眼/硬雞眼 heloma durum

硬脊膜/脊硬膜 spinal dura mater
硬脊膜动静脉瘘/硬脊膜動靜脈瘻 spinal dural arteriovenous fistula
硬脊膜外脓肿/硬脊膜外膿腫 spinal epidural abscess
硬脊膜外血肿/硬脊膜外血腫 spinal epidural hematoma
硬[脊]膜外阻滞/硬膜外阻滯 epidural block
硬脊膜下脓肿/硬脊膜下膿腫 spinal subdural abscess
硬脊膜下血肿/硬脊膜下血腫 spinal subdural hematoma
硬胶囊剂/硬膠囊[劑] hard capsule
硬结/硬結 scleroma
硬结的/硬結的 indurated
硬结红斑/硬結性紅斑 erythema induratum
硬结性肾炎/硬結性腎炎 indurative nephritis
硬结性心肌炎/硬結性心肌炎 indurative myocarditis
硬金属尘肺症/硬金屬塵肺症 hard-metal lung disease
硬膜/硬[腦脊]膜 dura mater
硬膜的/硬膜的 dural
硬膜内出血/硬膜內出血 intradural hemorrhage
硬膜内的/硬腦膜內的 intradural
硬膜内脂肪瘤/硬腦膜內脂肪瘤 intradural lipoma
硬膜外/硬膜上的,硬膜外的 epidural
硬膜外出血/硬膜外出血 epidural hemorrhage
硬膜外的/硬膜外的 extradural
硬膜外麻醉/硬膜周圍麻醉法 peridural anesthesia
硬膜外脓肿/硬膜外膿瘍,硬腦膜外膿腫 epidural abscess
硬膜外腔造影术/硬膜外腔造影術 epidurography
硬膜外隙/硬膜外腔 extradural space
硬膜外血斑/硬膜外血斑 epidural blood patch
硬膜外造影术/硬腦膜周圍X光造影術 peridurography
硬膜外造影照片/硬腦膜周圍X光像 peridurogram
硬膜外镇痛/硬膜外鎮痛 epidural analgesia
硬膜外脂肪瘤/硬膜外脂肪瘤 epidural lipoma
硬膜外肿瘤/硬膜外腫瘤 epidural neoplasm
硬膜外注射/硬膜外注射 epidural injection
硬膜下/硬膜下的 subdural
硬膜下积脓/硬膜下積膿 subdural empyema
硬膜下积液/硬膜下積液 subdural effusion
硬膜下腔/硬膜下腔 subdural space
硬膜下水囊瘤/硬腦膜下水瘤 subdural hygroma
硬膜下隙/硬膜下腔,韌膜下隙 subdural space

硬膜下血肿/硬腦膜下血腫 subdural hematoma
硬脑[脊]膜成形术/硬膜成形術,硬膜造形術 duraplasty
硬脑[脊]膜内层炎/硬腦膜內層炎 internal meningitis
硬脑[脊]膜外层炎/硬腦膜外層炎,外硬腦膜炎 external meningitis
硬脑[脊]膜血肿/硬腦膜血腫 meningematoma
硬脑膜/硬腦膜 cerebral dura mater, dura mater of brain
硬脑膜动静脉瘘/硬腦膜動靜脈瘻 dural arteriovenous fistula
硬脑膜窦/硬腦膜竇 sinus of dura mater
硬脑膜外出血/脊椎管內硬腦膜外出血 extradural hemorrhage
硬脑膜外血肿/硬腦膜外血腫 epidural hematoma
硬脑膜下出血/硬腦膜下出血 subdural hemorrhage
硬脑膜下穿刺/硬腦膜下穿刺 subdural puncture
硬脑膜压下器/腦膜壓持器 decussorium
硬脑膜炎/硬腦膜炎 pachymeningitis
硬脑膜蛛网膜炎/硬膜蜘蛛膜炎 duroarachnitis
硬皮/硬皮 callous
硬皮病/硬皮病 scleroderma
硬皮病的/硬皮病的 sclerodermatous
硬皮病性皮肌炎/硬皮并硬皮肌炎 sclerodermatomyositis
硬皮病样迟发性皮肤卟啉病/硬皮病樣遲發性皮膚卟啉病 sclerodermoid porphyria cutanea tarda
硬皮心脏病/硬皮病心臟病 scleroderma heart disease
硬蜱科/硬蜱科 ixodidae
硬羟基磷灰石/硬羥基磷灰石 durapatite
硬式内镜/硬式內鏡 rigid endoscope
硬树脂/硬樹脂 copal
硬水/硬水 hard water
硬水综合征/硬水症候群 hard water syndrome
硬缩/硬縮,硬化性狹窄 sclerostenosis
[硬]下疳/硬下疳 hard sore
硬纤维袋反应/硬纖維反應 desmoid reaction
硬腺癌/硬腺癌 scirrhous adenocarcinoma
硬橡皮/硬[化]橡皮 vulcanite
硬性角膜接触镜/硬性角膜接觸鏡 hard corneal contact lens
硬性内障/硬性白内障 sclerocataracta
硬性乳头状瘤/硬性乳頭狀瘤 papilloma durum
硬[性]纤维瘤/硬纖維瘤 fibroma durum
硬药/硬藥 hard drug
硬脂的/硬脂的 stearic

硬脂瘤/硬脂瘤　lipoma durum
硬脂酸/硬脂酸　stearic acid
硬脂酸胆固醇/硬脂酸膽固醇　cholesteryl stearate
硬脂酸丁酯/硬酯酸丁酯　butyl stearate
硬脂酸钙/硬脂酸鈣　calcium stearate
硬脂酸红霉素/硬脂酸紅黴素　erythromycin stearate
硬脂酸类/硬脂酸類　stearic acids
硬脂酸铝/硬脂酸鋁　aluminium stearate
硬脂酸镁/硬脂酸鎂　magnesium stearate
硬脂酸钠/硬脂酸鈉　sodium stearate
硬脂酸鲨鱼肝油酯/硬脂酸鯊魚肝油酯　batyl monostearate
硬脂酸双酚A型环氧树脂酯/硬脂酸雙酚A型環氧樹脂酯　bisphenol A type epoxy resin stearate
硬脂酸辛酯/硬脂酸辛酯　2-ethylhexyl stearate
硬脂酸锌/硬脂酸鋅,脂蠟酸鋅　zinc stearate
硬脂酸盐/硬脂酸鹽　stearate
拥抱反射/擁抱反射　embrace reflex
拥挤现象/擁擠現象　crowding phenomenon
痈/癰　carbuncle, abscess disease
痈病/癰病　carbunculosis
痈·气血两虚证/癰·氣血兩虛證　abscess with qi-blood deficiency pattern
痈·热毒蕴结证/癰·熱毒蘊結證　abscess with heat-toxin amassment pattern
痈·热盛酿脓证/癰·熱盛釀膿證　abscess with pattern of suppuration due to heat exuberance
痈样的/癰樣的　carbunculoid
庸鲽鱼肝油/庸鰈魚肝油,比目魚肝油　halibut liver oil
庸医/庸醫　medicaster
永存玻璃体动脉/永存玻璃體動脈　persistent hyaloid artery
永存瞳孔膜/瞳孔膜存留　persistent pupillary membrane
永存性肠卵黄管/永存性腸卵黄管　persistent omphalomesenteric duct
永存性后肾管/永存性後腎管　persistent mesonephric duct
永存性脑咽管/永存性腦咽管　persistent craniopharyngeal duct
永存左上腔静脉/永存左上腔静脈　persistent left superior vena cava
永久充填/永久填補　permanent filling
永[久]磁铁/永久磁鐵　permanent magnet
永久性/永久性　permanent
永久性接触镜/永久性接觸鏡　extended-wear contact lens
永久性结肠造口术/永久性結腸造口術　permanent colostomy
永久性脱发/永久性禿髮　permanent alopecia
永久性心律不整/永久性心律不整　perpetual arrhythmia
永久性阈移/永久性閾移　permanent threshold shift
永久性种植体/永久性植入物　permanent implant
永久牙修复/永久牙修復　permanent dental restoration
永久硬度/永久硬度　permanent hardness
永停滴定法/永停滴定法　dead-stop titration
涌泉/湧泉　yongquan, KI1
[涌]吐法/[湧]吐法　emesis method
涌吐剂/湧吐劑　emetic formula
蛹婴/蛹嬰　chrysalis baby
用腹膜被覆/腹膜移補,腹膜覆蓋　peritonize
用户计算机接口/使用者電腦介面　user-computer interface
用力肺活量/用力肺活量　forced vital capacity
用力过度/過度用力　overexertion
用力呼气量/用力呼氣量　forced expiratory volume
用力呼气流速/用力呼氣流速　forced expiratory flow rate
用力呼气中段流量/用力呼氣中段流量　forced expiratory flow during middle half of FVC
用力性尿失禁/用力性尿失禁　exertional urinary incontinence
用奈氏试剂处理/以奈斯勒氏試劑處置　nesslerize
用麝香草脑处理/用麝香草腦處理　thymolize
用水蛭素防凝/使用水蛭素以抑制血液凝固　hirudinize
用药不足/用藥不足　under-medication
用药过度/用藥過度　over-medication
用药计划表/用藥計劃表　drug administration schedule
优境学/優境學　euthenics
优卡因/優卡因　eucaine
优霉素/優黴素　eumycin
优球蛋白/優球蛋白　euglobulin
优生流产/優生流產　eugenic abortion
优生论/優生論　eugenism
优生学/優生學　eugenics
优生学家/優生學家　eugenist
优生学绝育/優生學絕育法　eugenic sterilization
优生优境学/種族改良學　eugenothenics
优势[大脑]半球/優勢半球　dominant hemisphere
优势对数记分法/優勢對數記分法　lod score
优势构象/優勢構象　preferred conformation

优势抗原/優勢抗原　dominant antigen
优势卵泡/優勢卵泡　dominant follicle
优索液/優索液　Eusol
优先提供医疗服务组织/優先提供醫療服務組織
　　preferred provider organization
优种繁殖[法]/優種繁殖　stirpiculture
忧/憂　worry
忧恚无言/憂恚無言　Loss of Voice with
　　Acupuncture Therapy
忧伤肺/憂傷肺　anxiety impairing the lung
忧思伤心/憂思傷心　worry impairing the heart
忧为肺志/憂爲肺志　lung being associated with
　　worry
忧郁/憂鬱　stagnation pattern caused by worry
忧郁气质/憂鬱質　melancholic temperament
忧郁症/憂鬱病　melancholia
忧郁症患者/憂鬱病的　melancholic
忧中/憂中　stroke due to sorrow
幽闭恐怖/幽閉恐懼症　claustrophobia
幽居癖/幽閉嗜好，嗜幽癖　claustrophilia
幽门/幽門　①pylorus ②youmen, KI21
幽门闭锁/幽門閉鎖　pyloric atresia
幽门部/幽門部　pyloric part
幽门[部]的/幽門的　pyloric
幽门部分切除术/半幽門切除術　hemipylorectomy
幽门成形术/幽門成形術，幽門造形術　pyloroplasty
幽门窦/幽門竇　pyloric antrum
幽门梗阻/幽門梗阻　pyloric obstruction
幽门管/幽門管　pyloric canal
幽门管溃疡/幽門管潰瘍　pyloric canal ulcer
幽门后淋巴结/幽門後淋巴結　retropyloric lymph
　　node
幽门环变形/幽門環變形　deformity of pyloric ring
幽门肌切开术/幽門肌切開術　pyloromyotomy
幽门[及邻近部分胃]切除术/胃幽門部切除術
　　pylorogastrectomy
幽门痉挛/幽門痙攣　pylorospasm
幽门静脉/幽門静脈　pyloric vein
幽门镜检查/幽門檢視法　pyloroscopy
幽门扩张术/幽門擴張術　pylorodiosis
幽门括约肌/幽門括約肌　pyloric sphincter,
　　sphincter of pylorus
幽门淋巴结/幽門淋巴結　pyloric lymph node
幽门平面/幽門平面　transpyloric plane
幽门蹼/幽門蹼　pyloric web
幽门前瓣膜/幽門前瓣膜　prepyloric diaphragm
幽门前静脉/幽門前静脈　prepyloric vein
幽门切除术/胃幽門切除術　gastropylorectomy
幽门切开术/幽門切開術　pylorotomy
幽门上淋巴结/幽門上淋巴結　suprapyloric lymph
　　node
幽门十二指肠炎/幽門十二指腸炎　pyloroduodenitis
幽门痛/幽門痛　pyloralgia
幽门狭窄/幽門狭窄　pyloric stenosis
幽门下淋巴结/幽門下淋巴結　subpyloric lymph
　　node
幽门腺/幽門腺　pyloric gland
幽门炎/幽門炎　pyloritis
幽门造口术/幽門造口術　pylorostomy
尤尔特征/尤爾特徵　Ewart sign
尤因肉瘤/尤因肉瘤　Ewing sarcoma
由背向腹/從背面向腹側　dorsoventrad
由实转虚/由實轉虛　deficiency transformed from
　　excess
邮票状皮片/郵票狀皮片　stamp free skin graft
油/油　oil
油包水乳化佐剂/油包水乳化佐劑　water-in-oil
　　emulsion adjuvant
油包水乳剂/油包水乳劑　water-in-oil emulsion
油彩/油彩　paint
油彩皮炎/油彩皮炎　grease paint dermatitis
油纯度计/驗油器　oleometer
油的/油的　oily
油风/油風　alopecia areata
油风·肝肾两虚证/油風·肝腎兩虛證　alopecia
　　areata with liver-kidney deficiency pattern
油风·气血两虚证/油風·氣血兩虛證　alopecia
　　areata with qi-blood deficiency pattern
油风·气滞血瘀证/油風·氣滯血瘀證　alopecia
　　areata with pattern of qi stagnation and blood stasis
油风脱发/皮脂溢性脱髮　seborrheic alopecia
油风·血热生风证/油風·血熱生風證　alopecia
　　areata with pattern of blood heat generating wind
油管/油管　oil duct
油汗/油汗　sticky sweating
油剂/油劑　oil
油浸法/油浸法　oil immersion
油浸剂/油浸劑　oleoinfusion
油[浸]镜[头]/油浸鏡　oil immersion lens
油类/油類　oils
油疗法/油劑療法　eleotherapy
油醚麻醉/油醚麻醉　oil-ether anesthesia
油漆皮炎/油漆皮炎　paint dermatitis
油溶液剂/油劑溶液性　oily solution
油室/油室　oil cavity
油树脂/油樹脂　oleoresin

油酸/油酸　oleic acid
油酸汞/油酸汞　hydrargyrum oleatum
油酸类/油酸類　oleic acids
油酸酶/油酸酶　olease
油酸木馏油/油酸木餾油　oleocreosote
油酸双酚 A 型环氧树脂酯/油酸雙酚 A 型環氧樹脂酯　bisphenol A type epoxy resin oleate
油酸盐/油酸鹽　oleate
油酸乙酯/油酸乙酯　ethyl oleate
油糖剂/油糖劑　eleosaccharum
油调剂/油調劑　oil paste
油细胞/油細胞　oil cell
油性痤疮/油性痤瘡　oil acne
油性皮肤/油性皮膚　oil skin
油性皮脂溢/油性皮脂漏　seborrhea adiposa
油性肉芽肿/油性肉芽腫　oil granuloma
油硬脂酸盐/油硬脂酸鹽　oleostearate
油[脂]性腹水/脂肪性腹水　fatty ascites
油脂性基质/油脂性基質,脂性基劑　greasing base, greasy base
油脂[性]囊肿/油質囊腫　oil cyst
油制/油制　processed with oil
油肿/油質腫　elaioma
油棕榈酸盐/油軟脂酸鹽　oleopalmitate
疣/疣　wart, verruca
疣瘢瘤/疣瘢瘤　warty cicatricial tumor
疣病/疣病　verrucosis
疣病毒/疣病毒　wart virus
疣的/疣的　verrucous
疣痘/疣狀痘瘡　wartpox
疣化角化不良瘤/疣狀角化不良瘤　warty dyskeratoma
疣目/疣目　verruca vulgaris, wart
疣热治疗/疣熱治療　heat therapy of wart
疣性心炎/疣狀心臟炎　verrucous carditis
疣样穿通性胶原瘤/疣樣穿通性膠原瘤　collagenoma perforans verruciforme
疣样穿通性乳突内弹力瘤/疣樣穿通性乳突内彈力瘤　elastoma intrapapillare perforans verruciforme
疣状癌/疣狀癌　verrucous carcinoma
疣状白斑/疣狀白斑　verrucous leukoplakia
疣状表皮发育不良/疣狀表皮發育障礙　epidermodysplasia verruciformis
疣状的/疣狀的　verruciform
疣状发癣菌/疣狀毛癬菌　Trichophyton verrucosum
疣状核变形虫/疣狀核變形蟲　Amoeba verrucosa
疣状黄瘤/疣狀黄瘤　verruciform xanthoma
疣状结核/疣狀結核　tuberculosis verrucosa

疣状溃疡/疣狀潰瘍　warty ulcer
疣状脑/腦皮質之疣態　status verrucosus
疣状皮肤结核[病]/疣狀皮膚結核　tuberculosis verrucosa cutis
疣状皮结核/疣狀皮結核　tuberculosis verrucosa cutis
疣状皮炎/疣狀皮膚炎　dermatitis verrucosa, verrucous dermatitis
疣状瓶霉/疣狀瓶黴　Phialophora verrucosa
疣状湿疹/疣狀濕疹　eczema verrucosum
疣状天花/疣狀痘瘡,疣痘　variola verrucosa
疣状顽固性荨麻疹/疣狀頑固性蕁麻疹　urticaria perstans verrucosa
疣状心内膜炎/疣狀心内膜炎　endocarditis verrucosa
疣状血管瘤/疣狀血管瘤　verrucous hemangioma
疣状银屑病/疣狀乾癬　psoriasis verruciformis
疣状增生/疣狀增生　verrucous hyperplasia
疣状肢端角化病/疣狀肢皮角化症　acrokeratosis verruciformis
疣状痣/疣性痣　nevus verrucosus
疣状赘生物/心内膜疣性瘤　verrucous vegetation
铀化合物/鈾化合物　uranium compound
铀同位素分离器/鈾同位素分離器　calutron
铀性肾炎/鈾性腎炎　uranium nephritis
蚰蜒疮/蚰蜒瘡　centiped sore
游出/游出　emigration
游动孢子/游動芽孢　swarm spore
游动孢子囊/游動孢子囊　zoosporangium
游动胆囊/遊走性膽囊　floating gallbladder
游动肝/遊走肝　wandering liver
游动精子/游動精子　antherozoid
游动脾/浮動脾,遊走脾　floating spleen
游动心/游動心,徘徊心　wandering heart
游动性甲状腺肿/游動性甲狀腺腫　diving goiter
游动性水肿/游動性水腫　migratory edema
游离壁/游離壁　free wall
游离端固定桥/游離端固定橋　free-end fixed bridge
游离核糖体/游離[型]核糖體,游離核糖小體　free ribosome
游离肌皮瓣/游離肌皮瓣　free myocutaneous flap
游离甲状腺素指数/游離甲狀腺素指數　free thyroxin index
游离巨噬细胞/游離巨噬細胞,游走巨噬細胞　free macrophage
游离踇甲皮瓣/游離踇甲皮瓣　free great toe nail skin flap
游离皮瓣/游離皮瓣　free skin flap
游离皮肤移植/游離皮膚移植　free skin

transplantation
游离绒毛/游離絨毛　free villus
游离神经末梢/游離神經末梢　free nerve ending
游离水/游離水　free water
游离髓石/游離髓石　free denticle
游离性牙骨小体/游離性牙骨小體　free cementicle
游离移植物/游離移植物　free graft
游离龈/游離齦　free gingiva
游离龈沟/游離[牙]齦溝　free gingival groove
游离缘/游離緣　free border, free margin
游离组织移植术/游離組織移植術　free tissue grafting
游离组织移植物/游離組織移植物　free tissue graft
游蛇毒/游蛇毒　Colubridae venom
游戏疗法/遊戲療法　play therapy
游行性毛状圆虫/游行性毛狀圓蟲　strongylus subtilis
游泳池肉芽肿/游泳池肉芽腫　swimming pool granuloma
游泳者耳病/游泳者耳病,游泳者耳炎　swimmer ear
游泳者痒病/游泳者癢病　swimmer itch
游走的/遊走的,暫時的　fugitive
游走骨/遊走骨,浮動骨　wandering bone
游走肾/遊走腎,浮動腎　floating kidney
游走吞噬细胞/移動性吞噬細胞　mobile phagocyte
游走细胞/遊走細胞　migratory cell, wandering cell
游走性关节炎/遊走性關節炎　wandering arthritis
游走性甲状腺肿/遊走性甲狀腺腫　wandering goiter
游走性皮下结节/遊走性皮下結節　migratory subcutaneous nodule
游走性舌炎/遊走性舌炎　migratory glossitis
游走性痛/遊走[性]痛　wandering pain
游走性疣/暫時性疣　fugitive wart
游走性幼虫病/爬行[性蚴毒]疹　sandworm disease
有凹痕的/有凹痕的　pitted
有被膜的/有被膜的　tunicary
有被囊神经末梢/[有]被囊神經末梢　encapsulated nerve ending
有被小泡/有被小泡　coated vesicle
有壁细胞/[有]壁細胞　lepocyte
有柄子宫托/有柄子宮托,有杆子宮托　stem pessary
有[彩色]斑点的/有斑點的　guttate
有槽夹板/有槽夾板　hollow splint
有窗胎盘/有窗胎盤　fenestrated placenta
有创性方法/有創性方法　invasive method
有创压力监测/有創壓力監測　invasive pressure monitoring
有档针/有檔針　stop needle
有毒的/有毒的　toxiferous
有毒动物/有毒動物　poisonous animal
有毒植物/有毒植物　toxic plant
有发头皮/有髮頭皮　hairy scalp
有腹无头寄生畸胎/有腹無頭寄生畸胎,腹連無腦連胎　gastroacephalus
有感电阻/有感電阻　inductive resistance
有根苔/有根苔　rooted fur
有钩绦虫/有鉤條蟲　taenia solium
有关物质/有關物質　related substance
有汗/出汗　sweating
有汗性外胚层发育不良/有汗性外胚層發育不良　hidrotic ectodermal dysplasia
有核的/有核的　nucleated
有核红细胞血症/有核紅血球血症　pyrenemia
有核细胞/有核細胞　nucleated cell
有机铂化合物/有機鉑化合物　organoplatinum compound
有机锝化合物/有機錇化合物　organotechnetium compound
有机分析/有機分析　organic analysis
有机汞化合物/有機汞化合物　organomercury compound
有机硅化合物/有機矽化合物　organosilicon compound
有机合成/有機合成　organic synthesis
有机化学品/有機化學品　organic chemical
有机金属化合物/有機金屬化合物　organometallic compound
有机磷化合物/有機磷化合物　organophosphorus compound
有机硫磷化合物/有機硫磷化合物　organothiophosphorus compound
有机氯/有機氯　organochlorine
有机凝胶/有機凝膠　organogel
有机溶剂肾病/有機溶劑腎病　organic solvent nephropathy
有机酸/有機酸　organic acid
有机酸代谢病/有機酸代謝病　disorder of organic acid metabolism
有机酸尿症/有機酸尿症　organic aciduria
有机酸血症/有機酸血症　organic acidemia
有机体/有機體,生物體　organism
有机物元素/有機物元素,有機體元素　organogen
有机硒化合物/有機硒化合物　organoselenium compound
有机锡化合物/有機錫化合物　organotin compound
有机阳离子转运蛋白质类/有機陽離子轉運蛋白質

类 organic cation transport proteins
有机阴离子转运多肽 C/有機陰離子轉運多肽 C　organic anion transport polypeptide C
有机阴离子转运子/有機陰離子轉運子　organic anion transporter
有架夹/有架夾　bracketed splint
有角畸胎/有角畸胎,高額畸胎　megaloceros
有角夹板/有角夾板　angular splint
有节夹板/有節夾板　articulated splint
有节莎草/有節莎草,分節莎草　adrue
有节神经/有節神經,神經節神經　gangliated nerve
有节探针/有節探針,脊節型探針　vertebrated probe
有茎的/有莖的　pediculate
有茎露脑畸胎/有莖露腦畸胎　podencephalus
有空泡细胞/有空泡細胞　vacuolated cell
有孔的/有孔的　porous
有孔毛细血管/有孔毛細血管,有孔微血管　fenestrated capillary
有孔探针/有眼探針　eyed probe
有孔印模托盘/有孔印模托盤　perforated impression tray
有裂缝的/有裂隙的　rimose
有裂隙的/有裂隙的,裂開的　craquele
有卵石花纹的/有卵石花紋的,鵝卵石狀的　pebbly
有腔囊胚/有腔囊胚　coeloblastula
有乳头的/有乳頭的,含乳頭的,生乳頭的　papilliferous
有乳突的/有乳突的　papillose
有色鼻液溢/有色鼻液漏　chromorhinorrhea
有色溶液/有色溶液　colored solution
有色眼镜/有色眼鏡,著色眼鏡　tinted spectacles
有色杂质/有色雜質　foreign pigment
有神/有神　presence of vitality
有神经节的/有神經節的　ganglionated
有丝分裂/有絲分裂　mitosis
有丝分裂不分离/有絲分裂不分離　mitotic nondisjunction
有丝分裂纺锤体/有絲分裂紡錘體　mitotic spindle apparatus
有丝分裂辐射/有絲分裂輻射　mitogenic radiation
有丝分裂互换/有絲分裂互換　mitotic crossing over
有丝分裂期/有絲分裂期　mitotic phase
有丝分裂抑制剂/有絲分裂抑制劑,阻分裂毒　mitotic poison
有丝分裂原/有絲分裂原　mitogen
有丝分裂原受体/有絲分裂原受體　mitogen receptor
有丝分裂指数/有絲分裂指數,絲狀分裂指數　mitotic index

有髓鞘神经/有髓鞘神經　medullated nerve
有髓鞘神经瘤/有髓鞘神經瘤　fascicular neuroma
有髓[神经]纤维/有髓[神經]纖維　myelinated nerve fiber
有头疽/有頭疽,癰　carbuncle, headed carbuncle
有头疽·火毒蕴结证/有頭疽·火毒蘊結證　headed carbuncle with fire-toxin amassment pattern
有头疽·气虚毒滞证/有頭疽·氣虛毒滯證　headed carbuncle with pattern of qi deficiency and toxin stagnation
有头疽·湿热壅滞证/有頭疽·濕熱壅滯證　headed carbuncle with pattern of dampness-heat congestion and stagnation
有头疽·阴虚火旺证/有頭疽·陰虛火旺證　headed carbuncle with pattern of yin deficiency and fire effulgence
有外膜及栅栏状排列的神经瘤/有外膜及柵欄狀排列的神經瘤　palisading encapsulated neuroma
有隙并指/有隙并指,末端駢指畸形　acrosyndactyly
有隙并趾/有隙并趾,末端駢趾畸形　acrosyndactyly
有限外韧维管束/有限外韌維管束,閉鎖并立型韌維管束　closed collateral bundle
有限稀释技术/有限稀釋技術　limiting dilution technique
有限元分析/有限元分析　finite element analysis
有腺纲感染/有腺綱感染　adenophorea infection
有效波长/有效波長　effective wavelength
有效成分/有效成分　active principle
有效肾血浆流量/有效腎血漿流量　effective renal plasma flow
有效肾血流量/有效腎血流量　effective renal blood flow
有效碳数/有效碳數　effective carbon number
有效掩蔽/有效掩蔽　effective masking
有效直径/有效直徑　effective diameter
有性繁殖/有性繁殖　sexual propagation
有性生殖/有性生殖　sexual reproduction
有性世代/有性世代　gamobium
有旋毛虫的/有旋毛蟲的　trichinous
有氧训练/有氧訓練　aerobic training
有义链/有義鏈　sense strand
有益菌种/有益菌種　probiotics
有音肌阵挛/有聲肌陣攣　phonomyoclonus
有缘胎盘/有緣胎盤　placenta marginata
有月经者/有月經者,經期婦人,行經婦女　menstruant
有足[神经胶质]细胞/有足[神經]膠質細胞,有茎细胞　pediculated cell

右板/右板 right lamina
右半结肠切除术/右半結腸切除術 right hemicolectomy
右半心畸形/右半心畸形 hemicardia dextra
右半月瓣/右半月瓣 right semilunar valve
右苄替米特/右苄替米特 dexetimide
右部/右部 right part
右侧心力衰竭/右側心力衰竭 right sided heart failure
右肠系膜窦/右腸繫膜竇 right mesenteric sinus
右段间裂/右段間裂 right intersegmental fissure
右房静脉/右房静脈 right atrial vein
右房室瓣/右房室瓣 right atrioventricular valve
右房室瓣后尖/右房室瓣後尖 posterior cusp of right atrioventricular valve
右房室瓣前尖/右房室瓣前尖 anterior cusp of right atrioventricular valve
右房室口/右房室口 right atrioventricular orifice
右啡烷/右啡烷 dextrorphan
右肺/右肺 right lung
[右肺]底段上静脉/[右肺]底段上静脈 superior basal vein
[右肺]底段下静脉/[右肺]底段下静脈 inferior basal vein
右肺动脉/右肺動脈 right pulmonary artery
右肺动脉底部/右肺動脈底部 basal part of right pulmonary artery
右肺动脉后底支/右肺動脈後底支 posterior basal branch of right pulmonary artery
右肺动脉后降支/右肺動脈後降支 posterior descending branch of right pulmonary artery
右肺动脉后升支/右肺動脈後昇支 posterior ascending branch of right pulmonary artery
右肺动脉后支/右肺動脈後支 posterior branch of right pulmonary artery
右肺动脉尖支/右肺動脈尖支 apical branch of right pulmonary artery
右肺动脉内侧底支/右肺動脈内側底支 medial basal branch of right pulmonary artery
右肺动脉内侧支/右肺動脈内側支 medial branch of right pulmonary artery
右肺动脉前底支/右肺動脈前底支 anterior basal branch of right pulmonary artery
右肺动脉前降支/右肺動脈前降支 anterior descending branch of right pulmonary artery
右肺动脉前升支/右肺動脈前昇支 anterior ascending branch of right pulmonary artery
右肺动脉前支/右肺動脈前支 anterior branch of right pulmonary artery
右肺动脉上叶支/右肺動脈上葉支 superior lobar branch of right pulmonary artery
右肺动脉外侧底支/右肺動脈外側底支 lateral basal branch of right pulmonary artery
右肺动脉外侧支/右肺動脈外側支 lateral branch of right pulmonary artery
右肺动脉下叶上支/右肺動脈下葉上支 superior branch of inferior lobe of right pulmonary artery
右肺动脉下叶支/右肺動脈下葉支 inferior lobar branch of right pulmonary artery
右肺动脉中叶支/右肺動脈中葉支 middle lobar branch of right pulmonary artery
右肺副裂/右肺副裂 fissura accessoria pulmonis dextri
右肺上叶/右肺上葉 superior lobe of right lung
右肺上叶支气管/右肺上葉支氣管 right superior lobar bronchus
右肺水平裂/右肺水平裂 horizontal fissure of right lung
右肺下叶/右肺下葉 inferior lobe of right lung
右肺下叶支气管/右肺下葉支氣管 right inferior lobar bronchus
右肺中叶/右肺中葉 middle lobe of right lung
右肺中叶支气管/右肺中葉支氣管 right middle lobar bronchus
右芬氟拉明/右芬氟拉明 dexfenfluramine
右腹积证/右腹積證 amassment disease of right abdomen
右腹下神经/右腹下神經 right hypogastric nerve
右肝管/右肝管 ductus hepaticus dexter
右肝上间隙/右肝上間隙 right suprahepatic space
右肝下间隙/右肝下間隙 right subhepatic space
右睾丸静脉/右睾丸静脈 right testicular vein
右冠状动脉/右冠狀動脈 right coronary artery
[右冠状动脉]房室支/[右冠狀動脈]房室支 atrioventricular branch
右归丸/右歸丸 yougui pill
右归饮/右歸飲 yougui drink
右后外侧支/右後外側支 right posterolateral branch
右后叶/右後葉 right posterior lobe
右后叶上段/右後葉上段 superior segment of right posterior lobe
右后叶下段/右後葉下段 inferior segment of right posterior lobe
右甲状腺素/右甲狀腺素 dextrothyroxine
右脚/右腳 right crus
右结肠动脉/右結腸動脈 right colic artery

右结肠静脉/右結腸靜脉 right colic vein
右结肠淋巴结/右結腸淋巴結 right colic lymph node
右结肠旁沟/右結腸旁溝 right paracolic sulcus
右结肠曲/右結腸彎曲 right colic flexure
右颈干/右頸幹 right jugular trunk, right cervical trunk
右颈内动脉/右頸內動脈 right internal carotid artery
右颈内静脉/右頸內靜脈 right internal jugular vein
右颈外动脉/右頸外動脈 right external carotid artery
右颈总动脉/右頸總動脈 right common carotid artery
右肋间上静脉/右肋間上靜脈，右上肋間靜脈 right superior intercostal vein
右利手/右利手,慣用右手 right handedness
右淋巴导管/右淋巴導管 right lymphatic duct
右淋巴总干/右淋巴總幹 right common lymphatic trunk
右卵巢静脉/右卵巢靜脈 right ovarian vein
右吗拉胺/右嗎拉胺 dextromoramide
右美沙芬/右美沙芬 dextromethorphan
右美托咪啶/右美托咪啶 dexmedetomidine
右气管支气管上淋巴结/右氣管支氣管上淋巴結 right superior tracheobronchial lymph node
右髂内静脉/右髂內靜脈 right internal iliac vein
右髂外静脉/右髂外靜脈 right external iliac vein
右髂总静脉/右髂總靜脈 right common iliac vein
右前叶/右前葉 right anterior lobe
右前叶上段/右前葉上段 superior segment of right anterior lobe
右前叶下段/右前葉下段 inferior segment of right anterior lobe
右曲动脉/右曲動脈 right flexural artery
右三角韧带/右三角韌帶 right triangular ligament
右上肺静脉/右上肺靜脈 right superior pulmonary vein
右上肺静脉后支/右上肺靜脈後支 posterior branch of right superior pulmonary vein
[右上肺静脉后支]叶下部/[右上肺靜脈後支]葉下部 infralobar part
右上肺静脉尖支/右上肺靜脈尖支 apical branch of right superior pulmonary vein
右上肺静脉前支/右上肺靜脈前支 anterior branch of right superior pulmonary vein
右上肋间静脉/右上肋間靜脈 venae intercostales superior dextra
右肾动脉/右腎動脈 right renal artery
右肾静脉/右腎靜脈 right renal vein
右肾上腺静脉/右腎上腺靜脈 right suprarenal vein
右室房化/右室房化 atrialization of right ventricle
右室后静脉/右室後靜脈 posterior vein of right ventricle
[右室]漏斗部狭窄/[右室]漏斗部狹窄 漏斗狀狹窄 infundibular stenosis
右室前静脉/右室前靜脈 anterior vein of right ventricle
右室双出口/右室雙出口 double outlet right ventricle
右室异常肌束/右室異常肌束 anomalous muscle band of right ventricle
右束支/右束支 right bundle branch
右束支传导阻滞/右束支傳導阻滯 right bundle-branch block
右锁骨下动脉/右鎖骨下動脈 right subclavian artery
右锁骨下干/右鎖骨下幹 right subclavian trunk
右锁骨下静脉/右鎖骨下靜脈 right subclavian vein
右头臂静脉/右頭臂靜脈 right brachiocephalic vein
右位胃/右位胃 dextrogastria
右位心/右位心 dextrocardia
右位主动脉弓/右位主動脈弓 right aortic arch
右下肺静脉/右下肺靜脈 right inferior pulmonary vein
右下肺静脉前底支/右下肺靜脈前底支 anterior basal branch of right inferior pulmonary vein
右下肺静脉上支/右下肺靜脈上支 superior branch of right inferior pulmonary vein
右纤维环/右纖維環 right fibrous ring
右纤维三角/右纖維三角 right fibrous trigone
右心电图/右心電圖,右心动作描记波 dextrocardiogram
右心耳/右心耳 right auricle
右心房/右心房 right atrium
右心房功能/右心房功能 right atrial function
右心房梳状肌/右心房梳狀肌 pectinate muscle of right atrium
右心室/右心室 right ventricle
右心室肥大/右心室肥大 right ventricular hypertrophy
右心室功能/右心室功能 right ventricular function
右心室功能障碍/右心室功能障礙 right ventricular dysfunction
右心室后乳头肌/右心室後乳頭肌 posterior papillary muscle of right ventricle

右心室前乳头肌/右心室前乳頭肌 anterior papillary muscle of right ventricle
右心室双出口/右心室雙出口 double outlet of right ventricle
右心室中隔乳头肌/右心室中隔乳頭肌 musculi papillares septales ventriculi dextri
右心转流术/右心轉流術 right-heart bypass
右胸廓内动脉/右胸廓内動脈 right internal mammary artery
右旋苯丙胺/右旋苯丙胺,右旋安非他命 dextroamphetamine
右旋薄荷脑/右旋薄荷腦 dextromenthol
右旋泛醇/右旋泛[醯]醇 dexpanthenol
右旋化合物/右旋化合物 dextrocompound
右旋酒石酸/右旋酒石酸 dextrotartaric acid
右旋糖/右旋糖 dextrose
右旋糖酐/右旋糖酐 dextran
右旋筒箭毒碱/右旋筒箭毒鹼 d-tubocurarine
右旋心/右旋心 dextroversion of heart
右旋支/右旋支 right circumflex branch
右旋作用/右旋作用 dextrorotation
右眼/右眼 right eye
右腰干/右腰幹 right lumbar trunk
右腰淋巴结/右腰淋巴結 right lumbar lymph node
右叶/右葉 right lobe
右叶间裂/右葉間裂 right interlobar fissure
右移位/右错位 dextroposition
右缘/右緣 right border
右缘静脉/右緣静脈 right marginal vein
右缘支/右緣支 right marginal branch
右支/右支 right branch
右支气管/右支氣管 right bronchus
右支气管纵隔干/右支氣管縱隔幹,支氣管縱隔右幹 right bronchomediastinal trunk
右徵之人/右徵之人 atypicl-fire-phase person, more initiative
右主动脉弓/右主動脈弓,右主動脈弧 right aortic arch
右主支气管/右主支氣管 right principal bronchus
幼虫/幼蟲 larva
幼虫移行症/遊走性幼蟲病 larva migrans
幼单核细胞/前單核細胞 promonocyte
幼犊接触传染肺炎病毒/幼犢接觸傳染肺炎病毒 contagious pneumonia virus of young calves
幼儿喂养/幼兒餵養 infantile feeding
幼红细胞/幼紅細胞 erythroblast
幼红细胞岛/幼紅細胞島 erythroblastic islet
幼浆细胞/幼漿細胞,前漿細胞 proplasmacyte

幼巨核细胞/幼巨核細胞,前巨核細胞 promegakaryoblast
幼淋巴细胞/幼淋巴細胞,前淋巴球 prolymphocyte
幼B[淋巴]细胞/幼B[淋巴]細胞 immature B cell
幼T[淋巴]细胞/幼T[淋巴]細胞 immature T cell
幼淋巴细胞白血病/幼淋巴細胞白血病 prolymphocytic leukemia
幼年变形性关节炎/幼年變形性關節炎,青年型變形性關節炎 arthritis deformans juvenilis
幼年黑素瘤/幼年黑素瘤,青少年型黑色素瘤 juvenile melanoma
幼年期脊柱后凸/幼年期脊柱後凸,少年駝背 kyphosis dorsalis juvenilis
幼年透明性纤维瘤病/幼年透明性纖維瘤病 juvenile hyaline fibromatosis
幼年纤维瘤病/幼年纖維瘤病 juvenile fibromatosis
幼年纤维腺瘤/幼年纖維腺瘤 juvenile fibroadenoma
幼年型肌阵挛性癫痫/幼年型肌陣攣性癲癇 juvenile myoclonic epilepsy
幼年型类风湿关节炎/幼年型類風濕關節炎 juvenile rheumatoid arthritis
幼年型糖尿病/幼年型糖尿病 juvenile-onset diabetes
幼年型透明样/幼年型透明樣 juvenile hyaline
幼年型掌跖/幼年型掌蹠 juvenile palmoplantar
幼年性息肉/幼年性息肉 juvenile polyp
幼年性消瘦/幼年性消瘦 infantilis marasmus
幼年直肠息肉/幼年直腸息肉 juvenile rectal polyp
幼女妊娠/幼女妊娠 precocious pregnancy
幼禽肠炎死亡综合征/幼禽腸炎死亡症候群,家禽腸炎死亡症候群 poult enteritis mortality syndrome
幼胎/幼胎 neofetus
幼体生殖/幼體生殖,童體生殖 pedogenesis
幼稚[白]细胞/幼稚[白]細胞,未成熟白血球 immature leukocyte
幼稚白细胞过少症/幼稚白細胞過少症,未成熟白血球減少症 hyponeocytosis
幼稚白细胞增多症/幼稚白細胞增多症,未成熟白血球增多症 hyperneocytosis
幼稚红细胞血症/幼稚紅細胞血症,未成熟紅血球症 erythroneocytosis
幼稚型侏儒/幼稚型侏儒 infantile dwarf
幼稚症/幼稚症,幼稚病 infantilism
诱变/誘[發突]變 mutagenesis
诱变剂/誘變劑 mutagens
诱变力试验/誘變力試驗 mutagenicity test
诱变性/誘變性 mutagenicity
诱变育种/誘變育種 mutagenic breeding

诱导催眠/誘導催眠　hypnotization
诱导麻醉/誘導麻醉　induced anesthesia
诱导前期/誘導前期　pre-induction period
诱导物/誘導物,誘發物　inducer
诱导性心脏停搏/誘導性心臟停搏　induced cardiac arrest
诱导学说/誘導學説　induction theory
诱导抑制性T[淋巴]细胞/誘導抑制性T[淋巴]細胞　suppressor inducer T lymphocyte
诱发带/誘發帶　initiation zone
诱发电位/誘發電位　evoked potential
诱发反应测听法/誘發反應測聽法　evoked response audiometry
诱发高温/誘發高温　induced hyperthermia
诱发疟疾/誘發[性]瘧疾,人工瘧疾　induced malaria
诱发排卵/誘發排卵,誘導排卵　induced ovulation
诱发气胸/誘發氣胸　induced pneumothorax
诱发衰退/誘發衰退　induction decay
诱发突变/誘發突變,誘導性突變　induced mutation
诱发性变态反应/誘發性變態反應,誘發性過敏　induced allergy
诱发性癫痫/啟動性癲癇　activated epilepsy
诱发性吞噬作用/誘發性吞噬作用,誘導性吞噬作用　induced phagocytosis
诱发症状/誘發症狀　induced symptom
釉板/釉板　enamel lamella
釉丛/釉[質]叢　enamel tuft
釉冠/釉冠,齒冠　enamel cap
釉基质/釉基質,釉質層　enamel matrix
釉结/釉結　enamel knot
釉料/釉料　glaze
釉面横纹/釉面橫紋,釉質橫嵴　perikymata
釉胚/釉胚　enamel germ
釉上皮/釉上皮　enamel epithelium
釉梭/釉[質]梭　enamel spindle
釉索/釉[質]索　enamel cord
釉小皮/釉小皮,釉質薄膜　enamel cuticle
釉质/釉質　enamel
釉质白垩斑/釉質白堊斑　enamel opaque spot
釉质成形术/釉質成形術　enameloplasty
釉质代谢/釉質代謝　enamel metabolism
釉质的/[牙]釉質的　adamantine
釉质发生/釉質發生,釉質形成　amelogenesis
釉质发生不全/釉質發生不全,釉質生長不全　amelogenesis imperfect
釉质发育不全[症]/[齒]釉質發育不全　enamel hypoplasia
釉质钙化不全[症]/[齒]釉質鈣化不全　enamel hypocalcification
釉质棱柱的接合质/棱柱間質　cementing substance
釉质瘤/牙釉質瘤　adamantinoma
釉质母细胞腺瘤/釉質母細胞腺瘤　adamantinum adenoma
釉质母细胞腺瘤样肿瘤/釉質母細胞腺瘤樣腫瘤　ameloblastic adenomatoid tumor
釉质器/釉質器　enamel organ
釉质上皮瘤/釉質上皮瘤　epithelioma adamantinum
釉质生长线/釉質生長線　incremental line of enamel
釉质细胞/釉質細胞　enamel cell
釉质牙本质界/釉質齒質界　dentino-enamel junction
釉质牙骨质界/釉質牙骨質界　cemento-enamel junction
釉质牙瘤/釉質牙瘤,齒釉質瘤　osteo-odontoma
釉质增长型/釉質增長型,牙釉質漸層增生模式　incremental pattern of enamel
釉[质]珠/釉[質]珠　enamel pearl
釉柱/釉柱,齒釉質杆　enamel rod, enamel prism
釉柱间质/釉柱間質　interprismatic substance
釉柱鞘/釉[質]柱鞘　enamel rod sheath, enamel sheath
瘀斑/瘀斑　ecchymoses
瘀斑的/瘀斑的　ecchymotic
瘀斑状面色/瘀斑狀面色,瘀斑屍面　ecchymotic mask
瘀胆型肝炎/瘀膽型肝炎,膽汁瘀積性肝炎　cholestatic hepatitis
瘀点/瘀點　petechia
瘀点的/瘀點的,瘀斑的　petechial
瘀点疹/瘀斑[性]疹　petechial eruption
瘀积性溃疡/瘀積性潰瘍,瘀滯性潰瘍　stasis ulcer
瘀积性皮下硬化症/瘀積性皮下硬化症,瘀血性皮下硬化　stasis hypodermosclerosis
瘀积性皮炎/瘀積性皮膚炎,瘀血性皮膚炎　stasis dermatitis
瘀积性湿疹/瘀積性濕疹　eczema stasis
瘀积性紫癜/瘀積性紫癜,瘀血性紫癜　stasis purpura
瘀线/線狀瘀斑,瘀痕　vibex
瘀血脾/脾發紺　cyanosis lienis
瘀血肾/瘀血腎,紺色腎　cyanotic kidney
瘀血性低氧血症/瘀血性低氧血症,瘀血性缺氧　stagnant hypoxemia
瘀血性水肿/瘀血性水腫　stagnation edema
瘀滞/瘀滯,瘀積　stasis
瘀滞性血栓/瘀滯性血栓　stagnation thrombus
瘀热入络证/瘀熱入絡證　pattern of stagnant-heat

invading collaterals
瘀血/瘀血　static blood
瘀血流注/瘀血流注　deep multiple abscess due to static blood
瘀血流注·产后败瘀证/瘀血流注·産後敗瘀證　deep multiple abscess due to static blood with pattern of postpartum infection
瘀血流注·跌扑成瘀证/瘀血流注·跌撲成瘀證　deep multiple abscess due to static blood with pattern of falls and knocks
瘀血内结积证/瘀血内結積證　amassment disease with pattern of internal binding of static blood
瘀血痛/瘀血痛　static blood pain
瘀血肿/瘀血腫　ecchymoma, static blood swelling
瘀血阻络证/瘀血阻絡證　pattern of static blood blocking collaterals
瘀阻胞宫证/瘀阻胞宮證　pattern of static blood blocking in uterus, pattern of static blood blocking in womb
瘀阻胞脉证/瘀阻胞脈證　pattern of static blood blocking in uterine vessel
瘀阻冲任/瘀阻冲任　blood stasis blocking thoroughfare and conception channels
瘀阻脑络证/瘀阻腦絡證　pattern of blood stasis blocking brain
瘀阻胃络证/瘀阻胃絡證　pattern of static blood in stomach collaterals
瘀阻咽喉证/瘀阻咽喉證　pattern of static blood stagnated in throat
于蒂内尔病/Hutinel 氏病　Hutinel disease
余毒流注/餘毒流注　deep multiple abscess due to remnant toxin
余毒流注·毒邪炽盛证/餘毒流注·毒邪熾盛證　deep multiple abscess due to remnant toxin with blazing toxin pattern
余毒流注·火毒攻心证/餘毒流注·火毒攻心證　deep multiple abscess due to remnant toxin with pattern of fire-toxin attacking heart
余毒流注·气血两虚证/餘毒流注·氣血兩虛證　deep multiple abscess due to remnant toxin with qi-blood deficiency pattern
余毒未清证/餘毒未清證　pattern of remained toxicity
余甘子/餘甘子　Phyllanthus emblica
余热未清证/餘熱未清證　pattern of lingering heat
盂唇/盂唇，關節盂緣　glenoid labrum
盂肱韧带/盂肱韌帶　glenohumeral ligament
盂上结节/盂上結節　supraglenoid tubercle
盂下结节/盂下結節　infraglenoid tubercle
鱼/魚　fish
鱼鳔胶/魚[鰾]膠，鰾膠　isinglass
鱼刺中毒/魚刺中毒　ichthyoacanthotoxism
鱼蛋白质类/魚蛋白質類　fish proteins
鱼肝油醇/魚肝油醇　oleanol
鱼肝油化/魚肝油化，賦以魚肝油特性　jecorize
鱼肝油酸/魚肝油酸　morrhuic acid
鱼肝油酸钠/魚肝油酸鈉　sodium morrhuate
鱼肝油酸盐/魚肝油酸鹽　morrhuate
鱼纲/魚類　pisces
鱼钩状移位/魚鉤狀移位，魚鉤狀變位　fish-hook displacement
鱼际/魚際　①thenar, thenar eminence ②yuji, LU10
鱼际肌/魚際肌　thenar muscle
鱼际间隙/魚際間隙　thenar space
鱼际筋膜/魚際筋膜　thenar fascia
鱼酱样痰/魚醬樣痰　anchovy sauce sputum
鱼胶/魚膠　ichthyocolla
鱼精蛋白/魚精蛋白　protamine
鱼精蛋白核酸酯/魚精蛋白核酸酯　protamine nucleinate
鱼精激酶/魚精激酶　protamine kinase
鱼类毒液类/魚類毒液類　fish venoms
鱼鳞癣患者/魚鱗癬患者　porcupine man
鱼卵毒/魚卵毒　ichthyootoxin
鱼卵中毒/魚卵中毒　ichthyootoxism
鱼肉毒/魚肉毒，毒魚肉中所含的毒　ichthyosarcotoxin
鱼肉毒素类/魚肉毒素類　ciguatoxins
鱼肉中毒/魚肉中毒　fish poisoning
鱼石脂/魚石脂　ichthammol
鱼石脂铵/魚石脂銨　ammonium ichthyolate
鱼石脂磺酸/魚石脂磺酸，磺基魚石脂酸　ichthyolsulfonic acid
鱼石脂磺酸盐/魚石脂磺酸鹽　ichthyolsulfonate
鱼石脂软膏/魚石脂軟膏　ichthammol ointment
鱼藤酮/魚藤酮　rotenone
鱼尾纹/魚尾紋　fishtail line
鱼腥草/魚腥草　heartleaf houttuynia herb
鱼血毒/魚血毒　ichthyohemotoxin
鱼血中毒/魚血中毒　ichthyohemotoxism
鱼腰/魚腰　yuyao, EX-HN4
鱼油/魚油　fish oil
鱼中毒/中魚毒　ichthyotoxism
鱼状嘴/魚狀嘴　fish-like mouth
鱼子酱样斑/魚子醬樣斑　caviar spot

鱼子酱样舌/魚子醬樣舌　caviar tongue
鱼子石榴/魚子石榴　roe-pomegranate-like conjunctiva
鱼嘴样口/魚嘴樣口　carp-shaped mouth
鱼嘴状僧帽瓣狭窄/魚嘴狀僧帽瓣狹窄　fishmouth mitral stenosis
渔民病/漁民病,魚處理者病　fish-handler disease
逾期分娩/逾期分娩,晚産　postmature delivery
榆树/榆樹　elm
与年龄有关的/與年齡有關的　age-related
宇航病/宇航病,太空病　space sickness
宇宙辐射/宇宙輻射,宇宙放射　cosmic radiation
宇宙模拟/宇宙模擬　space simulation
宇宙线/宇宙[射]線　cosmic ray
宇宙医学/宇宙醫學,太空醫學　space medicine
羽红素/[鳥]羽紅素　turacin
羽红素卟啉/[鳥]羽紅素卟啉,鳥吡咯紫質　turacoporphyrin
羽毛/羽毛　feather
羽扇豆球蛋白/羽扇豆蛋白,莢豆蛋白　conglutin
羽扇豆中毒/羽扇豆中毒　lupinosis
羽样脆发病/羽樣脆髮病,羽毛狀髮　trichoptilosis
羽状肌/羽狀肌　pennate muscle, penniform muscle
雨蛙肽/雨蛙肽　caerulein
禹余粮/禹餘糧　limonite
语迟/語遲　retardation in speaking
谵词杂拌/諳詞雜拌,雜碎語症　word salad
语法倒错性言语障碍/語法倒錯性言語障礙　paragrammatism
语法缺失/語法缺失　agrammatism
语法性失语/語法性失語[症]　syntactical aphasia
语声低微/語聲低微　faint low voice
语声洪亮/語聲洪亮　sonorous voice
语声描记[法]/語聲描記[法]　phonautography
语声描记图/發音描記圖　phonautogram
语声商数/語聲商數　phonation quotient
语声重浊/語聲重濁　deep and harsh voice
语言发展/語言發展　language development
语言发展障碍/語言發展障礙　language development disorder
语言急促/言語急促　cluttering
语言謇涩/語言謇澀　sluggish speech, dysphasia
语言开导法/語言開導法　reasoning therapy
语言疗法/語言療法　language therapy
语言试验/語言試驗　language tests
语言学/語言學　linguistics
语言艺术/語言藝術　language art
语言障碍/語言障礙　language disorder

语言震颤/語[言震]顫　vocal fremitus
语义区别/語義區別　semantic differential
语义性失语/語義性失語,意義性失語　semantic aphasia
语音不清/語音不清　asaphia
语音参考/語音參考　phonetic reference
语音矫正法/語音矯正法　phoniatrics
语音矫正器/語音矯正器　speech aid appliance
语音矫正师/語音矯正專家　phoniatrician
语音描记器/發音描記器　phonautograph
语音评定/語音評定　speech evaluation
语音学/聲音學　phonetics
语音训练/語音訓練　voice training
语音增强/語響增強　pectorophony
语音障碍/語音障礙　voice disorder
语音质量/語音品質　voice quality
玉顶疽/玉頂疽　vertex carbuncle
玉门/玉門　hymen
玉米/玉米　corn
玉米蛋白/玉米蛋白,玉蜀黍蛋白　maisin
玉米蛋白分解[作用]/玉米蛋白分解[作用],玉蜀黍蛋白之分解　zeinolysis
玉米淀粉/玉米澱粉,玉蜀黍澱粉　corn starch
玉米黑粉病/玉米黑粉病,玉蜀黍黑穗病　corn smut
玉米黄质/玉米黃質　zeaxanthin
玉米素/玉米素　zeatin
玉米烯酮/玉米[赤黴]烯酮　zearalenone
玉米线条病毒/玉米線條病毒　maize streak virus
玉女煎/玉女煎　yunü decoction
玉屏风散/玉屏風散　yupingfeng powder
玉堂/玉堂　yutang, RN18
玉液/玉液　yuye, EX-HN13
玉真散/玉真散　yuzhen powder
玉枕/玉枕　yuzhen, BL9
玉竹/玉竹　fragrant solomonseal rhizome
芋螺毒素类/芋螺毒素類　conotoxins
郁病/鬱病,憂鬱　depression, depression disease
郁病·肝气郁结证/鬱病·肝氣鬱結證　depression with pattern of liver qi depression
郁病·肝阴虚证/鬱病·肝陰虛證　depression with pattern of liver yin deficiency
郁病·气郁化火证/鬱病·氣鬱化火證　depression with pattern of qi depression transforming into fire
郁病·痰气郁结证/鬱病·痰氣鬱結證　depression with pattern of phlegm-qi stagnation and binding
郁病·心脾两虚证/鬱病·心脾兩虛證　depression with pattern of heart-spleen deficiency
郁病·心神失养证/鬱病·心神失養證　depression

with pattern of malnutrition of heart spirit
郁病·心肾阴虚证/鬱病·心腎陰虛證 depression with pattern of yin deficiency of heart and kidney
郁病·心阴虚证/鬱病·心陰虛證 depression with pattern of heart yin deficiency
郁病·血瘀证/鬱病·血瘀證 depression with blood stasis pattern
郁病·阴虚火旺证/鬱病·陰虛火旺證 depression with pattern of exuberant fire due to yin deficiency
郁病·忧郁伤神证/鬱病·憂鬱傷神證 depression with pattern of anxiety injuring spirit
郁金/鬱金 turmeric root tuber
郁厥/鬱厥,暈厥 depression syncope, syncope due to stagnation pattern
郁李仁/鬱李仁 Chinese dwarf cherry seed
郁冒/鬱冒 oppressive feeling and dizziness
郁证/鬱證 stagnation pattern
育儿法/育兒法,育嬰法 infanticulture
育儿专家/育兒專家 puericulturist
育亨宾/育亨賓[皮素] Yohimbine
育龄妇女/育齡婦女 woman of child-bearing age
育龄期/育齡期,生育期 child-bearing period
育胚器/育胚器,造果器 archicarp
彧中/彧中 yuzhong, KI26
浴疗法/浴療法 balneotherapy
浴疗学/浴療學 balneology
浴痒病/浴癢病,沐浴搔癢症 bath itch
预包装/預包裝 prepackaging
预备性切开/預備性切開 precutting
预苯酸脱氢酶/預苯酸脱氫酶 prephenate dehydrogenase
预苯酸脱水酶/預苯酸脱水酶 prephenate dehydratase
预测的/預測的 predicted
预测[价]值/預測值 predictive value
预测最高心率/預測最高心率 predicted maximal heart rate
预产期/預產期 expected date of delivery, expected date of confinement
预成抗体/預成抗體 preformed antibody
预充步骤/預充步驟 priming procedure
预充液/預充液 priming fluid
预处理/預處理 pretreatment
预存抗体/預存抗體 preexisting antibody
预定命运/預定命運 prospective fate, prospective significance
预定[胚]区/預定[胚]區 prospective area, prospective region

预定潜能/預定潛能 prospective potency
预防/預防 prevention
预防法/預防療法 preventive treatment
预防接种/預防接種 vaccination, prophylactic immunization
预防精神病学/預防精神病學 preventive psychiatry
预防膜/預防膜,預膿膜 prophylactic membrane
预防卫生服务/預防衛生服務 preventive health service
预防性白细胞疗法/預防性白細胞療法,預防性白血球療法 preventive leukotherapy
预防性颈部清扫/預防性頸部清掃,預防性頸部廓清 prophylactic neck dissection
预防性康复/預防性康復 preventive rehabilitation
预防性扩展/預防性擴展 extension for prevention
预防性尿道炎/預防性尿道炎 prophylactic urethritis
预防性物质/預防性物質 preventive substance
预防牙科学/預防性牙科學 preventive dentistry
预防医学/預防醫學 preventive medicine
预防用麻疹蛋白/預防用麻疹蛋白,預防麻疹性蛋白質 prophylactic measles protein
预防用药/預防用藥 prophylactic
预防正畸学/預防正畸學 preventive orthodontics
预付费卫生计划/預付費衛生計劃 prepaid health plan
预构皮瓣/預構皮瓣 prefabricated skin flap
预后/預後 prognosis
预后性征状/預後[性]徵狀 prognostic
预激综合征/預激症候群 preexcitation syndrome
预期寿命/預期壽命 expectation of life
预示集/預示集,預示組 prediction set
预涂布板/預塗布板,預製板 precoated plate
预吸氧/預吸氧,預先吸氧作用 preoxygenation
预压制粒/預壓制粒 preliminary compression granulation
预兆呕吐/預兆嘔吐 anticipatory vomiting
预知子/預知子 akebia fruit
欲求调整法/欲求調整法 desire adjusting therapy
阈刺激/閾[界]刺激 threshold stimulus
阈剂量/閾劑量 threshold dose
阈叩诊/閾叩診,閾界叩法 threshold percussion
阈上刺激/閾上刺激 supraliminal stimulus
阈下刺激/閾下刺激 subliminal stimulus
阈限值/閾限值 threshold limit value
阈值/閾值 liminal value
阈值性状/閾值性狀 threshold trait
喻昌/喻昌 Yu Chang
御药院/禦藥院 Royal Drug Museum

愈创草/創傷草　vulnerary herb
愈创甘油醚/愈創甘油醚　guaifenesin
愈创木酚/愈創木酚　guaiacol
愈创木烷倍半萜类/愈創木烷倍半萜類　guaiane sesquiterpenes
愈创木脂/愈創木脂　guaiac
愈风宁心片/愈風寧心片　yufeng ningxin tablet
愈合/愈合,接合　union
愈合剂/愈合劑　consolidant
愈合期溃疡/愈合性潰瘍　healing ulcer
愈伤组织/愈傷組織　callus
鹬虻科/鷸虻科　Rhagionidae
鸢尾根酸/鳶尾酸　iridic acid
鸢尾属/鳶尾屬　Iris
鸢尾状塞子/鳶尾狀塞子　kite tail tampons
渊疽/淵疽　subaxillary tuberculosis
渊腋/淵腋　yuanye, GB22
元胡止痛片/元胡止痛片　yuanhu zhitong tablets
元气/元氣　primordial qi
元神/元神　mentality, primordial spirit
元神之府/元神之府　fu-viscera of mental activity, house of mentality
元素/元素　element
芫花/芫花　lilac daphne flower bud
芫花中毒/芫花中毒　lilac daphne poisoning
芜菁/蕪菁　Brassica rapa
芫荽/胡荽　Coriandrum
园艺/園藝　horticulture
园艺疗法/園藝療法　horticultural therapy
员针/員針　round-point needle
原/原　proto
原癌基因/原癌基因　proto-oncogene
原癌基因蛋白质类/原癌基因蛋白質類　proto-oncogene proteins
原白头翁素/原白頭翁黴菌素　protoanemonin
原壁菌病/原壁菌病,原藻病　protothecosis
原鞭毛虫/原鞭毛蟲,前鞭毛體　promastigote
原病毒/原病毒　provirus
原卟啉/原卟啉,原紫質　protoporphyrin
原卟啉尿/原卟啉尿,原紫質尿　protoporphyrinuria
原卟啉原/原卟啉原,生原紫質的　protoporphyrinogen
原卟啉原Ⅸ/原卟啉原Ⅸ,原紫質原Ⅸ　protoporphyrinogen Ⅸ
原卟啉原氧化酶/原卟啉原氧化酶,原紫質原氧化酶　protoporphyrinogen oxidase
原卟啉症/原卟啉症,初卟啉症,原紫質症　protoporphyria

原肠/原腸,初腸　archenteron
原肠胚/原腸胚　gastrula
原肠胚期/原腸[胚]期　gastrula period, gastrula stage
原肠胚外凸/原腸胚外凸,原腸胚外翻　exogastrulation
原肠胚形成/原腸胚形成　gastrulation
原肠中胚层/原腸中胚葉　gastral mesoderm
原虫/原蟲　protozoa
原虫孢子/原蟲孢子　protozoan spore
原虫病/原蟲病　protozoiasis
原虫蛋白质类/原蟲蛋白質類　protozoan proteins
原虫的/原蟲的　protozoal
原虫感染/原蟲感染　protozoan infection
原虫基因/原蟲基因　protozoan gene
原虫基因组/原蟲基因組　protozoan genome
原虫抗体/原蟲抗體　protozoan antibody
原虫抗原/原蟲抗原　protozoan antigen
原虫[性]痢疾/原蟲痢疾　protozoal dysentery
原虫性葡萄膜炎/原蟲性葡萄膜炎　protozoal uveitis
原虫性心肌炎/原蟲性心肌炎　protozoal myocarditis
原虫疫苗/原蟲疫苗　protozoan vaccine
原唇沟/原唇溝　primary labial groove
原代培养/原代培養,初次培養　primary culture
原代细胞/原代細胞,初細胞　primary cell
原单核细胞/原單核細胞,成單核細胞　monoblast
原地畸胎瘤/原地畸胎瘤,本處性畸胎瘤　autochthonous teratoma
原顶体/原頂體,頂胚葉,母尖體　acroblast
原顶体残余/原頂體殘餘,頂胚葉的殘留物　acroblastic remnant
原顶体粒/原頂體粒,原頭巾顆粒　proacrosomal granule
原动物鉴定/原動物鑒定　identification of original animal
原发癌/原發[性]癌　primary cancer, primary carcinoma
原发变应原/原發變應原　primary allergen
原发病/原發病　primary disease
原发病灶/原發病灶　primary lesion
原发不孕[症]/原發不孕[症]　primary infertility
原发肥大性骨关节病/原發肥大性骨關節病　primary hypertrophic osteoarthropathy
原发复合征/原發複徵,初期複徵　primary complex
原发骨/原發骨　primary bone
原发后肺结核病/原發後肺結核病　postprimary pulmonary tuberculosis

原发畸形/原發畸形　primary deformity
原发接种性结核/原發接種性結核　primary inoculation tuberculosis
原发进行性失语/原發進行性失語　primary progressive aphasia
原发孔型房间隔缺损/原發孔型房間隔缺損,心房中隔缺陷　ostium primum defect
原发耐药率/原發耐藥率　primary drug resistance rate
原[发]脓肿/原膿腫,母膿腫　mother abscess
原发脾性中性白细胞减少/原發脾性中性白細胞減少,原發性脾性嗜中性白血球減少病　primary splenic neutropenia
原发伤道/原發傷道　primary wound tract
原发型肺结核/原發型肺結核　primary pulmonary tuberculosis
原发性阿米巴脑膜脑炎/原發性阿米巴腦膜腦炎　primary amebic meningoencephalitis
原发性瘢痕挛缩/原發性瘢痕攣縮　intrinsic cicatricial contracture
原发性闭经/原發性閉經　primary amenorrhea
原发性侧索硬化/原發性側索硬化　primary lateral sclerosis
原发性出血/原發性出血　primary hemorrhage
原发性刺激性尿布皮疹/原發性刺激性尿布皮膚疹　primary irritant napkin dermatitis
原发性单纯疱疹/原發性單純皰疹　primary herpes simplex
原发性单株高丙球蛋白血症肾病/原發性單株高丙球蛋白血症腎病　primary monoclonal hypergammaglobulinemic nephropathy
原发性肺动脉高压/原發性肺動脈高壓　primary pulmonary hypertension
原发性肺泡换气不足/原發性肺泡換氣不足　primary alveolar hypoventilation
原发性干燥综合征/原發性乾燥症候群　primary desiccation syndrome
原发性高草酸尿症/原發性高草酸尿症　primary hyperoxaluria
原发性高血压/原發性高血壓　primary hypertension
原发性骨质溶解/原發性骨質溶解　essential osteolysis
原发性红细胞增多/原發性紅細胞增多,原發性紅血球過多症　primary polycythemia
原发性甲状旁腺功能亢进症/原發性甲狀旁腺功能亢進症　primary hyperparathyroidism
原发性甲状腺功能亢进/原發性甲狀腺機能亢進　primary hyperthyrodidsm

原发性腱鞘囊肿/原發性腱鞘囊腫　primary ganglion
原发性冷球蛋白血症肾病/原發性冷球蛋白血症腎病　primary cryoglobulinemic nephropathy
原发性淋巴水肿/原發性淋巴水腫　primary lymphedema
原发性毛细血管扩张/特發性毛細血管擴張　essential telangiectasia
原发性耐药/原發性耐藥　primary drug resistance
原发性皮肤骨瘤/原發性皮膚骨癌　primary cutaneous osteoma
原发性皮肤及皮下曲霉病/原發性皮膚及皮下麴黴菌病　primary cutaneous and subcutaneous aspergillosis
原发性皮肤浆细胞瘤/原發性皮膚漿細胞瘤　primary cutaneous plasmacytoma
原发性皮肤结核/原發性皮膚結核　primary cutaneous tuberculosis
原发性皮肤利什曼病/原發性皮膚利什曼病　primary dermal leishmaniasis
原发性皮肤淋球菌感染/原發性皮膚淋球菌感染,原發性皮膚淋病雙球菌病　primary cutaneous Neisseria gonorrhoeae infection
原发性皮肤毛霉菌病/原發性皮膚毛黴菌病,原發性皮膚白黴菌病　primary cutaneous mucormycosis
原发性皮肤球孢子菌病/原發性皮膚球孢子菌病　primary cutaneous coccidioidomycosis
原发性皮肤曲霉病/原發性皮膚麴黴菌病　primary cutaneous aspergillosis
原发性皮肤隐球菌病/原發性皮膚隱球菌病　primary cutaneous cryptococcosis
原发性皮肤组织胞浆菌病/原發性皮膚組織漿菌病　primary cutaneous histoplasmosis
原发性皮损/原發性皮損　primary lesion
原发性脾性嗜中性白细胞减少/原發性脾性嗜中性白血球減少　primary splenic neutropenia
原发性偏斜/原發性偏科,原偏向　primary deviation
原发性贫血/原發性貧血　primary anemia
原发性青光眼/原發性青光眼　primary glaucoma
原发性醛固酮[增多]症/原發性醛固酮[增多]症　primary aldosteronism
原发[性损]伤/原發[性損]傷　primary injury
原发性痛风/原發性痛風　primary gout
原发性痛经/原發性痛經　primary dysmenorrhea
原发性妄想/原發性妄想　primary delusion
原发性胃食管反流/原發性胃食管反流　primary gastroesophageal reflux
原发性心动过缓/原發性心動過緩,自發性心跳過慢　essential bradycardia

原发性牙本质/初生牙質　primary dentin
原发性阳痿/原發性陽痿　primary impotence
原发性移植肝无功能/原發性移植肝無功能　primary liver graft nonfunction
原发性移植肾无功能/原發性移植腎無功能　primary renal graft nonfunction
原发性粘连/原發性粘連　primary adhesion
原发血栓/原發性血栓　primary thrombus
原发作用/原發作用　primary action
原放线菌素/初放線菌素　proactinomycin
原粪卟啉症/原糞卟啉症,原糞紫質症　protocoproporphyria
原肛/原肛　primitive anus
原沟/原溝　primitive groove
原骨髓/原骨髓　primary marrow
[原]核融合/核融合,核接合　karyogamy
原核生物/原核生物　prokaryote
原核细胞/原核細胞　prokaryotic cell
原核细胞起始因子类/原核細胞起始因子類　prokaryotic initiation factors
原核状态/原核狀態　prokaryosis
原红细胞/原紅細胞,前母紅血球　proerythroblast
原花青素类/原花青素類　proanthocyanidins
原花色素/原花色素　proanthocyanidin
原黄素/原黄素　proflavine
原活质/原活質,細胞初質　idiophore
原肌球蛋白/原肌球蛋白　tropomyosin
原基/原基　anlage
原基异位性发育异常/原基異位性發育異常　chorista
原甲区/原甲區,原爪區　primary nail field
原尖/原[白齒]尖　protocone
原浆破坏/原漿破壞　plasmotropism
原浆性[神经]胶质细胞/原漿性[神經]膠質細胞,胞漿膠質　cytoplasmic glia
原浆性-纤维性星形胶质细胞/原漿性-纖維性星狀細胞　protoplasmic-fibrous astrocyte
原浆性星形胶质细胞/原漿性星形膠質細胞,原生質[性]星狀細胞　protoplasmic astrocyte
原胶原/原膠原,膠原單位　tropocollagen
原胶原酶/原膠原[蛋白]酶　procollagenase
原节间组织/原節間組織,原體節間部　interprotometamere
原结/原結　primitive knot, primitive node
原巨核细胞/原巨核細胞,巨核細胞母細胞,成巨核細胞　megakaryoblast
原口/原口　primitive mouth
原口凹/原口凹,原口溝　primary oral groove

原藜芦碱/原藜蘆素　protoveratrine
原粒细胞/原粒細胞,成髓細胞　myeloblast
原料/原料　raw material
原料药/原料藥　bulk drug, pharmaceutical product
原裂/原裂　primary fissure
原淋巴细胞/淋巴母細胞　lymphoblast
原B[淋巴]细胞/原B[淋巴]細胞　pro-B lymphocyte
原T[淋巴]细胞/原T[淋巴]細胞　pro-T lymphocyte
原卵/原[始小]卵　primitive ovule
原络配穴法/原絡配穴法　yuan-source points and collateral-points combination
原脑/原腦,初腦　archencephalon
原尿/原尿,初尿　crude urine
原皮质/原皮質,舊腦皮　archicortex
原皮质多形[细胞]层/原皮質多形[細胞]層　polymorphic layer of archicortex
原皮质分子层/原皮質分子層　molecular layer of archicortex
原皮质锥体[细胞]层/原皮質錐體[細胞]層　pyramidal layer of archicortex
原绒[毛]膜/原絨毛膜　mallochorion
原色/原色　primary color
原肾/原腎　archinephron
原肾管/原腎管　pronephric duct
原肾小管/原腎小管,原腎細管　pronephric tubule
原生生物学家/原生生物學家　protistologist
原生植物类/原生植物類　protophyta
原生质/原生質　protoplasm
原生质低减性肥胖/原生質低減性肥胖,胞漿不足性肥胖病　hypoplasmic obesity
原生质凝胶/原生質凝膠,凝膠狀胞質　plasmagel
原生质球/原生質球　spheroplast
原生质体/原生質體　protoplast
原生质体融合/原生質體融合　protoplast fusion
原生质体再生/原生質體再生　protoplast regeneration
原生中柱/原生中柱　protostele
原始齿沟/原[始]齒溝　primitive dental groove
原始的/原始的　primitive
原始肺泡/原始肺泡　primitive alveolus
原始苷/原始苷　primitive glycoside
原始横隔/原始橫隔　primitive septum transversum
原始后鼻孔/原始後鼻孔　primitive choana
原始记录/原始記錄　protocol
原始菌株/原始菌株　original strain
原始口腔/原始口腔初口　primitive oral cavity
原始卵泡/始基卵泡,原胚濾泡,初級濾泡　primordial follicle

原始霉素/原始黴素　pristinamycin
原始脑[脊]膜/原始腦[脊]膜　primitive meninx
原始脑泡/原始腦泡　primary cerebral vesicle
原始内胚层/原始內胚層　primitive endoderm
原始胚细胞/原始胚細胞,始基生殖细胞　primordial germ cell
原始皮质/原始皮質　primitive cortex
原始桑葚体/原始桑椹體　archimorula
原始神经外胚[层]瘤/原始神經外胚層腫瘤　primitive neuroectodermal tumor
原始神经元/原始神經元　archineuron
原始生殖管道/原始生殖管道,初级生殖管　primary genital duct
原始生殖细胞/原始生殖細胞,原[生]殖細胞　primordial germ cell
原始声门/原始聲門　primitive glottis
原始室管膜层/原始室管層　primitive ependymal layer
原始受精卵/原始受精卵　archicytula
原始体腔/原始體腔　primitive body cavity
原始头静脉/原始頭靜脈　primary head vein
原始外胚层/原始外胚層　primitive ectoderm
原始系膜/原始繫膜　primitive mesentery
原始细胞/原始細胞　primitive cell
原始细胞危象/原始細胞危象　blast crisis
原始小网膜囊/原始小網膜囊　primitive lesser sac
原[始]型/原始型　archetype
原始循环/原始循環　the first circulation
原始医学/原始醫學　primitive medicine
原始游走细胞/原始遊走細胞　primitive wandering cell
原始中心/原始中心　archicenter
原[始]主动脉/原主動脈　primitive aorta
原噬菌体/原噬菌體　prophage
原双星体/初雙星體　archamphiaster
原索/原索　primitive streak
原田病/原田病　Harada disease
原田综合征/Harada 氏症候群　Harada syndrome
原条/原條　primitive streak
原萜烷/原萜烷　protostane
原脱位/原始脫位　primitive dislocation
原位癌/原位癌,未侵襲癌　cancer in situ, preinvasive carcinoma
原位标记/原位標記　primed in situ labeling
原位定量法/原位定量法　quantitation in situ
原位多器官灌注/原位多器官灌注　in situ multiple organ perfusion
原位发生/原位發生　autochthon
原位发生的/原位發生的　autochthonous
原位肝移植/原位肝移植　orthotopic liver transplantation
原位灌注/原位灌注　in situ perfusion
原位旁肝移植/原位旁肝移植　paratopic liver transplantation
原位旁胰腺移植/原位旁胰腺移植　paratopic pancreas transplantation
原位缺口末端标记/原位缺口末端標記　in situ nick-end labeling
原位小肠移植/原位小腸移植　orthotopic small intestine transplantation
原位心脏移植/原位心臟移植　orthotopic cardiac transplantation
原位血栓/原位血栓,本處性血栓　autochthonous thrombus
原位杂交/原位雜交　in situ hybridization
原位杂交组织化学法/原位雜交組織化學法　in situ hybridization histochemistry method, ISHH method
原纹状体/原紋狀體　archistriatum
原窝/原窩　primitive pit
原纤维/原纖維　fibril
原纤维的/原纖維的　fibrillary
原纤维溶解/原纖維溶解　fibrillolysis
原纤维形成/原纖維形成,原纖維生成　fibrillogenesis
原纤维性颤搐/原纖維性牽搐　fibrillar twitching
原纤维性肾小球肾炎/原纖維性腎絲球腎炎　fibrillary glomerulonephritis
原小脑/原小腦　archicerebellum
原型/原型　prototype
原型药/原型藥　drug prototype
原穴/原穴　yuan-primary point
原养型/原養型,無機營養生物　prototroph
原叶绿素/原葉綠素,原葉綠質　protochlorophyll
原叶绿素酸酯/原葉綠素酸酯　protochlorophyllide
原因/原因　cause
原因不明发热/原因不明發熱　fever of unknown origin
原因不明性不孕/原因不明性不孕　unexplained infertility
原有丝分裂/原有絲分裂,準絲狀分裂　promitosis
原皂苷元/原皂苷元　prosapogenin
原褶/原褶,原始皺襞　primitive fold
原植物鉴定/原植物鑒定　identification of original plant
原质团分割/原質團分割　plasmotomy
原中心粒/原中心粒　procentriole

原转录本/原轉録本　primary transcript
原椎[骨]间凹痕/原椎骨間凹痕　metasomatome
原子分光亮度法/原子分光光度法　atomic spectrophotometry
原子辐射/原子輻射　atomic radiation
原子轨道/原子軌域　atomic orbital
原子核/原子核　nucleus of atom
[原子]核的/核的　nuclear
原子力显微镜检查/原子力顯微鏡檢查　atomic force microscopy
原子体积/原子體積　atomic volume
原子医学/原子醫學　atomic medicine
圆饼形阴囊/圓餅形陰囊　circumcrescent cake-like scrotum
圆窗/圓窗　round window
圆顶细胞/圓頂細胞　dome cell
圆二色性/圓二色性　circular dichroism, CD
圆环病毒科感染/圓環病毒科感染　Circoviridae infection
圆肌/圓肌　teres
圆肩/圓肩　round shoulder
圆酵母属/圓酵母屬，串狀酵母菌屬　*Torula*
圆孔/圓孔　foramen rotundum
圆利针/圓利針　round-sharp needle
圆盘电泳/圓盤電泳　disc electrophoresis
圆盘试纸放射免疫分析技术/圓盤試紙放射免疫分析技術　paper disc radioimmunoassay technique
圆偏振/圓偏極[化]　circular polarization
圆韧带/圓韌帶　ligamentum teres
圆韧带裂隙/圓韌帶裂隙　fissura ligamenti teres
圆韧带囊肿/圓韌帶囊腫　cyst of round ligament
圆韧带缩短术/圓韌帶縮短術　shortening of round ligament
圆苔状痰/圓苔狀痰　moss-agate sputum
圆体针/圓體針　round body needle
圆细胞/圓細胞　round cell
圆细胞癌/圓細胞癌　carcinoma roundocellulare
圆线虫病/圓線蟲病　strongyliasis
圆线目感染/圓線目感染　Strongylida infection
圆心病/圓心病　round heart disease
圆形/圓形　rotunda
圆形鼻孔/圓形鼻孔　circular nostril
圆形的/圓形的　round
圆形糠疹/圓形糠疹　pityriasis rotunda
圆形溃疡/胃之圓形潰瘍　round ulcer
圆形切除[术]/圓形切除[術]　circular excision
圆形切口/圓形切口，環狀切開　circular incision
圆形双边细胞/圓形雙邊細胞，圓形小體　corps rond

圆形缘纹孔/圓形緣紋孔　round bordered pit
圆癣/圓癬　tinea circinata
圆叶目/圓葉條蟲目　Cyclophyllidea
圆翳内障/圓翳内障　round nebular cataract, senile cataract
圆翳内障·肝热上扰证/圓翳内障·肝熱上擾證　round nebularcataract with pattern of liver-heat disturbing upward
圆翳内障·肝肾两虚证/圓翳内障·肝腎兩虛證　round nebularcataract with liver-kidney deficiency pattern
圆翳内障·脾胃气虚证/圓翳内障·脾胃氣虛證　round nebular cataract with spleen-stomach qi deficiency pattern
圆针/圓針　round needle
圆柱瘤/圓柱瘤　cylindroma
圆柱瘤的/圓柱瘤的　cylindromatous
圆柱瘤状汗腺腺瘤/圓柱瘤性汗腺腺瘤　cylindromatous spiradenoma
圆柱[体]/圓柱　cylinder
圆柱细胞上皮瘤/圓柱細胞上皮瘤　cylindrocellular epithelioma
圆柱形动脉瘤/圓柱狀動脈瘤　cylindroid aneurysm
圆柱状细胞癌/圓柱狀細胞癌　cylindrical carcinoma
圆柱状细胞乳头状瘤/圓柱狀細胞乳頭狀腺瘤　cylindrical-cell papilloma
圆锥动脉/圓錐動脈　conus artery
圆锥角膜/圓錐角膜　keratoconus
圆锥晶状体/圓錐晶狀體　lenticonus
圆锥乳头/圓錐乳頭　conical papillae
圆锥体/圓錐體　conoid
圆锥细胞/錐狀細胞　cone cell
缘层/[邊]緣層　marginal layer
缘带/緣帶　limbic band
缘的/緣的　limbal
缘嵴/緣嵴　marginal crest, marginal ridge
缘结节/緣結節　marginal tubercle
缘瘤/緣瘤　limbal tumor
缘上回/緣上迴　supramarginal gyrus
缘细胞/緣細胞　marginal cell
缘支/緣支　marginal ramus
缘中/緣中　yuanzhong, central rim
猿疾病/猿疾病　ape disease
猿疟原虫/猿瘧原蟲　*Plasmodium pitheci*
猿线/猿線　simian crease
猿[状]手/猿[狀]手，爪形手　monkey paw, ape hand
远部皮瓣/遠部皮瓣　remote skin flap

远部取穴/遠部取穴　distant point selection
远侧/末端　distal
远侧部/遠側部,前葉,端葉　pars distalis
远侧的/遠側的,遠端的　distal
远侧偏位/遠側偏位　distoclination
远侧血块/遠側血塊　distal clot
远侧中心粒/遠側中心粒　distal centriole, posterior centriole
远程病理学/遠程病理學　telepathology
远程放射学/遠端放射學　teleradiology
远程会诊/遠程會診　remote consultation
远程潜伏期/遠程潛伏期　distal latency
远程医学/遠程醫學,遠距醫學　telemedicine
远点/遠點　far point
远端肌病/遠端肌病,遠端型肌營養不良症　distal myopathy
远端肌营养不良症/遠端肌營養不良症,遠端肌病　distal myopathy
远端甲沟/遠端甲溝　distal nail groove
远端肾小管/遠端腎小管　distal kidney tubule
远端肾小管性酸中毒/遠端腎小管性酸中毒　distal renal tubular acidosis
远端小管/遠端小管,遠側小管　distal tubule
远端掌间韧带/遠端當間韌帶,遠側掌間韌帶　distal intermetacarpal ligament
远段输尿管不发育/遠段輸尿管不發育　distal ureteral aplasia
远复视像/遠複視像,交叉性複像　heteronymous image
远红外线疗法/遠紅外線療法　far-infrared therapy
远红外线美容仪/遠紅外線美容儀　far-infrared cosmetic apparatus
远节指骨/遠節指骨,遠側指節骨　distal phalanx
远节指骨粗隆/遠側指骨粗隆　tuberosity of distal phalanx
远节趾骨/遠節趾骨,遠側趾節骨　distal phalanx
远近配穴法/遠近配穴法　distal-proximal points association, distal-proximal points combination
远距[放射]疗法/遠距[放射]療法,遠隔治療　teletherapy
远距镭照射/遠距鐳照射　teleradium
远距离诊断/遠距診斷　telediagnosis
远距X射线[照]片/遠距X光照片　teleroentgenogram
远距X射线照相术/遠距X光攝影術　teleradiography
远距X射线治疗/遠距X光療法　teleroentgentherapy

远距听诊器/遠距聽診器　telesthetoscope
远距心电描记法/遠距心電描記法,遠距心電圖記錄法　telecardiography
远距心电描记器/遠距心電描記器　telelectrocardiograph
远距心音听诊器/遠距心音聽診器,心音遥聽器　telecardiophone
远期效应/遠期效應　remote effect
远视/遠視　hyperopia
远视·肝肾两虚证/遠視·肝腎兩虛證　hyperopia with liver-kidney deficiency pattern
远视力/視遠力　distant vision
远视力检查[法]/遠視力檢查[法]　examination of distant vision, distant vision test
远视·气血两虚证/遠視·氣血兩虛證　hyperopia with qi-blood deficiency pattern
远视散光/遠視散光　hyperopic astigmatism
远视[眼]/遠視[眼]　hypermetropia
远视者/遠視者　hypermetrope
远外侧入路/遠外側入路　far lateral approach
远位皮瓣/遠位皮瓣　distant skin flap
远心性丘疹性红斑/遠心性丘疹性紅斑　erythema papulatum centrifugum
远血/遠血　distant anal bleeding, proximal bleeding
远志/遠志　milkwort root
远志散/遠志散　polygala powder
远志酸/遠志酸　polygalic acid
远志汤/遠志湯　polygala decoction
远志饮子/遠志飲子　polygala drink
远志皂苷/遠志皂苷　senegin
远中唇的/遠中唇的,牙齒遠側唇面的　distolabial
远中唇切的/遠中唇切的,牙齒遠側唇近面的　distolabioincisal
远中错位/遠中錯位,偏遠位,遠側移位　distoversion
远中殆/遠中殆,齒遠側咬合　distal occlusion
远中殆的/遠中殆的　distoclusal
远中颊的/遠中頰的,齒之遠側頰面的　distobuccal
远中颊殆的/遠中頰殆的,遠側頰咬合面的　distobucco-occlusal
远中颊髓的/遠中頰髓的,遠側頰髓壁的　distobuccopulpal
远中面/遠中面　distal surface
远中磨牙/遠中磨牙　distomolar
远中舌的/遠中舌的,牙齒遠側舌面的　distolingual
远中舌殆的/遠中舌殆的,牙齒遠側舌咬面的　distolinguo-occlusal
远中舌切的/遠中舌切的,牙齒遠側舌近面的　distolinguoincisal

远中舌髓的/遠中舌髓的,牙齒遠側舌髓壁的 distolinguopulpal
远中髓唇的/遠中髓唇的,遠側髓唇壁的 distopulpolabial
远中髓的/遠中髓的,遠側髓壁的 distopulpal
远中髓舌的/遠中髓舌的,遠側髓舌壁的 distopulpolingual
远中[向]阻生/遠中[向]阻生 distoangular impaction
远中楔形瓣/遠中楔形瓣 distal wedge flap
远中移位/遠中移位,向遠側偏位 distoplacement
远中龈的/遠中齦的,牙齒遠側齦壁的 distogingival
远紫外线/遠紫外線 far ultraviolet
院内感染/院内感染 nosocomial infection
院内诊疗/院内診療 institutional practice
院前急救/院前急救 prehospital care
约翰松尿道成形术/約翰松尿道成形術 Johanson urethroplasty
约翰逊带环/Johnson 氏帶 Johnson band
约翰逊-史蒂文斯病/喬-史二氏病 Johnson-Stevens disease
约纳斯症状/強納斯氏症狀 Jonas symptom
约内病/Johne 氏病 Johne disease
约瑟夫病/Joseph 氏病 Joseph disease
约氏疟原虫/約氏瘧原蟲 Plasmodium yoelii
约束衣/約束衣,拘束衣 strait jacket
月骨/月骨 lunate bone
月骨软化/月骨軟化 lunatomalacia
月骨脱位/月骨脱位 lunate dislocation
月骨周围脱位/月[狀]骨周圍脱位 perilunar dislocation, perilunate dislocation
月光盲/月光盲 moon blindness
月桂/月桂 Laurus
月桂硫酸钠/月桂硫酸鈉 sodium lauryl sulfate
月桂酸类/月桂酸類 lauric acids
月桂酸盐类/月桂酸鹽類 laurates
月桂烯/月桂油烯 myrcene
月桂樱/月桂櫻 cherry laurel
月季花/月季花 Chinese rose flower
月见草属/月見草屬 Oenothera
月经/月經,行經 menstruation
月经病/月經病 emmeniopathy, menopathy
月经病脉/月經病脈 morbid pulse in menstruation
月经病诊法/月經病診法 menopathy diagnostics
月经不调/月經不調 menstrual disorder
月经常脉/月經常脈 regular pulse in menstruation
月经初潮/月經初潮,初經 menarche
月经的/月經的 menstrual

月经过多/月經過多 menorrhagia, profuse menstruation
月经过多·气虚证/月經過多·氣虛證 menorrhagia with qi deficiency pattern
月经过多·血热证/月經過多·血熱證 menorrhagia with blood heat pattern
月经过多·血瘀证/月經過多·血瘀證 menorrhagia with blood stasis pattern
月经过频/月經頻繁 epimenorrhea
月经过频过多/月經過多而頻繁 epimenorrhagia
月经过少/月經過少 hypomenorrhea
月经过少·肾虚证/月經過少·腎虛證 hypomenorrhea with kidney deficiency pattern
月经过少·痰湿证/月經過少·痰濕證 hypomenorrhea with phlegm-damp pattern
月经过少·血虚证/月經過少·血虛證 hypomenorrhea with blood deficiency pattern
月经过少·血瘀证/月經過少·血瘀證 hypomenorrhea with blood stasis pattern
月经后期/月經後期 retarded menstruation
月经后期·肝气郁结证/月經後期·肝氣鬱結證 delayed menstruation with pattern of liver qi depression
月经后期·脾虚湿困证/月經後期·脾虛濕困證 delayed menstruation with pattern of damp retention due to spleen deficiency
月经后期·肾精亏虚证/月經後期·腎精虧虛證 delayed menstruation with pattern of kidney essence insufficiency
月经后期·血寒凝滞证/月經後期·血寒凝滯證 delayed menstruation with pattern of blood stagnation and congelation due to cold
月经后期·血虚证/月經後期·血虛證 delayed menstruation with blood deficiency pattern
月经黄体/月經黄體 corpus luteum of menstruation
月经困难/月經困難 difficult menstruation
月经量过多/月經量過多,經血量過多 excessive menstruation
月经龄/月經齡 menstrual age
月经频发/月經頻發,月經次數過多 polymenorrhea
月经频繁[量]过多/月經頻數而量過多 polyhypermenorrhea
月经频繁[量]过少/月經頻數而量過少 polyhypomenorrhea
月经期/月經期 menstrual period
月经期口[黏膜]出血/月經期口出血 stomatomenia
月经期水肿/月經期水腫 menstrual edema
月经前痤疮/月經前痤瘡 premenstrual acne

月经前的/月經前的,行经前的　premenstrual
月经前期水肿/月經前期水腫　premenstrual edema
月经失调/月經失調　menstruation disturbance
月经史/月經史　menstrual history
月经稀发/月經稀發,月經來潮次數過少　oligomenorrhea
月经稀少/月經稀少　infrequent menstruation
月经先后无定期/月經先後無定期　irregular menstrual cycle
月经先后无定期·肝气郁结证/月經先後無定期·肝氣鬱結證　irregular menstruation with pattern of liver qi depression
月经先后无定期·肾气虚证/月經先後無定期·腎氣虛證　irregular menstruation with pattern of kidney qi deficiency
月经先期/月經先期　advanced menstruation, precocious menstruation
月经先期·肝郁化热证/月經先期·肝鬱化熱證　advanced menstruation with pattern of liver depression transforming into heat
月经先期·脾气虚证/月經先期·脾氣虛證　advanced menstruation with pattern of spleen qi deficiency
月经先期·肾气虚证/月經先期·腎氣虛證　advanced menstruation with pattern of kidney qi deficiency
月经先期·阳盛实热证/月經先期·陽盛實熱證　advanced menstruation with pattern of exuberant yang and excessive heat
月经先期·阴虚内热证/月經先期·陰虛内熱證　advanced menstruation with pattern of internal heat due to yin deficiency
月经性溃疡/月經性潰瘍　menstrual ulcer
月经学/月經學,月經論　emmenology
月经异常/月經異常　menoxenia
月经诱导药/月經誘導藥　menstruation-inducing agent
月经障碍/月經障礙,月經困難　paramenia
月经正常/月經正常　eumenorrhea
月经周期/月經週期　menstrual cycle
月状的/月狀的　lunate
月状沟/月狀溝　lunate sulcus
月状骨/月狀骨　lunar bone
月状面/月狀面　lunate surface
乐谱盲/樂譜盲　note blindness
阅读/閱讀　reading
阅读过慢/閱讀過慢,閱讀徐緩　bradylexia
阅读框/閱讀框　reading frame
阅读疗法/讀書療法　bibliotherapy
阅读试验/閱讀試驗　reading test

阅读障碍/閱讀障礙,拼讀及寫困難　dyslexia
越隔纤维/越隔纖維　transseptal fiber
越经传/越經傳　transmission of skipping to other channel
越鞠保和丸/越鞠保和丸　yueju baohe pill
越鞠丸/越鞠丸　pill for relieving stagnancy, yueju pill
晕厥/暈厥,昏厥　syncope
云门/雲門　yunmen, LU2
云母石状的/雲母石狀的　micaceous
云母状和角化性假上皮瘤性龟头炎/雲母狀和角化性假上皮瘤性龜頭炎　micaceous and keratotic pseudoepitheliomatous balanitis
云南白药/雲南白藥　yunnan baiyao powder
云杉属/雲杉屬　*Picea*
云室/雲室,霧室　cloud chamber
云雾移睛/雲霧移睛　fog moving before eye, vitreous opacity
云雾移睛·肝肾阴虚证/雲霧移睛·肝腎陰虛證　fog moving before eye with liver-kidney yin deficiency pattern
云雾移睛·气血两虚证/雲霧移睛·氣血兩虛證　fog moving before eye with qi-blood deficiency pattern
云雾移睛·气滞血瘀证/雲霧移睛·氣滯血瘀證　fog moving before eye with pattern of qi stagnation and blood stasis
云雾移睛·湿热蕴蒸证/雲霧移睛·濕熱蘊蒸證　fog moving before eye with pattern of dampness-heat amassing and steaming
云翳/雲翳　cloud nebula
匀浆/勻漿,均質物　homogenate
匀浆化/勻漿化,均質化　homogenization
匀浆器/勻漿器,均質機　homogenizer
匀质乳/均質乳　homogenized milk
芸香/芸香　rue
芸香[二]糖/芸香糖　rutinose
芸香酸/芸香酸　terebic acid
允许残留量/容許殘留量　allowable residue limit
允许误差/容許誤差　allowable error
孕妇/孕婦　gravida
孕妇贫血病/孕婦貧血病　sutika
孕激素/孕激素　progestogen
孕激素类/孕激素類　progestogens
孕龄/孕齡　gestational age
孕内发育/孕内發育　interior gestation
孕尿翳/孕尿翳,妊娠尿浮膜　cyestein
孕诺酮己酸酯/孕諾酮己酸酯　gestonorone caproate
孕期饮食/孕期飲食,産前飲食　prenatal diet

孕前保健/孕前保健　preconception care
孕三烯酮/孕三烯酮　gestrinone
孕势/孕勢,胎勢　ectogony
孕体/胚體　conceptus
孕酮/孕酮,黃體固酮　progesterone
孕酮还原酶/孕酮還原酶　progesterone reductase
孕酮结合球蛋白/孕酮結合球蛋白　progesterone-binding globulin
孕酮受体/孕酮受體　progesterone receptor
孕酮同源物/孕酮同源物　progesterone congener
孕吐/孕婦晨吐　morning sickness
孕外发育/孕外發育　exterior gestation
孕烷醇酮/孕烷醇酮　pregnanolone
孕烷二醇/孕烷二醇　pregnanediol
孕烷二酮类/孕烷二酮類　pregnanediones
孕烷类/孕烷類　pregnanes
孕烷三醇/孕烷三醇　pregnanetriol
孕烯醇酮/孕烯醇酮　pregnenolone
孕烯二酮类/孕烯二酮類　pregnenediones
孕烯类/孕烯類　pregnenes
孕烯诺龙酮腈/孕烯諾龍酮腈　pregnenolone carbonitrile
孕痈/孕癰　intestinal abscess during pregnancy
孕[甾]烷/孕烷　pregnane
孕[甾]烯/孕烯　pregnene
孕早期产前诊断/孕早期産前診斷　the first trimester prenatal diagnosis
运动/運動　motion
运动[表达]性精神疏泄/運動[表達]性精神疏泄,運動性精神發洩　motor abreaction
运动不能/運動不能　akinesia
运动不能发作/運動不能發作,無動性發作　akinetic seizure
运动不能性缄默症/運動不能性啞症　akinetic mutism
运动成形切断术/運動成形切斷術,造形截斷術　cinematization
运动处方/運動處方　exercise prescription
运动单位电位/運動單位電位　motor unit potential
运动单位动作电位/運動單位動作電位　motor unit action potential
运动倒错/運動倒錯,運動障礙　parakinesia
运动点/運動點　motion point
运动负荷试验/運動負荷試驗　exercise stress test
运动感觉/運動感覺,移動感覺　motion sense
运动感觉缺失/運動感覺缺失　akinesthesia
运动感受器/運動感受器,肌覺受器　motoceptor
运动根/運動根　motor root

运动功能减退/運動機能減退　hypokinesia
运动骨/運動骨　exercise bone
运动过度/運動過度　hyperkinesia
运动过度代谢/運動過度代謝,運動超額代謝　excess of exercise metabolism
运动过度征/運動過度徵　hyperkinesis sign
运动过强/運動過強,運動過度　hypermotility
运动活动/運動活動　motor activity
运动技能/運動技能　motor skill
运动技能障碍/運動技能障礙　motor skill disorder
运动交叉/運動[徑]交叉　motor decussation
运动觉/運動覺　kinesthetic sense
运动觉缺失/運動感覺缺失　kinanesthesia
运动觉训练/運動覺訓練　motor sensibility training
运动力/運動力　motoricity
运动疗法/運動療法　exercise therapy
运动密度测定法/運動密度測定法　cinedensigraphy
运动描记器/運動描記器,活動影像機　kinematograph
运动耐量/運動耐量　exercise tolerance
运动黏度/運動黏度　kinematic viscosity
运动皮肤病学/運動皮膚病學　sports dermatology
运动皮质/運動皮質　motor cortex
运动器/運動器　locomotorium
运动前区/運動前區　premotor area
运动强度/運動強度　exercise intensity
运动区/運動區　motion area
运动缺乏/運動缺乏　poverty of movement
运动设备/運動設備　sports equipment
运动神经/運動神經　motor nerve, motion nerve
运动神经传导速度/運動神經傳導速度　motor nerve conduction velocity
运动神经肌肉终板/運動神經肌肉終板　motor endplate
运动神经路径/運動神經路徑　motion nerve path
运动神经麻痹性膀胱/運動神經麻痺性膀胱　motor nerve paralytic bladder
运动神经末梢/運動神經末梢　motor nerve ending
运动[神经]细胞/運動神經細胞　motor cell
运动神经元/運動神經元　motor neuron
运动神经元病/運動神經元病　motor neuron disease
运动神经终板/運動神經終板　motion nerve plate
运动失调口吃/運動失調口吃　ataxic dysarthria
运动失调毛细管扩张综合征/運動失調毛細管擴張症候群　ataxia-telangiectasia syndrome
运动失调描记器/失調運動描記器　ataxiagraph
运动失调描记图/運動失調描記圖,失調運動曲線　ataxiagram

运动失调性失写症/運動失調性失寫症　atactic agraphia
运动失用症/運動失用症,自發動作無能　akinetic apraxia
运动时服用兴奋剂/運動時服用興奮劑　doping in sport
运动试验/運動試驗　exercise test
运动束/運動束,運動徑　motor tract
运动损伤/運動損傷,運動傷害　sports injury
运动伪差/運動偽差,移動性假象　motion artifact
运动细胞/運動細胞　motion cell
运动性白细胞/活動性白血球　motile leukocyte
运动性白细胞增多/運動性白血球增多　motile leukocytosis
运动性闭经/運動性閉經　exercise related amenorrhea
运动性蛋白尿/運動性蛋白尿　post-exercise proteinuria
运动性癫痫/運動性癲癇　rolandic epilepsy
运动性共济失调/運動[性共濟]失調　motor ataxia, locomotor ataxia
运动性末梢/運動性末梢　motion ending
运动[性]神经功能病/運動[性]神經功能病,運動神經官能症　kinesioneurosis
运动性失写[症]/運動性失寫[症]　motor agraphia
运动性失用[症]/運動性失用[症]　motor apraxia
运动性失语[症]/運動性失語[症]　motor aphasia
运动性消化不良/運動性消化不良　motor dyspepsia
运动性兴奋/運動性興奮　motion impulse
运动性荨麻疹/運動性蕁麻疹　exercise urticaria
运动徐缓/運動徐緩　bradykinesia
运动学/運動學　cinematics
运动压力试验/運動壓力試驗　exercise stress testing
运动医学/運動醫學　sports medicine
运动抑制剂/運動抑制劑,運動神經抑制藥　depressomotor
运动诱发电位/運動誘發電位　motor evoked potential
运动诱发性过敏/運動誘發性過敏　exercise-induced anaphylaxis
运动诱发性哮喘/運動誘發性哮喘　exercise-induced asthma
运动员病/運動員病　athlete's sickness
运动员心脏/運動員心臟　athlete heart
运动员足病/運動員足病　athlete foot
运动障碍/運動困難　dyskinesia
运动障碍的/運動困難的　dyskinetic
运动障碍综合征/運動障礙症候群　dyskinetic syndrome
运动知觉/運動知覺　motion perception
运动中枢/運動中樞　motion center
运动终板/運動終板　motor end plate
运动综合征/運動區症候群　motor syndrome
运皮质激素蛋白/運皮質激素蛋白　transcortin
运气/運氣　five evolutive phases and six climatic factors
运气不及/運氣不及　deficiency of five evolutive phases and six climatic factors
运气盛衰/運氣盛衰　rise and fall of five evolutive phases and six climatic factors
运气太过/運氣太過　excess of five evolutive phases and six climatic factors
运气相合/運氣相合　combined analysis of five evolutive phases and six climatic factors
运气学说/運氣學說　doctrine of five evolutive phases and six climatic factors
运输/運輸　transport
运用障碍/運用障礙,移動機能障礙　dyspraxia
晕/暈　halo
晕车[病]/暈車[病]　car sickness
晕船[病]/暈船[病]　sea sickness
晕动病/暈動病　motion sickness
晕细胞/暈細胞　halo cell
晕针/暈針　fainting during acupuncture
晕痣/暈痣　halo nevus
晕状脉络膜炎/暈狀脈絡膜炎　areolar choroiditis
熨法/熨法　hot packet method
熨剂/熨劑　compression formula
熨烙法/熨烙法　method of fomentation and cauterization

Z

杂多糖/雜多醣　heteropolysaccharide
杂发酵菌/雜發酵菌　heterofermenter
杂酚油/雜酚油　creosote
杂合抗生素/雜交抗生素　hybrid antibiotic
杂合性/雜合性,雜接合子性　heterozygosity
杂合子/雜合子,雜合體,異型合子　heterozygote
杂合子丢失/雜合子丢失　loss of heterozygosity
杂合子检测/雜合子檢測　heterozygote detection
杂合子筛查/雜合子篩查　heterozygote screening
杂化轨道/雜化軌道,混成軌域　hybrid orbital
杂环二环化合物/雜環二環化合物　heterocyclic bicyclo compound
杂环化合物/雜環化合物　heterocyclic compound
杂环酸类/雜環酸類　heterocyclic acids
杂环氧化物/雜環氧化物　heterocyclic oxide
杂环甾类/雜環甾類　heterocyclic steroids
杂货商痒病/雜貨商癬病　grocer itch
杂己聚糖/異己聚糖　heterohexosan
杂交/雜交　hybridization
杂交繁殖/雜交繁殖　outbreeding
杂交抗体/雜交抗體　hybrid antibody
杂交瘤/雜交瘤　hybridoma
杂交细胞/雜交細胞　hybrid cell
杂交育种/雜交育種　cross breeding
杂乱性失语[症]/亂雜性失語[症]　jargon aphasia
杂戊聚糖/異聚戊糖　heteropentosan
杂医科/雜醫科　department of miscellaneous diseases
杂音/雜音,嘈聲　bruit
杂原子/雜原子　heteroatom
杂质/雜質,異物　foreign matter
杂质检查/雜質檢查,異物檢查　determination of foreign matter
杂种/雜種　hybrid
杂种生物瓣/雜種生物瓣　hybrid bioprosthetic cardiac valve
杂种优势/雜種優勢　hybrid vigor
灾害救援/災害救援　disaster assistance
灾害医学/災害醫學　disaster medicine
灾难/災難　disaster
灾难反应/災難反應　catastrophic reaction
灾难性疾病/災難性疾病　catastrophic illness
甾醇/甾醇,固醇　sterol
甾醇蛋白/甾醇蛋白　sterol protein
甾醇硫酸酯酶/甾醇硫酸酯酶　steryl-sulfatase
甾醇 O-酰基转移酶/甾醇 O-醯基轉移酶　sterol O-acyltransferase
甾类/甾類　steroids
甾类堕胎药/甾類墮胎藥　steroidal abortifacient agent
甾类羟化酶类/甾類羥化酶類　steroid hydroxylases
甾类异构酶类/甾類異構酶類　steroid isomerases
甾体生物碱/甾體生物鹼　steroid alkaloid
甾体皂苷/甾體皂苷,類固醇皂苷　steroid saponin
甾体皂苷元/甾體皂苷元,類固醇皂苷元　steroid sapogenin
甾烷/甾烷　Gonanes
栽培/栽培　cultivation
再次肝移植/再次肝移植　secondary liver transplantation
再次免疫应答/再次免疫應答,次發性免疫反應　secondary immune response
再次肾移植/再次腎移植　secondary renal transplantation
再次心脏移植/再次心臟移植　cardiac retransplantation
再次移植/再次移植　secondary transplantation
再发性疱疹/再發性皰疹　herpes recurrens
再分化/再分化　redifferentiation
再感染/再傳染　reinfection
再感染肾盂肾炎/再感染腎盂腎炎　reinfectious pyelonephritis
再灌注/再灌注　reperfusion
再灌注损伤/再灌注損傷　reperfusion injury
再[呼]吸/再[呼]吸　rehalation
再获能/再獲能　recapacitation
再经/再經　disease involving other channel
再剖宫产术/再剖宮產術　repeat cesarean section
再燃/再燃　recrudescence
再入/再入　reentry
再上皮化/再上皮化　re-epithelialization
再摄取/再攝取　re-uptake

再生/再生　regeneration
再生过程/再生過程　super-regeneration
再生期脱发/再生期脫髮　anagen effluvium
再生医学/再生醫學　regenerative medicine
再生障碍性贫血/再生障礙性貧血,再生不能性貧血　aplastic anemia
再生[作用]/再生[作用]　regeneration
再手术/再手術　reoperation
再水化体液/再水化體液　rehydration solution
再吸入麻醉/再吸入麻醉　rehalational anesthesia
再循环/再循環　recirculation
再循环色谱法/再循環色譜法,再循環層析法　recycle chromatography
再训练/再訓練　retraining
再氧合/再氧合　reoxygenation
再氧化/再氧化　reoxidation
再造散/再造散　zaizao powder
再植/再植　replantation
再植入术/再植入法,補植法　reimplantation
再治疗/再治療　retreatment
在泉/在泉　qi in the earth
在线脱气设备/線上脫氣設備　on-line degasser
载黑[色]素细胞/載黑[色]素細胞　melanophore
载距突/載距突　sustentaculum tali
载台测微尺/載檯測微尺,載檯顯微量尺　stage micrometer
载体/載體　carrier, vector
载体蛋白/載體蛋白質　carrier protein
载体特异性/載體特異性　carrier specificity
载体效应/載體效應　carrier effect
载体转运/載體轉運,載體輸送　carrier transport
载药注射器/載藥注射器　prefilled syringe
载脂蛋白/載脂蛋白　apolipoprotein
载脂蛋白类/載脂蛋白類　apolipoproteins
载脂蛋白E类/載脂蛋白E類　apolipoproteins E
暂基托/暫基托　temporary base-plate
暂时充填/暫時充填,暫時填補　temporary filling
暂时磁铁/暫時磁鐵　temporary magnet
暂时情境性人格异常/暫時情境性人格障礙,短暫性處境人格障礙　transient situational personality disorder
暂时性/暫時性　fugax
暂时性肺炎/暫時性肺炎　ephemeral pneumonia
暂时性基模/暫時性基模　provisional matrix
暂时性棘层松解性皮肤病/暫時性棘層鬆解性皮膚病　transient acantholytic dermatosis
暂时性结肠造口术/暫時性結腸造口術　temporary colostomy
暂时性髋关节滑膜炎/暫時性髋關節滑膜炎　transient synovitis of hip joint
暂时性髋关节炎/暫時性髋關節炎　coxitis fugax
暂时性水肿/暫時性水腫　edema fugax, flying edema
暂时性新生儿甲状旁腺功能减退症/暫時性新生兒甲狀旁腺功能減退症　transitory neonatal hypoparathyroidism
暂时性医疗护理/暫時性醫療護理　respite care
暂时性义齿/暫時性義齒,臨時假牙　temporary denture
暂时性阈移/暫時性閾移　temporary threshold shift
暂时性躁狂/暫時性躁狂　transitory mania
暂时性眦成形术/暫時性眥成形術　provisional canthoplasty
暂时牙修复/暫時牙修復　temporary dental restoration
暂时硬度/暫時硬度　temporary hardness
暂时状态/暫時狀態,過渡狀態　transitory state
暂用假腿/暫用假腿　pillon
赞德细胞/Zander氏細胞　Zander cell
赞格迈斯特试验/怎格梅氏試驗　Zangemeister test
赞克试验/蔡克氏試驗　Tzanck test
赞克细胞/蔡克氏細胞　Tzanck cell
脏壁腹膜褶/臟壁腹膜褶,體壁腹膜皺襞　parietoperitoneal fold
脏壁[X射线]照相术/臟壁[X射線]照相術,臟壁透視術　parietography
脏壁中胚层/臟壁中胚層　splanchnic mesoderm
脏病及腑/臟病及腑　zang-viscera disease involving fu-viscera
脏层/臟層　visceral layer
脏毒/臟毒,肛門周膿瘍　anal cryptitis, perianal abscess
脏毒·脾虚气陷证/臟毒·脾虛氣陷證　anal cryptitis with pattern of spleen deficiency and qi sinking
脏毒·热毒蕴结证/臟毒·熱毒蘊結證　anal cryptitis with heat-toxin amassment pattern
脏毒·湿热下注证/臟毒·濕熱下注證　anal cryptitis with pattern of dampness-heat diffusing downward
脏腑/臟腑　zang-fu viscera
脏腑败坏/臟腑敗壞　corruption of zang-fu organs
脏腑辨证/臟腑辨證　pattern identification of zang-fu viscera
脏腑肌/臟腑肌,内臟肌　organic muscle
脏腑兼病辨证/臟腑兼病辨證　pattern identification of concurrent visceral manifestation
脏腑惊证/臟腑驚證　convulsion due to zang-fu

disorders
脏腑情志论/臟腑情志論 theory of zang-fu organs and emotions
脏腑相合/臟腑相合 interconnection of zang-fu organs
脏腑之气/臟腑之氣 qi of zang-fu viscera
脏腹膜/腹膜臟層 visceral peritoneum
脏结/臟結 binding of zang-viscera
脏厥/臟厥 zang-visceral cold limbs
脏连丸/臟連丸 zanglian pill
脏颅/臟顱 viscerocranium
脏面/内臟面 visceral surface
脏气清灵/臟氣清靈 keen visceral qi
脏器感觉/臟器感覺 visceral sense
脏器疗法/臟器療法 organotherapy
脏器[X射线]造影术/臟器[X射線]造影術, 内臟放射線攝影術 viscerography
脏象/臟象 visceral manifestation
脏象学说/臟象學說 theory of visceral manifestation
脏胸膜/[内]臟胸膜 visceral pleura
脏躁/臟躁 hysteria
脏躁·痰火交炽证/臟躁·痰火交熾證 hysteria with pattern of blazing of phlegm-fire
脏躁·心肝火旺证/臟躁·心肝火旺證 hysteria with pattern of exuberant fire of heart and liver
脏躁·心脾两虚证/臟躁·心脾兩虛證 hysteria with pattern of heart-spleen deficiency
脏躁·心肾不交证/臟躁·心腎不交證 hysteria with pattern of incoordination between heart and kidney
藏红/藏紅, 番紅 safranine
藏花精/藏紅精, 番紅花精 crocein
藏茴香油/藏茴香油 caraway oil
藏青果喉片/藏青果喉片 zangqingguo tablet
凿开状骨折/鑿開狀骨折, 鑿性骨折 chisel fracture
凿石工病/鑿石工病 stonecutter disease
凿状切牙/鑿狀切牙 screw-driver-shaped incisor
早搏心脏复合征/早搏心臟複合徵 premature cardiac complex
早产/早産 premature birth, premature delivery
早产儿/早産兒 premature, premature infant
早产儿皮肤松弛症/早産兒皮膚鬆弛症 anetoderma of permaturity
早产儿贫血/早産兒貧血 anemia of prematurity
早产儿视网膜病/早産兒視網膜病 retinopathy of prematurity
早发的/早發的 praecox
早发性白发及前磨牙发育不全并多汗症/早發性白髮及前白齒發育不全并多汗症 premature canities with premolar aplasia and hyperhidrosis
早发[性]痴呆/早發性失智 dementia praecox
早发性淋巴水肿/早發性淋巴水腫 lymphoedema praecox
早感受器电位/早感受器電位 early receptor potential
早接触/早接觸 premature contact
早老/早老 presenility
早老的/早老的 presenile
早老形象/早老形象, 早衰形象 geromorphism
早老性脱发/早老性脱髮, 壯年禿髮 alopecia prematura
早老症/早老症 progeria
早萌/早萌 premature eruption of tooth
早年脱发/早年脱髮, 早發性脱髮 premature baldness
早期充盈/早期充盈 early filling
早期干预/早期干預 early intervention
早期后除极/早期後除極 early afterdepolarization
早期减速/早期減速 early deceleration
早期鉴别/早期鑒別 preliminary identification
早期浸润癌/早期浸潤癌 early invasive carcinoma
早期流产/早期流産 early abortion
早期梅毒/早期梅毒 early syphilis
早期尿毒症/早期尿毒症 early stage uremia
早期前噬菌体/早期前嗜菌體, 潛性嗜菌體前期 prepropage
早期潜伏梅毒/早期潛伏梅毒, 早期隱性梅毒 early latent syphilis
早期神经梅毒/早期神經梅毒 early neurosyphilis
早期胎死/早期胎死 early fetal death
早期先天性梅毒/早期先天性梅毒 early congenital syphilis
早期修复/早期修復 early repair
早期诊断/早期診斷 early diagnosis
早日下床活动/早日下床活動 early ambulation
早熟/早熟 precocity, prematurity
早熟的/早熟的, 早成的 precocious
早熟青春期/早熟青春期, 性早熟 precocious puberty
早熟性巨生殖器巨体/早熟性巨生殖器巨體 macrogenitosomia precox
早衰综合征/早衰症候群 premature aging syndrome
早瘫性狂犬病/早癱性狂犬病 dumb rabies
早秃/早秃 premature alopecia
早现[遗传]/早現遺傳, 遺傳病逐代早發 anticipation
早泄[病]/早洩[病] premature ejaculation,

prospermia
早泄·肝经湿热证/早洩·肝經濕熱證 premature ejaculation with pattern of damp-heat in liver channel
早泄·肾气不固证/早洩·腎氣不固證 premature ejaculation with pattern of unconsolidated kidney qi
早泄·心脾两虚证/早洩·心脾兩虛證 premature ejaculation with pattern of heart-spleen deficiency
早泄·阴虚火旺证/早洩·陰虛火旺證 premature ejaculation with pattern of exuberant fire due to yin deficiency
早泄·阴阳两虚证/早洩·陰陽兩虛證 premature ejaculation with pattern of deficiency of both yin and yang
早孕/早孕 early pregnancy
早孕反应/早孕反應 early pregnancy reaction
枣花翳内障/棗花翳內障 date-flower cataract
枣仁远志汤/棗仁遠志湯 jujube seed and polygala decoction
蚤科/蚤科 Pulicidae
蚤属/蚤屬 Pulex
蚤咬状肾/蚤咬狀腎 flea-bitten kidney
藻胆色素/藻膽色素,藻色蛋白 phycobilin
藻胆体/藻膽體 phycobilisome
藻蛋白/藻蛋白 algin
藻蛋白质类/藻蛋白質類 algal proteins
藻红蛋白/藻紅蛋白,藻紅質 phycoerythrin
藻红细胞/藻紅細胞,藻紅血球 erythrosin cell
藻菌病/藻菌病 phycomycosis
藻类/藻類 alga
藻青蛋白/藻青蛋白,藻青苷 phycocyanin
藻色素/藻色素,藻色質 phycochrome
藻酸/藻[糖]酸 alginic acid
藻酸盐/藻酸鹽 alginate
藻酸盐印模材料/藻酸鹽印模材料 alginate impression material
藻样细胞/藻樣細胞 algoid cell
皂蛋白/皂蛋白 soap albumin
皂苷/皂苷 saponin
皂苷类/皂苷類 saponins
皂苷元/皂苷元 sapogenin
皂化/皂化 saponification
皂化剂/皂化劑 saponifier
皂基/皂基 soap base
皂角刺/皂角刺 Chinese honeylocust spine
皂角苷配基/皂角苷配基 sapogenins
皂泡样囊肿/皂泡樣囊腫 soapsuds cyst
皂树酸/[肥]皂樹酸,皂質樹酸 quillaic acid

皂土/皂土,水化矽酸鋁 bentonite
皂土-34/皂土-34 bentone-34
皂土絮凝试验/皂土絮狀試驗 bentonite flocculation test
造口术/造口術 ostomy
造瘘取石术/造瘻取石術 lithotony
造血的/造血的 hematogenic
造血干细胞/造血幹細胞 hematopoietic stem cell
造血干细胞动员/造血幹細胞動員 hematopoietic stem cell mobilization
造血干细胞移植/造血幹細胞移植 hematopoietic stem cell transplantation
造血[功能]不全/造血不全,造血不良 dyshematopoiesis
造血功能不足性贫血/造血機能不足性貧血 anhematopoietic anemia
造血管细胞/造血管細胞 vasoformative cell
造血器官/造血器官 hematopoietic organ, hemopoietic organ
造血溶血平衡/造血溶血平衡 hemogenic-hemolytic balance
造血生成因子/造血生成因子,促血球生成生長激素 haemopoietic growth factor
造血索/造血索 hematopoietic cord
造血系统/造血系統 hematopoietic system
造血细胞生长因子/造血細胞生長因子 hematopoietic cell growth factor
造血[诱导]微环境/造血[誘導]微環境 hematopoietic inductive microenvironment, hemopoietic inductive microenvironment
造血组织/造血組織 hematopoietic tissue, hemopoietic tissue
[造影]对比剂/對比劑,顯影劑 contrast agent
造影剂/造影劑 contrast media
造影剂肾病/造影劑腎病 radiographic contrast nephropathy
造影溶液/顯影溶液 contrast solution
造影注射/顯影注入 opacifying injection
噪声/噪音 noise
噪声性聋/雜訊性聾 noise-induced hearing loss
噪声性听觉丧失/雜訊性聽覺喪失 noise-induced hearing loss
噪音性神经功能病/雜訊病 echeosis
燥干清窍/燥乾清竅 dryness affecting clear orifices
燥剂/燥劑 dry formula
燥结/燥結 accumulation of dry feces
燥裂苔/燥裂苔 dry and cracked fur
燥气伤肺/燥氣傷肺 dry qi impairing lung

燥热/燥熱　dryness-heat
燥热伤肺/燥熱傷肺　dry-heat impairing lung
燥伤鼻窍证/燥傷鼻竅證　pattern of dryness invading nose
燥胜则干/燥勝則幹　predominant dryness causing withering
燥湿化痰/燥濕化痰　eliminating dampness and phlegm, drying the wetness-evil and eliminating phlegm
燥湿敛疮/燥濕斂瘡　eliminating dampness and astringing sores
燥苔/燥苔　dry fur
燥痰证/燥痰證　dry-phlegm pattern
燥邪/燥邪　dryness pathogen
燥邪犯肺证/燥邪犯肺證　pattern of dryness invading lung
燥性干涩/燥性乾澀　characteristic of dryness being dry and puckery, dryness being dry and puckery
燥易伤肺/燥易傷肺　dryness likely to injure lung
燥蝇属/燥蠅屬　Auchmeromyia
燥证/燥證　dryness pattern
躁烦/躁煩　restlessness
躁狂的/躁狂的　manic
躁狂患者/癲狂患者　phrenetic
躁狂性精神病/躁狂性精神病　manic psychosis
躁狂性谵妄/躁動性譫妄　active delirium
躁狂抑郁/躁鬱症　manic depressive
躁狂抑郁精神病/躁鬱精神病　manic-depressive psychosis
躁狂抑郁性［精神］障碍/躁鬱症　manic-depressive disorder
躁狂抑郁症/躁狂抑鬱症　manic-depressive illness
躁狂者/躁狂者　maniac
躁狂症/躁狂［症］　mania
躁狂状态评定量表/躁狂狀態評定量表　manic state rating scale
泽兰/澤蘭　hirsute shiny bugleweed herb
泽默林环/澤梅林環　Soemmerring ring
泽默林晶状体肿胀/Soemmerring 氏晶狀體腫脹　Soemmerring crystalline swelling
泽斯特锚凹附着体/澤斯特錨凹附著體　Zest anchor attachment
泽泻/澤瀉　oriental waterplantain rhizome
泽泻浸出物/澤瀉浸出物　alismin
曾特·吉厄尔吉维生素 C 反应/山蓋氏反應　Szent-Gyorgyi reaction
增白细胞药/增白細胞藥　leukopoietic
增大/增大　augmentation
增大性生长/增大性生長　auxetic growth
增感屏/增光影屏,強光屏　intensifying screen
增高/增高　raised
增积的/增積的　accrete
增剂疗法/增量療法,遞增療法　anatherapeusis
增加的/增加的　incremental
增加的血管穿透性/增加的血管穿透性　increased vascular permeability
增距立体 X 射线照相术/遠距式 X 射線立體攝影術　hyperstereoroentgenography
增力桥基/增力橋基　additional stresses abutment
增量调节/增量調節　up regulation
增敏/敏感化　sensitization
增强/增強　potentiation, accentuation
增强肌肉收缩药/增强肌肉收縮藥　positive inotropic drug
增强记忆药/增强記憶藥　memory enhancer
增强支抗/增强支抗　reinforced anchorage
增强子/增强子　enhancer
增强子元件/增强子元件　enhancer element
增溶剂/助溶劑　solubilizer
增溶作用/助溶作用　solubilization
增生/增生　proliferation
增生的/增生的　hyperplastic
增生期/增生期　proliferative phase
增生型天疱疮/增殖性天皰瘡　pemphigus vegetans
增生性/增生性　proliferating
增生性瘢痕/增生性瘢痕　hyperplastic scar
增生性玻璃体视网膜病/增生性玻璃體視網膜病　proliferative vitreoretinopathy
增生性胆囊炎/增生性膽囊炎　hyperplastic cholecystitis
增生性骨炎/增生性骨炎　productive osteitis
增生性滑膜炎/增生性滑膜炎　synovitis hyperplastica
增生性甲状腺肿/增生性甲狀腺腫　hyperplastic goiter
增生性筋膜炎/增生性筋膜炎　proliferative fasciitis
增生性毛根鞘瘤/增生性毛根鞘瘤　proliferative trichilemmoma
增生性囊肿/增生性囊腫　proliferative cyst
增生性脓皮病/增殖性膿皮病,增殖性皮膚炎　pyoderma vegetans
增生性皮炎/增殖性皮膚炎　dermatitis vegetans
增生性水疱性表皮松解症/增生性水皰性表皮鬆解症　epidermolysis bullosa hyperplastica
增生性胃病/增生性胃病　hyperplastic gastropathy
增生性息肉/增殖性息肉　hyperplastic polyp

增生性纤维变性/增生性纖維變性　fibrosis proliferativa
增生性序列性血管内皮瘤病/增生性序列性血管内皮瘤病　proliferating systematized angioendotheliomatosis
增生性血管内皮瘤病/增生性血管内皮瘤病　angioendotheliomatosis proliferans
增生性炎症/增生性炎症　proliferative inflammation, hyperplastic inflammation
增生性移植物/增生性移植物　hyperplastic graft
增生性龈炎/增生性齦炎　hyperplastic gingivitis
增生性支气管炎/增生性支氣管炎　productive bronchitis
增数性肥大/數量性肥大　numeric hypertrophy
增效剂/增效藥　synergist
增压曲线/增壓曲線　increasing pressure curve
增长期/增長期　epacme
增长期的/增長期的　epacmastic
增殖/增殖,繁殖　multiplication
增殖聚合/增殖聚合　proliferous polymerization
增殖细胞核抗原/增殖細胞核抗原　proliferating cell nuclear antigen
增殖腺/腺樣增殖[體]　adenoid
增殖腺扁桃体切除术/扁桃腺及增殖體切除術　adenotonsillectomy
增殖腺刀/腺樣增殖體切除刀　adenotome
增殖腺面容/腺樣增殖病面容　adenoid face
增殖腺[体]炎/腺樣增殖體炎　adenoiditis
增殖性/增殖性　vegetans
增殖性关节炎/增殖性關節炎　proliferating arthritis
增殖性红斑/紅斑瘤　erythroplasia
增殖性角化病/增殖性角化病　keratosis vegetans
增殖性结核/增殖性結核　hyperplastic tuberculosis
增殖性狼疮/增殖性狼瘡　lupus vegetans
增殖性类天疱疮/增殖性類天皰瘡　pemphigoid vegetans
增殖性毛外根鞘瘤/增生性毛根鞘囊腫瘤　proliferating trichilemmal tumor
增殖性囊肿/增殖性囊腫　proliferous cyst
增殖性脓性口炎/增殖性膿性口炎　pyostomatitis vegetans
增殖性肾炎/產出性腎炎　productive nephritis
增殖性生长/增殖性生長　multiplicative growth
增殖性视网膜炎/增生性視網膜炎　retinitis proliferans
增殖性心内膜炎/增殖性心内膜炎　vegetative endocarditis
增殖性溴疹/增殖性溴疹　vegetating bromoderma

扎格勒斯韧带/Zaglas 氏韌帶　Zaglas ligament
扎莫特罗/扎莫特羅　xamoterol
扎西他滨/扎昔他賓　zalcitabine
眨眼/瞬目,霎眼　blinking
眨眼动颌现象/頜動霎眼現象　jaw-winking phenomenon
乍醒垂睑/乍醒垂瞼　waking ptosis
乍醒麻木/乍醒麻木,覺醒無感覺　narcohypnia
诈病/詐病,裝病　malingering
栅栏/柵欄　palisade
栅栏细胞/柵狀細胞　palisade cell
栅栏形成/柵欄狀構造　palisade formation
栅栏状排列/柵欄狀排列　palisade arrangement
栅栏状皮肤纤维细胞瘤/柵欄狀皮膚纖維細胞瘤　palisading cutaneous fibrous histiocytoma
栅栏状肉芽肿/柵欄狀肉芽腫　palisading granuloma
栅栏组织/柵狀組織　palisade tissue
炸药性头痛/炸藥性頭痛　dynamite headache
痄腮/痄腮　mumps
痄腮·变证/痄腮·變證　deteriorated case of mumps
痄腮·常证/痄腮·常證　regular case of mumps
痄腮·毒窜睾腹证/痄腮·毒竄睾腹證　mumps with toxin attacking testes
痄腮·温毒袭表证/痄腮·溫毒襲表證　mumps with pattern of warm-toxin invading exterior
痄腮·温毒蕴结证/痄腮·溫毒蘊結證　mumps with accumulation and binding of warm-toxin pattern
痄腮·邪陷心肝证/痄腮·邪陷心肝證　mumps with pattern of pathogen invading heart and liver
榨出汁/壓出液　press juice
摘出[术]/摘出[術],剜出術　enucleation
摘除/摘除　plucking
窄面/面部狹長,狹面　leptoprosopia
窄面人/面部狹長者,狹面者　leptoprosope
窄谱抗生素/窄譜抗生素　narrow spectrum antibiotic
窄旋密螺旋体/狹迴螺旋體　Treponema stenogyratum
窄叶蛇头草/[窄葉]蛇頭草　balmony
粘连/粘連　synechia
粘连结合/粘連結合　adherens junction
粘连囊/粘連囊　adherent capsule
粘连舌/粘連舌,舌粘連　adherent tongue
粘连松解术/粘連分離術　adhesiolysis
粘连胎盘/粘連[性]胎盤　adherent placenta
粘连切离术/粘連切斷術　adhesiotomy
粘连性腹膜炎/粘連性腹膜炎　adhesive peritonitis
粘连性角膜白斑/粘連性角膜白斑　adherent leukoma of cornea

粘连性腱鞘炎/粘連性腱鞘炎　adhesive tenosynovitis
粘连性静脉炎/粘連性靜脈炎　adhesive phlebitis
粘连性溃疡/黏著性潰瘍　adherent ulcer
粘连性脑突出/粘連腦膨出　synencephalocele
粘连性疝/乾粘連性疝　dry hernia
粘连性消化不良/粘連性消化不良　adhesion dyspepsia
粘连性心包炎/粘連性心包炎　adhesive pericarditis
粘连性炎/粘連性炎[症],粘連性發炎　adhesive inflammation
粘连性中耳炎/粘連性中耳炎　adhesive otitis media
詹姆斯束/詹姆斯束　James tract
谵妄/譫妄　delirium
谵妄型疟/譫妄型瘧　delirious malaria
谵妄性休克/譫妄性休克　delirious shock
谵妄性忧郁症/譫妄性憂鬱病　melancholia with delirium
谵妄性躁狂/譫妄[性躁]狂　delirious mania
谵语/譫語,譫妄　delirious speech, delirium
展肌/展肌　abductor muscle
展旁核/展旁核　paraabducens nucleus
展青霉/開放青黴菌　Penicillium patulum
展神经/展神經　abducent nerve, abducens nerve
展神经核/外旋神經核　abducens nucleus, nucleus of abducent nerve
展神经疾病/展神經疾病　abducens nerve disease
展神经损伤/展神經損傷　abducens nerve injury
战场感染/戰場傳染　obsidional infection
战汗/戰汗　sweating following shiver
战壕背痛/戰壕背痛　trench back
战壕病/戰壕病　trench disease
战壕肺/戰壕肺[病]　trench lung
战壕口/戰壕口[病]　trench mouth
战壕热/戰壕熱　trench fever
战壕肾炎/戰壕腎炎　trench nephritis
战壕手病/戰壕手病　trench hand
战伤/戰傷　war wound
战伤外科学/戰傷外科學　war surgery
战时神经症/戰時神經[機能]病　combat disorder, combat neurosis
站/站　station
站立行走不能/起立步行不能　astasia-abasia
站立姿势/直立姿勢　usustatus
张肌韧带/張肌韌帶　tensor ligament
张景岳/張景岳　Zhang Jingyue
张口痉挛/張口痙攣　antitrismus
张口器/張口器　mouth gag
张力/張力　tension
张力过低/張力過低　hypotonia
张力过高/張力過強　hypertonia
张力计/[表面]張力計　tensiometer
张力亢进性肥大/張力亢進性肥大,數量性肥大　hypertonia hypertrophy
张力描记法/張力描記法　tonography
张力描记器/張力描記器,壓力描記器　tonograph
张力[描记]图/張力記錄　tonogram
张力缺乏的/無緊張的　atonic
张力缺乏性消化不良/鬆弛性消化不良　atonic dyspepsia
张力缺失/張力缺乏　atonia
张力失调/緊張度異常　dystonia
张力丝/張力絲　tonofilament
张力纤维/張力纖維　stress fiber, tonofibril
张力原纤维/張力原纖維　tonofibril
张力障碍/張力障礙　dystonic disorder
张仲景/張仲景　Zhang Zhongjing
章门/章門　zhangmen, LR13
樟碱/樟鹼　actinodaphnine
樟脑/樟腦　camphor
樟脑阿片酊/鴉片樟腦酊　camphorated opium tincture
樟脑草/貓薄荷草　cataria
樟脑5-单加氧酶/樟腦5-單加氧酶　camphor 5-monooxygenase
樟脑氯酚/樟腦氯酚　camphorated monochlorophenol
樟脑酸/樟腦[二]酸　camphoric acid
樟脑酸安替比林/樟腦酸安替比林　antipyrine camphorate
樟脑醑/樟腦醑　camphor spirit
樟脑中毒/樟腦中毒　camphorism
长势不能/長勢不能　failure to thrive
掌/[手]掌　palm, metacarpus
掌背侧骨间静脉/掌背側骨間靜脈　dorsal interosseous metacarpal vein
掌背动脉/掌背動脈　dorsal metacarpal artery
掌背静脉/掌背靜脈　dorsal metacarpal vein
掌侧副韧带/掌側副韌帶　volar accessory ligament
掌侧横掌骨间韧带/掌側橫掌骨間韌帶　volar transverse intermetacarpal ligament
掌侧韧带/掌側韌帶　palmar ligament
掌侧头韧带/掌側頭韌帶　volar capitular ligament
掌侧腕骨间韧带/掌側腕骨間韌帶　palmar intercarpal ligament
掌侧腕间韧带/掌側腕間韌帶　volar intercarpal ligament

掌侧腕掌骨韧带/掌側腕掌骨韌帶　palmar carpometacarpal ligament
掌侧腕掌韧带/掌側腕掌韌帶　volar carpometacarpal ligament
掌侧掌间韧带/掌側掌間韌帶　palmar intermetacarpal ligament
掌侧掌深动脉/掌側掌深動脈　deep volar metacarpal artery
掌长肌/掌長肌　palmaris longus, long palmar muscle
掌的/掌的　metacarpal
掌点凹/手掌點狀凹陷　palmar pit
掌短肌/掌短肌,短掌肌　palmaris brevis, musculus palmaris brevis, short palmar muscle
掌弓/掌弓　palmar arch
掌骨/掌骨　metacarpal bone
掌骨背侧韧带/掌骨背側韌帶　dorsal metacarpal ligament
掌骨底/掌骨底　base of metacarpal bone
掌骨骨间韧带/掌骨骨間韌帶　interosseous metacarpal ligament
掌骨骨折/掌骨骨折　fracture of metacarpal bone, metacarpal fracture
掌骨基底背侧韧带/掌骨基底背側韌帶　dorsal ligament of base of metacarpal bone
掌骨间动脉/掌骨間動脈　palmar intermetacarpal artery
掌骨间关节/掌骨間關節　intermetacarpal joint, articulations of metacarpal bones
掌骨间前韧带/掌骨間前韌帶　anterior intermetacarpal ligament
掌骨间隙/掌骨間隙　intermetacarpal space
掌骨髁/掌骨髁　condyle of metacarpal bone
掌骨切除术/掌骨切除術　metacarpectomy
掌骨深横韧带/掌骨深橫韌帶　deep transverse metacarpal ligament
掌骨体/掌骨體　shaft of metacarpal bone
掌骨头/掌骨頭　head of metacarpal bone
掌骨头间静脉/掌骨頭間靜脈　intercapital vein
掌骨掌侧韧带/掌骨掌側韌帶　palmar metacarpal ligament
掌黑癣/掌黑癬　tinea nigra
掌横弓/掌橫弓　transverse palmar arch
掌红斑/掌紅斑　erythema palmare
掌黄[色]瘤/掌黃[色]瘤　palmar xanthoma
掌肌/掌肌　musculus palmaris
掌棘皮病/掌棘皮病　acanthosis palmaris
掌腱膜/掌腱膜　palmar aponeurosis
掌腱膜横束/掌腱膜橫束　transverse fasciculi of palmar aponeurosis
掌腱膜挛缩/掌腱膜攣縮　dupuytren contracture
掌腱膜切除术/掌腱膜切除術　palmar aponeuroectomy
掌腱膜切开术/掌腱膜切開術　palmar aponeurotomy
掌颏反射/掌頦反射　plamomental reflex
掌拇指握法/掌拇指握法　palm and thumb grasp
掌拍法/掌拍　slapping
掌浅弓/掌淺弓　superficial palmar arch
掌浅横韧带/掌淺橫韌帶　superficial transverse metacarpal ligament
掌浅静脉弓/掌淺靜脈弓　superficial palmar venous arch
掌浅支/掌淺支　superficial palmar branch
掌韧带/掌韌帶　ligamentum palmaria
掌深弓/掌深弓　deep palmar arch
掌深弓静脉/掌深弓靜脈　deep palmar venous arch
掌深支/掌深支　deep palmar branch
掌条纹状黄变/掌條紋狀黃變　xanthochromia striata palmaris
掌腕背侧韧带/掌腕背側韌帶　dorsal carpometacarpal ligament
掌纹型/掌紋型　palm pattern
掌心动脉/掌心動脈　palmar metacarpal artery
掌心静脉/掌心靜脈,手掌側靜脈　palmar metacarpal vein
掌缘角化病/掌緣角化病　marginal keratoderma of palm
掌褶纹/掌褶紋　palmar flexion crease
掌跖扁平苔癣/掌蹠扁平苔癬　lichen planus of palm and sole
掌跖表皮松解性角化症/掌蹠表皮鬆解性角化症　epidermolytic keratosis palmaris et plantaris
掌跖的/掌蹠的　palmoplantar
掌跖点凹/掌蹠點狀凹陷　palmar and plantar pits
掌跖骨/掌蹠骨　metapodialia
掌[跖]骨过短/掌[蹠]骨過短　brachymetapody
掌跖过度角化症/掌蹠過度角化症　palmar and plantar hyperkeratosis
掌跖汗疱疹/掌蹠汗皰疹　palmoplantar pompholyx, cheiropompholyx
掌跖及黏膜黑色素瘤/掌蹠及黏膜黑色素瘤　palmoplantar mucosal melanoma
掌跖角化病/掌蹠角化病,手掌角化病　keratosis palmaris et plantaris, ichthyosis palmaris
掌跖角化过度[症]/掌蹠角化過度[症],手掌-足底角化過度,手掌-足蹠角化過度　hyperkeratosis of

palm and sole, palmar-plantar hyperkeratosis
掌跖角皮病伴黏膜白斑/掌蹠角皮症伴黏膜白斑　palmoplantar keratoderma with leukoplakia
掌跖角皮病伴牙周病/掌蹠角皮症伴牙周病　palmoplantar keratoderma with periodontosis
掌跖角皮症/掌蹠角皮症　palmoplantar keratodermia
掌跖角皮症伴角膜营养不良/掌蹠角皮症伴角膜營養不良　palmoplantar keratoderma with corneal dystrophy
掌跖角皮症伴食管癌/掌蹠角皮症伴食道癌　palmoplantar keratoderma with cancer of the esophagus
掌跖慢性水疱性皮炎/掌蹠慢性水皰性皮炎　chronic vesicular dermatitis of the palm and sole
掌跖梅毒疹/掌蹠梅毒疹　syphilid palmaris et plantaris
掌跖黏膜黄疸/黄病變性黄疸　xanthochromic jaundice
掌跖牛皮癣/掌蹠牛皮癬　psoriasis palmaris et plantaris
掌跖脓疱病/掌蹠膿皰症　palmoplantar pustulosis
掌跖脓疱型干癣/掌蹠膿皰型乾癬　palmar and plantar pustular psoriasis
掌跖皮肤角化病/掌蹠皮膚角化病　palmoplantar keratoderma
掌跖湿疹/掌蹠濕疹　palmoplantar eczema
掌跖疣/掌蹠疣　palmoplantar verruca
掌指关节/掌指關節　metacarpophalangeal joint, metacarpophalangeal articulation
掌指关节半脱位/掌指關節半脱位　subluxation of metacarpophalangeal joint
掌指关节背屈畸形/掌指關節背屈畸形　extension contracture of metacarpophalangeal joint
掌指关节侧副韧带/掌指關節側副韌帶　collateral ligament of metacarpophalangeal articulation
掌指关节脱位/掌指關節脱位　dislocation of metacarpal phalangeal joint, metacarpophalangeal dislocation
掌指关节外侧韧带/掌指關節外側韌帶　lateral ligament of metacarpophalangeal joint
掌中隔/掌中隔　palmar intermediate septum
掌中间隙/掌中間隙　midpalmar space
掌纵弓/掌縱弓　longitudinal palmar arch
帐弓/帳弓　tented arch
胀气/氣性膨脹　gaseous distention
胀痛/脹痛　bursting pain, distending pain
障/障　eye disease, ophthalmopathy, vision obstruction
障碍/障礙　disturbance
障碍阅读试验/尺讀試驗　bar-reading test
瘴毒的/瘴氣的　miasmatic
瘴疟/瘴癘,惡性瘧,凶險型瘧疾　malignant malaria, miasmatic malaria
瘴气/瘴氣,瘴毒　miana, miasma
瘴气病/瘴氣[性]病　miasmatic disease
瘴气传染/瘴氣傳染　miasmatic infection
招风耳/招風耳　bat ear
朝食暮吐/朝食暮吐　eating in morning but vomiting in evening
沼泽热/沼澤熱,螺旋體性黄疸　marsh fever
照海/照海　zhaohai, KI6
照射/照射　irradiation
照射后综合征/照射後症候群　postirradiation syndrome
照射剂量/照射劑量　exposure dose
照射疗法/照射療法　irradiation treatment
照射室/照射室　exposure cell
照相乳剂/攝影乳劑　photographic emulsion
照相用化学品/照相學之化合物　photographic chemical
照相纸式放射量计/感光紙輻射計　photographic radiometer
罩牙本质/罩牙本質　mantle dentin
遮盖片/遮蓋片　opaque disk
遮盖试验/覆蓋試驗　cover test
遮盖性弱视/遮蓋性弱視　occlusion amblyopia
折刀式强直/折刀式強直　clasp-knife spasticity
折刀式效应/彈簧刀作用　clasp-knife effect
折刀样强直/折刀狀強硬　clasp-knife rigidity
折刀状卧位/折刀狀臥位　jackknife position
折叠/折疊　folding
β折叠/β折疊　β-pleated sheet structure
折叠夹板/折疊夾板　hinge joint splint
折断/折斷　broken
折断面/折斷面　fracture surface
折返心律/折返心律,再回返節律　reciprocal rhythm, reentrant rhythm
折光测定法/折光測定法　refractometry
折仑诺/玉米赤黴醇　Zeranol
折射光/折射光　refracted light
折射器/折射器　refractor
折针/折針　breaking of inserted needle
辄筋/輒筋　zhejin, GB23
蛰伏脂瘤/越冬腺腫　hibernoma
赭石/赭石　hematite
赭石型突变/赭石型突變　ochre mutation

褶曲状盘片/褶曲狀碟片　convoluted discs
褶柱/皺襞柱　columns of ruga
浙贝母/浙貝母　thunberbg fritillary bulb
蔗尘肺/肺蔗塵沈著病　bagassosis
蔗聚糖/蔗聚糖　ficoll
蔗糖/蔗糖　sucrose
蔗糖化合物/蔗糖化合物　sucrate
蔗糖酶/蔗糖酵素,轉化酵素　sucrase
蔗糖酶异麦芽糖酶复合物/蔗糖酶異麥芽糖酶複合物　sucrase-isomaltase complex
蔗糖尿/蔗糖尿　saccharosuria
蔗糖血/蔗糖血　sucrosemia
贞芪扶正颗粒/貞芪扶正顆粒　zhenqi fuzheng granules
针/針　needle
针拨白内障/白內障摘除術　couching
针博士/針博士　erudite for acupuncture
针刺/針刺　acupuncture
针刺补泻/針刺補瀉　reinforcing and reducing manipulations of acupuncture therapy
针刺感/針刺感,荊棘感　acanthesthesia
针刺角度/針刺角度　needling angle
针刺疗法/針刺療法　acupuncture therapy
针刺麻醉/針刺麻醉　acupuncture anesthesia
针刺美容[术]/針刺美容[術]　acupuncture cosmetics
针刺伤/針刺傷　pricking wound
针刺试验/針刺試驗　pinprick test
针[刺]术/針[刺]術　stylostixis
针刺穴位/針刺穴位　acupuncture point
针刺镇痛/針刺鎮痛,針麻　acupuncture analgesia
针刀/針刀　akupotomye
针刀疗法/針刀療法　akupotomye treatment
针导/針導　needle guide
针电极/針電極　needle electrode
针动检影器/針動檢影器　velonoskiascopy
针感/針感　needling sensation
针罐法/針罐法　needling associated with cupping, needling combined with cupping
针迹瘢痕/針跡瘢痕　suture mark
针晶/針晶　acicular crystal, raphide
针灸处方/針灸處方　acumoxibustion prescription, acupuncture and moxibustion prescription
针灸大成/針灸大成　Compendium of Acupuncture and Moxibustion
针灸法/針灸法　acupuncture and moxibustion therapy
针灸甲乙经/針灸甲乙經　A-B Classic of Acupuncture and Moxibustion, The ABC Classic of Acupuncture and Moxibustion
针灸科/針灸科　department of acupuncture and moxibustion
针灸学/中醫針灸學　science of acupuncture and moxibustion of traditional Chinese medicine
针灸治疗学/針灸治療學　subject of acupuncture and moxibustion theraphy
针孔喷雾/針孔噴霧　needle spray
针孔片/針孔片　pinhole disk
针孔状瞳孔/針孔狀瞳孔,針眼狀瞳孔　pinhole pupil
针毛/針毛　aciculum
针扭转法/針扭轉法　acutorsion
针头共用/針頭共用　needle sharing
针头交换计划/針頭交換計劃　needle-exchange program
针吸活组织检查/針吸活組織檢查　needle biopsy
针线压迫法/針壓結扎法　acufilopressure
针形检影法/針動視網膜檢影法　belonoskiascopy
针压法/針壓[止血]法　acupression
针眼/針眼,麥粒腫　hordeolum, stye
针眼·风热客睑证/針眼·風熱客瞼證　stye with pattern of wind-heat lodging in eyelid
针眼·脾虚湿热证/針眼·脾虛濕熱證　stye with pattern of spleen deficiency and dampness-heat
针眼·热毒壅盛证/針眼·熱毒壅盛證　stye with pattern of heat-toxin congestion and excessiveness
针眼·正虚邪恋证/針眼·正虛邪戀證　stye with pattern of healthy qi deficiency and lingering pathogen
针止血法/針止血法　acuclosure
针状骨赘/針狀骨贅,骨刺　acidosteophyte
针钻/針鑽　pin punch
珍珠/珍珠　pearl
珍珠工骨髓炎/珍珠工骨髓炎,採蚌人骨髓炎　conchiolin osteomyelitis
珍珠明滴眼液/珍珠明滴眼液　zhenzhu ming eye drops
珍珠母/珍珠母　nacre
珍珠丸/珍珠丸　pearl pill
珍珠样阴茎丘疹/珍珠樣陰莖丘疹　pearly penile papules
珍珠状囊肿/珍珠狀囊腫　pearl cyst
真/真　true
真鞭毛虫纲/真鞭毛蟲類　Euflagellata
真毒素/真毒素　true toxin
真寒假热/真寒假熱　true cold disease with false heat manifestation

真寒假热证/真寒假熱證　pattern of true cold disease with false heat manifestation
真核生物/真核生物　eucaryote
真核细胞/真核細胞　eukaryotic cell
真核细胞起始因子类/真核細胞起始因子類　eukaryotic initiation factor
真核形成/真核形成　eucaryosis
真黑色素/真黑色素　eumelanin
真加绷带/Genga 氏繃帶　Genga bandage
真结/真結　true knot
真结合径/真結合徑　conjugate vera
真睛破损/真睛破損　ruptured wound of eyeball
真睛破损•风邪外袭证/真睛破損•風邪外襲證　ruptured wound of eyeball with pattern of external assault by wind
真睛破损•脓毒侵袭证/真睛破損•膿毒侵襲證　ruptured wound of eyeball with purulent toxin invasion pattern
真睛破损•气滞血瘀证/真睛破損•氣滯血瘀證　ruptured wound of eyeball with pattern of qi stagnation and blood stasis
真菌/真菌,黴菌　fungus, fungi
真菌孢子/真菌孢子　fungal spore
真菌病/真菌病　mycoses
真菌病理学/黴菌病理學　mycopathology
真菌成分/真菌成分　fungal component
真菌蛋白质类/真菌蛋白質類　fungal proteins
真菌的/真菌的,黴菌的　fungal
真菌霉素/真菌黴素　fungimycin
真菌毒素类/真菌毒素類　mycotoxins
真菌分型技术/真菌分型技術　mycological typing technique
真菌感染前/黴菌感染前　premycotic
真菌感染前期疹/黴菌感染前期疹　premycotic eruption
真菌纲/真菌綱　Eumycetes
真菌基因/真菌基因　fungal gene
真菌基因表达调控/真菌基因表達調控　fungal gene expression regulation
真菌基因组/真菌基因組　fungal genome
真菌菌苗/真菌菌苗　fungal vaccine
真菌抗体/真菌抗體　fungal antibody
真菌抗药性/真菌抗藥性　fungal drug resistance
真菌抗原/真菌抗原　fungal antigen
真菌染色体/真菌染色體　fungal chromosome
真菌性肺疾病/真菌性肺疾病　fungal lung disease
真菌性角膜炎/真菌性角膜炎　fungal keratitis
真菌性结膜炎/真菌性結膜炎　fungal conjunctivitis
真菌性脑膜炎/真菌性腦膜炎　fungal meningitis
真菌性葡萄膜炎/真菌性葡萄膜炎　mycotic uveitis
真菌性水肿/黴菌性水腫　mycotic edema
真菌性胃病/黴菌性胃酸過多　gastrosia fungosa
真菌性心包炎/黴菌性心包炎　fungal pericarditis
真菌性心肌炎/真菌性心肌炎　fungal myocarditis
真菌性心内膜炎/菌病性心內膜炎,黴菌性心內膜炎　mycotic endocarditis
真菌性眼感染/真菌性眼感染　fungal eye infection
真菌性主动脉瘤/真菌性主動脈瘤　mycotic aortic aneurysm
真菌学/真菌學,黴菌學　mycology
真菌血症/真菌血症,黴菌血症　fungemia
[真菌]缘饰体/緣飾體　lomosome
真菌中毒/黴菌毒病　mycotoxicosis
真菌子实体类/真菌子實體類　fungal fruiting bodies
真空刮宫术/真空刮宫術　vacuum curettage
真空吸引器/真空吸引器　vacuum suction
真空蒸馏/真空蒸餾　vacuum distillation
真空铸造机/真空鑄造機　vacuum casting machine
真肋/真肋,椎胸肋　true rib
真两性畸形/真兩性畸形,真兩性同體　true hermaphroditism
真两性同体/真兩性同體,真兩性畸形　true hermaphroditism
真密度/真密度　true density
真纳里带/Gennari 氏帶　Gennari band
真皮/真皮　dermis, corium, derma
真皮癌/真皮癌　carcinoma corium
真皮表皮的/真皮[與]表皮的　dermoepidermal
真皮表皮萎缩/真皮表皮萎縮　dermoepidermal atrophy
真皮床/真皮床　dermal bed
真皮的/[真]皮的　dermic
真皮发育不良/真皮發育不良　dermal hypoplasia
真皮汗管瘤/真皮汗管瘤　eccrine dermal duct tumor
真皮黑色素细胞错构瘤/真皮黑色素細胞錯構瘤　dermal melanocyte hamartoma
真皮及血管内筋膜炎/真皮及血管內筋膜炎　dermal and intravascular fasciitis
真皮胶原/真皮膠原　dermal collagen
真皮毛乳突/真皮毛乳突　dermal hair papilla
真皮内痣/真皮內痣　intradermal nevus
真皮片/真皮片　dermis graft
真皮鞘/真皮鞘　dermal sheath
[真皮]乳头层下的/乳突下的　subpapillary
真皮树突细胞脂肪存积/真皮樹突細胞脂肪存積　fat-storing of dermal dendrocyte

真皮树突细胞脂肪贮存错构瘤/真皮樹突細胞脂肪貯存錯構瘤 fat-storing hamartoma of dermal dendrocyte
真皮下血管网薄皮瓣/真皮下血管網薄皮瓣 subdermal vascular plexus thin skin flap
真皮下血管网皮片/真皮下血管網皮片 subdermal vascular plexus free skin graft
真皮移植片/真皮移植片 dermic graft
真皮移植术/真皮移植術 dermis grafting
真皮圆柱瘤/真皮圓柱瘤 dermal cylindroma
真皮造血/真皮造血 dermal hematopoiesis
真皮脂肪瓣/真皮脂肪瓣 dermis-fat flap
真皮脂肪移植术/真皮脂肪移植術 dermis-fat grafting
真皮脂肪移植物/真皮脂肪移植物 dermis-fat graft
真皮中层弹性组织溶解症/真皮中層彈性組織溶解 middermal elastolysis
真气/真氣 genuine qi
真热假寒/真熱假寒 true heat disease with false cold manifestation
真热假寒证/真熱假寒證 pattern of true heat disease with false cold manifestation
真人养脏汤/真人養臟湯 zhenren yangzang decoction
真疝/真疝 true hernia
真实假虚/真實假虛 true excess disease with false deficient manifestation
真实假虚证/真實假虛證 pattern of true excess disease with false deficient manifestation
真髓石/真髓石 true denticle
真胎盘/真胎盤 placenta vera
真糖/真糖 sucre actuelle
真绦虫类/真條蟲類 eucestoda
真头痛/真頭痛 intolerable headache, true headache
真网状细胞肉瘤/真性網狀細胞肉瘤 true reticulosarcoma
真涡虫/真渦蟲 Planarians
真武汤/真武湯 zhenwu decoction
真吸收/真吸收 true absorption
真相揭露/真相揭露 truth disclosure
真心痛/真心痛 true heart pain, angina pectoris, real heart pain
真心痛·寒凝心脉证/真心痛·寒凝心脈證 true heart pain with pattern of yang deficiency and cold congelation
真心痛·气虚血瘀证/真心痛·氣虛血瘀證 true heart pain with pattern of qi deficiency and blood stasis

真心痛·正虚阳脱证/真心痛·正虛陽脱證 true heart pain with pattern of vital qi deficiency and yang collapse
真性/真性 genuine
真性动脉瘤/真性動脈瘤 true aneurysm
真性肥大/真性肥大 true hypertropy
真性红细胞增多症/真性紅血球增多病,紅血球過多病,奥-維二氏病 polycythemia vera, polycythemia rubra vera, Osler-Vaquez disease
真性近视/真性近視 true myopia
真性眶距过宽/真性眶距過寬 true orbital hypertelorism
真性流感/真性流行性感冒 influenza vera
真性囊肿/真性囊腫 true cyst
真性失语/真性失語 true aphasia
真性胎块/真性胎塊 true mole
[真性]天花/真痘 variola vera
真性性早熟/真性性早熟 true precocious puberty
真性咽峡炎/真性咽峡炎 angina vera
真虚假实/真虛假實 true deficiency disease with false excessive manifestation
真虚假实证/真虛假實證 pattern of true deficiency disease with false excessive manifestation
真血浆/真血漿 true plasma
真牙/真牙 genuine tooth, wisdom tooth
真脏脉/真臟脈 critical pulse manifestation
真脏色/真臟色 genuine visceral complexion
砧镫关节/砧鐙關節 incudostapedial joint, incudostapedial articulation
砧镫脱位/砧鐙骨脱位 incudostapedial dislocation
砧骨/砧骨 incus
砧骨襞/砧骨褶 incudal fold
砧骨长脚/砧骨長腳 long crus of incus
砧骨短脚/砧骨短腳 short crus of incus
砧骨后韧带/砧骨後韌帶 posterior ligament of incus
砧骨切除术/砧骨切除術 incudectomy
砧骨韧带/砧骨韌帶 ligament of incus
砧骨上韧带/砧骨上韌帶 superior ligament of incus, ligamentum incudis superius
砧骨体/砧骨體 body of incus
砧骨窝/砧骨窩 incudal fossa
诊尺肤/診尺膚 examining skin of forearm
诊断/診斷[法] diagnosis
诊断的/診斷的 diagnostic
诊断检查服务/診斷檢查服務 diagnostic service
诊断模型/診斷[性]模型 diagnostic cast
诊断设备/診斷設備 diagnostic equipment
诊断试剂盒/診斷試劑盒 diagnostic reagent kit

诊断显像/診斷顯像　diagnostic imaging
诊断相关患者组/診斷相關患者組　diagnosis-related group
诊断性检查/診斷性檢查　diagnostic test
诊断性气胸/診斷氣胸　diagnostic pneumothorax
诊断性切开/證實切開術　confirmatory incision
诊断性纵隔积气/診斷性縱隔積氣　diagnostic pneumomediastinum
诊断学/診斷學　diagnostics
诊断用药/診斷用輔助藥　diagnostic agent
诊法/診法　diagnostic method
诊后病历/診後病歷,病後經過　catamnesis
诊籍/個案記錄,病志　case record
诊乳房/診乳房　palpating breast
诊室就医/診室就醫　office visit
诊虚里/診虛裡　examining xuli
枕/枕　zhen, AT 3, occiput
枕板障静脉/枕板障靜脈　occipital diploic vein
枕部的/枕部的,枕骨的　occipital
枕[部]肌节/枕[部]肌節　occipital myotome
枕部联胎/枕部連胎　iniodymus
枕部入路/枕部入路　occipital approach
枕部三头联胎/枕部三頭連胎　tri-iniodymus
枕[部]神经痛/枕[部]神經痛,枕骨神經痛　occipital neuralgia
枕大神经/枕大神經,大枕神經　greater occipital nerve
枕垫缝合/支墊縫線　bolster suture
枕动脉/枕[骨]動脈　occipital artery
枕动脉耳支/枕動脈耳支　auricular branch of occipital artery
枕动脉沟/枕動脈溝　sulcus for occipital artery, occipital groove
枕动脉降支/枕動脈降支　descending branch of occipital artery
枕动脉脑膜支/枕動脈腦膜支　meningeal branch of occipital artery
枕动脉乳突支/枕動脈乳突支　mastoid branch of occipital artery
枕动脉胸锁乳突肌支/枕動脈胸鎖乳突肌支　sternocleidomastoid branch of occipital artery
枕动脉枕支/枕動脈枕支　occipital branch of occipital artery, deep descending cervical artery
枕窦/枕竇　occipital sinus
枕窦沟/枕竇溝　sulcus for occipital sinus
枕额肌/枕額肌　occipitofrontalis, musculus occipitofrontalis
枕额肌额腹/枕額肌額腹　ventral frontalis musculi occipitofrontalis
枕腹/枕腹　occipital belly
枕盖/枕蓋　occipital operculum
枕骨/枕骨　occipital bone
枕骨板障静脉/枕骨板障靜脈　vena diploica occipitalis
枕骨侧部/枕骨側部　lateral part of occipital bone
枕骨侧窦沟/枕骨側竇溝　lateral groove for lateral sinus of occipital bone
枕骨大孔/枕骨大孔　foramen magnum of occipital bone
枕[骨]大孔脑膜瘤/枕[骨]大孔腦膜瘤　meningioma of foramen magnum
枕[骨]导静脉/枕導靜脈　occipital emissary vein
枕骨底部/枕骨底部　pars basilaris ossis occipitalis
枕骨底沟/枕骨基底溝　basilar groove of occipital bone
枕骨肌/枕骨肌　occipital muscle
枕骨嵴/枕嵴　occipital crest
枕骨角综合征/枕骨角症候群　occipital horn syndrome
枕骨髁/枕骨髁　occipital condyle
枕骨裂脑露畸胎/裂枕露腦畸胎　iniencephalus
枕骨裂脑露畸形/裂枕露腦畸形　iniencephaly
枕骨内隆凸/枕内隆凸　internal occipital protuberance
枕骨外隆凸/枕外隆凸　external occipital protuberance
枕骨斜坡/枕骨斜坡　clivus ossis occipitalis
枕骨圆枕/橫枕粗隆,枕骨隆凸　transverse occipital protuberance
枕核/枕核　pulvinar nucleus
枕横沟/枕橫溝　transverse occipital sulcus
枕后点/枕後點　opisthion
枕后位/枕骨向後　occipitoposterior
枕基底静脉/枕基底靜脈　occiptobasal vein
枕极/枕極　occipital pole
枕角/枕角　occipital angle
枕静脉/枕靜脈　occipital vein
枕淋巴结/枕淋巴結　occipital lymph node
枕鳞/枕鱗　occipital squama
枕隆起/枕隆凸　occipital eminence
枕内后结合/枕内後[軟骨]結合　posterior intraoccipital synchondrosis
枕内嵴/枕內嵴　internal occipital crest
枕内结合/枕内[軟骨]結合　intraoccipital synchondrosis
枕内隆凸/枕内粗隆　internal occipital protuberance

枕内前结合/枕内前[軟骨]結合　anterior intraoccipital synchondrosis
枕颞沟/枕顬溝　occipitotemporal sulcus
枕颞内侧回/枕顬內側迴　medial occipitotemporal gyrus
枕颞外侧回/枕顬外側迴　lateral occipitotemporal gyrus
枕颞支/枕顬支　occipitotemporal branch
枕平面/枕骨平面　occipital plane
枕前切迹/枕前切跡　preoccipital incisure
枕前位/枕骨向前　occipitoanterior
枕区/枕骨部　occipital region
枕乳突缝/枕乳突縫　occipitomastoid suture
枕软骨/枕軟骨　occipital cartilage
枕三角/枕三角　occipital triangle
枕上骨/枕上骨　supraoccipital bone
枕上旁线/枕上旁線　zhenshang pangxian, MS13, upper-lateral line of occiput
枕上正中线/枕上正中線　zhenshang zhengzhongxian, MS12, upper-middle line of occiput
枕生骨节/枕生骨節,生骨節　occipital sclerotome
枕头夹板/枕頭夾板　pillow splint
枕秃/枕秃　pillow bald
枕外嵴/枕外嵴　external occipital crest
枕外隆凸/枕外粗隆　external occipital protuberance
枕外隆凸尖/枕穴　inion
枕外软骨/枕外軟骨　exoccipital cartilage
枕下部/項部　napex
枕下肌/枕下肌　suboccipital muscle
枕下减压术/枕骨下壓力解除　suboccipital decompression
枕下静脉丛/枕下静脈叢　suboccipital venous plexus
枕下旁线/枕下旁線　zhenxia pangxian, MS14, lower-lateral line of occiput
枕下入路/枕下入路　suboccipital approach
枕下三角/枕下三角　suboccipital triangle
枕下神经/枕下神經　suboccipital nerve
枕小神经/枕小神經,小枕神經　lesser occipital nerve
枕囟门/枕囟門　occipital fontanelle
枕叶/枕葉　occipital lobe
枕叶内侧动脉/枕內側動脈　medial occipital artery
枕叶切除术/枕[骨]葉切除術　occipital lobectomy
枕叶外侧动脉/枕[骨]葉外側動脈　lateral occipital artery
枕叶性失语/枕葉性失語　occipital aphasia
枕缘/枕[側]緣　occipital border, occipital margin
枕支/枕支　occipital branch
枕支抗/枕支抗　occipital anchorage
枕最小神经/枕最小神經　least occipital nerve
疹/發疹,[皮]疹　exanthem, rash
疹的/[發]疹的　exanthematous
疹性坏死/[發]疹性壞死　exanthematous necrosis
阵发的/陣發的　paroxysmal
阵发快速/陣發快速　burst
阵发痛/陣發痛　paroxysmal pain
阵发型血管硬化性肌无力/陣發性血管硬化性肌無力　myasthenia paroxysmalis angiosclerotica
阵发性腹膜炎/陣發性腹膜炎　paroxysmal peritonitis
阵发性高血压/陣發性高血壓　episodic hypertension
阵发性呼吸困难/陣發性呼吸困難　paroxysmal dyspnea
阵发性疾病/陣發性疾病　paroxysmal disease
阵发性咳嗽/陣發性欬嗽　paroxysmal cough
阵发性冷性血红蛋白尿症/陣發性寒冷性血紅素尿　paroxysmal cold hemoglobinuria
阵发性手部血肿/陣發性手部血腫　paroxysmal hand hematoma
阵发性睡眠性血红蛋白尿症/陣發性夜間血色素尿　paroxysmal nocturnal hemoglobinuria
阵发性心动过速/陣發性心搏過速　paroxysmal tachycardia
阵发性眩晕/陣發性眩暈　paroxysmal vertigo
阵发性血管迷走神经性发作/陣發性血管迷走神經性發作　paroxysmal vasovagal attack
阵发性血红蛋白尿/陣發性血紅素尿　paroxysmal hemoglobinuria
阵发性夜间血尿症/陣發性夜間血尿症　paroxysmal nocturnal hemoglobinemia, PNH
阵挛/陣攣　clonus
阵挛发作/陣攣[性]發作　clonic seizure
阵挛描记器/陣攣描記器　clonograph
阵挛性/陣攣性,陣攣狀態　clonicity
阵挛性痉挛/陣攣性痙攣　clonic spasm
鸩酒毒/鴆酒毒　poisonous bird wine poisoning
振胞瘀痛/振胞瘀痛　contusion of palpebra, eyelid contusion
振荡/振盪　succuss
振荡电位/振盪電位　oscillatory potential
振荡器/振動器　oscillator
振荡损伤/振盪損傷　vibration injury
振荡音/振盪音　shaking sound
振动/振動　vibration
振动病/振動病　vibration disease
振动弛豫/振動弛緩　vibrational relaxation

振动[感]觉/振動[感]覺　palmesthesia
振动[感]觉减退/振動[感]覺減弱　pallhypesthesia
振动幻视/振動幻視,擺動幻視　oscillopsia
振动觉过敏/振動感覺過敏　hyperpallesthesia
振动觉减退/振動感覺遲鈍　hypopallesthesia
振动觉缺失/振動[感]覺缺失　pallanesthesia
振动疗法/振動療法　sismotherapy
振动偶合/振動偶合　vibrational coupling
振动器/振動器　vibrator
振动切片机/振動切片機　vibratome
振动性滑膜炎/振動性滑膜炎　vibration synovitis
振动性眼球震颤/振動狀眼球振顫　oscillating nystagmus
振动综合征/振動症候群　vibration syndrome
振法/振法　thumping manipulation, vibration manipulation
震颤/震顫　fremitus, tremor
震颤按摩法/震動按摩法　vibratory massage
震颤法/震顫法　needle-body trembling
震颤麻痹/震顫麻痺　paralysis agitans
震颤麻痹综合征/震顫麻痺症候群　paralysis agitans syndrome
震颤描记器/震顫記錄器　tremograph
震颤描记图/震顫描記波　tremorgram
震颤素/震顫素　tremorine
震颤性步行不能/震顫性步行不能　trembling abasia
震颤[性]麻痹/震顫麻痺,帕金森氏病　paralysis agitans
震颤性谵妄/震顫性譫妄　delirium tremens
震荡后综合征/腦震盪症候群　concussion syndrome
震荡培养/震盪培養　shake culture
震荡性脊髓病/震盪性脊髓病　concussion myelopathy
震荡性脊髓炎/震傷性脊髓炎　concussion myelitis
震动/震動,擺動　oscillation
震动性血管性水肿/震動性血管性水腫　vibratory angioedema
震力效应/震力效應　brisance effect
镇肝熄风汤/鎮肝熄風湯　zhengan xifeng decoction
镇痉药/鎮痙藥　antispastic
镇静/鎮静　sedative
镇静催眠药/鎮静催眠藥　sedative hypnotic
镇静剂/鎮静藥　calmative
镇咳合剂/鎮欬合劑　cough mixture
镇咳剂/鎮欬劑　cough remedy
镇咳药/鎮欬藥　antitussive agent
镇痛/鎮痛,止痛法　analgesia
镇痛剂肾病/鎮痛劑腎病　analgesic nephropathy
镇痛药/鎮痛藥　analgesic
镇吐药/鎮吐藥　anti-emetic
争胜行为/争勝行爲　agonistic behavior
怔忡/怔忡　severe palpitation
蒸/蒸　steaming
蒸发/蒸發　evaporation
蒸发残渣/蒸發殘渣　residue on evaporation
蒸发皿/蒸發碟　evaporating dish
蒸发失水/蒸發失水　evaporation water loss
蒸馏/蒸餾　distillation
蒸馏水/蒸餾水　distilled water
蒸气/蒸氣　vapor
蒸汽/蒸汽　steam
蒸汽变压按摩[法]/蒸汽按摩法　vapor massage
蒸汽烙术/[蒸]汽烙法　vapocauterization
蒸汽灭菌/蒸汽滅菌　steam sterilization
蒸汽帐/蒸汽幕　steam tent
蒸汽吸入疗法/蒸汽吸入療法　steam-inhaling therapy
蒸汽吸入损伤/蒸汽吸入損傷　steam inhalation injury
蒸汽浴/蒸汽浴　steam bath
蒸汽治疗/蒸汽療法　vapotherapy
蒸汽灼法/蒸汽烙法　zestocausis
蒸[制]/蒸煑　steaming
整倍配合/配子體結合　eugamy
整倍体/整倍體　euploid
整倍性/整倍性　euploidy
整臂易位/整臂易位　whole arm translocation
整复疗法/整復療法　reduction therapy
整复性角膜成形术/成形性角膜修補術　tectonic keratoplasty
整骨手法/整骨手法　osteopathic manipulation
整合酶类/整合酶類　integrases
整合酶抑制剂/整合酶抑制劑　integrase inhibitor
整合素类/整合素類　integrins
整合性医疗服务/整合性醫療服務　integrated delivery system of medical service
整合子类/整合子類　integrons
整理/整理　sorting
整理活动/整理活動　cooling-down
整容外科/美容外科　cosmetic surgery
整容牙科学/美容牙科學　cosmetic dentistry
整体保健/整體保健　holistic health
整体关系学/全體關係論　syzygiology
整体观念/整體觀念　holism
整体护理/整體護理　holistic nursing
整体康复/整體康復　integral rehabilitation

整体框架/整體框架　general frame
整体软骨支架/整體軟骨支架　solid block cartilage frame
整体[性]失调/整體性障礙　general disturbance
整体医学/全體醫學　holistic medicine
整形/整形　plastic
整形外科/整形外科,造形外科,補形外科　plastic surgery
正比计数器/正比計數器　proportional counter
正比例性白细胞减少[症]/白血球平均減少　hypo-orthocytosis
正比例性白细胞增多[症]/白血球平均增多　hyper-orthocytosis
正丙醇/正丙醇　N-propyl alcohol
正常促性腺素性闭经/正常促性腺素性閉經　normogonadotropic amenorrhea
正常促性腺素性功能减退症/正常促性腺激素性機能不足　normogonadotropic hypogonadism
正常的/正常的　normal
正常[动脉]血压/正常血壓　orthoarteriotony
正常灌注压突破/正常灌注壓突破　normal perfusion pressure breakthrough
正常𬌗/正常𬌗　normal occlusion
正常红细胞/正[常]紅血球　normocyte
正常红细胞性贫血/正紅血球性貧血　normocytic anemia
正常呼吸/正常呼吸　normal respiration
正常凝集素/正常凝[集]素　normal agglutinin
正常人类血清白蛋白/正常人類血清白蛋白　normal human serum albumin
正常人血浆/正常人血漿　normal human plasma
正[常]色红细胞/正色紅血球　normochromocyte
正常舌象/正常舌象　normal tongue manifestation
正常生活/正常生活　orthobiosis
正常视野/正常視野　normal visual field
正常位输尿管膨出/正常位輸尿管膨出　orthotopic ureterocele
正常温度/正常溫度,常温　normal temperature
正常细胞/正常細胞　normal cell
正常血清/正常血清,健康血清,正規血清　normal serum
正常血小板/正常血小板　orthoplastocyte
正常张力/正常張力　normal tension
正常压力脑积水/正常壓力腦積水　normal pressure hydrocephalus
正常眼压/正常眼壓　normal intraocular tension
正常侏儒/正常侏儒,生理侏儒　normal dwarf
正常组织学/正常組織學　normal histology
正成红细胞过多[症]/正母紅血球過度生成　normoblastosis
正氮平衡/正氮平衡　positive nitrogen balance
正电子/正電子　positron
正电子发射计算机体层扫描术/正[電]子發射斷層攝影術　positron emission tomography, PET
正电子脑瘤定位[描记]图/正電子腦掃描圖　positrocephalogram
正反馈/正反饋,正回饋　positive feedback
正分子疗法/正分子療法　orthomolecular therapy
正骨科/正骨科　department of bone orthopedics
正骨器/整骨器,矯骨器　orthotast
正骨手法/正骨手法　bone-setting manipulation
正骨水/正骨水　zhenggu mixture
正骨推拿/正骨推拿　massage for bone orthopedics
正𬌗法/校對咬合　check bite
正颌外科学/正頜外科學　orthognathic surgery
正颌学/正頜學　orthognathics
正畸保持器/正畸保持器　orthodontic retainer
正畸矫正器/正畸矯正器　orthodontic appliance
正畸矫正器设计/正畸矯正器設計　orthodontic appliance design
正畸矫治器/正畸矯治器　orthodontic appliance
正畸金属丝/正畸金屬絲　orthodontic wire
正畸力/正畸力　orthodontic force
正畸缺隙闭合/正畸缺隙閉合　orthodontic space closure
正畸托架/正畸托架　orthodontic bracket
正畸学/正畸學　orthodontics
正尖波/正尖波　positive sharp wave
正交函数法/正交函數法　orthogonal function method
正交设计/正交設計　orthogonal design
正交圆柱[透]镜/交叉柱面透鏡　crossed cylinder
正酒石酸盐/正酒石酸鹽　normal tartrate
正链/正鏈　plus strand
正亮氨酸/正白胺酸　norleucine
正磷酸/正磷酸　orthophosphoric acid
正磷酸二激酶丙酮酸盐/正磷酸二激酶丙酮酸鹽　orthophosphate dikinase pyruvate
正磷酸盐/正磷酸鹽　orthophosphate
正膦类/正膦類　phosphoranes
正漏/正漏　central corneal fistula with leakage
正梦/正夢　peaceful dream
正黏病毒科感染/正黏病毒科感染　Orthomyxoviridae infection
正疟/正瘧　regular malaria
正气/大氣　vital qi

正切暗点计屏/正切屏　tangent screen
正染色/正染色　positive staining
正视眼/正视眼,屈光正常　emmetropia
正视者/正视者　emmetrope
正数未成熟白细胞症/等數幼稚白血球症　normoskeocytosis
正水/正水　typical anasarca
正态分布/常態分配　normal distribution
正调节/正[性]調節　positive accommodation
正调节基因/正調節基因　positive regulator gene
正铁白蛋白/變血性白蛋白　methemalbumin
正铁化合物/高鐵化合物　ferric compound
正铁血红蛋白/正鐵血紅蛋白,變性血紅素　metahemoglobin
正铁血红蛋白尿/變性血紅素尿　methemoglobinuria
正铁血红蛋白血症的/變性血紅素血症的　methemoglobinemic
正铁血红素/正鐵血紅素,血黑質　hematosin
正铁血红素尿/血黑質尿　hematinuria
正铁血红素血症/血黑質血症　hematinemia
正铁血红素原/血黑質原　hematinogen
正突变株/正突變株　positive mutant
正位刺激物/正位刺激[物]　nomotopic stimulus
正位的/正位的　orthotopic
正位移植物/正位移植物　orthotopic graft
正弦电疗/正弦電療　sinusoidalization
正弦曲线的/正弦曲線的　sinusoidal
正相/正相　normal phase
正向流性/正向流性　positive rheotaxis
正邪相争/正邪分爭　struggle between vital qi and pathogen
正心汤/正心湯　heart qi regulating decoction
正性平衡/正性平衡　positive balance
正虚邪恋证/正虛邪戀證　pattern of lingering pathogen due to deficient vital qi
正虚瘀结积证/正虛瘀結積證　amassment disease with pattern of vital qi deficiency and binding of static blood
正压呼吸/正壓呼吸　positive-pressure respiration
正压换气/正壓換氣　positive-pressure ventilation
正压尿道造影[术]/正壓尿道造影[術]　positive pressure urethrography
正牙学/正牙學,牙科整形術　odontoplasty
正言疏导疗法/正言疏導療法　positive enlightening and consoling therapy
正营/正營　zhengying, GB17
正优生学/正優生學　positive eugenics
正治/正治　counteractive treatment

正治法/正治法　orthodox treatment
正中唇裂/正中唇裂,中裂唇　median cleft lip, median harelip
正中挡/正中擋　centric stop
正中的/正中的　median
正中动脉/正中動脈　median artery
正中额外牙/正中贅生齒,門齒間贅生齒　mesiodens
正中腭突/正中腭突　median palatine process
正中缝囊肿/正中縫囊腫　median raphe cyst
正中弓状韧带/正中弓狀韌帶　median arcuate ligament
正中沟/中間溝　median sulcus
正中关系/正中關係,中央性頜關係　centric relation
正中关系𬌗/正中關係𬌗　centric relation occlusion
正中关系弧/正中關係弧　centric relation arc
正中关系位/正中關係位　centric relation position
正中𬌗/正中𬌗,中央咬合　central occlusion
正中𬌗间记录/正中𬌗間記錄　centric interocclusal record
正中嵴/正中嵴　median bar
正中裂/正中裂　median fissure
正中菱形舌炎/中央菱形舌炎　median rhomboid glossitis
正中隆起/正中隆起　median eminence
正中面/正中面　mesion
正中磨牙症/中樞性夜間磨牙　centric bruxism
正中内皮垫/正中内皮墊　median endothelial cushion
正中旁的/正中旁的　paramedian
正中旁小叶/正中旁小葉　paramedian lobule
正中平衡/正中平衡　centric equilibration
正中平面/正中平面　midplane
正中切开/對切　medisect
正中切口/中間切開　median incision
正中上下颌[关系]记录/中心頜間記錄　centric maxillomandibular record
正中神经/正中神經　median nerve
正中神经病/正中神經病　median neuropathy
正中神经返支/正中神經返支　recurrent branch of median nerve
正中神经肌支/正中神經肌支　muscular branch of median nerve
正中神经内侧根/正中神經内側根　medial root of median nerve
正中神经外侧根/正中神經外側根　lateral root of median nerve
正中神经掌支/正中神經掌支　palmar branch of median nerve
正中神经指掌侧固有神经/正中神經指掌側指固有

神經　proper palmar digital nerve of median nerve
正中神经指掌侧总神经/正中神經指掌側總神經　common palmar digital nerve of median nerve
正中矢状面/正中矢狀面　median sagittal plane
正中锁/正中鎖　centric lock
正中位/中心位置　centric position
正中小叶/正中小葉　median lobule
正中胸骨切开术/正中胸骨切開術　median sternotomy
正中牙𬌗/正中牙𬌗　centric dental occlusion
正中支承点/中軸承點　central bearing point
正中直径/中直徑，前後徑　conjugata
正中自由区/正中自由區　centric free area
证/證　pattern
证候/症候群　syndrome
证候错杂/證候錯雜　intermingling pattern
证候禁忌/證候禁忌　incompatibility of drugs in pattern
证候相兼/證候相兼　concurrent pattern
证候真假/證候真假　true-false of pattern
证据/證據　evidence
证类本草/證類本草　Zhenglei Bencao
证治准绳/證治準繩　Standards for Diagnosis and Treatment
郑声/鄭聲　fading murmuring, unconscious murmuring
政和本草/政和本草　Zhenghe Bencao
症状/症狀　symptom
症状的/症狀的　symptomatic
症状记录/症狀記錄　semeiography
症状明显期/症狀明顯期　period of apparent manifestation
症状前诊断/症狀前診斷　presymptomatic diagnosis
症状性卟啉症/症狀性吡咯紫質沈著病　symptomatic porphyria
症状性多汗症/症狀性多汗症　symptomatic hyperhydrosis
症状性疾病/症候性病　symptomatic disease
症状性精神病/症候性精神病，附帶性精神病　symptomatic psychosis
症状性精索静脉曲张/症狀性精索静脈曲張　symptomatic varicocele
症状性溃疡/症狀性潰瘍　symptomatic ulcer
症状性皮肤划痕病/症狀性皮膚劃痕症　symptomatic dermatographism
症状性瘙痒/症狀性癢症　symptomatic pruritus
症状性脱发/症狀性禿髮　symptomatic alopecia
症状性哮喘/症狀性哮喘　symptomatic asthma
症状性侏儒症/症候性矮小　symptomatic nanism
症状性紫癜/症狀性紫癜[病]　purpura symptomatica
症状学/症狀學,症候學　semeiology
支/支　ramus
支撑足/支撐足　buttress foot
支持/支持,護具　support
支持骨/支持骨　support bone
支持区/支持區　supporting area
支持细胞/支持細胞　sustentacular cell
支持细胞连接复合体/支持細胞連接複合體　sertoli cell junction complex
[支持细胞]质膜下池/[支持細胞]質膜下池　subsurface cistern
支点/支點　fulcrum
支点线/支點線　fulcrum line
支点支柱牙/支點支柱牙　pier abutment
支点轴/支點軸　fulcrum axis
支顶孢病/支頂孢菌感染症　acremoniosis
支顶孢属/頂孢黴菌屬　*Acremonium*
支睾吸虫属/分支睾蟲屬　*Clonorchis*
支沟/支溝　zhigou, SJ6
支架保持器/支架保持器　frame retainer
支架带环/支架帶環　pier band
支架技术学/夾木技術學　splint technology
支架面/支架面　framework plane
支架式升支骨内植入体/支架式下頜支骨內植體　frame type of ramus endosseous implant
支架手术/[克尼格氏]支架手術　shelving operation
支架[术]/支架　stenting
支架移植/支架移植　structural transplantation
支链氨基酸代谢病/支鏈胺基酸代謝病　disorder of branched chain amino acid metabolism
支链氨基酸类/支鏈胺基酸類　branched-chain amino acids
支链淀粉/支鏈澱粉　amylopectin
支链淀粉病/澱粉黏膠質病　amylopectinosis
支链寡糖类/支鏈寡糖類　branched-chain oligosaccharides
支链脂肪酸/支鏈脂肪酸　branched-chain fatty acid
支气管/支氣管　bronchi, bronchia, bronchus
支气管癌/支氣管癌　bronchogenic carcinoma
支气管鼻窦炎/支氣管鼻竇炎　bronchosinusitis
支气管病/支氣管病　bronchopathy
支气管病学/支氣管病學　bronchology
支气管成形术/支氣管成形術　bronchoplasty
支气管出血/支氣管出血　bronchial hemorrhage
支气管胆道的/支氣管膽道的　bronchobiliary

支气管胆管瘘/支氣管膽管瘺　bronchobiliary fistula
支气管刀/支氣管刀　bronchotome
支气管的/支氣管的　bronchial
支气管动脉/支氣管動脈　bronchial artery
支气管肺病/支氣管肺病　bronchopneumopathy
支气管肺段/支氣管肺段　bronchopulmonary segment
支气管肺发育不良/肺支氣管發育不全　bronchopulmonary dysplasia
支气管肺隔离症/支氣管肺隔離症　bronchopulmonary sequestration
支气管肺量测定法/支氣管肺量測定法　bronchospirometry
支气管肺量计/支氣管肺量計　bronchospirometer
支气管肺量描记法/支氣管肺量描記法　bronchospirography
支气管[肺]螺旋体病/支氣管[肺]螺旋體病　bronchopulmonary spirochetosis
支气管肺门淋巴结/支氣管肺門淋巴結　bronchopulmonary hilar lymph node
支气管肺泡灌洗/支氣管肺泡灌洗　bronchoalveolar lavage
支气管肺泡灌洗液/支氣管肺泡灌洗液　bronchoalveolar lavage fluid
支气管肺泡呼吸/支氣管肺泡呼吸　bronchovesicular respiration
支气管肺泡呼吸音/支氣管肺泡呼吸音　bronchovesicular breathing sound
支气管肺性败血病/支氣管肺性敗血病　bronchopulmonary septicemia
支气管肺炎/支氣管肺炎　bronchopneumonia
支气管肺炎性结核/支氣管肺炎性結核　bronchopneumonic tuberculosis
支气管缝合术/支氣管縫合術　bronchorrhaphy
支气管干/支氣管幹　stem bronchus
支气管高反应性/支氣管高反應性　bronchial hyperreactivity
支气管灌洗/支氣管灌洗　bronchial lavage
支气管呼吸音/支氣管呼吸音　bronchial respiration
支气管激发试验/支氣管激發試驗　bronchial provocation test
支气管疾病/支氣管疾病　bronchial disease
支气管结石症/支氣管結石症　broncholithiasis
支气管痉挛/支氣管痙攣　bronchial spasm
支气管静脉/支氣管靜脈　bronchial vein
支气管静脉曲张/支氣管靜脈曲張　bronchial venous varix
支气管镜/支氣管鏡　bronchoscope
支气管镜检查/支氣管鏡檢查　bronchoscopy
支气管空洞呼吸音/支氣管空洞呼吸音　bronchocavernous respiration
支气管扩张/支氣管擴張　bronchodilation
支气管扩张药/支氣管擴張藥　bronchodilator
支气管扩张症/支氣管擴張症　bronchiectasis
支气管类癌肿瘤/支氣管類癌腫瘤　bronchial carcinoid tumor
支气管淋巴结炎/支氣管淋巴腺炎　bronchadenitis
支气管鳞癌/支氣管鱗癌　bronchial squamous cell carcinoma
支气管瘘/支氣管瘺　bronchial fistula
支气管啰音/支氣管性水泡音　bronchial rale
支气管螺旋体/支氣管螺旋體　Treponema bronchiale
支气管螺旋体病/出血性支氣管炎　hemorrhagic bronchitis
支气管麻痹/支氣管麻痺　bronchoplegia
支气管囊肿/支氣管囊腫　bronchocele
支气管内插管/支氣管內插管　endobronchial intubation
支气管内的/支氣管內的　endobronchial
支气管内麻醉/支氣管內麻醉　endobronchial anesthesia
支气管内膜结核/支氣管內膜結核　endobronchial tuberculosis
支气管黏膜炎/支氣管黏膜炎　endobronchitis
支气管黏液溢/支氣管黏液漏　bronchorrhea
支气管念珠菌病/支氣管念珠菌病　bronchocandidiasis
支气管脓溢/支氣管膿漏　bronchoblennorrhea
支气管诺卡放线菌病/支氣管土壤絲菌病　bronchonocardiosis
支气管憩室/支氣管憩室　bronchial diverticulum
支气管切开术/支氣管切開術　bronchotomy
支气管曲霉病/支氣管麴菌病　bronchoaspergillosis
支气管软骨缺损/支氣管軟骨缺損　bronchial cartilage deficiency
支气管软化/支氣管軟化　bronchomalacia
支气管食管肌/支氣管食道肌　bronchoesophageal muscle
支气管食管镜检查/支氣管食管鏡檢法　bronchoesophagoscopy
支气管食管瘘/支氣管食道瘺管　bronchoesophageal fistula
支气管收缩/支氣管收縮　bronchoconstriction
支气管收缩药/支氣管收縮藥　bronchoconstrictor agent

支气管树/支氣管樹,支氣管分支　bronchial tree
支气管刷检/支氣管刷檢　bronchial brushing
支气管危象/支氣管危象　bronchiocrisis
支气管狭窄/支氣管狹窄　bronchiarctia
支气管腺/支氣管腺　bronchial gland
支气管腺癌/支氣管性腺癌　bronchogenic adenocarcinoma
支气管腺瘤/支氣管腺瘤　bronchial adenoma
支气管哮喘/支氣管氣喘　bronchial asthma
支气管楔形切除术/支氣管楔形切除術　wedge resection of bronchus
支气管性震颤/支氣管性震顫　bronchial fremitus
支气管胸膜肺炎/支氣管胸膜肺炎　bronchopleuropneumonia
支气管胸膜瘘/支氣管胸膜瘻　bronchopleural fistula
支气管袖状肺叶切除术/支氣管袖狀肺葉切除術　bronchial sleeve lobectomy
支气管袖状切除术/支氣管袖狀切除術　sleeve resection of bronchus
支气管血流/支氣管血流　bronchial blood flow
支气管炎/支氣管炎　bronchitis
支气管炎的/支氣管炎的　bronchitic
支气管炎哮喘/支氣管炎哮喘　bronchitic asthma
支气管炎型斑疹伤寒/支氣管炎型斑疹傷寒　bronchotyphus
支气管炎型伤寒/支氣管炎型傷寒　bronchotyphoid
支气管羊鸣音/肺部羊鳴症　egophony
支气管异物/支氣管異物　foreign body in bronchus
支气管语音/支氣管聲　bronchophony
支气管原癌/支氣管原癌　carcinoma bronchogenic
支气管原的/支氣管原的　bronchogenic
支气管原性囊肿/支氣管原性囊腫　bronchogenic cyst
支气管杂音/支氣管雜音　bronchial murmur
支气管造口术/支氣管造口術　bronchostomy
支气管造影片/支氣管攝影片　bronchogram
支气管造影术/支氣管放射線攝影術　bronchography
支气管支/支氣管支　bronchial branch
支气管中层炎/支氣管中層炎　mesobronchitis
支气管肿瘤/支氣管腫瘤　bronchial neoplasm
支气管周[围]的/支氣管周[圍]的　peribronchial
支气管周炎/支氣管周[圍]炎　peribronchitis
支气管纵隔干/支氣管縱隔幹　bronchomediastinal trunk
支饮/支飲　thoracic fluid retention
支原体的/支原體的　mycoplasmal
支原体肺炎/支原體肺炎　mycoplasma pneumonia
支原体感染/支原體感染　mycoplasma infection
支原体目感染/支原體目感染　Mycoplasmatales infection
支原体[性]肺炎/支原體[性]肺炎　mycoplasmal pneumonia
支原体性尿道炎/支原體性尿道炎　mycoplasmal urethritis
支正/支正　zhizheng, SI7
支柱/支柱　abutment implant
支柱类似体/支柱類似體　abutment analog implant
支柱螺旋/支柱螺旋　abutment screw implant
支柱纤维/支持纖維　sustentacular fiber
支柱牙沟/支柱牙溝　abutment groove
支柱眼镜/支撐眼鏡　crutch glasses
汁/汁,液　juice
芝麻皮炎/芝麻皮炎　sesame seed dermatitis
枝状动脉瘤/枝狀動脈瘤　branching aneurysm
知柏地黄丸/知柏地黄丸　zhibai dihuang pills
知觉/知覺　perception
知觉闭合/知覺閉合　perceptual closure
知觉失真/知覺失真　perceptual distortion
知觉掩蔽/知覺掩蔽　perceptual masking
知觉障碍/知覺障礙　perceptual disorder
知母/知母　common anemarrhena rhizome
知情同意/知情同意　informed consent
肢/肢　extremity
肢带骨/肢帶骨　zonoskeleton
肢带[型]肌营养不良/肢帶[型]肌營養不良　limb-girdle muscular dystrophy
肢端白斑病/肢端白斑病　acroleukopathy
肢端持续性丘疹性黏蛋白沉积症/肢端持續性丘疹性黏液素病　acral persistent papular mucinosis
肢端点状角皮病/肢端點狀角皮病　acral punctate keratoderma
肢端肥大/肢端肥大　acral growth
肢端肥大的/肢端肥大的　acromegalic
肢端肥大性巨大畸形/肢端肥大性巨人症　acromegalogigantism
肢端肥大症/肢端肥大症　acromegaly
肢端感觉异常/肢端感覺異常　acroparesthesia
肢端感觉异常综合征/肢端感覺異常症候群　acroparesthesia syndrome
肢端骨质溶解/肢端骨質溶解　acro-osteolysis
肢端过度角化症/肢端過度角化症　acral hyperkeratosis
肢端过小症/肢端過小症,小手足畸形　acromicria
肢端汗管瘤/肢端汗管瘤　acral syringoma
肢端汗腺瘤/汗腺頂端汗腺瘤　acrospiroma

肢端黑变病/肢端黑變症　acromelanosis
肢端黑色素细胞痣/肢端黑色素細胞母斑　acral melanocytic nevus
肢端红斑/肢端紅斑　acroerythema
肢端红斑角皮症/肢端紅色角皮症　acroerythrokeratoderma
肢端红痛症/肢端紅痛症　erythermalgia
肢端厚皮病/肢端厚皮病　acropachyderma
肢端角化症/肢皮角化症　acrokeratosis
肢端黏液发炎性成纤维细胞肉瘤/肢端黏液發炎性成纖維母細胞肉瘤　acral myxoinflammatory fibroblastic sarcoma
肢端牛皮癣样半球形丘疹病/肢端乾癬樣半球形丘疹病　acral psoriasiform hemispherical papulosis
肢端脓疱病/肢端膿皰症　acropustulosis
肢端缺氧/肢端缺氧　acroasphyxia
肢端雀斑样痣黑[色]素瘤/肢端雀斑樣痣黑[色]素瘤　acral-lentiginous melanoma
肢端纤维角化瘤/肢端纖維角化瘤　acral fibrokeratoma
肢端纤细性侏儒/小肢侏儒　micromelic dwarf
肢端小动脉扩张/肢端小動脈擴張　acral arteriolar ectasia
肢端血管麻痹性/肢端血管麻痹性　acrovasoparalytica
肢端血管麻痹性厚皮症/肢端血管麻痹性厚皮症　pachydermia acrovasoparalytica
肢端血管皮炎/肢端血管性皮膚炎　acroangiodermatitis
肢端硬化病/肢端硬皮症　acroscleroderma
肢端着色斑性黑素瘤/肢端小痣性黑色素瘤　acral lentiginous melanoma
肢端紫癜/肢端紫瘢　acropurpura
肢根的/肢根的　rhizomelic
肢骨痛/肢骨痛　acrostealgia
肢骨纹状肥大/肢骨紋狀肥大　candle wax disease
肢关节炎/肢關節炎　acroarthritis
肢肌强直/肢肌強直　acromyotonia
肢畸形/肢畸形,畸肢　cacomelia
肢厥/肢厥　cold limbs
肢裂畸胎/肢裂畸胎　schistomelus
肢裂[畸形]/裂肢畸形　schistomelia
肢皮病/四肢皮病　acrodermatosis
肢皮炎/[四]肢皮炎　acrodermatitis
肢皮早老/肢端早衰症　acrogeria
肢缺损/肢缺損　loss of limb
肢体导联/肢導程　limb lead
肢体发育不全/肢體發育不全　hypomelia
肢体发育不全-少毛-颜面血管瘤综合征/肢體發育不全-少毛-顏面血管瘤症候群,羅伯茨氏症候群　hypomelia-hypotrichosis-facial hemangioma syndrome, Roberts syndrome
肢体感/肢覺　acrognosis
肢体感觉缺失/肢覺缺失　acragnosis
肢体痿废/肢體痿廢　disabled wilted limb
[肢体]压迫综合征/壓迫症候群　compression syndrome
肢体延长术/肢體延長術　limb lengthening
肢体语言/肢體語言　body language
肢体运动性失用症/四肢運動性失用症　limb kinetic apraxia
肢痛/肢痛　melagra
肢痛性红斑/肢痛性紅斑,肢端紅斑　acrodynic erythema
肢痛症/肢痛症　acrodynia
肢血管透视法/皮血管透視法　angiodiascopy
肢芽/肢芽　limb bud
织边绷带/織邊繃帶　webbing bandage
栀子/栀子　cape jasmine fruit
栀子豉汤/栀子豉湯　zhizichi decoction
脂醇/脂醇　lipidol
脂蛋白/脂蛋白　lipoprotein
脂蛋白受体/脂蛋白受體　lipoprotein receptor
脂蛋白脂酶/脂蛋白解酯酶　lipoprotein lipase
脂滴/脂滴　lipid droplet
脂多糖/脂多醣　lipopolysaccharide
脂多糖类/脂多醣類　lipopolysaccharides
脂肪/脂肪,脂質　fat
脂肪瓣/脂肪瓣　fat flap
脂肪变态/脂肪變態　fatty metamorphosis
脂肪变性/脂肪變性　adipose degeneration
脂肪潮/脂[肪]潮　fat tide
脂肪沉积/脂肪儲存病　lipidosis
脂肪抽吸[术]/脂肪抽吸[術]　suction lipectomy
脂肪醇/脂[肪]醇　fatty alcohol
脂肪代谢/脂肪代謝　fat metabolism, lipometabolism
脂肪代用品/脂肪代用品　fat substitute
脂肪的/脂肪的　fatty
脂肪分解/脂肪分解　steatolysis
脂肪分解不全/脂肪分解不全　hyposteatolysis
脂肪分解酶/脂肪分解酵素　lipolytic enzyme
脂肪分解性髓磷脂生成/髓鞘質變性　myelinosis
脂肪肝/脂肪肝　fatty liver
脂肪管型/脂肪圓柱　fatty cast
脂肪过多/脂肪過多　hyperliposis

脂肪过多症/脂肪過多症　liposis
脂肪过少/脂肪過少　hypoliposis
脂肪黑变性网状细胞增多症/脂肪黑變性網狀細胞增多症　lipomelanotic reticulosis
脂肪坏死/脂肪壞死　adiponecrosis
脂肪浸润/脂肪浸潤　fatty infiltration
脂肪颗粒移植术/脂肪顆粒移植術　fat granule grafting
脂肪颗粒注射移植[术]/脂肪顆粒注射移植[術]　fat granule injection grafting
脂肪类脂沉积症/脂肪類脂沈著病　lipolipoidosis
脂[肪]瘤的/脂瘤的　lipomatous
脂肪瘤性痣/脂瘤痣　lipomatous nevus
脂肪瘤样病/脂瘤症　lipomatosis
脂肪酶/脂[肪]酶,解脂酵素　lipase
脂肪囊/脂[肪]囊　fatty renal capsule
脂肪囊管/脂肪囊管　adipose duct
脂[肪]尿/脂尿症　lipuria
脂肪切除术/脂肪[組織]切除術　lipectomy
脂肪缺乏病/脂肪缺乏病　fat-deficiency disease
脂肪肉瘤/脂[肪]肉瘤　liposarcoma
脂肪肉芽肿/脂[肪]肉芽腫　lipogranuloma
脂肪肉芽肿病/脂[肪]肉芽腫症　lipogranulomatosis
脂肪软骨瘤/脂[肪]軟骨瘤,軟骨脂瘤　lipochondroma
脂肪疝/脂肪疝　fat hernia
脂肪疝形成/脂肪疝氣　fat herniation
脂肪[肾上腺]皮质激素类/脂肪類固醇　lipocorticoid
脂肪生成/脂肪生成,脂質生成　lipogenesis
脂肪栓塞/脂肪栓塞　oil embolism
脂肪水肿/脂[性]水腫　lipedema
脂肪酸/脂[肪]酸　fatty acid
脂肪酸合成酶复合物/脂肪酸合成酶複合物　fatty acid synthetase complex
ω-3 脂肪酸类/ω-3 脂肪酸類　omega-3 fatty acids
脂肪酸去饱和酶类/脂肪酸去飽和酶類　fatty acid desaturases
脂肪酸脱氢酶/脂肪酸脫氫酶　fatty acid dehydrogenase
脂肪体/脂肪體　fat body
脂肪痛/脂層痛　adiposalgia
脂肪突出/脂肪突出,脂肪性脫垂　adipocele
脂肪团/浮肉　cellulite
脂肪萎缩/脂性萎縮　adipose atrophy
脂肪萎缩型糖尿病/脂肪萎縮型糖尿病　lipoatrophic diabetes
脂肪系/脂肪系　fatty series
脂肪细胞/脂肪細胞　adipocyte, adipose cell, fat cell
脂肪纤维瘤/脂肪纖維瘤　adipofibroma
脂肪腺瘤/脂肪腺瘤　lipoadenoma
脂肪消化不良/脂質消化不良　fat indigestion
脂肪消散/脂肪消散　adipic resolution
脂肪泻/脂肪瀉　steatorrhea
脂肪形成/脂肪形成,脂肪生成　adipogenesis
脂肪性骨质疏松/脂肪性骨質疏鬆　adipose osteoporosis
脂肪性翼状胬肉/脂肪性翼狀胬肉　pimelopterygium
脂肪蓄积/脂肪蓄積[症]　lipopexia
脂肪氧化激素/脂肪氧化激素　adipokinin
脂肪移植/脂肪移植　fat transplantation, fat grafting
脂肪移植物/脂肪移植物　fat graft
脂肪乙醇氧化还原酶/脂肪乙醇氧化還原酶　fatty alcohol oxidoreductase
脂肪乙醛脱氢酶/脂肪乙醛去氫酶　fatty aldehyde dehydrogenase
脂肪油/脂肪油　fatty oil
脂肪诱发脂蛋白血症/脂肪引起之脂蛋白血症　fat-induced lipoproteinemia
脂肪增多/脂肪增多　lipotrophy
脂肪肿瘤/脂瘤　adipose tumor
脂肪族醇类/脂肪族醇類　fatty alcohols
脂肪族的/脂肪族的　aliphatic
脂肪族化合物/脂肪族化合物　aliphatic compound
脂肪组织/脂肪組織　fatty tissue, adipose tissue
脂肪组织炎/脂肪組織炎　steatitis
脂肪组织肿瘤/脂肪組織腫瘤　adipose tissue neoplasm
脂过氧化抑制药/脂過氧化抑制藥　lipid peroxidation inhibitor
脂褐素/脂褐質,脂色素　lipofuscin
脂褐质沉积症/脂褐質症　lipofuscinosis
脂褐质颗粒/脂褐質顆粒　lipofuscin granule
脂红质/脂紅質　liporhodin
脂环烃/脂環烴　alicyclic hydrocarbon
脂黄质/黄脂色素　lipoxanthine
脂肌瘤/脂肌瘤　lipomyoma
脂肌血管瘤/脂肌血管瘤　lipomyohemangioma
脂解酶/脂解酶　fat-splitting enzyme
脂解作用/脂肪分解　lipolysis
脂蓝质/脂藍質　lipocyanine
脂类/脂類　lipids
脂类分解/脂質分解　lipidolysis
脂类药物/脂類藥物　lipid drug
脂粒细胞/脂粒細胞　fatty granule cell
脂粒显现/脂粒顯現　lipophanerosis
脂瘤/脂瘤　adipose tumor, sebaceous cyst

脂瘤癌/脂瘤癌 carcinoma lipomatodes
脂瘤·痰气互结证/脂瘤·痰氣互結證 adipose tumor with pattern of intermingled phlegm and qi
脂瘤·痰湿化热证/脂瘤·痰濕化熱證 adipose tumor with pattern of phlegm-dampness transforming into heat
脂瘤性癌/脂瘤性癌 lipomatous cancer
脂瘤性睑下垂/脂肪瘤性垂瞼 ptosis lipomatosia
脂瘤性营养异常性巨大发育/脂瘤性巨體發育異常 macrodystrophia lipomatosa
脂瘤样癌/脂癌 lipomatous carcinoma
脂酶尿/脂肪酵素尿 lipasuria
脂酶试验/脂肪酶試驗 lipase test
脂膜/脂膜,脂層 fat membrane
脂膜炎/脂層炎 panniculitis
脂尿/脂[質]尿 lipoiduria
脂韧带/脂韌帶 adipose ligament
脂溶性维生素/脂溶性維生素 fat soluble vitamin
脂溶性学说/脂溶性學說 lipid solubility theory
脂肉瘤/脂肉瘤 adipose sarcoma
脂色素/脂色素 chromolipoid
脂色素原/脂色素原 lipochromogen
脂肾上腺/脂腎上腺 lipo-adrenal cortex
脂双层/脂雙層 lipid bilayer
脂酸尿/脂酸尿 lipaciduria
脂酸血/脂酸血[症] lipacidemia
脂酸乙二醇酯/脂酸乙二醇酯 ethyleneglycol fatty acid ester
脂肽/脂肽 lipopeptid
脂纹/脂紋 fatty streak
脂细胞/脂細胞 adipose cell
脂性粪/脂性糞 fatty stool
脂性腹水/脂性腹水 ascites adiposus
脂性黏液瘤/脂性黏液瘤 lipomatous myxoma
脂性上睑下垂/脂性上瞼下垂 ptosis adiposa
脂性肾病/脂質[性]腎病 lipoid nephrosis
脂性萎缩/脂肪萎縮 fatty atrophy
脂血[症]/脂血[症] lipidemia, lipemia
脂氧合酶/脂氧化酶 lipoxygenase
脂氧合酶抑制剂/脂氧合酶抑制劑 lipoxygenase inhibitor
脂氧素类/脂氧素類 lipoxins
脂氧素受体/脂氧素受體 lipoxin receptor
脂样糠疹/脂漏性糠疹 pityriasis steatoides
脂溢性痤疮/脂漏性痤瘡,油脂性痤瘡 acne sebacea
脂溢性睑炎/脂溢性瞼炎,非溃疡性眼瞼炎 seborrheic blepharitis
脂溢性角化病/脂漏性角化症,脂漏性角化疣 seborrheic keratosis, seborrheic wart
脂溢性毛囊炎/脂漏性毛囊炎 seborrheic folliculitis
脂溢性皮炎/皮脂溢性皮[膚]炎 seborrheic dermatitis
脂溢性湿疹/脂漏性濕疹 eczema seborrhoeicum
脂溢性脱发/皮脂溢性秃髮 alopecia seborrhoeica
脂溢性银屑病/脂漏性乾癬 sebopsoriasis
脂溢性疣/[皮]脂漏性疣 seborrheic verruca, seborrheic wart
脂溢性疣状棘皮瘤/脂漏性疣狀棘皮瘤 acanthoma verrucosa seborrhoeica
脂质/脂質 lipid
脂质 A/脂質 A lipid A
脂质代谢病/脂質代謝病 lipopathy
脂质过氧化作用/脂質過氧化作用 lipid peroxidation
脂质疾症/脂質病症 lipid disorder
脂质渐进性坏死/類脂質漸進性壞死 necrobiosis lipoidica
脂质体/[微]脂粒 liposome
脂质性肺炎/脂質性肺炎 lipid pneumonia
脂质移动/脂質移動 lipid mobilization
脂质疫苗/脂性疫苗 lipovaccine
脂质营养不良/脂質營養不良 lipodystrophy
脂质贮积病/脂質症 lipoidosis
脂族酯酶/脂族酯酶 abesterase
蜘蛛/蜘蛛 spider
蜘蛛毒/蜘蛛毒[素] spider venom
蜘蛛毒中毒/蜘蛛毒中毒 arachnidism
蜘蛛纲/蜘蛛網 Arachnida
蜘蛛纲媒介/蜘蛛網媒介 arachnid vector
蜘蛛恐惧症/蜘蛛恐懼症 arachnophobia
蜘蛛目/蜘蛛目 Araneae
蜘蛛母斑/蜘蛛母斑 nevus araneus
蜘蛛囊/蜘蛛囊 sac spider
蜘蛛细胞/蛛狀細胞 spider cell
蜘蛛性鼻炎/蜘蛛狀鼻炎 arachnorhinitis
蜘蛛样肾盂/蛛狀腎盂 spider pelvis
蜘蛛样指/蜘蛛樣指 arachnodactyly
蜘蛛咬伤/蜘蛛咬傷 spider bite
蜘蛛蜇伤/蜘蛛螫傷 spider sting
蜘蛛痣/蜘蛛痣 spider nevi
蜘蛛状的/蜘蛛狀的 araneous
蜘蛛状毛细管扩张症/蜘蛛狀毛細管擴張症 spider telangiectasis
蛛状痣癌/蛛狀痣癌 spider cancer
执业药师/執業藥師 licensed pharmacist
执业医生/開業醫生,開業醫師 medical practitioner

执照/執照　license
直背综合征/直背症候群　straight back syndrome
直鼻/直鼻　straight nose
直部/直部　straight part
直肠/直腸　rectum
直肠瓣/直腸瓣　rectal valve
直肠瓣切开术/直腸瓣切開術　rectal valvotomy
直肠闭锁/直腸閉鎖　rectal atresia
直肠病学/直腸病學　proctology
直肠病学家/直腸病專家　proctologist
直肠成形术/直腸成形術　proctoplasty
直肠弛缓不能/直腸弛緩不能　pelvirectal achalasia
直肠出血/直腸出血　hemoproctia
直肠丛/痔静脈叢　hemorrhoidal plexus
直肠刀/直腸刀　proctotome
直肠的/直腸的　rectal
直肠骶曲/直腸骶曲　sacral flexure of rectum
直肠缝合术/直腸縫合術　proctorrhaphy
直肠[肛门]麻痹/直腸麻痺　proctoparalysis
直肠隔/道格拉斯氏中隔　Douglas septum
直肠固定术/直腸固定術　proctopexy
直肠横襞/直腸橫[皺]襞　transverse folds of rectum
直肠后脓肿/直腸後膿腫　retrorectal abscess
直肠后拖出吻合巨结肠根治术/直腸後拖出吻合巨結腸根治術　duhamel procedure
直肠壶腹/直腸壺腹　ampulla of rectum, rectal ampulla
直肠环钳吻合术/直腸環鉗吻合術　ring clamp anastomosis of rectum
直肠会阴曲/直腸會陰曲　perineal flexure of rectum
直肠肌鞘拖出吻合巨结肠根治术/直腸肌鞘拖出吻合巨結腸根治術　soave procedure
直肠积粪/直腸積糞, 直腸鬱滯　proctostasis
直肠疾病/直腸疾病　rectal disease
直肠结肠镜检查/直結腸鏡檢法　proctocolonoscopy
直肠结肠切除术/直腸結腸切除術　proctocolectomy
直肠结肠炎/直腸結腸炎　proctocolitis
直肠痉挛/直腸痙攣　proctospasm
直肠静脉丛/直腸静脈叢　rectal venous plexus
直肠镜/直腸鏡　proctoscope
直肠镜检查/直腸鏡檢[法]　proctoscopy
直肠扩张/直腸擴張, 肛擴張　proctectasia
直肠扩张器/直腸擴張器　procteurynter
直肠扩张术/直腸擴張術　procteurysis
直肠阑尾瘘/直腸闌尾瘻　recto-appendicular fistula
直肠瘘/直腸瘻　rectal fistula
直肠麻醉/直腸麻醉　rectal anesthesia
直肠内壁疝/直腸內壁疝　hernia in recto

直肠内静脉丛/直腸內静脈叢　internal rectal plexus
直肠内切开术/肛内切開術　internal proctotomy
直肠尿道肌/直腸尿道肌　rectourethral muscle, musculus recto-urethralis
直肠尿道瘘/直腸尿道瘻　rectourethral fistula
直肠旁淋巴结/直腸旁淋巴結　pararectal lymph node
直肠旁窝/直腸旁陷凹　pararectal pouch
直肠膀胱成形术/直腸膀胱瘻造形術　proctocystoplasty
直肠膀胱膈/直腸膀胱膈　rectovesical septum
直肠膀胱肌/直腸膀胱肌　rectovesical muscle
直肠膀胱瘘/直腸膀胱瘻　rectovesical fistula
直肠膀胱切开术/直腸[式]膀胱切開術　proctocystotomy
直肠膀胱陷凹/直腸膀胱陷凹　rectovesical pouch, rectovesical excavation
直肠膀胱阴道瘘/直腸膀胱陰道瘻　recto-vesico-vaginal fistula
直肠前庭瘘/直腸前庭瘻　rectovestibular fistula
直肠前突/直腸前突, 成囊直腸　encysted rectum, rectocele
直肠前突·脾气虚证/直腸前突·脾氣虛證　rectocele with spleen qi deficiency pattern
直肠前突·气阴两虚证/直腸前突·氣陰兩虛證　rectocele with qi-yin deficiency pattern
直肠切除术/直腸切除術　proctectomy
直肠切开术/直腸切開術　proctotomy
直肠疝/直腸疝　rectal hernia
直肠上丛/直腸上叢　superior rectal plexus
直肠上动脉/直腸上動脈　superior rectal artery
直肠上静脉/直腸上静脈　superior rectal vein
直肠上淋巴结/直腸上淋巴結　superior rectal lymph node
直肠烧灼/直腸燒灼　rectal burning
直肠失禁/直腸失禁　rectal incontinence
直肠栓剂/直腸栓劑　rectal suppository
直肠损伤/直腸損傷　rectal injury
直肠投药/直腸投藥　rectal administration
直肠透析液/直腸透析液　rectal dialysis solution
直肠突出/直腸突出　proctocele
直肠脱垂/直腸脱垂　prolapse of rectum
直肠外静脉丛/直腸外静脈叢　external rectal venous plexus
直肠外切开术/肛外切開術　external proctotomy
直肠尾骨固定术/直腸尾骨固定術　proctococcypexy
直肠尾骨肌/直腸尾骨肌　rectococcygeal muscle
直肠息肉/直腸息肉　proctopolypus

直肠系膜/直腸繫膜 mesentery of rectum
直肠狭窄/直腸狹窄 stricture of rectum
直肠下丛/直腸下叢 inferior rectal plexus
直肠下动脉/直腸下動脈 inferior rectal artery
直肠下动脉阴道支/直腸下動脈陰道支 vaginal branch of inferior rectal artery
直肠下静脉/直腸下静脈 inferior rectal vein, venae rectales inferiores
直肠下神经/下直腸神經 nervi rectales inferiores
直肠性便秘/直腸性便秘，肛性便秘 proctogenous constipation
直肠炎/直腸炎 proctitis
直肠乙状结肠/直腸[和]乙狀結腸 proctosigmoid
直肠乙状结肠镜/直腸乙狀結腸鏡 proctosigmoidoscope
直肠乙状结肠镜检查[术]/直腸乙狀結腸鏡檢法 proctosigmoidoscopy
直肠乙状结肠切除术/直腸乙狀結腸切除術 proctosigmoidectomy
直肠乙状结肠炎/直腸乙狀結腸炎 proctosigmoiditis
直肠阴唇的/直腸陰唇的 rectolabial
直肠阴唇瘘/直腸陰唇瘻 rectolabial fistula
直肠阴道的/直腸陰道的 rectovaginal
直肠阴道隔/直腸陰道隔 rectovaginal septum
直肠阴道瘘/直腸陰道瘻 rectovaginal fistula
直肠阴道瘘成形术/直腸陰道瘻成形術 proctocolpoplasty
直肠阴道疝/直腸陰道疝 rectovaginal hernia
直肠造口术/直腸造口術 proctostomy
直肠指检/直腸指檢 digital rectal examination
直肠中丛/直腸中叢 middle rectal plexus
直肠中动脉/直腸中動脈 middle rectal artery
直肠中静脉/直腸中静脈 middle rectal vein
直肠肿瘤/直腸腫瘤 rectal neoplasm
直肠周围脓肿/直腸周圍膿腫 perirectal abscess
直肠周炎/直腸旁組織炎 paraproctitis
直肠注射/直腸注射 rectal injection
直肠子宫襞/直腸子宮[皺]襞 rectouterine fold
直肠子宫肌/直腸子宮肌 rectouterine muscle, musculus recto-uterinus
直肠子宫陷凹/直腸子宮陷凹 rectouterine pouch, rectouterine excavation
直肠子宫陷凹炎/道格拉斯氏陷凹炎 douglasitis
直尺试验/直尺試驗 ruler test
直刺/直刺 perpendicular insertion of needle
直电流/直流電 direct current
直动手机/直動手機 racer handpiece
直窦/直竇 straight sinus

直覆𬌗/垂直咬合過度 vertical overbite
直观解剖学/直觀解剖學 transcendental anatomy
直颌/直頜 orthognathism
直回/直迴 gyrus rectus
直集合小管/直集合[小]管 straight collecting tubule
直角夹板/直角夾板 right angle splint
直接暴力/直接暴力 direct violence, direct force
直接触染/直接觸染 direct contagion
直接刺激/直接刺激 direct excitation
直接刺激作用/直接刺激作用 direct stimulation
直接催吐药/直接催吐藥 direct emetic
直接法/直接檢查法 direct method
直[接反]应胆红素/膽囊膽紅素 cholebilirubin
直接范本假说/直接範本假說 direct template hypothesis
直接放射/直接放射 direct radiation
直接服务费用/直接服務費用 direct service cost
直接感觉束/感覺直徑 direct sensory tract
直接感染/直接傳染 direct infection
直接骨印模/骨直接壓跡 direct bone impression
直接骨折/直接骨折 direct fracture
直接固位/直接保持 direct retention
直接固位体/直接保持器 direct retainer
直接观察疗法/直接觀察療法 directly observed therapy
直接灌气法/直接充氣法 direct aeration method
直接喉镜/直接喉鏡 directoscope
直接喉镜检查[法]/直接喉鏡檢查 direct laryngoscopy
直接呼吸/直接呼吸 direct respiration
直接火花/直接火花 direct spark
直接检眼镜/直接檢眼鏡 direct ophthalmoscope
直接焦点照明法/直接焦點照明法 direct focal illumination
直接接触/直接接觸 direct contact
直接进样杆/直接進樣器 direct inlet probe, DIP
直接抗球蛋白试验/直接抗球蛋白試驗 direct antiglobulin test
直接叩诊/直接叩法 direct percussion
直接离心浮集法/直接離心漂浮法 direct centrifugal flotation method
直接皮瓣/直接皮瓣 direct skin flap
直接皮肤动脉/直接皮膚動脈 direct cutaneous artery
直接染色法/直接染色法 substantive staining
直接溶解因子/直接溶解因子 direct lytic factor
直接输血法/直接輸血法 immediate transfusion

直接填料树脂/直接填充性樹脂　direct filling resin
直接听诊/直接聽診法　direct auscultation
直接涂片法/直接塗片法　method of direct smear
直接压片/直接壓錠　direct compression
直接氧化酶/直接氧化酵素　direct oxidase
直接液体进样/直接液體進樣　direct liquid introduction, DLI
直接荧光抗体技术/直接螢光抗體技術　direct fluorescent antibody technique
直接诱变物/直接誘變物　direct acting mutagen
直接杂音/直接雜音　direct murmur
直接症状/直接症狀　direct symptom
直接致癌物/直接致癌物　directly acting carcinogen
直接转移/直接轉移　direct metastasis
直接作用/直接作用　direct action
直精小管/直精小管　straight tubule
直径/[真]直徑　anteroposterior diameter, true conjugate diameter
直举性肱骨脱位/肩之豎直性脱骱　luxatio erecta
直觉/直覺　intuition
直立的/直立的, 姿態性　orthostatic
直立倾斜检查/直立傾斜檢查　upright tilt testing
直立性蛋白尿/直立性蛋白尿　orthostatic proteinuria
直立性低血压/起立性血壓過低　orthostatic hypotension
直立性呼吸困难/直立性呼吸困難　orthostatic dyspnea
直立性心动过速/直立性心搏快速　orthostatic tachycardia
直立性紫癜/直立性紫瘢[病]　orthostatic purpura
直立猿人/直立猿人　Home erectus
直链淀粉/直鏈澱粉　amylose
直链六己糖/六元糖　hexamylose
直流电同步心律转复/直流電同步心律轉復　direct current synchronous cardioversion
直流电异步除颤/直流電非同步除顫　direct current nonsynchronous defibrillation
直流感应电检查/直流感應電檢查　galvanic-faradic current examination
直毛痣/直毛母斑　straight hair nevus
直喷浴/噴射沖洗　jet douche
直疝/直[接]疝　direct hernia
直视/直視　euthyphoria
直视二尖瓣成形术/直視二尖瓣成形術　open mitral valvoplasty
直视二尖瓣交界切开术/直視二尖瓣交界切開術　open mitral commissurotomy
直视下活检[术]/直視下活檢[術]　direct vision biopsy
直手机/直手機, 直機頭　straight handpiece
直头/直頭　straight head
直腿抬高加强试验/直腿抬高加強試驗　Bragard additional test
直腿抬高试验/直腿抬高試驗　straight leg raising test
直位叩诊板/直式叩診器　orthoplessimeter
直线加速器/直線加速器　linear accelerator
直线切口/直線切口　linear incision
直线笑/直線笑　straight smile
直小动脉/直小動脈　straight arteriole
直小静脉/直小靜脈　straight venule
直小血管/直[小]血管　vasa recta
直腰拾物器/遠距拾物器　teledactyl
直指叩诊法/正叩法, 直式叩診　orthopercussion
直中/直中　direct attack
直中三阴/直中三陰　direct attack of exogenous cold disease on three yin channels
直锥体束/錐體直徑　direct pyramidal tract
值/値　value
职业癌/職業癌　professional cancer
职业暴露/職業暴露　occupational exposure
职业病/職業病　occupational disease
职业病人关系/職業病人關係　professional-patient relation
职业的/職業的　occupational
职业技能训练/職業技能訓練　vocational skill training
职业家庭关系/職業家庭關係　professional-family relation
职业间关系/職業間關係　interprofessional relation
职业教育/職業教育　vocational education
职业痉挛/職業痙攣　occupation spasm
职业疗法/職業療法　occupational therapy
职业流动性/職業流動性　career mobility
职业伦理学/職業倫理學　professional ethics
职业皮肤病/職業皮膚病　occupational dermatosis
职业群体/職業群體　occupational group
职业事故/職業事故　occupational accident
职业损伤/職業損傷, 職業傷害　occupational injury
职业卫生/職業衛生　occupational health
职业卫生服务/職業衛生服務　occupational health service
职业卫生护理/職業衛生護理　occupational health nursing
职业性痤疮/職業性痤瘡　occupational acne, trade

acne
职业性共济失调/職業性共濟失調　professional ataxia
职业性喉炎/職業性喉炎　occupational laryngitis
职业性精神官能病/職業性精神官能病　occupation neurosis
职业性康复/職業性康復　vocational rehabilitation
职业性空气污染物/職業性空氣汙染物　occupational air pollutant
职业性麻痹/手工業麻痺　craft palsy
职业性盲/職業性盲　vocational blindness
职业性皮肤癌/職業性皮膚癌　occupational skin cancer
职业性皮肤病/職業性皮膚病　dermatergosis
职业性皮炎/職業性皮[膚]炎　occupational dermatitis
职业性神经症/職業性神經病,作業神經病　craft neurosis
职业性眼球震颤/職業性眼球震顫　occupational nystagmus
职业性厌倦/職業性厭倦　professional burnout
职业性硬皮症/職業性硬皮症　occupational scleroderma
职业性运动障碍/職業性運動困難　occupational dyskinesia
职业性噪声/職業性雜訊　occupational noise
职业选择/職業選擇　career choice
职业牙科学/職業牙科學　occupational dentistry
职业医学/職業醫學　occupational medicine
职业再训练/職業再訓練　vocational retraining
植虫/似植蟲,植動物　zoophyte
植木胶/植物纖維膠　phytoxylin
植入/植入　implantation, engraft
植入电极/植入電極　implanted electrode
植入片剂/植入錠劑　implant tablet
植入前诊断/植入前診斷　preimplantation diagnosis
植入窝/植入窝　implantation fossa
植入物/植入物　implant
植入物支持义齿/植入物支持義齒　implant-supported dental prosthesis
植入型除颤器/植入型除顫器　implantable defibrillator
植入型输注泵/植入型輸注泵　implantable infusion pump
植入性[畸胎]畸形/畸胎移植　teratic implantation
植入性囊肿/植入性囊腫　implantation cyst
植入性皮样囊肿/植入性皮囊瘤　implantation dermoid
植入性胎盘/植入性胎盤　placenta increta
植入性转移/植入性轉移　implantation metastasis
植入移植物/包埋移植物　implantation graft
植酸/植酸　phytic acid
植烷酸/植烷酸　phytanic acid
植烷酸贮积病/植烷酸貯積病　phytanic acid storage disease
植物/植物　plant
植物白蛋白/植物蛋白素　phytalbumin
植物半球/植物[性]半球　vegetal hemisphere
植物病毒/植物病毒　plant virus
植物病源的/植物病源的　plant-pathogenic
植物沉淀素/植物沈澱素　phytoprecipitin
植物雌激素类/植物雌激素類　phytoestrogens
植物促代谢素/植物促代謝素　phytochinin
植物促细胞分裂剂/植物細胞分裂素　phytomitogen
植物蛋白胨/植物蛋白腖　phytone
植物蛋白质类/植物蛋白質類　plant proteins
植物毒素/植物毒素　phytotoxin
植物发生/植物發生　phytogenesis
植物粪石/植物性胃結石,食物球,糞石　food ball
植物根/植物根　plant root
植物光照性皮炎/植物[性]光照性皮炎　phytophotodermatitis
植物过敏原/植物過敏原　phytoanaphylactogen
植物合成乳/蔬菜乳　vegetable milk
植物化学/植物化學　phytochemistry
植物化学分类学/植物化學分類學　plant chemotaxonomy
植物黄质/黄花色质　xanthin
植物基因/植物基因　plant gene
植物基因表达调控/植物基因表達調控　plant gene expression regulation
植物基因组/植物基因組　plant genome
植物激素/植物内泌素　phytohormone
植物极/植物極　vegetal pole, vegetative pole
植物茎/植物莖　plant stem
植物抗体/植物抗體　plantibody
植物抗肿瘤药/植物抗腫瘤藥　phytogenic antineoplastic agent
植物块茎/植物塊莖　plant tuber
植物蜡/植物蠟　vegetable wax
植物流行病/植物流行病　phytodemic
植物卵黄磷蛋白/植物卵黄磷蛋白　phytovitellin
植物螨/植物蟎　plant mite
植物毛粪石/植物[毛]糞石　phytotrichobezoar
植物名实图考/植物名實圖考　Plant Names and Illustrations

植物凝集素/植物性血球凝集素　phytohemagglutinin
植物凝集素类/植物凝集素類　plant lectins
植物皮炎/植物皮[膚]炎　phytodermatitis
植物球蛋白/植物球蛋白　phytoglobulin
植物染色体/植物染色體　plant chromosome
植物日光性皮炎/植物性日光接觸皮膚炎　phyto-photo-dermatitis
植物神经过敏者/自動過敏者　autophil
植物神经性共济失调/自主神經失調症　autonomic ataxia
植物生长调节物/植物生長調節物　plant growth regulator
植物树脂类/植物樹脂類　plant resins
植物提取物/植物提取物　plant extract
植物脱皮甾醇/植物脱皮甾醇　phytoecdysteroid
植物性/植物性　phyto
植物[性]蛋白/植物蛋白　vegetable protein
植物性肌浆球蛋白/植物性肌凝蛋白　vegetable myosin
植物性皮炎/植物引起的皮膚炎　plant-induced dermatitis
植物性胰岛素/植物性胰島素　vegetable insulin
植物芽/植物芽　plant shoot
植物药理学/植物藥理學　phytopharmacology
植物药疗法/植物藥療法,本草療法　phytotherapy
植物胰岛素/植物胰島素　plant insulin
植物引起的/植物引起的　plant-induced
植物油类/植物油類　plant oils
植物原[因]病/植物原病,植物性病　phytonosis
植物源的/植物源的,植物性的　phytogenic
植物甾醇/植物膽固醇　phytocholesterol
植物甾醇苷/植物脂醇苷　phytosterolin
植物甾醇类/植物甾醇類　phytosterols
植物蒸腾作用/植物蒸騰作用　plant transpiration
植物制剂/植物製劑　plant preparation
植物致病性真菌/植物致病性真菌　plant-pathogenic fungi
植物肿瘤/植物腫瘤　plant tumor
植物肿瘤诱导质粒/植物腫瘤誘導質粒　plant tumor-inducing plasmid
植物中毒/植物中毒　plant poisoning
植物状态/植物狀態　vegetative state
植物资源保护/植物資源保護　conservation of plant resource
植物组成部分/植物組成部分　plant component
植物组织培养/植物組織培養　plant tissue culture
植原体/植原體　phytoplasma

跖/蹠　metatarsus, plantar
跖背动脉/蹠[骨]背動脈　dorsal metatarsal artery
跖背静脉/蹠背靜脈,趾背靜脈　dorsal metatarsal vein
跖部沟状角化病/足底溝狀角化病　keratoma plantare sulcatum
跖部神经瘤/蹠部神經瘤　plantar neuroma
跖侧跟骰韧带/蹠側跟骰韌帶　plantar calcaneocuboid ligament
跖侧骨间肌/蹠側骨間肌　musculi interossei plantares
跖侧骰舟韧带/足底骰舟韌帶　plantar cuboscaphoid ligament
跖垫/蹠墊　plantar cushion
跖方肌/蹠方肌　quadrate muscle of sole
跖沟状角皮病/足底溝狀角皮病　chaluni
跖骨/蹠骨　metatarsal bone
跖骨背侧韧带/蹠骨背側韌帶　dorsal metatarsal ligament
跖骨背动脉/蹠骨背動脈　dorsal metatarsal artery
跖骨的/蹠骨的　metatarsal
跖骨底/蹠骨底　base of metatarsal bone
跖骨底动脉/蹠骨底動脈　planter metatarsal artery
跖骨骨间韧带/蹠骨骨間韌帶　interosseous metatarsal ligament
跖骨骨折/蹠骨骨折　fracture of metatarsus, metatarsus fracture
跖骨过短/蹠骨過短　brachymetatarsia
跖骨基底背侧韧带/蹠骨基底背側韌帶　dorsal ligament of base of metatarsal bone
跖骨间关节/蹠骨間關節　intermetatarsal joint, articulations of metatarsal bone
跖骨间隙/蹠骨間隙　intermetatarsal space
跖骨间远端足底韧带/遠側蹠側蹠間韌帶　disral plantar intermetatarsal ligament
跖骨切除术/蹠切除術　metatarsectomy
跖骨深横韧带/蹠骨深橫韌帶　deep transverse metatarsal ligament
跖骨体/蹠骨體　shaft of metatarsal bone
跖骨头/蹠骨頭　head of metatarsal bone
跖骨头间静脉/蹠骨頭間靜脈　intercapital vein
跖骨足底韧带/蹠骨蹠側韌帶　plantar metatarsal ligament
跖管综合征/蹠管症候群　metatarsal tunnel syndrome
跖汗疱/足汗皰疹　podopompholyx
跖肌/蹠肌　plantaris, musculus plantaris
跖间足底横韧带/足底横蹠間韌帶　plantar

transverse intermetatarsal ligament
跖间足底近侧韧带/足底近側蹠間韌帶　plantar proximal intermetatarsal ligament
跖腱膜/蹠腱膜　plantar aponeurosis
跖腱膜纤维瘤病/足蹠纖維瘤病　plantar fibromatosis
跖筋膜炎/蹠筋膜炎　plantar fasciitis
跖内侧趾底固有神经/蹠內側神經趾底固有神經　proper plantar digital nerve of medial plantar nerve
跖浅横韧带/蹠淺橫韌帶　superficial transverse metatarsal ligament
跖韧带/蹠韌帶　plantar ligament
跖痛症/蹠痛[症]　metatarsal pain, pain in metatarsus, metatarsalgia
跖外侧趾底固有神经/蹠外側神經趾底固有神經　proper plantar digital nerve of lateral plantar nerve
跖疣/蹠疣　plantar wart, verruca plantaris
跖趾关节/蹠趾關節　metatarsophalangeal joint, metatarsophalangeal articulation
跖趾关节侧副韧带/蹠趾關節側副韌帶　collateral ligament of metatarsophalangeal joint
跖趾关节脱位/蹠趾關節脫位　dislocation of metatarsal-phalangeal joint, metatarsophalangeal dislocation
跖趾关节外侧韧带/蹠趾關節外側韌帶　lateral ligament of metatarsophalangeal joints
跖足底总动脉/蹠足底總動脈　common plantar metatarsal artery
止汗/止汗　hidroschesis
止汗剂/止汗劑　antiperspirants
止汗药/止汗藥　anhidrotic
止痉散/止痙散　zhijing powder
止渴剂/止渴劑　adipsa
止泡药/止泡藥　antifoaming agent
止嗽散/止嗽散　zhisou powder
止痛剂/止痛劑　analgesic
止痛胶/止痛膠　anodyne colloid
止痛药/止痛藥，鎮痛藥　acesodyne
止吐的/止吐的　antiemetic
止吐药/止吐藥　antiemetics
止涎剂/止涎藥　antisialagogue
止泻药/止瀉藥　antidiarrheal
止血/止血，出血遏制　arrest of hemorrhage, haemostasis
止血带/止血帶　tourniquet
止血带试验/止血帶試驗　tourniquet test
止血带止血法/止血帶止血法　hemostasis with tourniquet
止血的/止血的　hemostatic
止血技术/止血技術　hemostatic technique
止血剂/止血劑　hemodent, blood-stanching formula
止血棉/止血棉　styptic cotton
止血器/止血器　hemostat
止血钳/止血鉗　hemostatic forcep
止血药/止血藥　hemostatic, bleeding-arresting preparation
止痒药/止癢藥　antipruritic
纸/紙　paper
纸币样皮肤/紙鈔樣皮膚　paper money skin
纸电泳/紙[上]電泳　paper electrophoresis
纸电泳法/紙電泳法　paper electrophoresis
纸碟式放射量计/小盤輻射計　pastille radiometer
纸片法/紙片法　paper disk method
纸片敏感度/紙片敏感度　disk susceptibility
纸[上色]层分析法/紙層析法，濾紙色層分析法　paper chromatography
纸箱样音/薄板箱音　bandbox sound
纸样胎/紙樣胎[兒]　papyraceous fetus
纸状皮/紙狀皮　paper skin
指/指　①finger ②zhi, SF1
指背动脉/指背動脈　dorsal digital artery
指背腱膜/指背腱膜　aponeurosis dorsalis digiti
指背静脉/掌背指靜脈　dorsal digital vein
指背神经/指背神經　dorsal digital nerve
指不全畸胎/指不全畸胎　perodactylus
指部分切除术/半指骨切除術　hemiphalangectomy
指寸定位法/指寸定位法　finger-cun measurement
指的/指的　digital
指等长/[手]指等長　isodactylism
指垫/指髓　digital pulp
指动脉/[手]指動脈　digital artery
指端/指端　finger tip
指端并指/指端并指　syndactyly of finger tip
指端粉碎性骨折/指端粉碎性骨折，叢簇骨折　tuft fracture
指副韧带/指副韌帶　accessory ligament of digits of hand
指腹/指腹　finger pulp
指骨/指骨　phalanx, phalangeal bone of hand
指骨的/指骨的　phalangeal
指骨底/指骨底　base of phalanx
指骨骨折/指骨骨折　phalangeal fracture, fracture of phalanges of finger, phalanx fracture of hand
指骨过短/指骨過短　brachyphalangia
指骨滑车/指骨滑車　trochlea of phalanx
指骨间关节/指骨間關節　interphalangeal joint of

hand, interphalangeal articulation of finger, phalangeal articulation
指骨切除术/指骨切除術　phalangectomy
指骨体/指骨體　shaft of phalanx
指骨头/指骨頭　head of phalanx
指骨炎/指[節]骨炎　phalangitis
指关节/指關節　articulation of digits of hand
指关节屈曲畸形/指關節屈曲畸形　flexion deformity of interdigital joint
指关节外侧韧带/指關節外側韌帶　lateral ligament of joint of finger
指关节粘连/指關節融合　synphalangism
指过小/指過小, 小指　microdactyly
指滑膜鞘/指滑膜鞘　synovial sheath of finger
指环状韧带/指環狀韌帶　annular ligament of digits of finger
指簧/指簧　finger spring
指甲/指甲　nail of finger, nail
指甲髌骨综合征/指甲髕骨症候群　nail-patella syndrome
指甲病理学/指甲病理學　onychopathology
指甲脆弱/指甲脆弱　nail brittle
指甲的/指甲的　ungual
指甲肥大/指甲肥大　onychauxis
指甲肥厚/指甲肥厚　nail hypertrophy
指甲分离/指甲分離　nail splitting
指甲过度弯曲/指甲過度彎曲　over curvature of the nail
指甲过小/指甲過小, 指甲小畸形　micronychia
指甲花/指甲花　henna
指甲基质-指甲甲床痣/指甲母質和指甲床母斑, 指甲母質和指甲床痣　naevi of the nail matrix and bed
指甲疾病/指甲疾病　nail disease
指甲毛细管搏动描记器/指甲毛細管搏動描記器　onychograph
指甲毛细管搏动图/指甲毛細管搏動描記圖　onychogram
指甲磨光/指甲磨光　nail buffing
指甲皮肤带/指甲皮膚帶　onychodermal band
指甲鞘囊肿/指甲鞘囊腫　onycholemmal cyst
指甲脱落/指甲脱落　nail shedding
指甲下的/指甲下的　subungual
指甲异色/色甲症　chromonychia
指甲异位/指甲異位　onychoheterotopia
指甲硬化/指甲硬化　scleronychia
指甲营养不良/指甲發育異常　onychodystrophy
指甲周围疾患/指甲周圍疾病　periungual disorder
指甲周围纤维瘤/指甲周圍纖維瘤　periungual fibromata
指甲周围疣/指甲周圍疣　periungual wart
指尖水疱/指尖水皰　fingertip bullae
指间关节/指間關節　articulation of finger joints
指间关节侧副韧带/指間關節側副韌帶　collateral ligament of interphalangeal articulation of hand
指间关节脱位/指間關節脱位　interphalangeal dislocation
指间隙/指間隙　interdigit
指腱交叉/指腱交叉　chiasm of digits of hand
指腱鞘/指腱鞘　tendinous sheath of finger
指痉挛/指痙攣　dactylospasm
指矫形术/指矯形術　orthodigita
指节/指節, Knuckle 氏　Knuckle
指节垫/指節小墊　knuckle pad
指静脉/指靜脈　plantar digital vein
指叩诊/指叩法　finger percussion
指扩张术/[用]指擴張術　digital dilatation
指黏液囊肿/指黏液囊腫　digital mucous cyst
指蹼间隙/指蹼間隙　finger web space
指浅屈肌/屈指淺肌　flexor digitorum superficialis, musculus flexor digitorum superficialis
指浅屈肌肱尺头/指淺屈肌肱尺頭　humeroulnar head of flexor digitorum superficialis
指浅屈肌桡骨头/指淺屈肌橈骨頭　radial head of flexor digitorum superficialis
指切进针法/指切進針法　fingernail-pressure needle inserting
指丘疹性钙化性弹力纤维变性/指丘疹性鈣化性彈力纖維變性　digital papular calcific elastosis
指曲痛/指曲痛, 手指彎痛　dactylocampsodynia
指三叉/指三叉　digital triradius
指伸肌/伸指肌　extensor digitorum, extensor muscle of finger
指伸肌和示指伸肌腱鞘/伸指肌及伸食指肌腱鞘　tendinous sheath of extensor digitorum and extensor indicis
指深屈肌/屈指深肌　deep flexor muscle of finger
指神经阻滞/指神經阻斷　digital nerve block
指十字韧带/指十字韌帶　crucial ligament of finger
指示变量/指標變數　indicator variable
指示电极/指示電極　indicating electrode
指示剂/指示劑　indicator
指示剂稀释法/指示劑稀釋法　indicator-dilution method
指示剂稀释技术/指示劑稀釋技術　indicator-dilution technique

指示性咨询/指示性諮詢　directive counseling
指数性近视/折射異常性近視　index myopia
指数性屈光不正/指數性不正視　index ametropia
指数性散光/指數性散光　index astigmatism
指数性远视/指數性遠視　index hypermetropia
指水肿/手指腫　dactyledema
指损伤/指水腫,指損傷　finger injury
指体积描记器/指體積描記器　digital plethysmography
指头纤维骨性假瘤/指頭纖維骨性假瘤　fibro-osseous pseudotumor of the digit
指弯曲/指彎曲　streblodactyly
指腕动度测量器/手指、手腕運動度測定器　kinomometer
指纹/指紋　fingerprint
指纹法/指紋法　fingerprinting
指纹鉴定法/指紋鑒定法　dactyloscopy
指纹区/指紋區　fingerprint region
指纹型/指紋型　fingerprint pattern
指纹学/指紋學　dactylography
指细胞/指[狀]細胞　phalangeal cell
指纤维瘤/指纖維瘤　digital fibroma
指纤维鞘/指纖維鞘　fibrous sheath of finger
[指]纤维鞘环状部/[指]纖維鞘環狀部　annular part of fibrous sheath
指纤维性肿胀/指纖維[性]腫脹　digital fibrous swelling
指线/指線　digital ray
指压法/指壓法　digital compression
指压推拿/指壓推拿　finger-pressing massage
指压止痛法/指壓止痛法　method of finger pressing for relieving pain
指压止血法/指壓止血法　digital pressure hemostasis
指炎/指炎　dactylitis
指硬皮病/指硬化病　sclerodactyly
指掌侧固有动脉/指掌側固有動脈　proper palmar digital artery
指掌侧静脉/指掌側靜脈,掌指靜脈　palmar digital vein
指掌侧支动脉/指掌側支動脈　collateral digital artery
指掌侧总动脉/指掌側總動脈　common volar digital artery
指掌侧总静脉/指掌側總靜脈　common palmar digital vein
指掌侧总神经/指掌側總神經　common palmar digital nerve
指掌总动脉/指掌總動脈　common palmar digital artery
指针疗法/針壓法,指壓按摩　acupressure
指诊眼压测量法/眼球內壓之指測法,眼指壓測法　digital tonometry
指征/指徵,指示症狀　indicant
指周皮炎/指周圍皮膚炎　peridigital dermatitis
指状副银屑病/指狀類乾癬　digitate parapsoriasis
指状皮肤病/指狀皮膚病　digitate dermatosis
指状[突]的/指狀的　digitate
指状疣/指狀疣　verruca digitata
指总伸肌/伸指總肌　common extensor muscle of digits
趾/趾　toe, zhi, AH2
趾背动脉/趾背動脈　dorsal digital artery of foot
趾背静脉/趾背靜脈　dorsal digital vein of foot
趾背神经/趾背神經　dorsal digital nerves of foot
趾不全畸胎/趾不全畸胎　perodactylus
趾部分切除术/半趾骨切除術　hemiphalangectomy
趾长屈肌/屈趾長肌　flexor digitorum longus, long flexor muscle of toe
趾长屈肌腱鞘/屈趾長肌腱鞘　tendinous sheath of flexor digitorum longus
趾长伸肌/伸趾長肌　extensor digitorum longus, long extensor muscle of toe
趾长伸肌腱鞘/伸趾長肌腱鞘　tendinous sheath of extensor digitorum longus
趾的/趾的　digital
趾底静脉/趾底靜脈　venae digitales plantares
趾垫/趾墊,趾髓　digital pulp
趾端粉碎性骨折/趾端粉碎性骨折,叢簇骨折　tuft fracture
趾短屈肌/屈趾短肌　flexor digitorum brevis, musculus flexor digitorum brevis
趾短伸肌/伸趾短肌　extensor digitorum brevis, musculus extensor digitorum brevis
趾骨/趾骨　phalange of toe, bone of toe, phalange of foot
趾骨的/趾骨的　phalangeal
趾骨底/趾骨底　base of phalanx
趾骨骨折/趾骨骨折　phalangeal fracture, toe fracture
趾骨过短/趾骨過短　brachyphalangia
趾骨滑车/趾骨滑車　trochlea of phalanx
趾骨间关节/趾骨間關節　interphalangeal joint of foot, interphalangeal articulation of toe
趾骨切除术/趾骨切除術　phalangectomy
趾骨体/趾骨體　shaft of phalanx
趾骨头/趾骨頭　head of phalanx

趾骨炎/趾[節]骨炎　phalangitis
趾关节/趾關節　articulation of digits of foot
趾关节外侧韧带/趾關節外側韌帶　lateral ligament of joint of toe
趾过小/趾過小，小趾　microdactyly
趾滑膜鞘/趾滑膜鞘　synovial sheath of toe
趾环状韧带/趾環狀韌帶　annular ligament of digits of foot
趾甲/趾甲　toe nail
趾甲病理学/趾甲病理學　onychopathology
趾甲部分移植术/趾甲部分移植術　partial toe nail grafting
趾甲的/趾甲的　ungual
趾甲肥大/趾甲肥大　onychauxis
趾甲肥厚/趾甲肥厚　nail hypertrophy
趾甲分离/趾甲分離　nail splitting
趾甲复合移植术/趾甲複合移植術　compound toe nail grafting
趾甲过度弯曲/趾甲過度彎曲　over curvature of the nail
趾甲过小/趾甲過小，趾甲小畸形　micronychia
趾甲疾病/趾甲疾病　nail disease
趾甲溃疡/趾甲潰瘍　toenail ulcer
趾甲皮肤带/趾甲皮膚帶　onychodermal band
趾甲鞘囊肿/趾甲鞘囊腫　onycholemmal cyst
趾甲全部移植术/趾甲全部移植術　total toe nail grafting
趾甲脱落/趾甲脫落　nail shedding
趾甲移植术/趾甲移植術　toe nail grafting
趾甲移植物/趾甲移植物　toe nail graft
趾甲异位/趾甲異位　onychoheterotopia
趾甲营养不良/趾甲發育異常　onychodystrophy
趾甲硬化/趾甲硬化　scleronychia
趾甲周围疾病/趾甲周圍疾病　periungual disorder
趾甲周围纤维瘤/趾甲周圍纖維瘤　periungual fibromata
趾甲周围疣/趾甲周圍疣　periungual wart
趾尖点/趾尖點　acropodion
趾间关节侧副韧带/趾間關節側副韌帶　collateral ligament of interphalangeal articulation of foot
趾间关节脱位/趾間關節脫位　dislocation of interphalangeal joint, interphalangeal dislocation of foot
趾间隙/趾間隙　interdigit
趾腱鞘/趾腱鞘　tendinous sheath of toe
趾矫形术/趾矯形術　orthodigita
趾痉挛/趾痙攣　dactylospasm
趾静脉/趾靜脈　plantar digital vein
趾黏液囊肿/趾黏液囊腫　digital mucous cyst

趾神经阻滞/趾神經阻斷　digital nerve block
趾十字韧带/趾十字韌帶　cruciate ligament of toe
趾水肿/趾水腫，腳趾腫　dactyledema
趾下垂/垂趾　drop toe
趾纤维瘤/趾纖維瘤　digital fibroma
趾纤维鞘/趾纖維鞘　fibrous sheath of toe
趾炎/趾炎　dactylitis
趾总静脉/趾總靜脈　common digital vein of foot
趾足底固有动脉/趾足底固有動脈　proper plantar digital artery
趾足底固有神经/趾足底固有神經　proper plantar digital nerve
趾足底总神经/趾底總神經　common plantar digital nerve
趾足底总神经趾足底固有神经/趾足底總神經趾足底固有神經　proper plantar digital nerve of common plantar digital nerve
枳壳/枳殼　orange fruit
枳实/枳實　immature orange fruit
枳实导滞丸/枳實導滯丸　zhishi daozhi pill
枳实消痞丸/枳實消痞丸　zhishi xiaopi pill
枳实薤白桂枝汤/枳實薤白桂枝湯　zhishi xiebai guizhi decoction
枳术丸/枳尤丸　zhizhu pill
酯/酯　ester
酯化/酯化[作用]　esterification
酯化雌激素类/酯化雌激素類　esterified estrogens
酯类/酯類　esters
酯酶/酯[皂化]酵素　esterase
C1酯酶缺乏/C1酯酶缺乏　C1 esterase deficiency
C1酯酶抑制合成缺乏/C1酯酶抑制合成缺乏　C1 esterase inhibitor deficiency
酯树胶/酯膠　ester gum
酯水解[作用]/酯解　esterolysis
至宝丹/至寶丹　most treasured bolus, zhibao minipill
至恶心为度/至噁心爲止　ad nauseam
至阳/至陽　zhiyang, DU9
至阴/至陰　zhiyin, BL67
至真要大论篇/至真要大論篇　Treatise on Essentials in Medicine
志/志　will
志悲/志悲　profound sorrow
志达/志達　feeling optimistic
志愤/志憤　feeling angry
志贺毒素/志賀氏毒素　Shiga toxin
志贺菌疫苗/志賀菌疫苗　Shigella vaccine
志贺样毒素/志賀樣毒素　Shiga-like toxin

志苦/志苦　feeling depressed
志乐/志樂　feeling happy
志生/志生　feeling open-minded
志室/志室　zhishi, BL52
志意/志意　feeling easy
志愿卫生机构/志願衛生機構　voluntary health agency
制备色谱法/製備型層析法　preparative chromatography
制草乌/制草烏　prepared kusnezoff monkshood root
制川乌/制川烏　prepared common monkshood mother root
制大肠杆菌素/抗大腸桿菌素　colistatin
制动凝集[反应]/制動凝集[反應]　immobilization agglutination
制动试验/制動試驗　immobilization test
制革工病/製革工病　tanner disease
制何首乌/制何首烏　prepared fleeceflower root
制化/制化　restriction and generation
制菌剂/制菌劑　bacteriostatic
制菌作用/制菌作用,細菌繁殖受阻,細菌抑制　bacteriostasis
制麻风[菌]药/制麻風菌藥　leprostatic
制霉菌素/制黴菌素　nystatin
制霉[菌]药/制黴[菌]藥,制菌劑　mycostat
制霉素/制黴素　nysfungin
制念球菌素/制念球菌素　candidin
制尿/制尿,抗利尿　antidiuresis
制尿药/制尿藥　antidiuretic
制龋药/制齲藥　cariostatic agent
制乳剂/制乳劑　antigalactic
[制]霜/[制]霜　frost-like powder
制梭工人病/梭工病　shuttlemaker disease
制炭/制炭　carbonizing
制炭存性/制炭存性　burn as charcoal with function preserved
制药工程学/製藥工程學　pharmaceutical engineering
制药工业/製藥工業　pharmaceutic industry
制药工艺学/製藥工藝學　pharmaceutical technology
制欲剂/鎮欲藥,制欲藥　anaphrodisiac
质壁分离/原漿分離　plasmolysis
质壁分离复原/胞漿分離後復原　deplasmolysis
质地/質地　texture
质粒/質粒　plasmid
质粒介导耐药性/質粒介導耐藥性　plasmid-mediated resistance
质粒载体/質體載體　plasmid vector

质量保证/品質保證　quality assurance, QA
质量标准/質量標準　quality standard
质量分析/質量分析　quality analysis
质量分析检测器/質量分析檢測器　mass analyser detector
质量校正寿命/品質校正壽命　quality-adjusted life year
质量控制/品質管制,品管　quality control, QC
质量评价/品質評價　quality evaluation
质量吸收系数/品質吸收係數　mass absorption coefficient
质膜/質膜,細胞膜　plasmalemma
质膜内褶/質膜内褶　plasma membrane infolding
质判之人/質判之人　atypical fire-phase person, more free and contented
质谱法/質譜法　mass spectrometry
质谱图/質譜圖　mass spectrum
质谱仪/質譜儀　mass spectrograph
质体/質體　plastid
质体醌/質體醌　plastoquinone
质体蓝素/質體藍素　plastocyanin
质徵之人/質徵之人　atypical fire-phase person, more shallow and impetuous
质子泵/質子泵　proton pump
质子动力势/質子動力勢　proton-motive force
质子-磷酸协同转运/質子-磷酸協同轉運　proton-phosphate symporter
质子转运 ATP 酶类/質子轉運 ATP 酶類　proton-translocating ATPases
质子自递/自遞質子[作用]　autoprotolysis
炙甘草汤/炙甘草湯　zhigancao decoction
治崩三法/治崩三法　three methods for arresting massive uterine hemorrhage
治病求本/治病求本　treatment aiming at its root causes
治法/治法　method of treatment
治风法/治風法　dispelling wind method
治风化痰剂/治風化痰劑　formula for resolving phlegm with arresting wind
治风剂/治風劑　formula for wind disorder
治疗/治療　therapy, treatment
治疗比率/治療比率　curative ratio
治疗窗/治療窗　therapeutic window
治疗的/治療的　therapeutic
治疗等效/治療等效　therapeutic equivalency
治疗过程片断/治療過程片斷　episode of care
治疗接种/治療接種　curative inoculation
治疗结果/治療結果　treatment outcome

治疗配合禁忌/治療配合禁忌　therapeutic incompatibility
治疗失败/治療失敗　treatment failure
治疗失败率/治療失敗率　treatment failure rate
治疗完成率/治療完成率　completion rate of treatment
治疗性触摸/治療性觸摸　therapeutic touch
治疗性虹膜切除术/治療性虹膜切除術　therapeutic iridectomy
治疗性化学栓塞/治療性化學栓塞　therapeutic chemoembolization
治疗性抗血清/治療性抗血清　therapeutic antiserum
治疗性流产/治療性流產　therapeutic abortion
治疗性配伍禁忌/治療性配伍禁忌　therapeutic incompatibility
治疗性气胸/治療性氣胸　therapeutic pneumothorax
治疗性人类试验/治療性人類試驗　therapeutic human experimentation
治疗性栓塞/治療性栓塞　therapeutic embolization
治疗性文身/治療性文身　therapeutic tattoo
治疗性运动/矯治性運動　therapeutic exercise
治疗虚无主义/治療無爲主義　therapeutic nihilism
治疗学/治療學,治療法　therapeutics
治疗学家/治療[學]家　therapeutist
治疗药物监测/藥物治療監測　therapeutic drug monitoring
治疗应用/治療應用　therapeutic use
治疗用抗原/治療性抗原　therapeutic antigen
治疗诱发疟/治療性瘧　therapeutic malaria
治疗指数/治療指數　therapeutic index
治疗作用/治療作用　therapeutic action
治肾病药/治腎病藥　nephritic
治痛风药/治痛風藥　arthrifuge
治未病/治未病　preventive treatment of disease
治痈疡法/治癰瘍法　method for treating sores and carbuncles
治愈性治疗/有效療法,治愈療法　curative treatment
治则/治則　principle of treatment
治灼伤剂/治灼傷藥　antipyrotic
栉头蚤属/頭梳蚤屬　Ctenocephalides
桎羽之人/桎羽之人　atypical water-phase person, more calm and composed
致癌病毒/致癌病毒　cancer-inducing virus
致癌的/致癌的　carcinogenic
致癌逆转录病毒科蛋白质类/致癌逆轉錄病毒科蛋白質類　oncogenic retroviridae proteins
致癌物[质]/致癌物[質]　carcinogen, carcinogenic substance
致癌性/致癌性　carcinogenicity
致癌性试验/致癌性試驗　carcinogenicity test
致癌性烃/致癌性烴　carcinogenic hydrocarbon
致癌原/致癌[性物]質　carcinogen
致癌作用/致癌作用　carcinogenesis
致白细胞溶解剂/白血球崩解藥　leukocytolytic
致白血病物质/白血病原質　leukemogen
致病力/致病性　pathogenicity
致病物质/致病物質,成病物質　materies morbi
致病性/致病性　pathogenicity
致喘的/氣喘原的　asthmagenic
致喘剂/致喘藥　asthmogenic
致痤疮物[质]/致痤瘡物質　acnegen
致癫痫病灶/致癲癇病灶　epileptogenic focus
致动脉粥样化膳食/致動脈粥樣化膳食　atherogenic diet
致佝偻病饮食/致佝僂[病]飲食　rachitic diet
致幻剂/幻覺劑,致幻藥　hallucinogen
致幻觉药/迷幻藥　hallucinogenic, psychotomimetic, psychedelic
致黄疸性/黄疸生成性　icterogenicity
致畸剂/致畸劑　teratogens
致畸临界期/致畸臨界期　critical period to teratogenic agent
致畸敏感期/致畸敏感期　sensitive period to teratogenic agent
致畸性/致畸性　teratogenecity
致畸易感性/致畸易感性　susceptibility to teratogenic agent
致畸因子/致畸[胎]因子,致畸原　teratogen
致畸原/致畸原,致畸[胎]因子　teratogen
致畸作用/致畸作用　teratogenesis
致痉物/致痙物　spasmogen
致冷/冷凍,冷卻　refrigeration
致瘤病毒/致瘤病毒　oncogenic virus
致密斑/致密斑　macula densa
致密板/致密板　lamina densa
致密部/致密部　compact part
致密层/致密層　stratum compactum
致密沉积物病/密度沈積病　dense deposit disease
致密的/致密的,皺縮的　pyknotic
致密结缔组织/致密結締組織　dense connective tissue
致密[全能]原浆/致密無核胞漿　pyknoplasson
致密水肿/致密水腫　compact edema
致密细胞/皺縮細胞　pyknotic cell
致密性骨炎/凝縮性骨炎　condensing osteitis

致密性髂骨炎/致密性髂骨炎 osteitis condensans ilii
致密组织/致密組織 compact tissue
致免疫物/致免疫物 immunizator
致敏的/致敏的 sensitized
致敏剂量/致敏劑量 priming dose
致敏淋巴细胞/致敏淋巴細胞 primed lymphocyte
致敏绵羊[红]细胞试验/敏感化綿羊血球試驗 sensitized sheep cell test
致敏素/起敏素 sensitin
致敏物质/致敏物質 substance sensibilisatrice
致敏细胞/致敏細胞 sensitized cell
致敏性注射/致敏性注射 sensitizing injection
致敏作用/致敏[感]作用,感應作用,過敏性 sensitization
致命的/致命的 fatal
致命性结局/致命性結局 fatal outcome
致命性麻疹/劇性麻疹 serempion
致命性中线肉芽肿/致命性中線肉芽腫 lethal midline granuloma
致脑炎性蛋白质/致腦炎性蛋白質 encephalitogenic protein
致龋膳食/致齲膳食 cariogenic diet
致龋物/致齲物 cariogenic agent
致龋性/齲蛀形成性 cariogenicity
致热钩端螺旋体/致熱螺旋體 Leptospira pyrogenes
致热射线/熱射線 caloric ray
致热药/發熱劑 pyrectic
致伤物/致創傷物 vulnerant
致伤因素/致傷因素 causative factor of injury
致肾炎菌株/致腎炎菌株 nephritogenic strain
致湿物/致濕物 humectant
致湿[作用]/致濕作用 humectation
致衰弱剂/致衰弱劑 hypostheniant
致死当量/致死當量 lethal equivalent
致死的/致死的 lethal
致死基因/致死基因 lethal gene
致死量/致死量 fatal dose
致死率/致死率 fatality rate
致死突变/致死突變 lethal mutation
致死性发育不良/致死性發育不良 thanatophoric dysplasia
致死性家族性失眠症/致死性家族性失眠症 fatal familial insomnia
致死性紧张症/致死性緊張症 lethal catatonia
致突变原/突變原 mutagen
致突眼物质/致凸眼物質 exophthalmos producing substance

致心律失常/新心律不整,藥物致心律不整 proarrhythmia
致心律失常性/致節律不整形成 arrhythmogenic
致休克注射/致休克注射 shocking injection
致谵妄药/譫妄藥 delirifacient
致肿瘤核糖核酸病毒/致瘤核糖核酸病毒 oncorna virus
致肿瘤性/生瘤性 oncogenicity
秩边/秩邊 zhibian, BL54
掷弹者骨折/擲彈兵骨折 grenade-thrower fracture
痔/痔[瘡] hemorrhoid
痔的/痔的 hemorrhoidal
痔环/痔環 anal verge
痔绞痛/痔絞痛 hemorrhoidal colic
痔瘘/痔瘻疾病 hemorrhoid and fistula
痔切除术/痔切除術 hemorrhoidectomy
痔脱垂/痔脱垂 prolapse of hemorrhoid
窒息/窒息 suffocation
窒息的/窒息的 asphyctic
窒息毒气/窒氣 choke damp
窒息剂/窒息藥 asphyxiant
窒息性甲状腺肿/窒息性甲狀腺腫 suffocative goiter
窒息性日射病/窒息性日射症 asphyxial insolation
窒息性胸廓发育不良/先天性胸部發生不全 asphyxiating thoracic dysplasia
窒息综合征/窒息症候群 asphyctic syndrome
蛭纲/水蛭綱 Hirudinea
智/智 wisdom
智齿/智齒,遲齒 opsigenes
智齿水平位/智齒水平位 horizontal position of the wisdom tooth
智力/智力 intelligence
智力薄弱症/精神薄弱病 hypophrenosis
智力测验/智力測驗 intelligence test
智力测验器/智力測驗器 mentimeter
智力迟钝/智力遲鈍 baryencephalia
智力年龄/心智年齡 mental age
智力商数/智商 intelligence quotient
智力障碍/智力障礙 dysgnosia, intellectual dysfunction
痣/痣 naevus
痣黄内皮瘤/痣黄内皮瘤 nevoxanthoendothelioma
痣细胞痣/痣細胞痣 nevocytic nevus
痣性精神错乱/斑痣性精神錯亂症 nevoid amentia
痣样的/痣樣[的] nevoid
痣样基底细胞癌综合征/痣樣基底細胞癌症候群 nevoid basal cell carcinoma syndrome

痣样囊肿/痣狀囊腫 nevoid cyst
痣样象皮病/痣性象皮病 nevoid elephantiasis
痣样周围白癜风/痣樣周圍白斑 perinevoid vitiligo
痣周白斑/痣周白斑 perinevic vitiligo
痣状角化病/痣狀角化病 nevoid keratosis
滞产/滯產 prolonged labor
滞留死胎/死胎不下,失産 missed labor
滞留胎盘/滯留胎盤 retained placenta
滞留性月经/滯留性月經 retained menstruation
滞脉/[遲]滯脈 pulsus tardus
滞弹性纤维痣/缺彈性纖維母斑 nevus anelasticans
滞针/滯針 stucking of needle
置放急救识别卡/置放急救識別卡 tagging
置换/置換 replacement
置换法/置換法 displacement method
置换骨/置換骨,替代骨 replacement bone
置换关节成形术/置換關節成形術 replacement arthroplasty
置换价/置換價 displacement value
置换术/置換術 replacement
置信区间/置信區間 confidence interval
稚阳/稚陽 tender yang
稚阴/稚陰 tender yin
中傍人事/中傍人事 consideration of personal factors in emotional therapy
中鼻道/鼻中道 middle nasal meatus
中鼻道前房/鼻中道前房 atrium of middle meatus
中鼻甲/中鼻甲 middle nasal concha
中波疗法/中波療法 medium wave therapy
中卟啉/中卟啉 mesoporphyrin
中卟啉类/中卟啉類 mesoporphyrins
中部亚洲/中部亞洲 Central Asia
中草药/中草藥 Chinese herbal medicine
中层钙化/中層鈣化 medial calcification
中层坏死/中層[性]壞死,中膜壞死 medial necrosis
中肠/中腸 midgut
中肠扭转/中腸扭轉 midgut volvulus
中肠襻/中腸襻 midgut loop
中成药/中成藥 Chinese patent medicine, traditional Chinese patent medicines and simple preparations
中冲/中沖 zhongchong, PC9
中床突/中床突 middle clinoid process
中胆红素/新膽紅質 mesobilirubin
中胆色素/新膽汁鹽 mesobilin
中胆紫素/中膽紫素,新膽菫菜素 mesobiliviolin
中等身材/中等身材,中型身材 mesosoma
中[等以]上身材/中[等以]上身材 hypermesosoma
中[等以]下身材/中[等以]下身材 hypomesosoma

中等照明视力/中等照明視力 mesopia
中动脉/中動脈 medium-sized artery
中都/中都 zhongdu, LR6
中渎/中瀆 zhongdu, GB32
中度近视/中度近視 medium myopia
中度淋巴瘤/中度淋巴瘤 intermediate-grade lymphoma
中度锚基空隙合拢/中度錨基空隙合攏 moderate anchorage space closure
中度妊高征/中度妊高徵 moderate PIH
中度伤/中度傷 moderate injury
中度烧伤/中度燒傷 moderate degree burn
中度拥挤/中度擁擠 moderate crowding
中度远视/中度遠視 medium hypermetropia
中段/中段 midpiece, middle piece
中段中胚层/中間中胚層 intermediate mesoderm
中恶/中惡 noxious pathogen attack
中耳/中耳 middle ear
中耳胆脂瘤/中耳膽脂瘤 middle ear cholesteatoma
中耳[负压]吸液法/波利澤氏吸出法 negative politzerization
中耳通气/中耳通氣 middle ear ventilation
中耳压力计/中耳壓力計 pneumophone
中耳炎/中耳炎 otitis media
中耳[炎]性脑炎/耳病性腦炎 otocerebritis
中分法/中分法 bisecting technique
中封/中封 zhongfeng, LR4
中缝背核/中縫背核 nucleus raphes dorsalis
中缝苍白核/中縫蒼白核 nucleus raphes pallidus
中缝大核/中縫大核 nucleus raphes magnus
中缝核/中縫核 rapheal nucleus, raphe nucleus
中缝核群/中縫核群 rapheal nuclear group
中缝核中间线形核/中縫核中間線形核 nucleus linearis intermedius of rapheal nuclear group
中缝核中央上核/中縫核中央上核 superior central nucleus of rapheal nuclear group
中缝核嘴侧线形核/中縫核嘴側線形核 nucleus linearis rostralis of rapheal nuclear group
中缝隐核/中縫隱核 nucleus raphes obscurus
中府/中府 zhongfu, LU1
中腑中风/中腑中風 apoplexy involving fu-viscera
中副动脉/中副動脈 middle collateral artery
中腹部/中腹部 mid-abdomen
中干/中幹 middle trunk
中隔/中隔 septum
中隔处女膜/分隔性處女膜 septate hymen
中隔脓肿/中隔膿腫 septal abscess
中隔缺损/中隔缺損 septal defect

中隔乳头状肌/中隔乳頭狀肌　septal papillary muscle
中隔细胞/中隔細胞　septal cell
中隔缘束/中隔緣徑　septomarginal tract
中跟关节面/跟骨中關節面　middle calcanean articular surface
中骨盆平面/中骨盆平面　mid plane of pelvis
中骨盆狭窄/中骨盆狹窄　contracted midpelvis
中国传统医学/中國傳統醫學　Chinese traditional medicine
中国肺结核病分类法/中國肺結核病分類法　Chinese classification of pulmonary tuberculosis
中国九分法/中國九分法　Chinese Rule of Nine
中国民族医药学会/中國民族醫藥學會　China Medical Association of Minorities
中国镍钛矫正线/中國鎳鈦矯正線　Chinese nickel-titanium wire
中国医学史/中國醫學史　Chinese medical history
中国针灸学会/中國針灸學會　China Association of Acupuncture-Moxibustion
中国中西医结合学会/中國中西醫結合學會　Chinese Association of the Integrative Medicine
中果皮/中果皮　mesocarp
中和/中和　neutralization
中和机理/中和機理　neutralizing mechanism
中和结核菌素［皮肤反应］抗体/中和結核菌素［皮膚反應］抗體　anticutin
中和抗体/中和［性］抗體　neutralizing antibody
中和试验/中和試驗　neutralization test
中和［作用］/中和作用　neutralization
中横棒/中橫棒　Crepis
中厚皮片/中厚皮片　intermediate thickness free skin graft
中华沼螺/中華沼螺　Parafossarulus sinensis
中华中医药学会/中華中醫藥學會　China Association of Chinese Medicine
中黄卵/中黃卵　medialecithal egg, mesolecithal ovum
中基质/［胚胎］中基質　mesostroma
中极/中極　zhongji, RN3
中间部/中間部　intermedius
中间代谢/中間代謝　intermediary metabolism
中间带/中間帶,中間區　intermediate zone
中间的/中間的,中層的,正中的　intermediate, medial
中间固位桥基/中間固位橋基　intermediate retaining
中间腱/中間腱　intermediate tendon
中间粒径/中位粒徑　median diameter

中间连接/中間連接　intermediate junction
中间内侧核/中間內側核　nucleus intermediomedialis
中间凝胶技术/中間凝膠技術　intermediate gel technique
中间盘/中間板　intermediate disc
中间葡萄膜炎/中間葡萄膜炎　intermediate uveitis
中间期出血/中間期出血　intermediate hemorrhage
中间桥基/中間橋基　intermediate abutment
中间清醒期/中間清醒期,神志清明期　lucid interval
中间缺失/中間缺失　intercalary deletion
中间神经/中間神經　intermediate nerve, intermediary nerve
中间神经节/中間神經節　intermediate ganglia
中间神经腮腺丛/正中神經鵝足叢　plexus anserinus nervi mediani
中间神经元/中間神經元　interneuron
中间丝/中間絲　intermediate filament
中间丝蛋白质类/中間絲蛋白質類　intermediate filament proteins
中间宿主/中間宿主　intermediate host
中间体/中間體　intermediate
中间外侧核/中間外側核　nucleus intermediolateralis
中间外侧束/中間外側徑　intermediolateral tract
中间微动脉/中間小動脈　meta-arteriole
中间窝/中間窩　middle fossa
中间线/中間線　intermediate line, central stratum
中间线形核/中間線形核　nucleus linearis intermedius
中间楔骨/中間楔骨　intermediate cuneiform bone, middle cuneiform
中间型肌纤维/中間型肌纖維　intermediate muscle fiber
中间型麻风/中間型麻風　borderline leprosy
中间型细胞癌/中間型細胞癌　intermediate-cell carcinoma
中间牙骨质/中間牙骨質　intermediate cementum
中间腰淋巴结/中間腰淋巴結　intermediate lumbar lymph node
中间［与］外侧的/中間與外側的　intermediolateral
中间运动/中間運動　intermediary movement
中间诊疗设施/中間診療設施　intermediate care facility
中间支/中間支　intermediate branch
中间种植体/中間種植體　intermediary implant
中焦/中焦　middle jiao
中焦如沤/中焦如漚　middle jiao being organ of soaking
中焦湿热/中焦濕熱　dampness-heat in middle jiao

中焦湿热证/中焦濕熱證　pattern of dampness-heat in middle jiao
中焦实热证/中焦實熱證　pattern of excessive-heat in middle jiao
中节指骨/中指節骨　middle phalanx
中节趾骨/中趾節骨　middle phalanx
中结肠动脉/中結腸動脈　middle colic artery
中结肠静脉/中結腸靜脈　middle colic vein
中结肠淋巴结/中結腸淋巴結　middle colic lymph node
中介的/仲介的　mesomeric
中介核/中介核　intercalatus nucleus
中介子/仲介子　neutretto
中经中风/中經中風　apoplexy involving channel
中颈心神经/中頸心神經　middle cervical cardiac nerve
中静脉/中靜脈　medium-sized vein
中距关节面/距骨中關節面　middle talar articular surface
中客/中客　infantile convulsive seizure due to fright of seeing straigers
中客忤/中客忤　infantile convulsive seizure due to fright of seeing straigers
中空的/中空的,凹陷,空洞　hollow
中空树脂泡/中空樹脂泡　hollow acrylic bulb
中空纤维膜式氧合器/中空纖維膜式氧合器　hollow fiber membrane oxygenator
中空纤维型透析器/中空纖維型透析器　hollow fiber dialyser
中魁/中魁　zhongkui, EX-UE4
中肋横突韧带/中肋橫突韌帶　middle costotransverse ligament
中联合去骨术/中聯合去骨術　midsymphyseal ostectomy
中髎/中髎　zhongliao, BL33
中淋巴细胞/中淋巴細胞　medium-sized lymphocyte
中膂俞/中膂俞　zhonglüshu, BL29
中氯化血红素/新血晶素　mesohemin
中络中风/中絡中風　apoplexy involving collateral
中美毒葛藤碱/中美毒葛藤鹼　vellosine
中门齿/[正]中門齒　central incisor
中南非洲回归热螺旋体/中南非洲回歸熱螺旋體,突頓氏螺旋體　Borrelia duttonii
中脑/中腦　midbrain, mesencephalon
中脑被盖/中腦蓋膜　tegmentum mesencephali
中脑被盖综合征/大腦腳蓋症候群　tegmental syndrome
中脑出血/中腦出血　midbrain hemorrhage

中脑导水管/中腦導水管　mesencephalic aqueduct, aqueduct of midbrain
中脑导水管周围灰质/導水管周邊灰質　periaqueductal gray matter, PAG
中脑的/中腦的　mesencephalic
中脑顶盖/中腦頂蓋　tectum of midbrain
中脑动脉/中腦動脈　mesencephalic artery
中脑核/中腦核　mesencephalic nucleus
中脑静脉/中腦靜脈　mesencephalic vein
中脑切开术/中腦切開術　mesencephalotomy
中脑曲/中腦曲　mesencephalic flexure
中脑水管/中腦水管　mesencephalic aqueduct
中脑炎/中腦炎　mesencephalitis
中内裂球/中内[分]裂球　mesentomere
中内胚层/中内胚葉　mesentoderm
中年人/中年人　middle aged
中黏蛋白酶/新黏液素酶　mesomucinase
中颞动脉沟/中顳動脈溝　sulcus arteriae temporalis mediae
中胚层/中胚層,中胚葉　mesoderm
中胚层带/中胚葉帶　mesodermal band
中胚层的/中胚葉的　mesodermal
中胚层混合瘤/中胚葉混合瘤　mesodermal mixed tumor
中胚层肌/中胚葉肌　mesodermal muscle
中胚层节/中胚葉外節　epimerite
中胚层维持/中胚葉維持　mesodermal maintenance
中胚层细胞/中胚葉細胞　mesoblastema
中胚层脏腑层细胞/中胚葉臟腑層細胞　splanchnic cell
中胚层肿瘤/中胚葉[混合]瘤　mesodermal tumor
中胚层综合征/中胚葉症候群　mesodermal syndrome
中胚叶上皮层/中胚葉上皮層　desmepithelium
中胚叶肾瘤/中胚葉腎瘤　mesoblastic nephroma
中频电疗法/中頻電療法　medium frequency electrotherapy
中频电诊断法/中頻電診斷法　medium frequency electrodiagnosis
中品/中品　medium grade drug
中期/中期,轉變期　metaphase
中期分裂/中期分離　metacinesis
中期染色体/中期染色體　metaphase chromosome
中期胎死/中間死胎,中期死胎　intermediate fetal death
中气/中氣　middle qi
中切牙孔/正中門齒孔,史卡帕氏孔　median incisor foramen

中清之腑/中清之腑 fu-viscera with clear juice
中泉/中泉 zhongquan, EX-UE3
中筛斑/中篩斑 middle macula cribrosa
中筛窦/中篩竇 middle ethmoidal sinus
中上牙槽神经/中上齒槽神經 middle superior alveolar nerve
中舌窦/中舌竇 medial lingual sinus
中肾/中腎 mesonephros
中肾管/中腎管 mesonephric duct
中肾瘤/中腎瘤 mesonephroma
中肾旁管/副中腎管 paramesonephric duct
中肾小管/中腎細管 mesonephric tubule
中肾小球/中腎小球 mesonephric glomerulus
中肾褶/中腎皺襞 mesonephric fold
中湿啰音/中濕啰音 medium rales
中实肠胚/初期胚 mesomula
中枢/中樞 zhongshu, DU7
中枢刺激/中樞刺激 central stimulation
中枢淋巴[样]器官/中樞淋巴樣器官, 初級淋巴器官 central lymphoid organ
中枢神经系统/中樞神經系統, 中央神經系 central nervous system, CNS
中枢神经系统艾滋病动脉炎/中樞神經系統愛滋病動脈炎 central nervous system AIDS arteritis
中枢神经系统白血病/中樞神經系統白血病 central nervous system leukemia
中枢神经系统病毒感染/中樞神經系統病毒感染 central nervous system viral disease
中枢神经系统刺激剂/中樞神經系統刺激劑 central nervous system stimulant
中枢神经系统感染/中樞神經系統感染 central nervous system infection
中枢神经系统疾病/中樞神經系統疾病 central nervous system disease
中枢神经系统寄生虫感染/中樞神經系統寄生蟲感染 central nervous system parasitic infection
中枢神经系统结核/中樞神經系統結核 central nervous system tuberculosis
中枢神经系统静脉血管瘤/中樞神經系統靜脈血管瘤 central nervous system venous angioma
中枢神经系统狼疮/中樞神經系統狼瘡 central nervous system lupus, CNS lupus
中枢神经系统狼疮血管炎/中樞神經系統狼瘡血管炎 central nervous system lupus vasculitis
中枢神经系统囊肿/中樞神經系統囊腫 central nervous system cyst
中枢神经系统蠕虫病/中樞神經系統蠕蟲病 central nervous system helminthiasis
中枢神经系统细菌感染/中樞神經系統細菌感染 central nervous system bacterial infection
中枢神经系统血管畸形/中樞神經系統血管畸形 central nervous system vascular malformation
中枢神经系统血管炎/中樞神經系統血管炎 central nervous system vasculitis
中枢神经系统药物/中樞神經系統藥物 central nervous system agent
中枢神经系统原虫感染/中樞神經系統原蟲感染 central nervous system protozoal infection
中枢神经系统真菌感染/中樞神經系統真菌感染 central nervous system fungal infection
中枢神经系统肿瘤/中樞神經系統腫瘤 central nervous system neoplasm
中枢神经兴奋药/中樞神經興奮藥 central nervous stimulant
中枢神经抑制药/中樞神經抑制藥 central nervous depressant
中枢神经元/中樞神經單位, 中央神經單位 central neuron
中枢衰竭/中樞衰竭 central failure
中枢兴奋状态/中樞刺激狀態 central excitatory state
中枢性暗觉/中樞性暗覺 centraphose
中枢性感觉缺失/中樞性感覺缺失 central anesthesia
中枢性共济失调/中樞性運動失調 central ataxia
中枢性光幻觉/中樞性光幻覺, 中心影幻視 centrophose
中枢性黑矇/中樞性黑矇 central amaurosis
中枢性换气不足/中樞性換氣不足 central hypoventilation
中枢性肌松弛药/中樞性肌鬆弛藥 central muscle relaxant
中枢性惊厥/中樞性驚厥 central convulsion
中枢性聋/中樞性聾症 central deafness
中枢性失语/中樞性失語症 central aphasia
中枢性睡眠呼吸暂停/中樞性睡眠呼吸暫停 central sleep apnea
中枢性听觉疾病/中樞性聽覺疾病 central auditory disease
中枢性听觉丧失/中樞性聽覺喪失 central hearing loss
中枢性听觉障碍/中樞性聽覺障礙 central auditory dysfunction
中枢性痛/中樞性疼痛 central pain
中枢性心动过缓/中樞性心搏過緩 central bradycardia

中枢性眼球震颤/中心眼球震顫　central nystagmus
中枢性运动/中樞性運動　centrocinesia
中枢性紫绀/中樞性發紺　central cyanosis
中枢[性]总和/中樞性積聚　central summation
中枢抑制状态/中樞抑制狀態　central inhibition state
中枢支/中樞支　central branch
中枢作用佐剂/中樞作用佐劑　central acting adjuvant
中庭/中庭　zhongting, RN16
中途结/中途結　bouton en passant(法)
中途突触/中途突觸　synapse en passant(法)
中外胚层/中外胚層　mesectoderm
中脘/中脘　zhongwan, RN12
中脘痈/中脘癰　Zhongwan abscess
中微子/中微子　neutrino
中纬板小体/中緯板小結　dermatosome
中纬[卵]裂/中緯[卵]裂,赤道面分裂　equatorial cleavage
中位差/中位差　median deviation
中位产钳术/中位產鉗術,中位產鉗產　mid forceps delivery
中位构造/中位構造　mesostructure
中位钳/中位產鉗　mid forceps
中位数检验/中位數檢定　median test
中位微笑/中位微笑　median smile
中西医结合/中西醫結合　integration of traditional Chinese medicine and western medicine
中下丘脑/中下丘腦　middle hypothalamus
中线/中線　midline
中线核群/中線核群　midline nuclear group
中线融合/中線融合　midline fusion
中线致死性肉芽肿/中線致死性肉芽腫　midline lethal granuloma
中向人格/内外兼向人格　ambiversion
中向人格者/内外兼向人格者　ambivert
中消/中消　middle consumption
中消·气阴两虚证/中消·氣陰兩虛證　middle consumption with pattern of deficiency of both qi and yin
中消·湿热中阻证/中消·濕熱中阻證　middle consumption with pattern of damp-heat blocking middle jiao
中消·胃燥津伤证/中消·胃燥津傷證　middle consumption with pattern of fluid damage and stomach dryness
中小脑脚/中小腦腳　middle cerebellar peduncle
中小学生护理/中小學生護理　school nursing

中小学生卫生保健服务/中小學生衛生保健服務　school health service
中小学牙科保健/中小學牙科保健　school dentistry
中楔骨/中楔骨　mesocuneiform bone
中斜角肌/中斜角肌　scalenus medius, middle scalene muscle
中心暗点/中心暗點　central scotoma
中心保持咬头/中心保持咬頭　centric holding cusp
中心登记/中心登記　central registry
中心电端/中心電端　central electric terminal
中心纺锤体/中心紡錘體　central spindle
中心关系𬌗/中心關係咬合　centric relation bite
中心关系记录值/中心關係記錄值　centric relation record value
中心核综合征/中心核症候群　central cord syndrome
中心颌关系记录/中心頜關係記錄　centric jaw relation record
中心滑动/中心滑動　slide in centric
中心腱/中心腱　central tendon, phrenic center
中心降温/中心降溫　core cooling
中心静脉导管插入术/中心靜脈導管插入術　central venous catheterization
中心静脉压/中心靜脈壓　central venous pressure
中心粒/中心粒　centriole
中心母细胞/中心母細胞　centroblast
中心耐受/中心耐受　central tolerance
中心器/中心器　central apparatus
中心球/中心球　centrosphere
中心上下颌关系/中心上下頜關係　centric maxillomandibular relation
中心射线/中心射線　central ray
中心视力/中央視覺,中央視力　central vision
中心视力检查法/中心視力檢查法　examination of central vision
中心视野/中心視野　central visual field
中心束/中心[光]束　central beam
中心体/中心體　centrosome
中心微管/中心微管　central microtubule
中心细胞/中心細胞　centrocyte
中心线/中心線　centrage
中心小窝/中心小窩　central pit
中心性坏死/中心性壞死　central necrosis
中心性脊髓炎/中心性脊髓炎　central myelitis
中心咬合/中心咬合,正中咬合　centric bite
中心支承/中軸承　central bearing
中心支承描绘装置/中軸承描軌器　central bearing tracing device

中心支承器/中軸承器　central bearing device
中心质/中心[體]漿　centroplasm
中心周围暗点/中心周圍暗點　pericentral scotoma
中心注视/中心注視　central fixation
中心自由/中心自由　freedom in centric
中行者/中行者　person with impartial character
中型动脉/中型動脈　medium-sized artery
中型腭的/中型懸雍垂的　mesostaphyline
中型颌的/中型頜的　mesognathous
中型颌头颅/中型頜頭顱　mesognathous skull
中型眶/中型眼眶　mesoconch
中型淋巴细胞/中型淋巴球,中等大淋巴球　mesolymphocyte
中型面头颅/中型面頭顱　mesoprosopic skull
中型头/中型頭　mesaticephaly
中型头的/中型頭的　mesocranic
中型牙/中型齒　mesodontism
中型[颜]面的/中型面的　mesoprosopic
中性氨基酸类/中性胺基酸類　neutral amino acids
中性氨基酸转运系统/中性胺基酸轉運系統　neutral amino acid transport system
中性白细胞/中性白細胞　neutrophils
中性白细胞过多性白细胞减少/嗜中性白血球之比例異常增加的白血球減少症　hyperhypocytosis
中性白细胞过多性白细胞增多/中性白血球過多性白血球增多症　dihypercytosis
中性白细胞减少[症]/嗜中性白血球減少症　neutrocytopenia
中性白细胞浸润/中性白細胞浸潤　neutrophil infiltration
中性白细胞趋向性/嗜中性白血球趨性　neutrotaxis
中性半抗原/中性半抗原　neutral hapten
中性带/中性區　neutral zone
中性的/中性的　neutral
中性碘/中性碘　neutral iodine
中性分叶核粒细胞/中性分葉核粒細胞　neutrophilic granulocyte segmented form
中性杆状核粒细胞/中性杆狀核粒細胞　neutrophilic granulocyte band form
中性焊媒/中性焊劑　neutral flux
中性𬌗/中性𬌗　neutral occlusion
中性红/中性紅　neutral red
中性精蛋白锌胰岛素/混合胰島素　neutral protamine hagedorn insulin
中性粒细胞/中性粒細胞　neutrophilic granulocyte
中性粒细胞减少性小肠结肠炎/中性粒細胞減少性小腸結腸炎　neutropenic enterocolitis
中性皮肤/中性皮膚　neutral skin

中性糖苷神经鞘脂类/中性糖苷神經鞘脂類　neutral glycosphingolipids
中性晚幼粒细胞/中性後髓細胞　neutrophilic metamyelocyte
中性盐血浆/加鹽血漿　salt plasma
中性早幼粒细胞/中性前髓細胞　neutrophilic promyelocyte
中性脂肪/中性脂肪　neutral fat
中性中幼粒细胞/中性骨髓細胞　neutrophilic myelocyte
中央凹/中央凹　fovea centralis, central fovea
中央凹发育不良/中央凹發育不良　foveal hypoplasia
中央凹反射/中央凹反射　foveal reflex
中央部/中央部　central part
中央动脉/中央動脈　central artery
中央肺炎/中央肺炎,中心肺炎　central pneumonia
中央沟/中央溝　central sulcus
中央沟动脉/中央溝動脈　artery of central sulcus
中央骨/中央骨　central bone
中央管/中央管　central canal
中央核/中央核　central nucleus
中央核肌病/中央核肌病　central core myopathy, centronuclear myopathy
中央后沟/中央後溝　postcentral sulcus
中央后沟动脉/中央後溝動脈　artery of postcentral sulcus
中央后回/中央後迴　postcentral gyrus
中央后静脉/中央後靜脈　postcentral vein
中央后区/中央後區　postcentral area
中央后支/中央後支　postcentral branch
中央灰质/中央灰質　central gray
中央尖/中央尖　central cusp
中央静脉/中央靜脈　central vein
中央巨噬细胞/中央巨噬細胞　central macrophage
中央淋巴结/中央淋巴結　central lymph node
中央脑系统/中央腦系統　centrencephalic system
中央内侧核/中央內側核　central medial nucleus
中央旁沟/中央旁溝　paracentral sulcus
中央旁核/中央旁核　paracentral nucleus of thalamus
中央旁小叶/中央旁小葉　paracentral lobule
中央前沟/中央前溝　precentral sulcus
中央前沟动脉/中央前溝動脈　artery of precentral sulcus
中央前回/中央前迴　precentral gyrus
中央前静脉/中央前靜脈　precentral vein
中央前置胎盘/中央前置胎盤　placenta praevia centralis
中央鞘/中央鞘　central sheath

中央乳糜管/中央乳糜管　central lacteal
中央上核/中央上核　superior central nucleus
中央胎盘/中央胎盤　central placenta
中央外侧核/中央外側核　central lateral nucleus
中央窝/中央窩　central fossa
中央细胞/中央細胞　central cell
中央消退/中央消退　central clearing
中央小叶/中央小葉　central lobule
中央小叶翼/中央小翼葉　ala of central lobule
中央中核/中央中核　centromedian nucleus
中央轴承点/中央軸承點　centric bearing point
中央轴空病/中央軸空病　central core disease
中腰联胎/[中]腰連胎,中段連胎　anacatadidymus
中药/中藥　Chinese materia medica, traditional Chinese drug
中药毒/中藥毒　drug eruption
中药化学/中藥化學　chemistry of Chinese materia medica
中药鉴别学/中藥鑒別學　identification of Chinese materia medica
中药炮制学/中藥炮製學　science of processing Chinese materia medica
中药师/中藥師　traditional Chinese pharmacist
中药学/中藥學　Chinese materia medica
中药药剂学/中藥藥劑學　pharmacy of Chinese materia medica
中药药理学/中藥藥理學　pharmacology of Chinese materia medica
中药制剂/中藥製劑　Chinese material medica preparation
中药制剂分析/中藥製劑分析　analysising drug form of Chinese materia medica
中叶/中葉　middle lobe
中叶素/垂體中間部內泌素,中間素　intermedin
中叶支/中葉支　branch of middle lobe, middle lobar branches
中叶综合征/右肺中葉症候群　middle lobe syndrome
中医/中醫　traditional Chinese medicine, traditional Chinese physician
中医儿科学/中醫兒科　pediatrics of traditional Chinese medicine
中医耳鼻喉科学/中醫耳鼻喉科學　otorhinolaryngology of traditional Chinese medicine
中医妇科学/中醫婦科學　gynecology of traditional Chinese medicine
中医肛肠科学/中醫肛腸科學　proctology of traditional Chinese medicine

中医各家学说/中醫各家學說　theories of schools of traditional Chinese medicine
中医骨伤科学/中醫骨傷科學　osteology and traumatology of traditional Chinese medicine
中医护理学/中醫護理學　science of nursery of traditional Chinese medicine
中医基础理论/中醫基礎理論　basic theory of traditional Chinese medicine
中医急诊学/中醫急診學　science of emergency of traditional Chinese medicine
中医康复学/中醫康復學　science of rehabilitation of traditional Chinese medicine
中医内科学/中醫內科學　internal medicine of traditional Chinese medicine
中医皮肤科学/中醫皮膚科學　dermatology of traditional Chinese medicine
中医情志疗法/中醫情志療法　emotional therapy in Chinese medicine
中医师/中醫[師]　traditional Chinese physician
中医推拿学/中醫推拿學　science of tuina of traditional Chinese medicine
中医外科学/中醫外科[學]　surgery of traditional Chinese medicine
中医文献学/中醫文獻　Chinese medical literature
中医心理治疗/中醫心理治療　TCM psychological treatment
中医学/中醫學　traditional Chinese medicine
中医眼科学/中醫眼科學　ophthalmology of traditional Chinese medicine
中医养生学/中醫養生學　science of health maintenance of traditional Chinese medicine
中医药/中醫藥　traditional Chinese medicine and pharmacy
中医药学/中醫藥學　traditional Chinese medicine and pharmacy
中医药周期疗法/中醫藥週期療法　menstrual cycle therapy with Chinese medicine
中医诊断学/中醫診斷學　diagnostics of traditional Chinese medicine
中硬度金合金/中硬度金合金　medium gold alloy
中幼红细胞/嗜多色素性母紅血球　polychromatophilic erythroblast
中幼粒细胞/中幼粒細胞,骨髓細胞　myelocyte
中脏中风/中臟中風　apoplexy involving zang-viscera
中正之官/中正之官　fu-viscera with decisive character, gallbladder as the decision-maker organ
中支描记器/中支描記器　central-bearing tracing device

中支器/中支器　central-bearing device
中指/中指　middle finger
中指同身寸/中指同身寸　middle finger cun, proportional unit of middle finger
中置式移植骨/中置式移植骨　interpositional bone graft
中轴/中轴　neutral axis
中轴骨骼/中軸骨骼　axial skeleton
中轴肌/中軸肌　axial muscle
中轴阶度/軸性梯度　axial gradient
中渚/中渚　zhongzhu, SJ3
中注/中注　zhongzhu, KI15
中柱/中柱　stele
中着丝粒染色体/中著絲粒染色體　centric chromosome
中子/中子　neutro
中子俘获疗法/中子俘獲療法　neutron capture therapy
中子活化分析/中子活化分析　neutron activation analysis
中子射线/中子射線　neutron ray
中子衍射/中子衍射　neutron diffraction
中纵隔/中縱隔　middle mediastinum
终板/終板　lamina terminalis, end-plate
终板电位/終板電位　end plate potential
终[板]膜/終膜　telolemma
终板旁回/終板旁迴　paraterminal gyrus
终板入路/終板入路　lamina terminalis approach
终板血管器/終板血管器　organum vasculosum of lamina terminalis, OVLT
终板噪声/終板雜訊　end plate noise
终变期/終變期　diakinesis stage
终部/終部　terminal part
终产物调节/終產物調節　end-product regulation
终池/終池　terminal cisterna
终点测定/終點測定　endpoint determination
终动脉/終動脈　end artery
终端/終端　end
终端肺泡/終端肺泡　terminal alveolus
终核/終核　terminal nucleus
终环/終環　end ring
终极前体/最終前驅物　ultimate precursor
终结/終結　terminal bouton
终扣/終扣　terminal bouton
终蕾/終蕾　end bud
终毛/終毛,恆久毛　terminal hair
终模型/終模型　final cast
终末潮气/終末潮氣　end tidal gas

终末囊泡期/終末囊泡期　terminal sac period
终末期固缩肾/終末期固縮腎　end-stage-contracted kidney
终末网/閉鎖網,終網　terminal web
终末细胞/終末細胞　cell of termination, end cell, terminal cell
终末细支气管/終末細支氣管　terminal bronchiole
终末血尿/終末血尿　terminal hematuria
终末圆锥/終末圓錐　conus terminalis
终脑顶突/終腦頂突　paraphasis
终期分裂/終期核分裂　teleomitosis
终期梅毒/終期梅毒　telesyphilis
终期性乐/性交後期快感　end-pleasure
终球/終球　end bulb
终身一胎[现象]/一次生殖,單次繁殖　semelparity
终神经/終神經　terminal nerve
终神经节/終神經節　terminal ganglion
终室/終室　terminal ventricle
终树突/終樹突　end-brush
终丝/終絲　filum terminale
终宿主/終宿主　definitive host
终位性眼球震颤/終位性眼球震顫　endposition nystagmus
终纹/終紋　terminal stria
终纹床核/終紋床核　bed nucleus of stria terminalis, BNST
终印模/最後壓模　final impression
终止/終止　termination
终止带/終止帶　termination zone
终止核/終止核　terminal nucleus
终止密码子/終止密碼子　termination codon, terminator codon
终止区/終止區　terminator region
终止子/終止子　terminator
终致癌物/終致癌物　ultimate carcinogen
终轴突/終軸索,軸突終端　teleneurite
终足/終足　end foot
钟摆样反射/鐘擺樣反射　pendular reflex
钟摆状节律/[心音之]鐘擺狀節律　pendulum rhythm
钟情妄想/鍾情妄想　delusion of being loved
钟乳石/鐘乳石　stalactite
钟乳体/鍾乳體　cystolith
钟响/鐘響　bell-metal resonance
钟音/鐘音　bell sound
钟状期/鐘狀期　bell stage
肿/腫　swelling
肿大/腫大　tumefaction

肿的/腫的　tumid
肿度测定器/腫度計,脹度計　turgometer
肿节风/腫節風　sarcandra twig and leaf
肿块/腫塊　lump
肿块切开术/腫瘤切開術　oncotomy
肿瘤/腫瘤　tumour
肿瘤标记/腫瘤標記　tumor marker
肿瘤病/腫瘤病　oncosis
肿瘤病毒/[致]腫瘤病毒　tumor virus
肿瘤病毒感染/腫瘤病毒感染　tumor virus infection
肿瘤蛋白质类/腫瘤蛋白質類　neoplasm proteins
肿瘤分期/腫瘤分期　neoplasm staging
肿瘤辅助疗法/腫瘤輔助療法　neoadjuvant therapy
肿瘤负荷/腫瘤負荷　tumor burden
肿瘤干细胞/腫瘤幹細胞　tumor stem cell
肿瘤干细胞测定/腫瘤幹細胞測定　tumor stem cell assay
肿瘤黑[色]素/腫瘤色素　phymatorhusin
肿瘤护理/腫瘤護理　oncologic nursing
肿瘤坏死因子/腫瘤壞死因子　tumor necrosis factor
肿瘤坏死因子受体/腫瘤壞死因子受體　tumor necrosis factor receptor
肿瘤基因表达调控/腫瘤基因表達調控　neoplastic gene expression regulation
肿瘤浸润淋巴细胞/腫瘤浸潤淋巴細胞　tumor-infiltrating lymphocyte
肿瘤抗体/腫瘤抗體　neoplasm antibody
肿瘤抗药性/腫瘤抗藥性　neoplasm drug resistance
肿瘤抗原/腫瘤抗原　neoplasm antigen
肿瘤免疫学/腫瘤免疫學　tumor immunology
肿瘤扑落音/腫瘤撲落音　tumor plop
[肿瘤]切除术/[腫瘤]切除術,結節除術　tylectomy
肿瘤侵润/腫瘤侵潤　neoplasm invasiveness
肿瘤妊娠并发症/腫瘤妊娠并發症　neoplastic pregnancy complication
肿瘤溶解综合征/腫瘤溶解症候群　tumor lysis syndrome
肿瘤逃逸/腫瘤逃逸　tumor escape
肿瘤特异性抗原/腫瘤特異性抗原　tumor specific antigen
肿瘤细胞系/腫瘤細胞系　tumor cell line
肿瘤细胞转化/腫瘤細胞轉化　neoplastic cell transformation
肿瘤相关抗原/腫瘤相關抗原　tumor associated antigen
肿瘤形成过程/腫瘤形成過程　neoplastic process
肿瘤性秃发/腫瘤性禿髮　alopecia neoplastica
肿瘤性心包炎/腫瘤性心包炎　neoplastic pericarditis
肿瘤性肢端角化症/腫瘤性肢端角化症　acrokeratosis neoplastica
肿瘤学/腫瘤學　oncology
肿瘤循环细胞/腫瘤循環細胞　neoplasm circulating cell
肿瘤压迫/腫瘤壓迫,瘤壓　oncothlipsis
肿瘤移植/腫瘤移植　neoplasm transplantation
肿瘤遗传学/腫瘤遺傳學　tumor genetics
肿瘤抑制蛋白质类/腫瘤抑制蛋白質類　tumor suppressor proteins
肿瘤抑制基因/腫瘤抑制基因　tumor suppressor gene
肿瘤治疗/腫瘤治療　oncotherapy
肿瘤治疗方案/腫瘤治療方案　antineoplastic protocol
肿瘤种植/腫瘤種植　neoplasm seeding
肿疡/腫瘍,膿腫,膿瘍　abscess, swollen sore
肿疡作痒/腫瘍作癢　itching due to swollen sore
肿胀/腫脹　swell
肿胀的/腫脹的　tumefaciens
肿胀技术吸脂术/腫脹技術吸脂術　tumescent liposuction
肿胀舌/腫脹舌　swollen tongue
肿胀星形细胞/膨脹星[形]細胞　bloated cell
肿胀性鼻炎/腫脹性鼻炎　turgescent rhinitis
肿胀性狼疮/腫脹性狼瘡　lupus tumidus
种间杂交/種間雜交　intervarietal hybridization
种免疫/種免疫[性],族免疫性　species immunity
种群/種群,菌落　colony
种特性丧失/失去種性,種性偏差　despeciation
种特异性/種屬特異性　species specificity
种系/種系　germ line
种系发生/種系發生　phylogeny
种质/種質　germ plasm
种质变异/胚漿演變　blastation
种质演变/胚芽演變,胚芽進化　blastogeny
种子/種子　seed, promoting conception
种子罐/種子罐　seed tank
种子植皮术/種子植皮術　seed skin grafting
种子状移植物/種子狀移植物　seed graft
种族/種族　race
种族关系/種族關係　race relation
种族灭绝/種族滅絕　genocide
中毒/中毒　intoxication
中毒病/中毒病　toxicosis, nosotoxicosis, poisoning
中毒病性/中毒病性　nosotoxicity
中毒剂量/中毒劑量　toxic dose
中毒控制中心/中毒控制中心　poison control center

中毒型痢疾/中毒型痢疾　toxic dysentery
中毒性白内障/中毒性白內障　toxic cataract
中毒性白细胞增多/中毒性白血球增多　toxic leukocytosis
中毒性表皮坏死松解症/中毒性表皮壞死鬆解症　toxic epidermal necrolysis
中毒性病/中毒病,毒物病　toxicopathy
中毒性发绀/中毒性發紺　toxic cyanosis
中毒性肝炎/中毒性肝炎　toxipathic hepatitis
中毒性肝硬化/毒物性肝硬變　toxic cirrhosis
中毒性和生理性秃发/中毒性和生理性秃髮　toxic and physiologic alopecia
中毒性黑矇/中毒性黑矇　toxic amaurosis
中毒性黑皮炎/中毒性黑變皮[膚]炎　melanodermatitis toxica
中毒性红斑/毒物性紅斑　toxic erythema
中毒性黄疸/中毒性黄疸　toxic jaundice
中毒性精神病/毒物性精神病　toxic psychosis
中毒性痉挛/毒物性痙攣　toxic spasm
中毒性巨结肠/中毒性巨結腸　toxic megacolon
中毒性皮病/中毒性皮病　toxicoderma
中毒性皮炎/中毒性皮[膚]炎　dermatitis venenata
中毒性葡萄膜炎/中毒性葡萄膜炎　toxic uveitis
中毒性肾[变]病/中毒性腎症　toxic nephrosis
中毒性肾损害/中毒性腎損害　nephrotoxicity
中毒性肾炎/中毒性腎炎　toxic nephritis
中毒性视神经炎/中毒性視神經炎　toxic optic neuritis
中毒性水肿/中毒性水腫　toxic edema
中毒性苔藓状黑皮炎/中毒性苔蘚狀黑皮炎　melanodermatitis toxica lichenoides
中毒性脱发/中毒性秃髮　toxic alopecia
中毒性心肌炎/毒物性心肌炎　toxic myocarditis
中毒性休克综合征/中毒性休克症候群　toxic shock syndrome
中毒性眩晕/中毒性眩暈,毒物性眩暈　toxemic vertigo, toxic vertigo
中毒性眼球震颤/中毒性眼球震顫　toxic nystagmus
中毒[性]谵妄/毒物[性]譫妄　toxic delirium, intoxication delirium
中毒性紫癜/毒物性紫瘢　purpura toxica, toxic purpura
中毒疹/中毒疹　toxic eruption
中风/中風　apoplexy
中风闭证/中風閉證　apoplexy with blocking pattern
中风的/中風的　apoplectic
中风·风火闭窍证/中風·風火閉竅證　apoplexy with pattern of wind-fire blocking orifices
中风·风火上扰证/中風·風火上擾證　apoplexy with pattern of upward disturbance of wind-fire
中风·风痰火亢证/中風·風痰火亢證　apoplexy with pattern of hyperactivity of wind-phlegm-fire
中风·风痰瘀阻证/中風·風痰瘀阻證　apoplexy with pattern of blockade of wind-phlegm-static blood
中风后遗症/中風後遺症　sequelae of apoplexy, sequela of apoplexy
中风·气虚血瘀证/中風·氣虛血瘀證　apoplexy with pattern of qi deficiency and blood stasis
中风·痰火闭窍证/中風·痰火閉竅證　apoplexy with pattern of phlegm-fire blocking orifices
中风·痰火瘀闭证/中風·痰火瘀閉證　apoplexy with pattern of blockade caused by phlegm-fire stasis and blocade
中风·痰热腑实证/中風·痰熱腑實證　apoplexy with pattern of excessive fu-viscera caused by phlegm-heat
中风·痰湿蒙窍证/中風·痰濕蒙竅證　apoplexy with pattern of phlegm-damp clouding orifices
中风·痰湿蒙神证/中風·痰濕蒙神證　apoplexy with pattern of phlegm-damp clouding orifices
中风·痰浊瘀闭证/中風·痰濁瘀閉證　apoplexy with pattern of blockade of phlegm-turbidity and static blood
中风脱证/中風脫證　apoplectic collapse
中风型/中風型　apoplectic type
中风性囊肿/中風性囊腫　apoplectic cyst
中风休克/中風休克　apoplectic shock
中风样败血症/中風樣敗血病　apoplectiform septicemia
中风·阴虚动风证/中風·陰虛動風證　apoplexy with pattern of wind stirring due to yin deficiency
中风·中经络/中風·中經絡　apoplexy involving channel and collateral
中风·中脏腑/中風·中臟腑　apoplexy involving zang and fu-viscera
中风状脊髓炎/中風狀脊髓炎　apoplectiform myelitis
中暑/中暑　heat-stroke, summerheat stroke
仲醇/二級醇　secondary alcohol
众羽之人/眾羽之人　atypical water-phase person, more self-disciplined
种痘后脑炎/接種[疫苗]後腦炎　postvaccinal encephalitis
种植桥基固定桥/種植橋基固定橋　implant fixed bridge
种植体固位/種植體固位　implant retention

种植牙周膜/種植牙周膜　implant periodontal membrane
种植义齿/種植義齒,植入假牙　implant denture
种植义齿美学/種植義齒美學　implant denture aesthetics
种植义齿组织内部结构/種植義齒組織內部結構　substructure of implant denture
种植义齿组织外部结构/種植義齒組織外部結構　superstructure of implant denture
种植桩/種植樁　implant post
重病/重病　advanced disease
重大感染/重大傳染　mass infection
重大医疗保险/重大醫療保險　major medical insurance
重氮苯/重氮苯　diazobenzene
重氮苯磺酸/二偶氮苯磺酸　diazobenzene-sulfonic acid
重氮丝氨酸/重氮之醯絲胺基酸　azaserine
重氮反应/重氮反應　diazo reaction
重氮化合物/重氮化合物　diazo compound
重氮化[作用]/重氮化　diazotization, diazotize
重氮磺苯/重氮磺苯　diazosulfobenzol
重氮甲烷/重氮甲烷　diazomethane
重的/重的　gravis
重度妊高征/重度妊高徵　severe pregnancy-induced hypertension syndrome
重度伤/重度傷　severe injury
重度烧伤/重度燒傷　severe degree burn
重度消瘦型营养不良/重度消瘦型營養不良　marasmus
重铬酸钾/重鉻酸鉀,二鉻酸鉀　potassium dichromate
重铬酸盐/重鉻酸鹽　bichromat
重剂/重劑　heavy formula
重金属/重金屬　heavy metal
重金属中毒性肾病/重金屬中毒性腎病　heavy metal nephropathy
重晶石/重晶石　barite
重酒石酸甲基异吡唑/重酒石酸二甲基二嘧唑啉　lysidine bitartrate
重酒石酸肾上腺素眼溶液/重酒石酸腎上腺素眼用溶液　epinephrine bitartrate ophthalmic solution
重觉/重覺　weight perception
重叩诊/深叩法,重叩法　deep percussion
重离子/重離子　heavy ions
重力/重力　gravity
重力电池/重力電池　gravity cell
重力灌注/重力灌注　gravity perfusion
重力性[下垂]改变/重力性[下垂]改變　gravitational change
重力性休克/引力性休克　gravitation shock
重力性椎管出血/重力性椎管積血　gravitating hemorrhage
重力引流/重力引流　gravity drainage
重力知觉/重力知覺　gravity perception
重链/重鏈　heavy chain
重链病/重鏈[蛋白質]病　heavy chain disease
重链可变区/重鏈可變區　variable region of heavy chain
重链类/重鏈類　heavy chain class
重链亚类/重鏈亞類　heavy chain subclass
重量/重量　weight
重量失认[症]/重覺缺失,壓覺缺失　baragnosis
重硫酸奎宁/雙硫酸奎寧　quinine bisulfate
重氢/重氫　heavy hydrogen
重碳酸钠/重碳酸鈉　bicarbonate sodium
重碳酸盐血/重碳酸鹽血症　bicarbonatemia
重听/重聽　hard of hearing, hearing impairment
重痛/重痛　heavy pain
重物/重物　heavy
重型天花/重症天花　variola major
重性精神病/重性精神病　major psychosis
重性抑郁[症]/重性抑鬱[症]　major depression
重氩/重氬　metargon
重阳必阴/重陽必陰　extreme yang changing into yin
重阳之人/重陽之人　person with excessive yang
重氧/重氧　heavy oxygen
重阴必阳/重陰必陽　extreme yin changing into yang
重阴之人/重陰之人　person with excessive yin
重龈/重齦　swollen gums
重躁狂/重躁狂　acromania
重镇安神/重鎮安神　tranquilization with heavy materials, tranquillization with heavy prescription
重症地中海贫血/重型海洋型貧血　thalassemia major
重症多形[性]红斑/史-强二氏症候群　Stevens-Johnson syndrome
重症黄疸/重症黃疸　icterus gravis
重症肌无力[综合征]/重症肌無力症　myasthenia gravis syndrome, myasthenia gravis
重症监护/加强醫護　intensive care
重症监护病房/重症監護病房　intensive care unit
重症监护急救车/重症監護急救車　mobile intensive care unit
重症监护治疗病房/重症監護治療病房　intensive care unit

重症结肠炎/重症結腸炎,溃疡性结肠炎 colitis gravis
重症联合免疫缺陷/重症聯合免疫缺陷 severe combined immunodeficiency
重[症]痒疹/重型癢疹 prurigo agria
重[症]躁狂/重躁狂病 hypermania
舟车丸/舟車丸 zhouche pill
舟骨粗隆/舟骨粗骨 tuberosity of navicular bone
舟骨关节面/舟骨關節面 navicular articular surface
舟骨结节/舟骨結節 tubercle of scaphoid bone
舟骨炎/舟[狀]骨炎 scaphoiditis
舟甲角/舟甲角 scaphoconchal angle
舟状的/舟狀的 navicular
舟状腹/舟狀腹 boat-shaped abdomen, scaphoid abdomen
舟[状]骨/舟[狀]骨 navicular bone, scaphoid bone
舟[状]骨关节炎/舟[狀]骨關節炎 navicular arthritis
舟[状]肩胛/舟[狀]肩胛 scaphoid scapula
舟状头/舟狀頭 scaphocephaly
舟状头脑积水/舟狀水腦 scaphohydrocephalus
舟状窝/舟狀窩 scaphoid fossa
舟状窝瓣/舟狀窩瓣 valve of navicular fossa
舟状心/舟狀心 boat-shaped heart
周痹/周痺 bi disease with general pain, general arthralgia
周边/周邊 peri
周边的/周邊的,末梢的 peripheral
周边虹膜切除术/周邊虹膜切除術 peripheral iridectomy
周边虹膜切开术/周邊虹膜切開術 peripheral iridotomy
周边视野/周邊視野 peripheral visual field
周边室/周邊室 periphery compartment
周边性嗜中性白细胞减少病/周邊性嗜中性白血球減少病 peripheral neutropenia
周边性秃/周邊性秃髮 alopecia marginalis
周边阻滞/周邊阻滯 parietal block
周径纤维缩短率/周徑纖維縮短率 circumferential fiber shortening rate
周邻症状/鄰近症狀 neighborhood symptom
周皮/周皮 periderm
周皮的/周皮的 perithelial
周皮上皮瘤/外被上皮瘤 periepithelioma
周皮细胞/外被細胞,外被組織,外皮細胞 pericyte, perithelial cell
周皮细胞瘤/周皮細胞瘤 pericytoma
周皮性血管肉瘤/周皮性血管肉瘤 perithelial angiosarcoma
周期/週期 cycle
周期的/週期的 cyclic
周期内线/週期内線 intraperiod line
周期外排卵/額外排卵 paracyclic ovulation
周期性/週期性 periodicity
周期性鼻炎/週期性鼻炎 periodic rhinitis
周期性出血/週期性出血 cyclic hemorrhage
周期性关节痛/週期性關節痛 periodic arthralgia
周期性呼吸/週期性呼吸 periodic respiration
周期性疾病/週期性[疾]病 cyclic disease, periodic disease
周期性甲脱落/週期性甲脱落 periodic shedding of nails
周期性精神病/週期性精神病,更替性精神病 circular psychosis, periodic psychosis
周期性呕吐/週期性嘔吐 cyclic vomiting
周期性水肿/週期性水腫 periodic edema
周期性瘫痪/週期性麻痺 periodic paralysis
周期性透析/週期式透析 periodic dialysis
周期性胃痛/週期性胃病,胃週期痛 gastroperiodynia
周期性中性白细胞减少/週期性嗜中性白血球減少 cyclic neutropenia
周期性紫癜/週期性紫癜 periodic purpura
周染细胞/周染細胞 perichrome
周韧维管束/周韌型維管束 amphicribral vascular bundle
周荣/周榮 zhourong, SP20
周视镜片/周視透鏡 periscopic lens
周视眼镜/周視眼鏡 periscopic spectacle
周围暗点/外周暗點 peripheral scotoma
周围动脉[动脉]瘤/末梢性動脈瘤 peripheral aneurysm
周围二联微管/周圍二聯微管 peripheral diplomicrotubule
周围淋巴[样]器官/周圍淋巴樣器官,次級淋巴器官 peripheral lymphoid organ
周围神经/周圍神經 peripheral nerve
周围神经病变/周邊神經病變 peripheral neuropathy
周围神经卡压症/周圍神經卡壓症 peripheral entrapment neuropathy
周围神经手术/周圍神經手術 operation on peripheral nerve
周围神经痛/周圍神經痛,末梢神經痛 peripheral neuralgia
周围神经系统/周圍神經系統 peripheral nervous system, PNS

周围神经系统疾病/周圍神經系統疾病　peripheral nervous system disease
周围神经系统药/周圍神經系統藥　peripheral nervous system agent
周围神经系统肿瘤/周圍神經系統腫瘤　peripheral nervous system neoplasm
周围性感觉缺失/末梢性感覺缺失　peripheral anesthesia
周围性眩晕/末梢性眩暈　peripheral vertigo
周围支/周圍[神經]支　peripheral branch
周围紫绀/周圍[性]發紺　peripheral cyanosis
周细胞/周細胞　pericyte
周相运动/周相運動　phase motion
粥样斑/粥瘤　atheroma
粥样斑块/粥樣斑塊　atheromatous plaque
粥样角膜溃疡/粥樣角膜潰瘍　atheromatous corneal ulcer
粥样泻性幼稚型/粥狀瀉性幼稚型　celiac infantilism
粥样[硬]化性溃疡/粥瘤性潰瘍　atheromatous ulcer
Y轴/Y軸　Y axis
轴壁/軸壁　axial wall
轴测器/測軸器　axometer
轴的/軸的　axial
轴后肌/軸後肌　postaxial muscle
轴-棘突触/軸-棘[神經元]突觸　axo-spinous synapse
轴流/軸流　axial current
轴面/軸面　axial surface
轴膜/軸膜　axolemma
轴旁中胚层/軸旁中胚層　paraxial mesoderm
轴偏心/軸偏向　axis deviation
轴牵引/軸牽引　axis traction
轴前肌/軸前肌　preaxial muscle
轴丘/軸丘　axon hillock
轴三叉/軸三叉　axial triradius
轴上躯干肌/軸上[軀幹]肌　epiaxial muscle
轴-树突触/軸-樹突觸　axo-dendritic synapse
轴丝/軸[纖]絲　axial filament, axoneme
轴索/軸索　neurite, axis-cylinder
轴-体突触/軸-體突觸　axo-somatic synapse
轴突/軸突　axon
轴突变性/軸突變性　axonal degeneration
轴突蛋白/軸突蛋白　neuronin
轴突的/軸突的　axonal
轴突断伤/軸突斷傷　axonotmesis
轴突反射/軸突反射　axon reflex
轴突反应/軸突反應　axon reaction
轴突海绵质/軸突海綿狀質　axospongium
轴突颈/軸突頸　cervix of axon
轴突裂支/軸突裂支　schizaxon
轴突起始段/軸突起始段　initial segment of axon
轴突切断术/軸突切除術　axotomy
轴突神经病/軸突神經病變　axonal neuropathy
轴突输送/軸突運輸　axonal transport
轴[突]系膜/軸突繫膜,中軸索,中軸類　mesaxon
轴突运输/軸突運輸　axonal transport
轴伪足/有軸偽足　axiopodium
轴下躯干肌/軸下[軀幹]肌　hypaxial muscle
轴小体/軸小體　axile corpuscle
轴心复合体/軸心複合體　core complex
轴型皮瓣/軸型皮瓣　axial pattern skin flap
轴型血管/軸型血管　axial pattern blood vessel
轴性近视/軸性近視　axial myopia
轴性屈光不正/軸性不正視　axial ametropia
轴性视神经炎/軸性視神經炎　axial optic neuritis
轴性远视/軸性遠視　axial hypermetropia
轴右偏心电图/右描記波　dextrogram
轴质/軸質,軸漿　axoplasm
轴质流/軸質流,軸漿流　axoplasmic flow
轴周间隙/軸周間隙　periaxonal space
轴-轴突触/軸-軸突觸　axo-axonic synapse
轴状动脉瘤/軸狀動脈瘤　axial aneurysm
肘/肘　elbow, zhou, SF3
肘部筋伤/肘部筋傷　injury of elbow fascia
肘尺韧带/肘尺韌帶　cubitoulnar ligament
肘的/肘的　cubital
肘反射/肘反射　elbow jerk
肘骨间囊/肘骨間囊　interosseous cubital bursa
肘骨折/肘骨折　cubital fracture
肘拐/肘拐　elbow crutch
肘关节/肘關節　elbow joint, cubital joint, articulation of elbow
肘关节病/肘關節病　olecranarthropathy
肘关节肌/肘關節肌　articularis cubiti
肘关节结核/肘關節結核　tuberculosis of elbow joint
肘关节囊状隐窝/肘關節囊狀隱窩　accessory recess of elbow
肘关节脱位/肘關節脱位,曲肘骱出　dislocation of elbow joint, elbow dislocation
肘关节网/肘關節網　cubital articular rete, articular cubital rete
肘关节炎/肘關節炎　anconitis
肘管综合征/肘管症候群　cubital tunnel syndrome, elbow tunnel syndrome
肘后备急方/肘後備急方　Handbook of Prescriptions for Emergency

肘后肌/肘後肌　musculus anconeus
肘后区/肘後部　posterior cubital region
肘后三角/肘後三角　posterior cubital triangle
肘后窝/肘後窝　posterior cubital fossa
肘肌/肘肌　anconeus, anconeus muscle
肘尖点/肘尖點　olecranon point
肘尖[穴]/肘尖[穴]　zhoujian, EX-UE1
肘髎/肘髎　zhouliao, LI12
肘淋巴结/肘淋巴結　cubital lymph node
肘内侧韧带/肘内側韌帶　medial ligament of elbow
肘内翻/肘内翻　cubitus varus
肘前区/肘前部　anterior cubital region
肘浅淋巴结/肘淺淋巴結　superficial cubital lymph node
肘屈曲前旋畸形/肘屈曲前旋畸形　flexion pronation deformity of elbow
肘桡韧带/肘橈韌帶　cubitoradial ligament
肘深淋巴结/肘深淋巴結　deep cubital lymph node
肘痛风/肘痛風　pechyagra
肘痛风症/肘關節痛　anconagra
肘外侧三角/肘外側三角　lateral cubital triangle
肘外翻/肘外翻　cubitus valgus
肘窝/肘窩　cubital fossa, antecubital fossae
肘痈/肘癰　elbow abscess
肘正中静脉/肘正中静脈　median cubital vein
帚霉病/小帚樣黴菌病　scopulariopsosis
帚霉属/小帚樣黴菌屬　Scopulariopsis
咒禁博士/咒禁博士　erudite for exorcism
绉布绷带/縐布繃帶　crepe bandage
昼间的/晝間的　diurnal
昼间尿频/晝尿症，白晝多尿　diuria
昼惊/晝驚　pavor diurnus
昼盲/晝盲　day blindness
昼盲者/晝盲[患]者　hemeralope
昼暝/晝暝　no energy in daytime
昼现幼丝虫/晝現幼絲蟲　Filaria diurna
昼夜的/晝夜的　nyctohemeral
昼夜节律/晝夜節律　circadian rhythm
昼夜节律性睡眠障碍/晝夜節律性睡眠障礙　circadian rhythm sleep disorder
昼夜性节律/晝夜性律動　nyctohemeral rhythm
昼遗[精]/晝遺精　diurnal pollution
皱襞/皺襞　fold, plica
皱襞缝术/皺襞縫術　plicating suture
皱襞集中/皺襞集中　converging fold
皱襞舌/溝狀舌　lingua plicata
皱痕/皺褶　crease
皱眉肌/皺眉肌　corrugator supercilii
皱缩变性/皺縮變性　crenation degeneration
皱缩耳/皺縮耳　atelectatic ear
皱缩红细胞症/皺縮紅血球症　crenocytosis
皱胃/皺胃　abomasum
皱纹/皺紋　wrinkle
皱纹皮肤综合征/皺紋皮膚症候群　wrinkly skin syndrome
皱纹整形术/皺紋整形術　rhytidoplasty
皱褶/褶皺　crease
皱褶性厚皮症/皺褶性厚皮症　pachydermia plicature
皱褶缘/皺褶緣　ruffled border
骤进暴露疗法/驟進暴露療法　flooding therapy
朱厄特钉/朱爾特氏釘　Jewett nail
朱[姆布希]氏型全身性脓疱性银屑病/聰布施型全身性膿皰性乾癬　Zumbusch psoriasis
朱砂/朱砂　cinnabar
朱砂安神丸/朱砂安神丸　sedative bolus, zhusha anshen pill
朱砂点/朱砂點　spot of oil cavity
朱砂掌/朱砂掌　cinnabar palm
朱震亨/朱震亨　Zhu Zhenheng
侏儒/侏儒[症]　dwarf, dwarfism
侏儒节细胞/侏儒節細胞　midget ganglion cell
侏儒菌落/侏儒菌叢　dwarf colony
侏儒双极细胞/侏儒雙極細胞　midget bipolar cell
侏儒症/侏儒狀態，侏儒病　dwarfism
β-珠蛋白基因/乙型球蛋白基因　beta-globin gene
珠蛋白基因簇/珠蛋白基因簇　globin gene cluster
珠蛋白锌胰岛素/球蛋白鋅胰島素　globin zinc insulin
珠蛋白胰岛素/球蛋白胰島素　globin insulin
珠突出眶/珠突出眶　eyeball protrusion related to head position
珠样小结/牛結核病結　pearly nodule
珠中气动/珠中氣動　vitreous opacity
珠子参/珠子參　largeleaf Japanese ginseng rhizome
诸病源候论/諸病源候論　General Treatise on Causes and Manifestations of All Diseases, Treatise on Causes and Symptoms of Diseases
猪鼻支原体/豬鼻黴漿菌　Mycoplasma hyorhinis
猪草属/豬草屬　Ambrosia
猪肠道孤病毒/豬腸道孤病毒　enteric cytopathogenic swine orphan virus
猪丹毒/豬丹毒　swine erysipelas
猪胆汁白蛋白/豬霍亂弧菌蛋白　sucholoalbumin
猪的/豬的　porcine
猪甘氨胆酸/豬甘膽酸　hyoglycocholic acid
猪霍乱病毒/豬霍亂病毒　hog cholera virus

猪苓/豬苓　zhuling
猪苓汤/豬苓湯　zhuling decoction
猪流行性感冒/豬流行性感冒　swine influenza
猪毛菜碱类/豬毛菜鹼類　salsoline alkaloids
猪囊尾蚴病/豬囊尾蚴病　cysticercosis cellulosae
猪肉/豬肉　pork
猪饲养员病/豬飼養員病　swineherd disease
猪牙皂/豬牙皂　Chinese honeylocust abnormal fruit
蛛毒溶血素/蜘蛛溶血素　arachnolysin
蛛毒中毒/蜘蛛[咬]中毒　arachnoidism
蛛网膜/蛛網膜　arachnoid mater, arachnoid
蛛网膜[颗]粒/蛛[網]膜粒　arachnoid granulation
蛛网膜囊肿/蛛網膜囊腫　arachnoid cyst
蛛网膜绒毛/蛛網膜絨毛,蜘蛛膜絨毛　arachnoid villi, villi of arachnoid
蛛网膜下的/蛛網膜下的　subarachnoid
蛛网膜下池/蛛網膜下池　subarachnoid cistern
蛛网膜下腔/蛛網膜下腔　subarachnoid cavity
蛛网膜下腔出血/蛛網膜下腔出血　subarachnoid hemorrhage
蛛网膜下腔麻醉/蛛網膜下腔麻醉[法]　subarachnoid anesthesia
蛛网膜下腔阻滞/蛛網下膜阻斷　subarachnoid block
蛛网膜下隙/蛛網膜下隙　subarachnoid space
蛛网膜下液/蛛網膜下液　subarachnoid fluid
蛛网膜炎/蛛網膜炎　arachnoiditis
蛛网状孔/蛛網狀孔　arachnoid foramen
蛛状腹/蛛狀腹　arachnogastria
蛛状毛细血管扩张/蛛狀毛細血管擴張　spider telangiectasia
蛛状痣/蛛狀痣　nevus araneus
潴留囊肿/瀦留囊腫　retention cyst
潴留性黄疸/停滯性黃疸　retention jaundice
潴留性尿毒症/滯留性尿素症　retention uraemia
竹罐/竹罐　bamboo jar
竹节发/竹樣毛　bamboo hair
竹节参/竹節參　Japanese ginseng
竹节样脊柱/竹狀椎骨　bamboo spine
竹节样结节/竹節樣結節　bamboo-like node
竹节状发炎性浸润/竹節狀發炎性浸潤　bamboo-like inflammatory infiltrate
竹林寺女科/竹林寺女科　Bamboo Forest Temple's Secret on Women's Diseases
竹茹/竹茹　bamboo shavings
竹桃霉素/夾竹桃黴素　Oleandomycin
竹叶石膏汤/竹葉石膏湯　zhuye shigao decoction
竹叶汤/竹葉湯　Lophatherum decoction
逐步判别分析/逐步判別分析　stepwise discriminate analysis
逐水剂/逐水劑　drastic diuretics formula
主成分/主成分　main constituent
主成分分析/主成分分析　principal component analysis, PCA
主成分回归法/主成分回歸法　principal component regression method
主[导]基因/主[導]基因,主控基因　master gene
主动安乐死/主動安樂死　active euthanasia
主动病例发现/主動病例發現　active case finding
主动过敏反应/主動過敏性　active anaphylaxis
主动肌/催動肌　agonistic muscle
主动脉/主動脈　aorta
[主动脉]半月瓣弧缘/[主動脈]半月瓣弧緣　lunula of semilunar valve
[主动脉]半月瓣小结/[主動脈]半月瓣小結　nodule of semilunar valve
主动脉瓣/主動脈瓣　aortic valve
主动脉瓣闭锁/主動脈瓣閉鎖　aortic atresia
主动脉瓣反流/主動脈[口]反流　aortic regurgitation
主动脉瓣关闭不全/主動脈瓣閉鎖不全　aortic incompetence
主动脉瓣后半月瓣/主動脈瓣後半月瓣　posterior semilunar valve of aortic valve
主动脉瓣环扩大成形术/主動脈瓣環擴大成形術　aortic annulus plastic enlargement
主动脉瓣口面积/主動脈瓣口面積　aortic valve orifice area
主动脉瓣脱垂/主動脈瓣脫垂　aortic valve prolapse
主动脉瓣狭窄/主動脈瓣狹窄　aortic valve stenosis
主动脉瓣右半月瓣/主動脈瓣右半月瓣　right semilunar valve of aortic valve
主动脉瓣与二尖瓣置换术/主動脈瓣與二尖瓣置換術　aortic and mitral valve replacement
主动脉瓣杂音/主動脈[瓣]雜音　aortic murmur
主动脉瓣左半月瓣/主動脈瓣左半月瓣　left semilunar valve of aortic valve
主动脉病/主動脈病　aortopathy
主动脉部分切除术/主動脈部分切除術　aortectomy
主动脉插管[术]/主動脈插管[術]　aortic cannulation
主动脉杈/主動脈杈　aortic bifurcation
主动脉肠瘘/主動脈腸瘺[管]　aortoenteric fistula
主动脉成形术/主動脈整型術　aortoplasty
主动脉窗/主動脈窗　aortic window
主动脉丛/主動脈叢　plexus aorticus
主动脉的/主動脈的　aortic
主动脉窦/主動脈竇　aortic sinus

主动脉窦瘤/主動脈竇瘤　aneurysm of aortic sinus
主动脉窦瘘管/主動脈竇瘻管　aortic sinus fistula
主动脉肺动脉窗/肺主動脈窗　aorticopulmonary window
主动脉肺动脉隔/主動脈肺動脈隔　aorticopulmonary septum
主动脉肺动脉间隔缺损/主動脈肺動脈間隔缺損,主動脈肺動脈間隔缺陷　aortopulmonary septal defect
主动脉缝合术/主動脈縫合術　aortorrhaphy
主动脉干/主動脈幹,大動脈幹　truncus aortae
主动脉根/主動脈根　aortic root
主动脉弓/主動脈弓　aortic arch, arch of aorta
主动脉弓病/主動脈弓病　aortic arch disease
主动脉弓节/主動脈弓節　aortic knuckle
主动脉弓离断/主動脈弓離斷　interruption of aortic arch
主动脉弓淋巴结/主動脈弓淋巴結　lymph node of aortic arch
主动脉弓延长/主動脈弓延長　elongation of aortic arch
主动脉弓综合征/主動脈弓症候群　aortic arch syndrome
主动脉沟/主動脈溝　aortic sulcus
主动脉固定术/主動脈固定術　aortopexy
主动脉冠状动脉大隐静脉旁路移植术/主動脈冠狀動脈大隱靜脈旁路移植術　aortocoronary arterial saphenous vein bypass grafting
主动脉冠状动脉动脉管道旁路移植术/主動脈冠狀動脈動脈管道旁路移植術　aortocoronary arterial conduit bypass grafting
主动脉冠状动脉分流术/主動脈冠狀動脈分流術　aortocoronary bypass
主动脉冠状动脉腹壁下动脉旁路移植术/主動脈冠狀動脈腹壁下動脈旁路移植術　aortocoronary inferior epigastric artery bypass grafting
主动脉冠状动脉旁路移植术/主動脈冠狀動脈旁路移植術　aortocoronary bypass grafting
主动脉冠状动脉桡动脉旁路移植术/主動脈冠狀動脈橈動脈旁路移植術　aortocoronary radial artery bypass grafting
主动脉冠状动脉胃网膜动脉旁路移植术/主動脈冠狀動脈胃網膜動脈旁路移植術　aortocoronary gastroepiploic artery bypass grafting
主动脉冠状动脉胸廓内动脉旁路移植术/主動脈冠狀動脈胸廓內動脈旁路移植術　aortocoronary internal mammary artery bypass grafting
主动脉横断/主動脈橫斷　transection of aorta
主动脉横断钳闭术/主動脈橫斷鉗閉術　aortic cross clamping
主动脉后淋巴结/主動脈後淋巴結　postaortic lymph node
主动脉环扩张症/主動脈環擴張　annuloaortic ectasia
主动脉疾病/主動脈疾病　aortic disease
主动脉夹层/主動脈夾層　dissection of aorta
主动脉夹层[动脉]瘤/主動脈夾層[動脈]瘤　dissecting aneurysm of aorta
主动脉口/主動脈口　aortic orifice
主动脉裂孔/主動脈裂孔　aortic hiatus
主动脉瘤/主動脈瘤　aortic aneurysm
主动脉瘤间置修复术/主動脈瘤間置修復術　interposition repair of aortic aneurysm
主动脉内膜炎/主動脈內膜炎　endaortitis
主动脉内球囊泵/主動脈內球囊泵　intraaortic balloon pumping
主动脉内球囊反搏/主動脈內球囊反搏　intraaortic balloon counterpulsation
主动脉旁体/主動脈旁體　paraaortic body
主动脉破裂/主動脈破裂　aortic rupture
主动脉髂动脉分流术/主動脈髂動脈分流術　aortoiliac bypass
主动脉前淋巴结/主動脈前淋巴結　preaortic lymph node
主动脉切开术/主動脈切開術　aortotomy
主动脉球/主動脈球　aortic bulb, bulb of aorta
主动脉神经/主動脈神經　aortic nerve
主动脉肾神经节/主動脈腎神經節　aorticorenal ganglion
主动脉松开钳闭综合征/主動脈鬆開鉗閉症候群　aortic declamping syndrome
主动脉梭/主動脈梭　aortic spindle
主动脉缩窄/主動脈縮窄　aortic coarctation
主动脉缩窄切除术/主動脈縮窄切除術　resection of coarctation of aorta
主动脉体/主動脈體　aortic body
主动脉痛/主動脈痛　aortalgia
主动脉外侧淋巴结/主動脈外側淋巴結　lateral aortic lymph node
主动脉峡/主動脈峽　aortic isthmus
主动脉狭窄/主動脈狹窄　aorta stenosis
主动脉下淋巴结/主動脈下淋巴結　subaortic lymph node
主动脉小球/主動脈小球　aortic glomera
主动脉心室成形术/主動脈心室成形術　aortoventriculoplasty
主动脉血流/主動脈血流　aortic flow

主动脉血流阻断/主動脈血流阻斷　aortic occlusion
主动脉压/主動脈壓　aortic pressure
主动脉炎/主動脈炎　aortitis
主动脉硬化/主動脈硬化　aortosclerosis
主动脉造影术/主動脈 X 光攝影法　aortography
主动脉震颤/主動脈震顫　aortic thrill
主动脉周围炎/主動脈周圍炎　periaortitis
主动脉阻塞/主動脈阻塞　aortic obstruction
主动免疫/主動免疫　active immunity
主动免疫疗法/主動免疫療法　active immunotherapy
主动生物转运/主動生物轉運　active biological transport
主动性白细胞增多/主動性白血球增多　active leukocytosis
主动性违拗/主動拒絕症,主動違拗症　active negativism
主动性运动/主動性活動　active motion
主动运动/自動練習　active exercise
主动助力运动/主動助力運動　active assistant exercise
主动转运/主動轉運,主動運輸　active transport
主段/主段　principal piece
主观的/主觀的　subjective
主观性耳鸣/自覺性耳鳴　subjective tinnitus
主观眩晕/自體性眩暈　subjective vertigo
主观状态/主觀狀態　subjective state
主基因/主基因　major gene
主径/主徑　principal tract
主静脉/主靜脈　cardinal vein
主客配穴法/主客配穴法　host-guest points association, host-guest points combination
主链/主鏈　backbone
主模型/主模型　master cast
主脑说/主腦説　theory of the brain dominating mental activity
主凝集素/主凝集素　principal agglutinin
主气/主氣　host climatic qi
主桥基/主橋基　primary abutment
主任医师/主任醫師　chief physician
主韧带/主韌帶　cardinal ligament
主色/主色　governing complexion
主视检查器/主視檢查器　manoptoscope
主题词/主題詞　subject heading
主题理解测验/主題自覺試驗　thematic apperception test
主题性逻辑倒错/專題性錯論症　thematic paralogia
主细胞/主細胞　principal cell, chief cell

主纤维/主纖維　principal fiber
主线/主線　main line
主线横向指数/主線橫向指數　main line index of transversality
主线指数/主線指數　main line index
主心说/主心説　theory of the heart dominating mental activity
主要代谢产物/基本代謝產物　essential metabolite
主要疾病/主要疾病　principal disease
主［要］凝集［反应］/主凝集　chief agglutination
主要症状/主要症狀　cardinal symptom
主要组织相容性复合体基因/主要組織相容性複合體基因　major histocompatibility complex gene
主要组织相容性复合物/主要組織相容性複合物　major histocompatibility complex
主要组织相容性系统/主要組織相容性系統　major histocompatibility system
主胰管/主胰管　main pancreatic duct
主缢痕/主縊痕　primary constriction
主运/主運　host evolutive phase
主支气管/主支氣管　primary bronchus
主致密线/主致密線　major dense line
主［轴］平面/主軸平面　principal plane
煮沸疫苗/煮沸疫苗　koktigen
煮散/煮散　boiled powder, powder for boiling
煮［制］/煮［製］,煮沸　boiling
助癌剂/助癌劑　cocarcinogen
助产杠杆/助產槓杆,彎槓杆　vectis
助产士/助產士　nurse midwife
助产学/助產學,産科學　midwifery
助感器/助感器　sensory aid
助理护士/助理護士　nurse's aide
助力运动/助力運動　assistant exercise
助流剂/助滑劑　glidant
助滤器/助濾器　filter aid
助色团/增色團　auxochrome
助视器/助視器　visual acuity aid
助听器/助聽器　hearing aid
助听器皮炎/助聽器皮［膚］炎　hearing-aid dermatitis
助消化药/消化藥［劑］,健胃腸藥　digestant, digestive tonic
助行器/助行器　walker
助悬剂/助懸劑　suspending agent
助阳解表/助陽解表　reinforcing yang to relieve exterior
助荧光物/增螢光質　auxoflore
助孕药/助孕劑　proconceptive
住根异皮线虫/住根異皮線蟲,附根線蟲

Heterodera radicicola
住院/住院　hospital admission
住院保险/住院保險　hospitalization insurance
住院病人/住院病人　inpatient
住院儿童/住院兒童　hospitalized child
住院期间审核/住院期間審核　concurrent review
住院青少年/住院青少年　hospitalized adolescent
住院时间/住院時間　length of stay
住院外科医师/外科住院醫師　house surgeon
住院医师/住院醫師　house physician
贮藏/貯藏,備藏,貯積　storage
贮存/貯存　depot
贮积病/貯積病,沈著病　thesaurismosis disease
贮积症/貯積症　thesaurosis
贮气囊/貯氣囊　reservoir bag
贮脂细胞/貯脂細胞　fat-storing cell
注气疗法/氣胭療法　emphysatherapy
注射/注射　injections
注射泵/注射泵　syringe pump
注射法/注射法　injection method
注射过速性休克/注射過速性休克　speed shock
注射剂/注射[劑]　injection
注射器/注射器,注射筒　injector, syringe
注射[器]针[头]/注射器針頭　syringe needle
注射用灭菌制品/注射用無菌製品　sterile product for injection
注射用容器/注射用容器　container for injection
注射[用溶]液/注射用溶液　parenteral solution
注射用水/注射用水　water for injection
注视点/注視點　point of fixation
注视角/定向角　angle of direction
注视平面/注視平面　plane of regard
注视眼/注視眼　fixating eye
注视抑制指数/注視抑制指數　ocular fixation index
注水解剖术/注水解剖術　hydrotomy
注意过强/注意力過度,注意力增強　hyperprosexia
注意力/注意力　attention
注意力缺陷障碍伴多动/注意力缺陷障礙伴多動　attention deficit disorder with hyperactivity, attention deficit hyperactivity disorder
注意力障碍/注意力障礙　disturbance of attention
驻车丸/駐車丸　zhuche pill
柱/柱　columna
柱超载/柱超載　column overload
柱后衍生化/[管]柱後衍生化　post-column derivatization
柱间区/柱間區　interprismatic region
柱间物质/齒釉質之釉柱間質　interprismatic substance
柱晶/柱晶　styloid
柱晶白霉素类/柱晶白黴素類　leucomycins
柱镜片/柱面透鏡　cylindrical lens
柱前衍生化/[管]柱前衍生化　pre-column derivatization
柱切换/柱切換　column switching
柱上检测器/柱上檢測器　on-column detector
柱上进样器/管柱進樣器　on-column injector
柱状的/[圓]柱狀的　cylindrical
柱状关节/柱狀關節,筒狀關節　cylindrarthrosis
柱状上皮/柱狀上皮　columnar epithelium
柱状上皮癌/柱狀上皮癌　carcinoma cylindrocellulare
柱状上皮瘤/柱狀上皮瘤　cylindrical epithelioma
柱状细胞/[圓]柱狀細胞　columnar cell, cylindrical cell
柱状细胞癌/柱狀細胞癌　carcinoma cylindrical
柱状细胞的/柱狀細胞的　cylindrocellular
柱子/[支]柱　pillar
祝福状手/祝福狀手　benediction hand
祝说病由/祝說病由　prayer-healing incantation and talisman
祝由/祝由　prayer-healing incantation and talisman
祝由科/祝由科　department of incantation and psychology, prayer-healing incantation and talisman
疰夏/疰夏　summer non-acclimation, summer non-acclimatization
蛀节疔/蛀節疔　ding of finger condyle
铸道针/鑄道針　sprue pin
铸工热/黄銅匠熱,金屬煙熱　brass chill
铸液/鑄液　cast dressing
铸造唇杆/鑄造唇桿　casting labial bar
铸造顶盖/鑄造頂蓋　casting coping
铸造冠/鑄造冠　cast crown
铸造冠夹板/鑄造冠夾板　cast cap splint
铸造卡环/鑄造卡環　cast clasp
铸造蜡/鑄造蠟　casting wax
铸造圈/鑄造圈　casting ring
铸造型盒/鑄造型盒　casting flask
筑宾/築賓　zhubin, KI9
抓痕/抓痕　scratch mark, scratch
抓伤/抓破　scratching
抓伤恐惧症/抓傷恐懼症　amychophobia
抓握反射/抓握反射　grasping reflex
爪/爪[形]　claw
爪蟾/有爪蟾蜍　Xenopus laevis
爪蟾蛋白质类/爪蟾蛋白質類　xenopus proteins
爪甲毛发发育异常/爪甲毛髮發育異常

onychotrichodysplasia
爪切法/爪切法　nail pressing needle inserting
爪形手/爪形手　claw hand deformity
爪形趾/爪形趾　claw toe
爪形足/爪形足　claw foot
爪状挖匙/爪針　cleoid
专家委员会/專家委員會　professional staff committee
专家系统/專家系統　expert system
专科医院/專科醫院　special hospital
专利药/專利藥[品]　patent drug, patent medicine
专卖药/專賣藥　patented medicine
专门订制化学品/專門訂制化學品　custom chemical
专门订制中间体/專門訂制中間體　custom intermediate
专性寄生物/專性[活物]寄生物　obligatory parasite
专业机构康复/專業機構康復　institution-based-rehabilitation
专业教育/專業教育　professional education
专业人员关系/專業人員關係　interprofessional relationship
专业委员会/專業委員會　specialty board
专一性/專一性　specificity
专用化学品/專用化學品　specialty use of chemical
专用食品/專用食品　specialized food
转氨酶类/轉氨酶類　transaminases
转白反应/褪色反應　blanching reaction
转白现象/褪色現象　blanching phenomenon
转变的/轉變的,過渡的　transitional
转变温度/轉變溫度　transition temperature
转呆丹/轉呆丹　dementia treatment pill
转导/轉導　transduction
转导素/轉導蛋白　transducin
转导子/轉導子　transductant
转谷酰胺酶/轉穀醯胺酶　transglutaminases
转钴胺素类/轉鈷胺素類　transcobalamins
转归/轉歸　sequelae
转化/轉化　transformation
转化基因/轉化基因　transformed gene
转化克隆/轉化克隆　transformed clone
转化瘤/轉變瘤　transition tumor
转化酶/轉化酶　convertase
转化生长因子/轉化生長因子　transforming growth factor
转化糖/轉化糖　invertose
转化体/轉化體,轉移體　transformant
转化细胞系/轉化細胞系　transformed cell line
转化子/轉化子　transformant

转换部位/轉換部位　switch site
转换反应/轉化反應　conversion reaction
转换寄生/異種寄生,易主寄生　metaxeny
转换区/轉換區　switch region
转换性癔病/轉換性癔病　conversion hysteria
转[性]障碍/轉換[性]障礙　conversive disorder, conversion disorder
转基因/轉基因　transgene
转基因动物/轉基因動物,基因轉殖動物　transgenic animal
转流前滤器/轉流前濾器　pre-bypass filter
转录/轉錄　transcription
转录沉默子/轉錄沈默子　transcriptional silencer element
转录酶/轉錄酶　transcriptase
转录启动子/轉錄啟動子　transcription initiation site
转录起始位点/轉錄起始位點　transcriptional start site
转录学说/轉錄學說　transcription theory
转录延伸因子类/轉錄延伸因子類　transcriptional elongation factors
转录因子/轉錄因子　transcription factor
转录终止区/轉錄終止區　transcription termination region
转录子/轉錄子　transcripton
转醛醇酶/轉醛醇酶　transaldolase
转染/轉[移感]染　transfection
转输细胞/轉輸細胞　transfusion cell
转胎位术/倒轉術　version
转糖苷作用/轉酶苷作用,糖基轉移作用　transglycosidation
转铁蛋白/運鐵蛋白,鐵傳遞蛋白　transferrin
转铁蛋白缺乏/運鐵蛋白缺乏　transferrin deficiency
转铁蛋白受体/轉鐵蛋白受體　transferrin receptor
转铁结合蛋白质类/轉鐵結合蛋白質類　transferrin-binding proteins
转酮醇酶/轉酮醇酶,酮醇基轉移酶　transketolase
转位不全/轉位不全　arrested rotation
转位皮瓣/轉位皮瓣　transposition skin flap
转卧呼吸/轉臥呼吸,折身呼吸　trepopnea
转续宿主/[替代]中間宿主　paratenic host
转移/轉移　metastasizing
转移癌/轉移癌　metastatic cancer
转移 RNA 氨酰化/轉移 RNA 胺醯化　transfer RNA aminoacylation
转移到神经/轉移到神經　metastasis ad nervos
转移的/轉移的　metastatic
转移盖/轉移蓋　transfer coping

转移活动/轉移活動　transfer activity
转移酶/轉移酶　transferase
转移细胞/轉移細胞　emigrated cell
转移[性]癌/轉移性癌　metastatic carcinoma
转移性败血病/轉移性敗血病　metastasizing septicemia
转移性肺炎/轉移性肺炎　metastatic pneumonia
转移性睾丸炎/轉移性睾丸炎　metastatic orchitis
转移性脑膜炎/轉移性腦膜炎　metastatic meningitis
转移性脓毒败血病/轉移性膿毒敗血病　metastatic septicopyemia
转移性脓肿/轉移性膿腫　metastatic abscess
转移性腮腺炎/轉移性腮腺炎　metastatic mumps
转移性肾炎/轉移性腎炎　metastatic nephritis
转移性视网膜炎/遷徙性視網膜炎　metastatic retinitis
转移性炎症/遷徙性炎症　metastatic inflammation
转移因子/轉移因子　transfer factor
转移组件/轉移元件　transition element
转译蛋白质修饰/轉譯蛋白質修飾　translational protein modification
转院协议/轉院協議　transfer agreement
转运小泡/轉運小泡　transport vesicle
转座/轉座　transposition
转座酶类/轉座酶類　transposases
转座子/轉座子　transposon
转座子解体酶类/轉座子解體酶類　transposon resolvases
转座组件/轉座組件　transposable element
转矩成形钳/轉矩成形鉗　torque bending plier
转矩辅弓/轉矩輔弓　torquing auxiliary arch
转矩托槽/轉矩托槽　torque slot bracket
转轮镊/轉輪鑷　roller forcep
转门法/轉門法　swing-door method
转陀螺样杂音/轉陀螺狀雜音　humming-top murmur
转子成形术/轉子成形術，粗隆成形術　trochanterplasty
转子的/轉子的，粗隆的　trochanteric
转子骨折/轉子骨折　trochanteric fracture
转子间嵴/粗隆間嵴　intertrochanteric crest
转子间线/粗隆間線　intertrochanteric line
转子流速计/轉子流速計　rotameter
转子皮下囊/轉子皮下囊　subcutaneous trochanteric bursa
转子窝/粗隆凹　trochanteric fossa
转子下切骨术/粗隆下截骨術　subtrochanteric osteotomy

转筋/痙攣　spasm
桩冠/合釘繼續牙冠　post crown
桩核技术/樁核技術　post and core technique
装盒/裝型盒　flasking
装甲心/裝甲心，盔甲心　armour heart
装胶囊/膠囊貯藥，膠囊製劑　capsulation
装量差异/含量均一度　content uniformity
装相/刻板式舉動，頰板式言行，習癖　mannerism
装置/裝置，配備　device, fitting
壮/壯　one moxa-cone
壮骨关节丸/壯骨關節丸　zhuanggu guanjie pill
壮观霉素/壯觀黴素　spectinomycin
壮年期/壯年期，繼青春期　postadolescence
壮年人/年青成人　postadolescent
壮年秃发/早老性秃髮　alopecia presenilis
壮热/壯熱　high fever
壮水制阳/壯水制陽　strengthening governor of water for restraining hyperactivity of yang
壮阳/壯陽　strengthening yang
状态/狀態　state
撞击力/撞擊力　impact force
撞击伤/撞擊傷　impact injury
撞击伤目/撞擊傷目　ocular contusion
撞击伤目·风热犯目证/撞擊傷目·風熱犯目證　ocular contusion with pattern of wind-heat assailing eye
撞击伤目·气滞血瘀证/撞擊傷目·氣滯血瘀證　ocular contusion with pattern of qi stagnation and blood stasis
撞击性耳鸣/滴答狀耳鳴　clicking tinnitus
椎板成形术/椎板成形[手]術　laminoplasty
椎板切除术/椎板切除術　laminectomy
椎板切开术/椎板切開術　laminotomy
椎底动脉供血不足/椎底動脈供血不足　vertebrobasilar insufficiency
椎动脉/椎動脈　vertebral artery
椎动脉丛/椎動脈叢，[交感神經系]脊椎叢　vertebral plexus
椎动脉沟/椎動脈溝　groove for vertebral artery
椎动脉横突部/椎動脈橫突部　transverse part of vertebral artery
椎动脉寰椎部/椎動脈寰椎部　atlantic part of vertebral artery
椎动脉肌支/椎動脈肌支　muscular branch of vertebral artery
椎动脉脊支/椎動脈脊支　spinal branch of vertebral artery
椎动脉颈段狭窄/椎頸動脈狹窄　caroticovertebral

stenosis
椎动脉颅内部/椎動脈顱内部　intracranial part of vertebral artery
椎动脉脑膜支/椎動脈腦膜支　meningeal branch of vertebral artery
椎动脉破裂/椎動脈破裂　vertebral artery dissection
椎动脉三角/椎動脈三角　triangle of vertebral artery
椎动脉神经/椎動脈神經　vertebral nerve
椎动脉型颈椎病/椎動脈型頸椎病　vertebral artery type of cervical spondylosis
椎动脉椎前部/椎動脈椎前部　prevertebral part of vertebral artery
椎弓/椎弓　vertebral arch
椎弓板/椎弓板　lamina of vertebral arch
椎弓根/椎弓根　pedicle of vertebral arch
椎骨/椎骨　vertebra
椎骨多关节炎/脊椎多關節炎　vertebral polyarthritis
椎骨关节面切除术/椎骨關節面切除術　facetectomy
椎骨关节韧带/椎骨關節韌帶　articular ligament of vertebrae
椎骨关节突/椎骨關節突,聯軛凸　zygapophysis
椎骨骺炎/椎骨骺炎　vertebral epiphysitis
[椎骨]横突切除术/[椎骨]橫突切除術　transversectomy
[椎骨]横突切开术/[椎骨]橫突切開術　transversotomy
椎[骨]间的/椎間的　intervertebral
椎骨连结/椎骨連結,椎骨關節　vertebral joint
椎骨切除术/椎骨切除術　vertebrectomy
椎骨乳状突/椎骨凸　metapophysis
椎骨上关节突/椎骨前關節突　prezygapophysis
椎骨式/脊椎动物公式　vertebral formula
椎[骨]体/椎體　vertebral body
椎骨图/椎骨圖　osteogram
椎骨外[静脉]丛/椎骨外静脈叢　extraspinal plexus
椎骨下切迹/椎骨下切跡,椎骨大切跡　inferior vertebral incisure
椎骨胸骨的/椎骨[與]胸骨的　vertebrosternal
椎骨胸骨肋/真肋,椎胸骨肋　vertebrosternal rib
椎骨周炎/椎骨周[圍]炎　perispondylitis
椎关节病变/椎關節病變　spondylarthropathy
椎关节强硬的/椎關節粘連的　spondylotic
椎关节突关节/椎關節突關節　zygapophyseal joint
椎关节炎/椎關節炎　spondylarthritis
椎管/椎管　spinal canal
椎管闭合不全/脊管閉合不全　spinal dysraphism
椎管穿刺注气法/椎管充氣穿刺術　pneumorachicentesis
椎管积水/脊髓积水　hydrorachis
椎管脊/椎管脊　intraspinal spur
椎管内出血/椎管内出血　hematorrhachis
椎管内脓肿清除术/椎管内膿腫清除術　evacuation of intraspinal abscess
椎管内肿瘤切除术/椎管内腫瘤切除術　excision of intraspinal tumor
椎管狭窄/椎管狭窄,骨狭窄　spinal stenosis
椎基底动脉供血不足/椎基底動脈供血不足　vertebrobasilar artery insufficiency
椎基[底]动脉缺血/脊柱基底局部缺血　vertebrobasilar ischemia
椎间板/椎間板　intervertebral disk
椎间静脉/椎間静脈　intervertebral vein
椎间孔/椎間孔　intervertebral foramina, intervertebral foramen
椎间孔挤压试验/椎間孔擠壓試驗　spurling test
椎间孔切开术/椎間孔切開術　foraminotomy
椎间联合/椎間聯合　intervertebral symphysis
椎间面/椎間面　intervertebral surface
椎间盘/椎間盤　intervertebral disc
椎间盘病/椎間盤病　discopathy
椎间盘化学松解术/椎間盤化學鬆解術　intervertebral disk chemolysis
椎间盘切除术/椎間板切除術　diskectomy
椎间盘X射线造影术/椎間板X光攝影術　diskography
椎间盘X射线[照]片/椎間盤X光照相　discogram
椎间盘突出/椎間盤突出　herniated intervertebral disc
椎间盘移位/椎間盤移位　intervertebral disk displacement
椎间盘综合征/椎間盤症候群　disc syndrome
椎间前孔/椎間前孔　anterior intervertebral foramen
椎间切迹/椎間切跡　intervertebral notch
椎静脉/椎静脈　vertebral vein
椎孔/椎孔　vertebral foramen
椎肋/椎肋　vertebral rib
椎肋的/椎骨與肋骨的　vertebrocostal
椎内后静脉丛/椎内後静脈叢　posterior internal vertebral venous plexus
椎内前静脉丛/椎内前静脈叢　anterior internal vertebral venous plexus
椎旁神经节/椎旁神經節　paravertebral ganglion
椎旁神经节阻滞术/椎旁神經節阻滯術　paravertebral nerve ganglion block
椎前部/椎前部　prevertebral part
椎前层/椎前層　prevertebral layer

椎前间隙/椎前間隙　prevertebral space
椎前静脉/椎前靜脈　anterior vertebral vein
椎前淋巴结/椎前淋巴結　prevertebral lymph node
椎前神经节/椎前神經結　prevertebral ganglion
椎上切迹/椎[骨]上切跡　superior vertebral notch
椎神经/[脊]椎神經　vertebral nerve
椎神经节/椎神經結　vertebral ganglion
椎体钩/椎體鉤　uncus of vertebrate body
椎体环状突/椎體環狀突　annular apophysis of vertebral body
椎体静脉/椎體靜脈　basivertebral vein
椎体两极细胞/錐體兩極細胞　cone bipolar
椎外后静脉丛/椎外後靜脈叢　posterior external vertebral venous plexus
椎外前静脉丛/椎外前靜脈叢　anterior external vertebral venous plexus
椎下肌/椎下肌　subvertebral muscle
椎下切迹/椎[骨]下切跡　inferior vertebral notch
椎胸膜韧带/椎胸膜韌帶　vertebropleural ligament
锥虫/錐蟲　trypanosome
锥虫变异表面糖蛋白类/錐蟲變異表面糖蛋白類　trypanosoma variant surface glycoproteins
锥虫病/錐蟲病　trypanosomiasis
锥虫病疹/錐蟲[病]疹　trypanosomid
锥虫番红/錐蟲黃樟油精　trypasafrol
锥虫蓝/錐藍　trypan blue
锥虫肿胺/有機性砷劑　tryparsamide
锥虫属/錐蟲屬　*Trypanosoma*
锥虫样鞭毛型/錐蟲樣鞭毛型　trypomastigote
锥蝽/錐鼻蟲　cone-nosed bug
锥蝽锥虫/錐蝽錐蟲　Trypanosoma triatomae
锥骨/錐骨　pyramidal bone
锥隆起/錐隆凸　pyramidal eminence
锥体/棱錐[體],角錐[體]　pyramid
锥体虫属/錐體蟲屬　*Trypanosoma*
锥体底/錐底　base of pyramid
锥体辐射线/錐放線　pyramidal radiation
锥体肌样部/視錐肌樣質　cone myoid
锥体交叉/錐體交叉　decussation of pyramid
锥体前的/錐體前的　prepyramidal
锥体前束/錐體前徑　anterior pyramidal tract, prepyramidal tract
锥体束/錐體徑　pyramidal tract
锥体束切断术/錐體束切斷術　pyramidotomy
锥体束外的/錐體束外的　extrapyramidal
锥体束外综合征/椎體[束]外症候群　extrapyramidal syndrome
锥体束征/錐體束徵[象]　pyramidal sign

锥体外侧束/錐體外側徑　pyramidolateral tract
锥体外束/錐體外束　extrapyramidal tract
锥体外系/錐體外系　extrapyramidal system
锥体外系副作用评定量表/錐體外系副作用評定量表　rating scale for extrapyramidal side effect
锥体外系疾病及运动异常疾患/錐體外系疾病及運動異常疾患　disease of extrapyramidal system and movement disorder
锥体外障碍/錐體外障礙　extrapyramidal disorder
锥体系/錐體系　pyramidal system
锥体细胞/錐狀細胞　pyramidal cell
锥体[细胞]层/錐體[細胞]層　pyramidal layer
锥痛/錐痛　boring pain
锥突/錐突　pyramidal process
锥形白内障/錐形白內障　pyramidal cataract
锥形切除术/[圓]錐形切除法　conization
锥形韧带/[圓]錐狀韌帶　conoid ligament
锥形小塔螺/錐形小塔螺　Pirenella conica
锥形牙/錐形牙　cone-shaped tooth
锥状肌/錐狀肌　pyramidalis
锥状结节/錐狀結節　conoid tubercle
锥状叶/錐體葉　pyramidal lobe
坠积性肺炎/沈積性肺炎　hypostatic pneumonia
坠积性脓肿/沈積性膿腫　hypostatic abscess
坠积性皮炎/沈積性皮膚炎　dermatitis hypostatica
坠积性[血管]扩张/積血性血管擴張　hypostatic ectasia
坠睛/墜睛　downward eye deviation
坠痛/墜痛　bearing-down pain
缀合蛋白质/結合蛋白質　conjugated protein
赘骨/贅骨　splint bone
赘肉/贅肉,浮肉　carnosity
赘肉性溃疡/贅肉性潰瘍　exuberant ulcer
赘生变形性关节炎/贅生變形性關節炎　arthritis deformans neoplastica
赘生物/贅疣　excrescence
赘生指/贅指,多指,額外指　supernumerary finger
赘余畸形/贅餘畸形,贅生　pleonasm
赘状瘢痕/贅狀瘢痕　pedunculated scar
准备/準備　preparation
准备性虹膜切除术/準備性虹膜切除術　preliminary iridectomy
准备注射/準備注射　preparatory injection
准分子激光/準分子雷射　excimer laser
准分子离子/準分子離子　quasi-molecular ion
准确质量/準確質量　exact mass
准显性/準顯性　quasi-dominance
准性殖循环/準性殖循環　parasexual cycle

灼热足/足底灼痛　burning foot
灼热足综合征/腳底燒灼症候群　burning feet syndrome
灼烧/灼燒　burn
灼痛/灼痛,燒痛　burning pain
浊度减低单位/濁度潔淨單位　turbidity reducing unit
浊响/濁響　dull resonance
啄痛/啄痛　pecking pain
啄治法/啄治法　knife pecking method
着痹/著痺　arthralgia caused by damp pathogen, stationary bi
着床/[卵]著床,營巢　nidation
着肤灸/明灸,直接灸　direct moxibustion
着色斑病/棕斑症　lentiginosis
着色不足/著色不足　hypochromatism
着色的/著色的,色素的　pigmentosus
着色剂/著色劑　coloring agent
着色细胞/著色細胞　cytochrome cell
着色性干皮病/色素性乾皮[樣]病　pigmented xerodermoid
着色真菌病/著色真菌病　chromoblastomycosis
着丝粒/著絲粒　centromere
着丝粒融合/著絲粒湊合　centric fusion
着丝粒显带/著絲粒顯帶　centromeric banding
着丝粒异染色质/著絲粒異染色質　centromeric heterochromatin
着丝粒指数/中央節指數　centromeric index
着相/著相　pursuit for entity
咨询/諮詢　counseling
咨询干预/諮詢介入　counseling intervention
咨询者/顧問醫師,諮商醫師　consultant
姿势肌/姿勢肌　postural muscle
姿势描记[法]/姿勢描記[法]　posturography
姿势性脊柱侧凸/姿勢性脊柱側彎　postural scoliosis
姿势训练/姿勢訓練　postural training
资源/資源　resource
滋补肺肾/滋補肺腎　nourishing lung and kidney
滋补肺胃/滋補肺胃　nourishing lung and stomach
滋补肺阴/滋補肺陰　nourishing lung yin
滋补肝肾/滋補肝腎　nourishing liver and kidney
滋补肝胃/滋補肝胃　nourishing liver and stomach
滋补肝阴/滋補肝陰　nourishing liver yin
滋补脾胃/滋補脾胃　nourishing spleen and stomach
滋补脾阴/滋補脾陰　nourishing spleen yin
滋补肾精/滋補腎精　nourishing kidney essence
滋补肾阴/滋補腎陰　nourishing kidney yin
滋补心肺/滋補心肺　nourishing heart and lung
滋补心肾/滋補心腎　nourishing heart and kidney
滋补心阴/滋補心陰　nourishing heart yin
滋肺润肠/滋肺潤腸　nourishing lung and clearing intestine
滋肝明目/滋肝明目　nourishing liver for improving eyesight
滋水清肝饮/滋水清肝飲　water nourishing and liver clearing decoction
滋养层/滋養層,滋胚層　trophoblast
滋养层盖/滋養層蓋　trophoblastic operculum
滋养层甲状腺功能亢进症/滋養層甲狀腺功能亢進症　trophoblastic hyperthyroidism
滋养层腔隙/滋養層腔隙,滋養層間隙　trophoblastic lacuna
滋养层细胞/滋養層細胞　trophoblastic cell
滋养层肿瘤/滋養層腫瘤　trophoblastic neoplasm
滋养动脉/滋養動脈　nutrient artery
滋养管/滋養管　nutrient canal
滋养孔/滋養孔　nutrient foramen
滋养体/滋養體　sporadin
滋养外胚层/滋養外胚層　trophectoderm
滋养细胞/滋養細胞　nutrient cell
滋养质溶解/卵滋質破壞　deutoplasmolysis
滋阴/滋陰　nourishing yin
滋阴安神/滋陰安神　nourishing yin and calming mind
滋阴补血/滋陰補血　nourishing yin and tonifying blood
滋阴补阳/滋陰補陽　nourishing yin and tonifying yang
滋阴降火/滋陰降火　nourishing yin for lowering fire
滋阴降火法/滋陰降火法　nourishing yin and descending fire
滋阴解表/滋陰解表　nourishing yin to relieve exterior pattern
滋阴平肝/滋陰平肝　nourishing yin and supressing liver yang, nourish yin and calm the liver
滋阴潜阳/滋陰潛陽　nourishing yin for suppressing hyperactive yang
滋阴清热/滋陰清熱　nourishing yin and clearing heat
滋阴柔肝/滋陰柔肝　nourishing yin for softening liver
滋阴润燥/滋陰潤燥　nourishing yin for moistening dryness
滋阴疏肝/滋陰疏肝　nourishing yin and soothing liver
滋阴息风/滋陰息風　nourishing yin for calming

endogenous wind
滋阴益胃/滋陰益胃　nourishing yin for benefiting stomach
子孢子率/種蟲率　sporozoite rate
子孢子体/種蟲　oxyspore
子病及母/子病及母　illness of child viscera affecting mother one
子代/子[世]代　filial generation
子烦/子煩　gestational dysphoria, restlessness during pregnancy
子烦•痰火内蕴证/子煩•痰火内蘊證　gestational dysphoria with pattern of internal retention of phlegm-fire
子烦•阴虚火旺证/子煩•陰虛火旺證　gestational dysphoria with pattern of exuberant fire due to yin deficiency
子宫/子宮　uterus
子宫白带/子宮白帶　metroleukorrhea
子宫闭锁/子宮閉鎖　atresia uteri
子宫病/子宮病　metropathia
子宫部/子宮部　uterine part
子宫残角妊娠/子宮殘角妊娠　pregnancy in rudimentary horn
子宫测量/子宮測量　uterometry
子宫测量器/子宮測量器　hysterometer
子宫肠瘘/子宮腸瘻　utero-intestinal fistula
子宫成形术/子宮整形術　hysteroplasty
子宫出血/子宮出血　uterine hemorrhage
子宫穿孔/子宮穿孔　uterine perforation
子宫次根治性切除术/子宮次根治術　subradical hysterectomy
子宫次全切除术/次全子宮切除術,大部分子宮切除術　subtotal hysterectomy
子宫刀/子宮刀　hysterotome
子宫的/子宮的　uterine
子宫底/子宮底　fundus of uterus
子宫底切除术/子宮底切除術　defundation
子宫底输卵管切除术/子宮底輸卵管切除術　acrohysterosalpingectomy
子宫底胎盘/底部胎盤　fundal placenta
子宫骶骨韧带缩短术/子宮骶骨韌帶縮短術　shortening of uterosacral ligament
子宫骶韧带/子宮骶韌帶　uterosacral ligament
子宫动脉/子宮動脈　uterine artery
子宫动脉卵巢支/子宮動脈卵巢支　ovarian branch of uterine artery
子宫动脉螺旋支/子宮動脈螺旋支　spiral branch of uterine artery

子宫动脉输卵管支/子宮動脈輸卵管支　tubal branch of uterine artery
子宫动脉阴道支/子宮動脈陰道支　vaginal branch of uterine artery
子宫毒素/子宮毒素　metrotoxin
子宫端/子宮端　uterine extremity
子宫发育不全/子宮發育不全　uterine hypoplasia
子宫分段/子宮分段　uterine segment
子宫附件/子宮附屬器　adnexa uteri
子宫附件固定术/子宮附屬器官固定術　tuboadnexopexy
子宫附件疾病/子宮附屬器疾病　adnexal disease
[子宫]附件切除术/子宮附屬器官切除術　adnexectomy
子宫附件炎/子宮附屬器官發炎　adnexitis
子宫复旧/子宮復舊　involution of uterus
[子宫]复旧不全/復舊不全　subinvolution
子宫腹膜的/子宮腹膜的　metroperitoneal
子宫腹膜瘘/子宮腹膜瘻管　metroperitoneal fistula
子宫腹膜炎/子宮腹膜炎　metroperitonitis
子宫根治术/子宮根治術　radical hysterectomy
子宫功能不全/子宮機能不全　uterine insufficiency
子宫骨盆韧带/子宮骨盆韌帶　uteropelvic ligament
子宫固定术/子宮懸吊術　suspension of uterus
子宫横纹肌瘤/子宮橫紋肌瘤　rhabdomyoma uteri
子宫肌层/子宮肌層　myometrium
子宫肌[层]炎/子宮肌[層]炎　myometritis
子宫肌瘤/子宮肌瘤　hysteromyoma
子宫肌瘤切除术/肌瘤切除術　myomectomy
子宫肌切开术/子宮肌切開術　hysteromyotomy
子宫积恶露/子宮惡露不下　lochiometra
子宫积脓/子宮積膿　pyometra
子宫积脓气/子宮積膿氣,膿氣子宮　pyophysometra
子宫积气/子宮積氣,氣子宮　physometra
子宫积气水/氣水子宮　pneumohydrometra
子宫积水/子宮積水　hydrometra
子宫积水气/子宮積水氣　hydrophysometra
子宫积血/子宮積血　hematometra
子宫积血气/子宮積氣血,氣血子宮　physohematometra
子宫疾病/子宮疾病　uterine disease
子宫监测/子宮監測　uterine monitoring
子宫绞痛/子宮絞痛　uterine colic
子宫颈/子宮頸　neck of uterus, cervix, cervix uteri
子宫颈癌/子宮頸癌　carcinoma of the uterine cervix, cervical cancer
子宫颈癌•肝气郁结证/子宮頸癌•肝氣鬱結證　cervical cancer with pattern of liver qi depression

子宫颈癌•肝肾阴虚证/子宫頸癌•肝腎陰虛證 cervical cancer with pattern of liver-kidney yin deficiency
子宫颈癌•脾肾阳虚证/子宫頸癌•脾腎陽虛證 cervical cancer with pattern of yang deficiency of spleen and kidney
子宫颈癌•湿热瘀毒证/子宫頸癌•濕熱瘀毒證 cervical cancer with pattern of poisonous damp-heat and static blood
子宫颈闭锁/子宫頸閉鎖 atresia of cervix
子宫颈成形术/宫颈整形術 hysterotracheloplasty
子宫颈缝术/子宫頸縫補術 hysterotrachelorrhaphy
子宫颈管/子宫頸管 canal of cervix of uterus
[子宫]颈管内的/[子宫]頸管內的 intracervical
子宫颈积血/子宫頸積血 hematotrachelos
[子宫颈]痉挛性强直/子宫之痙攣性強硬 spasmodic rigidity
子宫颈扩张袋/子宫頸擴大球 metreurynter
子宫颈扩张术/子宫頸擴張術 hysterotrachelectasia
子宫颈流产/子宫頸流產 cervical abortion
子宫颈糜烂/子宫頸糜爛 cervical erosion
[子宫颈]纳[博特]氏囊肿/子宫頸腺囊腫 Nabothian cyst
子宫颈内瘘/子宫頸內瘻管 intracervical fistula
子宫颈内膜/子宫頸內膜 endocervix
子宫颈内膜炎/子宫頸內膜炎 endocervicitis
子宫颈旁组织/子宫頸旁組織 paracervix
子宫颈切除术/子宫頸切除術 cervicectomy
子宫颈切开术/子宫頸切開術 hysterotrachelotomy
子宫颈韧带/子宫頸韌帶 cervical ligament of uterus
子宫颈神经节/子宫頸神經節 uterine cervical ganglion
子宫颈腺囊肿/子宫頸腺囊腫 Naboth cyst
子宫颈阴道部/子宫頸陰道部 vaginal part of cervix
子宫颈阴道瘘/子宫頸陰道瘻管 fistula cervicovaginalis
子宫颈阴道上部/子宫頸陰道上部 supravaginal part of cervix
子宫颈阴道炎/子宫頸陰道炎 cervicocolpitis
子宫颈与阴道/子宫頸與陰道 cervicovaginallis
子宫痉挛/子宫痙攣 hysterospasm
子宫静脉/子宫靜脈 uterine vein
子宫静脉丛/子宫靜脈叢 uterine venous plexus
子宫静脉炎/子宫靜脈炎 metrophlebitis
子宫口/子宫口 orifice of uterus
子宫口闭合术/子宫口閉合術 hysterocleisis
子宫口刀/子宫口刀,子宫頸刀 hysterostomatome
子宫口扩张器/子宫口擴張器 hystereurynter
子宫口扩张术/子宫口擴張術 hystereurysis
子宫口切开术/子宫口切開術 stomatomy
子宫宽韧带疝/子宫廣韌帶疝 hernia of the broad ligament of the uterus
子宫扩张/子宫擴張 metrectasla
子宫阔韧带/子宫闊韌帶 broad ligament of uterus
子宫鳞癣/子宫[魚]鱗癣 ichthyosis uteri
子宫卵巢静脉曲张/子宫卵巢靜脈腫 uteroovarian varicocele
子宫卵巢韧带/子宫卵巢韌帶 uteroovarian ligament
子宫麻痹/子宫麻痺 metroparalysis
子宫囊肿形成/子宫囊腫形成 metrocystosis
子宫内儿哭/子宫內兒啼 vagitus uterinus
子宫内翻/子宫內翻 inversion of uterus
子宫内截断/子宫內截斷 intrauterine amputation
子宫内镭管支持器/子宫內鐳管支持器 hysterostat
子宫内膜/子宫內膜 endometrium
子宫[内膜]癌/子宫內膜癌 hysterocarcinoma
子宫内膜不规则脱落/子宫內膜不規則脫落 irregular shedding of endometrium
子宫内膜的/子宫內膜的 endometrial
[子宫内膜]功能层/功能層 functional layer
[子宫内膜]海绵层/海綿層 spongy layer
子宫内膜基质/子宫內膜基質 endometrial stroma
[子宫内膜]基质细胞/間質細胞,基質細胞 stroma cell
子宫内膜[基质]异位/子宫基質病 stromatosis
子宫内膜间质肉瘤/子宫內膜基質肉瘤 endometrial stromal sarcoma
子宫内膜间质细胞瘤/子宫內膜間質細胞瘤 endometrial stromal tumor
子宫内膜结核/子宫內膜結核 endometrial tuberculosis
子宫内膜瘤/子宫內膜瘤 endometrioma
子宫内膜囊腺状增生/子宫內膜囊腺狀增生 cystic-glandular hyperplasia of the endometrium
子宫内膜囊肿/子宫內膜囊腫 endometrial cyst
子宫内膜切除术/子宫內膜切除術 endometrectomy
子宫内膜炎/子宫內膜炎 endometritis
子宫内膜样癌/子宫內膜樣癌 endometrioid carcinoma
子宫内膜样的/子宫內膜樣的 endometrioid
子宫内膜异位囊肿/子宫內膜異位囊腫 endometrial implantation cyst
子宫内膜增生/子宫內膜增生 endometrial hyperplasia
[子宫内膜]致密层/[子宫內膜]緊密層 compact layer

子宫内膜肿瘤/子宮內膜腫瘤　endometrial neoplasm
子宫内生活/子宮內生活　intrauterine life
子宫内输血/子宮內輸血　intrauterine blood transfusion
子宫内腺肌病/子宮內肌腺症　adenomyosis interna
子宫内压/子宮內壓　intrauterine pressure
子宫内注射/子宮內注射　intrauterine injection
子宫旁淋巴结/子宮旁淋巴結　parauterine lymph node
子宫旁血囊肿/子宮旁血囊腫，子宮後血囊腫　parametric hematocele
子宫旁组织/子宮旁組織　parametrium
子宫旁组织炎/子宮旁組織炎　parametritis
子宫膀胱的/子宮膀胱的　uterovesical
子宫膀胱缝术/子宮膀胱瘻閉合術　hysterocystocleisis
子宫膀胱瘘/子宮膀胱瘻　uterovesical fistula
子宫破裂/子宮破裂　rupture of uterus
子宫气鼓/子宮氣鼓　tympania uteri
子宫腔/子宮腔　cavity of uterus, uterine canal
子宫腔粘连综合征/子宮腔粘連症候群　Asherman syndrome
子宫切除术/子宮切除術　hysterectomy
子宫切开术/子宮切開術　hysterotomy
子宫全部脱垂/子宮全部脫出　frank prolapse
子宫全切术/全部子宮切除術　total hysterectomy
子宫三角韧带/子宮三角韌帶　triangular ligament of uterus
子宫疝/子宮疝　uterine hernia
子宫[X射线]造影术/子宮 X 射線攝影術　uterography
子宫[X射线]照相/子宮 X 光像　hysterogram
子宫渗血/子宮滲血　metrostaxis
子宫石/子宮石，子宮鈣化　hysterolith
子宫收缩/子宮收縮　uterine contraction
子宫[收缩]电[流]描记法/子宮電圖測定　electrohysterography
子宫收缩过度/子宮收縮過度　hyperdynamia uteri
子宫收缩剂/子宮強壯藥　uterotonic
子宫收缩描记器/子宮收縮描記計　hysterograph
子宫收缩松解术/産道鬆解術　tocolysis
子宫收缩松解药/子宮收縮鬆解藥　tocolytic agent
子宫收缩药/子宮收縮藥　uterotonic
子宫输卵管卵巢切除术/子宮輸卵管卵巢切除術　hysterosalpingo-oophorectomy
子宫输卵管切除术/子宮輸卵管切除術　hysterosalpingectomy
子宫输卵管吻合术/子宮輸卵管吻合術　uterosalpingostomy
子宫输卵管炎/子宮輸卵管炎　metrosalpingitis
子宫输卵管造影术/子宮輸卵管 X 光攝影法　hysterosalpingography
子宫输卵管周炎/子宮腹膜輸卵管炎　perimetrosalpingitis
子宫松弛药/子宮鬆弛藥　uterorelaxant
子宫松解术/子宮鬆解術　hysterolysis
子宫胎盘/子宮胎盤　placenta uterina
子宫胎盘卒中/子宮胎盤性中風　uteroplacental apoplexy
子宫探子/子宮探針　uterine probe
子宫体/子宮體　body of uterus
子宫体癌/子宮體癌　corpus carcinoma
子宫体切开剖腹产术/標準剖腹產術，子宮體切開剖腹生產術　corporeal cesarean section
子宫痛/子宮痛　hysteralgia
子宫托/子宮托　pessary
子宫脱垂/子宮脫垂　prolapse of uterus
子宫外膜/子宮外膜　perimetrium
子宫外妊娠/子宮外妊娠　extra-uterine gestation
子宫外腺肌病/子宮外肌腺症　adenomyosis externa
子宫外孕/子宮外孕，異位妊娠，子宮外妊娠　exfetation
子宫萎缩/子宮萎縮　metratrophia
子宫温度测量法/子宮溫度測量法　hysterothermometry
子宫系膜/子宮繫膜　mesometrium
子宫系膜襞/中子宮皺襞　mesouterine fold
子宫峡/子宮峽　isthmus of uterus
子宫狭窄/子宮狹窄　metrostenosis
子宫下段剖宫产术/子宮下段剖宮產術　low-segment cesarean section
子宫纤维变性/子宮纖維變性　fibrosis uteri
子宫纤维瘤/子宮纖維瘤　metrofibroma
子宫纤维瘤切除术/子宮纖維瘤切除術　fibroidectomy
子宫腺/子宮腺　uterine gland
子宫腺肌病/子宮肌腺症　adenomyosis
子宫腺肌炎/類腺瘤增生性子宮炎　adenomyometritis
子宫兴奋药/子宮興奮藥　uterus stimulant
子宫性闭经/子宮性閉經　uterine amenorrhea
子宫性咳嗽/子宮性欬嗽　uterine cough
子宫性痛经/子宮性痛經　uterine dysmenorrhea
子宫[穴]/子宮[穴]　zigong, EX-CA1
子宫学/子宮[病]學　hysterology
子宫炎/子宮炎　metritis

子宫炎的/子宫炎的 metritic
子宫炎性滑膜炎/子宫炎性滑膜炎 metritic synovitis
子宫液溢/子宫溢液，子宫漏 metrorrhea
子宫阴道肠疝/子宫陰道腸疝 hysterovagino-enterocele
子宫阴道丛/子宫陰道叢 uterovaginal plexus
子宫阴道积水/子宫陰道積水 hydrometrocolpos
子宫阴道镜/子宫陰道鏡 hysterocolposcope
子宫阴道切除术/子宫陰道切除術 hysterocolpectomy
子宫阴道突出/子宫陰道脫疝 metrocolpocele
子宫阴道原基/子宫陰道原基 uterovaginal primordium
子宫右角/子宫右角 right horn of uterus
子宫右缘/子宫右緣 right margin of uterus
子宫圆韧带/子宫圓韌帶 round ligament of uterus, ligament teres uteri
子宫圆韧带动脉/子宫圓韌帶動脈 artery of round ligament of uterus
子宫杂音/子宫雜音 uterine souffle
子宫直肠骶骨韧带/子宫直腸骨骶韌帶 uterorectosacral ligament
子宫直肠陷凹切开术/後穹窿切開術 culdotomy
子宫肿瘤/子宫腫瘤 uterine neoplasm
子宫珠蛋白/子宫珠蛋白 uteroglobin
子宫棕榈襞/子宫棕櫚皺襞 arbor vitae uteri
子宫左角/子宫左角 left horn of uterus
子宫左缘/子宫左緣 left margin of uterus
子核/子核 daughter nucleus
子菌落/子菌落 daughter colony
子淋/子淋 gestational stranguria, stranguria during pregnancy
子淋•膀胱湿热证/子淋•膀胱濕熱證 gestational stranguria with pattern of damp-heat in bladder
子淋•心火炽盛证/子淋•心火熾盛證 gestational stranguria with pattern of blazing heart fire
子淋•阴虚内热证/子淋•陰虛内熱證 gestational stranguria with pattern of internal heat due to yin deficiency
子瘤/子瘤 daughter tumor
子满/子滿 gestational edema and panting, hydramnios
子满•脾气虚证/子滿•脾氣虛證 hydramnios with pattern of spleen qi deficiency
子满•气滞湿阻证/子滿•氣滯濕阻證 hydramnios with pattern of qi stagnation and damp retention
子母弹伤/子母彈傷 cluster bomb wound
子囊/子囊 ascus
子囊孢子/子囊芽孢 ascospore
子囊果/子囊果 ascocarp
子囊菌/子囊菌 sac fungi
子囊菌纲/子囊菌綱 Ascomycetes
子囊壳/子囊殼，芽孢器 perithecium
子囊盘/子囊盤 apothecium
子囊肿/子囊腫 daughter cyst
子气/子氣 child qi
子死腹中/子死腹中 dead fetus in uterus
子嗽/子嗽 cough during pregnancy, gestational cough
子嗽•痰饮犯肺证/子嗽•痰飲犯肺證 gestational cough with pattern of phlegm-fluid invading lung
子嗽•阴虚肺燥证/子嗽•陰虛肺燥證 gestational cough with pattern of yin deficiency and lung dryness
子痰/子痰 tuberculosis of epididymis
子痰•气血两虚证/子痰•氣血兩虛證 tuberculosis of epididymis with qi-blood deficiency pattern
子痰•湿痰凝结证/子痰•濕痰凝結證 tuberculosis of epididymis with pattern of dampness-phlegm coagulating and intermingling
子痰•阳虚痰凝证/子痰•陽虛痰凝證 tuberculosis of epididymis with pattern of yang deficiency and phlegm coagulation
子痰•阴虚内热证/子痰•陰虛内熱證 tuberculosis of epididymis with pattern of yin deficiency and internal heat
子午流注法/子午流注法 midnight-noon ebb-flow acupoint selection, point selection by midday-midnight flowing of qi-bloodpoint
子午圈像差/子午圈像差 meridional aberration
子细胞/子細胞，兒細胞 daughter cell
子痫/子癇 eclampsia, convulsions during pregnancy
子痫的/子癇的 eclamptic
子痫发作期/子癇發作期 attacking stage of eclampsia
子痫•肝风内动证/子癇•肝風内動證 eclampsia with pattern of internal stirring of liver wind
子痫前毒血症/初期子癇性毒血症 preeclamptic toxemia
子痫•痰火扰神证/子癇•痰火擾神證 eclampsia with pattern of phlegm-fire disturbing spirit
子痫性尿毒症/子癇性尿毒病 eclamptic uremia
子悬/子懸 chest and abdominal fullness during pregnancy, distention in chest during pregnancy, gestational suspension

子悬·肝气犯脾证/子懸·肝氣犯脾證　gestational suspension with pattern of liver qi invading spleen
子悬·心肾不交证/子懸·心腎不交證　gestational suspension with pattern of incoordination between heart and kidney
子眩/子眩　dizziness during pregnancy, pregnancy vertigo
子岩/子巖　testicle cancer
子叶状胎盘/子葉狀胎盤　placenta cotyledonata
子喑/子喑　aphonia during pregnancy, gestational aphonia
子喑·肺阴虚证/子喑·肺陰虛證　gestational aphonia with pattern of lung yin deficiency
子喑·肾阴虚证/子喑·腎陰虛證　gestational aphonia with pattern of kidney yin deficiency
子隐/子隱　undescended testis
子痈/子癰　epididymitis and orchitis, testicular abscess
子痈·气滞痰凝证/子癰·氣滯痰凝證　testicular abscess with pattern of qi stagnation and phlegm coagulation
子痈·湿热下注证/子癰·濕熱下注證　testicular abscess with pattern of dampness-heat diffusing downward
子痈·阳虚寒凝证/子癰·陽虛寒凝證　testicular abscess with pattern of yang deficiency and cold congelation
子疣/子疣　seed wart
子晕/子暈　gestational vertigo
子晕·肝肾阴虚证/子暈·肝腎陰虛證　gestational vertigo with pattern of liver-kidney yin deficiency
子晕·肝阳上亢证/子暈·肝陽上亢證　gestational vertigo with pattern of liver yang hyperactivity
子晕·脾虚肝旺证/子暈·脾虛肝旺證　gestational vertigo with pattern of spleen deficiency and liver hyperactivity
子晕·气血两虚证/子暈·氣血兩虛證　gestational vertigo with pattern of deficiency of both qi and blood
子肿/子腫,懷孕水腫　gestational anasarca, gestational edema
子肿·脾虚证/子腫·脾虛證　gestational anasarca with spleen deficiency pattern
子肿·气滞证/子腫·氣滯證　gestational anasarca with qi stagnation pattern
子肿·肾虚证/子腫·腎虛證　gestational anasarca with kidney deficiency pattern
姊妹细胞/姊妹細胞　sister cell
籽骨/子骨,種子狀骨　sesamoid bone
籽骨炎/種子骨炎　sesamoiditis
籽软骨/子軟骨　sesamoid cartilage
紫白癜风/紫白癜風,花斑癬,汗斑　purple vitiligo, tinea versicolor
紫癍/紫癍　purple macula
紫草/紫草　Lithospermum, arnebia root, gromwell root
紫草萃取液/紫草萃取液　comfrey extract
紫草膏/紫草膏　zicao soft plaster
紫癜[病]/紫癜[病]　purpura
紫癜的/紫癜性　purpuric
紫癜风/紫癜風,扁平苔癬　lichen planus
紫癜风·风热阻络证/紫癜風·風熱阻絡證　lichen planus with pattern of wind-heat obstructing collateral
紫癜风·风湿蕴肤证/紫癜風·風濕蕴膚證　lichen planus with pattern of wind-dampness amassing in skin
紫癜风·气滞血瘀证/紫癜風·氣滯血瘀證　lichen planus with pattern of qi stagnation and blood stasis
紫癜风·热伤络证/紫癜風·熱傷絡證　purpura with pattern of wind-heat injuring collaterals
紫癜风·虚火上炎证/紫癜風·虛火上炎證　lichen planus with pattern of deficiency-fire flaring upward
紫癜肝病/肝性紫癜　peliosis hepatis
紫癜·气不摄血证/紫癜·氣不攝血證　purpura with pattern of failure of qi to keep blood
紫癜·血热妄行证/紫癜·血熱妄行證　purpura with pattern of bleeding due to blood heat
紫癜·阴虚火旺证/紫癜·陰虛火旺證　purpura with pattern of exuberant fire due to yin deficiency
紫绀型心脏病/發紺性心臟病　cyanotic heart disease
紫宫/紫宫　zigong, RN19
紫河车/紫河車　human placenta
紫红色[的]/苯胺紫　mauve
紫花地丁/紫花地丁　Tokyo violet herb
紫花洋地黄苷/紫色洋地黄苷　purpureaglycoside
紫花洋地黄苦素/洋地黄苦質　picrin
紫幻视/紫幻視　ionophose
紫碱/紫鹼　viologen
紫金锭/紫金錠　zijin troch
紫堇碱/紫堇鹼　corydaline
紫堇块茎碱/紫堇塊茎鹼　corytuberine
紫螺属/紫螺屬　*Murex purpurea*
紫螺紫素/紫螺紫素　punizin
紫霉素/紫黴素　viomycin
紫膜/紫膜　purple membrane

紫苜蓿/紫苜蓿　Medicago sativa
紫尿酸/紫尿酸　violuric acid
紫尿酸铵/紫尿酸銨　ammonium purpurate
紫色带/紫色帶　lilac band
紫色盲/紫色盲　anianthynopsy
紫杉酚/紫杉酚　paclitaxel
紫杉碱/觀音杉素　taxine
紫杉烷类/紫杉烷類　taxoids
紫舌/紫舌　purplish tongue
紫石英/紫石英　fluorite
紫苏属/紫蘇屬　Perilla
紫苏梗/紫蘇梗　perilla stem
紫苏叶/紫蘇葉　perilla leaf
紫苏子/紫蘇子　perilla fruit
紫檀碱类/紫檀鹼類　pterocarpans
紫外辐射/紫外線輻射　ultraviolet radiation
紫外线/紫外線,超紫線　ultraviolet ray
紫外线测量计/紫外線測量計　uviometer
紫外线灯/紫外線燈　ultraviolet lamp
紫外线分光光度法/紫外線分光光度法　ultraviolet spectrophotometry
紫外线红斑/紫外線紅斑　ultraviolet erythema
紫外线疗法/紫外線療法　ultraviolet therapy
紫外线色素沉着作用/紫外線色素沈著作用　ultraviolet pigmentation effect
紫外线杀菌作用/紫外線殺菌作用　ultraviolet germicidal effect
紫外线显微镜检查/紫外線顯微鏡檢查　ultraviolet microscopy
紫外线显微吸收分光术/紫外線顯微吸收分光術　ultraviolet microscopic absorption spectroscopy
紫外线消毒乳/紫外線消毒乳　uviol milk
紫外线照射/紫外線照射［法］　ultraviolet irradiation
紫外线照血法/紫外線照血法　ultraviolet blood irradiation
紫菀/紫菀　tatarian aster root
紫菀属植物/紫菀屬植物　Aster plant
紫纹/紫紋　purple striae
紫雪/紫雪　zixue powder
紫罂粟次碱/藤荷包牡丹定鹼　adlumidine
紫罂粟碱/紫罌粟鹼　adlumine
紫质病/紫質病　porphyrism
紫朱草［根］/紫朱草根,牛舌草根　alkanet
紫锥花属/紫花馬藺菊屬　Echinacea
自卑感/自卑感　sense of inferiority
自病记录/自病記錄　autopathography
自残/自殘　self-mutilation
自插导管［法］/自插導管　autocatheterism

自动安瓿灌封机/自動安瓿充填熔封機　automatic ampule filling and sealing machine
自动比浊计/自動比濁計　automated nephelometric
自动充血/主動性充血　active congestion
自动倒转/自然轉向,胎自轉向　spontaneous version
自动定量视野计/自動定量視野計　automatic quantitative perimeter
自动反应素试验/自動反應素試驗　automated reagin test
自动供氧人工呼吸器/自動供氧人工呼吸器　pulmotor
自动聚合［作用］/自體聚合作用　autopolymerization
自动模式识别/自動模式識別　automated pattern recognition
自动破坏［作用］/自體破壞　autodestruction
自动数据处理/自動資料處理　automatic data processing
自动脱水包埋机/自動脫水包埋機　automatic dewatering embedding machine
自动行为/自發行為　automatic behavior
自动性/自發性　automaticity
自动性失禁/自動性失禁　active incontinence
自动性舞蹈病/自動性舞蹈病　automatic chorea
自动性运动/自動性運動　automatic movement
自动性运动描记器/自動性運動描記器　automatograph
自动验光仪/自動驗光儀　autorefractomer
自动氧化［作用］/自動氧化　auto-oxidation
自动音量控制/自動音量控制　automatic volume control
自动长出/自動長出　active eruption
自动症/自動症　automatism
自动症性霍乱/自動症性霍亂　automatic cholera
自动致敏/自動性致敏作用　active sensitization
自发变［态反］应性/自發性過敏　spontaneous allergy
自发病/自發病　autopathy
自发的/自發的,自體的　autogenous, autologous, spontaneous
自发反应/自發反應　operant
自发回忆/自然回憶　automnesia
自发凝集反应/自發凝集反應　spontaneous agglutination
自发凝集素/自發凝集素,自發凝素　idioagglutinin
自发溶素/自發溶素　idiolysin
自发通气/自發通氣　spontaneous ventilation
自发同种凝集素/自發同種凝集素　idioisoagglutinin
自发同种溶素/自發同族溶素　idioisolysin

自发突变/自發性突變　spontaneous mutation
自发性搏动/自發性搏動　automatic beat
自发性出血/自發性出血　autogenous hemorrhage
自发性动脉瘤/自發性動脈瘤　spontaneous aneurysm
自发性耳声发射/自發性耳聲發射　spontaneous otoacoustic emission
自发[性]反射/自發[性]反射　idioreflex
自发性腹膜炎/自發性腹膜炎　spontaneous peritonitis
自发性骨折/自發性骨折　spontaneous fracture
自发性黑色素性黏膜增生/本態性黑色素性黏膜增生　essential melanotic mucosal hyperplasia
自发性肌收缩/肌本質性收縮　myoidism
自发性进行性毛细血管扩张症/本態性進行性微血管擴張症　essential progressive telangiectasia
自发性脓毒败血病/自發性膿毒敗血病　spontaneous septicopyemia
自发性脓肿/自發性膿腫　idiopathic abscess
自发性破裂/自發性破裂　spontaneous rupture
自发性气胸/自發性氣胸　spontaneous pneumothorax
自发性瘙痒/特發性搔癢　essential pruritus
自发性神经瘤/自發性神經瘤　spontaneous neuroma
自发性神经痛/自發性神經痛　idiopathic neuralgia
自发性肾炎/自發性腎炎　idiopathic nephritis
自发性食物过敏/自發性食物過敏　idioblapsis
自发性痛经/特發性痛經　essential dysmenorrhea
自发性胃穿孔/自發性胃穿孔　spontaneous perforation of stomach
自发性吸收/自發性吸收　idiopathic resorption
自发性哮喘/自發性哮喘　essential asthma
自发性心包炎/自發性心包炎　idiopathic pericarditis
自发性眩晕/自發性眩暈　spontaneous vertigo
自发性血胸/自發性血胸　spontaneous hemothorax
自发性胰岛素过多症/自發性胰島素過多症　spontaneous hyperinsulinism
自发性杂音/自發性雜音　spontaneous murmur
自发性指脱落/自發性指脱落　dactylolysis spontanea
自发性趾脱落/自發性趾脱落　dactylolysis spontanea
自发性子宫出血/自發性子宮出血　essential uterine hemorrhage
自发性紫癜/自發性紫癜病　idiopathic purpura
自发演化/自發演化　spontaneous evolution
自发异种凝集素/自發異族凝集素　idioheteroagglutinin
自发异种溶素/自發異族溶素　idioheterolysin
自发荧光/自體螢光　autofluorescence
自发运动/自發運動　automatic motion
自分泌作用/自分泌作用　autocrine action
自感/自感　self-inductance
自感劳累分级/自感勞累分級　rating of perceived exertion
自感应/自感應　self-induction
自汗[病]/自汗[病]　spontaneous sweating
自汗·肺脾气虚证/自汗·肺脾氣虛證　spontaneous sweating with pattern of qi deficiency of lung and spleen
自汗·气阴两虚证/自汗·氣陰兩虛證　spontaneous sweating with pattern of deficiency of both qi and yin
自汗·邪热郁蒸证/自汗·邪熱鬱蒸證　spontaneous sweating with pattern of stagnation and steaming of pathogenic heat
自汗·心肾两虚证/自汗·心腎兩虛證　spontaneous sweating with pattern of deficiency of both heart and kidney
自汗·阴虚火旺证/自汗·陰虛火旺證　spontaneous sweating with pattern of exuberant fire due to yin deficiency
自汗·营卫不和证/自汗·營衛不和證　spontaneous sweating with pattern of disharmony between nutrient and defense phases
自耗营养/自耗營養　allogotrophia
自[己]灌洗胃/自己洗胃　autolavage
自记温度计/自記溫度計,記錄溫度計　recording thermometer
自[家]溶[解]/自溶　autolysis
自检喉镜检查/自體喉鏡檢查　autolaryngoscopy
自检听诊器/自體聽診器　autechoscope
自检眼底镜/自體眼底器　autofundoscope
自检眼底镜检查/眼底自檢法　autofundoscopy
自检眼镜/自體檢眼鏡　auto-ophthalmoscope
自检眼镜检查/自體檢眼鏡檢查　auto-ophthalmoscopy
自洁区/自潔區　self-cleaning area
自解词/自解詞　idiolog
自解[言]语症/獨語症　idioglossia
自觉性震颤/主觀震顫　subjective fremitus
自窥癖/自窺癖　extrospection
自利清水/自利清水　watery stool
自恋癖/自體觀察欲,自戀狂　narcissism
自流注射器/自流唧筒　fountain syringe
自律的/自律的,自主的　autonomic

自泌激活/自泌活化　autocrine activation
自描听力计/自描聽力計　automatic recording audiometer
自尿疗法/自尿療法　auto-urotherapy
自凝树脂/自乾樹脂　self-curing resin
自皮移植片/自皮移植物　autodermic graft
自启效应/自啟效應　self-priming effect
自然的/自然的,天然的　natural
自[然发]生/自[然發]生　autogenesis
自[然发]生的/自生的　autogenetic
自然法则/自然法則　natural law
自然分解/自然分解　physiolysis
自然分娩/自然分娩　natural childbirth
自然感染/天然傳染　natural infection
自然换气法/天然換氣法　natural ventilation
自然科学/自然科學　natural science
自然疗法/自然療法,放任療法　physiocracy
自然流产/自然流產　spontaneous abortion
自然杀伤细胞/自然殺傷細胞　natural killer cell
自然铜/自然銅　pyrite
自然突变/自然突變　natural mutation
自然消退/自然消退　spontaneous regression
自然选育/自然選育　natural selection
自然选择/自然淘汰,天擇　natural selection
自然选择学说/自然選擇學説　natural selection theory
自然医术/自然療法　naturopathy
自然语言处理/自然語言處理　natural language processing
自然哲学/自然哲學　natural philosophy
自然资源保护/自然資源保護　conservation of natural resource
自燃/自燃　spontaneous combustion
自溶产物/自溶産物　autolysate
自溶的/自溶的　autolytic
自溶酶/自解酵素　autolytic enzyme
自溶性腹膜炎/自溶性腹膜炎　autolytic peritonitis
自溶[作用]/自溶[作用]　autolysis
自杀/自殺　suicide
自杀未遂/自殺未遂　attempted suicide
自伤/自傷,自製損害　autolesion
自伤性皮肤病/自傷性皮膚病　self-inflicted dermatosis
自身标志假说/自身標志假説　self-marker hypothesis
自身部位失认[症]/定位覺缺失,部位覺缺失　autotopagnosia
自身定向力障碍/自身定向力障礙　autopsychic disorientation
自身反应性/自體反應性　autoreactivity
自身肺氧合/自身肺氧合　autogenous lung oxygenation
自身分化/本身分化,内在控制分化　self-differentiation
自身分泌活动因子/自身分泌活動因子　autocrine motility factor
自身分泌性细胞交流/自身分泌性細胞交流　autocrine communication
自身过敏性/自體過敏性　autoanaphylaxis
自身红细胞致敏/自體紅血球敏感化　autoerythrocyte sensitization
自身红细胞致敏综合征/自體紅血球過敏作用症候群　autoerythrocyte sensitization syndrome
自身活性物质/自泌素　autacoid
自身接种/自體接種　autoinoculation
自身抗体/自身抗體,自體抗體　autoantibody
自身抗原/自身抗原,自體抗原　autoantigen
自身玫瑰花结/自身玫瑰花結　autorosette
自身免疫/自體免疫　autoimmunity
自身免疫病/自體免疫病　autoimmune disease
自身免疫的/自體免疫的　autoimmune
自身免疫性多内分泌腺病/自體免疫多内分泌病　autoimmune polyendocrine disease
自身免疫性多内分泌腺综合征/自體免疫多腺體性症候群　autoimmune polyglandular syndrome
自身免疫性肝炎/自體免疫性肝炎　autoimmune hepatitis
自身免疫性甲状旁腺炎/自體免疫性甲狀旁腺炎　autoimmune parathyroiditis
自身免疫性甲状腺炎/自體免疫性甲狀腺炎　autoimmune thyroiditis
自身免疫性溶血性贫血/自體免疫性溶血性貧血　autoimmune hemolytic anemia
自身免疫性孕酮皮炎/自體免疫黄體激素皮膚炎　autoimmune progesterone dermatitis
自身免疫应答/自體免疫反應　autoimmune response
自身敏感性皮炎/自體過敏性皮膚炎　autosensitization dermatitis
自身耐受性/自身耐受性　self-tolerance
自身凝集/自體凝集　autoagglutination
自[身]溶酶体/自溶酶體　autolysosome
自[身]溶素/自溶[血]素　autolysin
自身识别/自身識別　self-recognition
自身受体/自體受體　autoreceptor
自身输血/自體輸血[術]　autotransfusion
自身吞噬作用/自體吞噬作用　autophagocytosis

自身修饰假说/自身修飾假説 altered self-hypothesis
自身血清疗法/自體血清療法 autoserous treatment
自身血清肿凡纳明疗法/自體血清砷劑療法 autoserosalvarsan treatment
自身牙根种植体/自體牙根種植體 autologous root implant
自身牙移植术/自體牙移植術 autogenous tooth transplantation
自身移植的/自體移植的 autoplastic
自身移植术/自體移植法 autografting
自身移植物/自體移植物 autograft
自身疫苗/自身疫苗,自體疫苗 autogenous vaccine
自身致敏/自體致敏 autosensitization
自适应最小二乘/自適應最小平方 adaptive least square
自诉病史/自陳病歷 autoanamnesis
自体白细胞疗法/自體白血球療法 autoleukocytotherapy
自体败血病/自體敗血病 autosepticemia
自体孢子/自體孢子 autospore
自体变态反应的/自體過敏的 autoallergic
自体变应性肝炎/自體過敏性肝炎 autoallergic hepatitis
自体表皮移植术/自體表皮移植術 auto-epidermal grafting
自体导电法/自體傳導法 autoconduction
自体导液法/自體引流,自身洩液法 autodrainage
自体电子发射/自體電子發射 auto-eletronic emission
自体毒物/自體毒物 autointoxicant
自体锻炼/自體鍛煉 autogenic training
自体感觉/自體感覺 self-feeling
自体骨髓移植/自體骨髓移植 autologous bone marrow transplantation
自体红细胞敏感性紫癜/自體紅血球敏感性紫瘢症 purpura autoerythrocytica
自体幻视/自見幻覺 autoscopic hallucination
自体活化/自體促動作用 autoactivation
自体激素破坏/自體内分泌素破壞 autohormonoclasis
自体甲状旁腺移植/自體甲狀旁腺移植 parathyroid autotransplantation
自体检查/自體檢查 autoscopy
自体角膜移植术/自體角膜造形術 autokeratoplasty
自体免疫多内分泌念珠菌病综合征/自體免疫多内分泌念珠菌病症候群 autoimmune polyendocrine-candidiasis syndrome
自体免疫性脂膜炎/自體免疫性脂層炎 autoimmune panniculitis
自体皮肤的/自體皮膚的 autodermic
自体皮移植术/自體皮移植術 autologous skin grafting
自体脾移植/自體脾移植 autologous spleen transplantation
自体上皮移植物/自體上皮移植物 autoepidermic graft
自体肾毒素/自體腎毒素 autonephrotoxin
自体湿疹化/自體濕疹化,自傳濕疹 autoeczematization
自体实验/自體實驗 autoexperimentation
自体噬菌体/自體噬菌體 autobacteriophage
自体受精/自體受精 autogamy
自体输血/自體輸血 autologous blood transfusion
自[体吞]泡/自體吞噬泡 autophagic vacuole
自体吞噬红细胞作用/自體吞噬紅血球作用 autoerythrophagocytosis
自[体吞]噬体/自噬小體 autophagosome
自体外周血干细胞移植/自體外周血幹細胞移植 autologous peripheral blood stem cell transplantation
自体小肠移植/自體小腸移植 autologous small intestine transplantation
自体悬吊法/自體懸吊法 self-suspension
自体血浆疗法/自體血漿療法 autoplasmotherapy
自体血清肿凡纳明/自體血清阿斯凡納明 autoserosalvarsan
自体氧化物质/自體氧化物質 auto-oxidizable substance
自体药理学/自體藥理學 autopharmacology
自体移植/自體移植 autoplastic transplantation
自体移植膀胱成形术/自體移植膀胱造形術 autocystoplasty
自体移植物/自體移植物 autogenous graft, autoplastic graft
自体有效物质/自體有效物質 autacoid
自体中毒/自體中毒 autointoxication
自体中毒性精神病/自體中毒性精神病 autointoxication psychosis
自体[组织]放射照片/自體放射攝影 autohistoradiograph
自听增强/自覺聲高 autophonia
自慰/自慰,手淫,自淫 masturbation
自我暗示/自我暗示 autosuggestion
自我暗示性/自我暗示性 autosuggestibility
自我本能/自我本能 ego instinct

自我表露/自我揭露　self-disclosure
自我持续序列复制/自我持續序列複製　self-sustained sequence replication
自我刺激/自我刺激　self-stimulation
自我催眠/自己催眠　autohypnosis
自我概念/自我概念　self-concept
自我护理/自我護理　self-care
自我护理病房/自我護理病房　self-care unit
自我检查/自我檢查　self-examination
自我理解不能/不能自我瞭解　akatanoesis
自我评估/自我評估　self-assessment
自我评价方案/自我評價方案　self-evaluation program
自我[人格]变换[妄想]/自他混合，偽裝他人　appersonification
自我伤害行为/自我傷害行爲　self-injurious behavior
自我疏泄/自行精神發洩　autocatharsis
自我投药法/自我投藥法　self-medication
自我效验/自我效驗　self-efficacy
自我心理学/自我心理學　self-psychology
自我训练/自我訓練　autotraining
自我遵嘱服药/自我遵囑服藥　self-administration
自吸收/自吸收　self-absorption
自行车测力计/自行車測力器　bicycle ergometer
自行车疗法/自行車療法　cyclotherapy
自行车运动/自行車運動　bicycling
自[行]断离/自我截斷　autoamputation
自行缓解/自行緩解　spontaneous remission
自行性肿瘤消退/自行性腫瘤消退　spontaneous neoplasm regression
自旋标记物/自旋標記物　spin label
自旋捕获/自旋捕獲　spin trapping
自旋密度/旋轉密度　spin density
自血激素疗法/血液激素療法　hemocrinotherapy
自养[畸]胎/自養畸胎　autositic monster
自异体皮混合移植术/自異體皮混合移植術　intermingled transplantation of auto and allogeneic skin
自由场测听[法]/自由場測聽[法]　free-field audiometry
自由电子/游離電子　free electron
自由基/自由基　free radical
自由基负离子/自由基陰離子　radical anion
自由基清除剂/自由基清除劑　free radical scavenger
自由基学说/自由基學說　free radical theory
自由基正离子/自由基陽離子　radical cation
自由狂/自由狂　eleuteromania

自由联想/自由聯想　free association
自由能/自由能　free energy
自由容积学说/自由容積學說　free volume theory
自由上肢/自由上肢　free upper limb
自由上肢骨/自由上肢骨　bone of free upper limb
自由上肢连结/自由上肢連結　joint of free upper limb
自由态药物/自由態藥物　free drug
自由下肢/自由下肢　free lower limb
自由下肢骨/自由下肢骨　bone of free lower limb
自由下肢连结/自由下肢連結　joint of free lower limb
自愈力/自[然治]愈力　vis medicatrix naturae
自愿性脱位/自由意志脱位　voluntary dislocation
自知力/自覺力,內省力　insight
自制自用中间体/自製自用中間體　captive intermediate
自主/自主　autonomy
自主的/自主的　autonomic
自主反射障碍/自主反射障礙　autonomic dysreflexia
自主分化/自我分化　self-differentiation
自主复制序列/自主複製序列　autonomous replication sequence
自主膀胱/自主性膀胱　autonomous bladder
自主神经/自主神經　autonomic nerve, automatic nerve
自主神经病变/自主神經病變　autonomic neuropathy
自主神经传导阻滞/自主神經傳導阻滯　autonomic nerve block
自主神经丛/自主神經叢　autonomic plexus
自主神经腹部/自主神經腹部　abdominal portion of autonomic nerve
自主神经节/自主神經節　autonomic ganglia
自主神经盆部/自主神經盆部　pelvic portion of autonomic nerve
自主神经去神经支配/自主神經去神經支配　autonomic nervous denervation
自主神经通路/自主神經通路　autonomic nervous pathway
自主神经系统/自主神經系統　autonomic nervous system
自主神经系统疾病/自主神經系統疾病　autonomic nervous system disease
自主神经系统障碍/自主神經系統障礙　autonomic nervous system disorder
自主神经胸部/自主神經胸部　thoracic portion of autonomic nerve

自主神经药物／自主神經藥物　autonomic nervous agent
自主神经支／自主神經支　autonomic branch
自主性高功能甲状腺结节／自主性高功能甲狀腺結節　autonomous hyperfunctional thyroid nodule
自主性膀胱／自主性膀胱，自動性膀胱　automatic bladder, autonomic bladder
自助器／自助器　self-help device
自助小组／自助小組　self-help group
自助装置／自助裝置　self-help device
Y 字绷带／Y 字繃帶　Y-shaped bandage
字盲／字盲　word blindness
8 字形绷带／8 字形繃帶　figure-of-8 bandage
T 字形骨折／T 字形骨折　T fracture
V-Y 字形皮瓣／V-Y 字形皮瓣　V-Y flap
字序性书写不能／寫字不能　literal agraphia
眦／眥，眼角　canthus
眦病／眥病　canthus disease
眦部睑缘炎／眥部瞼緣炎　angular blepharitis
眦成形术／眥成形術，眥造形術　canthoplasty
眦错位／眥錯位　dystopia canthi
眦缝合术／眥縫合術　canthorrhaphy
眦固定术／眥固定術　canthopexy
眦结膜炎／眥病結膜炎　angular conjunctivitis
眦切除术／眥切除術　canthectomy
眦切开术／眥切開術，眥鬆解術　cantholysis
眦韧带／眥韌帶　canthal ligament
眦炎／眥炎　canthitis
宗教疗法／祈禱療法　theotherapy
宗教性忧郁症／宗教性憂鬱病，天譴憂鬱病　melancholia religiosa
宗教医院／宗教醫院　religious hospital
宗筋／宗筋　convergent tendon, penis and testes
宗气／宗氣　pectoral qi
综合保健／綜合保健　comprehensive health care
综合化学疗法／綜合化學治療　polychemotherapy
综合疗法／綜合療法　combined modality therapy
综合性／周全性　comprehensiveness
综合性老年评估／周全性老年評估　comprehensive geriatric assessment
综合性牙病防治／綜合性牙病防治　comprehensive dental care
综合牙科学／一般牙醫學　general dentistry
综合医院／綜合醫院　general hospital
综合预防／綜合預防　universal precaution
综合征／綜合症狀，症候群，複合症狀　symptom complex, syndrome
XYY 综合征／XYY 性染色體異常症候群　XYY syndrome
综合治疗医师／普遍性治療家　pantherapist
棕黑素／嗜黑色素　phaeomelanin
棕花蛛咬中毒／棕蜘蛛中毒　loxoscelism
棕榈／棕櫚　fortune windmillpalm petiole
棕榈襞／棕櫚皺襞　palmate fold
棕榈醇／十八烷醯基醇　palmityl alcohol
棕榈酸／棕櫚酸，軟脂酸　Palmitic Acid
棕榈酸辛酯／棕櫚酸辛酯　octyl palmitate
棕榈酸盐类／棕櫚酸鹽類　palmitates
棕榈酰辅酶 A／棕櫚醯輔酶 A　palmitoyl coenzyme A
棕榈酰肉毒碱／棕櫚醯卡尼丁　palmitoyl carnitine
棕榈酰 CoA 水解酶／棕櫚醯 CoA 水解酶　palmitoyl-CoA hydrolase
棕色毒毛旋花子素／棕色毒毛旋花子素　onaye
棕色瘤／棕色［腫］瘤　brown tumor
棕色内障／棕色内障　brown cataract
棕色水肿／棕色水腫　brown edema
棕色隐居蜘蛛咬伤／棕色隱居蜘蛛咬傷　brown recluse spider bite
棕色脂肪瘤／棕色脂肪瘤　brown fat tumor
棕色脂肪组织／棕色脂肪組織　brown adipose tissue
腙／腙　hydrazone
鬃／鬃　bristle
总按／總按　simultaneous palpations with three fingers
总产程／總產程　total stage of labor
总代谢／總代謝　total metabolism
总胆管／總膽管　common bile duct
总胆管的／總膽管的　choledochal
总氮量／總氮量　nitrogen content
总抚养率／總撫養率　total dependency ratio
总骨脚／總骨腳　common bony crus
总固体／總固體　total solid
总和／總和　summation
总灰分／總灰分　total ash
总腱／共同腱　common tendon
总腱环／腱總環　common tendinous ring
总浸出物／總抽提物　total extractive
总卵黄管／總卵黃管　common vitelline duct
总膜脚／總膜腳　common membranous crus
总死亡率／總死亡率　all-cause mortality
总体表面积／總體表面積　total body surface area
总体反射／集團反射　mass reflex
总体评定量表／總體評定量表　global assessment scale
总吸收量／總吸收量　integral absorbed dose

总远视/完全遠視　total hypermetropia
总指嵴数/總指嵴數　total finger ridge count
总主静脉/總主靜脈　common cardinal vein
总转化产量/總轉化産率　overall conversion yield
纵层/縱層　longitudinal layer
纵产式/縱産式　longitudinal lie
纵隔/縱隔　mediastinum
纵隔部/縱隔部　mediastinal part
纵隔肠囊肿/縱隔腸囊腫　enteric cyst of mediastinum
纵隔充气造影照片/縱隔充氣照片　pneumomediastinogram
纵隔的/縱隔的　mediastinal
纵隔蜂窝[组]织炎/縱隔蜂窩[組]織炎　mediastinal cellulitis
纵隔后动脉/後縱隔動脈　posterior mediastinal artery
纵隔后淋巴结/縱隔後淋巴結　posterior mediastinal lymph node
纵隔积气/縱隔積氣,氣縱隔　pneumomediastinum
纵隔积血/縱隔積血　hematomediastinum
纵隔疾病/縱隔疾病　mediastinal disease
纵隔间隙/縱隔間隙　mediastinum space
纵隔静脉/縱隔靜脈　mediastinal vein
纵隔镜/縱隔鏡　mediastinoscope
纵隔镜检查/縱隔鏡檢法,縱隔檢視法　mediastinoscopy
纵隔淋巴结结核/縱隔淋巴結結核　mediastinal lymphonode tuberculosis
纵隔囊肿/縱隔囊腫　mediastinal cyst
纵隔脓肿/縱隔膿腫　mediastinal abscess
纵隔皮样囊肿/縱隔皮樣囊腫　dermoid cyst of mediastinum
纵隔扑动/縱隔撲動　mediastinal flutter
纵隔气肿/縱隔氣腫　mediastinal emphysema
纵隔前动脉/前縱隔動脈　anterior mediastinal artery
纵隔前淋巴结/縱隔前淋巴結　anterior mediastinal lymph node
纵隔前淋巴结上群/縱隔前淋巴結上群　superior group of anterior mediastinal lymph node
纵隔切开术/縱隔切開術　mediastinotomy
纵隔乳糜症/縱隔乳糜症,乳糜縱隔　chylomediastinum
纵隔疝/縱隔疝　mediastinal hernia
纵隔X射线照片/縱隔X線照片,縱隔X光圖　mediastinogram
纵隔X射线照相术/縱隔X光攝影　mediastinography
纵隔神经源性肿瘤/縱隔神經源性腫瘤　mediastinal neurogenic tumor
纵隔嗜铬细胞瘤/縱隔嗜鉻細胞瘤　mediastinal pheochromocytoma
纵隔纤维化/縱隔纖維化　mediastinal fibrosis
纵隔心包炎/縱隔心包炎　mediastinal pericarditis
纵隔胸膜/縱隔胸膜,胸膜縱隔部　mediastinal pleura
纵隔血管滤泡性淋巴节增生/縱隔血管濾泡性淋巴節增生　angiofollicular mediastinal lymph node hyperplasia
纵隔炎/縱隔炎　mediastinitis
纵隔移位/縱隔移位　mediastinal displacement
纵隔支/縱隔支　mediastinal branch
纵隔肿瘤/縱隔腫瘤　mediastinal neoplasm
纵沟/縱溝　longitudinal groove
纵骨折/縱骨折　longitudinal fracture
纵火狂/縱火癖　incendiarism
纵肌/縱肌　longitudinalis, longitudinal muscle
纵裂/縱裂　longitudinal fissure
纵切片/縱切片　longitudinal section
纵韧带/縱韌帶　longitudinal ligament
纵褥式缝合/垂直墊褥狀縫合法　vertical mattress suture
纵束/縱束　longitudinal band
纵纤维/縱纖維　longitudinal fiber
纵向的/縱[向]的　longitudinal
纵向分辨率/縱向解析度　longitudinal resolution
纵向分离/縱向分離　longitudinal dissociation
纵小管/縱小管　longitudinal tubule
纵欲不节/縱欲不節　indulgence in sensual pleasure without restraint
走罐/走罐　moving cupping
走黄/走黄　running yellow, carbuncle complicated by septicemia, toxemia and septicemia
走黄·热毒内闭证/走黄·熱毒内閉證　running yellow with pattern of internal blockage of heat-toxin
走黄·热毒入血证/走黄·熱毒入血證　running yellow with pattern of heat-toxin entering blood phase
走黄·壮热亡阴证/走黄·壯熱亡陰證　running yellow with pattern of yin exhaustion due to high fever
走火/走火　fire deviate from course
走火入魔/走火入魔　fire deviate from course and entrance of demons
走马疳/走馬疳,口頰壞疽　acute gangrenous stomatitis, noma

奏乐器不能/奏樂器不能　instrumental amusia
足/足　foot, pes
足背/足背　dorsum of foot
足背侧骨间静脉/足背側骨間静脈　dorsal interosseous vein of foot
足背动脉/足背動脈　dorsal artery of foot
足背筋膜/足背筋膜　dorsal fascia of foot
足背静脉丛/足背静脈叢　dorsal venous plexus of foot
足背静脉弓/足背静脈弓　dorsal venous arch of foot
足背静脉网/足背静脈網　dorsal venous rete of foot
足背内侧皮神经/足背內側皮神經　medial dorsal cutaneous nerve of foot
足背外侧皮神经/足背外側皮神經　lateral dorsal cutaneous nerve of foot
足背系韧带/足背繫韌帶　fundiform ligament of foot
足背中间皮神经/足背中間皮神經　intermediate dorsal cutaneous nerve of foot
足背中皮神经/足背中皮神經　intermediate dorsal cutaneous nerve of foot
足病/足病　pedopathy
足部骨骼/足部骨骼　foot bone
足部舟状骨/足部舟狀骨　scaphoid bone of foot
足颤/足顫　tremor of feet
足长度/足長度　foot length
足充填器/足形充填器　foot plugger
足的/足的　pedal
足底/足底　sole of foot
足底板/足底板　sole plate
足底长韧带/蹠側長韌帶　long plantar ligament
足底疔/足底疔　ding of sole, furuncle on sole
足底方肌/足底方肌,蹠方肌　quadratus plantae, musculus quadratus plantae
足底敷用药/足底貼用藥　suppedania
足底弓/足底弓　plantar arch
足底弓穿支/足底弓穿支　perforating branch of plantar arch
足底腱膜/足底腱膜,蹠腱膜　plantar aponeurosis
足底筋膜炎/足底筋膜炎　plantar fasciitis
足底静脉弓/足底静脈弓　plantar venous arch
足底静脉网/足底静脈網　plantar venous rete
足底内侧动脉/足底內側動脈　medial plantar artery
足底内侧动脉浅支/足底內側動脈淺支　superficial branch of medial plantar artery
足底内侧动脉深支/足底內側動脈深支　deep branch of medial plantar artery
足底内侧神经/足底內側神經　medial plantar nerve
足底胼胝/足底胼胝　plantar callus
足底浅弓/足底淺弓,蹠淺弓　superficial plantar arch
足底韧带/蹠側韌帶　plantar ligament
足底深动脉/足底深動脈　deep plantar artery
足底深弓/足底深弓,蹠深弓　deep plantar arch
足［底］神经痛/足底神經痛　pododynia
足底痛/足底痛,蹠痛　plantalgia
足底外侧动脉/足底外側動脈　lateral plantar artery
足底外侧神经/外蹠神經　lateral plantar nerve
足底外侧神经浅支/足底外側神經淺支　superficial branch of lateral plantar nerve
足底外侧神经深支/足底外側神經深支　deep branch of lateral plantar nerve
足底外动脉/足底外動脈　external plantar artery
足底疣/足底疣,蹠疣　verruca plantaris
足发背/足發背　cellulitis of foot dorsum, pyogenic carbuncle of back of foot
足发背·湿热下注证/足發背·濕熱下注證　cellulitis of foot dorsum with pattern of dampness-heat diffusing downward
足发背·虚火灼筋证/足發背·虛火灼筋證　cellulitis of foot dorsum with pattern of deficiency-fire scorching tendon
足反射/足反射　foot reflex
足副舟骨/足副舟骨　accessory navicular bone
足跟点/足跟點　pternion
足跟疽/足跟疽　tuberculosis of heel
足跟轻叩/跟部輕叩,叩跟反射　heel tap
足跟痛/足跟痛　painful heel, heel pain
足弓形动脉/足弓形動脈　arcuate artery of foot
足骨/足骨　bones of foot
足骨间背侧肌/足骨間背側肌　dorsal interosseous of foot
足骨炎/足骨炎　pedal osteitis
足关节/足關節　joint of foot, articulations of foot
足关节炎/足關節炎　podarthritis
足汗/足汗　foot sweating
足后段/足後段　hindfoot
足踝疽/足踝疽　ankle abscess
足畸形/足畸形　foot deformities
足疾病/足疾病　foot disease
足迹法/足跡法　footprinting
足尖/足尖　foot tip
足厥阴肝经/足厥陰肝經　Jueyin Liver Channel of Foot, Jueyin Liver Meridian of Foot
足菌肿/足菌腫,足菌病　mycetoma
足溃疡/足潰瘍　foot ulcer
足量/足量　quantum satis
足临泣/足臨泣　zulinqi, GB41

足霉菌/足[分枝]黴菌　foot fungus
足内侧缘/足内側緣　medial border of foot
足内翻/足内翻　strephenopodia
足内翻试验/足内翻試驗　inversion stress test, varus stress test
足皮肤病/足皮膚病　foot dermatosis
足窍阴/足竅陰　zuqiaoyin, GB44
足球员膝病/足球膝病　football knee
足软/足軟　flaccidity of feet
足三里/足三里　zusanli, ST36
足三阳经/足三陽經　three yang channels of foot, three yang meridians of foot
足三阴经/足三陰經　three yin channels of foot, three yin meridians of foot
足少阳胆经/足少陽膽經　Shaoyang Gallbladder Channel of Foot, Shaoyang Gallbladder Meridian of Foot
足少阴肾经/足少陰腎經　Shaoyin Kidney Channel of Foot, Shaoyin Kidney Meridian of Foot
足水肿/足水腫　podedema
足损伤/足損傷　foot injury
足太阳膀胱经/足太陽膀胱經　Taiyang Bladder Channel of Foot, Taiyang Bladder Meridian of Foot
足太阴脾经/足太陰脾經　Taiyin Spleen Channel of Foot, Taiyin Spleen Meridian of Foot
足通谷/足通谷　zutonggu, BL66
足痛/足痛　podalgia, foot pain
足突/足突　foot process
足突型肾病/足突型腎病　foot process nephrosis
足外侧缘/足外側緣　lateral border of foot
足外翻/足外翻　convex foot
足外翻试验/足外翻試驗　eversion stress test, valgus stress test
足外踝征/外踝徵象，伽達克氏徵象　external malleolar sign
足五里/足五里　zuwuli, LR10
足细胞/足細胞　foot cell, podocyte
足下垂/足下垂　drop foot
足先露/足产式,足位生产　footling presentation
足现象/足現象　foot phenomenon
足小头间静脉/足小頭間靜脈　intercapitular vein of foot
足心动脉/蹠骨底側動脈　plantar metatarsal artery
足心静脉/蹠底靜脈　plantar metatarsal vein
足癣/足癬　tinea of feet
足雅司病/足雅司病　foot yaws
足阳明胃经/足陽明胃經　Yangming Stomach Channel of Foot, Yangming Stomach Meridian of Foot
足医/足醫　podiatrist
足医术/足醫術　podiatry
足蚓状肌/足蚓狀肌　lumbrical muscle of foot
足印/足印,足跡　ichnogram
足印器/足痕器,足紋器　podograph
足硬/足硬　stiff foot
足浴/足浴　pediluvium
足月的/足月的,滿期的　full-term
足月儿/足月兒　term infant
足月分娩/足月分娩　term birth
足阵挛/足陣攣　clonus foot, foot clonus
足跖臭汗症/足蹠臭汗症　plantar bromidrosis
足趾/[足]趾　toe
足趾背面/足趾背面　dorsal surface of toe
足趾底面/足趾底面　plantar surface of toe
足趾征/趾徵象,巴賓司基氏反射　toe sign
足中段/足中段　midfoot
足舟骨/舟骨　navicular bone
足舟骨骨折/足舟[狀]骨骨折　fracture of scaphoid of foot, scaphoid fracture of foot
足舟状骨/足舟狀骨　navicular bone of foot
阻断变异株/阻斷變異株　blocked mutant
α-阻断剂/甲型阻斷劑　alpha blocker
阻断疗法/阻斷療法　withholding treatment
阻断性胸膜炎/阻斷性胸膜炎　blocked pleurisy
阻断正畸学/阻斷正畸學　interceptive orthodontics
阻遏/阻遏　repression
阻遏蛋白/阻遏蛋白　repressor protein
阻遏酶/阻遏酶　repressible enzyme
阻遏物蛋白/阻遏物蛋白　aporepressor
阻抗/阻抗　impedance
阻抗体积描记术/阻抗體積描記術　impedance plethysmography
阻抗心动描记术/阻抗心動描記術　impedance cardiography
阻尼扭摆旋转试验/阻尼扭擺旋轉試驗　damped torsion swing test
阻塞器/填器　obturator
阻塞性动脉疾病/阻塞性動脈疾病　obstructive arterial disease
阻塞性肺疾病/阻塞性肺疾病　obstructive lung disease
阻塞性肺炎/阻塞性肺炎　obstructive pneumonia
阻塞性黄疸/阻塞性黃疸　obstructive jaundice
阻塞性角化病/[外耳道之]阻塞性角化病　keratosis obliterans
阻塞性静脉膨胀/靜脈膨脹　phlebismus

阻塞性栓塞/[全]阻塞性栓塞 obturating embolism
阻塞性栓子/阻塞性栓子 obturating embolus
阻塞性睡眠呼吸暂停/阻塞性睡眠呼吸暫停 obstructive sleep apnea
阻塞性通气障碍/阻塞性通氣障礙 obstructive ventilatory disorder
阻塞性小气道病/小氣道阻塞性疾病 obstructive small airways disease
阻生磨牙/臼齒嵌閉 impacted molar
阻生牙/嵌閉齒 impacted tooth
阻睡药/妨睡藥,防睡劑 agrypnode
阻滞/阻滯 block
阻滞剂/阻滯劑 retarder
阻滞麻醉/阻斷麻醉 block anesthesia
阻滞物/阻斷劑 blocker
阻滞性胃积气/食道痙攣性胃積氣 blocked aerogastria
阻滞药/阻斷藥 blocade, blocker
阻滞长出/阻生萌牙 impeded eruption
组氨醇/組胺醇 histidinol
组氨醇磷酸酶/組胺醇磷酸酶 histidinol-phosphatase
组氨酸/組胺酸 histidine
组氨酸氨基裂合酶/組[織]胺酸溶酶 histidine ammonia-lyase
组氨酸 tRNA 连接酶/組[織]胺酸 tRNA 連接酶 histidine-tRNA ligase
组氨酸酶/組[織]胺酸酶 histidase
组氨酸酶缺乏/組[織]胺酸解壞酶缺乏 ahıstıdasıa
组氨酸尿/組[織]胺酸尿 histidinuria
组氨酸脱羧酶/組[織]胺酸去碳酶 histidine decarboxylase
组氨酸血症/組[織]胺酸血症 histidinemia
组胺/組[織]胺 histamine
组胺代谢药/組[織]胺代謝藥 histamine metabolism drug
组胺分泌因子/組[織]胺分泌因子 histamine-releasing factor
组胺激动药/組[織]胺激動藥 histamine agonist
组胺 N-甲基转移酶/組[織]胺 N-甲基轉移酶 histamine N-methyltransferase
组胺 H1 拮抗剂/組[織]胺 H1 拮抗劑 histamine H1 antagonist
组胺拮抗药/組[織]胺拮抗藥 histamine antagonist
组胺类药/組[織]胺類藥 tissue amine drug
组胺试验/組[織]胺試驗 histamine test
组胺释放/組[織]胺釋放 histamine release
组胺释放试验/組[織]胺釋放試驗 histamine-release test

组胺受体/組[織]胺受體 histamine receptor
组胺 H1 受体/組[織]胺 H1 受體 histamine H1 receptor
组胺 H2 受体拮抗药/組[織]胺 H2 受體拮抗藥 histamine H2 receptor antagonist
组胺性头痛/組[織]胺性頭痛 histamine cephalalgia
组胺休克/組[織]胺休克 histamine shock
组胺血[症]/組[織]胺血症 histaminemia
组胺抑制因子/組[織]胺抑制因子 histamine suppressor factor
组成/組成 composition
组成[结构]蛋白/組成蛋白[質] constitutive protein
组成性异染色质/體質性異染色質 constitutive heterochromatin
组蛋白/組[織]蛋白 histone
组蛋白赖氨酸 N-甲基转移酶/組蛋白賴胺酸 N-甲基轉移酶 histone-lysine N-methyltransferase
组蛋白类/組蛋白類 histones
组蛋白密码/組蛋白密碼 histone code
组蛋白脱乙酰基酶类/組蛋白脱乙醯基酶類 histone deacetylases
组蛋白锌胰岛素/組[織]蛋白鋅胰島素 histone zinc insulin
组分/組[成]分 component, constituent
组合化学技术/組合化學技術 combinatorial chemistry technique
组合皮瓣/組合皮瓣 combined skin flap
组合性牙瘤/組合性牙瘤 compound odontoma
组合运动模式/組合運動模式 mass movement pattern
组句不能/連句不能,連語不能 aphrasia
组牙功能殆/組牙功能殆 group functional occlusion
组织/組織 tissue
组织包埋/組織包埋 tissue embedding
组织胞浆菌病/組織漿菌病,網狀內皮細胞菌病 histoplasmosis
组织胞浆菌素/組織漿菌素 histoplasmin
组织保存/組織保存 tissue preservation
组织变态/組織變化,組織變形 tissue metamorphosis
组织变形性滑液囊肿/組織變形性滑液囊腫 metaplastic synovial cyst
组织病理学/組織病理學,病理組織學 histopathology
组织成分/組織成分,組織要素 tissue element
组织处理技术/組織處理技術 tissue management technique
组织存活/組織存活 tissue survival

组织代用品/組織代用品　tissue substitute
组织胆固醇沉着/膽脂醇沈著　cholesterohistechia
组织蛋白/組織蛋白　tissue protein
组织蛋白酶/組織蛋白酶,蛋白分解酵素　cathepsin
组织蛋白尿/組織蛋白尿　histonuria
组织蛋白胰岛素/組織蛋白胰島素　histone insulin
组[织]滴虫病/組織滴蟲病　histomoniasis
组织毒的/組織毒的　histotoxic
组织多肽抗原/組織多肽抗原　tissue polypeptide antigen
组织发生/組織發生　histogenesis
组织方针/組織方針　organizational policy
组织分布/組織分布　tissue distribution
组织分化/組織分化　histo-differentiation
组织分型/組織分型　tissue typing
组织改革/組織改革　organizational innovation
组织工程/組織工程　tissue engineering
组织供者/組織供者　tissue donor
组织构成缺陷/組織構成缺陷,缺陷瘤　hamartia
组织构造学/組織構造學,組織構成學　tectology
组织固定/組織固定　tissue fixation
组织管理模型/組織管理模型　organizational model
组织含水过多/組織含水過多　histohydria
组织呼吸/組織呼吸　tissue respiration
组织化学/組織化學　histochemistry
组织化学疗法/組織化學療法　histochemotherapy
组织激肽释放酶类/組織激肽釋放酶類　tissue kallikreins
组织间吸收/間質吸收　interstitial absorption
组织间隙液压/組織間隙液壓　interstitial fluid pressure
组织库/組織庫　tissue bank
组织扩张/組織擴展　tissue expansion
组织扩张器/組織擴展器　tissue expander
组织隶属关系/組織隸屬關係　organizational affiliation
组织疗法/組織療法　tissue therapy
组织瘤/組織瘤　histioma
组织面/組織面　tissue surface
组织内放射/間質輻射　interstitial radiation
组织内氯[化物]过多/高氯症　chlorhistechia
[组织内]氧过多/氧過多　hyperoxia
组织内脂肪消失/組織脂肪消失　lipohistiodieresis
组织[内]贮留/組織[内]滞留　historetention
组织黏合剂/組織黏合劑　tissue adhesive
组织凝血酶/組織凝血酶　histothrombin
组织培养/組織培養[法]　tissue culture
组织培养技术/組織培養技術　tissue culture technique
组织配型/組織配型　tissue matching
组织破碎/組織破裂　historrhexis
组织气肿/組織氣腫　tissue emphysema
组织汽化/組織汽化　tissue vaporization
组织切片/組織切片　tissue slice
组织切片机/組織切片機　histotome
组织切片术/組織切片術　histotomy
组织缺氧[症]/組織缺氧[症]　histanoxia
组织溶解/組織溶解　histolysis
组织溶解物/組織溶解產物　histolysate
组织射线照相术/組織放射照相術　historadiography
组织生理学/組織生理學　histophysiology
组织损害/組織[學的]損害,微小病竈　histologic lesion
组织弹性测定器/組織彈性計　elastometer
组织糖分过多/組織含糖過多　hyperglycistia
组织糖原/組織糖原　tissue glycogen
组织提取物/組織提取物　tissue extract
组织调整/組織調整　tissue conditioning
组织细胞/組織細胞　histiocyte
组织细胞的/組織細胞的　histiocytic
组织细胞化学/組織細胞化學　histocytochemistry
组织细胞坏死性淋巴结炎/組織細胞壞死性淋巴結炎　histiocytic necrotizing lymphadenitis
组织细胞瘤/組織細胞瘤,組織球瘤　histiocytoma
组织细胞瘤病/組織細胞瘤病,多發組織細胞瘤　histiocytomatosis
组织细胞肉瘤/組織細胞肉瘤　histiosarcoma
组织细胞吞噬性脂膜炎/組織細胞吞噬性脂膜炎　histiocytic cytophagic panniculitis
组织细胞性白血病/組織細胞白血病　histiocytic leukemia
组织细胞性淋巴瘤/組織細胞性淋巴瘤　histiocytic lymphoma
组织细胞学制备技术/組織細胞學製備技術　histocytological preparation technique
组织细胞增多症/組織細胞增多症　histocytosis
组织相容性/組織相容性,組織適應　histocompatibility
组织相容性复合体/組織相容性複合體　histocompatibility complex
组织相容性基因/組織相容性基因　histocompatibility gene
组织相容性基因复合体/組織相容性基因複合體　histocompatibility gene complex
组织相容性基因座/組織適合性位元點　histocompatibility locus

组织相容性抗原/組織相容性抗原 histocompatibility antigen
组织相容性Y抗原/組織相容性Y抗原 histocompatibility Y antigen
组织相容性试验/組織相容性試驗 histocompatibility test
组织效率/組織效率 organizational efficiency
组织形成液/組織成型液 enchyma
组织形态学/組織形態學 histomorphology
组织型生长/組織型生長 histiotypic growth
组织型纤溶酶原激活物/組織型纖溶酶原啟動物 tissue plasminogen activator
组织型纤维蛋白溶酶原活化剂/組織漿胞素原活化劑 tissue-type plasminogen activator
组织修复/組織修復 tissue repair
组织学/組織學 histology
组织学技术/組織學技術 histological technique
组织学技术员/組織學技術員 histology technician
组织学类型肿瘤/組織學類型腫瘤 neoplasms by histologic type
组织学诊断/組織學診斷［法］,組織檢診法 histodiagnosis
组织血原性/組織原及血原的 histohematogenous
组织氧过少/組織含氧過少 histohypoxia
组织样的/組織樣的 histoid
组织样瘤/組織樣新生物 histoid neoplasm
组织样麻风瘤/組織樣麻風瘤 histoid leproma
组织移植/組織移植 tissue transplantation
组织荧光/組織螢光 histofluorescence
组织营养质/組織營養質 histotroph
组织运动/組織運動 histokinesis
组织再生/組織再生 tissue regeneration
组织增生/組織增生［過度］ hyperblastosis
组织增生过多/組織增生過多 hamartoplasia
组织张力/組織張力 tissue tension
组织者/發育誘導組織,胚胎之機化質 organizer
组织针/組織針 harpoon
组织阵列分析/組織陣列分析 tissue array analysis
组织中心/組織中心,形成中心 organization center
组织终变/細胞最後分化 histoteliosis
组织中毒性缺氧/組織中毒性缺氧 histotoxic hypoxemia
组织贮存/組織貯存 tissue storage
组织状况研究/組織狀況研究 organizational case study
组织着色病/組織著色病 histochromatosis
祖德克-勒里什综合征/蘇-勒二氏症候群 Sudeck-Leriche syndrome
祖德克萎缩/Sudeck氏萎縮 Sudeck atrophy
祖克坎德尔静脉/Zuckerkandl氏静脈 Zuckerkandl vein
祖先/祖先 antecedent
钻穿性脓/穿洞性膿 burrowing pus
钻骨［露髓］术/鑽骨［露髓］術 bone drilling operation
钻取活组织检查/鑽鑿式活組織檢查法 punch biopsy
钻石样皮肤病/鑽石樣皮膚病 diamond-skin disease
钻牙机/齒科機械 dental engine
嘴侧线形核/嘴側線形核 nucleus linearis rostralis
嘴刺目感染/嘴刺目感染 Enoplida infection
最长肌/最長肌 longissimus, longissimus muscle
最大长度/最大長度 greatest length
最大功能容量/最大功能容量 maximal functional capacity
最大呼气流量-容积曲线/最大呼氣流量-容積曲線 maximal expiratory flow-volume curve
最大呼气流速/最大呼氣流速 maximal expiratory flow rate
最大加速期/最大加速期 maximum acceleration phase
最大耐受剂量/最大耐受劑量 maximum tolerated dose, MTD
最大耐受浓度/最大耐受濃度 maximum tolerated concentration, MTC
最大容许量/最大容許［劑］量 maximum permissible dose
最大收缩高/最大收縮高 apex height
最大酸排出量/最大酸排出量 maximal acid output
最大通气量/最大通氣量 maximal voluntary ventilation
最大氧耗量/最大氧耗量 maximal oxygen consumption
最大运动心率/最大運動心率 maximal exercise heart rate
最大中期呼气流速/最大中期呼氣流速 maximal mid-expiratory flow rate
最大做功能力/最大做功能力 maximal work capacity
最低肺泡有效浓度/最低肺泡有效濃度 minimum alveolar concentration
最低抑菌浓度/最低抑菌濃度 minimum inhibitory concentration, MIC
最低装量/最小充填量 minimum fill
最高容许浓度/最高容許濃度 maximum allowable concentration

最广泛接触的牙尖交错殆/最廣泛接觸的牙尖交錯殆　maximum contacted intercuspal occlusion
最广泛接触牙尖交错位/最廣泛接觸牙尖交錯位　maximum contacted intercuspal position
最后区/最後區　area postrema
最佳的/最適合的　optimal
最佳膳食/最適當飲食　optimal diet
K-最近邻域法/K-最近鄰法　K-nearest neighbor method
最上鼻甲/最上鼻甲　supreme nasal concha, supreme ethmoidal concha
最上鼻甲骨/最上鼻甲骨　concha nasalis suprema
最上项线/最上項線　highest nuchal line
最适pH/最適酸鹼值　optimum pH
最适宿主/最適宿主　host of predilection
最适温度/最適溫度　optimum temperature
最适响度级/最適響度級　most comfortable loudness level
最外囊/最外囊　extreme capsule
最小蛋白量/最小蛋白質　minimum protein
最小抵抗部/最小抵抗部　locus minoris resistentiae
最小二乘法/最小平方法　least square method
最小红斑量/最小紅斑量　minimal erythema dose
最小偏向/最小偏向　minimum deviation
最小球差单透镜/對側透鏡　crossed lens
最小视角/最小視角　minimum visual angle
最小腰围/最小腰圍　minimum waist circumference
最小致死量/最小致死量　minimum lethal dose
最小致死浓度/最小致死濃度　minimum lethal concentration, MLC
最优化方法/最適化方法　optimization method
最终产物/最終產物　end product
最终原因/最終原因,最後原因　ultimate cause
罪恶妄想/罪惡妄想　delusion of sin
醉汉/醉漢　inebriate
醉[状]/醉　inebriation
左板/左板　left lamina
左半结肠切除术/左[側]半結腸切除術　left hemicolectomy
左半球/左半球　left hemisphere
左半心畸形/左半心畸形　hemicardia sinistra
左半月瓣/左半月瓣　left semilunar valve
左布诺洛尔/左布諾洛爾　levobunolol
左侧心力衰竭/左側心力衰竭　left-sided heart failure
左肠系膜窦/左腸繫膜竇　left mesenteric sinus
左段间裂/左段間裂　left intersegmental fissure
左房壁折叠术/左房壁折疊術　left atrial wall plication
左房静脉/左房靜脈　left atrial vein
左房前静脉/左房前靜脈　anterior vein of left atrium
左房升主动脉联合切口/左房昇主動脈聯合切口　combined left atrio-aortic incision
左房室瓣/左房室瓣　left atrioventricular valve
左房室瓣后尖/左房室瓣後尖　posterior cusp of left atrioventricular valve
左房室瓣连合尖/左房室瓣連合尖　commissural cusp of left atrioventricular valve
左房室瓣前尖/左房室瓣前尖　anterior cusp of left atrioventricular valve
左房室口/左房室口　left atrioventricular orifice
左房斜静脉/左房斜靜脈　oblique vein of left atrium
左房血栓清除术/左房血栓清除術　left atrial thrombectomy
左啡诺/左啡諾　levorphanol
左肺/左肺　left lung
[左肺]底段上静脉/[左肺]底段上靜脈　superior basal vein
[左肺]底段下静脉/[左肺]底段下靜脈　inferior basal vein
左肺动脉/左肺動脈　left pulmonary artery
左肺动脉底部/左肺動脈底部　basal part of left pulmonary artery
左肺动脉后底支/左肺動脈後底支　posterior basal branch of left pulmonary artery
左肺动脉后支/左肺動脈後支　posterior branch of left pulmonary artery
左肺动脉尖支/左肺動脈尖支　apical branch of left pulmonary artery
左肺动脉内侧底支/左肺動脈內側底支　medial basal branch of left pulmonary artery
左肺动脉前底支/左肺動脈前底支　anterior basal branch of left pulmonary artery
左肺动脉前降支/左肺動脈前降支　anterior descending branch of left pulmonary artery
左肺动脉前支/左肺動脈前支　anterior branch of left pulmonary artery
左肺动脉上舌支/左肺動脈上舌支　superior lingular branch of left pulmonary artery
左肺动脉上叶支/左肺動脈上葉支　superior lobar branch of left pulmonary artery
左肺动脉舌支/左肺動脈舌支　lingular branch of left pulmonary artery
左肺动脉外侧底支/左肺動脈外側底支　lateral basal branch of left pulmonary artery
左肺动脉下舌支/左肺動脈下舌支　inferior lingular

branch of left pulmonary artery
[左肺动脉]下叶上支/[左肺動脈]下葉上支　superior branch of inferior lobe
左肺动脉下叶支/左肺動脈下葉支　inferior lobar branch of left pulmonary artery
左肺静脉/左肺靜脈　left pulmonary vein
左肺毛细血管/左肺微血管　left pulmonary capillary
左肺上叶/左肺上葉　superior lobe of left lung
左肺上叶支气管/左肺上葉支氣管　left superior lobar bronchus
左肺下叶/左肺下葉　inferior lobe of left lung
左肺下叶支气管/左肺下葉支氣管　left inferior lobar bronchus
左肺小舌/左肺小舌　lingula of left lung
左肺心切迹/左肺心切跡　cardiac notch of left lung
左腹积证/左腹積證　amassment disease of left abdomen
左腹下神经/左腹下神經　left hypogastric nerve
左肝管/左肝管　ductus hepaticus sinister
左肝上后间隙/左肝上後間隙　posterior left suprahepatic space
左肝上间隙/左肝上間隙　left suprahepatic space
左肝上前间隙/左肝上前間隙　anterior left suprahepatic space
左肝下后间隙/左肝下後間隙　posterior left subhepatic space
左肝下间隙/左肝下間隙　left infrahepatic space
左肝下前间隙/左肝下前間隙　anterior left subhepatic space
左睾丸静脉/左睾丸靜脈,睾丸左靜脈　left testicular vein, vena testicularis sinistra
左宫之人/左宫之人　atypical earth-phase person, more on one's own
左冠状动脉/左冠狀動脈　left coronary artery
左冠状动脉窦房结支/左冠狀動脈竇房結支　branch of sinuatrial node of left coronary artery
左冠状动脉外侧支/左冠狀動脈外側支　lateral branch of left coronary artery
左冠状动脉圆锥支/左冠狀動脈圓錐支　branch of left coronary arterial conus
左冠状静脉/左冠狀靜脈　left coronary vein
左归丸/左歸丸　zuogui pill
左归饮/左歸飲　zuogui drink
左后分支阻滞/左後分支阻滯　left posterior hemiblock
左奇静脉/左奇靜脈　left azygos vein
左脚/左腳　left crus
左结肠动脉/左結腸動脈　left colic artery

左结肠静脉/左結腸靜脈　left colic vein, vena colica sinistra
左结肠淋巴结/左結腸淋巴結　left colic lymph node
左结肠旁沟/左結腸旁溝　left paracolic sulcus
左金丸/左金丸　zuojin pill
左颈干/左頸幹　left jugular trunk
左颈内静脉/左頸內靜脈　left internal carotid vein
左颈外静脉/左頸外靜脈　left external jugular vein
左角之人/左角之人　atypical wood-phase person more obedient
左肋间上静脉/左上肋間靜脈　left superior intercostal vein
左利手/善用左手　left handedness
左卵巢静脉/左卵巢靜脈　left ovarian vein
左洛啡烷/左洛啡烷　levallorphan
左美丙嗪/左美丙嗪　methotrimeprazine
左内叶/左內葉　left medial lobe
左脐静脉/左臍靜脈　left umbilical vein
左气管支气管上淋巴结/左氣管支氣管上淋巴結　left superior tracheobronchial lymph node
左髂内动脉/左髂內動脈　left internal iliac artery
左髂外动脉/左髂外動脈　left external iliac artery
左前分支阻滞/左前分支阻滯　left anterior hemiblock
左腔静脉皱襞/左腔靜脈皺襞　fold of left vena cava
左腔静脉韧带/左腔靜脈韌帶　ligament of the left vena cava
左炔诺孕酮/左炔諾孕酮　levonorgestrel
左三角韧带/左三角韌帶　left triangular ligament
左上肺静脉/左上肺靜脈　left superior pulmonary vein
左上腔静脉韧带/左上腔靜脈韌帶　ligament of left superior vena cava
左肾动脉/左腎動脈　left renal artery
左肾上腺静脉/左腎上體靜脈　left suprarenal vein
左矢状窝/左矢狀窩　fossa sagittalis sinistra
左室充盈压/左室充盈壓　left ventricular filling pressure
左室辅助搏动/左室輔助搏動　left ventricular assist pulsation
左室后静脉/左[心]室後靜脈　posterior vein of left ventricle
左室后支/左室後支　posterior branch of left ventricle
左室前静脉/左室前靜脈　anterior vein of left ventricle
左束支/左束支,左[房室束]脚　left bundle branch

左束支传导阻滞/左束支傳導阻滯 left bundlebranch block
左锁骨下动脉/左鎖骨下動脈 left subclavian artery
左锁骨下干/左鎖骨下幹 left subclavian trunk
左锁骨下静脉/左鎖骨下靜脈 left subclavian vein
左头臂静脉/左頭臂靜脈 left brachiocephalic vein
左外叶/左側葉 left lateral lobe
左外叶上段/左外葉上段 superior segment of left lateral lobe
左外叶下段/左外葉下段 inferior segment of left lateral lobe
左位阑尾炎/左側闌尾炎 left-sided appendicitis
左位心/左心性臟器異位 levocardia
左下肺静脉/左下肺靜脈 left inferior pulmonary vein
左纤维环/左纖維環 left fibrous ring
左纤维三角/左纖維三角 left fibrous trigone
左心/左心 left heart
左心耳/左心耳,心左耳 left auricle, left auricle of heart
左心耳结扎术/左心耳結扎術 ligation of left atrial appendage
左心发育不全综合征/左心發育不全症候群 hypoplastic left heart syndrome
左心房/左心房 left atrium
左心房功能/左心房功能 left atrial function
左心房梳状肌/左心房梳狀肌 pectinate muscle of left atrium
左心房斜静脉/左心房斜靜脈 oblique vein of left atrium
左心室/左心室 left ventricle
左心室的/左心室的 left ventricular
左心室肥大/左心室肥大 left ventricular hypertrophy
左心室功能/左心室功能 left ventricular function
左心室功能障碍/左心室功能障礙 left ventricular dysfunction
左心室后静脉/左心室後靜脈 vena ventriculi sinistri posterior
左心室后乳头肌/左心室後乳頭肌 posterior papillary muscle of left ventricle
左心室后乳头状肌/左心室後乳頭狀肌 musculus papillaris posterior ventriculi sinistri
左心室品质指数/左心室品質指數 left ventricular mass index
左心室破裂/左心室破裂 left ventricle rupture
左心室前乳头肌/左心室前乳頭[狀]肌 anterior papillary muscle of left ventricle
左心室收缩压/左心室收縮壓 left ventricular systolic pressure
左心室双出口/左心室雙出口 double outlet of left ventricle
左心室心电图/左心室波 levocardiogram
左心引流/左心引流 left heart venting
左心转流术/左心轉流術 left heart bypass
左心转流系统/左心轉流系統 left heart bypass system
左胸廓内动脉/左胸廓内動脈 left internal mammary artery
左旋多巴/左旋多巴 L-dopa
左旋甲状腺素/左旋甲狀腺素 levothyroxine
左旋酒石酸/左旋酒石酸 levotartaric acid
左旋门冬酰胺醇/左旋門冬醯胺醇 leucogenenol
左旋咪唑/左旋咪唑 levamisole
左旋糖/左旋糖 sinistrose
左旋心/左旋心 levoversion of heart
左旋眼/眼球左旋 levoclination
左眼/左眼 left eye
左氧氟沙星/左氧氟沙星 levofloxacin
左腰干/左腰幹 left lumbar trunk
左腰淋巴结/左腰淋巴結 left lumbar lymph node
左叶/左葉 left lobe
左叶间裂/左葉間裂 left interlobar fissure
左右配穴法/左右配穴法 left-right points association, left-right points combination
左右转位/左右轉位 situs inversus
左缘静脉/左緣靜脈 left marginal vein
左缘支/左緣支 left marginal branch
左支/左支 left branch
左支气管纵隔干/支氣管縱隔左幹 left bronchomediastinal trunk
左主支气管/左主支氣管 left principal bronchus
佐剂诱发性关节炎/佐劑誘發性關節炎 adjuvant-induced arthritis
佐药/佐藥 assistant drug
佐-泽综合征/Zollinger-Ellison 二氏症候群 Zollinger-Ellison syndrome
佐制药/佐製藥 supplementary inhibitory medicine
佐助药/佐助藥 supplementary drug
作呕/作嘔 gagging
作业简化/作業簡化 work simplification
作用/作用 action
作用部位/作用部位 site of action
作用簇/凝集族 ergophore group
作用电极/作用電極 active electrode
作用方式/作用方式 mode of action

作用受遏/作用受遏　arrest of action
坐板疮/坐板瘡　seat sore
坐骶韧带/坐骶韌帶　ischiosacral ligament
坐股韧带/坐骨韌帶　ischiofemoral ligament
坐骨/坐骨　ischium, ischial bone
坐骨病性脊柱侧凸/坐骨脊柱側彎　ischiatic scoliosis
坐骨丛/坐骨叢　ischiadic plexus
坐骨大孔/坐骨大孔　greater sciatic foramen
坐骨大切迹/坐骨大切跡　greater sciatic notch
坐骨的/坐骨的　ischiadic
坐骨肛门窝/坐骨直腸窩　ischioanal fossa, ischiorectal fossa
坐骨肛门窝脂体/坐骨直腸窩脂體　adipose body of ischioanal fossa
坐骨海绵体肌/坐骨海綿體肌　ischiocavernous muscle
坐骨棘/坐骨棘　ischial spine
坐骨棘间径/坐骨棘間徑　bi-ischial diameter
坐骨寄生肢畸胎/三足畸胎　ischiomelus
坐骨结节/坐骨結節　ischial tuberosity
坐骨结节滑囊炎/坐骨結節滑囊炎　synovitis of ischiac tubercle
坐骨结节间径/坐骨結節間徑　intertuberous diameter
坐骨结节炎/坐骨粗隆炎　ischionitis
坐骨孔疝/坐骨孔疝　ischiatic hernia
坐骨联胎/坐骨連胎　ischiadelphus
坐骨联胎畸形/坐骨連胎畸形　ischiodymia

坐骨前列腺韧带/坐骨前列腺韌帶　ischioprostatic ligament
坐骨神经/坐骨神經　①sciatic nerve, ischiadic nerve ②zuogushenjing, AH6
坐骨神经伴行动脉/坐骨神經伴行動脈　accompanying artery of ischiadic nerve
坐骨神经病/坐骨神經病　sciatic neuropathy
坐骨神经牵拉试验/坐骨神經牽拉試驗　sciatic stretch test
坐骨神经痛/坐骨神經痛　sciatic neuralgia
坐骨神经痛性脊柱侧凸/坐骨神經痛性脊柱側彎　sciatic scoliosis
坐骨体/坐骨體　body of ischium
坐骨臀大肌囊炎/坐骨臀大肌囊炎　ischiogluteal bursitis
坐骨小孔/坐骨小孔　lesser sciatic foramen
坐骨小切迹/坐骨小切跡　lesser sciatic notch
坐骨支/坐骨支　ramus of ischium
坐骨直肠[的]/坐骨直腸的　ischiorectal
坐骨直肠窝脓肿/坐骨直腸窩膿腫　ischiorectal abscess
坐骨直肠窝疝/坐骨直腸窩疝　ischiorectal hernia
坐忘/坐忘　oblivion when sitting still in qigong practice, sitting and forgetting
坐浴/坐浴　sitz bath
唑拉西泮/唑拉西泮　zolazepam
做作性障碍/做作性障礙　factitious disorder

附录

国际单位制

1. 国际单位制(Le Système International d'Unités)及其国际简称 SI 是在 1960 年第 11 届国际计量大会上通过的。国际单位制单位由基本单位、导出单位(包括辅助单位在内的具有专门名称的导出单位和组合形式的导出单位,组合形式的导出单位本附录不予收录)及其倍数单位构成。

2. 圆括号中的名称,是它前面的名称的同义词。

3. 无方括号的量的名称与单位名称均为全称。方括号中的字,在不致引起混淆、误解的情况下,可以省略。去掉方括号中的字即为其名称的简称。

表 1　基本单位

量的名称	单位名称	单位符号
大陆名/台湾名	大陆名/台湾名	
长度/長度	米/公尺	m
质量/質量	千克(公斤)/公斤	kg
时间/時間	秒/秒	s
电流/電流	安[培]/安培	A
热力学温度/熱力學溫度	开[尔文]/克耳文	K
物质的量/物[質]量	摩[尔]/莫耳	mol
发光强度/發光強度	坎[德拉]/燭光	cd

表 2　包括辅助单位在内的具有专门名称的导出单位

量的名称	导出单位		换算关系
	单位名称	单位符号	
大陆名/台湾名	大陆名/台湾名		
[平面]角/[平面]角	弧度/弧度,弳度	rad	$1\ rad=1\ m/m=1$
立体角/立體角	球面度/立弳	sr	$1\ sr=1\ m^2/m^2=1$
频率/頻率	赫[兹]/赫	Hz	$1\ Hz=1\ s^{-1}$
力/力	牛[顿]/牛頓	N	$1\ N=1\ kg\cdot m/s^2$
压力,压强,应力/壓力,壓強,應力	帕[斯卡]/帕斯卡	Pa	$1\ Pa=1\ N/m^2$
能[量],功,热量/能[量],功,熱[量]	焦[耳]/焦耳	J	$1\ J=1\ N\cdot m$
功率,辐[射能]通量/功率,輻射能通量	瓦[特]/瓦特	W	$1\ W=1\ J/s$
电荷[量]/電荷量	库[仑]/庫侖	C	$1\ C=1\ A\cdot s$
电压,电动势,电位,(电势)/電壓,電動勢,電位,(電勢)	伏[特]/伏特	V	$1\ V=1\ W/A$
电容/電容	法[拉]/法拉	F	$1\ F=1\ C/V$
电阻/電阻	欧[姆]/歐姆	Ω	$1\ \Omega=1\ V/A$
电导/電導	西[门子]/西門	S	$1\ S=1\ \Omega^{-1}$

量的名称	导出单位		
	单位名称	单位符号	换算关系
大陆名/台湾名	大陆名/台湾名		
磁通[量]/磁通量	韦[伯]/韋伯	Wb	1 Wb=1 V·s
磁通[量]密度,磁感应强度/磁通[量]密度,磁感應強度	特[斯拉]/特士拉	T	1 T=1 Wb/m²
电感/電感	亨[利]/亨利	H	1 H=1 Wb/A
摄氏温度/攝氏温度	摄氏度/攝氏温度	℃	1 ℃=1 K
光通量/光通量	流[明]/流明	lm	1 lm=1 cd·sr
[光]照度/照度	勒[克斯]/勒克斯	lx	1 lx=1 lm/m²

表 3　由于人类健康安全防护需要而确定的具有专门名称的导出单位

量的名称	导出单位		
	单位名称	单位符号	换算关系
大陆名/台湾名	大陆名/台湾名		
[放射性]活度/放射活性	贝可[勒尔]/贝克	Bq	1 Bq=1 s⁻¹
吸收剂量/吸收劑量 比授[予]能/比授能 比释动能/比釋動能	戈[瑞]/戈雷	Gy	1 Gy=1 J/kg
剂量当量/等價劑量,當量劑量	希[沃特]/西弗	Sv	1 Sv=1 J/kg

表 4　国际单位制词头

因数	词头名称	词头符号
	大陆名/台湾名	
10^{24}	尧[它]/佑	Y
10^{21}	泽[它]/皆	Z
10^{18}	艾[可萨]/艾	E
10^{15}	拍[它]/拍	P
10^{12}	太[拉]/太,兆	T
10^{9}	吉[咖]/吉,十億	G
10^{6}	兆/百萬	M
10^{3}	千/千	k
10^{2}	百/百	h
10^{1}	十/十	da
10^{-1}	分/分	d
10^{-2}	厘/厘	c

(续表)

因数	词头名称 大陆名/台湾名	词头符号
10^{-3}	毫/毫	m
10^{-6}	微/微	μ
10^{-9}	纳[诺]/奈	n
10^{-12}	皮[可]/披,微微	p
10^{-15}	飞[母托]/飛,毫微微	f
10^{-18}	阿[托]/阿,微微微	a
10^{-21}	仄[普托]/介	z
10^{-24}	幺[科托]/攸	y

注:词头与基本单位、导出单位共同组成一个新单位,即构成倍数单位。词头只用于构成倍数单位,不单独使用。

表 5 可与国际单位制单位并用的计量单位

量的名称 大陆名/台湾名	单位名称 大陆名/台湾名	单位符号	换算关系
时间/時間	分/分	min	1 min=60 s
	[小]时/[小]時	h	1 h=60 min=3 600 s
	日,(天)/日,天	d	1 d=24 h=86 400 s
[平面]角/[平面]角	度/度	°	$1°=(\pi/180)$ rad
	[角]分/[角]分	′	$1′=(1/60)°=(\pi/10\ 800)$ rad
	[角]秒/[角]秒	″	$1″=(1/60)′=(\pi/648\ 000)$ rad
体积/體積	升/公升	L,(l)	$1\ L=1\ dm^3=10^{-3}\ m^3$
质量/質量	吨/公噸	t	$1\ t=10^3$ kg
	原子质量单位/原子質量單位	u	$1\ u≈1.660\ 540×10^{-27}$ kg
旋转速度/轉速	转每分/每分鐘轉速	r/min	$1\ r/min=(1/60)\ s^{-1}$
长度/長度	海里/海里,浬	n mile	1 n mile=1 852 m(只用于航行)
速度/速度	节/節	kn	1 kn=1 n mile/h=(1 852/3 600) m/s (只用于航行)
能/能	电子伏/電子伏[特]	eV	$1\ eV≈1.602\ 177×10^{-19}$ J
级差/位準差	分贝/分貝	dB	
线密度/線密度	特[克斯]/德士	tex	$1\ tex=10^{-6}$ kg/m
面积/面積	公顷/公頃	hm^2	$1\ hm^2=10^4\ m^2$

注:1. 平面角单位度、分、秒的符号,在组合单位中采用(°)、(′)、(″)的形式。例如,不用°/s,而用(°)/s。
2. 升的符号中,小写字母 l 为备用符号。
3. 公顷的国际通用符号为 ha。

希腊字母表

大写	小写	名称	大写	小写	名称
A	α	阿尔法	N	ν	纽
B	β	贝塔	Ξ	ξ	克西
Γ	γ	伽马	O	o	奥米克戎
Δ	δ	德尔塔	Π	π	派
E	ε	艾普西隆	P	ρ	柔
Z	ζ	泽塔	Σ	σ	西格马
H	η	伊塔	T	τ	陶
Θ	θ	西塔	Υ	υ	宇普西隆
I	ι	约(yāo)塔	Φ	φ	斐
K	κ	卡帕	X	χ	希
Λ	λ	拉姆达	Ψ	ψ	普西
M	μ	谬	Ω	ω	奥米伽

地质年代表

宙 Eon	代 Era	纪 Period	世 Epoch	生物发展阶段 Development of Organisms	距今时间(百万年) Time(Ma BP)
显生宙(PH) Phanerozoic	新生代(Kz) Cenozoic	第四纪(Q) Quaternary	全新世(Q_h) Holocene	现代人类出现。	0.0117
			更新世(Q_p) Pleistocene	生物绝大部分与现在类似。智人出现。	2.58
		新近纪(N) Neogene	上新世(N_2) Pliocene	生物面貌与现在接近,哺乳类形体变大。直立人出现。	5.333
			中新世(N_1) Miocene	类人猿出现。	23.03
		古近纪(E) Paleogene	渐新世(E_3) Oligocene	哺乳类迅速发展,被子植物繁盛。	33.9
			始新世(E_2) Eocene		56.0
			古新世(E_1) Paleocene		66.0
	中生代(Mz) Mesozoic	白垩纪(K) Cretaceous		被子植物出现,末期恐龙等大批生物绝灭。	~145.0
		侏罗纪(J) Jurassic		鸟类出现,爬行类及苏铁等裸子植物繁盛。	201.3±0.2
		三叠纪(T) Triassic		哺乳类出现。	251.902±0.024
	古生代(Pz) Paleozoic	二叠纪(P) Permian		无脊椎动物和裸子植物发展。	298.9±0.15
		石炭纪(C) Carboniferous		爬行类出现,蕨类植物繁盛。	358.9±0.4
		泥盆纪(D) Devonian		昆虫、原始鱼类、蕨类和原始裸子植物出现。	419.2±3.2
		志留纪(S) Silurian		原始鱼类、原始陆生植物出现。	443.4±1.5
		奥陶纪(O) Ordovician		无颌类脊椎动物出现,海生藻类发育。	485.4±1.9
		寒武纪(∈) Cambrian		小壳动物出现,藻类、三叶虫开始繁盛。	541.0±1.0
前寒武纪 Precambrian	元古宙(PT) Proterozoic			藻类、细菌繁盛,软躯体无脊椎动物出现。	2500
	太古宙(AR) Archean				4000
	冥古宙 Hadean				~4600

注:本表各地质时代的距今时间按国际地层委员会 2018 年 8 月资料。其中未经全球地质年龄测定的标准方法确定的用近似值表示(数字前加"~")。

元素周期表

(Periodic Table of the Elements)

注:
1. 标准原子量的数值选自 Pure Appl. Chem. 85, 1047-1078 (2013) 中的表 4 (http://dx.doi.org/10.1351/PAC-REP-13-03-02)。
2. 族号 1/IA,前者为国际纯粹与应用化学联合会 (IUPAC) 推荐标准,后者为中国大陆比较为通用的标准。
3. 元素"铝"和"铯"的英文名称 "aluminium"、"cesium" 和 "caesium" 都可使用。